August 12–16, 2012
Portland, Oregon, USA

AF762064

Association for
Computing Machinery

Advancing Computing as a Science & Profession

SIGIR'12 Vol. 1 of 2

The Proceedings of the International ACM SIGIR Conference on
Research & Development in Information Retrieval

Sponsored by:
ACM SIGIR

Supported by:
Microsoft Research, Baidu, Google Research, Yahoo! Labs, IBM Research, eBay, Oracle, Morgan & Claypool Publishers, Springer, Cambridge University Press, University of Oregon Applied Information Management Prorgram, Now Publishers, and Oregon Health & Science University

Association for
Computing Machinery

Advancing Computing as a Science & Profession

The Association for Computing Machinery
2 Penn Plaza, Suite 701
New York, New York 10121-0701

Copyright © 2012 by the Association for Computing Machinery, Inc. (ACM). Permission to make digital or hard copies of portions of this work for personal or classroom use is granted without fee provided that copies are not made or distributed for profit or commercial advantage and that copies bear this notice and the full citation on the first page. Copyright for components of this work owned by others than ACM must be honored. Abstracting with credit is permitted. To copy otherwise, to republish, to post on servers or to redistribute to lists, requires prior specific permission and/or a fee. Request permission to republish from: permissions@acm.org or Fax +1 (212) 869-0481.

For other copying of articles that carry a code at the bottom of the first or last page, copying is permitted provided that the per-copy fee indicated in the code is paid through www.copyright.com.

Notice to Past Authors of ACM-Published Articles
ACM intends to create a complete electronic archive of all articles and/or other material previously published by ACM. If you have written a work that has been previously published by ACM in any journal or conference proceedings prior to 1978, or any SIG Newsletter at any time, and you do NOT want this work to appear in the ACM Digital Library, please inform permissions@acm.org, stating the title of the work, the author(s), and where and when published.

ISBN: 978-1-4503-1658-3 (Digital)

ISBN: 978-1-4503-2000-9 (Print Vol.1)

Additional copies may be ordered prepaid from:

ACM Order Department
PO Box 30777
New York, NY 10087-0777, USA

Phone: 1-800-342-6626 (USA and Canada)
+1-212-626-0500 (Global)
Fax: +1-212-944-1318
E-mail: acmhelp@acm.org
Hours of Operation: 8:30 am – 4:30 pm ET

ACM Order Number: 606121

Printed in the USA

Welcome from the General Conference Chair

Welcome to Portland, Oregon, USA for the 35th Annual ACM SIGIR Conference on Research and Development in Information Retrieval. SIGIR is the premier international forum for the presentation of new research results and the demonstration of new systems and techniques in the field of information retrieval, also known as search. My colleagues and I from Oregon Health & Science University (OHSU) are pleased to be hosting this year's SIGIR, and we hope that you enjoy your stay in Portland as well as the technical and social programs that we have arranged.

Successfully organizing a conference of the size and scope of SIGIR would not be possible without the dedicated work of a great many individuals. First and foremost, I thank the Program Committee Chairs, Jamie Callan, Yoelle Maarek, and Mark Sanderson, who together with Posters & Demos Chairs Falk Scholer, Mark Smucker, and Andrew Turpin put together an excellent main technical program. I also thank Henning Müller, who organized our slate of tutorials; Eugene Agichtein and Vanessa Murdock, who organized the workshops; Udo Kruschwitz and Su-Lin Wu, who organized the industry track; Maarten de Rijke and Mounia Lalmas, who organized the doctoral consortium; Doug Oard, who served as mentoring chair; and ChengXiang Zhai, who chaired the outstanding paper awards committee. Collectively, these individuals were largely responsible for the technical events that most SIGIR participants will attend, and I thank them for their tremendous efforts.

Many other individuals worked largely behind the scenes to ensure that SIGIR 2011 would be a success, including treasurer, Javed Mostafa; publicity chair, Jayashree Kalpathy-Cramer; publications chair, Elmer Bernstam; and local arrangements chair, Justin Fletcher. I also thank Aaron Cohen, who coordinated sponsorship, and Chris Weldon, who served as the webmaster.

Finally, I am indebted to others for the invaluable help and advice they have provided, especially James Allan, SIGIR Chair, and Ian Soboroff, SIGIR Treasurer.

SIGIR 2012 is, of course, sponsored by ACM, but has also received generous support from numerous companies and organizations. Microsoft Research, Baidu, and Google were all particularly generous with support at the Gold level, with Yahoo! Labs providing support at the Silver level and eBay, IBM Research, and Oracle providing support at the Bronze level. In addition, Morgan & Claypool, Springer, Cambridge University Press, the University of Oregon Applied Information Management Program, and Now Publishers all made arrangements to support and exhibit at the conference. The organization of SIGIR 2012 also would not have been possible without the support of the Department of Medical Informatics & Clinical Epidemiology at OHSU. Finally, logistical aspects of the conference were handled with excellence by Kim Lepin of the Division of Continuing Medical Education at OHSU.

Welcome to Portland, and I hope that you enjoy the conference and your stay in Oregon.

William Hersh
SIGIR 2012 Conference Chair
Oregon Health & Science University
Portland, Oregon, USA

Welcome from the Program Chairs

We are delighted to welcome you to the 35th edition of SIGIR, the ACM International Conference on Research and Development in Information Retrieval. The conference continues its tradition of being the premier forum for research and development information retrieval, the computer science discipline behind what many call "search". The high number of submitted papers, this year again, demonstrates both the breadth and depth of the research being done in this vibrant field, both in academia and industry. We have done our best to ensure that these papers meet high standards of quality in terms of technical contribution, innovation, presentation, reference to previous work, and methodology. At the same time, we have tried to be flexible in the application of these criteria in order to consider papers describing novel and innovative work that may be somewhat unconventional.

The conference received 483 full paper submissions this year. Examining the country code of the paper's contact author, we found that 185 (38%) come from the Americas; 158 (33%), Asia and Pacific region; and 140 (29%) from Europe, the Middle East and Africa. Of these, 98 (20%) were accepted, essentially the same as last year's acceptance rate and up from the 16.7% rate of the year before. There was almost no difference in the acceptance rates across the three broad regions. The top five countries in terms of accepted papers were the U.S.A. (36), China (14), the U.K. & Spain (both 7), and the Netherlands (6). In addition, 208 short papers were submitted to the poster track, of which 76 (36.5%) were accepted. In the other categories, there were 17 (47.2%) demonstrations, 4 workshops, and 16 tutorials accepted. The top five technical areas (as inferred from the primary keyword assigned by the authors) covered by the accepted papers, were queries and query analysis (18%), retrieval models and ranking (14%), web IR & social media search (13%), document representation and content analysis (11%), and users and interactive IR (9%). This was a small re-ordering of the topics from last year.

SIGIR this year again used a two-tier double-blind reviewing approach. In a first stage, at least three reviewers read every paper and provided ratings and comments. Then, in a second stage, the primary and secondary Area Chairs ensured the quality of the reviewing process by studying, validating, and summarizing these reviews, and adding their own feedback and ratings. When required, Area Chairs initiated a discussion among the reviewers to resolve any controversial issues or significant differences of opinion. Once the discussion stage was completed, the two Area Chairs made the final decisions for nearly all submitted papers. At the program committee meeting held in Haifa, Israel, the Program Chairs and the attending Area Chairs went over the reviews, verified the process, gathered additional input, and made decisions in the few cases for which assistance had been requested.

The success of the conference depends on the numerous volunteers who, every year, devote large amounts of their time to reviewing and assisting in the organization of the program. We would like to acknowledge the tremendous work of the 200 general program committee members, representing more than 30 countries, and the effort and dedication of the 47 Area Chairs. They should be credited for the high quality of the program this year.

We also acknowledge the tremendous job done by the Posters Chairs in handling the short papers, and the great work done by the other Chairs with their tasks. We thank the general chair Bill Hersh, who was a wonderful partner in getting this program together. We are grateful to Yahoo! Labs for graciously hosting the Program Committee meeting in Haifa and to Thomas Preuss for his support of the ConfMaster system throughout the entire reviewing process.

Finally, we are in debt to the authors and attendees. They are the ones who make this conference possible. We hope that you will find this program interesting and thought-provoking. Our goal is not only to give you the opportunity to share ideas with other researchers and practitioners from around the world, but also to foster new research and innovation in this fascinating and ever-evolving domain.

Jamie Callan
Program Chair
Carnegie Mellon University

Yoelle Maarek
Program Chair
Yahoo! Research, Israel

Mark Sanderson
Program Chair
RMIT University, Australia

Table of Contents

Session 2A: Evaluation 1

Session 2B: Structured Data

Session 2C: Recommender Systems 1

Session 3A: Users 1: Personalization and User Modeling

Session 3B: Architectures 1

Session 3C: Search Log Analysis

Session 4A: User Intent

Session 4B: Efficiency

Session 4C: Spam and Abuse

Session 5A: Users 2: Exploratory Search

Session 5B: Multimedia 2

Session 5C: Recommender Systems 2

Session 6A: Query Expansion and Reformulation

Session 6B: Social Media 1

Session 8B: Entities

Session 8C: Learning to Rank

Session 9A: Community QA

Session 9B: Federated Search

Session 9C: Diversity 2

Session 10A: Evaluation 2

Session 10B: Representation

Session 10C: Classification

Doctoral Submissions

Demonstrations

Industry Talk Abstracts

Poster Abstracts

Tutorial Presentations

SIGIR 2012 Organizing Committee

General Chair: William Hersh *(Oregon Health & Science University, USA)*

Program Chairs: Jamie Callan *(Carnegie Mellon University, USA)*
Yoelle Maarek *(Yahoo! Research, Israel)*
Mark Sanderson *(Royal Melbourne Institute of Technology, Australia)*

Treasurer: Javed Mostafa *(University of North Carolina-Chapel Hill, USA)*

Posters & Demos Chairs: Falk Scholer *(Royal Melbourne Institute of Technology, Australia)*
Mark Smucker *(University of Waterloo, Canada)*
Andrew Turpin *(University of Melbourne, Australia)*

Tutorials Chair: Henning Müller *(University of Applied Sciences Western Switzerland, Switzerland)*

Workshops Chairs: Eugene Agichtein *(Emory University, USA)*
Vanessa Murdock *(Yahoo! Research, Spain)*

Industry Track Chairs: Udo Kruschwitz *(University of Essex, United Kingdom)*
Su-Lin Wu *(Yahoo! Labs, USA)*

Doctoral Consortium Chairs: Mounia Lalmas *(Yahoo! Research, Spain)*
Maarten de Rijke *(University of Amsterdam, The Netherlands)*

Mentoring Chair: Douglas Oard *(University of Maryland, USA)*

Best Papers Chair: ChengXiang Zhai *(University of Illinois - Champaign-Urbana, USA)*

Publications Chair: Elmer Bernstam *(The University of Texas Health Science Center at Houston, USA)*

Local Arrangements Chair: Justin Fletcher *(Oregon Health & Science University, USA)*

Publicity Chair: Jayashree Kalpathy-Cramer *(Oregon Health & Science University, USA)*

Sponsorships Chair: Aaron Cohen *(Oregon Health & Science University, USA)*

Webmaster: Chris Weldon *(Oregon Health & Science University, USA)*

SIGIR 2012 Committees

Senior Program Committee

Jamie Callan *(Carnegie Mellon University - USA) – Chair*
Yoelle Maarek *(Yahoo! Research - Israel) – Chair*
Mark Sanderson *(RMIT University - Australia) – Chair*

Eugene Agichtein *(Emory University - USA)*
James Allan *(University of Massachusetts Amherst - USA)*
Sihem Amer-Yahia *(QCRI and CNRS - France)*
Ricardo Baeza-Yates *(Yahoo! Research - Spain)*
Andrei Broder *(Yahoo! Research - USA)*
Peter Bruza *(Queensland University of Technology - Australia)*
David Carmel *(IBM Research - Israel)*
Ben Carterette *(University of Delaware - USA)*
Carlos Castillo *(Qatar Computing Research Institute - Qatar)*
Tat Seng Chua *(National University of Singapore - Singapore)*
Charles L. A. Clarke *(University of Waterloo - Canada)*
Kevyn Collins-Thompson *(Microsoft Research - USA)*
Nick Craswell *(Microsoft - USA)*
W. Bruce Croft *(University of Massachusetts Amherst - USA)*
Fernando Diaz *(Yahoo! Research - USA)*
Susan Dumais *(Microsoft Research - USA)*
Evgeniy Gabrilovich *(Google - USA)*
Eric Gaussier *(Université Joseph Fourier - France)*
Shlomo Geva *(Queensland University of Technology - Australia)*
Djoerd Hiemstra *(University of Twente - The Netherlands)*
Xian-Sheng Hua *(Microsoft - USA)*
Gareth Jones *(Dublin City University - Ireland)*
Franciska de Jong *(University of Twente - The Netherlands)*
Vanja Josifovski *(Yahoo! Research - USA)*
Diane Kelly *(University of North Carolina at Chapel Hill - USA)*
Wessel Kraaij *(Radboud University Nijmegen and TNO - The Netherlands)*
Oren Kurland *(Technion - Israel)*
Mounia Lalmas *(Yahoo! Research - Spain)*
Elizabeth D. Liddy *(Syracuse University - USA)*
Wei-Ying Ma *(Microsoft Research Asia - China)*
Donald Metzler *(USC/ISI - USA)*
Isabelle Moulinier *(Thomson Reuters - USA)*
Edleno S. Moura *(UFAM - Brazil)*
Marc Najork *(Microsoft Research - USA)*
Tao Qin *(Microsoft Research Asia - China)*
Maarten de Rijke *(University of Amsterdam - The Netherlands)*
Ian Ruthven *(University of Strathclyde - UK)*
Tetsuya Sakai *(Microsoft Research Asia - China)*
Fabrizio Silvestri *(Information Science and Technology Institute - Italy)*
Andrew Trotman *(University of Otago - New Zealand)*
Ellen Voorhees *(NIST - USA)*
Arjen P. de Vries *(Centrum Wiskunde & Informatica - The Netherlands)*
Ryen White *(Microsoft Research - USA)*
Yiming Yang *(Carnegie Mellon University - USA)*
Elad Yom-Tov *(Yahoo! Research - USA)*
Yi Zhang *(University of California at Santa Cruz - USA)*
Ming Zhou *(Microsoft Research Asia - China)*

Program Committee

Omar Alonso *(Microsoft - USA)*
Gianni Amati *(Fondazione Ugo Bordoni - Italy)*
Avi Arampatzis *(Democritus University of Thrace - Greece)*
Jaime Arguello *(University of North Carolina at Chapel Hill - USA)*
Javed A. Aslam *(Northeastern University - USA)*
Leif Azzopardi *(University of Glasgow - UK)*
Peter Bailey *(Microsoft - USA)*
Krisztian Balog *(Norwegian University of Science and Technology - Norway)*
Hannah Bast *(University of Freiburg - Germany)*
Nicholas J. Belkin *(Rutgers - The State University of New Jersey - USA)*
Ron Bekkerman *(LinkedIn - USA)*
Michael Bendersky *(University of Massachusetts Amherst - USA)*
Klaus Berberich *(Max-Planck Institute for Informatics - Germany)*
Bodo Billerbeck *(Microsoft - Australia)*
Roi Blanco *(Yahoo! Research - Spain)*
Toine Bogers *(Royal School of Library and Information Science - Denmark)*
Edward Bortnikov *(Yahoo! Labs - Israel)*
Mohand Boughanem *(University Paul Sabatier - France)*
Martin Braschler *(Zurich University of Applied Sciences - Switzerland)*
Eric W. Brown *(IBM Research - USA)*
Chris Buckley *(Sabir Research - USA)*
Stefan Buettcher *(Google - USA)*
B. Barla Cambazoglu *(Yahoo! Research - Spain)*
Yunbo Cao *(Microsoft Research Asia - China)*
Jaime Carbonell *(Carnegie Mellon University - USA)*
James Caverlee *(Texas A&M University - USA)*

Raman Chandrasekar *(Evri - USA)*
Kevin C. Chang *(University of Illinois at Urbana-Champaign - USA)*
Yi Chang *(Yahoo! Labs - USA)*
Longbin Chen *(Microsoft - USA)*
Ye Chen *(Microsoft - USA)*
Pu-Jen Cheng *(National Taiwan University - Taiwan)*
Ed H. Chi *(Google Research - USA)*
Paul Clough *(University of Sheffield - UK)*
Michael Cole *(Rutgers University - USA)*
Jack G. Conrad *(Thomson Reuters - Switzerland)*
Gordon V. Cormack *(University of Waterloo - Canada)*
Ingemar Cox *(University College London - UK)*
Marco Cristo *(FUCAPI - Brazil)*
J. Shane Culpepper *(RMIT University - Australia)*
Altigran S. da Silva *(Universidade Federal do Amazonas - Brazil)*
Brian D. Davison *(Lehigh University - USA)*
Gianluca Demartini *(University of Fribourg - Switzerland)*
Ludovic Denoyer *(University Pierre et Marie Curie - France)*
Debora Donato *(Yahoo! Labs - USA)*
Gideon Dror *(Yahoo! Research - Israel)*
Gregory Druck *(Yahoo! Research - USA)*
Georges Dupret *(Yahoo! Labs - USA)*
Miles Efron *(University of Illinois - USA)*
David Eichmann *(University of Iowa - USA)*
Hui Fang *(University of Delaware - USA)*
Henry Feild *(University of Massachusetts Amherst - USA)*
Dennis Fetterly *(Microsoft Research - USA)*
Marcus C Fontoura *(Google - USA)*
Luanne Freund *(University of British Columbia - Canada)*
Ophir Frieder *(Georgetown University - USA)*
Ingo Frommholz *(University of Bedfordshire - UK)*
Norbert Fuhr *(Universität Duisburg-Essen - Germany)*
Patrick Gallinari *(Universite Pierre et Marie Curie - France)*
Bin Gao *(Microsoft Research Asia - China)*
Fredric Gey *(University of California at Berkeley - USA)*
C. Lee Giles *(Pennsylvania State University - USA)*
Aristides Gionis *(Yahoo! Research - Spain)*
Ayse Goker *(City University London - UK)*
Sreenivas Gollapudi *(Microsoft Research - USA)*
Marcos Goncalves *(UFMG - Brazil)*
Gregory Grefenstette *(3DS Exalead - France)*
Jiafeng Guo *(Chinese Academy of Sciences - China)*
Qi Guo *(Emory University - USA)*
Maxim Gurevich *(Google - USA)*
Cathal Gurrin *(Dublin City University - Ireland)*
Karl Gyllstrom *(Katholieke Universiteit Leuven - Belgium)*
Sanda M. Harabagiu *(University of Texas at Dallas - USA)*
Donna Harman *(NIST - USA)*
Claudia Hauff *(Delft University of Technology - The Netherlands)*
David Hawking *(Funnelback and Australian National University - Australia)*
Daqing He *(University of Pittsburgh - USA)*
Qi He *(IBM Almaden Research Center - USA)*
Marti Hearst *(University of California at Berkeley - USA)*
Monika Henzinger *(University of Vienna - Austria)*
Katja Hofmann *(University of Amsterdam - Netherlands)*
Eric Horvitz *(Microsoft Research - USA)*
Jimmy Huang *(York University - Canada)*
Jing Jiang *(Singapore Management University - Singapore)*
Thorsten Joachims *(Cornell University - USA)*
Hideo Joho *(University of Tsukuba - Japan)*
Joemon M. Jose *(University of Glasgow - UK)*
Jaap Kamps *(University of Amsterdam - The Netherlands)*
Noriko Kando *(National Institute of Informatics - Japan)*
Evangelos Kanoulas *(Google - Switzerland)*
Jussi Karlgren *(Gavagai - Sweden)*
Gabriella Kazai *(Microsoft Research Cambridge - UK)*
Irwin King *(The Chinese University of Hong Kong - Hong Kong, SAR)*
Jinyoung Kim *(University of Massachusetts Amherst - USA)*
Marijn Koolen *(University of Amsterdam - The Netherlands)*
Yehuda Koren *(Yahoo! Research - Israel)*
Alexander Kotov *(Emory University & Georgia Tech - USA)*
Giridhar Kumaran *(Microsoft - USA)*
Wai Lam *(The Chinese University of Hong Kong - Hong Kong, SAR)*
Birger Larsen *(Royal School of Library and Information Science - Denmark)*
Martha Larson *(Delft University of Technology - Netherlands)*
Ray R. Larson *(University of California at Berkeley - USA)*
Dawn Lawrie *(Loyola University Maryland - USA)*
Matthew Lease *(University of Texas at Austin - USA)*
Miro Lehtonen *(University of Helsinki - Finland)*
Jochen L. Leidner *(Thomson Reuters Global Resources - Switzerland)*
Anton Leuski *(University of Southern California - USA)*
David D. Lewis *(David D. Lewis Consulting - USA)*
Hang Li *(Microsoft Research - China)*
Yuefeng Li *(Queensland University of Technology - Australia)*
Edo Liberty *(Yahoo! Research - Israel)*
Christina Lioma *(University of Copenhagen - Denmark)*
Chao Liu *(Microsoft Research - USA)*
Tie-Yan Liu *(Microsoft Research Asia - China)*
David Losada *(University of Santiago de Compostela - Spain)*
Jie Lu *(IBM Research - USA)*
Robert W. P. Luk *(The Hong Kong Polytechnic University - Hong Kong, SAR)*
Hao Ma *(Microsoft Research - USA)*
Craig Macdonald *(University of Glasgow - UK)*
Andrew MacFarlane *(City University London - UK)*
Eren Manavoglu *(Yahoo! Labs - USA)*
R. Manmatha *(University of Massachusetts Amherst - USA)*
Stephane Marchand-Maillet *(University of Geneva - Switzerland)*
Yosi Mass *(IBM Research Haifa - Israel)*
James Mayfield *(Johns Hopkins University - USA)*
Paul McNamee *(Johns Hopkins University - USA)*

Edgar Meij *(University of Amsterdam - The Netherlands)*
Natasa Milic-Frayling *(Microsoft Research - UK)*
Mandar Mitra *(Indian Statistical Institute - India)*
Prasenjit Mitra *(Pennsylvania State University - USA)*
Marie-Francine Moens *(Katholieke Universiteit Leuven - Belgium)*
Alistair Moffat *(University of Melbourne - Australia)*
Josiane Mothe *(Université de Toulouse - France)*
Vanessa Murdock *(Yahoo! Research - Spain)*
Sung Hyon Myaeng *(Korea Advanced Institute of Science and Technology - Korea)*
Gonzalo Navarro *(University of Chile - Chile)*
Michael L. Nelson *(Old Dominion University - USA)*
Hwee Tou Ng *(National University of Singapore - Singapore)*
Charles Nicholas *(University of Maryland Baltimore County - USA)*
Jian-Yun Nie *(University of Montreal - Canada)*
Alexandros Ntoulas *(Microsoft Research - USA)*
Douglas W Oard *(University of Maryland - USA)*
Sandeep Pandey *(Yahoo! Research - USA)*
Bo Pang *(Yahoo! Labs - USA)*
Laurence Park *(University of Western Sydney - Australia)*
Gabriella Pasi *(University of Milano-Bicocca - Italy)*
Jan Pedersen *(Microsoft - USA)*
Jian Pei *(Simon Fraser University - Canada)*
Anselmo Peñas *(UNED - Spain)*
Raffaele Perego *(ISTI-CNR - Italy)*
Jeremy Pickens *(Catalyst Repository Systems - USA)*
Benjamin Piwowarski *(CNRS - University Paris 6 - UK)*
Barbara Poblete *(University of Chile - Chile)*
John Prager *(IBM Research - USA)*
Kunal Punera *(RelateIQ - USA)*
Filip Radlinski *(Microsoft - UK)*
Hema Raghavan *(IBM Research - USA)*
Edie Rasmussen *(University of British Columbia - Canada)*
Berthier Ribeiro-Neto *(Federal University of Minas Gerais - Brazil)*
Thomas Roelleke *(Queen Mary, University of London - UK)*
Haggai Roitman *(IBM Research Haifa - Israel)*
Dmitri Roussinov *(University of Strathclyde - UK)*
Stefan Rueger *(The Open University - UK)*
Daniel M Russell *(Google - USA)*
Ralf Schenkel *(Saarland University - Germany)*
Falk Scholer *(RMIT University - Australia)*
Jangwon Seo *(Google - USA)*
Pavel Serdyukov *(Yandex - Russian Federation)*
Chirag Shah *(Rutgers University - USA)*
Shuming Shi *(Microsoft Research Asia - China)*
Milad Shokouhi *(Microsoft - UK)*
Anna Shtok *(Technion - Israel)*
Luo Si *(Purdue University - USA)*
David A. Smith *(University of Massachusetts Amherst - USA)*
Mark D. Smucker *(University of Waterloo - Canada)*
Ian Soboroff *(NIST - USA)*
Aya Soffer *(IBM - Israel)*
Oren Somekh *(Yahoo! Labs - Israel)*
Dawei Song *(Robert Gordon University - UK)*
Torsten Suel *(Polytechnic Institute of NYU - USA)*
Jian-Tao Sun *(Microsoft Research Asia - China)*
Neel Sundaresan *(eBay Research Labs - USA)*
Krysta M Svore *(Microsoft Research - USA)*
Idan Szpektor *(Yahoo! Research - Israel)*
Jie Tang *(Tsinghua University - China)*
Jinhui Tang *(Nanjing University of Science and Technology - China)*
Martin Theobald *(Max Planck Institute for Informatics - Germany)*
Paul Thomas *(CSIRO - Australia)*
Paul Thompson *(Dartmouth College - USA)*
Qi Tian *(Microsoft Research Asia - USA)*
Anastasios Tombros *(Queen Mary, University of London- UK)*
Elaine Toms *(University of Sheffield - Canada)*
Dolf Trieschnigg *(University of Twente - Netherlands)*
Ming-Feng Tsai *(National Chengchi University - Taiwan)*
Theodora Tsikrika *(University of Applied Sciences Western Switzerland - Switzerland)*
Andrew Turpin *(University of Melbourne - Australia)*
Antti Ukkonen *(Yahoo! Research - Spain)*
Olga Vechtomova *(University of Waterloo - Canada)*
Emre Velipasaoglu *(Yahoo! Labs - USA)*
Robert Villa *(University of Sheffield - UK)*
Nina Wacholder *(Rutgers University - USA)*
Xiaojun Wan *(Peking University - China)*
Jingdong Wang *(Microsoft Research Asia - China)*
Jun Wang *(University College London - UK)*
Lidan Wang *(University of Maryland at College Park - USA)*
Meng Wang *(Hefei University of Technology - China)*
William Webber *(University of Maryland - USA)*
Ingmar Weber *(Yahoo! Research - Spain)*
Wouter Weerkamp *(University of Amsterdam - Netherlands)*
Ji-Rong Wen *(Microsoft Research Asia - China)*
Thijs Westerveld *(Teezir Search Solutions - The Netherlands)*
Max L. Wilson *(University of Nottingham - UK)*
Zhong Wu *(Microsoft - USA)*
Grace Hui Yang *(Georgetown University - USA)*
Linjun Yang *(Microsoft Research Asia - China)*
Emine Yilmaz *(Microsoft Research Cambridge - UK)*
Hongyuan Zha *(Georgia Institute of Technology - USA)*
Zhengjun Zha *(NUS - Singapore)*
ChengXiang Zhai *(University of Illinois at Urbana-Champaign - USA)*
Lei Zhang *(Microsoft Research Asia - China)*
Min Zhang *(Tsinghua University - China)*
Le Zhao *(Carnegie Mellon University - USA)*
Dengyong Zhou *(Microsoft Research - USA)*
Jinfeng Zhuang *(Microsoft - USA)*
Nivio Ziviani *(Federal University of Minas Gerais - Brazil)*
Guido Zuccon *(CSIRO - Australia)*

Additional Paper Reviewers

Alvaro Barreiro *(University of A Coruña - Spain)*
Jennifer Bayzick *(Lehigh University - USA)*
Wladmir Brandao *(Federal University of Minas Gerais - Brazil)*
Guillaume Cabanac *(University of Toulouse - France)*
Ethem F. Can *(University of Massachusetts Amherst - USA)*
Bin Cao *(Microsoft Research Asia - USA)*
Maria Christoforaki *(Polytechnic Institute of NYU - USA)*
Costas Dimopoulos *(Polytechnic Institute of NYU - USA)*
Christos Diou *(Centre for Research and Technology Hellas - Greece)*
Matt Ekstrand-Abueg *(Northeastern University - USA)*
Victor Fresno *(UNED - Spain)*
Yan Fu *(Beijing Normal University - China)*
Peter Golbus *(Northeastern University - USA)*
Liangjie Hong *(Lehigh University - USA)*
Vivian Hu *(York University - Canada)*
Somayeh Khatiban *(City University London - UK)*
Haiming Liu *(University of Bedfordshire - UK)*
Qiang Lu *(Kore Federal - USA)*
Wei Lu *(Wuhan University - China)*
Pavel Metrikov *(Northeastern University - USA)*
Jun Miao *(York University - Canada)*
Sergey Nepomnyachiy *(Polytechnic Institute of NYU - USA)*
Virgil Pavlu *(Northeastern University - USA)*
Maria-Hendrike Peetz *(University of Amsterdam - Netherlands)*
Anisio Lacerda *(Federal University of Minas Gerais - Brazil)*
Joaquin Perez-Iglesias *(UNED - Spain)*
Shahzad Rajput *(Northeastern University - USA)*
Marco Tulio Ribeiro *(Federal University of Minas Gerais - Brazil)*
Calum Robertson *(Sirca Ltd - Australia)*
Alvaro Rodrigo *(UNED - Spain)*
Nuzhah Gooda Sahib *(Queen Mary, University of London-UK)*
Rodrygo Santos *(University of Glasgow - UK)*
Yue Shi *(Delft University of Technology - Netherlands)*
Adriano Veloso *(Federal University of Minas Gerais - Brazil)*
Zaihan Yang *(Lehigh University - USA)*
Zheng Ye *(York University - Canada)*
Jeonghee Yi *(Microsoft - USA)*
Ismet Zeki Yalniz *(University of Massachusetts Amherst - USA)*
Jianwen Zhang *(Microsoft Research Asia - USA)*
Jessie Zhao *(York University - Canada)*
Arkaitz Zubiaga *(City University of New York - USA)*

Poster Committee

Falk Scholer *(RMIT University - Australia) – Chair*
Mark D. Smucker *(University of Waterloo - Canada) – Chair*
Andrew Turpin *(University of Melbourne - Australia) – Chair*

Eytan Adar *(University of Michigan - USA)*
Mikhail Ageev *(Moscow State University - Russian Federation)*
John Akinyemi *(University of Waterloo - Canada)*
Elif Aktolga *(University of Massachusetts Amherst - USA)*
Omar Alonso *(Microsoft - USA)*
Robin Aly *(University of Twente - Netherlands)*
Peter Anick *(Brandeis University - USA)*
Jaime Arguello *(University of North Carolina at Chapel Hill - USA)*
Azin Ashkan *(University of Waterloo - Canada)*
Javed Aslam *(Northeastern University - USA)*
Hany Azzam *(Queen Mary, University of London-UK)*
Niranjan Balasubramanian *(University of Massachusetts Amherst - USA)*
Krisztian Balog *(Norwegian University Science and Technology - Norway)*
Alberto Barrón - Cedeño *(Universidad Politécnica de Valencia - Spain)*
Paul N. Bennett *(Microsoft Research - USA)*
Gerald Benoit *(Simmons College - USA)*
Roi Blanco *(Yahoo! Research - Spain)*
Eric Brown *(IBM Research - USA)*
Rui Cai *(Microsoft Research, Asia - China)*
Silvia Calegari *(University of Milan - Bicocca - Italy)*
Fazli Can *(Bilkent University - Turkey)*
Robert Capra *(University of North Carolina at Chapel Hill - USA)*
Annalina Caputo *(University of Bari - Italy)*
Mark Carman *(Monash University - Australia)*
Ben Carterette *(University of Delaware - USA)*
Marc - Allen Cartright *(University of Massachusetts Amherst - USA)*
Carlos Castillo *(Qatar Computing Research Institute - Qatar)*
Yi Chang *(Yahoo labs - USA)*
Francine Chen *(FX Palo Alto Laboratory - USA)*
Yi Chen *(Dublin City University - Ireland)*
Yun Chi *(NEC Laboratories America - USA)*
Paul Clough *(University of Sheffield - UK)*
Michael Cole *(Rutgers University - USA)*
Kevyn Collins - Thompson *(Microsoft Research - USA)*
Gao Cong *(Nanyang Technological University - Singapore)*
Eli Cortez *(Federal University of Amazonas - Brazil)*

Bin Cui *(Peking University - China)*
Sally Jo Cunningham *(Wakaito University - New Zealand)*
Altigran da Silva *(UFAM - Brazil)*
Na Dai *(Lehigh University - USA)*
Lorand Dali *(Jožef Stefan Institute - Slovenia)*
Jeff Dalton *(University of Massachusetts Amherst - USA)*
Kareem Darwish *(Microsoft Research - Egypt)*
Emanuele Di Buccio *(University of Padova - Italy)*
Giorgio Maria Di Nunzio *(University of Padova - Italy)*
Debora Donato *(Yahoo! Labs - USA)*
Georges Dupret *(Yahoo! Labs - USA)*
Miles Efron *(University of Illinois - USA)*
Koji Eguchi *(Kobe University - Japan)*
David Eichmann *(U. Iowa - USA)*
David Elsweiler *(Friedrich - Alexander Universitaet Erlangen - Germany)*
Jianping Fan *(UNC - Charlotte - USA)*
Fabio Faria *(University of Campinas - Brazil)*
Shaolei Feng *(Siemens Corporate Research Labs - USA)*
Nicola Ferro *(University of Padova - Italy)*
Ingo Frommholz *(University of Bedfordshire-UK)*
Xin Fu *(Microsoft - USA)*
Norbert Fuhr *(Universität Duisburg - Essen - Germany)*
Atsushi Fujii *(Tokyo Institute of Technology - Japan)*
Bin Gao *(Microsoft Research Asia - China)*
Wei Gao *(Qatar Computing Research Institute - Qatar)*
Susan Gauch *(University of Arkansas - USA)*
Shima Gerani *(University of Lugano - Switzerland)*
Shlomo Geva *(Queensland University of Technology - Australia)*
Fredric Gey *(University of California, Berkeley - USA)*
Brigitte Grau *(LIMSI - CNRS & ENSIIE - France)*
Mark A. Greenwood *(University of Sheffield - UK)*
Daniel Gruhl *(IBM Research - USA)*
Cao Guihong *(Microsoft - USA)*
Qi Guo *(Emory University - USA)*
Karl Gyllstrom *(K.U. Leuven - USA)*
Stephanie Haas *(University of North Carolina at Chapel Hill - USA)*
Preben Hansen *(Swedish Institute of Computer Science - Sweden)*
Donna Harman *(NIST - USA)*
Morgan Harvey *(University of Erlangen - Nuremberg - Germany)*
Claudia Hauff *(TU Delft - The Netherlands)*
Daqing He *(University of Pittsburgh - USA)*
Jiyin He *(Centrum Wiskunde & Informatica - The Netherlands)*
Ben He *(Graduate Univ. of Chinese Academy of Sciences - China)*
Andreas Henrich *(University of Bamberg - Germany)*
Djoerd Hiemstra *(University of Twente - Netherlands)*
Katja Hofmann *(University of Amsterdam - Netherlands)*
Frank Hopfgartner *(International Computer Science Institute - USA)*
Vivian (Qinmin) Hu *(York University, Canada - Canada)*
Jimmy Huang *(York University, Toronto, Ontario, Canada - Canada)*
Alvaro Francisco Huertas - Rosero *(University of Glasgow-UK)*
Yoshiyuki Inagaki *(Yahoo! Labs - USA)*
Giacomo Inches *(University of Lugano, USI - Switzerland)*
Diana Inkpen *(SITE, University of Ottawa - Canada)*
Jagadeesh Jagarlamudi *(University of Maryland - USA)*
Adam Jatowt *(Kyoto University - Japan)*
Jiwoon Jeon *(Google - USA)*
Jing Jiang *(Singapore Management University - Singapore)*
Daxin Jiang *(Microsoft Research Asia - China)*
Rong Jin *(Michigan State University - USA)*
Hideo Joho *(University of Tsukuba - Japan)*
Leszek Kaliciak *(Robert Gordon University - UK)*
Jaap Kamps *(University of Amsterdam - The Netherlands)*
Noriko Kando *(National Institute of Informatics - Japan)*
Nattiya Kanhabua *(L3S Research Center - Germany)*
Evangelos Kanoulas *(Google - Switzerland)*
Sarvnaz Karimi *(CSIRO - Australia)*
Maryam Karimzadehgan *(University of Illinois at Urbana - Champaign - USA)*
Mostafa Keikha *(University of Lugano - Switzerland)*
Diane Kelly *(University of North Carolina Chapel Hill - USA)*
Jinyoung Kim *(University of Massachusetts, Amherst - USA)*
Seokhwan Kim *(Institute for Infocomm Research - Singapore)*
Jin-Dong Kim *(Database Center for Life Science - Japan)*
Donald Kraft *(Department of Computer Science - USA)*
Anagha Kulkarni *(Carnegie Mellon University - USA)*
Giridhar Kumaran *(Microsoft Corporation - USA)*
Oren Kurland *(Technion - Israel)*
Dmitry Lagun *(Emory University - USA)*
Mounia Lalmas *(Yahoo! Research - Spain)*
Ni Lao *(Carnegie Mellon University - USA)*
Guy Lapalme *(Université de Montréal - Canada)*
Ray Larson *(University of California, Berkeley - USA)*
Neal Lathia *(University of Cambridge - UK)*
Matthew Lease *(University of Texas at Austin - USA)*
Gary Geunbae Lee *(POSTECH - Republic of Korea)*
Jung-Tae Lee *(Korea University - Republic of Korea)*
Teerapong Leelanupab *(University of Glasgow-UK)*
Miro Lehtonen *(University of Helsinki - Finland)*
Elizabeth Liddy *(iSchool, Syracuse University - USA)*
Xia Lin *(Drexel University - USA)*
Christina Lioma *(University of Copenhagen - Denmark)*
Ting Liu *(Harbin Institute of Technology - China)*
Nathan Liu *(HKUST - Hong Kong, SAR)*
Robert Luk *(The Hong Kong Polytechnic University - Hong Kong, SAR)*
Yuanhua Lv *(UIUC - USA)*
Hao Ma *(Microsoft Research - USA)*
Andrew MacFarlane *(City University London - UK)*
Takuya Maekawa *(Osaka University - Japan)*
Prasenjit Majumder *(DAIICT - India)*
Yi Mao *(Microsoft - USA)*
Ilya Markov *(University of Lugano - Switzerland)*
Paul McNamee *(Johns Hopkins University - USA)*
Edgar Meij *(University of Amsterdam - Netherlands)*

Donald Metzler *(USC/ISI; USA - USA)*
Einat Minkov *(University of Haifa - Israel)*
Mandar Mitra *(Indian Statistical Institute - India)*
Stefano Mizzaro *(University of Udine - Italy)*
Marie - Francine Moens *(Katholieke Universiteit Leuven - Belgium)*
Alistair Moffat *(University of Melbourne - Australia)*
Yashar Moshfeghi *(University of Glasgow - UK)*
Vanessa Murdock *(Yahoo! Research - Spain)*
Preslav Nakov *(Qatar Computing Research Institute - Qatar)*
Michael Nelson *(Old Dominion University - USA)*
Charles Nicholas *(UMBC - USA)*
Jian - Yun Nie *(DIRO - University of Montreal - Canada)*
Tae - Gil Noh *(Heidelberg University - Germany)*
Jahna Otterbacher *(Illinois Institute of Technology - USA)*
Virgil Pavlu *(Northeastern University - USA)*
Jan Pedersen *(Microsoft - USA)*
Fuchun Peng *(Microsoft - USA)*
Karen Pinel - Sauvagnat *(IRIT - France)*
Tamara Polajnar *(University of Glasgow - UK)*
Luca Pretto *(University of Padova - Italy)*
Xiaoguang Qi *(Lehigh University - USA)*
Filip Radlinski *(Microsoft-UK)*
Hema Raghavan *(IBM Research - USA)*
Edie Rasmussen *(University of British Columbia - Canada)*
John Riedl *(University of Minnesota - USA)*
Adam Roegiest *(University of Waterloo - Canada)*
Haggai Roitman *(IBM Research Lab, Haifa - Israel)*
Dan Rose *(A9.com - USA)*
Jun Sakuma *(University of Tsukuba - Japan)*
Fabrizio Sebastiani *(Consiglio Nazionale delle Ricerche - Italy)*
Kazuhiro Seki *(Kobe University - Japan)*
Jangwon Seo *(Google Inc. - USA)*
Chirag Shah *(Rutgers University - USA)*
James G. Shanahan *(Church and Duncan Group Inc. - USA)*
Milad Shokouhi *(Microsoft - UK)*
Gianmaria Silvello *(University of Padova - Italy)*
Fabrizio Silvestri *(Information Science and Technology Institute - Italy)*
Khe Chai Sim *(National University of Singapore - Singapore)*
David Smith *(University of Massachusetts Amherst - USA)*
Padmini Srinivasan *(The University of Iowa - USA)*
Vassilios Stathopoulos *(University College London-UK)*
Juliane Stiller *(Humboldt Universitaet zu Berlin - Germany)*
Aixin Sun *(Nanyang Technological University - Singapore)*
Mingxuan Sun *(Georgia Institute of Technology - USA)*
Shanu Sushmita *(University of Glasgow - UK)*
S.M.M. Tahaghoghi *(Microsoft - USA)*
John Tait *(johntait.net Ltd. - UK)*
Bin Tan *(Amazon - USA)*
Carla Teixeira Lopes *(University of Porto - Portugal)*
Simone Teufel *(University of Cambridge - UK)*
Ulrich Thiel *(Fraunhofer - Germany)*
James Thom *(RMIT - Australia)*
Paul Thomas *(CSIRO - Australia)*
Paul Thompson *(Dartmouth College - USA)*
Qi Tian *(University of Texas at San Antonio - USA)*
Anastasios Tombros *(Queen Mary, University of London- UK)*
Ricardo Torres *(University of Campinas (UNICAMP) - Brazil)*
Andrew Trotman *(University of Otago - New Zealand)*
Sarah Tyler *(University of California, Santa Cruz - USA)*
Sumithra Velupillai *(Stockholm University - Sweden)*
Vitaliy Vitsentiy *(Ternopil National Economic University - Ukraine)*
Stephen Wan *(CSIRO - Australia)*
Xiaojun Wan *(Peking University - China)*
Taifeng Wang *(Microsoft Research Asia - China)*
Changhu Wang *(Microsoft Research Asia - China)*
Lidan Wang *(University of Maryland, College Park - USA)*
Xin - Jing Wang *(Microsoft Research Asia - China)*
Mengqiu Wang *(Stanford University - USA)*
Wouter Weerkamp *(University of Amsterdam - Netherlands)*
John Whissell *(University of Waterloo - Canada)*
Tak - Lam Wong *(The Hong Kong Institute of Education - Hong Kong, SAR)*
Jun Xu *(Microsoft Research Asia - China)*
Xiaobing Xue *(University of Massachusetts, Amherst - USA)*
Grace Hui Yang *(Georgetown University - USA)*
Jiang - Ming Yang *(Microsoft - China)*
Emine Yilmaz *(Microsoft Research Cambridge - UK)*
Minoru Yoshida *(University of Tokyo - Japan)*
Xiaojun Yuan *(University at Albany, SUNY - USA)*
Dell Zhang *(Birkbeck, University of London - UK)*
Zhongfei Zhang *(State University of New York at Binghamton - USA)*
Min Zhang *(Tsinghua University - China)*
Peng Zhang *(Robert Gordon University, Aberdeen - UK)*
Lanbo Zhang *(University of California, Santa Cruz - USA)*
Dong Zhou *(Trinity College Dublin - Ireland)*
Guido Zuccon *(CSIRO - Australia)*

Additional Poster Reviewers

Marco Bressan *(University of Padova - Italy)*
Peter Golbus *(Northeastern University - USA)*
Xiang - Fei Jia *(University of Otago - New Zealand)*
Anne - Laure Ligozat *(LIMSI - CNRS & ENSIIE - France)*
Xian - Ming Liu *(Harbin Institute of Technology - China)*
David Milne *(CSIRO - Australia)*
Xinmei Tian *(University of Science and Technology of China - China)*
Wengang Zhou *(University of Texas at San Antonio - USA)*

Demonstrations Committee

Falk Scholer *(RMIT University - Australia) – Chair*
Mark D. Smucker *(University of Waterloo - Canada) – Chair*
Andrew Turpin *(University of Melbourne - Australia) – Chair*

Mikhail Ageev *(Moscow State University - Russian Federation)*
John Akinyemi *(University of Waterloo - Canada)*
Omar Alonso *(Microsoft - USA)*
Hany Azzam *(Queen Mary, University of London - UK)*
Alberto Barrón-Cedeño *(Universidad Politécnica de Valencia - Spain)*
Steve Beitzel *(Applied Communication Sciences - USA)*
Kevyn Collins-Thompson *(Microsoft Research - USA)*
Silviu Cucerzan *(Microsoft Research - USA)*
Sally Jo Cunningham *(Wakaito University - New Zealand)*
Giorgio Maria Di Nunzio *(University of Padova - Italy)*
Debora Donato *(Yahoo! Labs - USA)*
Georges Dupret *(Yahoo! Labs - USA)*
Jianping Fan *(UNC Charlotte - USA)*
Jiyin He *(Centrum Wiskunde & Informatica - Netherlands)*
Ben He *(Graduate University of Chinese Academy of Sciences - China)*
Vivian (Qinmin) Hu *(York University - Canada)*
Jiwoon Jeon *(Google - USA)*
Joemon Jose *(University of Glasgow - UK)*
Leszek Kaliciak *(Robert Gordon University - UK)*
Nattiya Kanhabua *(L3S Research Center - Germany)*
Jinyoung Kim *(University of Massachusetts, Amherst - USA)*
Giridhar Kumaran *(Microsoft - USA)*
Jochen Leidner *(Thomson Reuters - Switzerland)*
Christina Lioma (*University of Copenhagen - Denmark)*
Ting Liu *(Harbin Institute of Technology - China)*
Vibhu Mittal *(Root-1 - USA)*
Filip Radlinski *(Microsoft - UK)*
Edie Rasmussen *(University of British Columbia - Canada)*
Chirag Shah *(Rutgers University - USA)*
Rao Shen *(Yahoo! - USA)*
Milad Shokouhi *(Microsoft - UK)*
Juliane Stiller *(Humboldt Universitaet zu Berlin - Germany)*
Bin Tan *(Amazon - USA)*
Carla Teixeira Lopes *(University of Porto - Portugal)*
Ulrich Thiel *(Fraunhofer Gesellschaft - Germany)*
Anastasios Tombros *(Queen Mary, University of London-UK)*
Ricardo Torres *(University of Campinas - Brazil)*
John Whissell *(University of Waterloo - Canada)*
Jiang-Ming Yang *(Microsoft - China)*
Minoru Yoshida *(University of Tokyo - Japan)*
Dell Zhang *(Birkbeck, University of London - UK)*

Tutorial Committee

Henning Müller *(HES-SO, Sierre - Switzerland) - Chair*

Paul Clough *(University of Sheffield – United Kingdom)*
Allan Hanbury *(Technical University of Vienna - Austria)*
Preben Hansen *(SICS, Stockholm - Sweden)*
Jaap Kamps *(University of Amsterdam – The Netherlands)*
Liadh Kelly *(Dublin City University – Ireland)*
Birger Larsen *(Royal School of Library Science Copenhagen – Denmark)*
Jochen Leidner *(Linguit Ltd. - USA)*

Workshop Committee

Eugene Agichtein *(Emory University - USA) – Chair*
Vanessa Murdock *(Yahoo! Research - Spain) – Chair*

Best Paper Awards Committee

ChengXiang Zhai *(University of Illinois at Urbana-Champaign - USA) – Chair*

Tat-Seng Chua *(National University of Singapore - Singapore)*
Evgeniy Gabrilovich *(Google - USA)*
Shlomo Geva *(Queensland University of Technology - Australia)*
Paul B. Kantor *(Rutgers University - USA)*
Iadh Ounis *(University of Glasgow – United Kingdom)*
Luo Si *(Purdue University - USA)*
Ellen Voorhees *(NIST - USA)*
Arjen P. de Vries *(Centrum Wiskunde & Informatica - The Netherlands)*

Doctoral Consortium Committee

Maarten de Rijke (*University of Amsterdam - Netherlands*) - Chair
Mounia Lalmas (*Yahoo! Research - Spain*) - Chair

Peter Bruza *(Queensland University of Technology, Australia)*
Kevyn Collins-Thompson *(Microsoft Research - USA)*
David Hawking *(Funnelback and Australian National University - Australia)*
Gareth Jones *(Dublin City University - Ireland)*
Joemon Jose *(University of Glasgow – United Kingdom)*
Noriko Kando *(National Institute of Informatics - Japan)*
Oren Kurland *(Technion - Israel)*
Wai Lam *(The Chinese University of Hong Kong - Hong Kong, SAR)*
Prasenjit Majumder *(DAIICT - India)*
Isabelle Moulinier *(Thomson Reuters - USA)*
Jian-Yun Nie *(Université de Montréal - Canada)*
Tetsuya Sakai *(Microsoft Research Asia - China)*
Luo Si *(Purdue University - USA)*
Andrew Trotman *(University of Otago - New Zealand)*
Ellen Voorhees *(NIST - USA)*
Arjen P. de Vries *(Centrum Wiskunde & Informatica - The Netherlands)*
Cong Yu *(Google Research - USA)*
Yi Zhang *(University of California Santa Cruz - USA)*

Mentoring Committee

Douglas W. Oard *(University of Maryland - USA)* - Chair

Avi Arampatzis *(Democritus University of Thrace - Greece)*
Jimmy Lin *(University of Maryland - USA)*
Charles K. Nicholas *(University of Maryland, Baltimore County - USA)*

SIGIR 2012 Sponsors & Supporters

Sponsors

SIGIR
Special Interest Group
on Information Retrieval

Association for
Computing Machinery

Advancing Computing as a Science & Profession

Corporate Supporters

Gold Supporters

Microsoft® Research

Baidu 百度

Google™

Silver Supporter

YAHOO! LABS

Bronze Supporters

ebay® Research Labs

IBM Research

ORACLE®

Friends

MORGAN & CLAYPOOL PUBLISHERS

Springer
the language of science

CAMBRIDGE UNIVERSITY PRESS

UNIVERSITY OF OREGON
Applied Information Management
Master's Degree Program

now
the essence of knowledge

Other Supporters

OREGON HEALTH & SCIENCE UNIVERSITY

Salton Award Lecture
Information Retrieval as Engineering Science

Norbert Fuhr
Faculty of Engineering Sciences
University of Duisburg-Essen
Duisburg, Germany
norbert.fuhr@uni-due.de

Categories and Subject Descriptors

H.3.0 [**Information Storage and Retrieval**]: General

General Terms

Theory, Experimentation

Keywords

theoretic foundations, explanations, standardized testing

Extended Abstract

First, let me say how pleased I am to receive the Gerard Salton Award from SIGIR. His pioneering work strongly influenced our field for several decades. I had lively discussions with him at several occasions, especially during his stay with our research group in Darmstadt in 1988. We were following different theoretic approaches—he as inventor of the vector space model, myself as a young researcher being enthusiastic about probabilistic models—but the discussions with him improved my understanding of the commonalities and differences of both approaches, such as the role of representations, underlying assumptions and theoretic justifications.

Like my predecessors, here I want to give my personal view on information retrieval, by first presenting my own definition of the field, and then pointing out some areas for future research.

For me, IR deals with *vagueness and imprecision in information systems.* The imprecision is usually caused by the imperfection in the representation of the semantics and pragmatics of the objects stored, which are typically (multimedia) documents. Vagueness, on the other hand, is due to the fact that the user is not able to formulate her information need in a precise way; this leads to an iterative search process (which might even occur with databases for formatted data, like e. g. in product search in a Web shop).

This definition does not make the usual distinction between database (DB) and IR systems. In fact, in a certain aspect, I view IR as a kind of generalization of the former: The logical DB view interprets query processing as the task of finding those objects o for a query q for which the implication $o \to q$ holds. Rijsbergen defined IR as being based on uncertain inference, i.e. determining the probability $P(d \to q)$ that document d implies the query. Thus, from a querying point of view, classic DBs can be regarded as a special case of IR (though probabilistic DBs have become a major research topic in the DB field in recent years).

However, the major difference between DB and IR lies in the consideration of the pragmatic level: The major goal of an IR system is to support the user in solving her current problem or fulfilling her task at hand. Thus, standard IR evaluation is based on the concept of relevance or, in the case of user-based experimentation, on task-related criteria like task time or success rate. In contrast, the DB field delegates the pragmatic aspects to the application layer, which is beyond the DB scope.

Now let me turn to the major topic of this paper: IR as an engineering discipline. Certainly, many people working in this field would feel themselves as IR "engineers", i.e. they apply and extend known methods for solving new problems. However, a civil engineer planning a new building, a mechanical engineer constructing a new machine or an electrical engineer designing a new device—they all build upon a rich portfolio of basic findings and theoretic models, which not only allow them to solve the problem, but also make predictions about the result of their efforts (as well as knowing the limits of their methods). In analogy, assume an IR "engineer" being confronted with the task of designing a system for a new collection of documents and a new type of information needs—would she be able to guarantee a certain MAP or an average search task completion time? Rather not—instead, the standard practice is to try out some of the existing methods and tune them for the specific case—then an evaluation will show if and how well this system works.

So we might wonder what is required for constructing an IR system like in other engineering disciplines? I think we need two things that allow us to build upon, namely 1) theoretic models, and 2) solid empirical evidence.

On the theory side, the basis is rather small. E.g., for the case of ad-hoc retrieval, we have the probability ranking principle, various models based on it (like the classical probabilistic models, the principle of uncertain inference, and language models / divergence from randomness), and the term weighting axioms. These frameworks tell us *how* to achieve good or even optimum retrieval performance, provided that the underlying assumptions hold. However, we hardly have theories that tell us *why* certain methods work and others don't. From an engineering perspective, we would like to know how document features like length, language, domain, genre, structure or the term definition (single words, phrases, named entities etc.) affect quality

Copyright is held by the author/owner(s).
SIGIR'12, August 12–16, 2012, Portland, Oregon, USA.
ACM 978-1-4503-1472-5/12/08.

(and why)—and in a similar way, also for the topic characteristics as well as the relevance definition. Alas, we can hardly answer any of these questions.

On the empirical side, we have a vast amount of papers presenting numerous variants of existing models and methods, along with experimental results. This is partly a consequence of favoring experimental over theoretic work in our field. However, in the light of our general theme of IR as engineering science, this development was not helpful, for two major reasons:

1. We are not able to give a fully satisfying explanations of the outcomes of the experiments performed. Since we are mainly focusing on retrieval quality, too little attention is paid to the different factors affecting the results, like e. g. the representation used, the various assumptions underlying the retrieval model, the method used for estimating the model parameters, or the specific properties of the test collections used; often, good or bad performance is attributed to 'the model', without investigating its various components or the influence of the other factors (or their combination).

2. We can not predict to what extent these findings can be generalized to other settings: For a single collection, it is impossible to tell how far we can generalize from this single point of observation. Even with multiple collections, given that each one represents a point in a high-dimensional parameter space (and we even don't know what the crucial parameters are), we can hardly define the area where interpolation is reasonable—plus the problem that these are stochastic experiments anyway, and we would need more observations to get a statistically significant result.

In order to draw any useful conclusions from experimental results, we need standardized test environments and test procedures for being able to aggregate knowledge from larger numbers of experimental studies. I know only of a single meta-study [1] that looked at papers proposing specific methods for improving the quality of ad-hoc retrieval, which used some of the official TREC and CLEF collections. Although all of the considered papers claimed some performance improvements over previous work, hardly any of them was actually able to beat the best official run for the corresponding collection—the authors had been cheating by using poor baselines for comparison. This experience calls for more standardized experimentation, so that experimental results can be compared immediately.

Unfortunately, in recent years, we have seen a trend in the opposite direction: A large fraction of the papers at the top IR venues publish experimental results using proprietary collections. Thus, the experiments presented cannot be repeated by other researchers. This procedure does not satisfy the basic requirements for empirical scientific work, and it is kind of surprising how the IR community tolerates this violation of scientific standards. Proprietary data not only eases cheating (as we are no longer able to find out, this might even increase the frequency of this kind of misconduct), the major problem is the impediment of scientific progress: If someone has an idea on how to improve over the method presented in a paper (and the vast majority of our research is of that kind), then there is no possibility to perform this research, since the data used for the previous work is inaccessible. Some people claim that it would be sufficient to describe the major characteristics of the data used, so that other researchers could set up a similar test collection to perform that work. However, we are far away from such an approach—we just don't know the relevant features that determine retrieval quality and thus would allow for repeating IR experiments with different collections.

However, even with the best experimental standards, it is mainly theoretic work that will move our field forward towards an engineering discipline: A good theoretic model has a high explanatory power, and it is based on explicit assumptions. The former allows us to make predictions, and the latter specifies the conditions under which the model is applicable. A more detailed discussion of experimental vs. theoretic work in computer science can be found in [2], where the main conclusion can be summarized in the somewhat paradox statement "There is empirical evidence that the most important contributions to our field are not the experimental ones".

The above discussion has focused on classical, system oriented IR approaches, but it also holds for user-oriented approaches ([3, p. 105] calls for engineering in information seeking) as well as for new research areas in IR [?].

Empirical research is necessary, but it must be accompanied by strong theoretic models. IR evaluations should focus more on answering the *why* questions, and less on *how* to achieve good performance for the test collections at hand. Only this kind of research will put an IR engineer into the position to judge whether or not a specific model is applicable in a given situation, and then use it for making predictions about the properties of the system she is designing.

1. REFERENCES

[1] T. G. Armstrong, A. Moffat, W. Webber, and J. Zobel. Improvements that don't add up: ad-hoc retrieval results since 1998. In D. W.-L. Cheung, I.-Y. Song, W. W. Chu, X. Hu, and J. J. Lin, editors, *CIKM*, pages 601–610. ACM, 2009.

[2] G. Génova. Is computer science truly scientific? *Commun. ACM*, 53(7):37–39, 2010.

[3] P. Ingwersen and K. Järvelin. *The turn: integration of information seeking and retrieval in context.* Springer-Verlag New York, Inc., Secaucus, NJ, USA, 2005.

Keynote Talk

Retrieving Information from the Book of Humanity: The Personalized Medicine Data Tsunami Crashes on the Beach of Jeopardy

Daniel R. Masys
Affiliate Professor
Biomedical and Health Informatics
University of Washington
Seattle, Washington
dmasys@u.washington.edu

Abstract

From a mute but eloquent alphabet of 4 characters emerges a complex biological 'literature' whose highest expression is human existence. The rapidly advancing technologies of 'nextgen sequencing' will soon make it possible to inexpensively acquire and store the characters of our complete personal genetic instruction set and make it available for health assessment and disease management. This uniquely personal form of 'big data' brings with it challenges that will be discussed in this keynote presentation. Topics will include a brief introduction to the linguistic challenges of 'biology as literature', the impact of personal molecular variation on traditional approaches to disease prevention, diagnosis and treatment, and the challenges of information retrieval when a large volume of primary observations is made that is associated with an evanescent and rapidly changing corpus of scientific interpretation of those primary observations. Experience with extracting high quality pheonotypes from electronic medical records has shown that Natural Language Processing capability is an essential information extraction function for correlation of clinical events with personal genetic variation. Any powerful set of information can be used or misused, and put those who depend upon it in jeopardy. These issues, and a lesson from the long running Jeopardy TV series, will be discussed.

Categories and Subject Descriptors

J.3 [**Life and Medical Sciences**] Biology and Genetics, Medical Information Systems, H.3.1 [**Content Analysis and Indexing**] Linguistic Processing

General Terms

Algorithms, Management, Languages, Theory

Keywords

Human genome, personalized medicine, genotypes, phenotypes.

Copyright is held by the author/owner(s).
SIGIR'12, August 12–16, 2012, Portland, Oregon, USA.
ACM 978-1-4503-1472-5/12/08.

Bio

Dr. Daniel R. Masys is an Affiliate Professor of Biomedical and Health Informatics in the Department of Biomedical Informatics and Medical Education at the University of Washington, Seattle, School of Medicine. Previously he served as Professor and Chair of the Department of Biomedical Informatics and Professor of Medicine at the Vanderbilt University School of Medicine. An honors graduate of Princeton University and the Ohio State University College of Medicine, he completed postgraduate training in Internal Medicine, Hematology and Medical Oncology at the University of California, San Diego, and the Naval Regional Medical Center, San Diego. He served as Chief of the International Cancer Research Data Bank of the National Cancer Institute, National Institutes of Health, and was also Director of the Lister Hill National Center for Biomedical Communications, which is a computer research and development division of the National Library of Medicine. He also served as Director of Biomedical Informatics at the University of California, San Diego School of Medicine, Director of the UCSD Human Research Protections Program, and Professor of Medicine.

Dr. Masys is an elected member of the Institute of Medicine of the National Academy of Sciences. He is a Diplomate of the American Board of Internal Medicine in Medicine, Hematology, and Medical Oncology. He is a Fellow of the American College of Physicians, and Fellow and Past President of the American College of Medical Informatics. His research interests include development of informatics infrastructure for conducting clinical and translational research, genome-phenome correlation using phenotype data derived from electronic medical records data, and approaches to incorporating genomic data effectively into clinical systems.

Adaptation of the Concept Hierarchy Model with Search Logs for Query Recommendation on Intranets

Ibrahim Adeyanju
IDEAS Research Institute
The Robert Gordon University
St Andrews Street, Aberdeen
AB25 1HG, Scotland, UK
i.adeyanju@rgu.ac.uk

Dawei Song
School of Computer Science
Tianjin University, China &
Department of Computing
Open University, UK
dawei.song@open.ac.uk

M-Dyaa Albakour
School of Computer Science
and Electronic Engineering
University of Essex
Colchester C04 3SQ, UK
malbak@essex.ac.uk

Udo Kruschwitz
School of Computer Science
and Electronic Engineering
University of Essex
Colchester C04 3SQ, UK
udo@essex.ac.uk

Anne De Roeck
Centre for Research in
Computing
Open University, Walton Hall
Milton Keynes MK7 6AA, UK
a.deroeck@open.ac.uk

Maria Fasli
School of Computer Science
and Electronic Engineering
University of Essex
Colchester C04 3SQ, UK
mfasli@essex.ac.uk

ABSTRACT

A concept hierarchy created from a document collection can be used for query recommendation on Intranets by ranking terms according to the strength of their links to the query within the hierarchy. A major limitation is that this model produces the same recommendations for identical queries and rebuilding it from scratch periodically can be extremely inefficient due to the high computational costs. We propose to adapt the model by incorporating query refinements from search logs. Our intuition is that the concept hierarchy built from the collection and the search logs provide complementary conceptual views on the same search domain, and their integration should continually improve the effectiveness of recommended terms. Two adaptation approaches using query logs with and without click information are compared. We evaluate the concept hierarchy models (static and adapted versions) built from the Intranet collections of two academic institutions and compare them with a state-of-the-art log-based query recommender, the Query Flow Graph, built from the same logs. Our adaptive model significantly outperforms its static version and the query flow graph when tested over a period of time on data (documents and search logs) from two institutions' Intranets.

Categories and Subject Descriptors

H.3.3 [**Information Systems**]: Information Search and Retrieval

Keywords

Log Analysis, Query Suggestions, Concept Hierarchy

Permission to make digital or hard copies of all or part of this work for personal or classroom use is granted without fee provided that copies are not made or distributed for profit or commercial advantage and that copies bear this notice and the full citation on the first page. To copy otherwise, to republish, to post on servers or to redistribute to lists, requires prior specific permission and/or a fee.
SIGIR'12, August 12–16, 2012, Portland, Oregon, USA.
Copyright 2012 ACM 978-1-4503-1472-5/12/08 ...$10.00.

1. INTRODUCTION

The need to assist a user in finding relevant information has led to continuous changes in the functionalities of search engines. Prominent internet search engines now provide user-friendly features such as query auto-completion, query refinement lists and visual representation of related concepts to the query in addition to the typical ranked list of retrieved documents (e.g. Google, Bing and Yahoo! Web search engines). These extra features are expected to make it easier and quicker for a user's information need to be satisfied. We focus on the techniques used for generating suitable refinements to a current (or an initial) query, known as *query recommendation*, which is one of the interactive features in modern search engines.

Although lots of models have been proposed for recommending query refinement terms, most have exploited the document collection or previous search logs but not both. Our intuition is that these two approaches to query recommendation provide complementary conceptual views on the same search domain. Recommendations from the collection typically discover relationships between terms based on statistical analysis giving a conceptual view of the domain. On the other hand, the search logs provide a conceptual view of the domain based on collective user intelligence. Each approach also has its inherent weakness. For instance, the search logs approach might not be able to give any suggestions for new queries that were never used in the past. On the other hand, the document collection approach might give too many unsuitable suggestions for current queries that have a very high document frequency leading to a statistical relationship with many of the terms in the collection. Therefore, our hypothesis is that the integration of the two approaches will improve the query recommendation quality and in turn the retrieval performance. A conceptual view of the search domain would be a natural bridge and common foundation for the two approaches.

Specifically, we propose the integration of these two approaches by continuously adapting the concept hierarchy model built from a document collection with user interactions derived from query logs. The concept subsumption hierarchy [24] is a good choice as a simple but effective approach to query recommendation. Our research focuses on Intranet search which (similar to Enterprise search) is different from Web search [15]. The document collection on an Intranet is relatively small and changes less frequently. It is thus feasible to build a domain model to reflect the conceptual structure within the collection. In this scenario, the topic structure generated by the concept hierarchy might map onto a pre-defined structure in the organisation. For example, a concept hierarchy model generated from documents in an academic institution's Intranet might show the relationship between lecturers and the courses they teach, research students and their supervisors, or academic staff and their research interests. On an Intranet, it can also be expected that identical queries are more likely to be related to the same user information need since the context of search is more limited than in Internet search. Therefore, previous user interactions can be used to improve a new user search by suggesting query refinement terms from a previous session with a similar query. Query terms used in the same session also implies that they are related and can be used to improve query recommendation models.

In this paper, we propose a novel method to adapt the model with search logs and compare with its static equivalent as a baseline which does not incorporate any previous user interactions. We also compare these hierarchy models (static and adaptive) with a state-of-the-art adaptive query recommendation approach called the query flow graph model [6] which is built solely from search logs. We test the effectiveness of these models using an automated evaluation based on query log data by experimenting with search logs obtained from two academic institutions' search engines.

Section 2 discusses related work on query recommendation and utilization of search logs to improve information seeking. We then provide in-depth details of the concept hierarchy model, how we utilise it for generating query refinement terms and our proposed method for adaptation with search logs in Sections 3, 4 and 5. Section 6 explains our experimental set-up while evaluation results are discussed in Section 7. We conclude the paper in Section 8 by outlining our main contributions and plans for future work.

2. RELATED WORK

Recommendation of refinements to queries is a common feature of modern search engines, both general and specialised ones. Determining the best terms to recommend remains a challenge as this depends on the combination of several factors. However, studies have indicated that users prefer having suggestions regardless of their usefulness [23, 26, 27]. Knowledge of the query's context, which can be a function of the user's knowledge about the domain, previous search queries, etc., is a crucial factor when suggesting terms that help a user find specific information faster. The two main resources available for query recommendation are the document collection (including anchor logs) [28, 24, 10, 18, 20, 13] and search logs [3, 19, 12, 4, 17, 6, 5, 7, 8], which can also be used as forms of implicit or explicit feedback to re-rank retrieved documents.

The approaches that utilise the collection discover relationships between terms using all documents (global) [9, 13] or those retrieved as relevant to a query (local) [24, 10]. Terms considered as related to the query are then recommended for query refinement or automatically used for query expansion. These techniques are therefore less dependent on any user feedback (implicit or explicit) but require updates to their recommendation models when there is a significant change in the underlying collection if their suggestions are mined from all documents. This method is perhaps most useful for new search engines with little or no query logs.

Query search logs, on the other hand, provide real user experience which can be mined to discover useful local or global patterns. Query recommendations can be said to be local if they are based only on each user's previous searches [19], while global recommendations are derived from a group of users or all users [6, 8]. The main drawback is that logs have to be collected over a period of time before such techniques can be applied since data from one search engine might not be easily applicable to others, especially for Intranets.

Mining post-query click behaviour has been studied and applied in information retrieval tasks. For example, using landing page information to derive query suggestions [12] and mining user search trails for search result ranking [26], where the presence of a page on a trail increases its query relevance. Click graphs were also used to derive labels to short-cut search trails to help users reach target pages efficiently [25]. Since users are typically reluctant to provide explicit feedback on the usefulness of ranked results returned for a search query, automatic extraction of implicit feedback has continued to be exploited by researchers. Click-through data is one form of implicit feedback left by users, which can be used to learn the retrieval ranking function [17]. Queries and clicks can be interpreted as "soft relevance judgements" [11] to find out the user's actual intention and interests. Query recommendations can then be derived, for example, by looking at submitted queries and building query flow graphs [6, 7], query-click graphs [11], cover graphs [4] or association rules [14]. Mining query logs has also been combined with query similarity measures to derive query modifications [19].

The Query flow graph model (QFG) [6] has been successfully applied to mine query suggestions from query logs. It is a directed graph, which contains a set of nodes consisting of all distinct queries submitted to a search engine, while the edges between two nodes represent a user query refinement. Edges are weighted primarily based on the frequency of such refinements, though the actual weighting function depends on the application. Recommendations can be made for a query if it is found in any of the QFG nodes by obtaining terms at the end of all edges that emerge from the query node. These terms can then be ranked based on the weights of the edges leading to them from the query node. In this paper, we compare the concept hierarchy used in our work to QFG since they are both directed graph structures but one is typically built from a document collection while the other is built from query logs.

3. CONCEPT HIERARCHY MODEL

The concept hierarchy model [24] was initially introduced to assist users to browse the top documents returned by a search engine by showing the topic structure in the retrieved documents. A hierarchical tree, where specialised concepts or terms are subsumed by more generic ones, is generated automatically using an unsupervised algorithm based on a statistical co-occurrence measure. Hence, we adopt the acronym SHReC (**S**ubsumption **H**ierarchy for **Re**sult

Clustering) of an existing implementation[1] and use this to refer to the concept hierarchy model in this paper. Although SHReC was introduced for clustering retrieval results, it can easily be applied to an Intranet collection. This model can be utilised for suggesting terms for query refinements (addition or replacement) by showing a sub-tree from the initial hierarchy encapsulating the given query as used in [18]. A more intuitive way to utilise the model for query refinement is to transform terms in the sub-tree encapsulating the query into a ranked list based on the strength/closeness of their links to the query in the SHReC graph.

3.1 Building the SHReC Model

The SHReC model is automatically derived as a hierarchical organization of concepts from a set of documents without using training data or standard clustering techniques [24]. The basic idea is to use term co-occurrence to create a subsumption hierarchical tree. The generality or specificity of a term (or concept) in the model is determined mainly by its document frequency. The more documents a term appears in, the more general it is assumed to be. The conditions for subsumption are therefore dependent on document frequencies. It should be noted that a term as used in this paper for the SHReC model is the equivalent of a concept and does not necessarily mean a single keyword. A term could be an entire query which can be formulated as a word, keyword, phrase or n-grams. A term 'x' is said to subsume 'y' when Equation 1 is met; where α is the strength of subsumption.

$$P(x \mid y) \geq \alpha \wedge P(y \mid x) < 1 \quad (1)$$

The relationship between 'x' and 'y' are derived from statistical probabilities of their co-occurrence in the collection. Operationally, if *df* is a function that returns the document frequency of a given term, $df(x) > df(y)$ and $df(x \wedge y)/df(y) \geq \alpha$. Although $\alpha = 1$ is ideal for a complete subsumption, a slightly smaller value can be chosen in order to allow few occurrences of term 'y' with other terms other than 'x'. $\alpha = 0.8$ was chosen in [24] based on empirical studies and we used the same α value in our work.

3.2 SHReC from an Intranet collection

Although the original SHReC model was built from top documents returned by a search engine given a query, we extended this to build the model from a substantial crawl of an Intranet collection. SHReC can be viewed as a directed graph $G_{SHReC} = (V, E, w)$ where:

- V is a set of nodes containing all the unique concepts or terms derived from documents in the Intranet collection with a special node 'SHReC root' representing the root of the graph tree;
- $E \subset V \times V$ is the set of directed edges;
- $w : E \rightarrow (0..1]$ is a weighting function that assigns to every pair of terms $(x, y) \in E$ a weight $w(x, y)$.

Generating a list of suitable candidate terms or concepts (V) to occur in the model is not trivial in our case since unlike in the original subsumption hierarchy approach, we do not have a current query to guide the selection of related terms. We must therefore ensure that our candidate terms cover a reasonable proportion of the vocabulary that users might employ to formulate their queries. Meanwhile, the computational complexity associated with building a SHReC model must also be considered. This is because each candidate term should be compared with all other terms to obtain their co-occurrence document frequency. For example, a list of 50,000 candidate terms will require about 2.5 billion (50000^2) co-occurrence checks between terms while building the model.

A generic approach will be to extract all unique keywords found in the collection as candidate terms. Additional candidates can then be generated by extracting n-grams (phrases) from documents in the collection that contain these unique keywords to cater for queries that contain more than one keyword. The maximum size of n in each n-gram should be limited to a small number (≤ 5) as users are less likely to use longer phrases from an analysis of the query logs available to us. The extracted n-grams can also be restricted to those that match a particular syntactic pattern (e.g. Noun Preposition Noun for a 3-gram) [21].

[1]http://shrec.sourceforge.net/

4. SHReC AS A QUERY RECOMMENDER

We employ the SHReC model for suggesting useful terms for query refinement in order to satisfy a user's information need. We propose to do so by finding a given query in the model and suggesting more generalised (immediate ancestor) and specialised (immediate descendants) terms related to the query in the hierarchy. These terms are ranked based on the weighting function shown in Equation 2. The function implicitly combines the subsumption ratio ($df(x \wedge y)/df(y)$) and document frequency ratio ($df(y)/df(x)$) between any two terms ('x' subsumes 'y') in the model. The subsumption ratio is the quotient of the co-occurrence document frequency ($df(x \wedge y)$) and the child's document frequency, and is used to determine subsumption between terms in the hierarchy (see Equation 1). The document frequency ratio is the ratio of the document frequencies of two connected terms in SHReC. It ensures that the closer the document frequencies of two directly linked terms, the more useful they are as a refinement for one another.

$$\text{If 'x' subsumes 'y', then } w(x, y) = df(x \wedge y)/df(x) \quad (2)$$

Figure 1 shows a sample SHReC model to illustrate its use for query recommendation. We only show the computation of weights for the link between terms 'A' and others to avoid cluttering the diagram. Given a query such as term 'F' in the figure, our technique will suggest terms 'H', 'C', 'G', 'B' and 'A', ranked in order of their computed weights (w).

The example above assumes that term 'F' would be found in the model irrespective of whether it is a keyword or phrase. This is not intuitive as it means that a lot of queries might not be matched in the model. Since many queries are likely to be formulated as phrases and might contain more than one word, one or more of the query words might occur separately in the model. Therefore when a query is not found in the model, its keywords are extracted and suggestions are provided by aggregating the recommendations from each of this keyword. The combined recommendations are re-ranked based on magnitude of their weights with respect to the keyword that recommend them. This should reduce the number of times a suggestion is not made, since previous works [27, 26] have found that users prefer to be provided suggestions regardless of their usefulness.

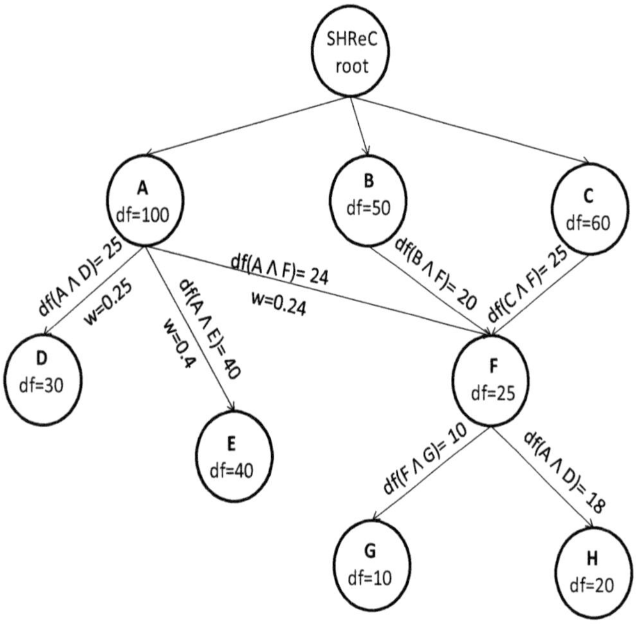

Figure 1: An example SHReC model

5. ADAPTIVE SHReC MODEL

In order to improve the effectiveness of query refinement recommendations from the SHReC model, we propose its adaptation with users' search logs. This ensures that query terms not captured during the creation of the SHReC model are incorporated into the model. Adaptation with query logs can be seen as an amalgamation of the query flow graph model [6] (see Section 2) and SHReC. The adaptation process is carried out for pairs of query refinements found at periodic intervals (e.g. every week) to minimise its computational cost. In a live system, such adaptation will be programmed to take place at a time when the search engine is least busy such as past midnight on Sunday morning in preparation for the new week. We start with an initial SHReC model built as described in Section 4 and then continuously update the model with the refinement terms found in the search logs. The weight of each refinement in the log is computed as shown in Equation 3. Such refinements might be restricted to only those in which there was at least a click after refining the current query or all refinements found in the logs for the adaptation period. The total frequency is cumulative so that collective user intelligence is taken into account rather than those for just that periodic interval.

$$\text{for x} \rightarrow \text{y}, \ logWeight(x,y) = \frac{totalFrequency(x \rightarrow y)}{totalFrequency(x \rightarrow *)} \quad (3)$$

where * is any term apart from 'x' found as a refinement of 'x' in the logs from inception of SHReC adaptation. Function *totalFrequency* is also computed cumulatively from the beginning of the adaptation process.

The adaptation process is formalised with the pseudo-code listed in Algorithm 1. It starts with the normalisation (as listed in Algorithm 2) of weights w for each edge in the initial SHReC built from the document collection only (Lines 1-3 of Algorithm 1), so that the total weight of all edges originating from a term node sums up to 1. The weights of new refinement terms added to the model from the logs will also have values between 0 and 1. The function $norm(G_{SHReC})$ therefore ensures that the weights of newly added terms are comparable to those already in the SHReC graph. The weights of edges from the initial SHReC are kept in w' for updates with the log weights. This ensures the original SHReC weights remain influential and comparable to the log weights.

Each unique query refinement (reformulation) pair found in the query logs between the periodic interval used for adaptation is then incorporated into the model. We cater for all possible scenarios as shown by the conditional statements listed on Lines 5, 7, 9 and 11 of the main adaptation algorithm. We update the weights between refinement terms in the model if both already exist by adding the weight calculated from the query logs to the current normalised SHReC weights (Line 6). When only one of the terms exist in the current SHReC, the other term is added (as parent or child) with the weights of the edge between them initialised to the computed weights from the logs (Line 8 & 10). Both

Algorithm 1 Adapting SHReC with query logs

Require: $G_{SHReC} = (V, E, w)$, a concept hierarchy graph
Require: $G_{normSHReC}$, normalised SHReC
Require: $R = \{r_1, \ldots, r_n\}$, reformulations in test period
Require: $r_i = x \rightarrow y$, query 'x' reformulated as query 'y'
Require: $lw(r_i) = logWeight(x, y)$, log weights (Eqn 3)
1: **if** (Inception of original SHReC's adaptation) **then**
2: $G_{normSHReC}{=}norm(G_{SHReC}){=}\ (V, E, w_{adapted}, w')$ (from Algorithm 2)
3: **end if**
4: **for each** $r_i \in R$ **do**
5: **if** $x \in V$ AND $y \in V$ **then**
6: $G_{normSHReC}$.updateweights$(x, y, lw(r_i))$ i.e. $w_{adapted}(x, y) \leftarrow w'(r_i) + lw(r_i)$
7: **else if** $x \in V$ AND $y \notin V$ **then**
8: $G_{normSHReC}$.addDescendant$(x, y, lw(r_i))$ i.e. $w_{adapted}(x, y) \leftarrow lw(r_i)$
9: **else if** $x \notin$ SHReC AND $y \in$ SHReC **then**
10: $G_{normSHReC}$.addAscendant$(y, x, lw(r_i))$ i.e. $w_{adapted}(x, y) \leftarrow lw(r_i)$
11: **else**
12: $G_{normSHReC}$.add$(x, y, lw(r_i))$ i.e. $w_{adapted}(x, y) \leftarrow lw(r_i)$
13: **end if**
14: **end for**

Algorithm 2 Function $norm(G_{SHReC})$

Input: $G_{SHReC} = (V, E, w)$, a concept hierarchy graph
Output: $G_{normSHReC} = (V, E, w_{adapted}, w')$
w' stores normalised weights for terms in original SHReC
1: **for each** $v \in V$ **do**
2: $sum \leftarrow 0$
3: OUT $\leftarrow$ getAllOutNodes(v), where $OUT \subset V$
4: **for each** $o \in OUT$ **do**
5: $sum += w(v, o)$
6: **end for**
7: **for each** $o \in OUT$ **do**
8: $w'(v, o) \leftarrow w(v, o)/sum$
9: **end for**
10: **end for**
11: **return** $G_{normSHReC}$

terms are added into the graph if they do not currently exist using weights computed from logs (Line 12). We do not re-normalise after updates because w' is always from the original SHReC and the weights from the logs are computed from cumulative frequency. Normalising and adding cumulative log weights will mean that refinements in previous adaptation periods contribute more than to the weight updates thereby giving them undue advantage.

Figure 2(i) illustrates the normalisation step of the adaptation process using a sub-tree from Figure 1. The sum of w' from node 'A' equals to 1. We then exemplify other steps of the adaptation process in Figure 2(ii). Here, the refinements from the query logs during the adaptation period from inception are assumed to be the three shown in the rectangle at the top-right corner of the figure with the log weights calculated using Equation 3. The effect of the adaptation is that the link to 'F' is given more weights than others because this refinement is found in both the logs and SHReC model: $w_{adapted}(A, F) \leftarrow w'(A, F) + lw(A, F)$ from Line 6 of Algorithm 1. The ranking of the recommendation also changes since some of the log weights are higher than those from the original SHReC. For instance, term 'Q' will be ranked higher than 'D' during query recommendation.

6. EXPERIMENTAL SETUP

Our aim is to improve a user's search experience by suggesting refinement terms related to a current query. Recommended terms can be useful as they can assist users in choosing the right query terminology that leads them to most relevant documents. The expectation is that the refined query will result in more relevant results than the current query, thereby making it easier and quicker for a user to find required information. We evaluate the effectiveness of query refinement terms recommended by the following three models.

1. S_SHReC, static SHReC built from only the Intranet document collection (see Section 4) and is not updated in any form throughout the test period.

2. A_SHReC, our adaptive SHReC discussed in Section 5 in which refinements extracted from search logs are continually incorporated at periodic intervals. Two forms of adaptation are carried out.

    (a) Using query logs without click information. In this case, we use all refinements from the query irrespective of whether or not there is a click on resulting documents after refinement.

    (b) Using query logs with click information. In this case, we consider the click information as another signal for implicit feedback where we use only refinements in which there is at least one click on results immediately after refinement.

3. QFG, a Query Flow Graph[6] discussed in Section 2 built continually at periodic intervals from the same search logs. Our version of QFG ranks only the immediate nodes coming out of a query node rather than all nodes in the graph. This is because the top ranked recommendations are always those nearest to the query node and we are able to reduce the expensive computational costs associated with ranking all nodes in the graph for the query. It also ensures that QFG's recommendation method is comparable to SHReC's, extracted only from immediate nodes related to a query node in SHReC. QFG was built using all refinements in the logs as well as only those in which there was at least one click immediately after reformulation, for comparison with the adaptive SHReC versions. Lastly, when a query is not found in the model, it is tokenised into keywords (just like SHReC) and suggestions aggregated from the recommendations that resulted from each of its token. The combined recommendations are then re-ranked based on magnitude of their weights with respect to the tokens that recommend them.

These models are evaluated extensively with an automated evaluation methodology which utilises real user logs. The datasets (web crawl and search logs for two academic institutions' Intranets) used in our experiments are described in Section 6.1. Our evaluation methodology is described in Section 6.2, followed by specific details of how we built the SHReC model used in our experiments in Section 6.3.

6.1 Datasets

The data (documents collection and search logs) used in our experiments were obtained from the Intranets of two UK academic institutions namely University of Essex and The Open University, referred to as *Essex* and *OU* respectively. The document collections were created by crawling the main websites of the institutions with Nutch[2]. We limited each crawl to a maximum depth of fifteen and simulated the Intranet search engines of the institutions on our machines using Apache Solr[3]. This allows us to obtain the document frequency of any term and co-occurrence document frequency of any two terms required for SHReC creation. The crawls for *Essex* and *OU* were done in July 2011 and October 2011 containing 77,841 and 220,059 documents respectively.

The search log data used in our experiments are obtained from the Intranet search engines of *Essex* and *OU*. Each search record contains the user query, a transaction time stamp, a session identifier and URLs visited by the user. Query refinements are extracted from queries in each session based on their time stamp. We used logs of 12 weeks between February and May 2011 for our evaluation. The total number of queries entered during this period were 32,212 and 117,358 for *Essex* and *OU* respectively.

6.2 Evaluation methodology

We use an automated evaluation framework, *AutoEval*, which measures the effectiveness of query recommendations over a period of time based on actual query logs [2]. The evaluation framework was validated with a user study which showed that scores from the automated evaluation correlated highly with user evaluation of the recommendations. The query recommender models are evaluated automatically by comparing the actual refinements observed in the log files, for which there is at least one user click on results after refinement, to those proposed by a model. In other words, we interpret a user click after a reformulation as presence of a relevant suggestion.

Each model is evaluated continuously at periodic intervals. In our experiments, this is done on a weekly basis. The logs

[2]http://nutch.apache.org/

[3]http://lucene.apache.org/solr/

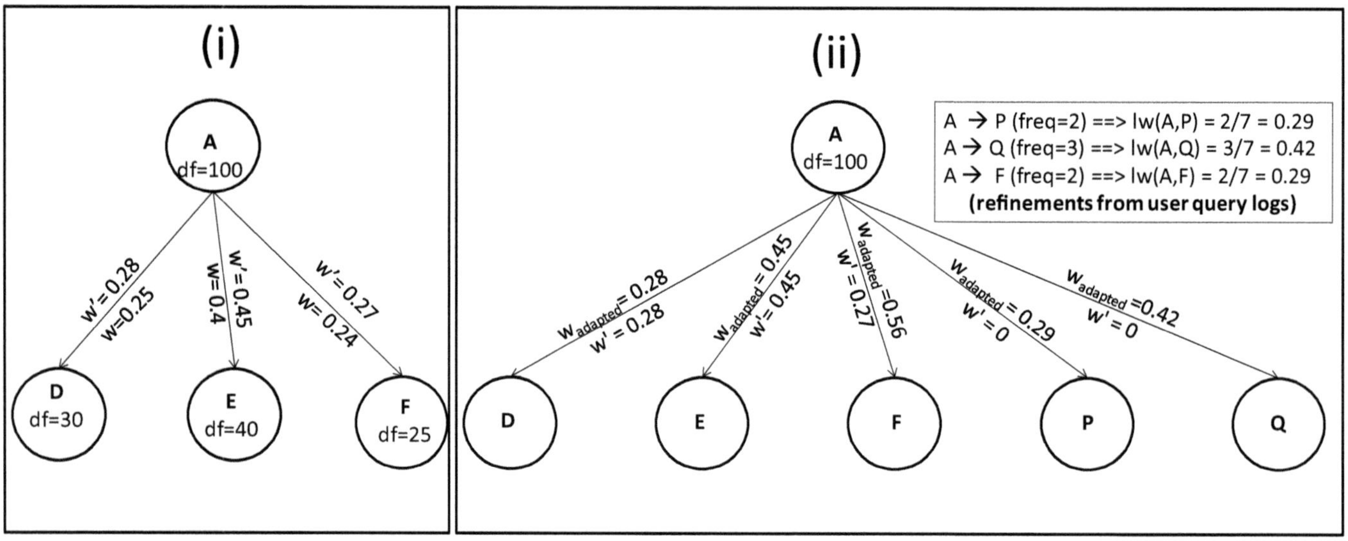

Figure 2: Adaptation of SHReC with search logs

for each successive week are used for training and testing respectively. In other words, we adapt the models with week i's log refinements (training) and use the logs from week $i+1$ as test data; where $1 \leq i \leq n$, the number of weeks in the test period. The training and test data are therefore different for each week. The model is first evaluated on a particular weekly batch and then updated from the logs of the same batch. The evaluation methodology is not circular as the data is first used for evaluation then for learning.

For all Q, i.e. query refinements with user clicks found in the query logs for a particular week, we compute each model's Mean Reciprocal Rank (MRR) score as shown in Equation 4. The evaluation process results in a score for each logged week. Overall, the process produces a series of scores for each query recommendation model being evaluated. These scores allow the comparison between different models. One query recommender model can therefore be considered superior over another if a statistically significant improvement can be achieved over the specific period.

$$MRR = \frac{1}{Q}(\sum_{i=1}^{Q} \frac{1}{r_i}) \quad (4)$$

where r_i is the rank of an actual query refinement in the list of refinements recommended by the model. Note that when the actual query refinement is not included in a model's list of recommended terms, then $1/r$ is set to zero.

6.3 SHReC creation

Creation of a SHReC model for an Intranet requires two main resources: a collection of documents and a list of candidate terms. The main challenge is in generating the list of suitable candidates that should occur in the model. As discussed earlier in Section 3.1, the computational complexity of the creation process necessitates that the size of the list is manageable. In order to determine the reasonable size of candidate terms based on the trade-off between computational cost and effectiveness of recommendations, we tested different sets of candidates extracted from *Essex*'s collection. Firstly, we extracted all keywords from the collection and up to two other words around each keyword to form bi-grams and tri-grams leading to 54,830 unique candidates. This set is labelled as CS_{all} (candidate set for all terms). CS_{15k} consists of 15,086 terms from the list of keywords with document frequency between 20 and 13,226 (the maximum document frequency), and terms not in this set occurred in less than 0.026% (20/77,841) of the crawled Intranet collection. We also created CS_{10k}, CS_{5k} and CS_{1k} consisting of 10,148, 5,005 and 1,002 terms respectively. The terms with the least document frequency were 35, 89 and 631 for CS_{10k}, CS_{5k} and CS_{1k}.

Table 1 shows a comparison of the candidate sets across some important features. The number of subsumptions increases with the size of candidate set although there is no direct proportionality. For example, whilst the number of candidates in CS_{all} is more than triple of those in CS_{15k}, the proportion of subsumptions is just about twice. This might mean that the most important terms for subsumption are those with medium document frequencies. The computational cost on the other hand is like a geometric progression of the number of terms. The cost here refers to the time it takes to completely build a SHReC model on an Intel Duo core CPU (3GHz each), 4GB RAM with Windows 7 enterprise edition OS running 64-bit Java codes and using 4GB virtual memory. A candidate set of a thousand terms (CS_{1k}) takes less than 30mins to complete, while a candidate set ten times bigger (CS_{10k}) completes its SHReC creation in over 36hrs, which is about seventy-two times the amount of time. This is due to the amount of co-occurrence document frequency checks whose time complexity is $O(n^2 - n)$.

The average MRR results from the automated evaluation of the SHReC built from these candidate sets over a 12 weeks test period are also shown in Table 1. The query recommendations from the static SHReC built from CS_{all} are significantly better than those from the other candidate sets (paired t-test at 95% confidence). However, there is only a marginal difference among the adaptive versions of the models after 12 weeks of adaptation with all observed refinements from search logs. This implies that though the size of candidate set is important for the original static SHReC, its

Table 1: Comparison of different *Essex* candidate sets for SHReC creation

	CS_{all}	CS_{15k}	CS_{10k}	CS_{5k}	CS_{1k}
Minimum document frequency	2	20	35	89	631
Maximum document frequency	13,226	13,226	13,226	13,226	13,226
Size of Candidate set	54,830	15,086	10,148	5,005	1,002
Number of subsumption in SHReC	4,275,737	2,281,606	1,284,458	444,129	25,084
Computational Cost (approx.)	8weeks	4days	36.5hrs	10hrs	25mins
Average MRR of Static SHReC	**0.0109**	0.0006	0.0004	0.0005	0.0002
MRR in 12th week of adaptation	0.1298	0.1292	0.1272	0.1276	0.1274

Table 2: Comparison of different *OU* candidate sets for SHReC creation

	CS_{15k}	CS_{10k}	CS_{5k}	CS_{1k}
Minimum document frequency	85	157	451	4,487
Maximum document frequency	134,505	134,505	134,505	134,505
Size of Candidate set	15,018	10,000	5,001	1,000
Number of subsumption in SHReC	196,406	171,711	57,039	13,959
Computational Cost (approx.)	3days 6hrs	38.5hrs	7.5hrs	29mins
Average MRR of Static SHReC	0.0003	0.0005	0.0007	0.0007
MRR in 12th week of adaptation	0.1618	0.1619	0.1620	0.1619

adaptation with search logs minimises the effect of the size of candidates when utilised for query recommendation.

We obtained identical patterns for similar candidate sets extracted from *OU* as shown in Table 2. The candidate set for all terms which had over 11,8820 terms was not tested as this would not be practical. Based on the above analysis of different candidate sets across the two datasets, especially with respect to the trade-off between time complexity and effectiveness, we selected CS_{10k} whose SHReC is used for further analysis and comparison to the QFG in the next section.

7. RESULTS AND DISCUSSION

Evaluation results from our experiments are analysed in this section. Firstly, we discuss results related to a comparative analysis of Static SHReC (S_SHReC), QFG and Adaptive SHReC (A_SHReC) which uses all query refinements found in the search logs for the test in Section 7.1. We then analyse results from experiments when SHReC is adapted with only refinements where there is a user click immediately after the refinement in Section 7.2. We also compare this adaptive SHReC to a query flow graph (equivalent to the query click graph [11]) which also uses only refinements with user clicks.

7.1 Adaptation with all query log refinements

Experimental results of the query recommendation models for the two Intranets are plotted on graphs shown in Figures 3 and 4. The average weekly MRR evaluation across the 12 weeks test period are given in Table 3. The values in bold font are significantly better than others across the same evaluation metric at 95% confidence, while the underlined values are significantly worse. We employed a non-parametric measure (Kruskal-Wallis) since a plot of our results deviated from the normal distribution. The z-values are also shown in the Tables to indicate other levels of significance. For example, a z-value above 2.58 indicates a significantly better or worse result at 99% confidence depending on polarity (positive or negative). It should be noted that QFG evaluation results are always one week less than those from the SHReC models. This is because QFG is built cumulatively on a weekly basis from the search logs and therefore has no evaluation in the first week. SHReC is first built from a collection and can be evaluated with the query logs from the first week as test data before its subsequent adaptation for other weeks.

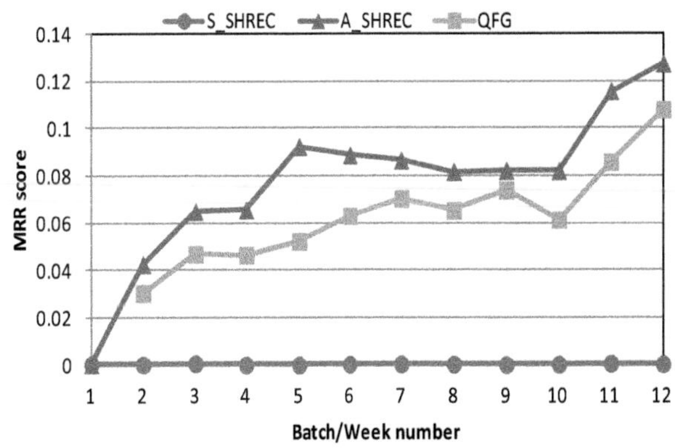

Figure 3: *Essex* evaluation results for adaptation with all query log refinements

Static SHReC (S_SHReC) was significantly worse than adaptive SHReC and QFG at 99% confidence ($z < -2.58$) as shown in Table 3. Its performance in proposing suitable query refinement terms is about the same with very little fluctuations every week throughout the evaluation for both *Essex* and *OU* (Figures 3 and 4). A possible reason for the low performance of S_SHReC might be that the statistical co-occurrence led to lots of noisy subsumptions between terms. The evaluation method might also have adversely affected S_SHReC since queries from search logs are used for the automated testing. Popular queries are likely to be

Table 3: Evaluation scores for adaptation with all query log refinements

Model	Average MRR (*Essex*)	MRR in 12th week (*Essex*)	Average MRR (*OU*)	MRR in 12th week (*OU*)
S_SHReC	0.00044 (z=-4.45)	0.00042	0.00078 (z=-4.45)	0.00066
A_SHReC	**0.07750** (z=3.23)	0.12717	**0.11038** (z=2.99)	0.16196
QFG	0.06400 (z=1.24)	0.10776	0.09764 (z=1.49)	0.14694

repeated often by different users thereby giving advantage to models that utilise the logs for their recommendation.

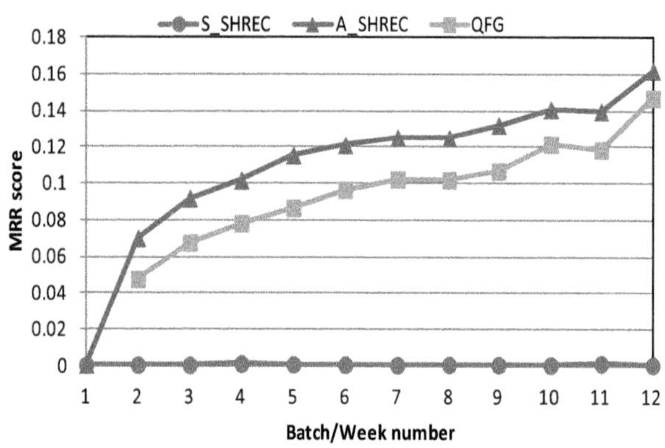

Figure 4: Evaluation results for *OU* for adaptation with all query log refinements

Our adaptive SHReC (A_SHReC) is significantly better than QFG from the evaluation results across both datasets as can also be seen in Table 3. This is mainly due to the fact that it is able to effectively integrate suggestions mined from both document collection and search logs. Users are therefore able to benefit from other previous users with similar information needs as reflected by their queries. The superior performance of A_SHReC over the other two models verifies our hypothesis that the collection and search logs are complementary sources for query recommendation. The continuous increase in MRR on every week is an indication that our adaptation method supports gradual learning and the increase is likely to continue for a long period afterwards. Although, the average MRR score was about 8% for *Essex*, a MRR score of about 13% in the 12th week of adaptation (Table 3) means that the average value might not give a true picture of the model's effectiveness. This is because the MRR score in the first week was very low, same as S_SHReC's. The same analysis applies to *OU* where the difference between the average score and score in the 12th week is over 5%. The MRR score from the second week onwards varied between 7-16%. The slightly higher scores obtained from *OU* compared to *Essex* is likely to be due to the availability of a bigger search log which enable more of the model's suggestions to be matched during evaluation.

The behaviour of the A_SHReC as compared to S_SHReC is similar to the decision stump [16] and its boosted version in machine learning. The decision stump on its own has a very low accuracy but a far better accuracy with boosting, performing better than or equivalent to some of the then state-of-the-art machine learning models. There is generally an increase in evaluation score every week for both A_SHReC and QFG with occasional decreases across the two Intranets. However, the graph of A_SHReC is generally above QFG for the two datasets throughout the test period (see Figures 3 and 4). This supports the fact that A_SHReC's performance is not solely due to its adaptation with search logs since QFG also learns from the same logs. The suggestions from the S_SHReC are therefore useful but their performance is boosted after adaptation with the logs.

The generally low MRR scores might be due to the harsh gold standard (a user's immediate refinement with click) employed in the automated evaluation framework compared to what might be obtained in a user study where users are asked to rate the suggestions as relevant or not. The context of the ground truth refinements are also not fully captured by the evaluation framework and this context might have changed based on the resulting documents shown to the user by the search engine.

Table 4: Average weekly queries for models

	Test	S_SHReC	A_SHReC	QFG
Essex	1340	1067	1181	581
OU	5523	3727	4868	2711

Table 4 shows the average number of weekly queries used in our evaluation and how many of these queries for which the models were able to recommend at least one term for reformulation. A_SHReC is able to provide suggestions about 88% of the time on the average compared to 46% and 74% for QFG and S_SHReC respectively across both datasets. We observe that quite a few of the terms used in creating our initial SHReC model were found directly in the query logs. This is because the difference in the number of queries for which a suggestion was made between A_SHReC and S_SHReC is far smaller than that of QFG. For instance, only an average of 104 (1181 − 1067) new refinements were added into the SHReC model for *Essex* though an average of 581 new refinements were added to QFG every week. This means that the weights on the links between 477 terms already existing in the SHReC and other nodes were strengthened by the adaptation on a weekly basis. An identical trend is observed for *OU*. Nevertheless, users will still not get a suggestion 12% of the time from A_SHReC. This can be reduced further extracting similar terms to those in the graph from dictionaries or domain glossaries.

7.2 Incorporating Clicks for Adaptation

Figures 5 and 6 show results from our evaluation of the query recommendation models for the *Essex* and *OU* where only log refinements with at least one user click are used for SHReC adaptation as well as creation of QFG. The average values are also given in Table 5.

The results trends are very similar to those from the previous section, with A_SHReC significantly better than both S_SHReC and QFG. However, the evaluation scores for both

Table 5: **Evaluation scores for adaptation with refinements having user clicks after reformulation**

Model	Average MRR (*Essex*)	MRR in 12th week (*Essex*)	Average MRR (*OU*)	MRR in 12th week (*OU*)
S_SHReC	0.00044 (z=-4.54)	0.0004	0.00078 (z=-4.54)	0.00066
A_SHReC	**0.06453** (z=3.11)	0.1204	**0.10078** (z=3.15)	0.15474
QFG	0.05146 (z=1.46)	0.09697	0.08709 (z=1.42)	0.13904

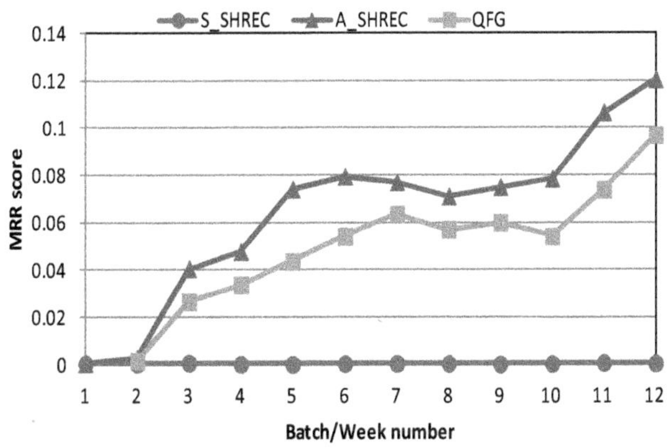

Figure 5: Evaluation results for *Essex* for adaptation with log refinements having user clicks

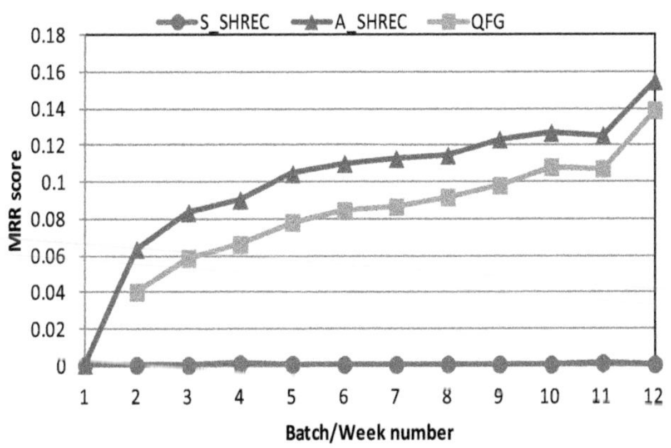

Figure 6: Evaluation results for *OU* for adaptation with log refinements having user clicks

A_SHReC and QFG when only log refinements with user clicks are used for adaptation are smaller than those for which all refinements in the logs are used (see Tables 3 and 5). For instance, the average MRR for *Essex* when adaptation is carried out with all logs is 0.0775 compared to 0.06453 for using only those with clicks. The same applies to *OU* (0.11038 versus 0.10078). This implies that users will benefit more from the models when all log refinements are used for adaptation rather than only those with clicks. Although this initially seems counter intuitive, a good explanation is that users do not necessarily have to click on the resulting documents before modify their queries even though they might have read the result snippets or titles which give hints on how to better formulate their queries.

7.3 Evaluation with click based metrics

A recent study showed that a better retrieval performance is obtained when users are able to reformulate their queries to more successful queries [1]. This was estimated by metrics which rely on click through data such as those introduced in [22]. Furthermore, we also found out that increase or decrease in the retrieval performance of the original query can be a good indication of the quality of query recommendation. This suggests we can automatically assess the quality of query recommendation through these quality metrics before involving real users.

buraries, midwifery courses, masters courses,
payday, foundation courses, copy shop,
credits, academic reference, study skills,
summer term, human rights centre, phd courses,
short courses, language lingistics,graduate diploma,
exam papers, pre sessional course, performing arts,
undergraduate admissions, extenuating cercumstances

Figure 7: Sample twenty (20) queries used for click based quality evaluation

Therefore, we conducted a further evaluation based on that finding to assess the recommendation coming from both A_SHReC and QFG models. The models were first trained (adapted) on all refinements in the log data for *Essex* between October and December 2010. For testing, fifty queries of medium frequency between 5 and 15 are sampled from the logs of *Essex* between February and May 2011. This is similar to the sampling approach in [6] where frequent and rare queries are avoided. We then selected the worst performing 20 queries (see Figure 7[4]) out of these queries using the MRR_C[5] quality metric. Here, MRR_C refers to the mean value of $\sum_i 1/r_i$ of all clicks on each occurrence of the specific query in the logs; r_i is the rank of document clicked within the result list displayed to the user. The intuition behind selecting the least performing queries is that they present a more challenging scenario for the query recommender models as they are the ones where the user is most likely to reformulate. For each of the 20 queries, we selected up to three recommendations from each recommender model, i.e. A_SHReC and QFG. For each model, query q and recommendation r, we calculate the difference $\Delta(MRR_C) = MRR_C(r) - MRR_C(q)$.

The averages are shown in Table 6. We observe that overall both models are capable of recommending queries that can increase the observed retrieval quality estimated by click through data. We also see that the adaptive concept hierarchy model outperformed the query flow graph model reinforcing our previous evaluation.

[4]Some of these queries are actually mis-spellings.
[5]MRR_C should not be confused with the MRR scores used in Equation 4.

Table 6: Retrieval performance differences achieved by recommendations from both models

	Mean $\Delta(MRR_C)$ for top 10 recommendations	$\Delta(MRR_C)$ for top 3 recommendations
A_SHReC	+0.1738	+0.069
QFG	+0.070	+0.059

Remark: Although we discussed only MRR results, other evaluation metrics such as MAP & Recall as well as using only the top ten recommendations gave results with identical trends to the ones discussed in this paper.

8. CONCLUSIONS AND FUTURE WORK

We have proposed a novel method for adaptation of the concept hierarchy model with query refinements from search logs on Intranets for query refinement recommendation. Experimental results indicate that our adaptive model improves in its query recommendation performance over a period of time and is significantly better than its static version as well as the query flow graph which is a state-of-the-art adaptive query recommender model. We also discovered that it was better to adapt the concept hierarchy model with all log refinements irrespective of whether there were user clicks or not. We intend to further validate our automated evaluation results with user studies, incorporate our model in a live system and compare its effectiveness to other query recommendation models.

Acknowledgements

This work is part of the AutoAdapt research project funded by EPSRC grants EP/F035357/1 and EP/F035705/1.

9. REFERENCES

[1] M.-D. Albakour, U. Kruschwitz, N. Nanas, I. Adeyanju, D. Song, M. Fasli, and A. De Roeck. Analysis of query reformulations in a search engine of a local web site. In *ECIR'12*, pages 517–521, 2012.

[2] M.-D. Albakour, N. Nanas, U. Kruschwitz, M. Fasli, Y. Kim, D. Song, and A. De Roeck. Autoeval: An evaluation methodology for evaluating query suggestions using query logs. In *ECIR'11*, pages 605–610. Springer, 2011.

[3] P. Anick. Using terminological feedback for web search refinement - a log-based study. In *SIGIR '03*, pages 88–95. ACM, 2003.

[4] R. Baeza-Yates and A. Tiberi. Extracting semantic relations from query logs. In *SIGKDD'07*, pages 76–85, 2007.

[5] R. Baraglia, F. Cacheda, V. Carneiro, D. Fernandez, V. Formoso, R. Perego, and F. Silvestri. Search shortcuts: a new approach to the recommendation of queries. In *RecSys'09*, pages 77–84. ACM, 2009.

[6] P. Boldi, F. Bonchi, C. Castillo, D. Donato, A. Gionis, and S. Vigna. The query-flow graph: model and applications. In *CIKM*, pages 609–618. ACM, 2008.

[7] I. Bordino, C. Castillo, D. Donato, and A. Gionis. Query similarity by projecting the query-flow graph. In *SIGIR'10*, pages 515–522. ACM, 2010.

[8] D. Broccolo, L. Marcon, F. M. Nardini, R. Perego, and F. Silvestri. Generating suggestions for queries in the long tail with an inverted index. *Information Processing and Management*, 48:326–339, 2012.

[9] J. Callan, B. W. Croft, and S. M. Harding. The inquery retrieval system. In *Proceedings of the Third International Conference on Database and Expert Systems Applications*, pages 78–83. Springer, 1992.

[10] D. Carmel, E. Farchi, Y. Petruschka, and A. Soffer. Automatic query refinement using lexical affinities with maximal information gain. In *SIGIR '02*, pages 283–290. ACM, 2002.

[11] N. Craswell and M. Szummer. Random walks on the click graph. In *SIGIR '07*, pages 239–246. ACM, 2007.

[12] S. Cucerzan and R. W. White. Query suggestion based on user landing pages. In *SIGIR'07*, pages 875–876. ACM, 2007.

[13] V. Dang and W. B. Croft. Query reformulation using anchor text. In *WSDM'10*, pages 41–50, 2010.

[14] B. M. Fonseca, P. B. Golgher, E. S. de Moura, and N. Ziviani. Using association rule to discover search engines related queries. In *Proceedings of the First Latin American Web Congress*, pages 66–71, 2003.

[15] D. Hawking. Enterprise search. In R. Baeza-Yates and B. Ribeiro-Neto, editors, *Modern Information Retrieval*, pages 641–683. Addison-Wesley, 2011.

[16] W. Iba and P. Langley. Induction of one-level decision trees. In *ICML*, pages 233–240. M. Kaufmann, 1992.

[17] T. Joachims and F. Radlinski. Search engines that learn from implicit feedback. *IEEE Computer*, 40(8):34–40, 2007.

[18] H. Joho, M. Sanderson, and M. Beaulieu. Hierarchical approach to term suggestion device. In *SIGIR '02*, pages 454–454. ACM, 2002.

[19] R. Jones, B. Rey, and O. Madani. Generating query substitutions. In *WWW '06*, pages 387–396, 2006.

[20] R. Kraft and J. Zien. Mining anchor text for query refinement. In *WWW'04*, pages 666–674, 2004.

[21] U. Kruschwitz. *Intelligent Document Retrieval: Exploting Markup Structure*. Springer, 2005.

[22] F. Radlinski, M. Kurup, and T. Joachims. How does clickthrough data reflect retrieval quality? In *CIKM'08*, pages 43–52. ACM, 2008.

[23] I. Ruthven. Re-examining the potential effectiveness of interactive query expansion. In *SIGIR '03*, pages 213–220. ACM, 2003.

[24] M. Sanderson and B. Croft. Deriving concept hierarchies from text. In *SIGIR'99*, pages 206–213. ACM, 1999.

[25] R. White and R. Chandrasekar. Exploring the use of labels to shortcut search trails. In *SIGIR'10*, pages 811–812. ACM, 2010.

[26] R. W. White, M. Bilenko, and S. Cucerzan. Studying the use of popular destination to enhance web search interaction. In *SIGIR'07*, pages 159–166. ACM, 2007.

[27] R. W. White and I. Ruthven. A study of interface support mechanisms for interactive information retrieval. *JASIST*, 57(7):933–948, 2006.

[28] J. Xu and W. B. Croft. Query expansion using local and global document analysis. In *SIGIR'96*, pages 4–11. ACM, 1996.

Adaptive Query Suggestion for Difficult Queries*

Yang Liu*, Ruihua Song†, Yu Chen†, Jian-Yun Nie‡ and Ji-Rong Wen†
* Beijing Institute of Technology,† Microsoft Research Asia,‡University of Montreal
yan9liu@gmail.com, {rsong,yu.chen,jrwen}@microsoft.com, nie@iro.umontreal.ca

ABSTRACT

Query suggestion is a useful tool to help users formulate better queries. Although this has been found highly useful globally, its effect on different queries may vary. In this paper, we examine the impact of query suggestion on queries of different degrees of difficulty. It turns out that query suggestion is much more useful for difficult queries than easy queries. In addition, the suggestions for difficult queries should rely less on their similarity to the original query. In this paper, we use a learning-to-rank approach to select query suggestions, based on several types of features including a query performance prediction. As query suggestion has different impacts on different queries, we propose an adaptive suggestion approach that makes suggestions only for difficult queries. We carry out experiments on real data from a search engine. Our results clearly indicate that an approach targeting difficult queries can bring higher gain than a uniform suggestion approach.

Categories and Subject Descriptors

H.3.3 [**Information Search and Retrieval**]: query formulation

General Terms

Algorithms, Experimentation, Measurement

Keywords

Difficult queries, adaptive query suggestion, query suggestion evaluation

1. INTRODUCTION

It is often difficult for users to compose appropriate queries in Web search. Even if a query expresses well the right information need from the point of view of human beings, the query can still fail to retrieve the desirable documents. This is the case for the query "what's in fashion", which clearly describes the information need on learning the current fashion trends. However, most top search results are irrelevant, as shown in the top results from Google (`http://www.google.com`) in Table 1: the second result is irrelevant while the third one is not authoritative enough. The query is difficult because the current search methods cannot find the desired documents effectively. To be general, we consider all the queries with a low NDCG score *difficult queries* as in [17]. The low NDCG scores could be due to several reasons: the query's key terms mismatch those in the desired documents; the query is too general, the query is too narrow, and so on. No matter what the underlying reason is, one can alleviate the problem by suggesting appropriate alternative queries to the user, which can perform better in search.

Query suggestion is a technique which can assist users to interactively refine queries. However, most previous work on query suggestion, such as [29, 23, 7, 8], tries to identify alternative queries that bear a strong similarity or relevance to the original query. For easy queries, the suggested queries can often result in good search results, as is also the case for the original query. In such cases, query suggestion is less crucial, and can even be annoying sometimes (imagine, for example, the case when a user submits a very good query, but becomes uncertain when a number of alternatives are suggested). However, for difficult queries, it is critical but much harder to suggest queries that perform well. For example, for the same example query "what's in fashion", the suggestions "what's in fashion 2010" and "what's in fashion for men" are both relevant , but they are not more effective than the original query, as will be shown in Table 4. To be useful, a suggested query should not only be relevant to the original query, but also allow to better retrieve the desired documents.

Query reformulation is another technique aiming at improving the relevance of search results. Different from query suggestion, query reformulation is performed automatically on the original query without explicit interactions with the user. In such a setting, one should make sure that the automatic reformulation has a high precision. In practice, it is often limited to replacing some original query terms by correcting misspelled words, or suggesting some more frequently used terms that are slightly different from the original terms in morphology. However, such a replacement does not apply to the difficult queries we target in this paper such

*The work was done when the first author was visiting Microsoft Research Asia.

Permission to make digital or hard copies of all or part of this work for personal or classroom use is granted without fee provided that copies are not made or distributed for profit or commercial advantage and that copies bear this notice and the full citation on the first page. To copy otherwise, to republish, to post on servers or to redistribute to lists, requires prior specific permission and/or a fee.
SIGIR'12, August 12–16, 2012, Portland, Oregon, USA.
Copyright 2012 ACM 978-1-4503-1472-5/12/08 ...$10.00.

Table 1: One example of a difficult query, a better suggestion, and their top three search results returned by Google in November 4, 2011.

Query: "what's in fashion"	Suggestion: "latest fashion trends"
Fashion - Women's **Fashion** - **Fashion** Website Get a look at 2011 women's fashion. ELLE is the leading ... *www.elle.com/Fashion*	**Fashion** - Women's **Fashion** - **Fashion** Website Get a look at 2011 women's fashion. ... for seasonal ... *www.elle.com/Fashion*
Quiz: **What's** Your **Fashion** Style? What's Your Fashion Style? Find out what your likes ... *www.lhj.com/lhj/quiz.jsp?quizId=/.../WhatsYourStyleQuiz...*	**Fashion Trends** and News on Style.com NEW ON STYLE.COM. fashion shows. Spring 2012 ... *www.style.com/trendsshopping/*
Celebrity **Fashion**|**What's** hot|High Street Style Tips... OUR Fashion Ed's top fashion and beauty picks ... *www.thesun.co.uk/.../Celebrity-Fashion-Whats-hot-High-S...*	Trends - **Fashion Trends** (Vogue.com UK) Get a look at 2011 women's fashion. ... for seasonal ... *www.vogue.co.uk/fashion/trends*

as "what's in fashion", in which all the words are spelled correctly and are quite frequent.

In this paper, we do not intend to design a system that solves the problem of difficult queries alone; rather we propose an interactive suggestion method that adaptively suggests alternative queries when this is necessary or useful, namely for difficult queries. The goal is to suggest more effective queries for them. As an example, a good suggestion for the original query "what's in fashion" is "latest fashion trends", which both corresponds well to the original search intent and leads to better search results, as shown in Table 1.

As we hinted earlier, query suggestion can be useful in some cases (especially difficult queries), but annoying in some others (especially easy queries). It is then natural to determine when it is useful to perform query suggestion and to use it only for the useful cases. To do this, we use a regression model to predict the retrieval performance of queries and then return suggestions according to the query difficulty. Experimental results show that our adaptive query suggestion approach significantly improves the uniform query suggestion.

In addition to proposing an effective query suggestion method that targets difficult queries, we also propose some new measures to evaluate the quality of query suggestion, which we call Max@n (the maximal NDCG using the first n suggestions) and SDCG@n (the discounted cumulative gain using the first n suggestions). Compared to the measures used in previous studies, these measures can better reflect the use of query suggestions by end users.

The contributions of this work are twofold. First, to our best knowledge, it is the first time that query suggestion is studied specifically to help difficult queries. Second, we successfully demonstrate that our adaptive approach significantly improves the retrieval effectiveness of original queries and outperforms the current state of the art.

The remainder of this paper is organized as follows. We briefly review related work in Section 2. We propose two new evaluation measures in Section 3. Then, we describe our proposed approach for difficult queries in Section 4 and evaluate the approach in Section 5. The adaptive query suggestion approach is described and tested in Section 6. Finally, we present concluding remarks and future work in Section 7.

2. RELATED WORK

Our work is related to query suggestion, query reformulation and query performance prediction. We will review some work in these three areas.

2.1 Query Suggestion

In the past decade, many approaches have been proposed to perform query suggestion. Much work takes advantage of click-through information from query logs and leverages co-clicked URLs to identify related queries. For example, [6] constructed a bipartite graph based on click-through and clusters similar queries by assuming that queries for which the same documents are clicked on are similar. Here, clicked documents are considered as representing the user's search intent. [32] further extended the approach by also taking into account the content words of the queries. Therefore, queries in the same cluster are both similar to each other and share the same search intent. Baeza-Yates et al. [2] proposed to cluster similar queries by considering queries along with the text of their clicked URLs. Given an initial query, the queries from its cluster can be considered as possible suggestions.

In recent years, other types of useful information have been included into the bipartite graph. Mei et al. [24] proposed to compute hitting time on a large-scale bipartite graph mined from click-through data. Then candidate queries are ranked by the hitting time. Cao et al. [8] clustered queries into concepts and then by mapping user query sessions to concept sessions, they enhanced query suggestion by considering enriched contextual information. In [23], the authors proposed a query suggestion framework including two parts: The offline part builds a query similarity graph by user-query and query-click bipartite graphs; The online part applies a ranking algorithm to the query similarity graph and then suggests latent semantically relevant queries to users. To tackle the problem of rare query suggestion, Song et al. [28] built two bipartite graphs by leveraging both click and skip information from query logs and used an optimal random walk and combination model to determine query correlations.

Most of these approaches focus on enhancing user search experiences by providing related queries to expand searches [29]. The evaluation measure commonly used reflects whether the suggested queries are relevant to the original query. As we argued, a useful query suggestion is not only relevant, but also more effective. This is particularly important for difficult queries. To cope with this requirement, we will propose a new evaluation methodology in this paper.

2.2 Query Reformulation

Query reformulation techniques are widely used to modify user queries in order to improve retrieval effectiveness. Traditional methods include pseudo relevance feedback, which adds some terms extracted from the top ranked documents into the query [22, 30, 33]. Recent work exploits query logs to collect reformulation candidates. In [20], the authors identify query-level and phrase-level candidate substitutions for user queries by mining session data. Candidates are ranked according to two relevance measurements, i.e., "precise rewriting" and "broad rewriting". To address the problem of term mis-specification and under-specification within a query, Wang and Zhai [31] define two novel term association patterns, i.e., context-sensitive term substitution and term additions, and propose a method to discover these patterns by analyzing term co-occurrences in query logs. Gao et al. [15] propose a ranker-based search query speller that gathers correction candidates from query logs and then use a ranker trained from manually annotated data to rank the candidates. Guo et al. [16] propose a unified CRF model for query refinement by incorporating four independent techniques for query correction.

Anchor text is an alternative data source for query reformulation. It has been observed that there is a similarity between search queries and anchor texts [13]. Therefore, Kraft and Zien [21] propose a method to generate refinements for queries by mining anchor texts. They also employ a ranking algorithm for combining multiple factors to select query refinements. By using anchor texts to simulate click-through data of query log, Dang and Croft [12] employ the approaches described in [25, 31] to reformulate queries. Their results show that anchor texts are at least as effective as a real query log for this purpose.

The refinement work usually outputs alternative queries that will most likely change the user query's search results. To ensure high precision, the previous work often performs changes that are safe and hesitates to do risky refinements. The same technique can be hardly applied to difficult queries, for which more different suggestions are needed.

2.3 Query Performance Prediction

Query performance prediction is the task of estimating the quality of the search results for a query. Recently, a number of predictors have been proposed for this task [11, 1, 34, 10, 35, 36]. Carmel et al. [9] conducted a comprehensive comparison among these predictors over several TREC benchmarks and further discussed several methods for combing different predictors to obtain performance enhancement. Different from previous predictors evaluated on TREC-like collections, Balasubramanian et al. [5] propose an effective and efficient query performance prediction technique for real Web search that uses aggregates of retrieval scores and retrieval features. Our work is in the same setting. Therefore, we will use a similar approach to determine difficult queries in Section 6.

3. QUERY SUGGESTION AND QUALITY MEASURES

In this section, we first formulate the problem of query suggestion for difficult queries. Then we define measures to evaluate how good a suggestion list is for a difficult query.

3.1 Query suggestion problem

Query suggestion can be formulated as a two-step process: First, given a query q, a set of candidate queries $C = \{c_1, c_2, \ldots, c_m\}$ for suggestion are identified; then the candidates are ranked according to some quality criterion. Similar to the Probability Ranking Principle (PRP) [27], the best suggestion list can be seen as the one in which the suggested queries are ranked in decreasing order of their relevance probability $P(rel = 1|q, c)$, in which $rel = 1$ means relevance, q is the original query and c refers to a candidate. We then choose at most n ($n < m$) top candidate as suggestions to q, denoted by $C_s =< c_{s1}, c_{s2}, \ldots, c_{sn} >$. The key problem is to find an optimal function $r(q, c_i)$ to estimate $P(rel = 1|q, c_i)$.

This is the standpoint taken in many previous studies. The measurements proposed are based on direct human judgments [29, 23, 7, 28, 8] or indirect human judged resources like Open Directory Project (ODP) data [23, 3]. For example, for each pair of the original query and a suggestion, assessors are given the queries and their corresponding search result pages side-by-side, and asked to make a binary decision of whether two queries are related [29].

As we discussed previously, a useful suggestion should be the one that improves the search effectiveness. Therefore, we change the previous relevance probability to the usefulness probability $P(useful = 1|q, c)$. For example, although both "what's in fashion for men" and "latest fashion trends" are relevant to the query "what's in fashion", the latter is more effective, thus its usefulness is higher. We will define two measures to reflect the usefulness in the next subsection.

Some measures in a similar vein have been used in query reformulation. For example, [12] used the metric precision@n, which is the fraction of top n retrieved documents that are relevant, to measure the quality of a refined query. In this paper, we will assume that our goal is to improve NDCG@k. Accordingly, we propose two measurements Max@n and SDCG@n to measure the effectiveness of a suggestion list.

3.2 Quality measures

3.2.1 *Evaluating an individual suggestion*

We use the judged document set of an original query q, which is pooled from several popular search engines, to evaluate a query suggestion c_{s_i}. Instead of precision@n, we choose NDCG to evaluate an individual suggestion, which is commonly used for Web search. Given an original query q, we have a set of documents, denoted as D, judged by human assessors. Then, NDCG@k is defined as $\frac{DCG@k}{IDCG@k}$, where DCG@k is calculated by as follows:

$$DCG@k = \sum_{i=1}^{k} \frac{2^{rating(i)} - 1}{log(1 + i)} \tag{1}$$

Here $rating(i)$ is the relevance rating of the document at position i. In our experiments, we have five grades of relevance, i.e., perfect, excellent, good, fair, and bad, corresponding to the ratings 4, 3, 2, 1, and 0, respectively. IDCG@k is the ideal discounted cumulated gain which is produced by the perfect ordering of D.

We evaluate the retrieval performance of a suggestion c_{s_i} by calculating NDCG@k measure for the list of retrieved documents $S(c_{s_i})$ based on the judgments of D. Note that although on average there are more than 100 documents judged for each original query, there are still some un-judged documents retrieved by suggested queries. We regard these un-judged documents as irrelevant, or bad, as is commonly done in IR evaluation.

3.2.2 *Evaluating a suggestion list*

Based on the NDCG measure of a single suggestion, we can measure the quality of a suggestion list. Usually search engines show at most ten suggestions for a query in rows at the bottom of search results or a list on the left side bar. The suggestion list is usually short so that the users can easily go through it and choose a suggestion that looks promising. Given a list of n suggestions, it is impossible to tell which of them will be selected by the user. Therefore, we use the maximum NDCG@k achievable by these n suggestions, denoted by Max@n, as a quality measure of the list.

For example, for an original query, the NDCG@3 values of its top five suggestions are:

$$< 0.4, 0.6, 0.5, 0.7, 0.2 >$$

Then Max@1 is 0.4; Max@2 is 0.6; Max@3 is 0.6; Max@4 is 0.7; and Max@5 is 0.7. By connecting these Max@n points, we can use a monotonically increasing curve to describe these values.

We also use the metric SDCG@n to measure the overall quality of a suggestion list, which assumes that the user scans the suggestion list from top to bottom. This is similar to the assumption used in the general DCG measure. SDCG@n is defined as follows:

$$SDCG@n = \sum_{i=1}^{n} \frac{NDCG@k(i)}{log(1+i)} \tag{2}$$

Here n is the total number of suggestions in a suggestion list and NDCG@k(i) is the quality of the suggestion at position i.

As search engines often return less than ten suggestions for a query, it is unfair to compare them with our methods if they return less suggestions. Thus, we choose Max@n and SDCG@n with $n \leq 5$ as our main metrics and use the queries with at least five suggestions in our experiments.

4. OUR APPROACH

In this section, we describe our approach to address the problem of query suggestion for difficult queries. Figure 1 shows the work flow of our approach.

Given a query q, we first retrieve candidates based on clicks and query terms. Then we use a search system to obtain search result pages for the original query q and candidates $\{c_1, c_2, \ldots, c_m\}$ [1]. For each pair of q and c_i, we extract features to predict how well the candidate will perform. Our proposed features are extracted from queries, candidates, and their search result pages. Next, we apply a ranking model $f(\mathbf{x}_{c_i})$ to estimate $P(useful = 1|q, c_i)$. The model is learned on a training set composed of difficult queries. Finally, we sort the candidates by their estimated scores and return top n candidates as suggestions.

We will describe the above processes in detail in the following subsections.

4.1 Retrieving Candidates

Candidates can be collected from many data sources. In our work, we mine query clusters from click-through data and retrieve candidates based on query clusters.

First, we build a click-through bipartite graph from the search logs collected on Bing (`http://www.bing.com`) from

[1]Note that the search results of the candidates can be prefetched offline.

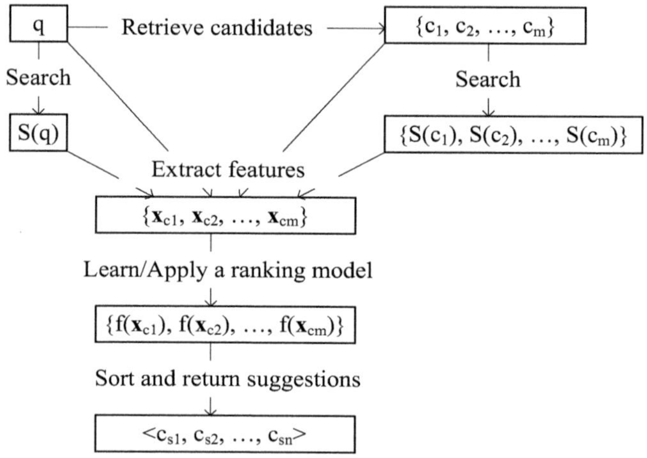

Figure 1: Flowchart of generating suggestions for a query

January 1st to March 25th, 2010. An edge e_{ij} is created between a query node q_i and a URL node u_j if u_j has been clicked when users issued q_i. The weight w_{ij} of edge e_{ij} is the aggregated click number. The query q_i is then represented as an L_2-normalized vector, in which each dimension corresponds to a URL. If edge e_{ij} exists, the value of the dimension is normalized w_{ij}; otherwise, it is zero.

Second, we apply the clustering method proposed in [8]. The algorithm creates a set of clusters as it scans through the queries. For each query q, the algorithm first finds the closest cluster C, and then tests the diameter of $C \cup \{q\}$. If the diameter is not larger than D_{max}, q is merged into C. Otherwise, a new cluster is created with q as its first member.

Third, we divide queries in each query cluster into intent groups. When examining query clusters, it is observed that the search intents of some queries in a query cluster are almost the same. Despite the slight difference in their forms, they can be safely treated as duplicates to one another. This phenomenon is mainly caused by misspellings, with or without stop words, different tenses, equivalent syntax, and so on. For example, "jet bleu", "jetbue" and "jetb" share the same intent with "jetblue". It is annoying if we show these misspelled or duplicate queries as suggestions. To solve this problem, we apply a sequence of transformation operations, such as spelling correction, stop words removal, stemming, and term sorting, to all queries in each cluster and then group two queries together if their edit distance after the transformation operations is less than a threshold. Then, we select the most frequent query in each group to be the group leader, which will be returned as a candidate on behalf of the whole group.

Given an original query q, we identify the query-cluster map to find the cluster containing q. All the group leaders in the cluster are returned as candidates for q.

4.2 Extracting Features

We extract some features to measure how well candidate c_i performs. These features will be used within a learning-to-rank framework (see the next section). The features are extracted from $\langle q, S(q), c_i, S(c_i)\rangle$, where $S(q)$ and $S(c_i)$ are search results returned by Bing for q and c_i respectively. In our experiments, we use the first page containing top ten search results for each query.

Our proposed features can be divided into four categories: match features, cross match features, similarity features and an estimated NDCG feature.

4.2.1 Match Features

The match features aim to measure how well a candidate matches its own search result. Our intuition is that only well-matched candidates are qualified to be suggestions.

Match features are extracted from c_i and $S(c_i)$. As each result in $S(c_i)$ is usually composed of three parts: title, snippet, and URL, we calculate match features for each of them. Take title as an example. Given the candidate c_i and a title $T_{i,j}$, which is the title of the j-th result in $S(c_i)$, we first remove stop words by Fox's list [14] and stem terms by Porter Stemmer [26]. Then we count how many times a term t_k of c_i occurs in the title and normalize the term frequency (TF) by the length of title in words:

$$MatchScore(c_i, T_{i,j}) = \sum_{t_k \in c_i} \frac{TF(t_k, T_{i,j})}{length(T_{i,j})} \quad (3)$$

Finally, we calculate the feature of TitleMatch by aggregating all titles from the top N results and discounting MatchScore by the position of the title as follows:

$$TitleMatch = \sum_{j=1}^{N} \frac{MatchScore(c_i, T_{i,j})}{log(j+1)} \quad (4)$$

Similar to TitleMatch, we also calculate the features of SnippetMatch and URLMatch. The three features compose our match features.

4.2.2 Cross Match Features

The cross match features aim to measure how well a candidate's search result $S(c_i)$ matches the original query q. The intuition is that a search result $S(c_i)$ that matches better the original query is more likely to correspond the original query's information need.

Cross match features are extracted from q and $S(c_i)$. Similar to the match features, we calculate three features based on title, snippet, and URL. For example, $MatchScore(q, T_{i,j})$ represents the cross match feature on the title of the j-th result in $S(c_i)$. TitleCrossMatch can be computed as:

$$TitleCrossMatch = \sum_{j=1}^{N} \frac{MatchScore(q, T_{i,j})}{log(j+1)} \quad (5)$$

SnippetCrossMatch and URLCrossMatch can be computed similarly.

4.2.3 Similarity Features

The similarity features are other features trying to measure the similarity between a candidate and the original query. This similarity is measured on the candidate's search result $S(c_i)$ and the original query's search result $S(q)$. On the one hand, as we want $S(c_i)$ to satisfy the original query's information need, the topic of $S(c_i)$ should not drift too much away from $S(q)$. On the other hand, $S(c_i)$ would fail to provide new and better results if it is too similar to $S(q)$.

To cover the two aspects, we extract three similarity features on the result pages, URLs and domains. PageSimilarity tries to prevent from a possible topic drift. It is calculated by the cosine similarity between the vectors of $S(q)$ and $S(c_i)$. The vectors are formed by terms in the search results after stopword removal and stemming. TF-IDF formula is used to weigh the terms. URLSimilarity is estimated by the number of common URLs between $S(q)$ and $S(c_i)$ and DomainSimilarity is based on the number of common domains, which are derived from URLs, between the two search results.

4.2.4 Estimated NDCG Feature

As we discussed earlier, difficult queries are more in need of suggestions. The estimated NDCG feature tries to capture, to some extent, how relevant a set of search results is to the original query, by which we want to reflect the difficulty of the query. This estimate is made using the sets of search results from different query formulations. The intuition is that, if a document appears in the top search results of many candidates, a.k.a. voted by many candidates, it is very likely to be relevant. Therefore, an estimate of relevance can be obtained for each search result.

Given q, the top search results of q's candidates form a search result collection $\bigcup_{i=1}^{m} S(c_i)$. For each unique document in the collection, we count the number of times that the candidates return it among top ten as the document's estimated relevance ratings. For a candidate c_i, every document in $S(c_i)$ will have an estimated rating. Consequently, we can calculate the estimated NDCG for the candidate using Equation 1, in which $rating(i)$ is the estimated relevance rating instead.

4.3 Learning to Rank Suggestions

We use a pairwise learning-to-rank method, RankSVM [19] to rank the candidates. RankSVM focuses on the relative order between two items in a ranking list and its objective of learning is to directly minimize the number of item pairs with reverse order. Given a list of candidates, RankSVM outputs the prediction score for each candidate, which can be used to rank candidates by sorting them on the prediction score in descending order.

Formally, suppose a candidate set $\mathcal{C} = \{(\boldsymbol{x_i}, y_i) | \boldsymbol{x_i} \in \mathbb{R}^d, y_i \in R^1\}$ and let y_i be the retrieval performance, e.g., NDCG@3, of a candidate $\boldsymbol{x_i}$. The ranking function has the form:

$$f(\boldsymbol{x}) = \sum_{i=1}^{l} (-\alpha_i) y_i K(\boldsymbol{x_i}, \boldsymbol{x}) + b^* \quad (6)$$

where $K(\cdot)$ is the kernel function. In our experiments, we choose the RBF (radial basis function) kernel. Notice that RankSVM tries to rank queries according to its search effectiveness (y_i) rather than their relevance or relatedness to the original query. A higher-ranked candidate is the one that is more effective in search. This allows us to capture the desired usefulness.

We define the error function for incorrect pairwise ordering as follows [4]:

$$\Theta_f(\boldsymbol{x_i}, \boldsymbol{x_j}) = \begin{cases} 1, & \text{if sign}((f(\boldsymbol{x_i}) - f(\boldsymbol{x_j})) \neq \text{sign}(y_i - y_j) \\ 0, & \text{otherwise} \end{cases} \quad (7)$$

Then, the optimal ranking function f^* can be learned by minimizing the overall ranking errors:

$$f^* = \underset{f}{\text{argmin}} \sum_{\boldsymbol{x_i} \in \mathcal{C}} \sum_{\boldsymbol{x_j} \in \mathcal{C}} \Theta_f(\boldsymbol{x_i}, \boldsymbol{x_j}) \quad (8)$$

Note that we only use the difficult queries, which perform worse than a threshold (e.g., 0.4 in this paper) in terms of NDCG@3, in a training set to learn ranking models.

5. EXPERIMENTS ON SUGGESTION APPROACHES

In this section, we conduct experiments on a set of real Web search queries to evaluate the effectiveness of our proposed approach and compare it with several baseline approaches.

5.1 Data Collection

The dataset collected contains about 10,000 real Web queries from the search logs of Bing. On average, each query has more than 100 documents judged in five relevance grades. As our evaluation will use the top 5 suggestions, to be fair, we discard the queries for which the baseline approaches or our approach returns less than five suggestions. Finally we have 4,068 queries for experimentation.

We fetch top three search results from Bing for each of the original 4,068 queries, and calculate NDCG@3 to measure how difficult each original query is. We divide the original queries into 10 bins according to their NDCG@3 values: $[0, 0.1), [0.1, 0.2), \ldots, [0.9, 1]$. The number of queries in each bin is shown in Figure 2. As we can see, there are a quite large number of queries (1,019) in the four lowest bins below 0.4. These queries account for around 25% of the total queries. Their low NDCG values indicate that it is difficult to retrieve relevant documents for them with the original queries, and they need better suggestions to improve search.

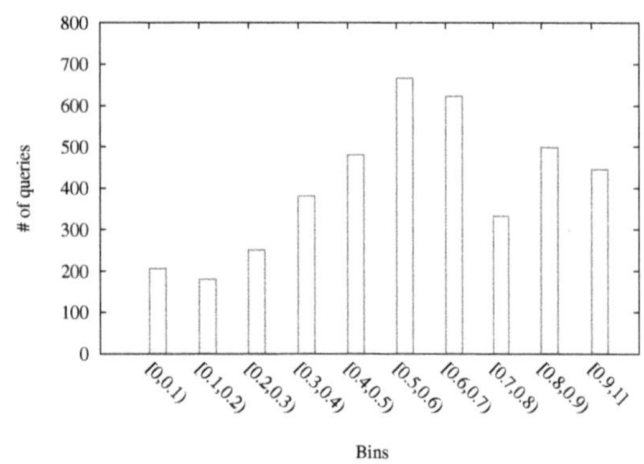

Figure 2: Distribution of original queries in different bins of retrieval performance

For all the 4,068 original queries, our approach identifies 638,391 suggestion candidates from the three-month search log. On average, each original query has about 157 candidates. Again, we fetch the top three search results from the search engine for each candidate and compute their NDCG@3 values based on the relevance judgments of the original query. If a candidate has a higher NDCG@3 value than its original query, it is an *improved candidate*. Figure 3 shows the average number of candidates and improved candidates per original query in each NDCG bin. As we can see, there are a larger number of improved queries in the lower bins than in the higher bins. For the $[0, 0.1)$ bin, each query has 33 improved candidates on average. The number of improved candidates decreases progressively as the original queries become easier. For the original queries in the bins of $[0.8, 0.9)$ and $[0.9, 1]$, almost none of their candidates is better than the original ones. This is not a surprise because search engines already perform very well in returning relevant documents for the easy queries, and hence there is less space left for further improvement. The above observation supports our conjecture that query suggestion is more necessary for difficult queries. It is on difficult queries that we can obtain large improvements on search effectiveness.

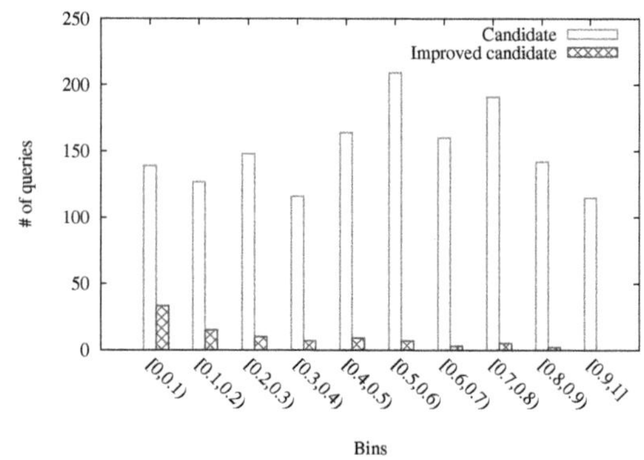

Figure 3: Number of candidates per query and number of improved candidates per query in different bins

As additional baselines, we also evaluate the suggestions from two commercial search engines, SE1 and SE2, for the original queries. For a suggestion from SE1 or SE2, we fetch the top three search results from them to evaluate its effectiveness in NDCG@3 .

5.2 Evaluating Ranking Models

We first conduct experiments to investigate the ranking models that are learnt from different types of features. The 4,068 original queries are randomly divided into ten subsets, and we conduct ten-fold cross validation for all learning experiments in this paper. In each trial, the queries in nine subsets are used as the training set, and the remaining subset as the testing set. In order to train a RankSVM model specifically for difficult queries, we only preserve the queries whose NDCG values are below 0.4 in the training set. For testing, however, we use all the original queries in order to reflect the fact that we cannot know their NDCG values in advance. The reported performance measures are averaged on the ten trials.

Figure 4 shows the results measured by Max@1 for the first six bins. Due to limited space, we do not show the results for original queries in other bins and other Max@n, but the trend is similar and has been clearly presented in Figure 4. First, we find that cross match features perform consistently better than match features. This observation is intuitive because the cross match features capture how well a candidate matches the original query. Second, we observe that the estimated NDCG feature is the most significant type in the bin of $[0, 0.1)$, more effective than the similarity measures. This is interesting and consistent with our assumption that for difficult queries we need to suggest queries that are more different from the original queries. In contrast, when queries become easier, the similarity measures stand out as the most effective criteria. This is also intuitive — easy queries do not need suggestions that are very different from the original ones; otherwise, there is a high risk of topic drift. However, we also observe that the combined approach that uses all types of feature (**All**) does not always outperform the one using the similarity measures only, namely in the bins $[0.3, 1]$. This can be explained by the fact that the models are trained on the difficult queries only (from bins below 0.4). During the training process, some of the features may be over-used and their possible negative impact on the queries in other bins may not be observed during the training. It would be more appropriate to use all the queries in the training in order to separate a model for difficult queries from the one for easy queries. We will leave this to future work.

The very good performance of similarity measures for easy queries does provide a good indication that these measures can be used as a good model for easy queries. It is then intuitive to combine the model trained on all the features (which performs well on difficult queries) and the one with similarity features only.

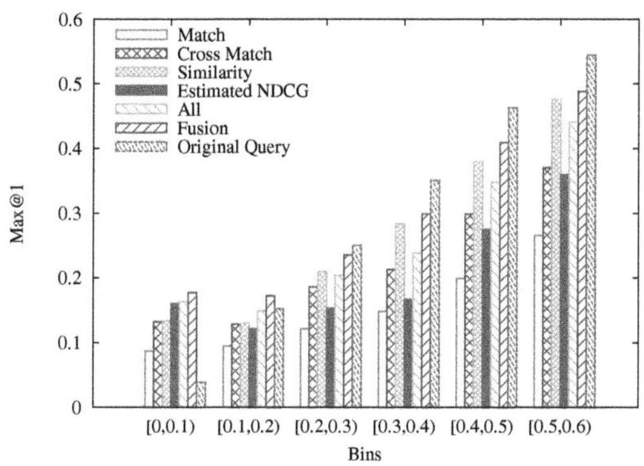

Figure 4: Evaluating ranking models based on different type of features over original queries in different bins

We propose using a variant of Borda's ranking fusion method [18] to combine the two models as follows:

$$Score(c) = \lambda \frac{1}{\sqrt{r_a(c)+1}} + (1-\lambda)\frac{1}{\sqrt{r_s(c)+1}} \quad (9)$$

where r_a is the position of candidate c in the list of suggestions returned by the model based on all features, and r_s is the position of c in the list returned by the model based on similarity features. λ is a trade-off parameter to balance the two models. The experimental results show that for a wide range of λ, from 0.3 to 0.7, the fusion outperforms both models. In our remaining experiments, we empirically set λ to 0.5.

The fusion method is consistently the best among our proposed methods as shown in Figure 4. This indicates that the simple fusion method is capable of taking advantage of both models for difficult and easy queries. We also calculate the difference between the fusion method and the two separate models in terms of Max@1-5 for all queries and SDCG@5 for queries in different bins. The results are shown in Table 2 and Table 3 respectively. In all the cases except one, the fusing approach improves the two separate models, and the improvements are statistically significant. Therefore, we use the fusion method as our query suggestion approach in remaining experiments.

5.3 Comparing Our Approach with Baselines

We compare our fusion approach with several baseline approaches. We collect suggestions from **SE1** and **SE2** as two additional baselines representing the current state of the art for query suggestion in commercial search engines. Also we randomly choose five queries from candidates to form suggestions. We denote this baseline as **Random**. The comparison results are evaluated by Max@1-5 and SDCG@5, shown in Table 2 and Table 3. As our method contains a candidate identification step followed by a candidate selection step, in order to see the impact of each of them, we also report the case when 5 suggestions are randomly chosen from the identified candidates (Random), i.e. we only use the first step.

As shown in the two tables, our fusion approach is dramatically better than any baseline in terms of all Max@1-5 and SDCG@5. The differences are statistically significant. This indicates that the existing query suggestion technologies used in commercial search engines have not well solved the problem of difficult queries. A possible reason may be that too much emphasis is put on the similarity between the suggestions and the original query. As we observed, the similarity criterion does not work well for difficult queries. To illustrate this, we show two examples in Table 4. In each example, we show an original query and top five suggestions returned by three approaches along with their NDCG@3 values. Given the query "what's in fashion", SE1 and SE2 provide some related queries that are subtopics of the query by adding a few key terms. Unfortunately, they fail to find better results on fashion because of the ineffective original query terms. Our approach suggests queries that are more different, such as "latest fashion trends" and "fashion now", which remove some ineffective key terms, like "what's in", and add a few better ones, like "trends", "latest", and "now". In terms of NDCG@3, our suggestions can improve the retrieval performance from 0.1564 to 0.5307. For the query "gallery furniture", SE1 and SE2 provide specific furniture brands that are related to the original query. However, there is a clear topic drift. Our fusion approach is more effective and the suggestions are more specific and within the scope of the original query.

In Table 2, we observe that although our approach is the best one among all suggestion approaches, it performs worse than original queries in terms of Max@1 and Max@2, meaning that we have to use at least 3 suggestions in order to catch up and improve the original queries. In order to better understand the situation, we have a closer look into the six bins in Figure 5. It turns out that our fusion approach works better for queries that are more difficult. For the most difficult queries (in the bins of $[0, 0.2)$) there is already improvements on Max@1, i.e. the first suggestion is already better than the original queries. When we extend to larger bins in $[0, 0.3)$, it still achieves improvement starting from Max@2. For easier queries, it becomes more difficult to improve the result by one or two suggestions only. However, it consistently improves the original queries from Max@3. This means that the approach is capable of proposing better queries for these bins when we allow at least 3 suggestions.

Nevertheless, we observe a clear trend: the easier the original query, the more difficult to propose a better suggestion. It is then intuitive to suggest queries according to the difficulty of the query. We investigate such an approach in the next section.

Table 2: Max@1-5 of suggestion approaches over all 4,068 queries. We conduct paired t-test for the difference between our fusion method with any other method and bold face indicates statistically significant with $p < 0.01$.

Max@n	1	2	3	4	5
Fusion	0.497	0.553	0.58	0.594	0.604
All	**0.442(-11%)**	**0.504(-9%)**	**0.536(-8%)**	**0.558(-6%)**	**0.573(-5%)**
Similarity	**0.485(-2%)**	**0.541(-2%)**	**0.568(-2%)**	**0.585(-2%)**	**0.596(-1%)**
Random	**0.205(-59%)**	**0.307(-44%)**	**0.372(-36%)**	**0.413(-30%)**	**0.443(-27%)**
SE1	**0.214(-57%)**	**0.296(-46%)**	**0.347(-40%)**	**0.386(-35%)**	**0.415(-31%)**
SE2	**0.172(-65%)**	**0.252(-54%)**	**0.299(-48%)**	**0.331(-44%)**	**0.357(-41%)**
Original Queries	0.572(15%)	0.572(3%)	**0.572(-1%)**	**0.572(-4%)**	**0.572(-5%)**

Table 3: SDCG@5 of suggestion approaches over queries in different bins. We conduct paired t-test for the difference between our fusion method with any other method and bold face indicates statistically significant with $p < 0.01$.

SDCG@5	$[0, 1]$	$[0, 0.1)$	$[0.1, 0.2)$	$[0.2, 0.3)$	$[0.3, 0.4)$	$[0.4, 0.5)$	$[0.5, 0.6)$
Fusion	1.358	0.456	0.451	0.63	0.805	1.104	1.36
All	**1.255(-8%)**	0.481(5%)	**0.427(-5%)**	**0.585(-7%)**	**0.694(-14%)**	**1.008(-9%)**	**1.271(-7%)**
Similarity	**1.329(-2%)**	**0.343(-25%)**	**0.406(-10%)**	**0.575(-9%)**	**0.766(-5%)**	**1.062(-4%)**	**1.338(-2%)**
Random	**0.618(-54%)**	**0.245(-46%)**	**0.22(-51%)**	**0.315(-50%)**	**0.357(-56%)**	**0.482(-56%)**	**0.634(-53%)**
SE1	**0.556(-59%)**	**0.265(-42%)**	**0.242(-46%)**	**0.305(-52%)**	**0.386(-52%)**	**0.486(-56%)**	**0.574(-58%)**
SE2	**0.429(-68%)**	**0.250(-45%)**	**0.265(-41%)**	**0.321(-49%)**	**0.329(-59%)**	**0.39(-65%)**	**0.372(-73%)**

Table 4: Two queries and their suggestions returned by our fusion approach, SE1, and SE2 together with their NDCG@3. All suggestions are changed to lowercase.

Our Approach		SE1		SE2	
Query: what's in fashion (NDCG@3=0.1564)					
latest fashion trends	0.5307	what in fashion 2011	0	fashion trends	0
fashion now	0.4693	fashion what in 2010	0	what's in fashion 2010	0.2961
hottest casual fashion trends women	0.2346	what's in fashion now 2010	0	what's in fashion for men	0
fashion trends women	0.2961	what's in fashion fall 2010	0.1564	what's in fashion for teens	0
styles cool fashion	0	what in fashion this summer	0	what's in fashion 2009	0.1564
Query: gallery furniture (NDCG@3=0.2939)					
gallery furniture address	0.3728	carson pirie scott furniture gallery	0	fingers furniture	0
gallery furniture bedroom	0.2939	ashley furniture gallery	0	ashley furniture	0
gallery furniture sales you money card	0.2346	the dump furniture store	0	star furniture	0
gallery furnisher	0.2387	macy's furniture galleries	0	furniture store	0
gallery furniture post oak	0.2387	fingers furniture	0	hilton furniture	0

6. ADAPTIVE QUERY SUGGESTION

To make good suggestions for all the queries, it is important to distinguish difficult queries from easy ones. A key problem is to predict how difficult a query is. Although we have used a simple feature (Estimated NDCG) to reflect the query difficulty in the learning-to-rank model, there is still the need to determine query difficulty with a more sophisticated method and explicitly use it to vary the strategy of query suggestion. We will carry out experiments using such a prediction of query difficulty.

6.1 Learning to Predict Difficult Queries

Various methods have been proposed to predict query difficulty. Any effective predictor can be used in our experiments. We choose to use the RAPP method proposed in [5]. The key idea behind this approach is to use the ranking scores, as well as the features that are used for ranking documents (e.g. BM25, click and PageRank), to predict the quality of the results. We re-implement the approach of [5].

We conduct three-fold cross validation to train a regressor using all queries, including easy queries and difficult queries. The predicted difficulty value for a query q is denoted by $g(q)$. If the query q is judged as difficult according to $g(q)$, we return suggestions that are generated by our fusion approach to users. This leads to an adaptive approach for query suggestion, i.e. more query suggestions for difficult queries than for easy queries.

6.2 Experiments on Adaptive Query Suggestion

To quantitatively test the idea, we assume that a certain suggestion budget (the number of suggestions) is allowed for the entire query set, and our goal is to distribute the budget on different queries according to their difficulty. The budget is defined by m suggestion slots per query on average. The total suggestion slots available for all our test queries is then defined by $4,068 \times m$. To make our test easier, we will assume that whenever a query is considered to be worthy for suggestions, we propose 5 suggestions. This is in line with our evaluation method that uses the top 5 suggestions. Therefore, we will select to perform query suggestion on $n = 4,068 \times m \div 5$ most difficult queries. For the other queries, no suggestion will be provided. This evaluation schema is of course a simplification of the real situation; but it does reflect the latter to some extent.

For a budget of m slots per query, we evaluate our adaptive query suggestion approach and the fusion approach on the Max@ns metric. Here ns is the total number of the

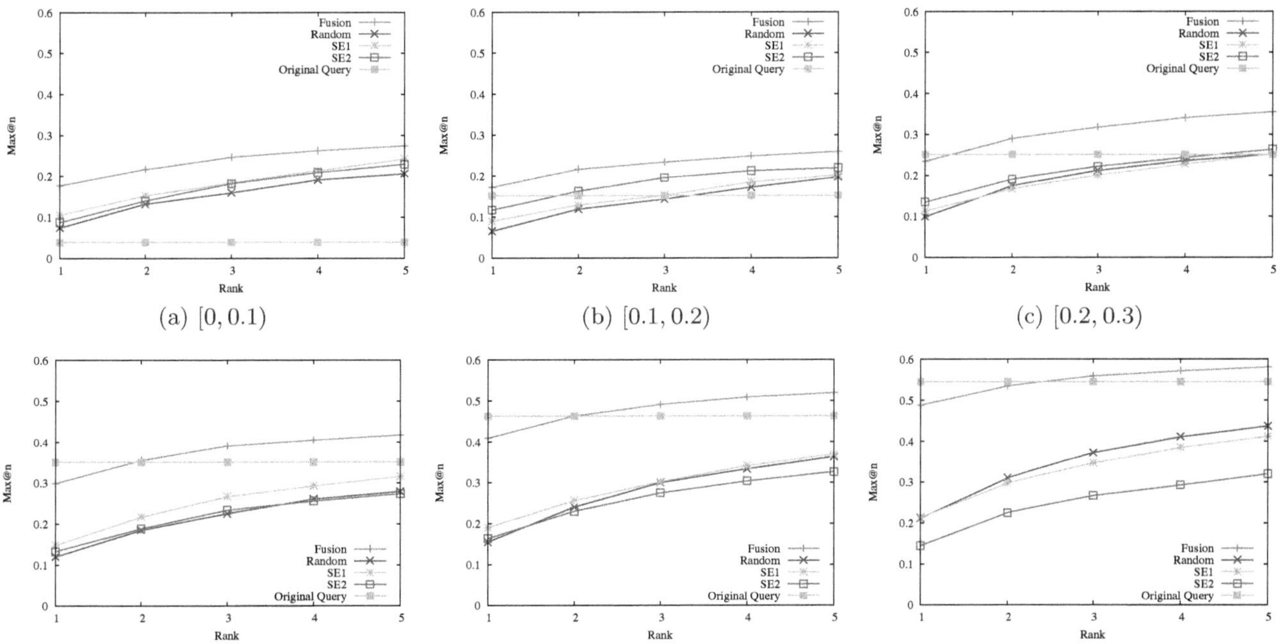

(a) $[0, 0.1)$ (b) $[0.1, 0.2)$ (c) $[0.2, 0.3)$

(d) $[0.3, 0.4)$ (e) $[0.4, 0.5)$ (f) $[0.5, 0.6)$

Figure 5: Effectiveness comparison among different approaches in different bins

suggestions assigned to a query. For the queries without suggestion, we use NDCG@3 of the original query to calculate Max@ns. Figure 6 shows the average Max@ns scores of the adaptive approach (**Adaptive**) and the fusion approach (**Fusion**), along with different number of suggestions: $m = 1 \dots 5$. We also plot the average NDCG@3 values of all original queries (**Original Query**) in the figure.

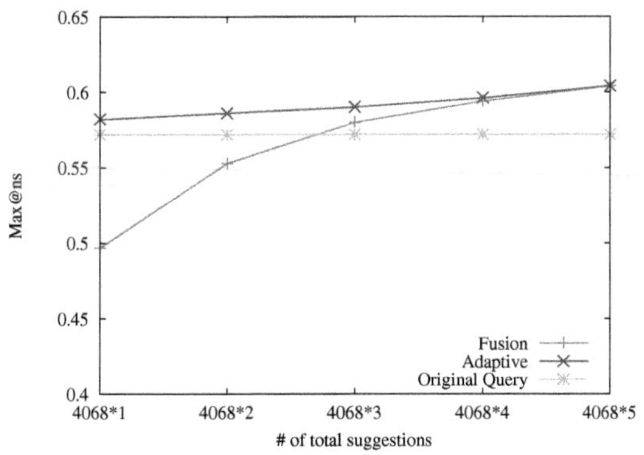

Figure 6: Comparing adaptive query suggestion with the fusion approach and the original queries with budget control

As shown in Figure 6, our adaptive approach consistently outperforms the fusion approach and the original queries. Specifically, when m is small (one or two), the fusion approach cannot suggest queries better than the original ones. One can only find better queries when there are 3 slots or more. This is because the slots are uniformly distributed over all the queries, including on easy queries which do not need suggestions. The adaptive approach successfully avoids this problem. It can target more difficult queries for which query suggestion is more useful. Its improvements over the original queries are statistically significant for all budget settings.

The above simulation provides a good indication that one can gain more in targeting difficult queries for query suggestion. However, we assumed an equal number (5) of suggestions for all the queries whose $g(q)$ is lower than a threshold. In practice, this strategy can be improved by proposing different numbers of suggestions according to $g(q)$. We will leave this to future work.

7. CONCLUSION

Query suggestion is widely used by search engines. Although it is found useful, the method is used uniformly on all the queries. In this paper, we show that query suggestion is more beneficial for difficult queries than for easy queries. To the best of our knowledge, this is the first investigation of query suggestion according to query difficulty.

In this paper, we used a learning-to-rank method to learn to rank suggestion candidates by using different features. Then an adaptive approach is proposed to provide suggestions according to the estimation on query difficulty. The experiments reported in this paper show that:

1. There is much more to gain in proposing query suggestions for difficult queries;
2. To be useful, the suggestions for more difficult queries should be less similar to the original query;
3. An adaptive suggestion according to query difficulty is the most useful approach;

In addition to the above conclusions, we also proposed two new evaluation measures that take into account the possible improvements in NDCG by the suggested queries, as well as their ranking in the suggestion list. These measures can better reflect the use of suggestions by end users than the previous measures.

This work is a first step towards adaptive query suggestion. There is much room for future improvements. First, in order to gain more insights on query suggestion for the whole spectrum of queries, we may need to train different, difficulty-dependent, query suggestion models. That is, for each category of queries, a specific model is trained to predict whether it is useful to suggest queries and what type of query is the most useful. Second, the true usefulness of different query suggestion methods should be tested with true users. Third, the proposed method can be used in different tasks. For example, as we have shown, some suggested queries lead to better search results. It is then possible to utilize our suggestions to automatically re-rank the search results of difficult queries.

8. REFERENCES

[1] G. Amati, C. Carpineto, and G. Romano. Query difficulty, robustness, and selective application of query expansion. In *ECIR*, pages 127–137, 2004.

[2] R. A. Baeza-Yates, C. A. Hurtado, and M. Mendoza. Query recommendation using query logs in search engines. In *EDBT Workshops*, pages 588–596, 2004.

[3] R. A. Baeza-Yates and A. Tiberi. Extracting semantic relations from query logs. In *KDD*, pages 76–85, 2007.

[4] N. Balasubramanian, G. Kumaran, and V. R. Carvalho. Exploring reductions for long web queries. In *SIGIR*, pages 571–578, 2010.

[5] N. Balasubramanian, G. Kumaran, and V. R. Carvalho. Predicting query performance on the web. In *SIGIR*, pages 785–786, 2010.

[6] D. Beeferman and A. L. Berger. Agglomerative clustering of a search engine query log. In *KDD*, pages 407–416, 2000.

[7] S. Bhatia, D. Majumdar, and P. Mitra. Query suggestions in the absence of query logs. In *SIGIR*, pages 795–804, 2011.

[8] H. Cao, D. Jiang, J. Pei, Q. He, Z. Liao, E. Chen, and H. Li. Context-aware query suggestion by mining click-through and session data. In *KDD*, pages 875–883, 2008.

[9] D. Carmel and E. Yom-Tov. Estimating the query difficulty for information retrieval. In *SIGIR*, page 911, 2010.

[10] D. Carmel, E. Yom-Tov, A. Darlow, and D. Pelleg. What makes a query difficult? In *SIGIR*, pages 390–397, 2006.

[11] S. Cronen-Townsend, Y. Zhou, and W. B. Croft. Predicting query performance. In *SIGIR*, pages 299–306, 2002.

[12] V. Dang and W. B. Croft. Query reformulation using anchor text. In *WSDM*, pages 41–50, 2010.

[13] N. Eiron and K. S. McCurley. Analysis of anchor text for web search. In *SIGIR*, pages 459–460, 2003.

[14] C. Fox. Lexical analysis and stoplists. *Information Retrieval - Data Structures & Algorithms*, pages 102–130, 1992.

[15] J. Gao, X. Li, D. Micol, C. Quirk, and X. Sun. A large scale ranker-based system for search query spelling correction. In *COLING*, pages 358–366, 2010.

[16] J. Guo, G. Xu, H. Li, and X. Cheng. A unified and discriminative model for query refinement. In *SIGIR*, pages 379–386, 2008.

[17] K. Järvelin and J. Kekäläinen. Cumulated gain-based evaluation of ir techniques. *ACM Trans. Inf. Syst.*, 20(4):422–446, 2002.

[18] J.C.Borda. Mémoire sur les élections au scrution. *Histoire de l'Acadêmie Royal des Sciences*, 1781.

[19] T. Joachims. Optimizing search engines using clickthrough data. In *KDD*, pages 133–142, 2002.

[20] R. Jones, B. Rey, O. Madani, and W. Greiner. Generating query substitutions. In *WWW*, pages 387–396, 2006.

[21] R. Kraft and J. Y. Zien. Mining anchor text for query refinement. In *WWW*, pages 666–674, 2004.

[22] V. Lavrenko and W. B. Croft. Relevance-based language models. In *SIGIR*, pages 120–127, 2001.

[23] H. Ma, H. Yang, I. King, and M. R. Lyu. Learning latent semantic relations from clickthrough data for query suggestion. In *CIKM*, pages 709–718, 2008.

[24] Q. Mei, D. Zhou, and K. W. Church. Query suggestion using hitting time. In *CIKM*, pages 469–478, 2008.

[25] F. Peng, N. Ahmed, X. Li, and Y. Lu. Context sensitive stemming for web search. In *SIGIR*, pages 639–646, 2007.

[26] M. Porter. An algorithm for suffix stripping. *Program: electronic library and information systems*, 14(3):130–137, 1980.

[27] S. E. Robertson. The probability ranking principle in ir. *Journal of Documentation*, 33:130–137, 1977.

[28] Y. Song and L. wei He. Optimal rare query suggestion with implicit user feedback. In *WWW*, pages 901–910, 2010.

[29] Y. Song, D. Zhou, and L. wei He. Post-ranking query suggestion by diversifying search results. In *SIGIR*, pages 815–824, 2011.

[30] T. Tao and C. Zhai. Regularized estimation of mixture models for robust pseudo-relevance feedback. In *SIGIR*, pages 162–169, 2006.

[31] X. Wang and C. Zhai. Mining term association patterns from search logs for effective query reformulation. In *CIKM*, pages 479–488, 2008.

[32] J.-R. Wen, J.-Y. Nie, and H. Zhang. Clustering user queries of a search engine. In *WWW*, pages 162–168, 2001.

[33] J. Xu and W. B. Croft. Improving the effectiveness of information retrieval with local context analysis. *ACM Trans. Inf. Syst.*, 18(1):79–112, 2000.

[34] E. Yom-Tov, S. Fine, D. Carmel, and A. Darlow. Learning to estimate query difficulty: including applications to missing content detection and distributed information retrieval. In *SIGIR*, pages 512–519, 2005.

[35] Y. Zhou and W. B. Croft. Ranking robustness: a novel framework to predict query performance. In *CIKM*, pages 567–574, 2006.

[36] Y. Zhou and W. B. Croft. Query performance prediction in web search environments. In *SIGIR*, pages 543–550, 2007.

Learning to Suggest: A Machine Learning Framework for Ranking Query Suggestions

Umut Ozertem*
Speech @ Microsoft
Mountain View, CA
umuto@microsoft.com

Olivier Chapelle*
Criteo
Palo Alto, CA
o.chapelle@criteo.com

Pinar Donmez*
Salesforce
San Francisco, CA
pdonmez@salesforce.com

Emre Velipasaoglu
Yahoo! Labs
Sunnyvale, CA
emre_velipasaoglu@yahoo.com

ABSTRACT

We consider the task of suggesting related queries to users after they issue their initial query to a web search engine. We propose a machine learning approach to learn the probability that a user may find a follow-up query both useful and relevant, given his initial query. Our approach is based on a machine learning model which enables us to generalize to queries that have never occurred in the logs as well. The model is trained on co-occurrences mined from the search logs, with novel utility and relevance models, and the machine learning step is done without any labeled data by human judges. The learning step allows us to generalize from the past observations and generate query suggestions that are beyond the past co-occurred queries. This brings significant gains in coverage while yielding modest gains in relevance. Both offline (based on human judges) and online (based on millions of user interactions) evaluations demonstrate that our approach significantly outperforms strong baselines.

Categories and Subject Descriptors

H.3.3 [**Information Search and Retrieval**]: Query Formulation, Retrieval Models

Keywords

search assistance, query suggestion, machine learning, query log mining

1. INTRODUCTION

Query suggestions are an integral part of the modern search experience. Here we are concerned with query reformulation suggestions that are presented the users after they submit their query, rather than query completion suggestions. The latter is useful in helping the user formulate an original query by aiding in spelling and term selection while typing in the query. Query reformulation suggestions, on the other hand, are useful for changing direction once a search query has been already issued. The needs for such an action could include disambiguation once the user realizes after inspection of the results that the concept he had in mind had possibly other stronger meanings different than his. Or, the user may want to formulate an even more precise and succinct query to hone in on better answers. It could also involve modification of the information need based on the information gained by inspection of the search result, to either dive deeper into research or move to a different aspect of a task. The needs are much varied.

Past scientific research is focused on a few main methods to address most user needs for query reformulation. A large group of methods are based on leveraging the "wisdom of crowds" by analyzing the search logs. Another group of methods use term semantics to derive new queries from existing ones. The former group of methods can be divided into those that exploit query co-occurrences in the search logs, and those that leverage the document click information such as random walks over query-document bipartite graphs. In the latter group, a number of query synthesis methods exist, either synthesizing new queries with active user participation, or directly without any user input. We delve into a review of these existing methods in the related works section, and contrast them with our method.

There are a few fundamental shortcomings of these methods, (i) the utility of a query reformulation suggestion to the user's search task is indirectly handled (ii) all co-occurrences in the query logs are treated equally, without modeling the probability that the pair of queries belong to the same search task or not (iii) models that are solely based on collocated queries in the past logs will have limited coverage.

In this paper, we develop a machine learning framework which addresses the above shortcomings. First, the utility argument is handled explicitly by building a utility model that takes into account positions of URLs that are common to result sets of the original query and the suggestions. Second, we propose an implicit task boundary method to model whether a following query is a *continuation* of the preceding queries; as a result, co-occurrences in the search logs are not

*This work was completed while the author was at Yahoo! Labs.

Permission to make digital or hard copies of all or part of this work for personal or classroom use is granted without fee provided that copies are not made or distributed for profit or commercial advantage and that copies bear this notice and the full citation on the first page. To copy otherwise, to republish, to post on servers or to redistribute to lists, requires prior specific permission and/or a fee.
SIGIR'12, August 12–16, 2012, Portland, Oregon, USA.
Copyright 2012 ACM 978-1-4503-1472-5/12/08 ...$10.00.

treated equally, but weighted with the probability that they belong to the same task. Finally, we learn to predict the utility of suggestion by using a rich feature space including lexical and result set features that capture the salient factors of why a suggestion could be useful to the user given his initial query, rather than only relying on the observed query co-occurrences in the past. We train this machine learning model with a learning target derived from the past query co-occurrences rather than relying on human judgments. This allows us to generalize the knowledge trained on the past query co-occurrences and the machine learned model can generate both relevant and useful (query,suggestion) pairs that have never observed in the past logs, leading to a significant increase in coverage. Also, it avoids the costly and time consuming human labeling process. Furthermore, the machine learning framework also has the advantage of providing the apparatus that can effectively blend disparate sources of query suggestion candidates such as those based on wisdom of crowds and those based on synthesis, which has been addressed in an ad-hoc fashion at best so far.

In the next section, we review the existing literature and contrast our method with related works. In Section 3, we describe the proposed framework in more detail. Section 4 dives into the description of how we address utility explicitly by constructing a suitable learning target. Section 5 describes the feature space, the training set and the learning method. Section 6 talks about one strength of this method which can score and blend in synthetic suggestion candidates as well as query extensions observed in the search logs that are too rare for the collocation based methods to capture. These are followed by experimental results in section 7 and conclusions in section 8.

2. RELATED WORK

Leveraging "wisdom of crowds" has been very popular in generating query suggestions. A large set of research articles focused on leveraging the session structure and other information to find alternate queries to suggest. The main idea is to find pairs of queries that frequently co-occur in users' search sessions and use them as suggestions for each other. For example, Huang et al. [10] find such co-occurrences and rank the suggestions for an input query by frequency of co-occurrence, $freq(q_1, q_2)$, where q_1 is the input query and q_2 is a suggestion candidate (within a certain time window in the same user session). Jensen et al. [12] considered *point-wise mutual information* (PMI) along with frequency of co-occurrence. PMI is defined as

$$\text{PMI}(q_2, q_1) = \log\left(\frac{\Pr(q_2, q_1)}{\Pr(q_1)\Pr(q_2)}\right) \quad (1)$$

For a particular q_1, the $\Pr(q_1)$ term is constant for all the possible suggestion candidates, and ordering given by PMI only depends on the ratio of the frequency of q_2 conditioned on q_1 divided by the marginal frequency of q_2. While, frequency of co-occurrence is not a test of dependence, PMI is a valid test of independence. However, PMI favors rare events [24]. A preferred test of collocations in text corpora has been G^2 *log-likelihood-ratio* (LLR), introduced to NLP by Dunning [7]. Moore gives several formulations of G^2 in [17] and shows it is equivalent to *mutual information* (MI)

$$\begin{aligned}\text{MI}(q_2, q_1) = {} & \Pr(q_2, q_1)\text{PMI}(q_2, q_1) + \Pr(q_2, \overline{q}_1)\text{PMI}(q_2, \overline{q}_1) \\ & + \Pr(\overline{q}_2, q_1)\text{PMI}(\overline{q}_2, q_1) + \Pr(\overline{q}_2, \overline{q}_1)\text{PMI}(\overline{q}_2, \overline{q}_1)\end{aligned} \quad (2)$$

where $\overline{q}$ denotes the set of all queries except q. MI addresses the bias of PMI by taking into account the probabilities of the complement events as well. LLR was found to be among the best performing statistical tests of dependence by Thanopoulos et al. [24] for extracting collocations. LLR was used by Jones et. al. [13] as a feature in a machine learning framework to expand queries for matching advertisements to an input query.

Boldi et al. [3] move to a more structured processing of the sessions by building a query-flow graph where the nodes are queries and edges are associated with weights that capture how likely a user is to move from one query to the next within a session. Then, neighbors with the largest edge weights are selected as suggestions for an input query. In [2], they also classified the transitions as specializations which are essentially query extensions, generalizations which are usually contractions, errors corrections and lateral moves, and use these categories for selecting suggestions for different purposes.

Another group of methods focused on leveraging the clicked documents by building a query-document bipartite graph. Assumption here is that similar queries have larger overlap between their respective clicks. For example, Mei et al. [15] use a random walk over the bipartite graph to find similar queries. Beeferman et al. [1] use hierarchical agglomerative clustering iteratively to find groups of queries that are similar and can be used as suggestions for one another, however, this is expensive. Baeza-Yates et al. [21] used an efficient k-means algorithm to find similar queries, but it requires the number clusters ahead of time. Sadikov et al. [22] combined the query-flow graphs with document click information to find query suggestions.

Query synthesis methods looked into generating suggestions by leveraging search logs as well as external information sources. Szpektor et al. [23] use a template generation method by leveraging WordNet [16]. Use of all token boundaries in segmentation of the queries leads to many poor suggestion candidates. Jain et al. [11] use Conditional Random Fields to segment to queries, yielding better results. They also use a machine learned stage to filter bad suggestions but they do not address blending the suggestions with other methods such as those based on session analysis. Both in [11] and [13] the machine learning for suggestion scoring is based on editorial labels, whereas in our method we use probabilities estimated from the query logs as regression target.

3. PROPOSED FRAMEWORK

This section gives an overview of our proposed pipeline. The detailed description of each component follows in the subsequent sections. Below is a brief summary of each component.

- **Target Generation**: The first step deals with estimating a scoring function that measures how useful and relevant is a follow-up query to a given query. We estimate this score by a probabilistic utility function that relies on the query co-occurrence. We discuss different definitions of the query co-occurrence in the next section. The scores are used as the target values in our machine learning model. This is a discriminating advantage of our method and one of our main contributions since it saves the costly and time consuming human labeling process.

- **Features**: The next step of the pipeline is to create the feature vector representation of each query pair in the data. We use two sets of features, namely lexical and result set based features. They are designed to capture the semantic similarity and helpfulness of the suggestion to the original query which is formally defined in the following section. Since the features do not depend on the session logs, it allows our system to handle synthetically generated suggestion candidates. This is another differentiator of our approach when learning query suggestions.

- **Ranking Model**: Once the target scores are estimated and the features are generated, we perform regression using Gradient Boosted Decision Tree (GBDT). This model enables us to rank the suggestion candidates for a given a query, and eliminate the irrelevant and useless ones.

- **Candidates**: The candidate suggestions we tested the ranking model on come from various sources including query logs. However, query logs provide only limited number of candidates especially for rare queries. To address the sparsity, we use additional candidate queries that are either synthetically generated or extended queries. Our feature space is appropriate to blend in such candidates with those obtained from query logs.

4. TARGET GENERATION

4.1 Query Co-occurrence

The targets to be used in our machine learning model depend on $\Pr(q_2, q_1)$, namely the probability of *query co-occurrence*. In this paper, we define query co-occurence as when two queries are manually[1] issued by the same user within the same *session*. We define the user session as all the user activity within a time window limited by 10 minutes of inactivity. Nevertheless, the models we develop in this paper do not strictly depend on this definition and can be used with other timeout limits or other definitions of user session.

A first design choice is whether to consider all pairs of queries within the same session or consecutive queries only. The latter option makes the query co-occurrence set robust to intent drift in the search session. The intent drift can be defined as the gradual change in user's intent as the search session progresses, and perhaps can be explained best by an example. Here is a real search session: "lost cast" → "dexter cast" → "michael c. hall" → "michael c. hall cancer". The argument against restricting to consecutive pairs is that the majority of sessions do not have such intent drift and it results in a significant decrease in coverage. We will provide experiments with both of these choices.

The simplest approach for scoring suggestion candidates is to measure the reformulation probabilities from the frequency counts in the logs and pick the queries with the highest reformulation probabilities $\Pr(q_2 \mid q_1)$,

$$\Pr(q_2 \mid q_1) = \frac{\Pr(q_2, q_1)}{\Pr(q_1)} \qquad (3)$$

[1]We ignore queries suggested by the system because they may introduce a *presentation bias*.

Here $\Pr(q_2, q_1)$ is the probability that q_2 occurs after q_1 within the same session and $\Pr(q_1)$ is the marginal probability of q_1. There are two problems with this approach. First it could be that the query q_2 is unrelated to q_1. This happens when q_1 and q_2 belong to different *tasks* that the user wants to solve. One way to address that issue would be to consider only queries within the same task, but this requires a system for detecting task boundaries [2] which itself can be prone to errors. In this paper we propose a solution that does not rely on task boundary detection. The second problem is that the result page associated with query q_2 may not be useful, for example if the documents that q_2 retrieves are identical of those of the original query q_1.

For these reasons, we say that, given a query pair (q_1, q_2), the query q_2 was a *helpful* reformulation of query q_1 if and only if the following two conditions are satisfied:

1. The query q_2 is a *continuation* of q_1. If the query q_2 is the beginning of a new task and has nothing to do with q_1, we should not consider q_2 to be a helpful reformulation for q_1.

2. The query q_2 has a positive *utility*, that is the search results returned for that query are useful to the user.

The details of these two conditions are described in the next two sections.

4.2 Utility of Reformulations

When trying to assess the utility of a reformulation, a simple criterion is to say that reformulations that lead to a click in the result page of q_2 are useful, and the others are not useful. In the extreme case, a query for which the search engine does not return any results cannot be a good suggestion by definition.

But reformulations followed by a click are not always useful. Consider the following query reformulations that appear frequently in query logs "bank of america" → "bank of america online" or "facebook" → "facebook login". Although co-occurrences like these lead to a click on the result set of the second query q_2, they do not likely take the user to a destination URL that is not already directly accessible from the original query q_1. We thus define a reformulation to be useful only if it leads to a click on a URL that either is not existing in the search result page of q_1 or that is ranked higher than that in the search result page of q_1.

For formalizing this idea we compare the ranks of the same URLs in q_1 and q_2 (if any) and use the rank discounts that DCG uses. Let D_c be the set of clicked documents on the result page of q_2 and $r(q, d)$ returns the rank of the given document $d \in D_c$ for the given query q and returns $+\inf$ if the URL is not ranked. The total difference in discounts of the clicked documents Δ is defined as

$$\Delta = \sum_{d \in D_c} \left(\frac{1}{\log r(q_2, d)} - \frac{1}{\log r(q_1, d)} \right) \qquad (4)$$

When there was a click on q_2, the reformulation is defined to be useful if $\Delta > 0$. This occurs only if at least one of the two conditions above holds for one of the clicked url.

In addition to the condition in (4), we also consider the queries that can address the user need directly in the search result page (without any clicks) as useful [5]. For example, weather information in the weather direct answer module for the query "lake tahoe weather", or current stock quote

Table 1: Effect of the implicit session model (see section 4.3).

$\Pr(q_2 \mid q_1)$		$\Pr(q_2 \mid q_1, c=1)$	
facebook	0.0286	rei	0.0431
ebay	0.0244	nordstrom	0.0342
amazon	0.0225	dicks	0.0307
rei	0.0214	columbia	0.0281
nordstrom	0.0191	macys	0.0274

q_1 = northface

$\Pr(q_2 \mid q_1)$		$\Pr(q_2 \mid q_1, c=1)$	
facebook	0.0794	chase	0.0993
chase	0.0415	capital one	0.0558
wells fargo	0.0227	wells fargo	0.0530
capital one	0.0223	american express	0.0404
google	0.0185	bank of america online	0.0281

q_1 = bank of america

and other details in the finance module for the query "amzn" are examples of such queries, where the user does not need any clicks to get to the desired information. Therefore in addition to the condition in (4), if there is no further query reformulation in the session, and if the final query of the session contains such direct answer modules, we consider these queries to be useful reformulations as well.

To sum up, we define a query reformulation to be useful if either there was at least a click on q_2 and $\Delta > 0$; or there was no click on q_2, the result page of q_2 contained a direct answer module and there was no further reformulation afterwards.

4.3 Implicit Task Boundary Detection

Remember that we want to compute the probability that q_2 follows q_1 under the condition that q_2 is a continuation of q_1 (denoted by $c = 1$) and that it is useful (denoted by $u = 1$) as defined in the previous section; that is,

$$\Pr(q_2 \mid q_1, c = 1, u = 1). \tag{5}$$

First, note that u is an observed variable, while c is not. It is in particular straightforward to compute $\Pr(q_2 \mid q_1, u = 1)$ by simply filtering out the pairs for which $u = 0$. In the rest of this section, we will thus assume that all probabilities are implicitly conditioned on $u = 1$ and will drop that conditioning from the equations.

The following equation holds:

$$\begin{aligned}\Pr(q_2 \mid q_1) = \Pr(q_2 \mid q_1, c = 0) \Pr(c = 0 \mid q_1) \\ + \Pr(q_2 \mid q_1, c = 1) \Pr(c = 1 \mid q_1).\end{aligned} \tag{6}$$

Let us denote $\mu = \Pr(c = 0 \mid q_1)$. In the case that the user issues an unrelated query ($c = 0$), q_1 and q_2 are independent and thus $\Pr(q_2 \mid q_1, c = 0) = \Pr(q_2 \mid c = 0)$ that we approximate as the marginal distribution $\Pr(q_2)$. Equation (6) becomes:

$$\Pr(q_2 \mid q_1) = \mu \Pr(q_2) + (1 - \mu) \Pr(q_2 \mid q_1, c = 1). \tag{7}$$

In equation (7), both $\Pr(q_2 \mid q_1)$ and $\Pr(q_2)$ are known distributions and the distribution that we want to compute is $\Pr(q_2 \mid q_1, c = 1)$. At a high level, this can be achieved by subtracting $\mu \Pr(q_2)$ from $\Pr(q_2 \mid q_1)$. But we cannot do this subtraction naively as this could lead to negative probabilities. The correct way of computing $\Pr(q_2 \mid q_1, c = 1)$ is a maximum likelihood estimation as explained below.

Let us consider for now that μ is known and fixed. For a given query q_1, let us denote the n unique queries q_2 that co-occured with q_1 as $q^1, \ldots, q^n$ and let N_{q^i} be the number of co-occurences. With these notations, we have that $\Pr(q_2 = q^i \mid q_1) \propto N_{q^i}$. Finally, let $p_i = \Pr(q_2 = q^i \mid q_1, c = 1)$ be the probabilities that we want to evaluate. The maximum likelihood estimate can be formulated as the solution of the following optimization problem:

$$\max_{p_i} \sum_{i=1}^{n} N_{q^i} \log[\ \mu\ \Pr(q_2 = q^i) + (1 - \mu)\ p_i\ ], \tag{8}$$

under constraints,

$$\sum_i p_i = 1, \quad p_i \geq 0.$$

In practice, in order to avoid solving a constrained optimization problem, we perform the following change of variables,

$$p_i = \frac{\exp(x_i)}{\sum_j \exp(x_j)},$$

and we are left with a convex and unconstrained optimization problem on x_i which can be solved using standard optimization techniques such as non-linear conjugate gradient descent.

Note that in the extreme case $\mu = 0$, the optimal solution of (8) is $p_i = N_{q^i} / \sum_j N_{q^j} = \Pr(q_2 = q^i \mid q_1)$, which concurs with equation (7).

The only part left is how to select, for each q_1, $\mu = \Pr(c = 0 \mid q_1)$. We use the following intuition: $\Pr(q_2)$ has a very large entropy, but the entropy of $\Pr(q_2 \mid q_1, c = 1)$ should be much smaller because there are only a limited number of queries that users are likely to type as a continuation of q_1. Our heuristic to select μ is to find the value such that the resulting distribution p_i has minimum entropy. On top of this entropy criterion, we add a Beta(1,10) prior on μ, reflecting that for most queries q_1, the following query q_2 is unrelated (large μ).

The importance of conditioning on $c = 1$ is illustrated in table 1. Without this conditioning, irrelevant but frequent queries such as "facebook" tend to have a high $\Pr(q_2 \mid q_1)$ value.

5. MACHINE LEARNING

This section first discusses the feature space that the ranking model uses and then the training process.

5.1 Features

We use two main categories of features: lexical features and result set features as shown in Tables 2 and 3. Most of the features are intuitively simple and the short descriptions are enough, and the rest is detailed here. We do not use session log features because they are not defined for synthetic suggestions as well as other candidate suggestions.

The lexical features use the query strings themselves, like number of words in each query, number of words or characters they share in the beginning or at the end, and Levenshtein distance [14] between the two queries.

In the result set features, there are mainly two types: those that consider the quality of the results and those that

Table 2: Lexical features

Feature	Short Description
LEV	Levenshtein distance between q_1 and q_2
LQ1	length of q_1
LQ2	length of q_2
LDIFF	LQ1-LQ2
ABSLDIFF	abs(LDIFF)
ABSLDIFFN	ABSLDIFF/LQ1
NW1	number of tokens in q_1
NW2	number of tokens in q_2
COMMONW	number of tokens in common in q_1 and q_2
COMMONWN	COMMONW/NW1
COMMONWP	tokens in common in the beginning
COMMONWS	tokens in common at the end
COMMONCP	characters in common in the beginning
COMMONCS	characters in common at the end

consider the overlap of the two result sets. For assessing the quality of the results we use scores given by a learning to rank system (LTR), but any other relevance score such as BM25 could have been used. Queries that have better results should have higher average LTR scores. We use the LTR scores themselves, as well as the difference and the ratio, intuitively, a high quality query suggestion should have good results, even better if it has better results than the original query, which creates assisted paths to relevant and well formed queries.

Another group of features is the number of common URLs and domains in top K ranks. These aim to determine the overlap in the result sets of q_1 and q_2, which has been used as a query-pair level relevance metric [20, 8]. We typically expect the predictions to be high when the values of these features are in a medium range: when the overlap between queries is too small, they are probably not related; and when it is too large, the query q_2 does not contain any new information relative to q_1 (see section 4.2). Number of common URLs gives a strong signal but it is non-zero for only a very small portion of query pairs. To overcome this sparsity issue, we also use the number of common domains. One clear observation is that having results from the same domain is much more informative if the domain is a tail one. As the domain becomes more generic such as `wikipedia.org` or `cnn.com` having such a domain in common becomes less meaningful. To capture this intuition, we use inverse query frequency (IQF) [6], similar to the inverse document frequency well-known in TF-IDF. IQF of a given domain d is

$$\mathrm{IQF}(d) = \log\left(\frac{|Q|}{|q : d \in q|}\right) \quad (9)$$

In words, this is the log of the ratio of number of all queries to the number of queries that lead to at least one result with the given domain d. We generate another set of features using the sum of IQF of the common domains in top K ranks.

Result set aboutness: Aboutness vector similarity is by far the most important (and also the most complicated) result set feature that we use and merits special attention. The problem with the result set overlap based measures is that although they are effective at identifying queries that are very close in meaning (almost synonymous), the overlap drops very sharply to zero when the compared queries are relevant, but not almost identical in meaning. In the context of query suggestions, it is important to identify relevant queries not only almost identical ones. CODOMAINIQF solves this problem up to some extent. Yet, one needs compare not only whether the pair of queries return the same results, but also whether the two queries have results that are not identical but are about the same or similar concept. This will give an idea on the semantic relation between a pair of queries.

Table 3: Result set features

Feature	Short Description
LTR11	LTR score of the top result for q_1
LTR21	LTR score of the top result for q_2
LTR15	average LTR score at top 5 for q_1
LTR25	average LTR score at top 5 for q_2
LTR110	average LTR score at top 10 for q_1
LTR210	average LTR score at top 10 for q_2
LTRRATIO1	LTR11/LTR21
LTRDIFF1	LTR11-LTR21
LTRRATIO5	LTR15/LTR25
LTRDIFF5	LTR15-LTR25
LTRRATIO10	LTR110/LTR210
LTRDIFF10	LTR110-LTR210
COURLCOUNT1	boolean, URLs in top result are the same
COURLCOUNT5	number of the same URLs in top 5
COURLCOUNT10	number of the same URLs in top 10
CODOMAINCOUNT1	boolean, domains of the top results are the same
CODOMAINCOUNT5	number of same domains in top 5
CODOMAINCOUNT10	number of same domains in top 10
CODOMAINIQF1	IQF of of the domain at top result, if the same
CODOMAINIQF5	total IQF of the common domains in top 5
CODOMAINIQF10	total IQF of the common domains in top 10
ABOUTNESS	cosine similarity over the aboutness vectors

For example, "toyota prius" and "toyota yaris" are quite related and would be considered good suggestions although have no results in common in top 10, based on the results returned by a web search engine. Hence, the result set overlap is insufficient to assess relevance. This particular one is an example that CODOMAINIQF cannot also handle, because although the queries are quite relevant, the common domains that they have are quite popular domains with low IQF scores (`toyota.com`, `autos.yahoo.com`, `autos.msn.com`, `wikipedia.org`).

To build a semantic similarity metric, we construct an aboutness vector of each query, which can be considered as a bag-of-words representation based on the web results, which consists of the *concepts*—that are part of a predefined concept dictionary—in the documents returned for this query. This is based on previous work [19] which computed for each concept and each document an aboutness score defined as the probability that a user interested in this concept would find the document relevant. Algorithm 1 explains how to extend the computation of this aboutness score from documents to query. The score for a query is a weighted sum of the scores of the documents returned for that query, where the weights put more emphasis on documents ranked higher. Finally the aboutness similarity of a query pair is the cosine similarity between the corresponding aboutness vectors. Table 4 shows examples of queries, and their top 20 concept terms ranked in descending order with respect to $S(t)$, the aboutness score of the concept term t. Although quite related, the pairs of queries presented here have zero results in common.

Algorithm 1 Algorithm to compute the aboutness vector

Require: Concept dictionary D, query q.
Retrieve set R of top-k results for q.
for concept $t \in D$ **do**
  $S(t) = 0$
  for $i = 1, .., k$ **do**
    $d = i$-th document in R.
    if concept t is in d **then**
      $a =$ aboutness score of concept t in D [19].
      $S(t) = S(t) + 0.9^{i-1} a$.
    end if
  end for
end for
Set $S(t)$ to 0 for the concepts t that are not in the top 20 highest scores.
Aboutness vector: $\mathbf{a}(q) := [\ldots, S(t), \ldots]$

Table 4: Examples of the aboutness vector

Query	Terms in the aboutness vector (ordered)
iphone 4	iphone, store, 4, camera, phone, apps, inc, facetime, mode, recording, software, 3gs, resolution, battery, shop, network, ios, 3g, broadband, ipod
blackberry storm	blackberry, smartphone, verizon, touchscreen, 3g, storm, rim, blackberry, blackberry curve, iphone, vodafone, blackberry pearl, battery, apps, gps, camera, 2, battery life, gsm, research in motion
toyota prius	hybrid, car, prius, toyota, mpg, photo, price, sales, specs, vehicle, yaris, cars, review, reviews, msrp, specification, milage, model, economy, research
toyota yaris	yaris, hatchback, car, price, hybrid, toyota, models, spec, mpg, liftback, dealer, model, vehicles, review, photo, reviews, city, prius, transmission, vehicle

5.2 Learning

We first compute all probabilities of co-occurences $\Pr(q_1, q_2)$ based on one year of a commercial search engine logs. For each query pair, we use the utility and the implicit task boundary detection models to compute the training targets $\Pr(q_2 \mid q_1, c = 1, u = 1)$, and the features as explained above.

Since training a model on all query pairs would be time consuming, the pairs are subsampled as follows. We first select a subset of queries q_1. Each query q_1 is included in that set with probability $\min(1, c_1 \Pr(q_1))$, where c_1 is a constant. This results in a set of 13,220 queries q_1. Similarly, for each q_1, we select a subset of q_2 with probability $\min(1, c_2 \Pr(q_2 \mid q_1))$. This sampling insures, at both levels, that the head queries are selected as well as some of the tail queries. The median size of q_2 for a given q_1 is 30 and the total number of training instances is 382,740.

The learning algorithm is Gradient Boosted Decision Trees (GBDT) [9]. All the hyperparameters of this algorithm—number of trees, number of nodes, shrinkage factor—are tuned on a separate validation set.

6. SUGGESTION CANDIDATES

We review in this section the three different sources of candidates that will be scored by our model.

6.1 Query logs

The most obvious source of candidates come from the co-occurences in the logs. In order to reduce the number of suggestions, for head queries in particular, we only consider the queries q_2 which co-occured at least 3 times with q_1.

But relying only on query logs still limits the coverage of query suggestions and many queries with a low query log frequency will remain with a few or no suggestions. To further increase the coverage, we use additional sources of information as well, and the rest of this section briefly presents these sources; synthetic suggestions [11], and most frequent specializations.

6.2 Synthetic Suggestions

Here we use a recent work on a synthetic query suggestion generation method that combines a number of unit level operations such as dropping words or several ways of word replacements, to build synthetic query suggestions. Below we give a very brief summary of the method, and for further details please refer to the original paper [11]. Also, note that there is nothing in the relevance model or the feature space that is specifically tuned for this particular method, and one could have used any other query suggestion generation method as well [16, 23]. This is one of the biggest advantages of the proposed framework since it is flexible to work with any type of suggestion candidates since the features do not require historical data from the past session logs.

The first step of the synthetic query generation method we use is a unit importance model, which segments the query into units and assigns importance weights to each unit. Afterwards, less important units of the query are dropped, or replaced with other contextually relevant units. The unit replacements come from sources like: (i) queries that co-occur frequently (same as in PMI, LLR) (ii) phrases from queries that lead to clicks to same URLs ("thanksgiving recipe" and "turkey recipe" lead to clicks on same documents, then "thanksgiving" and "turkey" are substitutable units in the context of "recipe").

Probably the best way to briefly explain how the synthetic query generation works is walking through a few examples. The query "big lots store" does not have many good suggestions as compared to "big lots", due to much lower frequency. Here, after the importance model decides the term "store" can be dropped, it brings the queries that are frequently co-occurring with "big lots" as suggestions for the query "big lots store". The query "cost cutters new jersey" does not have any suggestions, again due to low frequency. The importance model decides "cost cutters" is more important, and drops "new jersey". Queries that frequently co-occur with "cost cutters" are identified and the dropped place name is added back to these to generate synthetic suggestions like "supercuts new jersey", "great clips new jersey". For details on the importance models determines which terms to drop and so on, please refer to the original paper [11].

6.3 Most Frequent Extensions

A significant portion of the query reformulations are extensions, where the user adds more terms to the original query. Even in the cases without a reliable co-occurrence signal, in many cases the most frequent queries that contain the current query can be relevant and useful suggestions. In fact, this idea also has been the backbone of the query completion features in the search industry. The drop-down table that suggests completions of the query as the user is typing is based on the most frequent queries that contain the user entered portion of the query.

We will use up to 20 most frequent queries that contains the original query as a suggestion source, but with one modification; we use a word boundary condition to bring these completions where the query is a full word, so that if the query is "awk" it is not completed to "awkward family pictures" or "awkward tv moments" as it would in query completion, but rather bring suggestions like "awk example" or "awk tutorial".

Although it does not bring nonsensical queries as in the synthetic suggestions method, this can also bring many irrelevant suggestions and again cannot be used directly. For example for the query "dream", among many good suggestions like "dream interpretations" or "dream dictionary" this also brings "dream theater", a progressive rock band that has nothing to do with the meaning of the original query. We use the machine learning model to get rid of such irrelevant suggestions.

7. EVALUATION

We conducted a careful, thorough analysis of the proposed system to verify its effectiveness. In this section, we first review the experimental setup and then offer the empirical analysis through the discussion of the major findings.

7.1 Experimental Setup

Query Set: We collected a random sample of 912 fully anonymized queries issued on a commercial search engine according to their frequency.

Manual Annotation: All manual annotation tasks described were performed by a group of eight professional search engine quality evaluators experienced with assessing the quality of query suggestions and search results.

Annotation Guidelines: Professional annotators provided 4-level ratings (excellent, good, fair, bad) for the ranked suggestions for these 912 unique queries. Annotators were asked to base their judgement after looking at the results page and comparing those for the query and the suggestion; this is important to capture the utility of a suggestion.

Variations of the system: We designed a systematic evaluation where we tested different versions of our system against the baseline. We briefly review each version below:

`B`: As a baseline, the candidates are ranked according to mutual information (2). Only the suggestions with a score larger than 50 are kept, and the threshold value is set empirically by optimizing the trade-off between the quality and coverage.

`10M`: Score of a suggestion is directly computed by the utility estimation $\Pr(q_2 \mid q_1, u = 1, c = 1)$. There is no machine learning model and only the suggestions from the query logs are considered. Co-occurrence of all query pairs are considered within a session of 10 minutes, as described in Section 4.

`10M-ML`: Scores are predicted by the GBDT model. Only the suggestions from the query logs are considered

`10M-ML-SY`: Same as `10M-ML` with the difference that synthetic suggestions (section 6.2) and most frequent specializations (section 6.3) are also scored.

`10MC, 10MC-ML, 10MC-ML-SY`: Same as the above three models except that only consecutive pairs in a session are treated as co-occurrences -to avoid the intent drift in the sessions.

We did not consider a baseline trained on the labeled data alone as an interesting baseline to report on. The reasons can be summarized as follows. With the exception of query substitutions work of Jones et. al. [13], most notable query suggestion research focused on sources other than editorial labels for training machine learning systems. Editorial data is expensive, and generalizing to the tail at web scale requires a lot of labeled data. Search result ranking is probably a simpler problem than query suggestion ranking since, the latter attempts to learn utility left over from the current search. Yet, state of the art methods for learning to rank search results utilize tens of thousands of labeled examples (see Yahoo! Learning to Rank Challenge [4]). Learning to suggest properly would probably require more. Jones et. al. can do with a training set of 1000 query pairs because their task is bid term generation which is much simpler than suggesting queries for various reasons. First, the task is designed to retrieve query substitutions for the current search (so ad coverage can be increased), rather than utility for subsequent searches. Second, non-sensical substitutions are filtered by matching to the advertisers' bid terms. And last but not least, even the surviving ones are not shown to the user directly. Training on the session data holds other advantages as well. User feedback on additional utility of a suggestion given the current search is directly captured, which is difficult in the editorial data. Our system, on the other hand, does not rely on a large set of labeled data but rather simulates target labels based on the likelihood of the suggestions.

Offline Evaluation: The offline analysis relies on the editorial judgments and there are two major criteria that we deem important to measure. First is the ability of the system to rank the good quality suggestions higher. The second measures the number of queries for which the system is not able to bring any suggestions. These two criteria is analogous to the precision-recall tradeoff in standard document retrieval problems. We adopt DCG and Precision at various cut-off points to measure the quality of the ranked suggestions.

$$\mathrm{DCG}@k = \sum_{i=1}^{k} \frac{2^{l_q^i} - 1}{\log(1+i)}$$

$$P@k = \frac{\sum_{i=1}^{k} r_q^i}{k} \tag{10}$$

where $l_q^i \in \{0, 1, 2, 3\}$ is the graded relevance (3 is the best) of the suggestion ranked at position i for a given query q. r_q^i is the binary version where the good and excellent labels are transformed into 1 and the rest is assigned 0. The overall DCG and Precision are calculated by averaging over all the queries in the test data.

We defined the *coverage* as the ratio of the number of queries the system could bring suggestions for to the total number of test queries. Coverage measures the likelihood of a system to find suggestions for a given query. Therefore, it complements the DCG and Precision metrics.

Online Evaluation: For the online analysis, we conducted an A/B test where we tested and compared the proposed system (`10M-ML-SY` implementation) against the baseline on live traffic. Both systems are tested on randomly sampled user populations without imposing any bias towards a particular group of users. The suggested queries appear as related searches at the bottom of the result page. Users interactions

Table 5: Coverage, DCG, and Precision improvement compared to the mutual information baseline.

	depth = 1	depth=3	depth=5	depth=7	depth=9	depth=12
Coverage						
10M	-9%	2%	2%	4%	34%	294%
10MC	-9%	0%	0%	2%	33%	282%
10M-ML	-13%	-3%	-1%	2%	32%	289%
10MC-ML	-17%	-7%	-6%	-4%	25%	269%
10M-ML-SY	17%	28%	35%	40%	85%	381%
10MC-ML-SY	17%	28%	34%	40%	84%	365%
DCG on common coverage						
10M	2%	5%	5%	6%	9%	4%
10MC	2%	9%	8%	8%	9%	7%
10M-ML	5%	8%	8%	8%	9%	10%
10MC-ML	5%	7%	8%	9%	10%	9%
10M-ML-SY	7%	9%	8%	9%	10%	10%
10MC-ML-SY	8%	8%	7%	10%	12%	11%
Precision on common coverage						
10M	4%	10%	9%	10%	14%	11%
10MC	8%	13%	11%	12%	15%	11%
10M-ML	7%	10%	10%	11%	12%	12%
10MC-ML	6%	8%	10%	13%	13%	12%
10M-ML-SY	8%	11%	10%	11%	13%	14%
10MC-ML-SY	8%	11%	10%	13%	16%	16%

Table 6: Coverage and CTR improvements of the 10M-ML-SY system in the online test.

	depth = 1	depth=3	depth=5	depth=7	depth=9	depth=12
Coverage	10%	31%	40%	40%	35%	91%
CTR	42%	41%	38%	37%	50%	49%

with the suggested queries are logged in the query logs for a period of one week. To ensure production quality and sufficient diversity of the suggestions, we further remove the low utility queries that are near-duplicates of already suggested queries. The duplicate elimination method is identical in both baseline and test buckets; the details of the model is explained in detail in [18]. We measured the CTR on the suggestions that our system ranked and compared it against the CTR on those ranked by a MI baseline. Here CTR at position k is defined as number of clicks within the first k suggestions divided by number of result pages with at least k suggestions.

A/B tests are expensive in the sense that they require engineering resources to build the necessary online platform to do a full comparison. For this reason, instead of implementing online tests for each variation of the model, for the online test we picked 10M-ML-SY, one of the best performing models in the offline comparisons, with respect to coverage and the quality metrics based on human judgments.

7.2 Results

In Table 5, we show the relative performance of different versions of the proposed system against the baseline with respect to DCG, Precision and Coverage metrics at various cut-off points (depths). The DCG and Precision values are calculated on the queries that both systems bring suggestions at the specified depth; hence we refer to it as common coverage in Table 5. Generally, the performance gap increases with depth where the largest gaps occur at depths 9 and 12. At depths 9 and 12, the best performer in terms of DCG against the baseline is 10MC-ML-SY followed by 10M-ML-SY and 10M-ML. The same is also true in terms of Precision. This suggests that i) the machine learned models outperform the systems that directly uses estimated target scores $\Pr(q_2 \mid q_1, u = 1, c = 1)$ without any learning, ii) the system is able to blend the additional candidates very well that the overall quality of the suggestions are as good as the organic counterpart. Furthermore, the performance of the proposed approach (in both DCG and Precision) either outperforms or is comparable to the strong MI (Mutual Information) baseline at all depths.

The coverage remains relatively flat across different methods at small depths. This is not surprising since all methods are effective in bringing at least a few suggestions for a given query. However, the coverage difference becomes more evident at larger depths where the real benefit of the implicit task boundary model and the machine learning step can be assessed. At depths 9 and 12, the best coverages are those of 10M-ML-SY and 10MC-ML-SY. We are quite encouraged by this result since it demonstrates that our approach can blend the additional candidates into organic ones without hurting the performance while maintaining a high coverage. The coverage of 10MC-ML is quite low compared to these two, since the higher quality is suffered by a loss in coverage for 10MC-ML. The coverage of the baseline, on the other hand, is significantly lower than the rest at larger depths even though it has comparable coverage to others at smaller depths.

In Figure 1 we demonstrate how the editorial judgments are distributed for the baseline, and the full machine learning model 10M-ML-SY that is used in the online test. To be able to show how much of the gain comes from the implicit task boundary model, and how much of it comes from the machine learning step, we present the grade distributions of the implicit task boundary model 10M as well. We compared the grade distribution at different cut-off points from top 1 to top 12. Also, the grades presented in the histograms are computed over the each individual coverage of the methods, hence they are different than those in 5, which compares the relevance over the common coverage. A few things to note in Figure 1 are: (i) 10M and 10MC-ML-SY do perform better not only with respect to the common coverage (as presented in Table 5) but also over their entire coverage, which is significantly bigger than the common coverage with the baseline. (ii) At every rank cut-off, the ratio of good and excellent suggestions are higher and the ratio of fair and bad suggestions are lower for both 10M and 10MC-ML-SY, hence the grade distributions are more skewed towards better grades. (iii) Although the implicit task boundary model 10M is better than the baseline in terms of total number of good or excellent suggestions, the machine learning step has a more important contribution in bringing a lot more good quality suggestions without increasing the ratio of bad suggestions.

The results of the online analysis are similarly encouraging. We compared our system against the MI baseline in terms of both CTR and coverage. We note that the definition of coverage and CTR in the online evaluation is slightly different that those used in the offline analysis. In the online version, the coverage is weighted by query frequency. On the other hand, the click ratios are calculated separately for each system on the respective queries where there is a suggestion. The results are presented in table 6. They show that our system not only increases the chance of finding suggestions for a given query, it also ensures a significantly higher quality of these suggestions. Additionally, we report a 0.9% decrease in the next-page clicks using our system. Users' needs for a suggestion are higher at the bottom of a page since they view the top 10 results before they see the related searches at the bottom. The fact that the CTR increases and the next-page clicks decreases indicate to some extent that the suggestions were useful.

To understand what the model does, it is instructing to look at which features were the most relevant in the GBDT model. Overall result set features are much more important than lexical features, with ABOUTNESS and some LTR based scores being the most relevant ones. This is not surprising since the result set features are more sophisticated features. Among the lexical features LEV and more generally features that depend on both q_1 and q_2 were more heavily used by the GBDT model.

Finally Table 7 lists the results of the two models for a few sample queries.

Table 7: sample queries and their suggestions for 10M and the baseline

query	odd couple
B	tony randall
10-M	jack klugman, tony randall, odd couple movie, tony curtis, youtube, john fiedler, jack lemmon, imdb, grumpy old men, odd couple theme, taxi
query	al di meola
B	al di meola discography, al di meola tabs, john mclaughlin, paco de lucia, twitter
10-M	john mclaughlin, youtube, stanley clarke, paco de lucia, lee ritenour, return to forever, jeff beck, amazon, al di meola youtube
query	skateboard wheels
B	cheap skateboard wheels, spitfire skateboard wheels
10-M	longboard wheels, ccs, skateboard, skateboards, amazon, cheap skateboard wheels, skateboard trucks, skateboard decks, soft skateboard wheels, big 5, purple skateboard wheels, sports authority
query	sigir
B	-
10-M	sigar, sigir 2012, special inspector general for iraq, sigir current news
query	Balvenie
B	balvenie scotch
10-M	glenlivet, glenfiddich, balvenie doublewood, glenmorangie, talisker, macallan, balvenie scotch, lagavulin, scotch
query	wool sweater
B	-
10-M	ll bean, women wool sweater, women's wool sweater, ping pong table

8. CONCLUSIONS

In this paper we present an end-to-end query suggestion method that implements novel ideas such as incorporating usefulness of reformulations, an implicit session boundary model, and a machine learning model to further improve the suggestion relevance and be able to add more sources of suggestions beyond the co-occurrences in query logs. The idea of incorporating usefulness into the query co-occurrence models is not specific to our particular selection of target, and it can be used directly with PMI, LLR, and other similar measures as well. Even without the machine learning step, the reformulation relevance model shows significant improvements over MI, significant gains in coverage and modest gains in relevance. The feature generation and machine learning step brings some further relevance improvement, and allows us to add other candidate sources, which significantly increases the coverage. This is a particular advantage of our approach against the related work in the literature. We trained the machine learning model with targets generated from session logs via the utility and implicit task boundary models, which removes the dependency on large labeled data. The offline as well as the online evaluation demonstrate the effectiveness of the proposed framework against MI. We observed significant improvements in coverage and quality metrics. The click through rates on the online tests are very promising and we plan to extend this work with personalization and further diversification of suggestions.

9. REFERENCES

[1] D. Beeferman and A. Berger. Agglomerative clustering of a search engine query log. In *Proceedings of the sixth ACM SIGKDD International Conference on Knowledge Discovery and Data Mining*, pages 407–416. Acm Press, 2000.

[2] P. Boldi, F. Bonchi, C. Castillo, D. Donato, A. Gionis, and S. Vigna. The query-flow graph: model and applications. In *Proceedings of the 17th ACM conference on Information and knowledge management*, CIKM '08, pages 609–618, New York, NY, USA, 2008. ACM.

[3] P. Boldi, F. Bonchi, C. Castillo, D. Donato, and S. Vigna. Query suggestions using query-flow graphs. In *Proceedings of the 2009 workshop on Web Search Click Data*, WSCD '09, pages 56–63, New York, NY, USA, 2009. ACM.

[4] O. Chapelle and Y. Chang. Yahoo! learning to rank challenge overview. *Journal of Machine Learning Research - Proceedings Track*, 14:1–24, 2011.

[5] L. B. Chilton and J. Teevan. Addressing people's information needs directly in a web search result page. In *Proceedings of the 20th international conference on World wide web*, WWW '11, pages 27–36, 2011.

[6] H. Deng, I. King, and M. R. Lyu. Entropy-biased models for query representation on the click graph. In *Proceedings of the 32nd international ACM SIGIR conference on Research and development in information retrieval*, SIGIR '09, pages 339–346, New York, NY, USA, 2009. ACM.

[7] T. Dunning. Accurate methods for the statistics of surprise and coincidence. *Comput. Linguist.*, 19:61–74, March 1993.

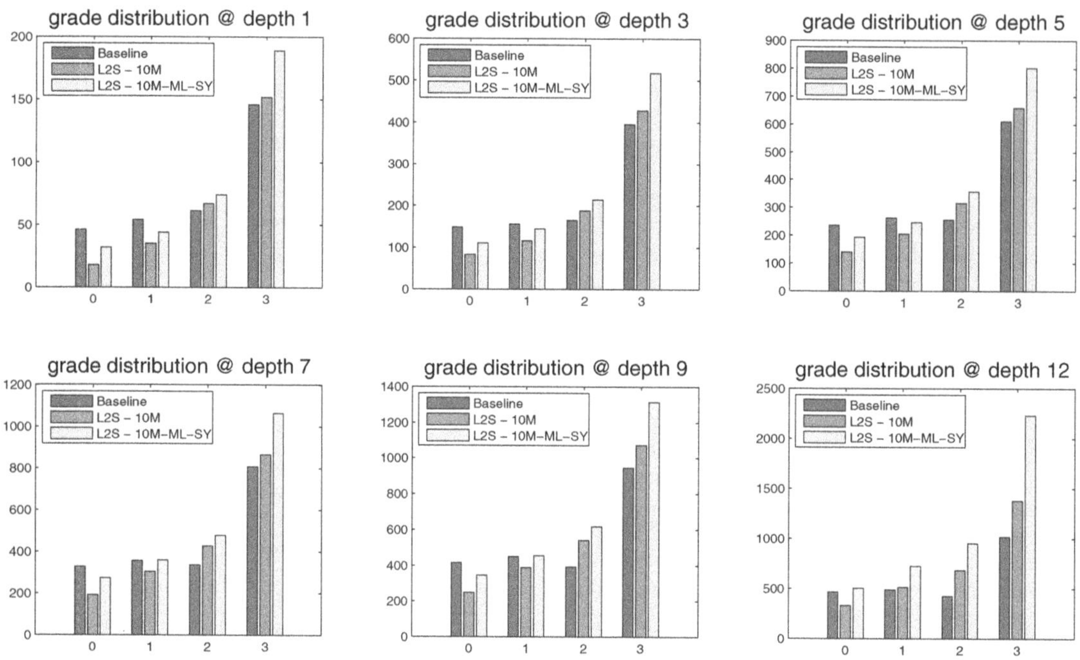

Figure 1: Grade distributions (3=Excellent, 2=Good, 1=Fair, 0=Bad) at different ranks for `10M` and `10M-ML-SY` versus the baseline.

[8] L. Fitzpatrick and M. Dent. Automatic feedback using past queries: social searching? In *Proceedings of the 20th annual international ACM SIGIR conference on Research and development in information retrieval*, SIGIR '97, pages 306–313, New York, NY, USA, 1997. ACM.

[9] J. H. Friedman. Greedy function approximation: A gradient boosting machine. *Annals of Statistics*, 29, 2000.

[10] C. Huang, L. Chien, and Y. Oyang. Relevant term suggestion in interactive web search based on contextual information in query session logs. *Journal of the American Society for Information Science and Technology*, 54:638–649, 2003.

[11] A. Jain, U. Ozertem, and E. Velipasaoglu. Synthesizing high utility suggestions for rare web search queries. In *Proceedings of the 34th international ACM SIGIR conference on Research and development in Information*, SIGIR '11, pages 805–814, 2011.

[12] E. C. Jensen, S. M. Beitzel, A. Chowdhury, and O. Frieder. Query phrase suggestion from topically tagged session logs. In H. L. Larsen, G. Pasi, D. O. Arroyo, T. Andreasen, and H. Christiansen, editors, *Flexible Query Answering Systems, 7th International Conference, FQAS 2006, Milan, Italy, June 7-10, 2006, Proceedings*, volume 4027 of *Lecture Notes in Computer Science*, pages 185–196. Springer, 2006.

[13] R. Jones, B. Rey, O. Madani, and W. Greiner. Generating query substitutions. In *Proceedings of the 15th international conference on World Wide Web*, WWW '06, pages 387–396, New York, NY, USA, 2006. ACM.

[14] V. I. Levenshtein. Binary codes capable of correcting deletions, insertions, and reversals. *Soviet Physics Doklady*, (10), 1966.

[15] Q. Mei, D. Zhou, and K. Church. Query suggestion using hitting time. In *Proceeding of the 17th ACM conference on Information and knowledge management*, CIKM '08, pages 469–478, New York, NY, USA, 2008. ACM.

[16] G. A. Miller. Wordnet: A lexical database for english. *Communications of the ACM*, 38:39–41, 1995.

[17] R. C. Moore. On Log-Likelihood-Ratios and the Significance of Rare Events. In *Proceedings of the 2004 Conference on Empirical Methods in Natural Language Processing (EMNLP'04)*, 2004.

[18] U. Ozertem, E. Velipasaoglu, and L. Lai. Suggestion set utility maximization using session logs. In *Proceedings of the 20th international ACM Conference on Information and Knowledge Management*, CIKM '11, 2011.

[19] D. Paranjpe. Learning document aboutness from implicit user feedback and document structure. In *CIKM '09: Proceeding of the 18th ACM conference on Information and knowledge management*, pages 365–374. ACM, 2009.

[20] V. V. Raghavan and H. Sever. On the reuse of past optimal queries. In *Proceedings of the ACM SIGIR Conference on Research and Development in Information Retrieval*, pages 344–350. ACM Press, 1995.

[21] C. H. Ricardo Baeza-Yates and M. Mendoza. Query recommendation using query logs in search engines. In *Trends in Database Technology - EDBT 2004 Workshops*, 2005.

[22] E. Sadikov, J. Madhavan, L. Wang, and A. Halevy. Clustering query refinements by user intent. In *Proceedings of the 19th international conference on World wide web*, WWW '10, pages 841–850, New York, NY, USA, 2010. ACM.

[23] I. Szpektor, A. Gionis, and Y. Maarek. Improving recommendation for long-tail queries via templates. In *Proceedings of the 20th international conference on World wide web*, WWW '11, pages 47–56, New York, NY, USA, 2011. ACM.

[24] A. Thanopoulos, N. Fakotakis, and G. Kokkinakis. Comparative evaluation of collocation extraction metrics. In *Proceedings of the 3rd Language Resources Evaluation Conference*, pages 620–625, 2002.

Privacy-Aware Image Classification and Search

Sergej Zerr*, Stefan Siersdorfer*, Jonathon Hare**, Elena Demidova*
*L3S Research Center, Hannover, Germany
{zerr,siersdorfer,demidova}@L3S.de
**Electronics and Computer Science, University of Southampton, Southampton, UK
jsh2@ecs.soton.ac.uk

ABSTRACT

Modern content sharing environments such as Flickr or YouTube contain a large amount of private resources such as photos showing weddings, family holidays, and private parties. These resources can be of a highly sensitive nature, disclosing many details of the users' private sphere. In order to support users in making privacy decisions in the context of image sharing and to provide them with a better overview on privacy related visual content available on the Web, we propose techniques to automatically detect private images, and to enable privacy-oriented image search. To this end, we learn privacy classifiers trained on a large set of manually assessed Flickr photos, combining textual metadata of images with a variety of visual features. We employ the resulting classification models for specifically searching for private photos, and for diversifying query results to provide users with a better coverage of private and public content. Large-scale classification experiments reveal insights into the predictive performance of different visual and textual features, and a user evaluation of query result rankings demonstrates the viability of our approach.

Categories and Subject Descriptors

H.3.5 [**Online Information Services**]: Web-based services

General Terms

Algorithms, Human Factors

Keywords

image analysis, privacy, classification, diversification

1. INTRODUCTION

With increasing availability of content sharing environments such as Flickr, and YouTube, the volume of private multimedia resources publicly available on the Web has drastically increased. In particular young users often share private images about themselves, their friends and classmates without being aware of the consequences such footage may have for their future lives [4, 26]. Photo sharing users often lack awareness of privacy issues. A recent study revealed that more than 80% of the photos publicly shared by young people are of such a private nature that they would not show these images to their parents and teachers [26]. The popular Facebook platform allows its users not only to publish photos, but also to mark the names of the depicted people. In this way, even people who did not publish any compromising information, can leave discoverable footprints on the Web.

(a) Top-3 public photos (b) Top-3 private photos

Figure 1: Top-3 search results with original Flickr ids for the query "ronaldo" (a) in the original ranking, and (b) obtained through our privacy-oriented search method (status: Oct. 2010).

Existing sharing platforms do not support users in making adequate privacy decisions in multimedia resource sharing. On the contrary, these platforms quite often employ rather lax default configurations, and mostly require users to manually decide on privacy settings for each single resource. Given the amount of shared information this process can be tedious and error-prone. In this paper we tackle the problem of supporting users in making privacy decisions in the context of image sharing (especially for large batch uploads). To this end, we first exploit an average community notion of privacy gathered through a large-scale social annotation game. We then employ the obtained community feedback to build classification models on selected visual features and textual metadata, and apply these models to estimate adequate *privacy settings* for newly uploaded images and search results. Such alert systems could be directly integrated into social photo sharing applications like Flickr or Facebook, or provided as a browser plugin.

Permission to make digital or hard copies of all or part of this work for personal or classroom use is granted without fee provided that copies are not made or distributed for profit or commercial advantage and that copies bear this notice and the full citation on the first page. To copy otherwise, to republish, to post on servers or to redistribute to lists, requires prior specific permission and/or a fee.
SIGIR'12, August 12–16, 2012, Portland, Oregon, USA.
Copyright 2012 ACM 978-1-4503-1472-5/12/08 ...$15.00.

A second aspect that we study in this paper is *privacy-oriented search.* Existing systems do not enable users to directly search for private content in a systematic way. The motivation for enabling privacy-oriented search is two-fold: First, users should be able to retrieve resources about themselves (or about their children or other relatives) published by third parties at an early stage, so that measures such as contacting owners of servers or providers can be taken. Second, the degree of privacy of the information need behind a query can be ambiguous for a search engine. For example, a user querying "*ronaldo*" could be interested in photos showing either professional or private life of this football star. In this paper, we use classifier outputs to conduct privacy-oriented search, which enables users to directly discover private information about a specific topic (see Figure 1 for an example). In addition, we perform *privacy-based diversification* of search results (i.e. retrieving a "mixture" of private and public content) to minimize the risk of user dissatisfaction in cases where queries are ambiguous with respect to the privacy aspect of the information need. The motivation for this is analogous to topic-related diversification [11]: to cover different information needs and provide an overview over the whole search result space rather than just a list of top-ranked results.

We are aware that building alarm systems for private content and enabling privacy-oriented search can be seen as contradicting goals; privacy-oriented search is not negative per se, as it can be used for retrieving private content users are comfortable to share, and, more importantly, can help with the early discovery of privacy breaches. However, as with almost every technology, it requires sensible handling and constructive usage.

The remainder of this paper is organized as follows: In Section 2 we discuss related work in the context of security and privacy in social networks, image analysis as well as classification and diversification techniques. In Section 3 we describe our data collection and labeling method which enabled us to obtain a large dataset for the privacy-based image classification. We analyze visual and textual image features in Section 4. In Section 5 we describe the classification approach, and present ranking and diversification techniques which provide an overview of the available search results taking into account their privacy as estimated by the classifier. We evaluate our techniques for privacy-based classification, ranking and diversification in Section 6. In Section 7 we conclude and show directions for future work.

2. RELATED WORK

With emergent Web 2.0 applications, various security and privacy aspects in social networks have attracted increasing research attention. There are several works studying user privacy attitudes in social networks, privacy decisions upon sharing multimedia resources, and possible risks. In their early work [12], Gross and Aquisti study privacy settings in a large set of Facebook users, and identify privacy implications and possible risks. Lange [18] studies user behavior with respect to revealing personal information in video sharing. All of these papers point out lack of user awareness regarding exposure of aggregated contextual information arising from users' resource sharing habits. In this work, we provide a way to automatically identify privacy-relevant content of images to increase user awareness and support privacy decisions.

There is a plethora of work dealing with the problem of establishing suitable access policies and mechanisms in social Web environments. Caminati and Ferrari [6], for example, propose collaborative privacy policies as well as techniques for enforcing these policies using cryptographic protocols and certificates. Felt and Evans [9] suggest to limit access to parts of the social graph and to certain user attributes. Squicciarini et al. [27] introduce privacy mechanisms in social web environments where the resources might be owned by several users. In [3], the authors discuss the problem of defining fine-grained access control policies based on tags and linked data. The user can, for instance, create a policy to specify that photos annotated with specific tags like "party" can only be accessed by the friends specified in the user's Friend of a Friend (FOAF) profile. In this paper, we do not focus on access mechanisms or policies. Instead, we concentrate on the *automatic* identification of private resources (more specifically, photos) and on privacy-oriented search.

Vyas et al. [32] utilize social annotations (i.e. tags) to predict privacy preferences of individual users and automatically derive personalized policies for shared content. These policies are derived based on a semantic analysis of tags, similarity of users in groups, and a *manually* defined privacy profile of the user. Ahern et al. [2] study the effectiveness of tags as well as location information for predicting privacy settings of photos. To this end, tags are *manually* classified into several categories such as Person, Location, Place, Object, Event, and Activity. In comparison, we do not require these manual steps, and, in addition, make use of the image content which allows us to utilize visual features to determine adequate privacy settings even for resources that do not have any associated tags.

Analysis of visual and textual image (meta-)data is applied to tackle a variety of problems, such as determining attractiveness [25] or quality [33] of photos, search result diversification [19], and others. Figueiredo et al. [10] analyze the quality of textual features available in Web 2.0 systems and their usefulness for classification. In comparison to these works, we study textual and visual features in the context of *privacy-oriented* classification and search.

Classification is a well-studied area with a variety of probabilistic and discriminative models [7]. The popular SVM-light software package [15], for instance, provides various kinds of parameterizations and variations of classification techniques (e.g., binary classification, SVM regression and ranking, transductive SVMs, etc.). In this paper we apply classification techniques in a novel context to automatically determine image privacy.

There is a large body of work on diversification of document search results and adaptation of evaluation schemes in this context - see e.g. [5, 8, 11]. Several of these papers perform diversification of search results as a post-processing or re-ranking step of document retrieval. These methods first retrieve the relevant search results, and then filter or re-order result lists to achieve diversification. In this paper, we do not deal with topic-related search result diversification but, instead, adapt and apply diversification techniques for *privacy-oriented* search.

In comparison to previous work, we are the first to analyze various visual features and textual annotations in the context of image privacy, and to conduct a study of their applicability in the context of privacy-oriented classification and search.

3. DATA

An individual's notion of privacy is prone to continuous change. For example, something a 16 year old youth may not consider sensitive may later lead to a rejection of his job application. Therefore, independent opinions can be very useful in order to support the user for adequate privacy judgment, and we build on an average community notion of privacy collected in this study. Our intent is to automatically suggest images with potentially sensitive content (and leave the final decision to the user), rather than images that a particular person would not share with the world.

In order to obtain an appropriate dataset with labeled private and public image examples, we performed a user study in which we asked external viewers to judge the privacy of the photos available online. To this end, we crawled 90,000 images from Flickr[1], using the "most recently uploaded" option to gather photos uploaded in the time period from January to April 2010. As we planned to investigate whether textual annotations can help us automatically selecting suitable privacy settings for an image, we only crawled images annotated with at least five English tags.

Of course, Flickr does not provide access to photos explicitly declared as private by other users; therefore, in this work we focus on private images that are publicly available on the Web. However, we think that classification and feature engineering techniques employed in this paper are general enough to be also applied to learn classification models from hidden private content.

As labeling a large-scale image dataset requires considerable manual effort, we conducted the user study as an annotation game (cf. Figure 2). Social annotation games are popular tools for solving tasks that are difficult for machines, and easy for human users, such as image labeling [31]. At each step of the game we presented five photos to a participant of the study. For each photo, the participants had to decide if, in their opinion, the photos belonged to the private sphere of the photographer. To this end, we asked the participants to imagine that images presented to them were photos they took with their own cameras, and mark these images as "private", "public", or "undecidable". We provided the following guidance for selecting the label: "*Private* are photos which have to do with the private sphere (like self portraits, family, friends, your home) or contain objects that you would not share with the entire world (like a private email). The rest is *public*. In case no decision can be made, the picture should be marked as *undecidable*." If the user could not decide at first glance, she could choose to display metadata of the photo or use a link to see the photo in its original context on Flickr. To obtain sufficient evidence for the privacy label assignments, each photo was shown to at least two different users. In case of a disagreement, the photo was queued to be shown to additional users. Users gathered points for each classified photo. As incentive for providing accurate answers, credit was not just given for the number of labeled images, but also for inter-user agreement. The more similar the choices of the user and the other players (their assessments, of course, not being visible to the user in advance), the higher was the score of the user. Our privacy game had an unlimited number of levels and was online over the course of two weeks. We asked our participants to complete at least one level of the game with 1000 pictures; in addition, the users could continue playing to gather more points for themselves and their teams. Over the course of the experiment, 81 users between ten and 59 years of age worked in six teams. For example, one of the teams consisted of graduate computer science students working together at a research center; other teams contained users of social platforms including facebook and some online forums[2]. Altogether 83,820 images were annotated[3]. After cleaning (remove unregistered users and photos annotated by less than two different people) 37,535 images remained. This set was used for our experiments.

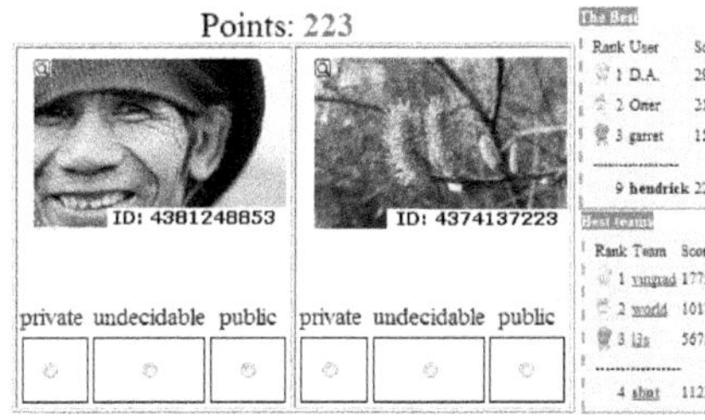

Figure 2: User interface of the privacy game. The user marks each photo as either "private", "public" or "undecidable". The system displays the current score of the user and the scores of the competing user teams.

Our analysis revealed that in the cleaned dataset around 70% of photos were labeled as public or undecidable by all of the participating judges. This relatively high percentage is expected as we originally crawled only images publicly available on the Web. Around 13% of the images were labeled as "private" by all the judges, and 28% received "private" votes from at least one of the judges. Overall the dataset contained 4,701 images labeled as private, and 27,405 ones labeled as public by 75% of the judges, which we use as ground truth for our classification experiments in Section 6.1. Thus, depending on the voting-based threshold applied, our sample indicates that a publicly available set of images from Flickr can contain 13-28% of private images.

We computed the inter-rater agreement using the Fleiss κ-measure [13], a statistical measure of agreement between individuals for qualitative ratings. Note that according to Fleiss' definition, $\kappa < 0$ corresponds to no agreement, $\kappa = 0$ to agreement by chance, and $0 < \kappa \leq 1$ to agreement beyond chance. We measured κ on a randomly selected subset of 100 images from the ground truth set labeled by 36 users, where every user rated each of those images, and obtained κ=0.6.

4. FEATURES

Image privacy is a very subjective concept. It is influenced by a number of different factors such as place, objects and persons on the photo as well as the point in time the photo was taken.

Content-based features of an image like the presence of edges, faces, or other objects may give some insights about its degree of privacy. In particular, in this work, apart from

[1] All rights on pictures published in this paper are reserved to the image owners. The pictures were available on Flickr in May 2012. The pictures are supplied with their Flickr ids. These ids can be used for obtaining further legal information.

[2] `facebook.com`, `forum.vingrad.ru`, `forum.sbnt.ru` and others.

[3] The anonymized data as well as some of the applications based on the described classification techniques are presented at `http://l3s.de/picalert`

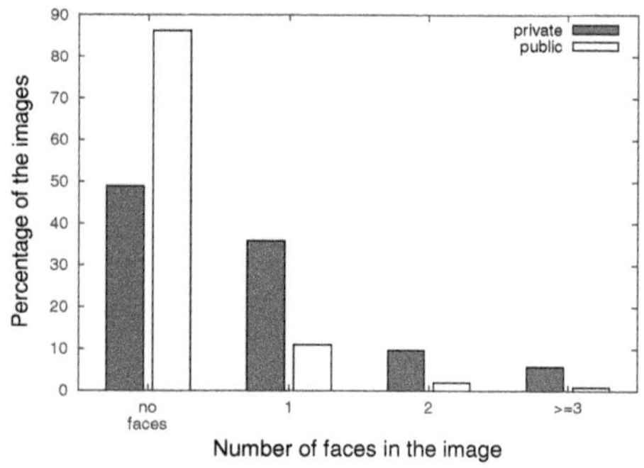

Figure 3: The distribution of human faces among private and public photos

textual features such as title and tags, we have selected image features which can help discriminate between natural and man-made objects/scenes (the EDCV feature) and features that can indicate the presence or absence of particular objects (SIFT). We have also selected features that measure the colors within the image (color-histograms), and a feature that measures the presence or absence of faces within the image.

Visual features and associated metadata are later used for training of models for privacy classification. Note that, similar to other machine learning scenarios, "hints" provided by individual features do not suffice for predicting the privacy character of all photos; however, in Section 6.1 we will show that the *combined evidence* of multiple features yields applicable results.

4.1 Visual Image Privacy Features

Digital images are internally represented as two-dimensional arrays of color pixels. This representation is difficult to use directly for classification because it is highly multidimensional and subject to noise. Instead, a process known as feature extraction is typically used to make measurements about the image content. Image features come in many forms, from the very low-level, to so-called high-level features. Low-level features are typically formed from statistical descriptions of pixels, whilst high-level features are those that have a directly attributable semantic meaning. For this study, we have selected a range of image features that could potentially be used in building a classifier that can discriminate public and private images automatically.

In the following descriptions of the visual features, we attempt to discuss theoretical motivations for the use of the particular feature, and also describe some observations from the use of the features for classification experiments within our privacy image dataset. Please note that many of the illustrations need to be viewed in color (with a quality printer or as PDF) in order to understand them fully.

4.1.1 Face detection

We first study the hypothesis that there might be a relationship between the occurrence of faces in an image and the background of the scene with respect to privacy. Figure 3 denotes the correlation between the number of detected faces in a photo and its privacy value in our dataset.

We observe that the occurrence of faces in a picture is strongly associated with a high degree of privacy although a considerable number of faces also can be found in public images. The detection of faces within an image is a high-level feature extraction operation.

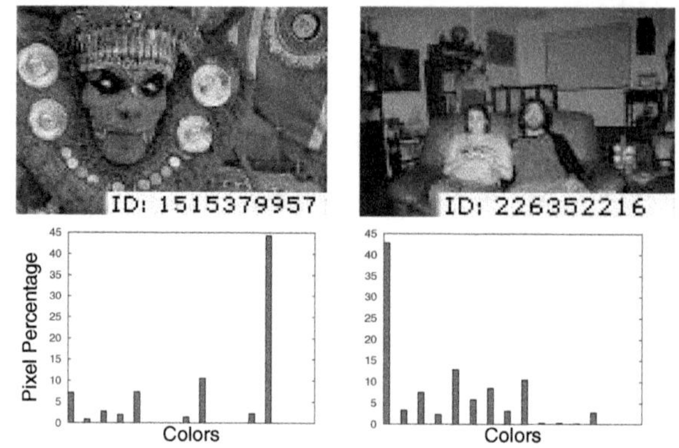

(a) Public photo (b) Private photo

Figure 4: Example of a public photo with a few dominant colors and a private photo.

Figure 5: The top row show the most discriminative colors for public images and the bottom row for private images from our dataset. The colors have been arranged by hue to aid visualization. It can be seen that the discriminative colors of public images are more saturated (i.e. more vibrant) than for private images.

In order to find faces in images we used an implementation of the Viola-Jones face detector [30], which uses a boosted cascade of weak classifiers to detect frontal and profile faces within the image. Two types of summary feature were generated using the face detector; the first is a single numeric feature that counts the number of faces detected within the image. The second is a variable-length vector that encodes the relative area of the bounding box around each detected face. Note that private photos do not necessarily show persons (e.g. photos of letters and private workspaces); furthermore, faces are partially not recognized from certain angles or if parts of the faces are hidden.

4.1.2 Color Histograms

Intuitively, color may be an indicator for certain types of public and private image. For example, public images of landscape scenes are very likely to have a specific color distribution.

The global color histogram of an image is one of the simplest forms of image feature. The histogram is constructed by assigning each pixel in the image to a histogram bin based on its color. The global color histogram completely discards all information about how the colors appear spatially within the image.

In this study, the histogram was calculated in the HS (Hue, Saturation) color space with each color-dimension split evenly into four segments, resulting in a histogram consisting of 16 bins.

Previous studies have shown that skin-tones across ethnicities are tightly clustered in HS space [24], so HS histograms should be particularly good at efficiently modeling skin tones and predicting the presence or absence of people, which can be observed to be a high indicator of privacy. We also observed, as shown in Figure 4 that public photos often contain a few very strong discrete colors (resulting in a *spiky* histogram) whereas in private photos the colors are

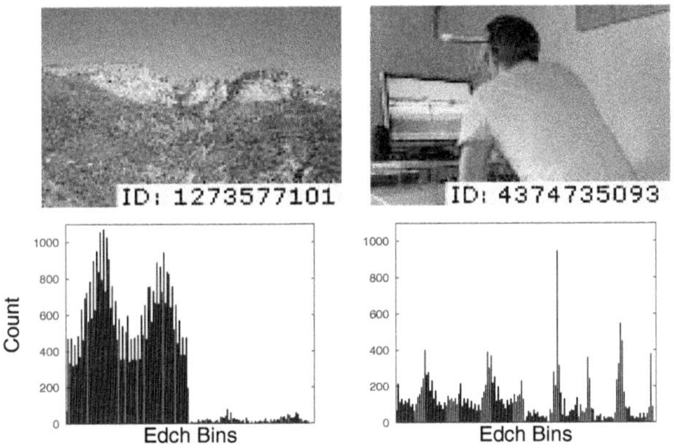

(a) Public photo (b) Private photo

Figure 6: Example of a public photo dominated by incoherent edges and a private photo of a working place with a mix of coherent and incoherent edges.

distributed more uniformly. The former might correspond to artistic make up and an artificial environment, whilst the latter is typical for amateur photos. More specifically, as shown in Figure 5, which was generated from the weights of the classifiers discussed in Section 5.1, we perceive that public images tend to contain more fully saturated colors (vibrant colors), whilst the colors in private images tend to be more desaturated. We also observed that black and white photos correspond to private portraits in most cases.

4.1.3 Edge-Direction Coherence Vector

The edges within an image are a very powerful feature for discriminating between different types of scene, and thus might be useful for privacy classification.

In particular it has been shown previously that edge-based features can be a particularly good discriminator of indoor and outdoor images [16]. Images taken in artificial environments tend to be dominated by strong, straight, near-vertical lines, whilst those of natural environment tend to predominantly contain shorter and weaker edges in all directions [29]. The check of the top 100 positive and negative images, correctly classified using the edge feature revealed that just 20% of private photos were taken outdoor whereas 11% of public ones were taken indoor.

The edge-direction coherence vector (EDCV) [29] consists of a pair of histograms that encode the lengths and directions of edges within the image. The first histogram encodes incoherent edges, whilst the second histogram encodes coherent edges. Coherent edges are edges within the image that are relatively straight and long, whilst incoherent edges are short and/or non-straight. Each bin of the histograms represents a small range of edge directions, whilst the magnitude of the bin is proportional to the summed lengths of all the coherent (or incoherent) edges with that particular direction in the image. We implemented the algorithm described in [28], where edges and their directions are found using the Canny edge detector. Coherent edges are those that deviate in direction by less than five degrees over their length, and have a pixel length greater than 0.002% of the image area. In terms of privacy classification, the EDCV feature of public images depicting landscape scenes is likely to be dominated by incoherent edges. Private images are much more likely to contain a mixture of both coherent and incoherent edges from a mixture of the presence of people (mostly incoherent) and

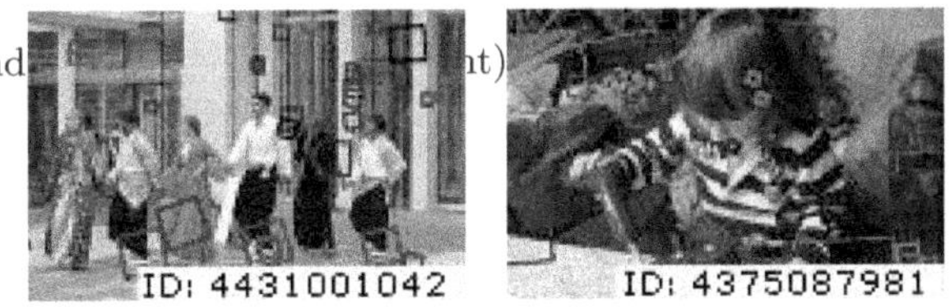

(a) Public photo (b) Private photo

Figure 7: Examples of public and private photos. The most dominating features are surrounded with boxes; the brightness of the boxes is proportional to the strength of the features.

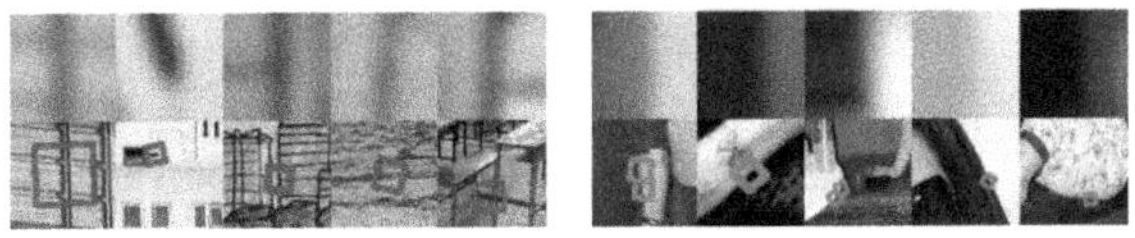

(a) Public features (b) Private features

Figure 8: Some discriminative public and private SIFT features along with example snippets from the original images.

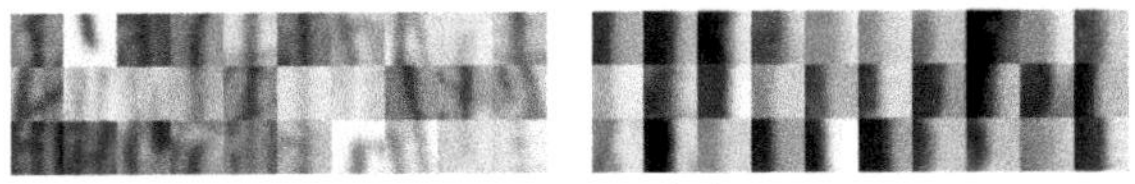

(a) Public features (b) Private features

Figure 9: Top-30 discriminative public and private SIFT features

This is illustrated in Figure 6 where the two histograms are shown as one larger histogram with the incoherent vector on the left and coherent vector on the right. Public images of cityscapes, that contain some natural features (i.e. trees or people) would also contain a mix of both coherent and incoherent edges, however, there might be some changes in the distribution of these edges with respect to their orientation.

4.1.4 Quantized SIFT Features

Private and public photos typically tend to be taken in specific contexts. For example, pictures can be taken in public places like stadiums, supermarkets and airports, or in private places like home, car, or garden. Accordingly the objects contained in a photo, like sport equipment, furniture, human and animal body parts could be different and thus give us some insights about an image's privacy. Examples of features dominating the classification decision using the machine learning model described in Section 5.1 are visualized in Figure 7. Recent advancements in low-level image description have led to approaches that are based on the detection and description of locally interesting or salient regions depicting objects and textured regions. Many region detection and description approaches have been proposed, however, the SIFT [20] descriptor remains the most popular descriptor currently. The SIFT descriptor is a 128 dimensional vector that describes local texture. Because the application of an interest point detector can lead to a variable number of SIFT features for different images, a popular technique for using SIFT features for classification is to quantize the features into a small vocabulary of "visual terms", and to create sparse, fixed length vectors for each image that encode the number of occurrences of each type of visual term. In this study, we detected interest regions in each image by detecting peaks in a difference-of-Gaussian pyramid [20]. Approximate k-means [22] was used to learn a 12000 term

Table 1: Top-50 stemmed terms according to their Mutual Information values for "public" vs. "private Photos" in Flickr

Terms for Private photos				
studio	photograph	sexi	strobist	februari
blond	kid	hat	love	woman
year	smile	black	eye	famili
white	fun	portrait	selfportr	peopl
dress	valentin	day	friend	parti
femal	boy	birthday	face	model
fashion	daughter	children	coupl	self
babi	cute	child	girl	beauti
me	nikon	pretti	hair	man
photographi	young	lip	happi	wed

Terms for Public photos				
craft	mountain	natur	rock	draw
sky	tree	snow	jan	flower
januari	art	paint	lake	winter
view	citi	car	moon	landscap
anim	cat	road	north	build
frozen	island	full	ice	bridg
water	abstract	hdr	park	sea
hous	boat	fire	bird	handmad
architectur	sunset	sunris	cloud	macro
night	dog	illustr	design	river

codebook for vector quantization from a random sample of one million SIFT features from the dataset.

SIFT-based features are commonly used for generic object recognition because similar combinations of SIFT features will often occur in different images of the same class of object. As public and private images often have very different types of objects depicted in them, SIFT-based features have the potential to be a powerful discriminator. Figure 8 shows some examples of the discriminative public and private visual terms within the context of an image from which the term occurs. In order to obtain the most discriminative features, we computed the Mutual Information (MI) measure [21] from information theory, which measures how much the joint distribution of features (visual terms) and categories deviates from a hypothetical distribution in which features and categories ("private" and "public" in our case) are independent of each other. Figure 9 visualizes the top-30 discriminative SIFT features for public and private images. Typically, SIFT features correlated to public images are observed to be of highly textured regions, whilst those corresponding to private images tend to depict more linear features such as edges. More specifically, as can be seen from Figure 8, SIFT features corresponding to public features tend to come from regions containing text and symbolic shapes, and also from patterns like in the case of an image containing flowers. Conversely, many SIFT features associated with private features correspond to human body parts or items like furniture, typically occurring in private environments.

4.1.5 Brightness and Sharpness

We also studied features like brightness and sharpness that have been shown to be an indicator of photo attractiveness [25]. In the same study, private amateur photos were also not found very attractive by a community of users. Our *brightness* feature is a single valued number that is calculated by averaging the luminance values of all the pixels in the image.

4.2 Textual Image Privacy Features

In addition to visual features, the textual annotation of images available in Web 2.0 folksonomies such as Flickr can provide additional clues on the privacy of photos. This holds partly due to correlations of topics with privacy-related image content.

Table 1 shows the top-50 **stemmed** tags automatically extracted from our labeled data set of private and public photos described in Section 3 using MI in a similar way as in Section 4.1.4. Obviously the majority of tags used in images falling into the private category describe personal concepts like family (babi, famili, child), emotions and sentiment (happi, love, beauti), and concepts related to the human body (hair, face, eye), whereas tags in the public category mostly refer to nature motives (snow, sunset, tree), architecture (bridg, build, architect), and inanimate objects (car, rock). This result indicates that privacy decisions can be correlated with specific terms found in tag annotations, and illustrates the potential merit of additional textual metadata for privacy prediction tasks.

5. PRIVACY EXPLORER

In this section we describe the Privacy Explorer system, which provides two types of privacy-based search mechanisms: 1) *privacy-oriented search* retrieving the most private search results, and 2) *privacy-based search result diversification* providing an overview of search results with varying degree of privacy.

5.1 Classification Model

In order to predict the privacy of photos we use a supervised learning paradigm which is based on training items (photos in our case) that need to be provided for each category. Both training and test items, which are later given to the classifier, are represented as multi dimensional feature vectors. These vectors can be constructed using tf or $tf \cdot idf$ weights of tags or titles, and the visual features described above. Photos labeled as "private" or "public" are used to train a classification model, using probabilistic or discriminative models (e.g., SVMs).

In our classification experiments we use linear support vector machines (SVMs) classifiers. SVMs construct a hyperplane $\vec{\omega} * \vec{x} + b = 0$ that separates the set of positive training examples (photos manually tagged as "private" in our case) from a set of negative examples (photos tagged as "public") with maximum margin. SVMs have been shown to perform very well for various classification tasks [21].

For combining multiple features, a normalization step for the input vectors is needed, since the ranges of absolute values for different features can vary and are not directly comparable. One possible normalization technique is to employ a trained sigmoid function which maps feature values from arbitrary range into the range $[0, 1]$. After this transformation the dimensions of the different input vectors are in the same range and can be combined. SVMs provide as output a value which determines the distance of a new test image from the separating hyper plane. We used Platt's method [23] to transform this output into a probability value.

5.2 Privacy-Oriented Search

In order to enable users to get an overview of the most private images relevant to a query, privacy-oriented search retrieves a set of relevant images, and re-orders them according to descending degree of privacy (see Figure 1 in the Introduction). In order to create a list of images ranked by privacy, we can estimate the likelihood of image privacy using the output of the SVM classifier trained on a set of images labeled as "public" or "private" by the users. We described the training process of the classifier and feature selection in Section 4.

5.3 Privacy-Based Diversification

A privacy-aware image search engine should provide an overview of the available search results, taking into account their privacy. For example, for a query "wedding make-up pictures", users might want to retrieve some professional images from wedding catalogs, examples of private wedding photos, or recent wedding photos of the user's personal friends available on Web 2.0 platforms. In contrast to Web image search, which focuses on a few relevant results, privacy-based diversification can minimize the risk of user's dissatisfaction in such scenarios. In what follows, we describe a framework to handle diversity in image search with respect to the privacy dimension. This framework enables us to obtain result sets of images covering a broad range of privacy degrees from publicly available images to private photos of personal friends.

5.3.1 Diversification Quality and Estimates

The relevance of a search result is typically evaluated using the standard nDCG measure [14] that accumulates the gain of each individual search result throughout the result set. α-nDCG [8] is a standard evaluation measure to balance relevance of search results with their novelty. α-nDCG views a search result (i.e. an image or a document) as a set of mutually independent binary information nuggets. Each nugget represents the presence of a different aspect of the user's information need, such as a fact, or topicality of the document [8].

Compared to the standard nDCG measure, the computation of the gain $G[k]$ of a search result at rank k in α-nDCG is extended with a parameter $\alpha \in (0,1]$ to trade off relevance and novelty of a search result:

$$G[k] = \sum_{n_i \in N} J(d_k, n_i) \times (1-\alpha)^{\sum_{j=1}^{k-1} J(d_j, n_i)}, \quad (1)$$

where $N = \{n_1, \ldots, n_m\}$ is the space of the possible information nuggets, $J(d_k, n_i)$ is a binary user judgment of containment of nugget n_i in the result d_k, and $\sum_{j=1}^{k-1} J(d_j, n_i)$ is the number of higher ranked results judged to contain nugget n_i. The resulting gain $G[k]$ is discounted by its position k, and accumulated over the positions $[1, k]$ to obtain the discounted cumulative gain DCG$[k]$:

$$\text{DCG}[k] = \sum_{j=1}^{k} \frac{G[j]}{\log_2(1+j)}. \quad (2)$$

Finally, the DCG$[k]$ is normalized by the ideal discounted cumulative gain vector DCG$'[k]$: nDCG$[k] = \frac{\text{DCG}[k]}{\text{DCG}'[k]}$.

We now describe how α-nDCG, originally defined in the context of topic-based diversification, can be adapted to the privacy-based diversification. In topic-based diversification, information nuggets represent some mutually independent binary properties of documents [8]. In contrast, probability of image privacy has a continuous range of values. In our context, we interpret the notion of information nugget $n_i \in [0,1]$ as a numeric property of the image with $n_i = 1$ being the most private. In our user study the values of the privacy nuggets are directly judged by the users. For the automatic diversification we used the classifier output described in Section 5.1 as estimate for the privacy nuggets values.

In this scenario we cannot assume privacy-related information nuggets in different search results to be mutually independent. Therefore, we propose a more general α-nDCG-G measure that takes into account similarity of the information nuggets contained in the kth result to the information nuggets contained in the higher ranked search results:

$$G[k] = \sum_{n_i \in N} J(d_k, n_i) \times (1-\alpha)^{\sum_{j=1}^{k-1} \sum_{n_y \in N} J(d_j, n_y) \times \text{sim}(n_i, n_y)}, \quad (3)$$

where in the equation $G[k]$ is the kth element of the gain vector, $N = \{n_1, \ldots, n_m\}$ is the space of the possible nuggets, $J(d_k, n_i)$ is a binary judgment of containment of nugget n_i in search result d_k, $\alpha \in (0,1]$ is a factor to trade off relevance and novelty of a search result, and sim(n_i, n_y) is the similarity between the nuggets n_i and n_y.

In general, Equation 3 relaxes the nugget independence assumption of the standard α-nDCG. This equation can be applied to estimate quality of a search result in presence of information nuggets with continuous range of values. As in this paper we perform diversification only with respect to the privacy dimension and image d_k only contains one particular privacy nugget n_k, we can simplify Equation 3 for this particular scenario as follows:

$$G[k] = (1-\alpha)^{\sum_{j=1}^{k-1} \text{sim}(n_k, n_j)}, \quad (4)$$

where n_k and n_j are the privacy nuggets in images d_k and d_j respectively. A possible estimate for similarity of the privacy nuggets n_k and n_j is the difference in their privacy values: sim$(n_k, n_j) = 1 - |n_k - n_j|$.

5.3.2 Diversification Algorithm

For automatic diversification, nugget privacy values n_k and n_j required for the gain computation in Equation 4 are computed with probability estimates obtained through the classification methods described in Section 5.1.

Algorithm 1 Proc Select Diverse Images

Require: list L of top-k images ranked by relevance, number r of diverse images to be selected.
Ensure: list R of the relevant and diverse images.

$R \leftarrow \emptyset$
while $|R| < r$ **do** {less than r elements selected}
  $i^* \leftarrow \text{argmax}_{i \in L \setminus R} G[i]$
  $L \leftarrow L \setminus \{i^*\}$
  $R \leftarrow R \cup \{i^*\}$
end while

Let L be the list of top-k images sorted by the probability of their relevance to the user's information need. Analogous to [1, 11] Algorithm 1 starts with the most relevant image at

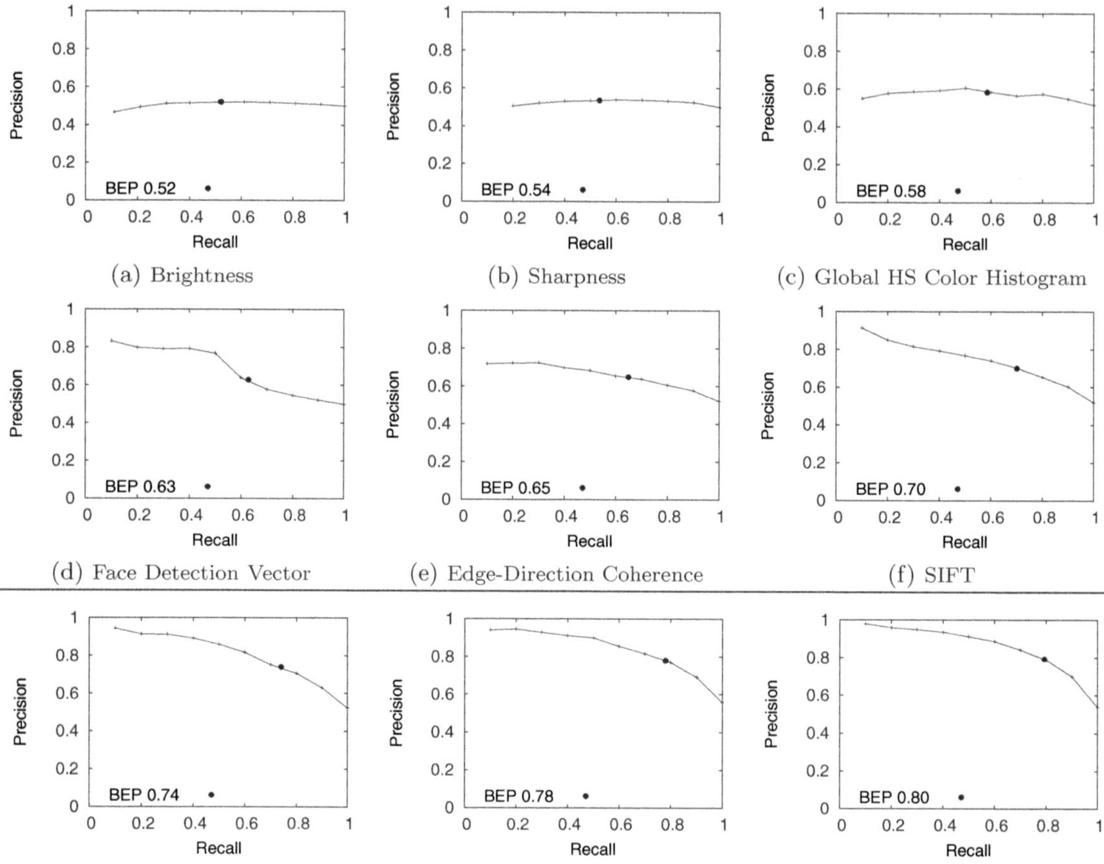

(a) Brightness (b) Sharpness (c) Global HS Color Histogram
(d) Face Detection Vector (e) Edge-Direction Coherence (f) SIFT
(g) Visual Features (h) Textual Features (Tags & Title) (i) Textual & Visual Features

Figure 10: Precision-recall curves for textual and visual features.

the top of L, and selects subsequent candidates by greedily optimizing the estimated gain in Equation 4. The worst case complexity of Algorithm 1 is $O(l \times r)$, where l is the number of images in L and r is the number of images to be selected for the result list.

6. EVALUATION

We now elaborate on the quantitative results of different experiments for classification, privacy-oriented search, and diversification using the visual and textual features motivated in the previous sections.

6.1 Classification

For our classification experiments, we used the SVM-light [15] implementation of linear support vector machines (SVMs) with default parameterization.

Our dataset described in Section 3 contained 4,701 images labeled as private, and 27,405 ones labeled as public by 75% of the judges. In order to obtain a balanced set, we randomly restricted the set of public photos to a subset of 4,701 images, so that the number of private images was equal to the number of public ones. From this set, we randomly selected 60% as training data for building our classifiers, and 40% as test data, with each data set containing an equal proportion of public and private instances.

We conducted our classification experiments on balanced data sets, which is commonly done the literature (see e.g. [33, 25]) in order to capture general classifier properties independent of the a priori class probabilities on a particular dataset. Our quality measures are the precision-recall curves as well as the precision-recall break-even points for these curves. The break-even point (BEP) is the precision/recall value at the point where precision equals recall, which is equal to the F_1 measure, the harmonic mean of precision and recall, in that case. The results of the classification experiments for selected visual features described in Section 4 and the combination of visual and textual features are shown in Figure 10. The main observations are:

- Visual features like sharpness, brightness and color histograms that have been shown to be relevant in the context of photo attractiveness classification in previous work [25] do not achieve significant discriminative performance in our scenario.
- Experiments with object related visual features, however, presented in the second row, show a substantial improvement. The occurrence of faces in photos is an intuitive indicator for privacy, reflected by a BEP of 0.63 for the face feature. The edge-direction coherence feature performs slightly better, and achieves a BEP of 0.65. In our experiments, SIFT features outperform all of the other visual features (BEP = 0.70).

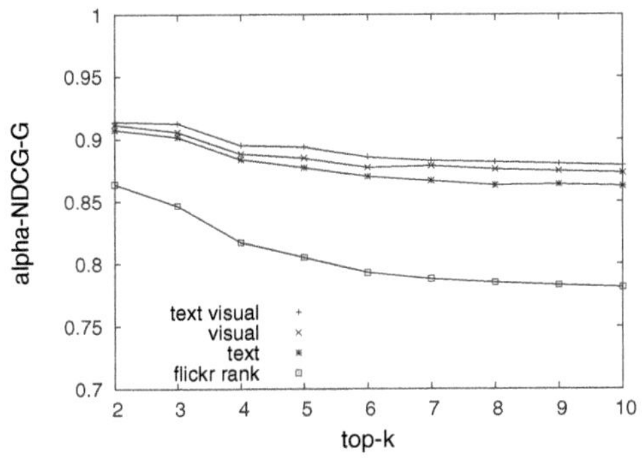

Figure 11: alpha-nDCG-G for the initial Flickr ranking and top-10 diversified search results using textual and visual image features for classification

- The *combination of all available visual features* further increases the BEP to 0.74.
- The pictures we used for classification experiments, contained good quality textual metadata (e.g titles and at least three English tags). Thus the *text features* could provide a short but concise summary of the image content and result in a BEP of 0.78.
- Finally, the *combination of the visual and textual features* leads to an additional performance boost with a BEP of 0.80, showing that textual and visual features can complement each other in the privacy classification task. However, classification with only visual features alone also produces promising results, and can be useful if no or insufficient textual annotations are available as is the case for many photos on the web.

Note, that it is possible to trade recall against precision for sensitive applications. For instance, we obtain prec=0.88 for recall=0.6, and prec=0.93 for recall=0.4 for a combination of textual and visual features; even when restricting ourselves to *only visual features* we still obtain practically applicable results (prec=0.82 for recall=0.6, and prec=0.89 for recall=0.4). This is useful for finding specifically strong candidates of private photos in large photo sets. In the context of photo sharing applications this might allow for tuning the sensitivity of personal "privacy warning" systems according to individual preferences.

Although privacy is a subjective concept, our data annotation captures an aggregated community perception of privacy, which turns out to be correlated to textual and visual features in a plausible way, and can be predicted.

6.2 Ranking and Diversification

6.2.1 Query Set

In order to obtain queries for ranking and diversification experiments, we filtered a set of image-related queries from an MSN search engine query log[1] based on their target URLs. To this end, we considered only queries containing the term "image" or "photo" in these URLs.

We manually filtered out queries related to adult content, and randomly selected 50 queries for our experiments (examples being "picture of a power plant", or "fall pictures"). For each of these, we retrieved photos and corresponding metadata from the top-1000 Flickr search results.

To assess the quality of privacy-based ranking and diversification in a real-world scenario, we performed a user study with 30 participants. We presented the keyword queries and their top-10 results retrieved by different ranking methods to the users in random order. Users were asked to judge the privacy level for each image on a 4-point Likert scale, with 1 corresponding to "clearly public" and 4 to "clearly private". Apart from the modified Likert scale the user assessment was a replication of the game described in Section 3.

6.2.2 Ranking by Privacy

For each query, we computed privacy-oriented rankings as described in Section 5.2. The list of test photos in descending order of their user-assigned privacy value was considered as ground truth for our experiments. We compared the order of the automatically generated rankings using Kendall's Tau-b [17]. We chose the Tau-b version in order to avoid a systematic advantage of our methods due to many ties produced by the high number of photos with equal user ratings.

The main observations are:

- The original Flickr ranking does not consider the privacy of the images in the search results. This was reflected by a small τ_b value of -0.04. In contrast, our methods show a clear correlation with the user-based privacy ranking.
- Since not all of the photos in the set contained usable metadata, ranking based on text with (τ_b= 0.26) is outperformed by ranking using visual features (τ_b=0.31).
- Finally the combination of textual and visual features provides the best ranking performance (τ_b=0.33). However, ranking with only visual features can still be useful for cases and applications where no or insufficient textual photo annotation is available.

The results of the pairwise t-test between the different ranking types confirm their statistical significance for a confidence level of 95%. We obtained good classification results with default parameters for SVM. Although the tuning options such as soft-margin parameter C or alternative kernels might lead to further improvements, this is outside of the focus of this work.

6.2.3 Diversification

We used α-nDCG-G in order to measure the quality of privacy-based image diversification described in Section 5.3. In our experiments we used an α value of 0.5 to balance the amount of re-ranking of the original search result with respect to the privacy dimension. The (hypothetical) optimal ranking for normalizing DCG was obtained through diversifying images directly by their user defined privacy scores.

The main result observations shown in Figure 11 are:

- Our diversification approaches clearly help to diversify Flickr query results according to the privacy dimension, and, compared to the original Flickr rank, achieve an improvement of 8.7% using textual and 9.8% using visual features.
- The combination of visual and textual features leads to a further average improvement (10.5%).

For each ranking position $k \geq 2$ we conducted pairwise t-tests between the different ranking methods for a confidence level of 95%. The tests between the original rank and other methods confirm the statistical result significance. The difference between the textual features and the combination of the textual and visual features is significant for $k \geq 5$.

[1] `http://research.microsoft.com/en-us/um/people/nickcr/wscd09/`

7. CONCLUSIONS AND FUTURE WORK

In this paper we applied classification using various visual and textual features to estimate the degree of privacy of images. Classification models were trained on a large-scale dataset with privacy assignments obtained through a social annotation game. We made use of classifier outputs to compute ranked lists of private images as well as search results diversified according to the privacy dimension. Our classification and ranking experiments show the best performance for a hybrid combination of textual and visual information. However, the approach of using only visual features shows applicable results as well and can be applied in scenarios where no textual annotation is available (e.g. personal photo collections or mobile phone pictures).

Regarding future work, we aim to study additional features in the privacy context such as color-SIFT, or applying and testing various alternative machine learning approaches for classification and ranking. For gathering additional training data, techniques like active learning algorithms, which take intermediate user feedback into account, might help to further optimize the choice of sample images presented to human assessors. As the perception of "privacy" is highly subjective and user-dependent, we would like to study recommender mechanisms, such as collaborative filtering, to account for individual user preferences, and to provide personalized results.

8. ACKNOWLEDGMENTS

This work is partly funded by the European Commission under the grant agreement 270239 (ARCOMEM), 248984 (GLOCAL), and 231126 (LivingKnowledge) as well as by the NTH School for IT Ecosystems.

9. REFERENCES

[1] R. Agrawal, S. Gollapudi, A. Halverson, and S. Ieong. Diversifying search results. In *WSDM'09*.

[2] S. Ahern, D. Eckles, N. Good, S. King, M. Naaman, and R. Nair. Over-exposed?:privacy patterns and considerations in online and mobile photo sharing. In *CHI'07*.

[3] C. M. Au Yeung, N. Gibbins, and N. Shadbolt. Providing access control to online photo albums based on tags and linked data. In *SSW'09*.

[4] S. B. Barnes. A privacy paradox: Social networking in the united states. *First Monday*, 11(9), Sept. 2006.

[5] J. Carbonell and J. Goldstein. The use of mmr, diversity-based reranking for reordering documents and producing summaries. In *SIGIR'98*.

[6] B. Carminati and E. Ferrari. Privacy-aware collaborative access control in web-based social networks. In *LCNS Springer(2008), 5094, 81-96.*

[7] S. Chakrabarti. *Mining the Web: Discovering Knowledge from Hypertext Data.* M.Kaufmann, 2002.

[8] C. L. Clarke, M. Kolla, G. V. Cormack, O. Vechtomova, A. Ashkan, S. Büttcher, and I. MacKinnon. Novelty and diversity in information retrieval evaluation. In *SIGIR'08*.

[9] A. Felt and D. Evans. Privacy protection for social networking platforms. In *Web 2.0 SP'08*.

[10] F. Figueiredo, F. Belém, H. Pinto, J. Almeida, M. Gonçalves, D. Fernandes, E. Moura, and M. Cristo. Evidence of quality of textual features on the web 2.0. In *CIKM'09*.

[11] S. Gollapudi and A. Sharma. An axiomatic approach for result diversification. In *WWW'09*.

[12] R. Gross and A. Acquisti. Information revelation and privacy in online social networks. In *WPES '05*.

[13] K. Gwet. *Handbook of Inter-Rater Reliability.* Advanced Analytics, LLC, second edition, 2010.

[14] K. Järvelin and J. Kekäläinen. Cumulated gain-based evaluation of ir techniques. *ACM Trans. Inf. Syst.*, 20(4):422–446, 2002.

[15] T. Joachims. Making large-scale support vector machine learning practical. *Advances in kernel methods: support vector learning*, pages 169–184, 1999.

[16] W. Kim, J. Park, and C. Kim. A novel method for efficient indoor-outdoor image classification. *JSPS'10*.

[17] W. H. Kruskal. Ordinal measures of association. *Journal of the American Statistical Association*, 53(284):814–861, 1958.

[18] P. G. Lange. Publicly private and privately public: Social networking on youtube. *JCMC'08*.

[19] R. Leuken, L. Garcia, X. Olivares, and R. Zwol. Visual diversification of image search results. In *WWW'09*.

[20] D. Lowe. Distinctive image features from scale - invariant keypoints. *IJCV*, 60(2):91–110, Jan. 2004.

[21] C. D. Manning, P. Raghavan, and H. Schütze. *Introduction to Information Retrieval.* Cambridge University Press, 1 edition, July 2008.

[22] J. Philbin, O. Chum, M. Isard, J. Sivic, and A. Zisserman. Object retrieval with large vocabularies and fast spatial matching. In *IEEE CVPR'07*.

[23] J. C. Platt. Probabilistic outputs for support vector machines and comparisons to regularized likelihood methods. In *Advances in Large Margin Classifiers*, pages 61–74. MIT Press, 1999.

[24] Y. Raja, S. J. McKenna, and S. Gong. Tracking and segmenting people in varying lighting conditions using colour. In *FG '98*, Washington, USA, 1998.

[25] J. San Pedro and S. Siersdorfer. Ranking and classifying attractiveness of photos in folksonomies. In *WWW '09*.

[26] V. Schleswig-Holstein. Statistische erfassung zum internetverhalten jugendlicher und heranwachsender. In *A study of the consumer organization in Schleswig-Holstein, Germany*, March 2010.

[27] A. Squicciarini, Mohamed, and F. Paci. Collective privacy management in social networks. In *WWW'09*.

[28] M. Tuffield, S. Harris, D. Dupplaw, A. Chakravarthy, C. Brewster, N. Gibbins, K. O'Hara, F. Ciravegna, D. Sleeman, Y. Wilks, and N. Shadbolt. Image annotation with photocopain. In *SWAMM'06*.

[29] A. Vailaya, A. Jain, and H. J. Zhang. On image classification: City images vs. landscapes. *Pattern Recognition*, 31(12):1921 – 1935, 1998.

[30] P. Viola and M. Jones. Robust real-time object detection. *IJCV*, 57(2):137–154, 2002.

[31] L. von Ahn and L. Dabbish. Labeling images with a computer game. In *SIGCHI '04*.

[32] N. Vyas, A. Squicciarini, C. Chang, and D. Yao. Towards automatic privacy management in web 2.0 with semantic analysis on annotations. In *CollCom'09*.

[33] C.-H. Yeh, Y.-C. Ho, B. A. Barsky, and M. Ouhyoung. Personalized photograph ranking and selection system. In *MM '10*, New York,USA, 2010.

Manhattan Hashing for Large-Scale Image Retrieval

Weihao Kong
Shanghai Key Laboratory of Scalable Computing and Systems
Department of Computer Science and Engineering
Shanghai Jiao Tong University
Shanghai, China
kongweihao@cs.sjtu.edu.cn

Wu-Jun Li
Shanghai Key Laboratory of Scalable Computing and Systems
Department of Computer Science and Engineering
Shanghai Jiao Tong University
Shanghai, China
liwujun@cs.sjtu.edu.cn

Minyi Guo
Shanghai Key Laboratory of Scalable Computing and Systems
Department of Computer Science and Engineering
Shanghai Jiao Tong University
Shanghai, China
guo-my@cs.sjtu.edu.cn

ABSTRACT

Hashing is used to learn binary-code representation for data with expectation of preserving the neighborhood structure in the original feature space. Due to its fast query speed and reduced storage cost, hashing has been widely used for efficient nearest neighbor search in a large variety of applications like text and image retrieval. Most existing hashing methods adopt Hamming distance to measure the similarity (neighborhood) between points in the hashcode space. However, one problem with Hamming distance is that it may destroy the neighborhood structure in the original feature space, which violates the essential goal of hashing. In this paper, Manhattan hashing (MH), which is based on Manhattan distance, is proposed to solve the problem of Hamming distance based hashing. The basic idea of MH is to encode each projected dimension with multiple bits of *natural binary code* (NBC), based on which the Manhattan distance between points in the hashcode space is calculated for nearest neighbor search. MH can effectively preserve the neighborhood structure in the data to achieve the goal of hashing. To the best of our knowledge, this is the first work to adopt Manhattan distance with NBC for hashing. Experiments on several large-scale image data sets containing up to one million points show that our MH method can significantly outperform other state-of-the-art methods.

Categories and Subject Descriptors

H.3.3 [**Information Systems**]: Information Search and Retrieval

General Terms

Algorithms, Measurement

Keywords

Hashing, Image Retrieval, Approximate Nearest Neighbor Search, Hamming Distance, Manhattan Distance

Permission to make digital or hard copies of all or part of this work for personal or classroom use is granted without fee provided that copies are not made or distributed for profit or commercial advantage and that copies bear this notice and the full citation on the first page. To copy otherwise, or republish, to post on servers or to redistribute to lists, requires prior specific permission and/or a fee.
SIGIR'12, August 12–16, 2012, Portland, Oregon, USA.
Copyright 2012 ACM 978-1-4503-1472-5/12/08... $15.00.

1. INTRODUCTION

Nearest neighbor (NN) search [28] has been widely used in machine learning and related application areas, such as information retrieval, data mining, and computer vision. Recently, with the explosive growth of data on the Internet, there has been increasing interest in NN search in massive (large-scale) data sets. Traditional brute force NN search requires scanning all the points in a data set whose time complexity is linear to the sample size. Hence, it is computationally prohibitive to adopt brute force NN search for massive data sets which might contain millions or even billions of points. Another challenge faced by NN search in massive data sets is the excessive storage cost which is typically unacceptable if traditional data formats are used.

To solve these problems, researchers have proposed to use hashing techniques for efficient approximate nearest neighbor (ANN) search [1, 5, 7, 19, 30, 38, 39, 41]. The goal of hashing is to learn binary-code representation for data which can preserve the neighborhood (similarity) structure in the original feature space. More specifically, each data point will be encoded as a compact binary string in the hashcode space, and similar points in the original feature space should be mapped to close points in the hashcode space. By using hashing codes, we can achieve constant or sub-linear search time complexity [32]. Moreover, the storage needed to store the binary codes will be dramatically reduced. For example, if each point is represented by a vector of 1024 bytes in the original space, a data set of 1 million points will cost 1GB memory. On the contrary, if we hash each point into a vector of 128 bits, the memory needed to store the data set of 1 million points will be reduced to 16MB. Therefore, hashing provides a very effective way to achieve fast query speed with low storage cost, which makes it a popular candidate for efficient ANN search in massive data sets [1].

To avoid the NP-hard solution which directly computes the best binary codes for a given data set [36], most existing hashing methods adopt a learning strategy containing two stages: projection stage and quantization stage. In the projection stage, several projected dimensions of real values are generated. In the quantization stage, the real values generated from the projection stage are quantized into binary codes by thresholding. For example, the widely used single-bit quantization (SBQ) strategy adopts one single bit to quantize each projected dimension. More specifically, given a point $\mathbf{x}$ from the original space, each projected dimension i will be associated with a real-valued projection function $f_i(\mathbf{x})$. The ith hash bit of $\mathbf{x}$ will be 1 if $f_i(\mathbf{x}) \geq \theta$. Otherwise, it will be 0. Here, θ is a threshold, which is typically set to 0 if the data have been normalized to have zero mean. Although a lot of projection methods have been proposed for hashing, there exist only two quantization methods. One is the SBQ method stated above, and the other is the hierarchical quantization (HQ) method in anchor graph hashing (AGH) [18]. Rather than using one bit, HQ divides each dimension into four regions with three thresholds and uses two bits to encode each region. Hence, HQ will associate each projected dimension with two bits. Figure 1 (a) and Figure 1 (b) illustrate the results of SBQ and HQ for one projected dimension, respectively. Till now, only one hashing method, AGH in [18], adopts HQ for quantization. All the other hashing methods adopt SBQ for quantization.

Currently, almost all hashing methods adopt Hamming distance to measure the similarity (neighborhood) between points in the hashcode space. The Hamming distance between two strings of equal length is the number of positions at which the corresponding symbols are different [1]. As will be stated below in Section 3.1, neither SBQ nor HQ can effectively preserve the neighborhood structure under the constraint of Hamming distance. Hence, although the projection functions in the projection stage can preserve the neighborhood structure, the whole hashing procedure will still destroy the neighborhood structure in the original feature space due to the limitation of Hamming distance. This will violate the goal of hashing and consequently satisfactory performance cannot be easily achieved by traditional Hamming distance based hashing methods.

In this paper, we propose to use Manhattan distance for hashing to solve the problem of existing hashing methods. The result is our novel hashing method called Manhattan hashing (MH). The main contributions of this paper are briefly outlined as follows:

- Although a lot of hashing methods have been proposed, most of them focus on the projection stage while ignoring the quantization stage. This work will systematically study the effect of quantization. We find that the quantization stage is at least as important as the projection stage. A good quantization strategy combined with a bad projection strategy may achieve better performance than a bad quantization strategy combined with a good projection strategy. This finding is very interesting, which might stimulate other researchers to move their attention from the projection stage to the quantization stage, and finally propose better methods simultaneously taking both stages into consideration.

- MH encodes each projected dimension with multiple bits of *natural binary code* (NBC), based on which the Manhattan distance between points in the hashcode space is calculated for nearest neighbor search. MH can effectively preserve the neighborhood structure in the data to achieve the goal of hashing. To the best of our knowledge, this is the first work to adopt Manhattan distance with NBC for hashing.

- Experiments on several large-scale image data sets containing up to one million points show that our MH method can significantly outperform other state-of-the-art methods.

The rest of this paper is organized as follows. In Section 2, we introduce the related work of our method. Section 3 describes the details of our MH method. Experimental results are presented in Section 4. Finally, we conclude the whole paper in Section 5.

2. RELATED WORK

Due to the promising performance in terms of either speed or storage, hashing has been widely used for efficient ANN search in a large variety of applications with massive data sets, such as text retrieval [33, 39], image retrieval [6, 20], audio retrieval [2], and near-duplicate video retrieval [29]. As a consequence, many hashing methods have been proposed by researchers. In general, the existing methods can be roughly divided into two main classes [6, 39]: data-independent methods and data-dependent methods [2].

The representative data-independent methods include locality-sensitive hashing (LSH) [1, 5] and its extensions [3, 16, 17, 21, 24]. The hash functions of these methods are just some simple random projections which are independent of the training data. Shift invariant kernel hashing (SIKH) [24] adopts projection functions which are similar to those of LSH, but SIKH applies a shifted cosine function to generate hash values. Many applications, such as image retrieval [24] and cross-language information retrieval [38], have adopted these data-independent hashing methods for ANN. Generally, data-independent methods need longer codes than data-dependent methods to achieve satisfactory performance [6]. Longer codes means higher storage and computational cost. Hence, the data-independent methods are less efficient than the data-dependent methods.

Recently, data-dependent methods, which try to learn the hash functions from the training data, have attracted more and more attentions by researchers. Semantic hashing [25, 26] adopts a deep generative model based on restricted Boltzmann machine (RBM) [9] to learn the hash functions. Experiments on text retrieval demonstrate that semantic hashing can achieve better performance than the original TF-IDF representation [27] and LSH. AdaBoost [4] is adopted by [2] to learn hash functions from weakly labeled positive samples. The resulting hashing method achieves better performance than LSH for audio retrieval. Spectral hashing (SH) [36] uses spectral graph partitioning strategy for hash function learning where the graph is constructed based on the similarity between data points. To learn the hash functions, binary reconstruction embedding (BRE) [15] explicitly minimizes the reconstruction error between the distances in the original feature space and the Hamming distances of the corresponding binary codes. Semi-supervised hashing (SSH) [34, 35] exploits both labeled data and unlabeled data for hash function learning. Self-taught hashing [39] uses some self-labeled data to facilitate the supervised hash function learning. Complementary hashing [37] exploits multiple complementary hash tables learned sequentially in a boosting manner to effectively balance the precision and recall. Composite hashing [38] combines multiple information sources into the hash function learning procedure. Minimal loss hashing (MLH) [22] tries to formulate the hashing problem as a structured prediction problem based on the latent structural SVM framework. SPICA [8] tries to find independent projections by jointly optimizing both accuracy and time. Hypergraph hashing [42] extends SH to hypergraph to model the high-order relationships between social images. Active hashing [40] is proposed to actively select the most informative labels for hash function learning. Iterative quantization (ITQ) [6] tries to learn an orthogonal rotation matrix to refine the initial projection matrix learned by principal component analysis (PCA) [13]. Experimental results show that ITQ can achieve better performance than most state-of-the-art methods.

Few of the existing methods discussed above have studied the effect of quantization. Because existing quantization strategies can not effectively preserve the neighborhood structure under the constraint of Hamming distance, most existing hashing methods still can not achieve satisfactory performance even though a large number of sophisticated projection functions have been designed by

[1] `http://en.wikipedia.org/wiki/Hamming_distance`

[2] In [39], data-independent is called data-oblivious while data-dependent is called data-aware. It is obvious that they have the same meaning.

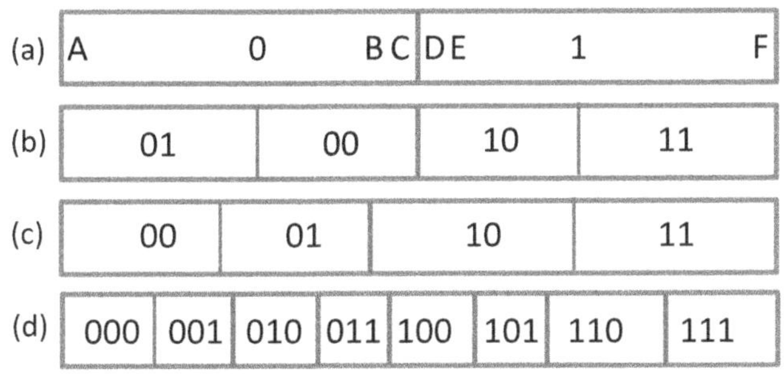

Figure 1: Different quantization methods: (a) single-bit quantization (SBQ); (b) hierarchical quantization (HQ); (c) 2-bit Manhattan quantization (2-MQ); (d) 3-bit Manhattan quantization (3-MQ).

researchers. The work in this paper tries to study these important factors which have been ignored by existing works.

3. MANHATTAN HASHING

This section describes the details of our Manhattan hashing (MH) method. First, we will introduce the motivation of MH. Then, the Manhattan distance driven quantization strategy will be proposed. After that, the whole learning procedure for MH will be summarized. Finally, we will do some qualitative analysis about the performance of MH.

3.1 Motivation

Given a point $\mathbf{x}$ from the original feature space $\mathbb{R}^d$, hashing tries to encode it with a binary string of c bits via the mapping $h : \mathbb{R}^d \rightarrow \{0,1\}^c$. As said in Section 1, most hashing methods adopt a two-stage strategy to learn h because directly learning h is an NP-hard problem. Let's first take SBQ based hashing as an example for illustration. In the projection stage, c real-valued projection functions $\{f_k(\mathbf{x})\}_{k=1}^c$ are learned and each function can generate one real value. Hence, we have *c projected dimensions* each of which corresponds to one projection function. In the quantization stage, the real-values are quantized into a binary string by thresholding. More specifically, $h_k(\mathbf{x}) = 1$ if $f_k(\mathbf{x}) \geq \theta$. Otherwise, $h_k(\mathbf{x}) = 0$. Here, we assume $h(\mathbf{x}) = [h_1(\mathbf{x}), h_2(\mathbf{x}), \cdots, h_c(\mathbf{x})]^T$, and θ is a threshold which is typically set to 0 if the data have been normalized to have zero mean. Figure 1 (a) illustrates the result of SBQ for one projected dimension. Currently, most hashing methods adopt SBQ for the quantization stage. Hence, the difference between these methods lies in the different projection functions.

Till now, only two quantization methods have been proposed for hashing. One is SBQ just discussed above, and the other is HQ which is adopted by only one hashing method AGH [18]. Rather than using one bit, HQ divides each projected dimension into four regions with three thresholds and uses two bits to encode each region. Hence, to get a c-bit code, HQ based hashing need only $c/2$ projection functions. Figure 1 (b) illustrates the result of HQ for one projected dimension.

To achieve satisfactory performance for ANN, one important requirement of hashing is to preserve the neighborhood structure in the original space. More specifically, close points in the original space $\mathbb{R}^d$ should be mapped to similar binary codes in the code space $\{0,1\}^c$.

We can easily find that with Hamming distance, both SBQ and HQ will destroy the neighborhood structure in the data. As illustrated in Figure 1 (a), point 'C' and point 'D' will be quantized into 0 and 1 respectively although they are very close to each other in the real-valued space. On the contrary, point 'D' and point 'F' will be quantized into the same code 1 although they are far away from each other. Hence, in the code space of this dimension, the Hamming distance between 'F' and 'D' is smaller than that between 'C' and 'D', which obviously indicates that SBQ can destroy the neighborhood structure in the original space.

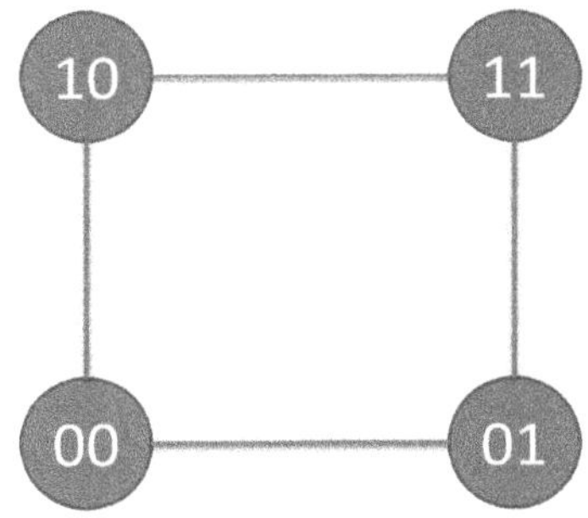

(a) Hamming distance

(b) Decimal distance with NBC

Figure 2: Hamming distance and Decimal distance between 2-bit codes. The distance between two points (i.e., nodes in the graph) is the length of the shortest path between them.

HQ can also destroy the neighborhood structure of data. Let $d_h(x,y)$ denote the Hamming distance between binary codes x and y. From Figure 1 (b), we can get $d_h(A,F) = d_h(A,B) = d_h(C,D) = d_h(D,F) = 1$, and $d_h(A,D) = d_h(C,F) = 2$. Hence, we can find that the Hamming distance between the two farthest points 'A' and 'F' is the same as that between two relatively close points such as 'A' and 'B'. The even worse case is that $d_h(A,F) < d_h(A,D)$, which is obviously very unreasonable.

The problem of HQ is inevitable under the constraint of Hamming distance. Figure 2 (a) shows the Hamming distance between different 2-bit codes, where the distance between two points (i.e., nodes in the graph) is equivalent to the length of the shortest path between them. We can see that the largest Hamming distance between 2-bit codes is 2. However, to keep the relative distances between 4 different points (or regions), the largest distance between two different 2-bit codes should be at least 3. Hence, no matter how we permute the 2-bit codes for the four regions in Figure 1 (b), we cannot get any neighborhood-preserving result under the constraint of Hamming distance. One choice to overcome this problem of HQ is to design a new distance measurement.

3.2 Manhattan Distance Driven Quantization

As stated above, the problem that HQ cannot preserve the neighborhood structure in the data is essentially from the Hamming distance. Here, we will show that Manhattan distance with natural binary code (NBC) can solve the problem of HQ.

The Manhattan distance between two points is the sum of the differences on their dimensions. Let $\mathbf{x} = [x_1, x_2, \cdots, x_d]^T$, $\mathbf{y} = [y_1, y_2, \cdots, y_d]^T$, the Manhattan distance between $\mathbf{x}$ and $\mathbf{y}$ is defined as follows:

$$d_m(\mathbf{x}, \mathbf{y}) = \sum_{i=1}^{d} |x_i - y_i|, \quad (1)$$

where $|x|$ denotes the absolute value of x.

To adapt Manhattan distance for hashing, we adopt a q-bit quantization scheme. More specifically, after we have learned the real-valued projection functions, we divide each projected dimension into 2^q regions and then use q bits of *natural binary code* (NBC) to encode the index of each region. For example, if $q = 2$, each projected dimension is divided into 4 regions, and the indices of these regions are $\{0, 1, 2, 3\}$, the NBC codes of which are $\{00, 01, 10, 11\}$. If $q = 3$, the indices of regions are $\{0, 1, 2, 3, 4, 5, 6, 7\}$, and the NBC codes are $\{000, 001, 010, 011, 100, 101, 110, 111\}$. Figure 1 (c) shows the quantization result with $q = 2$ and Figure 1 (d) shows the quantization result with $q = 3$. Because this quantization scheme is driven by Manhattan distance, we call it *Manhattan quantization* (MQ). The MQ with q bits is denoted as q-MQ.

Another issue for MQ is about threshold learning. Badly learned thresholds will deteriorate the quantization performance. To achieve the neighborhood-preserving goal, we need to make the points in each region as similar as possible. In this paper, we use k-means clustering algorithm [14] to learn the thresholds from the training data. More specifically, if we need to quantize each projected dimension into q bits, we use k-means to cluster the real values of each projected dimension into 2^q clusters, and the midpoint of the line joining neighboring cluster centers will be used as thresholds.

In our MH, we use the *decimal distance* rather than the Hamming distance to measure the distances between the q-bit codes for each projected dimension. The decimal distance is defined to be the difference between the decimal values of the corresponding NBC codes. For example, let $d_d(\mathbf{x}, \mathbf{y})$ denote the decimal distance between $\mathbf{x}$ and $\mathbf{y}$, then $d_d(10, 00) = |2 - 0| = 2$ and $d_d(010, 110) = |2 - 6| = 4$. Figure 2 (b) shows the decimal distances between different 2-bit codes, where the distance between two points (i.e., nodes in the graph) is equivalent to the length of the shortest path between them. We can see that the largest decimal distance between 2-bit codes is 3, which is enough to effectively preserve the relative distances between 4 different points (or regions). Figure 1 (c) shows one of the encoding results which can preserve the relative distances between the regions. Figure 1 (d) is the results with $q = 3$. It is obvious that the relative distances between the regions are also preserved. In fact, it is not hard to prove that this nice property will be satisfied for any positive integer q. Hence, our MQ strategy with $q \geq 2$ provides a more effective way to preserve the neighborhood structure than SBQ and HQ.

Given two binary codes $\mathbf{x}$ and $\mathbf{y}$ generated by MH, the Manhattan distance between them is computed from (1), where x_i and y_i correspond to the ith projected dimension which should contain q bits. Furthermore, the difference between two q-bit codes of each dimension should be measured with decimal distance. For example, if $q = 2$,

$$\begin{aligned} d_m(000100, 110000) &= d_d(00, 11) + d_d(01, 00) + d_d(00, 00) \\ &= 3 + 1 + 0 \\ &= 4. \end{aligned}$$

If $q = 3$,

$$\begin{aligned} d_m(000100, 110000) &= d_d(000, 110) + d_d(100, 000) \\ &= 6 + 4 \\ &= 10. \end{aligned}$$

It is easy to see that when $q = 1$, the results computed with Manhattan distance are equivalent to those with Hamming distance, and consequently our MH method degenerates to the traditional SBQ-based hashing methods.

3.3 Summary of MH Learning

Given a training set, the whole learning procedure of MH, including both projection and quantization stages, can be summarized as follows:

- Choose a positive integer q, which is 2 in default;
- Choose an existing projection method or design a new projection method, and then learn $\lfloor \frac{c}{q} \rfloor$ projection functions;
- Use k-means to learn 2^q clusters, and compute $2^q - 1$ thresholds based on the centers of the learned clusters;
- Use MQ in Section 3.2 to quantize each projected dimension into q bits of NBC code based on the learned thresholds;
- Concatenate the q-bit codes of all the $\lfloor \frac{c}{q} \rfloor$ projected dimensions into one long code to represent each point.

One important property of our MH learning procedure is that MH can choose an existing projection method for the projection stage, which means that the novel part of MH is mainly from the quantization stage which has been ignored by most existing hashing methods. By combining different projection functions with our MQ strategy, we can get different versions of MH. For example, if PCA is used for projection, we can get 'PCA-MQ'. If the random projection functions in LSH are used for projection, we can get 'LSH-MQ'. Both PCA-MQ and LSH-MQ can be seen as variants of MH. Similarly, we can design other versions of MH.

3.4 Discussion

Because the MQ for MH can better preserve the neighborhood structure between points, it is expected that with the same projection functions, MH will generally outperform SBQ or HQ based hashing methods. This will be verified by our experiments in Section 4.

The total training time contains two parts: one part is for projection, and the other is for quantization. Compared with SBQ, although MQ need extra $O(n)$ time for k-means learning, the total time complexity of MH is still the same as that of SBQ based methods because the projection time is at least $O(n)$. Here n is the number of training points. Similarly, we can prove that with the same projection functions, MH has the same time complexity as HQ based methods.

It is not easy to compare the absolute training time between MH and traditional SBQ based methods. Although extra training time is needed for MH to perform k-means learning, the number of projection functions will be decreased to $\lfloor \frac{c}{q} \rfloor$ while SBQ based methods need c projection functions. Hence, whether MH is faster or not depends on the specific projection functions. If the projection stage is very time-consuming, MH might be faster than SBQ based methods. But for other cases, SBQ based methods can be faster than MH. The absolute training time of HQ based methods is about the same as that of MH with $q = 2$ because HQ also need to learn the thresholds for quantization. For $q \geq 3$, whether MH is faster than HQ base methods or not depends on the specific projection functions because MH need fewer projection functions but larger number of thresholds.

As for query procedure, the speed of computing hashcode for query in MH is expected to be faster than SBQ based methods because the number of projection operations for MH with $q \geq 2$ is only $\lfloor \frac{c}{q} \rfloor$ of that for SBQ. The query speed of MH with $q = 2$ is the same as that of HQ based methods. When $q \geq 3$, the speed of computing hashcode of MH will be faster than HQ based methods due to the smaller number of projection operations.

4. EXPERIMENT

4.1 Data Sets

To evaluate the effectiveness of our MH method, we use three publicly available image sets, LabelMe [32][3], TinyImage [31][4], and ANN_SIFT1M [12] [5].

The first data set is *22K LabelMe* used in [22, 32]. LabelMe is a web-based tool designed to facilitate image annotation. With the help of this annotation tool, the current LabelMe data set contains as large as 200,790 images which span a wide variety of object categories. Most images in LabelMe contain multiple objects. *22K LabelMe* contains 22,019 images sampled from the large LabelMe data set. As in [32], we scale the images to have the size of 32x32 pixels, and represent each image with 512-dimensional GIST descriptors [23].

The second data set is *100K TinyImage* containing 100,000 images randomly sampled from the original 80 million Tiny Images [31]. TinyImage data set aims to present a visualization of all the nouns in the English language arranged by semantic meaning. A total number of 79,302,017 images were collected by Google's image search engine and other search engines. The original images have the size of 32x32 pixels. As in [31], we represent them with 384-dimensional GIST descriptors [23].

The third data set is *ANN_SIFT1M* introduced in [10, 11, 12]. It consists of 1,000,000 images each represented as 128-dimensional SIFT descriptors. ANN_SIFT1M contains three vector subsets: subset for learning, subset for database, and subset for query. The learning subset is retrieved from Flickr images and the database and query subsets are from the INRIA Holidays images [11]. We conduct our experiments only on the database subset, which consists of 1,000,000 images each represented as 128-dimensional SIFT descriptors.

Figure 3 shows some representative images sampled from LabelMe and TinyImage data sets. Please note that the authors of *ANN_SIFT1M* provide only the extracted features without any original images of their data. From Figure 3, it is easy to see that LabelMe and TinyImage have different characteristics. The LabelMe data set contains high-resolution photos, in fact most of which are street view photos. On the contrary, the images in TinyImage data set have low-resolution.

4.2 Baselines

As stated in Section 3.3, MQ can be combined with different projection functions to get different variants of MH. In this paper, the most representative methods, ITQ [6], SIKH [24], LSH [1], SH [36], and PCA [6, 13], are chosen to evaluate the effectiveness of our MQ strategy. ITQ, SH, and PCA are data-dependent methods, while SIKH and LSH are data-independent methods. These chosen methods are briefly introduced as follows:

- **ITQ:** ITQ uses an iteration method to find an orthogonal rotation matrix to refine the initial projection matrix learned by PCA so that the quantization error of mapping the data to the vertices of binary hypercube is minimized. Experimental results in [6] show that it can achieve better performance than most state-of-the-art methods. In our experiment, we set the iteration number of ITQ to be 100.
- **SIKH:** SIKH uses random projections to approximate the shift-invariant kernels. As in [6, 24], we use a Gaussian kernel whose bandwidth is set to the average distance to the 50th nearest neighbor.
- **LSH:** LSH uses a Gaussian random matrix to perform random projection.
- **SH:** SH uses the eigenfunctions computed from the data similarity graph for projection.
- **PCA:** PCA uses the eigenvectors corresponding to the largest eigenvalues of the covariance matrix for projection.

All the above hashing methods can be used to provide projection functions. By adopting different quantization strategies, we can get different variants of a specific hashing method. Let's take PCA as an example. 'PCA-SBQ' denotes the original PCA hashing method with single-bit quantization, 'PCA-HQ' denotes the combination of PCA projection with HQ quantization [18], and 'PCA-MQ' denotes one variant of MH combining the PCA projection with Manhattan quantization (MQ). Because the threshold optimization techniques for HQ in [18] can not be used for the above five methods, we use the same thresholds as those in MQ. All experiments are conducted on our workstation with Intel(R) Xeon(R) CPU X7560@2.27GHz and 64G memory.

4.3 Evaluation Metrics

We adopt the scheme widely used in recent papers [6, 24, 36] to evaluate our method. More specifically, we define the ground truth to be the Euclidean neighbors in the original feature space. The average distance to the 50th nearest neighbors is used as a threshold to find whether a point is a true positive or not. All the experimental results are averaged over 10 random training/test partitions. For each partition, we randomly select 1000 points as queries, and leave the rest as training set to learn the hash functions.

Based on the Euclidean ground truth, we can compute the precision, recall and the mean average precision (mAP) [6, 18] which are defined as follows:

$$Precision = \frac{\text{the number of retrieved relevant points}}{\text{the number of all retrieved points}},$$

$$Recall = \frac{\text{the number of retrieved relevent points}}{\text{the number of all relevent points}},$$

$$mAP = \frac{1}{|Q|}\sum_{i=1}^{|Q|}\frac{1}{n_i}\sum_{k=1}^{n_i} Precision(R_{ik}),$$

where $q_i \in Q$ is a query, n_i is the number of points relevant to q_i in the data set, the relevant points are ordered as $\{x_1, x_2, \cdots, x_{n_i}\}$, R_{ik} is the set of ranked retrieval results from the top result until you get to point x_k.

4.4 Results

The mAP values for different methods with different code sizes on *22K LabelMe*, *100K TinyImage*, and ANN_SIFT1M are shown in Table 1, Table 2, and Table 3, respectively. The value of each entry in the tables is the mAP of a combination of a projection function with a quantization method under a specific code size. The best mAP among SBQ, HQ and MQ under the same setting

[3] `http://labelme.csail.mit.edu/`

[4] `http://groups.csail.mit.edu/vision/TinyImages/`.

[5] `http://corpus-texmex.irisa.fr/`.

(a) LabelMe

(b) TinyImage

Figure 3: Sample images from LabelMe and TinyImage data sets.

is shown in bold face. To study the effect of q which is the length of NBC for each projected dimension, we evaluate our MH methods on *22K LabelMe* and *100K TinyImage* by setting the q to three different values (2, 3, and 4). From Table 1 and Table 2, we find that $q = 2$ (2-MQ) achieves the best performance for most cases. Hence, unless otherwise stated, $q = 2$ is a default setting.

From Table 1, Table 2, and Table 3, it is easy to find that our MQ method achieves the best performance under most settings, which means that our MQ with Manhattan distance does be very effective. Furthermore, we can also find that HQ achieves better performance than SBQ under most settings. Because both HQ and our MQ methods adopt more than one bit to encode each projected dimension, it may imply that using multiple bits to encode each projected dimension can be better than using just one single bit. This phenomenon has also been observed by the authors of AGH [18]. The essential difference between HQ and 2-MQ lies in the difference between Hamming distance and Manhattan distance. Hence, the better performance of MQ (compared with HQ) shows that Manhattan distance is a better choice (compared with Hamming distance) to preserve the neighborhood (similarity) structure in the data.

Figure 4 and Figure 5 show the precision-recall curves on *22K LabelMe* and ANN_SIFT1M data sets, respectively. Once again, we can easily find that our MQ based MH variants significantly outperform other state-of-the-art methods under most settings.

5. CONCLUSION

Most existing hashing methods focus on the projection stage while ignoring the quantization stage. This work systematically studies the effect of quantization. We find that the quantization stage is at least as important as the projection stage. This work might stimulate other researchers to move their attention from the projection stage to the quantization stage, and finally propose better methods simultaneously taking both stages into consideration.

The existing quantization methods, such as SBQ and HQ, will destroy the neighborhood structure in the original space, which violates the goal of hashing. In this paper, we propose a novel quantization strategy called Manhattan quantization (MQ) to effectively preserve the neighborhood structure among data. The MQ based hashing method, call Manhattan hashing (MH), encodes each projected dimension with multiple bits of *natural binary code* (NBC), based on which the Manhattan distance between points in the hashcode space is calculated for nearest neighbor search. MH can effectively preserve the neighborhood structure in the data to achieve the goal of hashing. To the best of our knowledge, this is the first work to adopt Manhattan distance with NBC for hashing. The effectiveness of our MH method is successfully verified by experiments on several large-scale real-world image data sets.

Table 1: mAP on *22K LabelMe* data set. The best mAP among SBQ, HQ, 2-MQ, 3-MQ and 4-MQ under the same setting is shown in bold face.

# bits	32					64				
	SBQ	HQ	2-MQ	3-MQ	4-MQ	SBQ	HQ	2-MQ	3-MQ	4-MQ
ITQ	0.2771	0.3166	**0.3537**	0.2860	0.2700	0.3283	0.4303	0.4881	**0.5163**	0.4803
SIKH	0.0487	0.0512	**0.0722**	0.0457	0.0339	0.1175	0.1024	**0.1700**	0.1242	0.0906
LSH	**0.1563**	0.1210	0.1382	0.0961	0.0684	0.2577	0.2507	**0.2833**	0.2514	0.1998
SH	0.0802	0.1540	**0.2207**	0.2103	0.2026	0.0988	0.1960	0.3237	0.3440	**0.3441**
PCA	0.0503	0.1414	0.1913	0.2064	**0.2092**	0.0388	0.1585	0.2233	0.3177	**0.3303**
# bits	128					256				
	SBQ	HQ	2-MQ	3-MQ	4-MQ	SBQ	HQ	2-MQ	3-MQ	4-MQ
ITQ	0.3559	0.5203	0.5905	**0.6968**	0.6758	0.3731	0.5862	0.6496	0.8053	**0.8062**
SIKH	0.2673	0.2125	**0.3669**	0.2736	0.2274	0.4109	0.3994	**0.5704**	0.4984	0.4139
LSH	0.3310	0.4360	**0.4596**	0.4423	0.3863	0.3955	0.5768	0.6115	**0.6321**	0.5833
SH	0.1644	0.2553	0.4367	0.4627	**0.4747**	0.2027	0.2671	0.4418	**0.5563**	0.5520
PCA	0.0298	0.1669	0.2114	0.3221	**0.3653**	0.0226	0.1549	0.1710	0.2288	**0.2814**

Table 2: mAP on *100K TinyImage* data set. The best mAP among SBQ, HQ, 2-MQ, 3-MQ and 4-MQ under the same setting is shown in bold face.

# bits	32					64				
	SBQ	HQ	2-MQ	3-MQ	4-MQ	SBQ	HQ	2-MQ	3-MQ	4-MQ
ITQ	**0.4936**	0.3963	0.4279	0.3185	0.3746	0.5811	0.5513	**0.5908**	0.4859	0.5109
SIKH	0.1354	0.1388	**0.2209**	0.1419	0.0868	0.3041	0.2789	**0.4037**	0.3197	0.2023
LSH	**0.3612**	0.3010	0.3396	0.2266	0.2161	0.4843	0.4747	**0.5183**	0.4445	0.4059
SH	0.1173	0.1870	**0.2372**	0.2271	0.1749	0.1934	0.3330	**0.4463**	0.4416	0.3445
PCA	0.0459	0.2124	**0.2569**	0.2566	0.1924	0.0405	0.3316	0.3845	**0.4196**	0.3139
# bits	128					256				
	SBQ	HQ	2-MQ	3-MQ	4-MQ	SBQ	HQ	2-MQ	3-MQ	4-MQ
ITQ	0.6227	0.6882	**0.7346**	0.6853	0.6671	0.6404	0.7877	0.8270	**0.8472**	0.8153
SIKH	0.5077	0.4239	**0.6311**	0.5139	0.3884	0.6625	0.6342	**0.7643**	0.6954	0.5892
LSH	0.5663	0.6421	**0.6856**	0.6474	0.5799	0.6145	0.7678	**0.7855**	0.7854	0.7219
SH	0.3044	0.4610	**0.5664**	0.5620	0.5062	0.4069	0.5643	0.6568	**0.6573**	0.5399
PCA	0.0360	0.4608	0.4896	**0.5137**	0.4533	0.0325	0.5267	0.5348	**0.5382**	0.5157

6. ACKNOWLEDGEMENTS

This work is supported by the NSFC (No. 61100125), the 863 Program of China (No. 2011AA01A202, No. 2012AA011003), and the Program for Changjiang Scholars and Innovative Research Team in University of China (IRT1158, PCSIRT).

7. REFERENCES

[1] A. Andoni and P. Indyk. Near-optimal hashing algorithms for approximate nearest neighbor in high dimensions. *Commun. ACM*, 51(1):117–122, 2008.

[2] S. Baluja and M. Covell. Learning to hash: forgiving hash functions and applications. *Data Min. Knowl. Discov.*, 17(3):402–430, 2008.

[3] M. Datar, N. Immorlica, P. Indyk, and V. S. Mirrokni. Locality-sensitive hashing scheme based on p-stable distributions. In *Proceedings of the ACM Symposium on Computational Geometry*, 2004.

[4] Y. Freund and R. E. Schapire. Experiments with a new boosting algorithm. In *Proceedings of International Conference on Machine Learning*, 1996.

[5] A. Gionis, P. Indyk, and R. Motwani. Similarity search in high dimensions via hashing. In *Proceedings of International Conference on Very Large Data Bases*, 1999.

[6] Y. Gong and S. Lazebnik. Iterative quantization: A procrustean approach to learning binary codes. In *Proceedings of Computer Vision and Pattern Recognition*, 2011.

[7] J. He, W. Liu, and S.-F. Chang. Scalable similarity search with optimized kernel hashing. In *Proceedings of the ACM SIGKDD International Conference on Knowledge Discovery and Data Mining*, 2010.

[8] J. He, R. Radhakrishnan, S.-F. Chang, and C. Bauer. Compact hashing with joint optimization of search accuracy and time. In *Proceedings of Computer Vision and Pattern Recognition*, 2011.

[9] G. E. Hinton. Training products of experts by minimizing contrastive divergence. *Neural Computation*, 14(8):1771–1800, 2002.

[10] H. Jegou, M. Douze, and C. Schmid. Hamming embedding and weak geometric consistency for large scale image search. In *Proceedings of the European Conference on Computer Vision*, 2008.

[11] H. Jegou, M. Douze, and C. Schmid. Improving bag-of-features for large scale image search. *International Journal of Computer Vision*, 87(3):316–336, 2010.

[12] H. Jégou, M. Douze, and C. Schmid. Product quantization for nearest neighbor search. *IEEE Trans. Pattern Anal. Mach. Intell.*, 33(1):117–128, 2011.

[13] I. Jolliffe. *Principal Component Analysis*. Springer, 2002.

Table 3: mAP on ANN_SIFT1M data set. The best mAP among SBQ, HQ and 2-MQ under the same setting is shown in bold face.

# bits	32			64			96			128		
	SBQ	HQ	2-MQ	SBQ	HQ	2-MQ	SBQ	HQ	2-MH	SBQ	HQ	2-MQ
ITQ	0.1657	0.2500	**0.2750**	0.4641	0.4745	**0.5087**	0.5424	0.5871	**0.6263**	0.5823	0.6589	**0.6813**
SIKH	0.0394	0.0217	**0.0570**	0.2027	0.0822	**0.2356**	0.2263	0.1664	**0.2768**	0.3936	0.3293	**0.4483**
LSH	0.1163	0.0961	**0.1173**	0.2340	0.2815	**0.3111**	0.3767	0.4541	**0.4599**	0.5329	0.5151	**0.5422**
SH	0.0889	0.2482	**0.2771**	0.1828	0.3841	**0.4576**	0.2236	0.4911	**0.5929**	0.2329	0.5823	**0.6713**
PCA	0.1087	0.2408	**0.2882**	0.1671	0.3956	**0.4683**	0.1625	0.4927	**0.5641**	0.1548	0.5506	**0.6245**

[14] T. Kanungo, D. M. Mount, N. S. Netanyahu, C. D. Piatko, R. Silverman, and A. Y. Wu. An efficient k-means clustering algorithm: Analysis and implementation. *IEEE Trans. Pattern Anal. Mach. Intell.*, 24(7):881–892, 2002.

[15] B. Kulis and T. Darrell. Learning to hash with binary reconstructive embeddings. In *Proceedings of Neural Information Processing Systems*, 2009.

[16] B. Kulis and K. Grauman. Kernelized locality-sensitive hashing for scalable image search. In *Proceedings of International Conference on Computer Vision*, 2009.

[17] B. Kulis, P. Jain, and K. Grauman. Fast similarity search for learned metrics. *IEEE Trans. Pattern Anal. Mach. Intell.*, 31(12):2143–2157, 2009.

[18] W. Liu, J. Wang, S. Kumar, and S. Chang. Hashing with graphs. In *Proceedings of International Conference on Machine Learning*, 2011.

[19] W. Liu, J. Wang, Y. Mu, S. Kumar, and S.-F. Chang. Compact hyperplane hashing with bilinear functions. In *Proceedings of International Conference on Machine Learning*, 2012.

[20] Y. Mu, J. Shen, and S. Yan. Weakly-supervised hashing in kernel space. In *Proceedings of Computer Vision and Pattern Recognition*, 2010.

[21] Y. Mu and S. Yan. Non-metric locality-sensitive hashing. In *Proceedings of AAAI Conference on Artificial Intelligence*, 2010.

[22] M. Norouzi and D. J. Fleet. Minimal loss hashing for compact binary codes. In *Proceedings of International Conference on Machine Learning*, 2011.

[23] A. Oliva and A. Torralba. Modeling the shape of the scene: A holistic representation of the spatial envelope. *International Journal of Computer Vision*, 42(3):145–175, 2001.

[24] M. Raginsky and S. Lazebnik. Locality-sensitive binary codes from shift-invariant kernels. In *Proceedings of Neural Information Processing Systems*, 2009.

[25] R. Salakhutdinov and G. Hinton. Semantic Hashing. In *SIGIR workshop on Information Retrieval and applications of Graphical Models*, 2007.

[26] R. Salakhutdinov and G. E. Hinton. Semantic hashing. *Int. J. Approx. Reasoning*, 50(7):969–978, 2009.

[27] G. Salton and C. Buckley. Term-weighting approaches in automatic text retrieval. *Inf. Process. Manage.*, 24(5):513–523, 1988.

[28] G. Shakhnarovich, T. Darrell, and P. Indyk. *Nearest-Neighbor Methods in Learning and Vision: Theory and Practice*. The MIT Press, 2006.

[29] J. Song, Y. Yang, Z. Huang, H. T. Shen, and R. Hong. Multiple feature hashing for real-time large scale near-duplicate video retrieval. In *ACM Multimedia*, 2011.

[30] B. Stein. Principles of hash-based text retrieval. In *Proceedings of the International ACM SIGIR Conference on Research and Development in Information Retrieval*, 2007.

[31] A. Torralba, R. Fergus, and W. T. Freeman. 80 million tiny images: A large data set for nonparametric object and scene recognition. *IEEE Trans. Pattern Anal. Mach. Intell.*, 30(11):1958–1970, 2008.

[32] A. Torralba, R. Fergus, and Y. Weiss. Small codes and large image databases for recognition. In *Proceedings of Computer Vision and Pattern Recognition*, 2008.

[33] F. Ture, T. Elsayed, and J. J. Lin. No free lunch: brute force vs. locality-sensitive hashing for cross-lingual pairwise similarity. In *Proceedings of the International ACM SIGIR Conference on Research and Development in Information Retrieval*, 2011.

[34] J. Wang, O. Kumar, and S.-F. Chang. Semi-supervised hashing for scalable image retrieval. In *Proceedings of Computer Vision and Pattern Recognition*, 2010.

[35] J. Wang, S. Kumar, and S.-F. Chang. Sequential projection learning for hashing with compact codes. In *Proceedings of International Conference on Machine Learning*, 2010.

[36] Y. Weiss, A. Torralba, and R. Fergus. Spectral hashing. In *Proceedings of Neural Information Processing Systems*, 2008.

[37] H. Xu, J. Wang, Z. Li, G. Zeng, S. Li, and N. Yu. Complementary hashing for approximate nearest neighbor search. In *Proceedings of International Conference on Computer Vision*, 2011.

[38] D. Zhang, F. Wang, and L. Si. Composite hashing with multiple information sources. In *Proceedings of the International ACM SIGIR Conference on Research and Development in Information Retrieval*, 2011.

[39] D. Zhang, J. Wang, D. Cai, and J. Lu. Self-taught hashing for fast similarity search. In *Proceedings of the International ACM SIGIR Conference on Research and Development in Information Retrieval*, 2010.

[40] Y. Zhen and D.-Y. Yeung. Active hashing and its application to image and text retrieval. *Data Mining and Knowledge Discovery*, 2012.

[41] Y. Zhen and D.-Y. Yeung. A probabilistic model for multimodal hash function learning. In *Proceedings of the ACM SIGKDD International Conference on Knowledge Discovery and Data Mining*, 2012.

[42] Y. Zhuang, Y. Liu, F. Wu, Y. Zhang, and J. Shao. Hypergraph spectral hashing for similarity search of social image. In *ACM Multimedia*, 2011.

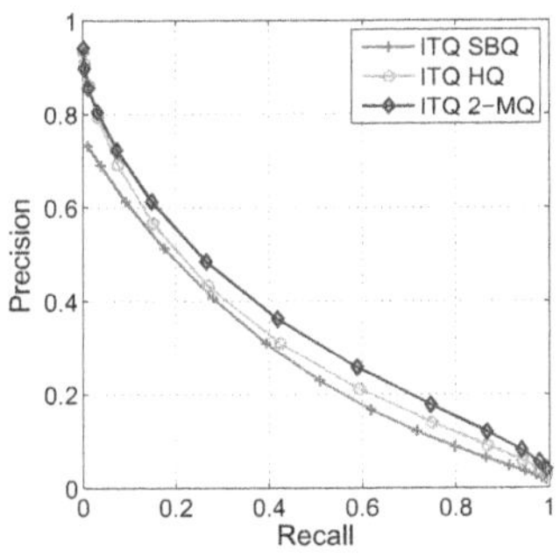

ITQ 32 bits

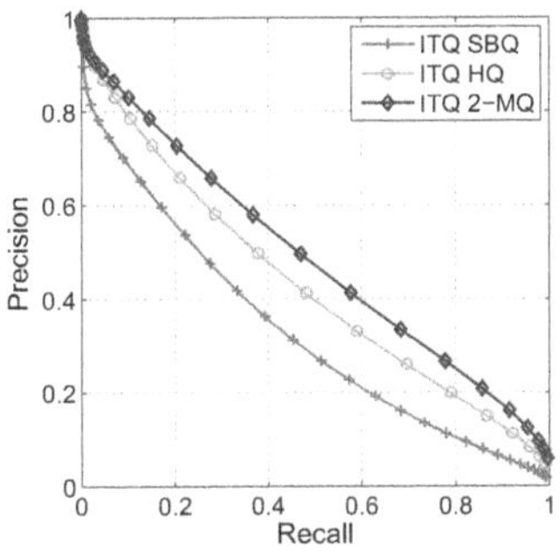

ITQ 64 bits

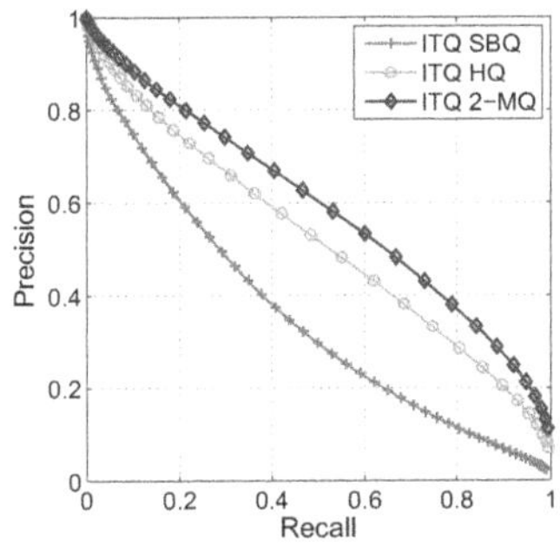

ITQ 128 bits

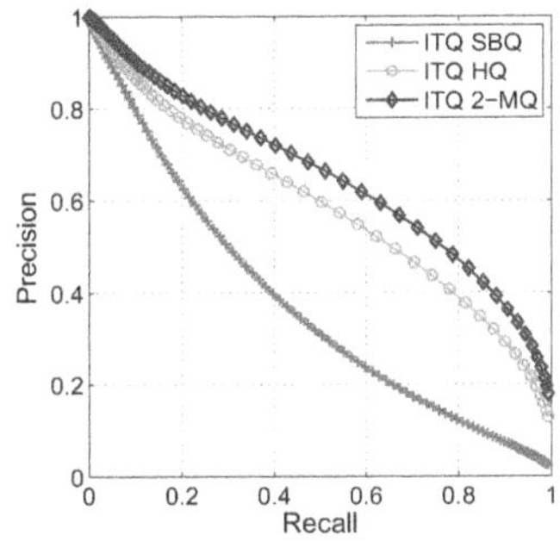

ITQ 256 bits

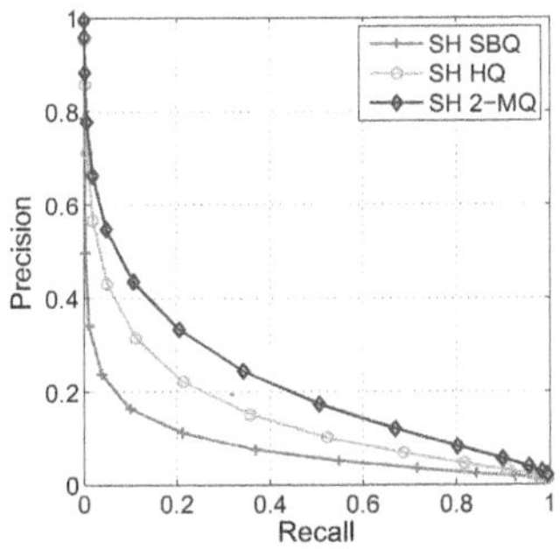

SH 32 bits

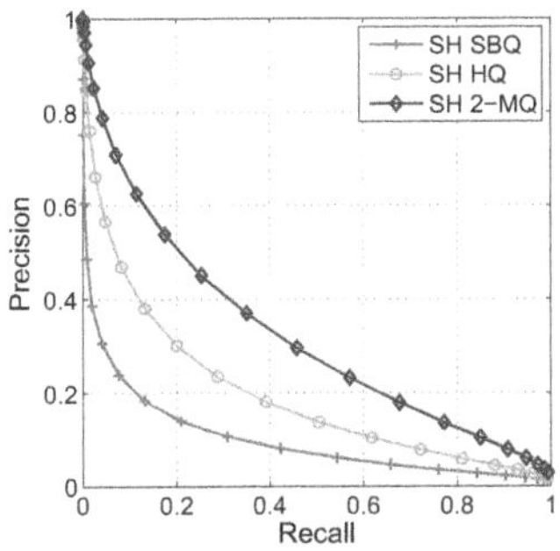

SH 64 bits

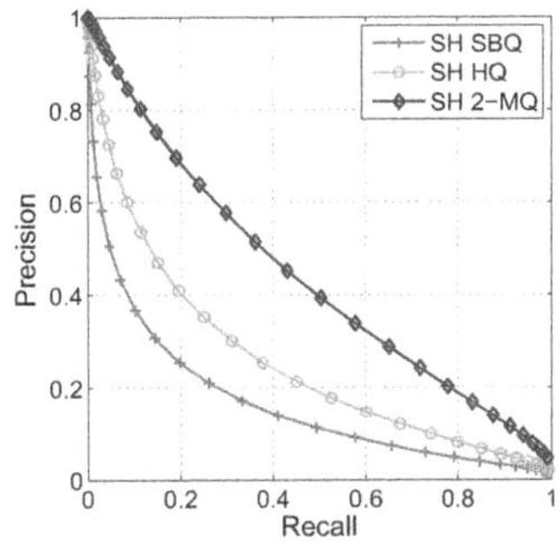

SH 128 bits

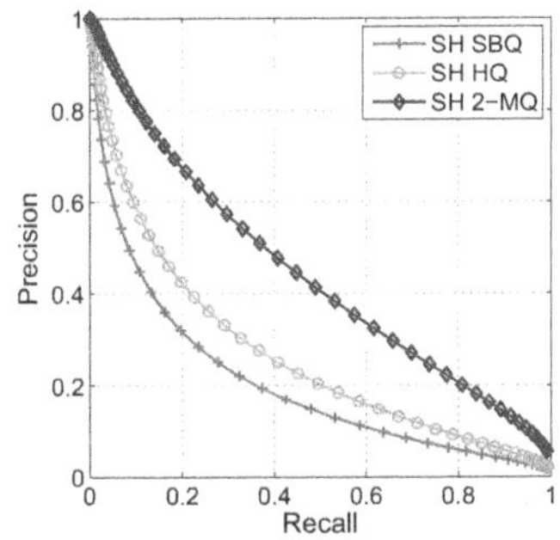

SH 256 bits

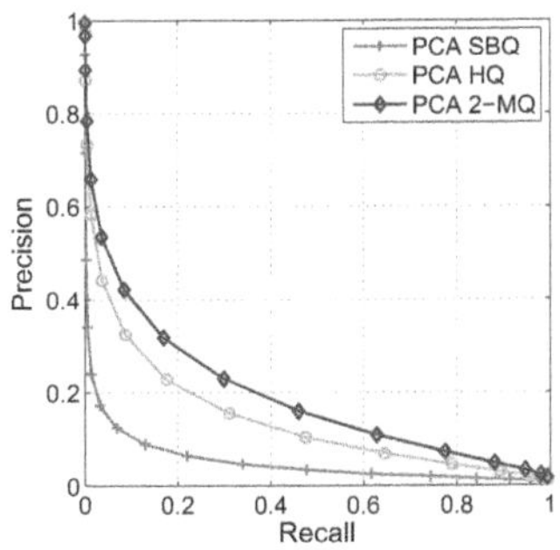

PCA 32 bits.

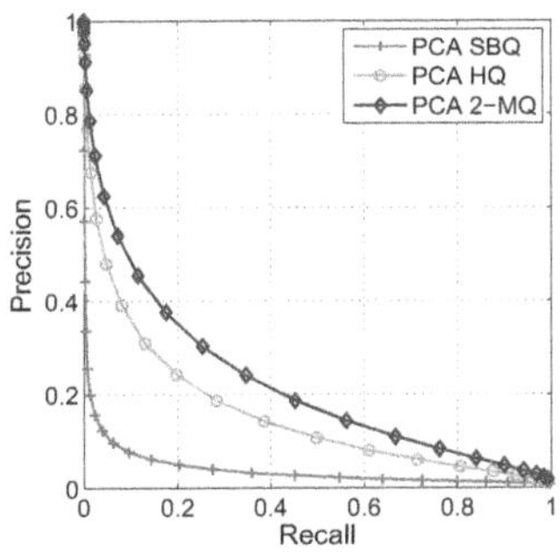

PCA 64 bits.

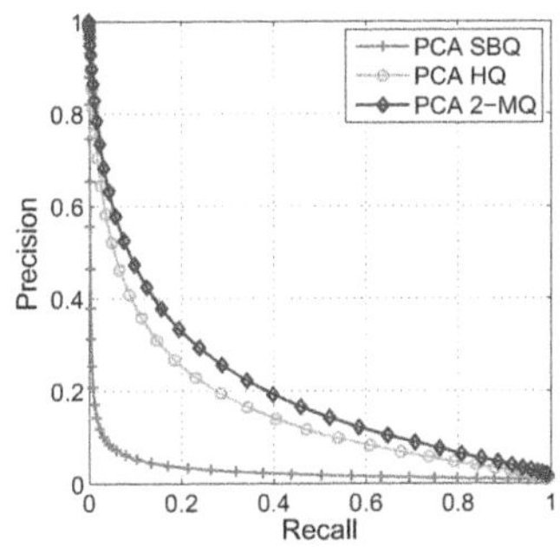

PCA 128 bits.

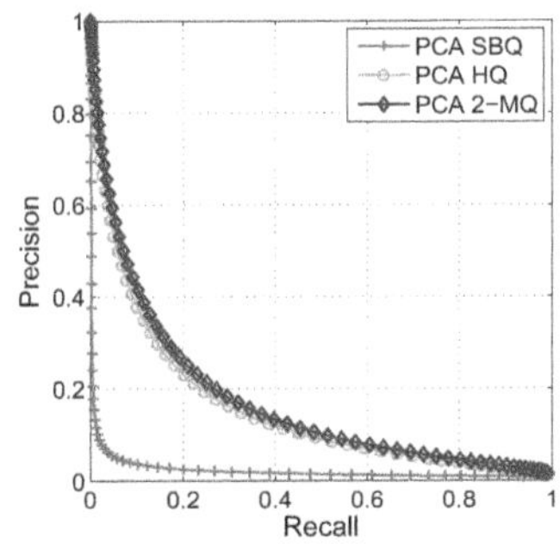

PCA 256 bits.

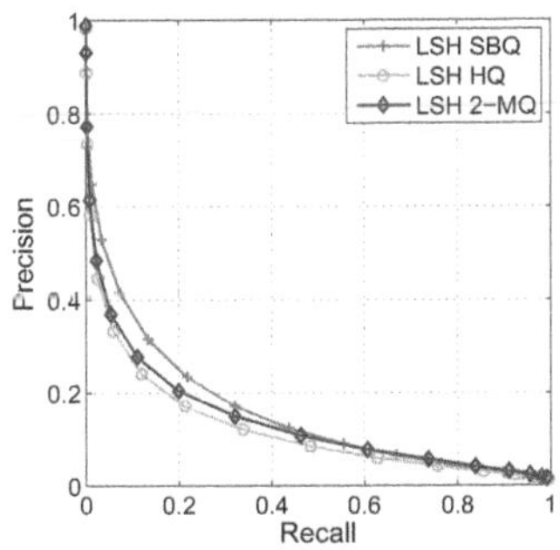

LSH 32 bits

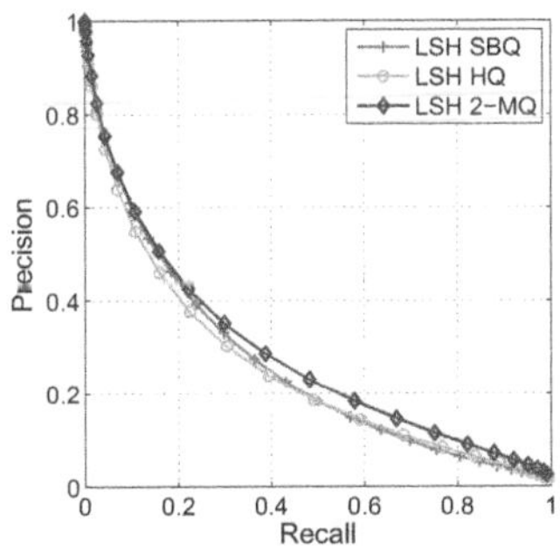

LSH 64 bits

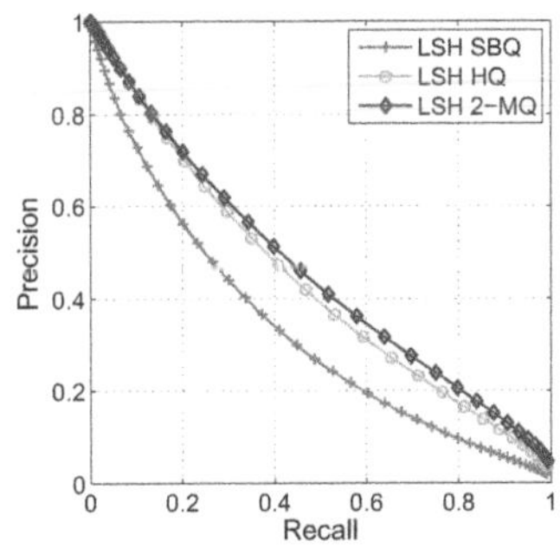

LSH 128 bits

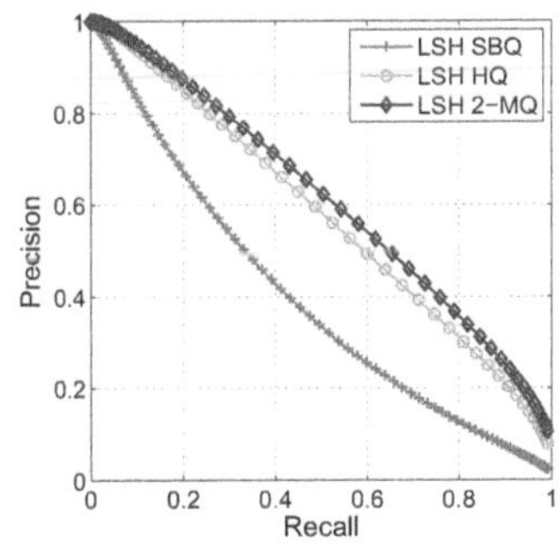

LSH 256 bits

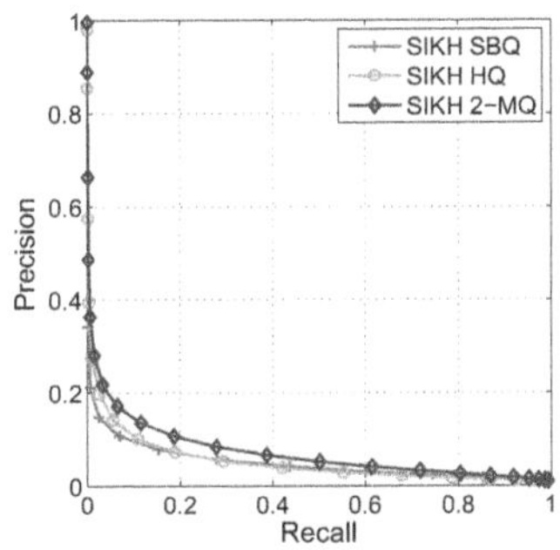

SIKH 32 bits

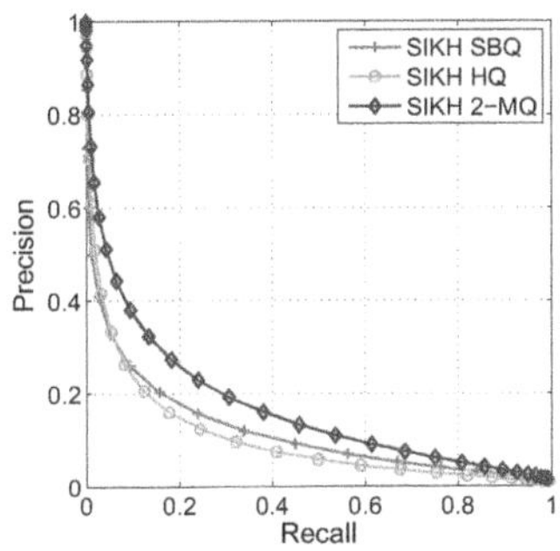

SIKH 64 bits

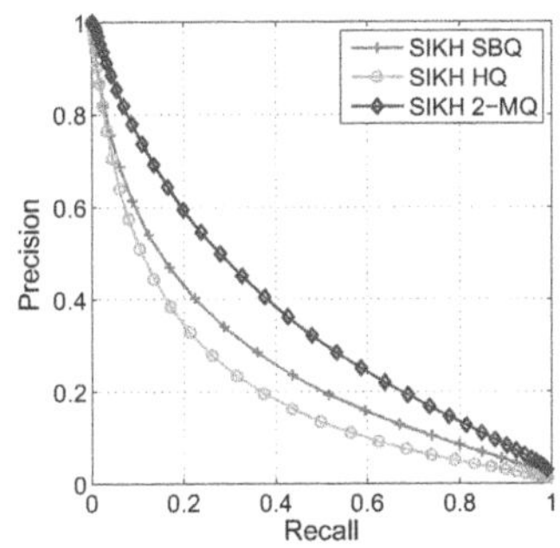

SIKH 128 bits

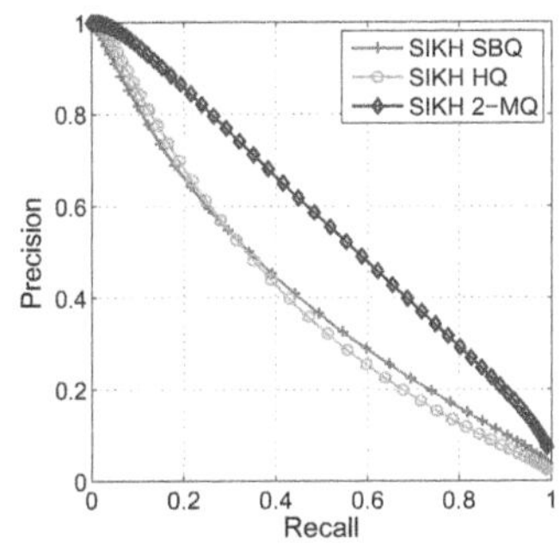

SIKH 256 bits

Figure 4: Precision-recall curve on *22K LabelMe* data set

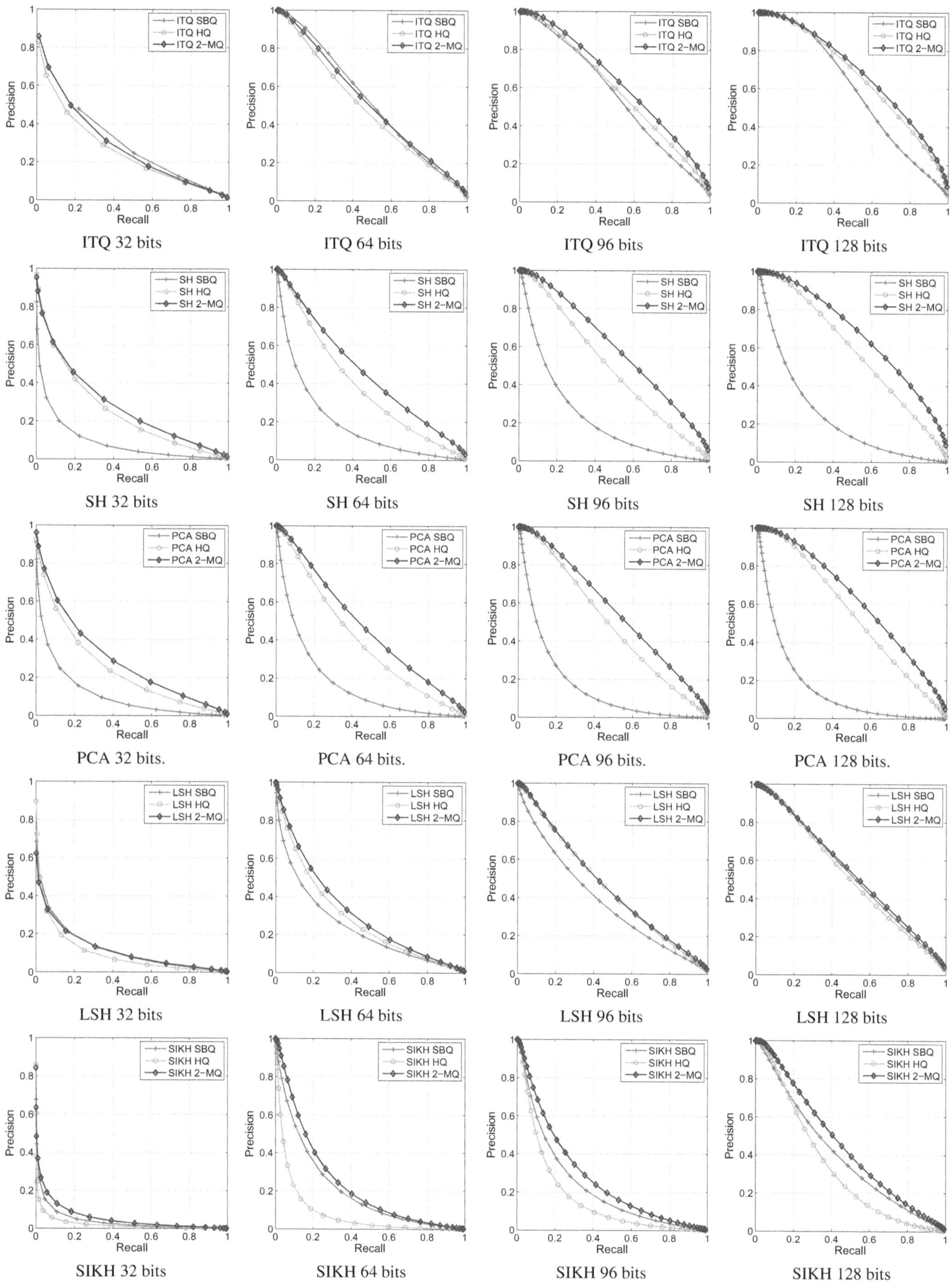

Figure 5: Precision-recall curve on ANN_SIFT1M data set

Boosting Multi-Kernel Locality-Sensitive Hashing for Scalable Image Retrieval

Hao Xia, Pengcheng Wu, Steven C.H. Hoi
School of Computer Engineering
Nanyang Technological University
Singapore 639798
{xiah0002,wupe0003,chhoi}@ntu.edu.sg

Rong Jin
Computer Science and Engineering Dept.
Michigan State University
East Lansing, MI, 48824
rongjin@cse.msu.edu

ABSTRACT

Similarity search is a key challenge for multimedia retrieval applications where data are usually represented in high-dimensional space. Among various algorithms proposed for similarity search in high-dimensional space, Locality-Sensitive Hashing (LSH) is the most popular one, which recently has been extended to Kernelized Locality-Sensitive Hashing (KLSH) by exploiting kernel similarity for better retrieval efficacy. Typically, KLSH works only with a single kernel, which is often limited in real-world multimedia applications, where data may originate from multiple resources or can be represented in several different forms. For example, in content-based multimedia retrieval, a variety of features can be extracted to represent contents of an image. To overcome the limitation of regular KLSH, we propose a novel Boosting Multi-Kernel Locality-Sensitive Hashing (BMKLSH) scheme that significantly boosts the retrieval performance of KLSH by making use of multiple kernels. We conduct extensive experiments for large-scale content-based image retrieval, in which encouraging results show that the proposed method outperforms the state-of-the-art techniques.

Categories and Subject Descriptors

H.3.3 [**Information Storage and Retrieval**]: Retrieval models; H.2.8 [**Database Applications**]: Image databases

General Terms

Algorithms, Experimentation

Keywords

Image Retrieval, High-dimensional indexing, Locality-sensitive hashing, Kernel methods

1. INTRODUCTION

Similarity search, or Nearest Neighbor (NN) search, plays a critical role in Content-Based Image Retrieval (CBIR) systems [33, 24]. Typically, images in a CBIR system are represented in a high-dimensional space, and the size of an image database can easily be over millions or even billions for large-scale real-world applications. These two aspects have made CBIR an open grand challenge although it has been extensively studied for decades.

A variety of data structures have been proposed for indexing and searching data points in a low-dimensional space [31, 7, 2, 29]. These approaches work well for low dimensional data. But, when the number of dimensions grows, they often become less efficient, a phenomenon known as the *curse of dimensionality*. Specifically, the time or space requirements of these approaches often grow exponentially with the dimensionality.

Since exact NN search is hard to scale for high-dimensional data, recent studies mainly focus on *approximation* approaches [20, 14, 25, 1], which aim to remove the exponential dependence on dimensionality. Instead of finding the nearest point p to a query point q, approximate NN search allows to return any point within the distance of $(1+\epsilon)$ times the distance from q to p. Recent studies have shown that by adopting the approximation, the complexity of NN search is reduced from exponential to polynomial in terms of its dependence on the dimensionality. Several recent studies have successfully applied the random projection idea for approximate NN search over high-dimensional data. One of the most well-known techniques in this direction is Locality-Sensitive Hashing (LSH) [20, 14, 6], which has been actively studied and successfully applied to many applications [20, 10, 1].

One limitation of regular LSH is that they require explicit vector representation of data points. Kernelized LSH (KLSH) [23] addresses this limitation by employing kernel functions to capture similarity between data points without having to know their explicit vector representation. KLSH has been shown effective empirically, but there is no formal analysis of KLSH in theory. In this paper, we first analyze the theoretical property of KLSH to better understand the behavior and capacity of KLSH in similarity search. Second, we address the limitation of KLSH. Despite the success, most existing KLSH techniques only adopt a single kernel function. This significantly limits its application to many real-world image retrieval tasks [40, 18], where images are often analyzed by a variety of feature descriptors and are measured by a wide class of diverse similarity functions.

To this end, we propose a novel Boosting Multi-Kernel Locality-Sensitive Hashing (BMKLSH) framework, which improves KLSH by learning a combination of multiple kernels. The key challenge of multi-kernel LSH is to determine an optimal combination of multiple kernels by determining appropriate bit size to each of the multiple kernels. To overcome the challenge, we propose a boosting scheme to greedily find a good solution in an efficient approach. Our extensive experiments show that BMKLSH significantly en-

Permission to make digital or hard copies of all or part of this work for personal or classroom use is granted without fee provided that copies are not made or distributed for profit or commercial advantage and that copies bear this notice and the full citation on the first page. To copy otherwise, to republish, to post on servers or to redistribute to lists, requires prior specific permission and/or a fee.
SIGIR'12, August 12–16, 2012, Portland, Oregon, USA.
Copyright 2012 ACM 978-1-4503-1472-5/12/08 ...$15.00.

hances the performance of KLSH in exploring the power of multiple kernels for CBIR.

The rest of this paper is organized as follows. Section 2 reviews related work. Section 3 gives our analysis of KLSH, and Section 4 presents the proposed BMKLSH method. Section 5 discusses our experiments. Finally Section 6 concludes this work.

2. RELATED WORK

This section reviews related work in approximate nearest neighbor (NN) search with the focus on image retrieval applications.

In literature, developing efficient techniques for indexing high dimensional images has been studied extensively in information retrieval, multimedia, and database communities [4, 5, 9]. Spatial data structure approaches (e.g., kd-tree [2, 29] or metric tree [35]) were used to handle the NN search problem; however, they scale poorly with data dimensionality. In practice, if the number of dimensions is large enough, kd-tree and other similar data structures require an expensive inspection in the data set, thereby perform no better than an exhaustive linear search that simply compares a query to every data point in the database.

Instead of solving the exact similarity search for high dimensional indexing, recent years have witnessed active studies of approximate high-dimensional indexing techniques [20, 14, 25, 3, 8, 11]. The key of most techniques is to exploit random projection to tackle the curse of dimensionality issue, such as Locality-Sensitive Hashing (LSH) [20], a very well-known and highly successful technique in this area. In general, we can group most of existing approaches into two major categories: linear projection methods and kernel-based methods. Below we briefly review the first category and then focus on discussing the second category.

For the first category, one of the most notable techniques is LSH [20], which utilizes a family of locality sensitive hashing functions which map similar items to same bucket with high probability, and dissimilar items to same bucket with low probability. With such a hash function, one can easily search within the bucket a query point belongs to in order to find nearest neighbors of the query. LSH efficiently solves the approximate similarity search problem and achieves query time in the worst case $O(dn^{1/\epsilon})$. Gionis et al. [14] improved the techniques and achieved significant query time $O(dn^{1/(1+\epsilon)})$. Recently, many studies have attempted to improve upon the regular LSH technique. For example, [25] introduced multi-probe LSH methods that reduce the space requirement of the basic LSH method. Tao et al. [34] proposed the locality-sensitive B-tree technique that mainly concerns the performance improvement of I/O disk access. Besides, there are many other existing works that accommodate LSH functions in tackling different issues, including Hamming distance [20], inner products [6], ℓ_p-norms [10], normalized partial matching [15], learned Mahalanobis metrics [27], and so on. Last but not least, there are also many recent studies of learning compact binary codes inspired by the idea of LSH [39, 16, 36, 22].

Our study is more related to the second category of kernel-based methods. In particular, kernel-based LSH (KLSH) [23] was recently proposed to overcome the limitation of the regular LSH technique that often assumes the data come from a multidimensional vector space and the underlying embedding of the data must be explicitly known and computable. KLSH provides a powerful framework to explore arbitrary kernel/similarity functions where their underlying embedding only needs to be known implicitly. In [28], the authors proposed a variant of KLSH which aims to force the expected Hamming distance between the binary codes of two vectors is related to the value of a shift-invariant kernel. In [17], the authors proposed an improved algorithm for learning binary codes with kernel to speed up the KLSH technique. Despite being studied actively, most existing kernel-based hashing methods [23, 28, 17, 26] only consider a single kernel, which cannot fully explore the potential of multiple kernel functions in a real CBIR application.

Symbol	Meaning
d	number of dimensions of input data
n	number of image examples in database
$\mathbf{X}$	$d \times n$ matrix of n image examples
$\mathbf{q}$	query image example
$\mathbf{x}_i$	i-th image example in database
K	kernel matrix
n_q	number of training query examples
m	number of different kernel functions
κ_l	l-th kernel function
b	length of a hash key
p	number of data points sampled in KLSH
t	number of indices selected in KLSH
D_t	distribution at the t-th round
T	number of boosting rounds

Table 1: Summary of notation used in this paper

Very recently, some emerging study has attempted to apply KLSH by exploring multiple kernels. In [37], they proposed a simple solution named MKLSH by applying the existing KLSH algorithm for each specific kernel individually, and then combining the outputs of these KLSH processes. Our work however differs from their method in several aspects. First of all, their naive approach to combining multiple kernels simply treats each kernel equally, which fails to fully explore the power of combining multiple diverse kernels in KLSH. Second, their technique is essentially unsupervised, which does not fully explore the data characteristics and thus cannot achieve the optimal indexing performance. In contrast, our technique is in general supervised and is able to learn the optimal combination of multiple kernels from training data to maximize the indexing performance.

3. ANALYSIS OF KERNELIZED LSH

In this section, we first review the algorithm of Kernelized Locality-Sensitive Hashing (KLSH), and then present our analysis of KLSH.

Let $\mathbf{X} \in \mathbb{R}^{d\times n}$ be the collection of data points to be searched. Given a query $q \in \mathbb{R}^d$, to efficiently find the k nearest neighbors, LSH projects each data point into a low-dimensional binary space, referred to as the *hash* key. The hash keys are constructed by applying b binary-valued hash functions $h_1, \dots, h_b$ to the data points in $\mathbf{X}$. KLSH generalizes LSH by introducing a kernel function $\kappa(\mathbf{x}_i, \mathbf{x}_j)$ to map a data point $\mathbf{x}_i$ to a functional space through a nonlinear feature mapping $\phi(\mathbf{x}_i)$ that satisfies the condition $\kappa(\mathbf{x}_i, \mathbf{x}_j) = \phi^\top(\mathbf{x}_i)\phi(\mathbf{x}_j)$. To build the hash function, KLSH first randomly selects a subset of p data points from $\mathbf{X}$, denoted as $S = \{\mathbf{x}_1^s, \dots, \mathbf{x}_p^s\}$, and forms a kernel matrix K over the sampled data points; it then generates b random vectors $\mathbf{e}_S^1, \dots, \mathbf{e}_S^b$ and computes a hashing function for each random vector $\mathbf{e}_S^k$ as

$$h_k(\phi(\mathbf{x})) = \text{sign}\left(\sum_{j=1}^{p} w_j^k \kappa(\mathbf{x}, \mathbf{x}_j^s)\right),$$

where $\mathbf{w}^k = (w_1^k, \dots, w_p^k)^\top$ is given by $\mathbf{w}^k = K^{-1/2}\mathbf{e}_S^k$. Algorithm 1 outlines the key steps of KLSH, where b is a critical parameter that determines the length of hash key to be constructed in KLSH.

Although KLSH is proved to be effective empirically, no theoretical analysis is provided for the properties of KLSH. To bound approximation error of KLSH, we introduce a few notations. De-

Algorithm 1 KLSH

INPUT:
- an image database: $\{\mathbf{x}_i | i = 1, \ldots, n\}, \mathbf{x}_i \in \mathbb{R}^d$
- length of the hash key: b
- a kernel function: $\kappa(\cdot, \cdot)$

randomly select p data points $S = \{\mathbf{x}_j^s | j = 1, \ldots, p\}$
$K = [\kappa(\mathbf{x}_i^s, \mathbf{x}_j^s)]_{p \times p}$
for $k = 1, \ldots, b$ **do**
  form $\mathbf{e}_S^k$: select t indices at random from $[1, \ldots, p]$
  form $\mathbf{w}^k = K^{-1/2}\mathbf{e}_S^k$
  construct hash function:
  $h_k(\phi(\mathbf{x})) = \text{sign}(\sum_{j=1}^p w_j^k \kappa(\mathbf{x}, \mathbf{x}_j^s))$
end for

OUTPUT: a set of b hash functions $\mathcal{H} = \{h_k | k = 1, \ldots, b\}$

fine $\mathbf{h}_i \in \mathbb{R}^b$ as

$$\mathbf{h}_i = \left(\sum_{j=1}^p w_j^1 \kappa(\mathbf{x}_i, \mathbf{x}_j^s), \ldots, \sum_{j=1}^p w_j^b \kappa(\mathbf{x}_i, \mathbf{x}_j^s) \right)^\top$$

and $H = (\mathbf{h}_1, \ldots, \mathbf{h}_n)$. Let $K_a = [\kappa(\mathbf{x}_i, \mathbf{x}_j)]_{n \times n}$ be the Gram matrix for all data points in $\mathbf{X}$, and $K_b = [\kappa(\mathbf{x}_i, \mathbf{x}_j^s)]_{n \times p}$ be the kernel matrix between data points in $\mathbf{X}$ and the sampled data points in S. Let $\lambda_1, \ldots, \lambda_n$ be the eigenvalues of K_a ranked in the descending order. We first bound the error caused by the random vectors $\{\mathbf{e}_S^k\}_{k=1}^b$.

THEOREM 1. *With a probability at least $1 - \delta$, we have*

$$\left| \frac{t}{p} K_b K^{-1} K_b^\top - \frac{1}{b} H^\top H \right|_F \leq \sqrt{\frac{2t \ln(2/\delta)}{b}} |K_b K^{-1} K_b^\top|_F$$

PROOF. Let us define A as $A = \frac{1}{b}\sum_{k=1}^b \mathbf{e}_S^k [\mathbf{e}_S^k]^\top$. It is easy to see that $\mathrm{E}[A] = \frac{t}{p} I$. According to the concentration inequality of linear operator [32], we have, with a probability $1 - \delta$, that

$$\left| A - \frac{t}{p} I \right|_F \leq \sqrt{\frac{2t \ln(2/\delta)}{p}}$$

We complete the proof by the using the fact

$$\left| \frac{t}{p} K_b K^{-1} K_b^\top - \frac{1}{b} H^\top H \right|_F = \left| K_b K^{-1/2} \left(\frac{t}{p} I - A \right) K^{-1/2} K_b^\top \right|_F$$
$$\leq \left| \frac{t}{p} I - A \right|_F |K_b K^{-1} K_b^\top|_F$$

□

THEOREM 2. *Assume $\kappa(\mathbf{x}, \mathbf{x}) \leq 1$ for any $\mathbf{x}$. Let $k \in \mathbb{Z}$ and $\epsilon \in (0, 1)$ be any two numbers satisfying $k/\epsilon^4 \leq p/[64\eta^2]$, where $\eta = 1 + \sqrt{8 \log(1/\delta)}$. Then, with a probability at least $1 - 2\delta$, we have*

$$\frac{1}{n^2} \sum_{i,j=1}^n \left(\kappa(\mathbf{x}_i, \mathbf{x}_j) - \frac{p}{tb} \mathbf{h}_i^\top \mathbf{h}_j \right)^2 \leq \frac{3}{n} \sum_{i=1}^{n-k} \lambda_{k+i}^2 + 3\epsilon + \frac{6p^2 \ln(2/\delta)}{bt}$$

PROOF. According to Theorem [12], with a probability $1 - \delta$, for any $\epsilon \in [0, 1]$ and $k \in \mathbb{Z}$ that satisfy

$$\frac{k}{\epsilon^4} \leq \frac{p}{64\eta^2}$$

where $\eta = 1 + \sqrt{8 \log(1/\delta)}$, we have

$$|K_a - K_b K^{-1} K_b^\top|_F \leq \sqrt{\sum_{i=1}^{n-k} \lambda_{k+i}^2 + \epsilon n}$$

where $|\cdot|_F$ stands for the Frobenius norm. Using the triangle inequality of Frobenius norm, we have

$$\left| \frac{t}{p} K_a - \frac{1}{b} H^\top H \right|_F$$
$$\leq \frac{t}{p} \left| K_a - K_b K^{-1} K_b^\top \right|_F + \left| \frac{t}{p} K_b K^{-1} K_b^\top - \frac{1}{b} H^\top H \right|_F$$

Combining the result from Theorem 1, we have, with a probability $1 - 2\delta$,

$$\left| \frac{t}{p} K_a - \frac{1}{b} H^\top H \right|_F$$
$$\leq \frac{t}{p} \sum_{i=1}^{n-k} \lambda_{k+i} + \frac{t}{p} \epsilon n + \sqrt{\frac{2t \ln(2/\delta)}{b}} |K_b K^{-1} K_b^\top|_F$$

We complete the proof by using the fact $|K_b K^{-1} K_b|_F \leq |K_a|_F \leq \sum_{i=1}^n \lambda_i \leq n$ and the definition of Frobenius. □

As indicated by Theorem 2, on average, kernel similarity $\kappa(\mathbf{x}_i, \mathbf{x}_j)$ is well approximated by $\frac{p}{tb} \mathbf{h}_i^\top \mathbf{h}_j$, and the approximation error decreases as the number of bits b increases. Furthermore the approximation error is related to the eigenvalues of kernel matrix K_a. In particular, the skewed the eigenvalues of K_a, the smaller the approximation error.

Theorem 2 shows that different types of kernels will lead to very different approximation errors, depending on their eigenvalue distributions. Hence, some kernels will have good retrieval accuracy but rather poor approximation performance while the others may have the opposites. Thus, combining multiple kernels could potentially avoid relying too much on a single kernel that could be of neither poor approximation nor low retrieval accuracy. To make a good tradeoff between retrieval accuracy and approximation error, we propose a boosting scheme to combine multiple kernels for KLSH in order to obtain both high retrieval accuracy and low approximation error.

4. LEARNING TO COMBINE MULTIPLE KERNELS FOR KLSH

4.1 Overview

In this section, we propose a framework of learning the combination of multiple kernels for Kernelized Locality-Sensitive Hashing, which aims to boost KLSH by making use of a combination of multiple kernels. One key question is how to determine the weights for kernel combination. A straightforward approach is to assign equal weight to each kernel function, and apply KLSH with the uniformly combined kernel function. Such an approach might not fully explore the power of multiple kernels.

To address this limitation, we propose a scheme to assign each kernel a different number of bits so as to reflect the importance of the kernel. The key challenge of this scheme is thus how to optimize the bit size allocation with respect to different kernel functions. Figure 1 illustrates the proposed framework, which consists of two key steps: (i) bit allocation optimization, and (ii) the multi-kernel hashing as shown in Algorithm 2.

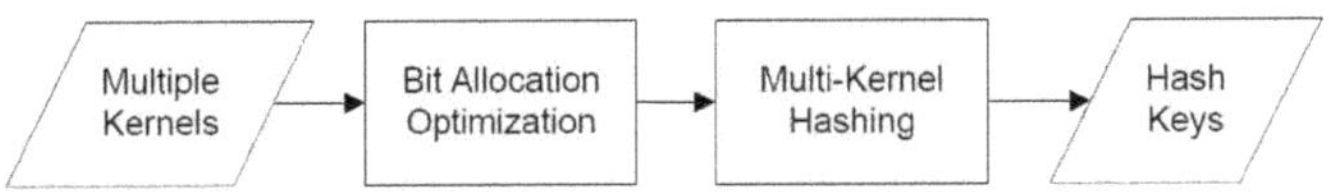

Figure 1: The proposed framework of learning to combine multiple kernels for improving kernel LSH

Algorithm 2 The Multi-Kernel Hashing scheme

INPUT:

- an image database: $\{\mathbf{x}_i | i = 1, \dots, n\}$, $\mathbf{x}_i \in \mathbb{R}^d$
- a set of m different kernels: $\{\kappa_l | l = 1, \dots, m\}$
- bits allocation vector $[b_1, \dots, b_m]$

```
k = 0
randomly select p data points S = {x_j^s | j = 1, ..., p}
for l = 1, ..., m do
    K_l = [κ_l(x_i^s, x_j^s)]_{p×p}
    for r = 1, ..., b_l do
        k = k + 1
        form e_S^k: select t indices at random from [1, ..., p]
        form w^k = K_l^{-1/2} e_S^k
        construct hash function:
        h_k(φ(x)) = sign(Σ_{j=1}^p w_j^k κ_l(x, x_j^s))
    end for
end for
```

OUTPUT: a set of b hash functions $\mathcal{H} = \{h_k | k = 1, \dots, b\}$

Unlike the regular KLSH that adopts a single kernel, BMKLSH employs a set of m kernels for the hashing scheme. Besides, a key difference between BMKLSH and some existing Multi-Kernel LSH (MKLSH) [37] is the bit allocation optimization step to find the parameter $[b_1, \dots, b_m]$ that determines the allocations of bit sizes for a set of m kernels. Unlike the existing MKLSH approach [37] that simply assigns the same number of bits to each kernel, leading to a uniform combination of multiple kernels, we develop two supervised learning algorithms (WMKLSH and BMKLSH), described below, that effectively learn the importance of individual kernels, and consequentially determine the appropriate number of bits for each kernel.

4.2 WMKLSH by Weighted Bit Allocation

We first propose a Weighted Multi-Kernel Locality-Sensitive Hashing (WMKLSH) scheme by a supervised learning approach to determine the allocation of bit size, where a kernel is assigned a larger size of bits if it better captures the similarity between data points.

In order to learn the importance weights of different kernels for the retrieval tasks, we assume a small training data set is available for our learning task. The training set consists of a small set of queries and their relevance judgements, which usually can be easily collected in a real-life CBIR system via the relevance feedback mechanism [30, 19].

For the WMKLSH algorithm, we begin by testing the retrieval performance of KLSH with a set of m kernels on the given training set. After that, we can obtain the retrieval performance in terms of mean Average Precision (mAP), As a result, we can compute the weights based on the retrieval performance of each kernel, i.e., $\alpha_l = e^{mAP_l}, l = 1, \dots, m$. Finally, the bit sizes of the kernels are allocated proportionally according to their importance weights.

4.3 BMKLSH for Optimizing Bit Allocation

To further improve the above learning scheme, we propose a boosting scheme, referred to as BMKLSH, to learn the optimal allocation of bit sizes, which adopts the similar idea of boosting algorithms for classification [13]. Let us denote by n_q the number of queries, and $AP_l(i), l \in [m], i \in [n_q]$, be the Average Precision performance of applying the l-th kernel $\kappa_l(\cdot, \cdot)$ to retrieve vectors for the i-th query. In order to find the optimal allocation of bit sizes, we cast it into the following optimization problem:

$$\max_{b_1,\dots,b_m \in [b]} \sum_{i=1}^{n_q} \exp\left(\sum_{l=1}^{m} AP_l(i)\right) \text{subject to} \sum_{l} b_l = b \quad (1)$$

Since each b_l is an integer variable, the above problem is essentially an integer programming task, which is NP-hard. To find an efficient solution, we approximate the above optimization problem by introducing a set of combination weights $\alpha_l, l \in [m]$, each of which represents the importance of each kernel so as to determine each bit size b_i. In order to learn the optimal weights, we turn the above optimization into the following optimization problem

$$\max_{\alpha \in \mathbb{R}_+^m, \alpha^\top \mathbf{1} = 1} \sum_{i=1}^{n_q} \exp\left(\sum_{l=1}^{m} \alpha_l AP_l(i)\right) \quad (2)$$

Given the learned weights α, we assign to the l-th kernel $b\alpha_l$ bits, where b is the total number of bits.

To efficiently solve the problem in (2), we adopt a boosting based strategy. Following the similar procedure of Adaboost algorithm [13], we introduce a distribution of weights D_t to indicate the retrieval difficulty of the instances in the training data set. At each boosting round, we measure the retrieval performance (e.g. average precision) of each kernel based on the existing KLSH algorithm (shown in Algorithm 1), and select the best kernel with the largest weighted Average Precision (wAP) performance over the current distribution D_t, which is defined as:

$$wAP_l = \sum_{i=1}^{n_q} D_t(i) AP_l(i) \quad (3)$$

At the end of each boosting round, an importance weight is computed for the selected kernel based on its retrieval performance, and the weights of each poorly retrieved query example will be increased such that the next selected kernel will focus more on those hardly retrieved examples. The boosting procedure will be repeated T times. Finally, we allocate a bit size to each kernel based on its cumulative weight in all the T boosting rounds. The details of the proposed algorithm are given in Algorithm 3.

4.4 Time Complexity Analysis

First of all, assume the length of hash key b is fixed, both WMKLSH and BMKLSH algorithms have the same querying time cost as that of KLSH and MKLSH. Next we focus on discussing training and indexing time cost.

As supervised methods, WMKLSH and BMKLSH algorithms need to test the performance for all training instances with all kinds of kernels once. For BMKLSH, at each boosting round, it only updates the distribution of training instances and computes the weight for each round based on the distribution. The updating step is in general linear. Thus, the main time cost consumed mostly falls into the process of validating the performance of training instances.

5. EXPERIMENTS

We conduct extensive experiments to examine the efficacy of the proposed algorithms for scalable content-based image retrieval.

5.1 Experimental Testbed

We perform experiments on two well-known public image databases which have been widely used for benchmark image retrieval tasks. Besides, we downloaded 1,000,000 social images from Flickr to form a background class and combine it with the second database to form a large scale data set. We briefly introduce some details of the two data sets below.

The first data set is the INRIA Holidays data set[1], which has been widely used for benchmark evaluation of image retrieval performance [21]. It contains 500 image groups, each of which repre-

[1] `http://lear.inrialpes.fr/~jegou/data.php`

Algorithm 3 BMKLSH: Boosting Multi-Kernel LSH algorithm for optimizing the bit size allocation

INPUT:

- an image database: $\{\mathbf{x}_i | i = 1, \ldots, n\}$, $\mathbf{x}_i \in \mathbb{R}^d$
- length of the hash key: b
- a set of m different kernels, $\{\kappa_l | l = 1, \ldots, m\}$
- a set of n_q training instances $\{\mathbf{x}_i^t | i = 1, \ldots, n_q\}$ with additional feedback info (positive and negative lists)
- number of boosting rounds: T
- initial distribution: $D_1(i) = 1/n_q, i = 1, \ldots, n_q$

for $t = 1, \ldots, T$ **do**
  for $l = 1, \ldots, m$ **do**
    obtain $AP_l(i), l = 1, \ldots, m, i = 1, \ldots, n_q$ by testing on the training set based on Algorithm 1
    $wAP_l = \sum_{i=1}^{n_q} D_t(i) AP_l(i)$
    $\alpha_t^l = e^{wAP_l}$
  end for
  $\alpha_t^l \leftarrow \frac{\alpha_t^l}{\sum_{i=1}^{m} \alpha_t^i}, l = 1, \ldots, m$
  $l^* = \arg \max_{l \in \{1,2,\ldots,m\}} \alpha_t^l$
  $\alpha_t \leftarrow \alpha_t^{l^*}, AP_t \leftarrow AP_{l^*}, wAP_t \leftarrow wAP_{l^*}$
  update the distribution of the training instances:

$$D_{t+1}(i) = \frac{D_t(i)}{Z_t} \times \begin{cases} e^{-\alpha_t} & if\ AP_t(i) \geq wAP_t \\ e^{\alpha_t} & if\ AP_t(i) < wAP_t \end{cases}$$

  Z_t is a normalization factor to make D_{t+1} a distribution
end for
$\alpha_l = \sum_{t=1}^{T} \alpha_t^l, l = 1, \ldots, m$
allocate bits to m kernels $[b_1, \ldots, b_m]$ based on the weights α_l
Multi-Kernel Hashing($[b_1, \ldots, b_m]$)

sents a distinct scene or object. The first image of each group is the query image and the correct retrieval results are the other images of the group. There are 1491 images in total, including 500 queries and 991 corresponding relevant images.

The second data set is a large-scale data set, which consists of both the ImageCLEF database[2] and the collection of 1,000,000 images crawled from Flickr (named as "Flickr1M"). ImageCLEF is a medical image database, which was also used in [38]. For all the categories, we randomly select 10% images as the query pool, the other images as database pool. For the Flickr photos, we treat all of them as the background noisy photos, which are mainly used to test the scalability of our algorithms. We denote this data set as the "ImageCLEF + Flickr1M" data set or "ImageCLEFFlickr" for short.

5.2 Experimental Setup

We present our experimental results by showing the percentage of database items searched with the hashing function instead of measuring the exact search time in order to avoid the unfairness from different implementations of the codes. To achieve this purpose, we have to set a parameter for the LSH search, i.e., ρ, which is used to control the fraction of nearest neighbors to be linearly scanned.

For performance metric, we evaluate the retrieval performance based on mean Average Precision (mAP) and top-n ($n = 1, 2, \ldots, 5$) retrieval accuracy. The Average Precision (AP) value is the area under precision-recall curve for a query. The mAP value is calculated based on the average AP value of all the queries. The precision value is the ratio of relevant examples over the total retrieved examples, while recall is the ratio of the relevant examples retrieved over the total relevant examples in the database.

[2]http://www.imageclef.org

Our objective is to achieve fast and accurate image retrieval. As LSH can only return a portion of images, only the top returned images (Hit Items) are needed to be evaluated. Based on this concern, the mAP performance reported in our experiments is based on the mAP over all the returned items (except for the experiments of parameter sensitivity evaluation, where we adopt the top-10 mAP performance to enable a fair evaluation of different parameter settings). It is worth mentioning that in some previous works they usually reported mAP values for the whole data set. As we know, the more the image examples retrieved the higher the mAP value obtained. Thus, it is not totally fair to directly compare the exact value of our results with the results of the previous works. In our experiments, we have implemented all the compared methods including our algorithms under the same evaluation criterion to enable fair comparisons. Nonetheless, from the experimental results, we found that the mAP results we achieved are higher than some of the others's reported results, although we are actually based on a criterion that generates relatively lower mAP values.

As the proposed algorithms need some training data, we split the original query set into two parts, each time we select one part for query, and the other part for training. The final result is obtained by computing the average of the results over the two splits. Finally, we conduct the evaluations of all the algorithms 10 times and average the results over these 10 runs to obtain a stable result.

5.3 Image Descriptors and Kernel Functions

5.3.1 *Image Descriptors*

We adopt both global and local feature descriptors for representing images in our experiments. We have some preprocessing by resizing all images to 500×500 pixels while keeping the aspect ratio unchanged. For global features, we extract five kinds of features, including (1) Color histogram and color moments, (2) Edge direction histogram, (3) Gabor wavelets transform, (4) Local Binary Pattern, and (5) GIST. For local features, we extract the bag of visual words features based on two types of descriptors: SIFT and SURF. In particular, for SIFT: we adopt the Hessian-Affine interest region detector with threshold 500 and the SIFT descriptor; for SURF: we use SURF detector with threshold 500 and SURF descriptor. For the clustering, we adopt a forest of 16 kd-trees and search 2048 neighbor to speed up the clustering task. Finally, we use TF-IDF to generate the bag of visual words to represent the local features. In total, with different vocabulary sizes, we extracted four kinds of local features, including SIFT200, SIFT1000, SURF200 and SURF1000.

5.3.2 *Kernel Functions*

From the above, we represent each image by 9 types of different features. We then build kernel functions for these 9 types of features. Before we compute the kernels, we normalize the feature vectors to zero mean (each dimension) and unit length (each point). We adopt the RBF kernel:

$$\kappa(\mathbf{x}, \mathbf{x}') = exp(-\gamma^{-1} d(\mathbf{x}, \mathbf{x}')) \quad (4)$$

where $d(\cdot, \cdot)$ is the distance and γ is selected as the mean of the pairwise distance where the distance is computed using L2 distance. In total, we have a set of 9 kernels for our retrieval tasks. Finally, we note that all kernel matrices are normalized to unit trace to balance different kernels.

5.4 Comparison Algorithms

To extensively examine the efficacy of the proposed algorithms, we have implemented several different solutions for adopting KLSH

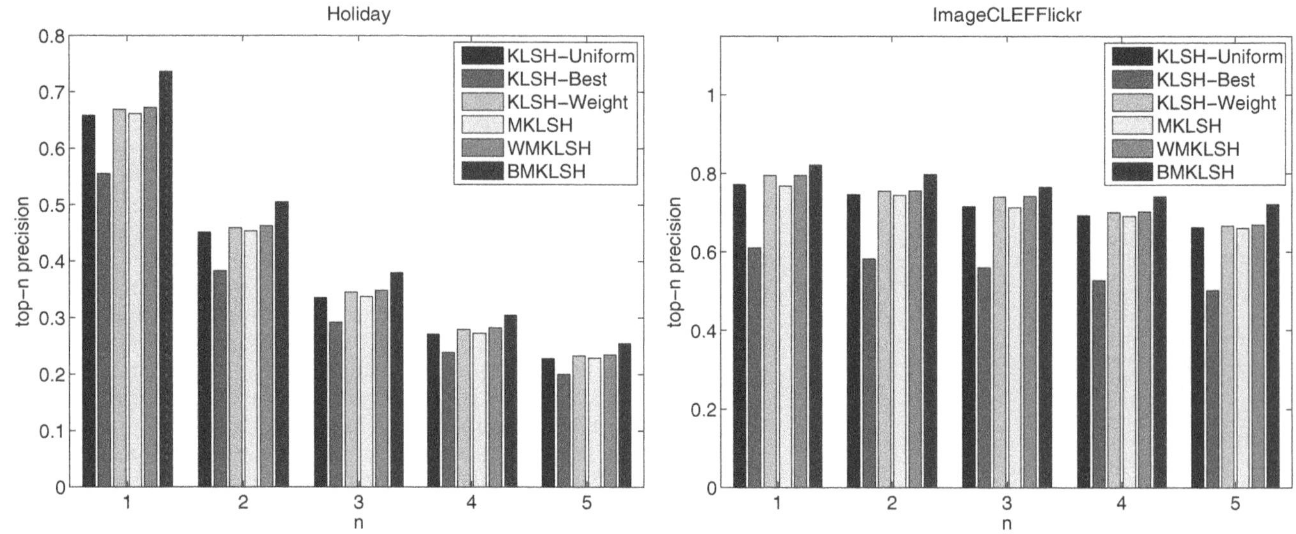

(a) "Holiday" data set

(b) "ImageCLEFFlickr" data set

Figure 2: Evaluation of average top-n precision of retrieval results by different algorithms.

with multiple kernels. In particular, we have implemented the following algorithms:

- KLSH-Uniform: a baseline method that uniformly combines the m kernels, i.e., $\kappa = \sum_{l=1}^{m} \frac{1}{m}\kappa_l$, and adopts this combined kernel for KLSH.
- KLSH-Best: We test the retrieval performance of all kernels, evaluate their mAP values on the training set, and then select the best kernel (with the highest mAP value). We adopt this best kernel for KLSH.
- KLSH-Weight: We evaluate the mAP performance of all kernels on the training set, calculate the weight of each kernel w.r.t. their mAP values: $\alpha_l = e^{mAP_l}$ (the same weight function as WMKLSH and BMKLSH), and finally normalize the weights (sum to be 1). Finally, we adopt the weighted combination of the m kernels: $\kappa = \sum_{l=1}^{m} \alpha_l \kappa_l$ for KLSH.
- MKLSH [37]: an existing KLSH approach that uses multiple kernels by a uniform bit size allocation.
- WMKLSH: the proposed algorithm by using a weighted bit size allocation for multiple kernels, as described in Section 4.2.
- BMKLSH: the proposed BMKLSH algorithm by optimizing bit size allocation via boosting as shown in Algorithm 3.

5.5 Experimental Results

We now present the performance evaluation results on the data sets. We measure the performance in terms of top-n ($n = 1, 2, \ldots, 5$) precision and the mAP value of all returned Hit items. For this experiment, we fix the parameters as follows: $\rho = 0.1$, $b = 300$, $p = 300$, $t = 30$, and $T = 20$. We will evaluate the sensitivity of these parameters in the subsequent section. We summarize the experimental results of mAP performance of the compared algorithms on the two data sets in Table 2, and illustrate the details of the top-n precision results in Figure 2. Below we discuss the empirical observations from these results.

To examine statistical significance of the comparisons, for the experimental results reported below, we highlight the best result in each group in bold font by conducting student t-tests with the significance level $\alpha = 0.05$.

Table 2: Experimental results of mAP performance.

Algorithm	Metric	Holiday	ImageCLEFFlickr
KLSH-Uniform	mean	0.58506	0.16902
	std	± 0.00258	± 0.00100
KLSH-Best	mean	0.50361	0.09813
	std	± 0.00364	± 0.00018
KLSH-Weight	mean	0.59986	0.17823
	std	± 0.00321	± 0.00156
MKLSH	mean	0.58994	0.16761
	std	± 0.00110	± 0.00086
WKLSH	mean	0.60562	0.17621
	std	± 0.00037	± 0.00064
BKLSH	mean	**0.66867**	**0.20460**
	std	± **0.00337**	± **0.00400**

5.5.1 *On the "Holiday" Data Set*

From the experimental result shown in Table 2 and Figure 2, we can draw several observations. First of all, by comparing the three different KLSH algorithms with different kernels, it seems a bit surprising to find that KLSH-Uniform, a simple uniform combination of all kernels, outperformed KLSH-Best, which is based on the best kernel chosen from the training set. But when thinking further, it is not difficult to explain the result as KLSH-best only explores a single kernel, while KLSH-Uniform jointly exploits multiple kernels. This result is further verified when we examine the result of KLSH-Weight, which outperform both KLSH-Best and KLSH-Uniform. These observations show that it is very important to explore the power of multiple kernels for KLSH in some real-world applications.

Second, by comparing the proposed WMKLSH and BMKLSH algorithms against the KLSH and MKLSH algorithms, we found that the proposed algorithms generally perform better than the KLSH and MKLSH algorithms, and the proposed BMKLSH algorithm attained the best result among all the compared algorithms, which was significantly better than the other algorithms. These promising results showed that the proposed BMKLSH technique is more effective to explore the power of multiple kernels for enhancing the image retrieval performance.

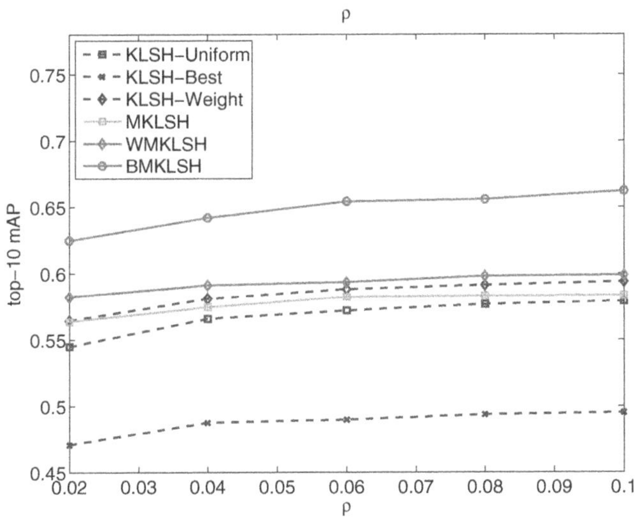

(a) parameter ρ

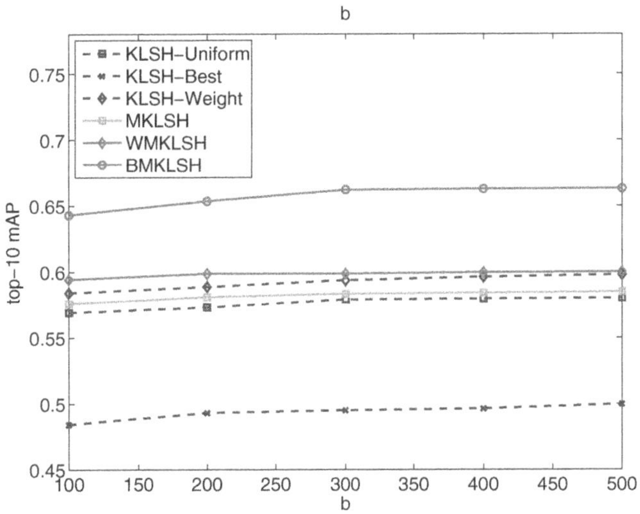

(b) parameter b

Figure 3: Evaluation of parameter ρ and b on the "Holiday" data set

5.5.2 On the "ImageCLEF+Flickr1M" Data Set

The experimental results of this data set are shown in the last column of Table 2 and the right of Figure 2. By examining the results of the three KLSH algorithms, i.e., KLSH-Uniform, KLSH-Best, KLSH-Weight, we found that the situation is the same as that on the "Holiday" data set. Further, by comparing the proposed WMKLSH and BMKLSH algorithms with the KLSH and MKLSH algorithms, we found the similar observation where the proposed BMKLSH achieved the best result among all the compared schemes. This result indicates that by the proposed boosting scheme, the BMKLSH algorithm is to effectively identify the best kernel and achieve a good tradeoff between the best kernel and the optimal combination of multiple kernels.

5.6 Parameter Sensitivity Evaluation

In this section, we aim to examine the parameter sensitivity of the proposed BMKLSH scheme for image retrieval tasks. Specifically, there are several important parameters, including (1) ρ, the parameter that controls the fraction of nearest neighbors to be linearly scanned, (2) **b**, the bit length of hash key, (3) the parameter **t** used in KLSH, which is to choose t indices for forming vector $\mathbf{e}_S$, (4) the parameter **p** used in KLSH, which is to choose a subset of p examples for computing the kernel matrix in KLSH, and (5) the number of rounds **T** used in the boosting algorithm.

For the rest of the experiments, when varying one of the parameters for evaluation, the others will remain fixed at the following default settings: $\rho = 0.1$, $b = 300$, $t = 30$, $p = 300$, and $T = 20$. We adopt the top-10 mAP performance for evaluation in this section.

5.6.1 Evaluation of ρ and b

The ρ and b are two key parameters for the LSH algorithm. Figure 3 (a) and (b) show the evaluation of two parameters ρ and b, respectively. From the experimental results, it is not difficult to see that increasing the value of ρ in general leads to increase of the top-10 mAP performance. This is not difficult to understand as the larger the ρ value, the more examples in the database will be inspected, thus more relevant image examples can be likely retrieved. Similarly, we also observe that increasing the value of hash key length b also leads to the increase of the top-10 mAP performance. This is easy to understand as the larger the hash key length, the more information can be encoded, which thus could lead to more accurate results. Finally, similar to the previous observations, for all different values of these two parameters, BMKLSH consistently outperformed the other algorithms.

5.6.2 Evaluation of parameter p and t in KLSH

The parameter p and t are two parameters in the KLSH algorithm. Figure 4 (a) and (b) show the evaluation of two parameters p and t, respectively. From the results, we can see that increasing the p value in general leads to better performance of all the algorithms. This is reasonable as more examples are sampled we are able to obtain a more accurate estimate of the distribution for KLSH. However, when p is large enough (e.g., $p > 200$), the improvement of increasing p becomes not significant. In practice, to trade off the performance and efficacy, we can choose any value between 200 and 400 for this situation. On the other hand, for the parameter t, we found that increasing the value of t does not always lead to improvement of the performance. In some cases, a large t value could slightly degrade the performance. Nonetheless, all the algorithms are generally not very sensitive to this parameter.

5.6.3 Evaluation of the number of boosting rounds T

We now examine how the number of boosting rounds affects the performance of the proposed BMKLSH algorithm. Figure 5 shows the evaluation results. From the results, we can see that the performance of BMKLSH algorithm in general increases with respect to the increase of T. The performance of the BMKLSH algorithm becomes saturated when T is sufficiently large, e.g., $T >= 20$.

5.7 Analysis of Bit Allocation Weights

Figure 6 illustrates the bit allocation weights by three algorithms on the two data sets. The x, y, z-axis denotes the index of kernel used, the algorithm, and the weight assigned to each kernel, respectively. From this figure, we can see that MKLSH assigns equal weights to all the kernels, WMKLSH assigns different weights according to their performance and the weights are non-zero, while the weights assigned by BMKLSH are sparse, i.e., it focuses on those kernels which are more beneficial to the retrieval tasks. Specifically, for the "Holiday" dataset, the weights learned by BMKLSH

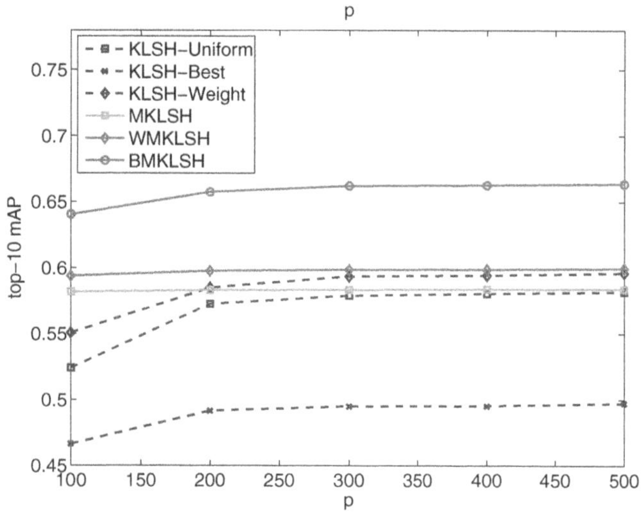

(a) parameter p

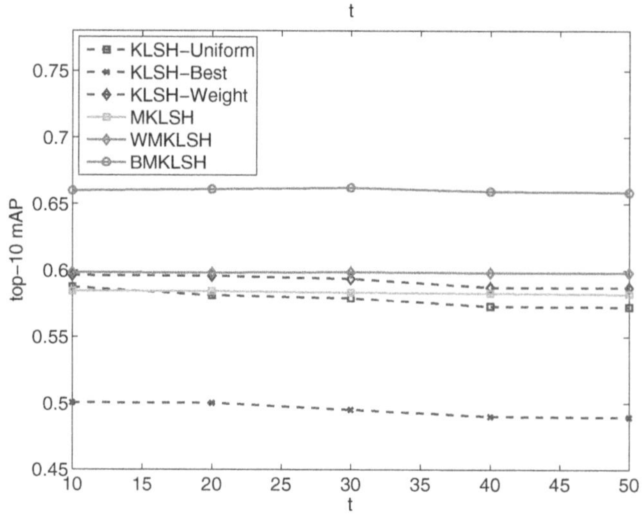

(b) parameter t

Figure 4: Evaluation of two parameters p and t used in the KLSH algorithm

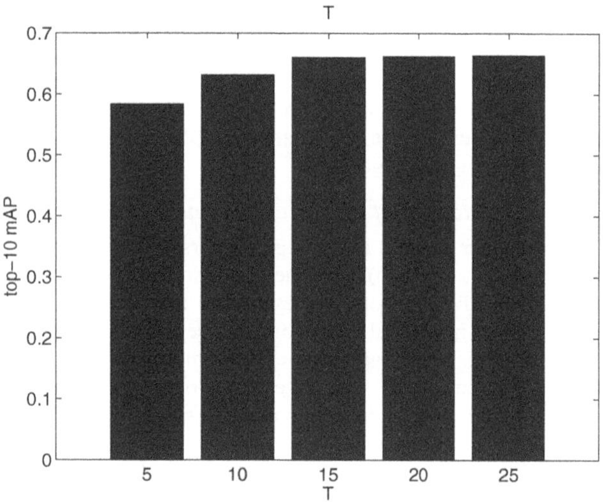

Figure 5: Evaluation of the number of boosting rounds (T) in the proposed BMKLSH algorithm.

are mainly assigned to Color, GIST, SIFT1000 and SURF1000; while for the "ImageCLEFFlickr" dataset, BMKLSH allocates all the weights to only GIST and SURF1000. This is reasonable as most of the medical images in the "ImageCLEF" dataset are gray-level images and contain rich texture contents, which thus favor GIST features instead of color features. Moreover, it is interesting to observe that for the "Holiday" data set, the weight of Color is less than SIFT200 and SURF200 assigned with WMKLSH, but BMKLSH filters SIFT200 and SURF200 while keeps Color. This is also quite reasonable as SIFT1000 and SURF1000 are somewhat redundant with SIFT200 and SURF200, but they are complementary to Color. These observations indicate that BMKLSH can learn an effective and sparse combination of multiple kernels.

5.8 Evaluation of Time Efficiency

Finally, we evaluate the efficiency of all the six algorithms on the "Holiday" data set. The experiments were running in Matlab on a Linux machine with 3GHz Intel CPU and 16GB RAM. As we analyzed before, all the compared algorithms share the same querying time given a fixed bit size b. In our experiments, typically for $b = 300$, the average retrieval time per query is about 0.65ms for all the compared algorithms. In the following, we focus on the evaluation of training and indexing time efficiency.

Figure 7 shows the evaluation results of the total amount of training and indexing time cost on the holiday data set, which were averaged over 10 runs. Among all the algorithms, it is not surprising that WMKLSH and BMKLSH took more time cost for training and indexing because of the nature of their supervised learning processes. Such additional overhead is however acceptable since the training process typically is done in an offline manner. To further examine if the training and indexing process is scalable, we examine the relationship of their time cost with respect to the bit size b, and found that they generally follow a linear relationship. Besides, we also vary the number of boosting rounds T for the BMKLSH algorithm. From the results, we can see that the time cost only increases slightly w.r.t. the increase of T, which is almost neglected.

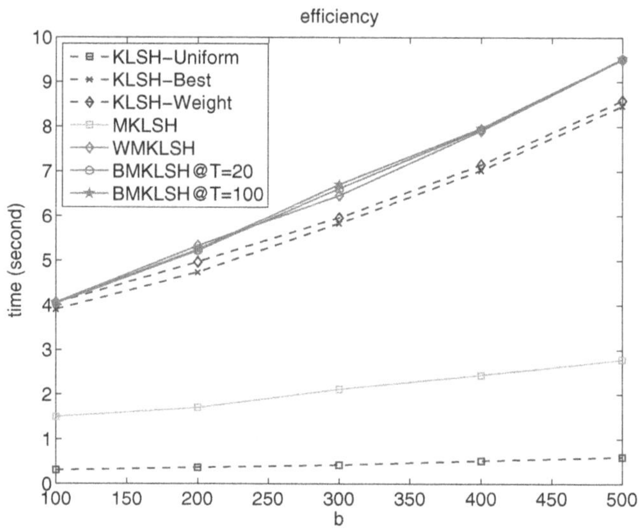

Figure 7: Evaluation of training and indexing time efficiency.

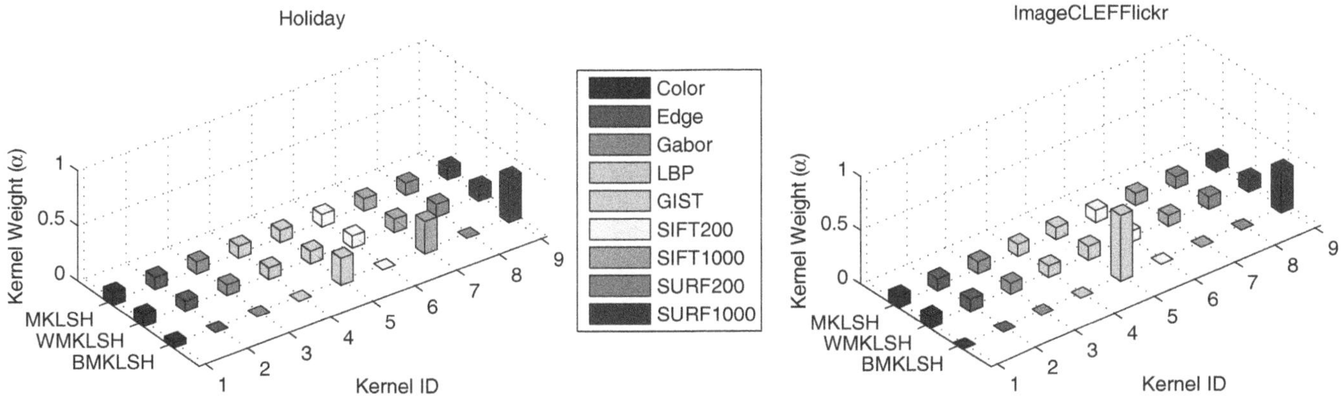

Figure 6: Visualization of bit allocation weights obtained by three different algorithms.

5.9 Evaluation of Qualitative Performance

Finally, we illustrate the qualitative retrieval performance by randomly choosing some query images from the database. Figure 8 shows the retrieval results by different algorithms. This figure includes four retrieval cases of different queries, each of which shows the top-3 retrieved results by three representative algorithms: KLSH-Best, MKLSH, and BMKLSH. From the qualitative results, we can see that the proposed BMKLSH algorithm in general is able to return more relevant results than the other algorithms.

6. CONCLUSIONS

This paper investigated a framework of Multi-Kernel Locality-Sensitive Hashing by exploring multiple kernels for efficient and scalable content-based image retrieval. We first analyzed the theoretical property of kernel LSH (KLSH). We further emphasized that it is of crucial importance to develop a proper combination of multiple kernels for determining the bit allocation task in KLSH, although KLSH and MKLSH with naive use of multiple kernels have been proposed in literature. We thus proposed two new algorithms: (i) WMKLSH that combines multiple kernels via a simple weighted combination, and (ii) BMKLSH that employs a boosting-like scheme to optimize the bit allocation of multiple kernels for KLSH. We have conducted an extensive set of experiments to evaluate the performance of the proposed algorithms, in which the encouraging results showed that the proposed BMKLSH algorithm using the boosting approach is able to considerably surpass a number of baseline methods. Future work will apply our technique to tackle other problems, such as search-based image annotation.

Acknowledgments

This work was in part supported by Singapore MOE tier 1 project (RG33/11), Microsoft Research grant (M4060936), and US Army Research Office (W911NF-11-1-0383).

7. REFERENCES

[1] S. Arya, T. Malamatos, and D. M. Mount. Space-time tradeoffs for approximate nearest neighbor searching. *J. ACM*, 57(1):1–54, 2009.

[2] J. L. Bentley. Multidimensional binary search trees used for associative searching. *Commun. ACM*, 18(9):509–517, 1975.

[3] S. Berchtold, D. A. Keim, and H.-P. Kriegel. The x-tree: An index structure for high-dimensional data. In *VLDB*, pages 28–39, San Francisco, CA, USA, 1996.

[4] C. Böhm, S. Berchtold, and D. A. Keim. Searching in high-dimensional spaces: Index structures for improving the performance of multimedia databases. *ACM Comput. Surv.*, 33(3):322–373, 2001.

[5] G.-H. Cha, X. Zhu, P. Petkovic, and C.-W. Chung. An efficient indexing method for nearest neighbor searches in high-dirnensional image databases. *IEEE Transactions on Multimedia*, 4(1):76–87, 2002.

[6] M. Charikar. Similarity estimation techniques from rounding algorithms. In *STOC*, pages 380–388, 2002.

[7] K. L. Clarkson. A randomized algorithm for closest-point queries. *SIAM J. Comput.*, 17(4):830–847, 1988.

[8] B. Cui, B. C. Ooi, J. Su, and K.-L. Tan. Indexing high-dimensional data for efficient in-memory similarity search. *IEEE Trans. on Knowl. and Data Eng.*, 17(3):339–353, 2005.

[9] I. Daoudi, K. Idrissi, S. E. Ouatik, A. Baskurt, and D. Aboutajdine. An efficient high-dimensional indexing method for content-based retrieval in large image databases. *Image Commun.*, 24(10):775–790, 2009.

[10] M. Datar, N. Immorlica, P. Indyk, and V. S. Mirrokni. Locality-sensitive hashing scheme based on p-stable distributions. In *Proc. 20th annual symposium on Computational geometry (SCG'04)*, pages 253–262. New York, NY, 2004.

[11] W. Dong, M. Charikar, and K. Li. Asymmetric distance estimation with sketches for similarity search in high-dimensional spaces. In *SIGIR*, pages 123–130, 2008.

[12] P. Drineas and M. W. Mahoney. On the nystrom method for approximating a gram matrix for improved kernel-based learning. *Journal of Machine Learning Research*, 6:2005, 2005.

[13] Y. Freund and R. E. Schapire. A decision-theoretic generalization of on-line learning and an application to boosting. *J. Comput. Syst. Sci.*, 55(1):119–139, 1997.

[14] A. Gionis, P. Indyk, and R. Motwani. Similarity search in high dimensions via hashing. In *VLDB*, 1999.

[15] K. Grauman and T. Darrell. Pyramid match hashing: Sub-linear time indexing over partial correspondences. In *CVPR*, 2007.

[16] J. He, S.-F. Chang, R. Radhakrishnan, and C. Bauer. Compact hashing with joint optimization of search accuracy and time. In *CVPR*, pages 753–760, 2011.

[17] J. He, W. Liu, and S.-F. Chang. Scalable similarity search with optimized kernel hashing. In *KDD*, pages 1129–1138, 2010.

[18] S. C. H. Hoi and M. R. Lyu. A multimodal and multilevel ranking

Figure 8: Comparison of qualitative retrieval performance on the "Holiday" dataset. This figure shows four examples. For each query, we show the top-3 retrieved images by three representative methods, i.e., KLSH-Best, MKLSH, and BMKLSH, respectively.

scheme for large-scale video retrieval. *IEEE Transactions on Multimedia*, 10(4):607–619, 2008.

[19] S. C. H. Hoi, M. R. Lyu, and R. Jin. A unified log-based relevance feedback scheme for image retrieval. *IEEE Trans. KDE*, 18(4):509–204, 2006.

[20] P. Indyk and R. Motwani. Approximate nearest neighbor: Towards removing the curse of dimensionality. In *STOC*, pages 604–613, 1998.

[21] H. Jegou, M. Douze, and C. Schmid. Hamming embedding and weak geometric consistency for large scale image search. In *ECCV (1)*, pages 304–317, 2008.

[22] A. Joly and O. Buisson. Random maximum margin hashing. In *CVPR*, pages 873–880, 2011.

[23] B. Kulis and K. Grauman. Kernelized locality-sensitive hashing for scalable image search. In *ICCV*, 2009.

[24] M. S. Lew, N. Sebe, C. Djeraba, and R. Jain. Content-based multimedia information retrieval: State of the art and challenges. *ACM Trans. Multimedia Comput. Commun. Appl.*, 2(1):1–19, 2006.

[25] Q. Lv, W. Josephson, Z. Wang, M. S. Charikar, and K. Li. Multi-probe lsh: efficient indexing for high-dimensional similarity search. In *VLDB*. Vienna, Austria, 2007.

[26] Y. Mu, J. Shen, and S. Yan. Weakly-supervised hashing in kernel space. In *CVPR*, pages 3344–3351, 2010.

[27] B. K. P. Jain and K. Grauman. Fast image search for learned metrics. In *CVPR*, 2008.

[28] M. Raginsky and S. Lazebnik. Locality-sensitive binary codes from shift-invariant kernels. In *NIPS*, pages 1509–1517, 2009.

[29] J. T. Robinson. The k-d-b-tree: A search structure for large multi-dimensional dynamic indexes. *SIGMOD*, pages 10–18, 1981.

[30] Y. Rui, T. S. Huang, M. Ortega, and S. Mehrotra. Relevance feedback: A power tool in interactive content-based image retrieval. *IEEE Trans. CSVT*, 8(5):644–655, Sept. 1998.

[31] M. Shamos and D. Hoey. Closest-point problems. In *Proc. 16th Annual IEEE Symposium on Foundations of Computer Science (FOCS)*, pages 151–162, 1975.

[32] S. Smale and D.-X. Zhou. Geometry on probability spaces. *Constr Approx*, 30:311–323, 2009.

[33] A. W. M. Smeulders, M. Worring, S. Santini, A. Gupta, and R. Jain. Content-based image retrieval at the end of the early years. *IEEE Trans. PAMI*, 22(12):1349–1380, 2000.

[34] Y. Tao, K. Yi, C. Sheng, and P. Kalnis. Quality and efficiency in high dimensional nearest neighbor search. In *SIGMOD Conference*, pages 563–576, 2009.

[35] J. K. Uhlmann. Satisfying general proximity/similarity queries with metric trees. *Information Processing Letters*, 40:175–179, 1991.

[36] J. Wang, O. Kumar, and S.-F. Chang. Semi-supervised hashing for scalable image retrieval. In *CVPR*, pages 3424–3431, 2010.

[37] S. Wang, S. Jiang, Q. Huang, and Q. Tian. S3mkl: scalable semi-supervised multiple kernel learning for image data mining. In *ACM Multimedia*, pages 163–172, 2010.

[38] L. Yang, R. Jin, L. B. Mummert, R. Sukthankar, A. Goode, B. Zheng, S. C. H. Hoi, and M. Satyanarayanan. A boosting framework for visuality-preserving distance metric learning and its application to medical image retrieval. *IEEE Trans. Pattern Anal. Mach. Intell.*, 32(1):30–44, 2010.

[39] D. Zhang, J. Wang, D. Cai, and J. Lu. Self-taught hashing for fast similarity search. In *SIGIR*, pages 18–25, 2010.

[40] J. Zhuang, T. Mei, S. C. H. Hoi, X.-S. Hua, and S. Li. Modeling social strength in social media community via kernel-based learning. In *ACM Multimedia*, pages 113–122, 2011.

Diversity by Proportionality: An Election-based Approach to Search Result Diversification

Van Dang and W. Bruce Croft
Center for Intelligent Information Retrieval
Department of Computer Science
University of Massachusetts
Amherst, MA 01003
{vdang, croft}@cs.umass.edu

ABSTRACT

This paper presents a different perspective on diversity in search results: diversity by proportionality. We consider a result list most diverse, with respect to some set of topics related to the query, when the number of documents it provides on each topic is proportional to the topic's popularity. Consequently, we propose a framework for optimizing proportionality for search result diversification, which is motivated by the problem of assigning seats to members of competing political parties. Our technique iteratively determines, for each position in the result ranked list, the topic that best maintains the overall proportionality. It then selects the best document on this topic for this position. We demonstrate empirically that our method significantly outperforms the top performing approach in the literature not only on our proposed metric for proportionality, but also on several standard diversity measures. This result indicates that promoting proportionality naturally leads to minimal redundancy, which is a goal of the current diversity approaches.

Categories and Subject Descriptors

H.3.3 [**Information Storage and Retrieval**]: Information Search and Retrieval – retrieval models

General Terms

Algorithms, Measurement, Performance, Experimentation.

Keywords

Search result diversification, proportional representation, proportionality, redundancy, novelty, Sainte-Laguë.

1. INTRODUCTION

Search result diversification techniques have been studied as a method of tackling queries with unclear information needs. Standard retrieval models and evaluations are based on the assumption that there is a single specific topic associated with the relevant documents for a query. Diversification models [4, 1, 26], on the other hand, identify the probable "aspects" of the query and return documents for each of these aspects, making the result list more diverse. Aspects denote the multiple possible intents, interpretations, or subtopics associated with a given query. By explicitly representing and providing diversity in the result list, these models can increase the likelihood that users will find documents relevant to their specific intent and thereby improve effectiveness.

This problem of finding a diverse ranked list of documents, with respect to the aspects of the query, has been studied primarily from the perspective of minimizing *redundancy*. In other words, existing work focuses on penalizing result lists with too many documents on the same aspect, which increases the redundancy of coverage, and promoting lists that contain documents covering multiple aspects. Most of the effectiveness measures for diversity [7, 8] are also based on this notion of redundancy. They penalize the redundancy in a ranked list of documents by judging each of the documents given the context of those retrieved at earlier ranks [9].

In this paper, we approach the same task from a different perspective. We view the problem of finding a good result list of any given size as the task of finding a representative sample of the larger set of ranked documents. Hence, the quality of the subset (a result list) should be measured by how well it represents the whole set (a much larger sample of the ranking). Using a simple (and well-worn) example, in a ranked list for a query "java", 90% of the documents may be about the programming language and 10% about the island. From our perspective, a result list containing ten documents where only one of them was about the island would be more representative than a result list containing five documents on each subtopic. Consequently, we treat the problem of finding a diverse result of documents as finding a *proportional representation* for the document ranking.

Finding a *proportional representation* is a critical part of most electoral processes. The problem is to assign a set of seats in the parliament to members of competing political parties in a way that the number of seats each party possesses is proportional to the number of votes it has received. In other words, the members in the elected parliament must be a *proportional representation* of these parties. If we view each position in our ranked list as a "seat", each aspect of the

Permission to make digital or hard copies of all or part of this work for personal or classroom use is granted without fee provided that copies are not made or distributed for profit or commercial advantage and that copies bear this notice and the full citation on the first page. To copy otherwise, to republish, to post on servers or to redistribute to lists, requires prior specific permission and/or a fee.
SIGIR'12, August 12–16, 2012, Portland, Oregon, USA.
Copyright 2012 ACM 978-1-4503-1472-5/12/08 ...$10.00.

query as a "party" and the aspect popularity as the "votes" for this "party", the problem of diversification becomes very similar to this seat allocation problem.

Based on the above analogy, we propose a novel technique for search result diversification. It is an adaptation of the Sainte-Laguë method, a standard technique for finding proportional representations that is used in the official election in New Zealand[1]. Generally, our technique starts with an empty ranked list of a certain size. It sequentially visits each "seat" in the list and determines for each of them to which aspect it should be allocated in order to maintain proportionality. Then it selects the best document for the selected aspect to occupy this "seat". In addition, we also present a new effectiveness measure that captures *proportionality* in search results. We demonstrate empirically that our method is more effective than the top performing approach in the diversity literature not only according to the proportionality measure but also using several standard metrics including α-NDCG [7] and NRBP [8] that existing work has been designed to optimize. This indicates that optimizing search results for proportionality naturally leads to minimal redundancy and a diverse, effective result list.

In the next section, we briefly mention some related work. Section 3 presents our approach to proportionality and the effectiveness measure based on it. Section 4 describes in detail our proportionality-driven framework for search result diversification. Section 5 and 6 contains the experimental setup and results, as well as analyses and discussions. Finally, Section 7 concludes.

2. RELATED WORK

The literature of diversification has been concentrating on the notion of *novelty* and *redundancy*. These two notions are considered under the context of user behavior with the assumption that users examine the result lists top down and eventually stop reading. Therefore, a document at any rank providing the same information as those at earlier ranks is considered *redundant*. Likewise, a *novel* document is one that provides information that has not been covered by any of the previous documents. As a result, a ranked list is considered more diverse if it contains less redundancy, or equivalently, more novelty.

This is clearly demonstrated through several standard effectiveness metrics such as α-NDCG [7] and NRBP [8]. They measure the diversity of a ranked list by explicitly rewarding novelty and penalizing redundancy observed at every rank. Similarly, diversification techniques [4, 29, 1, 5, 26] attempt to form a diverse ranked list by repeatedly selecting documents that are different to those previously selected. In other words, they try to accommodate novelty at every position in the list.

In this paper, we present a different perspective on diversity. This view of diversity emphasizes proportionality, which is the property that the number of documents returned for each of the aspects of the query is proportional to the overall popularity of that aspect. Consequently, the framework we derive is driven by this notion of proportionality, thus is different from the existing work.

Several metrics have been proposed to measure the proportionality in the outcome of an electoral process, an excellent summary of which is provided by Gallagher and Lijphart [17, 19]. They can be classified into two broad categories: the first concentrates on the absolute difference between the percentage of seats and the percentage of votes, the second focuses on the the ratio between them. These measures appear mathematically simple but attempt to address complex specific issues of elections that are not always relevant to our context. As a result, we apply Gallagher's Index [17], or the least square index, which is reasonably suited to our problem.

For completeness, we will provide a brief survey of techniques in the current literature of diversification. They can be classified as either implicit or explicit approaches. The former [4, 29] assumes that similar documents cover similar aspects without modelling the actual aspects. They iteratively select documents that are similar to the query but different to the previously selected documents in terms of vocabulary [4] or divergence from one language model to another [29]. More recent work [25, 22] applies the portfolio theory to document ranking, which views diversification as a mean of risk minimization. Explicit approaches [23, 1, 5, 26], on the other hand, explicitly models aspects of a query with a taxonomy [1], top retrieved documents [5] or query reformulations [23, 26] and thus can directly select documents that cover different aspects. Experimentally, explicit approaches have been demonstrated to be superior to implicit approaches [26].

3. PROPORTIONALITY

In this paper, we view the task of diversification as finding a proportional representation for a document ranking. In this section, we will explain the notion of *proportionality* as well as describing an effectiveness measure for it.

3.1 Definition of Proportionality

Let $T = \{t_1, t_2, ..., t_n\}$ indicate a set of aspects for a query q and D denote a large set of documents related to q. Let p_i indicate the popularity of the aspect $t_i \in T$, which is the percentage of documents in D covering this aspect. Additionally, let S be any subset of D. We define S to be *proportional to D*, or a *proportional representation* of D, with respect to T if and only if the number of documents in S that is relevant to each of the aspects $t_i \in T$ is proportional to its popularity p_i.

Let us revisit the example in Section 1, in which there are 90% of documents in D about the "java" programming language and the rest 10% is about an island named "java". Let $\{x, y\}$ denote any subset of D with x documents about programming and y documents about the island. In this case, $\{9, 1\}$ is proportional and thus is a proportional representation of D. While $\{8, 2\}$ is not proportional, it is more proportional than $\{7, 3\}$.

Let R indicate a ranking of documents in D and S now represent a sub-ranking of R. We define S to be proportional to R if the subset of documents S provides at every rank is a proportional representation of D.

3.2 Effectiveness Measure

This notion of proportionality is, in fact, frequently used in evaluating the outcome of elections in which seats are assigned to members of competing political parties. This problem can be stated as follows. We have a limited number of seats in the parliament and a number of competing parties. Each party has its own members. Through election

[1] http://www.elections.org.nz/voting/mmp/sainte-lague.html

campaigns, each party obtains a number of votes from people around the country. The goal is to assign members of different parties to the seats such that the number of seats each party gets is proportional to the votes it receives.

Several metrics have been proposed to measure such proportionality. Most of them are based on the difference between the percentage of votes each party receives and the percentage of seats it gets. Among those, the least square index (LSq) [17] is one of the standard metrics for measuring dis-proportionality:

$$LSq = \sqrt{\frac{1}{2}\sum_i (v_i - s_i)^2} \simeq \sum_i (v_i - s_i)^2$$

where v_i and s_i are the percentage of votes and the percentage of seats the i-th party received. Let us illustrate this with an example in which we have *ten* seats and *three* competing parties, namely A, B and C. Let us assume both A and B receive 50% of the votes and C gets 0%. Clearly, the proportional assignment which provides A and B each with *five* seats and C with *none* will result in $LSq = 0$. The value for LSq will increase when the seat assignment becomes more disproportional.

We will now turn our attention to the proportionality of a retrieved list of *ten* documents for the query "satellite", which we assume to have two aspects: "satellite internet" and "satelilte phone" with equal popularity of 50%. Due to the possible presence of non-relevant documents, we have to create a third "aspect" to account for non-relevant documents. As a result, proportionality requires this list to contain *five* relevant documents for each of the two aspects and *zero* documents for the "non-relevant" aspect. This situation seems to be very similar to the election described above. Unfortunately, we cannot apply LSq to measure the dis-proportionality of this result list due to two differences.

First, each member typically belongs to exactly one political party. As a result, one party gets more seats than it should always indicates that some other party is getting less than they deserve. A document, however, might be related to multiple aspects of a query. It then is possible that an aspect can be "rewarded" with additional documents while others still have as many relevant documents as they deserve.

Second, it is equally bad for any party to get any more seats than it should. In our case, however, selecting for the result list a document that is relevant to an aspect that already has enough relevant documents in the list is not as bad as selecting a non-relevant document.

Taking both differences into consideration, we argue that LSq, since is designed for the seat allocation problem, puts too much penalty on overly representing query aspects. LSq fails to recognize that some of these situations do not create any undesirable consequences in our setting, and thus should not be penalized. Therefore, we propose a new metric, dis-proportionality at rank K, calculated as follows:

$$DP@K = \sum_{aspect\ t_i} c_i (v_i - s_i)^2 + \frac{1}{2} n_{NR}^2 \qquad (1)$$

where v_i is the number of relevant documents that the aspect t_i should have, s_i is the number of relevant documents the system actually found for this aspect, n_{NR} is the number of non-relevant documents, and

$$c_i = \begin{cases} 1 & v_i \geq s_i \\ 0 & \text{otherwise} \end{cases}$$

Formula (1) has two important properties. The first is that it penalizes a result set for under-representing any aspect of the query ($s_i < v_i$) but not for over-representing them ($s_i > v_i$), which addresses the first issue associated with LSq. The second is that while the over-representation of a query aspect is not penalized, the over-representation of the "non-relevant" aspect ($n_{NR} > 0$) is, which overcomes the second issue associated with LSq.

A perfectly disproportional set of documents in the context of information retrieval would be a set with all non-relevant documents. Thus, the Ideal-DP is given by:

$$Ideal\_DP@K = \sum_{aspect\ t_i} v_i^2 + \frac{1}{2}K^2$$

The last step is to derive our proportionality measure by normalizing the DP score with Ideal-DP in order to make it comparable across queries:

$$PR@K = 1 - \frac{DP@K}{IDeal\_DP@K}$$

Finally, the Cumulative Proportionality (CPR) measure for rankings is calculated as follows:

$$CPR@K = \frac{1}{K}\sum_{i=1}^{K} PR@i$$

4. PROPOSED METHOD

In this section, we first introduce the Sainte-Laguë method, a standard technique for finding proportional representations that is used to solve the seat allocation problem described in Section 3.2. We then demonstrate the analogy between this problem and our problem of propotionality-based diversification, which helps us derive our technique from the Sainte-Laguë method.

4.1 The Sainte-Laguë Method

This method considers all of the available seats iteratively. For each of them, it computes a *quotient* for all of the parties based on the votes they receive and the number of seats they have taken. This seat is then assigned to the party with the largest quotient, which helps maintain the overall proportionality. We assume the selected party will then assign one of its members to this seat. Finally, it increases the number of seats assigned to the chosen party by one. The process repeats until all seats are assigned. Pseudo code for this procedure is provided as Algorithm 1. In this procedure, $P = \{P_1, P_2, ..., P_n\}$ is the set of parties and $M_i = \{m_1^{(i)}, m_2^{(i)}, ..., m_{l_i}^{(i)}\}$ is the set of members of the party P_i. v_i and s_i indicate the number of votes P_i receives and the number of seats that have been assigned to P_i so far.

Algorithm 1 The Sainte-Laguë method for seat allocation

$s_i \leftarrow 0, \forall i$
for all available seats in the parliament **do**
  for all parties P_i **do**
    $quotient[i] = \frac{v_i}{2s_i+1}$
  end for
  $k \leftarrow \arg\max_i quotient[i]$
  $m^* \leftarrow$ the best member of P_k
  Assign the current seat to m^*
  $M_k \leftarrow M_k \setminus \{m^*\}$
  $s_k \leftarrow s_k + 1$
end for

4.2 Diversity by Proportionality

4.2.1 Framework

Let q indicate the user query, $T = \{t_1, t_2, ..., t_n\}$ indicate the aspects for q whose popularity is $\{p_1, p_2, ..., p_n\}$. In addition, let $R = \{d_1, d_2, ..., d_m\}$ be the ranked list of documents returned by an initial retrieval and $P(d_i|t_j)$ indicate some estimate of the probability that the document d_i is relevant to the aspect t_j. The task is to select a subset of R to form a diverse ranked list S of size k.

As mentioned earlier, existing techniques [1, 26] generally favor an S with smaller redundancy. Our idea, on the other hand, is to favor an S with higher proportionality. The optimal S, consequently, is a ranked list in which the number of relevant documents for each of the aspects t_i is proportional to its popularity p_i. This objective is, in fact, very similar to that of the seat allocation problem above. As a result, we derive a general proportionality framework for diversification directly from the procedure presented above, which is described as Algorithm 2.

This framework can be explained as follows. We start with a ranked list S with k empty seats. For each of these seats, we compute the quotient for each aspect t_i following the Sainte-Laguë formula. We then assign this seat to the aspect t_{i^*} with the largest quotient, which marks this seat as a place holder for a document about the aspect t_{i^*}. After that, we need to employ some mechanism to select the actual document with respect to t_{i^*} to fill this seat. Depending on that mechanism, we then need to update the number of seats occupied by each of the aspects t_i accordingly. This process repeats until we get k documents for S or we are out of candidate documents. The order in which each document is put into S determines its ranking. Assuming each document selected for t_i is truly relevant to t_i, the Sainte-Laguë method guarantees proportionality in the final set of documents.

Different choices of document selection mechanisms, which subsequently determine the choices of seat occupation update procedures, will result in different instantiations of our framework. We now present two such instantiations.

Algorithm 2 A Proportionality Framework

```
s_i ← 0, ∀i
for all available seats in the ranked list S do
    for all aspects t_i ∈ T do
        quotient[i] = v_i / (2s_i + 1)
    end for
    i* ← arg max_i quotient[i]
    d* ← find the best document with respect to t_i*
    S ← S ∪ {d*}
    update s_i, ∀i accordingly
end for
```

4.2.2 A Naive Adaptation

We first present a straightforward adaptation from the seat allocation problem above. The Sainte-Laguë method assumes that each member belongs to exactly one party. When a member is assigned to a certain seat, the party naturally takes up the entire seat. Directly applying this technique to our context means assuming each document is associated with a single aspect. As such, we have to determine the aspect for each of the documents $d_j \in R$, which we assume to be the aspect $t_i \in T$ to which d_j is most relevant:

$$\arg\max_{t_i \in T} P(d_j|t_i)$$

As a result, we construct for each aspect t_i a list of documents associated with it in decreasing order of relevance, noted as $M_i = \{d_1^{(i)}, d_2^{(i)}, ..., d_{l_i}^{(i)}\}$ where l_i is the number of documents in M_i. It follows naturally that the best document for an aspect t_i is the first in the list M_i. We refer to this native adaptation as PM-1 and codify it as Algorithm 3.

Algorithm 3 PM-1

```
s_i ← 0, ∀i
for all seats in the ranked list S do
    for all aspects t_i ∈ T do
        quotient[i] = v_i / (2s_i + 1)
    end for
    i* ← arg max_i quotient[i]
    d* ← pop M_i*
    S ← S ∪ {d*}
    s_i* ← s_i* + 1
end for
```

4.2.3 A Probabilistic Interpretation

We now provide a probabilistic interpretation of the Sainte-Laguë method, which removes the naive assumption that a document can only be associated with a single aspect. Instead, we assume all documents $d_j \in D$ are relevant to all aspects $t_i \in T$, each with a probability $P(d_j|t_i)$. This probabilistic interpretation, which we call PM-2, is described by Algorithm 4.

A first point to note is that PM-2 has a different mechanism for document selection. Once a seat is given to the aspect t_{i^*} with the largest quotient, we need to assign to this seat a document that is relevant to t_{i^*}. In the context of multi-aspect documents, however, among several documents all of which are relevant to t_{i^*}, it is sensible to promote documents that may be slightly less relevant to t_{i^*} but are at the same time relevant to other aspects, compared to those that are slightly more relevant to t_{i^*} but are non-relevant to all others. This is, after all, what motivates diversification: we want more users to be able to find what they want. Therefore, PM-2 introduces the parameter λ:

$$d^* \leftarrow \arg\max_{d_j \in R} \lambda \times qt[i^*] \times P(d_j|t_{i^*}) + (1-\lambda) \sum_{i \neq i^*} qt[i] \times P(d_j|t_i)$$

that trades relevance to t_{i^*} with relevance to more aspects. We abbreviate $quotient[i]$ to $qt[i]$ due to the space limitation.

A second point is that when a document d^* is selected for the current seat, since it is assumed to be relevant to all aspects $t_i \in T$, each aspect occupies a certain "portion" of this seat as opposed to a single aspect taking up the entire seat as previously. Intuitively, the degree of occupation of the seat is proportional to the normalized relevance to d^*:

$$s_i \leftarrow s_i + \frac{P(d^*|t_i)}{\sum_{t_j \in T} P(d^*|t_j)}$$

where s_i is the "number", which is now better regarded as "portion", of seats occupied by t_i.

PM-2 can be summarized as a two-step procedure as follows. For each of the k seats in S, it first employs the Sainte-Laguë formula to determine which aspect this seat should go to in order to best maintain the proportionality. Then,

Algorithm 4 PM-2

$s_i \leftarrow 0, \forall i$
for all seats in the ranked list S **do**
  for all aspects $t_i \in T$ **do**
    $quotient[i] = \frac{v_i}{2s_i+1}$
  end for
  $i^* \leftarrow \arg\max_i quotient[i]$
  $d^* \leftarrow \text{argmax}_{d_j \in R}\ \lambda \times quotient[i^*] \times P(d_j|t_{i^*}) + (1-\lambda)\sum_{i \neq i^*} quotient[i] \times P(d_j|t_i)$
  $S \leftarrow S \cup \{d^*\}$
  $R \leftarrow R \setminus \{d^*\}$
  for all aspects $t_i \in T$ **do**
    $s_i \leftarrow s_i + \frac{P(d^*|t_i)}{\sum_{t_j} P(d^*|t_j)}$
    Since d^* is assumed relevant to all aspects, each of these aspects will take up a certain "portion" of this seat
  end for
end for

it selects the document that, in addition to being relevant to this aspect, is relevant to other aspects as well. Finally, it updates the "portion" of seats in S occupied by each of the aspects t_i according to how relevant it is to the selected document.

5. EXPERIMENTAL SETUP

Query and Retrieval Collection. Our query set consists of 98 queries, 50 of which are from the diversity task of the TREC 2009 Web Track (WT-2009) [10] and the other 48 are from TREC 2010 Web Track (WT-2010) [11]. Our evaluation is done on the ClueWeb09 Category B retrieval collection[2], which is also used in both WT-2009 and WT-2010. This collection contains approximately 50 million web pages in English. During query and indexing time, both the query and the collection are stemmed using the Porter stemmer. In addition, we perform stopword removal using the standard INQUERY stopword list.

Baseline Retrieval Model. We use the standard query-likelihood model within the language modeling framework [14] to conduct the initial retrieval run. This run serves both as a mean to provide a set of documents for the diversity models to diversify and a baseline to verify their usefulness. We also use this model as the estimate of relevance $P(d_j|t_i)$ between the document d_j and the aspect t_i.

Spam filtering is known to be an important component of web retrieval [3]. Following Bendersky et al. [3], we use a spam filtering technique as described by Cormack et al. [12] with the publicly available Waterloo Spam Ranking for the ClueWeb09 dataset, which assigns a "spamminess" percentile $S(d)$ to each document d in the collection. In particular, let $p(d_i|q)$ indicate the score the retrieval model assigns to the document d_i, the final score of d_i is given by:

$$P(d_i|q) = \begin{cases} p(d_i|q) & \text{if } S(d_i) \geq 60 \\ -\infty & \text{otherwise} \end{cases}$$

Diversity Models. We evaluate PM-2, the proportionality-aware model we propose for search result diversification. In addition, we will also present results obtained by PM-1 for comparison. Our first diversity baseline model for comparison is MMR [4], which is considered standard in the diversity literature. Since the explicit approach for diversification is generally superior to the implicit approach, we also compare our models to xQuAD, which has been demonstrated to outperform many others in this class [26]. In fact, xQuAD is among the top performers in both diversity tasks of TREC 2009 and TREC 2010 [10, 11]. In addition to these two baselines, we also compare our results to those published by TREC whenever appropriate.

Experiment Design. We use Lemur/Indri [3] to conduct the baseline query-likelihood retrieval run with the toolkit's default parameter configuration. All of the diversification approaches under evaluation are applied on the top-K retrieved documents. All of these models except for PM-1 has a single parameter λ to tune. Readers should refer to the original papers [4, 26] for the interpretation of this parameter in the respective models. We consider for λ values in the range $\{0.05, 0.1, 0.15, ..., 1.0\}$. Our two-fold cross validation enforces complete separation between tuning and testing. In particular, each system is tuned on WT-2009 and tested on WT-2010 and vice versa. We present the result averaged across two folds unless stated otherwise. PM-1, since it is parameter-free, has no tuning involved.

As for the parameter K, we tested $K \in \{50, 100, 500, 1000\}$ and found that all four models achieved their best at $K = 50$. Therefore, all results presented here are achieved with $K = 50$.

Evaluation Metric. We first report our results using CPR, the proportionality metric we propose in Section 3. Since this metric certainly favors our models as they are designed to capture proportionality in the search results, we also report the results of several standard metrics that existing work was designed to optimize. This includes those used in the official evaluation of the diversity task WT-2010 [11]: α-NDCG [7], ERR-IA (a variant of ERR [6]) and NRBP [8]. These measures penalize redundancy at each position in the ranked list based on how much of that information the user has seen and how likely it is that the user is willing to scan down to that position. In addition, we also report our results using Precision-IA [1] and subtopic recall, which indicate respectively the precision across all aspects of the query and how many of those aspects are covered in the results. Last but not least, all of these measures are computed using the top 20 documents each model retrieves also to be consistent with the official TREC evaluation [10, 11].

[2]http://boston.lti.cs.cmu.edu/Data/clueweb09/

[3]http://www.lemurproject.org

Query Aspects. Explicit approaches such as xQuAD and PM-2 assume the availability of the query aspects and their popularity. We first consider the official sub-topics identified by TREC's assessors for each of the queries as its aspects. This simulates the situation where we know exactly what aspects the query has and provides a controlled environment to study the effectiveness of different diversification approaches. As for the aspect popularity, since it is not available in TREC's judgment data, we assume uniform probability for all aspects, which is also consistent with existing work [26, 27, 28].

In order to simulate more practical settings in which we do not know but have to guess the aspects of the query, we follow Santos et al. [26] by adopting suggestions provided by a commercial search engine as aspect representations. However, the search engine is unable to provide suggestions for *four* of the queries in our set. As a result, these experiments are conducted on the subset of 94 queries for which we can obtain aspect representation. We also assume uniform aspect distribution since it was demonstrated to be the most helpful [26].

It is worth noting that the aspects obtained from the search engine certainly do not completely align with the judged aspects provided by TREC assessors. In other words, there will be overlap between the two sets but there will also be generated aspects that are not in the judged set. We will refer to this problem as the misalignment between different sets of aspects and we do not attempt to evaluate the relevance of these misaligned aspects (those that are not in the judged set) in this paper.

6. RESULTS

6.1 Proportionality

In this section, we evaluate how well different methods maintain proportionality in the search results using both TREC sub-topics and suggestions from a commercial search engine as aspect descriptions. Table 1 shows the Cumulative Proportionality score for each system as well as the Win/Loss ratio – the number queries each system improves and hurts respectively. The letters Q, M, X and P indicate statistically significant differences (p-value < 0.05) to Query-likelihood, MMR, xQuAD and PM-1 respectively.

From Table 1, we first notice that although all diversity models are able to provide improvement over the initial retrieval, the magnitude of improvement is very different. The improvement from MMR, for example, is insignificant while the improvement from the other three is more substantial.

Among the four diversity models, PM-2 outperforms all others on both sets of aspects with statistical significance, which demonstrates the effectiveness of our method at capturing proportionality. MMR is the least effective since it is completely unaware of the query aspects, and thus is unable to capture the proportionality among them. xQuAD, on the other hand, does take into account the query aspects to penalize redundancy. For each document selected, xQuAD downweights each of the aspects based on the degree of its relevance to the selected document so that the aspects that have less relevant documents will have higher priority in the next round. Further details about xQuAD can be found in [26]. Hence, xQuAD indeed has the effect of implicitly promoting proportionality, which explains why it significantly outperforms query-likelihood, and also MMR on one of the

Table 1: Performance of all techniques in CPR. The letters Q, M, X and P indicate statistically significant differences to Query-likelihood, MMR, xQuAD and PM-1 respectively (p-value < 0.05).

		CPR	Win/Loss
Sub-topics	Query-likelihood	0.4012	
	MMR	0.4018	36/32
	xQuAD	$0.4534_{Q,M}$	48/31
	PM-1	$0.4462_{Q,M}$	46/34
	PM-2	$\mathbf{0.4771}^{X,P}_{Q,M}$	49/33
Suggestions	Query-likelihood	0.3977	
	MMR	0.4016	36/26
	xQuAD	0.4242_{Q}	41/29
	PM-1	0.4067	34/40
	PM-2	$\mathbf{0.4696}^{X,P}_{Q,M}$	48/31

aspect sets. PM-2, despite the conceptual difference, can be explained using xQuAD's framework of reweighting aspects as well. From this perspective, the biggest difference between the two is that PM-2 uses a more proportionality aware aspect weighting function which is based on the Sainte-Laguë algorithm. This result indeed confirms the effectiveness of this proportionality-driven aspect weighting function.

It is worth noting that PM-1, despite being a parameter-free naive version of PM-2, is comparable to xQuAD. There is no statistically significant difference between these two. Comparing PM-1 to PM-2, however, reveals the weakness of its naive assumption. PM-1 associates each of the documents with exactly one aspect, thus it has the risk of associating documents with the wrong aspects. In addition, PM-1 fails to promote documents relevant to multiple aspects. Both of these account for its inferiority to PM-2 with both sets of aspects.

6.2 Standard Redundancy-based Metrics

We now compare our proposed techniques to MMR and xQuAD using standard metrics from the diversity literature as mentioned earlier. Instead of showing the results averaged across two folds, we show the results obtained in each fold separately so that we can compare our results with the official results from TREC. It should be noted that the comparison between our results and those from TREC should be taken as indicative only, since our systems and theirs use different initial retrieval run. Table 2 shows the results for all of the techniques we studied as well as the best performing system on ClueWeb09 Category B reported by TREC. In addition to the scores in each metric, Table 2 also presents the Win/Loss ratio each system achieves over the query likelihood baseline in terms of α-NDCG.

The first observation from Table 2 is that all systems perform worse in all metrics on WT-2009 than they do on WT-2010. The effectiveness of all systems certainly depends on the quality of documents retrieved by the initial retrieval run. Since all of our systems rerank the top 50 returned documents for each query, we examine these documents in both precision-IA and sub-topic recall. The former indicates how many relevant documents for each aspect we have for reranking and the latter indicates how many of the aspects for which we have relevant documents. The results are shown in Table 3, which suggests that the top 50 documents for queries in WT-2009 cover less topics (i.e. many sub-

Table 2: Performance of all techniques in several standard redundancy-based measures. The Win/Loss ratio is with respect to α-NDCG. The letters Q, M, X and P indicate statistically significant differences to Query-likelihood, MMR, xQuAD and PM-1 respectively (p-value < 0.05).

		α-NDCG	Win/Loss	ERR-IA	Prec-IA	S-Recall	NRBP
WT-2009							
Sub-topics	Query-likelihood	0.2979		0.1953	0.1146	0.4327	0.1689
	MMR	0.2963	16/19	0.1922	**0.1221**	0.4447	0.1657
	xQuAD	$0.3300_{Q,M}$	23/15	$0.2207_{Q,M}$	0.1190	**0.4700**	$0.1950_{Q,M}$
	PM-1	0.3076	18/17	0.2027	0.1140	0.4440	0.1738
	PM-2	$\mathbf{0.3473}^{P}$	19/19	$\mathbf{0.2407}^{P}$	0.1197	0.4633	**0.2172**
Suggestions	Query-likelihood	0.2875		0.1895	0.1095	0.4212	0.1634
	MMR	0.2926	16/15	0.1919	0.1108	0.4351	0.1655
	xQuAD	0.2995	14/19	0.1973	0.1089	0.4403	0.1700
	PM-1	0.2870	16/18	0.1830	0.0929^{X}	0.4111	0.1560
	PM-2	**0.3200**	17/19	**0.2139**	$\mathbf{0.1123}^{P}$	**0.4472**	**0.1884**
WT-2009 Best (uogTrDYCcsB) [10]		0.3081	N/A	0.1922	N/A	N/A	0.1617
WT-2010							
Sub-topics	Query-likelihood	0.3236		0.2081	0.1713	0.5479	0.1656
	MMR	0.3349_{Q}	19/14	0.2161	0.1740	0.5694_{Q}	0.1750
	xQuAD	$0.4074_{Q,M}$	29/14	$0.2671_{Q,M}$	0.2028	$0.6410_{Q,M}$	$0.2206_{Q,M}$
	PM-1	$0.4323^{X}_{Q,M}$	32/13	$0.3071^{X}_{Q,M}$	0.1827	$0.6323_{Q,M}$	$0.2654^{X}_{Q,M}$
	PM-2	$\mathbf{0.4546}^{X,P}_{Q,M}$	34/10	$\mathbf{0.3271}^{X}_{Q,M}$	**0.2030**	$\mathbf{0.6503}_{Q,M}$	$\mathbf{0.289}^{X}_{Q,M}$
Suggestions	Query-likelihood	0.3268		0.2131	0.1730	0.5355	0.1722
	MMR	0.3361_{Q}	17/14	0.2206	0.1746	0.5507	0.1819
	xQuAD	$0.3582_{Q,M}$	31/6	$0.2372_{Q,M}$	0.1785	0.5775_{Q}	0.1964_{Q}
	PM-1	0.3664^{X}	25/15	0.2409	0.1654	0.5996	0.1952
	PM-2	$\mathbf{0.4374}^{X,P}_{Q,M}$	33/10	$\mathbf{0.3087}^{X,P}_{Q,M}$	**0.1841**	$\mathbf{0.6279}^{X}_{Q,M}$	$\mathbf{0.2690}^{X,P}_{Q,M}$
WT-2010 Best (uogTrB67xS) [11]		0.4178	N/A	0.2980	N/A	N/A	0.2616

Table 3: Quality of the baseline run for the WT-2009 and WT-2010 query sets in sub-topic recall and precision-IA.

	S-Recall@50	Prec-IA@50
WT-2009	0.54	0.0821
WT-2010	0.7003	0.1486

topics do not get any relevant documents) and also contain considerably less relevant documents for each of the topics than WT-2010. Therefore, there is far less room for improvement on WT-2009 than there is on WT-2010, which leads to the fact that all systems perform better on WT-2010.

Regarding the comparison among diversification techniques, we see a very similar trend as in the previous case with proportionality. In particular, MMR is least effective method due to its lack of awareness of the query aspects. PM-2, on the other hand, outperforms all other methods in almost all metrics with statistically significant improvement in many cases. PM-2 with automatically generated aspects even outperforms the best performing system in TREC evaluation. It should be noted that the best performing system in TREC 2010 of which results we report also use suggestions generated by a search engine as aspect descriptions. This further confirms the effectiveness of PM-2: it provides results with not only a higher degree of proportionality but also a lower degree of redundancy.

6.3 Improvement Analysis

The analyses in this section are conducted on the entire query set as there is no need to consider WT-2009 and WT-2010 separately. In addition, we only present our analyses with the manually generated set of aspects because we have similar findings with the other set, only to a slightly lesser extent due to the aspect misalignment problem.

We are interested in two aspects of the improvement each technique provides over the initial retrieval: (1) the robustness [21] of the improvement, and (2) the reasons that account for this improvement. Robustness refers to the number of queries each technique improves and hurts together with the magnitude of the performance change. To understand the robustness of each model, we provide a more detailed view of the Win/Loss ratio that was provided earlier in Table 1 and Table 2. In particular, instead of showing how many queries each system improves and hurts over the entire query set, we now look at these numbers with respect to the percentage of the improvement. The histogram in Fig. 1 shows, for various ranges of relative increases (positive ranges) and decreases (negative ranges) in CPR and α-NDCG, the number of queries improved and hurt with respect to the query likelihood baseline.

It can be seen from Fig. 1 that most of the performance changes resulting from using MMR is in the two low ranges −[0%,25%] and +[0%, 25%], which indicates that MMR rarely improves or hurts a query drastically. Combined with the fact that it helps and hurts about the same number of queries (35/33), MMR can only provide slight improvement over the baseline.

In contrast, PM-2 and xQuAD provide substantial improvement (> +100%) for several queries. In addition, compared to MMR, these two models hurt about the same number of queries but they improve many more. As a result, PM-2 and xQuAD significantly outperform MMR in most cases. Comparing PM-2 and xQuAD, although they help and hurt about the same number of queries, PM-2 has a much larger magnitude of improvement. This is demon-

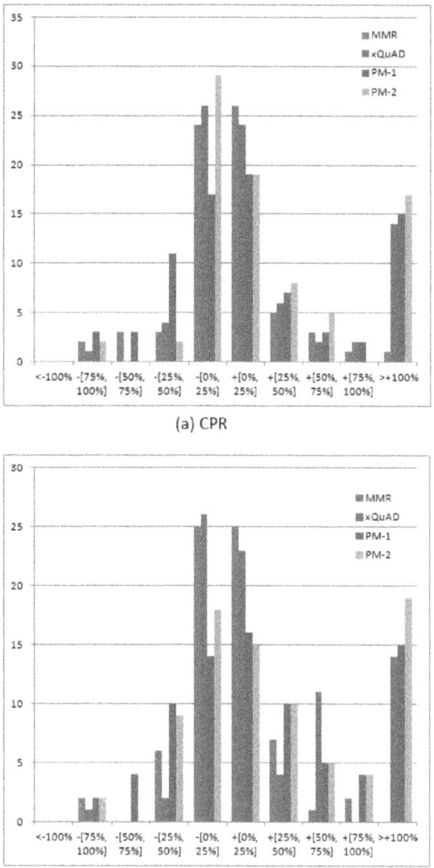

(a) CPR

(b) α-NDCG

Figure 1: Robustness of all techniques with respect to the baseline query-likelihood.

strated through Fig. 1 with the fact that PM-2 has more queries in the highest range (>+100%).

The effectiveness of each model depends on two factors: the quality of the initial retrieved set of documents and the model's power to select a diverse subset from that pool of documents. Since all models operate on the same pool, the former factor becomes irrelevant. As for the model power, the key component of both our method and xQuAD is the query likelihood estimate of relevance $P(d_j|t_i)$ between an aspect t_i and a document d_j. While xQuAD uses $P(d_j|t_i)$ to penalize redundancy at every rank, PM-2 uses it to accommodate proportionality. Intuitively, the more accurate $P(d_j|t_i)$ is at telling which document is relevant to which of the aspects of the query, the more diverse the final ranked list will be. In this experiment, we study how well these techniques perform at different level of accuracy $P(d_j|t_i)$ provides.

In order to quantify the accuracy of $P(d_j|t_i)$, we do as follows. Let D be the set of top 50 documents returned for the query q, which has a set of aspects $\{t_1, t_2, ..., t_n\}$. We rank all documents $d_j \in D$ for each of the aspects t_i with $P(d_j|t_i)$ and record the NDCG score. We then use the average of NDCG across all aspects as the measure of accuracy of $P(d_j|t_i)$. Table 4 presents the absolute improvement each model has over the baseline (in both CPR and α-NDCG separately) on different ranges of accuracy of $P(d_j|t_i)$. We

Table 4: CPR and α-NDCG breakdown by ranges of accuracy of $P(d_j|t_i)$.

	$Acc._{P(d_j \mid t_i)}$	[0,0.1)	[0.1, 0.2)	[0.2, 0.3)	[0.3, 1.0]
	#q	28	21	26	23
CPR	QL	0.1049	0.4152	0.5296	0.6040
	MMR	−0.0142	+0.0249	−0.0015	−0.0013
	xQuAD	+0.0062	+0.0326	+0.0666	+0.1097
	PM-1	+0.0028	+0.0286	+0.0500	+0.1059
	PM-2	+0.0193	+0.0613	+0.0903	+0.1417
α-NDCG	QL	0.07	0.3078	0.4143	0.4885
	MMR	−0.0079	+0.0146	+0.0133	+0.0013
	xQuAD	+0.0202	+0.0509	+0.0768	+0.0863
	PM-1	+0.0212	+0.0221	+0.0677	+0.1252
	PM-2	+0.0288	+0.0616	+0.1189	+0.1548

also show the number queries and how the baseline query likelihood performs in each of these ranges.

Since MMR does not use $P(d_j|t_i)$, its performance obviously does not correlate with the accuracy of $P(d_j|t_i)$. PM-2 consistently provides larger improvement than xQuAD across all ranges of accuracy and metrics. In addition, the gap between the improvement in both CPR and α-NDCG of PM-2 and xQuAD is generally larger as the accuracy of $P(d_j|t_i)$ increases. This clearly indicates using $P(d_j|t_i)$ to optimize proportionality is much more effective than to minimize redundancy, which explains the all-round superiority of PM-2.

In summary, we have demonstrated that MMR is the least effective because it helps and hurts about the same number of queries. PM-2 and xQuAD both help more queries than they hurt, but PM-2 is able to provide substantially larger improvement over the baseline than xQuAD, helping PM-2 to be statistically significantly better than xQuAD even though they both outperform MMR and the baseline. The reason for PM-2's superiority over xQuAD is that PM-2 uses $P(d_j|t_i)$ to accommodate proportionality at every rank, which is more effective than using it to penalize redundancy. The results obtained with PM-2 contain not only a higher degree of proportionality but also a lower degree of redundancy.

6.4 Failure Analysis

Our techniques sequentially go over all "seats" in the result ranked list and decide for each of them which aspect it should go to. After the aspect is determined, PM-1 simply chooses the best document for this aspect according to $P(d_j|t_i)$ while PM-2 might promote documents that are slightly less relevant to this aspect but relevant to other aspects as well.

The problem arises when the initial retrieval fails to find relevant documents for some of the aspects. When a "seat" is assigned to an aspect without relevant documents, $P(d_j|t_i)$ will mistakenly provide some false positive non-relevant documents to fill in that seat, leading to undesirable results. In this section, we will investigate this effect.

Sub-topic recall of the baseline run is certainly the best metric for studying the effect of coverage. Table 5 shows how different systems behave on different ranges of sub-topic recall of the top 50 documents retrieved by the baseline run. For each of the sub-topic recall ranges, Table 5 provides the percentage of queries that each system helps and hurts (marked as "%Q+" and "%Q-" respectively) together with the its relative improvement ("%Imp.") in both CPR and α-NDCG with respect to the baseline. We also show for each range the number of queries as well as the performance of the baseline for references.

We first examine the percentage of queries helped and hurt by each system. At the low recall range ([0,0.5)), both PM-1 and PM-2 hurt more queries than they improve. As the recall goes up, these numbers improve. This trend is especially clear with α-NDCG. This clearly demonstrates the effect sub-topic recall has on our techniques.

xQuAD by its nature does not have the same problem. As a result, the negative effect of low subtopic recall on xQuAD is smaller than it is on our methods: xQuAD has better Win/Loss ratios than both PM-1 and PM-2 on low ([0,0.5)) and medium ([0.5,0.75)) recall range. This helps further explain what we saw earlier in Table 2: although the same techniques perform worse on WT-2009 than they do on WT-2010, PM-1 and PM-2 are the ones with the largest performance difference in terms of Win/Loss ratio. The reason is the subtopic recall of the baseline for WT-2009 is considerably lower than that for WT-2010 (as demonstrated previously in Table 3), which affects our systems the most.

MMR despite not having this problem, it hurts about the same number of queries as our techniques in the low and medium recall ranges due to its overall ineffectiveness. In addition, it helps significantly less queries compared to ours.

With respect to the relative improvement over the baseline, even though xQuAD has better Win/Loss ratios than PM-2 on the low and medium recall ranges, PM-2 still manages to provide larger improvement than xQuAD. Additionally, the gap between the two models becomes substantially larger in the high recall range. This provides additional evidences to support the effectiveness of PM-2.

In summary, even though our proportionality-aware method PM-2 is very effective overall, it depends critically on the coverage of the baseline run.

6.5 Discussion: On Noisy Aspect Descriptions

Given that automatically generated aspects can be helpful for diversification, it is important to know how to generate them. Using query suggestions from commercial search engines in effect is using a "black box" for this important component. Hence, this section aims to provide a preliminary discussion on whether we can use aspects generated by existing work in query suggestion and reformulation for diversification.

While most of those reformulation techniques focus on making user queries more effective [2, 18, 24, 20, 15], some aim to generate reformulations that cover different aspects of the original query [16]. We have adapted these techniques [16] to generate a set of clusters for each of our queries, where each cluster is assumed to represent an aspect of the original query. Details can be found in [16]. We concatenate all queries in each cluster to form a "document", from which we then construct a language model. Finally, we use Indri's weighted query representation of this model as the aspect description and the frequency of the cluster as the popularity of the aspect. The resulting query set consists of 77 queries for which the reformulation technique can provide clusters.

We now re-evaluate all of our techniques using this set of aspects. The results are presented in Table 6. Interestingly, we observe that the performance of xQuAD, PM-1 and PM-2 is substantially lower than with the previous two aspect sets. We observe that this set of aspects, in comparison with the set obtained from the search engine, contains (1) considerably less of the TREC sub-topics and more of other aspects that are not identified by TREC's assesors, and also (2) some unclear aspect descriptions. The low performance of all systems, in fact, clearly demonstrates the aspect misalignment issue and the noisiness of this set.

With these noisy aspects, PM-2 is still better than xQuAD with most of the metrics. The performance of xQuAD is, in fact, even lower than that of the query likelihood baseline in both CPR and α-NDCG. PM-2 still manages to provide improvement, but it is more comparable to MMR. Interestingly, PM-1 is now the best performing approach.

To conclude, aspects generated by the current query reformulation technique are generally not very "effective" for diversification. This notion of "effectiveness", however, has to be taken with care. We have been penalizing all systems for finding documents for aspects that are different to TREC sub-topics. In practice, these unjudged aspects might be relevant to the query as well. This raises the question of how reliable the current evaluation paradigm is that relies on pre-defining a fixed set of aspects for each queries. We will investigate this issue in future work.

7. CONCLUSIONS AND FUTURE WORK

In this paper, we present a different perspective on search result diversification: diversity by proportionality. We consider a result list to be more diverse if the number of documents relevant to each of the aspects is proportional to the overall popularity of that aspect. We then propose Cumulative Proportionality (CPR), an effectiveness measure for proportionality which is based on metrics commonly used for evaluating outcomes of elections. Motivated by the Sainte-Laguë method for assigning seats in a parliament to members of competing political parties, we also present a proportionality-driven framework for diversification. It sequentially determines for each of the "seats" in the result list the aspect that best maintains the overall proportionality with respect to the previously selected topics. It then determines for this seat the best document with respect to that topic. Using this framework, we derive PM-1 – a naive adaptation of the seat allocation mechanism, from which we then develop the probabilistic interpretation, which we called PM-2.

Our results have demonstrated that, with both manually and automatically generated aspect descriptions, PM-2 is statistically significantly better than the top performing redundancy-based technique not only in CPR, but also on several other standard redundancy-based measures. This indicates that promoting proportionality will result in minimal redundancy, as desired by the current standard in diversity.

For future work, we will compare the aspects generated by existing reformulation techniques to the TREC sub-topics in order to quantify the aspect misalignment problem. If many of these misaligned aspects are indeed sensible, we might have to re-examine if predefining a set of topics for each query is a valid strategy for evaluating diversification techniques. In addition, Santos et al. has pointed out that learning to dynamically provide different diversification strategies for different queries based on how ambiguous they are [27] and what intent they have [28] significantly improves the performance of xQuAD. We plan to investigate these approaches since they are potentially beneficial for our model.

Table 5: Performance breakdown by S-Recall of the initially retrieved documents. "%Q+" and "%Q-" indicate respectively the percentage of queries helped and hurt by each technique. "%Imp." indicates the relative improvement of each technique over the baseline query likelihood (QL).

	S-Recall Ranges	[0,0.5)			[0.5,0.75)			[0.75,1.0]		
	#Queries	39			27			32		
		%Q+	%Q-	%Imp.	%Q+	%Q-	%Imp.	%Q+	%Q-	%Imp.
CPR	QL (CPR)	0.2504			0.4689			0.5279		
	MMR	10%	41%	−6%	56%	26%	+4%	53%	28%	+1%
	xQuAD	26%	36%	−6%	74%	19%	+15%	56%	38%	+22%
	PM-1	23%	41%	−5%	63%	30%	+6%	63%	31%	+25%
	PM-2	23%	41%	0%	67%	30%	+18%	69%	28%	+31%
α-NDCG	QL (α-NDCG)	0.1610			0.3791			0.4349		
	MMR	13%	38%	+5%	48%	33%	+3%	53%	28%	+3%
	xQuAD	31%	33%	+6%	74%	22%	+19%	63%	31%	+24%
	PM-1	31%	33%	+5%	56%	37%	+7%	72%	22%	+34%
	PM-2	28%	36%	+8%	67%	30%	+24%	75%	22%	+42%

Table 6: Performance of all techniques with noisy aspect descriptions. Q, M and X indicate significant difference to Query-Likelihood, MMR and xQuAD respectively.

	CPR	α-NDCG	ERR-IA	Prec-IA	S-Recall	NRBP
Query-likelihood	0.3669	0.2637	0.1644	0.1113	0.4107	0.1332
MMR	0.3824	0.2769	0.1722	**0.1353**$_Q$	**0.4450**	0.1387
xQuAD	0.3598	0.2601	0.1620	0.1169$_M$	0.4052	0.1299
PM-1	**0.3943**	**0.2944**$_X$	**0.1961**$_X$	0.1306	0.4189	**0.1685**$_X$
PM-2	0.3703	0.2828	0.1888	0.1157$_M$	0.4010	0.1641

8. ACKNOWLEDGMENTS

This work was supported in part by the Center for Intelligent Information Retrieval, and in part by Vietnam Education Foundation. Any opinions, findings and conclusions or recommendations expressed in this material are those of the authors and do not necessarily reflect those of the sponsor.

9. REFERENCES

[1] R. Agrawal, S. Gollapudi, A. Halverson, and S. Ieong. Diversifying search results. In *Proceedings of WSDM*, pages 5-14, 2009.

[2] R. Baeza-Yates, C. Hurtado and M. Mendoza. Query recommendation using query logs in search engines. In *The ClustWeb Workshop*, pages 588-596, 2004.

[3] M. Bendersky, D. Fisher, and W.B. Croft. UMass at TREC 2010 Web Track: Term dependence, spam filtering and quality bias. In *Proceedings of TREC*, 2010.

[4] J. Carbonell and J. Goldstein. The use of MMR, diversity-based reranking for reordering documents and producing summaries. In *Proceedings SIGIR*, pages 335-336, 1998.

[5] B. Carterette and P. Chandar. Probabilistic models of ranking novel documents for faceted topic retrieval. In *Proceedings of CIKM*, pages 1287-1296, 2009.

[6] O. Chapelle, D. Metlzer, Y. Zhang, and P. Grinspan. Expected reciprocal rank for graded relevance. In *Proceedings of CIKM*, pages 621-630, 2009.

[7] C.L.A. Clarke, M. Kolla, G.V. Cormack, O. Vechtomova, A. Ashkan, S. Buttcher, and I. MacKinnon. Novelty and diversity in information retrieval evaluation. In *Proceedings of SIGIR*, pages 659-666, 2008.

[8] C.L.A. Clarke, M. Kolla, and O. Vechtomova. An effectiveness measure for ambiguous and underspecified queries. In *Proceedings of ICTIR*, pages 188-199, 2009.

[9] C.L.A. Clarke, N. Craswell, I. Soboroff, and A. Ashkan. A comparative analysis of cascade measures for novelty and diversity. In *Proceedings of WSDM*, pages 75-84, 2011.

[10] C.L.A. Clarke, N. Craswell, and I. Soboroff. Overview of the TREC 2009 Web track. In *TREC*, 2009.

[11] C.L.A. Clarke, N. Craswell, I. Soboroff, and G.V. Cormack. Overview of the TREC 2009 Web track. In *TREC*, 2009.

[12] G.V. Cormack, M.D. Smucker, and C.L.A. Clarke. Efficient and effective spam filtering and re-ranking for large web datasets. Apr 2010.

[13] N. Craswell, O. Zoeter, M.J. Taylor, and B. Ramsey. An experimental comparison of click position-bias models. In *Proceedings of WSDM*, pages 87-94, 2008.

[14] W.B. Croft, D. Metzler, and T. Strohman. Search Engines: Information Retrieval in Practice. *Addison-Wesley*, 2009.

[15] V. Dang and W.B. Croft. Query reformulation using anchor text. In *Proceedings of WSDM*, pages 41-50, 2010.

[16] V. Dang, X. Xue, and W.B. Croft. Inferring query aspects from reformulations using clustering. In *Proceedings of CIKM*, pages 2117-2120, 2011.

[17] M. Gallagher. Proportionality, disproportionality and electoral systems. In *Electoral Studies*, 10(1):33-51, 1991.

[18] R. Jones, B. Rey and O. Madani. Generating query substitutions. In *Proceedings of WWW*, pages 387-396, 2006.

[19] A. Lijphart. Electoral systems and party systems: A study of twenty-seven democracies, 1945-1990. *Oxford University Press*, 1994.

[20] Q. Mei, D. Zhou and K. Church. Query suggestion using hitting time. In *Proceedings of CIKM*, pages 469-477, 2008.

[21] D. Metzler and W.B. Croft. Latent concept expansion using markov random fields. In *Proceedings of SIGIR*, pages 311-318, 2007.

[22] D. Rafiei, K. Bharat and A. Shukia. Diversifying web search results. In *Proceedings of WWW*, page 781-790, 2010.

[23] F. Radlinski and S. Dumais. Improving personalized web search using result diversification. In *Proceedings of SIGIR*, pages 691-692, 2006.

[24] X. Wang and C. Zhai. Mining term association patterns from search logs for effective query reformulation. In *Proceedings of CIKM*, pages 479-488, 2008.

[25] J. Wang and J. Zhu. Portfolio theory of information retrieval. In *Proceedings of SIGIR*, pages 115-122, 2009.

[26] R. L. T. Santos, C. Macdonald, and I. Ounis. Exploiting query reformulations for web search result diversification. In *Proceedings of WWW*, pages 881-890, 2010.

[27] R. L. T. Santos, C. Macdonald, and I. Ounis. Selectively diversifying web search results. In *Proceedings of CIKM*, pages 1179-1188, 2010.

[28] R. L. T. Santos, C. Macdonald, and I. Ounis. Intent-aware search result diversification. In *Proceedings of SIGIR*, pages 595-604, 2011.

[29] C. Zhai, W.W. Cohen, and J. Lafferty. Beyond independent relevance: Methods and evaluation metrics for subtopic retrieval. In *Proceedings of SIGIR*, pages 10-17, 2003.

Explicit Relevance Models in Intent-Oriented Information Retrieval Diversification

Saúl Vargas, Pablo Castells and David Vallet
Universidad Autónoma de Madrid
Escuela Politécnica Superior, Departamento de Ingeniería Informática
{saul.vargas,pablo.castells,david.vallet}@uam.es

ABSTRACT

The intent-oriented search diversification methods developed in the field so far tend to build on generative views of the retrieval system to be diversified. Core algorithm components –in particular redundancy assessment– are expressed in terms of the probability to observe documents, rather than the probability that the documents be relevant. This has been sometimes described as a view considering the selection of a single document in the underlying task model. In this paper we propose an alternative formulation of aspect-based diversification algorithms which explicitly includes a formal relevance model. We develop means for the effective computation of the new formulation, and we test the resulting algorithm empirically. We report experiments on search and recommendation tasks showing competitive or better performance than the original diversification algorithms. The relevance-based formulation has further interesting properties, such as unifying two well-known state of the art algorithms into a single version. The relevance-based approach opens alternative possibilities for further formal connections and developments as natural extensions of the framework. We illustrate this by modeling tolerance to redundancy as an explicit configurable parameter, which can be set to better suit the characteristics of the IR task, or the evaluation metrics, as we illustrate empirically.

Categories and Subject Descriptors

H.3.3 [**Information Search and Retrieval**]: Information Search and Retrieval – *retrieval models*

General Terms

Algorithms, Measurement, Performance, Experimentation, Theory

Keywords

Diversity, relevance models, language models, generative models

1. INTRODUCTION

The value of diversity as a fundamental dimension of information utility has started to be cared for in the Information Retrieval (IR) research community for over a decade [4]. Diversity-enhancement methods have been developed [1,7,21,27,29], diversity evaluation methodologies and metrics have been proposed [1,8,24,29], and a diversity task has been included in the latest TREC campaigns [9]. Theories of IR diversity build on a revision of the classic document independence assumption in IR: the marginal utility of a document indeed highly depends on –in general, decreases with– the relevance of the documents the user has previously seen. Considering this, IR systems' output diversification is posited as an effective strategy to cope with the uncertainty (ambiguity and/or incompleteness) involved in user queries, as imperfect expressions of true user needs. By trading diminishing marginal relevance for increased query aspect coverage, diversification strategies seek to maximize the range of users (the precise potential intents behind the query) who will get at least some relevant document, thereby improving the overall gain [1,7,10,21].

Two trends can be broadly distinguished in the diversification methods reported in the literature, based on whether or not they use an explicit representation of query intents [22]. Whereas intent-oriented methods include an explicit query aspect space in their formulation, implicit diversification schemes typically rely at some level on inter-document similarity, under the assumption that dissimilar documents should cover diverse query aspects. Interestingly, intent-implicit approaches generally build –as far as their formalization goes– on an explicit relevance model, often lending from the Probability Ranking Principle [7,27,29]. Whereas, in contrast, the intent-explicit methods tend to elaborate, in their problem statement, formalization, and algorithmic formulation, on generative views of the retrieval system to be diversified, where relevance is implicit [1,21,25]. Core algorithm components –in particular redundancy assessment– are expressed in such approaches in terms of the probability to observe documents, rather than the probability that the documents be relevant. This has been sometimes described as a view considering the selection of a single document in the underlying task model [28].

In this paper we propose an alternative formulation of aspect-based diversification algorithms which explicitly includes a formal relevance model. Our research has a theoretical motivation in seeking an alternative, nuanced understanding of the intent-explicit diversity problem, and the resulting variants in the formulation and development of aspect-based diversification methods. On the other hand, the explicit relevance approach has advantages of its own. We report experiments in search and recommendation tasks where the approach shows competitive or better performance than its original counterparts. Moreover, the relevance-based formulation opens the way for further extensions and elaborations with models involving an explicit representation of relevance. As a particular case, we show that the framework provides a sound basis for tuning redundancy penalization in a principled way, as a smooth consistent extension of the diversity model.

The rest of the paper is organized as follows. We briefly introduce and discuss intent-oriented diversification schemes in the next section, paying specific attention to their document-oriented gen-

Permission to make digital or hard copies of all or part of this work for personal or classroom use is granted without fee provided that copies are not made or distributed for profit or commercial advantage and that copies bear this notice and the full citation on the first page. To copy otherwise, or republish, to post on servers or to redistribute to lists, requires prior specific permission and/or a fee.
SIGIR'12, August 12–16, 2012, Portland, Oregon, USA.
Copyright 2012 ACM 978-1-4503-1472-5/12/08...$15.00.

erative formal foundation. We introduce our relevance-based revision of such schemes after that in section 3, including details for the development, estimation and computation of the components of our resulting diversification framework. We empirically test the effectiveness of our approach in section 4. Section 5 describes a formal extension of the proposed framework to model and adjust the diversification to different degrees of tolerance to redundancy. We discuss the results and implications of our approach in section 6, and conclude with a summary and final comments in section 7.

2. RELEVANCE MODELS VS. GENERATIVE MODELS

The different views on relevance implied by the Probability Ranking Principle (PRP) [20] and the Language Modeling (LM) approaches to IR [16] raised interest and debate in the research community by the turn of the past decade [23]. The absence of a clear explicit notion of relevance in the early LM formulations has been often considered to involve an underlying assumption of single relevant document selection [3]. Even though –or precisely because– there does not seem to be a unique common understanding on such issues in the field, and a unique view on whether or how LM actually capture relevance, we see theoretical –and potentially practical– interest in exploring new formulations of the diversity problem –and the derivation of algorithms thereupon– which explicitly build on the probability of relevance.

As stated in the introduction, we focus on approaches to diversity which are founded on an explicit representation of query intents. As two prototypical representative instances of this approach, we focus on IA-Select [1] and xQuAD [21] as the algorithms of reference for our study. Both have proved to be quite effective in IR diversity tasks, outperforming prior non-explicitly intent-oriented approaches (see [22] for a comprehensive empirical analysis and comparisons). We start by briefly reviewing the formulation of these diversification schemes, and the fundamental principles on which they build, in order to contrast them later to a relevance-based alternative.

The definition of the IA-Select approach is developed in [1] around a quality component $V(d|q,c)$ broadly defined as the likelihood that a document d satisfies the query q given the user intent c. The diversification problem is stated as finding a subset of documents –of a given size– that maximizes the probability that at least one of them is relevant. This is formulated as finding the set S that minimizes:

$$p(S|q) = \sum_c p(c|q)\left(1 - \prod_{d\in S}(1 - V(d|q,c))\right) \quad (1)$$

While solving this problem is NP-Hard, the authors provide a practical approximation to the optimal solution by greedily re-ranking a baseline set of documents picking one document at a time that maximizes the following objective function:

$$g(d|q,c,S) = \sum_c p(c|q)\, V(d|q,c) \prod_{d'\in S}(1 - V(d'|q,c)) \quad (2)$$

where S is the set of documents that were selected in the previous iterations. Agrawal et al generically describe $V(d|q,c)$ as a term quantifying to what extent the document d responds to the user need expressed by q when the intended sense of the query is c. The authors do not enforce a strict probabilistic rigor in the development of this component, and in fact omit an explicit specification, thus leaving its implementation somewhat open to different realizations of the expressed principle. For their own experiments, the implementation of $V(d|q,c)$ is hinted as the product of a baseline retrieval scoring function (the system to be diversified) by the probability that d belongs to category c –which may be read as $p(c|d)$. No explicit probability of relevance is introduced in their development and –if we may indulge on a rather informal note– one might find in the $V(d|q,c)$ notation some reminiscence of a probability distribution over documents.

xQuAD does have a quite precise probabilistic formulation [21]. It is stated and developed upon a document generative model formulation, whereby the resulting key terms of the algorithms reflect the probability to observe documents, rather than the explicit probability of the latter to be relevant. Specifically, the xQuAD scheme consists of a greedy algorithm with the same essential structure as IA-Select, but with a differently defined objective function:

$$g(d|q,c,S) = (1-\lambda)\, p(d|q) + \lambda\, p(d,\neg S|q) \quad (3)$$

That is, the objective is a linear combination of the probability to observe a document given the query (which may be understood as the baseline retrieval function), and the probability to observe the document given the query, assuming –strictly sticking to the probabilistic notation– no previously selected document had be observed given the query (which represents the marginal utility of the document). The marginal utility component is in turn developed by marginalizing over the set of query intents, which after some Bayesian derivations and mild conditional independence assumptions results in:[1]

$$p(d,\neg S|q) \sim \sum_c p(c|q)\, p(d|c,q) \prod_{d'\in S}(1 - p(d'|c,q))$$

Thus the xQuAD algorithm is formulated and developed upon (conditional) document distributions, as ultimately embodied in the $p(d|q)$ and $p(d|c,q)$ components.

Therefore neither IA-Select, nor xQuAD, or other explicitly intent-oriented diversification schemes that we are aware of, include relevance as an explicit magnitude or random variable.

3. RELEVANCE-BASED DIVERSIFICATION ALGORITHMS

3.1 Relevance-Based IA-Select

Taking up from a more literal interpretation of Agrawal's initial problem statement, we investigate a revision of the IA-Select formulation by defining $V(d|q,c) \equiv p(r|d,q,c)$, where r is the binary relevance random variable (and r is used as a shorthand for $r = 1$). With this formulation, the objective function to be maximized in the problem statement (equation 1) then explicitly becomes:

$$p(S|q) = \sum_c p(c|q)\left(1 - \prod_{d\in S}(1 - p(r|d,q,c))\right)$$

[1] The original version of xQuAD [21] would use $p(d|c)$ rather than $p(d|q,c)$. Later publications [22] present however the latter form, which we have also found to work better in our experiments, whereby we favor it here. Our analysis and considerations apply just the same to both variants in any case.

And the marginal utility objective function for the greedy approximation algorithm (equation 2) gets then defined as:

$$g(d|q,c,S) = \sum_{c} p(c|q)\, p(r|d,q,c) \prod_{d' \in S} (1 - p(r|d',q,c)) \quad (4)$$

In order to implement this formulation we need a means to estimate $p(r|d,q,c)$. Before addressing that, we formulate a similar revision of the xQuAD algorithm.

3.2 Relevance-Based xQuAD

For this algorithm we actually reconsider the own initial formulation of the approach. Rather than expressing the objective function in terms of document probabilities as in equation 3, we define the objective function on an explicit relevance model, as:

$$g(d|q,c,S) = (1-\lambda)\, p(r_d|q) + \lambda\, p(r_d, \neg r_S|q) \quad (5)$$

where r_d means d is relevant –that is, $p(r_d|q) \stackrel{\text{def}}{=} p(r|d,q)$– and $\neg r_S$ means no document in S is relevant. Taking this starting point, by similar steps to the original xQuAD, we derive:

$$p(r_d, \neg r_S|q) = \sum_{c} p(c|q)\, p(r_d, \neg r_S|q,c)$$

$$= \sum_{c} p(c|q)\, p(r|d,c,q) \prod_{d' \in S} (1 - p(r|d',c,q))$$

where we have assumed r_d and r_S are conditionally independent given q and c. Substituting all this in the objective function gives:

$$g(d|q,c,S) = (1-\lambda)\, p(r|d,q) +$$

$$+ \lambda \sum_{c} p(c|q)\, p(r|d,q,c) \prod_{d' \in S} (1 - p(r|d',q,c))$$

It is easy to see that the above function becomes the relevance-based version of IA-Select (equation 4) when $\lambda = 1$. We hence notably find that, on a relevance model foundation, xQuAD turns out to be a generalization of IA-Select. We shall thus deal with the two reformulations as a single approach henceforth.

We now turn to the problem of estimating the two models involved in the new objective function, so as to come up to an effectively computable form for the latter.

3.3 Aspectual Relevance Model

Two main components: the aspect model $p(c|q)$, and the relevance model $p(r|d,q,c)$, need to be estimated in order to compute the objective function $g(d|q,c,S)$ of our diversification approach.

First, for the relevance model, by applying Bayes' rule we have:

$$p(r|d,q,c) = \frac{p(c|d,q,r)\, p(r|d,q)}{p(c|d,q)}$$

The $p(r|d,q)$ component can be obtained from the retrieval system, as we shall discuss later in the next subsection.

The marginalization of the conditional aspect distribution with respect to relevance gives $p(c|d,q) = p(c|d,q,r)\, p(r|d,q) + p(c|d,q,\neg r)\, \big(1 - p(r|d,q)\big)$. Therefore by substitution in the numerator above, the relevance model can be rewritten as:

$$p(r|d,q,c) = \frac{p(c|d,q) - p(c|d,q,\neg r)\, \big(1 - p(r|d,q)\big)}{p(c|d,q)} \quad (6)$$

Now we assume that under non-relevance, aspects are independent from documents and queries, that is $p(c|d,q,\neg r) \sim p(c|\neg r)$. In other words, given non-relevance, we consider there is no particular relation the aspect is enforced to meet with respect to the query and the document –other than not forming a relevant tuple. Since most aspect / document / query tuples are not related in practice, as relevance is highly sparse, such negative condition can be considered as negligible. Comparable assumptions can be found in probabilistic developments in the literature (see e.g. [29]) –only with no aspect variable involved. Furthermore, we assume no particular bias between aspects towards relevance or non-relevance, i.e. we approximate $p(c|\neg r) \sim p(c)$. The aspect prior can be estimated from the coverage of aspects in the document collection, if the latter is considered as a fair representative sample space for users' information need intents. Or, in the absence of further information, the prior can be taken as uniform.

Now, $p(c|d,q)$ for equation 6 can be approximated in different ways, depending on the nature of the aspect space and the available observations. When aspects consist of categorical data in such a way that $p(c|d)$ can be directly estimated from the data, we use the approach:

$$p(c|d,q) \sim \frac{p(c|d)\, p(c|q)/p(c)}{\sum_{c'} p(c'|d)\, p(c'|q)/p(c')}$$

using Bayes' rule, marginalization over aspects (in the denominator), and assuming again conditional independence of documents and queries given a query aspect (if a uniform aspect prior is assumed, $p(c)$ and $p(c')$ further cancel out). In our experiments, we take this approximation when ODP is used as the aspect space for search diversification (see section 4.1). We use it in movie and music recommendation tasks as well, where movie genres and artist tags, respectively, are taken as the aspect space (section 4.2).

When aspects belong to the query space, $p(d|c)$ can be estimated from the baseline retrieval function (as suggested e.g. in [21,22]), in a similar way as $p(d|q)$ is estimated for queries (see equation 8 below). In that case, we take the approach:

$$p(c|d,q) \sim \frac{p(d|c)\, p(c|q)}{p(d|q)} \quad (7)$$

using Bayes' rule and assuming conditional independence of documents and queries given a query aspect. Note that this independence assumption is rather mild in this context, since the estimation of $p(d|c)$ applies to documents sampled from the result set for q –i.e. $p(d|c)$ in practice is meaning $p(d|c,R_q)$, which is a form of blind relevance feedback approximation to $p(d|c,q)$, R_q being the set of documents returned for q that are to be diversified. In our experiments, we shall use this approximation when TREC subtopics (manually provided by human assessors for each query) are taken as the aspect space by the diversification algorithm (see section 4.1).

The generative model $p(d|q)$ in equation 7 can be either estimated (more or less) directly from the baseline search system –when the retrieval function implements a language model– or it can be approximated from a relevance model as (see e.g. [3] for this type of derivation):

$$p(d|q) \sim \frac{p(r|d,q)}{\sum_{d' \in R_q} p(r|d',q)} \quad (8)$$

Finally, as to the estimation of $p(c|q)$, we consider two alternatives. For categorical aspects, we marginalize over documents in the result set:

$$p(c|q) \sim \sum_{d \in R_q} p(c|d)\, p(d|q)$$

where we assume conditional independence of query aspects and queries given a document in R_q, and we use the estimate for $p(d|q)$ discussed above (e.g. equation 8). For manually-provided query subtopics (TREC data), we assume a uniform distribution $p(c|q) \sim 1/n_q$, where n_q is the number of subtopics of query q.

3.4 Relevance Model Estimation

Estimating the explicit probability of relevance of a document for a query has been researched in the IR literature from different points of view, distinguished from each other by the source from which relevance distributions are estimated.

Retrieval systems based on the PRP rank documents by decreasing probability of relevance $p(r|d,q)$ given a query [20]. However, rather than directly estimating this probability, these systems compute a function that is equivalent in rank to $p(r|d,q)$, and easier to estimate. The retrieval function is obtained by a series of monotonous operations on the probability of relevance, which involve lossy transformations, in the sense that it is not possible to recover $p(r|d,q)$ back from the final expression. There is thus not in general an analytic approach to obtain an explicit relevance model from a PRP retrieval system [3].

On the other hand, a number of studies have researched the relation between retrieval function score distributions and relevance [2], and some have devised approaches to estimate the probability of relevance from score values [18]. In essence, these approaches analyze the distribution of the scoring function, and their correspondence with known relevance information, thus training a model of relevance given system scores, by regression on the available data [18].

We propose a similar but quite easier approach to estimate the probability of relevance, which just requires the availability of either precision estimates, or click statistics, for the retrieval system being diversified. Rather than mapping scores to probabilities of relevance, we use a common relevance estimate for all queries, based only on the position of documents. Namely, we estimate the probability of relevance by:

$$p(r|d,q) \sim p_s(r|\tau_s(d,q),q)$$

where $\tau_s(d,q)$ is the rank position of document d in the result list returned by the baseline retrieval s in response to query q. Note that this step involves, in a way, a form of rank-based retrieval system output normalization where (similarly to e.g. rank-sim normalization [17]) we only use the document order τ_s returned by the system, regardless of the score values. After this step, estimating the probability of relevance of a document for a query amounts to estimating the probability of relevance at each rank position $p_s(r|k,q)$ for the retrieval system s. To simplify the notation, we shall henceforth drop the 's' subscript from $p_s(r|k,q)$, but it should be implicitly understood, as this distribution estimate is system-dependent.

3.4.1 Estimate on Relevance Judgments

If relevance judgments are available to train the relevance model or, equivalently, we have an estimate of precision at k of the retrieval system (for k ranging up to the size of the document set to be diversified), the positional relevance probability can be estimated as:

$$p(r|k,q) \sim k\, P_q@k - (k-1)\, P_q@(k-1) \tag{9}$$

where $P_q@k$ denotes the precision at k of the system on query q. In our experiments we estimate precision by splitting the set of test queries (with their relevance judgments) into two disjoints subsets of equal size for 2-fold cross-validation. For the queries in one subset, we approximate $p(r|k,q) \sim p(r|k)$ using an average precision estimate $P_q@k \sim P@k$, computed in the complementary query subset.

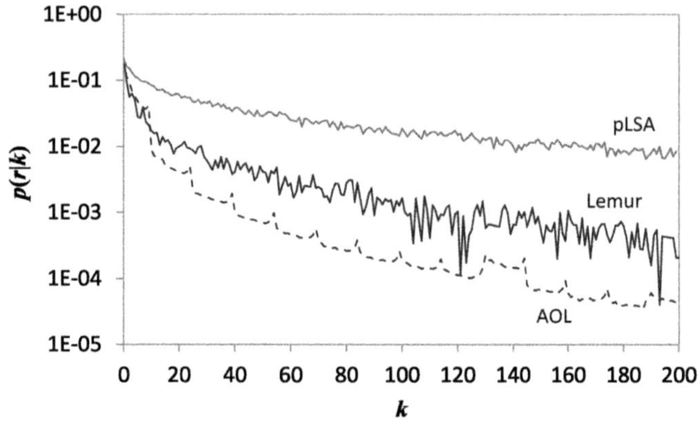

Figure 1. Relevance distribution estimate on the top 200 positions for different retrieval systems on different datasets (*y* axis displayed in log scale). The estimates for Lemur and pLSA are based on $P@k$ measurements, whereas the AOL curve is derived from click statistics from the AOL query log. The Lemur curve is computed on TREC 2009/10 diversity task data. The relevance curve of pLSA is derived from a recommendation task on MovieLens data (see section 4.2).

As an illustrative example, Figure 1 shows the average relevance distribution estimate resulting for the Lemur Indri search system and the pLSA recommender –which we use as baselines in our experiments in section 4. The precision estimates are taken from the TREC 2009/10 diversity task data for Lemur, and from the MovieLens[2] dataset for pLSA (more details in section 4.2). For Lemur, the distribution decreases from $p(r|1) \sim 0.21$ to around 10^{-4} by $k = 200$. pLSA displays a higher relevance probability due to the nature of the recommendation task on this dataset. Compared to more involved methods such as the regression techniques described in [18], this approach is equivalent to simply using the raw relevance data (a histogram of positional relevance) without regularization, rather than a parameterized fit (e.g. by a logistic function).

3.4.2 Estimate on Click Statistics

A positional relevance model $p(r|k)$ can also be built from simple click statistics for the baseline retrieval system [19]. Assuming a cascade browsing model [15], and the simplifying assumption that a document is clicked if and only if it is relevant, we may consider the approximation:

$$p(click|k) \sim p(\neg stop|k-1)\, p(r|k) \tag{10}$$

where $p(click|k)$ is the probability that a document at position k is clicked, and $p(\neg stop|k-1)$ denotes the event that the user continues (does not stop) browsing after position $k-1$. This term can in turn be decomposed by marginalization into the relevance and non-relevance cases:

[2] http://www.grouplens.org/node/73

$$p(\neg stop|k) = p(\neg stop|k,r)\, p(r|k) + \\ + p(\neg stop|k,\neg r)\,\big(1 - p(r|k)\big) \quad (11)$$

Assuming the probability to stop is independent from the position of the document given its relevance, and combining equations 10 and 11 we get:

$$p(r|k) \sim \frac{p(click|k)}{p(\neg stop|r)p(r|k-1) + p(\neg stop|\neg r)\big(1 - p(r|k-1)\big)}$$

Starting from $p(r|1) \sim p(click|1)$, the above equation provides a recursive means to estimate the probability of relevance at each position in the ranking by just having some statistics (e.g. from a query log) of the ratio of clicks at each position, i.e. a background estimate of $p(click|k)$. The two remaining parameters represent a user model (as has been well-studied before, see e.g. [15]), where $p(\neg stop|\neg r)$ reflects the user's "patience", and $p(\neg stop|r)$ is related to how many relevant documents the user is willing to get. This user model allows to account for the position bias in click statistics, and can be estimated in different ways. In the absence of specific data or criteria about this, a simplification such as $p(stop|r) = 1$ –a single relevant document is enough– and $p(stop|\neg r) = 0$ –the user never gives up until finding a relevant document– has been found to be acceptable for many purposes [8,15], which in our case just yields:

$$p(r|k) \sim \frac{p(click|k)}{1 - p(r|k-1)} \quad (12)$$

If click data became too sparse below a certain position, $p(click|k)$ might be estimated by regression techniques from this point on, since we need an estimate of $p(r|k)$ for as many positions as the diversification system is intended to rerank.

As an illustrative example, Figure 1 shows the relevance curve derived from the AOL query log dataset using this approach, which we shall also test in our experiments. The curve is not significantly far below Indri on TREC 2009/10 (in fact it is above it in the top ten). Since AOL can be assumed to be a well optimized engine, this (small) difference can be attributed to a divergence in user behavior beyond the first web search results page (i.e. the behavior on the first and subsequent pages do not fit the same model), and/or the imprecision of the model. On the other hand, the AOL curve reflects practical (and personal) utility for real Web users, which is probably more demanding than topical (less subjective) relevance as applied by TREC assessors.

The estimation of relevance models continues to be a research topic in the IR field, and our approach might benefit from any improvement on this point –the more accurate the relevance model, the better the diversification algorithm can be expected to perform. Interestingly however, even with rough relevance probability estimates like the ones described here, the relevance-based diversification method seems to achieve good performance. Testing our framework with simple approaches as defined in equations 9 and 12, we already observe comparable or better results than the formulations based on generative models, as we report in the next section.

4. EXPERIMENTAL RESULTS

We have tested our relevance-based diversification framework on two IR domains: ad-hoc search, as defined in the TREC Web track diversity task [9], and movie recommendation [24].

4.1 Search Diversity

In order to test our framework on search diversity, we use the data from the TREC diversity task, namely, the ClueWeb collection category B, the topic data, and the relevance assessments from the TREC 2009 and 2010 editions [9]. We use the Lemur Indri retrieval model[3] (version 5.2) as the baseline search engine.

We rerank the top 100 documents returned by the search system by the original a) IA-Select and b) xQuAD algorithms, and c) by our relevance-based reformulation. We test two query aspect spaces for diversification: 1) the Open Directory Project (ODP) categories as in [1], and 2) the subtopics manually provided in the TREC 2009/10 diversity task, as a reference for comparison. We do not apply an exhaustive optimization or tuning of the diversifiers, since the goal of the experiment is the comparison of alternatives, rather than reaching the maximum performance possible. To this respect, our results are roughly comparable in range to those reported e.g. in [21].

With ODP categories, we use the Textwise[4] classification service to estimate $p(c|d)$, by normalization of the score returned by the classifier. For TREC subtopics, we derive an estimate by submitting them as queries to the baseline search system, as discussed earlier in section 3.3. We use a simple uniform aspect prior estimate, and compute the rest of components as described in that section. We test both equations 9 and 12 to estimate the rank-relevance model $p(r|k)$, using relevance judgments from the TREC dataset and AOL click statistics, respectively. TREC relevance information is used in a 2-fold cross-validation, where the relevance judgments of TREC 2009 are used to estimate $P@k$ and derive $p(r|k)$ in TREC 2010 topics, and vice-versa.

Figure 2 compares the performance of the original xQuAD algorithm and the relevance-based reformulation (RxQuAD, using relevance judgments –equation 9– for the $p(r|k)$ estimate), measured by ERR-IA, for λ ranging from 0 to 1. It can be seen that the relevance-based approach consistently outperforms the original xQuAD version. The plots also give an idea of the sensitiveness of the algorithms to the choice of the λ parameter. It is interesting to notice that using TREC subtopics, the best result is reached for $\lambda = 1$, that is with maximum diversity. This makes sense, as the diversifiers use a "relevance-safe" aspect space, inasmuch as

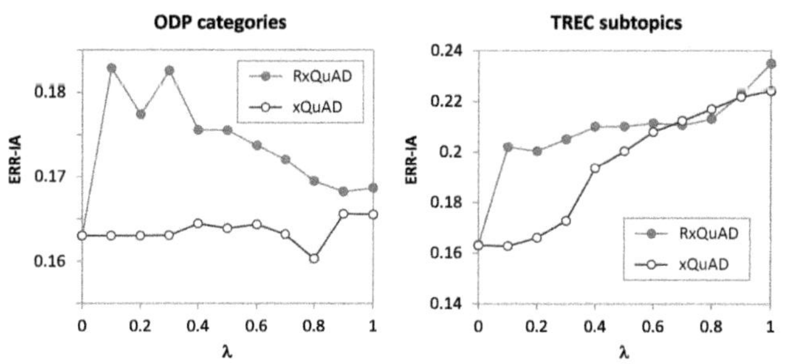

Figure 2. Comparative performance (measured by ERR-IA) of relevance-based diversification (RxQuAD) and xQuAD, ranking over values of λ. The algorithms are tested on TREC 2009/10 data for ClueWeb category B, using ODP (left) and TREC subtopics (right) as the query aspect space, and TREC relevance judgments for the $p(r|k)$ estimate.

[3] http://lemurproject.org/indri

[4] http://textwise.com

Table 1. Comparative evaluation on TREC 2009/10 data for ClueWeb category B, using ODP categories (above) and TREC subtopics (below). The best result for each metric (in the ODP and TREC blocks respectively) is highlighted in bold. For our RxQuAD scheme, we show the results with $p(r|k)$ estimates from the TREC relevance judgments (Qrels), and click statistics from AOL (Clicks). The value of λ that is used for xQuAD and RxQuAD is indicated on the corresponding row. Values marked with $^\blacktriangle$ and $^\triangle$ indicate, respectively, significant and non-significant improvements over IA-Select and xQuAD (in this order). Similar convention with $^\blacktriangledown$ and $^\triangledown$ indicates values below xQuAD or IA-Select. Statistical significance is established by Wilcoxon $p < 0.05$ in all cases.

			λ	α-nDCG @20	ERR-IA @20	nDCG-IA@20	S-precision @r	S-recall @20
	Lemur		-	0.2587	0.1630	0.2396	0.0788	0.4636
ODP categories	IA-Select		-	0.2651	0.1681	0.2423	0.0935	0.4483
	xQuAD		0.9	0.2675	0.1656	0.2451	0.0893	0.4864
	RxQuAD	Qrels	0.1	**0.2858**$^{\triangle\blacktriangle}$	0.1828$^{\triangle\blacktriangle}$	**0.2655**$^{\triangle\blacktriangle}$	**0.1045**$^{\triangle\blacktriangle}$	**0.4898**$^{\blacktriangle\triangle}$
		Clicks	0.4	0.2841$^{\blacktriangle\triangle}$	**0.1831**$^{\triangle\triangle}$	0.2605$^{\triangle\blacktriangle}$	0.1036$^{\triangle\blacktriangle}$	0.4830$^{\blacktriangle\triangledown}$
TREC subtopics	IA-Select		-	0.3541	0.2346	**0.3213**	**0.1300**	**0.5787**
	xQuAD		1.0	0.3445	0.2241	0.3127	0.1149	0.5704
	RxQuAD	Qrels	1.0	**0.3543**$^{\triangle\triangle}$	**0.2349**$^{\triangle\triangle}$	0.3192$^{\triangledown\triangle}$	0.1205$^{\blacktriangledown\triangle}$	0.5782$^{\triangledown\triangle}$
		Clicks	1.0	0.3512$^{\triangledown\triangle}$	0.2320$^{\triangledown\triangle}$	0.3166$^{\triangledown\triangle}$	0.1185$^{\blacktriangledown\triangle}$	0.5748$^{\triangledown\triangle}$

subtopics are tightly related to the query, and therefore diversifying for them does not result in such a potential relevance loss tradeoff as with ODP categories.

Table 1 shows the comparative results on a more complete set of diversity metrics, computed with the evaluation script from the TREC diversity task. We also show subtopic precision at r (S-precision@r) [29] where r is the subtopic recall (S-recall) in the set of documents being diversified. In other words, S-precision@r is the number of subtopics in the reranked set, divided by the first position where all the subtopics have been covered –it thus complements S-recall@20 with a measure of how early in the ranking all possible aspects are covered. Note that α-nDCG, ERR-IA, and nDCG-IA account for both diversity and relevance, whereas S-recall and S-precision@r are pure diversity metrics. For xQuAD and our approach, the results correspond to the best λ in terms of ERR-IA, selected manually with a precision of 0.1.

It can be seen that the relevance-oriented approach improves the two original diversifiers with ODP categories on all metrics (except on subtopic recall for the click-based configuration against xQuAD). With TREC subtopics, IA-Select is considerably effective –which we believe is due to the mostly single-valued aspect coverage per document, a situation where IA-Select seems to work particularly well–, and has similar effectiveness to our approach, with some advantage on S-precision@r. Our approach performs better than xQuAD on this aspect space in all cases though. In general, the best results for our framework are obtained with the baseline-specific estimate of $p(r|k)$ (equation 9) on TREC relevance judgments ('Qrels' rows in Table 1), as one might expect. We may however observe that the results obtained with the AOL click statistics ('Clicks' rows) are almost as good as the results with the relevance judgments. This suggests that our approach is not particularly demanding or sensitive to the nature of the required relevance information to estimate $p(r|k)$.

4.2 Recommendation Diversity

In order to test our approach on a different domain other than ad-hoc search, we conduct additional experiments on recommender system tasks. For this purpose we use two well-known datasets: the 1M version of the MovieLens collection, which includes one million ratings (on a 1-5 scale) by 6,040 users for 3,900 items; and an extract from Last.fm provided by Ò. Celma [6], including the full listening history of 992 users up till May 2009. The Last.fm data involves 176,948 artists and a total of 19,150,868 user accesses to music tracks. We use two recommender system baselines: a probabilistic Latent Semantic Analysis (pLSA) recommender [14], which is among the top performing on this data; and a simple non-personalized recommender which recommends movies by popularity (i.e. by the number of ratings), which has shown to be competitive in these settings [11].

We follow the adaptation of the diversity problem to recommendation scenarios proposed in [25], by which items (here movies and music artists) are taken as the equivalent of documents, and users play the part of queries. Movie genre is used as the equivalent of query aspects in MovieLens, and social tags (assigned to artists by Last.fm users) are used for the same purpose in the music dataset. MovieLens includes 19 genres, whereas in Last.fm we use a total of 123,819 different tags.

The user-item interaction data (user ratings in MovieLens, artist playcounts in Last.fm) is split into training and test sets, following common experimental practice in the Recommender Systems field [13], where the test data are used as the equivalent of relevance judgments. In our experiments we take five random 80-20% splits of the MovieLens data and repeat for 5-fold cross-validation. In Last.fm we do a temporal 60-40% data split of the song access records based on their timestamp (see [6] for further details on the evaluation methodology we adhere to).

Since the aspect space is categorical, and aspects are associated to items in a binary way (movies either belong or do not belong to a genre, and similarly for artist tags), we take the simple approximation $p(c|d) \sim [d \in c]/\sum_{c'}[d \in c']$, where $[d \in c] = 1$ when d "has" the aspect (genre or tag) c, and zero otherwise. In other words, we assume a uniform conditional aspect distribution among the set of aspects covered by each item. Different from the search setting, we estimate the background aspect prior from the overall distribution of aspects in the set of items, given that the item-aspect association is explicit, manual, reliable, and therefore can be considered fairly informative. We estimate $p(r|k)$ by equation 9, using test ratings as relevance judgments for the computation of $P@k$, with a random 2-fold split of test users. We use very slight variations of the derivations in section 3.3, better suit-

Table 2. Comparative evaluation on MovieLens (left) and Last.fm (right) data, for diversification over a pLSA recommender baseline (top block), and recommendation by item popularity (bottom). The best result of each metric is highlighted in bold for each block. The improvement of the baselines is statistically significant in all cases. Improvements with respect to IA-Select and xQuAD (in this order) are marked with ▲ when statistically significant, and △ otherwise. Values with ▼ indicate a significant decrease respect to them. Statistical significance is established by Wilcoxon $p < 0.001$ in all cases. The value of λ that is used for xQuAD and RxQuAD is indicated next to each row and dataset block.

		MovieLens						Last.fm				
	λ	α-nDCG @20	ERR-IA @20	nDCG-IA @20	S-precision @r	S-recall @20	λ	α-nDCG @20	ERR-IA @20	nDCG-IA @20	S-precision @r	S-recall @20
pLSA	-	0.3108	0.1880	0.2189	0.0658	0.6448	-	0.1209	0.0684	0.1566	0.2710	0.0738
IA-Select	-	0.3079	0.1885	0.2195	0.0684	0.6567	-	0.1198	0.0778	0.1795	0.2669	0.0727
xQuAD	0.9	**0.3564**	0.2053	**0.2415**	0.0959	0.7453	1.0	0.1264	0.0794	0.1857	0.2866	0.0765
RxQuAD	0.5	0.3467▲▼	**0.2116▲△**	0.2294▲▼	**0.1195▲▲**	**0.7806▲▲**	1.0	**0.1428▲▲**	**0.1030▲▲**	**0.1914▲△**	**0.3543▲▲**	**0.0906▲▲**
Item popularity	-	0.1944	0.1013	0.1101	0.0677	0.7205	-	0.1329	0.0849	0.2022	0.1468	0.0604
IA-Select	-	0.2239	0.1448	0.1377	0.0666	0.7045	-	0.1250	0.0910	0.2139	0.1471	0.0602
xQuAD	0.9	0.2315	0.1243	0.1343	0.1010	0.7893	1.0	0.1345	0.0947	**0.2284**	0.1587	0.0641
RxQuAD	0.9	**0.2413▲▲**	**0.1494▲▲**	**0.1429▲▲**	**0.1947▲▲**	**0.8413▲▲**	1.0	**0.1421▲▲**	**0.1058▲▲**	0.2136▲▼	**0.2096▲▲**	**0.0790▲▲**

ed for model estimation on recommendation input data. We also found it effective to normalize the top-level diversity component in the xQuAD schemes before its linear combination with $p(r|d,q)$ (equations 3 and 5). We use a distribution-based normalization technique [12] for both versions (the original xQuAD and our variation) which showed to be effective in our experiments.

Figure 3 shows the performance of our relevance-based algorithm (RxQuAD) compared to xQuAD on MovieLens (left) and Last.fm (right), in terms of ERR-IA, for λ ranging from 0 to 1. The two collections are quite different both in their volumetric statistics (size, etc.), the nature of the user-item interaction data (movie ratings vs. music track playcounts), and the nature and distribution of item aspects (editorial genres vs. community-contributed tags), which accounts for the different behavior of the algorithms with respect to the λ parameter. In particular, the performance of our approach shows a drastic drop from λ = 0.9 to 1 in MovieLens, whereas it improves consistently with λ on Last.fm, peaking at λ = 1 (which corresponds, as pointed out in section 3.2, to the relevance-based version of IA-Select). We attribute this difference to the fact that the baseline performance on Last.fm is quite low, whereby diversifying involves a lower relevance loss (hence the optimum improvement with maximum diversification). MovieLens allows for better baseline performance, whereby moderating the diversity degree is more appropriate, and an extreme diversification results in a drastic accuracy loss. Overall the improvement respect to xQuAD is clear.

Table 2 shows results on further metrics, showing also the diversification of the popularity-based recommender baseline, in addition to pLSA. As in the experiments in search diversity, the λ parameter in xQuAD and RxQuAD is chosen to optimize for ERR-IA on each dataset. We see that our approach is consistently better in most cases. Only over pLSA in MovieLens we observe mixed results, with xQuAD producing better values on α-nDCG and nDCG-IA respectively, while RxQuAD is best on ERR-IA, and pure diversity –as measured by S-precision@r and S-recall. RxQuAD achieves clearer improvements on the popularity baseline. So it does on Last.fm for both baselines –except on nDCG-IA against popularity. This suggests that RxQuAD finds more room for improvement over the original algorithms on weak baselines (popularity recommendation vs. pLSA) and/or difficult datasets (Last.fm compared to MovieLens), with a low baseline effectiveness, whereas on a strong baseline run, there is no clear winner. We also observe that the IA-Select algorithm is not always effective on these recommendation tasks. We attribute this to the strong redundancy penalization of IA-Select (as we shall discuss later), which may involve a loss of relevant documents, particularly over a strong baseline like pLSA. The ineffectiveness is mostly observed in terms of α-nDCG, a metric which (by a default α = 0.5) applies a softer redundancy discount which IA-Select may mismatch. Furthermore, because of the $p(c|d)$ term, items with multiple aspects (which abound in Last.fm) are demoted by IA-Select, which explains some low subtopic recall values.

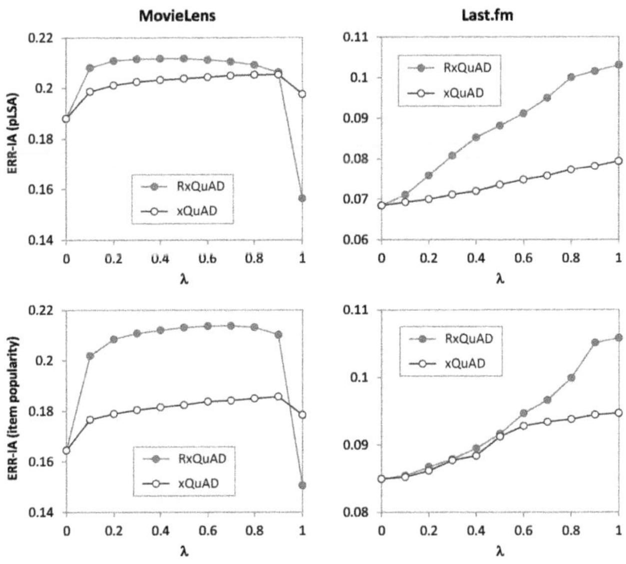

Figure 3. Comparative performance (measured by ERR-IA) of relevance-based diversification (RxQuAD) and xQuAD, ranging over values of λ. The algorithms are tested on the MovieLens 1M dataset (left), using movie genre as the query aspect space; and Last.fm (right) using social tags as information need aspects. pLSA is the baseline recommender system diversified in the two top graphics, and the popularity-based item recommender in the bottom ones.

5. RELEVANCE-BASED REDUNDANCY MANAGEMENT

Beyond the interest and potential advantages of the relevance-based diversification model as a stand-alone development, an explicit relevance model provides the basis for the introduction and derivation of further extensions on a formal probabilistic basis. We show this by extending our framework with an explicit model of the tolerance to redundancy: different tasks, or different users, introduce different conditions on how redundancy should be handled and penalized. We show next how this can be accounted for by a smooth generalization of our framework.

5.1 Tolerance to Redundancy

Let $stop$ denote, as in section 3.4, a binary random variable that is true when a user, in some retrieved document list browsing context, stops reading documents. And let $stop_S$ denote the fact that a user stops browsing at some point after reading some documents in a set S. We may refine the xQuAD diversity component as $p(r_d, \neg stop_S | q)$, where the marginal utility of the document d is defined in terms of the user stopping before reaching d. This results into a nuanced reformulation of the objective function:

$$g(d|q,c,S) = (1-\lambda)\, p(r|d,q) + \\ + \lambda \sum_c p(c|q)\, p(r|d,c,q) \prod_{d' \in S} \big(1 - p(stop|d',c,q)\big)$$

This form of the objective generalizes the original one by abstracting from the reasons why a document d –in the context of a particular ranking– would not add value to the effective utility of the result list.

Now, as we did in section 3.4 (equation 11, but here with further conditioning variables), we may marginalize the stopping probability with respect to relevance:

$$p(stop|d',c,q) = p(stop|d',c,q,r)\, p(r|d',c,q) + \\ + p(stop|d',c,q,\neg r)\, p(\neg r|d',c,q)$$

where again different simplifications can be considered. First, within the objective function for greedy document selection, we should consider $p(stop|d',c,q,\neg r) = 0$ for $d' \in S$, as the utility of the next document (which the objective function means to assess) would not be an issue if the user had stopped browsing already somewhere in S. Another reasonable simplification is to assume the user's decision to stop at a specific document only depends on finding relevance, i.e. $p(stop|d',c,q,r) \sim p(stop|r)$, whereby the model reduces to:

$$p(stop|d',c,q) \sim p(r|d',c,q)\, p(stop|r)$$

This way the original diversification algorithm is generalized to a form where an additional parameter $p(stop|r)$ represents the user tolerance to redundancy –or in some sense, how many documents it takes for the user to be satisfied:

$$g(d|q,c,S) = (1-\lambda)\, p(r|d,q) + \\ + \lambda \sum_c p(c|q)\, p(r|d,c,q) \prod_{d' \in S} \big(1 - p(r|d',c,q)\, p(stop|r)\big)$$

The introduction of this additional parameter allows to better match this characteristic of users and/or retrieval tasks. It allows to control (raise or soften) the penalization that should be applied to documents possessing aspects that are already covered in the original formulation of xQuAD. The latter implicitly assumes $p(stop|r) = 1$, that is, the user stops as soon as he finds a relevant document (zero tolerance to redundancy), which reflects again an implicit assumption that users are willing to select a single document –which is often not the case.

An equivalent parameter might be inserted in the original xQuAD formulation to soften redundancy penalization, but it would lack the formal justification that the relevance-based approach enables. Furthermore, the xQuAD redundancy penalization is already rather mild compared to RxQuAD, since the discounting term of the novelty component is based on document probabilities $p(d|c)$, which tend to range on much lower values (since they should sum to 1 over all documents covering an aspect) compared to a Bernoulli relevance distribution $p(r|d,c,q)$. The addition of a tolerance parameter to xQuAD would only make this worse –unless it ranged beyond [0,1], which would bring the scheme even farther from a formal probabilistic basis.

On the other hand, tolerance to redundancy has also been explicitly modeled and introduced in the context of metric formalization upon user models [5,8,15,24]. Therefore the use of this parameter in our diversification algorithm has the potential of a better optimization for such metrics by bringing the diversification model closer to the principles and assumptions which are built into the metrics.

5.2 Empirical Observation

In order to illustrate the effect of adjustable redundancy, we display as a heat map in Figure 4 the performance values of the generalized RxQuAD with different values of $p(stop|r)$, measured by α-nDCG with different values of α (also reflecting different degrees of redundancy tolerance). For this test, we select the TREC subtopics in the search task (with $p(r|k)$ estimated on relevance judgments), and the MovieLens dataset for the recommendation task. We keep the same values for λ as were selected in the previous experiments, and the pLSA baseline in the recommendation task. It can be observed that the redundancy penalization effect of $p(stop|r)$ is consistent with the equivalent parameter in the metric, i.e. the values evolve on a diagonal pattern: higher $p(stop|r)$ values in the algorithm perform better for higher α in the metric, and vice versa. The MovieLens graphic is smoother as the results are averaged over about 6,000 users (vs. 100 topics in TREC), and averaged again over 5 folds.

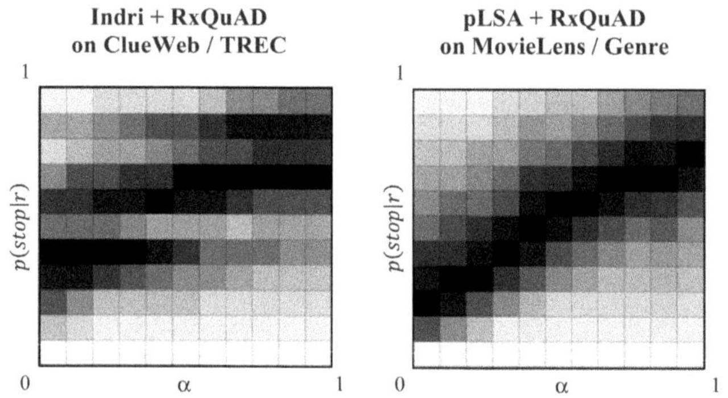

Figure 4. Parameterized tolerance to redundancy in the RxQuAD diversification algorithm by $p(stop|r)$, evaluated with corresponding metric configurations (α parameter in α-nDCG), by increments of 0.1. The values are displayed as a heat map where the darker colors (rank-normalized per column) represent higher α-nDCG values. The left map shows results for search diversity (over Indri) on ClueWeb with TREC subtopics, and the right map shows results recommendation diversity (over pLSA) on MovieLens with genres. A diagonal trend can be observed in the relative metric values.

6. DISCUSSION

In practical terms, using a relevance model in the redundancy component results in a higher redundancy penalization than is applied with a document generation model in xQuAD, as discussed in the previous section. Adding to one over all documents, the variations of $p(d|c)$ are quite small compared to $p(c|q)$, whereby subtopic coverage may tend to overdo redundancy in the overall effect of the algorithm. In contrast, the conditional Bernoulli relevance distribution $p(r|d,c,q)$ does not add to one in general over documents (unless the model assumes a unique relevant document), and may thus range over a significantly higher scale. Our relevance-oriented formulation hence enables a stronger redundancy penalization. This strength can be softened if needed, by the generalization for redundancy adaptation described in the previous section.

Compared to the original xQuAD, IA-Select goes to the opposite extreme in redundancy penalization: according to the approach described by Agrawal et al [1], redundancy is penalized by $p(c|d)$, which may have values close to 1 when documents cover a single aspect with high probability. The effect is that once an aspect is covered by some document in S, any other document covering this aspect is considered to add near zero marginal utility [28]. As a particular consequence, there is little discrimination between degrees of redundancy (i.e. an aspect that has been covered just once vs. further times before), and once all aspects have been covered, the diversified ranking degrades to the original order defined by the baseline retrieval system (see [26] for further analysis). Our relevance-oriented formulation does not result in such extremes either, as far as the probability of relevance, even at the high rank positions does usually not get as close to 1 as $p(c|d)$ may get. In practice, IA-Select may also soften the penalization by multiplying $p(c|d)$ by the baseline retrieval function. The penalization is also milder when documents cover several aspects, in which case $p(c|d)$ ranges over lower values. The algorithm implementation designer has no explicit control over these factors though –in contrast with our proposed extension for redundancy adjustment–, which may also account for the instability of IA-Select across heterogeneous experiments observed in section 4.

Besides these considerations, a relevance-based redundancy assessment better matches the structure of redundancy-sensitive metrics such has ERR-IA and α-nDCG, which are formalized in terms of probabilities of relevance [8]. This may partly account for the observed improved performance. The introduction of an explicit redundancy control parameter allows further gauging how aggressive the novelty-seeking component should be, enabling a finer adjustment to the role of redundancy in specific IR tasks and metrics.

Modeling tolerance to redundancy illustrates the potential advantages that an explicit relevance model brings about. Tolerance to redundancy could be introduced in the original formulations of IA-Select and xQuAD as well e.g. as a scalar parameter in the redundancy penalization component, but it is not clear how this might be given a principled –not simply heuristic– justification. As noted by Welch et al [28], "*common to a majority of prior research* [on search diversification] *is the single relevant document assumption*", which makes it difficult to explicitly formalize variable degrees of acceptable redundancy. The lack of this limitation might be credited as a virtue of an explicit relevance model. Though it has also been argued that a document generative model does not intrinsically negate the selection of several relevant documents [16], it is not clear how this multiple selection could be explicitly reflected upon a generative model. Welch et al [28] actually address this by explicitly modeling the number of relevant documents that the user is seeking to get. The alternative we show here has a considerably simpler development and does not require the introduction of this additional, somewhat artificial variable (the number of sought documents). Instead, our approach builds on models of user behavior, which are being extensively researched in the field (e.g. [8,15] among many other works).

A tradeoff of the relevance model is that it needs to be trained on relevance information –a tradeoff which is shared with PRP approaches in contrast to language modeling to build information retrieval systems. We have shown however that the need for training in our framework is not demanding in terms of the involved complexity, the data requirements, or the required accuracy, since a simple approach with few data proves to be good enough to produce quite competitive results. Furthermore, a rough rank-relevance estimate from a commercial search engine click log showed to be sufficient to obtain almost as good results as with expensive editorial relevance judgments.

7. CONCLUSION

IR diversification approaches proposed so far in the field use either an explicit representation of information need aspects, or an explicit relevance model, but not both. We have proposed and developed a revision of prior intent-oriented diversification schemes with the introduction of an explicit relevance model in the formulation of the approach. We observe that an explicit relevance model results in comparable or even better performance than prior approaches in terms of diversity evaluation metrics, in different application domains (search and recommendation) on different datasets. The approach thus favorably compares to its original alternatives, and might open new lines for effectiveness improvements.

From a theoretical standpoint, the relevance-oriented formulation provides an alternative –perhaps more direct– description of the diversity problem, whereupon the algorithmic scheme can be directly derived. The relevance-based foundation may be better suited for the description of diversification processes and their underlying principles: marginal utility, diminishing returns, relative value of documents, and so forth. Concepts such as relevance and utility find clear, unambiguous and more direct reflection in the framework itself. Furthermore, the formulation provides a more direct match of metric schemes in which relevance models underlie [5,8,15,24], therefore potentially providing for a better optimization against such metrics.

An additional side-effect of the relevance-oriented formulation is the unification of the IA-Select and xQuAD approaches into a common scheme. The proposed framework opens moreover new directions for further formal developments where relevance is an intrinsic variable. As a particular case, we show the formal extension of our framework to describe and adjust the algorithm to different degrees of tolerance to redundancy, the consistency of which is empirically validated.

8. ACKNOWLEDGMENTS

This work was supported by the national Spanish projects TIN2011-28538-C02-01 and S2009TIC-1542.

9. REFERENCES

[1] Agrawal, R., Gollapudi, S., Halverson, A., and Ieong, S. Diversifying search results. 2nd ACM International Conference on Web Search and Data Mining (WSDM 2009). Barcelona, Spain, February 2009, 5-14.

[2] Arampatzis, A. and Robertson, S. Modeling score distributions in information retrieval. Information Retrieval 14(1), 2011, 26-46.

[3] Bache, R., Baillie, M., and Crestani, F. Language models, probability of relevance and relevance likelihood. ACM International Conference on Information and Knowledge Management (CIKM 2007). Lisbon, Portugal, 2007, 853-856.

[4] Carbonell, J. G. and Goldstein, J. The Use of MMR, Diversity-Based Reranking for Reordering Documents and Producing Summaries. 21st Annual International ACM Conference on Research and Development in Information Retrieval (SIGIR 1998). Melbourne, Australia, August 2998, 335-336.

[5] Carterette, B. An analysis of NP-completeness in novelty and diversity ranking. Information Retrieval 14(1), February 2011, 89-106.

[6] Celma, Ò. and Herrera, P. A New Approach to Evaluating Novel Recommendations. 2nd ACM International Conference on Recommender Systems (RecSys 2008). Lausanne, Switzerland, 2008, 179-186.

[7] Chen, H. and Karger, D. R. Less is More. 29th Annual International ACM Conference on Research and Development in Information Retrieval (SIGIR 2006). Seattle, WA, USA, August 2006, 429-436.

[8] Clarke, C. L. A., Craswell, N., Soboroff, I., and Ashkan, A. A Comparative Analysis of Cascade Measures for Novelty and Diversity. 4th ACM International Conference on Web Search and Data Mining (WSDM 2011). Hong-Kong, China, February 2011, 75-84.

[9] Clarke, C. L. A., Craswell, N., Soboroff, I, and Cormack, G. V. Overview of the TREC 2010 Web Track. TREC 2010, Gaithersburg, MD, USA.

[10] Clarke, C. L. A., Kolla, M., Cormack, G. V., Vechtomova, O., Ashkan, A., Büttcher, S., and MacKinnon, I. Novelty and diversity in information retrieval evaluation. 31st Annual International ACM Conference on Research and Development in Information Retrieval (SIGIR 2008). Singapore, July 2008, 659-666.

[11] Cremonesi, P., Koren, Y., Turrin, R. Performance of recommender algorithms on top-n recommendation tasks. 4th ACM International Conference on Recommender Systems (RecSys 2010). Barcelona, Spain, September 2010, 39-46.

[12] Fernández, M., Vallet, D., and Castells, P. Using Historical Data to Enhance Rank Aggregation. 29th Annual International ACM Conference on Research and Development in Information Retrieval (SIGIR 2006). Seattle, WA, USA, August 2006, pp. 643-644.

[13] Herlocker, J. L., Konstan, J. A., Terveen, L. G., and Riedl, J. T. Evaluating collaborative filtering recommender systems. ACM Transactions on Information Systems 22, 1, 2004, 5-53.

[14] Hofmann, T. Latent semantic models for collaborative filtering. ACM Transactions on Information Systems 22(1), January 2004, 89-115.

[15] Hu, B., Zhang, Y., Chen, W., Wang, G., and Yang, Q. Characterizing Search Intent Diversity into Click Models. 20th International Conference on World Wide Web (WWW 2011). Hyderabad, India, March 2011, 17-26.

[16] Lafferty, L., Zhai, C. Probabalistic Relevance Models Based on Document and Query Generation. In Croft W.B. and Lafferty J. (Eds.), Language Modeling for Information Retrieval. Kluwer Academic Publishers, Dordrecht, Netherlands, 2003.

[17] Lee, J. H. Analyses of multiple evidence combination. 20th ACM SIGIR Conf. on Research and Development in Information Retrieval (SIGIR 1997). Philadelphia, PA, USA, July 1997, 267-276.

[18] Nottelmann, H. and Fuhr, N. From Retrieval Status Values to Probabilities of Relevance for Advanced IR Applications. Information Retrieval 6(3-4), September 2003, 363-388.

[19] Pan, B., Hembrooke, H., Joachims, T., Lorigo, L., Gay, G., and Granka, L.A. In Google We Trust: Users' Decisions on Rank, Position, and Relevance. Journal of Computer-Mediated Communication 12(3), June 2007, 801-823.

[20] Robertson, S. E. The Probability Ranking Principle in IR. Journal of Documentation 33(4), 1977, 294-304.

[21] Santos, R. L. T., Macdonald, C., and Ounis, I. Exploiting query reformulations for web search result diversification. 19th International Conference on World Wide Web (WWW 2010). Raleigh, NC, USA, April 2010, 881-890.

[22] Santos, R. L. T., Macdonald, C., and Ounis, I. On the Role of Novelty for Search Result Diversification. Information Retrieval. In Press.

[23] Spark-Jones, K., Robertson, S. E., Hiemstra, D., Zaragoza, H. Language Modelling and Relevance. In Croft W.B. and Lafferty J. (Eds.), Language Modeling for Information Retrieval. Kluwer Academic Publishers, Dordrecht, Netherlands, 2003.

[24] Vargas, S. and Castells, P. Rank and Relevance in Novelty and Diversity Metrics for Recommender Systems. 5th ACM Int. Conf. on Recommender Systems (RecSys 2011). Chicago, IL, October 2011, 109-116.

[25] Vargas, S., Castells, P., and Vallet, D. Intent-Oriented Diversity in Recommender Systems. 34th Annual International ACM SIGIR Conference on Research and Development in Information Retrieval (SIGIR 2011). Beijing, China, August 2011, 1211-1212.

[26] Vargas. S., Castells, P., and Vallet, D. On the Suitability of Intent Spaces for IR Diversification. International Workshop on Diversity in Document Retrieval (DDR 2012) at the 5th ACM International Conference on Web Search and Data Mining (WSDM 2012). Seattle, WA, USA, February 2012.

[27] Wang, J. and Zhu, J. Portfolio theory of information retrieval. 32nd Annual International ACM SIGIR Conference on Research and Development in Information Retrieval (SIGIR 2009). Boston, MA, USA, July 2009, 115-122.

[28] Welch, M. J., Cho, J., and Olston, C. Search result diversity for informational queries. 20th International Conference on World Wide Web (WWW 2011). Hyderabad, India, March 2011, 237-246.

[29] Zhai, C., Cohen, W. W., and Lafferty, J. Beyond independent relevance: Methods and evaluation metrics for subtopic retrieval. 26th Annual International ACM SIGIR Conference on Research and Development in Information Retrieval (SIGIR 2003). Toronto, Canada, July 2003, 10-17.

AspecTiles: Tile-based Visualization of Diversified Web Search Results

Mayu Iwata*
Microsoft Research Asia, China
Osaka University, Japan
iwata.mayu@ist.osaka-u.ac.jp

Tetsuya Sakai
Microsoft Research Asia, China
tetsuyasakai@acm.org

Takehiro Yamamoto
Microsoft Research Asia, China
Kyoto University, Japan
tyamamot@dl.kuis.kyoto-u.ac.jp

Yu Chen
Microsoft Research Asia, China
Yu.Chen@microsoft.com

Yi Liu
Microsoft Research Asia, China
lewisliu@microsoft.com

Ji-Rong Wen
Microsoft Research Asia, China
jrwen@microsoft.com

ABSTRACT

A diversified search result for an underspecified query generally contains web pages in which there are answers that are relevant to different aspects of the query. In order to help the user locate such relevant answers, we propose a simple extension to the standard Search Engine Result Page (SERP) interface, called AspecTiles. In addition to presenting a ranked list of URLs with their titles and snippets, AspecTiles visualizes the relevance degree of a document to each aspect by means of colored squares ("tiles"). To compare AspecTiles with the standard SERP interface in terms of usefulness, we conducted a user study involving 30 search tasks designed based on the TREC web diversity task topics as well as 32 participants. Our results show that AspecTiles has some advantages in terms of search performance, user behavior, and user satisfaction. First, AspecTiles enables the user to gather relevant information significantly more efficiently than the standard SERP interface for tasks where the user considers several different aspects of the query to be important at the same time (*multi-aspect tasks*). Second, AspecTiles affects the user's information seeking behavior: with this interface, we observed significantly fewer query reformulations, shorter queries and deeper examinations of ranked lists in multi-aspect tasks. Third, participants of our user study found AspecTiles significantly more useful for finding relevant information and easy to use than the standard SERP interface. These results suggest that simple interfaces like AspecTiles can enhance the search performance and search experience of the user when their queries are underspecified.

*This research was conducted while the first author was an intern at Microsoft Research Asia.

Permission to make digital or hard copies of all or part of this work for personal or classroom use is granted without fee provided that copies are not made or distributed for profit or commercial advantage and that copies bear this notice and the full citation on the first page. To copy otherwise, to republish, to post on servers or to redistribute to lists, requires prior specific permission and/or a fee.

SIGIR'12, August 12–16, 2012, Portland, Oregon, USA.

Copyright 2012 ACM 978-1-4503-1472-5/12/08 ...$10.00.

Categories and Subject Descriptors

H.3.3 [**Information Search and Retrieval**]; H.5.2 [**Interfaces**]: [Evaluation/methodology]

General Terms

Experimentation, Human Factors

Keywords

Diversified Search, Search Result, Visualization, User Study

1. INTRODUCTION

Search queries are often *ambiguous* ("office" may mean a workplace or a Microsoft product) or *underspecified* ("harry potter" may mean the books, the films or the main character) [7]. Given such queries, *search result diversification* aims to cover different search *intents* of the query in a single ranked list of retrieved documents [1]. We are particularly interested in underspecified queries as every query is arguably underspecified to some extent unless it is a perfect representation of the underlying information need. One possible way to explicitly represent these different intents would be to use *information types*, which we refer to as *aspects*[1]. For example, desired aspects of an underspecified query "elliptical trainer" (a stationary exercise machine) may include *product names*, *benefits* and *reviews*. The present study concerns what kind of interface would be effective for presenting a diversified ranked list of results obtained in response to such a query.

An underspecified query may possibly represent an information need for a specific aspect of a topic or for various aspects of a topic. For example, with the aforementioned "elliptical trainer" query, the user may be looking for *product names* of the elliptical trainer, or he may be looking for not only product names, but also *benefits* and *reviews* of elliptical trainers. Thus, we make a distinction between *single-aspect tasks* and *multi-aspect tasks* in our study. This is because the effectiveness of a search result presentation interface may depend on the variety of aspects that the user desires. Another possible viewpoint for categorizing search tasks would be the number of relevant answers the user requires (e.g. home page findings vs. recall-oriented search) [3, 17], but this study primarily concerns

[1]This usage of "aspect" is different from TREC, where it was used synonymously with "instance." [11, 12]

recall-oriented search where several answers that match a certain aspect of the query need to be collected by the user.

To help the user efficiently and effectively locate retrieved relevant answers that match the desired aspects within the Search Engine Result Page (SERP), we propose a simple extension to the standard SERP interface, which we call *AspecTiles*. Figure 1 shows a screenshot of the AspecTiles interface. As can be seen, AspecTiles visualizes which of the ranked web pages are relevant to which aspects by means of colored squares ("tiles") that are shown to the left of each document in the SERP. Moreover, the color represents the degree of relevance to an aspect. We believe that this line of research is important but missing in current search result diversification studies: even though most diversification systems rely on explicit identification of different search intents, a standard SERP interface does not tell the user which document is likely to be relevant to which of the intents, and to what degree. We hypothesized that a more informative interface such as AspecTiles will help web search engine users.

In this study, we conduct a user study involving 30 search tasks designed based on the TREC web diversity task topics as well as 32 participants to address the following Research Questions:

- RQ1: Does AspecTiles enable users to gather relevant information more effectively and efficiently when compared to the standard SERP interface?
- RQ2: Does AspecTiles affect the user's information seeking behavior? In what way?

RQ1 is the central question addressed in this paper. Compared to the standard SERP interface, AspecTiles provides the additional information of which documents are relevant to which aspects and to what degree. Thus, we expect the user to quickly scan the ranked list and locate relevant documents that match the desired aspects. Moreover, we would like to clarify under what conditions AspecTiles can be beneficial. For example, it is possible that AspecTiles may be more useful for multi-aspect tasks than for single-aspect tasks, as it can highlight the difference between a document that covers multiple aspects and one that covers only one aspect. Moreover, other factors such as the number of tiles displayed, the quality of the aspects represented as tiles and the accuracy of the estimated degree of relevance represented by the tile color may affect the outcome.

While RQ1 concerns user performance, RQ2 concerns user behavior. For example, we can hypothesize that, if the displayed aspects match well with the user's desired aspects, then the user can locate desired information without reformulating his query many times. Another possible hypothesis would be that, since AspecTiles enables the user to skip documents that are seemingly irrelevant to the desired aspects while scanning the ranked list, it may guide the user to documents that lie deeper in the ranked list.

The remainder of this paper is organized as follows. Section 2 discusses related work. Section 3 describes our experimental design for evaluating AspecTiles, and Section 4 presents our results. Finally, Section 5 concludes this paper and discusses future work.

2. RELATED WORK

Information visualization takes advantage of the user's visual information processing abilities by generating graphical representations of data or concepts for presenting textual information [21], and is known to be useful for quantitative comparisons [15]. Thus, many search result visualization methods have been proposed to provide the user with a quick overview of the retrieved documents. According to Turetken and Sharda [20], web documents can be visualized based on content (e.g., title and term frequency) [4, 9, 10, 14, 16, 23], connectivity (e.g., number of incoming and outgoing links), and others (e.g., metadata like document size and the web domain) [4, 10]. Our AspecTiles falls into the first category, as it visualizes the relevance of each retrieved web page with respect to each displayed aspect.

The TileBar interface proposed by Hearst [9] and the simpler HotMap interface proposed by Hoeber and Yang [14] are visually somewhat similar to AspecTiles. In TileBar, each retrieved document is represented by a rectangle, where the query terms are arranged vertically and the document length is represented horizontally. For each query term, its term frequency within each section of a document is represented in grayscale. In HotMap, a row of squares are shown to the left of each retrieved document, where each square represents a particular query term and its within-document term frequency. The user experiments by Hoeber and Yang suggested that HotMap is useful for effective and efficient information gathering. Our AspecTiles is different from TileBar and HotMap in that (a) the row of squares (which we call *tiles*[2]) represent possible aspects or intents of the query rather than the individual query terms of that query; and (b) the color of each tile represents the degree of relevance of the document to that particular aspect rather than term frequency. Thus, AspecTiles requires the backend search engine to provide a set of possible aspects given a query, and estimated per-aspect relevance scores. To our knowledge, our work is the first to study this kind of interface for the purpose of presenting diversified search results.

There are other ways to visualize search engine results, such as *glyph-based* and *graph-based* methods. Glyph-based approaches include the work by Heimonen and Jhaveri [10] who used document-shaped icons, and the work by Chau [4] who used a flower metaphor for representing statistics such as term frequency and document length. Graph-based approaches include bar charts of Reiterer *et al.* [16], and the radar charts of Yamamoto and Tanaka [23]. The radar charts were used for visualizing a fixed set of credibility criteria (accuracy, objectivity, authority, currency, and coverage). None of these studies was to do with multiple intents/aspects and search result diversification.

Brandt *et al.* [2] describe a method for dynamically presenting diversified search results. The main idea is to present a tree of web pages and dynamically recomputing it based on the nodes expanded by the user instead of showing a flat static list. While this rich presentation approach may have benefits, it is radically different from the standard SERP, and may be difficult to prevail. Moreover, its usability (e.g. the cognitive load of making the user backtrack within a tree, that of rearranging documents that the user has seen or has yet to see, etc.) is unknown. In contrast, AspecTiles lets the user go through a list just like traditional SERP, and is arguably easier for existing web search engines to adopt.

Our choice of using simple tiles (i.e. colored squares) for representing per-aspect relevance of retrieved documents is based on findings from previous research in user interface studies including the aforementioned ones. In particular, the user evaluation of HotMap [14] suggested that the simple interface offers effective and efficient information access as well as high user satisfaction. While HotMap users may quickly skip documents that are nonrelevant to the query and locate relevant documents with high query term frequencies, AspecTiles users may quickly skip documents that are nonrelevant to the *desired aspects of the query* and even locate relevant documents that cover multiple desired aspects. Fur-

[2]Note that Hearst's "tiles" refer to nonoverlapping text segments [9].

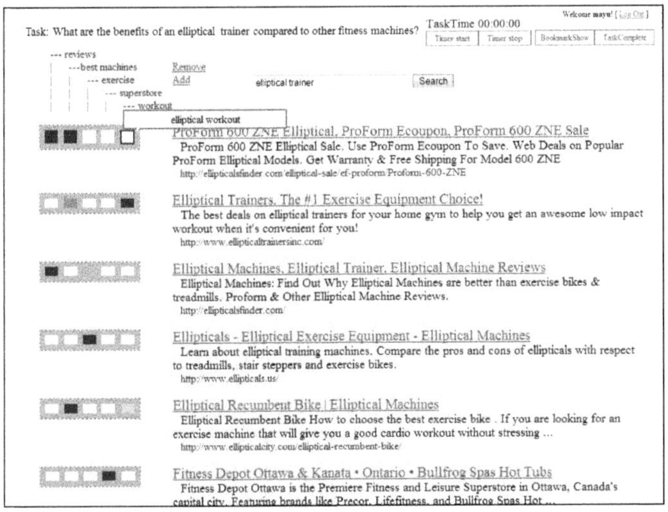

Figure 1: Screenshot of AspecTiles with five tiles (elliptical trainer).

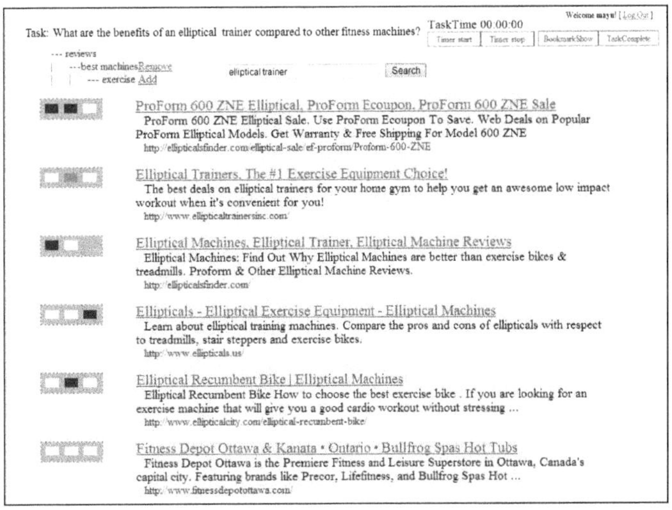

Figure 2: Screenshot of AspecTiles with three tiles (elliptical trainer).

thermore, Xiang *et al.* [22] compared a tree view and a list view to visualize criminal data relations, and reported that users may find it difficult to use unfamiliar interfaces like the tree view. Chen and Yu [5] conducted a meta-analysis of six information visualization usability studies for IR and also reported that users perform better with simple visual interfaces than with complex ones.

Regarding the underlying search engine that SERP interfaces require, a number of effective search result diversification algorithms have been proposed recently [1, 8, 18]. Any of these algorithms could be used with our AspecTiles presentation interface, provided that an explicit set of aspects of the given query and per-aspect relevance scores for each retrieved document are available. In this study, we use as input the diversified web search system described by Dou *et al.* [8]. This system was a top performer in the Japanese Document Ranking (search result diversification) subtask of the recent NTCIR-9 INTENT task [19].

3. EXPERIMENTAL DESIGN

This section describes a user study that we designed to address the research questions mentioned in Section 1: Is AspecTiles more effective and efficient than the standard SERP? How does it affect the user's search behavior?

3.1 Interfaces

We compared three prototype interfaces in our user experiments: AspecTiles with five tiles, AspecTiles with three tiles and a baseline interface with no tiles. The number of tiles refers to the *initial* setting – participants were allowed to change the number of displayed tiles during their search tasks, as we shall explain later. We initially displayed either five or three tiles because (a) too many tiles would mean a wide left margin for the SERP and therefore waste of space; and (b) showing too much information may have adverse effects on the user performance and satisfaction. Note, for example, that current web search engines typically show no more than eight query suggestions at a time.

Figures 1, 2 and 3 show screenshots of our three interfaces for the query "elliptical trainer." All interfaces show the title, snippet and URL of each ranked document. In addition, the two AspecTiles interfaces show (a) *aspect labels* (e.g. "reviews", "best machines", "exercise" etc.) at the top of SERP; (b) a colored tile for each displayed aspect, whose color represents the per-aspect relevance of the document in five-point scale (dark blue means highly relevant and light blue means marginally relevant); and (c) a popup text when the mouse is placed over a tile, which reminds the user of the aspect label. In addition, the user can freely adjust the number of displayed aspects to any number between zero and eight during the experiment, by clicking the Add or the Remove button. For example, if a user of the three-tile AspecTiles interface finds that none of the displayed aspects is useful, he may choose to click Add to show more aspects, some of which may turn out be relevant to his needs. Whereas, the baseline interface is very similar to popular search engines such as Google and Bing.

The three experimental interfaces share the same underlying diversification algorithm. When a query is issued, its top 300 search results and *query suggestions* are obtained using Bing API[3]. In our study, we treated these query suggestions as the aspects to be displayed on the interface, as they are easy to obtain, reasonably accurate and were effective for search result diversification with Dou *et al.*'s algorithm [8] at the NTCIR-9 INTENT task [19]. To save space, the aforementioned aspect labels were obtained after removing all query terms from each query suggestion; whereas, the original query suggestion string was shown in the popup text (e.g. "reviews" for the former and "elliptical trainer reviews" for the latter). A more sophisticated method that is dedicated to finding accurate aspects (information types) for AspecTiles deserves to be explored, but this is beyond the scope of our study: we focus on the usefulness of AspecTiles in a realistic situation where the displayed aspects do not perfectly overlap with the desired aspects.

Using the aspects thus obtained, we used the algorithm by Dou *et al.* to compute per-aspect relevance scores and to rerank the SERP obtained by Bing API. Our future plan includes letting the user click the tiles (as well as the aspect labels) on the AspecTiles interface and thereby dynamically rerank documents, but this is beyond the scope of the present study. Our current focus is to examine the effect of *showing* the tiles to the user rather than that of interacting with the tiles as well as with the aspect labels (query suggestions).

[3]http://www.bing.com/toolbox/bingdeveloper/

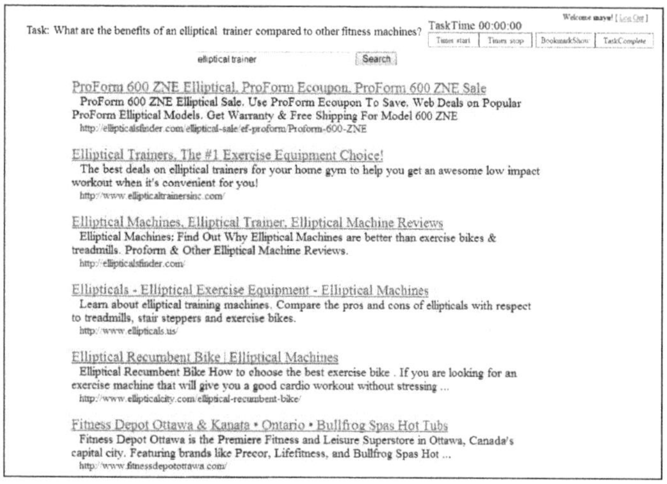

Figure 3: Screenshot of the baseline interface (elliptical trainer).

3.2 Tasks

As we hypothesized that AspecTiles may be more useful for multi-aspect tasks (e.g. Find *product names*, *benefits* and *reviews* of the elliptical trainer) than for single-aspect tasks (e.g. What are the *benefits* of an elliptical trainer?), we devised 15 multi-aspect tasks and 15 single-aspect tasks shown in Table 1. For this purpose, we carefully examined the TREC 2009 web diversity task topics and selected 15 *faceted* (i.e. underspecified) topics that had *informational* subtopics [6], so that each selected topic could be used as a resource for creating exactly one multi-aspect task and exactly one single-aspect task [4]. Figure 4 shows a selected topic: it contains a query field, a description field and several informational subtopics. From this topic, we created a multi-aspect task: "Find information about elliptical trainer machines. (reviews, benefits, product names)." The words in parenthesis correspond to the *desired aspects*, i.e., the types of information that the participants are asked to collect. In this example, these desired aspects correspond to informational subtopics 1, 3 and 4: for every multi-aspect task, we selected exactly three desired aspects. When more than three informational subtopics were available, we carefully selected three desired aspects from them so that the overlap between the selected aspects and the *displayed* aspects (i.e. query suggestions) are neither too high nor too low. As we mentioned earlier, we wanted to examine the realistic situation where the displayed aspects are of *reasonable* accuracy. In fact, the average number of informational subtopics per faceted topic was 3.8, so we used up most of the informational subtopics in the faceted topics. On the other hand, from the same topic, we created one single-aspect task: "What are the benefits of an elliptical trainer compared to other fitness machines?" Note that this is exactly subtopic 3. In summary, we prepared 15 multi-aspect tasks that require participants to look for exactly three aspects (e.g. reviews, benefits and product names), and 15 single-aspect tasks that require them to look for exactly one aspect (e.g. benefits).

[4]TREC diversity topics also have *navigational* subtopics, which we did not utilize as our focus was on collecting multiple answers that are relevant to each aspect.

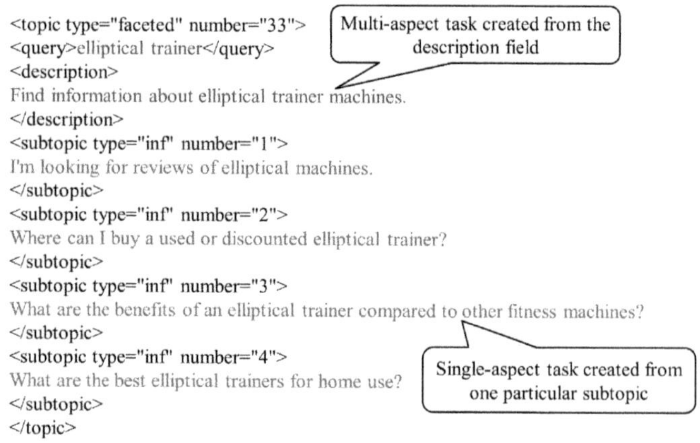

Figure 4: A sample topic from the TREC 2009 web diversity task.

3.3 Procedure

We hired 32 participants for our user study. 21 of them were male and 11 were female; 24 were students in computer science; four were researchers in computer science and the other four were desk workers. The average age of the participants was 26.18 years, with a standard deviation of 4.34.

Then we formed an experimental design similar to that of the TREC interactive track [13]. Each participant performed a total of six tasks (three multi-aspect and three single-aspect): two using the five-tile AspecTiles, two using the three-tile AspecTiles and the other two using the baseline. The choice and the order of systems and tasks were randomized for each participant.

Prior to the actual user experiment, each participant went through a training task to become familiar with the interfaces and the tasks. Each training session took approximately ten minutes.

For each of the six tasks, the participants were provided with a printed task description document that contained the initial query (e.g. "elliptical trainer"), a short explanation of the topic (e.g. "a stationary exercise machine"), (for multi-aspect tasks only) the three desired aspects (e.g. "reviews," "benefits" and "product names.") and some additional information if required. For the elliptical trainer example, the short explanation indicated that it is a kind of stationary exercise machine (description obtained from Wikipedia) and a sample picture of an elliptical trainer was shown to the participants as additional information. This is because the tasks that originate from TREC are not real information needs of the participants, and therefore the participants were not necessarily familiar with all of the tasks.

In each task session, the participant used one of the aforementioned three interfaces to collect as many *answers* as possible within ten minutes (for single-aspect tasks) or fifteen minutes (for multi-aspect tasks). An answer is a relevant instance that matches one of the desired aspects (e.g. a particular product name of elliptical trainer). When the participant clicked on a URL within the interface, a special landing page window popped up, from which he could extract arbitrary part of the HTML by a mouse drag and *bookmark* it. A single bookmark can contain multiple text segments from the same webpage, as well as images and links. A single *relevant* bookmark may contain one or multiple answers, and may even cover multiple desired aspects. For example, one bookmark may contain a product name of elliptical trainer, its review as well as its picture. Note that we used a special browsing interface to facilitate collection of answers rather than a standard web browser.

Table 1: Task list.

Topic	S: single-aspect task, M: multi-aspect task (three desired aspects)
elliptical trainer	S: What are the benefits of an elliptical trainer compared to other fitness machines? M: Find information about elliptical trainer machines. (reviews, benefits, product names)
disneyland hotel	S: What hotels are near Disneyland? M: Find information about hotels near Disneyland Resort in California. (packages, reviews, coupons)
getting organized	S: Find catalogs of office supplies for organization and decluttering. M: Find tips, resources, supplies for getting organized and reducing clutter. (tips, resources, supplies)
dinosaurs	S: I'm looking for free pictures of dinosaurs. M: I want to find information about and pictures of dinosaurs. (pictures, names, games)
poker tournaments	S: Find books on tournament poker playing. M: I want to find information about live and online poker tournaments. (schedules, game names, books)
volvo	S: Where can I find Volvo semi trucks for sale (new or used)? M: I'm looking for information on Volvo cars and trucks. (reviews, dealers, product names)
rick warren	S: I want to see articles and web pages about the controversy over Rick Warren's invocation at the Obama inauguration. M: I'm looking for information on Rick Warren, the evangelical minister. (biography, articles, books)
diversity	S: What is cultural diversity? What is prejudice? M: Find information on diversity, both culturally and in the workplace. (management methods, definition, poems)
starbucks	S: Find the menu from Starbucks, with prices. M: Find information about the coffee company Starbucks. (menu, calories, coupons)
diabetes education	S: Find free diabetes education materials such as videos, pamphlets, and books. M: I'm looking for online resources to learn and teach others about diabetes. (materials, diet, classes)
atari	S: I want to read about the history of the Atari 2600 and other Atari game consoles. M: Find information about Atari, its game consoles and games. (history, classic games, arcade games)
cell phones	S: What cell phone companies offer Motorola phones? M: Find information about cell phones and cellular service providers. (provider names, prices, reviews)
hoboken	S: Find restaurants in Hoboken. M: Find information on the city of Hoboken, New Jersey. (restaurants, history, real estate)
orange county convention center	S: What hotels are near the Orange County Convention Center? M: Looking for information about the Orange County Convention Center in Orlando, Florida. (event schedules, hotels, restaurants)
the secret garden	S: Find reviews of the various TV and movie adaptations of The Secret Garden. M: Find information and reviews about The Secret Garden book by Frances Hodgson Burnett as well as movies and the musical based on it. (reviews, summary, music)

But this condition was the same across the three interfaces that we wanted to compare.

The query field of the original TREC topic served as the initial query for each task, so that each participant began his task by looking at a diversified search result. However, participants were also allowed to freely reformulate the query. As was mentioned earlier, they were allowed to change the number of displayed aspects to an arbitrary number between zero and eight in the AspecTiles interfaces during the experiment.

Participants were also allowed to finish their task sessions prior to the time limit if they felt that their collected answers were complete. After each task session, they were asked to fill out a post-task questionnaire. After completing all of the six task sessions, they were asked to fill out an exit questionnaire. The entire procedure for one participant took approximately one hour.

4. RESULTS

Section 4.1 discusses the results for RQ1 (search performance); 4.2 discusses the results for RQ2 (search behavior); and 4.3 discusses the questionnaire results.

4.1 Search performance

4.1.1 Bookmark relevance assessment

Through 192 task sessions (32 participants, each with 6 tasks), a total of 1,262 bookmarks were obtained. In order to evaluate user performance for these task sessions, three annotators independently assessed all of these bookmarks. Figure 5 is a screenshot of the assessment tool we developed for that purpose: the left panel shows a particular bookmark (a part of an HTML file) to be assessed with radio buttons for selecting a relevance grade ("highly relevant," "somewhat relevant" or "not relevant"). For multi-aspect tasks, if a bookmark was judged relevant, then the assessors were also asked to check on one or more of the desired aspects that the bookmark contained. The inter-assessor agreement was quite high (Fleiss' kappa: 0.666). Based on the three assessment sets, we constructed two ground-truths: *strict* and *lenient* sets. In the former, the relevance grade of each bookmark reflects the lowest relevance grade for that bookmark among the three assessors, and the matched aspects of that bookmark are obtained by taking the intersection of the three assessors' selected aspects. In the latter, the relevance grade of each bookmark reflects the highest relevance grade for that bookmark among the three assessors, and the matched aspects of that bookmark are obtained by taking the union of the three assessors' selected aspects. Thus, the strict set reflects the view: "nothing is relevant unless all three assessors say that it is relevant" while the lenient set reflects the view: "anything is relevant if at least one assessor says that it is relevant."

4.1.2 Effectiveness and Efficiency

Using the strict and lenient sets of ground truths, we compared the user effectiveness and efficiency for AspecTiles and for the baseline interface. For each task session, let n be the number of relevant bookmarks found by a particular user. Then precision is n divided by the number of bookmarks found by that user for that task session, and recall is n divided by the total number of known relevant bookmarks for that task session. As measures of search efficiency, we also measured the time taken to obtain the *first relevant* bookmark ("Time-FirstRel"), the number of document clicks before the first relevant bookmark was obtained

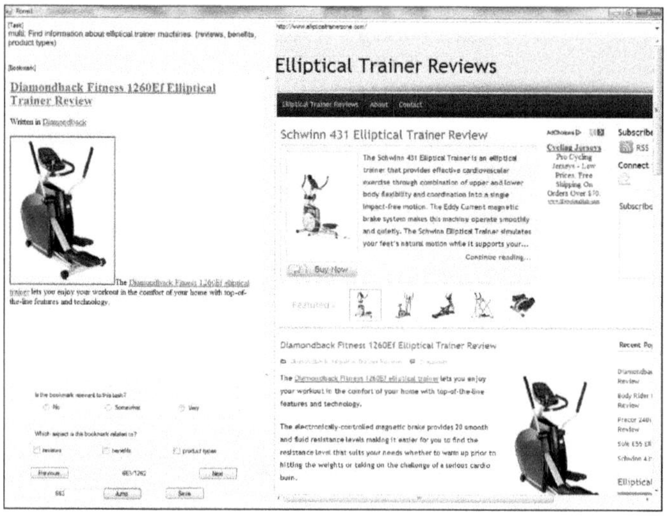

Figure 5: Screenshot of the assessment tool. The left panel shows a bookmark (containing a picture, a product name and its review) and the right panel shows the entire page from which the bookmark was extracted.

("DocClick-FirstRel"), the average time between obtaining a relevant bookmark and obtaining the next relevant bookmark ("Time-TwoRel"), and the average number of document clicks between obtaining a relevant bookmark and obtaining the next relevant bookmark ("DocClick-TwoRel"). Clearly, all of these statistics should be low for an ideally efficient interface. For multi-aspect tasks that require three aspects, we also compute aspect coverage, i.e. the fraction of desired aspects covered by the user's bookmarks (which can range from $0/3$ to $3/3$).

Tables 2 and 3 show the user effectiveness and efficiency results with the strict and lenient sets, respectively. For both task types (single-aspect and multi-aspect), we conducted a two-factor (interface and task) ANOVA at $p \leq 0.05$ for all types of measurements. For single-aspect tasks, only the task effect was significant for Precision, Time-FirstRel, DocClick-FirstRel, Time-TwoRel, and DocClick-TwoRel; none of the effects was significant for Recall. For multi-aspect tasks, only the task effect was significant for Precision and Aspect coverage, and only the system effect was significant for Recall, Time-FirstRel, DocClick-FirstRel, Time-TwoRel, and DocClick-TwoRel. If a significant interaction was found, we also conducted a Bonferroni post-hoc test at $p \leq 0.05$ between two interfaces. In the tables, statistically significant differences with the baseline are shown in bold.

In multi-aspect tasks, it can be observed that the five-tile AspecTiles demonstrated significantly higher recall than the baseline. Moreover, although not statistically significant, it can be observed that Precision and Aspect Coverage values also tend to be higher with AspecTiles. On the other hand, it can be observed that AspecTiles is significantly better than the baseline in terms of Time-FirstRel, DocClick-FirstRel, Time-TwoRel and DocClick-TwoRel. The latter two statistics in particular show that even the three-tile AspecTiles is advantageous over the baseline. Thus, we can conclude that, for multi-aspect tasks, AspecTiles lets the user collect relevant pieces of information in shorter time using fewer clicks than the baseline, while keeping the user effectiveness at least comparable. In addition, note that, for multi-aspect tasks, the measurements for five-tile AspecTiles are consistently better than those for three-tile AspecTiles. Although the differences are not statistically

Table 2: Effectiveness and efficiency results (strict). The average of all 32 task sessions is reported, with the standard deviation in parenthesis. Significant differences with the baseline at $p \leq 0.05$ according to the Bonferroni post-hoc test are shown in bold.

Task type		Baseline	Three-tile AspecTiles	Five-tile AspecTiles
Single	Precision	0.498	0.496	0.469
		(0.387)	(0.409)	(0.395)
	Recall	0.143	0.154	0.152
		(0.127)	(0.193)	(0.145)
	Time -FirstRel	187.5	193.4	183.8
		(96.8)	(108.4)	(100.9)
	DocClick -FirstRel	2.500	1.655	2.258
		(2.502)	(1.738)	(2.065)
	Time -TwoRel	99.8	89.3	113.4
		(63.6)	(70.1)	(76.9)
	DocClick -TwoRel	2.631	2.234	2.997
		(1.348)	(1.061)	(1.742)
Multi	Precision	0.684	0.685	0.717
		(0.248)	(0.252)	(0.232)
	Recall	0.130	0.184	**0.214**
		(0.088)	(0.178)	(0.204)
	Aspect Coverage	0.644	0.741	0.759
		(0.315)	(0.233)	(0.250)
	Time -FirstRel	166.9	130.3	**118.0**
		(117.0)	(92.7)	(120.6)
	DocClick -FirstRel	3.345	1.963	**1.714**
		(3.199)	(1.055)	(0.897)
	Time -TwoRel	115.5	**82.4**	**69.3**
		(77.1)	(77.0)	(48.4)
	DocClick -TwoRel	2.808	**2.087**	**1.997**
		(1.607)	(1.270)	(0.598)

significant in our experiment, this suggests that displaying tiles is beneficial.

For single-aspect tasks, we cannot claim that AspecTiles is effective as there are no significant differences observed. We attribute this mainly to the fact that for single-aspect tasks, the chance of finding the desired aspect within the displayed aspects is smaller compared to multi-aspect tasks. For example, for both the single-aspect task "What cell phone companies offer Motorola phones?" and the multi-aspect task "Find information about cell phones and cellular service providers. (provider names, prices, reviews)," the initial query automatically issued by the system was "cell phones." As a result, in both tasks, the initially displayed aspects (obtained from query suggestions in response to "cell phones") were "providers, verizon, sprint" in three-tile AspecTiles, and additionally "prepaid, cheap" in five-tile AspecTiles. While the displayed aspects such as "providers" and "cheap" are probably directly useful for the multi-aspect task as it requires "provider names" and "prices," they are probably not useful for the particular single-aspect task as "motorola" is not included in them. We manually counted the number of initially displayed aspects that are actually relevant to the desired aspects for all task sessions: it was 0.683 for single-aspect tasks and 1.113 for multi-aspect tasks on average. The next section investigates this effect of quality of the displayed aspects in more detail.

Table 3: Effectiveness and efficiency results (lenient). The average of all 32 task sessions is reported, with the standard deviation in parenthesis. Significant differences with the baseline at $p \leq 0.05$ according to the Bonferroni post-hoc test are shown in bold.

Task type		Baseline	Three-tile AspecTiles	Five-tile AspecTiles
Single	Precision	0.615 (0.425)	0.581 (0.441)	0.649 (0.383)
	Recall	0.136 (0.107)	0.148 (0.151)	0.185 (0.149)
	Time -FirstRel	176.2 (100.0)	183.9 (105.3)	155.8 (87.7)
	DocClick -FirstRel	2.188 (2.086)	2.207 (2.555)	1.871 (1.408)
	Time -TwoRel	94.1 (65.4)	107.9 (91.2)	90.8 (54.1)
	DocClick -TwoRel	2.461 (1.354)	2.758 (2.328)	2.285 (1.170)
Multi	Precision	0.772 (0.245)	0.802 (0.285)	0.849 (0.221)
	Recall	0.127 (0.081)	0.173 (0.103)	**0.213** (0.194)
	Aspect Coverage	0.733 (0.296)	0.828 (0.262)	0.828 (0.246)
	Time -FirstRel	165.3 (117.4)	124.3 (87.8)	**114.0** (118.0)
	DocClick -FirstRel	3.333 (3.188)	1.926 (1.072)	**1.643** (0.870)
	Time -TwoRel	110.6 (76.0)	**72.9** (62.5)	**66.6** (47.3)
	DocClick -TwoRel	2.749 (1.615)	**1.987** (1.211)	**1.920** (0.564)

4.1.3 *Effect of Quality of Displayed Aspects and Relevance Estimation Accuracy*

AspecTiles requires as input (a) a set of aspects to be displayed in response to a query; and (b) per-aspect relevance score for each retrieved document. In this study, we chose to use query suggestions for (a), and a state-of-the-art diversified web search system [8] for (b), so that we can study the advantages of AspecTiles in a practical situation. Thus, in our study, both the quality of the displayed aspects and the estimated per-aspect relevance score (shown as colors of the tiles) are far from perfect. In this section, we investigate their effects on user effectiveness.

To investigate the effect of displayed aspect quality on user effectiveness, we computed precision, recall and (for multi-aspect tasks only) aspect coverage of the bookmarks at the *query level* rather than the task session level as was done in Section 4.1.2. This is because participants can issue multiple queries during a task session, and the displayed aspects (and therefore their quality) change accordingly within the task session. For each issued query, let n be the number of relevant bookmarks found by a particular user for that query. Then *per-query* precision is n divided by the number of bookmarks found by that user for that query, *per-query* recall is n divided by the total number of known relevant bookmarks for that query. We also compute *per-query* aspect coverage, i.e. the fraction of desired aspects covered by the user's bookmarks for that query. The quality of each set of displayed aspects was computed automatically: if a displayed aspect had at least one overlapping word with the task sentence, it was regarded as relevant; the quality of the displayed aspects set was defined as the fraction of such relevant displayed aspects.

Table 4: Spearman's rank correlation between user effectiveness (strict) and the quality of displayed aspects / relevance estimation accuracy.

Task type		Displayed aspect quality	Relevance estimation accuracy
Single	Precision	0.334	0.496
	Recall	0.300	0.490
Multi	Precision	0.434	0.506
	Recall	0.324	0.516
	Aspect Coverage	0.369	0.506

On the other hand, to investigate the effect of relevance estimation accuracy, we computed precision, recall and (for multi-aspect tasks only) aspect coverage of the bookmarks *for every clicked document*. This is because the quality of estimated per-aspect relevance score for each clicked document change accordingly within the task session. For each clicked document, let n be the number of relevant bookmarks found by a particular user on that document. Then *per-document* precision is n divided by the number of bookmarks found by that user within a particular document, *per-document* recall is n divided by the total number of known relevant bookmarks within that document. We also compute *per-document* aspect coverage, i.e. the fraction of desired aspects covered by the user's bookmarks within that document. For example, if two bookmarks were saved from a clicked document and only one of them was relevant, the precision for this document is 0.5. For computing these metrics, the first author of this paper manually examined all 1,483 clicked documents obtained in our experiments, and identified *false alarms*: a false alarm is a document-aspect pair that AspectTiles presented as relevant even though in fact the document content suggested otherwise. (Whereas, she did not check for *misses*: relevant document-aspect pairs which AspecTiles failed to present as relevant.)

Tables 4 and 5 show the Spearman's rank correlation values between user effectiveness and the aspect quality / relevance estimation accuracy with the strict and lenient sets, respectively. Recall that the user effectiveness values were computed per query for the displayed aspect quality and per document for the relevance estimation accuracy. It can be observed that user effectiveness (precision, recall and aspect coverage) is indeed correlated with the quality of displayed aspects and with the accuracy of estimated per-aspect relevance scores. The correlation is especially high for the latter. These results suggest that AspecTiles would be even more effective if the underlying search system can provide more appropriate selection of aspects to be displayed, as well as accurate per-aspect relevance scores. Note that showing innacurate relevance scores (in the form of colors) may seriously mislead the user: if the system fails to indicate that a document is relevant from a certain aspect, the user may skip the document; conversely, if the system shows a false positive for a certain aspect, the user may be forced to visit a document that is not useful to him.

4.2 Search Behavior

Now we discuss RQ2: how does AspecTiles affect the user's information seeking behavior? For this purpose, we recorded the participants's every operation performed on the three interfaces during the aforementioned experiments.

Table 5: Spearman's rank correlation between user effectiveness (lenient) and the quality of displayed aspects / relevance estimation accuracy.

Task type		Displayed aspect quality	Relevance estimation accuracy
Single	Precision	0.320	0.522
	Recall	0.287	0.506
Multi	Precision	0.411	0.555
	Recall	0.392	0.542
	Aspect Coverage	0.327	0.523

4.2.1 *Search Behavior Measurements*

Table 6 summarizes the number of query reformulations, the average query lengths (including the initial query and the queries reformulated by the participants), the average rank of clicked documents ("Rank-All"), the average rank of clicked documents that contain at least one relevant bookmark in the strict set ("Rank-Rel (strict)"), and the average rank of clicked documents that contain at least one relevant bookmark in the lenient set ("Rank-Rel (lenient)"). As before, for both task types (single-aspect and multi-aspect), we conducted a two-factor (interface and task) ANOVA at $p \leq 0.05$ for all types of measurements. For multi-aspect tasks, the interface effect was significant for all measures; for single-aspect tasks, none of the effects was significant. We thus conducted a Bonferroni post-hoc test at $p \leq 0.05$ between two interfaces for multi-aspect tasks; significant differences with the baseline are shown in bold. It can be observed that, when the participants used AspecTiles for multi-aspect tasks, they performed significantly fewer query reformulations, issued shorter queries, and clicked documents that are deeper in the ranked list, compared to the baseline interface. Though not statistically significant, similar trends can be observed for single-aspect tasks, except for the query length. We also examined other measurements such as the number of clicked documents and the time to complete the task session, but did not find any clear trends.

The above significant differences between AspecTiles and the baseline interface are quite intuitive. With AspecTiles, users perform fewer query reformulations probably because the displayed aspects serve as an alternative to forming new queries. For example, if the displayed aspects represent more specific information needs than the current query, then the user may not have to add a new query term to the current query to explicitly specialize his need. This is also reflected in the significant differences in the average query length. Moreover, with AspecTiles, users dig deeper in the ranked lists, probably because AspecTiles lets the user quickly skip documents that appear to be irrelevant to the desired aspects. That is, provided that the choice of displayed aspects and the per-aspect relevance shown in colors are both sufficiently accurate, AspecTiles may be able to let the user reach the desired documents efficiently. Moreover, note that five-tile AspecTiles outperforms three-tile AspecTiles in all of these measurements, though the differences are not statistically significant.

4.2.2 *Search Behavior Sample*

Section 4.2.1 discussed the summary statistics that represent user behavior. We now discuss the actual operation sequences of the participants. Figure 6 shows some typical user operations handpicked from our multi-aspect tasks; similar data for single-aspect tasks are omitted due to lack of space. Each box represents a particular user operation on the interface, and a row of boxes represent a

Table 6: Number of query reformulations, query length, and the average rank of clicked documents. The average and interquartile range values are reported. Significant differences with the baseline at $p \leq 0.05$ according to the Bonferroni post-hoc test are shown in bold.

Task type		Baseline	Three-tile AspecTiles	Five-tile AspecTiles
Single	Query reform	2.313 (0-8)	1.724 (0-5)	1.548 (0-5)
	Query length	2.585 (1-7)	2.532 (1-5)	2.646 (1-8)
	Rank-All	7.502 (1-46)	8.899 (1-49)	8.285 (1-47)
	Rank-Rel (strict)	6.968 (1-27)	10.025 (1-39)	8.511 (1-47)
	Rank-Rel (lenient)	7.132 (1-27)	9.929 (1-39)	9.155 (1-47)
Multi	Query reform	3.900 (0-13)	2.370 (0-10)	**1.552** (0-9)
	Query length	2.741 (1-7)	2.347 (1-5)	**2.189** (1-5)
	Rank-All	7.229 (1-70)	**10.785** (1-81)	**13.152** (1-95)
	Rank-Rel (strict)	7.294 (1-40)	**12.426** (1-61)	**13.725** (1-86)
	Rank-Rel (lenient)	7.282 (1-40)	**12.108** (1-61)	**13.347** (1-86)

particular participant's task session over a timeline. The operations shown are: "select a highly/somewhat relevant bookmark of the lenient set" (number of aspects covered by the bookmark is shown); "select a Nonrelevant answer of the lenient set" (indicated by **N**)); "reformulating a Query" (**Q**); "click a Document" (**D**); "put mouse over a tile to show the Popup label" (**P**); and "increase number of Tiles" (**T**).

Figure 6 confirms some of our aforementioned findings more qualitatively, and offers some additional insights into user behavior. For example, by comparing the rows of five-tile AspecTiles with those of the baseline, it can be observed not only that the latter contains more query reformulation operations (**Q**'s), but that participants often reformulated queries at the very beginning of the search interactions with the baseline interface (See lines (1) and (4)). With the baseline interface, the number of sessions beginning with an immediate query reformulation was 17 for single-aspect tasks and 12 for multi-aspect tasks; in contrast, with five-tile AspecTiles, the same statistic was 8 for single-aspect tasks and 4 for multi-aspect tasks. Moreover, it can be observed that the number of clicked documents before finding the first relevant bookmark (**D**'s to the left of the first square with a number) tends to be smaller with AspecTiles, which is again in line with our quantitative results. Furthermore, it can be observed that, with AspecTiles, participants tend to find a larger number of relevant bookmarks and relevant aspects, although these trends were not statistically significant in our quantitative results.

Next, we discuss typical usage patterns of AspecTiles, which we have observed physically during the user experiments and also from the operation logs that we analyzed postmortem. An AspecTile user typically begins a session by checking the aspect labels of the initial search result. If the displayed aspects seem appropriate, he utilizes the tiles, i.e. place a mouse over a tile and see the aspect label as a popup text, and clicks the document. In Figure 6, this can

Topic	Line	Interface	Operation sequence
atari	(1)	Baseline	Q D N D D D D Q D D Q D D D D D N D D 2 2 D 2 2 D 2
atari	(2)	Three-tile	P D D 3 3 3 3 3 3 3 D D D D 3 2 2 1 2 1 D D 2 3 P Q D 2 2 2 P D 3
atari	(3)	Five-tile	P D P D N N N N N N P D 1 1 1 2 2 2 1 2 D
disneyland hotel	(4)	Baseline	Q D Q D D 1 D D D Q D N D 1 Q Q D Q D 1 D D D Q Q D
disneyland hotel	(5)	Three-tile	Q P D N Q D 1 D P D 1 P D 1 Q D D N D 1 D N N Q D N D 2 D D 1 1 1
disneyland hotel	(6)	Five-tile	D 1 1 1 P D D P D 1 P D P D 1 P D P D P D P D P D N P D 1
rick warren	(7)	Baseline	D D D Q D D D D D 1 Q Q D D D 1 D D D Q Q D D D
rick warren	(8)	Three-tile	T T D D 1 D 1 D 1 D D D 2 2 D 1 D D P D 1
rick warren	(9)	Five-tile	D 1 D 1 P T T T P D P D P D 2 D D P Q D P Q D P D P

Figure 6: The participants' operation sequences in nine task sessions. The operations shown are: "select a highly/somewhat relevant bookmark of the lenient set" (number of aspects covered by the bookmark is shown); "select a Nonrelevant answer of the lenient set" (indicated by N)); "reformulating a Query" (Q); "click a Document" (D); "put mouse over a tile to show the Popup label" P; "increase number of Tiles" T.

be seen as a repetition of **P**'s and **D**'s (See lines (2), (3) and (6)). On the other hand, if the displayed aspects look unsatisfactory, the user often increases tiles and reformulate queries, as represented by **T**'s and **Q**'s in the figure (See lines (5) and (8)). For example, line (8) represents a multi-aspect task for "I'm looking for information on Rick Warren, the evangelical minister. (biography, articles, books)," where the initially displayed aspect labels were "controversy, obama, sermons." As the user judged that these displayed aspects did not directly match the three desired aspects, he immediately increased the number of displayed aspects (two **T**'s at the beginning of the session). Again, this example suggests that the quality of the displayed aspects is important. Moreover, Figure 6 line (3) contains many nonrelevant bookmarks (**N**'s), and this was because the document clicked by the user had a high estimated relevance to the aspect "(atari) classic games" even though it in fact discussed many other types of games besides Atari. Thus the user was misled by the color displayed by AspecTiles. Again, this highlights the importance of providing accurate relevance per-aspect estimates to the user.

As an additional and inconclusive remark, it appeared that while participants with high computer skills (e.g. researchers) tended to actively reformulate queries without referring to the tiles, those with relatively lower computer skills tended to rely on the tiles. While it is possible that AspecTiles may be more helpful to the latter class of users, we will have to design a new experiment with a larger set of participants to pursue this new research question.

4.3 User Satisfaction

Finally, we discuss the results of the exit questionnaire, which we summarized in Table 7. The participant's answer to each question was on a five point scale: from 1 (strongly disagree) to 5 (strongly agree). The Mann-Whitney's U test at $p \leq 0.05$ was used to compare AspecTiles with the baseline. Note that only Question 6 was asked separately for three-tile and five-tile AspecTiles. It can be observed that the participants found AspecTiles useful for finding relevant information, easy to use and that they are willing to use it again, compared to the baseline (Q1-Q3). Moreover, participants seemed to prefer the five-tile version to the three-tile version (Q6), although the difference is not statistically significant. Recall that the user effectiveness was indeed generally higher with five-tile AspecTiles than with the three-tile version.

We also received some additional feedback from participants. Five participants remarked that they wanted to select or create their own aspects to display; other five remarked that reranking the search result by a selected aspect would be very useful. In summary, AspecTiles was generally popular with the participants, and some of them wanted even more advanced features in it.

For the results of the post-task questionnaire, we asked the participants to answer four questions: "Are you familiar with this topic?," "Was it easy to do the search on this topic?," "Are you satisfied with your search results?" and "Did you have enough time to do an effective search?," but we could not find any clear trends among the three interfaces.

5. CONCLUSIONS

In this study, we proposed a simple extension to the standard SERP interface for presenting a diversified search result for an underspecified query. AspecTiles shows a row of tiles to the left of each retrieved document, where each tile represents a particular aspect of the query and the per-aspect relevance degree of that document. To compare AspecTiles with the standard SERP interface in terms of usefulness, we conducted a user study involving 30 search tasks designed based on the TREC web diversity task topics as well as 32 participants. Our main findings are:

- In multi-aspect tasks, participants were significantly more efficient with AspecTiles than with the baseline interface, in terms of time to find the first relevant bookmark, number of documents clicked before finding the first relevant bookmark, the average time between finding two relevant bookmarks, and the average number of document clicks between finding two relevant bookmarks. On the other hand, the search effectiveness with AspecTiles was at least as high as that with the baseline: in fact, the five-tile AspecTiles significantly outperformed the baseline in terms of recall as well.

- In multi-aspect tasks, AspecTiles users used significantly fewer query reformulations, shorter queries, and dug deeper in the ranked list, compared to users of the baseline interface.

- Participants of our user study found AspecTiles significantly more useful for finding relevant information, easier to use, and were more willing to use it again than the baseline interface.

These results suggest that simple interfaces like AspecTiles can enhance the search performance and search experience of the user when their queries are underspecified. While we did not obtain statistically significant results for single-aspect tasks, the general trend suggests that AspecTiles may help these cases as well.

Table 7: Exit questionnaire results. The average and standard deviation values are reported. Significant differences with the baseline at $p \leq 0.05$ according to the Mann-Whitney's U test are shown in bold.

<table>
<tr><th>Questions</th><th>Baseline</th><th>Three-tile AspecTiles</th><th>Five-tile AspecTiles</th></tr>
<tr><td>Q1: Did you find the interface useful for finding relevant information?</td><td>2.875 (0.941)</td><td colspan="2">3.718 (0.581)</td></tr>
<tr><td>Q2: Was it easy to use the interface?</td><td>3.156 (0.919)</td><td colspan="2">3.562 (0.800)</td></tr>
<tr><td>Q3: Do you want to use the interface again?</td><td>2.875 (0.906)</td><td colspan="2">3.593 (0.837)</td></tr>
<tr><td>Q4: Was the color information intuitive?</td><td>-</td><td colspan="2">3.218 (1.099)</td></tr>
<tr><td>Q5: Were the aspect labels appropriate?</td><td>-</td><td colspan="2">3.812 (0.997)</td></tr>
<tr><td>Q6: Was the number of displayed aspects appropriate?</td><td>-</td><td>3.437 (0.877)</td><td>3.562 (0.913)</td></tr>
</table>

As our future work, we plan to enable the aspect-based reranking feature that was mentioned in Section 4.3, to enable both more efficient and more exploratory search. Moreover, as our results show that the quality of displayed aspects and the accuracy of per-aspect relevance estimates are important for maximizing the benefit of AspecTiles, we plan to improve the backend search system. Finally, as we discussed in Section 4.2.2, we would like to identify the class of users for which interfaces like AspecTiles would be most helpful.

6. ADDITIONAL AUTHOR

Shojiro Nishio
(Osaka University, Japan, email: nishio@ist.osaka-u.ac.jp)

7. REFERENCES

[1] R. Agrawal, S. Gollapudi, A. Halverson, and S. Leong. Diversifying Search Results, In *Proc. of WSDM 2009*, pages 5–14, 2009.

[2] C. Brandt, T. Joachims, Y. Yue, and J. Bank. Dynamic Ranked Retrieval, In *Proc. of WSDM 2011*, pages 247–256, 2011.

[3] A. Broder. A Taxonomy of Web Search, *ACM SIGIR Forum*, 36(2):3–10, 2002.

[4] M. Chau. Visualizing Web Search Results Using Glyphs: Design and Evaluation of a Flower Metaphor, *ACM Transactions on Management Information Systems*, Vol. 2, No. 1, Article 2, 2011.

[5] C. Chen and Y. Yu. Empirical Studies of Information Visualization: A Meta-Analysis, *Int'l Journal of Human-Computer Studies*, 53(5):851–866, 2000.

[6] C. L. Clarke, N. Craswell, and I. Soboroff. Overview of the TREC 2009 Web Track, In *Proc. of TREC 2009*, 2010.

[7] C. L. Clarke, M. Kolla, and O. Vechtomova. An Effectiveness Measure for Ambiguous and Underspecified Queries, In *Proc. of ICTIR 2009*, pages 188–199, 2009.

[8] Z. Dou, S. Hu, K. Chen, R. Song, and J. -R. Wen. Multi-Dimensional Search Result Diversification, In *Proc. of WSDM 2011*, pages 475–484, 2011.

[9] M. A. Hearst. TileBars: Visualization of Term Distribution Information in Full Text Information Access, In *Proc. of CHI 1995*, pages 59–66, 1995.

[10] T. Heimonen and N. Jhaveri. Visualizing Query Occurrence in Search Result Lists, In *Proc. of IV 2005*, pages 877–882, 2005.

[11] W. Hersh, A. M. Cohen, P. Roberts, and H. K. Rekapalli. TREC 2006 Genomics Track Overview, In *Proc. of TREC 2006*, pages 52–78, 2006.

[12] W. Hersh and P. Over. Interactivity at the Text Retrieval Conference (TREC), *Information Processing and Management*, 37(3):365–367, 2001.

[13] W. Hersh and P. Over. TREC-9 Interactive Track Report, In *Proc. of TREC-9*, pages 41–50, 1999.

[14] O. Hoeber and X. D. Yang. A Comparative User Study of Web Search Interfaces: HotMap, Concept Highlighter, and Google, In *Proc. of WI 2006*, pages 866–874, 2006.

[15] J. Mackinlay. Automating the Design of Graphical Presentations of Relational Information, *ACM Transactions on Graphics*, 5(2):110–141, 1986.

[16] H. Reiterer, G. Tullius. and T. M. Mann. INSYDER: A Content-based Visual-Information-Seeking System for the Web, *Int'l Journal on Digital Libraries*, 5(1):25–41, 2005.

[17] T. Sakai. Evaluation with Informational and Navigational Intents, In *Proc. of WWW 2012*, pages 499–508, 2012.

[18] R. L. T. Santos, C. Macdonald, and I. Ounis. Exploiting Query Reformulations for Web Search Result Diversification, In *Proc. of WWW 2010*, pages 881–890, 2010.

[19] R. Song, M. Zhang, T. Sakai, M. P. Kato, Y. Liu, M. Sugimoto, Q. Wang, and N. Orii. Overview of the NTCIR-9 INTENT Task, In *Proc. of NTCIR-9*, pages 82–105, 2011.

[20] O. Turetken and R. Sharda. Visualization of Web Spaces: State of the Art and Future Directions, *ACM SIGMIS Database*, 38(3):51–81, 2007.

[21] C. Ware. Information Visualization: Perception for Design, *Morgan Kaufmann*, 2000.

[22] Y. Xiang, M. Chau, H. Atabakhsh, and H. Chen. Visualizing Criminal Relationships: Comparison of a Hyperbolic Tree and a Hierarchical List, *Decision Support Systems*, 41(1):69–83, 2005.

[23] Y. Yamamoto and K. Tanaka. Enhancing Credibility Judgment of Web Search Results, In *Proc. of CHI 2011*, pages 1235–1244, 2011.

Time-Based Calibration of Effectiveness Measures

Mark D. Smucker
Department of Management Sciences
University of Waterloo, Canada
mark.smucker@uwaterloo.ca

Charles L. A. Clarke
School of Computer Science
University of Waterloo, Canada
claclark@plg.uwaterloo.ca

ABSTRACT

Many current effectiveness measures incorporate simplifying assumptions about user behavior. These assumptions prevent the measures from reflecting aspects of the search process that directly impact the quality of retrieval results as experienced by the user. In particular, these measures implicitly model users as working down a list of retrieval results, spending equal time assessing each document. In reality, even a careful user, intending to identify as much relevant material as possible, must spend longer on some documents than on others. Aspects such as document length, duplicates and summaries all influence the time required. In this paper, we introduce a *time-biased gain* measure, which explicitly accommodates such aspects of the search process. By conducting an appropriate user study, we calibrate and validate the measure against the TREC 2005 Robust Track test collection. We examine properties of the measure, contrasting it to traditional effectiveness measures, and exploring its extension to other aspects and environments. As its primary benefit, the measure allows us to evaluate system performance in human terms, while maintaining the simplicity and repeatability of system-oriented tests. Overall, we aim to achieve a clearer connection between user-oriented studies and system-oriented tests, allowing us to better transfer insights and outcomes from one to the other.

Categories and Subject Descriptors

H.3.4 [**Information Storage and Retrieval**]: Systems and Software—*Performance evaluation (efficiency and effectiveness)*

General Terms

Experimentation, Human Factors, Measurement

Keywords

Information retrieval, search evaluation

Permission to make digital or hard copies of all or part of this work for personal or classroom use is granted without fee provided that copies are not made or distributed for profit or commercial advantage and that copies bear this notice and the full citation on the first page. To copy otherwise, to republish, to post on servers or to redistribute to lists, requires prior specific permission and/or a fee.
SIGIR'12, August 12–16, 2012, Portland, Oregon, USA.
Copyright 2012 ACM 978-1-4503-1472-5/12/08 ...$10.00.

1. INTRODUCTION

System-oriented tests and user-oriented studies represent competing approaches to search engine evaluation. A system-oriented test typically develops a set of relevance judgments to determine the quality of ranked document lists returned in response to a query [39]. Effectiveness measures computed over these ranked lists provide a method for tuning search engines and comparing one engine to another. In contrast, a user-oriented study examines actual user behavior during interactive retrieval sessions. These studies span a spectrum from intensive laboratory investigations involving a relatively small number of subjects [18] to large-scale analyses of interaction logs capturing the search activities of millions of people [9, 42, 43].

The value of a user-oriented study lies in its ability to reflect many aspects of the search process, including interaction and presentation. Unfortunately, user studies can be complex and costly. Running subjects through a laboratory experiment can require substantial time and money, and we may need to repeat experiments as elements of the interface and engine change. On the other hand, interaction logs are noisy, uncontrolled, and capture only a portion of the user experience.

The value of a system-oriented test lies in its simplicity and repeatability. Effectiveness measures isolate and evaluate a single element of the search engine, i.e., the quality of its ranked list. Once we develop a set of relevance judgments, evaluation measures can be re-computed with little additional expense or effort. As software developers modify and train ranking algorithms, effectiveness measures may be applied over and over again, as often as needed.

Various researchers [7, 10, 43] suggest a generic framework that encapsulates many of the effectiveness measures in current use, including Normalized Discounted Cumulative Gain (nDCG) [17], Rank Biased Precision (RBP) [23], and Expected Reciprocal Rank (ERR) [9]. All of these measures can be expressed as a sum over documents in a ranked list,

$$\frac{1}{\mathcal{N}} \sum_{k=1}^{\infty} g_k d_k, \qquad (1)$$

where g_k represents the *gain* associated with the document appearing at rank k, and d_k represents a *discount* associated with rank k, which is independent of the document. In practice, we either compute the sum to some fixed but arbitrary depth K or until we know its value within some ϵ. The normalization factor $\mathcal{N}$ is optional, but if it is present, it serves to map the value of the sum into the range $[0:1]$, which may be required for averaging over multiple queries.

RBP uses the discount formula $d_k = \beta^{k-1}$, where β is a constant in the range $[0 : 1]$. Gain values for RBP are binary, with $g_k = 1$ if the document at rank k is judged relevant, and $g_k = 0$ if it is not judged relevant. ERR uses a reciprocal rank discount formula of $d_k = 1/k$, and nDCG uses the discount formula $d_k = 1/(\log_2(1+k))$. For both of these measures, a gain value may be interpreted as a relevance probability, i.e., the probability that a user viewing the document would judge it to be relevant. When applying these measures, the probabilities are estimated from graded relevance judgments, e.g., "definitive", "excellent", "good", etc. [24]. In the case of ERR, the gain value of a document at rank k depends on the gain values of the documents at ranks 1 to $k-1$, with gain values increasingly attenuated when more relevant documents appear at higher ranks.

All of these measures may be interpreted in terms of a simple user model: The user starts at the first document and works their way down the list, eventually stopping when they become tired or bored. The discount d_k indicates the probability that the user continues to rank k, and the gain g_k represents the benefit (i.e., utility) to the user of viewing the document at rank k. Thus, the sum in Equation 1 can be understood as the expected total benefit experienced by the user, with the various gain values and discount formulae corresponding to different assumptions about user needs and behaviors. In particular, the attenuated gain values in ERR correspond to the idea that, after viewing each relevant document, the user derives less benefit from viewing additional relevant documents.

Underlying this user model is an implicit assumption that the user views documents at a constant rate, spending the same time assessing each one. Because of this assumption, these effectiveness measures can fail to accommodate aspects of the search process that directly impact the quality of the ranked list as experienced by the user. For example, most modern search engines provide captions, or summaries, that describe each of the documents [36]. A user scanning these summaries might quickly skip those results that are obviously not relevant to their needs, without ever viewing the contents of the associated documents. Similarly, we might expect shorter documents to take less time to assess than longer documents, since a user may spend less time skimming them. In addition, when a document is similar in content to a document a user has already viewed, it may be easy to assess quickly, regardless of its length. Once a user recognizes the duplicated content, they can immediately return to the result list and continue to the next result.

In this paper, we propose a framework for evaluation measures based on time, allowing us to directly accommodate aspects of the search process ignored by standard effectiveness measures. We retain the simple model of a user working their way down a result list, but with both gain and discount now expressed in terms of time. As the user works their way down the list, let $G(t)$ be the cumulative gain experienced by the user at time t. In other words, if the user invests time t in assessing the result list, they will derive a total benefit of $G(t)$. We model the possibility that the user stops at some point by a *decay* function $D(t)$, which indicates the probability that the user continues until time t. Thus, $D(0) = 1$ and decreases monotonically to 0 as $t \to \infty$. Under this model, an equivalent of Equation 1 may be expressed as

$$\frac{1}{\mathcal{N}} \int_0^\infty \frac{dG}{dt} D(t) dt. \tag{2}$$

Of course, measuring instantaneous gain would prove difficult in practice, and we quickly return to considering gain values one document at a time, but retaining decay as a function of time. By smearing gain equally across each document and converting $D(t)$ into a step function, we may approximate Equation 2 with

$$\frac{1}{\mathcal{N}} \sum_{k=1}^{\infty} g_k D(T(k)), \tag{3}$$

where $T(k)$ is the expected time it would takes for a user to reach rank k and begin to assess the document. Although we have returned to a summation over ranks, we now explicitly consider time as a part of the measure.

We refer to Equation 3 as *time-biased gain*, and we spend the remainder of this paper developing and exploring this effectiveness measure. In its development, we face the potentially controversial and complex problem of providing a realistic estimate for $T(k)$. Ideally, for use in an effectiveness measure, the estimate should be straightforward both to compute and to comprehend. Competing with this requirement is the need for a clear connection back to actual user behavior, so that the effectiveness measure provides a meaningful guide for training and tuning ranking algorithms.

We note that setting $T(k) = c(k-1)$, for some constant c, reduces Equation 3 back to Equation 1, which corresponds to a scenario in which the user views documents at a constant rate. To move beyond this simple scenario, we need to examine user behavior in a realistic context, calibrating our estimate of $T(k)$ against the actions of these users. As a result, time-biased gain is more closely tied to a usage scenario than traditional evaluation measures. Moving to a different scenario requires a different calibration of the evaluation measure, a price we pay for the closer connection to user behavior.

After a review of related work, we discuss the calibration and validation of time-biased gain against the test collection employed in the TREC 2005 Robust Track experiments [39]. As part of this calibration, we report a user study in which we presented subjects with an interface styled after a modern web search engine, including a result page with ten query-biased summaries, and instructed them to find and save as many relevant documents as possible in the time allowed, while making as few mistakes as possible. The associated scenario is of a careful and determined user, with a topical information need, intending to identify as much relevant material as they can in the time they have available.

We believe this scenario is appropriate for the TREC Robust Track, and similar experiments, where a document is considered relevant if it contains any relevant material at all, and evaluation measures traditionally consider documents that are relatively deep in the result list. For other scenarios, a different calibration might be appropriate. For example, in the context of web search, where users may interact with fewer results and rarely dig as deeply in the result list, calibration might be based on interaction logs taken from the search engine itself.

After developing a $T(k)$ function appropriate to our usage scenario, we consider other components of our time-biased gain measure, including the choice of a decay function. We explore properties of the measure and compare it to other evaluation measures. Finally, we end the paper with a discussion of extensions and future work.

2. RELATED WORK

We may interpret many current effectiveness measures in terms of the simple user model outlined in the introduction [7, 9, 17, 23, 43]. While all of these measures implicitly assume that a user progresses down the ranked list at a constant rate, they incorporate different assumptions about when and why the user will stop, and how much benefit or utility they can be expected to gain. All of these measures may be expressed in form of Equation 1 [7, 43]. Even precision at k may be interpreted in terms of a user who always views exactly the top k documents, and no more. Along the same lines, Robertson [26] retrofits a similar user model into the venerable Mean Average Precision (MAP) effectiveness measure, which may also be extended to incorporate graded relevance values similar to those employed by nDCG [15, 27, 30].

Turpin et al. [37], Yilmaz et al. [42], and Dupret [14] have gone beyond this simple model by explicitly incorporating summaries into their user models and thus into their metrics. An important difference between their work and ours is that we explicitly model time in addition to the click decisions. Summaries are designed to, and do speed the rate at which users find relevant documents [20, 36]. We believe it is important that metrics reflect the value of summaries by having a user model that incorporates the time required to separately evaluate summaries and documents. Time is important to users. Su [35] found from interviews with 40 users that the success category of "Efficiency - Time" was ranked first with the highest frequency of mention.

Turpin and Hersh [38] hypothesized that the time to read documents was a reason why batch-style and user evaluations produce different results. In their study, Turpin and Hersh found that the baseline system, which had a lower MAP, ranked shorter documents higher than the *improved* system. The *improved* system had a pivoted length normalization [31] component that preferred longer documents — longer TREC documents have a higher prior probability of being relevant. Turpin and Hersh found that users of the baseline system were able to read more documents than the users of the *improved* system. As a result, users of the baseline system were able to compensate for its lower precision and find equal amounts of relevant material in the same amount of time. Our time-biased gain metric explicitly takes document length into consideration, for we have also found that users take longer to judge longer documents. Yang and Lad [41] and Arvola et al. [2] also consider the cost of reading in the evaluation of IR systems.

Our time-biased gain metric aligns well with Fuhr's probability ranking principle for interactive IR [16]. Fuhr carefully outlines that users of interactive IR systems have to make a series of decisions and that these decisions each have their own cost. For our metric, cost is measured in time, and both cost and gain are directly tied to the series of probabilistic decisions made by the user.

Much of this work can be viewed as following a framework for evaluation laid out by Cooper [11, 12] and Dunlop [13]. Cooper believed that effectiveness measures should be based on the utility a user personally gains from a retrieval system. A critical part of Cooper's plan was the use of *validation experiments* to measure the ability of an evaluation measure to predict utility. Dunlop built on and refined the ideas of Cooper. Rather than subjectively measure a user's utility, Dunlop established the use of HCI methods to predict user performance in terms of the number of relevant documents found in a given amount of time.

Efforts to relate evaluation measures to models of user behavior can be seen as an attempt to bridge the gap between system-oriented tests and user-oriented studies. In these cases, the goal is to move system-oriented measures closer to user-oriented studies. Working from the other direction, efforts have been made to simulate the use of interactive retrieval systems in order to determine their quality [1, 4, 21, 40]. Efforts related to this approach includes the use of simulation to better understand interactive retrieval behavior [3, 19]. We see these two directions of research merging as system-oriented measures continue to increase the resolution of their user models [8].

3. CALIBRATION

At the core of our new metric, time-biased gain, is the computation of the time to reach rank k of a ranked list, which we will refer to as the function $T(k)$. Given that we are retaining the traditional model of a user working down a ranked list in order, we need to estimate the amount of time it takes to process a given document. As such, we need to consider what is a reasonable process that a user would go through to determine if a document is relevant.

The majority of search interfaces now present a ranked list in two parts. The first part is the display of a series of document summaries that are intended to help the user decide if the corresponding full documents should be viewed or skipped. The second part is the full document itself.

Faced with this interface, the user must first examine the document summary and decide whether to click and view the full document or not. While it is certainly possible that a user may realize benefit from viewing the summary alone, we believe that for TREC-style topics and information needs, that a user needs to view the full document in order to realize gain from finding relevant material in the document.

Thus, we need to model the decision of whether to click or not and produce both an estimate of the time the decision takes to be made as well as an estimate of what the decision will be. If the user decides to click on a summary, then the user must study the document and make a decision about the document's relevance. Only if the user clicks on a relevant document's summary and then decides the document is relevant will the user realize any gain. Gain cannot be obtained from non-relevant documents nor from skipped relevant documents. As with the summary, we need to estimate time spent on the full document and the final relevance decision of the user.

There are nearly endless variables that could be taken into consideration in the models of decision making for summaries and documents. In this paper, we choose to focus on a few variables that are most likely to affect user decisions.

The most obvious variables affecting these decisions are the user and the topic. While users vary greatly and contribute large amounts of variance to user studies, we do not attempt to model different user strategies for processing ranked lists. Instead, our user model is an idealized individual representing the population as a whole. As for the topic, at this time we do not see an easy way to identify a priori how a topic will affect users' behavior, and we are forced to treat all topics the same.

After the user and topic, the document itself is likely the most important variable to consider. We consider two attributes of the document to use in our model: the relevance of the document and the document's length. Relevance should be a strong indicator of how likely summaries will be clicked and whether or not the document will be recognized by users to be relevant [37]. The time to make decisions based on textual items is likely to be dependent on their length.

Given that summaries tend to be short and of nearly equal length, we will assume they are all assessed in the same amount time, T_S seconds. For documents, let $T_D(l) = al + b$, be the time in seconds to assess a document of length l, where l is measured in words. $T_D(l)$ models an evaluation process of scanning the document at a rate of a seconds per word and then a constant amount of time, b seconds, to account for carefully assessing a small amount of text and the overhead of making a decision about relevance. As we will justify, if a user views a duplicate of a document later, then we treat that duplicate as if it had zero length ($l = 0$).

We use a document's relevance to predict the probability that a summary will be clicked and to predict the probability that when viewed, a full document is recognized as relevant. Formally, let $P(C|R)$ be the probability of a click given NIST relevance, where C and R are binary random variables. Also, let $P(S|R)$ be the probability of saving a viewed document as relevant given NIST relevance, where S and R are binary random variables. Saving a document is the equivalent of recognizing a document to be relevant.

Putting both the time to make decisions and the probabilities of the decisions together, we have a model of the time it takes to process a document in the ranked list and can now estimate the time to reach rank k, i.e. $T(k)$.

Let l_i be the length of the document at rank i. Let r_i be the NIST binary relevance judgment associated with the document at rank i, where $r_i = 1$ if the document is relevant, $r_i = 0$ otherwise. Then, we estimate the expected time for the user to reach rank k as:

$$T(k) = \sum_{i=1}^{k-1} T_S + T_D(l_i)P(C = 1|R = r_i) \qquad (4)$$

Not present in $T(k)$ are the probabilities of the user saving a document as relevant, which are only needed for computation of the gain.

With Equation 4 in hand, we need to calibrate it to produce estimates in line with actual human behavior. We next explain how we calibrated $T(k)$ and estimated $P(S|R)$ based on a user study.

3.1 User Study

To calibrate our metric, we need actual user data that involves the processing of ranked lists. We utilize data collected as part of the user study conducted by Smucker and Jethani [34].

The user study presented participants with a user interface styled after modern web search engines. The interface had two types of web pages. One page looked like a search engine results page with 10 query-biased document summaries. Clicking on a summary took a participant to a page with the full document. On the full document page, participants could decide to save the document as relevant or simply use the web browser's back button to return to the summaries page. At the bottom of the summaries page, participants could click a link to obtain the next 10 results. The system recorded all clicks and times spent on the pages as well the decisions to save documents as relevant. The user interface only allowed participants to search the given ranked list of documents. No query reformulation was possible.

The study used 8 topics from the TREC 2005 Robust track, which used the AQUAINT newswire document collection. The topics (310, 336, 362, 367, 383, 426, 427, 436) were selected to be of possible interest to study participants.

48 participants worked on 4 search topics for 10 minutes each. Topics were balanced across participants, list precision, and task order. The study instructed participants to find and save as many relevant documents as possible in the 10 minutes while making as few mistakes as possible. In cases of technical issues affecting data collection, or when it was apparent that participants did not follow instructions, these participants were removed and new participants were recruited until the study was a fully balanced design with 48 participants.

The user study had dual purposes. One purpose was to investigate the effect of precision on user performance, and the other was to provide behavioral data for calibration of our time-biased gain metric. As a result, the ranked lists of documents had a uniform precision of either 0.6 or 0.3, which were representative of the precision at rank 10 performance of the best and lower performing systems in the TREC 2005 Robust track. By uniform, we mean that for every 10 documents shown, either 6 or 3 were relevant. The construction of the result lists placed both relevant and non-relevant documents at ranks reflective of their overall likelihood of being ranked highly by retrieval systems. The result was that we were able to control the precision, and the study participants still had a realistic task of distinguishing between highly ranked relevant and non-relevant documents. Full details of the result lists construction, screenshots of the user interface, and other study details, can be found in [34], which also reports on the results of the precision component of the study.

3.2 Calibration Values

Given the user study, we can estimate the time it takes users to process a document summary and a full document. At first glance, computing these times would appear to be as simple as taking the average of each, for each user, and reporting the user average. Instead, since we are interested in computing gain versus time for a population, we need to compute harmonic means, or as we do in this paper, weighted averages where each weight reflects the amount of a user's activity in the study.

From the user study, we have measurements of the time participants spent on the summaries page before they clicked on a summary or the next link. Likewise, we have measured the time spent viewing documents before leaving the page.

To compute the population average for the time spent on a summary, we need to consider that we can only measure the time spent on the summaries page before clicking on a summary. Without eyetracking we cannot know for certain how much time is spent on each individual summary. Thus, we compute the amount of time per summary for a participant to be the sum of all time spent on the summaries page divided by the maximum rank of a clicked summary. In this way, we spread the time out over both the summaries clicked and not clicked. To compute the population average time on a single summary, we weight the individual partici-

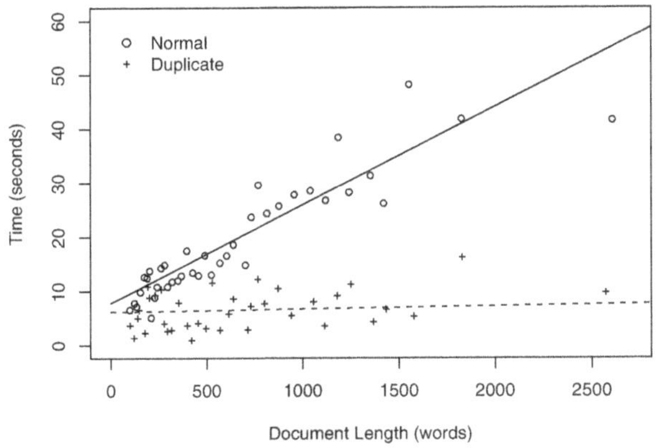

Figure 1: Time to judge document relevance with linear fits to 4212 data points that have been binned and averaged for visualization purposes.

Parameter	Description	Value
P(C=1|R=1)	Probability of click on relevant summary	0.64
P(C=1|R=0)	Probability of click on non-rel. summary	0.39
P(S=1|R=1)	Prob. of save/judge relevant document as rel.	0.77
P(S=1|R=0)	Prob. of save/judge non-relevant doc. as rel.	0.27
T_S	Time to evaluate a summary (seconds)	4.4 s
$T_D(l)$	Time in seconds to judge doc. of l words. Duplicates treated as $l = 0$.	$0.018 \cdot l + 7.8$

Table 1: Calibration values. P(S=1|R=0) is not used by the metric, but is shown for completeness.

pant's time by the maximum rank. As such, the population average time per summary is:

$$T_S = \sum_p \frac{\sum_i S_{ip}}{M_p} \frac{M_p}{\sum_p M_p} = \frac{1}{\sum_p M_p} \sum_p \sum_i S_{ip} \quad (5)$$

where S_{ip} is the i-th time spent by participant p on the summary page and M_p is the maximum click rank by participant p. For our data, $T_S = 4.4$ seconds. If we did not compute a weighted average, the average would be 5.3 seconds.

For the time spent viewing a full document before saving it as relevant or clicking the web browser's back button to return to the summaries page, we take all of the recorded times and fit a linear model to the time in terms of the document's length. By using all of our participants' data, we will obtain a model of the time to judge a document's relevance that is weighted based on the level of activity of that participant.

Figure 1 show a plot of time to judge document relevance vs. document length. We measured document length as the number of word occurrences in a document as parsed by Indri [32]. For the purposes of the plot, we binned the individual data points such that approximately 15 documents were in each bin. Each single document was judged by an average of 9.1 participants, and thus each plotted data point represents the average of many document lengths and times. Averaging the data points in the plot hides the considerable variation in time to judge documents.

In Figure 1, we have separately plotted the times for documents when first viewed by a participant, and the times for a participant's later views of document duplicates. We identified near duplicates in the AQUAINT collection with a variant of Broder's duplicate detection algorithm [5], and only considered documents with the highest possible similarity to be duplicates of each other, i.e. all shared shingles are identical. We refer to these near duplicates as duplicates. We found 10.1% of the documents to be duplicates.

The linear fits to all of the first-viewed documents (3614 data points) and the duplicate views (598 points) are shown in Figure 1. The linear model for first-viewed documents is given by: $T_D(l) = 0.018 \cdot l + 7.8$, and has an adjusted R-squared of 0.12, which means that 12% of the variance is explained by the model. We looked at including the relevance of the documents and/or the precision of the lists in the linear regression, but neither increased the adjusted R-squared.

The linear fit to the *duplicates* does not explain any of the variance in the time to judge a duplicate, and as such the time to judge a duplicate can be estimated equally well by taking the mean, which gives a result of 6.8 ± 0.5 seconds. The constant in the fit to the first viewed documents is 7.8 ± 0.7. Since the standard errors of the mean duplicate time and the constant term of the linear fit overlap, there is no significant difference between the two, and we simply treat duplicates as zero length documents.

Lorigo et al. [22] found that on information style tasks, participants spent 40% of their time looking at the search results and the remainder elsewhere (presumably at the full web pages). Our participants spent 33% of their time on the summaries and 67% on the full documents.

Of note, user studies typically report user averages. For example, with our data, the average participant took 26.5 seconds per viewed document. In contrast, for the same set of document viewings, the mean of $T_D(l)$ is 18.9 seconds. The difference comes about because the participants who worked faster, took less time per document and also viewed more documents in the same amount of time. If we used the participant averages, we would overestimate the amount of time it takes our population to reach rank k. This difference also means that most statistics reported by user studies cannot be directly used in metrics like ours.

We obtained the parameter settings for the probabilities of clicking on summaries and documents in a straightforward fashion. For both the probability to click on a summary given the relevance, $P(C|R)$, and the probability to save a document as relevant given given relevance, $P(S|R)$, we calculate them as weighted averages. We know the relevance of each document as given by the NIST assessors and can calculate the fraction of views on relevant documents that result in a document being saved, $P(S = 1|R = 1)$, as well as the fraction of views on non-relevant documents that result in a save, $P(S = 1|R = 0)$. For calculating the probability of a click on a summary given the document's relevance, $P(C|R)$, we make the assumption that all summaries up to the maximum clicked rank are viewed. Given this assumption, we can calculate the probabilities of clicking on sum-

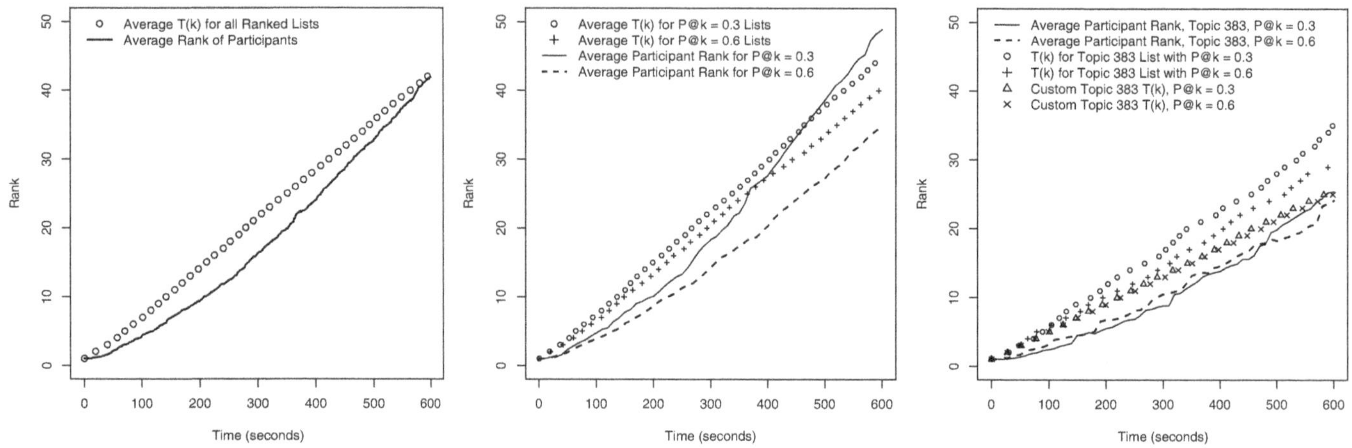

Figure 2: These plots show the predicted time to rank k, $T(k)$, vs. the measured time to rank k for the 48 participants in the user study. Please see the text for a detailed description of each plot.

maries in the same fashion as for documents. In the case of computing the weighted average for documents, we weight a participant's $P(S|R)$ by the number of documents viewed during a search task. In the case of summaries, we weight a participant's $P(C|R)$ by the participant's maximum clicked rank. Table 1 shows the computed probabilities.

Yilmaz et al. [42] reported for a commercial web search engine the probabilities of users clicking on documents of varying relevance: Bad: 0.49, Fair: 0.45, Good: 0.55, Excellent: 0.71, and Perfect: 0.94. In comparison, our probability of clicking on a relevant document is 0.64 and falls in-between "Good" and "Excellent", which seems appropriate. Our probability of clicking on a non-relevant document is 0.39 and falls below "Bad", and shows that our summaries on average provided the study participants with an ability to discriminate between relevant and non-relevant documents. Like Yilmaz et al., we find that a significant fraction of low-quality or non-relevant documents are clicked on.

The probabilities for saving a document show that given a full document, participants are better able to discriminate between relevant and non-relevant as compared to summaries, but that they still have a true positive rate, $P(S = 1|R = 1) = 0.77$ less than one. In other words, not all relevant documents are recognized as such, and this makes sense given a population of users as opposed to modeling the single NIST assessor. Given constraints on time and abilities, not all users will detect when a document is relevant.

4. VALIDATION

In Section 3 we proposed a method to estimate the time it takes a user population to reach rank k, i.e. $T(k)$. Our $T(k)$ consists of Equation 4 and the calibration values for $T(k)$ estimated from a 48 participant user study. Table 1 shows a summary of the calibration values.

Our $T(k)$ is a simple model of user behavior for what is a task of considerable complexity. In processing a ranked list of documents, users must make complex decisions regarding the time they devote to summaries and full documents and the accuracy with which they make decisions. In the user study data that we used to calibrate time-biased gain, there is considerable variation in observed user strategies for the searching of ranked lists [33]. For example, some users quickly select summaries to click while others take 2-3 times longer to make their selection. Another example is that while the study participants primarily moved forward (down) the ranked lists with 94% of the average participant's clicks being on a summary lower ranked than the previously clicked summary, not all movement is forward.

In this section we discuss the ability of our $T(k)$ to make reasonable estimates of the time it takes the population to reach rank k. In the user study, participants searched for relevant documents in 16 ranked lists of documents. Each of 8 topics had two lists. One of the two lists had a precision of 0.3 and the other a precision of 0.6. The design of the study meant that 12 participants worked on each list. Participants worked for 10 minutes on each list.

Figure 2 shows three plots comparing $T(k)$ and actual participant behavior. The far left plot averages $T(k)$ for all 16 of the ranked lists and 192 traces of participant behavior. On average, $T(k)$ produces a linear rate of progress down a ranked list. Given how we produced the calibration values, this average behavior for the 16 ranked lists is expected. As we will show briefly, $T(k)$ produces non-linear predictions for individual ranked lists. At 600 seconds, the average $T(k)$ matches the average rank of the participants and shows that our calibration on average works. If we had not used weighted averages to produce the calibration values, $T(k)$ would have underestimated the rank reached at 600 seconds.

We also see in the far left plot of Figure 2 that the study participants increased their rate as they progressed down the ranked lists. This speedup makes sense given that participants will take some time to learn a model of what is and is not relevant. We also noticed that participants working down some of the 0.3 precision lists dramatically increased their rate of work once getting past the first page of 10 results. Our $T(k)$ is an average of the slower initial behavior and the faster behavior found later in the search process. We leave for future work the possibility of having the parameters of $T(k)$ vary with time.

IR user interfaces employ document summaries as a mechanism to allow users to find relevant material faster. The better the document summaries are, the easier it is for users

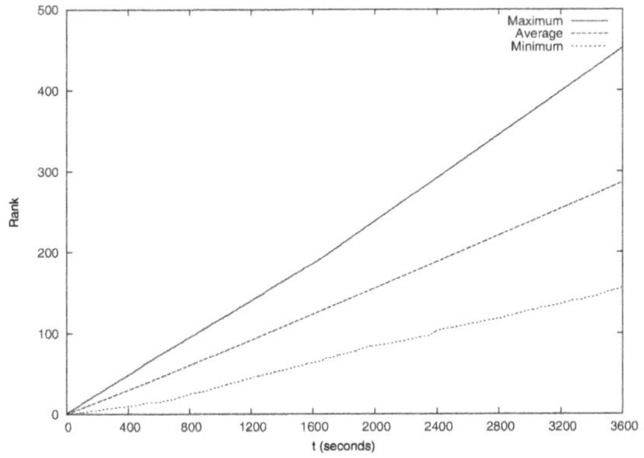

Figure 3: Maximum, average, and minimum rank at time t over all queries and runs from the TREC 2005 Robust Track.

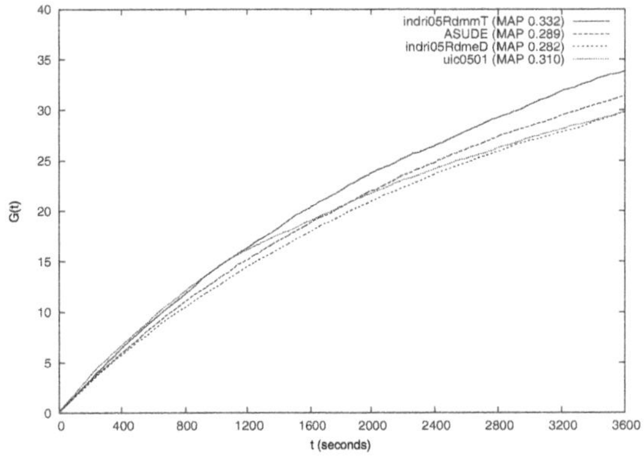

Figure 4: $G(t)$, cumulative gain at time t, for top scoring runs from the TREC 2005 Robust Track.

to save time by skipping non-relevant results. In the center plot of Figure 2, we see that the study participants processing the 0.3 precision list do process more of the lists compared to the 0.6 precision lists. $T(k)$ only models precision in the form of different summary click probabilities given the relevance of the document, but it too predicts that the population will reach a larger rank k with a lower precision list as compared to a higher precision list in the same amount of time. At 600 seconds, the predictions of $T(k)$ fall between the actual ranks reached by the participants.

As mentioned in Section 3, our study design precluded us from using the search topic as part of our model even though it is well-known that topics vary considerably. In the far right plot of Figure 2, we show the participants' behavior for the 0.3 and 0.6 precision lists of Topic 383 (mental illness drugs). Topic 383 requires that a relevant document name an actual drug. The documents in the result list tend to be long documents. As the far right plot shows, the participants work down the ranked list at a much slower rate than on average (far left plot). In addition, the participants show little difference in rank reached for the 0.3 and 0.6 lists. Also shown in the plot are the predictions of $T(k)$ for these two ranked lists. As can be seen here, $T(k)$ is not simply a linear function of rank. The different documents with their differing ranks and relevance judgments produce unique $T(k)$ values for each ranked list.

While our $T(k)$ correctly estimates a slower rate for Topic 383, it does overestimate the rate of progress, and it also predicts a gap between the ranks reached for the 0.3 and 0.6 lists. To illustrate the degree to which modeling of the topic could help future versions of $T(k)$, we calibrated $T(k)$ using only Topic 383. In the far right plot, we label this version of $T(k)$ the "Custom Topic 383 T(k)." As shown, the custom calibrated $T(k)$ much better reflects the actual participant behavior on Topic 383.

Given the importance of modeling the topic, a possibility for producing per-topic, custom calibrated versions of $T(k)$ would be to assign multiple assessors to a topic during test collection construction. The behavior of the assessors could be recorded and packaged alongside the relevance judgments, and then each topic could have its own $T(k)$.

To what extent does $T(k)$ vary on actual runs? Figure 3 shows the maximum, average, and minimum rank at time t for all of the submitted runs to the TREC 2005 Robust Track. As shown, there is a considerable range of ranks at a given time. In terms of Equation 3, this result means that at a given rank k, different ranked lists will vary in their predicted time to reach that rank and will have different amounts of decay, $D(t)$, applied at that rank.

5. TIME-BIASED GAIN

In this section, we pull together the pieces of the time-biased gain measure defined in Equation 3, suggesting specific formulae for the remaining components, including gain, decay and normalization.

5.1 Gain

For the remainder of the paper, we define

$$g_k = \begin{cases} P(C=1|R=1)P(S=1|R=1) & \text{if } r_i = 1 \\ 0 & \text{if } r_i = 0 \end{cases}$$

Under this definition, if the document at rank k is relevant, the gain is equivalent to the probability of viewing it and saving it. If the document is not relevant, the gain is zero. This definition is consistent with the binary relevance values typical of TREC tasks and adopted for our calibration process. In principle, we could adopt the graded gain values employed by nDCG, the attenuated gain values employed by ERR, or even gain values that take document length and other features into account. We leave the exploration of these ideas for future work.

Ignoring decay for now, we combine gain values with $T(k)$, our formula for estimated rank at time t, allowing us to compute $G(t)$ for individual runs. Figure 4 shows $G(t)$ for four runs taken from the TREC 2005 Robust Track, along with their official MAP values [39]. All four runs performed well, with `indri05RdmmT` and `uic0501` being the best and second-best title-only runs, and `ASUDE` and `indri05RdmeD` being the best and second-best description-only runs. For three of these runs, their relative cumulative gain remains consistent over the full time period. The story for `uic0501` is different. It leads the other runs for the first twenty minutes, but begins to fall behind after that, providing some insight into its behavior. While similar insight might be gained from a standard recall-precision plot, calibrating gain against time may provide a better sense of the performance experienced by a user.

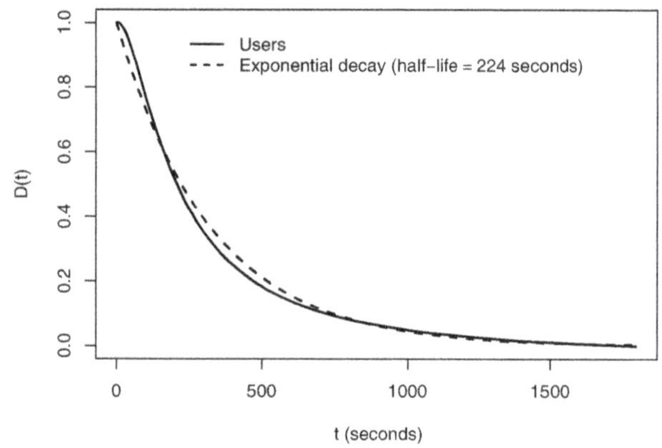

Figure 5: User data and fitted decay curve for $D(t)$.

5.2 Decay

Our calibration process provides no guidance regarding the form of the decay function $D(t)$, but standard exponential decay provides one possibility:

$$D(t) = e^{-t\frac{\ln 2}{h}}, \tag{6}$$

where h is the "half-life" of users, i.e., the time at which half of the initial users have stopped scanning the result list.

To support this choice of decay function, we turn to an interaction log taken from a commercial search engine, in this case from the MSN search engine. This anonymized log was made available to selected researchers across the information retrieval community during 2006 and 2007. For example, Zhang et al. [43] employed it to validate the discount function appearing in RBP. The log contains user interaction data for 5 million searches during May 2006.

We treat the time between the query and its last click as a proxy for the time spent scanning the result list and viewing documents, allowing us to estimate $D(t)$. Since our scenario assumes a careful and determined user, we try to filter out users with navigational needs, etc., by eliminating searches with less than five clicks. We also filter out searches that take longer than 30 minutes.

Figure 5 plots the $D(t)$ estimated from this log. As shown in the figure, exponential decay with a half-life of 224 seconds provides a good fit to this data. We use this half-life in the remainder of the paper.

We note that it should be possible to employ log data to estimate $T(k)$, as well as $D(t)$, although we would need document length and other data not present in this log. This approach would be particularly appropriate for calibration in the context of web search. We leave this idea for future work.

5.3 Interpretation

Before we move on to the normalization factor, we pause in our development of time-biased gain to consider one way in which the measure may be interpreted. Recall that g_k represents the *expected* gain at rank k and $T(k)$ represents the *expected* time to reach rank k. Let G_k be a random variable indicating the *actual* gain experienced by a particular user from the document at rank k, and let T_k be a random variable indicating the *actual* time taken by a user to reach rank k. Thus, we have

$$\sum_{k=1}^{\infty} g_k D(T(k)) = \sum_{k=1}^{\infty} E[G_k] D(E[T_k]) \tag{7}$$

$$\leq \sum_{k=1}^{\infty} E[G_k] E[D(T_k)] \tag{8}$$

$$= \sum_{k=1}^{\infty} E[G_k D(T_k)] \tag{9}$$

$$= E\left[\sum_{k=1}^{\infty} G_k D(T_k)\right]. \tag{10}$$

Equation 8 holds by Jensen's inequality, since exponential decay is convex. Equation 9 holds since G_k and T_k are independent. Equation 10 is the number of documents a user is expected to save as relevant. Hence, if we ignore normalization by setting $\mathcal{N} = 1$, we may interpret the measure as a lower bound on this value.

5.4 Normalization

Evaluation measures are typically normalized so that their values fall into the range [0:1]. Depending on the measure, this normalization may be required for the measure to be reasonably averaged over multiple queries, at least if an arithmetic mean is used. For example, the raw summation appearing in MAP is normalized by dividing it by the number of known relevant documents, so that it treats "all queries equally" [25].

The nDCG measure bases its normalization on the set of known relevant documents. It computes a maximum value for the summation in Equation 1 over a ranked list of these documents, which becomes the value for $\mathcal{N}$. If we know all relevant documents in the collection, we may follow a similar approach for time-biased gain, ranking these relevant documents in the order that maximizes Equation 2. Under this approach, the value for $\mathcal{N}$ varies from topic to topic, according to the set of relevant documents known for that topic. Unfortunately, as it does for nDCG, this approach suffers from the need to know all relevant documents, and the value of the measure will change if new relevant documents surface.

RBP bases its normalization on an idealized collection containing an unlimited number of relevant documents. We may follow a similar approach for time-biased gain by assuming an unlimited number of zero-length relevant documents. If we set $T_x = T_S + T_D(0)P(C = 1|R = 1)$, then over this idealized collection we have $T(k) = T_x \cdot (k - 1)$, so that

$$\mathcal{N} = \sum_{k=1}^{\infty} g_k D(T(k)) \tag{11}$$

$$= P(C = 1|R = 1)P(S = 1|R = 1) \sum_{k=0}^{\infty} e^{-T_x k \frac{\ln 2}{h}}$$

$$= \frac{P(C = 1|R = 1)P(S = 1|R = 1)}{1 - e^{-T_x \frac{\ln 2}{h}}}$$

Under this approach, $\mathcal{N}$ is now constant across all queries. For our calibration values, $\mathcal{N} \approx 17.1$.

Given our interpretation of time-biased gain as a lower bound on the number of documents a user is expected to save as relevant, normalization may not be necessary, and in this paper, we set $\mathcal{N} = 1$. The creators of ERR, who

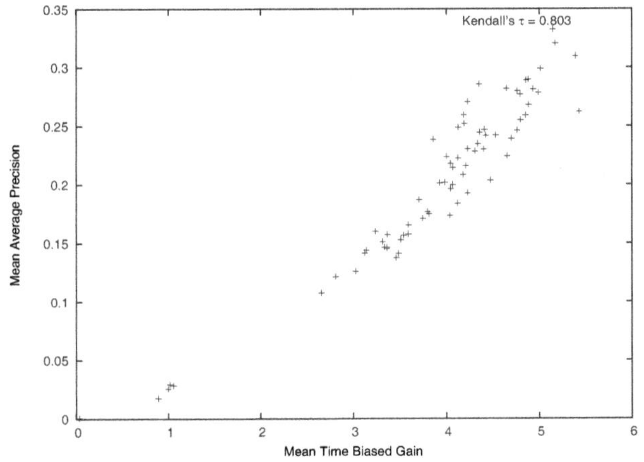

Figure 6: Time-biased gain compared against MAP over runs from the TREC 2005 Robust Task.

emphasize a similar interpretation, do not normalize that measure. In addition, normalization is not required if we average over topics using a geometric mean [25, 39]. We leave further exploration of normalization for future work.

6. COMPARISON

In this section, we provide a brief comparison between time-biased gain and other effectiveness measures used at TREC and elsewhere. Apart from time-biased gain, these measures are computed by the standard TREC evaluation program (`trec_eval`). All measures are computed over the runs submitted to the TREC 2005 Robust Track.

Figure 6 presents a scatter plot of MAP vs. time-biased gain. The measures are correlated, with a Kendall's τ of 0.794. Due to exponential decay, time-biased gain tends to emphasize early gain, a point illustrated by the run `uic0501`. Reflecting the behavior seen in Figure 4, it achieves the second-best performance, a time-biased gain value of 5.39 vs. a MAP value of 0.310, outperforming runs with higher MAP values.

With the best time-biased gain value of 5.43, and a MAP value of only 0.262, the run `sab05ror1` forms an interesting case study [6]. This run was trained on TREC vol. 4 & 5 qrels and documents and had very mixed performance across topics as measured by average precision. While the attempt appeared to fail when measured by MAP, the run's status as an obvious outlier suggests that the attempt may have succeeded after all (or at least warrants further investigation).

Sakai [29] proposes *discriminative power* as one method for assessing the behavior of effectiveness measures. While high discriminative power does not necessarily indicate a good measure, low discriminative power would raise questions about the measure. To calculate discriminative power, we compute a significance test between each pair of runs submitted to an experimental task, such as the TREC Robust Track. Discriminative power is the number of pairs that are significant at some fixed level. Table 2 compares the discriminative power of time-biased gain against several standard measures. MAP is known to have high discriminative power, due to the depth at which relevant document can influence its value. However, time-biased gain provides good discriminative power when compared to simple precision@10 and nDCG@K, for typical values of K.

Measure	t-test	Randomization	Bootstrap
MAP	66.0%	66.4%	67.2%
precision@10	51.6%	51.4%	52.7%
nDCG@10	49.5%	49.6%	51.0%
nDCG@20	54.5%	54.6%	55.6%
time-biased gain	57.5%	57.5%	58.8%

Table 2: Discriminative power of measures according a two-tailed paired t-test, a randomization test, and a bootstrap test (significance level 0.05).

7. CONCLUDING DISCUSSION

Equation 2 lies at the heart of our work. The remainder of the paper represents only one possible route for developing this equation. In following this route, we have adhered as closely as possible to the typical assumptions underlying a TREC task. We adopt the scenario of a careful and determined user, with a topical information need, intending to identify as much relevant material as they can in the time they have available. In another context, such as web search, another scenario will be more appropriate, requiring different calibration of the measure.

In following this route, we have also adhered as closely as possible to the typical assumptions underlying the creation of evaluation measures. Similar to the generic framework of Equation 1, time-biased gain is structured as a normalized sum over discounted gain values. Our primary innovation is to discount by time instead of rank.

However, a better numeric approximation to Equation 2 might be achieved through simulation. The user model described in Section 3 could easily be adapted for this purpose. By simulating thousands of users interacting with a result list, we may approximate both expected gain and variance. We leave this idea for future work.

Time-based calibration allows us to accommodate aspects of the search process that are ignored by traditional effectiveness measures. For example, in TREC collections longer documents are more likely to be relevant than shorter documents [31]. During the early years of TREC, considerable effort was made to adjust ranking functions according to document length [28, 31]. In light of the greater time required to judge longer documents, it may be that adjustment of the evaluation measures was also required.

We recognize that our approach to duplicates rewards behavior that might be viewed as undesirable by many users. Since we are following typical TREC guidelines for relevance, our calibration of time-biased gain rewards a system for returning duplicate documents, since they are faster to assess. In other contexts, it is likely that duplicates should provide no gain, thus penalizing runs through the extra time required to assess them. We considered following this approach in this paper, but decided to stay as true as possible to the TREC guidelines.

In this paper we focused on the population level behavior of determined, informational searchers. In future work, it would be good to study different classes of user behavior, and produce for each class a calibrated time-biased gain.

8. ACKNOWLEDGMENTS

We thank all of the anonymous reviewers for their comments. In particular, we thank Reviewer 3 for providing several pages of thoughtful feedback. Like Reviewer 3, we recognize the limitations of this paper's version of time-biased gain, and we plan to address these limitations in future work. Thanks to Ben Carterette and Falk Scholer for their helpful feedback on an early version of this paper. David Hu wrote the software to compute the sets of near-duplicate documents.

This work was supported in part by the Natural Sciences and Engineering Research Council of Canada (NSERC), in part by GRAND NCE, in part by Google, in part by an Amazon Web Services in Education Research Grant, in part by the facilities of SHARCNET, and in part by the University of Waterloo.

9. REFERENCES

[1] I. J. Aalbersberg. Incremental relevance feedback. In *SIGIR*, pp. 11–22. 1992.

[2] P. Arvola, J. Kekäläinen, and M. Junkkari. Expected reading effort in focused retrieval evaluation. *Information Retrieval*, 13:460–484, 2010.

[3] L. Azzopardi. The economics in interactive information retrieval. In *SIGIR*, pp. 15–24, 2011.

[4] L. Azzopardi, K. Järvelin, J. Kamps, and M. D. Smucker. Report on the SIGIR 2010 workshop on the simulation of interaction. *SIGIR Forum*, 44:35–47, 2011.

[5] A. Broder. On the resemblance and containment of documents. In *Compression and Complexity of Sequences*, pp. 21–29, 1997.

[6] C. Buckley. Looking at limits and tradeoffs: Sabir Research at TREC 2005. In *TREC*. 2005.

[7] B. Carterette. System effectiveness, user models, and user utility: A conceptual framework for investigation. In *SIGIR*, pp. 903–912, 2011.

[8] B. Carterette, E. Kanoulas, and E. Yilmaz. Simulating simple user behavior for system effectiveness evaluation. In *CIKM*, pp. 611–620, 2011.

[9] O. Chapelle, D. Metlzer, Y. Zhang, and P. Grinspan. Expected reciprocal rank for graded relevance. In *CIKM*, pp. 621–630, 2009.

[10] C. L. Clarke, N. Craswell, I. Soboroff, and A. Ashkan. A comparative analysis of cascade measures for novelty and diversity. In *WSDM*, pp. 75–84, 2011.

[11] W. S. Cooper. On selecting a measure of retrieval effectiveness. *JASIS*, 24(2):87–100, Mar/Apr 1973.

[12] W. S. Cooper. On selecting a measure of retrieval effectiveness: Part II. implementation of the philosophy. *JASIS*, 24(6):413–424, Nov/Dec 1973.

[13] M. D. Dunlop. Time, relevance and interaction modelling for information retrieval. In *SIGIR*, pp. 206–213. 1997.

[14] G. Dupret. Discounted cumulative gain and user decision models. In *SPIRE*, pp. 2–13. 2011.

[15] G. Dupret and B. Piwowarski. A user behavior model for average precision and its generalization to graded judgments. In *SIGIR*, pp. 531–538, 2010.

[16] N. Fuhr. A probability ranking principle for interactive information retrieval. *Information Retrieval*, 11:251–265, 2008.

[17] K. Järvelin and J. Kekäläinen. Cumulated gain-based evaluation of IR techniques. *ACM TOIS*, 20(4):422–446, 2002.

[18] D. Kelly. *Methods for Evaluating Interactive Information Retrieval Systems with Users*, now Publishers, 2009.

[19] H. Keskustalo, K. Järvelin, T. Sharma, and M. L. Nielsen. Test collection-based IR evaluation needs extension toward sessions: A case of extremely short queries. In *AIRS*, pp. 63–74, 2009.

[20] R. Khan, D. Mease, and R. Patel. The impact of result abstracts on task completion time. In *Workshop on Web Search Result Summarization and Presentation, WWW'09*.

[21] J. Lin and M. D. Smucker. How do users find things with PubMed? Towards automatic utility evaluation with user simulations. In *SIGIR*, pp. 19–26. 2008.

[22] L. Lorigo, M. Haridasan, H. Brynjarsdóttir, L. Xia, T. Joachims, G. Gay, L. Granka, F. Pellacini, and B. Pan. Eye tracking and online search: Lessons learned and challenges ahead. *JASIS*, 59(7):1041–1052, 2008.

[23] A. Moffat and J. Zobel. Rank-biased precision for measurement of retrieval effectiveness. *ACM TOIS*, 27(1):1–27, 2008.

[24] M. A. Najork, H. Zaragoza, and M. J. Taylor. HITS on the Web: How does it compare? In *SIGIR*, pp. 471–478, 2007.

[25] S. Robertson. On GMAP: and other transformations. In *CIKM*, pp. 78–83, 2006.

[26] S. Robertson. A new interpretation of average precision. In *SIGIR*, pp. 689–690, 2008.

[27] S. E. Robertson, E. Kanoulas, and E. Yilmaz. Extending average precision to graded relevance judgments. In *SIGIR*, pp. 603–610, 2010.

[28] S. E. Robertson and S. Walker. Some simple effective approximations to the 2-Poisson model for probabilistic weighted retrieval. In *SIGIR*, pp. 232–241, 1994.

[29] T. Sakai. Evaluating evaluation metrics based on the bootstrap. In *SIGIR*, pp. 525–532, 2006.

[30] T. Sakai and S. Robertson. Modelling a user population for designing information retrieval metrics. In *EVIA*, pp. 30–41, 2008.

[31] A. Singhal, G. Salton, M. Mitra, and C. Buckley. Document length normalization. *IPM*, 32(5):619–633, 1996.

[32] T. Strohman, D. Metzler, H. Turtle, and W. B. Croft. Indri: A language-model based search engine for complex queries (extended version). Tech Report IR-407, CIIR, University of Massachusetts Amherst, 2005.

[33] M. D. Smucker. An analysis of user strategies for examining and processing ranked lists of documents. In *HCIR*, 2011.

[34] M. D. Smucker and C. Jethani. Human performance and retrieval precision revisited. In *SIGIR*, pp. 595–602, 2010.

[35] L. T. Su. Evaluation measures for interactive information retrieval. *IPM*, 28:503–516, March 1992.

[36] A. Tombros and M. Sanderson. Advantages of query biased summaries in information retrieval. In *SIGIR*, pp. 2–10, 1998.

[37] A. Turpin, F. Scholer, K. Järvelin, M. Wu, and J. S. Culpepper. Including summaries in system evaluation. In *SIGIR*, pp. 508–515. 2009.

[38] A. H. Turpin and W. Hersh. Why batch and user evaluations do not give the same results. In *SIGIR*, pp. 225–231, 2001.

[39] E. M. Voorhees. Overview of the TREC 2005 Robust Retrieval Track. In *TREC*, 2005.

[40] R. W. White, I. Ruthven, J. M. Jose, and C. J. van Rijsbergen. Evaluating implicit feedback models using searcher simulations. *ACM TOIS*, 23(3):325–361, 2005.

[41] Y. Yang and A. Lad. Modeling expected utility of multi-session information distillation. In *ICTIR*, pp. 164–175, 2009.

[42] E. Yilmaz, M. Shokouhi, N. Craswell, and S. Robertson. Expected browsing utility for web search evaluation. In *CIKM*, pp. 1561–1564, 2010.

[43] Y. Zhang, L. A. Park, and A. Moffat. Click-based evidence for decaying weight distributions in search effectiveness metrics. *Information Retrieval*, 13:46–69, 2010.

Time Drives Interaction: Simulating Sessions in Diverse Searching Environments

Feza Baskaya, Heikki Keskustalo, Kalervo Järvelin
School of Information Sciences
FI-33014
University of Tampere, Finland
{ Feza.Baskaya, Heikki.Keskustalo, Kalervo.Jarvelin }@uta.fi

ABSTRACT

Real life information retrieval takes place in sessions, where users search by iterating between various cognitive, perceptual and motor subtasks through an interactive interface. The sessions may follow diverse strategies, which, together with the interface characteristics, affect user effort (cost), experience and session effectiveness. In this paper we propose a pragmatic evaluation approach based on scenarios with explicit subtask costs. We study the limits of effectiveness of diverse interactive searching strategies in two searching environments (the scenarios) under overall cost constraints. This is based on a comprehensive simulation of 20 million sessions in each scenario. We analyze the effectiveness of the session strategies over time, and the properties of the most and the least effective sessions in each case. Furthermore, we will also contrast the proposed evaluation approach with the traditional one, rank based evaluation, and show how the latter may hide essential factors that affect users' performance and satisfaction - and gives even counter-intuitive results.

Categories and Subject Descriptors

H.3.3 [**Information Search and Retrieval**]: Search process

Keywords

Session-based evaluation, simulation, time-based evaluation

1. INTRODUCTION

Interaction through search interface and environment greatly affects the user behavior, user experience, and user performance.

Many earlier studies have extended the traditional Cranfield view of IR and discussed various aspects of interactive searching (see, e.g., [4], [5], [6], [13], [21]), user interaction, and query modification (see, e.g., [3], [10], [14], [28]).

During interaction the user selects between *subtasks*, e.g., whether to scan the result or launch a new query instead, and how to construct the query. Such selections obviously affect session gains. However, different subtasks also have costs, e.g., they take time. This is important because real life IR often takes place under (time) constraints. In particular, keeping the overall session cost reasonable may be essential for end users.

The costs of subtasks may vary for many reasons between searching environments. For example, regarding the query side, small devices and touch screens are inconvenient for typing [11]. Recently, novel kinds of searching devices, including personal phone-based mobile devices, have become increasingly popular.

In order to minimize the overall session costs, a mobile phone user might e.g., avoid typing and prefer result scanning. Low input costs might change the situation from the user's point of view, leading to longer queries. Therefore, if we assume two users having identical needs and identical cost constraints regarding the overall session time, it is possible that different devices render different subtask combinations optimal in searching.

Traditional IR evaluation focuses on the quality of the ranked output. In this view, the costs of posing queries are non-problematic, even uninteresting. In this paper we will utilize simple scenarios to bring time factors into the research setting. Scenarios formalize and quantify the gains and costs of interactive sessions. We construct two cases – a personal desktop computer (PC) and a smart phone (SP) case, with subtask costs derived from the literature. We will simulate session interaction involving multiple queries based on prototypical but empirically grounded query modification strategies using a test collection. We then explore the effectiveness of searching via the exhaustive set of querying-scanning combinations possible, and evaluate the effectiveness of both scenarios in terms of Cumulated Gain (CG) [16] under time constraint (overall session time). We use non-normalized metrics, because normalized metrics may yield misleading results, especially if time is taken into account.

Early papers on IR evaluation had a comprehensive approach to interactive IR evaluation. Cleverdon et al. [8] pointed out, among others, physical and intellectual user effort as an important factor in IR evaluation. Salton [24] identified user effort measures in the context of IR evaluation. More recently Su [30] gave a comparison of 20 different evaluation measures for interactive IR, including actual cost of search, several utility measures, and worth of search results vs. time expended. The interactive aspect of IR requires attention because previous studies have repeatedly shown that discrepancy exists between interactive and non-interactive evaluation results. Hersh et al. [12] showed that a weighting scheme giving maximum improvement over the baseline in non-interactive batch evaluation failed to surpass others when real users performed a simulated task. Turpin and Hersh [31] observed that a system superior over the baseline in batch evaluation, measured by mean

Permission to make digital or hard copies of all or part of this work for personal or classroom use is granted without fee provided that copies are not made or distributed for profit or commercial advantage and that copies bear this notice and the full citation on the first page. To copy otherwise, or republish, to post on servers or to redistribute to lists, requires prior specific permission and/or a fee.
SIGIR'12, August 12-16, 2012, Portland, Oregon, USA.
Copyright 2012 ACM 978-1-4503-1472-5/12/08…$10.00.

average precision, was not superior in an interactive situation. Turpin and Scholer [32] found no significant relationship between the search engine effectiveness measured by mean average precision and real user success in a precision-oriented task. Smith and Kantor [25] observed that users of degraded systems were as successful as those using non-degraded systems. They suggested that users achieved this by altering their behavior.

Dunlop [9] proposed "time-to-view" graphs, which incorporate user interface and system as well as the time component into the same framework for evaluation of system effectiveness. However he did not analyze time constraints, query modification strategies and different devices.

Smucker [26] brought time factors into the traditional Cranfield setting by augmenting it with the use of the GOMS [7] model (acronym for Goals, Operators, Methods, and Selections). He suggests a user model for IR where the search process is seen as a sequence of actions (e.g., typing; clicking; evaluating a summary; waiting for the results to load) with associated times and probabilities (e.g., whether the simulated user will click on a relevant summary). He used the model in a simulated study to demonstrate the impact of changes in the IR system interface (e.g., when the speed and accuracy of the summary evaluation is varied) on user performance (the number of relevant documents read within a given time frame). While his experiment was limited to single query situations, the approach can be extended to multiple query scenarios, e.g., for computing the costs of specific query reformulations.

Azzopardi [2] addressed the cost aspect by treating interactive IR as an *economical* problem and studied the trade-off between querying and browsing while maintaining a given level of normalized CG (NCG) [15] in sessions. His analysis focused on querying – scanning depth combinations for various formal retrieval methods that deliver a given level of NCG.

Our approach in the present paper differs from earlier studies. Our study is based on the simulation of multiple-query sessions generated with various query modification and scanning strategies in different searching environments.

In the next section we start by discussing session generation with costs, and present the research questions. In Section 3 we describe the research setting. In Section 4 we will run an experiment in a test collection based on scenarios and discuss the results. We close the paper by discussing the significance of our approach in the last section.

2. CONSTRUCTION OF SESSIONS

A *use case* is "a relatively informal description of system's behavior and usage, intended to capture the functional requirements of the system by describing the interaction between the outside actors and the system, to reach the goal of the primary actor" [19]. We utilize simplified use cases, which we call scenarios, to present an alternative way to look at the effectiveness of IR approaches based on the user viewpoint. The next subsections will first explain the session generation formally, and then explain the specific query modification (QM) and scanning strategies utilized in the scenarios.

2.1 Session generation

For session simulation, we first formally generate all possible sessions under constraints. We will represent sessions as sequences of actions with costs. For example the tuple $<(a_1,c_1), (a_2,c_2), \ldots, (a_n,c_n)>$ is a session of *n* actions and each pair (a_i,c_i) in the session representation represents an action a_i and its cost c_i. The elementary action types are:

- Initial query, represented as ('iq', ic), where 'iq' is the action label and ic ($\in$R) the cost in seconds.
- Query reformulation ('q', qc), where 'q' is the action label and qc ($\in$R) the cost in seconds.
- Document snippet scan ('s', sc), where 's' is the action label and sc ($\in$R) the cost in seconds.
- Next page request ('n', nc), where 'n' is the action label and nc ($\in$R) the cost in seconds.

The constraints are:

- MaxSLen, maximum session length in terms of elementary actions, here 50 actions.
- MaxSCost, maximum session cost (seconds), here 60, 90 or 120 seconds.
- A session always begins with an initial query.
- All queries (initial and reformulation) are followed by at least one snippet scan.
- The longest scan sequence we consider is a scan of 10 snippets (i.e. one typical result page).

In effect, the shortest possible session therefore is initial action IA = <(iq, ic),(s, sc)>, consisting of an initial query followed by the scan of one snippet (with costs). To generate longer sessions, we define the set NA for the possible subsequent actions:

$$NA = \{<(q, qc), (s, sc)>, <(s, sc)>, <(n,nc), (s,sc)>\}$$

Note here that the next actions are tuples of one or two elementary actions; a scan may appear individually, while a reformulation / next page requires a scan to follow. Sessions are generated by concatenating next actions to the initial action. Concatenation of two tuples $S_1 = <e_1, e_2, \ldots, e_n>$ and $S_2 = <f_1, f_2, \ldots, f_m>$ is denoted by $<S_1, S_2> = <e_1, e_2, \ldots, e_n, f_1, f_2, \ldots, f_m>$. This operation generalizes over a set of session tuples S_i, denoted as:

$$\times_{i=1\ldots n} S_i = <<\ldots <<S_1, S_2>, S_3>, \ldots>, S_n>.$$

The cost of a session S is, informally, the sum of its action costs. More formally, we derive this cost by the function *s-cost* as follows:

$$s\text{-}cost(S) = \sum_{(a,c) \in S} c$$

[N.B. we extend the definition of the set membership operator from sets to tuple components in an obvious way.] For example, the cost of the session S1 = <('iq', ic),('s', sc), ('q', qc),('s', sc)> is *s-cost*(S1) = ic+sc+qc+sc.

The condition of maximum scan length of *n* in a session S is enforced by the Boolean predicate *max-scan*(S, *n*). It yields 'true' for a given session S if S does not contain a subsequence of scan actions $<(\text{'s'}, sc)_1, (\text{'s'}, sc)_2, \ldots, (\text{'s'}, sc)_n>$, otherwise 'false' (formal definition here omitted for brevity).

To generate sessions, we first generate all sessions up to the max number of actions MaxSLen. This session set is MLS:

$$MLS = \bigcup_{i=1\ldots MaxSLen} \{<IA, \times_{j=1\ldots i} ac_j > \mid ac_j \in NA\}$$

We then select the subset of sessions fulfilling the time constraint MaxSCost and the scan length constraint as follows. All sessions in MLS with maximal cost MaxSCost (or less) form the set MCS:

$$MCS = \{S \in MLS \mid s\text{-}cost(S) \leq MaxSCost \wedge max\text{-}scan(S, 11)\}$$

Note that this approach does not define the query contents or modifications in sessions. However, it keeps them within constraints and guarantees that the last action is a document snippet scan. In our experiments, we excluded the next page action from NA due to the max scan length constraint of 10. The next two sub-sections explain and justify the query modification and scanning strategies used in the experiment.

2.2 Query Modification Strategies

We will simulate interactive search sessions as querying-scanning iterations having a goal, a procedure to reach the goal, and constraints regarding the procedure. We define the goal in terms of maximizing CG during the session under the constraint on the overall session time available. The procedure is defined in terms of QM and scanning strategies.

The previous section did not define any particular QM strategies. We assume that a set of individual words $\{w_1, w_2, w_3, w_4, w_5\}$ is available for each particular topic, and QM strategies determine how elements from this set are combined to form queries (either the initial query, or one of the subsequent queries). In other words, given a set of individual search words for the topic, the QM strategy defines how to form a sequence of queries.

Five QM strategies (S1 – S5) were used in the experiment. These prototypical strategies are based on term level changes which have grounding in the observed real life behavior and are justified by literature (see [1], [20], [33]):

- **S1**: an initial one-word query (w_1) is followed by repeatedly varying the search word :
  Q_1: w_1 -> Q_2: w_2 ->Q_3: w_3 ->Q_4: w_4 ->Q_5: w_5
- **S2**: an initial two-word query ($w_1\,w_2$) is followed by queries formed by repeatedly varying the second word :
  Q_1: $w_1\,w_2$ -> Q_2: $w_1\,w_3$ -> Q_3: $w_1\,w_4$ -> Q_4: $w_1\,w_5$
- **S3**: an initial three-word query ($w_1\,w_2\,w_3$) is followed by queries formed by repeatedly varying the third word :
  Q_1: $w_1\,w_2\,w_3$ -> Q_2: $w_1\,w_2\,w_4$ -> Q_3: $w_1\,w_2\,w_5$
- **S4**: an initial one-word query (w_1) is followed by adding one word to each subsequent query :
  Q_1: w_1 -> Q_2: $w_1\,w_2$ -> Q_3:$w_1\,w_2\,w_3$ -> Q_4:$w_1\,w_2\,w_3\,w_4$ -> ...
- **S5**: an initial two-word query ($w_1\,w_2$) is followed by adding one word to each subsequent query :
  Q_1: $w_1\,w_2$ -> Q_2: $w_1\,w_2\,w_3$ -> Q_3: $w_1\,w_2\,w_3\,w_4$ -> ...

This means that the sessions consist of at most 3 to 5 queries; this reflects real life behavior [22]. Generally speaking, constructing a query entails a cost due to the cognitive user load plus the edit costs. We will return to the cost factors in Section 2.4.

2.3 Scanning Strategies

The user may simply scan one or more documents after each query before formulating the next query candidate or ending the session. After a *single* query Q_i a sequence of one or more document snippets may be scanned:

Q_1->s_{11}->s_{12}->s_{13}->...

The cost of this session manifests as:

$qc_1 + sc_{11} + sc_{12} + sc_{13} + ...$

When a *set* of queries is available for one topic, the user can scan varying numbers of document snippets after any particular query, leading to a vast number of possible querying-scanning *sessions*, e.g.,

Q_1->s_{11}->Q_2->s_{21}->Q_3->s_{31}-> ... or

Q_1->s_{11}->s_{12}->Q_2->s_{21}->... or

Q_1->s_{11}->s_{12}->s_{13}->Q_2->s_{21}-> s_{22}->Q_3->s_{31}->... etc.

In real life a session typically continues until the user has found what he was looking for, at least partially, and/or when he runs out of time or queries. The scanning lengths may fluctuate for many reasons. In this paper we study the properties of optimal and less optimal interactive behaviors in sessions below the given overall time constraint. Therefore we produced *all* possible sessions as follows. For all five QM strategies we formed all possible combinations of scanning lengths exhaustively (from 1 to 10 documents) using a sequence of all possible queries available per topic (cf. equation MCS in Section 2.1). We focus on the top documents because only few top documents may be inspected by the user in real life [14], [23], and only these may matter for the user [1]. As we had 5 words for each topic, sessions had at most 5 queries, controlled by the QM strategy and time constraint. As the query words were ordered by quality (see 3.1), the query words were used in that particular order, not permuted.

2.4 Cost Factors

There is a cost involved with the subtasks of formulating the query and scanning. We assume that the *absolute cost* is partially determined by the scenario. Empirical studies show that it takes significantly more time to enter queries by using a small smart phone keypad than by using an ordinary keyboard [17]. To study the significance of subtask costs under overall session cost constraint we define two scenarios, i.e., a Desktop PC scenario (PC) and a Smart phone scenario (SP). These scenarios have different subtask costs. This is justified because the properties of the devices partially determine the subtask costs [17].

Obviously, also forming queries under different QM strategies S1 – S5 have very different *relative costs.* All queries in strategies S1, S2 and S3 have a fixed query length in sessions (one, two or three words, correspondingly) while in strategies S4 and S5 the queries grow longer. In real life the typing speed is affected by, e.g., the experience and knowledge of the person, the size of the keyboard, the layout of the keyboard (e.g., nine-key multi-tap vs. qwerty keyboard) [17], [18], and whether predictive text feed is available and used. We used literature to derive the cost values in scenarios PC and SP regarding the initial query cost and the subsequent query cost (Table 1).The query costs in S1 – S5 in the Desktop PC case are based on the typing costs of 3.0 seconds per word. The corresponding Smart Phone costs are based on [17]. The authors performed a large-scale log analysis of cell phone usage and observed that an average smart phone query length was 2.56 words and the average query-entry time was 39.8 seconds (average typing cost of 15.5 seconds per word). We assume in our simulations that the cost of *adding* one word to a query (that is, S4 and S5) or *replacing* one word at the end of the previous query (that is, S1, S2, S3) is a constant, i.e., either 3.0 or 15.5 seconds depending on the scenario.

Table 1. Average subtask costs (in seconds) of five QM strategies (S1-S5) for two scenarios: (i) initial query cost, (ii) subsequent query cost, and (iii) the cost of scanning one document snippet

Scenario 1: Desktop PC					
QM strategy	**S1**	**S2**	**S3**	**S4**	**S5**
Initial query	3.0	6.0	9.0	3.0	6.0
Subsequent query	3.0	3.0	3.0	3.0	3.0
Snip. scanning cost	3.0	3.0	3.0	3.0	3.0
Scenario 2: Smart Phone					
QM Strategy	**S1**	**S2**	**S3**	**S4**	**S5**
Initial query	15.5	31.0	46.5	15.5	31.0
Subsequent query	15.5	15.5	15.5	15.5	15.5
Snip. scanning cost	3.0	3.0	3.0	3.0	3.0

To check whether these costs are reasonable we also performed a small-scale experiment where four test persons typed the initial and subsequent queries according to strategies S1-S5 using two types of interfaces (Desktop PC and Smart Phone) for three test topics. The experiment corroborated that the query time estimates were reasonable.

The document snippet scanning costs in real life are affected by the motor and perceptual costs plus the cognitive load related to the task. In this study we assume that the document snippet scanning cost is constant in both scenarios and across the searching strategies S1 – S5 (see Table 1). In the SP case we defined a scanning cost of three seconds per snippet. We justify this by an observation by Kamvar and Baluja [17] that the average cell phone user used 30 seconds to scan the search results before selecting one, after receiving 10 search results. For the snippet scanning costs in the Desktop PC case we decided to use the same value. Obviously, our methodology is well-suited to experiment with different costs. The overall cost constraint of a session was defined as 60, 90, or 120 seconds. In the simulations all subtasks (querying and scanning) had to be performed within this time constraint. We excluded the eventual thinking time in producing query words.

2.5 Research questions

We set forth the following research questions:

1. How effective are the five QM strategies (S1 to S5) in terms of CG when we compare the Desktop PC and the Smart Phone scenarios under overall time constraint?
2. What are the characteristics of the best and the worst sessions achieved in terms of average scan length, and average number of queries?
3. How stable are the observed trends when the overall time constraint changes? Can we recommend QM strategies based on the scenario - what to do, and what not to do, assuming a specific time constraint?
4. What is proper evaluation methodology when time is part of the evaluation setting?

3. RESEARCH SETTING

3.1 Test Collection and Search Engine

We used a subset of the TREC 7-8 document collection with 41 topics for the experiment. The documents have graded relevance assessments on a four-point scale with respect to the topics. [27]

The present authors obtained query words for session generation for the test topics from [20] where the authors used real test persons to suggest keywords of various lengths for queries on the 41 topics. The test persons were asked to directly propose good search words from topic descriptions (descriptions and narratives) in a structured way. Among others, they produced query versions of various lengths: (i) one word, (ii) two words, and (iii) three or more words. These were collected per topic as ordered word lists of 5 words for each topic. During the query formulation experiment the test persons did not interact with a real retrieval system. While this may have affected negatively the quality of queries, Keskustalo and colleagues [20] suggest that the test persons were able to construct the query words in a descending order of effectiveness.

Retrieval system *Lemur* with language modeling and two-stage smoothing options was used in the experiment.

3.2 Session Data

For each topic we utilized a minimum of 1 query and a maximum of 5 queries in each session. A minimum of 1 document snippet and a maximum of 10 document snippets were scanned per query.

In Table 2, the number of possible scanning paths is given for consecutive queries. If the session comprises at most 2 queries, first there are 10 possible paths after the first query, and for every path there are 10 possible paths after the second query. So the combinations of these at most two queries sum up to 10+10*10 =110 possible paths. In our experiment design, users can pose up to 5 queries depending on session strategy; this presents altogether 111,110 possible paths, which are taken into consideration.

Table 2. Number of possible sessions per number of queries, when at most 10 documents can be scanned after each query

Queries	1	2	3	4	5	Σ
Possible sessions	10	100	1000	10,000	100,000	111,110

We ran all 41 topics * 5 QM strategies * Q queries, $Q \in \{3, 4, 5\}$ depending on the strategy, and collected their results. Then we generated all 111K possible sessions from the query results, pruned the ones exceeding the time constraint in each scenario, and by using the recall base (qrels), evaluated the CG of the scanned snippets for each session. For example, for the session Q_1->s_{11}-> s_{12}->s_{13}->Q_2->s_{21}->s_{22}->Q_3->s_{31}, the CG is calculated on the basis of the snippet sequence s_{11}, s_{12}, s_{13}, s_{21}, s_{22}, s_{31}. Altogether about 45 million sessions (41 topics * 5 QM strategies* 111,110 possible scanning sessions * 2 scenarios) were evaluated. As the collection has graded relevance assessments, CG was incremented by 3 points for the highly relevant documents, 2 points for the fairly relevant documents and 1 point for the marginal ones. Whenever a duplicate was retrieved by a subsequent query in a session, its gain was nullified. Finally, we ranked all sessions within a topic and a strategy by their CG scores. In this data set per topic, strategy and time constraint, each session is represented by its tuple of actions (see 2.1) and its gain.

3.3 Data Analysis

The action tuples allow the analysis of the number of queries and the length of each scan in a session. The ranked order of sessions allows identification of the best and the worst session across topics, strategy, scenario, and time constraint. We analyze the sets of 10 best sessions, and 10 worst sessions per topic as averages instead the single best or worst session. This approach smoothes minor random variations in human behavior and thus the set of top (bottom) 10 sessions provide more reliable measurements compared to the single best/worst session when we explore their properties under varying conditions. Since the present study does not aim to prove one retrieval method better than another, we report the findings without tests on significance of statistical differences.

4. EXPERIMENTS

4.1 Results for the 60 Seconds Time Frame

First we discuss the CG results under the two scenarios, PC and SP. We present the best case and worst case results regarding all querying-scanning sessions based on the five QM strategies: S1 (*sequence of individual* words); S2 (*two-words;* last word varied); S3 (*three-words;* last word varied); S4 (incremental extension starting from *one* word); and S5 (incremental extension starting from *two* words). Table 3 gives the averaged CG values, the number of queries and scans per query for 10 best and 10 worst cases for every QM strategy for the 60 second time constraint, which are utilized in the following figures in this section.

Table 3. Averaged CG, number of Queries (#q) and Scans per Query (s/q) for scenarios PC and SP, for 5 strategies for the 10 best (b) and 10 worst (w) sessions, time constraint 60 seconds

Time	Environment		Query Modification Strategies				
(60 s)	best/worst		S1	S2	S3	S4	S5
avg. CG	PC	b	4.9	8.3	8.5	7.9	8.1
		w	1.2	5.4	7.1	4.7	6.0
	SP	b	2.8	3.6	2.3	4.4	3.7
		w	1.2	2.8	2.3	2.0	2.9
avg. #q	PC	b	2.7	2.6	2.5	4.2	3.0
		w	5.0	4.0	3.0	5.0	4.0
	SP	b	1.9	1.5	1.0	2.0	1.5
		w	2.7	1.7	1.0	2.6	1.7
avg. s/q	PC	b	6.4	6.3	6.2	3.8	5.3
		w	3.0	3.8	5.0	3.0	3.8
	SP	b	4.7	3.6	2.5	4.0	3.6
		w	1.6	2.5	2.5	1.7	2.5

Table 4 and Table 5 are equivalent to Table 3 but for the time constraints 90 and 120 seconds, respectively. Figure 1 shows the CG of the best (worst) sessions for each strategy in both scenarios under the overall cost constraint of 60 seconds. Note that all sessions require 60 seconds or less if no further action fits in (the absolutely worst imaginable session without any time requirement, in terms of the CG, would naturally consist of the initial action (IA) only). In other words, regarding the worst results, we report CG for the worst possible 60 second performance.

When the best sessions of the PC and SP cases are compared in Figure 1, the PC case performs at a considerably higher level (average CG is above 8 in three strategies) than the SP case (average CG is below 5 in all strategies).

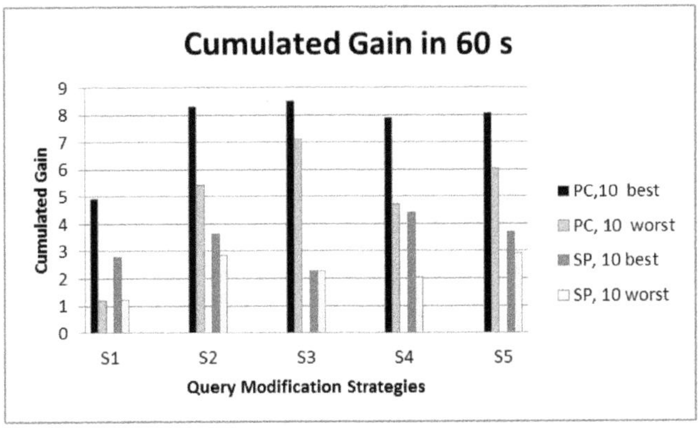

Fig 1. Cumulated Gain under cost constraint of 60 seconds.

Second, when the best and the worst cases are compared within the scenarios, not surprisingly, the best case results are typically clearly better than the worst case results except in SP case for S3. In the latter case both the best and the worst session may not contain more than one query because of high query entry cost.

Third, among the best cases for PC the strategies S2 and S3 are almost equally good. For the SP case, the strategy S2 (varying the second word), S4 (extending from one word), and S5 (extending from two words) lead to much higher gain than S1 and S3. An interesting trade-off in the SP scenario can be observed when the scanning length is considered. In the best case the gain reached increases from S1 to S2. However, the average scanning length decreases (Fig. 2). In other words, a better result is achieved using the longer queries although a smaller number of documents are scanned on the average; the ranking is simply better.

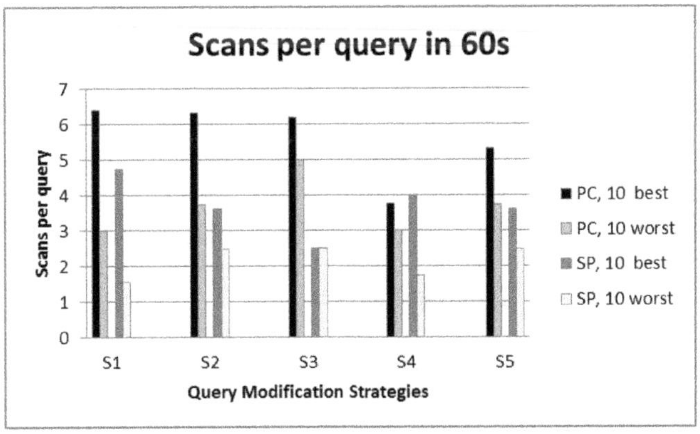

Fig 2. Average number of scanned document snippets per query under cost constraint of 60 seconds.

Table 4. Averaged CG, number of Queries (#q) and Scans per Query (s/q) for scenarios PC and SP, for 5 strategies for the 10 best (b) and 10 worst (w) sessions, time constraint 90 seconds

Time (90 s)	Environment best/worst		S1	S2	S3	S4	S5
avg. CG	PC	b	5.8	10.5	10.4	10.4	10.5
		w	1.9	7.6	10.3	7.6	8.7
	SP	b	5.0	7.3	6.0	7.1	7.0
		w	0.9	2.5	3.0	2.5	2.6
avg. #q	PC	b	3.8	3.5	3.0	5.0	4.0
		w	5.0	4.0	3.0	5.0	4.0
	SP	b	2.0	2.0	1.9	2.5	2.0
		w	4.1	3.4	2.6	4.1	3.4
avg. s/q	PC	b	6.9	7.3	8.3	5.0	6.3
		w	5.0	6.3	8.3	5.0	6.3
	SP	b	8.8	6.8	4.7	6.3	6.8
		w	1.6	1.4	1.7	1.4	1.4

(Columns S1–S5: Query Modification Strategies)

4.2 Results for the 90 Seconds Time Frame

Figure 3 shows the CG results when the sessions take 90 seconds. In this case, the observations comply with the 60 second case. Difference between S3's best and worst CG values is closing in the PC scenario; this is because of lacking further scanning options, there is now enough time to scan almost all 10 documents for each query. S3 strategy has a maximum of 3 queries to execute before the 5 keywords run out. This in turn confines the possible scanning space. It is also conspicuous that the difference between best and worst CG values in SP case is much larger than in PC case.

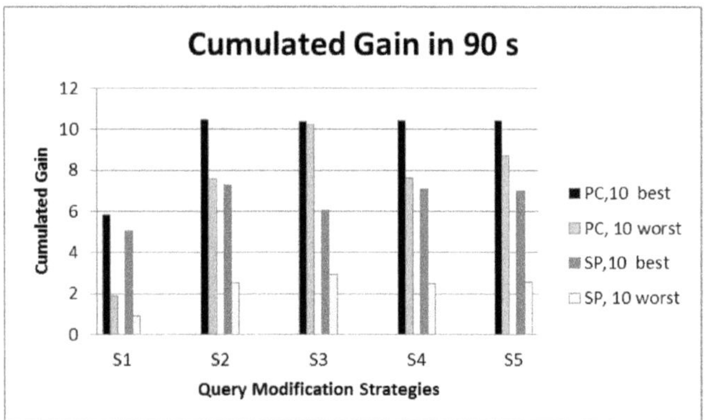

Fig 3. Cumulated Gain under cost constraint of 90 seconds.

When scanning in the best sessions of the PC and SP cases is compared (Fig. 4), we notice that even though the scans per query values for SP case are higher than or similar to the PC case, the CG values are always poorer (Fig. 3). This is due to the smaller number of posed queries in SP case than in PC case. This follows from the trade-off between query vs. scan costs.

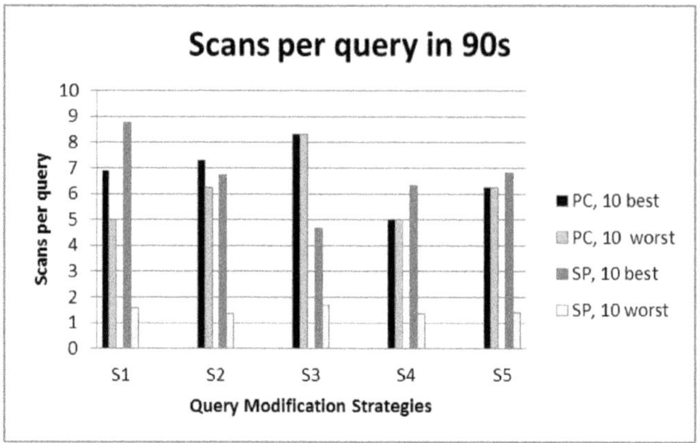

Fig 4. Average number of scanned document snippets per query under cost constraint of 90 seconds.

Interestingly, the difference between the best and the worst sessions both in terms of gain and average scan length remains great in SP case, but fades away in PC case. In the latter, 90 seconds allows the searcher to launch almost all queries and scan the best results in all cases. When the results are compared between different strategies, the strategy S4 with on average 5 scans in PC case and approximately 6 scans in SP case (Fig. 4) produce similar CG values as the other QM strategies (Fig. 3). Again, larger queries yield better rankings. On the other hand, S3 in SP case has less than 5 scans per query, and still achieves slightly better CG results than S1 strategy.

Table 5. Averaged CG, number of Queries (#q) and Scans per Query (s/q) for scenarios PC and SP, for 5 strategies for the 10 best (b) and 10 worst (w) sessions, time constraint 120 seconds

Time (120 s)	Environment best/worst		S1	S2	S3	S4	S5
avg. CG	PC	b	6.4	11.1	11.4	11.7	11.5
		w	3.4	10.5	11.4	10.0	10.9
	SP	b	5.6	9.1	9.2	9.1	8.9
		w	1.1	5.1	6.7	4.5	5.7
avg. #q	PC	b	4.8	4.0	3.0	5.0	4.0
		w	5.0	4.0	3.0	5.0	4.0
	SP	b	3.0	2.9	2.0	3.0	2.9
		w	5.0	4.0	3.0	5.0	4.0
avg. s/q	PC	b	7.3	8.8	10.0	7.0	8.8
		w	7.0	8.8	10.0	7.0	8.8
	SP	b	7.6	6.6	8.8	7.6	6.5
		w	2.8	3.5	4.7	2.8	3.5

(Columns S1–S5: Query Modification Strategies)

4.3 Results for the 120 Seconds Time Frame

Figure 5 shows the CG values under the cost constraint of 120 seconds. In the PC case, the gaps between the best and worst CG values are diminishing. This can be explained so that every strategy except S1and S4 has enough time to pose all the queries and employ much scanning. According to the experiment design, worst cases must also use up the allocated time, and this results in that there is enough time to launch all queries and scan the results. When the best sessions of the PC and SP cases are compared, we notice that there are no large differences. Again, in Figure 6 we can see as many scans per query (S/Q) for S1 and S4 in the SP case as in the

PC case for best sessions. Besides all the strategies for PC case show the same S/Q for 10 best and 10 worst sessions. Although in SP case S/Q values diverge from each other, Figure 6 exhibits similar patterns as Figure 4. From Figure 5 one can conclude that, if there is enough time for searching, one should use at least two word queries for good results. If the queries are of lower quality like S1, then scanning matters. In short, the more you scan, the more you get.

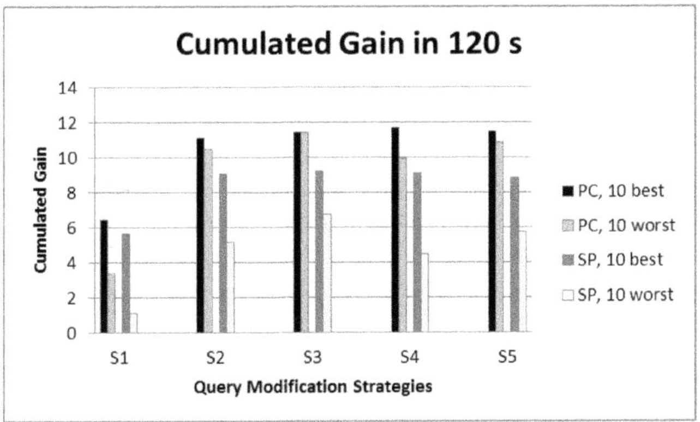

Fig 5. Cumulated Gain under cost constraint of 120 seconds.

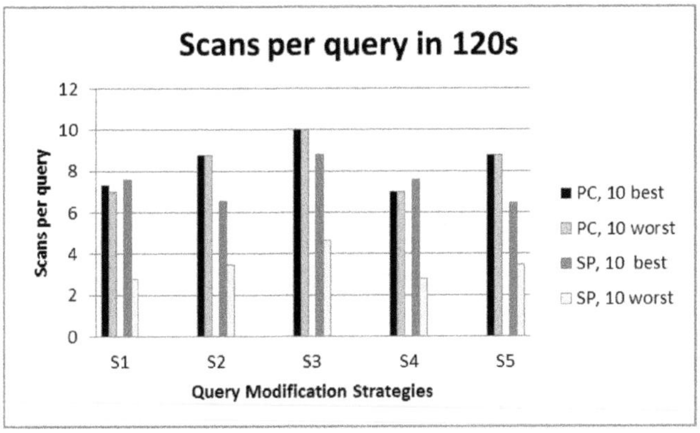

Fig 6. Average number of scanned document snippets per query under cost constraint of 120 seconds.

5. DISCUSSION

We had three empirical and one methodological research question. The three empirical ones were about effectiveness of different QM strategies under time constraints, characteristics of the best and the worst QM sessions, and the stability of the observed trends. The methodological one was about proper evaluation of sessions under time constraints. We will consider each of the questions below.

Strategy effectiveness. Given a stringent time frame in the PC scenario, the user cannot use the entire vocabulary (all queries) and perform exhaustive scanning for all queries. Short queries (strategy S1) are clearly inferior regarding session effectiveness. It seems reasonable to invest on two to three word queries (S2, S3) because the evidence thereby added for ranking significantly improves the quality of the results. This can also be seen in strategies S4 and S5, when they have enough time to advance beyond the first query. When more time is allocated to searching, the weaker strategies catch up because there is more time for scanning the results and the weaker ranking effectiveness is not that critical.

In the SP scenario the rules of the game change a bit. In a stringent time frame there is no time for tedious query input, and one must compromise toward short scanning of weaker quality rankings. The more effective strategies cannot be applied at all due to high query input cost. Again, when more time is allocated, weaker strategies catch up. In the longest sessions of S2-S5, the gap between the best vs. worst sessions begins to close.

Session characteristics. In the PC scenario, under stringent time constraints, the best sessions involved less queries and longer scans than the worst sessions (Table 3). However, as the time allocation grows, the differences disappear. Between the best strategies in the PC case, both the number of queries and the average scan lengths increase as time allocation grows (Tables 3-5). Correspondingly, in the worst sessions, the number of queries does not change as time grows, but the scan lengths grow. This is because the worst sessions consume all possible queries even under the shortest time frame. Similarity with best sessions grows.

In the SP scenario, under stringent time constraints, the best sessions also involved less queries and longer scans than the worst sessions (Table 3). As the time allocation grows, the differences remain, probably due to shortage of time even in the longer sessions. Between the best strategies in the SP case, both the number of queries and the average scan lengths increase as time allocation grows, the latter dramatically between 60 and 90 seconds (Tables 3-4). Correspondingly, in the worst sessions, the number of queries grows along time, but the scan lengths remain low. The worst behavior here means investing the effort in query input. Also here there were interesting differences in scan lengths between queries in sessions.

All in all, if time allows, two to three first query words that one identifies, followed by a longer scan, seem to provide reasonable performance, no matter what the strategy among S2-S5 is.

Effect of time. With limited time allowance, it seems important to make a good compromise between providing evidence for ranking (longer queries) and scanning the search results. The compromise depends on the overall cost levels related to the stringency of the time frame and on the relations between cost types. This depends on the searching device. Expensive input favors scanning at length, cheap input favors better queries. The more time is available the less it matters how one searches – there will be time to identify the relevant documents.

Evaluation methodology. Typical IR evaluation metrics are based on the quality of ranking alone. In session-based evaluation they must be applied with great care because they may be insufficient or even misleading. They may be partially insensitive to the user's experience and observed costs and benefits. This is particularly critical, when user's costs (time expenditure) are taken into account and the metric employs normalization, i.e. scaling the measurements to a predefined range such as [0, 1]. For example, the popular NDCG metric [15] and its non-discounted counterpart NCG should be avoided in any comparisons between searching environments, and between strategies within a given searching environment *when* input costs are taken into account. This is because the ideal gain vector used for normalization is read to vastly different lengths between strategies or environments. For example, consider Figure 7, which plots NCG over time for strategy S2 in the two scenarios.

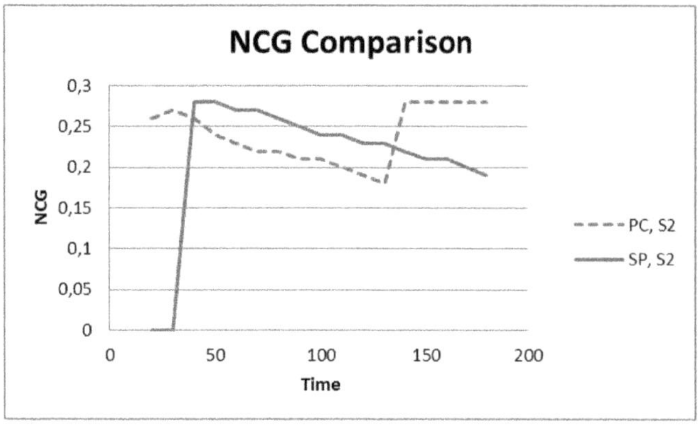

Fig 7. NCG vs. time comparison of PC and SP for S2 (41 Topics).

Due to normalization (division by the ideal cumulated gain vector) the SP scenario seems to have better performance in the time frame from 40 to 135 seconds. This is due to (a) ranking being somewhat effective, and (b) the number of documents seen in each session: in the PC case the user sees 15 to 35 documents, but in the SP case only 5 to 20 documents in the indicated time frame. Figure 8 plots CG with the corresponding data and makes the difference clear.

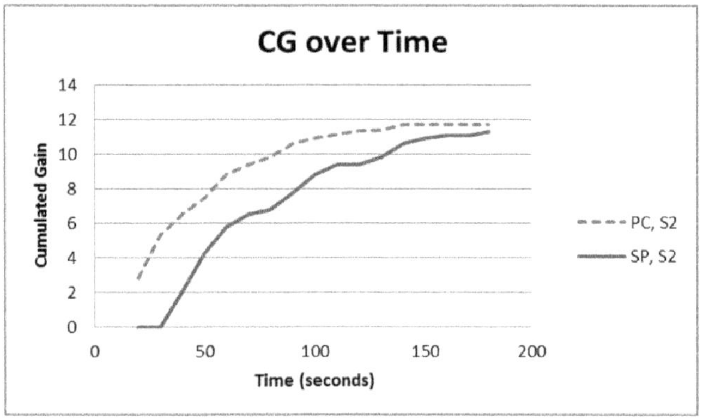

Fig 8. CG over time for S2 in scenarios PC and SP (41 Topics).

Similar pitfalls also plague the most classic metric, MAP. Consider the following two rankings observed for a given topic in two scenarios and/or strategies under the same time constraint (say, one minute; queries omitted and binary relevance for simplicity):

r1: 0 0 0 0 0 0 0 0 1 1

r2: 1 0 0 0 0

Further, assume that there are three relevant documents for the topic. The MAP for the ranking r1 is (1/9 + 2/10 + 0)/3 = 0.103 and for r2 (1 + 0 + 0)/3 = 0.333. Arguably, r2 is the better ranking, but if both require one minute, what is the user's opinion? The first session collected twice as many relevant documents.

Even within the un-normalized metric, such as CG, incorporating time in session-based evaluation has profound effects. Consider Figures 9 and 10. The former gives traditional cumulated gain over ranks for strategies S1 and S3 for the 41 topics. The latter gives CG over time in the two scenarios.

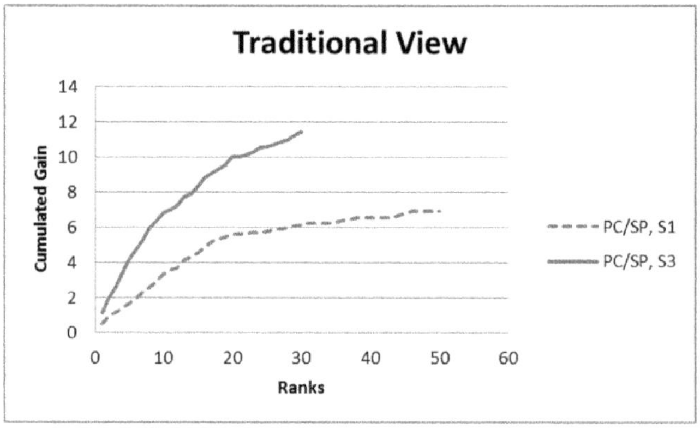

Fig 9. Traditional View, CGs over ranks for 41 topics, scenarios PC and SP for strategies S1 (allowing 5 queries) and S3 (allowing only 3 queries).

In Figure 9, both scenarios PC and SP have the same observed effectiveness, because the evaluation focuses on the gain (CG) over the result ranks, no matter how long it takes to retrieve the documents. The two strategies S1 and S3 differ in effectiveness, S3 providing far better effectiveness than S1. However, when time is taken into account (Fig. 10), the scenarios and strategies differ greatly from each other. Up to 60 seconds, S3 in the SP case is the worst strategy and this is entirely due to the high input cost of the long query. With enough time (180 sec.), S3 in SP catches up S3 in PC case. Also, PC and SP do not much differ for S1 due to the relatively low input cost and weak result quality. Comparing Figures 9 and 10, it is easy to see that time drives interaction and profoundly affects both user experience and effectiveness in sessions in different scenarios.

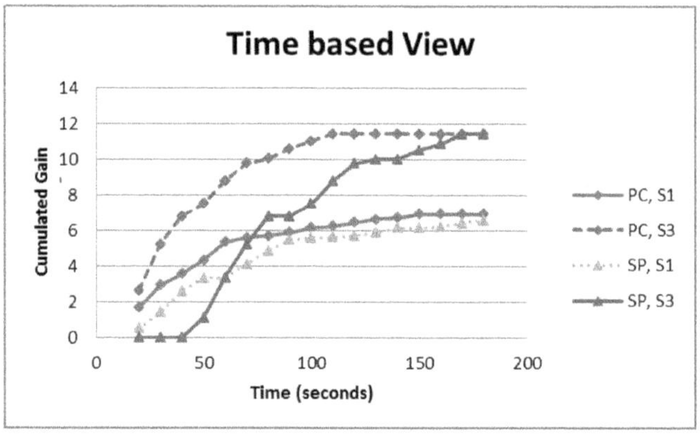

Fig 10. Time based View, CGs over time for 41 topics, scenarios PC and SP for strategies S1 and S3.

Limitations. In our study we did not take into account the time, which users spend for pondering about possible query words. One might argue that the more words one needs to identify, the harder (and slower) per word it comes. However, the thinking time is the same between sessions using the same number of words. In addition, this could be taken into account by revising subsequent query costs (Table 1). We have chosen to short-cut here in order to avoid too much complexity at this stage. Furthermore, we do not consider the time users spend in examining documents. This may depend on the device used. This can be seen as an artificial limitation. Tackling it would, however, complicate analysis, and this is therefore left for later study. We did not simulate user's learning during a session. Admittedly, learning from snippets and seen documents take place.

This is not impossible to simulate but some challenges remain to be solved.

We employed in the evaluation relatively limited query vocabularies, simple bag-of-word queries, and relatively short time frames. The query vocabularies and structure are justified by query length statistics in many search environments [14], [29], and the time frames by our simulation capabilities. However, the time frames are for *effective search time in sessions,* excluding thinking and document examination time. While the query vocabularies are short, they are human-generated for this collection, and therefore more realistic than words mined, e.g., from known relevant documents (in qrels).

We did not cover all the imaginable complex sessions. However we employed idealized and literature-based sessions, which shed the light on the peculiar evaluation problems beyond the traditional rank-based evaluation. This is a step forward while we are not suggesting that anyone follows a single strategy consistently in real life.

Our initial results are promising. First, the scenario, and to a large extent the device itself, dictate what kind of interactive behavior can be successful. Because real users do have limited resources and they use various devices having different properties, our methodology has unquestionable user relevance and potential pragmatic value for the industry. Measuring the effectiveness of systems from the pragmatic point of view may increase the validity of the results achieved. This may lead to greater user satisfaction. Secondly, our experimental results suggest that strict time constraints determine some session strategies as the best strategies as they maximize CG. The strengths of our approach are:

- The QM strategies S1-S5 have an empirical real life grounding
- The query vocabularies were generated by real test persons, and only thereafter used in automatic simulation
- We were able to evaluate over 20M sessions in each scenario; this is clearly intractable both physically, intellectually and economically with human test persons.

We have only taken the first steps. In future, we will study the dimensions of variation related to users, systems, information sources and sessions to construct more fine-grained scenarios explicating hypotheses about user goals, learning, and behaviors to validate evaluation measures used. [19]

6. CONCLUSIONS

In this study, we have shown the necessity of a pragmatic evaluation approach based on scenarios with explicit subtask costs under an overall time constraint. Effectiveness of various query modification and scanning strategies for two scenarios, namely, PC and SP is analyzed. Furthermore, the characteristics of the best and the worst interactive search sessions are examined. Expensive input favors scanning at length, cheap input favors better queries. The more time is available the less it matters how one searches – there will be time to identify the relevant documents. We have shown that the effort required by searching devices and the overall search time allocation drive interaction and profoundly affect both user experience and effectiveness in sessions in different scenarios. Moreover, we have also pointed out the inapt use of all normalized rank-based measures. Thus, we hope we could instigate new evaluation metrics for time-based comparisons.

7. ACKNOWLEDGMENT

This research was funded by Academy of Finland grant number 133021.

8. REFERENCES

[1] Azzopardi, L. 2007. Position Paper: Towards Evaluating the User Experience of Interactive Information Access Systems. In *SIGIR'07 Web Information-Seeking and Interaction Workshop*, 5 p.

[2] Azzopardi, L. 2011. The economics of interactive information retrieval. In *Proceedings of the 34th Annual International ACM SIGIR Conference on Research and Development in Information Retrieval*, 15-24.

[3] Bates, M. J. 1979. Information search tactics. *Journal of the American Society for Information Science,* 30(4), 205-214.

[4] Bates, M. J. 1989. The Design of Browsing and Berrypicking Techniques for the Online Search Interface. *Online Review*, 13(5), 407-424.

[5] Beaulieu, M. 2000. Interaction in Information Searching and Retrieval. *Journal of Documentation*, 56(4), 431-439.

[6] Belkin, N. L. 1980. Anomalous States of Knowledge as a Basis for Information Retrieval. *Canadian Journal of Information and Library Science*, 5, 133-143.

[7] Card, S. K., Moran, T. P., and Newell, A. 1983. *The Psychology of Human-Computer Interaction.* L. Erlbaum Assoc. Inc., Hillsdale, NJ, USA.

[8] Cleverdon, C.W., Mills, L., and Keen, M. 1966. Factors determining the performance of indexing systems, vol. 1-design. In *Aslib Cranfield Research Project*, Cranfield.

[9] Dunlop, M. D. 1997. "Time Relevance and Interaction Modeling for Information Retrieval". In *Proceedings of the 20th Annual International ACM SIGIR Conference on Research and Development in Information Retrieval*, Philadelphia,206-213.

[10] Fidel, R. 1985. Moves in online searching. *Online Review*, 9 (1), 62-74.

[11] Hearst, M. A. 2011. "Natural" Search User Interfaces. *Communications of the ACM*, vol. 54, 60-67.

[12] Hersh, W., Turpin, A., Price, S., Chan, B., Kraemer, D., Sacherek, L., and Olson, D. 2000. Do Batch and user Evaluations Give the Same Results? In *Proceedings of the 23rd Annual International ACM SIGIR Conference on Research and Development in Information Retrieval*, 17-24.

[13] Ingwersen, P. and Järvelin, K. 2005. *The Turn: Integration of Information Seeking and Retrieval in Context.* Heidelberg, Springer.

[14] Jansen, M. B. M., Spink, A., and Saracevic, T. 2000. Real Life, Real Users, and Real Needs: A Study and Analysis of User Queries on the Web. *Information Processing & Management*, 36(2), 207-227.

[15] Järvelin, K. and Kekäläinen, J. 2002. Cumulated Gain-Based Evaluation of IR Techniques. *ACM Transactions on Information Systems,* 20(4), 422-446.

[16] Järvelin, K. and Kekäläinen, J. 2000. IR evaluation methods for retrieving highly relevant documents. In *Proceedings of the 23rd Annual International ACM SIGIR Conference on Research and Development in Information Retrieval*, Athens, Greece, 41-48.

[17] Kamvar, M. and Baluja, S. 2007. Deciphering Trends in Mobile Search. *Computer,* 40(8), 58-62.

[18] Karat, C-M., Halverson, C., Horn, D., and Karat, J. 1999. Patterns of entry and correction in large vocabulary continuous

speech recognition systems. In *ACM Conference on Human Factors in Computing Systems*, 568-575.

[19] Karlgren, J., Järvelin, A., Eriksson, G, and Hansen, P. 2011. Use cases as a component of information access evaluation. In *DESIRE'11 workshop, October* 28, 2011, Glasgow, Scotland, UK.

[20] Keskustalo, H., Järvelin, K., Pirkola, A., Sharma, T. and Lykke, M. 2009. Test Collection-Based IR Evaluation Needs Extension Toward Sessions – A Case of Extremely Short Queries. In *Proceedings of the 5th Asia Information Retrieval Symposium* (AIRS'09), 63-74.

[21] Kuhlthau, C. C. 1991. Inside the Search Process. *Journal of the American Society for Information Science*, 42(5), 361-371.

[22] Price, S.L., Nielsen, M.L., Delcambre, L.M.L., and Vedsted, P. 2007. Semantic Components Enhance Retrieval of Domain-specific Documents. In *Proceedings of the 16th ACM CIKM*, 429-438.

[23] Ruthven, I. 2008. Interactive Information Retrieval. In *Annual Review of Information Science and Technology*, vol. 42, 2008. 43-91.

[24] Salton, G. 1970. Evaluation Problems in Interactive Information Retrieval. *Information Storage and Retrieval,* 6, 29-44.

[25] Smith, C. L. and Kantor, P. B. 2008. User Adaptation: Good Results from Poor Systems. In *Proceedings of the 31st Annual International ACM SIGIR Conference on Research and Development in Information Retrieval*, 147-154.

[26] Smucker, M. D. 2009. Towards Timed Predictions of Human Performance for Interactive Information Retrieval Evaluation. In *Third Workshop on Human-Computer Interaction and Information Retrieval* (HCIR'09), October 23, 2009, Washington DC, USA.

[27] Sormunen, E. 2002. Liberal Relevance Criteria of TREC – Counting on Negligible Documents? In *Proceedings of the 25th Annual International ACM SIGIR Conference on Research and Development in Information Retrieval*, Tampere, 324-330.

[28] Spink, A. 1997. Study of Interactive Feedback during Mediated Information Retrieval. *Journal of the American Society for Information Science*, 48(5), 382-394.

[29] Stenmark, D. 2008. Identifying Clusters of User Behavior in Intranet Search Engine Log Files. *Journal of the American Society for Information Science*, 59(14), 2232-2243.

[30] Su, L.T. 1992. Evaluations Measures for Interactive Information Retrieval. *Information Processing & Management* 28(4), 503-516.

[31] Turpin, A. and Hersh, W. 2001. Why Batch and User Evaluations Do Not Give the Same Results. In *Proceedings of the 24th Annual International ACM SIGIR Conference on Research and Development in Information Retrieval*, 225-231.

[32] Turpin, A. and Scholer, F. 2006. User Performance versus Precision Measures for Simple Search Tasks. In *Proceedings of the 29th Annual International ACM SIGIR Conference on Research and Development in Information Retrieval*, 11-18.

[33] Vakkari, P. 2000. Cognition and changes of search terms and tactics during task performance. In *Proceedings of RIAO 2000 Conference*, Paris: C.I.D., 894-907.

Evaluating Aggregated Search Pages

Ke Zhou
University of Glasgow
Glasgow, United Kingdom
zhouke@dcs.gla.ac.uk

Ronan Cummins
National University of Ireland
Galway, Ireland
ronan.cummins@nuigalway.ie

Mounia Lalmas
Yahoo! Labs
Barcelona, Spain
mounia@acm.org

Joemon M. Jose
University of Glasgow
Glasgow, United Kingdom
joemon.jose@glasgow.ac.uk

ABSTRACT

Aggregating search results from a variety of heterogeneous sources or *verticals* such as news, image and video into a single interface is a popular paradigm in web search. Although various approaches exist for selecting relevant verticals or optimising the aggregated search result page, evaluating the quality of an aggregated page is an open question. This paper proposes a general framework for evaluating the quality of aggregated search pages. We evaluate our approach by collecting annotated user preferences over a set of aggregated search pages for 56 topics and 12 verticals. We empirically demonstrate the fidelity of metrics instantiated from our proposed framework by showing that they strongly agree with the annotated user preferences of pairs of simulated aggregated pages. Furthermore, we show that our metrics agree with the majority user preference more often than the current diversity-based information retrieval metrics. Finally, we demonstrate the flexibility of our framework by showing that personalised historical preference data can improve the performance of our proposed metrics.

Categories and Subject Descriptors

H.3.3 [**Information Systems**]: Information Search and Retrieval

General Terms

Measurement, Experimentation

Keywords

aggregated search, evaluation, performance metric, diversity

1. INTRODUCTION

With the emergence of various vertical search engines dedicated to certain media types and genres, such as news, image, video, it is becoming popular to present results from a set of specific verticals dispersed throughout the standard "general web" results, for example by adding image results to the ten blue links for the query "pictures of flowers". This new search paradigm is often known as *aggregated search* [4]. The three main challenges that arise in realising such systems are vertical selection (**VS**), item selection (**IS**), and result presentation (**RP**). Vertical selection deals with deciding which verticals are implicitly intended by a query. Item selection deals with selecting a subset of items from each vertical to present on the aggregated page. Result presentation deals with organising and embedding the various types of items on the result page. The most common presentation strategy for aggregated search is to merge the results into one ranked list of so-called *blocks*, and is now the 'de facto' standard in many search engines.

Although various approaches exist for selecting relevant verticals [4, 5] and for optimising aggregated search pages [2, 17], evaluating the quality of aggregated search pages is still a challenge. Consider the query "yoga poses" which suggests that a visual element in the result page would be useful to many users. Furthermore consider that 75% of users who issue this query would prefer "image" results, 60% would prefer "video" results, and 10% would prefer "news" results, to "general web" results. Figure 1 shows three possible aggregated search pages[1] (A, B, and C) for the sample query. It is clearly difficult to objectively ascertain the aggregated search page that represents a more effective returned set, as there are a variety of compounding factors that could affect a user preference. A user may prefer a page because of his/her preference towards a specific vertical (vertical preference). In such a case, a user may prefer page A because it contains more images. A user who prefers a result set with more items that are topically relevant might prefer page C, whereas a user who prefers more relevant items towards the top of the page (presentation preference) might prefer page B. Furthermore, a user who desires a more diverse returned set (vertical diversity) may prefer page C. Any combination of those factors can influence the perceived quality and user preference of the pages.

In this paper, we propose a general framework for instantiating metrics that can evaluate the quality of aggregated search pages in terms of both *reward* and *effort*. Specifically, we develop an approach that uses both topical-relevance and vertical-orientation information to derive the utility of any

[1]R and N represent a Relevant or Non-relevant result respectively.

Permission to make digital or hard copies of all or part of this work for personal or classroom use is granted without fee provided that copies are not made or distributed for profit or commercial advantage and that copies bear this notice and the full citation on the first page. To copy otherwise, to republish, to post on servers or to redistribute to lists, requires prior specific permission and/or a fee.
SIGIR'12, August 12–16, 2012, Portland, Oregon, USA.
Copyright 2012 ACM 978-1-4503-1472-5/12/08 ...$15.00.

Page A (Image+Web) | Page B (Web) | Page C (News+Web+Video)

Figure 1: Three Examplar Aggregated Search Pages for the Query "yoga poses".

given aggregated search page. Our approach is flexible and takes into account any combination of items retrieved, any combination of verticals selected, and the positions of those results on the presented page.

This paper makes several contributions: (i) we propose a framework for the evaluation of aggregated search pages that capture both effort and reward in a formal way; (ii) we outline a novel approach for simulating aggregated search pages and collect a large set of user preferences over page pairs; (iii) we demonstrate the effectiveness of the metrics derived from our framework by comparing them with several existing IR metrics; and (iv) we show that our metrics can be personalised for each user and, therefore, can be further improved using training data.

Related work is reviewed in Section 2. In Section 3, we formally outline the problem of aggregated search evaluation and list the assumptions made in this work. In Section 4, we propose a general framework from which we derive a number of metrics. A method for collecting the page preferences of users is outlined in Section 5. Subsequently in Section 6, these are used to evaluate the performance of our metrics against baseline ones. We also show how the performance of our metrics can be improved using training data. Conclusions and future work are discussed in Section 7.

2. RELATED WORK

Various works evaluating one component of an aggregated search system in isolation exist. Vertical selection in aggregated search has been studied in [4, 5, 15, 26]. Much of this research aims to measure the quality of the set of selected verticals, compared with an annotated set obtained by collecting manual labels from assessors [4, 5, 26] or derived from user interaction data [15]. The annotation can be binary [4, 5] or graded [26]. The quality of a particular vertical selection approach is mostly evaluated with standard measures of precision and recall using the binary annotated set. Our work also evaluates this key component by utilising graded vertical-orientation information derived from a multi-assessor preferred vertical annotation set [26], as this allows for a more refined evaluation scheme.

Recent attempts to evaluate the utility of the whole aggregated search page [3, 17] consider the three key components of aggregated search (**VS**, **IS**, **RP**) together. Our work takes a similar holistic approach and proposes a general evaluation framework for measuring aggregated search page quality. For example, [17] evaluate the utility of a page based on a user engagement metric (CTR). This evaluation framework requires large-scale user interaction data, which may not always be available. In addition, it is not feasible to collect user interaction data for all possible page combinations. Others [6] evaluate the utility of the page by asking annotators to make assessments based on a number of criteria (e.g. relevance, diversity). Although this work is a comprehensive way to evaluate aggregated pages, it remains costly to gather assessments for all possible aggregated pages.

The most similar work [3] to ours collects preferences on block pairs from users and measures the page quality by calculating the distance between the page in question and the ideal (reference) page; the shorter the distance, the better the page. One advantage is that any possible combination of vertical blocks that form an aggregated page can be tested, from a block-oriented point of view (without regard to item selection). However, when the results retrieved for a vertical (block) change, the assessments previously gathered may not be reusable, as the preference will undoubtedly change accordingly. As our work follows the Cranfield paradigm, once the assessments (both item topical-relevance and vertical-orientation) are gathered, it can be applied to evaluate any possible aggregated search page (any combination of vertical selection, item selection and result presentation). Therefore, our work leads to a more robust, inexpensive, and reusable approach for evaluating aggregated search pages.

Topical diversity is an important topic. Various diversity-aware IR metrics have been proposed [8, 10, 18], capturing the importance of each subtopic, the degree to which an item represents the subtopic, and the topical-relevance of the item. Diversity-based metrics can promote returned sets that are both topically relevant and diverse. A simplistic way of adapting these metrics to aggregated search is to treat subtopics as verticals and subtopic importance as vertical-orientation. In this way, all existing diversity-based IR metrics can be adapted to evaluate aggregated search. Although in principle suitable to evaluate aggregated search, diversity-based metrics are not appropriate for use with block-based pages where user behaviour is different; for instance user browsing behavior within a block containing images may be different to that within a block containing "general web" results. Furthermore, the various types of items (text, image, etc.) that need to be accounted for in an aggregated search scenario are not explicitly modelled in diversity-based metrics. For example, the effort in reading a piece of text is greater than the effort in viewing a picture. Our framework is better adapted to the task of aggregated search, and models all key components simultaneously.

Others [20] have proposed an aggregated search metric that captures both vertical diversity and topical diversity. It can be noted that the framework developed in this paper can also be extended to incorporate topical diversity, but due to space limitations, we will leave this as future work.

3. PROBLEM FORMULATION

We introduce some formal notation and outline some of the main assumptions used throughout this work.

3.1 Aggregated Page Composition

An aggregated search page P is composed of a set of blocks $\{B_1, B_2, ...B_n\}$, where each block B_i consists of a set of items $\{I_{i1}, I_{i2}, ...I_{im}\}$. An item can be a "general web" page or a vertical result. Only snippets of each item appear on the aggregated search page. We make several assumptions[2] about the page P: (i) results are presented into blocks from top to bottom, and within each block, items are shown either from left to right (Image, Video) or from top to bottom (News, Recipe); (ii) each block B_i consists of items originating from only one vertical; (iii) only one block of each type is placed on a page (with the exception of "general web" blocks); and (iv) a block consists of one 'general web' item or k vertical items. This is different to previous work [3, 17] where vertical block could be embedded into only three positions of "general web" results (top of the page, middle of the page, bottom of the page). We relax this assumption and allow a vertical block to be slotted between *any* two "general web" blocks on the page.

3.2 Relevance and Orientation

Our objective is to develop metrics that measure the quality of any possible aggregated search page. The metrics must work regardless of the selected verticals, the items retrieved from each vertical, and where the vertical results are positioned on the page. To achieve this, we assume that the following two types of relevance assessments are available:

- The topical-relevance of each item, which is an assessment indicating whether a given item I_{ij} within block B_i is topically relevant to a topic q[3]. This is denoted $qrel(I_{ij}|q)$.
- The user specific vertical-orientation [26], which is a value between zero and one indicating the fraction of users that prefer a page to contain items from the vertical V_i rather than "general web" results for a topic q. This is denoted $orient(V_i|W, q)$.

The two relevance assessments are assumed to be made independently. The concept of vertical-orientation [26] reflects the perceived usefulness of a vertical from the user perspective prior to viewing vertical results and without regard to the quality of the vertical results. The vertical-orientation assessment is obtained by comparing each vertical in turn to the reference "general web" vertical, by asking users whether items from this vertical are likely to improve the quality of a standard web page. Consequently, the vertical orientation of the Web ($orient(W|W, q)$) is deemed to be 0.5, as we can imagine that a user would randomly select a page when presented with two similar "general web" pages. The topical-relevance assessment of each item contributes to the measurement of relevance for each retrieved result. This type of assessment can be made using similar pooling techniques [13] to those used in TREC.

With these two assessment types, we assume that a user obtain the highest reward by reading the most topically relevant item, originating from the most highly oriented vertical, first. With this assumption, only the vertical (or verticals) with a higher orientation than the "general web" ($orient(V|W, q) > 0.5$) should be presented on the aggregated search page; all other verticals should be suppressed.

3.3 User Interaction Behaviour

We make some assumptions about how users interact with an aggregated search page P:

- The user examines each page one block at a time. When the user reads page P, a block B_i on the page P has a certain probability of being examined. This probability denoted $Exam(B_i)$ is estimated depending on the type of browsing model assumed.
- After the user decides to examine a block B_i, we assume a static user browsing behavior within the block; the user reads all the items I_{i1} to I_{im} within that block.

Given that our metrics are based on average user and that there is usually only a limited number of items per block, this simple within block user browsing model is appropriate.

4. EVALUATION FRAMEWORK

We aim to develop metrics that evaluate an aggregated search page similarly to how a user might. Given two pages P_1 and P_2, we wish to measure their effectiveness in satisfying a user information need using a utility function $Util(P)$. If a user prefers P_1 over P_2 for a given query, the utility measure should lead to $Util(P_1) > Util(P_2)$.

Following [11], the utility of a page is determined by *reward* and *effort*. A page with a high utility should satisfy the average user information need with relatively little effort. We define the utility metric $Util(P)$ of the page P based on all blocks $\{B_1, B_2, ...B_n\}$ on the page. When a user reads page P, a block B_i on the page P has a certain probability $Exam(B_i)$ of being examined. This probability might depend on the position of the block presented, the snippet type of the items (image, text) within the block, or the satisfaction level after reading previous blocks B_1 to B_{i-1}. The probability $Exam(B_i)$ can be estimated depending on the type of browsing model assumed.

After the user decides to read block B_i, he/she will be rewarded with some gain $G(B_i)$ coming from reading all the items I_{i1} to I_{im} within that block. Here we assume that the topical-relevance of the item snippet is a good indication of the relevance of the item itself. Therefore, by reading all the items within the block B_i, the user will also have spent some effort $E(B_i)$ in reading this block. Therefore, based on our assumptions, we define the utility of the page $Util(P)$ as

[2]These assumptions are made in accordance with existing aggregated search systems.

[3]In this work, we assume that topical-relevance assessments are binary.

the expected gain of reading a page divided by the expected effort spent:

$$Util(P) = \frac{\sum_{i=1}^{|P|} Exam(B_i) \cdot G(B_i)}{\sum_{j=1}^{|P|} Exam(B_j) \cdot E(B_j)} \quad (1)$$

where $|P|$ is the number of blocks on page P. To ensure suitable normalisation over a set of queries, we define a normalized utility score $nUtil(P)$, similar to $nDCG$ [12]. We normalise the score of the utility of page P by that of the ideal page P_{ideal}:

$$nUtil(P) = \frac{Util(P)}{Util(P_{ideal})} \quad (2)$$

Until now, we have defined a general evaluation framework for any aggregated search page that considers both reward and effort simultaneously. Consequently, for two pages P_1 and P_2, we can say P_1 is better than the other when $nUtil(P_1) > nUtil(P_2)$. In the following sections, we instantiate the gain $G(B_i)$, the effort $E(B_i)$, and the examination probability $Exam(B_i)$ of the blocks. We then outline how to normalise the $Util(P)$ metrics by constructing an ideal page. Finally, we incorporate a simple personalisation parameter that captures the degree to which a user prefers vertical diversity on an aggregate search page.

4.1 Gain of Reading a Block

Given a block B_i containing a set of items (I_{i1}, I_{i2}, ... I_{im}) originating from vertical V_j, we would expect that if the vertical is highly oriented given the query, the user will achieve a higher gain. We denote this block orientation as *Orient*, which is related to the task of *vertical selection*. Furthermore, we would expect that the more topically relevant items a block contains, the higher the gain for the user. We denote the topical-relevance of the block as *Topic*. Before combining these two factors, we define the gain relating to the vertical-orientation of the block B_i:

$$Orient(B_i, \alpha) = g(orient(V_j|W, q), \alpha) \quad (3)$$

where $orient(V_j|W, q)$ is a value between 0 and 1. The function $g()$ is used so that the relative gain of the vertical can be altered using a tuning parameter α. The $orient(V_j|W, q)$ value is defined as the fraction of users that would prefer the vertical V_j to be added to the "general web" results W. As the "general web" is the pivot to which verticals are added, if $orient(V_j|W, q) > 0.5$, then adding the vertical should be rewarded. If $orient(V_j|W, q) < 0.5$, the gain of the block should be less than the "general web" results (i.e. 0.5). Therefore, we use a pivot at the 0.5 value through which $g()$ must pass. The following function satisfies these criteria:

$$g(x, \alpha) = \frac{1}{1 + \alpha^{-log_{10}(x/(1-x))}} \quad (4)$$

A graph of the function $g(x, \alpha)$ is shown in Figure 2. This function controls how much the gain increases as the vertical-orientation level increases. When α is small ($1 < \alpha < 10$), we obtain a more steep curve; highly oriented verticals are more rewarded, and conversely, low orientated verticals are more penalised. When α equals to 10, the reward is exactly the same as the vertical orientation $orient(V_j|W, q)$.

Now we define the gain relating to topical-relevance of the items within B_i:

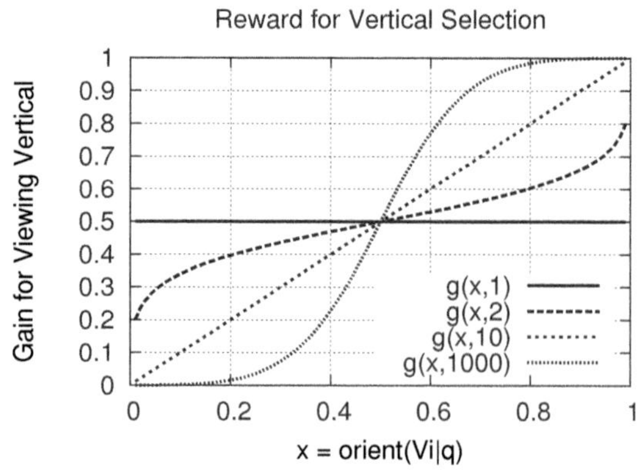

Figure 2: Function $g()$ for Controlling Reward on Orientation with Various Parameter α.

$$Topic(B_i) = \sum_{k=1}^{|B_i|} qrel(I_{ik}|q) \quad (5)$$

$|B_i|$ is the number of items within block B_i and $qrel(I_{ik}|q)$ is the binary relevance assessment of the item I_{ik}. In short, we use the sum of the binary relevance judgments of the items as the topical-relevance gain of all the items within the block B_i.

Now that we have defined the gain of a block in terms of both vertical-orientation and topical-relevance, we combine these in a suitable manner. Specifically, we combine the gain based on the above two criteria:

$$G(B_i) = Orient(B_i, \alpha) \cdot Topic(B_i) \quad (6)$$

where α is the tuning parameter as described above. We combine these two factors in an independent manner as both vertical-orientation and topical-relevance are related to the quality of the block. Either a low oriented block (low $Orient(Bi)$) or a topically irrelevant item (low $Topic(Bi)$) would result in an unsatisfied user.

4.2 Effort of Reading a Block

We now consider the effort $E(B_i)$ spent in examining a block B_i. Based on the assumed block-based user browsing behavior, the effort of examining a block is defined as the accumulative effort of reading all the items within it:

$$E(B_i) = \sum_{k=1}^{|B_i|} E(I_{ik}) \quad (7)$$

where $|B_i|$ is the number of items within block B_i, $E(I_{ik})$ is the effort spent in reading the item I_{ik}.

Several factors may affect the effort spent in examining an item $E(I_{ik})$: the media type of the snippet (text, image) or the size of the snippet (text length). We assume that there are only three categories of item snippet ("image", "text" and "video"). Furthermore, we assume that "image", "text" and "video" have a standard size. Based on [23], the time taken to assess the relevance of an image is estimated 2.34 seconds, while the time taken to assess a text snippet is 7.02 seconds. We extrapolate that a video takes twice as much

Table 1: Effort of Reading each Category.

Snippet Category	"image"	"text"	"video"
Effort	1	3	6

time to assess as a text[4] (14 seconds). Therefore, the relative effort taken to examine each snippet type is shown in Table 1 and is used as the unit of effort. These settings are not optimal and have been chosen heuristically after a review of the literature. Identifying more optimal settings is outside the scope of this work.

4.3 Examination Probability for a Block

We concentrate on defining the user browsing model for examining a block $Exam(B_i)$ on a page. Several models exist [8, 9, 16] that aim to predict the probability with which a user will examine an item. Position models [16] use only the position of the item in a result set. The cascade model [8] uses the relevance of the items previously examined, the intuition being that a sufficiently satisfied user will not continue to examine extra items. Motivated by the fact that users tend to be attracted by vertical results and the visual attention on them will increase the examination probability of other nearby web results, the attention model [9] aims to capture the visual attractiveness of the page. We do not propose a new user browsing model for aggregated search. Rather, we adopt these different models and incorporate them into our framework, namely the position examination models **DCG** [12] and **RBP** [16], the cascade model **ERR** [8], and the attention model **ATT** [9].

To adapt **ERR** to block examination, we assume that the satisfaction of viewing previous blocks is defined as the average gain of viewing each item within the block. For **ATT**, β_{dist} is the distance between the item under consideration and the closest vertical that has the attention bias (image and video). As we do not have access to query logs to accurately estimate the attention bias parameter ζ, instead of assuming that ζ is a position-specific parameter, we assume that ζ is a global variable that is constant for all positions. In addition, there will be attention-bias only when results from image or video verticals are presented on the page. The standard ζ is obtained by exploring the optimal setting in a development set.

4.4 Normalisation Using the Ideal Page

A summary of the non-normalised utility metrics that can be instantiated in our framework are listed in Table 2. We have a suite of metrics that reward pages that contain highly oriented verticals, contain topically-relevant items, promote topically-relevant blocks earlier on the page, for less effort. The utility metrics must be normalised by the ideal aggregated page. To obtain the latter, we require a brute-force approach that calculates the metric score for all pages, and then selects the page with the maximal score as the ideal page ($arg\_max(Util(P))\forall P$). This approach is not viable, given the number of possible combinations of various components of aggregated search. Therefore, we use a greedy algorithm to select a subset of aggregated pages from all the pages that exist, and only select the optimal page from this set. The idea is to use a simple metric for each component, and only select the pages that perform optimally for all those components. This is described in Section 5.2, where the simulation of aggregated page pairs is discussed.

4.5 Personalised Utility Metrics

Previous research [26] has shown that different users have different preferences with regard to the type of vertical. A vertical with low orientation to a query for the average user may still be beneficial to users that prefer a very diverse information space. Therefore, we define a personalised vertical diversity preference factor to capture this scenario. We achieve this by linearly combining the normalised utility of the page with the vertical recall. This introduces a personalised preference parameter λ_i:

$$I\_Util(P, \lambda_i) = (1 - \lambda_i) \cdot nUtil(P) + \lambda_i \cdot vRecall(P) \quad (8)$$

where λ_i is a parameter between 0 and 1 for user i, and controls the trade-off between vertical diversity and the quality of the aggregated search page. $vRecall(P)$ represents the fraction of all verticals that are presented on page P. The larger λ_i is, the more the user prefers a page with items originating from different verticals (high vertical diversity).

5. COLLECTING PAIRWISE PREFERENCE ASSESSMENTS

To validate the fidelity of our metrics (how they agree with actual user preferences of aggregated search pages), we collected a set of pairwise preference assessments over aggregated page pairs. We first present the data and material used for this purpose. We then simulate a set of aggregated search pages that vary in different levels of quality for each topic. Afterwards, we select a set of page pairs (two simulated pages) for each topic. Finally, we collect preference assessments for the page pairs for all topics. We outline some statistics and analysis of the assessments gathered.

5.1 Data

We use an aggregated search test collection [25] created by reusing the existing web collection ClueWeb09. This test collection consists of a number of verticals (listed in Table 3), each populated by items of that vertical type, a set of topics (320) expressing information needs relating to one or more verticals, and assessments indicating the topical-relevance of the items and the perceived user-oriented usefulness of their associated verticals to each of the topics. The verticals are created either by classifying items in the web collections into different genres (e.g. Blog, News) or by adding items from other multimedia collection (e.g. Image, Video). The topics and topical-relevance assessments of items that vary in genres are obtained by reusing assessments developed in TREC evaluation tasks (TREC Web Track and Million-Query Track). The vertical-orientation information of each topic [26] is obtained by only providing the vertical names (with a description of their characteristics) and asking a set of assessors to make pairwise preference assessments, comparing each vertical in turn to the reference "general web" vertical ("is adding results from this vertical likely to improve the quality of the ten blue links?").

We select a subset of topics from which to collect assessments. We ensure that this subset of topics still conforms to the real-world distribution of aggregated search covering a wide range of needs with different highly oriented verticals. Therefore, we selected 56 topics detailed in Table 4.

[4]We assume that users need to open and view the video item to assess its topical-relevance.

Table 2: Summarisation of Utility Metrics for Aggregated Search.

Metric	Examination Model $Exam(k)$	Parameter	Utility
AS_{DCG}	$\frac{1}{log(k+1)}$	α	
AS_{RBP}	β^{k-1}	α, β	$Util(P) = \frac{\sum_{i=1}^{\|P\|} Orient(B_i) \cdot Exam(i)}{\sum_{j=1}^{\|P\|} E(B_j) \cdot Exam(j)}$
AS_{ERR}	$\frac{\prod_{j=1}^{k-1}(1-\frac{G(B_j)}{\|B_j\|})}{k}$	α	
AS_{ATT}	$[(1-\frac{1}{log(k+1)}) \cdot \beta_{dist} + \frac{1}{log(k+1)}] \cdot \zeta$	α, ζ	

Table 4: Distribution of Number of Selected Topics Assigned to Various Highly Oriented Verticals.

Verticals	Image	Video	Recipe	News	Book	Blog	Ans	Shop	Disc	Schol	Wiki	Web-only	Total Qrys
Topic Num	4	3	3	4	3	3	3	3	5	3	12	10	56

Table 3: Verticals Used in this Paper.

Vertical	Document	Type
Image	online images	media
Video	online videos	
Recipe	recipe page	genre
News	news articles	
Books	book review page	
Blog	blog articles	
Answer	answers to questions	
Shopping	product shopping page	
Discussion	discussion thread from forums	
Scholar	research technical report	
Reference/Wiki	encyclopedic entries	
General web	standard web pages	

5.2 Simulating Aggregated Search Pages

For each topic, we simulate a set of aggregated search pages. As indicated in Section 3, we assume that a page consists of ten "general web" blocks (one "general web" page is a block) and up to three vertical blocks dispersed throughout those ten blocks (where each vertical block consists of a fixed number of three items). Recall that there are three key components of an aggregated search system that can be varied: (i) Vertical Selection (**VS**); (ii) Item Selection (**IS**); and (iii) Result Presentation (**RP**). We generate pages by simulating an aggregated search system in which the three components vary in quality.

The assessments for vertical-orientation were created by gathering annotations across several users. For the process of varying **VS**, for a given vertical V_i and query q, we consider the vertical to have a high vertical orientation if $orient(V_i|W, q)$ is greater than 0.75 [5]. We simulate four different vertical selection strategies, namely *Perfect*, *ReDDE*, *CORI*, *Bad*. *Perfect* selects all the highly oriented verticals, while *Bad* randomly selects the maximum number (three) of lowly oriented verticals. *ReDDE* and *CORI* rank the verticals according to the ReDDE [21] and CORI [7] resource selection approaches, and select the top K ranked verticals.

[5]We select the threshold as 0.75 as 75% assessors majority preference is a suitable percentage whereby the assessments are neither too noisy (50%) or stringent (100%). Furthermore, it creates a vertical intent distribution across the topics that realistically conforms to the real-world [4].

For **IS** we simulate three potentially different levels of relevance. These are *Perfect*, *BM25*, and *TF*. *Perfect* selects all items in the vertical that are topically relevant. *BM25* and *TF* select the top three ranked items from the rankings provided by the BM25 and a simple TF (term frequency) weighting respectively, with the PageRank score as a prior for both *BM25* and *TF*.

For **RP**, we simulate three different result presentation approaches: *Perfect*, *Random* and *Bad*. *Perfect* places the vertical blocks on the page so that gain could potentially be maximised, i.e. all the relevant items are placed before non-relevant items. However, if these items are part of a vertical, we position the highest orientated vertical first. *Random* randomly disperses the vertical blocks on the page while maintaining the position of the "general web" blocks. *Bad* reverses the perfectly presented page.

By varying the quality of each of the three key components, we can vary the quality of the result pages created by an aggregated search system in a more controlled way. For each topic, we can create 36 ($4 \times 3 \times 3$) pages[6]. In addition, the snippet of each item is automatically generated by the Lemur Toolkit and the presentation style conforms with typical search page presentation (presenting the vertical name in front of vertical results). Using this approach we can create a near ideal aggregated page for a query by using *Perfect* **VS**, *Perfect* **IS**, and *Perfect* **RP**. This is a greedy approach to the problem and is used as our method of normalisation for $nUtil$.

5.3 Constructing and Selecting Page Pairs

We now describe the selection of page pairs so that they can be presented to a user for judgment. One way to achieve this is to randomly sample two aggregated search pages, and collect a sufficient set of user preference judgments. However, following [3], we attempt a broad categorisation of the aggregated search pages into "bins" according to page quality, i.e. H (High), M (Middle) and L (Low). We can then provide a more in depth analysis of the performance of the metrics over different regions of the page space.

Although we do not know the quality of all the pages, we can roughly estimate the page quality using the quality of

[6]Certain combinations of VS, IS, and RP do not create unique simulated pages.

the components that created the page. We estimate this by assuming that the three components contribute equal importance to the quality of the page. We then evaluate each component respectively using a suitable metric. The quality score of the page is determined by linearly combining the metric score for each component. This is a coarse approach of determining the quality of the page. We use the F-measure (VS), Mean Precision (IS), and Kendall-tau correlation (RP). We then rank all the pages according to the three linearly combined metrics and evenly categorise the pages in the ranking into "H", "M" and "L" bin respectively.

We now have a method of comprehensively analysing how various metrics perform over the whole page space by selecting pages from these pre-assigned bins. Specifically, we have six bin pairs, H-H, H-M, H-L, M-M, M-L, L-L, which uniformly represent all the entire page space for the queries (albeit in coarse intervals). For each pair of bins, we randomly select 8 page pairs from it. Consequently, we select in total 48 (6×8) page pairs for each topic.

5.4 Collecting Pairwise Preference Assessments

Our preference assessment data is collected over the Amazon Mechanical Turk crowd-sourcing platform, where each worker was compensated $0.01 for each assessment made. A page pair was presented with the topic (title and description) shown in the upper position of the assessment page. This was followed by a pair of aggregated pages shown side-by-side. The assessor was provided with three options when making the assessments: "left page is better", "right page is better" and "both are bad". The latter option captures the scenario where a user is confused due to the poor page quality[7]. For each page pair, we collect four assessments (from four different assessors). The total number of assessments made during this preference collection process was 10752 ($56 \times 48 \times 4$). Following [19], a quality control was ensured by including 500 "trap" HITs. Each "trap" HIT consists of a triplet (q, i, j) where either page i or j was taken from a query other than q. We interpreted an assessor preferring the set of extraneous results as evidence of malicious or careless assessments and assessors who failed more than two trap HITs were discarded.

5.5 Analysis of Assessments

Of the 203 assessors who contributed HITs, 39 had their assessments removed from the assessment pool due to failing more than 2 trap HITs. For the remaining 164/203, participation followed a power law distribution where about 12% (20/164) of the assessors completed about 60% (6522/10752) of our HITs. We also found out that assessors rarely select the "both are bad" options provided as only 7% (684/10752) of the assessments are of this option.

We want to answer the following question: **RQ1** Do users agree with each other when assessing aggregated search pairs? Therefore, we measured annotator agreement of preferences of aggregated page pairs using Fleiss' Kappa [24] (denoted by K_F), which corrects for agreement due to chance. Fleiss' Kappa is convenient because it ignores the identity of the assessor-pair, and is designed to measure agreement over instances labeled by different (even disjoint) sets of assessors. The results are shown in Table 5.

[7]The option "Both are good" is not included because this information can be potentially obtained by investigating inter-assessor agreement for definite preferences.

Table 5: Statistics of User Preference Assessment Agreement over Various Quality Bins.

bins	4/4	3/4	Kappa agreement
all	2231	8051	0.241
H-H	347	1396	0.238
H-M	427	1354	0.283
H-L	461	1318	0.317
M-M	287	1424	0.192
M-L	394	1327	0.261
L-L	315	1332	0.210

We observe that assessor agreement on presentation-pairs was $K_F = 0.241$, which is considered *fair* agreement [24]. This result is similar to previous research [3, 26], which reaffirm that evaluating aggregated search is not an easy task, and that various users have their own assumptions about what a good page is. Of all 10752 aggregated page-pairs, 8051 (74.8%) had a majority preference of at least 3/4 and only 2231 (20.7%) had a perfect 4/4 majority preference. It is perhaps not surprising that assessor agreement is not high as agreement on page-pairs requires that assessors make similar assumptions about the cost of different types of errors. Furthermore, the low inter-assessor agreement may be explained by the fact that users make different assumptions regarding the importance of each aggregated search component (**VS**, **IS**, **RP**). Alternatively, it may be that assessors have a hard time distinguishing between good presentations. Following previous research [3], given this low level of inter-assessor agreement, rather than focusing on the metrics agreement with each individual preference, we focus on their agreement with the majority preference (3/4 or greater, and 4/4) in the evaluation.

6. EVALUATION

We investigate the fidelity[8] [22] of the proposed metrics. We leave an investigation on the reliability of the metric (discriminative power [18]) for future work. We aim to answer the following questions:

1. **RQ2** With standard parameter settings, are the standard diversity metrics suitable for aggregated search, and do our proposed metrics accurately predict user preferences for aggregated search pages?
2. **RQ3** Can we learn personalised parameters from historical data and, subsequently, provide a higher agreement with the user preferences?

To demonstrate the fidelity of our four metrics (AS_{DCG}, AS_{RBP}, AS_{ERR} and AS_{ATT}), we compare them with existing IR metrics. We utilise both user-oriented IR metrics capturing topical-relevance (*nDCG* [12], *P@10*), and diversity-aware metrics (α-*nDCG* [10], *D-nDCG* [18], *D#-nDCG* [18], *IA-nDCG* [1]) which we adapt to incorporate vertical diversity. We select the latter as they are the most prevalent user-oriented IR metrics. Their adaptation is as follows: (i) we replace subtopic importance with $orient(V|W, q)$; (ii) we substitute the user model for ranks to the one that applies to blocks; and finally (iii) we normalise according to the ideal aggregated search page.

[8]The extent to which an evaluation metric measures what it is intended to measure.

To measure the performance of the metrics, we calculate the percentage of agreement (percentage of those pairs for which the metric agrees with the majority preference of users). The larger the percentage of agreement, the more accurately the metric can predict the user preference of any aggregated search page pairs, and the higher the metric fidelity. A two-tailed t-test (significant at the $p < 0.01$ level, denoted by ▲ or ▼) is used to show which metric correlates more significantly with the user preferences[9].

6.1 Standard Parameter Settings

To answer **RQ2**, we carry out a set of experiments where we employ the prevalent standard parameter settings for the metrics used in IR experiments. We utilise the standard log discount function for all DCG related metrics (AS_{DCG}, $nDCG$, α-$nDCG$, D-$nDCG$ and $D\#$-$nDCG$). We set the α parameter in α-$nDCG$ to 0.5 and γ to 0.5 for $D\#$-$nDCG$. For our proposed metrics, we set $\alpha = 10$ (a linearly increasing vertical-orientation function) and $\lambda_i = 0.0$ (no personalised vertical diversity preference) as the standard parameters. For the user persistence parameter in AS_{RBP}, we set $\beta = 0.8$ as this value best correlates with the user browsing behavior from a real-world query-log data [16]. These standard settings instantiate a simple metric (e.g. AS_{DCG}) similar to existing topical diversity-aware metrics that incorporate subtopic importance probability (D-$nDCG$). The standard ζ of AS_{ATT} is obtained by exploring the optimal setting in a development set that contained 500 preference page pairs that contain visually attractive results (results coming from Image and Video).

Our evaluation, the fidelity of the metrics, thus focuses on the agreement (of each metric) with the user preferences over the set of aggregated search results. As we have already categorised page pairs into various quality "bins" (H-H, H-M, H-L, M-M, M-L, L-L), we report the experimental results over different bin pairs, in order to understand each metric performance over the whole evaluation space. Our experiments have two parts: (i) when fixing the assumed user browsing model (e.g. DCG), we compare the performance of our proposed metrics with existing IR metrics; (ii) under the proposed framework, we compare user models to investigate which ones make more accurate prediction of the user preferences on aggregated page pairs.

6.1.1 *Comparison of Metrics*

We present results for a majority preference of 3/4 or greater, or 4/4, in Table 6. The significance is calculated in comparison with one of the proposed metrics, AS_{DCG}. Our metrics have higher agreement with user preferences for the H-M, H-L and M-L bins compared to the less discriminative bins (H-H, M-M, or L-L). In addition, for page pairs with higher majority user agreement (4/4 instead of 3/4), our metrics tend to make more accurate prediction of the user preferences. After closer examination, we observe that the metrics agreement with the majority user preference is higher on pairs where there is greater consensus between assessors. This is similar to reported in [3].

We also observe that overall the proposed aggregated search metrics (AS_{DCG}) work better than existing IR metrics ($nDCG$ and $P@10$). They have a significantly better performance across almost the entire metric space. This is not surprising given that the proposed metrics incorporate aspects unique to aggregated search (vertical-orientation), which can affect user preferences. Indeed, when the page quality is expected to be high, traditional IR metrics that do not consider vertical-orientation perform worse than the proposed metrics. But it is worth noting that $nDCG$ performs significantly better than other metrics on L-L page pairs. This might be because as the returned verticals are of low orientation, and for these types of page pairs, simply measuring topical relevance of items might correlate more with the user browsing behavior than considering the additional vertical orientation; when assessing two low-quality pages, the user is trying to find more topically relevant items, without regard to the orientation of the vertical.

For the diversity-aware metric, α-$nDCG$ performs significantly worse than the proposed metrics. This is because α-$nDCG$ implicitly penalises the within vertical redundancy of items. This evaluation strategy is not appropriate when presenting results from the same vertical in a block. A close examination shows that this degraded performance is due to the over-penalisation for items within each vertical. Although recent research [14] has suggested that α may be tuned on a per query basis to either promote or discount extra items from the same sub-topic (vertical), we leave this for future work. In addition, instead of fully utilising the graded $orient(V|W,q)$ information, α-$nDCG$ treats relevant verticals in a binary sense, another reason that may cause the degraded performance.

The other existing diversity-aware metric D-$nDCG$ performs comparably well. This is not surprising as when employed with standard parameter setting, D-$nDCG$ is most similar to the proposed aggregated search metrics (AS_{DCG}). The major difference is that AS_{DCG} captures the effort of examining result snippets of different types. $D\#$-$nDCG$ performs significantly worse than D-$nDCG$ over the entire simulated page space used for evaluation in the context of aggregated search. This proves that simply promoting vertical diversity without considering vertical-orientation can degrade the evaluation performance. In addition, as we will see later, because of the various users vertical diversity preference, personalised vertical diversity can be a better strategy for the evaluation of aggregated search. Finally, IA-$nDCG$ also performs considerably worse than AS_{DCG}. A close examination suggests that this is due to the over-rewarding of the vertical results in a page.

When we assume a uniform effort distribution of the resulting snippets, which can be of various types, the metric performances decrease from 67.3% to 65.6%. However, this decrease is not statistically significant. This might be due to the small number of topics promoting image or video vertical results. Estimation of the efforts associated with reading snippet of various types on a large-scale dataset is needed.

6.1.2 *Comparison of User Models*

For the proposed metrics with various user models (AS_{DCG}, AS_{RBP}, AS_{ERR} and AS_{ATT}), their agreements with the users majority preference (3/4 or greater) are shown in Table 7[10]. We observe that the metric agreements are com-

[9] We also used the sign test [3]. For all page pairs with majority of preference, our proposed metrics performed significantly better than random. Since we are interested in comparing metrics, we do not report the sign test outcomes.

[10] The results of metric agreement with 4/4 users majority preference is similar and is, therefore, not included due to space limitations.

Table 6: Metric Agreements with Various User's Majority Preference: Proposed Metric vs. Baseline Metrics.

majority preference	bins	AS_{DCG}	D-$nDCG$	$D\#$-$nDCG$	IA-$nDCG$	α-$nDCG$	$nDCG$	$P@10$
3/4 or greater	all	67.3%	65.9%	62.9%▼	64.3%	62.4%▼	60.1%▼	53.9%▼
	H-H	61.4%	60.4%	57.2%▼	57.0%▼	54.0%▼	53.3%▼	49.5%▼
	H-M	74.3%	72.3%▼	68.8%	71.1%	60.5%▼	63.1%▼	61.2%▼
	H-L	78.0%	78.4%	76.3%	75.8%	73.3%▼	67.9%▼	58.3%▼
	M-M	64.7%	62.7%▼	64.2%	64.8%	64.9%▼	61.1%▼	51.2%▼
	M-L	72.4%	68.1%	67.1%▼	65.8%▼	70.2%▼	67.3%▼	55.1%▼
	L-L	51.3%	52.6%	53.2%	53.1%	51.7%	54.7%▲	47.3%▼
4/4	all	71.1%	69.4%	64.8%▼	67.7%	63.1%▼	60.9%▼	54.1%▼
	H-H	68.2%	65.4%	56.3%▼	62.1%▼	53.1%▼	52.4%▼	52.3%▼
	H-M	76.3%	76.0%	70.1%▼	78.2%	62.0%▼	64.8%▼	58.1%▼
	H-L	77.6%	78.9%	76.9%	78.3%	74.1%	65.9%▼	56.7%▼
	M-M	67.3%	65.1%	65.1%	63.7%	63.4%	62.5%	49.4%▼
	M-L	75.2%	72.4%	66.5%▼	68.4%▼	72.0%	68.3%▼	57.2%▼
	L-L	61.1%	57.8%▼	51.3%▼	54.5%▼	51.9%▼	52.6%▼	52.3%▼

paratively similar; although, overall, the metrics based on position-based user models (AS_{DCG} and AS_{RBP}) perform consistently better than the adapted cascade model metric AS_{ERR} or the attention-based model AS_{ATT}.

We further see that comparatively AS_{ERR} performs better on H-M and H-L bins and worse on others. The degraded performance might be due to the fact that only binary topical-relevance assessments (of items) are available and the metric largely rewards the top relevant results. This also partly explains why AS_{ERR} performs particularly well between high quality pages (highly oriented and relevant results are presented at the top of the page) and low quality pages. It is most likely that instead of considering the entire page, most assessors looked only at the early results of the page when assessing.

However, surprisingly, by incorporating attention bias (of visually attractive vertical results) into the position-based model, the performance of the metric AS_{ATT} degrades, compared with AS_{DCG}. This might be due to the inaccurate estimation of the attention bias ζ from our small-scale experiments. After closer examination, it may be that assessors have a considerable preference bias on pages that contain visually attractive results (image, video) [3]. Therefore, the preference assessment between pages containing image and video verticals may be noisier, which could result in a natural bias for those types. Further experiments are needed to explain and understand this bias and its effect.

In comparing AS_{DCG} and AS_{RBP}, although it is observed that AS_{RBP} performs slightly better for page pairs consisting of pages with high quality agreements, the result is not significant. As the only difference between AS_{DCG} and AS_{RBP} is the position-based discounting factor (the user browsing model), the slight improvement is caused by the different user model. This user browsing modelling factor is examined in more detail later.

6.1.3 Summary

Although the results of our proposed metrics are promising when compared with existing IR metrics, the results should be treated with caution as the agreement is not substantial (the best performance is 67.7% from our proposed metric AS_{RBP}). After a close examination of the user preferences, compared with the metric prediction, the reasons for this include: (i) the vertical-orientation annotations [26] may not fully agree with the real user preference of verticals (they are noisy estimations); and (ii) although three key components of aggregated search are captured, we have only used simple default values for some of the parameters. This motivates further experiments that aim to learn personalisation parameters from historical data.

Table 7: Proposed Metric Agreements with 3/4 User Majority Preferences: Comparison of User Examination Models.

bins/metrics	AS_{DCG}	AS_{RBP}	AS_{ERR}	AS_{ATT}
all	67.3%	67.7%	63.8%▼	66.9%
H-H	61.4%	62.1%	53.1%▼	60.5%
H-M	74.3%	75.4%	78.2%▲	72.1%▼
H-L	78.0%	80.3%	79.1%	77.4%▼
M-M	64.7%	65.2%	56.7%▼	66.3%
M-L	72.4%	71.9%	64.9%▼	70.0%
L-L	51.3%	48.8%▼	54.1%	54.5%

6.2 Learning for Metrics

We can improve the performance of our metrics by learning suitable parameter settings using training data, thus addressing the research question **RQ3**. We only use AS_{RBP} as an example. We recall that AS_{RBP} has three parameters: α that controls the degree to which vertical orientation is rewarded; β that controls the user browsing behavior in terms of user persistence; and λ_i that controls the degree to which a user prefers a diverse aggregated page.

Training is done in two stages. First, we learn suitable values for α and β independently of λ_i. We categorised the user preference data into five sets and use five-fold cross validation for training and testing. We set $\lambda_i = 0.0$ (users do not prefer vertical-based diverse results unless the vertical provides better results) and iterate through different settings of values: α (from 1 to 100) and β (from 0.5 to 1.0). The optimal combination is obtained with $\alpha = 7.0$ and $\beta = 0.85$ indicating that users generally favour results that contain highly-oriented verticals, and that users do not have a persistent browsing behaviour (they care more about the results returned in a high position in the page). The corresponding results are shown in Table 8. The performance of the metric is improved over the standard parameter settings from 67.7% to 72.6%. This improvement is due to the better estimation of two parameters α and β concerned with two main aspects of aggregated search, vertical selection and result presentation. By learning from historical data, AS_{RBP} (and other metrics) can better capture these two aspects. Second, we fix the optimal settings for α and β and learn personalised

Table 8: Learned AS_{RBP} Metric Agreements with User's Majority Preferences for All Page Pairs.

Parameter	Standard	Optimal α and β	Optimal α, β and λ_i
Agreement	67.7%	72.6%▲	75.9%▲

user preference parameters for diversity (λ_i). Although not optimal, this is sufficient to analyse the "personalisable" parameter independently of others.

As we need sufficient data for learning the parameter, we only test this over the top twenty "head" assessors who made most of the assessments. Like with previous setting, for each assessor, we separate assessor data into five sets and use five-fold cross validation to train and test. For the overall performance, we average the performance for all those assessors. The results are also shown in Table 8. The optimal setting for λ_i varies from 0.15 to 0.4 among different assessors whereas the average optimal setting for those assessors is 0.23. Similar to [26], this demonstrates that each user has his/her own understanding and preference over the diversity of the results. We can report that by using this personalised parameter, the prediction of the metric agreement with the majority of user preference is improved significantly, from 72.6% to 75.9%. This effectively illustrates that aggregated search can be improved if we have a better understanding of each user preference over the diversity of results. This is particularly useful for systems that can gather personalised interaction data for their users.

7. CONCLUSIONS AND FUTURE WORK

We introduced a general evaluation framework that captures several traits unique to aggregated search. We instantiated a suite of metrics for evaluating aggregated search pages from this framework. We presented a methodology to collect user preferences over aggregated pages, which allowed us to measure various aspects of our proposed metrics. We did this by simulating aggregated search pages of different quality for a range of topics. The approach allowed us to analyse different parts of the aggregated page pair space. Furthermore, we showed that the proposed metrics correlate well with the majority user preferences and that traditional IR metrics are not well suited to the task. In addition, while some diversity-based metrics can be adapted to measure the preference between page pair, they are not ideal. By instantiating several non-tuned versions of metrics from our framework, we showed that these metrics are at least comparable to diversity-based IR metrics. We also showed that our metrics have the ability to tune their behaviour for pages for which personalised preference data is available.

Future work will involve extending and setting several parameters of the metrics so that they more closely correlate with user preferences for the sets of page pairs. In particular, when query-log data is available, we can further extend the framework by proposing new user browsing models for aggregated search and investigate their values. We will also devise new approaches to utilise the available implicit user feedback data to better estimate the parameters. Another interesting challenge will be to compare the effectiveness and weakness of existing diversity-aware metrics for evaluating aggregated search, and study the ability of our framework to generalise them.

Acknowledgments This work was supported partially by both the EU LiMoSINe project (288024) and by the Irish Research Council's INSPIRE (FP7 COFUND) programme. Any opinions, findings, and recommendations expressed in this paper are the authors' and do not necessarily reflect those of the sponsors.

8. REFERENCES

[1] R. Agrawal, S. Gollapudi, A. Halverson, and S. Ieong. Diversifying search results. *WSDM*, 2009.
[2] J. Arguello, F. Diaz, and J. Callan. Learning to aggregate vertical results into web search results. *CIKM*, 2011.
[3] J. Arguello, F. Diaz, J. Callan, and B. Carterette. A methodology for evaluating aggregated search results. *ECIR*, 2011.
[4] J. Arguello, F. Diaz, J. Callan, and J.-F. Crespo. Sources of evidence for vertical selection. *SIGIR*, 2009.
[5] J. Arguello, F. Diaz, and J.-F. Paiement. Vertical selection in the presence of unlabeled verticals. In *SIGIR*, 2010.
[6] P. Bailey, N. Craswell, R. W. White, L. Chen, A. Satyanarayana, and S. M. M. Tahaghoghi. Evaluating whole-page relevance. *SIGIR*, 2010.
[7] J. P. Callan, Z. Lu, and W. B. Croft. Searching distributed collections with inference networks. *SIGIR*, 1995.
[8] O. Chapelle, D. Metlzer, Y. Zhang, and P. Grinspan. Expected reciprocal rank for graded relevance. *CIKM*, 2009.
[9] D. Chen, W. Chen, H. Wang, Z. Chen, and Q. Yang. Beyond ten blue links: enabling user click modeling in federated web search. *WSDM*, 2012.
[10] C. L. Clarke, M. Kolla, G. V. Cormack, O. Vechtomova, A. Ashkan, S. Büttcher, and I. MacKinnon. Novelty and diversity in information retrieval evaluation. *SIGIR*, 2008.
[11] G. Dupret. User Models to Compare and Evaluate Web IR Metrics. In *SIGIR 2009 Workshop on The Future of IR Evaluation*, 2009.
[12] K. Järvelin and J. Kekäläinen. Cumulated gain-based evaluation of ir techniques. *TOIS*, 2002.
[13] K. S. Jones and C. J. Rijsbergen. Report on the need for and the provision of an 'ideal' information retrieval test collection. British Library Research and Development Report No. 5266, 1975.
[14] T. Leelanupab, G. Zuccon, and J. M. Jose. A query-basis approach to parametrizing novelty-biased cumulative gain. In *ICTIR*, 2011.
[15] X. Li, Y.-Y. Wang, and A. Acero. Learning query intent from regularized click graphs. In *SIGIR*, 2008.
[16] A. Moffat and J. Zobel. Rank-biased precision for measurement of retrieval effectiveness. *TOIS*, 2008.
[17] A. K. Ponnuswami, K. Pattabiraman, Q. Wu, R. Gilad-Bachrach, and T. Kanungo. On composition of a federated web search result page: using online users to provide pairwise preference for heterogeneous verticals. *WSDM*, 2011.
[18] T. Sakai and R. Song. Evaluating diversified search results using per-intent graded relevance. *SIGIR*, 2011.
[19] M. Sanderson, M. L. Paramita, P. Clough, and E. Kanoulas. Do user preferences and evaluation measures line up? *SIGIR*, 2010.
[20] R. L. T. Santos, C. Macdonald, and I. Ounis. Aggregated search result diversification. *ICTIR*, 2011.
[21] L. Si and J. Callan. Relevant document distribution estimation method for resource selection. *SIGIR* 2003.
[22] E. M. Voorhees. Overview of the trec 2003 question answering track. In *TREC*, 2003.
[23] X.-B. Xue, Z.-H. Zhou, and Z. M. Zhang. Improving web search using image snippets. *ACM Trans. Internet Technol.*, 8:21, 2008.
[24] J. Fleiss. Measuring nominal scale agreement among many raters. *Psychological Bulletin.*, 76(5), 1971.
[25] K. Zhou, R. Cummins, M. Lalmas, and J. M. Jose. Evaluating large-scale distributed vertical search. In *LSDS-IR workshop in CIKM*, 2011.
[26] K. Zhou, R. Cummins, M. Halvey, M. Lalmas and J. M. Jose. Assessing and Predicting Vertical Intent for Web Queries. In *ECIR*, 2012.

Combining Inverted Indices and Structured Search for Ad-hoc Object Retrieval

Alberto Tonon, Gianluca Demartini, and Philippe Cudré-Mauroux
eXascale Infolab
U. of Fribourg—Switzerland
{firstname.lastname}@unifr.ch

ABSTRACT

Retrieving semi-structured entities to answer keyword queries is an increasingly important feature of many modern Web applications. The fast-growing Linked Open Data (LOD) movement makes it possible to crawl and index very large amounts of structured data describing hundreds of millions of entities. However, entity retrieval approaches have yet to find efficient and effective ways of ranking and navigating through those large data sets. In this paper, we address the problem of Ad-hoc Object Retrieval over large-scale LOD data by proposing a hybrid approach that combines IR and structured search techniques. Specifically, we propose an architecture that exploits an inverted index to answer keyword queries as well as a semi-structured database to improve the search effectiveness by automatically generating queries over the LOD graph. Experimental results show that our ranking algorithms exploiting both IR and graph indices outperform state-of-the-art entity retrieval techniques by up to 25% over the BM25 baseline.

Categories and Subject Descriptors

H.3.3 [**Information Storage And Retrieval**]: Information Search and Retrieval—*retrieval models*; H.3.4 [**Information Storage And Retrieval**]: Systems and Software—*performance evaluation (efficiency and effectiveness)*

General Terms

Algorithms, Experimentation, Performance

Keywords

Ad-hoc Object Retrieval, Entity Search, LOD

1. INTRODUCTION

Many modern websites, such as Web portals or news aggregators, are today including entity-centric functionalities. Common examples include the aggregation of all pieces of content related to a given person, or the extraction of the most important entities appearing in a given article. Some companies, like the New York Times, manually maintain a directory of entities and ask human experts to create links between their resources (e.g., news articles) and the corresponding entities (e.g., celebrities appearing in the articles). Increasingly, however, websites are turning to automated methods due to the sheer size of the resources they have to analyze, and the large number of entities they have to consider.

Recently, the Linked Open Data (LOD) movement[1] started an effort to make entity data openly available on the Web. In this initiative, Uniform Resource Identifiers[2] (URIs) are used to identify entities. Each entity can be looked up (*dereferenced*) online, where it is described and linked to further entities using the Resource Description Framework[3] (RDF). The fundamental difference between LOD and standard entity datasets like, for instance, Wikipedia, lies in the inherent structure of the data. On the LOD cloud, the data is provided by uncorrelated parties and is given as a giant graph of semi-structured data.

In the context of online entity search, the TREC Entity track [3] has studied two related search tasks: "Related Entity Finding" (i.e., finding all entities related to a given entity query) and "Entity List Completion" (i.e., finding entities with common properties given some examples). The SemSearch challenge[4] focused on Ad-hoc Object Retrieval (AOR), that is, finding the entity identifier of a specific entity described by a user query [20].

This paper focuses on Ad-hoc Object Retrieval over semi-structured data. We propose a novel search architecture that exploits both IR and graph data management techniques to effectively and efficiently answer AOR queries. Specifically, we propose a hybrid solution that starts by retrieving an initial list of results from an inverted index using a ranking function, and then re-ranks and extends the result list by exploiting the underlying graph representation of the data. Our extended experimental evaluation performed over standard collections shows that our proposed solution significantly improves the effectiveness (up to 25% improvement over the chosen baseline) while maintaining very low query execution times. We consider our results as especially promising since the LOD test collections that are

Permission to make digital or hard copies of all or part of this work for personal or classroom use is granted without fee provided that copies are not made or distributed for profit or commercial advantage and that copies bear this notice and the full citation on the first page. To copy otherwise, to republish, to post on servers or to redistribute to lists, requires prior specific permission and/or a fee.
SIGIR'12, August 12–16, 2012, Portland, Oregon, USA.
Copyright 2012 ACM 978-1-4503-1472-5/12/08 ...$15.00.

[1] `http://linkeddata.org/`
[2] `http://tools.ietf.org/html/rfc3986`
[3] `http://www.w3.org/RDF/`
[4] `http://semsearch.yahoo.com`

today available are noisy and incomplete, and since we expect both the quality and the coverage of LOD datasets to rapidly improve in the future.

In summary, the main contributions of this paper are:

- A comparison of entity search techniques for AOR tasks including state-of-the-art IR techniques such as query extension and pseudo relevance feedback.
- A new hybrid search architecture for AOR that combines IR and graph data management techniques exploiting the graph structure of the underlying data.
- A new, fairer and continuous evaluation methodology for relevance assessment based on iterative crowsdsourcing.
- An extensive evaluation of our novel search system for AOR using two standard test collections.

The rest of the paper is structured as follows. We discuss related work, focussing on Entity Search and AOR approaches, in Section 2. We briefly introduce the Linked Open Data movement in Section 3. Section 4 is devoted to a high-level description of our hybrid system. We describe several approaches for AOR based on inverted indices and NLP techniques in Section 5, and describe complementary techniques based on structured queries and graph data management techniques in Section 6. In Section 7, we experimentally compare the performance of our hybrid approach to a series of state-of-the-art AOR approaches on two standard test collections. Finally, we present our conclusions in Section 8.

2. RELATED WORK

Searching for entities instead of documents or Web pages is a recent trend in IR. Early approaches focused on single-type entity search, for example in the context of the expert finding task at the TREC Enterprise track [4], where standard IR approaches such as language modeling [1] have been applied. Complex entity search tasks have been addressed more recently. For instance, the INEX Entity Ranking track [12] studied the problem of finding entities matching a keyword query (e.g., "Countries where I can pay in Euro") using Wikipedia. The Entity track at TREC [3] evaluated the *Related Entity Finding* task, which aims at finding entities related to a given entity (e.g., "Airlines using the Boeing 747") using both a collection of Web pages as well as a collection of RDF triples. Several effective approaches for this task focus on entity type and co-occurrence information [7, 17]. The task of ranking entities appearing in one document taking into account the time dimension has been studied in [13].

2.1 Ad-hoc Object Retrieval

The main goal of the SemSearch Challenge is to create evaluation collections for the task of Ad-hoc Object Retrieval [20] on the Web of data. This task consists in retrieving entity identifiers (i.e., URIs) given a keyword query describing the single entity the user is looking for (e.g., "harry potter"). Evaluation collections for this task have been created by crowdsourcing relevance judgements [5].

The first approaches for AOR exploited standard IR techniques that had previously been used for other entity search tasks such as expert finding. The basic idea is to construct an entity profile by collecting and aggregating all information available about an entity and to index the resulting collections of entity profiles with standard IR techniques in order to answer entity search queries. Looking back at previous work from entity search, several techniques can be applied to improve the effectiveness of the AOR task. For example, different data types can be used to rank entities for AOR based on an inverted index and BM25F [21] as a ranking function [6].

Various methods already proposed for different entity search tasks can be exploited for AOR as well, such as approaches exploiting probabilistic models [2]. In [11], Demartini *et al.* adopt structured and Natural Language Processing approaches to improve the effectiveness of entity search. We suggest further AOR approaches relying on recent IR techniques in Section 5.

The contribution of this work is a novel hybrid approach that benefits both from known IR ranking functions as well as from an analysis of the graph structure of the entities. We compare below our novel approach against state-of-the-art entity search techniques.

2.2 Hybrid Search

A number of hybrid search systems have already been developed. In [14], Elbassuoni and Blanco propose ranking models for keyword queries over RDF data. Their task is different from AOR as they aim at selecting subgraphs matching the query and then ranking them by means of statistical language models. CE^2 [23] is a hybrid IR-DBMS system that provides ranking schemes for hybrid queries (i.e., keyword queries that describe joins and predicates between entities) over RDF data. $Beagle^{++}$ [18] is a desktop search engine that exploits both an inverted index and a structured repository for file metadata to provide more effective search functionalities to the desktop user. SIREn [10] is a hybrid Web search framework that supports keyword as well as structured queries over RDF data. SIREn focuses on scalability and efficiency through novel indexing schemes that can index data and answer user queries efficiently by using an inverted index. Instead, we propose methods to improve ranking effectiveness for AOR.

3. LOD PRIMER

LOD is an online movement whose origins can be traced back to a note[5] published by Tim Berner-Lee a few years ago. LOD suggests to publish data on the Web following four principles: i) using URIs to identify things ii) using HTTP URIs such that things can be dereferenced online (using for example a Web browser) iii) providing useful, structured information about the things when they are dereferenced, using for example RDF/XML and iv) including links to other, related URIs in the exposed data to foster data aggregation and discovery.

Hence, LOD can be seen as a grassroots effort leveraging on the current architecture of the Web (HTTP, URIs, Content Negotiation, XML, RDF, webservers and browsers) to publish data. Figure 1 below includes on the right-hand side a macroscopic view on the LOD cloud as of September 2011, where each node depicts a separate data set and the edges symbolize links between the data sets[6]. As of Septem-

[5] `http://www.w3.org/DesignIssues/LinkedData.html`

[6] Linking Open Data cloud diagram, by Richard Cyganiak and Anja Jentzsch. `http://lod-cloud.net/`

ber 2011, the LOD cloud contains approximatively 300 data sets and more than 30 billion RDF triples[7]. In our context, each RDF triple can be seen as a simple sentence, connecting a *subject* (an entity URI), a *property* (a predicate URI) and an *object* (which can be either a URI or a literal). The following triple, for instance

```
(example.net/Alice, foaf:age, ''17'')
```

encodes the fact that Alice (as identified by the URI `example.net/Alice`) is 17 years old.

Since the same URI can be used as a subject or object in different triples, RDF naturally forms labelled graphs that connect entities to values and further entities. In the following, we make a distinction between object properties—linking entities to other entities—and datatype properties—associating values to a given entity[8].

Large collections of triples are typically stored in a database system (such as Oracle 11g[9], Virtuoso[10] or RDF-3X [19]). LOD data sets are typically referenced online (e.g., on CKAN[11]) and can be queried or crawled over HTTP using the SPARQL[12] declarative query language.

4. SYSTEM ARCHITECTURE

We describe the architecture of our hybrid search system in the following. Our approach is based on an inverted index that supports full text search on one hand, and on a structured repository, which maintains a graph representation of the original data, on the other hand. The ability to query an inverted index and to obtain a ranked list of results allows us to retrieve an initial set of entities that match the user query. Starting from this set of retrieved entities, we take advantage of algorithms exploiting the graph structure of the data thanks to our structured repository: retrieved entities are nodes in the data graph that can be used as starting points for graph traversals and neighborhood queries. Thus, the structured repository is used to refine the original IR-based results by navigating the data-graph, selecting potentially new entities or reinforcing the relevance of the results selected through the inverted index.

Figure 1 illustrates the main components of our system and their interactions. The search process proceeds as follows. First, a user initiates an entity search through a keyword query. The query is parsed and extended (see below Sections 5.2 and 5.3). A first set of results is retrieved using the expanded query and an inverted index on the LOD data. Several mechanisms can be used at this stage to improve ranking effectiveness, such as a multi-field index with BM25F scoring, NLP, or pseudo-relevance techniques (see below Section 5 for a detailed discussion on that point.)

This first set of results is then enriched using structured queries on (a subset of) the LOD graph. We take advantage of two types or graph queries in that context: scope queries following datatype properties (see Section 3), and graph traversal queries following object properties. Both types of queries start from the LOD nodes corresponding to the first set of results, and retrieve additional information (sets of literals and sets of entities respectively) to refine the results. As the LOD graph is highly connected (i.e., there are many properties that connect entities among themselves or that connect entities to literals), we must at this stage identify the most effective properties to follow in order to limit the scope of the graph queries. The details of our graph approach are given in Section 6.1. At this point, new entities may be added to the result set and previously identified entities may change position in the rankings due to the new information gathered. Finally, the top-k results are sent back to the querier.

5. INVERTED INDEX AND AD-HOC OBJECT RETRIEVAL TECHNIQUES

The first approach to index graph-structured datasets such as those found in the LOD cloud is to aggregate all information attached to the entities. Thus, we create *entity profiles* by building an inverted index on the entity labels. We consider each entity profile as a document (similarly to candidate-centric expert finding approaches [1]) containing all versions of the entity name directly attached to it in the graph. This index structure considering entity profiles as bag-of-words combined with a BM25 ranking function will be our baseline approach. We describe below three further approaches we propose to improve this baseline. These are based on a structured inverted index, on NLP techniques (query expansion), and on pseudo-relevance feedback.

5.1 Structured Inverted Index

First, we consider a structured inverted index approach, which separately indexes different values attached to the entity. In order to create a structured inverted index, we index separately different types of information attached to the entity. This is similar to previous work [6]. Specifically, we create a structured inverted index for the three following pieces of information:

URI First we tokenize the URI identifying the entity in the LOD cloud. As the URI often contains the entity name (e.g., `http://dbpedia.org/page/Barack_Obama`), this field often matches the user query well.

Labels We also consider a list of manually selected datatype properties (i.e., *label, title, name, full-name, family-name, given-name, has-pretty-name, prefLabel, given-name, nickname,* which frequently occur in various LOD datasets) that point to a label or textual description of the entity.

Attributes Finally, we consider all the other datatype properties (i.e., non-label attributes) and attach their values to the entity.

Once the indices are created, we obtain a ranked list of results by means of various ranking functions such as BM25F.

5.2 Query Expansion

Natural Language Processing techniques have been applied to other entity search tasks. In this paper, we exploit query expansion and relevance feedback techniques on top of the BM25 baseline for the AOR task.

[7] `http://www4.wiwiss.fu-berlin.de/lodcloud/state/`

[8] We hence follow the vocabulary introduced by the Web Ontology Language OWL, see `http://www.w3.org/TR/owl-ref/`

[9] `http://www.oracle.com/technetwork/database/options/semantic-tech/index.html`

[10] `http://virtuoso.openlinksw.com/`

[11] `http://thedatahub.org/group/lodcloud`

[12] `http://www.w3.org/TR/rdf-sparql-query/`

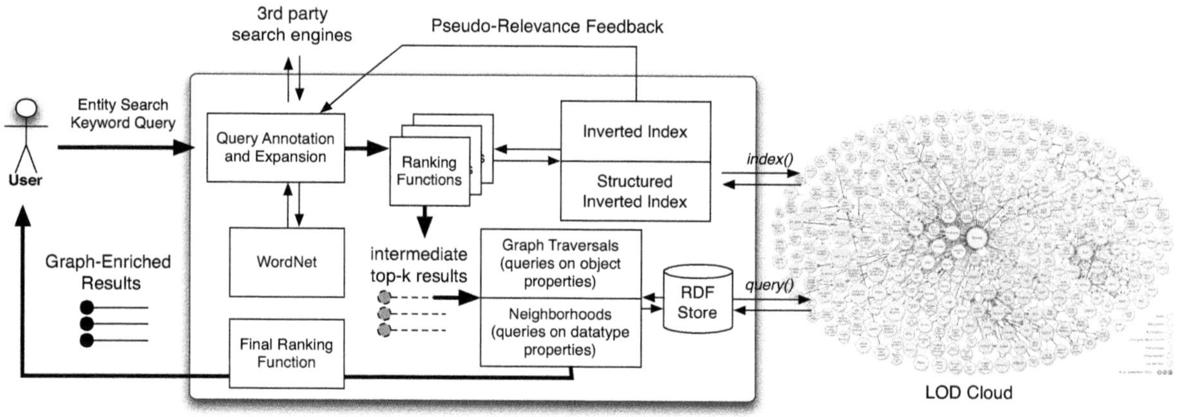

Figure 1: Our hybrid search system, where results retrieved from an inverted index are refined through structured graph queries.

Specifically, given a disjunctive keyword query q we extend it by adding additional related terms such as synonyms, hypernyms, and hyponyms from Wordnet [15]. This makes the query (e.g., "New York") retrieve additional results including different ways of referring to the specified entity (e.g., "Big Apple").

In addition, we exploit commercial search engines query autocompletion features to obtain additional keywords, given the original user query. Specifically, we send the original query q to a commercial search engine (Google) and we expand it by appending the first 5 terms the autocompletion algorithm suggests for q (e.g., "New York Times").

5.3 Pseudo-Relevance Feedback

Finally, we also implement pseudo-relevance feedback techniques on top of the baseline approach by first running the original query q and then considering the labels of the top-3 retrieved entities to expand the user query. For instance, the query "q=NY" can be expanded to "New York", "New York City" and "North Yorkshire" (labels of the top-3 entities retrieved for the original query q).

We report evaluation results comparing those various techniques on standard AOR collections in Section 7.

6. GRAPH-BASED ENTITY SEARCH

All the techniques described above neglect two key characteristics of LOD data: i) LOD entities are *interlinked*, in the sense that related entities are often connected, and ii) data values are *clustered* in the graph, such that many relevant values can be retrieved by following series of links iteratively from a given entity. In this section, we describe how we can leverage structured graph queries to improve the performance of our system taking advantage of those two characteristics.

As previously mentioned, our hybrid ranking solution consists of two steps. The first step (described in the preceding section) uses the IR infrastructure to obtain an initial ranking of entity identifiers. In the second step, the graph structure is exploited. We use the first set of entities from the original ranking as seeds in the graph. From those initial points, we traverse the graph following promising edges, that is, we follow object property edges potentially leading to additional results, and datatype properties leading to additional values.

Let $Retr = \{e_1, e_2, .., e_n\}$ be the ranked list of entities resulting from the query to the inverted index. Our goal is to define a set of functions that use the top-N elements of $Retr$ to create an improved list of results $StructRetr = \{e'_1, e'_2, .., e'_m\}$. This new list of results may contain entities from $Retr$ as well as new entities discovered when traversing the LOD graph. To obtain $StructRetr$, we exploit top LOD properties that are likely to lead to relevant results[13].

Once $StructRetr$ is obtained, we create a final result set and return it to the user. We adopt a simple model that linearly combines the two entity rankings:

$$finalScore(e') = \lambda \cdot BM25(q, e) + (1 - \lambda)(score(q, e, e'))$$

where q is the user query, $score(q, e, e')$ is our new ranking function (see below Section 6.2), and $BM25(q, e)$ is the initial score of the entity $e \in Retr$ (or of the entity in $Retr$ that lead to $e' \in StructRetr$ by following RDF properties).

6.1 Entity Graph Traversals Using SPARQL Queries

We describe below how we take advantage of SPARQL queries to retrieve additional results by following object property links in the LOD graph.

Structured Queries at Scope One.

Our simplest graph traversal approach looks for candidate entities directly attached to entities that have already been identified as relevant (i.e., entities in $Retr$). First, we need to ensure that only meaningful edges are followed. The object property `<dbpedia:wikilink>`, for instance, represents links between entities in Wikipedia. As an example, the entity 'dbpedia:Stevie_Wonder' has a `<dbpedia:wikilink>` pointing to 'dbpedia:Jimi_Hendrix'. Since the AOR task aims at finding all the identifiers of one specific entity, this kind of links is not very promising.

[13]It is possible to obtain such a list of properties by means of a training test collection. In this paper, we perform cross validation across the two different AOR test collections in order to identify the most promising properties.

On the other hand, the `<owl:sameAs>` object property is used to connect identifiers that refer to the same real world entity. For instance, the entity '<dbpedia:Barack_Obama>' links via `<owl:sameAs>` to the corresponding Freebase entity '<fbase:Barack_Obama>'. This object property is hence most probably valuable for improving the effectiveness of AOR in a LOD context.

To obtain a list of object properties worth following, we rank all properties in the dataset by their observed likelihood of leading to a relevant results[14]. Table 1 gives the top object property scores for the SemSearch collections. Using such a ranked list of properties as a reference, we define a series of result extension mechanisms exploiting structured queries over the data graph to identify new results. At this stage, we focus on recall rather than precision in order to preserve all candidate entities. Then, we rank candidate entities by means of a scoring function.

The first and simplest approach (SAMEAS) we consider is to follow exclusively the `<owl:sameAs>` links. Specifically, for each entity <e> in the top-N retrieved results, we issue the following query:

```
SELECT ?x
WHERE { { <e> <owl:sameAs> ?x }
        UNION
        { ?x <owl:sameAs> <e> }
      }
```

which returns all entities that are directly linked to <e> via a `<owl:sameAs>` object property.

Our second approach is based on the property scores defined above and exploits information from DBPedia. As DBPedia originates from Wikipedia, it contains disambiguation and redirect links to other entities. For example, 'dbpedia:Jaguar' links via `<dbpedia:disambiguates>` to 'dbpedia:Jaguar_Cars' as well as to 'dbpedia:Jaguar_(computer)' and others. Our second approach (S1_1) also follows such links to reach additional relevant entities. Thus, we define the following structured query:

```
SELECT ?x
WHERE { { <e> <owl:sameAs> ?x } UNION
        { ?x <owl:sameAs> <e> } UNION
        { <e> <dbpedia:disambiguates> ?x } UNION
        { ?x <dbpedia:redirect> <e> }
      }
```

which extends SAMEAS queries with two additional triple patterns.

Our third scope one approach (S1_2) includes properties that are more specific to the user queries. In addition to the generic properties of the previous two approaches, we add to the list of links to follow object properties like `<dbpedia:artist>`, `<skos:subject>`, `<dbpedia:title>`, and `<foaf:homepage>`, that appear in Table 1 and which lead to more general (albeit still related) entities.

The final scope one approach we propose (S1_3) extends S1_2 by adding matching patterns using the `<skos:broader>` property that links to more general entities. In addition to those four approaches, we additionally evaluated more complex query patterns based on the property scores defined above but did not obtain significant improvements over our simpler approaches.

[14]We compute the property scores by counting the number of times a property represents a path from a retrieved to a relevant entity (or the other way around) and dividing the result by the total number of such paths.

Structured Queries at Scope Two.

An obvious extension of the above approach is two look for related entities further in the graph by following object property links iteratively. In the following, we describe a few scope two approaches following pairs of links.

The number of potential paths to follow is increasing exponentially with the scope of the queries. To reduce the search space, we rank object property *pairs* by their likelihoods of leading to relevant entities[15].

The first strategy (S2_1) to retrieve potentially interesting entities at scope two is based on structured join queries containing top-two property pairs. The query issued to the structured repository looks as follows:

```
SELECT ?y
WHERE { { <e> <dbpedia:wikilink> ?x .
          ?x <skos:subject> ?y } UNION
        { <e> <dbpedia:wikilink> ?w .
          ?w <owl:sameAs> ?y } UNION
        [...]
      }
```

The second approach (S2_2) uses a selection of the top-two property pairs considering the starting entity e both as a subject as well as an object of the join queries. Finally, the third scope two approach (S2_3) applies a join query with the most frequent property pairs that do not include a `<dbpedia:wikilink>` property. The assumption is that due to the high frequency of this type of links[16] too many entities are retrieved, which produces a noisy result set. On the other hand, by focusing on non-frequent properties we aim at reaching few high-quality entities.

We note that it would be straightforward to generalize our graph traversal approach by considering scopes greater than two, or by considering transitive closures of object properties. Such approaches impose however a higher overhead and only marginally improve on scope one and scope two techniques from our experience.

6.2 Neighborhood Queries and Scoring

Once a new set of entities (*StructRetr*) has been reached, there is the need to 1) rank them by means of a scoring function and 2) merge the original ranking *Retr* with *StructRetr*. Given an entity $e' \in StructRetr$ and the entity $e \in Retr$ from which e' originated, we compute the e' ranking score by defining a function $score(q, e, e')$ that is used to rank all entities in *StructRetr*.

Our scoring function exploits a text similarity metric applied to the query and the literals directly or indirectly attached to the entity by means of datatype properties. As noted above, related literals are implicitly clustered around entities in the LOD cloud. While many literals are directly attached to their entities (e.g., `age`, `label`), some are attached indirectly, either through RDF blank nodes (e.g., `name-> firstname`, `address->zip code`), or are attached to related entities.

[15]Due to space limitations, we do not report here the list of such property pairs which was computed in the same way as for scope one queries.

[16]As described at `http://vmlion25.deri.ie/` this is the most frequent property in the test collection.

Table 1: Top object properties in the SemSearch collections by estimated likelihood (Recall) of connecting retrieved and relevant entities.

	From retrieved (x) to relevant entities (y)			From relevant (y) to retrieved entities (x)		
	Object Property	Recall	Prec	Object Property	Recall	Prec
SemSearch 2010	<http://dbpedia.org/property/wikilink>	82.10%	0.81%	<http://dbpedia.org/property/wikilink>	67.73%	0.52%
	<skos:subject>	11.75%	0.7%	<http://dbpedia.org/property/redirect>	7.47%	0.44%
	<http://www.w3.org/2002/07/owl#sameAs>	1.60%	1.54%	<http://www.w3.org/2002/07/owl#sameAs>	2.93%	0.76%
	<http://dbpedia.org/ontology/artist>	0.98%	15.42%	<http://dbpedia.org/property/disambiguates>	1.60%	3.85%
	<http://dbpedia.org/property/disambiguates>	0.68%	1.98%	<skos:subject>	1.33%	1.87%
	<http://dbpedia.org/property/title>	0.55%	1.81%	<http://xmlns.com/foaf/0.1/homepage>	1.33%	2.95%
	<http://dbpedia.org/ontology/producer>	0.43%	2.87%	<http://dbpedia.org/ontology/artist>	0.80%	1.97%
	<http://dbpedia.org/property/region>	0.43%	8.37%	...		
	<http://dbpedia.org/property/first>	0.37%	7.32%			
	<http://dbpedia.org/property/redirect>	0.25%	3.91%			
SemSearch 2011	<http://dbpedia.org/property/wikilink>	89.50%	0.44%	<http://dbpedia.org/property/wikilink>	37.50%	0.41%
	<skos:subject>	4.42%	0.22%	<skos:subject>	37.50%	0.32%
	<http://www.w3.org/2002/07/owl#sameAs>	1.66%	1.66%	<http://www.w3.org/2002/07/owl#sameAs>	10.71%	0.7%
	<http://dbpedia.org/property/disambiguates>	1.10%	0.89%	<skos:broader>	7.14%	0.93%
	<skos:broader>	1.10%	0.67%	<http://xmlns.com/foaf/0.1/homepage>	1.79%	2.08%
	<http://swat[...]/nsfaward.owl#piOrg>	1.10%	67.44%	<http://dbpedia.org/property/reference>	1.79%	1.75%
	<http://xmlns.com/foaf/0.1/page>	0.55%	0.13%	<http://rdfs.org/sioc/ns#links_to>	1.79%	0.04%
	...			<http://dbpedia.org/property/redirect>	1.79%	0.24%

We use neighborhood queries to retrieve all literals attached to a given entity through datatype properties, either at scope one or at scope two, e.g.,

```
SELECT ?S
WHERE { { <e> <datatypeproperty> ?S } UNION
        { <e> ?x ?y .
        ?y <datatypeproperty> ?S }
      }.
```

To minimize the overhead of such queries, we only retrieve the most promising literals. Table 2 lists the datatype properties whose values are most similar to the user queries. We adopt here the Jaro-Winkler (JW) similarity metric, which fits the problem of matching entity names well [9].

Additionally, we adopt a modified version of this scoring function by applying a threshold τ on the value of $JW(e', q)$ to filter entities that do not match well. Thus, only entities e' for which $JW(e', q) > \tau$ are included in the result set. Also, we check the number of outgoing links of each entity in *StructRetr* and only keep those entities having at least one outgoing link. The assumption (which was also made by the creators of the AOR evaluation collections) is that entities with no literals attached and that are not the subject of any statement are not relevant.

The final results are then constructed by linearly combining the Jaro-Winkler scores with the original entity score as noted above. The following section gives more information about this combination and compares the performance of several ranking methods.

7. EXPERIMENTAL EVALUATION

We present below the results of a performance evaluation of our hybrid approaches for AOR. Our aim was to evaluate the overall effectiveness and efficiency of our approach as well as the impact of the various parameters involved. More specifically, we investigated the impact of the following parameters:

- N, the number of top entities from the IR method which are used as a seed for the structured queries;
- *score*(), the scoring function used to rank entities from the structured repository;
- τ, the threshold on the text similarity measure to consider an entity description a match to the query;
- λ, the weight used to linearly combine the results from the IR and the structured query approaches.

In addition, we report results for different IR methods using BM25 scoring, structured IR indices using BM25F scoring, and graph traversals using scope one and two approaches over the structured repository combined with the IR baseline. We conclude this section with a few efficiency remarks on the overhead generated by our two-phase hybrid approach.

7.1 Experimental Setting

In order to evaluate and compare the proposed approaches, we adopt standard collections for the AOR task. We use the testsets created in the context of the SemSearch challenge for the 2010 and 2011 editions[17]. This allows us to compare the different variants we proposed with previous work that has been evaluated on the same collections.

The underlying dataset used in the testset is the Billion Triple Challenge 2009 dataset which consists of 1.3 billions RDF triples crawled from different domains of the LOD cloud. The two test collections contain 50 and 92 queries respectively, together with relevance judgements on a 3-level scale obtained by crowdsourcing the assessment task.

We adopt the official evaluation metrics from the SemSearch initiative and from previous work: Mean Average Precision (MAP), Normalized Discounted Cumulative Gain (NDCG), and early Precision (P10). Statistical significance is measured against the BM25 baseline by means of a two-tailed paired t-test by considering a difference significant when $p < 0.05$.

7.2 Evaluation Collections Based on Crowdsourcing

The AOR evaluation collections created in the context of the SemSearch initiative used crowdsourcing techniques to create relevance judgements for the entities by asking anony-

[17]`http://km.aifb.kit.edu/ws/semsearch10/` for 2010 and `http://km.aifb.kit.edu/ws/semsearch11/` for 2011.

Table 2: Top datatype properties with 10+ occurrences ranked by $JW(e', q)$ text similarity on the 2010 collection.

Datatype Property	JW(e',q)	Occurrences
<http://www.w3.org/2006/03/wn/wn20/schema/lexicalForm>	0.8449	19
<http://dbpedia.org/property/county>	0.8005	17
<http://www.daml.org/2003/02/fips55/fips-55-ont#name>	0.7674	27
<http://www.geonames.org/ontology#name>	0.7444	78
<http://www.aktors.org/ontology/portal#full-name>	0.7360	55
<http://dbpedia.org/property/wikiquoteProperty>	0.7096	10
<http://www.w3.org/2004/02/skos/core#prefLabel>	0.6911	158
<http://purl.org/dc/elements/1.1/title>	0.6711	236
<http://sw.opencyc.org/concept/Mx4rwLSVCpwpEbGdrcN5Y29ycA>	0.6680	48
<http://dbpedia.org/property/officialName>	0.6623	54

mous Web users to judge entity relevance for a small economic reward. Such a novel approach to relevance judgement triggers obvious questions about the reliability of the results. In [5], Blanco *et al.* experimentally show how such an approach is reliable and, most importantly, repeatable.

Traditional effectiveness evaluation methods (e.g., based on the Cranfield paradigm) have been largely used in TREC initiatives. Document collections, queries, and relevance judgements form test collections, which are typically made available to foster repeatable and comparable experiments. Because of the increasing size of the corpora and the impossibility of manually judging all documents, a pooling methodology is typically used: top retrieved results from each run submitted to the evaluation initiative are judged; non-judged results are assumed to be not relevant. Such an approach has been shown to be fair for comparing participants but unfair with respect to any following systems evaluated on the same collection "because the non-contributors will have highly ranked unjudged documents that are assumed to be not relevant" [22]. Zobel [25] showed that TREC collections can still be used to provide an unbiased comparison. To overcome the limitations of pooling, novel measures taking judgement incompleteness into account (e.g., bpref [8]) or adopting sampling to delve deeper into the ranked list (e.g., infAP [24]) have been proposed. Such refinements are also needed because the coverage of the judgement pools gets smaller over time as the size of the collection grows (e.g., 300,000 documents with a pool depth of 100 in TREC-5 and 1 billion documents with a pool depth of 20 in TREC 2011).

The recent trend of crowdsourcing relevance judgments enables an alternative approach. As shown in [5], the results obtained by crowdsourcing relevance judgements for the same collection at different points in time empirically demonstrates the repeatability of such experiments. Based on this important result and on the vision of "evaluation campaigns that run *continuously*" [5], we propose an approach to fair comparison of different IR systems running on the same evaluation collection.

Assuming systems A, B, and C participated in an evaluation initiative and, therefore, contributed to the assessment pool with their top-10 results, then each result of A in the top-10 will be judged while results beyond rank 10 may be judged or not (they will only be judge if retrieved by B or C in their top-10). On the other hand, a new system D appearing after the evaluation initiative may retrieve in its top-10 results many unjudged results that are typically considered as not relevant. This strongly penalizes runs which retrieve results that are very different from the original results that were part of the evaluation initiative. Instead, new systems should exploit crowdsourcing to obtain the missing judgements by running the same micro-tasks that provided the original (crowdsourced) relevance judgements.

One key advantage of this approach is that subsequent runs created after the initial evaluation campaign can be judged on a fair basis as if they were part of the original results. One drawback however is that the number of relevant results changes (i.e., increases) in this way, thus making measures that take this into account (e.g., MAP) incomparable with the ones computed originally by the evaluation initiative. Anyhow, the availability of the original retrieved results (i.e., the submitted runs which are available for all tasks at TREC) allows the authors of later approaches to recompute the measures and compare them against previous approaches.

As the approach proposed in this paper substantially differs from the approaches run during the evaluation campaign, both in terms of system architecture and retrieved results (see Table 3), we decided to adopt this new approach to obtain fair relevance judgements for the top-10 results of our various approaches. Thus, in the remainder of this paper, we report evaluation measures computed over relevance judgements complemented with additional crowdsourced judgements.

7.3 Completing Relevance Judgement through Crowdsourcing

In order to obtain additional relevance judgements for unjudged entities in the top-10 results of our runs, we published micro-tasks (HITs) on Amazon MTurk. We followed the same task design and setting as the ones used to create the test collections for the AOR task at SemSearch (as described in [5, 16]). We asked the crowd to judge a total of 1583 additional query-entity pairs for the 2010 collection and 1183 for the 2011 collection.

We split the tasks in batches of 10 entities per HIT, which were rewarded 0.20$ each and assigned to 3 different workers. The overall number of relevant entities increased by +8% (passing from 2028 to 2193) for the 2010 collection and by 17% (from 470 to 551) for the 2011 collection[18].

As a consequence, Precision@10 for our approach is comparable to the original SemSearch submissions as it is com-

[18]The extended assessment files we created together with the script to generate them from MTurk output are available at `http://diuf.unifr.ch/xi/HybridAOR`

Table 3: New retrieved results that were *not* retrieved by the BM25 baseline for top-10 results of IR and graph-based approaches in both collections.

	Approach	New Retr.	New Rel.	New Not-judged
SemSearch 2010	Extension	266	1	262
	Query Autoc.	308	2	303
	PRF3	220	0	218
	SAMEAS	92	11	76
	S1_1	211	29	162
	S1_2	312	19	281
	S1_3	312	19	281
	S2_1	15	3	12
	S2_2	16	3	13
	S2_3	16	3	13
SemSearch 2011	Extension	179	0	175
	Query Autoc.	216	2	212
	PRF3	153	0	152
	SAMEAS	20	8	12
	S1_1	56	14	39
	S1_2	103	9	97
	S1_3	103	9	92
	S2_1	2	1	1
	S2_2	2	1	1
	S2_3	4	4	0

puted on fully judged results. On the other hand, absolute values of MAP will be lower when computed with the extended relevance judgements as the number of relevant results has increased. In any case, the baseline we adopted closely matches the approaches used so far for the AOR task evaluated in SemSearch. Moreover, we compare below our proposed hybrid solution against a plethora of standard IR approaches like query extension and pseudo-relevance feedback.

7.4 Evaluation of Entity Ranking Techniques

Table 4 gives the results obtained by using BM25 scoring[19] on the inverted index built on all the literals attached to the entity (entity profile). We compare this baseline approach against standard IR techniques such as query extension using related words (Extension), query autocompletion as provided by commercial Web search engines (Query Autoc.), and Pseudo Relevance Feedback using top-3 retrieved entities (PRF3). We experimented with various approaches to handle the terms in the query and in the end opted for a disjunctive approach (i.e., we take each term in the query separately and 'OR' the results) since it performed best. The only exception is for the approaches based on a structured index and BM25F scoring for which we adopt a conjunctive approach. As we can see, the BM25 baseline performs best on both test collections. This indicates that methods working well for other entity search tasks may not be directly applicable to the AOR task due to the specific semantics of the user query, meant to uniquely describe one specific entity. Anyhow, we observe that the query autocompletion method obtains an Average Precision of 1.0 for a query (q16 of 2011), for which all other methods performed poorly (0.02). This originates from a misspelling in the original query, which was corrected by the external autocompletion functionality.

Table 5 gives results for the structured inverted index approach (see Section 5.1). The table lists results for indices built on entity profiles constructed using different types of literals. When compared to the baseline index (which aggregates all literals directly attached to the entities in a single *document*), we observe that structured indices perform better. Specifically, when a conjunctive query and BM25F ranking is used over a structured inverted index, effectiveness increases. The best results are obtained by the index encompassing all three fields, that is, URI, Label, and Attributes (ULA).

[19]The parameter b in BM25 has been selected by cross-validation on the 2010 and 2011 testsets.

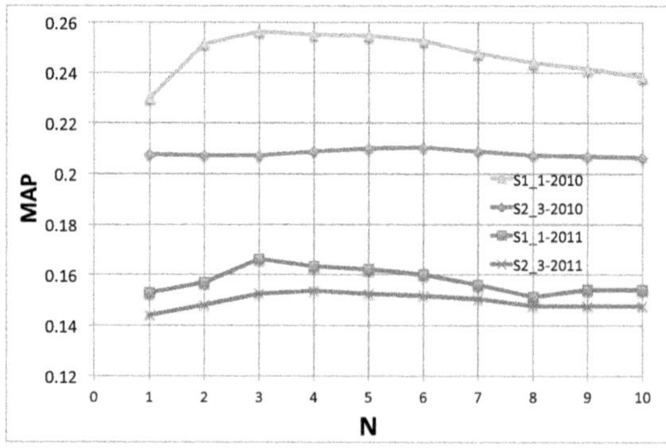

Figure 2: Effectiveness values varying the number of top-N entities retrieved by IR approaches.

7.5 Evaluation of Graph Query Techniques

Parameter Analysis.

Figure 2 shows how effectiveness (MAP) varies when varying the parameter N indicating the number of entities considered as input for the structured queries, both for the 2010 and 2011 collections. We observe that the best number of entities to consider lies between 3 and 4 in most cases, therefore we fix this parameter to 3 for the following experiments.

Moreover, we observe that high values (i.e., $0.8 - 0.9$) for the threshold τ used to discard entities lead to higher MAP in all cases. The optimal value for λ varies for scope one and two approaches. Interestingly, for the best performing method S1_1, the optimal value for λ is 0.5 for both the 2010 and 2011 collections: for such an approach, our hybrid system reaches an optimal tradeoff between IR and graph data management techniques.

Table 6 gives the performance of different functions used to compute $score(q, e, e')$. As we can see, the most effective method is the one that exploits the original BM25 score of e to score e'. This is the scoring function we use to compute the final results of the hybrid system as reported in Table 8.

Table 6: MAP values for S1_1 and S2_3 obtained by means of different instantiation of $score(q, e, e')$ using $\lambda = 0.5$ on the 2010 collection.

score(q,e,e')	S1_1	S2_3
Count $JW(e', q) > \tau$	0.2585	0.2076
Avg count $JW(e', q) > \tau$	0.2509	0.2075
Sum JW(e',q)	0.2558	0.2074
Avg JW(e',q)	0.2571	0.2075
Sum $BM25(e, q) - \epsilon$	0.2586	0.2113

Table 4: Standard ER approaches over the inverted index.

	2010 Collection			2011 Collection		
	MAP	P10	NDCG	MAP	P10	NDCG
BM25	**0.2070**	**0.3348**	**0.5920**	**0.1484**	**0.2020**	**0.4267**
Extension	0.1417	0.2152	0.4912	0.1131	0.16	0.3953
Query Autoc.	0.085	0.1717	0.4301	0.1298	0.1640	0.4136
PRF3	0.13	0.2152	0.5078	0.0998	0.1720	0.3642

Table 5: Approaches based on a structured inverted index with BM25 and BM25F scoring.

		2010 Collection			2011 Collection		
		MAP	P10	NDCG	MAP	P10	NDCG
BM25	URI only	0.2113	0.3120	0.5904	0.1141	0.1600	0.3562
	Label only	0.1156	0.2130	0.4911	0.1018	0.1660	0.3575
	Attrib. only	0.2070	**0.3348**	0.5920	0.1487	0.2020	0.4274
BM25F	URI-Label	0.2209	0.3239	**0.6083**	0.1502	0.2120	**0.4277**
	Label-Attrib.	0.2011	0.3033	0.5411	0.1431	0.1980	0.3966
	URI-Attrib.	0.2238	0.3130	0.5445	0.1538	0.2080	0.3988
	ULA	**0.2307**	0.3326	0.5450	**0.1628**	**0.2140**	0.3973

Table 7: Average query execution time (ms) on the 2011 dataset.

Approach	IR time	RDF time	Total time
BM25 Baseline	285	-	285
Extension	580	-	580 (+104%)
Query Autoc.	1447	-	1447 (+408%)
PRF3	2670	-	2670 (+837%)
SAMEAS	285	30	315 (+11%)
S1_1	285	48	333 (+17%)
S1_2	285	84	369 (+29%)
S1_3	285	86	371 (+30%)
S2_1	285	1746	2031 (+613%)
S2_2	285	2192	2477 (+769%)
S2_3	285	105	390 (+37%)

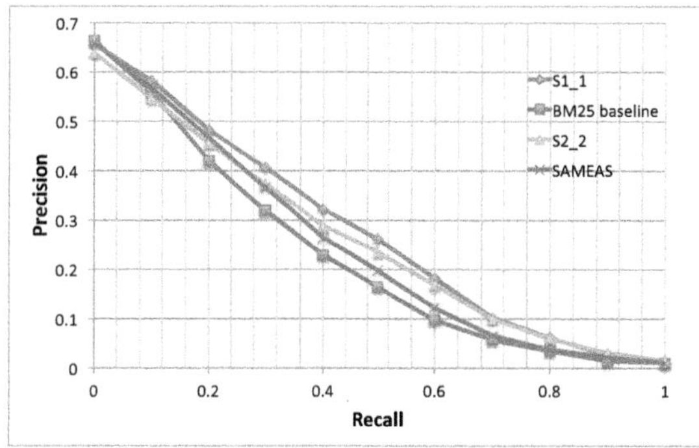

Figure 3: Precision/Recall curves for graph-based approaches on the 2010 collection.

Evaluation of Hybrid Approaches.

Table 8 gives results for the graph-based extension of the baseline ranking. We observe that most approaches based on scope one queries significantly improve over the baseline BM25 ranking. The simple S1_1 approach, which exploits `<owl:sameAs>` links plus Wikipedia redirect and disambiguation information, performs best obtaining a 25% improvement of MAP over the baseline on the 2010 dataset. Figure 3 shows Precision/Recall curves for the baseline BM25 ranking and for graph-based approaches. Again, we can see how S1_1 outperforms other approaches. The S1_2 approach performs best in terms of MAP on the 2011 dataset, although not significantly better than the baseline.

7.6 Efficiency Considerations

Table 7 shows execution times for the different components of our system and for various approaches[20]. Quite naturally, the IR baseline is faster than more complex approaches. Interestingly, we observe that structured approaches based on scope one queries perform very well, only adding a very limited overhead to the inverted index approach. The S1_1 approach, which is the best in terms of effectiveness, adds a cost of only 17% in terms of execution time to the BM25 baseline. The approaches based on scope two queries that use `<dbpedia:wikilink>` are more costly and would require a specific effort to make them scalable over large datasets. The scope two approach S2_6, which uses less frequent object properties, has still a reasonable overhead (37%).

In terms of storage consumption, the original collection containing 1.3 billions statements occupies 253GB. The baseline inverted index created with MG4J[21] is 8.9GB, the structured index used with BM25F scoring is 5GB, while the graph index created with RDF-3X[22] is 87GB. We note that the graph index could easily be optimized by discarding all the properties that are not used by the graph traversals and neighborhood queries (we could save considerable space this way, from 50% to 95% approximatively depending on the graph approaches used).

8. CONCLUSIONS

As more datasets become available on the Web, novel applications can exploit semi-structured data to build entity-centric functionalities. In this paper, we present a hybrid system for effectively and efficiently solving Ad-hoc Object Retrieval tasks. Our approach is based on the combination of results from an inverted index storing entity profiles and from a structured database storing graph data.

[20]We did not put any emphasis on improving the efficiency of our system. Experiments were run on a single machine with a cold cache and disk-resident indices for both the inverted indices and the structured repository.

[21]`http://mg4j.dsi.unimi.it/`

[22]`http://code.google.com/p/rdf3x/`

	2010 Collection			2011 Collection		
	MAP	P10	NDCG	MAP	P10	NDCG
BM25	0.2070	0.3348	0.5920	0.1484	0.2020	0.4267
SAMEAS	0.2293* (+11%)	0.363* (+8%)	0.5932 (+0%)	0.1612 (+9%)	**0.2200** (+9%)	0.4433 (+4%)
S1_1	**0.2586*** (+25%)	**0.3848*** (+15%)	0.5965 (+1%)	0.1657 (+12%)	0.2140 (+6%)	0.4426 (+4%)
S1_2	0.2305* (+11%)	0.3217 (-4%)	0.5724* (-3%)	**0.1731** (+17%)	0.2180 (+8%)	**0.4532** (+6%)
S1_3	0.2306* (+11%)	0.3217 (-4%)	0.5721* (-4%)	0.1716 (+16%)	0.2140 (+6%)	0.4501 (+5%)
S2_1	0.2118 (+2%)	0.3370 (+1%)	0.5971 (+1%)	0.1550 (+4%)	0.2060 (+2%)	0.4376 (+3%)
S2_2	0.2118 (+2%)	0.3370 (+1%)	0.5965 (+1%)	0.1555 (+5%)	0.2080 (+3%)	0.4379 (+3%)
S2_3	0.2113 (+2%)	0.3402 (+2%)	**0.5978** (+1%)	0.1589 (+7%)	0.2120 (+5%)	0.4385 (+3%)

Table 8: Graph-based approaches with scope one and two queries compared to the IR baseline. * indicates statistically significant difference against the BM25 baseline.

Our extensive experimental evaluation over two different evaluation collections shows that the use of structured search on top of standard IR approaches can lead to significantly better results (up to 25% improvement over the BM25 baseline in terms of Mean Average Precision). This comes at the cost of incorporating additional components in the system architecture and of implementing additional merging and ranking functions in the processing pipeline. In any case, our measurements show that the overhead caused by the graph data management components is surprisingly limited and only represents 17% for the most effective approach.

We consider our initial hybrid results as very promising, especially given that the LOD sample data sets used in the test collections were extremely noisy and incomplete (automated data cleaning and entity linking are two prominent research topics in the LOD community, which should hopefully alleviates those issues on the medium term). As future work, we plan to focus on further user queries (e.g, Entity List Completion queries and queries specifying the category of the entity sought) and on improving the efficiency of our proposed hybrid system in distributed and cloud settings.

9. ACKNOWLEDGMENTS

We would like to thank the anonymous reviewers for their helpful comments. This work was supported by the Swiss National Science Foundation under grant number PP00P2_128459, and by the Haslerstiftung in the context of the Smart World 11005 (MemOrles) project.

10. REFERENCES

[1] K. Balog, L. Azzopardi, and M. de Rijke. A language modeling framework for expert finding. *Inf. Process. Manage.*, 45(1):1–19, 2009.

[2] K. Balog, M. Bron, and M. De Rijke. Query modeling for entity search based on terms, categories, and examples. *ACM Trans. Inf. Syst.*, 29:22:1–22:31, 2011.

[3] K. Balog, P. Serdyukov, and A. P. de Vries. Overview of the TREC 2011 entity track. In *TREC 2011.*

[4] K. Balog, I. Soboroff, P. Thomas, N. Craswell, A. P. de Vries, and P. Bailey. Overview of the TREC 2008 enterprise track. In *TREC 2008.*

[5] R. Blanco, H. Halpin, D. M. Herzig, P. Mika, J. Pound, H. S. Thompson, and D. T. Tran. Repeatable and reliable search system evaluation using crowdsourcing. In *SIGIR*, pages 923–932, 2011.

[6] R. Blanco, P. Mika, and S. Vigna. Effective and Efficient Entity Search in RDF Data. In *International Semantic Web Conference (1)*, pages 83–97, 2011.

[7] M. Bron, K. Balog, and M. de Rijke. Ranking related entities: components and analyses. In *CIKM*, pages 1079–1088, New York, NY, USA, 2010. ACM.

[8] C. Buckley and E. M. Voorhees. Retrieval evaluation with incomplete information. In *SIGIR*, pages 25–32, New York, NY, USA, 2004. ACM.

[9] W. W. Cohen, P. Ravikumar, and S. E. Fienberg. A comparison of string metrics for matching names and records. In *KDD Workshop On Data Cleaning And Object Consolidation*, 2003.

[10] R. Delbru, N. Toupikov, M. Catasta, and G. Tummarello. A Node Indexing Scheme for Web Entity Retrieval. In *ESWC (2)*, pages 240–256, 2010.

[11] G. Demartini, C. S. Firan, T. Iofciu, R. Krestel, and W. Nejdl. Why finding entities in Wikipedia is difficult, sometimes. *Inf. Retr.*, 13(5):534–567, 2010.

[12] G. Demartini, T. Iofciu, and A. P. de Vries. Overview of the INEX 2009 Entity Ranking Track. In *INEX*, pages 254–264, 2009.

[13] G. Demartini, M. M. S. Missen, R. Blanco, and H. Zaragoza. TAER: time-aware entity retrieval-exploiting the past to find relevant entities in news articles. In *CIKM*, pages 1517–1520, 2010.

[14] S. Elbassuoni and R. Blanco. Keyword search over RDF graphs. In *CIKM*, pages 237–242, 2011.

[15] C. Fellbaum. Wordnet. *Theory and Applications of Ontology: Computer Applications*, pages 231–243, 2010.

[16] H. Halpin, D. M. Herzig, P. Mika, R. Blanco, J. Pound, H. S. Thompson, and D. T. Tran. Evaluating Ad-Hoc Object Retrieval. In *International Workshop on Evaluation of Semantic Technologies (IWEST 2010) at ISWC2010.*

[17] R. Kaptein, P. Serdyukov, A. De Vries, and J. Kamps. Entity ranking using Wikipedia as a pivot. In *CIKM*, pages 69–78, New York, NY, USA, 2010. ACM.

[18] E. Minack, R. Paiu, S. Costache, G. Demartini, J. Gaugaz, E. Ioannou, P.-A. Chirita, and W. Nejdl. Leveraging personal metadata for desktop search: The beagle^{++} system. *J. Web Sem.*, 8(1):37–54, 2010.

[19] T. Neumann and G. Weikum. The RDF-3X engine for scalable management of RDF data. *The VLDB Journal*, 19:91–113, February 2010.

[20] J. Pound, P. Mika, and H. Zaragoza. Ad-hoc object retrieval in the web of data. In *WWW*, pages 771–780, New York, NY, USA, 2010. ACM.

[21] S. E. Robertson and H. Zaragoza. The Probabilistic Relevance Framework: BM25 and Beyond. *Foundations and Trends in Information Retrieval*, 3(4):333–389, 2009.

[22] E. M. Voorhees. The philosophy of information retrieval evaluation. In *CLEF'01*, pages 355–370.

[23] H. Wang, T. Tran, C. Liu, and L. Fu. Lightweight integration of IR and DB for scalable hybrid search with integrated ranking support. *Web Semant.*, 9:490–503, 2011.

[24] E. Yilmaz and J. A. Aslam. Estimating average precision with incomplete and imperfect judgments. In *CIKM*, pages 102–111, 2006.

[25] J. Zobel. How reliable are the results of large-scale information retrieval experiments? In *SIGIR*, pages 307–314, New York, NY, USA, 1998. ACM.

Retrieving Similar Discussion Forum Threads: A Structure Based Approach

Amit Singh Deepak P Dinesh Raghu
IBM Research - India, Bangalore, India
{amitkumarsingh,deepak.s.p,dinraghu}@in.ibm.com

ABSTRACT

Online forums are becoming a popular way of finding useful information on the web. Search over forums for existing discussion threads so far is limited to keyword-based search due to the minimal effort required on part of the users. However, it is often not possible to capture all the relevant context in a complex query using a small number of keywords. Example-based search that retrieves similar discussion threads given one exemplary thread is an alternate approach that can help the user provide richer context and vastly improve forum search results. In this paper, we address the problem of finding similar threads to a given thread. Towards this, we propose a novel methodology to estimate similarity between discussion threads. Our method exploits the thread structure to decompose threads in to set of weighted overlapping components. It then estimates pairwise thread similarities by quantifying how well the information in the threads are mutually contained within each other using lexical similarities between their underlying components. We compare our proposed methods on real datasets against state-of-the-art thread retrieval mechanisms wherein we illustrate that our techniques outperform others by large margins on popular retrieval evaluation measures such as NDCG, MAP, Precision@k and MRR. In particular, consistent improvements of up to 10% are observed on all evaluation measures.

Categories and Subject Descriptors

H.3.3 [**Information Storage and Retrieval**]: Information Search and Retrieval—*Retrieval Models*

Keywords

Forums, Threads, Retrieval, Similarity

1. INTRODUCTION

Online forums are fast becoming a very popular data source on the web. They are an easy way to publish knowledge since composing a post in a forum is much easier than composing a web page. Further, forums are interactive spaces where many people contribute and hence are *live* (as against web pages that are often static); making them more attractive to contribute to. Forums are monitored by many people making spurious information easy to detect and point out; hence, it may be expected that contributors would exercise some caution to ensure that the information that they post is correct and useful. It may also be observed that forums mostly contain subjective knowledge (e.g., opinions) and hence are often complimentary to other knowledge sources such as Wikipedia[1]. Despite such uniqueness, there have been only a few forum search engines[2 3] and searching forum threads is still only an emerging topic [28, 10, 12].

In this paper, we consider the problem of *finding similar threads to a given thread.* Threads in online discussion forms are collections of posts that are posted in response to a common starting post. Finding similar data objects in other popular data sources such as text collections [13], web documents [8], images [34], websites[4], social network profiles [15], linked entities [19] and relational data [9] have been a subject of much research. *However, finding similar threads in online forums, to the best of our knowledge, has not received enough attention.*

Applications: Much like finding similar objects in other knowledge sources, finding similar threads has many potential applications. For example, a user browsing a thread in a discussion forum could be provided links to *similar threads* for a more detailed reading on the same or related topic. Likewise, links to *related threads* (much like grouping of news articles in systems such as *Google News*[5]) could be of use in thread retrieval systems [12]. A notion of similarity among threads would also help developing a clustered interface for search results (e.g., Yippy[6]) in thread retrieval. A *knowledge author* who seeks to read through discussions forums (e.g., developer forums) and document problems and solutions from them would most likely prefer to read through similar threads together since that would help minimize context switch, by enabling her to cover one type of problems in entirety before moving to the next. Though finding similar threads has many potential applications as outlined above, we focus on the scenario of providing a functionality of *finding similar threads* to a given thread (e.g., the thread the

Permission to make digital or hard copies of all or part of this work for personal or classroom use is granted without fee provided that copies are not made or distributed for profit or commercial advantage and that copies bear this notice and the full citation on the first page. To copy otherwise, to republish, to post on servers or to redistribute to lists, requires prior specific permission and/or a fee.
SIGIR'12, August 12–16, 2012, Portland, Oregon, USA.
Copyright 2012 ACM 978-1-4503-1472-5/12/08 ...$15.00.

[1]http://en.wikipedia.org
[2]http://www.boardreader.com
[3]http://www.boardtracker.com
[4]http://www.similarsites.com/
[5]http://news.google.com
[6]http://search.yippy.com

user is reading currently) and evaluate the effectiveness of the similarity measure that we propose, using classical Information Retrieval evaluation measures.

<table>
<tr><td colspan="2">User:0
My Beetel 220 modem has suddenly stopped working.
The data led has stopped blinking. Can somebody help?</td></tr>
<tr><th>Thread T1</th><th>Thread T2</th></tr>
<tr><td>User:1
You could restart the modem and see whether it works. Else, it may be due to some problem in the splitter. Try connecting the line directly to modem</td><td>User:2a
It would most likely be solved by a modem restart.</td></tr>
<tr><td></td><td>User:2b
If the above solution doesnt work, try connecting the line directly without splitter.</td></tr>
</table>

Table 1: Example Thread Patterns.

Challenges vis-a-vis Document Similarity: Threads in discussion forums, despite being largely composed of textual content, have various properties that distinguish them from regular text documents such as newswire articles. The latter are mostly authored by a single author, whereas discussion forum threads involve many contributors. This makes them less coherent, and more vulnerable to abrupt jumps in topics. Further, discussion forum threads have an inherent structure; this could be visualized as a tree structure where posts form nodes and edges linking posts to their replies. The intuitive method of estimating similarity that considers *each thread as a large document comprising of all the component posts* followed by usage of traditional similarity metrics such as tf.idf cosine would obviously lead to large posts being able to influence similarity more than smaller ones; this is undesirable since the length of a post is more often related to other factors such as author's style than the utility of the post. At the other end of the fragmentation spectrum, is that of *considering each thread as a bag of posts*, with similarity between them being quantified as an aggregate of the pairwise similarities between the posts. Consider two hypothetical threads T1 and T2 spawned out of the same first question in Table 1. Despite being very similar due to the nature of content posted, no pair of posts (one from each thread) have a high lexical similarity. This is due to the content in the single post in T1 getting split across two posts in T2. Such fragmentation is common in discussion forums due to varying expertise levels of content authors and dents the effectiveness of the bag of posts approach. The third solution is that of *selecting highly informative words to form summaries of each thread* and using them as a keyword query in keyword search systems that operate on forums [28, 10, 12]. However, such selection of words is often hard making it difficult to capture the entire context of the query thread. We address the above challenges in developing a methodology for finding similar threads.

Our specific contributions are as follows:

- We propose a novel methodology for estimating pairwise similarities for discussion forum threads that leverages structural information of threads by decomposing threads into weighted overlapping components. For our choice of component types, we show that the similarity computation can be performed efficiently.
- An extensive empirical evaluation that illustrates that our methodology outperforms state-of-the-art baselines.

2. PROBLEM DEFINITION

Consider a discussion forum thread X and a set of threads $\mathcal{Y}$. We would like to develop a method that heuristically estimates the similarity between X and each thread in $\mathcal{Y}$. Given such a method $S(.,.)$, one can rank the threads in $\mathcal{Y}$ in the non-increasing order of similarity with X, such that the following condition is satisfied:

$$\forall y \in \mathcal{Y} - \{Y_1, Y_2, \ldots, Y_{i-1}\}, S(X, Y_i) \geq S(X, y)$$

where Y_i denotes the ith thread when threads in $\mathcal{Y}$ are arranged in the non-increasing order of similarity wrt X. The above condition simply suggests that Y_i has a score at least as much as any of threads not ahead of it in the ranking.

2.1 Thread and Posts

Since we will make many references to threads and posts, we hereby informally outline what we mean by them. We define a post as the smallest unit of communication in online forums that consists of content posted by a user. Each post has associated meta-data such as user ID of the user posting the post, time of posting the post etc. A thread starts off with a post (that we call as the *first post*, whose title is the thread title too), and comprises all posts in reply to the initial posts. There is a recursiveness in the definition in that it includes all posts in reply to posts already in the thread. A thread tree is formed by the posts in the thread as nodes, and with a directed edge from a post to all direct replies to it. In such a thread tree represented in Figure 1(b), B2 is a direct reply to B1 whereas B4 was posted in reply to B2. In most online discussion forums, the thread structure is apparent due to the restrictions imposed (a reply having to be attached a specific post); if not, the thread structures could be identified heuristically [25].

2.2 Thread Components

Threads being composed of posts, an intuitive way to model thread similarity would be to consider a thread as a bag of posts, wherein the scoring function could be posed as an aggregate of the pairwise similarity between posts. However, such a formulation would not be robust to fragmentation of information across posts, as seen in Section 1. In short, we would do better by allowing for collections of posts in a one thread to be mapped to collections of posts in another, while performing similarity calculations. Thread substructures have been exploited for online community search in [28] where four substructures were considered viz., the *entire thread*, *single posts*, *post-reply pairs* and *the dialogue* (a chain of posts from root to a leaf). The results therein suggest that the dialog substructure was not very useful. Based on such conclusions, we also opt to consider *single posts* and *post-reply pairs* as the substructures for consideration. For this choice of substructure types, we will show in a later section, that our similarity computation is very efficient. Though we only consider the above two types of

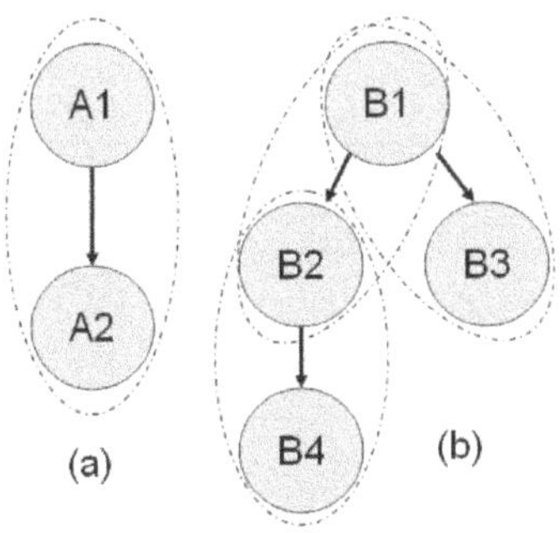

Figure 1: Threads with Post-Reply Substructures.

substructures, the framework of our methodology is generic and can accommodate any kinds of substructures.

For a thread represented by nodes as posts and reply-to relations as edges, in addition to the individual posts, the set of substructures would include the pairs indicated by the ovals as shown in Figure 1. Consider the thread in Example 1(b); the component substructures would then be $\{B1, B2, B3, B4, [B1, B2], [B1, B3], [B2, B4]\}$. It may be noted that such a modeling does not fully solve the information fragmentation issue since it does not allow a set of three posts to match to a single post, even if that happens to be the real nature of fragmentation in a specific case. However, it goes one step forward than matching posts to posts, and could allow for matching the two posts in T2 in Table 1 to map to the single post in T1. We will use post and post-reply substructures (which we refer to, as components, hereon) in estimating similarity between threads in Section 3.

3. OUR APPROACH

We now describe the techniques that we propose for estimating thread similarity; we will first describe a framework and then go on to describe instantiations of the framework that we use in our empirical evaluation. The basic problem is that of estimating the similarity between two threads X and Y. Once we have a means of estimating such thread pairwise similarities, it is easy to build a retrieval engine that finds the top-k similar threads to a given query thread, as seen in Section 2.

3.1 Modeling Thread Similarity

We now outline our concerns in modeling the similarity between threads, $S(X, Y)$. *Firstly*, threads in discussion fora, due to intervention by many people, could steer away from the main topic in the course of time and digress to tangential topics; all posts are typically not equally important to the central topic of discourse. Thus, a methodology for estimating thread similarity would have to weigh posts differentially, based on heuristics such as relevance to the central topic(s) or author reputation. *Secondly*, a thread is a collection of posts, and the number of posts in a thread could vary very widely. For example, a thread in a technical discussion forum could be composed of just 2 posts (e.g., the statement of a problem, followed by a reply with the solution), or could be a long drawn discussion (involving scores of posts) between participants that culminates in finding the solution to the problem posed in the first post. In finding similar threads to a given query thread, one may have to compare threads of widely varying sizes. Due to these properties of *thread posts having to be weighted differentially*, and *threads being composed of widely varying number of posts*, we find it very intuitive to decompose the notion of thread pairwise similarity into two distinct components; one that measures how well the information in X is subsumed in Y (where Y could contain other extra information), and another that measures how well Y is subsumed in X. Towards this, as detailed in Section 2.2, we decompose threads into a set of potentially overlapping components with an associated weight for each, weights indicating the importance of the component to the thread in consideration.

For a pair of threads, X and Y, our estimate of similarity between them (that we denote by $S(X, Y)$) would consider three factors:

- $P_S(X, Y)$, a score that denotes how well the thread X is subsumed by (i.e., contained in) Y.
- $P_S(Y, X)$, an analogous score that estimates how well Y is subsumed by X.
- $Sim(X_{headpost}, Y_{headpost})$, the similarity between the titles and the first posts of the threads.

$X_{headpost}$ denotes the document formed by collating the title and the first post of the thread X. We use several popular text similarity metrics in estimating $Sim(.,.)$.

3.1.1 Estimating Subsumption

In estimating how well X *is being subsumed by* Y, *we roughly try to find the best matching component of* Y *for* **each** *component in* X. In particular, many of Y's components may be left unmatched; this is because while estimating how well X is contained in Y, we would intuitively not want to penalize Y for the extra information that it may contain. To recollect, the components of the thread in Example 1(b) (which we refer to as X) are $\{B1, B2, B3, B4, [B1, B2], [B1, B3], [B2, B4]\}$. We associate a score with each component X_i w.r.t Y:

$$Score_Y(X_i) = max\{Sim(X_i, Y_j) | Y_j \in Y\} \quad (1)$$

where $Sim(.,.)$, the similarity between components, denotes the text similarity and X_i denotes the text document formed by putting together the text from posts within X_i. Essentially, for each component of X, we estimate the maximal similarity with any component in Y.

As can be seen, $B2$ has its representation in 3 of these 7 components of X; it is easy to see that a post would have representation in as many pairs as it has immediate children (if not a root, it is also represented in a pair with its parent). However, we would not like to allow certain posts to influence the $P_S(X, Y)$ score more than others by design. *In particular, we want to choose a set of components of* X *such that each post is only represented once across the set.*

Figure 2 represents a graph with the components of the thread X as nodes; we call it the *component graph*. We induce an edge between components that share a node. The scores (computed as described above) are shown against the nodes. Now, our problem reduces to finding the *maximum weight independent set*[7] (MWIS)[27] of such a graph. The non-adjacency property of the MWIS set ensures that no post is counted twice, due to the nature of inducing edges.

To be fair in comparison between components that contain single posts and those that contain two, we use an intuitive weighting scheme where the score of each component is

[7]http://en.wikipedia.org/wiki/Maximal_independent_set

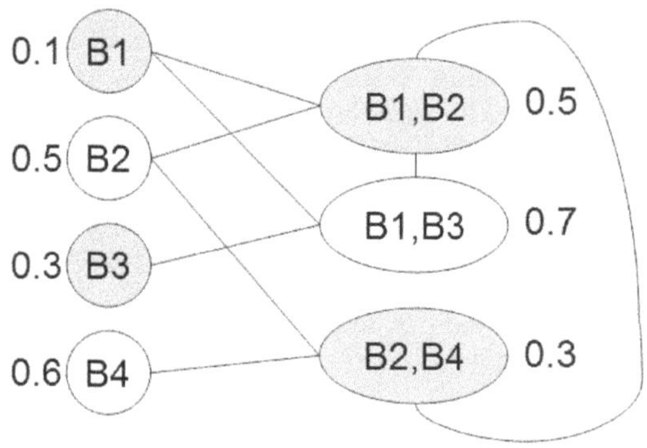

Figure 2: Component Graph.

weighed as much as the number of posts it contains. Thus, the MIS shown in white in Figure 2 would have a score of $0.5 + 0.6 + 0.7 * 2 = 2.5$; for the graph in our example, the white nodes denote the MWIS as well.

THEOREM 3.1. *For the component graph of a thread, the MWIS can be computed in polynomial time and always covers each post exactly once.*

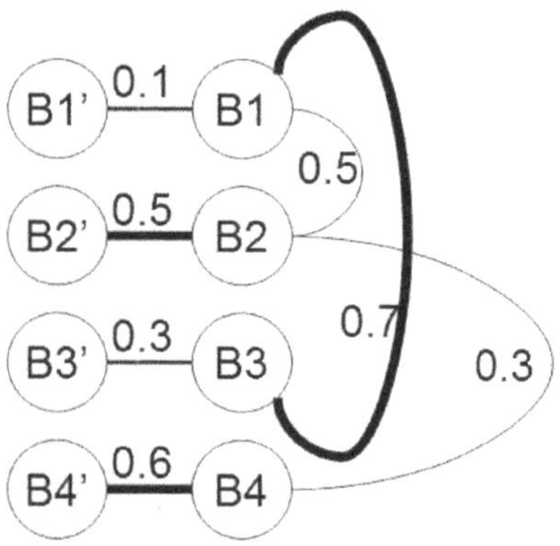

Figure 3: Transformed Graph.

Proof: In Figure 2, we used nodes as components for the sake of simplicity. Now, we illustrate a new graph where the nodes in the component graph (i.e., components of the thread) are translated to edges; this is given in Figure 3. In this graph, we use two nodes to represent each post p, one node to stand for a post (that we denote as p itself, at the risk of overloading notation), and another one that we use as a pseudo-node, p' to avoid self-edges (since we are about to talk about matching and most literature on matching is silent about graphs that contain self-edges). A pair component $\{p_1, p_2\}$ is represented by the edge $p_1 - p_2$ whereas the edge $p_1 - p_1'$ represents the singleton component $\{p_1\}$. Now, the MWIS problem for component graphs corresponds to the problem of finding the Maximum Weighted Matching (MWM) in the transformed graphs like in Figure 3. This transformation is possible since we have modeled the component graph as one where each component can *at most* contain two posts, thanks to our choice of components that can at most span two posts. The MWM problem is known to be solvable in polynomial time [14]; this proves the first part of the theorem.

We now informally clarify as to why the maximum matching of the new graph would cover every post exactly once. A post is deemed to be covered in a matching if the matching contains an edge that is incident of a node *or* the pseudo-node of the post. Matching, by definition, would not allow for covering a node (either of p or p') multiple times. Our informal proof as to why every post is covered works by contradiction. Let us assume that an MWM does not cover post p. This implies that neither the node p, nor p' (the pseudo-node), is included in it. Hence, we can simply add the edge connecting p and p' to the matching without violating the property of it being a matching (no node incident on multiple edges). Since we assume (like in most cases in literature) that edge weights are non-negative, this can only improve the weight of the matching, and also includes more nodes. This negates the initial premise that the matching that excluded p was the MWM and completes the proof. ∎

Our formulation of $P_S(X, Y)$ is now the following:

$$P_S(X,Y) = \frac{\sum_{X_i \in MWIS(X,Y)} w_X(X_i) \times Score_Y(X_i)}{\#\ posts\ in\ X}$$

where $MWIS(X,Y)$ denotes the MWIS for the component graph constructed from thread X w.r.t thread Y and $Score_Y(X_i)$ is computed as in Equation 1. Normalizing the sum by the number of posts in X is kosher since each post is represented exactly once in one of the terms in the numerator (the one corresponding to the component in $MWIS(X,Y)$ that contains the post). The only term that has not yet been introduced yet is $w_X(X_i)$; we delve deeper into this weighting parameter in the following subsection.

Complexity of finding MWIS(X,Y): As we have already illustrated, the problem of finding MWIS(X,Y) reduces to finding the Maximum Weighted Matching in our case. MWM is solvable in $\mathcal{O}(m\sqrt{n})$ where m denotes the number of edges, and n denotes the number of vertices in the transformed graph. However, very fast approximations have been proposed recently [11], thus making the computational expense not of much concern.

3.1.2 *Differentially Weighting Components*

Consider a thread about a technical issue (e.g., *bluetooth not connecting in symbian*) and two posts from it, one of which talks about the core issue (e.g., *bluetooth fix for symbian*), whereas the other talks about a tangential issue (e.g., *comparsion of iphone with android and symbian*); we would intuitively want to weigh the former higher since it is *more central* to a topic. This is all the more important for generic posts (e.g., *please help me solve the problem*) that would have to be weighed lower to limit their influence. To enable this sort of weighting, we represent post as a mixture of topics.

$$w_X(X_i) = \sum_{topic \in X} P(X_i|topic) \times P(topic|X)$$

Now, $P(X_i|topic)$ can be interpreted as the likelihood of the topic model generating component X_i under the "bag-of-words" assumption. Similarly, $P(topic|X)$ measures the importance of the topic to the thread. We estimate these weights over a specified number of topics (that are maximally represented in the thread) with the number of topics taken as a system parameter.

3.1.3 Putting it all together

Having described our formulation of $P_S(X,Y)$ (and thus, the analogous $P_S(Y,X)$), we now describe how we combine the three factors outlined in Section 3.1. Since we are interested in finding similar threads, similarity being quantified by means of containing similar content, we would intuitively prefer finding such Ys (in response to a query thread X) which have to high values of $P_S(X,Y)$ and $P_S(Y,X)$. Either of these being low is a strong indication of the asymmetry, and thus, we choose to give the lower of the two values more preference by using the lowest of the three means (harmonic, geometric and arithmetic) to aggregate these. Our measure of similarity then takes the following form:

$$S(X,Y) = \lambda\ harmonic\_mean(P_S(X,Y), P_S(Y,X))$$
$$+(1-\lambda)\ Sim(X_{headpost}, Y_{headpost}) \quad (2)$$

λ balances the weight given to the subsumption term against that given to the *headpost* similarity. It may be noted that though we model similarities using feature sets like in [33], we stick to a symmetric notion of similarity as is popular for similarities between textual entities.

3.2 Approach Instantiations

In modeling thread similarities, we have outlined how we exploit substructures and differentially weigh them using topics. To show the incremental utility of substructures and topics, we consider four different techniques:

- **SUB:** This denotes the subsumption based thread similarity approach where we do not consider post-pairs as components (thus, the only components would be individual posts) and weigh them all equally.
- **SUB-TOP:** While considering only individual posts as components, we now harness the topic clusters to weigh each component (i.e., post) differentially.
- **SUB-STR:** This improves upon the SUB approach by considering post-pairs as components (in addition to individual posts); however, we weigh all components equally (do not use topics).
- **SUB-STR-TOP:** This denotes the full-fledged approach where the set of components is made up of both individual posts and post-pairs and components are weighed using the topics.

4. BASELINE METHODS

Since the problem that we are addressing in this paper has not been subject of prior research (Ref. Section 6), we outline a series of intuitive methods to estimate thread similarities. We outline the techniques under two heads; one in which the query thread summaries or extracts are used as queries to retrieve threads harnessing state-of-the-art thread retrieval models, and another in which the threads are directly compared against each other.

4.1 Using Thread Retrieval Models

4.1.1 Pseudo Cluster Selection (PCS)

The title and the first post of a thread are important since they are very influential in setting the agenda of the thread; they have been found useful for thread retrieval [2]. We put together the title and the first post of the query thread as a query and employ the Pseudo Cluster Selection (PCS) model for thread retrieval (proposed in [28]) with the system parameter k set to 5.

4.1.2 Summarization Techniques

Summarization techniques [22] process a document and produce a concise version encompassing the most important concepts in the document. We use those to summarize the query thread to a text snippet; the snippet is then passed to the PCS thread retrieval model to retrieve similar threads.

We use two popular summarization techniques. MMR [6] focusses on increased diversity (and thus, reduced redundancy) while choosing sentences from the document to add to the summary. Submodular [21] is a recently proposed technique that models the summarization problem as that of maximizing a submodular function under a budget constraint. We denote these approaches as $Q.MMR$ or $Q.SM$ depending on what summarization technique is used (Q indicates that the query thread alone is summarized).

4.2 Comparing Threads

Here, we outline intuitive techniques (based on current trends in text processing) to find similar threads.

4.2.1 Bag Of Words (BOW)

The most widely used model for representing documents in Information Retrieval is that of considering a document as a collection (i.e., a bag) of the component words [1]. In this baseline, we consider a thread as a large document (under the large document model [12]) formed by putting together the text from all the component posts. Now, the similarities between threads can be estimated as the similarities between such documents as assessed using one of the popular text similarity measures that use the bag of words (BOW) model. We will experiment with measures such as cosine similarity of term frequency vectors, cosine similarity of tf.idf vectors [16] and Jaccard similarity co-efficient[17].

$$BOW(X,Y) = Sim(X,Y) \quad (3)$$

where $Sim(.,.)$ stands for the text similarity between the document representations of the threads.

4.2.2 Bag of Posts (BOP)

In this method, we consider each thread as a bag of the component posts [12]. Now, to compute thread pairwise similarity, we aggregate the postwise BOW similarities (between a pair of posts, one from each thread) using the arithmetic mean to arrive at a single measure of thread pair similarity.

$$BOP(X,Y) = mean\{BOW(t_x,t_y)|t_x \in X, t_y \in Y\} \quad (4)$$

Such aggregation of pair-wise similarities using the arithmetic mean is used in methods such as UPGMA and (Average-Link) Hierarchical Agglomerative Clustering [18].

4.2.3 Title and First Post (HeadPost)

Since the first post of the thread initiates the thread, it is intuitive for the thread initiator to provide a representative title for it to attract relevant attention from the forum. In many threads like those in support forums, the first post conveys the problem and subsequent posts typically contain solutions or (requests for) more elaborate descriptions of the problem. The contents of the first post and its title can be thought of *setting the agenda* of the thread, and thus being more representative of the thread than other posts [2]. Here, we estimate the similarity between threads as a function of the similarity between their titles and the first posts.

$$HeadPost(X,Y) = Sim(X_{headpost}, Y_{headpost}) \quad (5)$$

where $X_{headpost}$ and $Y_{headpost}$ denote the text documents formed by putting together the title and the first post of the thread X and Y respectively.

4.2.4 BOP+HeadPost

This denotes a linear combination of BOP and HeadPost.

$$BOP + HeadPost(X,Y) = \alpha BOP(X,Y) + (1-\alpha) HeadPost(X,Y) \quad (6)$$

We set $\alpha = 0.45$ since that was empirically found to be the choice yielding the best performance.

4.2.5 Maximum Similarity between Posts (MAX)

The BOP method (Section 4.2.2) may not be very robust to noise. Consider comparing a long thread with a thread containing just two posts, one of which is a noisy post; the noisy post would then affect half of the values on which the arithmetic mean is computed, and thus reduce the thread pairwise similarity considerably. Such considerations lead us to the MAX method that uses the maximum *BOW* similarity between a pair of posts to estimate similarity.

$$MAX(X,Y) = max\{BOW(t_x, t_y) | t_x \in X, t_y \in Y\} \quad (7)$$

This method is analogous to the similarity computation used in the popular Single-Link Hierarchical Agglomerative Clustering method [18].

4.2.6 Top-k Similarities (Top-k)

Instead of considering just the max similarity (like we do in MAX above), we now consider the mean of the top-k pairwise similarities.

$$Top\text{-}k(X,Y) = mean(top\text{-}k\{BOW(t_x, t_y) | t_x \in X, t_y \in Y\}) \quad (8)$$

where the top-k(.) method, when applied to a set of scores, returns the subset of top-k values.

4.2.7 Central Post Similarity (Central)

In this method, we use a UPGMC [23] style aggregation of pairwise similarities. Unlike UPGMC that computes the similarity between centroids of collections (i.e., threads), we choose to use the similarity between the *central* posts of the two threads (similar to using the most central entity to represent the collection in K-medoids [26]), centrality estimated by mechanisms such as those outlined in [12]. This leads to:

$$Central(X,Y) = BOW(X_{central}, Y_{central}) \quad (9)$$

where $X_{central}$ denotes the most central post in X.

4.2.8 Summarization Techniques

Unlike Section 4.1.2 where the query thread alone was summarized, we now summarize each of the threads in the corpus to separate documents. We then retrieve similar documents using traditional IR techniques using the query thread summaries as queries. Based on the summarization technique used, we denote the technique as either *All.MMR* or *All.SM* (*All* denotes that the query as well as the corpora are summarized). For each of the summarization technique, we summarize each corpus thread to between 25 and 50 words and pick the summary size that yields best performance; it turns out that the best performance was consistently achieved for summaries between 30 and 40 words.

HeadPost	threadID
Safari Crashing : ...safari is crashing almost every 5 minutes while surfing the web. I get immediately returned to the homepage and have to start over.....	1033829
Light leakage: Just upgraded from an original iPhone on Sunday to the iPhone 3g....I noticed that all down the left side between the iPhone casing ad the glass screen.. there is light leaking through..,	1968289
iPhone 4 Speaker Volume: ....earpiece volume on each has been astoundingly bad...speakerphone function is basically worthless and seems no louder whether it is on or off...	2459984
No sound in one earbud: .. when I play my music, no sound is emitted to one of the earbuds. ...	2537835
iPhone 4 in endless reboot: ..If I plug it into a USB power adapter .. connect to iTunes.. unplug the phone from the USB power adapter it shuts off ...get the endless reboot if I plug it into my MBP	2475944

Table 2: Sample queries. "threadID" is used to identify the thread in online apple discussion forums

5. EXPERIMENTAL EVALUATION

We now describe the empirical evaluation where we compare our techniques (listed in Section 3.2) against the baseline techniques detailed in Section 4. We use several standard measures (NDCG, MAP, MRR, Precision) in evaluation. We measure NDCG and Precision at various rank cut-offs of the search results (5, 10 and 15 results). We first describe the dataset used followed by describing an exhaustive set of results across techniques and performance measures, with all techniques using the tf.idf cosine similarity measure to model the *Sim*(.,.) function. We then analyze the techniques across other popular similarity measures and varying values of algorithm parameters.

	Total	Query	Annotated
Total number of Threads	147,000	38	3412
Avg #posts per Thread	6	11	12
Avg #words per posts	76	81	91
Avg #words in title	7	6	8
Avg #words in first post	79	78	84

Table 3: Summary statistics of dataset used

5.1 Dataset

We crawled a dataset consisting of ~147K threads from Apple Discussion Forums (*https://discussions.apple.com/*),

Apple's official discussion forum for sharing tips and solutions with other users. All the crawled web-pages were preprocessed and posts present in different webpages but belonging to the same thread were identified. For each thread, the crawl contained information such as title, firstpost, other posts, author information, reply-to link and time stamp.

The queries (threads) for this dataset were generated by identifying threads related to popular issues[8] in iPhone. In total, we generated 38 queries[9]. Some of the sample query threads are listed in Table 2. For each query thread, we query the collection using the keywords in the query thread to identify candidate threads. For a given query thread, we sought the help of human labelers to assign ternary relevance judgments to each candidate thread; 2 for *high relevance*, 1 for *partial relevance* and 0 for *irrelevant*. We had $\sim$ 85 candidate threads per query for the final evaluation and the labeling effort was roughly 60-80 minutes per query thread, leading to a total of 45 hours of human effort spent in labeling. It was often difficult to distinguish between *high relevance* and *partial relevance* threads; hence we combined these two relevance levels to give a binary labelling (*relevant/irrelevant*), used to evaluate our system. Inter-annotator agreement of 89% and 61% with Kappa coefficient of 0.68 & 0.42 was observed for the binary and ternary relevance judgements respectively.

5.2 Evaluation on Cosine tf.idf Similarity

Table 4 presents the performance of the various techniques considered, when the tf.idf cosine similarity is used for estimating text similarity within each of them. Under each measure, we highlight the best performing technique. All the approaches that use thread retrieval techniques are seen to be competitive to each other, with minor variations among performance trends. The better approaches among the ones that compare threads (i.e. BOP, HeadPost and BOP+HeadPost) significantly outperform the thread retrieval baselines. This is expected since thread retrieval techniques work with thread summaries (or excerpts such as first posts) whereas the thread comparison techniques such as BOP, HeadPost and BOP+HeadPost have the entire query thread at their disposal. MAX, Top-K and Central, techniques that use only a few pairwise post similarities are seen to not perform as well as BOP; this is likely to be because of certain generic posts (e.g., *help me please*) in the query thread that could spuriously boost the thread similarity estimates with those threads that also contain such posts. More significantly, the subsumption based approaches that we propose significantly outperform all the other techniques. Among them, the SUB-STR-TOP that uses both substructures and topics is found to perform the best in seven out of the eight evaluation measures considered.

5.3 Evaluation on other Similarity Measures

We considered two other similarity measures in our evaluation; the cosine similarity between normalized term-frequency vectors, and the Jaccard similarity co-efficient[17]. The performance trends on these similarity measures are largely similar to those observed in Table 4; hence, we plot only the NDCG@10, MAP and MRR values. The performance on the Cosine Similarity and Jaccard measures are given in

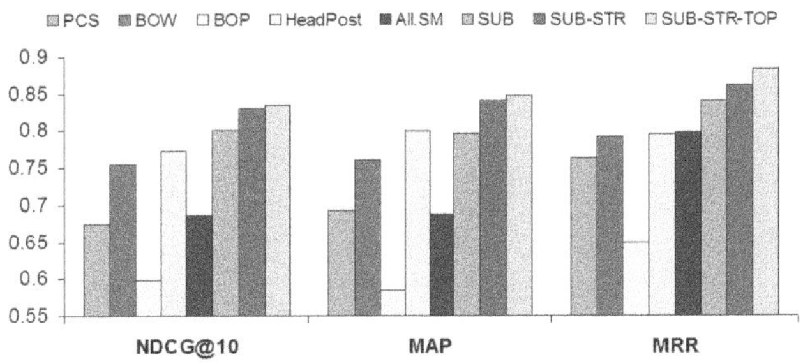

Figure 4: Results on Cosine Similarity

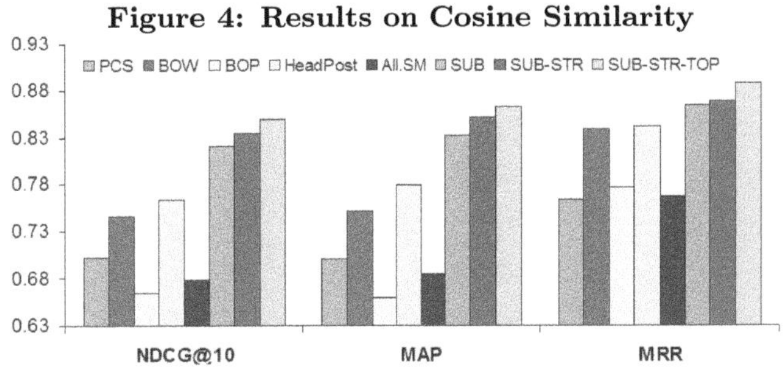

Figure 5: Results on Jaccard Similarity

Figure 4 and 5 respectively. BOW is seen to consistently beat BOP in these charts unlike in Table 4; this is expected since the lack of idf while comparing small text documents (BOP compares posts) could spuriously enhance similarities of dissimilar posts that contain common words. Our techniques are seen to be outperforming the others on all the evaluation measures with SUB-STR-TOP being consistently the best among on all the three evaluation measures.

5.4 Value of Usage of Components

Our technique incorporates the HeadPost-style similarity and the subsumption based assessment to arrive at an overall measure of similarity between threads. Usage of weighted post and post-reply pairs as components in subsumption-based similarity assessment is at the core of the technique that we propose. In this section, we isolate and analyze the benefit of using components in subsumption based similarity assessment independent of other factors such as HeadPost-style similarity and topic-based weighting.

Table 5 compares ranking of some selected candidate threads for the HeadPost and SUB-STR$^-$ (which denotes SUB-STR without the HeadPost i.e., the setting $\lambda = 1$) systems; the starred ones were judged as relevant by human labelers. For these chosen threads, title is indicative of their first post content; hence we have only shown title of the candidate threads. As evident for threads 1 and 2, highly similar title (and first posts) could mean that the threads are very similar; thus, the top few threads based on HeadPost similarity end up being relevant to the query thread. It is, hence, natural to expect that HeadPost would perform very well when the top few results alone are considered, such as indicated by NDCG@5 and MAP@5 measures. The effectiveness of HeadPost, however, deteriorates when threads with very similar titles and first posts are exhausted. This can be seen for candidates 5, 6 and 7 (that are all relevant) that have minimum title overlap with the query thread, thus falling behind in the ranking. Thus, HeadPost is less effective when more results are considered. This is indicative of the complementary nature of the thread content based similarity assessment and the HeadPost based similarities.

Figure 6 compares various techniques: BOP, SUB-STR$^-$,

[8]http://www.iphonefaq.org/faq

[9]Please contact the first or second author to obtain a copy of the dataset with queries and relevance judgements.

Method	NDCG@5	NDCG@10	NDCG@15	P@5	P@10	P@15	MAP	MRR
PCS	0.741	0.737	0.703	0.775	0.738	0.695	0.771	0.779
Q.MMR	0.712	0.729	0.714	0.734	0.727	0.691	0.737	0.754
Q.SM	0.735	0.692	0.699	0.754	0.710	0.675	0.758	0.770
BOW	0.727	0.693	0.678	0.749	0.679	0.644	0.752	0.851
BOP	0.808	0.791	0.765	0.841	0.801	0.770	0.809	0.857
HeadPost	0.820	0.773	0.749	0.851	0.786	0.748	0.801	0.864
BOP+HeadPost	0.831	0.812	0.789	0.855	0.824	0.783	0.825	0.871
MAX	0.695	0.684	0.688	0.729	0.717	0.696	0.731	0.780
Top-K	0.706	0.707	0.721	0.759	0.749	0.724	0.765	0.819
Central	0.710	0.683	0.655	0.737	0.699	0.636	0.742	0.770
All.MMR	0.730	0.720	0.717	0.758	0.727	0.685	0.751	0.767
All.SM	0.763	0.727	0.719	0.774	0.746	0.694	0.771	0.808
SUB	0.851	0.836	0.811	0.866	0.831	0.799	0.851	0.909
SUB-TOP	0.872	0.846	0.830	0.871	0.847	0.809	0.870	0.914
SUB-STR	0.874	0.851	0.833	0.870	**0.850**	0.811	0.875	0.910
SUB-STR-TOP	**0.901**	**0.895**	**0.855**	**0.885**	0.844	**0.827**	**0.907**	**0.932**

Table 4: Experiment Results with tf.idf Cosine Similarity Measure.

Id	Title	HeadPost	SUB-STR$^-$
1*	SIM card not found message	1	4
2*	No SIM card installed msg	5	7
3	Sim card not supported	6	9
4	swap out the micro sim into a another phone?	47	11
5*	My phone had been LOCKED! Help plsssss....	59	8
6*	iPhone disabled.	69	6
7*	problems with iphone 3G update to OS 4.0.1	77	67
8	Import Contacts isnt working	82	23

Table 5: Ranking of candidate threads for a sample query thread with title "sim card not installed". * indicates that the candidate was adjudged relevant by the annotators.

HeadPost (i.e., SUB-STR with $\lambda = 0$), BOP+HeadPost and SUB-STR. BOP+HeadPost and SUB-STR are able to leverage the complementarity of the HeadPost and content based similarity aspects to beat approaches that consider only either of them. While SUB-STR outperforms BOP+HeadPost consistently, SUB-STR$^-$ is also competitive to BOP+HeadPost thereby indicating effectiveness of component based approach. SUB-STR$^-$ system has its own pitfalls due to not considering the HeadPost similarity, for e.g., it fails for cases when there is high lexical similarity between the candidate thread and the query thread but different aspects are discussed. This is evident from candidate 4 and 8 that are ranked high by SUB-STR$^-$, where a different issue related to iphone sim is discussed. This confirms the complementarity of HeadPost and content based similarities, and underlines that our notion of components is able to achieve significant gains over just considering threads as Bag Of Posts.

5.5 Significance Tests

Table 6 presents results of randomization tests [29], conducted for the most competitive baselines (i.e., BOP, BOP + HeadPost) and the various configurations of our techniques. While our techniques provide results that are statistically significant at a p-value < 0.05 over the baselines, it is interesting to note that SUB-STR-TOP's performance is statistically significant on each of MRR, NDCG@10, MAP wrt all the other techniques.

To further verify the utility of the post-reply pair substructure, we conducted another statistical significance test where in, apart from single posts, random post pairs were fed to SUB-STR as post-reply pairs; we call it SUB-STR$_{\text{Random}}$. The null-hypothesis that SUB-STR and SUB-STR$_{\text{Random}}$ are equivalent was rejected easily with a two-sided p-value $<$ 0.015, thus empirically establishing the utility of real post-reply pairs over random post-pairs.

5.6 Effect of System Parameters

Our approaches have two parameters, λ, the relative weighting between subsumption based similarity and HeadPost similarity and then, the number of topics being considered. In this section, we analyze the sensitivity of our approaches to variations in these parameters and illustrate that our techniques are insensitive to variations on these parameters over a large range of their values.

5.6.1 *Sensitivity to* λ

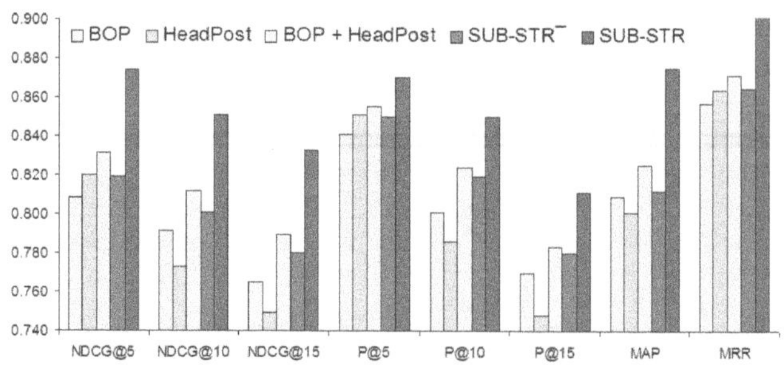

Figure 6: Effect of Usage of Components

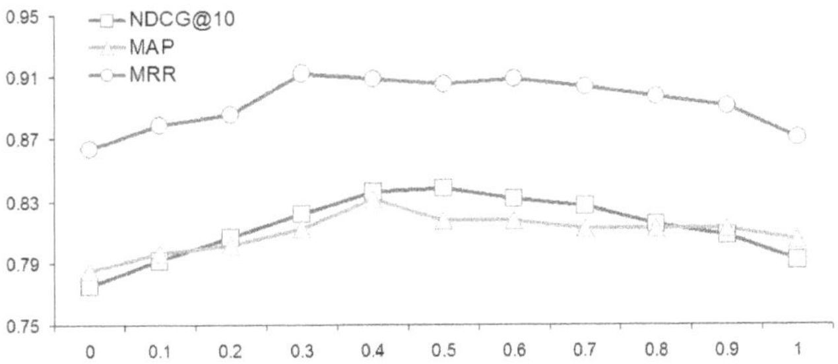

Figure 7: Sensitivity to λ

To enable analyze the effect of λ independent of the number of topics and usage of post-pairs as components, we plot the performance of SUB across varying values of λ in Figure 8. When $\lambda = 0$, the approach degenerates to the HeadPost technique, whereas at the other extreme, it discards the title and first post based similarity altogether. More interestingly, it fairs better than HeadPost (the left-most point of the curves) for any non-zero value of λ and is rather insensitive to λ values between 0.3 and 0.8.

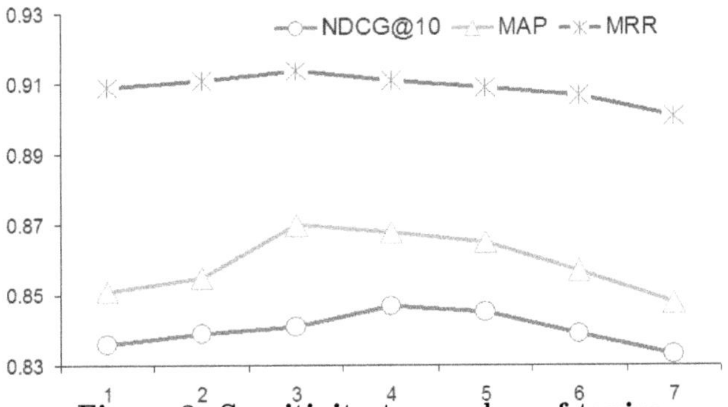

Figure 8: Sensitivity to number of topics

5.6.2 Sensitivity to number of topics

Selecting the right number of topics is an important problem in topic modeling [30]. Nonparametric models like the Chinese Restaurant Process [3] are not scalable to large datasets as can be expected in thread retrieval scenarios. Due to the popularity of generative approaches in topic modeling, we used LDA [4] for representing a component (and hence the entire thread) as mixture of topics. One could potentially use any other method for doing the same. To estimate the topic distribution for each component, we built our LDA model over a collection of 20000 threads with *#topics* = 100. This is an offline process. Since we use topics to weigh the components, the number of topics in a component is another important parameter for our system. We plot the performance of the SUB-TOP on varying number of topics (restricting the component to belong to at most k topics). Similar to the observations for λ, the approach is largely insensitive to variations between 2 and 5.

6. RELATED WORK

The problem of finding threads similar to a given thread, to the best of our knowledge, has not been considered before, in literature. In this section, we provide a brief review of related literature. Firstly, we describe literature dealing with processing of discussion threads. Secondly, we review prior works focussing on finding similarities between semi-structured content such as XML (we will see shortly that discussion threads may be considered as semi-structured data).

Work on Discussion Threads: A forum thread, unlike text documents, are authored by multiple people and contain discussions on a particular topic. Upto 75% of the links from forums are found to link to noise pages like user profiles and login pages [35]; this makes traditional web page ranking techniques like PageRank [5] and HITS [20] inapplicable since such links are not indicative of recommendations. Thread/forum retrieval, the task of identifying relevant threads or posts within them in response to a user query (e.g., a phrase or 3-4 words), has been of much interest in recent years. One of the early works on forum retrieval attempted to adapt the random surfer model to induce links with content information (to content-wise similar pages) to rank forum pages better [35]. An extension to this model that utilizes information about common posters for link induction was presented in [7]. Subsequent works on thread retrieval moved away from the considering threads as collections of pages to considering them as collections of posts. [12] shows that thread retrieval improves by considering only some relevant posts, instead of all the posts in a thread. [28] illustrates that considering the post-reply pair (a post along with a reply to it) substructure in threads improves accuracy in thread retrieval. Though the problem that we address is significantly different in that we attempt to rank threads based on similarity to a *given thread* (which, unlike a user query, is typically larger and has a well-formed structure), we have evaluated our technique against adaptations of thread retrieval methods (in Section 5).

Work on XML Similarity: A forum thread may be represented as a tree with posts as nodes where a parent-child relationship exists between a post and it's reply. Additionally, siblings (multiple replies to the same post) may be ordered based on the temporal ordering. Each of these nodes (posts) could have attributes like time and poster id. It is intuitive to think of an XML schema to represent such threads due to the hierarchical nature (i.e., the tree). This leads to the question whether we can use XML similarity measures to estimate similarities between threads. However, traditional XML similarity measures make heavy use of the structural similarity [24] whereas we may not want to rely too much on structural similarity in estimating thread similarities. This is so since the content is likely to be more important than structure; the example in Table 1 shows two threads that are very similar despite the structural dissimilarity. Though macro-level structural similarity clearly cannot be used off-the-shelf to estimate thread similarities, certain types of substructures (e.g., post-reply pair) have been found to be useful in thread processing [28]. In this context, it is useful to note that research on XML similarity has gone beyond plain structural similarity [24] to hybrid methods that make use of semantic similarity of content [31]. A survey of XML similarity methods appears in [32]. In short, we argue that estimating thread similarities is different from estimating similarities between XML data since the notion of thread similarity relies more on content and certain sub-structures (unlike XML similarity where the similarities between macro-level structures is seen to be useful).

7. CONCLUSIONS AND FUTURE WORK

In this paper, we considered the problem of finding similar discussion forum threads to a query thread. Similarity Search on threads has numerous applications such as an enabler to providing links to similar threads in discus-

Method	BOP	BOP+Headpost	SUB	SUB-STR	SUB-TOP	SUB-STR-TOP
SUB	*mrr,ndcg,map*	*mrr,ndcg,map*	–			
SUB-STR	*mrr,ndcg,map*	*mrr,ndcg,map*	*map*	–		
SUB-TOP	*mrr,ndcg,map*	*mrr,ndcg,map*	*map*		–	
SUB-STR-TOP	*mrr,ndcg,map*	*mrr,ndcg,map*	*mrr,ndcg,map*	*mrr,ndcg,map*	*mrr,ndcg,map*	–

Table 6: Randomization Test Results. The measures on which the left column method is significant over the top row method at a p-value < 0.05 are indicated in the appropriate cell. We consider the *mrr*, *mdcg* (NDCG @ 10) and *map* evaluation measures.

sion forums and providing a clustered interface to present results in thread retrieval systems. Our similarity measure revolves around the notion of how well the threads being compared are mutually contained within each other. To estimate pairwise thread similarities, we model threads as a set of weighted overlapping components, whereby containment is quantified by the lexical similarity between components from the threads under consideration. Specifically, we use the post-reply component that has been found to be useful in discussion forum search, in addition to using individual posts as components; we proved that our similarity computation can run in polynomial time for this choice of component types. We outlined several intuitive methods that use thread retrieval techniques and direct thread comparison and evaluated our approaches against them. Through an extensive series of experiments on real world data, we established the effectiveness of our technique on popular similarity measures such as NDCG, MAP, Precision and MRR. Specifically, our techniques are seen to outperform the baselines by approximately 10% on an average on each of the measures.

We have considered two kinds of sub-structures, individual posts and post-pairs, in our technique. Incorporating more sophisticated structural components may enable better quality retrieval possible at the expense of increased similarity computation costs. Devising indexing techniques that could enable looking at just a subset of threads in response to a query thread could enhance performance. We are currently exploring ways to build a parameterized thread similarity measure that could be continuously tuned in response to user feedback. In email discussion groups, a single post may involve replies to multiple previous posts. Identifying such relationships and utilizing them in similarity modeling could potentially improve the retrieval quality.

Acknowledgements

We thank Srujana Merugu for discussions that helped us improve the final presentation.

8. REFERENCES

[1] R. A. Baeza-Yates and B. Ribeiro-Neto. *Modern Information Retrieval.* Addison-Wesley Longman Publishing Co., Inc., Boston, MA, USA, 1999.

[2] S. Bhatia and P. Mitra. Adopting inference networks for online thread retrieval. In *AAAI*, 2010.

[3] D. M. Blei, T. L. Griffiths, M. I. Jordan, and J. B. Tenenbaum. Hierarchical topic models and the nested chinese restaurant process. In *NIPS.* MIT Press, 2004.

[4] D. M. Blei, A. Y. Ng, M. I. Jordan, and J. Lafferty. Latent dirichlet allocation. *Journal of Machine Learning Research*, 3:2003, 2003.

[5] S. Brin and L. Page. The anatomy of a large-scale hypertextual web search engine. *Comput. Netw. ISDN Syst.*

[6] J. Carbonell and J. Goldstein. The use of mmr, diversity-based reranking for reordering documents and producing summaries. SIGIR '98, pages 335–336, 1998.

[7] Z. Chen, L. Zhang, and W. Wang. postingrank: bringing order to web forum postings. AIRS'08, pages 377–384, 2008.

[8] J. Dean and M. R. Henzinger. Finding related pages in the world wide web. *Computer Networks*, 31(11-16), 1999.

[9] P. M. Deshpande, D. P, and K. Kummamuru. Efficient online top-k retrieval with arbitrary similarity measures. EDBT '08, pages 356–367, 2008.

[10] H. Duan and C. Zhai. Exploiting thread structures to improve smoothing of language models for forum post retrieval. In *ECIR*, pages 350–361, 2011.

[11] R. Duan and S. Pettie. Approximating maximum weight matching in near-linear time. FOCS '10, pages 673–682, 2010.

[12] J. L. Elsas and J. G. Carbonell. It pays to be picky: an evaluation of thread retrieval in online forums. In *SIGIR*, pages 714–715, 2009.

[13] G. Forman, K. Eshghi, and S. Chiocchetti. Finding similar files in large document repositories. In *KDD*, pages 394–400, 2005.

[14] H. N. Gabow. *Implementation of algorithms for maximum matching on nonbipartite graphs.* PhD thesis, Stanford, CA, USA, 1974. AAI7413628.

[15] J. Golbeck. Trust and nuanced profile similarity in online social networks. *ACM Trans. Web*, 3:12:1–12:33, September 2009.

[16] A. Huang. Similarity measures for text document clustering. pages 49–56, 2008.

[17] P. Jaccard. The Distribution of the Flora in the Alpine Zone. *New Phytologist*, 11(2):37–50, 1912.

[18] A. K. Jain and R. C. Dubes. *Algorithms for clustering data.* Prentice-Hall, Inc., Upper Saddle River, NJ, USA, 1988.

[19] G. Jeh and J. Widom. Simrank: a measure of structural-context similarity. In *KDD*, pages 538–543, 2002.

[20] J. M. Kleinberg. Authoritative sources in a hyperlinked environment. *J. ACM*, 46:604–632, September 1999.

[21] H. Lin and J. Bilmes. Multi-document summarization via budgeted maximization of submodular functions. HLT '10, pages 912–920, 2010.

[22] I. Mani and M. T. Maybury. *Advances in Automatic Text Summarization.* 1998.

[23] F. Murtagh. A survey of recent advances in hierarchical clustering algorithms. *Computer Journal*, 26(4):354–359, 1983.

[24] A. Nierman and H. V. Jagadish. Evaluating structural similarity in xml documents. In *WebDB*, pages 61–66, 2002.

[25] D. P, D. Garg, and V. Varshney. Analysis of enron email threads and quantification of employee responsiveness. In *TextLink Workshop at IJCAI*, 2007.

[26] H.-S. Park and C.-H. Jun. A simple and fast algorithm for k-medoids clustering. *Expert Syst. Appl.*, 36, March 2009.

[27] S. Sanghavi, D. Shah, and A. Willsky. Message passing for max-weight independent set. In *In NIPS*, 2007.

[28] J. Seo, W. B. Croft, and D. A. Smith. Online community search using thread structure. In *CIKM*, pages 1907–1910, 2009.

[29] M. D. Smucker, J. Allan, and B. Carterette. In *CIKM*, Lisboa, Portugal, 2007.

[30] M. Steyvers and T. Griffiths. *Probabilistic Topic Models.* Lawrence Erlbaum Associates, 2007.

[31] J. Tekli, R. Chbeir, and K. Yétongnon. A hybrid approach for xml similarity. In *SOFSEM (1)*, pages 783–795, 2007.

[32] J. Tekli, R. Chbeir, and K. Yétongnon. An overview on xml similarity: Background, current trends and future directions. In *Computer Science Review 3(3)*, 2009.

[33] A. Tversky. Features of Similarity. In *Psychological Review*, volume 84, pages 327–352, 1977.

[34] R. C. Veltkamp and M. Tanase. Content-based image retrieval systems: A survey. Technical report, 2000.

[35] G. Xu and W.-Y. Ma. Building implicit links from content for forum search. In *SIGIR*, pages 300–307, 2006.

Summarizing Highly Structured Documents for Effective Search Interaction

Lanbo Zhang, Yi Zhang, Yunfei Chen
School of Engineering
University of California, Santa Cruz
Santa Cruz, CA 95064 USA
{lanbo, yiz, ychen}@soe.ucsc.edu

ABSTRACT

As highly structured documents with rich metadata (such as products, movies, etc.) become increasingly prevalent, searching those documents has become an important IR problem. Unfortunately existing work on document summarization, especially in the context of search, has been mainly focused on unstructured documents, and little attention has been paid to highly structured documents. Due to the different characteristics of structured and unstructured documents, the ideal approaches for document summarization might be different. In this paper, we study the problem of summarizing highly structured documents in a search context. We propose a new summarization approach based on query-specific facet selection. Our approach aims to discover the important facets hidden behind a query using a machine learning approach, and summarizes retrieved documents based on those important facets. In addition, we propose to evaluate summarization approaches based on a utility function that measures how well the summaries assist users in interacting with the search results. Furthermore, we develop a game on Mechanical Turk to evaluate different summarization approaches. The experimental results show that the new summarization approach significantly outperforms two existing ones.

Categories and Subject Descriptors

H.3.3 [**Information Storage and Retrieval**]: Information Search and Retrieval

Keywords

Summarization, Structured Documents, Facets, Facet Selection, Summary Evaluation

1. INTRODUCTION

To deal with the information overload problem, search engines help users filter out the majority of useless information by returning documents that are likely to be relevant. However, users still need to judge which documents in the returned results are most useful to them based on the summaries of the retrieved documents. Based on their judgments, users will determine which particular search results they should navigate to. In this perspective, summaries of retrieved documents are important since they will directly influence the user's decision on how to interact with the search results.

Color:	Color
Country:	USA
Director:	Cameron, James (I)
Distributor:	Twentieth Century Fox Film Corporation [us] - (2014) (USA) (theatrical)
Genres:	Action Adventure Sci-Fi
Language:	English
Related movie:	Avatar (2009)
Release date:	USA 2014
Title:	Avatar 2 (2014)
Url:	http://www.imdb.com/Title?Avatar 2 (2014)

Figure 1: A faceted document example (a movie)

Highly structured documents with rich metadata are becoming increasingly prevalent on the Internet and in various verticals. An important trait of highly structured documents is that the major part of a document is composed of metadata. Examples of this type of documents are those representing different kinds of entities, such as products, movies, persons, corporations, etc. In these documents, each metadata field characterizes a specific facet of the entity, and may be assigned with one or several values which are usually short, but contain very important information. In this paper, we use the phrase **faceted documents** to refer to this type of documents, and we call each metadata field a **facet**, a metadata field assigned with a particular value a **facet-value pair**. For simplicity, we sometimes use the term "FVP" to denote "facet-value pair". Figure 1 shows a faceted document example (a movie), where the bold words are different facets, each of which is followed by the value(s) of the facet. In this document, the facet "genre" has three values: "Action", "Adventure", and "Sci-Fi", which correspond to three facet-value pairs respectively: "genre: Action", "genre: Adventure", and "genre: Sci-Fi".

Although search engines for faceted documents are becoming increasingly prevalent (e.g., Amazon/eBay/IMDB Search), there has been little research on summarization of faceted documents. There has been a large volume of work on document summarization in the last several decades.

Permission to make digital or hard copies of all or part of this work for personal or classroom use is granted without fee provided that copies are not made or distributed for profit or commercial advantage and that copies bear this notice and the full citation on the first page. To copy otherwise, or republish, to post on servers or to redistribute to lists, requires prior specific permission and/or a fee.
SIGIR'12, August 12–16, 2012, Portland, Oregon, USA.
Copyright 2012 ACM 978-1-4503-1472-5/12/08... $15.00.

However, most of the existing work has been focused on the summarization of unstructured documents. In this paper, we study the problem of summarizing faceted documents in the retrieval context, where the key question is: given a query and a retrieved document composed of a group of facet-value pairs (e.g., Figure 1), how should the system select a small number of facet-value pairs that fit the space (i.e. size) constraint, while delivering as much useful information about the document to the search engine user?

The simplest approach is to manually select a few important facets, and only facet-value pairs of those facets will be included in the summary. This method is query-independent and widely used by many commercial search engines including Amazon Search. For almost all searches on Amazon, the returned product summaries always contain the same facets including title, price, rating, and the shipping information. This solution may not be sufficient, since different users may care about different aspects of a product. Ideally, summaries should be tailored to individual searches. For example, for the query "15-inch silver laptop by Lenovo", the product facets "screen size", "color", "category", and "maker" are very important information to the user, and thus should be included in each product summary so that the user can judge the quality of each retrieved result more accurately.

An alternative approach is to adapt summarization approaches initially developed for unstructured documents (e.g., query-biased approaches) to faceted documents. Most of the existing query-biased summarization approaches select relevant sentences from the original document, and generate the summary by compressing the relevant sentences. To use the existing approaches, we can treat each facet-value pair as a sentence, and use existing sentence-selection approaches to select the best facet-value pairs. However, this approach suffers from two major problems. First, structural information of faceted documents might be ignored. For example, this approach cannot distinguish between different facets, which may not be equally important to the user. Second, since most query-biased approaches tend to select segments/sentences with query terms, some important facet-value pairs without query terms might never be shown in the summary. For example, for the query "15-inch silver laptop by Lenovo", the facet-value pair "color: black" is unlikely to be shown in the summary using existing approaches. However, it is in fact very useful information for the searcher to identify that this document is actually non-relevant.

In this paper, we propose a new summarization approach specifically designed for faceted documents. We observe that a query searching for faceted documents usually implicitly or explicitly involves one or several facet-value pairs that jointly define the information need behind the query. If we can identify the relevant facet-value pairs, we will be able to know which facets might be important for the query, and thus be able to generate better summaries for the user based on those facets. For example, for the query "15-inch silver laptop by Lenovo", we can learn that "color: silver" might be a relevant facet-value pair, thus "color" might be an important facet, and thus we probably should show this facet for all retrieved documents whatever the corresponding value is. In order to discover the relevant facet-value pairs, we propose a learning-based approach for ranking facet-value pairs. To evaluate our approach, we propose a utility-based summary evaluation framework, and compare our summarization approach with two existing ones. The major contributions of this paper include:

1. We propose a new summarization approach for faceted documents based on query-specific facet selection. In particular, we propose a learning-based approach and a set of useful features for ranking facet-value pairs.

2. We argue that a good summary should assist the user in interacting with the search engine. Accordingly, we propose a utility-based evaluation framework for document summarization in the retrieval context.

3. Motivated by research in Experimental Economics, we design a game for crowdsourcing the evaluation of summarization approaches with Mechanical Turk.

4. We compare our new summarization approach with two existing approaches using the game we design on Mechanical Turk.

2. RELATED WORK

Query-biased summarization approaches have been shown to perform better than generic summarization approaches in retrieval tasks. In [23], Tombros et al. compared the query-biased summaries with the static summaries composed of the title and first few sentences of retrieved documents, and found that query-biased summaries can help users improve the speed and accuracy in identifying relevant documents. Similar results were found in [27]. Major search engines including Google, Yahoo, and Bing usually summarize a search result by including the web page title, URL, and a query-biased snippet in the summary [5].

Previous work on document summarization has been largely focused on unstructured documents, where the key question is how to select good sentences from the original document. There has been a large volume of work focused on sentence selection for document summarization [23, 27, 10, 25, 19, 15, 26, 17, 3]. The commonly used attributes of sentences include their positions in the document, the words and query terms they contain, linguistic cues, relationships between sentences, etc. Some approaches take into account the diversity and coverage of a summary while selecting sentences [4, 15].

There has been little work on summarizing structured documents until recently. Huang et al. explored the snippet generation problem in XML search in 2008 [12]. Their approaches are designed based on the assumption that a query result snippet should: 1) be a self-contained and meaningful information unit, 2) be able to differentiate itself from other query results, and 3) be representative of the query result. The snippet retrieval track of INEX 2011 focuses on how best to generate informative snippets for XML search results, in which the Wikipedia corpus is used.

Different from existing work, in this paper, we are focusing on summarizing highly structured documents (i.e. faceted documents) which contain very few texts, and are mainly composed of metadata. Summarization of this type of documents is no longer a sentence selection problem, but a metadata selection problem. To the best of our knowledge, there has been very little work on metadata selection for document summarization.

Traditionally, the evaluation of summarization systems involves measuring quantitative attributes of the summaries, such as the similarity between automatically generated summaries and human-created ones [6, 14, 22]. In 1990s, there had been attempts to develop schemes that measure qualitative features of the systems in a task-based environment [11, 20, 18, 24]. During the last decade, a commonly used scheme for the evaluation of summarization systems has been to ask subjects to do relevance judgments based on document summaries, where the precision, recall, and speed of user judgments, and the number of references to the full document are used as the major metrics [23, 27]. In this paper, we propose a new unified evaluation measure based on the utility of summaries to the user.

There has been some work on selecting relevant facet-value pairs of queries. In [28], Zhang et al. proposed a few heuristic approaches for selecting facet-value pairs from semi-structured documents in a faceted feedback mechanism. In the data-centric track of INEX 2011 [8], one task is to select facet-value pairs of movies for users to provide feedback. Our work is different in that we try to tackle the FVP-ranking problem using a learning-based approach and we propose and study a number of features of different sorts for FVP ranking.

3. EXISTING APPROACHES

In this section, we review two existing approaches that can be used for summarizing faceted documents. The first approach is currently used by commercial search engines, and the other one was initially proposed for summarizing unstructured documents, which can be adapted to faceted documents.

3.1 Manual Facet Selection

In this approach, a fixed set of presumably important facets are manually selected for summarization of all documents. To summarize a document, the facet-value pairs of the selected facets in the document will be chosen to form the summary. There might be different ways to select the fixed set of facets, for example, based on domain knowledge or other considerations such as to maximize click-throughs, purchases, or conversion rates. This approach has been widely used in commercial search engines (such as Amazon Search, IMDB search, etc.).

3.2 Maximum Marginal Relevance (MMR)

A typical approach of query-biased summarization is an incremental sentence selection approach based on the criterion of Maximum Marginal Relevance [4]. At each step, MMR selects a sentence that is similar to the query but dissimilar to the already selected sentences in the summary.

MMR can be adapted to faceted documents by treating each facet or each facet-value pair as an information unit. Algorithm 1 shows the summarization process for a document, and Equation 1 shows how to select the next information unit at each step.

$$\mathrm{u}_{k+1} = \arg\max_{\mathrm{u}_i \in \mathbf{U} \setminus \mathbf{U}_k} \left\{ \lambda * \mathrm{sim}_1(\mathrm{u}_i, \mathrm{Q}) - (1-\lambda) * \max_{\mathrm{u}_j \in \mathbf{U}_k} \{\mathrm{sim}_2(\mathrm{u}_i, \mathrm{u}_j)\} \right\} \quad (1)$$

In Equation 1, u_{k+1} denotes the next information unit we will select, $\mathbf{U}$ denotes the set of all information units in the document, $\mathbf{U}_k$ denotes the set of information units that have been selected in the previous k steps, Q is the user query, sim_1 and sim_2 can be any similarity functions such as cosine similarity, TFIDF, etc., λ is the coefficient to trade off between relevance and diversity.

Algorithm 1 : Summarization based on MMR

Input:
Q: the user query
$\mathbf{U}$: the set of all information units in document d
M: the maximum number of information units allowed
1) Initialize: $k = 0$; $\mathbf{U}_0 = \emptyset$
2) While the size of $\mathbf{U}_k$ is smaller than M
3) Select the next unit u_{k+1} according to Equation 1
4) $\mathbf{U}_{k+1} = \mathbf{U}_k \cup \{\mathrm{u}_{k+1}\}$
5) $k = k + 1$
6) end
Output: the set of selected information units ($\mathbf{U}_k$)

When applied to faceted documents, MMR suffers from two major drawbacks. One is that MMR ignores structural information of documents, which might be crucial for determining the relevance of a document. For example, for the query "movie with Tom Cruise", MMR cannot distinguish between "actor: Tom Cruise" and "producer: Tom Cruise". In fact, the user is more likely to search for movies with Tom Cruise as an actor. The other drawback of MMR (and other query-biased approaches as well) is that some important information units without any query terms are less likely to be included in the summary. In the previous query example, if a movie has no Tom Cruise as an actor, the facet "actor" usually won't be included in its summary although this facet is an important indicator to show that this movie is actually non-relevant.

4. SUMMARIZATION BASED ON QUERY-SPECIFIC FACET SELECTION

In a search application for faceted documents, the information need behind a query is usually related to a group of facet-value pairs. Sometimes, the information need can even be totally represented by one or several facet-value pairs. For example, the query "15-inch silver laptop by Lenovo" can be represented using four facet-value pairs: "category: laptop", "screen size: 15 inches", "color: silver", and "maker: Lenovo". Intuitively, the corresponding facets of those related facet-value pairs ("category", "screen size", "color", "maker" in the example) should be shown in a summary since the relevance of a retrieved document largely depends on its value(s) on those facets. For example, a returned product with "screen size: 12-inch" or "color: black" is obviously non-relevant. A good summary should include those important facets in order to help the user determine the relevance of a document quickly.

Most of the existing query-biased summarization approaches contain two major steps. First, select sentences that are most relevant to the query. Second, build the summary by compressing the sentences to maximize certain criteria (query term coverage, novelty, readability, etc.) while meeting the space constraint [19]. In our approach, we introduce a new step of facet selection for summarizing faceted documents. As we mentioned, the information need behind a query might be related to some important facets. When summarizing a document, it is helpful to show the important facets, even if those facets of the document do not "look" relevant to the query (e.g., without any query terms). In the previous query example, the facet-value pair "color: black" of a document is very useful information to show that this document is in fact non-relevant. However, by using existing approaches, this facet-value pair is unlikely to be chosen since it does not contain any query terms. Existing approaches do not have the intelligence to predict that the facet "color" is in fact an important facet for this query. In other words, if we are able to learn the important facets for individual queries, we will be able to generate better summaries, which is exactly the goal of our approach.

Our approach has three major steps. First, we use a learning-based approach to rank all facet-value pairs according to their relevance to the query. Second, given the ranked FVPs, we further rank facets according to their importance. Finally, we generate summaries for each retrieved document based on the most important facets we learn in the previous step. The following subsections describe each step in detail.

4.1 Ranking Facet-Value Pairs

Given a query searching for faceted documents, how can we learn the related facet-value pairs? This task can be viewed as an attempt to understand the hidden information need behind a query. In our previous work, we proposed several heuristic approaches for ranking facet-value pairs in the context of semi-structured documents [28]. In this paper, our approach is different in two aspects. First, we are focusing on faceted documents where metadata dominates a document. The ideal approaches for highly-structured faceted documents might be different from those for semi-structured documents where unstructured text is dominating. Secondly, we use a learning-based instead of heuristic approach for ranking facet-value pairs. Compared with heuristic approaches, learning-based approaches generally perform better for the advantage of being able to combine multiple evidences. In fact, some of the features we propose in this paper are equivalent to the best approaches used in [28], and our experimental results show that the performance can be dramatically improved by using a learning-based approach (Table 3).

In our work, to obtain training data for FVP ranking, we hire a human assessor to judge the relevance of facet-value pairs. To combine multiple features, we use the well-known Gradient Boosted Trees (GBT) [7] as the learning model, which has the advantage of being able to handle deep interactions among features, and has been shown to perform well in other tasks such as learning to rank [16] and sentence selection for document summarization [19].

4.1.1 Features

We use a number of features to measure the relevance between a query and a facet-value pair. These features can be categorized into seven categories based on what type of information they depend on. Table 1 summarizes all the features we use.

1) Query Features

This type of feature only depends on the query. We use two features: the query length (number of words), and the average IDF of all query words. The average IDF is used to measure the uniqueness of a query.

2) Facet Features

This type of feature only depends on the facet. The first (F.Type) is a categorical feature that identifies the facet (the number of unique facets is usually small). The second feature (F.NumValues) is the number of unique values the facet has in the whole corpus. The third feature (F.NumOccrs) is the total number of occurrences of all facet-value pairs of this facet in the whole corpus.

3) Value Features

This type of feature only depends on the value. Two features of this type are used: V.Length is the number of words contained in the value, and V.AvgIDF is the average IDF of all value words.

4) FVP Features

This type of feature depends on the facet-value pair as a whole. P.NumDocs is the number of documents containing this facet-value pair. P.IDF is the Inverse Document Frequency of this FVP.

5) Query-Facet Features

This type of feature measures the similarity between the query and the facet. QF.TFIDF is the TFIDF score between the query and the facet name. This feature might be useful based on the intuition that some users might use the facet name to express the faceted constraint of their information need. For example, the query "movies directed by James Cameron" is related to the facet "director".

6) Query-Value Features

This type of feature measures the similarity between the query and the value. We use four features based on four traditional IR scoring methods. QV.BM25 and QV.TFIDF are the BM25 and TFIDF scores between the query and the value. QV.SIDF is different from QV.TFIDF by ignoring the term frequency. QV.CosSim is the cosine similarity score, where the query and value vectors are calculated using the TFIDF weighting method. Comparing these four features, QV.BM25 and QV.CosSim have a penalty mechanism for long values while the other two do not.

7) Query-FVP Features

This type of feature depends on both the query and the facet-value pair, which are mainly based on the frequency of the FVP occurring in the top retrieved documents. QP.DFN measures how many documents in the top N retrieved ones contain the FVP, where we set N = 10, 100, 1000, and the number of all retrieved documents respectively. QP.DFIDFN is the product of QP.DFN and the IDF of the FVP. This group of features might be useful based on the intuition that a facet-value pair occurring frequently in the top retrieved documents while less frequently in the whole corpus are more likely to be relevant to the query.

4.2 Ranking Facets

A facet is more likely to be important to the query if its facet-value pair(s) are relevant to the query. Based on the predicted relevance scores of all facet-value pairs in previous step, we can further rank facets according to their importance to the query. Specifically, we use the following Equation for facet ranking:

$$\mathrm{s}(\mathrm{f}_i, \mathrm{Q}) = \max_{\mathrm{p}_j \in \mathbf{P}(\mathrm{f}_i)} \{\mathrm{s}(\mathrm{p}_j, \mathrm{Q})\} \tag{2}$$

where $\mathbf{P}(\mathrm{f}_i)$ is the set of all facet-value pairs of facet f_i, $\mathrm{s}(\mathrm{p}_j, \mathrm{Q})$ is the relevance score of facet-value pair p_j, which is calculated in the previous step.

Table 1: Features for ranking facet-value pairs

Type	ID	Detail
Query	Q.Length	Number of words in the query
	Q.AvgIDF	Average IDF of query words
Facet	F.Type	The facet type (categorical)
	F.NumValues	Number of unique values of this facet
	F.NumOccrs	Number of occurrences of all values of this facet
Value	V.Length	Number of words in the value
	V.AvgIDF	Average IDF of value words
FVP	P.NumDocs	Number of documents containing this FVP
	P.IDF	IDF of this FVP
Query-Facet	QF.TFIDF	TFIDF score between the query and the facet name
Query-Value	QV.TFIDF	TFIDF score between the query and the value
	QV.BM25	BM25 score between the query and the value
	QV.SIDF	Sum of IDFs of the overlapped words between the query and the value
	QV.CosSim	Cosine similarity between the query and the value
Query-FVP	QP.DF10	FVP frequency in the top 10 retrieved documents
	QP.DFIDF10	QP.DF10 * IDF of the FVP
	QP.DF100	FVP frequency in the top 100 retrieved documents
	QP.DFIDF100	QP.DF100 * IDF of the FVP
	QP.DF1000	FVP frequency in the top 1000 retrieved documents
	QP.DFIDF1000	QP.DF1000 * IDF of the FVP
	QP.DFAll	FVP frequency in all retrieved documents
	QP.DFIDFAll	QP.DFAll * IDF of the FVP

4.3 Summarizing Documents

A faceted document (as shown in Figure 1) can be abstracted as a set of facet-value pairs. To summarize a faceted document is thus to answer the following question: which facets or which facet-value pairs should we choose from the original document? In this paper, we focus on facet selection instead of FVP selection based on two considerations. First, a facet is important to show if only there is at least one relevant (to the query) facet-value pair of this facet in the whole corpus, no matter whether the current document contains the relevant facet-value pair(s) or not. Secondly, a summary interface for faceted documents is usually organized by facets with each facet shown in a single line. It seems more natural to generate summaries by facet selection in order to have a better control on the generated summary. For example, it will be easier to control the maximum number of facets in a summary.

4.3.1 Summarization Based on QSFS

Given the ranked facets, we select the most important facets in a document to generate the summary. To determine which values of a selected facet to show, we can use many existing sentence-selection approaches. The whole process for summarizing all retrieved documents of a query is shown in Algorithm 2. To differentiate our approach from Manual Facet Selection (MFS), we will call our approach Query-Specific Facet Selection (QSFS) in the rest of this paper.

Algorithm 2 : Summarization based on Query-Specific Facet Selection (QSFS)

Input:
Q: the user query
C: the whole corpus
D: the set of retrieved documents to summarize
M: the maximum number of facets allowed in a summary
1) Rank all facet-value pairs occurring in **C** based on Q
2) Rank all facets according to Equation 2
3) For each document d in **D**
4) Initialize $\mathbf{S}_d = \emptyset$
5) Initialize $\mathbf{F}_d$: the set of facets available in d
6) While the number of facets in $\mathbf{S}_d$ is less than M
7) $f = \arg\max_{f_i \in \mathbf{F}_d} \{s(f_i, Q)\}$
8) $\mathbf{S}_d = \mathbf{S}_d \cup \{f\}$
9) $\mathbf{F}_d = \mathbf{F}_d \setminus \{f\}$
10) End while
11) For each facet in S_d
12) Determine which values to show in the summary
13) End for
14) End for
Output: the summary of each document

4.3.2 Integrating MMR and QSFS

MMR and QSFS are two distinct approaches with very different characteristics. MMR aims to include as many relevant information units in the summary, while keeping low redundancy in the summary. To summarize a document, MMR depends only on the unstructured sentences of the document: it does not use any structural information of the document, nor does it use any information from other documents. QSFS aims to discover the hidden important facets of a query by identifying the relevant facet-value pairs. In contrast to MMR, QSFS takes into account a large number of documents and facet-value pairs occurring in the corpus. From this point of view, MMR is a **local** method focusing on the current document, and QSFS is a **global** method focusing on the query and the whole corpus. Given the different characteristics of MMR and QSFS, we expect that their combination will further improve the summary quality.

The combined approach is similar to QSFS (Algorithm 2) except for two positions. First, we use a new method to choose the next facet in line 7) of Algorithm 2, which is shown in Equation 3. $s_{MMR}(f_i, Q)$ denotes the score of facet f_i based on MMR (Equation 4), $s_{QSFS}(f_i, Q)$ denotes the score of facet f_i based on QSFS (Equation 2). c is the coefficient to trade off between MMR and QSFS, which can be tuned in practice. Second, we need to change the order of facet selection (line 6-10) and value selection (line 11-13) in order to calculate the MMR score of each facet.

$$f = \arg\max_{f_i \in \mathbf{F}_d} \{c * s_{MMR}(f_i, Q) + (1 - c) * s_{QSFS}(f_i, Q)\} \quad (3)$$

The calculation of $s_{MMR}(f_i, Q)$ (Equation 4) is similar to Equation 1 except that we are treating facets as the basic information units instead of sentences. In Equation 4, $v(f_i, d)$ denotes all the values of facet f_i in document d, which are treated as a single sentence when calculating the similarities.

$$s_{MMR}(f_i, Q) = \lambda * sim_1(v(f_i, d), Q) - (1 - \lambda) * \max_{f_j \in S_d} \{sim_2(v(f_i, d), v(f_j, d))\} \quad (4)$$

5. A UTILITY-BASED EVALUATION FRAMEWORK

Evaluation of summaries in search is a very challenging problem that has not been well studied. Some previous work has been using the precision and recall of subjects' relevance judgments [23, 27] as the metrics. However, it's not clear how to trade off between precision and recall when we need to choose the best from several summarization approaches. More importantly, it does not directly measure the utility of the summary for each search engine user.

To measure the utility of the summaries in a search session, we need to examine how the summaries are used by the user. A user guesses which documents in the returned results might be relevant based on the summaries of retrieved documents. The user will skip (not click) documents considered not relevant and navigate to (click) documents considered relevant. If a clicked document is relevant, the user gains some utility. If a clicked document is not relevant, the user incurs some loss due to the waste of time and cognitive efforts. If a skipped document is relevant, the user also incurs some loss for missing useful information.

Accordingly and motivated by the well-known linear utility measure used in the TREC adaptive filtering task [21], we propose a utility-based framework for the evaluation of summarization approaches. Specifically, for a relevant document clicked by the user (i.e. the user guesses it is relevant), the user utility increases by A; for a non-relevant document clicked by the user, the user utility decreases by B; for a relevant document skipped (i.e. not clicked) by the user, the user utility decreases by C; for a non-relevant document skipped by the user, the user utility increases by D. We summarize the parameters of our utility function in Table 2.

Table 2: The utility function

	Document: +	Document: −
User: click (guess +)	A	$-B$
User: not click (guess -)	$-C$	D

The amounts of utility obtained or lost in different cases (A, B, C, D) depend on the specific application and user. The system or the user can adjust the values of A, B, C, D to fit each specific scenario. For example, in an application needs high recalls, we can increase the penalty for missing a relevant document (C); while in an application needs high precisions, we can increase the penalty for clicking on (i.e. misjudging) a non-relevant document (B).

However, it's worth mentioning that this evaluation framework is based on several assumptions. First, we assume a user will read every document summary in the result list. Second, we assume a user can recognize the relevant document after clicking on and accessing the full document. Third, we assume a user will click on a document if the user guesses the document is relevant (+) based on the summary. This assumption is not always true, especially if a user's information need is already satisfied by the summary (e.g., a user searches for a telephone number and the summary contains the answer). However, this assumption is true in many real world scenarios where the utility of a relevant document is realized through actions (e.g. purchasing, reading, etc.) after clicking on the search result. In general, the utility-based evaluation framework seems a better match of the real retrieval scenario, and it provides a single unified measure for comparing different summaries, in contrast to the measures of precision and recall that are hard to tradeoff in practice [23, 27].

6. EVALUATION METHODOLOGY

6.1 Experimental Goals

We design experiments to answer the following questions:

1. How does the proposed summarization approach based on query-specific facet selection perform? Is it better than existing summarization approaches? We will implement and compare four summarization approaches: 1) Manual Facet Selection (MFS), 2) Maximum Marginal Relevance (MMR), 3) Query-Specific Facet Selection (QSFS), and 4) the combination of MMR and QSFS (MMR-QSFS). MFS and MMR are two existing approaches, while QSFS and MMR-QSFS are two approaches we propose.

2. How does the proposed facet-value-pair ranking approach perform? The performance of the FVP-ranking approach will largely influence the quality of the generated summaries. Specifically, we are interested in: 1) the general performance of the learning-based approach, 2) whether the proposed features are useful, and 3) whether the learning algorithm (GBT) combines multiple features effectively.

6.2 The Data Set

Our data set is from the data-centric track of INEX 2010 [9], which consists of: 1) the IMDB data set including 1,594,513 movies; 2) 26 query topics (keywords, description, and narrative) created by the track participants (in the final version); and 3) relevance judgments of query-document pairs.

We refined this data set to make it more suitable for our experiments. To make it easier for subjects to make relevance judgments and without loss of generality, we focus on one genre of documents by using only those documents representing movies, and remove those non-movie documents such as TV series, etc. This leaves a total of 490,075 movies in our data set. Besides, we observed that the relevance judgments provided by the INEX track participants contain some mistakes. To reduce the influence of those wrong relevance judgments, we hired a graduate student to scrutinize all relevance judgments and correct those obvious mistakes. [1]

To prepare the training and test data for our FVP-ranking approach, we ask the same graduate student to do relevance judgments on query-FVP pairs. To obtain FVP candidates,

[1] Visit http://users.soe.ucsc.edu/~lanbo for the data

all FVPs are ranked based on the BM25 score between the query and the value (feature QV.BM25 in Table 1), and the top 100 FVPs of each query are selected for relevance judging. As a result, we have a total number of 2600 query-FVP relevance judgments, among which there are 148 relevant ones. [2]

6.3 User Study on Mechanical Turk

We use Amazon Mechanical Turk to evaluate the generated summaries. The subjects are asked to guess (i.e. judge) the relevance of each document based on its summary. One problem is that the Turks are motivated by monetary payoffs rather than any information needs, and thus may not make judgments carefully as we hope. Similar problems have been addressed by experimental economists who often work with paid subjects. The general idea of their solution is to incentivize subjects with real monetary payoffs through a game, in which subjects need to do what researchers hope them do in order to maximize their payoffs [13]. We use the same solution in our experiments, and we pay a subject an amount of bonus depending on his/her judging performance. The amount of bonus is calculated based on the utility function described in Table 2, where we set $A = B = 4$ cents, $C = D = 2$ cents.

For each query, we show the subject the keywords, description, and narrative of the topic, and a list of summaries of up to 15 relevant documents and up to 15 non-relevant documents which are ranked highest by our document retrieval algorithm. For each summary, the subject needs to make a choice among three options: "relevant", "non-relevant", or "not sure" (Figure 2). The subject won't get or lose any cents if he/she chooses "not sure". To ensure a reasonably large sample of users, we hire a total number of around 100 subjects on Mechanical Turk. For each subject working on a specific query, we will randomly choose a summarization approach. In our game, we make sure no subject works on different summarization approaches of the same topic. For each combination of a query and a summarization approach, we have 4 subjects to work on it, and the average utility to the 4 subjects will be used to measure the performance of the summarization approach on this particular query.

In our game, we randomly assign 5~10 queries to each subject. A subject can choose to continue or stop after he/she completes 5 queries. In our experiments, we find almost all subjects completed all 10 queries, and some subjects particularly expressed their great interests in the game by sending emails to the task organizer. Besides, we find the proportion of documents labeled as "not sure" by Turks is very low (less than 5%) among all judged documents. These facts imply that our evaluation approach is quite effective in terms of attracting participants on crowdsourcing websites.

6.4 Evaluation Metrics

6.4.1 Mean Average Normalized Utility (MANU)

We measure a summarization approach based on the average utility its summaries bring to the users, namely, the average amount of bonus the subjects who have worked on this approach earned. Specifically, we propose the **Mean** (across topics) **Average** (across subjects) **Normalized Utility**

[2]Visit http://users.soe.ucsc.edu/~lanbo for the data

Title: **Avatar** (2008)
Stars: Murden, Tony; Arad, Natalie; Mills, Rebecca (III)
Writer: Pickles, **James** (II)
* Based on the above summary, do you think this movie is relevant, not relevant, or not really sure?

Figure 2: A Document Summary Example

(**MANU**) as the major metric.

$$\text{MANU} = \frac{1}{|\mathbf{Q}|}\sum_{q\in\mathbf{Q}}\frac{1}{|\mathbf{U}_q|}\sum_{u\in\mathbf{U}_q}\text{NU}(q,u) \tag{5}$$

In Equation 5, q denotes a query, $\mathbf{Q}$ denotes the set of all queries, u denotes a user (subject), $\mathbf{U}_q$ denotes the set of subjects that work on query q, and NU(q, u) denotes the Normalized Utility of user u on query q, which is calculated as:

$$\text{NU}(q, u) = \frac{\text{U}(q, u) - \text{MinU}(q)}{\text{MaxU}(q) - \text{MinU}(q)} \tag{6}$$

where U(q, u) is the total utility (bonus) subject u gets on query q, MaxU(q) and MinU(q) are the maximum and minimum possible utility of query q, namely, the amount of bonus one gets when he/she correctly (incorrectly) judges all documents of query q.

6.4.2 Existing IR Metrics

For the evaluation of our FVP-ranking approach, we use the Mean Average Precision (**MAP**) as the major metric. In the comparison of different summarization approaches, we will also report the performance of each approach in terms of traditional IR metrics including macro **Precision** and macro **Recall**, which are calculated as follows:

$$\text{Precision} = \frac{1}{|\mathbf{Q}|}\sum_{q\in\mathbf{Q}}\frac{1}{|\mathbf{U}_q|}\sum_{u\in\mathbf{U}_q}\text{Precision}(q,u) \tag{7}$$

$$\text{Recall} = \frac{1}{|\mathbf{Q}|}\sum_{q\in\mathbf{Q}}\frac{1}{|\mathbf{U}_q|}\sum_{u\in\mathbf{U}_q}\text{Recall}(q,u) \tag{8}$$

where Precision(q, u) is defined as the ratio of relevant documents among all documents judged as relevant by u, Recall(q, u) is defined as the ratio of documents judged as relevant by u among all relevant documents.

6.5 Summary Constraints

When generating summaries, we use the following constraints for all summarization approaches: 1) at most 3 facets can be included in a summary; 2) the values of each facet cannot be longer than 100 characters (in order to fit in a single line); and 3) each facet can have at most 4 values (so as not to overwhelm users with too many values). In our user study, we organize each document summary into three lines with each facet shown in a single line. Figure 2 shows a document summary example, where the bold words are those occurred in the query.

6.6 Settings of FVP-Ranking Approaches

We use the package from [1] for learning gradient boosted trees. To determine the best number of trees in GBT, we use the best MAP instead of the smallest error on the validation set. Regarding the parameters of GBT, we use the Bernoulli distribution, a maximum of 3000 trees, an interaction depth of 5, a minimum number of observations of 10 in each tree node, and a shrinkage parameter of 0.01. These parameters are not tuned since the performance is not very sensitive to them [2]. We use 10-fold cross validation to evaluate our approach, and the average performance on all folds will be reported.

6.7 Settings of Summarization Approaches

Four summarization approaches are implemented and compared in our experiments: Manual Facet Selection (MFS), Maximum Marginal Relevance (MMR), Query-Specific Facet Selection (QSFS), and the Combination of MMR and QSFS (MMR-QSFS). For all approaches, we use the first 13 topics for training and parameter tuning, and the remaining 13 topics for test.

Manual Facet Selection (MFS): To ensure a reasonably good performance of this approach, we select facets based on the collected relevance judgments of facet-value pairs. Those facets with most relevant facet-value pairs to queries in the training set are chosen. The top five facets we get in this way are "title", "actor", "director", "keyword", "genre", which are consistent with our common sense on the important facets of movies.

Maximum Marginal Relevance (MMR): For an individual document, we view each facet with the corresponding values as an information unit when applying MMR. Each facet is treated as a bag of words when calculating the similarity in Equation 1. In our experiments, we use the conventional TFIDF method to measure the similarities. To set the parameter λ used in Equation 1, four different values (0.3, 0.5, 0.7, 1) are tried on the training set, and the value that leads to the best summary utility (0.5) is used for testing.

Query-Specific Facet Selection (QSFS): In this approach, we first rank all facets for each query according to Equation 2, then we summarize each retrieved document by selecting the most important facets from the document.

Combination of MMR and QSFS (MMR-QSFS): To set the parameter c in Equation 3, five values (0, 0.3, 0.5, 0.7, 1) are tried on the training set and the best value (0.3) is used for testing. For λ, we use the same value as the one tuned in the MMR approach (0.5).

6.8 More Details

We use the BM25 algorithm implemented in Lemur as the document retrieval approach throughout our experiments. Before scoring a document, we remove all XML tags, and treat it as an unstructured document. We did not use a more sophisticated retrieval method since that is not the focus of this paper.

In our experiments, only the query keywords are allowed to be used for all approaches. The query descriptions and narratives are only used when showing the query to the subjects to help them understand the information need.

7. EXPERIMENTAL RESULTS

In this section, we show the performances of our FVP-ranking approaches, and the performances of different summarization approaches.

7.1 FVP-Ranking Approaches

First, we look at the performances of our FVP-ranking approaches, since the accuracy of the top-ranked FVPs will significantly influence the quality of the generated summaries. Table 3 shows the ranking performance (using four commonly used IR metrics) of each FVP-ranking approach, where GBT is the learning-based approach that integrates all features proposed in Table 1, and all the other 12 approaches are based on individual features[3].

Table 3: Performances of different FVP-ranking approaches. GBT is the learning-based approach, and the other approaches use individual features. GBT significantly outperforms all the other approaches under a paired t-test (p-value < 0.05).

Approach	MAP	R-Prec	P@5	P@R=1
QV.TFIDF	0.18	0.09	0.08	0.11
QV.SIDF	0.18	0.15	0.14	0.10
QP.DF10	0.30	0.25	0.22	0.23
QP.DFIDF10	0.32	0.28	0.22	0.24
QP.DFAll	0.33	0.21	0.30	0.21
QP.DFIDFAll	0.33	0.21	0.30	0.21
QV.CosSim	0.37	0.24	0.33	0.23
QV.BM25	0.42	0.29	0.34	0.28
QP.DF1000	0.48	0.38	0.29	0.36
QP.DFIDF1000	0.51	0.43	0.29	0.38
QP.DFIDF100	0.53	0.43	0.29	0.37
QP.DF100	0.53	0.44	0.29	0.37
GBT	**0.73**	**0.61**	**0.45**	**0.55**

Based on Table 3, we have several findings. First, GBT dramatically outperforms all individual features, which demonstrates the superiority of the learning-based approach, and implies that the features we proposed are quite complementary with each other. Second, QP (Query-FVP) features generally perform better than QV (Query-Value) features, which implies that the frequency among top retrieved documents (measured by QP features) is a stronger signal than the pure text match between the value and the query. Third, among all QP features, QP.DF100 and QP.DFIDF100 perform the best, which implies that 100 might be a reasonable cutoff for top retrieved documents. Fourth, among all QV features, QV.BM25 and QV.CosSim outperform QV.TFIDF and QV.IDF significantly. Note that the major difference between these features is that QV.BM25 and QV.CosSim normalize term frequency based on the value length of the FVP while the other two do not. Given the dramatically different performances, it seems that length normalization is very important for FVP ranking, and this might be generalized to other short-text-ranking problems as well.

7.2 Summarization Approaches

The performances of four summarization approaches are shown in Table 4. Different metrics are reported, while MANU is our major measure. The results show that our proposed approaches (QSFS and MMR-QSFS) are significantly better than the two baselines (MFS and MMR). We discuss each summarization approach in detail in the following subsections.

[3]We didn't use the other features since they do not measure the relevance between a query and an FVP directly, and thus are not suitable for FVP ranking individually.

Table 4: Performances of Different Summarization Approaches. ∗ and ◇ denote a significant improvement over MFS and MMR respectively (p-value < 0.05).

Approach	MANU	Precision	Recall
MFS	0.813	0.871	0.708
MMR	0.887	0.867	0.859∗
QSFS	0.923∗◇	0.921◇	**0.887∗**
MMR-QSFS	**0.929∗◇**	**0.933∗◇**	0.886∗

7.2.1 *Manual Facet Selection (MFS)*

Although widely used in commercial search engines, MFS performs significantly worse than the other approaches. This is not surprising since it's not adapted to individual queries. If we take a further look at the Precision and Recall, we find that the poor performance of MFS is mainly due to the low Recall, while the Precision is reasonably good and very close to that of MMR. One possible reason is as follows. Due to the fact that the majority of retrieved documents are non-relevant, subjects tend to be cautious when judging a document as relevant. They usually won't judge a document as relevant unless they observe enough evidences. The major drawback of MFS is that some important facets of a document may not be shown in its summary. As a result, subjects will judge the document as non-relevant by default due to the lack of enough evidences to show that the document might be relevant.

7.2.2 *Maximum Marginal Relevance (MMR)*

MMR works significantly better than MFS in terms of Recall, which is not surprising given that MMR is more likely to show facets that contain query terms. However, MMR does not perform significantly better than MFS in terms of MANU, and even slightly worse in terms of Precision. There are two possible reasons. First, some important facets without query terms are less likely to be selected by MMR, while they might be selected by MFS. Second, more query terms shown in the summary might mislead the subjects so that they guess the document is relevant even if it is in fact non-relevant, and this might be one possible reason why MMR does not have a good Precision.

7.2.3 *Query-Specific Facet Selection (QSFS)*

QSFS significantly outperforms both MFS and MMR in terms of the major measure MANU. It's not surprising that QSFS outperforms MFS since QSFS adapts to each individual query and can learn query-specific important facets. However, it's interesting to investigate why QSFS outperforms MMR. One big problem of MMR (and probably most existing query-biased summarization approaches) is that a facet of a document without any query terms is less likely to be shown in the summary, even if this facet is in fact crucial for users to make relevance judgments. QSFS does not suffer from this problem since it aims to discover important facets for each individual query, and the important facets of a document will be shown in the summary no matter whether they contain query terms or not.

Let's consider the query example "movies with Tom Cruise", by which the user is looking for movies acted by Tom Cruise. Assume there is a movie which has Tom Cruise as a producer, and none of the other facets of the movie (including "actor") contain "Tom Cruise". To summarize this movie, MMR will select the facet "producer" but probably not the facet "actor". As a result, there is no evidence in the summary generated by MMR that can verify this document is in fact non-relevant, and some users may even guess this document as "relevant" in order to maximize their utility. Even if some users judge such a summary as "non-relevant" by default, they still could make mistakes. For example, for a movie with Tom Cruise as both an actor and a producer, there is a possibility that MMR will select the facet "producer" but not the facet "actor" in order to ensure a diversity in the summary. QSFS does not suffer from this problem since it will rank both the facet "actor" and "producer" high using our proposed facet-ranking approach.

As we mentioned, the performance of QSFS will largely depend on the performance of the FVP-ranking approach. According to the results reported in Section 7.1, our FVP-ranking approach performs reasonably well on the data set we use, which also explains why QSFS performs well.

7.2.4 *Combining MMR and QSFS (MMR-QSFS)*

The combination of MMR and QSFS further improves the summarization performance. However, the improvement is not significant. One reason could be that QSFS already works very well on our data set (note that both Precision and Recall are around 90%), so that the space for improvement is limited. Considering the complementary characteristics of MMR and QSFS, the improvement might be more significant on data sets where MMR and QSFS do not perform well individually. We will further explore this approach on more data sets in our future work.

8. CONCLUSIONS AND FUTURE WORK

The task of summarizing highly structured documents in retrieval has not been addressed by prior work, probably due to the lack of a clear definition of good summaries and the lack of an appropriate evaluation methodology. In this research, we assume good document summaries should be informative enough so that a search engine user can judge the utility of the returned results quickly and navigate to the relevant documents without the cost of clicking on many non-relevant URLs/documents. To achieve this goal, a summary should include not only facet-values pairs that match certain query term(s), but also facet-value pairs that make it clear if the underlying document is non-relevant.

We proposed a new summarization approach based on query-specific facet selection, and compared it with a commonly used approach in industry (i.e. MFS) and a well-known approach (i.e. MMR) for summarizing unstructured documents. Also, we proposed a utility-based evaluation framework to measure the effectiveness of summaries in terms of assisting users in interacting with the search results. We developed a game on Mechanical Turk to evaluate the quality of the generated summaries in this framework. The experimental results show that the summaries generated by the new approach are significantly better than those generated by the two baselines. To our knowledge, this is the first paper that focuses on summarizing highly structured documents, which is an important problem given the increasing prevalence of such kind of data.

The work reported in this paper is our first step for summarizing highly structured documents, and can be extended in several directions. For example, the summarization approach proposed in this paper, especially the FVP-ranking component, learns from labeled data instead of user interactions. In the future, we will explore how user interactions can be used to train the model so that the summarization approach can directly optimize the utility measure (i.e. MANU).

It is worth mentioning that two components of our work can be used in other applications besides the summarization of highly structured documents. In order to select important facets, we propose a learning-based approach for ranking facet-value pairs. Specifically, we propose a set of features that are complementary with each other. The experimental results show that the proposed features are useful for FVP ranking, and the learning-based approach can further improve the performance over the best individual feature by integrating multiple features. This approach might be valuable in other applications where FVP-ranking task is involved (e.g., faceted search, faceted query suggestion, etc.). Besides, the utility-based evaluation measure and the crowdsourcing game can be used for the evaluation of unstructured-document summarization as well.

9. ACKNOWLEDGEMENTS

This work was funded by National Science Foundation IIS-0953908, IIS-1144564, UCSC/LANL ISSDM. Any opinions, findings, conclusions or recommendations expressed in this paper are the authors', and do not necessarily reflect those of the sponsors.

10. REFERENCES

[1] The gbm package. http://cran.r-project.org/web/packages/gbm/.

[2] Generalized boosted models: A guide to the gbm package. http://cran.r-project.org/web/packages/gbm/vignettes/gbm.pdf.

[3] L. L. Bando, F. Scholer, and A. Turpin. Constructing query-biased summaries: a comparison of human and system generated snippets. IIiX '10, 2010.

[4] J. Carbonell and J. Goldstein. The use of mmr, diversity-based reranking for reordering documents and producing summaries. SIGIR '98, 1998.

[5] C. L. A. Clarke, E. Agichtein, S. Dumais, and R. W. White. The influence of caption features on clickthrough patterns in web search. SIGIR '07, 2007.

[6] H. P. Edmundson. New methods in automatic extracting. *J. ACM*, 16:264–285, April 1969.

[7] J. H. Friedman. Greedy function approximation: A gradient boosting machine. *The Annals of Statistics*, 29(5):pp. 1189–1232, 2001.

[8] S. Geva, J. Kamps, and R. Schenkel. Inex 2011 workshop pre-proceedings, 2011.

[9] S. Geva, J. Kamps, R. Schenkel, and A. Trotman. Inex 2010 workshop pre-proceedings, 2010.

[10] J. Goldstein, M. Kantrowitz, V. Mittal, and J. Carbonell. Summarizing text documents: sentence selection and evaluation metrics. SIGIR '99, 1999.

[11] T. F. Hand. A proposal for task-based evaluation of text summarization system., 1997.

[12] Y. Huang, Z. Liu, and Y. Chen. Query biased snippet generation in xml search. SIGMOD '08, 2008.

[13] J. Kagel and A. E. Roth, editors. *The Handbook of Experimental Economics*. Princeton University Press, 1995.

[14] J. Kupiec, J. Pedersen, and F. Chen. A trainable document summarizer. SIGIR '95, 1995.

[15] L. Li, K. Zhou, G.-R. Xue, H. Zha, and Y. Yu. Enhancing diversity, coverage and balance for summarization through structure learning. WWW '09, 2009.

[16] P. Li and C. J. C. Burges. Learning to rank using classification and gradient boosting. NIPS '06, 2006.

[17] D. E. Losada. Statistical query expansion for sentence retrieval and its effects on weak and strong queries. *Inf. Retr.*, 13(5):485–506, Oct. 2010.

[18] I. Mani and E. Bloedorn. Multi-document summarization by graph search and matching. AAAI'97/IAAI'97, 1997.

[19] D. A. Metzler and T. Kanungo. Machine learned sentence selection strategies for query-biased summarization. In *SIGIR 2008 Workshop on Learning to Rank for Information Retrieval*, 2008.

[20] S. Miike, E. Itoh, K. Ono, and K. Sumita. A full-text retrieval system with a dynamic abstract generation function. SIGIR '94, 1994.

[21] S. E. Robertson and D. A. Hull. The trec-9 filtering track final report. 2000.

[22] G. Salton, A. Singhal, M. Mitra, and C. Buckley. Automatic text structuring and summarization. *Inf. Process. Manage.*, 33:193–207, March 1997.

[23] A. Tombros and M. Sanderson. Advantages of query biased summaries in information retrieval. SIGIR '98, 1998.

[24] A. Turpin, F. Scholer, K. Jarvelin, M. Wu, and J. S. Culpepper. Including summaries in system evaluation. SIGIR '09, 2009.

[25] R. Varadarajan and V. Hristidis. A system for query-specific document summarization. CIKM '06, 2006.

[26] C. Wang, F. Jing, L. Zhang, and H.-J. Zhang. Learning query-biased web page summarization. CIKM '07, 2007.

[27] R. W. White, J. M. Jose, and I. Ruthven. A task-oriented study on the influencing effects of query-biased summarisation in web searching. *Inf. Process. Manage.*, 39:707–733, September 2003.

[28] L. Zhang and Y. Zhang. Interactive retrieval based on faceted feedback. SIGIR '10, 2010.

TFMAP: Optimizing MAP for Top-N Context-aware Recommendation

Yue Shi[a]*, Alexandros Karatzoglou[b], Linas Baltrunas[b], Martha Larson[a], Alan Hanjalic[a], Nuria Oliver[b]
[a]Delft University of Technology, Netherlands; [b]Telefonica Research, Spain
[a]{y.shi, m.a.larson, a.hanjalic}@tudelft.nl, [b]{alexk, linas, nuriao}@tid.es

ABSTRACT

In this paper, we tackle the problem of top-N context-aware recommendation for implicit feedback scenarios. We frame this challenge as a ranking problem in collaborative filtering (CF). Much of the past work on CF has not focused on evaluation metrics that lead to good top-N recommendation lists in designing recommendation models. In addition, previous work on context-aware recommendation has mainly focused on explicit feedback data, *i.e.*, ratings. We propose TFMAP, a model that directly maximizes Mean Average Precision with the aim of creating an optimally ranked list of items for individual users under a given context. TFMAP uses tensor factorization to model *implicit feedback* data (*e.g.*, purchases, clicks) with contextual information.

The optimization of MAP in a large data collection is computationally too complex to be tractable in practice. To address this computational bottleneck, we present a fast learning algorithm that exploits several intrinsic properties of average precision to improve the learning efficiency of TFMAP, and to ensure its scalability. We experimentally verify the effectiveness of the proposed fast learning algorithm, and demonstrate that TFMAP significantly outperforms state-of-the-art recommendation approaches.

Categories and Subject Descriptors

H.3.3 [**Information Storage and Retrieval**]: Information Search and Retrieval—*Information Filtering*

Keywords

Collaborative filtering, context-aware recommendation, mean average precision, implicit feedback, tensor factorization

1. INTRODUCTION

Collaborative Filtering (CF) methods are at the core of most recommendation engines. Most of the data traces left by online users come in the form of implicit feedback, *i.e.*, we know which items a user interacted, *e.g.*, purchased, used, or clicked, etc., and possibly also the count of each interaction; however, we do not have an explicit rating, *i.e.*, a relevance score, that represents the strength of the user's interest in that item [13]. Learning the suggestion function from implicit feedback data, such as purchase or usage logs, can either be considered a classification problem, where items are classified to relevant or irrelevant, or a ranking problem where an optimal list of items is to be computed.

Top-N recommendation has recently attracted increased research interest because it generates a ranked list of results, which is directly connected to the end-user satisfaction [9]. Conventionally, recommender systems have been optimized to produced scores. A predicted score reflects the system's hypothesis of the strength of a particular user's preference for a particular item. In an overwhelmingly large number of recommender system use scenarios, users do not want preference strength information on all the items in the collection, but rather a compact list of top recommended items.

Although ranking-oriented CF approaches have been proposed for explicit feedback domains, e.g., EigenRank [19] and CoFiRank [34], those approaches are difficult to apply to implicit feedback domains, since they require training examples that are derived from the users ratings on various items. In particular, implicit feedback is often binary in nature. We notice that in top-N recommendation, the quality of a recommendation list that contains items of binary relevance can be quantified using Mean Average Precision (MAP), a well known evaluation measure in the information retrieval (IR) community. MAP provides a single-figure measure of quality across recall levels, has especially good discrimination and stability properties, and roughly corresponds to the average area under the precision-recall curve [21]. It is thus a good measure of performance when a short list of the most relevant items is shown to users [27]. A state-of-the-art approach, Bayesian Personalized Ranking (BPR) [24], has been recently proposed to train recommendation models by optimizing the measure of the Area Under the ROC Curve (AUC), which is based on pairwise comparisons between items. Note that in the AUC measure mistakes at the top of the list carry equal weight to mistakes in the bottom of the recommendation list. In contrast to AUC, MAP is a list-wise measure, for which mistakes in the recommended items at the top of the list carry a higher penalty than mistakes at the bottom of the list [10, 39]. Users typically consider only few (5 -10) top-ranked items in the recommendation list, it is thus particularly important to get the recommendations at the top of the list right. The top-heavy bias of MAP is thus particularly important in the recommendation problem. For this reason, we propose a recommendation model for implicit feedback domains by directly optimizing MAP.

*This work was conducted when the first author was an intern at Telefonica Research, Barcelona.

Permission to make digital or hard copies of all or part of this work for personal or classroom use is granted without fee provided that copies are not made or distributed for profit or commercial advantage and that copies bear this notice and the full citation on the first page. To copy otherwise, to republish, to post on servers or to redistribute to lists, requires prior specific permission and/or a fee.
SIGIR'12, August 12–16, 2012, Portland, Oregon, USA.
Copyright 2012 ACM 978-1-4503-1472-5/12/08 ...$10.00.

Typically, recommender systems have access to additional information about the user-item interactions, such as the *context* that is associated with the user-item interaction [1]. The context could be the location where the user listened to a song on his/her mobile phone or the time of the user-item interaction. Context-aware recommendations (CARs) are a new paradigm that can significantly improve the recommendation relevance and quality, compared to conventional recommendations solely based on user-item interactions [1, 4, 14, 25]. In this paper we present a generic CF model that is based on a generalization of matrix factorization to address context-aware recommendations. We extend the concept of matrix factorization to *tensor factorization*. A tensor is a generalization of the matrix concept to multiple dimensions. In the example above the user-item two-dimensional matrix is converted into a three-dimensional tensor of user-item-location interactions (see Figure 1).

Two key issues need to be considered in CARs: (1) *Context Integration*. The contextual information needs to be integrated in the recommendation model to be able to benefit the quality of the recommendation; and (2) *Optimization Function*. The recommendation model needs to be optimized under an objective function that corresponds to the recommendation quality for each user under each given context. Previous work in CARs has extensively studied the *context integration* issue, such as using tensor factorization [14] (TF) and factorization machines [25]. However, the second issue (*optimization function*) has only been addressed in a simplistic way. In the work of [14] and [25], the objective function in the recommendation model consists of minimizing the rating prediction error. This is an effective strategy where explicit feedback data is available from users, however, optimizing this objective is infeasible for scenarios with only implicit feedback data. In these scenarios, the quality of a recommendation list for a user is solely dependent on the positions of the relevant items in the list under the given context.

Here we propose a new context-aware recommendation approach based on tensor factorization for MAP maximization (TFMAP) that is designed to work with implicit feedback datasets. Taking insights from the area of *learning to rank*, TFMAP directly optimizes MAP for learning the model parameters, *i.e.*, latent factors/features of users, items and context types, which are then used to generate item recommendations for users under different types of context.

Directly optimizing MAP across all the users in a data collection is an expensive and non-trivial task. Therefore, we also propose a fast learning algorithm that exploits several properties of the average precision (AP) measure. We show that the computational complexity of the fast learning algorithm for TFMAP is linear in the number of observed items in a given data collection. Our contributions in this paper can be summarized as: 1) We propose a new generalized CF approach, TFMAP, that directly optimizes for MAP and leverages contextual information when available. We demonstrate that TFMAP outperforms state-of-the-art context-aware and context-free approaches. We observe significant improvements not only in MAP but also in precision at the top-N ranked recommendations. 2) To the best of our knowledge, TFMAP is also the first approach that can exploit datasets with implicit user feedback and contextual information. 3) We propose a fast learning algorithm that ensures the scalability of TFMAP and that exploits several properties of the AP measure.

The paper is organized as follows: in Section 2 we discuss the most relevant previous work and position our paper with respect to it. The research problem and the terminology used throughout the paper are presented in Section 3. In Section 4, we present the detail of TFMAP and the fast learning algorithm. Our experimental evaluation is reported in Section 5. Finally, Section 6 summarizes our main contributions and highlights a few areas of future work.

2. RELATED WORK

The work in this paper closely relates to three research areas: CF with implicit feedback, context-aware recommendation, and learning to rank. In the following, we present the most relevant related work in each of them.

CF with Implicit Feedback. Most CF approaches in the literature deal with the rating prediction problem, as defined in the Netflix prize competition[1]. A common approach to CF is to fit a latent factor model to the data, *e.g.*, latent semantic models [12, 28], and matrix factorization models, which learns a latent feature/factor vector for each user and item in the dataset such that the inner product of these features minimizes an explicit or implicit loss function [5]. Factor models have been shown to perform well in terms of predictive accuracy and scalability [2, 18, 26].

One of the first studies that used latent factor models for large implicit feedback datasets was introduced in [13]. It uses a least squares loss function and exploits the structure of the data (dominated by zero entries that correspond to negative preference), such that observed user-item interactions are weighted proportionately to the count of the interactions. Some extensions following this approach are introduced in [23] and [29]. In [24] a factorization approach based on the optimization of a smoothed pairwise ranking objective function was proposed. Optimizing the proposed objective function corresponds to maximizing the AUC. In this paper, we propose to learn a recommendation model by optimizing MAP, whose top-bias property is a significant advantage over AUC for recommender systems, as discussed in Section 1. In addition, our work is substantially different from the aforementioned work, since various types of contextual information are exploited for the recommendation.

Context-aware recommendation (CAR). Early work in CAR utilized contextual information for pre-processing, where context drives data selection, or post-processing, where context is used to filter recommendations [1, 4]. Recent work has focused on building models that integrate contextual information with the user-item relations and model the user, item and context interactions directly. Two state-of-the-art approaches have been proposed to date, one based on tensor factorization [14, 35] and the other on factorization machines [25] (FM). However, both approaches have been designed for the *explicit* rating prediction problem.

In this paper we utilize a tensor factorization approach, *i.e.*, the CANDECOMP/PARAFAC (CP) model [15], to represent the interactions among the user, the item and the context type. Our approach includes two substantial innovations, compared to the state of the art in CARs: (1) It targets recommendation scenarios with implicit feedback; and (2) it takes the evaluation metric (MAP) into account for learning the recommendation model.

Note that recommendation approaches have been proposed to take into account additional information (also referred as metadata, side information, or attributes) about users or items, *e.g.*, collective matrix factorization [30], localized fac-

[1] http://www.netflixprize.com/

tor models [3] and graph-based approaches [16]. However, this type of information would go beyond our definition of "context", since we refer to context as information that is associated with both the user and the item at the same time. Finally, note that a recommended item set from a recommender is regarded as the "context" of user choice in the work of [38]. However, this type of context is still extracted from the user-item relations, and thus, does not fall in the scope of the context studied in this paper.

Learning to Rank. Learning to rank has been an attractive research topic in both the machine learning and the information retrieval communities [20]. Our work in this paper is closely related to recent research where proxies for common IR evaluation measures, such as NDCG and MAP, are used as the objective functions. The main difficulty of directly optimizing evaluation measures lies in their non-smoothness [7], *i.e.*, they are dependent on the rank values of ranked documents/items but not directly on the predicted relevance scores.

Ranking approaches can be broadly classified into two categories, those that implicitly optimize the IR measure and those that formulate an explicit approximation of the measure. LambdaRank [7] is a popular implicit optimization method, which was proposed to apply gradient descent on an implicit loss function, that is related to IR measures. Methods that explicitly optimize IR measures include structured estimation techniques [32] that minimize convex upper bounds of loss functions based on evaluation measures [37], *e.g.*, SVM-MAP [39] and AdaRank [36]. In the case of CF, CoFiRank [34] introduced a matrix factorization method where structured estimation was used to minimize over a convex upper bound of NDCG. SoftRank [31] was the first approach that proposed an explicit smoothed version of an evaluation measure, in which a rank distribution was employed, resulting in the expected values of document ranks that are smooth to the predicted relevance scores. In addition, a more general extension of SoftRank was presented by Chapelle et al. [8].

In this paper, we also employ an explicit approximation of MAP, which is a smooth function of model parameters. Our work is different from aforementioned research, since we target context-aware recommendation rather than query-document search, and we propose a fast learning algorithm, which is critical for large-scale recommender systems.

3. PROBLEM AND TERMINOLOGY

The research problem studied in this paper is stated as follows: *Given implicit feedback and contextual information on user-item interactions, recommend to each user and under a given context, an optimal (from a MAP perspective) item list.*

We denote the implicit feedback data from M users to N items under K types of context as a binary tensor Y, *i.e.*, a 3-dimensional tensor, with $M \times N \times K$ entries which are denoted with y_{mik}: (1) $y_{mik} = 1$ indicates that user m has interacted (*i.e.* purchased, used) with item i under context type k. We can thus assume that the user has a preference for this item; and (2) $y_{mik} = 0$ indicates the absence of an interaction and thus the preference of user m to item i under context type k is unknown. $|Y|$ denotes the number of nonzero entries in Y. Y_{mk} denotes a binary vector that indicates the user m's preference on all the items under context type k.

As mentioned in Section 2, the main idea behind factor models is to fit the original user-item interaction matrix with a low rank approximation. In this work we use tensor factorization (TF) as a generalization of the classical matrix factorization methods that accommodates for the contextual information. The latent features are stored in three matrices $U \in \mathcal{R}^{M\times D}$, $V \in \mathcal{R}^{N\times D}$ and $C \in \mathcal{R}^{K\times D}$ that correspond to users, items, and context types, respectively. We use U_m to denote a D-dimensional row vector, which represents the latent features for user m. Similarly, V_i represents the latent features of item i, and C_k represents the latent features of context type k.

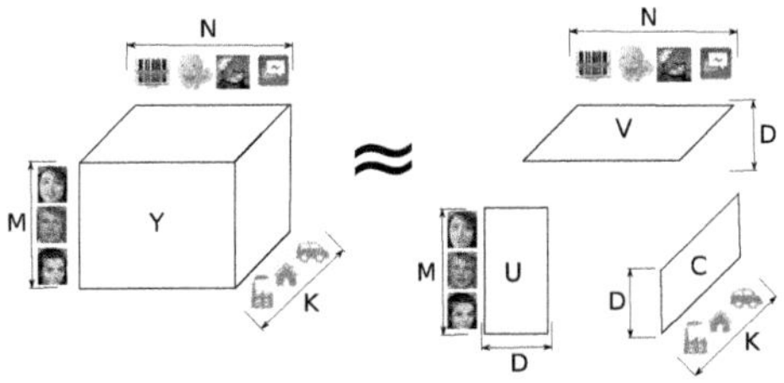

Figure 1: CP tensor factorization model.

We use the CP model [15], as illustrated in Fig. 1, for tensor factorization, in which user m's preference to item i under context type k is factorized as the inner product of the latent feature vectors, as shown below:

$$f_{mik} = \langle U_m, V_i, C_k \rangle = \sum_{d=1}^{D} U_{md} V_{id} C_{kd} \tag{1}$$

Based on user's m preference over all the items under context type k, we can then generate a recommendation list by ranking all the items in a descending order of the computed scores. Then, the AP of this list is defined as:

$$AP_{mk} = \frac{1}{\sum_{i=1}^{N} y_{mik}} \sum_{i=1}^{N} \frac{y_{mik}}{r_{mik}} \sum_{j=1}^{N} y_{mjk} \mathbb{I}(r_{mjk} \leq r_{mik}) \tag{2}$$

where r_{mik} denotes the rank of item i in the list of user m under context type k and $\mathbb{I}(\cdot)$ is an indicator function, which is equal to 1 if the condition is satisfied, and otherwise 0.

The MAP is defined as the average of AP across all the users and all the context types, as shown below:

$$MAP = \frac{1}{MK} \sum_{m=1}^{M} \sum_{k=1}^{K} \frac{\sum_{i=1}^{N} \frac{y_{mik}}{r_{mik}} \sum_{j=1}^{N} y_{mjk} \mathbb{I}(r_{mjk} \leq r_{mik})}{\sum_{i=1}^{N} y_{mik}} \tag{3}$$

4. TFMAP

In this section, we present the main technical contributions of this paper: (1) our proposed *smooth approximation of MAP*, its *optimization* and associated complexity analysis; and (2) a novel *fast learning algorithm* for optimizing over the smooth MAP measure in a context-aware setting.

4.1 Smoothed Mean Average Precision

It is apparent from Eq. (2) and (3), that AP (or MAP) depends on the rankings of the items in the recommendation lists. The rankings of the items change in a non-smooth way with respect to the predicted user preference scores and thus, the AP measure ends up being a non-smooth function with respect to the latent features of users, items and context types. We thus cannot use any of the standard optimization methods that require smoothness in the objective function.

As previously mentioned, significant progress has been made in the area of learning to rank regarding the explicit optimization of evaluation metrics, such as MAP. The key issue is to approximate r_{mik} and $\mathbb{I}(r_{mjk} \leq r_{mik})$ in Eq. (2) and (3) by smoothed functions with respect to the model parameters, *i.e.*, U, V, and C.

Based on insights in [8], we approximate $\mathbb{I}(r_{mjk} \leq r_{mik})$ by the following logistic function:

$$\mathbb{I}(r_{mjk} \leq r_{mik}) \approx g(f_{mjk} - f_{mik}) = g(\langle U_m, V_j - V_i, C_k \rangle) \tag{4}$$

where $g(x) = 1/(1+e^{-x})$. The basic assumption is that the condition of item j being ranked higher than item i is more likely to be satisfied, if item j has relatively higher relevance score than item i. The authors in [8] also proposed a sophisticated approximation for r_{mik}, which, to the best of our knowledge, has not been deployed in practice. In the case of MAP, we argue it is not necessary to approximate r_{mik}, since only $1/r_{mik}$ is in use. For this reason, we propose to directly approximate $1/r_{mik}$ with another logistic function:

$$\frac{1}{r_{mik}} \approx g(f_{mik}) = g(\langle U_m, V_i, C_k \rangle) \tag{5}$$

Note that the larger the predicted relevance score f_{mik} the closer $g(f_{mik})$ gets to 1, resulting in a low value of r_{mik}. Reversely, the lower f_{mik}, the larger is r_{mik}. Substituting Eq. (4) and (5) into Eq. (3), we obtain a smoothed approximation of MAP:

$$MAP = \frac{1}{MK} \sum_{m=1}^{M} \sum_{k=1}^{K} \frac{1}{\sum_{i=1}^{N} y_{mik}} \sum_{i=1}^{N} y_{mik} g(\langle U_m, V_i, C_k \rangle) \times \sum_{j=1}^{N} y_{mjk} g(\langle U_m, V_j - V_i, C_k \rangle) \tag{6}$$

4.2 Optimization

Since Eq. (6) is smooth with respect to U_m, V_i, and C_k, we can now optimize it using standard methods, such as gradient ascent. In order to avoid overfitting , we add the Frobenius norms of the latent factors for regularization. Hence, the resulting TFMAP objective function is given by:

$$L(U,V,C) = \sum_{m=1}^{M} \sum_{k=1}^{K} \frac{1}{\sum_{i=1}^{N} y_{mik}} \sum_{i=1}^{N} y_{mik} g(\langle U_m, V_i, C_k \rangle) \times \sum_{j=1}^{N} y_{mjk} g(\langle U_m, V_j - V_i, C_k \rangle) - \frac{\lambda}{2}(\|U\|^2 + \|V\|^2 + \|C\|^2) \tag{7}$$

Note that we neglect the constant coefficient in MAP, since it has no influence on the optimization. Given a set of training data Y, a local maxima of Eq. (7) can be obtained by alternatively performing gradient ascent on one of the latent feature vectors at each step, while keeping the other latent vectors fixed. The gradients with respect to U, C, and V are given by Eq. (8~10). Note that for notation convenience, we have performed the following substitutions: $f_{mik} := \langle U_m, V_i, C_k \rangle$, $f_{m(j-i)k} := \langle U_m, V_j - V_i, C_k \rangle$, $\delta := g'(f_{mik}) \sum_{j=1}^{N} y_{mjk} g(f_{m(j-i)k}) - g(f_{mik}) \sum_{j=1}^{N} y_{mjk} g'(f_{m(j-i)k})$.

$$\frac{\partial L}{\partial U_m} = \sum_{k=1}^{K} \frac{1}{\sum_{i=1}^{N} y_{mik}} \sum_{i=1}^{N} y_{mik} \big[\delta(V_i \odot C_k) + g(f_{mik}) \sum_{j=1}^{N} y_{mjk} g'(f_{m(j-i)k})(V_j \odot C_k)\big] - \lambda U_m \tag{8}$$

$$\frac{\partial L}{\partial C_k} = \sum_{m=1}^{M} \frac{1}{\sum_{i=1}^{N} y_{mik}} \sum_{i=1}^{N} y_{mik} \big[\delta(U_m \odot V_i) + g(f_{mik}) \sum_{j=1}^{N} y_{mjk} g'(f_{m(j-i)k})(U_m \odot V_j)\big] - \lambda C_k \tag{9}$$

$$\frac{\partial L}{\partial V_i} = \sum_{m=1}^{M} \sum_{k=1}^{K} \frac{y_{mik}(U_m \odot C_k)}{\sum_{i=1}^{N} y_{mik}} \sum_{j=1}^{N} y_{mjk} \big[g'(f_{mik}) g(f_{m(j-i)k}) + \Big(g(f_{mjk}) - g(f_{mik})\Big) g'(f_{m(j-i)k})\big] - \lambda V_i \tag{10}$$

where $\odot$ denotes element-wise product, and $g'(x)$ denotes the derivative of $g(x)$. Note that since neither U_m or C_k is coupled with other latent feature vectors as in Eq. (6), the derivation of Eq. (8) and (9) is straightforward. However, V_i is coupled with other latent feature vectors in Eq. (6), resulting in a more complicate derivation of Eq. (10). We leave the detailed derivation of Eq. (10) in the Appendix.

In order to understand the practical utility of TFMAP, we analyze the complexity of the learning process for one iteration. Given the data sparseness in the tensor Y and the fact that we usually have $|Y| >> M, K$, the computational complexity of calculating the gradients in Eq. (8) and (9) is $O(D|Y|)$, which is linear to the number of observed user-item interactions in the given tensor. Hence, the computation of the gradients with respect to the latent user features and latent context features is tractable, and able to scale up for large-scale use cases. However, the complexity of Eq. (10) is $O(DN|Y|)$. Considering that we usually have $|Y| >> N$, this complexity is even larger than quadratic in the number of items in the given collection. Thus, the computation of gradients regarding latent item features could be intractable in practice.

In the next section, we propose a novel *fast learning algorithm* to address the computational bottleneck in Eq. (10), reducing its complexity to $O(D|Y|)$.

4.3 Fast Learning

The proposed fast learning algorithm is outlined in Algorithm 1. Note that according to the definition of AP in Eq. (2), it is not necessary to optimize the latent features of all the items in order to maximize AP (as explained below).

The key idea of speeding up the learning process is to optimize, for each fixed pair of user m and context type k, the latent features of only a *set of representative* items, denoted as a buffer B_{mk}.

The gradient of the objective in Eq. (7) with respect to the latent features of item i in B_{mk} can be computed as:

$$\frac{\partial L}{\partial V_i} = \sum_{m=1}^{M} \sum_{k=1}^{K} \frac{y_{mik}(U_m \odot C_k)}{\sum_{i \in B_{mk}} y_{mik}} \sum_{j \in B_{mk}} y_{mjk} \big[g'(f_{mik}) g(f_{m(j-i)k}) + \Big(g(f_{mjk}) - g(f_{mik})\Big) g'(f_{m(j-i)k})\big] - \lambda V_i \tag{11}$$

The computational complexity then depends on the size of the buffer, *i.e.*, the number of items selected for each pair of user-context type. When all items are included in the buffer, Eq. (11) is equal to Eq. (10), while selecting fewer items in the buffer results in lower complexity.

The key issue with this approach is finding the *right* items to include in the buffer, as the quality of the learning process and hence the resulting model directly depends on the items included in the buffer. The buffer needs to be constructed in such a way that it both reduces the computational complexity of the learning algorithm and conserves the necessary information to yield a high quality model.

4.3.1 *Representative Item Selection*

Relevant Items. For each user in a given context, we first include in the buffer all the items that have been observed by the user in that context, *i.e.*, for which we have the user's implicit feedback. These items are the basis for the computation of AP. Note that AP is defined based on the ranks of relevant items. Updating the latent features of relevant items should improve (*i.e.*, reduce) their rankings, thus, resulting in improved AP.

Irrelevant Items. Note that the ranking of irrelevant items influences AP indirectly, since their rankings are relative to the rankings of relevant items. Updating the latent features of irrelevant items will also improve (*i.e.*, raise) their rankings, thus, resulting in overall improved AP.

However, in practice, there are many more irrelevant items than relevant items for a user under a given context. The quantity of irrelevant items thus becomes the computational bottleneck in the learning algorithm of TFMAP.

For this reason, we choose to select only a relatively small number of irrelevant items in the buffer, n_{mk}, for user m and context type k. AP is a top-heavy list-wise ranking measure such that the lower the ranking of an item (the closer it is to the top of the list), the higher its influence in the final score. Top-ranked irrelevant items are the most influential items for AP optimization, yielding the following lemma:

LEMMA 1. *If we try to improve the AP of a ranking list by optimizing (*i.e.*, raising) the ranks of n irrelevant items, then raising the ranks of the top n irrelevant items should yield the largest improvement in AP.*

The proof in the case of $n = 1$ is provided in the Appendix. The proof for the case of $n > 1$ can be obtained in a similar way. Note that we could first sort all the irrelevant items for user m under context k in a descending order, according to the preference scores computed by the current model, *i.e.*, U_m, V and C_k in current iteration, and then select the top-ranked n_{mk} irrelevant items into the buffer.

In this work, we choose the set of irrelevant items in the buffer, n_{mk}, to be equal to the number of observed/relevant items for user m under context k, resulting in a total of $2n_{mk}$ items in the buffer.

We now optimize Eq. (7) for the latent features of the items within the buffer only. The complexity of Eq. (11) over each iteration is $O(2\tilde{n}^2MKD)$, where $\tilde{n}$ denotes the average number of observed items per user and context type. Note that we have $\tilde{n}MK = |Y|$ and $|Y| >> \tilde{n}$. Therefore, the complexity of Eq. (11) is $O(D|Y|)$, which is linear to the number of observed items in the given collection.

4.3.2 *Efficient Buffer Construction*

In order to select the top-ranked irrelevant items in each iteration, we need to make a prediction for each item and sort them according to the current predicted scores. Considering that most recommender systems contain large numbers of items, the computational cost for the prediction and sorting process would be very high. For this reason, we propose to sample a small set of irrelevant items and to select the top-ranked irrelevant items within the sampled set into the buffer.

We can maintain the representativeness of the top-ranked irrelevant items from the sampled set by using a key property

ALGORITHM 1: Fast Learning TFMAP

Input: Training set Y, regularization parameter λ, sampling size n, learning rate γ, and the maximal number of iterations $itermax$.
Output: The learned latent features U, V, and C.
Initialize $U^{(0)}$, $V^{(0)}$, and $C^{(0)}$ with random values, and $t = 0$;
$p_0 = MAP$ based on Y and $U^{(0)}$, $V^{(0)}$, $C^{(0)}$;
repeat
  for $m = 1, 2, \ldots, M$ **do**
    $U_m^{(t+1)} = U_m^{(t)} + \gamma \frac{\partial L}{\partial U_m^{(t)}}$ based on Eq. (8);
  for $k = 1, 2, \ldots, K$ **do**
    $C_k^{(t+1)} = C_k^{(t)} + \gamma \frac{\partial L}{\partial C_k^{(t)}}$ based on Eq. (9);
  for $m = 1, 2, \ldots, M$ **do**
    for $k = 1, 2, \ldots, K$ **do**
      B_{mk} = **BufferConstruct**$(Y_{mk}, U_m^{(t)}, V, C_k^{(t)}, n)$;
      for $i \in B_{mk}$ **do**
        $V_i^{(t+1)} = V_i^{(t)} + \gamma \frac{\partial L}{\partial V_i^{(t)}}$ based on Eq. (11);
  $t = t + 1$;
  $p = MAP$ based on Y and $U^{(t)}$, $V^{(t)}$, $C^{(t)}$;
  if $p - p_0 \leq 0$ **then**
    break ;
  $p_0 = p$;
until $t \geq itermax$;
$U = U^{(t)}$, $V = V^{(t)}$, $C = C^{(t)}$

ALGORITHM 2: BufferConstruct

Input: User m's preference on all the items under context type k, i.e., Y_{mk}, and U_m, V, C_k, and sampling size n.
Output: B_{mk}.
$B_{mk} = \emptyset$;
$B_{mk} = B_{mk} \cup \{i | y_{mik} = 1\}$;
$n_{mk} = cardinality(B_{mk})$;
$p = \min_{i, y_{mik}=1} \langle U_m, V_i, C_k \rangle$;
$S = \{i | y_{mik} = 0\} \cap \{i | \langle U_m, V_i, C_k \rangle > p\}$;
Randomly sample n items from S as Q;
Descendingly sort items in Q, according to $\langle U_m, V_i, C_k \rangle, i \in Q$;
Set top-ranked n_{mk} items in Q as B^-;
$B_{mk} = B_{mk} \cup B^-$;

of AP: *The items below the last relevant item in a ranked list have no contribution to AP.* This property can be easily understood from the definition of AP (see Equation 2).

Therefore, for each user under a given context type, we first find the relevant item with the lowest score. This operation is computationally cheap since the number of relevant items is usually very small. We then sample n_s irrelevant items from those irrelevant items (assuming that most unobserved items are irrelevant) that have higher predicted relevance scores than the minimum predicted relevance score of the relevant items. This sampled set has higher probability to contain the globally top-ranked irrelevant items than a randomly sampled set. Note that the relevance scores are calculated by the model in each iteration. We illustrate the buffer construction for user m under context type k in an single iteration in Fig. 2.

In addition, since the model will become more accurate with each iteration, the minimum predicted score of the relevant items will also increase gradually. In other words, the position of the last relevant item in the ranked list will gradually move to the top of the list. As another by-product, this effect also helps to reduce the buffer construction time

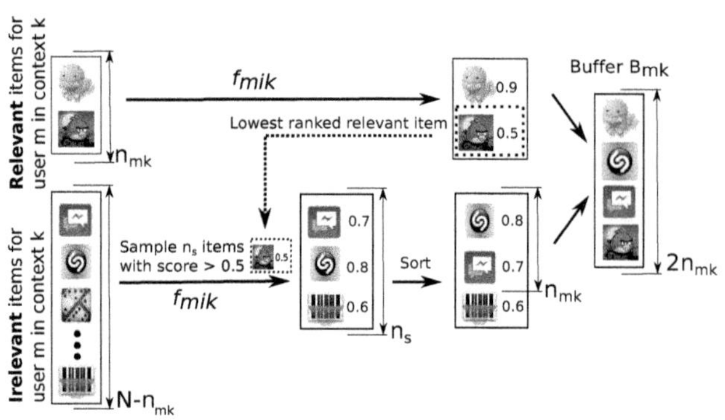

Figure 2: Illustration of buffer construction.

with each iteration. An experimental analysis confirming this property will be presented in Section 5.

Note that the sampling size for the irrelevant items does not only influence the buffer construction time, but also the quality of the learned latent item features. We investigate this tradeoff between buffer size (i.e., computational cost) and performance in Section 5.

4.3.3 Termination Criterion

Since Eq. (6) is an approximation of MAP for the training data Y, we can use MAP (given by Eq. 3) as another termination criterion apart from conventional criteria, such as the number of iterations or the convergence rate. We stop the optimization process when we observe deteriorating values of MAP. Degrading values of MAP on the training data indicates that further optimizing the approximation of MAP as in Eq. (6) may not contribute to raising the true MAP.

5. EXPERIMENTAL EVALUATION

In this section we present a collection of experiments that evaluate the proposed TFMAP. We first give a detailed description of the datasets and setup that are used in the experiments. Then, we investigate the impact of several parameters in the proposed fast learning algorithm that are critical for TFMAP, as mentioned in Section 4.3. Finally, we evaluate the recommendation performance of TFMAP, compared to several baselines, and analyze its scalability.

The experiments were designed to address the following research questions: 1) Does the proposed fast learning algorithm benefit TFMAP in achieving MAP maximization? 2) Does TFMAP outperform state-of-the-art context-aware and context-free approaches? 3) Is TFMAP scalable for large-scale context-aware recommendation?

5.1 Experimental Setup

5.1.1 Dataset

The main dataset we use in this paper is from the *Appazaar* project[2] [6]. *Appazaar* recommends mobile applications to users from the Android Market. The application usage data is recorded in the form of implicit feedback since *Appazaar* logs which apps are run by each user. In addition, *Appazaar* also tracks available contextual information from the phone sensors, such as motion sensor and GPS. We use two contextual factors in the experiments, i.e., motion (unavailable, slow, fast) and location (workplace, home, elsewhere). Note that both of the contextual factors were inferred from a GPS trace. Hence, the context variable has 9 possible types that take into account all the combinations of the two contextual factors, *i.e.*, $K = 9$ for C in Eq. (1). For example, context type "1" denotes that implicit feedback about a user running an application was observed when the user was at work and his/her motion status was unavailable. Finally, we represent one observation in the dataset as a triplet $(UserID, ItemID, ContextTypeID)$. The dataset contains 300469 triplets, 1767 users, 7701 items, 9 combinations of contextual features. On average, there are 18.9 app usage events per user and context type. A more detailed description of the dataset and its collection procedure can be found in [6].

Note that conventional CF benchmark datasets, *e.g.*, Netflix dataset, are not enriched with contextual information. Although the *Appazaar* dataset is not as large as these benchmark datasets, it is still much larger than datasets that have been used in previous context-aware recommendation work [14, 25]. Moreover, the datasets previously used in the CAR literature are all based on explicit ratings rather than implicit feedback, thus, not ideal for our study.

5.1.2 Experimental Protocol

We separate the dataset into a training set and a test set, according to the timestamps. The training set consists of the first 80% implicit feedback data, while the test set contains the remaining 20% data. The target is to use the training set to learn a recommendation model, *i.e.*, U, V and C, which is then used to generate recommendation lists for each user under each type of context.

We use the MAP measure as in Eq. (3) to evaluate on the testset $\tilde{Y}$. Note that in order to have fair comparison with context-free approaches, we only preserve one context type for each user in the test set, *i.e.*, we randomly select one context type for each user in the test set and preserve the user's feedback within the selected context type, while excluding all the user's feedback data under other context types. To further clarify this design choice, we give a negative example in which a user in the test set has implicit feedback on the items under two different types of context. In this case, the MAP of context-aware approaches, such as TFMAP, should be measured according to AP under the two different types of context, while context-free approaches would only calculate AP based on the items and ignore the context. For this reason, our choice is necessary in order to attain fair comparative results to other context-free approaches.

In addition, note that since we only have implicit feedback from users, we cannot treat all the items that have no feedback in the test set as irrelevant/negative ones, in which case the recommendation performance could be severely underestimated. For this reason, we adopt a conventional widely-used evaluation strategy [9, 17], in which we randomly select 1000 items that have no feedback as irrelevant ones for each user in the test set. The performance is measured according to the recommendation list that only contains these 1000 items together with relevant items, *i.e.*, the items for which there is implicit feedback for that user.

In order to carry out our validation experiments, we randomly select 10% of all the implicit feedback data available in the training set. In our validation experiments we investigate the impact of the parameters and the fast learning algorithm in TFMAP.

Finally, note that we empirically tune the following conventional parameters so they yield the best performance in the validation test: regularization parameter λ=0.001, latent dimensionality D=10, and learning rate γ=0.001.

[2]http://appazaar.net/

5.1.3 Setup for Comparison to FM

As mentioned in Section 2, the state-of-the-art context-aware approaches, such as FMs [25], are designed to tackle the rating prediction problem (explicit feedback), and hence they are difficult, if not impossible, to apply to implicit feedback data. For this reason, we use another dataset, *Food* dataset [22], which has also been used in the work on FMs [25]. This dataset contains ca. 6K 5-scale ratings from 212 users on 20 menus/items, and each rating is associated with 2 contextual factors, *i.e.* one factor about whether the user's feeling about hunger is real or virtual (2 values: real, virtual) when she rated a menu, and the other factor about the user's hunger degree (3 values: normal, hungry and full). By taking into account all the combinations of the two contextual factors, we obtain 6 types of context in the Food dataset.

In our experiments, we randomly select 80% of the ratings as the training set and the remaining ratings as the test set. Items with a rating higher than 3 in the test set are considered to be relevant. Note that a different rating threshold could be set to define the relevant items. Under this setting, we use FM approach to first predict the ratings of the users on the items under each context type, and then generate the recommendation list according to the predicted ratings. For TFMAP, we train the model by converting the training set to an *implicit feedback* dataset, in which each rated item is regarded as an indicator of implicit feedback (*i.e.*, the user tried the food item).

5.2 Validation: Impact of Fast Learning

We investigate the properties of the fast learning algorithm in TFMAP, presented in Section 4.3. The experimental results reported in this subsection are measured on the validation set previously described.

5.2.1 Impact of Sampling Size

By varying the sampling size in the fast learning algorithm of TFMAP, we investigate the buffer construction time and the performance variation in terms of MAP in the validation set, *i.e.*, an issue discussed in Section 4.3.2. We measure the buffer construction time cumulatively across all the users under all the context types in the training set over one iteration. The result is shown in Fig. 3.

Note that the buffer construction time increases almost linearly as the sampling size increases. Hence, with a relatively small sampling size, we could significantly reduce the buffer construction time compared to the case where all the irrelevant items for each user under a given context need to be ranked. For example, in the *Appazaar* dataset we have over 7000 items, which means that a sampling size of 200 could save over 50% of the buffer construction time, as illustrated in Fig. 3. Also note that the recommendation performance in terms of MAP increases sharply as the sampling size increases up to 200, and then saturates. Therefore, even with a relatively small size of irrelevant items, *e.g.*, 200, (compared to all the irrelevant items), the top-ranked irrelevant items within the sampled set are sufficiently representative to be used for MAP optimization.

In sum, these results empirically verify the selection of a small set of irrelevant items to create the buffer in the fast learning algorithm of TFMAP and justify our algorithm design choices. For the remaining experiments we will keep a sampling size of 200.

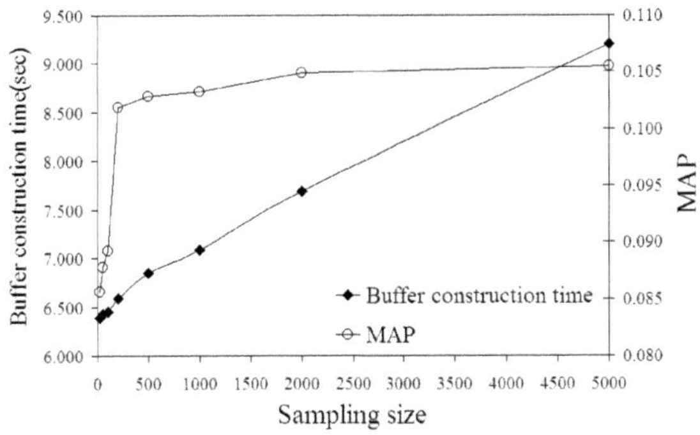

Figure 3: The impact of sampling size on buffer construction time and MAP of TFMAP.

5.2.2 Impact of Representative Irrelevant Items

Here we aim to understand the the effectiveness of choosing the representative irrelevant items in the buffer. Rather than selecting representative irrelevant items to construct the buffer, an alternative is to use randomly selected irrelevant items. To test the random procedure we abandoned the ordering step of the algorithm and instead we randomly selected n_{mk} irrelevant items from the sampled set of size 200. In this case the accuracy yields a MAP of 0.083, dropping by 18.6% compared to the case where top-ranked irrelevant items are selected, i.e., MAP of 0.102 as shown in Fig. 3. Increasing the sampling size further emphasizes the benefit of carefully selecting the representative items. When we choose to sample 5000 irrelevant items, the benefit over the random strategy is 21.7%. This experiment validates the benefit of using representative irrelevant items in the buffer, as discussed in Section 4.3.1.

5.2.3 Effect of the Lowest-ranked Relevant Item

As discussed in Section 4.3.2, it is not necessary to sample from all the irrelevant items in order to construct the buffer for a user in a given context, since the items ranked below the lowest-ranked relevant item have no influence on AP. Thus, the sampling process could be more efficient by neglecting the items ranked below the lowest-ranked relevant item.

Here, we present an experimental study that examines the change of the position of the lowest-ranked relevant item, *i.e.*, the maximal rank of relevant items in a recommendation list, during iterations, and also the change in the corresponding buffer construction time, as shown in Fig. 4. Note that this experiment is conducted on the validation set, with sampling size of 200 in TFMAP, and the results shown in Fig. 4 are the average values across all the users under all context types in each iteration.

We observe that the maximal rank of relevant items decreases with each iteration as the model is gradually optimized, *i.e.*, the model is more likely to rank relevant items higher in the list along iterations. This observation provides empirical evidence that exploiting the lowest-ranked relevant item in the sampling process does contribute to improving the quality of the representative irrelevant items, and also the efficiency of the buffer construction with each iteration. For example, the buffer construction time reduces by over 10% in the second iteration, compared to the first iteration.

5.2.4 Effectiveness of the Termination Criterion

Our final validation experiment investigates the effectiveness of the proposed termination criterion for the fast learning algorithm, as discussed in Section 4.3.3. We show the MAP measured in both the training (excluding the valida-

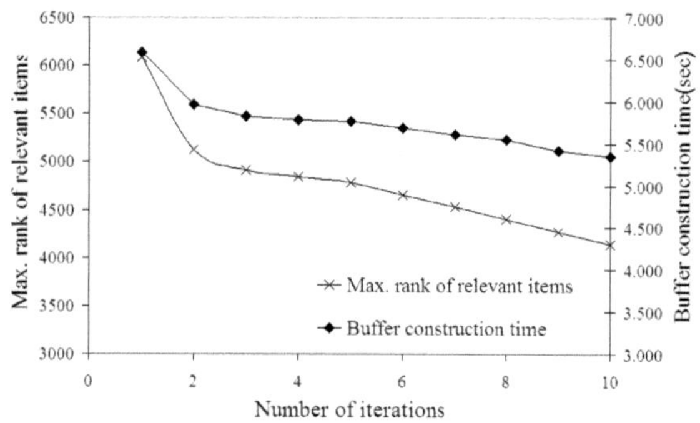

Figure 4: The average maximal rank of relevant items and the buffer construction time along iterations.

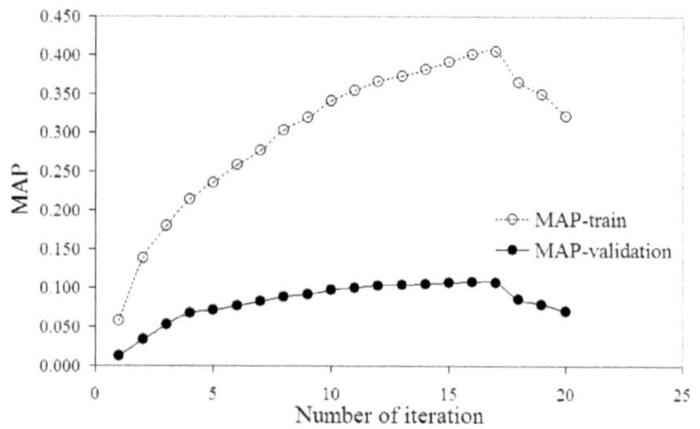

Figure 5: The MAP of the training set and the validation set in the learning process

tion set) and the validation sets across the iterations, as in Fig. 5. Both MAP measures gradually improve towards an optimal value with only a few iterations (less than 20), indicating that TFMAP effectively learns latent features for users, items and context types for MAP optimization. Also note that both MAP measures start dropping consistently after a few iterations, indicating that it is effective to use the MAP measured in the training set as a termination criterion for the learning process to avoid model overfitting.

From all the findings described in this section, we can give a positive answer to our first research question.

5.3 Performance Comparison

We now compare the performance of TFMAP with that of 5 baseline algorithms, according to the recommendation performance measured on the test set. The baseline approaches involved in this comparative experiment are listed below:

- **Pop**. A naive baseline that recommends items in terms of their popularity (*i.e.*, the number of observations from all the users) under the given context.
- **iMF**. A state-of-the-art CF approach proposed by Hu et al [13] for implicit feedback data.
- **BPR-MF**. Bayesian personalized ranking (BPR) represents another state-of-the-art optimization framework of CF for implicit feedback data [24]. BPR-MF represents the choice of using matrix factorization (MF) as the learning model with BPR optimization criterion. Note that the implementation of this baseline is done with the publicly available software MyMediaLite [11]. Although various learning models are available to be used with BPR, we find BPR-MF gives the best performance.
- **TFMAP-noC**. A variant of the proposed TFMAP, in which contextual information,*i.e.*, C, is not involved in the learning algorithm. Note that iMF, BPR-MF and TFMAP-noC are context-free methods, *i.e.*, the contextual information has no influence on the recommendations to individual users.
- **FM**. Factorization machine (FM) is a state-of-the-art context-aware approach [25]. As mentioned in Section 5.1.3, the comparison between FM and TFMAP is conducted on the *Food* dataset, due to the applicability of FM. Note that the implementation of FM is done with the publicly available software libFM[3].

Table 1: Performance comparison of TFMAP and context-free baselines on Appazaar dataset

	MAP	P@1	P@5	P@10
Pop	0.090	0.312	0.292	0.227
iMF	0.577	0.698	0.642	0.583
BPR-MF	0.612	0.800	0.712	0.602
TFMAP-noC	0.629	0.834	0.720	0.602
TFMAP	**0.659**	**0.879**	**0.732**	**0.611**

Table 2: Performance comparison of TFMAP and FM on Food dataset

	MAP	P@1	P@5	P@10
FM	0.152	0.036	0.050	0.055
TFMAP	**0.219**	**0.089**	**0.075**	**0.059**

Based on the Appazaar dataset, the recommendation performance of TFMAP and all the baselines except FM is shown in Table 1, from which we obtain three observations.

First, the context-free version of the proposed TFMAP, *i.e.*, TFMAP-noC significantly outperforms the other baselines in terms of MAP. Note that in our experiments, statistical significance is measured based on AP and precision values of all the users in the test set, according to Wilcoxon signed rank significance test with p<0.01. This result indicates that in the case that contextual information is unavailable, directly optimizing MAP as proposed in TFMAP could still lead to substantial improvement over state-of-the-art context-free approaches, such as iMF and BPR-MF.

Second, we can see that both BPR-MF and TFMAP-noC attain dramatic improvement in MAP over the other two baselines, Pop and iMF. As mentioned in Section 2, BPR is designed to optimize the evaluation metric AUC. The superior performance of BPR-MF and TFMAP-noC suggests that directly optimizing an evaluation metric that measures the recommendation performance in implicit feedback systems would yield significant improvements in the recommendation performance. In addition, note that TFMAP-noC achieves a significant improvement in MAP of 3% over BPR-MF, and 4% improvement of P@1. This result indicates that optimizing MAP is a better choice for recommender systems than optimizing AUC, since the top-heavy bias in MAP is a critical factor that provides substantial benefit for the recommendation performance.

Third, as can be seen, TFMAP achieves an additional significant improvement over TFMAP-noC, *e.g.*, 5% in MAP and P@1. This result indicates that TFMAP succeeds in utilizing contextual information together with user-item implicit feedback for maximizing MAP. In addition, the exploitation of context could greatly improve implicit feedback recommenders; a similar conclusion was reached by previous work on CAR with explicit feedback [25, 14].

As mentioned before, we compare TFMAP with FM using the Food dataset, according to the protocol described in Section 5.1.3. The results are shown in Table 2. As can be observed, TFMAP significantly improves over FM to a large

[3]http://www.libfm.org/

extent, i.e., by more than 40% in MAP, 100% in P@1 and 50% in P@5 and 8% in P@10, showing a great competitiveness for top-N context-aware recommendation. From all the experimental results presented in this section, we confirm a positive answer to our second research question.

5.4 Scalability

The last experiment investigates the scalability of TFMAP by measuring the model training time against the amount of data used for training the model. We use from 10% to 100% of the training data (the observed implicit feedback data in the training set) for learning the latent features, and the corresponding training times are shown in Fig. 6. Note that we have normalized the training time by the time that is required for training the model with all the data in the training set. It can be observed that the training time increases almost linearly with the amount of the training data, empirically verifying the property of linear computational complexity. This finding also allows us to answer our last research question positively.

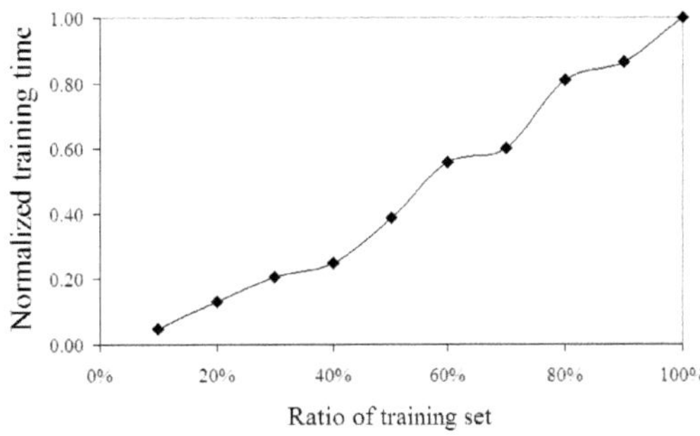

Figure 6: Scalability analysis of TFMAP

6. CONCLUSIONS AND FUTURE WORK

We have presented TFMAP, a novel top-N context-aware recommendation approach for implicit feedback domains. This approach utilizes tensor factorization to model each user's preference for each item under each type of context, and the factorization model is learned by directly optimizing MAP. We also propose a fast learning algorithm that exploits several properties of AP to keep the complexity of TFMAP linear to the number of implicit feedback data in a given collection, thus, making TFMAP scalable. Our experimental results verify the effectiveness of the proposed fast learning algorithm for TFMAP, and demonstrate that TFMAP could outperform several state-of-the-art context-aware and context-free recommendation approaches.

Taking insights from recent statistical analysis on evaluation measures [33], one line of our future work is to investigate the potential of optimizing other measures for context-aware recommendation, since different measures may represent different aspects of the recommendation quality. Another interesting topic of future work is to integrate contextual information together with metadata of users and items, as discussed in Section 2, to further advance the state-of-the-art in recommender systems.

7. ACKNOWLEDGEMENTS

We are very grateful to Matthias Böhmer for making the Appazzar data available. This work is funded as part of a Marie Curie Intra European Fellowship for Career Development (IEF) awards held by Alexandros Karatzoglou (CARS, PIEF- GA-2010-273739).

8. REFERENCES

[1] G. Adomavicius, R. Sankaranarayanan, S. Sen, and A. Tuzhilin. Incorporating contextual information in recommender systems using a multidimensional approach. *ACM Trans. Inf. Syst.*, 23:103–145, January 2005.

[2] D. Agarwal and B.-C. Chen. Regression-based latent factor models. KDD '09, pages 19–28, 2009.

[3] D. Agarwal, B.-C. Chen, and B. Long. Localized factor models for multi-context recommendation. KDD '11, pages 609–617, 2011.

[4] L. Baltrunas and F. Ricci. Context-based splitting of item ratings in collaborative filtering. RecSys '09, pages 245–248, 2009.

[5] J. Basilico and T. Hofmann. Unifying collaborative and content-based filtering. ICML '04, pages 65–72, 2004.

[6] M. Böhmer, B. Hecht, J. Schöning, A. Krüger, and G. Bauer. Falling asleep with angry birds, facebook and kindle - a large scale study on mobile application usage. In *Proc. of Mobile HCI '11*, 2011.

[7] C. J. C. Burges, R. Ragno, and Q. V. Le. Learning to Rank with Nonsmooth Cost Functions. NIPS '06, pages 193–200, 2006.

[8] O. Chapelle and M. Wu. Gradient descent optimization of smoothed information retrieval metrics. *Inf. Retr.*, 13:216–235, June 2010.

[9] P. Cremonesi, Y. Koren, and R. Turrin. Performance of recommender algorithms on top-n recommendation tasks. RecSys '10, pages 39–46, 2010.

[10] J. Davis and M. Goadrich. The relationship between precision-recall and roc curves. ICML '06, pages 233–240, 2006.

[11] Z. Gantner, S. Rendle, C. Freudenthaler, and L. Schmidt-Thieme. MyMediaLite: a free recommender system library. RecSys '11, pages 305–308, 2011.

[12] T. Hofmann. Latent semantic models for collaborative filtering. *ACM Trans. Inf. Syst.*, 22:89–115, January 2004.

[13] Y. Hu, Y. Koren, and C. Volinsky. Collaborative filtering for implicit feedback datasets. ICDM '08, pages 263–272, 2008.

[14] A. Karatzoglou, X. Amatriain, L. Baltrunas, and N. Oliver. Multiverse recommendation: n-dimensional tensor factorization for context-aware collaborative filtering. RecSys '10, pages 79–86, 2010.

[15] T. G. Kolda and B. W. Bader. Tensor decompositions and applications. *SIAM Rev.*, 51:455–500, August 2009.

[16] I. Konstas, V. Stathopoulos, and J. M. Jose. On social networks and collaborative recommendation. SIGIR '09, pages 195–202, 2009.

[17] Y. Koren. Factorization meets the neighborhood: a multifaceted collaborative filtering model. KDD '08, pages 426–434, 2008.

[18] Y. Koren, R. Bell, and C. Volinsky. Matrix factorization techniques for recommender systems. *Computer*, 42:30–37, August 2009.

[19] N. N. Liu and Q. Yang. Eigenrank: a ranking-oriented approach to collaborative filtering. SIGIR '08, pages 83–90, 2008.

[20] T.-Y. Liu. Learning to rank for information retrieval. *Foundations and Trends in Information Retrieval*, 3(3):225–331, 2009.

[21] C. D. Manning, P. Raghavan, and H. Schütze. *Introduction to information retrieval*. Cambridge Univ. Press, Cambridge [u.a.], 1. publ. edition, 2008.

[22] C. Ono, Y. Takishima, Y. Motomura, and H. Asoh. Context-aware preference model based on a study of difference between real and supposed situation data. UMAP '09, pages 102–113, 2009.

[23] R. Pan and M. Scholz. Mind the gaps: weighting the unknown in large-scale one-class collaborative filtering. KDD '09, pages 667–676, 2009.

[24] S. Rendle, C. Freudenthaler, Z. Gantner, and S.-T. Lars. Bpr: Bayesian personalized ranking from implicit feedback. UAI '09, pages 452–461, 2009.

[25] S. Rendle, Z. Gantner, C. Freudenthaler, and L. Schmidt-Thieme. Fast context-aware recommendations with factorization machines. SIGIR '11, pages 635–644, 2011.

[26] R. Salakhutdinov and A. Mnih. Probabilistic matrix factorization. volume 20 of *NIPS '08*, 2008.

[27] G. Shani and A. Gunawardana. Evaluating recommendation systems. In F. Ricci, L. Rokach, and B. Shapira, editors, *Recommender Systems Handbook*, pages 257–298. 2010.

[28] L. Si and R. Jin. Flexible mixture model for collaborative filtering. ICML '03, pages 704–711, 2003.

[29] V. Sindhwani, S. S. Bucak, J. Hu, and A. Mojsilovic. One-class matrix completion with low-density factorizations. ICDM '10, pages 1055–1060, 2010.
[30] A. P. Singh and G. J. Gordon. Relational learning via collective matrix factorization. KDD '08, pages 650–658, 2008.
[31] M. Taylor, J. Guiver, S. Robertson, and T. Minka. Softrank: optimizing non-smooth rank metrics. WSDM '08, pages 77–86, 2008.
[32] I. Tsochantaridis, T. Joachims, T. Hofmann, and Y. Altun. Large margin methods for structured and interdependent output variables. *J. Mach. Learn. Res.*, 6:1453–1484, 2005.
[33] J. Wang and J. Zhu. On statistical analysis and optimization of information retrieval effectiveness metrics. SIGIR '10, pages 226–233, 2010.
[34] M. Weimer, A. Karatzoglou, Q. Le, and A. Smola. Cofirank - maximum margin matrix factorization for collaborative ranking. NIPS '07, pages 1593–1600, 2007.
[35] L. Xiong, X. Chen, T.-K. Huang, J. Schneider, and J. G. Carbonell. Temporal collaborative filtering with bayesian probabilistic tensor factorization. In *SDM'10*, pages 211–222, 2010.
[36] J. Xu and H. Li. Adarank: a boosting algorithm for information retrieval. SIGIR '07, pages 391–398, 2007.
[37] J. Xu, T.-Y. Liu, M. Lu, H. Li, and W.-Y. Ma. Directly optimizing evaluation measures in learning to rank. SIGIR '08, pages 107–114, 2008.
[38] S.-H. Yang, B. Long, A. J. Smola, H. Zha, and Z. Zheng. Collaborative competitive filtering: learning recommender using context of user choice. SIGIR '11, pages 295–304, 2011.
[39] Y. Yue, T. Finley, F. Radlinski, and T. Joachims. A support vector method for optimizing average precision. SIGIR '07, pages 271–278, 2007.

APPENDIX

A. DERIVATION OF EQ. (10)

Note that in the following derivation, we leave out the derivative of the regularization term, i.e., $-\lambda V_i$, due to the space limit.

$$\frac{\partial L}{\partial V_i} = \sum_{m=1}^{M}\sum_{k=1}^{K}\frac{y_{mik}(U_m \odot C_k)}{\sum_{i=1}^{N} y_{mik}}\Big(g'(f_{mik})\sum_{j=1}^{N} y_{mjk}g(f_{m(j-i)k}) - g(f_{mik})\sum_{\substack{j=1\\ j\neq i}}^{N} y_{mjk}g'(f_{m(j-i)k}) + \sum_{\substack{p=1\\ p\neq i}}^{N} y_{mpk}g(f_{mpk})g'(f_{m(i-p)k})\Big)$$

Since we have $g'(-x) = g'(x)$, we obtain:

$$\frac{\partial L}{\partial V_i} = \sum_{m=1}^{M}\sum_{k=1}^{K}\frac{y_{mik}(U_m \odot C_k)}{\sum_{i=1}^{N} y_{mik}}\Big(g'(f_{mik})\sum_{j=1}^{N} y_{mjk}g(f_{m(j-i)k}) + \sum_{\substack{p=1\\ p\neq i}}^{N} y_{mpk}g(f_{mpk})g'(f_{m(p-i)k}) - g(f_{mik})\sum_{\substack{j=1\\ j\neq i}}^{N} y_{mjk}g'(f_{m(j-i)k})\Big)$$

By replacing index "p" by "j", we obtain:

$$\frac{\partial L}{\partial V_i} = \sum_{m=1}^{M}\sum_{k=1}^{K}\frac{y_{mik}(U_m \odot C_k)}{\sum_{i=1}^{N} y_{mik}}\Big(g'(f_{mik})\sum_{j=1}^{N} y_{mjk}g(f_{m(j-i)k}) + \sum_{\substack{j=1\\ j\neq i}}^{N} y_{mjk}\big(g(f_{mjk})g'(f_{m(j-i)k}) - g(f_{mik})g'(f_{m(j-i)k})\big)\Big)$$

Since the term in the last summation is 0 when $j = i$, we obtain:

$$\frac{\partial L}{\partial V_i} = \sum_{m=1}^{M}\sum_{k=1}^{K}\frac{y_{mik}(U_m \odot C_k)}{\sum_{i=1}^{N} y_{mik}}\Big(g'(f_{mik})\sum_{j=1}^{N} y_{mjk}g(f_{m(j-i)k}) + \sum_{j=1}^{N} y_{mjk}\big(g(f_{mjk})g'(f_{m(j-i)k}) - g(f_{mik})g'(f_{m(j-i)k})\big)\Big)$$

$$= \sum_{m=1}^{M}\sum_{k=1}^{K}\frac{y_{mik}(U_m \odot C_k)}{\sum_{i=1}^{N} y_{mik}}\sum_{j=1}^{N} y_{mjk}\Big(g'(f_{mik})g(f_{m(j-i)k}) + \big(g(f_{mjk}) - g(f_{mik})\big)g'(f_{m(j-i)k})\Big)$$

B. PROOF OF LEMMA 1

For the case of $n = 1$, consider that $r = [r_1, r_2, \ldots, r_N]$ denotes the current ranks of all N items in a ranked list and r' denotes their ranks after some optimization. We can optimize the latent features of a single irrelevant item a using a very small step size until its rank would increase from $r_a = q$ to $r'_a = q + 1$. Consequently, the rank of item b that was ranked $q + 1$ would now be ranked q, i.e., $r_b = q + 1$ and $r'_b = q$. Now the Lemma can be proved by proving that $\Delta AP = AP_{r'} - AP_r$ is a non-increasing function of q. It follows that the largest improvement ΔAP can be achieved by raising the rank of the irrelevant item with the lowest rank. Note that this proof is not related to a user or a context, so we simplify the notations. The ΔAP can be expressed as:

$$\Delta AP = \frac{1}{N_R}\sum_{i=1}^{N}\frac{y_i}{r'_i}\sum_{j=1}^{N} y_j \mathbb{I}(r'_j \le r'_i) - \frac{1}{N_R}\sum_{i=1}^{N}\frac{y_i}{r_i}\sum_{j=1}^{N} y_j \mathbb{I}(r_j \le r_i)$$

where N_R denotes the number of relevant items. Since we have the condition: $r_i = r'_i$, if $i \neq a, b$, we can obtain

$$\Delta AP = \frac{1}{N_R}\Big(\frac{y_a}{r'_a}\sum_{j=1}^{N} y_j \mathbb{I}(r'_j \le r'_a) + \frac{y_b}{r'_b}\sum_{j=1}^{N} y_j \mathbb{I}(r'_j \le r'_b) - \frac{y_a}{r_a}\sum_{j=1}^{N} y_j \mathbb{I}(r_j \le r_a) - \frac{y_b}{r_b}\sum_{j=1}^{N} y_j \mathbb{I}(r_j \le r_b)\Big)$$

Since we also have $y_a = 0$ as known, we further obtain:

$$\Delta AP = \frac{1}{N_R}\Big(\frac{y_b}{r'_b}\sum_{j=1}^{N} y_j \mathbb{I}(r'_j \le r'_b) - \frac{y_b}{r_b}\sum_{j=1}^{N} y_j \mathbb{I}(r_j \le r_b)\Big)$$

Substituting $r_b = q + 1$ and $r'_b = q$, we have:

$$\Delta AP = \frac{1}{N_R} y_b \sum_{j=1}^{N} y_j\Big(\frac{1}{q}\mathbb{I}(r'_j \le q) - \frac{1}{q+1}\mathbb{I}(r_j \le q+1)\Big)$$

Again, when $j \neq a, b$, we have $r_j = r'_j$, and:

$$\mathbb{I}(r'_j \le q) = \mathbb{I}(r_j \le q+1) = 1, \quad if \quad r'_j \le q$$
$$\mathbb{I}(r'_j \le q) = \mathbb{I}(r_j \le q+1) = 0, \quad if \quad r'_j > q+1$$

Accordingly, we obtain:

$$\sum_{j=1, j\neq a,b}^{N} y_j\Big(\frac{1}{q}\mathbb{I}(r'_j \le q) - \frac{1}{q+1}\mathbb{I}(r_j \le q+1)\Big) = N_q\Big(\frac{1}{q} - \frac{1}{q+1}\Big)$$

where N_q denotes the number of relevant items within top-q items. Finally, we obtain:

$$\begin{aligned}\Delta AP = \frac{1}{N_R} y_b \Big(&\sum_{j=1, j\neq a,b}^{N} y_j\big(\frac{1}{q}\mathbb{I}(r'_j \le q) - \frac{1}{q+1}\mathbb{I}(r_j \le q+1)\big)\\ &+ y_a\big(\frac{1}{q}\mathbb{I}(r'_a \le q) - \frac{1}{q+1}\mathbb{I}(r_a \le q+1)\big)\\ &+ y_b\big(\frac{1}{q}\mathbb{I}(r'_b \le q) - \frac{1}{q+1}\mathbb{I}(r_b \le q+1)\big)\Big)\\ = \frac{1}{N_R} y_b \Big(&N_q\big(\frac{1}{q} - \frac{1}{q+1}\big) + y_b\big(\frac{1}{q} - \frac{1}{q+1}\big)\Big)\\ = \frac{1}{N_R}&\frac{N_q y_b + y_b^2}{q(q+1)}\end{aligned}$$

Note that $N_q \le q$ and $y_b \in \{0, 1\}$. We complete the proof with ΔAP is a non-increasing function of q. A similar proof can be deduced for the case of $n > 1$.

Increasing Temporal Diversity with Purchase Intervals

Gang Zhao, Mong Li Lee, Wynne Hsu and Wei Chen
School of Computing, National University of Singapore
13 Computing Drive, NUS, Republic of Singapore, 117417
{zhaogang,leeml,whsu,weichen}@comp.nus.edu.sg

ABSTRACT

The development of Web 2.0 technology has led to huge economic benefits and challenges for both e-commerce websites and online shoppers. One core technology to increase sales and consumers' satisfaction is the use of recommender systems. Existing product recommender systems consider the order of items purchased by users to obtain a list of recommended items. However, they do not consider the time interval between the products purchased. For example, there is often an interval of 2-3 months between the purchase of printer ink cartridges or refills. Thus, recommending appropriate ink cartridges one week before the user needs to replace the depleted ink cartridges would increase the likelihood of a purchase decision. In this paper, we propose to utilize the purchase interval information to improve the performance of the recommender systems for e-commerce. We design an efficient algorithm to compute the purchase intervals between product pairs from users' purchase history and integrate this information into the marginal utility model. We evaluate our approach on a real world e-commerce dataset. Experimental results demonstrate that our approach significantly improves the conversion rate and temporal diversity compared to state-of-the-art algorithms.

Categories and Subject Descriptors

H.3.3 [**Information Storage and Retrieval**]: [Information Search and Retrieval]

General Terms

Algorithms, Experimentation, Measurement, Performance

Keywords

Recommender System, E-commerce, Personalization, Temporal Diversity, Utility Theory, Purchase Intervals

Permission to make digital or hard copies of all or part of this work for personal or classroom use is granted without fee provided that copies are not made or distributed for profit or commercial advantage and that copies bear this notice and the full citation on the first page. To copy otherwise, to republish, to post on servers or to redistribute to lists, requires prior specific permission and/or a fee.
SIGIR'12, August 12–16, 2012, Portland, Oregon, USA.
Copyright 2012 ACM 978-1-4503-1472-5/12/08 ...$10.00.

1. INTRODUCTION

Advances in Web 2.0 technology has resulted in huge economic benefits and challenges for e-commerce websites . A report in [7] reveals that the sales volume of B2C (business-to-Consumer) in China market is about 47 billion RMB yuan (7.5 billion US dollar) in 2011, and is expected to reach 650 billion RMB yuan (103 billion US dollar) in 2013. E-service providers are keen to invest in technologies that help users make purchase decisions and increase the satisfaction of users' online shopping experiences.

One core technology in e-commerce is the use of recommender systems to produce a list of recommendations that users may be interested to buy. Research in recommender systems build models to characterize items (content-based filtering [19]) or users (collaborative filtering [4, 17, 12]) or both (hybrid recommender systems [13, 15]) so as to predict the rating or preference that a user would give to an item. Items with the highest predicted ratings are then recommended to the user. These models assume that the value of an item for a user does not change over time.

The works in [9, 16, 22] examine the temporal dynamics in recommendation systems. [16] consider the order of the items purchased and apply the Markov Chain theory to predict the next item that a user will purchase. [9, 22] design models to capture changes in user preferences for products over time due to external events such as new product offerings, seasonal changes or festive holidays (short-term bias) as well as long term interest. Note that these works have low temporal diversity [10] since they will repeatedly recommend the same top-k items to a user if s/he does not make purchases often.

Figure 1 shows the purchase histories of 5 users for products a, b, c, d, e. We use H_i to denote the purchase history of user u_i. Suppose we want to recommend some products to user u_5 at time point 24. Since u_5 has previously bought products a and c, the algorithms in [16, 22] would recommend product d to u_5. This is because based on the purchase order and short-term bias, both users u_1 and u_3 buy d after purchasing c. From the long term interest of users [22], we see that users who purchase product c always purchase d. Further, suppose u_5 does not buy d at time point 24. When s/he logs into the system at time points 19 and 21, the algorithms in [16, 22] will still recommend d to u_5.

In this work, we advocate that the intervals between user purchases may influence a user's purchase decision. A quick survey reveals that users who purchase an iphone usually purchase apps one week later, after they have setup the new phone and become familiar with its use. Thus recommend-

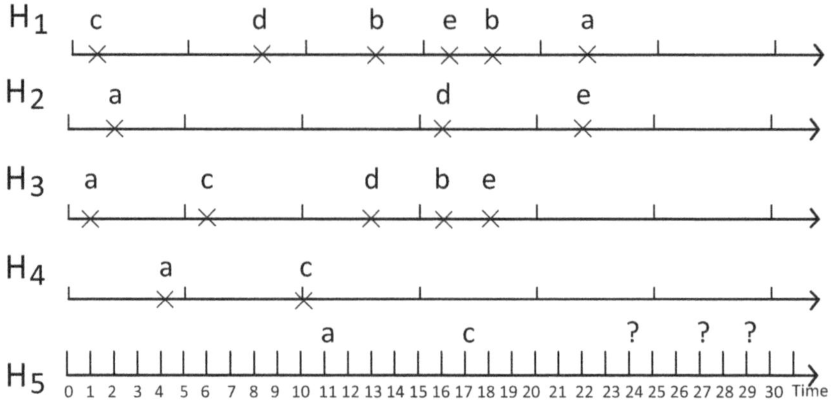

Figure 1: Example of Users' Purchase History

ing apps to a new iphone user a day after is not likely to increase sales, whereas pushing apps 5-6 days later is probably more effective.

Consider again our example in Figure 1. For illustrative purposes, let us assume that the interval between each time point is a day. We observe that user u_2 buys product d 14 days after s/he has bought a, while user u_3 buys d 12 days after s/he has bought a. We could conclude that, on average, users are likely to purchase d 13 days after s/he has purchased a. Assuming that all the users u_1 to u_5 are similar, we can summarize the average purchase interval between product pairs from their purchase histories as shown in Table 1. Based on Table 1, if u_5 logs into the system at time point 24, then we will recommend product d since s/he has bought a 13 days ago. However, if s/he logs into the system at time point 27, then we will recommend product b to him/her because we see that users who bought c tend to buy b 11 days later. Similarly, our approach will recommend e to u_5 if s/he logs into the system at time point 29.

Theories in economics and consumer behavior postulate that the value of certain products may change over time, especially if the user has recently purchased them. This is known as the Law of Diminishing Marginal Utility [1]. For example, a user is less likely to buy a second computer or mobile phone if s/he has recently bought one. In contrast, products such as milk, bread and eggs are likely to be purchased over and over again. Thus the value or marginal utility of a product for a user depends on his/her purchase history. Recent works have applied these theories to recommender systems [11, 21]. The authors in [21] incorporate marginal utility into product recommender systems. They adapt the widely used Cobb-Douglas utility function [3] to model product-specific diminishing marginal return and user-specific basic utility to personalize recommendation.

Here, we propose a framework that incorporates purchase intervals for product recommendation. The model in our framework will combine purchase interval information in users' purchase histories with marginal utility. This enables us to increase the temporal diversity of the recommended items which is an important facet of product recommender systems [10]. Given the scale of users, products and purchase history in any e-commerce website, we design an algorithm to efficiently compute the purchase interval between pairs of product for all users. We evaluate our method on a real world data set obtained from an e-commerce B2C website Jingdong in China. The experimental results show that our approach improves the conversion rate, precision and recall of the state-of-the-art utility-based recommendation algorithm [21]. Further, we can achieve a significantly higher temporal diversity compared to traditional recommender systems.

Table 1: Average Purchase Intervals

	a	b	c	d	e
a	-	15	5.7	13	18.5
b	4	-	-	-	2.5
c	-	11	-	7	13.5
d	14	3	-	-	6.3
e	6	2	-	-	-

The rest of the paper is organized as follows. Section 2 gives the background of the concepts used in this paper. Section 3 describes our proposed framework. Section 4 gives the results of our experimental study. Section 5 discuss related works and we conclude in section 6.

2. PRELIMINARIES

In this section, we provide the background for the economics concepts used in our proposed model. We review the notions of utility, utility surplus and the law of diminishing marginal utility and discuss how these concepts are adapted to model product-specific diminishing marginal return and user-specific utility for personalized recommendation.

2.1 Utility and Utility Surplus

Utility and Utility Surplus are two fundamental concepts from economics. *Utility* can be defined as a measure of the satisfaction obtained from the consumption or purchase of various goods and services. The utility of a product i, denoted as δ_i, can be modeled as the weighted sum of k characteristics or features of the product as follows:

$$\delta_i = \sum_k \beta^k * c_i^k \qquad (1)$$

where c_i^k is the kth feature of product i and β^k is its weight.

Utility surplus determines the excess utility one gets by purchasing a product. It is defined as the gain in the utility of a product minus the cost/price of the product as follows:

$$US(i) = \delta_i - \alpha \cdot price_i \quad (2)$$

where $price_i$ is the price of product i and α is the marginal net utility of money.

Equations 1 and 2 assume that users have the same preference for the features of a product. In reality, users may have different preferences for a product's features. In order to personalize product recommendations, we revise the above equations to allow user-specific preferences for product features as follows:

$$\delta_{u,i} = \sum_k \beta_u^k * c_i^k \quad (3)$$

$$US(u,i) = \delta_{u,i} - \alpha_u \cdot price_i \quad (4)$$

where β_u^k is the user u's preference for the kth feature of product i and α_u is the sensitivity of user u to the product price.

Consumer behavior theory shows that a person usually makes a purchase decision depending on a product's utility surplus. Hence, our goal is to find the list of products that maximizes the utility surplus for users.

2.2 Law of Diminishing Returns

The Law Of Diminishing Marginal Utility states the marginal utility of product drops as the consumption of the product increases. Thus, each product will have a product-specific diminishing rate γ_i. [21] use the well-known Constant elasticity of substitution(CES) to capture this property. If a user has already purchased X_i quantity of product i, then then the marginal utility of buying an additional unit of i is $(X_i + 1)^{\gamma_i} - X_i^{\gamma_i}$.

By taking into consideration the Law Of Diminishing Marginal Utility, we can refine the utility surplus as follows:

$$US(X_i, i, u) = \delta_{u,i} \cdot ((X_i + 1)^{\gamma_i} - X_i^{\gamma_i}) - \alpha_u \cdot price_i \quad (5)$$

Note that in Equation 5, the utility surplus is decreased due to the diminishing effect.

3. PROPOSED FRAMEWORK

Our proposed framework incorporates the information of purchase intervals into the utility surplus model. It has three main phases:

Phase I: Generate Purchase Interval Cube. This phase computes a purchase interval matrix M_u for each user from his/her purchase history. Each cell $M_u[i,j]$ stores the interval between the purchase of products i and j for user u. We obtain a purchase interval cube when we combine the purchase interval matrix of all the users. Section 3.1 gives the computational details of this phase.

Phase II: Build Model. This phase uses the SVD matrix factorization method [8] to learn the feature vectors of users and products from the training data. Then we can learn the optimal settings for the parameters in our purchase interval enhanced utility based model. We discuss how to incorporate the purchase interval information into the utility model in Equation 5 in Section 3.2 and estimate its parameters in Section 3.3.

Phase III: Recommendation. When a user logs into the system at time t, we use our model to compute the utility surplus of each product at this time point t and rank them. A list of top K products that the user is most likely to purchase is recommended to the user.

3.1 Purchase Interval Cube

An e-commerce database D consists of a set of users U, product items I and purchase histories of users H. Each entry in the purchase history is a tuple $< u, i, t >$ which records the time t at which user u purchase item i.

Let H_u be the purchase history of user u and I_u be the set of products purchased by a user u over a time window ω. For each pair of products i, $j \in I_u$, we want to find the average time interval when u would purchase j after purchasing i. Since u may purchase products i and j multiple times, we let T_i and T_j be the sets of time stamps at which u bought i and j respectively. For each $t_j \in T_j$, we find the $t_i \in T_i$ such that $t_j - t_i$ is the smallest and is less than ω. Let $\Phi = \{[t_{i_1}, t_{j_1}], [t_{i_2}, t_{j_2}], \cdots, [t_{i_n}, t_{j_n}]\}$ be the set containing such pairs of time stamps. Then the average purchase interval $d_{u,i,j}$ where a user u buys product j after buying product i can be determined as follows:

$$d_{u,i,j} = \frac{\sum_{[t_{i_r}, t_{j_r}] \in \Phi} t_{j_r} - t_{i_r} / (log_2(2 + count(t_{j_r}, t_{i_r}))}{\sum_{[t_{i_r}, t_{j_r}] \in \Phi} 1/(log_2(2 + count(t_{j_r}, t_{i_r}))} \quad (6)$$

where the function $count(t_{i_r}, t_{j_r})$ returns the number of products purchased by the user between time stamps t_{i_r} and t_{j_r}.

Note that Equation 6 considers both the time interval between the purchase of the two products i and j, as well as the number of products bought in between i and j. We penalize the interval that has more purchases in between by taking the *log*.

Given the huge amount of user purchase histories and the large number of users and products, we need an efficient method to compute the purchase intervals between product pairs. Algorithm 1 gives the details of generating the purchase interval cube that captures the purchase interval between pairs of products for all users.

The algorithm takes as input the set of user purchase histories H and the window size ω. Each entry e in the user purchase history is a 3-tuple consisting of the user id u, product id *id* and a time stamp t. The output is a purchase interval cube M that stores the purchase intervals of products for all users. We denote the purchase history and purchase interval matrix for each user u as H_u and M_u respectively.

For each user, we slide a window of size ω over his/her purchase history H_u and use a list Q to maintain the purchases which occur in the current window. The list R stores tuples containing product pairs and their smallest purchase intervals. Each entry in R is a 4-tuple $< i, j, x, c >$ where i and j are product ids, x is the purchase interval between i and j, and c is the number of products purchased between i and j. In order to reduce computation, we use two lists R_w and R'_w to temporally store the interval pairs corresponding to the purchase entries in Q. These lists are initialized in lines 1-4. For each entry e in the user purchase history, we compare the timestamps between e and the oldest entry e' in Q. If the purchase interval exceeds the window size ω, we remove e' from Q and all the records that has the same product *id* as e' from the list R_w, that is, we do not need to

```
Algorithm 1: Generate Purchase Interval Cube
   input  : Set of purchase histories H = {H_1, ..., H_n},
            Window size ω
   output : Purchase interval cube M = {M_1, ..., M_n}
1  foreach u ∈ U do
2      Initialize list Q ← ∅; /* to store entries e */
3      /* e is a 3-tuple < u, id, t > */
4      Initialize lists R, R_w, R'_w ← ∅; /* to store records r */
5      /* r is a 4-tuple < i, j, x, c > where i and j are product
       ids, x is the purchase interval between i and j, and c is
       the number of products purchased between i and j.*/
6      foreach e ∈ H_u do
7          /* remove records whose purchase interval exceeds ω
           */
8          while (e.t - e'.t) > ω where e' is the first entry in
           Q do
9              remove e' from Q;
10             remove all tuples r from R_w where r.i = e'.id;
11         /* update purchase interval and count of products */
12         Let e' be the last entry in Q;
13         x' ← e.t - e'.t;
14         if x' > 0 then
15             c' ← 1;
16         else
17             c' ← 0;
18         /* handle the case e.id occur more than once in ω */
19         if ∃ e' in Q s.t. e'.id = e.id then
20             while r.i <> e.id where r is the first entry in
               R_w do
21                 create r' ← (r.i, e.id, r.x + x', r.c + c');
22                 add r' to R'_w;
23                 remove r from R_w;
24         /* create new interval records */
25         foreach r ∈ R_w do
26             create r' ← (r.i, e.id, r.x + x', r.c + c');
27             add r' to R'_w;
28             add r' to R;
29         R_w ← R'_w;
30         R'_w ← ∅;
31         if ∃ e' in Q s.t. e'.id = e.id then
32             remove e' from Q;
33             remove all tuples r from R_w where r.i = e.id ;
34         create a tuple r ← < e.id, e.id, 0, 0 >;
35         add r to list R_w;
36         push e to queue Q;
37     Use Equation 6 to obtain M_u from R;
```

consider this pair of products $e'.id$ and $e.id$ further (Lines 8-10).

Based on the latest entry e' in Q and the records in R_w, we update the interval and count of products purchased between $r.i$ and $e.id$ (Lines 12-33). If a user has purchased the product $e.id$ more than once in the window ω, then we remove records whose time intervals are not the smallest (Lines 19-23 and 31-33). Otherwise, we generate new interval records r' and store them in both R and R'_w (Lines 25-28). Note that we only need to update the interval records in R_w with the time difference between e and the latest entry e' in Q (line 12-17). Lines 34-36 creates an interval record r for each entry e and inserts e into Q.

Finally, R stores the list of purchase intervals between product pairs for a user u. We apply Equation 6 to compute $d_{u,i,j}$. Each cell $M_u[i,j]$ stores the value of $d_{u,i,j}$ (Line 37). The purchase interval matrix of all users $u \in U$ will form a purchase interval cube M. Figure 2 shows the purchase interval cube obtained for our example in Figure 1.

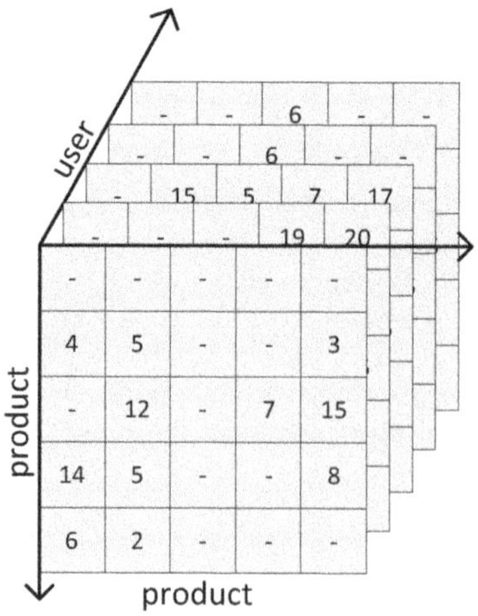

Figure 2: Purchase Interval Cube obtained from Figure 1

Let us illustrate Algorithm 1 with user u_1's purchase history in Figure 1. Suppose ω is set to 20. The first entry e is $< u_1, c, 1 >$. Since all the lists are initially empty, we create a record $r < c, c, 0, 0 >$ and add it to R_w. We also insert e into Q. When we process the second entry $< u_1, d, 8 >$, we compare its timestamp with that of the first entry $< u_1, c, 1 >$ in Q to check whether their purchase interval exceeds ω. Since it does not, we will compute the interval $x' = 8$ and $c' = 1$ and generate a new record $< c, d, 7, 1 >$. We insert this record into R and update R_w. R_w now has two records, $< c, d, 7, 1 >$ and $< d, d, 0, 0 >$. The third and fourth entries in H_{u_1} are similarly processed. Figure 3(a) shows the lists Q, R_w and R obtained.

When we process the entry $< u_1, b, 16 >$ in H_{u_1}, we find that there is another entry for product b in Q. We create new records $< b, b, 5, 2 >$ and $< e, b, 2, 1 >$ for the product pairs (b, b) and (e, b). We also remove the older entry $< u_1, b, 13 >$ from Q and insert $< u_1, b, 18 >$ into Q. Figure 3(b) shows the updated lists.

When we process the last entry $< u_1, a, 22 >$, we find that its timestamp and that of the first entry $< u_1, c, 1 >$ in Q exceeds the window size ω. Hence, we remove $< u_1, c, 1 >$ from Q and the corresponding records $< c, b, 17, 3 >$ from R_w. We only need to create 3 new records for R (see Figure 3(c)).

Algorithm 1 only needs to scan the user purchase history once. It has a complexity of $O(|U| \times m \times n)$ where m is the maximum number of purchase entries in the window size ω and $n = max(|H_u|)$.

In order to ensure that we only consider frequently purchased product pairs, we will do a post-processing of the purchase interval cube M obtained from the user history as follows. For each product pair i and j, we count the number of users u such that $M_u[i,j]$ is nonzero. If the number of users that purchase this pair of products is less than some threshold, then we will discard this pair of products and set $M_u[i,j]$ to a null value.

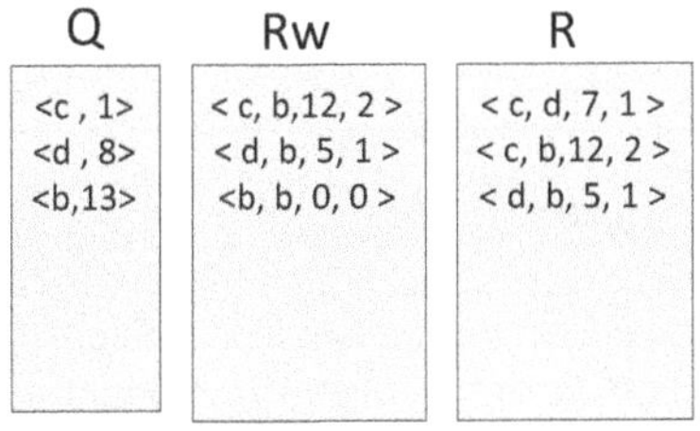

(a) Lists obtained after $< u_1, e, 16 >$

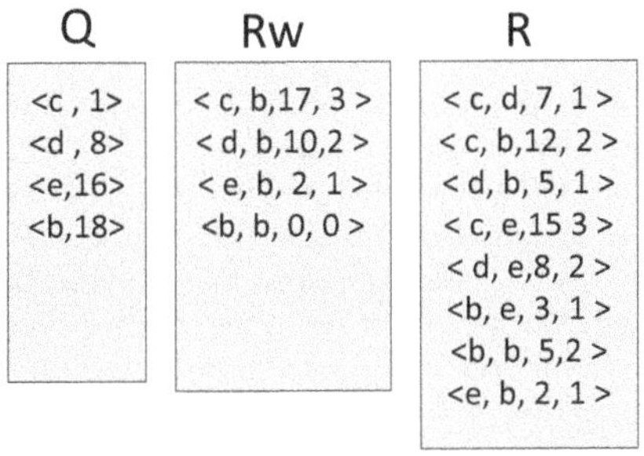

(b) Lists obtained after $< u_1, b, 18 >$

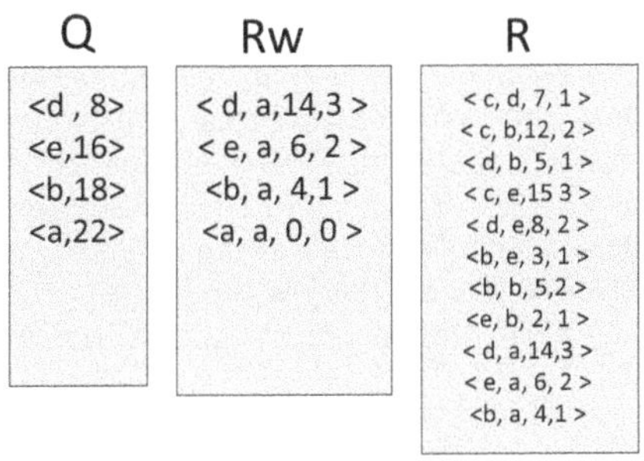

(c) Lists obtained after $< u_1, a, 22 >$

Figure 3: Example to Illustrate Algorithm 1

3.2 Utility Model with Purchase Intervals

Due to the sparsity problem, it is impossible to generate all the intervals between pairs of products from a user's own purchase history. We address this by using the purchase history of similar users to estimate the purchase interval information. We denote the similarity between user u and u' as $sim(u, u')$. Then the average purchase interval between two products i and j for user u can be estimated as follows:

$$d'_{u,i,j} = \frac{\sum_{u' \in U} d_{u',i,j} * (1 + sim(u, u'))}{\sum_{u' \in U} (1 + sim(u, u'))} \quad (7)$$

The similarity between users can be obtained by using some existing latent factor based methods. In our experiments, we use the degree of overlap in the users' purchase histories as a measure of their similarity.

Having obtained the average purchase interval between product pairs for each user, the next step is to incorporate the interval factor into the utility plus model. Suppose a user u has already purchased a set of products I_u and s/he logs into the system at time t. Before we recommend some product j, we want to consider the effect of the interval between a product $i \in I_u$ and j. We model this purchase interval factor $PI(u, i, j)$ as follows:

$$PI(u, i, j) = \frac{1}{log_2(|t - t_i - d'_{u,i,j}| + 2)} \quad (8)$$

Equation 8 reduces the effect of purchase intervals by the distance between $(t - t_i)$ and $d_{u,i,j}$. For example, suppose we have estimated that u typically buys product j $d'_{u,i,j}$ days after buying product i. Then we will recommend product j to u if $|(t - t_i)$ - $d'_{i,j,u}| < \epsilon$.

We can now modify the utility surplus function to include the purchase interval factor as follows:

$$\begin{aligned} US^+(X_i, i, u) = & \quad (9) \\ & \delta_{u,i} \cdot ((X_i + 1)^{\gamma_i} - X_i^{\gamma_i}) \cdot (1 + max_{j \in H_u} PI(u, j, i))^{\mu_i} \\ & -\alpha_u \cdot price_i \end{aligned}$$

In Equation 9, $\delta_{u,i}$ is the basic utility of product i to user u and α_u is the sensitivity of u to the product price p_i. The term $((X_i + 1)^{\gamma_i} - X_i^{\gamma_i})$ considers the return rate γ_i for product i, while the term $(1 + max_{j \in H_u} PI(u, j, i))^{\mu_i}$ accounts for the purchase interval factor. Note that we find the product pair (j, i) that has the largest purchase interval effect and add an product-specific parameter μ_i to tune the effect of each product.

3.3 Parameter Estimation

In this section, we discuss how we estimate the parameters $\delta_{u,i}$, γ_i, μ_i and α_u in Equation 9. Recall that

$$\delta_{u,i} = \sum_k \beta_u^k * c_i^k$$

We use the SVD matrix factorization method [8] to learn the user preference for the product features. Given a $|U| \times |I|$ user-product matrix A, each entry $a_{u,i}$ in A can be estimated as

$$\hat{a}_{u,i} = \left\langle q_i^T, p_u \right\rangle \quad (10)$$

With this, we replace β_u^k and c_i^k in Equation 10 with p_u and q_i respectively. We have $\delta_{u,i} = \hat{A}_{u,i}$ This allows us to use SVD to estimate the utility of a product to a user.

Similar to [21], we define the joint probability of these parameters as:

$$\begin{aligned} JP = & \prod_u Pr(p_u) \prod_i Pr(q_i) \prod_u Pr(\alpha_u) \prod_i Pr(\gamma_i) \prod_i Pr(\mu_i) \\ & \prod_{u,i,t} Pr(r_{u,i,t} | US(X_i, i, u)) \quad (11) \end{aligned}$$

where $Pr(r_{u,i,t} | US^+(X_i, i, u))$ denotes the conditional probability of a user u making the decision to purchase product i at time t given the utility surplus value $US^+(X_i, i, u)$ at time t.

Here, we define

$$Pr(r_{u,i,t} | US^+(X_i, i, u)) = \frac{1}{1 + e^{-r_{u,i,t} \cdot US^+(X_i, i, u)}} \quad (12)$$

where $r_{u,i,t} = 1$ if user u purchase i at time t. Otherwise $r_{u,i,t} = -1$. Note that a higher utility surplus value indicates that the user is more likely to purchase the product i.

The parameters can be estimated by maximizing the joint probability. We assume Gaussian priors on all the model parameters $N(\varphi, \frac{1}{\lambda})$. For p_u and q_i, we have $\varphi_{p_u} = \varphi_{q_i} = 0$ and variance λ_1. The mean and variance for α, γ and μ are $\varphi_\alpha, \varphi_\gamma$, φ_μ and $\lambda_\alpha, \lambda_\gamma$, λ_μ respectively. Then maximizing the joint probability is equivalent to minimizing the negative log likelihood as follows:

$$
\begin{aligned}
(p_u, q_i, \alpha_u, \gamma_i, \mu_i) &= argmin[-logJP] \\
&= argmin\frac{1}{2}\lambda_1 \sum_u ||p_u||^2 + \frac{1}{2}\lambda_1 \sum_i ||q_i||^2 + \\
&\frac{1}{2}\lambda_\alpha \sum_u (\alpha_u - \varphi_\alpha)^2 + \frac{1}{2}\lambda_\gamma \sum_i (\gamma_i - \varphi_\gamma)^2 + \\
&\frac{1}{2}\lambda_\mu \sum_i (\mu_i - \varphi_\mu)^2 + \sum_{u,i,t} log(1 + e^{-r_{u,i,t} \cdot US(X_i, i, u)})
\end{aligned}
$$

We use the stochastic gradient descent method to find the optimal values for the parameters. Our learning algorithm updates the parameters by using the following first order derivatives:

$$
\begin{aligned}
p_u &= p_u - \theta_1 \cdot \frac{\partial(-logJP)}{\partial p_u} \\
q_i &= q_i - \theta_1 \cdot \frac{\partial(-logJP)}{\partial q_i} \\
\alpha_u &= \alpha_u - \theta_2 \cdot \frac{\partial(-logJP)}{\partial \alpha_u} \\
\gamma_i &= \gamma_i - \theta_3 \cdot \frac{\partial(-logLJP)}{\partial \gamma_i} \\
\mu_i &= \mu_i - \theta_4 \cdot \frac{\partial(-logJP)}{\partial \mu_i}
\end{aligned} \tag{13}
$$

At each iteration, the learning rate is controlled by θ_1, θ_2, θ_3 and θ_4. The values of θ_1, θ_2, θ_3, θ_4, λ_1, $\lambda_\alpha, \lambda_\gamma$ and λ_μ can be set by cross-validation.

4. EXPERIMENTAL STUDY

In this section, we report the results of the experiments we have carried out to evaluate the effectiveness of our proposed approach. We call our method SVD_{pi}. We also compare the performance of our method with three algorithms:

1. *TopPop*. This is a baseline algorithm which recommends the top-K most popular products to users;
2. SVD [8]. SVD is a widely used recommendation algorithm based on latent factors and matrix factorization.
3. SVD_{util} [11]. SVD_{util} is the state-of-the-art recommendation algorithm for e-commerce which incorporates marginal net utility and the law of diminishing returns into SVD.

Since SVD, SVD_{util} and SVD_{pi} all have a learning phase to set the optimal values for their parameters, we use the first 90% of each user's purchase history for training and the remaining 10% for testing. We associate each user u and each product i with a feature vector p_u and q_i respectively. We set the dimension of the latent factor is 50.

We use both positive and negative training points. Each purchase record is a positive point. Given that the density of e-commerce data set is usually much lower than that of movie or music rating dataset [5], we randomly sample 0.1% of the missing entries and set them to 0 to train the SVD model. For SVD_{util} and SVD_{pi}, we randomly sample 1% from the missing entries as negative points.

4.1 Experiment Dataset

We collect a dataset from Jingdong which is one of the biggest B2C e-commerce websites in China. We crawled products that belong to the electronic category. The dataset consists of 197,025 users, 98,302 products and 2,610,279 purchase records from January 2010 to November 2011. The density of the dataset is 0.013%.

We pre-process the dataset to remove products that have less than 10 purchase records, as well as users who have purchased less than 10 products. The clean dataset D has 96,882 users, 6,921 products and 2,302,066 purchase records. The density of this dataset is now 0.34%. We sort the purchase records according to the users to form their purchase history. Records in each user purchase history are ordered by their time stamps. Figure 4 shows the distribution of the number of distinct number of products bought by users and the popularity of the products. As expected, there is a long tail in the products purchased.

4.2 Evaluation Metrics

Our evaluation metrics include temporal diversity, conversion rate, precision and recall. Temporal diversity measures the differences between two lists of recommendations when a user logs into the system at different times. For example, suppose a user is given a set of 5 recommended products at time t. If he logs into the system later and only 1 of the 5 recommendations is different, then the diversity between the two lists is $1/5 = 0.2$. [10] derives the diversity between two lists L_t and $L_{t'}$ from their set theoretic difference as follows:

$$L_{t'} \setminus L_t = \{x \in L_{t'} | x \notin L_t\} \tag{14}$$

$$diversity(L_t, L_{t'}, K) = \frac{|L_{t'} \setminus L_t|}{K} \tag{15}$$

where K is the number of products in each list. If the two lists are exactly the same, then diversity is 0.

Conversion rate is a commonly used metric in e-commerce to determine if a user has obtained at least one good recommendation. If the user purchased at least one product from the recommended top K list, then we say that the user has switched from a browser to a buyer. If L is the list of recommended products and L' is the list of products actually purchased by the user, then the conversion rate is given by:

$$conversion\ rate@K = \begin{cases} 1 & \text{if } |L \cap L'| > 0 \\ 0 & \text{otherwise} \end{cases} \tag{16}$$

We compare the conversion rate of the various algorithms by taking the average of values computed for each test user.

The standard definitions for precision and recall are as follows:

$$recall@K = \frac{|L \cap L'|}{|L'|} \tag{17}$$

$$precision@K = \frac{|L \cap L'|}{K} \tag{18}$$

4.3 Results and Analysis

We first examine the effect of the window size ω on the conversion rate, recall and precision of the various algo-

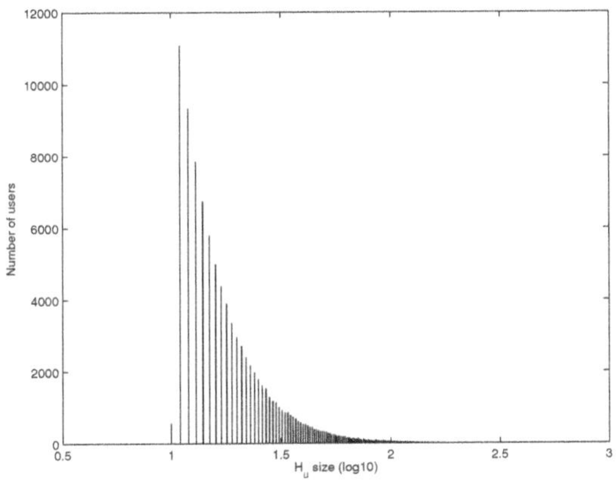

(a) # Distinct Products

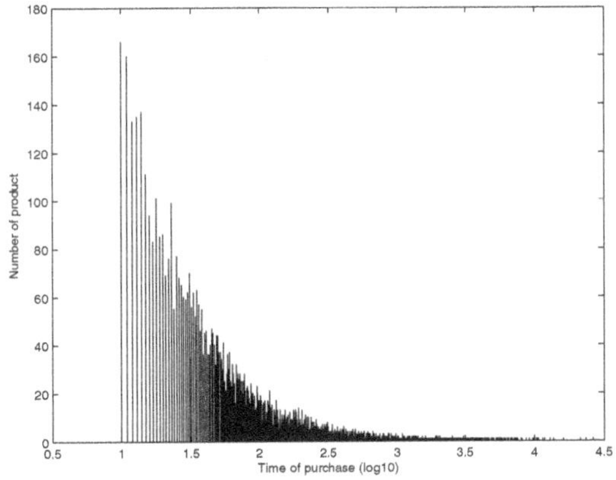

(b) Product Popularity

Figure 4: Characteristics of Dataset

rithms. We set ω to 7, 14, 21, 28 and 35 days. This implies that the purchase intervals generated are less than or equals to ω. Table 2 shows the accumulated density of the purchase interval matrix generated by Algorithm 1 for the different values of ω. We observe that the density increases as we consider larger purchase intervals.

Figure 5 gives the results of this experiment for different values of K. We see that the conversion rate increases as K increases. Similar observations are made for the precision and recall graphs. The best result is obtained when $\omega = 28$. We use this window size for the rest of the experiments.

Next, we compare the performance of our algorithm SVD_{pi} to *TopPop*, SVD and SVD_{util}. Figure 6 shows the results. Since *TopPop* recommends the most popular products and is not personalized, it has the lowest conversion rate compared to the personalized SVD-based methods. When we compare SVD_{pi} with SVD and SVD_{util}, we see that using purchase intervals significantly improves the conversion rate, recall and precision of the recommendations.

We give an example of the results obtained. Table 3 gives the products corresponding to the product IDs. Table 4 shows a sample of the purchase intervals between the products 229040002 (DVD-ROM) and 24101000e (Wireless Router) computed from the dataset. We observe that users typically purchase a DVD-ROM about 25 days after purchasing a Wireless Router.

Table 5 shows a sample of user $U_{10370829}$'s purchase history in the training data. The first entry in the testing data for this user is $< 229040002, 2010-07-16 >$ indicating that s/he purchases the product 229040002 (DVD-ROM) at time $2010-07-16$. Upon examining the list of products recommended by the various algorithms, we find that our method SVD_{pi} also recommends this product 229040002 (DVD-ROM) to the user, whereas both SVD and SVD_{util} recommend the product 23d010004 (Internet Cable). From the user purchase history data, we find that users either purchase the products 24101000e (Wireless Router) and 23d010004 (Internet Cable) together, or purchase Internet Cable 1-2 days after buying Wireless Router. Since SVD and SVD_{util} do not consider the purchase intervals, both of them recommend the product Internet Cable to user $U_{10370829}$.

Table 2: Effect of ω on the Density of Purchase Interval Matrix

ω	7	14	21	28	35
Density	0.41%	0.59%	0.65%	0.74%	0.83%

Table 3: Sample Products

Product ID	Product Title
22306000e	Galaxy GT430 512MB DDR5 Graphics Card
229040002	LITEON 18X DVD-ROM
23d010004	PHILIPS SWA1938/93-5 Internet Cable 5M
23d02000e	CHOSERL Q505 VGA Cable 1.5M
24101000e	TP-LINK WR340G+ 54M Wireless Router

Table 4: Sample Purchase Intervals (in days)

Product ID	Product ID	Interval
24101000e	229040002	22
24101000e	229040002	25
24101000e	229040002	25
24101000e	229040002	27
24101000e	229040002	27
24101000e	229040002	29
24101000e	229040002	22
24101000e	229040002	23
24101000e	229040002	26
24101000e	229040002	27

Table 5: Sample of User $U_{10370829}$'s Purchase History in Training Data

Product ID	Purchase time
23d02000e	2010-03-19
23201000d	2010-03-30
23d100002	2010-04-20
23d060003	2010-04-26
233020011	2010-05-25
24101000e	2010-06-19
22306000e	2010-06-26

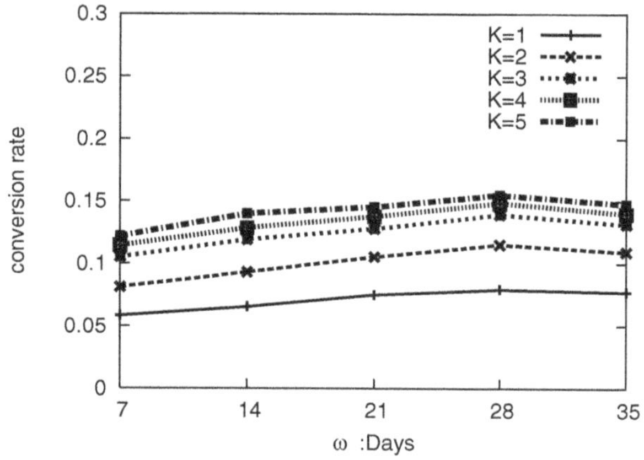

(a) Conversion Rate

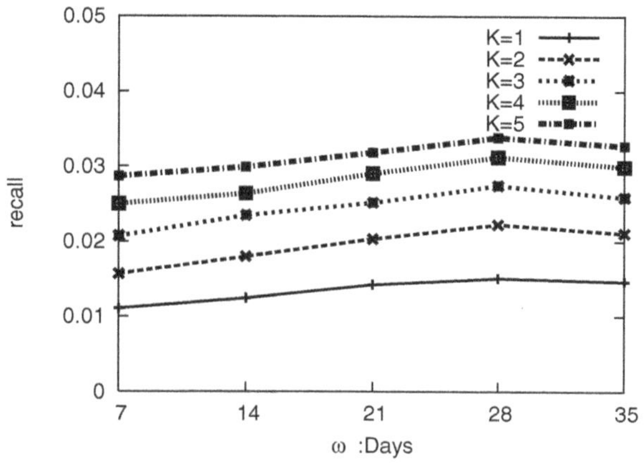

(b) Recall

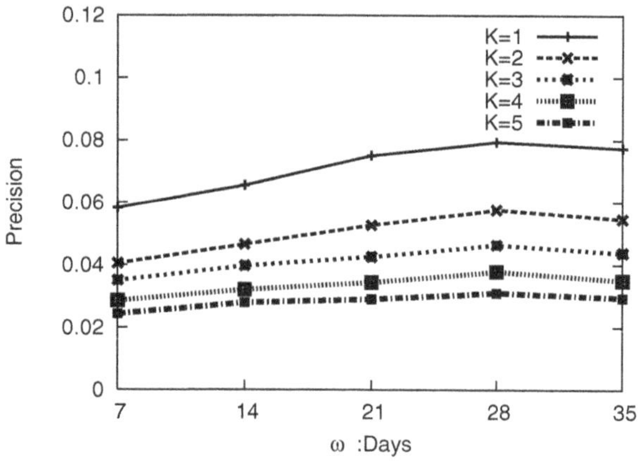

(c) Precision

Figure 5: Effect of Window Size ω

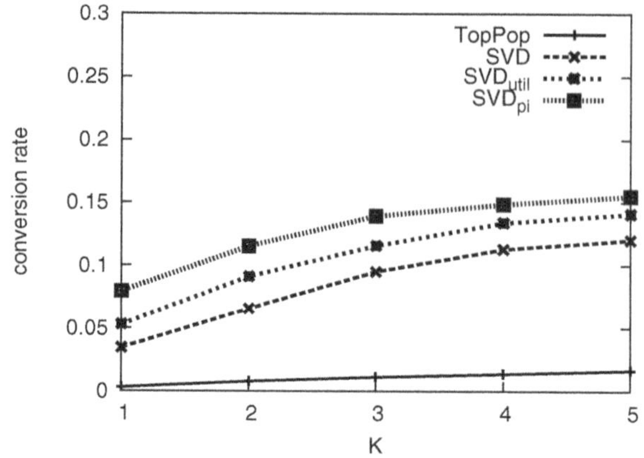

(a) Conversion Rate

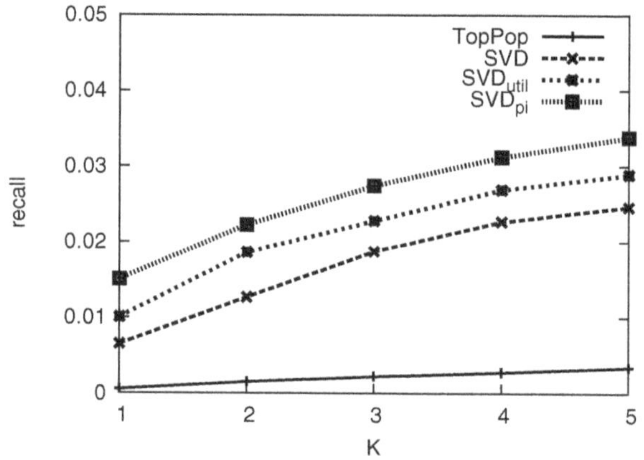

(b) Recall

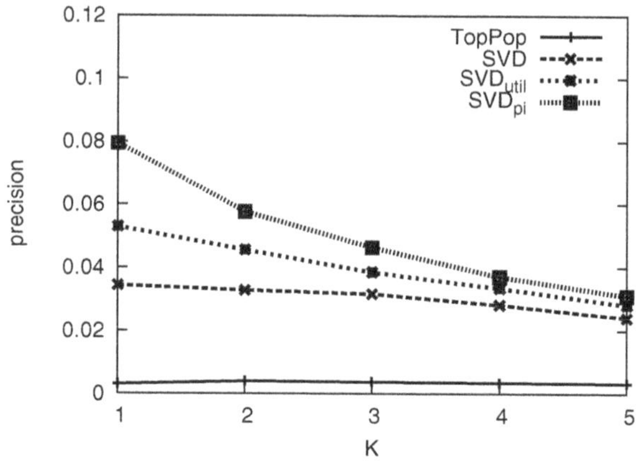

(c) Precision

Figure 6: Comparative Study

4.4 Temporal Diversity

We also investigate the temporal diversity of the various algorithms. We obtain the first recommendation list L at the time stamp of the first entry in the testing data. Then we partition the testing data into two and put the first partition into the training data. We re-run the algorithms on this larger training data and obtain a second recommendation list L' at the time stamp of the first entry in the second partition.

Figure 7 shows the temporal diversity result for the top-5 and top-10 recommended items. The temporal diversity of $TopPop$ is 0 because both its recommendation lists contains the same popular products. Our proposed method SVD_{pi} has the highest temporal diversity compared to SVD and SVD_{util} since the products recommended depends on the time at which the user logs into the system.

Based on the results, we envisage that our proposed approach would be useful in email-based or message-based marketing applications. At different time points, when we want to push some products to consumers, we can determine the products that would be most attractive to consumers at that time point instead of only products that consumers may potentially like.

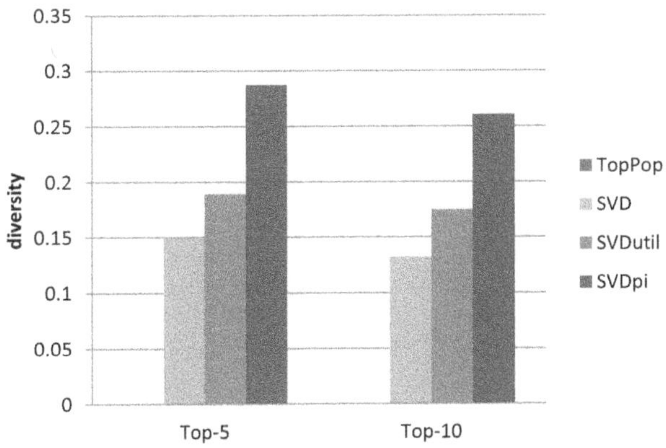

Figure 7: Top-5 and Top-10 Temporal Diversity for $TopPop, SVD, SVD_{util}, SVD_{pi}$

4.5 Effect of Taxonomy

Finally, we study the effect of taxonomy on the various algorithms. Based on the original e-commerce website, products are classified under various levels of category, e.g., both the products *"DELL V3400R-426S 14 inch laptop"* and *"DELL V3400R-426S 13.3 inch laptop"* fall under the same brand *"Dell"* which is under the product type *"Laptops"*. The product type *"Laptops"* is under *"Computers"* which is under *"Computers & Software"*. Thus, we could consider both models of the Dell laptops as the same product type.

In this experiment, we replace specific product models by their product type and brand, that is, we generalize *"DELL V3400R-426S 14 inch laptop"* and *"DELL V3400R-426S 13.3 inch laptop"* to a more general product called *"DELL Laptops"*. Then we re-generate the purchase interval cube and learn a new model for recommendation. Note that we drop the product price term from Equation 9 since we would not have the price of the generalized product.

Figure 8 gives the conversion rate and temporal diversity of the algorithms on this dataset. We observe that all the methods show improvement in the conversion rate. The temporal diversity of all the algorithms decrease slightly because the total number of distinct products is reduced when we merge the individual product models of the same brand to their product type. The gap between SVD_{pi} and the other algorithms widens as the density of the purchase interval cube increases with the use of taxonomy.

5. RELATED WORKS

There has been a long stream of research in recommender systems. Collaborative filtering (CF) has been widely used in these systems. Works in CF can be divided into two categories: memory-based CF and model-based CF. Memory-based CF utilizes the entire user-item-rating data to predict user preferences of new items by identifying similar users. The similarity computation employs measures such as TF-IDF. Representative memory-based CF algorithms include item-based and user-based KNN algorithms [4, 17, 12]. However, memory-based CF algorithms cannot handle data sparsity well and are not scalable.

Model-based approaches have been proposed to alleviate these problems. A model-based CF technique typically uses the user-item-rating data to learn a model for prediction [2]. Well known model-based CF include Bayesian belief nets(BNs) CF models [2, 14, 20], latent factor models [6] and clustering CF models [18]. Research on model-based CF reached a peak in the Netflix movie recommendation competition where a matrix factorization-based CF approach such as SVD is used to learn the model.

In product recommender systems, users' preference tend to change over time. The work in [16] combines the latent factor model and Markov chain model to predict the next basket of products that may be purchased by users. This method utilizes the order of products purchased as the temporal information. Liang et. al [22] propose that the score of each product should be determined by both the long-term preference and short-term bias due to external events such as seasonal festivities. The long-term preference is defined as user similarity when they purchase the same products, while the short-term bias consider the product similarity over a short period of time. The work in [9] design a method to learn the temporal changes of users and items.

The work in [11] highlights that product recommender systems differ from the music or movie recommender systems as the former should take into account the utility of products in their ranking. The authors employ the utility and utility surplus theories from economics and marketing to improve the list of recommended product. [10] use the SVD model to learn the features of products and enhance the model with the Law of Diminishing Marginal Utility. In our work, we combine the notions of purchase intervals and utility surplus to obtain a model that increases the temporal diversity of products recommended.

6. CONCLUSION

In this paper, we have investigated how purchase intervals are able to increase the temporal diversity and conversion rate in product recommender systems. Existing works have primarily considered the order of items purchased by users and do not consider the time interval between the products purchased. We have designed a model that combines purchase interval information in users' purchase history with

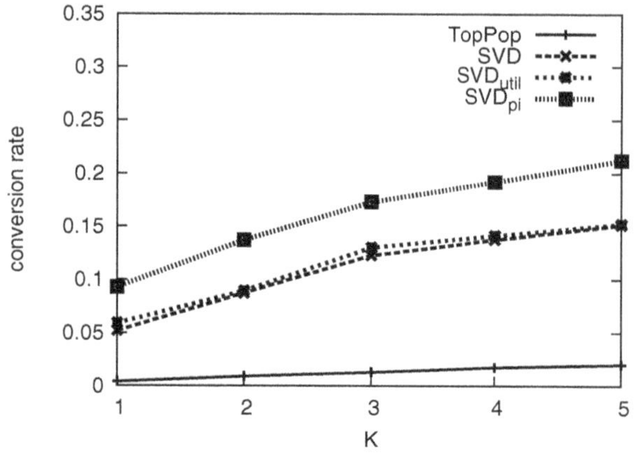

(a) Conversion Rate

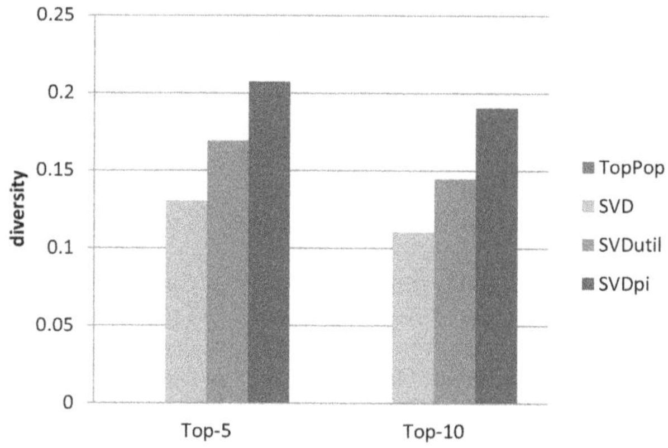

(b) Temporal Diversity

Figure 8: Effect of Taxonomy

marginal utility and the Law of Diminishing Returns. We have also devised an efficient algorithm to generate a purchase interval cube by scanning users' purchase history once. Experimental results on a real world data set obtained from an e-commerce B2C website Jingdong in China demonstrate that the proposed approach improves the precision, recall, conversion rate of the state-of-the-art recommendation algorithms. It also significantly improves the temporal diversity which is essential for product recommendation systems. Future work includes enhancing our model with user purchase data from multiple e-commerce websites and using MapReduce to increase the scalability of our algorithms.

7. REFERENCES

[1] W.J. Baumol and A.S. Blinder. *Microeconomics: Principles and Policy.* 2008.

[2] J.S. Breese, D. Heckerman, and C. Kadie. Empirical Analysis of Predictive Algorithms for Collaborative Filtering. In *Microsoft Technical Report*, pages 43–52, 2007.

[3] C. Cobb and P. Douglas. Latent semantic models for collaborative filtering. *American Economic Review*, 18:139–165, 1928.

[4] K. Goldberg, T. Roeder, D. Gupta, and C. Perkins. Eigentaste: A constant time collaborative filtering algorithm. *Information Retrieval*, 4:133–151, 2001.

[5] J.L. Herlocker, J.A. Konstan, L.G. Terveen, and J.T. Riedl. Evaluating collaborative filtering recommender systems. *ACM TOIS*, 22, 2004.

[6] T. Hofmann. Latent semantic models for collaborative filtering. *ACM TOIS*, 22:89–115, 2004.

[7] http://news.imeigu.com/a/1315461895947.html. Market share and sales growth situation of jingdong mall., September 2011.

[8] Y. Koren. Factorization meets the neighborhood: a multifaceted collaborative filtering model. In *ACM SIGKDD*, pages 426–434, 2008.

[9] Y. Koren. Collaborative filtering with temporal dynamics. pages 89–97, 2009.

[10] N. Lathia, S. Hailes, L. Capra, and X. Amatriain. Temporal diversity in recommender systems. In *ACM SIGIR*, pages 210–217, 2010.

[11] B. Li, A. Ghose, and P.G. Ipeirotis. Towards a theory model for product search. In *WWW Conference*, pages 327–336, 2011.

[12] M.R. McLaughlin and J.L. Herlocker. A collaborative filtering algorithm and evaluation metric that accurately model the user experience. In *ACM SIGIR*, pages 329–336, 2004.

[13] P. Melville, R.J. Mooney, and R. Nagarajan. Content-boosted collaborative filtering for improved recommendations. In *National Conference on Artificial intelligence*, pages 187–192, 2002.

[14] K. Miyahara and M.J. Pazzani. Collaborative filtering with the simple bayesian classifier. In *PRICAI*, pages 679–689, 2000.

[15] D.Y. Pavlov and D.M. Pennock. A maximum entropy approach to collaborative filtering in dynamic, sparse, high-dimensional domains. In *Neural Information Processing Systems*, pages 1441–1448, 2002.

[16] S. Rendle, C. Freudenthaler, and L. Schmidt-Thieme. Factorizing personalized markov chains for next-basket recommendation. In *WWW Conference*, pages 811–820, 2010.

[17] B. Sarwar, G. Karypis, J. Konstan, and J. Reidl. Item-based collaborative filtering recommendation algorithms. In *WWW Conference*, pages 285–295, 2001.

[18] S.H. Seng, S. Chee, J. Han, and K. Wang. Rectree: An efficient collaborative filtering method. In *DaWaK*, pages 141–151, 2001.

[19] L. Si and R. Jin. Flexible Mixture Model for Collaborative Filtering. In *ICML*, pages 704–711, 2003.

[20] X. Su and T.M. Khoshgoftaar. Collaborative filtering for multi-class data using belief nets algorithms. In *IEEE ICTAI*, pages 497–504, 2006.

[21] J. Wang and Y. Zhang. Utilizing marginal net utility for recommendation in e-commerce. In *ACM SIGIR*, pages 1003–1012, 2011.

[22] L. Xiang, Q. Yuan, and S. et. al. Zhao. Temporal recommendation on graphs via long- and short-term preference fusion. In *ACM SIGKDD*, pages 723–732, 2010.

Adaptive Diversification of Recommendation Results via Latent Factor Portfolio

Yue Shi[a], Xiaoxue Zhao[b]*, Jun Wang[b], Martha Larson[a], Alan Hanjalic[a]
[a]Delft University of Technology, Netherlands; [b]University College London, United Kingdom
{x.zhao, j.wang}@cs.ucl.ac.uk, {y.shi, m.a.larson, a.hanjalic}@tudelft.nl

ABSTRACT

This paper studies result diversification in collaborative filtering. We argue that the diversification level in a recommendation list should be adapted to the target users' individual situations and needs. Different users may have different ranges of interests – the preference of a highly focused user might include only few topics, whereas that of the user with broad interests may encompass a wide range of topics. Thus, the recommended items should be diversified according to the interest range of the target user. Such an adaptation is also required due to the fact that the uncertainty of the estimated user preference model may vary significantly between users. To reduce the risk of the recommendation, we should take the difference of the uncertainty into account as well.

In this paper, we study the adaptive diversification problem theoretically. We start with commonly used latent factor models and reformulate them using the mean-variance analysis from the portfolio theory in text retrieval. The resulting Latent Factor Portfolio (LFP) model captures the user's interest range and the uncertainty of the user preference by employing the variance of the learned user latent factors. It is shown that the correlations between items (and thus the item diversity) can be obtained by using the correlations between latent factors (topical diversity), which in return significantly reduce the computation load. Our mathematical derivation also reveals that diversification is necessary, not only for risk-averse system behavior (non-adpative), but also for the target users' individual situations (adaptive), which are represented by the distribution and the variance of the latent user factors. Our experiments confirm the theoretical insights and show that LFP succeeds in improving latent factor models by adaptively introducing recommendation diversity to fit the individual user's needs.

Categories and Subject Descriptors

H.3.3 [**Information Storage and Retrieval**]: Information Search and Retrieval—*Information Filtering*

*The first two authors have equal contribution to this work.

Permission to make digital or hard copies of all or part of this work for personal or classroom use is granted without fee provided that copies are not made or distributed for profit or commercial advantage and that copies bear this notice and the full citation on the first page. To copy otherwise, to republish, to post on servers or to redistribute to lists, requires prior specific permission and/or a fee.
SIGIR'12, August 12–16, 2012, Portland, Oregon, USA.
Copyright 2012 ACM 978-1-4503-1472-5/12/08 ...$10.00.

Keywords

Collaborative filtering, diversity, latent factor model, mean-variance, portfolio theory

1. INTRODUCTION

Collaborative Filtering (CF) is a popular technique to provide users with personalized suggestions of information items, including movies, music, books, news articles to name just a few [1]. An intuition behind CF is that users who had similar preferences in the past are likely to have similar preferences in the future; the more similar they were in the past, the more likely they will agree with each other in the future [26]. Although the underlying mechanism of CF is very different from algorithms used for text retrieval and Web search, recommendation results are often presented to users in the same form as retrieval results, i.e., as a ranked list. The list contains items that have been recommended for a given target user (profile), ranked in order of their predicted preference scores (relevance). Parallel to text retrieval and Web search, diversification of the results list has recently been identified as a critical factor that significantly influences end-user satisfaction with a recommender system [13, 19, 29, 36].

In the past, researchers not only have investigated various means to approach diversification (i.e., to answer the question, "How to diversify?"), but, most importantly, have explored the rationale behind it (i.e., to answer the question, "Why diversify the results?"). In text retrieval, some authors regard diversifying the search results as a way of reducing redundancy and improving information novelty in the results [6, 8], as in work on sub-topic retrieval [35], whereas others consider it as a means of managing uncertainty and risk in the ranked list [7, 32].

However, given the fact that there is a balance between diversification and other criteria such as relevance [6, 8, 32], the third question now emerges, that is, "When to diversify?". More specifically, do we need to make diversification adaptive to different retrieval/recommendation situations? If yes, what is the appropriate diversification level in each of the situations? A recent study on Web search has found that different queries could benefit from different diversification strategies [23, 24]. In recommendation, it is even more useful to make the diversification adaptive to individual user's tastes. The usefulness of adaptive diversification has two aspects: First, user tastes have different scope and coverage of the underlying topics/factors, indicated by the rated items. Some users' tastes are more specific to a few topical areas, while others are more diversified across various top-

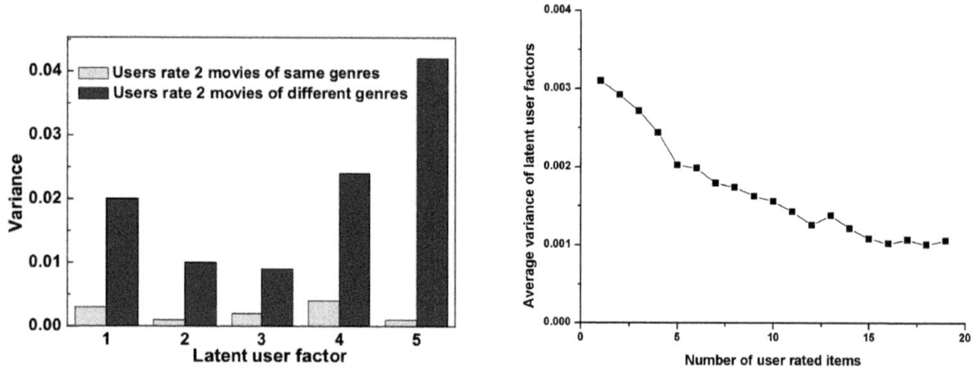

Figure 1: PureSVD (with latent dimensionality 5) [4] on the MovieLens 1M dataset [12]. Left: The variance of each latent user factor for users who rated 2 movies with same or different genres. Right: The relationship between the average variance of latent user factors against the number of movies that the user rated.

ics. To see this, consider the following example in which two movies favored by a user are chosen as a sample that serves as a reflection of the user's overall movie tastes. Suppose a user favors two movies, "Underworld" and "Twilight". For that user, we may provide a recommendation list containing less diversified items as it is likely that the user's taste is more concentrated on a few specific topical areas (likely to prefer Fantasy and Thriller kind movies). By contrast, if the user likes "The Social Network" and "Taken", then a more diversified recommendation would fit the user's taste better, implied by the fact that the preferred two movies are in quite different genres. These examples suggest that the diversification level should rely on the underlying topic distribution and the specificity of the individual user's taste. Second, a target user's "true" taste is hidden and inferred from the rated items of that user (the user profile). Thus, our understanding of the target user's taste varies and depends on the ambiguity of the provided user profile. If a user just rated a small number of items, which may not provide enough information to infer the user's exact taste, a more diversified recommendation would be a safer bid.

Fig. 1 further illustrates our intuition by employing a latent factor model on a movie rating data set. The uncertainty of learned user tastes was measured by their variances (the exact definition can be found later in Section 3.1). First, we can see that the variances of the latent user factors are obviously higher for the users who favored two movies with the same genre, than for the users who favored two movies with different genres. Second, we can also see that the variance of latent user factors decreases as the user rates more items[1].

The above examples represent the typical aspects that need to be addressed in order to successfully answer the "when" question. Taking them into account, this paper proposes a new recommendation framework, called Latent Factor Portfolio (LFP), by connecting latent factor models [9, 17, 18, 22, 34] with portfolio retrieval [30]. Latent factor models construct latent user factors/topics from user profile data, and use them to predict the unknown ratings. They have been widely used for CF, due to their accuracy and scalability. Our focus in this paper is, however, not on predicting user ratings, but on capturing the uncertainty of latent factors and subsequently employing it to infer the diversification level. In the proposed framework, the coverage of a user's preference is modelled by the distribution of latent factors and the uncertainty is represented by using the variances of latent factors. Our derivation then shows that the distribution and the uncertainty of latent factors in a user profile determine the final diversity of the ranked list. If we want to control the final uncertainty at a certain level, the diversification level should reflect the variance (uncertainty) of latent factors in a user profile that has been given. Note that the novelty of our study does not lie only in the combination of latent factor models and portfolio retrieval, but also, importantly, in the insights and understandings of the adaptive diversification, which otherwise would not be derived from either approach independently.

The paper is organized as follows. We present the detail of the proposed LFP in Section 2, after which we discuss the related previous work in Section 3. Our experimental evaluation is reported in Section 4, and Section 5 summarizes and concludes the paper.

[1]It should be emphasized that more ratings in a profile may not necessarily give us more information about the user preference. It also depends on what items the user has rated, since some ratings may be more informative than others [11].

2. LATENT FACTOR PORTFOLIO

2.1 Uncertainty in Latent Factors

In latent factor models, a rating from user u for item i is decomposed as the inner product of the latent user factors and the latent item factors, as expressed by:

$$r_{ui} = \sum_{a=1}^{A} V_{ia} U_{ua} \tag{1}$$

where V_{ia} denotes the extent to which the ith item is associated with the ath latent factor, and U_{ua} denotes the extent that user u is interested in the ath latent factor. A is the number of latent factors that are employed in the model. Assuming that the representation of items is independent of individual users, and the latent item factors can be learned beforehand, in practice, we can regard the latent item factors as constants. In this paper, our focus is on the uncertainty of the user factors given a user profile, however, the uncertainty of the item factors could be analogously derived. The expected value of a rating r_{ui} is thus expressed as:

$$E(r_{ui}) = \sum_{a=1}^{A} V_{ia} E(U_{ua}) \tag{2}$$

We also derive the variance of rating r_{ui} and the covariance between rating r_{ui} and r_{uj} as follows:

$$\begin{aligned} Var(r_{ui}) &= E[r_{ui} - E(r_{ui})]^2 \\ &= E[\sum_{a=1}^{A} V_{ia} U_{ua} - \sum_{a=1}^{A} V_{ia} E(U_{ua})]^2 \\ &= E[\sum_{a=1}^{A} V_{ia} (U_{ua} - E(U_{ua}))]^2 \\ &= E[\sum_{a=1}^{A} \sum_{l=1}^{A} V_{ia} V_{il} (U_{ua} - E(U_{ua})) (U_{ul} - E(U_{ul}))] \\ &= \sum_{a=1}^{A} V_{ia}^2 \sigma_{ua}^2 \end{aligned} \tag{3}$$

$$\begin{aligned} Cov(r_{ui}, r_{uj}) &= E[(r_{ui} - E(r_{ui})) (r_{uj} - E(r_{uj}))] \\ &= E[\sum_{a=1}^{A} V_{ia} (U_{ua} - E(U_{ua})) \sum_{a=1}^{A} V_{ja} (U_{ua} - E(U_{ua}))] \\ &= E[\sum_{a=1}^{A} \sum_{l=1}^{A} V_{ia} V_{jl} (U_{ua} - E(U_{ua})) (U_{ul} - E(U_{ul}))] \\ &= \sum_{a=1}^{A} V_{ia} V_{ja} \sigma_{ua}^2 \end{aligned} \tag{4}$$

where σ_{ua}^2 denotes the variance of the ath latent factor of user u, i.e., $\sigma_{ua}^2 = E[U_{ua} - E(U_{ua})]^2$. The variance of each rating in terms of latent factors represents the uncertainty. Note that in the derivation of Eq. (3) and (4), we make use of the property that the user's interest in different latent factors are uncorrelated, as shown:

$$E[(U_{ua} - E(U_{ua}))(U_{ul} - E(U_{ul}))] = 0, a \neq l \tag{5}$$

This property is a common assumption in latent factor models, in which each latent factor represents one aspect independent of all the others. We have two insights from the above formulation in Eqs. (3) and (4). First, as seen in Eq. (3), the variance (uncertainty) of the user preference score (the rating) is associated with the variance in the latent factors, indicating that taking into account the uncertainty in the latent factors could contribute to modelling the user preference. Second, as seen in Eq. (4), the covariance (proportionate to the correlation) between a user's preferences of two items is also associated with the variance of the latent factors, indicating that it is feasible to exploit the uncertainty of latent factors to regulate the recommended items in order to satisfy the user's demand on the diversity and the coverage of recommended items.

Ideally, the variance of a latent user factor, e.g., σ_{ua}^2, is estimated from a number of observations of U_{ua}, which means we need to sample the rated items from user u multiple times. However, this estimation could be infeasible in practice, since 1) multiple observations of user profiles are typically unavailable, thus, requiring heuristic sampling strategy, 2) it requires training the model multiple times

ALGORITHM 1: Latent Factor Portfolio

Input: a given user u and its latent factors $\mathbf{U_u}$, latent item factors $\mathbf{V}$, weighting coefficients $w_n, n = 1, 2, \ldots, N$, and parameter b
Output: A local optimal ranked item list for user u.
$C = \{1, 2, \ldots, N\}$;
$S = \emptyset$;
Select the item with index idx, i.e.,
$idx = \arg\max_{c(n), n=1,2,\ldots,N} \sum_{a=1}^{A} U_{ua} V_{c(n)a}$ to be ranked in the first position;
$S = S \cap \{idx\}$;
$k = 2$;
repeat
  for *each* $x \in C \& x \notin S$ **do**
    Compute $\Delta F(x)$ according to Eq. (11);
  end
  $c(k) = \arg\max_x \Delta F(x)$;
  $S = S \cap \{c(k)\}$;
  $k = k + 1$;
until $k > N$;

according to different observations of user profiles, thus, inflating the computational cost. For this reason, we propose an approximation for the variance of each latent user factor, based on the latent factors of the items that have been rated by the user, as shown below:

$$\sigma_{ua}^2 = \frac{1}{|N_u|} \sum_{i \in N_u} (U_{ua} - V_{ia})^2 \tag{6}$$

where N_u represents the set of items rated by user u, and $|N_u|$ denotes its cardinality. This approximation satisfies our basic assumptions about the properties of uncertainty as follows. In the case that a user prefers two or more similar items, i.e., the items could be expected to be represented by similar latent factors, the estimated variance with respect to those latent factors could be low. Conversely, if two rated items are quite different, i.e., the items could be expected to be represented by far different latent factors, the corresponding variance of the latent user factors could be high.

2.2 Latent Factor Portfolio Ranking

Taking into account the ranking positions of the items, we can express the overall relevance of a recommendation list based on latent factors as below:

$$R_{uN} = \sum_{n=1}^{N} w_n r_{uc(n)} = \sum_{n=1}^{N} w_n \sum_{a=1}^{A} V_{c(n)a} U_{ua} \tag{7}$$

in which w_n is a weighting coefficient for rank position n and it is a monotonically decreasing function of the ranking position. The most common function for w_n is $w_n = 1/2^{n-1}$ [15], which is also used in this paper. Here, we introduce a rank function $c(n)$ that returns the item index of the nth item in the ranking list. R_{uN} denotes the overall relevance of N recommended items for user u.

2.2.1 From Factor Level to Rank Level

Taking into account Eqs. (2)- (4) and (7), we obtain the expected value of the relevance of the ranked list as:

$$E(R_{uN}) = \sum_{n=1}^{N} w_n \sum_{a=1}^{A} V_{c(n)a} E(U_{ua}) \tag{8}$$

and the variance of the ranked list as:

$$Var(R_{uN}) = \sum_{n=1}^{N} w_n^2 \sum_{a=1}^{A} V_{c(n)a}^2 \sigma_{ua}^2 + \sum_{n=1}^{N} \sum_{\substack{m=1 \\ m \neq n}}^{N} w_n w_m \sum_{a=1}^{A} V_{c(n)a} V_{c(m)a} \sigma_{ua}^2 \quad (9)$$

where, for the readability, we skip the detailed derivation from the topic variance to the rank list variance, and leave it to Appendix A. Note that the uncertainty of the recommendation list is represented by the variance in terms of latent factors. We have two insights from the two terms of Eq. (9). The first term reflects that the variance of a recommendation list is also top-biased. In other words, if the variance of a latent user factor, e.g., σ_{ua}^2, is given, then the latent factor of top-ranked items would have larger influence on the uncertainty of the recommendation list than the low-ranked items. In this sense, in order to reduce the uncertainty of the recommendation list, we need to rank the item relatively higher if its latent factor, e.g., $V_{c(n)a}$, is large and the variance of the corresponding latent user factor, i.e., σ_{ua}^2, is low. The second term indicates that the relative rank positions of any two items in the recommendation list influence the overall uncertainty. For example, if the variance of a latent user factor is large and the user has shown interest in an item whose corresponding latent factor is also large, then ranking another item with also a large corresponding latent factor at the higher position leads to the larger uncertainty. Conversely, if the variance of a latent user factor is small, then ranking the two items higher would not lead to large increase of the overall uncertainty. Note that the variances of all the latent user factors need to be taken into account for an aggregated impact on the overall uncertainty. Summarizing, it is evident that by exploiting the uncertainty of the latent factors, recommendation diversification can be attained adaptively.

2.2.2 Sequential Ranking

Following the portfolio theory of IR [32], we can attain an optimal recommendation list by taking into account the tradeoff between the mean relevance of the recommended items and the corresponding variance. As a result, the objective function is expressed as:

$$F(R_{uN}) = E(R_{uN}) - bVar(R_{uN}) \quad (10)$$

in which b is a risk-reward tradeoff parameter. As we shall see later, parameter b is a system level parameter and does not contribute to the user adaptive adjustment of the diversification level. Instead, the diversification level in the ranked list will automatically be adjusted according to the uncertainty of the user factors and their distribution (in other words, rely on how much we understand the target user from the provided ratings). By maximizing this objective function, an optimal ranking can be achieved, which attains an optimal mean-variance balance. In this paper, we adopt the sequential ranking algorithm as used in [30] to solve the optimization problem in Eq. 10. Again, for readability, we leave the exact derivation in Appendix B and give the final item ranking rule at rank k as:

$$\begin{aligned} c^*(k) &= \arg\max_{c(k)} \{\Delta F(R_{uk})\} = \arg\max_{c(k)} \{F(R_{uk}) - F(R_{uk-1})\} \\ &= \arg\max_{c(k)} \Big\{ \sum_{a=1}^{A} \Big(V_{c(k)a} U_{ua} - b w_k \sigma_{ua}^2 V_{c(k)a}^2 \\ &\quad - 2b\sigma_{ua}^2 \sum_{m=1}^{k-1} w_m V_{c(k)a} V_{c(m)a} \Big) \Big\} \end{aligned} \quad (11)$$

where we have dropped w_k from Appendix B since it is a constant for rank k. We call the above formulation *latent factor portfolio ranking*, since both the mean and the variance are defined on latent factors of users and items, as reflected in the summation over the factor space a. The most important characteristic in LFP is the introduction of the variances of the latent factors σ_{ua}^2, which introduces the adaptation. Combining σ_{ua}^2 and b, topic diversity in the ranked list is adjusted in two levels. At the *system level*, the need for diversification is due to the risk-averse behaviour of the system and it is adjusted at parameter b. As shown in [33], the risk-averse behaviour is query (user profile)-independent and related to the utility of the system, defined by the used IR metric. At the *user profile level*, the need for diversification is related to the level of absolute certainty about the latent topics that the target user is interested in. The uncertainty is represented by the variances σ_{ua}^2 of the latent factors in the formula. Combined with b, it adaptively balances the mean and reward tradeoff in the user profile level, thus making the topic diversification adapted to each individual users's need.

In the next section, we position the proposed LFP with respect to related work, and discuss its contribution.

3. RELATED WORK AND DISCUSSION

Latent factor models have become a dominating branch among CF approaches, due to their superiority in terms of accuracy and scalability, as shown in Netflix competition [17]. Matrix Factorization (MF) forms a group of the most well-known latent factor models, e.g., Singular Value Decomposition (SVD) [18], SVD++ [16]. Probabilistic Matrix Factorization (PMF) was proposed to carry out the rating factorization from a probabilistic view [22], which leads to the most widely used regularized L2-norm regression model. Additionally, logistic regression was also proposed to learn latent factors [2]. The latest developments in recommender systems have explored different criteria to improve user satisfaction based on latent factor models, such as modelling user choice process [34] and the marginal net utility [31].

From Eq. (11), we observe that: on one hand, compared to the latent factor models (e.g., [17] and [22]), LFP ranks an item at position k based on not only its rating predictions, i.e., the first term in Eq. (11), but also its uncertainty in terms of the latent item factors, i.e., the second term, and the correlation between this item and the items ranked before it, i.e., the third term. Therefore, we can regard LFP as a general extension for latent factor models that introduces the tradeoff with respect to the uncertainty of recommended items. Note that in our derivation we only consider the uncertainty from user latent factors. One can also consider the randomness of both the user factors and items factor simultaneously, but the study is worth a full attention and is beyond the scope of this paper. We thus leave the detailed discussion and research for future work.

Diversity is realized as one of the most important aspects for the recommendation quality [13, 19, 29, 36]. It is the key factor to help users to explore new interests that they might not discover by themselves and thus enhance user experience. Ziegler et al. proposed a re-ranking algorithm to bring topic diversification, which balances the ranking list according to user's complete spectrum of interests [36]. According to their studies, diversity of a recommendation list may hamper precision to some degree, but will improve user satisfaction as a whole. Then, Zhang and Hunley formalized the intra-list topic diversification problem by addressing a multi-objective optimization problem on diversity and preference similarity [13]. On the other hand, Lathia et al. considered the recommender system as a temporally evolving system that gives diversified recommendations over time [19]. They provided a hybrid algorithm that can offer dynamic recommendations, and they also discovered the negative correlation between user profile length and the degree of recommendation diversity. The issue of evaluating the novelty and the diversity of recommendations has also been raised [29]. In addition, we note that diversifying search results has been extensively studied in the IR community [6, 8, 10, 20, 23, 24, 25], resulting in a fruitful set of diversification methods.

It is also of interest to specifically compare the proposed LFP as in Eq. (11) with other adaptive diversification methods recently proposed in text retrieval [23, 24]. In [23], the diversification trade-off of an unseen query was obtained by mapping it to the known queries whose optimal diversification level is known a priori. By contrast, our method is fully unsupervised and the diversification level is naturally adapted to the latent topics that the target user is interested in and also how many of them we have already obtained in the ranked list. As shown by the first term of Eq. (11), an item is promoted if it has the same topic as the user's. However its rank score will be penalized if the same topic has already appeared in the lower ranks (see the product $V_{c(k)a}V_{c(m)a}$ in the third term). In [24], an intent-aware search result diversification method was proposed. This study was focused on the first term in our formula. In their approach, query aspect intents are classified into two categories (factors): informational and navigational, and a machine learning algorithm is used to rank documents with respect to the categories.

The other branch of research related to our work exploits portfolio theory for various information retrieval and recommendation tasks. The importance of such approaches has recently been underlined in a talk by Resnick [21], who projects the usefulness and the necessity of portfolio theory in personalized systems. The application of portfolio theory in information retrieval and recommendation was first proposed by Wang et al. [30, 32]. Recent increasing attention to exploiting principles in economics for IR [3] may also fall under the same direction.

In the original portfolio retrieval formulation, the uncertainty about the overall relevance of a ranked list is linked to the co-variances between individual documents (relevancies) [30, 32]. However, as they are conditioned on a given query or user profile, exactly, how to obtain such a co-variance matrix remains an open question. In practice, the covariance between two relevance scores is approximated by the covariance with respect to their document term occurrences or user ratings. Computationally, this approach is expensive because every document or item pair needs to be considered. In this paper, we solve this issue by providing a better explanation of the correlation: document or items are correlated because of their underlying topics and latent factors. As shown in Eq. (11), LFP ranks items by taking into account item correlations based on their latent factors/topics, i.e., the products between item factors, which are not exploited in the original model. For example, when ranking a movie in position k, LFP (in the case of $b > 0$) would perfer a movie with a genre (assumed to be represented by a latent factor) that was not contained by the movies ranked before position k, in order to maximize Eq. (11). In this sense, we can regard LFP as a general extension for the original retrieval model, where when $A = 1$, LFP returns to the original retrieval model in [32].

4. EXPERIMENTAL EVALUATION

In this section we present a series of experiments to evaluate the proposed adaptive diversification method. We specifically focuse on the following aspects: 1) As discussed, user tastes have different scope and coverage, reflected by their rated items: some are more specific, while others have wider interests. The question is whether our method is able to adapt the diversification level to the taste of each user. 2) The number of rated items provided by users varies. As a result, we have different accuracy and uncertainty about the users' "true" taste. We intend to investigate whether our method could adjust the diversification level of the ranked list to the uncertainty. 3) If we consider the overall recommendation quality is an aggregated effect from both the relevance and the diversity, whether LFP could benefit for improving the overall recommendation quality?

4.1 Experimental Framework

4.1.1 Dataset

The publicly available dataset MovieLens-1M is used in our experimental evaluation. The dataset contains 1M ratings (scale 1-5, 5 for the best, and 1 for the worst) from about 6K users on about 3.7K movies/items. The data sparseness is 95.5%. Each user in the dataset has at least 20 ratings. In addition, the genre information of movies is provided. There are in total 18 genres, and each movie can be associated with multiple genres. The average number of genres per movies is 1.62. Note that our focus in this paper is not on the performance comparison against the state-of-the-art baselines, but on investigating how the proposed method could diversify recommendation results under different conditions of user profiles (tastes). The choice of a moderate size dataset enables an efficient exploration of experimental results under various settings.

In order to create the training set (for estimating the latent factor models) and the test set (for evaluation), we split the data into a large set containing 80% of the users and a small set the remaining 20%. For each user profile length (UPL) that we investigate in the experiments, we create a test set containing users with that UPL, by randomly selecting the desired number of items (i.e., UPL=2,3,5 and 10) from each user in the small set. The remaining items from each profile in the small set are added to the complete large set to form the training set.

4.1.2 Evaluation Metrics

In our experiments, we adopt a common metric in text retrieval, Mean Average Precision (MAP), to measure the effectiveness of the ranked recommendation list. In order to calculate MAP, we set the relevance threshold as rating 4. In other words, we regard items with ratings equal to or larger than 4 as relevant.

For the investigation of the trade-off (and combination) of the relevance and the diversity in Section 4.2.4, we utilize another evaluation metric from text retrieval, αNDCG [8]. We use movie genres as "nuggets" in calculating αNDCG. The exact definition of αNDCG is expressed below:

$$\alpha NDCG@K = \frac{\alpha DCG@K}{\alpha IDCG@K} \tag{12}$$

in which,

$$\alpha DCG@K = \sum_{k=1}^{K} \frac{\sum_{l=1}^{L} J_{kl}^{u}(1-\alpha)^{q_{l,k-1}^{u}}}{log_2(1+k)} \tag{13}$$

J_{kl}^u is an indicator function that is equal to $r_{uc(k)}$ (i.e., the rating of the kth movie in the list for user u), if the kth movie in the recommendation list of user u contains genre l, otherwise 0. $q_{l,k-1}^u$ denotes the number of movies ranked up to position $k-1$ that contain genre l in the recommendation list for user u. α is a constant set to control the magnitude of penalty for the redundancy of the recommended items. The value of α can be within the range $[0,1]$, in which the higher value indicates the larger penalty. In our experiments, we use $\alpha = 0.5$ as a moderate choice for measuring diversity. αIDCG@K denotes the highest possible value of αDCG@K in the case that the top K recommendation list contains "ideally" diversified relevant items. Thus, αNDCG is normalized to be [0,1]. Note that αNDCG depends on both the movie ratings and genres, representing a suitable metric for our purpose of evaluating the trade-off between the relevance and the diversity. Since we particularly focus on the top-ranked items in recommender systems, we use $K = 5$ in the experiments.

To solely measure the recommendation diversity in a ranked list, we also introduce a simple diversity measure called DNG@K. It measures the number of genres in the top-K ranked list. The number is discounted according to the position of the corresponding movie in order to consider the rank bias. Specifically, we define DNG@K as:

$$DNG@K = \sum_{k=1}^{K} w_k G(k) \tag{14}$$

in which $G(k)$ denotes the number of genres that the kth movie have and that are not included in the top $k-1$ movies. w_k is a discount factor that is set as $w_k = 1/2^{k-1}$. Similar to αNDCG, we focus our evaluation with $K = 5$. The reported DNG is an average across all the test users. Note that DNG is different from other proposed diversity measures that take into account the relevance of recommended items, such as the work in [29].

4.1.3 Latent Factor Models

In collaborative filtering, there are various ways of obtaining latent factors in Eq. (1), either by non-probabilistic approaches [16, 17, 18] or from a probabilistic viewpoint [22]. In our experiment, we choose one representative from each of the two categories, briefly described as follows:

PureSVD: It is the basic form of singular value decomposition [4], as show in Eq. (15). Supposing the user-item rating matrix R consists of M users and K items, the rating matrix R can be decomposed into three low-rank matrices, $P^{M\times A}$, $S^{A\times A}$, and $Q^{K\times A}$. Then, the latent factors of users can be denoted as $\mathbf{U}$, and the latent factors of items can be denoted as $\mathbf{V}$, as shown in Eq. (16). Each column vector in $\mathbf{U}$ (e.g., $\mathbf{U_u}$ for user u) or $\mathbf{V}$ (e.g., $\mathbf{V_i}$ for item i) represents the corresponding user or item. Although PureSVD features the most basic latent factor model, the recommendation performance for top-N tasks is competitive according to a recent empirical study [9]. For this reason, we choose it as a representative of non-probabilistic latent factor models.

$$\mathbf{R} = PSQ^T \tag{15}$$

$$\mathbf{U} = (PS^{1/2})^T, \mathbf{V} = S^{1/2}Q^T \tag{16}$$

PMF: We use probabilistic matrix factorization [22] (PMF) as one of the state-of-the-art latent factor models in CF. PMF estimates the latent factors of users and items by maximizing the posterior, which is the conditional probability of the latent factors given the observed ratings R and hyper-parameters Θ, as shown below:

$$\mathbf{U},\mathbf{V} = \arg\max_{\mathbf{U},\mathbf{V}} \quad p(\mathbf{U},\mathbf{V}|R,\Theta) \tag{17}$$

The resulting objective function of PMF is expressed as:

$$\mathbf{U},\mathbf{V} = \arg\min_{\mathbf{U},\mathbf{V}} \frac{1}{2}\sum_{u=1}^{M}\sum_{j=1}^{K} I_{uj}\left(r_{uj} - g(\mathbf{U_u^T V_j})\right)^2 + \frac{\lambda_U}{2}\|\mathbf{U}\|_F^2 + \frac{\lambda_V}{2}\|\mathbf{V}\|_F^2 \tag{18}$$

The latent factors of users and items are learned from the user-item ratings (normalized to $[0,1]$), and the magnitudes of latent factors are penalized in order to alleviate overfitting. $g(x)$ is a logistic function, i.e., $g(x) = 1/(1+\exp(-x))$, that serves to bound the range of the inner product of latent factors. A simplification is usually made to set $\lambda = \lambda_U = \lambda_V$, which is also used in this paper.

4.2 Results and Analysis

4.2.1 System-level Diversity

As discussed, our LFP model implies that the need for diversification in a ranked list comes from two levels. Our first experiment is to investigate the system level diversity, which is controlled by the parameter b in Eq. (11). In our experiment, we use the training set to train the latent factor models, and for each user in the test set, we randomly select 2 rated items, i.e., User Profile Length (UPL=2), as user profiles, and use the remaining rated items as ground truth. By varying the value of parameter b in LFP, we evaluate its influence on the recommendation performance of different latent factor models, which is shown in Fig. 2. As can be seen, for both PureSVD and PMF, the diversity measure DNG@5 generally increases as the value of b in LFP increases, while MAP decreases. Note the baseline latent factor models are equivalent to the case that we set $b = 0$. The figures show that a positive value of b could contribute to diversifying the recommendation results, and the magnitude of diversification is controlled by its value. However, a

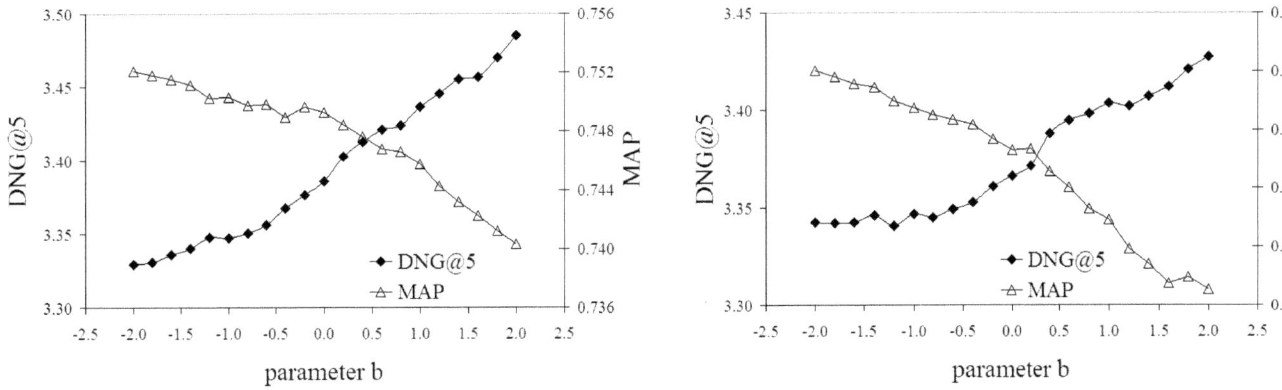

(a) LFP for PureSVD

(b) LFP for PMF

Figure 2: The system level diversity: the impact of parameter b on DNG@5 and MAP.

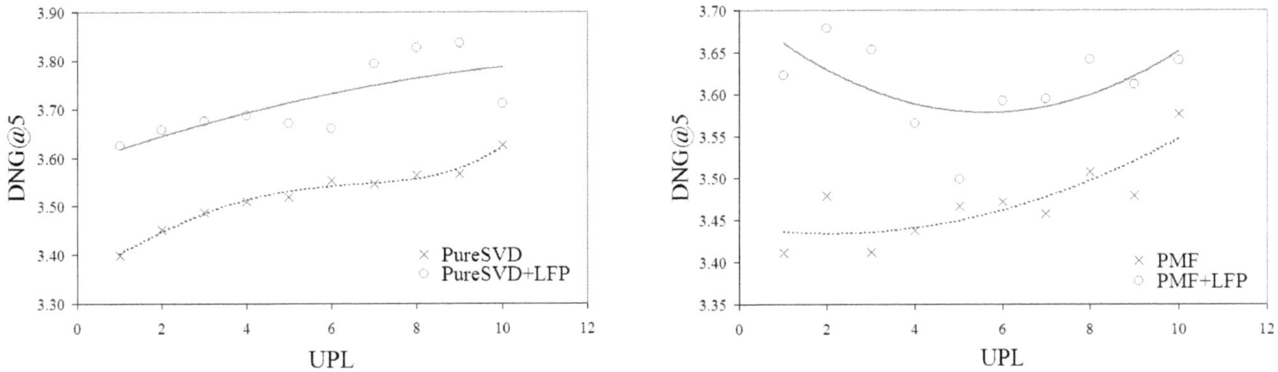

(a) LFP for PureSVD

(b) LFP for PMF

Figure 3: The diversity that depends on the target user profiles: the number of rated items.

Table 1: The diversity DNG@5 adapted to the target user profiles: the range of interests.

	UPL=2		UPL=3	
	Focused	Broad	Focused	Broad
PureSVD	3.148	3.419	3.174	3.386
PureSVD+LFP	3.293	**3.641**	3.304	**3.608**
p-value	0.096	0.000*	0.026	0.000*
PMF	3.353	3.400	3.373	3.432
PMF+LFP	3.415	**3.494**	3.449	**3.570**
p-value	0.335	0.006*	0.411	0.002*

positive value of b could reduce the MAP, indicating that it may degrade the end-user satisfaction when the results are over-diversified. The observation is consistent to the study in text retrieval in [33]. Because the parameter is a constant across target users, it serves to adjust the diversity of recommendation at the system level, and its optimal value depends on the evaluation metrics used (in other words, the utility of the recommendation system).

4.2.2 *Adaptive diversity: the num. of rated items*

We have discussed in Section 1 that the observed numbers of rated items are different across users. As illustrated in Fig. 1, the number of user rated items influences the uncertainty of the learned latent user factors–the more information we have about the user, the less uncertain our model is about the user's hidden tastes. In the following experiment, we evaluate the impact of the model uncertainty on the diversity of recommended items, where the model uncertainty is indicated by the number of rated items provided in the user profile. We generate the user profile length (UPL) from 1 to 10, and randomly select the rated items as user profile items. As in our dataset, each user has at least rated 20 items. Setting UPL up to 10, we ensure that there are at least 10 rated items per user used for testing.

From Fig. 3, we observe that the LFP models succeed in consistently increasing the diversity of recommendation results for both PureSVD and PMF. Note that the increases are all statistically significant, according to Wilcoxon signed rank significance test with $p<0.01$. This indicates that LFP could effectively capture the uncertainty of latent factors and use it to diversify recommendation results.

In addition, the diversity achieved by both our LFP and each of the basic latent factor models, PureSVD and PMF, generally increases as the users rated more items. At a first glance, the result seems to contradict with the idea that adding ratings in the user profile would reduce the uncertainty of the user model and thus the need for diversifying the results. A closer look, however, suggests that this is intuitively correct because when there are few rated items known from the users, the recommended items could be strongly biased toward the few known items, and thus less diversified, whereas when more rated items are known from the users, the recommended items could be more likely to cover different aspects of user interest, and are thus more diversified.

Table 2: Example recommendation results for five movies using the two different types of user profiles. We refer "Ac" to *Action*, "Ad" to *Adventure*, "C" to *Comedy*, "D" to *Drama*, "H" to *Horror*, "R" to *Romance*, "SF" to *Sci-Fi*, "T" to *Thriller*, and "W" to *War*. LFP with PureSVD is used.

Type	User with *Focused* interest		User with *Broad* interests	
Profile	Chariots of Fire (D) Erin Brockovich (D)		American Pie (C) The Blair Witch Project (H)	
Rank	PureSVD	PureSVD+LFP	PureSVD	PureSVD+LFP
1	Second Best(D)	Second Best(D)	Big Daddy(C)	Big Daddy(C)
2	Saving Private Ryan(Ac,D,W)	North by Northwest(D,T)	Bowfinger(C)	The Mask of Zorro(Ac,Ad,R)
3	North by Northwest(D,T)	The Truman Show(D)	Parasite(H,SF)	Baby Geniuses(C)
4	The Truman Show(D)	Saving Private Ryan(Ac,D,W)	Baby Geniuses(C)	Parasite(H,SF)
5	Jakob the Liar(D)	Jakob the Liar(D)	The Mask of Zorro(Ac,Ad,R)	Bowfinger(C)
DNG@5	2.25	1.75	1.69	2.75

Finally and most importantly, we also observe that the increase of diversity introduced by LFP generally decreases as the number of user rated items increases. As shown, the diversity increase brought by LFP with PureSVD tends to be constant as the UPL increases, and the diversity achieved by using LFP with PMF tends to be closer to that of using only PMF as the UPL increases. When the UPL is small, LFP automatically provides relatively larger increase of diversity against the basic latent factor models. In other words, when the users rated only a few items, the basic latent factor models tend to recommend items based on highly uncertain latent factors. LFP addresses the risk of the basic latent factor models by providing more diversified results.

4.2.3 *Adaptive diversity: the range of interests*

We now focus on the evaluation by considering the users with different ranges of interests. To make our study focused and controlled, we are particularly interested in two types of users, i.e., the users who rated movies with the same genre (denoted as the "Focused" type), and the users who rated movies with the non-overlapped genres (denoted as the "Broad" type). The first type of user profiles represents a typical situation in which the target user has a specific range of interests and as a result, the diversification is less required, while the second type represents the opposite situation in which diversification is more desired. Also as demonstrated in the previous section, LFP could be most beneficial for diversifying recommendation results for the users who only rated a limited number of items. For this reason, we use UPL 2 and 3 in this investigation. For each UPL, we classify a user into the "Focused" type if all his or her rated items contain the same genre, and into the "Broad" type if all rated items are associated with genres different from each other.

The results are shown in Table 1, from which we have two observations. First, for both PureSVD and PMF, the diversity of the "Focused" type is lower than the "Broad" type for most of the cases. This result is in accordance with our understanding, as discussed in Section 1, that the commonality of the items in the user profile has a significant impact on the user need for diversification. In the case of the "Focused" type of user profiles, the latent user factors are learned from the items that have the same or similar topics (in this case genres), and the latent factors of those movies could be similar. As a result, the uncertainty and variance of the latent user factors could be low, and those latent user factors would promote to recommend movies with the same or similar genres as the movies that the user has already watched, i.e., a less diversified recommendation. By contrast, a more diversified recommendation would be promoted to the "Broad" type of user profiles.

Second, we observe that for both PureSVD and PMF, and

Table 3: Relevance vs. diversity (with PureSVD).

	MAP	DNG@5	αNDCG@5
UPL=2			
PureSVD	0.749	3.483	0.845
PureSVD+LFP ($b=-1$)	**0.751**	3.341	0.833
PureSVD+LFP ($b=1$)	0.738	**3.645**	**0.858**
UPL=5			
PureSVD	0.764	3.533	0.854
PureSVD+LFP ($b=-1$)	**0.772**	3.417	0.841
PureSVD+LFP ($b=1$)	0.741	**3.683**	**0.866**
UPL=10			
PureSVD	0.769	3.555	0.857
PureSVD+LFP ($b=-1$)	**0.774**	3.456	0.845
PureSVD+LFP ($b=1$)	0.745	**3.706**	**0.870**

Table 4: Relevance vs. diversity (with PMF).

	MAP	DNG@5	αNDCG@5
UPL=2			
PMF	0.787	3.412	0.846
PMF+LFP ($b=-1$)	**0.791**	3.361	0.839
PMF+LFP ($b=1$)	0.758	**3.500**	**0.864**
UPL=5			
PMF	0.807	3.515	0.863
PMF+LFP ($b=-1$)	**0.814**	3.415	0.851
PMF+LFP ($b=1$)	0.763	**3.611**	**0.874**
UPL=10			
PMF	0.818	3.538	0.865
PMF+LFP ($b=-1$)	**0.826**	3.462	0.855
PMF+LFP ($b=1$)	0.774	**3.610**	**0.872**

for both UPL=2 and UPL=3, LFP has a significant increase of diversity for the "Broad" type of user profiles, while introducing a slight change of diversity for the "Focused" type. The result indicates that LFP could effectively exploit the distribution of latent user factors to adaptively determine the level of diversification. This is further illustrated by the example in Table 2. We clearly see that LFP automatically adjusts the diversity of recommendations according to the different range of interests learned from the user profiles.

4.2.4 *Combining Relevance and Diversity*

Our final experiment investigates how LFP can benefit the end-user satisfaction by considering both the relevance and diversity of recommended items. We test the recommendation performance in terms of relevance, as measured by MAP, and the performance in terms of diversity, as measured by DNG@5, under two different settings of parameter b in LFP, i.e., $b=-1$ and 1. Note that as shown in Section 4.2.1, a positive value of b tends to increase the recommendation diversity, while decreasing the recommendation relevance. The opposite results can be observed in the case of a negative value of b. The results are shown in Table 3 and 4. We first observe that LFP could improve the relevance of recommendations for the users who have broad interests. When $b=-1$, LFP improves MAP for both PureSVD and PMF. This result indicates that in the case that LFP increases the similarity among the recommended items based on latent item factors, it could contribute to improving the relevance of the recommendation. The empirical result is also consistent with the statistical mean-variance analysis of MAP conducted in [33]. Second, LFP could achieve a trade-off between the recommendation relevance and the diversity. As can be seen, when $b = 1$, LFP diversifies the recommendation results and results in an improved DNG@5 for both PureSVD and PMF, while degrading the relevance performance as measured by MAP. However, on the whole, αNDCG is substantially improved, indicating that the degraded relevance is compensated by a payoff in the overall quality of recommendation when both relevance and diversity are taken into account. Although here αNDCG could only serve as an approximation of the end-user satisfaction for the recommended items, the results are evident that we can use LFP to adjust the trade-off between the relevance and the diversity of recommendations from latent factor models, allowing us to give a positive answer to our final research question.

5. CONCLUSION AND FUTURE WORK

We proposed a new recommendation framework, called Latent Factor Portfolio (LFP), specifically for adaptively diversifying recommendation results for individual users. We exploited the variance of the latent user factors to capture the range of user interests and uncertainty of the user profiles and use them as the basis for indicating users' needs for diversity. Through our experiments, we demonstrated the effectiveness of LFP for adapting result diversification to the users' needs without accessing to explicit item properties. In addition, we also showed that LFP is capable of effectively adjusting the trade-off between the relevance and the diversity of recommended items, and thus could further contribute to the overall recommendation quality.

Our future work involves several possible directions. First, we are interested in alternative optimization algorithms to improve the portfolio selection process. Second, we will extend the basic latent factor models and explore various ways of estimating the variances of latent factors of both users and items, possible through Bayesian approaches [5]. Third, we are also interested in investigating the possibility to develop dynamic LFP that could instantly modify recommendations through the interactions with users [14, 27]. Finally, we would like to extend our work to adaptive search result diversification in text retrieval [28] and compare our work with other diversification approaches.

6. REFERENCES

[1] G. Adomavicius and A. Tuzhilin. Toward the next generation of recommender systems: A survey of the state-of-the-art and possible extensions. *IEEE Transactions on Kowledge and Data Engineering*, 17(6):734–749, 2005.

[2] D. Agarwal and B.-C. Chen. Regression-based latent factor models. KDD '09, pages 19–28, 2009.

[3] L. Azzopardi. The economics in interactive information retrieval. SIGIR '11, pages 15–24, 2011.

[4] R. Bambini, P. Cremonesi, and R. Turrin. *Recommender Systems Handbook*, chapter Recommender Systems for a IPTV Service Provider: A Real Production Environment. Springer, 2010.

[5] D. M. Blei, A. Y. Ng, and M. I. Jordan. Latent dirichlet allocation. *J. Mach. Learn. Res.*, 2003.

[6] J. Carbonell and J. Goldstein. The use of MMR diversity-based reranking for reordering documents and producing summaries. SIGIR '98, pages 335–336, 1998.

[7] H. Chen and D. R. Karger. Less is more: probabilistic models for retrieving fewer relevant documents. SIGIR '06, 2006.

[8] C. L. Clarke, M. Kolla, G. V. Cormack, O. Vechtomova, A. Ashkan, S. Büttcher, and I. MacKinnon. Novelty and diversity in information retrieval evaluation. SIGIR '08, pages 659–666, 2008.

[9] P. Cremonesi, Y. Koren, and R. Turrin. Performance of recommender algorithms on top-N recommendation tasks. RecSys '10, pages 39–46, 2010.

[10] S. Guo and S. Sanner. Probabilistic latent maximal marginal relevance. SIGIR '10, pages 833–834, 2010.

[11] A. S. Harpale and Y. Yang. Personalized active learning for collaborative filtering. SIGIR '08, pages 91–98, 2008.

[12] J. L. Herlocker, J. A. Konstan, A. Borchers, and J. Riedl. An algorithmic framework for performing collaborative filtering. SIGIR '99, pages 230–237, 1999.

[13] N. Hurley and M. Zhang. Novelty and diversity in top-N recommendation – analysis and evaluation. *ACM Trans. Internet Technol.*, 10:14:1–14:30, March 2011.

[14] T. Jambor, J. Wang, and N. Lathia. Using control theory for stable and efficient recommender systems. WWW '12, pages 11–20, 2012.

[15] K. Järvelin and J. Kekäläinen. Cumulated gain-based evaluation of IR techniques. *ACM Trans. Inf. Syst.*, 20:422–446, October 2002.

[16] Y. Koren. Factorization meets the neighborhood: a multifaceted collaborative filtering model. KDD '08, pages 426–434, 2008.

[17] Y. Koren, R. Bell, and C. Volinsky. Matrix factorization techniques for recommender systems. *Computer*, 42:30–37, August 2009.

[18] M. Kurucz, A. A. Benczúr, and K. Csalogány. Methods for large scale svd with missing values. In *Proceedings of KDD Cup and Workshop*, 2007.

[19] N. Lathia, S. Hailes, L. Capra, and X. Amatriain. Temporal diversity in recommender systems. SIGIR '10, pages 210–217, 2010.

[20] F. Radlinski and S. Dumais. Improving personalized web search using result diversification. SIGIR '06, pages 691–692, 2006.

[21] P. Resnick. Personalized filters yes; bubbles no. http://presnick.livejournal.com/21239.html, July 2011.

[22] R. Salakhutdinov and A. Mnih. Probabilistic matrix factorization. NIPS '08, 2008.

[23] R. L. Santos, C. Macdonald, and I. Ounis. Selectively diversifying web search results. CIKM '10, pages 1179–1188, 2010.

[24] R. L. Santos, C. Macdonald, and I. Ounis. Intent-aware search result diversification. SIGIR '11, pages 595–604, 2011.

[25] B. Sarwar, G. Karypis, J. Konstan, and J. Reidl. Item-based collaborative filtering recommendation algorithms. WWW '01, pages 285–295, 2001.

[26] U. Shardanand and P. Maes. Social information filtering: algorithms for automating 'word of mouth'. CHI '95, pages 210–217, 1995.

[27] M. Sloan and J. Wang. Dynamical information retrieval modelling: a portfolio-armed bandit machine approach. WWW '12, pages 603–604, 2012.

[28] J. Teevan, S. T. Dumais, and E. Horvitz. Potential for personalization. *ACM Trans. Comput.-Hum. Interact.*, 17(1):4:1–4:31, Apr. 2010.

[29] S. Vargas and P. Castells. Rank and relevance in novelty and diversity metrics for recommender systems. RecSys '11, pages 109–116, 2011.

[30] J. Wang. Mean-variance analysis: A new document ranking theory in information retrieval. ECIR '09, pages 4–16, 2009.

[31] J. Wang and Y. Zhang. Utilizing marginal net utility for recommendation in e-commerce. SIGIR '11, pages 1003–1012, 2011.
[32] J. Wang and J. Zhu. Portfolio theory of information retrieval. SIGIR '09, pages 115–122, 2009.
[33] J. Wang and J. Zhu. On statistical analysis and optimization of information retrieval effectiveness metrics. SIGIR '10, pages 226–233, 2010.
[34] S.-H. Yang, B. Long, A. J. Smola, H. Zha, and Z. Zheng. Collaborative competitive filtering: learning recommender using context of user choice. SIGIR '11, pages 295–304, 2011.
[35] C. X. Zhai, W. W. Cohen, and J. Lafferty. Beyond independent relevance: methods and evaluation metrics for subtopic retrieval. SIGIR '03, pages 10–17, 2003.
[36] C.-N. Ziegler, S. M. McNee, J. A. Konstan, and G. Lausen. Improving recommendation lists through topic diversification. WWW '05, pages 22–32, 2005.

APPENDIX

A. TOPICAL VS. RANK VARIANCES

We present the detailed derivation of $Var(R_{uN})$ in Eq. (9) below. Let us start with

$$Var(R_{uN}) = E[R_{uN} - E(R_{uN})]^2.$$

Taking into account Eq. (7), we have:

$$\begin{aligned}
&Var(R_{uN})\\
=&E[\sum_{n=1}^{N} w_n \sum_{a=1}^{A} V_{c(n)a}U_{ua} - \sum_{n=1}^{N} w_n \sum_{a=1}^{A} V_{c(n)a}E(U_{ua})]^2\\
=&E[\sum_{n=1}^{N} w_n \sum_{a=1}^{A} V_{c(n)a}\left(U_{ua} - E(U_{ua})\right)]^2\\
=&E[\sum_{n=1}^{N} w_n^2 \sum_{a=1}^{A}\sum_{l=1}^{A} V_{c(n)a}V_{c(n)l}(U_{ua} - E(U_{ua}))(U_{ul} - E(U_{ul}))\\
&+\sum_{n=1}^{N}\sum_{\substack{m=1\\ m\neq n}}^{N} w_n w_m\\
&\times \sum_{a=1}^{A}\sum_{l=1}^{A} V_{c(n)a}V_{c(m)l}(U_{ua} - E(U_{ua}))(U_{ul} - E(U_{ul}))].
\end{aligned}$$

Using the property as in Eq. (5), we obtain:

$$\begin{aligned}
&Var(R_{uN})\\
=&\sum_{n=1}^{N} w_n^2 \sum_{a=1}^{A} V_{c(n)a}^2 E[(U_{ua} - E(U_{ua}))^2]\\
&+\sum_{n=1}^{N}\sum_{\substack{m=1\\ m\neq n}}^{N} w_n w_m \sum_{a=1}^{A} V_{c(n)a}V_{c(m)a}E[(U_{ua} - E(U_{ua}))^2].
\end{aligned}$$

The Eq. (9) is obtained as above with the definition of σ_{ua}^2.

B. SEQUENTIAL RANKING

The detailed derivation of $\Delta F(R_{uk})$ in Eq. (11) is given below:

$$\Delta F(R_{uk}) = F(R_{uk}) - F(R_{uk-1})$$

$$\begin{aligned}
=&\sum_{n=1}^{k} w_n \sum_{a=1}^{A} V_{c(n)a}U_{ua} - b(\sum_{n=1}^{k} w_n^2 \sum_{a=1}^{A} V_{c(n)a}^2\sigma_{ua}^2\\
&+\sum_{n=1}^{k}\sum_{\substack{m=1\\ m\neq n}}^{k} w_n w_m \sum_{a=1}^{A} V_{c(n)a}V_{c(m)a}\sigma_{ua}^2)\\
&-\Big(\sum_{n=1}^{k-1} w_n \sum_{a=1}^{A} V_{c(n)a}U_{ua} - b(\sum_{n=1}^{k-1} w_n^2 \sum_{a=1}^{A} V_{c(n)a}^2\sigma_{ua}^2\\
&+\sum_{n=1}^{k-1}\sum_{\substack{m=1\\ m\neq n}}^{k-1} w_n w_m \sum_{a=1}^{A} V_{c(n)a}V_{c(m)a}\sigma_{ua}^2)\Big)\\
=&w_k \sum_{a=1}^{A} V_{c(k)a}U_{ua} - b\Big(w_k^2 \sum_{a=1}^{A} V_{c(k)a}^2\sigma_{ua}^2\\
&+\sum_{n=1}^{k}\sum_{\substack{m=1\\ m\neq n}}^{k} w_n w_m \sum_{a=1}^{A} V_{c(n)a}V_{c(m)a}\sigma_{ua}^2\\
&-\sum_{n=1}^{k-1}\sum_{\substack{m=1\\ m\neq n}}^{k-1} w_n w_m \sum_{a=1}^{A} V_{c(n)a}V_{c(m)a}\sigma_{ua}^2\Big)\\
=&w_k \sum_{a=1}^{A} V_{c(k)a}U_{ua} - b\Big(w_k^2 \sum_{a=1}^{A} V_{c(k)a}^2\sigma_{ua}^2\\
&+\sum_{m=1}^{k-1} w_k w_m \sum_{a=1}^{A} V_{c(k)a}V_{c(m)a}\sigma_{ua}^2\\
&+\sum_{n=1}^{k-1}\sum_{\substack{m=1\\ m\neq n}}^{k} w_n w_m \sum_{a=1}^{A} V_{c(n)a}V_{c(m)a}\sigma_{ua}^2\\
&-\sum_{n=1}^{k-1}\sum_{\substack{m=1\\ m\neq n}}^{k-1} w_n w_m \sum_{a=1}^{A} V_{c(n)a}V_{c(m)a}\sigma_{ua}^2\Big).
\end{aligned}$$

Combining the last two terms results in:

$$\begin{aligned}
\Delta F(R_{uk}) =&w_k \sum_{a=1}^{A} V_{c(k)a}U_{ua} - b\Big(w_k^2 \sum_{a=1}^{A} V_{c(k)a}^2\sigma_{ua}^2\\
&+\sum_{m=1}^{k-1} w_k w_m \sum_{a=1}^{A} V_{c(k)a}V_{c(m)a}\sigma_{ua}^2\\
&+\sum_{n=1}^{k-1} w_n w_k \sum_{a=1}^{A} V_{c(n)a}V_{c(k)a}\sigma_{ua}^2\Big).
\end{aligned}$$

Note that in above m and n are interchangeable. We, thus, have:

$$\begin{aligned}
\Delta F(R_{uk}) =&w_k \sum_{a=1}^{A} V_{c(k)a}U_{ua} - b\Big(w_k^2 \sum_{a=1}^{A} V_{c(k)a}^2\sigma_{ua}^2\\
&+2\sum_{m=1}^{k-1} w_k w_m \sum_{a=1}^{A} V_{c(k)a}V_{c(m)a}\sigma_{ua}^2\Big).
\end{aligned}$$

Swapping the summation order over space m and a in the last term, we obtain Eq. (11):

$$\begin{aligned}
\Delta F(R_{uk}) =&w_k \sum_{a=1}^{A} \Big(V_{c(k)a}U_{ua} - bw_k\sigma_{ua}^2 V_{c(k)a}^2\\
&-2b\sigma_{ua}^2 \sum_{m=1}^{k-1} w_m V_{c(k)a}V_{c(m)a}\Big).
\end{aligned}$$

Modeling the Impact of Short- and Long-Term Behavior on Search Personalization

Paul N. Bennett[1], Ryen W. White[1], Wei Chu[2], Susan T. Dumais[1],
Peter Bailey[2], Fedor Borisyuk[3], and Xiaoyuan Cui[2]
Microsoft Research[1], Microsoft Bing[2], Microsoft Server & Tools[3]
One Microsoft Way, Redmond, WA 98052 USA
{pauben, ryenw, wechu, sdumais, pbailey, fedbor, xcui}@microsoft.com

ABSTRACT

User behavior provides many cues to improve the relevance of search results through personalization. One aspect of user behavior that provides especially strong signals for delivering better relevance is an individual's history of queries and clicked documents. Previous studies have explored how short-term behavior or long-term behavior can be predictive of relevance. Ours is the first study to assess how short-term (session) behavior and long-term (historic) behavior interact, and how each may be used in isolation or in combination to optimally contribute to gains in relevance through search personalization. Our key findings include: historic behavior provides substantial benefits at the start of a search session; short-term session behavior contributes the majority of gains in an extended search session; and the combination of session and historic behavior out-performs using either alone. We also characterize how the relative contribution of each model changes throughout the duration of a session. Our findings have implications for the design of search systems that leverage user behavior to personalize the search experience.

Categories and Subject Descriptors

H.3.3 [**Information Storage and Retrieval**]: Information Search and Retrieval – *search process*; *selection process*.

Keywords

Personalization; Web search.

1. INTRODUCTION

Search personalization improves retrieval effectiveness by tailoring the ranking of results for individual users based on models of their interests [24][28][29]. To construct the profiles necessary for search personalization, evidence of a user's interests can be mined from observed past behaviors. This behavior can be sourced from the short-term (e.g., the current search session) [34] or the long-term (e.g., across many previous sessions) [25]. These studies have shown that personalization is important but often care must be taken in how it is applied, e.g., we may only want to personalize queries which have high click entropy [11][30].

An important determinant of the success of personalization is the behavioral information that is used to construct user profiles. Although there has been some work examining the effect of different contextual sources for modeling user interests [22][33], another critical aspect of personalization is the timespan of the behavioral information used for profile construction. Short-term profiles capture recent interactions but lack users' long-term interests.

Permission to make digital or hard copies of all or part of this work for personal or classroom use is granted without fee provided that copies are not made or distributed for profit or commercial advantage and that copies bear this notice and the full citation on the first page. To copy otherwise, or republish, to post on servers or to redistribute to lists, requires prior specific permission and/or a fee.
SIGIR'12, August 12–16, 2012, Portland, Oregon, USA.
Copyright 2012 ACM 978-1-4503-1472-5/12/08...$15.00.

Long-term profiles represent long-term interests but may not adequately represent searcher needs for the current task. Earlier attempts to address this challenge leveraged different representations for each source [18] or made ad hoc decisions around how to weight distant actions [27]. A principled investigation of the impact of short- and long-term behavior on search personalization is lacking and we address that shortcoming with the research presented here.

In this paper, we investigate how users' long-term search activity history interacts with their short-term search session behavior. We characterize these interactions using a framework for modeling behavior from different timespans and predicting search relevance. We explore the effectiveness of user profiles developed based on different temporal views. Although each model makes use of sets of search activity gathered over different durations, the same feature set is used for each time span to remove that source of variation, and decay factors (among other things) are studied in a principled manner. We evaluate the success of these models via a large search log containing queries, results, and clicks, enabling us to compare the performance of each personalized ranker relative to that of a high quality commercial search engine in a manner similar to previous personalization research [8][25][34]. We make the following unique contributions with this research:

- Propose a novel unified modeling framework that provides an integrative view of different parameters of personalization and controls key aspects such as the features generated from behavior and decay factors employed.
- Study dynamics in the relative contribution to personalization of short- and long-term models over the course of a session. As part of our analysis, we confirm intuitions that long-term behavior is useful at the start of a session and that short-term models yield benefit as the session proceeds.
- Provide new findings on search personalization, such as the special properties of the first query in the session, and the strong performance of models that *learn* to combine short- and long-term features for each query, rather than simply aggregating all features; suggesting that individual queries differentially benefit from short- and long-term personalization.

The remainder of this paper is structured as follows. Section 2 presents related work on model-based user behavior analysis for search personalization. Section 3 describes our unified framework for combining a user's (long-term) historical behavior with their (short-term) session activity and outlines the features and model training. Section 4 describes the experiment, including the data and methodology. We present findings in Section 5, discuss them and their implications in Section 6, and conclude in Section 7.

2. RELATED WORK

There is growing interest in the information retrieval (IR) community in examining how knowledge of a searcher's interests and context can be used to improve various aspects of search such as ranking or query suggestion. Here we review prior research that examines the use of implicit user profiles generated using a user's searching and browsing actions (queries, clicks on search results, and subsequent navigation) to personalize Web search.

Recent investigations that employ a user's search and browse actions to influence search personalization include those based on: a user's location [1], a user's history of search activity [25], the ability of a user to read at differing levels of complexity [8] and patterns of re-finding the same search result [31]. Others discuss how different forms of context and search activity may be used to cast search behavior as a prediction problem [22][33].

Several research groups have investigated personalizing search results using user profiles that comprise topical representations of users' search interests. Gauch et al. [14] learned user profiles from browsing history, Speretta and Gauch [26] built profiles using search history, and Chirita et al. [7] and Ma et al. [19] used profiles that users specified explicitly. In all cases, interest profiles were compared with those of search results and used to affect the order in which results were presented to individuals. Bennett et al. [2] demonstrated how category features from the Open Directory Project (ODP, dmoz.org) could be used to improve search ranking in the aggregate for all users but not for individual searchers.

The context of search activities within the current session has been used to build richer models of interests and improve how the search system interprets the user's current query. Cao et al. [4][5] represented search context within a session by modeling the sequence of user queries and clicks. They learned sequential prediction models from large-scale log data, and applied the models to URL recommendation, query suggestion, and query categorization. Mihalkova and Mooney [21] used similar search session features to disambiguate the current search query. White et al. [34] constructed topical models of searcher's interests using the current query and recent search activities such as queries and hyperlink clicks, and used these models to predict future interests. Models of short-term interests based on search queries and result clicks have also been used to improve search quality [9][24][36]. For example, Xiang et al. [36] developed heuristics to promote search results with the same topical category if successive queries in a search session were related by general similarity, and were not specializations, generalizations or reformulations.

Much of the work on search personalization focuses on longer-term models of user interests. Teevan et al. [29] developed rich long-term user models based on desktop search activities to improve ranking. Matthijs and Radlinski [20] developed models of users' interests using browsing behavior and evaluated their ranking improvements using an interleaving methodology (merging original and personalized rankings and observing SERP clicks). Sontag et al. [25] developed generative and discriminative probabilistic models using ODP category models from historical click data. They learned parameters based on the divergence of individual user behaviors from normative behaviors to re-rank search results and found the largest gains for an ensemble of the two models. Tan et al. [28] studied long-term language model-based representations of users' interests based on queries, documents and clicks. They considered different amounts of history and found that for fresh queries recent history was the most important, but for recurring queries longer-term history was more important.

Although long-term models described above include short-term information, few explicitly study it separately. Dou et al. [11] learned both click-based and topic-based user models over a 12-day period. Personalization was most effective for queries with high click entropy (as has also been observed by Teevan et al. [30]). Topic profiles resulted in highly variable performance across queries, and personalization was more effective for users with more historical information. Li et al. [18] modeled short- and long-term user activities but used different representations for each. They built long-term profiles using topics from the Google Directory of previously-clicked results and short-term models using a cache of recently-clicked results. They compared re-ranking based on user models with Google Directory and observed some advantages of personalization for users with varied profiles (so-called ambiguous users). However the study involved only 12 users over a ten-day period, and they were instructed to search for specific topics, hobbies and to repeat queries. Sugiyama et al. [27] modeled users' interests with both ephemeral short-term preferences and persistent long-term preferences, with an exponential decay on the importance of older information. They observed small improvements for personalized methods.

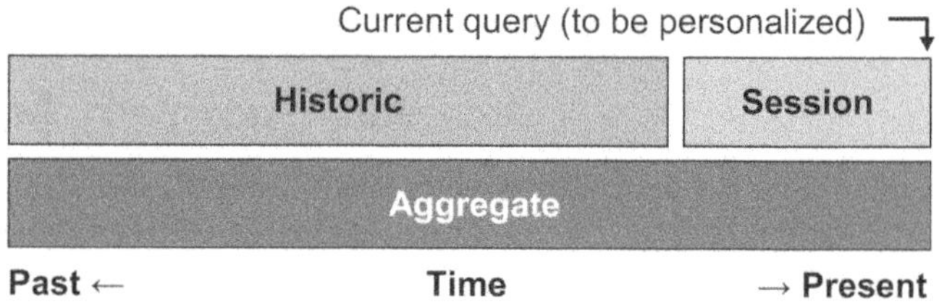

Figure 1. An illustration of how we create profiles from recent (*Session*), past (*Historic*), or a combination (*Aggregate*).

The research presented in this paper differs from previous work in several important ways. First, we present a unified framework over how interests are represented (as topics or URLs) and how short- and long-term temporal dynamics are modeled. Second, we examine the effects of the query position within a session on how these behavior models change in their relative contribution. Third, we show how to learn models that effectively combine short- and long-term behavior to create improved personalization models. Finally, our evaluation is conducted on large-scale logs from a major search engine over a two-month timespan, thus addressing scale and representativeness issues inherent in smaller studies.

3. PERSONALIZATION FRAMEWORK

We can model users' preferences from different temporal *views* of their history of interaction with the search engine. Figure 1 illustrates the relationship between each of the three temporal views that comprise the framework. The figure also shows the position of the current query which we would like to personalize. We can build a model based only on recent interactions in an attempt to capture the user's current focus. One such approach used previously, and which we adopt in this work, is to look at *session* interaction [34]. Additionally, we consider the *historic* interactions that a user had with the search engine prior to the current session, potentially comprising many days or weeks of activity. This long-term information may be useful in disambiguating underspecified queries by preferring results on topics known to be historically of interest to the user [25]. In addition, since information seeking tasks may extend across many sessions [17] the current task (session) may relate to previous sessions. This suggests a model that *aggregates* all history over a shifting time window, effectively combining short- and long-term interests.

To compare the contributions of the three different temporal views, we need a framework that yields comparable features in each of them. Otherwise, the success of one view may simply be an artifact of having modeled a component in one view that is missing from the other views. To do this, we present a novel framework that incorporates both functions that correspond to the temporal views depicted in Figure 1 and time-weighting functions. We use two representations that are commonly studied in the literature: topics and URLs [14][20][25] and show how features often studied in prior research emerge from our framework.

We now present our framework and explain how it incorporates the following factors that are understood to affect personalization quality [28][31][34]: recency; the similarity of the current query to past user queries; the similarity of a document to be ranked for the current query to the documents previously returned to a user; and how the user interacted with those past results.

3.1 Framework Overview

Within the context of personalizing search based on past behavior, we consider a number of different factors. For example, given the user has issued query q, from the temporal view on the user's past search interactions, $\text{view}(u_l)$, we can consider all related queries, $\text{related}(q, u_l)$ where u_l is the set of the user's past issued queries, the search results, and any behavioral interactions the user had with the results. We focus on clicks but skips (explicitly ignoring a result) and misses (failing to notice a result) can also be considered. The function $\text{related}(q, u_l)$ returns a set of queries that are related to q. For each related query, q_r, we also model the strength of its relationship to the current query for this user, $\text{w}(q_r, q, u_l)$, which we abbreviate as w_{q_r}. For each related query, the search engine returns a set of results, $\text{results}(q_r)$, whose elements we refer to as d_{q_r}, the documents returned for the related query. For each d_{q_r} we consider both its similarity, $\text{sim}(d_{q_r}, \text{d})$, to a document, d, for the current query when determining how we should estimate the relevance of d, and we may also consider what action, denoted as $\text{action}(q_r, d_{q_r})$, the user took with respect to the document (e.g., a satisfied click serving as an indication that the document is relevant [12][13]). We can write a family of features related to personalization parameterized by choices for the related query function, the relationship weight, the similarity and the action. One such simple formulation that considers all of these factors to generate a feature value from a $\langle q, d, u_l \rangle$ triple is:

$$f(q, d, u_l) = \sum_{q_r \in \text{related}(q, u_l) | q_r \in \text{view}(u_l)} w_{q_r} \sum_{d_{q_r}} \text{sim}(d_{q_r}, \text{d}) \, \text{action}(q_r, d_{q_r})$$

Given appropriate choices for the related query function, the weighting, similarity, and action, one can derive many commonly studied features for personalization. For example, when the set of related queries comprises all queries in the user's past interaction, the relationship weight is uniformly 1, the similarity function returns 1 for identical URLs and 0 otherwise, and the action is whether or not the user clicked on the document from the related query, then the resulting feature is simply the number of times the user has clicked on d. With the same choices except where the related queries are only queries from the past interactions that are identical, then one obtains the number of previous times the user clicked on d when issuing q, a quantity highly indicative of refinding in personalization research [31].

This framework is useful for studying different temporal views because it allows us to vary the weight and related query functions to capture temporal effects while ensuring each time view has comparable features. Furthermore, it is amenable to choosing multiple types of similarity functions and yielding comparable feature families. For example, given a representation of a document, d, as a vector of topic probabilities then one reasonable similarity function would be the inner product between the current document and the document from the related query, d_{q_r}. Again assuming that all queries in a user's history are uniformly weighted and the action is a click, then the resulting feature is the inner product between the topics of results that the user has clicked on in the past and the topics of the current document.

Seeing how this amounts to the inner product over all clicked on topics and d's topics is instructive in understanding how these features could be computed efficiently in practice. For any similarity function that can be written as the inner product of two documents by using a representation of the document, $\Phi(d)$, such that $\text{sim}(d_{q_r}, d) = \langle \Phi(d_{q_r}), \Phi(d) \rangle$, we can rewrite the inner product as an inner product of d and an aggregated weight vector:

$$f(q, d, u_l) = \langle \Phi(d), \sum_{q_r \in \text{related}(q, u_l) | q_r \in \text{view}(u_l)} w_{q_r} \sum_{d_{q_r}} \Phi(d_{q_r}) \, \text{action}(q_r, d_{q_r}) \rangle$$

$$= \langle \Phi(d), \omega(q, d, u_l) \rangle$$

where $\omega(q, d, u_l)$ is shorthand for the weight vector derived from the sum. This new weight vector is more convenient to work with because it can be updated simply by adding in the most recent interactions for any case where the relationship weight does not change based on the overall interaction history. Even when the related queries selection is more complex such as including all queries that are a superset of the current query, this can be computed efficiently by constructing an inverted index for each user mapping query words to weight vectors, $\omega(q, d, u_l)$.

When the representation $\Phi(\cdot)$ returns a document's topic vector, one obtains quantities commonly used in studying personalization by topic [25]. When the representation is based on identical URLs, we capture that by defining $\Phi(\cdot)$ as a sparse vector over all URLs (i.e., 1 for the argument URL and 0 elsewhere).

Now that we have laid the foundations for the framework and shown that it can be used to represent several previously-proposed personalization features, we address the problems of choosing functions for related queries, relationship weight, similarity, and actions motivated by literature on personalized search. Each combination of these will yield a feature which we use as input to the machine-learned ranker examined in this study.

3.2 Query Selection and Weighting

3.2.1 *Temporal Selection*

We now return to our depiction of time views of a profile in Figure 1 and define concretely how we represent these views. We represent the *Session*, *Historic*, and *Aggregate* views as choices of the $\text{view}(u_l)$ function. That is, the *Session* view returns the queries from the current session. If the related function is "identical queries", then together with the *Session* view filter the sum is over "identical queries within the session." Likewise, the *Historic* view returns queries before the current session, and the *Aggregate* view returns all queries in the user's past interactions. Thus, given choices for the parameterization of weight, similarity, and action, instead of having a single feature, we now have three features: a session version, a historic version, and an aggregate version. When we turn to modeling later in the paper, we separate the features and build models using only features from each view enabling us to study each view and compare the views with the same number and types of features in each.

Note that we chose to make a session distinction since sesssions have been commonly used as a proxy to identify task boundaries [15][17]. Session has been used in the context of personalization to predict short-term activity [33][34], and it is currently of broad interest to the IR community as a track in the Text Retrieval Conference [16]. For our purposes a session is demarcated by 30 minutes of user inactivity as described in [32].

3.2.2 Temporal Weighting

In addition to the session boundary, we may also posit that recent interactions of a user matter more than distant ones. This has been captured in personalization by introducing a decay function on past interactions [10][23][27][34]. We introduce a similar decay into our framework by setting the relationship weighting function, w_{q_r}, to a decay value. Let $p(q_r)$ refer to the number of queries in the time view (session, historic, aggregate) by which the related query precedes the current query. Thus $p(q_r)=1$ is the most recent previous query (in session, history, and aggregate respectively). Then we choose $c^{p(q_r)-1}$ as the decay, where c is a decay factor. Rather than emphasizing absolute time, this emphasizes recent activity. Figure 2 shows the weights for various decay factors over previous queries. For experiments reported in this paper, we chose c=0.95 (shown as a red dotted line in the figure) because it lies between the extremes of massively emphasizing recent activity and uniformly emphasizing all actions. We also used simple uniform weighting (c=1), shown as the blue solid horizontal line at the top of Figure 2.

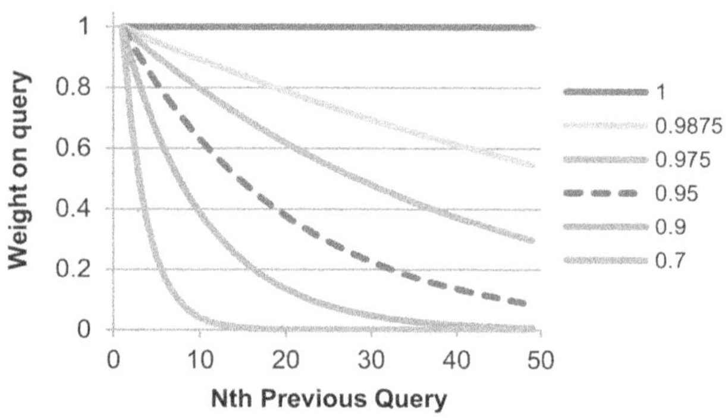

Figure 2. Query decay weights given various decay factors.

3.2.3 Query Generalization and Specialization

Various studies have demonstrated that users interact differently with results if they have recently generalized a query (reformulated by dropping words) or specialized it (reformulated by adding words) [36]. Because of this we introduce four choices for the $\text{related}(q, u_l)$ function: (1) all queries in the user's profile (generated using $\text{view}(u_l)$), giving rise to features that capture the user's preference for a document independent of the current query, q; (2) all queries exactly matching q in the user's profile, which captures specific interactions; (3) all queries in the profile that are (improper) subsets of q, which captures behavior on generalizations of q (i.e. a subset has fewer words and is therefore more general); (4) all queries in the profile that are (improper) supersets of q, which captures behavior on all specializations of q. The subsets and supersets were determined after stopwords were removed and had to share at least one non-stopword with q (i.e., empty sets were not permitted).

3.3 URL Representation

As noted in Section 3.1, the user's interaction with a particular document is a useful predictor for personalization as an indicator of re-finding behavior. Therefore, we use one choice of $\Phi(\cdot)$ which returns a sparse vector over URLs (document IDs) that is 1 for the dimension corresponding to the URL of Φ's argument and 0 elsewhere. As further discussed in Section 3.1, this gives rise to a variety of useful features depending on the remaining parameter choices, e.g., the user's preference (measured as number of clicks) for a document: (1) across all queries; (2) for the current query, q; (3) for generalizations of q; and (4) for specializations of q.

3.4 Topical Representation

Topical representations of documents are commonly used in personalization studies (e.g., [14][25][34]). To obtain such a topic representation for this study, we labeled each document with a vector of probabilities of categories from the top two levels of the ODP hierarchy using a text-based classifier. Each document's vector was restricted to the three most probable classes. The classifier has a micro-averaged F1 value of 0.60 and is described more fully in [2]. As mentioned in Section 3.1, given appropriate choices for the remaining parameters, this representation will yield features that capture the user's preference for the topics of d: (1) across all queries; (2) for the current query, q; (3) for generalizations of q; and (4) for specializations of q. To measure the similarity between the document's topical representation and $\omega(q, d, u_l)$ resulting from the topic parameterization we use the cosine similarity, which is commonly used in the literature.

3.5 Search Actions

While a variety of behavioral signals have been studied in the literature, we restrict our choice for the $\text{action}(q_r, d_{q_r})$ function to *satisfied* (SAT) clicks on the search engine result page. A SAT click involves a user dwelling on the result for at least 30 seconds or one which terminates the search session [12][13]. We focus on SAT clicks since research indicates that dwell time is indicative of relevance and that clicks with short dwell times ("quick backs") are unlikely to be relevant [37].

3.6 Profile Information Measures

Personalization studies have also commonly introduced features that measure the amount of information known about the user or the appropriateness of personalizing for a query [1][8][30][34]. Similar notions also emerge from our framework. When the choice of relationship weight, the representation, and action are all non-negative, then $\omega(q, d, u_l)$ can be treated as describing a probability space over the representation space, $\Phi(\cdot)$, by normalizing across the feature dimensions. In fact, if we further summed across all users when the relationship is exact query match, with the URL representation, and click actions, then the entropy of the resulting vector is *QueryClickEntropy*, commonly referred to as click entropy in earlier personalization research [11][30]. To simplify the personalized versions because tracking all URLs for a user can be costly, we make a simplifying assumption and compute this entropy over (clicked) rank positions instead of URLs. If the same query always returns the same search results in the same rank order, then the personalized click entropy for a query (*UserQueryPositionEntropy*) is the same as a personalized computation for standard click entropy.

Likewise, we use the topical representation and compute entropy of the resulting $\omega(q, d, u_l)$. In which case if we sum across users, we obtain *QueryTopicEntropy* (used to identify ambiguous queries for personalization in [25]), conditional on the user across all queries we obtain *UserTopicEntropy*, conditional on user and query we obtain *UserQueryTopicEntropy*, and similarly for subset and superset. Because these entropy-based features derive from the appropriate parameterization of $\omega(q, d, u_l)$, they can depend on each time view and use decay or uniform weighting.

Table 1. Summary of Features. For each parameterized feature, the feature type action(q_r, d_{q_r}) = SAT click. When a row has the "Temporal Selection" box checked then a version is instantiated for each value of view(u_I) = *Session*, *Historic*, *All*. When a row has the weight box checked then a version is instantiated for each value of w_{q_r} = uniform, decay. Thus rows with both temporal selection and temporal decay correspond to 3 views × 2 weight = 6 features.

Temporal Selection	Weight	Feature	Description
		Query-Doc-User Features	
×	×	*DocTopicCosineUserTopicProfile* : cosine of $\Phi(d), \omega(q, d, u_I)$ with related(q, u_I)=all, $\Phi(\cdot)$ = Topic	Topic similarity of overall user's history to this URL
×	×	*UserClicksOnUrl* : inner prod. of $\Phi(d), \omega(q, d, u_I)$ with related(q, u_I)=all, $\Phi(\cdot)$ = URL	Click count of overall user's history to this URL
×	×	*DocTopicCosineUserTopicProfileForQuery* : cosine of $\Phi(d), \omega(q, d, u_I)$ with related(q, u_I)=q, $\Phi(\cdot)$ = Topic	Class similarity of selected user history (exact query) to this URL
×	×	*UserClicksOnUrlForQuery* : inner prod. of $\Phi(d), \omega(q, d, u_I)$ with related(q, u_I)=q, $\Phi(\cdot)$ = URL	Click count of selected user history (exact query) to this URL
×	×	*DocTopicCosineUserTopicProfileForSubsetQuery* : cosine of $\Phi(d), \omega(q, d, u_I)$ with related(q, u_I)=subset q, $\Phi(\cdot)$ = Topic	Class similarity of selected user history (subset of query after stopword removal) to this URL
×	×	*UserClicksOnUrlForSubsetQuery* : inner prod. of $\Phi(d), \omega(q, d, u_I)$ with related(q, u_I)=subset q, $\Phi(\cdot)$ = URL	Click count of selected user history (subset of query after stop-word removal) to this URL
×	×	*DocTopicCosineUserTopicProfileForSupersetQuery* : cosine of $\Phi(d), \omega(q, d, u_I)$ with related(q, u_I)=superset q, $\Phi(\cdot)$ = Topic	Class similarity of selected user history (superset of query after stopword removal) to this URL
×	×	*UserClicksOnUrlForSupersetQuery* : inner prod. of $\Phi(d), \omega(q, d, u_I)$ with related(q, u_I)=superset q, $\Phi(\cdot)$ = URL	Click count of selected user history (superset of query after stop-word removal) to this URL
		Query Features	
Query Ambiguity Measures			
		QueryClickEntropy (commonly called click entropy in the literature)	Measures the diversity of clicks across users. Higher entropy indicates queries with more intents
		QueryTopicEntropy	Higher entropy indicates topically ambiguous.
Query Difficulty Measures			
		PositionInSession	Easy queries come early in a session with reformulations later
		QueryLength	Query length has been shown to be predictive of query difficulty
		QueryFrequency	More frequent queries often have more click information
Query-Doc			
		Rank	Rank of base ranker – non-personalized estimate of relevance
		Query-History Features	
Query Number Features in Profile (not quite analogs)			
×		*NumberOfQueries*	Number of distinct queries in interaction view
×		*NumberOfSessionsWithQuery*	Number of sessions in view containing this query
×		*NumberOfSubsetQueries*	Number of distinct queries in view matching subset relation
×		*NumberOfSupersetQueries*	Number of distinct queries in view matching superset relation
Focus of User Profile			
×	×	*UserTopicEntropy:* entropy of normalized $\omega(q, d, u_I)$ with related(q, u_I)=all, $\Phi(\cdot)$ = Topic	Measures diversity of the user's observed needs
×	×	*UserQueryTopicEntropy:* entropy of normalized $\omega(q, d, u_I)$ with related(q, u_I)=q, $\Phi(\cdot)$ = Topic	Measure of diversity of topics that have satisfied the user's need for this exact query in the past
×	×	*UserSubsetQueryTopicEntropy:* entropy of normalized $\omega(q, d, u_I)$ with related(q, u_I)=subset q, $\Phi(\cdot)$ = Topic	Measures diversity of topics that have satisfied the user's need for the selected (subset) history
×	×	UserSupersetQueryTopicEntropy: entropy of normalized $\omega(q, d, u_I)$ with related(q, u_I)=superset q, $\Phi(\cdot)$ = Topic	Measure of diversity of topics that have satisfied the user's need for the selected (super) history
×	×	*UserPositionEntropy:* entropy of normalized $\omega(q, d, u_I)$ with related(q, u_I)=all, $\Phi(\cdot)$ = Position	Higher positional entropy means that the user is not always satisfied by results in the top position
×	×	*UserQueryPositionEntropy:* entropy of normalized $\omega(q, d, u_I)$ with related(q, u_I)=q, $\Phi(\cdot)$ = Position	Higher positional entropy means that the user is not always satisfied by results in the top position for this query. If the results for a query are always stable, this is personalized click entropy

We also introduce simple features that measure the number of queries or sessions containing the query in each view. We use these features in our model and describe them in detail in Table 1.

3.7 Additional Features and Summary

In addition to the features listed thus far, we also have a number of other non-personalized features of the query and the search results that we use in our models. These include the query click entropy and query class entropy (whose relationship to the framework is described in Section 3.6), which measures the diversity of clicks across users, and the diversity of topics in the search results for the current query, both derived from historic log data. Other features such as the length of the query and the rank position of each of the result URLs, as determined by the baseline ranker, are also included. A full description with additional motivation of each of these additional features, as well as all features described in text above, is provided in Table 1.

In summary, we consider several features, 3 temporal views and 2 weights. There are 14 rows in the table that depend both on temporal selection *and* weight accounting for 14×3×2=84 features. There are four features that depend *only on* temporal selection accounting for 4×3=12 features, and there are 6 features that have no temporal selection or weight – resulting in 102 features total. Restricting the set of features used to a single temporal view yields 14×2+4+6=38 features.

4. EXPERIMENTAL METHODOLOGY

Using the models described in the previous section, we aim to answer questions about the relative performance of each of the temporal views. In this section we describe the method that we followed for our experiments. We begin by describing the set of research questions that we answer in our study.

4.1 Research Questions

The study investigates the following conditions, each specifying the amount and type of search history used for personalization:

1. **Session:** All previous actions in current search session. The full set of features in Table 1 instantiated for the *Session* view yielding 38 features.
2. **Historic:** All previous actions apart from those in the current session. The full set of features in Table 1 instantiated for the *Historic* view yielding 38 features.
3. **Aggregate:** All previous actions before the current query. The full set of features in Table 1 instantiated for the *Aggregate* view yielding 38 features.
4. **Union** of *Session*, *Historic*, and *Aggregate*: Combines the sets of features associated with each of the three other views. The full set of features in Table 1 instantiated for the each of the *Session*, *Historic*, and *Aggregate* views yielding 102 features (32 temporal selection features × 3 + the 6 additional features).

Adding the *Union* condition allows the ranker to determine how much weight to put on each of the three possible time views.

Using these four conditions, we train models that re-rank the top Web search results provided by a large commercial search engine. The baseline used for our experiments is the original ranking of the top ten results provided by the engine. Note that this baseline is highly competitive and outperforming it is very challenging.

We address the following three research questions:

1. Do short- and long-term models both provide evidence for improved personalization? (Session, Historic vs. baseline)

Training	Wk 1	Wk 2	Wk 3	Wk 4	Wk 5	Wk 6	Wk 7	Wk 8
Testing	Wk 1	Wk 2	Wk 3	Wk 4	Wk 5	Wk 6	Wk 7	Wk 8

Profile generation	Example generation

Figure 3. Illustration of our usage of data to profiles relative to the training and testing sets.

- Which one provides more? (Session vs. Historic)
- Do they provide additive information? (Union vs. the best-performing model of Session and Historic)

2. Does aggregating all activity (with or without a decay factor emphasizing recent activity) capture the full interaction of short- and long-term models? (Aggregate vs. Union)
3. Do some features act differently in short- versus long-term models? (Can the performance of Union be explained by any of Session, Historic, or Aggregate?)

Answers to these questions provide valuable insight about the relative utility of the time views and help inform decisions about when and how to use these views for search personalization.

4.2 Data Set and Evaluation Methodology

The primary source of data for this study is a proprietary data set comprising anonymized logs of users of the Microsoft Bing search engine. The logs contained a unique user identifier, a search session identifier, the query, the top-10 URLs returned by the search engine for that query, and clicks on the results. We used eight weeks of log data gathered from July and August 2011 to train and evaluate our different models. Logs were collected from flights where other personalization support was disabled, so as to not bias our results with other personalization signals.

For evaluation, we need a personalized relevance judgment for each result. Obtaining many explicit relevance judgments from real users is impractical, and there is no known approach to train expert judges to provide reliable judgments that reflect real user preferences. Hence we obtained these judgments using a log-based methodology inspired by [12] and similar to that used in [2][8]. Specifically, we assign a positive judgment to one of the top 10 URLs if it is a *satisfied result click* (SAT click). We define a SAT click in a similar way to previous work [12] as either a click followed by no further clicks for 30 seconds or more, or the last result click in the session. We also assign a positive judgment to a URL if it is a SAT click in one of the following two queries in the session -- as long as all queries up to the SAT click share at least one URL in the top 10 with the original query. The remaining top-ranked URLs receive a negative judgment. This gives us a positive or negative judgment for each of the top-10 URLs for each query. The rank positions of the positive judgments are used to evaluate retrieval performance before and after re-ranking. Specifically, we measure our performance using the mean average precision (MAP) of the re-ranked lists. This is the mean of the average precision attained for each of the queries across the top-10 results retrieved before re-ranking (for the baseline) and after re-ranking (for each of the views of interest). Queries for which we cannot assign a positive judgment to any top-10 URL are excluded from the dataset.

We used a modified form of five-fold cross validation by user for training and testing, splitting based on user identifier. This is modified in the sense that during each fold 80% of the users were used for training and 20% of the users were held out for testing, but all of the test data came from the week after the training data. Splitting on user meant that there are no overlapping users between training and test. We did this because we wanted to ensure that the predictive patterns we learned also apply to users not seen during model training (as would be the case when deploying such models in practice). Figure 3 demonstrates how we extracted training and test data from the logs. Both training (week 7) and testing (week 8) data use the six weeks immediately prior to each to ensure feature distributions between train and test are based on the same amount of profile information. For each query in week seven, the historic features are computed based on actions from up to six weeks before that query (weeks 1–6). For users in the test fold (week 8), we used data from weeks 2–7 to build the profiles. Because we aim to compare the contributions of both historic and recent activity, if users lack search activity in a timespan then reliably comparing our experimental outcomes becomes challenging. We leave studying how this tradeoff changes with the amount of available history from a user as future work. Therefore, we restricted users to those with at least one SAT click in each of the six weeks before the week of interest (note this only uses weeks 1–7 and does *not* use knowledge of week 8 when selecting users). Over the 8 week period, the selection process resulted in around 155K user profiles over 10.4M sessions with an average of 174.40 (σ=181.49) queries/user and 2.61 queries/session (σ=3.36). All MAP results are means of performance across the five folds.

4.3 Experiments

Using the described dataset, we train a ranking model using the LambdaMART learning algorithm [35] for re-ranking the top ten results of the query. LambdaMART is an extension of LambdaRank [3] based on boosted decision trees. LambdaMART has been shown to be one of the best algorithms for learning to rank. Indeed, an ensemble model in which LambdaMART rankers were the key component won Track 1 of the 2010 Yahoo! *Learning to Rank Challenge* [6]. However, we note the choice of learning algorithm is not central to this work, and any reasonable learning to rank algorithm would likely provide similar results.

We use LambdaMART with 500 decision trees. We did a grid search using cross-validation by user over a 5 percent sample of the *training* set using the Union feature set. We used a range of number of leaves $\in$ {35, 70, 140, 280, 560}, minimum instances in a leaf node $\in${200, 400, 800, 1600, 2000}, learning rate $\in$ {0.075, 0.15, 0.30, 0.60}, and number of trees in the ensemble $\in${50, 100, 200, 400}. There was relative insensitivity in the area where number of leaves $\leq$ 100, learning rate $\leq$ 0.3, minimum instances in a leaf node $\leq$ 2000, and number of trees $\in$ [50,200]. We broke ties arbitrarily and used number of leaves = 70, minimum instances in a leaf node = 2000, learning rate = 0.3, and number of trees = 50. After sweeping to determine parameters, we used the same parameters for all other models. We did this because we wish to understand how each model/feature set behaves in combination with the other parameters. For each fold, 10% of the training set is used as validation for model selection.

5. RESULTS

In this section we present the findings of our analysis. We focus on comparing the performance of the models constructed using the four conditions listed in Section 4.1. We begin by describing the overall performance of the models across all queries, then focus only on queries for which there is a measurable difference in search performance (e.g., where MAP changes) since those more clearly illustrate performance differences (although mask coverage effects, which we also explore). We report the change in performance from the baseline ranking – a highly competitive top Web search engine. We also conducted paired t-tests to compare the performance of the models with each other and the baseline.

5.1 Overall Performance

We begin by analyzing the overall performance of the models over the baseline. We measured the change (difference) in MAP from the baseline non-personalized search engine ranking's MAP across all queries for each of the four experimental conditions. For proprietary reasons, we only report the change from the baseline's MAP, rather than reporting absolute performance.

5.1.1 Performance on All Queries

Figure 4 presents the change in overall MAP for each model from the baseline. Error bars denote standard error of the mean in this chart and all other charts in the remainder of the paper.

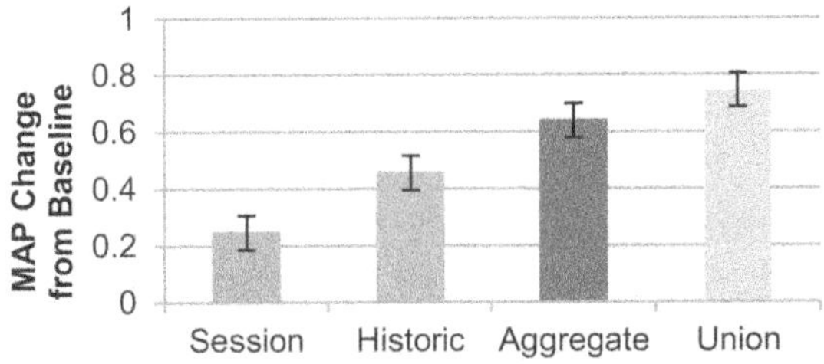

Figure 4. Average change in MAP from baseline ranker MAP

As seen in Figure 4, all methods improve over the baseline (i.e., all reported changes are positive). All gains over the baseline and differences between methods are significant with paired t-tests at $p < .01$. The figure shows increasing amounts of profiling information leads to greater improvements in retrieval performance. Interestingly using all sets of features (*Union*) and allowing the ranker to learn how the time views should be used for each query leads to the largest improvements over the baseline. This suggests that how personalization should be applied may be more nuanced than simple aggregation can capture (e.g., there may be times when we want to ignore historic data for personalization if the task is atypical of the user). We emphasize that while greater profiling information leads to better performance, this is not a foregone conclusion. For example, if every session was a new task unlike anything a user has previously done, then we would expect *Session* to outperform *Historic*. Likewise, if simple combinations of long- and short-term data could fully summarize the information available, then *Union* would not outperform *Aggregate*.

5.1.2 Effect of Query Position in Session

During search sessions, searchers reformulate their queries and adapt their information needs based upon exposure to information. We wanted to study whether this had an effect on the performance of the models. Figure 5 shows the average change in MAP from the baseline, broken out by the query position in the session, from the first to the fifth query and all remaining queries thereafter.

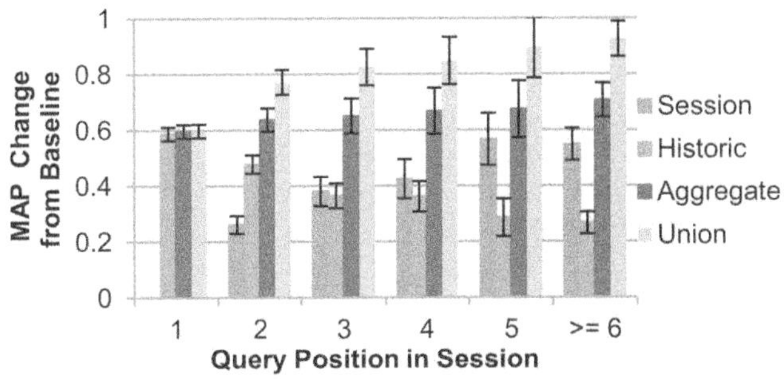

Figure 5. Avg. change in MAP by position of query in session.

From Figure 5, we see the *Session*-based personalization steadily increases its gains as more session information becomes available and seems to stabilize around 0.55 gain in MAP. On the other hand, *Historic* quickly decreases its gains as the information from the current session is not captured and the searcher's immediate interests may not be reflected in their long-term interests. It is interesting to note that by the fifth query, the session information accounts for half the gains in personalization (*Aggregate* vs. *Historic*). Looking at *Union* we can see that allowing the ranker to learn how to combine short- and long-term history leads to the best gains versus simple aggregation of the two profile sources. Note that the gains of *Union* over the other models are significant at $p < .01$ across all queries in the session except the first. For the first query in a session, the three models incorporating historic information have access to the same information, and as expected, their performance is nearly statistically identical. Overall this implies that re-finding and personalization are likely qualitatively different in the short term versus long term – otherwise simple aggregation would likely capture the behavior.

5.2 Performance When Measurably Different

Until now, we have focused on the effect on overall retrieval performance. However, since personalization may only be appropriate for a subset of queries, a more sensitive measure of the relative performance of the temporal views is to consider only performance on queries where personalization resulted in a different MAP score (i.e., non-zero difference) than the baseline – which we call *measurably different* queries for brevity. This provides important insight into the relative precision that each personalization method has independent of the fraction of queries that they affect. We present results from that analysis in this section.

5.2.1 All Measurably Different Queries

We begin by examining the change in MAP for the measurably different queries. Figure 6 shows the average change for each of the four profiling methods.

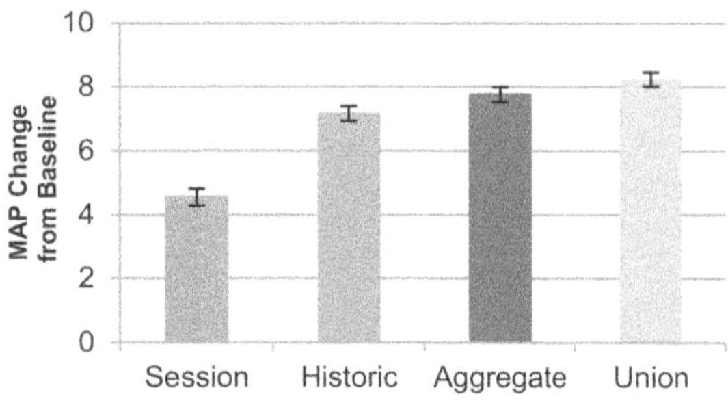

Figure 6. Average change in MAP given measurably different.

The figure shows that the gains are much larger when we focus on the measurably different queries (e.g., for *Session*, the MAP gain is more than 4 vs. 0.2 in Figure 4). The relative ordering of the sources is the same as presented in Figure 4, although the performance of the three models which incorporate historic information are more similar between themselves and more noticeably different from *Session* than when looking at changes in overall MAP. Differences are significant with paired t-tests at $p < .01$ for all comparisons apart from the *Aggregate* versus *Union* comparison, which is significant at $p < .10$.

5.2.2 Effect of Query Position in Session

In a similar way to earlier, we also study the effect of query position in session on the change in MAP for the measurably different queries. Figure 7 shows the gain over the baseline as the session proceeds. We see the gains per query are quite large, ranging from 3 points to 13 points of MAP. Several observations can be made from these differences. Again we see that the gain from *Session* increases then plateaus and that the gain from *Historic* decreases as the session progresses. Differences between *Session* and *Historic* are significant at $p < .01$ apart from at queries 3 and 4 where the gains in MAP that they offer cross.

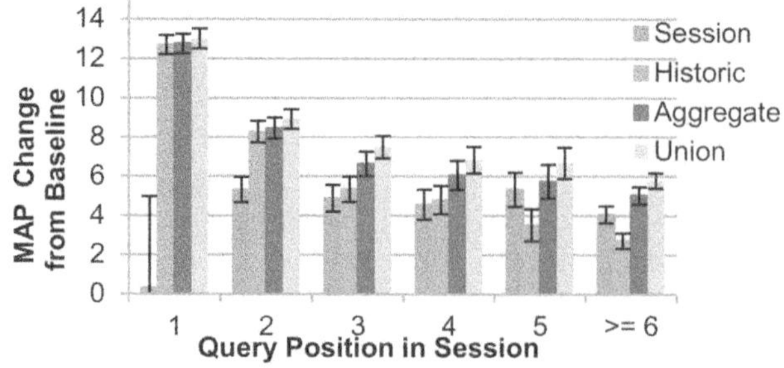

Figure 7. Average change in MAP on measurably different queries for each temporal view vs. position of query in session.

Next, we see that the gains of *Aggregate* and *Union* over measurably different queries are comparable in all positions (*Union* is better but generally not significant, other than at queries 3 and 5 ($p < .05$)). Since *Union* outperforms *Aggregate* overall (see Section 5.1.1) this implies the query volume impacted is the key difference (also see Figure 9) and suggests that being able to differentially weight short-term and long-term behavior can personalize different sets (i.e., it is not simply a gain in precision over the same queries).

Finally, the large increase in MAP in the first position for the methods using long-term information suggests that more ambiguous queries, which personalization most benefits [11][30], may be more likely to happen as the first query in the session. This intuitively makes sense since much session behavior is captured by refinement and reformulation after the first query.[1] In Figure 8 we examine several important properties of the queries in each position in the session to help us interpret such differences. We report Z-scores to highlight how the queries in each position differ from the mean of all positions.

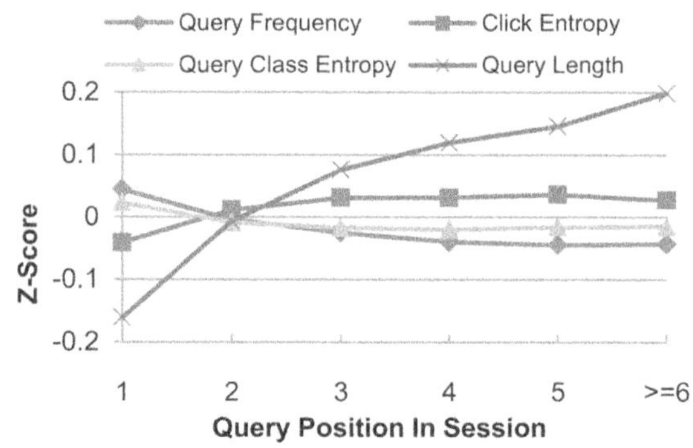

Figure 8. Mean of query properties for queries in a position normalized by their overall mean and standard deviation. Below/above zero is below/above average. Y-axis units are standard deviations (represented as the Z-score).

[1] The small gains with large variance of *Session* in position one results from a small number of queries that improve from the non-personalization features (e.g., query frequency, length) that are always available. It is clear from the error bars, that this is non-significant.

From Figure 8, we see the first position consists of very short queries that are frequent and have lower than average click entropy with higher than average topic ambiguity. Perhaps this is the reason why long-term profiles are so successful in the first position since they can frequently provide disambiguation. The most clear trend observable in the graph is for query length. Typically short queries start a session but the query length increases dramatically later in the session. While the low click entropy at the first position may seem contradictory to having ambiguous queries at the start of a session, this is an effect of the frequency of short sessions containing primarily navigational intents. For example, if we focus simply on sessions of length five or more, the z-score of the click entropy in the first position of such long sessions is 0.04 – well above the average. The decrease in ambiguity and increase in complexity (length) later in the session may explain why observed gains in MAP across the impacted queries are lower as we extend further into the session.

5.2.3 Query Volume Impacted by Personalization

Since personalization is not applied to all queries, it is important to understand the fraction of queries that can be affected by each of the time views. Overall the query volume impacted (percentage of measurably different queries) for the methods ranges from 5.42% (*Session*) to 9.05% (*Union*). However, there are some interesting effects when we consider the position of the query in the session. Figure 9 presents the fraction of queries with impacted performance at different query positions in the session.

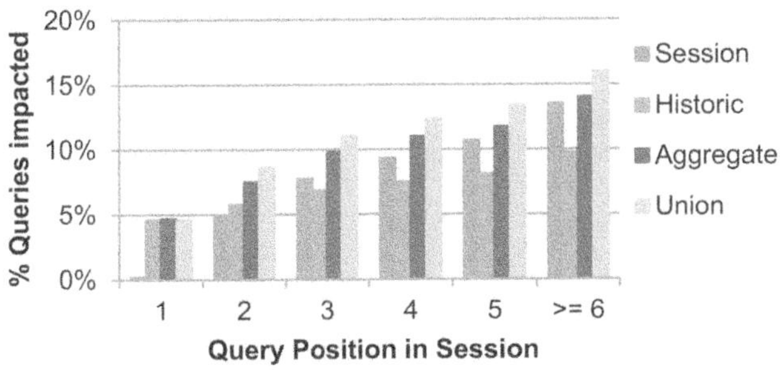

Figure 9. Percentage of queries with performance different than baseline vs. position of query in session.

In examining the impact percentages reported in Figure 9, we see that all of the methods personalize more often later in the session. This rate of impact rises most rapidly for the *Session* personalization as more information becomes available to it. Interestingly, impact rate also rises for the *Historic* method even though that method does not incorporate information from the current session. This suggests that long sessions may be *a priori* more likely to come from a user's prototypical interests although this observation requires further study. Changes in impact rate as the session proceeds may indeed be related to changes in query properties such as query length and popularity as the session proceeds and searchers' needs become more narrowly focused. As we saw in Figure 8, properties of the queries change over the course of the search session, and these changes may affect the percentage of queries that are amenable to personalization.

5.3 Effects of Other Conditions

As well as measuring the effect of time view on the performance of the model, we also explored the effects of other conditions mentioned in Section 3. Given the representation, one possibility is that the uniform weight or the decay weighting is crucial. For all of the features that use a weight we ran an ablation study that only used uniform weighted features, decay-weighted, or both and we observed no significant differences (not shown for space).

It is also interesting to consider whether these temporal aspects that happen using all features (*All*) are due only to topical effects (*Topic*) or to URL effects (*URL*). We summarize these conditions in Figure 10, normalizing each of them by the maximum performance within condition to focus on the temporal trend within condition.

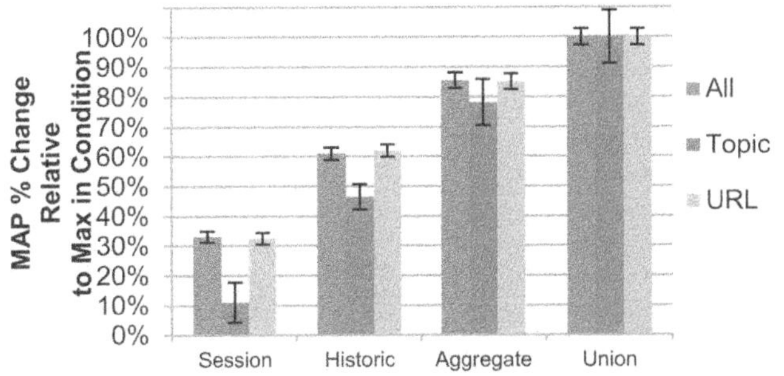

Figure 10. Changes in performance for other model conditions relative to the best performing time view and condition pair.

We see the same trends observed overall also hold within each of these conditions. This implies that the tradeoffs between short- and long-term aspects are not simply due to effects seen under one representation but are more general across representation choices. Both for space and because our emphasis here is on temporal aspects, we do not focus on comparing performance across conditions and address that in future work.

6. DISCUSSION AND IMPLICATIONS

We have studied how short-term (session) behavior and long-term (historic) behavior interact, and how each may be used in isolation or in combination to optimally contribute to gains in relevance through search personalization. Through a large-scale analysis of search logs, we have shown: that historic behavior provides substantial benefits at the start of a search session; that short-term session behavior contributes the majority of gains in an extended search session; and that the combination of session and historic behavior outperforms either using just session behavior alone or using simple aggregations. Importantly, we also showed that by learning a combination of the three views, the model can determine which should be weighted most highly given the current query and prior behavior. These results have important implications for search personalization, which has typically only studied short- or long-term behaviors independently. We show there is value from carefully considering interactions between them.

We observe that over the course of a search session there are variations in query properties such as query length and query ambiguity. These query changes may also affect the potential for personalization. As the session proceeds, we observe that more queries can be impacted by personalization since there may be more evidence of searcher interests resulting in increasing overall utility, but smaller gains in retrieval effectiveness for queries that do change, perhaps because the queries are more difficult.

Our research improves the understanding of how short- and long-term behaviors can be used by search engine designers to improve the performance of search personalization. For example, based on the position of the current query in a session, the search engine could use a particular source (e.g., historic data early in the session, session data as the session proceeds). However, we have also shown we can learn a model that can outperform any source in isolation and appropriately choose behaviors from each time view to attain better retrieval performance. Future work will extend this research, including actions beyond clicks (e.g., skips) and other query similarity measures. We will also quantify the impact of short-term modeling for the cold-start problem of providing personalization to users with no previously observed interactions.

7. CONCLUSIONS

Previous work in search personalization has leveraged short-term or long-term behaviors to construct models of searcher interests. However, little is known about how these behaviors interact and when we should be leveraging them separately or in combination. In this paper we investigated the interaction between short- and long-term interests, and how this information can be combined to learn performant search personalization models. We demonstrated the benefits of historic behavior: at the outset of a session, short-term models yield benefit as the session proceeds; and allowing the ranker to learn weights for short-term features, long-term features, and their combination models searcher interests more effectively. This work makes an important step toward unifying prior work on personalization. Future work will explore further aspects of the interaction between different feature durations as well as other conditions from the framework that we only touched on briefly here (e.g., topic vs. URL), all focusing on how best to improve search performance through personalization.

8. ACKNOWLEDGMENTS

We would like to thank Dan Schwartz, Sebastian de la Chica, and Yi Mao for contributing to early prototypes of the research here. We would also like to thank Filip Radlinski for discussions around the implications for session-based personalization.

REFERENCES

[1] Bennett, P.N., Radlinski, F., White, R.W., and Yilmaz, E. (2011). Inferring and using location metadata to personalize web search. *SIGIR*, 135–144.

[2] Bennett, P., Svore, K., and Dumais, S. (2010). Classification-enhanced ranking. *WWW*, 111–120.

[3] Burges, C.J.C., Ragno, R., and Le, Q.V. (2006). Learning to rank with non-smooth cost functions. *NIPS*, 193–200.

[4] Cao, H., Jiang, D., Pei, J., He, Q., Liao, Z., Chen, E., and Li, H. (2008). Context-aware query suggestion by mining click-through and session data. *KDD*, 875–883.

[5] Cao, H., Hu, D.H., Shen, D., Jiang, D., Sun, J.-T., Chen, E., and Yang, Q. (2009). Context-aware query classification. *SIGIR*, 3–10.

[6] Chapelle, O., Chang, Y., and Liu, T.-Y. (2010). The Yahoo! learning to rank challenge. *http://learningtorankchallenge.yahoo.com.*

[7] Chirita, P., Nejdl, W., Paiu, R., and Kohlschutter, C. (2005). Using ODP metadata to personalize search. *SIGIR*, 178–185.

[8] Collins-Thompson, K., Bennett, P.N., White, R.W., de la Chica, S., and Sontag, D. (2011). Personalizing web search results by reading level. *CIKM*, 403–412.

[9] Daoud, L. Tamine-Lechani, L., Boughanem, M., and Chebaro, B. (2009). A session based personalized search using an ontological user profile. *SOC*, 1732–1736.

[10] Downey, D., Dumais, S., Liebling, D. and Horvitz, E. (2008). Understanding the relationship between searchers' queries and information goals. *CIKM*, 449–458.

[11] Dou, Z., Song, R. and Wen, J-R. (2007). A large-scale evaluation and analysis of personalized search strategies. *WWW*, 581–590.

[12] Fox, S., Kuldeep, K., Mydland, M., Dumais, S., and White, T. (2005). Evaluating implicit measures to improve Web search. *ACM TOIS, 23(2)*: 147-168.

[13] Gao, J., Yuan, W., Li, X., Deng, K., and Nie, J-Y. (2009). Smoothing clickthrough data for web search ranking. *SIGIR*, 355–362.

[14] Gauch, S., Chaffee, J., and Pretschner, A. (2003). Ontology-based user profiles for search and browsing. *WIAS*, 219–234.

[15] Jones, R. and Klinkner, K.L. (2008). Beyond the session timeout: automatic hierarchical segmentation of search topics in query logs. *CIKM*, 699–708.

[16] Kanoulas, E., Carterette, B., Clough, P., and Sanderson, M. (2010). Session track overview. *TREC 2010.*

[17] Kotov, A., Bennett, P.N., White, R.W., Dumais, S.T., and Teevan, J. (2011). Modeling and analysis of cross-session search tasks. *SIGIR*, 5–14.

[18] Li, L., Yang, Z., Wang, B. and Kitsuregawa, M. (2007). Dynamic adaptation strategies for long-term and short-term user profile to personalize search. *APWeb/WAIM*, 228–240.

[19] Ma, Z., Pant, G., and Sheng, O. (2007). Interest-based personalized search. *ACM TOIS, 25(1)*: Article 5.

[20] Matthijs, N. and Radlinski, F. (2011). Personalizing web search using long term browsing history. *WSDM*, 25–34

[21] Mihalkova, L. and Mooney, R. (2009). Learning to disambiguate search queries from short sessions. *ECML*, 111–127.

[22] Piwowarski, B. and Zaragoza, H. (2007). Predictive user click models based on click-through history. *CIKM*, 175–182.

[23] Shen, X., Dumais, S.T., and Horvitz, E. (2005). Analysis of topic dynamics in Web search. *WWW*, 1102–1103.

[24] Shen, X., Tan, B., and Zhai, C. (2005). Context-sensitive information retrieval using implicit feedback. *SIGIR*, 43–50.

[25] Sontag, D., Collins-Thompson, K., Bennett, P.N., White, R.W., Dumais, S.T., and von Billerbeck, B. (2012). Probabilistic models for personalizing web search. *WSDM*, 433-442.

[26] Speretta, M. and Gauch, S. (2005). Personalizing search based on user search histories. *WI*, 622-628.

[27] Sugiyama, K., Hatano, K., and Yoshikawa, M. (2004). Adaptive web search based on user profile constructed without any effort from users. *WWW*, 675–684.

[28] Tan, B., Shen, X. and Zhai, C. (2006). Mining long-term search history to improve search accuracy. *KDD*, 718–723.

[29] Teevan, J., Dumais, S.T., and Horvitz, E. (2005). Personalizing search via automated analysis of interests and activities. *SIGIR*, 449–456.

[30] Teevan, J., Dumais, S.T., and Liebling, D.J. (2008). To personalize or not to personalize: modeling queries with variation in user intent. *SIGIR*, 163–170.

[31] Teevan, J., Liebling, D., and Geetha, G.R. (2011). Understanding and prediction personal navigation. *WSDM*, 85–94.

[32] White, R.W. and Drucker, S.M. (2007). Investigating behavioral variability in Web search. *WWW*, 21–30.

[33] White, R.W., Bailey, P., and Chen, L. (2009). Predicting user interests from contextual information. *SIGIR*, 363–370.

[34] White, R.W., Bennett, P.N. and Dumais. S.T. (2010). Predicting short-term interests using activity-based search context. *CIKM*, 1009–1018.

[35] Wu, Q., Burges, C. J.C. Svore, K. M., and Gao, J. (2008). Ranking, boosting, and model adaptation. *Microsoft Research Technical Report MSR-TR-2008-10.*

[36] Xiang, B., Jiang, D., Pei, J., Sun, X., Chen, E., and Li, H. (2010). Context-aware ranking in Web search. *SIGIR*, 451–458.

[37] Zhong, F., Wang, D., Wang, G., Chen, W., Zhang, Y., Chen, Z., and Wang, H. (2010). Incorporating post-click behaviors into a click model. *SIGIR*, 355–362.

Improving Searcher Models Using Mouse Cursor Activity

Jeff Huang
Information School
University of Washington
sigir2012@jeffhuang.com

Ryen W. White
Microsoft Research
Redmond, WA 98052
ryenw@microsoft.com

Georg Buscher
Microsoft Bing
Bellevue, WA 98004
georgbu@microsoft.com

Kuansan Wang
Microsoft Research
Redmond, WA 98052
kuansanw@microsoft.com

ABSTRACT

Web search components such as ranking and query suggestions analyze the user data provided in query and click logs. While this data is easy to collect and provides information about user behavior, it omits user interactions with the search engine that do not hit the server; these logs omit search data such as users' cursor movements. Just as clicks provide signals for relevance in search results, cursor hovering and scrolling can be additional implicit signals. In this work, we demonstrate a technique to extend models of the user's search result examination state to infer document relevance. We start by exploring recorded user interactions with the search results, both qualitatively and quantitatively. We find that cursor hovering and scrolling are signals telling us which search results were examined, and we use these interactions to reveal latent variables in searcher models to more accurately compute document attractiveness and satisfaction. Accuracy is evaluated by computing how well our model using these parameters can predict future clicks for a particular query. We are able to improve the click predictions compared to a basic searcher model for higher ranked search results using the additional log data.

Categories and Subject Descriptors

H.3.3 [**Information Storage and Retrieval**]: Information Search and Retrieval—*Retrieval models*

Keywords

cursor data, scrolling, searcher models, click data, user interactions, search result examination

1. INTRODUCTION

Web search engines allow users to search and retrieve relevant documents from billions of Web pages. The user issues a query and the search engine returns a list of results, generally ranked in order of relevance. The relevance of the results is based on a number of factors: how well a document matches the query, a document's reputation, and more recently, implicit feedback in the form of past behaviors for that query from many users. Records of these user behaviors are commonly sourced from query logs containing users' queries and the corresponding clicks, if any. Query logs are easy to collect, since they typically already exist as web server access logs without modification to the search engine.

Being able to compute relevance scores from implicit feedback allows a search engine to better rank the search results for future queries. Clicks (in the aggregate) provide a clear signal that users were attracted to the search result, and numerous studies have used click data in searcher models to infer relevance scores. These searcher models (e.g., [4, 7, 34]) track the user's state as they examine search results and use the observable events (e.g., clicks) to infer search result attractiveness and document relevance. However, query logs possess inherent limitations, some of which have been noted in the literature [11, 24]. They are unable to reveal actual user intent, provide little data about uncommon queries, and omit many interactions. Furthermore, they are uninformative for queries that have no clicks, i.e., abandoned queries.

In this paper, we introduce richer interaction data that can be used to supplement query and click data. This richer data comprises cursor movements and scrolling on the search engine results page (SERP), data which is not collected by commercial search engines but may be potentially useful. We believe cursor movements and scrolling can be additional implicit signals of relevance. These interactions can be captured at scale and can be recorded without disrupting the user, as shown in Huang et al. [21]. Actions such as cursor hovering and scrolling can be translated into implicit relevance feedback when overlaid on the SERP. In this work, we explore techniques to extend searcher models by using cursor hovering and scrolling activity to reveal latent variables in these searcher models to more accurately infer search result attractiveness and document relevance. As far as we are aware, this is the first study that explores the potential of cursor and scrolling interactions for use in searcher models.

Our primary contribution in this work is our study of extending a popular searcher model by adding hover and scroll data, informed by our analysis of replays of user interactions on the search results page. We find qualitative evidence that from a human observer's perspective, hovering and scrolling provide insight into the user's intentions and attention as they examine the SERP. We find that we

Permission to make digital or hard copies of all or part of this work for personal or classroom use is granted without fee provided that copies are not made or distributed for profit or commercial advantage and that copies bear this notice and the full citation on the first page. To copy otherwise, to republish, to post on servers or to redistribute to lists, requires prior specific permission and/or a fee.
SIGIR'12, August 12–16, 2012, Portland, Oregon, USA.
Copyright 2012 ACM 978-1-4503-1472-5/12/08 ...$10.00.

can improve searcher models by estimating whether a search result was viewed based on cursor hover and scroll behavior.

The remainder of the paper is structured as follows. In Section 2 we describe related work that characterizes cursor interactions with SERPs and searcher models. Section 3 describes the cursor data that we used in our study. We present an initial exploratory analysis of the data, which was useful in informing decisions about model features, in Section 4. In Section 5 we describe an extension to the searcher model using the cursor hover and scroll data, and present results of experiments using them in Section 6. We discuss the findings, their implications, and limitations of the method in Section 7, and conclude in Section 8.

2. RELATED WORK

Two lines of prior research are related to the work described in this paper: (i) studies characterizing how people interact with search result pages using their cursor, and (ii) searcher models primarily using click data.

2.1 Cursor Tracking on the Web and in Search

Buscher et al. investigated the use of gaze tracking to predict salient regions of Web pages [2] and the use of visual attention as implicit relevance feedback to personalize search [3]. To avoid eye-tracking studies, cursor tracking has been evaluated as an alternative to eye tracking for determining attention on the Web page. Initial studies established a close correspondence between gaze and cursor position [16, 21, 29, 30]. An early study by Chen et al. [5] showed that the distance between gaze and cursor was markedly shorter in regions of encountered pages to which users attended. More recent work has focused on the relationship between cursor and gaze on search tasks. In a study involving 32 subjects performing 16 search tasks each [29, 30], Rodden et al. identified a strong alignment between cursor and gaze positions. They found that the distance between cursor and gaze positions was longer along the x-axis than the y-axis, and was generally shorter when the cursor was placed over the search results. Guo and Agichtein [16] reported similar findings in a smaller study of ten subjects performing 20 search tasks each. Like Rodden et al., Guo and Agichtein noticed that distances along the x-axis tended to be longer than the distances along the y-axis. They could predict with 77% accuracy when gaze and cursor were strongly aligned using cursor features. Huang et al. [21] similarly found a correlation in cursor and gaze positions, and noted that the correlation was stronger on SERPs than on other Web pages. Huang et al. [20] determined when alignment occurred based on factors of time and cursor behavior. They showed that the alignment between cursor and gaze is stronger as the user is more active with the cursor.

Guo and Agichtein [14] captured cursor movements using a modified browser toolbar and found differences in cursor travel distances between informational and navigational queries. Furthermore, a decision tree could classify the query type using cursor movements more accurately than using clicks. Guo and Agichtein also used interactions such as cursor movement, hovers, and scrolling to accurately infer search intent and interest in search results [15]. They focused on automatically identifying a searcher's research or purchase intent based on features of the interaction. Rodden et al. [30] identified four general uses of the cursor in Web search—neglecting the cursor while reading, using the cursor as a reading aid (either horizontally or vertically), and using the cursor to mark interesting results. In a large-scale study, Huang et al. [21] conducted an analysis of cursor activity (including clicks on hyperlinks, clicks on non-hyperlinks, hover behavior) and its relation to Web search behavior. They also showed how cursor activity could be used to estimate the relevance of search results and to differentiate between good and bad search abandonment. Rather than tracking the cursor unobtrusively via cursor tracking, Lagun and Agichtein [25] presented a method to estimate gaze position by blurring the SERP and only revealing a region proximal to the cursor. They found that result viewing and clickthrough patterns agree closely with unrestricted viewing of results, as measured by eye-tracking equipment.

One line of related research has explored the use of cursor movements, clicks, and gaze as implicit indicators of interest on Web pages. In early work, Goecks and Shavlik modified a Web browser to record themselves browsing hundreds of Web pages [10]. They found that a neural network could predict variables such as the amount of cursor activity on the SERP, which they considered surrogate measurements of user interest. Claypool et al. [6] developed the "curious browser", a custom Web browser that recorded activity from 75 students browsing over 2,500 Web pages. They found that cursor travel time was a positive indicator of a Web page's relevance, but could only differentiate highly irrelevant Web pages. They also found that the number of clicks on a page did not correlate with its relevance. Hijikata [19] used client-side logging to monitor five subjects browsing a total of 120 Web pages. They recorded actions such as text tracing and link pointing using the cursor. The findings showed that these behaviors were good indicators for interesting regions of the Web page, around 1.5 times more effective than rudimentary term matching between the query and regions of the page. Shapira et al. [31] developed a special Web browser and recorded cursor activity from a small number of company employees browsing the Web. They found that the ratio of cursor movement to reading time was a better indicator of page quality than cursor travel distance and overall length of time that users spend on a page. Liu and Chung [26] recorded cursor activity from 28 students browsing the Web. They noticed patterns of cursor behaviors, including reading by tracing text. Their algorithms predicted users' cursor behaviors with 79% accuracy.

2.2 Searcher Models Using Click Data

Searcher models have been developed from two main hypotheses that are commonly used as assumptions in the models. Since users are biased towards clicking search results that are more highly ranked [23], the **examination hypothesis** is used to isolate a search result's attractiveness from its position. This hypothesis, originally formulated in Richardson et al. [28], states that the likelihood that a user will click on a search result is influenced only by 1) whether the user examined the search result and 2) its attractiveness. In other words, a user must examine a search result before potentially clicking that result. By making this assumption, a search result's attractiveness can be computed independent to its position in the ranking, i.e.,

$$P(C_i = 1) = P(E_i = 1)P(C_i = 1|E_i = 1),$$

where the term $P(E_i = 1)$ is the position bias and the term $P(C_i = 1|E_i = 1)$ is the search result's attractiveness.

To determine whether a user examined the search result, some searcher models draw from the **cascade hypothesis** [7] which dictates the search results a user has examined. The cascade hypothesis states that a user always examines search results sequentially and goes from top-to-bottom on the SERP. A user decides whether to click a result before examining the next result, preventing scenarios where the user returns to a higher-ranked search result after passing it by. Therefore, if users do not examine a particular search result, they will not examine any search results below it, i.e.,

$$P(E_1 = 1) = 1,$$
$$P(E_{i+1} = 1 | E_i = 0) = 0.$$

While the original cascade model stipulated that once a user clicked, they would no longer examine any search results, extensions of this hypothesis have sidestepped that assumption. The Dependent Click Model [13] allows for query sessions comprising multiple clicks: it possesses a parameter representing the probability that the clicked document is irrelevant and that the user returns to examining more search results. The Click Chain Model [12] and Dynamic Bayesian Network Model (DBN) [4] both extend this by adding an additional parameter representing the probability that a user abandons a query session without clicking, thus circumventing the cascade hypothesis's side effect that users are assumed to examine every search result in abandoned queries. Later in the paper, we will describe our extension to the DBN model, which we selected because of its popularity in the literature and its good performance. Additionally, the inference step could be simplified and the model itself was conducive to the inclusion of cursor data due to a separate examination state; these are two more reasons this model was particularly suited to our study.

Other searcher models such as the User Browsing Model [9] and the Partially-Observable Markov Model [34] avoid the cascade hypothesis entirely by allowing that the user jumps between search results non-sequentially in their examination. However, these models must possess more parameters representing the probabilities of transitions between search result positions. This makes the inference particularly difficult when there are fewer query sessions with clicks from which to learn.

The research presented in this paper intersects the two categories of prior work presented in this section by extending **searcher models** using **cursor tracking**.

3. CURSOR DATA

We recorded interaction data directly on the SERP of the Bing Web search engine. Log data were gathered over a period of 13 days between May 26, 2011 and June 7, 2011 during an external experiment on a small fraction of user traffic, primarily from English-speaking countries. We sampled by user, storing every query from each user in the experiment. In total, our data comprised around 1.8 million queries, averaging eight queries per searcher (median = 3 queries).

To record user interactions with the SERP at scale without the need to install any browser plugins, we used an efficient and scalable approach similar to that used by Huang et al. [21]. We implemented entirely JavaScript-based logging functions that were embedded into the HTML source code of the SERP. To obtain a detailed understanding of user interactions with the SERP, we deployed methods to measure and record a variety of interactions with the page as well as page characteristics, such as the layout of elements on the page. We recorded information on cursor movements, clicks, scrolling, as well as bounding boxes of certain components on the SERP and the browser's viewport size.

↓ Time	
	Query: lady gaga concert tickets
	Cursor moves from top to hover over 3rd search result
	Cursor pauses for 3 seconds
	Text "Tour Dates Only" is hovered with the cursor
	Cursor moves to the 4th search result, pausing 1s
	User scrolls to the 5th search result, pausing 3s
	Cursor returns to the 4th search result and clicks
	Click: Result 4 [http://gaga.com/tix/]

Figure 1: A user searches for "lady gaga concert tickets", examines the first page of results, and clicks the 4th search result. Typical query logs contain only query and click data (bold).

↓ Time	
	Query: flourless cake recipe
	Cursor moves to the bottom-right over whitespace
	No activity for 4 seconds
	Cursor moves over to the scrollbar
	User scrolls down half a screen
	No activity for 2 seconds
	User scrolls down half a page
	Cursor makes left-right motions over the 6th result
	User scrolls to the bottom of the page
	User quickly scrolls back up to the top
	Cursor moves to the top-right over the page
	User closes the page

Figure 2: A user searches for "flourless cake recipe" and scrolls to the bottom of the page, then scrolls back up and closes the window.

Figure 1 presents a fictional query along with the corresponding click data and client-side interactions. In this and many other cases, the cursor and scrolling data reveals more information about the user's intent. In the above scenario, the query logs only show that a query was issued, and that some time later, the 4th result was clicked. This is useful information, but the interaction data supplement this by showing that the user was active the whole time examining several results and that the user likely examined the 5th result and returned to the 4th result, indicating the 1–3 and 5th results may have been less relevant than the 4th result.

Figure 2 presents a fictional query that has no clicks. In typical query logs, the only recorded data would be the query text itself. The richer cursor and scrolling data here shows that the user did indeed scroll all the way to the bottom. We also see that the user paused to read through the results[1]. In this particular case, it seems reasonable to assume the user abandoned the query because they did not find what they were seeking. Thus, this query can be labeled as unsatisfying in a user-centered analysis of the logs.

[1]Query logs can compute the dwell time of a click, but only if another recorded event occurs after the click.

When logging any additional type of user interaction data beyond clickthrough, a tradeoff has to be made between: (i) level of detail (e.g., temporal and spatial resolution), (ii) the impact of any additional JavaScript code on page weight, page load time, and therefore the user experience, which can be sensitive to even small increases in load time, and (iii) the amount of data transferred (and hence bandwidth consumed) between the client and the remote server, as well as log volume created on the backend server. We negotiated a tradeoff between these dimensions by: (i) reasonably coarsening the log resolution, (ii) compressing the JavaScript code down to around three kilobytes, and (iii) compressing the log data as well as using a buffering approach for its transferal via Ajax to the backend server. We now describe in more detail the fields recorded in our log data and the methods used to record them.

3.1 Cursor Positions

The JavaScript function for logging cursor positions periodically checked the cursor's x- and y-coordinates within the Web page relative to its top-left corner of the page every 250 milliseconds. Whenever the cursor had been moved more than 8 pixels away from its previously logged position, its new coordinates were sent to the backend server. Eight pixels correspond to approximately half a line of text on the SERP. Since cursor tracking was relative to the document, we captured cursor alignment to SERP content regardless of how the user got to that position (e.g., by scrolling, or keyboard). Therefore, this approach was compatible with other behaviors such as scrolling or keyboard input. In previous cursor tracking studies, the cursor position was polled at particular time intervals, such as every 50 milliseconds (ms) [15] or every 100ms [29]. This is impractical at a large scale because of the large amount of data to transfer from the user's computer to the server. Our approach is similar to Huang et al. [21], who found that a 40ms pause provided a reasonable tradeoff between data quantity and granularity of the recorded events. However, we elected to record the cursor position every 250ms since we were sending data to the remote server every eight pixels of cursor movement, rather than every two seconds. As such we wanted to minimize the data gathered and transmitted to avoid adversely affecting the user experience with delays associated with log data capture and data transmission to the remote server.

3.2 Clicks

Clicks were recorded using the JavaScript onMouseDown event handling method. Thus, the backend server received log entries with location coordinates for every click, no matter whether the click occurred on a link or elsewhere on the page (even on white space containing no content that appears adjacent to or between SERP elements). In order to identify clicks on hyperlinks and differentiate them from clicks on inactive page elements, we also extracted and logged unique hyperlink identifiers that were embedded in the SERP, along with the corresponding URL of the hyperlink. The URL helped identify the actual search result because different query sessions could have different search results or the same search results ranked differently.

3.3 Scrolling

We also recorded the current scroll position, i.e., the y-coordinate of the uppermost visible pixel of the SERP in the browser viewport. This coordinate was checked three times per second and was recorded whenever it had changed more than 40 pixels compared to the last logged scroll position. Forty pixels correspond to the height of about two lines of text. From this coordinate we were able to gain a number of insights into scrolling activity, including whether the user was scrolling up or down, and the maximum scroll depth in the result page, in order to understand how far down the page the user had scrolled.

3.4 Page Layout

Simply logging the text of what was displayed on the SERP is insufficient for reconstructing its layout since SERPs vary per query (depending on what kinds of SERP elements are shown, etc.), font sizes, and other browser preferences. To reconstruct the exact SERP layout as it was rendered in the user's browser, we recorded the positions and sizes of certain regions. The specific regions in which we were interested in were as follows: (i) top and bottom search boxes, (ii) left rail and its contained related searches, search history, and query refinement areas, (iii) mainline results area and its contained result entries, including advertisements and instant answers, and (iv) right rail.

For each region bounding box, we determined and logged the coordinates of its upper left corner as well as its width and height in pixels. Using this information, we could later map the positions of cursor positions and clicks to specific regions of the page. The recorded data also contained the size of the user's Web browser window, which combined with the scrolling activity could deduce information about the parts of the page that were visible at a particular time during the query session.

Figure 3 presents a screenshot of the page layout of a reconstructed SERP taken from a query session replay. Important components are outlined in light blue boxes; the user's cursor position is shown as a gray pointer; and the green area represents parts of the Web page not visible in the browser window on the user's screen at the current time.

4. EXPLORATORY ANALYSES

Before constructing any searcher models, we wanted to obtain a deeper understanding of the recorded cursor and scrolling activity since this type of data was relatively unexplored. This included both a qualitative perspective and a more traditional quantitative analysis of the data. The findings here inform the approach we take in enhancing the searcher model.

4.1 Qualitative Observations

We began by reconstructing the SERP layout from the recorded logs, and developed a tool to replay the entire sequence of cursor interactions on the page in great detail. This included an outline highlighting the viewable area of the Web page (based on the dimensions of the Web browser viewport), since this would change according to the users' screen resolution and their scrolling. One of the authors then visually investigated a random sample of over a hundred replays of interactions on the search result pages made by real users. During the replays, the author put himself in the users' place to determine their intent. His judgments of their intents were informed by the cursor behaviors described in prior literature. These qualitative observations were a rich

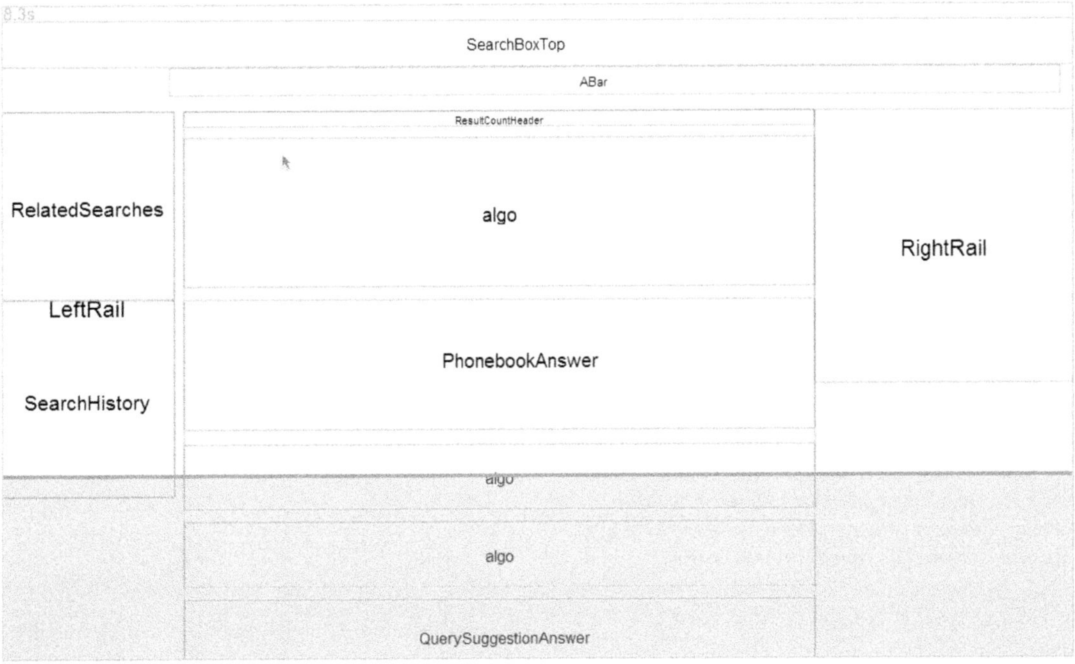

Figure 3: The reconstructed SERP during a query session replay. Light blue boxes outline important components, a grey pointer represents the user's cursor position, and the green area overlays off-screen portions of the Web page. The number in the top-left is the time elapsed since the start of the query session.

way of truly understanding the data and provided a number of key insights that were difficult to quantify.

First, we saw that many users could only view a small portion of the Web page initially, which only displayed ads or an "Answer" element (such as the PhonebookAnswer, which shows local results and contact information, in Figure 3); these users would often scroll down a bit to view at least a couple of search results. The time spent pausing after a scroll suggested that they indeed examined those newly revealed search results. We were less confident that the user had examined all the visible search results if they did not scroll, since they often clicked a link or abandoned the query immediately after the page loaded.

Second, while we could not see where the user was actually looking, the cursor would commonly move around the page from top-to-bottom while hovering over particular areas, and then move to the scrollbar to reveal more search results, corresponding nicely with the *linear traversal hypothesis* [23]. This behavior seemed to suggest that whenever a user hovered over a search result, they had at least examined that result and the search results above it.

Third, we observed some users moving their cursor back-and-forth horizontally which we believed to be them following the cursor as they read text; some users would do this quite frequently in a single query session. This corroborates previous work that observed this behavior in lab settings [20, 26, 30], and suggests that this behavior is specific to individual users.

Finally, we observed many sessions in which the user would move their cursor quickly and directly from the search box to the first search result, without scrolling down to view any of the lower-ranked search results. This happened often in navigational queries, so this provoked the question whether interaction data would be more or less useful in navigational queries; we explore this later in Section 6.2.2.

4.2 Quantitative Summary

As described in an earlier section, the raw interaction events comprised cursor positions, clicks, window scrolls, and page layout. Statistics specific to the different types of interaction data logged include:

Cursor: Users hovered over multiple search result captions (mean = 2.6, median = 2), even for navigational queries when it was clear that a single search result will suffice. This pattern of behavior has been observed in previous studies of eye tracking [8], as well as previous work on large-scale cursor tracking [21].

Clicks: Mouse clicks were collected regardless of whether they were navigational clicks (clicks on a hyperlink) or interactive clicks on controls in the page (17.1% of clicks). 64.7% of all clicks were hyperlink clicks and 35.2% were non-hyperlink clicks, including re-query events (estimated from clicks on the upper or lower search boxes) totaling around 11% of all queries.

Scrolling: Window scrolling is a client-side interaction that is rarely captured in the context of Web search. Of the queries in our set, 29.7% contained at least one scroll event. 61.8% of logged interaction sequences for a query ended on a downwards scroll. As expected, there were more downward scrolls than upward scrolls, and the majority of scrolled queries (54.8%) comprised only downward scrolls. This suggests that most queries do not result in the user returning to the top of the SERP to examine search results that may be hidden following scrolling.

Figure 4 contrasts queries in which the user has scrolled with queries where the user did not scroll. As expected,

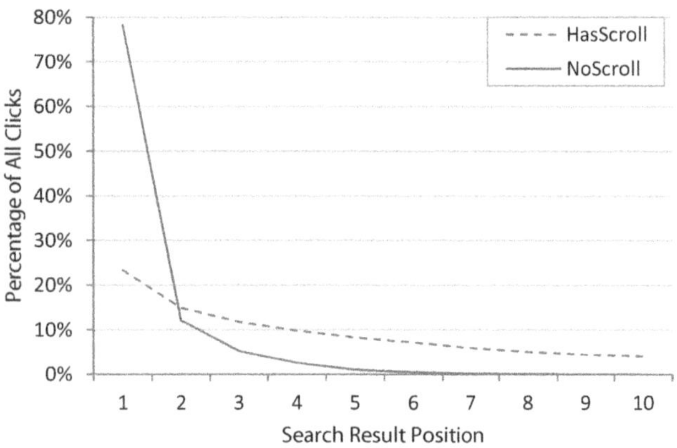

Figure 4: The click distributions for cases in which the user does not scroll, and when there is at least one scroll event during the query session. The distribution is heavily skewed when there is no scrolling, and almost linear when the user has scrolled.

when the user has not scrolled, the click distribution is significantly more skewed towards higher-ranked search results. The difference between the click distributions is quite drastic: in query sessions where the user has scrolled, search results in lower-ranked positions have a fairly good chance of being selected. This is consistent with the examination hypothesis mentioned earlier, and supports a hypothesis that scrolling towards a set of search results makes it likely the user has examined those results.

The observations informed the following two hypotheses that we wanted to apply to searcher models: 1) when a user scrolled down, they have already examined the search results in their viewing area and those above it, and 2) when a user hovered over a search result, they have examined it and the search results above it. In the next section, we validate these hypotheses by implementing them in a traditional searcher model that uses only clicks.

5. EXTENDING A SEARCHER MODEL

Searcher models are structured based on theoretical knowledge of a user's search examination process. Their internal parameters are inferred from observable data, which in turn can be applied to compute relevance label scores for search results. Label scores are position-independent and computed from the model for every query × search result. The search results can then be re-ranked using these labels for future occurrences of the same query. Thus, a better searcher model can compute more accurate relevance labels for search ranking.

We replicate the Dynamic Bayesian Network (DBN) model [4] as the baseline model to which we compare against. The DBN model is the most cited searcher model since the Cascade Model (which compared favorably to all models before it). It compares favorably to the Cascade Model [4, 36], and fares well compared to other models (e.g., [36, 37]). Thus, the DBN model serves as a solid baseline for our purposes; it provides an example searcher model in which we can focus on whether cursor data can improve a model, rather than outperforming all models, i.e., more of an analysis of the value of cursor data than strictly model development.

The DBN model is a graphical model where the nodes represent states of the user examining the search results. The model is represented formally as follows:

- E_i: the user examined the search result
- C_i: the user clicked the search result
- A_i: the search result attracted the user
- S_i: the landing page satisfied the user (relevance)

$$
\begin{aligned}
A_i = 1, E_1 = 1 &\Leftrightarrow C_i = 1 \\
P(A_i = 1) &= a_u \\
P(S_i = 1 | C_i = 1) &= s_u \\
C_i = 0 &\Rightarrow S_i = 0 \\
S_i = 1 &\Rightarrow E_{i+1} = 0 \\
P(E_{i+1} = 1 | E_i = 1, S_i = 0) &= \lambda \\
E_i = 0 &\Rightarrow E_{i+1} = 0
\end{aligned}
$$

In this model, users examine search results from top to bottom, assessing at each result whether or not it is attractive enough to click (cascade hypothesis), which depends only on the attractiveness of the link a_u (examination hypothesis). If they click, there is some probability s_u they will be satisfied and stop the search process; if they are not satisfied, they either return to the search results page to examine the next search result with probability λ, or abandon the search. Figure 5 enumerates the user states and decisions in the DBN model; the "hover above and scroll towards" state was a new observable event generated from the cursor data. Examining a search result could emit this event, but the events are not a precondition of examining a result.

During the exploratory analysis phase, we saw that scrolling towards a set of search results led to a higher chance of those results being examined. Additionally, hovering over a search result similarly suggested that result and those above it were examined. These assumptions were incorporated into the searcher model by adding the following constraint:

$$(\exists h \in H : i \leq h) \vee i \in V \Rightarrow P(E_i = 1),$$

where H is the set of search result positions the user hovered over, and V is the set of all search results shown when the user scrolled. These events would reveal that the user had examined the search results, but a user examining a search result would not necessarily emit a corresponding hover or scroll event.

We reimplement the DBN model with $\lambda = 1$, labeled *Algorithm 1* in Chapelle and Zhang [4], to simplify the inference of latent variables. Then we incorporate the additional examination constraint to validate the observations in the exploratory analyses.

6. EXPERIMENT

In this section, we describe an experiment comparing the baseline DBN model with the modified DBN model incorporating cursor data for computing relevance labels. We define the click perplexity metric used to evaluate the model and report the experiment and results.

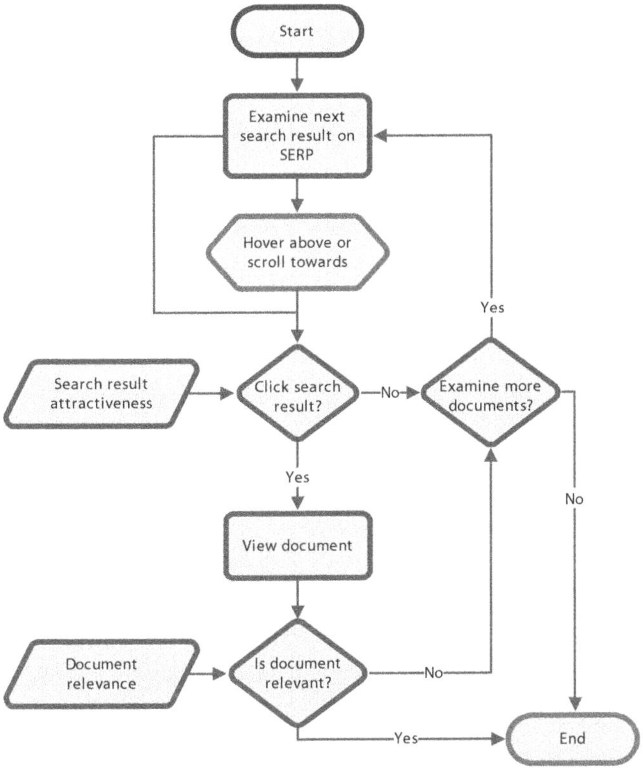

Figure 5: Flow diagram of the users' states in the modified Dynamic Bayesian Network model enhanced with cursor hover and scrolling data. The hexagon represents the new potentially observable events that can be captured in interaction logs.

6.1 Evaluation

While we cannot evaluate unobserved events in a searcher model, we can test how well the model predicts clicks, the observable events. Click perplexity was evaluated in a number of other searcher model studies [9, 12, 35, 36, 37] as a measure of predicting click-through rates. Our evaluation used a similar methodology as the past studies in literature: query sessions were divided evenly into training and test sets, each comprising at least 5 query sessions; we only accepted one query session from each user for a particular query to prevent a small number of users from dominating the data. There were 7,341 queries in which at least 10 unique users issued the query; this filtered out queries with insufficient data.

We compared *the DBN model with only click data*, as it is implemented in the literature, with *the DBN model with click and cursor data* from our logs. These data were used to train the searcher model, and the trained model was used to predict clicks in the test set[2]. Better prediction of clicks in the test set implies that the searcher model (and its inferred parameters) better reflects the result examination process. The click perplexity quantifies how much the test data surprises the trained model; it is computed for each combination of query and position as,

$$p_i = 2^{-\frac{1}{N}\sum_{n=1}^{N}(C_i^n log_2 q_i^n + (1-C_i^n) log_2(1-q_i^n))}$$

where p_i is the perplexity in the ith position, N is the number of links, and q_i^n is the predicted click probability for the nth query session. The exponent represents the cross-entropy estimated from a probability distribution. The lowest perplexity is 1, meaning the trained model perfectly predicted the test data, while a larger perplexity means the model was less accurate in predicting the test data. Because the lower bound of the perplexity depends on the click-through rate of the query, the perplexity varies substantially depending on the position of the search result. Therefore, we computed a separate perplexity value for each of the top ten rank positions.

6.2 Results

We now report on the results of our experiments. Figure 6 shows the computed perplexities for each position on the SERP. The baseline searcher model comprising only click data did not perform as well as the searcher model incorporating both click and scrolling data. The latter model was further improved when incorporating hover data as well, although the improvement was small since there is an overlap between the search results the user scrolls to, and the search results at or above that which the user hovers above.

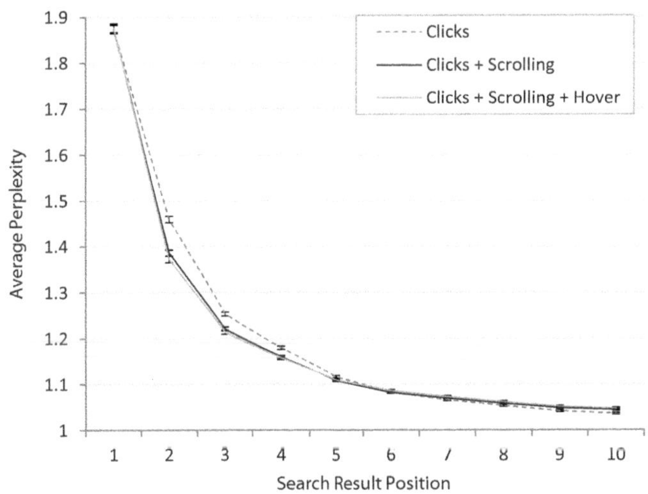

Figure 6: A comparison between 3 variations of the DBN model: 1) the baseline model using only click data, 2) a modified model also incorporating scrolling data, and 3) a modified model incorporating clicks, scrolling, and hover data. Lower click perplexity represents better prediction. Error bars represent the standard error of the mean.

It is clear that the additional cursor data improves relevance labels for search results in positions 2–5, but the prediction is slightly worse for search results in positions 6–10. However, users benefit more from the better prediction accuracy for the search results in higher positions since users consider them more important, so we believe there is an overall improvement. More accurate click predictions signify that the document relevance and search result at-

[2]The cursor data was only used for training the searcher model, and not for testing, i.e., we did not try to predict cursor movements and scrolling.

tractiveness labels are more likely to be close to true objective values of these parameters. For search results in positions 6–10, there appears to be a slight decrease in accuracy for predicted clicks in the models incorporating cursor data. We are unsure whether this is due to overfitting or noise in the data. The difference in perplexity for using clicks only compared to clicks + scrolling was significant at the $t(7340) \geq 8.26, p < 0.001$ level at positions 2–5. The difference in perplexity for using clicks + scrolling data compared to clicks + scrolling + hover data was significant at the $t(7340) \geq 3.07, p < 0.002$ level at positions 2 and 3, as the perplexity drops from 1.46 to 1.37 in position 2 and from 1.25 to 1.21 in position 3. Both differences were significant even after applying the Bonferroni correction.

We performed two additional sets of analyses of our results designed to better understand the nature of our gains. We studied the distribution of gains and losses across the top 10 rank positions. We also studied the effect of query types (navigational versus non-navigational) on our click prediction accuracy. We now report the findings of each.

6.2.1 Gains and Losses

For each of the 7,341 queries in our set, and for each rank position, we determined whether the DBN model with full cursor data (clicks + scrolling + hovers) outperformed the model with only clicks. We then computed the percentage of queries for which the model with cursor data attained a perplexity value above, below, or equal to the clicks-only model. Note that to simplify the analysis, we ignored the magnitude of difference between the models for a query. Figure 7 highlights the change in click prediction performance for different positions.

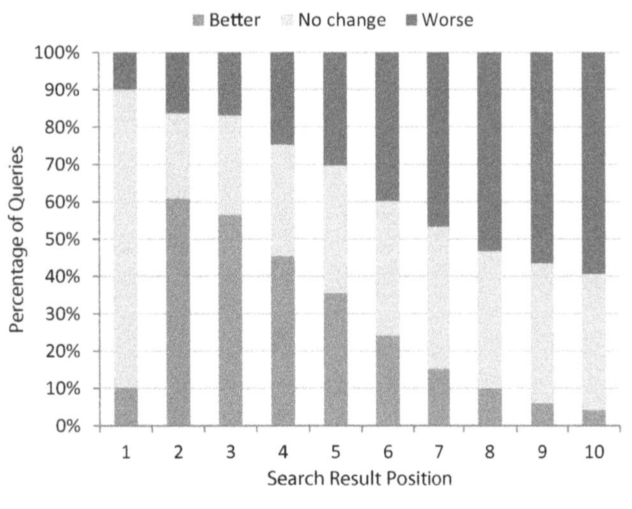

Figure 7: The percentage of queries whose click perplexity was helped or hurt by adding cursor hover and scroll data to the DBN searcher model.

The findings reveal a number of things. First, there was generally no change for the first rank position. Second, the biggest gains from the cursor model came at position 2, where over 60% of queries were benefited by using the additional cursor data. Third, the fraction of queries for which the cursor model performed best decreased fairly rapidly with rank, ending with only 5% of queries benefiting from cursor data for at rank position 10. One possible explanation is that since users only scroll for a third of queries, we possess less hover and scrolling evidence from which to learn user preferences at lower ranks. Finally, for the second rank position onwards, the fraction of queries for which there is no change remains fairly constant in the 20–35% range (increasing gradually with rank). Although there were no immediately noticeable patterns in those queries, they need more analysis since they may represent an opportunity for additional gains, especially further down the ranking, where they represent a sizeable fraction of queries.

6.2.2 Effect of Query Intent

We also segmented the queries into navigational and non-navigational query types to see if performance differences existed between different query intents in our models. Teevan et al. adopted a metric of click entropy as a threshold to classify navigational and non-navigational query types [33]. They showed that navigational queries classified in this manner exhibited differences in user behavior. We used the same method to segment the queries in our set, and identified 2,407 navigational queries and 3,509 non-navigational queries. The remaining 1,426 queries had a click entropy value between the navigational and non-navigational thresholds, and were removed from this part of the analysis.

Originally, we hypothesized that cursor and scrolling data may be less useful for navigational queries, since the clicks can be determined more easily. However, our findings (summarized in Figure 8) showed that click prediction improved when cursor data was added in both navigational and non-navigational queries, particularly in higher-ranked positions; the click predictions were almost evenly improved in navigational queries as in non-navigational queries. Differences in click perplexity between all four combinations—navigational and non-navigational queries, with and without cursor data—were statistically significant at the $t(5915) \geq 7.63, p < .001$ level after applying the Bonferroni correction. We also inspected the individual queries for which the additional cursor data helped and hurt click prediction; the queries exhibited no discernible pattern. It appears that the improvements were uniform and not particular to one type of query.

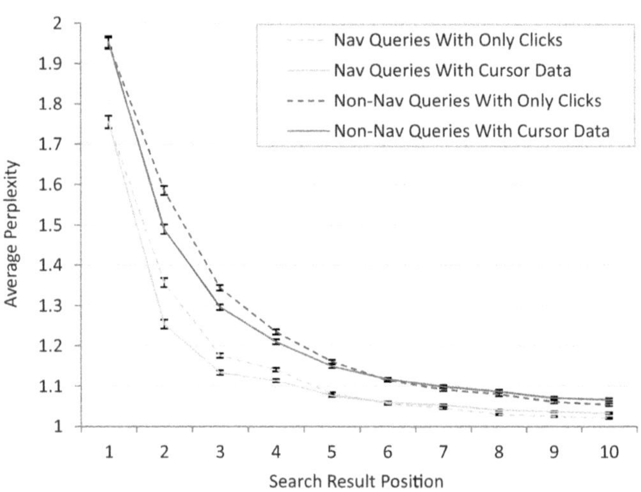

Figure 8: Comparison in click prediction between navigational and non-navigational queries, with and without cursor data. Lower click perplexity represents better prediction.

7. DISCUSSION

Initial exploratory findings have given us key insights. The replays and aggregate analyses have suggested that users seem to examine the search results they scroll towards, and the search results they hover over. We were able to convert these findings into constraints in the DBN model, a popular searcher model. An experiment comparing the DBN model with only click data to the DBN model with hover and scrolling as examination signals showed that the additional data helped predict clicks. After further disentangling the queries into navigational and non-navigational query intents, we found little difference between the two types of queries, and visually inspecting the queries themselves sustained our confidence that better relevance labels can be inferred across all types of queries. Our experiments have shown that by augmenting query logs with richer interaction data attainable at scale (in our case, cursor hover and scrolling), we can realize improvements in existing searcher models. The better searcher models can compute more accurate attractiveness and relevance labels for pairs of query $\times$ search result, which in turn lead to position-independent search result scores that can be ranked.

This work has implications for the design of search systems. Search companies have been processing query logs for some time now, and the amount of query logs that can be collected is limited—they cannot obtain more query and click data from a fixed number of users. However, companies can scalably and efficiently collect more search data such as cursor movements and scrolling. These can be used to improve searcher models by generating more accurate attractiveness and relevance labels for search results. Search engineers can then leverage these labels to supplement existing scoring factors for ranking the search results, such as document and link analyses algorithms. Additionally, the labels can be used for analytics and to answer questions such as "Which search results are highly attractive but are not actually relevant?" or "For which queries are users likely to abandon because of unattractive search results?"

In other data-intensive computer science areas such as natural language processing and data mining, there has been evidence that collecting and mining additional data can be more useful than improving algorithms. A study by Banko and Brill [1] compared various learning algorithms for disambiguating natural language. They showed that increasing the amount of data by 10-fold would make even the worst algorithm better than the best algorithm. A recent article published by Google researchers about "The Unreasonable Effectiveness of Data" [17] highlights the power of web-scale data for machine translation. Rajaraman presented anecdotal evidence to argue that, "adding more, independent data usually beats out designing ever-better algorithms to analyze an existing data set" in an article titled "More data usually beats better algorithms" [27]. A similar phenomenon may be occurring in Web search, where growing dependence on user-generated search logs makes it more important going forward to collect more independent data. Cursor interactions and scrolling activity are new types of data that are more difficult to interpret but can supplement existing query logs. We may be able to improve ranking in the future, as well as user assistance interface features, by modeling interaction on different interface features.

We acknowledge several limitations in our study which may be addressed in future work. Our searcher model was fairly simple since our goal was to demonstrate the value of new interaction data rather than develop the best overall searcher model. Our searcher model does not take advantage of several metrics that have been shown to improve searcher models: click order [22], the duration between clicks [18], and temporally changing relevance of search results [32]. Another limitation is that SERPs in commercial search engines are becoming richer and more interactive. While SERPs have greatly evolved from 10 blue links, features such as *hover preview* and interactive customized displays for many types of search results have changed how users behave. Finally, the extensions we made to the searcher model were informed by an exploratory analysis of replays of user sessions; the results show that there can be benefit to incorporating non-click data in searcher models, but we have not investigated what other forms of data may similarly improve them. These limitations can be addressed in future work, perhaps with searcher models beyond the DBN model, incorporating previously mentioned factors such as click order, duration, and temporal relevance.

8. CONCLUSIONS

We have conducted exploratory analyses of recorded user interactions on the SERP with both qualitative and quantitative approaches. These analyses suggested that scrolling towards a set of search results and hovering over search results are related to whether a user examined them. By adding these interactions as constraints in a popular searcher model, we were able to infer attractiveness and relevance labels for search results. We evaluated newly generated labels from the revised searcher model by comparing it to the searcher model using only click data. The searcher model with the additional cursor data was able to better predict future clicks, implying that the labels are more accurate.

Click data in query logs are but one source of user behavior data that can be used for ranking. We have shown that collecting richer data in the form of client-side interactions can be useful. Cursor and scrolling activity is only a subset of recordable interaction data, and using new independent data may be a fruitful avenue to pursue. As we previously referenced, researchers in data mining and machine translation have found that simply adding more data can result in an order of magnitude of greater improvement in the system than making incremental improvements to the processing algorithms. We have yet to see if richer data will make such an impact in the application of ranking from searcher models, but our experiment suggests the possibility.

9. ACKNOWLEDGMENTS

The authors thanks Katherine Ye for editing earlier drafts of the paper. The first author of the paper is supported by a Google Research Award and Facebook Fellowship.

10. REFERENCES

[1] M. Banko and E. Brill. Scaling to very very large corpora for natural language disambiguation. In *Proceedings of ACL*, pp. 26–33, 2001.

[2] G. Buscher, E. Cutrell, and M. R. Morris. What do you see when you're surfing?: using eye tracking to predict salient regions of web pages. In *Proceedings of CHI*, pp. 21–30, 2009.

[3] G. Buscher, A. Dengel, and L. van Elst. Eye movements as implicit relevance feedback. In *CHI Extended Abstracts*, pp. 2991–2996, 2008.

[4] O. Chapelle and Y. Zhang. A dynamic bayesian network click model for web search ranking. In *Proceedings of WWW*, pp. 1–10, 2009.

[5] M. C. Chen, J. R. Anderson, and M. H. Sohn. What can a mouse cursor tell us more?: correlation of eye/mouse movements on web browsing. In *CHI Extended Abstracts*, pp. 281–282, 2001.

[6] M. Claypool, P. Le, M. Wased, and D. Brown. Implicit interest indicators. In *Proceedings of IUI*, pp. 33–40, 2001.

[7] N. Craswell, O. Zoeter, M. Taylor, and B. Ramsey. An experimental comparison of click position-bias models. In *Proceedings of WSDM*, pp. 87–94, 2008.

[8] E. Cutrell and Z. Guan. What are you looking for?: an eye-tracking study of information usage in web search. In *Proceedings of CHI*, pp. 407–416, 2007.

[9] G. E. Dupret and B. Piwowarski. A user browsing model to predict search engine click data from past observations. In *Proceedings of SIGIR*, pp. 331–338, 2008.

[10] J. Goecks and J. Shavlik. Learning users' interests by unobtrusively observing their normal behavior. In *Proceedings of IUI*, pp. 129–132, 2000.

[11] C. Grimes, D. Tang, and D. M. Russell. Query logs alone are not enough. In *WWW Workshop on Query Log Analysis*, 2007.

[12] F. Guo, C. Liu, A. Kannan, T. Minka, M. Taylor, Y.-M. Wang, and C. Faloutsos. Click chain model in web search. In *Proceedings of WWW*, pp. 11–20, 2009.

[13] F. Guo, C. Liu, and Y. M. Wang. Efficient multiple-click models in web search. In *Proceedings of WSDM*, pp. 124–131, 2009.

[14] Q. Guo and E. Agichtein. Exploring mouse movements for inferring query intent. In *Proceedings of SIGIR*, pp. 707–708, 2008.

[15] Q. Guo and E. Agichtein. Ready to buy or just browsing?: detecting web searcher goals from interaction data. In *Proceedings of SIGIR*, pp. 130–137, 2010.

[16] Q. Guo and E. Agichtein. Towards predicting web searcher gaze position from mouse movements. In *Proceedings of CHI*, pp. 3601–3606, 2010.

[17] A. Halevy, P. Norvig, and F. Pereira. The unreasonable effectiveness of data. *IEEE Intelligent Systems*, 24(2):8 –12, 2009.

[18] Y. He and K. Wang. Inferring search behaviors using partially observable markov model with duration (pomd). In *Proceedings of WSDM*, pp. 415–424, 2011.

[19] Y. Hijikata. Implicit user profiling for on demand relevance feedback. In *Proceedings of IUI*, pp. 198–205, 2004.

[20] J. Huang, R. White, and G. Buscher. User see, user point: gaze and cursor alignment in web search. In *Proceedings of CHI*, pp. 1341–1350, 2012.

[21] J. Huang, R. W. White, and S. Dumais. No clicks, no problem: using cursor movements to understand and improve search. In *Proceedings of CHI*, pp. 1225–1234, 2011.

[22] S. Ji, K. Zhou, C. Liao, Z. Zheng, G.-R. Xue, O. Chapelle, G. Sun, and H. Zha. Global ranking by exploiting user clicks. In *Proceedings of SIGIR*, pp. 35–42, 2009.

[23] T. Joachims, L. Granka, B. Pan, H. Hembrooke, and G. Gay. Accurately interpreting clickthrough data as implicit feedback. In *Proceedings of SIGIR*, pp. 154–161, 2005.

[24] R. Kohavi, R. Longbotham, D. Sommerfield, and R. Henne. Controlled experiments on the web: survey and practical guide. *Data Mining and Knowledge Discovery*, 18(1):140–181, 2009.

[25] D. Lagun and E. Agichtein. Viewser: Enabling large-scale remote user studies of web search examination and interaction. In *Proceedings of SIGIR*, pp. 365–374, 2011.

[26] C.-C. Liu and C.-W. Chung. Detecting mouse movement with repeated visit patterns for retrieving noticed knowledge components on web pages. *IEICE - Trans. Inf. Syst.*, E90-D(10):1687–1696, October 2007.

[27] A. Rajaraman. More data usually beats better algorithms. `http://anand.typepad.com/datawocky/2008/03/more-data-usual.html`, 2008.

[28] M. Richardson, E. Dominowska, and R. Ragno. Predicting clicks: estimating the click-through rate for new ads. In *Proceedings of WWW*, pp. 521–530, 2007.

[29] K. Rodden and X. Fu. Exploring how mouse movements relate to eye movements on web search results pages. In *SIGIR Workshop on Web Information Seeking and Interaction*, pp. 29–32, 2007.

[30] K. Rodden, X. Fu, A. Aula, and I. Spiro. Eye-mouse coordination patterns on web search results pages. In *CHI Extended Abstracts*, pp. 2997–3002, 2008.

[31] B. Shapira, M. Taieb-Maimon, and A. Moskowitz. Study of the usefulness of known and new implicit indicators and their optimal combination for accurate inference of users interests. In *Proceedings of SAC*, pp. 1118–1119, 2006.

[32] R. Srikant, S. Basu, N. Wang, and D. Pregibon. User browsing models: relevance versus examination. In *Proceedings of KDD*, pp. 223–232, 2010.

[33] J. Teevan, S. T. Dumais, and D. J. Liebling. To personalize or not to personalize: modeling queries with variation in user intent. In *Proceedings of SIGIR*, pp. 163–170, 2008.

[34] K. Wang, N. Gloy, and X. Li. Inferring search behaviors using partially observable markov (pom) model. In *Proceedings of WSDM*, pp. 211–220, 2010.

[35] Y. Yang, X. Shu, and W. Liu. A probability click tracking model analysis of web search results. In *Proceedings of ICONIP*, pp. 322–329, 2010.

[36] Y. Zhang, D. Wang, G. Wang, W. Chen, Z. Zhang, B. Hu, and L. Zhang. Learning click models via probit bayesian inference. In *Proceedings of CIKM*, pp. 439–448, 2010.

[37] F. Zhong, D. Wang, G. Wang, W. Chen, Y. Zhang, Z. Chen, and H. Wang. Incorporating post-click behaviors into a click model. In *Proceedings of SIGIR*, pp. 355–362, 2010.

Personalization of Search Results Using Interaction Behaviors in Search Sessions

Chang Liu
School of Communication and Information, Rutgers University
4 Huntington Street,
New Brunswick, NJ 08901, USA
changl@eden.rutgers.edu

Nicholas J. Belkin
School of Communication and Information, Rutgers University
4 Huntington Street,
New Brunswick, NJ 08901, USA
belkin@rutgers.edu

Michael J. Cole
School of Communication and Information, Rutgers University
4 Huntington Street,
New Brunswick, NJ 08901, USA
m.cole@rutgers.edu

ABSTRACT

Personalization of search results offers the potential for significant improvement in information retrieval performance. User interactions with the system and documents during information-seeking sessions provide a wealth of information about user preferences and their task goals. In this paper, we propose methods for analyzing and modeling user search behavior in search sessions to predict document usefulness and then using information to personalize search results. We generate prediction models of document usefulness from behavior data collected in a controlled lab experiment with 32 participants, each completing uncontrolled searching for 4 tasks in the Web. The generated models are then tested with another data set of user search sessions in radically different search tasks and constrains. The documents predicted useful and not useful by the models are used to modify the queries in each search session using a standard relevance feedback technique. The results show that application of the models led to consistently improved performance over a baseline that did not take account of user interaction information. These findings have implications for designing systems for personalized search and improving user search experience.

Categories and Subject Descriptors

H.3.3 [Information Storage and Retrieval]: Information Search and Retrieval – relevance feedback.

General Terms

Measurement, Human Factor

Keywords

Implicit feedback, search behaviors, document usefulness, task type, personalization

1. INTRODUCTION

User search interactions are complex, but they are also coherent over segments of a search session, for example when evaluating results from a query. Overall, one expects the actions of a user to reflect their task goal and the process they carry out to achieve that goal. It is reasonable, then, to think that evidence of the user's search interests and task goal may be available in observations of their behaviors during the search session. In this study, we investigate the effectiveness of using the observation of people's behaviors during information-seeking sessions for improving and personalizing their interactions with information. We generated document usefulness prediction models from a laboratory experiment of the influence of different types of tasks on task search session behaviors, including a general model and several specific models tailored to different types of tasks. Then these prediction models were applied to TREC 2011 Session Track data to evaluate their retrieval performance.

Permission to make digital or hard copies of all or part of this work for personal or classroom use is granted without fee provided that copies are not made or distributed for profit or commercial advantage and that copies bear this notice and the full citation on the first page. To copy otherwise, or republish, to post on servers or to redistribute to lists, requires prior specific permission and/or a fee.
SIGIR'12, August 12–16, 2012, Portland, Oregon, USA.
Copyright 2012 ACM 978-1-4503-1472-5/12/08...$15.00.

Our study makes several contributions to the literature. First, we examined user behavioral measures as predictors of document usefulness and built prediction models. Second, we demonstrate the prediction models perform well on an entirely different dataset of user interactions. Third, we found that the prediction accuracy of document usefulness and some of users' search behaviors are positively related to the consistent increase in retrieval performance by the personalization model.

2. RELATED WORK

2.1 Sources for Implicit Relevance Feedback

Users of information retrieval systems can provide explicit information about their interests and task intent via relevance feedback. However, users may not be willing to provide explicit relevance feedback, so research has concentrated on techniques to gain relevance feedback information via implicit processes. These implicit relevance feedback (IRF) techniques observe user search behaviors unobtrusively and infer the relevance/usefulness of documents and other information objects from the user interactions. Evidence for IRF comes from various measures of user search behaviors while interacting with individual content pages, search result pages, and other behaviors during a search session [11] [9].

Document usefulness for IRF may be learned from behaviors such as dwell time on each content page, the number of clicks and scrolling on each content page, number of visits to each content page, and further usage of content pages [9]. User behaviors on search result pages have been found to be good indicators of user document preferences [9]. These behaviors include the time on a search result page before the first click, total time on a search result page, click-through and click order of each content page on the search result page, and so on [1] [7]. There is also evidence that the nature of query reformulation during a search episode can be predictive of document usefulness, and perhaps of task type [13]. In the research to date, these sources for IRF have typically been investigated individually, with little work integrating multiple user behaviors over all types of Web pages to predict document usefulness.

2.2 Implicit Relevance Feedback

Correlation of individual measures of user behavior with users' document preferences have been found to vary for different task types [10] [16] and in different search stages [14]. White and Kelly [16] analyzed retrieval performance after implementing an IRF system based on dwell time on content pages when task type information was considered and when the user information was considered. They found that dwell time combined with knowledge of task information improved retrieval performance. White, Ruthven and Jose [18] examined the effect of search stages on the utility of implicit relevance feedback (IRF) and explicit relevance feedback (ERF) in two separate systems. Their results showed that in the IRF system, IRF is used more in the middle of the search than at the beginning or end, whereas in ERF system, ERF is used more towards the end. Liu and Belkin [14] examined the interaction between decision time on content pages, search stage, and document usefulness, and found knowledge of search stage could help improve the interpretation of decision time as IRF, as could knowledge of task and topic. This work suggests that a high performance search personalization model should predict document usefulness taking account of the users' search context, including task type, user task and topic knowledge, search stage, and so on. Generally, the performance of a personalization algorithm should be improved if it incorporates the ability to predict aspects of the user's task and knowledge.

3. USER EXPERIMENT

3.1 Experimental Design

For our initial study, we recruited 32 participants from a domain relevant to our work/search tasks. They were informed in advance that they would receive $20 for participation. To ensure they treated their assigned tasks seriously, they were told that the top 25% who saved the best set of pages for all four tasks, as judged by an external expert, would receive an additional $20.

The participants were undergraduates at Rutgers university majoring in journalism and were between 18 and 27 years old (26 female, and 6 male). Most were native English speakers (78%) with the balance indicating a high proficiency in English. Participants had an average search experience of 8.85 years using a range of browsers (IE, Firefox, Safari, Chrome, and others). Generally, participants rated their search experience high with more Web search experience as compared to online library catalog search. They were generally positive about their average success when conducting online searches.

Each participant was given a tutorial as a warm-up task and then performed four Web search tasks (described in section 3.2). A pre-search questionnaire elicited their prior familiarity with each task, and their knowledge of the task topic. Participants were asked to search using IE 6.0 on our lab computer, were free to go anywhere on the Web to search for information, and were asked to continue the search until they had gathered enough information to accomplish the task. There was a time limit of 20 minutes for each task.

For each task, participants were asked to **save** content pages that were useful for accomplishing the assignment, and could delete saved pages that were later found to be not useful. When participants decided they had found and saved enough information objects for purposes of the task, they were then asked to evaluate the usefulness of the information objects they saved, or saved and then deleted, through replaying the search using a screen capture program. An online questionnaire was then administered to ask about their searching experience, including their subjective evaluation of their performance, and reasons for that evaluation. The order of the four tasks was systematically rotated for each participant following a Latin Square design. After completing four different tasks, an exit questionnaire was administered asking about their overall search experience.

3.2 Search Tasks

The four work tasks and associated search tasks that we identified are presented below. These tasks follow the normal scenario practice as proposed by Borlund [4], and are couched in journalism terms; that is, journalists are typically given an assignment, and an associated task to complete. Each task was constructed using the faceted task classification scheme proposed by Li & Belkin [12], (modified slightly by us) in order to vary tasks systematically by facet values. In the task descriptions, below we identify the facet values for each (indicated in *italics*). These are also specified in Table 1.

Background Information Collection (BIC)

Your assignment: You are a journalist for the New York Times, working with several others on a story about "whether and how changes in US visa laws after 9/11 have reduced enrollment of international students at universities in the US". You are supposed to gather background information on the topic, specifically, to find what has already been written on this topic. **Your task**: Please find and save all the stories and related materials that have already been published in the last two years in the Times on this topic, and also in five other important newspapers.

The BIC task is a *Mixed Product* because identifying "important" newspapers is intellectual, but finding topical documents is factual. It is *Document Level* because whole stories are judged. It has the *Specific Goal* of finding documents on a well-defined topic, but *Unnamed* because the search targets are not specifically identified (compare with CPE, below).

Interview Preparation (INT)

Your assignment: Your assignment editor asks you to write a news story about "whether state budget cuts in New Jersey are affecting financial aid for college and university students. **Your Task:** Please find the names of two people with appropriate expertise that you are going to interview for this story and save just the pages or sources that describe their expertise and how to contact them.

INT is a *Mixed Product*, because defining expertise is intellectual, and contact information is a fact. It is at the *Document Level*, because expertise is determined by a whole page. The *Goal Quality is Mixed*, because determining expertise is amorphous but contact information is specific. It is *Unnamed* because the search targets are not specifically identified in the task.

Copy Editing (CPE)

Your assignment: You are a copy editor at a newspaper and you have only 20 minutes to check the accuracy of the three underlined statements in the excerpt of a piece of news story below.

Topic: New South Korean President Lee Myung-bak takes office

Body: Lee Myung-bak is the 10th man to serve as South Korea's president and the first to come from a business background. He won a landslide victory in last December's election. He pledged to make the economy his top priority during the campaign. Lee promised to achieve 7% annual economic growth, double the country's per capita income to US$4,000 over a decade and lift the country to one of the topic seven economies in the world. Lee, 66, also called for a stronger alliance with top ally Washington and implored North Korea to forgo its nuclear ambitions and open up to the outside world, promising a better future for the impoverished nation. Lee said he would launch massive investment and aid projects in the North to increase its per capita income to US$3,000 within a decade "once North Korea abandons its nuclear program and chooses the path to openness."

Your Task: Please find and save an authoritative page that either confirms or disconfirms each statement.

CPE is a *Factual Product*, because facts have to be identified. It is at the *Segment Level*, because items within a document need to be found. It has the *Specific Goal* of confirming facts, and it is *Named* because the search targets are specified.

Advance Obituary (OBI)

Your assignment: Many newspapers commonly write obituaries of important people years in advance, before they die, and in this assignment, you are asked to write an advance obituary for a famous person. **Your task**: Please collect and save all the information you will need to write an advance obituary of the artist Trevor Malcolm Weeks.

OBI is a *Factual Product*, because facts about the person are needed. It is at the *Document Level* because entire documents need to be examined. It is *Unnamed* because the search targets are not specifically identified in the task. The *Goal Quality is Amorphous* because "all the information" is undefined.

Table 1 Variable facet values for the search tasks

Task	Naming	Product	Level	Goal (quality)
BIC	Unnamed	Mixed	Document	Specific
CPE	Named	Factual	Segment	Specific
INT	Unnamed	Mixed	Document	Mixed
OBI	Unnamed	Factual	Document	Amorphous

3.3 Data Collection and Behavioral Measures

During the search, all of the participants' interactions with the computer system were logged during the searches on the client side: eye-tracking; mouse movement capture; clicks and URL requests; scrolling; keystrokes; queries and other behaviors. This logging required multiple systems, including Tobii eyetracking software, UsaProxy, the Morae screen-capture program [3], as well as our own software. From these logs, we extracted a variety of measures of the users' search behaviors on search result pages (SERPs) and content pages throughout the session, and during query intervals. A query interval is defined as the interval between two successive queries issued in one search session; and the last query interval is the period after issuing the last query till the completion of the task. The behavioral variables used in the work reported here are listed in Table 2. We classified these behaviors into two groups: behavioral measures on the clicked documents and behavioral measures during the query intervals.

Table 2 Behavioral measures considered for learning predictive models

Behavioral measures	Definition
Behavioral measures on clicked documents	
dwell time	the dwell time on the document, from the point the page is opened till the point the page is closed
number.of. mouseclick	the number of mouse clicks, including Left button down, Right button down, and scrolling, while the page is opened
number.of. keystrokes	the number of keystrokes while the page is opened
visit_id	the number of times a content page has been visited during one search session
Behavioral measures during query intervals	
time_to_first_click	the time before first click on pages after issuing a query
content_mean	the average dwell time on content pages during the query interval
content_sum	the total dwell time on content pages during the query interval
content_count	the total number of content pages visited during the query interval
serp_mean	the average dwell time on SERPs during the query interval
serp_sum	the total dwell time on SERPs during the query interval
serp_count	the total number of SERPs examined during the query interval
prop_content	the proportion of time on content pages of the total dwell time during the interval
interval_time	the total time in each query interval
diff_content	the difference between the dwell time on a content page and the average dwell time on all content pages during the query interval

4. GENERATION OF PREDICTION MODELS

4.1 Building the Models

We used binary recursive partitioning analysis [5] to identify the most important predictors of useful pages. Recursive partitioning is a stochastic learning technique for non-parametric classification problems. It grows decision trees by examining all independent variables and splits a node using the variable that best distinguishes the remaining data in the collection. The tree is grown until all of the data has been assigned to a node. Recursive partitioning has an intuitive interpretation as a collection of rules to classify the dataset. An example (illustrative only) might be "The document is useful if dwell time > 20 seconds and the time to the first click < 34 seconds and there are fewer than 5 SERPs in the query interval". This method has not been used much in identifying predictors of document usefulness or user interests.

Recursive partitioning may be superior to logistic regression when the goal is to correctly classify members rather than optimize overall accuracy. Recursive partitioning can take account of the possible interactions between predictor variables natively in the algorithm.

We used recursive partitioning analysis to generate prediction models of document usefulness based on the potentially important behavioral variables listed in Table 2. Decision trees were generated using these predictors, and we identified the cutoff points based on the observed distribution of the variables in the dataset. To better learn the behavioral measures, we made a training collection that balanced the number of saved pages and not-saved pages by sampling the larger not-saved pages pool. In this way, ten balanced training sets were constructed, each sharing the same saved pages pool. The recursive partitioning method was applied to each sample to generate the prediction model. We then compared the variables and cutoff values in these generated models to identify the repeated variables and cutoff values for the decision-tree based prediction model.

4.2 General Prediction Models

We first built the general prediction model when considering all tasks in the experiment, without taking account of the task type. In this model, three behavioral measures were identified as the important factors: *visit_id*, *dwell time* and *time to first click*.

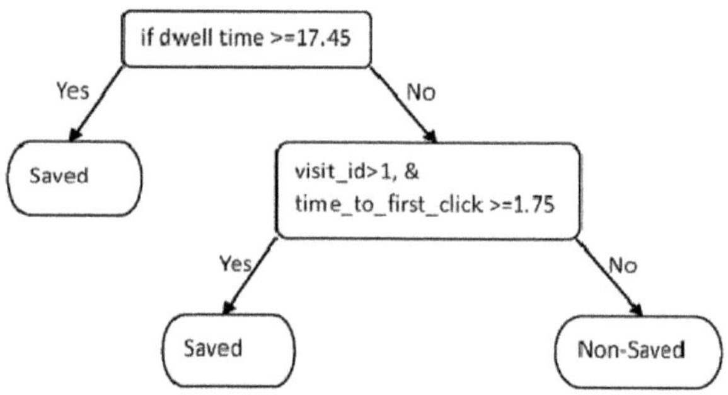

Figure 1 General prediction model

Among these three variables, the *dwell time* on documents is the most important variable in the general prediction model. Examining the distribution of dwell time in the dataset, we found that the model cutoff (17.45 seconds) is the third quarter of the dwell time in all the data. At the same time, we found users saved one quarter of all the visited pages in the assigned task, so it is reasonable to infer that the cutoff point for the dwell time variable depends upon the proportion of saved documents among all visited documents. If the relative frequency of saved documents is not clear in a new dataset, the median dwell time can be adopted as used in White and Kelly [17]. Not many documents were visited more than once by users in one search session, so the model specifies that if a page has been visited more than once, even though the dwell time is shorter than the median, the page is predicted to be useful. Finally, the cutoff time for time to first click is close to the first quarter of the distribution in the dataset. We will apply these cutoff points in our test dataset to evaluate the prediction model.

4.3 Specific Prediction Models

We also conducted 10 random sampling and recursive partitioning analyses on each of the individual tasks to see if tasks of different types would lead to different combinations of important predictors and prediction models. Following the procedure in section 4.1, for each task, we made balanced pools of saved and non-saved pages with the total number of saved pages, and then generated the prediction models using recursive partitioning. Because the CPE task and OBI task in our user experiment differ the most from one another as task types, we present the specific prediction models for CPE (Figure 2) and OBI (Figure 3).

These tree models show that *dwell time* on documents is still the most important predictor. However, the cutoff point for each task is very different, i.e. 30.65 seconds in CPE and 17.5 seconds in OBI. This result indicates that appropriate cutoff points are needed for different types of tasks, as White and Kelly [16] suggested. As for the general model, we suggest the median as the cutoff point for each task. The CPE model also identifies visit time of the page, number of mouse clicks on the page, and the proportion of time spent on content pages during the query interval (*prop_content*) as important variables. Among them, the number of mouse clicks was negatively related to the saved documents, and the *prop_content* was positively related to the saved documents. The OBI model looks very similar to the general model, except that it specifies a range for the *variable time to first click*, which is close to the first quarter to the median value for that variable in the dataset.

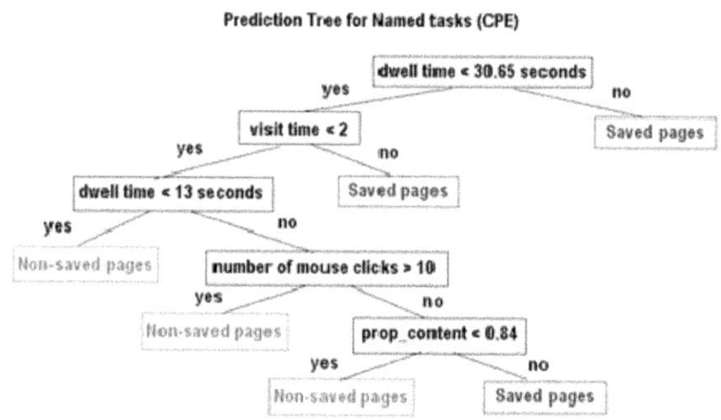

Figure 2. Specific prediction model for CPE

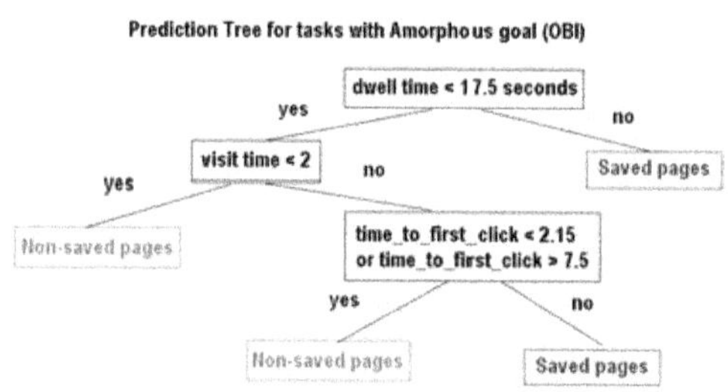

Figure 3. Specific prediction model for OBI

5. IMPLEMENTATION OF PREDICTION MODELS

In order to evaluate the prediction models (both the general model and the specific models) generated from the user experiment, we applied our models to the data collected for the TREC 2011 Session Track. The Session Track [8] aims to provide test collections and evaluation measures for studying information retrieval based on previous user interactions during a search session, rather than one-time queries. The track used the ClueWeb09 collection (English only) [1], and the topics were

[1] lemurproject.org/clueweb09

defined in the usual TREC ad hoc sense, with a title, description, and narrative. Sessions of real user interactions were recorded, including users' queries, clicks on search result pages, and associated time stamps. There were search sessions for 76 topics in total.

5.1 Task Classification

Before implementing the prediction models, we first classified the tasks in the TREC 2011 Session Track using our modification of the Li & Belkin [12] task classification scheme. The 76 sessions were classified into 4 types of tasks according to the task facets. From Table 3 we can see that all of the 76 tasks required searching for factual information, so the product for them is *Factual.* In addition, 66 of the 76 sessions can be classified as searching for information on the *Segment* level, with *Specific* goal, with search targets *Named* (SSN). There are very few examples of three other types of tasks (i.e. SSU, DSN, DAN) in the data set. When we tried to match these task types with the task classification in our user experiment (Table 1), we found that the SSN type of task was mostly similar to CPE, and DSN and DAN types of tasks were very similar to OBI, so we used these specific models for those tasks. We applied the General model for the SSU task type.

Table 3 Task classification of the search tasks in TREC 2011 Session Track

Task type	SSN	SSU	DSN	DAN
Level	Segment	Segment	Document	Document
Goal(quality)	Specific	Specific	Specific	Amorphous
Naming	Named	Unnamed	Named	Named
Product	Factual	Factual	Factual	Factual
Model applied	CPE	General model	OBI	OBI
number of tasks	66	4	4	2

5.2 Prediction Models on the TREC Dataset

The general model for the TREC dataset was based on the general model we built from the user experiment and the threshold was determined based on the targeted dataset.

The general model (decision tree) is:

if (visit_id > 1),{then it is a useful page};
else if (dwell time > 28.55 seconds), {then it is a useful page};
else if (6.33 seconds < **time-to-first-click <14.55** seconds), {then it is a useful page};
else {non-useful pages}.

The implementation of specific models in the TREC dataset is based on our task classification (Table 3). The CPE specific model is used for SSN type of task, the OBI specific model is used for DSN and DAN types of task, and the other task types use the general model. Since the interaction log for the TREC 2011 Session Track was collected on the server side, and did not include any user interactions on the documents (i.e. content pages), the variable *number of mouse clicks* was not included in the specific models..

The specific model (decision tree) is:

if (visit_id > 1), then useful pages
if (task type = SSN)
{if (dwell time >=28.84 #Median dwell time for this type of task)
{then useful pages }
else if (prop_content>=0.6 #Median for this type of task)
{then useful pages }
else { then non-useful pages }}

else if (task type = SSU)
{if (dwell time >=17 #Median dwell time for this type of task)
{then useful pages }
else if (task type = DSN or DAN,
{if (dwell time >=32.82 #Median dwell time for these types of task)
{then useful pages}
else if (time_to_first_click > 6.33 & time_to_first_click < 14.55)
{then useful pages }
else {non-useful pages }}}

5.3 Relevance Feedback Technique

For evaluation of the various prediction models in this paper, we use only one of the three types of query modification specified in the TREC 2011 Session Track, which uses the maximum amount of behavioral data obtained during the search session [8]. Since the Session Track's basic concept was to compare the search results of the final query in a search session using a baseline system with no behavioral data, to the results of a final query using such data, we used the results of our document usefulness prediction models to modify the last query but one (*last -1*) in the session, using both positive and (positive + negative) relevance feedback (RF). The TREC 2011 Session Track database, Clueweb09 English only [8] was the searched collection, and was the source for documents and terms for RF.

From the prediction of document usefulness for each of our models, we generated a pool of "relevant" documents that occurred during each search session, and calculated the term frequency for each term in the pool, and in the equivalent corpus of non-useful documents. The observed term frequency was then discounted by the prior of the expectation of appearance in a random document in the English language using the Brown corpus [15].

With respect to the number of useful and non-useful terms for query expansion, we used the approach described in Belkin et al. [2], in which a negative RF system was implemented. The number of suggested feedback terms was determined by the formula:

> $5n + 5$, where n = number of judged documents to a maximum of 25 suggested terms.

The query was parsed as a weighted sum, using the default Lemur[2] weighting for RF term addition for positive terms, and adding the negative terms under the InQuery "NOT" operator, with 0.6 weight.

[2] lemurproject.org

Two relevance feedback methods were implemented:

Positive relevance feedback only: In the runs with positive RF only, the predicted "useful" documents were used to calculate the term frequency, the top 25 terms were selected to expand the *last -1* query in the session.

Both positive and negative relevance feedback: In the runs with both positive and negative RF, the predicted "useful" documents were used to calculate the term frequency for "useful" terms and the top 15 terms were selected to be "useful" terms; the predicted "non-useful" documents were used to calculate the term frequency for "non-useful" terms and the top 10 terms were selected to be "non-useful" terms. We then combined the *last-1* queries with the 15 "useful" terms (with positive weight 1.0), and the 10 "non-useful" terms (with negative weight 0.6) using the Indri query language.

Therefore, we have four prediction models of document usefulness generated and evaluated in this study:

- General model with Positive RF only (GP)
- General model with Positive and Negative RF (GPN)
- Specific model with Positive RF only (SP)
- Specific model with Positive and Negative RF (SPN)

5.4 Baseline model

Our baseline model used Pseudo Relevance Feedback on the last queries issued by the users in each session. The default parameters in the Indri Retrieval System were used as follows:

Parameters for Pseudo Relevance Feedback:

```
int fbDocs = _param.get( "fbDocs" , 10 );
int fbTerms = _param.get( "fbTerms" , 10 );
double fbOrigWt = _param.get( "fbOrigWeight", 0.5 );
double mu = _param.get( "fbMu", 0 );
```

We compare the retrieval performance of our personalized models with the baseline system, to evaluate whether the personalized models based on users' interactions in the search session improve results over pseudo relevance feedback that does not take account of users' interaction behaviors.

6. EVALUATION OF PREDICTION MODELS

6.1 Prediction Accuracy of Document Usefulness

We evaluated the prediction accuracy of document relevance against the TREC assessors' relevance judgments [8]. The relevance judgments ranged from -2 to 3 (-2 stands for spam document, 0 stands for not relevant, 1 for relevant, 2 for highly relevant, and 3 means the document is a key to the information need). Since we used binary relevance ratings in our prediction models, we grouped TREC assessors' judgments into two groups: ratings that were -2 or 0 were grouped as "not-relevant", and ratings of 1 to 3 were grouped as "relevant".

Table 4 and Table 5 show the prediction accuracy of the general model and the specific models on the document relevance. They demonstrate that the general model achieved better prediction performance than the specific model for the TREC 2011 Session Track data.

Table 4 Prediction accuracy of the general model

		TREC assessment		
		not- relevant	relevant	total
General model predicted	not-relevant	29 (53%)	45(Type I error)	74
	relevant	26 (Type II error)	83 (65%)	109
	total	55	128	183
Overall accuracy				61%

Table 5 Prediction accuracy of the specific model

		TREC assessment		
		not- relevant	relevant	total
Specific model predicted	not-relevant	24 (44%)	55 (Type I error)	69
	relevant	31(Type II error)	73 (57%)	102
	total	55	128	183
Overall accuracy				53%

6.2 Retrieval Performance Comparison

6.2.1 Overall performance

We first calculated the mean of the retrieval performance over 76 sessions by each of the models (Table 6). Our results demonstrate that all of the four models improve over the baseline, on almost all the measures provided by TREC 2011 Session Track [8].

Table 6 Overall retrieval performance

	Baseline	GPN	GP	SPN	SP
ERR[3]	0.20	0.28	0.29	0.27	0.28
ERR@10	0.19	0.28	0.29	0.26	0.28
nERR[4]	0.29	0.44	0.45	0.41	0.42
nERR@10	0.27	0.43	0.45	0.40	0.42
nDCG[5]	0.30	0.24	0.25	0.24	0.25
nDCG@10	0.20	0.34	0.35	0.32	0.33
AP[6]	0.09	0.09	0.09	0.08	0.09
GAP[7]	0.08	0.09	0.09	0.09	0.09

6.2.2 Retrieval performance by sessions

Expected Reciprocal Rank (ERR) [6] was chosen for the following analysis because the user model underlying the ERR measure matches the user model underlying our prediction models. When examining results by search sessions, we found, as usual,

[3] ERR: Expected Reciprocal Rank;

[4] nERR: ERR normalized by the maximum ERR per query;

[5] nDCG: normalized discounted cumulative gain;

[6] AP: Average Precision

[7] GAP: Graded Average Precision;

that there is great variety in evaluation results for any single technique between sessions. For example, the GP model had better retrieval performance on ERR in 42 sessions, but had worse performance on ERR in 32 sessions.

Table 7 Retrieval performance change over baseline on ERR

Run / Measures	All sessions			
	GP	GPN	SP	SPN
Mean ERR	0.29	0.28	0.28	0.27
Percent improvement over baseline (ERR=0.20)	44%	38%	38%	32%
Number of sessions that improve the baseline	40	40	36	36
Number of session that decrease from the baseline	29	32	32	34
Number of session that did not change the baseline	7	4	8	6

6.2.3 The relationship between prediction accuracy and retrieval performance

Among the 76 sessions, there were 12 sessions in which users did not click on any documents. We first compare the retrieval performance and the change over baseline between the sessions that did not contain any clicked documents (N=12) with the sessions that contained at least one clicked document (N=64).

Table 8 Comparison between two types of sessions

Models	Sessions that do not contain clicked documents (N=12)	Sessions that contain clicked documents (N=64)	Mann-Whitney test
	Mean (SD) of retrieval performance evaluated using ERR measure	Mean (SD) of retrieval performance evaluated using ERR measure	p
GPN	0.08 (0.15)	0.32 (0.25)	<0.05
GPN change over baseline	-0.07 (0.3)	0.11 (0.31)	<0.05
GP	0.15 (0.28)	0.32 (0.25)	<0.05
GP change over baseline	0.01 (0.13)	0.11 (0.31)	<0.05
SPN	0.08 (0.15)	0.31 (0.27)	<0.05
SPN change over baseline	-0.07 (0.3)	0.09 (0.32)	<0.05
SP	0.15 (0.28)	0.31 (0.27)	<0.05
SP change over baseline	0.01 (0.13)	0.09 (0.32)	0.095

Table 8 shows that the retrieval performance of our four models and the improvement of our models over baseline (except SP) is significantly better in the sessions that contain clicked documents than in sessions that did not contain any clicked documents. This result shows that our models need clicked document data to improve search results.

Since we are using users' interactions during sessions to build the prediction models of document usefulness, in the following analysis, we present results for sessions that contain at least one clicked document (N=64) to evaluate the performance of our prediction models. We then examine the relationship between prediction accuracy and retrieval performance, by three types of change (decrease, no change, and increase) in retrieval performance compared with the baseline.

We compare the amount of user interaction in each session, and the prediction accuracy of document usefulness by the *general model* among the three groups (Table 9). The amount of user interactions is defined as the sum of the number of queries, the number of search result pages, and the number of content pages visited. Our results show that the prediction accuracy of document usefulness in the sessions for which use of the general model increased the retrieval performance over the baseline was as high as 75%. In contrast, the prediction accuracy was only 51% in the sessions that where personalization decreased the retrieval performance. The Kruskal Wallis test revealed that the differences in the overall accuracy was significant ($p<.05$). Neither the number of clicked documents nor the number of interactions was significantly different among three groups.

Table 9 Comparison of behaviors and prediction in the general model

	Sessions that decrease from the baseline	Sessions that did not change the baseline	Sessions that increase from the baseline	Kruskal-Wallis Test
	Mean	Mean	Mean	p
Number of clicked documents in the session	2.87	2.33	2.84	0.82
Number of interaction s in the session	12.57	9.67	12.39	0.70
Overall accuracy of the general model	**51%**	**53%**	**75%**	**<.05**

We also compared the amount of user interaction in each session, and the prediction accuracy of document usefulness by the *specific model* among the three groups (Table 10). As with the general model, we found that the sessions that increased retrieval performance over the baseline by the specific model had significantly higher prediction accuracy of document usefulness (64%) with the specific model as compared to the sessions that decreased the retrieval performance (34%). Again, neither the number of clicked documents nor the number of interactions was significantly different among three groups.

Table 10 Comparison of behaviors and prediction in the specific model

	Sessions that decrease from the baseline	Sessions that did not change the baseline	Sessions that increase from the baseline	Kruskal-Wallis Test
	Mean	Mean	Mean	p
Number of clicked documents in the session	2.4	2.4	3.21	0.70
Number of interaction s in the session	11.44	9.8	13.35	0.45
Overall accuracy of the general model	**0.34**	**0.41**	**0.64**	**.009**

In general, when applying our prediction models on the TREC Session Track 2011 dataset, our results indicate that the better the prediction accuracy, the greater the improvement of retrieval performance over the baseline.

6.2.3.1 When to personalize?

Figure 4 and Figure 5 show the ERR values for each search session for the baseline and for each of our personalization methods. It is clear there are specific search sessions which will benefit from our personalization methods, and others for which such personalization is either not worth the effort, or harmful.

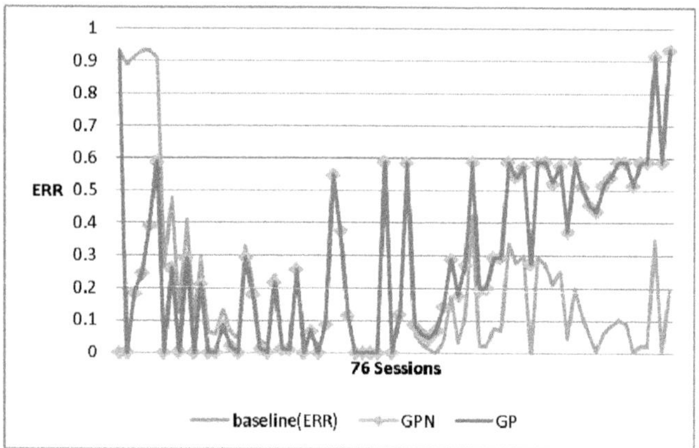

Figure 4 When to personalize using the general model (sessions ordered according to increasing positive difference between GPN and baseline)

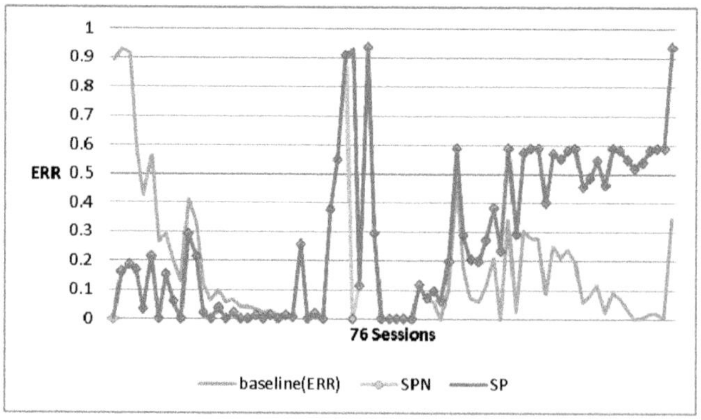

Figure 5 When to personalize using the specific model (sessions ordered according to increasing positive difference between SPN and baseline)

The question is when should one apply personalized models? (cf. [16]) In practice we need to identify these sessions from the observable user interactions during the search session. To accomplish this we focus on interaction behaviors that are associated with sessions where our models were particularly good and particularly bad. Specifically, we look at the behaviors in sessions where our models improved retrieval performance by greater than 0.20 on ERR and for sessions where the models did worse than-0.05 on ERR. We compare the behavioral variables in the search sessions between the two extremes in retrieval performance defined by the GP model in Table 11. For the sessions in which retrieval performance benefited a lot from the personalization model, users spent significantly more dwell time on each content page (51.25 seconds) than in the other group of sessions where the performance was decreased (34.61 seconds). They also spent a relatively greater proportion of task time on reading content pages (43%) than in the other group of sessions (29%). These results, in particular the former, suggest that it is possible to identify search sessions which would benefit from personalization relatively early in the course of the search session.

Table 11 Comparison of behavioral measures between two groups defined by GP model

Behavioral measures	Decrease d group (N=13)	Benefit group (N=24)	Mann-Whitne y test
	Mean	Mean	p
Total time on task (seconds)	354.27	317.35	1
Total time on content pages (seconds)	102.78	141.71	.19
Total time on SERPs	223.03	141.73	.18
Mean dwell time on each content page (seconds)	**34.61**	**51.25**	**<.05**
Mean dwell time on each SERPs (seconds)	37.43	24.00	.31
Number of query	4.23	3.96	.37
Time to first click (seconds)	33.47	22.44	.19
Query interval time (seconds)	86.97	86.64	.52
Proportion of time spent on content pages in the session	**29%**	**43%**	**<.05**

7. DISCUSSION

In this study, we generated document usefulness prediction models based on a laboratory experiment of the influence of different types of tasks on task session behaviors. We constructed a general prediction model and several specific prediction models tailored to different types of tasks. Recursive partitioning analysis was used to generate decision tree models based on users' interaction behaviors during search sessions. Our models identified three main behavioral measures as important predictors of document usefulness: *dwell time* on document, the number of times a page has been visited in the session (*visit_id*), and the time before first click after issuing a query (*time to first click*). Besides the positive relationship between dwell time and document usefulness, we found that, in all but one case, the *visit_id* and *time_to_first_click* to be positively related to document usefulness. The specific models for different types of tasks show major differences by task type for both the predictors and the rules. For example, in the specific prediction model for CPE, *number of mouse clicks* on the document was negatively related to document usefulness, and the proportion of time spent on content pages during query interval (*prop_content*) was positively related to document usefulness. However, neither of these two measures and associated rules was useful in the specific model for OBI. Furthermore, although all models included dwell time as a significant factor, cut-off points for dwell time to predict usefulness differed between the different tasks, and from that of the general model.

A primary focus of this study was to evaluate whether the prediction models generated from our user experiment could improve retrieval performance, so we applied our models to the TREC 2011 Session Track data. The comparison of the prediction by the different models against TREC assessors' relevance judgments showed the general model had higher accuracy than the specific models. One reason for this is that there is a great imbalance in task type in the TREC 2011 Session Track data. The vast majority of the tasks were of a task type similar to the CPE task in our experiment. Our specific model for CPE contains *number of mouse clicks* on the documents as one of the predictors, but such data was not available in the server-side logs in the TREC 2011 Session Track. The task type imbalance also meant that not enough data was available (10 sessions in total) for three of the four types of tasks (SSU, DSN, DAN). Consequently, one can expect the specific models will fail when they try to adapt to the individual task types. In addition, other facets of the task types may present in the TREC Session Track that differ from those in the user experiment in our lab. Such facets could influence users' behaviors in different ways. For example, users were given 20 minutes for searching in our experiment, whereas in the crowdsourced search sessions in the TREC Session Track, users were given only 5 minutes for searching. Users were likely to have searched with an awareness of time-pressure which might not have been the case during our experiment.

With respect to retrieval performance, all of our models improved a great deal from the baseline which used pseudo relevance feedback on the last queries users issued in each session. Our general model had somewhat better retrieval performance than the specific model on both of the two relevance feedback methods. The models with positive relevance feedback performed only slightly better than the models with both positive and negative relevance feedback. This suggests that using negative IRF may not be worth the effort, although perhaps the limited size of the data set for the TREC Session Track mitigates this conclusion. In addition, we found that the better the prediction accuracy of document usefulness, the more likely that the model could improve retrieval performance.

Teevan, Dumais & Horvitz [16] examined users' clicks and explicit judgments for the same queries and found they differed greatly from one another. They proposed that the *potential for personalization* could be defined by the gap between how well search engines could perform if they were to tailor results to the individual, and how well they currently perform by returning results designed to satisfy everyone. In our study, we also addressed the question of *when to apply personalization models* by presenting the retrieval difference between our models and the baseline. We found our prediction models consistently improved retrieval performance over the baseline in some sessions, but consistently decreased the performance of the baseline line in some other sessions. We compared some users' behavioral measures during these sessions, and found significant differences between the two extreme groups. In particular, users spent significantly more dwell time on each content page and a greater proportion of task time on content pages for the sessions where the personalization models we applied were beneficial. Dwell time on content pages has been proven to be positively related to document relevance, and one explanation for our results is that users were visiting more useful documents in the sessions where the models performed well and that query expansion based on the useful documents helped users to articulate their information needs. Therefore, IRF based on the predicted useful documents achieved better results than using the top *n* returned documents, as in pseudo relevance feedback. Further work is needed to investigate when the system should apply personalization models to improve retrieval performance.

Because the data that we used for our personalization models should be applicable to any general retrieval system, one might expect that our levels of improvement would be applicable to techniques with much higher baseline performance, resulting in higher absolute performance levels. It is also the case that our usefulness prediction models were used as input to quite standard, and rather simple relevance feedback techniques. More sophisticated use of the models could result in better overall performance improvement.

8. CONCLUSION

In this study, we used searchers' interaction behavioral measures derived from a laboratory experiment to build prediction models of document usefulness. We then evaluated the prediction accuracy and retrieval performance of these models by applying them to the TREC 2011 Session Track data set, where users search interactions were generated in radically different search sessions. We found several behavioral measures, e.g. dwell time, visit time, time to first click, proportion of time on content pages, and others could be potential predictors of document usefulness. We also found different combinations of variables and rules of prediction models based on these measures for different types of tasks. The results demonstrate that the prediction models we generated from our user experiment improve the performance over a baseline that did not take account of user interaction information in search sessions with quite different characteristics than those from which the prediction models were developed. The positive "transfer" effect leads us to believe the models we have developed may be used for personalization of retrieval in a variety of searching circumstances, and that we could expect even greater performance benefit when richer, client-side data that our prediction models depend upon are applied.

ACKNOWLEDGMENTS

The research that led to this work was funded by the IMLS, under grant number LG-06-07-0105-07. We thank all of the members of the Personalization of the Digital Library Experience (PoODLE) research team at Rutgers University, without whose efforts this work could not have been accomplished. Thanks to Si Sun for assistance in TREC 2011 Session Track. Thanks to Jingjing Liu for validating task classification as the third coder. Thanks to David Pane at CMU, who helped us greatly and generously in performing the Indri runs.

REFERENCES

[1] Agichtein, E., Brill, E., Dumais, S., & Ragno, R. (2006). Learning user interaction models for predicting web search result preferences. In *Proceedings of the 29th Annual International ACM SIGIR Conference on Research and Development in Information Retrieval*. (pp. 3-10). Seattle, Washington, USA.

[2] Belkin, N. J., Carballo, J. P., Cool, C., Lin, S., Park, S. Y., Rieh, S. Y., et al. (1998). Rutgers' TREC-6 interactive track experience. *Proceedings of the Sixth Text REtrieval Conference*, 597-610.

[3] Bierig, R., Cole., M.J., & Gwizdka, J. (2009). A user centered experiment and logging framework for interactive information retrieval. In N.J. Belkin, R. Bierig, G. Buscher, L. van Elst, J. Gwizdka, J. Jose, et al. (Eds), CEUR Workshop Proceedings: 512. Proceedings of the SIGIR 2009 Workshop on Understanding the User: Logging and interpreting user interactions in information search and retrieval, UIIR'2009 (pp. 8-11). Aachen, Germany: CEUR Workshop Proceedings.

[4] Borlund, P. (2003). The IIR evaluation model: A framework for evaluation of interactive information retrieval systems. *Information Research*, 8(3), paper no. 152. Retrieved from http://informationr.net/ir/8-3/paper152.html.

[5] Breiman, L. (1984). *Classification and Regression Trees*. Boca Raton: Chapman & Hall/CRC.

[6] Chapelle, O., Metzler, D., Zhang, Y., and Grinspan, P. (2009). Expected reciprocal rank for graded relevance. In *Proceedings of the 18th ACM Conference on Information and Knowledge Management (CIKM)*, 2009, 621-630.

[7] Fox, S., Karnawat, K., Mydland, M., Dumais, S., & White, T. (2005). Evaluating implicit measures to improve web search. *ACM Transactions on Information Systems*, 23(2), 147-168.

[8] Kanoulas, E., Hall, M. Clough, P. Carterette, B., & Sanderson, M. (2012) Overview of the TREC Session Track. In: *The Twentieth Text REtrieval Conference Proceedings (TREC 2011)*. Gaithersburg, MD: National Institute of Standards and Technology. Retrieved on 20 May 2012 at http://trec.nist.gov/pubs/trec20/t20.proceedings.html.

[9] Kelly, D. (2005). Implicit feedback: Using behavior to infer relevance. In A. Spink and C. Cole (Eds.) *New Directions in Cognitive Information Retrieval* (pp.169-186). Netherlands: Springer Publishing.

[10] Kelly, D. & Belkin, N.J. (2004). Display time as implicit feedback: Understanding task effects. *In Proceedings of the 27th annual international ACM SIGIR conference on Research and development in information retrieval (SIGIR '04)*. ACM, New York, NY, USA, 377-384. DOI= http://doi.acm.org/10.1145/1008992.1009057

[11] Kelly, D. & Teevan, J. (2003). Implicit feedback for inferring user preference: A bibliography. *SIGIR Forum*, 37(2), 18-28.

[12] Li, Y. & Belkin, N.J. (2008). A faceted approach to conceptualizing tasks in information seeking. *Inf. Process. Manage.* 44, 6 (November 2008), 1822-1837. DOI=10.1016/j.ipm.2008.07.005 http://dx.doi.org/10.1016/j.ipm.2008.07.005

[13] Liu, C., Gwizdka, J., & Liu, J. (2010). Helping identify when users find useful documents: examination of query reformulation intervals. In *Proceeding of the third symposium on Information interaction in context (IIiX '10)*. ACM, New York, NY, USA, 215-224. DOI= http://doi.acm.org/10.1145/1840784.1840816

[14] Liu, J. & Belkin, N.J. (2010). Personalizing information retrieval for multi-session tasks: The roles of task stage and task type. In *Proceedings of the 33rd Annual International ACM SIGIR Conference on Research & Development on Information Retrieval (SIGIR '10)*. Geneva, Switzland, July 19-23, 2010.

[15] Loper, E. and Bird, S. (2002). NLTK: The Natural Language Toolkit. *Proceedings of the ACL02 Workshop on Effective tools and methodologies for teaching natural language processing and computational linguistics,* Volume 1, July, 2002 Association for Computational Linguistics.

[16] Teevan, J., Dumais, S.T., and Horvitz, E. (2010). Potential for personalization. *ACM Trans. Comput.-Hum. Interact.* 17, 1, 1-31.

[17] White, R. W. & Kelly, D. (2006). A study on the effects of personalization and task information on implicit feedback performance. In *Proceedings of the 15th ACM international conference on Information and knowledge management* (pp. 297-306). Arlington, Virginia, USA.

[18] White, R.W., Ruthven, I., and Jose, J.M. (2005). A study of factors affecting the utility of implicit relevance feedback. In *Proceedings of the 28th annual international ACM SIGIR conference on Research and development in information retrieval (SIGIR '05)*. ACM, New York, NY, USA, 35-42.

User Evaluation of Query Quality

Wan-Ching Wu
SILS
University of North Carolina
Chapel Hill, NC, 27599 USA
wanchinw@email.unc.edu

Diane Kelly
SILS
University of North Carolina
Chapel Hill, NC, 27599 USA
dianek@email.unc.edu

Kun Huang
School of Management
Beijing Normal University
Beijing, China, 100875
huangkun@bnu.edu.cn

ABSTRACT
Although a great deal of research has been conducted about automatic techniques for determining query quality, there have been relatively few studies about how people judge query quality. This study investigated this topic through a laboratory experiment with 40 subjects. Subjects were shown eight information problems (five fact-finding and three exploratory) and asked to evaluate queries for these problems according to several quality attributes. Subjects then evaluated search engine results pages (SERPs) for each query, which were manipulated to exhibit different levels of performance. Following this, subjects reevaluated the queries, were interviewed about their evaluation approaches and repeated the rating procedure for two information problems. Results showed that for fact-finding information problems, longer queries received higher ratings (both initial and post-SERP), and that post-SERP query ratings were more affected by the proportion of relevant documents viewed to all documents viewed rather than the ranks of the relevant documents. For exploratory information problems, subjects' ratings were highly correlated with the number of relevant documents in the SERP as well as the proportion of relevant documents viewed. Subjects adopted several approaches when evaluating query quality, which led to different quality ratings. Finally, during the reliability check subjects' initial evaluations were fairly stable, but their post-SERP evaluations significantly increased.

Categories and Subject Descriptors
H.3 [**Information Storage and Retrieval**]: Information Search and Retrieval - query formulation, search process.

General Terms
Experimentation, Human Factors

Keywords
Query quality, query recommendation, query evaluation

1. INTRODUCTION
Query performance prediction (QPP) is the task of estimating the expected quality of search results for a query in the absence of relevance feedback [4, 8]. The basic goal is to predict when a query will perform poorly so that some intervention can occur before results are returned. For example, additional information might be elicited from the user or term expansion might be used to enhance the query. QPP approaches are classified into two types: pre-retrieval and post-retrieval [4, 8]. Pre-retrieval approaches estimate query performance based on features of the query while post-retrieval approaches consider the results retrieved by the query. Pre-retrieval approaches are further subdivided into those that exploit the linguistic structure of the query, including the morphological, syntactical and semantic properties of the query, and those that use term statistics, including specificity, similarity, coherency and relatedness. Post-retrieval approaches include measures such as clarity and robustness, and score analysis.

Permission to make digital or hard copies of all or part of this work for personal or classroom use is granted without fee provided that copies are not made or distributed for profit or commercial advantage and that copies bear this notice and the full citation on the first page. To copy otherwise, or republish, to post on servers or to redistribute to lists, requires prior specific permission and/or a fee.
SIGIR'12, August 12–16, 2012, Portland, Oregon, USA.
Copyright 2012 ACM 978-1-4503-1472-5/12/08...$10.00.

Although a great deal of research has been conducted about QPP, there have been relatively few studies about the relationship among QPPs and users' evaluations of query difficulty. Hauff et al. [10] note "while most QPP methods have been motivated and developed based on how a user might rate a query, these intuitions have never been empirically validated" (pg. 980). To address this limitation, Hauff et al. [9, 10] compared the query performance ratings made by humans with performance scores estimated by a suite of QPP methods. Results showed that user ratings and QPPs were mostly uncorrelated, suggesting that QPP methods are not representative of how users evaluate query quality. Lioma et al. [12] found that users could not reliably identify pre-determined query difficulty ratings associated with a set of 420 queries, but were able to identify some features that would make a query difficult for a search system.

While these previous studies provide some insight about the relationship among QPPs and users' evaluations of query difficulty, they do not reveal insight about how people actually judge query quality. In one of the studies reported by Hauff et al. [10], assessors were provided with queries and information need descriptions and asked to judge the queries based on what they expected the results to be if they submitted the queries to a Web search engine. Assessors made their judgments using a 5-point scale, where 1=poor quality query and 5=high quality query. The researchers did not report assessors' experiences using this scale to evaluate query quality, although it was noted that their ratings varied considerably. Lioma et al. [12] asked assessors to rate queries using three categories (easy, medium, hard). In both studies, assessors evaluated queries without inspecting results. Neither study probed people about how they judged query quality.

People rate a variety of objects in daily life (e.g., movies, restaurants, books), but it is unlikely that many people have rated queries. How would people approach this task? What factors would they consider when evaluating query quality? How would they make decisions about which numeric ratings to assign to which queries? In this paper we explore these questions. We are not concerned with the relationship between QPPs and people's evaluations of query quality, but instead seek to address more fundamental questions about how people make evaluations of query quality. Specifically, our research questions are (RQ1)

How do people make judgments about query quality? (RQ2) How are people's judgments related to features of the query, information problem and search results? (RQ3) How reliable are people's judgments?

Understanding how people evaluate query quality is important for several reasons. A better understanding of how people evaluate query quality might provide data on which to model future QPPs, or it might help researchers better understand the differences between automatic QPPs and human QPP. Although QPPs leverage collection-based statistics and should not necessarily be correlated with users' query evaluations, understanding how people view query quality might be helpful in modeling computer-human interaction regarding QPP. Understanding how people evaluate query quality is also important in the context of another popular IR technique: query suggestion. Traditionally, query suggestions are presented to users without any information about their potential goodness or quality. However, it might be useful to allow users to provide query *recommendations* to others, that is, query suggestions that have rating information associated with them in a manner similar to that provided by recommendation services such as Amazon and Netflix. It might also be useful for an information system to elicit query ratings from users so that it can make more personalized recommendations in the future. While *suggestion* and *recommendation* are often used as synonyms in the literature, in this study we distinguish between these two terms to demarcate a difference between the provision of unrated and rated suggestions, respectively. We pose one additional question to better understand what people think of the idea of query recommendation: (RQ4) What are people's perceptions of query recommendations? This is a natural question to ask in the context of an experiment that focuses on how people evaluate query quality, since this would presumably underlie query recommendation.

2. BACKGROUND

This study is related to three major areas of research: query performance predictors (QPPs), query suggestion, and online recommendations. Because this paper is not focused on automatic QPPs, this research is not reviewed (see [4] for an overview).

In a series of studies, Hauff and colleagues [9, 10] explored the relationship between QPPs and users' evaluations of query quality. This work was motivated by the observation that underlying most QPP methods are assumptions about how users evaluate query quality, despite a lack of research about how users make decisions about queries and suggestions. In a series of studies, Hauff and colleagues found few strong correlations between assessors' query quality evaluations and QPPs. The researchers first collected pre-retrieval ratings from 18 assessors for a set of 50 topics. Assessors were shown information need descriptions and queries and asked to indicate their expectations of the quality of the search results.

Hauff et al. [9, 10] found great variability is assessors' query ratings, and few direct correlations between these ratings and a set of QPP pre-retrieval measures. Hauff et al. also compared pre-retrieval and post-retrieval QPP measures with assessors' pre- and post-retrieval query quality ratings of a set of query suggestions. While assessors could distinguish between high and low quality suggestions, their ratings were uncorrelated with the automatic QPP measures. Across all experiments, the QPP measure that was most correlated with assessors' ratings was the pre-retrieval predictor *SumSCQ* which assigns higher quality scores to more specific queries. Typically queries that contain more terms are associated with a higher *SumSCQ*; this suggests that people's pre-retrieval query quality judgments might be influenced by query length. Similarly, Lioma et al [12] found that people were fairly good at identifying features that were correlated with query difficulty, including queries that were "too vague" or "too short," but were unable to reliably assess query difficulty using a rating scale of easy, medium and hard.

In addition to these studies, two studies have examined the relationship between QPPs and user performance [18, 19]. While these studies focused on different research questions than the ones on which we focus, their results showed that user performance was unrelated to several QPP measures. Turpin and Hersh [18] found that the clarity scores of queries created by their users were much lower on average than those reported in system-based QPP evaluations where queries were automatically created. Turpin and Hersh further found that there was no correlation between the *clarity* of a user's query (a post-retrieval QPP) and the user's actual performance on the search task. Zhao and Scholer [19] examined nine pre-retrieval QPPs and found that they were not useful predictors of when users experienced search difficulties.

A portion of Hauff et al.'s [10] work was a secondary analysis of data collected in a study investigating the extent to which users could be induced to take bad query suggestions because they believed many others had taken the suggestions [11]. Kelly et al. [11] did not find an effect for "query popularity," but did find that users selected significantly more high quality than low quality query suggestions. Although this research was not conducted in the context of QPP, it does provide some indirect evidence that people make predictive judgments about query quality when selecting among a set of suggestions and that these judgments are often accurate. Like QPP research, query suggestion research is an area that might benefit from an increased understanding of how people evaluate query quality.

Increasing amounts of research have been published about query suggestion within the last ten years [15] and query suggestion is now a common feature of many information search systems. When users issue queries to most major commercial search services, they receive search results and query suggestions. However, they do not receive information about how the query suggestions were selected. While these query suggestions are likely identified through a combination of techniques based on aggregated query log data, details about the usage and frequency of various queries are not displayed to users. In social and collaborative search systems, query suggestions come from fellow users who belong to a community or specialized group with a common set of information needs [1, 16, 17]. These suggestions are also free-standing in the sense that users only know that they have been suggested or used, but nothing about their potential quality or usefulness. Thus, it seems that an important opportunity might exist in allowing users to associate ratings with query suggestions. In recent work, Baraglia et al. [2] proposed the idea of machine-rated query suggestions where queries would be rated with a 10-point scale (10=positive, 5=neutral and 1=negative), but their research was focused on algorithms for selecting and rating suggestions, rather than user ratings or interpretations of ratings.

In this paper we distinguish between query suggestions and query recommendations. The key difference between the two is the presence (*recommendation*) or absence (*suggestion*) of rating information. While suggestions can be generated by both systems and humans, ratings are, in most cases, associated with humans. The basic act of associating ratings with items is one with which most people are familiar. However, rating behavior, in general, is not a well-understood topic, even in the recommender system literature [7]. A recent call for a special issue of *ACM Transactions on Interactive Intelligent Systems (TiiS)* states that little research has focused on the decision-making processes of users. Instead, research has focused on algorithms for identifying recommendations and eliciting and modeling users' preferences[1].

Rating behavior has been studied more extensively in the consumer behavior literature. This research has primarily focused on consumer bias, cultural differences, brand loyalty and receiver experience and expertise in relation to commercial products [c.f., 6, 14]. A typical way these studies conceptualize objects that are rated, and people's subsequent use of ratings for making decisions about these objects, is by classifying them into *search* and *experience* goods [13]. *Search goods* are goods that are characterized by product attributes for which full information can be acquired before purchase. Search goods (e.g., dishwasher) are typically evaluated using objective criteria (e.g., capacity, noise level). Institutional-based ratings (e.g., *Consumer Reports*) often guide purchasing behavior. *Experience goods* (e.g., wine, movies, and books) are goods whose ratings are dominated by subjective attributes. For these types of goods, user ratings (instead of institutional ratings) often guide purchasing behavior.

We submit that query recommendations have more in common with experience goods. As with most experience goods, users need to *experience* the item before rating it; we are not suggesting that people blindly rate other people's queries, but rather rate their own queries after they have finished searching. It is an open question as to how people would approach this task and if they would even find recommendations useful. Furthermore, previous research has found the stability of people's ratings of experience goods somewhat brittle and influenced by the ratings of others [20]; thus, another open question concerns the stability of people's ratings.

3. METHOD

A laboratory experiment was conducted using a classic pre-test/post-test design. The pre-test allowed us to observe how subjects would rate query quality before viewing search results (pre-retrieval), while the post-test allowed us to observe if and how these evaluations changed as a result of viewing search results (post-retrieval). We manipulated search result quality to determine if specific performance levels could be mapped to specific query quality scores.

Subjects were instructed that they would be shown other people's information problems and queries and then provide evaluations of query quality. Subjects completed three major steps: (1) *initial query evaluation* where they were shown an information problem description and query and asked to evaluate the query according to several attributes; (2) *search result evaluation* where they were shown a list of 10 search results and asked to evaluate these results; and (3) *post-SERP query evaluation* where they were once again presented with the information problem description and query and asked to re-evaluate the query. These steps were completed for eight information problems. After the evaluation, subjects were interviewed about the strategies they used to evaluate queries and their opinions about the usefulness of query recommendations. Following this, subjects were asked to repeat the rating procedure for two information problems/queries they had previously seen. This functioned as a reliability check to test the stability of subjects' query quality evaluations.

3.1 Information Problems and Queries

Eight information problems were used in this study. Five of the information problems were fact-finding information problems (FF) and were based on the navigational tasks used in [3]. Three were exploratory information problems (EX) and were created based on topics used in the TREC Aquaint collection (although results were from the Web, not the Aquaint corpus). Each information problem was associated with one query. Query length for FF information problems ranged from one to five words, while for EX information problems, it remained fixed at three words.

Subjects completed the FF and EX problems in blocks (all the FF problems were in one block and all the EX problems were in another). Subjects were randomly assigned to receive either the FF block or EX block first. Within each block, information problems were rotated using a Latin-square. Examples of information problems and queries are shown in Table 1. The full set of queries is shown in Table 2. The full set of information problems and queries can be viewed online at (http://ils.unc.edu/sigir2012queryrating/).

Table 1. Examples of information problems and queries.

Information Problem Description	Query	Task Type
Bob is interested in researching the history of motorcycles. To start his research, he decides to find out when each major motorcycle company was founded. Specifically, he wants to determine the year in which Harley Davidson motorcycles was founded.	harley davidson	FF
Janet is planning a boat convention for her company which will be held next year in Las Vegas and needs to select a hotel. She has heard positive things about the Bellagio hotel, but first wants to find out how many guest rooms are available.	bellagio hotel las vegas rooms	FF
Carol is planning to fly to Amsterdam next month and would like to learn more about the body scanners that are being used in many airports as part of routine security procedures. Specifically, she is interested in gathering a range of information and opinions about these scanners and any privacy or health issues related to their use.	airport body scanners	EX

Table 2. Information problem IDs, queries and length.

Information Problem IDs	Query	Length
FF1	billiards	1
FF2	harley davidson	2
FF3	bank savings rates	3
FF4	statue of liberty spikes	4
FF5	bellagio hotel las vegas rooms	5
EX1	black bear attacks	3
EX2	modern day piracy	3
EX3	airport body scanners	3

[1] http://tiis.acm.org/pdf/human-decision-making-and-recommder-systems.pdf

3.2 Initial Query Evaluation

During the initial query evaluation, subjects were presented with an information problem and query along with four questions about query quality (Table 3). The query quality questions assessed the subject's beliefs about the representativeness of the query, the likelihood it would retrieve useful results, the extent to which the subject would recommend the query to others, and the subject's star-rating of the query. The first three items were measured using a 5–point scale and the star-rating scale ranged from 1 star to 5 stars. This latter type of rating was selected because of its ubiquity in online computing environments.

Table 3. Initial query evaluation items.

Item	Scale
How well do you think the query represents the information problem?	1=not at all; 3=somewhat; 5=very well
How useful do you expect the search to be?	1=not at all; 3=somewhat; 5=very useful
How likely would you be to recommend this query to someone else searching for the same information problem?	1=not at all; 3=somewhat; 5=very likely
Please select the star rating that best reflects your opinion of the potential quality of the query.	

3.2 Search Result Evaluation

After subjects completed the initial query evaluation, they were directed to a search engine results page (SERP) containing a list of ten search results. We collected 10 search results for each information problem using the Google search engine. Search results were carefully screened until the relevance of each search result was agreed upon by two authors of the study. On the SERP, each result was represented by a title, snippet, and URL (Figure 1). To enhance the realism of the search result environment, the SERP was deliberately designed to mimic Google's SERP. Subjects were debriefed at the end of the experiment about this manipulation. We modified snippets so that they did not contain answers to the information problems. The information problem was visible at the bottom of the page (omitted from screen shot to conserve space).

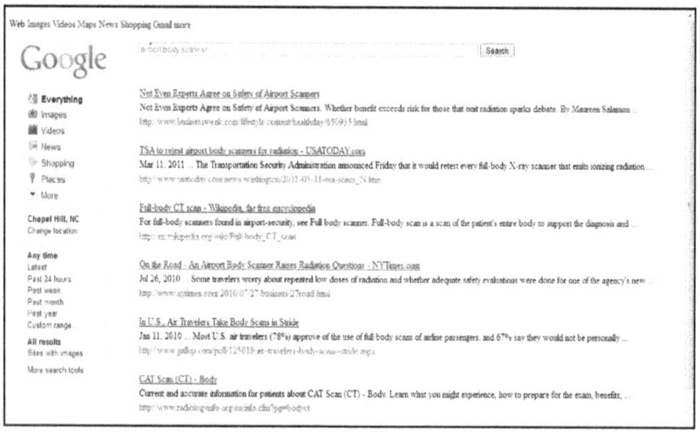

Figure 1. Artificial SERP constructed for study.

When presenting search results of FF information problems, subjects were randomly assigned to a high or a low condition, measured by Reciprocal Rank (RR) – the inverse of the rank of the first relevant search result in a list. For each FF information problem, only one relevant search result appeared in the search results list. For subjects assigned to the high condition, the relevant search result appeared at positions 1 through 5 for FF1-FF5 and for subjects in the low condition the relevant search result appeared at positions 6 through 10. The performance conditions can be viewed in Table 4. Each FF information problem was associated with two performance conditions.

Table 4. Performance conditions for FF problems.

Information Problem	Reciprocal Rank (High Condition)	Reciprocal Rank (Low Condition)
FF1	1.000	0.167
FF2	0.500	0.143
FF3	0.330	0.125
FF4	0.250	0.111
FF5	0.200	0.100

For each EX information problem, subjects were randomly assigned to one of three performance conditions: low, medium, or high. The conditions varied in terms of both number of relevant results presented and the positions of the relevant results, resulting in variations in Normalized Discounted Cumulated Gain (nDCG) from 0.31 to 1. The three conditions for any single EX information problem only differed in terms of where relevant search results were ranked, but different EX information problems differed in the number of relevant results shown on a result list. The performance conditions are shown in Table 5.

Table 5. Performance conditions for EX problems.

Information Problem	Number Relevant	Performance Condition	nDCG
EX1	2	Low	0.31
		Medium	0.51
		High	1.00
EX2	4	Low	0.42
		Medium	0.59
		High	0.80
EX3	6	Low	0.65
		Medium	0.73
		High	0.91

For each search result viewed, subjects were asked two questions: (1) Does the webpage contain the exact information needed? (Yes, No) and (2) Do you think the webpage was useful to the person who typed the query? (1=not at all; 3=somewhat; 5=very useful). Only when both questions were answered could they return to the SERP. Subjects were not required to examine all 10 results and could examine the results in any order. Once they felt they had gathered enough information from the result list to evaluate the query, they proceeded to the post-SERP query evaluation.

3.3 Post-SERP Query Evaluation

During the post-SERP query evaluation, subjects were shown the information problem and query again, and asked the following: (1) How likely would you be to recommend this query to someone else searching for the same information problem? (1=not at all; 3=somewhat; 5=very likely) and (2) Based on the documents you've examined on the search result list, please select the star rating that best reflects your opinion of the actual quality of the query (subjects were presented with the 5-star rating widget). Both of these questions were from the initial query evaluation and functioned as post-test questions. While the first question was identical to one of the initial query evaluation questions, the second contained slight word changes to indicate that subjects should consider their experiences evaluating search results.

3.4 Exit Interview

After subjects completed the evaluations, semi-structured interviews were conducted to obtain qualitative data about the strategies subjects took to evaluate queries and their perceptions of the usefulness of query recommendations. Interviews were tape-recorded and the interview scheme was composed of four parts: questions regarding how subjects judged the quality of queries on their own, questions regarding how search results affected subjects' judgments of query quality, questions regarding evaluation strategies used for different information problem types and questions regarding subjects' opinions of query recommendations in the context of online searching.

3.5 Reliability Check

After the interviews, subjects were asked to re-evaluate the last information problem they were given from the first task block and the first information problem from the second task block. For each problem, subjects repeated the initial query evaluation, search results evaluation and post-SERP query evaluation. Subjects did not have access to their previous ratings.

3.6 Subjects

Subjects were recruited through the staff mailing list at our university. Forty-one subjects participated. From the interview session it was found that one subject misunderstood the study instructions and was therefore excluded from analysis.

Before starting the query evaluations, subjects completed a Demographic Questionnaire. The vast majority of respondents were females (70.73%), 26.83% were males, and 2.44% did not answer this question. Their ages ranged from 18-66 years old (M=39.6, SD=14.0). With respect to the status of participants, 25 (62.5%) were university staff; nine (22.5%) had both student and staff status; two (5%) were students and three (7.5%) were neither university staff nor student, and the status of one subject was unknown. For subjects who were university staff or full-time professionals (37, 92.5%), their occupations ranged from research assistant, project manager/director, programmers/analyst, administrative assistant or manager, financial counselor, business manager, lecturer, editor, teacher, to masseuse.

Subjects' search experience was measured with the Search Self-Efficacy Scale [5]. The Search Self-Efficacy Scale is a 14-item scale used to characterize search expertise. Subjects indicate their confidence in completing a series of activities using a 10 point scale where 1=totally unconfident and 10=totally confident. Subjects scored an average of 7.38 (SD=1.42) on the Search Self-Efficacy Scale, indicating moderate to high search experience. Because we slightly modified the wording of some items from the original scale to make them more contemporary, Cronbach's alpha was computed using subjects' responses to these items. This was found to be 0.947, demonstrating high reliability.

4. RESULTS

The research questions we addressed were (RQ1) How do people make judgments about query quality? (RQ2) How are people's judgments related to features of the query, information problem and search results? (RQ3) How reliable are people's judgments? And (RQ4) What are people's perceptions of query recommendations?

4.1 Initial Query Evaluation

In this section, we investigate how subjects' initial evaluations varied according to information problem type and query length (RQ2). Pearson product-moment correlation coefficients were first computed to assess the relationships among the four initial query evaluation items. Results showed that there was a high correlation among subjects' responses to the items (Table 6).

Table 6. Correlations among initial query evaluation items.

	Rep	Useful	Rec	Rating
Representativeness	-	.869**	.865**	.843**
Useful	.869**	-	.866**	.859**
Recommendation	.865**	.866**	-	.885**
Rating	.843**	.859**	.885**	-

**Correlation is significant at the 0.01 level (2-tailed).

Figures 2 and 3 show subjects' initial query quality ratings for the fact-finding (FF) and exploratory (EX) information problems, respectively. The two figures show that while the initial query evaluations across the four items were virtually identical for different EX information problems, these values increased for FF information problems as query length increased from one word to four words. The figures also show that subjects were generally more conservative with their *recommendation* and *star-ratings* judgments. It was found that for FF information problems there was a significant difference in subjects' judgments of representativeness ($F(4,195)=23.21$, $p<.001$), usefulness ($F(4,195)=22.34$, $p<.001$), recommendation ($F(4,195)=30.11$, $p<.001$) and star-rating ($F(4,195)=22.41$, $p<.001$). Post-hoc tests indicate that the ratings given to FF1 were significantly lower than those given to FF2, FF3, FF4 and FF5; that the ratings given to FF2 were significantly lower than those given to FF4 and FF5; and the ratings given to FF3 were significantly lower than those given to FF4 and FF5. There were no significant differences in subjects' ratings of FF4 and FF5. For EX information problems, there were no significant differences for any of the initial query ratings (representativeness: $F(2, 78)=.27$, $p=.762$; usefulness: $F(2, 78)=.10$, $p=.907$; recommendation: $F(2,78)=.16$, $p=.852$; star-rating: $F(2, 78)=.04$, $p=.959$)

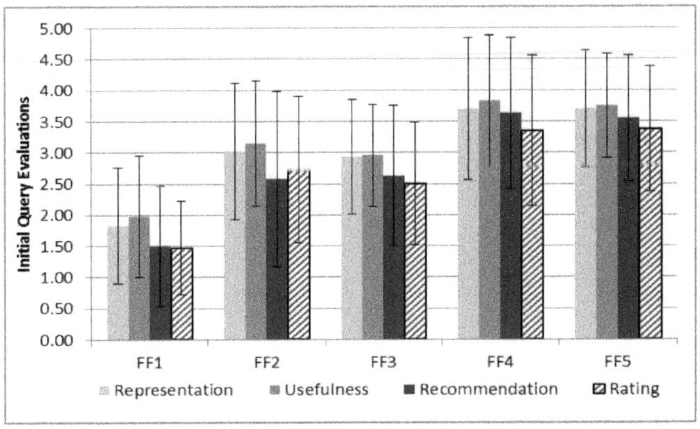

Figure 2. Initial evaluations of FF information problem queries (error bars represent +/-1 standard deviation).

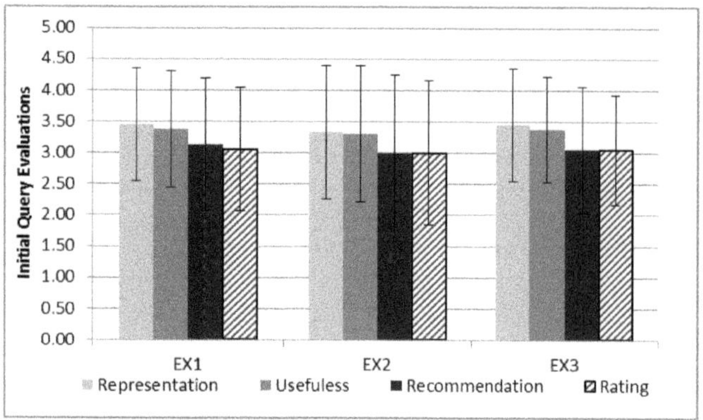

Figure 3. Initial evaluations of EX information problem queries (error bars represent +/-1 standard deviation).

Since all EX information problems were represented by three-word queries, EX information problems were compared to FF3 to examine whether there was a difference in how people rated queries according to information problem type. It was found that overall subjects rated the three-term EX queries higher on all four initial query evaluation items than the three-term FF query. Subjects found EX three-term queries to be more representative (EX: M=3.41, SD=.65; FF3: M=2.93, SD=.92) and the searches to be more useful (EX: M=3.35, SD=.64; FF3: M=2.95, SD=.81); subjects were more likely to recommend three-term EX queries to other people (EX: M=3.06, SD=.76; FF3: M=2.63, SD=1.13) and also assigned more stars to these queries (EX: M=3.03, SD=.70; FF3: M=2.50, SD=.99). Paired-samples t-tests were conducted to compare the means between EX and FF3 on all four items and the results show that three-term queries for EX information problems were rated as significantly more representative ($t(39)=-2.65$, $p=.012$), more useful ($t(39)=-2.53$, $p=.015$) and received significantly more stars than FF3 ($t(39)=-2.85, p=.007$).

4.2 Search Result Evaluation

RQ2 also asked about how people's judgments are affected by the quality of the search results. Before we examine this, we first examine the extent to which our performance manipulations worked. During the search result evaluation stage a total of 1479 result clicks were made, which represented 46.22% of the total search results shown to subjects. Figure 4 shows the percentage of times subjects' explicit relevance judgments corresponded with the judgments made by the researchers and the *click rate* for each information problem. *Click rate* is defined as the percentage of web results clicked from a ten-result SERP. If a web result prejudged by the researchers as relevant was clicked and also judged by a subject as relevant, it was counted as an instance of *correspondence*. Note that we are not measuring inter-rater reliability (as is common in the IR literature), but rather whether our experimental manipulations worked. This is why we use the term *correspondence* and report percent agreement. The figure shows that all of the information problems had an 80% or above correspondence rate except for FF3, which had only a 65% correspondence rate. FF3 also received the highest click rate among a range of click rates from 0.40 to 0.57. Even though the information problem had a well-defined goal (locate a bank with a particular savings rate), subjects might have had a difficult time processing the results and understanding if results were relevant.

Figures 5 and 6 compare subjects' *experienced performance* (EP) (according to their clicks and explicit relevance judgments) with the manipulated performance, or the *performance intended* by the researchers (IP). EP for FF information problems, measured by RR, was computed by taking the inverse of the rank of the first clicked result. The greatest disagreement occurred for FF3, which was expected given the results in Figure 4. EP for EX information problems was measured by nDCG of the ten returned results; unclicked results were scored as irrelevant. Despite the disagreement between EP and IP for EX information problems, subjects experienced the intended relative performance conditions except for EX3. For this topic, there were 6 relevant documents in the list and for the high condition this meant that most of these were concentrated near the top of the list. It is likely that subjects stopped reviewing the list once they found a few relevant documents, which would lead to lower EP nDCG scores for high performance conditions. Overall, the mismatch between IP and EP for EX information problems is likely related to the varying number of documents opened by subjects and a discrepancy between their judgments and the researchers' judgments.

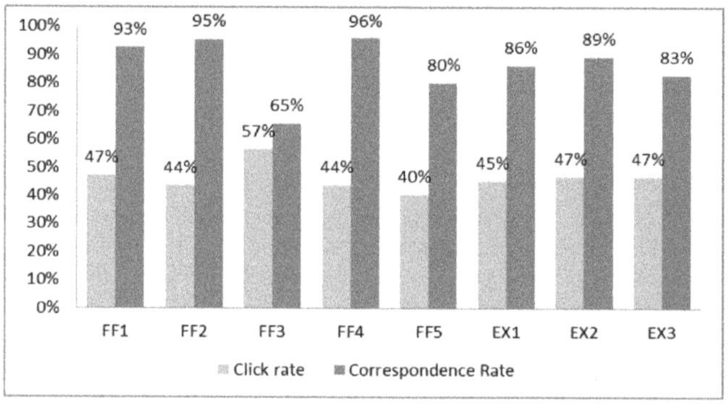

Figure 4. Search results click rate and correspondence rate.

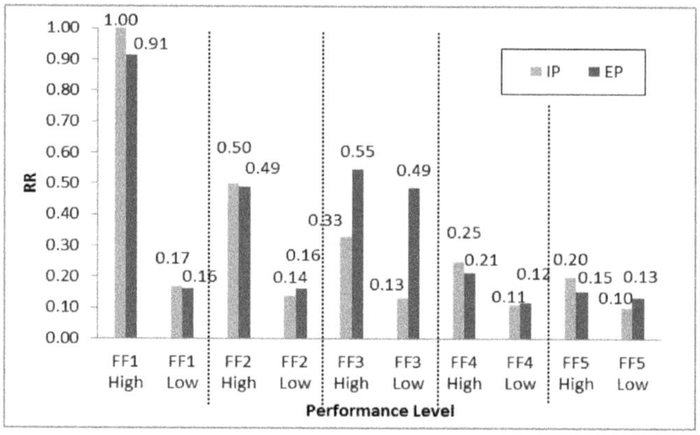

Figure 5. Comparison of intended performance (IP) and experienced performance (EP) for FF information problems.

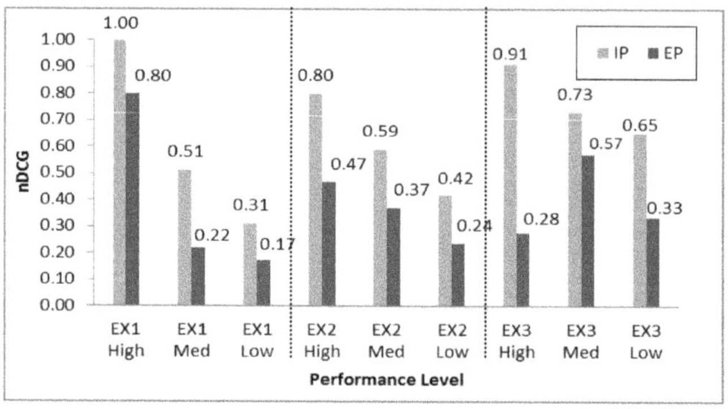

Figure 6. Comparison of intended performance (IP) and experienced performance (EP) for EX information problems.

Results also provide some initial insight into RQ1: How do people make judgments about query quality? In considering subjects' evaluation approaches for each information problem type (Figure 7), we see that for FF information problems most subjects either took an *exhaustive approach*, evaluating all 10 (22%) search results or a *selective approach* only evaluating 1-3 (50%) results. For EX information problems, we see greater diversity in the number of results evaluated. Sixty-one percent of subjects evaluated 1-4 results, while about 18% evaluated all 10 results. In Section 4.4, we examine the relationship between evaluation approach (*exhaustive* vs. *selective*) and subjects' post-SERP query evaluations in more depth.

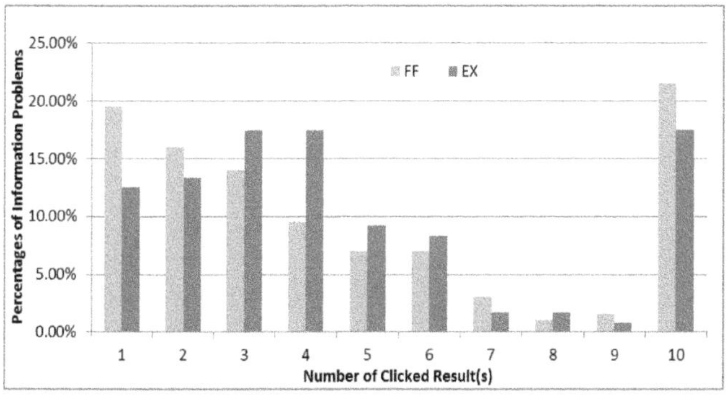

Figure 7. Distribution of number of clicked results according to information problem type.

The order in which search results were clicked was analyzed to investigate whether there was a relationship between click order, rank of result and subjects' relevance judgments. Click order was positively correlated with rank of search result (r=.56, p<.001), and subjects tended to click results ranked higher first. Click order was negatively correlated with perceived usefulness of a search result (r= -.46, p<.01); the search results subjects clicked earlier in time were evaluated as more useful than the ones clicked later.

4.3 Post-SERP Evaluation

After investigating subjects' interactions with the search results, we can now investigate how perceived quality of the search results impacted subjects' ratings (RQ2). During the post-SERP evaluation, subjects were asked again how likely they would be to recommend a query and how many stars they would assign it. The star-ratings assigned and likelihood to recommend the query were positively correlated (r=.88, p<.001). Thus, in subsequent analysis, we only include results related to one of these measures.

4.3.1 FF Information Problem Post-SERP Ratings

Figure 8 shows the relationship between subjects' initial query quality ratings and their post-SERP ratings for the FF information problems. The post-SERP ratings are further divided according to intended performance level (recall that FF information problems were grouped into high and low performance sets). Queries associated with higher performance levels consistently received higher post-SERP ratings than those associated with lower levels. Subjects in the low performance group evaluated an average of 4 documents, while those in the high performance group evaluated an average of 7 documents. Many subjects in the low performance group likely gave-up without finding a relevant document; this might explain the lower post-SERP ratings of this group. Independent-samples t-tests were applied to compare the means in post-SERP ratings between the high (n=21) and low performance groups (n=19) for each FF information problem. None of pairs was significant (FF1: t(38)=-1.96, p=0.056; FF2: t(38)=-0.76, p=0.46; FF3: t(38)=-0.67, p=0.51; FF4: t(38)=-1.80, p=.08; t(38)=-0.32, p=.75).

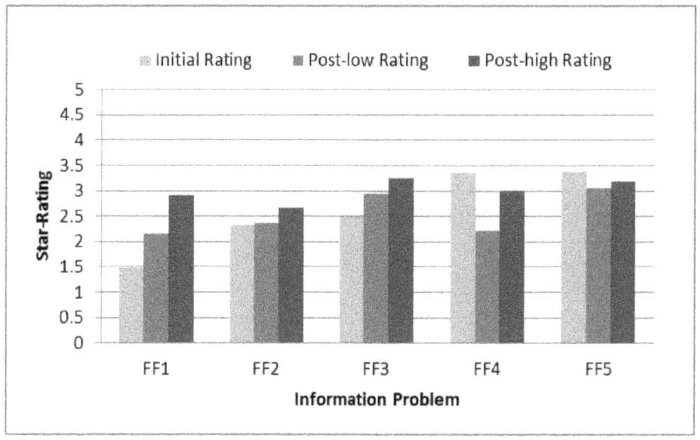

Figure 8. Comparisons of initial and post-SERP ratings for FF information problems according to performance.

The post-SERP ratings were higher than the initial ratings for all information problems except FF4 and FF5. Paired-samples t-tests were conducted to compare initial ratings to post-SERP ratings. Results showed that the only times that initial and post-SERP ratings were significantly different from each other were when FF1 and FF3 information problems were coupled with the high performance levels: FF1-H (t(20)=-5.45, p<.001); FF3-H (t(20)=-2.72, p=.013) and when FF4 was coupled with the low performance level (t(18)=2.79, p=.012).

During the search result evaluations, subjects were allowed to view any number of search results and in any order. To better understand the relationship between subjects' evaluation behaviors and their query quality ratings, we examine *interactive precision,* or the ratio of number of documents marked relevant to number of documents evaluated (Figure 9). In general, post-SERP ratings increased as *interactive precision* went up; the two variables were significantly correlated (r(198)=.57, p<.001).

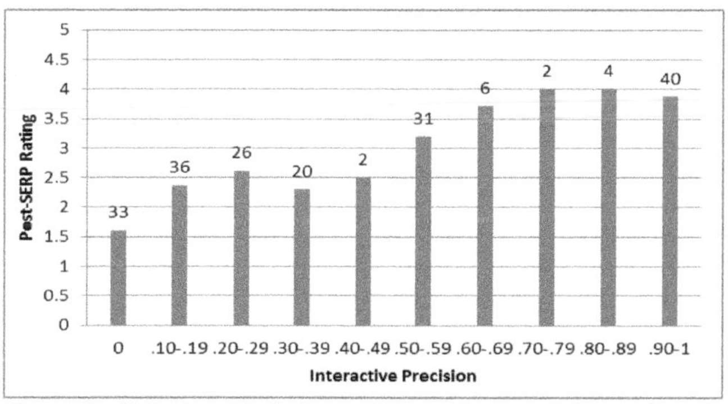

Figure 9. Relationship between interactive precision and post-SERP ratings for FF information problems (data labels represent number of information problems).

Multiple linear regression analysis was used to model the post-SERP ratings given to FF information problems. Since in most cases, the initial and post-SERP ratings did not differ significantly from each other, query length was considered to be a predictor along with number of relevant search results experienced, and *interactive precision*. A stepwise method was used and two models were derived. The first model showed that *interactive precision* was the single best predictor in post-SERP ratings, β= .57, t(198) = 9.72, p < .001. *Interactive precision* also explained a significant proportion of variance in post-SERP rating (adjusted R^2=.32, F (1, 197) = 94.49, p<.001). In the second model both *interactive precision* and length significantly predicted post-SERP ratings (interactive precision: $\beta = .58$, $t(198) = 10.00$, $p < .001$; length: $\beta = .16$, $t(197) = 2.75$, $p = .001$); they explained 34.1% of variance in post-SERP rating (F (2, 197) = 52.58, p<.001).

4.3.2 EX Information Problems Post-SERP Ratings

While in FF information problems the descriptive statistics show that higher post-SERP ratings followed high performance levels, the trend was not observed for EX information problems. When post-ratings were grouped individually by *interactive precision*, post-SERP ratings significantly increased with *interactive precision* (Figure 10) ($r(118)$=.61, p<.001).

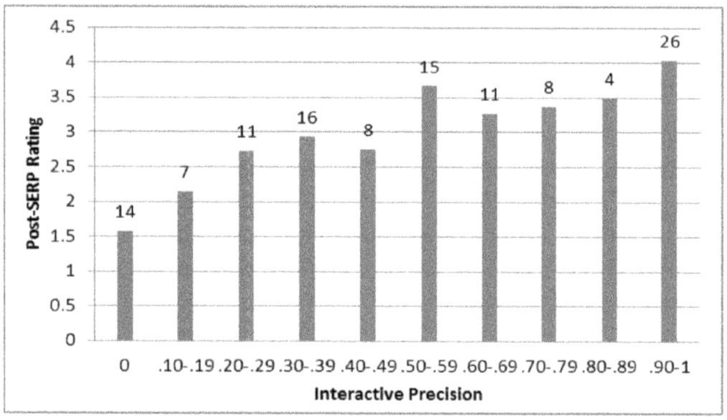

Figure 10. Relationship between interactive precision and post-SERP ratings for EX information problems (data labels represent number of information problems).

Initial ratings and post-SERP ratings of query quality for EX information problems are displayed in Figure 11. Paired-samples t-tests found that the initial and post-SERP ratings were only significantly different for the medium performance level in EX3 ($t(13)$=-3.24, p=.006). At first glance it might seem unusual that the difference between the initial and post-SERP ratings were not also significant for the low group for EX3. Paired-sample t-tests were conducted, so there was likely a difference between the initial ratings of those who received the low and medium performance levels for this problem.

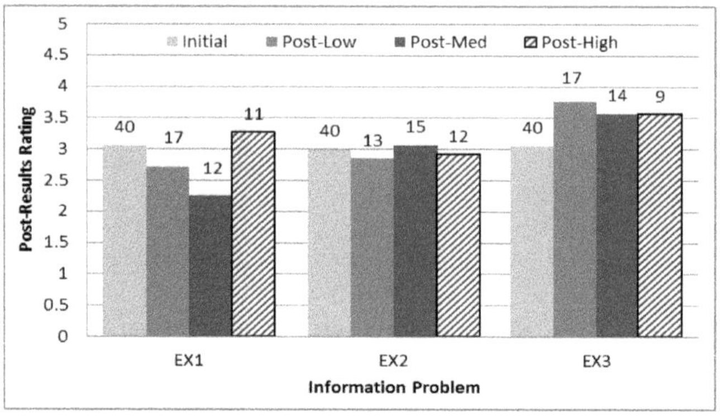

Figure 11. Comparisons of initial and post-SERP ratings for EX information problems by information problem and performance level (data labels represent number of subjects).

Figure 12 shows the differences in subjects' initial ratings and their post-SERP ratings as number of relevant search results experienced increased. Overall, subjects were more consistent in the direction of rating adjustment when they encountered few relevant search results. In cases where subjects identified no relevant documents at all, in most information problems the post-SERP ratings decreased (12 out of 14). In cases where subjects found one or two relevant results, the direction of the differences were not as predictable. When subjects identified more than three relevant search results, in most cases, subjects' post-SERP ratings were higher than their initial ratings.

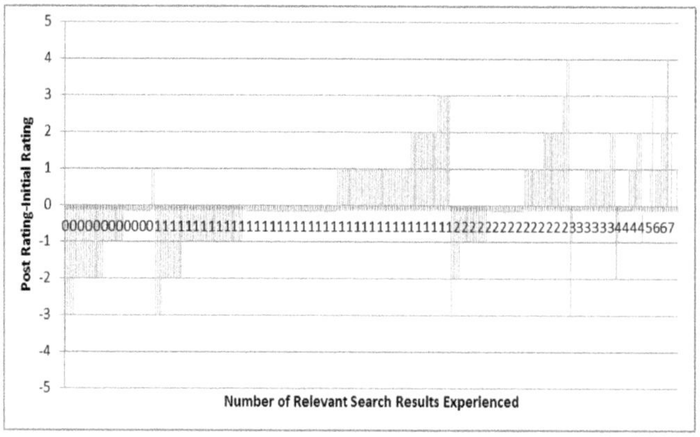

Figure 12. Relationship between number of relevant search results experienced and difference in initial and post-SERP ratings for EX information problems.

A regression analysis was also conducted for EX information problems to better understand which factors most influenced subjects' ratings. *Interactive precision*, number of relevant search results found, and experienced performance were entered into a stepwise regression. Results showed that *interactive precision* was the best predictor of post-SERP ratings, $\beta = .61$, $t(118) = 8.44$, p<.001; it also explained a significant proportion of variance in post-SERP ratings (adjusted R^2=.371, $F(1, 118)$=71.25, p<.001).

4.4 Query Quality Evaluation Approaches

RQ1 asked how people make judgments of query quality. In Section 4.2, it was shown that subjects seemed to take different strategies when evaluating search results. In order to examine whether different approaches had any influence on post-SERP ratings, we classified and compared subjects' evaluation approaches. For FF information problems, we classified subjects' evaluation approaches into two types: *Selective* and *Exhaustive*. Subjects using the *Selective* approach only examined one search result, while those using an *Exhaustive* approach examined all ten search results. For EX information problems subjects took more varied approaches resulting in three groups: *Selective*, *Persistent* and *Exhaustive*. The *Selective* approach represented cases where subjects examined 1-3 results, the *Persistent*, 4 to 7 results, and the *Exhaustive*, 8 to 10 results. These evaluation approaches were examined in the context of subjects' post-SERP ratings.

Results show that for FF information problems, those using the *Exhaustive* evaluation approach gave lower ratings to queries (M=2.14, SD=1.04, n=43) than those using the *Selective* approach (M=3.26, SD=1.27, n=39). An independent-samples t-test indicated this difference was significant ($t(1,80)$=4.38, p<.001). For EX information problems, those using the *Exhaustive* approach assigned the highest star-ratings (M=3.17, SD=0.96, n=24), followed by the *Persistent* (M=3.07, SD=1.04, n=44) and the *Selective* (M=3.12, SD=1.34, n=52), but the differences were not significant ($F(2, 117)$=.06, p=0.95).

In addition to examining subjects' evaluation behaviors, we asked subjects during the exit interview how they initially evaluated queries and then re-evaluated them after viewing search results (RQ1). With respect to the criteria subjects used to assign the initial query ratings, most stated that the specificity of the query was the most important factor. Some mentioned that they compared queries to what they would put in a search box; if they could think of better expressions they would rate the queries worse, and vice versa. Subjects took more varied approaches to assigning post-SERP ratings. Some mentioned they based their ratings on the number of relevant results they had found, some relied on the positions of relevant search results, and others considered both factors. Yet rarely did subjects differentiate between approaches taken to evaluate queries for FF and EX information problems. Although some indicated they spent more time on EX information problems because they wished to gather more background information on the topic, many of them said that for FF problems they kept looking for other search results even when they had successfully identified the answer. The motivation for the latter came from the fear that they could miss something, the answer could be wrong, they had personal interests in some topics, or simply out of habit.

We also asked subjects how they felt about using star-ratings during real-world searching (RQ4). When asked whether they would consider using a system which provides rated query suggestions, many said yes because it would save time and benefit people who are not experienced with searching. Some said it depended on who rated the query suggestions and how well they could formulate queries by themselves. People who said they would not use such systems expressed doubt because systems or other people could not predict their information needs, or even if they could some subjects believed star-ratings were very subjective and they would rather have descriptions about why a query could be useful. Subjects constantly associated query star-ratings with hotel and restaurant stars and other product reviews and ratings such as those that appear in Netflix and Amazon. Their familiarity with these common usages resulted in a general agreement on the concept: the more stars there were, the higher the quality. The majority of the subjects believed 5-star query suggestions would lead to the most relevant results, some mentioned that they would expect these queries to also help them find information the quickest. Subjects said they would interpret 3-star queries as those that lead to information that was buried in the search results and would take some time to discover. Finally, subjects said they would interpret 1-star queries as useless and unhelpful; most said they would not use 1-star queries.

4.5 Reliability Check

To examine the consistency of subjects' evaluations (RQ3), subjects were asked to repeat the evaluation procedures for the last information problem they were given from the first task block and the first information problem from the second task block; thus, subjects reevaluated one FF and one EX information problem. Note that they did not have access to their previous ratings in this stage. Paired-samples t-tests were conducted to examine the differences in subjects' evaluations of FF and EX information problems (Table 7). Results demonstrated that subjects' initial ratings in the reliability check did not significantly differ from those in the main study session for both FF and EX information problems, but subjects' post-SERP ratings in the reliability check were significantly higher than those in the main study session for both information problem types. We note that subjects clicked on fewer search results during the reliability check (M_{FF}=3.05, M_{EX}=3.60) than the study session (M_{FF}=4.15, M_{EX}=4.68) and that the distributions of the clicked results were significantly different (FF:Z=-6.50, p<.001; EX:Z=-6.51, p<.001).

Table 7. Relationship between subjects' ratings during the main study and reliability check (*p<.05; **p<.01).

	FF: Initial Rating	FF: Post-SERP Rating	EX: Initial Rating	EX: Post-SERP Rating
Main Study	2.60 (1.32)	2.70 (1.49)	3.10 (1.13)	2.80 (1.29)
Reliability Check	2.80 (1.10)	3.10 (1.34)	3.30 (1.04)	3.23 (1.19)
t-statistic	-1.11	-2.58**	-1.31	-2.21*

5. DISCUSSION

Our study conceptualized query evaluation as a two-stage process: initial evaluation and post-SERP evaluation, a distinction drawn from pre-retrieval and post-retrieval QPP approaches. Queries were first assessed based on impressions of query strings, and further refined after SERPs were examined. We found that by first impression, longer queries led to higher query quality for FF information problems; this was supported by the concept of "specificity" solicited from subjects during the interviews. This result also aligns with Hauff et al. [10] who found that assessors' query quality ratings were moderately correlated with the pre-retrieval predictor *SumSCQ* which assigns higher quality scores to more specific queries and with Lioma et al. [12] whose subjects identified vague and short queries as problematic for systems.

We found that subjects rated queries associated with EX information problems higher in quality compared with FF queries of the same length. Subjects' post-SERP evaluations of queries for EX information problems were also higher than for FF problems. These results might be explained by the vagueness of EX information problems as mentioned by subjects; subjects probably did not pose as strict evaluation standards on open information needs than on more defined information needs. It is also likely that subjects viewed themselves as more open to ideas when searching for EX information problems. This suggests that perhaps query recommendations would have the greatest potential for these types of information problems.

When examining how result quality affected query quality, it appeared that *interactive precision,* the number of relevant search results found to the number of documents viewed was the best predictor of post-SERP ratings of query quality for both types of information problems. This is in contrast with what we expected, which is that reciprocal rank would be a better predictor of subjects' post-SERP evaluations of query quality for FF information problems. Rather, our finding implies that regardless of information problem type, people expected that a good quality query would retrieve more than one relevant result.

For FF information problems, we found that query length was positively correlated with subjects' initial query ratings as well as their post-SERP ratings. We also observed that in most cases, subjects' initial ratings of query quality did not significantly differ from their post-SERP ratings. Only when a relatively long query was followed by a low quality SERP and when a relatively short query was followed by a good SERP did subjects change their ratings of queries. In cases of EX information problems where query length was held constant, people were also more consistent in how they adjusted their ratings when no relevant results or when many relevant results were found.

With respect to evaluation approaches, we found that subjects either took a selective or exhaustive approach when evaluating queries for FF information problems, and a selective, persistent or exhaustive approach when evaluating queries for EX information problems. This was slightly contrary to what we expected; we expected that most subjects would take a selective approach when evaluating FF information problem queries since the resolution of such problems only requires a single result. Subjects who took an exhaustive approach when evaluating FF problems assigned lower ratings to queries than those who took a selective approach, while the reverse was true for EX problems. In the Exit Interviews, subjects did not differentiate between FF and EX information problems, which was surprising since much is made about the differences in these types of tasks in the research community.

Finally, we found that the initial quality evaluations subjects gave to queries were fairly stable, changing very little during the reliability check. However, their post-SERP evaluations of queries for both types of information problem significantly increased during the reliability check. We found that subjects viewed significantly fewer documents and even clicked on different documents. While this might have been caused by fatigue, it is an open question as to whether query quality evaluations are stable or, if like ratings of other experience goods they are, by nature, brittle.

This study had several limitations; perhaps the most important was the limited number of topics and queries. This study was an initial exploration of this problem space. Using only one query per information problem and holding query length constant for information problems was necessary so that the number of experimental conditions would be manageable. Using a larger combination would have compromised our abilities to collect qualitative data, through interviews, about subjects' ratings. In the future, collecting a larger number of ratings for a larger number of topics and queries would likely enhance our understanding of users' evaluations of query quality.

6. CONCLUSION

Our work explored how people make judgments about query quality; how these judgments are related to features of the query, information problem and search results; how reliable these judgments are; and what people's perceptions are of query recommendation. To our knowledge, this was one of the first systematic studies of how people make query quality evaluations. Our findings provide a useful starting-point for future user-oriented studies of query quality evaluation and recommendation, and might also provide fodder for those working on automatic QPP methods. Future research will examine mechanisms for allowing users to express and share query quality ratings, and develop models of users' decision-making processes regarding query recommendations.

7. ACKNOWLEDGMENTS

We thank Max Felsher for his assistance with data collection.

8. REFERENCES

[1] Amershi, S., & Morris, M. R. (2008). Cosearch: A system for co-located collaborative Web search. *Proceedings of CHI '08*, 1647-1656.

[2] Baraglia, R., Cacheda, F., Carneiro, V., Fernandez, D., Formoso, V., Perego, R., & Silvestri, F. (2009). Search shortcuts: A new approach to recommendation of queries. *Proceedings of RecSys '09*, New York, NY, 77-84.

[3] Buscher, G., Dumais, S. & Cutrell, E. (2010). The good, the bad and the random: An eye-tracking study of ad quality in Web search. *Proceedings of SIGIR '10*, 42-49.

[4] Carmel, D., & Yom-Tov, E. (2010). Estimating the query difficulty for information retrieval. *Synthesis Lectures on Information Concepts, Retrieval and Services, #15.*

[5] Debowski, S., Wood, R. & Bandura, A. (2001). The impact of guided exploration and enactive exploration on self-regulatory mechanisms and information acquisition through electronic enquiry. *Journal of Applied Psychology, 86*(6), 1129-1141.

[6] Duan, W., Gu, B., & Whinston, A. B. (2008). Do online reviews matter? An empirical investigation of panel data. *Decision Support Systems, 45*, 1007-1016.

[7] Ekstrand, M. D., Riedl, J. T., & Konstan, J. A. (2010). Collaborative filtering recommender systems. *Foundations and Trends in Human-Computer Interaction, 4*(2), 81-173.

[8] Hauff, C., Hiemstra, D., & de Jong, F. (2008). A survey of pre-retrieval query performance predictors. *Proceedings of CIKM '08*, 1419-1420.

[9] Hauff, C., Kelly, D., & Azzopardi, L. (2010). Query quality: User ratings and system predictions. *Proceedings of SIGIR'10*, 743-744.

[10] Hauff, C., Kelly, D., & Azzopardi, L. (2010). A comparison of user and system query performance predictors. *Proceedings CIKM '10*, 979-988.

[11] Kelly, D., Cushing, A., Dostert, M., Niu, X., & Gyllstrom, K. (2010). Effects of popularity and quality on the usage of query suggestions during information search. *Proceeding of CHI '10*, 45-54.

[12] Lioma, C., Larsen, B., & Schutze, H. (2011). User perspectives on query difficulty. *Proceedings of ICTIR*, 3-14.

[13] Nelson, P. (1970). Information and consumer behavior. *Journal of Political Economy, 78*(2), 311-329.

[14] Senecal, S. & Nantel, J. (2004). The influence of online product recommendations on consumers' online choices. *Journal of Retailing, 80*(2), 159-169.

[15] Silvestri, F. (2010). Mining query logs: Turning search usage data into knowledge. *Foundations and Trends in Information Retrieval, 4*(1-2), 1-174.

[16] Smyth, B., Balfe, E., Freyne, J., Briggs, P., Coyle, M., & Boydell, O. (2004). Exploiting query repetition and regularity in an adaptive community-based Web search Engine. *User Modeling and User-Adapted Interaction, 14*(5), 382-423.

[17] Smyth, B., Coyle, M. & Briggs, P. (2011). Communities, collaboration, and recommender systems in personalized Web search. *Recommender Systems Handbook*, 579-614.

[18] Turpin, A. & Hersh, W. (2004). Do clarity scores for queries correlate with user performance? *Proceedings of the 15th Australasian Database Conference (ADC '04)*, 85-91.

[19] Zhao, Y., & Scholer, F. (2007). Predicting query performance for user-based search tasks. *Proceedings of the Australasian Database Conference (ADC '07)*, 112-115.

[20] Zhu, H., Huberman, B., & Luon, Y. (2012). To switch or not to switch: Understanding social influence in online choices. *Proceedings of CHI '12*, 2257-2266.

Efficient In-Memory Top-k Document Retrieval

J. Shane Culpepper
School of CS & IT
RMIT University
Melbourne, VIC, 3001,
Australia
shane.culpepper@rmit.edu.au

Matthias Petri
School of CS & IT
RMIT University
Melbourne, VIC, 3001,
Australia
matthias.petri@rmit.edu.au

Falk Scholer
School of CS & IT
RMIT University
Melbourne, VIC, 3001,
Australia
falk.scholer@rmit.edu.au

ABSTRACT

For over forty years the dominant data structure for ranked document retrieval has been the inverted index. Inverted indexes are effective for a variety of document retrieval tasks, and particularly efficient for large data collection scenarios that require disk access and storage. However, many efficiency-bound search tasks can now easily be supported entirely in-memory as a result of recent hardware advances.

In this paper we present a hybrid algorithmic framework for in-memory bag-of-words ranked document retrieval using a self-index derived from the FM-Index, wavelet tree, and the compressed suffix tree data structures, and evaluate the various algorithmic trade-offs for performing efficient queries entirely in-memory. We compare our approach with two classic approaches to bag-of-words queries using inverted indexes, *term-at-a-time* (TAAT) and *document-at-a-time* (DAAT) query processing. We show that our framework is competitive with state-of-the-art indexing structures, and describe new capabilities provided by our algorithms that can be leveraged by future systems to improve effectiveness and efficiency for a variety of fundamental search operations.

Categories and Subject Descriptors

H.3.1 [**Information Storage and Retrieval**]: Content Analysis and Indexing—*indexing methods*; H.3.2 [**Information Storage and Retrieval**]: Information Storage—*file organization*; H.3.3 [**Information Storage and Retrieval**]: Information Search and Retrieval—*query formulation, retrieval models, search process*; I.7.3 [**Document and Text Processing**]: Text Processing—*index generation*

Keywords

Text Indexing, Text Compression, Data Storage Representations, Experimentation, Measurement, Performance

1. INTRODUCTION

Top-k retrieval algorithms are important for a variety of real world applications, including web search, on-line advertising, relational databases, and data mining. Efficiently ranking answers to queries in large data collections continues to challenge researchers as the collection sizes grow, and the ranking metrics become more intricate. Despite recent hardware advances, inverted indexes remain the tool of choice for processing efficiency-bound search tasks [17]. However, large memory systems also provide new opportunities to explore another class of indexing algorithms derived from the *suffix array* to potentially improve the efficiency of various in-memory ranked document retrieval tasks [25, 27].

In this paper we present a hybrid algorithmic framework for in-memory bag-of-words ranked document retrieval using a self-index derived from the *FM-Index*, *wavelet tree*, and the *compressed suffix tree* data structures [12, 20, 27, 22], and evaluate the various algorithmic trade-offs for performing efficient in-memory ranked querying. We compare our approach with two classic approaches to bag-of-words queries using inverted indexes, *term-at-a-time* (TAAT) and *document-at-a-time* (DAAT) query processing. We show that our framework is competitive with state-of-the-art indexing structures, and describe new capabilities provided by our algorithms that can be leveraged by future systems to improve efficiency and effectiveness for various document retrieval tasks.

Permission to make digital or hard copies of all or part of this work for personal or classroom use is granted without fee provided that copies are not made or distributed for profit or commercial advantage and that copies bear this notice and the full citation on the first page. To copy otherwise, to republish, to post on servers or to redistribute to lists, requires prior specific permission and/or a fee.
SIGIR'12, August 12–16, 2012, Portland, Oregon, USA.
Copyright 2012 ACM 978-1-4503-1472-5/12/08 ...$15.00.

Our contributions. Firstly, we propose a hybrid approach to solving a subset of important top-k document retrieval problems – *bag-of-words* queries. Secondly, we present a comprehensive efficiency analysis comparing in-memory inverted indexes with top-k self-indexing algorithms for bag-of-words queries on text collections an order of magnitude larger than any other prior experimental study. To our knowledge, this is the first comparison of this new algorithmic framework for realistic sized text collections using a standard similarity metric – BM25. Finally, we describe how our algorithmic framework can be extended to efficiently and effectively support other fundamental document retrieval tasks.

2. PROBLEM OVERVIEW

In this paper, we investigate the use of self-indexing algorithms to solve the **top-k document search problem**. A document collection $\mathcal{T}$ is a contiguous string drawn from an alphabet Σ, where $\sigma = |\Sigma|$ is the number of distinct "terms" or strings. In practice, Σ can be characters (UTF8 or ASCII), bytes, integers, or even phrases. Each document in $\mathcal{T}$ is separated by a unique end of document symbol defined to be lexicographically smaller than any $s \in \Sigma$.

DEFINITION 1. *A* **top-k document search** *takes a query* $q \in \Sigma$, *an integer* $0 < k \leq d$, *and a text* $\mathcal{T} \in \Sigma$ *partitioned into* d *documents* $\{\mathcal{D}_1, \mathcal{D}_2, \ldots, \mathcal{D}_d\}$, *and returns the top-$k$ documents ordered by a similarity measure* $S(q, \mathcal{D}_i)$.

In this work, we focus primarily on bag-of-words queries, so our baseline $S(q, \mathcal{D}_i)$ ranking function is BM25. Our $S(q, \mathcal{D}_i)$ ranking function has the following formulation:

$$\textbf{BM25} = \sum_{t \in q} \log\left(\frac{N - f_t + 0.5}{f_t + 0.5}\right) \cdot \text{TF}_{\textbf{BM25}}$$

$$\text{TF}_{\textbf{BM25}} = \frac{f_{d,t} \cdot (k_1 + 1)}{f_{d,t} + k_1 \cdot ((1-b) + (b \cdot \ell_d / \ell_{avg}))}$$

Here, N is the number of documents in the collection, f_t is the number of distinct document appearances of t, $f_{d,t}$ is the number of occurrences of term t in document d, $k_1 = 1.2$, $b = 0.75$, ℓ_d is the number of symbols in the dth document, and ℓ_{avg} is the average of ℓ_d over the whole collection. The free parameters k_1 and b can be tuned for specific collections to improve effectiveness, but we use the standard Okapi parameters suggested by Robertson et al. [36].

3. ALGORITHMS

We now present an overview of the key data structures and algorithms used in our framework. Here, we only outline the key properties and features of wavelet trees and suffix arrays used in our search engine; for a more in-depth tutorial, see, for example Navarro and Mäkinen [30] and the references therein. Efficient operations in succinct data structures depend on two fundamental operations over a bitvector $\mathcal{B}[0, n-1]$:

$\text{RANK}_{0/1}(\mathcal{B}, i)$:	Return the number of 0's/1's in $\mathcal{B}[0, i]$.
$\text{SELECT}_{0/1}(\mathcal{B}, i)$:	Return the position of the ith of 0's/1's in $\mathcal{B}$.

Both operations can be performed in constant time. A simple constant time $\text{RANK}_{0/1}$ solution uses $o(n)$ space in addition to storing $\mathcal{B}$ [23]. More space efficient $\text{RANK}_{0/1}$ algorithms are possible [35].

3.1 Wavelet Trees

Efficient RANK_s and SELECT_s over an alphabet of size $\sigma > 2$ can be performed using a wavelet tree [20]. A wavelet tree decomposes the RANK_s and SELECT_s operations over $[0, \sigma-1]$ into $\text{RANK}_{0/1}$ and $\text{SELECT}_{0/1}$ operations on a binary alphabet using a binary tree. The root of the tree represents the whole alphabet. Its children represent each half of the alphabet of the parent node. Each leaf node in the tree represents one symbol in $[0, \sigma-1]$. When answering the RANK_s query for a specific symbol s, we perform $\text{RANK}_{0/1}$ operations at each level in the tree until we arrive at the leaf node representing s. The overall $\text{RANK}_s(\mathcal{T}, i)$ can be computed by combining the $\text{RANK}_{0/1}$ results at each tree level in $\mathcal{O}(\log \sigma)$ time. Any symbol $s = \mathcal{T}[i]$ is also computed in time $\mathcal{O}(\log \sigma)$ with a similar algorithm; we call this operation $\text{ACCESS}(\mathcal{T}, i)$. Using a succinct representation of $\text{RANK}_{0/1}$ and $\text{SELECT}_{0/1}$ [35], a wavelet tree requires $nH_0 + o(n \log \sigma)$ bits of space, where $H_0 \leq \log \sigma$ is the zero-order entropy of $\mathcal{T}$.[1]

Wavelet trees are a surprisingly versatile data structure, and have attractive time and space bounds for many primitive operations in self-indexing algorithms [14]. As a result, many top-k document retrieval approaches rely heavily on wavelet trees. A subset of important wavelet tree operations include:

$\text{RANK}_s(\mathcal{T}, s, sp, ep)$:	Return the number of occurrences of symbol s in a range $\mathcal{T}[sp, ep]$.
$\text{SELECT}_s(\mathcal{T}, s, j, sp, ep)$:	Return the position of the jth occurrence of symbol s in a range $\mathcal{T}[sp, ep]$.
$\text{ACCESS}(\mathcal{T}, i)$:	Return symbol $\mathcal{T}[i]$.
$\text{RMQ}(\mathcal{T}, sp, ep)$:	Return the smallest symbol s in a range $\mathcal{T}[sp, ep]$.
$\text{RQQ}(\mathcal{T}, k, sp, ep)$:	Return the kth smallest symbol s in a range $\mathcal{T}[sp, ep]$.

[1]We assume logarithms are in base 2.

3.2 Self-indexing

A suffix array $\text{SA}[0, n-1]$ over $\mathcal{T}$ stores the offsets to all suffixes in $\mathcal{T}$ in lexicographical order. Any pattern $\mathcal{P}$ of length m occurring in $\mathcal{T}$ is a prefix of one or more suffixes in SA. These suffixes, due to the lexicographical order within SA, are grouped together in a range $\text{SA}[sp, ep]$. To determine $\text{SA}[sp, ep]$, we perform two binary searches over SA and $\mathcal{T}$. Each binary search comparison requires up to m symbol comparisons in $\mathcal{T}$, for a total of $\mathcal{O}(m \log n)$ time. Using additional auxiliary data structures this cost can be reduced to $\mathcal{O}(m + \log n)$ [25]. Suffix array construction is a well studied problem, and many solutions with various time and space trade-offs exist in the literature [34]. However, searching for a pattern $\mathcal{P}$ in $\mathcal{T}$ using only a suffix array requires $\mathcal{O}(n \log n)$ bits to store both $\mathcal{T}$ and SA, which in practice is at least 5 times the text size.

By replacing $\mathcal{T}$ with the Burrows-Wheeler Transform (BWT) permuted text, the key operations of a basic SA can be emulated with much less space, close to the size of $\mathcal{T}$ in compressed form. The Burrows-Wheeler Transform [7] – also known as the block-sorting transform – produces a permutation of a string T, denoted T^{BWT}, by sorting the n cyclic rotations of T into full lexicographical order, and taking the last column of the resulting $n \times n$ matrix. The resulting string T^{BWT} tends to be more compressible as symbols are grouped together based on their context in $\mathcal{T}$, which makes the BWT an important part in many state of the art compression systems [26]. To produce T^{BWT} for a given text $\mathcal{T}$, it is not necessary to construct $\mathcal{M}$ as there is a duality between T^{BWT} and the SA over a text $\mathcal{T}$: $T^{\text{BWT}}[i] = \mathcal{T}[\text{SA}[i] - 1 \bmod n]$.

The original text $\mathcal{T}$ can be recovered from T^{BWT} in linear time without the need for any additional information. To recover $\mathcal{T}$ from only T^{BWT} we first recover the first column, F, in $\mathcal{M}$ by sorting the last column ($L = T^{\text{BWT}}$), in lexicographical order. By mapping the symbols in L to their respective positions in F so $L[i] = F[j]$ (usually referred to as the LF mapping, $j = \text{LF}(i)$) we can recover $\mathcal{T}$ backwards as $\mathcal{T}[n-1] = T^{\text{BWT}}[0] = \$$ and $\mathcal{T}[j-1] = T^{\text{BWT}}[\text{LF}(i)]$ if and only if $\mathcal{T}[j] = T^{\text{BWT}}[i]$. Since F is simply a sort of the n characters of the string in lexicographical order, it can be represented succinctly as a lookup table of alphabet characters along with the count of all symbols that appear before the current character c. The LF mapping is computed using the equation

$$\text{LF}(i) = \text{LF}(i, c) = C[c] + \text{RANK}_s(T^{\text{BWT}}, i) \quad (1)$$

where c is the symbol $T^{\text{BWT}}[i]$, and $C[c]$ stores the number of symbols in T^{BWT} smaller than c.

Performing a search in $\mathcal{T}$ using the BWT permuted text is straightforward. Recall that all rows are sorted in lexicographical order in $\mathcal{M}$. Therefore, for a pattern $\mathcal{P}$, all occurrences of $\mathcal{P}$ in $\mathcal{T}$ must have a corresponding row in $\mathcal{M}$ within a range $\langle sp, ep \rangle$. To determine the range within $\mathcal{M}$, we first determine the range $\langle sp_m, ep_m \rangle$ within $\mathcal{M}$ that corresponds to $\mathcal{P}_m$ using $C[\,]$. Then, for each symbol $j = m-1 \ldots 0$ in $\mathcal{P}$, we iteratively find $\langle sp_j, ep_j \rangle$ by calculating the number of rows within $\langle sp_{j+1}, ep_{j+1} \rangle$ that are preceded by the symbol $\mathcal{P}_j$ in $\mathcal{T}$. For a given row j, the LF mapping can be used to determine the row in $\mathcal{M}$ representing the symbol preceding j in $\mathcal{T}$. The preceding row is determined by counting the number of occurrences of $c = T^{\text{BWT}}[j]$ *before* the current row and ranking these occurrences within $C[s]$. Assume we have located $\langle sp_{j+1}, ep_{j+1} \rangle$, which corresponds to the rows prefixed by $\mathcal{P}[j+1, m]$. Then

$$sp_j = \text{LF}(sp_{j+1} - 1, p_j) \quad (2)$$

will calculate the position in F of the first occurrence of $\mathcal{P}_j$ within $\langle sp_{j+1}, ep_{j+1} \rangle$, and thus compute the start of our range of rows within $\mathcal{M}$ that correspond to $\mathcal{P}[j, m]$. Similarly, we compute

$$ep_j = \text{LF}(ep_{j+1}, p_j) - 1. \quad (3)$$

Once the area $\langle sp, ep \rangle$ is determined, self-indexes offer a way to find any occurrence position $\text{SA}[j]$, for $sp \leq j \leq ep$. This is accomplished by sampling $\mathcal{T}$ at regular intervals, and marking positions of SA that point to sampled text positions in a bitmap $E[0, n-1]$. Sampled suffix array positions are stored in an array $G[\text{RANK}_1(E, j)] = \text{SA}[j]$ if $E[j] = 1$. Given a target value $\text{SA}[j]$, the successive values $i = 0, 1, \ldots$ are evaluated until $E[\text{LF}^i(j)] = 1$, producing the desired answer of $\text{SA}[j] = \text{SA}[\text{LF}^i(j)] + i$. If every κth text position is sampled, we guarantee i can be found for every $0 \leq i < \kappa$, and sampling requires $\mathcal{O}((n/\kappa) \log n)$ extra bits for G (and for E in compressed form [35]), and computes any entry of SA within κ applications of LF.

Similarly, in order to recover any text substring $\mathcal{T}[l, r-1]$ (including the whole $\mathcal{T}$), we can use the same sampling of text position multiples of κ, and store $H[i] = \text{SA}^{-1}[i \cdot \kappa]$. Thus, we extend the range to $T[l, r'-1]$, for $r' = \kappa \cdot \lceil r/\kappa \rceil$ and display from the suffix array position $j = \text{SA}^{-1}[r']$. Then, we can display the area backwards as $T^{\text{BWT}}[j], T^{\text{BWT}}[\text{LF}(j)], T^{\text{BWT}}[\text{LF}^2(j)], \ldots$. Each step requires one RANK_s and one ACCESS operation, which has the same cost as LF. Therefore, we can display $\mathcal{T}[l, r-1]$ within $\mathcal{O}(r - l + \kappa)$ probes of LF.

In practice self-indexes can be reduced to a wavelet tree over T^{BWT} with auxiliary information to emulate F (the C array) and the sampling information. This representation of a self-index is referred to as an *FM-Index* [12, 13]. A wavelet tree built over T^{BWT} uses $nH_k(\mathcal{T}) + o(n \log \sigma)$ bits [24] for any $k \leq \alpha \log_\sigma(n) - 1$ and constant $\alpha < 1$, so the space requirements are reasonable. Here $H_k(\mathcal{T}) \leq H_{k-1}(\mathcal{T}) \leq \ldots \leq H_0(\mathcal{T}) \leq \log \sigma$ is the k-th order entropy of $\mathcal{T}$ [26], a measure of the performance of any compressor using k-th order statistical modeling on $\mathcal{T}$. Many other self-indexing variations exist with different time / space trade-offs [30, 15]. In principle, any of these approaches are compatible with the framework we present here, as long as the method returns a $\langle sp, ep \rangle$ range of matching suffixes.

4. TOP-K DOCUMENT RETRIEVAL USING SELF-INDEXES

In order to efficiently solve the **top-k document search problem**, unadorned self-indexing algorithms are not sufficient. Two approaches to enhance the self-index have been proposed. The first is to use a *document array*, that is, a mapping between every suffix in $\mathcal{T}$ to its corresponding document identifier [10, 18, 27, 41]. The second is to store, in addition to the global self-index, one self-index of each individual document in the collection [22, 37]. These alternatives offer different theoretical frameworks that are not directly comparable, but experimental studies [10, 31] have consistently shown that the first approach offers better space and time performance in practice.

Representing the document array with a single wavelet tree can provide additional important advantages. For example, the list of distinct documents where a substring $\mathcal{P}$ appears, with the corresponding term frequencies, can be obtained without any additional structure [18], in $\mathcal{O}(\log d)$ time per document retrieved, once the self-index has given the suffix array range of $\mathcal{P}$. This information

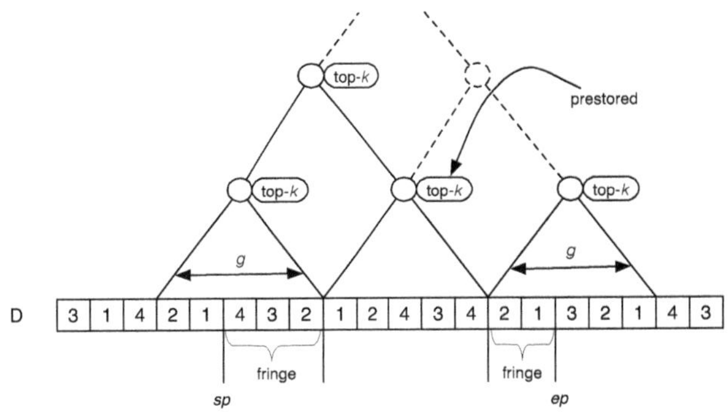

Figure 1: Precomputed top-k results over fixed intervals g stored in a skeleton succinct suffix tree using the HSV approach. Only the fringe leaves are processed for a given $\langle sp, ep \rangle$ range.

can then be used to calculate simple TF×IDF based $S(q, \mathcal{D}_i)$ metrics at query time [37]. In addition, several other operations such as Boolean intersection can be performed efficiently using only the wavelet tree over the document array [19].

Culpepper et al. [10] showed how to use the same wavelet tree to find the top-k documents (with raw term frequency weights) for a string $\mathcal{P}$. Among all of the strategies proposed, the heuristic algorithm **GREEDY** worked best in practice. Despite the lack of worst-case theoretical guarantees, they show unadorned wavelet trees are efficient in time and space for this task. Hon et al. [22] presented a technique with worst-case performance guarantees. The **HSV** approach builds on the same document listing strategy originally proposed by Sadakane [37]. While **HSV** was originally described using individual self-indexes for each document as in Sadakane's approach [37], the method can be applied on top of either document-listing solution in practice. The key insight of the **HSV** method is to precompute the top-k results for the lowest suffix tree nodes in a predetermined sampling range. Figure 1 shows a **HSV** tree over D. In this example, a $\langle sp', ep' \rangle$ range of size g is precalculated and stored in a succinct suffix tree. An arbitrary query $\langle sp, ep \rangle$ is received. The bulk of the query result is already precomputed as $\langle sp', ep' \rangle$. The remainder of the query can then be processed using RQQ queries over the *fringe* ranges to generate the final top-k counts.

Using g samples guarantees that any suffix array interval $\langle sp, ep \rangle$ for a given $\mathcal{P}$ falls into one of three categories: (1) The range is completely covered by the sampled interval, and the top-k answer is precomputed; (2) The range is partially covered, and at most $2g$ fringe leaves must to be processed at query time and merged with the sample; or (3) The range is too small to be covered. For Case (3), the complete $\langle sp, ep \rangle$ range must be processed at runtime, but is guaranteed to be smaller than $2g$.

Navarro and Valenzuela [31] demonstrated that implementing **HSV** over a document array, and using the **GREEDY** approach of Culpepper et al. [10] to speed up document listing, is more efficient than using either **GREEDY** or **HSV** in isolation. The hybrid approach requires additional space to support **HSV** on top of **GREEDY**, but efficiency is significantly improved by limiting the number of rank queries required at query time. This approach as well as other trade-offs are explored more fully in this paper.

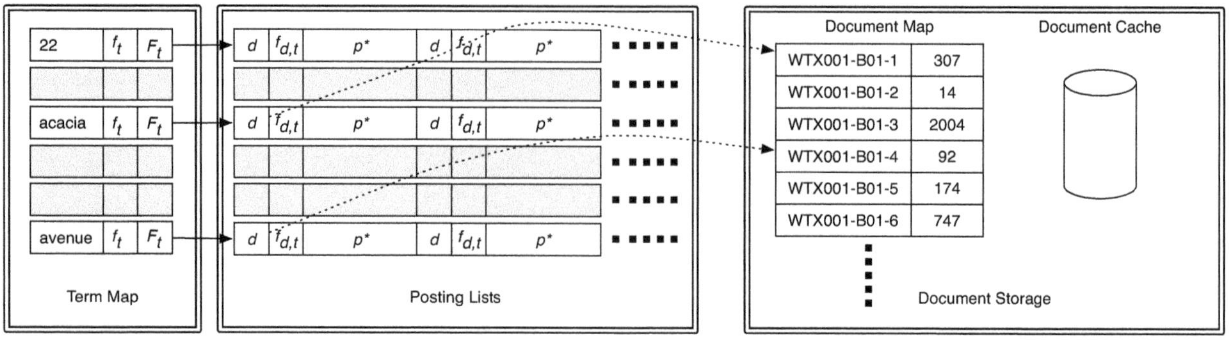

Figure 2: The three fundamental components of an inverted index. Each term in the vocabulary is mapped to a posting list of $\langle d, f_{d,t} \rangle$ tuples. For each tuple, the position offsets p^* are also stored to support phrase or term proximity queries.

5. INVERTED INDEXES

Traditional approaches to the **top-k document search problem** rely on *inverted indexes*. Inverted indexes have been the dominant data structure for a variety of ranked document retrieval tasks for more than four decades [44]. Despite various attempts to displace inverted indexes from their dominant position for document ranking tasks over the years, no alternative has been able to consistently produce the same level of efficiency, effectiveness, and time / space trade-offs that inverted indexes can provide (see, for instance Zobel et al. [45]).

Figure 2 shows a typical inverted indexing system. The system contains three key components: (1) *Term Map* - The vocabulary of terms, along with the number of documents containing one or more occurrence of the term (f_t), the number of occurrences of the term in the collection (F_t), and a pointer to the corresponding posting list. (2) *Posting Lists* - An ordered list of tuples, $\langle d, f_{d,t} \rangle$, containing the document identifier and the frequency of the term in document d. For each tuple, the ordered position offsets, p^* are also maintained in order to support phrase queries. For indexes that do not require phase queries, p^* can be omitted. (3) *Document Storage* - A document map to match d to the document name, and a pointer to the document in a document cache.

Ranked document retrieval requires that only the top-k documents are returned, and, as a result, researchers have proposed many heuristic approaches to improve top-k efficiency [1, 4, 5, 6, 32, 38]. These approaches can be classified in two general categories: *term-at-a-time* (**TAAT**) and *document-at-a-time* (**DAAT**). Each of these approaches have various advantages and disadvantages.

5.1 Term-at-a-Time Processing (TAAT)

For **TAAT** processing, a fixed number of accumulators are allocated, and the rank contribution incrementally calculated for each query term in increasing document order. When inverted files are stored on disk, the advantages of this method are clear. The inverted file for each term can be read into memory, and processed sequentially. However, when k is small relative to the total number of matching documents in collection, **TAAT** can be inefficient, particularly when the number of terms in the query increases, since all of the inverted lists must be processed before knowing the full rank score of each document. In early work, Buckley and Lewit [6] proposed using a heap of size k to allow posting lists to be evaluated in **TAAT** order. Processing is terminated when the sum of the contributions of the remaining lists cannot displace the minimum score in the heap.

Moffat and Zobel [29] improved on this pruning approach with two heuristics: **STOP** and **CONTINUE**. The **STOP** strategy is somewhat similar to the method of Buckley and Lewit, but the terms are processed in order of document frequency from least frequent to most frequent. When the threshold of k accumulators is reached, processing stops. In contrast, the **CONTINUE** method allows the current accumulators to be updated, but new accumulators cannot be added. These accumulator pruning strategies only approximate the true top-k result list.

If approximate results are acceptable, the **TAAT** approach can be made even more efficient using *impact ordering* [1, 2, 33]. The key idea of impact ordering is to precompute the TF for each document a term appears in. Next, quantize the TF values into a variable number of buckets, and sort the buckets (or blocks) for each term in decreasing impact order. Now, the top-k representative can be generated by sequentially processing each of the highest ranking term contribution blocks until a termination threshold is reached. The authors refer to this blockwise processing method as *score-at-a-time* processing. Despite not using the full TF contribution for each term, Anh and Moffat [1] demonstrate that the effectiveness of impact ordered indexes is not significantly reduced, but efficiency is dramatically improved.

5.2 Document-at-a-Time Processing (DAAT)

The alternative approach is to process all of the terms simultaneously, one document at a time [8]. The advantage of this approach is that the final rank score is known as each document is processed, so it is relatively easy to maintain a heap containing exactly k scores. The disadvantage is that all of the term posting lists are cycled through for each iteration of the algorithm requiring non-sequential disk reads for multi-word queries. However, our focus in this paper is *in-memory* ranked retrieval, so **DAAT** tends to work very well in practice.

Pruning strategies to further increase efficiency also exist for **DAAT** processing. The most widely used pruning strategy for **DAAT** is **MAXSCORE**. Turtle and Flood [40] observed that the **BM25** TF component can never exceed $k_1 + 1 = 2.2$. So, the total score contribution for any term is at most $2.2 \cdot \log(N/N_t)$. Using this observation, Turtle and Flood present an algorithm that allows posting values below the threshold to be skipped. As the minimum bounding score in the heap slowly increases, more and more postings can be omitted. Enhanced **DAAT** pruning strategies similar in spirit to **MAXSCORE** have been shown to further increase efficiency [4, 38].

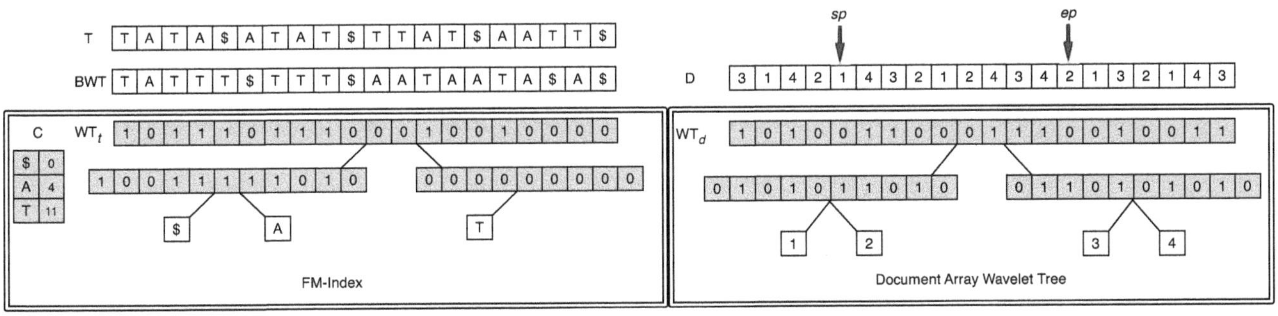

Figure 3: Given the text collection $\mathcal{T}$ = TATA\$ATAT\$TTAT\$AATT\$ of four documents, a self-indexing system requires two wavelet trees. The first wavelet tree supports backwards search over the BWT permuted text, and the second supports statistical calculations over the document array. Note that only the items in grey are stored and used for query operations.

Turtle and Flood also describe a similar approach to improve the efficiency of **TAAT** strategies. However, the **TAAT** variant is more complex than the **DAAT** approach as it requires an ordered candidate list of k documents to be maintained. The candidate list is used to skip document postings in each term list which could not possibly displace the current top-k documents once the heap contains k items.

Fontoura et al. [17] compare several **TAAT** and **DAAT** based in-memory inverted indexing strategies. The authors present novel adaptations of **MAXSCORE** and **WAND** [4] to significantly improve query efficiency of in-memory inverted indexes. The authors go on to show further efficiency gains in **DAAT** style processing by splitting query terms into two groups: rare terms and common terms. The exact split is based on a fixed threshold selected at query time. For our baselines, we use **WAND** for **DAAT** query processing, and **MAXSCORE** for **TAAT** query processing.

6. SELF-INDEXING APPROACHES

We now describe our general approach to in-memory indexing and retrieval. Figure 3 shows the key components of our retrieval system: an FM-Index and the document array wavelet tree, WT_d. In addition, our system requires a *Document Map* to map document identifiers to human readable document names (or URLs). No document cache is required and the original documents or snippets around each match can be recreated directly from the FM-Index by extracting the required text positions using the suffix array sampling. Only the items in grey are stored and used for character-based top-k document retrieval. All other components are shown for illustration purposes only.

ALGORITHM **GREEDY-TAAT**

INPUT	A sorted list t of q terms.
OUTPUT	A list of k documents in rank order.

1: Initialize a max-heap $R \leftarrow \{\}$
2: **for** $i \leftarrow 1$ **to** q **do**
3:     Determine $\langle sp, ep\rangle$ for term t_i
4:     $A_i \leftarrow$ **GREEDY**(sp, ep, k')
5: **end for**
6: **for** $i \leftarrow 1$ **to** q **do**
7:     **for** $j \leftarrow 1$ **to** k' **do**
8:         **if** $A_i[j] \in R$ **then**
9:             **UPDATE**$(R, A_i[j], score)$
10:         **else**
11:             **ADD**$(R, A_i[j], score)$
12:         **end if**
13:     **end for**
14: **end for**
15: **return** $R[1 \ldots k]$

FUNCTION **GREEDY** (sp, ep, k)
1: $\ell \leftarrow \text{WT}_d$.root
2: A max-heap, sorted by $ep - sp$, $h \leftarrow$ **PUSH**$(\ell, [sp, ep])$
3: A priority queue PQ $\leftarrow \{\}$.
4: $i \leftarrow 0$
5: **while** $h \neq \emptyset$ **and** $i < k$ **do**
6:     $\ell, [sp', ep'] \leftarrow$ **POP**(h)
7:     **if** ℓ is leaf **then**
8:         PQ $\leftarrow$ **ENQUEUE**$(\ell.\text{docid}, ep' - sp' + 1)$
9:         $i \leftarrow i + 1$
10:     **else**
11:         $[s_0, e_0] \leftarrow [\text{RANK}_0(\mathcal{B}_\ell, sp'), \text{RANK}_0(\mathcal{B}_\ell, ep')]$
12:         $[s_1, e_1] \leftarrow [\text{RANK}_1(\mathcal{B}_\ell, sp'), \text{RANK}_1(\mathcal{B}_\ell, ep')]$
13:         **if** $e_0 - s_0 > 0$ **then** $h \leftarrow$ **PUSH**$(\ell.\text{left}, [s_0, e_0])$
14:         **end if**
15:         **if** $e_1 - s_1 > 0$ **then** $h \leftarrow$ **PUSH**$(\ell.\text{right}, [s_1, e_1])$
16:         **end if**
17:     **end if**
18: **end while**
19: **return** PQ

A simple bag-of-words search using a self-index retrieval system is outlined in Algorithm **GREEDY-TAAT**. Recall that the sp and ep range for any string can be found using a backwards search in the BWT permuted text using only a wavelet tree over $\mathcal{T}^{\text{BWT}}$ and C. So, the $\langle sp, ep\rangle$ for each query term in Line (3) can be calculated in $\mathcal{O}(|t_i| \log \sigma)$ time using an FM-Index. Now, a wavelet tree over the document array WT_d can be used to retrieve exactly k documents in frequency order for each term using **GREEDY** or **QUANTILE** [10]. This algorithm is analogous to **TAAT** processing, and is referred to as **GREEDY-TAAT**. Note that Function **GREEDY** can also be augmented with **HSV** as described in Section 4 to further increase the efficiency of constructing A_i for each query term.

We also present several variations on this general strategy. First, we consider the addition of **HSV** style precomputations over WT_d as described by Navarro and Valenzuela [31]. Instead of storing the top-k most frequent symbols in the skeleton suffix tree, we store

Query length	TREC 7 & 8 queries			TREC WT10G queries		
	Total	Matches	Average n_i	Total	Matches	Average n_i
$\lvert q \rvert$	Queries	('000)	('000)	Queries	('000)	('000)
1	100	9.9	9.9	100	3.3	4.7
2	100	24.8	12.5	100	68.6	42.5
3	100	104.5	38.5	100	292.8	123.2
4	100	238.1	69.0	100	601.1	166.6
5	100	351.2	95.1	100	866.5	228.5
6	100	408.7	107.8	100	1041.9	280.4
7	100	463.8	126.2	100	1149.7	319.6
8	100	489.8	148.3	100	1171.8	339.2
random sample	800	234.9	70.0	800	621.5	181.2

Table 1: Statistics of the queries used in experiments (sampled based on query length, or sampled from the filtered MSN query log), reporting the number of queries run, the mean number of documents that contained one or more of the query terms, and the mean length of the inverted lists processed.

the top-k most important symbols sorted by term impact for each interval g to improve effectiveness. In order to capture k-values commonly used in IR systems ($k = 10, 100, 1000$), we prestore values of any k that is a power of 2 up to 8192 in term contribution order. Note that we go higher than 1024 since the values of k' necessary to ensure good effectiveness can be greater than the desired k.

Observe that in typical bag-of-words query processing over English text, the size of the vocabulary is often small relative to the total size of the collection. As such, we also present a new hybrid approach to top-k bag-of-words retrieval using a *Term Map* and WT_d. If we assume the vocabulary is fixed for each collection, then the $\langle sp, ep \rangle$ range for each term can be precalculated and retrieved using a term map, as in the inverted indexing solution. This means that the FM-Index component is no longer necessary when processing bag-of-words queries. We refer to these hybrid approaches as **SEM-GREEDY** and **SEM-HSV**. These methods reduce the overall space requirements of our approach, but also limit the full functionality of some auxiliary operations. For example, the text can no longer be reproduced directly from the index, so snippets cannot be generated on the fly, and phrase queries are no longer natively supported. However, for classic bag-of-words queries, our hybrid approach provides an interesting trade-off to consider. Our final variation is to support a term-based self-index. We refer to this approach as **FM-TERM**.

It is also possible to support a **DAAT** query processing strategy in our retrieval system, but this would require efficiently supporting RMQ over the document array. Our approach currently supports a generalization of RMQ – RQQ. But, the cost of RQQ is $\mathcal{O}(\log d)$ per k value extracted, while constant time solutions for RMQ currently exist [16]. However, an RMQ style approach as presented by Fischer and Heun [16] incurs an additional $2n$ bits of space, and so we do not explore the possibility further in this work.

Also note the current top-k bag-of-words approach shown in **GREEDY-TAAT** is based entirely on the frequency counts of each item. This means that our current implementation only approximates the top-k items. This is a well-known problem in the inverted indexing domain. This limitation holds for any character-based bag-of-words self-indexing system that does frequency counting at query time since we can not guarantee that item $k + 1$ in any of the term lists does not have a higher score contribution than any item currently in the top-k intermediate list. A method of term contribution precalculation is required in order to support **BM25** or language-model ranking. Without the term contribution scoring, **WAND** and **MAXSCORE** enhancements are not possible, and therefore every document in the $\langle sp, ep \rangle$ must be evaluated in order to guarantee the final top-k ordering. However, this limitation can be mitigated by using **HSV** since we can precalculate the impact contribution for each sample position and store this value instead of storing only the frequency ordering. Top-k guarantees are also possible using a term-based self-indexing system where each distinct term is mapped to an integer using **HSV** or other succinct representations of term contribution preprocessing. In future work, we intend to fully examine all of the possibilities for top-k guarantees using self-indexes in various bag-of-words querying scenarios.

When using character-based self-indexing approaches for bag-of-words queries, there is another disadvantage worth noting. For self-indexes, there is an efficiency trade-off between locating the top-k $f_{d,t}$ values and accurately determining f_t since the index can extract exactly k $f_{d,t}$ values without processing every document. For a fixed vocabulary, f_t is easily precomputed, and can be stored in the term map with the $\langle sp, ep \rangle$ pairs. But, in general it is not straightforward to determine f_t for arbitrary strings over WT_d without auxiliary algorithms and data structures to support calculating the value on the fly. The **FM-HSV** approach allows us to prestore f_t for each sampled interval which can be be used to calculate f_t over $\langle sp, ep \rangle$ more efficiently by only processing potential fringe leaves. Calculating f_t using only WT_d for arbitrary strings in near constant time using no additional space remains an open problem.

7. EXPERIMENTS

In order to test the efficiency of our approach, two experimental collections were used. For a small collection, we used the TREC 7 and 8 *ad hoc* datasets. This collection is composed of 1.86 GB of newswire data from the *Financial Times*, *Federal Register*, *LA Times*, and *Foreign Broadcast Information Service*, and consists of around 528,000 total documents [42]. For a larger in-memory collection, we used the TREC WT10G collection. This collection consists of 10.2 GB of markup text crawled from the internet, totalling 1,692,096 documents [21].

All of the algorithms described in this paper were implemented using C/C++ and compiled with gcc 4.6.1 with -O3 optimizations. For our baselines, we have implemented the in-memory variant of **WAND** as described by Fontoura et al. [17] for **DAAT**, and an in-memory variant of **MAXSCORE** for **TAAT**. Experiments were run on a single system with 2× Intel Xeon E5640 Processors with a 12 MB smart cache, 144 GB of DDR3 DRAM, and running Ubuntu Linux 11.10. Times are reported in milliseconds unless otherwise

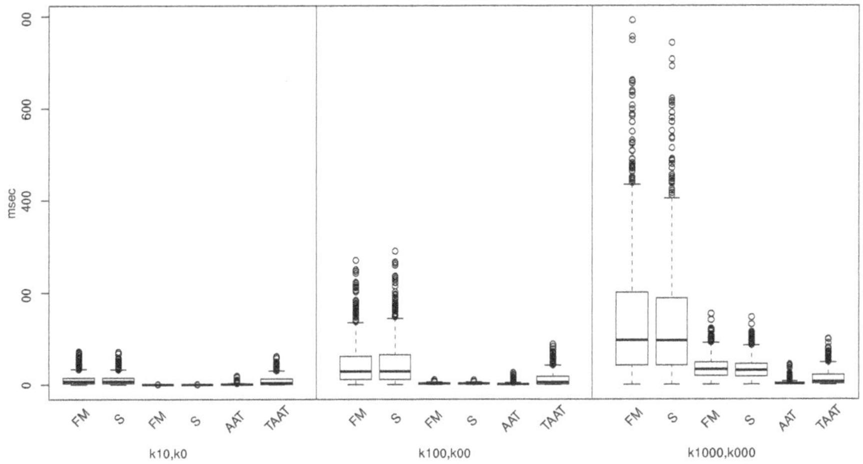

Figure 4: Efficiency for 1,000 randomly sampled MSN queries against the TREC 7 & 8 collection.

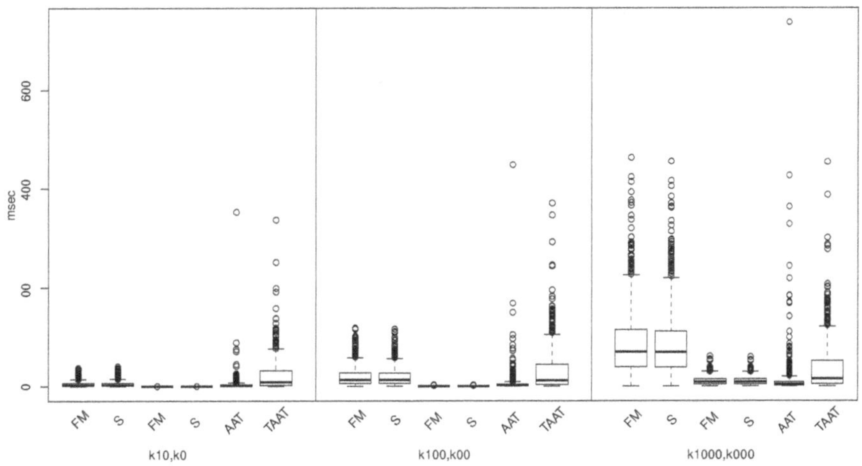

Figure 5: Efficiency for 1,000 randomly sampled MSN queries against the the TREC WT10G collection.

noted. All efficiency runs are reported as the mean and median of 10 consecutive runs of a query, and all necessary information is preloaded into memory.

Note that we do not carry out an full evaluation of the effectiveness of the algorithms presented in this paper. In previous work, we showed that the BM25 ranking and query evaluation framework used in our approach can be as effective as other state-of-the-art open source search engines when using $k' > k$, and do not repeat those experiments here [11]. In these experiments, we use the minimum k' values that result in retrieval performance that is comparable to the effectiveness obtained through exhaustive processing. In all experiments we use $k' = 8 * k$ for the TREC 7 & 8 dataset, and $k' = 2 * k$ for the TREC WT10G dataset. These values for k' give results for the MAP and P@10 effectiveness measures that are not statistically significantly different compared to exhaustive processing, for both collections (paired t-test, $p > 0.05$). We intend to pursue additional efficiency and effectiveness trade-offs in future work.

7.1 Experimental Setup

In order to test the efficiency of our algorithms, queries of varying length were extracted from a query log supplied by Microsoft. Each query was tested against both TREC collections, and the filtering criteria used was that every word in the query had to appear in at least 10 distinct documents, resulting in a total of 656,172 unique queries for the TREC 7 & 8 collection, and a total of 793,334 unique queries for the TREC WT10G collection. From the resulting filtered query sets, two different query samples were derived.

First, 1000 queries of any length were randomly sampled from each set, to represent a generic query log run. The 1,000 sampled queries for TREC 7 & 8 have an average query length of 4.224, and the average query length of the WT10G sample set is 4.265 words per query. For the second set of experiments, 100 queries for each query length 1 to 8 were randomly sampled from the same MSN query sets. Table 1 shows the statistical properties of the sampled queries that were used in the second experimental setup, including the average number of documents returned for each query for each query length, and the average length of postings lists processed for each query, computed as $(\sum_{i=1}^{|q|} n_i)/|q|$.

7.2 Average Query Efficiency

In order to test the efficiency of our algorithms, two experiments were performed on each of the collections. The first experiment is designed to measure the average efficiency for each algorithm,

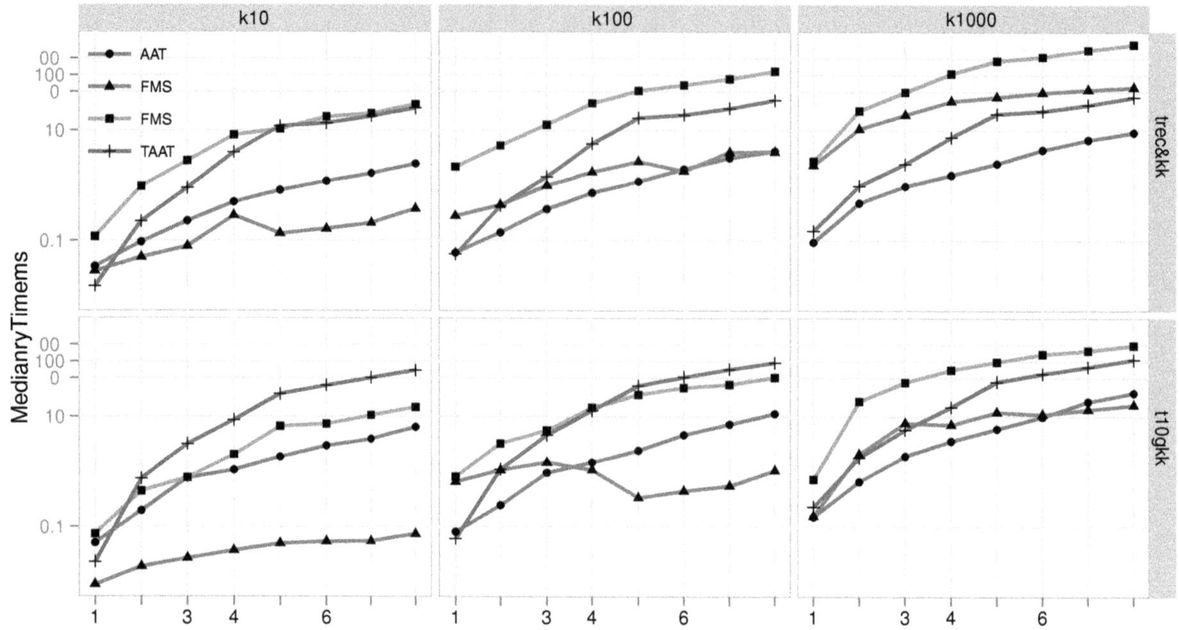

Figure 6: Efficiency of query length of 1 to 8 on the TREC 7 & 8 collection (top row) and TREC WT10G collection (bottom row) for *k*=10,100 and 1000. For each query length, 100 randomly sampled queries are used from the MSN query log set.

given a sampling of normal queries. For this experiment, the length of the queries was not bounded during sampling, and had an average query length of just over 4 words per query as mentioned in Section 7.1.

Figures 4 and 5 show the relative efficiency of each method averaged over 1,000 randomly sampled MSN queries for TREC 7 & 8, and TREC WT10G. Each boxplot summarizes the time values as follows: the solid line indicates the median; the box shows the 25th and 75th percentiles; and the whiskers show the range, up to a maximum of 1.5 times the interquartile range, with outliers beyond this shown as separate points. In both figures, the following abbreviations are used for the algorithms: **FM-GREEDY** (**FM**), **SEM-GREEDY** (**SE**), **FM-HSV** (**FM-H**), **SEM-HSV** (**SE-H**), **DAAT** , and **TAAT**.

We report the timings for all of the self-indexing methods using the *character-based* indexes. We also ran the same experiments using our *term-based* indexes, but the performance was identical. This result is not surprising since the dominant cost in the self-indexing method is traversing the wavelet tree over the document array, and is dictated by the depth of the wavelet tree and not the overall length. Since the depth depends only on the number of documents, both approaches consistently produce similar running times. So, the only efficiency difference between character-based and term-based indexes is in space-usage which is discussed in Section 7.

We see that the self-indexing methods which must calculate all frequency scores (**FM** and **SE**) incur the most overhead as k increases. This is largely due to the multiplicative effect of collating many consecutive k values. For example, when collating frequency values from WT_d, the number of rank operations is proportional to the depth of the wavelet tree. In the case of the TREC WT10G collection, which contains around 1.6 million documents, the depth of the wavelet tree is 24. So, the number of random rank probes in wavelet tree begins to significantly degrade the performance for larger k.

This effect can be marginalized by augmenting WT_d with **HSV**. Since an **HSV** style index has a portion of each $\langle sp, ep\rangle$ ranges, only the *fringe* positions for each range need to be calculated at runtime, reducing the total number of page faults. For all k, the **HSV** indexes are efficient and remarkably resilient to outliers. In general, the **WAND** variant of **DAAT** is more efficient for large values of k, but can perform poorly for certain queries. For example, the query "`point out the steps to make the world free of pollution`" on the WT10G collection consistently performed poorly in our **DAAT** framework.

7.3 Efficiency based on Query Length

We now break down the efficiency of each of our algorithms relative to two parameters: k and q, where q is the number of terms in a query. Figure 6 shows the average of 10 runs of 100 queries per query length, q. For one-word queries, for all values of k, the inverted indexing approaches **DAAT** and **TAAT** are superior. This is not surprising since only a single term posting must be traversed to calculate **BM25**, and the algorithms have excellent locality of access. Still, the **HSV** variant is the most efficient for small k.

For $|q| > 1$, the results also depend on k. For $k = 10$ and $k = 100$, the self-indexing methods are more efficient than **TAAT** since the methods can extract exactly k values. Since the sample rates in the lower regions of the **HSV** methods are close to k, very little work needs to be done by the indexes. The **WAND**-based **DAAT** method remains remarkably efficient for all values of k. As k increases, the performance of the **HSV**-based approaches begins to degrade since the sample size for the precalculated top-k orderings grows exponentially. The performance degradation at large k is equivalent to Case (3) as described in Section 4. In essence, most of the $\langle sp, ep\rangle$ ranges turn out to be much smaller than any of the samples, so the complete $\langle sp, ep\rangle$ range must be computed at runtime, reducing the performance to **FM-GREEDY** when an appropriate sample is not available. Note that the performance of **HSV** for TREC 7 & 8 is worse than for WT10G for two reasons. First, k'

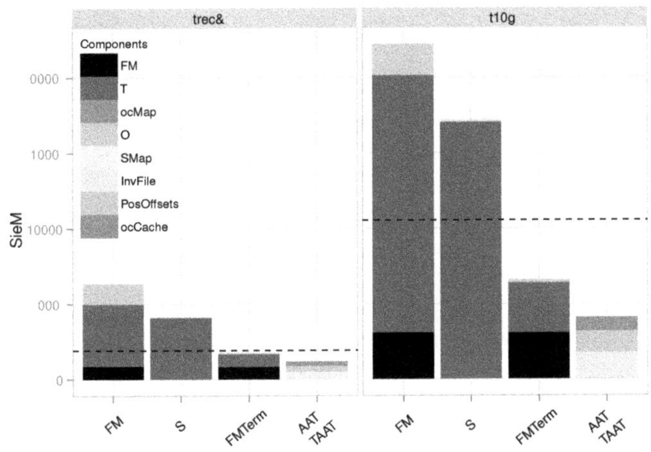

Figure 7: Space usage for each component in the three indexing approaches presented in this paper for the TREC 7 & 8 collection (left) and the TREC WT10G collection (right). The dashed line in both graphs represents the total space usage of the original uncompressed text for the collection.

is four times larger in TREC 7 & 8 resulting in fewer sample points. Secondly, if only a partial match is found, the self-index approach must retrieve 8 times more intermediate documents for scoring than in the inverted indexing approaches.

Note that none of our self-indexing approaches currently employ **MAXSCORE** or other methods to guide scoring. In principle our approach could also benefit from similar enhancements. We intend to explore the benefits and drawbacks of various early termination and impact scoring approaches for self-indexes in future work.

7.4 Space Usage

We now address the issue of space usage for the different algorithmic approaches. Inverted indexes are designed to take advantage of a myriad of different compression techniques. As such, our baselines also support several state-of-the-art byte and word aligned compression algorithms [3, 9, 28, 39, 43]. So, when we report the space usage for an inverted index, the numbers are reported using compressed inverted indexes and compressed document collections.

Figure 7 presents a break down of space usage for each component of the inverted indexing and self-indexing approaches. From a functionality perspective, there are several different componentization schemes to consider. First, consider the comparison of an inverted index method (including the term map, the postings list with p^* offsets, the document map, and the compressed document cache) with an FM-Index (including WT_d, the document map, and any other precomputed values – for instance the **HSV** enhancement). We consider these two in-memory indexes as functionally equivalent, as both can support bag-of-words or phrase queries, and can recreate snippets or even the original uncompressed document. The character based variant **FM** is significantly larger, but able to support a range of special character and arbitrary substring queries that term-based indexes do not support. Therefore, the term-based self-indexing variant **FM-TERM** is much closer to the inverted indexing variant in space usage and functionality.

The second alternative are indexes that support *only* bag-of-words queries. Now, an inverted index method requires only the term map, the postings list *without* p^* offsets, and the document map. The character-based self-indexes are essentially the same, but the FM-Index component is replaced with a term map component. Note that the **FM** component of **FM-TERM** is only required for phrase queries, and can also be dropped if only bag-of-words queries are required. When considering all of the current self-indexing options presented in this paper, using an FM-Index component instead of a term map appears to offer the most flexible configuration for character-based self-indexes, while the term-based variant is competitive in both time, space, and functionality with an inverted index.

8. CONCLUSION

We have presented an algorithmic framework for in-memory bag-of-words query processing that is efficient in practice. We have compared and contrasted our framework with industry and academic standard inverted indexing algorithms. Our approach shows great promise for advancing the state-of-the-art in exciting new directions.

However, several challenges must be overcome before these algorithms can reach widespread acceptance. For instance, recent work has dramatically reduced the space required for self-indexing algorithms, there are still opportunities to further reduce space usage in self-indexes. Another shortcoming of bag-of-words querying with self-indexing algorithms is providing top-k guarantees. While good solutions exist for providing top-k guarantees on singleton pattern queries, optimally merging multiple queries remains problematic.

However, self-indexing algorithms can also efficiently provide functionality that is notoriously inefficient, and sometimes even impossible, using inverted indexes. In addition to basic bag-of-words queries, our approach has the capability to perform phrase queries of any length, as well as the ability to support complex statistical calculations at query time, with no additional indexing costs. In fact, phrase queries were shown to be significantly faster using **FM-GREEDY** than when using inverted indexing approaches in prior work [10]. Self-indexes also inherently preserve term proximity. So, not only can each term be found quickly, but the n-terms surrounding the keyword can quickly be extracted, tabulated, and used for on-the-fly statistical calculations. Applications of this functionality include more efficient relevance feedback algorithms, construction of higher order language models in ranking metrics, or term dependency extraction and query expansion. In summary, all of the disadvantages outlined in this paper for self-indexing paper warrant further research, as the potential benefits of this new approach are compelling indeed.

In future work, we will explore new algorithmic approaches to reduce space usage, and to further improve efficiency for larger values of k. We also intend to investigate the combination of efficient phrase querying and proximity calculations to produce and evaluate novel ranking metrics. Finally, we will design and evaluate new approaches to support distributed in-memory query processing in order to scale our system to terabyte size collections.

9. ACKNOWLEDGMENTS

This work was supported in part by the Australian Research Council. We thank Gonzalo Navarro and Daniel Valenzuela for insightful discussions on the **HSV** method. We also thank Alistair Moffat for valuable feedback on a draft of this paper.

References

[1] V. N. Anh and A. Moffat. Pruned query evaluation using pre-computed impacts. In *SIGIR*, pages 372–379, 2006.

[2] V. N. Anh, O. de Kretser, and A. Moffat. Vector-space ranking with effective early termination. In *SIGIR*, pages 35–42, 2001.

[3] N. R. Brisaboa, A. Fariña, G. Navarro, and M. F. Esteller. (S, C)-dense coding: An optimized compression code for natural language text databases. In *SPIRE*, volume 2857 of *LNCS*, pages 122–136, 2003.

[4] A. Z. Broder, D. Carmel, H. Herscovici, A. Soffer, and J. Zien. Efficient query evaluation using a two-level retrieval process. In *CIKM*, pages 426–434, 2003.

[5] E. W. Brown. Fast evaluation of structured queries for information retrieval. In *SIGIR*, pages 30–38, 1995.

[6] C. Buckley and A. F. Lewit. Optimization of inverted vector searches. In *SIGIR*, pages 97–110, 1985.

[7] M. Burrows and D. J. Wheeler. A block-sorting lossless data compression algorithm. Technical Report 124, Digital Equipment Corporation, Palo Alto, California, May 1994.

[8] S. Büttcher, C. L. A. Clarke, and G. V. Cormack. *Information Retrieval: Implementing and evaluating search engines.* MIT Press, Cambridge, Massachusetts, 2010.

[9] J. S. Culpepper and A. Moffat. Enhanced byte codes with restricted prefix properties. In *SPIRE*, volume 3772 of *LNCS*, pages 1–12, November 2005.

[10] J. S. Culpepper, G. Navarro, S. J. Puglisi, and A. Turpin. Top-k ranked document search in general text databases. In *ESA, Part II*, LNCS 6347, pages 194–205, 2010.

[11] J. S. Culpepper, M. Yasukawa, and F. Scholer. Language independent ranked retrieval with NeWT. In *ADCS*, pages 18–25, December 2011. See `http://goanna.cs.rmit.edu.au/~e76763/publications/cys11-adcs.pdf`.

[12] P. Ferragina and G. Manzini. Opportunistic data structures with applications. In *FOCS*, pages 390–398, 2000.

[13] P. Ferragina and G. Manzini. Indexing compressed text. *Journal of the ACM*, 52(4):552–581, 2005. A preliminary version appeared in FOCS 2000.

[14] P. Ferragina, R. Giancarlo, and G. Manzini. The myriad virtues of wavelet trees. *Information and Computation*, 207:849–866, 2009.

[15] P. Ferragina, R. Gonzaález, G. Navarro, and R. Venturini. Compressed text indexes: From theory to practice. *Journal of Experimental Algorithmics*, 13:12.1–12.31, 2009.

[16] J. Fischer and V. Heun. Space-efficient preprocessing schemes for range minimum queries on static arrays. *SIAM Journal on Computing*, 40(2):465–492, 2011.

[17] M. Fontoura, V. Josifovski, J. Liu, S. Venkatesan, X. Zhu, and J. Zien. Evaluation strategies for top-k queries over memory-resident inverted indexes. *Proceedings of the VLDB Endowment*, 4(12):1213–1224, 2011.

[18] T. Gagie, S. J. Puglisi, and A. Turpin. Range quantile queries: Another virtue of wavelet trees. In *SPIRE*, pages 1–6, 2009.

[19] T. Gagie, G. Navarro, and S. Puglisi. New algorithms on wavelet trees and applications to information retrieval. *Theoretical Computer Science*, 426:25–41, 2012.

[20] R. Grossi, A. Gupta, and J. S. Vitter. Higher-order entropy-compressed text indexes. In *SODA*, pages 841–850, 2003.

[21] D. Hawking. Overview of the TREC-9 web track. In *TREC-8*, pages 87–102, 1999.

[22] W.-K. Hon, R. Shah, and J. S. Vitter. Space-efficient framework for top-k string retrieval problems. In *FOCS*, pages 713–722, 2009.

[23] G. Jacobson. *Succinct static data structures.* PhD thesis, Carnegie Mellon University, 1988.

[24] V. Mäkinen and G. Navarro. Implicit compression boosting with applications to self-indexing. In *SPIRE*, LNCS 4726, pages 229–241, 2007.

[25] U. Manber and E. W. Myers. Suffix arrays: A new method for on-line string searches. *SIAM J. Comp*, 22(5):935–948, 1993.

[26] G. Manzini. An analysis of the Burrows-Wheeler transform. *Journal of the ACM*, 48(3):407–430, May 2001.

[27] S. Mithukrishnan. Efficient algorithms for document retrieval problems. In *SODA*, pages 657–666, 2002.

[28] A. Moffat and V. N. Anh. Binary codes for non-uniform sources. In *DCC*, pages 133–142, 2005.

[29] A. Moffat and J. Zobel. Self indexing inverted files for fast text retrieval. *ACM TOIS*, 14(4):349–379, 1996.

[30] G. Navarro and V. Mäkinen. Compressed full-text indexes. *ACM Computing Surveys*, 39(1):2–1 – 2–61, 2007.

[31] G. Navarro and D. Valenzuela. Space-efficient top-k document retrieval. In *SEA*, LNCS 7276, pages 307–319, 2012.

[32] M. Persin. Document filtering for fast ranking. In *SIGIR*, pages 339–348, 1994.

[33] M. Persin, J. Zobel, and R. Sacks-Davis. Filtered document retrieval with frequency sorted indexes. *JASIST*, 47(10):749–764, 1996.

[34] S. J. Puglisi, W. F. Smyth, and A. H. Turpin. A taxonomy of suffix array construction algorithms. *ACM Comp. Surv.*, 39(2):4.1–4.31, 2007.

[35] R. Raman, V. Raman, and S. S. Rao. Succinct indexable dictionaries with applications to encoding k-ary trees and multisets. In *SODA*, pages 233–242, 2002.

[36] S. E. Robertson, S. Walker, S. Jones, M. Hancock-Beaulieu, and M. Gatford. Okapi at TREC-3. In *TREC-3*, 1994.

[37] K. Sadakane. Succinct data structures for flexible text retrieval systems. *J. Discr. Alg.*, 5(1):12–22, 2007.

[38] T. Strohman, H. Turtle, and W. B. Croft. Optimization strategies for complex queries. In *SIGIR*, pages 219–225, 2005.

[39] A. Trotman. Compressing inverted files. *Information Retrieval*, 6(1): 5–19, 2003.

[40] H. Turtle and J. Flood. Query evaluation: strategies and optimizations. *Information Processing and Management*, 31(6): 831–850, 1995.

[41] N. Välimäki and V. Mäkinen. Space-efficient algorithms for document retrieval. In *CPM*, LNCS 4580, pages 205–215, 2007.

[42] E. M. Voorhees and D. K. Harman. Overview of the Eighth Text REtrieval Conference (TREC-8). In *TREC-8*, pages 1–24, 1999.

[43] H. Yan, S. Ding, and T. Suel. Compressing term positions in web indexes. In *SIGIR*, pages 147–154, 2009.

[44] J. Zobel and A. Moffat. Inverted files for text search engines. *ACM Comp. Surv.*, 38(2):6–1 – 6–56, 2006.

[45] J. Zobel, A. Moffat, and K. Ramamohanarao. Inverted files versus signature files for text indexing. *ACM TODS*, 23(4):453–490, 1998.

Index Maintenance for Time-Travel Text Search

Avishek Anand[†], Srikanta Bedathur[‡], Klaus Berberich[†], Ralf Schenkel[*]

[†]Max-Planck Institute for Informatics, Saarbrücken, Germany
[‡]IIIT-Delhi, New Delhi, India
[*]Saarland University, Saarbrücken, Germany

{aanand,kberberi}@mpi-inf.mpg.de, bedathur@iiitd.ac.in, schenkel@mmci.uni-saarland.de

ABSTRACT

Time-travel text search enriches standard text search by temporal predicates, so that users of web archives can easily retrieve document versions that are considered relevant to a given keyword query and existed during a given time interval. Different index structures have been proposed to efficiently support time-travel text search. None of them, however, can easily be updated as the Web evolves and new document versions are added to the web archive.

In this work, we describe a novel index structure that efficiently supports time-travel text search and can be maintained incrementally as new document versions are added to the web archive. Our solution uses a sharded index organization, bounds the number of spuriously read index entries per shard, and can be maintained using small in-memory buffers and append-only operations. We present experiments on two large-scale real-world datasets demonstrating that maintaining our novel index structure is an order of magnitude more efficient than periodically rebuilding one of the existing index structures, while query-processing performance is not adversely affected.

Categories and Subject Descriptors

H.3.3 [**Information Search & Retrieval**]: Search process

General Terms

Experimentation, Algorithms, Performance

Keywords

Time-Travel Text Search, Index Maintenance, Web Archives

1. INTRODUCTION

In recent years, there has been an increasing awareness that born-digital contents, such as those on the Web, are ephemeral but often worth preserving. Organizations involved in the preservation of web contents include non-profits (e.g., the Internet Archive [1] and the Internet Memory Foundation [2]), for-profit companies, as well as national libraries and universities. The motivations behind such web archives are diverse and range from preservation of cultural heritage to compliance with legal requirements.

Web archives typically contain multiple versions of every document that reflect the evolution of its content over time. Interfaces provided to users in order to access archived contents, though, are still limited, for instance, to URL-based lookup & browsing as in the Internet Archive's Wayback Machine or simple keyword search. Motivated by this, *time-travel text search* has been proposed as an extension of standard text search by temporal predicates. Users can thus combine a keyword query (e.g., financial crisis) with a time interval (e.g., `[2006, 2008]`) to retrieve all document versions from the archive that are considered relevant to the given keywords and existed during the given time interval. Different index structures [3, 4, 7] have been proposed to efficiently support time-travel text search, incurring controllable overhead either in terms of index size or response time when compared to standard text search.

However, none of the existing index structures for time-travel text search can easily be updated when additional document versions are archived. To keep up with the state of the web archive, they thus have to be rebuilt periodically. While this used to be the case as well for standard inverted indexes, their maintenance in the presence of *insertions*, *modifications*, and *deletions* of documents is now fairly well-understood [11, 19, 24].

Our approach put forward in this work efficiently supports time-travel text search and handles additions of new document versions to the archive. It distinguishes between *active versions*, as the most recent and still current document versions, and *archive versions*, as the document versions already superseded by a more recent version of the same document. To search the active versions, a standard incrementally updatable inverted index [11, 18] is employed, which we will not discuss further. Our focus instead is on searching the archive versions. We propose a novel index structure to this end, building on our own sharded index for time-travel text search [4], and describe how it can be maintained incrementally when document versions are superseded and thus need to be migrated from the active index.

The original sharded index for time-travel text search relies on a method to horizontally partition each index list, so that any time-travel query can be processed without sequentially reading index entries that do not overlap with the query time-interval. It then relaxes the horizontal partitions

Permission to make digital or hard copies of all or part of this work for personal or classroom use is granted without fee provided that copies are not made or distributed for profit or commercial advantage and that copies bear this notice and the full citation on the first page. To copy otherwise, to republish, to post on servers or to redistribute to lists, requires prior specific permission and/or a fee.
SIGIR'12, August 12–16, 2012, Portland, Oregon, USA.
Copyright 2012 ACM 978-1-4503-1472-5/12/08 ...$10.00.

determined (the so-called *shards*), taking into account the I/O characteristics of the storage infrastructure, encoded as a parameter η reflecting the cost ratio between random seeks and sequential reads. The method guarantees for every *relaxed shard* that the *expected number* of wastefully read index entries is bounded by η. We are more stringent in this work and consider the worst case by bounding the *maximum number* of wastefully read index entries instead. This allows us to develop an online incremental sharding algorithm that keeps only a small in-memory buffer for every shard in the archive index. We show that our online algorithm is within an approximation factor of $(2 - \frac{2}{\eta+2})$ and hence results in at most two times the optimal number of relaxed shards.

We conducted experiments on the revision history of the English Wikipedia and the UKGOV web archive, as two large-scale real-world datasets. Our results show that incrementally maintaining our novel index structure is an order of magnitude more efficient than periodically rebuilding a sharded index for time-travel text search. Query processing performance, in addition, is not adversely affected and even improves in some cases. We therefore believe that the proposed approach provides the best of both worlds – update ability and efficient query processing – two key features needed when searching web archives but missing so far.

The rest of this paper unfolds as follows: Section 2 introduces our model and notation. Section 3 recaps key ideas behind the sharded index that we build upon. Section 4 describes our incremental sharding method to maintain the index. Section 5 presents the overall architecture of our system. Our experimental evaluation is the subject of Section 6. Finally, we relate to existing research in Section 7 and conclude in Section 8.

2. DATA AND QUERY MODEL

We consider a collection $\mathcal{D}$ of versioned documents that change over time. Each document d is uniquely identified by an identifier id_d. At time t, document d may have an active version d^* and zero or more archive versions $\langle d^1, d^2, \ldots \rangle$. Each (active or archive) version d^i of d comes with a valid-time interval $I(d^i) = [\, begin(d^i),\ end(d^i)\,)$ that denotes when that version was the active version of d; for d^*, $end(d^*) = \infty$ and $t \in I(d^*)$. We furthermore assume that all the $I(d^i)$ are disjoint.

The active version of a document turns into an archive version when the document is re-crawled and either a new active version is found or the document was removed from the Web. In both cases, the end time of the old version is set to the current time.

We consider time-travel queries over $\mathcal{D}$ that consist of a set of terms $Q = \{q_1, \ldots, q_m\}$ and a time interval $[b_Q, e_Q]$. When evaluated, this query retrieves the set of document versions that satisfy the keyword query Q and existed at any time during the time interval $[b_Q, e_Q]$.

3. INDEX ORGANIZATION

We now describe our index organization and briefly recap the sharded index for time -travel text search [4] that we build upon in this work.

Our system distinguishes between *active versions*, as those that are the most recent and still current version of a document, and *archive versions*, as those that have already been superseded by a more recent version of the same document. To search them, our system employs separate indexes, coined *active index* and *archive index*.

Both our indexes are based on the established inverted index [28] that associates each term with an *index list*. Each entry in the index list, $\langle id_d, I(d^i), s \rangle$, consists of a document identifier id_d, a valid-time interval, $I(d^i) = [begin(d^i), end(d^i)]$, and a payload s. The specifics of the payload depend on the retrieval model and the types of queries to be supported – it can be empty, a scalar value (e.g., capturing term frequency), or include positional information. When no confusion arises, we simply use $begin(p)$ and $end(p)$ of an index entry p to refer to the valid-time interval boundaries of the corresponding document version.

Queries that only ask for current information contained in active versions can be processed using only the active index, which corresponds to the live index that search engines maintain on the current Web. Time-travel queries that also ask for information from the past contained in archive versions are processed using both the active index and the archive index in combination.

The active index is implemented as an incrementally updatable inverted index [11, 18]. Depending on the fraction of time-travel queries among all queries posed to the system, index lists in the active index can be organized to efficiently support queries on active versions or time-travel queries. For the former, index entries may be ordered by their document identifier to allow for more efficient query processing, possibly together with additional structures [8, 12, 21, 26]. For the latter, index entries may be ordered by the begin boundary of their valid-time interval to support efficient filtering of too recent document versions.

The archive index is implemented as a sharded index [4], whose key ideas we now briefly recap. The sharded index distributes entries in an index list over disjoint partitions coined *shards*. Entries within a shard are ordered by the begin boundary of their valid-time interval. In addition, each shard comes with an *impact list* that maintains, for every possible begin boundary b_Q of a query time-interval, the position of the earliest entry in the shard whose valid-time interval contains the begin boundary b_Q. In practice, impact lists can be represented compactly and kept in main memory, as described in [4].

When processing a time-travel query, all shards for the query terms in Q are read from the position stored in their impact list for the begin boundary b_Q of the query time-interval, as opposed to, from their beginning. Per shard this involves one random seek to get to the indicated position followed by a number of sequential reads. One can safely stop reading a shard once the first index entry with a begin boundary larger than e_Q has been seen. The query processing cost thus depends on the number of shards, each of which is accessed with a random seek, and the total number of index entries that are read sequentially. Every method that assigns index entries to shards has to consider these two factors.

We now describe how index entries can be assigned to shards so as to optimize query processing cost. Since the assignment of index entries to shards solely depends on their valid-time intervals, we describe it as an interval-to-shard assignment problem and use the notions index entry and interval interchangeably. Let us first introduce some basic notation for intervals that we need in what follows. An interval I_j is associated with a begin time $begin(I_j)$ and an end time $end(I_j)$. We say that an interval I_1 subsumes an interval I_2 (for short: $I_1 \sqsupset I_2$), if:

$$begin(I_2) > begin(I_1) \wedge end(I_2) < end(I_1) .$$

An index entry is said to be a wasted read, if it is accessed during query processing although its valid-time interval does not overlap with the query time-interval. Such a wasted read may be caused when an interval I_1 *subsumes* another interval I_2 in the same shard. Assuming that a shard contains only these two intervals, the impact list entry for a begin boundary b_Q of the query time-interval after the end of I_2 will point to I_1 which is stored before I_2, and I_2 will be read even though it does not qualify as query result.

Since all shards for a term are accessed for any time-travel query including the term, the cost incurred due to random seeks is proportional to the number of shards per term. The cost for random seeks and sequential reads can be traded-off with two extremes. On one hand we can eliminate the cost for all but one random seek by having only a single shard per term. On the other hand, we can eliminate wasted reads altogether by creating idealized shards. *Idealized sharding* avoids subsumption entirely, i.e., there are no two intervals I_1 and I_2 with $I_1 \sqsupset I_2$ in a shard. The minimal number of idealized shards for a given set of intervals can be determined using a greedy algorithm, as described in [4].

The best performing solution is usually in between these two extremes, taking into account the I/O characteristics of the storage infrastructure housing the index. *Cost-aware sharding* developed in [4] systematically allows for interval subsumptions, while minimizing the overall number of shards. It thus trades some additional wasted sequential reads for a reduced number of random seeks. The method minimizes the number of shards per index list (and hence the number of random seeks) by systematically merging idealized shards. It thereby ensures that the expected number of wasted sequential reads per shard is below a threshold η encoding the cost ratio between random seeks and sequential reads.

4. INCREMENTAL SHARDING

Incremental sharding takes into account the relative costs of random and sequential accesses by a more restrictive bound on the number of subsumptions for a given shard. It bounds the absolute number of subsumptions for a given shards. This is opposed to cost aware sharding in [4] where the number of subsumptions per shard were on an average limited to a system-wide parameter. A bound on the number of subsumptions per shard translates to bounding the number of sequential wasted reads. We term this restriction as the *bounded subsumption* property. A shard is said to exhibit a bounded subsumption property if an interval in that shard does not subsume more than η intervals, where η is a system-wide constant same as before. Formally,

DEFINITION 1 (BOUNDED SUBSUMPTION). *A shard S is said to satisfy the bounded subsumption property of limit η if each interval $I_i \in S$ does not subsume more than η intervals:*

$$\forall I_i \in S : |\{I_j \in S \mid I_j \neq I_i \wedge I_i \sqsupset I_j\}| \leq \eta .$$

The problem of minimizing the number of random accesses with a limited number of wasted sequential accesses can be redefined in terms of minimizing the overall number of shards such that each shard exhibits the bounded subsumption. Thus, the problem definition becomes:

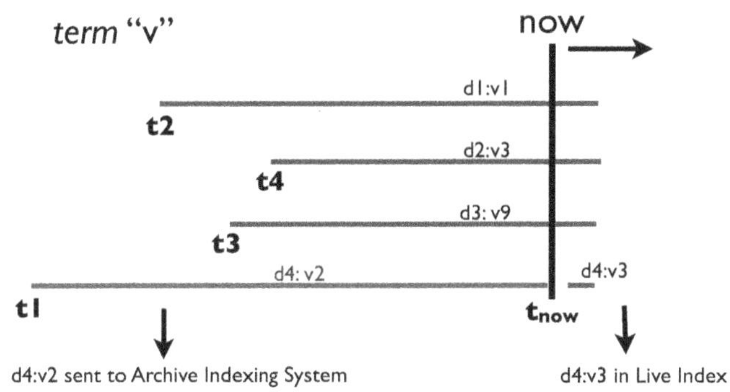

Figure 1: End time order of finalizing versions

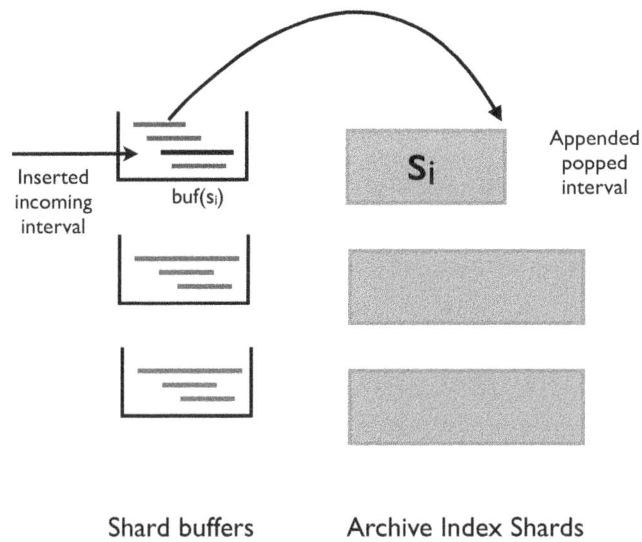

Figure 2: Incremental sharding

DEFINITION 2. *Given a set of intervals $\mathcal{I}$, partition $\mathcal{I}$ into a* minimal set *of shards $\mathcal{S} = \{S_1, \ldots, S_m\}$, $\forall I_k \in S_i,\ I_k \in \mathcal{I}$ where:*

$$S_i \cap S_j = \emptyset \qquad \forall S_i, S_j \in \mathcal{S},\ i \neq j$$
$$\bigcup_i S_i = \mathcal{I}$$
$$\text{s.t.} \quad \forall S_i \in \mathcal{S} \ : S_i \text{ satisfies bounded subsumption.}$$

Before attempting to solve the above problem let us discuss certain properties in an archive indexing setting. Firstly, the archive setting is very specific in terms of arrival of the input sequence, i.e., in the order of arrival of new versions to the archive index. Whenever the end time of an existing version is determined, it is sent to the archive indexing system (refer Figure 1). Since versions are generated in the end time order, the input intervals also follow the same order.

Secondly, we do not deal with deletions of versions since a deletion of a document results in an entry in the archive index for that document, and existing versions are never removed. This means that the index steadily grows over time with the older collection indexed by the archive index being a subset of the current collection.

Finally, from the indexing point of view it is preferable to have an updating scheme which appends newly created postings at the end of the index list. The major benefit of an append operation is that the indexes built for the older indexes can be used as partial solutions to build an up-to-date archive index efficiently thus avoiding recomputation. Recomputation of shards with a non-append based technique (say cost-aware sharding) is expensive because it involves processing the entire input (existing data along with the new updates) thus limiting its applicability to an update aware indexing system.

Another benefit with an append operation is the avoidance of the expensive decompression and compression cycles in building the new updated index. While merging two index lists by employing recomputation the corresponding shards of each term are completely decompressed to form usable input for the sharding algorithm. After recomputing the new set of shards are compressed back again for storage. The most popular compression algorithms used in index list compression are based on gap-encoding schemes which are local schemes and hence append friendly. Hence, rather than optimally solving the problem we look for an approach which is based on an append only operation to the existing shards and exploits the end time order of input arrival. In the following subsection we introduce the *incremental sharding* algorithm which apart from being incremental also has an approximation guarantee.

4.1 Incremental Sharding Algorithm

We present the *incremental sharding algorithm* which is an update aware incremental algorithm with a factor $(2 - \frac{2}{\eta+2})$ approximation algorithm(cf. Algorithm 1). Apart from having the natural benefit of being an append only algorithm it also exploits the end time arrival order of the intervals by processing the intervals in that order thus avoiding expensive sort operations on the input.

The algorithm processes intervals in the end time order (cf. line 1) and creates or updates shards incrementally. It follows a scheme of immediate assignment but deferred append of an interval to a shard. For each shard we maintain a *shard buffer* of size $\eta + 1$ and an *shard begin time*. The assignment of the interval to a shard is based on the begin time of the shard and the shard buffer defers the actual writing or appending of the interval of the shard to satisfy the bounded subsumption property. In other words the shard buffer maintains the interval until it deems it right to be appended to the end of the shard.

When an interval, $I[i]$, is processed it is either assigned to an existing shard based on the interval and shard begin times (cf. line 15) or it results in the creation of a new shard (lines 7-10). The creation of a new shard involves setting the begin time of the shard to zero and placing the chosen interval in its shard buffer. Until the buffer reaches its capacity of η the begin time of the shard remains zero. The shard begin time is first updated only when the an interval is popped out of it after the buffer reaches its capacity $\eta + 1$. When the assignment for the interval is decided, say S_t, it is placed in the respective shard buffer $buf(S_t)$ (cf. line 19). The incremental sharding chooses the shard whose begin time has the least difference with the begin time of the incoming interval (cf. line 15).

The shard buffers determine the relative position of the intervals in the shard where it will be finally stored. The insertions into the buffer are made to preserve the begin time order (cf. line 19) which in turn ensures a begin time order when intervals are removed from it. This is diagramatically shown in Figure 2. Only the first interval or the interval with the minimum begin time is removed from the buffer to limit the buffer size to $\eta + 1$ (line 23) and it is appended to the end of its corresponding shard S_t. The shard buffers also ensure that no interval in a shard subsumes more than η intervals. This is done by setting the begin time of a shard $S_t.begin$ to the first interval $begin(first(buf(S_t)))$(or the interval with the least begin time) of the shard buffer as in line 24. The interval with the minimum begin time in the shard can subsume the maximum number of intervals and any interval with a begin time lesser than it is dissallowed.

Note the use $\cup$ in lines 23 and 30 to indicate the *append* operation on the shard that is logically organized as a list of intervals in their begin time order.

Algorithm 1 Incremental Sharding Algorithm

1: *Input:* (i)η, (ii)$\mathcal{I}$ sorted in increasing order of end times
2: $\mathcal{S} = \emptyset$ // incremental sharding
3:
4: **for** $i = 1 \,..\, |\mathcal{I}|$ **do**
5: //creates new shard
6: **if** $\neg\exists S \in \mathcal{S} : S.begin \leq begin(I[i])$ **then**
7: create **new shard** S_{new} and $buf(S_{new})$
8: $S_{new}.begin = 0$
9: **add** $I[i]$ to $buf(S_{new})$
10: $S = \mathcal{S} \cup \{S_{new}\}$
11: **end if**
12:
13: //find the best candidate shard for assignment
14: $S_{cand} = \{S_i \mid S_i \in \mathcal{S} \wedge S_i.begin \leq begin(I[i])\}$
15: $S_t = \underset{g \in S_{cand}}{argmin}\ (begin(I[i]) - g.begin)$
16:
17: //update buffers and begin times of shards
18: **if** $S_t \neq S_{new}$ **then**
19: **insert** $I[i]$ into $buf(S_t)$ in begin time order
20: **end if**
21: **if** $|buf(S_t)| = \eta + 1$ **then**
22: //first element in the buffer finalized
23: $S_t = S_t \cup removefirst(buf(S_t))$
24: $S_t.begin = begin(first(buf(S_t)))$
25: **end if**
26: **end for**
27:
28: //finally append the buffer intervals to the shards
29: **for** $S \in \mathcal{S}$ **do**
30: $S = S \cup buf(S)$
31: **end for**
32:
33: *Output:* $\mathcal{S}$ is the incremental sharding.

4.2 Approximation Guarantee

THEOREM 1. *Incremental sharding is a* $(2 - \frac{2}{\eta+2})$ *approximation.*

We approach the proof by first proving two lemmas. Assuming that incremental sharding produces m shards, we construct a worst case scenario. For notational convenience let us assume that shards are numbered according to their creation times in incremental sharding, i.e., S_1 was created before S_2 and so on.

LEMMA 1 (DESCENDING BEGIN TIMES). *If incremental sharding created a shard S_{i+1} after S_i, then $S_i.begin > S_{i+1}.begin$.*

PROOF. We prove this property by induction over increasing number of intervals $I_i \in \mathcal{I}$ which are added in in end time order, i.e, $end(I_{i+1}) > end(I_i)$.

$i = 1$: For the first interval I_1 the property holds since there are no earlier shards.

$i \to i+1$: Let there be n existing shards $\mathcal{S} = \{S_1 \cdots S_n\}$. Depending on the begin time of the $(i+1)$th interval $begin(I_{i+1})$ we consider the following two cases:

Case 1: If $begin(I_{i+1}) < S_k.begin$, $1 \leq k \leq n$, then I_{i+1} forms a new shard S_{new} and the begin of the shard $S_{new}.begin$ is less than all the existing shard begin times. This proves the claim.

Case 2: Assuming $\exists S_k : begin(I_{i+1}) \geq S_k.begin$ and on addition of I_{i+1} to S_k there is a violation of the descending begin time order of shards, i.e. , $S_k.begin > S_{k-1}.begin$. This means that $S_{k-1}.begin < begin(I_{i+1})$ and I_{i+1} should have been assigned to S_{k-1} due to a smaller difference according to the induction hypothesis of $S_{k+1}.begin > S_k.begin$, $\forall 1 \leq k < n$. □

LEMMA 2 (INCREMENTAL SUBSUMPTION). *An interval added to S_i subsumes at least $(i-1)(\eta+1)$ intervals.*

PROOF. Note that $S_i.begin$ refers to the time of the first interval in the buffer of shard S_i or the earliest begin time in the shard buffer $buf(S)$. By Lemma 1 we know that there is an ordering of the shard begin times. Hence for an interval I assigned to S_i the following holds – $begin(I) < S_{i-1}.begin < \cdots < S_1.begin$. Since we assume end time arrival order of intervals it subsumes all intervals in $i-1$ shards buffers, which are $S_1, ..., S_{i-1}$. Further the fixed buffer size of $\eta+1$ results in making the subsumptions lower bounded by $(i-1)(\eta+1)$. □

We recollect the *Staircase Property* of a shard as introduced in [4] as a property which requires the intervals to be in their begin time order and additionally disallowing subsumptions among any pair of intervals in the shard. We further need to introduce the notion of *stalagtite sets* and *stalagtite groups*. A *stalagtite set* Λ_s is a set of time intervals such that,

$$\forall p, q \in \Lambda_s, begin(p) \leq begin(q) \Rightarrow end(p) > end(q).$$

Stalagtite groups (cf. Figure 3) are a collection of sets of intervals such that choosing one interval from each of these sets results in a *stalagtite set*.

LEMMA 3 (STALAGTITE GROUPING). *Stalagtite grouping with a staircase property in each shard is the worst case for incremental sharding.*

PROOF. From the previous lemma, any input resulting in m shards from incremental sharding will have at least intervals with $\eta+1$, $2(\eta+1)$, $\cdots$, $(m-1)(\eta+1)$ subsumptions in $S_2, S_3, \cdots, S_m$ respectively. Let us suppose that the set of subsumed intervals when the first interval added to S_i be represented as $sub(S_i)$. To reduce the overall number of shards we should strive for a configuration with minimum number of subsumptions. This is possible when $sub(S_1) \subseteq sub(S_2) \subseteq \cdots \subseteq sub(S_m)$ and $|S_i| = \eta+1, \forall i = 1, \ldots, m$. This arrangement forms a *stalagtite group*(cf. Figure 3) with each of the groups having a cardinality of $\eta+1$.

Additionally, each of these stalagtite groups should have a staircase arrangement to allow for the maximum capacity - η - out of place insertions. Any additional interval or misaligned interval either increases subsumption or reduces capacity for out of place insertions. Any removal of intervals on the other hand result in contradiction to the original assumption that there are m shards from incremental sharding. □

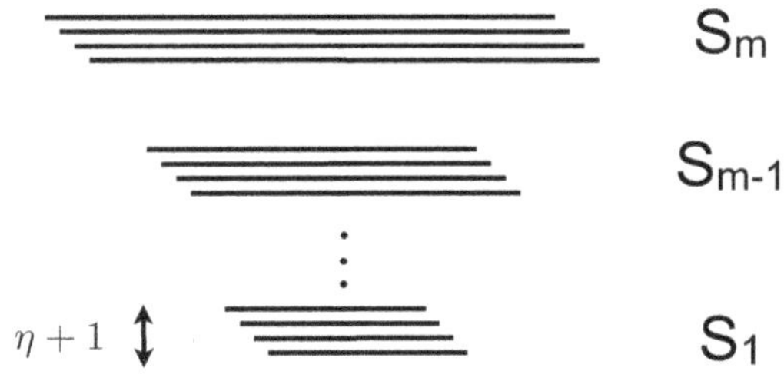

Figure 3: Stalagtite groups

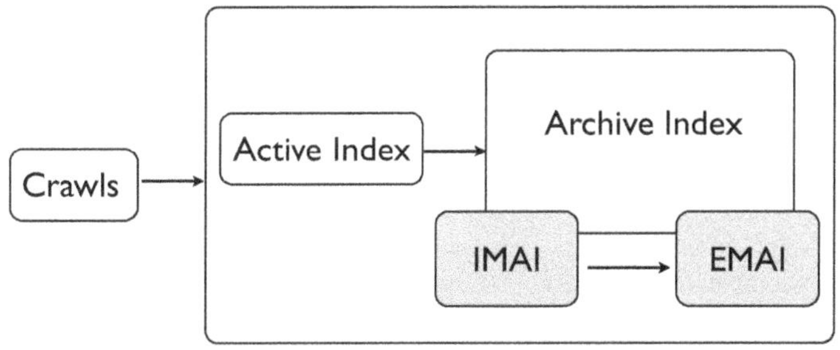

Figure 4: System architecture

Now we can complete the proof for Theorem 1.

PROOF. From the Lemma 3 we know that there are m stalagtite groups with each group residing in the shards formed from incremental sharding. It is easy to see that none of the optimal shards will have more than $2\eta+1$ intervals. Thus we choose an assignment where we try to minimize minimum number of shards, i.e., choose as many shards with $2\eta+1$ intervals as possible. One such assignment is when we assign η of the $\eta+1$ intervals of S_i to S_{m+1-i}, $\forall i \leq \frac{m}{2}$. The remaining $\frac{m}{2}$ intervals (an interval from each S_i) can then be placed in $\frac{m}{2(\eta+1)}$ shards. Hence for m shards created by incremental sharding we get a minimum of $\frac{m}{2} + \frac{m}{2(\eta+1)}$ shards. Notice that we can have other arrangements which give the same number of minimum shards. The ratio

$$\frac{|S|}{OPT} = \frac{m}{\frac{m}{2} + \frac{m}{2(\eta+1)}} = 2\left(1 - \frac{1}{\eta+2}\right)$$

proves that incremental sharding is a factor $(2 - \frac{2}{\eta+2})$ approximation algorithm. □

5. SYSTEM ARCHITECTURE

Figure 4 shows a high-level overview of the architecture of a search engine using our incremental sharding method. It consists of

- The *active index* for all active versions of documents, consisting of an in-memory inverted list for each term that keeps the active versions of documents containing this.
- The *archive index* for all archive versions of documents, consisting of an inverted list for each term that is

organized in shards. The archive index consists of an in-memory index *IMAI* and an on-disk index *EMAI*, both organized in shards.

- A *crawler* that continuously crawls the target Web sites, for example a predefined set of domains or the complete Web.

When the crawler encounters a new document that has been unknown so far, it adds it to the active index; this is an inexpensive operation since the active index is in main memory. When a document is found again, it is checked for changes (using, for example, a fingerprinting technique such as [9, 16]). If changes are detected, the active version of that document turns into an archive version (with end time equal to the crawl time) and is sent to the archive index, and index entries for the new active version are added to the active index.

The archived version is then added to the in-memory archive index by first creating the corresponding postings for each term, which are then added to the in-memory archive index using the incremental technique from Section 4. Figure 1 shows an example for this, where in a crawl at time t_{now} a new version v_3 for document $d4$ is detected. This results in firstly adding a new version $d4 : v3$ with a begin time t_{now} to the affected terms in the active index. Secondly, the end time of $v2$ is finalized and the posting $\langle d4 : v2, [t_1, t_{now}], score \rangle$ with the complete interval information is send to the archive indexing system. In the archive indexing system this posting is processed by placing it in the shard buffer of term "v" and updating the IMAI from the popped posting in the buffer as shown in Figure 2. As soon as the in-memory index IMAI is full, entries are merged into the disk-based archive index EMAI, merging corresponding shards; this essentially corresponds to incremental maintenance of standard inverted lists.

6. EXPERIMENTAL EVALUATION

All our algorithms were implemented in Java 1.6, within the time-travel indexing system presented earlier in [4]. Experiments were conducted on Dell PowerEdge M610 servers, with 48 GB of main memory, and attached to a large disk array through iSCSI.

The two data collections used in our experiments are: (i) the English Wikipedia revision history, referred to as the **WIKI** collection, which contains the edit history from January 2001 until December 2005 excluding all the minor edits, and (ii) a web archive, referred to as the **UKGOV** collection, provided by the Internet Memory Foundation (previously European Archive), consisting of weekly crawls of 11 government websites within U.K. during 2004 and 2005. The characteristics of these two collections are briefly summarized in Table 1. For the ease of experimentation, we rounded the time-stamps of versions to the nearest day for all datasets.

6.1 Index Management

We build indexes based on incremental sharding (INC) and cost-aware sharding as in [4] (CA) algorithms with relaxation parameter(η) values 10, 100 and 1000. All sharded indexes are stored on disk in flat files containing both the lexicon (i.e., pointers to the shards for each term) as well as sharded term lists. At run time, the lexicon is read completely into memory, and for a given query the appropriate shards are retrieved from disk. For compression we employ 7-bit + gap encoding [20].

We simulate the index updates needed for our incremental index maintenance as follows: we first created partial indexes for each month containing postings of only those versions that have end time within that month. The index is incremented, starting from an empty index, by merging partial index of each month in sequence. We employed *immediate-merging* [10] to create one consolidated index at the end of every monthly merge operation, and each sharded posting list in the index is incrementally maintained using our INC algorithm. We compared this with CA sharding, which recomputes the entire sharding for the combined index every time from scratch. In other words, all shards of a posting list in the currently merged index are read and decompressed, the corresponding list from the partial index for the next month is also read and decompressed, these two are combined, and finally, a new sharding is generated using the CA algorithm for the merged index which is written in compressed form to disk.

6.2 Query Workloads and Execution

We compiled one query workload for each dataset, by extracting frequent queries from the AOL query logs that were temporarily available during 2006. For querying the WIKI dataset, we extracted the 300 most frequent queries which had a result click on the domain `en.wikipedia.org`; similarly for UKGOV, we compiled 50 queries which had result hit on `.gov.uk` domains. Using these keyword queries, we generated a time-travel query workload with 5 instances each for the following three different temporal predicate granularities: *week*, *month* and *year*.

For query processing we employed conjunctive query semantics i.e., query results contain documents that include all the query terms. We use wall-clock times (in milliseconds) to measure the query processing performance. The runtimes were measured on warm caches using only a single core. Specifically, each query was executed five times in succession and the average of the last four runs was taken for a more stable and accurate measurement of the query runtime.

6.3 Results

Index Maintenance Performance

Figures 5 and 6 show results of our experiments on index maintenance with WIKI and UKGOV datasets respectively. Note the log-scale used on the y-axis in these charts, which represents the time-taken for the consolidated sharded index to be built in milliseconds. It is quite evident from these charts that the INC algorithm for maintaining the index is an order of magnitude faster than CA. Note that for UKGOV we report maintenance times for the first seven months only which is already smaller than time taken to merge the entire index for two years using INC. This efficiency comes from two advantages that INC enjoys over CA: first, recomputing the sharding by CA on the merged index takes much of the time and grows as the index size grows. Since INC does not recompute the sharding, its performance improves significantly. Second, it does not have to decompress, merge and shard the entire list before writing do the disk. Instead, it has to just read two posting lists in parallel and append corresponding shards (without decompressing), and write to the disk. From

Dataset	Coverage	Size (in GB)	$\mathcal{N}$	$\mathcal{V}$	μ/σ
WIKI	2001 to 2005	~700	1,517,524	15,079,829	9.94 / 46.08
UKGOV	2004 to 2005	~400	685,678	17,297,548	25.23 / 28.38

Datasets with no. of documents $\mathcal{N}$, no. of versions $\mathcal{V}$, average number of versions per documents μ, and standard deviation σ.

Table 1: Characteristics of datasets used

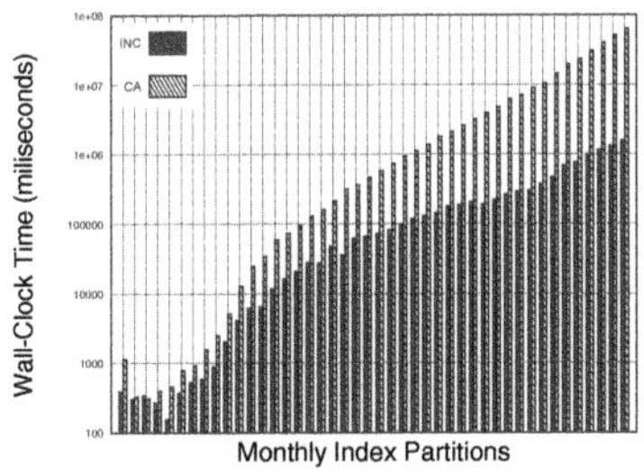

(a) $\eta = 10$

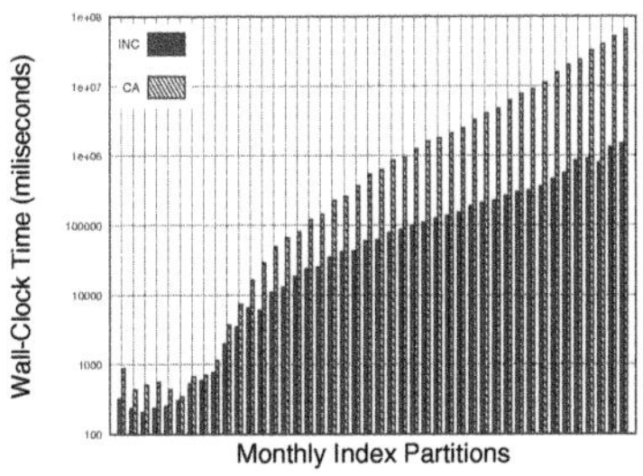

(b) $\eta = 100$

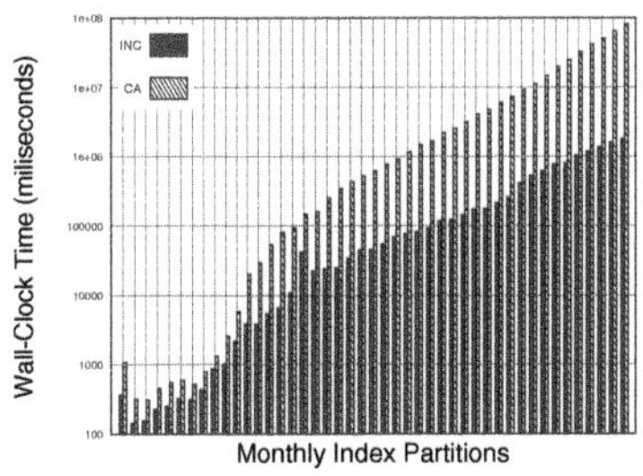

(c) $\eta = 1000$

Figure 5: Performance of index maintenance - WIKI

our experiments we observe that recomputation of shards accounts for an average of 45% of the entire maintenance time. Compression and decompression take upto 15% of the overall time but since we use 7-bit encoding for compression we expect that a more involved compression technique would only increase the maintenance time. It should be noted that in our simulation we do not perform an append, instead we resort to creating a new index file in each step – incurring additional overheads. Thus, the performance of INC can be further improved by carefully implementing advanced index merging methods.

		Sharding	
Dataset	η	INC	CA
	10	23.37	32.83
WIKI	100	13.32	11.41
	1000	5.83	4.42
	10	10.93	13.16
UKGOV	100	6.84	10.35
	1000	4.14	4.79

Table 2: Average number of shards per term

Effect on Query Processing

To assess the effect of using INC for index maintenance on query processing performance, we used the final index computed for each dataset – i.e., after merging the last partial index at end of 5 years in case of WIKI and after the last partial index at the end of 2 years in case of UKGOV. We compared the performance of answering queries using this index against the query performance over a newly created *archive index* for the entire collection, sharded using CA. Since the active index, as mentioned in 5 is common to both INC and CA, we omitted the query processing time over the active index from our measurements. We considered indexes obtained using three relaxation parameter values η = 10, 100, 1000. We report runtimes, measured in milliseconds, averaged over queries for three granularities of temporal predicates we considered – *week*, *month* and *year*, as described in Section 6.2. Results are shown in Figures 7 and 8 for WIKI and UKGOV datasets respectively.

As one can observe from these charts, the sharded index generated using INC compares quite favorably with the combined sharded index computed using CA. This behavior is consistent across all the granularities of temporal predicate for all values of η parameter. In some small number of cases, the performance of INC is slightly better than that of CA, and is never worse. Further, we also compared the average number of shards generated by both the algorithms with different values of η. These results are summarized in Table 2. As these results show, using INC in most cases generates fewer number of shards on average for each posting list, reducing the number of random accesses required during query processing. So, when the underlying storage system has high cost of random accesses, then it seems more beneficial to query processing performance to use INC to maintain the index than using CA.

7. RELATED WORK

We now put our work in context with existing research. This can be categorized into (a) work on maintaining inverted indexes when faced with changes in the document collection and (b) approaches that make search aware of temporal information associated with documents. No work, to the best of our knowledge, has been done at the intersection of the two categories.

Given that the construction of inverted indexes is well understood and can easily be parallelized, one existing maintenance strategy has been to rebuild the index periodically. Returning stale query results, most of the time, is an obvious disadvantage of this approach. For a long time, though, this has been the approach taken by major search engines on the Web. Only lately, Peng et al. [24] have addressed

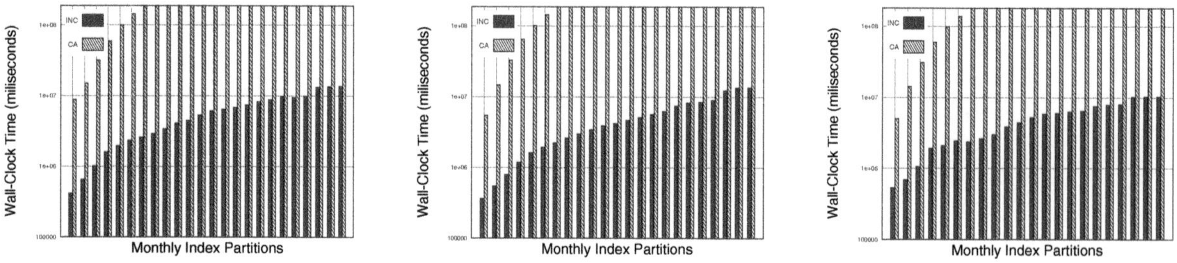

(a) $\eta = 10$ (b) $\eta = 100$ (c) $\eta = 1000$

Figure 6: Performance of index maintenance – UKGOV

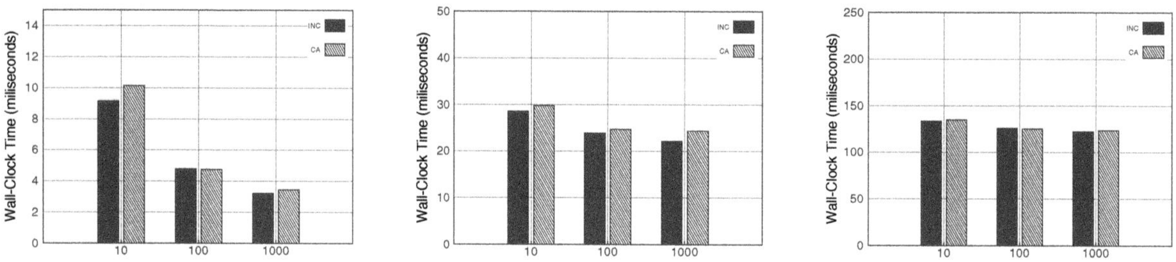

(a) Week (b) Month (c) Year

Figure 7: Query processing performance with varying granularity of temporal predicate – WIKI

the issue of handling updates in web-scale indexes. Instead of rebuilding the index, Lester et al. [19] suggest to collect updates in an in-memory index that is then merged, from time to time to amortize costs, with a disk-resident inverted index. This merge can either be performed in-situ, thus modifying posting lists at their current location, or by storing entirely new posting lists. A hybrid approach that chooses between these alternatives is described by Büttcher et al. [11]. Guarajada and Kumar [13] can be seen as another extension that leverages query logs to determine terms whose posting lists mandate eager maintenance. In a spirit similar to log-structured methods [23], Lester et al. [18] propose to keep multiple indexes of geometrically increasing size and merge them, when they overflow, in a rolling manner. Query results reflecting the current state of the document collection can be obtained in these approaches by executing queries both on in-memory and disk-resident indexes. For more detailed discussions of inverted index maintenance, we refer to the recent textbooks by Büttcher et al. [10] and Manning et al. [20], as well as, the survey by Zobel and Moffat [28].

Constructing indexes for (versioned) document collections with a high degree of redundancy has been an active area of research lately. Anick and Flynn [5], as the earliest approach, applies techniques from version-control systems to a text index. Zhang and Suel [27] propose a two-level index that avoids repeatedly indexing redundant content. Herscovici et al. [17] employ a sequence-alignment formulation to address the same problem. Berberich et al. [7] present the idea of time-travel text search, incorporating temporal predicates into text search, and describe a vertically partitioned (or, sliced) inverted index to support it efficiently. Anand et al. [4], as the work that our methods build upon, show that time-travel text search can be supported equally efficiently by building a horizontally partitioned (or, sharded) inverted index. He et al. [14, 15] have focused on improving compression techniques for inverted indexes on versioned document collections. As a final note, the problem of indexing and querying data with associated temporal information has been studied intensively in the database community – a survey of existing approaches is given by Salzberg and Tsotras [25] present. Becker et al. [6], being based on the B^+-Tree, and Muth et al. [22], as a log-structured method inspired by the LSM-Tree [23], are two database approaches that explicitly deal with updates.

8. CONCLUSIONS

This paper presented incremental sharding, an efficient maintenance technique for indexes in web archives. It uses only cheap append operations to add newly arrived versions to the existing index. It can be smoothly integrated into a search engine for both live and archived documents. Experiments demonstrated that the technique is an order of magnitude more efficient than recomputing the index.

Our future work will focus on an full-fledged implementation of our proposed system. We will further study the influence of different techniques for inverted list maintenance.

Acknowledgments

Partially supported by the EU within the 7th Framework Programme under contract number 258105 "Longitudinal Analytics of Web Archive data (LAWA)".

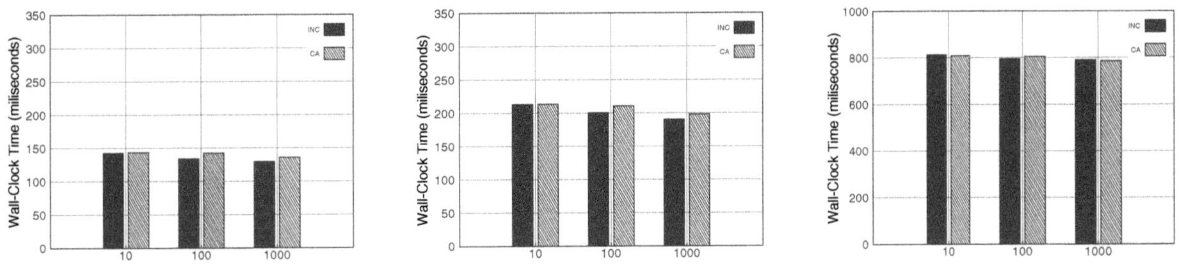

(a) Week (b) Month (c) Year

Figure 8: Query processing performance with varying granularity of temporal predicate – UKGOV

9. REFERENCES

[1] Internet Archive. http://archive.org.

[2] Internet Memory Foundation. http://www.internetmemory.org.

[3] Avishek Anand, Srikanta J. Bedathur, Klaus Berberich, and Ralf Schenkel. Efficient temporal keyword search over versioned text. In *CIKM*, pages 699–708, 2010.

[4] Avishek Anand, Srikanta J. Bedathur, Klaus Berberich, and Ralf Schenkel. Temporal index sharding for space-time efficiency in archive search. In *SIGIR*, pages 545–554, 2011.

[5] Peter G. Anick and Rex A. Flynn. Versioning a full-text information retrieval system. In *SIGIR*, pages 98–111. ACM, 1992.

[6] B. Becker, S. Gschwind, T. Ohler, B. Seeger, and P. Widmayer. An asymptotically optimal multiversion b-tree. *VLDB J.*, 5(4), 1996.

[7] K. Berberich, S. Bedathur, T. Neumann, and G. Weikum. A Time Machine for Text Search. In *SIGIR*, pages 519–526, 2007.

[8] Andrei Z. Broder, David Carmel, Michael Herscovici, Aya Soffer, and Jason Y. Zien. Efficient query evaluation using a two-level retrieval process. In *CIKM*, pages 426–434, 2003.

[9] Andrei Z. Broder, Steven C. Glassman, Mark S. Manasse, and Geoffrey Zweig. Syntactic clustering of the web. *Computer Networks*, 29(8-13):1157–1166, 1997.

[10] S. Büttcher, C.L.A. Clarke, and G.V. Cormack. *Information Retrieval: Implementing and Evaluating Search Engines*. The MIT Press, 2010.

[11] Stefan Büttcher and Charles L. A. Clarke. Hybrid index maintenance for contiguous inverted lists. *Inf. Retr.*, 11(3):175–207, 2008.

[12] Shuai Ding and Torsten Suel. Faster top-k document retrieval using block-max indexes. In *SIGIR*, pages 993–1002, 2011.

[13] Sairam Gurajada and P. Sreenivasa Kumar. On-line index maintenance using horizontal partitioning. In *CIKM*, pages 435–444, 2009.

[14] Jinru He, Hao Yan, and Torsten Suel. Compact full-text indexing of versioned document collections. In *CIKM*, pages 415–424, 2009.

[15] Jinru He, Junyuan Zeng, and Torsten Suel. Improved index compression techniques for versioned document collections. In *CIKM*, pages 1239–1248, 2010.

[16] Monika Rauch Henzinger. Finding near-duplicate web pages: a large-scale evaluation of algorithms. In *SIGIR*, pages 284–291, 2006.

[17] Michael Herscovici, Ronny Lempel, and Sivan Yogev. Efficient indexing of versioned document sequences. In *ECIR*, pages 76–87, 2007.

[18] Nicholas Lester, Alistair Moffat, and Justin Zobel. Efficient online index construction for text databases. *ACM Trans. Database Syst.*, 33(3), 2008.

[19] Nicholas Lester, Justin Zobel, and Hugh E. Williams. Efficient online index maintenance for contiguous inverted lists. *Inf. Process. Manage.*, 42(4):916–933, 2006.

[20] Christopher D. Manning, Prabhakar Raghavan, and Hinrich Schütze. *Introduction to information retrieval.* Cambridge University Press, 2008.

[21] Alistair Moffat and Justin Zobel. Self-indexing inverted files for fast text retrieval. *ACM Trans. Inf. Syst.*, 14(4):349–379, 1996.

[22] Peter Muth, Patrick E. O'Neil, Achim Pick, and Gerhard Weikum. The LHAM Log-Structured History Data Access Method. *VLDB J.*, 8(3-4):199–221, 2000.

[23] Patrick E. O'Neil, Edward Cheng, Dieter Gawlick, and Elizabeth J. O'Neil. The log-structured merge-tree (lsm-tree). *Acta Inf.*, 33(4):351–385, 1996.

[24] Daniel Peng and Frank Dabek. Large-scale Incremental Processing Using Distributed Transactions and Notifications. In *SOSP*, 2010.

[25] B. Salzberg and V. Tsotras. Comparison of Access methods for Time-evolving Data. *ACM Computing Surveys*, 31(2):158–221, 1999.

[26] Trevor Strohman and W. Bruce Croft. Efficient document retrieval in main memory. In *SIGIR*, pages 175–182, 2007.

[27] Jiangong Zhang and Torsten Suel. Efficient search in large textual collections with redundancy. In *WWW*, pages 411–420, 2007.

[28] Justin Zobel and Alistair Moffat. Inverted files for text search engines. *ACM Comput. Surv.*, 38(2), 2006.

Optimizing Positional Index Structures for Versioned Document Collections

Jinru He*
Facebook Inc.
1601 Willow Road
Menlo Park, CA, 94025
jihe@fb.com

Torsten Suel
CSE Department
Polytechnic Institute of NYU
Brooklyn, NY, 11201
suel@poly.edu

ABSTRACT

Versioned document collections are collections that contain multiple versions of each document. Important examples are Web archives, Wikipedia and other wikis, or source code and documents maintained in revision control systems. Versioned document collections can become very large, due to the need to retain past versions, but there is also a lot of redundancy between versions that can be exploited. Thus, versioned document collections are usually stored using special differential (delta) compression techniques, and a number of researchers have recently studied how to exploit this redundancy to obtain more succinct full-text index structures.

In this paper, we study index organization and compression techniques for such versioned full-text index structures. In particular, we focus on the case of positional index structures, while most previous work has focused on the non-positional case. Building on earlier work in [32], we propose a framework for indexing and querying in versioned document collections that integrates non-positional and positional indexes to enable fast top-k query processing. Within this framework, we define and study the problem of minimizing positional index size through optimal substring partitioning. Experiments on Wikipedia and web archive data show that our techniques achieve significant reductions in index size over previous work while supporting very fast query processing.

Categories and Subject Descriptors

H.3.3 [**INFORMATION STORAGE AND RETRIEVAL**]: Information Search and Retrieval.

Keywords

Inverted index, index compression, versioned documents, positional index structures, redundancy elimination.

1. INTRODUCTION

Large search engines now have to process thousands of queries per second over tens of billions of documents, resulting in very significant hardware and energy costs. Query processing algorithms in these engines are based on inverted index structures, and a large amount of research over the last decade has focused on how to better organize, compress, and access such indexes. This has contributed to significant increases in algorithmic efficiency that, together with increases in CPU speeds and counts, have allowed the major engines to keep up with the ever increasing user demands [9].

In this paper, we study how to organize and compress inverted index structures. However, we focus here on the case of versioned document collections, i.e., collections where each document is represented by multiple versions. Such versioned document collections occur in a number of search applications, such as search in the web collection of the Internet Archive, consisting of more than 150 billion snapshots (versions) of web pages collected since 1996, or in Wikipedia, which retains the complete edit history of all articles. Other important scenarios are version control systems, document management systems, and versioned file systems, which retain all past versions of the files they manage. The goal in indexing versioned document collections is to build full-text index structures that allow keyword search across all versions.

The primary challenge is that because all past versions are retained, a versioned document collection is much larger than a collection that only keeps the latest version. For example, the English language part of Wikipedia contained about 2.4 million articles in January 2008, but each article had 35 versions on average. An inverted index that simply indexes each version separately would thus be much larger than an index that only considers the latest versions. However, versioned document collections also have very significant redundancies between the different versions, which could be exploited by suitable compression techniques. In fact, there has been a large amount of research on delta (or differential) compression and other redundancy elimination techniques for storage systems and networks (see, e.g., [23, 16, 27, 19, 29, 28]), and many systems now use such techniques to store their collections.

There has also been some amount of work on how to exploit these redundancies to better compress full-text indexes for versioned document collections [4, 7, 32, 15, 5, 11, 12, 8]. Note that this is a different problem and that compression schemes for content do not directly imply how to compress an inverted index, though some basic ideas are useful in both scenarios. Most previous work on indexing has focused on non-positional index structures storing document IDs and maybe term frequencies or quantized impact scores, while only [32, 8] consider positional index structures that also store the locations of term occurrences inside the document versions.

We focus here on such positional index structures. Positional indexes are used by most search engines and other IR systems to enable better ranking and for features such as phrase searches. However, positional indexes are typically about 3 to 5 times larger than non-positional ones. An additional challenge arises in the versioned case, in that a single insertion or deletion of a term produces a shift in the position information for all subsequent terms in the new doc-

*Work performed while this author was a PhD student at Polytechnic Institute of NYU

Permission to make digital or hard copies of all or part of this work for personal or classroom use is granted without fee provided that copies are not made or distributed for profit or commercial advantage and that copies bear this notice and the full citation on the first page. To copy otherwise, or republish, to post on servers or to redistribute to lists, requires prior specific permission and/or a fee.
SIGIR'12, August 12–16, 2012, Portland, Oregon, USA.
Copyright 2012 ACM 978-1-4503-1472-5/12/08... $15.00.

ument version. This problem does not exist in the non-positional case, where we can simply add or remove one posting, and as a result, techniques for the positional case are very different from those for non-positional indexes.

In this paper, we propose improved techniques for positional indexing in versioned document collections, building on the approach described in [32]. In particular, we describe a framework for efficient query processing with non-positional and positional index structures that combines the approaches in [32] and [12]. Within this framework, we study the problem of optimizing positional index size by modeling it as a substring partitioning problem. We then describe heuristic optimization algorithms for this problem that can scale to large document collections. Our experiments on large versioned data sets from Wikipedia and the Internet Archive show significant reductions in index size over [32] and [8] with very fast access speeds.

The remainder of the paper is organized as follows. Next, we provide some technical background and discuss related work. Section 3 summarizes our contributions. Section 4 describes our overall indexing and query processing framework and provides some baseline experimental results. Sections 5 and 6 describe algorithms for document partitioning and our lookup mechanism for accessing position data. Finally, Section 7 provides some concluding remarks.

2. BACKGROUND AND RELATED WORK

We now provide some background and describe related work. We first introduce inverted indexes and index compression methods. Then we discuss previous work on indexing and querying versioned document collections. Finally, we provide background on redundancy elimination using content-dependent partitioning methods.

2.1 Inverted Index Structures

Most search engines and other textual IR systems use inverted index structures to support keyword queries. For a given document collection C, let $w_0, \ldots, w_{m-1}$ be the set of all distinct terms in C. An inverted index I_C for C contains an inverted list I_{w_i} for every i. Each inverted list I_{w_i} is a list of index *postings*, where each posting contains the ID (called docID) of a document containing w_i, and additional information such as the number of occurrences of w_i in d (called frequency), or the locations of each occurrence of w_i in the document (called positions). An index structure is called *positional* if it contains position information, and non-positional otherwise. In this paper, we focus on indexes with docIDs, frequencies, and positions. We refer to [33] for a survey of inverted indexing techniques and applications.

There are several ways inverted index structures can be laid out on disk or in memory. A direct layout would place each posting's docID next to the corresponding frequency and position values, but in practice this is rarely done. Better performance is usually achieved by either keeping docIDs, frequencies, and positions in separate layers with their own access structures, or at least interleaving larger chunks of values (e.g., 128 docIDs followed by their associated frequencies). We will use separate layers for docIDs, frequencies, and positions.

Index compression: The postings in inverted lists are usually sorted by docID and then compressed [33]. To obtain better compression, most approaches store not the actual docIDs, but the differences between consecutive docIDs in the list, called *d-gaps*. The same is also done for different position values within the same document. Of course, this requires summing up these differences again during decompression. To support fast random access, inverted lists (or their individual layers) are often organized into blocks of, say, 128 values, such that each block can be individually accessed and decompressed by searching in an auxiliary array containing the last (or first) docID of each block in uncompressed form.

Many inverted index compression algorithms have been proposed. In our experiments, we use the OPT-PFD method proposed in [31], which belongs to the *PForDelta* [13, 34] family of compression methods. OPT-PFD achieves very high decompression rates (up to more than a billion integers per second and per core on current CPUs). It also achieves a very small compressed index size, particularly for highly clustered data sets. OPT-PFD was previously used to compress non-positional indexes for versioned collections in [11, 12]. Some moderate additional reductions in index size could be obtained by using the Interpolative Coding techniques (IPC) in [22], at the cost of slower position lookups.

Query processing and positions: Very simple ranking functions such as BM25 or the Cosine measure can be implemented by intersecting (conjunctive queries) or merging (disjunctive queries) the inverted lists of the query terms, and then computing a score based on the frequency data in the postings and other information such as document sizes and term frequencies. However, it is known that position data can be used to obtain significantly better result rankings than those achievable using only frequency data (see, e.g., [21]).

Fetching the position data for all postings in the intersection or union of the inverted lists would be quite expensive. Instead, a widely used approach [24] first applies a simple non-positional ranking function (e.g., BM25), and then determines the top-k results under the positional ranking by fetching position data only for the top k' results under the simple function, for some $k' > k$. This significantly reduces the cost of fetching positions, such that positional ranking can be performed in almost the same time as non-positional ranking. One consequence of this approach is that accesses to positional index data are much sparser than accesses to docIDs and frequencies.

2.2 Indexing Versioned Collections

A versioned document collection C is a set of documents $d_0, \ldots, d_{n-1}$ where each document d_i consists of m_i versions $d_i^1, \ldots, d_i^{m_i}$. For simplicity, we assume a linear history of versions; however, our techniques also apply to collections with branches (forks) in the revision history. For a general overview of challenges in building large-scale archival systems for versioned data, see [3, 26]. There is some amount of recent work on indexing and searching in versioned document collections that can be split into three subsets, as follows.

Non-positional versioned indexing: A number of compression methods for non-positional versioned indexes have been proposed [4, 15, 7, 5, 11, 12, 8]. The first work on this problem appears to be the work of Anick and Flynn in [4], which proposes a scheme based on the idea of indexing the delta between consecutive document versions and then adjusting query processing suitably. The last few years have seen several new techniques that achieve much better compression. While our focus in this paper is on positional index structures, our complete query processor also requires an additional non-positional index. This index is used to first compute a simple ranking function that determines which items need to be fetched from our positional structure, as discussed at the end of the previous subsection.

We employ a non-positional index structure proposed in [12], which appears to achieve a very good trade-off between size and speed. This structure is based on a two-level approach, inspired by an earlier idea in [1] for a related but different problem. In a nutshell, the idea is to use two levels of indexing, a small first-level index that only stores whether a term occurs anywhere in a document (plus quantized upper-bound scores for each document in the case of disjunctive queries), and a larger second-level index that stores which versions contain the term and what their frequencies are. Query processing involves accessing the first level to perform filtering, and then selectively those parts of the second level that are still needed.

However, other non-positional structures could also be used with our approach.

Positional versioned indexing: There has been much less work on positional indexes for versioned collections. We note that there are basic differences between the positional and non-positional case. Non-positional indexes can use a set- or bag-oriented approach to model differences between consecutive versions of a document. In the positional case, however, we need to think in terms of common substrings. This way a change in position information due to an insertion or deletion before the start of the substring can be handled by changing the offset of the substring in the document, following an idea first proposed in [20] for index updates. Thus, techniques for non-positional indexes are of limited help for the positional case.

We are aware of two previous approaches for positional indexing of versioned collections [32, 8]. The basic idea in [32] is to use a content-dependent partition technique such as Karp-Rabin fingerprints [18] or *Winnowing* [25] to split document versions into fragments during indexing. Then each unique fragment is only indexed once. This is done by computing for each fragment a hash value that is compared to those of the already indexed fragments. In addition, extra meta data structures are built, and appropriate changes in the query processor made, in order to translate fragment-based matches back to document versions during query processing.

Thus, the performance of the method in [32] depends on finding a high-quality partition of document versions into fragments, such that the total size of the distinct fragments is minimized. In this paper, we follow the approach in [32], and our main goal is to come up with new fragment selection and optimization mechanisms that improve significantly over the Winnowing technique used in [32].

The approaches in [8], on the other hand, are based on very different techniques such as Lempel-Ziv compression, re-pairing, and self-indexing structures. We will provide an experimental comparison with results in [32] and [8] in later sections.

Range and Aggregation Queries: Several recent papers have studied query operations other than standard ranked queries for versioned collections. In particular, [2, 10] looked at how to support temporal range queries over versioned collections, where queries are restricted to a certain interval of time. Also, [30] proposed a query operator called *durable search* that returns documents that consistently rank highly over some time period, thus aggregating scores over multiple versions.

We note here that these operations are orthogonal to our approach, and could be easily integrated into our framework by suitably modifying the non-positional part of the index and query processor. In general, we try to sidestep the question of what the best ranking function and query operations are, and in our experiments we just use a fairly simple ranking function (BM25) in the non-positional part in order to drive the lookups into our positional structure.

2.3 Content-Dependent String Partitioning

A large amount of research in operating systems and networking has focused on how to detect and eliminate redundancies in large data collections; see, e.g., [23, 16, 27, 19, 29, 28]. While the proposed methods utilize a number of interesting algorithmic techniques, one technique, *content-dependent string partitioning*, is of particular interest to us here.

In a nutshell, the goal is to divide each file into substrings (or fragments) such that files that contain a lot of similarity have a lot of common substrings. Note that if we simply split files into fixed-size fragments, we might not see any common fragments at all even if the files differ by only a single insertion or deletion at the beginning of the file, due to misalignments of the fragment boundaries in the files. Thus, the goal is to come up with partitioning methods that are robust to small changes due to insertions and deletions, and that can be applied independently on the various files, which might in fact be located on different machines.

Several approaches have been proposed in the literature which all use hash values on small local substrings to determine fragment boundaries. This means that any long common substrings in different files (or versions) are partitioned in the same way, resulting in common fragments. The first and best known partitioning technique is based on Karp-Rabin (KR) fingerprints [18], and works as follows: We first slide a window of some size c through the file and compute a hash value $h(s)$ for each substring s of length c. We then declare a fragment boundary before any substring s such that $h(s)$ is $x \, mod \, y$ for some fixed choice of x and y. Two more recent techniques, the Winnowing (WIN) approach in [25] and the 2-way Min (2MIN) approach in [29], follow the same idea of hashing substrings of fixed size, but use different conditions for defining fragment boundaries.

While all three approaches are used in the literature, experimental results suggest that 2MIN [29] results in more (and overall longer) common substrings, thus identifying more redundancy. The technique works as follows: As before, we compute hash values for all substrings of some fixed size c, say $c = 10$ or $c = 20$. This gives us an array of integer hash values $h[0 \cdots n-c]$. We then set a fragment boundary before position i in the input file if $h[i]$ is strictly smaller than all other $h[j]$ with $i-w \leq j < i+w$ for some fixed w that we select. In other words, we set a boundary wherever the hash value is the smallest value within a neighborhood of radius w. This results in an average fragment size of about $2w$. The process is illustrated in Figure1:

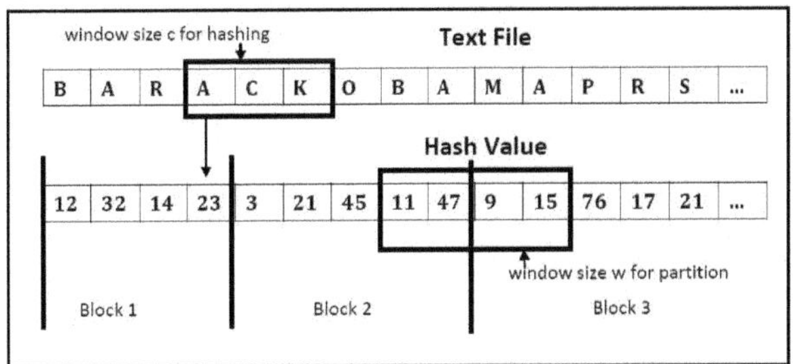

Figure 1: Example of the 2MIN file partition techniques in [29]. A small window of size $c = 3$ moves over the input file (top) to create an array of hash value (bottom). Then we select fragment boundaries using $w = 2$.

3. OUR CONTRIBUTIONS

In this paper, we study the problem of organizing and compressing positional index structures for versioned collections. In particular, our main contributions are as follows:

- We describe a complete framework for full-text indexing and querying in versioned document collections. This framework combines ideas from [32] and [12], and enables fast top-k query processing with succinct index structures.
- We study the problem of finding good partitionings of document versions into fragments. Our methods differ from strictly local methods such as KR, WIN, and 2MIN in that we can exploit knowledge of the edit history of a document.
- We describe a multi-level optimization approach for finding good partitionings that scales to very large data sets.
- Finally, we perform an experimental evaluation of our approach based on large document collections from Wikipedia and the Internet Archive. The results show significant reductions in index size over previous work while maintaining very fast query processing.

4. VERSIONED INDEXING FRAMEWORK

We now describe our general framework for indexing and querying versioned document collections. The framework further develops earlier ideas in [32], and combines them with ideas for the non-positional case in [12]. We first give a high-level description of our positional indexing approach, and then show how to combine positional and non-positional indexes to support query processing. Finally, we provide some experimental results for several baseline methods.

In the following, we use the term *fragment* to refer to any substring generated by some partitioning of the document versions, based on the content-dependent partitioning schemes in Subsection 2.3 or other techniques. All our partitioning schemes and fragments respect word boundaries, such that no word is cut in the middle; this is done by first replacing words with word IDs, and then hashing each sequence of c word IDs. Each occurrence of a fragment f is called an application of f. We assume that each document is identified by a *docID*, each version of a document by a *vID* (which could consist of a docID and a version number), and each fragment by a *fragID*.

4.1 Positional Index Structure

Now we describe our positional index structure for versioned document collections.

Positional indexing process: We first describe the indexing process assuming that we directly apply one of the content-dependent partitioning techniques in section 2.3, as in [32]; we later discuss how to accommodate the new partitioning schemes used in this paper. To build the positional index, we partition each new version of a document into fragments. For each fragment, we then compute an MD5 hash over the entire fragment, and check a table to see if the same fragment was previously encountered in the same document. If the fragment has not occurred before, we assign it a new fragID, and then index the fragment as if it were a separate document, creating postings consisting of a fragID and the position of a term within the fragment. Note that there is no frequency stored in the postings since most such frequencies are 1; it is more efficient to repeat the fragID in several postings if needed, at least after index compression. The resulting posting lists are ordered by fragID, where fragments in the same document are assigned a common range of fragIDs. The fragment-based position index is then compressed using standard techniques. In particular, we use OPT-PFD on blocks of 128 values for both fragIDs and positions within fragments, thus allowing efficient random lookups into the lists.

Meta data structures: To support positional lookups on this index structure, we need additional data structures that allow us to map between positions in fragments and positions in document versions. Thus, we maintain a *version/frag table* that stores, for each version, the number of fragment applications in the version and the list of fragIDs in the order in which the fragments occur in the version. This table is compressed using suitable techniques, as described later. In addition, we store the size of each fragment (in words) in a separate *frag size table*. Note that these two tables, which we call meta data, are kept completely in main memory during query execution.

All the major structures are shown in Figure 2. Our meta data structures are similar to, but different from, those described in [32]. Note that we are not showing the table of fragment hashes mentioned earlier. The reason is that this table is only useful for index updates when directly applying the content-dependent partitioning schemes in Subsection 2.3. Our goal in later sections is to come up with new partitioning schemes that exploit the history of a document for better compression; however, the update scheme based on a hash table will not apply in this case anymore. We discuss this issue later.

Performing position lookups: Accesses to the positional index structure are in the form of lookups containing a term and a vID, asking for the positions of all occurrences of the term in a version. A lookup is performed by first obtaining the range of fragIDs assigned to the document – recall that each document has its own contiguous range of fragIDs, though this is not true for each version. Then we access the inverted lists to get all fragIDs within this range that contain the term. Next, we access the version/frag table and fetch and uncompress the entry for the version. Finally, we use this information to check which fragIDs returned by the index occur in the requested version, and for those that do, we translate the position within the fragment back to a position within the version.

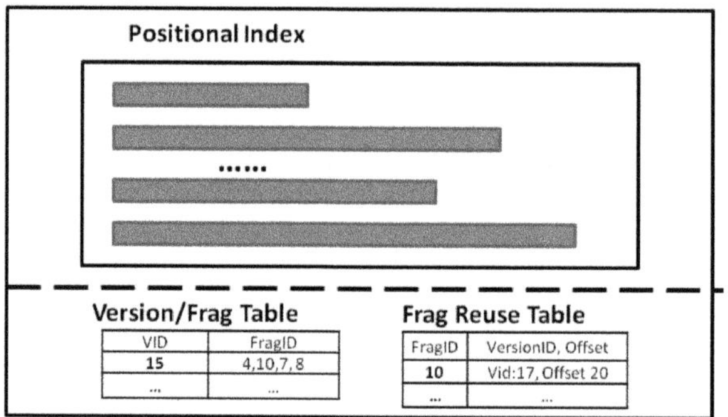

Figure 2: Major data structures in the positional index, including the inverted lists (top) and the meta data (bottom).

Note that if several versions of the same document need to be looked up for the same term, we can do this faster by passing a list of vIDs and performing only one lookup into the inverted list. Finally, when accessing several inverted lists for the same vID (as would happen as part of a multi-term query), we could try to fetch and uncompress the corresponding entry in the version/frag table only once, but the benefits of this are very small.

4.2 Query Processing

Next we describe how to integrate the positional index structure into our overall framework for positional query processing over versioned document collections. For this, we add a non-positional index structure. In particular, we implemented a two-level index structure called 2R-MSA described in [12], which supports fast ranked top-k queries under simple non-positional ranking functions such as BM25. The resulting structure is sketched in Figure 3, showing the two levels of the non-positional index on the left, and the positional index and meta data on the right.

Note that only the meta data needs to be kept in memory during query processing, while all layers of the inverted lists can be kept on disk or partially cached in main memory using any state-of-the-art caching policy. Also, the first-level, second-level, and positional inverted lists for each term are actually laid out next to each other on disk, such that all three structures can be fetched with a single disk seek. Finally, we note that in principle the non-positional index is not even required to perform query processing, as all necessary information is also contained in the positional index and meta data. However, each such query would take hundreds of ms to complete, while the non-positional two-level index (which is much smaller than the positional index) accelerates it to a few ms.

Using this setup, a top-k keyword query for a positional ranking function is executed by first issuing the query to the non-positional index structures to return the top k' results (vIDs) for some $k' > k$. This is done by using DAAT query processing over the first level, and lookups into the second level, as described in [12]. In the second stage, we perform lookups into the positional index for these k' results, and then use the positional data to rerank the results and return the top k results.

Note that there is a natural trade-off between meta data size and positional index size that is present in both our work here and [32].

Basically, using smaller fragments results in more meta data but also more common fragments between versions and thus (up to a point) a smaller index. Our goal in this paper is to obtain the best trade-off between meta data and index size. A smaller meta data size means that less memory is needed to store this data, and that more main memory is available for caching the other index data, an issue that we will explore later.

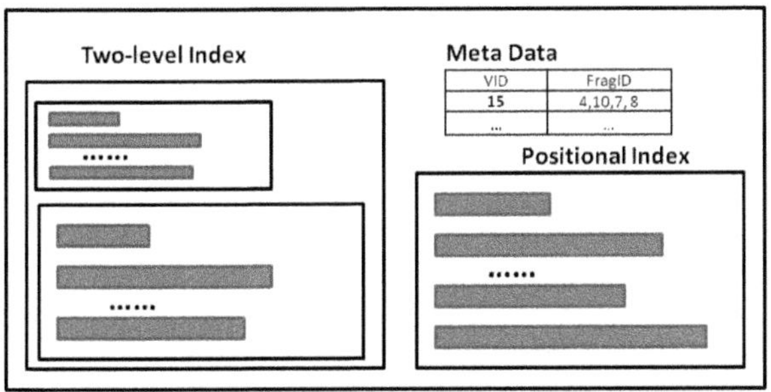

Figure 3: Major data structures in our indexing framework.

One feature of our framework is that it separates positional and non-positional query processing issues. Thus, for example, the decision on whether to perform disjunctive or conjunctive query processing only impacts query processing in the non-positional part. It is also easy to support temporal range queries by applying the techniques in [10] in the non-positional index. Aggregate operations such as the durable search operator in [30] can also be handled in the first level. Finally, when performing searches in versioned document collections, it is often desirable to limit the number of results from the same document that are returned, say, returning only the highest-scoring version of each document. This is also easy to do in our setup.

4.3 Preliminary Experimental Results

In this section, we first describe the data sets used in this paper. Then we present some preliminary experimental results comparing existing approaches, thus setting a baseline over which to improve in subsequent sections.

Data sets: We use a versioned document collection from Wikipedia (WIKI) and a data set from the Internet Archive. The Wikipedia data consists of 240,000 distinct documents with on average 35 versions per document. The documents were selected as a 10% random sample from a complete snapshot of the English language Wikipedia from Jan 2001 to Jan 2008. The Internet Archive data consists of 1.06 million documents from the Irish web domain collected between 1996 to 2006. Only documents with at least 10 distinct versions were selected, and each document has 15 versions on average. Similar data sets were also used in [30, 12, 8].

Experimental results: We now present preliminary experimental results on our data sets. We compare three basic approaches, the one in [32] (ZS), the best approach in [8] based on VByte and LZMA (CFMN), and a trivial baseline where all versions are treated as separate documents (no sharing). For the ZS approach, we explore three different content-dependent partitioning techniques: KR, WIN (used in [32]), and 2MIN.

We set the parameter $w = 20$ for the 2MIN version of ZS, resulting in a total of $348,548,098$ fragment applications. To enable a fair comparison with ZS-KR and ZS-WIN, we selected parameters for those methods such that they result in approximately the same number of applications and the same meta data size. For CFMN, we report the best result presented in [8]. CFMN and the trivial baseline do not have a distinction between meta data and the actual index.

Table 1 shows the index size, meta data size (if applicable), total index size, and number of indexed positions for each method, for the WIKI data set. All methods except CFMN use OPT-PFD to compress the positional index. As we see, all methods achieve significant improvements over the trivial baseline. Both ZS-WIN (used in [32] and ZS-2MIN) achieve a smaller size than CFMN, with ZS-2MIN outperforming ZS-WIN by about 10%. Surprisingly, ZS-KR is much worse than the other methods, showing that the choice of content-dependent partitioning technique can make a big difference in practice.

	index	meta	total	millions of positions
No sharing	19053	-	-	14404
ZS-KR	2762	96	2858	1880
ZS-WIN [32]	1479	96	1575	971
ZS-2MIN	1324	96	1420	867
CFMN [8]	-	-	1954	-

Table 1: Comparison of resulting index sizes for different baseline methods on the Wikipedia data. Shown from left to right are index size, meta data size, and total index size in MB, and the number of positions indexed in millions.

	index	meta	total	millions of positions
No sharing	13026	-	13026	9885
ZS-KR	4820	84	4904	3391
ZS-WIN [32]	3708	84	3792	2422
ZS-2MIN	3618	84	3702	2386

Table 2: Comparison of resulting index sizes for different baseline methods on the Internet Archive data set. Shown from left to right are index size, meta data size, and total index size in MB, and the number of positions indexed in millions.

Table 2 shows results for the Internet Archive data set. For this data set, no results for CFMN were available. Here, the reduction in size over the trivial baseline is smaller but still substantial (up to a factor of 3.6). This is probably because the average number of versions per document is smaller than for Wikipedia. Again, ZS-2MIN achieves the smallest index size of all. Thus in the remainder of the paper, we use ZS-2MIN as the baseline over which we need to improve.

5. IMPROVED PARTITIONING METHODS

In this section, we describe new algorithms for selecting good fragments, i.e., for partitioning versions into substrings in a way that obtains a good trade-off between index and meta data size.

We start by defining the problem more formally. To model index size, we assume (for now) that it is proportional in the number of positions that are indexed, that is, the sum of the sizes of all distinct fragments that are created in the partitioning. On the other hand, the size of the meta data is proportional to the total number of fragment applications. This is because the meta data size is dominated by the version/frag table, which needs to store at least one fragID for each application. Note that fragments in our setup are only reused within versions of a single document, and thus we perform fragment selection separately in each document. For a document d with versions $d^1, \ldots, d^m$, the problem of minimizing index size given an upper bound on meta data size can be formulated as follows:

Problem: Given strings $d^1, \ldots, d^m$ and an integer t, find a set of strings F minimizing $\sum_{f \in F} len(f)$ such that every d^i can be partitioned into a multiset of substrings C^i with $\sum_i |C^i| \leq t$ and $set(C^i) \subset F$.[1]

The problem discussed here is similar to the *Minimum Substring Cover Problem* studied by Hermelin et al. [14], which was motivated by applications in Computational Biology and Formal Language Theory. The main difference is that in [14] the bound t is on the size of each C^i, rather than the sum of the sizes. This changes the structure of the problem, and thus the algorithms in [14] and their proof of NP Completeness do not extend to our case. (We con-

[1] $set(C^i)$ is the set corresponding to multiset C^i.

jecture that our problem is also NP Complete, but are still working on a proof.)

Note that the numbers of postings and fragment applications do not provide a precise model for the sizes of the index and meta data structures, respectively. The meta data contains an additional frag size table that is not accounted for in this model, and both structures are compressed using a technique (OPT-PFD) that defies easy analysis. However, we found that this simplistic model is usually good enough to guide our optimization methods towards good solutions (though we introduce a slightly refined model later).

In the following subsections, we describe several methods for finding good partitionings via careful selection of fragments, given a limitation on the number of fragment applications. Most of our methods follow the same overall structure, consisting of several levels of optimization. On the top level, we need to decide how much of the allowed meta data size (or number of applications) should be allocated to each document, and on the lower level we optimize fragment selection in each document given a bound on the number of applications. This fragment selection method greedily selects fragments from a pool of candidate fragments, and the main overall challenge is how to generate a limited-size pool of promising candidate fragments, given that putting all possible substrings into the pool is not a feasible option. Due to space constraints we can only sketch some of the methods.

The main idea motivating our work here is that standard content-dependent partitioning techniques such as KR, WIN, and 2MIN choose boundaries using only local information, and are thus blind to version history. In fact, this is a major advantage in many applications, where boundaries have to be chosen independently, e.g., for similar files located on different machines. But in our case, we have all the different versions available during indexing, and thus we should be able to select better fragments by looking beyond a single version and peeking into earlier and later versions of the same document. While this seems intuitive, it turns out to be quite challenging to really outperform the results obtained by just applying 2MIN to the approach in [32].

5.1 A Simple Improvement

We start out with a simple improvement over ZS-2MIN that demonstrates some of the issues we have to address. Recall that the 2MIN partitioning uses a parameter w that determines the average fragment size. However, it is not obvious what the best choice of w is, as this depends on the amount of redundancy between different versions. More significantly, we should not expect the best overall trade-off from using the same parameter w for all documents – we may get much better results by using a smaller w for some documents and a larger for others.

ZS-MF: This leads to the first improved heuristic, ZS-MF. We start out by partitioning every document several times using 2MIN with different parameters w, and storing the number of postings generated and the number of fragment applications for each w. This results in a small table such as Table 3 showing a trade-off between postings and fragment applications. We generate such a table for each document in the collection.

w	# of frag. applications	# of dist. frags	# of positions
no sharing	-	-	68906
50	4832	483	51580
42	5518	509	46112
34	6641	552	41056
26	9003	608	34167
18	12538	713	27762
10	21844	956	21420

Table 3: An example of an actual position/meta data trade-off table for a document, where w is varied from 10 to 50.

Note that there is no obvious best choice for w based on the above table, as the best choice depends on choices available in other documents. To deal with this, we optimize across all different documents as follows. We first select in all documents the largest value of w. If this already results in more applications than the global budget, then we would fail, so we make sure to choose a large enough maximum value for w. Now we repeatedly select one document and decrease its w value, resulting in an increase in the number of applications but a decrease in index size, until we reach the limit for the number of applications. In fact, we greedily select the document, and the new smaller value of w, that gives us the largest benefit, defined as the ratio of index size decrease and meta data increase.

To do this, we initialize a heap structure containing an entry for every possible choice of document and new value of w. Elements in the heap are organized by their benefit. Now we repeatedly extract the element with the largest benefit, update our overall counts of fragment applications and positions, and then update any other elements in the heap whose benefit is changed due to our choice. In the example table above, if we decrease w from 50 to 34, we would delete the entry for $w = 42$ from the heap, and update the benefits of $w = 26$, $w = 18$, and $w = 10$ to reflect the new starting point $w = 34$. (Only entries for the same document need to be deleted or updated.) We continue this process until we have exhausted our fragment application budget.

The simple heuristic used in ZS-MF already gives measurable improvements over ZS-2MIN, as we will see in the later experimental results. Note that the heap-based optimization across different documents using trade-off tables is also used in all our subsequent algorithms. Finally, we note that partitioning files using many different values of w does not have to be expensive at all, due to an interesting property of the 2MIN partitioning scheme. In particular, any boundary selected using w will also be a boundary for any $w' < w$, fragments obtained using different values of w form a hierarchical partitioning, and we can compute the boundaries for all possible values of w in a single computation using some simple data structures.

5.2 Hierarchical Fragment Selection

We now present the next set of heuristics for further improvements. While the approach in the previous subsection tried different values of w, in the end we selected one single value of w in each document. However, one would expect that updates between versions are not uniformly distributed over files, and that it might be beneficial to use different fragment sizes in different parts of the file (e.g., smaller or larger fragments at the start or end of the file, or in earlier or later versions). In fact, a similar idea was used in [17] in the context of removing redundancy in network transmissions.

Implementing this requires a new mechanism that allows us to select a mix of fragments of different sizes. Our high-level approach for this is as follows: We start out by generating a large pool of candidate fragments for each document. Then we greedily select good fragments from the pool until all versions are completely covered, as discussed further below. The main problem is how to create a good candidate pool. We propose two simple approaches for this:

ZS-MFS: We use 2MIN partitioning in order to define a hierarchical partitioning, by varying w from a small value w_0 to some maximum value, and defining the candidate pool as containing all fragments on all the levels. We note that this number is linear in the number of bottom-level fragments.

ZS-MOF: This approach attempts to create a larger and richer candidate pool by using a hierarchy that contains additional partially overlapping fragments on some levels. In particular, we first select all fragments for the smallest value of w_0. Then we add to the pool new artificial fragments consisting of any consecutive k fragments from the bottom level, for $k = 2, 3, 4$ up to some k_{max}. Above this level, we simply continue as in ZS-MFS. Thus, in ZS-MOF we put all candidate fragments from ZS-MFS into the pool, and then add additional overlapping (shifted) fragments at the lower levels. As we will see, in practice $k_{max} = 3$ or 4 is enough, and thus the candidate pool does not get overly large. (We also tried other schemes for creating larger candidate pools of overlapping fragments, but this simple approach did almost as well as the best.)

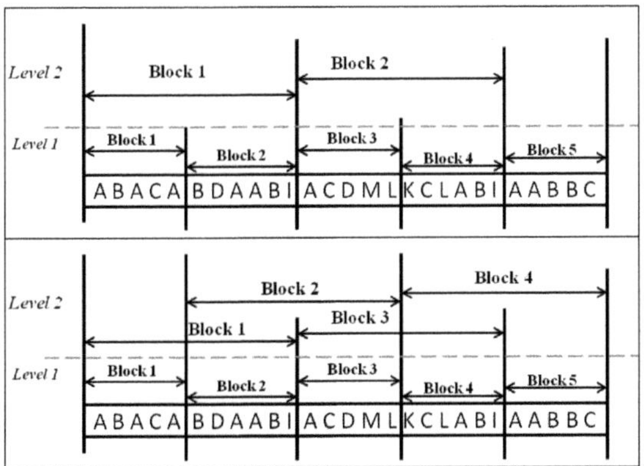

Figure 4: Example of the candidate fragments considered in ZS-MFS (top) and ZS-MOF (bottom), showing only the bottom two layers. As shown, ZS-MOF adds additional overlapping fragments in Level 2. Note that we use characters instead of word IDs for the underlying terms, to simplify the figure.

The ZS-MFS and ZS-MOF schemes are illustrated in Figure 4. We now describe how to select fragments from the candidate pools. We first insert all fragments in the pool into a heap, organized by a fragment score s, and then greedily select the fragments with the highest scores from this heap. To define the score s, we first need to introduce three other values for each fragment:

- the coverage $c = l \times m$ where m is the number of times the fragment occurs in the document AFTER removing all occurrences that intersect with previously chosen fragments.
- the index cost, which we define as $i_c = 1.0$ (one unit per position value).
- the meta data cost, which we define as $m_c = 1.0 + z \times m$ for some constant z (we choose $z = 1.0$).

Then the score of a fragment is defined as $s = c/(i_c + x \times m_c)$. Here, the value x determines how much we value meta data size versus index size, and running the optimization with a larger x results in a solution with a smaller meta data size. Thus, by trying several different values of x we can again get a trade-off table as in ZS-MF, and then run a global optimization across documents as before.

Note that after each extraction of a fragment from the heap, we need to update the s-scores of all other fragments that overlap the chosen fragment somewhere in some version of the document. This is done by keeping for each fragment a list of conflicting (overlapping) other fragments and then updating only these after an extraction. The overall problem of selecting the fragments given a candidate pool and a value x is sketched in Algorithm 1, with some details omitted due to space constraints:

Algorithm 1 optimize(frags, x)

```
Output: results
  results ← ∅;
  h ← ∅;
  for i = 0 to frags.size() do
    frags[i].score = getScore(frags[i], x);
    h.push(frags[i]);
  end for
  while not (h.empty()) do
    f ← h.pop();
    results.insert(f);
    flist ← findConflictFragments(f);
    for i = 0 to frags.size() do
      flists[i].count ← flists[i].count−1;
      if flists[i].count = 0 then
        h.remove(flists[i]);
      else
        /* update count and score for flists[i] in the h */
        flists[i].score = updateScore(flists[i], x);
        h.update(flists[i]);
      end if
    end for
  end while
  return results
```

5.3 Frequency-Based Partitioning

In the previous subsection, we explained how to obtain better partitionings by creating a suitable pool of candidate fragments and then greedily selecting from this pool. For efficiency reasons, the size of the pool had to be limited; thus it is not feasible to place all substrings of all sizes occurring anywhere in the document into the pool, as some documents are quite large. Instead, we attempted to create sparse but rich enough sets of fragments for the pool.

However, all of the candidate fragments were derived from a 2MIN-based partitioning, and all the fragment boundaries occur as boundaries in 2MIN for some w. But there is really no reason to believe that a random hash function (as used in 2MIN) is very good as picking exactly the right fragment boundaries. Thus, given that we can look at the entire history of the document, can we come up with a better and different way to determine fragment boundaries?

In this subsection, we describe such a way. We note that we still take the general approach from the previous subsections. Thus, we have a candidate pool from which fragments are greedily selected based on their s-score, and we also have the global optimization across documents using the trade-off tables.

Consider the first step in 2MIN partitioning, as described in Subsection 2.3, where we slide a window of some size c over a file and compute a hash value for each window. Now however, instead of choosing cuts based on this hash value, we choose cuts based on the frequency (multiplicity) of the hash value which, ignoring collisions, is equal to the number of times this substring of size c occurs in entire document. In particular, we place a cut whenever we see a large change in this frequency from one window position to the next. In particular, when we see a sharp increase, we use the left boundary of the current window to make a cut, and when we see a sharp decrease we use the right boundary of the previous window for the cut.

The intuition for this is quite simple: A high frequency indicates that the content is shared by many versions and thus good material for fragment candidates, while a low frequency indicates content that had a much shorter lifetime. Placing boundaries this way should thus allow us to choose fragments of maximum size that are undisturbed by edits, or more informally, we identify and cut out the bad parts that limit the number of applications that a fragment sees. Also, we have a good chance of getting consistent cuts in different versions, avoiding misalignment problems as discussed in Subsection 2.3 in the context of fixed-size blocks.

To implement this, we need to add two details. First, we need to define when a difference in frequency is significant enough to merit placing a cut; this is determined by a value x. Second, we need a safety valve for cases when the frequency-based approach creates some very large fragments. We do this by using 2MIN to cut any fragment of size greater than some value y, say $y = 100$ or more.

This gives us a partitioning of the versions into basic fragments. We now create additional candidate fragments as in ZS-MFS and

ZS-MOF, by combining several consecutive base fragments into larger candidate fragments. This gives us our candidate pool, and then the rest of the method is as before. We refer to the resulting method as ZS-FREQ.

5.4 Experimental Results

We now evaluate the different partitioning schemes by looking at the resulting index sizes and index construction costs. We compare the four new methods, ZS-MF, ZS-MFS, ZS-MOF, and ZS-FREQ, and the ZS-2MIN method from Section 4. As before, we use OPT-PFD to compress the resulting positional indexes.

Overview of results: We start with the positional index size, total number of positions, and total number of distinct fragments for the various methods, shown in Table 4. To allow a fair comparison, we set the target budget for fragment applications as the number of fragment applications in ZS-2MIN for $w = 20$. The numbers given are for the best choices of various parameters; we investigate some of these choices later. We can make the following observations: First, all methods achieve decreases in total index size and in the number of positions compared to ZS-2MIN. The best result is obtained by ZS-FREQ, which reduces index size by about 22% over ZS-2MIN, followed by ZS-MOF, ZS-MFS and ZS-MF. Second, the total number of distinct fragments is also reduced in these methods. Since the number of fragment applications is fixed, this means that the produced fragments are used more frequently on average (which is of course the whole point).

	index	meta	total size	positions	distinct frags
ZS-2MIN	1324	96	1420	867	20.3
ZS-MF	1238	96	1334	771	18.9
ZS-MFS	1121	97	1218	702	16.7
ZS-MOF	1089	97	1186	661	15.8
ZS-FREQ	1035	97	1133	623	15.4

Table 4: Comparison of the different partitioning methods on the Wikipedia data. Shown from left to right are the index size, meta data size, and total index size in MB, and the total number of positions and distinct fragments in millions.

In Table 5, we show results for selected methods on the Internet Archive data. As before, the reductions in size are more limited, due to the smaller number of versions per document. We observe that ZS-FREQ achieves a roughly 18% smaller index size than ZS-2MIN.

	index	meta	total size	positions	distinct frags
ZS-2MIN	3618	85	3703	2386	55.6
ZS-MOF	3125	86	3211	2060	40.8
ZS-FREQ	2971	86	3057	1893	38.2

Table 5: Comparison of selected partitioning methods on the Internet Archive data.

In Table 6, we show the time needed to build the index structures for the trivial baseline, ZS-2MIN, and ZS-FREQ. All runs were performed on a single core of an Intel Xeon E5520 processor running at 2.26 Ghz, using the Wikipedia data with a total of about 8 million versions and about 19 billion term occurrences. We divide the index construction into three phases: First, the time for selecting good fragments; this applies only to ZS-FREQ (and the other new techniques). Second, the time for parsing and creating postings, which in the case of ZS-2MIN also includes the cost of running the 2MIN partitioning (for ZS-FREQ, this cost is mostly included in the time for the first phase). Third, the cost of merging the postings into a final index.

We see that ZS-FREQ spends most of its time in the selection phase, which is not surprising. Most of this time is spent inside the **optimize()** algorithm, and we expect this could be brought down somewhat through additional optimizations. We note that the time for ZS-MOF and ZF-MFS is similar to that of ZS-FREQ, while that for ZS-MF is closer to ZS-2MIN. ZS-2MIN spends a lot of time in the 2MIN partitioning code, but then is much faster than the trivial baseline during the merge, as much less position data needs to be processed in this phase.

	No sharing	ZS-2MIN	ZS-FREQ
Selection	-	-	18hours
Parsing	93 mins	2hours 40mins	10mins
Merging	65 mins	5 mins	5mins
Total	2hours 38 mins	2hours 45mins	18hours 15 mins

Table 6: Index construction time for different algorithms on the Wikipedia data.

Choosing parameters: Next, we present results on how to tune the various parameters. In Figure 5, we show the trade-off between positional index size and meta data size for the various methods on Wikipedia. To obtain the results, we first use ZS-2MIN with window sizes ranging from 20 to 40. Then we run the other algorithms using the number of fragment applications from ZS-2MIN as an upper bound. We see from Figure 5 that as the meta data size increases, positional index size decreases for all methods, as expected. Our new partitioning methods all achieve a better trade-off than ZS-2MIN, with ZS-FREQ consistently achieving the best results. We note that even the largest meta data size chosen, about 97 MB for our 10% data set, would result in a meta data size of slightly less than 1 GB on the complete Wikipedia data of 2.4 million articles and over 80 million versions. Keeping this amount of data in main memory is clearly feasible on many current systems.

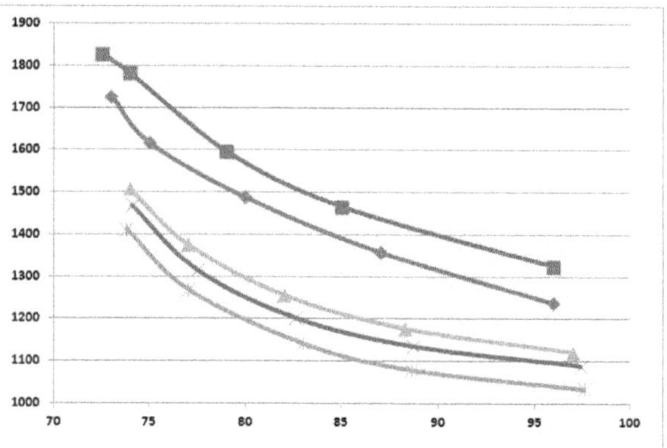

Figure 5: Trade-off between index and meta data size for the various algorithms on the Wikipedia data. The x-axis shows the compressed meta data size in MB, while the the y-axis shows the positional index size in MB.

Next, we investigate some more parameter choices. For the ZS-MOF method, we had to choose a parameter k_{max} that limits how many levels of overlapping fragments are put into the candidate pool, and we suggested that a value of 3 or 4 is sufficient. This issue is explored in Figure 6, where we show the index size and index construction time of ZS-MOF for different choices of k_{max}. For this data, we used a subset of only 1% of Wikipedia (i.e., 10% of our set), as these runs were quite time consuming. We see that index construction time increases with k_{max}, but index size is already close to optimal for $k_{max} = 3$.

Next, Figure 7 shows the impact of choosing different values for the x (left) and y (right) parameter in ZS-FREQ. These experiments were again run on a 1% subset due to time constraints. In both charts, we have the meta data size in MB on the x-axis, and the index size in MB on the y-axis. We see that choices of $x = 15$ and $y = 100$ appear to get good results over the entire range.

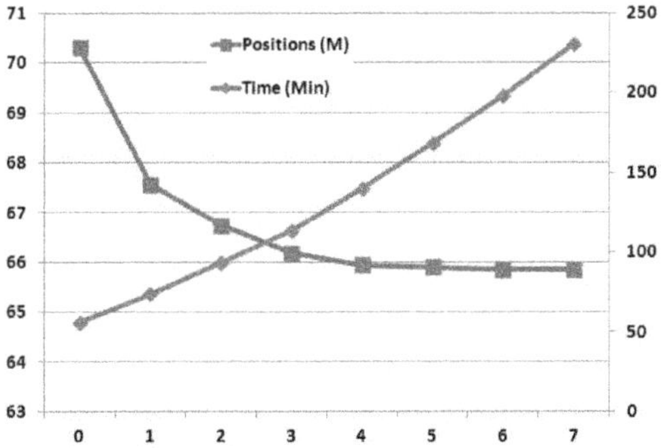

Figure 6: Index size and index construction time for ZS-MOF with different values of k_{max}, on a sample of the Wikipedia data. The y-axis on the left shows the index size in MB, and the y-axis on the right shows the index construction time in minutes.

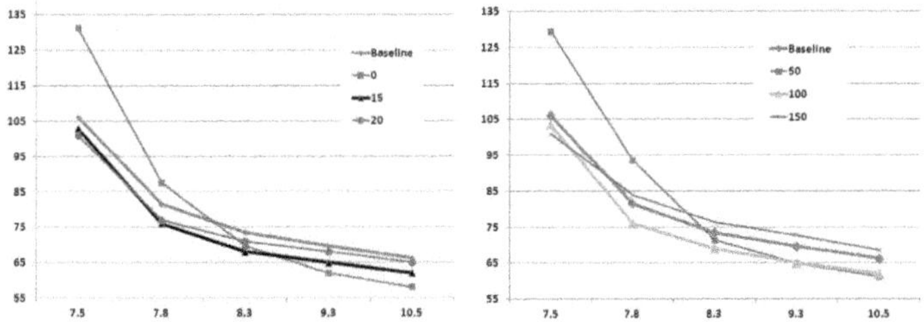

Figure 7: Selecting parameters x and y for the ZS-FREQ method.

6. QUERY PROCESSING

In this section, we describe how to support fast positional lookups during query processing, and then provide some experimental results.

Position lookups: As discussed in Section 4, we assume that a query first executes a simple ranking operation on a non-positional index structure. Afterwards, position lookups are performed for a limited number (a few hundred or a thousand) of the most promising documents that were returned. This means that position lookups are fairly sparse and essentially random accesses into the positional lists. (However, given the characteristics of hard disks, we still have to fetch the entire position list into main memory if it is not cached, as skips in the accesses are rarely large enough to justify extra disk seeks.)

Recall the version/frag table, which is assumed to be held in memory. Then a lookup for the positions of a term within a version consists of three steps: (1) determining the range of the fragIDs assigned to a document, (2) fetching all position data for this range from the position list for this term, and (3) fetching the entry for the version from the version/frag table and using that information plus the data from the frag size table to translate positions within fragments into positions within the version. When performing lookups for several versions of the same document, all vIDs are passed to the lookup mechanism in one call, enabling faster batch processing of these lookups.

The range of fragIDs assigned to a document can be stored in a simple table with one entry per document containing a base fragID for this document. The frag size table is also easily stored as an array of unsigned chars (if fragments are of size at most 256) or shorts otherwise. Some more work is needed to store and compress the version/frag table, which is the largest of the structures. Here, we store the first fragID of each version as an offset from the base fragID of the document, and each subsequent fragID as a gap from the previous fragID (with an additional bit for the sign of the gap). These values are then organized in blocks of 128 and compressed using OPT-PFD, with an appropriate lookup structure that allows fetching of the list of fragIDs for a particular version. A further improvement exploits the fact that the list of fragIDs in consecutive versions is often very similar, by using the list of the preceding version as a reference for encoding the next list (similar to what is commonly done to compress adjacency lists in web graphs [6]). Overall, this results in significant size reductions that are crucial for a good trade-off between meta data and index size.

Lookup performance: We present some performance results for position lookups in Table 7. The results are based on the ZS-FREQ method, but similar numbers hold for all partitioning methods since lookup costs are fairly insensitive to the quality of the partitioning. In the results, we exclude the cost of the initial traversal of the non-positional index, and only count the costs of the positional lookups.

From top to bottom, Table 7 shows the number of positions per query that are returned, the time for finding the first fragID in the relevant fragID range in the index, the time for decoding index data, the time for translating fragment positions back into version positions, and the total time, all in ms per query. Finally, at the bottom we see the cost per position fetched, in microseconds. This is for the case where we allow each document to be represented by multiple versions in the top-k results. As we see, lookups are quite efficient, and costs are around 2.5 ms when we fetch positions for the top-1000 results returned by the non-positional index.

Table 8 shows how lookup times increase as we limit the number of versions per document that are allowed in the top-k results. The motivation for this is that the user may not be interested in receiving 10 results that are all different versions of the same document, and thus a query processor may decide to limit the number of versions from the same document (similar to the way in which search engines may limit the number of results from the same web site). We would expect this to result in slower lookups into our structure as there is less access locality, and less opportunity for batching accesses as discussed. However, even when fetching position information for 1000 versions from 1000 distinct documents, costs are moderate at about 6.44 ms per query.

	Top-10	Top-100	Top-1000
# of decoded positions	130	306	2700
Seek time	0.1	0.24	1.87
Decode time	0.03	0.08	0.29
Translation time	0.02	0.03	0.38
Total time	0.15	0.35	2.54
Cost per position in us	1.2	1.1	0.9

Table 7: Performance of our positional lookup mechanisms. All times are in ms per query, except for the cost per position which is in microseconds.

	Top-10	Top-100	Top-1000
1	0.22	0.92	6.44
5	0.21	0.80	6.25
10	0.15	0.65	5.56
20	0.15	0.51	4.83
40	0.15	0.41	3.79
60	0.15	0.38	2.78
no limit	0.15	0.35	2.54

Table 8: Performance of our positional lookup mechanisms when we limit the number of versions per document allowed in the top-k, in ms per query.

Impact of caching: In the above experiments, we assumed that the positional index is in main memory. We also performed experiments in a scenario where the index resides on disk but is partially cached in main memory, as is the case in many real systems. As expected, all methods benefited significantly from caching, with ZS-FREQ again outperforming the other methods.

7. CONCLUSIONS

In this paper, we have studied how to build succinct positional full-text index structures for versioned document collections. We described a general framework for indexing and querying based on document partitioning, and then proposed new techniques for selecting good partitionings. Our experimental results showed that the proposed methods achieve significant reductions in index size while also supporting very fast query processing.

There are a number of open issues that we are trying to resolve. First, we believe that additional refinements in the ZS-FREQ approach could result in additional index size decreases and much faster index building methods. The current approach with its reliance on the x and y parameters seems somewhat ad-hoc. Second, we are looking at how to best update our structures. One of the benefits of the approach in [32] was that updates could be handled easily through use of a hash table mechanism, but this breaks down with the new partitioning techniques. Part of this is fundamental: Since our goal is to exploit the entire history of a document, any incremental updates are bound to eventually degrade the performance of the scheme. However, we believe that some of these drawbacks can be ameliorated.

Acknowledgments

This research was supported by NSF Grant IIS-0803605 "Efficient and Effective Search Services over Archival Webs", and by a grant from Google. We also thank the Internet Archive for providing access to the Ireland data set.

8. REFERENCES

[1] I. Altingovde, E. Demir, F. Can, and O. Ulusoy. Incremental cluster-based retrieval using compressed cluster-skipping inverted files. *ACM Trans. on Information Systems*, 26(3), June 2008.

[2] A. Anand, S. Bedathur, K. Berberich, and R. Schenkel. Efficient temporal keyword search over versioned text. In *Procóf the 19th ACM Int. Conf. on Information and Knowledge Management*, 2010.

[3] A. Anand, S. Bedathur, K. Berberich, R. Schenkel, and C. Tryfonopoulos. Everlast: a distributed architecture for preserving the web. In *Proc. of the 9th ACM/IEEE Joint Conference on Digital Libraries*, 2009.

[4] P. G. Anick and R. A. Flynn. Versioning a full-text information retrieval system. In *Proc. of the 15th Annual Int. ACM SIGIR Conf. on Research and Development in Information Retrieval*, 1992.

[5] K. Berberich, S. Bedathur, T. Neumann, and G. Weikum. A time machine for text search. In *Proc. of the 30th Annual Int. ACM SIGIR Conf. on Research and Development in Information Retrieval*, pages 519–526, 2007.

[6] P. Boldi and S. Vigna. The webgraph framework I: compression techniques. In *Proc. of the 13th Int. World Wide Web Conference*, 2004.

[7] A. Broder, N. Eiron, M. Fontoura, M. Herscovici, R. Lempel, J. McPherson, R. Qi, and E. Shekita. Indexing shared content in information retrieval systems. In *Proc. of the 10th Int. Conf. on Extending Database Technology*, pages 313–330, 2006.

[8] F. Claude, A. Fariña, M. Martínez-Prieto, and G. Navarro. Indexes for highly repetitive document collections. In *Proc. 20th ACM International Conference on Information and Knowledge Management (CIKM)*, 2011.

[9] J. Dean. Challenges in building large-scale information retrieval systems. In *Proceedings of the Second ACM International Conference on Web Search and Data Mining*, 2009.

[10] J. He and T. Suel. Faster temporal range queries over versioned text. In *Proc. of the 34th Annual Int. ACM SIGIR Conf. on Research and Development in Information Retrieval*, 2011.

[11] J. He, H. Yan, and T. Suel. Compact full-text indexing of versioned document collections. In *Proc. of the 18th ACM Int. Conf. on Information and Knowledge Management*, 2009.

[12] J. He, J. Zeng, and T. Suel. Improved index compression techniques for versioned document collections. In *Proc. of 18th ACM Int. Conf. on Information and Knowledge Management*, 2010.

[13] S. Heman. Super-scalar database compression between RAM and CPU-cache. MS Thesis, Centrum voor Wiskunde en Informatica, Amsterdam, July 2005.

[14] D. Hermelin, D. Rawitz, R. Rizzi, and S. Vialette. The minimum substring cover problem. *Information and Computation*, 206(11), 2008.

[15] M. Herscovici, R. Lempel, and S. Yogev. Efficient indexing of versioned document sequences. In *Proc. of the 29th European Conf. on Information Retrieval*, 2007.

[16] J. Hunt, K.-P. Vo, and W. Tichy. Delta algorithms: An empirical analysis. *ACM Trans. on Software Engineering and Methodology*, 7, 1998.

[17] U. Irmak and T. Suel. Hierarchical substring caching for efficient content distribution to low-bandwidth clients. In *Proc. of the 14th Int. World Wide Web Conference*, May 2005.

[18] R. Karp and M. Rabin. Efficient randomized pattern-matching algorithms. *IBM J. of Research and Development*, 31(2):249–260, 1987.

[19] P. Kulkarni, F. Douglis, J. LaVoie, and J. Tracey. Redundancy elimination within large collections of files. In *USENIX Annual Technical Conference*, 2004.

[20] L. Lim, M. Wang, S. Padmanabhan, J. S. Vitter, and R. Agarwal. Dynamic maintenance of web indexes using landmarks. In *Proc. of the 12th Int. World Wide Web Conference*, 2003.

[21] D. Metzler and W. Bruce. A markov random field model for term dependencies. In *Proc. of the 28th Annual Int. ACM SIGIR Conf. on Research and Development in Information Retrieval*, 2005.

[22] A. Moffat and L. Stuiver. Binary interpolative coding for effective index compression. *Information Retrieval*, 3:25–47, July 2000.

[23] A. Muthitacharoen, B. Chen, and D. Mazières. A low-bandwidth network file system. In *Proc. of the 18th ACM Symp. on Operating Systems Principles*, pages 174–187, October 2001.

[24] Y. Rasolofo and J. Savoy. Term proximity scoring for keyword-based retrieval systems. In *Proc. of the 25th European Conference on Information Retrieval*, 2003.

[25] S. Schleimer, D. Wilkerson, and A. Aiken. Winnowing: Local algorithms for document fingerprinting. In *Proc. of ACM SIGMOD Conf. on Management of Data*, pages 76–85, 2003.

[26] S. Song and J. Jaja. Archiving temporal web information: Organization of web contents for fast access and compact storage. In *Technical Report UMIACS-TR-2008-08*, 2008.

[27] N. Spring and D. Wetherall. A protocol independent technique for eliminating redundant network traffic. In *Proc. of the ACM SIGCOMM Conference*, 2000.

[28] T. Suel and N. Memon. Algorithms for delta compression and remote file synchronization. In K. Sayood, editor, *Lossless Compression Handbook*. Academic Press, 2002.

[29] D. Teodosiu, N. Bjorner, Y. Gurevich, M. Manasse, and J. Porkka. Optimizing file replication over limited bandwidth networks using remote differential compression. TR2006-157-1, Microsoft, 2006.

[30] L. U, N. Mamoulis, K. Berberich, and S. Bedathur. Durable top-k search in document archives. In *Proc. of ACM SIGMOD Conf. on Management Of Data*, 2010.

[31] H. Yan, S. Ding, and T. Suel. Inverted index compression and query processing with optimized document ordering. In *Proc. of the 18th Int. World Wide Web Conference*, 2009.

[32] J. Zhang and T. Suel. Efficient search in large textual collection with redundancy. In *Proc. of the 16th Int. World Wide Web Conference*, 2007.

[33] J. Zobel and A. Moffat. Inverted files for text search engines. *ACM Computing Surveys*, 38(2), 2006.

[34] M. Zukowski, S. Heman, N. Nes, and P. Boncz. Super-scalar RAM-CPU cache compression. In *Proc. of the Int. Conf. on Data Engineering*, 2006.

To Index or not to Index: Time-Space Trade-Offs in Search Engines with Positional Ranking Functions

Diego Arroyuelo*
Dept. of Informatics,
Univ. Técnica F. Santa María
Yahoo! Labs Santiago, Chile
darroyue@inf.utfsm.cl

Senén González†
University of Chile.
Yahoo! Labs Santiago, Chile
sgonzale@dcc.uchile.cl

Mauricio Marin‡
University of Santiago, Chile
Yahoo! Labs Santiago, Chile
mmarin@yahoo-inc.com

Mauricio Oyarzún
University of Santiago, Chile
Yahoo! Labs Santiago, Chile
mauricio.silvaoy@usach.cl

Torsten Suel§
CSE Department
Polytechnic Institute of NYU
Brooklyn, NY, 11201
suel@poly.edu

ABSTRACT

Positional ranking functions, widely used in web search engines, improve result quality by exploiting the positions of the query terms within documents. However, it is well known that positional indexes demand large amounts of extra space, typically about three times the space of a basic nonpositional index. Textual data, on the other hand, is needed to produce text snippets. In this paper, we study time-space trade-offs for search engines with positional ranking functions and text snippet generation. We consider both index-based and non-index based alternatives for positional data. We aim to answer the question of whether one should index positional data or not.

We show that there is a wide range of practical time-space trade-offs. Moreover, we show that both position and textual data can be stored using about 71% of the space used by traditional positional indexes, with a minor increase in query time. This yields considerable space savings and outperforms, both in space and time, recent alternatives from the literature. We also propose several efficient compressed text representations for snippet generation, which are able to use about half of the space of current state-of-the-art alternatives with little impact in query processing time.

Categories and Subject Descriptors

H.3.3 [**Information Storage and Retrieval**]: Information Search and Retrieval; H.2.4 [**Systems**]: Textual databases

*Partially funded by Fondecyt Grant 1-110066.
†CONICYT Thesis Work Support Code 78100003.
‡Partially supported by FONDEF D09I1185.
§Supported by NFS Grants IIS-0803605 and IIS-1117829.

Permission to make digital or hard copies of all or part of this work for personal or classroom use is granted without fee provided that copies are not made or distributed for profit or commercial advantage and that copies bear this notice and the full citation on the first page. To copy otherwise, to republish, to post on servers or to redistribute to lists, requires prior specific permission and/or a fee.
SIGIR'12, August 12–16, 2012, Portland, Oregon, USA.
Copyright 2012 ACM 978-1-4503-1472-5/12/08 ...$15.00.

General Terms

Algorithms, Experimentation, Performance

Keywords

Positional indexing, text compression, index compression, wavelet trees, snippet generation.

1. INTRODUCTION

Web search has become an important part of day-to-day life, affecting even the way in which people think and remember things [35]. Indeed, *web search engines* are one of the most important tools that give access to the huge amount of information stored in the web. The success of a web search engine mostly depends on its efficiency and the quality of its ranking function. To achieve efficient processing of queries, search engines use highly optimized data structures, including inverted indexes [6, 10, 25]. State-of-the-art ranking functions, on the other hand, combine simple term-based ranking schemes such as BM25 [10], link-based methods such as Pagerank [7] or Hits [24], and up to several hundred other features derived from documents and search query logs.

Recent work has focused on *positional ranking functions* [32, 27, 36, 28, 33, 40, 10] that improve result quality by considering the positions of the query terms in the documents. Thus, documents where the query terms occur close to each other might be ranked higher, as this could indicate that the document is highly relevant for the query. To support such positional ranking, the search engine must have access to the position data. This is commonly done by building an index for all term positions within documents, called a *positional index.* The goal is to obtain an index that is efficient in terms of both index size and access time.

As shown in [32], positional ranking can be carried out in two phases. First, a simple term-based ranking scheme (such as BM25) defined over a Boolean filter is used to determine a set of high-scoring documents, say, the top 200 documents. In the second phase, the term positions are used to rerank these documents by refining their score values. (Additional third or fourth phases may be used to do further reranking according to hundreds of additional features [38], but this is orthogonal to our work.) Once the final set of top-scoring documents has been determined (say, the top 10), it is necessary to generate appropriate *text snippets*, typically text surrounding the term occurrences, to return as part of the result page. This requires access to the actual text in the indexed web pages. It is well known [40, 21] that storing position data requires a considerable amount of space, typically about 3 to 5 times the space of an inverted index storing only document identifiers and term frequencies. Furthermore, storing the documents for snippet generation requires significant additional space.

This paper focuses on alternative approaches to performing the above two-step document ranking process and the query snippet-generation phase. The aim is to optimize both space and query processing time. One important feature of position data is that it only needs to be accessed for a limited number of promising documents, say a few dozens or hundreds of documents. This access pattern differs from that for document identifiers and term frequencies, which are accessed more frequently, making access speed much more important. For position data, on the other hand, we could consider somewhat slower but smarter alternative representations without losing too much efficiency at query time [40].

In this paper, we push this idea further and consider not storing the position data (i.e, the positional index) at all. Instead, we compute positions *on the fly* from a compressed representation of the text collection. We will study two alternative approaches to compressing the text collection: (1) *wavelet trees* [23], which are succinct data structures from the combinatorial pattern matching community, and (2) compressed document representations that support fast extraction of arbitrary documents. It has been shown that, compared to positional indexes, web-scale texts can often be compressed in much less space [21]. More importantly, these representations can be used for both positional reranking and snippet generation. One concern is how these alternatives impact query processing speed, and thus we will study the resulting trade-offs between running time and space requirement.

Thus, *to index or not to index position data*, that is the research question that we hope to answer in this paper. To our knowledge, such alternative approaches for implementing positional ranking functions have not been rigorously compared before. Our main result is that we can store all the information needed for query processing (i.e., document identifiers, term frequencies, position data, and text) using space close to that of state-of-the-art positional indexes (which only store position data and thus cannot be used for snippet creation), with only a minor increase in query processing time. Thus, we provide new alternatives for practical compression of position and text data, outperforming recent approaches in [34].

Following current practice in search engines [21, 14], we assume a scenario where there is enough space to maintain index data structures completely in main memory, in compressed form. In this scenario, large text collections are usually partitioned over a number of nodes in a cluster, such that each partition fits into the memory of its node. This paper focuses on how to organize data within each partition, as also assumed in previous work such as [21, 14].

2. BACKGROUND AND RELATED WORK

Let $\mathcal{D} = \{D_1, \ldots, D_N\}$ be a document collection of size N, where each document is represented as a sequence $D_i[1..n_i]$ of n_i terms from a vocabulary $\Sigma = \{1, \ldots, V\}$. Notice that every term is represented by an integer, hence the documents are just arrays of integers. We also identify each document D_i with a unique document identifier (docID) i. Given a term $t \in \Sigma$ and a document $D_i \in \mathcal{D}$, the *in-document positions* of t in D_i is the set $\{j | D_i[j] = t\}$.

Throughout this paper, we assume that all term separators (like spaces, ',', ';', '.', etc.) have been removed from the text. Also, we assume that all terms in the vocabulary have been represented in a case-insensitive way. This is in order to facilitate the search operations that we need to carry out over the documents in order to compute (on the fly) the positions of a given query term. To be able to retrieve the original text (with separators and the original case) one can use the *presentation layer* introduced by Fariña et al. [17, Section 4]. This also supports removing stopwords and the use of stemming, among other vocabulary techniques. This extra layer requires extra space on top of that of the compressed text, as well as extra time to obtain the original text. However, this scheme must be used on all the alternatives that we consider in this paper, and thus we disregard the overhead introduced by the presentation layer and focus only on the low-level details of compression (but keeping in mind that the original text can still be retrieved).

2.1 Inverted Index Compression

The efficiency of query processing in search engines relies on *inverted indexes*. These data structures store a set of *inverted lists* $I_1, \ldots, I_V$, which are accessed through a *vocabulary table*. The list I_t maintains a *posting* for each document containing the term $t \in \Sigma$. Usually, a posting in an inverted list consists of a docID, a term frequency, and the in-document positions of the term. (In real systems, the docIDs, term frequencies and in-document positions are often stored separately.) Indexes whose postings store in-document positions are called *positional inverted indexes*.

We assume that an inverted list I_t is divided into blocks of 128 documents each — the particular choice of 128 documents per block is an implementation issue. Given a block of I_t, the term-position data for all the documents in that block are stored in a *separate* block of variable size. The inverted lists of the query terms are used to produce the result for the query. Since the query results are usually large, the result set must be ranked by relevance.

For large document collections, the data stored in inverted indexes requires considerable amounts of space. Hence, the indexes must be compressed. To support efficient query processing (such as DAAT [10], WAND [9] or BMW OR [15]) and effective compression in the inverted lists, we sort them by increasing docID. Let $d_t[1..|I_t|]$ denote the sorted list of docIDs for the inverted list I_t. Then, we replace $d_t[1]$ with $d_t[1] - 1$, and $d_t[i]$ with $d_t[i] - d_t[i-1] - 1$ for $i = 2, \ldots, |I_t|$. In the case of frequencies, every f_i is replaced with $f_i - 1$, since $f_i > 0$ always holds. For the positions, each $p_{i,j}$ is replaced with $p_{i,j} - p_{i,j-1} - 1$. Then these values are encoded with integer compression schemes that take advantage of the resulting smaller integers.

There has been a lot of progress on compressing docIDs and frequencies, with many compression methods available [41, 10]. Some of them achieve, in general, a very good compression ratio, but at the expense of a lower decompression speed [10], for example Elias γ and δ encodings

[16], or Golomb/Rice parametric encodings [22], interpolative encoding [30]. Other methods achieve a (slightly) lower compression ratio, though with much higher decompression speed, for example VByte [39], S9 [3], and PForDelta [42], among others [10]. The best compression method depends on the scenario at hand.

2.2 Positional Indexes

Unfortunately, the scenario is not the same for compressing term positions, which is a problem where it has been difficult to make much progress. For instance, previous work [40] concludes that term positions in the documents do not follow simple distributions that could be used to improve compression (as is the case of, for instance, docIDs and frequencies). As a result, a positional index is about 3 to 5 times larger than a docID/frequency index, and becomes a bottleneck in index compression. Another important conclusion from [40] is that we may only have to access a limited amount of position data per query, and thus it might be preferable to use a method that compresses well even if its speed is slightly lower.

Positions in inverted indexes are used mainly in two applications, phrase searching and positional ranking schemes. In this paper we study positional ranking, where the positions of the query terms within the documents are used to improve the performance of a standard ranking such as BM25. The rationale is that documents where the query terms appear close together could be more relevant for the query, so they should get a better score. Although we focus only on positional ranking functions, the compression schemes used in this paper allow for phrase searching as well. This scenario is left for future work.

A recent work on positional indexing is that of Shan et al [34]. They propose to use the *flat position indexes* [11, 14] as an alternative of positional inverted indexes. The result is that docIDs, term frequencies and position data can be stored in space close to that of positional inverted lists, yielding a reduction of space usage. However, this index does not store the text, which makes it less suitable in scenarios where text snippets must be generated.

2.3 Snippet Generation

Besides providing a ranking of the most relevant documents for a query, search engines must show query snippets and support accessing the "in-cache" version of the documents. Each snippet shows a portion of the result document, in order to help the user judge its likely relevance before accessing it. Turpin et al. [37] introduce a method to compress the text collection and support fast text extraction to generate snippets. However, to achieve fast extraction, they must use a compression scheme that uses more space than usual compressors. In a more recent work, Ferragina and Manzini [21] study how to store very large text collections in compressed form, such that the documents can be accessed when needed, and show how different compressors behave in such a scenario. One of their main concerns was how compressors can capture redundancies that arise very far apart in very long texts. Their results show that such large texts can often be compressed to just 5% of their original size.

2.4 Compressed Text Self-Indexes

Succinct or *compressed* data structures use as little space as possible to support operations as efficiently as possible. Thus, large data sets (like graphs, trees, and text collections) can be manipulated in main memory, avoiding the secondary storage. In particular, we are interested in compressed data structures for text sequences. A *compressed self-index* is a data structure that represents a text in compressed space, supports indexed search capabilities on the text, and is able to obtain any text substring efficiently [31]. It can be seen as compression tools with indexed search capabilities.

Given a sequence $T[1..n]$ over an alphabet $\Sigma = \{1, \ldots, V\}$, we define operation $\mathsf{rank}_c(T, i)$, for $c \in \Sigma$, as the number of occurrences of c in $T[1..i]$. Operation $\mathsf{select}_c(T, j)$ is defined as the position of the j-th occurrence of c in T. A *wavelet tree* [23] (WT for short) is a succinct data structure that supports rank and select operations, among many virtues [19].

A WT representing a text T is a balanced binary search tree where each node v represents a contiguous interval $\Sigma^v = [i..j]$ of the sorted set Σ. The tree root represents the whole vocabulary. Σ^v is divided at node v into two subsets, such that the left child v_l of v represents $\Sigma^{v_l} = [i..\frac{i+j}{2}]$, and the right child v_r represents $\Sigma^{v_r} = [\frac{i+j}{2} + 1..j]$. Each tree leaf represents a single vocabulary term. Hence, there are V leaves and the tree has height $O(\log V)$. For simplicity, in the following we assume that V is a power of two.

Let T^v be the subsequence of T formed by the symbols in Σ^v. Hence, $T^{root} = T$. Node v stores a bit sequence B^v such that $B^v[l] = 1$ if $T^v[l] \in \Sigma^{v_r}$, and $B^v[l] = 0$ otherwise. Given a WT node v of depth i, $B^v[j] = 1$ iff the i-th most-significant bit in the encoding of $T^v[j]$ is 1. In this way, given a term $c \in \Sigma$, the corresponding leaf in the tree can be found by using the binary encoding of c. Every node v stores B^v augmented with a data structure for rank/select over bit sequences [31]. The number of bits of the vectors B^v stored at each tree level sum up to n, and including the data structure every level requires $n + o(n)$ bits. Thus, the overall space is $n \log V + o(n \log V)$ bits [23, 31].

Since a WT replaces the text it represents, we must be able to retrieve $T[i]$, for $1 \leq i \leq n$. The idea is to navigate the tree from the root to the leaf corresponding to the unknown $T[i]$. To do so, we start from the root, and check if $B^{root}[i] = 0$. If so, the leaf of $T[i]$ is contained in the left subtree v_l of the root. Hence, we move to v_l looking for the symbol at position $\mathsf{rank}_0(B^{root}, i)$. Otherwise, we move to v_r looking for the symbol at position $\mathsf{rank}_1(B^{root}, i)$. This process is repeated recursively, until we reach the leaf of $T[i]$, and runs in $O(\log V)$ time as we can implement the rank operation on bit vectors in constant time. To compute $\mathsf{rank}_c(T, i)$, for any $c \in \Sigma$, we proceed mostly as before, using the binary encoding of c to find the corresponding tree leaf. On the other hand, to support $\mathsf{select}_c(T, j)$, for any $c \in \Sigma$, we must navigate the upward path from the leaf corresponding to term c. Both operations can be implemented in $O(\log V)$ time; see [31] for details.

The space required by a WT is, in practice, about 1.1–1.2 times the space of the text [12]. In our application to IR, this would produce an index larger than the text itself, which is excessive. To achieve compression, we can generate the Huffman codes for the terms in Σ (this is a *word-oriented Huffman coding* [29]) and use these codes to determine the corresponding tree leaf for each term. Hence, the tree is not balanced anymore, but has a Huffman tree shape [12] such that frequent terms will be closer to the tree root than less frequent ones. This achieves a total space of $n(H_0(T)+1) + o(n(H_0(T)+1))$ bits, where $H_0(T) \leq \log V$ is the zero-order empirical entropy of T [26]. In practice, the space is about 0.6 to 0.7 times the text size [12]. However, notice that we have no good worst-case bounds for the operations, as the length of the longest Huffman code assigned to a symbol could be $O(V)$.

2.5 Self-Indexes for IR Applications

There have been some recent attempts to apply alternative indexing techniques, such as self-indexes, in large-scale IR systems. In particular, we mention the work by Brisaboa et al. [8] and Arroyuelo et al. [5, 4]. The former [8] concludes that WT are competitive when compared with an inverted index for finding all the occurrences of a given query term within a single text. The latter [5, 4] extends [8] by supporting more IR-like operations on a WT. The result is that a WT can represent a document collection using $n(H_0(T) + 1) + o(n(H_0(T) + 1))$ bits while supporting all the functionality of an inverted index. The experimental results in [5] compare with an inverted index storing just docIDs, which of course yields a smaller index. However, WTs also store extra information, such as the term frequencies and, most important for us here, the compressed text and thus the term-position data.

Recent work [21] also tried to use (among other alternatives) a compressed self-index to compress web-scale texts, in order to allow decompression of arbitrary documents. Their conclusion is that compressed self-indexes still need a lot of progress in order to be competitive with standard compression tools, both in compression ratio and decompression speed. A contribution of our present work is a compressed self-index that is able to store web-scale texts and is competitive with the best state-of-the-art compressors. We think that this is a step forward in closing the gap between theory and practice in this area [20].

3. CONTRIBUTIONS

In this paper we study what are the best ways to organize in-document positions and textual data, in order to efficiently support positional ranking and snippet generation in text search engines. One of our main conclusions is that some compressed representations of the textual data — which are needed to support snippet generation — can also be used to efficiently obtain the term positions needed by positional ranking methods. Therefore, *no positional index is needed in many cases*, thus saving considerable space at little cost in terms of running time.

Our main contributions can be summarized as follows:

1. A study of several trade-offs for compressing position data. Rather than storing a positional index, we propose to compute the term positions from a compressed representation of the text. We explore and propose several compression alternatives. Our results significantly enhance current trade-offs between running time and memory space usage, enabling in this way more design choices for web search engines. One of our most interesting results is that both position and textual data can be stored in about 71% the space of current positional inverted indexes.

2. A study of several alternatives for compressing textual data, extending the alternatives studied in previous work [21]. In particular, we show that using the scheme in [37] (to compress text and support efficient snippet generation) before using a standard compressor yields good time-space trade-offs, extending the alternatives introduced in [18]. It is important to note that variants of the scheme in [37] have been adopted by some commercial search engines, which makes our results of practical interest.

3. We propose several improvements over wavelet trees [23], in order to make them competitive for representing document collections. We show how to improve the compression ratio by compressing the sequence associated to every node of the tree with standard compressors. The result is a practical web-scale compressed self-index that is competitive with the best state-of-the-art compressors.

4. COMPRESSING TERM-POSITION AND TEXTUAL DATA

Compressing in-document positions, i.e., the positions where each term occur within a document, has been recognized as a difficult task [40, 21]. Indeed, positions have become a bottleneck for compression compared to docIDs and frequencies. Moreover, recent work shows that the textual data can be compressed better than positions [21]. There are two main reasons for this. First, positions have a different distribution than docIDs and frequencies [40]. Second, since positions are stored separately for each term (recall Section 2.1), the local context for terms that is exploited by text compression schemes is not available in the positional inverted lists. Usually, positions require about 3 to 5 times the space of an inverted index storing docIDs and frequencies. Thus, efficient compression of in-document positions is an important challenge.

Positional inverted indexes are the standard solution to this problem [25, 10, 6]. In particular, [40] shows a detailed study of alternative ways to compress positional inverted indexes. However, it is not clear that using the methods in [40] is the best one can do. Notice that the in-document position data can be obtained (at query time) by searching for the query terms in the documents — a simple scan of the document suffices. Since textual data can be compressed much better than positions, this could decrease the space usage of positions. However, the question is how this impacts query performance. We investigate this issue in this paper. We assume that positions are used to support *positional ranking* as described in [10, 40].

Another important issue in web search engines is the ability to generate snippets for the query results that allow users to decide which of the result documents they should visit. In this context, snippets have been shown to improve the effectiveness of search engines. To provide snippets, a search engine must store a (simplified) version of the documents in the collection. In the case of web search engines, this means the entire textual web, which requires a considerable amount of resources. Thus, the textual data must be compressed [21].

4.1 Basic Query Processing Steps for Positional Ranking and Snippet Extraction

From now on we assume a search engine where positional ranking is used to score documents, and where snippets must be generated for the top-scoring documents. Thus, solving a query involves the following steps:

1. **Query Processing Step:** Given a user query, use an inverted index to get the top-k_1 documents according to some standard ranking function (e.g., BM25).

2. **Positional Ranking Step:** Given the top-k_1 documents from the previous step, get the positions of the query terms within these documents. Then rerank the results using a positional ranking functions [10, 40].

3. **Snippet Generation Step:** After the re-ranking of previous step, get snippets of length s for the top-k_2 documents, for a given $k_2 \leq k_1$.

For instance, $k_1 = 200$ (as in [40]) and $k_2 = 10$ (as in most commercial search engines) are typical values for them. We assume $s = 10$ in this paper. The different values for these parameters should be chosen according to the trade-off between query time and search effectiveness that we want to achieve. Step 2 is usually supported by a positional inverted index [25, 10, 40]. Step 3 is supported by compressing the document collection and supporting the extraction of arbitrary documents. Our focus here is on alternative ways to implement the last two steps.

4.2 The Baseline: Positional Inverted Lists and Compressed Textual Data

This section describes and evaluates baseline approaches to support term positions indexing and snippet extraction.

4.2.1 Positional Inverted Lists

Positional inverted lists (`PIL`s, for short) are the standard approach for indexing in-document position data in search engines [25, 10, 6]. In particular, we assume the representation explained in Section 2.1. To obtain position data at query time, given the docIDs of the top-k_1 results for a given query, we identify the PIL blocks containing the desired positional index entries. Then these blocks are *fully decompressed*, and the corresponding positions are obtained. A drawback here is that we need to decompress the entire `PIL` block, even if we only need a single entry in it. Thus, we might end up decompressing, in the worst case, k_1 blocks in each of the inverted lists involved in the query. Afterwards, these positions are used to rerank the top-k_1 documents, as in [40].

The access pattern for position data is much sparser than that for docIDs and frequencies, since positions must be obtained only for the top-k_1 documents. Thus, just a few positions are decompressed from the `PIL` in each query. Given this sparse access pattern and the high space requirement of positions (as discussed above), it is better to use compression methods with a good compression ratio, like Golomb/Rice compression. These are slower to decompress, yet the fact that only a few positions are decompressed should not impact in the overall query running time.

4.2.2 Compressed Textual Data

To compress the text collection and support decompressing arbitrary documents, a simple alternative that is used by several state-of-the-art search engines — for instance Lucene [13] — is to divide the whole collection into smaller text blocks, which are then compressed separately. The block size offers a time-space trade-off: larger blocks yield better compression, although decompression time is increased. Given the popularity [13, 21] and simplicity of this approach, we use it as the baseline for the compressed text.

4.2.3 Baseline Experiments

Experimental Setup.
We show now experiments for the baseline approaches. For this we use an HP ProLiant DL380 G7 (589152-001) server, with a Quadcore Intel(R) Xeon(R) CPU E5620 @ 2.40GHz processor, with 128KB of L1 cache, 1MB of L2 cache, 2MB of L3 cache, and 96GB of RAM, running version 2.6.34.8-68.fc13.i686.PAE of Linux kernel.

We use the TREC GOV2 collection, with about 25.2 million documents and about 32.86 million terms in the vocabulary. We work just with the text content of the collection (that is, we ignore the html code from the documents). This requires about 127GB in ASCII format. When we represent the terms as integers, the resulting text uses 91,634 MB. We use a subset of 10,000 random queries from the query log provided with the TREC GOV2 collection. All methods were implemented using C++, and compiled with `g++ 4.4.5`, with the full optimization flag `-O5`.

Experiments for Step 1.
In Table 1 we show the average query time (in milliseconds per query) for the initial query processing step (Step 1 of Section 4.1). We show results for two types of queries: traditional AND queries (using DAAT query processing and BM25 ranking) and the BMW OR approach from [15], which is one of the most efficient current solutions for disjunctive queries (using a two-layer approach, which yields slightly faster query times [15]). The index for docIDs and frequencies required 9,739 MB of space, using PForDelta compression for docIDs and S16 for frequencies. Notice that the query time for AND is almost constant (within two decimal digits) with respect to k_1. The process to obtain the top-k_1 documents uses a heap (of size k_1). However, operating the heap takes negligible time, compared to the decompression of docIDs and the DAAT process. BMW OR, on the other hand, is an early-termination technique, and thus k_1 impacts the query time.

Table 1: Experimental results for the initial query processing step (Step 1) for AND and OR queries.

top-k_1	DAAT AND (ms/q)	BMW OR [15] (ms/q)
50	14.75	35.70
100	14.77	43.39
150	14.80	47.90
200	14.81	51.74
300	14.81	58.19

Experiments for Step 2.
In Table 2 (first two rows) we show experimental results for obtaining positions with the baseline `PIL`s, using two compression schemes: Rice and S16, which offer the most interesting trade-offs [40]. We also show query times for different values of k_1, namely 50, 100, 150, 200 and 300 (the experiments in [40] only use $k_1 = 200$). As we can see, Rice

requires only about 90% the space of S16, but takes twice as much time. Comparing the query times of Step 2 for Rice and S16 with the query times of Step 1 in Table 1, we can see that position extraction is a small fraction of the overall time. Hence, we can use Rice to compress PILs and obtain a better space usage with only a minor increase in query time. For Rice, PILs use 2.91 times the space of the inverted index that stores docIDs and frequencies. For S16, this number is 3.22.

Experiments for Step 3.

Table 3 shows experimental results for the baseline for compressed textual data. Just as in [21], we divide the text into blocks of 0.2MB, 0.5MB or 1.0MB, and compress each block using different standard text compression tools. In particular, we show results for `lzma` (which gives very good results in [21]) and Google's `snappy` compressor [1], which is an LZ77 compressor that is optimized for speed rather than compression ratio. These two compressors offer the most interesting trade-offs among the alternatives we tried. As it can be seen, `lzma` achieves much better compression ratios than `snappy`. The compressed space achieved for the whole text is 8,133 MB for `lzma` and 27,388 MB for `snappy`.

The differences in extraction time are also considerable, with `snappy` being much faster. Note that [21] reports a decompression speed of about 35MB/sec for `lzma`. However, to obtain a given document we must first decompress the entire block that contains it. Hence, most of the 35MB per second do not correspond to any useful data. In other words, this does not measure effective decompression speed for our scenario, and thus we report per-query times rather than MB/s for both methods.

4.3 Computing Positions and Snippets from the Compressed Document Collection

We explore next the alternative of obtaining position data directly from the compressed text. This implies that in Step 2 of the query process, k_1 documents must be decompressed, rather than only k_2 in Step 3, as in the baseline.

Using Standard Text Compressors.

Our first approach is to obtain positions using the baseline for generating snippets from Section 4.2.2. In rows 3 and 4 of Table 2 we show the time-space trade-offs for this approach, using `lzma` and `snappy` compressors, and blocks of size 0.2 MB. We conclude that using `lzma` we can store positions and text in about half the space of PIL(the latter just storing positions). However, this approach is two orders of magnitude slower than the positional index. If we use `snappy` instead, we obtain an index that is 21.86% larger than PIL (Rice), and running times to obtain positions that are about an order of magnitude slower (this might be acceptable in some cases). In the following, we try to improve on both of these techniques.

Zero-order Compressors with Fast Text Extraction.

An alternative to compressing the text that could support faster position lookups is the approach from Turpin et al. [37]. The idea is to first sort the vocabulary according to the term frequencies, and then assign term identifiers according to this order. In this way, the term identifier `0` corresponds to the most frequent term in the collection, `1` to the second most frequent term, and so on. The document collection is then represented as a single sequence of identifiers, where each term identifier is encoded using VByte [2]. Note that the 128 most frequent terms in the collection are thus encoded in a single byte. Actually, [37] uses a move-to-front strategy to store the encodings: the first time a term appears in a document, it is encoded with the original code assigned as before; the remaining appearances are represented as an offset to the previous occurrence of the term. We also use this approach in our experiments.

By using an integer compression scheme (such as VByte) for the text, we are able to decompress *any text portion* very efficiently (no text blocks are needed this time). Table 2 shows the resulting trade-offs for this alternative (see the row for "VByte"). Notice that we improve the query time significantly, making it competitive with PILs. The higher space usage is a concern, but note that we also represent the text within this space, not just the position data as in PILs. We also tried other compression schemes, such as PForDelta and S9, obtaining poorer compression ratios and similar decompression speed. The only method that improved the compression ratio is VNibble, a variant of VByte that represents any integer with a variable number of nibbles (i.e., half bytes). As in VByte, one bit of each nibble is used as a continuation bit, so only 3 bits of each nibble are used to represent the number. The results of Table 2 show space savings of about 10% over VByte. Also, notice that we are now able to use space close to that of `snappy` (with blocks of 0.2 MB), yet with a better query time.

The fast query time is due to two facts. First, methods like VByte and VNibble are able to decompress hundred of million integers (which in our case correspond to terms) per second [41]. Second, VByte and VNibble are able to decompress just the desired documents, without negative impact on compressed size. However, this is basically zero-order compression, and hence we are still far from the space usage of, for instance, `lzma`. We address this next.

Natural-Language Compression Boosters.

To obtain higher-order compression, we propose to use a so-called natural-language compression booster [18]. The idea is to use first a zero-order compressor on the text, then this compressed text is further compressed using some standard compression scheme. It has been shown that this can yield better compression ratios than just just using a standard compression scheme [18] (especially for smaller block sizes). In our case, we propose using Turpin et al's approach [37] as booster (using VByte and VNibble as we explained above) on the sequence of term identifiers, rather than Word Huffman or End-Tagged as in [18]. Our experiments indicate that the former are faster and use only slightly more space than the latter.

In Table 2 we show the trade-offs for this approach (see the rows for approach "Compression Boosters"). We show results for blocks of size 0.001, 0.01, 0.05, and 0.2 MB of VByte and VNibble compressed text. Overall, the reduction in space usage (compared to the original VByte approach) is considerable. Compared to `lzma` (0.2 MB), the result is a reduction in space usage of 16.68% (12,486 MB vs 14,987 MB), but at the cost of twice the running time as the original `lzma`. When using smaller blocks, however, the time to obtain positions rapidly improves, while the size does not increase too much. For `snappy`, on the other hand, we obtain a

Table 2: Experimental results for extracting term-position data (Step 2).

Approach	Compression Scheme	Space Usage (MB)	Position extraction time (ms/q) $k_1 = 50$	$k_1 = 100$	$k_1 = 150$	$k_1 = 200$	$k_1 = 300$
Positional indexes	PIL(Rice)	28,373	1.28	2.22	3.05	3.27	5.57
	PIL(S16)	31,338	0.74	1.12	1.43	1.75	2.51
Text compressors	`lzma` (0.2 MB)	14,987	137.60	260.36	375.21	482.09	684.94
	`snappy` (0.2 MB)	34,576	9.47	18.00	25.95	33.49	47.74
Zero-order Compressors	VByte	38,339	0.95	1.91	2.86	3.81	5.72
	VNibble	34,570	1.86	3.71	5.57	6.75	8.10
Compression Boosters	VByte + `lzma` (0.2 MB)	12,486	256.16	484.35	716.41	906.54	1,284.87
	VByte + `lzma` (0.05 MB)	13,981	70.32	133.18	192.09	246.94	351.71
	VByte + `lzma` (0.01 MB)	16,762	19.26	36.51	52.67	68.00	97.04
	VByte + `lzma` (0.001 MB)	22,340	6.11	11.60	16.80	21.72	31.10
	VByte + `snappy` (0.2 MB)	20,158	9.71	18.86	26.41	34.01	48.69
	VByte + `snappy` (0.05 MB)	20,366	2.36	4.48	6.47	8.36	11.95
	VByte + `snappy` (0.01 MB)	22,086	0.82	1.56	2.25	2.91	4.17
	VByte + `snappy` (0.001 MB)	27,919	0.45	0.86	1.24	1.60	2.30
Compressed self-indexes	WT(7 KB)	40,534	1.94	3.68	5.30	6.85	9.80
	WT(1 KB)	56,917	0.33	0.62	1.04	1.15	1.75
	WT(7 KB) + `lzma`	19,628	19.25	36.59	52.83	68.36	97.71
	WT(1 KB) + `lzma`	42,359	7.22	13.54	19.44	24.97	35.57
	WT(7 KB) + `snappy`	25,122	14.35	23.76	39.38	51.02	74.56
	WT(1 KB) + `snappy`	46,778	2.07	3.61	5.88	7.32	10.47

Table 3: Experimental results for compressing the document collection (Step 3).

Compressor	Block size (MB)	Space usage (MB)	Compression Ratio	Snippet extraction time (ms/q) $k_2 = 10$	$k_2 = 30$	$k_2 = 50$
`lzma`	0.2	14,987	16.35	29	84	136
	0.5	13,489	14.72	63	181	292
	1.0	12,682	13.84	117	335	540
`snappy`	0.2	34,576	37.73	2	6	9
	0.5	34,426	37.57	5	14	23
	1.0	34,390	37.53	10	28	46

reduction of 41.69% in space for blocks of size 0.2 MB, with a very minor increase in query time. When we reduce the block size to 0.05 MB, the query time improves even more, and becomes competitive with the time to obtain positions from PIL (Rice). We note that using more advanced techniques from [40] we could obtain about 21 to 22 GB of space for PIL, making both techniques competitive in both space and time. However, VByte + `snappy` also contains the text within this space, allowing for use during snippet generation. Thus, we are able to store both text and positions in a representation that uses less space than PIL, which stores only positions.

4.4 A Compressed Self-Index for Positions and Snippets

Let T be the text obtained from the concatenation (in arbitrary order) of the documents in the collection. We represent T with a WT to obtain term positions and text snippets. Given a position i in T, one can easily obtain both the docID of the document that contains $T[i]$ and the starting position of a given document j by means of operations rank and select [5], assuming a table of document lengths.

Byte-Oriented Huffman WT.

Instead of a bit-oriented WT (as the ones explained in Section 2.4), we use the byte-oriented representation from [8], using the Plain Huffman encoder, which is the most efficient alternative reported in there. The idea is to first assign a Huffman code to each vocabulary term [29]. Then, we store the most significant *byte* of the encoding of each term in array B^{root}. That is, each WT node v stores an array of bytes B^v, instead of bit arrays as in Section 2.4. Next, each term in the text is assigned to one of the children of the root, depending on the first byte in the encodings. Notice that in this way the WT is 256-ary. See [8] for details.

To support rank and select, we use the simple approach from [8]. Given a WT node v, we divide the corresponding byte sequence B^v into superblocks of s_b bytes each. For each superblock we store 256 *superblock counters*, one for each possible byte. These counters tell us how many occurrences of a given byte there are in the text up to the last position of the previous superblock. Also, each superblock is divided into blocks of b bytes each. Every such block also stores 256 *block counters*, similarly as before. The difference is that the values of these counters are local to the superblock, hence less bits are used for them. To compute $\mathsf{rank}_c(T, i)$, we first compute the superblock j that contains i, and use the superblock counter for c to count how many c there are in T up to superblock $j-1$. Then we compute the block i' that contains i and add (to the previous value) the block counter for c. Finally, we must count the number of c within block i'. This is done with a sequential scan over block i'. This block/superblock structure allows for time-space trade-offs. In our experiments we use $s_b = 2^{16}$. Hence, superblock counters can be stored in 16 bits each. We consider $b = 1$ KB, $b = 3$ KB and $b = 7$ KB. Operation select is implemented by binary searching the superblock/block counters; thus no extra information is stored for this [8].

To obtain position data assume that, given docID i for a top-k_1 document and a query term t, we want to obtain the positions of t within D_i. A simple solution could be to extract document D_i from the `WT`, and then search for t within it (as in Section 4.3). However, the decompression speed of a `WT` is much slower than that of the schemes used in Section 4.3, so we must use a more efficient way. An idea is to use operation select to find every occurrence of t within D_i, hence working in time proportional to the number of occurrences of the term. Let d be the starting position for document D_i in T. Hence, there are $r \leftarrow \mathsf{rank}_t(T, d)$ occurrences of t before document D_i, and the first occurrence of t within D_i is at position $j \leftarrow \mathsf{select}_t(T, r+1)$, the second occurrence at position $j' \leftarrow \mathsf{select}_t(T, r+2)$, and so on. Overall, if o is the number of occurrences of t within D_i, then we need 1 rank and $o+1$ selects to find them.

In Table 2 we show the experimental trade-offs for `WT`, for the different block sizes tested. As it can be seen, `WT` (7 KB) requires space close to (though slightly larger than) that of the VByte approach. `WT` (3 KB) and `WT` (1 KB) obtain better times, but requiring even more space. Moreover, `WT` (7 KB) is slower than `PIL` (Rice) and uses more space. The `WT`, on the other hand, includes the textual data, but still this space usage could leave it out of competition. Next, we introduce extra improvements to make them more competitive.

Achieving Higher-Order Compression with the `WT`.

Basically, `WT`s are zero-order compressors, which explains their high space usage. To achieve higher-order compression, notice that B^{root} contains the most significant byte of the Huffman encodings of the original terms. Thus, the original text structure is at least partially preserved in the structure of B^{root}, which might thus be as compressible as the original text. A similar behavior can be observed in internal nodes. Thus, we propose to compress the blocks of B^v in each `WT` node v by using some standard compressor.

Table 2 shows results for `lzma` and `snappy`, the best compressors we tried. Notice that `WT` (7 KB) + `lzma` achieves 19,628 MB, almost half the space used by `WT` (7 KB). The time to obtain positions becomes, on the other hand, an order of magnitude larger. `WT` (7 KB) + `snappy` achieves slightly better times, but using more space. Also, `WT` (7 KB) + `lzma` uses slightly less space than VByte + `snappy` (0.2 MB), but is somewhat slower. Overall, this significant reduction in space could make `WT`competitive.

5. EXPERIMENTAL RESULTS

We now show the time-space trade-offs for the overall solution space we explored. We use here the same basic setup as in Section 4.2.3, with the same parameters (block sizes) for each alternative. We consider the most competitive indexing alternatives from previous sections for positions and snippet generation, described in Table 4. All results include the time and space of the inverted index to carry out Step 1 of the query process, as well as of all structures used in Steps 2 and 3.

Table 4: Glossary of the indexing schemes used in Figure 1. All schemes include the inverted index.

Indexing Scheme	Description
Scheme 1	`WT` for positions and text.
Scheme 2	`WT` compressed with `lzma` for positions and text.
Scheme 3	`WT` compressed with `snappy` for positions and text.
Scheme 4	Text compressed with VByte/ VNibble for positions and text.
Scheme 5	VByte compression booster on `snappy` for positions and text.
Scheme 6	`PIL` (Rice) for positions and VByte/ VNibble for text.

Note that only Scheme 6 stores an index for position data. Figure 1 shows the different trade-offs for DAAT AND queries with BM25 ranking. Conclusions for OR queries are similar to that for AND. We only show results for $k_1 = 200$ and $k_2 \in \{10, 50\}$, which are representative of other values we tested.

As can be seen, Scheme 6, which uses `PIL` for positions and Turpin et al [37] for snippets, has one of the fastest query times among all alternatives, but space usage is high compared to other methods. This is because this scheme needs to store positions and text separately. The two points for Scheme 6 that are plotted correspond to using VByte (higher space usage) and VNibble.

Scheme 1 also offers a competitive query time (among the fastest alternatives), but still uses a considerable amount of space. The time-space trade-offs for the schemes that use `WT` are obtained for different block sizes within the `WT` nodes (1 to 7 KB). Scheme 2 and Scheme 3 compress the byte sequences of each `WT` node (as proposed in Section 4.4). As can be seen, the space usage is improved significantly, in some cases by a factor of two. However, query time degrades, making these alternatives less compelling.

Scheme 4 is very competitive in query time, but again its space usage is high. Scheme 5 corresponds to the compression boosters proposed in Section 4.3, and it obtains a very impressive trade-off. One of the most interesting settings is for blocks of size 0.05 MB. In this case, the overall space usage is 1.06 times the space of `PIL` (Rice), with a query time 1.21 times higher than Scheme 4 and 1.23 times higher than Scheme 6 (which uses `PIL`). For blocks of size 0.01 MB, Scheme 5 requires 1.12 times the space of `PIL` (Rice), with a query time that is 0.96 times the one of Scheme 4, and 0.98 the one of Scheme 6. Thus, using only slightly more space than `PIL` (Rice) (recall the results in Table 2), Scheme 5 includes everything needed for query processing: docIDs, frequencies, term positions, and the text needed to gener-

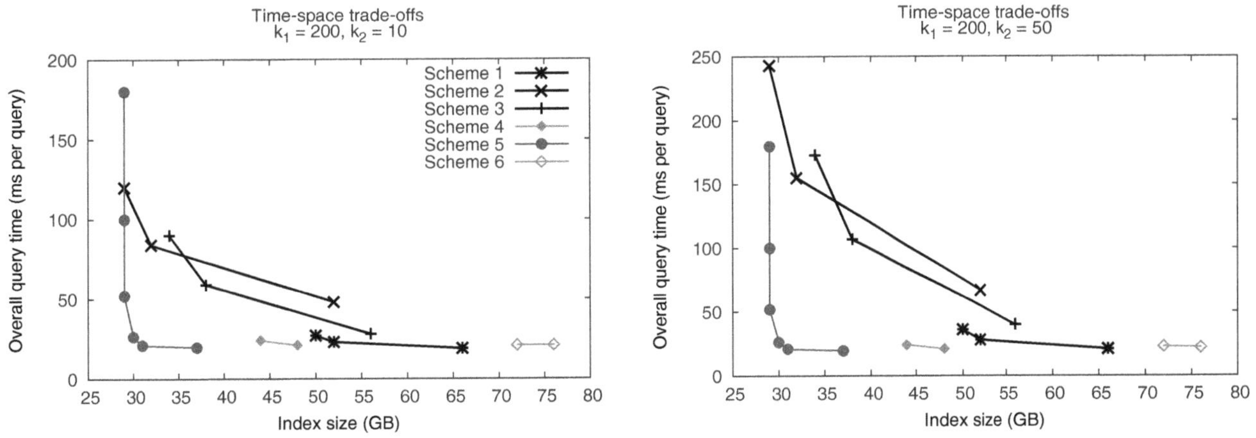

Figure 1: Time-space trade-offs for the overall query process for the GOV2 collection, including positional ranking and snippet generation. The size of each alternative includes the size of inverted index with docIDs and frequencies, which for the TREC GOV2 collection requires 9,739MB.

ate snippets. This is one of the most important conclusions in this paper, that "not to index" can be a real alternative for positional data in practical scenarios. As stated in Section 4.3, the space usage of `PIL`s can be reduced to about 21 GB–22 GB for the TREC GOV2 collection [40]. However, we would still need to add the inverted index and the compressed text to that space in order to support all query processing steps.

Finally, the smallest space alternatives we tested (which are not shown in Figure 1) are the ones that use the inverted index for query processing and `lzma` compression for positions and snippets. This achieves about 22,225 MB of space. This scheme includes everything needed for query processing, and uses only 78% the space of `PIL`. However, query processing time increases significantly, to more than 400 ms per query. This scheme could be useful in some cases where the available memory space is very restricted, such that a larger index would mean going to disk.

A recent alternative [34] proposes to use *flat positional indexes* [11, 14] to support phrase querying; this index could also be used for positional ranking. This is basically a positional index from which docID and frequency information can also be obtained. The results reported for the GOV2 collection in [34] give an index of size 30,310 MB that includes docIDs and frequencies, but not the text needed for snippet generation, making this approach uncompetitive for our scenario.

6. CONCLUSIONS

From our study we can conclude that there exists a wide range of practical time-space trade-offs, other than just the classical positional inverted indexes. We studied several alternatives, trying to answer the question of whether it is necessary to index position data or not. As one of the most relevant points in the trade-off, we propose a compressed document representation based on the approach in [37] combined with Google's `snappy` compression [1]. This allows us to compute position and snippet data using less space than a standard positional inverted index that only stores position data. Even if we include the space used for document identifiers and term frequencies, this approach uses just 1.12 times the space of a positional inverted index, with the same or slightly better query time.

This means that in many practical cases, "not to index" position data may be the most efficient approach. This provides new practical alternatives for positional index compression, a problem that has been considered difficult to address in previous work [40, 21]. Finally, we also showed that compressed self-indexes such as wavelet trees [23] can be competitive with the best solutions in some scenarios.

7. REFERENCES

[1] `http://code.google.com/p/snappy/`.

[2] V. N. Anh and A. Moffat. Compressed inverted files with reduced decoding overheads. In *Proc. of 21st Annual Int. ACM SIGIR Conf. on Research and Development in Information Retrieval*, pages 290–297, 1998.

[3] V. N. Anh and A. Moffat. Inverted index compression using word-aligned binary codes. *Inf. Retr.*, 8(1):151–166, 2005.

[4] D. Arroyuelo, V. Gil-Costa, S. González, M. Marin, and M. Oyarzún. Distributed search based on self-indexed compressed text. *Information Processing and Management*, 2012. To appear.

[5] D. Arroyuelo, S. González, and M. Oyarzún. Compressed self-indices supporting conjunctive queries on document collections. In *SPIRE*, LNCS 6393, pages 43–54, 2010.

[6] R. Baeza-Yates and B. Ribeiro-Neto. *Modern Information Retrieval - the Concepts and Technology Behind Search, Second Edition.* Pearson Education Ltd., Harlow, England, 2011.

[7] S. Brin and L. Page. The anatomy of a large-scale hypertextual web search engine. *J. of Computer Networks*, 30(1-7):107–117, 1998.

[8] N. Brisaboa, A. Fariña, S. Ladra, and G. Navarro. Implicit indexing of natural language text by reorganizing bytecodes. *Information Retrieval*, 2012. To appear.

[9] A. Z. Broder, D. Carmel, M. Herscovici, A. Soffer, and J. Zien. Efficient query evaluation using a two-level

retrieval process. In *Proc. of 12th International Conference on Information and Knowledge Management*, pages 426–434. ACM, 2003.

[10] S. Büttcher, C. Clarke, and G. Cormack. *Information Retrieval: Implementing and Evaluating Search Engines.* MIT Press, 2010.

[11] C. Clarke, G. Cormack, and F. Burkowski. An algebra for structured text search and a framework for its implementation. *Computer Journal*, 38(1):43–56, 1995.

[12] F. Claude and G. Navarro. Practical rank/select queries over arbitrary sequences. In *SPIRE*, LNCS 5280, pages 176–187. Springer, 2008.

[13] D. Cutting. Apache Lucene. `http://lucene.apache.org/`.

[14] J. Dean. Challenges in building large-scale information retrieval systems: invited talk. In *WSDM*, page 1, 2009.

[15] S. Ding and T. Suel. Faster top-k document retrieval using block-max indexes. In *Proc. of 34th Annual Int. ACM SIGIR Conf. on Research and Development in Information Retrieval*, pages 993–1002, 2011.

[16] P. Elias. Universal codeword sets and representations of the integers. *IEEE Transactions on Information Theory*, 21(2):194–203, 1975.

[17] A. Fariña, N. Brisaboa, G. Navarro, F. Claude, A. Places, and E. Rodríguez. Word-based self-indexes for natural language text. *ACM Transactions on Information Systems (TOIS)*, 30(1):article 1, 2012.

[18] A. Fariña, G. Navarro, and J. Paramá. Boosting text compression with word-based statistical encoding. *Computer Journal*, 55(1):111–131, 2012.

[19] P. Ferragina, R. Giancarlo, and G. Manzini. The myriad virtues of wavelet trees. *Information and Computation*, 207(8):849–866, 2009.

[20] P. Ferragina, R. González, G. Navarro, and R. Venturini. Compressed text indexes: From theory to practice. *ACM Journal of Experimental Algorithmics*, 13, 2008.

[21] P. Ferragina and G. Manzini. On compressing the textual web. In *WSDM*, pages 391–400, 2010.

[22] S. Golomb. Run-length encoding. *IEEE Transactions on Information Theory*, 12(3):399–401, 1966.

[23] R. Grossi, A. Gupta, and J. S. Vitter. High-order entropy-compressed text indexes. In *SODA*, pages 841–850, 2003.

[24] J. M. Kleinberg. Authoritative sources in a hyperlinked environment. *J. of ACM*, 46(5):604–632, 1999.

[25] C. Manning, P. Raghavan, and H. Schütze. *Introduction to Information Retrieval.* Cambridge University Press, 2008.

[26] G. Manzini. An analysis of the Burrows-Wheeler transform. *J. ACM*, 48(3):407–430, 2001.

[27] D. Metzler and W. B. Croft. A markov random field model for term dependencies. In *Proc. of 28th Annual Int. ACM SIGIR Conf. on Research and Development in Information Retrieval*, 2005.

[28] G. Mishne and M. Rijke. Boosting web retrieval through query operations. In *Proc. of 27th European Conference on IR Research*, 2005.

[29] A. Moffat. Word-based text compression. *Software, Practice, and Experience*, 19(2):185–198, 1989.

[30] A. Moffat and L. Stuiver. Binary interpolative coding for effective index compression. *Inf. Retr.*, 3(1):25–47, 2000.

[31] G. Navarro and V. Mäkinen. Compressed full-text indexes. *ACM Computing Surveys*, 39(1), 2007.

[32] Y. Rasolofo and J. Savoy. Term proximity scoring for keyword-based retrieval systems. In *Proc. of 25th European Conference on IR Research*, 2003.

[33] R. Schenkel, A. Broschart, S. Hwang, M. Theobald, and G. Weikum. Efficient text proximity search. In *14th String Processing and Information Retrieval Symposium*, 2007.

[34] D. Shan, W. X. Zhao, J. He, R. Yan, H. Yan, and X. Li. Efficient phrase querying with flat position index. In *CIKM*, pages 2001–2004, 2011.

[35] B. Sparrow, J. Liu, and M. Wegner. Google effects on memory: Cognitive consequences of having information at our fingerprints. *Science*, 333(6043):776–778, 2011.

[36] T. Tao and C. Zhai. An exploration of proximity measures in information retrieval. In *Proc. of 30th Annual Int. ACM SIGIR Conf. on Research and Development in Information Retrieval*, 2007.

[37] A. Turpin, Y. Tsegay, D. Hawking, and H. Williams. Fast generation of result snippets in web search. In *Proc. of 30th Annual Int. ACM SIGIR Conf. on Research and Development in Information Retrieval*, pages 127–134, 2007.

[38] L. Wang, J. J. Lin, and D. Metzler. A cascade ranking model for efficient ranked retrieval. In *Proc. of 34th Annual Int. ACM SIGIR Conf. on Research and Development in Information Retrieval*, pages 105–114, 2011.

[39] H. Williams and J. Zobel. Compressing integers for fast file access. *Computer Journal*, 42(3):193–201, 1999.

[40] H. Yan, S. Ding, and T. Suel. Compressing term positions in web indexes. In *Proc. of 32nd Annual Int. ACM SIGIR Conf. on Research and Development in Information Retrieval*, pages 147–154, 2009.

[41] H. Yan, S. Ding, and T. Suel. Inverted index compression and query processing with optimized document ordering. In *WWW*, pages 401–410, 2009.

[42] M. Zukowski, S. Héman, N. Nes, and P. Boncz. Super-scalar ram-cpu cache compression. In *ICDE*, page 59, 2006.

Studies of the Onset and Persistence of Medical Concerns in Search Logs

Ryen W. White
Microsoft Research
One Microsoft Way
Redmond, WA 98052
ryenw@microsoft.com

Eric Horvitz
Microsoft Research
One Microsoft Way
Redmond, WA 98052
horvitz@microsoft.com

ABSTRACT
The Web provides a wealth of information about medical symptoms and disorders. Although this content is often valuable to consumers, studies have found that interaction with Web content may heighten anxiety and stimulate healthcare utilization. We present a longitudinal log-based study of medical search and browsing behavior on the Web. We characterize how users focus on particular medical concerns and how concerns persist and influence future behavior, including changes in focus of attention in searching and browsing for health information. We build and evaluate models that predict transitions from searches on symptoms to searches on health conditions, and escalations from symptoms to serious illnesses. We study the influence that the prior onset of concerns may have on future behavior, including sudden shifts back to searching on the concern amidst other searches. Our findings have implications for refining Web search and retrieval to support people pursuing diagnostic information.

Categories and Subject Descriptors
H.3.3 [**Information Storage and Retrieval**]: Information Search and Retrieval – *search process, information filtering*

Keywords
Health search; medical search; cyberchondria.

1. INTRODUCTION
People often turn to the Web to find information about medical concerns. A recent study found that 80% of Web users have performed online medical searches [12]. Framed by the popularity of health-related search, we seek to better understand how users find medical information online, with the goal of developing tools to better support search for medical information. Researchers have investigated the search behavior of medical domain experts (e.g., [5]) and the reliability of online medical content (e.g., [11]). Search log data provides unique insight into the natural search behaviors of search engine users, and a number of studies have used that type of data to investigate how users find medical information. Studies to date have largely focused on medical search behavior within one session and examined issues such as the escalation of basic symptoms to more serious concerns [24] or decisions about when to seek a consultation with a health professional [25]. However, medical searches span multiple sessions and are connected over time, as people monitor symptoms and adapt their lines of inquiry based on exposure to information found on the Web and other sources (e.g., professional diagnoses) [2].

Permission to make digital or hard copies of all or part of this work for personal or classroom use is granted without fee provided that copies are not made or distributed for profit or commercial advantage and that copies bear this notice and the full citation on the first page. To copy otherwise, or republish, to post on servers or to redistribute to lists, requires prior specific permission and/or a fee.
SIGIR'12, August 12–16, 2012, Portland, Oregon, USA.
Copyright 2012 ACM 978-1-4503-1472-5/12/08...$15.00.

We explore how medical concerns emerge over time and how these concerns persist after their onset. Within-session analysis is limited in this context as it may not capture the behavior preceding the onset of searches for a condition, meaning that we may not observe changes from *symptoms* (i.e., an observed departure from normal function or feeling such as headache or chest pain) to *conditions* (i.e., a disease or disorder such as brain tumor or heart attack) within session boundaries. Indeed as we show in our analysis of large-scale search logs, about 60% of medical search sessions start directly with a condition query[1]. The relationship between log-based signs of the onset of concerns and longer-term search behavior following a search diagnostic on the implications of a symptom may or may not be tightly linked; search on conditions may be initiated by external factors such as diagnosis provided by a medical professional or prior searching (in the log data in our study, around 95% of sessions originating with a condition had medical searches in previous sessions). Regardless, a better understanding of the behavior may provide valuable clues about searchers' medical trajectories that search engines might use to help searchers (e.g., by predicting emerging concerns and personalizing the search experience).

We analyze search and browsing data gathered from a sample of approximately 170 thousand consenting toolbar users over a three-month period. Contributions extending from the analysis include:

- Characterizing how health-related concerns emerge in search activity over time, including key aspects of this process such as escalations in the severity of conditions searched.
- Analyzing aspects of the persistence of concerns after the onset, including associated interruptions to future search tasks and changes in the searcher's focus of attention thereafter.
- Construction and evaluation of machine-learned models to predict medical condition onset, escalations, and likely interruptions in future sessions given a user's search history.
- Proposal of design implications based on our findings that can help inform the development of search tools to monitor and proactively support online medical searching.

Through improved understanding and modeling of emerging concerns, we can help searchers make better decisions on their own health seeking and guide engagement with medical professionals.

The remainder of this paper is structured as follows. Section 2 describes related work in such areas as medical search and long-term user profiling. Section 3 describes the data and how we use it to build the long-term user profiles necessary for our study. In Section 4, we present findings of our analysis characterizing the onset and persistence of medical concerns over time. Section 5 focuses on predicting: (i) the onset on concerns, (ii) escalations to searches about serious illnesses, and (iii) interruptions of future

[1]For 81% of search sessions containing terms indicating a specific medical condition, the session started with the same condition.

searches on other topics with returns to the healthcare concern at focus. Section 6 discusses our findings, their implications, and opportunities for future study. We conclude in Section 7.

2. RELATED WORK

Web interaction logs have been used previously to study medical Web search behavior. Bhavnani *et al.* [6] demonstrated that Web page term co-occurrence of medical symptoms and disorders can reasonably predict the degree of influence on search behavior. Spink *et al.* [17] characterized healthcare-related queries issued to Web search engines and showed that users were gradually shifting from general-purpose search engines to specialized Web sites for medical- and health-related queries. White and Horvitz [24] used a log-based methodology to study escalations in medical concerns during Web search (shifts from search on common symptoms to searches on serious ailments) a behavior that they termed *cyberchondria*. Their work highlighted the potential influence of several biases of judgment demonstrated by people and search engines themselves, including base-rate neglect and availability. In a follow-up study, White and Horvitz [25] examined the occurrence of escalation from symptoms to searches for local medical professionals and facilities such as nearby hospitals. Cartright *et al.* [8] studied differences in search behaviors associated with diagnosis vs. more general health-related information seeking. They decomposed health information seeking into evidence-based (search on relevance of signs and symptoms) and hypothesis-based (search on conditions and treatments), and studied how medical foci evolve during exploratory health search sessions.

The research described above largely focused on medical search behavior within a single session. Several pieces of prior work explore the pursuit of health information across multiple sessions. White and Horvitz [24] framed directions with longer-term analyses including a study of the recurrence of concerns over multiple sessions and interruptions of non-medical searches with return to the pursuit of a health concern. They showed that 13.5% of the medical searchers in the logs they studied exhibited recurrence in medical searches, mainly for symptoms (50.8% of users reissued queries for the same symptoms over multiple sessions). In other cross-session research, White and Horvitz [25] show how using evidence drawn from multiple search sessions can enhance the performance of a classifier that predicts the search for local healthcare resources. Another study of medical search behavior over time was conducted by Ayers and Kronenfeld [2] who used Web log data in a multiple regression analysis exploring the relationship between chronic medical conditions and frequency of Web use, as well as changes in health behavior associated with Web usage. Their findings suggest that Web use was influenced not only by the presence of one particular chronic illness but by the total number of chronic conditions. They also found that the more often someone uses the Web as a source of health information, the more likely they will alter their health behavior based on the information they encounter online.

Prior research has used long-term histories more generally to improve search and recommendation effectiveness, typically learning a user's profile from either browsing or search history. White *et al.* [21] investigated the utility of different contextual sources and their combinations for a URL recommendation task. They found that models constructed from historic data for each user most accurately predict users' longer-term future interests. Piwowarski and Zaragoza [15] explored three different predictive click models using historical and social contexts, in a Web search setting trying to predict relationships between queries and documents. Teevan *et al.* [20] constructed user profiles from indexed desktop documents and showed that this information could be used to re-rank search results and improve relevance for individuals. Matthijs and Radlinski [14] constructed user profiles using users' browsing histories, and evaluated their approach using an interleaving methodology. Tan *et al.* [18] focused only on the most relevant prior queries and constructed language models for this task. Although this work has been carried out in the context of general Web search, it has special applicability to medical search.

The medical community has studied the effects of health anxiety disorders, including hypochondriasis, over time [1], but not in the context of Web search. Health anxiety is problematic since it is often maladaptive (i.e., out of proportion with the degree of medical risk) and amplified by the fact that those affected are often undiscerning about the source of their medical information [19]. Such anxiety usually persists even after an evaluation by a physician and reassurance that concerns about symptoms lack an underlying medical basis. Beyond interactions with medical professionals, patients' health concerns may manifest in other ways such as search behavior, an assertion supported by [23], which showed that those whom self-identified as hypochondriacs searched more often for health information than average Web searchers.

Despite the popularity of medical Web content, there is a need for improved information services to the medical information consumer. Cline and Haynes [7] present a review of work in this area that suggests that public health professionals should be concerned about online health seeking, consider potential benefits, synthesize quality concerns, and identify criteria for evaluating online health information. Eysenbach and Kohler [11] used focus groups and naturalistic observation to study users attempting assigned search tasks on the Web. They found that the credibility of Web sites (in terms of source, design, appearance, language used, and ease of use) was important in the focus group setting, but that, in practice, many participants largely ignored source. Some organizations have already started efforts to improve the general quality of medical information on the Web, such as the Health on the Net Foundation [12]. Others have studied enhancing Web pages or search results with tools to support credibility assessment [16]. Eastin and Guinsler [10] showed that an individual's level of health anxiety moderates the relationship between health seeking and healthcare utilization decisions. White and Horvitz [26] demonstrated a relationship between the nature and structure of Web page content and the likelihood that users would escalate their concerns as observed in downstream behavior (e.g., the order in which serious and non-serious explanations for symptoms appeared on the page and the distance between these mentions).

We believe that much more can be learned from studying health information-seeking behaviors over time, and we perform a longitudinal study with that focus. Our work differs from prior research in a number of ways. First, we study the emergence, onset, and the persistence of medical concerns over time as observable in search queries. Second, we leverage a log-based methodology that provides data in the wild from a large sample of consenting users over many search sessions, rather than relying on running user studies, or within-query and within-session log analysis. Finally, we develop predictive models of whether onsets will occur, the nature of the onset, and its persistence, rather than immediate health-related actions such as within-session escalations.

3. BUILDING USER PROFILES

To study long-term medical search behavior, we needed to build long-term search profiles for each user in our log data. We begin by describing the data and profile construction method.

3.1 Data

We use anonymized logs of URLs visited by users who consented to provide data through a widely distributed browser toolbar. We gathered data over a three-month period (January 2011 – March 2011). Log entries included a unique user identifier, a timestamp for each page view, and the URL of the page visited. We excluded intranet and secure (https) URL visits at the source. To remove variability caused by cultural and linguistic variation in search behavior, we only include log entries generated by users in the English-speaking United States locale. From these logs, we extracted search sessions on Google, Yahoo!, and Bing via a similar methodology to White and Drucker [22]. Search sessions comprised queries, clicks on search results, and pages visited during navigation once users left the search engine. Search sessions ended after a period of user inactivity exceeding 30 minutes.

We assigned topical labels to extracted URLs to identify which were medically related. We assigned URLs in our dataset to categories in the Open Directory Project (ODP, dmoz.org) in an automated manner using a content-based classifier, described and evaluated in [4]. The classifier employs logistic regression to predict the ODP category for a Web page, resulting in a label for each page such as *Health/Medicine*. To lessen the impact of small differences in assigned labels, we use only 219 categories at the top two levels of the ODP hierarchy. The findings in [4] revealed that, when optimized for the score in each category, the content-based classifier has a micro-average F1 of 0.60, which we believed was sufficient for our purposes.

3.2 Long-Term Profile Generation

To identify searchers showing evidence of health-seeking intent, we constructed profiles for a randomly selected subset of users who had visited at least one URL labeled with the *Health* category of the ODP[2]. We removed outlier users (approximately the most active 1% of users) who visited large numbers of URLs in the study duration (as likely traffic generated by robotic systems). The resultant set of approximately 170,000 users, conducted over 25 million search sessions and visited over one billion URLs over the three-month duration of study. The average number of browsing sessions per user was around 240 (of which around 150 were search sessions), spanning on average 76 days per participant.

In addition to labeling URL content using a text classifier, we also automatically labeled the search queries issued by users based on whether they contain symptoms (e.g., headache), benign explanations (e.g., caffeine withdrawal), serious illnesses (e.g., brain tumor), or some combination of these types of medical concern. To perform the labeling, we leveraged lists of relatively common symptoms, as well as benign and more serious illnesses. Specifically, we used the following sources for each class of concern:

- *Symptoms*: Symptom list from the Merck medical dictionary. The same list of symptoms has been used in previous analysis of search behavior [8] to identify health-related sessions.
- *Benign explanations*: List of commonly occurring conditions, as defined in [24] and used in that study for a log-based analysis of online search behavior. The wordlist is based on the *International Classification of Diseases 10th Edition* (ICD-10) published by the World Health Organization.
- *Serious illnesses*: List of serious conditions defined in [24].

In the log-centric analysis, we also used synonyms of symptoms and conditions to increase coverage (e.g., including "tiredness" in addition to "fatigue"). Synonyms for each symptom or condition

[2]We excluded URLs in the *Health/Animals* category.

Table 1. Summary statistics of long-term medical profiles. Mean and standard deviation (SD) are reported.

Statistic (n=169,513)	Mean	SD
# queries	1076.31	1112.32
# medical queries (click)	36.67	60.29
% queries medical (click)	3.4%	4.3%
# medical queries (wordlist)	10.31	17.90
# queries with serious illnesses	4.60	8.68
# unique serious illnesses	1.69	1.60
# queries with benign explanations	1.86	5.81
# unique benign explanations	0.70	1.05
# queries with symptoms	4.15	11.39
# unique symptoms	1.23	1.75
# URLs	5738.76	5968.84
# medical URLs	190.65	317.53
% URLs that are medical	3.9%	4.6%
# search sessions	153.40	91.55
# medical sessions	37.04	32.05

were identified via a two-step walk on the search engine click graph using an approach similar to that described in [3]. The automatically-generated lists of synonyms were reviewed by the authors to remove erroneous list entries (e.g., all astrology-related synonyms were removed for the serious illness "cancer"). To count as a match on one or more of the concern types, a query needed to be an exact match against the concern or one of its synonyms as generated using the walk described above. We avoided substring matches to ensure high precision in labeling queries.

The user profiles conducted as described in this section were used to pursue answers to three research questions:

Q1: What are some key characteristics of the long-term profiles generated to study health seeking over time?

Q2: What are characteristics of how health-related concerns emerge in search activity *over time*, including key aspects of this process such as escalations in the severity of conditions searched?

Q3: How do searches for the condition persist following evidence of an initial onset of concern, in terms of related medical searches and specifics such as interruptions in future search sessions and changes in searchers' focus of attention?

Answers to these questions could provide valuable insights to search system designers.

4. CHARACTERIZING BEHAVIORS

We divide this section into three parts: (i) we provide an overview of medical search behavior in the data set (Section 4.1), (ii) we characterize aspects of the onset of medical conditions (Section 4.2), and (iii) we analyze the persistence of the condition searching following the condition onset (Section 4.3).

4.1 Medical Searching Over Time (Q1)

We begin with an overview of medical search behavior over time, averaged on a per-user basis. Table 1 lists summary statistics over the available log data in the three-month period studied. Note that for the purposes of this analysis, a *medical session* is defined as a search session where the user has issued a medical search query or visited a URL labeled with the *Health* category of the ODP (or a sub-category). A *medical query* is defined in two ways: *wordlist* –

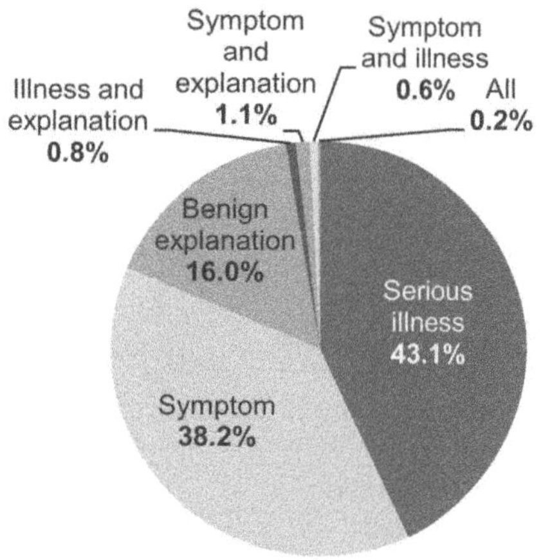

Figure 1. Distribution of medical queries per concern type. Queries are labeled using the wordlist method.

query contains at least one of the symptoms, benign explanations, or serious illnesses defined earlier, or *click* – a query resulting in a search engine result page (SERP) click on a page labeled in the `Health` category of the ODP. The click method has better coverage since it does not depend on string matching. However, since much of our analysis uses the wordlist method (since it is more precise and already broken into conditions, symptoms, etc.), we also report statistics on that.

From the findings presented in Table 1, we can see the average user in our dataset issued 10–15 queries per day. Of those queries, around 3% are medically related. It is worth noting the high standard deviation values for some of the medical statistics, such as the *# medical queries*. As noted previously [23], there are users who may be more likely to search for medical information (e.g., those affected by health anxiety). We retained these and other outliers to more fully represent the distribution of Web searchers.

Table 1 also shows that users are querying more often for symptoms and serious illnesses than common, benign explanations. It is important to understand the composition of medical queries that users are issuing since it has direct implications for the type of support that search engines should offer. With that in mind, we performed further analysis of the queries in medical sessions.

4.1.1 *Query Composition*

Figure 1 shows the fraction of medical queries (from those that could be labeled according to our wordlist method) that contain each of the seven possible combinations of the three concern types. The figure shows that searching for a single concern type is most common, with 97.3% of labeled medical queries containing only a single *type* of concern (and 94.6% of those queries containing only a single concern). Serious illnesses and symptoms are the most popular concern types that searchers pursue. Interestingly, and somewhat concerningly, searches for serious illnesses occur around two-and-a-half times as often as searches for benign explanations, even though the benign explanations of symptoms are typically much more likely given prevalence statistics.

4.1.2 *Symptoms and Conditions*

Turning our attention to the role of symptoms and conditions in the medical sessions, we found that 80.7% of sessions that contain a medical condition (serious or benign), start with that condition immediately. In contrast only, 49.8% of the sessions containing a medical symptom start with a symptom. If we compute the percentages across all medical sessions, regardless of whether they contain a medical symptom, the differences between symptoms and conditions are amplified. Overall, 17.6% of medical sessions start with a symptom and 57.8% of medical sessions start with a condition. As suggested in previous work [8], searchers may begin with a hypothesis and refine that based on evidence gathered during the session. The longitudinal methodology provides us with insight into user behavior before the session that can help us to better understand how these concerns first emerge.

4.2 Condition Onset (Q2)

We now explore the search behavior of users prior to the first occurrence of a particular condition of interest across the three-month study duration. We refer to the first query that the user issues related to this condition as the *condition onset*. In identifying the onset, we randomly selected one condition per user from that user's long-term profile. Although the onset is the first instance of the selected condition in the user's long-term search history, their pre-onset history can contain *other* conditions that may have been searched for before the onset. Allowing users to explore multiple conditions more accurately reflects real Web search behavior than, say, limiting our analysis to the first instance of *any* condition in the long-term profiles. That said, this may not have been hugely impactful since 83% searched for at most one other condition prior to onset (61% searched for none).

For each randomly selected onset condition, we extracted all queries and URL visits before its onset, extending back to the beginning of the available search logs for that user. We also extracted the behavior for that user after the condition onset, and we use that to study aspects of the estimated impact of the condition on future search behavior, as described later in the paper. The extraction process yielded 158,917 pre-onset histories, one per user. We begin by studying the search behavior in these histories.

4.2.1 *Pre-Onset Search Behaviors*

We look at a number of variables capturing users' medical search behavior. From pre-onset behavior, we computed the following:

- *Number of queries*
- *Number of URLs*: Number of non-SERP URLs visited.
- *Number of medical queries*: Number of medical queries, defined using the wordlist and click methods from earlier.
- *Number of medical URLs*: Number of non-SERP URLs that are labeled as being in the `Health` category of the ODP.
- *Fraction of URLs medical*: Fraction of all non-SERP URLs that are labeled as being medical.
- *Total time to onset*: Total timespan to the onset of the condition from the start of the log data for that user.
- *Total time online*: Total time that user spends searching online (sum of all dwell time for pages in search sessions).
- *Fraction time online*: Fraction of the time between the start of the log data and the onset that the user spends online.
- *Fraction online time on medical URLs*
- *Number of search sessions*
- *Number of medical search sessions*

We also compute the same four features for the symptoms and conditions observed in the pre-onset history, e.g., for symptoms:

- *Number of queries with symptoms*
- *Number of unique symptoms*
- *Symptom persistence*: Time for which a symptom persists, computed as timespan between its first and last occurrence.
- *Number of symptom sessions*: Number of sessions that contained at least one query with a symptom.

The mean (M) and standard deviation (SD) pre-onset variable values for all conditions are reported in the *All* column in Table 3. There were about 50 days of user behavior in our logs on average before the onset of the condition of interest. Users performed around 20 medical search sessions in that time, spent 8% of their total time searching online and they spent around 3% of their online time examining medical content. Users generally focused on a single symptom and a single condition in the pre-onset phase. Symptom searches persisted for around four days on average, whereas condition searches persisted for around six days.

To understand the relatedness between the symptoms observed in user search histories and the onset conditions, we used the serious-illness→symptom and common-explanation→symptom mappings from a prior study by White and Horvitz [24]. In that study, the authors mapped 12 commonly occurring symptoms (e.g., chest pain, dizziness) to one or more of over 100 conditions based on a review of medical literature. In this study, we first extracted all onset-condition→symptom pairs from each user's search history, computed synonyms for each using the method described earlier, and filtered to retain pairs with one of the 12 common symptoms from [24]. In total, 79.5% of the filtered condition-symptom pairs observed for a user comprised a correct mapping from a symptom to a condition likely to cause it. The high match shows that across many sessions, the symptoms and the onset-condition are strongly related; even if it takes time for queries mentioning the condition directly to be visible in the query stream, there are indications that its emergence extends back over time.

4.2.2 *Effects of Other Factors*

In addition to behavior over all onsets, we also studied the effect of two marginalizations: condition severity and transition type.

4.2.2.1 *Condition Severity*

From all of pre-onsets available, we selected those where the onset condition was a serious illness or a benign explanation; the 7,104 onsets based on queries containing both severity types were removed for this marginalization analysis. The feature values for each of the classes are reported in third and fourth data columns of Table 3. Given the large sample sizes, all differences between severity types across all variables were significant using one-way multivariate analyses of variance (MANOVA) ($F(2,310727) = 5.81$, $p < .01$). All paired differences for each variable between the severity types were also significant at $p < .013$ using Tukey post-hoc testing. There are some noteworthy differences seen with searchers starting with benign versus serious conditions. We found that the *% medical queries*, *# symptom queries*, *# condition queries*, and *# medical queries* features show that the onset of benign explanations was typically preceded by more medical searching than preceded serious illnesses and *All* (e.g., *% medical queries* is 4% for benign explanations but only 3.2% and 3% for *All* and serious illnesses respectively). One explanation is that Web search is contributing as a causal influence (rather than just reflecting user concerns), and that these users are better informed from reading more Web pages, and hence able to make better decisions about the condition(s) to which they should transition.

4.2.2.2 *Transition Type*

As well as studying the severity of the onset condition, we also examined the effect of the type of transition that the user makes between symptoms in the pre-onset phase and the onset condition. Prior work examined *within-session* escalations in medical concerns [24], where users were observed to transition from searches on common symptoms such as twitching, to serious illnesses such as amyotrophic lateral sclerosis (also referred to as ALS, motor neuron disease, and Lou Gehrig's disease), and within-session non-escalations, where users transition from querying about symptoms to benign explanations, such as muscle strain and anxiety. However, given the large volume of medical sessions that begin with a condition directly (around 60% as reported earlier in the paper), it is important to also consider another transition type: *between-session* escalations and non-escalations, where the onset condition is still related to a preceding symptom, but that symptom occurs outside of the current session. Figure 2 illustrates the two types of escalation. Queries are represented as circles, Web pages by rectangles, and different types of escalation by single-line arrows (e.g., [lump]→[cancer] within a single session).

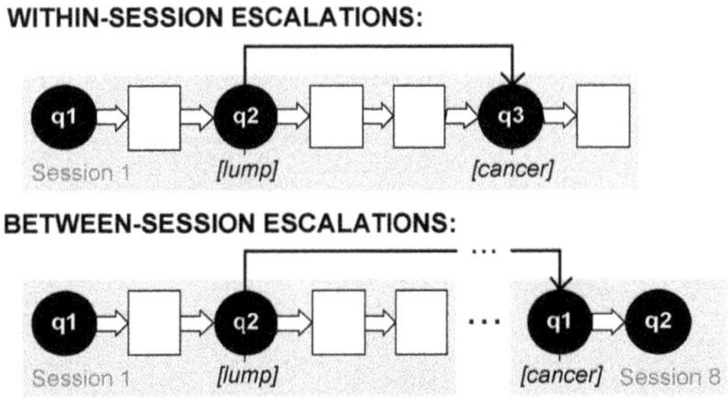

Figure 2. Examples of different escalation types.

To reduce the likelihood that the symptom is unrelated to the condition, we used the serious illness→symptom and benign explanation→symptom mappings described earlier (that restricts the condition-symptom pairs considered to those with a known association) and required that the gap between the symptom and the illness/explanation be at most seven days. We found that within-session escalations occur within three minutes of the symptom query (M=2.57 minutes, SD=4.33 minutes) similar to previous work [24], whereas between-session escalations typically happen within 2–3 days of the symptom (M=2.28 days, SD=1.94 days). We show later that observing escalations leads to better predictive models of the onset condition and post-onset interruptions.

We also computed the values of the features described in the previous section for cases where the onset is a between-session escalation and a between-session non-escalation. The results of this analysis are shown in Table 3. All differences were again significant using a one-way MANOVA ($F(6,321226) = 4.38$, $p < .01$). We can see from Table 3 that escalating and non-escalating users were typically more active searchers on average (*# queries*, *# URLs*), as well as more active in searching for medical information generally (e.g., *% medical queries, # medical sessions*). These users also appear more concerned about symptoms and conditions, as indicated by features such as *# symptom queries* and *# condition sessions*. Focusing on the four transition types, we see that histories ending with a between-session escalation or non-escalation had search behavior that differed most significantly from the overall average. The *Between* columns are highlighted in Table 3 for reference. Between-session escalations and non-escalations may result from long-term concerns which affect medical searching behavior over time, or external diagnosis, where pre-diagnoses concerns are evident in the search log data. Within-session transitions may be a more local phenomenon that is to a lesser extent are reflected in long-term online behaviors.

Table 3 presents statistics over all the pre-onset history, irrespective of where the activity occurred. Since prior work has shown that health behavior changes over time [2], it may also be valuable to understand the temporal dynamics in these features over the course of the pre-onset history and proximal to the onset itself.

4.2.3 *Temporal Dynamics*

We now focus on two temporal aspects of medical searching during the pre-onset behavior: (i) trends over time, and (ii) clusters containing evidence of periodic medical searching.

Table 3. Features of pre-onset search behaviors across all onsets and marginalizations. All differences between groups—All vs. marginalizations, and between and within marginalizations—are statistically significant at $p < .05$. For cells with two entries, first is mean (M) and the second is standard deviation (SD). Bold text denotes features explicitly discussed in the body of the paper.

		All (n=158,917)		Marginalizations					
				Condition Severity		Transition Type			
	Feature	M SD	Gradient of best-fit line	Serious illness (n=117389)	Benign explanation (n=34424)	Escalation		Non-escalation	
						Within (n=1022)	Between (n=8434)	Within (n=439)	Between (n=608)
General health seeking	# queries	611.95 756.86	−0.0140	614.13 740.20	608.79 803.52	**660.93** **672.35**	**778.22** **888.44**	**733.73** **797.96**	**847.14** **880.68**
	# URLs	4148.02 4750.56	**−0.0085**	3985.72 4698.06	3875.80 4887.60	**4298.50** **4897.93**	**4659.43** **5089.18**	**4666.40** **5129.73**	**4863.70** **5181.13**
	# medical queries (wordlist)	5.90 13.11	**+0.1150**	**5.30** **12.12**	**7.69** **15.48**	12.55 32.96	11.64 23.55	13.98 27.07	15.16 33.33
	# medical queries (click)	19.52 41.04	**+0.1230**	**18.02** **39.58**	**24.58** **44.65**	29.10 73.25	35.13 87.25	31.83 63.23	39.06 69.21
	% queries medical (click)	3.2% 3.8%		**3.0%** **4.0%**	**4.0%** **4.2%**	**4.4%** **5.2%**	**4.5%** **4.3%**	**4.3%** **4.8%**	**4.6%** **4.9%**
	Time to onset (days)	**49.50** **26.21**		51.46 25.96	42.84 26.08	50.35 26.24	45.46 26.07	49.57 25.69	46.64 25.11
	Time online (days)	3.89 4.02	**−0.0009**	3.93 4.01	3.70 4.03	4.03 3.87	4.28 4.23	4.46 4.27	4.61 4.27
	% time online (of time to onset)	**7.9%** **8.2%**		7.6% 8.3%	8.6% 9.3%	8.0% 9.2%	9.4% 9.8%	9.0% 9.4%	9.9% 10.3%
	% online time on medical URLs	**2.3%** **2.1%**		2.3% 2.5%	2.4% 2.4%	2.5% 2.9%	2.9% 3.2%	2.6% 3.0%	3.3% 3.8%
	# medical sessions	**21.17** **23.34**	+0.0761	21.09 23.00	21.33 24.50	22.72 27.59	29.23 27.87	24.52 27.27	30.15 26.46
Symptoms	# unique symptoms	**0.63** **1.21**		0.59 1.15	0.72 1.33	**2.08** **1.57**	**2.40** **1.88**	**2.18** **1.94**	**2.64** **2.15**
	# symptom queries	1.98 6.96	**+0.1320**	**1.81** **6.43**	**2.34** **7.58**	**7.38** **11.83**	**9.53** **22.32**	**9.22** **20.34**	**12.38** **22.97**
	Symptom persistence (days)	**3.41** **8.78**		3.33 8.75	3.43 8.55	4.12 10.70	4.76 9.84	4.05 8.90	6.02 9.41
	# symptom sessions	0.74 1.75	+0.0932	0.68 1.61	0.86 1.94	**2.38** **2.41**	**3.09** **3.98**	**2.73** **4.11**	**3.65** **4.76**
Conditions	# unique conditions	**0.74** **1.41**		0.69 1.36	0.89 1.55	**1.09** **1.74**	**1.49** **2.01**	**1.29** **2.01**	**1.64** **2.00**
	# condition queries	1.88 5.68	**+0.1570**	**1.74** **5.36**	**2.27** **6.36**	**3.05** **7.78**	**4.19** **8.09**	**4.26** **10.77**	**5.36** **16.43**
	Condition persistence (days)	**6.04** **12.37**	+0.0400	5.96 12.46	6.13 12.08	5.96 12.39	6.92 13.53	8.06 13.95	5.87 9.55
	# condition sessions	0.94 2.15	+0.0910	0.87 2.05	1.13 2.43	**1.34** **2.50**	**2.01** **3.19**	**1.83** **3.47**	**2.29** **3.85**

4.2.3.1 Trends

For each feature, we computed its daily value (sum or average) across all days in the pre-onset history. If there was no data for a day, then a value of zero was recorded. The result was a time series for each feature value. We then computed the line of best fit for the data and recorded the gradient of the line. If the gradient was positive, then the feature value increased over the time prior to the onset (negative: decreased and zero: constant). The average gradient values for features described in the previous section are shown in Table 3 under the *All* column for applicable variables. In the table, we see that non-medical features such as *# URLs* or *time spent online* are more or less static over the course of the pre-onset phase. In contrast, the features of the medical search behavior, particularly those focused on symptoms and conditions (*# symptom queries*, *# condition queries*) increase over the duration of the pre-onset history, perhaps as the onset condition and related symptoms received a greater focus of attention from the searcher.

As well as computing the average gradient across all conditions, we also studied the gradients by condition to obtain more detailed insight into temporal effects. Figure 3 shows the average gradient values for the *# symptom queries* (which had one of the highest average gradients in Table 3) across all conditions observed in our data occurring 100 or more times. Serious illnesses are marked in dark gray and benign explanations appear in light gray. We can see that benign explanations generally have a lower gradient than the serious illnesses, signifying that there may be more gradual increases in symptom-search frequency related to conditions of that type. Two more noteworthy observations can be made

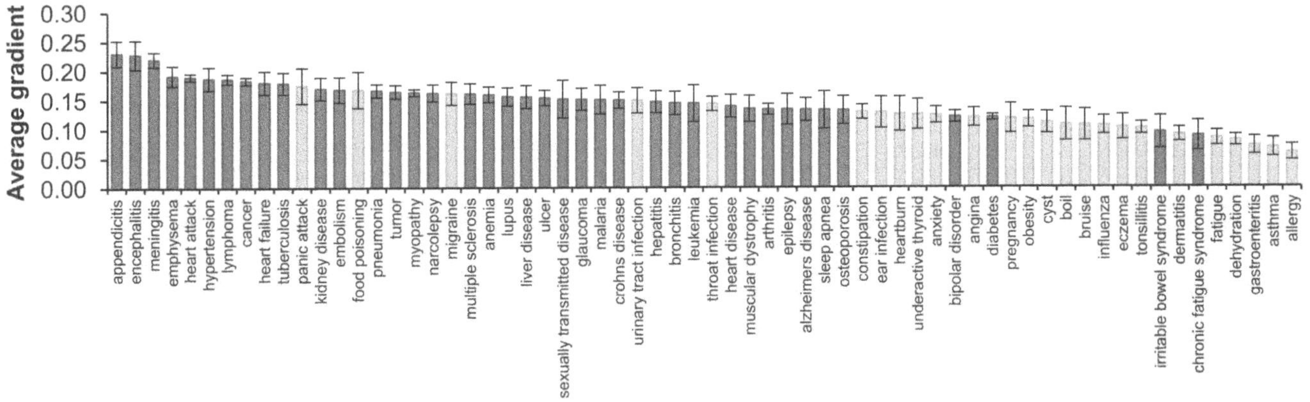

Figure 3. Distribution of gradients of best fit lines for # *symptom queries* (per onset condition). Error bars denote standard error.

from the figure: (i) there is an increase in the acuity of the conditions as average gradient increases and (ii) benign explanations appearing on the left-hand side of the figure are acute conditions such as panic attacks and food poisoning, whereas the serious illnesses on the right-hand side are chronic syndromes and diseases which are stable over time, e.g., diabetes. This analysis shows that we can estimate some important properties of the onset condition by looking at trends in preceding symptom searching. As we will show later, these trends have strong predictive value.

4.2.3.2 Periodicities in Medical Searching

Considering only temporal trajectories tells us little about how the features are distributed temporally. Previous work [24] briefly described the presence of periodicities in medical searching, with periods of no medical search interspersed with clusters of intense activity. Here, we identified such clusters for pre-onset histories.

We define a *cluster* as a sequence of consecutive medical queries with at least one symptom or condition query per day. A gap of a day or more leads to the creation of a new cluster. The average number of clusters per pre-onset history is 2.83 (SD=2.43), the average cluster length is around 2.54 days (SD=2.32 days), and the average periodicity of the clusters is around two weeks (M=14.50 days, SD=12.70 days). To determine whether periodicity changed as the onset approached, we computed the Pearson correlation coefficient (r) between the time between the clusters and the time from the onset. There was a fairly strong positive correlation between these variables (r=0.55) showing that as we move further back in time away from the onset the distance between the clusters increases. In addition, as the time until the condition onset drops, average cluster duration increases (r=−0.64). Trends in both of these measures suggest that the intensity of the medical searching increases as the condition onset nears.

4.2.4 Summary

So far, we have explored aspects of the pre-onset search behavior. Among other things, we showed that: (i) the nature of the condition and the symptom-onset transition may affect medical search behavior, and (ii) that symptom and condition searches increase prior to condition onset (varying by condition type), with an observed increase in the intensity of medical searching. These insights may be useful in predicting outcomes such as condition onsets, something that we explore in more detail later in the paper.

4.3 Persistence of Conditions (Q3)

We now turn attention to post-onset search activity, including important issues such as the amount of time that searchers spend searching related to the onset condition, interruptions to subsequent search activity that are related to that condition, and changes in the conditions that searchers' attend to over time.

4.3.1 Post-Onset Search Behavior

We computed the same features for post-onset behavior as we did for onset (Table 4). We also show the relative percentage change between pre-onset and post-onset behaviors in the last column and features for the onset condition (highlighted), including the number of times the condition recurred post-onset and the total time spent on the onset condition, the sum of the dwell times of all pages on click trails following each instance of a condition query.

The results of this analysis suggest that users are more active medical searchers once they focus on a particular condition. All differences between pre- and post-onset values of the variables in Table 4 are significant (independent t-tests, Bonferroni correction, all $p \leq .002$). We observe a drop in symptom searching, perhaps because they are now focused on a specific condition. The number of unique conditions actually rises because only 39% of users perform condition searching pre-onset; post-onset condition searching is much more common, centered on a single condition.

We now study ways in which the onset might persist in subsequent search behavior: as interruptions to unrelated search tasks and in changes to users' focus of attention over time.

4.3.2 Interruptions

Interruptions refer to a suspension of an ongoing activity and have been studied in detail in the human-computer interaction and psychology communities (e.g., [9]). The analysis of interruptions to search activities associated with persistent health concerns was first introduced in [27]. That research focused on interruptions caused by escalations or health anxiety, and found that interruptions were largely occurred as recurrent searches for symptoms. In this paper, we extend our previous work to consider the all interruptions associated with the onset condition (irrespective of the cause) and the specifically focus on the cost of the interruptions in terms of time users spent and frequency of occurrence in the logs.

To study interruptions in our log-based context, we needed a way to automatically label interruptions so as to be reasonably confident that the user was being interrupted by medical concerns. To do this, we used the following definition: Given a search session containing queries and URLs, an interruption comprises at least one search for the onset condition sandwiched between two series of one or more non-medical searches. Analysis of the post-onset data revealed that 30.3% of users were interrupted in this way. Of those who experienced an interruption, there were 2.39 interrup-

Table 4. Features of post-onset search behaviors. Degree of change from pre-onset behaviors are also shown.

Feature	% or M ±SD	% change fm pre-onset
% URLs medical	4.9%	+88.5
% queries medical	4.2%	+31.3
% online time on medical pages	8.0%	+247.8
# unique symptoms	0.50 ±1.01	−20.6
Symptom persistence (days)	2.46 ±3.42	−27.9
# unique conditions	1.04 ±1.29	+40.5
Condition persistence (days)	7.57 ±12.49	+25.3
# onset condition recurrence	2.72 ±4.79	n/a
Time on onset condition (hours)	1.43 ±2.11	n/a
Onset condition persistence	9.97 ±18.69	n/a
# onset condition sessions	1.78 ±1.67	n/a

tion events and they spent a total of 2 hours 16 minutes searching for the onset condition (SD=2 hours 31 minutes, max=30 hours 48 minutes). Around 6% of search sessions were interrupted and on average 2.68 days (of the on-average 27 post-onset days) contained an interruption per user. It seems that the onset of concern about a condition does have an impact that is in part manifested as interruptions to other future search behavior. Further evidence for which the onset condition may affect post-onset behavior is found by examining what has the user's focus of attention over time.

4.3.3 *Focus of Attention*

Focus of attention in our context refers to the conditions and/or symptoms that the searcher is targeting during health seeking. Cartright *et al.* [8] studied this concept with a single search session. We expand that research by examining searcher foci post-onset and spanning multiple search sessions, specifically looking at the extent to which searchers focus only on the onset condition.

We explored the post-onset data for evidence of a narrow (single) focus of attention once the onset emerged. In particular, we focus on cases where we observed users searching for at least two unique conditions (N=27,016), including the onset condition, and then after condition onset, *the user no longer performs any symptom searches and only searches for the onset condition.* In analyzing our data, we observe that 27.9% of users exhibited evidence of such narrowing of their attentional focus post-onset. The effect is amplified given particular transition types such as escalations.

Table 5 shows the percentage of users with a narrower focus of attention in their post-onset search behavior, broken down by transition direction and by transition distance. The findings summarized in the table suggest that a singular focus of attention is much more likely following escalations, and in particular, following between-session escalations. This may be caused by the escalation, an accumulation of medical information from the Web, or from real-world sources such as diagnosis or prognosis by a medical professional. If escalations provide clues on the future behavior of users, then they may be useful for predicting search behaviors and in developing tools to proactively support health seeking.

4.3.4 *Summary*

In this subsection we have studied aspects of the persistence of onset condition and associated behavior. We show that there is a significant increase in health-search behavior following the emergence of the onset condition, as well as other changes such as a drop in symptom searching. There is also evidence of interruptions related to the onset condition, as well as a narrowing of the

Table 5. Percentage of users who exhibit a narrower focus of attention post onset.

Direction	Distance	
	Within-session	Between-session
Escalation	23.8%	32.7%
Non-escalation	12.6%	16.6%

focus of attention following the condition onset. These are examples of the types of insights that can only be made through our novel examination of long-term search behavior.

The paper so far has presented a descriptive analysis of long-term health-seeking behavior on the Web. We believe that such characterizations are valuable to learn how people pursue medical information online, and can benefit search providers and other researchers working in this area. Although insights can be gleaned from such analysis that can assist in the design of search systems, to have direct practical value to search engine users an application is required. We envision that predictive models based on long-term search behavior will play an increasing role in search systems, monitoring search intentions and managing system intervention. We now explore such predictions in more detail.

5. PREDICTING ONSET & PERSISTENCE

We focus on three tasks: (i) whether users will transition from symptom searching to condition searching, (ii) whether users will escalate between-session to a particular condition, and (iii) whether users will be interrupted by the condition post-onset.

5.1 Feature Generation

The features used in the prediction are in four classes: (i) *queries*, (ii) *pages*, (iii) *temporal* – trends, clusters, and persistence of symptoms or conditions over time, and (iv) *onset* – features of the condition onset, used only in the third task to predict interruptions.

Query features: The query length, number of queries, the number and fraction of queries that are medical, the number of symptoms, serious illnesses, and benign explanation queries. Counts of the various escalation and non-escalation types are also included.

Page features: The total number of pages, the number and fraction of pages that are medical, the number of unique medical ODP categories visited, the total time spent in medical pages, the fraction of the total time online that was spent on medical pages.

Temporal features: Total timespan of the pre-onset history, trends in the feature values over time, and cluster features, such as their duration and periodicity. Also included is the persistence of symptoms and conditions over time (time between instances of them).

Onset features (only used for prediction task (iii)): Features of the type of transition, the type of condition, and the distance from the most recent symptom to the onset, if available.

5.2 Methodology and Findings

We constructed classifiers to address each of the three prediction tasks. We built models using logistic regression, shown to be an effective classifier for similar tasks in the online medical search domain [25]. Since the methodology used differed for each task, we describe the method and the findings separately.

5.2.1 *Onset*

This task involved predicting whether a user will transition from symptom searching to condition searching. In the analysis presented so for in this paper, we know when the onset has occurred. By that point, it might be too late for a search engine to intervene, and being able to predict whether the onset of a condition will occur in the future could be useful. To do this, we required training data containing all features minus anything condition-related (since we wanted to predict condition presence) and a label indicating whether the user transitioned to a condition in the future.

To construct the training set, we started at the beginning of the available log data for each user and determined whether they had transitioned to a condition search at some point in the future. If the user had transitioned, then we took the time of the first condition onset (which was on average 45 days from the beginning of the logs, denoted as M_C), subtracted a random number of days (between one and seven) from that time (so that we were not always making the prediction immediately before the onset), and used data in the resultant timespan to create features. For users who did not transition to a condition at any point in their log data, we used M_C and subtracted a random number of days (from $1-7$ days) from that data. This gave us positive examples (search history→onset) and negative examples (search history→no onset), one example per user. We selected 5000 examples with an equal number of positive and negatives, such that the accuracy of a marginal model that always predicted positive was 50%. We measured classifier accuracy and used ten-fold cross validation.

The findings of the experiments showed that we were able to predict whether a user would transition to a condition with an accuracy of 75.5%, averaged across 100 experimental runs. Important features included the volume of medical content viewed. Figure 4 shows the receiver-operator characteristic (ROC) curve for the onset prediction task averaged across all runs. Also shown in the figure are the curves for the other tasks, which we now describe. Note that all models perform significantly better than the marginal model using t-tests on the 100 runs ($t(198) \geq 3.34$, $p < .01$).

5.2.2 *Escalations*

In the analysis presented earlier in the paper, we showed that between session escalations have the potential to cause lasting long-term impact on search behavior. Therefore, we investigated the prediction of between-session escalation given prior search behavior. The methodology employed is similar to that for the onset prediction task and the classifier only had access to symptom features. The positive examples resulted in between-session escalations and the negative examples did not. Once again, we selected 5000 examples for training and test and equally split positive examples (search history→between-session escalation) and negative examples (search history→no between-session escalation), and we used ten-fold cross validation. We attain 76.4% accuracy, and the most useful features were temporal (especially the symptom gradients) and unique symptom query counts.

5.2.3 *Interruptions*

The final task involves predicting whether a future interruption is going to occur given that we have already observed the onset of a particular condition. Interruptions are defined as in Section 4.3.2. For this task, we can use all features preceding the onset and also the features of the onset itself, such as the condition type (e.g., serious illness or benign explanation), the transition (e.g., escalation or non-escalation), and the time taken to perform the transition. As before, we selected 5000 random examples, with an equal number of positives (search history+onset→interruption) and negatives (search history+onset→no interruption).

The results of our analysis show that we were able to attain a prediction accuracy of 80.6% for this task. The features that were most valuable in making the prediction were related to the nature of the onset, suggesting that with knowledge of those features (and no long-term history of search behavior) we would be able to

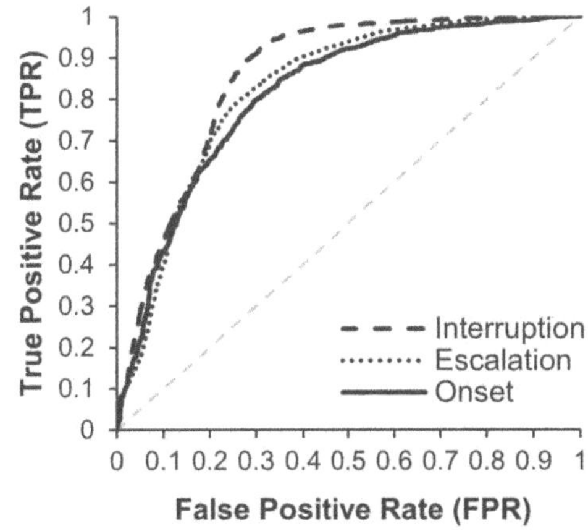

Figure 4. ROC curves for each prediction task. Performance of the marginal model shown as dotted line.

predict whether the user would be interrupted in their future searching. Indeed, we experimented with only restricting the features used to those in the onset class and found that we were able to predict with 71.2% accuracy that the user would be interrupted at some later date by a return to the onset condition.

The models and experiments described in this section demonstrate how key aspects of the condition onset and its estimated impact can be predicted with good accuracy. As we discuss in the next section, accurate predictive modeling capabilities afford a range of possibilities for search engines to better help medical searchers.

6. DISCUSSION AND IMPLICATIONS

We studied the onset and persistence of medical concerns over time as observed from search log data. This is the first study of its kind to focus on long-term medical search. During this study we explored features of the pre-onset search behavior and investigated trends in the feature values and changes in their intensity over the pre-onset phase. Among other things, we found that:

- Many pre-onset symptoms were related to the onset condition, even though they could be issued weeks beforehand.
- Symptom and condition searching increases with proximity to the appearance of evidence of the onset of interest in a specific condition, and the trends are affected by condition acuteness.
- The nature of the onset, measured in this study in terms of severity and transition type (escalations and non-escalations) affect pre-onset search behavior.
- Medical search behavior post-onset differs from pre-onset, e.g., symptom searching drops, condition searches increase.
- Interruptions and a narrowing of the focus of attention succeeding and related to the onset condition occur frequently.

We also showed that we can predict several aspects of the medical search process, such as condition onset, between-session escalation, and related interruptions to future search activities.

Several refinements of search are suggested by the results. On one, we can foresee the use of onset occurrence as a cue for a search engine to leverage that user's previous clicks for related-symptom queries as implicit feedback to enhance the current ranking (similar to [18]). If the search engine *predicts* the onset it could also use the set of symptoms previously searched to estimate the condition that the user is likely to transition to and adjust the search experience based, for example, on severity or incidence rates. The between-session escalation predictor could be used to inform the user *before* they escalate. If the engine can reliably estimate that the user is heading toward an escalation, it could intervene and help the user make an informed decision about what condition to focus on, perhaps offering a set of common benign explanations instead, or more generally, prior and posterior probabilities of serious (rarer) illnesses, conditioning the posterior probabilities on key demographics (e.g., age and gender) and related symptoms, family history, etc. Alternatively, since users may lose time task switching during interruptions [9], the engine could anticipate future interruptions given an onset and proactively gather other information to lessen the lag time when the user returns to a condition search, or provide special support to simplify task switching. The challenge lies in leveraging predictions in a way that respects the highly sensitive nature of medical information, does not overstate their role or their value, and guides users to qualified medical professionals where appropriate.

Although our findings are promising, we acknowledge several limitations of our research. Even though we have a user identifier, it may not actually be a single user who is performing the searches, especially for shared machines. We also did not filter out medical professionals' search data, which is likely to differ from novices [5]. By focusing on a single onset condition for each user we could not dive more deeply into key structural aspects of medical concerns over time, such as transitions between concerns, or how searching and browsing activity associated with common and less common symptoms, benign versus serious disorders, etc. influences these transitions. The association between pre-onset behavior and the onset condition could also have been made clearer by requiring that the onset condition occur within a time window of initial searches for medical concerns; discarding users from our analysis who did not meet this criterion. Also, we did not seek to distinguish the behavior of people with (potentially inappropriate) health anxieties and those wrestling with a diagnosed or yet to be diagnosed serious illness. User attributes, such as levels of health anxiety [23], may influence search behavior. We studied interruptions and focus-of-attention at scale in a naturalistic setting, but used limited definitions of each. More work is needed to refine those definitions for more accurate detection of interruption, attention, and biases. Finally, we need to work with users directly, in addition to their logs, to understand the medically-relevant events in their lives (e.g., professional diagnoses or prognoses), and study how those events affect their search behavior.

7. CONCLUSIONS

We presented a log-based longitudinal study of medical search behavior on the Web. We characterized aspects of search behavior and temporal changes in that behavior before the onset of a condition, and we showed that there are differences in behavior associated with the nature of the onset condition and the transition to that condition from symptom searching. We also studied post-onset behaviors and found evidence of interruption effects and focus narrowing associated with the onset condition. Search engines could monitor long-term search behavior and provide support in advance of the onset or to lessen its impact on search behavior. To this end, we developed predictive models to accurately estimate when concerns are likely to escalate and the impact that their onset can have. Our findings support the development of tailored support for medical search, to help those turning to the Web for medical matters better manage their health seeking.

REFERENCES

[1] Asmundson, G.J.C., Taylor, S., and Cox, B.J. (2001). *Health Anxiety: Clinical and Research Perspectives on Hypochondriasis and Related Conditions*. Wiley.

[2] Ayers, S. and Kronenfeld. J. (2007). Chronic illness and health-seeking information on the Internet. *Health*, 11(3): 327–347.

[3] Beeferman, D. and Berger, A. (2000). Agglomerative clustering of a search engine query log. *KDD*, 407–416.

[4] Bennett, P., Svore, K. and Dumais, S. (2010). Classification enhanced ranking. *WWW*, 111–120.

[5] Bhavnani, S.K. (2002). Domain-specific search strategies for the effective retrieval of healthcare and shopping information. *SIGCHI*, 610–611.

[6] Bhavnani, S.K. *et al.* (2003). Exploring the distribution of online healthcare information. *SIGCHI*, 816–817.

[7] Cline, R.J. and Haynes, K.M. (2001). Consumer health information seeking on the Internet; the state of the art. *Health Education Research*, 16(6): 671–692.

[8] Cartright, M., White, R.W., and Horvitz, E. (2011). Intentions and attention in exploratory health search. *SIGIR*, 65-74

[9] Czerwinski, M., Horvitz, E., and Wilhite, S. (2004). A diary study of task switching and interruptions. *SIGCHI*, 175–182.

[10] Eastin, M.S. and Guinsler, N.M. (2006). Worried and wired: effects of health anxiety on information-seeking and health care utilization behaviors. *Cyber. and Behav.*, 9(4): 494–498.

[11] Eysenbach, G. and Kohler, C. (2002). How do consumers search for and appraise health information on the world wide web? qualitative studies using focus groups, usability test, and in-depth interviews. *Brit. Med. J.*, 324: 573–577.

[12] Fox, S. (2011). Health topics: 80% of internet users look for health information online. *Pew Internet & Amer. Life Project*

[13] Health on the Net Foundation. www.hon.ch/HONcode/Pro.

[14] Matthijs, N. and Radlinski, F. (2011). Personalizing web search using long-term browsing history. *WSDM*, 25−34.

[15] Piwowarski, B. and Zaragoza, H. (2007). Predictive user click models based on click-through history. *CIKM*, 175-182.

[16] Schwarz, J. and Morris, M.R. (2011). Augmenting web pages and search results to support credibility assessment. *SIGCHI*, 1245–1254.

[17] Spink, A. *et al.* (2004). A study of medical and health queries to Web search engines. *Health Info. and Lib. J.*, 21: 44–51.

[18] Tan, B., Shen, X., and Zhai, C. (2006). Mining long-term search history to improve search accuracy. *KDD*, 718–723.

[19] Taylor, S. and Asmundson, G.J.C. (2004). *Treating Health Anxiety: A Cognitive-Behavioral Approach*. Guilford Press.

[20] Teevan, J., Dumais, S.T., and Horvitz, E. (2005). Personalizing search via automated analysis of interests and activities. *SIGIR*, 449−456.

[21] White, R.W., Bailey, P., and Chen, L. (2009). Predicting user interests from contextual information. *SIGIR*, 363−370.

[22] White, R.W. and Drucker. S.M. (2007). Investigating behavioral variability in web search. *WWW*, 21–30.

[23] White, R.W. and Horvitz, E. (2009). Experiences with web search on medical concerns and self-diagnosis. *AMIA*, 696−700.

[24] White, R.W. and Horvitz, E. (2009). Cyberchondria: studies of the escalation of medical concerns in web search. *TOIS*, 27(4): 23.

[25] White, R.W. and Horvitz, E. (2010). Web to world: predicting transitions from self-diagnosis to the pursuit of local medical assistance in web search. *AMIA*, 882–886.

[26] White, R.W. and Horvitz, E. (2010). Predicting escalations of medical queries based on web page structure and content. *SIGIR*, 769–770.

A Semi-Supervised Approach to Modeling Web Search Satisfaction

Ahmed Hassan
Microsoft Research
Redmond, WA
hassanam@microsoft.com

ABSTRACT

Web search is an interactive process that involves actions from Web search users and responses from the search engine. Many research efforts have been made to address the problem of understanding search behavior in general. Some of this work focused on predicting whether a particular user has succeeded in achieving her search goal or not. Most of these studies have faced the problem of the lack of reliable labeled data to learn from. Unlike labeled data, unlabeled data recording behavioral signals in Web search is widely available in search logs. In this work, we study the plausibility of using labeled and unlabeled data to learn better models of user behavior that can be used to predict search success more effectively. We present a semi-supervised approach to modeling Web search satisfaction. The proposed approach can use either labeled data only or both labeled and unlabeled data. We show that the proposed model outperforms previous methods for modeling search success using labeled data. We also show that adding unlabeled data improves the effectiveness of the proposed models and that the proposed method outperforms other strong semi-supervised baselines.

Categories and Subject Descriptors

H.3.3 [**Information Search and Retrieval**]: Search Process

Keywords

search engine evaluation, user behavior models, semi-supervised learning

1. INTRODUCTION

Finding effective evaluation metrics for information retrieval systems has always received plenty of attention. The need for good evaluation metrics increases as information retrieval systems advance leaving smaller rooms for improvements. Traditionally, per-query metrics such as Mean Average Precision (MAP), Precision @k, and Normalized Discounted Cumulative Gain (NDCG) have been widely used. Recently, researchers started using behavioral signals for evaluating information retrieval systems. Some of this work still considered query-level evaluation [25], while other looked at goal success [12]. Goal level success prediction is related to another body of work that tries to understand different patterns of user behavior in Web search like understanding the behavioral differences between novice and expert users [27], and studying how behavior changes in difficult search tasks [4].

A major problem facing these research efforts is the lack of labeled data to train effective learning algorithms. Hence, most of this work has either been limited to small-scale studies [8], or large-scale analysis of unlabeled data [27, 4]. Labeled data consists of all behavioral signals collected from a user in a search goal and a label indicating whether the user's information need was satisfied or not.

Some approaches have been proposed to overcome the limited availability of labeled data by building frameworks for collecting realistic labeled data. Hassan et al. [13] created a toolbar that monitors search behavior and collects explicit satisfaction ratings from users when they normally use Web search. The toolbar asks users to rate their search experience after every search goal. The main problem with this approach is the low adoption rates of users and the difficulty of keeping users engaged with the toolbar. Ageev et al. [1] suggested using a game like strategy where study participants are competing to find answers to questions using Web search in a given amount of time. Like the first approach, this approach suffers from the low adoption rates. It also creates artificial information needs, rather than monitoring the information needs of real user; which may affect user behavior. Human judges were used to collect labeled search goals in [12]. This process is noisy because judges have no information about the actual intent underlying the information need. Moreover, it is expensive and time consuming. Hence, it does not scale when a large amount of annotated data is needed.

Unlike labeled data, unlabeled data of behavioral signals is readily available in search logs. In unlabeled data, we have access to several signal describing the user behavior, but we do not know whether the user succeeded in satisfying her information goal or not. This suggests that algorithms that can learn from both labeled and unlabeled data could be very effective in modeling search success.

In this work, we look into ways of predicting success in search by modeling user behavior. We introduce a new ap-

Permission to make digital or hard copies of all or part of this work for personal or classroom use is granted without fee provided that copies are not made or distributed for profit or commercial advantage and that copies bear this notice and the full citation on the first page. To copy otherwise, to republish, to post on servers or to redistribute to lists, requires prior specific permission and/or a fee.
SIGIR'12, August 12–16, 2012, Portland, Oregon, USA.
Copyright 2012 ACM 978-1-4503-1472-5/12/08...$15.00.

proach that can use either labeled data only, or labeled and unlabeled data in a semi-supervised setting. We compare the proposed method to previous work on Web search success prediction using labeled data. We also compare it to strong baselines that apply other semi-supervised learning frameworks to the same problem. We discuss the advantages and limitations of the proposed method, and highlight the performance gains the proposed method achieves both in the supervised and semi-supervised settings. We also show empirically that adding unlabeled data improves prediction accuracy.

The rest of this paper will proceed as follows. In Section 2, we discuss related work. We provide a formal definition of our problem is Section 3. In Section 4, we describe a generative model for predicting success and show how it can be extended to the semi-supervised case. Finally we present experiments in Section 6, discussions in Section 7 and we conclude in Section 8.

2. RELATED WORK

Evaluating information retrieval is a challenging problem that received a lot of attention. Traditionally, search engines have been evaluated using classical methodologies that use query sets and relevance judgments. One of the most frequently used metrics for evaluating ad hoc information retrieval is Mean Average Precision (MAP). MAP is optimized to cover both recall and precision while taking the entire search result ranking into consideration. State of the art measurements of query result relevance use discounted cumulative gain (DCG) [18]. The intuition behind DCG is that users are only interested in the first few results and hence high early precision is desirable [14]. DCG metrics lend themselves to a user model of scanning a ranked list of results to some depth. DCG can be calculated using manual query URL relevance judgments, or estimated query URL relevance [2, 21]. Later, DCG evolved into the Normalized Discounted Cumulative Gain (NDCG) [17]. NDCG normalizes DCG across queries by sorting documents of a result set by relevance, computing the ideal DCG, and normalizing DCG with with the ideal DCG. DCG is additive in nature and assumes that documents are independent. Expected Reciprocal Rank [6] is another metric inspired by the cascade model that alleviates these problems. It is defined as the expected reciprocal length of time that the user will take to find a relevant document. Other metrics have been also used like Precision @k.

All those methods are query based metrics. They evaluate an information retrieval system by evaluating individual queries. However, a single user information need may result in one or more queries, and the same query may have different underlying information needs. Hence, individual query URL relevance may not always correlate with user satisfaction. Moreover, all these metrics use human relevance judgments which is expensive to collect and may be noisy because human judges do not know the exact intent behind an information need.

Mining search logs has been extensively studied by various researchers. For example, Jansen et al. [16] studied user query distribution, information needs, and sessions. Beitzel et al. [5] studied the change in popularity of topically categorized queries. White et al. [28] studied search trails including queries and page navigation from toolbar logs.

More specifically, other research has looked at mining search logs for measuring search quality. Fox et al. [9] found that a strong correlation exists between search log features and user satisfaction. They used Bayesian modeling and decision trees to model explicit satisfaction ratings using several kinds of features. They used clickthrough rate features, dwell time features, and features describing how users end their search sessions.

Huffman and Hochster [15] studied the correlation between user satisfaction and simple relevance metrics. They reported a relatively strong correlation between user satisfaction and linear models encompassing the query URL relevance of the first three results for the first query in the search task.

Radlinski et al. [26] showed that interleaving the results of two ranking functions and presenting the interleaved results to users is a good predictor of relative search engine performance. They also looked at using metrics including abandonment rate, reformulation rate, and time to first click to predict relative performance. They found out that those metrics do not perform as well as interleaving results. Using aggregated features extracted from user behavior is certainly correlated with satisfaction. However, it has been shown that modeling the transitions between actions performed by users during search is a stronger predictor of satisfaction [12].

White and Morris [27] tried to understand the behavioral differences between novice and expert users. They define expert users as those who use advanced operators. They show that the behavior of expert users is different compared to non-expert ones. Aula et al. [4] studied how user behavior changes in difficult search tasks. They performed a user study to understand how users behave with difficult search tasks. They found out that when faced with a difficult search tasks, users tend to use more diverse queries, use advanced operators, and spend more time on the search results page. These studies provide many interesting observations about user behavior. However, they do not try to model or predict success due to the lack of labeled data about goals and success.

Hassan et al. [12] showed that modeling action sequences representing user behavior is better than models based on the query URL relevance of the first three results for the first query. The main reasons are that different information needs sometimes underlie the same query, and that the first query does not tell the complete picture in terms of the entire search task. A user study where firsthand satisfaction ratings were directly collected from users, who opted in to use a special toolbar, was presented in [13].

Piwowarski et al. [24] presented a model that uses Bayesian Networks to predict document relevance in the absence of document content models. They presented a Bayesian Network approach to holistically model user behavior interactions, and used it to identify distinct patterns of search behaviors. These patterns, along with a list of custom features, were used to predict the relevance of a set of query document pairs.

Ageev et al. [1] proposes an extension of the Markov Model approach, described in [12], by augmenting the Markov Model with additional search features. They also used a game like strategy for collecting labeled data where they ask participants to find answers to questions using Web search. None of those methods has considered using unlabeled data to improve the effectiveness of the success prediction models. They all faced the problem of the lack of labeled data and came up with different solutions: human judges [12], toolbars [13], and games [1]. The amount of data collected is still relatively small and does not allow further developments targeting specific types of information needs, verticals, or users.

Semi-supervised learning is a special form of machine learning where both labeled and unlabeled data are used in the learning process. Labeled data is usually expensive, and hard to obtain. This resulted in a huge interest in learning techniques that can use unlabeled data as well as labeled data. Semi-supervised learning is a very well established area. Some of the earliest semi-supervised methods in the literature is the self training wrapper algorithm which retrains a supervised model using unlabeled data that have been labeled by the same model with high confidence [3, 10]. The closely related concept of transductive inference has been studied in [11]. A very good introduction and survey of semi-supervised learning techniques could be found in [31, 7, 29]. We will show in this work how semi-supervised learning techniques can improve the effectiveness of success prediction algorithms by using labeled and unlabeled data.

3. PROBLEM DEFINITION

We start by defining some terms that will be used throughout the paper:

Definition: A *search goal/task* is a single information need that may result in one or more queries [20, 12].

Definition: *A search trail* is an ordered sequence of actions performed by the user during a search goal.

Definition: A *labeled dataset* is a collection of search goals associated with success labels. Every goal in the labeled data is labeled as successful or unsuccessful either by a human judge or by collecting firsthand labels from users conducting the search.

Definition: An *unlabeled dataset* is a collection of search goals without success labels. This data is easier to collect and does not need any human judges , or any special software to collect labels (i.e. browser plugins).

Assume we have a stream of queries submitted to a search engine. In response to each query, the engine returns a search results page. The user may decide to interact with this page by clicking on results, other search engine features, or by reformulating the query. Every query is a part of a *search goal* with the objective of satisfying a particular information need. Every search goal is represented with a search trail. A search trail is represented by an ordered sequence of user actions. Actions include all types of interactions performed by the users while using the search engine. Following [12], we use the set of actions described in Table 1. Examples of a successful and an unsuccessful goals are shown in Tables 2 and 3 respectively. In the successful goal, the user started with the query *"van gogh self portrait"*, and quickly decided to click on an image results. She spent some time examining the result then she successfully ended her search. In the unsuccessful goal, the user typed a query, and briefly clicked on two search results. After that, she decided to switch to the images vertical, but the image vertical still did not have any relevant results so she reformulated her query. Apparently, that still did not satisfy her information need, and hence she gave up and ended her search.

The labeled data was collected during a user study where search behavioral signals and explicit success ratings were collected directly from users. This will be described in details in Section 5. This is better than asking human annotators to judge whether a user was successful with his search or not because judges do not have access to information about the actual user intent.

Action	Description
START	the user starts a new goal
Q	a query submission
RL	a related Search Click
SP	a spelling Suggestion Click
SR	a search result click
AD	a sponsored search result click
TB	a switch to a different tab (search vertical)
END	the user ends the search goal

Table 1: A list of possible user actions

Action	
Query	van gogh self portrait
IMG CLICK	url1
END	

Table 2: An Example of a Successful Goal

So given a search goal, our objective is to predict whether that goal ended up being successful or not. We adopt a semi-supervised learning approach to address this problem. Our training data X can be divided into X_l, for which labels Y_l are provided, and X_u, for which no labels are provided.

4. APPROACH

Generative models specify a joint probability distribution over observations and labels. Generative models are often used in machine learning for classification. A conditional distribution is formed from a generative model by use of Baye's rule. In this section, we define a generative model for user behavior and describe how it can be used for both supervised and semi-supervised learning.

4.1 A Generative Model for User Behavior

We assume that search trails are generated by a mixture model. The mixture model has two mixture components corresponding to *success* and *failure*. Every trail is generated using a probability distribution defined by the parameters of the mixture mode, denoted θ. Let there be a set of classes $C = [c_s, c_f]$ corresponding to the *success* and *failure* cases.

Actions in a search trail x_i are generated using the selected mixture component. Every trail x_i is generated according to a distribution $P(x_i|c, \theta)$. Hence the likelihood of seeing a trail x_i is the sum of its probability over the *success* and *fail* mixture components:

$$P(x_i|\theta) = \sum_{c \in [c_s, c_f]} P(c|\theta) P(x_i|c; \theta) \quad (1)$$

Every search trail x_i consists of a set of actions. For every action we chose the next action by drawing from the mixture distributions. Assuming every trail consists of a set of actions: $x = \{a_1, a_2, ..., a_n\}$ and that every action is dependent only on the previous action and independent of the trail length, then we can write:

$$P(x|c, \theta) \propto \prod_{j=1}^{n} P(a_j|a_{j-1}; c; \theta) \quad (2)$$

	Action
Query	steven colbert painting
CLICK	url1
CLICK	url2
TAB SWITCH	IMAGES
Query	steven colbert recursive painting
END	

Table 3: An Example of an Unsuccessful Goal

This leaves us with a set of parameters $\theta_{a,a',c} \equiv P(a'|a;c;\theta)$ for every pair of actions a and a', and every class c. In addition we have two more parameters θ_{c_s} and θ_{c_f} corresponding to the prior class probabilities $P(c_s|\theta)$ and $P(c_f\theta)$. Hence, the probability of generating any search trail x is:

$$P(x|\theta) \propto \sum_{c\in\{c_s,cf\}} P(c|\theta) \prod_{j=1}^{n} P(a_j|a_{j-1};c;\theta) \quad (3)$$

where x is a search trail consisting of a set of actions $x = \langle a_1, a_2, \ldots, a_n, \rangle$, n is the number of actions in trail x, and a_j is action number j in x . In our experiments, we model the trail length by introducing one multinomial distribution for each possible length. Alternatively, we can assume that trail length is identically distributed to reduce the number of parameters.

4.2 Supervised Classification

To use this model for classification, we need to learn an estimate $\hat{\theta}$ of the model parameters. To estimate these parameters, we may use maximum likelihood estimation (MLE) or maximum a posterior (MAP) estimates. One potential problem with MLE is that it may result in zero estimates of some parameters if the corresponding transition has not been seen in the training data. This problem is usually solved by smoothing. Alternatively, we can use MAP estimates with Dirichlet priors, which is identical to MLE with Laplace smoothing. Hence, the action transition parameters are estimated as:

$$\hat{\theta}_{a_i,a_j,c} \equiv P(a_i|a_{i-1};c;\hat{\theta}) = \frac{1 + N_{a_i,a_j,c}}{|A| + N_{a_i,c}} \quad (4)$$

where $N_{a_i,a_j,c}$ is the empirical count of transitions from a_i to a_j in trails in class c, $N_{a_i,c}$ is the empirical count of a_i in the same trails, and $|A|$ is the total number of actions. Similarly, the class probabilities are estimated as:

$$\hat{\theta}_c \equiv P(c|\hat{\theta}) = \frac{1 + N_c}{2 + N} \quad (5)$$

where N_c is the fraction of trails in the training data with class c, and N is the size of the training set.

Given these parameters we can derive a conditional probability distribution to classify new instances given the generative model:

$$P(c|x_i, \hat{\theta}) = \frac{P(c|\hat{\theta})P(x_i|c;\hat{\theta})}{P(x_i|\hat{\theta})} \quad (6)$$

To classify a new trail we just need to compute:

$$PRED(x_i) = arg\,max_{c\in\{c_s,c_f\}} P(c|x_i, \hat{\theta}) \quad (7)$$

This model has three advantages compared the one presented in [12]: (1) the model proposes a more principled way of modeling user behavior, (2) the Markov model presented in [12] makes decisions based on trail likelihood ($P(x|c;\theta)$), while the model we present here uses posterior class probabilities instead ($P(c|x,\theta)$). We will show later the advantages of taking the prior distribution into consideration, and (3) this model can be extended to the semi-supervised case as will be shown in the next sections.

4.3 Modeling Time

We tried two different approaches to modeling time. In the first approach, we treat transition time as a continuous variable drawn from a Gamma distribution with parameters k, and θ. We compute the distribution parameters for every class (i.e. success or failure), and every transition. Then, the probability of some value given a class, $P(t = v|c)$, can be computed by plugging v into the equation for the Gamma distribution parameterized by the parameters we computed earlier.

In the second approach, we replace every click action (e.g. algorithmic result click, sponsored result click, etc.) with one of three different actions based on the click dwell time. For example instead of the action *"SR"*, which denote a search result click, we have *"SR-short"* , *"SR"*, and *"SR-long"*. Long clicks are defined to have a dwell time for longer than 30 seconds and have been shown to correlate with satisfaction, as in previous work [9]. Similarly, short clicks are clicks with a quick bounce back to the SERP and have dwell time on the landing page of under 15 seconds [9]. SERP view actions (e.g. query submission, related search click, etc.) are replaced with one of two actions: short if dwell time is less than 20 seconds, and long otherwise. Short time to first click, which is the difference between the timestamp from serving up the page and the timestamp of the first user click on the page, has been previously shown to be correlated with satisfaction [26].

4.4 Semi-Supervised Classification

The model we described in the previous subsections uses labeled data only to estimate the model parameters. Due to the high cost of obtaining labeled data for this task, and the wide availability of unlabeled data, we would like to extend the model such that it uses labeled and unlabeled data for learning. The model parameters, $\hat{\theta}$ have been estimated using MAP estimations. This cannot directly handle unlabeled data. However, we can do so by using the expectation maximization (EM) algorithm. Semi-supervised classification with EM has been successfully applied to different domains before, including text categorization [23].

The EM algorithm is an iterative algorithms which can be used to find the MAP estimates of parameters in statistical modeling. The algorithm has two main steps: the *Expectation* step and the *Maximization* step. The Expectation (E) step of the algorithm computes the expectation of the missing values; in this case the class membership distribution of the unlabeled data. The Maximization (M) step re-estimates the parameters by maximizing the likelihood of the parameters using the previously computed expectations. The algorithm works as follows:

- Estimate the parameters $\hat{\theta}$ from labeled data only
- Loop while the parameters improve:
  - **E:** Use the current classifier to estimate $P(c_s|x_i;\hat{\theta})$, and $P(c_f|x_i;\hat{\theta})$ for all unlabeled trails.

- **M**: Re-estimate model parameters, $\hat{\theta}$, using the labeled data and the component memberships of the unlabeled.

To take the component membership of the unlabeled data into consideration during training, we modify Equation 4 to:

$$\hat{\theta}_{a_i,a_j,c} \equiv P(a_i|a_{i-1};c;\hat{\theta}) = \frac{1 + \sum_{x_i \in X} \delta(x_i,c) N(x_i,a,a')}{|A| + \sum_{x_i \in X} \delta(x_i,c) N(x_i,a)} \quad (8)$$

where X is the set of training data, $N(x_i, a, a')$ is the number of transitions from a to a' in x_i, and $N(x_i, a)$ is the number of occurrences of a in x_i. For the labeled data, $\delta(x_i, c)$ is 1 if x_i is in class c and 0 otherwise. For the unlabeled data, $\delta(x_i, c)$ is the component membership probabilities calculated in the previous E step.

5. DATA

Our data includes search behavioral signals and explicit success ratings collected directly from users. This data was collected during a user study where firsthand success ratings were collected from users. This is better than traditional ways of collecting data that use annotators to judge whether a user has been successful or not [12]. The latter method introduces more noise in the labels because judges lack information about the actual intent behind the search goal.

Study participants were instructed to install a toolbar. The toolbar detects when a user submits a query to Google, Bing, or Yahoo search engines. It then monitors and records all actions performed by the user during search. Participants were instructed to submit a binary success rating at the end of every search goal. Participants were also allowed to ignore a search goal, in which case, no data was collected about that goal.

Every log entry contained a user identifier, a time-stamp for every page view, and the URL of the visited page. Page views included query submission, search result clicks, navigation beyond the search results page originating from clicks on links in a search result, and clicks on other search engine features (e.g. spelling corrections, related searches, etc.). Secure (https) URLs have not been collected and any identifiable information was removed from the data prior to any analysis.

More than 10k unique searches were collected a long with a label indicating whether the search was successful or not. Every record included a search trail, and a success label. A search trail originates with the submission of a query to a search engine and contains all queries and post-query navigation trails [27]. A search trail always begins with a query and ends when the information seeking activity stops. A search trail is represented by an ordered sequence of user actions as described earlier.

6. EXPERIMENTS

6.1 The Supervised Setting

6.1.1 Baselines

We compare the proposed approach to three baselines in the supervised setting. The first baseline poses the problem as a classic machine learning problem where a set of features

Features
Number of queries
Number of clicks of all types
Number of algorithmic results clicks
Number of sponsored results clicks
Number of answer results clicks
Number of pagination clicks
Number of spell suggestion clicks
Number of related queries clicks
Average time between clicks
Time span of goal
Average time to first click
Average dwell time

Table 4: Static features for predicting success.

adopted from previous work, [26, 12], are used to train a logistic regression classifier . The set of features we used are summarized in Table 4

The second baseline is the Markov model approach described in [12]. In this approach, two Markov models are trained to characterize the behavior of users in successful and failed goals. Features are described by a sequence of actions as described earlier. A new goal x is classified as successful if $P(x|success) > P(x|failure)$.

The last baseline uses Conditional Random Fields to model success [1]. We ran our approach on the data used in [1]; which was made publicly avaiable. We will report the results from [1] and the results obtained by our approach using the same data.

6.1.2 Experimental setup

We perform experiments using the data described in Section 5. We used four supervised methods; the generative model presented in this paper and three baselines. To compare supervised methods, we report accuracy using 10-fold cross-validation. Folds were created based on user ids. We used the entire dataset described in Section 5. Users reported success in approximately 80% of the goals in this dataset and the rest reported failure. A different dataset was used for the comparison against the CRF method, presented in [1], as will be described later.

6.1.3 Results

We start by comparing the two approaches we described for modeling time and found that the difference in performance was not statistically significant at the 0.05 level according to the Wicoxon *p-value*. We will use the approach based on time discretization in all following experiments.

We then compared the performance of all supervised methods using 10-fold cross validation over the entire dataset. Figure 1 shows the performance of the proposed method and the two baselines. We notice that the proposed approach outperforms the two baselines and the difference is statistically significant at the 0.05 level. We notice that the static features baseline has the worst performance. This agrees with findings reported in previous work because the static features describe an aggregate view of user behavior and misses many important pieces of information. We also see performance gains compared to the Markov model approach. Modeling the posterior probability of search goals ($P(c|x, \theta)$ yields better results that modeling the likelihood ($P(x|c, \theta)$ especially because the dataset is unbalanced with respect to the proportion of successful and failed goals This imbalance is typical in any random sample of query impressions because most users achieve their search goals and dissatisfaction is usually the exception. For example, Ageev et al. [1] performed a study where users were asked to find answers to specific questions using Web search. In 87% of the tasks, users reported success by finding and reporting an answer. Hassan et al. [12] asked judges to label search goals as successful or not and reported that more than 70% of the goals were labeled as successful. In our dataset, where first-hand success labels were collected from users, approximately 80% of the goals ended with users reporting that their information need was satisfied. When we had a closer look at the performance of the proposed generative model and the Markov model of [12], we noticed that the performance slightly improved for the majority class (satisfied goals) and significantly improved by over for the minority class (dissatisfied goals).

We also compared the performance of our approach to the CRF approach presented in [1]. We used the same dataset and the same experimental setup described in [1]. They used a game like strategy where study participants are competing to find answers to questions using Web search in a given amount of time. The data was collected in 4 different game rounds. We used 4-fold cross-validation where the data from three games was used for training and the data from the fourth was used for testing. Ageev et al. [1] defined four different success criteria: 1) the user submitted an answer and the answer was correct, 2) the user submitted an answer that could be correct or not, 3) the user visited a good URL that has relevant information to the question, and 4) the user visited a good URL and it was last in the search session. Like [1], we measured accuracy and macro-averaged F-measure over the successful and unsuccessful results. For the Markov model and the generative model approaches. We modeled time using the discrete approach described in Section 4.3. The results are shown in Table 5. The table shows that both the CRF model and the generative model outperform the Markov model. The gap between the performance of the generative model and the Markov model increases as the data imbalance increases as expected. The performance of the CRF and the generative model depends on the success definition. The former is better for some definitions and the latter is better for others. The difference in performance is very small in all cases.

6.2 The semi-supervised setting

We compare the proposed approach to two baselines. The first baseline is a transductive discriminative model trained on features describing the transition between different actions. The second baseline is a graph based algorithm based on random fields and harmonic functions. In the rest of this section, we describe the baselines, experimental setup and results.

6.2.1 Baseline 1: Transductive SVM

In this baseline, we can use the action transitions (i.e. transition from a to a' in search trails) as features and train a discriminative model. The objective of this model is to classify each search trail into one of two categories (success or failure). The first step in this process is to transform search trails into a representation suitable for the classification task. One way to approach this problem is to compute a set of aggregate features to describe the user behavior from the search trail (e.g. number of clicks, number of queries, average dwell time, etc.). Hassan et al. [12] looked at this approach and showed that directly modeling transitions is better than using aggregate features. They also showed that transitions subsume information in aggregate features.

Instead of using aggregate features, we can derive features that directly represents the search trail without losing much information. We can use the transition between every two consecutive actions as a feature. For example, given the search trail: *"Q Q SR END"* where *Q*, *SR*, and *END* correspond to query submission, search result click, and goal termination respectively, we can extract the following three features: *Q-Q*, *Q-SR*, and *SR-END*.

Generally, we will have $|A|^2$ features where A is the set of possible actions. Every feature corresponds to a possible transition between two states. Every trail will be represented using those features. Feature values are simply the number of times every transition has been observed in the trail. The feature vector is expected to be sparse with most of the features having a zero value. Transductive support vector machines [19] extend SVMs in that they could handle both labeled and unlabeled data in a semi-supervised setting. SVMs use a set of labeled data, X_l, and a set of corresponding labels Y_l. SVM training algorithm builds a model that assigns new examples into one category or the other. In that, SVMs try to induce a general decision function for the learning task. Transductive SVMs use an unlabeled set X_u along with X_l, and Y_l. TSVMs take into account a particular set of unlabeled data, X_u, and try to minimize misclassification of this set of unlabeled data.

Joachims [19] used TSVMs for text classification and proposed an algorithm for training TSVMs efficiently. Joachims [19] argues that TSVMs are suitable for text classification because of the high dimensional input space and the feature vector sparseness. Although our feature space is smaller than typical feature spaces in text classification, we believe TSVMs is a strong baseline for this problem.

6.2.2 Baseline 2: Harmonic Functions

Another popular class of semi-supervised learning algorithms is the graph based methods. Graph based learning algorithms rely on building a graph representation of labeled and unlabeled data points. Edges in the graph encode pairwise similarities between points. Graph based algorithms have been successfully applied to a range of problems in natural language processing, computer vision, and computational biology. Graph based methods are discriminative and transductive in nature.

We construct a graph $G(V, E)$, where V is the list of labeled and unlabeled trails. E is a set of edges connecting similar points. Inspired by the bag of words model for representing text documents, we represent every trail using a bag of transitions. Every transition has a count associated with it. Each transition corresponds to a dimension in high dimensional space, and every trail is a vector in that space. The frequency of every transition is used as its weight. Let A be the set of possible user actions, $|A|$ be the number of such possible actions, and $N(x_i, a, a')$ be the number of transitions from a to a' in x_i. Then every trail can be represented as vector as follows

$$\vec{x_i} = (N(x_i, a_1, a_1), N(x_i, a_1, a_2), \ldots, N(x_i, a_n, a_n)) \quad (9)$$

We use the popular Cosine similarity measure to compute similarity between user behavior in different goals. The vector representation of trails allows us to use the Cosine similarity measure to compute similarity between any two given trails. The Cosine metric measures the similarity by computing the cosine of the angle between the two vectors representing the search trails. Formally, this can be written as:

$$Cos(\vec{x_a}, \vec{x_b}) = \frac{\vec{x_a} \cdot \vec{x_b}}{|\vec{x_a}| \times |\vec{x_b}|} \tag{10}$$

To construct the graph, we create a node for every search trail. Every pair of nodes is connected by an edge. The weight of edges comes from one of the similarity measure described above. The graph could be also represented by an $n \times n$ symmetric matrix, where n is the number of search trails. Every element $M(i, j)$ represents the similarity between trail x_i and trail x_j.

Zhu et al. [30] presented a semi-supervised graph learning approach based on Gaussian random fields and harmonic functions. The similarity graph we described earlier is used to represent both labeled and unlabeled data. The learning problem is then formulated using the Gaussian random field on this graph, with the mean of this field characterized using harmonic functions [30].

The method assumes n data points, l of which are labeled, and the rest u are unlabeled. Consider the graph $G = (V, E)$ built as described above. We represent the graph using a symmetric $n \times n$ matrix W. The objective of this method is to compute a real valued function $f : V \to \mathbb{R}$. The values of f are fixed for labeled data and equal the class label. The value of f for unlabeled data will be computed and used to assign labels to unlabeled data. Zhu et al. shows that the function f that minimizes the eneregy function $E(f)$ is harmonic [30]. It is intuitive that the function f is expected to have similar labels to points that are close in the graph. Hence, they used the quadratic energy function:

$$E(f) = \frac{1}{2} \sum_{i,j} w_{ij} (f(i) - f(j))^2 \tag{11}$$

The harmonic solution is computed explicitly as follows:

- Let $D = diag(d_i)$ be the diagonal matrix with entries $d_i = \sum_j w_{ij}$, where $W = [w_{ij}]$ is the weight matrix.
- Because f is harmonic, it can be expressed as $f = Pf$, where $P = D^{-1}W$.
- Split W, and similarily D and P into 4 blocks:
$$W = \begin{bmatrix} W_{ll} & W_{lu} \\ W_{ul} & W_{uu} \end{bmatrix}$$
- Let $f = \begin{bmatrix} f_l \\ f_u \end{bmatrix}$, where f_u denotes the values of f for the unlabeled data.
- The harmonic solution is given as:
$$f_u = (D_{uu} - W_{uu})^{-1} W_{ul} f_l = (I - P_{uu})^{-1} P_{ul} f_l$$

6.3 Experimental Setup

We perform experiments using the data described in Section 5. We compare the performance of three semi-supervised methods. The first is the proposed approach that uses expectation maximization to extend a generative mode to handle labeled and unlabeled data. The second uses Transductive Support Vector Machines (TSVMs), and the third is a graph based model that uses Gaussian random fields and harmonic functions. We carried out the experiments in the transductive settings, following [7]. In this setting, the test set coincides with the set of unlabeled points (50% of the data). This has two main advantages. First, it is economical in terms of the required data. Second, it allows us to compare different methods including those that are naturally transductive. We compare every semi-supervised method to a corresponding supervised method to assess the benefit of adding the unlabeled data. We also compare the semi-supervised methods to one another. To make sure that the reported results are independent of labeled points selection, we select 10 different sets of labeled data for every number of labeled data points at random and report the average of the 10 runs.

6.4 Results

In this section, we assess the benefit of using unlabeled data for every model. We compare every semi-supervised method (the proposed method and the baselines) to a corresponding supervised method. We compare the supervised and the semi-supervised versions of the proposed approach. We compare the Trasductive SVM baseline to an inductive SVM classifier, and the harmonic functions baseline to a k-neaerest neighbor method using the same graph. The objective of this experiment is to estimate the benefit of using unlabeled data regardless of the semi-supervised model used. We start with SVM and TSVM. Figure 2 compares the performance of both methods while varying the amount of labeled data. We notice a consistent improvement over using labeled data only when unlabeled data is introduced. The improvement is bigger when the number of labeled points is small and gets smaller quickly as more labeled data is introduced.

We notice similar behavior when we compare semi-supervised learning using harmonic functions to the K-nearest neighbor method in Figure 3. Interestingly, we notice that adding the unlabeled data hurts the performance when the number of labeled points is very small. Otherwise, adding labeled data improves performance. Like TSVM, the benefit of adding unlabeled data decreases as more labeled data is introduced. The benefit of using harmonic functions with labeled and unlabeled data over using KNN is considerably bigger than the benefits of using TSVM over SVM.

Figure 4 compares the performance of the semi-supervised generative model that uses EM and the supervised generative mode. We notice similar behavior to the two previous cases where using EM and unlabeled data improves performance. Unlike the graph based model, the improvement is consistent regardless of the amount of labeled data. The improvement is also considerably larger than the TSVM case.

We also compare the performance of the three semi-supervised learning algorithm in Figure 5. The figure compares the performance of the generative model with EM, the Transductive Support Vector Machines (TSVMs) model, and the graph based model that uses Gaussian random fields and harmonic functions using a Cosine similarity graph. We notice that the graph based model performs poorly when the amount of labeled data is limited. The two other methods

Success Definition	Majority		MM		GM		CRF	
	Acc	F1	Acc	F1	Acc	F1	Acc	F1
Answer Correct	65	40	68	61	67	60	68	60
Answer Sub.	87	47	83	64	88	65	86	64
Good URL	83	45	78	60	83	65	80	57
Good URL Last	60	38	67	66	67	67	68	66

Table 5: The Majority Baseline (MB) vs. the Markov Model (MM) approach vs. the Generative Model (GM) approach vs. the CRF approach using data from [1].

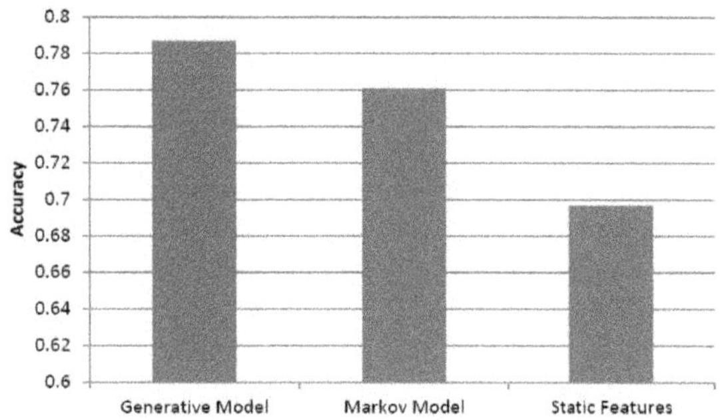

Figure 1: Performance of all supervised methods using 10 fold cross validation.

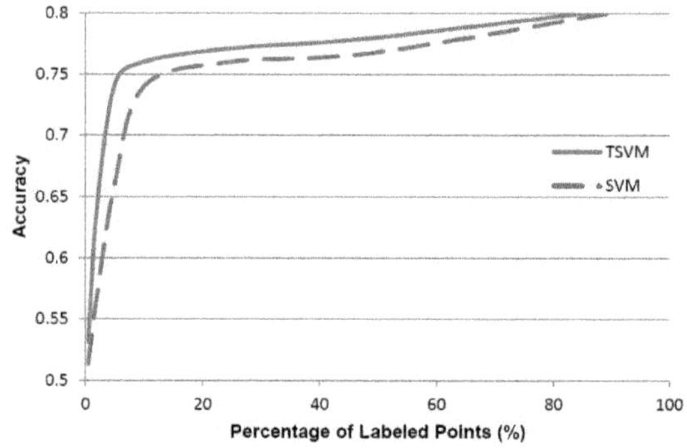

Figure 2: Performance of SVM vs. TSVM for different numbers of labeled data points.

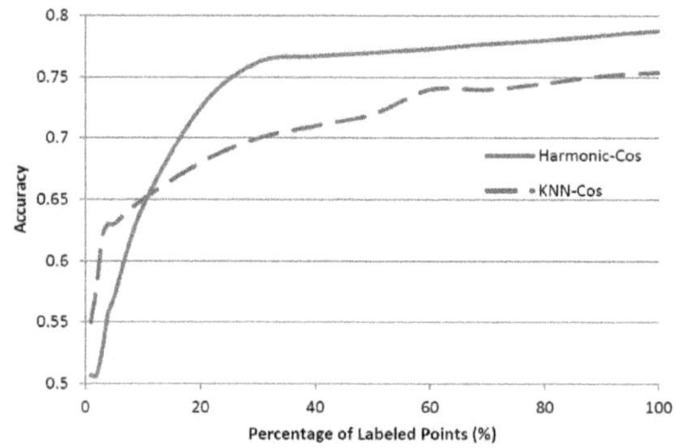

Figure 3: Performance of Harmonic Functions vs. KNN for different numbers of labeled data points.

perform better with the the generative model with EM outperforming all other models with a large margin. As more labeled data is introduced the improvement margin starts to decrease.

The experiments show that adding unlabeled data considerably increases the prediction power of the models. This gain is achieved regardless of which semi-supervised model is used. When we compare the three semi-supervised mode, we notice that both the EM model and the TSVM model perform better than the other baseline and their performance is pretty close to one another. The EM model has an advantage over the TSVM and the graph based models which are transductive in nature. Transductive models need to be retrained for every new test set. The generative EM model does not suffer from this limitation.

Adding more unlabeled data points is shown to improve performance in Figure 6. In this experiment, we fixed the number of labeled points at 250, varied the number of unlabeled points and observed the performance. The figure indicates that adding more unlabeled data improves performance for all methods.

In summary, we have shown that using a semi-supervised framework improves performance regardless of the algorithm. We have also shown that the EM model and the TSVM model perform better than the graph based model, and that the EM model has an advantage over the other models because it does not have to operate in a transductive setting.

7. DISCUSSION

We studied the problem of Web search success prediction. Our study is different from previous work in that the methods we proposed can learn from both labeled and unlabeled data. The area of using behavioral signals to model success in Web search is rather new. All previous work has posed the problem as a supervised learning problem where labeled data is used to train a model that can be used later for predictions. We have discussed the problems associated with collecting labeled data for search success prediction and how the process is time consuming, expensive, and sometimes not very reliable. In the meantime, unlabeled data could be easily and quickly collected. We showed how learning from labeled and unlabeled data can improve the performance of search success prediction models. We proposed different methods for incorporating unlabeled data in the learning process. We showed that adding unlabeled data significantly improves performance. We also compared the performance of different methodologies for learning from labeled and unlabeled data and highlighted the strength and weakness of every method. In addition, we also proposed a novel supervised learning model for search success prediction. We showed that this model outperforms or achieves a comparable perfromance compared to the state of the art methods for predicting search success.

We performed several experiments comparing the performance of several supervised and semi-supervised models for predicting success in search. Now, we try to summarize our finding for both the supervised and the semi-supervised cases. For the supervised case, the proposed model, and the Markov model [12] perform much better than a classifier that used a set of static features. The static features classifier aggregates features describing the user behavior. It performs poorly compared to the other models because the other models have a more accurate picture of user behavior by modeling action sequences. The proposed model is more

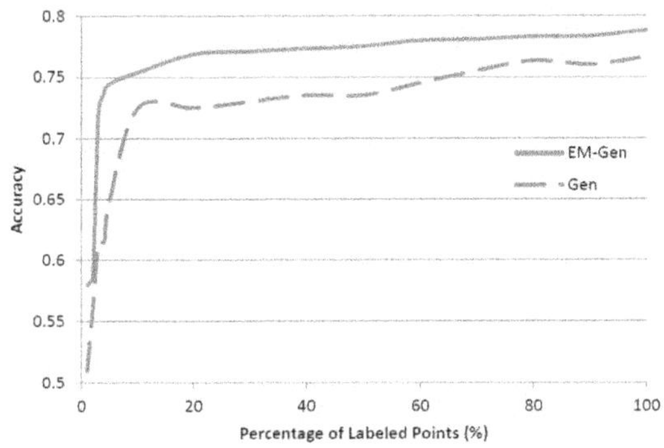

Figure 4: Performance of Generative Model vs. Generative Model with Expectation Maximization for different numbers of labeled data points.

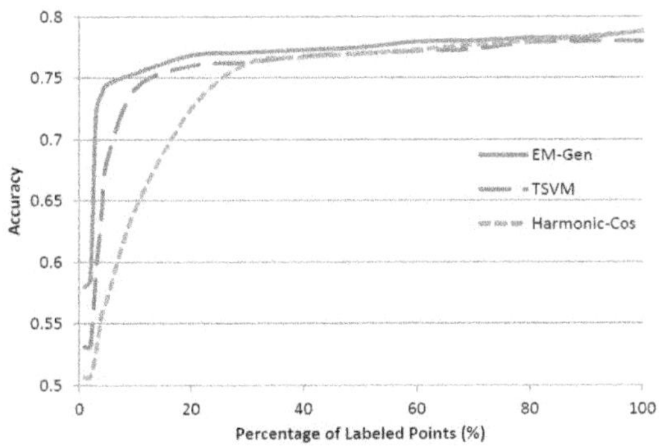

Figure 5: Performance of all semi-supervised models for different numbers of labeled data points.

principled and performs better than the Markov model [12]. The Markov model is intuitive and powerful, but it uses the likelihood of the action sequence representing a search goal, rather than the posterior probability as is the case with the proposed method. The posterior probability takes the prior into consideration which was shown to be important especially because of the inherent imbalance in the data distribution.

In the semi-supervised case, the generative model with EM performs best when the the labeled data is scarce. This is consistent with [22] that states that generative models have superior performance when only a few training examples are available. When the number of labeled data is increased, the performance of all algorithms is similar. One advantage for the generative model with EM over TSVM is that TSVMs are very slow to train and cannot handle large amounts of data. The graph based model is also pretty slow because it involves computing a pairwise similarities for all data points. Another advantage for the generative model is that it is inductive by nature. However, other models may be used in an inductive setting as well but possibly with some performance loss.

Our results show that incorporating unlabeled data in the user satisfaction prediction task improves classification. Previous work on user satisfaction prediction and other related tasks have faced the problem of the limited avaiability of labeled data for supervised learning. Our results suggest that

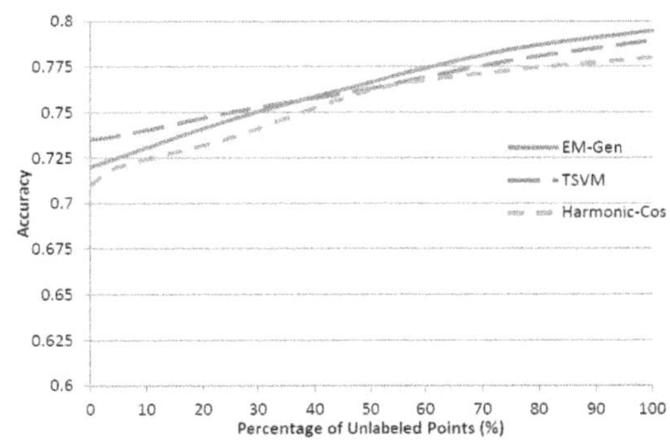

Figure 6: Performance of All Semi-supervised methods for different numbers of unlabeled data points.

semi-supervised methods in general, not only the proposed one, should be seriously considered in the future to predict satisfaction and other similar tasks.

Our findings suggest several lines of future directions for this work. The fact that adding unlabeled data can improve the performance will allow us to build more specific success prediction models that target specific verticals or specific types of queries. Moreover, this may allow us to build personalized success models tailored to the behavior of different users. We also plan to compare the predictive power of different transitions along the search trail. A preliminary study showed that looking at the entire trail is more informative that any parts of it, but we believe that we can develop better models by further studying this problem. One other direction of future research is to try to incorporate other query and SERP features like the ones presented in [1] in the semi-supervised models.

8. CONCLUSIONS

We presented novel methodologies for predicting success in Web search by analyzing user behavior. Collecting large amounts of labeled data for search success prediction is time consuming and sometimes not reliable. We showed that using semi-supervised methods, where both labeled and unlabeled data are used, improves the prediction acuracy. We presented several methods for incorporating unlabeled data and we discussed the advantages nad disadvantages of each. The results suggest that semi-supervised methods in general should be considered in the future for this task and other similar tasks.

9. REFERENCES

[1] M. Ageev, Q. Guo, D. Lagun, and E. Agichtein. Find it if you can: a game for modeling different types of web search success using interaction data. In *Proceedings of the 34th international ACM SIGIR conference on Research and development in Information*, SIGIR '11, pages 345–354, New York, NY, USA, 2011. ACM.

[2] E. Agichtein, E. Brill, and S. T. Dumais. Improving web search ranking by incorporating user behavior information. In *SIGIR 2006: Proceedings of the 29th annual international ACM SIGIR conference on Research and development in information retrieval*, pages 19–26, New York, NY, USA, 2006. ACM.

[3] A. Agrawala. Learning with a probabilistic teacher. *Information Theory, IEEE Transactions on*, 16(4):373 – 379, jul 1970.

[4] A. Aula, R. M. Khan, and Z. Guan. How does search behavior change as search becomes more difficult? In *Proceedings of the 28th international conference on Human factors in computing systems*, CHI '10, pages 35–44, New York, NY, USA, 2010. ACM.

[5] S. M. Beitzel, E. C. Jensen, A. Chowdhury, D. Grossman, and O. Frieder. Hourly analysis of a very large topically categorized web query log. In *Proceedings of the 27th annual international ACM SIGIR conference on Research and development in information retrieval*, SIGIR '04, pages 321–328, New York, NY, USA, 2004. ACM.

[6] O. Chapelle, D. Metlzer, Y. Zhang, and P. Grinspan. Expected reciprocal rank for graded relevance. In *Proceeding of the 18th ACM conference on Information and knowledge management*, CIKM '09, pages 621–630, New York, NY, USA, 2009. ACM.

[7] O. Chapelle, B. Schölkopf, and A. Zien, editors. *Semi-Supervised Learning*. MIT Press, Cambridge, MA, 2006.

[8] H. A. Feild, J. Allan, and R. Jones. Predicting searcher frustration. In *Proceeding of the 33rd international ACM SIGIR conference on Research and development in information retrieval*, SIGIR '10, pages 34–41, New York, NY, USA, 2010. ACM.

[9] S. Fox, K. Karnawat, M. Mydland, S. Dumais, and T. White. Evaluating implicit measures to improve web search. *ACM Transactions on Information Systems*, 23, 2005.

[10] S. Fralick. Learning to recognize patterns without a teacher. *Information Theory, IEEE Transactions on*, 13(1):57 – 64, jan 1967.

[11] A. Gammerman, V. Vovk, and V. Vapnik. Learning by transduction. In *In Uncertainty in Artificial Intelligence*, pages 148–155. Morgan Kaufmann, 1998.

[12] A. Hassan, R. Jones, and K. L. Klinkner. Beyond dcg: user behavior as a predictor of a successful search. In *WSDM '10: Proceedings of the third ACM international conference on Web search and data mining*, pages 221–230, New York, NY, USA, 2010. ACM.

[13] A. Hassan, Y. Song, and L.-w. He. A task level metric for measuring web search satisfaction and its application on improving relevance estimation. In *Proceedings of ACM 20th Conference on Information and Knowledge Management (CIKM 2011)*, 2011.

[14] D. Hawking, N. Craswell, P. Thistlewaite, and D. Harman. Results and challenges in web search evaluation. In *Proc of WWW '99*, pages 1321–1330, 1999.

[15] S. B. Huffman and M. Hochster. How well does result relevance predict session satisfaction? In *Proceedings of the 30th annual international ACM SIGIR conference on Research and development in information retrieval*, pages 567–574, 2007.

[16] B. J. Jansen, A. Spink, and T. Saracevic. Real life, real users, and real needs: a study and analysis of user queries on the web. *Inf. Process. Manage.*, 36:207–227, January 2000.

[17] K. Järvelin and J. Kekäläinen. Ir evaluation methods for retrieving highly relevant documents. In *Proceedings of the 23rd annual international ACM SIGIR conference on Research and development in information retrieval*, SIGIR '00, pages 41–48, New York, NY, USA, 2000. ACM.

[18] K. Järvelin and J. Kekäläinen. Cumulated gain-based evaluation of ir techniques. *ACM Trans. Inf. Syst.*, 20(4):422–446, 2002.

[19] T. Joachims. *Making large-scale support vector machine learning practical*, pages 169–184. MIT Press, Cambridge, MA, USA, 1999.

[20] R. Jones and K. Klinkner. Beyond the session timeout: Automatic hierarchical segmentation of search topics in query logs. In *Proceedings of ACM 17th Conference on Information and Knowledge Management (CIKM 2008)*, 2008.

[21] S. Jung, J. L. Herlocker, and J. Webster. Click data as implicit relevance feedback in web search. *Information Processing and Management (IPM)*, 43(3):791–807, 2007.

[22] T. M. Mitchell. *Machine Learning*. McGraw-Hill, Inc., New York, NY, USA, 1 edition, 1997.

[23] K. Nigam, A. Mccallum, and T. M. Mitchell. *Semi-Supervised Text Classification Using EM*, chapter 3. MIT Press, 2006.

[24] B. Piwowarski, G. Dupret, and R. Jones. Mining user web search activity with layered bayesian networks or how to capture a click in its context. In *Proceedings of the Second ACM International Conference on Web Search and Data Mining*, 2009.

[25] F. Radlinski, M. Kurup, and T. Joachims. How does clickthrough data reflect retrieval quality? In *Proceeding of the 17th ACM conference on Information and knowledge management*, CIKM '08, pages 43–52, New York, NY, USA, 2008. ACM.

[26] F. Radlinski, M. Kurup, and T. Joachims. How does clickthrough data reflect retrieval quality? In J. G. Shanahan, S. Amer-Yahia, I. Manolescu, Y. Zhang, D. A. Evans, A. Kolcz, K.-S. Choi, and A. Chowdhury, editors, *CIKM*, pages 43–52. ACM, 2008.

[27] R. W. White and S. M. Drucker. Investigating behavioral variability in web search. In *Proceedings of the 16th international conference on World Wide Web*, 2007.

[28] R. W. White and J. Huang. Assessing the scenic route: measuring the value of search trails in web logs. In *Proceeding of the 33rd international ACM SIGIR conference on Research and development in information retrieval*, SIGIR '10, pages 587–594, 2010.

[29] X. Zhu. Semi-supervised learning literature survey. University of Wisconsin-Madison - Computer Science TR 1530.

[30] X. Zhu, Z. Ghahramani, and J. D. Lafferty. Semi-supervised learning using gaussian fields and harmonic functions. In *International Conference on Machine Learning*, 2003.

[31] X. Zhu and A. B. Goldberg. Introduction to semi-supervised learning. *Synthesis Lectures on Artificial Intelligence and Machine Learning*, 3(1):1–130, 2009.

Social Annotations: Utility and Prediction Modeling

Patrick Pantel, Michael Gamon
Microsoft Research
One Microsoft Way
Redmond, WA, USA
{ppantel,mgamon}@microsoft.com

Omar Alonso, Kevin Haas
Microsoft Corp
1065 La Avenida
Mountain View, CA, USA
{omalonso,kevinhaa}@microsoft.com

ABSTRACT

Social features are increasingly integrated within the search results page of the main commercial search engines. There is, however, little understanding of the utility of social features in traditional search. In this paper, we study utility in the context of social annotations, which are markings indicating that a person in the social network of the user has liked or shared a result document. We introduce a taxonomy of social relevance aspects that influence the utility of social annotations in search, spanning query classes, the social network, and content relevance. We present the results of a user study quantifying the utility of social annotations and the interplay between social relevance aspects. Through the user study we gain insights on conditions under which social annotations are most useful to a user. Finally, we present machine learned models for predicting the utility of a social annotation using the user study judgments as an optimization criterion. We model the learning task with features drawn from web usage logs, and show empirical evidence over real-world head and tail queries that the problem is learnable and that in many cases we can predict the utility of a social annotation.

Categories and Subject Descriptors

H.3.3 [**Information Storage and Retrieval**]: Information Search and Retrieval

General Terms

Algorithms, Design, Experimentation, Measurement

Keywords

Social relevance, social aspects, web search

1. INTRODUCTION

Social offerings are becoming table stakes for the major search engines. Querying for your local pizza restaurant on Bing or Google may yield reviews from your friends about the restaurant, or about nearby restaurants liked by your friends. A query for "*maui hotels*" may yield a result indicating that your colleagues like the *Royal Lahaina Resort* on Facebook and a query for "*luau history*" may yield a social annotation on the result "Hawaii Luau History" stating that your friend has liked or shared the document.

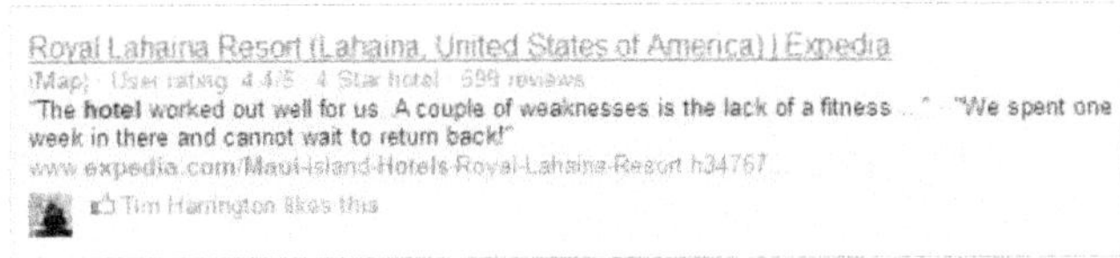

Figure 1: Example social annotation for the query "*maui hotels*".

The user can benefit from such social experiences in various ways, including: (a) discovery of socially vetted recommendations; (b) personalized search results; (c) connecting to the lives of their friends; (d) result diversity; and (e) emotionally connecting with an otherwise static and impersonal search engine. There is, however, very little understanding whether these social features are useful or detrimental to the whole-page user experience, or, for that matter, how to even measure the utility of social features.

Consider a **social annotation** feature, such as the one depicted in Figure 1, where some results on the search results page (SERP) are enriched with markings indicating some of your friends that have previously `liked` or `shared` that result[1]. Are such endorsements from dearest friends more relevant to the user than from acquaintances or coworkers? Are expert opinions or those from friends who live in the vicinity of the restaurant more valuable? Do annotations on irrelevant results amplify their negative perception?

Studying such aspects and their effect on social relevance form the basis of this paper. We begin by enumerating a taxonomy of social relevance aspects, i.e. cues or criteria that influence the perceived utility of social annotations. We consider aspects related to the user query, the social connection, and the relevance of the related content (e.g., a document returned by the search engine). We then define measures of social annotation utility and present the results of a large controlled user study of the interplay between each of these aspects on head and tail queries drawn from several months of real-world queries issued to a commercial search

Permission to make digital or hard copies of all or part of this work for personal or classroom use is granted without fee provided that copies are not made or distributed for profit or commercial advantage and that copies bear this notice and the full citation on the first page. To copy otherwise, to republish, to post on servers or to redistribute to lists, requires prior specific permission and/or a fee.
SIGIR'12, August 12–16, 2012, Portland, Oregon, USA.
Copyright 2012 ACM 978-1-4503-1472-5/12/08 ...$10.00.

[1]Social networks have different terms to indicate explicit positive user interest of a document, such as *like*, *+1*, and *tag*. Herein we use the term `like` generically to indicate any of these, and `dislike` to indicate negative interest.

engine. We show evidence that social annotations add perceived utility to users in varying degrees according to the social relevance aspects. Finally, we turn our attention to the task of automatically predicting the utility of a social annotation. We model the prediction task using a multiple additive regression tree model over features available to a standard search engine. We show empirical evidence that the task is learnable and that we can automatically predict the utility of a social annotation. The major contributions of our research are:

- We introduce a taxonomy of social relevance aspects, drawn from the query, social connection and content, which influence the utility of social annotations on the search results page.
- We conduct a user study to quantify the influence and interplay of the social relevance aspects, over real-world social annotation impressions drawn from a commercial search engine.
- We propose a machine learned discriminative model for predicting the expected added value of a social annotation in an online scenario.
- We empirically show that our model can accurately predict the relevance of a social annotation.

2. RELATED WORK

Most relevant to our work is that of Muralidharan et al. [18] who show through user studies and eyetracking analysis that the presentation of the social annotation, such as the size of the profile thumbnail, greatly impacts user engagement of the annotation. Through anecdotal feedback, participants from their studies conjectured that annotations would be useful in certain social and subjective topics (e.g., restaurant and shopping queries) or when presented by friends believed to be topical authorities (e.g., a fitness trainer annotating a fitness web document) or when in a close relationship with the searcher; but for other situations the participants believed annotations were not helpful, such as when there is no label explaining why an annotation was present. In this paper, we build upon their work by exploring a taxonomy of influential social relevance aspects, including query class, content relevance, and social network aspects; and quantifying their utility and interplay.

2.1 Social Features in Web Search

Evans and Chi [9] performed a detailed user study about the role that social interactions play in collaborative search tasks. Outside of collaborative search, social signals have primarily been explored as implicit ranking features hidden deep inside the ranking functions [20, 26], for example by examining how users would benefit from personalized search results considering implicit behavior similarity attributes such as from click-based measures [22, 23, 1]. Bao et al. [2] further argue that the quality of a web page can be improved by the amount of del.icio.us annotations and Carmel et al. [6] show that personalized search improves the quality of intranet search results. For traditional web search, Heymann et al. [13] predicted that while social bookmarks can provide ancillary data not present in the web page, the majority of tags are also present in the document, or inlinks/outlinks, and therefore would have limited use as ranking features.

Recently, social features are appearing as explicit user-facing features such as in: (1) **annotations**, where interest by the searcher's social network is visibly marked on an existing search result (v.s. Figure 1); (2) **injected results**, where social data, such as tweets or status posts, are presented in a manner similar to and within the existing search results, but sourced outside of the web corpus; and (3) **independent results**, where the social data is presented in a manner not to be mistaken for one of the web search results, such as in a web answer or direct display. This paper specifically focuses on measuring utility in the context of social annotations and leaves the analysis of other visualizations to future work.

2.2 Measuring the Utility of a Search Result

Relevance is a multidimensional dynamic concept and there is a wide range of factors that influence a user's perception of relevance. Via an extensive user study, Barry and Schamber proposed a set of categories capturing users' relevance criteria or *cues* (e.g., accuracy, specificity, expertise, presentation, etc.) in the context of an information seeking task [3]. More recently, Borlund provided a framework for examining relevance in the context of information retrieval evaluation [4]. The relevance and usefulness of results returned by web search engines are typically evaluated using variants of nDCG [16], expected reciprocal rank [7], mean average precision, relative information gain, and a variety of click/feedback metrics [25, 15], such as (1) clicks on lower-ranked documents indicate that higher-ranked documents are less relevant for the query; and (2) clicks to documents which are quickly abandoned by the user for other search results are deemed less relevant for the query. However, use of these traditional metrics can present challenges when personalizing and annotating web search results, as higher-ranked search results may be passed up for lower-ranked search results with social annotations. As shown in [8] and [12], annotations and other modifications to captions can alter the success rate for users independent of where the document was ranked in the result set. Fidel and Crandall [10] show factors beyond the document that affect the perception of relevance, including recency, detail, and genre; but they do not discuss social factors. This paper extends their work and also proposes metrics by which the utility of a social annotation feature can be measured.

2.3 Predicting Relevance

At the core of a search engine is the ability to learn to rank candidate documents according to their relevance to a user query. As such there is a plethora of work on modeling, feature extraction, selection, and model adaptation, see Liu [17] for a comprehensive survey and Burges et al. [5] for a description of the system that won the recent Yahoo! Learning to Rank Challenge. In our work, we introduce a complementary task, that of learning to predict the relevance of a social annotation. As such, we make use of a state-of-the-art learning algorithm [27] and predict social relevance based on runtime features from web usage logs and query classifiers commonly used in web search ranking, as well as social relevance cues defined in this paper.

3. ASPECTS OF SOCIAL RELEVANCE

Consider a search results page consisting of ranked content (e.g., documents, videos, images) in response to a user query. Formally, we define a **social annotation** as a tuple, $\{q, u, c, v\}$, consisting of a query q, content u, a social network connection c and the connection's interest valence v in the content (e.g., `like`, `dislike` or `share`). For example, Figure 1 illustrates such a social annotation impression where q is "*maui hotels*", u is a relevant Expedia hotel page, c is "*Tim Harrington*" and v is `like`.

In this section we propose a taxonomy of aspects that influence the utility of a social annotation, spanning the query, the social connection, and the content.

3.1 Query Aspects (QA)

3.1.1 *Query Intent* (QA-INT)

We divide queries into two sets based on whether they are **navigational (nav)** or **non-navigational (nnv)**. We expect that social annotations will be less valuable when the user is simply looking for the url of a web page she wants to reach. Other possible intents that are not explicitly studied in this paper include informational and transactional intents, which we grouped within our nnv intent, and which partially overlap with our QA-CLS aspects described next.

3.1.2 *Query Class* (QA-CLS)

The utility of a social annotation may be influenced by the class of the issued query. For example, although one might find value in knowing the interest of a social connection when querying for a movie, song, or book, we may expect only certain connections such as experts to be of interest for a health query. Similarly for local queries, interest from connections in the vicinity of the target location are likely more valuable than distant connections.

We focus our analysis on the following query classes covering the majority of social annotations found on a commercial search engine:

- **Commerce (com)**: Product-related queries seeking specifications, prices, comparisons, transactions, and reviews.
- **Health (hea)**: Queries on health-related topics such as symptoms, procedures, and treatments.
- **Movies (mov)**: Movie title queries.
- **Music (mus)**: Queries for musical artists, bands, and song lyrics.
- **Restaurant (res)**: Local queries related to restaurants, cafes, and drinking establishments.

3.2 Social Connection Aspects (SA)

The social network connection is at the heart of the social annotation and it clearly influences its utility. Consider the query "*korean restaurant*" and a set of resulting links to nearby korean restaurants. We expect that a connection who is an expert on korean cuisine may increase the utility of an annotation, and that a connection living near the localized neighborhood is more important than one far away. A dear friend's interest in the restaurant may also hold more weight than a more distant work colleague. And finally, the interest valence, whether positive, negative or neutral might affect relevance. Below we summarize each of these aspects and their value ranges.

3.2.1 *Circle* (SA-CIR)

The circle of a connection refers to the relation of the connection to the searcher. Intuitively, a co-worker's interest in an article related to the workplace might hold more value than a family member or friend's interest. We consider the following circles: **work colleague (wkc)**, **family member (fam)**, and **friend (frn)**. Other interesting circles out of scope for this paper include school friends, college friends, church friends, and sports club friends.

3.2.2 *Affinity* (SA-AFF)

The affinity between a searcher and a connection refers to their degree of closeness. Although affinity has a continuous range, in this paper we consider two affinities: **close (cls)** and **distant (dst)**. As conjectured in [18] we generally expect the closeness of a connection to greatly influence the perceived utility of a social annotation.

3.2.3 *Expertise* (SA-EXP)

Whether a connection is an **expert (exp)** or **non-expert (nex)** on the search topic may influence the value of a social annotation especially when issuing informational or transactional queries. Other possible values not considered in this paper include hobbyist and enthusiast.

3.2.4 *Geographical Distance* (SA-GEO)

For local queries, we expect that a connection living **near (nea)** the target location will add more value than if living **far (far)**. For non-local queries, the value of this aspect is **not applicable (n/a)**. One might also consider the geographic distance between the searcher and the connection, but we leave this aspect for consideration in future work.

3.2.5 *Interest Valence* (SA-INT)

Social annotations require both a social network connection and the interest valence of that connection with respect to the annotated search result. Most experiences today classify the valence as either a **like (lik)** or a **share (shr)**, i.e. that the user has shared the document with someone. In this paper, we also consider a third valence, **dislike (dis)**.

3.2.6 *Out of Scope Aspects*

Other aspects may influence the value of a social annotation, such as the connection's gender, age, and general interests. We leave these for further study in future work.

3.3 Content Aspects (CA)

Finally, the social annotation is influenced by the relevance of the document to the intent of the user query. We consider graded relevance according to the following scale, similar to that proposed by Järvelin and Kekäläinen [16]:

- **Perfect (per)**: The page is the definitive or official page that strongly satisfies the most likely intent.
- **Excellent (exc)**: The page satisfies a very likely or most likely intent.
- **Good (goo)**: The page moderately satisfies a very likely or most likely intent.
- **Fair (fai)** The page weakly satisfies a very likely or most likely intent.
- **Bad (bad)**: The page does not satisfies the intent.
- **Detrimental (det)**: The page contains content that is inappropriate for a general audience.

4. SOCIAL RELEVANCE

This section presents the results of a user study quantifying the utility of a social annotation. We analyze the interplay between the social relevance aspects presented in Section 3 and identify situations where a social annotation is more relevant than others. Our approach is to sample social annotation impressions on a commercial search engine and to have human annotators judge the utility of each impression. In the following sections, we describe our process for sampling social annotation impressions (i.e., $\{q, u, c, v\}$-tuples) and the guidelines for judging their relevance. Then, in Sections 4.4 and 4.5, we present our analysis.

4.1 Query-URL Sampling

We define $\mathcal{U}$ as the universe of all social annotation impressions observed on a commercial search engine during three weeks spanning three months of US English web usage logs: 10/7/2011-10/14/2011, 11/4/2011-11/11/2011, and 12/2/2011-12/9/2011. We admitted only queries that were classified by the search engine to be in our domains of interest, namely commerce, health, movies, music, or restaurants (see Section 3.1.2). We applied a low classification threshold to admit a larger number of queries since we later manually annotate the query class of all queries in our test set. We further rejected any query suspected of being bot-generated.

We define the head of $\mathcal{U}$ as all tuples where q is in the top-20% of the most frequent queries, and the tail as all tuples where q is in the bottom 30%. A query-frequency weighted sample of queries from both sets yield our test queries, referred to as `HEAD` and `TAIL` consisting of 2388 and 1375 queries respectively.

For each query in `HEAD` and `TAIL`, we randomly selected one url from $\mathcal{U}$ using an impression-weighted sampling (i.e., a url with many social annotation impressions in the usage logs for the query is more likely to be chosen than a url with fewer social annotation impressions for the query).

We used a crowdsourcing tool to have each query in `HEAD` and `TAIL` manually classified according to the query classes defined in Section 3.1.2 as well as an `other` class. We obtained three judgments per query (7526 judgments) from a total of 32 independent annotators and kept the majority vote. The inter-annotator agreement as measured by Fleiss' κ was 0.495 (moderate agreement).

We further manually judged the relevance of each url to the associated query in `HEAD` and `TAIL`. The relevance categories and guidelines are those listed in Section 3.3. As this task is known to be more difficult than query classification, we employed seven professional independent annotators with experience in search engine relevance testing. The observed inter-annotator agreement as measured by Fleiss' κ was 0.176 (slight agreement).

4.2 Social Annotation Sampling

In order not to bias the social annotations to the specific social networks of our human annotators, we simulated a social network for our judges. We used this network to create the connections c and interest valences v for our random query-url pairs in `HEAD` and `TAIL`.

Figure 2 illustrates the virtual social network. It consists of twelve connections spanning the social circles and affinities defined in Section 3.3. We assume in this network that `family members` always have a `close` affinity whereas `work`

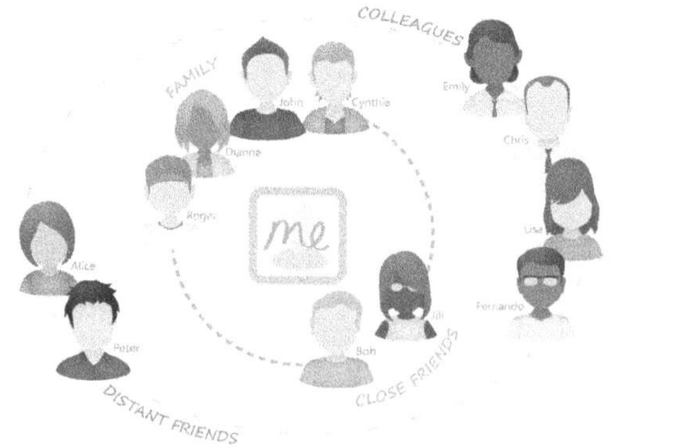

Figure 2: Simulated social network.

`colleagues` have a `distant` affinity. `Friends` can have affinity either `close` or `distant`.

For each query-url pair in `HEAD` and `TAIL` we assigned a social annotation as follows. First, we randomly sampled a circle (either `work colleague`, `family`, or `friend`). Then, we randomly selected an individual from that circle, which also determines the affinity of the connection (either `close` or `distant`). Next, we randomly picked whether the connection was an `expert` or `non-expert` with respect to the document and we randomly chose the interest valence (either `like`, `dislike` or `share`). Finally, if the query was annotated as a local query, we randomly determined if the connection lived `near` or `far` from the intended target location. Otherwise, we set the geo-distance aspect to `n/a`.

Deploying our user study over the actual social networks of the participants is preferable, however several problems arise that make this infeasible, most notably privacy concerns. Also, since our study requires significant training and expertise, we found it necessary to hire professional annotators, thus limiting the total number of independent annotators. Using their personal networks would not only cause privacy concerns, but it would also bias towards a non-representative set of search users. Simulating a social network as we do carries its own risks. Firstly, we expect people's personal social networks to vary in terms of attribute value distributions (for example, some people have only work colleagues in their network while others have mostly friends and family) as well as diversity distribution. Although in our setup we assumed uniform priors for all attributes, if given the true priors it is trivial to reweight the findings. Secondly, the degree of an individual in their social network (i.e., average number of network connections) is significantly larger than the twelve in our virtual network, and also varies significantly[2]. To balance the cognitive load on our judges, the reliability of judgments, and reducing the risks of simulating a social network, we chose to keep the connection degree small enough whilst ensuring diversity in age, gender, and ethnicity. Finally, by explicitly drawing the judges' attention to social aspects, there is a risk of overemphasizing their importance and thus influencing the judgments, though we expect this influence to be minimal.

4.3 Annotation Task

The judges were presented with the following scenario:

[2]Hill and Dunbar [14] estimate the average connection degree at 153 and Ugander et al. [24] measured the median degree of Facebook users in May 2011 at 99.

	HEAD			TAIL		
	Oct'11	Nov'11	Dec'11	Oct'11	Nov'11	Dec'11
Test Cases	770	823	795	423	486	466
Judgments	1540	1646	1590	846	972	932
sig-util	402	634	428	273	363	225
some-util	734	610	785	397	341	449
no-util	364	377	315	164	241	225
dont-know	5	10	11	1	22	0
error	35	15	51	11	5	33

Table 1: Summary of the test datasets and the human labels broken down by judgment category.

> *Imagine you issue a search query to a commercial search engine. Amongst the results set, you see the result below, which someone in your social network has either liked, disliked or shared. Your task is to judge the utility of this social annotation. Value can be assessed on that the annotation is relevant to you, is useful to you, or is generally interesting to you.*

The annotators were also presented with their virtual social network from Figure 2 along with a textual description of each of the twelve individuals in the network. For each test case, the social annotation was graphically presented as though returned from a search engine, similar to what is illustrated in Figure 1. A textual description of the annotation is also presented to the annotator, stating the connection's circle, affinity, expertise, interest valence and geo-distance (if the query was a local query, such as for a restaurant).

For each $\{q, u, c, v\}$ tuple in `HEAD` and `TAIL` the annotation task is to assess the utility of the social annotation according to the following guidelines:

- **Significant utility** (`sig-util`). The annotation is substantially relevant, useful, or of interest to you.
- **Some utility** (`some-util`). The annotation is somewhat relevant, useful or of interest to you.
- **No utility** (`no-util`). The annotation is not relevant, useful or of interest to you.
- **Don't know** (`dont-know`). I don't have enough information to assess this annotation.
- **Non English/Service error** (`error`). Can't judge because content is non-English or there is a service error (e.g., 404 message, image didn't load, etc.)

Annotators were encouraged to enter a comment justifying their judgments and were required to do so if their judgment was `dont-know` or `error`.

Each test tuple in `HEAD` and `TAIL` was annotated by two judges randomly drawn from a pool of seven paid professional independent annotators, for a total of 7532 judgments. We trained the judges by iterating on the guidelines over an independent dataset [3]. In cases where the judges disagreed, we adjudicated as follows. If one judge added a comment that we determined clearly justified the judgment, we adjudicated the test tuple to that judge's decision. If both judges added a comment deemed clearly justifying their decision or if both judges omitted a comment, then we retained the disagreeing judgments.

[3]The training phase was necessary to achieve a fair inter-annotator agreement. As such, although it would have been desirable to crowdsource the judgments we deemed the task too difficult and that paid professional independent judges were necessary.

R(T)	ω function definition
$\mathbf{R_{Rel}(T)}$	$\omega_{Rel} = \begin{cases} \texttt{sig-util}: & 1 \\ \texttt{some-util}: & 0.5 \\ \texttt{no-util}: & 0 \end{cases}$
$\mathbf{R_{Prec}(T)}$	$\omega_{Prec} = \begin{cases} \texttt{sig-util}: & 1 \\ \texttt{some-util}: & 1 \\ \texttt{no-util}: & 0 \end{cases}$

Table 2: Utility metrics of social annotations.

Table 1 summarizes the breakdown of the resulting judgments. Inter-annotator agreement as measured by Fleiss' κ on this annotation task was 0.395 (0.487 on `HEAD` and 0.236 on `TAIL`), considered moderate to fair agreement. For our final datasets `HEAD` and `TAIL` we omit the 2.7% of the judgments that were judged as `dont-know` and `error`.

4.4 Utility Analysis

Let T be a set of test tuples, such as those from `HEAD` and `TAIL`, where $t_i = \{q_i, u_i, c_i, v_i\}$, let A be a set of aspect values and T_A be the subset of tuples in T matching an aspect value in A. For example, if A = {`QA-CLS-hea`, `SA-CIR-fam`, `SA-INT-lik`}, then T_A is the set of all test tuples in `HEAD` and `TAIL` where q is a health query, and c is a family connection that has liked u. Finally, let $J(t)$ be the set of judges that annotated a test tuple t.

We define $R(T)$, the expected utility of social annotations in T, as the average utility of each tuple in T:

$$R(T) = \frac{\sum_{t \in T} \frac{\sum_{j \in J(t)} \omega(t,j)}{|J(t)|}}{|T|} \tag{1}$$

where $\omega: \mathbb{J} \rightarrow \mathbb{R}$ is a real-valued utility function mapping judgments $\mathbb{J}$ to real numbers in the range [0,1], where $\mathbb{J}$ is the set {`sig-util`, `some-util`, `no-util`} defined in Section 4.3.

Table 2 lists the two variants of $R(T)$ that we report on in this paper. $\mathbf{R_{Rel}(T)}$, our relevance utility metric, assigns a graded utility score to each judgment similar to that done for query-url relevance judgments [16]. $\mathbf{R_{Pre}(T)}$ expresses a binary utility where a social annotation has positive utility if it is judged as either significantly or somewhat relevant, otherwise negative utility. $R_{Pre}(T)$ can be thought of as a measure of social annotation precision.

Table 3 lists the overall utility and per aspect utility breakdown, over the `HEAD` and `TAIL` data sets[4]. The expected overall relevance, at 0.543 indicates that social annotations are generally somewhat relevant, useful or of interest to users. Each individual aspect, however, influences the utility in very different ways. Those aspects with significantly more utility are bolded with a ‡ symbol and those with less utility are bolded with a † symbol.

Overall, we observe no statistically significant difference between the expected utility of head vs. tail queries (note that health queries and restaurant queries seem to have higher utility on tail, but this is not statistically significant). It is surprising that the query class aspects (`QA-CLS`) generally do not show different utility with respect to the average, however further analysis in Section 4.5 reveals significantly differentiated influence in combination with social aspects. Also counter to our expectations, judges found equal utility between navigational and non-navigational queries. For the content aspects (`CA`), although we observe no statistical

[4]`CA-det` had too few judgments to report results.

		HEAD			TAIL		
		Samples	R_{Rel}	R_{Prec}	Samples	R_{Rel}	R_{Prec}
	ALL	2388	0.543 ± 0.011	0.771 ± 0.013	1375	0.541 ± 0.014	0.763 ± 0.016
QA	QA-INT-nav	785	0.539 ± 0.019	0.775 ± 0.022	93	0.513 ± 0.054	0.753 ± 0.066
	QA-INT-nnv	1603	0.545 ± 0.014	0.769 ± 0.015	1282	0.543 ± 0.015	0.764 ± 0.017
	QA-CLS-com	701	0.544 ± 0.021	0.785 ± 0.023	208	0.556 ± 0.035	0.784 ± 0.039
	QA-CLS-hea	169	0.549 ± 0.040	0.772 ± 0.047	36	0.611 ± 0.073	0.847 ± 0.085
	QA-CLS-mov	233	0.526 ± 0.037	0.740 ± 0.041	61	0.549 ± 0.070	0.762 ± 0.077
	QA-CLS-mus	674	0.570 ± 0.020	**0.809‡ ± 0.023**	762	0.532 ± 0.019	0.755 ± 0.022
	QA-CLS-res	159	0.524 ± 0.045	0.730 ± 0.052	51	0.608 ± 0.073	0.843 ± 0.069
	QA-CLS-oth	452	0.517 ± 0.027	**0.723† ± 0.030**	257	0.531 ± 0.034	0.745 ± 0.041
SA	SA-CIR-wkc	818	**0.494† ± 0.016**	0.782 ± 0.021	470	**0.498† ± 0.022**	0.779 ± 0.027
	SA-CIR-fam	788	**0.654‡ ± 0.019**	**0.841‡ ± 0.019**	431	**0.625‡ ± 0.024**	**0.810‡ ± 0.027**
	SA-CIR-frn	782	**0.484† ± 0.021**	**0.690† ± 0.025**	474	0.508 ± 0.026	**0.706† ± 0.031**
	SA-AFF-cls	1169	**0.657‡ ± 0.015**	**0.845‡ ± 0.015**	689	**0.622‡ ± 0.020**	**0.804‡ ± 0.021**
	SA-AFF-dst	1219	**0.434† ± 0.014**	**0.701† ± 0.019**	686	**0.460† ± 0.019**	0.722 ± 0.025
	SA-EXP-exp	1194	**0.635‡ ± 0.016**	**0.819‡ ± 0.016**	686	**0.609‡ ± 0.020**	0.799 ± 0.022
	SA-EXP-nex	1194	**0.451† ± 0.014**	**0.723† ± 0.019**	689	**0.474† ± 0.019**	0.728 ± 0.025
	SA-GEO-nea	57	0.469 ± 0.067	0.711 ± 0.087	13	**0.673‡ ± 0.098**	**0.923‡ ± 0.098**
	SA-GEO-far	75	0.593 ± 0.063	0.787 ± 0.070	17	0.588 ± 0.081	0.853 ± 0.108
	SA-GEO-n/a	2256	0.543 ± 0.012	0.772 ± 0.013	1345	0.539 ± 0.015	0.761 ± 0.017
	SA-INT-dis	740	0.570 ± 0.019	**0.818‡ ± 0.021**	454	0.526 ± 0.024	0.771 ± 0.029
	SA-INT-lik	853	**0.620‡ ± 0.018**	**0.861‡ ± 0.017**	498	**0.628‡ ± 0.024**	**0.827‡ ± 0.024**
	SA-INT-shr	795	**0.436† ± 0.019**	**0.631† ± 0.024**	423	**0.455† ± 0.025**	**0.680† ± 0.032**
CA	CA-per	63	0.603 ± 0.075	0.786 ± 0.075	86	**0.628‡ ± 0.059**	0.826 ± 0.055
	CA-exc	390	0.561 ± 0.025	0.809 ± 0.028	215	**0.627‡ ± 0.032**	**0.877‡ ± 0.031**
	CA-goo	644	0.572 ± 0.021	**0.816‡ ± 0.023**	337	0.582 ± 0.029	0.812 ± 0.033
	CA-fai	577	0.535 ± 0.023	0.758 ± 0.025	235	0.547 ± 0.032	0.783 ± 0.037
	CA-bad	710	**0.509† ± 0.021**	**0.719† ± 0.025**	496	**0.458† ± 0.024**	**0.660† ± 0.030**
	CA-det	4	–	–	6	–	–

Table 3: Utility of social annotation on SERP vs. social relevance aspects from the query, network connection, and content, with 95% confidence intervals. Bold indicates statistical significance over all test tuples (ALL) with † indicating lower utility and ‡ indicating higher utility. (-) indicates too few judgments.

significance within the class, the descending utility trend follows the graded relevance judgments, with higher utility on both HEAD and TAIL for perfect and excellent content versus lower utility for fair and bad content.

The social aspects SA generally have significant differentiating influence. The social affinity (SA-AFF) shows the most influence on utility followed by expertise (SA-EXP) and connection circle (SA-CIR), where colleagues and friends have equal utility but family members have much higher expected utility. For interest valence (SA-INT), knowing that a connection has liked (lik) a link shows more utility than average, but a share (shr) shows a negative utility influence. Interestingly, disliking a link (dis) has little effect on utility, which is further confirmed in our analysis in Section 4.5. Since only 7% of the queries in HEAD and 4% in TAIL were local queries, our sampling resulted in too few geo-distance (SA-GEO) instances that were near or far. The result is large confidence bounds and the only statistically significant utility difference is shown in the TAIL where knowing near-ness is more valuable than not. Further investigation on this aspect is warranted because we expect geographical distance to have influence on social annotations of local queries.

We performed feedback analysis by inspecting a random sample of the comment boxes filled by our judges. For the no-util judgment, the feedback was mainly split between poor content matches or vague queries, and connections of very poor perceived utility. For the latter, expertise was the main discussed social cue followed by affinity and interest valence. Example feedback includes: "Because he is a distant friend, neutral and a non-expert, his opinion is not going to be useful to me." and "Even though the connection is a family member, being a non-expert and neutral on the page would make me think that they do not know a lot on the result." For the some-util judgment, feedback mainly revolved around the circle and dislike aspects as the driving cues for utility. Example comments include: "Chris' dislike might get me to click another link, even though it's what I'm looking for, it could be a bad quality link."; "Even though Bob is neutral, since he's an expert there is added value in his annotation."; and "Anytime one of my friends 'dislikes' a website, it might make me dig further to see why." Finally, for the sig-util judgment, expertise and affinity drove the utility cues. Example feedback includes: "There is a lot of added value to this annotation because Bob is my close friend and an expert." and "She is only a colleague, but she is an expert on the result and her opinion matters to me because she knows what she is talking about."

Finally, we further analyzed the utility of all pairwise combinations of aspects. We list the top-20 and bottom-20 in terms of R_{Rel} utility in Table 4, computed over $T_{\text{HEAD}\cap\text{TAIL}}$. The main conclusion from this analysis is that social annotations have very large variations in utility depending on the aspects defined in Section 4, with relevance utility ranging from 0.336-0.754 in pairwise combinations. These should be leveraged in deciding when to impress a social annotation to a user.

4.5 Aspect Interplay Analysis

We turn now to measuring the interplay between social relevance aspects. In a production system, some aspects are more expensive than others to obtain. For example, most search engines will already have query classifiers in place whereas it may be harder to obtain some of the social aspect values such as a connection's affinity or expertise. In this section, we are interested in answering the question: what is the value of a set of aspects if we know another set of aspects?

Top-20 Pairs by R_{Rel}			
SA-AFF-cls ∩ CA-per	0.754	SA-AFF-cls ∩ CA-exc	0.683
SA-CIR-fam ∩ CA-per	0.736	SA-CIR-fam ∩ CA-goo	0.680
SA-AFF-cls ∩ SA-INT-lik	0.734	SA-AFF-cls ∩ CA-goo	0.679
SA-AFF-cls ∩ SA-EXP-exp	0.731	SA-AFF-cls ∩ SA-GEO-far	0.679
SA-CIR-fam ∩ SA-INT-lik	0.727	SA-EXP-exp ∩ CA-per	0.674
SA-CIR-fam ∩ SA-EXP-exp	0.726	SA-AFF-cls ∩ QA-CLS-res	0.671
SA-EXP-exp ∩ SA-INT-lik	0.713	SA-INT-lik ∩ CA-exc	0.669
SA-INT-lik ∩ CA-per	0.696	SA-GEO-far ∩ SA-INT-lik	0.669
SA-CIR-fam ∩ SA-GEO-far	0.689	SA-CIR-fam ∩ QA-CLS-res	0.668
SA-CIR-fam ∩ CA-exc	0.686	SA-EXP-exp ∩ CA-goo	0.667
Bottom-20 Pairs by R_{Rel}			
SA-CIR-frn ∩ CA-bad	0.422	SA-EXP-nex ∩ SA-GEO-nea	0.396
SA-EXP-nex ∩ CA-bad	0.417	SA-AFF-dst ∩ CA-bad	0.396
SA-INT-shr ∩ QA-CLS-mov	0.412	SA-GEO-nea ∩ CA-fai	0.395
SA-CIR-frn ∩ SA-EXP-nex	0.410	SA-CIR-frn ∩ SA-INT-shr	0.394
SA-CIR-wkc ∩ SA-EXP-nex	0.410	SA-CIR-frn ∩ SA-GEO-nea	0.388
SA-AFF-dst ∩ QA-CLS-mov	0.409	SA-GEO-nea ∩ SA-INT-shr	0.385
SA-CIR-wkc ∩ SA-INT-shr	0.405	SA-AFF-dst ∩ SA-EXP-nex	0.363
SA-INT-shr ∩ CA-bad	0.397	SA-EXP-nex ∩ SA-INT-shr	0.355
SA-EXP-nex ∩ SA-GEO-nea	0.396	SA-AFF-dst ∩ SA-INT-shr	0.355
SA-AFF-dst ∩ CA-bad	0.396	SA-CIR-frn ∩ SA-AFF-dst	0.336

Table 4: Top-20 and Bottom-20 social relevance aspect combinations in terms of R_{Rel} utility.

4.5.1 Relative Gain

More formally, given a corpus of tuples T and a set of aspect values A_1, we are interested in the expected relative gain or loss in social annotation utility, $RG_T(A_2 \parallel A_1)$, if we learn another set of aspect values A_2:

$$\mathbf{RG_T}(A_2 \parallel A_1) = \frac{R(T_{A_1} \cap T_{A_2}) - R(T_{A_1})}{R(T_{A_1})} \quad (2)$$

Consider for example $A_1 = \{\texttt{health}\}$ (query class) and $A_2 = \{\texttt{family}\}$ (circle). Using Eq. 1, we can compute the expected utility of a social annotation in $T_{\{\texttt{health}\}}$ as $R(T_{\{\texttt{health}\}})$. We can similarly compute the expected utility if we also knew the **`family`** aspect, $R(T_{\{\texttt{health}\}} \cap T_{\{\texttt{family}\}})$. Eq. 2 measures the ratio between these two utilities, which captures the expected gain or loss of knowing **`family`** given that we knew **`health`**. RG_T is non symmetric, that is $\mathbf{RG}(T_{A_1} \parallel T_{A_2}) \neq \mathbf{RG}(T_{A_2} \parallel T_{A_1})$. Positive gain is indicated by the sign of RG_T, and no gain is observed if $RG_T = 0$.

Relationship to information gain.

The interplay between social relevance aspects can also be expressed in terms of information gain. Although we report only values of RG_T in this paper and prefer its interpretability (it can be directly interpreted as the expected ratio increase in utility), for completeness we derive the information gain criteria. First, let $P_T(v)$ be the probability that a tuple $t \in T$ is judged as $v \in \mathbb{J}$:

$$\mathbf{P_T}(v) = \frac{\sum_{t \in T} \sum_{j \in J(t)} \phi_j(t, v)}{\sum_{t \in T} \sum_{j \in J(t)} 1} \quad (3)$$

where $\phi_j(t, v)$ indicates if tuple t is judged as v by annotator j. Then the information gain of A_2 given A_1 is defined as:

$$\mathbf{IG_T}(A_1, A_2) = H(T_{A_1}) - H(T_{A_1} \cap T_{A_2}) \quad (4)$$

$$\mathbf{H}(T) = -\sum_{v \in \mathbb{J}} P_T(v) \log_2 P_T(v) \quad (5)$$

4.5.2 Results

We focus our analysis on the relative gain of social aspects with respect to each other, the query class aspects (**`QA-CLS`**) and content aspects (**`CA`**). We omit the geo-distance aspect for lack of space and since very few gains were significant.

Table 5 and Table 6 list the relative utilty gains of **`SA`** vs. **`QA-CLS`** and **`CA`**, respectively. Bolded entries indicate statistically significant gains. The value of any cell can be interpreted as the utility gain or loss (in terms of R_{Rel} and R_{Prec}) over both **`HEAD`** and **`TAIL`** of knowing the row aspect given the column aspect, i.e. $RG_{\texttt{HEAD} \cup \texttt{TAIL}}(\texttt{row} \parallel \texttt{column})$. For example, given the query class **`movie`**, knowing that the connection is in the **`family`** circle increases the relevance utility by a factor of 0.27, whereas if it is in the **`work colleague`** circle reduces the relevance utility by a factor of 0.132. Dashed entries represent either <0.001 utility gain/loss or impossible combinations (e.g., since family members are always considered to have close affinity in our setting then $T_{\texttt{family} \cap \texttt{distant}}$ is an empty set).

Generally, knowing all social aspects with the exception of **`friend`** and **`dislike`** yields significant utility gain (or loss) over the query classes and content relevance aspects. The top-3 social aspects resulting in the most overall gains are the **`family`** circle and the **`affinity`** aspects. We computed RG between all combinations of **`affinity`** and **`circle`** aspects (table omitted for lack of space). We found that if we knew the **`circle`** then further knowing **`affinity`** leads to a utility difference of a factor of 0.319. In contrast, if we knew first the **`affinity`**, then further knowing the **`circle`** leads to a utility difference of a factor of only 0.243. Clearly **`circle`** and **`affinity`** are not independent. Hence, if one has to choose, investing in obtaining the **`affinity`** of a connection is more valuable than obtaining **`circle`**. If the affinity is known to be **`close`** then there is no value in also knowing that the circle is a **`friend`** (i.e., a social annotation from a close friend or family member has equal utility in our data). If the affinity is **`distant`**, however, then there is significant value in determining if the circle is **`work colleague`** (0.116 gain) or **`friend`** (0.243 loss).

Expertise, as expected, affects utility relatively more than other social aspects for **`health`** queries. With respect to **`music`** queries, **`expertise`** along with **`affinity`**, **`interest`** and the **`family`** circle equally most influence utility. Content that was **`shared`** has more influence on utility than other social aspects for **`music`** queries.

5. PREDICTING SOCIAL RELEVANCE

In the previous sections we have identified and examined the influence of social relevance aspects on the utility of social annotations, and our user study confirmed that this influence is of a differentiated and complex nature. In this section we aim to build on these results by asking the question: can we predict automatically whether a social annotation adds utility to a search result? To address this question, we develop discriminative models by learning from signals obtained in two different ways: (1) **offline** features, obtained from the social relevance aspects used in our user study in Section 4; and (2) **online** features, obtained from signals available at runtime in a commercial search engine, to examine how well we can perform in our prediction task in a real-world scenario without access to features such as a connection's **`circle`** and **`affinity`** or gold judgments on **`query class`** and **`content relevance`**.

5.1 Offline Features

Our 16 **offline** features are derived from the social relevance aspects presented in Section 3. The query class aspects (**`QA-CLS`**) are mapped to five binary features, namely **`commerce`**, **`health`**, **`movie`**, **`music`**, and **`restaurant`**. The social aspects each become a categorical feature as follows: **`circle`** = {*wkc*, *fam*, *frn*}; **`affinity`** = {*cls*, *dst*}; **`expertise`** = {*exp*, *nex*}; **`geo-distance`** = {*nea*, *far*, *n/a*}; and

	QA-CLS-com		QA-CLS-hea		QA-CLS-mov		QA-CLS-mus		QA-CLS-res	
	RG_{Rel}	RG_{Prec}	RG_{Rel}	RG_{Prec}	RG_{Rel}	RG_{Prec}	RG_{Rel}	RG_{Prec}	RG_{Rel}	RG_{Prec}
SA-CIR-wkc	**−0.124**	−0.011	−0.029	0.043	−0.132	−0.019	−0.059	0.037	−0.092	−0.011
SA-CIR-fam	**0.215**	**0.093**	0.14	0.056	**0.27**	**0.148**	**0.144**	**0.059**	**0.247**	**0.15**
SA-CIR-frn	−0.078	**−0.074**	−0.081	−0.091	−0.103	−0.12	**−0.086**	**−0.096**	−0.139	−0.132
SA-AFF-cls	**0.211**	**0.089**	0.16	0.063	**0.237**	**0.118**	**0.145**	**0.057**	**0.251**	**0.134**
SA-AFF-dst	**−0.213**	**−0.09**	−0.125	−0.049	**−0.225**	−0.112	**−0.154**	**−0.061**	**−0.208**	−0.111
SA-EXP-exp	**0.159**	0.052	**0.169**	0.062	0.141	0.056	**0.141**	**0.05**	**0.191**	0.075
SA-EXP-nex	**−0.161**	−0.053	**−0.167**	−0.062	−0.126	−0.05	**−0.137**	−0.048	−0.161	−0.063
SA-INT-dis	0.028	0.057	−0.022	0.02	0.044	0.063	0.012	0.029	0.034	0.062
SA-INT-lik	**0.149**	**0.112**	0.146	**0.129**	**0.189**	**0.143**	**0.14**	**0.084**	0.133	0.119
SA-INT-shr	**−0.185**	**−0.17**	−0.134	−0.155	**−0.193**	**−0.174**	**−0.188**	**−0.138**	−0.184	**−0.199**

Table 5: Relative utility gain (R_{Rel} and R_{Prec}) of social aspects (rows) vs. query aspects (columns) over HEAD **∪** TAIL**. Bold indicates that the relative utility gain is statistically significant with 95% confidence.**

	CA-per		CA-exc		CA-goo		CA-fai		CA-bad	
	RG_{Rel}	RG_{Prec}	RG_{Rel}	RG_{Prec}	RG_{Rel}	RG_{Prec}	RG_{Rel}	RG_{Prec}	RG_{Rel}	RG_{Prec}
SA-CIR-wkc	−0.052	0.042	−0.039	0.041	**−0.093**	−0.014	**−0.102**	0.014	**−0.09**	0.039
SA-CIR-fam	**0.248**	**0.153**	**0.126**	0.056	**0.172**	**0.08**	**0.186**	**0.081**	**0.235**	**0.09**
SA-CIR-frn	−0.107	−0.123	−0.072	**−0.09**	−0.082	−0.064	−0.075	**−0.091**	**−0.151**	**−0.15**
SA-AFF-cls	**0.247**	**0.143**	**0.153**	**0.068**	**0.175**	**0.09**	**0.183**	**0.066**	**0.209**	**0.074**
SA-AFF-dst	**−0.193**	−0.112	**−0.14**	−0.063	**−0.192**	**−0.098**	**−0.189**	−0.068	**−0.188**	−0.067
SA-EXP-exp	0.129	0.044	**0.154**	0.036	**0.159**	**0.063**	**0.151**	**0.061**	**0.145**	0.057
SA-EXP-nex	−0.146	−0.049	**−0.149**	−0.034	**−0.155**	**−0.062**	**−0.174**	**−0.071**	**−0.135**	−0.053
SA-INT-dis	−0.066	−0.004	–	0.046	0.018	0.047	0.026	0.039	0.044	0.043
SA-INT-lik	0.166	0.074	**0.153**	**0.08**	**0.169**	**0.108**	**0.159**	**0.115**	**0.11**	**0.108**
SA-INT-shr	−0.101	−0.072	**−0.16**	**−0.122**	**−0.215**	**−0.176**	**−0.215**	**−0.176**	**−0.158**	**−0.155**

Table 6: Relative utility gain (R_{Rel} and R_{Prec}) of social aspects (rows) vs. content aspects (columns) over HEAD **∪** TAIL**. Bold indicates that the relative utility gain is statistically significant with 95% confidence.**

`interest-valence` = {*lik*, *shr*, *dis*}. Finally, the content relevance aspects (`CA`) are mapped to six binary features, namely `perfect`, `excellent`, `good`, `fair`, `bad`, `detrimental`.

5.2 Online Features

We turn now to features that are available to a search engine at runtime, which we call **online** features. Although no human annotator can provide relevance or query classification judgments at runtime, most search engines today have proxies from automatic query classifiers [21] and content rankers [19]. Social aspects are also generally unavailable at runtime. However, there are a multitude of other measurements computed by search engines, and usage logs are routinely collected. The total number of features we collect in our **online** models runs at over 150. Below we describe the major classes of features and list examples.

- **Query Classes**: Our search engine evaluates each query by a set of automatic query classifiers, which assign a score to each query/class pair. We selected 55 of these classes as real-valued features, including `is-commerce`, `is-local`, `is-health`, and `is-movie`. While these automatic classifiers are not perfectly accurate, they serve as a proxy for the coarser (but more reliable) query-class annotation in our user study.
- **Session Metrics**: For user sessions containing the query, we measure features such as `average session duration` and `average page view count`.
- **User Metrics**: For users that have issued the query, we measure features such as `average click count` and `average page view count`.
- **Query Metrics**: We measure query-level aggregate features such as `average dwell time`, `average time to first click`, and `issues per day`.
- **Result Metrics**: We measure query-url aggregate metrics such as `average dwell time` and `abandonment`.

5.3 Model

For all our prediction experiments we use the Multiple Additive Regression Trees (MART) [27] algorithm, which is based on the Stochastic Gradient Boosting paradigm [11]. We used log-likelihood as the loss function, steepest-descent as the optimization technique and binary decision trees as the fitting function. MART offers a range of crucial advantages: it has been proven to yield high accuracy, it does not require any feature normalization and can handle any mix of real-valued, multi-valued and binary features, and finally, through its use of decision trees it can handle non-linear dependencies between the features. The latter advantage is of particular importance in our case since we have already found in Section 4 that combinations of social relevance aspects are predictive for social relevance. We cast our task as a supervised learning problem for predicting the utility of a social annotation $t = \{q, u, c, v\}$ (see Section 3). For reasons of simplicity, we cast the prediction task as a binary task (i.e., a social annotation is either relevant or not).

5.4 Experimental Setup

We use the data produced by our user study in Section 4. For each judged social annotation tuple t in the data, we extract a feature vector according to Sections 5.1 and 5.2. The online aggregate features are extracted from US English Web search usage logs from the same 3-month period as the samples drawn for our user study (see Section 4.1). The online features are directly obtained from the annotated tuples from our user study. We retain a total of 2380 `HEAD` tuples and 1371 `TAIL` tuples[5].

For each tuple, we mapped the two annotator judgments from the space $\mathbb{J}$ to a binary value indicating whether the social annotation in the tuple was relevant (1) or not (0). To this end, we use a conservative minimum-based approach, where we label any tuple as relevant if the minimum anno-

[5] 12 of the 3763 tuples were discarded where online feature extraction failed.

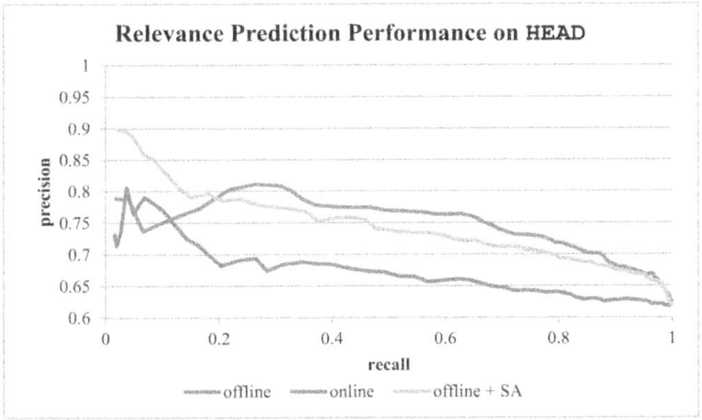

Figure 3: Prediction performance on HEAD using feature sets: offline, online, online + social aspects.

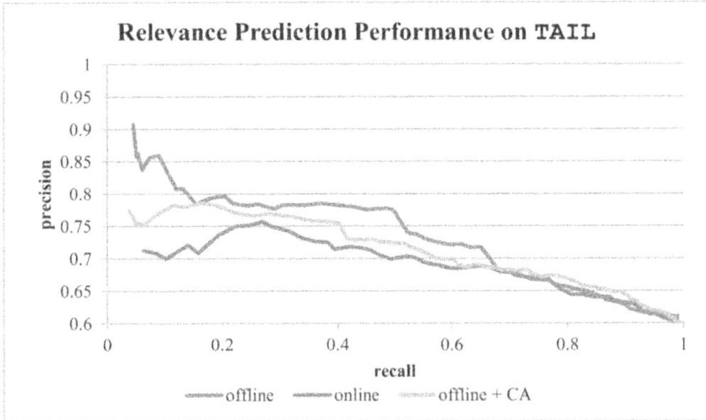

Figure 4: Prediction performance on TAIL using feature sets: offline, online, online + social aspects.

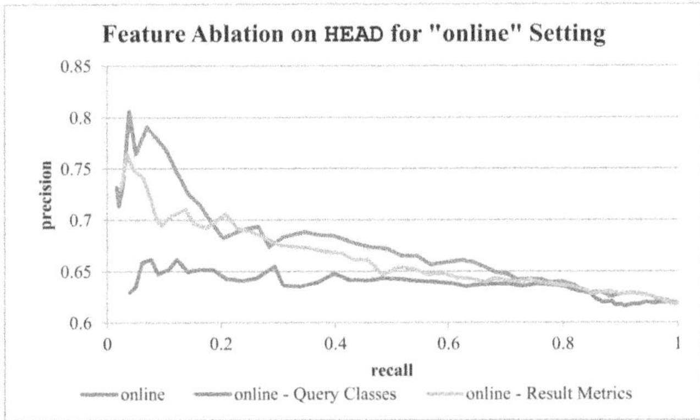

Figure 5: Ablation of two most predictive online feature familes on HEAD: Query Classes and Results Metrics.

tated utility is `some-util`, i.e. where none of the judges has labeled the case as `no-util`. In `HEAD` this results in 909 class 0 (non-relevant) examples and 1471 class 1 (relevant) examples. In `TAIL` we have 552 non-relevant and 819 relevant examples.

For the MART learner, we train for 100 iterations (resulting in 100 trees) and restrict the decision tree stumps to 10 leaf nodes that cover a minimum of 25 samples. All reported results are based on 10-fold cross-validation.

5.5 Results

We present the results of our prediction experiments separately for `HEAD` and `TAIL` tuples since we observe systematically different behavior between the two in our prediction task. Figures 3 and 4 illustrate the precision-recall characteristics of the relevance prediction with different feature sets. Overall, the task is learnable and as could be expected, the prediction model that uses **offline** features outperforms all other models on both `HEAD` and `TAIL`.

It is common in practice to impress a social annotation anytime one is available for a query-url context. Looking at the split between positive and negative examples in the test data, one would achieve 61.8% relevance precision on `HEAD` and 59.7% relevance precision on `TAIL` by impressing every available social annotation to a user. Using our **offline** model on `HEAD`, one could increase the rate of relevance by a factor of 13% while maintaining 88% recall, or by a factor of 25% at 50% recall. On `TAIL`, the same model would increase the rate of relevance by a factor of 7% at 87% recall, or by a factor of 29% at 50% recall.

We analyzed the importance of the offline features in our model by observing the weights assigned by MART in its training log files. For `HEAD`, the social aspects were consistently ranked highest: circle, affinity and expertise are the three most important features, followed by content relevance judgments. For `TAIL`, the picture is different. Here, the content relevance features are dominant. The top-ranked feature is whether the content relevance is marked as `bad`, which is not surprising since instances of non-relevant urls are higher in `TAIL` and social annotations on irrelevant documents have less utility. This relevance feature is followed in the importance ranking by a number of social aspects (affinity, circle and expertise), followed by whether the content relevance is `excellent`, followed by query class features.

We also observe that there is enough signal in the **online** features for predictions up into the 70-75% precision range, albeit at much lower recall rate than for offline features. Prediction ability is highest on `TAIL` nearly achieving the performance of offline features. Somewhat surprisingly, in both `HEAD` and `TAIL`, we observed that the **Query Class** features were by far the most predictive, followed by the **Results Metrics** features - see ablation results in Figure 5 for `HEAD` (`TAIL` omitted for lack of space). In fact for `HEAD` queries, only using query class features produces results close to those using all online features. In `TAIL`, the picture is more differentiated, where adding other online features to the query classifier features improves results.

Based on this analysis of feature importance and the finding that online features are predictive but not as predictive as offline features, we also experimented with adding the most predictive offline features (aspect family) to the set of online features. For `HEAD` queries we added the social aspect features (`circle`, `affinity`, `expertise`, etc.), and for `TAIL` queries we added the content relevance features (`perfect`, `excellent`, `fair`, etc.) Results are also shown in Figures 3 and 4. We observe that we can increase the performance of online features by adding social aspects and content relevance features. We take this as an encouraging result since proxies of both these feature families may be made available at runtime. Content relevance features such as PageRank scores can be assessed, which - while not as accurate as human judgments - may provide additional signal. Similarly, social relevance features could be amenable to statistical modeling from observable data such as social network characteristics or profile modeling at runtime, an area that we plan to investigate in future research.

6. CONCLUSION AND FUTURE WORK

We presented a taxonomy of aspects that influence the perceived utility of social annotations in a Web search scenario, drawn from the query, social connection, and content relevance. Via a user study, we took a first step at quantifying the utility of social annotations and gained insights on the complex interplay between the social relevance aspects. We concluded that there are large variations in utility depending on the aspects in play and that these should be leveraged when deciding to impress a social annotation to a user. We learned that social aspects are most influential in perceived utility, in particular affinity, expertise and interest valence. We further established that close social connections and experts in the search topic provide the most utility, whereas distant friends and friends that show no positive or negative interest valence provide the least utility, by a factor of over 50%.

We also showed that we can automatically predict whether a social annotation is relevant for a given query/url pair. We cast the task as a binary supervised learning problem over a stochastic gradient boosting model. In an offline experiment, we drew features from the manually labeled user study and established that we can accurately predict social utility. In a configuration simulating an online scenario, we drew session-, query-, document-, and user-level features from query classifiers and web usage logs, which can be computed at runtime by commercial web search engines. In this online setting, we established the prediction task as learnable and approaching the performance of the offline model. Finally, by adding the social aspects and content relevance aspects from the offline features to the online features, we gained predictive performance over just the online features.

A promising avenue of future work is to develop social aspects classifiers in order to increase our ability to predict the utility of a social annotation. Other directions include investigating the influence of other social aspects such as age, gender, user location, and school; and applying our framework to other social features such as interleaved results. Perhaps most valuable, however, is to broaden our concept of utility, which we have limited to a search result, to the whole-page user experience, as outlined in Section 1, and further our understanding of how social features affect the overall information seeking, discovery, and sensemaking processes.

7. REFERENCES

[1] E. Agichtein, E. Brill, and S. Dumais. Improving web search ranking by incorporating user behavior information. In *SIGIR*, 2006.

[2] S. Bao, G. Xue, and X. e. a. Wu. Optimizing web search using social annotations. In *WWW*, 2007.

[3] C. L. Barry and L. Schamber. Users' criteria for relevance evaluation: A cross-situational comparison. *Inf. Process. Manage.*, 34(2-3):219–236, 1998.

[4] P. Borlund. The concept of relevance in ir. *JASIST*, 54(10):913–925, 2003.

[5] C. J. C. Burges, K. M. Svore, P. N. Bennett, A. Pastusiak, and Q. Wu. Learning to rank using an ensemble of lambda-gradient models. *Journal of Machine Learning Research*, 14:25–35, 2011.

[6] D. Carmel, N. Zwerdling, I. Guy, S. Ofek-koifman, N. Har'el, I. Ronen, E. Uziel, S. Yogev, and S. Chernov. Personalized social search based on the user's social network. In *CIKM*, pages 1227–1236, 2009.

[7] O. Chapelle, D. Metlzer, Y. Zhang, and P. Grinspan. Expected reciprocal rank for graded relevance. In *CIKM*, pages 621–630, 2009.

[8] C. Clarke, E. Agichtein, S. Dumais, and R. White. The influence of caption features on clickthrough patterns in web search. In *SIGIR*, 2007.

[9] B. M. Evans and E. H. Chi. An elaborated model of social search. *Inf. Process. Manage.*, 46(6):656–678, 2010.

[10] R. Fidel and M. Crandall. Users' perception of the performance of a filtering system. In *SIGIR*, 1997.

[11] J. Friedman. Greedy function approximation: a gradient boosting machine. *Annals of Statistics*, 29, 2001.

[12] K. Haas, P. Mika, P. Tarjan, and R. Blanco. Enhanced results for web search. In *SIGIR*, 2011.

[13] P. Heymann, G. Koutrika, and H. Garcia-Molina. Can social bookmarking improve web search. In *WSDM*, 2008.

[14] R. A. Hill and R. I. M. Dunbar. Social network size in humans. *Human Nature*, 14(1):53–72, 2003.

[15] S. Huffman and M. Hochster. How well does result relevance predict session satisfaction? In *SIGIR*, 2007.

[16] K. Järvelin and J. Kekäläinen. Cumulated gain-based evaluation of ir techniques. *ACM Trans. Inf. Syst.*, 20:422–446, October 2002.

[17] T.-Y. Liu. Learning to rank for information retrieval. *Foundations and Trends in Information Retrieval*, 3:225–331, March 2009.

[18] A. Muralidharan, Z. Gyongyi, and E. H. Chi. Social annotations in web search. In *SIGCHI*, 2012.

[19] L. Page, S. Brin, R. Motwani, and T. Winograd. The pagerank citation ranking: Bringing order to the web. In *WWW*, 1998.

[20] J. Pitkow and H. e. a. SchÂĺutze. Personalized search. In *ACM*, volume 45(9), 2002.

[21] D. Shen, J. Sun, Q. Yang, and Z. Chen. Building bridges for web query classification. In *Proceedings of SIGIR*, 2006.

[22] J. Teevan, S. Dumais, and D. Liebling. To personalize or not to personalize: Modeling queries with variation in user intent. In *SIGIR*, 2008.

[23] J. Teevan, S. T. Dumais, and E. Horvitz. Personalizing search via automated analysis of interests and activities. In *SIGIR*, pages 449–456, 2005.

[24] J. Ugander, B. Karrer, L. Backstrom, and C. Marlow. The anatomy of the facebook social graph. *CoRR*, abs/1111.4503, 2011.

[25] K. Wang, T. Walker, and Z. Zheng. Pskip: estimating relevance ranking quality from web search clickthrough data. In *SIGKDD*, 2009.

[26] S. Wedig and O. Madnani. A large-scale analysis of query logs for assessing personalization opportunities. In *SIGKDD*, 2006.

[27] Q. Wu, C. J. Burges, K. M. Svore, and J. Gao. Ranking, boosting and model adaptation. *Microsoft Research Technical Report*, 2008.

An Exploration of Ranking Heuristics in Mobile Local Search

Yuanhua Lv
Department of Computer Science
University of Illinois at Urbana-Champaign
Urbana, IL 61801, USA
ylv2@uiuc.edu

Dimitrios Lymberopoulos [†], Qiang Wu [‡]
[†] Microsoft Research
[‡] Microsoft
Redmond, WA 98052, USA
{dlymper, qiangwu}@microsoft.com

ABSTRACT

Users increasingly rely on their mobile devices to search local entities, typically businesses, while on the go. Even though recent work has recognized that the ranking signals in mobile local search (e.g., distance and customer rating score of a business) are quite different from general Web search, they have mostly treated these signals as a black-box to extract very basic features (e.g., raw distance values and rating scores) without going inside the signals to understand how exactly they affect the relevance of a business. However, as it has been demonstrated in the development of general information retrieval models, it is critical to explore the underlying behaviors/heuristics of a ranking signal to design more effective ranking features.

In this paper, we follow a data-driven methodology to study the behavior of these ranking signals in mobile local search using a large-scale query log. Our analysis reveals interesting heuristics that can be used to guide the exploitation of different signals. For example, users often take the *mean* value of a signal (e.g., rating) from the business result list as a "pivot" score, and tend to demonstrate different click behaviors on businesses with lower and higher signal values than the pivot; the clickrate of a business generally is *sublinearly* decreasing with its distance to the user, etc. Inspired by the understanding of these heuristics, we further propose different transformation methods to generate more effective ranking features. We quantify the improvement of the proposed new features using real mobile local search logs over a period of 14 months and show that the mean average precision can be improved by over 7%.

Categories and Subject Descriptors

H.3.3 [**Information Search and Retrieval**]: Miscellaneous

General Terms

Algorithms, Human Factors, Measurement

Keywords

Mobile local search, search log analysis, ranking heuristics

Permission to make digital or hard copies of all or part of this work for personal or classroom use is granted without fee provided that copies are not made or distributed for profit or commercial advantage and that copies bear this notice and the full citation on the first page. To copy otherwise, to republish, to post on servers or to redistribute to lists, requires prior specific permission and/or a fee.
SIGIR'12, August 12–16, 2012, Portland, Oregon, USA.
Copyright 2012 ACM 978-1-4503-1472-5/12/08 ...$15.00.

1. INTRODUCTION

The wide availability of internet access on mobile devices, such as phones and personal media players, has allowed users to search and access Web information while on the go. According to a recent report from comScore [1], as of July 2011, there were over 234 million mobile users in U.S., with nearly 50 percent searching on their mobile devices. The availability of continuous fine-grained location information on these devices has enabled mobile local search, which employs user location as a key factor to search for local entities, to overtake a significant part of the query volume. Sohn et al.'s study [34] found that 38% of mobile information needs are local. This is also evident by recent reports by BIA/Kelsey [2] which show that 30% of all search volume will be local in nature by 2015, as well as by the rising popularity of location-based search applications such as Google Local, Bing Local, and Yelp.

Even though mobile local search is similar to general Web search in that they both boil down to a similar problem of relevance/click prediction and result ranking, there are two fundamental differences and also challenges in developing effective ranking functions for mobile local search.

First, the ranking signals in mobile local search are quite different from general Web search. On the one hand, Web search handles a wide range of Web objects, particularly webpages, while mobile local search focuses mostly on ranking local businesses (e.g., restaurants). Therefore, special domain knowledge about the ranking objects in mobile local search could be exploited to improve ranking accuracy. For instance, businesses may receive *ratings* and *reviews* from their customers thanks to the Web 2.0 services, which have been shown to be useful signals for ranking businesses [3, 43]. On the other hand, local search users generally prefer businesses that are physically close to them; this is particularly critical for mobile users who are on the go and their range of reach might be limited. For example, a user would be more likely to visit a restaurant within 1 kilometer than another one within 2 kilometers to get breakfast, if the two restaurants are similarly good on other aspects. The *distance* between the result business and the user's location has been recognized as an important ranking signal in mobile local search [17, 3, 26]. In fact, the customer rating score, the number of reviews, and the distance are all shown explicitly to users in the search result user interface of mobile local search, as shown in Figure 1, and therefore play an important role in influencing the user's click decision.

[1]http://www.comscore.com/
[2]http://www.biakelsey.com/

Figure 1: Sample mobile local search result.

Properly studying and modeling how this information affects user click behavior is arguably the key to improving ranking accuracy.

In spite of the recognition of these new ranking signals, previous work has mostly treated them as a black-box to extract very basic features (e.g., raw rating scores and distance values) without going inside the signals to study how exactly they affect the relevance or clickrate of a business. For example, it is unclear how the clickrate of a business changes with its rating score: does a lower rating score necessarily lead to a lower clickrate? In the aforementioned restaurant example, a 1 kilometer difference in distances may lead to significantly different clickrates of two restaurants, but would the same 1 kilometer distance difference also cause similar clickrate difference of another two restaurants that are further away from user's location, e.g., 10 and 11 kilometers instead of 1 and 2 kilometers away? It is critical to understand the underlying behaviors/heuristics of a ranking signal, which would guide us to design more effective ranking features; this has been demonstrated extensively in the development of retrieval functions for general Web search, e.g., [30, 33, 11, 25].

Second, similarly to personalization in Web search [32, 36, 35, 13, 37, 28], personal preference affects user click behavior and can therefore constitute an important ranking signal for mobile local search [38]. For instance, knowing that a mobile user searching for restaurants prefers Chinese food, we can rank more Chinese restaurants on the top to avoid bothering the user with other types of restaurants. However, conversely to Web search, it is non-trivial to build user profiles for capturing personal preference of different businesses in mobile local search. On the one hand, the text associated with each business is often very sparse so that it would be hard to build content-based user profiles proposed previously [32, 36]. On the other hand, due to the local nature, a user tends to only click nearby businesses, so it is hard to find users who live far away from each other but share similar business click patterns, making it difficult to apply the collaborative filtering approaches (e.g., [35, 13]) or statistical topic modeling approaches (e.g., [20, 4, 27]), for user profiling.

Inspired by the understanding of these challenges, in this paper, we explore the ranking heuristics behind these new signals in mobile local search to develop more effective ranking features. Specifically, our contributions are threefold.

First, we follow a data-driven methodology to study the behavior of the new ranking signals in mobile local search using a large-scale query log. Our analysis reveals interesting heuristics that can be used to guide the exploitation of different signals. For example, we reveal a common phenomenon for all signals involved in our study, i.e., users often take the *mean* value of a signal from the business result list as a "pivot" score, and tend to demonstrate different click behaviors on businesses with lower and higher signal values than the pivot; the clickrate of a business generally is *sublinearly* decreasing with its distance to the user, etc. Motivated by these heuristics, we further propose different normalization methods to generate more effective ranking features.

Second, we exploit domain knowledge of businesses, i.e., business category information used in a commercial search engine, and employ a back-off strategy to estimate the user preference of business categories instead of specific businesses: two users from different locations, though hardly co-clicking any specific business, may still be interested in similar business categories. We study how such a user preference signal affects the clickrate of a business and design effective strategies to generate personalization features.

Third, we develop a clickrate prediction function to leverage the complementary relative strengths of various signals, by employing a state-of-the-art predictive modeling method, MART [15, 16, 40]. In doing this, we hope to exploit the strength of machine learning to quantify the improvement of the proposed features. We evaluate the performance of the proposed new features using real mobile local search logs over a period of 14 months, with an emphasis on those difficult queries, and show that the mean average precision can be improved by over 7%.

2. RELATED WORK

There have been several large scale studies in the past on mobile query log analysis for deciphering mobile search query patterns [22, 23, 9, 41, 8, 38]. The goal of these studies is to provide quantitative statistics on various aspects of mobile search that can help gain better insight on the mobile users' information needs. However, few of these efforts have provided insight about the ranking issue.

In early studies of local search or geographic search, some work attempted to identify queries that may not contain an explicit geographic reference (e.g., a city name) but have a "geo-intent" nevertheless [39, 2, 42], while some others focused on improving the query processing and ranking efficiency [7, 12, 10]. They are all orthogonal to our work in that we study how to improve the ranking accuracy for "geo-intent" queries.

Recently, the task of improving the ranking accuracy of mobile local search has also begun to attract efforts [1, 24, 3, 26] which have already recognized that the ranking signals in mobile local search (e.g., distance and rating score of a business) are quite different from general Web search. However, these studies have mostly treated such ranking signals as a black-box to extract very basic features (e.g., raw distance values and rating scores). Although some statistics of these signals are also often used as complementary features, such as the average distance and the standard deviation of distance in the current location [26], existing work relies purely on machine learning techniques to combine all features without going inside the signals to understand how exactly they affect user click behaviors. In contrast to existing studies, our work is a first attempt at understanding the behaviors and heuristics of these ranking signals for click prediction in mobile local search.

It has been previously demonstrated that understanding the behaviors/heuristics of a ranking signal is critical in the development of retrieval functions for Web search [30, 33, 14, 11, 25]. For example, the term frequency signal, which assigns a higher score to a document if it contains more occurrences of the query term, should be normalized to prevent the contribution of repeated occurrences from growing too large due to the burstiness phenomenon [30, 14], and the term frequency signal should also be normalized by document length since long documents tend to use the same terms repeatedly [30, 33, 14]. All effective retrieval models in Web search have implemented these heuristics [14], and previous work has also shown that a retrieval function tends to work poorly if any desirable retrieval heuristic is violated [14, 25]. Inspired by the successes and lessons from the development of retrieval models, we thus explore the ranking heuristics in mobile local search and try to understand how exactly a ranking signal in mobile local search is related to the clickrate/relevance of a business.

Additionally, opinionated content has also been exploited in some existing search tasks. For example, in opinion retrieval [29], the goal of the task is to locate documents (primarily blog posts) that have opinionated content; Ganesan and Zhai [18] studied the use of the content of customer reviews to represent an entity (e.g., business) in entity ranking; Zhang et al. [43] proposed different methods to aggregate the counts of thumb-ups and thumb-downs for rating prediction, etc. Different from previous work, our work aims at understanding the relationship between the clickrate of a business and its rating score and number of reviews in mobile local search.

Personalized search has attracted much attention in Web search [32, 36, 13, 28, 38]. To the best of our knowledge, no previous work has exploited personalization for mobile local search. In this paper, we design appropriate approaches to exploiting personalization in mobile local search and quantify their impact on ranking accuracy using real mobile local query logs.

3. EXPERIMENTAL SETTING

3.1 Dataset

To the process of acquiring relevance judgments and evaluating mobile local search is a challenging problem. First, the Cranfield style evaluation that has been used in the evaluation of many traditional information retrieval tasks [31] would not work here, since the relevance judgments in mobile local search are particularly dependent on the search context, e.g., location of the user [24, 26]. Second, asking users to make explicit relevance judgments can be very costly because it is necessary to cover a diverse set of queries in different contexts. Third, although Joachims et al. have developed methods for extracting relative relevance judgments from user clickthrough data in general Web search [21], it is unclear if these methods also work for mobile local search where the position bias of clickthrough and the interpretation of clickthrough may be different from general Web search. Due to these problems in applying traditional evaluation methods, in our work, we choose to follow the previous work on mobile local search [3, 26] and simply use clicks to approximate the relevance judgments. Although each individual user click may not be very reliable, the aggregation of a great number of user clicks from a large-scale query log could still provide powerful indicator of relevance. Thus, it is very likely that features that help improve click prediction will be useful in ranking as well.

Therefore our task is, given a query, to predict if a candidate business would be clicked, and then rank the candidate businesses based on the click prediction. In our experiments, the query is sampled from the search log, while the candidate businesses are all those businesses that were shown to the user for that query. To learn and evaluate a click prediction model, we split the query log into four parts. The first 9 months of data is kept out as the "history" data, and is used purely for estimating the popularity of a business and the user's personal preference. We sample queries from the next 3, 1, and 1 months of data respectively for training, validating, and testing the click prediction models.

We apply three preprocessing steps to make these four datasets more practical and representative: (1) We exclude queries that did not receive any click or received clicks for every candidate business, since these queries will not influence the average ranking performance in the experiments. (2) We identify and filter out queries that match a business name exactly, e.g., "Starbucks"; solving such kind of queries is a relatively easy task, since users usually have clearer information needs (e.g., visiting a nearby Starbucks) as compared to other more general queries, e.g., "Coffee". In doing this, we place an emphasis on difficult queries in our study. (3) We empirically remove queries (from all the four datasets) by "users" who issued more than 1000 queries in total in the training, validation, and test datasets, because such "users" are more likely to be robots. Finally, we obtain 60475, 18491, and 23152 queries as the training, validation, and test queries; the average number of clicks and the average number of candidate businesses for each query are 1.34 and 17 respectively.

3.2 Learning Model for Click Prediction

Since we need to leverage multiple signals for click prediction, we seek help from machine learning. We adopt MART [40], a learning tool based on Multiple Additive Regression Trees, to provide a common learning framework on top of which we can compare the performance of different ranking heuristics and ranking features. MART is based on the stochastic gradient boosting approach described in [15, 16] which performs gradient descent optimization in the functional space. In our experiments on click prediction, we used the log-likelihood as the loss function, used steepest-decent (gradient descent) as the optimization technique, and used binary decision trees as the fitting function.

We construct a training instance for each query-business pair, which consists of a set of features (e.g., distance, rating, etc.) and a click label which indicates if the user clicks the business (1 for click and 0 otherwise). The training and validation data are fed into MART to build a binary classification model, which we use to estimate the probability of clicks in the test data.

Note that the choice of machine learning algorithms is not critical in our paper: we only take machine learning as a black-box tool to evaluate the proposed heuristics and features. We chose MART mainly because it can potentially handle non-linear combination of features, and it is widely adopted in current commercially available search and advertisement ranking engines.

The main goal of our experiments is to explore and evaluate effective ranking heuristics for boosting the special ranking signals in mobile local search. Our baseline feature set contains 6 representative features that are selected based on previous research studies [17, 24, 26]. These features are: (1) the distance between the query and the business locations, (2) the popularity measure of the business as defined by the number of clicks in the history search logs, (3) the clickrate of the business in the history data as defined by the

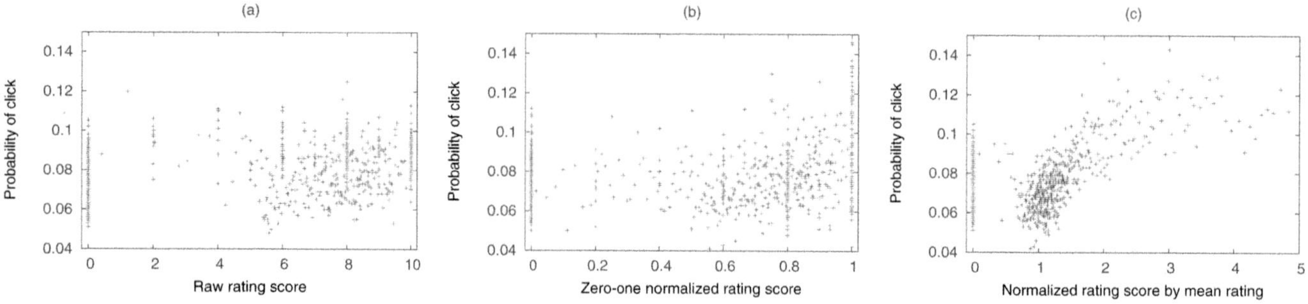

Figure 2: Probability of click for businesses from a bin, plotted against the mean rating score of this bin.

Distance	1	Rating	0.3794
#Clicks	0.7193	#Reviews	0.3462
ClickRate	0.9976	TimeFrame	0.1752

Table 1: Relative feature importance in baseline

number of clicks divided by the number of impressions and defined as 0 if it did not occur in the history data, (4) the customer rating score of the business in a range of [0, 10], (5) the number of customer reviews of the business, and (6) a time code that represents both the time frame within a day (one out of five time frames) that the query was submitted and the day of the week that the query was submitted (weekend or weekday). Since we only re-rank top-ranked businesses from a commercial mobile local search engine, and those businesses that do not match the query keywords at all have already been eliminated, we thus do not involve any textual matching feature and focus only on the special signals of mobile local search.

We evaluate the retrieval performance in terms of MAP (Mean Average Precision) and the precision at different recall levels. Because we are only re-ranking a set of top-ranked businesses in response to a query, the recall score will be the same for any ranking model. In other words, MAP will be only influenced by the positions of the relevant results. So we believe that, in our study, MAP is a good measure to capture the ranking accuracy of top-ranked results. Besides, we also compare the importance of each feature in constructing the MART model, following the relative importance measure proposed in [15].

4. RANKING SIGNALS AND HEURISTICS

In mobile local search, the rating score, the number of reviews, and the distance are not only the key back-end ranking signals, but also important information displayed explicitly in the search result UI as shown in Figure 1. Although the "personal preference" signal is not explicitly shown to users, users certainly know their own preference. That being said, these four ranking signals are directly observable to users, and users' click behaviors presumably would be heavily dependent on these signals. Therefore, understanding how exactly a user's decision relates to these signals would potentially lead to better ways of modeling these signals and thus to improving mobile local search. In this section, we study in detail these four ranking signals.

4.1 Customer Rating

Intuitively, the customer rating score of a business would significantly affect users' click behaviors in mobile local search, since users are used to consulting other people's ratings and opinions about an entity to help make their own decision [29]. To verify this intuition, we trained a click prediction model using the baseline features described in the previous section and examined the relative importance of the different features. The results shown in Table 1 indicate that conversely to our intuition, the importance of the rating score as a feature is relatively low in our baseline system.

4.1.1 Likelihood of Click/Relevance

To examine this observation, we analyze the likelihood of relevance (i.e., clickrate) of businesses of all rating scores, and plot these likelihoods against the rating score to obtain a "click pattern". Intuitively, the likelihoods should increase monotonically with the rating score.

To estimate these likelihoods, we sort all the businesses in the training data in order of increasing rating score, and divide them into several equal sized (i.e., 1000) "bins", yielding 1032 different bins. We select the mean rating score in each bin to represent the bin on the graphs used in later analysis. We can then compute the probability of a randomly selected business from the ith bin getting clicked, which is the ratio of the number of clicked businesses from the ith bin, and the bin size. In terms of conditional probability, given a business b, this ratio of the ith bin can be represented by $p(b \text{ is clicked} \mid b \in Bin_i)$.

Figure 2(a) shows how the probabilities obtained from the above analysis relate to the mean rating score in a bin. Surprisingly, there seems to be no clear relationship between the likelihood of click and the rating score.

This anti-intuitive observation could be possibly caused by the potentially incomparable rating scores across different queries: result businesses retrieved by some queries may have higher rating scores than that retrieved by some other queries. To verify this, we adopt the popular zero-one score normalization method, which linearly normalizes the rating scores of every query to a range of [0, 1]. Such a normalization strategy has been widely used for feature normalization in many learning to rank tasks, e.g., [6]. After that, we do a similar analysis of the probabilities of click, but against the normalized rating score. The results are shown in Figure 2(b). Unfortunately, there is still no clear relationship, suggesting that the ineffectiveness of the rating score as a feature is not purely caused by the incomparable score range.

4.1.2 The "Mean" Normalization Scheme

To diagnose the problem, we further look into the distribution of rating scores of businesses that get clicked. Since the distribution of rating scores is intuitively related to the

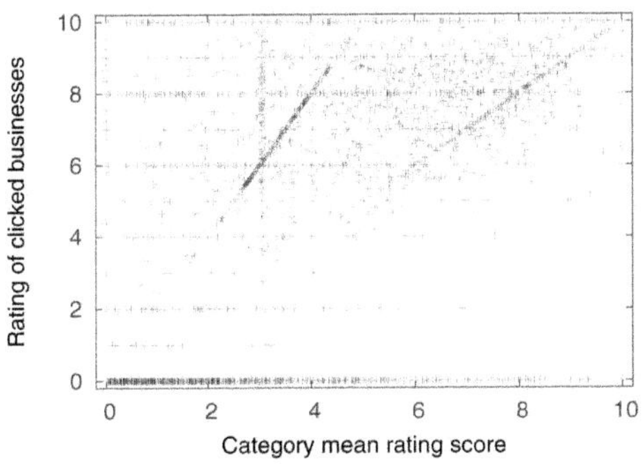

Figure 3: Rating of clicked businesses, plotted against the mean rating score of the corresponding business category.

type/category of businesses, we do this analysis in a category-aware way. Specifically, we compare the rating score of a clicked business with the mean rating score of all businesses from the same category. In doing this, we hope to understand if the clicked businesses are among the highly rated businesses in a category. The comparison results are illustrated in Figure 3, in which we show 10% of randomly selected *clicked* businesses from the training data.

Interestingly, we can see that the rating scores of most of the clicked businesses are above their corresponding category mean rating score. For example, when the category mean rating score is 4, few businesses with a rating score lower than 4 get clicked. This shows that the rating score is indeed useful and is directly related to users' click behaviors. However, how does a user know the mean rating score of a category so as to click businesses above this score?

In reality, we expect that users do not really know the mean score of a category. However, users may be able to have an approximate estimation of this mean score through looking over the retrieved business list: the retrieved businesses for a query often belong to the same category, and thus could be used as a sample set of businesses from that category, the mean rating score of which can be viewed as approximately the mean category rating. If the above assumption is true, it may suggest that, users often take the mean rating score from the business result list as a "pivot" score, and tend to click businesses with higher scores than this pivot. This intuitively makes sense: a user's click decision, although influenced by the rating score, is not entirely based on it, but if the rating of a business is above his/her expectation (i.e., the pivot) which is learned from the result list in an ad hoc way, the business would be more likely to be clicked.

Inspired by this analysis, we propose to normalize rating scores using the mean rating score of the retrieved businesses. A straightforward approach is to divide the original rating score using this mean value, which not only makes the rating scores more comparable across queries but also aligns them at the corresponding mean rating score of each query. We plot the probabilities of click against the normalized rating score in Figure 2(c). It is clear that the probability of click increases monotonically with the normalized rating when the normalized rating is larger than 1 (i.e., the mean point), while the probability tends to be random when the normalized rating is lower than 1. This is an empirical

Methods	MAP	P@0.3	P@0.5	P@0.8
Baseline	.419	.441	.434	.403
ZeroOneNorm	.419	.442	.434	.403
MeanNorm*	$.425^{bz}$	$.448^{bz}$	$.440^{bz}$	$.409^{bz}$
AutoNorm-C	$.422^{b}$	$.445^{b}$	$.437^{b}$	$.406^{b}$
AutoNorm-Q*	$.431^{mc}$	$.454^{mc}$	$.446^{mc}$	$.415^{mc}$
RatingPred*	$.428^{b}$	$.451^{b}$	$.443^{b}$	$.413^{b}$
Norm+Pred	$.438^{qr}$	$.461^{qr}$	$.453^{qr}$	$.421^{qr}$

Table 2: Comparison of methods for modeling rating scores. "Norm+Pred" combines methods tagged using $*$. $b/z/m/c/q/r$ indicates the significance over Baseline, ZeroOneNorm, MeanNorm, AutoNorm-C, AutoNorm-Q, and RatingPred respectively, at the 0.001 level using the Wilcoxon non-directional test.

verification of the fact that users tend to take the mean rating score from the observed results as a "pivot" score, and a clear demonstration of different click behaviors on businesses with lower and higher scores than the pivot score.

To examine if the proposed simple mean normalization scheme can really improve ranking accuracy, we use the normalized rating score to replace the original rating score and learn a new model, labeled as "MeanNorm", and compare its performance with the baseline model. In addition, we also take the widely used zero-one strategy for rating normalization as another baseline run, which is labeled as "ZeroOneNorm". The comparison results are reported in Table 2, and show that the mean normalization scheme works the best, achieving significant improvement over both baseline runs. At the same time, the zero-one normalization does not improve the accuracy of the baseline model. This suggests that we can improve ranking performance by pointing out the mean rating value.

Another approach to explicitly normalizing the rating of a business with the mean rating of all result businesses would be to encode the mean rating of result businesses as an additional feature and let the training algorithm itself decide how to do the normalization. To evaluate this approach, we train a new model, labeled as "AutoNorm-Q", by adding the mean rating score of businesses from the same single *query* into the baseline feature set. We also train another model, labeled as "AutoNorm-C", in which we add the mean rating score of businesses from the same *category* into the baseline. We present the performance of these two runs in Table 2. The results demonstrate that AutoNorm-Q works much better than AutoNorm-C, confirming our analysis that users select the "pivot" from the businesses shown to them. AutoNorm-Q improves over the baseline by approximately 3%. Moreover, AutoNorm-Q improves over MeanNorm, suggesting that the mean normalization scheme can be boosted by optimizing the way of exploiting the "mean" in a supervised manner.

4.1.3 Cluster-based Smoothing of Ratings

It is often the case that a business does not receive any customer rating. In the presence of missing rating scores, a default value of 0 is often used, which, however, may be inaccurate: (1) a business that does not receive any customer rating does not necessarily mean that it should be rated low; (2) it could be unfair to use the same default rating score for all businesses. Even if a business receives a rating score, it may still be inaccurate if the rating is only contributed by a very small number of customers. Therefore, more accurate prediction/smoothing of ratings could potentially improve ranking accuracy, and we propose a cluster-based method to predict/smooth rating values.

The basic idea is based on the cluster hypothesis [19], and averages rating scores $r(x)$ from all businesses x in the same cluster C to smooth the rating $r(b)$ of business b so as to obtain an updated rating $r'(b)$. The intuition is that businesses in the same cluster should receive similar ratings, and the rating stability of a cluster would benefit an individual business. Formally,

$$r'(b) = f\left(r(b), \frac{1}{|C|} \sum_{x \in C, b \in C} r(x)\right) \quad (1)$$

where f is a function to control rating update. The key component is thus the business cluster. We use two types of clusters: business category and business chain. The former allows us to use the rating of all businesses in a given category to estimate the rating of an unrated business in that category (e.g. use all businesses in the "Coffee & Tea" category to estimate the rating score of a Starbucks business). The latter approach, allows us to estimate the rating score of a business by exploiting the rating score of other businesses belonging to the same chain (e.g. use different Strabucks coffeehouses rating scores to estimate the rating score of an unrated Starbucks coffeehouse).

There are two challenges with this approach: how to choose function f and how to leverage the evidences from two types of clusters. Inspired by the effective performance of automatic feature normalization in the previous section, we also let the learning algorithm optimize these two factors in a supervised way. Specifically, we provide both a category mean rating and a business-chain mean rating as two separate features to the learning algorithm. In addition, we also introduce two description variables for these two new features, i.e., the size of the category and the size of the business chain, to the learning algorithm.

This method is labeled as "RatingPred", and we present the experiment results in Table 2. We can see that RatingPred improves over the baseline significantly, suggesting the proposed cluster-based smoothing can indeed improve rating values. Furthermore, we combine RatingPred with the proposed feature normalization methods, leading to a new run labeled as "Norm+Pred". It is observed from Table 2 that Norm+Pred outperforms either single method alone, suggesting that smoothing ratings and normalizing ratings are complementary to each other. Norm+Pred improves over the baseline by more than 4.5%.

4.2 Review Count

The count of reviews represents another signal from the opinionated content, which can intuitively reflect the popularity of a business. However, we find that the importance of this signal is also low in the baseline model, as shown in Table 1. Similarly to the rating score analysis, we reveal that this is because users often take the mean review count from their observed businesses as a "pivot", and demonstrate different click patterns on businesses with lower and higher review count than the pivot. However, the learning algorithm fails to capture this important information. To better exploit the strengths of this signal, we need to feed this pivot number (i.e., mean review count) to the learning algorithm. That is, we should either manually normalize the review count using the pivot, or introduce the pivot as an additional feature for automatic normalization.

Methods	MAP	P@0.3	P@0.5	P@0.8
Baseline	.419	.441	.434	.403
ZeroOneNorm	.421	.444	.436	.405
MeanNorm*	$.425^{bz}$	$.448^{bz}$	$.441^{bz}$	$.409^{bz}$
AutoNorm-C	$.423^{b}$	$.445^{b}$	$.438^{b}$	$.407^{b}$
AutoNorm-Q*	$.431^{mc}$	$.454^{mc}$	$.446^{mc}$	$.414^{mc}$
ReviewsPred*	$.429^{b}$	$.451^{b}$	$.443^{b}$	$.413^{b}$
Norm+Pred	$.438^{qr}$	$.461^{qr}$	$.453^{qr}$	$.421^{qr}$

Table 3: Comparison of methods for modeling review counts. "Norm+Pred" combines methods tagged using $*$. The description of notations $b/z/m/c/q/r$ are the same as Table 2.

The experimental results presented in Table 3 show that the ranking performance can be significantly improved by the "mean" normalization scheme. Different notations in the table are defined similarly to their counterparts in Table 2 but applied to normalize review count. Specifically, the simple mean normalization method (i.e., MeanNorm) performs significantly better than the widely used score normalization method (i.e., ZeroOneNorm) which does not leverage the mean value; also, automatic normalization (i.e., AutoNorm-Q) works more effectively than manual normalization (i.e., MeanNorm).

In addition, similar to the rating score, we can also improve ranking performance by smoothing review count based on the cluster hypothesis to make it more accurate (this run is labeled as "ReviewsPred"). The mean normalization scheme and the cluster-based smoothing can be leveraged together (i.e., Norm+Pred) to further improve performance, achieving 4.5% improvement in MAP.

4.3 Distance

Local search differs from other search tasks mainly because its ranking signals feature geographical distance. In fact, distance has also been shown to be one of the most important features in both previous work, e.g., [26], and our work, as shown in Table 1.

To understand how distance affects the click patterns of users, we first plot in Figure 4 (left) the likelihood of click for a business against its distance from the user. Interestingly, there is indeed a monotonically decreasing trend of the likelihood with respect to distance; this may explain why distance appears to be the most important feature in our experiments. Furthermore, we observe that the likelihood is decreasing sub-linearly with distance: the likelihood decreases with distance, but the decreasing speed drops as distance becomes large. This intuitively makes sense: a restaurant within 1 mile would have clear advantages over another similar restaurant within 2 miles, but two restaurants within 9 miles and 10 miles may not have much difference. That is, the relevance of a business is more sensitive to its distance when the distance value is smaller.

With the Box-Cox transformation analysis [5], we find there is approximately a logarithm transformation. To illustrate it, we plot the likelihood of click with respect to the logarithm transformation of distance in Figure 4 (right).

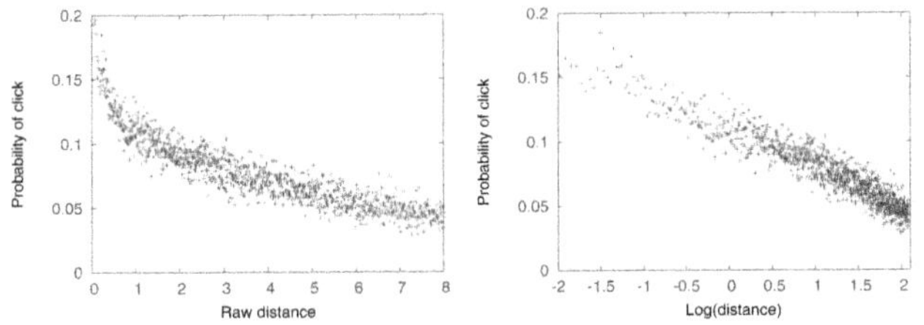

Figure 4: Probability of click for businesses from a bin, plotted against the mean distance (left) and Log(distance) (right) scores of this bin.

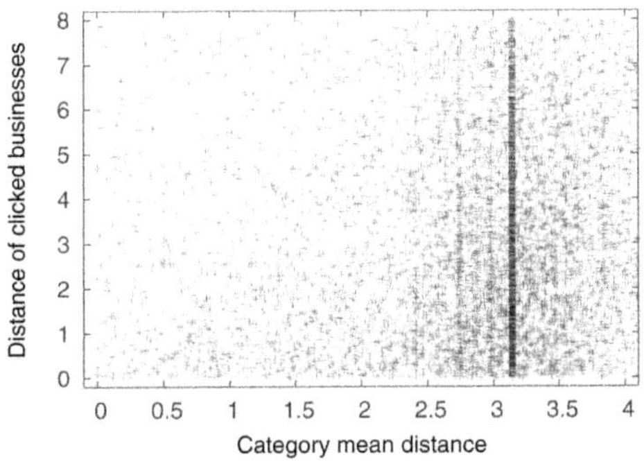

Figure 5: Distance of clicked businesses, plotted against the mean (traveling) distance of the corresponding business category.

Linear scaling in distance would overly penalize businesses that are relatively far away from the user, while the logarithm transformation generally improves modeling distance.

Similar to ratings and review counts, distance is also observable to users. One interesting question is if there is also a "pivot" click phenomenon. To answer this question, we plot the distance of clicked businesses against the mean traveling distance to businesses in the same category, as shown in Figure 5. Indeed, the plot shows that users tend to click businesses closer than the category mean distance, suggesting that the "mean" normalization scheme could also be applicable in the case of the distance feature. Yet, the "pivot" phenomenon of distance is not as clear as that of ratings and review counts. One possible reason is that users can generally understand distance better than ratings and review counts, because distance is a concrete concept, while ratings and review counts appears to be more abstract and subjective; as a result, users tend to rely more on the statistics of the observed business list to make sense of ratings and review counts, but absolute distance itself may have already made much sense. This is also consistent with our previous observation that there is a clear relationship between raw distance values and the probability of click, as shown in Figure 4 (left).

We now verify our analysis using empirical experiments, the results of which are reported in Table 4. We first apply the simple mean normalization method to divide distance by the mean distance value of all observed businesses for the same query. This run is labeled as "MeanNorm". We can see it improves over the baseline system significantly, which suggests that feature normalization still helps even though absolute distance values are already largely comparable. We next compare "MeanNorm" with "MeanNorm+" in which the simple mean normalization method is applied to *log*(distance). Apparently, "MeanNorm+" works more effectively, confirming our analysis that the logarithm transformation is useful for better modeling distance. In addition, we create another run "ZeroOneNorm+" which differs from "MeanNorm+" in that the zero-one normalization is used. We observe that "ZeroOneNorm+" works significantly worse than "MeanNorm+", confirming our analysis that the "mean" normalization scheme works well for distance, and suggesting that users would also like to click businesses with a distance smaller than the pivot (i.e., mean distance in the result list).

Methods	MAP	P@0.3	P@0.5	P@0.8
Baseline	.419	.441	.434	.403
MeanNorm	$.429^{b}$	$.451^{b}$	$.443^{b}$	$.414^{b}$
ZeroOneNorm+	$.428^{b}$	$.451^{b}$	$.443^{b}$	$.413^{b}$
MeanNorm+	$.435^{mz}$	$.457^{mz}$	$.449^{mz}$	$.420^{mz}$
AutoNorm	$.434^{m}$	$.456^{m}$	$.449^{m}$	$.419^{m}$
AutoNorm+	$.435^{ma}$	$.457^{ma}$	$.450^{ma}$	$.420^{ma}$

Table 4: Comparison of methods for modeling distance. Methods with an indicator "+" applies logarithm transformation. $b/z/m/a$ indicates the significance over Baseline, ZeroOneNorm+, MeanNorm, and AutoNorm respectively, at the 0.05 level using the Wilcoxon non-directional test.

Finally, we also evaluate two automatic mean normalization runs, namely "AutoNorm" and "AutoNorm+", where we introduce the mean value of distance and *log*(distance) in the search results as additional features into the training process to let the learning algorithm automatically normalize the distance and the *log*(distance) features respectively. First, "AutoNorm+" outperforms "AutoNorm", though the improvement is small; this suggests that sub-linear transformation of distance is beneficial, yet its advantage tends to be weakened as we use automatic feature normalization, because MART can potentially handle non-linear combination automatically. Second, by comparing "AutoNorm(+)" with "MeanNorm(+)", we can see that automatic normalization can work better than or comparable to the simple mean normalization. Overall, both automatic normalization and manual normalization can improve over baseline by approximate 4% with the proposed new features.

4.4 Personal Preference

Our goal is to build user profiles so that we can compute the user preference of a business so as to rank businesses in a user adaptive way. However, it is non-trivial to build content-based user profiles [32, 36] in mobile local search, since the text associated with each business is often very sparse. Thus, we choose to use the collaborative filtering approach [20, 27, 4], based on the history click data, to estimate the likelihood that a user u likes business b, formally the conditional probability $P(b|u)$. Yet there is another challenging problem: due to the local nature of the task, a user tends to only click nearby businesses, so the co-occurrences are also of local nature and thus very sparse. For example, it is very hard to find users who live far away from each other but share similar business click patterns. To solve this problem, we exploit the domain knowledge of businesses and instead estimate the likelihood that a user u

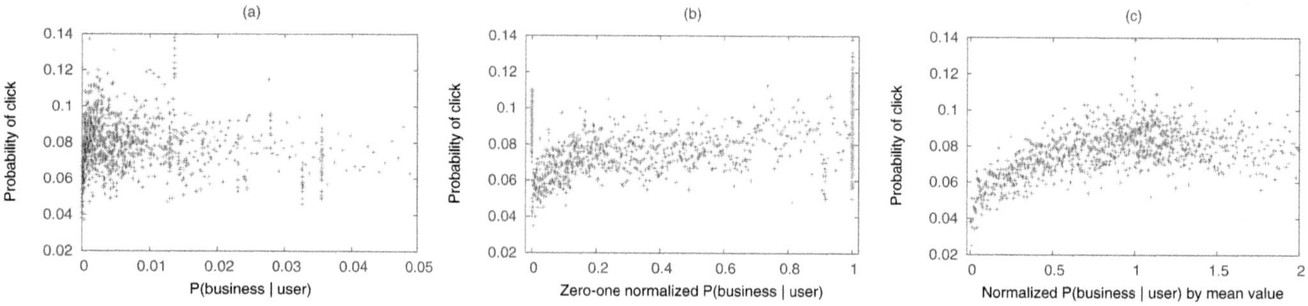

Figure 6: Probability of click for businesses from a bin plotted against the mean user preference of this bin.

likes business category c, i.e., $P(c|u)$: as a business category can cover businesses from different locations, co-occurrences of categories and users can happen across locations. As a by-product, the number of categories, which is about 3000, is only about 1/5000 of the number of businesses, significantly reducing the dimension. Our experiments show that we can build profiles for 1 million users in several hours on a single machine.

Although the category information of a business that the user has clicked can be obtained directly from the history data, due to the data sparseness problem of many users, we follow the idea of statistical topic modeling to estimate $P(c|u)$ in a more smoothing way. First, we introduce hidden variables Z with states z for every user-category pair. The possible set of states z is assumed to be finite and of size k. We empirically set $k = 100$ in our work. We can map our problem to the standard topic modeling problem: the original document-term matrix is replaced by a user-category matrix, and the original co-occurrence relationship is replaced by a click. In our work, we adopt PLSA [20] and LDA [4]. Since these two models perform similarly effectively in our experiments, we only show the results based on PLSA.

Considering observations in the form of clicks (c, u) of categories and users, PLSA models the probability of each click (i.e., a user u clicks a business of category c) as a mixture of conditionally independent multinomial distributions:

$$P(c, u) = \sum_z P(z)P(u|z)P(c|z) = P(u) \sum_z P(z|u)P(c|z) \quad (2)$$

Since our problem is to estimate user preference, we will work with the conditional model

$$P(c|u) = \sum_z P(z|u)P(c|z) \quad (3)$$

The model can be estimated using the Expectation Maximization (EM) algorithm to obtain parameters $P(z|u)$ and $P(c|z)$. Now, we have constructed a user profile $P(c|u)$. Then given any business b, since b may belong to multiple categories, we average the conditional probabilities of these corresponding categories as the user preference of a business, i.e., $P(b|u)$.

Some users may have more history clicks, and the profiles of these users would intuitively be more reliable than that of some other users who make fewer clicks. In order to make the model more intelligent so as to be able to automatically learn how much personalization we should apply for each user, we encode both the user preference, i.e., $P(b|u)$, and the number of history clicks of the user into the learning algorithm. We do not do any normalization, and this run is labeled as "NoNorm". We compare it with the baseline and observe that, though "NoNorm" outperforms the baseline significantly, the improvement is indeed minor.

Personalization	MAP	P@0.3	P@0.5	P@0.8
Baseline	.419	.441	.434	.403
NoNorm	$.420^{b}$	$.442^{b}$	$.434^{b}$	$.404^{b}$
MeanNorm	$.420^{b}$	$.442^{b}$	$.434^{b}$	$.404^{b}$
MeanNorm+	$.428^{nm}$	$.450^{nm}$	$.442^{nm}$	$.411^{nm}$
AutoNorm	$.427^{nm}$	$.450^{nm}$	$.442^{bm}$	$.411^{bm}$
AutoNorm+	$.428^{nm}$	$.450^{nm}$	$.443^{nm}$	$.412^{nm}$

Table 5: Comparison of methods for modeling user preference. Methods with an indicator "+" applies logarithm transformation. $b/n/m$ indicates the significance over Baseline, NoNorm, and MeanNorm respectively, at the 0.01 level using the Wilcoxon non-directional test.

To examine the reason, we follow Section 4.1.1, and plot the probability of click for businesses against the user preference, as shown in Figure 6 (a). We can see that the probability of click generally does not vary a lot when the user preference changes; this may be one possible reason why "NoNorm" does not work very well. We then apply the zero-one normalization and generate another plot in Figure 6 (b). It shows that the zero-one normalization essentially stretches the plot along the x-axis. There also appears to be an increasing trend only when the user preference is very small. Next, we try the mean normalization method in Figure 6 (c). It shows clearly that when the user preference is below the mean value (i.e., $x = 1$) of the current search results, the probability of click increases monotonically with user preference and the increasing speed decreases as the user preference approaches its mean value. However, after the user preference reaches the mean value, the probability of click even has a tendency to decrease slightly. Again, this observation shows that users choose the mean value as a pivot score and have different click behaviors on the two sides of the pivot. Furthermore, it is interesting to see that the probability of click is maximized when the user preference is around the mean value: too low preference may mean that the business is not interesting to the user (i.e., irrelevant business), while too high preference may indicate that the business could be too similar to what the user clicked before (i.e., redundant business). The pivot observation seems to demonstrate that a user's decision may like an exploration-exploitation tradeoff: exploit what he/she knows but meanwhile explore what he/she does not know.

Methods	MAP	P@0.3	P@0.5	P@0.8
Baseline	.419	.441	.434	.403
All	.449	.472	.464	.433
All-Rating	.448	.471	.463	.432
All-Reviews	.449	.472	.464	.433
All-Distance	.441	.464	.456	.425
All-Personalization	.448	.471	.463	.431
All-Rating-Reviews	.442	.464	.456	.426
All-Rating-Reviews -Personalization	.436	.458	.450	.420

Table 6: Sensitivity analysis. It shows that combining the proposed new features (i.e., "All") can improve the Baseline over 7%.

Inspired by the analysis above, we develop a manual mean normalization run ("MeanNorm") and an automatic mean normalization run ("AutoNorm") for feature normalization. According to the results shown in Table 5, "AutoNorm" improves over both the baseline and "MeanNorm" significantly, while "MeanNorm" does not perform very well. We hypothesize that this could be because of the sublinear increasing curve of the mean normalization method, as shown in Figure 6 (c): similar to our observations of distance normalization, automatic normalization using MART can potentially handle non-linear combination well, while manual normalization cannot. To verify our intuition, we first apply a logarithm transformation based on the Box-Cox transformation analysis [5] onto user preference and then add the two normalization methods on top of the transformed feature, leading to two new runs "MeanNorm+" and "AutoNorm+". Table 5 shows that these two runs perform similarly well and the best among all methods, verifying our hypothesis and also showing the necessity of sublinear transformation. Overall, by normalizing the personalization features, we can obtain over 2% MAP improvements.

4.5 Sensitivity Analysis

We combine the most effective modeling methods for all the four signals into our final model, including "Norm+Pred" from Table 2 for modeling the customer rating, "Norm+Pred" from Table 3 for modeling the review count, "AutoNorm+" and "MeanNorm+" from Table 4 for modeling distance, and "AutoNorm+" and "MeanNorm+" from Table 5 for modeling user preference. The final model is labeled as "All" and shown in Table 6. Table 7 lists the 23 features in the "All" model as well as where each feature comes from. We can see that the "All" model outperforms the baseline by more than 7%, suggesting that understanding the behaviors and heuristics behind ranking signals can indeed lead to better modeling methods and thus improving ranking accuracy.

We have shown that the selected modeling methods (now as components in the final "All" model) perform very well in modeling each individual signal. Now we turn to examine how sensitive of these methods when we combine them together. We remove some new modeling method(s) at a time, while keeping all other modeling methods and the baseline features. For example, "All-Rating" in Table 6 is constructed by excluding from the "All" model the proposed novel features in the "Norm+Pred" method for rating modeling, while the features occurring in other models, including all baseline features, are kept. From Table 6, we can see that when we remove "Distance", the performance drops clearly, suggesting that "Distance" is very sensitive in the final model and its effect cannot be replaced. However, when we exclude "Rating", "Reviews", or "Personalization", the performance only decreases slightly or even does not change. It suggests that the effect of these signals may have a large overlap; as a result, although they perform well as individual signals, their performance could not add together.

	Features	Imp.	Contributor
1	MeanNorm_Log_Distance	1	Distance
2	ClickRate	0.5859	Baseline
3	#Clicks	0.5152	Baseline
4	#Reviews_Mean	0.3692	Reviews
5	Log_UserPref_Mean	0.3646	Personalization
6	Rating_Mean	0.3453	Rating
7	MeanNorm_#Review	0.3137	Reviews
8	|BusinessChain|	0.3132	Rating&Reviews
9	Log_MeanNorm_UserPref	0.2897	Personalization
10	MeanNorm_Rating	0.2242	Rating
11	|Category|	0.2229	Rating&Reviews
12	Log_Distance_Mean	0.1814	Distance
13	#CategoryReviews	0.1731	Reviews
14	CategoryRating	0.1665	Rating
15	User_#Clicks	0.1651	Personalization
16	Log_Distance	0.1434	Distance
17	#BusinessChainReviews	0.1394	Reviews
18	Distance	0.1122	Baseline
19	BusinessChainRating	0.1100	Rating
20	Rating	0.1071	Baseline
21	Log_UserPref	0.1057	Personalization
22	#Reviews	0.0686	Baseline
23	TimeFrame	0.0660	Baseline

Table 7: Relative feature importance in the final model

To go a step further, we remove "Rating" and "Reviews" at the same time, and find that its performance degrades much more than that of "All-Rating" and "All-Reviews". This observation confirms that ratings and review counts are highly redundant to each other, which intuitively makes sense. After removing "Rating" and "Reviews", we also remove "Personalization" in the last row of Table 6. We can see the performance degradation is much larger than when we remove "Personalization" from the "All" model, suggesting that the personalization features also tend to be redundant to "Rating" and "Reviews". This is interesting, which may suggest that personal preference tends to have significant overlap with global preference of a business.

Finally, we go in depth to the feature level to analyze what are the relative importance of each feature, as shown in Table 7. Apparently, distance, with the proposed normalization method, appears to be the most important feature. The two popularity measures from the Baseline are the second and the third most important features. These observations are consistent with the findings from previous work (e.g., [26]) that distance and popularity dominate the ranking signals of mobile local search. However, other signals have also contributed many useful features. For example, the top-6 features covers all feature contributors.

Two particularly interesting observations are that (1) three mean values are ranked very high, and (2) 8 out of the top-12 features are directly related to the mean normalization scheme, suggesting that the proposed "mean" normalization scheme indeed helps model signals in mobile local search. Due to the effectiveness of the proposed new features, many features from the baseline have been pushed to the bottom of Table 7.

5. CONCLUSIONS

In this paper, we follow a data-driven methodology to study the ranking heuristics/behaviors of multiple ranking signals, including the customer rating score, the number of reviews, the geographic distance, and the user preference, in mobile local search using a large-scale query log.

Our analysis reveals interesting heuristics that can be used to guide the exploitation of different signals. First, we reveal a common phenomenon for all these four signals: users often take the mean value of a signal from the business result list as a "pivot" score, and tend to demonstrate different click behaviors on businesses with lower and higher signal values than the pivot. Inspired by this understanding, we proposed a "mean" normalization scheme to encode the pivot information into feature normalization or into model training, which has been shown to improve modeling these signals significantly. Second, we find that the clickrate of a business is increasing/decreasing sublinearly with user-preference/distance; as a result, linear scaling in these signals would bias to/against some particular businesses. In order to overcome this problem, we propose sublinear transformation methods for modeling these signals based on power transformation analysis, which work very well. We quantify the improvement of the proposed methods using real mobile local search logs over a period of 14 months and show that the mean average precision can be improved significantly.

6. REFERENCES

[1] A. Amin, S. Townsend, J. Ossenbruggen, and L. Hardman. Fancy a drink in canary wharf?: A user study on location-based mobile search. In *INTERACT '09*, pages 736–749, 2009.

[2] L. Backstrom, J. Kleinberg, R. Kumar, and J. Novak. Spatial variation in search engine queries. In *WWW '08*, pages 357–366, 2008.

[3] K. Berberich, A. C. König, D. Lymberopoulos, and P. Zhao. Improving local search ranking through external logs. In *SIGIR '11*, pages 785–794, 2011.

[4] D. M. Blei, A. Y. Ng, and M. I. Jordan. Latent dirichlet allocation. *J. Mach. Learn. Res.*, 3:993–1022, 2003.

[5] Box, G. E. P. and Cox, D. R. An analysis of transformations. *Journal of the Royal Statistical Society. Series B (Methodological)*, 26(2):211–252, 1964.

[6] O. Chapelle and Y. Chang. Yahoo! learning to rank challenge overview. *Journal of Machine Learning Research - Proceedings Track*, 14:1–24, 2011.

[7] Y.-Y. Chen, T. Suel, and A. Markowetz. Efficient query processing in geographic web search engines. In *SIGMOD '06*, pages 277–288, 2006.

[8] K. Church and N. Oliver. Understanding mobile web and mobile search use in today's dynamic mobile landscape. In *MobileHCI '11*, pages 67–76, 2011.

[9] K. Church, B. Smyth, P. Cotter, and K. Bradley. Mobile information access: A study of emerging search behavior on the mobile internet. *ACM Trans. Web*, 1, May 2007.

[10] G. Cong, C. S. Jensen, and D. Wu. Efficient retrieval of the top-k most relevant spatial web objects. *Proc. VLDB Endow.*, 2:337–348, August 2009.

[11] N. Craswell, S. Robertson, H. Zaragoza, and M. Taylor. Relevance weighting for query independent evidence. In *SIGIR '05*, pages 416–423, 2005.

[12] I. De Felipe, V. Hristidis, and N. Rishe. Keyword search on spatial databases. In *ICDE '08*, pages 656–665, 2008.

[13] Z. Dou, R. Song, and J.-R. Wen. A large-scale evaluation and analysis of personalized search strategies. In *WWW '07*, pages 581–590, 2007.

[14] H. Fang, T. Tao, and C. Zhai. A formal study of information retrieval heuristics. In *SIGIR '04*, pages 49–56, 2004.

[15] J. H. Friedman. Greedy function approximation: A gradient boosting machine. *Annals of Statistics*, 29:1189–1232, 2000.

[16] J. H. Friedman. Stochastic gradient boosting. *Comput. Stat. Data Anal.*, 38:367–378, February 2002.

[17] J. Froehlich, M. Y. Chen, I. E. Smith, and F. Potter. Voting with your feet: An investigative study of the relationship between place visit behavior and preference. In *Ubicomp'06*, pages 333–350, 2006.

[18] K. Ganesan and C. Zhai. Opinion-based entity ranking. *Information Retrieval*, 2011.

[19] M. A. Hearst and J. O. Pedersen. Reexamining the cluster hypothesis: scatter/gather on retrieval results. In *SIGIR '96*, pages 76–84, 1996.

[20] T. Hofmann. Probabilistic latent semantic indexing. In *SIGIR '99*, pages 50–57, 1999.

[21] T. Joachims, L. Granka, B. Pan, H. Hembrooke, F. Radlinski, and G. Gay. Evaluating the accuracy of implicit feedback from clicks and query reformulations in web search. *ACM Trans. Inf. Syst.*, 25, April 2007.

[22] M. Kamvar and S. Baluja. A large scale study of wireless search behavior: Google mobile search. In *CHI '06*, pages 701–709, 2006.

[23] M. Kamvar and S. Baluja. Deciphering trends in mobile search. *Computer*, 40:58–62, August 2007.

[24] N. D. Lane, D. Lymberopoulos, F. Zhao, and A. T. Campbell. Hapori: context-based local search for mobile phones using community behavioral modeling and similarity. In *Ubicomp '10*, pages 109–118, 2010.

[25] Y. Lv and C. Zhai. Lower-bounding term frequency normalization. In *CIKM '11*, pages 7–16, 2011.

[26] D. Lymberopoulos, P. Zhao, A. C. König, K. Berberich, and J. Liu. Location-aware click prediction in mobile local search. In *CIKM '11*, 2011.

[27] B. Marlin. Modeling user rating profiles for collaborative filtering. In S. Thrun, L. Saul, and B. Schölkopf, editors, *Advances in Neural Information Processing Systems 16*, Cambridge, MA, 2004. MIT Press.

[28] N. Matthijs and F. Radlinski. Personalizing web search using long term browsing history. In *WSDM '11*, pages 25–34, 2011.

[29] I. Ounis, C. Macdonald, M. de Rijke, G. Mishne, and I. Soboroff. Overview of the trec 2006 blog track. In *TREC*, 2006.

[30] S. E. Robertson and S. Walker. Some simple effective approximations to the 2-poisson model for probabilistic weighted retrieval. In *SIGIR '94*, pages 232–241, 1994.

[31] M. Sanderson. Test collection based evaluation of information retrieval systems. *Foundations and Trends in Information Retrieval*, 4(4):247–375, 2010.

[32] X. Shen, B. Tan, and C. Zhai. Context-sensitive information retrieval using implicit feedback. In *SIGIR '05*, pages 43–50, 2005.

[33] A. Singhal, C. Buckley, and M. Mitra. Pivoted document length normalization. In *SIGIR '96*, pages 21–29, 1996.

[34] T. Sohn, K. A. Li, W. G. Griswold, and J. D. Hollan. A diary study of mobile information needs. In *CHI '08*, pages 433–442, 2008.

[35] K. Sugiyama, K. Hatano, and M. Yoshikawa. Adaptive web search based on user profile constructed without any effort from users. In *WWW '04*, pages 675–684, 2004.

[36] B. Tan, X. Shen, and C. Zhai. Mining long-term search history to improve search accuracy. In *KDD '06*, pages 718–723, 2006.

[37] J. Teevan, S. T. Dumais, and E. Horvitz. Potential for personalization. *ACM Trans. Comput.-Hum. Interact.*, 17:4:1–4:31, April 2010.

[38] J. Teevan, A. Karlson, S. Amini, A. J. B. Brush, and J. Krumm. Understanding the importance of location, time, and people in mobile local search behavior. In *MobileHCI '11*, pages 77–80, 2011.

[39] L. Wang, C. Wang, X. Xie, J. Forman, Y. Lu, W.-Y. Ma, and Y. Li. Detecting dominant locations from search queries. In *SIGIR '05*, pages 424–431, 2005.

[40] Q. Wu, C. J. Burges, K. Svore, and J. Gao. Ranking, boosting, and model adaptation. Technical Report MSR-TR-2008-109, Microsoft Research, 2008.

[41] J. Yi, F. Maghoul, and J. Pedersen. Deciphering mobile search patterns: a study of yahoo! mobile search queries. In *WWW '08*, pages 257–266, 2008.

[42] X. Yi, H. Raghavan, and C. Leggetter. Discovering users' specific geo intention in web search. In *WWW '09*, pages 481–490, 2009.

[43] D. Zhang, R. Mao, H. Li, and J. Mao. How to count thumb-ups and thumb-downs: user-rating based ranking of items from an axiomatic perspective. In *ICTIR'11*, pages 238–249, 2011.

Mining Query Subtopics from Search Log Data

Yunhua Hu
Microsoft Research Asia
Beijing, China
yuhu@microsoft.com

Yanan Qian
SPKLSTN Lab, Xi'an Jiaotong University, Xi'an, China
yanan.qian@stu.xjtu.edu.cn

Hang Li
Microsoft Research Asia
Beijing, China
hangli@microsoft.com

Daxin Jiang
Microsoft Research Asia
Beijing, China
djiang@microsoft.com

Jian Pei
Simon Fraser University
Burnaby, BC, Canada
jpei@cs.edu.ca

Qinghua Zheng
SPKLSTN Lab, Xi'an Jiaotong University, Xi'an, China
qhzheng@mail.xjtu.edu.cn

ABSTRACT

Most queries in web search are ambiguous and multifaceted. Identifying the major senses and facets of queries from search log data, referred to as query subtopic mining in this paper, is a very important issue in web search. Through search log analysis, we show that there are two interesting phenomena of user behavior that can be leveraged to identify query subtopics, referred to as 'one subtopic per search' and 'subtopic clarification by keyword'. One subtopic per search means that if a user clicks multiple URLs in one query, then the clicked URLs tend to represent the same sense or facet. Subtopic clarification by keyword means that users often add an additional keyword or keywords to expand the query in order to clarify their search intent. Thus, the keywords tend to be indicative of the sense or facet. We propose a clustering algorithm that can effectively leverage the two phenomena to automatically mine the major subtopics of queries, where each subtopic is represented by a cluster containing a number of URLs and keywords. The mined subtopics of queries can be used in multiple tasks in web search and we evaluate them in aspects of the search result presentation such as clustering and re-ranking. We demonstrate that our clustering algorithm can effectively mine query subtopics with an F1 measure in the range of 0.896-0.956. Our experimental results show that the use of the subtopics mined by our approach can significantly improve the state-of-the-art methods used for search result clustering. Experimental results based on click data also show that the re-ranking of search result based on our method can significantly improve the efficiency of users' ability to find information.

Categories and Subject Descriptors

H.3 [**INFORMATION STORAGE AND RETRIEVAL**]: Information Search and Retrieval

Permission to make digital or hard copies of all or part of this work for personal or classroom use is granted without fee provided that copies are not made or distributed for profit or commercial advantage and that copies bear this notice and the full citation on the first page. To copy otherwise, to republish, to post on servers or to redistribute to lists, requires prior specific permission and/or a fee.

SIGIR'12, August 12–16, 2012, Portland, Oregon, USA.

Copyright 2012 ACM 978-1-4503-1472-5/12/08 ...$15.00.

General Terms

Algorithms, Experimentation

Keywords

Search Log Mining, User Behavior, Query Subtopics, Clustering, Search Result Clustering

1. INTRODUCTION

Understanding the search intent of users is essential for satisfying a user's search needs. How to best represent query intent is still an ongoing research problem. One consensus among the researchers is that the intents of queries can be characterized along multiple dimensions. The intents of a query can be represented by its search goals, such as informational, navigational, and transactional [7]. It can also be represented by semantic categories or topics [8, 23, 24]. Furthermore, it can be represented by subtopics (cf., [14]), denoting multiple senses or multiple facets of the query.

Most queries are ambiguous or multifaceted [14]. For example, 'harry shum' is an ambiguous query, which may refer to an American actor, a vice president of Microsoft, or another person named Harry Shum. 'Xbox' is a multifaceted query. When people search for 'xbox', they may be looking for information on different facets of an Xbox, such as 'online game', 'homepage', and 'marketplace'. Note that a query can be both ambiguous and multifaceted. The more frequent a query is, the more likely that it has multiple senses or facets. The major difference between the topics and subtopics of a query is that the former is more coarse-grained and related to other queries, while the latter is fine-grained and is only about the query in question.

Identifying the major subtopics of a query is very important for many search tasks such as personalized search, query suggestion, and search result presentation including clustering, re-ranking, and diversification. In this paper, we aim to automatically mine the major subtopics (senses and facets) of queries from the search log data. Although there is some related work, the subtopic mining problem as defined in this paper does not seem to have been studied previously.

We performed a comprehensive study of the two phenomena, referred to as 'one subtopic per search' (OSS) and 'subtopic clarification by additional keyword' (SCAK) respectively. We show that we can mine the subtopics of queries from search log data by effectively using the phenomena. We then represent the senses or facets of a query by a number of URLs and keywords. We observe that this can be done with high accuracy for head queries. Although the phenomena have been observed or mentioned in previous work (cf., [26]), there has not been a detailed study conducted on them, as far as we know.

If a user clicks multiple URLs after submitting a query (the multiple URLs are also referred to as multi-clicks in this paper), then the clicked URLs tend to represent the same subtopic, which is called one subtopic per search (OSS). Figure 1 shows an example of search results for the query 'harry shum' on a web search engine. The result contains URLs about two Harry Shum's. The search log data indicates that URLs 1, 3, and 5 are usually clicked together in individual searches, and URLs 2 and 4 are clicked together. Each group of URLs actually corresponds to one sense, i.e., one subtopic. Gale and Church discovered a similar phenomenon in natural language texts, called 'one sense per discourse' [19], which means an ambiguous word usually only has one sense in a specific context. Users often add ad-

Figure 1: Search result for query 'Harry Shum'.

ditional keywords (in most cases, one additional keyword) to a query to expand the query in order to clarify its subtopic. This phenomenon is called subtopic clarification by additional keyword (SCAK). As a result, the URLs clicked after searching both with the original and the expanded queries tend to represent the same subtopic and the keyword also tends to be indicative of the subtopic. For example, people may submit 'harry shum microsoft' as an expanded query to specify the subtopic. The URLs clicked in searches for both 'harry shum' and 'harry shum microsoft' usually represent the same subtopic, Harry Shum from Microsoft, and therefore 'microsoft' becomes a keyword of the subtopic.

We employ a clustering algorithm to group URLs as well as keywords into clusters, where each cluster represents one subtopic of a query. For example, one cluster for query 'harry shum' may contain the home page of the Microsoft Harry Shum, his wiki profile, and the keywords 'microsoft' and 'bing'. The clustering is performed based on the two phenomena of user behavior, as described above. Specifically, for each query and its expanded queries (the original query plus keywords), the related click log data is collected. Clustering is then carried out on all the clicked URLs. If two URLs are clicked together many times in the click data, then they are likely to be clustered together. If two URLs are clicked both under the original and expanded queries, then they are likely to be clustered together. We employ a special data structure consisting of a prefix tree and a suffix tree to facilitate recursive execution of the clustering algorithm on the log data. In this way, the mining of subtopics can be conducted very efficiently.

We conducted experiments to measure the accuracy of our clustering method on a TREC data set and a new data set in which the subtopics of both queries are labeled. For ambiguous subtopics, our method can achieve a B-cubed F1 from 0.925 to 0.956. For multifaceted subtopics, our method can achieve a B-cubed F1 from 0.896 to 0.930 in terms of B-cubed F1. The results indicate that our method can effectively perform query subtopic mining.

We also evaluated our method in search result clustering. We compared our method with a state-of-the-art method of search result clustering. Experimental results show that our method can significantly improve accuracy. The improvements are 5.4% in terms of B-cubed precision and 6.1% in terms of B-cubed recall. When compared side-by-side with human generated results, we also find that our method is significantly better than the baseline.

We further evaluated our method on search result re-ranking, in which the user is confirmed with the subtopic she has in mind and re-ranking of search results based on user feedback is performed. We used the average click position in the log data as the evaluation measure. The results show that our method can boost the average click position 0.61 points higher, which implies a promising improvement in the user experience.

There are three major contributions in our work:

1. We have analyzed two phenomena in user search behavior that can be utilized to identify query subtopics.
2. We have developed a clustering method that can effectively and efficiently mine the subtopics on the basis of the phenomena and use them to represent query subtopics.
3. We have successfully applied the mined results to two tasks: search result clustering and re-ranking.

The rest of the paper is organized as follows. Section 2 introduces related work. Section 3 describes the detailed analysis of user behavior in the log data for subtopic mining. Section 4 explains our approach to subtopic mining and Section 5 presents the experimental results. Section 6 presents two applications of our subtopic mining algorithm. Section 7 concludes the paper.

2. RELATED WORK

2.1 Search Log Mining

The intent of a query can be characterized along several dimensions, including search goals [7], semantic classes [5], topics [4], and subtopics [14]. The search goals can be informational, navigational, or transactional. The semantic classes of a query can be represented by ODP categories[1]. The topics or subtopics of a query can be represented by a number of queries or URLs. Topics are usually more coarse-grained and can cover multiple queries, while subtopics are more fine-grained and associated with a specific query [14]. For example, for the query 'xbox', all aspects related to Xbox including online game, market place, and even other game consoles are usually included in the topic of the query. In contrast, each aspect of Xbox is represented by one subtopic of the query.

Mining topics from search log data has been intensively

[1]Open Directory Project: http://www.dmoz.org/.

studied[2]. Click-through bipartite graph data can be used for clustering queries and URLs. Specifically queries which share the same clicked URLs are considered similar. Methods for performing the task have been proposed (e.g., [4, 10, 15, 18, 21, 25, 27]). Beeferman et al. [4], for example, proposed conducting clustering on a click-through bipartite graph and viewing the obtained clusters as topics covering multiple queries. Radlinski et al. [25] proposed first using search session data to find similar queries, and then using a click-through bipartite graph to refine the discovered queries that are similar, and finally grouping the similar queries into the same clusters. The clusters containing the same query are then regarded as topics of the query.

There are some similarities but also significant differences between our work and Radlinski et al.'s work. 1) The problem settings are different. In their work, a subtopic is represented by multiple queries, while in our work a subtopic is represented by keywords and URLs. 2) The information used for subtopic mining is different. They used search sessions to find frequently co-occurring query pairs, considered them candidates of similar query pairs, and finally used a click-through bipartite graph to filter unlikely queries. 3) The goals are also different. The mined results in their work were utilized for manual creation of TREC data. In this paper, we quantitatively evaluated our method on two search tasks, namely search result clustering and re-ranking.

Methods for utilizing a user's click behavior in individual searches have been developed, e.g., [12, 15]. Existing work aimed at modeling and predicting a user's click behavior while our work attempts to find the subtopics of queries. The exploitation of the prefix and suffix relationship between queries was also considered in the previous work, e.g., [26]. In our work, we not only use the prefix and suffix relationship between queries, but also the clicked URLs of the queries and our goal is to conduct query subtopic mining.

2.2 Search Result Presentation

When a query is ambiguous or multifaceted, presenting its search result by sense or facet to users would improve the search experience [9]. Many methods have been proposed, including search result clustering and dynamic ranking.

Search result clustering attempts to cluster the search results according to semantic classes, topics, or subtopics [11]. For example, Chen and Dumais [13] proposed using text classification technologies to classify search results into predefined categories. Zeng proposed using text clustering techniques to cluster a research result based on the titles and snippets of web pages [29]. See also [2, 16, 17]. The major characteristic of these methods is that they use the content of documents in search result clustering.

Wang and Zhai further extended the idea and proposed exploiting the search results of the current query as well as the search results of similar queries [26]. They first build query relationships. For each query, similar queries are found from previous search sessions. They then perform clustering on the clicked URLs of the query and its similar queries. They use the titles and snippets of web pages for similarity calculation. The major difference between their work and our work is that they did not consider mining and utilization of query subtopics. In this paper, we use Wang and Zhai's method as the baseline for search result clustering.

Recently, Brandt et al. proposed a new search UI called dynamic ranking model [6]. The mined subtopics by our method can also be used in the dynamic ranking model. Specifically, when the user hovers the mouse on an URL in the UI, we can dynamically show the other URLs in the same subtopic under the mouse-hovered URL.

[2]The topics or subtopics of queries cannot be obtained by simply clustering the search results (documents) of queries [25].

Table 1: Multi-clicks in search logs of 'harry shum'

Multi-clicks	Frequency
"http://research.microsoft.com/en-us/people/hshum", "http://en.wikipedia.org/wiki/Harry_Shum", "http://www.microsoft.com/presspass/exec/Shum/"	50
"http://en.wikipedia.org/wiki/Harry_Shum,_Jr", "http://www.imdb.com/name/nm1484270/"	95

3. TWO PHENOMENA

3.1 One Subtopic per Search

One subtopic per search (OSS) means that the jointly clicked URLs in a specific search are likely to represent the same subtopic. We conducted analysis on the phenomenon with a search log data set from a commercial web search engine (DataSetA as described in Table 8) and validated the correctness of this hypothesis. Our explanation of the phenomenon is: 1) Search users are rational and they do not randomly click on search results (cf., [1, 20]). 2) Users *usually* have one single subtopic in mind for a particular search.

Table 1 shows two groups of multi-clicked URLs (i.e., the multiple URLs clicked by a user in a query) from search logs for the query 'harry shum'. The three URLs in the first group are about one sense and the two URLs in the second group are about another sense. Users may accidently click URLs belonging to two different groups, but such cases are rare. This is reasonable, because if a user searches for a specific person then she usually would only click the URLs about the person and skip the URLs about other people. We call such user behavior 'one subtopic per search'. We examined the accuracy of using one subtopic per search as a rule for subtopic identification. By accuracy we mean the percentage of the multi-clicks that share the same subtopics among all multi-clicks. We sampled 10,000 groups of multi-clicks of individual queries in DataSetA, which are labeled based on the sense or facet. When all the URLs within the multi-clicks are about the same sense or facet, we consider that the rule has correctly identified a subtopic. Table 2 shows the accuracy versus the number of multi-clicks. We can see that the average accuracy of one subtopic per search is about 84%, suggesting that it is very helpful for identifying the subtopics of queries. Table 2 also shows that the accuracy will decrease when the number of URLs in a group of multi-clicks increases. That is to say, the more URLs there are clicked in a search, the less likely that the URLs share the same subtopic. Clicking many URLs in one query may indicate that the user is uncertain about what she is looking

Table 2: Accuracy of rule v.s. number of clicks

# of Clicks	2	3	4	≥ 5	Avg.
Accuracy	0.902	0.824	0.741	0.683	0.842

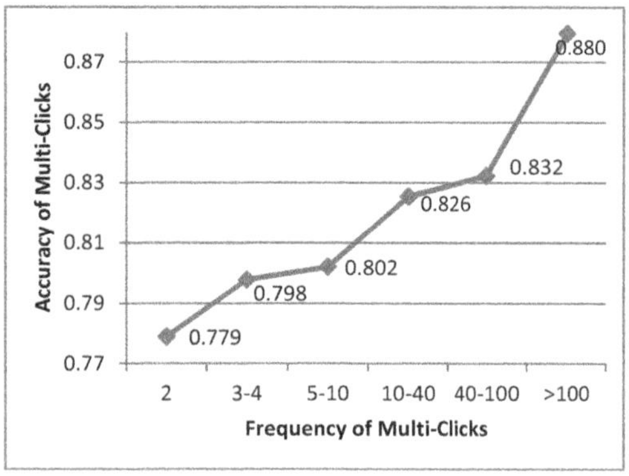

Figure 2: Accuracy of rule vesus frequency.

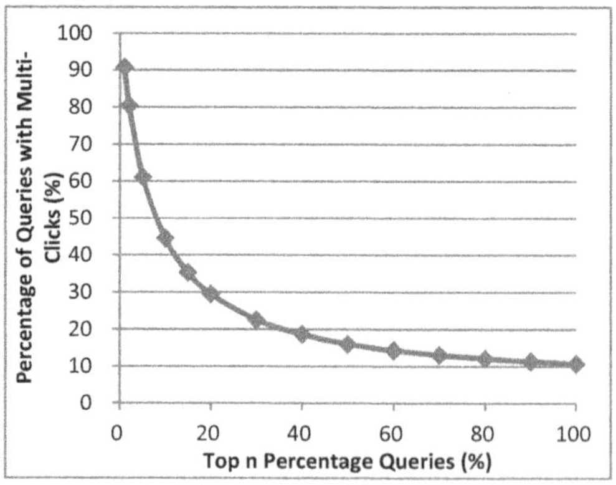

Figure 3: Distribution of top n% queries having multi-clicks.

for or wants to learn about all aspects of the query. We also observe that the higher the frequency a group of multi-clicks has, the more likely they share the same subtopic. Figure 2 shows the relation between accuracy and frequency. When a multi-click is only observed twice in the log data, the average accuracy is 0.779. In contrast, when it happens more than 100 times, the accuracy can be as high as 0.880. We

Table 3: Accuracy of rule v.s. click position

	Same subtopic	Different subtopic	All
# of Multi-clicks	8,421	1,579	10,000
Ave. Position	3.57	3.63	3.50
Ave. Click Intervals	3.23	3.27	3.20

investigated the relationship between the click positions and the accuracy of the rule. Table 3 shows the results. 'Same subtopic' means that the rule is correct and the results represent the same subtopic. 'Different subtopic' means that the rule is incorrect and the results represent different topics. We can see that click positions do not affect the one subtopic per search phenomenon.

Figure 3 shows the percentages of queries with multi-clicks. The queries with higher frequencies in search log data are more likely to have multi-clicks. For example, for the top 1% frequent queries in the search logs (corresponding to about 50% of search traffic), more than 90% of them have multi-clicks. Therefore, the phenomenon of one subtopic per search can help query subtopic mining for head queries.

3.2 Subtopic clarification by Additional Keyword

Many short queries are simply noun phrases, and long queries often contain short queries plus additional keywords, in which the keywords clarify the subtopics of the short queries. We refer to a short query as the original query, and longer queries containing the short query as expanded queries. The clicked URLs after searching with the original query and the expanded queries tend to represent the same subtopic. The keywords can also become labels of the subtopic. This is the phenomenon of subtopic clarification by additional keyword. The phenomenon can be explained in the following ways: 1) Search users are rational users. 2) Sometimes users tend to add additional keywords to specify the subtopics in their minds. We have also empirically validated the correctness of this hypothesis.

Table 4 shows the expanded queries and their clicks with respect to the query 'harry shum' in the search log data. From the table, we can see that the clicked URLs of query 'microsoft harry shum' also appear in the former group of URLs corresponding to Harry Shum of Microsoft. The clicked URLs of 'harry shum jr' can be found in the latter group of URLs corresponding to the actor Harry Shum. The keywords 'microsoft' and 'jr' can be used to represent the two groups (subtopics) respectively. Therefore, each expanded query covers one subtopic of the original query with the keyword as the label of the subtopics.

We conducted analysis on the patterns of queries. We classified queries into four types. If the query is a single phrase, usually a noun phrase, then the type is 'Q'. The other three types are '$Q + W$', '$W + Q$', and 'Others', where 'W' denotes a keyword and 'Q' denotes a phrase. We estimated the distribution of the four types. We randomly selected 1,000 queries from the search log data. For each query, we checked whether it might be an expansion of another query. More specifically, we enumerated all queries that could be expanded from the considered query. The most reasonable query-expanded query pair is selected and then the query type is labeled. The clicked URLs were also used to help make the judgments. The distribution of query types is presented in Table 5. From the table, we can see that the types '$Q + W$' and '$W + Q$' consist of about 42% of the queries. '$Q+W$' is more popular than '$W+Q$'. We further examined

Table 5: Distribution of Query Types

Query Type	'Q'	'$Q + W$'	'$W + Q$'	'Others'
Percentage	0.455	0.255	0.165	0.125

whether the subtopics of the expanded queries are covered by those of the original queries. In other words, given two queries with the types 'Q' and '$Q + W$', we judged whether the subtopics of the latter are contained in the subtopics of the former. We randomly selected 500 pairs of queries with the forms 'Q' and '$Q + W$', where the queries in Q form are from DataSetA, and studied the relationship between the subtopics of the original query and expanded query. If subtopics of an expanded query are contained in subtopics of the original query, then we say there is 'subtopic overlap'

Table 4: Search logs of 'harry shum' ignoring click frequency

Query	Clicked URLs
harry shum	"http://research.microsoft.com/en-us/people/hshum", "http://en.wikipedia.org/wiki/Harry_Shum", "http://www.microsoft.com/presspass/exec/Shum/"
harry shum	"http://en.wikipedia.org/wiki/Harry_Shum,_Jr", "http://www.imdb.com/name/nm1484270/"
microsoft harry shum	"http://research.microsoft.com/en-us/people/hshum", "http://www.microsoft.com/presspass/exec/Shum/"
harry shum jr	"http://en.wikipedia.org/wiki/Harry_Shum,_Jr"
harry shum glee	"http://en.wikipedia.org/wiki/Harry_Shum,_Jr", "http://www.imdb.com/name/nm1484270/"

between the two. We also checked whether two queries share identical clicked URLs, and if so we call it 'URL overlap'. In the investigation we found there is no significant difference between the results of queries in the forms '$Q+W$' and '$W+Q$'. Thus, we merged the two types. Table 6 shows

Table 6: Relation of subtopic overlap and URL overlap between query and expanded query pair

	URL overlap	None URL overlap
All query pairs	0.814	0.186
Subtopic overlap	0.801	0.199
None subtopic overlap	0.183	0.817

the results. From the results, we can see that 81.4% of expanded queries have URL overlap with the original queries, and 18.6% of expanded queries do not. For the expanded queries with URL overlap, 80.1% of them have subtopic overlaps with the original queries. For the expanded queries without URL overlap, 81.7% of them do not have subtopic overlap with the original queries. For example, 'beijing' and 'beijing duck', 'fast' and 'fast food', and 'computer science' and 'computer science department' do not have URL overlap, and they do not have subtopic overlap either. Hence we can exploit URL overlap to filter out unrelated 'expanded queries' (they are not 'true' expanded queries), and use the subtopics of the remaining expanded queries to help identify the subtopics of the original queries. This becomes another rule for subtopic mining.

We also investigated the percentage of queries the rule can be applied. Figure 4 shows the more popular (frequent) a query is, the more likely the rule is applicable. For the top 1% frequent queries (about 50% of search traffic), about 88% have expansions, and on average there are 89 expanded queries for each query. The results indicate the identification by keyword rule can be used for subtopic mining.

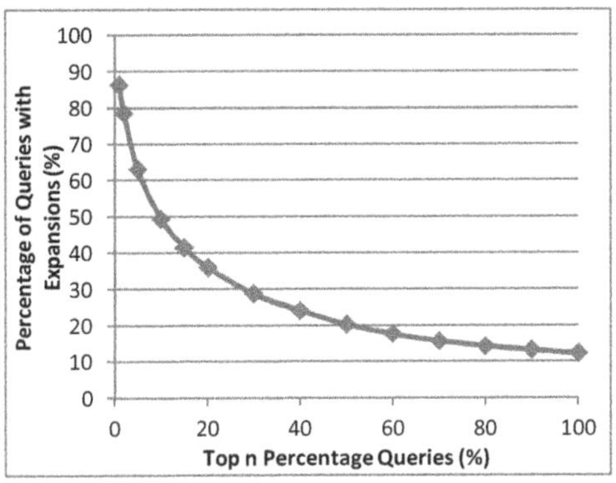

Figure 4: Distribution of top n% queries having expanded queries.

4. CLUSTERING METHOD

We employ a clustering method to mine subtopics of queries leveraging the two phenomena and search log data. The flow of the method is shown in Figure 5. In the preprocessing stage, we build an index to store all the queries and their clicked URLs. False expanded queries are then pruned from the index. In the clustering stage, the URLs associated with a query and its expanded queries are grouped into clusters, each representing one subtopic. In the post-processing stage, keywords are assigned to the clusters (subtopics) to enrich the representations of subtopics.

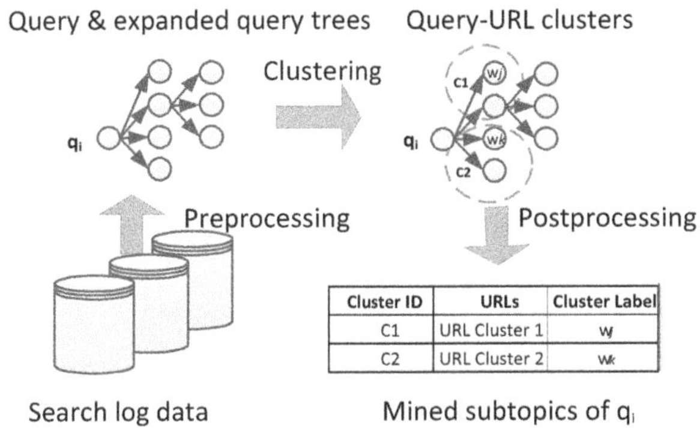

Figure 5: The flow of clustering method.

4.1 Preprocessing

4.1.1 Indexing

We first index all the queries in an index consisting of a prefix tree and a suffix tree to facilitate efficient clustering. We only consider queries in three forms ('Q', '$Q+W$' and '$W+Q$'), as discussed in Section 3.2.

We then segment queries and index them. In the prefix tree, query 'Q' and its expanded queries 'Q+W' are indexed in a father node and child nodes respectively. Search log data of each query is also stored in its node. With the prefix tree, we can easily find the expanded queries of any query. In the suffix tree query 'Q' and its expanded queries 'W+Q' are indexed as a father node and child nodes respectively. Figure 6 illustrates the data structure. For query 'harry shum', we can easily find its expanded queries 'Q+W' from the prefix tree, such as 'harry shum jr', 'harry shum glee', and 'harry shum bing'. We can also easily find its expanded queries 'W+Q' from the suffix tree, such as 'microsoft harry shum' and 'actor harry shum'.

4.1.2 Pruning

We then remove the false expanded queries from the prefix and suffix trees by using a heuristic rule: If a query 'Q' does not have URL overlap with its expanded queries 'Q+W'

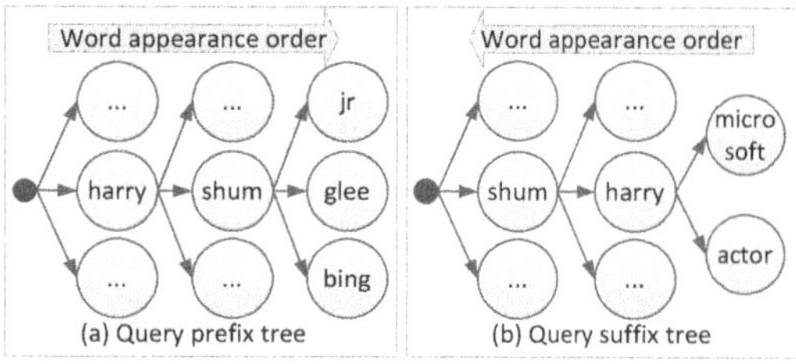

Figure 6: The data structures to index search logs.

and 'W+Q' (i.e., there is no clicked URL shared by the queries), then those expanded queries will be viewed as false expanded queries and pruned from the trees. For example, 'fast food' and 'fast' do not have URL overlap, and thus 'fast food' will be pruned as a child node of 'fast'. Similarly, 'hot dog' and 'dog' do not have URL overlap so 'hot dog' will be pruned as child node of 'dog'. This heuristics is based on the discussions in Section 3.2. After pruning, only the 'true' expanded queries are stored in the prefix and suffix trees.

4.2 Clustering

We conduct clustering on the clicked URLs of each query and its expanded queries. Since all the queries are indexed in the trees, the clustering can be performed locally and recursively on the trees. The clustering of clicked URLs is guided by the two phenomena described in Section 3. After clustering, each group of clustered URLs is taken as one subtopic of the query in the father node.

4.2.1 *Similarity Function*

The clustering is repeatedly conducted on the clicked URLs of a query and its expanded queries on the trees. The similarity function between two clicked URLs is defined as a linear combination of three similarity sub-functions.

Specifically, the similarity function between URLs u_i and u_j is defined as

$$S(u_i, u_j) = \alpha S_1(u_i, u_j) + \beta S_2(u_i, u_j) + \gamma S_3(u_i, u_j) \quad (1)$$

Here S_1 is a similarity function based on the OSS phenomenon, S_2 is based on the SCAK phenomenon, S_3 is based on string similarities, with α, β, and γ as weights.

S_1 is defined as

$$S_1(u_i, u_j) = \frac{\vec{m}_{u_i} \cdot \vec{m}_{u_j}}{||\vec{m}_{u_i}||_2 ||\vec{m}_{u_j}||_2} \quad (2)$$

where $\vec{m}_{u_i}$ and $\vec{m}_{u_j}$ denote the vectors of multi-clicks of u_i and u_j respectively, '$\cdot$ ' denotes the dot product, and $|| \cdot ||_2$ denotes the L_2 norm. Each element of the vector corresponds to one multi-click pattern, and its value represents the frequency of the multi-clicks. Intuitively, URLs u_i and u_j will become similar if they frequently co-occur.

S_2 is defined as

$$S_2(u_i, u_j) = \frac{\vec{w}_{u_i} \cdot \vec{w}_{u_j}}{||\vec{w}_{u_i}||_2 ||\vec{w}_{u_j}||_2} \quad (3)$$

where $\vec{w}_{u_i}$ and $\vec{w}_{u_j}$ denote the vectors of keywords associated with u_i and u_j respectively, $\cdot$ denotes the dot product, and $|| \cdot ||_2$ denotes the L_2 norm. Note that there is a null keyword, which is associated with the original query (father node). Intuitively, URLs u_i and u_j will become similar if they are clicked in searches of expanded queries containing the same keywords. Figure 7 shows the clustering of URLs u_1, u_2, u_3, etc on query q and its expanded queries $q + w1$, $q + w2$, and $q + w3$. The URLs are represented by vectors with each element corresponding to one keyword. S_3 simply represents the similarity between u_i and u_j as strings.

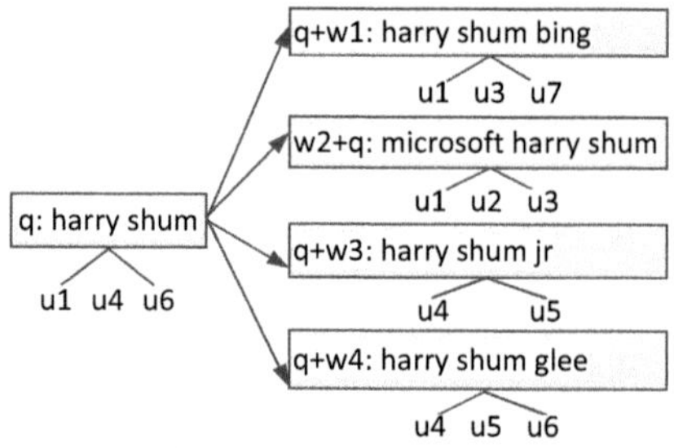

(a) Query and expanded queries

	q	q+w1	w2+q	q+w3	q+w4
u1	1	1	1		
u2			1		
u3		1	1		
u4	1			1	1
u5				1	1
u6	1				1
u7		1			

(b) Vectors of keywords associated with URLs

Figure 7: Example of clustering using subtopic clarification by keyword.

Intuitively, two URLs will be viewed as similar if there are many words shared by the two URLs [22]. To conduct a similarity calculation, we segment a URL into tokens based on the slash symbols, and calculate the cosine similarity of the tokens as S_3.

4.2.2 *Algorithm*

We employ an agglomerative clustering algorithm to perform clustering. The algorithm has the advantage of ease of implementation. One can also consider employing other clustering algorithms. The specific algorithm is as follows:

Step 1: Select one URL and create a new cluster containing the URL.

Step 2: Select the next URL u_i, and make a similarity comparison between the URL and all the URLs in the existing clusters. If the similarity between URL u_i and URL u_j in one of the clusters is larger than threshold θ, then move u_i into the cluster. If u_i cannot be joined to any existing clusters, create a new cluster for it.

Step 3: Finish when all the URLs are processed.

4.3 Postprocessing

The output of the clustering process is clusters of URLs for each query and its expanded queries. The clusters which consist of only one URL are excluded. Each cluster represents one subtopic of the query. We further extract keywords from the expanded queries and assign them to the corresponding cluster as subtopic labels. As a result, each cluster not only consists of URLs but also retains keywords as cluster labels. The subtopic popularity can be further estimated from the frequency of clicked URLs in each cluster.

Table 7 shows the mined search subtopics of query 'harry shum'. The first subtopic has three keywords and two URLs and the second subtopic has three keywords and three URLs.

Table 7: Examples about mined subtopics of 'harry shum'

Subtopic ID	Keywords with frequency	URLs with frequency
1	'harry shum microsoft' : 201	"http://en.wikipedia.org/wiki/Harry_Shum": 961
	'harry shum bing' : 80	"http://research.microsoft.com/en-us/people/hshum/": 317
	'microsoft harry shum' : 22	"http://www.microsoft.com/presspass/exec/Shum/" : 98
2	'harry shum jr' : 2746	"http://en.wikipedia.org/wiki/Harry_Shum,_Jr." : 2999
	'harry shum glee' : 371	"http://harryshumjr.com/" : 845
	'harry shum junior' : 43	"http://www.imdb.com/name/nm1484270/" : 327

5. EXPERIMENTS ON ACCURACY

5.1 Data Sets

We carried out experiments on the accuracy of our method with three data sets. The first dataset (TREC Data) is from the TREC search result diversification track[3] in 2009. About 7% of URLs in the data set are not accessible on the web now, so we removed them and added new URLs in the search results of the queries at a commercial search engine. The remaining two datasets consist of queries and URLs randomly sampled from the logs of the commercial search engine in the EN-US market from June 1st, 2010 to March 31st 2011. To reduce the data size, we selected queries which occurred at least two times in one week during a year.

Human assessors labeled the subtopics by grouping the URLs associated with the queries. The guideline for the labeling is exactly the same as that in TREC. For ambiguous queries, it is usually easy to make distinctions between the subtopics of the queries. For multifaceted queries, it is sometimes difficult to make distinctions between the subtopics. We asked the assessors to refer to the examples in the TREC data as a spec in their data labeling. Table 8 gives the statistics of the datasets. 'Mixed queries' means that the queries are both ambiguous and multi-faceted.

Table 8: Statistics of three data sets

# of items	TREC	DataSetA	DataSetB
Queries	50	100	50
URLs	6,498	9,657	4,899
Subtopics	243	1,415	/
Ambiguous queries	11	57	20
Multifaceted queries	39	19	24
Mixed queries	0	24	6

5.2 Setting

The quality of a clustering algorithm is usually measured in terms of purity and inverse purity. Recently, Amigo et al. [3] showed that B-cubed precision, recall and F1 are more suitable for the evaluation of clustering results, thus we adopted those measures for evaluation.

We split DataSetA into three parts and used 1/3 of them for parameter tuning and 2/3 of them for evaluation. The entire TREC dataset was used for evaluation. There are four parameters in our algorithm: α, β, and γ in the similarity function, and θ in the clustering algorithm. We tune the parameters heuristically. First, we set all parameters at the value 0.3. Then we increase or decrease the parameter value in increments of 0.05. After several rounds of tuning, we found the final α, β, γ, and θ were 0.35, 0.4, 0.25, and 0.3, respectively.

[3]http://trec.nist.gov/data/webmain.html

5.3 Results

Table 9 shows the accuracy of our methods on the two data sets for ambiguous queries, multifaceted queries, and mixed queries. The experimental results indicate that our approach performs quite well in the subtopic mining task. To understand the effect of each similarity sub-function, we conducted another experiment with the two datasets combined together and Table 10 reports the results. We can see that all three similarity sub-functions can achieve high precision, which indicates that the two phenomena described in Section 3 really exist. The recalls of the three functions are not so high, however, mainly due to the sparseness of the available data. By combining the uses of all the similarity sub-functions, we can significantly improve the recalls while maintaining high precision.

Table 9: Accuracy of subtopic mining for different types of queries

Data Set	Query Type	B-cubed Precision	B-cubed Recall	B-cubed F1
TREC	Ambiguous	0.918	0.932	0.925
	Multifaceted	0.893	0.899	0.896
DataSetA	Ambiguous	0.961	0.951	0.956
	Multifaceted	0.937	0.924	0.930
	Mixed	0.952	0.941	0.946

Table 10: Accuracy of subtopic mining with different similarity functions on the 'Combined' data set

Similarity Function	B-cubed Precision	B-cubed Recall	B-cubed F1
OSS phenomenon	0.945	0.681	0.791
SCAK phenomenon	0.915	0.778	0.841
URL string	0.976	0.517	0.676
All	0.928	0.922	0.925

The clustering accuracy in Table 10 differs from the accuracy in finding subtopics using the two rules in Section 3. There are two main reasons for this. First, different evaluations are made. Table 10 shows the accuracy of subtopic mining using clustering. Section 3 shows the accuracy of individual rules without using clustering. Second, different evaluation measures are utilized.

6. APPLICATIONS OF SUBTOPIC MINING

We consider two applications, search result clustering and re-ranking, and evaluate our method within the applications.

6.1 Search Result Clustering

Search result clustering is about grouping the URLs in the search result of a query by subtopics. Many methods have

Table 11: Accuracy comparison between our method and baseline

Data set	Query Type	B-cubed Precision		B-cubed Recall		B-cubed F1	
		Our Method	Baseline	Our Method	Baseline	Our Method	Baseline
TREC Data	Ambiguous	0.926	**0.944**	**0.924**	0.792	**0.925**	0.861
	Multifaceted	0.864	**0.872**	**0.905**	0.808	**0.884**	0.839
DataSetA	Ambiguous	**0.963**	0.874	**0.935**	0.878	**0.949**	0.876
	Multifaceted	**0.936**	0.840	**0.913**	0.906	**0.927**	0.877
	Mixed	**0.952**	0.839	**0.933**	0.920	**0.942**	0.878
Improvement		+5.4%		+6.1%		+5.9% ($p \leq$ 4.58E-06 in the sign test)	

Table 12: Accuracy comparison from various perspectives

		Purity	Diversity	Coverage	Granularity	Average
Assessor 1	Baseline	2.88	2.35	2.52	2.73	2.62
	Our method	3.41	3.27	3.60	3.25	3.39
Assessor 2	Baseline	3.15	2.46	2.75	3.08	2.86
	Our method	3.60	3.29	4.27	3.44	3.65
Average	Baseline	3.02	2.41	2.64	2.91	**2.74**
	Our method	3.51	3.28	3.94	3.35	**3.52**

been proposed for search result clustering. Wang and Zhai's method [26] can be viewed as state-of-the-art and we take it as a baseline. We conduct comparisons in two settings: accuracy comparison and side by side comparison.

6.1.1 Our Method

Our method conducts query subtopic mining offline and stores the mined results in a database. Once the search results for a query are given by the search system, our method performs search result clustering online. Specifically, our method first refers to the database and finds the subtopics of the query, each of which may contain several URLs. For each search result, our method then takes the subtopics of the query as seed clusters. There might be some URLs which do not belong to any of the mined subtopics. We calculate cosine similarity between them and the URLs in the existing clusters by using the TFIDF of terms in titles and snippets. We then assign those URLs to the existing clusters or create new clusters on the basis of the calculated similarities and regard them as the final search result clusters.

6.1.2 Accuracy Comparison

We compared our method with the baseline method on ambiguous queries, multifaceted queries, and mixed queries, respectively. Table 11 shows the detailed comparison between our method and the baseline.

From the results, we can see that our method outperforms the baseline method. When combining the two datasets, the improvement of our method over the baseline is 5.4% in terms of B-cubed precision, 6.1% in terms of B-cubed recall, and 5.9% in terms of B-cubed F1 respectively.

6.1.3 Side-by-Side Comparison

We also compared our method with the baseline side-by-side. We created a new dataset referred to as DataSetB. DataSetB contains 50 queries and includes all three types of queries. First we applied both our method and the baseline to each query to obtain two sets of clustering results. Then, we showed the two results to two assessors to perform side by side evaluations. To avoid bias, we randomly swapped the sides of the two results. The assessors could not figure out which result was from which approach.

Several measures were used for evaluation of the results by each method: purity, diversity, coverage, and granularity. Purity is similar to precision and coverage is similar to recall. Diversity shows the difference between clusters. Granularity means how specific the cluster is. An ideal clustering should have high purity, high diversity, high coverage and fine granularity. We asked the assessors to give a score (1 to 5) for each measure.

Table 12 shows the average scores of the methods in terms of the measures for all 50 queries. The results show that our approach is much better than the baseline. The overall improvement is about 28%.

Table 13 shows the side-by-side evaluation results averaged over the 50 queries. When conducting an evaluation, the assessors made judgments on which result was better using three labels: 'better than,' 'equally good,' and 'worse than.' The results show that for about 60% of the queries, our method is better than the baseline; for about 21% of the queries, our method is equal to the baseline. We found that the clusters generated by our method are easier for humans to understand than the baseline.

Table 13: Side-by-Side Comparison

	Better than	Equal to	Worse than
Assessor 1	32	10	8
Assessor 2	30	11	9
Average	31	10.5	8.5

6.1.4 Discussion

When analyzing the results, we found the clusters generated by our approach are more accurate and natural (easy to understand) than the clusters generated by the baseline. This indicates that the clustering of URLs from a user's perspective (log mining based) can achieve better results than from a content creator's perspective (content based).

Our approach outperforms the baseline approach in terms of F1 measure for ambiguous, multifaceted, and mixed queries. The improvements of our approach on recall are larger than the improvements on precision. This is because our approach starts from the mined subtopics that cover the main subtopics of queries. On the contrary, the baseline has no such information, and it tends to generate larger clusters.

The improvement of our method over the baseline on the TREC data is not as high as those on DataSetA. Because in the TREC data, each subtopic consists of about 26.7 URLs while in DataSetA each subtopic only consists of about 6.8 URLs. In other words, DataSetA has finer grained subtopics than the TREC data. When the granularity of subtopics is coarser, our method can benefit less from log mining.

Here we show three examples of results given by the two methods. For simplicity, we only show the labels (subtopics) of URLs in each cluster. The first example is an ambiguous query, the second is a multifaceted query, and the third is a mixed query. We can see that our method often gives more specific clusters (subtopics) while the baseline tends to produce more general clusters (subtoipcs).

Table 14: Examples of comparison between our approach and baseline

Query	Our method	Baseline
Black swam (Ambiguous)	C1: black swan movie	C1: black swan movie
	C2: black swan diet	black swan reviews
	C3: black swan inn	C2: black swan yoga
	C4: black swan yoga	black swan theory
	C5: black swan wine	C3: black swan reviews
Video game (Multifaceted)	C1: video game reviews	C1: video game reviews
	C2: video game cheats	video game cheats
	C3: video game stores	video game stores
	C4: video game addiction	C2: video game wiki
	C5: video game trailers	video game history
Manchester (Mixed)	C1: Manchester united	C1: Manchester England
	C2: Manchester college	Manchester tourism
	C3: Manchester history	Manchester news
	C4: Manchester news	C2: Manchester united
	C5: Manchester tourism	Manchester soccer

6.2 Search Result Re-Ranking

We consider another search task for the evaluation of our subtopic mining method, namely, search result re-ranking. We chose to do so because we can easily use click-through data to conduct quantitative evaluation.

6.2.1 *Our Method*

When the search system provides the results to the user, there might be multiple ways to present it if the query contains multiple subtopics, i.e., it is ambiguous or multifaceted. These include simple ranking, clustering of URLs by subtopics, dynamic ranking of URLs belonging to the same topic, as well as re-ranking of URLs by subtopics.

Re-ranking is conducted in the following way. The user is first asked which subtopic she is interested in, with the subtopics shown at the top of the results page. When the user selects a subtopic, the URLs belonging to the subtopic will be moved to the top (re-ranked). The relative order between URLs inside and outside of the subtopic will be kept. The subtopics are assumed to be represented by keywords of subtopics mined with our method.

Figure 8 shows an example UI in which re-ranking is performed for the query 'harry shum.' The second subtopic of the query is selected and all the URLs belonging to it are re-ranked at the top. This will significantly improve a user's experience compared with the conventional approach (Figure 1). Although re-ranking is a simple, interactive approach to search results presentation (cf., [28]), there seems to be no study before on the approach to the best of our knowledge. Note that re-ranking can only be done for head queries, because it is based on log data mining, which is a shortcoming that any data mining method may suffer from.

6.2.2 *Evaluation*

We collected search log data of 20,000 randomly selected searches at the commercial search engine, for which the query has at least two subtopics mined by our method. The search log data contains the ranking results of URLs as well as the clicks on URLs in the searches. We used the data to estimate how much the cost of users' searches can be saved by re-ranking based on our subtopic mining method.

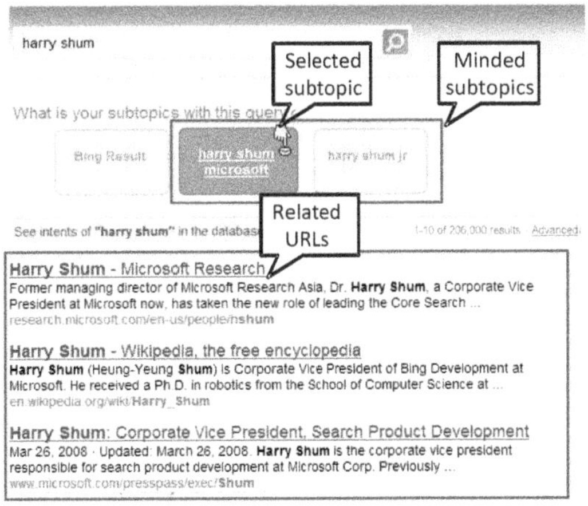

Figure 8: Example of search result re-ranking.

We first calculated the average position of last clicked URLs in the 20,000 searches. The result is 3.41. The number indicates the average cost of finding information in the conventional search UI based on ranking.

Next, we used the same log data to estimate the cost for users based on re-ranking. We assumed that the cost for the user to check the subtopics and click one of them is 1.0, because the subtopics are shown in one line at the top, and examining them is almost equivalent to examining the title and snippet of a URL. The cost of finding the last click within each selected subtopic can be calculated by using the search log data, because within the subtopic the ranking order is preserved. Note that because of the one subtopic per search phenomenon, the clicked URLs in a search usually belong to the same subtopic. We calculated the average position of last clicked URLs belonging to the same subtopics in the 20,000 searches and found that it is 1.80.

The cost saved in the re-ranking may be calculated as

$$\Delta = 3.41 - 1.80 - 1 = 0.61$$

This is the result for the saved cost per search. Similarly, we can estimate the saved cost per query, which is 0.7. We can conclude, therefore, that the re-ranking method can reduce a user's effort in finding information, and thus our method of subtopic mining is effective.

7. CONCLUSIONS AND FUTURE WORK

In this paper, we have studied the problem of query subtopic mining. Specifically, we have discovered two phenomena of user search behavior that can be used as signals to mine major senses and facets of ambiguous and multifaceted queries. One is called one subtopic per search and the other subtopic clarification by additional keyword. We have developed a clustering algorithm that can effectively and efficiently mine query subtopics on the basis of the two phenomena. We have evaluated the effectiveness of the proposed approach. On the TREC dataset, the F1-measure is 0.925 for finding ambiguous subtopics and 0.896 for finding multifaceted subtopics. When applied to search result clustering, our method can improve precision by 5.4% and recall by 6.1%. The effectiveness of our method has also been verified in search result re-ranking, using click data.

There are several issues we want to further explore to enhance our current work. First, only three types of features were used in the current clustering algorithm. We plan to investigate the use of other features to further improve the accuracy. Second, we only tried one clustering algorithm as an example. Other existing algorithms can be applied as well. Third, the mined subtopics by our method were only applied to two applications, and they can be useful in other applications as well. We also plan to try some other applications such as personalized search and search result diversification. Finally, our method can only be employed when there is enough search log data, which is also a drawback for most log mining algorithms. How to apply the approach in tail queries is also an issue we need to consider.

8. ACKNOWLEDGEMENTS

This research was done when the second author was visiting MSRA, her research was supported by the SPKLSTN Lab (National Science Foundation of China under Grant No. 60825202, 61173112, and Cheung Kong Scholar's Program).

Jian Pei's research is supported in part by an NSERC Discovery Grant, a BCFRST NRAS Endowment Research Team Program project, and a GRAND NCE project.

9. REFERENCES

[1] E. Agichtein, E. Brill, and S. Dumais. Improving web search ranking by incorporating user behavior information. In *Proceedings of SIGIR'06*, pages 19–26, 2006.

[2] O. Alonso and M. Gertz. Clustering of search results using temporal attributes. In *Proceedings of SIGIR'06*, 2006.

[3] E. Amigó, J. Gonzalo, J. Artiles, and F. Verdejo. A comparison of extrinsic clustering evaluation metrics based on formal constraints. *Inf. Retr.*, 12:461–486, August 2009.

[4] D. Beeferman and A. L. Berger. Agglomerative clustering of a search engine query log. In *Proceedings of SIGKDD'00*, pages 407–416, 2000.

[5] S. Beitzel, E. Jensen, A. Chowdhury, and O. Frieder. Varying approaches to topical web query classification. In *Proceedings of SIGIR'07*, pages 783–784. ACM, 2007.

[6] C. Brandt, T. Joachims, Y. Yue, and J. Bank. Dynamic ranked retrieval. In *Proceedings of WSDM'11*, pages 247–256, 2011.

[7] A. Z. Broder. A taxonomy of web search. *Sigir Forum*, 36:3–10, 2002.

[8] A. Z. Broder, M. Fontoura, E. Gabrilovich, A. Joshi, V. Josifovski, and T. Zhang. Robust classification of rare queries using web knowledge. In *Proceedings of SIGIR'07*, pages 231–238, 2007.

[9] M. Burt and C. L. Liew. Searching with clustering: An investigation into the effects on users' search experience and satisfaction. *Online Information Review*, 36, 2012.

[10] H. Cao, D. Jiang, J. Pei, Q. He, Z. Liao, E. Chen, and H. Li. Context-aware query suggestion by mining click-through and session data. In *Proceeding of KDD'08*, 2008.

[11] C. Carpineto, S. Osiński, G. Romano, and D. Weiss. A survey of web clustering engines. *ACM Computing Surveys (CSUR)*, 41(3):17, 2009.

[12] O. Chapelle and Y. Zhang. A dynamic bayesian network click model for web search ranking. In *Proceedings of WWW'09*, pages 1–10, 2009.

[13] H. Chen and S. Dumais. Bringing order to the web: automatically categorizing search results. In *Proceedings of CHI'00*, pages 145–152, 2000.

[14] C. L. A. Clarke, N. Craswell, and I. Soboroff. Overview of the trec 2009 web track. In *Proceedings of TREC'09*, pages 1–9, 2009.

[15] N. Craswell and M. Szummer. Random walks on the click graph. In *Proceedings of SIGIR'07*, pages 239–246, 2007.

[16] H. Deng, I. King, and M. Lyu. Entropy-biased models for query representation on the click graph. In *Proceedings of SIGIR'09*, pages 339–346. ACM, 2009.

[17] P. Ferragina and A. Gulli. A personalized search engine based on web-snippet hierarchical clustering. *Software: Practice and Experience*, 38(2):189–225, 2008.

[18] S. Fujita, K. Machinaga, and G. Dupret. Click-graph modeling for facet attribute estimation of web search queries. In *Adaptivity, Personalization and Fusion of Heterogeneous Information*, pages 190–197, 2010.

[19] W. Gale, K. Church, and D. Yarowsky. One sense per discourse. In *Proceedings of the workshop on Speech and Natural Language*, pages 233–237. Association for Computational Linguistics, 1992.

[20] T. Joachims. Optimizing search engines using clickthrough data. In *Proceedings of KDD'02*, pages 133–142, 2002.

[21] R. Jones and K. Klinkner. Beyond the session timeout: Automatic hierarchical segmentation of search topics in query logs. In *Proceedings of CIKM'08*, pages 699–708, 2008.

[22] M. Kan and H. Thi. Fast webpage classification using url features. In *Proceedings of the 14th ACM international conference on Information and knowledge management*, pages 325–326. ACM, 2005.

[23] Y. Li, Z. Zheng, and H. K. Dai. Kdd cup-2005 report: facing a great challenge. *SIGKDD Explor. Newsl.*, 7:91–99, December 2005.

[24] H.-T. Pu, S.-L. Chuang, and C. Yang. Subject categorization of query terms for exploring web users' search interests. *J. Am. Soc. Inf. Sci. Technol.*, 53:617–630, August 2002.

[25] F. Radlinski, M. Szummer, and N. Craswell. Inferring query intent from reformulations and clicks. In *Proceedings of WWW'10*, pages 1171–1172, 2010.

[26] X. Wang and C. Zhai. Learn from web search logs to organize search results. In *Proceedings SIGIR'07*, pages 87–94, 2007.

[27] J.-R. Wen, J.-Y. Nie, and H.-J. Zhang. Clustering user queries of a search engine. In *Proceedings of WWW'01*, pages 162–168, 2001.

[28] X. Yuan and N. J. Belkin. Supporting multiple information-seeking strategies in a single system framework. In *Proceedings of SIGIR'07*, pages 247–254, 2007.

[29] H. Zeng, Q. He, Z. Chen, W. Ma, and J. Ma. Learning to cluster web search results. In *Proceedings of SIGIR'04*, pages 210–217. ACM, 2004.

Search, Interrupted: Understanding and Predicting Search Task Continuation

Eugene Agichtein*
Emory University
Atlanta, GA, USA
eugene@mathcs.emory.edu

Ryen W. White, Susan T. Dumais, and Paul N. Bennett
Microsoft Research
Redmond, WA, USA
{ryenw, sdumais, pauben}@microsoft.com

ABSTRACT

Many important search tasks require multiple search sessions to complete. Tasks such as travel planning, large purchases, or job searches can span hours, days, or even weeks. Inevitably, life interferes, requiring the searcher either to recover the "state" of the search manually (most common), or plan for interruption in advance (unlikely). The goal of this work is to better *understand*, *characterize*, and *automatically detect* search tasks that will be continued in the near future. To this end, we analyze a query log from the Bing Web search engine to identify the types of *intents*, *topics*, and *search behavior* patterns associated with long-running tasks that are likely to be continued. Using our insights, we develop an effective prediction algorithm that significantly outperforms both the previous state-of-the-art method, and even the ability of human judges, to predict future task continuation. Potential applications of our techniques would allow a search engine to pre-emptively "save state" for a searcher (e.g., by caching search results), perform more targeted personalization, and otherwise better support the searcher experience for interrupted search tasks.

Categories and Subject Descriptors

H.3.3 [**Information Storage and Retrieval**]: Information Search and Retrieval – *search process; selection process*

Keywords

Search session analysis; Search behavior; Personalization.

1. INTRODUCTION

As Web search becomes increasingly important for planning and decision making, the complexity and scope of search tasks performed on search engines is increasing. Search engines are now often used for tasks such as travel planning, job hunting, or real estate searching. However, these tasks require significantly more effort and time to complete [10][21][24][25], potentially spanning days, weeks, or even months. While existing commercial Web search engines such as Bing and Google now provide tools to help users maintain and manage their search histories, the support they provide is not sufficient and the tools are not specifically designed to allow searchers to resume tasks that may been interrupted.

A challenge for search engines is to detect when a searcher is performing a long-running search task and *predict* whether they will continue it in the future. To this end, we analyze a query log from Bing to understand the types of *intents*, *motivations*, *topics*, and *search behaviors* associated with long-running tasks that are likely to be continued. Specifically, we try to understand search task continuation by analyzing tasks that were and were not continued by over a thousand Web searchers.

For example, consider the task of planning a wedding. The searcher might begin by checking recommended venues and their availabilities. However, at that point the task could be interrupted, as it requires checking dates and venues with the immediate family. When the task is continued the next day, the searcher has to restart from the beginning, unless the user planned for this event, and manually saved the most promising intermediate results. Indeed, there has been previous work on system support that lets users explicitly record promising content [10][27]. However, a perfect search engine could save the user the trouble if it could reliably detect that a suspended search session is likely to be continued at a later time.

While previous studies have considered long running tasks spanning multiple sessions (e.g., [10][21][24][25]), we dive deeper into the problem of task continuation to analyze the intent, motivation, and topics of these tasks. The more extensive analysis we perform allows for a fuller understanding of which tasks are most commonly resumed, in turn resulting in more accurate task continuation prediction. Potential applications include pre-emptively "saving state" for a searcher (e.g., by caching search results), more targeted personalization, and otherwise better supporting the searcher experience for long-running searches.

More formally, our problem is *predicting task continuation*:

> *Given* an active search task that has been suspended, *predict* whether the searcher will continue the task in the near future (e.g., within the next five days).

This problem is challenging, since it requires a search engine to make predictions about the kinds of tasks that tend to be continued, which intuitively would require substantial knowledge about the world. Yet, this work presents techniques to make these predictions automatically as well as, and often better than, experienced human annotators. Our contributions are threefold:

- A large-scale characterization of the intents, motivations, and topics associated with long-running search tasks (Section 3).
- Novel features to effectively capture these characteristics for automated prediction of task continuation (Section 4).
- Techniques for accurate prediction of continuation that outperform both a state-of-the-art automatic baseline and human predictions, coupled with the analysis of the most effective features used by the predictive algorithms (Section 5).

Next, we present related work to put our contributions in context.

2. RELATED WORK

Prior research that relates to what we describe in this paper falls into four main areas: (i) behavioral analysis and modeling of search, (ii) understanding search intent, (iii) analysis of cross-session tasks, and (iv) task switching and interruptions.

* Work done while visiting Microsoft Research.

Permission to make digital or hard copies of all or part of this work for personal or classroom use is granted without fee provided that copies are not made or distributed for profit or commercial advantage and that copies bear this notice and the full citation on the first page. To copy otherwise, or republish, to post on servers or to redistribute to lists, requires prior specific permission and/or a fee.
SIGIR'12, August 12–16, 2012, Portland, Oregon, USA.
Copyright 2012 ACM 978-1-4503-1472-5/12/08...$15.00.

Search behavior has been studied intensely in recent years. Log data from search engines have proven to be extremely valuable in studying how people search in naturalistic settings across a wide variety of different search intents. Most previous work has focused on search behavior analysis and prediction within a single search session [1][7][42], and related queries within a session can be part of a *search goal* [16][19], which try to represent the more abstract concept of search intent given only observable events. However, there is growing interest in using long-term search log data to build models of users' interests [39] and improve search result ranking [34].

An important part of representing search intent is understanding the various types of search tasks and the different motivations that searchers may have for pursuing their information goals. Earlier work on understanding search behavior focused on classifying queries into high-level search goals, such as informational, navigational and transactional [6][8][32]. Kellar *et al.* [20] conducted a field study in which they logged detailed Web usage and asked participants to provide task categorizations of their Web usage based on the following categories: fact finding, information gathering, browsing, and transactions. They showed differences in search behavior per task type. In particular, information gathering tasks were the most complex; participants spent more time completing this task, viewed more pages, and used the Web browser functions most heavily during this task. Li and Belkin [23] review and discuss previously-proposed task classifications and develop a faceted classification that can be used to describe searchers' work tasks and information search tasks. They identify essential facets and categorize them into generic task facets (e.g., source, product, and goal) and common task attributes (e.g., task characteristics and user perceptions). Rather than characterizing the nature of the search intent, Radlinski *et al.* [30] model search intent from queries and clicks in a way that could be directly consumed by search engines. Goals and related constructs (such as search intent) have also been widely studied in psychological research. Austin and Vancouver [4] review the theoretical development of the structure and properties of goals, goal establishment and striving processes, and goal-content taxonomies, which we use to motivate the selection of task dimensions to analyze. In fact, to our knowledge, our research is the first attempt to bring theory of motivation from psychology to bear on search intent analysis.

In this paper we focus on tasks extending across multiple sessions. Search behavior can be analyzed over time to identify queries that express the same underlying information need. Previous work has tried to automatically identify queries on the same task. Mei *et al.* [26] proposed a framework to study sequences of search activities and focused on simple prediction and classification tasks, ranging from predicting whether the next click will be on an algorithmic result to segmenting the query stream into goals and missions. Teevan *et al.* [37] showed, via query log analysis, that nearly 40% of queries were attempts to re-find previously encountered results. Aula *et al.* [3] studied the search and information re-access strategies of experienced Web users using a survey. They found that people often have difficulty remembering the queries they used originally to discover information of interest. MacKay and Watters [25] explored a variety of Web-based information seeking tasks and found that almost 60% of complex information gathering tasks continued across sessions. Liu and Belkin [24] examined the structure (parallel or dependent) of tasks that extend across different search sessions. Jones and Klinker [19] proposed methods to partition a query stream into research missions and goals, where each mission corresponds to a set of related information needs and may include multiple search goals. Morris *et al.* [27] developed *SearchBar*, a system that proactively and persistently stores query histories, browsing histories, and users' notes and ratings. SearchBar supports multi-session investigations by assisting with task context resumption and information re-finding. Donato *et al.* [10] developed *SearchPad*, a system that automatically identifies research missions and presents a search workspace comprising previous queries and results related to the mission. SearchPad uses measures of topic coherence between pairs of consecutive queries and user engagement to identify such research missions. This work was further extended by Aiello *et al.* [2] to group queries into mission-coherent clusters based on searcher behavior. However, none of the research described so far specifically addressed the important challenge of predicting search task continuation.

The most similar research to this paper is that of Kotov *et al.* [21]. In that paper, the authors describe research on modeling cross-session information needs, and address the challenge of identifying all previous queries in a user's search history on the same task as the current query, and predicting whether a user will return to the task in future sessions. Kotov *et al.* developed classifiers for these two tasks and through evaluation using labeled data from search logs showed that their classifiers can perform both tasks effectively. We use these classifiers as a baseline for some of the analysis presented later in the paper.

Also relevant to this work is previous research on task switching and interruptions. Multi-tasking and external factors such as interruptions have been previously associated with prolonged search tasks. Spink [35] studied the multi-tasking behavior of a single searcher in a public library using diary, observation and interviews and found that switching between tasks was common. On the basis of that study, she then developed a model of information multi-tasking and information task switching. Czerwinski *et al.* [9] present the findings of a week-long diary study of task interleaving admist interruptions, following eleven information workers in a non-search setting. They show that task complexity, task duration, length of absence, interruption count, and task type influence the perceived difficulty of switching back to tasks with participants reporting that it was most difficult to recommence complex tasks. The features we devise to represent tasks adapt and operationalize these ideas.

The research presented in this paper extends previous work in a number of ways. First, we perform a detailed descriptive analysis of the cross-session search tasks that maps task intents and motivations derived from the information science and psychology literatures to evidence of task continuation mined from search logs and labeled by trained human annotators. Second, we propose new features to model characteristics of cross-session search tasks, focusing on future task continuation, using features of search behavior mined from annotated log data. Third, we show that these features can improve continuation modeling and prediction over a previously-reported state-of-the-art baseline, and even over experienced human annotators attempting to perform the same prediction task.

3. UNDERSTANDING CROSS-SESSION TASKS: DESCRIPTIVE ANALYSIS

This section describes the data collection (Section 3.1), the human data annotation for the dimensions hypothesized to be related to search task continuation (Section 3.2), and presents analysis of task characteristics (Sections 3.4-3.5) based on both manual annotation of the tasks and an extended set of search log data.

3.1 Data Collection

The data were gathered from the Microsoft Bing commercial Web search engine by sampling a set of sessions over a one-week period for more than 1,000 users. Similar to [21], we study what have been previously defined as "early dominant" tasks identified for each user. An early dominant task is defined as having at least two distinct queries issued within a two-day period at the beginning of the week of interest. Some of these tasks are continued later during the week, while others are not. The data that we used for our study are summarized in Table 1.

Users and tasks (1 early-dominant task per user)	1,191
Unique queries	28,474
Active period	Last week of February 2010
Prior history	2 weeks prior
Continued tasks	683 (57%)

Table 1. Search log data used in this study.

Additionally, the data above were augmented by extracting up to an additional two weeks of prior history for each user in the sample, from the two weeks immediately before the week of interest. This history contained search sessions determined based on a 30-minute inactivity timeout [40], as well as the queries and URLs issued and visited. This allowed us to study the potential for utilizing additional profile information to predict task continuation.

3.2 Data Annotation

We annotated the characteristics of early dominant search tasks (defined above) according to a range of dimensions derived from information and cognitive science literatures, following the procedure in Section 3.3. Our goals were: (1) to analyze the relationship of task characteristics to task continuation and (2) to learn to automatically identify these characteristics for better search continuation modeling and prediction. In particular, we wished to investigate how task *intent* and *motivation*, as well as other contextual factors such as task *urgency*, relate to the likelihood of continuing a search task (within the one-week horizon that we used in our study). In the remainder of this subsection we define the dimensions on which we annotated tasks.

Intent Type: The type of the task, derived from previous studies in the information science literature (e.g., [20][23]). The hypothesis is that some task types, such as information gathering or transactions, are associated with task continuation. The specific intent types chosen for labeling were:

- *Fact finding (focused)*: Find specific piece(s) of information (e.g., a query such as "mc gilvery oil wolsey").
- *Information gathering (exploration)*: Find information on a topic rather than for a specific fact (e.g., "english comedy").
- *Undirected browsing*: Explore a site or the Web without an obvious goal (e.g., "portland craigs list").
- *Transaction*: Accomplish a task or perform a transaction online (e.g., "pay discover card bill")
- *Communication (social)*: Read or interact in online social sites such as forums.
- *Information maintenance or update*: Monitor information on a running topic and possibly update a Web resource.

Motivation: The cognitive or affective motivation inferred to be behind the task, derived and simplified from cognitive science and psychology literature [4]. Our intuition was that some motivations are more likely to associate with task continuation than others. The motivations selected for labeling were:

- *Affective*: Based on emotion or feeling, with sub-categories of *Arousal* (e.g., adult content), *Tranquility* (e.g., viewing art), *Happiness*, and *Physical well-being* (e.g., verifying health information).
- *Cognitive*: Learning about the world or about the self, with sub-categories of *Exploration*, *Understanding*, and *Positive self-evaluation*.
- *Self-assertive*: Individual relationship between person and the environment, with sub-categories of *Individuality, Self-Determination, Superiority,* and *Approval* (e.g., posting on a support forum).
- *Social*: Integrative social relationships, with sub-categories of *Belongingness* (maintaining social relationships), *Social Responsibilities*, or providing *Social Support*.

If none of the specific subtypes seemed appropriate, the annotators had an option to pick a generic motivation (e.g., "Social").

Complexity: The complexity of the task, measured by the number of goals required to find the needed information. We hypothesized that more complex tasks, with multiple goals, are more likely to be continued. The options for complexity were:

- *Single goal*: A task that can be theoretically satisfied by a single web page (e.g., "women's suffrage 1922").
- *Multiple goals*: A task that is expected to require aggregating information from multiple web pages (e.g., "cheap flights").
- *Undirected*: No evident goal (may be undirected exploration).

We asked annotators to specify the number of goals (if the task was not labeled as "undirected") based on their estimates of the number of Web pages required to fulfill the searcher's information need (one=single goal, many=multiple goals).

WorkOrFun: Does the task appear to be necessary for work or life or is it more for fun? We hypothesized that fun-related tasks are more likely to be continued than those considered to be work-related.

Time Sensitivity: How urgent or time sensitive is the information need, and is it likely to disappear/expire in a short time? Naturally, we hypothesized that highly time-sensitive tasks are less likely to be continued.

Continue or Not?: Finally, we asked the annotators to predict how likely they think a task is to continue within the week's data horizon. The following four response options were available: [*very likely, likely, unlikely, very unlikely*]. We hypothesized that human judges would be able to use their world knowledge and intuition to reasonably estimate the likelihood of task continuation, given the information available to them from the first two days of search behavior (e.g., all of the queries that users had issued, the URLs they had clicked, and the time of these events). These manually-generated estimates serve as a baseline for the performance of the predictive models developed in this paper.

3.3 Annotation Procedure and Agreement

The human annotations were performed at the *task* level, where each task was previously identified as "early dominant" by a human annotator (defined in Section 3.1 above), using a separate manual annotation process described in detail in reference [21]. For each of these tasks, the annotators were shown the sequences of queries, clicks, and date/times, with corresponding session identifiers, as well as all other search actions of that user (regardless of the task)The actual labeling was performed only for the early-dominant tasks. The four annotators reviewed the guidelines for the above intents and motivations and worked through more than 20 example search tasks together, to ensure consistent interpretation and application of the guidelines. Annotators labeled an average of nearly 300 search tasks each, with three of them contributing over 90% of the labels.

An additional sample of 100 tasks was labeled by the three annotators responsible for the bulk of the labeling, for the purposes of computing inter-annotator agreement statistics. The average annotator agreement and the free-marginal Fleiss Kappa statistic [31] are reported in Table 2[1].

Dimension	*Average Agreement*	*Free-marginal Kappa*
Intent	0.649	0.591
Motivation	0.649	0.532
Complexity (# goals)	0.712	0.568
Time sensitivity	0.698	0.547
Work or Fun?	0.677	0.516

Table 2. Inter-annotator agreement for goal/intent labels (across the additional 100 tasks).

The agreement ranges from 0.65 to 0.71, with *Kappa* values between 0.52 for "WorkOrFun" to 0.59 for "Intent". These values are acceptable for such a difficult and potentially-subjective task.

3.4 Task analysis: Intent and Motivation

The majority of tasks were labeled as *information gathering (exploratory)* (56%), examples of which included research, school work, shopping, and travel planning. The other tasks were labeled as *fact finding (focused)* (20%), and *transaction* (13%), with the remainder of the search intents comprising 2-4% each.

The task continuation statistics for these intents are reported in Figure 1. Information maintenance tasks were most likely to be continued (85%), followed by undirected browsing (78%). Both of these may reflect hobbies and other longer term interests of the users in our study. Interestingly, *transaction* and *communication* were also likely to be continued (both over 70-75%). One possible confound is that transaction tasks include a small fraction of *navigational re-finding*, even though by requiring at least two unique queries we attempted to filter out navigational queries. With 52% and 48% return rates, *information gathering* and *fact finding* tasks were less likely to be continued, perhaps because most these tasks were fairly simple and could be completed within a single session.

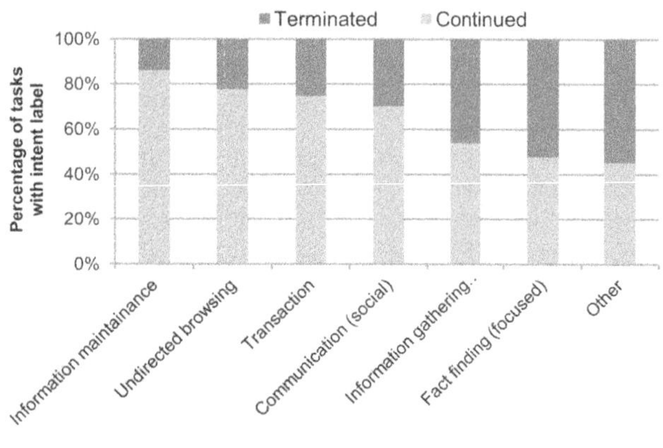

Figure 1. Task continuation for broad search intents.

[1] We use free-marginal Multi-rater Kappa since it is appropriate for typical agreement studies in which raters' distributions of cases into categories are unrestricted.

Figure 2 reports the task continuation statistics for different motivations for the tasks, in decreasing order by the likelihood of continuation. It appears that affectively motivated tasks are more likely to be continued, with arousal (typically, adult content) the most likely to be continued. Interestingly, *self-assertive* and *social* motivations were almost equally likely to result in task continuation, while tasks motivated by *cognitive: understanding* and *affective: physical wellbeing* were the least likely tasks to be continued. Tasks with these motivations do not typically persist over time, presumably because they involved episodic lookups of facts or health-related information that does not require follow-up.

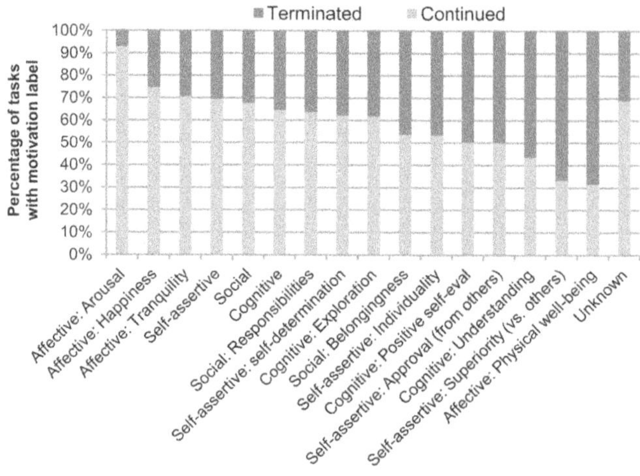

Figure 2. Task continuation for different search motivations.

In addition to analyzing variations in task continuation likelihoods associated with different intents and motivations, we were also interested in the impact of task complexity on the likelihood that users would continue. Figure 3 shows the relationship between the number of goals identified and the task continuation likelihood.

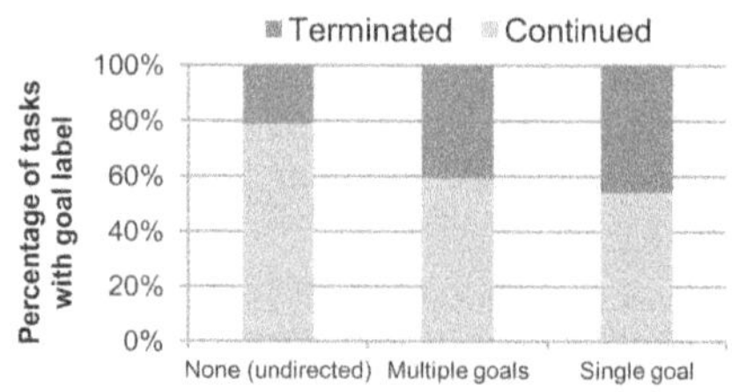

Figure 3. Task continuation by task complexity (number of goals).

Interestingly, the number of task goals (Figure 3) is not strongly associated with task continuation. In fact, the tasks that appear to be undirected (e.g., without a clear goal page or information nugget), are more likely to be continued. These include browsing employment opportunities, real estate listings, or adult content. Furthermore, tasks judged to be time-sensitive (Figure 4a), are more likely to be continued, compared to tasks judged to be not time-sensitive. Also tasks being attempted for pleasure (fun) rather than necessity (work-related) are also slightly more likely to be continued (Figure 4b). While this seems counter-intuitive, one explanation could be that when searching by necessity, users are more likely to satisfice once the (minimum) sufficient information is found, whereas curiosity- or pleasure-driven exploration are less likely to be satisfied as quickly, and is likely to be more aligned with the searcher's long-term interests. We explore this observation further in the next section.

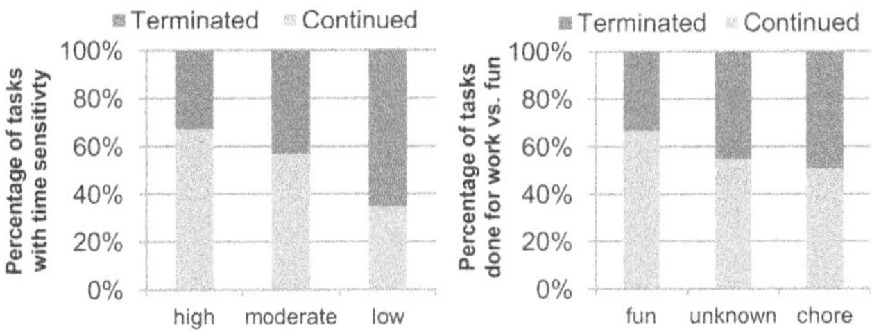

Figure 4. Task continuation by (a) time sensitivity and (b) work or fun task types.

We have seen in this section that several factors are associated with the likelihood of task continuation. In particular, tasks that give searchers pleasure and align with the users' interests are more likely to be continued, at least within the one-week period analyzed in this study, as we explore in more detail next.

3.5 Search Topic Analysis: Repeat History

We hypothesized that certain topical categories of tasks are more likely to be resumed than others (see also [10]). To identify topical category, we use automatic query classification into the top two levels of the Open Directory Project (ODP, dmoz.org) hierarchy. The classifier has a micro-averaged F1 value of 0.60 and is described more fully in reference [5]. To obtain a topic representation for queries labeled as belonging to the task of interest, we obtained the top ten results for each query from Bing and categorized each result by running the text classifier on its content. The result is a vector of topic probabilities, which we restricted to the three most probable classes. For each task, we obtained the most probable ODP category by merging the distributions for all associated queries.

Figure 5 reports that search tasks in some ODP categories, such as "adult", "kids and teens" and "news", are very likely to be continued, while search involvement with other topics, such as "home", "health", and "science" appear to be more episodic and less likely to be continued over time. Note that the search topic is distinct from the search intent (e.g., a task associated with "news" topics may be either *information maintenance*, or *fact finding*). Importantly, this demonstrates that the ODP category labels may be useful for automatically predicting task continuation. We explore the utility of this representation for prediction later in the paper.

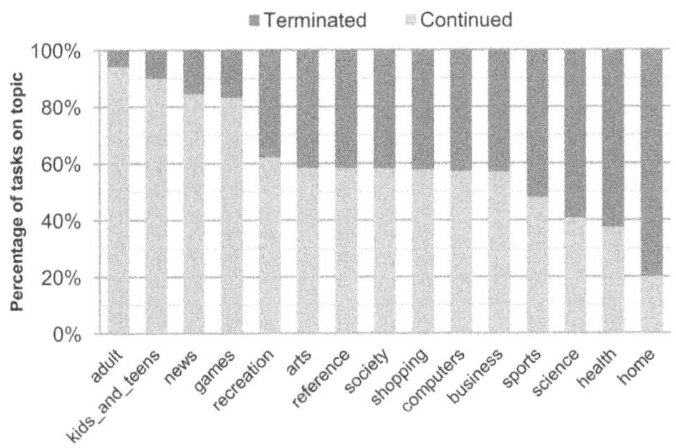

Figure 5. Task continuation by top-level ODP category.

The potential utility of the ODP category labels for task continuation prediction is not surprising, and indeed we observed anecdotally in our data that some topics were more likely to be repeated over time. These topic repeatability statistics could be considered as a "prior" for the task continuation likelihood, and could be exploited in the absence of any other information about the user.

Class Repeats: Specific Categories	*Repeat Prob.*
Most Likely	
Computers/Internet	0.639
Arts/Television	0.562
Adult/Computers	0.543
Arts/Radio	0.521
Adult/Image_Galleries	0.515
Games/Board_Games	0.503
Shopping/Antiques_and_Collectibles	0.483
Games/Video_Games	0.482
Arts/Music	0.469
Adult/World	0.469
Games/Card_Games	0.431
Shopping/General_Merchandise	0.431
Sports/Baseball	0.421
Adult/Arts	0.415
Shopping/Vehicles	0.413
Least Likely	
Shopping/Visual_Arts	0.047
Recreation/Living_History	0.042
Computers/Consultants	0.041
Recreation/Birding	0.041
Recreation/Climbing	0.040
Science/Instruments_and_Supplies	0.039
Arts/Writers_Resources	0.038
Reference/Museums	0.035
Society/Holidays	0.032
Recreation/Scouting	0.029
Health/Animal	0.029
Society/Gay,_Lesbian,_and_Bisexual	0.027
Business/International_Business_and_Trade	0.027
Arts/Illustration	0.022
Sports/Tennis	0.020

Table 3. Highest and lowest repeat probabilities for different ODP topical categories (large-scale sample).

To examine this observation in more detail we analyzed the probability that a given topical category will be observed in a future session for the same user within a week (similar to the setting used for this study). To do this, we used a separate set of Bing search logs for a period of three weeks that did not overlap with the one week of data used for our study. From these logs we extracted over 100 million search sessions for over five million unique users. Search sessions were defined using a 30-minute inactivity timeout [40]. The results are summarized in Table 3, and show that topics such as *Computers/Internet*, *Arts/Television*, and *Adult/Computers* are the most likely to be observed in subsequent search sessions, while topics such as *Sports/Tennis* or *Reference/Museums* are likely to be used in one session but not to appear in future sessions for the same user within the following week. The former set of categories may be more likely to reflect users' longer-term, persistent interests, whereas the latter may be more transient and affected by immediate social responsibilities e.g., specific events such as a museum visit or a tennis tournament.

4. MODELING TASK CONTINUATION

In the previous section, we analyzed the task continuation data with a focus on the characteristics of the search tasks that are associated with task continuation. We now turn to modeling and automatically predicting task continuation. As described earlier, this is an important area for search providers trying to help users perform cross-session searching. We first describe the features used for task representation and then describe the algorithms and training procedure that we adopted in this study (Section 4.2).

4.1 Features

We represent a task using *topical*, *user engagement*, *user history profile*, and *topic and query priors* feature groups, described in more detail below and shown in Table 4. We use these features to predict task continuation.

Baseline features. We began by re-implementing the most important features reported in [21], which forms our baseline system in the prediction experiments. These features capture the basic lexicographic and behavior properties of the search session, such as query overlap, number of clicks on results returned by the search engine, and time between queries. Reference [21] provides more detailed descriptions of these features.

In addition to the baseline features, we also added four groups:

Search topic. These new features aim to capture the topical categories of the task derived from the automated classifier trained on ODP data and described in Section 3.5. Additional measures include the entropy of the topic distribution (for both the first- and second-level categories of the ODP hierarchy) to capture the degree of topical focus in the task. We conjectured that tasks that span fewer distinct ODP topics are more likely to be continued

User engagement. These new features aim to capture the searcher's level of engagement in the task they are performing, going far beyond the baseline features described above. Features of note include the estimated satisfaction and dissatisfaction with the results (based on estimates of the amount of time that users spent dwelling on clicked results, per [13]), the span of time and effort invested in the task, the amount of "multi-tasking" interspersed with the task, as well as other metrics of effort and user activity. We hypothesized that if a user is heavily engaged with a task and that effort is focused, they will be more likely to continue.

User profile history. In addition to analyzing the current search task, we also aim to capture historical information about the user. To do this we used two weeks of log data from the time period before the week of interest for each of the users in our study. Features generated from this profile include the topic distribution of previous search sessions, queries, overlap with the current task, and other profile information such as the time of the day and day of the week when the task was started. We hypothesized that topics or query terms that interested the user in the past, are more likely to be continued in the future.

Repeat priors on topic and query repetition. In addition to the random sample of the nearly 1,200 users under study, we make use of global query and ODP category statistics computed over the query log described in Section 3.5. We hypothesized that topics and query terms that tend to re-appear globally could provide additional evidence for task continuation.

4.2 Classifiers

We experimented with two different classifiers for the problem of predicting task continuation. The two classifiers used were Logistic Regression [15] (which was shown to be effective for task continuation prediction in reference [21]). We refer to this method as **Baseline** in subsequent experiments.

Our main experiments were performed using a gradient-**B**oosted Decision **T**ree classifier, based on the MART algorithm [14], with a logistic penalty, so that we can evaluate the importance of richer feature combinations. We refer to this classifier as **BT** (for Boosted Tree) in subsequent experiments, typically listed in combination with either all the features in Table 4 ("BT: All") or feature subsets. The classification task is to predict whether a search task, previously identified to be early-dominant for a user, will be continued in the future (positive class) or not (negative class). All experimental results reported below were performed using 5 runs of 10-fold cross validation, randomized for each method.

Name	Description
Baseline features	
BASE_SameQueryHist, BASE_NumSessHist, BASE_NumDomQueriesHist, BASE_AvgInterQTimeHist, BASE_FreqDomQueriesHist, BASE_NumDwell30Hist, BASE_NumQueryHist, BASE_NumTop10ClickQuery BASE_AvgInterQTimeSess BASE_NumClickHist BASE_NumQueryChars BASE_SubQueryHist BASE_SupQueryHist BASE_SubQuerySess BASE_SupQuerySess	Implemented as described in reference [21]
Topic	
NumClassifierLeafs	Number of distinct classifier topics clicked on task
NumODPCats	Number distinct ODP categories clicked
NumODPLeafs	Number distinct ODP leafs clicked
TopClassifierLeaf	Most frequent topic
TopOdpCat	Most frequent ODP category
TopODPLeaf	Most popular ODP leaf
OdpDomCatEntropy	Entropy of dominant task ODP categories
OdpDomLeafEntropy	Entropy of dominant task ODP leafs
ClassifierDomEntropy	Entropy of dominant task classifier leafs
Engagement Effort and Focus	
AvgClickPosQuery	Average position of result clicks for last query
TotalSkipPosQuery	Sum of skip positions for last query
AvgDomClickPos	Avg click pos for all dom task queries
TotalDomSkipPos	Sum of skip positions for all dom task queries
AvgClickPosSess	Avg click position for all queries in session
TotalSkipPosSess	Sum of skip positions for all queries in session
NumDomClickBacks	Total number of on-task click-backs
AvgDomClickBacks	Avg number of click backs per session
NumDomTaskSessions	# sessions that had at least one dom task query
NumOffTaskQueriesSess	Number off-task queries in last session
NumTaskSwitchHist	#off/on- task switches over recent history
NumTaskSwitchSess	#off/on- task switches over last session
OnTaskQueriesRatioSess	Fraction of on-task to total queries in last session
OnTaskSessionsRatio	Fraction of on-task to off-task sessions
TaskSpanTime	Time from first to last occurrence of dominant task
TaskSpanSessions	Sessions spanned by the dominant task
TaskSpanDays	Number of days for the task
NumDomResClicks	Total number of clicks on dominant task queries
AvgDomResClicks	Avg # clicks per query on dominant task
NumSATClicks	Clicks on dominant task with > 60 sec dwell time
NumDSATClicks	Clicks on dominant task with < 30 sec dwell time
User Profile	
SameQueryPriorHist	1 if last dom task query appeared in prior history
DomQueriesPriorHist	Number of dom task queries in prior history
NumDomTopicPriorHist	Number of dom topics in prior history
FracDomTopicsPriorHist	Fraction of dom task topics in prior history
FracPriorHistDomTopics	Fraction of topics in prior history also in dom task
NumTopicPriorHist	Total number unique topics in prior history
ProbPriorHistDomTopics	Sum of dom task topic probabilities
TopDomTopicsInPriorHist	Top K (k=10) most popular topics in prior history
TaskStartDayOfWeek	Day of week (Sun=0) for the start of the task
TaskStartTimeOfDay	Time of day (midnight=0) for the start of the task.
Repeat Priors	
CatRepeatPrior	Probability of category repeat for the same user
QueryRepeatPrior	Probability of query repeat for the same user
TermRepeatPrior	Probability of term repeat for the same user

Table 4. Features used to represent cross-session search tasks.

4.3 Evaluation Metrics

To compare the performance of the classification methods we use the following standard performance measures: (1) accuracy, (2) precision and recall for the positive class (task continuation), and (3) area under the receiver-operator-characteristic curve (AUC). Statistical significance between performance values was calculated using two-tailed independent sample *t*-tests where appropriate.

5. RESULTS AND DISCUSSION

This section first reports the human performance on the task, to indicate that predicting continuation is challenging even for human judges (Section 5.1). We then report the results of automatic continuation predictors (Section 5.2), followed by extensive analysis of the feature groups and individual features that are most strongly predictive of task continuation (Section 5.3). Finally, we present the findings of a failure analysis which suggests future improvements to our predictive models.

5.1 Human Prediction of Task Continuation

Table 5 reports the performance of the classifier trained on individual task dimensions (manually labeled as described above), as well as on the explicit human judgment of task continuation, and a classifier trained on the combination of all of the manual annotations. In other words, we attempt to create the best "hybrid" human and machine prediction possible, by using the labels provided by the human judges as features. These labels were expected to augment the explicitly labeled "continue or not" prediction (which was considered positive when the response was "very likely" or "likely", and negative otherwise). Recall, that the annotators were able to see the first two days of the user's search history, but did not have access to the longer-term User Profile features above). So, the humans' predictions were performed based on two days of data as well as world knowledge and intuition about the nature of search tasks. As Table 5 indicates, humans can definitely predict continuation more accurately than the naïve Majority baseline that always picks "continue", or than any individual intent or motivation label. However, there is an even stronger signal in the *combination* of the manual dimension labels, resulting in the best prediction possible based on the human judgments data.

Method (Human Annotations)	*Accuracy*	*Precision*	*Recall*	*AUC*
Majority baseline ("continue")	0.573	0.573	1.000	0.573
Task type	0.586	0.591	0.842	0.566
Motivation	0.629	0.660	0.738	0.628
Complexity	0.572	0.575	0.986	0.506
WorkOrFun	0.550	0.574	0.852	0.579
Continue prediction	0.677	0.730	0.703	0.692
BT: All human labels	**0.678**	**0.704**	**0.764**	**0.729**

Table 5. Human task annotations vs. search continuation.

In addition to computing the predictive value of the task dimensions and their combination, we were also interested in the relationship between the nature of the human judges' estimation of continuation likelihood and whether users were observed to be continuing the search task. We did this to help us to understand their ability to make the explicit prediction (rather than using their prediction as a feature for learning). Figure 6 shows the predicted versus actual outcomes for each of the four rating options.

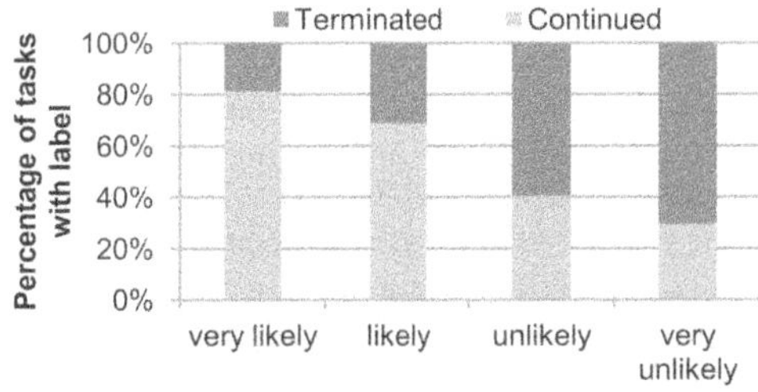

Figure 6. Predicted vs. actual task continuation by human annotators.

As Figure 6 indicates, when human judges were sure of the prediction (i.e., rated a task to be "very likely" or "very unlikely" to be continued), their prediction accuracy was 80% and 75%, respectively. However, for the majority of cases, the annotators provided more tentative labels ("likely" and "unlikely"), and in those cases the predictions had substantially lower accuracy..

We now focus on the predictive performance of the trained models, comparing them with the human predictive performance.

5.2 Comparing Prediction Methods

Table 6 reports the performance of a human prediction of task continuation, against our implementation of the state-of-the-art baseline described in [21], and our extended method *BT:All* (using all classifier features and two weeks of prior history as described above). Both classifiers substantially outperform the human annotators; furthermore, *BT:All* substantially and significantly outperforms the baseline in terms of accuracy, precision, and AUC metrics with $p < 0.01$.

Method	*Accuracy*	*Precision*	*Recall*	*AUC*
Human prediction	0.677	0.730	0.703	0.692
Baseline	0.697	0.728	0.761	0.752
BT: All Features	**0.751** (+8%)**	**0.786** (+8%)**	**0.783 (+3%)**	**0.829** (+10%)**

Table 6. Predicting search continuation (* and ** indicate statistical significance at $p \leq 0.05$ and $p \leq 0.01$ compared to the Baseline, respectively, using unpaired t-test).

We augment the quantitative analysis in Table 6 by plotting the precision-recall curve for each of the methods in Figure 7.

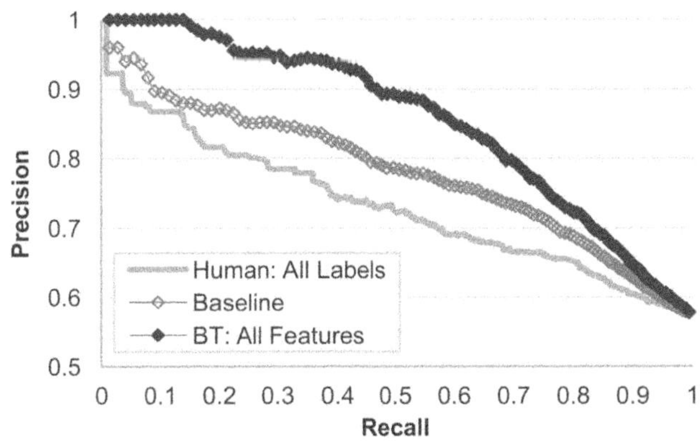

Figure 7. Precision-Recall curve for predicting search continuation for the Baseline, BT:All, and the Human prediction methods.

As Figure 7 indicates, both the automated *Baseline* and our *BT:All Features* classifier substantially outperform human predictions. Furthermore, *BT:All* provides the biggest lift in AUC over the Baseline, at precision of at least 0.8 and remains acceptably high (≥ 0.75) until nearly 0.8 recall levels.

One factor that may affect the performance of the *BT:All* classifier is the availability of user history information. This information was not available to humans (although they can draw upon general world knowledge and their own search experiences) or Baseline. To quantify the contribution of user's history (profile) information to use for prediction, Table 7 reports the results of varying the amount of history data for each user included in the model from *None* (i.e., no user profile information prior to the two days at the beginning of prediction), to one week and two weeks.

Method	*Accuracy*	*Precision*	*Recall*	*AUC*
BT: All: No History	0.721	0.758	0.761	0.788
+ 1 Week History	0.731	0.766	0.768	0.791
+ 2 Weeks History	**0.751****	**0.786****	**0.783***	**0.829****

Table 7. Varying amount of history for user profile computation (* and ** indicate statistical significance at p≤0.05 and p≤0.01 compared to the *BT: All: No History* method, respectively, using unpaired t-test).

While adding one week of prior history improves performance slightly on all metrics, the improvements are not significant. However, the effects of adding an additional week of history (for two weeks total) are striking, providing substantial and significant improvements (with $p < 0.01$ for accuracy, precision, and AUC metrics, and $p < 0.05$ for Recall), compared to the same method with no prior user history. Having multiple weeks may more effectively capture the users' long-term interests or allow for recurring tasks (e.g., those that happen biweekly) to be observed and used to make predictions for the current week. More research is needed to determine whether such gains consistently increase with history length. Also note that even when we remove the history features, the performance of *BT:All: No History* is still substantially better than the performance of both Baseline and the human annotators. We discuss the differences between human and machine performance in more detail later in Section 5.4.

An important question in understanding the success of *BT:All* model is determining which feature groups contributed the most toward its strong performance. To this end, we now present some feature ablation analysis.

5.3 Feature Ablation Analysis

In order to determine the contribution provided by each of the feature groups, we perform feature ablation experiment, by starting with the full set of features (Table 4), and then systematically removing feature groups from the set, one group at a time. The results are reported in Table 8, averaging over five runs of randomized 10-fold cross validation.

Surprisingly, removing text features such as the most frequently used query terms, has negligible effect on performance. In contrast, removing the user profile features computed over the user history degrades performance significantly on the accuracy, precision, and AUC metrics. While other feature groups also appear to contribute, the single most valuable feature group is the user engagement effort and focus (listed in Table 4). Removing these features degrades performance significantly to roughly that of the original baseline. It appears that the more engaged the user is with the search task, the more likely they are to continue it in the one-week time span of our study.

Feature set	*Accuracy*	*Precision*	*Recall*	*AUC*
BT: All Features	**0.751**	**0.786**	**0.783**	**0.829**
– Topic	0.747	0.786	0.774	0.823
– **Engagement Effort and Focus**	0.703**	0.742**	0.746**	0.773**
– **User profile**	0.732**	0.770*	0.765	0.798**
– Repeat Priors	0.750	0.785	0.783	0.824

Table 8. Feature group ablation: task continuation prediction when removing one feature group at a time (* and ** indicate statistical significance at p≤0.05 and p≤0.01 compared to the *BT: All* method, respectively, using unpaired t-test).

5.3.1 Individual Features: Engagement and Focus

With the importance of the engagement features apparent in the feature-group ablation study, we set out to investigate how each of the individual engagement features correlates with task continuation. We computed the Pearson's correlation coefficient (r) between each of the engagement feature values and the task continuation label. The r values for the most and least correlated features are shown below in Table 9.

Engagement Feature	*r*
TaskSpanTime	**0.412**
NumDomTaskSessions	**0.387**
TaskSpanSessions	**0.364**
TaskSpanDays	**0.321**
OnTaskSessionsRatio	**0.230**
NumSATClicks	**0.178**
NumDomResClicks	0.162
TotalDomSkipPos	0.120
...	
NumOffTaskQueriesSess	-0.029
NumDomRepeatQueriesSess	-0.040
AvgDomClickBacks	-0.044
TotalSkipPosQuery	-0.052
OnTaskQueriesRatioSess	-0.055
NumTaskSwitchSess	**-0.148**

Table 9. Individual search engagement features vs. task continuation.

Table 9 reports that the most strongly correlated engagement features (from Table 4) include *TaskSpanTime*, *NumDomTaskSessions* (the number of on-task domain sessions), features such as the ratio of on-task vs. off-task sessions, and the number of SAT clicks (defined as clicks with dwell time ≥ 60). These features indicate that searchers tend to be more strongly focused on tasks that would be continued, and less involved in multi-tasking. In contrast, the *lack* of focus (e.g., increased multi-tasking during search as measured by the *NumTaskSwitchSess* feature), correlates negatively with task continuation. Interestingly, there is also a moderate correlation between search satisfaction (measured by the number of SAT clicks (defined in Table 4) and task continuation, and slightly negatively correlated to the number of "click-backs" or bounce-backs (*AvgDomClickBacks*), which are indicative of unsatisfying results. Indeed, Hu *et al.* [18] found a positive correlation between searcher satisfaction and search engine re-use on a week by week basis over a six-month period, although they just studied query volume and not task continuation.

To understand how the individual features contribute *in combination* with the other features for the BT classifier, Table 10 reports the individual features that contributed the most to reducing error during training – those with highest average relative reduction in residual squared error (averaged across the cross validation folds).

Feature	*Average Gain*
TaskSpanTime	1
DomQueriesPriorHist	**0.624**
BASE_NumQueryChars	**0.371**
TermRepeatPrior	**0.362**
BASE_AvgInterQTimeSess	**0.342**
BASE_AvgInterQTimeHist	**0.338**
BASE_NumQueryHist	**0.321**
TaskStartTimeOfDay	**0.289**
OnTaskQueriesRatioSess	**0.276**
OdpDomCatEntropy	**0.275**
FracPriorHistDomTopics	0.273
ClassifierDomEntropy	0.271
ProbPriorHistDomTopics	0.264
ClassRepeatPrior	0.260
BASE_FreqDomQueriesHist	0.252
NumTopicPriorHist	0.248
AvgDomClickPos	0.233
BASE_NumDwell30Hist	0.232
BASE_NumClickHist	0.224
BASE_NumSessHist	0.224
QueryRepeatPrior	0.218
AvgDomResClicks	0.210
BASE_SameQueryHist	0.208
NumDomTaskSessions	0.208
AvgDomClickBacks	0.201

Table 10. Feature importance: Top features, averaged across folds.

The single strongest predictor of continuation is *TaskSpanTime* – the amount of time the searcher already has spent on the task in the first two days. More interestingly, the next strongest indicator is *DomQueriesPriorHist*, the number of queries in the dominant task that were observed in the prior history for that user (hence pulling in information about the longevity of the task). The previously studied feature *BASE_NumQueryChars* (the number of characters in the query) is another strong indicator, perhaps because longer queries say something about the nature of the task or are suggestive of users' knowledge of a particular domain of interest. Previous studies have shown that users issue longer queries when searching in a domain about which they are knowledgeable [40]. Another new indicator of continuation is the *TermRepeatPrior* – the distribution of term repeat probabilities computed over more than five million users. This suggests that prior likelihoods of repetition computed independent of user may also be useful for predicting task continuation. Other strong indicators include the task start time of day, as well as the task focus and engagement features discussed above.

5.4 Analysis and Study Limitations

To gain additional insights into the task continuation prediction problem, we compared the task continuation predictions made by human annotators (using the labeling procedure described in Section 3.3), with those of the automated classifier, by focusing on the cases where the human and the classifier predictions differed. In these cases, humans were able to predict task *termination* more accurately (by about 25%) than task continuation. We conjecture that this could be partly explained to the data collection constraints, in that we required for a task to be resumed within one week in order to be marked "Continued". Furthermore, humans were able to predict continuation more accurately (by about 30%) for tasks labeled as difficult, compared to those labeled as easy or moderate. We also found that humans were most accurate in predicting task continuation within a day, which intuitively covers many transaction and planning tasks. Most remarkably, in cases where a task query previously occurred in a user's prior history, the classifier was 73% more likely to be correct than human judges, who did not have access to the long-term user profiles and had to rely on their intuition and world knowledge instead.

At this point it is appropriate to point out limitations of this study. As discussed earlier, to make this study feasible, the time horizon of task continuation was limited to one week. It is possible that some tasks are continued more than a week later. Another limitation is methodological: without asking the users directly, it was not possible for us to investigate the underlying causes of the search interruptions, i.e., whether the searchers were waiting for external input or simply ran out of time and had to switch to another task first. To get that information we will need to work with users directly and employ in-situ or retrospective methods to better understand the factors affecting their observed behaviors.

6. CONCLUSIONS

Many search tasks such as travel planning, making large purchases or job searches can span multiple search session extending over hours, days, or even weeks. The research reported in this paper is aimed at better understanding, characterizing, and automatically predicting search tasks that will be continued in the future – a task complementary to that of identifying previous related search sessions after the fact. We first annotated a query log from Bing to identify the types of search intents, motivations, and topics associated with search tasks that are continued. We then developed new features of search engagement and focus in search sessions, which we use as input for prediction. Finally we developed effective prediction algorithms that significantly outperform both the previous state-of-the-art method, as well as the ability of human judges to predict search continuation.

Our analysis of the task continuation yielded effective features that allow our prediction method to significantly outperform both a state-of-the-art baseline and predictions based on human judgments. We identified the groups of features (user prior history and task engagement) that most strongly predict task continuation. We also identified individual task characteristics, such as time span, user focus, and task start time that are most strongly correlated with continuation.

Future research directions include studying task continuations occurring beyond the one-week time frame studied here, as well as looking back further in time to build more complete historic profiles of users' search interests given the observed value of such historic information for task continuation prediction. We are also interested in applying task continuation predictions to improve search result ranking (e.g., by personalizing the results to the active task and not to the whole user's profile); and in better supporting searchers in resuming tasks (e.g., if a task is likely to be continued, saving the results already found for more convenient access once the task is continued). Thus, the work presented here forms an important advance towards developing a more personalized and intelligent solution for long-running, complex tasks – a key challenge for the information retrieval community.

7. ACKNOWLEDGMENTS

We thank Alexander Kotov and Jaime Teevan for collecting and labeling earlier data for this paper, and Dan Liebling and Shane Williams for assistance with data processing. We also thank Filip Radlinski for insights on quantifying complexity of search tasks.

REFERENCES

[1] E. Agichtein, E. Brill and S. Dumais. Improving Web search ranking by incorporating user behavior information. *SIGIR '06*, 19–26, 2006.

[2] L. M. Aiello, D. Donato, U. Ozertem, and F. Menczer. Behavior-driven clustering of queries into topics. *CIKM '11*, 1373–1382, 2011.

[3] A. Aula, N. Jhaveri and M. Käki. Information search and re-access strategies of experienced Web users. *WWW '05*, 583–592, 2005.

[4] J.T. Austin and J.B. Vancouver. Goal constructs in psychology: Structure, process, and content. *Psychological Bulletin, 120(3)*: 338–375, 1996.

[5] P.N. Bennett, K. Svore and S.T. Dumais. Classification-enhanced ranking. *WWW '10*, 111–120, 2010.

[6] A. Broder. A taxonomy of Web search. *SIGIR Forum, 32(2)*: 3–10, 2002.

[7] H. Cao, D. Jiang, J. Pei, Q. He, Z. Liao, E. Chen and H. Li. Context-aware query suggestion by mining click-through and session data. *KDD '08*, 875–883, 2008.

[8] Y.-S. Chang, K.-Y. He, S. Yu and W.-H. Lu. Identifying user goals from Web search results. *WWW '06*, 1038–1041, 2006.

[9] M. Czerwinski, E. Horvitz and S. Wilhite. A diary study of task switching and interruptions. *CHI '04*, 175–182, 2004.

[10] D. Donato, F. Bonchi, T. Chi and Y. Maarek. Do you want to take notes? Identifying research missions in Yahoo! Search Pad. *WWW '10*, 321–330, 2010.

[11] D. Downey, S.T. Dumais, D. Liebling and E. Horvitz. Understanding the relationship between searchers' queries and information goals. *CIKM'08*, 449–458, 2008.

[12] S. Dumais, G. Buscher and E. Cutrell. Individual differences in gaze patterns for web search. *IIiX '10*, 185–194, 2010.

[13] S. Fox, K. Karnawat, M. Mydland, S. T. Dumais and T. White. Evaluating implicit measures to improve the search experience. *TOIS, 23(2)*: 147–168, 2005.

[14] J. Friedman. MART boosted decision trees: Greedy function approximation: a gradient boosting machine. *Annals of Statistics, 25(5)*: 1189–1232, 2001.

[15] J. Friedman, T. Hastie and T. Tibshirani. Additive logistic regression: A statistical view of boosting. *Annals of Statistics, 28(2)*: 337–407, 2000.

[16] A. Hassan, R. Jones and K. Klinkner. Beyond DCG: User behavior as a predictor of a successful search. *WSDM '09*, 221–230, 2010.

[17] A. Hassan, Y. Song and L. He. A task level metric for measuring web search satisfaction and its application on improving relevance estimation. *CIKM'11*, 125–134, 2011.

[18] V. Hu, M. Stone, J. Pedersen and R.W. White. Effects of search success on search engine re-use. *CIKM'11*, 1841–1846, 2011.

[19] R. Jones and K. Klinkner. Beyond the session timeout: Automatic hierarchical segmentation of search topics in query logs. *CIKM '08*, 699–708, 2008.

[20] M. Kellar, C. Watters and M. Shepherd. A field study characterizing Web-based information-seeking tasks. *JASIST, 58(7)*: 999–1018, 2007.

[21] A. Kotov, P.N. Bennett, R.W. White, S.T. Dumais, and J. Teevan. Modeling and analysis of cross-session search tasks. *SIGIR'11*, 5–14, 2011.

[22] U. Lee, Z. Liu and J. Cho. Automatic indentification of user goals in Web search. *WWW '05*, 391–400, 2005.

[23] Y. Li and N.J. Belkin. A faceted approach to conceptualizing tasks in information seeking. *IP&M*, 44(6): 1822–1837, 2008.

[24] J. Liu and N.J. Belkin. Personalizing information retrieval for multi-session tasks: The roles of task stage and task type. *SIGIR '10*, 26–33, 2010.

[25] B. MacKay and C. Watters. Exploring multi-session Web tasks. *CHI '08*, 1187–1196, 2008.

[26] Q. Mei, K. Klinkner, R. Kumar and A. Tomkins. An analysis framework for search sequences. *CIKM '09*, 1991–94, 2009.

[27] D. Morris, M. Ringel Morris and G. Venolia. SearchBar: A search-centric Web history for task resumption and information re-finding. *CHI '08*, 1207–1216, 2008.

[28] B. Piwowarski and H. Zaragoza. Predictive user click models based on click-through history. *CIKM '07*, 175–182, 2007.

[29] F. Radlinski and T. Joachims. Query chains: Learning to rank from implicit feedback. *KDD '05*, 239–248, 2005.

[30] F. Radlinski, M. Szummer and N. Craswell. Inferring query intent from reformulations and clicks. *WWW '10*, 1171–1172, 2010.

[31] J.J. Randolph. Free-marginal multirater Kappa (multirater K free): an alternative to Fleiss' fixed-marginal multirater Kappa. *JULIS'05*, 2005.

[32] D.E. Rose and D. Levinson. Understanding user goals in Web search. *WWW '04*, 13–19, 2004.

[33] M.D. Smucker, J. Allan and B. Carterette. A comparison of statistical significance tests for information retrieval evaluation. *CIKM'07*, 623-632, 2007.

[34] D. Sontag, K. Collins-Thompson, P.N. Bennett, R.W. White, S.T. Dumais and B. Billerbeck. Probabilistic models for personalizing web search. *WSDM '12*, 433–442, 2012.

[35] A. Spink. Multitasking information behavior and information task switching: an exploratory study. *J. Documentation, 60(4)*: 336–351, 2004.

[36] B. Tan, X. Shen and C. Zhai. Mining long-term search history to improve search accuracy. *KDD '06*, 718–723, 2006.

[37] J. Teevan, E. Adar, R. Jones and M.A.S. Potts. Information re-retrieval: Repeat queries in Yahoo's logs. *SIGIR '07*, 151–158, 2007.

[38] E.G. Toms, L. Freund, R. Kopak and J.C. Bartlett. The effect of task domain on search. *CASON'03*, 303-312, 2003.

[39] R.W. White, P. Bailey and L. Chen. Predicting user interests from contextual information. *SIGIR '09*, 363–370, 2009.

[40] R.W. White and S.M. Drucker. Investigating behavioral variability in Web search. *WWW '07*, 21–30, 2007.

[41] R.W. White, S.T. Dumais, and J. Teevan. 2009. Characterizing the influence of domain expertise on Web search behavior. *WSDM '10*, 132–141.

[42] B. Xiang, D. Jiang, J. Pei, X. Sun, E. Chen, and H. Li. Context-aware ranking in Web search. *SIGIR'10*, 451–458, 2010.

Multi-Aspect Query Summarization by Composite Query*

Wei Song[1], Qing Yu[2], Zhiheng Xu[3], Ting Liu[1], Sheng Li[1], Ji-Rong Wen[2]
[1]School of Computer Science and Technology, Harbin Institute of Technology, Harbin, 150001, China
{wsong, tliu, lisheng}@ir.hit.edu.cn
[2] Microsoft Research Asia, Beijing, 100190, China
{qingyu, jrwen}@microsoft.com
[3] Institute of Automation, Chinese Academy of Sciences, Beijing, 100190, China
xuzhiheng19881130@gmail.com

ABSTRACT

Conventional search engines usually return a ranked list of web pages in response to a query. Users have to visit several pages to locate the relevant parts. A promising future search scenario should involve: (1) understanding user intents; (2) providing relevant *information* directly to satisfy searchers' needs, as opposed to relevant *pages*. In this paper, we present a paradigm for dealing with informational queries. We aim to summarize a query's information from different aspects. Query aspects are aligned to user intents. The generated summaries for query aspects are expected to be both specific and informative, so that users can easily and quickly find relevant information. Specifically, we use a *"Composite Query for Summarization"* method, which leverages the search engine to proactively gather information by submitting multiple composite queries according to the original query and its aspects. In this way, we could get more relevant information for each query aspect and roughly classify information. By comparative mining the search results of different composite queries, it is able to identify query (dependent) aspect words, which help to generate more specific and informative summaries. The experimental results on two data sets, Wikipedia and TREC ClueWeb2009, are encouraging. Our method outperforms two baseline methods on generating informative summaries.

Categories and Subject Descriptors

H.3.m [**Information Storage and Retrieval**]: Miscellaneous

General Terms

Algorithms, Experimentation

*This work was done when the first and third authors were visiting Microsoft Research Asia

Permission to make digital or hard copies of all or part of this work for personal or classroom use is granted without fee provided that copies are not made or distributed for profit or commercial advantage and that copies bear this notice and the full citation on the first page. To copy otherwise, to republish, to post on servers or to redistribute to lists, requires prior specific permission and/or a fee.
SIGIR'12, August 12–16, 2012, Portland, Oregon, USA.
Copyright 2012 ACM 978-1-4503-1472-5/12/08 ...$15.00.

Keywords

Query aspect, Query summarization, Composite query, Mixture Model

1. INTRODUCTION

Nowadays, accessing information on the Internet through search engines has become a fundamental life activity. Current web search engines usually provide a ranked list of URLs to answer a query. This type of information access does a good job for dealing with simple navigational queries by leading users to specific websites. However, it is becoming increasingly insufficient for queries with vague or complex information need. Many queries serve just as the start of an exploration of related information space. Users may want to know about a topic from multiple aspects. Organizing the web content relevant to a query according to user intents would benefit user exploration. In addition, a list of URLs couldn't directly satisfy user information need. Users have to visit many pages and try to find relevant parts within long pages, since the information may be scattered across documents. The long-standing goal of search engines should be providing relevant *information*, as opposed to relevant *documents*, to directly satisfy searchers' needs.

This paper presents a novel search paradigm that the system should automatically discover information and present an informative overview for a query from multiple aspects. We target on dealing with informational queries. A query represents a centric topic, and the query aspects are aligned to user intents covering diverse information needs. The query aspects could be specified explicitly by users through an interface or automatically mined from search logs or other resources [4, 18, 22, 25]. In this paper, we use simple methods to do aspect mining and mainly focus on ***multi-aspect oriented query summarization***: given a query and a set of aspects, generate a summary for each query aspect, which is expected to provide specific and informative content to users directly and helps for further exploration. Figure 1 shows an example of the system output.

We further formulate the multi-aspect oriented query summarization into 2 phases: *information gathering* and *summary generation*. Different from traditional text summarization where a set of documents to be summarized is given as a system input, we propose a *"Composite Query for Summarization"* method, which leverages the search engine to proactively gather related information. In addition to using the search result of the original query, we also composite a set of new queries and submit them to the search engine to

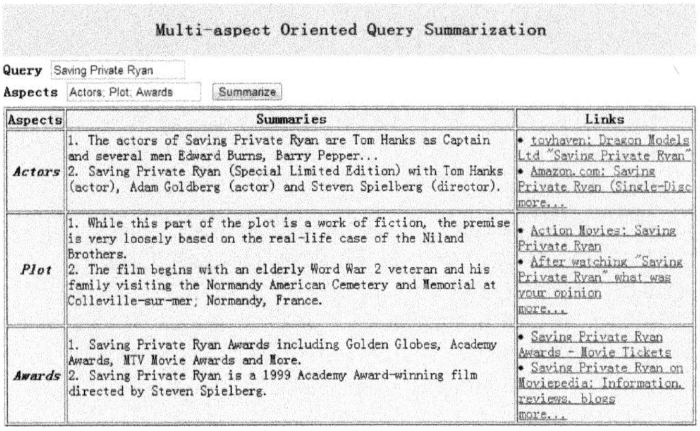

Figure 1: An example output of multi-aspect oriented query summarization.

collect query aspect related information. For example, by concatenating the original query and the keywords of an aspect as a query, we are able to get query dependent aspect information; by submitting the aspect keywords only as a query, we could get query independent aspect information. Our motivations are:

First, the search result of the original query may not contain enough information for all aspects that users care about, because the search engine returns documents only considering whether a document is relevant to the query keywords, rather than its aspects.

Second, for better aspect oriented exploration, the information for different query aspects should be as orthogonal as possible. It is important to distinguish the aspect specific information from the general information about the whole query. By using the composite queries, we could get more specific information for each aspect.

The flexible information gathering also helps for *summary generation* phase. By comparing the search results of different types of composite queries, query (dependent) aspect words can be identified without complex natural language processing, based on which more specific and informative summaries could be generated,

The contributions of this paper can be summarized as follows:

- We formulate the multi-aspect based query summarization task. In this scenario, the system proactively discovers information and aims to provide *multiple di mensional* and *direct* information seeking in response to informational queries.

- We propose a *"Composite Query for Summarization"* method for proactive information gathering, which is a key point for our task and differs from traditional search result organization and textual summarization.

- We emphasize generating specific and informative summaries to directly address searchers' needs on different aspects. To achieve this, we propose a simple method to identify query aspect dependent words by comparing the search results of different types of composite queries.

- We conduct experiments on both real web queries and large-scale pseudo queries based on Wikipedia[1]. Automatic evaluation and human judgements are used for measuring the quality of generated summaries.

The rest of the paper is organized as follows. First, we discuss related work in Section 2. In Section 3, we define the query aspect and briefly introduce optional approaches for query aspect mining. In Section 4, we detail the proposed "composite query" based method for both information gathering and aspect oriented summary generation. After that, we report our experimental results in Section 5. Section 6 states our conclusions.

2. RELATED WORK

2.1 Search Result Organization

Exploratory search becomes a new frontier in the search domain, which aims to provide additional support for information seeking beyond simple lookup [24]. Recent work has shown that well-organized search results are helpful for information exploration. For example, search result clustering [9, 11, 27], categorizing [1], facet based information exploration [6], representative queries [23] and tag clouds [10] are adopted for search result navigation. Clustering based approaches automatically group similar search result documents together [9, 11, 27]. Search result documents can also be classified into a manually constructed category taxonomy [1]. But the fixed hierarchy often lacks of flexibility to describe various user information needs. Faceted search aims to offer the ability for searchers to filter search results by specifying desired attributes [6]. However, the facets are usually pre-defined for some specific domain so that it is difficult to apply it to web search. Though most of the above methods organize search result documents into various aspects and improve user experience for information exploration, the content are still presented at document level, and users can't get relevant information directly.

2.2 Document Summarization

Single document summarization techniques have been successfully applied in web search engines (snippet generation) [19, 20]. A span of text gives users a first sight of the topics of a document. For efficiency, sentence extraction strategy is used for generating query dependent summaries [5].

Comparing with single document summarization, multi-document summarization is expected to generate a global picture for a set of documents which is given as input [15, 26]. Recently researchers utilize latent topics for multiple document summarization. For example, subtopics from the narrative of a topic (a description of a topic, which is provided by the DUC summarization track) is used to enhance summarization [17]. Wang uses topic model to extract subtopics and select sentences by topic words [21]. However, the latent topics used in these papers are usually mined unsupervised. As a result, the topics may fit to the data collection, rather than align to user intents.

Some work makes use of predefined aspects to provide (sentiment) summarization on reviews or comments [7, 14]. Our work is also inspired by [13], which incorporates user interaction into the summarization process. Given a corpus of documents, users predefine their interested facets and the

[1]http://en.wikipedia.org/

Figure 2: A snipping of returned documents for query "Saving Private Ryan" and two typical services provided by Bing Search.

system provides summaries according to the facets. The authors evaluate it on online reviews and Gene corpus (which are relatively "clean" data sets). In contrast, we focus on summarizing user intents related to a query rather than a given corpus. They don't consider the informativeness of the generated summaries, while one of our goals is to provide direct information to users.

Our work is based on query aspects but differs from existing work in several points. First, in our framework, query aspects could be mined from any resources but not limited to a set of documents to be summarized. Second, the traditional summarization task treats the documents as a given input to the system. However, in our scenario, we separate the information gathering and summarization generation phases. In this way, we view the whole web as a corpus and could proactively collect more related information for summarization. Third, we aim to generate both specific and informative content for each query aspect. Therefore, users could get relevant information directly.

3. QUERY ASPECT

Multi-aspect oriented query summarization depends on query aspects. In this section, we define the query aspect and briefly discuss query aspect mining methods both in literature and in realistic way.

An aspect represents a distinct information need relevant to the original query. Recently, various methods have been proposed for automatically discovering query intents [2, 4, 22, 25]. The NTCIR-9 Intent Task was organized to explore and evaluate the technologies of mining and satisfying different user intents for a vague query [18]. In these work, a query aspect is represented in different ways, such as a set of search queries related to the original query [2, 25], a set of query qualifiers [22] or a single intent string [18]. These definitions are in fact very similar. The main differences are: (1) Whether distinguish the original query and the query qualifier. (2) Whether select an exemplar (label) to represent a set of queries related to the same intent.

Inspired by previous work, we define an **aspect** as a query qualifier - keywords that are added to an **original query** to form a specific user intent. For example, "reviews" and "actors" could be seen as aspects for a movie. In this work, we mainly focus on multi-aspect oriented summary generation and use very simple method to mine query aspects. However, any existing method for mining query aspects could be incorporated.We can also use the services provided by search engines to get approximate query aspects. For example, search engines provide "query suggestion" or "related searches" features. Figure 2 shows a snipping of the search result from Bing Search page for query "Saving Private Ryan", a famous movie. Thus, the aspects could be easily identified using simple rules from related searches. We could also predefine some aspect templates for certain query classes, such as movie, travel, music, people, etc. We leave this as future work.

4. MULTI-ASPECT ORIENTED QUERY SUMMARIZATION

Now, we suppose the aspects are given and aim to summarize a query according to its different aspects. We expect to generate both *specific* and *informative* summary for each aspect instead of a set of documents so that the users could get relevant information directly. First, we explain the meaning of **specific** and **informative** by an example. Suppose that for the query "Saving Private Ryan", one of the user information needs is to know the "actors" of this movie. There are some candidate sentences:

(i) *"A movie page covers information about ne Steven Spielberg movie 'Saving Private Ryan' including actors film makers and behind the scenes "*

(ii) *"Saving Private Ryan cast are listed here including the Saving Private Ryan actresses and actors featured in the film "*

(iii) *"The actors of Saving Private Ryan are Tom anks as Captain and several men Ed ard Burns Barry Pep per "*

All the three sentences contain certain information about the aspect "actors". The first one talks about the general information about the query. It is Not specific to the desired aspect. The second sentence focuses on the desired aspect, however, it does not provide relevant information directly, only gives navigational information. We say it is specific but Not informative. The third sentence should be a good candidate which provides direct answers to the desired aspect, i.e., the names of the actors. It is both specific and informative.

As the example shows, the challenges of this task include: (1) Distinguish aspect specific information from general query information. (2) Identify informative content instead of navigational information only. We take the *Composite Query for Summarization* method to deal with above issue, which consists of 2 phases: information gathering and summary generation. First, we proactively get aspect specific information using composite queries. Then a mixture model is used to model different types of words which present query common information or aspect specific information. Finally, we rank the candidate sentences based on the mixture model and the redundancy in search results for generating summaries.

4.1 Information Gathering

Existing work on text summarization doesn't pay much attention on how to collect data. A natural way is to use query search result. However, there may be not enough information for certain query aspects, if we only use the search result of the original query. For example, some users wonder whether movie "Saving Private Ryan" tells a true story, but few top documents in the search result of "Saving Private Ryan" discuss this topic.

We present a composite query based method for information gathering. Formally, we denote the original query as Q and an aspect as A_k. For example, Q refers to the original query "Saving Private Ryan" and A_k refers to one aspect "actors". In information gathering phase, we composite a new query by concatenating the original query and the aspect words, denoted as $Q + A_k$. The composite query is "Saving Private Ryan actors". Therefore, we can submit the composite query to the search engine to get top ranked documents. Comparing with the search result of the original query, the search result of the composite query is much more specific for the query aspect. Also, we can submit the aspect A_k itself to the search engine to get information about the aspect which is query independent.

For a query with K aspects, we have a set of composite queries $\{Q, Q + A_1, ..., Q + A_K, A_1, ..., A_K\}$. We use the top returned documents for each composite query. The search result of Q (denoted as C_Q) provides overall information about the query; the search result of $Q + A_k$ (denoted as C_{Q+A_k}) provides the information about the aspect A_k of the query Q. The search result of A_k (denoted as C_{A_k}) provides information about the aspect itself which is query independent. The idea of using composite queries is straightforward and the benefits are two folded: (1) We collect more aspect related data which may be not contained in original query's search result. (2) The search engine helps us roughly classify information according to the query aspects.

Based on the collected data for query aspects, we identify aspect words by comparing the search results of different types of composite queries. These words are then used for assisting summary generation.

4.2 Summary Generation

4.2.1 Modeling Search Result

We assume the desired information for query aspect A_k is embedded in collection C_{Q+A_k}, which consists of 3 kinds of information: query general information, aspect information, irrelevant information. Correspondingly, the words in search results could be divided into 3 categories:

Query Common Words: They tend to occur frequently across multiple aspects, such as "movie", "TV", "IMDB" for "Saving Private Ryan".

Query Aspect Words: These words provide information for an aspect, such as "cast", "list" and "Tom Hanks" for the aspect "actors".

Global Background Words: These words distribute heavily on the Web. Mostly, they are stop words or high frequency non-discriminative words.

Figure 3 shows 3 types of words and their relationship in search results of the original query and the composite

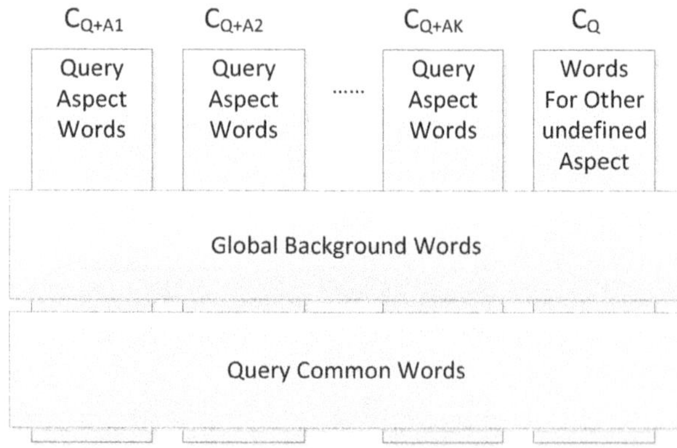

Figure 3: The illustration of the relationship between the search results of different composite queries and different types of words.

queries. We assume that the query aspect words describing the aspect A_k of query Q will occur more in C_{Q+A_k}, while the query common words will occur frequently across multiple aspects. Based on the collected data by using composite queries, the observations support the assumption. Therefore, we adopt a mixture model to describe each type of words. Formally, θ_k represents the *query aspect ords* model for aspect A_k. θ_B represents the *query common ords* model. θ_G represents the *global background ords* model which is to draw globally high frequency terms. All these models are multinomial probability distributions over vocabulary.

The collection C_{Q+A_k} could be generated by the mixture model. Each word w in C_{Q+A_k} is generated according to:

$$p_k(w) = \lambda_G p(w|\theta_G) + (1 - \lambda_G) \times (\alpha_B p(w|\theta_B) + (1 - \alpha_B) p(w|\theta_k)) \quad (1)$$

where $p_k(w)$ represents the probability of a term occurrence w in collection C_{Q+A_k}, λ_G and α_B are fixed parameters. The generative process could be seen as 2 steps: first decide whether this word is from θ_G, and then decide it comes from θ_B or θ_k. To estimate the aspect word model θ_k, we first estimate θ_G and θ_B. θ_G is estimated using maximum likelihood estimator based on document frequency which is computed on a large collection of web pages. θ_B is estimated by combining the search results of the original query and all query aspects, i.e., $C_Q \cup \{C_{Q+A_k}\}$. We use C_Q to catch the general content of the query and the unknown aspects which are not defined explicitly or mined already. θ_B could be estimated according to:

$$p(w|\theta_B) = \frac{tf(w, C_Q) + \sum_k tf(w, C_{Q+A_k})}{\sum_{w'} (tf(w', C_Q) + \sum_k tf(w', C_{Q+A_k}))} \quad (2)$$

where $tf(w, \cdot)$ represents the term frequency in a collection. After deriving $p(w|\theta_B)$ and $p(w|\theta_G)$, $p(w|\theta_k)$ could be estimated using the expectation maximization (EM) algorithm [3] by maximizing the log-likelihood of the collection C_{Q+A_k}:

$$L(C_{Q+A_k}) = \sum_w \log tf(w, C_{Q+A_k}) p_k(w) \quad (3)$$

For each term w in C_{Q+A_k}, the updating formulas of the E-step and the M-step are shown below:

E-Step:

$$p_w(z=G) = \frac{\lambda p(w|\theta_G)}{\lambda p(w|\theta_G)+(1-\lambda)((1-\alpha_B)p(w|\theta_k)+\alpha_B p(w|\theta_B))}$$

$$p_w(z=k) = \frac{(1-\alpha_B)p(w|\theta_k)}{(1-\alpha_B)p(w|\theta_k)+\alpha_B p(w|\theta_B)}$$

M-Step:

$$p(w|\theta_k) = \frac{tf(w\ C_{Q+A_k})(1-p_w(z=G))p_w(z=k)}{\sum_{w'} tf(w'\ C_{Q+A_k})(1-p_{w'}(z=G))p_{w'}(z=k)}$$

where z is a latent variable introduced to represent which type a word is assigned to. $p(z=G)$ and $p(z=k)$ are corresponding probabilities. In this way, we distinguish the *query aspect ords* from the *query common ords*. The words with high probabilities in θ_k represent the specific query aspect better.

Next, we consider to identify more informative aspect words. We divide the query aspect words into 2 categories: *query dependent aspect ords* which provide direct information for the aspect, such as "Tom Hanks" and "Edward Burns" for aspect "actors"; *query independent aspect ords* which are query independent and reflect the characteristics of the aspect itself, like "actor", "actress", and "cast" for aspect "actors". We distinguish these 2 types of query aspect words by the assumption that query dependent aspect words occur in $C_{Q+\ \ _k}$, and query independent aspect words occur in both $C_{Q+\ \ _k}$ and $C_{\ \ _k}$. The $C_{\ \ _k}$ is the search result of the aspect A_k itself, which contains many words related to the aspect. However, these words can be used for any query with such aspect, but don't bring direct information for a specific query. So we identify query dependent aspect words as $QDW_k = \{t|t \in C_{Q+\ \ _k}$ and $t \notin C_{\ \ _k}\}$. The words occur in $C_{Q+\ \ _k}$ that suggests they are related to the query aspect, but don't occur in $C_{\ \ _k}$ that indicates they are query dependent. The relative importance of the query dependent aspect words could be read out from $p(w|\theta_k)$.

4.2.2 Sentence Selection

To summarize aspect A_k for query Q, we extract sentences from the content of the search result documents in $C_{Q+\ \ _k} \cup C_Q$. The candidate sentences are then ranked based on their specificity, redundancy and informativeness. The top ranked sentences are used as a summary for the desired aspect.

Candidate sentence filtering based on specificity. Only part of the sentences within the search result are related to the desired aspect. We select a candidate sentence for a desired aspect only if it is closer to the desired aspect than to any other aspects. To measure this, we classify each sentence to one of the aspects:

$$k^* = \underset{i \in \{1\ 2\ \ldots\ K\ B\ G\}}{\text{argmax}} \prod_{w \in s} p(w|\theta_i) \qquad (4)$$

where θ_i is an estimated *query aspect ords* model or the *query common ords* model or the *global background ords* model. A sentence within $C_{Q+\ \ _k} \cup C_Q$ is chosen as a candidate only if k^* equals to k. Thus, all the selected candidate sentences are more specific to the desired aspect.

Sentence clustering. The candidate sentences are selected from multi-documents. Redundancy is particular important. On one hand, the same information conveyed by sentences from different documents indicates its importance. On the other hand, it is not good to show duplicate sentences to users. Due to the above reasons, the candidate sentences are grouped into clusters according to lexical features. We adopt a hierarchical clustering approach. Each single sentence is initiated as a cluster. If two clusters are close enough, they are merged. This procedure repeats until the smallest distance between all remaining clusters is larger than a threshold. Edit distance is used to measure the distance between two sentences. We use $U(s)$ to represent the cluster, which the sentence s belong to. The size of this cluster $U(s).size$ indicates the popularity of this cluster or the redundancy of the information this cluster conveys.

Measuring informativeness. Since informative summaries are expected, we measure the informativeness of a sentence based on:

$$info(s|\theta_k) = (1-\beta) \sum_{\substack{w \in s \\ w \in QDW_k}} p(w|\theta_k) + \beta \sum_{\substack{w \in s \\ w \notin QDW_k}} p(w|\theta_k) \qquad (5)$$

where QDW_k represents the query dependent aspect words for aspect A_k; β is a parameter to tune the impact of the query dependent aspect words.

Sentence ranking. In each cluster, we select one sentence with highest $info(s|\theta_k)$ as the exemplar to represent the cluster. The exemplars selected from all clusters are ranked according to $Weight_k(s)$:

$$Weight_k(s) = log(1 + U(s).size) \times info(s|\theta_k) \qquad (6)$$

5. EXPERIMENTS

In the experiments, we assume the query aspects are given and focus on evaluating the quality of generated summaries for query aspects. The data sets we used already contain aspects for each query. Our method and baseline methods take both query and aspects as input.

5.1 Data Sets

To the best of our knowledge, few public data set can be used to evaluate the multi-aspect oriented query summarization. We constructed two data sets from well-known data sources, Wikepedia and TREC. We will introduce the data sets and experimental results in following sections.

5.1.1 Wikipedia Data

Each topic page in Wikipedia is composed of a title and a list of sub sections, which describe the topic from different aspects. For example, the title of a page is "Saving Private Ryan", and the page includes subheadings like "Plot", "Cast" and "Production". In our experiments, we treated the title of a page as a query, the meaningful subheadings (top level) as query aspects. We filtered out the meaningless subheadings like "Notes", "References" and "Further Readings" by rules. We also filtered out pages with less than 3 or larger than 10 aspects to avoid noise. We used the textual content under a subheading as the golden reference for the corresponding aspect. In all, we sampled 1000 pages (queries) from an English Wikipedia dump which was collected in January 2011. The statistics of the sampled data is listed in Table 1.

Table 1: The statistic of Wikipedia data set

Topics	1000
Average Length of Topics (words)	2.15
Average Aspects per Topic	5.15
Average Aspect Length (words)	798

We divided the sampled data into develop set and test set. The develop set containing 100 queries was used for parameter tuning. While the test set, which contains 900 queries, was used for comparing performance of different systems. Note that, since our method uses the search results of a search engine which may give Wikipedia pages as returned documents, we removed Wikipedia pages from the search results when doing experiments.

5.1.2 TREC 2009 Web Track Data

The trec data is widely used for search related experiment evaluation. We use the public available query set of TREC 2009 Web track. One goal of TREC 2009 Web Track is evaluating the search result diversity. The data set includes 50 topics and each topic has 3 to 8 manually edited subtopics to be covered. Each subtopic is a description of an information need. Figure 4 shows an example topic provided by TREC 2009 Web track.

We treated each topic as a query and derived query aspects from its subtopic descriptions by simple rules. We first extracted all nouns from a description. Then we excluded those terms which occur in original query, then used the remaining terms as an aspect. For example, for the query "Obama family tree", "mother information" was used as one aspect. In all, we got 50 queries and 4.9 aspects for each query on average.

```
<topic number="1" type="faceted">
  <query>obama family tree</query>
  <description>Find information on President Barack Obama's family
  history, including genealogy, national origins, places and dates of
  birth, etc.
  </description>
  <subtopic number="1" type="nav">
    Find the TIME magazine photo essay "Barack Obama's Family Tree".
  </subtopic>
  <subtopic number="2" type="inf">
    Where did Barack Obama's parents and grandparents come from?
  </subtopic>
  <subtopic number="3" type="inf">
    Find biographical information on Barack Obama's mother.
  </subtopic>
</topic>
```

Figure 4: An example topic in TREC 2009 web track.

5.2 Baselines

The proposed algorithm is denoted as `Q-Composite`. We compare it with 2 baselines. Baseline 1 is based on Ling et al [13], denoted as `Ling-2008`. This method first estimates an aspect prior distribution based on term co-occurrence in the corpus, then integrates the priors into a topic model, finally ranks sentences according to the distance between sentence language model and the aspect models. It is proved very effective for mining faceted summaries on relatively clean and formal data sets, like Gene corpus. But it is not oriented to the web search. Like traditional text summarization tasks, they just use a collection of documents related to the centric topic for summarization. We implemented this method and applied it to the multiple aspect based query summarization as a baseline. The aspect model of `Ling-2008` was estimated on the search result of each original query and the sentences for each aspect were extracted from the search results of both the original query and the composite query, which was the same as the input of our method.The second baseline is based on the top sentences in snippets, which are provided by a search engine for each composite query $Q+A_k$, denoted as `Snippet`. The number of the top sentences depends on the total summarization length limit. Though it is simple, it is very strong. These snippets are selected from the top relevant documents of the composite query, so that they are more likely specific to the query aspect. In addition, most snippet generation algorithms are based on single document summarization method, which tend to extract the sentences containing most relevant terms.

5.3 Parameter Settings

There are several parameters in our method. We tuned the parameters of our method and baselines on the develop set. In our experiments, λ_G was set to 0.95 in order to get more discriminative words. α_B was set to 0.8 to balance query common information and aspect specific information. The threshold used in sentence merging procedure was set to 0.7. The parameter β was set to 0.0, which means to rank sentences based on query dependent aspect words only. For each composite query, we used the top 50 documents from the search result. The words occurring in less than 3 documents were discarded.

5.4 Experiment Design and Evaluation

Due to the different characteristics of the two data sets, we adopt different evaluation strategies and metrics.

5.4.1 Evaluation on Wikipedia Data

For Wikipedia data, we generate the summaries based on real web data. We send both the original query and the composite queries to a commercial search engine and get the search result documents and snippets. For efficiency, we train the model using the snippets and extract sentences from the content of the documents. We use the ROUGE tool for evaluation on Wikipedia Data. ROUGE is a well-known tool for evaluating both single and multi-document summarization [12]. Basically, it is a recall-like metric. A higher ROUGE value means that more useful information is found. ROUGE-1 metric has been proved highly consistent with human judgements, so we take it for evaluation in our experiments. At evaluating time, the golden reference for each aspect is taken from the content of corresponding sub-heading in a Wikipedia page. Since the extracted sentences for summarization have different length, we let each system generate top sentences and the first 200, 400 and 600 words are used for evaluation.

5.4.2 Evaluation on TREC 2009 Data

For TREC data set, we generate summaries from the corpus provided by TREC rather than the whole Web, namely the ClueWeb09. Our method depends on the search engine's search result, so we need index ClueWeb09 and build a s-mall search engine. We use a simple ranking function to give search result based on BM25 [16], anchor text and stat-

Table 2: **Labeling guide and examples. The query is "Saving Private Ryan" and the aspect is "Actors"**

Label	Gain Value (Level)	Description	Examples
Informative and specific	5	The sentence focuses on the desired aspect and provides useful information which can help user to know something about the query aspect.	The actors of "Saving Private Ryan" include Tom Hanks, Tom Sizemor, Edward Burns.
Informative but not specific	4	The sentence conveys multi-aspect information about the query. And it does provide useful information for the desired aspect.	Saving Private Ryan is a 1998 American war film, directed by Steven Spielberg and it follows Tom Hanks as Captain John H. Miller.
Specific but not informative	2	The sentence talks about the desired aspect but doesn't provide much detail information.	Saving Private Ryan Cast and Details on TVGuide.com.
Not about this aspect but about the query	1	It provides some information about some aspects of the query but not related to the desired aspect.	Saving Private Ryan is a 1998 American epic war film set during the invasion of Normandy in World War II.
Not about this query	0	The sentence does not talk about the query.	Alphabetized and searchable index of real and fictional events, cast, and places related to films.

ic rank features. It generates snippets by selecting the top sentences which contain the most query terms.

Since the data does not provide golden reference at sentence level, we have to judge the quality of generated sentences manually. So it is necessary to clarify the standard for assessment. Ideally, a good query summary should make users get the desired information directly. In our scenario, we assess the summaries from two perspectives: specific and informative. First, we hope the summary can give specific information about an aspect rather than a general description covering multiple aspects. Second, it should give more direct information in contrast to navigational information so that users spend less time to obtain information.

Based on this standard, we asked labelers to label the generated sentences for 50 queries. For each system and each query aspect, the labelers had to evaluate the top 3 ranked sentences. Each sentence was assigned a gain value according to the guidelines shown in Table 2, which describes the labeling standard by using an example. Note that we skip the gain value 3, because we think that the "informative and specific" and "informative but not specific" sentences are useful to users for getting direct information, should be given higher bonus than other levels. The topic descriptions, as shown in Figure 4, were also presented to labelers as reference.

The normalized Discounted Cumulative Gain (nDCG) [8] is used to evaluate the performance. The nDCG is a metric that gives higher weights to well ranked objects. The average nDCG over all the test query aspects is used to measure the overall performance.

5.5 Experimental Results and Discussion

In this session, we present the experimental results on two data sets and analyze the performance of different systems and the impacts of key factors.

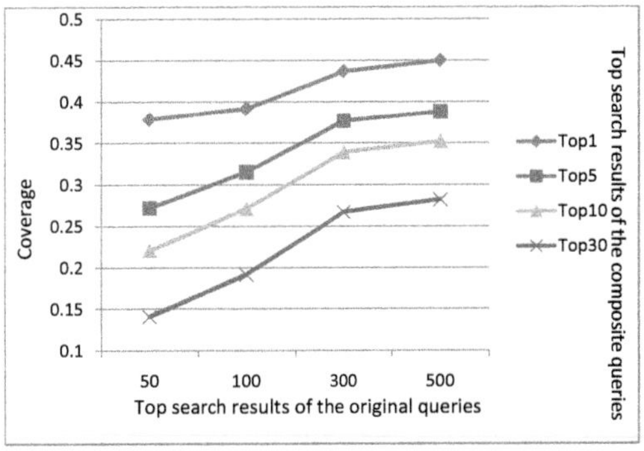

Figure 5: The average coverage of the search results of the original queries over the composite aspect queries.

5.5.1 Coverage of the Search Results of the Original Queries

Previous work focuses on organizing the search result of the original query into multiple aspects. We argue that the search result of an original query may not have enough information covering all query aspects. To verify this, we conduct a simple experiment to measure the coverage of the search results of the original queries on the corresponding composite queries. We sampled 100 queries from the Wikipedia data set. For each original query Q, we retrieved the set of top N URLs from a search engine, denoted as S_Q^N. For each composite query $Q + A_k$, we retrieved the set of top M URLs from the same search engine, denoted as $S_{Q+A_k}^M$. We measured the coverage of S_Q^N over $S_{Q+A_k}^M$, i.e., $\frac{|S_Q^N \cap S_{Q+A_k}^M|}{M}$.

The average coverage over all queries' aspects is shown in Figure 5. Intuitively, the search result of $Q + A_k$ should describe the query aspect better. However, the top documents in $S^{M}_{Q+\ k}$ rarely appear in S^{N}_{Q}. For example, more than 60% top 1 documents retrieved by composite queries are not in the top 100 returned documents for the corresponding original queries. When considering more top documents in $S^{M}_{Q+\ k}$, the coverage is even smaller. These observations indicate that, at the document level, the search results of the original queries couldn't cover most relevant information related to query aspects. By using composite queries, we could get much more relevant information. Next, we evaluate the quality of the fine-grained information units generated by systems.

5.5.2 System Comparisons

Figure 6 shows the performance comparisons of different systems on Wikipedia test set, varying the word number of summary length limit. We can see that `Q-Composite` outperforms both `Ling-2008` and `Snippet`. The results on TREC 2009 data have the similar trend, which are shown in Figure 7. We have found favorable results for Q-Composite on both NDCG@1 and NDCG@3. This shows proposed method is effective to extract more informative and aspect specific sentences. Especially, `Q-Composite` gains great improvement on NDCG@1, which is important for presenting condensing information on result pages.

To gain more insights, we analyze the label level distributions of the generated summary sentences of the 3 systems on TREC 20009 data set, as shown in Figure 8. The X-axis are label levels. The Y-axis is the distribution. We can see that our method provides more informative sentences (level 5 and level 4) compared with baselines. However, all systems still generate less specific and informative sentences than navigational sentences. This indicates the task is really challenging.

`Q-Composite` performs better than `Ling-2008`. The reasons may include: (1) `Ling-2008` estimates the aspect model on the search result of the original query. There may be not enough information covering all query aspects as shown in section 5.5.1. Therefore, for difficult aspects, it is unable to estimate accurate models. (2) In the search result of the original query, information related to multiple aspects often mixes together. It increases the difficulty to estimate discriminative aspect models. Therefore, it is more difficult to provide specific information for desired aspect. (3) The search result is so noisy that there are many navigational sentences. For example, sentences containing "actors" may also contain words like "cast", "list" and "actress". These words are very easy to have higher weights in aspect models and the sentences are ranked high as well. However, such sentences may only contain navigational information but can't provide direct information. Another reason affecting the performance of `Ling-2008` may be that we did not implement the variation with regularization, which is more complex but reported having better performance than the basic algorithm with Dirichlet model priors. In contrast, by using composite query based method, we are able to get more aspect specific information and roughly classify the information. By distinguishing query dependent aspect words and query independent aspect words, we give bonus to sentences that are aspect specific but also contain more information beyond aspect words.

`Snippet` performs well on Wikipedia data set. It is reasonable, since the snippet generation algorithm favorites the

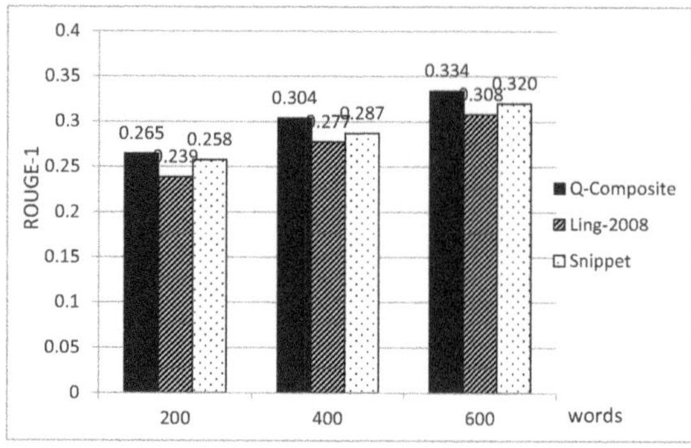

Figure 6: ROUGE-1 performance of Q-Composite and baseline systems on Wikipedia test data.

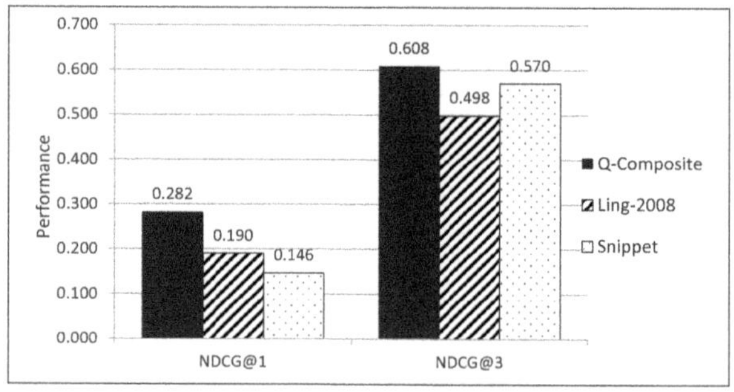

Figure 7: Performance comparisons between systems on TREC 2009 data set.

sentences containing many query terms. Thus the generated summaries match many query aspect terms, which benefits ROUGE-1 metric, especially when the length of summaries is short. However, the snippets don't show much informative information. From the Figure 8, we can see that `Snippet` provides more level 2 sentences (specific but not informative), but very few level 4 and level 5 sentences. The generated sentences usually lack of detail description about the query aspect, mostly are just navigational sentences which often fail to satisfy user information need directly. Our method could get more aspect specific information by comparing the search results of multiple composite queries. Highlighting query dependent aspect words also helps select more informative sentences. `Snippet` generates less irrelevant sentences. One reason is that most sentences in snippets contain original query terms, while other methods don't have such constraint. Another reason may be that using composite queries may lead to topic drift, if the search results of the composite queries contain much noise.

5.5.3 The Impact of Query Dependent Aspect Words

Our method distinguishes the query dependent aspect words and query independent aspect words. We examine the impact of these two types of words. We set the parameter β to be 0.5 in Equation 5 , which means we do not distinguish query dependent and independent aspect words. We denote it as `Q-Composite-AVG`. Since the human judgements on TREC 2009 data directly measure the informativeness of the generated summaries, we compare `Q-Composite` ($\beta = 0.0$) and `Q-Composite-AVG` on this data set. Figure 9 shows the level distributions of the generated top 1 sentences. We can

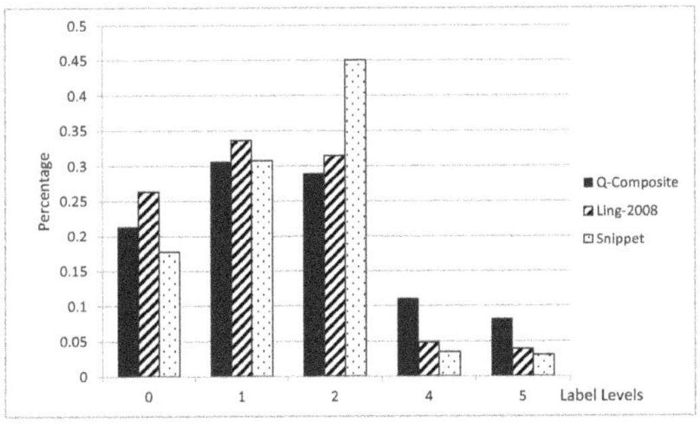

Figure 8: Level distributions of systems on TREC 2009 data set.

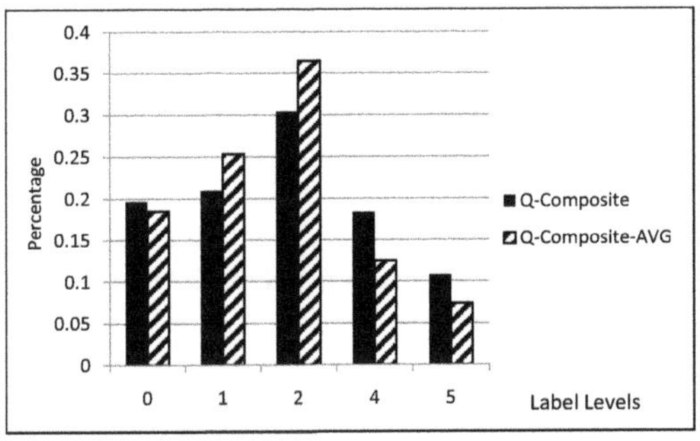

Figure 9: Level distributions of Q-Composite and Q-Composite-Avg on TREC 2009 data set.

see that `Q-Composite` generates more informative sentences (level 4 and level 5). In contrast, the `Q-Composite-AVG` generates more specific but non-informative sentences (level 2). That is because `Q-Composite` favorites the words not only related to the aspect but also related to the original query. The results show that distinguishing query dependent aspect words and independent words is useful for identifying more informative sentences. However, we also see that `Q-Composite` selects slightly more irrelevant sentences. This is because some composite queries bring in more noise, which leads to topic drift.

5.5.4 The Impact of Search Engine Result

Our method uses the search results returned by the search engine. In this section, we examine whether the quality of returned documents can affect system performance. We simulate some not very good results, by removing some documents from the search results or randomly picking documents. We test on the Wikipedia test set, since the evaluation can be done automatically. In details, we evenly `remove` 5 documents from the top 50 search results, denoted as `remove5`, namely the 1st, 11st, 21st, 31st and 41st documents. We construct the `remove15` in the same way. We also randomly sample 50 documents from the top 1000 results (denoted as `random`) and select the last 50 documents (denoted as `tail`).

The experimental results are shown in Figure 10. When the search results are not so bad (`remove5` or `remove15`), where most of the documents are relevant, the results are comparable. However, as the relevant documents reduce and noisy data increases, the models may be not very accurate. It shows worse results on `random` and `tail`. The results indicate our method depends on the quality of the search engine search results. For difficult composite queries, there may be no enough relevant candidate sentences for summarization. More noise may lead to topic drift as well.

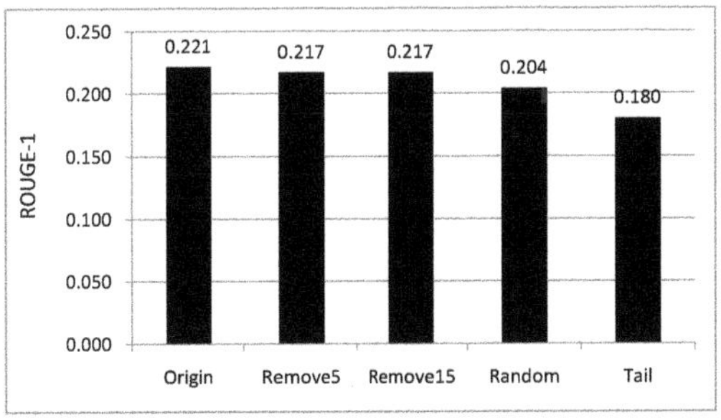

Figure 10: The impact of seach engine, on Wikipedia test set using ROUGE-1 performance.

6. CONCLUSIONS AND FUTURE WORK

In this paper, we presented a multi-aspect oriented query summarization task. This task aims to summarize a query from multiple aspects which are aligned to user intents. Ideally, the users could get relevant information satisfying their information needs directly. Specifically, we formulated the task into 2 main phases: information gathering and summary generation. In the information gathering phase, we proposed a composite query based strategy, which proactively gets information based on the search engine. This strategy differs from traditional search result organization and text summarization, where the set of documents to be deal with is seen as a given system input. In the summary generation phase, we took into consideration the specificity, informativeness and redundancy for sentence selection. We conducted experiments on 2 data sets. Both automatic evaluation and manually judgements were explored. We emphasized that the quality of aspect oriented summaries should be evaluated according to their specificity and informativeness. The experimental results showed that by using composite queries, much more aspect relevant information could be got and our method outperformed 2 baselines for generating informative summaries.

The proposed method attempts to directly provide well organized and relevant *information* to users, as opposed to relevant *documents*. We have several possible directions of future work. First, in this paper we assume the query aspects are given. We would examine the system performance when using automatically mined query aspects. Second, more advanced methods could be exploited to integrate multiple sources of information related to a query for generating more informative summaries. Third, the composite query strategy could be applied for search result diversification by retrieving more aspect related documents.

Acknowledgments

The 1st, 4th and 5th authors are supported by the National Natural Science Foundation of China under Grant No. 60736044, by the National High Technology Research and Development Program of China No. 2011ZX01042-001-001, by Key Laboratory Opening Funding of MOE-Microsoft Key

Laboratory of Natural Language Processing and Speech, Harbin Institute of Technology, HIT.KLOF.2009020.

7. REFERENCES

[1] H. Chen and S. T. Dumais. Bringing order to the web: automatically categorizing search results. In *C I*, pages 145–152, 2000.

[2] V. Dang, X. Xue, and W. B. Croft. Inferring query aspects from reformulations using clustering. In *Proceedings of the 20th ACM international conference on Information and kno ledge management*, CIKM '11, pages 2117–2120, New York, NY, USA, 2011. ACM.

[3] A. P. Dempster, N. M. Laird, and D. B. Rubin. Maximum likelihood from incomplete data via the em algorithm. *JOUR AL OF T E RO AL STATISTICAL SOCIET SERIES B*, 39(1):1–38, 1977.

[4] Z. Dou, S. Hu, K. Chen, R. Song, and J.-R. Wen. Multi-dimensional search result diversification. In *Proceedings of the 4th ACM WSDM*, pages 475–484, New York, NY, USA, 2011. ACM.

[5] J. Goldstein, V. Mittal, J. Carbonell, and M. Kantrowitz. Multi-document summarization by sentence extraction. In *Proceedings of the 2000 AACL A LP Workshop on Automatic Summarization*, pages 40–48, Stroudsburg, USA, 2000.

[6] M. A. Hearst. Clustering versus faceted categories for information exploration. *Commun ACM*, 49:59–61, April 2006.

[7] M. Hu and B. Liu. Mining and summarizing customer reviews. In W. Kim, R. Kohavi, J. Gehrke, and W. DuMouchel, editors, *Proceedings of the 10th ACM SIGKDD Seattle Washington USA August 22 25 2004*, pages 168–177. ACM, 2004.

[8] K. Järvelin and J. Kekäläinen. Ir evaluation methods for retrieving highly relevant documents. In *Proceedings of the 23rd annual international ACM SIGIR*, pages 41–48, New York, NY, USA, 2000. ACM.

[9] K. Kummamuru, R. Lotlikar, S. Roy, K. Singal, and R. Krishnapuram. A hierarchical monothetic document clustering algorithm for summarization and browsing search results. In *Proceedings of the 13th international conference on WWW*, pages 658–665, New York, NY, USA, 2004. ACM.

[10] B. Y.-L. Kuo, T. Hentrich, B. M. . Good, and M. D. Wilkinson. Tag clouds for summarizing web search results. In *Proceedings of the 16th ACM WWW*, pages 1203–1204, New York, NY, USA, 2007. ACM.

[11] D. J. Lawrie and W. B. Croft. Generating hierarchical summaries for web searches. In *Proceedings of the 26th ACM SIGIR*, pages 457–458, New York, NY, USA, 2003. ACM.

[12] C.-Y. Lin and E. Hovy. Automatic evaluation of summaries using n-gram co-occurrence statistics. In *Proceedings of the 2003 Conference of the AACL olume 1*, pages 71–78, Stroudsburg, PA, USA, 2003. Association for Computational Linguistics.

[13] X. Ling, Q. Mei, C. Zhai, and B. Schatz. Mining multi-faceted overviews of arbitrary topics in a text collection. In *Proceeding of the 14th ACM SIGKDD*, pages 497–505, New York, NY, USA, 2008. ACM.

[14] Q. Mei, X. Ling, M. Wondra, H. Su, and C. Zhai. Topic sentiment mixture: modeling facets and opinions in weblogs. In *Proceedings of the 16th international conference on World Wide Web*, pages 171–180, New York, NY, USA, 2007. ACM.

[15] A. Nenkova, L. Vanderwende, and K. McKeown. A compositional context sensitive multi-document summarizer: exploring the factors that influence summarization. In *Proceedings of the 29th Annual International ACM SIGIR Seattle Washington USA*, pages 573–580. ACM, 2006.

[16] S. Robertson and H. Zaragoza. The probabilistic relevance framework: Bm25 and beyond. *Found Trends Inf Retr* , 3:333–389, April 2009.

[17] C. Shen, D. Wang, and T. Li. Topic aspect analysis for multi-document summarization. In *Proceedings of the 19th ACM CIKM*, pages 1545–1548, New York, NY, USA, 2010. ACM.

[18] R. Song, M. Zhang, T. Sakai, M. Kato, Y. Liu, M. Sugimoto, Q. Wang, and N. Orii. Overview of the ntcir-9 intent task. In *TCIR 9 Proceedings*, pages 82–105. Morgan and Claypool, December 2011.

[19] A. Tombros and M. Sanderson. Advantages of query biased summaries in information retrieval. In *Proceedings of the 21st ACM SIGIR*, pages 2–10, New York, NY, USA, 1998. ACM.

[20] C. Wang, F. Jing, L. Zhang, and H.-J. Zhang. Learning query-biased web page summarization. In *Proceedings of the 6th ACM CIKM*, pages 555–562, New York, NY, USA, 2007. ACM.

[21] D. Wang, S. Zhu, T. Li, and Y. Gong. Multi-document summarization using sentence-based topic models. In *Proceedings of the ACL IJC LP 2009 Conference Short Papers*, pages 297–300, Stroudsburg, PA, USA, 2009. Association for Computational Linguistics.

[22] X. Wang, D. Chakrabarti, and K. Punera. Mining broad latent query aspects from search sessions. In *Proceedings of the 15th ACM SIGKDD*, pages 867–876, New York, NY, USA, 2009. ACM.

[23] X. Wang and C. Zhai. Learn from web search logs to organize search results. In *Proceedings of the 30th annual international ACM SIGIR*, pages 87–94, New York, NY, USA, 2007. ACM.

[24] R. White and R. Roth. Exploratory search. beyond the query-response paradigm. In *Synthesis Lectures on Information Concepts Retrieval and Services Series Gary Marchionini (ed) vol 3.* Morgan and Claypool, 2009.

[25] F. Wu, J. Madhavan, and A. Halevy. Identifying aspects for web-search queries. In *Journal of Artificial Intelligence Research*, pages 677–700, 2011 (40).

[26] W.-t. Yih, J. Goodman, L. Vanderwende, and H. Suzuki. Multi-document summarization by maximizing informative content-words. In *Proceedings of the 20th IJCAI*, pages 1776–1782, San Francisco, CA, USA, 2007. Morgan Kaufmann Publishers Inc.

[27] H.-J. Zeng, Q.-C. He, Z. Chen, W.-Y. Ma, and J. Ma. Learning to cluster web search results. In *Proceedings of the 27th annual international ACM SIGIR*, pages 210–217, New York, NY, USA, 2004. ACM.

Language Intent Models for Inferring User Browsing Behavior

Manos Tsagkias*
ISLA, University of Amsterdam
Amsterdam, The Netherlands
e.tsagkias@uva.nl

Roi Blanco
Yahoo! Research
Barcelona, Spain
roi@yahoo-inc.com

ABSTRACT

Modeling user browsing behavior is an active research area with tangible real-world applications, e.g., organizations can adapt their online presence to their visitors browsing behavior with positive effects in user engagement, and revenue. We concentrate on online news agents, and present a semi-supervised method for predicting news articles that a user will visit after reading an initial article. Our method tackles the problem using language intent models trained on historical data which can cope with unseen articles. We evaluate our method on a large set of articles and in several experimental settings. Our results demonstrate the utility of language intent models for predicting user browsing behavior within online news sites.

Categories and Subject Descriptors

H.3.3 [**Information Search and Retrieval**]: Retrieval Models

General Terms

Algorithm, Experiment

Keywords

Online news, article intent models, user, browsing, behavior

1. INTRODUCTION

Social media has changed the way news are produced and consumed, with well established news publishers having lost large share of their readers. The continuous decline in readership is also reflected in revenue, urging news publishers to seek new ways for monetizing their news articles. One of the many ways to do so is to increase the amount of time users spend on a news site. Central in achieving an increased user dwelling time within a site's property is the concept of *user engagement* [3], or quality of the user experience with an emphasis on the positive aspects of the interaction. Research on this area suggests that enhancing a web page with contextual information has positive impact on user engagement, and it has led to the development of a range of systems that address this phenomenon [9, 19]. A key ingredient here is to discover the right context for a web page, especially in a setting where user goals might change after the user visits the web page and new content is added continuously.

Context discovery can be cast as a task in the realm of semantics, personalization, or collaborative filtering, with the first being the most typical interpretation. Contextual information is drawn from a knowledge base built on a single source, e.g., news, Wikipedia or the web page's source domain, and typically remains relatively static over time. In the news domain, there is need for systems able to adapt, and discover the right sources of context in a dynamic fashion. As a working example, think of one news article announcing a forthcoming football game, and one reporting on the results of the game. In the first article a user might be interested in seeing information about the teams' setup, whereas in the second in the game highlights. Other examples are news articles reporting great natural disasters, e.g., Haiti's earthquake, or the tsunami in Japan, where users might want to see information about emergency services, the Red Cross, or weather reports.

Browsing behavior far outweighs direct search engine interaction as an information-gathering activity [26]. Given so, our focus is to recommend websites as opposed to search results. In contrast with previous approaches [26] which employ contextual sources for modeling a particular user's interests, we focus only on textual features extracted from the text of the articles browsed by the user and queries issued within a query session.

The main focus on in this paper is the *temporal context discovery* task: *For a given news article, and optionally a user, the system needs to discover webpages that the user is likely to visit after reading the article.* The task is challenging due to data sparsity issues that arise from the inherent volatility of the news domain, and the broad range of user intents, which lead to a heavy tailed distribution of user destinations after they visit a news article. To quantify this claim, we conducted an exploratory experiment. From a set of logical sessions extracted from query logs we identified web pages that are news articles, and classified them into categories, e.g., Science, Business, Entertainment. For each article we recorded the internet domains of the web pages that users visited after reading a news article, and assigned

*This work was conducted during a three-month internship at Yahoo! Research Barcelona.

Permission to make digital or hard copies of all or part of this work for personal or classroom use is granted without fee provided that copies are not made or distributed for profit or commercial advantage and that copies bear this notice and the full citation on the first page. To copy otherwise, or republish, to post on servers or to redistribute to lists, requires prior specific permission and/or a fee.
SIGIR'12, August 12–16, 2012, Portland, Oregon, USA.
Copyright 2012 ACM 978-1-4503-1472-5/12/08... $15.00.

these domains to the article's news category. We also record the popularity of a domain per category by counting the number of visits to the domain from articles in that category. Fig. 1 illustrates our findings on users navigational patterns after reading web pages in Yahoo! News. Red circles represent news categories, and white to blue shaded circles represent domains (white denotes least popular, and dark blue highly popular). News categories are laid out in space based on how they are connected to the domains. This results in an inner circle of news categories which forms a perimeter within which lie domains shared by these news categories, and outside of it are domains mostly unique to each category. The outer red dot perimeter includes categories that don't share common domains, i.e., Wikipedia, Yahoo! news, search engines, but share one or two rather "unique" domains attached to another category. Our findings suggest that there is a distinct set of domains where people navigate to depending on the category of the news article they read, forming a heavy tailed distribution of user navigational patterns. These challenges, i.e., data sparsity, and the cold start problem, restrain us from training robust recommendation models for articles that appear in user sessions, and make online recommendation virtually impossible for articles with no record in user sessions (we have to wait for at least one user trace).

Our approach to overcome these limitations is to cast the temporal context discovery task as an information retrieval problem, and develop methods for modeling user browsing intent in a query. These methods infer the user navigation patterns, by mapping the current article a users reads to a query into *intent space* which represents the content of articles likely to be clicked after the current one. This way, we aim to answer both challenges raised above; First, modeling article intent as proxy for user browsing intent helps to smooth out data sparsity issues. Second, modeling article intent allows for making predictions for unseen articles via the article intent space. Our experiments show that using text-based features and query session trails are able to achieve good performance for the task of temporal context discovery.

We envisage our methods to have concrete applications in enhancing user experience and engagement via dynamic link suggestion, result recommendation, and personalized web content optimization. Such applications can prove valuable to news agents, publishers, and consumers. News providers can leverage this information to generate focused recommendations via links to their consumers. In turn, consumers can save time completing their goal as relevant hyperlinks, or snippets from likely to visit web pages, and ads can be displayed on the same web page as the article.

The main contribution of this work is a model which uses historical data for making real-time predictions about the browsing patterns of users, for which little information is needed to be available at prediction time.

The rest of the paper is organized as follows. In the following section, Section 2, we present related work. In Section 3 we describe the problem definition, in Section 4 we outline our approach to the problem, in Section 5 and 6 we present our modeling and retrieval approaches, in Section 7 we describe our experimental setup, in Section 8 we report on results, in Section 9 we further discuss our findings, and in Section 10 we conclude.

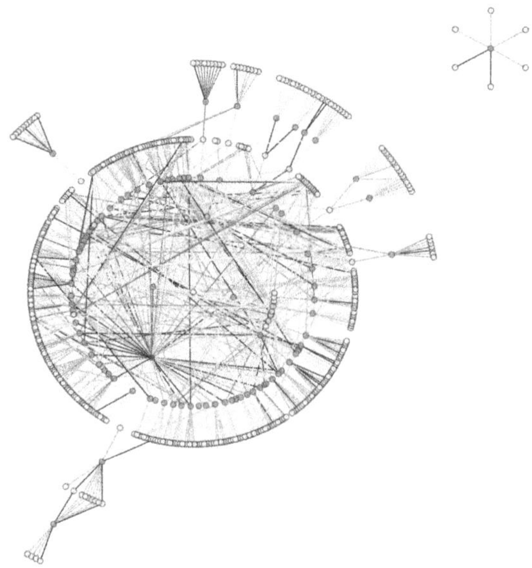

Figure 1: News categories show distinct patterns of where users navigate next after reading a news article. Red circles denote news categories, blue shaded circles denote internet domains; darker shades represent targets from many news categories. The two dark blue domains in the middle correspond to Wikipedia, and Yahoo! News.

2. RELATED WORK

The increased availability of query sessions coming from the logs of search engines has grown a research area that deals with studying, mining and making use of trails and user actions to improve search [12]. Search trails are sequences starting on a query and ending on a destination page, with a series of intermediate pages browsed by the user. For instance, these trails are a useful signal in order to learn a ranking function [1, 4] or to display the trails directly to the user [23] to help in the information seeking process. These approaches try to employ the query session information as implicit feedback in order to incorporate it into the ranking process. In contrast, our approach is targeted towards news article recommendation, using a mixture of the trail pages as a query.

There is an increased attention on techniques to identify the intent behind the query; this is one main challenge for modern search engines [7]. The first query classification was presented by Broder [6], in which queries were labeled as transactional, navigational or informational. However there are more sophisticated approaches, which take into account the multidimensionality of queries [10]. Approaches to classify web queries are mostly based on click-through data [15]. These methods are a key factor into identifying the real user's goals, and their applicability ranges from personalizing search results to predicting ad click-through [2], or search result diversification [8, 21].

Guo et al. [11] look at intent-aware query similarity for query recommendation. Intent is identified in search result snippets, and click-through data, over a number of latent topic models. Our approach differs in that the intent is modeled to capture the characteristics of the news domain and we do not recommend queries, but rather news articles. We also do not attempt to classify queries into a predefined set of categories, but rather we use the content of the clicked articles as an extended representation of the user intent.

Finally, there exists other possibilities for article recommendation, for instance those based on the explore-exploit framework like the one of Li et al. [16]. Those approaches require a significant amount of click-through traffic and in general are content-agnostic, using as similarity features clicks shared between users.

3. PROBLEM DEFINITION

We cast the problem of *temporal context discovery* as follows. Given a document $\alpha \in \mathcal{A}$, and a set of user sessions $\mathcal{T}$, find a ranked list of documents $\{\alpha\}_i \subseteq \mathcal{A}$ that a user is likely to read after reading α. The session set is defined as

$$\mathcal{T} := \{(q, \alpha, \ldots, o_j)\},$$

where $q \in Q$ represents a query, $\alpha \in \mathcal{A}$ is a document, and o_j is either a document $\alpha_j \in \mathcal{A}$ or another query $q_j \in Q$.

In this work, we reduce the complexity of the problem in two ways. First, we only focus on the news domain. In this respect, documents in $\mathcal{A}$ are news articles, and the majority of user queries we deal with is of informational type [6]. Second, we focus on methods that use only textual information derived from the articles' content. We do not use additional information from query logs or the web graph as signals for ranking, e.g., time spent on each document, hyperlinks between the documents. In particular, we omit the use of hyperlinks because they are not always present in news articles (see Section 1), and can potentially bias the evaluation as they reduce the recommendation space to the articles linked by the current one.

The problem at hand is similar to that of recommending similar articles to the article currently being read. However, in the current setting, the system has to probe user intent and recommend articles not only based on the user's cognitive model at the query issue time, but also on the changes that occur in their cognitive model after reading a news article. This requirement asks for an approach beyond recommending articles which are semantically or topically similar to α. In this setting, we face a challenging task as the recommendations have to adapt quickly and incrementally to reflect the ongoing process in the user's cognitive model.

To make things more tangible, consider a search session from a user υ that consists only of queries, and news articles. These query sessions [5] are records of the queries and the actions of the users of search engines, and they contain latent information about their interests, preferences, and behaviors. Let two users υ_1, and υ_2 issue the same informational query q to a search engine, and then click on a retrieved news article, possibly read it, then return to the search results, and click on another article. In the process, they may choose to refine their query with the current state of their cognitive model which has now possibly changed after visiting the retrieved news articles. This iterative process will generate the following traces:

$$\begin{aligned} \upsilon_1 &:= q_1 \to \alpha_1 \to \alpha_2 \to q_2 \to \alpha_3 \to \cdots \to \alpha_{\upsilon_1} \\ \upsilon_2 &:= q_1 \to \alpha_3 \to q_2 \to \alpha_1 \to \alpha_2 \to \cdots \to \alpha_{\upsilon_2} \end{aligned}$$

In these traces we see user υ_1 issuing a query, then visiting article α_1, then going back to the results page and selecting another article α_2. After visiting α_2, υ_1 decided to refine their query and issued q_2, and continued visiting other articles. A similar process occurs for user υ_2, however, the order υ_2 visits the article is different, and also, the position within the trace of the second query is different. The temporal context discovery task is defined as: predict $\alpha_2, \ldots, \alpha_\upsilon$ given q and α_1 for a user υ.

4. APPROACH

Our approach is to estimate a query model $\hat{q}$ that reflects user's browsing intent, namely, what article the user is likely to read after clicking α_1 and given their query trail τ_k. The rationale is that when $\hat{q}$ is submitted to an index of articles, a retrieval system will return documents that are likely to be read from user υ_k. To this end, our efforts are concentrated on modeling the query $\hat{q}$.

A key aspect here is to derive a robust method for modeling the user's browsing intent. We build on the intuition that user intent on a news article α can be captured by training models on the content of the articles that follow α. The rationale is that these models should capture the relation between content and patterns of user behavior using the query sessions. The query sessions define links between each article in the intent space. We call these models *article intent models* (AIMs). Fig. 2 illustrates this idea, and the steps we take afterwards.

Articles for which the system will make predictions do not necessarily exist in the news article pool, or have been recorded in user sessions which leaves them without intent models. We account for this issue by building on the assumption that similar articles lead to similar user traces. This way, articles that do not occur in user sessions are assigned the intent model of the most similar article that has one. This idea also helps assigning intent models to previously unseen articles, and allows coping with an expanding pool of articles.

With the article intent models in place, we estimate the query $\hat{q}$ using information from either the content of the article, its corresponding intent model, and a mixture of both. For the latter case, we derive several weighting methods which are explained in Section 5.4.

A retrieval system based on a widely used, state-of-the-art information retrieval method receives the query $\hat{q}$ and returns a ranked list of news articles. We consider two options for this. The first option submits the query to an index of articles, while the second option issues the query to an index of intent models, the ranked list of which is mapped to news articles.

Relevant articles are deemed those that follow α in user sessions. In order to ensure that the user has read the article in question, we discard articles in which users spent less than 30 seconds [14]. The system is evaluated on whether it manages to retrieve these relevant articles in early positions.

5. MODELING

We present the methods for addressing the steps involved in our approach: (a) Model the news article, (b) model article intent, and (c) model queries, which we consider as a mixture model of the first two steps.

We start with a pool of news articles $\mathcal{A} := \{\alpha_1, \ldots, \alpha_N\}$, where N is the size of the pool, and a list $\mathcal{T} := \{\tau_1, \ldots, \tau_K\}$

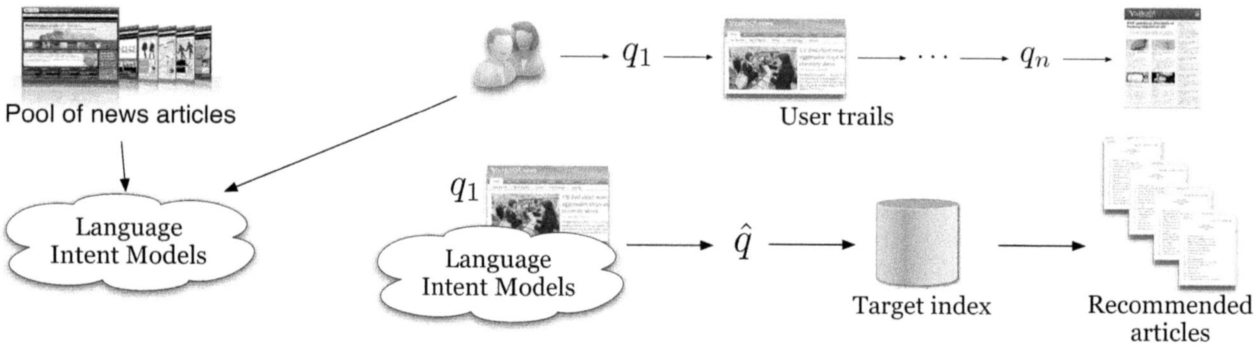

Figure 2: Our approach for recommending articles based on user intent.

Table 1: Description of the main symbols we use.

Symbol	Gloss
$\mathcal{A}$	Pool of news articles in the database
$\mathcal{T}$	Pool of user traces
τ_k	k trace in $\mathcal{T}$
υ_k	User identifier of trace k
q	Query
α_n	Article n in $\mathcal{A}$
w	token in a language model
${}_c\theta_n$	n-th article LM trained on content
${}_p\theta_n$	n-th article LM trained on persons
${}_o\theta_n$	n-th article LM trained on organizations
${}_l\theta_n$	n-th article LM trained on locations
${}_t\theta_n$	n-th article LM trained on time expressions
$\boldsymbol{\theta}_n$	n-th article language model vector
$\boldsymbol{\theta}^I_n$	n-th article intent model vector (AIM)
$P(w\|\theta_n)$	Probability of sampling w from n-th article LM
$P(w)$	A priori probability of sampling w
$n(w,\alpha_n)$	Frequency of w in n-th article
$sKL(\cdot)$	Symmetric KL divergence between α_1 and α_2
ξ	Weight parameter for LM linear combination

of user traces $\tau_k := (\upsilon_k, q, \alpha_1, \ldots, \alpha_{l_k})$, similar to the ones described in Section 3. K denotes the total number of user traces in our database, $k := \{1, \ldots, K\}$, υ_k is an anonymized user identifier, and l_k is the length of user trace k in clicks. Table 1 contains a list of symbols used throughout the paper.

5.1 Article models

Articles α_n are represented as language models drawn from ϕ different distributions, each one defined over its own event space. To reduce clutter, we refer to all ϕ language models as $\boldsymbol{\theta}_n$ to denote a vector of language models:

$$\boldsymbol{\theta}_n := \langle {}_1\theta_n, \ldots, {}_\phi\theta_n \rangle .$$

For achieving a rich representation of the textual content of the article, we focus on three families of sources for learning language models: (i) the unigrams of the news article, (ii) the named entities therein, and (iii) the time expressions mentioned in the article. We motivate the use of each source in turn.

Article content. The body of the news article itself is an important source of information for training language models that represent it [20, 24, 27], as witnessed from the successful previous work in probabilistic modeling for retrieval. We follow [18, 25] and use entire contents of article body, and title for training a unigram language model.

Named entities. A great majority of news refer to and discuss people, organizations, and locations. To this extent, we extract named entities, and train a language model per named entity type, i.e., persons, organizations, and locations. The rationale behind is that if an article focuses on a particular named entity, the named entity will occur many times in the article, resulting in a language model that emits this named entity with high probability.

Temporal expressions. Real world events are central to news reporting, and news articles connect the development of events through time expressions, e.g., "last week", "in one month". Using time expressions can help identify articles that discuss the same time period of an event [13]. We group time expressions into three classes, i.e., *past*, *present*, and *future* relative to the article's publication date. A language model trained on time expressions consists of these three classes, and the probability of emitting a class is proportional to the number of time expressions that belong to this class.

For every article α_n in $\mathcal{A}$ we train language models from the three different sources we described above: the article content, the named entities, and the temporal expressions. We assume that each article is drawn from three multinomial distributions, each one defined over its own event space $\mathcal{E}$ of token occurrences w. We smooth the number of times a token w is present in the article using Dirichlet priors, thus defining the probability of a token w to be generated from the language model n as:

$$P(w|\theta_n) = \frac{n(w,\alpha_n) + \mu P(w)}{|\alpha_n| + \mu},$$

where $n(w,\alpha_n)$ is the frequency of token w in α_n, $|\alpha_n|$ is the article length in tokens, $P(w)$ is the a priori probability of w, and μ the Dirichlet smoothing hyper-parameter [27].

5.2 Article intent models

Now, we shift from the content space to the intent space through the user traces in $\mathcal{T}$. An *article intent model* (AIM) $\boldsymbol{\theta}^I_n$ intends to capture the original user intent by using the articles that the user reads after α_n as proxy. More formally, $\boldsymbol{\theta}^I_n$ is defined as the combination of the language models of the articles users browsed afterwards,

$$\boldsymbol{\theta}^I_n = \sum_{k=1}^{K} \sum_{i=j}^{l_k} \lambda(i) \boldsymbol{\theta}_i,$$

where j is the position of α_n in trace τ_k, and $\lambda(i)$ a weighting function dependent on the position of an article within τ_k. $\lambda(i)$ is likely to be a exponential decay function, however, due to the sparseness of the dataset we set it to be uniform over all article models.

Noise in query logs, along with data sparsity, i.e., the small number of articles users visit after reading a news article (see Section 7 for a description of our dataset) can lead to poor article intent models. To account for this effect, we describe a method for assigning more than one AIM to an article. We work as follows. First, we compute the pairwise similarity of all articles in the pool that have associated article intent models. Then, we assign each article α_n a vector V_n of tuples that consist of an article intent model along with the similarity scores of the article intent model's associated article:

$$V_n := \left\langle (1, \boldsymbol{\theta}_n^I), \ldots, (s_\nu, \boldsymbol{\theta}_\nu^I) \right\rangle,$$

where $(1, \boldsymbol{\theta}_n^I)$ denotes the article intent model associated with α_n, and $(s_\nu, \boldsymbol{\theta}_\nu^I)$ is the article intent model for α_ν which has s_ν similarity with α_n.

Intent models for unseen articles. In many situations, the system will need to map articles that do not exist either in $\mathcal{A}$ (e.g., new article is added) or in $\mathcal{T}$ (e.g., the article has no logged visits yet) to the intent space. Given that we define all the models over the same event distributions, the method builds on the hypothesis that users reading similar articles are likely to have similar intent, and therefore produce a similar user trace.

Let α_n be an article with no AIM associated with it, we want to find similar articles to α_n for which there exist AIMs. If the intent models are generated from an unknown data distribution $P(\boldsymbol{\theta}^I)$, our goal is to find a model $\boldsymbol{\theta}_n^I$ such that the marginal probability computed over the whole intent model space is maximized:

$$P(\boldsymbol{\theta}_n^I) = \int P(\boldsymbol{\theta}_n^I|\boldsymbol{\theta}^I)P(\boldsymbol{\theta}^I)d\boldsymbol{\theta}^I.$$

We approximate the integral using the finite set of intent models generated from the articles in $\mathcal{A}$:

$$\sum_{j=1}^{|\mathcal{A}|} P(\boldsymbol{\theta}_j^I)P(\boldsymbol{\theta}_n^I|\boldsymbol{\theta}_j^I).$$

There are several possibilities for selecting $\boldsymbol{\theta}_j^I$; we make the assumption that documents with similar language models have similar intent models, and therefore $P(\boldsymbol{\theta}_n^I|\boldsymbol{\theta}_j^I) \propto sim(\boldsymbol{\theta}_n|\boldsymbol{\theta}_j)$. The article index selected is the one that maximizes

$$j = \underset{j \in \{0,\ldots,|\mathcal{A}|\}}{\text{argmax}} \; (sim(\boldsymbol{\theta}_n|\boldsymbol{\theta}_j)), \tag{1}$$

and $\hat{\boldsymbol{\theta}}_n^I = \boldsymbol{\theta}_j^I$. The final intent model is interpolated with the original model as:

$$\boldsymbol{\theta}_n^I = \xi\hat{\boldsymbol{\theta}}_n^I + (1-\xi)\boldsymbol{\theta}_n,$$

where ξ is a parameter defining the weight of each language model.

In order to select the most similar intent model in Eq. 1 we create an index of all the language models generated from $\mathcal{A}$, and rank them using $\boldsymbol{\theta}_n$ as a query, with the standard symmetric KL-divergence as a ranking function (defined in Section 6).

5.3 Query models

The previous sections have presented our approach to modeling news articles, and article intent models. We move on how to use them for estimating a query $\hat{q}$ for a user v_k. A straightforward way is to make the simplifying assumption that both the query issued by the user, and the article α_n they first read are representative for the user's intent. Formally, the estimated query can be written as:

$$\hat{q}^{ART} := \rho_q\theta_q + (1-\rho_q) \sum_{i \in \{c,p,o,l,t\}} \kappa_i \cdot {}_i\theta_n, \tag{2}$$

where ^{ART} denotes the estimation of the query using article models, and the original query model, ρ_q stands for the weight assigned to the query language model θ_q, κ_i denotes the weights for the different article language models ${}_i\theta_n$, i.e., content, named entities, temporal expressions. This user model operates in the vertical dimension in the sense that assumes that people are interested in reading similar articles to the one they first read, because, for example, they want to find more information about the topic of their interest. Although this assumption may stand true for certain users, it ignores the horizontal dimension, namely, users that want to read different aspects of the article they first read, or find information related to it but not directly.

We make the hypothesis that article intent models can serve this purpose, namely, model the user intent, for finding articles that users are likely to read afterwards. In this respect, we estimate the query $\hat{q}^{AIM}$ from article intent models associated with the article that the user visited first:

$$\hat{q}^{AIM} := \sum_{\nu}^{|V_n|} \beta_\nu \cdot \sum_{i \in \{c,p,o,l,t\}} \kappa_i \cdot {}_i\theta_n^I, \tag{3}$$

where ^{AIM} denotes the estimation of the query on article intent models, V_n is a vector with article intent models for α_n, and β_ν is a weight for each article intent model in V_n. The building block of these models depends on user trails extracted from query logs. Query logs are known to contain noise [22], and therefore using article intent models instead of article models may introduce topical shift, possibly degrading the quality of the list of suggested articles.

A natural way to tackle this problem is to model user intent as a mixture model of the user's query, the first article they read, and article intent models. We define a mixture model for modeling $\hat{q}$ as $\hat{q}^{ART+AIM}$:

$$\begin{aligned} \hat{q}^{ART+AIM} &:= \beta_{inc}\, \hat{q}^{ART} + \hat{q}^{AIM} \\ &= \beta_{inc}\, \hat{q}^{ART} + \sum_{\nu=1}^{|V_n|} \beta_\nu \cdot \sum_{i \in \{c,p,o,l,t\}} \kappa_i \cdot {}_i\theta_n^I, \end{aligned} \tag{4}$$

where β_{inc} is the weight regulating the importance of the user's query, and the first read article.

5.4 Weighting schemes

A straightforward procedure for estimating the weights in Eqs. (2)–(4) is to use supervised learning. In particular, without imposing any restriction in the parameters, the model could assign one weight per article in every trace, which asks for significant amounts of training data. This requirement renders supervised learning unsuitable for an online setting, where the pool of articles expands continuously, or where training data is scarce. The approaches we describe next aim at overcoming this problem by producing the query mixture model $\hat{q}^{ART+AIM}$ without the need for training. They build on knowledge derived from the distribution of similarities between the $\boldsymbol{\theta}_n^I$ vectors. The hypothesis is that the semantic similarity between an incoming article and its intent models is a good surrogate for regulating weights in query mixture models. To this end, we describe several strategies that create query mixture models for an article model, using one or several article intent models. We separate the two cases of *one* and *many* article intent models because of the implications in weighting.

Merge. We begin with a simple approach, namely, assign no weights to the article or to its article intent models, but merge their contents before training language models for content, named entities, and temporal expression. This can be generalized for any number of article intent models we want to consider.

Pairwise. This technique considers mixture models for an article and its most similar article intent model. We assign the incoming article intent model weight $1 - s_\nu$, and the intent model the weight s_ν, where $0 \leq s_\nu \leq 1$ is the semantic similarity between them. We also try the reverse, namely, the incoming article weights $1 - s_\nu$, and the intent model s_ν. We refer to this second approach as *Pairwise-R.*

Average. When it comes to add more than one AIM to the mixture model, we face the problem what weight to assign to the incoming article. One way is to assume that the incoming article language model is an article intent model trained only on itself and therefore its weight is set to 1. Then, we enforce the constraint on weights to sum up to 1:

$$\beta_{inc} + \beta_1 + \cdots + \beta_\nu = 1,$$

where $\beta_{inc} = 1$, which transforms the weights to:

$$\beta'_x = \frac{\beta_x}{\beta_{inc} + \beta_1 + \cdots + \beta_\nu}.$$

Median. The previous approach makes the assumption that an article model is semantically identical to an article intent model. We try to smooth this assumption by weighting the incoming article proportionally to the set of its article intent models. The weights of similar article intent models show a broad range of values, therefore their median value can be a good indicator for weighting the incoming article. In other words, if the median value is high, then we give preference to the article intent models as they are likely to bear more information, and vice-versa, if the median value is low, then we give preference to the incoming article as it is likely to be more informative for retrieval. Formally:

$$\beta_{inc} = 1 - m(\{\beta_1 + \cdots + \beta_\nu\}),$$

where $m()$ is the median value.

6. RETRIEVAL

All the formulation presented insofar builds comparable model representations. In order to retrieve articles, represented by either their language or intent models, as a response to a query $\hat{q}$ we use the symmetric Kullback-Leibler divergence. This is, given two vectors of models $\boldsymbol{\theta_t}$ and $\boldsymbol{\theta_n}$

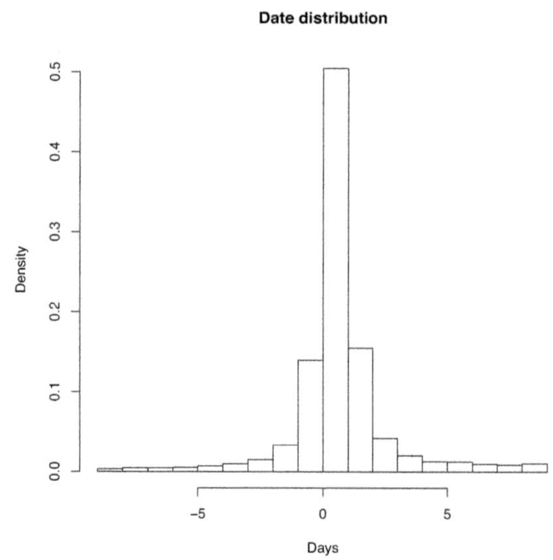

Figure 3: Distribution of the date difference in days between the articles users have clicked in a session, aggregated over all sessions. Positive difference indicates articles published prior to the input article. Showing differences less than 10 days for clarity.

we compute a score as

$$\begin{aligned} score(\boldsymbol{\theta_t}||\boldsymbol{\theta_n}) &:= sKL(\boldsymbol{\theta_t}|\boldsymbol{\theta_n}) \qquad (5)\\ &= \sum_{vc\in\{c,p,o,l,t\}} \left[\sum_w P(w|_{vc}\theta_t)\log\frac{P(w|_{vc}\theta_t)}{P(w|_{vc}\theta_n)}\right.\\ &\left. + \sum_w P(w|_{vc}\theta_n)\log\frac{P(w|_{vc}\theta_n)}{P(w|_{vc}\theta_t)}\right], \end{aligned}$$

where w is a token from the union of tokens in the respective language models.

In order to recommend articles, we need to rank $\hat{q}$ with respect to α_n. In this case $\hat{q}$ plays the role of $\boldsymbol{\theta_t}$ in Eq. 5 and $\boldsymbol{\theta_n}$ or $\boldsymbol{\theta_n^I}$ play the role of $\boldsymbol{\theta_n}$, when we consider the model of the article or its AIM respectively.

Temporal bias. Our ranking model assumes a uniform distribution over the likelihood of user preference on ranked documents. We examine whether this assumption holds by plotting the time difference of publication of articles that users visited after reading an initial article. Fig. 3 shows the user preference is biased towards articles published close to the first article they read. It has a strong peak at 0 days, rapidly decreasing in both sides, possibly due to the presentation bias in the search results. We model this phenomenon with the standard Cauchy distribution,[1] which introduces a bias towards articles visited shortly after the article at hand:

$$\lambda(i) = \frac{1}{\pi}\left[\frac{1}{(i-j)^2+1}\right].$$

[1]We experimented with modeling this distribution with a block exponential function, double exponential (Laplace distribution) and we found that among them using the Cauchy distribution gives the best retrieval effectiveness; see §9.

7. EXPERIMENTAL SETUP

In this section we describe our research questions, experiments, dataset and evaluation methodology. Our main research question we aim to answer is whether our query models can help in the task of temporal context discovery. We study this question in the following three dimensions:

Query modeling What is the effect in retrieval effectiveness when using our three query modeling approaches? What is the effect of temporal bias in the retrieval model?

Weighting What is the effect in performance of our weighting schemes?

Retrieval in intent space Can effectiveness be improved if we perform retrieval in the intent space instead of the article space?

To answer these research questions, we proceed as follows. First, we compare the three query models we presented in Section 5.3 which use either the query and the incoming article, or the article's intent model, or their combination. We study the effect of time in retrieval performance using retrieval models with and without temporal bias. Next, we focus on the weighting scheme for generating the query mixture models, and compare each of them. Finally, we change our index from articles to article intent models, and use our query models to retrieve article intent models which are then mapped to articles in a post-retrieval stage.

In Table 2 we list the alternatives we consider, along with their corresponding features. Runs that use only the article for modeling the query are denoted with ART, those using only article intent models AIM, and their combination ART + AIM. Query models on temporally biased retrieval modes have a superscript T, and different weighting methods are denoted in the subscript. For example, $\text{ART} + \text{AIM}^{\text{T}}_{\text{M}}$ is model that uses both the incoming article and the article intent models on a temporally biased retrieval model, using the Median weighting method for generating the query mixture model.

7.1 Dataset

Our dataset consists of 14,180 Yahoo! News items published in February 2011, and a parallel corpus of query logs from Yahoo! Search. We apply several preprocessing steps. We extract named entities using the SuperSense tagger,[2] and time expressions using the TARSQI Toolkit.[3] The query stream is segmented into several sets of related information seeking queries, i.e., logical sessions using the technique in [5]. The logical sessions are pruned to contain only queries and articles that exist in our article dataset.

Our experiments include a training, and a testing phase. We use 75% of the logical sessions for training article intent models for 3,060 articles, and the remaining 25% as ground truth for 434 query test articles.

7.2 Evaluation

We assemble our ground truth as follows. From the logical sessions in the test set we consider the first user query and article in the session as our input, and consider every following article as relevant to this input. This process results in a ground truth of 511 relevant documents (max/min/avg: 3/1/1.18 documents).

In our experiments we work as follows. Given the user query and the article, we generate a query $\hat{q}$ with our methods which we then use to retrieve articles from either an index of articles, or article intent models. We treat the user query and the input article equally as in Eq. (2). For query mixture models, we consider one article intent model, the most similar to the input article.

For our experiments we use the Indri framework [17]. We set the weights in an independent held-out data-set as follows: for named entities to 0.1, for temporal expressions to 0.1, and for the article content to 0.6. The smoothing parameter for Dirichlet smoothing is set to $\mu = 2500$, except otherwise stated. For articles without article intent models, we set $\xi = 0.5$. We report on standard IR measures: precision at 5 (P@5), mean reciprocal rank (MRR), mean average precision (MAP), and r-precision (Rprec). Statistical significance is tested using a two-tailed paired t-test and is marked as $^\blacktriangle$ (or $^\blacktriangledown$) for significant differences for $\alpha = .01$, or $^\vartriangle$ (and $^\triangledown$) for $\alpha = .05$.

8. RESULTS AND ANALYSIS

In this section we report on the results of our three experiments: (a) query models and temporal bias in retrieval, (b) weighting schemes for generating query mixture models, and (c) retrieval on article intent model index.

Query modeling. In our first experiment, we test our three query modeling methods we described in Section 5.3: (a) the incoming article (ART), (b) the article intent models (AIM), and (c) their combination (ART + AIM). These models are tested on two retrieval models, one with, and one without temporal bias. Models on the retrieval model with temporal bias are denoted with a superscript T. Our baseline is set to the method that uses only the incoming article (AIM, and ART^{T}).

In Table 3 we report on the performance of these systems with (top-half) and without (bottom-half) temporal bias in the retrieval process. In the retrieval setting without temporal bias, the baseline proves strong, and outperforms both AIM, and ART + AIM. In the retrieval setting with temporal bias the picture changes. ART^{T} outperforms AIM in MAP, MRR, and P@5. $\text{ART} + \text{AIM}^{\text{T}}$, the combination of incoming article, and the most similar article intent model, yields the best run, and outperforms the baseline in all metrics, statistically significantly so.

We explain the lower performance of AIM, and AIM^{T} (using only article intent models) by the fact that both models are dependent on the similarity of the incoming article to the article intent model. This dependency results in many instances to model the incoming user query–article pair with article intent models that are topically far away from the input pair. This sensitivity is smoothed out successfully in $\text{ART} + \text{AIM}^{\text{T}}$ where content from the input pair reduces the potential topical drift from the article intent model.

Weighting. In our second experiment we compare the effect of the weighting methods we describe in Section 5.4. We set the baseline to the best run so far, $\text{ART} + \text{AIM}^{\text{T}}$, which uses uniform weights. The retrieval method is temporally biased.

In Table 4 we report on results for our five weighting schemes. $\text{ART} + \text{AIM}^{\text{T}}$ marks the best performance, outperforming other weighting methods with statistical signifi-

[2] `http://sourceforge.net/projects/supersensetag/`

[3] `http://www.timeml.org/site/tarsqi/`

Table 2: Retrieval models we consider.

Model	Temp.Prior	Input model Article	Input model # AIM	Enhanced	Weighting scheme	Eq.
Models retrieve articles						
ART	—	✓	—	No	—	(2)
ART^{T}	✓	✓	—	No	—	(2)
AIM	—	—	1	No	—	(3)
AIM^{T}	✓	—	1	No	—	(3)
ART + AIM	—	✓	1	No	Merge	(4)
$\text{ART} + \text{AIM}^{\text{T}}$	✓	✓	1	No	Merge	(4)
$\text{ART} + \text{AIM}^{\text{T}}_{\text{P}}$	✓	✓	1	No	Pairwise	(4)
$\text{ART} + \text{AIM}^{\text{T}}_{\text{PR}}$	✓	✓	1	No	Pairwise-R	(4)
$\text{ART} + \text{AIM}^{\text{T}}_{\text{A}}$	✓	✓	N	No	Average	(4)
$\text{ART} + \text{AIM}^{\text{T}}_{\text{M}}$	✓	✓	N	No	Median	(4)
Models retrieve AIMs						
AIM − AIM	—	—	1	No	—	
$\text{AIM} - \text{AIM}_{\text{e}}$	—	—	1	Yes	—	

Table 3: Retrieval performance for three query modeling methods using: a) only the incoming article, b) only article intent models, c) a combination of the two, with and without temporal bias in retrieval. Boldface indicates best performance in the respective metric. Statistical significance tested against ART.

Run	Rel.Ret.	MAP	RPrec	MRR	P@5
Without temporal bias					
ART	239	0.2775	0.1916	0.2871	0.0889
AIM	200	$0.2349^{\triangledown}$	0.1778	0.2546	$0.0779^{\triangledown}$
ART + AIM	234	0.2619	0.1832	0.2800	0.0889
With temporal bias					
ART^{T}	253	0.3103	0.2216	0.3230	0.1009
AIM^{T}	193	$0.2450^{\blacktriangledown}$	$0.1790^{\triangledown}$	$0.2620^{\blacktriangledown}$	$0.0797^{\blacktriangledown}$
$\text{ART} + \text{AIM}^{\text{T}}$	261	$\mathbf{0.3385}^{\triangle}$	$\mathbf{0.2561}^{\triangle}$	$\mathbf{0.3568}^{\triangle}$	$\mathbf{0.1083}^{\triangle}$

Table 4: Retrieval performance for five weighting schemes for creating input article–article intent mixture models. Statistical significance tested against $\text{ART} + \text{AIM}^{\text{T}}$.

Run	Rel.Ret.	MAP	RPrec	MRR	P@5
$\text{ART} + \text{AIM}^{\text{T}}$	261	0.3385	0.2561	0.3568	0.1083
$\text{ART} + \text{AIM}^{\text{T}}_{\text{P}}$	252	0.3159	0.2289	$0.3284^{\triangledown}$	0.1037
$\text{ART} + \text{AIM}^{\text{T}}_{\text{PR}}$	252	$0.3110^{\triangledown}$	0.2254	$0.3238^{\blacktriangledown}$	$0.1014^{\triangledown}$
$\text{ART} + \text{AIM}^{\text{T}}_{\text{A}}$	253	$0.3116^{\triangledown}$	0.2289	$0.3252^{\triangledown}$	$0.1009^{\triangledown}$
$\text{ART} + \text{AIM}^{\text{T}}_{\text{M}}$	249	$0.3104^{\triangledown}$	0.2289	$0.3248^{\blacktriangledown}$	$0.1000^{\blacktriangledown}$

cant differences in most metrics. Among the rest of weighting schemes, performance hovers at similar levels. We believe this is a indication that the semantic similarity between the incoming article, and the article intent models may not be as discriminative as we hypothesized for assigning weights.

Retrieval in intent space. In our third experiment, we look at methods that retrieve article intent models instead of articles. We use Eq. (3) for query modeling. Then, we issue the query to an index of article intent models. The retrieved article models are mapped back to articles. We consider two methods for performing the mapping. AIM − AIM maps a retrieved article intent model to the most similar article in the dataset, and $\text{AIM} - \text{AIM}_{\text{e}}$ maps a retrieved article intent model to the I most similar articles.

Table 5: Retrieval performance for two systems retrieving article intent models, and then mapping them to articles.

Run	MAP	RPrec	MRR	P@5
AIM − AIM	0.1664	0.1025	0.1821	0.0659
$\text{AIM} - \text{AIM}_{\text{e}}$	0.1431	0.0895	0.1608	0.0512

In Table 5 we report on the performance of the two methods. The results are not directly comparable to those reported for retrieving articles because we are using a different index (an article intent model index), we observe a decrease in performance compared to the methods that directly retrieve articles. We foresee two reasons for the drop in performance. First, moving from an input article to an article intent model is an error prone process, because of the topical noise. This issue was also present in our first experiment when we used only article intent model for query modeling. Then, when we move back from the retrieved intent models to articles, additional noise is added multiplying the negative effects in retrieval effectiveness.

In sum, our experiments demonstrate the utility of our query models to capture user intent for predicting articles that a user will visit next. The most successful strategy is to use information from both the input query and article, and article intent models for query modeling. For mixing the two sources, uniform weighting proves the most effective. Performance is further improved with the user of temporally aware retrieval models. In the next section we further discuss our findings.

9. DISCUSSION

To better understand the performance of our methods, we take a closer look at the results, and we perform an analysis in the following directions: (a) temporal modeling, (b) the number of article intent models we consider, and (c) parameter optimization.

Temporal modeling. In our temporal aware retrieval models, we use the Cauchy distribution for modeling the bias of

Table 6: Retrieval performance for three temporal models using: (a) Cauchy distribution , (b) a block function, and (c) Laplace distribution. Statistical significance tested against ART + AIM^{T}.

Model	Rel.Ret.	MAP	RPrec	MRR	P@5
ART + AIM^{T}	261	0.3385	0.2561	0.3568	0.1083
Block	279	0.3214	0.2266$^{\triangledown}$	0.3398	0.1046
Laplace	251	0.3299$^{\triangledown}$	0.2527	0.3485$^{\triangledown}$	0.1041$^{\blacktriangledown}$

users towards recent news articles. We try to fit different temporal models on the distribution shown in Fig. 3. In particular, we look at a block function, and at Laplace distribution. From the shape of the distribution in Fig. 3 we derive the block function:

$$F(x) = \begin{cases} e^{-x+2}, & x > 2, \\ e^{x}, & 2 \leq x \leq 2, \\ e^{x-2}, & x < 2. \end{cases}$$

The Laplace distribution is defined as:

$$F(x) = \frac{1}{2b} \begin{cases} e^{-\frac{\mu - x}{b}}, & x < \mu, \\ e^{-\frac{x-\mu}{b}}, & x \geq \mu. \end{cases}$$

with $\mu = 0, b = 1$. We test the potential of these models on our best run, ART + AIM^{T}, replacing the Cauchy prior with a prior from the block function, and the Laplace distribution, respectively. The Cauchy prior marks the best performance among the temporal models. Comparing the Laplace distribution to the block function, the Laplace distribution recalls less documents, with higher precision (Rprec). The block function shows the opposite behavior; it shows the highest recall among all methods in expense of precision (see Table 6).

Number of article intent models. In our experiments for query mixture models we used one article intent model, the most similar to the input article. Here, we explore the effect on retrieval effectiveness by increasing the number of article intent models we consider.

In Table 7 we list the results from combining one, up to four article intent models with the input article. On average, increasing the number of article intent models leads to a decrease in performance for all methods. ART + AIM^{T} achieves the best performance across the board for $N = 1$. Each method peaks at different number of article intent models; ART + AIM$^{T}_{A}$ peaks at $N = 3$, and ART + AIM$^{T}_{M}$ at $N = 2$. The differences in performance at various N, however, for the later two models are small.

The performance of ART + AIM^{T} decreases quickly as N increases. A possible explanation can be due to the uniform weights assigned to the input article and to the article intent models. Uniform weights allow article intent models topically far away from the input article to be weighted equally, multiplying the effects of topical drift. The weighting schemes of ART + AIM$^{T}_{A}$ and ART + AIM$^{T}_{M}$ manage count for this effect, and show relatively stable performance for all N.

Parameter optimization. We explore the effect of the language model smoothing parameter on retrieval effectiveness. In our particular setting, the query models are much longer compared to traditional web search queries because they contain content of news articles, and for query mixture models, contain content from several news articles. We perform a parameter sweep on the Dirichlet priors smoothing parameter μ for two runs, ART, and ART + AIM^{T}. Fig. 4 illustrates the retrieval performance against μ. The differences in performance for different values are small. We believe this is due to the large size of the query, which lessens the smoothing effects.

Table 7: MAP scores for three weighting schemes for combining one to four article intent models with the incoming article. Boldface indicates best performance for the respective model.

Model	# Article intent models 1	2	3	4
ART + AIM^{T}	**0.3385**	0.2276	0.1878	0.1764
ART + AIM$^{T}_{A}$	0.3116	0.3106	**0.3141**	0.3037
ART + AIM$^{T}_{M}$	0.3104	**0.3107**	0.3085	0.2990

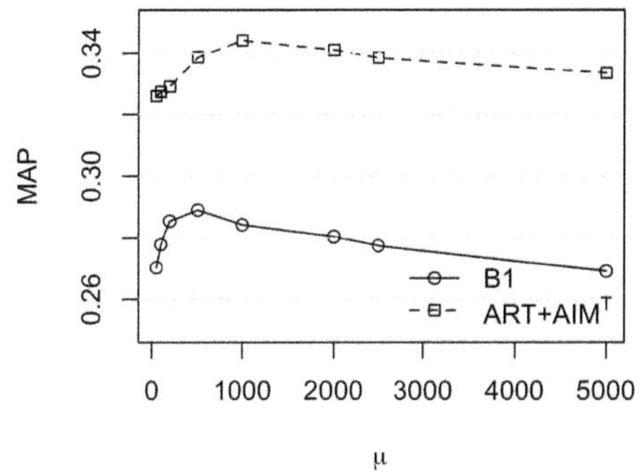

Figure 4: Retrieval effectiveness in MAP for the runs ART, and ART + AIM^{T} over a range of values of smoothing parameter μ.

10. CONCLUSIONS AND OUTLOOK

In this work we have introduced the task of temporal context discovery: Given a query from a user, and the first document they visit, the system aims to predict documents that are likely for the user to visit next. The task takes place in near real-time and systems need to suggest documents not necessarily seen before. The system tries to capture the user browsing intent, and to take into account the change in intent after the user visits the first document.

We focused on an instantiation of the task, and in particular on the news domain. We approached the task as a retrieval problem, and developed query modeling methods that aim to capture user intent. For this purpose, we introduced the *article intent models*, which are trained on the content of user queries and news articles that users have had visited, extracted from user trails in query logs. We presented methods for modeling article intent models with the input query and new article, and several weighting schemes for generating query mixture models. Our experiments demonstrate the utility of our methods for predicting news articles that are visited from users.

In future work, we envisage to enhance our query modeling methods with more elaborate term selection and weighting schemes. Also, we plan extending our query models for incremental updating so we are able to make suggestions given parts of a user trail. Finally, we would like to validate the models presented here with a user-based study, to determine whether the effect of the suggestions produce any behavioral difference in human readers. We believe this line of work is useful to online news agents for increasing the user engagement of their web presence.

Acknowledgments. The authors would like to thank the anonymous reviewers for their comments.

References

[1] E. Agichtein, E. Brill, and S. Dumais. Improving web search ranking by incorporating user behavior information. In *SIGIR '06*, pages 19–26, New York, NY, USA, 2006. ACM.

[2] A. Ashkan, C. L. Clarke, E. Agichtein, and Q. Guo. Classifying and characterizing query intent. In *ECIR '09*, pages 578–586, Berlin, Heidelberg, 2009. Springer-Verlag.

[3] S. Attfield, G. Kazai, M. Lalmas, and B. Piwowarski. Towards a science of user engagement (position paper). In *WSDM Workshop on User Modeling for Web Applications*, February 2011.

[4] M. Bilenko and R. W. White. Mining the search trails of surfing crowds: identifying relevant websites from user activity. In *WWW '08*, pages 51–60, New York, NY, USA, 2008. ACM.

[5] P. Boldi, F. Bonchi, C. Castillo, D. Donato, A. Gionis, and S. Vigna. The query-flow graph: model and applications. In *CIKM '08*, pages 609–618, New York, NY, USA, 2008. ACM.

[6] A. Broder. A taxonomy of web search. *SIGIR Forum*, 36:3–10, September 2002.

[7] L. Calderon-Benavides, C. Gonzalez-Caro, and R. Baeza-Yates. Towards a deeper understanding of the user?s query intent. *Search*, pages 1–4, 2010.

[8] O. Chapelle, S. Ji, C. Liao, E. Velipasaoglu, L. Lai, and S.-L. Wu. Intent-based diversification of web search results: metrics and algorithms. *Inf. Retr.*, 14 (6):572–592, dec 2011.

[9] M. Gamon, S. Basu, D. Belenko, D. Fisher, M. Hurst, and A. Konig. Blews: Using blogs to provide context for news articles. *Association for the Advancement of Artificial Intelligence*, 2008.

[10] C. N. González-Caro and R. A. Baeza-Yates. A multi-faceted approach to query intent classification. In R. Grossi, F. Sebastiani, and F. Silvestri, editors, *SPIRE*, volume 7024 of *Lecture Notes in Computer Science*, pages 368–379. Springer, 2011.

[11] J. Guo, X. Cheng, G. Xu, and X. Zhu. Intent-aware query similarity. In *CIKM '11*, pages 259–268, New York, NY, USA, 2011. ACM.

[12] T. Joachims. Optimizing search engines using clickthrough data. In *KDD '02*, pages 133–142, New York, NY, USA, 2002. ACM.

[13] N. Kanhabua, R. Blanco, and M. Matthews. Ranking related news predictions. In *SIGIR '11*, pages 755–764, New York, NY, USA, 2011. ACM.

[14] D. Kelly and N. J. Belkin. Display time as implicit feedback: understanding task effects. In *SIGIR '04*, pages 377–384, New York, NY, USA, 2004. ACM.

[15] U. Lee, Z. Liu, and J. Cho. Automatic identification of user goals in web search. In *WWW '05*, pages 391–400, New York, NY, USA, 2005. ACM.

[16] L. Li, W. Chu, J. Langford, and R. E. Schapire. A contextual-bandit approach to personalized news article recommendation. In *WWW '10*, pages 661–670, New York, NY, USA, 2010. ACM.

[17] D. Metzler and W. B. Croft. Combining the language model and inference network approaches to retrieval. *Inf. Process. Manage.*, 40:735–750, September 2004.

[18] D. Metzler, Y. Bernstein, W. B. Croft, A. Moffat, and J. Zobel. Similarity measures for tracking information flow. In *CIKM '05*, pages 517–524, New York, NY, USA, 2005. ACM.

[19] R. Mihalcea and A. Csomai. Wikify!: linking documents to encyclopedic knowledge. In *CIKM '07*, volume 7, pages 233–242, 2007.

[20] J. M. Ponte and W. B. Croft. A language modeling approach to information retrieval. In *SIGIR '98*, pages 275–281, New York, NY, USA, 1998. ACM.

[21] R. L. Santos, C. Macdonald, and I. Ounis. Intent-aware search result diversification. In *SIGIR '11*, pages 595–604, New York, NY, USA, 2011. ACM.

[22] C. Silverstein, H. Marais, M. Henzinger, and M. Moricz. Analysis of a very large web search engine query log. *SIGIR Forum*, 33:6–12, September 1999.

[23] A. Singla, R. White, and J. Huang. Studying trailfinding algorithms for enhanced web search. In *SIGIR '10*, pages 443–450, New York, NY, USA, 2010. ACM.

[24] M. Tsagkias, M. de Rijke, and W. Weerkamp. Hypergeometric language models for republished article finding. In *SIGIR '11*, pages 485–494, New York, NY, USA, 2011. ACM.

[25] M. Tsagkias, M. de Rijke, and W. Weerkamp. Linking online news and social media. In *WSDM '11*, pages 565–574, New York, NY, USA, 2011. ACM.

[26] R. W. White, P. Bailey, and L. Chen. Predicting user interests from contextual information. In *SIGIR '09*, pages 363–370, New York, NY, USA, 2009. ACM.

[27] C. Zhai and J. Lafferty. A study of smoothing methods for language models applied to information retrieval. *ACM Trans. Inf. Syst.*, 22:179–214, April 2004.

Efficient Query Recommendations in the Long Tail via Center-Piece Subgraphs

Francesco Bonchi
Yahoo! Research, Spain
bonchi@yahoo-inc.com

Raffaele Perego
ISTI - CNR, Pisa, Italy
r.perego@isti.cnr.it

Fabrizio Silvestri
ISTI - CNR, Italy; and
Yahoo! Research, Spain
f.silvestri@isti.cnr.it

Hossein Vahabi
IMT, Lucca, Italy
hossein.vahabi@imtlucca.it

Rossano Venturini
Dept. of Computer Science,
University of Pisa
rossano@di.unipi.it

ABSTRACT

We present a recommendation method based on the well-known concept of *center-piece subgraph*, that allows for the *time/space efficient* generation of suggestions also for *rare*, i.e., long-tail queries. Our method is scalable with respect to both the size of datasets from which the model is computed and the heavy workloads that current web search engines have to deal with. Basically, we relate terms contained into queries with highly correlated queries in a query-flow graph. This enables a novel recommendation generation method able to produce recommendations for approximately 99% of the workload of a real-world search engine. The method is based on a graph having *term* nodes, *query* nodes, and two kinds of connections: term-query and query-query. The first connects a term to the queries in which it is contained, the second connects two query nodes if the likelihood that a user submits the second query after having issued the first one is sufficiently high. On such large graph we compute the center-piece subgraph induced by terms contained into queries and we reduce the cost of this computation using a novel and efficient method based on an *inverted index* representation of the model. We experiment our solution on two real-world query logs and we show that its effectiveness is comparable (and in some case better) than state-of-the-art methods for head-queries. More importantly, the quality of the recommendations generated remains very high also for long-tail queries, where other methods fail even to produce any suggestion. Finally, we extensively investigate scalability and efficiency issues and we show the viability of our method in real world search engines.

Categories and Subject Descriptors

H.3.3 [**Information Search and Retrieval**]: Search process, Query formulation

Permission to make digital or hard copies of all or part of this work for personal or classroom use is granted without fee provided that copies are not made or distributed for profit or commercial advantage and that copies bear this notice and the full citation on the first page. To copy otherwise, or republish, to post on servers or to redistribute to lists, requires prior specific permission and/or a fee.
SIGIR'12, August 12–16, 2012, Portland, Oregon, USA.
Copyright 2012 ACM 978-1-4503-1472-5/12/08... $15.00.

General Terms

Algorithms, Experimentation, Measurement

Keywords

Query Recommender Systems, Web Search Effectiveness

1. INTRODUCTION

Much of the literature on query recommendation is devoted to propose novel "methods", or "models", that enhance *effectiveness.* Although this is, clearly, a fundamental issue, the other side of the coin, *efficiency,* has indeed been poorly addressed by the research community. The key idea behind query recommendation is that of exploiting the so-called *"wisdom of the crowds"*, i.e., the knowledge mined from search engine query logs which store all the past interactions of users with the search system. For this reason query recommenders are more effective when the information need of the user is a popular one, i.e., the same query has been been frequently submitted by other users in the past. Using common wording, these queries are *head queries* indicating that they are usually appearing in the head of the power-law-like curve typical of query popularity distribution. In this paper we introduce a novel recommendation method based on computing the *center-piece subgraph* [14] on a large graph-model. Our solution presents several enhancements with respect to the state-of-the art. Firstly, the method is scalable and efficient. It is scalable as the generation of the model is easily parallelizable and the model itself can be stored in a compressed form. Furthermore, we represent the model in an inverted index and we show that several engineering practices used for inverted indexes are inherited by our model as well. The inverted index representation has several advantages as, for instance, the possibility of exploiting the existing index processing infrastructure of search engines with small, or no, modifications. The suggestions generation time, also, is comparable to that taken by the query processing phase. Thus, generating recommendations does not represent a bottleneck even when rare, uncached queries are processed. Even if the main goal of this paper is that of designing an efficient and implementable system, we show that the quality of its suggestions is comparable (and sometimes even better) with respect to state-of-the-art method, query flow graph. Interestingly, the quality of the suggestions produced by our system is stable, almost independently of the frequency of the query in the query log used to learn the model. This is a key property which does not hold for the query flow graph. Query flow graph is, indeed, not able to generate suggestions for previously unseen or rare queries.

More in details, our method is based on a graph-model that we dub TQGraph (*Term-Query Graph*). A TQGraph extends the well-known Query Flow Graph [3] by considering two distinct sets of nodes: *Term* and *Query* nodes. Arcs connect a term node to all the query nodes containing it, while arcs between two query nodes expresses the likelihood that a user submits the second query after having issued the first one. We design such a structure so that we are able to generate recommendations for a query by extracting the *center-piece subgraph* [14] associated with terms of the query itself. It is important to remark that since we do not require a query to be present in the TQGraph, but only its terms, our method is able in principle to provide recommendations even for a never-seen-before query.

It is this term-centric perspective that allows us to provide a framework enabling suggestions to be efficiently generated on the fly during query processing. Finally, let us resume the original contributions of this paper:

- A novel method for query recommendation based on center-piece graph computation over the TQGraph [1] model. Being term-centric, our center-piece-based method does not suffer from the problem of sparsity of queries, being able to generate suggestions for previously-unseen queries as far as terms have been previously seen. Empirical assessment confirms that our method is able to generate suggestions for the vast majority (i.e., 99%) of queries and with a quality that is comparable to (and in some cases better than) the state-of-the-art method based on Query Flow Graph.

- After having proved the effectiveness our method, we are faced with its major but only apparent drawback: any suggestion pass through the computation of the center-piece subgraph from query terms. Given the very large size of the underlying graph, this task is clearly unfeasible for any system claiming to be real-time. We overcome to this limitation by introducing a novel and efficient way to compute center-piece subgraphs. This comes at the small cost of storing precomputed vectors that need to be opportunely combined to obtain the final results. The data structure we use is *inverted list-based* and thus it is particularly suitable for web search environments.

- The inverted-list-based data structure is compressed by using a *lossy compression* method able to reduce by an average of 80% the space occupancy of the uncompressed data structures. Furthermore, caching is exploited at the term-level to enable scalable generation of query suggestions. Being term-based, caching is able to attain hit-ratios of approximately 95% with a reasonable footprint (i.e., few gigabytes of main memory.) Furthermore, since the compression method is lossy, we have evaluated through a user study the loss in terms of suggestion quality, and we have found that this loss is negligible. We can claim that our method to generate suggestions is very effective (and efficient) also when a very aggressive lossy compression strategy is applied.

It should be noted that the last two research results, beyond enabling our model to be real-time, represent a more general achievement for what concerns the computation of center-piece subgraphs in very large graphs.

The paper is organized as follows. Section 2 presents related research results. Section 3 details the TQGraph model and presents the methods used to compute suggestions. In Section 4 we assess the quality of the recommendations computed by our method and we compare our results with state-of-the-art QFG. Sections 5 and 6 present and experimentally evaluate our scalability and efficiency enhancing techniques. Finally, in Section 7, we discuss future work and conclude.

2. RELATED WORK

Hanghan *et al.* in [14] propose the Center-Piece Subgraph, as the subgraph that best captures the connections of a set of nodes in a graph. The computation of the Center-Piece Subgraph is based on the *Hadamard* (i.e., component-wise) product of a set of vectors, where each vector is obtained by doing a random walk with restart from a single node. Due to the long processing time of random walks with restart, the method is unfeasible for real-time application on large graph. The authors themselves propose a way to speed up the process by precomputing a $n \times n$ matrix, where n is the number of nodes in graph. This technique helps on small graphs, but is unfeasible for large graphs due to space requirements. This paper contributes with a novel way to compute efficiently center-piece sub-graphs on large graphs. The technique requires to precompute probability distributions and storing them in an inverted index that need to be opportunely processed to obtain center-pieces. Moreover, several optimizations, namely pruning, bucketing, and compression can be applied in order to reduce the memory footprint.

The techniques proposed during last years for query recommendation are very different, yet they have in common the exploitation of usage information recorded in query logs.

Baeza-Yates *et al.* [1] exploit click-through data on query logs as a way to provide recommendations. The method is based on the concept of *Cover Graph* (CG). A CG is a bipartite graph of queries and URLs, where a query q and an URL u are connected if a user issued q and clicked on u that was an answer for the query. Suggestions for a query q are thus obtained by accessing the corresponding node in the CG and by extracting the related queries sharing more URLs.

Among the proposals exploiting the chains of queries stored in query logs, [7] use an association rule mining algorithm to devise frequent query patterns. These patterns are inserted in a query relation graph which allows "concepts" (queries that are synonyms, specializations, generalizations, etc.) to be identified and suggested. Jones *et al.* introduce the notion of query substitution or query rewriting, and propose a solution for sponsored search [9]. Such solution relies on the fact that in about half sessions the user modifies a query with another which is closely related. Such pairs of reformulated queries are mined from the log and used for query suggestion.

Boldi *et al.* introduce the *Query Flow Graph* [3] (QFG) model, which is a Markov chain-based representation of a

[1]A preliminary presentation of the idea of the TQGraph, was given in a poster at WWW'11 by the same authors: `http://www.www2011india.com/proceeding/companion/p15.pdf`.

query log. A QFG is a directed graph in which nodes are queries, and an edge $e = (q_1, q_2)$ exists if at least a user has issued q_2 after q_1. Furthermore, e is weighed by the probability of a user to issue q_2 after q_1. Given a query q, suggestions are generated by means of random walks from q on the QFG [4]. It is worth noting that the "central" part of our TQGraph (i.e, the subgraph induced by only the query nodes, without the term nodes) corresponds to a QFG, whose construction is discussed in detail in the next section.

The importance of rare query classification and suggestion recently attracted a lot of attention. Generating suggestions for rare queries is in fact very difficult due to the lack of information in the query logs. As it was pointed out by Downey *et al.* [6] trough an analysis on search behaviors, rare queries are very important, and their effective satisfaction is very challenging for search engines. The authors also study transitions between rare and common queries highlighting the difference between the frequency of queries and their related information needs.

Mei *et al.* propose a novel query suggestion algorithm based on ranking queries with the hitting time on a large scale bipartite graph [10]. The rationale of the method is to capture semantic consistency between the suggested queries and the original query. Empirical results on a query log from a real world search engine show that hitting time is effective to generate semantically consistent query suggestions. The authors show that the proposed method and its variations are able to boost long tail queries, and personalized query suggestion. Also a recent work by Yang *et al.* [12] proposes an optimal framework for rare-query suggestion leveraging on implicit feedbacks from users mined from the query logs.

Broder *et al.* [5] proposes an efficient and effective approach for matching ads against rare queries. The approach builds an expanded query representation by leveraging offline processing done for related popular queries. Xu and Xu [15] designes a way to learn similarity functions that are well suited for rare queries. The method leverages the knowledge extracted from past queries and build a locality sensitive hashing function thrugh which similarity of rare queries is estimated. Jain *et al.* [8] modifies the terms in rare queries in order to match more frequent queries in the query log.

All the previous proposals suffer from a main limitation which regards the granularity of the atomic items represented in the recommendation model. In the literature the granularity is always at the query level, and thus the suggestion algorithms can provide recommendations only to queries already seen in the past and present in the training log. This paper proposes a different solution in which the knowledge learned from the query log is coded at the granularity of the single terms present in the queries used for training. As a consequence, differently from competitors, our solution can generate suggestions even for queries not occurring in the training log and never submitted in the past. The only constraint is in fact on the presence in the training log of the terms used for expressing the query.

A totally orthogonal proposal to deal with query recommendations for long-tail queries has recently been presented by Szpektor *et al.* [13]. They propose to extract rules between *query templates* rather than individual query transitions, as currently done in session-based models. The method applies general rules learned from the log to rare queries fitting the rule. As an example, if the template $<$ *city* $>$ *hotels* $\rightarrow$ $<$ *city* $>$ *restaurants* holds strongly in the log, and *Montezuma* is recognized as a city in the rare query *Montezuma hotels*, then *Montezuma restaurants* is generated as possible query recommendation, even if it was not present it the training log.

Obviously this method extends the coverage of query recommendation to the long-tail from a different standpoint w.r.t. our proposal. While our method can not suggest *Montezuma restaurants* in the hypothetical case that the term *Montezuma* has never been seen before, the method based on query templates can only suggest recommendations for query for which templates exist. The two proposal are hence totally orthogonal and as such they could be potentially combined.

A second limitation common to some of the previous proposals is on efficiency. Query suggestions for most popular queries can be cached with query results themselves, but the time needed to generate relevant suggestions for queries that are not cached must necessarily be comparable to the query processing time. This need makes practically unusable all the methods requiring complex computations over large graphs, e.g., random walks over a huge QFG [4]. As discussed above, our novel solution to compute efficiently center-piece sub-graphs on large graphs solves this very important issue.

3. THE TQGRAPH MODEL

Let $Q = \langle q_1, \ldots, q_n \rangle$ be a query log, i.e., a set of queries each annotated with an anonymized *userid* and *timestamp* representing when the query has been submitted.

TQGraph is a digraph $G = (V, E)$ with vertices V and arcs E defined as follows. Let T be the set of all the distinct terms appearing in queries of Q. V contains a node for each term $t \in T$ and for each query $q \in Q$. In particular, let V_T be the set of *Term* nodes and V_Q be the set *Query* nodes, then $V = V_T \cup V_Q$. Likewise, E is the union of two different sets of arcs E_Q and E_{TQ}. Arcs in E_Q are defined as in QFG [3] and connect only nodes in V_Q. E_{TQ} contains arcs (t, q) where $t \in T$ is a term contained in query $q \in Q$. Finally, let $w : E \rightarrow (0..1]$ be a weighting function assigning to each arc $(u, v) \in E$ a value $w(u, v)$ defined as follows. For arcs $(t, q) \in E_{TQ}$, $\frac{w(t,q)=1}{d}$ where d is the number of distinct queries in which the t occurs, i.e., the number of outlinks of t. For arcs $(q, q') \in E_Q$ we follow QFG weighting scheme. In the original QFG paper, Boldi *et al.* [3] describe two distinct weighting schemes, namely *chaining probability* and *relative frequencies*. In the case of arc weighting it has been shown that *chaining probability* is the most effective scheme. Therefore, we resort to chaining probability for arcs in E_Q. To estimate such chaining probability, we extract for each arc $(q, q') \in E_Q$ a set of features. Such features are aggregated over all sessions in which queries q and q' appear consecutively and in this order. Finally, the chaining probability is computed by using logistic regression. Noisy arcs, i.e., arcs having a probability of being traversed lower than a minimum threshold value, are removed. In other words, query reformulations that are not likely to be made are not considered. For further details regarding the features and the model, we refer to the original work of Boldi et al. [3]. In particular, we have used the settings suggested in the original paper [3] for the values of the various parameters involved in QFG building.

3.1 Query suggestion method

Given our TQGraph G, the query suggestions for an incoming query q composed of terms $\{t_1, \ldots t_m\} \subseteq T$ are generated from G by extracting the center-piece subgraph [14]

	#queries	#terms	$\lvert V_Q\rvert$	$\lvert V_T\rvert$	dang.	$\lvert E_{TQ}\rvert$	$\lvert E_Q\rvert$	$\bar{d}_{TQ}$	$\bar{d}_Q$	#queries freq = 1	#terms freq = 1
Yahoo!	580,797,850	1,343,988,549	28,763,637	6,261,105	14.5%	83,808,761	56,250,874	13.38	1.95	162,221,967	5,099,145
MSN	14,899,247	35,697,149	6,488,713	2,014,547	35.2%	19,740,312	5,051,843	9.79	0.77	4,992,180	1,633,729

Table 1: Statistics of the two query logs and TQGraphs. Total number of queries and terms. Number of query nodes and term nodes. Percentage of dangling nodes. Number of arcs from terms to queries and from queries to queries, and corresponding average degrees. Number of queries and terms with frequency 1.

starting from the m Term nodes corresponding to terms $t_1, \ldots, t_m$. Given a directed graph and m of its nodes, the center-piece subgraph is informally defined as a small subgraph that best captures the connections between the m nodes. In our case the center-piece subgraph represent the set of queries that better represent terms of the original query q. It is important to point out, here, the following important fact: *in order to build a center-piece subgraph from q is not necessary that q is contained in the* TQGraph.

The center-piece subgraph for a query q composed of terms $\{t_1, \ldots t_m\} \subseteq T$ is obtained by performing a Random Walk with Restart (RWR) from *each one* of the m term nodes corresponding to terms in q. The resulting m stationary distributions are then multiplied component-wise. More formally, given an incoming query $q = \{t_1, \ldots, t_m\}$ we compute m RWRs from the m query-terms of q to obtain m vectors of stationary distribution $\mathbf{r}_{t_1}, \ldots, \mathbf{r}_{t_m}$. Then, we compute the *Hadamard* (i.e., component-wise) product of the m vectors $\mathbf{r}_{t_1} \circ \mathbf{r}_{t_2} \circ \ldots \circ \mathbf{r}_{t_m}$ to obtain the final scoring vector $\mathbf{r}_q$. Following the definition of Hadamard product, the i-th component of $\mathbf{r}_q$, i.e. $\mathbf{r}_q(i)$, is given by $\mathbf{r}_q(i) = \prod_{j=1}^{m} \mathbf{r}_{t_j}(i)$. Since each dimension of $\mathbf{r}$ corresponds to a query in Q, the TQGraph recommendation algorithm suggests the k queries having the k highest scores, where k is a parameter determining the maximum number of recommendations we want to show for each query. The reason for resorting to the product of the entries (namely, *Center-piece*) instead of their sum (namely, *Personalized PageRank*) is that we are interested in discovering queries that are "*strongly*" related to "*most of the terms*" in the starting query instead of queries that are highly related even to just few of them[2] It is also worth being remarked that, while Personalized PageRank could have been computed directly on the QFG, computing the center-piece subgraph related to the query terms can be done only on the TQGraph. Computing center-piece starting from the queries in QFGcontaining those terms, in fact, would prevent those queries themselves to be returned as suggestions. Obviously, this is not the case for the QFG-based model.

The following toy example shows how suggestions are computed using the center-piece-based TQGraph model. Consider a query log containing only two queries, q_1, q_2, made up from a vocabulary of three terms, t_1, t_2, t_3. Suppose that the RWR procedure described above leads to the following three stationary distributions: $\mathbf{r}_{t_1} = [0.9, 0.1]$; $\mathbf{r}_{t_2} = [0.3, 0.5]$; $\mathbf{r}_{t_3} = [0.09, 0.91]$. Finally, let k be equal to 1. According to this model, when a user submits a query containing terms (t_1, t_3) the system would compute the vector of scores $\mathbf{r}_q = [0.081, 0.091]$. Thus q_2, i.e., the top-1 center-piece subgraph, would be chosen as suggestion since, in this case, its score is greater than q_1 score.

4. EFFECTIVENESS

Ideally, a recommendation model has to produce high quality recommendations for the largest number of queries possible. The fraction of queries for which a method is able to generate recommendations, henceforth referred to as *coverage*, is of paramount importance in order to satisfy as much users requests as possible. It turns out that coverage is one of the major weak points of previously proposed solutions. As we shall see in the following our method is extremely robust w.r.t. this problem, and it is able to generate (useful) recommendations for a very large fraction of users' queries.

Unfortunately, defining and measuring quality of recommendations is not an easy task. It turns out to be, in fact, a subjective matter, usually measured on the basis of user-studies comparing a given method with some baselines. Following the prevailing custom, we will rely on an extensive user-study to assess effectiveness. Finally, to let the reader to appreciate the quality of our methods, we will discuss some anecdotal evidences on a small set of user-queries.

Query logs. We use two different query logs coming from two popular web search engines, namely Yahoo! and MSN.

- Yahoo! query log consists of approximately 600 millions of anonymized queries sampled from Yahoo! USA queries submitted within a short period of time in spring 2010. The TQGraph built on the Yahoo! log consists of $6,261,105$ term nodes and $28,763,637$ query nodes. The number of term-query arcs is $83,808,761$ whereas the number of arcs between query nodes is $56,250,874$.

- MSN is the Search Spring 2006 Query Log, released in the context of the 2009 Workshop on Web Search Click Data[3], containing approximately 15 millions queries from the USA search volume. The TQGraph built on this log consists of $2,014,547$ term nodes and $6,488,713$ query nodes, $19,740,312$ term-query arcs, and $5,051,843$ query-query arcs.

Table 1 reports some statistics on the two TQGraphs.

On coverage. Before describing recommendation effectiveness we discuss query coverage. As we have discussed before, the main advantage of our proposal over the state of the art, is the capability of providing useful recommendations also for "difficult" queries (i.e., rare or never-seen-before). Let us recall that, in order to produce recommendations for a given query, our method needs all the terms contained in the query to belong to the TQGraph. Or in other terms, our model fails to give a recommendation only when it receive a

[2]For the sake of completeness, a comparison of the suggestions produced by RWR from query nodes containing term queries and our TQGraph-based model is discussed in Section 4.

[3]`http://research.microsoft.com/en-us/um/people/nickcr/wscd09/`

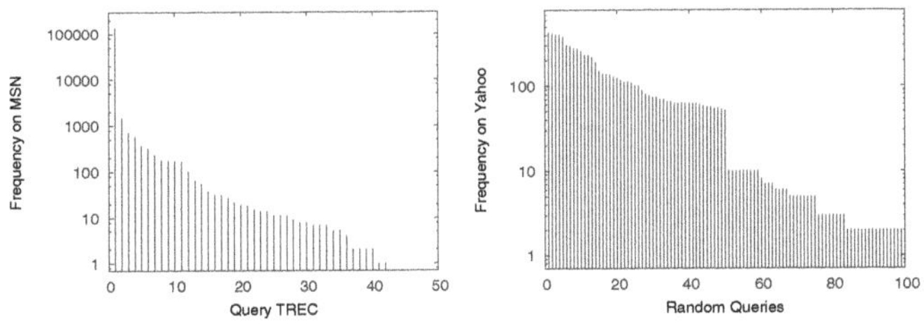

Figure 1: Frequency in the corresponding log of all the queries in the two testbeds.

never-seen-before term. While unique queries are quite frequent, unique terms are not. For instance, out of the 580.8 million of queries contained in the Yahoo! query log about 162.2 million of them are unique, in the same log the number of unique term is, instead, 5.1 million (see Table 1). Therefore, on this query log the coverage of our model is more than 99%, while the maximum coverage of QFG is 73% (i.e. the percentage of repeated queries).

User-study. Having pointed out the almost perfect coverage of our method, we next focus on evaluating the quality of the recommendations produced, evaluated by conducting a user-study. As a baseline for comparison we used recommendations provided by the state-of-the-art method QFG. To produce recommendations from the QFG we follow the method presented in [4]: recommendations are based on the probability of being at a certain node after performing a random walk over the QFG. This random walk starts at the node corresponding to the input query. At each step, the random walker either remains in the same node with probability 0.9, or follows one of the out-links with probability 0.1. in the latter case the links are followed with probability proportional to $w(i, j)$.

The user study was conducted on two different sets of queries. The first one is the composed by the 50 queries of the standard TREC Web diversification track testbed[4] that we use for the MSN query log. The second is a set of 100 queries randomly chosen from the Yahoo! query log. Figure 1 reports the distribution of the frequency of the queries in the two sets in the corresponding query log. We can observe that 8 queries in the TREC testbed do not appear at all in the MSN query log. The assessment was conducted by a group of 10 assessors (researchers not working on related topics). To reduce the load on our assessors we conducted only two, out of the four (2 query logs × 2 testbeds) possible user-studies. In particular we pair the Yahoo! set of queries up with the TQGraph and QFG models built over the same log (obviously the queries were randomly drawn by a portion of the log not used to build the suggestion models). Whereas, we pair TREC queries up with the models built on the MSN query log. In fact, the period from which TREC topics come, is close to the period in which MSN queries were collected.

We generated the top-5 recommendations for each query by using both the QFG and the TQGraph-based method with different parameters setting. Using a web interface each assessor was presented a random query followed by the list of all the different recommendations produced. Recommendations were presented shuffled, in order for the assessors to not be able to distinguish which system produced them. We give assessors the possibility to observe the search engine

[4]`http://trec.nist.gov/data/web09.html`

TREC on MSN	useful	somewhat	not useful
$\alpha = 0.9$	57%	16%	27%
$\alpha = 0.5$	32%	13%	55%
$\alpha = 0.1$	22%	12%	66%

100 queries on Yahoo!	useful	somewhat	not useful
$\alpha = 0.9$	48%	11%	41%
$\alpha = 0.5$	41%	20%	39%
$\alpha = 0.1$	37%	20%	43%

Table 2: TQGraph effectiveness on the two different set of queries and query logs, by varying α.

TREC on MSN	useful	somewhat	not useful
TQGraph $\alpha = 0.9$	57%	16%	27%
QFG	50%	9%	41%

100 queries on Yahoo!	useful	somewhat	not useful
TQGraph $\alpha = 0.9$	48%	11%	41%
QFG	23%	10%	67%

Table 3: TQGraph and QFG effectiveness on the two different testbeds.

results for the original query and the recommended query that was being evaluated. The assessors were asked to rate a recommendation using one of the following scores: *useful*, *somewhat useful*, and *not useful*[5].

In first instance we evaluate the impact of the α parameter (we recall here that α is the restart value of the RWR, from each term of the query to be recommended). Table 2 shows the effectiveness of our method when varying α among three different values $\alpha = 0.1, 0.5, 0.9$. Results show that the best quality is achieved when $\alpha = 0.9$. Table 3 reports the results of the user study comparing effectiveness of the TQGraph-based and QFG-based recommendations. TQGraph-based recommendations are globally of higher quality than QFG-based ones. We further investigate (see Table 4) the effectiveness of our method with respect to three different classes of MSN queries: unseen, dangling, and others. A query is unseen if it does not appear in the training query log. A query is dangling if its corresponding node in the QFG has no outgoing edges. The remaining queries belong to the class others. We observe that QFG is unable to provide suggestions for queries in the first two classes while our method provides

[5]The following very broad instruction was given to assessors: *A useful recommendation is a query such that, if the user submits it to the search engine, it provides new results that were not available using the original query, and that agree with the inferred user intent of the original query.* Of course there is a great deal of subjectivity in this assessment as the original intent is not known by the assessors.

TREC on MSN (unseen)	useful	somewhat	not useful
TQGraph $\alpha = 0.9$	46%	10%	44%
QFG	0%	0%	100%

TREC on MSN (dangling)	useful	somewhat	not useful
TQGraph $\alpha = 0.9$	60%	30%	10%
QFG	0%	0%	100%

TREC on MSN (others)	useful	somewhat	not useful
TQGraph $\alpha = 0.9$	59%	17%	24%
QFG	61%	13%	26%

Table 4: User study results on unseen, dangling and others queries.

suggestions of high quality. The two methods have almost the same quality for the third class of queries. A similar behavior has been observed in Yahoo! query log. We do not report the results due to space limitations.[6]

Anecdotal evidence. We next show an example of query recommendations. The query *"lower heart rate"* is one among the eight from the TREC testbed that does not appear at all in the MSN query log. Below we report the top 5 recommendations both using our TQGraph model and using RWR[7].

Query: lower heart rate

TQGraph **Suggestions**	**RWR Suggestions**
things to lower heart rate	broken heart
lower heart rate through exercise	prime rate
accelerated heart rate and pregnant	exchange rate
web md	bank rate
heart problems	currency exchange rate

We can observe that all the top-5 suggestions can be considered pertinent to the initial topic. Moreover, even if this is not an objective in this paper, they present some *diversity*: the first two are *how-to* queries, while the last three are queries related to finding information w.r.t. possible problems (with one very specific for pregnant women). The most interesting recommendation is probably *"web md"*, which makes perfect sense (WebMD.com is a web site devoted to provide health and medical news and information), and has a large edit distance from the original query. Recommendations produced by RWR are not relevant due to the effect we point out in Section 3.

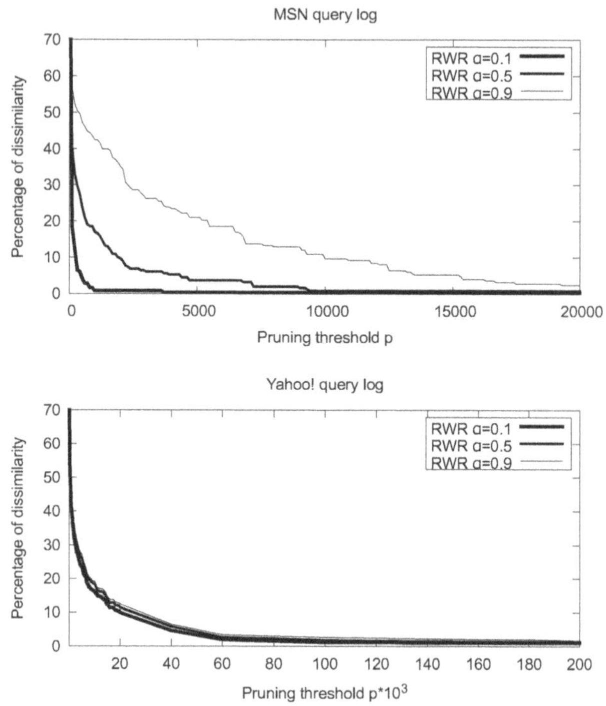

Figure 2: Dissimilarity (in percentage) for the top-5 suggestions as a function of the pruning threshold p, measured on the MSN (top) and Yahoo! (bottom) query logs. The curves refer to different values of the parameter α used in the RWR.

5. EFFICIENCY

Since query suggestions have to be served online, a query recommender must compute them efficiently, possibly in real-time. In this section we introduce some novel techniques allowing the efficient generation of recommendations at query time. Such techniques are peculiar of the TQGraph as they can only be achieved thanks to the term-centric perspective.

We recall that given an incoming query q, the generation of suggestions requires to compute RWRs on the TQGraph from the nodes associated with the terms occurring in the query. For each term t, the stationary probability distribution resulting from the RWR is represented by a vector $\mathbf{r}_t$ that scores queries in Q according to the probability of reaching them in a random walk on the TQGraph starting from t. As discussed in Section 3, given an incoming query $q = \{t_1, \ldots, t_m\}$, our recommender system returns the k queries having the largest probabilities in the Hadamard product $\prod_{i=1}^{m} \mathbf{r}_{t_i}$.

Before introducing our optimized solution we want to point out the major drawbacks of the two trivial approaches that can be used for computing suggestions using our model.

The most trivial approach consists in simply computing the RWR on the TQGraph for each term t_i in the incoming query as it arrives, and in multiplying the resulting stationary distributions.

[6]We observe that results in Table 3 and Table 4 are consistent because we considered as *not useful* the cases in which a method is not able to provide any suggestion.

[7]RWR corresponds to summing the entries of score vectors instead of computing the Hadamard product.

The second (less) trivial approach, instead, provides to store the precomputed stationary distributions for all the terms appearing in T. To improve efficiency, we can resort to use an index on which the stationary distribution of the random walks for terms in T are stored as lists of postings, where each posting is given by the identifier of the query (queryID), along with its probability. Recommendations for an incoming query are then computed by processing the posting lists associated with the terms composing the query.

Both approaches suffer from crucial time or space inefficiencies. The former approach requires $\Omega(m \cdot (|E| + |Q|))$ time for each suggestion, thus making it unusable in any online recommender system. As far as the latter approach is concerned, it has its main drawback in the space occupancy. Indeed, the algorithm for computing recommendations is significantly simpler and its time complexity is lower (i.e., $O(m \cdot |Q|)$). Storing all the stationary distributions requires to store $|T|$ different vectors of $|Q|$ entries each (namely, the ith entry of each vector is the probability of the i-th query in the stationary distribution of a term). The space required to store these $|T| \cdot |Q|$ entries is unfortunately prohibitive even for quite small query logs. For example, we notice that using such a approach for the TQGraph built over the relatively small MSN query log would ask to store a total of 13×10^{12} entries which is clearly not feasible in any real system.

In the following we show how the two above-mentioned drawbacks can be avoided by using three different optimizations, namely *pruning, bucketing,* and *compression.* The goal is to sensibly reduce space requirements, thus making our query suggestion method viable.

Pruning Lists. In order to reduce the space occupancy of the latter approach we consider to prune unnecessary entries in each list. The idea is to store only the probabilities of the top-p entries of each stationary distribution, where p is a user defined threshold. In this way we require to store p entries per term instead of $|Q|$.[8] The total number of entries to be stored becomes thus $p \cdot |T|$, with a large saving in space occupancy when $p \ll |Q|$. Obviously, this pruning phase comes at the price of introducing errors in the scores computed by the recommender. Assume that the k suggestions for a query $q = \{t_1, t_2, \ldots, t_m\}$ are the queries $q_1, q_2, \ldots, q_k$. The pruning phase introduces an error whenever one of these top-k queries has been pruned in the list of at least one of the terms $t_i \in q$.

We evaluated experimentally the effects of pruning, and report in Figure 2 the results of these tests. In particular we measured the average dissimilarities for the top-5 suggestions returned before and after pruning, by varying the number p of entries maintained for each term. Given two set A and B of size k, the **dissimilarity** among A and B is defined as $1 - \frac{|A \cap B|}{k}$. This experiment has been repeated by varying also the parameter α used in the RWR. In both cases the largest loss is obtained for RWR $\alpha = 0.9$. This is due to the fact that with this value of restart the most probable queries for a term are more likely to differ from the ones of other terms. This increases the chances for a query to be evicted from the list of at least a term of the user query. However, the experiments conducted show that relatively small values of p lead to a average similarity larger than 95% between the sets of top-5 results.

For example, it is possible to preserve the correctness of 97,6% of the top-5 results by setting $p = 20,000$ on the MSN query log. Note that on MSN 20,000 queries account for only 0.67% of the total number of queries $|Q|$ present in the log. For Yahoo! query log we can instead preserve 95.40% of the results by setting $p = 100,000$. In this case the number of non pruned queries is just 0.34% of $|Q|$. These figures show that about 97% of the queries in each list can be safely pruned away without remarkably affecting the quality of results. This phenomenon can be explained by observing that usually the terms in the user queries are highly related to each other. Thus, it should be not surprising that relevant queries have relatively high probabilities in the lists of all these terms.

Table 5 shows some figures related to the percentage of dissimilarity measured for some values of p on the two query logs. The average dissimilarity after pruning for the top-5 suggestions returned for all the queries in our testbeds, is computed by considering only those recommendations that have been deemed to be sufficiently good by assessors in the user study (namely, recommendations having been classified as *useful* or *somewhat useful* by at least an assessor). Dissimilarity, in percent, due to pruning for the whole lists of the top-5 recommendations is indicated between parenthesis.

As far as the space occupancy is concerned, we recall that the list of each term is formed by a pair of values, for each of the p most probable queries, i.e., the queryID and its probability. We represent each list in the form of a posting list. Firstly, we sort pairs by increasing queryIDs. Then, we encode differences between consecutive queryIDs by resorting to the well-known Elias' Delta coding (see [11] and references therein for more details on integers encoding methods). Finally, we encode the probability of each query in a fixed-length field of 8 bytes. The average number of bits required to store each pair ranges from 69 to 74 bits depending on the value of p. Complete experimental results are reported in parenthesis in Table 6. We observe that the larger the value of p, the denser are the lists for each term. This implies that gaps between queries IDs become smaller and, thus, each pair is more effectively encodable.

[8]The probability of a pruned query is assumed to be 0.

MSN query log

p	RWR $\alpha = 0.1$	RWR $\alpha = 0.5$	RWR $\alpha = 0.9$
5,000	1.18 (0.40)	5.31 (3.60)	13.66 (20.80)
10,000	1.18 (0.40)	1.77 (0.80)	7.10 (9.60)
15,000	1.18 (0.40)	1.77 (0.80)	6.01 (5.20)
20,000	1.18 (0.40)	1.77 (0.80)	3.28 (2.40)
100,000	1.18 (0.40)	0.88 (0.80)	0.00 (0.00)
200,000	1.18 (0.40)	0.00 (0.80)	0.00 (0.00)

Yahoo! query log

p	RWR $\alpha = 0.1$	RWR $\alpha = 0.5$	RWR $\alpha = 0.9$
5,000	21.75 (31.40)	24.26 (31.80)	25.08 (31.60)
10,000	15.09 (25,00)	18.69 (26.20)	18.31 (25.40)
15,000	11.93 (20.80)	15.74 (22.40)	14.58 (21.20)
20,000	11.23 (18.20)	13.77 (20.00)	13.22 (20.00)
100,000	1.05 (1.80)	2.30 (3.00)	2.37 (4.60)
200,000	1.05 (1.60)	1.64 (2.20)	1.36 (2.60)

Table 5: Average dissimilarity (in percentage) between the sets of top-5 suggestions computed with or without pruning as a function of p. The same measure computed by restricting to suggestions that have been considered "useful" or "somewhat useful" is reported between parenthesis.

MSN query log

p	RWR $\alpha = 0.1$	RWR $\alpha = 0.5$	RWR $\alpha = 0.9$
5,000	19.21 (73.63)	17.34 (73.98)	15.81 (73.71)
10,000	18.32 (73.31)	17.15 (73.44)	16.08 (73.44)
15,000	17.99 (73.16)	17.17 (73.16)	16.23 (73.32)
20,000	17.82 (73.03)	17.23 (72.96)	16.33 (73.21)
100,000	15.84(71.39)	16.09(71.28)	16.34(71.15)
200,000	15.43(70.22)	15.36(70.15)	15.21(70.05)

Yahoo! query log

p	RWR $\alpha = 0.1$	RWR $\alpha = 0.5$	RWR $\alpha = 0.9$
5,000	16.25 (72.17)	15.26 (72.26)	13.67 (72.33)
10,000	15.72 (71.43)	14.99 (71.54)	13.79 (71.63)
15,000	15.54 (71.17)	14.96 (71.29)	13.99 (71.42)
20,000	15.59 (71.03)	15.11 (71.17)	14.27 (71.32)
100,000	16.55 (70.47)	16.42 (70.67)	16.16 (70.87)
200,000	16.30 (69.94)	16.23 (70.12)	16.09 (70.30)

Table 6: Average bits per entry for our bucketing method ($\epsilon = 0.95$) and the baseline (between parenthesis) by varying p and α.

Approximating Probabilities. The above method allow to build a index of terms' RWRs, where the pruned list of queries for each term is coded as a postings list. The size of this index is used as baseline to assess the effectiveness of our more sophisticated solution that relies on approximations. We observed that the previous method spends most of its space in storing the probability $\mathbf{r}_t(q)$ for each query q

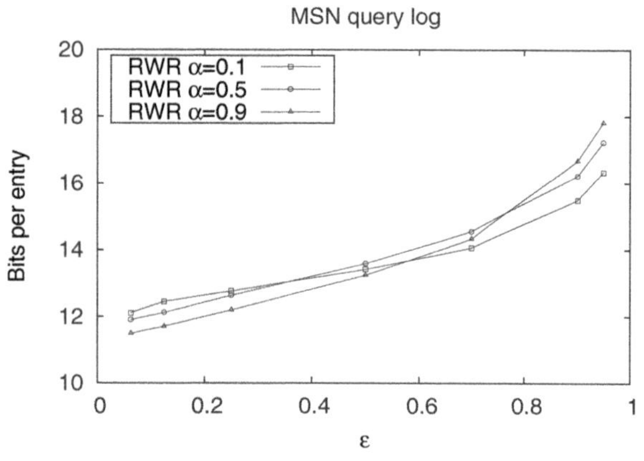

Figure 3: Average bits per entry on the MSN query log as a function of ϵ ($p = 20,000$).

in the stationary distribution $\mathbf{r}_t$. The idea is thus that of approximating each probability by a bucketing schema in a way that still preserves roughly indications of its magnitude. We start by choosing a parameter ϵ which is a real value in $(0, 1)$. We divide the query IDs in the list of a particular term t in buckets based on their probabilities. Let s be the smallest probability in the list. We have l buckets $B_0, B_1, \ldots, B_{l-1}$ where $\epsilon^{l-1} \leq s < \epsilon^l$. The i-th bucket B_i contains the IDs of the queries whose probabilities are in the range $[\epsilon^i, \epsilon^{i+1})$. The approximated probability $\hat{\mathbf{r}}_t(q)$ of a query q in bucket B_i is approximated with ϵ^i. This organization in buckets is particularly suitable for compression. In our scheme we sort queries IDs in each buckets, then we encode gaps between consecutive queries in the same bucket. Finally, we encode the index and the cardinality of each bucket. For simplicity, all the values have been encoded by resorting to Elias' Delta coding. Different choices are possible since the literature offers a great variety of different solutions for these aims [11]. According to our schema, the decoding is very simple: IDs of queries are obtained by decompressing each bucket, while their probabilities are set to be equal to ϵ^i where i is the index of the corresponding bucket.

By resorting to this bucketing technique, we are able to achieve high levels of compression as shown in Figure 3. In this figure we report the average number of bits per entry required by our method with $p = 20,000$, as a function of the values of ϵ and α. The number of bits per entry ranges between 11 and 19. These figures are reported for the MSN query log only since a very similar behavior was observed on the Yahoo! query log. Notice that the smaller the value of ϵ, the smaller is the average number of bits per entry. This expected effect is due to the fact that with smaller values of ϵ we obtain fewer different buckets which are more dense. Thus, query IDs become more compressible. Table 6 compares the average number of bits per entry required by our schema ($\epsilon = 0.95$), with those required by the baseline (pruned lists without bucketing). The comparison was made by using both the MSN and Yahoo! query logs by varying p for three different values of α in the RWR. The number of bits per entry for the baseline are reported between parenthesis. The table shows that our scheme is much more space-efficient than the baseline (namely, each entry requires roughly 4 times less space).

Clearly, our bucketing scheme may introduce approximations on the probabilities of each query. However, by construction, we are able to precisely bound the highest possible level of approximation. The approximated probability of any query q is in fact at most ϵ^{-1} times larger than its real probability (namely, $\mathbf{r}_t(q) \leq \hat{\mathbf{r}}_t(q) < \epsilon^{-1} \cdot \mathbf{r}_t(q)$). Thus, the larger is the value of ϵ, the better are the guarantees on the resulting approximations. Since recommendations are computed by using these approximated probabilities, there may exist differences between the top-k queries suggested by resorting to real probabilities and the ones obtained with approximated probabilities. In other words, a query that is among the top-k with real probabilities may be replaced by another query when we resort to approximations. However, we can prove that this event happens only if the two queries have a very close product of (real) probabilities. More formally, let $q = \{t_1, t_2, \ldots, t_m\}$ be the user query and let q' and q'' be any pair of candidate queries. Assume that

$$\mathbf{r}_{q'} = \prod_{i=1}^{m} \mathbf{r}_{t_i}(q') > \prod_{i=1}^{m} \mathbf{r}_{t_i}(q'') = \mathbf{r}''_{q}.$$

Thus, q' precedes q'' in the ranking for query q computed via real probabilities and, thus, q' should be preferred to q''. The relative order in the ranking between q' and q'' computed via the approximated probabilities differs if[9]

$$\hat{\mathbf{r}}_{q'} = \prod_{i=1}^{m} \hat{\mathbf{r}}_{t_i}(q') \leq \prod_{i=1}^{m} \hat{\mathbf{r}}_{t_i}(q'') = \hat{\mathbf{r}}_{q''}.$$

Therefore, a change in the relative order of these two queries is possible only if their products of probabilities are too close. More precisely, since $\mathbf{r}_{q'} < \hat{\mathbf{r}}_{q'}$, $\hat{\mathbf{r}}_{q'} \leq \epsilon^{-m}\mathbf{r}_{q''}$ and $\mathbf{r}_{q'} > \mathbf{r}_{q''}$, the relative order between q' and q'' cannot change whenever $\mathbf{r}_{q'} > \epsilon^{-m}\mathbf{r}_{q''}$. The quantity ϵ^{-m} is sufficiently small since the number of terms m in the input query is usually a value between 2 and 3. For example, the average number of terms per query in MSN query log is $m = 2.40$. Thus, it suffices that $\hat{\mathbf{r}}(q') > 1.131 \times \hat{\mathbf{r}}(q'')$ in order to preserve the relative order between q and q'' with $\epsilon = 0.95$.

Table 7 shows the percentage of dissimilarity achieved with pruning and bucketing with respect to the original results computing considering the whole lists. Once more dissimilarity is computed for the top-5 results restricted to those recommendations that have been considered sufficiently good in the user study discussed in Section 4. At the first glance, we can see that the percentage of dissimilarity is remarkable. For example, a percentage ranging between 47.12% and 28.14% of the useful suggestions generated using the whole lists built from the Yahoo! query log are lost due to pruning and approximation. We observe however, that we are measuring exact differences in sets of results. This measure might not actually capture the global quality of the set of suggestions provided. It could happen in fact (and we will see that it often actually happens), that a good query suggested by using the whole lists is evicted by the set of suggestions due to pruning and bucketing to make place to a different query of comparable quality. The differences in the probabilities among the queries retrieved which are close to the fifth position, are in fact so small that our approximation could swap two queries having a very similar probability. This has a negligible effect on the overall quality

[9]In case of tails between products of probabilities one of the queries is preferred arbitrarily.

MSN query log

p	RWR $\alpha = 0.1$	RWR $\alpha = 0.5$	RWR $\alpha = 0.9$
5,000	18.48 (8.47)	22.58 (14.11)	42.04 (40.32)
10,000	17.39 (8.47)	20.97 (12.50)	39.49 (30.65)
15,000	17.39 (8.47)	20.16 (12.10)	36.31 (25.40)
20,000	17.39 (8.06)	18.55 (11.29)	33.12 (22.18)
100,000	17.39 (8.06)	18.55 (11.29)	32.48 (21.77)
200,000	17.39 (8.06)	18.55 (11.29)	32.48 (21.77)

Yahoo! query log

p	RWR $\alpha = 0.1$	RWR $\alpha = 0.5$	RWR $\alpha = 0.9$
5,000	33.75 (40.30)	37.87 (42.22)	45.11 (47.12)
10,000	27.76 (34.12)	32.84 (36.89)	40.23 (42.22)
15,000	26.18 (31.13)	31.36 (34.33)	38.22 (39.23)
20,000	23.97 (27.72)	28.70 (31.56)	37.07 (38.38)
100,000	19.24 (17.48)	21.89 (20.26)	31.32 (28.78)
200,000	19.24 (17.70)	21.30 (19.62)	31.90 (28.14)

Table 7: Average dissimilarity (in percentage) between the sets of top-5 suggestions computed by resorting or not to bucketing (with $\epsilon = 0.95$) as a function of p. The same measure computed by restricting to suggestions that have been considered "useful" or "somewhat useful" is reported between parenthesis.

MSN query log

p	useful	somewhat	not useful
5,000	56%	17%	27%
20,000	55%	15%	30%
200,000	55%	15%	30%

Yahoo! query log

p	useful	somewhat	not useful
5,000	46%	29%	25%
20,000	47%	29%	24%
200,000	46%	28%	26%

Table 8: Effectiveness of the suggestions provided with pruning and bucketing as a function of p for $\epsilon = 0.95$ and $\alpha = 0.9$.

of the suggestions provided, but it accounts for a 20% error according to our metrics. In order to verify this hypothesis, we thus conducted a new user study to evaluate the recommendations generated with the index exploiting pruning ($p = 5,000; 20,000; 200,000$) and bucketing ($\epsilon = 0.95$).

Table 8 reports the results of this new user study, conducted exactly as discussed in Section 4. By comparing the figures reported in Table 3 and 8, we can see that the quality of recommendations as judged by our assessors does not change remarkably. The experiment confirms our hypothesis: *even if some of the lowest-ranked top-5 recommendations computed on the whole RWRs lists are lacking in the set of recommendations generated by using the pruned and approximated index, they are in most cases replaced with queries of similar quality even according to human judgements.*

6. SCALING UP SUGGESTION BUILDING

To further improve query suggestion response time in the case even the pruned and compressed index discussed above does not fit into the main memory of the computer used for generating suggestion, we can exploit caching to improve throughput and scalability. It is in fact worth remarking that while query popularity changes significantly over time, the usage of terms in queries presents a higher temporal locality [2].

As we have discussed in the previous section, our index is accessed by query terms. For each term t occurring in queries of the log, we have a posting list consisting of p pairs of query IDs and (approximated) steady-state probabilities of reaching such queries by performing a RWR from t. At recommendation-generation time, the lists corresponding to each term occurring in the incoming query are retrieved and their probabilities multiplied. Therefore, in order to speed-up the recommendation scoring phase we can adopt a cache to keep in memory a "working set" of "likely-to-be-used" lists. Each entry of the cache stores p bucketed queryIDs, and is accessed by using the associated term as the key. The cache can be managed with a simple "Least Recently Used" (LRU) policy consisting in replacing, when needed, the oldest list in the cache.

Experiments. In order to assess empirically the benefits of adopting such a caching mechanism, we consider two portions of the query logs not used to learn the TQGraph model. We extract from such portions the queries and we sort them by timestamp. From each query we parse the terms and we build the stream of term requests by keeping the order induced by query timestamps. Each time a term t appears in the stream, we check if the cache contains the associated list. If not we count a cache *miss* and we store t and the associated posting list in the cache, possibly evicting another entry according to the LRU policy. Three different values of $p = 5,000, 20,000, 200,000$ are considered in the experiments, while the relative average bits per entry b are set as reported in Table 6. As in the previous experiments the RWRs are computed by setting $\alpha = 0.9$. The number of entries fitting in a cache of s bits is thus given by $s/(p \cdot b)$.

Results. Figure 4 shows the percentage of cache misses measured on our LRU cache over the total number of requests. The first obvious observation is that bigger caches correspond to a smaller number of cache misses. Indeed, the cache miss curve has an asymptotic trend allowing us to estimate the most reasonable cache size for each query log.

For instance, in the case of the MSN query log, when p is equal to 5,000 and the average bit per entry is 15.81, we are able to obtain a cache miss ratio of 7.21% when the cache has a size of 4GB. On the other hand, by doubling the size of the cache (from 4GB to 8GB) we obtain a miss ratio of 6.20%, i.e., a decrease of just the 1.01%, a small gain if compared to the higher cost of allocating a bigger cache size.

Similar results can be observed in the case of the Yahoo! query log (> 1 billion terms) where almost 90% of the recommendations can be computed (when $p = 5,000$, and $\epsilon = 0.95$.) in memory by using a "small" 8GB cache. These figures strengthen further our proposal that results to be very scalable as it allows the fast generation of recommendations by using an in-memory approach for the vast majority of queries.

7. CONCLUSIONS AND FUTURE WORK

In this paper we shifted the common query-centric perspective over the problem of query recommendation, and by taking a term-centric perspective we achieved two important results. First a novel query recommendation method able to generate relevant query suggestions also for rare or previously unseen queries. Second, a framework to make our emthod extremely efficient and scalable, thanks to the use

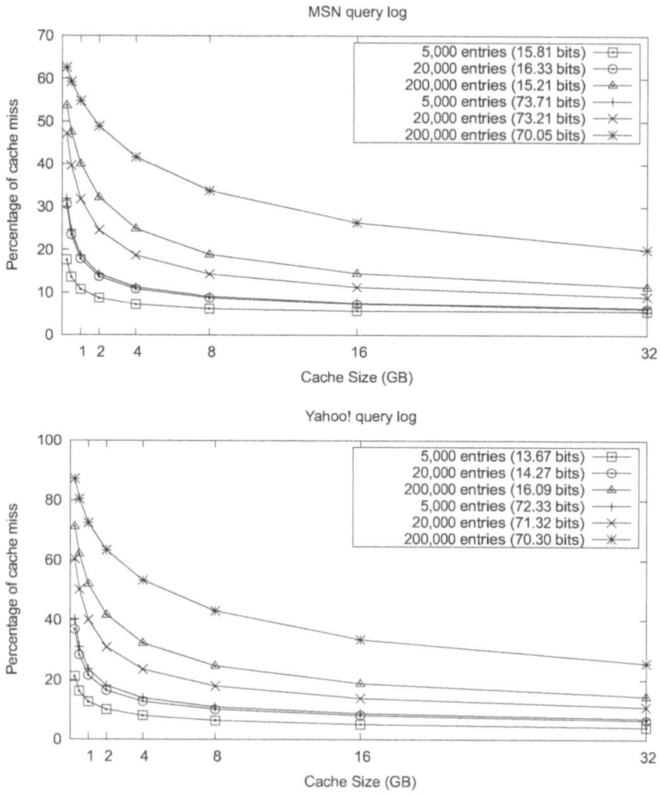

Figure 4: Miss ratio of our cache as a function of its size for different values of p. Results obtained on both the two query logs MSN (top) and Yahoo! (down) are reported.

of a optimized index data structure.

The proposed method is based on a graph model dubbed TQGraph, which has two sets of nodes: *Query* nodes, which are connected among them on the basis of the query reformulations observed in a historical query log, and *Term* nodes, which have only outgoing links pointing at the nodes corresponding to the queries in which the terms occur. Given a TQGraph, the suggestions for a incoming query are generated by performing RWRs starting from the nodes associated with query terms. The method we propose to efficiently compute on-the-fly query suggestions by exploiting a pruned and approximated index represents a more general contribution in the field of efficient computation of approximated random walks with restart, in particular of center-piece subgraphs. An accurate experimental evaluation was conducted to assess effectiveness and efficiency of our proposal. We firstly observed that the distribution of query terms allows our solution to provide suggestions for about the 99% of the queries encountered. The quality of TQGraph-based recommendations were judged higher than QFG-based ones in the user study conducted. Furthermore, we showed that the optimization techniques adopted are very effective, and safeguard the quality of suggestions provided also when aggressive pruning and lossy compression strategies are applied. Finally, a simple caching technique was proposed to enable scalable and fast in-memory generation of TQGraph-based recommendations.

There are various ideas that worth further investigation in order to improve our solution. Firstly, in our model the stationary distributions of the terms in the input query are multiplied together without considering their relative importance. Essentially, we are implicitly assuming that all the terms forming a query are equally important. Obviously, this is not the case. Thus, one could think to weight each vector based on the importance of the corresponding term. For example, we could increase the importance of the terms that better characterize the query at hand. This could be done by resorting to scoring mechanisms that recall known measures like TF/IDF.

Another aspect worth further exploration is the tuning of the length of the pruned lists and of the approximation level. In all the experiments conducted the values of these two parameters were equal for all the terms. Thus, we are again implicitly assuming that all the terms have the same importance. Instead, one should reserve more space for the lists of more important terms.

Acknowledgement

This research has been partially funded by the EU CIP PSP-BPN ASSETS Project, Grant Agreement no. 250527, and InGeoCloudS Project, Contract No 297300.

8. REFERENCES

[1] R. Baeza-Yates and A. Tiberi. Extracting semantic relations from query logs. In *Proc. KDD'07*.

[2] R. A. Baeza-Yates, A. Gionis, F. Junqueira, V. Murdock, V. Plachouras, and F. Silvestri. Design trade-offs for search engine caching. *TWEB*, 2(4), 2008.

[3] P. Boldi, F. Bonchi, C. Castillo, D. Donato, A. Gionis, and S. Vigna. The query-flow graph: model and applications. In *Proc. CIKM'08*.

[4] P. Boldi, F. Bonchi, C. Castillo, and S. Vigna. Query reformulation mining: models, patterns, and applications. *Inf. Retr.*, 14(3):257–289, 2011.

[5] A. Broder, P. Ciccolo, E. Gabrilovich, V. Josifovski, D. Metzler, L. Riedel, and J. Yuan. Online expansion of rare queries for sponsored search. In *Proc. WWW'09*.

[6] D. Downey, S. Dumais, and E. Horvitz. Heads and tails: studies of web search with common and rare queries. In *Proc. SIGIR'07*.

[7] B. M. Fonseca, P. Golgher, B. Pôssas, B. Ribeiro-Neto, and N. Ziviani. Concept-based interactive query expansion. In *Proc. CIKM'05*.

[8] A. Jain, U. Ozertem, and E. Velipasaoglu. Synthesizing high utility suggestions for rare web search queries. In *Proc. SIGIR'11*.

[9] R. Jones, B. Rey, O. Madani, and W. Greiner. Generating query substitutions. In *Proc. WWW'06*.

[10] Q. Mei, D. Zhou, and K. Church. Query suggestion using hitting time. In *Proc. CIKM'08*.

[11] F. Silvestri and R. Venturini. VSEncoding: efficient coding and fast decoding of integer lists via dynamic programming. In *Proc. CIKM'10*.

[12] Y. Song and L.-w. He. Optimal rare query suggestion with implicit user feedback. In *Proc. WWW'10*.

[13] I. Szpektor, A. Gionis, and Y. Maarek. Improving recommendation for long-tail queries via templates. In *Proc. WWW'11*.

[14] H. Tong and C. Faloutsos. Center-piece subgraphs: problem definition and fast solutions. In *Proc. KDD'06*.

[15] J. Xu and G. Xu. Learning similarity function for rare queries. In *Proc. WSDM'11*.

Supporting Efficient Top-k Queries in Type-Ahead Search

Guoliang Li† Jiannan Wang† Chen Li‡ Jianhua Feng†
† Department of Computer Science, Tsinghua National Laboratory for Information Science and Technology (TNList), Tsinghua University, Beijing 100084, China.
‡ Department of Computer Science, UC Irvine, CA 92697-3435, USA
liguoliang@tsinghua.edu.cn, wjn08@mails.tsinghua.edu.cn, chenli@ics.uci.edu, fengjh@tsinghua.edu.cn

ABSTRACT

Type-ahead search can on-the-fly find answers as a user types in a keyword query. A main challenge in this search paradigm is the high-efficiency requirement that queries must be answered within milliseconds. In this paper we study how to answer top-k queries in this paradigm, i.e., as a user types in a query letter by letter, we want to efficiently find the k best answers. Instead of inventing completely new algorithms from scratch, we study challenges when adopting existing top-k algorithms in the literature that heavily rely on two basic list-access methods: random access and sorted access. We present two algorithms to support random access efficiently. We develop novel techniques to support efficient sorted access using list pruning and materialization. We extend our techniques to support fuzzy type-ahead search which allows minor errors between query keywords and answers. We report our experimental results on several real large data sets to show that the proposed techniques can answer top-k queries efficiently in type-ahead search.

Categories and Subject Descriptors

H.3.3 [**Information Search and Retrieval**]: Retrieval models

General Terms

Algorithms, Experimentation, Performance

Keywords

Type-ahead search, top-k search, fuzzy search

1. INTRODUCTION

To give instant feedback when users formulate search queries, many information systems support *autocomplete* search, which shows results immediately after a user types in a partial keyword query. As an example, almost all the major search engines nowadays automatically suggest possible keyword queries as a user types in partial keywords. Most autocomplete systems treat a query with multiple keywords as *a single string*, and find answers with text that matches the string exactly. To overcome this limitation, a new type-ahead search paradigm has emerged recently [2, 13]. Using this paradigm, a system treats a query as a set of keywords, and does a *full-text* search on the underlying data to find answers including the keywords. We treat the last keyword in the query as a partial keyword the user is completing. For instance, a query "**`graph sig`**" on a publication table can find publication records with the keyword "**`graph`**" and a keyword that has "**`sig`**" as a prefix, such as "**`sigir`**", "**`sigmod`**", and "**`signature`**". In this way, a user can get instant feedback after typing keywords, thus can obtain more knowledge about the underlying data to formulate a query more easily.

Ji et al. [13] extended type-ahead search by allowing minor errors between queries and answers. As a user types in query keywords, the system can find relevant records with keywords *similar* to the query keywords. This feature is especially important when the user has limited knowledge about the exact representation of entities she is looking for. For instance, if a user types in a partial query "**`chritos falut`**", the system can find records approximately matching the two keywords despite the typo in the query, such as a record with keywords "Christos Faloutsos". Clearly these features can further improve user search experiences.

In this paper we study how to answer *ranking queries* in type-ahead search on large amounts of data. That is, as a user types in a keyword query letter by letter, we want to on-the-fly find the *most relevant* (or "top-k") records. One approach first finds records matching those query keywords, and then computes their ranking scores to find the most relevant ones. This approach is not efficient when there are a large number of candidate answers to compute and store. Existing type-ahead search approaches assume an index structure with a trie for the keywords in the underlying data, and each leaf node has an inverted list of records with this keyword, with the weight of this keyword in the record [13, 19]. As an example, Table 1 shows a sample collection of publication records. For simplicity, we only list some of the keywords for each record. Figure 1 shows the corresponding index structure. (More details about the index are in Section 3.)

Suppose a user types in a query "**`graph icdm li`**". For exact search, we find records containing the first two keywords and a word with prefix of "**`li`**", e.g., record r_5. For fuzzy search, we compute records with keywords *similar to* query keywords, and rank them to find the best answers. For each complete keyword, we find keywords *similar to* the query keyword. For instance, both keywords "**`icdm`**" and "**`icdl`**" are similar to the second query keyword. The last keyword

Permission to make digital or hard copies of all or part of this work for personal or classroom use is granted without fee provided that copies are not made or distributed for profit or commercial advantage and that copies bear this notice and the full citation on the first page. To copy otherwise, to republish, to post on servers or to redistribute to lists, requires prior specific permission and/or a fee.
SIGIR'12, August 12–16, 2012, Portland, Oregon, USA.
Copyright 2012 ACM 978-1-4503-1472-5/12/08 ...$15.00.

Table 1: Publication records with sample keywords.

Record ID	Record
r_0	graph icdm ...
r_1	graph group lui ...
r_2	gray icdl liu ...
r_3	graph icdl lin lui ...
r_4	graph group icdm lin liu ...
r_5	graph gray gross icdm lin liu ...
r_6	gray group icdm lin liu ...
r_7	gray gross group icdl lin ...
r_8	gross icdl liu ...
r_9	icdm liu ...

"li" is treated as a prefix condition, since the user is still typing at the end of this keyword. We find keywords that have a prefix similar to "li", such as "lin", "liu", and "lui". We access the inverted lists of these similar keywords to find records and rank them to find the best answers for the user.

A key question is: "how to access inverted lists on trie leaf nodes efficiently to answer top-k queries?" Instead of inventing completely new algorithms from scratch, we study how to adopt a plethora of algorithms in the literature for answering top-k queries by accessing lists (e.g., [21, 12]). These algorithms share the same framework proposed by Fagin [6], in which we have lists of records sorted based on various conditions. An aggregation function takes the scores of a record from these lists and computes the final score of the record. There are two methods to access these lists: (1) *Random Access*: Given a record id, we can retrieve the score of the record on each list; (2) *Sorted Access*: We retrieve the record ids on each list following the list order.

In this paper we study technical challenges when adopting these algorithms, and focus on new optimization opportunities that arise in our problem. In particular, we study how to support the two types of access operations efficiently by utilizing characteristics specific to our index structures and access methods. We make the following contributions: 1) In Section 3, we present a forward-list-based method for supporting random access on the inverted lists, and develop a heap-based method and list-materialization techniques to support sorted access efficiently. 2) In Section 4 we study fuzzy type-ahead search. We propose a list-pruning technique to improve the performance of sorted access, and study how to improve the techniques based on forward lists and list materialization for fuzzy search. Due to the challenging nature of the problem, our extensions are technically nontrivial. 3) In Section 5 we present our experimental results on real large data sets to show the efficiency of our techniques. We have deployed several systems using this paradigm, which have been used regularly and well accepted by users due to its friendly interface and high efficiency[1].

2. FORMULATION AND PRELIMINARIES

Type-Ahead Search: Let R be a collection of records such as the tuples in a relational table. Let D be the set of words in R. Let Q be a query the user has typed in, which is a sequence of keywords $\langle w_1, w_2, \ldots, w_m \rangle$. We treat the last keyword w_m as a partial keyword the user is completing, and other keywords as complete keywords the user has completed[2]. As a user types in a keyword query letter by letter, type-ahead search on-the-fly finds records that contain the first $m-1$ keywords and a word with the last keyword as a prefix.

[1] http://tastier.ics.uci.edu/

[2] Our method can be easily extended to the case that every keyword is taken as a partial keyword.

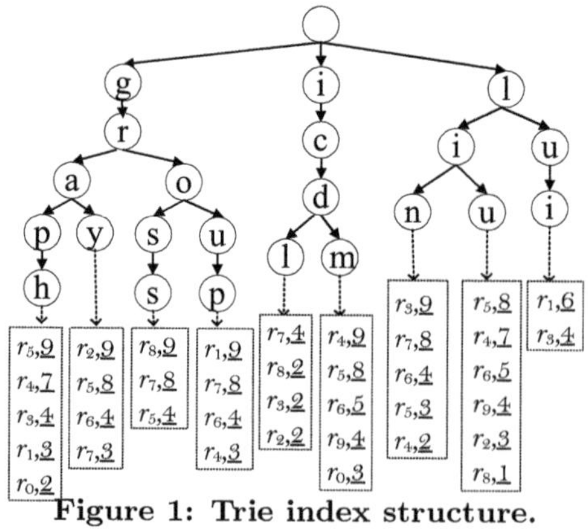

Figure 1: Trie index structure.

Without loss of generality, each string in the data set and a query is assumed to use lower-case letters. For example, in Table 1, $R = \{r_0, r_1, \ldots, r_9\}$, $D = \{$**graph**, **icdm**, **group**, **lui**, $\ldots\}$. Suppose a user types in a query "icdm gra". We treat "icdm" as a complete keyword and "gra" as a partial keyword. Records r_0, r_4, r_5, and r_6 are potentially relevant answers. For example, r_0 contains complete keyword "icdm" and word "graph" with a prefix of "gra". When the user types in more letters and submits query "icdm graph li", we treat "icdm" and "graph" as complete keywords and "li" as a partial keyword. Records r_4 and r_5 are potentially relevant answers.

Top-k Answers: We rank each record r in R based on its relevance to the query. Given a positive integer k, our goal is to compute the best k records in R ranked by their relevance to Q. Notice that our problem setting allows an important record to be in the answer, even if not all query keywords appear in the record (the "OR" semantics). Thus the algorithms in [13] cannot be used directly in our problem.

Ranking: In the literature there are many algorithms for answering top-k queries by accessing lists (e.g., [21, 12]). These algorithms share the same framework proposed by Fagin [6], in which we have lists of records sorted based on various conditions, such as term frequency and inverse document frequency ("tf*idf"). Each record has a score on a list, and we use an aggregation function to combine the scores of the record on different lists to compute its overall relevance to the query. The aggregation function needs to be *monotonic*, i.e., decreasing the score of a record on a list cannot increase the record's overall score. This approach has the advantage of allowing a general class of ranking functions. In this paper, we focus on an important class of ranking functions with the following property: the score $F(r, Q)$ of a record r to a query Q is a monotonic combination of scores of the query keywords with respect to the record r. Formally, we compute the score $F(r, Q)$ in two steps. In the first step, for each keyword w, we compute a score of the keyword with respect to the record r, denoted by $F(r, w)$. In the second step, we compute the score $F(r, Q)$ by applying a monotonic function on the $F(r, w)$'s for all the keywords w. The intuition of this property is that the more relevant an individual query keyword is to a record, the more likely this record is a good answer to this query. For example, we compute the score of a record to query "icdm graph li" by aggregating the scores of each of keywords with respect to the record.

Each complete keyword w has a weight associated with a record r, denoted by $W(r, w)$. This weight could depend

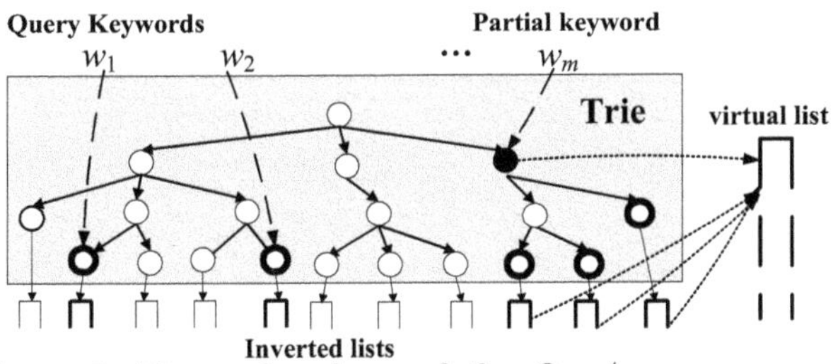

Figure 2: Type-ahead search for $Q = \langle w_1, w_2, \ldots, w_m \rangle$.

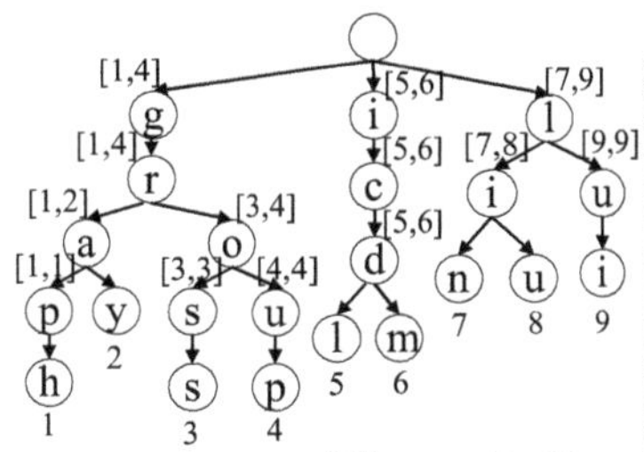

Forward index

Record	Forward list
r_0	$\langle 1,\underline{2}\rangle;\langle 6,\underline{3}\rangle$
r_1	$\langle 1,\underline{3}\rangle;\langle 4,\underline{9}\rangle;\langle 9,\underline{6}\rangle$
r_2	$\langle 2,\underline{9}\rangle;\langle 5,\underline{2}\rangle;\langle 8,\underline{3}\rangle$
r_3	$\langle 1,\underline{4}\rangle;\langle 5,\underline{2}\rangle;\langle 7,\underline{9}\rangle;\langle 9,\underline{4}\rangle$
r_4	$\langle 1,\underline{7}\rangle;\langle 4,\underline{3}\rangle;\langle 6,\underline{9}\rangle;\langle 7,\underline{2}\rangle;\langle 8,\underline{7}\rangle$
r_5	$\langle 1,\underline{9}\rangle;\langle 2,\underline{8}\rangle;\langle 3,\underline{4}\rangle;\langle 6,\underline{8}\rangle;\langle 7,\underline{3}\rangle;\langle 8,\underline{8}\rangle$
...	......

Figure 3: Forward lists.

on the keyword, such as the tf*idf value of the keyword in the record. As a specific case, it can also be independent from the keyword. For instance, if a record is a URL with tokenized keywords, its weight could be a rank score of the corresponding Web page. If a record is an author, we can use the number of publications of the author as a weight of this record. For the last partial keyword w_m, there could be multiple complete words. We compute the relevance score of w_m in the record, i.e., $F(r, w_m)$, based on the following property: $F(r, w_m)$ is the maximal value of the $W(r, d)$ weights for all the keywords d with respect to w_m in r, where d is a keyword in record r and has a prefix of w_m. This property states that we only look at the most relevant keyword in a record to the partial keyword when computing the relevance of the keyword to the record. It means that the ranking function is "greedy" to find the most relevant keyword in the record as an indicator of how important this record is to the partial keyword. As we can see in Section 3, this property allows us to do effective pruning when accessing the multiple lists of a query keyword. The following is an example function.

$$F(r, Q) = \sum_{i=1}^{m} F(r, w_i), \tag{1}$$

where

$$F(r, w_i) = \begin{cases} W(r, w_i) & if\ 1 \le i < m, \\ \max_{complete\ word\ d\ of\ w_m} \{W(r, d)\} & if\ i = m. \end{cases} \tag{2}$$

In Figure 1, consider query "**icdm graph li**" and record r_5. $F(r_5$, "**icdm**"$) = W(r_5$, "**icdm**"$) = 8$ and $F(r_5$, "**graph**"$) = W(r_5$, "**graph**"$) = 9$. The partial keyword "**li**" has two complete words "**lin**" and "**liu**". $F(r_5$, "**li**"$) = max\{W(r_5$, "**lin**"$), W(r_5$, "**liu**"$)\}=8$. $F(r_5$, "**icdm graph li**"$) = 25$.

3. EXACT TYPE-AHEAD SEARCH

In this section, we study efficient list-access methods to support *exact* type-ahead search, i.e., no mismatches between query keywords and answers.

Indexing: We construct a trie for the data keywords in the data D. A trie node has a character label. Each keyword in D corresponds to a unique path from the root to a leaf node[3] on the trie. For simplicity, a trie node is mentioned interchangeably with the keyword corresponding to the path from the root to the node. A leaf node has an inverted list of IDs of pairs $\langle rid, weight \rangle$, where rid is the ID of a record containing the leaf-node string, and $weight$ is the weight of the keyword in the record. Figure 1 shows the index structure in our running example. For instance, for the leaf node of keyword "**graph**", its inverted list has five elements. The first element "$\langle r_5, 9\rangle$" indicates that the record r_5 has this keyword, and the weight of this keyword in this record is "9", i.e., $W(r_5$, "**graph**"$) = 9$.

Searching: We compute the top-k answers to a query Q in two steps. As illustrated in Figure 2, in the first step, for each complete keyword $w_i (1 \le i \le m-1)$, we get its inverted list. For the last partial keyword, we locate the trie node of w_m and retrieve the inverted lists of the trie node's leaf descendants. For example, in Figure 1, consider a query "**icdm li**". The partial keyword "**li**" has two leaf-node keywords: "**lin**" and "**liu**". In the second step, we access the inverted lists to compute the k best answers.

Many algorithms have been proposed for answering top-k queries by accessing sorted lists [12, 6]. When adopting these algorithms to solve our problem, we need to efficiently support two basic types of access used in these algorithms: random access and sorted access on the lists.

3.1 Efficient Random Access

To support random access, we construct a forward index in which each record has a forward list of IDs of its keywords. We assume each keyword has a unique ID with respect to its leaf node on the trie, and the IDs of the keywords follow their alphabetical order. Figure 3 shows the forward lists. The element "$\langle 1, \underline{9}\rangle$" on the forward list of record r_5 shows that this record has a keyword with ID 1 and weight 9, which is keyword "**graph**" as shown on the trie.

Given a record and a complete keyword, we can get the corresponding weight by doing a binary-search on the forward list. For example, to get the weight of keyword "**icdm**" with ID 6 in r_5, we can do a binary search on r_5's forward list and get the corresponding weight 8. For the partial keyword, as it has multiple complete words, we need first locate its trie node and then enumerate its leaf-descendants to get the corresponding weights. This method could be expensive if the trie node has many leaf-descendants. To improve the performance, we can use an alternative method. For each trie node n, we can maintain a keyword range $[l_n, u_n]$, where l_n and u_n are the minimal and maximal keyword IDs of its leaf nodes, respectively [13]. An interesting observation is that a complete word with n as a prefix must have an ID in this keyword range, and each complete word in the data set with an ID in this range must have a prefix of n. In Figure 3, the keyword range of node "**g**" is $[1, 4]$, since 1 is the smallest ID of its leaf nodes and 4 is the largest one.

Based on this observation, this method verifies whether record r contains a keyword with a prefix of w_m as follows. We first locate the trie node w_m and then check if there is a keyword ID on the forward list of r in the keyword range $[l_{w_m}, u_{w_m}]$. Since we can keep the forward list of r sorted, this checking can be done efficiently. For instance, consider query "**graph icdm l**". For the first element on the inverted list of "**graph**", $\langle r_5, 9\rangle$, we can check whether

[3]A common "trick" to make each leaf node corresponds to a complete word and vice versa is to add a special mark to the end of each word. For simplicity we did not use this trick.

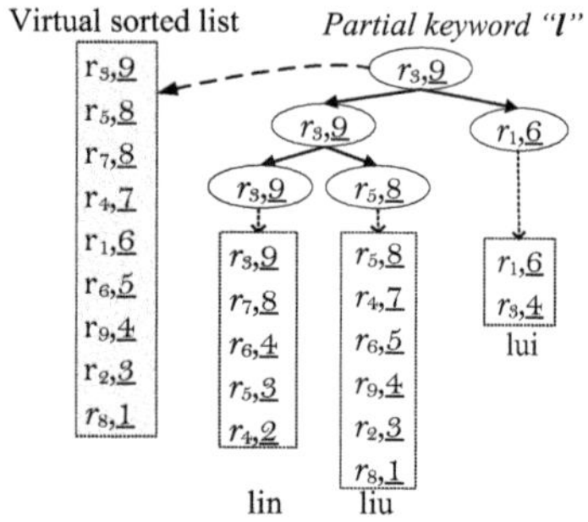

Figure 4: A heap-based method to compute the virtual sorted list of partial keyword "l".

r_5 contains other two keywords as follows. For complete keyword "**icdm**" with ID 6, we do a binary search on r_5's forward list and get weight 8. For partial keyword "**l**" with keyword range $[7, 9]$, using a binary search on r_5's forward list $(\langle 1, \underline{9}\rangle; \langle 2, \underline{8}\rangle; \langle 3, \underline{4}\rangle; \langle 6, \underline{8}\rangle; \langle 7, \underline{3}\rangle; \langle 8, \underline{8}\rangle)$, we find keyword IDs 7 and 8 in this range. Thus we know that the record indeed contains keywords with prefix "**l**", and compute the corresponding score $F(r_5, \text{"l"}) = max\{F(r_5, \text{"lin"}), F(r_5, \text{"liu"}), F(r_5, \text{"lui"})\} = 8$. Thus $F(r_5, \text{"graph icdm l"}) = 25$.

3.2 Efficient Sorted Access

To support sorted access, we can keep the elements on the inverted lists sorted based on their weights in a descending order. Thus, for the complete keyword, we can get an ordered list. For the partial keyword w_m, it has multiple leaf descendants and corresponding inverted lists. We use $U(w_m)$ to denote the union of those inverted lists, called *union list* of w_m. We need to support sorted access on $U(w_m)$ to retrieve the next most relevant record ID for w_m. Fully computing $U(w_m)$ using the keyword lists could be expensive in terms of time and space. In this section, we propose two techniques to support sorted access efficiently.

3.2.1 Heap-Based Method

We can support sorted access on $U(w_m)$ by building a max heap on the inverted lists of its leaf nodes. In particular, we maintain a cursor on each inverted list. The max heap initially consists of the record IDs pointed by the cursors so far, sorted on the weights of the keywords in these records. Notice that each inverted list is already sorted based on the weights of its keyword in the records. To retrieve the next best record, we pop the top element from the heap, increment the cursor of the list of the popped element by 1, and push the new element of this list to the heap. When popping all elements from the heap, we can get a sorted list for the partial keyword. For example, consider the partial keyword "**l**". It has three complete keywords "**lin**", "**liu**", and "**lui**". We can compute its union list as shown in Figure 4. Note that since our method does not need to compute the entire list of $U(w_m)$, $U(w_m)$ is a *virtual sorted list* of partial keyword w_m. On top of the inverted lists of complete keywords and the max heap of the partial keyword, we can adopt an existing top-k algorithm to find the k best records.

As an example, suppose we want to compute the top-1 best answer for query "**graph icdm l**" using sorted access only. We get the first elements of "**graph**" and "**icdm**", $\langle r_5, 9\rangle$ and $\langle r_4, 9\rangle$, pop the top element of the max heap in Figure 4, $\langle r_3, 9\rangle$, and compute an upper bound on the overall score of

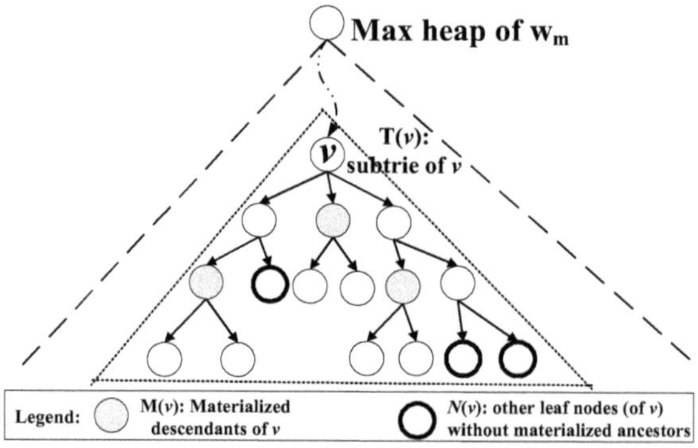

Figure 5: Benefits of materializing the union list $U(v)$ for node v with respect to partial keyword w_m.

an answer, i.e., 27. We get the next elements of "**graph**" and "**icdm**", $\langle r_4, 7\rangle$ and $\langle r_5, 8\rangle$. We increment the cursor of the list that produces the top element, push it into the heap, and retrieve the next top element: $\langle r_5, 8\rangle$. Based on the accessed elements, we have 1) The score of record r_5 is $9+8+8 = 25$; 2) The maximal score of record r_3 is $7 + 8 + 9 = 24$, and that of r_4 is $7+9+8 = 24$, while those of other records are at most $7+8+8 = 23$. Thus, record r_5 is the best answer.

3.2.2 List Materialization

We can further improve the performance of sorted access for the partial keyword w_m by precomputing and storing the unions of some of the inverted lists on the trie. Let v be a trie node, and $U(v)$ be the union of the inverted lists of v's leaf nodes, sorted by their record weights. If a record appears more than once on these lists, we choose its maximal weight as its weight on list $U(v)$. For example, $U(\text{"li"}) = \{\langle r_3, 9\rangle, \langle r_5, 8\rangle, \langle r_7, 8\rangle; \langle r_4, 7\rangle, \langle r_6, 5\rangle, \langle r_9, 4\rangle, \langle r_2, 3\rangle, \langle r_8, 1\rangle\}$. When using a max heap to retrieve records sorted by their scores for the partial keyword, this materialized list could help us build a max heap with fewer lists and reduce the cost of push/pop operations on the heap. Therefore, this method allows us to utilize additional memory space to answer top-k queries more efficiently. For instance, consider the index in Figure 1 and a query "**icdm gr**". For the partial keyword "**gr**", we access its data keywords "**graph**", "**gray**", "**gross**", and "**group**", and build a max heap on their inverted lists based on record scores with respect to this query keyword. If we materialize the union lists of "**gra**" and "**gro**", we can use their materialized lists, saving the time to traverse the four leaf nodes and some push/pop operations on the heap.

We next give a detailed cost-based analysis to quantify the benefit of materializing a node on the performance of operations on the max heap of w_m, for exact type-ahead search. Let B be a budget of storage space we are given to materialize union lists. Given a trie node v, let $U(v)$ be the union of inverted lists of leaf nodes in the subtrie of v. Our goal is to select trie nodes to materialize their union lists for maximizing the performance of queries. The following are naive algorithms for choosing trie nodes:

- Random: We randomly select trie nodes.
- TopDown: We select nodes top down from the trie root.
- BottomUp: We select nodes bottom up from leaf nodes.

Each naive approach keeps choosing trie nodes to materialize their union lists until the sum of their list sizes reaches the space limit B. One main limitation of these approaches is that they do not quantitatively consider the benefits of materializing a union list. To overcome this limitation, we propose a cost-based method called CostBased to do list materialization. Its main idea is the following.

For simplicity we say a node has been "*materialized*" if its union list has been materialized. For a query Q with a prefix keyword w_m, suppose some of the trie nodes have their union lists materialized. Let v be such a materialized node. If we can use $U(v)$ to construct the heap of w_m, we need not visit v's descendants and access the inverted lists of v's leaf descendants, and thus achieve the benefit of reducing the time of traversing the subtrie rooted at v and push/pop operations on the max heap of w_m. We say the materialized node v is *usable* for partial keyword w_m.

Next we discuss how to check whether a node v is usable for partial keyword w_m. If v is not a descendant of w_m, materializing v is unusable to w_m; otherwise, if no node on the path from v to w_m (including w_m) has been materialized, materializing v is usable to w_m. Notice that if v has a materialized ancestor v' on the path from v to w_m, then we can use the materialized list $U(v')$ instead of $U(v)$, and the list $U(v)$ will no longer be usable to w_m. To summarize, a materialized node v is *usable* for partial keyword w_m if,

1. v is a descendant of w_m; and
2. v has no materialized ancestor between v and w_m.

For example, consider a query "`icdm g`", materializing node "`l`" is unusable for partial keyword "`g`" as "`l`" is not a descendant of "`g`". Materializing "`gr`" is usable for "`g`" if "`g`" is not materialized. If "`gr`" is materialized, then materializing "`gra`" is unusable for "`g`" as we will use the materialized list of "`gr`" to build the max heap of "`g`", instead of using "`gra`".

If v is usable for w_m, materializing $U(v)$ has the following benefits for the heap of w_m. (1) We do not need to traverse the trie to access these leaf nodes and use them to construct the max heap; (2) Each push/pop operation on the heap is more efficient since it has fewer lists. Here we present an analysis of the benefits of materializing the usable node v. In general, for a trie node v, let $T(v)$ denote its subtrie and $|T(v)|$ denote the number of nodes in $T(v)$. The total time of traversing this subtrie is $\mathcal{O}(|T(v)|)$.

Now we analyze the benefit of materializing node v. As illustrated in Figure 5, suppose v has materialized descendants. Let $M(v)$ be the set of highest materialized descendants of v. These materialized nodes can help reduce the time of accessing the inverted lists of v's leaf nodes in two ways. First, we do not need to traverse the descendants of a materialized node $d \in M(v)$. We can just traverse $|T(v)| - \sum_{d \in M(v)} |T(d)|$ trie nodes. Second, when inserting lists to the max heap of w_m, we insert the union list of v into the heap and need not insert the union list of each $d \in M(v)$ and the inverted lists of $d' \in N(v)$ into the heap, where $N(v)$ denotes the set of v's leaf descendants having no ancestors in $M(v)$. Let $S(v) = M(v) \cup N(v)$. We quantify benefits of materializing node v:

1. *Reducing traversal time*: Since we do not traverse v's descendants, the time reduction is $B_1 = \mathcal{O}(|T(v)| - \sum_{d \in M(v)} |T(d)|)$.
2. *Reducing heap-construction time*: When constructing the max heap for keyword w_m, we insert the union list $U(v)$ into the heap, instead of the inverted lists of those nodes in $S(v)$. The time reduction is $B_2 = |S(v)| - 1$.
3. *Reducing sorted-access time*: If we insert the union list $U(v)$ to the max heap of w_m, the number of leaf nodes in the heap is $|S(w_m)|$. Otherwise, it is $|S(w_m)| + |S(v)| - 1$. The time reduction of a sorted access is $B_3 = \mathcal{O}(log(|S(w_m)| + |S(v)| - 1)) - \mathcal{O}(log(|S(w_m)|))$.

The following is the overall benefit of materializing v for the partial keyword w_m:

$$B_v = B_1 + B_2 + A_v * B_3, \tag{3}$$

where A_v is the number of sorted accesses on $U(v)$. A_v can be computed using the number of records in the union list $U(v)$, and the number of keywords in the query.

The analysis above is on a query workload. If there is no query workload, we can use the trie structure to count the probability of each node to be queried and use such information to compute the benefit of materializing a node. In this paper, we employ a no query workload setting.

4. FUZZY TYPE-AHEAD SEARCH

In this section, we first define the problem of top-k queries in fuzzy type-ahead search [13]. We then develop new techniques to support efficient list access to answer such queries by extending techniques developed in exact search.

4.1 Ranking

As a user types in a query letter by letter, fuzzy type-ahead search on-the-fly finds records with words *similar to* the query keywords. For example, consider the data in Table 1. Suppose a user types in a query "**`graph grose`**". We return r_5 as a relevant answer since it has a keyword "**`gross`**" similar to query keyword "**`grose`**". We use edit distance to measure the similarity between strings. Formally, the edit distance between two strings s_1 and s_2, denoted by $\mathsf{ed}(s_1, s_2)$, is the minimum number of single-character edit operations (i.e., insertion, deletion, and substitution) needed to transform s_1 to s_2. For example, $\mathsf{ed}(\mathtt{gross}, \mathtt{grose}) = 1$.

Similarity Function: Let π be a function that computes the similarity between a data string s and a query keyword w in $Q = \langle w_1, w_2, \ldots, w_m \rangle$. An example is:

$$\pi(s, w) = 1 - \frac{\mathsf{ed}(s, w)}{|w|},$$

where $|w|$ is the length of the query keyword w. We normalize the edit distance based on the query-keyword length in order to allow more errors for longer query keywords. Our results in the paper focus on this function, and they can be generalized to other functions using edit distance.

Let d be a keyword in the data set D. For each complete keyword w_i ($i = 1, 2, \ldots, m-1$) in the query, we define the similarity of d to w_i as:

$$\mathsf{Sim}(d, w_i) = \pi(d, w_i).$$

Since the last keyword w_m is treated as a prefix condition, we define the similarity of d to w_m as the maximal similarity of d's prefixes using function π, i.e.:

$$\mathsf{Sim}(d, w_m) = \max_{\text{prefix } p \text{ of } d} \{\pi(p, w_m)\}.$$

Let τ be a similarity threshold. We say a keyword d in D is *similar to* a query keyword w if $\mathsf{Sim}(d, w) \geq \tau$. We say a prefix p of a keyword in D is *similar to* the query keyword w_m if $\pi(p, w_m) \geq \tau$. We want to find the keywords in the data set that are similar to query keywords, since records with such a keyword could be of interest to the user.

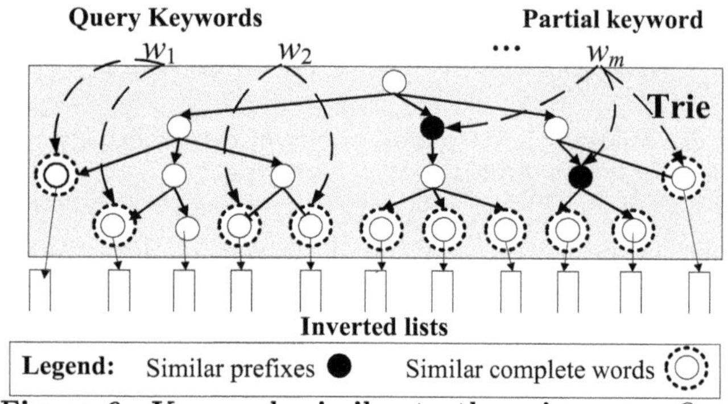

Figure 6: Keywords similar to those in query $Q = \langle w_1, w_2, \ldots, w_m \rangle$. Each query keyword w_i has similar keywords on leaf nodes. The last prefix keyword w_m has similar prefixes.

Let $\Phi(w_i)$ $(i = 1, \ldots, m)$ denote the set of keywords in D similar to w_i, and $P(w_m)$ denote the set of prefixes (of keywords in D) similar to w_m. We compute the top-k answers to the query Q in two steps. In the first step, for each keyword w_i in the query, we first compute an edit-distance upper bound based on the similarity function, i.e., $(1 - \tau) * |w_i|$, and then compute the similar keywords $\Phi(w_i)$ and similar prefixes $P(w_m)$ on the trie (shown in Figure 6). Ji et al. [13] developed an efficient algorithm for incrementally computing these similar strings as the user modifies the current query. A similar algorithm is developed in [5]. In the second step, we access the inverted lists of these similar data keywords to compute the k best answers.

For example, assume a user types in a query "`grose li`" letter by letter on the data shown in Table 1. Suppose the similarity threshold τ is 0.45. The set of prefixes similar to the partial keyword "`li`" is $P(\text{"li"}) = \{\texttt{l}, \texttt{li}, \texttt{lin}, \texttt{liu}, \texttt{lu}, \texttt{lui}, \texttt{i}\}$, and the set of data keywords similar to the partial keyword "`li`" is $\Phi(\text{"li"}) = \{\texttt{lin}, \texttt{liu}, \texttt{lui}, \texttt{icdl}, \texttt{icdm}\}$. In particular, "`lui`" is similar to "`li`" since $\mathsf{Sim}(\texttt{lui}, \texttt{li}) = 1 - \frac{\texttt{ed(lui,li)}}{|\texttt{li}|} = 0.5 \geq \tau$. The set of similar words for the complete keyword "`grose`" is $\Phi(\text{"grose"}) = \{\texttt{gross}\}$. Then we compute top-$k$ answers using the inverted lists of those words in $\Phi(\text{"grose"})$ and $\Phi(\text{"li"})$.

Ranking: We still assume the ranking function has the first property described in Section 2, which computes the score $F(r, Q)$ by applying a monotonic function on the $F(r, w_i)$'s for all the keywords w_i in the query. Given a complete keyword w_i and a record r, for exact search, we can use the weight of w_i in r, i.e., $W(r, w_i)$, to denote their relevancy $F(r, w_i)$. But for fuzzy search, the keyword w_i can be similar to multiple keywords in the record r, and different similar words have different similarities to w_i and different weights in r. A question is how to compute the relevance value of keyword w_i in record r, $F(r, w_i)$.

Let d be a keyword in record r such that d is similar to the query keyword w_i, i.e., $d \in \Phi(w_i)$. We use $F(r, w_i, d)$ to denote the relevance of this query keyword w_i in the record with respect to keyword d. The value should depend on both the weight of d in r, i.e., $W(r, d)$, as well as the similarity between w_i and d, i.e., $\mathsf{Sim}(d, w_i)$. Intuitively, the more similar they are, the more relevant w_i is to r in terms of d. For instance, $F(r, w_i, d) = \mathsf{Sim}(d, w_i) * W(r, d)$ is an example ranking function to evaluate the relevancy of w_i in the record with respect to keyword d. We use the following function with the second property in Section 2 to compute $F(r, w_i)$:

$$F(r, w_i) = \max_{\text{keyword } d \text{ (in } r\text{) similar to } w_i} \{F(r, w_i, d)\}. \quad (4)$$

4.2 Efficient Random Access

We first study how to support efficient random access for fuzzy type-ahead search. For simplicity, in the discussion we focus on how to verify whether the record has a keyword with a prefix similar to the partial keyword w_m. With minor modifications the discussion extends to the case where we want to verify whether r has a keyword similar to a complete keyword $w_i (1 \leq i \leq m - 1)$.

In each random access, given an ID of a record r, we want to retrieve information related to a query keyword w_i, which allows us to retrieve $W(r, d)$ for each of w_i's similar word d so as to compute the score $F(r, w_i)$. In particular, for a keyword w_i in the query, does the record r have a keyword similar to w_i? One naive way to get the information is to retrieve the original record r and go through its keywords. This approach has two limitations. First, if the data is too large to fit into memory and has to reside on hard disks, accessing the original data from the disks may slow down the process significantly. This costly operation will prevent us from achieving an interactive-search speed. The second limitation is that it may require a lot of computation of string similarities based on edit distance, which could be time consuming. In this section, we present two efficient approaches for solving this problem.

Method 1: Probing on Forward Lists: This method verifies whether record r contains a keyword with a prefix similar to w_m as follows. For each prefix p on the trie similar to w_m (computed in the first step of the algorithm as discussed above), we check if there is a keyword ID on the forward list of r in the keyword range $[l_p, u_p]$ of the trie node of p as discussed in Section 3.

Method 2: Probing on Trie Leaf Nodes: Using this method, for each prefix p similar to w_m, we traverse the subtrie of p and identify its leaf nodes. For each leaf node d, we store the fact that for the query Q, this keyword d has a prefix similar to w_m in the query. Specifically, we store

$$\langle \text{Query ID, partial keyword } w_m, \mathsf{Sim}(p, w_m) \rangle.$$

We store the query ID in order to differentiate it from other queries in case multiple queries are answered concurrently. We store the similarity between w_m and p to compute the score of this keyword in a candidate record. In case the leaf node has several prefixes similar to w_m, we only keep their maximal similarity to w_m. For each complete keyword w_i, we also store the same information for those trie nodes similar to w_i. Therefore, a leaf node might have multiple entries corresponding to different keywords in the same query. We call these entries for the leaf node as its collection of *relevant query keywords*. Notice that this structure needs very little storage space, since the entries of old queries can be quickly reused by new queries, and the number of keywords in a query tends to be small. We use this additional information to efficiently check if a record r contains a complete word with a prefix similar to the partial keyword w_m. We scan the forward list of r. For each of its keyword IDs, we locate the corresponding leaf node, and test whether its collection of relevant query keywords includes this query and

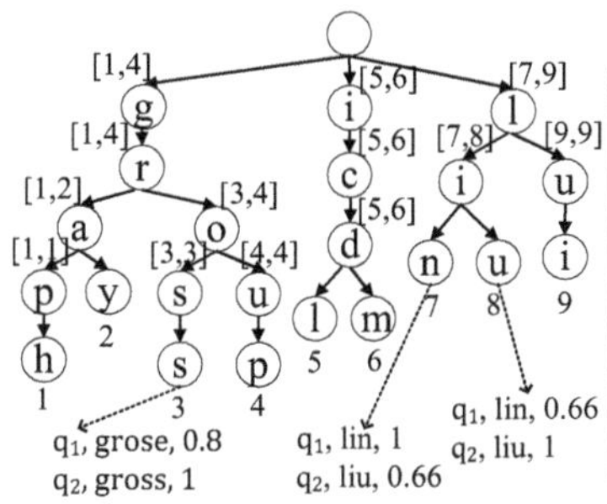

Forward index

Record	Forward list
r_0	⟨1,2⟩;⟨6,3⟩
r_1	⟨1,3⟩;⟨4,9⟩;⟨9,6⟩
r_2	⟨2,9⟩;⟨5,2⟩;⟨8,3⟩
r_3	⟨1,4⟩;⟨5,2⟩;⟨7,9⟩;⟨9,4⟩
r_4	⟨1,7⟩;⟨4,3⟩;⟨6,9⟩;⟨7,2⟩;⟨8,7⟩
r_5	⟨1,9⟩;⟨2,8⟩;⟨3,4⟩;⟨6,8⟩;⟨7,3⟩;⟨8,8⟩
...	......

Figure 7: Probing on trie leaf nodes.

the keyword w_m. If so, we use the stored string similarity to compute the score of this keyword in the query.

Figure 7 shows how we use this method in our running example, where the user types in a keyword query $q_1 = \langle \texttt{lin}, \texttt{grose} \rangle$. When computing the similar words of "**grose**", i.e., "**gross**", we insert the query ID (shown as "q_1"), the partial keyword "**grose**", and the corresponding prefix similarity to its collection of relevant query keywords. To verify whether record r_5 has a word with a prefix similar to "**grose**", we scan its forward list. Its third keyword is "**gross**". We access its corresponding leaf node, and see that the node's collection of relevant query keywords includes "**grose**". Thus we know that r_5 indeed contains a keyword similar to "**grose**", and can retrieve the corresponding prefix similarity.

Comparison: The time complexity of the forward-list based method (Method 1) is $\mathcal{O}(G * log(|r|))$, where G is the total number of similar prefixes of w_m and similar complete words of w_i's for $1 \leq i \leq m-1$, and $|r|$ is the number of distinct keywords in record r. Since the similar prefixes of w_m could have ancestor-descendant relationships, we can optimize the step of accessing them by considering the "highest" ones. The time complexity of the second method is

$$\mathcal{O}(\sum_{\text{smilar prefix } p \text{ of } w_m} |T(p)| + |r| * |Q|).$$

The first term corresponds to the time of traversing the subtries of similar prefixes, where $T(p)$ is the subtrie rooted at a similar prefix p. The second term corresponds to the time of probing the leaf nodes, where $|Q|$ is the number of query keywords. Notice that to identify the answers, we need access the inverted lists of complete words, thus the first term can be removed from the complexity. Method 1 is preferred for data sets where records have a lot of keywords such as long documents, while Method 2 is preferred for data sets where records have a small number of keywords such as relational tables with relatively short attribute values.

4.3 Efficient Sorted Access

Heap-Based Method: For a query keyword w, we want to support sorted access that can access record IDs based on the relevance of w to these records. As w has multiple similar words, we can support sorted access efficiently by building a max heap on the inverted lists of such similar words, as described in Section 3. Notice that, in exact search, each leaf node has the same similarity to w; but for fuzzy search, different leaf nodes could have different similarities. Thus, when pushing a record r from an inverted list of a similar word d to the heap, we maintain $\langle r, F(r,d) \rangle$ in the heap. We push/pop the record on the heap with the maximal $F(r,d)$.

Consider the query "**icdm li**". Figure 8 shows the two heaps for the two keywords. For illustration purposes, for

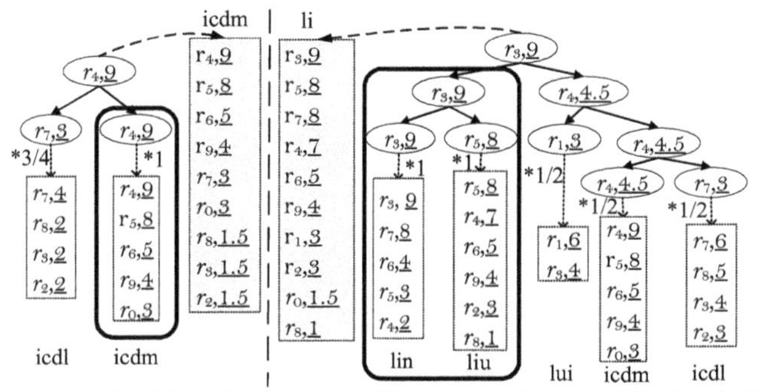

Figure 8: Max heaps for the query keywords "icdm" and "li". Each shaded list is merged from the underlying lists. It is "virtual" since we do not need to compute the entire list.

each keyword we also show the virtual merged list of records with their scores, and this list is only partially computed during the traversal of the underlying lists. Each record on a heap has an associated score of this keyword with respect to the query keyword, computed using Equation 4.

List Pruning: As there may be a large number of similar words for a query keyword, especially for the partial keyword, it could be expensive to construct a heap on the fly. We further improve the performance of sorted access on the virtual sorted list $U(w)$ by using the idea of "on-demand heap construction," i.e., we want to avoid constructing a heap for all the inverted lists of keywords similar to a query keyword. Suppose w has t similar words. Each push/pop operation on the heap of these lists takes $\mathcal{O}(log(t))$ time. If we can reduce the number of lists on the heap, we can reduce the cost of its push/pop operations. We have two observations about this pruning method. (1) As a special case, if those keywords matching query keywords *exactly* have the highest relevance scores, this method allows us to consider these records prior to considering other records with mismatching keywords. (2) The pruning can be more powerful if w is the last partial keyword w_m, since many of its similar keywords share the same prefix p on the trie.

Consider query "**icdm li**", Figure 8 illustrates how we can prune low-score lists and do on-demand heap constructions. The prefix "**li**" has several similar keywords. Among them, the two words "**lin**" and "**liu**" have the highest similarity value to the query keyword, mainly because they have a prefix matching the keyword exactly. We build a heap using these two lists. To compute the top-1 best answer, the lists of "**lui**", "**icdm**", and "**icdl**" are never included in the heap since their upper bounds are always smaller than the scores of popped records before the traversal terminates.

We next introduce how to do list pruning for the max-heap based methods in fuzzy type-ahead search. Given a keyword w, let $d_1, \ldots, d_t$ be its similar words and $L_1, \ldots, L_t$ be the corresponding inverted lists, respectively. We need not use all the inverted lists to build the max heap of w. Instead, we use those with higher similarities to w to "*on-demand build the max heap*". We first sort these inverted lists based on the similarities of their keywords to w, without loss of generality, suppose $\mathsf{Sim}(d_1, w) > \ldots > \mathsf{Sim}(d_t, w)$. We first construct the max heap using the lists with the highest similarity values and then include other lists on-demand.

Suppose L_i is a list not included in the heap so far. We can derive an upper bound u_i on the score of a record from L_i (with respect to the query keyword w) using the largest weight on the list and the string similarity $\mathsf{Sim}(d_i, w)$. Let r be the top record on the heap, with a score $F(r, w)$. If $F(r, w) \geq u_i$, then this list does not need to be included in the heap, since it cannot have a record with a higher score. Otherwise, this list needs to be included in the heap. Based on this analysis, each time we pop a record from the heap and push a new record r, we compare the score of the new record with the upper bounds of those lists not included in the heap so far. For those lists with an upper bound greater than this score, they need to be included in the heap from now on. Notice that this checking can be done very efficiently by storing the maximal value of these upper bounds, and ordering these lists based on their upper bounds. The pruning power can be even more significant if the keyword w is the partial keyword w_m, since many of its similar keywords share the same prefix p on the trie similar to w_m. We can compute an upper bound of the record scores from these lists and store the bound on the trie node p. In this way, we can prune the lists more effectively by comparing the value $F(r, w)$ with this upper bound stored on the trie, without needing to on-the-fly compute the bound.

List Materialization: For fuzzy search, the partial keyword w_m has multiple similar prefixes and each similar prefix has multiple similar words. The max heap of w_m is built on top of inverted lists of such similar words. Let d be such a similar word. Recall that the value $F(r, w_m, d)$ of a record r on the list of a similar word d with respect to w_m is based on both $W(d, r)$ and $\mathsf{Sim}(d, w_m)$. Let v be a materialized node. To use $U(v)$ to replace the lists of v's leaf nodes in the max heap, the following two conditions need to be satisfied:

- All the leaf nodes of v have the same similarity to w_m.
- All the leaf nodes of v are similar to w_m, i.e., their similarity to w_m is no less than the threshold τ.

When the conditions are satisfied, the sorting order of the union list $U(v)$ is also the order of the scores of the records on the leaf-node lists with respect to w_m. A materialized node v that satisfies the two conditions must be a descendant of a similar prefix of partial keyword w_m. We can prove this by contradiction. Suppose node v is not a descendant of any similar prefix of partial keyword w_m. Then node v and its ancestors are not similar prefixes of w_m, that is the leaf nodes of v are not similar keywords of w_m. This is contradicted with the second condition. Thus a materialized node v that satisfies the two conditions must be a descendant of a similar prefix of partial keyword w_m.

Suppose $p_1, p_2, \ldots, p_n$ are similar prefixes of w_m. We check whether their materialized descendants satisfy the two conditions as follows. Consider a materialized node v which has ancestors among $p_1, p_2, \ldots, p_n$. If node v has no descendants that are similar prefixes of w_m, v must satisfy the two conditions; otherwise suppose p_j is a descendant of v that is a similar prefix of w_m and has the largest similarity to v among all such descendants. Without loss of generality, let p_i be an ancestor of v and has the largest similarity with v among all similar prefixes. If $\mathsf{Sim}(v, p_j) \leq \mathsf{Sim}((v, p_i)$, v satisfies the two conditions; otherwise v will not. Thus we can find *usable* materialized nodes to construct the max heap of w_m and use our proposed techniques in Section 3.2.2 to do a cost-based analysis to select high-quality nodes for materialization.

5. EXPERIMENTS

We implemented our proposed techniques and compared with existing methods on three real data sets. (1) "DBLP": It included computer science publication records[4]. (2) "URL"[5]: It included 10 million URLs. (3) "Enron": It was an email collection[6]. Table 2 shows details of the data.

Table 2: Data sets and index costs.

Data Set	URL	DBLP	Enron
# of Records (millions)	10	1	0.5
Data size	1.1 GB	500 MB	1.4 GB
Avg. # of words/record	7.7	17.1	271.7
# of distinct keywords (millions)	1.79	0.392	1.26
Trie size	421 MB	31 MB	128 MB
Size of inverted lists	379 MB	83 MB	342 MB

For the DBLP data set, we selected 1000 real queries from the logs of our deployed systems and each query contained 1-6 keywords[7]. For the other two data sets, we generated 1000 queries with keywords randomly selected from the set of words used in the collection. We assumed the letters of a query were typed in one by one. For each keystroke, we measured the time of computing the top-k answers to this query. For exact search, we measured the total running time. For fuzzy search, we measured the time in two steps: in step 1 we computed keywords on the trie similar to the query keywords (using the algorithm described in [13]); in step 2 we found the top-k answers using the inverted lists of these similar keywords. Unless otherwise specified, $k = 10$.

We compared our method with state-of-the-art method [13]. We implemented the NRA algorithm described in [6] if we only do sorted access, and the Threshold Algorithm ("TA") if we can do both sorted access and random access.

All the indexes were built off-line and pre-loaded and full-resident in memory during all querying operations. All experiments were run on a Ubuntu Linux machine with an Intel Core processor (X5450 3.00GHz and 4 GB RAM).

5.1 Exact Search

Sorted Access Only: We implemented the following methods. (1) BinaryProbe [13]: We considered the inverted lists of the complete query keywords, and the union of the inverted lists for the complete keywords of the partial keyword. We chose the shortest list, and for each of its record IDs, we did binary probings on other lists. (2) NRA(Heap): We implemented the NRA algorithm using the heap-based technique. (3) NRA(Heap+Materialization[8]): We implemented the NRA algorithm using the heap-and-materialization-based techniques. Figure 9 shows the results on the Enron dataset, which showed that our method improved search efficiency. For instance, for queries with a partial keyword of length 2, NRA(Heap) reduced the query time of BinaryProbe from 128 ms to 10 ms. NRA(Heap+Materialization) further reduced the time to 2 ms. This is because 1) BinaryProbe first computed all results and then ranked them; 2) BinaryProbe on-the-fly computed the union list of the partial keyword. NRA(Heap) used the max heap to generate a sorted *partial* list and NRA(Heap+Materialization) used materialized lists to save push/pop operations on the heap.

Sorted Access + Random Access: We implemented the following methods. (1) BinaryProbe (Forward List)[13], we chose the shortest list, and for each of its record IDs, we verified whether the record ID contained other keywords

[4] http://dblp.uni-trier.de/xml/

[5] http://www.sogou.com/labs/dl/t-rank.html

[6] http://www-2.cs.cmu.edu/~enron/

[7] Details are omitted due to double-blind review.

[8] We used additional 50% space with respect to inverted index for materialization in the experiments.

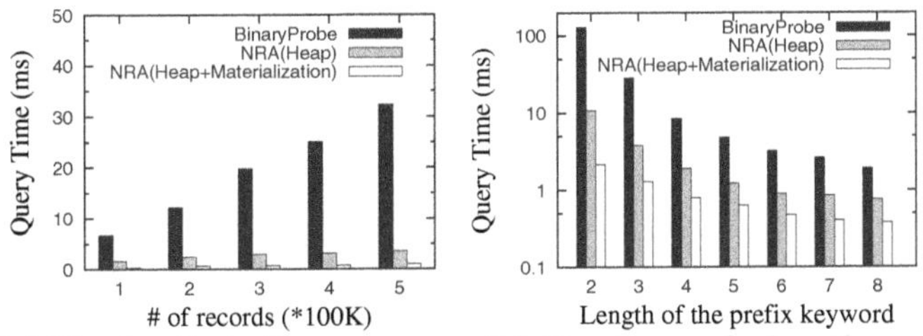

(a) Varying Data Size (b) Varying prefix length

Figure 9: Exact search using sorted access (Enron).

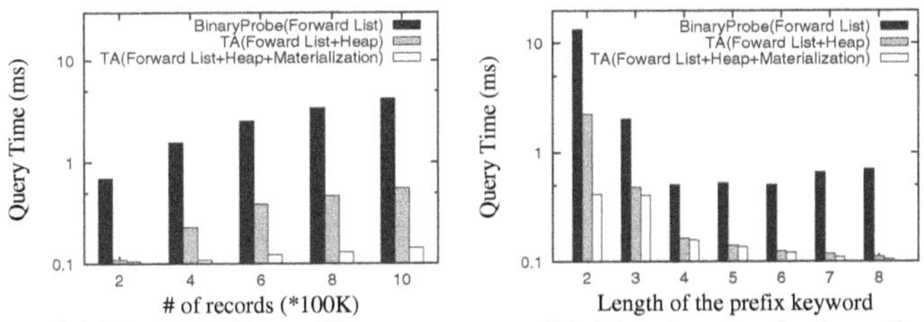

(a) Varying Data Size (b) Varying prefix length

Figure 10:Exact search using random access(DBLP).

using the forward list. (2) TA(Forward List+Heap): We implemented the TA algorithm using forward list for random access and max heap for sorted access. (3) TA(Forward List+Heap+Materialization): We implemented the TA algorithm using forward list, max heap, and list materialization. Figure 10 shows the results on the DBLP dataset. We can see that the random-access techniques indeed improved efficiency.

5.2 Fuzzy Search

Sorted Access Only: We first evaluated the effect of the list-pruning technique. Figure 11 shows the experimental results (including two steps). We can observe that list pruning indeed improved search efficiency. For the Enron dataset with 0.5M records, the method with pruning can reduce the time from 30 ms to 17 ms. The pruning technique was more effective on the Enron dataset than on the other two datasets mainly due to two reasons. First, the Enron dataset had more trie nodes due to its large number of distinct keywords in the emails. Thus a query keyword can have more similar prefixes on the trie. Second, the Enron dataset had fewer records, and the inverted lists were relatively shorter. During the list traversal, the NRA algorithm visited fewer records, and its higher score of the top record from the max heap helped us prune more lists.

List Materialization: We evaluated the improvement on sorted access using list materialization for fuzzy type-ahead search. We measured the amount of storage space for storing materialized lists as a percentage of the total size of the inverted lists on the trie. We varied this amount, and measured the average time of finding the top-10 answers using the NRA algorithm. Figure 12 shows the results. We can see that list materialization improved the search performance.

We implemented the different methods for list materialization, namely Random, TopDown, BottomUp, and CostBased as discussed in Section 3.2.2. Figure 13 shows the results. Among the three naive methods, Random gave the best results. The CostBased algorithm outperformed all the naive methods. This is because CostBased selected high-quality nodes for materialization using a cost-based analysis.

Sorted Access + Random Access: We implemented the TA algorithm using the two methods for random access and list pruning for sorted access (described in Section 4). Figure 14 shows the scalability results on the three datasets. The two random-access methods scaled well. Method 2 (probing on trie leaf nodes) outperformed Method 1 (probing on forward lists). This is because for the three data sets, there were many prefixes similar to the partial keyword, and Method 1 needed to consider all similar prefixes for each record on forward lists.

6. RELATED WORK

There are many studies on autocomplete and phrase prediction for user queries [22, 15, 9, 23, 7]. Google instant search was launched to support type-ahead search. It first suggested relevant queries based on user profiles and query logs and then answered the top queries. Chaudhuri et al. [5] studied how to find similar strings interactively as users type in a query string, using an approach similar to that in [13, 20]. They did not study the case where a query has multiple keywords that need list-intersection operations. The search paradigm studied in this paper is different since we support *fuzzy, full-text search* as users type in queries.

Bast et al. proposed techniques to support type-ahead search in their CompleteSearch systems [2, 3, 1]. Another study [19] is about type-ahead search on relational data graphs. Ji et al. [13] developed algorithms for fuzzy type-ahead search. Our work extends these studies by developing efficient algorithms to support top-k search.

Khoussainova et al. [14] proposed to suggest relevant SQL snippets as users type in SQL queries. Li et al. [18] studied how to use SQLs to support type-ahead search in databases. Feng et al. [8] studied fuzzy search on XML data. There have been many studies on supporting fuzzy search (e.g., [10, 17, 4, 11, 24, 16]). However these algorithms are inefficient for type-ahead search since they have low pruning power for short strings (partial keywords). The experiments in [13, 5] showed that these approaches are not as efficient as trie-based methods for fuzzy type-ahead search. Theobald et al. [25] proposed a heap-based method for query expansion. They used WordNet words and only utilized sorted access. We consider both sorted access and random access.

7. CONCLUSION

In this paper we studied how to efficiently answer top-k queries in type-ahead search. We focused on an index structure with a trie of keywords in a data set and inverted lists of records on the trie leaf nodes. We studied technical challenges when adopting existing top-k algorithms in the literature: how to efficiently support random access and sorted access on inverted lists? We presented two algorithms for supporting random access, and proposed optimization techniques using list pruning and materialization to support sorted access. Our techniques can be easily extended to support large datasets through data partition. For example, we have built a system to search on 20 million MEDLINE publication records using two machines.

Acknowledgement. The authors have financial interest in Bimaple Technology Inc., a company currently commercializing some of the techniques described in this publication. Chen Li is partially supported by the NIH grant 1R21LM010143-01A1 and the National Natural Science Foundation of China (No. 61129002). Guoliang Li, Jianan Wang, and Jianhua Feng were partly supported by the National Natural Science Foundation of China (No. 61003004), the National Grand Fundamental Research 973 Program of China (No. 2011CB302206), Tsinghua University (No. 20111081073), and the "NExT Research Center" funded by MDA, Singapore (No. WBS:R-252-300-001-490).

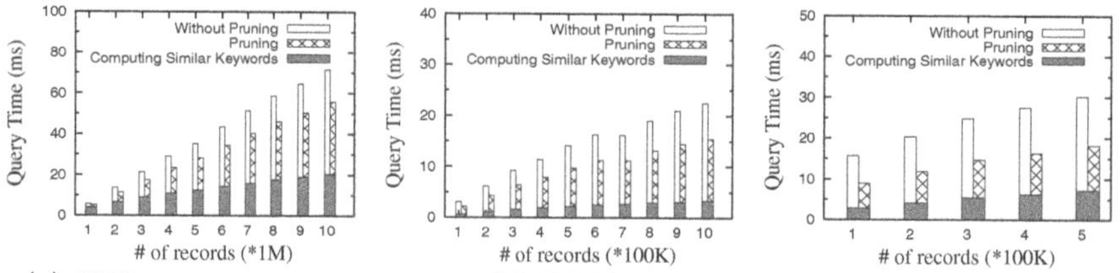

(a) URL (b) DBLP (c) Enron

Figure 11: Fuzzy search using list pruning (similarity threshold $\tau = 0.6$).

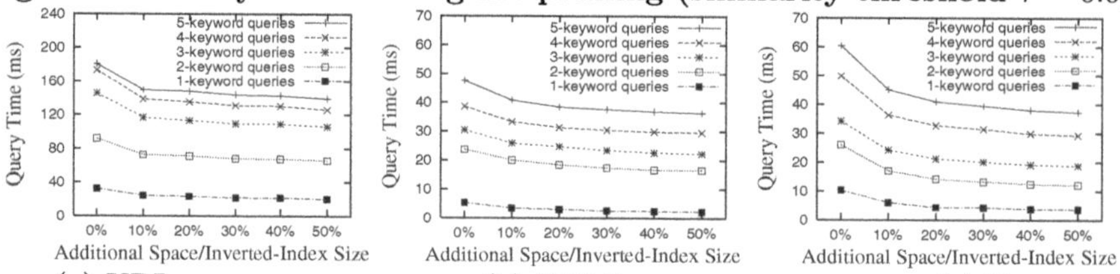

(a) URL (b) DBLP (c) Enron

Figure 12: Fuzzy search using list materialization (sorted access only, with list pruning, threshold $\tau = 0.6$).

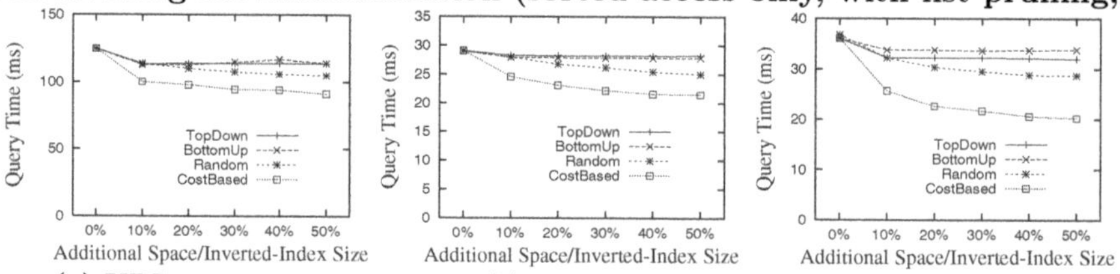

(a) URL (b) DBLP (c) Enron

Figure 13: Comparison of different materialization methods (similarity threshold $\tau = 0.6$).

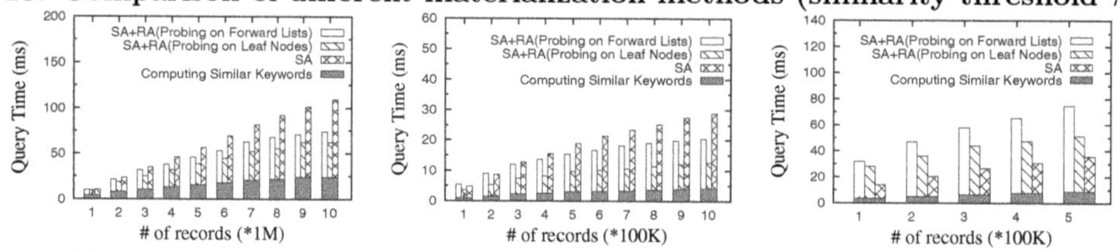

(a) URL (b) DBLP (c) Enron

Figure 14: Fuzzy search with sorted access ("SA") and random access ("RA") (similarity threshold $\tau = 0.6$).

8. REFERENCES

[1] H. Bast, A. Chitea, F. M. Suchanek, and I. Weber. Ester: efficient search on text, entities, and relations. In *SIGIR*, pages 671–678, 2007.

[2] H. Bast and I. Weber. Type less, find more: fast autocompletion search with a succinct index. In *SIGIR*, pages 364–371, 2006.

[3] H. Bast and I. Weber. The completesearch engine: Interactive, efficient, and towards ir& db integration. In *CIDR*, pages 88–95, 2007.

[4] S. Chaudhuri, V. Ganti, and R. Kaushik. A primitive operator for similarity joins in data cleaning. In *ICDE*, pages 5–16, 2006.

[5] S. Chaudhuri and R. Kaushik. Extending autocompletion to tolerate errors. In *SIGMOD Conference*, pages 707–718, 2009.

[6] R. Fagin, A. Lotem, and M. Naor. Optimal aggregation algorithms for middleware. In *PODS*, pages 102–113, 2001.

[7] J. Fan, G. Li, and L. Zhou. Interactive SQL query suggestion: Making databases user-friendly. *ICDE*, pages 351–362, 2011.

[8] J. Feng, and G. Li. Efficient Fuzzy Type-Ahead Search in XML Data. *IEEE TKDE*, 24(5):882–895, 2012.

[9] K. Grabski and T. Scheffer. Sentence completion. In *SIGIR*, pages 433–439, 2004.

[10] L. Gravano, P. G. Ipeirotis, H. V. Jagadish, N. Koudas, S. Muthukrishnan, and D. Srivastava. Approximate string joins in a database (almost) for free. In *VLDB*, pages 491–500, 2001.

[11] M. Hadjieleftheriou, A. Chandel, N. Koudas, and D. Srivastava. Fast indexes and algorithms for set similarity selection queries. In *ICDE*, pages 267–276, 2008.

[12] I. F. Ilyas, G. Beskales, and M. A. Soliman. A survey of top-k query processing techniques in relational database systems. *ACM Comput. Surv.*, 40(4), 2008.

[13] S. Ji, G. Li, C. Li, and J. Feng. Efficient interactive fuzzy keyword search. In *WWW*, pages 371–380, 2009.

[14] N. Khoussainova, Y. Kwon, M. Balazinska, and D. Suciu. Snipsuggest: Context-aware autocompletion for sql. *PVLDB*, 4(1):22–33, 2010.

[15] K. Kukich. Techniques for automatically correcting words in text. *ACM Comput. Surv.*, 24(4):377–439, 1992.

[16] H. Lee, R. T. Ng, and K. Shim. Extending q-grams to estimate selectivity of string matching with low edit distance. In *VLDB*, pages 195–206, 2007.

[17] C. Li, J. Lu, and Y. Lu. Efficient merging and filtering algorithms for approximate string searches. In *ICDE*, pages 257–266, 2008.

[18] G. Li, J. Feng, and C. Li. Supporting search-as-you-type using sql in databases. *IEEE TKDE*, 2012.

[19] G. Li, S. Ji, C. Li, and J. Feng. Efficient type-ahead search on relational data: a tastier approach. In *SIGMOD Conference*, pages 695–706, 2009.

[20] G. Li, S. Ji, C. Li, and J. Feng. Efficient fuzzy full-text type-ahead search. *VLDB J.*, 20(4):617-640, 2011.

[21] N. Mamoulis, K. H. Cheng, M. L. Yiu, and D. W. Cheung. Efficient aggregation of ranked inputs. In *ICDE*, page 72–83, 2006.

[22] H. Motoda and K. Yoshida. Machine learning techniques to make computers easier to use. *Artif. Intell.*, 103(1-2):295–321, 1998.

[23] A. Nandi and H. V. Jagadish. Effective phrase prediction. In *VLDB*, pages 219–230, 2007.

[24] J. Qin, W. Wang, Y. Lu, C. Xiao, and X. Lin. Efficient exact edit similarity query processing with the asymmetric signature scheme. In *SIGMOD Conference*, pages 1033–1044, 2011.

[25] M. Theobald, R. Schenkel, and G. Weikum. Efficient and self-tuning incremental query expansion for top-k query processing. In *SIGIR*, pages 242–249, 2005.

SimFusion+: Extending SimFusion Towards Efficient Estimation on Large and Dynamic Networks

Weiren Yu[†‡], Xuemin Lin[†♯], Wenjie Zhang[†], Ying Zhang[†], Jiajin Le[♮]

[†]The University of New South Wales, Australia [♯]East China Normal University, China

[‡]NICTA, Australia [♮]Donghua University, China

{weirenyu, lxue, zhangw, yingz}@cse.unsw.edu.au lejiajin@dhu.edu.cn

ABSTRACT

SimFusion has become a captivating measure of similarity between objects in a web graph. It is iteratively distilled from the notion that "the similarity between two objects is reinforced by the similarity of their related objects". The existing SimFusion model usually exploits the *Unified Relationship Matrix* (URM) to represent latent relationships among heterogeneous data, and adopts an iterative paradigm for SimFusion computation. However, due to the row normalization of URM, the traditional SimFusion model may produce the trivial solution; worse still, the iterative computation of SimFusion may not ensure the global convergence of the solution. This paper studies the revision of this model, providing a full treatment from complexity to algorithms. (1) We propose SimFusion+ based on a notion of the *Unified Adjacency Matrix* (UAM), a modification of the URM, to prevent the trivial solution and the divergence issue of SimFusion. (2) We show that for any vertex-pair, SimFusion+ can be performed in $O(1)$ time and $O(n)$ space with an $O(km)$-time precomputation done only once, as opposed to the $O(kn^3)$ time and $O(n^2)$ space of its traditional counterpart, where n, m, and k denote the number of vertices, edges, and iterations respectively. (3) We also devise an incremental algorithm for further improving the computation of SimFusion+ when networks are dynamically updated, with performance guarantees for similarity estimation. We experimentally verify that these algorithms scale well, and the revised notion of SimFusion is able to converge to a non-trivial solution, and allows us to identify more sensible structure information in large real-world networks.

Categories and Subject Descriptors

H.3.3 [**Information Search and Retrieval**]: Information Storage and Retrieval; G.2.2 [**Graph Theory**]: Discrete Mathematics

Keywords

Similarity Computation, SimFusion, Web Ranking Algorithm

1. INTRODUCTION

The conundrum of measuring similarity between objects based on hyperlinks in a graph has fueled a growing interest in the fields of information retrieval. This problem is also known as "link-based analysis" or "structural similarity search", and it has been extensively studied by different communities with a proliferation of emerging applications. Examples include collaborative filtering, hyper-text classification, graph clustering and proximity query processing. Recently, while the scale of the Web has dramatically increased our need to produce large graphs, the study of efficiently computing object similarity on such large graphs becomes a desideratum. In practice, an effective similarity measure should not only correlate well with human intuition but also scale well for large amounts of data.

Permission to make digital or hard copies of all or part of this work for personal or classroom use is granted without fee provided that copies are not made or distributed for profit or commercial advantage and that copies bear this notice and the full citation on the first page. To copy otherwise, to republish, to post on servers or to redistribute to lists, requires prior specific permission and/or a fee.
SIGIR'12, August 12–16, 2012, Portland, Oregon, USA.
Copyright 2012 ACM 978-1-4503-1472-5/12/08 ...$15.00.

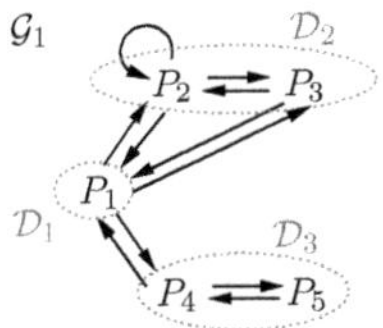

$$\lim_{k\to\infty}\mathbf{SimFusion}^{(k)} = \begin{array}{r} \mathcal{D}_1\{ \\ \mathcal{D}_2\{ \\ \\ \mathcal{D}_3\{ \\ \\ \end{array}\left[\begin{array}{ccccc} 1 & .219 & .219 & .219 & .219 \\ .219 & 1 & .219 & .219 & .219 \\ .219 & .219 & 1 & .219 & .219 \\ .219 & .219 & .219 & 1 & .219 \\ .219 & .219 & .219 & .219 & 1 \\ \underbrace{\quad}_{\mathcal{D}_1} & \multicolumn{2}{c}{\underbrace{\qquad\quad}_{\mathcal{D}_2}} & \multicolumn{2}{c}{\underbrace{\qquad\quad}_{\mathcal{D}_3}} \end{array}\right]$$

$$\lim_{k\to\infty}\mathbf{SimFusion+}^{(k)} = \left[\begin{array}{ccccc} 1 & .290 & .194 & .139 & .100 \\ .290 & 1 & .304 & .217 & .156 \\ .194 & .304 & 1 & .145 & .105 \\ .139 & .217 & .145 & 1 & .075 \\ .100 & .156 & .105 & .075 & 1 \\ \underbrace{\quad}_{\mathcal{D}_1} & \multicolumn{2}{c}{\underbrace{\qquad\quad}_{\mathcal{D}_2}} & \multicolumn{2}{c}{\underbrace{\qquad\quad}_{\mathcal{D}_3}} \end{array}\right]$$

Figure 1: Trivial SimFusion on Heterogeneous Domain

Among the existing metrics, SimFusion [1] can be regarded as one of the attractive ones on account of the following reasons. (i) Similar to PageRank [2] and SimRank [3], SimFusion is based on hyperlinks and follows the reinforcement assumption that "the similarity between objects is reinforced by the similarity of their related objects", which is fairly intuitive and conforms to our basic understandings. (ii) Unlike other measures (*e.g.,* PageRank and SimRank) that explore the linkage patterns merely from a single data space [2–4], SimFusion has the extra benefits of incorporating both inter- and intra-relationships from multiple data spaces in a unified manner to measure the similarity of heterogeneous data objects. (iii) SimFusion offers more intuitive and flexible ways of assigning weighting factors to each data space that reflects their relative importance, as opposed to the PageRank and SimRank measures that need to determine a damping factor. (iv) SimFusion provides a general-purpose framework for measuring structural similarity in a recursive fashion; other well-known measures, such as Co-Citation [5] and Coupling [6] are just special cases of SimFusion.

However, existing work on SimFusion has the following problems. Firstly, although the basic intuition behind the SimFusion model is appealing, it seems inappropriate to use the *Unified Relationship Matrix* (URM) to represent the relationships of heterogeneous objects. The main problem is that, according to the definition of URM $\mathbf{L}$ in [1], the sum of each row of $\mathbf{L}$ is always equal to 1. Since the product of $\mathbf{L}$ and the matrix $\mathbf{1}$ whose entries are all ones is equal to the matrix $\mathbf{1}$ of all ones, there always exists a trivial solution $\mathbf{S} = \mathbf{1}$ to the original SimFusion formula $\mathbf{S} = \mathbf{L} \cdot \mathbf{S} \cdot \mathbf{L}^T$ [1], as illustrated in Example 1. The same phenomena of yielding such a trivial solution may occur in our experimental results in Section 6. To address this issue, we shall revise the original SimFusion model.

EXAMPLE 1 (TRIVIAL SOLUTION). *Figure 1 depicts a graph $\mathcal{G}_1$ partly extracted from Cornell CS Department. Each vertex P_i*

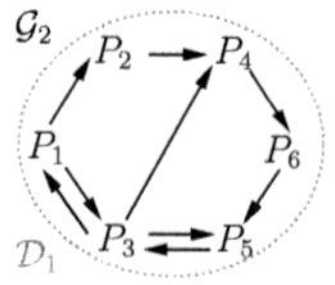

$$\lim_{k\to\infty}\mathbf{SimFusion}^{(2k)} = \begin{bmatrix} .46 & 0 & .46 & 0 & 0 & .46 \\ 0 & .38 & 0 & .38 & .38 & 0 \\ .46 & 0 & .46 & 0 & 0 & .46 \\ 0 & .38 & 0 & .38 & .38 & 0 \\ 0 & .38 & 0 & .38 & .38 & 0 \\ .46 & 0 & .46 & 0 & 0 & .46 \end{bmatrix} \neq \lim_{k\to\infty}\mathbf{SimFusion}^{(2k+1)} = \begin{bmatrix} .38 & 0 & .38 & 0 & 0 & .38 \\ 0 & .46 & 0 & .46 & .46 & 0 \\ .38 & 0 & .38 & 0 & 0 & .38 \\ 0 & .46 & 0 & .46 & .46 & 0 \\ 0 & .46 & 0 & .46 & .46 & 0 \\ .38 & 0 & .38 & 0 & 0 & .38 \end{bmatrix} \quad \lim_{k\to\infty}\mathbf{SimFusion+}^{(k)} = \begin{bmatrix} 1 & 0 & .25 & 0 & 0 & .25 \\ 0 & 1 & 0 & .25 & .18 & 0 \\ .25 & 0 & 1 & 0 & 0 & .18 \\ 0 & .25 & 0 & 1 & .25 & 0 \\ 0 & .18 & 0 & .25 & 1 & 0 \\ .25 & 0 & .18 & 0 & 0 & 1 \end{bmatrix}$$

Figure 2: Divergent SimFusion on Homogeneous Domain

denotes a web page, and each edge a hyperlink. There are three categories: $\mathcal{D}_1 = \{P_1\}$ (student), $\mathcal{D}_2 = \{P_2, P_3\}$ (staff), and $\mathcal{D}_3 = \{P_4, P_5\}$ (faculty). We want to retrieve the top-3 similar pairs of web pages in $\mathcal{G}_1$. However, the naive SimFusion fails to correctly find them. We observe that the SimFusion solution is a (trivial) matrix whose entries are all the same. In fact, vertices in $\mathcal{G}_1$ do not have the identical neighbor structures. Hence, the trivial solution is non-semantic in real communities.

Secondly, it is rather expensive to compute SimFusion similarities. The existing approach for SimFusion computation deploys a fixed-point iteration: $\mathbf{S}^{(k+1)} = \mathbf{L} \cdot \mathbf{S}^{(k)} \cdot \mathbf{L}^T$, which requires $O(kn^3)$ time and $O(n^2)$ space [1]. This impedes the scalability of SimFusion on large graphs. Worse still, the iterative computation of SimFusion do not always converge. The convergence of the SimFusion iterations heavily depends on the choice of the initial guess $\mathbf{S}^{(0)}$, as shown in Example 2.

EXAMPLE 2 (DIVERGENCE SIMFUSION). *Consider the disease transmission graph $\mathcal{G}_2$, where each vertex is an organism P_i which can carry the disease, and an edge represents one organism spreading it to another. One wants to find the three most similar organisms to P_2 in $\mathcal{G}_2$. However, the iterative computation of SimFusion does not work properly. We observe the following:*

(i) When $\mathbf{S}^{(0)}$ is set to an $n \times n$ identity matrix (according to [1]) the "even" and "odd" subsequences of $\{\mathbf{S}^{(k)}\}$ are convergent respectively, but they do not converge to the same limit, which makes the full sequence $\{\mathbf{S}^{(k)}\}$ divergent.

(ii) Choosing $\mathbf{S}^{(0)} = \mathbf{1}_n$ (i.e., an $n \times n$ matrix of all 1s) instead, we observe that the full SimFusion sequence $\{\mathbf{S}^{(k)}\}$ is always convergent to $\mathbf{1}_n$ regardless of the graph structure.

This suggests that the original SimFusion iterations may be divergent or converge to a trivial solution, not to mention its scalability. This highlights the need to find a feasible way to guarantee the convergence of the SimFusion iterations, but it is hard to devise an efficient algorithm for the revised SimFusion computation.

Thirdly, it is a big challenge to incrementally compute SimFusion on dynamic graphs. The traditional method [1] has to recompute the similarity from scratch when edges in a graph change over time, which is not adaptive to many evolving networks. Fortunately, we have an observation that the size of the areas affected by the updates is typically small in practice. To this end, we propose an incremental algorithm that fully utilizes these affected areas to compute SimFusion on dynamic graphs.

Contributions. This paper proposes SimFusion+, a revised notion of SimFusion, to provide a full treatment of SimFusion for the convergence issues and to improve its computational efficiency. In summary, we make the following contributions.

1. We formalize the problem of SimFusion+ computation (Section 2). The notion of SimFusion+ revises the divergence and non-semantic convergence worries of the traditional model [1].
2. We present optimization techniques for improving the computation of SimFusion+ to $O(1)$ time and $O(n)$ space for every pair of vertices, plus an $O(km)$-time precomputation run only once (Section 3).
3. We devise an efficient algorithm to compute the SimFusion+ similarity with better accuracy guarantees (Section 4). An error estimate is also given for the SimFusion+ approximation.
4. We devise an incremental algorithm for further optimizing the SimFusion+ computation when edges in networks are dynamically updated (Section 5). We show that the update cost of the incremental algorithm retains $O(\delta n)$ time and $O(n)$ space for handling a sequence of δ edge insertions or deletions.
5. We experimentally verify the effectiveness and scalability of the algorithms, using real and synthetic data (Section 6). The results show that SimFusion+ can govern the convergence towards a meaningful solution, and our algorithms achieve high accuracy and significantly outperform the baseline algorithms.

Related Work. The link-based similarity has become increasingly popular since the famous result of Google PageRank [2] on ranking web pages. Since then, there has been a surge of papers focusing on web link analysis. In particular, a growing interest has been witnessed in the SimFusion model over the past decade [1,7] as it provides a useful measure of similarity that supports different kinds of intra- and inter-node relations from multiple data spaces.

The iterative computation of SimFusion was proposed in [1] with several problems left open there. In comparison, this work extends [1] by (i) addressing the divergent and trivial solution of the original SimFusion, (ii) optimizing the time and space complexity of similarity computation, and (iii) supporting incremental update on evolving graphs, none of which was considered in [1].

It is worth mentioning that Jeh and Widom have proposed a similar structural measure called SimRank [3], predicated, as SimFusion is, on the idea that vertices are similar if they have similar neighbor structures. The essential difference between the two models is the notion of the convergence principle. SimFusion ensures the existence of the stationary distribution and ergodicity convergence to this distribution, whereas SimRank hinges on a damping factor $0 < c < 1$ to govern the convergence.

Optimization techniques have been devised for SimRank computation (*e.g.*, [8–11]). The best-known SimRank algorithm yields $O(k \min\{nm, \frac{n^3}{\log n}\})$ time [8]. The performance gain is mainly achieved by a partial sum function for amortization; as for SimFusion, the conventional matrix multiplication in its iterative formula misled its complexity, which was previously considered $O(kn^3)$ time and $O(n^2)$ space. The idea of the dominant eigenvector in this work significantly improves its computation to $O(km)$ time and $O(kn)$ space, which is more efficient than SimRank [8].

There has also been work on link-based similarity computation. A unified framework of link-based analysis was addressed in [7], which extends PageRank and HITS by (i) considering both inter- and intra-type relationships, and (ii) bringing order to data objects in different data spaces. It differs from this work in that the focus is on finding attribute values of a single object, rather than on improving the complexities for similarity estimation. Extensions of similarity reinforcement assumption were studied in [12], by spreading multiple relationship similarities over interrelated data objects to enhance their mutual reinforcement effects. Nevertheless, neither of these deduces rigorous mathematical formulae, and the rationales behind the integration approaches are different from this work. Recently, a closed-form solution to P-Rank (Penetrating-Rank) formula was addressed in [13]. Cai *et al.* [13] showed that when the damping factor $c = 1$ and weighting factor $\gamma = 0$, P-Rank can be reduced to SimFusion. However, this reasoning is based on the flawed assumption that the diagonal entries $\text{diag}(\mathbf{S})$ of the P-Rank similarity matrix were not considered. We argue that P-Rank is defined recursively, and hence, the omission of $\text{diag}(\mathbf{S})$ has an impact on the similarity of a vertex with itself, and recursively, it has an impact on the similarity of different pairs of vertices.

2. SIMFUSION ESTIMATION REVISED

In this section, we first revisit the definition of data space and data relation. We then introduce the notion of the *Unified Adjacency Matrix* (UAM) to revise the SimFusion model.

2.1 Data Space and Data Relation

Graphs studies here are digraphs having no multiple edges.

Data Space. A *data space* is the finite set of all data objects (vertices) with the same data type, denoted by $\mathcal{D} = \{o_1, o_2, \cdots\}$. $|\mathcal{D}|$ denotes the number of data objects in $\mathcal{D}$. Two nonempty data spaces $\mathcal{D}$ and $\mathcal{D}'$ are said to be *disjoint* if $\mathcal{D} \cap \mathcal{D}' = \varnothing$.

Throughout the paper, we shall use the following notations. (i) The *entire space* $\mathcal{D}$ in a network is the union of N disjoint data spaces $\mathcal{D}_1, \cdots, \mathcal{D}_N$ such that $\mathcal{D} = \bigcup_{i=1}^{N} \mathcal{D}_i$ and $\mathcal{D}_i \cap \mathcal{D}_j = \varnothing \;\; (i \neq j)$. (ii) The total size $|\mathcal{D}|$ of the entire space, denoted by n, is the sum of the number n_i of the data objects in each data space $\mathcal{D}_i$, *i.e.*, $n = \sum_{i=1}^{N} n_i$ with $n_i = |\mathcal{D}_i| \;\; (\forall i = 1, \cdots, N)$.

Intuitively, for heterogeneous networks, the distinct spaces $\mathcal{D}_i$ form a partition of $\mathcal{D}$ into classes. For homogenous networks, the partition of $\mathcal{D}$ is itself.

Data Relation. A *data relation* on $\mathcal{D}$ is defined as $\mathcal{R} \subseteq \mathcal{D} \times \mathcal{D}$, where $(o, o') \in \mathcal{R}$ is a connection (a directed edge) from object o to o'. Data objects in the same data space are related via *intra-type relations* $\mathcal{R}_{i,i} \subseteq \mathcal{D}_i \times \mathcal{D}_i$. Data objects between distinct data spaces are related via *inter-type relations* $\mathcal{R}_{i,j} \subseteq \mathcal{D}_i \times \mathcal{D}_j \;\; (i \neq j)$.

Intuitively, the intra-type relation carries connected information in each data space (*e.g.*, co-citation between web pages); the inter-type relation represents interlinked information between different data spaces (*e.g.*, making user requests). As an example, in Figure 1 there are three data spaces : $\mathcal{D} = \{P_1\} \cup \{P_2, P_3\} \cup \{P_4, P_5\}$, where $(P_2, P_2), (P_2, P_3), (P_3, P_2), (P_4, P_5), (P_5, P_4)$ are intra-type relations; $(P_1, P_2), (P_2, P_1), (P_3, P_1), (P_1, P_3), (P_1, P_4), (P_4, P_1)$ are inter-type relations.

2.2 Unified Adjacency Matrix

Let us now introduce the *unified adjacency matrix* (UAM). Consider a graph $\mathcal{G} = (\mathcal{D}, \mathcal{R})$ with data space $\mathcal{D}$ and data relation $\mathcal{R}$.

Unified Adjacency Matrix (UAM). The matrix $\mathbf{A} = \tilde{\mathbf{A}} + \mathbf{1}/n^2$ of size $n \times n$ is said to be a *unified adjacency matrix* of the relation $\mathcal{R}$ whenever

$$\tilde{\mathbf{A}} = \begin{pmatrix} \lambda_{1,1}\mathbf{A}_{1,1} & \lambda_{1,2}\mathbf{A}_{1,2} & \cdots & \lambda_{1,N}\mathbf{A}_{1,N} \\ \lambda_{2,1}\mathbf{A}_{2,1} & \lambda_{2,2}\mathbf{A}_{2,2} & \cdots & \lambda_{2,N}\mathbf{A}_{2,N} \\ \vdots & \vdots & \ddots & \vdots \\ \lambda_{N,1}\mathbf{A}_{N,1} & \lambda_{N,2}\mathbf{A}_{N,2} & \cdots & \lambda_{N,N}\mathbf{A}_{N,N} \end{pmatrix},$$

where (i) $\mathbf{1}$ is the $n \times n$ matrix of all ones; (ii) $\mathbf{A}_{i,j}$ is the submatrix of $\mathbf{A}$ whose (o, o')-entry equals 1 if there is an edge from data object o to o', *i.e.*, $\exists (o, o') \in \mathcal{R}$, $\frac{1}{n_j}$ if data object o has no neighbors in $\mathcal{D}_j$, or 0 otherwise; and (iii) $\lambda_{i,j}$ is called the *weighting factor* between data space $\mathcal{D}_i$ and $\mathcal{D}_j$ with $0 \leq \lambda_{i,j} \leq 1$ and $\sum_{j=1}^{N} \lambda_{i,j} = 1 \;(\forall i = 1, \cdots, N)$.

Intuitively, $\mathbf{A}_{i,j}$ represents the intra- $(i = j)$ or inter- $(i \neq j)$ relation from data space $\mathcal{D}_i$ to $\mathcal{D}_j$. $\lambda_{i,j}$ reflects the relative importance between data spaces $\mathcal{D}_i$ and $\mathcal{D}_j$.

EXAMPLE 3. *In Figure 1, the relative importance between data space $\mathcal{D}_i$ and $\mathcal{D}_j$ is denoted by a weighting matrix $\mathbf{\Lambda} = (\lambda_{i,j})_{3\times 3}$. Then, the UAM $\mathbf{A}$ of $\mathcal{G}_1$ can be derived from $\mathbf{A} = \tilde{\mathbf{A}} + \mathbf{1}/n^2$, where $\tilde{\mathbf{A}}$ is computed from $\mathbf{\Lambda}$ as follows.*

$$\mathbf{\Lambda} = \begin{matrix} & \mathcal{D}_1 & \mathcal{D}_2 & \mathcal{D}_3 \\ \mathcal{D}_1 & \frac{1}{2} & \frac{1}{6} & \frac{1}{3} \\ \mathcal{D}_2 & \frac{1}{6} & \frac{7}{12} & \frac{1}{4} \\ \mathcal{D}_3 & \frac{1}{3} & \frac{1}{4} & \frac{5}{12} \end{matrix} \Rightarrow \tilde{\mathbf{A}} = \begin{bmatrix} \frac{1}{2}[1] & \frac{1}{6}[1\,1] & \frac{1}{3}[1\,0] \\ \frac{1}{6}\begin{bmatrix}1\\1\end{bmatrix} & \frac{7}{12}\begin{bmatrix}1&1\\1&0\end{bmatrix} & \frac{1}{4}\begin{bmatrix}\frac{1}{2}&\frac{1}{2}\\\frac{1}{2}&\frac{1}{2}\end{bmatrix} \\ \frac{1}{3}\begin{bmatrix}1\\0\end{bmatrix} & \frac{1}{4}\begin{bmatrix}\frac{1}{2}&\frac{1}{2}\\\frac{1}{2}&\frac{1}{2}\end{bmatrix} & \frac{5}{12}\begin{bmatrix}0&1\\1&0\end{bmatrix} \end{bmatrix} = \left[\begin{array}{c|cc|cc} \frac{1}{2} & \frac{1}{6} & \frac{1}{6} & \frac{1}{3} & 0 \\ \hline \frac{1}{6} & \frac{7}{12} & \frac{7}{12} & \frac{1}{8} & \frac{1}{8} \\ \frac{1}{6} & \frac{7}{12} & 0 & \frac{1}{8} & \frac{1}{8} \\ \hline \frac{1}{3} & \frac{1}{8} & \frac{1}{8} & 0 & \frac{5}{12} \\ 0 & \frac{1}{8} & \frac{1}{8} & \frac{5}{12} & 0 \end{array}\right]$$

SimFusion+ Model. In light of the UAM $\mathbf{A}$, we next propose the revised model of SimFusion, termed SimFusion+, as follows:

$$\mathbf{S} = \frac{\mathbf{A} \cdot \mathbf{S} \cdot \mathbf{A}^T}{\|\mathbf{A} \cdot \mathbf{S} \cdot \mathbf{A}^T\|_2}, \tag{1}$$

where $\mathbf{S}$ is called the *Unified Similarity Matrix* (USM) whose (i, j)-entry represents the similarity score between object i and j.

The uniqueness and existence of the SimFusion+ solution $\mathbf{S}$ to Eq.(1) can be established by *the power iteration* [14, pp.381]. A detailed proof will be shown in Proposition 1 (Section 3).

The revised notion of SimFusion utilizes UAM (rather than URM) to represent data relations because UAM can effectively avoid divergent and trivial similarity solutions while well preserving the intuitive reinforcement assumption of the original model [1]. We observe that the root cause of the flawed solution to the original SimFusion is the "row normalization" of URM. Thus, by using UAM, we have an opportunity to postpone the operation of "row normalization" in a delayed fashion. To this end, we utilize the matrix 2-norm $\|\mathbf{A} \cdot \mathbf{S} \cdot \mathbf{A}^T\|_2$ to squeeze similarity scores in $\mathbf{S}$ into $[0, 1]$. The obtained similarity results in USM can not only prevent the divergence issue and the trivial solution but effectively capture the reliability of the similarity evidence between data objects. For instance, the SimFusion+ USMs in Examples 1 and 2 are nontrivial and intuitively explainable.

3. COMPUTING SIMILARITY VIA DOMINANT EIGENVECTOR

A conventional approach for finding the SimFusion+ solution $\mathbf{S}$ to Eq.(1) is to employ the following fixed-point iteration: [1]

$$\mathbf{S}^{(k+1)} = \frac{\mathbf{A} \cdot \mathbf{S}^{(k)} \cdot \mathbf{A}^T}{\|\mathbf{A} \cdot \mathbf{S}^{(k)} \cdot \mathbf{A}^T\|_2}. \tag{2}$$

However, as the matrix multiplication may contain $O(n^3)$ operations, it requires $O(kn^3)$ time and $O(n^2)$ space to compute Eq.(2) for k iterations, which may be quite expensive.

In this section, we study the optimization techniques to improve the computation of SimFusion+. Our key observation is that SimFusion+ computation can be converted into finding the dominant eigenvector of the UAM $\mathbf{A}$. The idea is to calculate the dominant eigenvector of $\mathbf{A}$ once, offline, for the preprocessing, and then it can be effectively memorized to compute similarity at query time.

We first revisit the definition of the dominant eigenvector.

DEFINITION 1 ([14, P.379]). *The dominant eigenvector of the $\mathbf{X}$ is an eigenvector, denoted by $\sigma_{\max}(\mathbf{X})$, corresponding to the eigenvalue λ of the largest absolute value of $\mathbf{X}$ such that*

$$\mathbf{X} \cdot \sigma_{\max}(\mathbf{X}) = \lambda \cdot \sigma_{\max}(\mathbf{X}) \;\; \textit{with} \;\; \|\sigma_{\max}(\mathbf{X})\|_2 = 1.$$

The dominant eigenvector of the UAM can be utilized for speeding up SimFusion+ computation based on the following proposition.

PROPOSITION 1. *Let $\mathbf{A}$ be the UAM of network $\mathcal{G} = (\mathcal{D}, \mathcal{R})$. The SimFusion+ matrix $\mathbf{S}$ can be computed as*

$$[\mathbf{S}]_{i,j} = [\sigma_{\max}(\mathbf{A})]_i \times [\sigma_{\max}(\mathbf{A})]_j, \tag{3}$$

where $[\star]_{i,j}$ denotes the (i, j)-entry of a matrix, and $[\star]_i$ denotes the i-th entry of a vector.

PROOF. We shall use the knowledge of Kronecker product ($\otimes$) and vec operator (see [15, p.139] for a detailed description).

(i) We first prove that $vec(\mathbf{S}) = \sigma_{\max}(\mathbf{A} \otimes \mathbf{A})$.

Taking $vec(\star)$ on both sides of Eq.(2) and applying Kronecker property $vec(\mathbf{BCD}^T) = (\mathbf{D} \otimes \mathbf{B}) \cdot vec(\mathbf{C})$ [15, p.147] yield

$$vec(\mathbf{S}^{(k+1)}) = \frac{(\mathbf{A} \otimes \mathbf{A}) \cdot vec(\mathbf{S}^{(k)})}{\|(\mathbf{A} \otimes \mathbf{A}) \cdot vec(\mathbf{S}^{(k)})\|_2}. \tag{4}$$

[1] Note that the uniqueness of the SimFusion+ solution guarantees that $\mathbf{S}$ is insensitive to the initial guess $\mathbf{S}^{(0)}$. For convenience, we choose $\mathbf{S}^{(0)} = \mathbf{1}$ of all 1s, which can be interpreted as "initially, no other vertex-pair is presumably more similar than itself".

Let $\mathbf{x}^{(k)} \triangleq vec(\mathbf{S}^{(k)})$ and $\mathbf{M} \triangleq \mathbf{A} \otimes \mathbf{A}$. Then Eq.(4) having the form $\mathbf{x}^{(k+1)} = \mathbf{M}\mathbf{x}^{(k)}/\|\mathbf{M}\mathbf{x}^{(k)}\|_2$ fits the *power iteration* paradigm [14, pp.381], which follows that the sequence $\{\mathbf{x}^{(k)}\}$ converges to the dominant eigenvector of $\mathbf{M}$. This in turn implies

$$vec(\mathbf{S}) \triangleq \lim_{k\to\infty} vec(\mathbf{S}^{(k)}) = \sigma_{\max}(\mathbf{A} \otimes \mathbf{A}).$$

One caveat is that the convergence of $vec(\mathbf{S}^{(k)})$ is ensured by the positivity of $\mathbf{A}\otimes\mathbf{A}$ [16, p.508] [2]. This is true because $\mathbf{A}$ is positive and the self-Kronecker product of two positive matrices preserves positivity.

(ii) We next show that $\sigma_{\max}(\mathbf{A} \otimes \mathbf{A}) = \sigma_{\max}(\mathbf{A}) \otimes \sigma_{\max}(\mathbf{A})$.

Since $\mathbf{A} \cdot \sigma_{\max}(\mathbf{A}) = \lambda \cdot \sigma_{\max}(\mathbf{A})$, it follows that

$$(\mathbf{A} \otimes \mathbf{A}) \cdot (\sigma_{\max}(\mathbf{A}) \otimes \sigma_{\max}(\mathbf{A})) = (\mathbf{A}\sigma_{\max}(\mathbf{A})) \otimes (\mathbf{A}\sigma_{\max}(\mathbf{A}))$$
$$= (\lambda \cdot \sigma_{\max}(\mathbf{A})) \otimes (\lambda \cdot \sigma_{\max}(\mathbf{A})) = \lambda^2 \cdot (\sigma_{\max}(\mathbf{A}) \otimes \sigma_{\max}(\mathbf{A})).$$

This implies that the dominant eigenvector of $\mathbf{A}\otimes\mathbf{A}$ is actually the self-Kronecker product of the dominant eigenvector of $\mathbf{A}$. Hence,

$$vec(\mathbf{S}) = \sigma_{\max}(\mathbf{A} \otimes \mathbf{A}) = \sigma_{\max}(\mathbf{A}) \otimes \sigma_{\max}(\mathbf{A}).$$

It can be noticed that the (i, j)-entry of the matrix $\mathbf{S}$ (*i.e.*, the $((i-1)\times n+j)$-th entry of the vector $vec(\mathbf{S})$) is exactly the product of the i-th and j-th entries of $\sigma_{\max}(\mathbf{A})$. Thus, Eq.(3) holds. □

Proposition 1 provides the efficient technique for accelerating SimFusion+ computation. The central point in optimizing $\mathbf{S}$ computation is that only *matrix-vector* multiplication is used for computing $\sigma_{\max}(\mathbf{A})$. Once calculated, the vector $\sigma_{\max}(\mathbf{A})$ is memorized and thus will not be recomputed when subsequently required, as opposed to the naive *matrix-matrix* multiplication in Eq.(2).

EXAMPLE 4. *Consider the graph $\mathcal{G}_1$ in Fig.1 with its UAM $\mathbf{A}$ already computed in Example 3. The dominant eigenvector of $\mathbf{A}$ is*

$$\sigma_{\max}(\mathbf{A}) = [.431 \quad .673 \quad .451 \quad .322 \quad .232]^T.$$

Then using Eq.(3) for computing $\mathbf{S}$ yields

$$\mathbf{S} = \begin{bmatrix} .186 & .290 & .194 & .139 & .100 \\ .290 & .453 & .304 & .217 & .156 \\ .194 & .304 & .203 & .145 & .105 \\ .139 & .217 & .145 & .104 & .075 \\ .100 & .156 & .105 & .075 & .054 \end{bmatrix}.$$

Note that $\sigma_{\max}(\mathbf{A})$ is calculated only once for the preprocessing and can be used for computing any entry of $\mathbf{S}$ at query time, e.g.,

$[\mathbf{S}]_{1,2} = [\sigma_{\max}(\mathbf{A})]_1 \times [\sigma_{\max}(\mathbf{A})]_2 = .431 \times .673 = .290.$

$[\mathbf{S}]_{1,3} = [\sigma_{\max}(\mathbf{A})]_1 \times [\sigma_{\max}(\mathbf{A})]_3 = .431 \times .451 = .194.$

Regarding computational complexity, our approach only needs $O(km)$ preprocessing time and $O(n)$ space to compute $\sigma_{\max}(\mathbf{A})$ by using the following *power iteration* [14, pp.381]:

$$\boldsymbol{\xi}^{(0)} = \mathbf{e}, \quad \boldsymbol{\xi}^{(k+1)} = \frac{\mathbf{A}\boldsymbol{\xi}^{(k)}}{\|\mathbf{A}\boldsymbol{\xi}^{(k)}\|_2} = \frac{\tilde{\mathbf{A}}\boldsymbol{\xi}^{(k)} + \gamma^{(k)}\mathbf{e}}{\|\tilde{\mathbf{A}}\boldsymbol{\xi}^{(k)} + \gamma^{(k)}\mathbf{e}\|_2}, \tag{5}$$

where $\mathbf{e} \triangleq (1, \cdots, 1)^T \in \mathbb{R}^n$ and $\gamma^{(k)} \triangleq \frac{1}{n^2}\sum_{i=1}^{n} [\boldsymbol{\xi}^{(k)}]_i$. [3] The existence and uniqueness of the dominant eigenvector $\sigma_{\max}(\mathbf{A})$ is guaranteed by the combination of Perron-Frobenius theorem [14, p.383] and the positivity of $\mathbf{A}$. Thus, by applying the power method, the sequence $\{\boldsymbol{\xi}^{(k)}\}$ converges to $\sigma_{\max}(\mathbf{A})$. Then, with $\sigma_{\max}(\mathbf{A})$ being memorized, only $O(1)$ time is required at query stage for computing each entry of $\mathbf{S}$ via Eq.(3). Indeed, due to $\mathbf{S}$ symmetry, only $n(n+1)/2$ entries $[\mathbf{S}]_{i,j}$ $(i \le j)$ need to be computed. In contrast to the $O(kn^3)$ time and $O(n^2)$ space of the conventional iterations, our approach is a significant improvement achieved by $\sigma_{\max}(\mathbf{A})$ computation.

Our method of memorizing $\sigma_{\max}(\mathbf{A})$ can extra accelerate SimFusion+ computation when only a small portion of similarity values of $\mathbf{S}$ need to be computed. Specifically, for certain applications like K-nearest neighbor (KNN) queries, given a vertex i as a query, one needs to retrieve the top-K ($\ll n$) most similar vertices in a graph by computing the i-th row of $\mathbf{S}$. Before Proposition 1 is introduced, computing the similarity of only one vertex-pair still requires $O(kn^3)$ time. In contrast, using the memorized $\sigma_{\max}(\mathbf{A})$, we only need $O(1)$ time for computing a single entry of $\mathbf{S}$ at query time. In fact, for KNN queries, after $\sigma_{\max}(\mathbf{A})$ is memorized with its entries sorted in an descending order for the preprocessing, it only takes constant time to retrieve the top-K results at query stage.

Proposition 1 also gives an interesting characterization of the SimFusion+ matrix.

COROLLARY 1. *The SimFusion+ matrix $\mathbf{S}$ is a rank 1 matrix.*

PROOF. Applying Eq.(3) to $\mathbf{S}$, we obtain that for any two rows of $\mathbf{S}$, $\exists\ \omega = [\sigma_{\max}(\mathbf{A})]_x/[\sigma_{\max}(\mathbf{A})]_y$ *s.t.* $[\mathbf{S}]_{x,*} = \omega \times [\mathbf{S}]_{y,*}$. Hence, the rank of $\mathbf{S}$ is 1. □

4. ESTIMATING SIMFUSION+ WITH BETTER ACCURACY

After the dominant eigenvector $\sigma_{\max}(\mathbf{A})$ has been suggested to speed up SimFusion+ computation, the algorithm presented in this section can guarantee more accurate similarity results.

The main idea of our approach is to leverage an orthogonal subspace for "upper-triangularizing" the UAM $\mathbf{A}$ ($n \times n$ dimension) into a *small* matrix $\mathbf{T}_k$ ($k \times k$ dimension) with $k \ll n$. Due to $\mathbf{T}_k$ small size and almost "upper-triangularity", computing the dominant eigenvector $\sigma_{\max}(\mathbf{T}_k)$ is far less costly than straightforwardly computing $\sigma_{\max}(\mathbf{A})$. We show that the choice of k provides a user-controlled accuracy over the similarity scores. The underlying rationale is that the dominant eigenvector of a matrix can be well-preserved by an orthogonal transformation.

We first use the technique of the Arnoldi decomposition [17] to build an order-k orthogonal subspace for the UAM $\mathbf{A}$.

LEMMA 1 ([17, PP.25-33]). *Let $\mathbf{A}$ be an $n \times n$ matrix. Then, for every $k = 1, 2, \cdots$, we have the following results.*

(a) There exists a unique $k \times k$ almost triangular matrix $\mathbf{T}_k$ s.t.

$$\mathbf{V}_k^T\mathbf{A}\mathbf{V}_k = \mathbf{T}_k, \tag{6}$$

where $\mathbf{V}_k = [\mathbf{v}_1 \,|\, \mathbf{v}_2 \,|\, \cdots \,|\, \mathbf{v}_k]$ is an $n \times k$ matrix consisting of k orthonormal column-vectors $\mathbf{v}_i \in \mathbb{R}^n$ $(i = 1, \cdots, k)$.

(b) The difference between $\mathbf{A}\mathbf{V}_k$ and $\mathbf{V}_k\mathbf{T}_k$ is a zero matrix except the last column. Precisely, there exist a small scalar δ_k and an orthonormal vector $\mathbf{v}_{k+1} \in \mathbb{R}^n$ such that

$$\mathbf{A}\mathbf{V}_k - \mathbf{V}_k\mathbf{T}_k = \delta_k\mathbf{v}_{k+1}\mathbf{e}_k^T, \tag{7}$$

where $\mathbf{e}_k = (0, \cdots, 0, 1)^T \in \mathbb{R}^k$ is a unit vector.

As depicted in Fig.3, by using the upper-triangularization process [4], the matrix $\mathbf{A} \in \mathbb{R}^{n\times n}$ can be transformed into the small almost triangular $\mathbf{T}_k \in \mathbb{R}^{k\times k}$ by the $n \times k$ orthonormal ma-

[2]According to the Perron-Frobenius theorem [14, p.383], the positivity of $\mathbf{A} \otimes \mathbf{A}$ ensures that there exists a unique dominant eigenvector of $\mathbf{A}\otimes\mathbf{A}$ associated with its eigenvalue being strictly greater in magnitude than its other eigenvalues.

[3]The correctness of Eq.(5) can be proved as follows:

$\mathbf{A}\boldsymbol{\xi}^{(k)} = (\tilde{\mathbf{A}}+\frac{1}{n^2}\mathbf{e}\mathbf{e}^T)\boldsymbol{\xi}^{(k)} = \tilde{\mathbf{A}}\boldsymbol{\xi}^{(k)}+\gamma^{(k)}\mathbf{e}$ with $\gamma^{(k)} = \frac{1}{n^2}\mathbf{e}^T\boldsymbol{\xi}^{(k)}$.

[4]From the computational viewpoint, $\mathbf{V}_k$, $\mathbf{T}_k$, $\mathbf{v}_k$ and δ_k in Eq.(7) can be obtained by an algorithm in our later developments.

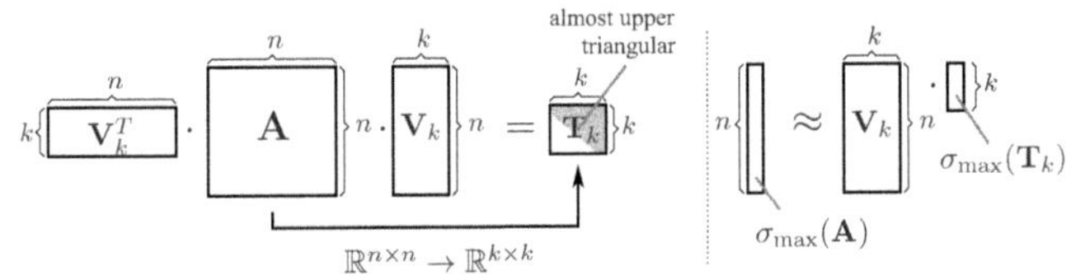

Figure 3: Upper Triangular Process of UAM

trix $\mathbf{V}_k$ for every iteration. As k increases, $\mathbf{T}_{k+1}$ can be iteratively obtained by bordering the matrix $\mathbf{T}_k$ at the last iteration (*i.e.*, $\mathbf{T}_{k+1} = \left[\begin{smallmatrix}\mathbf{T}_k & \star \\ \star & \star\end{smallmatrix}\right]$), and $\mathbf{V}_{k+1}$ by augmenting the matrix $\mathbf{V}_k$ at the last iteration with the vector $\mathbf{v}_{k+1}$ (*i.e.*, $\mathbf{V}_{k+1} = [\mathbf{V}_k \,|\, \mathbf{v}_{k+1}]$). When $k = rank(\mathbf{A})$, it follows that $\delta_k = 0$.

EXAMPLE 5. *Consider the network* $\mathcal{G}_1$ *in Fig.1 and its UAM* $\mathbf{A} = \tilde{\mathbf{A}} + \mathbf{1}/5^2$ *in Example 3. For* $k = 3$, $\exists\, \mathbf{V}_3 = [\mathbf{v}_1 \,|\, \mathbf{v}_2 \,|\, \mathbf{v}_3] \in \mathbb{R}^{5\times 3}$ *mapping* $\mathbf{A} \in \mathbb{R}^{5\times 5}$ *into* $\mathbf{T}_3 \in \mathbb{R}^{3\times 3}$ *s.t.* $\mathbf{T}_3 = \mathbf{V}_3^T \mathbf{A} \mathbf{V}_3$, *where*

$$\tilde{\mathbf{A}} = \begin{bmatrix} \frac{1}{2} & \frac{1}{6} & \frac{1}{6} & \frac{1}{3} & 0 \\ \frac{1}{6} & \frac{7}{12} & \frac{7}{12} & \frac{1}{8} & \frac{1}{8} \\ \frac{1}{6} & \frac{7}{12} & 0 & \frac{1}{8} & \frac{1}{8} \\ \frac{1}{3} & \frac{1}{8} & \frac{1}{8} & 0 & \frac{5}{12} \\ 0 & \frac{1}{8} & \frac{1}{8} & \frac{5}{12} & 0 \end{bmatrix}, \ \mathbf{T}_3 = \begin{bmatrix} 1.08 & .298 & 0 \\ .298 & .190 & .359 \\ 0 & .359 & -.083 \end{bmatrix}, \ \mathbf{V}_3 = \begin{bmatrix} .447 & .125 & -.089 \\ .447 & .750 & .044 \\ .447 & -.125 & .710 \\ .447 & -.125 & -.696 \\ .447 & -.625 & .032 \end{bmatrix}.$$

$\exists\, \delta_3 = .231, \mathbf{v}_4 = [-.881\ .328\ .137\ .280\ .135]^T$ *s.t. Eq.(7) holds. (see Example 7 for a detailed iterative process)*

In light of Lemma 1, we next provide an error estimate for SimFusion+ similarity when using $\sigma_{\max}(\mathbf{T}_k)$ to compute $\sigma_{\max}(\mathbf{A})$.

Error Estimation. We define a k-approximation similarity matrix $\hat{\mathbf{S}}_k$ over a low-order parameter k:

$$[\hat{\mathbf{S}}_k]_{i,j} = [\mathbf{V}_k \cdot \sigma_{\max}(\mathbf{T}_k)]_i \times [\mathbf{V}_k \cdot \sigma_{\max}(\mathbf{T}_k)]_j, \tag{8}$$

where $\mathbf{V}_k$ and $\mathbf{T}_k$ can be obtained from Lemma 1.

To differentiate $\hat{\mathbf{S}}_k$ from $\mathbf{S}$, we shall refer to $\mathbf{S}$ as *exact* similarity.

The following estimate for the approximate similarity $\hat{\mathbf{S}}_k$ with respect to the exact $\mathbf{S}$ can be established.

PROPOSITION 2. *For every* $k = 1, 2, \cdots$, *the following estimate holds:*

$$\|\hat{\mathbf{S}}_k - \mathbf{S}\|_2 \le \epsilon_k, \tag{9}$$

where

$$\epsilon_k = 2 \times |\delta_k \times [\sigma_{\max}(\mathbf{T}_k)]_k|, \tag{10}$$

and δ_k *is a small scalar given in Eq.(7);* $[\sigma_{\max}(\mathbf{T}_k)]_k$ *is the k-th entry of the dominant eigenvector of* $\mathbf{T}_k$.

(Please refer to the Appendix for a detailed proof.)

The parameter ϵ_k is intended as a user control over the difference between the approximate and the exact similarity matrices, and hence ϵ_k is generally chosen by a user. Provided that k is selected to satisfy Eq.(10), Proposition 2 states that the gap between the approximate and the exact similarity scores does not exceed ϵ_k.

EXAMPLE 6. *Consider the network* $\mathcal{G}_1$ *in Fig.1 and the matrix* $\mathbf{T}_3, \mathbf{V}_3, \delta_3$ *given in Example 5. For* $k = 3$, *we have*

$$\sigma_{\max}(\mathbf{T}_3) = [.945\ .316\ .089]^T.$$

Therefore, $\mathbf{V}_3 \cdot \sigma_{\max}(\mathbf{T}_3) = [.454\ .663\ .447\ .321\ .228]^T$. *Then applying Eq.(8) and the exact* $\mathbf{S}$ *in Example 4 yields*

$$\hat{\mathbf{S}}_3 = \{\textit{Using Eq.(8)}\} = \begin{bmatrix} .206 & .301 & .203 & .146 & .103 \\ .301 & .440 & .296 & .213 & .151 \\ .203 & .296 & .199 & .143 & .102 \\ .146 & .213 & .143 & .102 & .073 \\ .103 & .151 & .102 & .073 & .051 \end{bmatrix}$$

$$\hat{\mathbf{S}}_3 - \mathbf{S} = \{\textit{Using } \mathbf{S} \textit{ in Example 4}\} = .01 \times \begin{bmatrix} 2.02 & 1.09 & .83 & .67 & .34 \\ 1.09 & -1.33 & -.75 & -.41 & -.51 \\ .83 & -.75 & -.40 & -.21 & -.30 \\ .67 & -.41 & -.21 & -.09 & -.17 \\ .34 & -.51 & -.30 & -.17 & -.20 \end{bmatrix}$$

Algorithm 1: SimFusion+ $(\mathcal{G}, \epsilon, (u, v))$

Input : Network $\mathcal{G} = (\mathcal{D}, \mathcal{R})$, accuracy ϵ, vertex pair (u, v).
Output: Similarity score $s(u, v)$.

compute the matrix $\tilde{\mathbf{A}} \in \mathbb{R}^{n\times n}$ of the UAM $\mathbf{A}$ in $\mathcal{G}$;
initialize $\mathbf{e} \leftarrow (1, 1, \cdots, 1)^T \in \mathbb{R}^n$, and $\mathbf{v}_1 \leftarrow \frac{1}{\sqrt{n}}\mathbf{e}$;
foreach *iteration* $k = 1, 2, \cdots$ **do**
  initialize the auxiliary vector $\mathbf{w} \leftarrow \tilde{\mathbf{A}}\mathbf{v}_k + \frac{1}{n^2}(\mathbf{e}^T\mathbf{v}_k)\mathbf{e}$;
  for $i = 1, 2, \cdots, k-1$ **do**
    compute the almost upper triangular matrix $\mathbf{T}_k \in \mathbb{R}^{k\times k}$:
      $[\mathbf{T}_k]_{i,k-1} \leftarrow \mathbf{v}_k^T \cdot \mathbf{w}$;
    orthogonalize $\mathbf{w}$ *s.t.* $\mathbf{w} \perp span\{\mathbf{v}_1, \cdots, \mathbf{v}_k\}$:
      $\mathbf{w} \leftarrow \mathbf{w} - [\mathbf{T}_k]_{i,k-1} \cdot \mathbf{v}_{k-1}$;
  compute the residual scalar $\delta_k \leftarrow \|\mathbf{w}\|_2$;
  find the dominant eigenvector $\sigma_{\max}(\mathbf{T}_k)$;
  estimate the error $\epsilon_k \leftarrow 2 \times |\delta_k \times [\sigma_{\max}(\mathbf{T}_k)]_k|$;
  if $\epsilon_k \le \epsilon$ **then** exit for ;
  compute the residual vector $\mathbf{v}_{k+1}$:
    $\mathbf{w} \leftarrow \mathbf{w}/\delta_k$ and $\mathbf{v}_{k+1} \leftarrow \mathbf{w}$;
  free $\delta_k, \sigma_{\max}(\mathbf{T}_k)$;
free $\mathbf{w}, \mathbf{T}_k, \mathbf{v}_{k+1}, \delta_k$;
compute the approximate dominant eigenvector $\hat{\sigma}_{\max}(\mathbf{A})$
  $\hat{\sigma}_{\max}(\mathbf{A}) \leftarrow [\mathbf{v}_1 | \mathbf{v}_2 | \cdots | \mathbf{v}_k] \cdot \sigma_{\max}(\mathbf{T}_k)$;
free $\mathbf{v}_1, \cdots, \mathbf{v}_k, \sigma_{\max}(\mathbf{T}_k)$;
compute the approximate similarity score of (u, v)
  $\hat{s}(u, v) \leftarrow [\hat{\sigma}_{\max}(\mathbf{A})]_u \times [\hat{\sigma}_{\max}(\mathbf{A})]_v$;
return $\hat{s}(u, v)$;

We note that the gap between $\mathbf{S}$ *and* $\hat{\mathbf{S}}_k$ *for* $k = 3$ *is actually*

$$\|\hat{\mathbf{S}}_3 - \mathbf{S}\|_2 = .0257,$$

which is smaller than ϵ_k *(using Eq.(10) with* $\delta_3 = .231$*)*

$$\epsilon_k = 2 \times |.231 \times .089| = .0411.$$

Notice that if $k = rank(\mathbf{A})$ $(\ll n)$, [5] then $\epsilon_k = 0$ and the k-approximation similarity matrix $\hat{\mathbf{S}}_k$ becomes the conventional exact USM $\mathbf{S}$. From this perspective, the k-approximation similarity can be regarded as a generalization for the conventional similarity.

One of the possible ways of choosing an appropriate low order k for achieving the desired accuracy ϵ is to calculate the estimation error ϵ_k from Eq.(10) in an a-posteriori fashion after each iteration $k = 1, 2, \cdots$. [6] The iterative process stops once $\epsilon_k \le \epsilon$. Due to ϵ_k decreasing monotonicity, such k is the minimum low order *s.t.* $\|\hat{\mathbf{S}}_k - \mathbf{S}\|_2 \le \epsilon$. More concretely, the residual δ_k in Eq.(7) (Lemma 1) approaches 0 as k is increased to n, which implies

$$\epsilon_k = 2 \times |\delta_k| \times |[\sigma_{\max}(\mathbf{T}_k)]_k| \le 2 \times |\delta_k|.$$

Hence, the condition $\epsilon_k \le \epsilon$ (with ϵ_k being obtained from Eq.(10)) can be used as a stopping criterion for determining the minimum low order k needed for the desired accuracy ϵ.

Capitalizing on Eq.(8) and Proposition 2, below we provide an algorithm for SimFusion+ computation with accuracy guarantee.

Algorithm. SimFusion+ is shown in Algorithm 1. It takes as input a network $\mathcal{G} = (\mathcal{D}, \mathcal{R})$, a desired accuracy ϵ, and a vertex pair (u, v); it returns the approximate similarity $\hat{s}(u, v)$ such that $|\hat{s}(u, v) - s(u, v)| \le \epsilon$ with $s(u, v)$ being the exact value.

Before illustrating the algorithm, we first present the notations it uses. (a) $[\mathbf{T}_k]_{i,j}$ is the (i, j)-entry of the matrix $\mathbf{T}_k$, and $[\sigma_{\max}(\mathbf{T}_k)]_i$ is the i-th entry of the eigenvector $\sigma_{\max}(\mathbf{T}_k)$. (b)

[5] When k is set to $\text{argmin}_k\{\delta_k = 0\}$ (which is practically much smaller than $rank(\mathbf{A})$), $\epsilon_k = \epsilon_{k+1} = \cdots = \epsilon_n = 0$.

[6] As increased by 1 per iteration, the low order parameter k equals the iteration number.

#-line	time	memory	operation
4	$O(m)$	$O(n)$	sparse matrix-vector multiplication
6	$O(n)$	$O(n)$	vector dot product
7	$O(n)$	$O(n)$	vector addition and scalar multiplication
8	$O(n)$	$O(n)$	computing the 2-norm of a vector
9	$O(k)$	$O(k)$	using the power iteration
10	$O(1)$	$O(k)$	getting the vector component
12	$O(n)$	$O(n)$	scaling the vector

Table 1: Running Time & Memory Space Required per Iteration for Algorithm SimFusion+ in Lines 4-12

$span\{\mathbf{v}_1, \cdots, \mathbf{v}_k\}$ is the set of all linear combinations of vectors $\mathbf{v}_1, \cdots, \mathbf{v}_k$. (c) $\hat{\sigma}_{\max}(\mathbf{A})$ denotes the approximation of $\sigma_{\max}(\mathbf{A})$.

The algorithm SimFusion+ works as follows. It first computes $\mathbf{A}$ and initializes $\mathbf{v}_1$ (lines 1-2). Using $\mathbf{A}$, it then computes $\mathbf{T}_k$ (lines 4-6), δ_k (lines 7-8) and $\mathbf{v}_{k+1}$ (line 12) by orthonormalizing the vector $\mathbf{A}\mathbf{v}_k$ with respect to $\mathbf{v}_1, \cdots, \mathbf{v}_k$ for every iteration; SimFusion+ also calculates $\sigma_{\max}(\mathbf{T}_k)$ (line 9), and utilizes δ_k and $\sigma_{\max}(\mathbf{T}_k)$ to estimate the error ϵ_k (line 10). The process (lines 3-13) iterates until $\epsilon_k \le \epsilon$, *i.e.*, the minimum low order k is found *s.t.* ϵ_k meets the desired accuracy ϵ (line 11). For such k, the matrix-vector product $[\mathbf{v}_1|\mathbf{v}_2|\cdots|\mathbf{v}_k] \cdot \sigma_{\max}(\mathbf{T}_k)$ is used to approximate the dominant eigenvector of $\mathbf{A}$, and is memorized to compute $\hat{\sigma}_{\max}(\mathbf{A})$ (line 15). The product of the u-th and v-th entries of $\hat{\sigma}_{\max}(\mathbf{A})$ is collected in $\hat{s}(u,v)$, which is returned as the estimated similarity between vertex u and v (lines 17-18).

EXAMPLE 7. *We show how SimFusion+ estimates the similarity in $\mathcal{G}_1$ of Example 1. Given the desired accuracy $\epsilon = 0.05$, SimFusion+ first initializes the UAM $\mathbf{A}$ (in Example 3). It then iteratively computes $\mathbf{T}_k, \mathbf{v}_{k+1}, \delta_k, \sigma_{\max}(\mathbf{T}_k)$ and ϵ_k as follows:*

k	$\mathbf{T}_k$	$\mathbf{v}_{k+1}$	δ_k	$\sigma_{\max}(\mathbf{T}_k)$	ϵ_k
0	–	$[.447\ .447\ .447\ .447\ .447]^T$	–	–	–
1	$[1.08]$	$[.125\ .750\ -.125\ -.125\ -.625]^T$	*.298*	$[1]$	*.596*
2	$\begin{bmatrix} 1.08 & .298 \\ .298 & .190 \end{bmatrix}$	$[-.089\ .044\ .710\ -.697\ .032]^T$	*.359*	$\begin{bmatrix} .957 \\ .290 \end{bmatrix}$	*.208*
3	$\begin{bmatrix} 1.08 & .298 & 0 \\ .298 & .190 & .359 \\ 0 & .359 & -.083 \end{bmatrix}$	$[-.881\ .329\ .137\ .280\ .135\ .231]^T$	*.231*	$\begin{bmatrix} .945 \\ .316 \\ .090 \end{bmatrix}$	*.041*

The iteration terminates at $k = 3$ because the estimation error $\epsilon_3 = .041 \le \epsilon\,(= .05)$. SimFusion+ then memorizes $\hat{\sigma}_{\max}(\mathbf{A}) = [\mathbf{v}_1|\mathbf{v}_2|\mathbf{v}_3] \cdot \sigma_{\max}(\mathbf{T}_3)$ and returns the similarity $\hat{s}(u,v)$, i.e., the (u,v) entry of $\hat{\mathbf{S}}_3$, as shown in Example 6.

We next analyze the time and space complexity of SimFusion+ .

Running Time. The algorithm consists of two phases: preprocessing (lines 1-16), and on-line query (lines 17-18).

(i) For the preprocessing, (a) it takes $O(m)$ time to compute $\tilde{\mathbf{A}}$ (line 1) and $O(n)$ time to initialize $\mathbf{v}_1$ (line 2). (b) The total time of the **for** loop is analyzed in Table 1 (line 3-13), which is bounded by $O(m + 4n + k + 1)$ for each iteration. (c) It takes $O(kn)$ time to compute $\hat{\sigma}_{\max}(\mathbf{A})$ (line 15). Hence, the total time in this phase is $O(m + k(m+4n+k+1) + kn)$, which is bounded by $O(km)$.

(ii) The on-line query phase (lines 17-18) can be done in constant time for each query by virtue of $\hat{\sigma}_{\max}(\mathbf{A})$ memorization.

Combining (i) and (ii), the query time of SimFusion+ is in $O(1)$, plus an $O(km)$-time precomputation.

Memory Space. (i) In the precomputation, (a) initializing $\tilde{\mathbf{A}}$ and $\mathbf{v}_1$ takes $O(n)$ space (lines 1-2). (b) For each iteration k, the space complexity is analyzed in Table 1, which is bounded by $O(n)$ (line 3-13). (c) As the **for** loop terminates, only $\mathbf{v}_1, \cdots, \mathbf{v}_k$ and $\sigma_{\max}(\mathbf{T}_k)$ are kept in memory, yielding $O(kn + k)$ space; the other intermediate results can be freed (line 14). (d) Computing $\hat{\sigma}_{\max}(\mathbf{A})$ takes $O(k)$ space (line 15). Once computed, $\hat{\sigma}_{\max}(\mathbf{A})$ is memorized, yielding $O(n)$ space; $\mathbf{v}_1, \cdots, \mathbf{v}_k$ and $\sigma_{\max}(\mathbf{T}_k)$ are not used subsequently and thus can be freed (line 16).

(ii) For the on-line query (lines 17-18), $\hat{s}(u,v)$ can be computed in $O(n)$ space with $\hat{\sigma}_{\max}(\mathbf{A})$ memorized.

Taking (i) and (ii) together, the total space is bounded by $O(kn)$.

5. INCREMENTAL SIMFUSION+

For certain applications like social networks, graphs are frequently modified [9]. It is too costly to recalculate similarities every time when edges in the graphs are updated. This motivates us to study the following *incremental SimFusion+ estimating problem*.

Given a network $\mathcal{G}$, the eigen-information in $\mathcal{G}$, and a list $\bar{\mathcal{G}}$ of updates (edge deletions and insertions) to $\mathcal{G}$, it is to compute the new USM $\mathbf{S}'$ in $\mathcal{G}'$. Here $\mathcal{G}'$ is the updated $\mathcal{G}$, denoted by $\mathcal{G} + \bar{\mathcal{G}}$.

The idea is to maximally reuse the eigen-information in $\mathcal{G}$ when computing $\mathbf{S}'$. The observation is that $\bar{\mathcal{G}}$ is often small in practice; hence, $\mathbf{S}' (= \mathbf{S} + \bar{\mathbf{S}})$ is slightly different from $\mathbf{S}$. It is far less costly to find the change $\bar{\mathbf{S}}$ to the old $\mathbf{S}$ than to recalculate the new $\mathbf{S}'$ from scratch. The main result in this section is the following.

THEOREM 1. *The incremental SimFusion+ estimating problem is solvable in $O(\delta n)$ time and $O(n)$ space for every vertex pair, where δ is the number of edges affected by the update $\bar{\mathcal{G}}$.*

As we shall see later, δ captures the size of areas in a graph $\mathcal{G}$ that is affected by updates $\bar{\mathcal{G}}$; hence δ is much smaller than n when $\bar{\mathcal{G}}$ is small. That is, the incremental SimFusion+ can be performed more efficiently than computing similarities in $\mathcal{G}'$. This suggests that we compute the eigenvector of $\mathbf{A}$ in $\mathcal{G}$ once, and then incrementally compute SimFusion+ when $\mathcal{G}$ is updated.

To prove Theorem 1, we first introduce a notion of incremental UAM. We then devise an incremental algorithm for handling batch edge updates with the desired bound.

5.1 Incremental Unified Adjacency Matrix

Consider an old network $\mathcal{G} = (\mathcal{D}, \mathcal{R})$ and a new $\mathcal{G}' = (\mathcal{D}, \mathcal{R}')$.

Incremental UAM. The matrix $\bar{\mathbf{A}}$ is said to be the *incremental UAM* of the update $\bar{\mathcal{G}}$ $(= \mathcal{G}' - \mathcal{G}$, *i.e.*, a list of edge insertions and deletions) *iff* $\bar{\mathbf{A}} = \mathbf{A}' - \mathbf{A}$, where $\mathbf{A}$ and $\mathbf{A}'$ are the UAMs of the old network $\mathcal{G}$ and the new $\mathcal{G}'$, respectively.

Intuitively, the nonzero entries of $\bar{\mathbf{A}}$ can identify the edges in $\mathcal{G}$ that is affected by updates $\bar{\mathcal{G}}$. Typically, $\bar{\mathbf{A}}$ is a sparse matrix when δ is small. Indeed, the number of nonzero entries in $\bar{\mathbf{A}}$ is bounded by $O(\delta n)$, which represents the costs that are inherent to the incremental problem itself, *i.e.*, the amount of work absolutely necessary to be performed for the problem.

Using $\bar{\mathbf{A}}$, we next provide a strategy for incrementally computing SimFusion+ similarity.

PROPOSITION 3. *Given a network $\mathcal{G}$ and an update $\bar{\mathcal{G}}$ to $\mathcal{G}$, let $\mathbf{A}$ be the UAM of $\mathcal{G}$, and $\bar{\mathbf{A}}$ the incremental UAM of $\bar{\mathcal{G}}$. Then the new USM $\mathbf{S}'$ of the new network $\mathcal{G}'$ $(= \mathcal{G} + \bar{\mathcal{G}})$ can be computed as*

$$[\mathbf{S}']_{i,j} = [\boldsymbol{\xi}']_i \cdot [\boldsymbol{\xi}']_j \text{ with } [\boldsymbol{\xi}']_i = [\boldsymbol{\xi}_1]_i + \textstyle\sum_{p=2}^{n} c_p \times [\boldsymbol{\xi}_p]_i$$

$$c_p = \frac{\boldsymbol{\xi}_p^T \cdot \boldsymbol{\eta}}{\alpha_p - \alpha_1} \text{ and } \boldsymbol{\eta} = \bar{\mathbf{A}} \cdot \boldsymbol{\xi}_1. \tag{11}$$

where $\boldsymbol{\xi}_p$ is the eigenvector of $\mathbf{A}$ corresponding to the eigenvalue α_p with $\|\boldsymbol{\xi}_p\|_2 = 1$, and $\boldsymbol{\xi}_1$ is the dominant eigenvector of $\mathbf{A}$.

(Please refer to the Appendix for a detailed proof.)

The main idea in incrementally computing $\mathbf{S}'$ is to reuse $\bar{\mathbf{A}}$ and the eigen-pair $(\alpha_p, \boldsymbol{\xi}_p)$ of the original $\mathbf{A}$. From the computational perspective, memorization techniques can be applied to Eq.(11) for an extra speed-up in computing $[\boldsymbol{\xi}']_i$. Once $\boldsymbol{\eta}$ is computed, it can be memorized for computing $c_2, \cdots, c_n$. When $c_2, \cdots, c_n$ are calculated, they can be memorized for computing $[\boldsymbol{\xi}']_i$ and $[\boldsymbol{\xi}']_j$.

Algorithm 2: IncSimFusion+ $(\mathcal{G}, \mathbf{A}, (\alpha_p, \boldsymbol{\xi}_p), \bar{\mathcal{G}}, (u, v))$

Input : Network $\mathcal{G} = (\mathcal{D}, \mathcal{R})$, the old UAM $\mathbf{A}$ of $\mathcal{G}$, eigen-pairs $(\alpha_p, \boldsymbol{\xi}_p)$ of $\mathbf{A}$, the update $\bar{\mathcal{G}}$ to $\mathcal{G}$, query (u, v).
Output: New similarity score $s'(u, v)$.

```
1  compute the incremental UAM Ā for the update Ḡ :
     Ā ← UpdateA (G, A, Ḡ) ;
2  initialize a ← [ξ1]_u,   b ← [ξ1]_v ;
3  compute η ← Ā · ξ1 ;
4  free Ā, ξ1;
5  for p ← 2, ··· , n do
6     compute t ← ξp^T · η,   cp ← t/(αp − α1) ;
7     compute a ← a + cp × [ξp]_u,   b ← b + cp × [ξp]_v ;
8     free αp, ξp ;
9  free η, t ;
10 compute s'(u, v) ← a × b ;
11 return s'(u, v) ;
```

5.2 An Incremental Algorithm for SimFusion+

We next prove Theorem 1 by providing an incremental algorithm, referred to as IncSimFusion+, for handling δ edge updates.

Algorithm. The algorithm accepts as input a network $\mathcal{G}$, the UAM $\mathbf{A}$ of $\mathcal{G}$, the eigen-pairs $(\alpha_p, \boldsymbol{\xi}_p)$ of $\mathbf{A}$, an update $\bar{\mathcal{G}}$ (a list of edge insertions and deletions) to $\mathcal{G}$, and a vertex pair (u, v).

It works as follows. (a) IncSimFusion+ first computes the incremental UAM $\bar{\mathbf{A}}$ for the update $\bar{\mathcal{G}}$ by using procedure UpdateA (line 1). UpdateA incrementally finds all the changes to the old UAM $\mathbf{A}$ in the presence of a list of edge updates to $\mathcal{G}$. (b) For the given vertex pair (u, v), IncSimFusion+ initializes a and b based on the dominant eigenvector $\boldsymbol{\xi}_1$ of $\mathbf{A}$ (line 2) ; it computes $\boldsymbol{\eta}$ once and memorizes $\boldsymbol{\eta}$ for computing $c_2, \cdots, c_n$ (line 3). (c) Once computed, $c_2, \cdots, c_n$ are memorized for calculating the u-th and v-th entries of the dominant eigenvector $\boldsymbol{\xi}'$ of the new UAM,which is collected in a and b, respectively (lines 4-9). IncSimFusion+ returns $a \times b$ as the similarity $\hat{s}(u, v)$ (lines 10-11).

Edge Update. The procedure UpdateA is used for incrementally updating the UAM $\mathbf{A}$ by virtue of $\bar{\mathcal{G}}$. An update $\bar{\mathcal{G}}$ is represented as a sequence of 2-tuples $(\mathcal{D} \times \mathcal{D}, \mathsf{op})$ that records every single action of the edge update, in which $\mathcal{D} \times \mathcal{D}$ is a set of δ edges to be inserted or deleted, and op is either "+" (edge insertion) or "−" (edge deletion). For instance, after the edge (P_3, P_5) is added and (P_1, P_2) is removed from $\mathcal{G}_1$ in Fig.1, the update $\bar{\mathcal{G}}$ is denoted by

$$\bar{\mathcal{G}} = \{(P_3, P_5, +), (P_1, P_2, -)\}.$$

UpdateA identifies the incremental $\bar{\mathbf{A}}$ in two phases. (i) It first finds the affected nodes and the data spaces for each edge update in $\bar{\mathcal{G}}$ using a breadth-first search. (ii) It then updates the corresponding entries of $\bar{\mathbf{A}}$ based on the following. We abuse the notation $\mathcal{N}_{\mathcal{D}}(u)$ to denote all the neighbors of object u in the data space $\mathcal{D}$, *i.e.*,

$$\mathcal{N}_{\mathcal{D}}(u) = \{v \in \mathcal{D} |\ (u, v) \in \mathcal{R}\}.$$

Based on the partition of the entire data space $\mathcal{D} = \bigcup_{i=1}^{N} \mathcal{D}_i$ with $n_i = |\mathcal{D}_i|$, the incremental UAM $\bar{\mathbf{A}}$ can be accordingly partitioned into N^2 submatrices $\bar{\mathbf{A}}_{i,j}$.

- For each edge insertion $(u, v, +) \in \bar{\mathcal{G}}$ with $u \in \mathcal{D}_i$ and $v \in \mathcal{D}_j$, (i) we set all entries of $[\bar{\mathbf{A}}_{i,j}]_{u,\star}$ to $-\frac{\lambda_{i,j}}{n_j}$ except for their v-th entries to 0 if $\mathcal{N}_{\mathcal{D}_j}(u) = \varnothing$; (ii) we set all entries of $[\bar{\mathbf{A}}_{j,i}]_{\star,v}$ to $-\frac{\lambda_{j,i}}{n_i}$ except for their u-th entries to 0 if $\mathcal{N}_{\mathcal{D}_i}(v) = \varnothing$; (iii) we set $[\bar{\mathbf{A}}_{i,j}]_{u,v} = \lambda_{i,j}$ otherwise.
- For each edge deletion $(u, v, -) \in \bar{\mathcal{G}}$ with $u \in \mathcal{D}_i$ and $v \in \mathcal{D}_j$, (i) we set all entries of $[\bar{\mathbf{A}}_{i,j}]_{u,\star}$ to $\frac{\lambda_{i,j}}{n_j}$ except for their v-th entries to 0 if $|\mathcal{N}_{\mathcal{D}_j}(u)| = 1$; (ii) we set all entries of $[\bar{\mathbf{A}}_{j,i}]_{\star,v}$ to $\frac{\lambda_{j,i}}{n_i}$ except for their u-th entries to 0 if $|\mathcal{N}_{\mathcal{D}_i}(v)| = 1$; (iii) we set $[\bar{\mathbf{A}}_{i,j}]_{u,v} = -\lambda_{i,j}$ otherwise.

Complexity. The algorithm IncSimFusion+ is in $O(\delta n)$ time and $O(n)$ space for handling δ edge updates in $\bar{\mathcal{G}}$. (i) The procedure UpdateA can be bounded by $O(\delta n)$ time and $O(n)$ space (line 1). For each edge update in $\bar{\mathcal{G}}$, it is in at most $O(n)$ time and $O(n)$ intermediate space to update the corresponding entries of $\bar{\mathbf{A}}$. (ii) Computing $\boldsymbol{\eta}$ requires an $O(\delta)$-time and $O(n)$-space sparse matrix-vector multiplication $\bar{\mathbf{A}} \cdot \boldsymbol{\xi}_1$ (line 3). (iii) For every c_p, it takes $O(\delta)$ time and $O(n)$ space to calculate $\boldsymbol{\xi}_p^T \cdot \boldsymbol{\eta}$ (line 6) since $\boldsymbol{\eta}$ is a sparse vector with only $O(\delta)$ nonzeros; and $c_2, \cdots, c_p$ are memorized for computing $[\boldsymbol{\xi}']_i$, which requires $O(\delta n)$ time and $O(n)$ space in total. (iv) Computing a, b and $s'(u, v)$ needs constant time and space (lines 7 and 10). Thus, combining (i)-(iv) , the total complexity is bounded by $O(\delta n)$ time and $O(n)$ space.

EXAMPLE 8. *We show how IncSimFusion+ works. Consider the graph $\mathcal{G}_1$ in Fig.1 with its UAM $\mathbf{A}$ in Example 3. Suppose two edges (P_1, P_2) and (P_2, P_1) are removed from $\mathcal{G}_1$. The new USM $\mathbf{S}'$ is updated as follows.*

First, UpdateA is invoked for precomputing the incremental $\bar{\mathbf{A}}$ and the eigen-pairs $(\alpha_p, \boldsymbol{\xi}_p)$ of $\mathbf{A}$ in an off-line fashion:

$$\bar{\mathbf{A}} = \begin{bmatrix} 0 & -\frac{1}{6} & 0 & 0 & 0 \\ -\frac{1}{6} & 0 & 0 & 0 & 0 \\ 0 & 0 & 0 & 0 & 0 \\ 0 & 0 & 0 & 0 & 0 \\ 0 & 0 & 0 & 0 & 0 \end{bmatrix}$$

p	α_p	$\boldsymbol{\xi}_p$	c_p
1	1.184	$[.431\ .673\ .451\ .322\ .232]^T$	–
2	.503	$[.708\ {-.522}\ {-.242}\ .388\ .132]^T$	.062
3	-.480	$[-.256\ {-.020}\ .095\ .716\ {-.641}]^T$	-.018
4	-.366	$[-.021\ {-.507}\ .853\ {-.119}\ .017]^T$	-.025
5	.242	$[.497\ .127\ .037\ {-.467}\ {-.719}]^T$	.069

IncSimFusion+ next computes $\boldsymbol{\eta}$ from $\bar{\mathbf{A}}$ and $\boldsymbol{\xi}_1$ (line 3):

$$\boldsymbol{\eta} = \bar{\mathbf{A}} \cdot \boldsymbol{\xi}_1 = [-.112 \quad -.072 \quad 0 \quad 0 \quad 0]^T.$$

Then, c_p can be derived from the memorized $\boldsymbol{\eta}$ and $(\alpha_p, \boldsymbol{\xi}_p)$, e.g.,

$$\begin{aligned} c_2 &= \boldsymbol{\xi}_2^T \cdot \boldsymbol{\eta}/(\alpha_2 - \alpha_1) = -.0419/(.503 - 1.184) = .062, \\ c_3 &= \boldsymbol{\xi}_3^T \cdot \boldsymbol{\eta}/(\alpha_3 - \alpha_1) = .030/(-.480 - 1.184) = -.018. \end{aligned}$$

Once computed, $c_2, \cdots, c_5$ are memorized for calculating $[\boldsymbol{\xi}']_\star$:

$$\boldsymbol{\xi}' = \boldsymbol{\xi}_1 + \sum\nolimits_{p=2}^{5} c_p \times \boldsymbol{\xi}_p = [.327\ .703\ .485\ .326\ .266]^T.$$

Hence, applying $[\boldsymbol{\xi}']_\star$ to the new USM $\mathbf{S}'$ (line 10) yields

$$\mathbf{S}' = \begin{bmatrix} .107 & .230 & .159 & .107 & .087 \\ .230 & .494 & .341 & .230 & .187 \\ .159 & .341 & .235 & .158 & .129 \\ .107 & .230 & .158 & .107 & .087 \\ .087 & .187 & .129 & .087 & .071 \end{bmatrix}.$$

6. EXPERIMENTAL EVALUATION

In this section, a comprehensive empirical study of the proposed similarity estimating methods is presented.

6.1 Experimental Setting

Datasets. We used three real-life datasets and a synthetic dataset.

(1) MSN Data. [7] The MSN search log data were taken from "Microsoft Live Labs: Accelerating Search in Academic Research". This dataset was also used in the prior work [1]. It contains about 15M user queries from the United States in May 2006 and the corresponding clickthrough URLs. The dataset was formatted by showing each query, the URLs of the associated web pages, and the number of clickthroughs by query, as depicted below.

[7] http://research.microsoft.com/ur/us/fundingopps/RFPs/Search_2006_RFP.aspx

Query	URL	Clicks	URL	Clicks
Shopping	shopping.yahoo.com	2,375	www.ebay.com	1,859

The 15K most common queries in the search log were chosen, and the hyperlinks from the contents of the top 32K popular web pages were parsed. We built a network $\mathcal{G} = (\mathcal{D}, \mathcal{R})$, which consists of a web page space $\mathcal{D}_w$ and a query space $\mathcal{D}_q$.

(2) DBLP Data. [8] This dataset was derived from a snapshot of the computer science bibliography (from 2001 to 2010). We selected the research papers published in the following conference proceedings: "SIGIR", "KDD", "VLDB", "ICDE", "SIGMOD" and "WWW". Choosing a time step of two years, we built 5 DBLP web graphs $\mathcal{G}_i$ $(i = 1, \cdots, 5)$ with the sizes listed below:

	$\mathcal{G}_1$: 01-02	$\mathcal{G}_2$: 01-04	$\mathcal{G}_3$: 01-06	$\mathcal{G}_4$: 01-08	$\mathcal{G}_5$: 01-10
$\lvert\mathcal{D}\rvert$	1,838	3,723	5,772	9,567	12,276
$\lvert\mathcal{R}\rvert$	7,103	14,419	29,054	45,310	64,208

For each graph $\mathcal{G}_i = (\mathcal{D}_i, \mathcal{R}_i)$, two data spaces were used: paper space $\mathcal{D}_p^i$ and author space $\mathcal{D}_a^i$.

(3) WEBKB Data. [9] This dataset collects web pages from the computer science departments of four universities: Cornell (CO), Texas (TE), Washington (WA) and Wisconsin (WI). It was also used in the previous work [13] for link-based similarity estimation. For each university, a network $\mathcal{G}_{U_i} = (\mathcal{D}_i, \mathcal{R}_i)$ was built, in which (a) the web pages in $\mathcal{D}_i$ were classified into 7 categories (data spaces): student, faculty, staff, department, course, project and others, and (b) the UAM of $\mathcal{R}_i$ represented the hyperlink adjacency matrix. The sizes of these networks are as follows:

	U_1: CO	U_2: TE	U_3: WA	U_4: WI
$\lvert\mathcal{D}\rvert$	867	827	1,263	1,205
$\lvert\mathcal{R}\rvert$	1,496	1,428	2,969	1,805

(4) Synthetic Data. The data were produced by the C++ boost graph generator, with 2 parameters: the number of vertices and the number of edges. Varying the graph parameters, we used this dataset to represent homogenous networks for an in-depth analysis.

Compared Algorithms. The following algorithms were implemented in C++: (1) SimFusion+ and IncSimFusion+ ; (2) SF, a SimFusion algorithm via matrix iteration [1]; (3) CSF, a variant of SF, which leverages PageRank stationary distribution [13]; (4) SR, a SimRank algorithm via partial sums function [8]; (5) PR, a Penetrating-Rank algorithm encoding both in- and out-links [4].

Evaluation Metrics. For evaluating the performance of the algorithms, we used *Normalized Discounted Cumulative Gain* (NDCG) metrics [13]. The NDCG at a rank position p is defined as $\text{NDCG}_p = \frac{1}{\text{IDCG}_p} \sum_{i=1}^{p} \frac{2^{\text{rank}_i}-1}{\log_2(1+i)}$, where rank_i is the graded relevance of the similarity result at rank position i, and IDCG_p is the normalization factor to guarantee that NDCG of a perfect ranking at position p equals 1.

Twelve IT experts were hired to judge the similarity of the five algorithms. The final judgment was rendered by a majority vote.

All experiments were run on a machine with a Pentium(R) Dual-Core (2.00GHz) CPU and 4GB RAM, using Windows Vista. The algorithms were implemented in Visual C++. Each experiment was repeated over 5 times, and the average is reported here.

6.2 Experimental Results

6.2.1 Accuracy

We first evaluated the accuracy of SimFusion+ *vs.* SF, CSF, SR and PR in estimating the similarity, using real-life data.

We randomly chose 50 queries and 40 pages from the MSN query log, and compared the average NDCG_{10} (and NDCG_{30}) of the five

[8]http://www.informatik.uni-trier.de/~ley/db/

[9]http://www.cs.cmu.edu/afs/cs/project/theo-20/www/data/

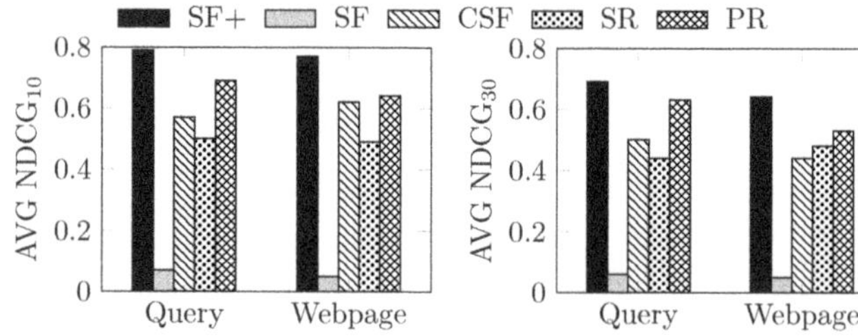

Figure 4: Comparing SimFusion+ with other ranking algorithms for the average NDCG_{10} and NDCG_{30} on MSN data

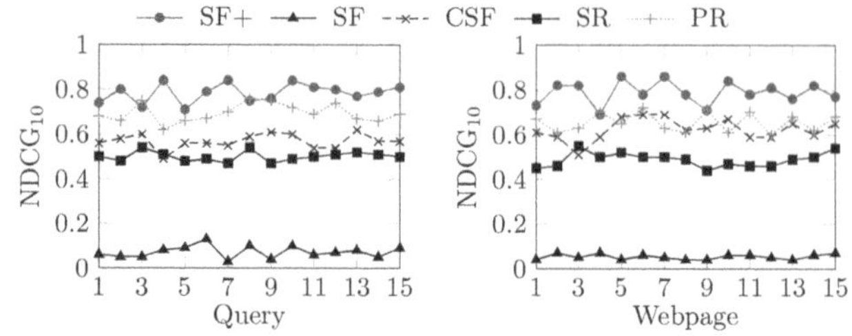

Figure 5: The detailed query-by-query and page-by-page comparisons for NDCG_{10} on MSN data

algorithms. The results are shown in Figure 4, in which the x-axis categorizes the objects according to query and web page. We find the following. (i) In most cases, SF seems hardly to get sensible similarities because with the increasing number of iterations, all the similarities of SF will asymptotically approach the same value. This verifies the convergence issue of the original model [1]. (ii) When SF did not fail, SimFusion+ always gave more accurate estimation on average than the other algorithms. For instance, for the top 10 queries, the average NDCG_{10} of SimFusion+ (0.79) is 10x better than SF (0.07), 39% better than CSF (0.57), 58% better than SR (0.50), and 15% better than PR (0.69), whereas for the top 30 web pages, the average NDCG_{30} of SimFusion+ (0.64) is 12x better than SF (0.05), 45% better than CSF (0.44), 33% better than SR (0.48), and 21% better than PR (0.53). This is because substituting UAM for URM effectively avoids divergent or trivial solutions, thus improving the quality and reliability of SimFusion+ similarity, as expected.

To further verify the accuracy, we randomly selected another 15 queries and 15 web pages from MSN data. In Figure 5, the query-by-query and page-by-page comparisons are shown for NDCG_{10} of the five algorithms. We observe that (i) for 12 out of 15 queries, SimFusion+ achieved highest accuracy of the five algorithms;for 13 out of 15 web pages, SimFusion+ outperformed the other algorithms in its accuracy, and was slightly less accurate than PR for only 2 pages. (ii) For all the queries and web pages, SimFusion+ showed the best accuracy performance on average, PR the second, and SF the worst. This is because SimFusion+ uses UAM to encode the intra- and inter-relations in a comprehensive way, thus making the results unbiased.

We also evaluated the performance of SimFusion+ on DBLP and WEBKB datasets. In DBLP experiments, 20 authors were randomly chosen from $\mathcal{G}_1$:01-02, $\mathcal{G}_3$:01-06 and $\mathcal{G}_5$:01-10 data, respectively. We compared the similarity of the top 10 authors in $\mathcal{G}_i$ $(i = 1, 3, 5)$ estimated by the five algorithms. The results of the average NDCG_{10} are depicted in Figure 6. It can be seen that SimFusion+ again achieved better accuracy on DBLP data. For instance, SimFusion+ (0.88) on $\mathcal{G}_3$:01-06 was 13x better than SF (0.06), 95% better than CSF (0.45), 26% better than SR (0.7), and 19% better than PR (0.74). In WEBKB experiments, we computed NDCG within 10 web pages for each object in each university data (CO,TE,WI,WA) and evaluated the average scores. Figure

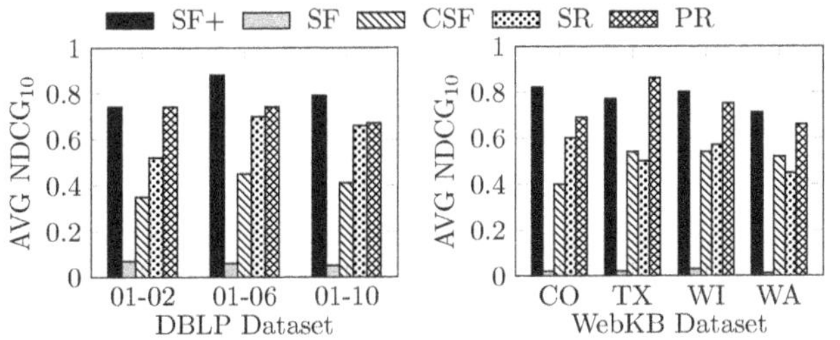

Figure 6: Comparing SimFusion+ with other ranking algorithms for the average NDCG$_{10}$ on DBLP and WEBKB data

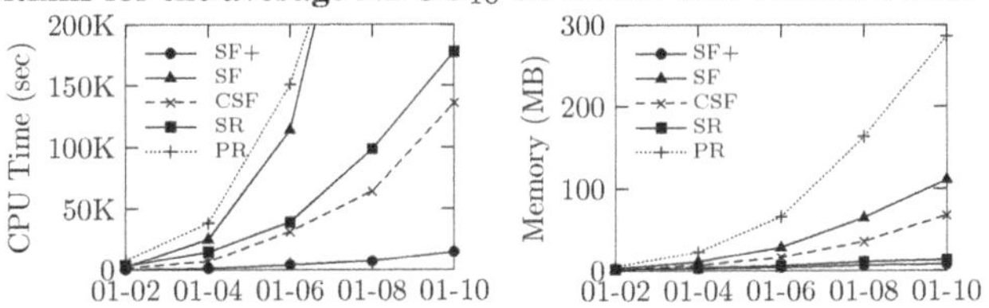

Figure 7: Comparing the CPU time and memory of the ranking algorithms on DBLP data

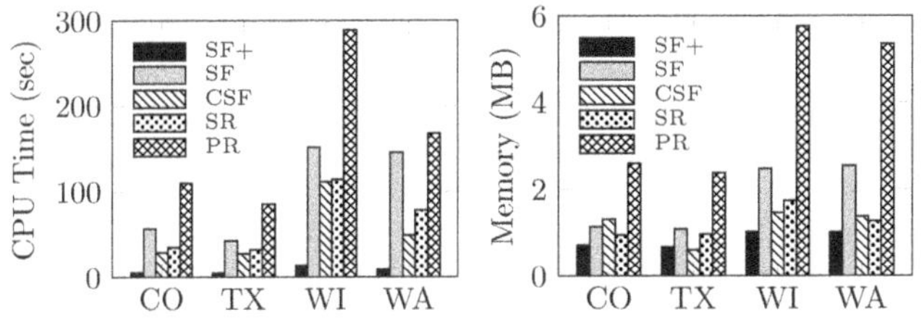

Figure 8: Comparing the CPU time and memory of the ranking algorithms on WEBKB data

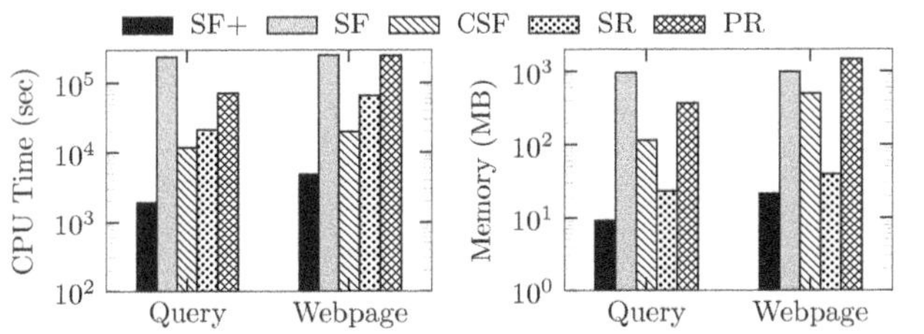

Figure 9: Comparing the CPU time and memory of the ranking algorithms for the given query and web page on MSN data

6 shows that SimFusion+ outperformed the other 4 algorithms on CO, WI and WA data, except that PR (0.8) did 6% better than SimFusion+ (0.75) on TX data. This tells that SimFusion+ accuracy performance is consistently stable on different experimental datasets.

6.2.2 *CPU Time & Memory Space*

We then evaluated the running time and memory space efficiency of SimFusion+ , SF, CSF, SR and PR using real datasets.

Figure 7 shows the CPU time and memory consumption for the five algorithms on DBLP. The total time and memory for each algorithm showed an increasing tendency with the growing size of DBLP. It can be noted that the time for SimFusion+ was at least one order of magnitude faster than CSF and SR on average, and more than 20x faster than PR and SF, whereas the space for SimFusion+ and SR increased linearly with the size of DBLP, in contrast with the quadratic increase in memory for SF, CSF, PR, as expected. This drastic speedup and decrease in RAM is due to the memorization of $\sigma_{\max}(\mathbf{T}_k)$ for computing USM, thus saving much time and space for repetitive matrix multiplications.

To further evaluate the efficiency, we compare the time and memory of the five ranking algorithms on WEBKB. In Figure 8, the results indicate that SimFusion+ took about 10x less time than SF and PR, and 6x less time than CSF and SR on average. The memory space for SimFusion+ was also efficient and scaled well with the size of WEBKB. It can be seen that SF also took small memory space (approx. 1M) when the data size was small (*e.g.,* CO and TX). However, when the data size increased (*e.g.,* WI and WA), SF was less useful since large memory storage (about 2.5M) was required to keep the intermediate result of the k-th iterative USM. In all the cases, SimFusion+ performed the best.

On large datasets, the effect of SimFusion+ is even more pronounced. Figure 9 reports the average time and memory of the five algorithms on MSN data, in which the y-axis is log-scale. We chose 50 queries and 40 web pages from $\mathcal{D}_q$ and $\mathcal{D}_w$, respectively. For each $o_q \in \mathcal{D}_q$ (*resp.* $o_w \in \mathcal{D}_w$), we estimated the similarity between o_q (*resp.* o_w) and other object $o \in \mathcal{D}_q \cup \mathcal{D}_w$. We see that SimFusion+ was highly efficient on large datasets (nearly 2 orders of magnitude than SF and PR, and 1 order of magnitude than CSF in both time and space). This validates that the performance of SimFusion+ is fairly stable among different datasets.

6.2.3 *Incremental Performance*

We next evaluated the incremental performance of IncSimFusion+ on real datasets. Given a sequence of edge updates (δ edge insertions and deletions in $\bar{\mathcal{G}}$), we compared the running time of IncSimFusion+ with that of SimFusion+ ; the latter had to recalculate the UAM when edges were updated, and the computational cost was counted. In these experiments, the eigen information of the old UAM can be preconditioned in an off-line fashion and shared by all the updated graphs for incremental computation, and hence their costs were not counted at the query stage. Due to space limitations, below we only reported the results on MSN dataset.

Varying δ (the number of the edges to be updated) from 600 to 3000, we first evaluated the running time of IncSimFusion+ and SimFusion+ over MSN data, respectively, for estimating all the similarities between the query objects in $\mathcal{D}_q$. Figure 10 shows that IncSimFusion+ outperformed SimFusion+ when $\delta < 2800$, but SimFusion+ performed better for larger δ, as expected. This is because the small value of δ often preserves the sparseness of the incremental UAM, and hence reduces the computational cost of η when the USM was incrementally updated.

To further validate the performance of IncSimFusion+ , we estimated the similarity among the web page in $\mathcal{D}_w$ and tested its CPU time on MSN data. In Figure 10, the result shows that IncSimFusion+ was highly efficient for the small number of edge updates. When $\delta > 7700$, SimFusion+ did better than IncSimFusion+ . This tells that increasing the number of updated edges induces more nonzeros in $\bar{\mathbf{A}}$, thus increasing the difficulty of incremental computation. We also noticed that the SimFusion+ time was less sensitive to the small number of updated edges, whereas the IncSimFusion+ time was linearly increased with δ, as expected. This is because once the edges are changed, SimFusion+ has to recompute all the similarities from scratch. In contrast, IncSimFusion+ only computes the similarities from the affected area of edge updates. In light of this, IncSimFusion+ scales well with δ.

6.2.4 *Effect of* ϵ

We used 9 web graphs with the number of vertices increased from 600K to 1.4M. We varied ϵ from 0.01 to 0.0001 and ran SimFusion+ on each graph. The results are reported in Figure 11. It can be seen that the computational time and memory consumption for SimFusion+ was sensitive to ϵ. The smaller the ϵ is, the larger amounts of the CPU time and memory space are, as expected. These confirmed our observation in Section 4, where we envisage that the small choice of ϵ imposes more iterations on computing $\mathbf{T}_k$ and $\mathbf{v}_k$, and hence increases the estimation costs.

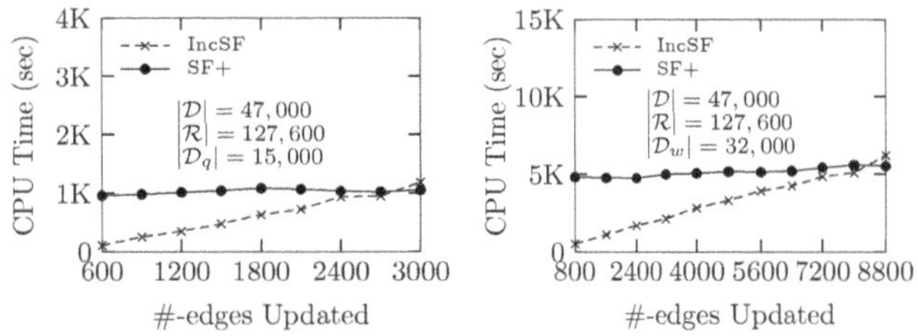

Figure 10: Comparing the CPU time of IncSimFusion+ with that of SimFusion+ on MSN data

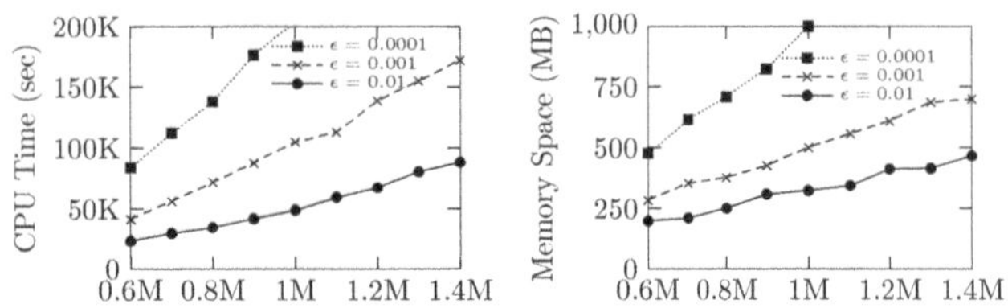

Figure 11: Effect of ϵ for SimFusion+ on synthetic data

7. CONCLUSIONS

We present SimFusion+, a revision of SimFusion, for preventing the trivial solution and the divergence issue of the SimFusion model. We propose efficient techniques to improve the time and space complexity of SimFusion+ computation with accuracy guarantees. We also devise an incremental algorithm to compute SimFusion+ similarity on dynamic graphs when edges are frequently updated. The empirical results on both real and synthetic datasets show that our methods achieve high performance and result quality.

We are currently studying the vertex-updating methods for incrementally computing SimFusion+. We are also to extend our techniques to parallel SimFusion+ computing on GPU.

8. REFERENCES

[1] W. Xi, E. A. Fox, W. Fan, B. Zhang, Z. Chen, J. Yan, and D. Zhuang, "SimFusion: Measuring similarity using unified relationship matrix," in *SIGIR*, pp. 130–137, 2005.

[2] L. Page, S. Brin, R. Motwani, and T. Winograd, "The PageRank citation ranking: Bringing order to the web," technical report, Stanford InfoLab, November 1999.

[3] G. Jeh and J. Widom, "SimRank: A measure of structural-context similarity," in *KDD*, pp. 538–543, 2002.

[4] P. Zhao, J. Han, and Y. Sun, "P-Rank: A comprehensive structural similarity measure over information networks," in *CIKM*, pp. 553–562, 2009.

[5] H. Small, "Co-citation in the scientific literature: A new measure of the relationship between two documents," *J. Am. Soc. Inf. Sci.*, vol. 24, no. 4, pp. 265–269, 1973.

[6] B. Jarneving, "Bibliographic coupling and its application to research-front and other core documents," *J. Informetrics*, vol. 1, no. 4, pp. 287–307, 2007.

[7] W. Xi, B. Zhang, Z. Chen, Y. Lu, S. Yan, W. Ma, and E. A. Fox, "Link Fusion: A unified link analysis framework for multi-type interrelated data objects," in *WWW*, pp. 319–327, 2004.

[8] D. Lizorkin, P. Velikhov, M. N. Grinev, and D. Turdakov, "Accuracy estimate and optimization techniques for SimRank computation," *VLDB J.*, vol. 19, no. 1, pp. 45–66, 2010.

[9] C. Li, J. Han, G. He, X. Jin, Y. Sun, Y. Yu, and T. Wu, "Fast computation of SimRank for static and dynamic information networks," in *EDBT*, pp. 465–476, 2010.

[10] G. He, H. Feng, C. Li, and H. Chen, "Parallel SimRank computation on large graphs with iterative aggregation," in *KDD*, pp. 543–552, 2010.

[11] W. Yu, W. Zhang, X. Lin, Q. Zhang, and J. Le, "A space and time efficient algorithm for SimRank computation," *World Wide Web*, vol. 15, no. 3, pp. 327–353, 2012.

[12] G. Xue, H. Zeng, Z. Chen, Y. Yu, W. Ma, W. Xi, and E. A. Fox, "MRSSA: An iterative algorithm for similarity spreading over interrelated objects," in *CIKM*, pp. 240–241, 2004.

[13] Y. Cai, M. Zhang, C. H. Q. Ding, and S. Chakravarthy, "Closed form solution of similarity algorithms," in *SIGIR*, pp. 709–710, 2010.

[14] G. Williams, *Linear Algebra with Applications*. Jones and Bartlett Publishers, 2007.

[15] A. J. Laub, *Matrix Analysis for Scientists and Engineers*. SIAM: Society for Industrial and Applied Mathematics, 2004.

[16] R. A. Horn and C. R. Johnson, *Matrix Analysis*. Cambridge University Press, February 1990.

[17] Y. Saad, *Iterative Methods for Sparse Linear Systems, Second Edition*. Society for Industrial and Applied Mathematics, 2 ed., April 2003.

Appendix: Proofs

Proof of Proposition 2.

PROOF. Let $\psi(\mathbf{x}) = \mathbf{A}\mathbf{x} - \alpha(\mathbf{x}) \cdot \mathbf{x}$ be a vector function of $\mathbf{x} \in \mathbb{R}^n$, with $\alpha(\mathbf{x})$ being a real function of $\mathbf{x}$. To simplify notations, we shall denote by α_k the dominant eigenvalue of $\mathbf{T}_k$, and

$$\boldsymbol{\eta}_k = \sigma_{\max}(\mathbf{T}_k), \quad \boldsymbol{\xi}_k = \mathbf{V}_k \cdot \sigma_{\max}(\mathbf{T}_k), \quad \boldsymbol{\xi} = \sigma_{\max}(\mathbf{A}).$$

Using $\mathbf{T}_k \boldsymbol{\eta}_k = \alpha_k \boldsymbol{\eta}_k$ and Eq.(7) in Lemma 1, we have

$$\begin{aligned}\psi(\boldsymbol{\xi}_k) &= \mathbf{V}_k \mathbf{T}_k \boldsymbol{\eta}_k + \delta_k \mathbf{v}_{k+1} \mathbf{e}_k^T \boldsymbol{\eta}_k - \alpha_k \mathbf{V}_k \boldsymbol{\eta}_k \\ &= \delta_k \mathbf{v}_{k+1} (\mathbf{e}_k^T \boldsymbol{\eta}_k) = \delta_k [\boldsymbol{\eta}_k]_k \mathbf{v}_{k+1},\end{aligned}$$

where $[\boldsymbol{\eta}_k]_k$ denotes the k-th entry of $\boldsymbol{\eta}_k$. Hence,

$$\|\boldsymbol{\xi}_k - \boldsymbol{\xi}\|_2 \le \|\psi(\boldsymbol{\xi}_k)\|_2 = |\delta_k [\boldsymbol{\eta}_k]_k| \|\mathbf{v}_{k+1}\|_2 = |\delta_k [\boldsymbol{\eta}_k]_k|.$$

Since $vec(\mathbf{S}_k) = \boldsymbol{\xi}_k \otimes \boldsymbol{\xi}_k$ and $vec(\mathbf{S}) = \boldsymbol{\xi} \otimes \boldsymbol{\xi}$, we have

$$\begin{aligned}\|\mathbf{S}_k - \mathbf{S}\|_2 &= \|vec(\mathbf{S}_k) - vec(\mathbf{S})\|_2 = \|\boldsymbol{\xi}_k \otimes \boldsymbol{\xi}_k - \boldsymbol{\xi} \otimes \boldsymbol{\xi}\|_2 \\ &= \|\boldsymbol{\xi}_k \otimes (\boldsymbol{\xi}_k - \boldsymbol{\xi}) + (\boldsymbol{\xi}_k - \boldsymbol{\xi}) \otimes \boldsymbol{\xi}\|_2 \\ &\le \underbrace{\|\boldsymbol{\xi}_k\|_2}_{\le 1} \cdot \|\boldsymbol{\xi}_k - \boldsymbol{\xi}\|_2 + \|\boldsymbol{\xi}_k - \boldsymbol{\xi}\|_2 \cdot \underbrace{\|\boldsymbol{\xi}\|_2}_{\le 1} \\ &= 2 \times \|\boldsymbol{\xi}_k - \boldsymbol{\xi}\|_2 \le 2 \times |\delta_k \times [\boldsymbol{\eta}_k]_k|,\end{aligned}$$

which completes the proof. □

Proof of Proposition 3.

PROOF. For the new graph $\mathcal{G}'$, let $\boldsymbol{\xi}'$ be the dominant eigenvector of $\mathbf{A}'$ with its eigenvalue α', and $\bar{\boldsymbol{\xi}}_1 = \boldsymbol{\xi}' - \boldsymbol{\xi}_1$, $\bar{\alpha}_1 = \alpha' - \alpha_1$, $\bar{\mathbf{A}} = \mathbf{A}' - \mathbf{A}$. Then, $\mathbf{A}'\boldsymbol{\xi}' = \alpha' \boldsymbol{\xi}'$ can be rewritten as

$$(\mathbf{A} + \bar{\mathbf{A}})(\boldsymbol{\xi}_1 + \bar{\boldsymbol{\xi}}_1) = (\alpha_1 + \bar{\alpha})(\boldsymbol{\xi}_1 + \bar{\boldsymbol{\xi}}_1).$$

Expanding the above equation, eliminating $\bar{\mathbf{A}}\bar{\boldsymbol{\xi}}_1$ and $\bar{\alpha}_1 \bar{\boldsymbol{\xi}}_1$ (the high-order infinitesimals of $\bar{\boldsymbol{\xi}}_1$), and using $\mathbf{A}\boldsymbol{\xi}_1 = \alpha_1 \boldsymbol{\xi}_1$, we have

$$\mathbf{A}\bar{\boldsymbol{\xi}}_1 + \boldsymbol{\eta} = \alpha_1 \bar{\boldsymbol{\xi}}_1 + \bar{\alpha}_1 \boldsymbol{\xi}_1 \text{ with } \boldsymbol{\eta} = \bar{\mathbf{A}} \boldsymbol{\xi}_1. \qquad (12)$$

Since $\boldsymbol{\xi}_1, \cdots, \boldsymbol{\xi}_n$ of $\mathbf{A}$ constitute a basis for $\mathbb{R}^n$, there exist scalars $c_1, \cdots, c_n$ *s.t.* $\bar{\boldsymbol{\xi}}_1 = c_1 \boldsymbol{\xi}_1 + \cdots + c_n \boldsymbol{\xi}_n$. Substituting this into Eq.(12) and pre-multiplying both sides by $\boldsymbol{\xi}_j^T$ produce

$$\boldsymbol{\xi}_j^T \sum_{i=1}^n c_i \alpha_i \boldsymbol{\xi}_i + \boldsymbol{\xi}_j^T \boldsymbol{\eta} = \alpha_1 \boldsymbol{\xi}_j^T \sum_{i=1}^n c_i \boldsymbol{\xi}_i + \bar{\alpha}_1 \boldsymbol{\xi}_j^T \boldsymbol{\xi}_1. \quad (j = 2, \cdots, n)$$

Due to $\boldsymbol{\xi}_i$ orthonormality $(i = 1, \cdots, n)$, we have

$$\underbrace{c_j \alpha_j \boldsymbol{\xi}_j^T \boldsymbol{\xi}_j}_{= c_j \alpha_j} + \boldsymbol{\xi}_j^T \boldsymbol{\eta} = \underbrace{c_j \alpha_1 \boldsymbol{\xi}_j^T \boldsymbol{\xi}_j}_{= c_j \alpha_1} + \underbrace{\bar{\alpha}_1 \boldsymbol{\xi}_j^T \boldsymbol{\xi}_1}_{= 0}.$$

Hence, $c_j = (\boldsymbol{\xi}_j^T \boldsymbol{\eta})/(\alpha_j - \alpha_1)$ with $\boldsymbol{\eta} = \bar{\mathbf{A}}\boldsymbol{\xi}_1 \quad (j = 2, \cdots, n)$.

To determine c_1, we use the identity $(\boldsymbol{\xi}_1 + \bar{\boldsymbol{\xi}}_1)^T (\boldsymbol{\xi}_1 + \bar{\boldsymbol{\xi}}_1) = 1$. Expanding the left-hand side, eliminating the high-order infinitesimal $\bar{\boldsymbol{\xi}}_1^T \bar{\boldsymbol{\xi}}_1$, and replacing $\bar{\boldsymbol{\xi}}_1$ with $c_1 \boldsymbol{\xi}_1 + \cdots + c_n \boldsymbol{\xi}_n$, we have

$$\underbrace{\boldsymbol{\xi}_1^T \boldsymbol{\xi}_1}_{= 1} + \underbrace{\boldsymbol{\xi}_1^T \sum_{i=1}^n c_i \boldsymbol{\xi}_i}_{= c_1} + \underbrace{\sum_{i=1}^n c_i \boldsymbol{\xi}_i^T \boldsymbol{\xi}_1}_{= c_1} = 1.$$

Due to $\boldsymbol{\xi}_1, \cdots, \boldsymbol{\xi}_n$ orthonormality, it follows that $c_1 = 0$. Thus,

$$vec(\mathbf{S}') = \boldsymbol{\xi}' \otimes \boldsymbol{\xi}' \text{ with } \boldsymbol{\xi}' = \boldsymbol{\xi}_1 + \bar{\boldsymbol{\xi}}_1 = \boldsymbol{\xi}_1 + \sum_{p=2}^n c_p \cdot \boldsymbol{\xi}_p,$$

$$c_p = \frac{\boldsymbol{\xi}_p^T \boldsymbol{\eta}}{\alpha_p - \alpha_1}, \text{ and } \boldsymbol{\eta} = \bar{\mathbf{A}} \boldsymbol{\xi}_1.$$

□

Group Matrix Factorization for Scalable Topic Modeling

Quan Wang
MOE-Microsoft Key Laboratory of Statistics&Information Technology
Peking University
v-quwan@microsoft.com

Zheng Cao
Dept. of Computer Science & Engineering
Shanghai JiaoTong University
mozeda@sjtu.edu.cn

Jun Xu, Hang Li
Microsoft Research Asia
No. 5 Danling Street
Beijing, China
{junxu,hangli}@microsoft.com

ABSTRACT

Topic modeling can reveal the latent structure of text data and is useful for knowledge discovery, search relevance ranking, document classification, and so on. One of the major challenges in topic modeling is to deal with large datasets and large numbers of topics in real-world applications. In this paper, we investigate techniques for scaling up the non-probabilistic topic modeling approaches such as RLSI and NMF. We propose a general topic modeling method, referred to as Group Matrix Factorization (GMF), to enhance the scalability and efficiency of the non-probabilistic approaches. GMF assumes that the text documents have already been categorized into multiple semantic classes, and there exist class-specific topics for each of the classes as well as shared topics across all classes. Topic modeling is then formalized as a problem of minimizing a general objective function with regularizations and/or constraints on the class-specific topics and shared topics. In this way, the learning of class-specific topics can be conducted in parallel, and thus the scalability and efficiency can be greatly improved. We apply GMF to RLSI and NMF, obtaining Group RLSI (GRLSI) and Group NMF (GNMF) respectively. Experiments on a Wikipedia dataset and a real-world web dataset, each containing about 3 million documents, show that GRLSI and GNMF can greatly improve RLSI and NMF in terms of scalability and efficiency. The topics discovered by GRLSI and GNMF are coherent and have good readability. Further experiments on a search relevance dataset, containing 30,000 labeled queries, show that the use of topics learned by GRLSI and GNMF can significantly improve search relevance.

Categories and Subject Descriptors: H.3.1 [Information Storage and Retrieval]: Content Analysis and Indexing

General Terms: Algorithms, Experimentation

Keywords: Matrix Factorization, Topic Modeling, Large Scale

1. INTRODUCTION

Topic modeling refers to machine learning technologies whose aim is to discover the hidden semantic structure existing in a large collection of text documents. Given a collection of text documents, a topic model represents the relationship between the terms and the documents through latent topics. A topic is defined as a probability distribution over terms or a cluster of weighted terms. A document is viewed as a bag of terms generated from a mixture of latent topics. Many topic modeling methods, such as Latent Semantic Indexing (LSI) [7], Probabilistic Latent Semantic Indexing (PLSI) [11], Latent Dirichlet Allocation (LDA) [5], Regularized Latent Semantic Indexing (RLSI) [26], and Non-negative Matrix Factorization (NMF) [13, 14] have been proposed and successfully applied to different applications in text mining, information retrieval, natural language processing, and other related fields.

One of the main challenges in topic modeling is to handle large numbers of documents and create large numbers of topics. For the probabilistic topic models like LDA and PLSI, the scalability challenge mainly comes from the necessity of simultaneously updating the term-topic matrix to meet the probability distribution assumptions. When the number of terms is large, which is inevitable in real applications, this problem becomes particularly severe. For the non-probabilistic methods of NMF and RLSI, the formulation makes it possible to decompose the learning problem into multiple sub-problems and conduct learning in parallel, and hence in general they have better scalability than the probabilistic methods[1]. Refer to [26] for detailed discussions.

The high scalability of non-probabilistic methods makes them easier to be employed in practice. However, to handle millions or even billions of documents, it is still necessary to further improve their scalability and efficiency. In this paper, we investigate the possibilities of further enhancing the scalability and efficiency of non-probabilistic methods such as RLSI and NMF.

The method, called Group Matrix Factorization (GMF), assumes that the documents have already been categorized into multiple classes in a predefined taxonomy. This assumption is practical and common in many real-world applications. For example, Wikipedia data contains a hierarchical taxonomy with 25 classes at the first layer. Each Wikipedia article falls into at least one of the classes. The ODP project[2] provides a taxonomy of semantic classes and about 4 million web pages manually classified into the classes. The data can be used for training a classifier and other webpages can be classified into the classes by the classifier [2]. GMF further assumes that there exists a set of class-specific topics for each of the classes, and there also exists a set of shared topics for all of the classes. Each document in the collection is specified by its classes, class-specific topics, as well as shared topics. In this way, the large-scale learning problem can be decomposed into small-scale sub-problems. We refer to the strategy as the divide-and-conquer technique.

Permission to make digital or hard copies of all or part of this work for personal or classroom use is granted without fee provided that copies are not made or distributed for profit or commercial advantage and that copies bear this notice and the full citation on the first page. To copy otherwise, to republish, to post on servers or to redistribute to lists, requires prior specific permission and/or a fee.
SIGIR'12, August 12–16, 2012, Portland, Oregon, USA.
Copyright 2012 ACM 978-1-4503-1472-5/12/08 ...$15.00.

[1]Note that LSI needs to be solved by SVD due to its orthogonality assumption and thus it is hard to be scaled up.
[2]http://www.dmoz.org/

In GMF, the documents in each of the classes are represented as a term-document matrix. The term-document matrix is then approximated as the product of two matrices: one matrix represents the shared topics as well as the class-specific topics, and the other matrix represents the document representations based on the topics. An objective function is defined to measure the goodness of prediction of the data with the model. Optimization of the objective function leads to the automatic discovery of topics as well as topic representations of the documents.

We show that GMF can be used to improve the efficiency and scalability of non-probabilistic topic models, using RLSI and NMF as examples. Specifically, we apply GMF to RLSI [26] and NMF [13, 14], obtaining the Group RLSI (GRLSI) and Group NMF (GNMF), respectively. Like in RLSI, the objective function of GRLSI consists of squared Frobenius norm as loss function, ℓ_1-regularization on topics, and ℓ_2-regularization on document representations. Similarly to NMF, GNMF also uses squared Frobenius norm as loss function and non-negative constraints on the topics and document representations. Algorithms for optimizing the loss functions of GRLSI and GNMF are given and theoretical justification of the algorithms is shown. Time complexity analysis show that GRLSI and GNMF can achieve P times of speedup on RLSI and NMF respectively, where P is the number of classes.

Experiments on two large datasets containing about 3 million documents have verified the following points. (1) Both GRLSI and GNMF can efficiently handle the documents on a single machine, and the number is larger than those which can be processed by most existing topic modeling methods. (2) GRLSI and GNMF are more scalable and efficient than RLSI and NMF respectively, especially when the number of topics is large. (3) In GRLSI and GNMF, the shared topics as well as the class-specific topics are coherent and meaningful. (4) Experiments on another relevance dataset show that GRLSI and GNMF can help significantly improve search relevance.

Exploiting the divide and conquer strategy in the non-probabilistic methods has been investigated in computer vision [16, 25]. However, it was not clear whether it works for text data. As far as we know, this is the first work on large scale text data. Our main contributions in this paper lie in that we have empirically verified the effectiveness of the divide and conquer strategy on text data, by specifically implementing and testing the GRLSI and GNMF methods in large scale experiments.

2. RELATED WORK

The goal of topic modeling is to automatically discover the latent topics in a document collection as well as model the documents by representing them with the topics. Methods for topic modeling fall into two categories: probabilistic approaches and non-probabilistic approaches. In the probabilistic approaches, a topic is defined as a probability distribution over terms and documents are viewed as data generated from mixtures of topics. To generate a document, one first chooses a topic distribution. Then, for each term in that document , one chooses a topic according to the topic distribution, and draws a term from the topic according to its term distribution. PLSI [11] and LDA [5] are two widely-used probabilistic approaches to topic modeling. Please refer to [3] for a survey on probabilistic topic models. In the non-probabilistic approaches, the term vectors of documents (term-document matrix) are projected into a topic space in which each axis corresponds to a topic. A document is then represented as a vector of topics in the space. These approaches are realized as factorization of the term-document matrix such that the matrix is approximately equal to the product of a term-topic matrix and a topic-document matrix under certain constraints. LSI [7] is a representative method, which performs the factorization under the assumption that the topic vectors are orthonormal. In NMF [13, 14], the factor matrices are assumed to be nonnegative, while in RLSI [26], the factor matrices are regularized with ℓ_1 and/or ℓ_2 norms.

It has been demonstrated that topic modeling is useful for knowledge discovery, search relevance ranking, and document classification (e.g., [19, 27, 26]). Topic modeling is actually becoming one of the most important technologies in text mining, information retrieval, natural language processing, and other related fields.

The topic modeling approaches that we have discussed so far are completely unsupervised. Recently, researchers have also proposed supervised or semi-supervised approaches to topic modeling. For example, Supervised Latent Dirichlet Allocation (SLDA) [4] and Supervised Dictionary Learning (SDL) [18] are methods for incorporating supervision into probabilistic and non-probabilistic topic models. In this paper, we assume that documents have already been classified into classes, and then we conduct topic modeling on the basis of the classification to enhance scalability and efficiency.

Using document classes in topic modeling has been studied in previous literature. For probabilistic approaches, Zhai et al.(2004), for example, proposed incorporating class labels into a multinomial mixture model in order to more accurately discover topics,such that some topics are shared by all classes and other topics are specific to individual classes [28]. The discriminatively training of LDA (DiscLDA) [12] and Partially Labeled Dirichlet Allocation (PLDA) [22] incorporate class labels into LDA to achieve similar goals. For the non-probabilistic approaches, Mairal et al. (2008) [17], Bengio et al. (2009) [1], and Wang et al. (2011) [25] proposed using class labels in Sparse Coding [15, 20], a special case of RLSI, in which a dictionary for each class (i.e., topics specific to each class) is learned first, after that a common dictionary over all classes (i.e., topics shared by all classes) is learned, and finally the common and class-specific dictionaries are learned simultaneously. Group Nonnegative Matrix Factorization (GNMF) [16] extends NMF in a similar way. Both extensions on non-probabilistic methods were conducted in computer vision. As can be seen, all the previous work was not motivated toward enhancing scalability and efficiency. In this paper, we also exploit class information in topic modeling and our goal is to enhance scalability and efficiency. As far as we know, this is the first time such an investigation is conducted on text data. We also note that the formulation of GNMF in this paper is different from that in [16].

3. GROUP MATRIX FACTORIZATION

We present the formulation of Group Matrix Factorization and provide a probabilistic interpretation of it.

3.1 Problem Formulation

Suppose that we are given a document collection $\mathcal{D}$ with size N, containing terms from a vocabulary $\mathcal{V}$ with size M. A document is represented as a vector $\boldsymbol{d} \in \mathbb{R}^M$ where each entry denotes the score of the corresponding term, for example, a Boolean value indicating occurrence, term frequency, tf-idf, etc. Each document is associated with a class label $y \in \{1, \cdots, P\}$. The N documents in $\mathcal{D}$ can be classified into P classes according to their class labels and represented as $\mathcal{D} = \{\mathbf{D}_1, \cdots, \mathbf{D}_P\}$. $\mathbf{D}_p = \left[\boldsymbol{d}_1^{(p)}, \cdots, \boldsymbol{d}_{N_p}^{(p)}\right] \in \mathbb{R}^{M \times N_p}$ is the term-document matrix corresponding to class p, in which each row stands for a term and each column stands for a document. N_p is the number of documents in class p such that $\sum_{p=1}^{P} N_p = N$.

A topic is defined as a subset of terms from $\mathcal{V}$ with important weights, and is also represented as a vector $\boldsymbol{u} \in \mathbb{R}^M$ with each entry corresponding to a term. Suppose that there are K_s shared topics, denoted as a term-topic matrix $\mathbf{U}_0 = \left[\boldsymbol{u}_1^{(0)}, \cdots, \boldsymbol{u}_{K_s}^{(0)}\right] \in \mathbb{R}^{M \times K_s}$, in which each column corresponds to a shared topic. Also, for each class p, there are K_c class-specific topics, which can also be represented by a term-topic matrix $\mathbf{U}_p = \left[\boldsymbol{u}_1^{(p)}, \cdots, \boldsymbol{u}_{K_c}^{(p)}\right] \in \mathbb{R}^{M \times K_c}$, where each column stands for a class-specific topic. Then, the total number of topics in the whole collection is $K = K_s + PK_c$ [3].

The documents in each class are then modeled by the shared topics as well as the topics specific to their own class. Specifically, given the shared topics $\mathbf{U}_0$ and the class-specific topics $\mathbf{U}_p$, document $\boldsymbol{d}_n^{(p)}$ in class p is approximately represented as a linear combination of these topics, i.e.,

$$\boldsymbol{d}_n^{(p)} \approx \tilde{\mathbf{U}}_p \boldsymbol{v}_n^{(p)} = \left[\mathbf{U}_0, \mathbf{U}_p\right] \boldsymbol{v}_n^{(p)}, \tag{1}$$

where $\tilde{\mathbf{U}}_p = \left[\mathbf{U}_0, \mathbf{U}_p\right] \in \mathbb{R}^{M \times (K_s + K_c)}$ is the concatenated term-topic matrix corresponding to class p, and $\boldsymbol{v}_n^{(p)} \in \mathbb{R}^{K_s + K_c}$ is the representation of document $\boldsymbol{d}_n^{(p)}$ in latent topic space. Since a document is represented only by the shared topics and the class-specific topics corresponding to its own class, GMF actually decomposes the large-scale matrix operations concerning all the topics into multiple small-scale ones concerning only subsets of the topics, and thus reduces the computational complexity.

Let $\mathbf{V}_p = \left[\boldsymbol{v}_1^{(p)}, \cdots, \boldsymbol{v}_{N_p}^{(p)}\right] \in \mathbb{R}^{(K_s+K_c) \times N_p}$ be the topic-document matrix corresponding to class p. We denote $\mathbf{V}_p^T = \left[\mathbf{H}_p^T, \mathbf{W}_p^T\right]$ such that $\tilde{\mathbf{U}}_p \mathbf{V}_p = \mathbf{U}_0 \mathbf{H}_p + \mathbf{U}_p \mathbf{W}_p$, where $\mathbf{H}_p \in \mathbb{R}^{K_s \times N_p}$ corresponds to shared topics $\mathbf{U}_0$ and $\mathbf{W}_p \in \mathbb{R}^{K_c \times N_p}$ corresponds to class-specific topics $\mathbf{U}_p$. Table 1 gives a summary of notations.

Thus, given a document collection together with the class labels, represented as $\mathcal{D} = \{\mathbf{D}_1, \cdots, \mathbf{D}_P\}$, GMF amounts to solving the following optimization problem:

$$\begin{aligned}
\min_{\{\boldsymbol{u}_k^{(0)}\}, \{\boldsymbol{u}_k^{(p)}\}, \{\boldsymbol{v}_n^{(p)}\}} \quad & \sum_{p=1}^{P} \sum_{n=1}^{N_p} \mathcal{L}\left(\boldsymbol{d}_n^{(p)} \| \tilde{\mathbf{U}}_p \boldsymbol{v}_n^{(p)}\right) + \theta_1 \sum_{k=1}^{K_s} \mathcal{R}_1\left(\boldsymbol{u}_k^{(0)}\right) \\
& + \theta_2 \sum_{p=1}^{P} \sum_{k=1}^{K_c} \mathcal{R}_2\left(\boldsymbol{u}_k^{(p)}\right) + \theta_3 \sum_{p=1}^{P} \sum_{n=1}^{N_p} \mathcal{R}_3\left(\boldsymbol{v}_n^{(p)}\right), \\
s.t. \quad & \boldsymbol{u}_k^{(0)} \in C_1, \quad k = 1, \cdots, K_s, \\
& \boldsymbol{u}_k^{(p)} \in C_2, \quad k = 1, \cdots, K_c, p = 1, \cdots, P, \\
& \boldsymbol{v}_n^{(p)} \in C_3, \quad n = 1, \cdots, N_p, p = 1, \cdots, P,
\end{aligned} \tag{2}$$

where $\mathcal{L}(\cdot\|\cdot)$ is a loss function that measures the quality of the approximation defined in Eq. (1); $\mathcal{R}_1(\cdot)$, $\mathcal{R}_2(\cdot)$, and $\mathcal{R}_3(\cdot)$ are regularization items on shared topics, class-specific topics, and document representations, respectively; C_1, C_2, and C_3 are feasible sets for shared topics, class-specific topics, and document representations, respectively; θ_1, θ_2, and θ_3 are coefficients.

3.2 Probabilistic Interpretation

We give a probabilistic interpretation of GMF, as shown in Figure 1. In the graphical model, shared topics $\boldsymbol{u}_1^{(0)}, \cdots, \boldsymbol{u}_{K_s}^{(0)}$ and class-specific topics $\boldsymbol{u}_1^{(p)}, \cdots, \boldsymbol{u}_{K_c}^{(p)}, p = 1, \cdots, P$, are parameters. All the shared topics are independent from each other, with prior $p\left(\boldsymbol{u}_k^{(0)}\right) \propto e^{-\theta_1 \mathcal{R}_1\left(\boldsymbol{u}_k^{(0)}\right)}$ and constraint $\boldsymbol{u}_k^{(0)} \in C_1$ on each $\boldsymbol{u}_k^{(0)}$. All the class-specific topics are independent from each other, with prior $p\left(\boldsymbol{u}_k^{(p)}\right) \propto e^{-\theta_2 \mathcal{R}_2\left(\boldsymbol{u}_k^{(p)}\right)}$ and constraint $\boldsymbol{u}_k^{(p)} \in C_2$ on each $\boldsymbol{u}_k^{(p)}$. Document representations $\boldsymbol{v}_1, \cdots, \boldsymbol{v}_N$ are regarded as latent variables, with prior $p(\boldsymbol{v}_n) \propto e^{-\theta_3 \mathcal{R}_3(\boldsymbol{v}_n)}$ and constraint $\boldsymbol{v}_n \in C_3$ on each $\boldsymbol{v}_n$. Class labels $y_1, \cdots, y_N$ are observed variables with a constant prior on each y_n. Documents $\boldsymbol{d}_1, \cdots, \boldsymbol{d}_N$ are also observed variables. Each document is generated according to a probability distribution conditioned on the shared topics, the class-specific topics, the corresponding class label, and the corresponding latent variable, i.e., $p\left(\boldsymbol{d}_n \middle| \left\{\boldsymbol{u}_k^{(0)}\right\}, \left\{\boldsymbol{u}_k^{(p)}\right\}, y_n, \boldsymbol{v}_n\right) = p\left(\boldsymbol{d}_n \middle| \left\{\boldsymbol{u}_k^{(0)}\right\}, \left\{\boldsymbol{u}_k^{(y_n)}\right\}, \boldsymbol{v}_n\right) \propto e^{-\mathcal{L}(\boldsymbol{d}_n \| \tilde{\mathbf{U}}_{y_n} \boldsymbol{v}_n)}$. Moreover, all triplets $(y_n, \boldsymbol{d}_n, \boldsymbol{v}_n)$ are independent given $\boldsymbol{u}_1^{(0)}, \cdots \boldsymbol{u}_{K_s}^{(0)}$ and $\boldsymbol{u}_1^{(p)}, \cdots, \boldsymbol{u}_{K_c}^{(p)}, p = 1, \cdots, P$. It can be easily shown that GMF formulation Eq. (2) can be obtained with Maximum A Posteriori approximation.

GMF can be applied to non-probabilistic methods to further enhance their scalability and efficiency. Next, as examples, we define Group RLSI (GRLSI) and Group NMF (GNMF) under the framework of GMF.

[3]A more general case is defining different numbers of class-specific topics for different classes, which can also be modeled by GMF.

Table 1: Table of notations.

Notation	Meaning
M	Number of terms in vocabulary
N	Number of documents in collection
P	Number of classes
N_p	Number of documents in class p
K_s	Number of shared topics
K_c	Number of class-specific topics for each class
K	Total number of topics
$\mathbf{D}_p \in \mathbb{R}^{M \times N_p}$	Term-document matrix corresponding to class p
$\boldsymbol{d}_n^{(p)} \in \mathbb{R}^M$	The n-th document in class p
$\mathbf{U}_0 \in \mathbb{R}^{M \times K_s}$	Term-topic matrix of shared topics
$\boldsymbol{u}_k^{(0)} \in \mathbb{R}^M$	The k-th shared topic
$\mathbf{U}_p \in \mathbb{R}^{M \times K_c}$	Term-topic matrix of class-specific topics for class p
$\boldsymbol{u}_k^{(p)} \in \mathbb{R}^M$	The k-th class-specific topic in class p
$\tilde{\mathbf{U}}_p = \left[\mathbf{U}_0, \mathbf{U}_p\right]$	Concatenated term-topic matrix corresponding to class p
$\mathbf{V}_p \in \mathbb{R}^{(K_s+K_c) \times N_p}$	Topic-document matrix corresponding to class p
$\boldsymbol{v}_n^{(p)} \in \mathbb{R}^{K_s+K_c}$	Representation of $\boldsymbol{d}_n^{(p)}$ in topic space
$\mathbf{H}_p$ and $\mathbf{W}_p$	Components of $\mathbf{V}_p$: $\mathbf{V}_p^T = \left[\mathbf{H}_p^T, \mathbf{W}_p^T\right]$

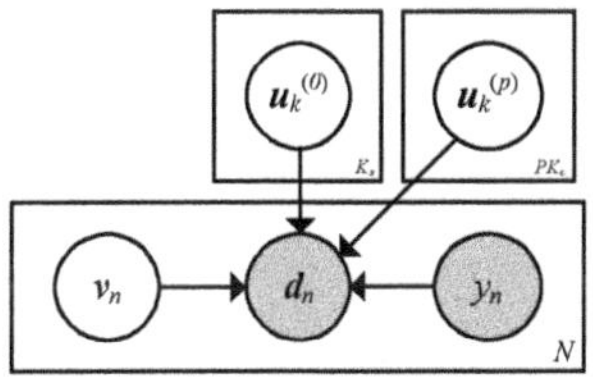

Figure 1: Graphical model of GMF.

4. GROUP RLSI

GRLSI adopts the squared Euclidean distance to measure the approximation quality and employs the same regularization schema as in RLSI [26], i.e., ℓ_1-regularization on both shared and class-specific topics and ℓ_2-regularization on document representations. The optimization problem of GRLSI is as follows:

$$\begin{aligned}
\min_{\{\boldsymbol{u}_k^{(0)}\}, \{\boldsymbol{u}_k^{(p)}\}, \{\boldsymbol{v}_n^{(p)}\}} \quad & \sum_{p=1}^{P} \sum_{n=1}^{N_p} \left\|\boldsymbol{d}_n^{(p)} - \tilde{\mathbf{U}}_p \boldsymbol{v}_n^{(p)}\right\|_2^2 + \lambda_1 \sum_{k=1}^{K_s} \left\|\boldsymbol{u}_k^{(0)}\right\|_1 \\
& + \lambda_1 \sum_{p=1}^{P} \sum_{k=1}^{K_c} \left\|\boldsymbol{u}_k^{(p)}\right\|_1 + \lambda_2 \sum_{p=1}^{P} \sum_{n=1}^{N_p} \left\|\boldsymbol{v}_n^{(p)}\right\|_2^2,
\end{aligned} \tag{3}$$

where λ_1 is the parameter controlling the ℓ_1-regularization, and λ_2

Algorithm 1 Group RLSI

Require: $\mathbf{D}_1, \cdots, \mathbf{D}_P$

for $p = 1 : P$ **do**
  $\mathbf{U}_p \leftarrow$ zero matrix
  $\mathbf{V}_p \leftarrow$ random matrix
end for
repeat
  $\mathbf{U}_0 \leftarrow \text{Update}U_0\left(\{\mathbf{D}_p\}, \{\mathbf{U}_p\}, \{\mathbf{V}_p\}\right)$
  for $p = 1 : P$ **do**
    $\mathbf{U}_p \leftarrow \text{Update}U_p\left(\mathbf{D}_p, \mathbf{U}_0, \mathbf{V}_p\right)$
    $\mathbf{V}_p \leftarrow \text{Update}V_p\left(\mathbf{D}_p, \mathbf{U}_0, \mathbf{U}_p\right)$
  end for
until convergence
return $\mathbf{U}_0, \mathbf{U}_1, \cdots, \mathbf{U}_P, \mathbf{V}_1, \cdots, \mathbf{V}_P$

is the parameter controlling the ℓ_2-regularization[4]. GRLSI decomposes the large-scale matrix operations in RLSI into multiple small-scale ones and thus can be solved more efficiently.

4.1 Optimization

Optimization Eq. (3) is convex with respect to one of the variables $\mathbf{U}_0, \mathbf{U}_1, \cdots, \mathbf{U}_P, V_1, \cdots, \mathbf{V}_P$ when the others are fixed. Thus we sequentially minimize the objective function with respect to shared topics $\mathbf{U}_0$, class-specific topics $\mathbf{U}_1, \cdots, \mathbf{U}_P$, and document representations $V_1, \cdots, \mathbf{V}_P$. This procedure is summarized in Algorithm 1.

4.1.1 Update of Matrix $\mathbf{U}_0$

Holding $\mathbf{U}_1, \cdots, \mathbf{U}_P, \mathbf{V}_1, \cdots, \mathbf{V}_P$ fixed, the update of $\mathbf{U}_0$ amounts to the following minimization problem:

$$\min_{\mathbf{U}_0} \sum_{p=1}^{P} \left\|\mathbf{D}_p - \mathbf{U}_0\mathbf{H}_p - \mathbf{U}_p\mathbf{W}_p\right\|_F^2 + \lambda_1 \sum_{m=1}^{M}\sum_{k=1}^{K_s} \left|u_{mk}^{(0)}\right|, \tag{4}$$

where $\|\cdot\|_F$ is the Frobenius norm and $u_{mk}^{(0)}$ is the mk-th entry of $\mathbf{U}_0$. Eq. (4) is equivalent to

$$\min_{\mathbf{U}_0} \|\mathbf{D} - \mathbf{U}_0\mathbf{H}\|_F^2 + \lambda_1 \sum_{m=1}^{M}\sum_{k=1}^{K_s} \left|u_{mk}^{(0)}\right|, \tag{5}$$

where $\mathbf{D}$ and $\mathbf{H}$ are defined as $\mathbf{D} = [\mathbf{D}_1 - \mathbf{U}_1\mathbf{W}_1, \cdots, \mathbf{D}_P - \mathbf{U}_P\mathbf{W}_P]$ and $\mathbf{H} = [\mathbf{H}_1, \cdots, \mathbf{H}_P]$, respectively. Let $\bar{\boldsymbol{d}}_m = (d_{m1}, \cdots, d_{mN})^T$ and $\bar{\boldsymbol{u}}_m^{(0)} = \left(u_{m1}^{(0)}, \cdots, u_{mK_s}^{(0)}\right)^T$ be the column vectors whose entries are those of the mth row of $\mathbf{D}$ and $\mathbf{U}_0$, respectively. Eq. (5) can be decomposed into M subproblems that can be solved independently, with each corresponding to one row of $\mathbf{U}_0$:

$$\min_{\bar{\boldsymbol{u}}_m^{(0)}} \left\|\bar{\boldsymbol{d}}_m - \mathbf{H}^T\bar{\boldsymbol{u}}_m^{(0)}\right\|_2^2 + \lambda_1 \left\|\bar{\boldsymbol{u}}_m^{(0)}\right\|_1, \tag{6}$$

for $m = 1, \cdots, M$.

Eq. (6) is an ℓ_1-regularized least squares problem, whose objective function is not differentiable and it is not possible to directly apply gradient-based methods. A number of techniques can be used here, such as interior point method [6], coordinate descent with soft-thresholding [9, 10], Lars-Lasso algorithm [8, 21], and feature-sign search [15]. Here we choose coordinate descent with soft-thresholding. To do so, we calculate $\mathbf{S}_0 = \mathbf{H}\mathbf{H}^T = \sum_{p=1}^{P} \mathbf{H}_p\mathbf{H}_p^T \in \mathbb{R}^{K_s \times K_s}$ and $\mathbf{R}_0 = \mathbf{D}\mathbf{H}^T = \sum_{p=1}^{P} \mathbf{D}_p\mathbf{H}_p^T - \sum_{p=1}^{P} \mathbf{U}_p\mathbf{W}_p\mathbf{H}_p^T \in \mathbb{R}^{M \times K_s}$, and then update $\mathbf{U}_0$ with the following update rule:

$$u_{mk}^{(0)} \leftarrow \frac{\left(\left|r_{mk}^{(0)} - \sum_{l \neq k} s_{kl}^{(0)} u_{ml}^{(0)}\right| - \frac{1}{2}\lambda_1\right)_+ \text{sign}\left(r_{mk}^{(0)} - \sum_{l \neq k} s_{kl}^{(0)} u_{ml}^{(0)}\right)}{s_{kk}^{(0)}},$$

where $s_{ij}^{(0)}$ and $r_{ij}^{(0)}$ are the ij-th entry of $\mathbf{S}_0$ and $\mathbf{R}_0$, respectively, and $(\cdot)_+$ denotes the hinge function. The algorithm for updating $\mathbf{U}_0$ is summarized in Algorithm 2.

[4]A more general case is setting different regularization parameters for shared topics and class-specific topics, for separately controlling the sparsity of shared topics and class-specific topics.

Algorithm 2 UpdateU_0

Require: $\mathbf{D}_1, \cdots, \mathbf{D}_P, \mathbf{U}_1, \cdots, \mathbf{U}_P, \mathbf{V}_1, \cdots, \mathbf{V}_P$

$\mathbf{S}_0 \leftarrow \sum_{p=1}^{P} \mathbf{H}_p\mathbf{H}_p^T$
$\mathbf{R}_0 \leftarrow \sum_{p=1}^{P} \mathbf{D}_p\mathbf{H}_p^T - \sum_{p=1}^{P} \mathbf{U}_p\mathbf{W}_p\mathbf{H}_p^T$
for $m = 1 : M$ **do**
  $\bar{\boldsymbol{u}}_m^{(0)} \leftarrow \mathbf{0}$
  repeat
    for $k = 1 : K_s$ **do**
      $x_{mk} \leftarrow r_{mk}^{(0)} - \sum_{l \neq k} s_{kl}^{(0)} u_{ml}^{(0)}$
      $u_{mk}^{(0)} \leftarrow \frac{\left(|x_{mk}| - \frac{1}{2}\lambda_1\right)_+ \text{sign}(x_{mk})}{s_{kk}^{(0)}}$
    end for
  until convergence
end for
return $\mathbf{U}_0$

Algorithm 3 UpdateU_p

Require: $\mathbf{D}_p, \mathbf{U}_0, \mathbf{V}_p$

$\mathbf{S}_p \leftarrow \mathbf{W}_p\mathbf{W}_p^T$
$\mathbf{R}_p \leftarrow \mathbf{D}_p\mathbf{W}_p^T - \mathbf{U}_0\mathbf{H}_p\mathbf{W}_p^T$
for $m = 1 : M$ **do**
  $\bar{\boldsymbol{u}}_m^{(p)} \leftarrow \mathbf{0}$
  repeat
    for $k = 1 : K_c$ **do**
      $x_{mk} \leftarrow r_{mk}^{(p)} - \sum_{l \neq k} s_{kl}^{(p)} u_{ml}^{(p)}$
      $u_{mk}^{(p)} \leftarrow \frac{\left(|x_{mk}| - \frac{1}{2}\lambda_1\right)_+ \text{sign}(x_{mk})}{s_{kk}^{(p)}}$
    end for
  until convergence
end for
return $\mathbf{U}_p$

4.1.2 Update of Matrix $\mathbf{U}_p$

Holding the other variables fixed, the update of $\mathbf{U}_p$ amounts to the following optimization problem:

$$\min_{\mathbf{U}_p} \left\|\mathbf{D}_p - \mathbf{U}_0\mathbf{H}_p - \mathbf{U}_p\mathbf{W}_p\right\|_F^2 + \lambda_1 \sum_{m=1}^{M}\sum_{k=1}^{K_c} \left|u_{mk}^{(p)}\right|, \tag{7}$$

where $u_{mk}^{(p)}$ is the mk-th entry of $\mathbf{U}_p$. Eq. (7) can be optimized with the same technique presented for optimizing Eq. (5). We calculate $\mathbf{S}_p = \mathbf{W}_p\mathbf{W}_p^T \in \mathbb{R}^{K_c \times K_c}$ and $\mathbf{R}_p = \mathbf{D}_p\mathbf{W}_p^T - \mathbf{U}_0\mathbf{H}_p\mathbf{W}_p^T \in \mathbb{R}^{M \times K_c}$, and then update $\mathbf{U}_p$ with the following update rule:

$$u_{mk}^{(p)} \leftarrow \frac{\left(\left|r_{mk}^{(p)} - \sum_{l \neq k} s_{kl}^{(p)} u_{ml}^{(p)}\right| - \frac{1}{2}\lambda_1\right)_+ \text{sign}\left(r_{mk}^{(p)} - \sum_{l \neq k} s_{kl}^{(p)} u_{ml}^{(p)}\right)}{s_{kk}^{(p)}},$$

where $s_{ij}^{(p)}$ and $r_{ij}^{(p)}$ are the ij-th entry of $\mathbf{S}_p$ and $\mathbf{R}_p$, respectively. The algorithm for updating $\mathbf{U}_p$ is summarized in Algorithm 3.

Algorithm 4 UpdateV_p

Require: $\mathbf{D}_p, \mathbf{U}_0, \mathbf{U}_p$

1: $\mathbf{\Sigma}_p \leftarrow \left(\tilde{\mathbf{U}}_p^T\tilde{\mathbf{U}}_p + \lambda_2\mathbf{I}\right)^{-1}$

2: $\mathbf{\Phi}_p \leftarrow \tilde{\mathbf{U}}_p^T\mathbf{D}_p$

3: **for** $n = 1 : N_p$ **do**

4: $\quad \boldsymbol{v}_n^{(p)} \leftarrow \mathbf{\Sigma}_p\boldsymbol{\phi}_n^{(p)}$, where $\boldsymbol{\phi}_n^{(p)}$ is the n-th column of $\mathbf{\Phi}_p$

5: **end for**

6: **return** $\mathbf{V}_p$

Table 2: Time complexity (per iteration) of RLSI and GRLSI.

	RLSI	GRLSI
Update **U**	$\frac{K^2N+\text{AvgDL}\times KN+IK^2M}{Q}$	$\frac{\frac{K^2N}{P}+\text{AvgDL}\times KN+IK^2M}{PQ}$
Update **V**	$\frac{\gamma^2K^2M+K^3+\text{AvgDL}\times\gamma KN+K^2N}{Q}$	$\frac{\gamma^2K^2M+\frac{K^3}{P}+\text{AvgDL}\times\gamma KN+\frac{K^2N}{P}}{PQ}$

4.1.3 *Update of Matrix* $\mathbf{V}_p$

The update of $\mathbf{V}_p$ with the other variables fixed is a least squares problem with ℓ_2-regularization. It can also be decomposed into N_p optimization problems, with each corresponding to one $\boldsymbol{v}_n^{(p)}$ and can be solved in parallel:

$$\min_{\boldsymbol{v}_n^{(p)}} \left\|\boldsymbol{d}_n^{(p)} - \tilde{\mathbf{U}}_p\boldsymbol{v}_n^{(p)}\right\|_2^2 + \lambda_2 \left\|\boldsymbol{v}_n^{(p)}\right\|_2^2,$$

for $n = 1, \cdots, N_p$. It is a standard ℓ_2-regularized least squares problem and the solution is:

$$\boldsymbol{v}_n^{(p)} = \left(\tilde{\mathbf{U}}_p^T\tilde{\mathbf{U}}_p + \lambda_2\mathbf{I}\right)^{-1}\tilde{\mathbf{U}}_p^T\boldsymbol{d}_n^{(p)}.$$

Algorithm 4 shows the procedure.

4.2 Time Complexity

The formulation of learning in GRLSI is decomposable and thus can be processed in parallel. Specifically, the **for**-loops in Algorithm 2 (i.e., line 3 to line 11), Algorithm 3 (i.e., line 3 to line 11), and Algorithm 4 (i.e., line 3 to line 5) can be processed in parallel. In this paper, we implement GRLSI as well as RLSI using multi-threaded programming and compare their time complexities. Table 2 shows the results, where Q is the number of threads, γ the topic sparsity, and AvgDL the average document length. For GRLSI, the "Update **U**" includes the update of $\mathbf{U}_0, \mathbf{U}_1, \cdots, \mathbf{U}_P$ and the "Update **V**" includes the update of $\mathbf{V}_1, \cdots, \mathbf{V}_P$. From the results, we can see that GRLSI is approximately P times faster than RLSI in terms of time complexity. Here we suppose that 1) the documents are evenly distributed to the P classes; 2) the number of class-specific topics in each class is similar to the number of shared topics; and 3) the topic sparsity of GRLSI is similar to the topic sparsity of RLSI.

4.3 Folding-in New Documents

Folding-in refers to the problem of computing representations of documents that were not contained in the original training collection. When a new document d, represented as $\boldsymbol{d} \in \mathbb{R}^M$ in the term space, is given, its representation in the topic space can be computed under two different conditions. First, if the class label of the document is given, denoted as y_d, we represent the document in the topic space as

$$\boldsymbol{v}_d = \arg\min_{\boldsymbol{v}} \|\boldsymbol{d} - \tilde{\mathbf{U}}_{y_d}\boldsymbol{v}\|_2^2 + \lambda_2\|\boldsymbol{v}\|_2^2. \quad (8)$$

Second, if the document label is unknown, we first define the error of classifying document d into class p as

$$\mathcal{E}\left(\boldsymbol{d}; \tilde{\mathbf{U}}_p\right) = \min_{\boldsymbol{v}} \left\|\boldsymbol{d} - \tilde{\mathbf{U}}_p\boldsymbol{v}\right\|_2^2 + \lambda_2 \|\boldsymbol{v}\|_2^2,$$

and predict the class label of document d by

$$y_d = \arg\min_p \mathcal{E}\left(\boldsymbol{d}; \tilde{\mathbf{U}}_p\right).$$

We then represent the document in the topic space with Eq. (8).

Algorithm 5 Group NMF

Require: $\mathbf{D}_1, \cdots, \mathbf{D}_P$

$\mathbf{U}_0 \leftarrow$ random matrix

for $p = 1 : P$ **do**

$\quad \mathbf{U}_p \leftarrow$ random matrix

$\quad \mathbf{V}_p \leftarrow$ random matrix

end for

repeat

$\quad \mathbf{U}_0 \leftarrow \mathbf{U}_0 * \frac{\sum_{p=1}^P \mathbf{D}_p\mathbf{H}_p^T}{\sum_{p=1}^P \mathbf{U}_0\mathbf{H}_p\mathbf{H}_p^T + \sum_{p=1}^P \mathbf{U}_p\mathbf{W}_p\mathbf{H}_p^T}$

$\quad$ **for** $p = 1 : P$ **do**

$\quad\quad \mathbf{U}_p \leftarrow \mathbf{U}_p * \frac{\mathbf{D}_p\mathbf{W}_p^T}{\mathbf{U}_p\mathbf{W}_p\mathbf{W}_p^T + \mathbf{U}_0\mathbf{H}_p\mathbf{W}_p^T}$

$\quad\quad \mathbf{V}_p \leftarrow \mathbf{V}_p * \frac{\tilde{\mathbf{U}}_p^T\mathbf{D}_p}{\tilde{\mathbf{U}}_p^T\tilde{\mathbf{U}}_p\mathbf{V}_p}$

$\quad$ **end for**

until convergence

return $\mathbf{U}_0, \mathbf{U}_1, \cdots, \mathbf{U}_P, \mathbf{V}_1, \cdots, \mathbf{V}_P$

5. GROUP NMF

Similarly we can define Group NMF (GNMF) by adopting the squared Euclidean distance to measure the approximation quality and employing the nonnegative constraints on shared topics, class-specific topics, and document representations, as in NMF [13, 14]. The optimization problem of GNMF is as follows:

$$\begin{aligned}
\min_{\left\{\boldsymbol{u}_k^{(0)}\right\}, \left\{\boldsymbol{u}_k^{(p)}\right\}, \left\{\boldsymbol{v}_n^{(p)}\right\}} \quad & \sum_{p=1}^{P}\sum_{n=1}^{N_p} \left\|\boldsymbol{d}_n^{(p)} - \tilde{\mathbf{U}}_p\boldsymbol{v}_n^{(p)}\right\|_2^2 \\
s.t. \quad & \boldsymbol{u}_k^{(0)} \geq 0, \quad k = 1, \cdots, K_s, \\
& \boldsymbol{u}_k^{(p)} \geq 0, \quad k = 1, \cdots, K_c, p = 1, \cdots, P, \\
& \boldsymbol{v}_n^{(p)} \geq 0, \quad n = 1, \cdots, N_p, p = 1, \cdots, P, \quad (9)
\end{aligned}$$

which decomposes the large-scale matrix operations in NMF into multiple small-scale ones and thus can be solved more efficiently.

5.1 Optimization

Optimization Eq. (9) is convex with respect to one of the variables $\mathbf{U}_0, \mathbf{U}_1, \cdots, \mathbf{U}_P, V_1, \cdots, \mathbf{V}_P$ while keeping the others fixed. We again sequentially minimize the objective function with respect to shared topics $\mathbf{U}_0$, class-specific topics $\mathbf{U}_1, \cdots, \mathbf{U}_P$, and document representations $V_1, \cdots, \mathbf{V}_P$. The procedure is summarized in Algorithm 5, where the operator "$*$" represents the entry-wise multiplication, and the division is also entry-wise.

The multiplicative update rules in Algorithm 5 were first proposed in [16] and then applied in [25]. However, neither [16] nor [25] gave sufficient evidence to demonstrate the correctness of them. Here, we theoretically justify Algorithm 5, showing that the objective in Eq. (9) is nonincreasing under the update rules in Algorithm 5. We first proof Proposition 1.

PROPOSITION 1. *Given* $\mathbf{X}, \mathbf{Y} \in \mathbb{R}_+^{M\times N}$ *and* $\mathbf{S} \in \mathbb{R}_+^{K\times N}$*, consider optimization problem* $\min_{\mathbf{A}\geq 0} \|\mathbf{X} - \mathbf{Y} - \mathbf{AS}\|_F^2$*. The objective is nonincreasing under the update rule*

$$\mathbf{A} \leftarrow \mathbf{A} * \frac{\mathbf{XS}^T}{\mathbf{ASS}^T + \mathbf{YS}^T},$$

where the operator "$*$" represents the entry-wise multiplication, and the division is also entry-wise.

A proof sketch of the proposition can be found in Appendix.

5.1.1 Update of Matrix $\mathbf{U}_0$

Holding $\mathbf{U}_1, \cdots, \mathbf{U}_P, \mathbf{V}_1, \cdots, \mathbf{V}_P$ fixed, the update of $\mathbf{U}_0$ amounts to the following minimization problem:

$$\min_{\mathbf{U}_0\geq 0} \sum_{p=1}^{P} \left\|\mathbf{D}_p - \mathbf{U}_0\mathbf{H}_p - \mathbf{U}_p\mathbf{W}_p\right\|_F^2,$$

which can be rewritten as

$$\min_{\mathbf{U}_0\geq 0} \|\mathbf{E} - \mathbf{F} - \mathbf{U}_0\mathbf{H}\|_F^2,$$

where $\mathbf{E}$, $\mathbf{F}$, and $\mathbf{H}$ are respectively defined as $\mathbf{E} = [\mathbf{D}_1, \cdots, \mathbf{D}_P]$, $\mathbf{F} = [\mathbf{U}_1\mathbf{W}_1, \cdots, \mathbf{U}_P\mathbf{W}_P]$, and $\mathbf{H} = [\mathbf{H}_1, \cdots, \mathbf{H}_P]$. It is easy to show that the objective is nonincreasing under the update rule

$$\mathbf{U}_0 \leftarrow \mathbf{U}_0 * \frac{\sum_{p=1}^{P} \mathbf{D}_p\mathbf{H}_p^T}{\sum_{p=1}^{P} \mathbf{U}_0\mathbf{H}_p\mathbf{H}_p^T + \sum_{p=1}^{P} \mathbf{U}_p\mathbf{W}_p\mathbf{H}_p^T},$$

according to Proposition 1.

5.1.2 Update of Matrix $\mathbf{U}_p$

Holding the other variables fixed, the update of $\mathbf{U}_p$ amounts to the following optimization problem:

$$\min_{\mathbf{U}_p\geq 0} \left\|\mathbf{D}_p - \mathbf{U}_0\mathbf{H}_p - \mathbf{U}_p\mathbf{W}_p\right\|_F^2.$$

According to Proposition 1 we get the multiplicative update rule:

$$\mathbf{U}_p \leftarrow \mathbf{U}_p * \frac{\mathbf{D}_p\mathbf{W}_p^T}{\mathbf{U}_p\mathbf{W}_p\mathbf{W}_p^T + \mathbf{U}_0\mathbf{H}_p\mathbf{W}_p^T},$$

which keeps the objective nonincreasing.

5.1.3 Update of Matrix $\mathbf{V}_p$

The update of $\mathbf{V}_p$ with the other variables fixed amounts to the following optimization problem:

$$\min_{\mathbf{V}_p\geq 0} \left\|\mathbf{D}_p - \tilde{\mathbf{U}}_p\mathbf{V}_p\right\|_F^2.$$

As demonstrated in [14], $\mathbf{V}_p$ can be updated with the following update rule:

$$\mathbf{V}_p \leftarrow \mathbf{V}_p * \frac{\tilde{\mathbf{U}}_p^T\mathbf{D}_p}{\tilde{\mathbf{U}}_p^T\tilde{\mathbf{U}}_p\mathbf{V}_p},$$

which keeps the objective nonincreasing.

5.2 Time Complexity

The multiplicative update rules of GNMF (i.e., line 7, line 9, and line 10 in Algorithm 5) can be processed in parallel since the multiplication and division are both entry-wise. In this paper, we implement GNMF as well as NMF using multithreaded programming and compare their time complexities. Table 3 shows the results, where Q is the number of threads and AvgDL is the average document length. For GNMF, the "Update $\mathbf{U}$" includes the update of $\mathbf{U}_0, \mathbf{U}_1, \cdots, \mathbf{U}_P$ and the "Update $\mathbf{V}$" includes the update of $\mathbf{V}_1, \cdots, \mathbf{V}_P$. From the results, we can see that GNMF are approximately P times faster than NMF in terms of time complexity. Here we also make the same assumptions as in Section 4.2.

Table 3: Time complexity (per iteration) of NMF and GNMF.

	NMF	GNMF
Update $\mathbf{U}$	$\frac{\text{AvgDL}\times KN+K^2M+K^2N}{Q}$	$\frac{\text{AvgDL}\times KN+K^2M+\frac{K^2N}{P}}{PQ}$
Update $\mathbf{V}$	$\frac{\text{AvgDL}\times KN+K^2M+K^2N}{Q}$	$\frac{\text{AvgDL}\times KN+K^2M+\frac{K^2N}{P}}{PQ}$

5.3 Folding-in New Documents

Given a new document $\boldsymbol{d} \in \mathbb{R}^M$, its representation in the topic space can be computed under two different conditions. First, if the class label y_d is also given, we can represent the document in the topic space as

$$\boldsymbol{v}_d = \arg\min_{\boldsymbol{v}\geq 0} \|\boldsymbol{d} - \tilde{\mathbf{U}}_{y_d}\boldsymbol{v}\|_2^2. \tag{10}$$

Second, if the document label is unknown, we first define the error of classifying document d into class p as

$$\mathcal{E}\left(\boldsymbol{d}; \tilde{\mathbf{U}}_p\right) = \min_{\boldsymbol{v}\geq 0} \left\|\boldsymbol{d} - \tilde{\mathbf{U}}_p\boldsymbol{v}\right\|_2^2,$$

and predict the class label of document d by

$$y_d = \arg\min_p \mathcal{E}\left(\boldsymbol{d}; \tilde{\mathbf{U}}_p\right).$$

We then represent the document in the topic space with Eq. (10).

6. RELEVANCE RANKING

Topic modeling can be used in a wide variety of applications. We apply GRLSI and GNMF to relevance ranking in search and evaluate their performances in comparison to RLSI and NMF respectively. The use of topic modeling techniques such as LSI was proposed in IR many years ago [7]. Two recent works [27, 26] demonstrated that improvements on relevance ranking can be achieved by using topic modeling.

The motivation of incorporating topic modeling into relevance ranking is to reduce "term mismatch". Traditional relevance models, such as VSM [24] and BM25 [23], are all based on term matching. The term mismatch problem arises when the author of a document and the user of a search system use different terms to describe the same concept, and in such a case the search may not be carried out successfully. For example, if the query contains the term "airplane" but the document contains the term "aircraft", then there is a mismatch and the document may not be viewed as relevant. In the topic space, however, it is very likely that the two terms are in the same topic, and thus the use of matching score in the topic space may help improve the relevance ranking. In practice it is beneficial to combine topic matching scores with term matching scores, to leverage both broad topic matching and specific term matching.

A general way of using topic models in IR is as follows. Suppose that there is a pre-learned topic model. Given a query q and a document d, we first represent them in the topic space as $\boldsymbol{v}_q$ and $\boldsymbol{v}_d$ respectively. Then we calculate the matching score between the query and the document in the topic space as the cosine similarity between $\boldsymbol{v}_q$ and $\boldsymbol{v}_d$. The topic matching score $s_{topic}(q, d)$ is then linearly combined with the term matching score $s_{term}(q, d)$ for final relevance ranking. The final relevance ranking score $s(q, d)$ is calculated as:

$$s(q, d) = \alpha s_{topic}(q, d) + (1 - \alpha)s_{term}(q, d), \tag{11}$$

Table 4: Sizes of Wikipedia and Web-I.

Dataset	# terms	# documents	# classes
Wikipedia	610,035	2,807,535	25
Web-I	530,905	3,184,138	204

Table 5: Statistics of Wikipedia and Web-I.

Dataset	Min	Max	R	Mean	STD	CV
Wikipedia	185	991,695	991,510	112301.4	200123.6	1.8
Web-I	226	29,999	29,773	15608.5	11152.0	0.7

where $\alpha \in [0, 1]$ is the coefficient. $s_{term}(q, d)$ can be calculated with any existing term-based model, for example, VSM and BM25.

7. EXPERIMENTS

We have conducted experiments to test the efficiency and effectiveness of GRLSI and GNMF.

7.1 Experimental Settings

We tested the efficiency and effectiveness of GRLSI and GNMF on two datasets[5]: Wikipedia dataset which consists of articles downloaded from the English version of Wikipedia and Web-I dataset which consists of webpages randomly sampled from a crawl of the Internet at a commercial search engine. The Wikipedia dataset contains 2,807,535 articles and the Web-I dataset contains 3,184,138 web documents. For both datasets, the titles and bodies were taken as the contents of the documents. Stop words in a standard list and terms whose total frequencies are less than 10 were removed. Table 4 lists the sizes of Wikipedia and Web-I datasets.

In the Wikipedia dataset, documents are associated with labels representing the categories of them. We adopted the 25 first-level categories in the Wikipedia hierarchy, i.e., each Wikipedia document is categorized into one of the 25 categories. The categories include "agriculture", "arts", "business", "education", "law", etc. In the Web-I dataset, similarly, all documents are categorized into one of the ODP categories by a built-in classifier at the search engine. There are 204 categories from the second-level ODP categories, including "arts/music", "business/management", "computer/graphics", "science/chemistry", "sports/baseball", etc. Table 5 gives the statistics of both Wikipedia and Web-I, where Min and Max stand for the minimal and maximal class sizes respectively, R is the range of class sizes, i.e., R = Max − Min, Mean and STD represent the mean value and the standard deviation of class sizes respectively, and CV is the coefficient of variance, i.e., CV = STD/Mean. One can see that Web-I has smaller R and CV values, indicating that it has a smaller degree of dispersion in the distribution of class sizes. From the table, we can see that although these two datasets have similar data sizes, the granularities of classes, i.e., number of classes and average number of documents per class, are very different.

We tested RLSI, NMF, GRLSI and GNMF on the Wikipedia dataset and Web-I dataset under different parameter settings. We used single machine implementations of the methods. Specifically, for the Wikipedia dataset, we set the number of class-specific topics per class and the number of shared topics in GRLSI and GNMF as $(K_s, K_c) = (10, 4)/(20, 8)/(50, 20)/(100, 40)$, resulting in $K = 110/220/550/1100$ total number of topics. (Note that the total number of topics in GRLSI and GNMF is $K_s + 25 \times K_c$, where 25 is the number of classes in the Wikipedia dataset.) We set the number of topics in RLSI and NMF as 110/220/550/1100 for fair comparison. For the Web-I dataset, we decided the number of class-specific topics per class and the number of shared topics in GRLSI and GNMF as $(K_s, K_c) = (10, 5)/(20, 10)/(40, 20)/(100, 50)$, resulting in $K = 1030/2060/4120/10300$ as the total number of topics. (The total number of topics in GRLSI and GNMF is $K_s + 204 \times K_c$, where 204 is the number of classes in the Web-I dataset.) As will be explained later, we found that it is not possible to run RLSI and NMF with such large numbers of topics on a single machine. Thus, we determined the number of topics in RLSI and NMF as 100/200/500/1000. Parameter λ_1 in GRLSI and RLSI, which controls the sparsity of topics, was selected from 0.01/0.02/0.05/0.1, for both datasets. Parameter λ_2 in GRLSI and RLSI was fixed to 0.1, following the experimental results in [26].

[5]We plan to release the two datasets to the research communities.

Table 6: Execution time (per iteration) of RLSI on Wikipedia.

Min.	$K = 110$	$K = 220$	$K = 550$	$K = 1100$
$\lambda_1 = 0.01$	19.49	44.13	110.35	342.59
$\lambda_1 = 0.02$	19.02	43.64	93.47	332.33
$\lambda_1 = 0.05$	16.73	34.63	90.45	318.27
$\lambda_1 = 0.1$	14.91	27.26	89.92	307.67

Table 7: Execution time (per iteration) of GRLSI on Wikipedia.

Min.	$K = 110$	$K = 220$	$K = 550$	$K = 1100$
$\lambda_1 = 0.01$	14.99	23.27	51.95	106.13
$\lambda_1 = 0.02$	14.01	22.88	50.17	104.13
$\lambda_1 = 0.05$	13.95	22.68	48.25	99.03
$\lambda_1 = 0.1$	14.05	22.47	48.07	97.13

We also conducted search relevance experiments to test the effectiveness of GRLSI and GNMF on another dataset, the Web-II dataset, which is obtained from the same web search engine. The dataset consists of 752,365 documents, 30,000 queries, and relevance judgments on the documents with respect to the queries. The relevance judgments are at five levels: "perfect", "excellent", "good", "fair", and "bad". There are in total 837,717 judged query-document pairs. The documents in Web-II are classified into 204 ODP categories with the same classifier as in Web-I. We randomly split the queries into validation/test sets, each has 15,000/15,000 queries. We used the validation set for parameter tuning and the test set for evaluation. We adopted MAP and NDCG at the positions of 1, 3, 5, and 10 as evaluation measures for relevance ranking. When calculating MAP, we considered "perfect", "excellent", and "good" as "relevant", and the other two as "irrelevant".

All of the experiments were conducted on a server with AMD Opteron 2.10GHz multi-core processor (2×12 cores), 96GB RAM. All the methods were implemented using C# multithreaded programming, with the thread number being 24.

7.2 Experiment 1

In this experiment, we evaluated the efficiency improvement of GRLSI and GNMF over RLSI and NMF on the Wikipedia dataset and the Web-I dataset. We ran all the methods in 100 iterations. For each method, the average execution time per iteration was recorded.

Table 6 and Table 7 report the average execution time per iteration for RLSI and GRLSI on Wikipedia, under different settings of topic numbers and λ_1 values. Figure 2 further shows average time per iteration of GRLSI and RLSI versus numbers of topics when $\lambda_1 = 0.01$. Figure 3 shows the average time per iteration of GNMF over NMF on Wikipedia, versus numbers of topics. From these results, we can conclude that GRLSI and GNMF consistently outperform RLSI and NMF, respectively, in terms of efficiency. More speedup can be achieved when total number of topics increases.

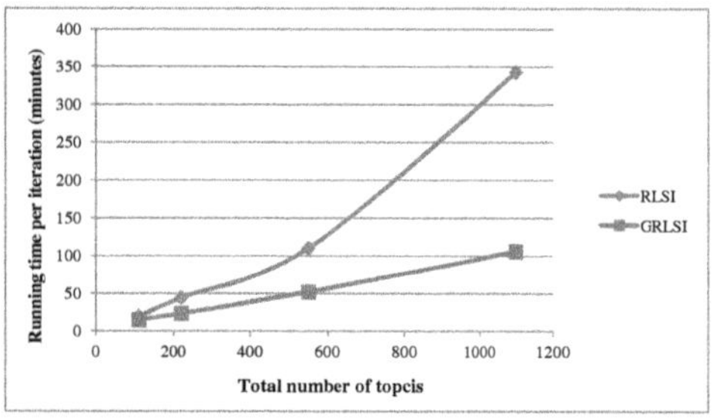

Figure 2: Execution time of RLSI and GRLSI on Wikipedia.

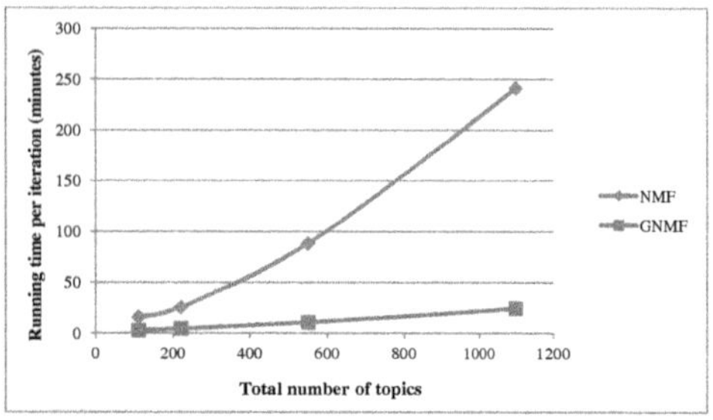

Figure 3: Execution time of NMF and GNMF on Wikipedia.

The results indicate that GRLSI and GNMF are superior to RLSI and NMF in terms of efficiency.

Table 8 and Table 9 report the average execution time per iteration for RLSI and GRLSI on Web-I with respect to different settings of topic numbers and λ_1 values. Figure 4 shows the average execution time per iteration of GRLSI and RLSI when λ_1 equals 0.01. Figure 5 shows the results of GNMF and NMF. In fact we were not able to run RLSI and NMF on the single machine, when the number of topics is larger than 1,000. The results indicate that GRLSI and GNMF have better efficiency and scalability, particularly when the number of topics gets large.

From the experimental results reported above, we can conclude that applying GMF to non-probabilistic methods of RLSI and NMF can significantly improve the efficiency and scalability of them. The proposed GRLSI and GNMF methods can handle much larger numbers of topics and much larger datasets.

Next, we evaluated the effectiveness of GRLSI and GNMF by checking the readability of the topics generated by them. As example, we show the topics generated by GRLSI and GNMF in the setting of $(K_s = 20, K_c = 8(10), \lambda_1 = 0.01, \lambda_2 = 0.1)$ for both Wikipedia and Web-I. Table 10 and Table 11 present example topics randomly selected from the topics discovered by GRLSI and GNMF on Wikipedia and Web-I. For each of the datasets and each of the methods, 3 shared topics and 9 class-specific topics are presented. The corresponding class labels are also shown for the class-specific topics. Top 6 weighted terms are shown for each topic. From all the results (including the results in other parameter settings), we found that (1) GRLSI and GNMF can discover readable topics. Both of the shared topics and the class-specific topics are coherent and easy to understand. (2) For each class, GRLSI and GNMF can discover class-specific topics that characterize the class. (3) GRLSI discovers compact topics (the average topic compactness AvgComp = 0.0032 for Wikipedia topics and AvgComp = 0.0018 for Web-I topics) [6] as expected.

[6]Average topic compactness is defined as average ratio of terms with non-zero weights per topic.

Table 8: Execution time (per iteration) of RLSI on Web-I.

Min.	$K = 100$	$K = 200$	$K = 500$	$K = 1000$
$\lambda_1 = 0.01$	26.57	49.79	123.45	324.58
$\lambda_1 = 0.02$	26.79	39.24	117.54	313.49
$\lambda_1 = 0.05$	23.23	34.64	110.67	303.24
$\lambda_1 = 0.1$	14.19	32.68	100.25	301.74

Table 9: Execution time (per iteration) of GRLSI on Web-I.

Min.	$K = 1030$	$K = 2060$	$K = 4120$	$K = 10300$
$\lambda_1 = 0.01$	35.48	57.50	104.37	438.29
$\lambda_1 = 0.02$	35.30	55.60	99.46	427.22
$\lambda_1 = 0.05$	35.36	52.63	94.78	414.37
$\lambda_1 = 0.1$	34.86	50.44	92.15	409.25

We further evaluated the shared topics discovered from Wikipedia (Table 10) and Web-I (Table 11). In the Web-I dataset, the shared topics seem to characterize general information. In the Wikipedia dataset some of the shared topics are similar to the class-specific topics in category "geography". We checked the Wikipedia dataset and found that this is because more than one third of Wikipedia articles fall into category "geography", and some geography related topics appear to be general in the document collection.

From the experimental results reported above, we can conclude that applying GMF to non-probabilistic methods of RLSI and NMF can maintain the same level of readability while significantly improving the efficiency and scalability. The resulting methods of GRLSI and GNMF can really find coherent and meaningful topics. This is true for not only class-specific topics, but also shared topics.

7.3 Experiment 2

In this experiment, we tested the effectiveness of GRLSI and GNMF by using the topics generated by them with the Web-I dataset in search relevance ranking on the Web-II dataset[7]. Specifically, for GRLSI, we combined the topic matching scores with the term matching scores given by BM25, denoted as "BM25+GRLSI". We took RLSI and CRLSI as baselines, denoted as "BM25+RLSI" and "BM25+CRLSI", respectively. In the former an RLSI model is trained for the whole Web-I dataset and in the latter an RLSI model is trained for each class. Similarly, for GNMF, we combined the topic matching scores with the term matching scores by BM25, denoted as "BM25+GNMF". We took NMF and CNMF as baselines, denoted as "BM25+NMF" and "BM25+CNMF", respectively. In the former an NMF model is trained for the whole Web-I dataset and in the latter an NMF model is trained for each class.

GRLSI, RLSI, GNMF, and NMF were trained on Web-I dataset with the same parameter settings in Section 7.1. For CRLSI and CNMF, we also trained the models on Web-I dataset under the same parameter settings in Section 7.1, except parameter K_s, as there exists no shared topic in CRLSI and CNMF.

To evaluate the relevance performance of these topic models on Web-II, we took a heuristic method for relevance ranking. Given a query q and a document d (and its label y_d), the method assigns the query into the same class that the document belongs to, i.e., class y_d, and then calculates the matching score between the query and the document in the topic space using the techniques described above for GRLSI and CRLSI (also GNMF and CNMF). The method then ranks the documents based on their relevance scores. The relevance score of a document is calculated as a linear combination of the BM25 score and the topic matching score

[7]We did not try to use the topics generated with Wikipedia, because the categories are not consistent with the categories in Web-II.

Table 10: Topics discovered by GRLSI (top) and GNMF (bottom) on Wikipedia.

	Shared topics			Arts			Geography			Politics		
GRLSI	commune	state	political	album	rock	groups	province	municipality	communes	elections	states	kingdom
	communes	highways	party	albums	american	musical	state	municipalities	commune	election	congressional	political
	department	route	colour	singers	musicians	music	village	gmina	department	weapon	delegations	parties
	places	highway	india	musicians	singers	rappers	villages	voivodeship	france	party	elections	country
	france	india	canada	track	country	metal	highways	population	departments	parties	united	party
	populated	brazil	australia	listing	english	heavy	united	germany	places	political	senate	fascism
GNMF	places	new	language	album	groups	rappers	village	district	department	elections	war	military
	populated	york	japanese	albums	rock	musicians	villages	germany	commune	election	world	country
	village	city	films	track	american	american	england	districts	communes	results	poland	units
	azerbaijan	zealand	cast	listing	musical	singers	india	town	france	members	weapons	formations
	population	jersey	chinese	released	metal	singles	population	administrative	departments	parties	conflict	army
	municipality	routes	english	band	musicians	wiley	central	towns	home	held	union	infantry

Table 11: Topics discovered by GRLSI (top) and GNMF (bottom) on Web-I.

	Shared topics			Arts/literature			Business/healthcare			Computers/internet		
GRLSI	video	business	games	poems	harry	book	dental	healthcare	care	chat	facebook	web
	phone	services	game	poetry	potter	chapter	dentist	practice	medical	teen	people	hosting
	mobile	company	cheats	poem	books	summary	care	test	health	online	connect	design
	tv	service	xbox	poets	rowling	books	dentistry	management	equipment	people	sign	website
	cell	products	ign	love	series	analysis	dentists	exam	ppo	friends	web	domain
	phones	management	pc	poet	children	author	health	patient	supplies	join	password	internet
GNMF	www	products	day	poems	harry	books	dentist	healthcare	medical	google	facebook	design
	http	product	october	quotes	potter	children	dentists	management	equipment	maps	people	web
	org	quality	september	shakespear	rowling	read	dentistry	patient	supplies	blog	connect	website
	website	buy	july	william	series	reading	dr	hospital	surgical	gmail	sign	development
	net	accessories	june	poetry	deathly	list	dental	solutions	patient	map	friends	marketing
	html	store	august	poets	hallows	readers	cosmetic	nursing	hospital	engine	password	graphic

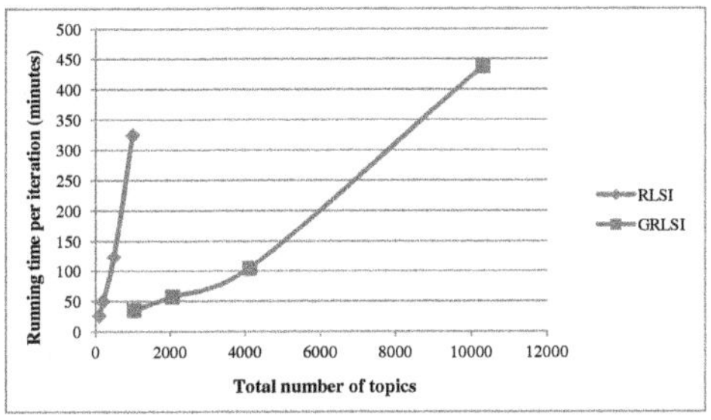

Figure 4: Execution time of RLSI and GRLSI on Web-I.

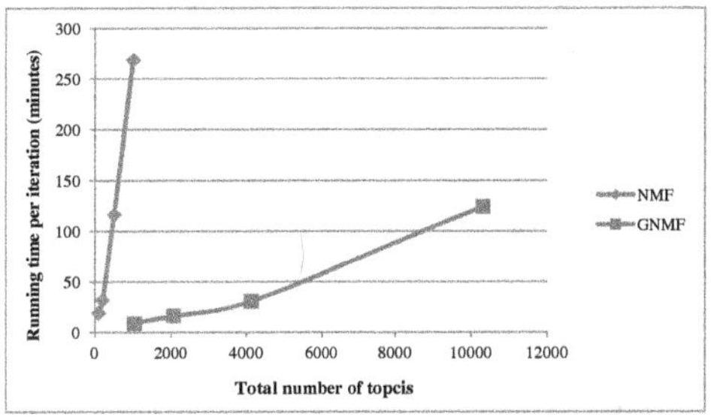

Figure 5: Execution time of NMF and GNMF on Web-I.

between the document and the query. For RLSI (also NMF), neither document labels nor query labels were needed. We directly calculated the matching score between a query and a document in the topic space using the techniques described in [26]. The trading-off parameter α in the linear combination was set from 0 to 1 in steps of 0.1 for all methods. The heuristic method of automatic assignment of a query into a class has the advantage of better efficiency in online prediction, given that usually the number of classes is large. Even though this is heuristic, our experimental results show that it is effective.

Table 12 and Table 13 show the retrieval performance of RLSI families and NMF families on the test set of Web-II respectively, obtained with the best parameter setting determined by the validation set. From the results, we can see that (1) all of these methods can *significantly* improve the baseline BM25 (t-test, p-value < 0.05). (2) GRLSI and GNMF perform *significantly* better than CRLSI and CNMF respectively (t-test, p-value < 0.05), indicating the effectiveness of Group Matrix Factorization, specifically, the use of shared topics. (3) GRLSI and GNMF perform slightly worse than RLSI and NMF, but they can achieve much higher efficiency and scalability, as described in Section 7.2. The decreases of accuracy by GRLSI and GNMF are very small, e.g., NDCG@1 drops only 0.0010 for GRLSI and 0.0011 for GNMF. (4) The NMF families perform better than the RLSI families. This is because we did not further tune the parameters for the RLSI families. The results in [26] show that with fine tuning RLSI can achieve high performances, and we anticipate that this is also the case for the other RLSI methods. We conclude that both GRLSI and GNMF are useful for relevance ranking with high accuracies.

8. CONCLUSIONS

In this paper, we have investigated the possibilities of further enhancing the scalability and efficiency of non-probabilistic topic modeling methods. We have proposed a general topic modeling technique, referred to as Group Matrix Factorization (GMF), which conducts topic modeling on the basis of existing classes of documents. Thus the learning of a large number of topics (i.e.,class-specific topics) can be performed in parallel. Although the strategy has been tried in computer vision, this is the first compre-

Table 12: Relevance performance of RLSI families on Web-II.

Method	MAP	NDCG@1	NDCG@3	NDCG@5	NDCG@10
BM25	0.3006	0.3043	0.3490	0.3910	0.4805
BM25+RLSI	0.3050	0.3076	0.3539	0.3943	0.4858
BM25+CRLSI	0.3027	0.3051	0.3509	0.3927	0.4840
BM25+GRLSI	0.3039	0.3066	0.3520	0.3934	0.4855

Table 13: Relevance performance of NMF families on Web-II.

Method	MAP	NDCG@1	NDCG@3	NDCG@5	NDCG@10
BM25	0.3006	0.3043	0.3490	0.3910	0.4805
BM25+NMF	0.3057	0.3091	0.3546	0.3960	0.4895
BM25+CNMF	0.3033	0.3055	0.3512	0.3934	0.4869
BM25+GNMF	0.3046	0.3080	0.3530	0.3955	0.4887

hensive study of it on text data, as far as we know. The GMF technique can be further specified in individual non-probabilistic methods. We have applied GMF to RLSI and NMF, obtaining Group RLSI (GRLSI) and Group NMF (GNMF), and theoretically demonstrated that GRLSI and GNMF are much more efficient and scalable than RLSI and NMF in terms of time complexity.

We have conducted experiments on two large datasets to test the performances of GRLSI and GNMF. Both datasets contain about 3 million documents. Experimental results show that GRLSI and GNMF are much faster and scalable than existing methods such as RLSI and NMF, especially when the number of topics is large. We have also verified that GMF can discover meaningful topics and the topics can be used to improve search relevance. As future work, we plan to implement GMF on distributed systems and perform experiments on even larger datasets.

9. REFERENCES

[1] S. Bengio, F. Pereira, and Y. Singer. Group sparse coding. In *NIPS*, pages 82–89, 2009.

[2] P. N. Bennett, K. M. Svore, and S. T. Dumais. Classification-enhanced ranking. In *WWW*, pages 111–120, 2010.

[3] D. Blei. Introduction to probabilistic topic models. *COMMUN ACM*, to appear, 2011.

[4] D. Blei and J. McAuliffe. Supervised topic models. In *NIPS*, pages 121–128, 2008.

[5] D. Blei, A. Y. Ng, and M. I. Jordan. Latent dirichlet allocation. *JMLR*, 3:993–1022, 2003.

[6] S. S. Chen, D. L. Donoho, and M. A. Saunders. Atomic decomposition by basis pursuit. *SISC*, 20:33–61, 1998.

[7] S. Deerwester, S. T. Dumais, G. W. Furnas, T. K. Landauer, and R. Harshman. Indexing by latent semantic analysis. *J AM SOC INFORM SCI*, 41:391–407, 1990.

[8] B. Efron, T. Hastie, I. Johnstone, and R. Tibshirani. Least angle regression. *ANN STAT*, 32:407–499, 2004.

[9] J. Friedman, T. Hastie, H. Hofling, and R. Tibshirani. Pathwise coordinate optimization. *ANN APPL STAT*, 1:302–332, 2007.

[10] W. J. Fu. Penalized regressions: The bridge versus the lasso. *J COMPUT GRAPH STAT*, 7:397–416, 1998.

[11] T. Hofmann. Probabilistic latent semantic indexing. In *SIGIR*, pages 50–57, 1999.

[12] S. Lacoste-Julien, F. Sha, and M. I. Jordan. Disclda: Discriminative learning for dimensionality reduction and classification. In *NIPS*, pages 897–904, 2008.

[13] D. D. Lee and H. S. Seung. Learning the parts of objects with nonnegative matrix factorization. *Nature*, 401:391–407, 1999.

[14] D. D. Lee and H. S. Seung. Algorithms for non-negative matrix factorization. In *NIPS 13*, pages 556–562. 2001.

[15] H. Lee, A. Battle, R. Raina, and A. Y. Ng. Efficient sparse coding algorithms. In *NIPS*, pages 801–808. 2007.

[16] H. Lee and S. Choi. Group nonnegative matrix factorization for eeg classification. In *AISTATS*, pages 320–327, 2009.

[17] J. Mairal, F. Bach, J. Ponce, G. Sapiro, and A. Zisserman. Discriminative learned dictionaries for local image analysis. In *CVPR*, 2008.

[18] J. Mairal, F. Bach, J. Ponce, G. Sapiro, and A. Zisserman. Supervised dictionary learning. In *NIPS*, pages 1033–1040. 2009.

[19] D. M. Mimno and McCallum. Organizing the oca: Learning faceted subjects from a library of digital books. In *JCDL*, pages 376–385, 2007.

[20] B. A. Olshausen and D. J. Fieldt. Sparse coding with an overcomplete basis set: a strategy employed by v1. *VISION RES*, 37:3311–3325, 1997.

[21] M. Osborne, B. Presnell, and B. Turlach. A new approach to variable selection in least squares problems. *IMA J NUMER ANAL*, 2000.

[22] D. Ramage, C. D. Manning, and S. Dumais. Partially labeled topic models for interpretable text mining. In *SIGKDD*, pages 457–465, 2011.

[23] S. E. Robertson, S. Walker, S. Jones, M. Hancock-Beaulieu, and M. Gatford. Okapi at trec-3. In *TREC'3*, 1994.

[24] G. Salton, A. Wong, and C. S. Yang. A vector space model for automatic indexing. *Commun. ACM*, 18:613–620, 1975.

[25] F. Wang, N. Lee, J. Sun, J. Hu, and S. Ebadollahi. Automatic group sparse coding. In *AAAI*, pages 495–500, 2011.

[26] Q. Wang, J. Xu, H. Li, and N. Craswell. Regularized latent semantic indexing. In *SIGIR*, pages 685–694, 2011.

[27] X. Wei and B. W. Croft. Lda-based document models for ad-hoc retrieval. In *SIGIR*, pages 178–185, 2006.

[28] C. Zhai, A. Velivelli, and B. Yu. A crosscollection mixture model for comparative text mining. In *SIGKDD*, pages 743–748, 2004.

Appendix

Proof sketch of Proposition 1. The proof will follow closely the proof given in [14] for the case $\mathbf{Y} = \mathbf{0}$. First note that the objective is decomposable in the rows of $\mathbf{A}$. Considering the case of a single row, denoted as $\bar{\boldsymbol{a}}$, leads to the objective

$$F(\bar{\boldsymbol{a}}) = \left\|\bar{\boldsymbol{x}} - \bar{\boldsymbol{y}} - \mathbf{S}^T\bar{\boldsymbol{a}}\right\|_2^2,$$

where $\bar{\boldsymbol{x}}$ and $\bar{\boldsymbol{y}}$ are the corresponding rows of $\mathbf{X}$ and $\mathbf{Y}$ respectively. Define the auxiliary function $G(\bar{\boldsymbol{a}}, \bar{\boldsymbol{a}}^t)$ as

$$G(\bar{\boldsymbol{a}}, \bar{\boldsymbol{a}}^t) = F(\bar{\boldsymbol{a}}) + (\bar{\boldsymbol{a}} - \bar{\boldsymbol{a}}^t)^T \nabla_{\bar{a}} F(\bar{\boldsymbol{a}}^t) + (\bar{\boldsymbol{a}} - \bar{\boldsymbol{a}}^t)^T \boldsymbol{\Omega}(\bar{\boldsymbol{a}}^t)(\bar{\boldsymbol{a}} - \bar{\boldsymbol{a}}^t),$$

where $\boldsymbol{\Omega}(\bar{\boldsymbol{a}}^t)$ is a diagonal matrix defined as

$$\omega_{ij}^t = \delta_{ij}\frac{\left(\mathbf{S}\mathbf{S}^T\bar{\boldsymbol{a}}^t\right)_i + (\mathbf{S}\bar{\boldsymbol{y}})_i}{(\bar{\boldsymbol{a}}^t)_i}.$$

Here, δ_{ij} is equal to 1 if $i = j$ and 0 otherwise. Then the update rule can be derived using the methods in [14]. □

Detecting Quilted Web Pages at Scale

Marc Najork
Microsoft Research
1065 La Avenida
Mountain View, CA 94043, USA
najork@microsoft.com

ABSTRACT

Web-based advertising and electronic commerce, combined with the key role of search engines in driving visitors to ad-monetized and e-commerce web sites, has given rise to the phenomenon of web spam: web pages that are of little value to visitors, but that are created mainly to mislead search engines into driving traffic to target web sites. A large fraction of spam web pages is automatically generated, and some portion of these pages is generated by stitching together parts (sentences or paragraphs) of other web pages. This paper presents a scalable algorithm for detecting such "quilted" web pages. Previous work by the author and his collaborators introduced a sampling-based algorithm that was capable of detecting some, but by far not all quilted web pages in a collection. By contrast, the algorithm presented in this work identifies all quilted web pages, and it is scalable to very large corpora. We tested the algorithm on the half-billion page English-language subset of the ClueWeb09 collection, and evaluated its effectiveness in detecting web spam by manually inspecting small samples of the detected quilted pages. This manual inspection guided us in iteratively refining the algorithm to be more efficient in detecting real-world spam.

Categories and Subject Descriptors

H.3.3 [**Information Search and Retrieval**]: Clustering, Information Filtering

General Terms

Algorithm, Experimentation, Measurement

Keywords

Web spam detection, phrase-level duplication, scalable algorithms

Permission to make digital or hard copies of all or part of this work for personal or classroom use is granted without fee provided that copies are not made or distributed for profit or commercial advantage and that copies bear this notice and the full citation on the first page. To copy otherwise, to republish, to post on servers or to redistribute to lists, requires prior specific permission and/or a fee.
SIGIR'12, August 12–16, 2012, Portland, Oregon, USA.
Copyright 2012 ACM 978-1-4503-1472-5/12/08 ...$10.00.

1. INTRODUCTION

Over the past 20 years, the World Wide Web has evolved from a way for scientists to exchange data and ideas to become the general population's medium of choice for information, communication, entertainment, and commercial transactions. Web-mediated electronic commerce in the United States is projected to reach close to $ 200 billion in 2011 [1]. Search engines such as Google and Bing form a key component of this web-based ecosystem, in that they enable users to locate content and services. The explosive rise in the popularity of the web and the volume of e-commerce, together with the key role of search engines, has given rise to the phenomenon of web spam: web content that is of little value to users, but created mainly to drive search engine traffic to particular target sites. Web spam creates a negative experience for search users, lowering the utility they derive from the search service. Consequently, web spam detection is an active area of research, both in search engines and in academia.

A substantial fraction of spam web pages is automatically generated, and some of that content is constructed out of all or parts of other web pages. In this paper, we introduce a technique for detecting all such web pages in a given collection, exhaustively and at large scale, using data-parallel infrastructure. We coin the term *quilted web page* to refer to a page that is "stitched" together out of "patches" taken from multiple other web pages. Figure 1 shows an example of such a quilted page (though arguably not spammy in nature) together with three of the source web pages that each donated a patch of words. The notion of quilted web page is congruent with our an earlier notion of *phrase-level replication* [9], but more constrained than the notion of *local text reuse* [15] introduced by Seo and Croft, which refers to portions of text shared between two documents, but does not insist on a large fraction of a document consisting of patches of multiple other documents.

The notion of textual similarity is at the heart of Information Retrieval, and there is a wide gamut of similarity-based problems, ranging from the retrieval problem (finding those documents in a collection that contain the – typically few – terms of a query) over local text reuse detection to the other extreme of near-duplicate detection (clustering a collection into classes of highly similar documents). The problem addressed in this paper is situated in the middle of the gamut (along with local text reuse detection), but it borrows ideas from the extreme end of the gamut, namely near-duplicate detection, and in particular *shingling*.

Figure 1: At the top left, a quilted web page, and around it, three of its source web pages.

The core idea of the seminal *shingling algorithm*, due to Broder *et al.*, is to segment each document into overlapping k-grams called *shingles* (drawing on the image of the overlapping shingles of a roof), to compact the shingles by hashing them, and to draw a consistent sample from the set of hashed shingles. In an early version of the algorithm [6], this was achieved by retaining all hash values h of a document where $h \bmod p = 0$ (with p fixed in advance), resulting in a variable-length vector of *shingleprints.* A refined version [5] employed randomly selected permutations and retained for each document those hash values that are minimal among all the document's hashes under a permutation, resulting in a fixed-sized shingleprint. Either scheme greatly reduces the amount of data required to represent each document, but neither addresses the time-complexity issues of document clustering, naive pair-wise comparison having quadratic complexity. A subsequent refinement (see [8] for a detailed description) combines groups of shingles into *megashingles* such that any two documents sharing a megashingle are with high probability near-duplicates of one another, thereby making it possible to cluster a set of documents into near-duplicate sets in linear time. Shingling is a purely *syntactic* technique; it does not presume any knowledge of the semantics of the document, and does not involve any language models. A competing approach to shingling, Charikar's locality-sensitive hashing scheme [7], is similarly syntactic in nature: Documents are tokenized through some extraneous mechanism (e.g. simple word-breaking or segmentation into overlapping k-grams), resulting in feature vectors that are viewed as points in a very high-dimensional space. A set of k hyperplanes in that high-dimensional space is fixed ahead of time. The algorithm determines for each point (document) and each hyperplane, what side of the hyperplane the point falls on, producing a bit per hyperplane and resulting in a k-bit hash value. Near-duplicate documents have, with high probability, highly similar hash values. The interested reader is referred to Henzinger's experimental comparison [10] of Broder's and Charikar's algorithms. Like these two algorithms, the algorithm described in this paper is purely syntactic. Moreover, it uses Broder's idea of segmenting each document into a sequence of overlapping k-grams.

There are multiple works addressing the middle portion of the gamut, detecting phrase-level replication. Fetterly, Manasse and Najork [9] attacked the problem by using core ideas of shingling – segmenting each document into overlapping k-grams and then performing a sequence of data reduction steps: hashing k-grams, collapsing near-duplicate documents (through shingling proper), eliminating popular k-grams, sampling the hashed k-grams of each document, and finally constructing sets of documents covering the surviving hashes of each document. Due to the sampling-based approach, their algorithm identifies some, but by no means all of the quilted pages in a collection, and some but not all of the "patch sources" of each quilted page. The algorithm described in this paper resembles our earlier attempt in many ways, but it is not probabilistic: given a collection, it will identify *all* quilted pages and *all* their source pages.

Baeza-Yates, Pereira and Ziviani [2] attacked the related problem of constructing a genealogical tree of web pages – deducing which web pages are derived from which other web pages – by segmenting pages into three-sentence shingles (as opposed to the more common work-level shingling), collapsing duplicate documents in a pre-processing stage, and finally deducing parent-child relationships between pages using a greedy algorithm. Their work is similar to ours in that it is not sampling-based, but differs in the choice of fingerprinting unit (three-sentence units vs. k-word units), the corpus size it was applied to (14 million vs. 503 million pages), and the underlying motivation.

Seo and Croft [15] describe an algorithm for detecting *local text reuse*, a document containing a patch of text taken from another document. Their algorithm (like both our earlier [9] and our current algorithm) is purely syntactic; documents are viewed as simple sequences of terms. It segments each document into non-overlapping sequences of terms using a technique called *hash-breaking*, and uses another technique called DCT (discrete-cosine transform) fingerprinting to make the algorithm less sensitive to small modifications of text. The algorithm outputs pairs of documents sharing a patch of text; unlike our algorithm it is not aimed at identifying quilted documents incorporating portions from multiple sources. Seo and Croft evaluated their algorithm empirically, and found precision and recall of text reuse to be good. It is difficult to ascertain the scalability of their approach. Their largest experiment processed a corpus of about 3 million blog posts; by comparison, the algorithm proposed in this paper was tested on a collection of over half a billion web pages.

More recently, Bendersky and Croft took [3] took another stab at the problem of detecting text reuse. Their approach is aimed at finding reuse in web-scale collections, and it assumes the existence of a retrieval system for that collection (say, a search engine). The algorithm does not aim to detect all instances of text reuse; rather, it takes a set of topical statements as input and aims to find all instances of text reuse related to these topics (leveraging the search engine to retrieve candidate documents for each topic). Another important difference to the previously described approaches is that theirs is not purely syntactic – it does involve language models, query likelihoods, and temporal information.

Another related line of work is that of Kolak and Schilit, who studied the problem of identifying quotations (short pieces of text excerpted from other documents) in a large collection of documents, namely the Google Books corpus. The underlying objective was to treat quotations as a form of "link" from the quoting to the quoted document. Like our past and present work, their algorithm borrows key ideas from shingling: documents are segmented into overlapping k-grams which are then hashed (core ideas of shingling), and hashes are added to an index to build up a collection of repeated text sequences. Their algorithm has been implemented in the MapReduce framework and appears to be highly scalable. While Kolak and Schilit's algorithm has many commonalities with the algorithm described in this paper, the two algorithms do compute different things: their algorithm identifies quotations (portions of text shared between documents) while ours identifies quilted web pages (web pages that consist largely of portions of other web pages).

Finally, it is worth pointing out that the problem of identifying quilted web pages is quite similar to that of identifying plagiarism. There exists a large body of work on plagiarism detection; two exemplary systems include COPS [4] and SCAM [16]. The interested reader is further referred to a study by Hoad and Zobel [11] comparing the effectiveness of various algorithmic approaches to plagiarism detection.

The remainder of the paper is structured as follows: Section 2 introduces a new algorithm for detecting quilted web pages, first by providing an intuitive explanation, then by framing the algorithm in a set-theoretic setting, and finally by sketching its implementation in DryadLINQ [17], a platform for data-parallel cluster computing that leverages LINQ, Microsoft's "language-integrated query" extension to the C# programming language. LINQ is based on list comprehensions, which in turn are closely related to set comprehensions, making the leap from specification to implementation quite small. Section 3 describes the experimental validation of our algorithm. It provides details on the data set and the computational infrastructure used in this study, and describes the runs we performed. We measured the effectiveness of the quilt detection algorithm in identifying spam web pages by manually inspecting a small sample of detected quilted pages (together with the source pages that provided the "patches" for each "quilt"). While (per definition) every detected page was indeed a quilt, only a small fraction of these pages was considered spam. Analyzing the nature of these false-positives guided us in refining our algorithm with several heuristics, which greatly reduced the rate of false positives. Finally, section 4 offers some concluding remarks and avenues for future research.

2. A SCALABLE QUILT DETECTION ALGORITHM

Our quilt detection algorithm takes a corpus of web pages as input, and outputs the set of all "quilted" web pages, together with the source web pages providing the textual "patches" that went into the quilt. Rather than considering only proper phrases as potential patches, we segment each n-word document into $n - k + 1$ overlapping k-grams. Discarding common k-grams that occur in more than m documents as well as unique ones that occur in only one document leaves us with a set of candidate *patch grams*. We consider a page to be *quilted* iff at least a θ fraction of its k-grams are patch grams, and if the minimum cover set of documents from which the patch grams are drawn contains at least c documents. So, our definition of quilted page involves the four parameters k, m, c and θ. The choice of these parameters impacts both the effectiveness (what fraction of quilted pages would be considered spam by human judges) and the efficiency (how long it takes to process the corpus) of the detection algorithm.

More formally, we consider a corpus D of documents (web pages). Each document $d \in D$ is a sequence of terms (words) $\langle t_1 \cdots t_n \rangle$, which can be grouped into $n-k+1$ overlapping k-grams, with $g_1 = \langle t_1 \cdots t_k \rangle$, $g_2 = \langle t_2 \cdots t_{k+1} \rangle$, etc. We write $grams_k(d)$ to denote the k-gram-set of document d, and $docs_k(g)$ to denote $\{d \in D : g \in grams_k(d)\}$, the set of documents containing k-gram g. We define the patch gram set of a document d (those k-grams of d that co-occur in at least one but fewer than m other documents) as follows:

$$pgrams_{k,m}(d) = \{g \in grams_k(d) : 1 < |docs_k(g)| \leq m\}$$

Obviously, $pgrams_{k,m}(d) \subseteq grams_k(d)$ for all d, k and m. We define the patch-fraction of a document d as the fraction of patch grams in the document's gram set:

$$patchfrac_{k,m}(d) = \frac{|pgrams_{k,m}(d)|}{|grams_k(d)|}$$

Moreover, we define $sources_{k,m}(d)$, the source documents contributing patch grams to a document d, as follows:

$$sources_{k,m}(d) = \text{minimal set } D' \subseteq D \text{ such that } pgrams_{k,m}(d) \subseteq \bigcup_{d' \in D'} pgrams_{k,m}(d')$$

In other words, $sources_{k,m}(d)$ is a (not necessarily unique) minimal set of documents whose combined patch grams cover all the patch grams of d. The set cover problem is NP-hard [12], but there is a well-known greedy approximation algorithm, detailed below. Using this notation, we define quilted web pages as follows:

Definition: A document d is said to be (k, m, c, θ)-*quilted* iff $patchfrac_{k,m}(d) \geq \theta$ and $|sources_{k,m}(d)| \geq c$.

Before describing the approximation algorithm for computing $sources_{k,m}(d)$, we first provide a few theorems concerning the role of the parameters in the definition of quiltedness:

Theorem 1 (Monotonicity in θ): A document that is (k, m, c, θ)-quilted is also (k, m, c, θ')-quilted for any $\theta' \leq \theta$.

Proof: Straightforward. For any document d, d is (k, m, c, θ)-quilted implies $|sources_{k,m}(d)| \geq c$ and $patchfrac_{k,m}(d) \geq \theta$, which implies $patchfrac_{k,m}(d) \geq \theta'$ since $\theta \geq \theta'$, which implies d is (k, m, c, θ')-quilted. □

Theorem 2 (Monotonicity in c): A document that is (k, m, c, θ)-quilted is also (k, m, c', θ)-quilted for any $c' \leq c$.

Proof: Straightforward. For any document d, d is (k, m, c, θ)-quilted implies $patchfrac_{k,m}(d) \geq \theta$ and $|sources_{k,m}(d)| \geq c$, which implies $|sources_{k,m}(d)| \geq c'$ since $c \geq c'$, which implies d is (k, m, c', θ)-quilted. □

Theorem 3 (Monotonicity in m): A document that is (k, m, c, θ)-quilted is also (k, m', c, θ)-quilted for any $m' \geq m$.

Proof: Assume $m' \geq m$, and consider a (k, m, c, θ)-quilted document d, so $patchfrac_{k,m}(d) \geq \theta$ and $|sources_{k,m}(d)| \geq c$. It is easy to see that $pgrams_{k,m'}(d) \supseteq pgrams_{k,m}(d)$, which implies that $patchfrac_{k,m'}(d) \geq patchfrac_{k,m}(d) \geq \theta$. Furthermore, since $pgrams_{k,m'}(d) \supseteq pgrams_{k,m}(d)$, and since $sources_{k,m}(d)$ is the *minimal* set of documents whose patch-grams cover $pgrams_{k,m}(d)$, the minimality property implies that $|sources_{k,m'}(d)| \geq |sources_{k,m}(d)| \geq c$. Taken together, this implies that d is (k, m', c, θ)-quilted. □

The attentive reader will notice that there is no Theorem 4 – (k, m, c, θ)-quiltedness is *not* monotonic in k. It is fairly easy to see why: choosing a very small value of k may render most k-grams common, i.e. occurring in more than m documents, while choosing a very large value of k may render most k-grams unique, i.e. occurring in only a single document. At either extreme, the average document will tend to have a smaller patch gram set, and hence a lower patch fraction, thereby reducing the number of documents d for which $patchfrac_{k,m}(d) \geq \theta$.

As mentioned above, the set cover problem is NP-hard. We compute $sources_{k,m}(d)$, the source documents contributing patch-grams to a document d, through the following greedy approximation algorithm:

$C \leftarrow \{(d', g) : d' \in D \setminus \{d\} \wedge g \in grams_k(d) \cap grams_k(d') \wedge$
$\quad 1 < |docs_k(g)| \leq m\}$
$sources_{k,m}(d) \leftarrow \emptyset$
while $C \neq \emptyset$ do
$\quad$ find a d' that maximizes $|\{g : (d', g) \in C\}|$
$\quad sources_{k,m}(d) \leftarrow sources_{k,m}(d) \cup \{d'\}$
$\quad C \leftarrow C \setminus \{(d'', g') \in C : g' \in \{g : (d', g) \in C\}\}$

It should be pointed out that Theorem 3 does not necessarily hold when $sources_{k,m}(d)$ is approximated rather than computed precisely. Nonetheless, even when using the above greedy approximation, we expect the set of quilted documents in a large collection to increase "mostly" monotonically as m increases.

We implemented the above set-theoretic definition of quiltedness using DryadLINQ [17], a data-parallel cluster computing platform that leverages LINQ, Microsoft's "language integrated query" extension to the C# programming language. LINQ is based on *list comprehensions*, a concept that originated in the functional programming community and that in turn is related to mathematical set notation (sometimes called set comprehensions). Because of the fairly close relationship between LINQ and set notations, it is reasonably straightforward to cast the above definitions in LINQ and C#. The entire implementation, shown in Figure 5 is just 74 lines of C# and LINQ, not counting utility libraries for hashing and mapping between textual and numeric ClueWeb09 document identifiers.

Functional programs in general and list comprehensions in particular can be efficiently evaluated in a data-parallel fashion, and DryadLINQ exploits that fact by executing any LINQ query on many machines in parallel. A DryadLINQ program is started on a single machine. Whenever the control flow encounters a LINQ query, DryadLINQ ships that query to available machines in a compute cluster, which

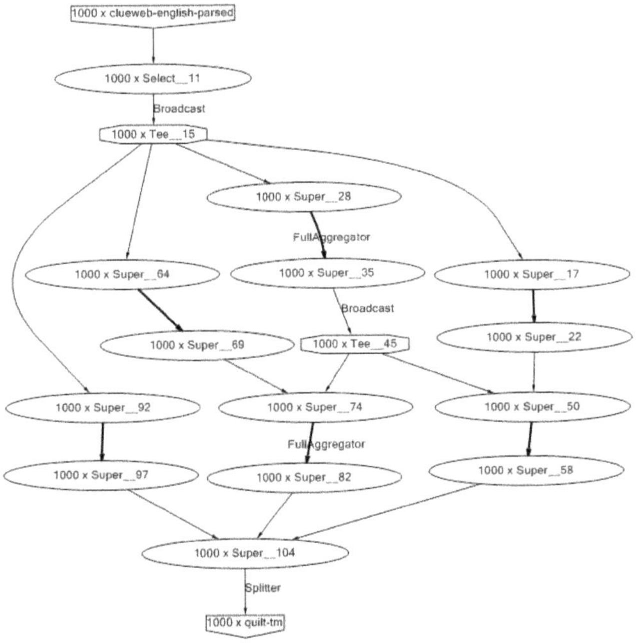

Figure 2: Data flow graph of the DryadLINQ implementation of our quilt detection algorithm.

also store the data (in our case, the corpus of documents) in a distributed fashion. Data is organized into *streams* segmented into multiple *partitions*, and the partitions of a stream are distributed across the cluster. A query is decomposed into multiple *stages*, each stage consisting of the maximal pipeline of operators (e.g. `Select`, `Where`, `GroupBy`, `Join`, `Partition` and `Merge`) that can be executed locally by reading and writing items in a streaming fashion. Each stage is executed in parallel, with the degree of parallelism determined by the partitioning of the input streams, and spread over the available machines in the cluster. A DryadLINQ computation can be characterized by a directed acyclic graph, with the nodes corresponding to stages and the edges corresponding to data flowing from one stage to the next. Figure 2 shows the data flow graph of the DryadLINQ implementation of our quilt detection algorithm. It contains 14 stages (represented as ovals), and completing each stage involves running 1000 processes distributed over the machines in the cluster. The processes in each stage are independent from each other and thus parallelizable; in practice, the DryadLINQ runtime runs just one such process per machine at any given time.

3. EXPERIMENTAL VALIDATION

The experiments described in this section were performed on a cluster of about 220 computers, each running the Windows Server 2003 64-bit operating system. Each machine had two dual-core AMD Opteron 2218 HE CPUs clocked at 2.6 GHz, 16 GB of DDR2 RAM, four 750 GB SATA drives, and a 1 Gbit/sec Ethernet NIC. Groups of about 25 computers were connected to a Blade RackSwitch G8052 48-port full-crossbar local switch; and the nine local switches were interconnected through a Blade RackSwitch G8264 switch, with 30 Gbit/sec full-duplex inter-switch bandwidth achieved via port aggregation.

For our experiments, we used the English-language subset of ClueWeb09 [14]. The collection was assembled through a web crawl conducted in 2009. The full collection consists of over a billion web pages, while the English-language subset is comprised of 503,898,901 pages. We segmented each page into individual words by embedding the Bing HTML parser into DryadLINQ and performing the parsing and word-breaking on our compute cluster. We subsequently performed several runs of the DryadLINQ implementation of our quilt detection algorithm, exploring various choices of the parameters k, m, c and θ. Typical runs took between 18 and 48 hours depending on parameter combinations as well as job competition. Since our compute cluster is shared among multiple users and a job's individual processes are routinely aborted by the cluster scheduler to accommodate other users, the aforementioned running times should only be viewed as upper bounds.

k	m	c	θ	# quilted	# sources
2	50	4	0.5	562,450	1114.78
3	50	4	0.5	4,865,307	27.75
4	50	4	0.5	33,904,401	21.58
5	50	4	0.5	58,002,718	22.35
6	50	4	0.5	58,526,481	16.49
7	50	4	0.5	52,926,434	12.14
8	50	4	0.5	47,158,399	9.78
9	50	4	0.5	42,278,205	8.53
10	50	4	0.5	38,479,113	7.82
5	50	2	0.5	82,832,986	16.37
5	50	3	0.5	68,103,596	19.48
5	50	4	0.5	58,002,718	22.35
5	50	5	0.5	50,251,757	25.18
5	50	6	0.5	44,206,465	27.94
5	50	7	0.5	39,444,093	30.59
5	50	8	0.5	35,611,760	33.12
5	50	9	0.5	32,453,725	35.57
5	50	10	0.5	29,797,202	37.94
5	10	4	0.5	16,924,347	15.16
5	20	4	0.5	31,492,573	17.87
5	30	4	0.5	42,267,988	19.85
5	40	4	0.5	50,849,031	21.32
5	50	4	0.5	58,002,718	22.35
5	60	4	0.5	64,145,058	23.16
5	70	4	0.5	69,434,726	23.84
5	80	4	0.5	74,062,259	24.41
5	50	4	0.4	93,141,485	28.68
5	50	4	0.5	58,002,718	22.35
5	50	4	0.6	33,040,377	16.79
5	50	4	0.7	15,700,171	12.71
5	50	4	0.8	4,650,478	9.38
5	50	4	0.9	439,044	6.95
5	50	4	1.0	209	4.75

Table 1: Percentage of (k, m, c, θ)-quilted pages in ClueWeb09 and average number of source pages, for various choices of k, m, c and θ.

The output of each quilt detection run is a stream containing the ClueWeb09 document IDs of all detected quilted

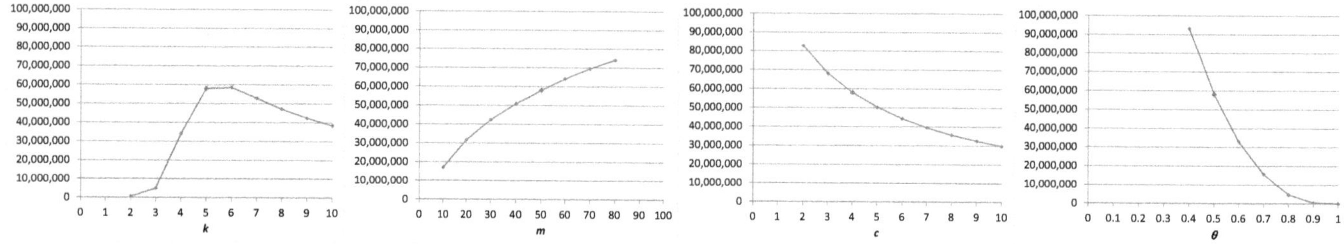

Figure 3: Number of quilted pages dependent on parameters setting. All plots have the common, highlighted pivot point $(k, m, c, \theta) = (5, 50, 4, 0.5)$, and each plots sweeps the parameter space in one dimension around that pivot point. From left to right, the parameters k, m, c and θ are varied.

pages, together with a minimal[1] set of source documents. We picked parameter combination $(k, m, c, \theta) = (5, 50, 4, 0.5)$ as a pivot point and varied the parameters around that pivot point, one dimension at a time. Table 1 shows the number of quilted pages in our corpus and the average number of source documents for each of the parameter combinations we explored. Figure 3 plots the number of quilted pages for each parameter sweep, giving credence to Theorems 1–3 stating the monotinicity in θ, c and m, as well as illustrating the non-monotonicity in k. The pivot point is highlighted in each plot.

In order to evaluate the effectiveness of our quilt detection algorithm at identifying spam web pages, we drew a small sample from the set of detected quilts, and extracted the words of each quilted page and their source documents from the ClueWeb09 corpus (again leveraging DryadLINQ). We then manually inspected each quilt and its sources and labeled them as *positive* (i.e. spam) or *negative* (not spam). Figure 4 shows a screen shot of the tool we used to perform this labeling.

Table 2 shows the results of labeling five of the runs described in Table 1,the first being the pivot point and the other four extreme choices of k, m, c, and θ. For each run, we sampled 100 (k, m, c, θ)-quilted pages and assessed them using the judging tool.

k	m	c	θ	spam
5	50	4	0.5	27%
10	50	4	0.5	22%
5	10	4	0.5	17%
5	50	10	0.5	19%
5	50	4	1.0	27%

Table 2: Percentage of sampled (k, m, c, θ)-quilted pages that are labeled as spam, for five choices of k, m, c and θ.

Among the five runs, the parameter combination we chose as the pivot point performed best. It is not clear how significant the observed differences in effectiveness are. The sample size is relatively small, but more importantly, our spam judgments are truly that: judgment calls. It was often quite hard to determine whether a given quilted page was spam or not. For one, a substantial fraction of web pages in the ClueWeb09 collection no longer exists in the wild; and often enough, the domain of the page either no longer exists or has been taken over by a "domain parking" service. In such cases, we had to judge the page solely based on its textual content, without considering embedded images or other pages in the same domain – two important cues in making spam judgments. Moreover, there is a fine line between low-quality content with commercial intent and outright spam. We might (somewhat arbitrarily) decide that an Amazon reseller engaging in keyword stuffing is pursuing a legitimate business, but a blog that is "reviewing" miracle patent medicines and monetizing this through a referral program is spam. It is hard to draw the line, and hard to do so consistently.

We were disappointed by the low percentage of quilted pages detected by our algorithm that would actually be considered spam by a human observer. By examining the many false positives, it became quickly clear that our algorithm identified the home pages of many blogs as quilted, with the full articles of the blog posts being the source documents contributing fragments to the blog home page. This observation guided us to add the following simple heuristic to our quilt detection algorithm: each source document should reside on a different web server than the quilted document. More formally, the initialization of C in the algorithm given in Section 2 is replaced by:

$$C \leftarrow \{(d', g) : d' \in D \setminus \{d\} \wedge g \in grams_k(d) \cap grams_k(d') \wedge 1 < |docs_k(g)| \leq m \wedge server(d) \neq server(d')\}$$

We refer to pages satisfying this refined definition of quiltedness as *foreign-sourced* quilted pages. There is some ambiguity as to what constitutes a web server: it could be identified by a symbolic host name, a paid domain name, an IP address, or even a domain registrar record. In our experiments, we treated paid domain names (such as `microsoft.com` or `cam.ac.uk`) as the identifiers of servers, and we insisted on source pages to originate from a different domain than the quilted page.

We ran this variant of our quilt detection algorithm on the same data set as before, with the parameters $(k, m, c, \theta) = (5, 50, 4, 0.5)$ that we had chosen as a pivot point. This run detected 20,576,548 quilted pages (a proper subset of about 35% of the pages detected by the unmodified quilt detection algorithm), each one incorporating an average of 28.26 foreign source pages. We labeled 100 pages drawn uniformly at random from the set of foreign-sourced quilted pages, and judged 34 of them as spam. This significantly increase in the fraction of quilted pages judged as spam provides some

[1]Or rather, approximately minimal, due to the greedy set cover approximation algorithm.

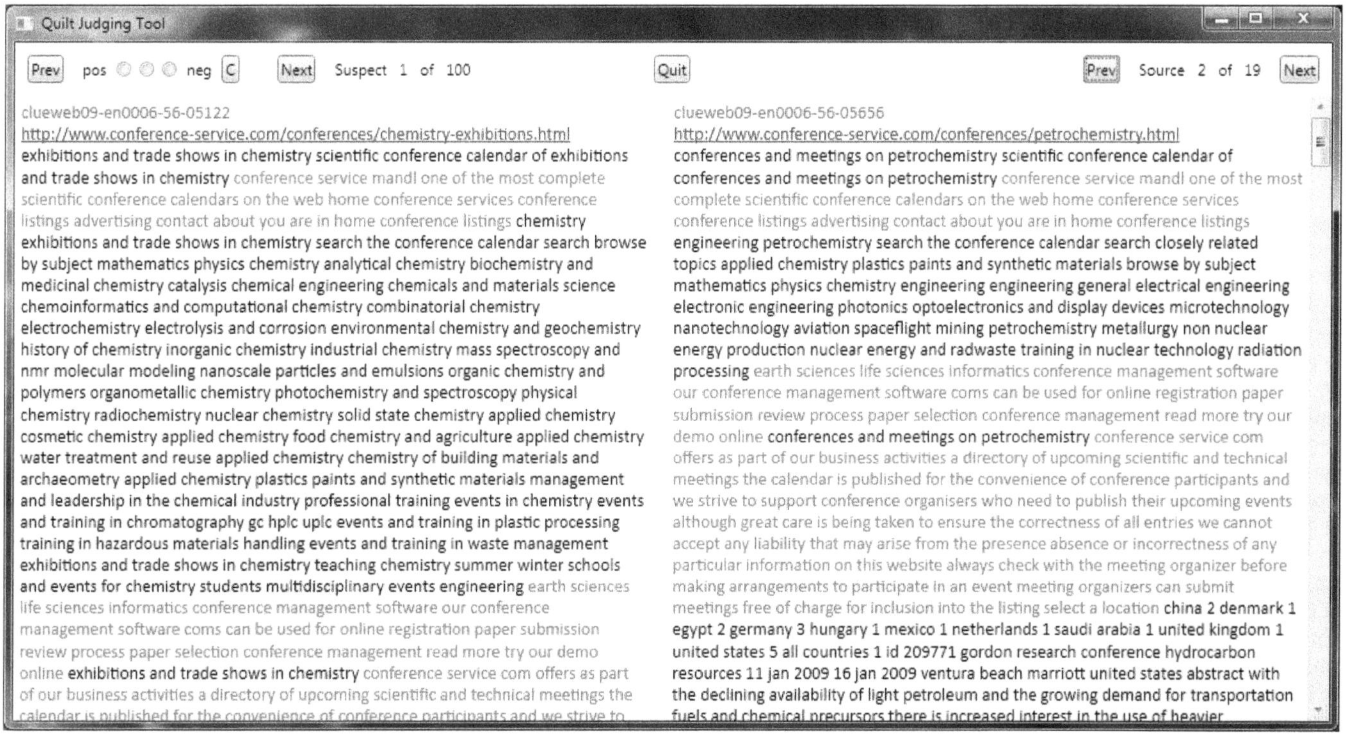

Figure 4: Tool used to view each quilt and its sources and label the quilt as spam or not spam.

evidence that the heuristic of requiring each source page to originate from a different server than the quilted page is indeed effective at surfacing spam.

None of the pages in our sample were of the blatant machine-generated variety we observed during our 2005 study, suggesting that spammers have become more sophisticated. However, our algorithm was very effective in surfacing web sites that appropriated semantically coherent parts of other web sites (say, a short essay) and used this content as "bait" to drive content to their own site, which was typically not topically related to the essay. Another pattern we observed repeatedly was "cookie-cutter" web sites, where apparently independent entities would offer essentially the same digital content, or sell the same products.

About two-thirds of the foreign-sourced quilted pages identified by our technique were not judged as spam. Within this set, we observed two notable patterns:

1. Publicly available documents (such as technical documents, standards, song lyrics, government notices, and biographic entries) are replicated on many sites, and most users would consider this content to be useful.

2. Some organizations (for example, Hartnell College) utilize multiple domains (`hartnell.edu` and `hartnell.cc.ca.us`), and serve similar pages on these domains.

The second class of false-positives accounted for about one-fifth of all false-positives. Spot-checking a few of them showed that most of these domains resolve to the same canonical IP address. For example, the symbolic host names `hartnell.edu` and `hartnell.cc.ca.us` resolve to `198.189.134.200`; and the symbolic host names `efinancialcareers.com`, `efinancialcareers.ie`, `efinancialcareers.be` resolve to `74.115.248.70`. Using IP addresses to represent web servers fits well into the data-parallel implementation of our algorithm. The alternative approach of leveraging the apparent textual similarity between these domain names, while feasible, is harder to shoe-horn into the DryadLINQ implementation. We implemented the former approach and tested it on the same data set as before, with the parameters $(k, m, c, \theta) = (5, 50, 4, 0.5)$ that we had chosen as a pivot point. This run detected 19,729,026 quilted pages, each one incorporating an average of 29.22 source pages hosted on web servers with different IP addresses than that of the quilted page. In other words, using this stricter notion of differing web servers has little impact on how many pages are detected as quilted. Again, we sampled 100 pages from this run and manually inspected them, finding 26 of them to be spam, which is noticeably lower than the 34% spam yield uncovered by the previous run. We attribute it to the imprecise nature of the assessment process.

In the course of assessing 100 samples each from 7 runs, we found that many quilted pages drew most of their patch-grams from just a few source pages, while most of the source pages contributed just one or a few patch grams. It would be interesting to modify the quilt detection algorithm (and the very definition of quiltedness) so as to ensure that each source page contributes at least a fraction of ϕ of the patch-grams in the quilted page. We leave this as an avenue for future work.

4. CONCLUSION

This paper builds on our earlier work on detecting phrase-level duplication on the web [9]. We give a formal definition of what constitutes a *quilted web page* (a web page that is stitched together out of textual patches taken from other web pages) and prove a few properties of that definition; we provide an algorithm for exhaustively detecting all quilted web pages in a given collection; we describe a data-parallel implementation of the algorithm that scales to very large collections; we evaluate the effectiveness of the algorithm in detecting web spam by applying it (with various parameterizations) to the half-billion page English-language subset of the ClueWeb09 collection [14] and judging samples of the detected quilted pages as to whether or not they indeed constitute spam; and we suggest a few heuristics to improve effectiveness.

A major area for future work will be to combine the syntactic approach of our algorithm with semantic (and domain-specific) techniques for spam detection. While the syntactic technique described in this paper (by virtue of its exhaustiveness) is fully effective at detecting all quilted web pages, the task of effectively identifying spam must ultimately incorporate semantic information. Our algorithm (correctly) identities news aggregation web sites to contain quilted pages (pages that collate opening paragraphs of news articles from other sources); but such news aggregation pages are not spam – users derive a real value from them. A potential semantic signal that distinguishes news aggregation from spam is *attribution* – a link from each excerpt to the underlying article.

The core ideas described in this paper are applicable not only to spam suppression in search engines, but also (and probably more so) to detecting plagiarism in web-scale corpora. Here again, semantic information (such as proper attribution) will be needed in addition to the purely syntactic approach of our technique.

Acknowledgments

This work grew out of a 2004 collaboration with Mark Manasse and Dennis Fetterly, and benefited from our many discussions. Dennis played a crucial role in the work described in this paper, by word-breaking the ClueWeb09 collection using the Bing HTML parser, supplying me with IP addresses for the URLs in the ClueWeb09 collection, providing me with a judging tool to adapt for this project, and patiently answering my many questions related to DryadLINQ. Thanks to the entire DryadLINQ team for building a system to make cluster-scale computing easy and fun, and particularly to Yuan Yu for being super-responsive in fixing bugs. Finally, thanks to Jamie Callan and his team at CMU for compiling the ClueWeb09 collection, which has arguably become the reference data set for reproducible web corpus research. I can hardly wait for ClueWeb12!

5. REFERENCES

[1] Jacqueline Anderson, Reineke Reitsma, Patti F. Evans, Samantha Y. Jaddou. Understanding Online Shopper Behaviors, US 2011. *Forrester Research*, 2011.

[2] Ricardo Baeza-Yates, Álvaro Pereira, and Nivio Ziviani. Genealogical Trees on the Web: A Search Engine User Perspective. In *17th International World Wide Web Conference*, 2008.

[3] Michael Bendersky and W. Bruce Croft. Finding Text Reuse on the Web. In *2nd ACM International Conference on Web Search and Data Mining*, 2009.

[4] Sergey Brin, James Davis, and Hector Garcia-Molina. Copy Detection Mechanisms for Digital Documents. In *ACM SIGMOD International Conference on Management of Data*, 1995.

[5] Andrei Z. Broder. On the Resemblance and Containment of Documents. In *Compression and Complexity of Sequences*, 1997.

[6] Andrei Z. Broder, Steven C. Glassmann, Mark S. Manasse, and Geoffrey Zweig. Syntactic Clustering of the Web. In *6th International World Wide Web Conference*, 1997.

[7] Moses S. Charikar. Similarity Estimation Techniques from Rounding Algorithms. In *34th Annual ACM Symposium on Theory of Computing*, 2002.

[8] Dennis Fetterly, Mark Manasse and Marc Najork. On the Evolution of Clusters of Near-Duplicate Web Pages. *1st Latin American Web Congress*, 2003.

[9] Dennis Fetterly, Mark Manasse and Marc Najork. Detecting Phrase-Level Duplication on the World Wide Web. In *28th Annual International ACM SIGIR Conference on Research and Development in Information Retrieval*, 2005.

[10] Monika Henzinger. Finding Near-Duplicate Web Pages: A Large-Scale Evaluation of Algorithms. In *29th Annual International ACM SIGIR Conference on Research and Development in Information Retrieval*, 2006.

[11] Timothy C. Hoad and Justin Zobel. Methods for Identifying Versioned and Plagiarised Documents. *Journal of the American Society for Information Science and Technology*, **54**(3):203–215, 2003.

[12] Richard M. Karp. Reducibility Among Combinatorial Problems. In *Symposium on the Complexity of Computer Computations*, 1972.

[13] Okan Kolak and Bill N. Schilit. Generating Links by Mining Quotations. In *19th ACM Conference on Hypertext and Hypermedia*, 2008.

[14] Lemur Project. The ClueWeb09 DataSet. Online at `http://lemurproject.org/clueweb09/`

[15] Jangwon Seo and W. Bruce Croft. Local Text Reuse Detection. In *31st Annual International ACM SIGIR Conference on Research and Development in Information Retrieval*, 2008.

[16] Narayanan Shivakumar and Hector Garcia-Molina. SCAM: A Copy Detection Mechanism for Digital Documents. In *2nd Annual Conference on the Theory and Practice of Digital Libraries*, 1995.

[17] Yuan Yu, Michael Isard, Dennis Fetterly, Mihai Budiu, Úlfar Erlingsson, Pradeep Kumar Gundar, and Jon Currey. DryadLINQ: a system for general-purpose distributed data-parallel computing using a high-level language. In *8th USENIX Conference on Operating Systems Design and Implementation*, 2008.

```
public class Doc : IEquatable<Doc> {
  public string url;
  public string docId;
  public string[] words;
  public override int GetHashCode() {
    return docId.GetHashCode();
  }
  public bool Equals(Doc other) {
    return docId.Equals(other.docId, StringComparison.Ordinal);
  }
}
public class QuiltFinder {
  public static ulong[] HashPatches(string[] words, int k) {
    var res = new ulong[Math.Max(0, words.Length - k + 1)];
    var sb = new StringBuilder();
    for (int i = 0; i < res.Length; i++) {
      for (int j = 0; j < k; j++) {
        if (j > 0) sb.Append(" ");
        sb.Append(words[i + j]);
      }
      res[i] = Hash(sb.ToString());
      sb.Clear();
    }
    return res;
  }
  public static IEnumerable<Pair<ulong,Pair<ulong,ulong>>> MakeDocGramDocTriple(ulong gram, ulong[] ids) {
    for (int i = 0; i < ids.Length; i++) {
      for (int j = 0; j < ids.Length; j++) {
        if (i != j) {
          yield return new Pair<ulong, Pair<ulong, ulong>>(ids[i], new Pair<ulong, ulong>(gram, ids[j]));
        }
      }
    }
  }
  public static ulong[] MinSourceDocSet(List<Pair<ulong, ulong>> gramIds) {
    List<ulong> res = new List<ulong>();
    while (gramIds.Count > 0) {
      var bestDoc = gramIds.OrderBy(x => x.Value)
                           .GroupBy(x => x.Value, x => x.Key, (k, g) => new Pair<ulong, int>(k, g.Count()))
                           .OrderByDescending(x => x.Value)
                           .First()
                           .Key;
      res.Add(bestDoc);
      var coveredGrams = gramIds.Where(x => x.Value == bestDoc).Select(x => x.Key).ToList();
      var dischargedGramDocs = gramIds.Join(coveredGrams, x => x.Key, y => y, (x,y) => x).ToList();
      gramIds = gramIds.Except(dischargedGramDocs).ToList();
    }
    return res.ToArray();
  }
  public static void FindQuilts(string inputStream, string outputStream, int k, int m, int c, double theta) {
    var docToGrams = PartitionedTable.Get<InitialParsedDocWithLinks>(inputStream)
                                     .Select(x => new { id = DocIdToULong(x.docId), grams = HashPatches(x.words, k) });
    var gramsPerDoc = docToGrams.Select(x => new { id = x.id, count = (double)x.grams.Length });
    var patchGrams = docToGrams.SelectMany(x => x.grams.Distinct())
                               .GroupBy(x => x, x => true, (gram, group) => new {gram = gram, count = group.Count()})
                               .Where(x => x.count > 1 && x.count <= m)
                               .Select(x => x.gram);
    var patchyDocs = docToGrams.SelectMany(x => x.grams.Select(y => new { id = x.id, gram = y }))
                               .Join(patchGrams, x => x.gram, y => y, (x, y) => x)
                               .GroupBy(x => x.id, x => x.gram, (id, group) => new { id = id, count = (double)group.Count() })
                               .Join(gramsPerDoc, x => x.id, y => y.id, (x, y) => new { id = x.id, frac = x.count / y.count })
                               .Where(x => x.frac >= theta)
                               .Select(x => x.id);
    var quilts = docToGrams.SelectMany(x => x.grams.Select(y => new { gram = y, id = x.id }))
                           .Join(patchGrams, x => x.gram, y => y, (x, y) => x)
                           .GroupBy(x => x.gram, x => x.id, (gram, group) => new { gram = gram, ids = group.Distinct().ToArray() })
                           .SelectMany(x => MakeDocGramDocTriple(x.gram, x.ids))
                           .Join(patchyDocs, x => x.Key, y => y, (x,y) => x)
                           .GroupBy(x => x.Key, x => x.Value, (id, group) => new { id = id, ids = MinSourceDocSet(group.ToList()) })
                           .Where(x => x.ids.Length >= c)
                           .Select(x => new Pair<string,string[]>(ULongToDocId(x.id), x.ids.Select(y => ULongToDocId(y)).ToArray()))
                           .ToPartitionedTable(outputStream);
  }
}
```

Figure 5: A DryadLINQ implementation of the quilt detection algorithm

Fighting against Web Spam: A Novel Propagation Method based on Click-through Data

Chao Wei, Yiqun Liu, Min Zhang, Shaoping Ma, Liyun Ru, Kuo Zhang

State Key Laboratory of Intelligent Technology and Systems,

Tsinghua National Laboratory for Information Science and Technology,

Department of Computer Science and Technology, Tsinghua University, Beijing, China, 100084

weichao053825@gmail.com, {yiqunliu,z-m,msp}@tsinghua.edu.cn,

lyru@vip.sohu.com, zhangkuo@sogou-inc.com

ABSTRACT

Combating Web spam is one of the greatest challenges for Web search engines. State-of-the-art anti-spam techniques focus mainly on detecting varieties of spam strategies, such as content spamming and link-based spamming. Although these anti-spam approaches have had much success, they encounter problems when fighting against a continuous barrage of new types of spamming techniques. We attempt to solve the problem from a new perspective, by noticing that queries that are more likely to lead to spam pages/sites have the following characteristics: 1) they are popular or reflect heavy demands for search engine users and 2) there are usually few key resources or authoritative results for them. From these observations, we propose a novel method that is based on click-through data analysis by propagating the spamicity score iteratively between queries and URLs from a few seed pages/sites. Once we obtain the seed pages/sites, we use the link structure of the click-through bipartite graph to discover other pages/sites that are likely to be spam. Experiments show that our algorithm is both efficient and effective in detecting Web spam. Moreover, combining our method with some popular anti-spam techniques such as TrustRank achieves improvement compared with each technique taken individually.

Categories and Subject Descriptors

H.3.3 [**Information Storage and Retrieval**]: Information Search and Retrieval; H.m [**Information SYSTEMS APPLICATIONS**]: Miscellaneous

Keywords

Spam detection, Web search engine, click-through data/bipartite graph, semi-supervised algorithm, label propagation

1. INTRODUCTION

Spamming refers to the malicious attempt to influence the outcome of ranking algorithms, and is usually aimed at obtaining an undeservedly high ranking for one or more Web pages [9]. Castillo and Davison [3] defined Web spam pages as those that benefit from spamming actions, including pages containing inappropriate material, pages with malware or viruses and pages that acquire undeserved traffic by spamming.

Permission to make digital or hard copies of all or part of this work for personal or classroom use is granted without fee provided that copies are not made or distributed for profit or commercial advantage and that copies bear this notice and the full citation on the first page. To copy otherwise, or republish, to post on servers or to redistribute to lists, requires prior specific permission and/or a fee.

SIGIR'12, August 12–16, 2012, Portland, Oregon, USA.

Copyright 2012 ACM 978-1-4503-1472-5/12/08 ...$15.00.

There are many reasons for Web spamming. The most important one is that some Web pages try to attract more user visits through search engines without improving content quality or search advertising. According to previous research [19], most users only look through the top results returned by search engines, which means that visitor traffic for a given page or site is highly correlated with its ranking in the results list. The incentive to drive traffic to Web sites as well as the dominant role of search engines is the reason for the ever-increasing amount of Web spam. Most Web spam is created for the purpose of making a profit. In 2005, Singhal [20] estimated that spammers expected to receive a few US dollars per sale for affiliate programs on Amazon, approximately $6 per sale of Viagra, and approximately $20-40 per new member of pornographic sites.

Different techniques are designed to fight against Web spam. State-of-the-art anti-spam techniques use Web page features [17], including both content-based [11] and hyper-link structure-based features [4], to construct Web spam classifiers. Other features, such as features that are extracted from search logs, and browsing logs [4] [5] [12], are also helpful for detecting spam. In fact, we can find spam more accurately by combining all of the signals of a given Web page/site from its content, links, search log features and browsing features [12][17]. In this framework, anti-spam engineers must perform additional work to design specific features and strategies that identify new types of spam by carefully examining characteristics of the spam pages/sites. The biggest limitation of this type of approach is that spammers will develop new spamming techniques immediately after the old tricks are identified. Web spam has evolved from term spamming and link spamming to more sophisticated techniques, such as JavaScript spamming techniques [6].

Existing studies focus mainly on identifying a variety of spam strategies. However, to fight against spam, it is useful and interesting to see how these spam pages attract traffic and make profits. We should notice that spam visiting mainly comes from search engines and its purpose is to draw as much traffic as possible. In other words, they use different spam techniques to cheat search engines, making their pages more "relevant" to specific queries, thus gaining traffic from those queries. These queries will be selected carefully by spammers. Usually, queries with two characteristics are selected. First, they are usually popular queries or reflect a high demand of users because spammers can gain much traffic if their strategies work. Popular queries are those queries that have high frequencies in search logs. Other queries may not be so popular, but they represent a common information need and thus have the potential to be popular, e.g. "How to lose weight?", "Are weight-loss pills effective?". Although different queries may be used, they reflect the same need for weight-loss strategies, which is interesting for many search users. Second, there are usually few key resources or authoritative results for these "spam oriented" queries because spam pages are unlikely to be ranked high in a search results list if there are many relevant and key resources for a given query. For example, few spammers will select the query "yahoo" or "nokia" as spamming contents because there exist authoritative pages for these contents as queries and it is almost impossible for spam pages to be ranked high in such result lists. With the second characteristic, spam pages may be ranked high in the result list, while the first characteristic makes sure the keyword draws much attention. Spamming contents with both characteristics help spam pages to gain user traffic.

Therefore, keywords that 1)are hot or reflect a heavy demand and 2) lack key recourses or authoritative results (we call these keywords spam-oriented queries in this paper) are more likely to be used by spammers and thus lead to spam pages. Web pages/sites that draw traffic mainly from these "spam" queries are more likely to be spam. These two observations indicate that we could use click-through logs to find Web spam. We construct a click-through bipartite graph with query nodes and URL nodes and employ an iterative method to propagate the "spamicity" scores based on the two characteristics of possible spamming contents. We found that a large number of spam pages can be identified by exploiting only the click-through data. This result shows that we could improve anti-spam performance by taking advantage of search logs.

The contributions of this paper are:

1, A label propagation algorithm on click-through bipartite graph is proposed to identify possible spam and its convergence is proven.

2, A thorough analysis of the click-through data is conducted to demonstrate that much can be accomplished with it to identify Web spam. To the best of our knowledge, few publications address the issue of finding spam by using only click-through data.

3, An experimental study on large-scale click-through log data is performed. Results show that the proposed algorithm can identify a variety of spam pages both effectively and efficiently.

The rest of this paper is organized as follows: Section 2 provides a brief review of related work. Section 3 presents our motivation in Web spam detection and formulates the label propagation problem. Section 4 discusses our label propagation problem in detail and proves convergence of our algorithm. In section 5, we perform an experimental validation of our techniques and demonstrate that we can detect spam pages in click-through data both effectively and efficiently. Section 6 gives some conclusion and future work.

2. RELATED WORK

2.1 Web Spamming Techniques and Detection Algorithms

Many spam techniques are emerging along with the development of search engines. Castillo and Davison [3] grouped spamming techniques into two categories: content and link spamming.

Content spamming, including term spamming and content-hidden techniques, refers to techniques that deliberately manipulate page contents and URL keywords to improve their rankings. Gyöngyi et al. [11] provided a list of different types of content spam, including term spam techniques such as repetition, dumping, weaving and stitching and content-hidden techniques such as cloaking [24], redirection spam [6] and visual cloaking [15]. Ntoulas et al. [17] introduced several content-based features to build spam classifiers, and their work is considered to be one of the most influential studies on detecting content spam. They found that spam pages contains more popular terms than non-spam pages. Other studies exploit additional text features to detect spam pages. Linguistic features [18] such as part-of-speech (POS) n-grams, textual features [2], language model features [14] and HTML patterns [22, 23] have been fully studied and were proven to be useful in spam detection.

Link spammers create certain hyper-link structures to boost their scores in typical link analysis, such as PageRank and HITS. Link farms [25], honey pots [11] and spam link exchange belong to this spamming technique. A variety of trust and distrust propagation algorithms such as Trustrank [10] and BadRank [21] and their variants [16] [26] are utilized and proven to be effective in terms of demoting spam. It has also been observed that spam sites often form dense sub-graphs and many works [4] [25] use link-based features, including the degree and spamicity of neighbors to detect them. Recently, Cheng et al. [7] used information from SEO forums to find spam site candidates and thus link farms.

2.2 Usage Data

To detect spam pages more efficiently and effectively, researchers usually combine different spam signals from different usage data, including browsing logs and search logs, to build classifiers.

Liu et al. [13] used browsing logs to estimate the importance of Web pages by defining a continuous-time Markov process on user browsing graph. They showed that their algorithm of BrowseRank is effective in demoting spam sites. Liu et al. [12] proposed a user behavior-oriented Web spam detection framework that was based on browsing logs (captured by a toolbar). They showed that spam sites' traffic relies almost completely on search engine-originated visits. Other features include the probability that a given page is a source page (i.e. people follow hyper-links on it) and the short-time navigation time (based on the assumption that most Web users would not visit many pages inside a spam Web site).

Search logs contain valuable information about queries and their corresponding URLs. However, there is no detailed analysis on how to utilize these data. Previous studies only created additional features from them [5] [12] [17] for content-based or link-based Web spam detection.

To sum up, state-of-the-art anti-spam techniques use content-based, link-based and user behavior features to construct Web spam classifiers. Anti-spam engineers must perform additional work to design specific features and strategies that can identify new types of spam by carefully examining spamming techniques. The biggest limitation of these approaches is that spammers will develop new Web spam techniques immediately after the old tricks are identified. Due to the fact that spammers often develop new Web spam techniques immediately after the old tricks are identified, the identification of spam and the resultant anti-spam techniques becomes a vicious cycle.

3. MOTIVATION AND PROBLEM FORMULATION

Traditional anti-spam techniques focus on identifying different spam techniques. These techniques fail to exploit how spam pages manage to gain traffic, in other words, how the spammers carefully select the keywords and boost the ranking of their pages/sites in corresponding results lists. The more traffic that spam sites receive, the more profit they will make and the more frustrated search engine users get.

Although spammers want to gain as much traffic as possible from search engines, it is not likely, as discussed in Section 1, for their spam pages/sites to rank high in all of the keywords for which they optimize.

Based on these observations, we design a label propagation algorithm on click-through data. Firstly, a small number of seed pages are selected and labeled as spam or non-spam. Then their labels are propagated on the click-through bipartite graph and other possible spam/non-spam pages are identified. The input consists of a) a set of labeled URLs (spam or non-spam), b) a set of unlabeled URLs and c) a set of constraints between URLs and the queries in the log. The goal is to find spam pages/sites from the unlabeled data.

We first give some definitions before formulating our problem.

Ⅰ. Search engine click-through data C and bipartite graph G.

The click log consists of triples $<q, u, f_{qu}>$, where q is a query, u is an URL representing a document on the Internet and f_{qu} is the number of times that URL u is clicked when query q is issued. Define $Q = \{q \mid q \text{ appears in } C\}$ and $U = \{u \mid u \text{ appears in } C\}$. Click-through data C has an equivalent form – a click-through bipartite graph G = (Q, U, E). There are two different types of nodes, queries and URLs in G. For every record $<q, u, f_{qu}>$ in C, there is an edge $(q, u) \in E$ with weight f_{qu}.

Each q/u is assigned with a probability p_q/p_u, which denotes how likely this q/u is to be a spam query/page or in other words, the spamicity of q/u.

Note that the click-through bipartite graph can be constructed either on page-level or site-level. In the latter form, u is replaced by its site but not the URL of itself. For example, <"Nokia", http://product.pcpop.com/Mobile/00283_1.html, 100> is replaced by <"Nokia", http://product.pcpop.com/, 100>.

Ⅱ. Labeled Seed URL set L.

L contains all of the pages/sites in C(G) that are manually labeled as spam or non-spam. More formally,

L = {u | u is labeled as a spam page/site or non-spam page/site}.

We will discuss the construction details of L in Section 5.2.

Ⅲ. URL result set RU and query result set QU.

RU and QU contain all the $<u, p_u>$ and $<q, p_q>$ pairs, respectively. After our algorithm ends, each URL u or query q in C (or G) will be assigned with a probability p_u/p_q, which denotes the probability that this URL or query is a spam page/site or query. More formally,

$$RU = \{<u, p_u> \mid p_u \text{ is the spamicity score for u}\}.$$

$$RQ = \{<q, p_q> \mid p_q \text{ is the spamicity score for q}\}.$$

Given G = (Q, U, E) and $L \subset U$, the goal of the spam pages/sites mining problem is to obtain the results set RU and RQ, which contain all of the possible spam pages/sites and queries in G, respectively.

4. A LABEL PROPAGATION ALGORITHM

4.1 Algorithm design

In this paper, we propose a label propagation (LP) algorithm to solve the problem that is defined in the previous section. More specifically, for every query q, we could calculate the probability p_q that q is a spam query by incorporating all of the label information of its neighbors. Similarly, we could calculate p_u for every URL u. We describe this procedure more formally as follows.

For $\forall q/u$, we use l_q/l_u to denote its label, which is S for spam and N for non-spam. Note that $P(l_u=N) = 1-P(l_u=S)$. Thus every URL u in labeled set L would have $P(l_u=S)=1$ or $P(l_u=S)=0$ initially and every URL u in the set U-L would have $P(l_u=S)=0$. Then we have

$$P(l_q=S)= \sum_{u:(q,u)\in E} \omega_{qu} P(l_u = S) \quad (1)$$

where

$$\omega_{qu} = \frac{f_{qu}}{\sum_{u:(q,u)\in E} f_{qu}}. \quad (2)$$

ω_{qu} can be interpreted as the transition probability from query q to URL u. It can be drawn from equation (1) and (2) that q's label is determined by all of its neighbors' labels. The bigger ω_{qu} is, the more influence its corresponding node has on determining the label of q.

Similarly, for each URL u in U\L, the probability $P(l_u=S)$ is computed as

$$P(l_u=S)= \sum_{q:(q,u)\in E} \omega_{uq} P(l_q = S) \quad (3)$$

where

$$\omega_{uq} = \frac{f_{qu}}{\sum_{q:(q,u)\in E} f_{qu}} \quad (4)$$

is the transition probability from URL u to query q.

Note that both ω_{qu} and ω_{uq} are not limited to the above form but arbitrary. The only requirement for them is they should have a probability interpretation, which means $\sum_{q:(q,u)\in E} \omega_{uq} = 1$ and

$\sum_{q:(q,u)\in E} \omega_{qu} = 1$. We can also interpret ω_{qu} and ω_{uq} as functions of features of queries and URLs and thus incorporate these features to extend our algorithm. We leave it as our future work.

Using Equation (1) and (3), we can obtain $P(l_q=S)$ and $P(l_u=S)$ recursively for all of the queries and URLs in the click-through bipartite graph. We can have a concise representation of this iterative process. Suppose that there are $|Q|$ queries: q_1, $q_2 \ldots q_{|Q|}$ and $|U|$ URLs: u_1, $u_2 \ldots u_{|U|}$. Define vectors:

$$\mathbf{P}_Q=(P(l_{q1}=S), P(l_{q2}=S)\ldots P(l_{q|Q|}=S))^T,$$

$$\mathbf{P}_U=(P(l_{u1}=S), P(l_{u2}=S)\ldots P(l_{u|U|}=S))^T,$$

and the transition probability matrixes:

$$\mathbf{M}_{qu}=(\omega_{qu})_{|Q|\times|U|}, \text{ and } \mathbf{M}_{uq}=(\omega'_{uq})_{|U|\times|Q|}.$$

Then in the ith iteration, we have

$$\mathbf{P}^i_Q=\mathbf{M}_{qu}\,\mathbf{P}^{i-1}_U$$

$$\mathbf{P}^i_U=\mathbf{M}_{uq}\mathbf{P}^i_Q$$

It should be noted that in each round of iteration, all of the URLs in seed set L should be re-assigned their initial labels. In this way, the algorithm converges. We will prove the convergence in section 4.4.

4.2 An Example

Consider a sample portion of a bipartite graph from a search engine click log, as shown in Figure 1.

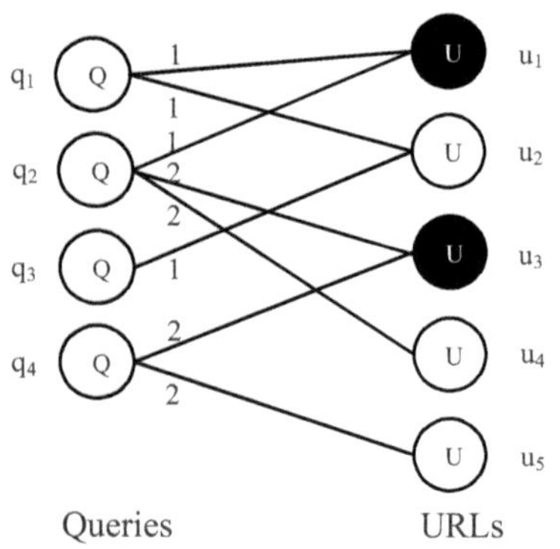

Figure 1. An example to demonstrate how the label propagation algorithm works

Assume that $L=\{u_1, u_3\}$ and both of the URLs are spam pages, as denoted in the shaded circle in Figure 1. Other nodes, including all of the query nodes and the remaining URL nodes, initially have $P(l=S)$ as 0. Then we have

$$\mathbf{P}^0_U=(1,0,1,0,0)^T,$$

$$M_{qu}=\begin{pmatrix} 0.5,0.5,0\ ,0\ ,0 \\ 0.2,0\ ,0.4,0.4,0 \\ 0\ ,1\ ,0\ ,0\ ,0 \\ 0\ ,0\ ,0.5,0\ ,0.5 \end{pmatrix}, \text{ and}$$

$$M_{uq}=\begin{pmatrix} 0.5,0.5,0\ ,0 \\ 0.5,0\ ,0.5,0 \\ 0\ ,0.5,0\ ,0.5 \\ 0\ ,1\ ,0\ ,0 \\ 0\ ,0\ ,0\ ,1 \end{pmatrix}$$

After the first iteration, we get

$$\mathbf{P}^1_Q=\mathbf{M}_{qu}\,\mathbf{P}^0_U=\begin{pmatrix} 0.5,0.5,0\ ,0\ ,0 \\ 0.2,0\ ,0.4,0.4,0 \\ 0\ ,1\ ,0\ ,0\ ,0 \\ 0\ ,0\ ,0.5,0\ ,0.5 \end{pmatrix}\begin{pmatrix} 1 \\ 0 \\ 1 \\ 0 \\ 0 \end{pmatrix}$$

$$=(0.5,0.6,0,0.5)^T$$

$$\mathbf{P}^1_U=\mathbf{M}_{uq}\mathbf{P}^1_Q=\begin{pmatrix} 0.5,0.5,0\ ,0 \\ 0.5,0\ ,0.5,0 \\ 0\ ,0.5,0\ ,0.5 \\ 0\ ,1\ ,0\ ,0 \\ 0\ ,0\ ,0\ ,1 \end{pmatrix}\begin{pmatrix} 0.5 \\ 0.6 \\ 0 \\ 0.5 \end{pmatrix}$$

$$=(0.55,0.25,0.55,0.6,0.5)^T$$

We notice that here both $P(l_{u1}=S)$ and $P(l_{u3}=S)$ are 0.55, which should be re-set to 1 before the we apply the next iteration.

4.3 The Positive Feedback Problem

Label propagation algorithms or random walks on click-through bipartite graphs have the positive feedback problems. Take u_5 in Figure 1 for example. $P(l_{u5}=S)$ is 0.5 after the first iteration. Because u_3 is a seed URL which are manually labeled as spam, we will set $P(l_{u3}=S)$ to be 1 before the second iteration begins. Therefore, it is easy to see that $P(l_{u5}=S)$ is 0.75 after the second iteration and converges to 1 if the algorithm continues. The reason is that edge $e = \langle q_4, u_5 \rangle$ is undirected and u_5 is a 1-degree node, which means that score of u_5 will flow back to q_4; from this process, it obtains its original spam score. We call this effect the positive feedback problem which would magnify the noise in the click-through bipartite graph and distort the final results.

Consider an extreme case given in Figure 2.

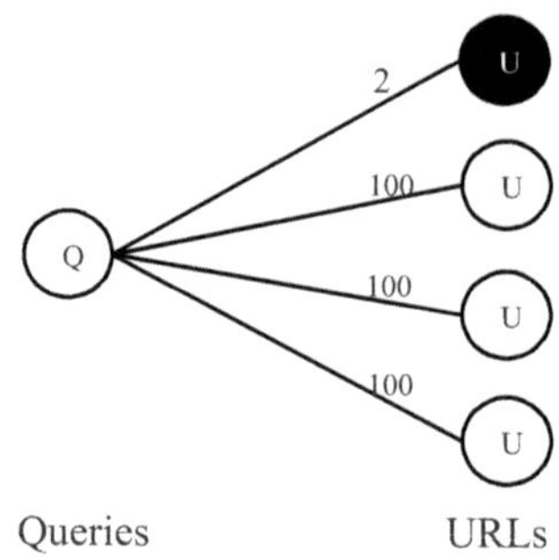

Figure 2. An extreme case for the positive feedback problem

Suppose that a non-typical user issues a query q to the search engine and then clicks a spam page while most of the other users use this query to navigate to high quality sites. All of the spam scores of the URLs will converge to 1 after our algorithms is applied on the graph, which contradicts the real explanation of the pages and this query.

It can be concluded from Figure 1 that this problem mainly affects those 1-degree nodes, such as u_4, u_5 and q_3. To solve this problem, we introduce the concept of confidence. We define the confidence of a node in the bipartite graph as a function of its degree d. More formally,

$$c(q)=f(d_q),\ c(u)=f(d_u),$$

where d_q and d_u are the degrees of node q and u, respectively. Then Equations 1 and 3 can be revised as follows.

$$P(l_q=S)=\sum_{u:(q,u)\in E}\omega_{qu}c(u)P(l_u=S)=\sum_{u:(q,u)\in E}\omega_{qu}P'(l_u=S)$$

$$P(l_u=S)=\sum_{q:(q,u)\in E}\omega_{uq}c(q)P(l_q=S)=\sum_{q:(q,u)\in E}\omega_{uq}P'(l_q=S)\cdot$$

It should be noted that function f here is arbitrary and we have many choices for function f. For simplicity, we use the indicator function in this paper.

Define

$$f(d)=\begin{cases}0\ , if\ d=1\\ 1\ ,else\end{cases}.$$

An intuitive interpretation for the indicator function is that before we obtain sufficient information to judge a 1-degree node if it is a spam page, we could treat it in the bipartite graph as pseudo normal page, forcing its spam score to be 0. Note that this constraint only applies to the unlabeled nodes since we need the seed-nodes to propagate their spamicity.

Now, applying the revised algorithm to Figure 2, we obtain $P(l_{q3}=S)$ = 2/302 and $P(l_{u3}=S) = P(l_{u4}=S) = P(l_{u5}=S)$ = 2/302, which are more reliable than the original algorithm.

The outline of the Label Propagation algorithm is shown in Figure 3.

The Label Propagation Algorithm:

Input: labeled seed set L, click-through data C(G)

Output: $P(l_u=S)$ and $P(l_q=S)$ for all URLs and queries in G

Begin

Do

for u∈L, set $P(l_u=S)$=1 or 0 according to their label by human assertors.

for all q∈Q do

$$P(l_q=S)=\sum_{u:(q,u)\in E}\omega_{qu}P'(l_u=S)$$

end for

for all u∈U\L do

$$P(l_u=S)=\sum_{q:(q,u)\in E}\omega_{uq}P'(l_q=S)$$

end for

until convergence

Output $P(l_u=S)$ for every URL u in U and $P(l_q=S)$ for every query q in Q

End

Figure 3. The label propagation algorithm

4.4 Convergence of the LP Algorithm

It is evident that $\mathbf{M_{qu}}$ and $\mathbf{M_{uq}}$ are right stochastic matrixes, each of whose rows consists of nonnegative real numbers, with each row summing to 1. Then consider $\mathbf{M_{uu}}=\mathbf{M_{uq}}\mathbf{M_{qu}}$. For each element m_{ij} in $\mathbf{M_{uu}}$, we have $m_{ij}=\sum_k \omega_{ik}\omega'_{kj}$ in $\mathbf{M_{uu}}$, where ω_{ik} and ω'_{kj} are elements $\mathbf{M_{uq}}$ and $\mathbf{M_{qu}}$, respectively. Thus we have

$$\begin{aligned}\sum_j m_{ij} &= \sum_j\sum_k \omega_{ik}\omega'_{kj}\\ &=\sum_k\sum_j \omega_{ik}\omega'_{kj}\\ &=\sum_k \omega_{ik}\sum_j \omega'_{kj}\\ &=\sum_k \omega_{ik}\\ &=1\end{aligned},$$

which means that $\mathbf{M_{uu}}$ is also a right stochastic matrix.

Now, if we are only interested in $\mathbf{P_U}$, the iteration process can be rewritten as

$$\mathbf{P^i_U}=\mathbf{M_{uu}P^{i-1}_U}=\mathbf{M_{uq}M_{qu}\ P^{i-1}_U},$$

where i denotes the iterations.

Suppose that there are |L| seed URLs in L, |C| 1-degree nodes and thus r = |U|-|L|-|C| remaining URLs in C. More specifically, let the probability vector $\mathbf{P_U}=(\mathbf{P_T}\ \mathbf{P_L})$ where $\mathbf{P_T}$ are the top |L|+|C| rows of $\mathbf{P_U}$(the labeled data and the pseudo labeled data) and $\mathbf{P_L}$ are the remaining r rows of $\mathbf{P_U}$(the unlabeled data). We split $\mathbf{M_{uu}}$ after the (|L|+|C|)th row and the (|L|+|C|)th column into 4 sub-matrixes

$$M_{uu}=\begin{pmatrix}M_{(|L|+|C|)(|L|+|C|)} & M_{(|L|+|C|)r}\\ M_{r(|L|+|C|)} & M_{rr}\end{pmatrix}.$$

Note that $\mathbf{P_T}$ never really changes. It can be shown that in our algorithm, $P_L=M_{rr}P_L+M_{r(|L|+|C|)}P_T$, which leads to $P_L=lim_{n\to\infty}M^n_{rr}P^0_L+[\sum_{i=1}^{n}M^{i-1}_{rr}]M_{r(|L|+|C|)}P_T$. Zhu and Ghahramani [27] proved that $\mathbf{P_L}$ converges to $(I-M_{rr})^{-1}M_{r(|L|+|C|)}P_T$ if $\mathbf{M_{uu}}$ is a right stochastic matrix. Thus the initial value of $\mathbf{P_L}$ is inconsequential.

Using the same approach, we could prove that $\mathbf{P_Q}$ also converges.

5. EXPERIMENT EVALUATION

The goal of the experiments is to evaluate how effective our algorithm is in detecting spam Web sites. Given a seed set L, the LP algorithm returns a list of pages/sites that are sorted according to their probability of being spam. Seed page/sites are not included in the list. We also obtain a list of queries that are sorted according to their probability of being used as a spam-oriented query. A detailed discussion of the queries and sites is in Section 5.6.

5.1 Bipartite Graph Construction

We collected query logs from March 1st, 2011 to March 9th, 2011 with the help of a famous commercial search engine company in

China. No private information was included in these logs. We pruned all of the query-URL pairs with just one click on any day in the log since they may contain noise and possible privacy information. After that, this click-through log consisted of 8,443,963 unique queries, with 12,470,865 unique URLs in 1,055,001 sites. Altogether, 17,660,907 query-URL pairs were collected and they were used in constructing the bipartite graph. The maximal component of the graph contains 2,111,135 (25.0%) unique queries, 3,614,514 (29.0%) URLs and 7,805,300 (44.2%) query-URL pairs. An interesting observation is that the second largest connected component contains only 326 queries, which is a much smaller number compared with the first component. It does not make sense to run the propagation process on such small connected graph. Therefore, we focus on the maximal component of the graph.

Although our algorithm can be applied on both the site-level and the page-level with click-through data, we applied it on the former mainly because of the sparsity problem. A single page usually has fewer queries or even only one query that is pointing to it, which makes it vulnerable to noise.

5.2 Seed Set Selection

5.2.1 Spam Seeds Selection

Seed set contains labeled sites for our LP algorithm. With the help of a famous commercial search engine in China, we obtained a spam site list. A total of 2,100 of these sites appear in our click-through data, and we use them as the spam section of seeds for our algorithms.

5.2.2 Non-spam Seeds Selection

We manually select several ordinary web sites as non-spam seeds according to two criteria. Firstly, these web sites should be famous. There are two reasons for this requirement: a) the more famous the site is, the less likely it will contain spam and b) these sites contain numerous key-resources and we need them to judge the spamicity of the queries. Secondly, sites that mainly consist of user-generated contents are removed because the quality of these contents cannot be guaranteed. For example, http://news.sina.com/ is a non-spam site because most of the pages in it are news articles. The contents will be posted after human examination. In contrast, http://bbs.sina.com.cn/ is not included in the seed set because it is a forum and its contents are not highly reliable. We manually selected 1,153 sites as non-spam section of the seeds.

At last, we constructed the seeds for the algorithm, including 2,100 spam sites and 1,153 non-spam sites. These two sites lists are available at http://www.thuir.cn/weichao/sigir2012/.

5.3 Performance Comparison

We have implemented the LP algorithm on the click-through bipartite graph constructed from search logs mentioned above, and we name it as LP.

Although the algorithm converges, it is not easy to decide when to end the algorithm. We observed that the spam probability changed little after 20 iterations. Specifically, in our experiment, there was little difference between the results after 20 iterations and 40 iterations. Thus, we ran the iteration process 20 times and then output the results.

We use two baselines in the experiment, namely PageRank and TrustRank. PageRank is widely used in ranking search engine results and TrustRank proves to be effective at detecting Web spam. With the help of the same commercial search engine, we constructed a Web link graph that contained 258,326,221 sites. For each hyperlink in page A that points to page B, we added a directed edge from A's site to B's site. Thus the link graph contains 4,883,760,072 edges. We implement the two methods that are completely based on this Web link graph, and they can be regarded as a representative of conventional content-independent anti-spam methods in a real Web environment. Also, we used the common α value of 0.85 in the implementations. We denote the above two baselines as PR and TRUST respectively.

Content-based anti-spam methods were not used in this paper because most of them work only for specific spam techniques. We can expect that they will not achieve a good performance because a variety of spam techniques are used by real spam sites.

Because our label propagation algorithm adopts a different type of information from state-of-the-art anti-spam techniques, it is interesting to combine these algorithms together, and we expect that this combination will achieve better performance than either algorithm. We use the method that is proposed in [1] to combine the results of different algorithms. Suppose L_u is the rank of site u in test set sorted by spamicity score obtained from the LP method, and O_u is the rank obtained from another anti-spam algorithm. Both the result lists are sorted in descending order by spamicity. Note that PageRank/TrustRank result is sorted by scores in ascending order since a lower PageRank/TrustRank score implies this site is more likely to be spam. The merged score S is calculated as follows:

$$S(\mathrm{u},\omega) = \omega \cdot \frac{1}{\mathrm{L_u}+1} + \frac{1}{O_{\mathrm{u}}+1},$$

where ω represents the importance of the LP algorithm's score. We set ω =1, indicating that both algorithms are equally important in the final rank calculation. Then the result list of LP is combined with PR and TRUST and we name them LP-PR and LP-TRUST respectively.

We ran the five algorithms and compared their performances on the test set with respect to the precision, recall, and AUC value, which are all common-used evaluation metrics for spam detection in previous studies [5][12].

5.4 Test Set and Labeling Criterion

Human annotators were recruited to label the URLs list that was returned by the algorithms. However, such labeling is not a trivial task. As discussed in Section 5.1, there are more than 1 million sites in the bipartite graph and it is therefore impossible to label all of them. Since we concern performance of the LP algorithm the most, we selected 3,000 sites uniformly from top half part of the LP results list and used them as our test set. The reason to focus on the top half of the LP results list is that the cost of mislabeling a reputable site as spam is much higher that the opposite. Two experienced human experts were asked to make spam judgments for them, according to the labeling criterion of Web Spam Challenge [28]. Based on the instructions, assessors will have four options for each site they have to tag:

- NONSPAM - The site does not contain spamming aspects.
- BORDERLINE - The site contains some aspects that

are suspicious of being spam.

- SPAM - The site contains spamming aspects.
- CAN'T CLASSIFY - The assessor could not classify the site.

It should be noted that we adopt a stricter judgment on spam sites when "BORDERLINE" and "CAN'T CLASSIFY" sites are labeled as NONSPAM. The reason is that the cost of mislabeling a normal site as spam is much higher than the opposite.

Another problem is that some of the sites may disappear from the Web for different reasons and could no longer be accessed. For these sites we send the URLs to a commercial search engine (http://www.sogou.com/) and obtain their snapshots. Then, they are labeled as "Spam", "Non-spam" or "Can't Access" based on these snapshots. Those whose snapshots did not exist were labeled as "Can't Access".

Each annotator was asked to label 1500 sites. Moreover, they were asked to label another 150 sites to evaluate their agreement. The Cohen's Kappa value is 0.856, which suggests a perfect agreement between the annotators.

Of all of the 3,000 sites, 1,490 are labeled as NONSPAM, 870 are labeled as SPAM and the remaining 640 sites can't be accessed now. We removed all of the inaccessible sites and used the 2,360 labeled sites as our test set (further information about these sites is available at http://www.thuir.cn/weichao/sigir2012/).

5.5 Experiment results

We performed the five algorithms and compared their performances on the test set by precision, recall, and AUC value. The experimental results are shown in Figure 4 and 5.

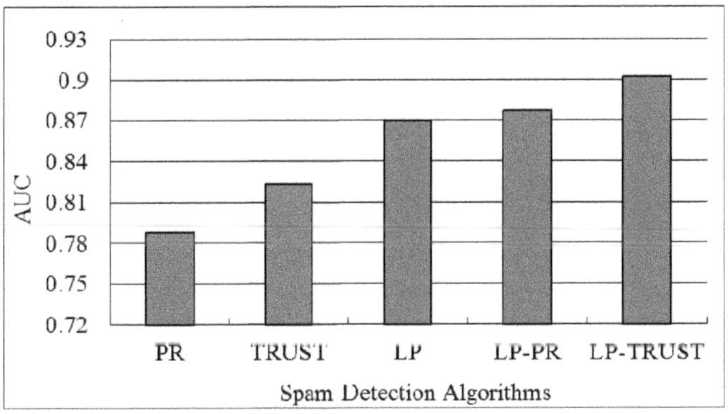

Figure 4. AUC value for different spam detection strategies

From the figures, we can see that all of the AUC values of the five algorithms are greater than 0.78, which suggests that they are effective in detecting Web spam. It is not surprising that PageRank performs the worst because spam sites can boost their PageRank scores using tricks such as the link-farm. TRUST works better than PR, which is consistent with previous research [10]. The AUC value of LP is 0.870, which is much better than both PR (0.788) and TRUST (0.823). This demonstrates our algorithm is effective in detecting Web spam sites. It is encouraging to see our LP algorithm performs better than TrustRank while the former is also less time-consuming. In our experiment, the LP algorithm based on our collected click-through data converged in less than 20 minutes. However, since Trustrank and Pagerank were performed on a complete Web graph that usually contains much more nodes than a click-through bipartite graph, it took more time for both of them to converge, e.g. 10 hours in our experiment.

LP-PR receives a higher AUC value (0.877) while the LP-TRUST approach is impressive in boosting the performance of Spam detection, which obtains a much higher AUC value (0.902) than all of the other algorithms. The precision of this approach can achieve as much as 90% with a recall of 50% and as much as 84.5% with a recall of 70%.

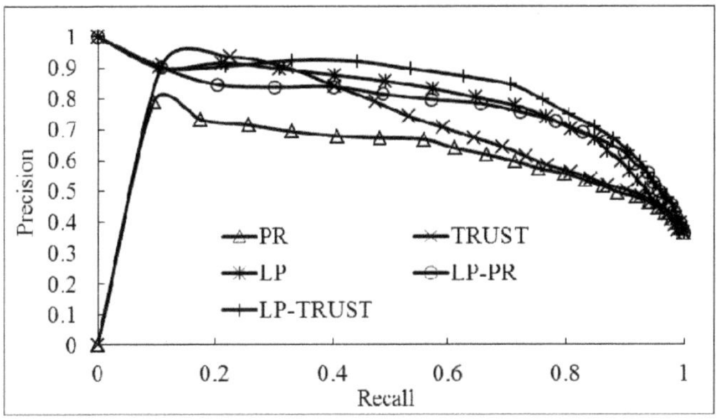

Figure 5. Precision-Recall Curve for different spam detection algorithms

We also conduct another experiment to see how robust our algorithm is. It is known that seed selection is truly important in semi-supervised algorithms such as TrustRank. We randomly split our Spam sites into 21 subsets (each with 100 seed sites) and then add them gradually into the seed set. The experiment results are summarized in Figure 6.

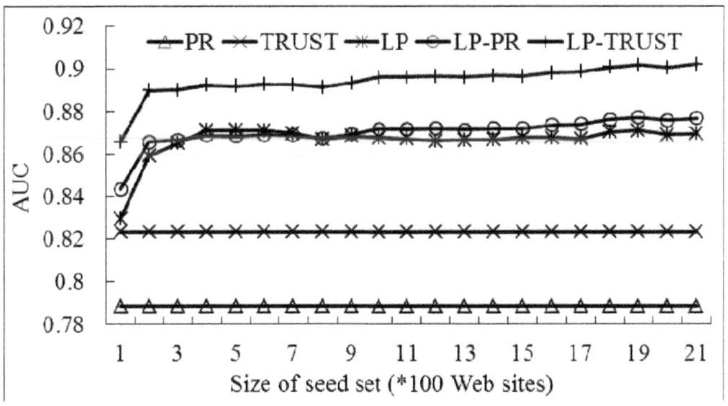

Figure 6. Algorithm performance with different seeds set

It can be seen that all of our algorithms are very robust. They can achieve a relatively high AUC value after only 400 sites are added into the seed sets. We also notice that LP performs consistently better than PR and TRUST. The AUC value of LP-PR is slightly smaller than LP when the size of spam seed sites is between 400 and 700. However, it consistently outperforms LP when more sites are added. LP-TRUST is always the best of all the algorithms.

One-side paired Wilcoxon-tests shows that LP, LP-PR and LP-TRUST are significantly better than TRUST and PR. LP-TRUST is significantly better than other methods. The detailed result is listed in Table 1.

Table 1 One-side paired Wilcoxon-test result (p-value indicates whether algorithm in the row is significantly better than algorithm in each column.)

Wilcoxon-test (p-value)	PR	TRUST	LP	LP-PR
TRUST	2.525e-06	NA	NA	NA
LP	3.206e-05	3.710e-05	NA	NA
LP-PR	3.206e-05	3.206e-05	0.000543	NA
LP-TRUST	3.206e-05	3.206e-05	3.206e-05	3.206e-05

The experiment shows that our novel algorithm is successful in detecting spam sites. Moreover, because we derive this algorithm from a totally different perspective from current anti-spam techniques, combining it with state-of-the-art techniques will result in a more powerful approach for detecting Web spam.

5.6 Discussions

5.6.1 Query analysis

We then conducted several experiments to see how our algorithm detects Web spam sites and why combining LP and TrustRank results in a significantly better performance. We selected the top 1,000 spamming queries and classified them into 7 categories manually: Porn, Game, Health, Entertainment, Software, Lottery and Others. The detailed composition is shown in Figure 7.

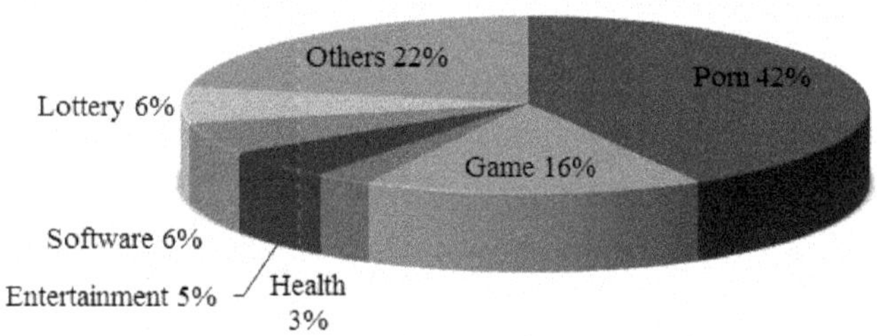

Figure 7. Composition for top spammy queries

We can see from Figure 7 that 42% of these queries are porn terms. Liu et al. [12] find that many of the queries that lead to spam site are porn terms. Spammers use these terms for optimization usually because they are always popular in search engine logs. Moreover, these queries often lack key-resources, which are "reputable" porn sites, because porn contents are illegal in many countries. This contradiction makes porn terms the first choice for spammers.

We notice that game related queries come at the second place, accounting for 16% of all of the 1,000 queries. This can be explained by the fact that quite a lot Internet users are relatively young and are prone to accessing online games. It is not surprising that they use the search engines to find the games. However, in contrast to queries that lead to reputable online games servers, most of these queries have illegal intents. For example, 64.2% of these game-related queries are about "private servers" for online games. These servers are illegal because they emulate online games without warranty. We find that sites that are targeted by these illegal queries usually adopt spam techniques. In contrast, ordinary game sites are not willing to take the risk using spam techniques because they will be put on the blacklist and thus cannot draw any traffic from search engines. Usually, they will adopt other strategies, such as sponsor searches, to draw the attention of potential users. However, things are different for illegal sites because search engines seldom provide services for them. For this reason, they turn to spam techniques. For example, we issued "私服", which means "private server" in Chinese to Google (http://www.google.com/) on October 28th, 2011 and found that almost all of the top 10 sites except for the 5th and the 10th are employing some spamming techniques. In fact, the 5th result is an entity of "私服" in an online encyclopedia site, similar to wikipedia.com and the 10th result is a news page of a famous Web site. This result suggests that illegal web sites are likely to use spam techniques. We list their URLs and spamming techniques in Table 2.

We conducted similar investigations on queries in other categories and find a similar conclusion (we do not list them here because of the space restrictions) that most of these queries meets the two criteria discussed in Section 1. First, they are hot or reflect a heavy demand of search engine users, such as online games or maintaining fitness. Secondly, they lack key resources or authoritative results. Several of these queries are even illegal.

Table 2 Top 10 results for query "私服"

Rank	URL	Spam or not
1	http://www.7774f.com/	Spam (dumping and weaving)
2	http://www.52dayu.com/	Spam (dumping, weaving and redirection)
3	http://www.cnnds.com/	Spam (repetition and stitching)
4	http://www.shiqi.cc/	Spam (link exchange)
5	http://baike.baidu.com/view/6975.htm	Not a spam (an online encyclopedia site)
6	http:// www.20zf.com/	Spam (link exchange)
7	http://www.wnlzj.com/	Spam (weaving and stitching)
8	http://www.luosisa.com/	Spam (weaving)
9	http://www.ipput.com/	Spam (weaving and stitching)
10	Vertical search result (News)	Not a spam

Previous research [5] suggests that monetizable queries are more likely to be spam keywords. However, we find that popular queries, such as porn terms, as well as queries with illegal intents are also more likely to be spam keywords. Two reasons can explain this. First, many spammers try to attract traffic to their sites so that they can increase revenue from advertisers instead of making profit directly from users by selling products. The more traffic or PageRank score their sites have, the more money the advertiser will pay them. Thus they try to gain traffic from popular queries and sometimes succeed in queries with little key-resources. Second, as for the illegal Web sites, they cannot improve their ranks in search engines by regular techniques such as sponsor search, which leads them to spam techniques.

5.6.2 Site analysis

We next examined the characteristics of the spam sites. When looking at the top ranked sites by the spam scores given by LP algorithm, we found that most of them contained illegal contents, such as pornography, private servers and online gambling, and that most used different spam techniques to draw traffic. Our algorithm can find them successfully because queries leading to these sites are more specific, containing porn terms or words such as "private server". Unlike porn sites, which mainly benefit from repetition and keywords stuff, private servers or online gambling sites often use dumping, weaving and stitching to attract traffic. Moreover, these sites often link to each other and hope to benefit from link-exchange. For example, http://www.uiop8.com/ uses almost all of the spam techniques that are listed above.

Other spam sites that we detected are more "general". Most of them would select a topic that they want to optimize and try to create as much spam content as possible, which appear to be relevant to as many queries as possible in this topic. The site http://www.hywww8.com/ is an example.

We also find that spam sites with few queries and clicks are more likely to be spam. Most of the top spam sites in the result list have only 1 query and 2 clicks (notice that 2 is the minimum number of clicks in our pruned click-through logs). This is consistent with our intuition. Reputable sites usually cover more topics and have more user clicks. As a result, when a site is clicked after a spammy query and it seldom appears in the click-through data which means it has few non-spammy queries, we have a bigger confidence that this is a spam site.

5.6.3 Combining label propagation with TrustRank

Although our method can discover a variety of spam sites, they have its own limitations. It is difficult to label ordinary sites with a rare number of queries. The main problem is that there is little information about these sites in the click-through data. However, other anti-spam techniques, such as TrustRank, could provide us with information about how trustworthy a site is, which could be used to boost the performance of our algorithms. In contrast, TrustRank also has its limitation. http://www.17646.com/, a private server for online games, manages to obtain a high TrustRank score, ranking the $86{,}000^{th}$ of all the 258,326,221 sites. Therefore, TrustRank fails to identify it as a spam site. However, it ranks the 80th for its spam score in our algorithm. By combining its spam rank and trust rank, we rank it at the 176th place in the final results list, which means that it is likely to be a spam site.

Because we use a completely different method to detect Web spam, we expect to obtain a much better performance by combining it with other state-of-the-art algorithms. We leave this promising task for our future work.

6. CONCLUSION AND FUTURE WORK

In this paper we have proposed a novel label propagation algorithm on click-through bipartite graphs to detect Web spam. Different from current approaches which focus on identifying predefined types of Web spam pages/sites, this algorithm exploits the characteristics of spam queries. The spamisity score propagates between queries and URLs iteratively on the click-through bipartite graph from a seed set that contains both spam and non-spam pages/sites. Experiment results show that our algorithm is both efficient and effective in detecting Web spam pages/sites. This algorithm introduces a novel perspective to fight against Web spam, and combining it with some current anti-spam techniques results in a much better performance.

For future work, we plan to investigate the following aspects. Firstly, we will attempt to solve the sparsity problem that was discussed in Section 5 by collecting more click-through data. We also notice that there are several small connected components except for the maximal one in the click-through log. Are there spam sites? How many spam sites exist in these components? We will try to answer these questions in future work. Secondly, our framework will be extended to embody other features, including content, hyperlink features and click-through features. For example, we found that even for those popular but not spammy queries, sites with few clicks are also suspicious. Query "戴尔官方网站" ("DELL official Website" in Chinese) appeared 6,159 times in the log and 39 different sites were clicked after it. Among these sits, spam site http://www.buydellonline.cn/ appeared only twice. Moreover, it appeared only 4 times in the click-through data. In contrast, http://www.dellenglish.com/ which appeared only 3 times after this query but had 38 clicks in query "English study", turned to be an ordinary site. This indicates such features can be used to boost the LP algorithm performance. Moreover, we notice that while some queries are generally more likely to be spam queries, some other queries are not likely to be spam queries, such as the name of a small company. Query taxonomy information is also a helpful feature. We will incorporate such information in our propagation process in our future work, too.

7. ACKNOWLEDGMENTS

This work was supported by Natural Science Foundation (60903107, 61073071), National High Technology Research and Development (863) Program (2011AA01A205) and Research Fund for the Doctoral Program of Higher Education of China (20090002120005).

8. REFERENCES

[1] Agichtein, E., Brill, E. and Dumais, S. 2006. Improving web search ranking by incorporating user behavior information. In *Proceedings of the 29th annual international ACM SIGIR conference on Research and development in information retrieval* (Seattle, Washington, August 6-11, 2006).SIGIR '06. ACM, New York, NY, 19-26.

[2] Attenberg, J. and Suel, T. 2008. Cleaning search results using term distance features. In *Proceedings of the 4th International Workshop on Adversarial Information Retrieval on the Web* (Beijing, China, April 22, 2008). AIRWeb '08. ACM, New York, NY, 21-24.

[3] Castillo, C. and Davison, B.D. 2011. *Adversarial Web Search.* Foundations and trends in Information Retrieval. 4, 5 (2011), 377-488.

[4] Castillo, C., Donato, D., Gionis, A., Murdock, V. and Silvestri, F. 2007. Know your neighbors: Web spam detection using the web topology. In *Proceedings of the 30th Annual International ACM SIGIR Conference on Research and Development in Information Retrieval* (Amsterdam, The Netherlands, July 23-27, 2007). SIGIR '07. ACM, New York, NY, 423-430.

[5] Chellapilla, K. and Chickering, D.M. 2006. Improving cloaking detection using search query popularity and monetizability. In *Proceedings of the 2nd International*

Workshop on Adversarial Information Retrieval on the Web (Seattle, Washington, August 10, 2006). AIRWeb '06. ACM, New York, NY, 17-24.

[6] Chellapilla, K., and Maykov, A. 2007. A taxonomy of JavaScript redirection spam. In *Proceedings of the 3rd International Workshop on Adversarial Information Retrieval on the Web* (Banff, Alberta, Canada, May 8, 2007). AIRWeb '07. ACM, New York, NY, 81-88.

[7] Cheng, Z., Gao, B., Sun, C., Jiang, Y. and Liu, T. 2011. Let Web Spammers Expose Themselves. In *Proceedings of the fourth ACM international conference on Web search and data mining* (Hong Kong, China, February 9-12, 2011). WSDM '11, ACM, New York, NY, 525-534.

[8] Erdélyi, M., Garzó, A. and Benczúr, A.A. 2011. Web spam classification: a few features worth more. In *Proceedings of the 2011 Joint WICOW/AIRWeb Workshop on Web Quality* (Hyderabad, India, March 28, 2011). WebQuality '11, ACM, New York, NY, 27-34.

[9] Gyöngyi, Z. and Garcia-Molina, H. 2005. *Spam: It's Not Just for Inboxes Anymore.* IEEE Computer Magzine. 38, 10 (2005), 28-34.

[10] Gyöngyi, Z., Garcia-Molina, H. and Pedersen, J. 2004. Combating Web Spam with TrustRank. *In Proceedings of the 30th International Conference on Very Large Data Bases* (Toronto, Canada, August 29 – September 3, 2004). VLDB '04. VLDB Endowment, US, 576-587.

[11] Gyöngyi, Z. and Garcia-Molina, H. 2005. Web spam taxonomy. In *Proceedings of the First International Workshop on Adversarial Information Retrieval on the Web* (Chiba, Japan, May 10, 2005). AIRWeb '05. ACM, New York, NY, 39-47.

[12] Liu, Y., Cen, R., Zhang, M., Ma, S., and Ru, L. 2008. Identifying Web spam with user behavior analysis. In *Proceedings of the 4th International Workshop on Adversarial Information Retrieval on the Web* (Beijing, China, April 22, 2008). AIRWeb '08. ACM, New York, NY, 9-16.

[13] Liu Y., Gao B., Liu TY., Zhang Y., Ma Z., He S. and Li H. 2008. BrowserRank: letting web users vote for page importance. In *Proceedings of the 31th Annual International ACM SIGIR Conference on Research and Development in Information Retrieval* (Singapore, July 20-24, 2008). SIGIR '08. ACM, New York, NY, 451-458.

[14] Martinez-Romo, J. and Araujo, L. 2009. Web spam identification through language model analysis. In *Proceedings of the 5th International Workshop on Adversarial Information Retrieval on the Web* (Madrid, Spain, April 21, 2009). AIRWeb '09. ACM, New York, NY, 21-28.

[15] Moshchuk, A., Bragin, T., Gribble, D.S. and Levy, M. H. 2006. A crawler-based study of spyware on the web. In *Proceedings of the thirteenth Annual Symposium on Network and Distributed System Security* (San Diego, California, US, February, 2006). NDSS '06.

[16] Nie, L., Wu, B. and Davison, D.B. 2007. Winnowing wheat from the chaff: Propagating trust to sift spam from the Web. In *Proceedings of the 30th Annual International ACM SIGIR Conference on Research and Development in Information Retrieval* (Amsterdam, The Netherlands, July 23-27, 2007). SIGIR '07. ACM, New York, NY, 869-870.

[17] Ntoulas, A., Najork, M., Manasse, M. and Fetterly, D. 2006. Detecting Spam Web Pages through Content Analysis. *In Proceedings of the 15th International Conference on World Wide Web* (Edinburgh, Scotland, May 23-26, 2006). WWW '06. ACM, New York, NY, 83-92.

[18] Piskorski, J., Sydow, M. and Weiss, D. 2008. Exploring linguistic features for Web spam detection: A preliminary study. In *Proceedings of the 4th International Workshop on Adversarial Information Retrieval on the Web* (Beijing, China, April 22, 2008). AIRWeb '08. ACM, New York, NY, 25-28.

[19] Silverstein, C., Marais H., Henzinger M., and Moricz M. 1999. Analysis of a Very Large Web Search Engine Query Log. *Association for Computer Machinery, SIGIR Forum, 33, 3.*

[20] Singhal, A. *Challenges in running a commercial search engine.* 2005. Keynote presentation at SIGIR 2005, August 2005.

[21] Sobek, M. 2002. PR0 — Google's PageRank 0 penalty, http://pr.efactory.de/e-pr0.shtml, 2002.

[22] Urvoy, T., Chauveau, E., Filoche, P. and Lavergne, T. Tracking Web spam with HTML style similarities. *ACM Transactions on the Web.* 2, 1 (February, 2008).

[23] Urvoy, T., Lavergne, T. and Filoche, P. 2006. Tracking Web spam with hidden style similarity. In *Proceedings of the 2nd International Workshop on Adversarial Information Retrieval on the Web* (Seattle, Washington, August 10, 2006). AIRWeb '06. ACM, New York, NY, 25-32.

[24] Wu, B. and Davison, D.B. 2006. Detecting semantic cloaking on the Web. *In Proceedings of the 15th International Conference on World Wide Web* (Edinburgh, Scotland, May 23-26, 2006). WWW '06. ACM, New York, NY, 819-828.

[25] Wu, B. and Davison, D. B. 2005. Identifying link farm spam pages. In *Special interest tracks and posters of the 14th International Conference on World Wide Web* (Chiba, Japan, May 10-14, 2005). WWW '05. ACM, New York, NY, 820 - 829.

[26] Wu, B., Goel, V. and Davison, D.B. 2006. Propagating trust and distrust to demote Web spam. In *Workshop on Models of Trust for the Web* (Edinburgh, Scotland, May 22, 2006). MTW '06.

[27] Zhu, X. and Ghahramani, Z. 2002. *Learning from Labeled and Unlabeled Data with Label Propagation.* CMU CALD technical report CMU-CALD-02-107.

[28] http://www.yr-bcn.es/webspam/datasets/uk2006-info/

Learning Hash Codes for Efficient Content Reuse Detection

Qi Zhang, Yan Wu, Zhuoye Ding, Xuanjing Huang
School of Computer Science, Fudan University
825 Zhangheng Road, Shanghai, P.R.China
{qi_zhang, 10210240075, 09110240024, xjhuang}@fudan.edu.cn

ABSTRACT

Content reuse is extremely common in user generated mediums. Reuse detection serves as be the basis for many applications. However, along with the explosion of Internet and continuously growing uses of user generated mediums, the task becomes more critical and difficult. In this paper, we present a novel efficient and scalable approach to detect content reuse. We propose a new signature generation algorithm, which is based on learned hash functions for words. In order to deal with tens of billions of documents, we implement the detection approach on graphical processing units (GPUs). The experimental comparison in this paper involves studies of efficiency and effectiveness of the proposed approach in different types of document collections, including ClueWeb09, Tweets2011, and so on. Experimental results show that the proposed approach can achieve the same detection rates with state-of-the-art systems while uses significantly less execution time than them (from 400X to 1500X speedup).

Categories and Subject Descriptors

H.3.3 [**Information Storage and Retrieval**]: Information Search and Retrieval - Information Search and Retrieval; H.3.7 [**Digital Libraries**]: Collection, Systems Issues

Keywords

Content Reuse Detection, GPUs, Learning to Hash

1. INTRODUCTION

There is a quick expansion in the popularity of user generated content in forums, microblogging sites, blogs, and other medius in recent years. These broadcast mediums provide opportunities for users to exchange content. According to the statistics, users in Twitter send 230 million tweets per day[8]. Technorati's State of the Blogosphere Report also showed that there are about 126 million blogs on the Internet in 2010. The development of these platforms has resulted in the number of user generated content (UGC) rapidly growing during the last few years.

While the increasing of UGC, *content reuse*, which is the practice of using existing content components, occurs frequently in these mediums. It contains various forms including duplicate, near-duplicate, and partial-duplicate. Exact duplicate documents can be easily identified by standard checksumming techniques. Near-duplicate web pages contain identical core content but are different in framing, navigation bar, advertisements, footer, or other non-content parts. Partial-duplicate, which is a more difficult problem, contains quoted phrases, sentences, or passages from other documents.

Duplicate or near-duplicate detection can help search engine to reduce storage costs and improve the quality of search indexes. It may also avoid users to see redundant documents in search results. Applications including plagiarism detection, information flow tracking, opinion mining, and so on may benefit from the partial-duplicate detection or involve it as the basis. Along with the increasing requirements, content reuse detection has received much attention in recent years. Many efficient and effective algorithms have been proposed [11, 15, 19, 23, 24, 25, 28, 33].

The challenges of content reuse detection include: 1) reuse may happen at different levels; 2) massive documents should be efficiently processed. Partial-duplicate detection may require different algorithms to the approaches proposed for resolving near-duplicate document detection. One of the main reason for this is that only a small part of a document is taken from others. Content reuse detection algorithms have to face with enormous documents, due to the rapid growth of the web. Thus, it is essential that content reuse detection methods should be efficient and scalable.

In this paper, we investigate a novel approach to detect sentence level content reuse by mapping sentence to a signature space. Signature of a sentence is created by taking the *bitwise-or* of all signatures of words occurs in the sentence. Rather than using traditional hash functions, which do not consider statistics of words or characters, to assign hash code for each word/character, we analyze the requirements of what the good codes should satisfy and formalize it as a constraint optimization problem. Since the task of finding optimal codes is NP hard, we relax the optimization problem and introduce a efficiency method to calculate the codes. With the signature generation method, sentences whose reuse scores are predicted to be less than a given threshold are eliminated. Experimental results show that the codes generated by the proposed method outperform

Permission to make digital or hard copies of all or part of this work for personal or classroom use is granted without fee provided that copies are not made or distributed for profit or commercial advantage and that copies bear this notice and the full citation on the first page. To copy otherwise, to republish, to post on servers or to redistribute to lists, requires prior specific permission and/or a fee.
SIGIR'12, August 12–16, 2012, Portland, Oregon, USA.
Copyright 2012 ACM 978-1-4503-1472-5/12/08 ...$10.00.

state-of-the-art approaches. In order to handle millions of documents, graphical processing units (GPUs) are used to implement the detection algorithm.

The contributions of this work are as follows: 1) We outline and discuss what makes good codes of words for content reuse detection. 2) Efficient optimization method is proposed based on several relaxation. 3) We provide parallel algorithm and its GPU implementation. 4) Evaluations on six large web collections in both English and Chinese are used to measure the efficiency and effectiveness.

The remaining of the paper is organized as follows: In section 2, we review a number of related work and the state-of-the-art approaches in related areas. Section 3 presents the proposed method. Experimental results in test collections and analyses are shown in section 4. Section 5 concludes this paper.

2. RELATED WORK

Our approach relates to three research areas: content reuse detection, learning to hash and parallel algorithms based on GPUs. In this section, we discuss the related work on these areas.

2.1 Content Reuse Detection

Content reuse detection has received much attention in the past several years. Previous studies on content reuse detection can be roughly divided into two research directions: representation and efficiency. The first one focuses on representing text in different levels with or without linguistic knowledge. With the growth of digital documents, efficiency, has also received much more attentions.

Shingling, which was proposed by Broder [4], uses contiguous subsequences to represent documents. It does not rely on any linguistic knowledge. If sets of shingles extracted from different documents are appreciably overlap, these documents are considered exceedingly similar, which are usually measured by Jaccard similarity. In order to reduce the complexity of shingling, meta-sketches was proposed to handle the efficiency problem [5].

In order to improve the robustness of shingle-like signatures, Theobald et al. introduced a method, SpotSigs. It provides more semantic pre-selection of shingles for extracting characteristic signatures from Web documents [28]. SpotSigs combines stopword antecedents with short chains of adjacent content terms. The aim of it is to filter natural-language text passages out of noisy Web page components. They also proposed several pruning conditions based on the upper bounds of Jaccard similarity.

Chowdhury et al. proposed I-Match [7], which filters the input document based on collection statistics and compute a single hash value for the remainder text. If the documents with same hash value, they are considered as duplicates. It hinges on the premise that removal of very infrequent terms and very common terms results good document representations for the near-duplicate detection task. Since I-Match signatures is respect to small modifications, Kołcz et al. [16] proposed the solution of several I-Match signatures, all derived from randomized versions of the original lexicon.

Different from the methods focused on document level, partial-duplicate detection was proposed by Zhang et al. [33]. They converted the task into two subtasks: sentence level near-duplicate detection and sequence matching. Except for the similarities between documents, the method can simultaneously output the positions where the duplicated parts occur. In order to handle the efficiency problem, they implement their method using three MapReduce jobs.

Local text reuse detection focus on identifying the reused and modified sentences, facts or passages, rather than whole documents. Seo and Croft [23] analyzed the task and defined six categories of text reuse. They proposed a general framework for text reuse detection. Several fingerprinting techniques for the framework were evaluated under the framework.

The most similar work to ours was proposed by Kim et al. [15]. They mapped sentences into a point in a high dimensional space and leveraged range searches in this space. However different with us, they simply use MD5 hash function for each word to generate signature file. In this paper, we outline and discuss what makes a good code for content reuse detection, and propose to use learned hash codes to capture the relations between words/characters to reduce the false matches.

2.2 Learning to Hash

Extensive research on similarity search have been proposed in recent years. Among them hash-based methods were received more attention due to its ability of solving similarity search in high dimensional space. Recently, several researches attempted to find good data-aware hash functions through machine learning.

Hinton and Salakhutdinov proposed to train a multilayer neural network with a small central layer to convert high-dimensional input vectors into low-dimensional codes [13]. They used a two-layer network called a Restricted Boltzmann machine(RBM) [14] to do it. Experimental results showed that it could accelerate document retrieval.

Spectral hashing [30] was defined to seek compact binary codes in order to preserve the semantic similarity between codewords. Weiss et al. defined the criterion for a good code which is related to graph partitioning and used a spectral relaxation to obtain a solution.

Norouzi and Fleet [20] introduced a method for learning similarity-preserving hash functions, which is based on latent structural SVM framework. They designed a specific loss function taking Hamming distance and binary quantization into account.

Zhang et al. introduced Self-Taught Hashing (STH) approach to semantic hashing [32]. They divided the problem of finding small codes into two stages. Firstly, they used unsupervised method, binarised-LapEig, to optimal l-bit binary codes for all documents in the given corpus. The classifiers were trained to predict the l-bit code for unseen documents.

Almost all the current methods for similarity-preserving hash functions attempt to map the high dimensional data, which represents the whole document or sentence, onto binary codes. In this paper, we seek good binary codes for words under the content reuse detection framework.

2.3 GPU-based Algorithms

Graphics programming units is designed for single instruction multiple data(SIMD) paradigm, which is different from general purpose microprocessors. Due to its advantages on massive parallel, high memory bandwidth, and powerful computing capacity, GPUs have been successfully used in numerical algorithms.

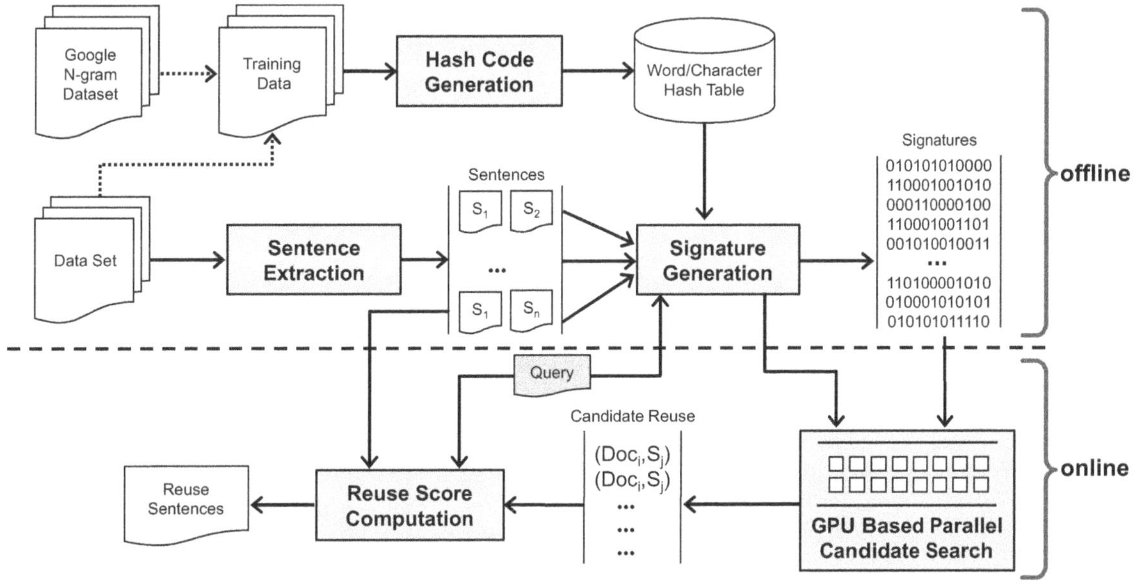

Figure 1: An overview of the proposed content reuse detection approach

Owens et al. [21] introduced their works on implementing three applications (protein folding simulation, scalable molecular dynamics, and calculating electrostatic potential maps). Through these examples, they demonstrated the potential of the GPU for delivering performance gains on real problems.

The emergence of the NVIDIA CUDA programming model speed up the trend of using GPUs to accelerate algorithms. Edelkamp et al. [9] introduced their work on accelerating state space search using GPUs. Linear algebra operators were also implemented to build blocks for more complex numerical algorithms [17]. The results of researches in sort [12], search [6], linear algebra [10], partial differential equations (PDEs) [3], and many other applications have demonstrated the performance and capabilities of GPUs.

F

3. OUR APPROACH

The processing flow of the proposed content reuse detection approach is shown in Figure 1. It consists of two distinct stages:*offline* and *online*. Given a collection of documents, the *sentence extraction* step splits the documents into sentences. *Hash code generation* step takes the training data calculated based on the given collections or open domain data set to generate data-aware hash codes for words or characters. *Signature generation* step uses the hash table to calculate hash code of sentences from both document corpus and given queries. The key algorithm of the online stage is *candidate searching*, which tries to filter the sentences whose reuse scores with the given query are guaranteed not bigger than a given threshold. The reuse sentences and their corresponding reuse scores are calculate in the final step.

Many similarity metrics have been proposed for content reuse detection. Jaccard similarity has been used in various works [4, 33]. Metzler et al. proposed to use weighted word overlap similarity to measure reuse score [18]. There are also a number of works to study the effect of cosine similarity [2, 31]. However, directly use these similarity metrics to detect content reuse in large collections would be very expensive. Because of this, in recent years, hash-based methods have been carefully studied and have demonstrated their advantageous for near similarity search in large document collections [27].

In this paper, we follow the method proposed by Kim et al. [15], which map sentence signature into a point in a high dimensional space. Within this method, each word (or character in Chinese corpus) is assigned a fixed-width bit string. The sentence signature is generated by taking *bitwise-or* of all signature of words in the sentence. Figure 2 shows an example of sentence signature generation process. $h(\cdot)$ represents hash function for words. In [15], two bits were set for each word using MD5 hash function [22] for 32-bit signatures.

Suppose $S_i = b_{i1}b_{i2}b_{i3}...b_{im}$, which consists of m-bits, represents a signature extracted from a sentence. We can map it into a point, $p_i = (b_{i1}, b_{i2}, b_{i3}, ..., b_{im})$, in m-dimensional space. Then the candidate sentences can be selected based on Euclidean distance between sentences, which can be calculated as follow:

$$Distance(p_i, p_j) = \sqrt{\sum_{k=1}^{m} (b_{ik} - b_{jk})^2}.$$

In other words, it also represents the number of bit different between the two sentences. Given a threshold $\sqrt{d}$, the points whose distances lie in the range are extracted as candidates.

3.1 Learning Hash Code

As mentioned above, signatures of sentences are generated based on the hash codes of words. Therefore, how to select hash codes for words has become one of the key problems in this task. In the following parts of this section, we discuss and describe our proposed method.

Sentence: Apple announces iPhone 4s.	
h(Apple)	= 0100 0010
h(announce)	= 1100 0010
h(iPhone)	= 1001 0000
h(4s)	= 0101 0011
Signature of Sentence (*bitwise-or*)	= 1101 0011

Figure 2: Example of sentence signature

3.1.1 *What good code should satisfy?*

The proposed approach tries to find as many as possible reuses under the given upper bound of false matches. In other words, it aims to maximize the recall rate, ρ_{rec}, on the given false positives rate ρ_{fp}. Under the same conditions, the number of bits, m, and the number, l, of bits set to 1 in the signature effect the detection recall and precision. In particular, m, l, and vocabulary size should follow the equation $\binom{m}{l} \geq w$ [15], and l is selected as the smallest value among all candidates. Hence, in order to save the code space, words which usually occur together should have the same hash code.

Based on the descriptions above, we seek hash codes which should satisfy the following properties: (1) the number of bits set to 1 in the word hash code is low; (2) the number of bits to code the vocabulary should be small; (3) words which usually occur together should have same hash codes. In this paper, we formalize the good code seeking task as a constraint optimization problem.

Let $\{y_i\}_{i=1}^{n}$ be the list of hash codes for n words. $y_i \in \{0,1\}^m$ represents m-bits binary vector. $\#(w_i)$ represents the number of sentences containing word w_i in the given corpus, $\#(w_i, w_j)$ indicates the number of sentences containing both word w_i and word w_j. s_{ij} measures the similarity between word w_i and w_j, which is formulated as following:

$$s_{ij} = \frac{\#(w_i, w_j)}{\sqrt{\#(w_i)}\sqrt{\#(w_j)}}.$$

s_{ij} equals to binary cosine similarity in which a dimension receives a score of 1 when the word appears in the sentence and 0 when it does not appear. The parameter l defines the number of bits set to 1 in the hash code. s_{ij} can be unsupervised generated based on given corpus. By incorporating all the constraints together, we obtain the following problem:

$$\begin{aligned} \text{minimize:} \quad & \sum_{ij} s_{ij} \left(\sum_{k=1}^{m} (y_{ik} - y_{jk})^2 \right) \\ \text{subject to:} \quad & y_i \in \{0,1\}^m, 1 \leq i \leq n \\ & \sum_{k=1}^{m} y_{ik} = l, 1 \leq i \leq n \end{aligned} \tag{1}$$

The property (1) is satisfied by $\sum_{k=1}^{m} y_{ik} = l$, where l is usually set to a small number (in this work, we set $l = \frac{1}{16}m$). The number of bits in hash code is predefined by m to follow the property (2). The property (3) is implemented as the objective function. If two words usually occur together in sentences and have different hash code, it would give negative impact of the objective function.

3.1.2 *Optimization*

The solving of equation (1) is 0-1 integer programming program, which is a special case of integer programming. It is known to be NP-hard. There is no easy solution for directly optimizing it. Since the number of bits required by equation (1) does not follow the restrictive assumption that the bits are uniformly distributed, the spectrum of the similarity matrix of the data can not be directly used to get the hash codes as spectral hashing [30]. Relaxation and approximation methods should be used to solve the large-scale problem.

First of all, the constraint $y_i \in \{0,1\}^m$ is replaced by $0 \leq y_i \leq 1$. By ignoring the integer constraints, the objective function in (1) is differentiable. In other words, the problem in (1) is relaxed as:

$$\begin{aligned} \text{minimize:} \quad & \sum_{ij} s_{ij} \left(\sum_{k=1}^{m} (y_{ik} - y_{jk})^2 \right) \\ \text{subject to:} \quad & 0 \leq y_i \leq 1, 1 \leq i \leq n \\ & \sum_{k=1}^{m} y_{ik} = l, 1 \leq i \leq n \end{aligned} \tag{2}$$

Since there are usually thousands of y_i and m is also bigger than 32 in practice, the number of parameters tend to be extremely large. The number of constraints is also linear in the size of vocabulary. Because of these, the problem in (2) can not be directly solved within acceptable time either.

In this work, we use an interior-point nonlinear programming algorithm based on a filter line search to solve the problem [29]. Based on it, the inequality constraints are converted to barrier functions which are combined with objective function. We combine the following barrier function with objective function to replace the constraint $0 \leq y_i \leq 1, 1 \leq i \leq n$:

$$-\mu \sum_{i}^{n} \sum_{k}^{m} (\ln(y_{ik}) + \ln(1 - y_{ik})) \tag{3}$$

,where μ is barrier parameter, which is decreased at each optimization iteration. The problem in equation 1 can now be formulated as a sequence of approximate maximization :

$$\begin{aligned} \text{minimize:} \quad & \sum_{ij} s_{ij} \left(\sum_{k=1}^{m} (y_{ik} - y_{jk})^2 \right) \\ & -\mu \sum_{i}^{n} \sum_{k}^{m} (\ln(y_{ik}) + \ln(1 - y_{ik})) \\ \text{subject to:} \quad & \sum_{k=1}^{m} y_{ik} - l = 0, 1 \leq i \leq n \end{aligned} \tag{4}$$

3.2 Reuse Detection

Algorithm 1 presents the pseudo-code for the detection part (marked as *online* in the figure 1) of the proposed reuse detection method. $SigCol$ represents a collection of sentence signatures extracted from a document collection. Given $SigCol$ and a query sentence, q, the *candidate search* step tries to identify a set of candidate sentences, $CSet$. The *candidate search* step selects sentences by searching the points whose distances between p_q are less than the given threshold $\sqrt{d}$. After that, if the candidate sentences set $CSet$ is not empty, the *reuse score computation* step calculates the reuse scores between query sentence with each

Algorithm 1 Pseudo-code of the Reuse Detection

INPUT: a query sentence, q, a distance threshold $\sqrt{d}$, and signatures of document collection, $SigCol$
OUTPUT: a set of detected reuse sentences, O_q

Candidate Selection:

1: Generate signature S_q for the given query q,
2: **for all** $S_i \in SigCol$ **do**
3: **if** $Distance(S_q, S_i) < \sqrt{d}$ **then**
4: $CSet = CSet \bigcup i$
5: **end if**
6: **end for**
7: **return** $CSet$

Reuse Score Computing:

1: **for all** $i \in CSet$ **do**
2: $Sim_{q,i} = Jaccard(S_q, S_i)$
3: **if** $Sim_{q,i} > \theta$ **then**
4: $O_q = O_q \bigcup < i, Sim_{q,i} >$
5: **end if**
6: **end for**
7: **return** Q_q

candidate based on Jaccard similarity. If the reuse score of a sentence is greater than the pre-defined threshold, the sentence and its corresponding document is added in the final list.

From analyzing the calculation consumption of algorithm 1, we observe that the most time consuming part is spent on step 3 of the candidate selection step. Since the number of sentences in $SigCol$ is usually tens of millions, $Distance(S_q, S_i)$ takes the most computing time of the whole algorithm. Fortunately, GPUs offered us an opportunity to accelerate the performance of the algorithm. Modern GPUs are massively parallel processors with extremely high memory bandwidth. Many operations can be performed in parallel. The distance calculation part is suitable for implementation on GPUs as it is fairly simple and consumes a huge part of computing resources.

The function executed GPUs in parallel is called *kernel*, which is driven by *threads* and grouped together in *blocks* and *grids*. In this work, we implement the step 3, 4, and 5 in *candidate selection* part as a kernel function. Based on the thread index and block index, different sentence signature S_i will be justified in different threads. Since signature file of the whole corpus is small enough (302MB for 10 million sentences), it can be easily loaded into the global memory of modern GPUs entirely at once.

The implement of the *candidate selection* is shown in figure 3. The first step is to copy signatures extracted from a collection into global memory. Different threads would parallel process different parts of signatures in stream processors. The step 2 and step 3 in the figure are iterated for each query. Because the bottleneck of this task on GPUs is the memory access rather than processing time, if multiple queries were processed at the same time, the acceleration ratio to CPU implementation would be further improved.

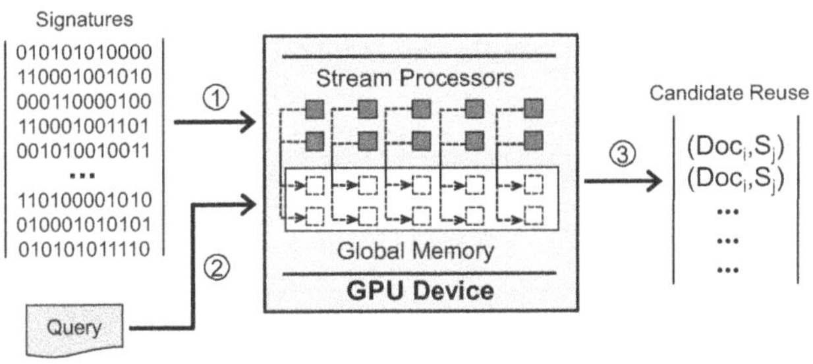

Figure 3: Implementation of GPU Based Parallel Candidate Search

4. EXPERIMENTS

4.1 Collections

We evaluate the proposed method with six corpora TIPSTER (Volume 1-3)[1], ClueWeb09-T09B[2], Tweets2011 Twitter [3], SogouT 2.0[4], Baidu Zhidao[5], Sina Weibo[6]. Table 1 shows the statistics of the six collections. TIPSTER collection contains news articles, discourse passages extracted from Associated Press (AP), Wall Street Journal (WSJ) and so on. It has been used for evaluations of information retrieval, entity extraction, and many other tasks. Tweets2011 Twitter collection is used by Trec 2011 microblog track, which contains about 16 million tweets sampled between January 23rd and February 8th, 2011 [7]. TREC Category B dataset (ClueWeb09-T09B), which is a subset of the ClueWeb09, contains 50 million English pages and has been used in various TREC tracks. Since the proposed approach is language independent, we also evaluate the proposed approach on three Chinese collections. Baidu Zhidao is one of the most popular community Q&A site in China. We crawled a portion of question and answer pairs of all categories from it, resulting in a local archive of about 33.5 million questions. Sina Weibo is the most popular and the largest Twitter-like micro-blog site in China. Messages or comments from approximate 1.78 million users are used in this work.

4.2 Implementation and Setup

We set the signature lengths(m) to 32 in this work. Following the parameters used in [15], the l is set 2 for 32 bits signature. For English collections, words are used as the basic units to assign hash codes. The basic units of Chinese collections are characters. We re-implemented the baseline **qSign** algorithm [15] using the MD5 [22] as hash function to assign hash codes for all the words/characters. It is labeled as "*MD5*" in the following tables and figures. To verify the proposed properties that good hash code should satisfy, we construct another hash code generation baseline, which set the same hash code for the words which often oc-

[1]http://www.ldc.upenn.edu/
[2]http://boston.lti.cs.cmu.edu/Data/clueweb09/
[3]http://trec.nist.gov/data/tweets/
[4]http://www.sogou.com/labs/dl/t.html
[5]http://zhidao.baidu.com
[6]http://www.weibo.com
[7]Since the data is crawled by ourselves with the tools and tweet lists provided by NIST, about 5.8% tweets are missed in our collection due to the user name change or other reasons.

Table 2: Detailed impact of different hash code generation methods. The reuse threshold θ is set to 0.8.

bits diff.	MD5			NER			OPT		
	#can.	P	R	#can.	P	R	#can.	P	R
$d = 0$	19,087	0.239	0.896	8,881	0.514	0.896	4,704	0.965	0.891
$d = 1$	17,2464	0.027	0.928	64,361	0.073	0.929	7,262	0.648	0.924
$d = 2$	992,403	0.005	0.965	416,552	0.012	0.968	27,060	0.182	0.966
$d = 3$	3,955,643	0.001	0.992	1,889,988	0.002	0.994	139,808	0.036	0.988
$d = 4$	12,049,613	0.000	1.000	6,472,842	0.001	1.000	632,570	0.008	0.998
$d = 5$	29,990,264	0.000	1.000	17,857,693	0.000	1.000	2,358,244	0.002	1.000

(a) TIPSTER

The total number of ground truth reuse sentences for 2,000 queries is 5,095.

bits diff.	MD5			NER			OPT		
	#can.	P	R	#can.	P	R	#can.	P	R
$d = 0$	15,686	0.611	0.394	15,205	0.631	0.394	15,773	0.623	0.403
$d = 1$	72,832	0.224	0.669	67,964	0.243	0.678	67,846	0.247	0.687
$d = 2$	310,708	0.071	0.907	258,559	0.085	0.906	242,141	0.091	0.907
$d = 3$	1,146,414	0.021	0.987	862,317	0.027	0.987	727,063	0.033	0.986
$d = 4$	3,775,472	0.006	0.998	2,654,901	0.009	0.998	2,001,083	0.012	0.998
$d = 5$	11,025,379	0.002	0.999	7,574,689	0.003	0.999	5,306,237	0.004	0.999

(b) SogouT 2.0

The total number of ground truth reuse sentences for 2,000 queries is 24,359.

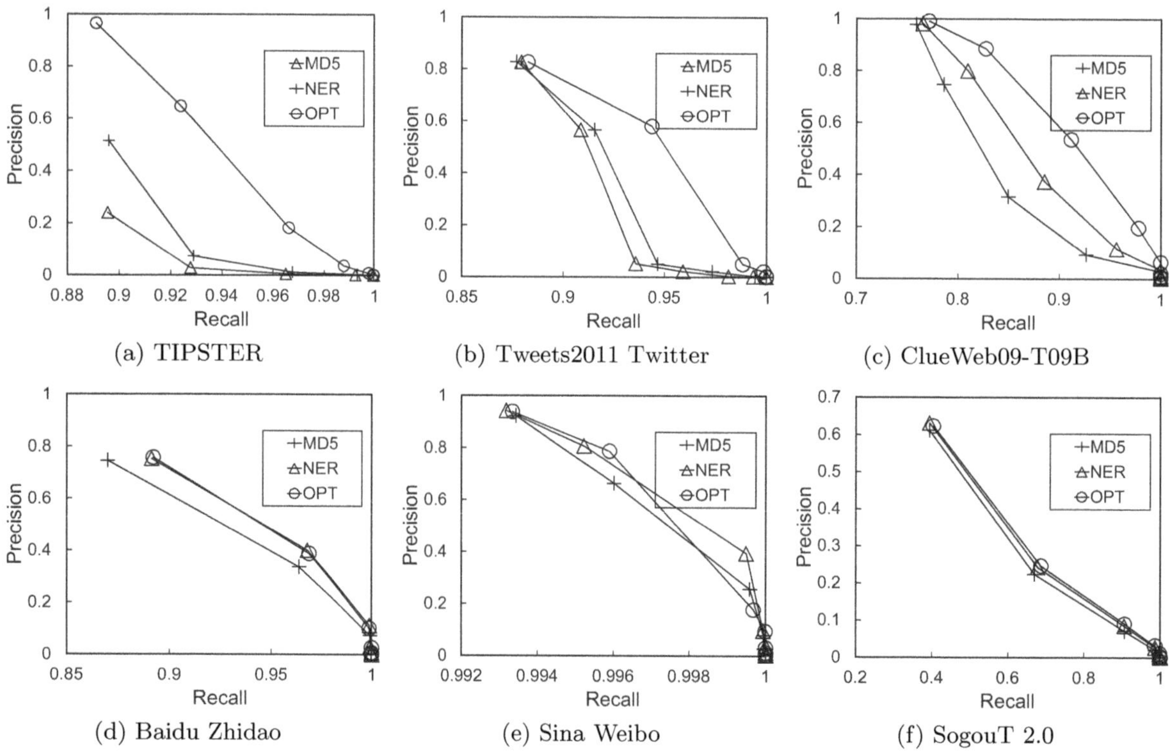

(a) TIPSTER (b) Tweets2011 Twitter (c) ClueWeb09-T09B

(d) Baidu Zhidao (e) Sina Weibo (f) SogouT 2.0

Figure 4: The precision-recall curves of candidate searching based on different hash code generation methods in all six corpora. The reuse threshold θ is set to 0.8.

Table 1: Statistics of the evaluation document collections

Corpus	Language	#Docs	Size
TIPSTER	English	1,078,925	3.25GB
Tweets2011 Twitter	English	15,204,939	2.13GB
ClueWeb09-T09B	English	50,220,423	490.4GB
Baidu Zhidao	Chinese	33,497,107	22.8GB
Sina Weibo	Chinese	267,612,493	418.6GB
SogouT 2.0	Chinese	37,205,218	558.0GB

cur together. "*NER*" is used to represent this method. For the proposed approach, although we have proposed several methods to reduce the computing consumption of the optimization problem, there would also be too many variables needed to optimize. In this work, we select top 3,000 words/characters to optimize according to their frequency. The similarity matrix is calculated based on 300,000 sentences extracted from each collection. The hash codes of the other words are generated based on MD5. We use "*OPT*" to represent this method in the following.

All the experiments were evaluated on a workstation with a 2.13G Intel Xeon quad-core processor, 4GB memory, and an NVIDIA Quadro 4000 graphics card with 2GB global memory and 256 stream processors. CUDA Toolkit version 4.1 is used to implement the algorithm. For sentence boundary detection, we used around 50 manually written rules to do it.

4.3 Effectiveness Evaluation

To compare the candidate searching with different hash code generation methods, for each corpus, we randomly selected 1 million sentences as evaluation data sets. As reuse detection queries, 2,000 sentences are randomly selected from them. The similarities between queries and sentences in the data set are calculated using cosine coefficient. The ground truth reuse sentences are obtained by comparing queries with all sentences in corresponding data set.

Table 2 illustrates the impact of candidate searching step with different hash code generation methods. We only list the detailed result in TIPSTER and SogouT 2.0, due to space limitations. Figure 4 summarizes results of all six corpora. In Table 2, d represents the d bits difference between query and reuse sentences. The reuse threshold θ is set to 0.8. "#can." represents the number of candidate sentences, which are selected using different hash code generation methods. From the results, we can observe that candidate searching step really benefits acceleration the reuse detection system. Instead of comparing with all sentences, the step can help reduce more than 90% calculation without losing any correct reuses in most cases.

From Table 2a, we can also observe that different hash code generation methods may highly impact the performance of candidate searching step. Although the baseline method, which is also used by previous work qSign [15], already achieves good results, the simple way which merge the hash code of similar words can further give more than 50% improvement in all bits difference level. Comparing to the baseline methods, hash codes generated based on the proposed learning based method achieve the best results. At the

Table 3: The average number of selected candidates per sentence at different recall level. The reuse threshold θ is set to 0.8.

Corpus	Recall Level	Gol.	MD5	NER	OPT
TIPSTER	0.89 (d=0)	2.5	9.5	4.4	**2.4**
	1.00 (d=4)	2.5	6024.8	3236.4	**316.3**
Twitter	0.88 (d=0)	1.5	1.6	1.6	**1.6**
	1.00 (d=4)	1.5	488.1	485.1	**477.4**
ClueWeb09	0.77 (d=0)	35.1	27.7	27.3	**26.9**
	1.00 (d=4)	35.1	1253.0	1006.4	**554.1**
Baidu Zhidao	0.75 (d=0)	2.6	3.0	3.0	**2.9**
	1.00 (d=3)	2.6	147.2	108.7	**94.5**
Sina Weibo	0.99 (d=0)	37.5	40.4	**39.5**	39.6
	1.00 (d=2)	37.5	145.8	95.0	**47.4**
SogouT 2.0	0.90 (d=2)	12.2	155.4	129.3	**121.1**
	1.00 (d=4)	12.2	1887.7	1327.5	**1000.5**

same recall level, the number of selected candidate sentences based the hash codes generated by the proposed methods is only 2.7% to 24.6% of the sentences selected based on MD5 hash code. This indicates that the proposed method can dramatically improve the effectiveness of candidate searching.

The precision-recall curves graph for all six collections are shown in Figure 4. The reuse threshold θ is also set to 0.8 in all the experiments for this figure. In almost all cases, the proposed approach achieves the best result among the three hash code generation methods. These results also demonstrate the observations described in the previous section. Although from the view precision-recall curve graph the precision improvement can not be easily noticed, at a recall level of 0.999, the proposed approach can further reduce around 51.9% sentences in SogouT 2.0, 55.4% in Sina Weibo and 27.7% in Baidu Zhidao over baseline method.

Table 3 shows the detailed performance of candidate searching step at different recall level in all six collections. The "Gol." column represents the average number of ground truth reuses per sentences. Since the recall level can only be controlled by the bits difference threshold, we list the parameter d in the bracket in the third column. From the table, we can observe that quotations are common in Web collections. While news articles also contain a large number of exact quotations. At almost all recall levels, the proposed hash code generation method achieves the best performance. It means that the proposed method can benefit the performance of candidate searching step.

In the above experiments, the documents used to calculate similarities between words for our approach are random selected from each collection. Since in-domain data may not be pre-collected in some cases, in this experiment we evaluate the performance of candidate selection with hash codes

Table 4: The average number of selected candidates per query sentence with in-domain and out-of-domain data. The reuse threshold θ is set to 0.8. The recall level is set to 100%, the corresponding bits difference d are in the bracket. "OPT_IN" represents hash codes generated based on in-domain data. "OPT_OUT" represents hash codes generated based on out-of-domain data.

Corpus	MD5	OPT_IN	OPT_OUT
TIPSTER (d=4)	6024.8	316.3	5482.1
Twitter (d=4)	488.1	477.4	492.1
ClueWeb09 (d=4)	1253.0	554.1	796.4
Baidu Zhidao (d=3)	147.2	94.5	88.1
Sina Weibo (d=2)	145.8	47.4	49.1
SogouT 2.0 (d=4)	1887.7	1005.5	1228.9

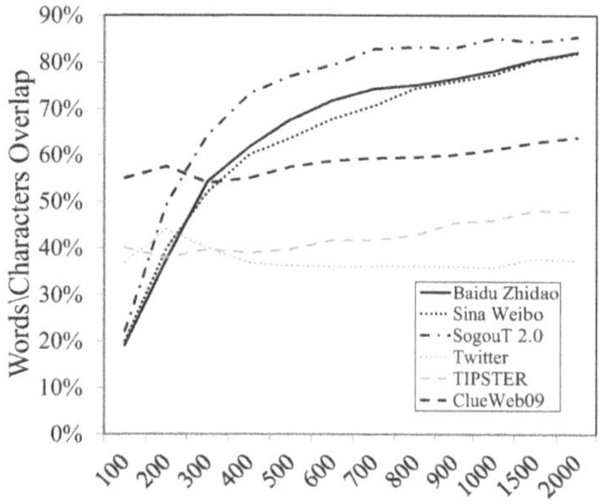

Figure 5: The overlap percentage of top frequency words/characters between corpora and "Web 1T 5-gram Corpus" or "Chinese Web 5-gram".

generated with similarities matrix calculated from open domain data sets. We use "Web 1T 5-gram Corpus[8]" and "Chinese Web 5-gram[9]" as the open domain data, where 5-grams are treated as sentences. They contain English and Chinese word n-grams and their observed frequency counts. Table 4 shows the performance candidate selection with these corpora. From the results, we can observe that in-domain data performs better than out-of-domain's in most cases. Out-of-domain data works better in Chinese than in English. For the corpus Baidu Zhidao, the performance of hash codes generated based on 5-grams is even better than in-domain data. We think that the main reason is that the words distributions in "Chinese Web 5-gram" are similar as Baidu Zhidao, which also contains documents from multiple domains. For English corpora, the performances of out-of-domain are not good as in-domains. In order to find the reason, we analysis the overlap of top frequency words. Figure 5 shows the overlap percentage of top frequency words/characters between corpora and "Web 1T 5-gram Corpus" or "Chinese Web 5-gram". From the statistics, we can observe the reason why out-of-domain data perform worse in English corpora than Chinese corpora. Distributions of words play an important role for the quality of generated hash codes from different domains.

4.4 Efficiency Evaluation

Due to the increasingly growing data, efficiency is another important issue we focused on in this paper. In this subsection, we compare the running time of our approach with state-of-the-art systems. We note that the running time of our approach composes of two steps: candidate selection and post-processing. Candidate selection step can be further divided into two steps: sentence feature generation and range searching. Because feature generation time for sentences are equal in different methods and the calculation consumption is small, we only evaluate the time of different range searching methods. To evaluate the impact of the number of selected candidates with different hash codes, we also evaluate the post-processing time.

Table 5 shows the running time of three different range searching methods. Brute force, which directly calculates all the distances between query and reference sentences, is implemented using a single thread CPU implementation and GPU implementation. We also adopt PM-Tree[10] [26] which is an indexing technique for efficient similarity searching. From the results, we can observe that indexing technique can improve searching efficiency. However, brute force method with GPU implementation can even achieve more than 1500 times speedup. Further more, the brute force methods do not need the index construction time. We think that the high memory bandwidth of GPU and naturally parallel algorithm are the main reason of the success of GPU implementation. Figure 6 shows the running time of GPU based candidate searching. We can observe that the processing time along the y axis increases as a linear function of the size of collection.

Figure 7 shows the post processing time at different recall level. We select two corpora "TIPSTER" and "SogouT 2.0" to evaluate the time using different hash codes. Figure 8 shows the post processing time with different hash codes generation methods. From these results, we can observe that the proposed hash code generation method can benefit the execution time of post processing. The number of selected candidates through different hash code generation methods impacts the execution time. Since our proposed method can filter more negative candidates than other methods, the running time are reduced.

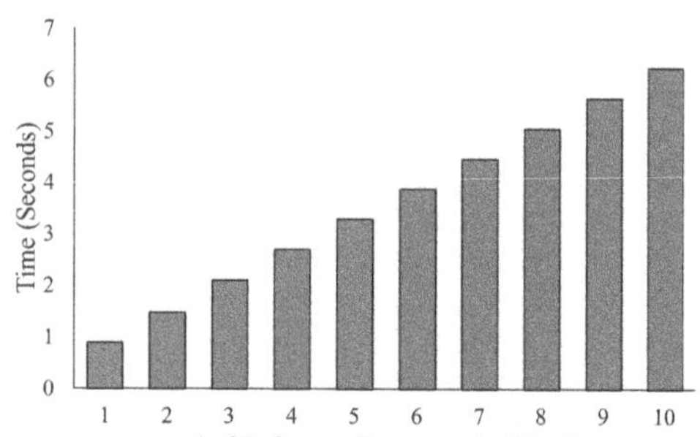

Figure 6: Total execution time of candidate selection implemented with GPU for 2,000 queries.

[8]LDC Catalog No. LDC2006T13

[9]LDC Catalog No. LDC2010T06

[10]We use the source code provided by Tomás Skopal. We set *pivot* to 20, and *pageSize* to 2048 in the experiments.

Table 5: Candidate selection time (seconds) for 2,000 queries using different range searching methods.

	0.1M	0.2M	0.3M	0.4M	0.5M	0.6M	0.7M	0.8M	0.9M	1M
Brute force (CPU)	468	939	1406	1873	2339	2807	3279	3749	4216	4685
PM-Tree (CPU)	152	297	433	569	704	852	979	1124	1258	1401
Brute force (GPU)	0.39	0.44	0.49	0.55	0.61	0.67	0.73	0.79	0.85	0.91

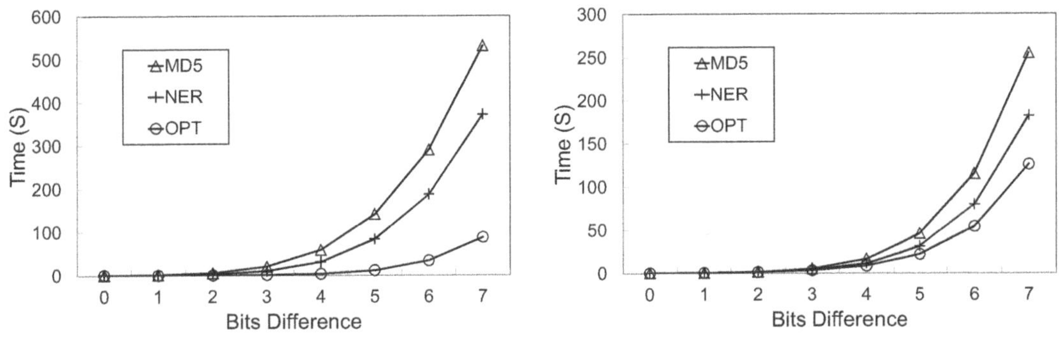

(a) TIPSTER (b) SogouT 2.0

Figure 7: The post processing time with different hash codes generation methods varies with recall level. The reuse threshold θ is set to 0.8. Each corpus contains 1 million sentences.

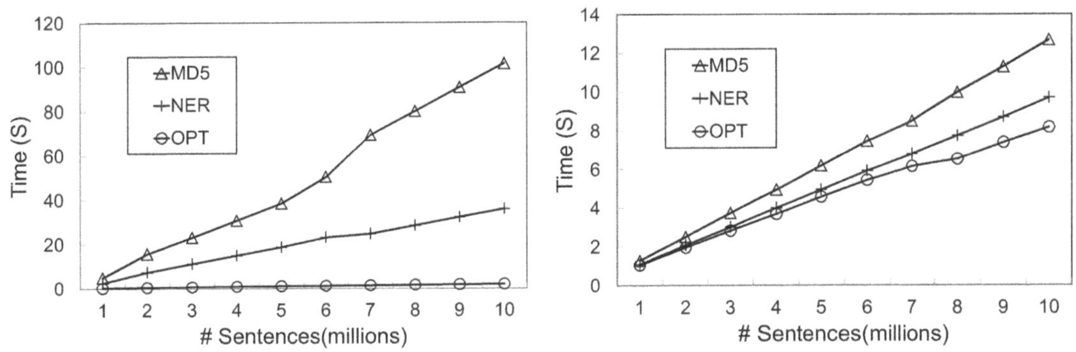

(a) TIPSTER (b) SogouT 2.0

Figure 8: The post processing time with different hash codes generation methods varies with corpus size. The reuse threshold θ is set to 0.8. The number of bits difference is set to 3.

5. CONCLUSIONS

In this work, we propose a novel approach which improves the efficiency and effectiveness of content reuse detection in two aspects. We introduce learning to hash method for generating hash codes of words/characters. We also propose to use GPU implementation to speedup the range searching task, which is the most time consuming part in candidate selection step. We evaluate the proposed approach in six different kinds of documents collections. Experimental results show that our method can significantly improve the efficiency of content reuse detection and would not impact the recall any more.

6. ACKNOWLEDGEMENT

The author wishes to thank the anonymous reviewers for their helpful comments. This work was partially funded by 973 Program (2010CB327900), National Natural Science Foundation of China (61003092, 61073069), Shanghai Leading Academic Discipline Project (B114), and "Chen Guang" project supported by Shanghai Municipal Education Commission and Shanghai Education Development Foundation (11CG05).

7. REFERENCES

[1] J. Aberdeen, J. Burger, D. Day, L. Hirschman, P. Robinson, and M. Vilain. Mitre: description of the alembic system used for muc-6. In *Proceedings of MUC6*, pages 141–155, Morristown, NJ, USA, 1995.

[2] R. J. Bayardo, Y. Ma, and R. Srikant. Scaling up all pairs similarity search. In *Proceedings of the 16th international conference on World Wide Web*, WWW '07, pages 131–140, 2007.

[3] J. Bolz, I. Farmer, E. Grinspun, and P. Schröoder. Sparse matrix solvers on the gpu: conjugate gradients and multigrid. *ACM Trans. Graph.*, 22:917–924, July 2003.

[4] A. Z. Broder. On the resemblance and containment of documents. In *Proceedings of SEQUENCES 1997*, page 21, Washington, DC, USA, 1997. IEEE Computer Society.

[5] A. Z. Broder. Identifying and filtering near-duplicate documents. In *Proceedings of COM 2000*, pages 1–10, London, UK, 2000. Springer-Verlag.

[6] B. Bustos, O. Deussen, S. Hiller, and D. Keim. A graphics hardware accelerated algorithm for nearest neighbor search. In V. Alexandrov, G. van Albada, P. Sloot, and J. Dongarra, editors, *Computational Science ĺC ICCS 2006*, volume 3994 of *Lecture Notes in Computer Science*, pages 196–199. Springer Berlin / Heidelberg, 2006.

[7] A. Chowdhury, O. Frieder, D. Grossman, and M. C. McCabe. Collection statistics for fast duplicate document detection. *ACM Trans. Inf. Syst.*, 20(2):171–191, 2002.

[8] L. Dugan. 230 million tweets per day, 50 million daily users and other twitter stats. *WWW.MEDIABISTRO.COM*, 2011.

[9] S. Edelkamp, D. Sulewski, and C. Yĺźcel. Perfect hashing for state space exploration on the gpu. In *ICAPS*, pages 57–64. AAAI, 2010.

[10] K. Fatahalian, J. Sugerman, and P. Hanrahan. Understanding the efficiency of gpu algorithms for matrix-matrix multiplication. In *Proceedings of the ACM SIGGRAPH/EUROGRAPHICS conference on Graphics hardware*, HWWS '04, pages 133–137, 2004.

[11] A. Gionis, P. Indyk, and R. Motwani. Similarity search in high dimensions via hashing. In *VLDB '99*, pages 518–529, San Francisco, CA, USA, 1999. Morgan Kaufmann Publishers Inc.

[12] N. K. Govindaraju, M. Henson, M. C. Lin, and D. Manocha. Interactive visibility ordering and transparency computations among geometric primitives in complex environments. In *Proceedings of the 2005 symposium on Interactive 3D graphics and games*, I3D '05, pages 49–56, 2005.

[13] G. Hinton and R. Salakhutdinov. Reducing the dimensionality of data with neural networks. *Science*, 313(5786):504 – 507, 2006.

[14] G. E. Hinton, S. Osindero, and Y.-W. Teh. A fast learning algorithm for deep belief nets. *Neural Comput.*, 18:1527–1554, July 2006.

[15] J. W. Kim, K. S. Candan, and J. Tatemura. Efficient overlap and content reuse detection in blogs and online news articles. In *Proceedings of the 18th international conference on World wide web*, WWW '09, pages 81–90, 2009.

[16] A. Kołcz, A. Chowdhury, and J. Alspector. Improved robustness of signature-based near-replica detection via lexicon randomization. In *Proceedings of SIGKDD 2004*, pages 605–610, 2004.

[17] J. Krüger and R. Westermann. Linear algebra operators for gpu implementation of numerical algorithms. In *ACM SIGGRAPH 2005 Courses*, SIGGRAPH '05, 2005.

[18] D. Metzler, Y. Bernstein, W. B. Croft, A. Moffat, and J. Zobel. Similarity measures for tracking information flow. In *Proceedings of the 14th ACM international conference on Information and knowledge management*, pages 517–524, 2005.

[19] K. Muthmann, W. M. Barczyński, F. Brauer, and A. Löser. Near-duplicate detection for web-forums. In *IDEAS '09*, pages 142–151, New York, NY, USA, 2009. ACM.

[20] M. Norouzi and D. Fleet. Minimal loss hashing for compact binary codes. In L. Getoor and T. Scheffer, editors, *Proceedings of the 28th International Conference on Machine Learning (ICML-11)*, pages 353–360, June 2011.

[21] J. D. Owens, M. Houston, D. Luebke, S. Green, J. E. Stone, and J. C. Phillips. GPU Computing. *Proceedings of the IEEE*, 96(5):879–899, 2008.

[22] R. Rivest. The md5 message-digest algorithm, 1992.

[23] J. Seo and W. B. Croft. Local text reuse detection. In *SIGIR '08*, pages 571–578, New York, NY, USA, 2008.

[24] N. Shivakumar and H. Garcia-Molina. Scam: A copy detection mechanism for digital documents. In *Digitial Library*, 1995.

[25] N. Shivakumar and H. Garcia-Molina. Finding near-replicas of documents and servers on the web. In *Proceedings of WebDB 1998*, pages 204–212, London, UK, 1999. Springer-Verlag.

[26] T. Skopal, J. Pokorný, and V. Snásel. Pm-tree: Pivoting metric tree for similarity search in multimedia databases. In *ADBIS (Local Proceedings)*, 2004.

[27] B. Stein. Principles of hash-based text retrieval. In *Proceedings of the 30th annual international ACM SIGIR conference on Research and development in information retrieval*, SIGIR '07, pages 527–534, 2007.

[28] M. Theobald, J. Siddharth, and A. Paepcke. Spotsigs: robust and efficient near duplicate detection in large web collections. In *SIGIR '08*, pages 563–570, New York, NY, USA, 2008. ACM.

[29] A. Wächter and L. T. Biegler. On the implementation of an interior-point filter line-search algorithm for large-scale nonlinear programming. *Mathematical Programming*, 106(1):25–57, Mar. 2006.

[30] Y. Weiss, A. Torralba, and R. Fergus. Spectral hashing. In D. Koller, D. Schuurmans, Y. Bengio, and L. Bottou, editors, *Advances in Neural Information Processing Systems*, pages 1753–1760. MIT Press, 2008.

[31] C. Xiao, W. Wang, X. Lin, and J. X. Yu. Efficient similarity joins for near duplicate detection. In *Proceeding of the 17th international conference on World Wide Web*, WWW '08, pages 131–140, 2008.

[32] D. Zhang, J. Wang, D. Cai, and J. Lu. Self-taught hashing for fast similarity search. In *Proceeding of the 33rd international ACM SIGIR conference on Research and development in information retrieval*, SIGIR '10, pages 18–25, 2010.

[33] Q. Zhang, Y. Zhang, H. Yu, and X. Huang. Efficient partial-duplicate detection based on sequence matching. In *Proceeding of the 33rd international ACM SIGIR conference on Research and development in information retrieval*, SIGIR '10, pages 675–682, 2010.

Explanatory Semantic Relatedness and Explicit Spatialization for Exploratory Search

Brent Hecht*, Samuel H. Carton*, Mahmood Quaderi*, Johannes Schöning†, Martin Raubal‡, Darren Gergle*§, Doug Downey*

*Northwestern University Dept. of Electrical Engineering and Computer Science, §Northwestern University Dept. of Communication Studies, †Independent Researcher, ‡ETH Zurich Institute of Cartography and Geoinformation

{brent,sam.carton,quaderi}@u.northwestern.edu, {dgergle,d-downey}@northwestern.edu, mail@johannesschoening.de, mraubal@ethz.ch

ABSTRACT

Exploratory search, in which a user investigates complex concepts, is cumbersome with today's search engines. We present a new exploratory search approach that generates interactive visualizations of query concepts using thematic cartography (e.g. choropleth maps, heat maps). We show how the approach can be applied broadly across both geographic and non-geographic contexts through *explicit spatialization,* a novel method that leverages any figure or diagram – from a periodic table, to a parliamentary seating chart, to a world map – as a spatial search environment. We enable this capability by introducing *explanatory semantic relatedness measures.* These measures extend frequently-used semantic relatedness measures to not only estimate the degree of relatedness between two concepts, but also generate human-readable explanations for their estimates by mining Wikipedia's text, hyperlinks, and category structure. We implement our approach in a system called Atlasify, evaluate its key components, and present several use cases.

Categories and Subject Descriptors

H.3.m [**Information Storage and Retrieval**]: Miscellaneous, H.5.m. [**Information interfaces and presentation (e.g., HCI)**]: Miscellaneous

General Terms

Algorithms, Measurement, Experimentation, Human Factors

Keywords

Semantic relatedness, exploratory search, spatialization, cartography, geography, Wikipedia, text mining, GIScience

1. INTRODUCTION

Exploratory search is an open-ended information seeking activity in which a user aims to better understand a complex concept [39, 40]. While exploratory search has historically accounted for roughly a quarter of Web search query volume [33], it remains challenging using today's search engines due to their focus on closed information requests and navigational queries [40].

In this paper, we leverage thematic cartography's well-known ability to communicate complex geographic distributions [2, 5, 6, 37] to help users understand the complex concepts encountered in exploratory search. While the benefits of cartography are usually limited to geographic inquiries, our approach is made domain-neutral by harnessing general relational knowledge mined from Wikipedia. This means that users can employ thematic cartography to explore concepts not only from a geographic perspective, but also from a chemistry perspective, a politics perspective, a music perspective, or a perspective from any other topic area (even user-defined topic areas).

We have implemented our exploratory search approach in a Web-based system called Atlasify. Given a query concept, Atlasify automatically generates an interactive thematic cartography layer (e.g. a choropleth or heat map) on top of a spatial *reference system* from any domain, such as a periodic table, a U.S. senate seating chart, or a world map. The layer illustrates the degree to which the query concept is related to each spatial entity in the reference system (e.g. chemical elements, senators, countries). By clicking on a spatial entity, users see natural language explanations of exactly how that entity or region is related to the query concept. Users can enter any query that corresponds to a Wikipedia article (i.e. a page title, anchor text, or redirect).

To make this process more concrete, consider the Atlasify use case in Figures 1–4. In Figure 1, a user who wants to learn about nuclear power has queried Atlasify for "Nuclear Power" and selected "Periodic Table" as the desired spatial reference system. As is typical with choropleth maps, the dark green areas in Figure 1 are very related to nuclear power, and the lighter green areas are less related. Exploring further, the user may wish to understand why, for example, plutonium is so strongly related to nuclear

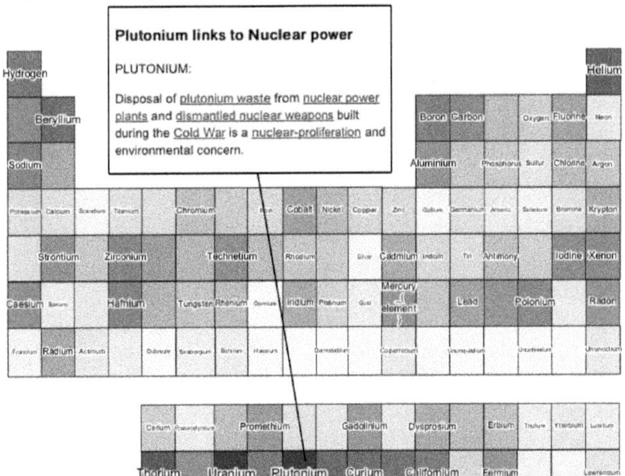

Figure 1. Atlasify's visualization of the query concept "Nuclear Power" on the "Periodic Table" spatial reference system. If users click on plutonium, they receive a list of explanations of how nuclear power and plutonium are related, a list that includes the above explanation.

Permission to make digital or hard copies of all or part of this work for personal or classroom use is granted without fee provided that copies are not made or distributed for profit or commercial advantage and that copies bear this notice and the full citation on the first page. To copy otherwise, or republish, to post on servers or to redistribute to lists, requires prior specific permission and/or a fee.
SIGIR'12, August 12–16, 2012, Portland, Oregon, USA.
Copyright 2012 ACM 978-1-4503-1472-5/12/08...$15.00.

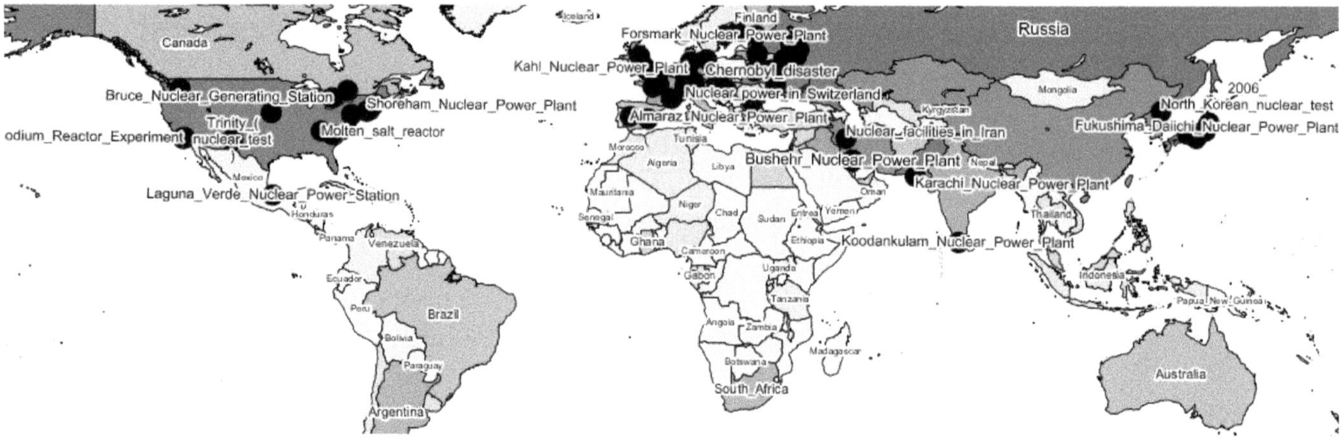

Figure 2. Atlasify visualizing the query concept "Nuclear Power" on the "World Map" reference system. The user is able to see that, for instance, sub-Saharan Africa is not very related to nuclear power, while the United States, Chernobyl, and Fukushima are quite related. The "World Map" reference system is the largest of Atlasify's spatial reference systems, with approx. 380,000 entities. For each query concept, the AtlasifySR+E *semantic relatedness between all entities and the query concept must be calculated.*

power. By clicking on plutonium in the visualization, the user is presented with natural language explanations of the relationships between nuclear power and plutonium. Seeking a geographic perspective on nuclear power, the user then changes to the "World Map" reference system (Figure 2). The user does the same for a temporal perspective in Figure 3 (the "Timeline" reference system) and a United States politics perspective in Figure 4 (the "U.S. Senate Seating Chart" reference system). Note that Atlasify correctly highlights Fukushima, Russia, and the United States in the world map, the various important eras in the history of nuclear power on the timeline, and so on. While this use case focuses on the query concept "Nuclear Power", Atlasify allows users to query for over 15 million articles from 25 different Wikipedia language editions. These Wikipedia-based concepts can currently be visualized on 13 different reference systems and adding new reference systems is straightforward.

The effectiveness of thematic cartography is well established in geographic domains (e.g. [2, 5, 6, 37]). The goal of our exploratory search approach is to extend the strengths of thematic cartography to the wide variety of domains and query concepts

Figure 3. "Nuclear Power" visualized on the "Timeline" reference system.

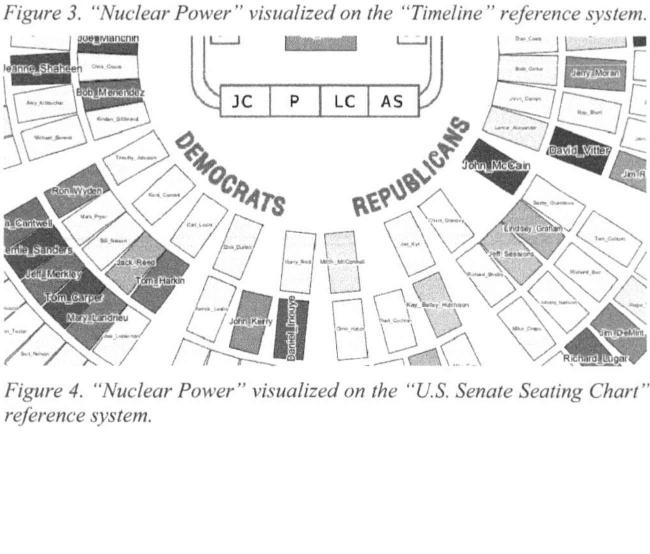

Figure 4. "Nuclear Power" visualized on the "U.S. Senate Seating Chart" reference system.

encountered in exploratory search. This goal can be broken down into three key challenges, the solutions to which are additional contributions of this paper and have implications outside of exploratory search.

The first challenge involves generalizing the visualization strategy used in Figure 2 to non-geographic reference systems (e.g. periodic tables, anatomical charts, timelines, and many other figures and diagrams). Our solution is *explicit spatialization* (ES), which enables cartographic and geographic information retrieval (GIR) methods to be applied in any figure or diagram. As discussed in Section 3, ES accomplishes this by "spatializing" concepts into pre-defined reference systems and generalizing the canonical model of geographic information to incorporate domain-neutral spatial information. In doing so, ES can extend the ongoing advances in online mapping and GIR to many domains outside of geography.

The second challenge involves automatically estimating the degree of relatedness between any of the millions of possible query concepts (e.g. "Nuclear Power") and every spatial entity in each reference system (e.g. chemical elements, countries). These estimates determine the value of the visual variables manipulated in thematic cartography, such as color and text size (e.g. the shades of green and font sizes in Figures 1–4). We show how Wikipedia-based semantic relatedness (SR) measures, which provide a numerical relatedness score for any pair of lexically expressed concepts, can solve this problem. We introduce a new SR measure, *AtlasifySR+E,* which uses a learned model to combine six separate SR measures, each capturing a different type of relationship. Experiments on several SR benchmarks show that *AtlasifySR+E* achieves state-of-the-art performance while also remaining language-neutral and using only open, easily accessible data, overcoming two limitations of the current state-of-the-art SR measure.

The final challenge concerns generating natural language explanations of the relationships between the query concept and any spatial entity. These explanations realize the key paradigm of modern interactive cartography that users be able to click on a part of a map to obtain additional details [34, 35]. To address this challenge, we introduce the notion of *explanatory semantic relatedness measures* (SR+E), which not only return a numeric estimate of the semantic relatedness between two entities, but also explain the identified relationships to end users. We show how Wikipedia-based SR measures can be made explanatory by using machine learning to mine informative snippets of Wikipedia text. Furthermore, we describe how our SR+E measure, *AtlasifySR+E*, uses machine learning to combine the explanations of its six constituent measures. Again, the approach of integrating the perspectives of each SR measure results in improved performance: our experiments demonstrate that *AtlasifySR+E*'s explanations outperform those of any single measure and other baselines.

In summary, this paper presents both a method for leveraging thematic cartography for domain-neutral exploratory search and the innovations in SR and information spatialization required to make that possible, namely (1) explicit spatialization, (2) improved SR estimation, and (3) explanatory SR measures. The remainder of this paper is organized as follows. After covering related work, we formally define explicit spatialization and discuss how it is implemented in the Atlasify system. Next, we introduce explanatory SR measures and describe methods for generating explanations for six separate SR measures. We then present our experiments, in which our approach and its components are evaluated up to the point where thematic cartography's well-understood methods take over. Finally, we conclude and discuss directions for future work.

2. RELATED WORK

In this section, we cover research related to this paper at a high level, with additional related work specific to each section of the paper discussed in context. Our research falls into the area of exploratory search. White et al. write that exploratory search systems aid users with information seeking problems that are "open-ended, persistent and multi-faceted" [40]. This stands in contrast to traditional Web search, which is primarily concerned with navigational queries and closed information requests. Despite the prevalence of exploratory queries, exploratory search is a relatively new research area with many open questions [40].

The field of cartography has identified several reasons why humans find thematic mapping useful for understanding complex geographic patterns. The known benefits of thematic maps are the communication of specific information [20, 37], the communication of regional/general information [20, 37], straightforward comparisons between maps showing different distributions [37], and straightforward comparisons between a mapped distribution and one's mental model of depicted entities and regions [24, 37]. We enable these benefits in a wide variety of domains outside geography. For instance, in Figure 1 it is easy to see that plutonium specifically is quite related to nuclear power, but so is the entire "region" of actinides (the bottom row). An Atlasify user may recall from chemistry class that actinides have to do with the atomic age, so the fact that this region is highlighted reinforces her mental model. Finally, comparing Figure 1 with a periodic table visualization of, say, coal power, it is easy to identify differences in the chemistry of the two concepts.

Our work within geographic reference systems is related to research in language models associated with geographic places For example, Google Correlate [12] provides an interface to models based on georeferenced query logs. Others have leveraged geographic language models to study the geographic distribution of *zeitgeist* terms [16], to explore the use of relatedness-like metrics in a geographic context [15, 28], and for various other applications (e.g. [7,19,27]). Some of this research has been echoed in the temporal domain (e.g. [28, 30]). We extend this work by generalizing the notion of geographic language models to arbitrary spatial reference systems, rather than just geographic and temporal ones. This research is also the first to our knowledge to (1) use geographic language models for exploratory search, (2) apply robust SR measures to geographic language models, and (3) use explanatory SR measures in this context (or any other).

3. EXPLICIT SPATIALIZATION

Explicit spatialization (ES) is a novel form of information spatialization that, diverging from the existing spatialization literature, uses *pre-defined* reference systems (e.g. maps, figures, and diagrams) instead of *data-driven* reference systems. While ES is essential to our exploratory search approach, it also has implications beyond this work. Namely, it provides a new means by which advances in online mapping and geographic information retrieval (GIR) can be extended to domains outside of geography.

3.1 Definition of Explicit Spatialization

Explicit spatialization (ES) "spatializes" or "projects" any object o into a pre-defined reference system such as a periodic table, map, or seating chart. More formally, ES defines a process that represents an object o in terms of the spatial entities E in a reference system rs according to the output of an ES function $f_{ES}(o, E)$. We clarify the key elements of this process below.

Let us consider Atlasify's implementation of explicit spatialization. In Atlasify, each object o is a query concept (e.g. "Nuclear Power") and the system's ES function is our SR+E measure *AtlasifySR+E*. The spatial entities considered include countries (and cities, landmarks, etc.) in the "World Map" reference system, chemical elements in the "Periodic Table" reference system, and so on. Atlasify therefore spatializes each query concept into each reference system by running *AtlasifySR+E* on each query concept/spatial entity pair.

In explicit spatialization, each spatial entity e □ E in a reference system rs is comprised of a tuple <**x**,**d**>, where **x** is a location (spatial footprint) in rs, and **d** is one or more data resources describing the entity. These data resources are mined by the ES function to spatialize the object o. In Atlasify, **d** consists of a single Wikipedia article describing each spatial entity.

The output of an ES function is a spatial distribution ("layer") whose data model is a generalization of the canonical model of geographic information [11] (see Figure 5). The canonical geographic model formalizes an atomic unit of geographic information as a tuple <**x**, **z**>, where **x** is a location in space-time of an entity on or near the surface of the Earth (e.g. its latitude / longitude coordinate or its polygonal representation) and **z** is a set of *attributes* corresponding to that entity (e.g. temperatures, population counts). ES generalizes the geographic information model by replacing "the Earth" with an arbitrary reference system

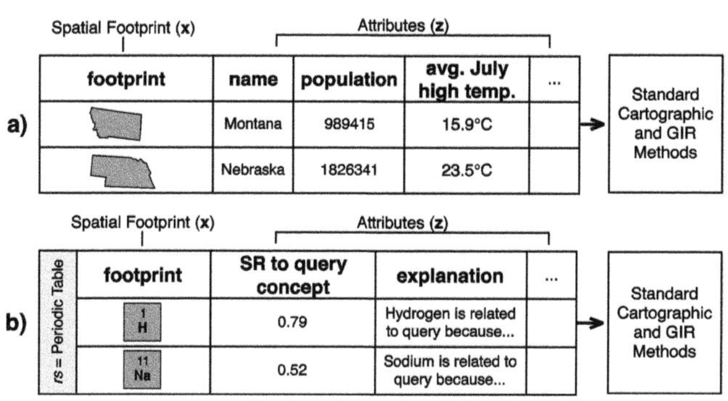

Figure 5. An example of the canonical data model of geographic information (a, top) and the explicit spatialization data model (b, bottom).

rs (such as the periodic table, an anatomical chart, etc.). The new model is equivalent to the geographic information model for a single fixed *rs* (except, of course, for the domain of the entities). It is via this reduction that ES can use traditional cartographic and GIR methods with little to no modification.

The flexibility of the ES data model makes it adaptable to nearly any reference system in any domain. As one example of ES's generality, consider a Web browser reference system that, as a user browses the web, shows heat maps visualizing relatedness to a persistent concept of interest. We have implemented a static proof-of-concept of this idea in Atlasify's "New York Times Homepage" reference system (Figure 6).

It is important to note that Atlasify's implementation of explicit spatialization is far from the only possible approach. Other ES functions could include topic detection techniques or an algorithm that calculates entity-level sentiment. Similarly, a projected object *o* could be a blog post, an academic paper, or even an entire document collection, and data resources **d** considered for each spatial entity could include tweets, images, or photo tags.

3.2 Relationship to Traditional Spatialization

Traditional spatialization produces data-driven, abstract reference systems generally by applying dimension reduction to document collections for the purpose of visualizing those collections (see [13, 36] for an overview). ES, on the other hand, leverages *existing* reference systems (e.g. the periodic table, the human body, the surface of the Earth) for general IR applications. As a result, ES avoids the pitfalls that can make traditional spatialization undesirable for search [13], such as the error introduced by dimension reduction [13, 17, 36] and the imposition of a single, static visualization for an entire document collection [13]. While a few commercial document visualization systems (e.g. [32]) have begun to explore extensible reference systems as in ES, they still rely on traditional spatialization as their primary paradigm.

3.3 Spatiotagging

Preparing a new reference system for an ES application like Atlasify is a straightforward process that we call *spatiotagging.* Spatiotagging is a generalization of geotagging to arbitrary spatial reference systems. To construct a reference system using spatiotagging, one simply identifies the spatial footprint (**x**) of the spatial entities in the reference system (e.g. chemical elements, Senate chamber seats, countries), and matches those entities to data resources (**d**) (e.g. corresponding Wikipedia articles). Spatial footprints can be identified by manually tracing the shapes of entities over a figure, diagram or image, obtaining pre-existing spatial representations (e.g. KML files or shapefiles), leveraging computer vision (e.g. OCR), or utilizing other techniques.

3.4 User-defined Reference Systems

While spatiotagging a new reference system is straightforward, it requires some effort. Further, users may not be able to find an existing reference system appropriate for their needs. In this section, we show how it is possible to extend ES to support ad-hoc, user-defined reference systems via the semantic relatedness work explained in detail later in the paper (Sections 4–5).

Figure 6. Atlasify's explicit spatialization of the query concept "Arab People" on the "New York Times Homepage" reference system. Atlasify correctly understands that the left column consists of Arab people-related stories. It also detects small increases in relatedness near "crude oil", etc.

Explicit spatialization enables the automatic construction of user-defined reference systems through three components: (1) predefined templates, which describe the general layout of the reference systems, (2) a category of concepts to act as spatial entities, and (3) SR algorithms. Figures 7 and 8 provide a small use case of user-defined reference systems generated in Atlasify using the "spectrum" and "simplex" predefined templates respectively. In both figures, the spatial entity concepts are members of the Wikipedia category "Grammy Award winners," and the SR algorithm is *AtlasifySR+E.*

Predefined templates and their "anchor concepts" make user-defined reference systems explicit. The "spectrum" template supports two anchor concepts and the "simplex" supports three. In Atlasify's implementation, users can set these anchor concepts to any concept covered by a Wikipedia article (e.g. "Rock music", "Hip hop music"). Note that a reference system defined by a given set of anchor concepts remains fixed, independent of which category of concepts (spatial entities) or query concept is plotted on it (i.e. it is not data-driven). As noted above, this is the key distinction between explicit and traditional spatialization.

In user-defined reference systems, the exact position of each spatial entity is defined by the SR between the corresponding concept and each of the anchor concepts. In other words, spatiotagging is done automatically in these reference systems using SR. If a spatial entity is very close to an anchor, this indicates that the corresponding concept is significantly more related to the nearby anchor than to the others. Only concepts that are non-trivially related to all anchors are included as spatial entities. In Atlasify's implementation, the category of concepts to act as spatial entities can be any Wikipedia category (Section 4).

As shown in Figure 8, user-defined reference systems are intended to be used as the basis for thematic cartography visualizations of query concepts just like standard ES reference systems. However, user-defined reference systems may also have value as exploratory search tools in and of themselves, without the thematic layer (e.g. Figure 7), but this more closely resembles traditional spatialization.

3.5 Spatial Information Retrieval

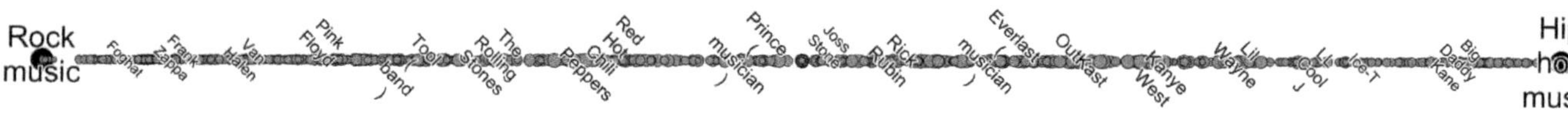

Figure 7: A spectrum user-defined reference system of Grammy Award winners plotted from "Rock music" to "Hip hop music". When used for thematic cartography visualizations, relatedness to the query concept is displayed in a similar fashion to Figure 3.

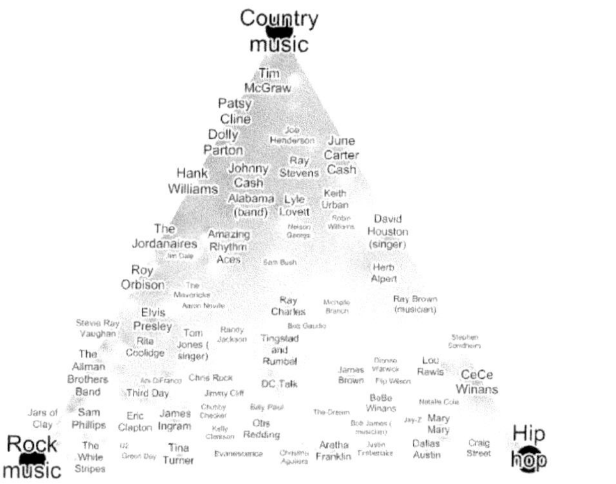

Figure 8. The query concept "Grand Ole Opry" is visualized on a simplex reference system defined by music genres, with the spatial entities being members of the Wikipedia category "Grammy Award Winners". It is clear that "Grand Ole Opry" is more related to country music than, say, rock music.

Our exploratory search approach focuses on the cartographic benefits of explicit spatialization, but ES also has GIR implications. Namely, ES generalizes GIR to *spatial information retrieval*[2] (SIR). In SIR, many GIR research areas – from understanding vague regions to toponym (place name) resolution to geographic relevance ranking to local search – can become relevant in non-geographic domains. For instance, Jones et al.'s work on modeling vague geographic regions [19] like the English Midlands could be applied to numerous other reference systems, e.g. to model the "belly" or "tummy" vague regions in an anatomical reference system.

To demonstrate the possibilities of SIR, we have implemented in Atlasify one of the most basic GIR features: the simple bounding box spatial query. Users can issue these spatial queries by clicking Atlasify's "What's Related Here" button. Users are then presented with a list of concepts ranked by relatedness to the spatial region defined by the current view frame, which can then be filtered by Wikipedia category. This allows users to, for example, find out the concepts most related to the actinide elements or to the longest-serving members of the Democratic caucus (in the middle left of the seating chart).

4. EXPLANATORY SEMANTIC RELATEDNESS MEASURES

In this section, we introduce *explanatory semantic relatedness measures* (SR+E). Like traditional semantic relatedness (SR) measures, SR+E measures return a value that summarizes the number and strength of relationships between a given pair of concepts (e.g. <Nuclear Power, Plutonium>)[14]. However, along with each value, SR+E measures also provide a ranked list of natural language *explanations* of the various relationships underlying the value, in descending order of informativeness.

As noted above, SR+E measures play an integral role in our exploratory search approach. Each spatial distribution that our approach visualizes with thematic cartography is made up of SR estimates between the query concept and all entities in a reference system. While these visualizations show users the degree to which a query concept is related to a given spatial entity, the natural language explanations produced by SR+E measures describe *why* they are related. In doing so, the explanations provide users with "details-on-demand" [35] for a clicked spatial entity, following the principles of interactive cartography [34].

We begin our detailed discussion of SR+E measures below by introducing methods for generating explanations for three popular existing SR measures – *WikiRelate* [38], *MilneWitten* [22], and *Explicit Semantic Analysis* [9] – and then do the same for several new measures. We describe how each resulting SR+E measure mines Wikipedia's text, links, or category structure to create explanations that reflect the relationships captured by the corresponding SR measure. We next cover *AtlasifySR+E*, the SR+E measure used in our exploratory search approach and implemented in the Atlasify system. *AtlasifySR+E* combines the benefits of the individual SR+E measures discussed above using a learned model. We hypothesized this ensemble approach could produce better SR estimates and explanations than any single measure alone. While we discuss the design of *AtlasifySR+E* here, our evidence that supports this hypothesis and descriptions of the related machine learning experiments are in Section 5.

Finally, we note that while our focus in this paper is on utilizing SR+E for exploratory search, we expect the explanation mechanisms and improved SR measures will have broader applicability as well. SR estimates are frequently utilized in NLP, AI, and IR [4, 9, 43], and have been applied in tasks such as information extraction [4], clustering [1, 30] and search [30].

4.1 Adding Explanations to SR Measures

4.1.1 Selecting SR Measures

There are many SR measures in the literature. Even limiting our attention to Wikipedia-specific SR measures, which have been shown to be better [30] or as good as WordNet-based measures [43], there are still quite a few to consider (e.g. [9, 22, 30, 38]). We focus on three such measures – *WikiRelate*, *MilneWitten*, and *Explicit Semantic Analysis* – because they are among the best-known SR measures and because each uses a different Wikipedia lexical semantic resource [44], thereby capturing different types of relationships between concepts. We also introduce new SR measures to take advantage of additional types of relationships that are not identified by published SR measures.

4.1.2 General Approach to Adding Explanations

Before discussing the details of how we added explanatory capabilities to each of the individual SR measures, we first cover the elements that apply across all measures.

As noted above, each SR+E measure must return a list of natural language relationship explanations ranked by informativeness. While there are other possible approaches, here we define the *informativeness* of each explanation to be based on two factors: the strength of the described relationship and the quality of the textual description. As such, each explanation must consist of natural language text, a relationship strength value, and a text quality value.

In all of our SR+E implementations, the text of relationship explanations is mined from Wikipedia. Several of the SR measures we considered implicitly calculate relationship strength when computing SR values. Where this is not true, we have developed strength metrics that are consistent with the SR measure's overall algorithm. As is described in Section 5, we utilize machine learning techniques to map features of the textual

[2] The term "Spatial Information Retrieval" has been used as a synonym of GIR in the literature, but not, to our knowledge, to refer to the generalization of GIR as it is used here.

explanations to an estimate of text quality, and combine this with relationship strength using heuristics to arrive at a final ranking. The heuristics differ for each SR+E measure, but they generally weigh relationship strength more heavily than text quality.

4.1.3 *WikiRelate*

WikiRelate [38] uses the Wikipedia Category Graph (WCG) structure as its lexical resource. In Wikipedia, each article can have 0 or more categories (they appear at the bottom of the article), and each of these categories can have 0 or more parents. The resulting graph is the WCG, which is a *folksonomy* [38].

WikiRelate leverages a variant of the WCG path length between the articles *a* and *b* to estimate SR(*a*,*b*). The insight behind this design is that each path represents a relationship between *a* and *b*, and the shorter the path, the stronger the relationship. We construct *WikiRelate* explanations to elucidate these relationship paths to the user in natural language. For example, Figure 9 displays a *WikiRelate* explanation for the strongest relationship between Chemistry and Mathematics (the shortest WCG path between the two articles). In the case of *WikiRelate*, text quality is not considered in the informativeness function as the natural language is automatically determined in the same way for all explanations.

Chemistry and Mathematics both belong to Category:Academic Disciplines

Chemistry

Chemistry is a member of Category:Natural sciences, which is a member of Category:Academic disciplines

Mathematics

Mathematics is a member of Category:Formal sciences, which is a member of Category:Academic disciplines

Figure 9. The top WikiRelate *explanation for the concept pair <Chemistry, Mathematics>. The format of this explanation and those in Figures 10 and 11 mimic that of the Atlasify interface.*

4.1.4 *MilneWitten, OutlinkOverlap, and WAGDirect*

The Wikipedia Article Graph (WAG) consists of Wikipedia articles and the links between them. There are several published WAG-based SR measures (e.g. [15, 22]). We implemented the measure by Milne and Witten [22], *MilneWitten*, as it has been used in popular web mining applications (e.g. [23]).

MilneWitten operates by comparing the set of articles that link to the articles *a* and *b*. The intuition is that if *a* and *b* share many inlinks, they should be assigned a high SR score.[3] The relationships considered here are indirect: a shared inlink means that an article *c* links to both *a* and *b*. Explanations based on *MilneWitten* must therefore elucidate the nature of these $a \leftarrow c \rightarrow b$ relationships. Figure 10a displays the most informative *MilneWitten* explanation for the concept pair <United States, Chocolate> (*c* = "Chocolate chip").

However, in order to establish that the explanation in Figure 10a was the top explanation – recall that explanations are ranked by informativeness, which is a function of strength and text quality – our *MilneWitten+E* implementation needed a way to measure the strength of each $a \leftarrow c \rightarrow b$ relationship. In other words, we required some method of determining that "Chocolate chip" represents a stronger $a \leftarrow c \rightarrow b$ relationship than, say, the article "List of Viva Piñata Episodes", which also links to both "Chocolate" and "United States". To solve this problem, we use bootstrapping to calculate $SR_{MilneWitten}(a,c)$ and $SR_{MilneWitten}(b,c)$. The strength of each $a \leftarrow c \rightarrow b$ relationship is then computed by taking $SR_{MilneWitten}(a,c) * SR_{MilneWitten}(b,c)$. This algorithm results in the relationship involving "Chocolate chip" being deemed the strongest relationship, with that involving "List of Viva Piñata Episodes" much further down the list.

Chocolate chip links to United States and Chocolate

CHOCOLATE CHIP:

Chocolate chips are small chunks of chocolate.

CHOCOLATE CHIP: AVAILABILITY

Today, chocolate chips are very popular as a baking ingredient in the United States and the chocolate chip cookie is regarded as a quintessential American dessert.

Cheese links to France

CHEESE: WORLD PRODUCTION AND CONSUMPTION:

The biggest exporter of cheese, by monetary value, is France; the second, Germany (although it is first by quantity)

Life and Death link to Organism

LIFE:

In biology, the science of living organisms, life is the condition that distinguishes active organisms from inorganic matter. Living organisms undergo metabolism, maintain homeostasis, possess a capacity to grow, respond to stimuli, reproduce and, through natural selection, adapt to their environment in successive generations.

DEATH:

Death is the termination of the biological functions that sustain a living organism.

Figure 10: (a, top) The top MilneWitten *explanation for <United States, Chocolate>, (b, middle) the top* WAGDirect *explanation for <Cheese, France>, (c, bottom) the top* OutlinkOverlap *explanation for <Life, Death>.*

We have also implemented a modified version of *MilneWitten*, *WeightedMW*, that more heavily weights the links that occur at the very beginning of overlapping articles (i.e. in the *gloss* of the article). The experiments in Section 5 show that this weighted measure estimates SR values somewhat better than our implementation of *MilneWitten*. Explanations are generated in the same fashion as in standard *MilneWitten*.

MilneWitten and *WeightedMW* ignore two important types of relationships present in the WAG. First and foremost, if *a* links directly to *b* ($a \rightarrow b$) or vice versa ($b \rightarrow a$), this link obviously represents a significant relationship between *a* and *b*. We implemented a new SR measure called *WAGDirect* to capture these relationships. *WAGDirect* considers only direct links between *a* and *b*, weighted by whether the link occurs in the gloss of the article and whether the link is bidirectional. Explanations of *WAGDirect* relationships thus consist of text snippets from article *a* that discuss *b*, and/or vice versa (Figure 10b), without any intermediary article *c*.

It was also important that we consider the inverse of *MilneWitten*: the overlap of the set of outlinks of *a* and *b*. This is done by our *OutlinkOverlap* measure, which is similar to other algorithms explored by Milne and Witten [21]. *OutlinkOverlap* uses the principle that, broadly speaking, if *a* and *b* share a significant number of outlinks, then *a* and *b* are quite related. *OutlinkOverlap* explanations thus describe how *a* and *b* discuss these mutually outlinked articles. In other words, they include text snippets from *a* and *b* that explicate the $a \rightarrow c \leftarrow b$ relationships considered by this SR measure (see Figure 10c). *OutlinkOverlap* relationship

[3] Our implementation of *MilneWitten* is slightly simplified from Milne and Witten's final measure; we only consider their "Google Distance-inspired" metric. They were able to gain modest but insignificant improvements by averaging in their "TFIDF-inspired" metric.

strengths are calculated in a similar manner as *MilneWitten* strengths.

4.1.5 Explicit Semantic Analysis

Explicit Semantic Analysis (*ESA*) [9,10] is a popular SR algorithm that uses Wikipedia text as its lexical resource. *ESA* models input concepts *a* and *b* "in terms of Wikipedia-based concepts" [9]. The measure is "explicit" because Wikipedia articles, which are understandable to humans, define this modeling space. *ESA*'s use of real concepts stands in stark contrast to the abstract concepts of methods like Latent Semantic Analysis (LSA), just as the real spaces of explicit spatialization differ from the abstract spaces of traditional spatialization (*Explicit Semantic Analysis* motivated the name of explicit spatialization).

Broadly speaking, to produce SR estimates, *ESA* considers the co-occurrence of *a* and *b* in a large number of Wikipedia articles *C*. Specifically, *ESA* represents *a* and *b* as vectors of bag-of-words similarity to each article *c* in *C*. It then compares these vectors using cosine similarity. The relationships considered by *ESA* are thus co-occurring mentions of *a* and *b* in each Wikipedia article in the concept space. Stronger relationships are defined by articles in *C* that more frequently mention both *a* and *b* (with consideration for document frequency as well), and strength can be estimated by comparing the combined values in each vector dimension while calculating the cosine similarity. Explanations derived from ESA thus describe the co-occurrence of mentions of *a* and *b* in each article *c* in *C* in a human-readable fashion (Figure 11).

Beer in Ireland discusses both Ireland and Beer

Though Ireland is better known for stout, 63% of the beer sold in the country is lager.

Figure 11: The top ESA *explanation for <Ireland, Beer>. In this case c = "Beer in Ireland".*

4.2 AtlasifySR+E

The SR+E measures discussed above capture distinct relationship types. *WikiRelate* tends to operate on classical relations [4] such as *isA* (hyponymy/hypernymy) and *hasA* (meronymy/holonymy) [38]. The WAG-based SR measures are more capable of discovering non-classical relations [4], such as *isTheBiggestExporterOf* (Figure 10b). Finally, *ESA* discovers the "distributional" relationships [4] inherent to text co-occurrence.

AtlasifySR+E, the algorithm employed in our exploratory search approach, combines all six previously discussed SR measures. The goal in doing so was to develop an SR+E measure that understands all three types of relationships. We hypothesized that such an ensemble measure would produce both (1) better SR estimates and (2) better relationship explanations. *AtlasifySR+E's* SR estimate for a pair of terms is the output of a learned model whose features include the estimates of each constituent SR measure as well as features like the word sense entropy of the pair. *AtlasifySR+E* generates explanations for these estimates using a different learned model to select the best explanation among those output by each constituent measure. *AtlasifySR+E* then iterates, choosing the next best explanation, resulting in a long ranked list of explanations.

The experiments section that follows (Section 5) describes in detail each of the learned models and their associated machine learning experiments. We also show in Section 5 that both of our hypotheses related to the combining of SR measures for improved performance were supported.

5. EVALUATION EXPERIMENTS

Evaluation of exploratory search systems is a notoriously difficult problem [39, 40]. In this paper, our evaluation strategy is to investigate the performance of the individual components of our exploratory search approach. Specifically, we focus the evaluation on our method of projecting query concepts into spatial distributions using SR+E's relatedness estimates and explanations. This has the added value of confirming these components as independent contributions. Once these spatial distributions have been created, thematic cartography's well-evaluated techniques (see [37] for an overview) can be employed.

Below, we first describe experiments that demonstrate the state-of-the-art accuracy of our SR estimates. Next, we discuss how we collected over 2,500 human judgments of explanation quality and used these judgments to train a ranker whose performance significantly exceeds baseline approaches.

5.1 SR Value Experiments

Accurate SR value estimates are integral to our exploratory search approach. The colors, text sizes, and other visual variables in Figures 1–4 and 7–8 are defined by *AtlasifySR+E*'s estimates of the SR between each spatial entity and the query concept. Our method for achieving high-quality SR is to combine the estimates of the six SR measures mentioned above using machine learning, and use the resultant trained model to generate *AtlasifySR+E*'s estimates. In this section, we describe this machine learning approach and evaluate the accuracy of *AtlasifySR+E*'s SR estimates against benchmark SR data sets.

We first ran an experiment to validate the performance of our implementations of SR measures from previous work. Following standard practice, we evaluated each implementation by comparing its SR estimates with datasets of human gold standard estimates using Spearman's r_s and Pearson's r (Table 1). These datasets consist of term pairs and associated SR values, which are averaged across all human annotators of a dataset. We used two long-standing SR datasets, *WordSim353* [8] and *MC30* [21], as well as *TSA287* [30] and *Atlasify240*[4], the SR dataset we developed as part of the experiment described in Section 5.2. The results in Table 1 indicate that our implementations are satisfactory, especially given Wikipedia-based SR measures' tendency to fluctuate in accuracy over time [26, 42].

Our approach to combining the estimates of each constituent SR measure was to use a regression model to predict the human gold standard judgments in *WordSim353*, the most common SR dataset in the literature. We then used this trained model[5] to predict the gold standard judgments in the four SR datasets discussed above. The regression model employed a variety of features, including the SR estimates produced by each constituent measure, along with numerous properties of the Wikipedia article corresponding to each term in a term pair (e.g. article length, link density). Our model also included as a feature the entropy of the word sense disambiguation task required to identify matching articles for each term. *AtlasifySR+E* uses a pairwise maximization approach for

[4] *Atlasify240* is available for download at http://www.cs.northwestern.edu/~ddowney/data_code.html

[5] Although *MC30* and *WordSim353* are frequently simultaneously used to evaluate SR measures, *MC30* is a subset of *WordSim353*. As such, prior to training the model on which we tested on *MC30*, we removed the 30 overlapping pairs from our training set (leaving 323 pairs available for training). We did the same for the 1 overlapping pair with TSA287.

SR Algorithm		MC30		WordSim353		TSA287		Atlasify240	
		r_s	r	r_s	r	r_s	r	r_s	r
WikiRelate	AtlasifySR+E	**.78**	**.82**	.49	.48	.40	.47	.52	.53
	Published	-	.57	-	.53	-	-	-	-
MilneWitten	AtlasifySR+E	**.64**	.65	.56	.52	.49	.45	.68	.69
	Published	**.70**	-	.69	-	-	-	-	-
WeightedMW		**.65**	.65	.66	.57	.53	.46	**.74**	**.72**
WAGDirect		**.71**	.73	.64	.58	.49	.53	.60	.56
OutlinkOverlap		**.64**	.67	.52	.42	.48	.42	.61	.51
ESA	AtlasifySR+E	**.74**	.77†	.72	.70†	**.58**	**.62†**	.71	**.72†**
	Published	**.72**	-	.75	-	-	-	-	-
TSA (*current SoA*)	Published	-	-	**.80**	-	**.63**	-	-	-
AtlasifySR+E		**.75**	**.81**	**.78‡**	**.76‡**	**.64**	**.68**	**.78**	**.77**
Inter-annotator Agreement		n/a	**.90**	n/a	**.55-.73**	n/a	-	n/a	**.77**

Table 1. The performance of the SR measures considered in this paper, in context with that of their published versions. Where inter-annotator agreement (InterAA) is available, bold indicates results with which we could not detect a significant difference with InterAA using the method in [10] *and* $p < 0.05$. *Where it is not available, bold indicates the top result and those with which we could not detect a significant difference with the top result. InterAA is not included for Spearman's* r (r_s) *due to the prevalence of ties* [43]. *Note that* AtlasifySR+E *is the only measure that is bold in all columns, including those for which there is data for the current state-of-the-art,* TSA. *A* ‡ *indicates that the model was trained on this dataset. A* † *indicates that the log of the estimates has been used for improved performance. Finally, a dash means that data was not reported.*

word sense disambiguation [22, 26], wherein word sense candidates are identified using anchor texts.

We found that a boosted implementation of Quinlan's M5 algorithm for smoothed trees of linear regression models achieved good performance using 10-fold cross validation (mean $r = 0.75$ with gold standard values). Among the most predictive features in the model were the SR scores generated by the constituent algorithms and the word sense entropy of the term pair. The constituent SR measure with the most predictive power was *ESA*.

We then evaluated the performance of our new *AtlasifySR+E* measure using the same experimental setup as above. The full results can be seen in Table 1. *AtlasifySR+E* performs better than all Wikipedia-specific measures on every dataset but *MC30* for both correlation metrics, and the *MC30* differences are not significant. Further, we could not detect a statistically significant difference between *AtlasifySR+E*'s Pearson's correlations and the inter-annotator agreement in every case.

We also could not detect a significant difference between the accuracy of SR estimates generated by *AtlasifySR+E* and those generated by *TSA*, which is the current state-of-the-art SR algorithm. *AtlasifySR+E* relies only on Wikipedia data while *TSA* additionally uses exogenous information in the form of a large set of *New York Times* abstracts stretching over decades. This data is language-specific, less accessible than Wikipedia, and less open. *AtlasifySR+E* may thus be preferable to *TSA* in, for example, for-profit settings, non-English contexts, and cross-language information retrieval, a popular application of semantic relatedness (e.g. [29]). Atlasify supports exploratory inquiry in 25 language editions of Wikipedia, and the multilingual nature of *AtlasifySR+E* is a major reason we were able to make Atlasify so universal. We also note that *AtlasifySR+E*'s ensemble approach – improving performance by combining different perspectives on the relatedness between concepts – can incorporate additional perspectives on relatedness, such as *TSA*'s temporal approach and future innovations.

5.2 Explanation Ranking Experiments

Each of *AtlasifySR+E*'s constituent SR+E measures returns a list of explanations ranked by their informativeness (Section 4.2). *AtlasifySR+E* must then consolidate and rank the explanations from each measure into a single list to return to the user when they click on a spatial entity. We approached this explanation ranking task as follows: given a concept pair and the up to six top-ranked (most informative) explanations from the constituent measures, *AtlasifySR+E* is to select the best explanation. *AtlasifySR+E* then iterates, removing the explanation it judged to be most interesting at each iteration and placing it in order in the list of explanations to be returned to the user. In the case of the constituent SR measure whose explanation was placed in the returned list, the next most informative explanation is considered in the subsequent iteration. Solving this ranking problem involved gathering a dataset from human judges and then using this dataset to train, develop, and test a ranker. We describe this effort below.

5.2.1 Data collection

Our training data was based on 268 manually selected concept pairs. Each concept mapped unambiguously to a Wikipedia article, and, following one approach in the literature (e.g. [8, 25]), concept pairs were hypothesized to uniformly cover the spectrum of semantic relatedness. While 28 of these concept pairs come from *WordSim353*, 240 are original pairs not seen before in the SR literature. These 240 pairs make up the *Atlasify240* dataset, which is focused on named entities. Named entities make up a large majority of concepts in spatial reference systems (e.g. "John McCain", "Israel", "Helium"). Existing datasets (e.g. [8, 21, 30]) include relatively few named entities, necessitating new concept pairs for our evaluation.

Each of the most informative (top-ranked) explanations from *AtlasifySR+E*'s constituent SR+E measures was generated for all of the 268 pairs and placed in a Web interface (when there was an explanation available). The interface allowed human annotators to rank the explanations for each pair of articles using drag-and-drop techniques. The presentation order of both the pairs and the explanations were randomized. Prior to ranking explanations for a pair, annotators were required to provide an SR estimate. Following the existing SR literature [25, 30], annotators were able to rank SR on a limited scale, in our case from 0 (not related) to 4 (very related). After ranking the available explanations, annotators were asked if they thought that their top-ranked explanation was a good explanation of a relationship between the two concepts.

Ten annotators finished all pairs. On average, annotators said 66% of their top-ranked explanations were good explanations of the relationship between the two concepts. As hypothesized, *WAGDirect* was by far the best algorithm, with 55% of its explanations being chosen as the best on average. However, *WAGDirect* was only able to produce an explanation in 26.8% of cases because only that many of the article pairs had at least one link between them. *WikiRelate* was lowest performing algorithm, but was still selected 13.8% of time when it was available. The *MilneWitten* algorithms were the most prolific and were each able to generate an explanation for over 80% of the samples.

For 18 (6.7%) pairs, no algorithm was able to generate an explanation. This is to be expected for pairs with very low SR; where there is no relatedness, there is no relationship to explain. Indeed the average mean SR judgment for these pairs was 0.52 (in a 0-4 range). In contrast, the average mean SR judgment for pairs for which all six algorithms generated explanations was 3.78.

5.2.2 Machine Learning

Using the hand-annotated ranks from our data collection process, we developed a dataset that consisted of numerous features for each explanation, including: (1) the SR value estimate from the constituent SR+E measure, (2) the textual quality of the explanation (described in Section 5.3), and (3) an indicator of which SR+E constituent measure produced the explanation. For each pair, we assigned the explanation with the lowest (i.e. best) mean rank a "1" and every other explanation a "2". We trained a ranker to predict the best ("1") explanation using SVMRank [18].

The results of this experiment can be found in Table 2. We report these results in terms of *coverage*, which is the percentage of pairs for which one or more explanations were available, and *precision*, which is the percentage of pairs for which *AtlasifySR+E* correctly identified the best explanation (when one or more were available).

Using 10-fold cross-validation, our best performing model had a precision of 56%, which is significantly better than random guessing ($\chi^2 = 13.2$, $p < .01$) and only 2% lower than mean inter-annotator agreement (58%). In other words, the model predicts the best explanation almost as well as humans agree on the best explanation. The difference between the model and the inter-annotator agreement is in fact not significant ($\chi^2 = 0.51$, $p = .48$). Moreover, this model results in a slightly better precision (insignificantly so) than *WAGDirect*, the best SR+E algorithm for explanations, and has a much higher coverage; it can return an explanation when *any* of the constituent algorithms can find an explanation. In our experiment, this was 93.3% of the time, compared to *WAGDirect*'s 26.8%.

It is important to note that a model based only on which SR+E method was used ("Measure indicators only") performs nearly as well as the full model, and the difference between them is not significant ($\chi^2 = 1.27$, $p = .15$). That is, the relative performance of the constituent SR+E explanation generators accounts for most of the predictive power of our ranking model.

Model features	***Precision***	***Coverage***
All features	56%	93%
Measure indicators only	51%	93%
Random	39%	93%
WAGDirect (Highest Precision Single SR Measure)	55%	27%
MilneWitten (Highest Coverage Single SR Measure)	35%	80%

Table 2. Results of our explanation ranking experiment.

5.3 Quality of Mined Text

The final machine learning experiment we will discuss assesses the quality of text mined from Wikipedia. This quality assessment, along with relationship strength estimates, is used to calculate the informativeness of the explanations for each of *AtlasifySR+E*'s constituent SR+E measures (Section 4). This informativeness is then used to rank explanations within each individual measure.

Hand-annotated data was supplied by four annotators, each of whom rated 500 snippets on a scale from 0 to 4 according to the quality of the natural language. Each snippet describes one "leg" of a relationship (e.g. Figures 10a and 10c have two snippets, while 10b has one). Quality was assessed using several factors, including readability and clarity of relationship described. Inter-annotator reliability was $r = 0.51$ (calculated with Fisher's z-value transformation [41]).

For training, each snippet was assigned two types of features: syntactic (e.g. lack of a verb) and contextual (e.g. at the top of the page). After experimenting with a variety of regression models, we found a linear regression model to be the most accurate. Using 10-fold cross-validation, this model was able to achieve a mean correlation of $r = 0.32$ (Table 3). While the combined model outperforms a model trained on only a single type of feature, models trained on either type of feature alone were not found to have significantly worse predictive power.

Model features	***r* with gold standard**
All features	0.32
Contextual features only	0.29
Syntactic features only	0.24
Human Inter-rater Agreement	*0.51*

Table 3. The results of our text snippet quality experiment.

6. CONCLUSION AND FUTURE WORK

In this paper, we showed how thematic cartography can be used for domain-neutral exploratory search, demonstrated this process in a working system called Atlasify, presented two use cases, and evaluated its key functions. We have also made three additional contributions that have implications outside of exploratory search. First, we presented explicit spatialization, which brings the benefits of online mapping and geographic information retrieval into domains beyond geography. Second, we introduced explanatory semantic relatedness (SR+E) measures, which extend popular SR measures to make them user-understandable. We built and evaluated an SR+E measure that produces explanations significantly better than those of baseline approaches. Finally, through its method of merging the benefits of its six constituent SR measures, our new SR+E measure produces SR estimates that are statistically indistinguishable from the state-of-the-art without relying on language specific or proprietary data.

Future work includes applying ES in traditional GIR applications and SR+E in traditional SR applications. We are also incorporating into *AtlasifySR+E* DBpedia's structured relationships, which are concise but of limited coverage. Finally, we are preparing a lab-based evaluation of Atlasify, an essential next step [40], as well as looking to the deploy the system more widely to see how our approach is leveraged by real users.

ACKNOWLEDGEMENTS

The authors thank Jeffrey Geiger for his spatiotagging work, our annotators, and our reviewers. Thanks also to Patti Bao and

Stephanie Hille. This work was supported by an NSF Graduate Fellowship (first author) and NSF Grant IIS-101675.

REFERENCES

[1] Bergstrom, T. and Karahalios, K. 2009. Conversation clusters: grouping conversation topics through human-computer dialog. *CHI '09*.

[2] Bertin, J. and Berg, W.J. 1989. *Semiology of Graphics*. University of Wisconsin Press.

[3] Bozzon, A., Brambilla, M., Ceri, S. and Fraternali, P. 2010. Liquid query: multi-domain exploratory search on the web. *WWW '10*.

[4] Budanitsky, A. and Hirst, G. 2006. Evaluating WordNet-based Measures of Lexical Semantic Relatedness. *Computational Linguistics*. 32, 1 (2006), 13–47.

[5] Card, S.K., Mackinlay, J.D. and Shneiderman, B. 1999. *Readings in Information Visualization: Using Vision to Think*. Morgan Kaufmann.

[6] Dodge, M., Kitchin, R. and Perkins, C. 2011. Introduction to The Map Reader. *The Map Reader: Theories of Mapping Practice and Cartographic Representation*. Wiley.

[7] Eisenstein, J., O'Connor, B., Smith, N.A. and Xing, Eric P. 2010. A Latent Variable Model for Geographic Lexical Variation. *EMNLP '10*.

[8] Finkelstein, L., Gabrilovich, E., Matias, Y., Rivlin, E., Solan, Z., Wolfman, G. and Ruppin, E. 2002. Placing Search in Context: The Concept Revisited. *ACM Transactions on Information Systems*. 20, 1 (2002), 116–131.

[9] Gabrilovich, E. and Markovitch, S. 2007. Computing Semantic Relatedness using Wikipedia-based Explicit Semantic Analysis. *IJCAI '07*.

[10] Gabrilovich, E. and Markovitch, S. 2009. Wikipedia-based Semantic Interpretation for Natural Language Processing. *JAIR*. 34, (2009), 443–498.

[11] Goodchild, M.F., Yuan, M. and Cova, T.J. 2007. Towards a general theory of geographic representation in GIS. *IJGIS*. 21, 3 (2007), 239–260.

[12] Google Correlate: *http://correlate.googlelabs.com/*. Accessed: 2011-07-28.

[13] Hearst, M.A. 2009. *Search User Interfaces*. Cambridge University Press.

[14] Hecht, B. and Gergle, D. 2010. The Tower of Babel Meets Web 2.0: User-Generated Content and Its Applications in a Multilingual Context. *CHI '10*.

[15] Hecht, B. and Raubal, M. 2008. GeoSR: Geographically explore semantic relations in world knowledge. *AGILE '08*.

[16] Hecht, B. and Schöning, J. 2008. Mapping the Zeitgeist. *GIScience '08 (Extended Abstracts)*.

[17] Hornbæk, K. and Frøkjær, E. 1999. Do Thematic Maps Improve Information Retrieval? *INTERACT '99* (1999), 1–8.

[18] Joachims, T. 2006. Training Linear SVMs in Linear Time. *KDD '06*.

[19] Jones, C.B., Purves, R.S., Clough, P.D. and Joho, H. 2008. Modelling Vague Places with Knowledge from the Web. *IJGIS*. 22, 10 (2008), 1045–1065.

[20] MacEachren, A.M. 1982. The Role of Complexity and Symbolization Method in Thematic Maps. *Annals of the Assoc. of American Geographers*. 72, 4 (1982), 495–513.

[21] Miller, G.A. and Charles, W.G. 1991. Contextual correlates of semantic similarity. *Language and Cognitive Processes*. 6, 1 (1991), 1–28.

[22] Milne, D. and Witten, I.H. 2008. An Effective, Low-Cost Measure of Semantic Relatedness Obtained from Wikipedia Links. *WIKI-AI '08*.

[23] Milne, D. and Witten, I.H. 2008. Learning to link with Wikipedia. *CIKM '08*.

[24] Montello, D.R. 2002. Cognitive Map-Design Research in the Twentieth Century: Theoretical and Empirical Approaches. *CAGIS*. 29, 3 (2002), 283–304.

[25] Pedersen, T., Pakhomov, S.V.S., Patwardhan, S. and Chute, C.G. 2006. Measures of semantic similarity and relatedness in the biomedical domain. *Journal of Biomedical Informatics*. 40, 3 (2006), 288–299.

[26] Ponzetto, S.P. and Strube, M. 2007. Knowledge Derived From Wikipedia For Computing Semantic Relatedness. *JAIR*. 30, (2007), 181–212.

[27] Popescu, A. and Grefenstette, G. 2010. Mining User Home Location and Gender from Flickr Tags. *ICWSM '10*.

[28] Popescu, A. and Grefenstette, G. 2010. Spatiotemporal mapping of Wikipedia concepts. *JCDL '10* (2010), 129–138.

[29] Potthast, M., Stein, B. and Anderka, M. 2008. A Wikipedia-based multilingual retrieval model. *ECIR '08*.

[30] Radinsky, K., Agichtein, E., Gabrilovich, E. and Markovitch, S. 2011. A Word at a Time: Computing Word Relatedness using Temporal Semantic Analysis. *WWW '11*.

[31] Rajaraman, A. 2009. Kosmix: High-Performance Topic Exploration using the Deep Web. *Proceedings of the VLDB Endowment*. 2, 2009 (2009), 1524–1529.

[32] Risch, J.S., Rex, D.B., Dowson, S.T., Walters, T.B., May, R.A. and Moon, B.D. 1997. The STARLIGHT information visualization system. *INFOVIS '97*.

[33] Rose, D.E. and Levinson, D. 2004. Understanding user goals in web search. *WWW '04*.

[34] Sheesley, B. 2009. Data Probing and Info Window Design on Web-based Maps. *Axis Maps Blog*. http://www.axismaps .com/blog/2009/07/data-probing-and-info-window-design-on-web-based-maps/. Accessed: 2012-06-04.

[35] Shneiderman, B. 1996. The eyes have it: a task by data type taxonomy for information visualizations. *IEEE Symposium on Visual Languages '96* (Sep. 1996), 336–343.

[36] Skupin, A. and Fabrikant, S.I. 2003. Spatialization Methods: A Cartographic Research Agenda for Non-geographic Information Visualization. *CAGIS*. 30, 2 (2003), 95–115.

[37] Slocum, T.A., McMaster, R.B., Kessler, F.C. and Howard, H.H. 2009. *Thematic Cartography and Geovisualization*. Prentice Hall.

[38] Strube, M. and Ponzetto, S.P. 2006. WikiRelate! Computing Semantic Relatedness Using Wikipedia. *AAAI '06*.

[39] White, R., Muresan, G. and Marchionini, G. 2006. Evaluating Exploratory Search Systems. *SIGIR '06 Workshop on Evaluating Exploratory Search* (2006).

[40] White, R., Roth, R. and Marchionini, G. 2009. *Exploratory search: beyond the query-response paradigm*. Morgan & Claypool.

[41] Zesch, T. and Gurevych, I. 2006. Automatically creating datasets for measures of semantic relatedness. *ACL-Workshop on Linguistic Distances*.

[42] Zesch, T. and Gurevych, I. 2010. The More the Better? Assessing the Influence of Wikipedia's Growth on Semantic Relatedness Measures. *LREC '10*.

[43] Zesch, T. and Gurevych, I. 2009. Wisdom of crowds versus wisdom of linguists – measuring the semantic relatedness of words. *Natural Language Engineering*. 16, 1 (2009), 25–59.

[44] Zesch, T., Gurevych, I. and Mühlhäuser, M. 2007. Analyzing and accessing Wikipedia as a lexical semantic resource. *Data Structures for Linguistic Resources and Applications*.

A Subjunctive Exploratory Search Interface to Support Media Studies Researchers

Marc Bron[1] Jasmijn van Gorp[2] Frank Nack[1]
Maarten de Rijke[1] Andrei Vishneuski[1] Sonja de Leeuw[2]
[1]ISLA, University of Amsterdam, Science Park 904, 1098 XH Amsterdam, The Netherlands
{m.m.bron, nack, derijke, a.vishneuski}@uva.nl
[2]TViT, Utrecht University, Muntstraat 2a, 3514 EV Utrecht, The Netherlands
{j.vangorp, j.s.deleeuw}@uu.nl

ABSTRACT

Media studies concerns the study of production, content, and/or reception of various types of media. Today's continuous production and storage of media is changing the way media studies researchers work and requires the development of new search models and tools. We investigate the research cycle of media studies researchers and find that it is an iterative process consisting of several search processes in which data is gathered and the research question is refined. Changes in the research question, however, trigger new data gathering processes. Based on these outcomes we propose a subjunctive exploratory search interface to support media studies researchers in refining their research question in an earlier stage of their research. To assess the subjunctive interface we conduct a user study and compare to a traditional exploratory search interface. We find that with the subjunctive interface users explore more diverse topics than with the standard interface and that users formulate more specific research questions. Although the subjunctive interface is more complex, this does not decrease its usability. These findings suggest that the subjunctive interface supports media studies researchers. The advantage of a subjunctive interface for exploration suggests a new direction for the development of exploratory search systems.

Categories and Subject Descriptors

H.3.3 [**Information Search and Retrieval**]: Search process; H.5.2 [**User Interfaces**]: Evaluation/methodology

Keywords

Exploratory search, subjunctive interface, humanities

1. INTRODUCTION

Media Studies can be situated both the humanities as well as in the social sciences and concerns the study of production, content and/or reception of various types of media, e.g., social media, film, and television [23]. Today's continuous production and storage of all types of media is changing the way humanities researchers work and the questions they seek to answer [3, 10, 27]. As a result, there is an increasing demand for tools to support exploration and analysis of this data [32, 33]. Tools to support humanities researchers exist but they are often not effective or remain unused [10, 34]. One reason is that, generally, tools are developed without looking at the context and complexity of the task [17]. Moreover, the level of detail at which available models of the research cycle describe search behavior is insufficient to design effective tools [32].

In this paper we start out by investigating the research cycle of media studies researchers. Through an analysis of a series of interviews about the research habits of media studies researchers we arrive at a model of the media studies research cycle. We compare our model to other models of the humanities research cycle, and find that it is consistent with existing models [4, 9] but that it is more detailed in identifying sequences of search processes and their influence on the research question.

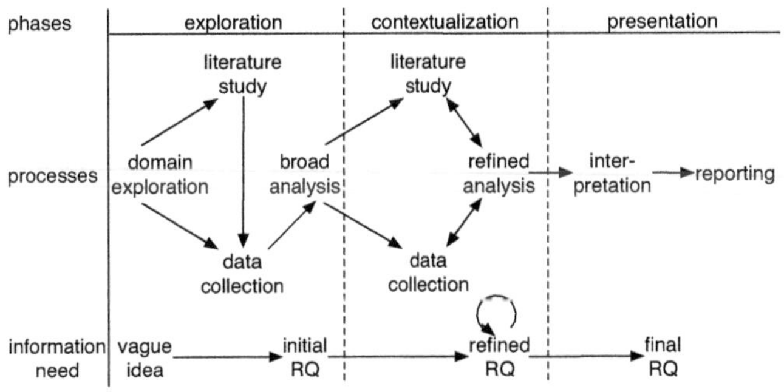

Figure 1: Overview of the phases in the media studies research cycle with associated search processes and changes in the research question (RQ). Arrows indicate possible sequences.

Figure 1 shows the phases in the media studies research cycle with the associated search processes and changes in the research question. We find that the research cycle of media researchers is an iterative process and that the research question is refined in each step. Take for example the following initial research question: "How are eastern European migrants represented on television," and its refinement: "How are children of USSR refugees represented in television programs for children from 1980 to 2000." Every change in the research question, however, triggers new data gathering processes. Changing the research question comes at a cost as new data has to be collected, organized and analyzed. We observe that factors influencing the research question are discovering alternative views

Permission to make digital or hard copies of all or part of this work for personal or classroom use is granted without fee provided that copies are not made or distributed for profit or commercial advantage and that copies bear this notice and the full citation on the first page. To copy otherwise, or republish, to post on servers or to redistribute to lists, requires prior specific permission and/or a fee.
SIGIR'12, August 12–16, 2012, Portland, Oregon, USA.
Copyright 2012 ACM 978-1-4503-1472-5/12/08... $15.00.

on a topic and discovering trends in the data. These observations suggest that an interface that supports these types of discovery in an early stage of the research cycle will reduce the number of iterations necessary to arrive at a final research question.

In this paper we focus on developing and assessing a search interface to support media studies researchers in refining their research question in the *exploration* phase of the research cycle. Requirements for such an interface are that it supports (i) exploring multiple views on a topic and (ii) discovering patterns in the data.

A number of exploratory search tools exist, that support various ways to explore collections, e.g., through filtering by facets, or relevance feedback, see [12, 29, 37] for overviews of systems and their capabilities. As work on exploratory search systems focuses on supporting exploration in a general setting, few have considered how exploratory search systems can support researchers in discovering alternative views and trends in the data during exploration. To support users in complex search tasks [17], investigating multiple aspects of a topic in a subjunctive interface was shown to reduce task complexity and task completion time [24, 35]. In the humanities, standard practices to discover patterns in data are organizing and comparing [26, 28, 33].

We propose to extend the traditional exploratory search system design in two ways: we incorporate two side-by-side versions of an exploratory search interface in a single interface and second, we add visualizations in which the characteristics of the result sets are shown and can be compared. An interface that incorporates multiple instances of the same search tool in a single interface is referred to as a subjunctive interface [24]. Given this subjunctive exploratory search interface we aim to answer the following research questions: (i) does the subjunctive exploratory search interface better support media studies researchers in a complex exploratory search task than a standard exploratory search interface; (ii) does the subjunctive exploratory search interface better support media studies researchers in refining a research question than a standard exploratory search interface; (iii) does the increase in complexity in terms of additional features affect the usability of the subjunctive interface as compared to a standard exploratory search interface?

In §2 we investigate the media studies research cycle. In §3 we describe the subjunctive exploratory search interface and in §4 the experimental design. In §5 we present the results of assessing the subjunctive interface, and provide a discussion in §6. Related work is discussed in §7 and we conclude in §8.

2. MEDIA STUDIES' RESEARCH CYCLE

To develop an exploratory search tool to support media studies researchers, it is necessary to gain insight into the user's information behavior and context of the task [16, 39]. Existing models of the humanities research cycle or scholarly search behavior [2, 11, 19, 39] are either too general for building tools [32], do not consider the context of increasing amounts of digital information [9], or focus on a different aspect of the research cycle [4].

We take a detailed look at the research habits of media studies researchers. We take a bottom-up approach and through a series of interviews identify changes in the research questions and search processes of media studies researchers during their research. We construct a model of their research cycle and link this to existing models of the humanities research cycle and information behavior.

2.1 Method

We interviewed seven media studies researchers from 3 different institutes with varying levels of experience: 1 PhD student, 4 post-doctoral researchers, 1 assistant-professor, and 1 full professor. Two interviewers conducted the interviews: a media studies researcher experienced in conducting interviews and a computer scientist with some interview experience. The interviewers' backgrounds supplement each other and limit the possibility of misunderstandings during the interview. The subjects were recruited during visits to 3 institutes and participation was voluntary.

The interview was conducted in a semi-structured style and consisted of three parts: (i) identification of a recent research project; (ii) open questions about search processes and research questions during the project; and (iii) an interactive part in which subjects wrote down the search processes on index cards and ordered them chronologically. This methodology is based on [9]. Interviews lasted about 30 minutes, were tape-recorded and later transcribed.

In our analysis of the interviews we used the following procedure: first we align the search process sequences produced by each of the interviewees by grouping cards with processes that exactly match in the same category. Each card that does not match is placed in a separate category. In the next step we apply coding, a qualitative categorization strategy [31], to the transcripts to identify categories of search processes in the interviews. Categories from the interviews that match with existing categories in the sequences are merged while newly identified categories are added to the sequences. This is an iterative process which is repeated until a stable set of categories emerges. The result is a sequence of categories showing the search processes over time, see Figure 1. Note that when using quotes, square brackets [..] indicate modifications to the original quote to improve understanding or to protect the anonymity of the subject. For identification purposes interviewees are assigned a number, i.e, I1 to I7.

2.2 Results

Three categories (phases) emerged from the analysis: exploration, contextualization, and presentation. Each phase consists of a number of search processes and affects the research question, see Figure 1. Below we describe each category in detail.

Exploration. In general a research project starts with exploration. All but one of the interviewees indicated that they started out with a broad question. One already started with specific research questions as these were defined in an earlier project (I6). With a broad question in mind researchers start an exploratory search for literature, relevant data or both. The goal of this phase is to arrive at an initial research question and to collect a broad sample of data. One researcher noted I1: "for me it starts with developing the research questions and data collection. This happens in parallel, so the question changes by the material you see" and another noted I2: "the data influences the research question, because the data is not available or because you start to see, oh this is so naïve."

Once a selection of relevant data has been made the initial analysis starts by organizing and structuring the collected material. This is a time consuming process in which material is watched, transcribed, and archived [28]. The goal is to get an overview and to formulate an initial research question, leading to the next phase.

Contextualization. The contextualization phase is the most iterative part of the research cycle. The arrows are going back and forth between analysis and data collection, and analysis and literature study in Figure 1, indicate that multiple iterations may be performed. In this phase a more focused data collection starts to place the initially collected material into context. We found various reasons for researchers to repeat the data collection step: getting a representative sample (I4: "so that [first analysis] was followed by collecting new data, using the methods identified in the literature and guided by insights from the earlier analysis"), getting context for a certain view (I5: "I needed to know the ethnic background of people [mentioned in tv-programs] for example"), and getting data to follow a new insight or direction (I3: "it was when I started having interviews that I realized that it is not so black and white and that is when the direction of my research changed completely"). These comments illustrate how analysis of the data leads to collection of additional data (I4, I5) and even completely new data (I3). These iterative steps suggest that initially researchers do not have specific criteria for data selection, only during analysis patterns emerge that lead to more specific search criteria. These changes in the search criteria manifest itself as a refinement in the research question.

After the new data has been collected another analysis follows, where, again, the material is inspected and relations between material are identified. The research question is further refined and will either lead to the next phase or another cycle of data collection and analysis. One researcher notes I1: "by organizing [the material] you create the story, I chose to use a chronological ordering, if I had organized my archive differently I would have written a different story. I could have organized it in supporters and opponents." In this case a certain view on the data was chosen and the data organized accordingly. The effort it takes to reorganize the data for a certain view constrains the number of alternatives that are investigated, suggesting that having an overview of the alternatives early in the research cycle can be beneficial. Another researcher states I2: "and then you return again to the data and sometimes the literature, while part of the data has already been collected, because you feel that something is there but it does not come out." In this case a certain contrast was expected in the data but did not appear after organization and analysis. This is another motivation for a more thorough exploration of views on the topic before analysis.

Presentation. The interviewees agree that at some point the data is fixed and the next phase starts. At this point a relevant sample of the data has been collected and this data is interpreted in the context of the refined research questions. This phase consists of analyzing and writing as the media studies researcher builds up a case to support his/her research questions by organizing the data and selecting appropriate qualitative evidence. After the analyses have been completed and the results have been written down, the findings are disseminated in publications and at conferences.

2.3 Relation to Other Models

We compare our model, as visualized in Figure 1, with previous work on describing the humanities research cycle. The model of literary critics describes six stages: preparation, elaboration, analysis and writing, dissemination, and further writing and dissemination [9]. The preparation stage corresponds with our exploration phase. The elaboration, and the analysis and writing stage correspond to our contextualization phase. While the dissemination, and further dissemination and writing stage corresponds to our presentation phase. That model, however, presents a cycle where all stages are completed in sequence while we find a number of shorter cycles in the initial stages. The shorter cycles serve to find a focus in the large amounts of available data. Another model proposes three phases: reading and annotation, developing interpretation, and presentation of interpretation [4], similar to our phases. The focus of this work, however, is on note taking and organizing processes and not on information seeking behavior. Additionally, we provide more detail about the search processes in which media studies researchers engage. There is work on describing the scholarly practices of humanities researchers [28], but while this work describes the possible processes, e.g., organizing, it does not describe how these processes influence the research questions during the research cycle. The value of our model is that it makes the sequences of search processes and the gradual refinement of the research questions in the media studies research cycle explicit. Information needs of media researchers have been classified in four phases: getting an overview, identifying boarderline exemplars, selection of specific programs and verification of facts [23]. These changes in information needs are consistent with our changes in the research question, but are not considered in the context of a research cycle and the possible repetition of information needs.

The relation of our model to search models [2, 11, 19], is that the stages and features associated with these models are observed in the media studies research cycle, but correspond to single processes, e.g., a data collection process. Our model describes the research cycle, the context of these search processes. The information behavior model by Wilson [39] provides a general framework to model users' information behavior in context. We do not consider all possible variables of the model as it is too broad. Instead, we focus on the search processes (information seeking behavior) and the change of the information need in the research cycle due to learning about characteristics of the data (intervening variables).

2.4 Discussion

We find that the research cycle of media studies researchers is an iterative process, where processes of data collection and analysis alternate, see Figure 1. In the *exploration* phase an initial data set is collected and analyzed. The analysis of data is an expensive process that consists of extracting and organization of material, but is necessary to get insight into the material and to refine the research question. In the *contextualization* phase a new data collection process starts and another analysis follows. If this analysis reveals that certain patterns or views on a topic have been missed the process repeats. Otherwise a process of analysis, writing, and dissemination follows, i.e., the *presentation* phase. Factors causing media studies researchers to adjust their research question are discovering alternative views on a topic, and discovering trends in the data. These observations suggest that an interface that supports these types of discovery in an earlier stage of the research cycle will reduce the number of iterations necessary to arrive at a final research question and so support media studies research.

3. A SUBJUNCTIVE INTERFACE

The model of the research cycle in §2 provides insight in the requirements for a successful search interface for media studies researchers. Below we describe the development process of our subjunctive exploratory search interface, simply referred to as *subjunctive interface* in the remainder of the paper, followed by a detailed description of the interface features.

3.1 Development Procedure

In developing the subjunctive interface care has been taken to follow user centered design principles [5]. Here, we motivate the initial design of the subjunctive interface, describe the data used in our prototype, and findings from two rounds of usability testing.

Initial design. We established two requirements for an interface for media studies researchers: (i) to provide users with support for exploration, i.e., support in formulating queries, query refinement and exploring various aspects of a topic; and (ii) to provide support for discovering patterns in the data, i.e, to compare alternatives and to observe trends in the data. A large body of work exists on interfaces for supporting exploratory search [7, 8, 21, 29, 38, 40]. Such interfaces provide support for the first requirement through visualizations, filters and facets. We start our interface development with the design of a prototypical exploratory search interface [7].

Not as well supported by this type of interface is the ability to compare alternatives. Subjunctive interfaces have been suggested for this purpose as this type of interface allows a user to perform multiple actions in parallel and compare the results, i.e., editing a document or searching a database. Typically multiple versions of a standard interface, e.g, a standard document editor, are presented side-by-side to create a subjunctive interface [24]. In web search, a multi-view interface has been proposed that supports multiple views of a traditional web search interface and allows users to explore more aspects of a topic than a single view variant [35]. Another requirement not as well supported is the discovery of trends in the data. Visualization laboratories, as those used in e-Science disciplines, are better suited for this purpose as these offer various visualization techniques, i.e., curves, scatter plots and renderings, to analyse large numerical datasets [15].

Given our requirements, we adapted the standard exploratory search interface design in two ways: (i) we extended the design to a subjunctive exploratory search interface by incorporating two side-by-side versions of a standard exploratory search interface; and (ii) we added a timeline visualization and a term statistics visualization in which the characteristics of the result sets obtained with each side of the interface are shown and can be compared.

Data set. Television studies (a sub-discipline of media studies) concerns the study of production and/or reception of television. From an audiovisual archive we obtained a catalogue of about 1.5M television program descriptions to serve as data set to be accessed through our interface. We use descriptions as the actual programs are often not directly accessible due to copyright legislation [23]. The program descriptions are created by archivists, and primarily consist of metadata fields describing the program. For example, keywords, summary, and fields with program production information, e.g., broadcast date and program creator. The back-end of the interface consists of a Lucene SOLR index, where stopwords have been removed and stemming has been applied. For retrieval the Lucene implementation of the Vector Space Model is used.[1]

Usability testing. In a first round of usability testing we presented a prototype of the subjunctive interface to two groups of media studies researchers, consisting of 12 and 16 subjects. A presentation with a walk-through of the interface was followed by a group interview. The three main findings are: (i) the importance of production information such as program broadcast date and program maker, next to the content of programs; (ii) program genre information is an essential subject in media studies; and (iii) television production/reception is often studied over time. We also received feature requests, i.e, the ability to exclude certain terms, to view the query history, and to load alternative archives such as news archives and television magazine collections.

After a new round of development we performed a usability study of the subjunctive interface. The subjects consisted of 30 first year information science students that participated as part of a class project. The main concerns of the subjects were with the cosmetics of the interface, the response time, and the size of the result snippets. After incorporating this feedback we performed a series of small pilot studies with media studies researchers to test the final design and to remove any further usability issues.

3.2 Subjunctive Interface Description

We start by describing an exploratory search interface that will serve as the basis for the subjunctive interface. In the remainder of the paper we refer to this interface as the *baseline* as it is used for comparison in our evaluation of the subjunctive interface described in §4. Figure 2 shows a schematic view of two interfaces: on the left-hand side the baseline and on the right-hand side the subjunctive

[1]http://lucene.apache.org/solr/

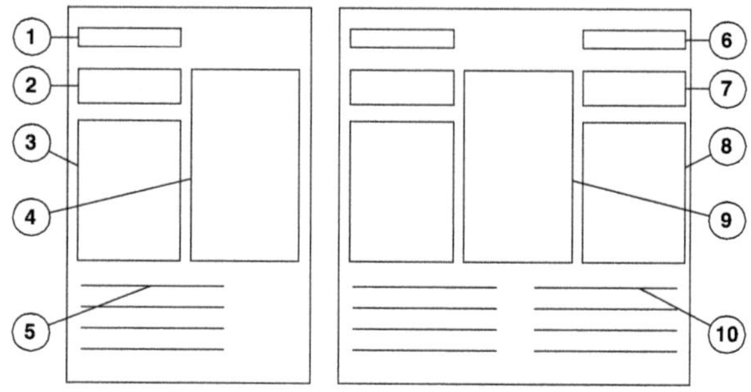

Figure 2: Schematic view of the baseline interface (left) and the subjunctive interface (right). Numbers are used for reference.

interface. We use the numbers (1, . . . , 10) in Figure 2 to reference specific components in the interfaces.[2]

Baseline. The baseline interface consists of a search box (1), two filters: a timeline (2) and a term-cloud filter (3), a timeline and term statistics chart (4), and a result list (5). The baseline interface provides traditional search functionality in that typing a query in the search box (1) results in a ranked list of document snippets (5). Each result snippet describes a program with a title, broadcast date, and a maximum of 40 words from the summary of the program. Next to each snippet, a bookmark button is available. Bookmarking a program adds it to the query history, available as drop-down list, showing for each query the programs bookmarked in its result set. When clicking on a snippet an *overlay* with the complete program description appears. In the result set 25 program snippets are shown per page and the result set is limited to a maximum of 500 programs to keep the interface responsive.

The filters (2, 3) enable a user to rapidly refine the result set returned for a query [36]. Each subsequent filter that is applied operates on the remaining program descriptions. Filters are reset by issuing a new query or pressing a "clear filter" button. The timeline filter removes programs with a broadcast date outside of the selected range, see top Figure 3.

The term-cloud filter enables a type of faceted search over the result set, see bottom Figure 3. Next to query refinement, faceted search also provides support for gaining insight in a topic [20, 36]. We decided on five facets based on the focus group interviews: *people* mentioned in a program, *makers* of a program, *channel* a program is broadcasted on, *words* are keywords characterizing the

[2]The interface is available at:
http://zookma.science.uva.nl/merdesdemo

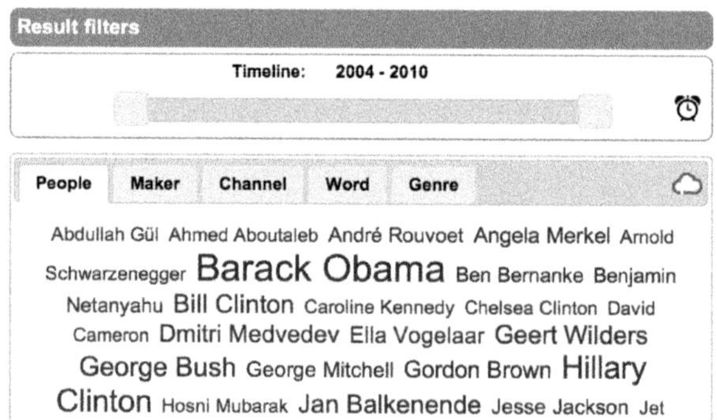

Figure 3: Screenshot of the timeline filter (top) and the term-cloud filter with the *people* facet selected (bottom).

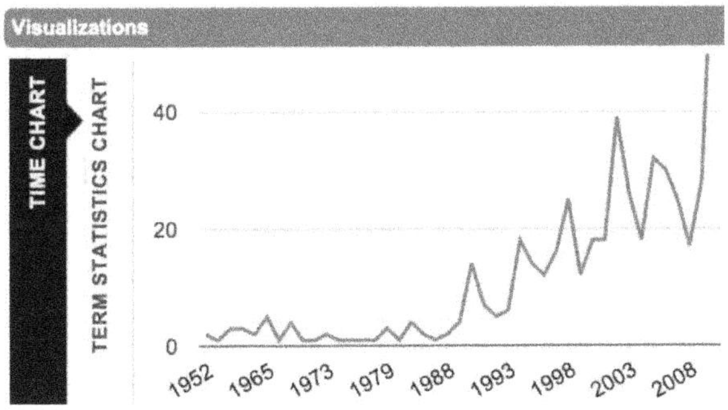

Figure 4: Timeline chart: y-axis showing the number of programs broadcasted per year; x-axis showing the years.

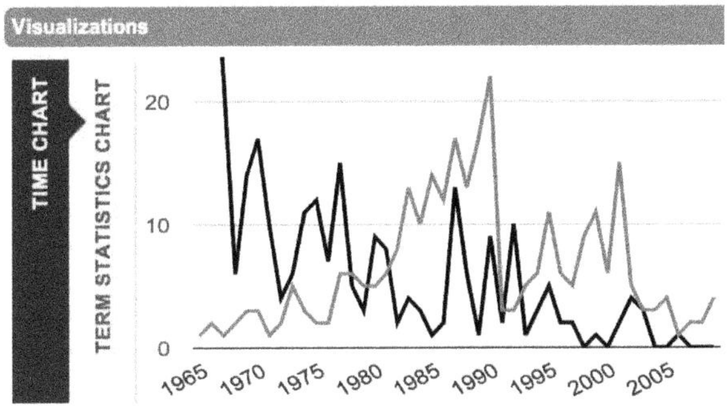

Figure 6: Subjunctive interface timeline chart: black corresponds to the result set for the query "protests", the lighter shade (red) to the query "riots". The axes are defined in Fig. 4.

program, and *genre* of a program. Each cloud provides two modes of filtering: *retain* and *remove*. To *retain* a user clicks a term and only program descriptions that contain the term are kept. To *remove*, a user clicks a term and holds the mouse button, drags it slightly and releases the mouse button causing program descriptions that contain the term to be removed. Repeating an action deactivates a filter and "un-hides" documents affected by this filter.

The final parts of the baseline interface are the timeline and term statistics charts (4). These visualizations offer support for discovering trends in the data. They are not shown simultaneously, but are accessed through a *slide deck*. The timeline chart, see Figure 4, is shown by default. By clicking on the *term statistics slide* an animation shows the term statistics chart "sliding" over and covering the timeline chart. The timeline chart is subsequently accessible through the *timeline slide*. An example of the term statistics chart is shown in Figure 5. A drop-down menu allows the user to select one of the facets (people, maker, channel, words, and genre) to inspect the terms that occur most frequently in the program descriptions.

Subjunctive exploratory search interface. The left-hand side of the subjunctive interface consists of the same features as the baseline interface. On the right side the subjunctive interface further consists of an additional search box (6), timeline and term-cloud filter (7, 8), and result list (10); see Figure 2. The two search boxes with their respective filters and result lists are independent and in essence provide the user with a second exploratory search interface. The visualizations in the subjunctive interface (9) differ from those in the baseline (4). The timeline chart shows two curves, one for each result set, see Figure 6. The curves are color coded black and red. Similarly, the search boxes are colored black and red on the left and right-hand side of the interface, respectively, to indicate their correspondence to the user. Analogously, the term statistics chart shows two bars per term, one for the frequency of the term in the left result set and one for its frequency in the right result set. The terms are required to occur in both result sets and are ordered by the total frequency in both sets, see Figure 7.

Note that although care has been taken in the design of the interface, we do not claim that this design is optimal. One suggestion for improvement is a tabbed view allowing a user to operate any number of instances of the interface and thus make any number of comparisons. Another issue arises from the term-cloud tabs, although offering faceted search the facets are hidden and only one facet is available at a time. Finally, we opted for cloud visualizations which have been found to be inferior to alphabetical listings [14]. The current design however satisfies the essential requirements for a subjunctive exploratory search interface and is suitable to answer our research questions.

4. USER STUDY

To assess the support provided by the subjunctive interface we conduct a user study with media studies researchers. Next, we describe the experimental design and our evaluation methodology.

4.1 Experimental Design

The experiment was set up as a remote user study with a between subjects design [18]. We decided on a remote user study to be able to

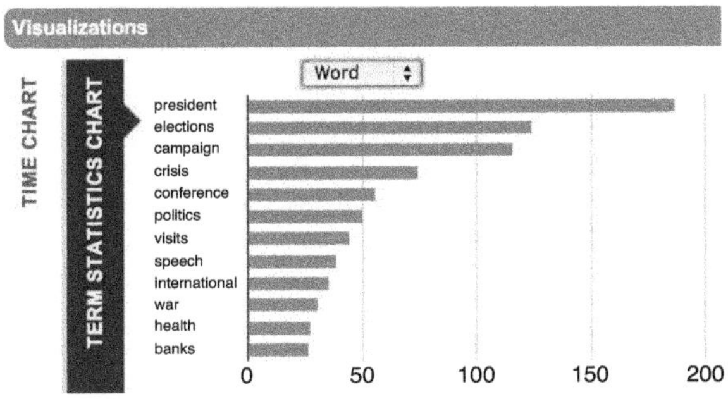

Figure 5: Term statistics chart: y-axis showing the terms with the highest frequency in the program descriptions of the current result set, x-axis showing the number of program descriptions that contain the term.

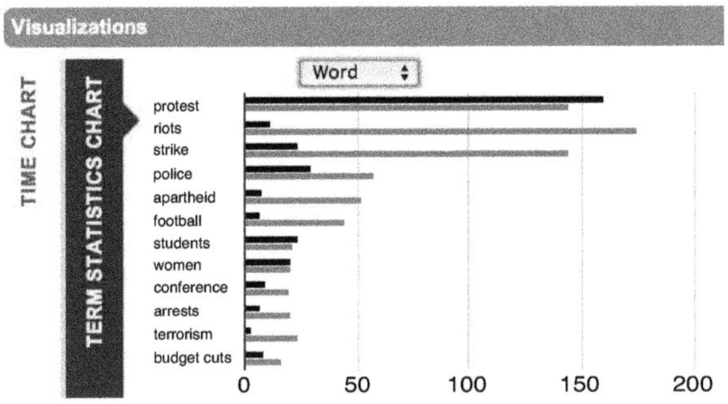

Figure 7: Subjunctive interface term statistics chart: y-axis showing terms with the combined highest frequency in the two result sets, x-axis showing the number of program descriptions that contain the term. Bar colors correspond to those in Fig. 6.

reach a wider audience of media studies researchers. A disadvantage is that there is less control over the setting of the study.

Study procedure. Subjects were recruited by spreading a URL among researchers and students at six media studies institutes. The URL directed subjects to a webpage explaining the experiment. Then subjects were presented with a consent form and a background questionnaire. Next, a three minute tutorial video of the interface was shown followed by a 3 minute practice session.

After practicing, subjects were given the following complex exploratory search task [17]: "As preparation for writing a research paper on the topic of migrants you investigate an audiovisual repository. You are interested in how migrants are represented on television. The goal of exploring the repository is to help you establish the initial research question for your paper." Subjects were instructed to bookmark programs deemed relevant to formulate their research question and given 30 minutes to search for relevant programs with one of the two interfaces. After 30 minutes, or when subjects pressed a done button, a form was presented in which subjects were asked to submit a research question. While formulating their research question the subjects had access to the program descriptions bookmarked earlier during search. The final step consisted of a usability questionnaire. A session took about 45 minutes per subject; as a reward, subjects received a 10 Euro gift certificate.

Subjects. The interface is developed to support media studies researchers, we therefore targeted subjects that had at least completed a Bachelor's degree in media studies. Out of 61 subjects, 38 completed the experiment. Two subjects that did complete the experiment were excluded from the experiment: one subject that spent a total of 26 seconds interacting with the interface and one subject that had not yet completed a Bachelor's degree. This left us with 36 subjects, 17 for the baseline and 19 for the subjunctive interface.

In terms of research experience, subjects are from a wide range of academic positions in media studies: 13 Master level students, 9 PhD students, 3 post doctoral researchers, 6 assistant professors, 1 full professor, and 4 research support staff. The research experience of subjects, in terms of the median (*MD*) and interquartile range (*IQR*), varies as subjects are a mix of researchers and students (*MD* = 3, *IQR* = 0–6.5). We asked subjects background questions using a 5 point Likert-type scale, where a one indicates no agreement and a five indicates extreme agreement. Subjects generally reported high levels of experience in general computer use (*MD* = 4, *IQR* = 4–5) and using online search tools (*MD* = 4, *IQR* = 4–5). Subjects had little previous experience with the topic of the search task, e.g., media and migration (*MD* = 2, *IQR* = 1–3). We found no significant differences between the groups in terms of these statistics.

4.2 Evaluation Methodology

We assess the support the subjunctive interface provides for media researchers in terms of three aspects: (i) support in exploration of different views of a topic; (ii) support in refining a research question; and (iii) general usability.

Exploration of different views. It is difficult to obtain a fixed set of relevance judgements for a complex exploratory search task, e.g., gathering documents that serve as basis to formulate a research question, as relevance is hard to determine in such a broad task [18]. Instead of using precision and recall, we evaluate support for exploration in terms of user interaction derived from server side log files. We hypothesize that an interface that provides better support for exploratorion will enable subjects to generate more query formulations and that subjects will bookmark more diverse documents.

Research question refinement. To evaluate subjects' research questions we asked three media researchers, experts in the field of media and migration, to act as assessors: an associate professor ($judge_1$), a full professor ($judge_2$), and a post-doctoral researcher ($judge_3$). Research questions were judged on five criteria: (i) general quality (g); (ii) extend to which a scope is defined, i.e., limiting the question to a certain person or time (s); (iii) clarity of formulation (f); (iv) embedding (e), i.e., the degree in which the research question relates to literature; and (v) originality (o). In the media studies research cycle the refinement of the research question is a manifestation of changes in data selection criteria. We therefore hypothesize that research questions formulated by subjects with the subjunctive interface will be judged higher on the scope criterion.

Table 1: Medians and interquartile ranges for user interactions with of the baseline (bl) and subjunctive (sj) interface.

interface feature	bl	sj
query formulations	3 (2–6)	**5 (3.3–7.8)**
bookmarks	9 (5.8–22.3)	9 (2.8–12.8)
document views	3 (1–7)	2 (0.3–5.3)
timeline filter	3.5 (2.5–9.5)	3 (0–8.5)
term-cloud filter	28 (13.5–41)	16 (9–36)
filter/analysis time (sec)	303 (204.8–589.3)	384 (222.5–544.3)
inspect result time (sec)	253 (51.3–438.8)	202 (94.8–385.3)
total time (sec)	532 (308–995)	575 (386.3–947.3)

Usability. Exploratory search systems are more complex than standard web search interfaces [36]. We introduce a subjunctive version of an exploratory search interface that essentially doubles the amount of features in the interface. We assess the subjunctive interface in terms of usability and use the following criteria: (i) usefulness, (ii) intuitiveness; (iii) ease of use; and (iv) interestingness, based on [22].

All judgements regarding the research questions and questions in the exit-questionnaire are given on a five point Likert-type scale, where the level of agreement is indicated in the range from one (not at all) to five (extremely). When reporting results the Wilcoxon ranksum test is used to determine significant differences between groups at the $\alpha < .05$ level. In tables significant differences are always in comparison to the baseline and indicated in bold face.

5. RESULTS

5.1 Exploratory Search Support

To answer our first research question we evaluate the performance of the baseline (bl) and subjunctive (sj) interface on a complex exploratory search task in terms of user interaction statistics and in terms of search patterns.

User interaction statistics. Our first hypothesis states that with the subjunctive interface subjects will formulate more queries and bookmark more diverse documents. We first compare subjects' interactions with the baseline and subjunctive interface, followed by an analysis of the diversity of the bookmarked documents.

Table 1 shows the medians (*MD*) and interquartile ranges (*IQR*), for interactions of subjects with features of the two interfaces. We find that the number of query formulations is higher for subjects using the subjunctive interface (bl *MD* = 3, sj *MD* = 5). The difference is significant as indicated by a Wilcoxon ranksum test ($W = 255.5$, $p < .05$) indicating that the subjunctive interface provides more support for generating new query formulations. We observe that subjects bookmark a similar number of documents with the interfaces (bl *MD* = 9, sj *MD* = 9). The high-end of the interquartile range for the baseline is higher but the difference is not significant. That subjects do not bookmark more documents may be due to the task description, i.e., the goal is to formulate a research question and not to bookmark as many relevant documents as possible.

The remaining interaction statistics demonstrate no apparent differences. We note that subjects spend a similar amount of time searching (bl $M = 532$, sj $M = 575$), but that users of the subjunctive interface spend more time operating the filters and/or analysing the visualizations (bl = 303, sj = 384). While in the baseline interface more time is spent inspecting results (bl = 254, sj = 202), i.e., reading result snippets and viewing documents. Although the difference is not significant it is to be expected that subjects spend more time analysing and filtering with the subjunctive interface as more information is presented. That subjects spent less time, or a similar amount of time inspecting results is surprising as the subjunctive interface presents twice as many results. We look further into this when analysing the interaction patterns.

Next we investigate whether there are differences in the diversity of bookmarked documents. We use cosine similarity as a distance measure and calculate the average pairwise cosine similarity of the documents bookmarked (D_s) by a subject (s):

$$avg\_sim(s) = \frac{1}{|P_s|} \sum_{(d,d') \in P_s} sim(d, d'),$$

here P_s is the set of pairs of documents bookmarked by a subject: $P_s = \{(d, d') : d, d' \in D_s, d \neq d'\}$ and $sim(d, d')$ is defined as:

$$sim(d, d') = \frac{\sum_{i=1}^{n} d_i \cdot d'_i}{\sqrt{\sum_{i=1}^{n} (d_i)^2} \cdot \sqrt{\sum_{i=1}^{n} (d'_i)^2}}.$$

The average similarities for subjects using the baseline (avg_sim $MD = .62$, $IQR = .56$–$.69$) are higher than the similarities of subjects using the subjunctive interface (avg_sim $MD = .52$, $IQR = .43$–$.63$) and this difference is significant ($W = 195$ $p = .05$). That documents bookmarked with the subjunctive interface are less similar than those bookmarked with the baseline indicates that with the subjunctive interface a more diverse set of documents are explored.

User interaction patterns. The interaction statistics suggest that the subjunctive interface provides more support for exploration than the baseline, if so we would expect to find differences in subjects' search behavior. We first describe the process of creating the interaction patterns based on maximal repeating patterns [30] and then analyze the patterns generated with the two interfaces.

An interaction pattern consists of all of a subject's search actions during a search session. We identify the following action types: submitting queries (Q), using filters (F), inspecting results (I), bookmarking (B), viewing program descriptions (D), paginating to new result pages (P), and closing the interface (S). Repeated actions are aggregated into a single action type, e.g., queries submitted in the left or right search box of the subjunctive interface are considered as a single query (Q) action. The purpose of the resulting interaction pattern is to reveal transitions between interaction types. Per subject group all occurrences of possible sub-patterns of at least two subsequent actions are counted to find the maximal repeated patterns (MRP) for each interface. For example, the sequence of actions: QFIFIQFI, contains the following MRP: QFI and FI, as these are the longest sequences that are repeated.

Table 2 shows the top 8 MRPs that start with a query action (Q), a filter action (F), or a bookmark action (B). In both interfaces the most frequent transition after submitting a query is to inspect the results (bl QI = 37, sj QI = 57). After this initial behavior, subjects using the subjunctive interface more often reformulate their query (bl QIQ = 12, sj QIQ = 22), while users of the baseline prefer filtering (bl QIF = 15, sj QIF = 13). This is consistent with the earlier finding, see Table 1, that the subjunctive interface provides more support for formulating new queries.

Table 2: Users' most frequent maximal repeated patterns with the baseline (bl) and subjunctive (sj) interface. Here Q is submitting queries, F is using filters, I is inspecting results, B is bookmarking, D is viewing documents, P is paginating to reach new result pages, and S is closing the interface.

Q starts pattern				F starts pattern				B starts pattern			
#	bl	#	sj	#	bl	#	sj	#	bl	#	sj
9	QFIF	12	QFQ	12	FIQ	18	FIFIFIF	8	BPBP	6	BIQ
9	QIQI	12	QIFI	14	FIFIF	19	FQ	10	BPB	7	BS
12	QIQ	13	QIF	15	FQ	23	FIB	11	BDB	8	BIB
13	QIFI	18	QIQI	15	FID	29	FIFIFI	13	BD	11	BDB
15	QIF	22	QIQ	25	FIB	34	FFIF	14	BFI	11	BFI
27	QFI	23	QFI	30	FIFI	55	FIFI	15	BP	14	BF
32	QF	37	QF	37	FIF	62	FIF	15	BI	18	BD
37	QI	57	QI	97	FI	116	FI	16	BF	22	BI

When starting with a filtering action and then inspecting the results (FI) subjects using the subjunctive interface tend to transition more from filtering actions to bookmarking or viewing documents (bl FIFI = 30, sj FIFI = 55). With the subjunctive interface subjects spend more time refining and inspecting result snippets (sj FIFIFI = 29); the number of times a filter and inspection sequence leads to a bookmark is comparable (bl FIB = 25, sj FIB = 23). The extra time spent refining and inspecting can be explained by the presence of the second result set in the subjunctive interface as subjects have a larger set of program descriptions at their disposal.

In the baseline interface a bookmark action is often followed by moving to the next result page (bl BP = 15) and (bl BPBP = 8), while in the subjunctive interface more often program descriptions are viewed (sj BD = 18). This suggests that subjects using the baseline interface are unable to formulate new queries or use filters to refine the result set and resort to browsing more result pages in the result set. This is consistent with the observation in the interaction statistics, see Table 1, that with the baseline more time is spent inspecting results; this is similar to the behavior observed in web search when users face a difficult search task [1]. Users of the subjunctive interface on the other hand, tend to bookmark documents on the first result page (sj BIB = 8) and (sj BDB = 11).

We have determined that there are differences in the interaction patterns of subjects using the baseline and subjunctive interface. Interaction patterns show that with the subjunctive interface subjects alternate more between formulating queries and inspecting results than subjects using the baseline interface. We also find that users of the baseline are more often unable to refine their information need and resort to an exhaustive search of the results.

5.2 Research Question Formulation Support

To address our second research question we evaluate how the exploration provided by the two interfaces affects the research questions formulated by the subjects. We perform two types of evaluation: (i) a quantitative evaluation where we use explicit judgements of the research questions; and (ii) a qualitative analysis where we divide research questions into phrases and classify these into several types to compare the composition of the research questions.

Research question formulation performance. Our second hypothesis states that research questions formulated by subjects with the subjunctive interface will be judged higher on the scope criterion. The top of Table 3 shows the medians and interquartile ranges for

Table 3: **Medians and interquartile ranges for judgements of the research questions on five criteria: general quality (g), scope (s), formulation (f), embedding (e), and originality (o), by three media researchers for the baseline (bl) and subjunctive (sj) interface.**

	$judge_1$		$judge_2$		$judge_3$	
	bl	sj	bl	sj	bl	sj
g	3 (2–4)	4 (3–4)	4 (2–4)	3 (2.3–4)	4 (3.8–4)	4 (3.3–5)
s	3 (2–4)	4 (3–4)	2 (2–4)	2 (2–3)	4 (3–4)	4 (2.3–4)
f	3 (3–4)	4 (2.3–4)	3 (2–4)	3 (2.3–4)	4 (4–4.3)	4 (4–4.8)
e	3 (3–4)	3 (2.3–4)	2 (2–3)	3 (2–3.8)	3 (1.8–4)	3 (2–4)
o	4 (3–4)	4 (3–4)	4 (3–4)	4 (3–4)	3 (2–4)	4 (2–4)

the judgements of the research questions on the five criteria, i.e, general quality (g), scope (s), formulation (f), embedding (e), and originality (o), by three media researchers. Overall agreement of the assessors on the criteria is low as indicated by Fleiss' Kappa ($\kappa < .2$). Agreement is stronger on the scope criterion ($\kappa = .2362$).

Subjects' research questions are judged to be good in terms of quality, formulation, and originality, for all three assessors (*MD* ≥ 3). The level of embedding is lower (*MD* ≤ 3), as researchers were unable to consult any literature during the experiment. The judgements for the scope of the research questions, are mixed. We observe, however, no apparent differences between the baseline and subjunctive interface for the judgement criteria.

That we observe no differences may be due to the open ended nature of the task of formulating a research question and the difficulty of judging research questions without any further context.

Research question composition. The research questions formulated by the media studies researchers provide a rich source of qualitative data. To investigate if there is a difference in the views and topics of the research questions, we perform a qualitative analysis of the phrases that define the scope in the research questions of the 36 subjects. We identify five types of phrases: defining (i) a program genre; (ii) a group to study; (iii) a focus on a theme or person; (iv) a time period; or (v) a part of the program production process.

Table 4 shows the number of occurrences of types of phrases that determine the scope of a research question. A similar number of phrases of type genre, period, and production is found in research questions generated with the baseline and subjunctive interface. There is a difference in the number of phrases of type group (bl = 14, sj = 17), but not in terms of unique phrases. Here, the phrase "migrants" is used to specify the population of study, most likely influenced by the use of the term in the search task. We observe that in research questions generated with the subjunctive interface more often phrases that describe a specific theme occur as compared to the baseline (bl = 8, sj = 12) and in most cases these themes are unique (bl = 7, sj = 11). This suggests that the subjunctive interface provides subjects with more support to explore different themes surrounding a topic and that they use this information to scope their research question. There is little influence on other types that determine the scope of a research question, e.g., a time period or television genre, as both interfaces provide users with the ability to spot trends through the timeline and term statistics chart.

Next we provide an example-based comparison to further illustrate the effect of the interfaces on the scope of the research questions. Table 5 shows the top 3 research questions for the baseline and subjunctive interface at the top and bottom respectively. Questions are ranked in terms of the sum of the three assessors' judgements on

Table 4: Number of occurrences (unique occurrences) of types of phrases that determine the scope of a research question.

interface	genre	group	theme	period	production
baseline	11 (6)	14 (8)	8 (7)	10 (10)	2 (2)
subjunctive	10 (7)	17 (8)	12 (11)	9 (9)	3 (3)

the scope criterion. We observe that when subjects use the baseline, questions are based on observations of trends in the timeline, i.e., the increase and decrease in the occurrence of a query term in programs. This leads to research questions that focus on a single topic during a certain period, i.e., the representation of the Islam (bl rq_1) and the representation of a political figure (bl rq_2). The ability to compare changes in frequency of query terms on a timeline in the subjunctive interface, however, inspires subjects to consider more views. This leads to research questions that include interactions between multiple aspects of a topic, e.g., representation of Muslims and the influence of terrorism (sj rq_1) and difference in representation of refugees' children in fictional programs compared to documentaries. In the last research questions (bl and sj rq_3) the effect of the subjunctive interface is most obvious. Although both questions follow the change in use of terminology over time, in the subjunctive interface a contrast is made between two terms.

5.3 Usability

To answer our third research question we look at the usability of the interfaces. Table 6 shows the medians and interquartile ranges of subjects' judgements of the usability of the two interfaces. Subjects indicate that both are intuitive (bl = 4, sj = 4) and that they are not difficult to use (bl = 2, sj = 2). Of the subjects, 75% do not find the subjunctive interface difficult to use (difficult ≤ 3). This suggests that subjunctivity can be added to exploratory interfaces with little cost to the difficulty and intuitiveness of the system. We further asked subjects if the interfaces were interesting to use and useful for media research. Subjects indicate that both interfaces are interesting (bl = 4, sj = 4) and useful, in case of the subjunctive interface subjects indicate it to be extremely useful (bl = 4, sj = 5). Regarding the visualizations subjects indicate a preference for the timeline chart. We suspect that the information in the term statistics chart is more difficult to interpret and therefore used less.

6. DISCUSSION

Regarding our first research question, we find significant evidence that with the subjunctive interface, media studies researchers exhibit different search behavior than with the baseline interface on a complex exploratory search task. Subjects are able to formulate more queries and bookmark more diverse documents than with a traditional exploratory search interface. Inspection of the interaction patterns confirms these findings. Users of the subjunctive interface follow a pattern of reformulating a query and inspecting results followed by another query reformulation and result inspection, while users of the traditional exploratory search interface formulate less queries and look through more result pages.

Table 6: Medians and interquartile ranges for the usability of the baseline (bl) and subjunctive (sj) interface.

question	bl	sj	question	bl	sj
intuitive	4 (4–4)	4 (3–4)	difficult	2 (2–2)	2 (2–3.8)
interesting	4 (4–5)	4 (4–5)	useful	4 (4–5)	5 (4–5)

Table 5: Top 3 research questions for the baseline (left) and subjunctive interface (right), ranked in terms of the scope criterion. Alterations to the research questions are indicated by [..] and serve to protect the anonymity of subjects or to improve clarity.

	Baseline	Subjunctive
rq_1:	How is the Islam represented in factual television genres during the period 2000–2010?	How are Muslim immigrants represented on television and what is the role of terrorism in this representation. Case study of several episodes of [$program_A$] and [$program_B$] about Muslims in [country].
rq_2:	How is [political figure] represented by the public broadcasting corporation during the elections for the house of representatives in 2010?	How are the experiences of refugees' children represented on television in fiction and documentaries from 1990 to 2010? Do we find any differences or changes and can these be explained?
rq_3:	Investigation of the evolution of the term integration in news and human interest programs broadcasted between 1992 and 2012.	In 1987 we observe a diminishing in the use of the term migrant worker and a rise in the use of the term immigrant. Is it possible to identify a cause in the broadcasting schedule of that time? Are there specific programs that started this development?

With regard to our second research question, we find that with both interfaces researcher are able to formulate high quality research questions. A qualitative analysis of the research questions shows that there is a difference in the research questions that subjects formulate. With the subjunctive interface subjects use more diverse themes to scope their research question. There is no influence on other types of defining the scope, e.g., a time period, as both interfaces provide users with the ability to spot trends in visualizations. An example based comparison of the top 3 research questions in terms of scope illustrates the difference in the number of views on a topic incorporated in the research questions.

Turning to the third research question, we find that although the complexity of the subjunctive interface in terms of features almost doubled compared to the standard exploratory search interface, most users indicate that the subjunctive interface is intuitive and not difficult to use. Users indicate that the subjunctive interface is interesting and judge it to be extremely useful for media research.

The subjunctive interface was developed to support the exploration phase in the media studies research cycle by supporting multiple views on a topic and discovering trends in the data. The above findings demonstrate that a subjunctive exploratory search interface can indeed provide this type of support for media studies research. A limitation of this study is that the time and data restrictions in the experiment make it an abstraction from the real research cycle; a longitudinal study where the subjunctive interface is used by media studies researches will have to be conducted. Another limitation is that the study of the research cycle is based on a small number of interviews. The development of the subjunctive interface, however, has been done in close co-operation with media studies researchers. Therefore the model and the ideas on which the subjunctive interface has been based, have repeatedly been under close examination from the targeted end users, thereby strengthening its foundation.

7. RELATED WORK

The work in this paper touches on various areas of research and we briefly highlight related work. Many specific related publications have already been cited earlier in the paper. We complement this with a brief and slightly more general discussion. As to exploratory search [25], many exploratory search tools have been suggested [6–8, 12, 13, 21, 29, 38, 40] which served as inspiration in the development of our interface.

Tools in the humanities exist for the analysis of data once it has been collected. Some of the more recent projects are: MONK[3] a data analysis laboratory that provides visualizations and data mining tools; TaPoR[4] an indexing and search tool to locate co-occuring phrases in texts; and Pliney [4] a tool for note taking and organizing to support insight generation. The Google ngram viewer is a tool that enables comparison of trends in term occurrences on a timeline in a large book collection supporting cultural analytics [27]. A limitation of these tools is the lack of support for exploration of different subsets of documents, e.g., query result sets.

Subjunctive interfaces have been proposed in a more general setting [24], e.g., to compare two documents in a side-by-side editor. For web search an interface with multiple views of a traditional web search interface was shown to be effective to support complex search tasks [35]. We extend this body of work by investigating the value of multiple views in a exploratory search interface.

8. CONCLUSION

In this paper we have presented a subjunctive exploratory search interface to support media studies research. By analysing the media studies research cycle we have found that media studies researchers require support in discovering multiple views on a topic and discovering trends in data to refine their research question in an earlier stage of the research cycle. We have developed a subjunctive exploratory search interface and performed a user study to assess its value for media studies researchers. We have found that with the subjunctive interface media studies researchers are able to formulate more queries and bookmark more diverse documents compared to a standard exploratory search interface. In a qualitative analysis of the research questions formulated by media studies researchers we have found evidence to suggest that the influence of the subjunctive interface is predominantly on the scope of the research question. Specificly, users of the subjunctive interface incorporate more views on a topic in their research question than users of the standard exploratory search interface. We have observed no advantage for other types of defining the scope as visualizations in both interfaces enable spotting trends in the data. In terms of usability, media studies researchers report that the subjunctive interface is intuitive and not difficult to use, suggesting that the additional complexity in terms of features in the subjunctive interface does not reduce its usability. These findings are important for media studies, but also have further implications. The continuous increase in data and its effect on the importance of exploration in the research cycle indicates a need to study this effect in other areas of the humanities. Additionally, with respect to exploratory search, the support provided by the subjunctive interface for exploration suggests a new direction for the development of exploratory search systems. In future work we plan to launch the subjunctive interface at a television archive to assess its value for media studies in a longitudinal study.

9. ACKNOWLEDGMENTS

This research was partially supported by the European Union's ICT Policy Support Programme as part of the Competitiveness and Innovation Framework Programme, CIP ICT-PSP under grant agree-

[3]http://monkproject.org/

[4]http://portal.tapor.ca/

ment nr 250430, the European Community's Seventh Framework Programme (FP7/2007-2013) under grant agreements nr 258191 (PROMISE Network of Excellence) and 288024 (LiMoSINe project), the Netherlands Organisation for Scientific Research (NWO) under project nrs 612.061.814, 612.061.815, 640.004.802, 380-70-011, 727.011.005, 612.001.116, the Center for Creation, Content and Technology (CCCT), the Hyperlocal Service Platform project funded by the Service the WAHSP and BILAND projects funded by the CLARIN-nl program, the Dutch national program COMMIT, and by the ESF Research Network Program ELIAS.

10. REFERENCES

[1] A. Aula, R. Khan, and Z. Guan. How does search behavior change as search becomes more difficult? In *SIGCHI'10*, pages 35–44, 2010.

[2] M. Bates. The design of browsing and berrypicking techniques for the online search interface. *Online review*, 13 (5):407–424, 1989.

[3] C. Borgman. The digital future is now: A call to action for the humanities. *Digital Humanities Quarterly*, 3(4), 2009.

[4] J. Bradley. Thinking about interpretation: Pliny and scholarship in the humanities. *Literary and linguistic computing*, 23(3):263–279, 2008.

[5] T. Brinck, D. Gergle, and S. Wood. *Usability for the Web: designing Web sites that work.* Morgan Kaufmann, 2002.

[6] M. Bron, J. van Gorp, F. Nack, and M. de Rijke. Exploratory search in an audio-visual archive: Evaluating a professional search tool for non-professional users. In *EuroHCIR 2011*, pages 3–6, Newcastle, 2011.

[7] R. Capra and G. Marchionini. The relation browser tool for faceted exploratory search. In *JCDL'08*, page 420, 2008.

[8] R. Capra, G. Golovchinsky, B. Kules, D. Russell, C. Smith, D. Tunkelang, and R. White. HCIR 2011. In *SIGIR Forum*, volume 45, pages 102–107, 2012.

[9] C. Chu. Literary critics at work and their information needs: A research-phases model. *Library & Information Science Research*, 21(2):247–273, 1999.

[10] E. Collins and J. Michael. How do researchers in the humanities use information resources? *Liber Quarterly*, 21(2), 2012.

[11] D. Ellis and M. Haugan. Modelling the information seeking patterns of engineers and research scientists in an industrial environment. *J. Doc.*, 53(4):384–403, 1997.

[12] G. Golovchinsky and J. Pickens. Interactive information seeking via selective application of contextual knowledge. In *IIiX'10*, pages 145–154, 2010.

[13] M. Hearst. Tilebars: visualization of term distribution information in full text information access. In *SIGCHI'95*, pages 59–66, 1995.

[14] M. A. Hearst and D. Rosner. Tag clouds: Data analysis tool or social signaller? In *HICSS '08*, pages 160–169, 2008.

[15] T. Hey and A. Trefethen. The data deluge: An e-science perspective. In *Grid computing*, pages 809–824, 2003.

[16] P. Ingwersen. Cognitive perspectives of information retrieval interaction: elements of a cognitive ir theory. *J. Doc.*, 52(1): 3–50, 1996.

[17] K. Järvelin and P. Ingwersen. Information seeking research needs extension towards tasks and technology. *Information Research*, 10(1):10–1, 2004.

[18] D. Kelly. Methods for evaluating interactive information retrieval systems with users. *FTNIR*, 3(1-2):1–224, 2009.

[19] C. Kuhlthau. Inside the search process: Information seeking from the user's perspective. *JASIS*, 42(5):361–371, 1991.

[20] B. Kules, R. Capra, M. Banta, and T. Sierra. What do exploratory searchers look at in a faceted search interface? In *JCDL'09*, pages 313–322, 2009.

[21] Y. Lin, J. Ahn, P. Brusilovsky, D. He, and W. Real. Imagesieve: Exploratory search of museum archives with named entity-based faceted browsing. *ASIST'10*, 47(1):1–10, 2010.

[22] A. Lund. Measuring usability with the use questionnaire. *Usability and User Experience*, 8(2):8, 2001.

[23] B. Lunn. User needs in television archive access: Acquiring knowledge necessary for system design. *JoDI*, 10(6), 2009.

[24] A. Lunzer and K. Hornbæk. Subjunctive interfaces: Extending applications to support parallel setup, viewing and control of alternative scenarios. *ACM TOCHI*, 14(4):17, 2008.

[25] G. Marchionini. Exploratory search: from finding to understanding. *Commun. ACM*, 49(4):41–46, 2006.

[26] L. Meho and H. Tibbo. Modeling the information-seeking behavior of social scientists: Ellis's study revisited. *JASIST*, 54(6):570–587, 2003.

[27] J. Michel, Y. Shen, A. Aiden, A. Veres, M. Gray, J. Pickett, D. Hoiberg, D. Clancy, P. Norvig, J. Orwant, et al. Quantitative analysis of culture using millions of digitized books. *Science*, 331(6014):176, 2011.

[28] C. Palmer. Scholarly work and the shaping of digital access. *JASIST*, 56(11):1140–1153, 2005.

[29] A. Shiri. Metadata-enhanced visual interfaces to digital libraries. *JIS*, 34(6):763–775, 2008.

[30] A. Siochi and R. Ehrich. Computer analysis of user interfaces based on repetition in transcripts of user sessions. *ACM TOIS*, 9(4):309–335, 1991.

[31] A. Strauss and J. Corbin. *Basics of qualitative research: Grounded theory procedures and techniques.* Sage Publications, Inc, 1990.

[32] E. Toms and H. O'Brien. Understanding the information and communication technology needs of the e-humanist. *J. Doc.*, 64(1):102–130, 2008.

[33] J. Unsworth. Scholarly primitives: what methods do humanities researchers have in common, and how might our tools reflect this. *Symposium on Humanities Computing: Formal Methods, Experimental Practice*, 2000.

[34] J. Unsworth. Tool-time, or 'haven't we been here already?' ten years in humanities computing. *Transforming Disciplines: The Humanities and Computer Science*, 2003.

[35] R. Villa, I. Cantador, H. Joho, and J. Jose. An aspectual interface for supporting complex search tasks. In *SIGIR*, pages 379–386, 2009.

[36] R. White and R. Roth. Exploratory search: Beyond the query-response paradigm. *Synthesis Lectures on Information Concepts, Retrieval, and Services*, 1(1):1–98, 2009.

[37] M. Wilson, R. White, et al. Evaluating advanced search interfaces using established information-seeking models. *JASIST*, 60(7):1407–1422, 2009.

[38] M. Wilson, B. Kules, et al. *From Keyword Search to Exploration.* Now Publishers, 2010.

[39] T. Wilson. Models in information behaviour research. *J. Doc.*, 55(3):249–270, 1999.

[40] K. Yee, K. Swearingen, K. Li, and M. Hearst. Faceted metadata for image search and browsing. In *SIGCHI'03*, pages 401–408, 2003.

Task Complexity, Vertical Display and User Interaction in Aggregated Search

Jaime Arguello, Wan-Ching Wu, Diane Kelly, Ashlee Edwards
School of Information and Library Science
University of North Carolina at Chapel Hill
Chapel Hill, NC, 27599-3360 USA
{jarguello, wanchinw, diane.kelly, aedwards}@unc.edu

ABSTRACT

Aggregated search is the task of blending results from specialized search services or *verticals* into the Web search results. While many studies have focused on aggregated search techniques, few studies have tried to better understand how users interact with aggregated search results. This study investigates how task complexity and vertical display (the blending of vertical results into the web results) affect the use of vertical content. Twenty-nine subjects completed six search tasks of varying levels of task complexity using two aggregated search interfaces: one that blended vertical results into the web results and one that only provided indirect vertical access. Our results show that more complex tasks required significantly more interaction and that subjects completing these tasks examined more vertical results. While the amount of interaction was the same between interfaces, subjects clicked on more vertical results when these were blended into the web results. Our results also show an interaction between task complexity and vertical display; subjects clicked on more verticals when completing the more complex tasks with the interface that blended vertical results. Subjects' evaluations of the two interfaces were nearly identical, but when analyzed with respect to their interface preferences, we found a positive relationship between system evaluations and individual preferences. Subjects justified their preference using similar rationales and their comments illustrate how the display itself can influence judgments of information quality, especially in cases when the vertical results might not be relevant to the search task.

Categories and Subject Descriptors

H.3.3 [**Information Storage and Retrieval**]: Information Search and Retrieval

General Terms

Performance, Experimentation, Human Factors.

Keywords

Aggregated search interfaces, search behaviors, evaluation, user study, interaction, task complexity

Permission to make digital or hard copies of all or part of this work for personal or classroom use is granted without fee provided that copies are not made or distributed for profit or commercial advantage and that copies bear this notice and the full citation on the first page. To copy otherwise, or republish, to post on servers or to redistribute to lists, requires prior specific permission and/or a fee.
SIGIR'12, August 12–16, 2012, Portland, Oregon, USA.
Copyright 2012 ACM 978-1-4503-1472-5/12/08...$15.00.

1. INTRODUCTION

In addition to Web search, commercial search companies (e.g., Google, Bing, Yahoo!) provide access to a wide range of specialized services known as *verticals* (e.g., images, video, news). There are two ways that users can access vertical results. If a user wants results from a particular vertical, the query can be issued directly to the vertical-specific search engine. In other cases, however, a user may not know that a vertical is relevant or may want results from multiple verticals at once. For these reasons, commercial systems often showcase vertical results alongside the Web results. Currently, this is done by blending a few of the vertical's results somewhere above, within, or below the Web results. The goal is to either satisfy the user with the blended results or to convey how the information need might be better satisfied by directly searching the vertical. The task of surfacing vertical results in response to a Web search query is known as *aggregated search*.

Most published research in aggregated search has focused on automatic methods for predicting which verticals to present (*vertical selection*) [4, 5, 11, 19] and where in the Web results to present them (*vertical presentation*) [2, 3, 23]. Evaluation of these systems has typically been conducted by using editorial vertical relevance judgements as the gold standard [2, 3, 4, 5, 19], or by using user-generated clicks on vertical results as a proxy for relevance [11, 23]. While these studies have greatly advanced the state of the art in aggregated search techniques, because users are far removed from the evaluation, they have contributed little insight about how users' higher-level objectives influence their engagement with vertical search results.

A few published studies have investigated user behavior with aggregated search interfaces [24, 25, 28]. Thus far, these studies show two major trends. First, when a vertical is relevant, users prefer to see its results towards to the top of the blended results [25, 28]. Second, there seems to be a click-bias in favor of visually appealing verticals such as *video* [25]. While these studies reveal important trends, several questions remain. Prior work shows that when completing more complex tasks users take longer, enter more queries, view more results, and use more sources than when completing less complex tasks [20]. Are these same effects *also* observed with aggregated search interfaces? What is the effect of task complexity on a user's demand for vertical results? Are more vertical results examined when the task is more complex? And, does it depend on whether the vertical results are blended into the web results? This study investigates these questions.

1.1. Research Questions

This study investigates how users interact with interfaces that vary the way that vertical results are displayed in response to a query. We investigated two different interfaces, referred to as the *blended interface* and the *non-blended interface*. Given the same query, both interfaces provided *indirect* access to the same set of Web and vertical results. Navigational tabs across the top and left side of both interfaces provided links to issue the query (or a new query) to only the Web search engine or only a particular vertical search engine. The only difference was that the blended interface showcased a few results from every vertical in the main search results page, while the non-blended interface did not.

In this work, we also focus on tasks of varying level of cognitive complexity and the effect these tasks have on users' interactions with vertical results *and* whether the amount of interaction depends on the blending of vertical results into the Web results. Prior work shows that when completing more complex tasks users take longer, enter more queries, view more search results, and use more sources than when completing less complex tasks [20]. However, no work has examined task complexity in the context of aggregated search. Specifically, we address the research questions in Table 1.

Table 1. Research Questions and Hypotheses

Research Question	Hypothesis
RQ1: How does task complexity affect search interaction in aggregated search?	**H1**: People will interact more when conducting more complex tasks.
RQ2: How does task complexity affect use of vertical search results?	**H2**: People will use more vertical results for more complex tasks.
RQ3: How does vertical display affect use of vertical results?	**H3**: People will use more vertical results when these are blended into the Web results.
RQ4: What are people's evaluations of the interfaces, perceptions of vertical results, and display preferences?	This question is primarily explored with no hypothesis.

2. RELATED WORK

2.1. Aggregated Search

The goal of aggregated search is to blend results from zero or more verticals into the Web search results. The task is typically decomposed into two subtasks: predicting which verticals to present (*vertical selection*) and predicting where in the Web results to present them (*vertical presentation*). Existing methods for vertical selection and presentation use machine learning to combine different types of predictive evidence: query-string features [2, 4, 5, 19, 23], vertical query-log features [2, 4, 5, 11, 23], vertical content features [2, 4, 5, 11], and implicit feedback features from previous presentations of the vertical [11, 23]. Model tuning and evaluation is typically done with respect to editorial relevance judgements [2, 3, 4, 5, 19] or, in a production environment, with respect to user-generated clicks and skips [11, 23]. In the first case, users do not actively participate in the evaluation. In the second case, their feedback is not *explicit*. Because users are far removed from the evaluation, this research has contributed little insight about how properties of the higher-level task (e.g., its complexity) influence users' interaction with and evaluation of the system.

A few user studies have investigated search and preference behavior with aggregated search interfaces [24, 25, 28]. Sushmita *et al.* [24] experimented with two aggregated search interfaces: one similar to our non-blended interface, which did not combine content from different sources in the main results, and a second interface that combined content from different sources in a two-dimensional blocked fashion. Subjects were asked to complete search tasks using both systems. Results showed significantly more clicks on vertical results using the aggregated interface. However, differences in the *inclusion* of cross-vertical content in subjects' response sheets and differences in subjects' system preferences were not significant.

In later work, Sushmita *et al.* [25] conducted a similar study with an aggregated interface similar to our blended interface and a blocked interface similar to the one used in Sushmita *et al.* [24]. Results showed that users clicked more on verticals that were presented higher in the blended results and on verticals that were more relevant to the task. Furthermore, a click bias was observed in favor of *video* results, which were more visually salient. That is, compared to the other verticals, users clicked more on video results irrespective of rank and relevance.

While the work above focused on different aggregated search interfaces, Zhu and Carterette [28] focused on where to blend results from a single vertical: *images*. They found a preference in favor of images ranked high in the blended results for queries with image intent.

To summarize, the work above reveals a few important trends. Users click more on verticals that are relevant and prefer layouts where the relevant verticals are ranked higher in the blended results. Additionally, aggregated search is not immune to click bias. Irrespective of relevance, users click more on verticals that are ranked high and are visually salient. Our work extends this previous work by focusing on the effect of task complexity and vertical display (the blending of vertical results into the main search results) on the use of vertical results and on users' evaluations of the system. Thus, one important aspect of our work is the manipulation of task complexity as an independent variable.

2.2 Tasks and Task Complexity

Toms [26] (quoting Hackman [12]) defines a task as a "set of assigned (a) goals to be achieved, (b) instructions to be performed, or (c) a mix of the two" ([26], pg. 45). Li and Belkin [17] define an information search task as "a task that users need to accomplish through effective interaction with information systems" ([17], pg. 1823). Information *search* tasks are usually distinguished from *work* tasks [7]. In this study we focus on *search* tasks. While task has always been an essential part of interactive search studies, it has been increasingly used as an independent variable and many studies have demonstrated that search behavior varies according to task and task characteristics [8, 14, 15, 20].

A large body of research has attempted to conceptualize and define tasks and task characteristics (e.g., [7, 9, 17, 26, 27]). Researchers have classified tasks according to type (e.g., open, factual, navigational, decision-making) and according to task properties (e.g., difficulty, urgency, structure, stage). Li and Belkin [17] present a faceted classification of tasks. This classification includes *generic* facets of tasks (e.g., source of task, time, product, process and goal) and *common* facets of tasks including characteristics (e.g., objective task complexity and interdependence) as well as users' perception of task (e.g., salience, urgency, difficulty, subjective task complexity and knowledge of task topic). Li [16] later found that the facets of *product* and *objective task complexity* had the most significant impact on search behavior. In a follow-up study, Li and Belkin [18] found that objective task complexity affected users' search interactions such as number of queries issued, mean query length, number of pages viewed, and number of sources consulted. Liu *et al.* [20] also found that objective task complexity (as measured by activities and information required) impacted search behavior. When completing more complex tasks, their subjects took longer, entered more queries, viewed more pages, and used more sources.

In this paper, we use cognitive complexity as a way to model differences between search tasks. We used three conceptualizations of task complexity to guide the creation of our search tasks (presented in Section 3.3). The first was described by Campbell [9] and later used by Li and Belkin [17]. In this model, four attributes determine complexity: (1) the number of potential paths to the desired outcome; (2) the presence of multiple desired outcomes; (3) the presence of conflicting interdependencies between paths; and (4) uncertainty regarding paths.

The second conceptualization is from Byström and J□rvelin [8], who define task complexity as the *a priori determinability* of tasks, which is the extent to which the searcher can deduce the required task inputs, processes, and outcomes based on the initial task statement. Although this conceptualization is based on subjective task complexity, Bell and Ruthven [6] used this model to create artificial search tasks with different levels of task complexity. The researchers reduced Byström and J□rvelin's five-level categorization into a three-level categorization and found that objective task complexity was correlated with users' subjective assessments of complexity.

The third conceptualization of task complexity we use comes from Jansen *et al.* [13] who used Anderson and Krathwohl's taxonomy of educational objectives [1] to design search tasks. Anderson and Krathwohl's taxonomy of educational objectives has two dimensions: a cognitive process dimension and a knowledge dimension. Jansen *et al.* created tasks reflecting six types of cognitive processes: *remember*, *understand*, *apply*, *analyze*, *evaluate* and *create* (see Table 2 in Section 3.3 for definitions). Although Jansen *et al.* [13] did not situate this work in the context of task complexity, they observed a number of significant differences in the amount of interaction users exhibited when completing different task types, including session duration, number of queries, and number of pages viewed.

3. Method

The present study used a within subjects design. Subjects were randomly assigned to use the non-blended or blended interface first. Subjects completed three search tasks of three levels of task complexity on a single domain with each interface (described in more detail below). The order of task complexity levels was fixed for each subject across interfaces but was counterbalanced using a Latin Square design among subjects. Each subject conducted tasks from a single domain on each interface and the order of task domains was counterbalanced using a Latin square. Search sessions were logged using the Lemur Query-Log Toolbar.[1]

3.1. Interfaces

Two aggregated search interfaces were compared in this study: the non-blended interface and the blended interface (Figure 1). Both interfaces provided access to a Web search engine and six different vertical search engines: *images*, *videos*, *news*, *blogs*, *community Q&A*, and *shopping*. All search engines were constructed using freely available APIs from Bing (*web*, *images*, *video*, *news*), Google (*blogs*), Yahoo! (*community Q&A*), and eBay (*shopping*). Search results of each type were displayed similar to how they are displayed in commercial systems. News results were presented by displaying the article title, news source, and publication date. Shopping results were presented by displaying an image of the product, its name, and its price. Video results were presented by displaying an image of the video, its title, and duration.

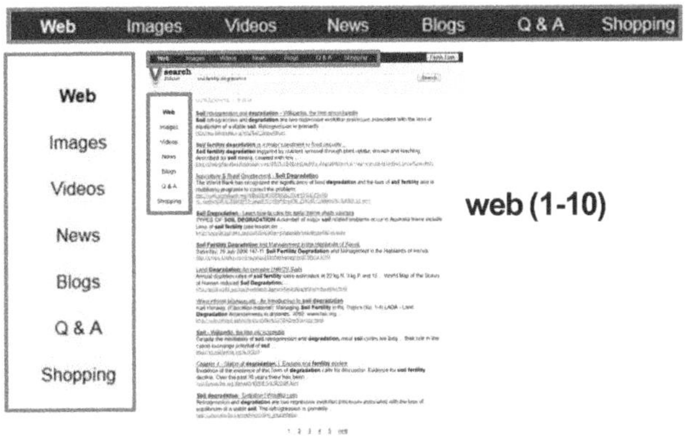

(a) Non-blended Interface

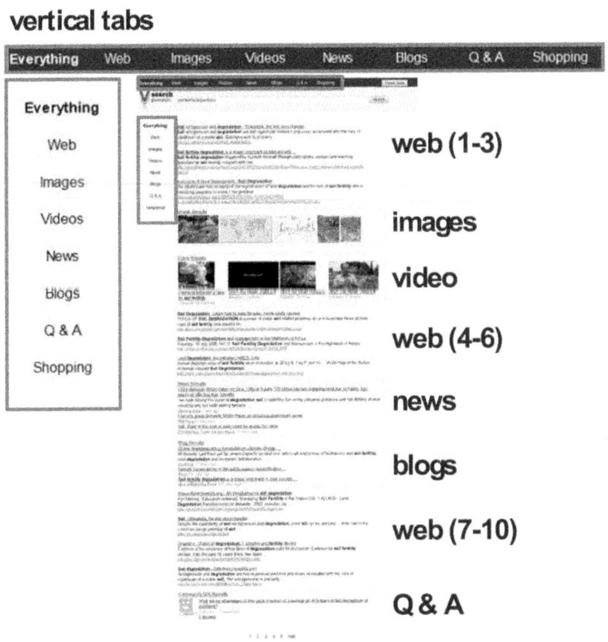

(b) Blended Interface

Figure 1. Screenshots of the (a) non-blended and (b) blended interface with the top and left navigational bars enlarged. The shopping vertical is not shown in the blended interface because it did not retrieve results for this query.

[1] http://www.lemurproject.org/querylogtoolbar/

Both interfaces were identical with one exception. The non-blended interface did not showcase vertical results in the main search results page. To see results from a particular vertical in the non-blended interface, users had to click on the vertical tab located on the top or left navigation bar. This functionality was also available in the blended interface. However, the blended interface also showcased a few results from each vertical in the main search results page. Each set of vertical results included a link to the vertical search engine. In both interfaces, users could click on a vertical tab and issue subsequent queries directly to the vertical-specific search engine. In the blended interface, verticals were displayed in the same position relative to the Web results. While commercial systems vary the presentation of verticals depending on the query, we wanted to keep the user experience with the blended interface as consistent as possible.

The blended interface represents the baseline, as this is how vertical results are typically presented by commercial systems. However, we are not putting the non-blended interface forward as a novel way to present vertical results. Rather, it allows us to study the effects of vertical display on behaviors and preferences.

3.2. Subjects

In this study, we wanted to focus on populations that have not been studied with great frequency in laboratory studies of information search. To achieve this goal, we recruited participants from Pittsboro, North Carolina, a nearby rural township located approximately 20 miles from our university. We describe the community using data from the 2010 US Census to provide setting context, not because we claim that our sample is representative of this population. According to 2010 US Census data, Pittsboro, NC has a population of 3,743 and a population density of 1,100.9/sq mi. The median age of community members is 41.4. About 72% of community members identified themselves as white, 20% as black or African American, 1.8% as Asian and 3.7% as some other race. In addition, about 9% identified themselves as Hispanic or Latino. With respect to educational attainment, about 15% are high school drop-outs, 30% have a high school degree only, 22% have some college, but no degree, and 29% of the population has a bachelor's degree or higher. The median household income is $40,056 and about 18% of all people live below the poverty line. About 63% are in the workforce.

Twenty-two flyers were posted around the community at places such as laundromats, restaurants, grocery stores, convenience stores, and the public library. An email recruitment notice was sent to a community mailing list. The flyers and recruitment notice specified three inclusion criteria: at least 18 years of age, at least two years of online search experience, and proficiency in reading and writing in English.

We conducted our study in private rooms at the community public library and college. The community college and public library are on the same campus; the public library serves as the library for students at the community college. The first 8 respondents were used as pilot subjects; an additional 29 respondents were used in the actual study. Because of a logging failure, one of these subjects was excluded from analyses.

Our subjects consisted of 12 men and 16 women. The average age of our subjects was 42 years old, and the median age was 38. Our youngest subject was 20, and our oldest subject was 74 years old. Fifty percent of our subjects were professionals, and 17% worked in the service industry. Three of our subjects were students, 3 were unemployed, and 3 were retired. With respect to highest level of educational attainment: 18% of subjects earned a high school degree or GED, 11% an Associate degree, 53% a bachelor's degree, 14% a master's degree, and 4% a doctorate. All participants spoke English as a first language.

Eighty-six percent of our subjects said they had been using desktop or laptop computers for 10 or more years, 11% said 4-6 years, and 1 person said they had used computers for less than 1 year. The majority of subjects (96%) said they use computers daily and have regular access to computers. Search engine use among our subjects was varied. Ninety–six percent of subjects use Google, 64% use Yahoo Search, 46% use Bing, and 21% use AOL Search. The most common tasks our subjects reported performing online were searching information and accessing email, followed by browsing and surfing the Internet.

Subjects' search experience was measured with a modified version of the Search Self-Efficacy Scale [10], which contained 14 items describing different search activities. Subjects indicated their confidence in completing each activity using a 10-point scale, where 1=totally unconfident and 10=totally confident. Items were then averaged for each subject to arrive at a composite measure of Search Self-Efficacy. Subjects' average Search Self-Efficacy was 7.59 (SD=1.53). Because the scale was slightly modified from its original form, two internal consistency estimates of reliability were computed: Cronbach's alpha and Spearman-Brown split-half coefficient. Both coefficients were high (Cronbach's alpha=0.932 and Spearman-Brown=0.937), indicating strong internal consistency.

3.3. Tasks

In two recent studies of vertical search, Sushmita *et al.* [24, 25] investigated different types of tasks. In Sushmita *et al.* [24] users were asked to complete non-navigational tasks that required them to compile information from several sources. The tasks (according to the example provided in Sushmita *et al.* [24]) included an indicative request which suggested that pictures and news about recent events would be useful information to collect. Thus, these tasks implicated the use of verticals. In Sushmita *et al.* [25], the researchers created tasks that had different source orientations. For example, some tasks implicated videos, while others implicated images. In this study, we wanted to create tasks that might require verticals, but we did not want to tell subjects to look for these types of results. We decided instead to construct tasks that we believed would require different amounts and diversity of information to complete and different amounts of search effort. In doing so, we turned to Anderson and Krathwohl's taxonomy of educational objectives [1] and the work of Jansen *et al.* [13].

We focus on the *cognitive process* dimension of Anderson and Krathwohl's taxonomy, which is presented in Table 2. Six types of cognitive processes are identified: *remember*, *understand*, *apply*, *analyze*, *evaluate* and *create*, with each type requiring increasing amounts of cognition and effort. While this taxonomy is traditionally used to create educational materials such as exercises and exam questions, we used it to construct search tasks similar to Jansen *et al.* [13]. We propose that the different dimensions in Table 2 reflect increasing levels of cognitive complexity. Our definition of complexity is similar to that proposed by Li and Belkin [17] and Campbell [9] who related objective task complexity to the number of possible paths that can be taken to solve a task, the number of possible solutions and outcomes, and the amount of uncertainty. Since we are using learning tasks, we also propose that task complexity is related to the amount of cognition and effort required to complete the tasks.

Table 2. Anderson and Krathwohl's Taxonomy of Learning Objectives (Cognitive Process Dimension) [1]

Dimension	Definition
Remember	Retrieving, recognizing, and recalling relevant knowledge from long-term memory.
Understand	Constructing meaning from oral, written, and graphic messages through interpreting, exemplifying, classifying, summarizing, inferring, comparing, and explaining.
Apply	Carrying out or using a procedure through executing, or implementing.
Analyze	Breaking material into constituent parts, determining how the parts relate to one another and to an overall structure or purpose through differentiating, organizing, and attributing.
Evaluate	Making judgments based on criteria and standards through checking and critiquing.
Create	Putting elements together to form a coherent or functional whole; reorganizing elements into a new pattern or structure through generating, planning, or producing.

For our tasks, we used all the cognitive processes except *apply* because we were unable to create search tasks for this category that were distinct from the other categories. We selected five domains to use when creating the tasks: health, e-commerce, entertainment, travel and science. In total, we created 25 tasks (one for each cognitive process/domain combination). Pilot tests with 6 people allowed us to refine the tasks. Ultimately, in this study we only used tasks that required three types of cognition: *remember*, *understand* and *analyze*. This decision was made because our pilot subjects could not complete all the tasks during the 1.5 hour time allotment. Thus, in total we used 15 search tasks representing three levels of complexity and five domains. Example tasks from two domains are displayed in Table 3.

Table 3. Example search tasks from two domains

Type	Complexity	Health	Science
Remember	Low	How many people in the U.S. are currently living with HIV?	What is the name of the deepest point in the ocean?
Understand	Medium	What are some long-term health risks faced by professional football players?	What are some human activities that can degrade soil fertility?
Analyze	High	What are some of the different types of artificial tanning methods? What health risks are associated with them?	You recently heard that a lot of trash ends up in the ocean. In which oceans or areas does most trash end-up and why?

3.4. User Experience Questionnaire

The sub-scales from O'Brien's Engagement Scale [21, 22] formed the basis of the sub-scales we used in this study to elicit subjects' system evaluations. The Engagement Scale [22] consists of a 31-item scale with 6 sub-scales which measure the following aspects of engagement (number in parenthesis indicates how many items are on each sub-scale): Focused Attention (7), Perceived Usability (8), Endurability (5), Novelty (3), Aesthetics (5) and Felt Involvement (3). For all scales, subjects respond by indicating their level of agreement with the items (1=strongly disagree; 5=strongly agree). Because the Engagement Scale was developed in the context of e-commerce applications, we reviewed the items and made the following modifications so that the sub-scales were better-suited for general search system evaluation: (1) replaced words such as "shopping" and "website" with "searching" and "system," respectively; (2) eliminated the *aesthetics* sub-scale because the general properties of our interfaces (e.g., color, fonts) were identical; (3) added a 5-item *Search Effectiveness* sub-scale because none of the original items were designed to evaluate vertical search and the quality of the search results; and (4) deleted one item from the *Focused Attention* sub-scale after three pilot subjects commented on its awkwardness and one item from the *Endurability* sub-scale that did not make sense given the study situation. Ultimately, we used the following sub-scales: Focused Attention, Felt Involvement, Perceived Usability, Endurability, and Search Effectiveness. The Search Effectiveness sub-scale consisted of the items in Table 4. Readers are referred to O'Brien [21] for the content of the other sub-scales. Reliability coefficients for all sub-scales are displayed in Table 5 along with the number of items for each sub-scale.

Table 4. Search Effectiveness Sub-Scale

No.	Item
1	The system provided enough information to help me solve the search tasks.
2	The system provided me with many different kinds of information.
3	The presentation of search results helped me easily combine different types of information.
4	The presentation of search results allowed me to easily identify relevant information.
5	The presentation of search results helped me get an overview of the types of information available.

Table 5. Reliability Coefficients for Sub-scales

Sub-Scale	No. of Items	Cronbach's Alpha
Focused Attention	4	.789
Felt Involvement	3	.714
Perceived Usability	7	.940
Endurability	4	.802
Search Effectiveness	5	.864

3.5. Exit Questionnaire

The Exit Questionnaire (Figure 2) contained a number of open and closed questions and used display logic to customize the questions depending on how subjects responded. Subjects were first asked if they noticed any differences between the two systems. Those who responded *Yes* were asked to describe the differences they noticed and then went to the next question. Those who responded *No* skipped the differences question and went to the next question which displayed a screen shot of the basic interface (with no results displayed) and identified the various options along the top and side as "verticals." Subjects were first asked if they noticed these verticals. Both those who responded *Yes* and *No* were then asked similar questions about their expectations about clicking on the verticals. Those who responded *No* initially were then routed to the last three questions. Those who responded *Yes* were first asked if they used the verticals. Those who responded *No* were asked why not, while those who responded *Yes* were asked if the verticals helped them during their searches. Subjects responding *Yes* were asked to describe how they helped. Subjects were then routed to the last three questions. The last three preference questions asked subjects to indicate which system (1) provided the best information, (2) was easier to use, and (3) they liked best. Subjects were provided with a no difference option and asked to explain their choices.

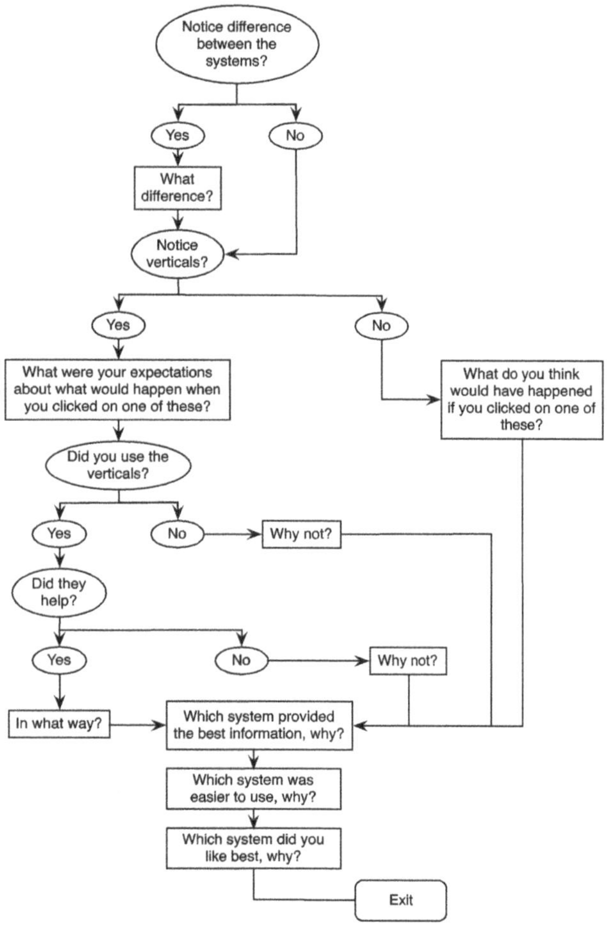

Figure 2. Exit Questionnaire Flow Diagram

3.6. Procedure

Once arriving to the study location, subjects were given an information sheet describing their rights as subjects and the basic procedure of the study. Subjects then completed an online entry questionnaire that collected information about demographics and computer and search experience. Next, subjects were given a set of written instructions. Following this, subjects completed a practice task using Google. The protocol required subjects to create responses to each search task in an auxiliary Word document. Subjects could type their response or use copy and paste. The purpose of the practice task was to acquaint subjects with this aspect of the study. Following the practice task, subjects were given their first search task and directed to use one of the interfaces. After completing three tasks, subjects completed the User Experience Questionnaire. Next, subjects repeated the entire sequence with another interface using different search tasks. Finally, subjects completed an Exit Questionnaire. The study took 1-1.5 hours to complete. Subjects were compensated $20 USD.

4. Results

We investigated four research questions: the effect of task complexity on search interaction (RQ1), the effect of task complexity on the use of vertical results (RQ2), the effect of vertical display on the use of vertical results (RQ3), and users' evaluations of each interface, their perceptions of verticals, and their interface preferences (RQ4).

4.1. Task Complexity & Interaction

With respect to RQ1, we hypothesized that more complex tasks would require a greater level of interaction (H1). While Anderson and Krathwohl's [1] taxonomy of learning tasks identifies six task-types, in this work, we focused on three (in ascending order of task complexity): *remember*, *understand*, and *analyze*. Search interaction was operationalized using five measures: time spent completing the task (time), number of queries issued (queries), number of search results clicked (clicks on SERP), and number of URLs visited (URLs). Subjects were asked to search naturally and, therefore, in several cases clicked on a search result and navigated far from the SERP. Thus, the number of URLs visited includes search results and URLs not directly linked to from the SERP. The number of SERP clicks included clicks on Web results as well as vertical results (in the blended interface).

Results showed a tendency for subjects to spend more time, issue more queries, click on more search results, and visit more URLs during tasks that were more complex (Table 6). A repeated measures ANOVA showed that all the differences were statistically significant.

Table 6. Interaction measures according to task complexity (Mean, St. Dev.)

	Time (sec)	Queries	Clicks on SERP	URLs
Remember	215.54 (185.26)	1.46 (0.83)	1.45 (1.09)	2.68 (3.61)
Understand	374.30 (221.53)	1.98 (1.51)	2.14 (1.73)	3.63 (3.15)
Analyze	491.93 (237.31)	2.88 (2.45)	2.79 (1.85)	4.75 (4.15)
$F(2,110)$, P-value	39.85, $p<.001$	11.69, $p<.001$	14.57, $p<.001$	6.17, $p=.003$
Bonferroni post-hoc comparisons	A>U>R	A>U, R	A>U>R	A> R

Bonferroni post-hoc tests were used to pinpoint the differences and found that for time and clicks on SERP, the differences between all pairs of tasks were statistically significant in the manner hypothesized, with tasks of increasing complexity requiring increasing amounts of time to complete and SERP clicks. For Queries, subjects entered significantly more when completing the *analyze* tasks than *understand* and *remember* tasks. For URLs, the significant difference was between *analyze* and *remember* tasks. To summarize, this analysis supports our hypothesis (H1) that more complex tasks are associated with greater levels of search interaction.

4.2. Task Complexity, Vertical Display & Vertical Usage

With respect to RQ2 and RQ3, we hypothesized that subjects would click on more vertical results for more complex tasks (H2) and that subjects would click on more vertical results using the blended interface (H3). While we do not have a hypothesis for an interaction effect between task complexity and vertical display, we wanted to explore whether the effect of task complexity on vertical usage is contingent on vertical results being blended into the Web results. To examine these hypotheses, a 3 x 2 two-way ANOVA was conducted on vertical clicks. Results show a main effect for vertical display ($F(1, 162)=10.25$, $p=.002$), but no main effect for task complexity ($F(2,162)=1.27$, $p=.282$) and no significant interaction between vertical display and task complexity ($F(2, 162)=2.61$, $p=.077$).

As shown in Table 7, subjects clicked on significantly more vertical results when using the blended interface (M=.17, SD=.43) than when using the non-blended interface (M=.01, SD=.11). This, combined with the significant main effect described above for vertical display, confirms hypothesis (H3) that people use more vertical results when these are blended into the Web results.

It is worth noting that the number of results (Web and vertical results) presented in the blended interface's main results page was greater than the number of results (only Web results) presented in the non-blended interface's main results page. It could be that subjects clicked on more vertical results using the blended interface because they clicked on more results in general. However, based on a two-way ANOVA, the main effect of interface on all SERP clicks (Web and vertical) was not significant ($F(1, 162)=.021$, $p=.885$). Given a similar number of total clicks, subjects seem to prioritize clicking on vertical results in the blended interface.

Table 7. Vertical clicks and total SERP clicks across task complexity and interfaces. Mean (St. Dev.)

	Vertical clicks			SERP Clicks		
	Non-Blended (n=28)	Blended (n=28)	Total	Non-Blended (n=28)	Blended (n=28)	Total
Remember	.04 (.19)	.04 (.19)	.04 (.19)	1.25 (.84)	1.64 (1.28)	1.45 (1.09)
Understand	.00 (.00)	.25 (.59)	.13 (.43)	2.29 (2.11)	2.00 (1.27)	2.14 (1.73)
Analyze	.00 (.00)	.21 (.42)	.11 (.31)	2.89 (2.13)	2.68 (1.54)	2.79 (1.85)
Total	.01 (.11)	.17 (.43)	.09 (.33)	2.14 (1.90)	2.11 (1.42)	2.13 (1.67)

Neither task complexity nor the interaction between task complexity and vertical display had a significant effect on the number of clicks on vertical results. However, it is interesting to note that for more complex tasks, almost all vertical clicks were made on the blended interface. In fact, of all 15 vertical clicks (across all tasks, subjects, and interfaces), only one was made on the non-blended interface. These results (visualized in Figure 3) suggest that during more complex tasks, subjects tend to examine more vertical results. However, they are prone to do so only when the vertical results are blended. While we consider this trend worthy of further investigation, the overall number of vertical clicks was low. We revisit this point in Section 5.

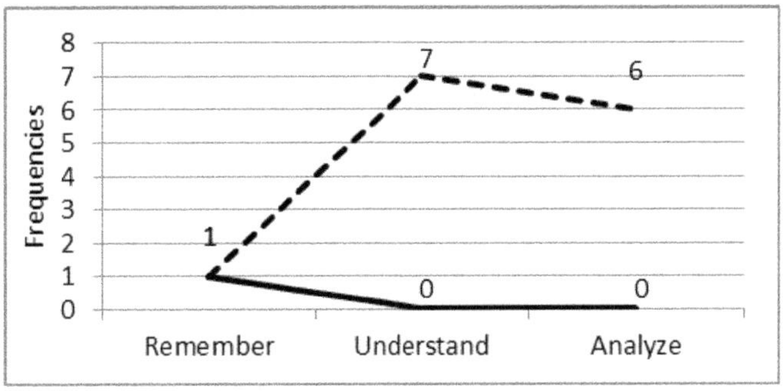

Figure 3. Comparison of vertical clicks on the blended (dashed line) and the non-blended interface (solid line)

4.3. Perceptions & Preferences

Our fourth research question explored users' evaluations of the interfaces, their perceptions of the verticals, and their display preferences.

After completing each set of tasks with one interface, subjects were asked to evaluate the system. Subjects' responses to the User Experience Questionnaire are shown in Table 8. There was little difference in subjects' ratings of the systems. For Perceived Usability, the mean ratings were identical. Paired samples t-tests were conducted and none of these differences were significant [Focused Attention: $t(27)=.953$, $p=.349$; Felt Involvement: $t(27)=.135$, $p=.894$; Perceived Usability: $t(27)=.000$, $p=1.000$; Endurability: $t(27)=-.325$, $p=.748$; and Search Effectiveness: $t(27)=-.747$, $p=.462$].

Table 8. Subjects' evaluations of each system (Mean, St. Dev.)

User Experience Sub-Scale	System	
	Non-blended	Blended
Focused Attention	2.96 (0.75)	2.83 (0.68)
Felt Involvement	3.50 (0.75)	3.48 (0.71)
Perceived Usability	3.69 (0.99)	3.69 (0.85)
Endurability	3.79 (0.77)	3.86 (0.72)
Search Effectiveness	3.54 (0.82)	3.71 (0.90)

After completing both sets of tasks (one set with each interface), subjects were asked about their perceptions of verticals and vertical results as well as their interface preferences.

As shown in Figure 2, subjects were first asked if they noticed any differences between interfaces. Twenty-three (82%) subjects claimed to notice differences. When asked what differences they noticed, the majority of subjects mentioned that the content of the results were more relevant for one system, others mentioned that the categories of search results were different, and others believed that the blended interface flowed better. A few subjects perceived blended vertical results as being advertisements.

Subjects were then asked whether they noticed the vertical tabs displayed on the top and left navigational bars. Twenty subjects (71%) said they noticed the verticals. Of these, the majority of subjects expected that clicking on a vertical tab would display a specific type of search result. Some said they expected the search engine to narrow the search results. One subject stated that he/she was concerned he/she would miss information by using the verticals. The 8 (29%) subjects that did not initially notice the verticals stated similar expectations, believing that the verticals would break down the search results by category.

Of the 20 subjects who noticed the verticals, only 7 (35%) said they used the verticals while searching. Of these, 3 thought the verticals were useful and 4 did not think they were useful either because they did not retrieve the right information or because they did not retrieve any results. People who did not use the verticals expressed that the search tasks did not require verticals; one subject said he/she was too preoccupied by the tasks to use verticals; another said that he/she did not usually use verticals.

Finally, at the end of the exit questionnaire, subjects were asked to express their preferences between interfaces in terms of information quality, ease of use, and overall experience (Figure 4). The preferences expressed by most subjects (n=22, 79%) were consistent across all three questions (information quality, ease of use, and overall). Only one subject favored different interfaces for different questions. Regarding information quality, 11 (39%) subjects preferred the non-blended interface, 12 (43%) preferred the blended interface, and the remaining five (18%) felt that both interfaces provided equal quality of information. For ease of use, 10 (36%) preferred the non-blended interface, 12 (43%) preferred the blended interface, and 6 (21%) stated no preference. Finally, in terms of overall preference, 11 (39%) preferred the non-blended interface, 13 (47%) preferred the blended interface, and 4 (14%) stated no preference. None of the chi-square tests were significant (information quality: $X^2(1) = 0.43$, $p = .84$; ease of use: $X^2(1) = 0.18$, $p = .67$; overall: $X^2(1) = 0.17$, $p = .68$).

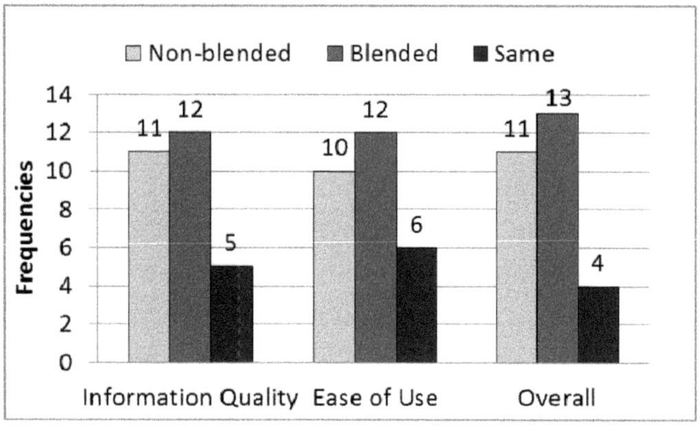

Figure 4. System Preferences

Given the clear division in system preferences, we reanalyzed subjects' evaluations of the systems (Table 8). Results showed that people who preferred the non-blended interface rated this interface higher than the blended on all the user experience sub-scales, while people who preferred the blended interface rated this interface higher than the non-blended interface (Table 9). These differences were especially pronounced for Perceived Usability and Endurability. We did not perform significance testing because of the small number of data points in each cell. However, these results suggest that the differences are not necessarily interface dependent, but rather person-dependent.

Table 9. Subjects' user experience ratings for each system according to their system preferences (Mean, St. Dev.)

User Experience Sub-Scale	People who preferred non-blended (n=11)		People who preferred blended (n=12)	
	Non-Blended	Blended	Non-Blended	Blended
Focused Attention	3.20 (.77)	2.83 (.70)	2.77 (.62)	2.83 (.74)
Felt Involvement	3.97 (.48)	3.06 (.78)	3.06 (.59)	3.75 (.75)
Perceived Usability	4.31 (.56)	2.83 (.73)	2.96 (.84)	4.08 (.46)
Endurability	4.32 (.30)	3.08 (.66)	3.25 (.70)	4.17 (.43)
Search Effectivenes s	3.8 (.83)	3.22 (.87)	3.32 (1.01)	4.02 (.73)

For each preference question, subjects were asked to justify their choices. The analysis of these responses showed a common set of rationales. Responses most often focused on the relevance of the information provided and the display of results. Because subjects often repeated their rationales across questions, responses are reported at the subject level to avoid misrepresenting the frequencies of certain rationales.

Subjects who preferred the non-blended system stated that it presented more relevant information (n=8), more credible information (n=3), and had a better layout (n=9). Subjects described the layout as "simple" and "intuitive" and stated that it helped them to more quickly identify relevant information (n=3) and was easier to use (n=4). Many subjects justified their preferences by commenting on what they did not like about the layout of the blended interface: "it spat everything out," "it was too visually overwhelming," and "it threw everything at you at once." Two subjects likened the verticals to commercial results stating that the non-blended interface had "fewer pulsing ads and screen garbage" and that the blended interface retrieved more "commercial results" from "less credible sources." These results illustrate how the display itself can influence judgments of information quality, especially in cases when the vertical results might not be relevant to the search query. Finally, one subject attributed her preference to experience, "I thought the [non-blended] was easier to navigate for me as a novice."

Subjects who preferred the blended system used similar rationales. Nine stated that the blended system provided more relevant information, although only one stated that it provided more credible information. With respect to layout, two subjects stated that the layout helped them to more quickly identify relevant information while one person stated that the system returned results faster. Comments regarding layout and ease of use were opposite of those expressed by subjects who preferred the non-blended system. Subjects who preferred the blended system thought the display was "visually pleasing" and "easier to use and more pleasant to look at." Subjects also liked that different types of results were presented and that they were "broken down into categories." Subjects commented that the display made "the subject matter easier to read and attain" and helped them be more efficient by "identifying different types of results." One subject described the vertical results as "illustrations," stating that "the illustrations made finding the information quicker and more entertaining." One subject justified his/her preference by stating that this display was the one which he/she was most familiar.

5. DISCUSSION

With respect to RQ1, more complex tasks required greater levels of search interaction: longer search sessions, more queries, more clicks on search results, and more webpages visited. Our results are consistent with results from Liu *et al* [13], who used three levels of objective task complexity, and consistent with Jansen *et al* [20], who used six levels of cognitive complexity (*remember*, *understand*, *apply*, *analyze*, *evaluate*, and *create*). Interestingly, Jansen *et al* [20] found that *evaluate* and *create* tasks required less search interaction than *analyze* tasks. However, with respect to the same cognitive complexity classes investigated in this work (*remember*, *understand,* and *analyze*), the trends are consistent.

When examining the effect of task complexity on the use of vertical results (RQ2), we observed a trend towards more clicks on vertical results for more complex tasks. However, the relationship was not significant. Our initial idea was to test five levels of task complexity (*remember*, *understand, analyze*, *evaluate*, and *create*), the hypothesis being that more complex tasks (and, in particular, the most complex: *evaluate* and *create*) would require increasing amounts and diversity of information to complete and would therefore require more use of vertical results. However, we discovered in our pilot tests that our target subjects could not complete 10 tasks in the time allotted (one task for each task-complexity/interface pair) and therefore decided to adjust the study design to include only tasks representing the first three levels of complexity (*remember, understand*, and *analyze*). While we did not find a significant main effect of task complexity on vertical usage, we found an interesting interaction between task complexity and vertical display (though, not significant, $p = 0.07$). Subjects clicked on more verticals when completing *understand* and *analyze* tasks with the blended interface. It is possible that we will find a significant effect of task complexity on vertical usage as well as an even stronger interaction effect between task complexity and vertical display when we examine the full range of task complexities, which we plan to do in future research.

Our findings regarding preferences between interfaces (RQ4) differ from Sushmita *et al.* [24], who found that subjects rated a blended interface more favorably than one where vertical results needed to be accessed by clicking on tabs. This difference might be the result of different study samples—Sushmita *et al.* [24] recruited subjects from the university and had a sample consisting of students, post-graduates and research staff. On the whole, these subjects were likely to be more technologically savvy than our subjects. Although Sushmita *et al.* [24] did not report the age of their subjects, they were likely younger than our subjects whose average age was 42 years. Moreover, the search tasks used in Sushmita *et al.* [24] implicated verticals, so this might also explain the difference.

Within our study, differences between subjects might also explain some of the variations in subjects' preferences and even in their use of verticals. For example, subjects with less search experience might prefer, and perform better with the non-blended interface because the results display is more parsimonious. Subjects with less search experience might find the blended display too visually overwhelming and distracting; this in turn, might impact their abilities to identify relevant information. While we measured Search Self-Efficacy (SSE), we did not initially design our experiment to test this variable. We conducted some preliminary analyses using this variable, but were not able to draw definitive conclusions because the search task domains were not distributed equally across the observed SSE scores and the SSE scores were slightly skewed. Future research should explore the potential relationship between search experience and vertical search display, along with other individual variables: people who are more visual thinkers might prefer the blended display or people who are novice users and/or have attention difficulties might prefer the non-blended display. If there are differences, then it might be useful for commercial search services to allow users to have more control over how verticals are displayed including the ability to turn-off verticals from a blended display.

6. CONCLUSION

We explored the relationship among task complexity, vertical display, and user interaction in aggregated search with research participants from our local community. Consistent with previous research, we found that more complex tasks were associated with greater interaction (i.e., longer sessions, more queries, more SERP clicks, and more pages visited). We also found that more complex tasks were associated with more clicks on vertical results. This is also consistent with previous research, which found that subjects used more sources during more complex tasks. Interestingly, however, users clicked on more vertical results during more complex tasks *only* when the vertical results were blended into the Web results. Finally, we found that subjects were divided in their preferences for vertical search displays. Differences between users (e.g., their search experience) may be an important factor in whether the blending of vertical results enhances or hinders the user experience. Future work will investigate tasks of additional complexity, a larger variety of presentation methods for verticals, and the effects of individual differences on display preferences.

This line of research has important implications for aggregated search systems. It may be worthwhile to consider *predicted* task complexity (predicted using session-level interaction signals) in vertical selection and presentation decisions. Furthermore, with respect to user preferences, personalization in aggregated search may be an interesting avenue to explore.

7. REFERENCES

[1] Anderson, L. W. and Krathwohl, D. A. (2001). *A taxonomy for learning, teaching and assessing: A revision of Bloom's taxonomy of educational objectives*. New York: Longman.

[2] Arguello, J., Diaz, F., and Callan, J. (2011). Learning to aggregate vertical results into web search results. In *Proceedings of CIKM*. ACM, 201–210.

[3] Arguello, J., Diaz, F., Callan, J. and Carterette, B. (2011). A methodology for evaluating aggregated search results. In *Proceedings of ECIR*. Springer-Verlag, 141–152.

[4] Arguello, J., Diaz, F., Callan, J. and Crespo, J.-F. (2009). Sources of evidence for vertical selection. In *Proceedings of SIGIR*. ACM, 315–322.

[5] Arguello, J., Diaz, F., and Paiement, J.-F. (2010). Vertical selection in the presence of unlabeled verticals. In *Proceedings of SIGIR*. ACM, 691-698.

[6] Bell, D. & Ruthven, I. (2004). Searcher's assessments of task complexity for Web searching. In *Proceedings of ECIR*. Springer-Verlag, 57–71.

[7] Byström, K. and Hansen, P. (2005). Conceptual framework for tasks in information studies. *Journal of the American Society for Information Science and Technology, 56*(10), 1050–1061.

[8] Byström, K. and Järvelin, K. (1995). Task complexity affects information seeking and use. *Information Processing and Management, 31*(2), 191–213.

[9] Campbell, D. J. (1988). Task complexity: A review and analysis. *Academy of Management Review, 13*(1), 40–52.

[10] Debowski, S., Wood, R., and Bandura, A. (2001). The impact of guided exploration and enactive exploration on self-regulatory mechanisms and information acquisition through electronic enquiry. *Journal of Applied Psychology, 86*(6), 1129–1141.

[11] Diaz, F. (2009). Integration of news content into web results. In *Proceedings of WSDM*. ACM, 182–191.

[12] Hackman, J. R. (1969). Toward understanding the role of task in behavioral research. *Acta Psychologica,* 31, 162–187.

[13] Jansen, B. J., Booth, D., & Smith, D. (2009). Using the taxonomy of cognitive learning to model online searching. *Information Processing & Management, 45*, 643–663.

[14] Kellar, M., Watters, C., and Shepherd, M. (2007). A field study characterizing Web-based information-seeking tasks. *Journal of the American Society for Information Science & Technology, 58*(7), 999–1018.

[15] Kim, J. (2006). Task difficulty as a predictor and indicator of web searching interaction. In *Proceedings of CHI*. ACM, 959–964.

[16] Li,Y. (2009). Exploring the relationships between work task and search task in information search. *Journal of the American Society for Information Science & Technology, 60*(2), 275–291.

[17] Li, Y. and Belkin, N. J. (2008). A faceted approach to conceptualizing tasks in information seeking. *Information Processing & Management, 44*, 1822–1837.

[18] Li, Y. and Belkin, N. J. (2010). An exploration of the relationship between work task and interactive information search behavior. *Journal of the American Society for Information Science & Technology, 61*(9), 1771–1789.

[19] Li, X., Wang, Y.-Y., and Acero, A. (2008). Learning query intent from regularized click graphs. In *Proceedings of SIGIR*. ACM, 339–346.

[20] Liu, J., Cole, M., Liu, C., Bierig, R. Gwizdka, J., Belkin, N.J., Zhang, J., and Zhang, X. (2010). Search behaviors in different task types. In *Proceedings of JCDL*. ACM, 69–78.

[21] O'Brien, H. L. (2010). The influence of hedonic and utilitarian motivations on user engagement: The case of online shopping. *Interacting with Computers, 22*, 344–352.

[22] O'Brien, H. L. and Toms, E. G. (2010). The development and evaluation of a survey to measure user engagement. *Journal of the American Society for Information Science & Technology, 61*(1), 50–69.

[23] Ponnuswami, A., Pattabiraman, K., Wu, Q., Gilad-Bachrach, R., and Kanungo, T. (2011). On composition of a federated web search result page: Using online users to provide pairwise preference for heterogeneous verticals. In *Proceedings of WSDM*. ACM, 715–724.

[24] Sushmita, S., Joho, H., and Lalmas, M. (2009). A task-based evaluation of an aggregated search interface. In *Proceedings SPIRE*. Springer–Verlag, 322–333.

[25] Sushmita, S., Joho, H., Lalmas, M., and Villa, R. (2010). Factors affecting click-through behavior in aggregated search interfaces. In *Proceedings of CIKM*. ACM, 519–528.

[26] Toms, E. G. (2011). Task-based information searching and retrieval. In I. Ruthven & D. Kelly (Eds.) *Interactive Information Seeking, Behaviour and Retrieval*. Facet Publishing, 43–59.

[27] Vakkari, P. (2003). Task-based information searching. *Annual Review of Information Science & Technology, 37*, 413–464.

[28] Zhu, D. and Carterette, B. (2010). An analysis of assessor behavior in crowdsourced preference judgements. In *Proceedings of SIGIR Workshop on Crowdsourcing for Search Evaluation*. ACM, 21–26.

Image Ranking Based on User Browsing Behavior

Michele Trevisiol*† Luca Chiarandini*† Luca Maria Aiello† Alejandro Jaimes†

{trevi, chiarluc, alucca, ajaimes}@yahoo-inc.com

*Web Research Group
Universitat Pompeu Fabra
Barcelona, Spain

†Yahoo! Research
Barcelona, Spain

ABSTRACT

Ranking of images is difficult because many factors determine their importance (e.g., popularity, quality, entertainment value, context, etc.). In social media platforms, ranking also depends on social interactions and on the visibility of the images both inside and outside those platforms. In this context, the application of standard ranking methods is not clearly understood, and neither are the subtleties associated with taking into account social interaction, internal, and external factors. In this paper, we use a large Flickr dataset and investigate these factors by performing an in-depth analysis of several ranking algorithms using both internal (i.e., within Flickr) and external (i.e., links from outside of Flickr) factors. We analyze rankings given by common metrics used in image retrieval (e.g., number of favorites), and compare them with metrics based on page views (e.g., time spent, number of views). In addition, we represent users' navigation by a graph and combine session models with some of these metrics, comparing with PageRank and BrowseRank. Our experiments show significant differences between the rankings, providing insights on the impact of social interactions, internal, and external factors in image ranking.

Categories and Subject Descriptors

H.3.3 [**Information Search and Retrieval**]: Information filtering; H.3.5 [**Online Information Services**]: Web-based services

General Terms

Agorithms, Experimentation

Keywords

Image Ranking, Social Browsing, Flickr, BrowseRank

Permission to make digital or hard copies of all or part of this work for personal or classroom use is granted without fee provided that copies are not made or distributed for profit or commercial advantage and that copies bear this notice and the full citation on the first page. To copy otherwise, to republish, to post on servers or to redistribute to lists, requires prior specific permission and/or a fee.
SIGIR'12, August 12–16, 2012, Portland, Oregon, USA.
Copyright 2012 ACM 978-1-4503-1472-5/12/08 ...$10.00.

1. INTRODUCTION

Many social media platforms function as somewhat independent ecosystems in which users carry out a number of social activities. In Flickr, in particular, users can share content and participate in multiple communities by submitting their photos to groups, by joining groups, and by performing several types of actions over Flickr content (*e.g.*, comment, add notes, favorite, *etc.*). The result of this is that the way the content is consumed is strongly influenced by all of the different social navigation paths that lead to it: a photo on Flickr, for example, can be linked to from a user's favorite photo collection, from several groups, galleries, and via other mechanisms, including the "external" web (*i.e.*, URLs outside of the Flickr domain).

As more social media platforms emerge, one of the key questions is whether traditional ranking algorithms, that may not take into account the subtleties of navigation patterns driven by social connections, can be successful within those ecosystems. In particular, the problem we are interested in addressing is the general ranking of images in Flickr (*i.e.*, as in PageRank, we would like to rank all of the images or a subset of them, in order of importance). Such ranking can have many applications, including retrieval, and information discovery, among others.

The importance of images in Flickr, or of "nodes" in similar social media platforms might depend on a number of *internal* and *external* factors. For example, an image that is very popular in a group that has a cult following, may have been marked by many users as a favorite image. The image has a large number of favorites because people within the Flickr community, and in particular, in the specific cult, view and favorite the image. In contrast, an image of an important real world event (*e.g.*, the British Royal Wedding) may get a high number of views, not by belonging to groups, but instead because it is linked to by multiple external (*i.e.*, outside of the Flickr domain) media outlets, and get comparatively few favorite marks. One of the key questions is thus what the impact of those external and internal factors is on ranking and selection of content.

In this paper, motivated by the scenario described above, we investigate the factors that affect image ranking by performing an in-depth analysis of the results of several ranking algorithms taking into account both internal (*i.e.*, within Flickr) and external (*i.e.*, links from outside the Flickr domain) factors. In particular, we analyze rankings given by common metrics used in image retrieval (*e.g.*, number of favorites), and compare them with metrics based on page views (*e.g.*, time spent, number of views). More specifically, in order to take into account the structure of Flickr in terms of navigation paths to and from specific images, we represent the user's navigation by a graph and combine session models with some of these metrics. We implement PageRank, BrowseRank, and compare them with different rankings.

Our main contributions can be summarized as follows:

- We compare five different implicit and explicit image ranking methods to a number of features. Our analysis gives insights into what aspects each ranking method emphasizes.
- We introduce a variation of the BrowseRank algorithm in which navigation patterns are used to assign a different damping factor to each node in the graph.
- We analyze the connectivity patterns of a large BrowseGraph extracted from Flickr. Results point to structural peculiarities that differentiate browsing graphs from other complex graphs like social and similarity networks.

To our knowledge, this is the most detailed comparison between image ranking algorithms in terms of number of baselines and features considered, and it is the first attempt to use BrowseRank for an image ranking task.

The rest of the paper is structured as follows. In Section 2 we discuss related work. In Section 3 we present the features of our Flickr dataset and we describe how we extract user session information. In Section 4 we describe our modified BrowseGraph. In Section 5 we compare our method with other baselines, highlighting their qualities and shortcomings.

2. RELATED WORK

Our work focuses on query-independent ranking of images. When dealing with the Web graph, or any other corpus of interlinked resources, the most popular ranking algorithms are PageRank [25], HITS (Hypertext Induced Topic Selection) [17] and SALSA (Stochastic Approach for Link-Structure Analysis) [18]. In addition, there are many extensions to PageRank, such as BrowseRank by Liu *et al.* [22, 23], in which pages are weighted not only by the number of incoming and outgoing links, but also by the time that users spend on each page.

Besides the ranking algorithm used, the quality of the ranking is heavily influenced by the graph that is used to model the relations between documents. The difference between the standard hyperlinks graph of webpages and the graph of the browsing data was studied by Liu *et al.* [24, 22]. Authors compare the efficiency of PageRank in both graph types, showing that a link analysis algorithm performs better on a user browsing graph than on the whole hyperlink graph. Moreover, they show that a browsing graph generated from about 15 days of data is stable enough to be reliable. As a result of its good performance, several variations and improvements of BrowseRank have been proposed in the recent past [33, 9, 5].

It is important to report that PageRank-like algorithms applied to a complete network or to any of its subnetworks yield very different results. This problem is defined as the *PageRank local ranking problem* [2, 3]. In our case, this drawback can occur because the Flickr links network is a subset of the entire Web. Therefore, a ranking performed by PageRank-like algorithms applied to the entire Web can present very different results compared to the same algorithms applied to our subnetwork. However, we avoid this issue considering a first level of external links in addition to the Flickr network, *i.e.,* the set of websites from which the users enter in Flickr. Moreover, we use this sets of external links to compute the exact values of *stop* and *reset* probabilities in our version of PageRank and BrowseRank (see Section 4.1).

Web ranking algorithms have also traditionally been used to rank images by using metatada associated with the images and/or by including content-based analysis. A number of alternatives has been explored to improve the result of the Web ranking task, including visual diversification [28, 31], near duplicate detection [8], query expansion [12], visual position [7], faceted detection [29], and re-rank based on click data [13].

Some authors have applied PageRank to image retrieval. A solution presented by Jean *et al.* [14, 15] based on the content of the images, is to extract the interest points from each image, classify the common ones, and create visual links between them. In that case, the hyperlinks are given by visual similarity among the images. Liu *et al.* [21] use a random walk algorithm for tag ranking in Flickr, to overcome the sparsity problem of the tags associated to the images inside the social network.

Much work has been made for image ranking inside a social network as Flickr, and in many cases they focus around the images with the highest number of favorites, as that is the clearest explicit action that users can make to show their interest for a specific photo. Pedro et al. [26] used the number of favorites in Flickr as relevance values for building and testing machine learning models. There are also studies that aim to detect favorite photos in Flickr or to predict the photos that a user is likely to favorite based on social, visual, and textual information [30].

Other papers investigate other explicit and implicit features that lead to similar results of the favorites. For instance, Prieur *et al.* [27] find a very high correlation between the number of favorites and the number of comments and views. Nevertheless, the reasons to select a picture as a favorite can be many[1] and they do not depend always on the user's interest. We want to show that using explicit features as favorites in an environment as Flickr, often leads to specific types of results.

The quality evaluation of any ranking of multimedia objects is not a trivial task due to the many quality dimensions at play. The attractiveness [10] and aesthetics [11, 16] of images retrieved always play an important role in user's satisfaction. Lerman *et al.* [20] for example, propose an automatic method to assign photo attractiveness values to photos by using textual and visual features. But in a specific environment such as an image-sharing social network, the relevance of the results may depend strongly on the social interactions. As many previous studies suggest [19, 4], social browsing and contact relationships are very important to model the interestingness of a resource in a socially connected environment.

In summary, although the literature in ranking is vast, we are not aware of work that specifically examines the ranking mechanisms we analyze in this paper and study those in relation to the image ranking task.

[1] `http://www.flickr.com/photos/pagedooley/6246688704/`

3. DATASET

For the purpose of this study, we took a sample of the *pageviews* of more than 10 million anonymous users from approximately two months of Flickr user log data, from August to October 2011. The pageviews are represented as plain text files that contain a line for each HTTP request satisfied by the Web server. For each pageview, our dataset contains the following fields:

$$\langle UserId, Time, ReferrerURL, CurrentURL, UserAgent \rangle$$

The *UserId* is a unique anonymized identifier computed from the Flickr userId in case of logged-in users and from a browser cookie otherwise. *CurrentURL* and *ReferrerURL* represent the current page the user is visiting and the page the user visited before arriving at the destination page. The *User-Agent* identifies the browser in use, and the *Timestamp* indicates when the page was visited. All of the data processing was anonymous and performed in aggregate. Flickr allows users to set specific pages to "private", but in our analysis we considered only public pages.

3.1 Pageview Filtering & Data Selection

In order to obtain a coherent dataset in terms of both timezone and activity, we focused on users who are located in the US by extracting the location of the IP address from the source of the HTTP request and filtering out non-US locations. We then removed traffic derived from Web crawlers by preserving only the entries whose User-Agent field contains a well-known browser identifier (*e.g.*, Firefox, Chrome). In spite of this filtering, there are cases in which the User-Agent field indicates that a legitimate browser was used, but the corresponding "users" have a very large number of pageviews. The frequency, however, suggests that such server requests could not have been made by humans, but instead were done automatically for malicious crawling. We therefore apply an additional filter by which we set a maximum threshold on the total number of pageviews per user. The threshold is set to remove a small percentage of the users (1% of the total amount). After applying the filtering steps described above, our sample contains approximately 309 Million pageviews.

3.2 Session Identification and Characteristics

Since user behavior varies over time, we group pageviews into *sessions*. A session consists of a sequence of events, typically requests made to the server by a user (*e.g.*, page views), over a specific period of time. To perform our analysis, we split the activity of a single user into different sessions when either of these two conditions hold:

- **Timeout:** the inactivity between two pageviews is longer than 25 minutes.
- **External url:** if a user visiting Flickr leaves the site and returns from a different domain, the current session ends even if previous visits are within the 25 minute threshold (we make the assumption that if a user is viewing a page on Flickr and visits another domain, then the session ends).

In the rest of the analysis we use the filtered dataset and sessions.

Figure 1: An example of pageviews that correspond to the entities of the browseGraph. Each row corresponds to a entity from top to bottom: user, group, photo

4. RANKING FROM BROWSEGRAPH

In this Section we explain how to create the BrowseGraph and we present a briefly analysis of the obtained graph. Furthermore, we describe the original BrowseRank algorithm and the modified version adapted to our domain.

4.1 Extraction of the BrowseGraph

The structure of a website is typically represented as a graph where nodes are pages and edges are the hyperlinks connecting them. In this model all the links have the same weight, disregarding how many times users go through them. The BrowseGraph [22, 23] is an alternative representation that captures the importance of the user navigation patterns by considering the actual transitions between one page to another, rather than hyperlinks.

The basic idea in our approach is that the navigation patterns within a social media platform have a strong impact on the importance of content. Therefore, we build a BrowseGraph based on our Flickr data: we create one node of the graph for each pageview that refers to one of three *entities* in Flickr, namely *users*, *groups*, and *photos*. Figure 1 shows examples of pages that are mapped to each entity, noting that all pageviews that show the same entity are condensed into a single node in the BrowseGraph. In other words, several types of pages are represented by a single node. For instance, since various URLs show the same image, all of those are mapped to a single node (fullscreen, slideshow, *etc.*).

The motivation behind this representation is that we are interested in ranking *the photographs* and those photographs may appear in multiple places (e.g., the photo appears prominently in the photo page, in the slide show, and in the photo favorites layouts of Figure 1), but since we are not interested in ranking each of the individual pages, we group them into a single node.

Flickr contains other page categories (*e.g.*, personal settings and photo upload pages) which we do not consider so we refer to them as non-entities and we do not create

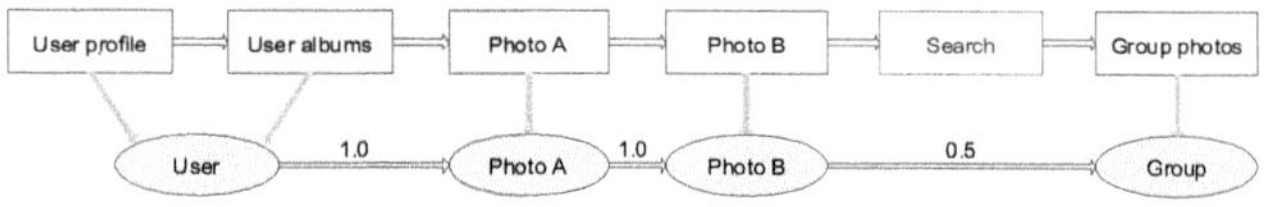

Figure 2: An example of a BrowseGraph. An example session is illustrated at the top, and the corresponding derived BrowseGraph is shown at the bottom. Gray arrows display the mapping between pageviews and browseGraph nodes.

Class	Examples	Ratio
search	search.yahoo.com, google.com	34.87%
social	facebook.com, tumblr.com	26.95%
mail	mail.yahoo.com, gmail.com	13.22%
aggregator	reddit.com, stumbleupon.com	7.76%
blog	blogspot.com, blogger.com	6.65%
photo	flickrhivemind.net, compfight.com	2.32%
microblog	twitter.com	2.26%
forum	discussion forums	2.00%
news	news.yahoo.com, cnn.com	1.67%
shop	ebay.com	0.85%

Table 1: Top ten most frequent external url classes in the dataset.

any nodes for them. The main reason to do so is that we are interested in the navigation between entities in Flickr. Therefore we need to discard some categories of traffic: *navigational* (*e.g.*, searching for photos), *configurational* (*e.g.*, changing settings, profile information) or *messaging*.

To build the browseGraph, we create the subgraph of each session and we then merge all subgraphs. Given a session $s = (p_1, p_2, ..., p_N)$ where p_n is a pageview, we map each entity pageview p_n to the vertex of the browseGraph and we connect them in the order they appear in the session. We then weight the arcs according to the number of non-entity pageviews between the source and the target. Intuitively, we would like to give the highest weight (namely 1) to the arcs that connect entities that appear in consecutive pageviews and a lower weight to pageviews that are more distant, to better express their actual proximity in the browsing activity. For example, in Figure 2, Photo A and Photo B are closer in the session than Photo B and Group. We do so by assigning the weight $w_{ij} = \frac{1}{NE(i,j)+1}$ where $NE(i, j)$ is the number of non-entity pageviews between i and j. We then compute the browseGraph by summing up all arcs with the same source and target.

A fragment of BrowseGraph is shown in Figure 2. The top row shows pageviews in a session, and the bottom part shows the resulting browseGraph. A vertex is created for each entity present in the session and gray arrows represent the mapping between pageviews and vertices. We can observe that the *Search* pageview, that displays the results of a query of the user and therefore does not refer to an entity, is not mapped to any BrowseGraph vertex but influences the weight of the corresponding edge of the BrowseGraph.

Modeling access from the Web (*i.e.*, domains different from Flickr) is important to detect the most frequently accessed entities from external sources. We therefore include in the graph also the nodes representing accesses to Flickr from external websites, derived from the *ReferrerURL* attribute of the first pageview of a session. However, since we are interested in understanding global navigation patterns, the full URL is too specific. For this reason we group external URLs in 17 classes as it was proposed by Chiarandini *et al.* [6]. Each class is detected by a set of regular expressions defined by manually inspecting the top 100 most popular referrer URLs. For example, the class "search" contains the URL of popular search engines (such as Yahoo!, Bing, and Google). The top ten most frequent classes are show in Table 1. The external URL classes cover around 99% of the total number of external URLs. For each class, we add a node to the BrowseGraph and we connect it to the nodes that correspond to the first entity of a session coming from the class.

	All	Photos	Groups	Users
#Nodes	49,275,691	46,569,946	183,996	2,521,749
$\langle k_{in} \rangle$	1.94	1.57	13.72	7.99
$\langle k_{out} \rangle$	1.94	1.51	13.69	9.05

Table 2: Browsegraph statistics, with detail on single node categories. $\langle k_{in/out} \rangle$ denote the average in- and out-degree.

	%Links			$\langle w \rangle$		
	Photos	Groups	Users	Photos	Groups	Users
Photos	0.6182	0.0098	0.1071	1.49	1.21	1.44
Groups	0.0114	0.0092	0.0057	1.54	1.44	1.65
Users	0.1332	0.0075	0.0979	1.48	1.41	1.32

Table 3: Flows and weights in browsegraph. Cells report the overall percentage of links flowing from a node type to another and the average weight $\langle w \rangle$ of edges according to the type of the endpoints.

4.2 Analysis of the BrowseGraph

The BrowseGraph we extract from the Flickr sessions has about 50 Million nodes 95 Million arcs, with in a very low graph density of around $3.8 \cdot 10^{-8}$. Statistics on average degree connectivity and graph size for the different Flickr entities are reported in Table 2. Higher degree of group and user nodes compared to photos suggests, as one might expect, that thematic groups and user profiles are hubs for the exploration of the website. The role of groups as navigation hubs is confirmed also by the inspection of the navigation flows between all of the possible pairs of node categories (Table 3), which shows that links from groups towards photos or users are on average used more often (*i.e.*, have higher weight) than other link types. Moreover, it appears that groups and user pages attract traffic from many sessions, but soon redirect this traffic to particular photos. This can be inferred by the fact the in-degree distribution for users and groups is heavier and broader than for photos, but the scenario is reversed when considering the distributions of the edge weights towards each node type (see Figure 3). In a nutshell, sessions end up in groups and user pages from anywhere in the network and from there they tend to converge to the most interesting or well positioned photos in the page.

Despite the important role of groups and user pages, the majority of arcs in the BrowseGraph are due to the navigation from one photo to another (62% of links, see Table 3). This is partially due to the disproportion in the cardinality of the three node categories (photo nodes account for 95%

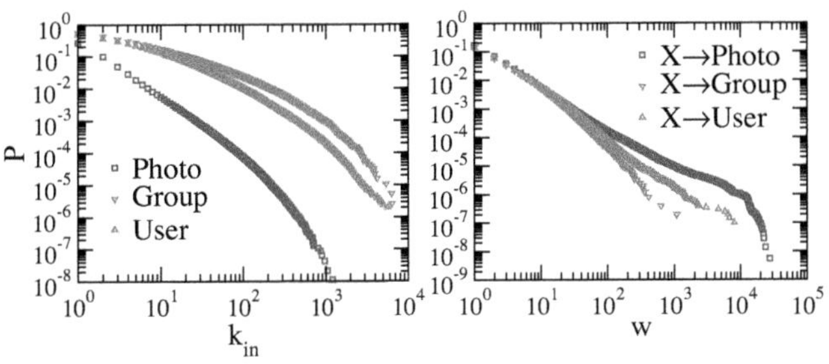

Figure 3: (Left) CCDF of the in-degree (k_{in}) for the three node types in the browsegraph. (Right) CCDF of arc weights for arcs terminating in nodes representing photos, groups or users.

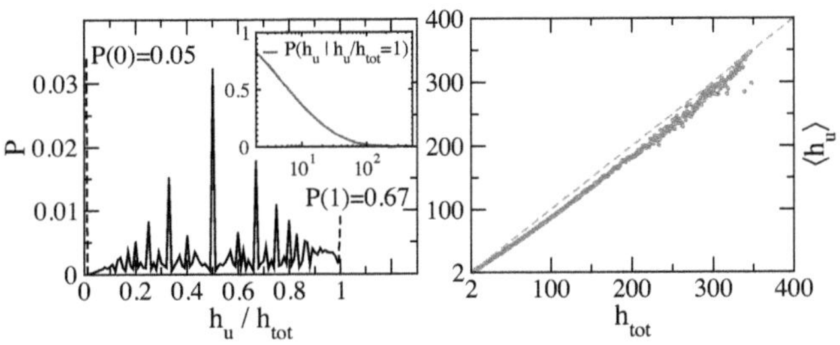

Figure 4: (Left) Distribution of ratio of session hops between two pictures belonging to the same owner (h_u) over the total number of hops (h_{tot}). The inset shows the CCDF of the number of hops for the sessions visiting only nodes of a single user, which constitutes the majority of cases. (Right) Average number of hops between pictures of the same owner $\langle h_u \rangle$ at fixed session length. Points lying almost on the diagonal mean very high correlation.

of nodes in the graph), but mainly it is the result of frequent navigation patterns. In fact, as shown in Figure 4, users very often browse photos of the same owner and this happens not only for short sessions, as highlighted by the rather broad distribution of session length for this case. This behavior is largely determined by the Flickr *photostream* at the top of every photo page, which shows a strip of 5 photos from the same owner, allowing easy navigation from one photo to another.

More generally, while surfing the Web, every user who visits a page eventually leaves following another link (or, more unlikely, end her session). As a result, a network created by the composition of such browsing patterns will have very high *balance* between in-and out-connectivity of nodes, as shown in Figure 5 (top). Such structural feature clearly differentiates navigation graphs from social graphs, in which popular individuals such as celebrities attract many connections and return a few back. The observed balance pattern gets slightly blurred only for very highly connected pages. Specifically, as shown in Figure 5 (bottom), well connected groups tend to have a higher in- than out-degree, while the distribution of the ratio of in-strength over out-strength for the most visited photos has a heavier tail towards values greater than one rather than towards zero. This confirms a scenario where the user navigation when not jumping from

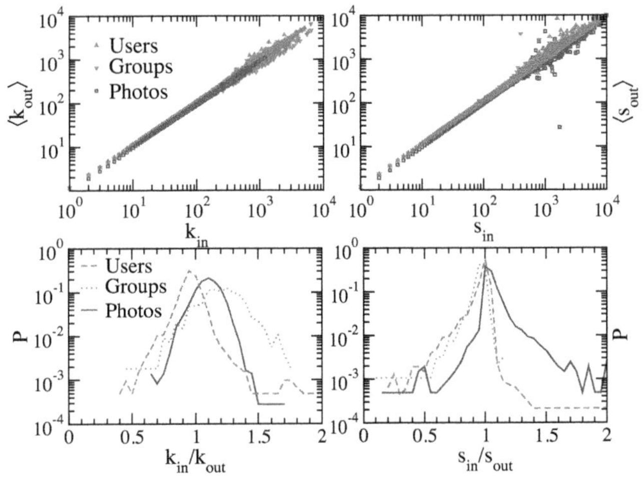

Figure 5: (Top) Average out-degree $\langle k_{out} \rangle$ and out-strength $\langle s_{out} \rangle$ at fixed values of in-degree k_{in} and in-strength s_{in}, for the three node types. Distribution of points almost perfectly aligned on the diagonal reveal the extremely high correlation between the amount of in and out session traffic which characterize navigation networks. (Bottom) Distribution of the ratio between in- and out-degree (in-and out-strength) for nodes with an in-degree (in-strength) higher than 500. The different skews of the distributions highlights the different roles of the three node types in browsing.

one photo to another, flows to hubs and gets redirected to popular photos.

Finally, a prevalent unidirectionality of browsing patterns can be evinced by the very low portion (0.17) of directed arcs $A \to B$ having a reciprocal $B \to A$, namely the reciprocation of the network. Again, this parameter is another footprint that discriminates navigation networks from social networks, which are on average highly reciprocated due to conventional social protocols.

4.3 Definition of Browserank

The BrowseGraph just outlined contains the information about user navigation paths and browsing behavior within Flickr. For example, the tendency to visit pictures in succession, moving directly from one photo to another, or exploiting the group and user nodes as hubs in order to select interesting photos and continue browsing.

Our goal is to use the computed BrowseGraph to rank entities inside Flickr. Since our BrowseGraph contains different types of nodes (photos, users, groups), not only photos are ranked. The obtained rank should capture well the global interest patterns leading the Web surfers to any of the entities considered. In this work we consider the rank for the photo nodes only, but in principle the rank scores obtained for user and group nodes can be used as well for different tasks.

Relying on the BrowseGraph structure alone may lead to a series of problems. Due to the low density of the graph (see Section 4.2), the ranking could be biased towards nodes with high degree (*e.g.*, a user with a large number of photos or spammers), regardless of the quality of the entities. Moreover, important node attributes such as the time spent on them or popularity would not taken into account. The ranking needs therefore to be adjusted using additional information. We applied and improved an algorithm that takes into account the time spent by the user on a page and uses this information to readjust the values returned by PageRank.

BrowseRank [22] is a ranking algorithm based on a continuous time Markov process model that exploits the link structure of the BrowseGraph. As opposed to the classic Markov process, BrowseRank takes into account the time that users spend on the page. In the context of Flickr, time spent on a photo could be a good indicator of interest by the user. Next, we describe the algorithm and the way in which we adapted it to the Flickr BrowseGraph.

4.3.1 Continuous-time Markov Model

As in [22], we use the Continuous-time Markov Model represented by the matrix $P(t) = [p_{nm}(t)]_{N\times N}$ where p_{nm} represents the transition probability from vertex v_n to v_m for time interval t.

The BrowseRank algorithm computes the stationary probability distribution $\{\pi_i\}$ by using the *transition rate matrix* $Q = [\frac{\partial}{\partial t}P(t)](0)$ and the Embedded Markov Chain (EMC). The EMC is a discrete Markov process derived from Q (for details see [22]). Given the stationary probability distribution of the EMC $\tilde{\pi}_i$, we can compute π_i using

$$\pi_i = \frac{\frac{\tilde{\pi}_i}{q_{ii}}}{\sum_{\{v_j\}}\frac{\tilde{\pi}_j}{q_{jj}}} \tag{1}$$

4.3.2 Embedded Markov Chain (EMC)

The EMC is a Markov Chain whose transition probabilities are based solely on the observed transitions between entities in the browseGraph $G = \langle\{v_i\}, \{e_{ij}\}, \{w_{ik}\}\rangle$ where $\{v_i\}$ is the set of vertexes, $\{e_{ij}\}$ is the set of edges and $\{w_{ij}\}$ the set of weights associated with the edges

In addition, for each node j, we compute the *reset probability* σ_j, *i.e.*, the probability of starting a new session in j as the number of sessions that start in j over the total number of sessions. Moreover, for each node j, we compute the *stop probability* α_j *i.e.* the probability of ending the session in j as the number of sessions that end in j over the total number of sessions that contain j. Both probabilities have been smoothed in order to avoid zero probabilities.

The transition probabilities of the EMC are computed in the following way:

$$emc_{ij} = \alpha_i \frac{w_{ij}}{\sum_{\{v_k\}} w_{ik}} + (1-\alpha_i)\sigma_j \tag{2}$$

Intuitively, Equation 2 indicates that as the user traverses node i of the graph, she may continue the navigation with probability α_i or randomly reset to any other node with probability $(1 - \alpha_i)$. In case she continues, the transition probability is computed based on the observed transitions. In case she resets, the probability of ending up in node j is the reset probabilty σ_j. Equation 2 looks similar to the weighted PageRank algorithm [32] but we are able to exploit additional information that is not available to web crawlers. By having the number of sessions starting and stopping in a given node, we are able to estimate the specific reset and stop probabilities σ_i and α_i for every page i. The estimation of these parameters makes the random walk more realistic since it models the navigation of the user in a more accurate way. Equation 2 differs also from Equation 8 in [22] in the fact that we are not only estimating the reset probability, but also the stop probability. The additional advantage of this parameter estimation is that it avoids to manually set any parameter prior to running of the algorithm.

After computing the EMC transition probabilities, we compute the stationary probabilities $\{\tilde{\pi}_i\}$. Up to this point we have not taken into account the time spent by the user on the entities. It is indeed interesting to compare the performance of the ranking with and without this information. We will therefore save the $\{\tilde{\pi}_i\}$ and we will refer to them simply as the *PageRank*.

4.3.3 BrowseRank

As a final step, we include the information about the time spent by the user on the entities to improve the result of the previous section. For each vertex of the browseGraph v_i we compute the duration of the visits of users as follows:

- For each pageview p_n with timestamp t_n belonging to session s, we compute its duration d_n as the difference between the timestamp of the next pageview and its timestamp $d_n = t_{n+1} - t_n$. As we are not able to compute the duration of the last action of a session, we decided to discard it.

- We then compute the *aggregate durations* by summing up the duration of consecutive pageviews that refer to the same browseGraph vertex v_i.

- Finally, for each v_i we compute the sample mean $\bar{Z}_i$ and the sample variance S_i^2 of its aggregate durations.

We apply the addictive noise model [22] to cope with noise deriving from different connection speeds and we compute q_{ii} by solving the optimization problem in Equation 3.

$$\begin{aligned} \min_{q_{ii}} \quad & ((\bar{Z} - \frac{1}{q_{ii}}) - \frac{1}{2}(S^2 - \frac{1}{q_{ii}^2}))^2 \\ s.t. \quad & q_{ii} < 0 \end{aligned} \tag{3}$$

We can now solve Equation 1 to compute the value of BrowseRank for every node.

The BrowseRank algorithm is straightforward to parallelize in Map-Reduce. In terms of complexity, the most demanding step is the computation of the stationary probability distribution of the EMC $\tilde{\pi}_i$. Using the power method, the overall complexity of the algorithm is $O(N\log(1/\epsilon))$, with N number of edges in the graph and ϵ a given degree of precision [1].

5. EVALUATION

We compare the top 1,000 Flickr photos ranked using five different importance scores, specifically:

- **Favorites**: absolute number of favorite marks assigned to a photo. Favorites can be assigned only by Flickr users.

- **Views**: absolute number of views of the photo page (this includes users that are not logged in).

- **Time**: cumulative time spent by all of the visitors of a photo page.

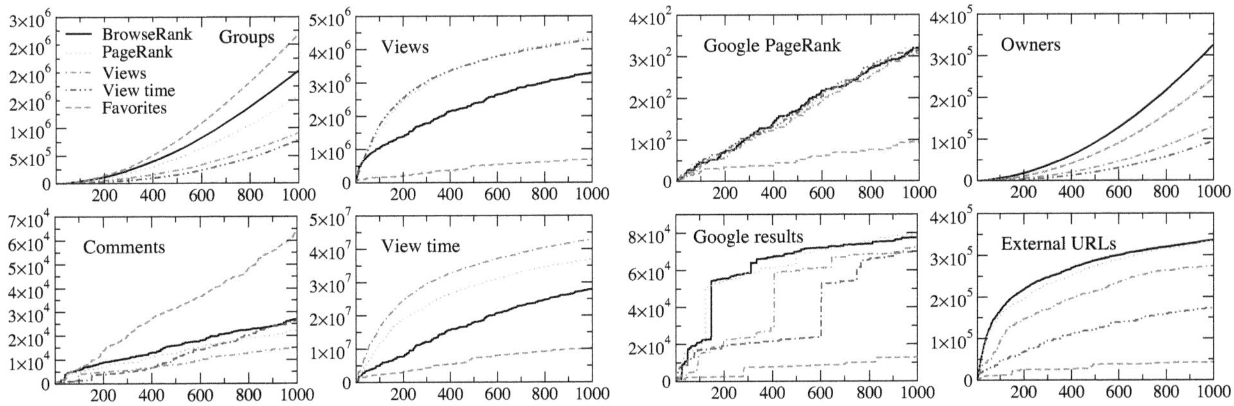

Figure 6: Comparison of the five ranking methods considered (BrowseRank, PageRank, Number of Views, View Time, Number of Favorites), according to eight features. Curves show the cumulative value of the feature up to the top $N \in [1, 1000]$ results in the ranking. The higher the curve, the more that feature is represented in the ranking. Columns from left to right depict results for number of distinct groups to which the photo in the ranking belongs, number of comments, number of views, view time, Google PageRank of the page containing the photo, number of Google results when using the page URL as search query, number of distinct owners of the photo, and number of external URLs from which the photo page has been reached. Number of views and view time are used as both ranking methods and features.

- **PageRank**: PageRank score of the photo page, with estimated start and stop probabilities as described in Section 4.3.2.
- **BrowseRank**: BrowseRank score of the photo page, with estimated start and stop probabilities as presented in Section 4.3.3.

The selected methods include a fairly general selection of explicit (Favorites), implicit (Views, Time) and centrality-based ranking techniques (Page/BrowseRank). The number of favorites has often been used as an evaluation baseline in Flickr photo ranking [26] as it is the most explicit indication of preference and the scores can easily be aggregated. Views and Time spent are also often used for ranking in photo sharing sites due to the ease of computation. Although quantitative correlations have been found between the visit count and the explicit user feedback on photos [20, 27], we show that all metrics behave in appreciably different ways.

5.1 Popularity, Interestingness, and Diversity

When comparing different picture sets, image quality is just one of the parameters. In particular, when images are embedded in dynamic social environments, the interest people have in particular photos can be determined (or influenced) more by the social dynamics of a community (*e.g.*, a group in Flickr) than by the inherent quality of the photos themselves. Similarly, interest can originate externally (*i.e.*, many photos in Flickr are linked from outside of Flickr) and thus be important independently of their aesthetic qualities (*e.g.*, photos of important events).

Given that several factors can be taken into account in considering a ranking of images, we identified four importance macro-notions and we list some quantitative *features* for each of them. All of the features were then used as evaluation parameters to compare the rankings.

- **Internal popularity**. Popularity of a photo inside the Flickr community. Popularity does not necessarily imply quality, but directly expresses the interest of users in a particular item. Features describing photo popularity are the number of *comments* the picture receives and the number of internal Flickr *groups* in which it appears[2].
- **External popularity**. We consider measures of external popularity: the *number of search results* obtained from a Google search using the photo page URL as a query, the *Google PageRank* of that URL, and the number of browsing sessions originating from an *external URL* that visit the photo page as the first Flickr page[3].
- **Collective attention**. Users not logged into Flickr as well as Flickr users who do not actively give feedback on photos, implicitly express their interest in specific photos by visiting the pages that contain them and by spending time on them. Therefore, we use the total *number of views* of a photo and the cumulative *time spent* on the photo as an aggregate measure of attention that a generic Web user, whether or not logged into Flickr, devotes to that image.
- **Diversity**. One of the applications of ranking a large-set of photos might be to display the most interesting ones. In this case, a very homogeneous set of pictures may result appealing to some user categories but are less likely to attract a wide public. Assuming that photos belonging to the same user are on average more homogeneous than pictures taken from different users,

[2]Although placing an image in multiple groups does not automatically make it popular, one can argue that photos that appear in multiple groups can be considered to be more popular because they have wider exposure

[3]For several queries, the Google search results were similar to those obtained by other search engines, so we used them as a representative metric

	$\frac{\vert photos_{tag}\vert}{\vert photos\vert}$	$\vert tags\vert$	$\vert set(tags)\vert$	$\langle tags\rangle$	H
BrowseRank	0.73	**7913**	**4347**	**7.93**	**11.23**
PageRank	0.75	7129	3583	7.39	10.57
Favorites	0.53	4164	2936	5.98	10.81
Time	0.80	6192	2245	6.20	9.31
Views	**0.83**	6523	2113	7.14	7.14

Table 4: Statistics on the tag diversity for the top 1000 photos in the rankings. Columns report, from left to right: fraction of tagged photos, number of tags, number of distinct tags, average number of tags per photo, and entropy H associated to the tag frequency distribution. Entropy is given in number of bits ($\log_2$). Highest values are highlighted in bold.

diversity can be estimated by the number of different *photo owners*. Additionally, an analysis on the diversity of the corpus of *tags* of the photos can be a measure of the variety of concepts represented.

We use the number of views and the view time as both ranking metrics and evaluation parameters to draw a more complete analysis of other rankings. We could have done the same for the number of comments, but we omitted to use it as a ranking metric because its performance was very similar to the Favorites. Cumulative values of each of the features defined are shown in Figure 6. To give a long-range overview of the behavior of the different ranking strategies, we show the feature values for the top 1k photos. Nevertheless, since many applications need much shorter ranked lists, we report that the relative position of the different curves is nearly unchanged for the top 20 and top 100 photos, for all the metrics considered.

Results reveal that most Favorites have good internal popularity, being the top metric in both number of groups and comments, but behave worse than any other metric in terms of external popularity and collective attention. In contrast, photos with top BrowseRank scores are less popular internally (even though their scores are comparable to favorites up to the top 100) but they attract relatively more collective attention and position above any other metric when counting external relevance and owner diversity. PageRank behaves worse than BrowseRank except for collective attention. Finally, Page views and Time perform reasonably well for external popularity and by definition in collective attention, but surprisingly the ranked photos have relatively little popularity in groups and receive few comments.

Diversity in terms of tag categories is explored separately in Table 4. The richness of the annotation corpora from the five rankings are evaluated in terms of number of (distinct) tags appearing in the corpus or on single photos. Furthermore, we computed the entropy on the tag frequency distribution as a measure of uncertainty of the type of tags attached to a randomly selected photo. BrowseRank clearly outperforms all other metrics.

5.2 Quality From Visual Inspection

Assessing the quality of photos by visually inspecting them is a challenging task due to the intrinsic subjective component of the evaluation. However, to gain insights into how different quantitative features impact the type of images shown, we show the top 10 images for all of the 5 ranks considered (Figure 7).

Albeit any manual classification is ultimately arbitrary,

	Art	Events	Series	Peculiar
BrowseRank	2,3,7,8	1,4,5	6	9,10
PageRank	4,5,7,9	2,3,6	1,8	10
Favorites	1,3,5,6	2,9	4,7,8,10	-
Time	5,9	10	1,2,3,4,6,7,8	-
Views	9	2,5	1,3,4,6,7,8,10	-

Table 5: Manual classification of top 10 ranked photos into four categories representing high-quality artistic images, natural and social events, picture series, and peculiar or fun images. Image numbers refer to Figure 7.

we partition the photos in four well-recognizable, high-level categories that help to better understand the nature of the top photos. The pictures shown are assigned to one of the following categories: 1) *artistic* high-quality landscapes or portraits 2) major natural and social *events*, 3) part of specific photo *series* or serial events, and 4) *peculiar* or curious shoots. Classification of each image is reported in Table 5.

At first glance, the Time and Views rankings are dominated by a majority of photos depicting scared visitors to a horror house[4]. Traces of the same series, plus a couple of pictures from a humorous calendar series are present also among the top Favorites; besides that, artistic pictures are prevalent, followed by two photos related to breaking news. BrowseRank and PageRank have an almost identical set of pictures, in different order. They both contain as many artistic images as Favorites but more images related to trending topics or natural events. Series-related pictures are present (*i.e.*, horror house and mosaics of electronic games characters) but just as singletons. Photos of peculiar art installation or entertainment activities complete the rank.

5.3 Discussion

The overall scenario emerging from the comparison shows that different metrics promote different types of photos. Rankings based on explicit feedback, namely Favorites, boost pictures that are well spread across Flickr groups and that receive attention from active Flickr users, but that may not have great impact outside of Flickr. Top rated images tend to belong to a small set of owners and convey a lower semantic variety than the pictures from centrality-based rankings. Artistic photos made by professionals are prevalent.

BrowseRank and PageRank, instead, overshadow a bit the very popular content *inside* Flickr to provide images with higher semantic variety and with apparently stronger interest from a broader part of the Web (outside of Flickr). This includes popular photos on trendy social events or pictures about popular fun facts or peculiar subjects. A positive side-effect of this is that photos that are related to popular memes just inside Flickr (*e.g.*, horror house pictures) are downgraded, and tend to disappear from the top ranking. Moreover, being based on the data from the navigation log only, centrality rankings are fully *implicit*. They do not need an active user base commenting or voting on the images. This means that BrowseRank and PageRank are effectively more able to pick up diverse image collections, and produced more balanced lists by considering external links to the photos. Such algorithms can be profitably parallelized, making efficient their computation even for big social media sites like Flickr.

[4]See http://www.nightmaresfearfactory.com/

Figure 7: Top 10 photos for the five ranking strategies considered. Pictures include: (F2) shot of an empty railroad station during a hurricane in US, (F4 and similar) pictures of visitors to a horror house, (F8,F10) fun calendar series, (F9) memorial potrait of Steve Jobs, (B1) portrait in support of gay marriage, (B4) rare natural phenomenon of water masses at different densities melting one into another (the photo was broadcast by several news media), (B5) arrests during the "Occupy Wall Street" movement demonstrations, (B6) mosaics of a popular electronic-game character, part of a wider series, (B9) close lion encounters tourist van, (B10,P10) art installations, (T10) mugshot of the youngest African-American sentenced to death in the US, (F1,B2, and more) artistic portraits, landscapes or photoart.

Simpler metrics such as time spent and number of views have the advantage of an easy computation, but overall they perform poorly compared to others, at least in terms of diversity of the results.

6. CONCLUSIONS AND FUTURE WORK

The problem of general ranking of images in social photo sharing services has not a widely-accepted solution and differences between different strategies have not been explored in depth so far.

To shed light on this matter, we compared five possible ranking strategies in Flickr: explicit feedback (number of favorites), implicit user information (number of views and time spent viewing), and graph-centrality methods (PageRank and BrowseRank) applied to the BrowseGraph, namely the graph of the user browsing sessions. In particular, we contribute to the definition of a customized version of the BrowseGraph that is limited to the navigation patterns inside the boundaries of the considered service, but that takes into account also the entry points of users navigating to Flickr from other domains. The purpose of such model is to express the complexity of navigation patterns in a meaningful way that captures the importance that images have outside of the social media platform being considered. Unlike previous work in PageRank-based algorithms, we estimate a different damping factor for each page from the user session information.

A comparison between rankings was performed on a large Flickr dataset along several axes including the internal and external popularity of ranked images, the overall attention that they attract from Web users, their diversity in terms of ownership, and semantic categories, and their visual appearance. Results show that the ranking based on explicit user feedback behaves better than simple implicit methods. Favorite-based ranking boosts mainly professional artistic photos that are very popular inside Flickr but they are limited in variety and have low impact on the external Web. On the contrary, centrality-based methods, BrowseRank in particular, promote images that have attracted interest of external Web services like news media and produce more diverse rankings, minimizing the noise due to serial but relatively uninteresting photos periodically popping out in Flickr.

As future work, we plan a refinement of general image ranking by combining different strategies and the production of personalized image ranking by processing the local browsing information occurring in the logical proximity of the activity of a user. The application of BrowseRank to query-dependent image ranking has to be studied as well. Possible developments include the application of our customized BrowseRank to other domains like news services, knowledge directories or general-purpose social media. Regarding the exploration of the inherent BrowseRank properties, interesting research lines include the analysis of the impact that temporal patterns have on the quality of the ranking and a thorough theoretical analysis of the effectiveness of our customized BrowseGraph model in the estimation of the global PageRank of a document in the Web.

7. ACKNOWLEDGMENTS

This research is partially supported by European Community's Seventh Framework Programme FP7/2007-2013 under the ARCOMEM and Social Sensor projects, by the Spanish Centre for the Development of Industrial Technology under the CENIT program, project CEN-20101037 "Social Media", and by Grant TIN2009-14560-C03-01 of the Ministry of Science and Innovation of Spain. Furthermore we would like to thank Paolo Boldi for his helpful suggestions.

8. REFERENCES

[1] M. Bianchini, M. Gori, and F. Scarselli. Inside PageRank. *ACM Transactions on Internet Technology*, 5(1):92–128, 2005.

[2] P. Boldi, M. Santini, and S. Vigna. Do Your Worst to Make the Best: Paradoxical Effects in PageRank Incremental Computations. *Algorithms and Models for the Web-Graph*, pages 168–180, 2004.

[3] M. Bressan and L. Pretto. Local computation of PageRank: the ranking side. In *Conference on Information and Knowledge Management*, pages 631–640. ACM, 2011.

[4] A. Capocci, A. Baldassarri, V. Servedio, and V. Loreto. Friendship, collaboration and semantics in Flickr: from social interaction to semantic similarity. In *MSM*, pages 8:1–8:4. ACM, 2010.

[5] M.-F. Chiang, W.-C. Peng, and P. Yu. Exploring latent browsing graph for question answering recommendation. *World Wide Web Internet And Web Information Systems*, pages 1–28, 2011.

[6] L. Chiarandini, M. Trevisiol, and A. Jaimes. Discovering Social Photo Navigation Patterns. In *ICME*. IEEE, 2012.

[7] F. Chierichetti and R. Kumar. Optimizing Two-Dimensional Search Results Presentation. *Science*, pages 257–266, 2011.

[8] O. Chum, J. Philbin, and A. Zisserman. Near duplicate image detection: min-hash and tf-idf weighting. In *BMVC*, volume 3, page 4, 2008.

[9] B. Gao, T.-Y. Liu, Y. Liu, T. Wang, Z.-M. Ma, and H. Li. Page importance computation based on Markov processes. *Information Retrieval*, 14(55):488–514, 2011.

[10] B. Geng, L. Yang, C. Xu, X. Hua, and S. Li. The role of attractiveness in web image search. In *Multimedia*, pages 63–72. ACM, 2011.

[11] R. Halonen, S. Westman, and P. Oittinen. Naturalness and interestingness of test images for visual quality evaluation. In *SPIE*, volume 7867, page 34, 2011.

[12] E. Hoque, O. Hoeber, and M. Gong. Evaluating the Trade-Offs between Diversity and Precision for Web Image Search Using Concept-Based Query Expansion. In *WI-IAT*, volume 3, pages 130–133. IEEE, 2011.

[13] V. Jain and M. Varma. Learning to Re-Rank: Query-Dependent Image Re-Ranking Using Click Data. In *WWW*, pages 277–286. ACM, 2011.

[14] Y. Jing. Pagerank for product image search. In *WWW*, pages 307–315. ACM, 2008.

[15] Y. Jing and S. Baluja. VisualRank: applying PageRank to large-scale image search. *IEEE Transactions on Pattern Analysis and Machine Intelligence*, 30(11):1877–90, Nov. 2008.

[16] H. Katti, K. Bin, T. Chua, and M. Kankanhalli. Pre-attentive discrimination of interestingness in images. In *ICME*, pages 1433–1436. IEEE, 2008.

[17] J. Kleinberg. Authoritative sources in a hyperlinked environment. *Journal of the ACM*, 46(5):604–632, 1999.

[18] R. Lempel and S. Moran. The stochastic approach for link-structure analysis (SALSA) and the TKC effect. *World Wide Web Internet And Web Information Systems*, 33:387–401, 2000.

[19] K. Lerman and L. Jones. Social Browsing on Flickr. In *ICWSM*, pages 1–4. ACM, 2007.

[20] K. Lerman, A. Plangprasopchok, and M. C. Wong. Personalizing Results of Image Search on Flickr. In *ITWP*. AAAI, 2007.

[21] D. Liu, X.-S. Hua, L. Yang, M. Wang, and H.-J. Zhang. Tag ranking. In *WWW*, pages 351–360. ACM, 2009.

[22] Y. Liu, B. Gao, T.-Y. Liu, Y. Zhang, Z. Ma, S. He, and H. Li. Browserank: letting web users vote for page importance. In *SIGIR*, pages 451–458, New York, NY, USA, 2008. ACM.

[23] Y. Liu, T.-Y. Liu, B. Gao, Z. Ma, and H. Li. A framework to compute page importance based on user behaviors. *Information Retrieval*, 13(1):22–45, 2009.

[24] Y. Liu, M. Zhang, and S. Ma. User browsing graph: Structure, evolution and application. In *WSDM (Late Breaking-Results)*. ACM, 2009.

[25] L. Page, S. Brin, R. Motwani, and T. Winograd. The PageRank Citation Ranking: Bringing Order to the Web. *World Wide Web Internet And Web Information Systems*, 54(2):1–17, 1998.

[26] J. S. Pedro, P. Street, and S. Sheffield. Ranking and Classifying Attractiveness of Photos in Folksonomies. In *WWW*, pages 771–780. ACM, 2009.

[27] C. Prieur, D. Cardon, J.-S. Beuscart, N. Pissard, and P. Pons. The Stength of Weak cooperation : A Case Study on Flickr. *arxiv.org*, 65(8):610–613, 2008.

[28] R. van Leuken, L. Garcia, X. Olivares, and R. van Zwol. Visual diversification of image search results. In *WWW*, pages 341–350. ACM, 2009.

[29] R. van Zwol and E. Al. Faceted exploration of image search results. In *WWW*, page 961. ACM, 2010.

[30] R. van Zwol, A. Rae, and L. Garcia Pueyo. Prediction of favourite photos using social, visual, and textual signals. In *Multimedia*, pages 1015–1018. ACM, 2010.

[31] O. Wu, W. Hu, and B. Li. Group ranking with application to image retrieval. In *Conference on Information and Knowledge Management*, pages 1441–1444. ACM, 2010.

[32] W. Xing and A. Ghorbani. Weighted PageRank algorithm. In A. A. Ghorbani, editor, *CNSR*, pages 305–314. IEEE, 2004.

[33] B. Zhou, Y. Liu, M. Zhang, Y. Jin, and S. Ma. Incorporating web browsing activities into anchor texts for web search. *Information Retrieval*, 14(3):290–314, 2010.

Modeling Concept Dynamics for Large Scale Music Search

Jialie Shen† HweeHwa Pang† Meng Wang‡ Shuicheng Yan⋆
† School of Information Systems, Singapore Management University, Singapore
{jlshen, hhpang}@smu.edu.sg
‡ Hefei University of Technology, Hefei, China
eric.mengwang@gmail.com
⋆ Department of ECE, National University of Singapore, Singapore
eleyans@nus.edu.sg

ABSTRACT

Continuing advances in data storage and communication technologies have led to an explosive growth in digital music collections. To cope with their increasing scale, we need effective Music Information Retrieval (MIR) capabilities like tagging, concept search and clustering. Integral to MIR is a framework for modelling music documents and generating discriminative signatures for them. In this paper, we introduce a multimodal, layered learning framework called $DMCM$. Distinguished from the existing approaches that encode music as an ensemble of order-less feature vectors, our framework extracts from each music document a variety of acoustic features, and translates them into low-level encodings over the temporal dimension. From them, $DMCM$ elucidates the concept dynamics in the music document, representing them with a novel music signature scheme called Stochastic Music Concept Histogram ($SMCH$) that captures the probability distribution over all the concepts. Experiment results with two large music collections confirm the advantages of the proposed framework over existing methods on various MIR tasks.

Categories and Subject Descriptors

H.3.3 [**Information Search and Retrieval**]: Query formulation, Search process; H.5.5 [**Sound and Music Computing**]: Systems

General Terms

Algorithms, Design, Experimentation, Human Factors

Keywords

Music Information Retrieval, Similarity Measure, Music Concepts

1. INTRODUCTION

The past decade has witnessed a tremendous growth in the availability of digital music on various application platforms. At the same time, the pervasiveness of social media and affordability of home media servers are bringing about a fundamental change in the way people enjoy and share music. Indeed, online music distribution has overtaken physical media like compact discs [2, 6, 7, 13], becoming the dominant distribution channel with consumers. These trends call for Music Information Retrieval (MIR) capabilities for tagging (for example to enable browsing and faceted retrieval), searching by concepts (in a similar manner as text search), and clustering/classification (to automatically organize the music library). Underpinning these capabilities is an effective framework for modeling rich musical content, so as to generate signatures that capture the distinct characteristics of individual music documents.

While music modeling has been a long-standing research topic, substantial scope remains for further advances. To illustrate the challenges involved, consider the song "Bohemian Rhapsody" by Queen - a British rock band. There are six sections in the song: intro, balla, guitar solo, opera, hard rock and outro. At various points, the song is performed by different singers and features different musical instruments like piano and guitar. Moreover, its tempo speeds up mid-way through. In characterizing the song, at the acoustic level the importance of the timbral, spectral and rhythmic features would vary over time. On a semantic level, the concepts associated with segments of the song, like "tender", "comforting" and "romantic", also vary as shown in Figure 1 [1].

Due to those challenges, music modeling goes beyond extraction of acoustic features, to learning their inter-play and, from there, deducing semantic concepts. However, existing approaches in [28, 34, 35, 33, 17, 25, 23] simply represent a music document as a bag of audio features and directly apply machine learning techniques on the features. Surprisingly, less attention has been paid on modeling the interaction or association among musical features, subpieces and dependency between different levels of concept. Moreover, the free-patch representation ignores information about temporal dynamics and order, which has been proven to be very important for accurate music search and analysis.

In this paper, we postulate three principles for an effective music modeling framework. First, the framework should capture both low-level acoustic features and high-level concepts. Second, the acoustic features and concepts may exhibit non-linear dependencies. Effectively modeling the complex associations between different concepts can be very helpful in improving system performance. Third, the characteristics of a music document are likely to vary over the temporal dimension. Building on the principles, we introduce a new Dynamic Musical Concept Mixture ($DMCM$) framework to facilitate comprehensive music modelling. To account for temporal variations, the framework splits each music doc-

[1] The wave form is generated using Audacity.

Permission to make digital or hard copies of all or part of this work for personal or classroom use is granted without fee provided that copies are not made or distributed for profit or commercial advantage and that copies bear this notice and the full citation on the first page. To copy otherwise, to republish, to post on servers or to redistribute to lists, requires prior specific permission and/or a fee.
SIGIR'12, August 12–16, 2012, Portland, Oregon, USA.
Copyright 2012 ACM 978-1-4503-1472-5/12/08 ...$15.00.

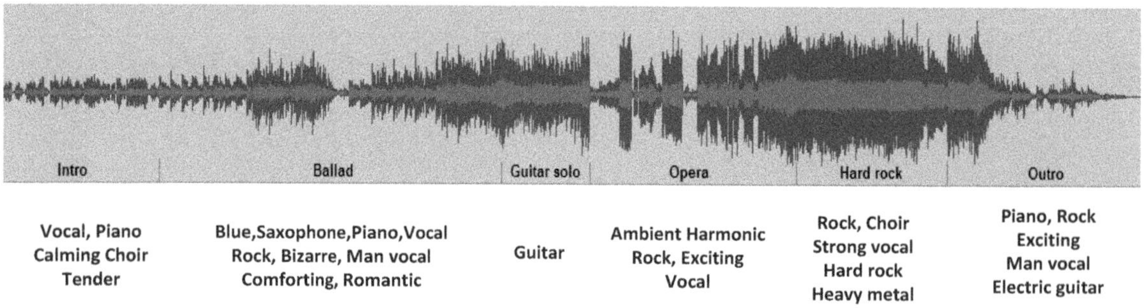

Figure 1: Various concepts related to song "Bohemian Rhapsody" by the British rock band Queen

ument by time into multiple segments, and derives a two-layer model for each segment:

- The *music preprocessing* layer extracts multiple acoustic features and maps them into an audio word from a pre-computed codebook.
- The *concept dynamics modeling* layer derives from the underlying audio words a Stochastic Music Concept Histogram ($SMCH$), essentially a probability distribution over the high-level concepts.

Thus, the music document is translated into a set of low-level audio words, and a corresponding set of high-level $SMCH$s. To the best of our knowledge, no prior work has adopted a similar approach as ours. To validate the effectiveness of the proposed framework, we have carried out a comprehensive set of experiment studies with two large music collections. A comparative analysis involving existing state-of-the-art methods confirms that our framework achieves substantial improvement in accuracy and robustness for various MIR tasks.

The rest of the paper is structured as follows: In Section 2, we review and analyze related work in the area of music signature generation. Their assumptions, limitations and application domains are discussed in detail. In Section 3, we introduce our feature extraction scheme and audio word generation process. Following that, Section 4 presents the proposed $DCMC$ framework. Section 5 reports our experiment configuration, including test collection, evaluation metrics and evaluation methodology. The experiment results are reported in Section 6. Finally, the article is concluded in Section 7.

2. LITERATURE REVIEW

Computing effective music signatures is an important but challenging problem. Various research communities have proposed approaches that built upon different musical features. They include textual labels for the title, performers, composers, style and symbolic representations of melody (e.g., MIDI and digital music scores). Due to space limitation, we focus on existing studies based on acoustic (content-based) features, which are the most relevant to our paper.

Music descriptor generation aims to derive effective content representation for information management or analysis applications (e.g., search, classification or tagging). While many systems exist for content-based speech recognition, there is much less effort on descriptive music feature extraction or modeling. Most of them directly treat low level spectral features as music signatures. Typical examples include the system developed by Nam and Berger [24], which applies three low-level acoustic features (spectral centroid, short time energy, and zero crossing rate) for automatic music genre classification. Another example is the work by Daudet [9] which applies pruned wavelet trees to model transients inside music signals. In [19], Lu et al. apply nine different audio features for audio classification. The feature set used in this study consists of MFCCs, zero crossing rates (ZCR), short time energy(STE), sub-band power distribution, brightness, bandwidth, spectrum flux (SF), band periodicity (BP) and noise frame ratio (NFR). Moreover, a support vector machine (SVM) is used for statistical classification. Tzanetakis et al. develop MARSYAS system - an advanced infrastructure for characterizing different acoustic properties of music signals [37]. The musical features extracted by MARSYAS include timbral texture, pitch content and rhythm. The features are combined linearly, and input to a SVM classifier. The study achieved a 61% classification accuracy on a small test collection.

More recently, Li et al. propose a DWCHs scheme to calculate Daubechies wavelet coefficients of music signal [16]. The key conjecture underlying the approach is that compared to conventional spectral analysis, a wavelet histogram technique is better able to capture both local and global temporal information inside the music signal. Their empirical results obtained on large scale test collections demonstrate that due to the wavelets' accurate summarization of the probability distribution over time and frequency domains, DWCHs outperforms MARSYAS with different machine learning classifiers for music genre classification.

The techniques described above rely on either one type of low level feature extracted using spectral analysis, or a linear concatenation of multiple acoustic features. It has been proven that such approaches generally do not produce a comprehensive and discriminative representation of music sequences. This is because the human auditory system senses and analyzes music sequences by integrating multiple characteristics in a nonlinear fashion. Consequently, any single type of acoustic feature is unlikely to contain sufficient information to represent the music effectively. Further, the acoustic features extracted from a music sequence are not weighted equally in human music perception and comprehension; in other words, the human hearing system gives different responses/weights to timber, rhythm and pitch. Thus, systems that assume a linear combination of acoustic features are inherently handicapped.

There is also an emerging stream of literature exemplified by Sheh et.al [27], Turnbull et.al [32] and Zhang et.al [39] that adopts statistical modeling to generate discriminative music descriptors from raw acoustic features. Shen et.al [30] develop the InMAF scheme, with a hybrid architecture that incorporates principal component analysis (PCA) and a multilayer perceptron neural network, to combine multiple musical properties in a nonlinear fashion. Experiment results obtained with two small data sets show its effectiveness and robustness against various kinds of audio alteration. Song et.al [31] propose a semi-supervised distance-based learning framework to integrate music features for genre classification.

Symbols	Definitions
$SMCH$	Stochastic music concept histogram
C	Total number of basic music concepts
S	Total number of music segments
R	Size of codebook
p_{cf}	Probability of music object belonging to concept c
$\Re^C$	Metric space generated by $SMCH$ with C dimensions
$\mathcal{M}$	A set of mappings modeled by $DMCM$
$\mathcal{CB}$	Audio codebook - a set of audio words
$\mathcal{T}$	A set of textual words to represent music concepts
$\mathcal{Z}$	A set of latent concepts
aw	Notation of audio word
$msim$	Notation of music similarity based on $SMCH$
A	Notation of feature for audio words
T	Notation of feature for textual words
P	A set of matching probabilities modelled by graph G
G	Notation of weighted bipartite graph for generative model
M	Notation of mapping between audio words and textual words
ϕ	Notation of kernel function for audio words
ϕ	Notation of kernel function for textual words
θ	Notation of system parameter for generative model

Table 1: Summary of symbols and definitions

Turnbull et.al [34, 35] propose a supervised multi-class labeling (SML) probabilistic scheme to generate semantic descriptors for large scale music retrieval; the framework builds upon GMMs. One of the common disadvantages suffered by the aforementioned methods is that feature vectors extracted from a music sequence are assumed to be independent and identically distributed (i.i.d.), and the music sequence is encoded as an ensemble of orderless feature vectors. Consequently, temporal dynamics in the music sequence are not accounted for properly. Motivated by the concerns, Coviello et.al [8] develop a dynamic texture model [10] to facilitate automatic music annotation and retrieval. It effectively accounts for not only temporal dynamics but also the timbral content in music. Experiment results obtained with the CAL500 dataset shows that the model improves the performance of music search and annotation significantly.

3. AUDIO WORD GENERATION

In this study, we represent audio features as a set of "audio words". To compute audio words to describe music sequences, raw input signal is firstly partitioned into several segments of equal length. From each segment, we extract five different kinds of features to form the low level music representation. They include timber, spectrum, rhythm, pitch and time as explained below.

- **Timbral features**: They characterize the timbral property of acoustic objects. In our system, short time Fourier transform is applied in the calculation. The timbral features computed include *Mel-Frequency Cepstral Coefficients* (MFCCs) [18], *Spectral Centroid, Rolloff, Flux, Low-Energy feature* [36], and *Spectral Contrast* [20]. The total dimensionality of the timbral features is 20.

- **Spectral features**: They characterize the spectral composition of music signal. In our implementation, each spectral feature vector contains *Auto-regressive (AR) features*; *Spectral Asymmetry, Kurtosis, Flatness, Crest Factors, Slope, Decrease, Variation*; *Frequency Derivative of Constant-Q Coefficients*; and *Octave Band Signal Intensities* [20]. The total dimensionality of these feature vectors is 20.

- **Rhythmic features**: They summarize the patterns of an acoustic object over a certain duration. The rhythmic features considered in this study include: *Beat Histogram* [36]; *Rhythm Strength, Regularity* and *Average Tempo* [20]. The total dimensionality is 12.

- **Wavelet features**: The wavelet transform provides a good scheme to divide raw signal into different frequency components over the temporal dimension. In our framework, the Daubechies wavelet filter with seven levels of decomposition is used for extracting a histogram of the wavelet coefficients at each subband [21]. For each subband, we compute the first three moments and the energy. Thus the dimensionality of the wavelet feature vectors is 28.

- **Time features**: Unlike traditional approaches, our system considers temporal coordinate information, which provides a more informative representation of local acoustic structure. Our time feature contains starting time, end time and the length of a sequence.

The k-mean algorithm is applied to cluster each of the feature spaces to form audio words [11]. The values of k are preconfigured to be 40 for timbral feature, 30 for spectral features, 35 for rhythmic features, 35 for wavelet features and 10 for time features. The whole process can be treated as a special transformation Φ:

$$\Phi_f : AF_f \rightarrow \boldsymbol{c}_f = \{c_{1f}, c_{2f}, ..., c_{kf}\}, \tag{1}$$

where c_{kf} denotes the centroid of cluster kf after k-means clustering on acoustic feature f. The audio word aw is defined as a sequence of audio feature cluster centroids and its representation is given as,

$$aw = [c_{ti}, c_r, c_{sp}, c_w, c_t] \tag{2}$$

where c_{ti}, c_r, c_{sp}, c_w, and c_t denote the cluster generated using timber feature, rhythm feature, spectral feature, wavelet feature and time feature respectively. Similar to keywords in text documents, we can construct an audio codebook $\mathcal{CB}$ containing R audio words,

$$\mathcal{CB} = \{aw_1, aw_2, ..., aw_R\} \tag{3}$$

where aw_r denotes audio word r in codebook $\mathcal{CB}$. In general, the music segments represented by the same set of audio words share certain levels of closeness and contain similar semantic concepts. Because huge variations are commonly encountered in raw music signal in practice, no existing scheme is able to group all the segments into one cluster based only on the temporal or (and) acoustic appearance. Thus, we employ the k-mean algorithm due to its simplicity and efficiency.

4. OUR METHOD

This section introduces a novel scheme to generate effective music descriptor for searching large scale music data collections. As depicted in Figure 2, the proposed system ($DMCM$) consists of two major components: 1) music preprocessing layer and 2) music concept modeling layer. In following sections, details of the system architecture and related algorithms are presented.

4.1 Music Preprocessing Layer

The key functionality of the music preprocessing layer is to calculate multiple acoustic features and project them onto an audio

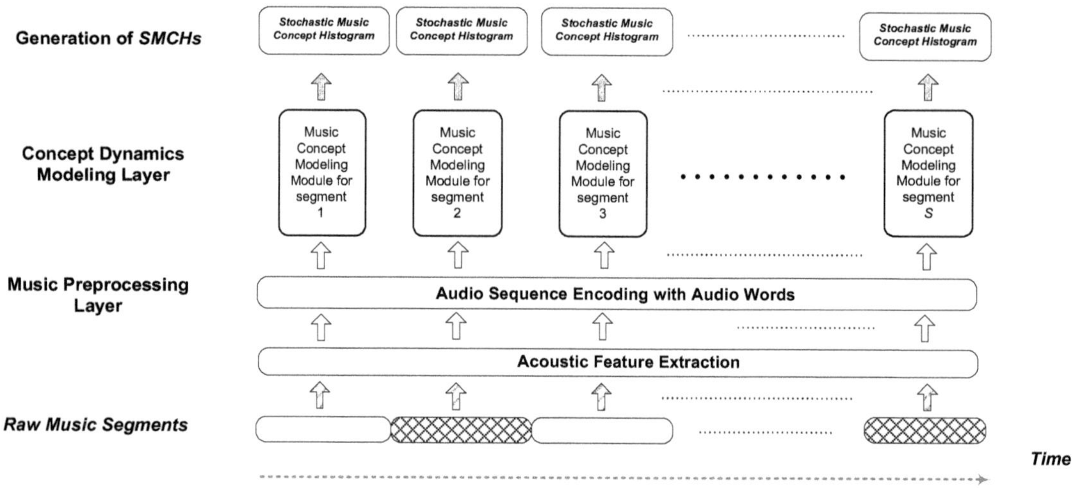

Figure 2: Architecture of the stochastic music concept modeling framework (DMCM). The output of this framework is a set of stochastic music concept histograms ($SMCH$s).

word from the codebook. Upon receiving the raw music signal, our system first decomposes it into multiple short segments with equal duration for the purpose of feature extraction. The number of segments S is preconfigured as a system parameter. Then, for each of the segments, based on four different kinds of features extracted, we find the most similar entry in the codebook and replace the index accordingly.

After this process, each input music is transformed into a sequence of indices or one-dimensional codes of audio words. The music document is now similar to a text document, which is a list of keywords. Under this paradigm, each music can be re-constructed by using the codebook of audio words.

4.2 Concept Dynamics Modeling Layer

The second layer of our system contains multiple music concept profiling modules developed based on generative learning principle. Each module corresponds to one music segment and outputs a stochastic music concept histogram - $SMCH$, describing the "probabilistic association" between the music and concepts at different levels. The set of $SMCH$s generated from this layer serves as signature of the input music for different MIR or content analysis applications. Before reviewing the architecture of this layer, we introduce the $SMCH$ music signature scheme.

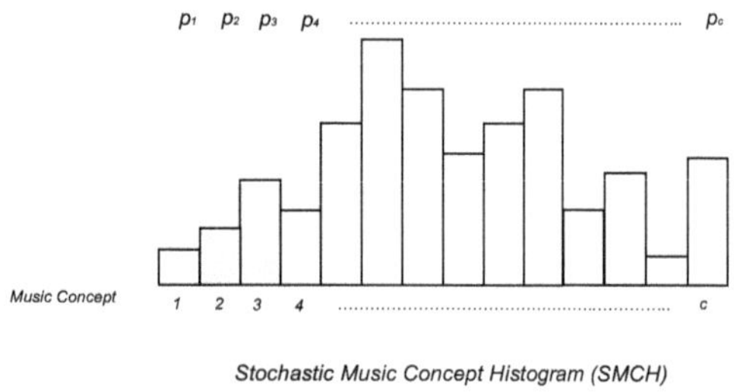

Figure 3: The structure of stochastic music concept histogram - $SMCH$

4.2.1 *Stochastic Music Concept Histogram*

Music concept representation is a crucial component of many music data management applications, including indexing, browsing, mining and retrieval. Here, we propose a unified scheme - stochastic music concept histogram ($SMCH$) as probabilistic representation of music documents. As demonstrated in Figure 3, it models the probability distribution of a music or a music segment over a set of predefined music concepts represented by audio words,

$$SMCH = \{p_1, p_2, ..., p_C\} \tag{4}$$

where $\sum_{c=1}^{C} p_c = 1$, C is the total number of musical concepts related to the music sequences, and p_c represents the probability of a given music object assigned to concept c. Since each $SMCH$ is a real-valued vector in metric feature space $\Re^C$, the distance between two music sequences ms_i and ms can be calculated using the normalized linear metric:

$$msim(SMCH_i, SMCH\ ) = \frac{\sum_{c=1}^{C} |p_{c\,i} - p_{c}\ |}{C} \tag{5}$$

where $msim(SMCH_i, SMCH\ ) \in [0, 1]$. The distance function for $SMCH$ enjoys the following properties,

- Positive definite: Given two music sequences ms_i and ms , $msim(SMCH_i, SMCH\ ) \geq 0$.
- Symmetry: Given two music sequences ms_i and ms , $msim(SMCH_i, SMCH\ ) = msim(SMCH\ , SMCH_i)$.
- Reflexivity: Given a music sequence ms , $vsim(SMCH\ , SMCH\ ) = 0$.
- Triangle inequality: Given three music sequences ms_i, ms and ms_l, $msim(SMCH_i, SMCH\ ) \leq msim(SMCH_i, SMCH_l) + msim(SMCH\ , SMCH_l)$.

For the properties shown above, the feature space based on $SMCH$ is a C-dimensional metric space $\Re^C$, and each $SMCH$ is a numeric vector in this space.

4.2.2 *Generative Model for Modelling Music Concepts*

The main goal of the multiclass probability estimation module is to derive a probabilistic distribution between a set of predefined

Algorithm 1 Generative Process to Learn Concept Mapping M.

Description:

1: Obtain prior about matching via sampling an n-to-1 mapping M;
2: **for** each matched edge (n, c) in graph G, where $n = 1, ..., N$ and c = $1, ..., C$:
3: Sample latent concept: $z_c \sim N(0, I_d)$, $\min\{d \ ,d \ \} \geq d \geq 1$
4: Sample features for audio words
5: $\phi \ (av_n) \sim N(W \ \ z_c + \mu \ \ , \Psi \ \ )$
6: Sample features for textual words
7: $\phi \ (t_c) \sim N(W \ \ z_c + \mu \ \ , \Psi \ \ )$
8: **for** each unmatched audio word n:
9: $\phi \ (av_n) \sim N(0, \sigma^2 I_{d_A})$
10: **for** each unmatched textual word c:
11: $\phi \ (t_c) \sim N(0, \sigma^2 I_{d_T})$

concepts (keywords) and a given music encoded with the audio codebook. In this study, we develop a generative model to facilitate the mapping process M based on canonical correlation analysis (CCA) [15].

As illustrated in Figure 4, the mappings M are treated as a weighted bipartite graph $G = (A, T, M, P)$. A and T are the feature vectors to describe audio words and textual keywords. For each audio word, we calculate the contextual feature - the co-occurrence counts of the word in neighboring music segments for audio words. Thus, we can generate a set of audio word feature vectors: $A = (av_1, ..., av_n)$, where $av_n \in \mathbb{R}^{d_A}$ for all n. To capture the text feature, the co-occurrence of different textual words is counted over the corpus. Hence we obtain a set of feature vectors $T = (t_1, ..., t_C)$ for C different music concept keywords. P is a set of the related probabilities (weights) estimated using the generative model. Given T and A, the learning process aims to derive an optimal mapping to translate words from the audio domain to a textual keyword (concept). It inputs feature matrices of the audio and textual words. **Algorithm 1** describes each step of the whole training process and the Figure 4 illustrates the abstract of the projection.

Different from the approach presented in [14], our algorithm samples an n-to-1 matching M from the prior mappings. We also restrict each audio word to occur only once but each text word can appear in multiple mapping pairs (line 1). The priors are assumed to be uniformly distributed. The approach underlying the learning algorithm is based on the probabilistic interpretation of CCA. It can be proved that the canonical correlation must be largest for the maximum likelihood estimates. Hence, a latent concept $z_c \sim N(0, I_d)$ can be generated for each matched edge (n, c) in the mapping M via sampling (line 3). I_d is a $d \times d$ identity matrix. Given the latent concept, samples of the audio words' feature vectors $\phi \ (aw)$ are drawn from a multidimensional Gaussian model with mean $W \ \ z_c + \mu$ and covariance Ψ (line 4 and line 5). W is a $d \ \ \times d$ matrix projecting concept z_c to the feature vector of audio words. A similar process is applied to the textual words (line 6 and line 7). Ψ and Ψ are covariance matrices to measure variations in two different domains. For unmatched words, we assume that the background distribution of audio and textual words can be used for mapping (line 8 - line 11).

4.2.3 Training Algorithm

Our training algorithm is developed on the principle of expectation-maximization (EM). It aims to find the maximum likelihood estimate via an iterative process. Given the statistical model introduced above, the log-likelihood of the training data is,

$$l(\theta) = log \sum_{M} p(av_n, t_c, M_{nc}|\theta) \tag{6}$$

where $\theta = (W \ \ , W \ \ , \Psi \ \ , \Psi \ \ )$ is a set of model parameters. The learning algorithm consists of two main steps,

- **E-step**: The posterior of all mappings is estimated by identifying the optimal n-to-1 mapping M in the graph G with weights P.
- **M-step**: Calculate the expected values of log-likelihood over all the possible pairs in the graph G. The weights P are updated with kernel Canonical Correlation Analysis (kCCA), which is trained on the best b mappings previously. In the first iteration of the EM estimation process, we do M-step computation using training matching pairs.

M-step: The goal of M-step is to optimize the values of θ so as to maximize the log-likelihood of all the mapping words from two different domains,

$$\max_{\theta} \sum_{(n \ \ c) \in M} logp(v_n, t_c, M_{nc}|\theta) \tag{7}$$

This learning goal is equivalent to maximizing the likelihood of the probabilistic KCCA model [3]. For two sets of samples, CCA seeks to find basis vectors which can (i) map the elements of the samples into the multidimensional space and (ii) maximize the correlation between sets of the projections. Because CCA is effective only for linear relationships, kCCA is applied to first project each data point into a multidimensional space with higher dimensionality, and CCA analysis is then carried out in the new feature space. Similar to kernel PCA [26], two kernels K and K are defined over A and T. With the kernels, the related function that we need to optimize is given by,

$$\max_{w_a \ w_t} \frac{w_a K \ \ K \ \ w_t}{\sqrt{w_a \ K^2 \ K^2 \ w_t}} \tag{8}$$

In order to avoid trivial learning, the process is regularized by introducing controlling the flexibility of the project. The partial least squares (PLS) is applied to penalized the norms of associated weights. Based on [4], a standard eigen problem can be obtained

$$\max_{w_a \ w_t} \frac{w_a K \ \ K \ \ w_t}{\sqrt{w_a \ K^2 \ K^2 \ w_t}} \tag{9}$$

E-step aims to calculate the expected value (posterior) over all the possible matching pairs in the graph G. It is easy to prove that the related computing process is P-complete [38]. Since the hard EM only needs to compute the b best mapping under the current model, we have:

$$M^{'} = \arg\max_{M_{1:b}} \log p(V, T, M|\theta) \tag{10}$$

where θ is current model parameter estimated for kCCA. The optimization process is casted as a maximum weighted bipartite matching problem. The goal is to project the vectors in two domains (audio and text) onto the latent space. Our system uses the Euclidean distance function to quantify similarity - $p_{a \ t}$ between the audio word a and textual word t. Meanwhile, $p_{a \ t}$ is interpreted as the matching probability or edge weight in the graph G for different pairs (a,t).

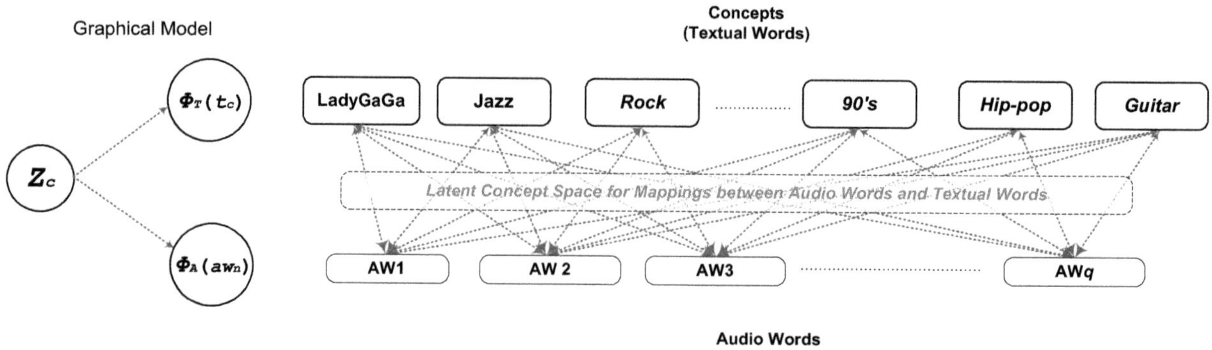

Figure 4: The goal of generative model is to derive the optimal mappings between audio words and various music concepts represented by textual words.

Algorithm 2 $SMCHs$ Computation

Description:

1: Divide the input song to S segments
2: Feature extraction over each music segment
3: Encode music with codebook
4: Calculate $SMCH$ for each segment using music concept modeling module in concept dynamics modeling layer
5: Output a set of $SMCHs$

$$p_{a\,t} = \|K\ (v_a)w_a - K\ (v_t)w_t\| \tag{11}$$

Using the equation, we calculate the matching probabilities for all possible mappings and find the best b pairs. Once the process is completed, we add the results into the kCCA learning examples and re-run the M-step. Our EM training procedure is similar to bootstrapping. Through iterations, the number of edges in graph G increases gradually. When the EM process stops, the matching probabilities obtained are used to compute $SMCH$.

4.3 Music Signature Generation with DMCM

The goal of $DMCM$ is to derive a set of $SMCHs$ to serve as signature of a given music. The $SMCHs$ can be applied in different MIR tasks. Using the system architecture introduced in the previous sections, we start with a training database where the codebook of audio words is generated. In the training stage, we process the songs in the database, extract features for each music and calculate the audio word codebook. Then, using **Algorithm 1** and the EM training procedure introduced above, we construct the concept dynamics modeling layer in our framework.

After the training phase, we proceed to compute the music signatures. The basic procedure is shown in **Algorithm 2** and consists of five main steps. For a given music item, the system initially partitions the input song into S segments (line 1). After that, the feature extraction procedure generates different kinds of features using the techniques described in Section 3 (line 2). Next, we apply the features to encode the input music sequence (line 3). A set of $SMCHs$ are calculated using the music concept modeling module in the second layer, one per generative model:

$$MSIG = \{SMCH_1, SMCH_2, ..., SMCH_S\} \tag{12}$$

where $SMCH_s$ is a set of the probabilities (weights) - P learned with the generative model for segment s.

5. EXPERIMENTAL CONFIGURATION

This section describes in detail our experiment configuration to facilitate large scale performance evaluation and comparison. First, an introduction of the evaluation metrics and methodology is given in Section 5.1. Next, Section 5.2 presents details of two different testbeds used in the empirical study. After that, the competing methods that are included in the performance comparison are introduced in Section 5.3. All the music descriptor generation schemes evaluated here have been fully implemented and tested on a Pentium (R) D, 3.20GHz, 1.98 GB RAM PC running the Windows XP operating system. The number of music segments in $DCMC$ is set to 20.

5.1 Evaluation Metrics and Methodology

Music signature generation is one of the most fundamental components in various kinds of MIR applications. In order to conduct a comprehensive performance comparison of different schemes, our proposed system and the competitors are tested and compared on three MIR related tasks. They are,

- Task I - Music tagging: For a given music sequence, how accurately different systems determine a set of recommended tags. We examine the quality of the tag sets with different number of tags (top 5 tags, top 10 tags, top 15 tags and top 20 tags). When applied to Task I, our proposed $DMCM$ first outputs a set of $SMCHs$, then the concept keywords (tags) with top k weights are selected as the tagging result.

- Task II - Music search (Content-based Music Retrieval): Using the music signature extracted from a query example, the system retrieves a list of music pieces from the database that are most similar. Here, the Euclidean distance function is used to quantify the similarity between two pieces of music. We examine the list of top-k results. k is set to 10 and 20.

- Task III - Music clustering: Based on the signature assigned to music clips, automatically cluster music documents. We apply the k-Means clustering algorithm due to its simplicity and efficiency [11, 22].

Two evaluation metrics are used for the music annotation task (Task I). They are mean per-tag precision and recall. The top 5, 10, 15, 20 and 25 tags are generated by the various systems for comparison. The per-tag recall and per-tag precision are formally given by

$$Precision = \frac{|t \quad _P|}{|t_G \quad |} \qquad Recall = \frac{|t \quad _P|}{|t \quad |} \tag{13}$$

where $|t_G \quad |$ is the number of songs annotated with the tags in the human-generated "ground truth" annotation and $t \quad _P$ is the number of music annotated correctly with the tags. A detailed explanation on how the "ground truth" information is generated will be given shortly.

To measure the performance of the various systems for music search (Task II), the mean average precision (MeanAP) and the area under the receiver operating characteristic curve (AROC) are adopted as assessment metrics. For comparing the performance of various clustering methods (Task III), the metric we used is the F-Measure F. The formula is given by

$$F = \frac{P \times R}{P + R} \tag{14}$$

where,

$$P = \frac{TP}{TP + FP} \qquad R = \frac{TP}{TP + FN} \tag{15}$$

TP is the true positive ratio, FP is the false positive ratio, and FN is the number of false negatives. In addition, to ensure result quality, tenfold cross validation is used to calculate the classification and clustering accuracy. This means the whole dataset is divided into ten disjoint subsets of (approximately) equal size. For testing, we train the algorithms on nine of the ten subsets and the remaining one is used for testing, each time leaving out a different subset. The process above is repeated for each system tested in our experiment study.

5.2 Music Testbeds

The test collections play a very important role in the empirical comparison study for MIR research. To ensure accuracy and fairness of the empirical results, we carefully develop or select two different test collections. Their details are as follows.

- TSI - This is the Computer Audition Lab 500-Song (CAL 500) data set developed by the CAL group [34, 35]. The collection consists of 500 modern western music documents performed by 500 different artists. Overall there are 174 'musically-relevant' tags categorized into six different semantic groups. They are mainly about instrumentation, vocal characteristics, genre, emotion, solo and usage terms. For this dataset, we use those six groups as high level musical concepts to train our statistical model. The text corpus used can be found in [1].

- TSII - As the size of the CAL500 data set is relatively small, we develop another test collection called TSII. It contains 6000 popular music items downloaded from Youtube or selected from the first author's CD collection. They are performed by 110 different singers, including 55 females and 55 males (such as Van Morrison, Michael Jackson, Elton John, Kylie Minogue, Madonna, Jennifer Lopez, Faith Hill, Lady Gaga etc.). We extract the lyrics of the songs and articles on the singers from Wikipedia and Last.fm as text corpus. 12 amateur musicians who are familiar with various music taxonomy and concepts were hired to create the ground truth for the tags in this collection. The ground truth was generated by attaching a tag to a music item if at least three people assigned the tag to the song. In cases where the respondents could not reach an agreement on a tag assignment, a similar resolution methodology as the one used in generating CAL500 is applied. At the end of the process, we obtain a total of 320 tags across 8 different categories. They are instrumentation, emotion, country, time, genre, vocal characteristics, speed, solo and usage terms.

Both TSI and TSII are used for testing the performance of different systems. TSII is applied for studying the performance of various signature generation schemes on music clustering and music search. For the purpose of acoustic feature extraction, we extract the audio tracks and convert them to 22050Hz, 16-bit, mono MP3 audio documents to ensure recording quality. The average length of the music clips is 120 seconds, the maximum length is 200 seconds and the shortest is about 100 seconds.

5.3 Competitors for Performance Comparison

For task I (music tagging), we compare the performance of our system against three state-of-the-art approaches including MMTagger [29], Autotagger [12, 5] and MSML [35, 34]. Acoustic feature considered by MSML is Mel-frequency cepstral coefficient (MFCC). Autotagger is evaluated based on three feature sets including MFCC delta, afeats and bfeats [2]. For MMTagger, we consider five low level feature configurations (timber features denoted by TF, rhythm features denoted by RF, spectral features denoted by SF, melody features denoted by MF and timber features+rhythm features+spectral features+melody features denoted by ALL.). Autotagger(MFCC delta), Autotagger(afeats) and Autotagger(bfeats) denote Autotagger with MFCC delta, afeats and bfeats respectively. MMTagger(TF), MMTagger(SF), MMTagger(MF), MMTagger(RF), MMTagger(ALL) denote our proposed model with timbral features, spectral features, rhythmic features, melody features and the combination of all four musical features.

To demonstrate the effectiveness of the music annotation generated by our system in search and clustering (Task II and Task III), we examine a wide range of methods for generating music descriptors, including CBIF [3], InMAF [30], DWCHs [16] and MARSYAS (denoted by MAR) [36].

6. EXPERIMENT RESULTS AND ANALYSIS

The music signatures generated by $DMCM$ are applicable to a wide range of MIR applications. This section presents a set of experiment studies to test and compare the performance of different systems on three MIR tasks including music tagging, music search and music clustering. How the systems are able to perform in a noisy environment is also evaluated.

6.1 On Music Tagging

In the first study, we test the performance of various tagging systems and $DMCM$ on the music tagging task. Table 2 and 3 report the empirical results of the systems with different feature configurations for the two testbeds. In this study, we test MMTagger and Autotagger with five and three feature settings respectively. The size of the tag set generated is configured to 10. The first row in both tables indicate how MSML performs on the tagging task using MFCC. Among the four systems tested, MSML demonstrates the lowest effectiveness. We believe there are two main reasons for the poor accuracy. Firstly, since music signals contain a rich set of acoustic features, effective music classification or annotation

[2][35] gives a detailed description of the feature sets.

[3]CBIF denotes the method proposed in [31].

cannot be achieved by considering only a single low-level acoustic feature. Moreover, the system does not consider temporal dynamics inside the music signal. Compared to MSML, Autotagger demonstrates a performance improvement though the accuracy gain is very limited. It is interesting to observe that MMTagger(SF) and MMTagger(MF) based on our learning framework could suffer from lower accuracies than Autotagger with certain acoustic feature configurations. This suggests the importance of music signature quality. On the other hand, the performance of MMTagger(ALL) is better than Autotagger using any feature combinations. A significant effectiveness gain ranging from 5% to 15% can be observed as different features are gradually integrated. The results clearly demonstrate that it is critical to combine features properly to achieve tagging effectiveness. The results obtained with both datasets clearly show that for the music tagging task, $DMCM$ significantly outperforms all the existing systems. For example, Table 2 shows that in comparison to MMTagger(ALL), our system achieves a precision gain of 0.351 to 0.413 for the CAL500 dataset, and 0.327 to 0.352 for the TSII collection. We also obtain similar improvements with the other two evaluation metrics.

Model	Precision	Recall
MSML	0.144	0.064
Autotagger(MFCC delta)	0.281	0.131
Autotagger(afeats)	0.266	0.094
Autotagger(bfeats)	0.291	0.153
MMTagger(ALL)	0.351	0.291
MMTagger(TF)	0.256	0.141
MMTagger(SF)	0.241	0.137
MMTagger(MF)	0.226	0.131
MMTagger(RF)	0.289	0.150
$DMCM$	**0.413**	**0.326**

Table 2: Comparison of tagging accuracy on test collection CAL500(TSI).

Model	Precision	Recall
MSML	0.121	0.043
Autotagger(MFCC delta)	0.257	0.102
Autotagger(afeats)	0.239	0.073
Autotagger(bfeats)	0.268	0.139
MMTagger(ALL)	0.327	0.241
MMTagger(TF)	0.231	0.117
MMTagger(SF)	0.220	0.116
MMTagger(MF)	0.207	0.103
MMTagger(RF)	0.262	0.125
$DMCM$	**0.352**	**0.278**

Table 3: Tagging accuracy on test collection TSII.

6.2 On Music Retrieval

Effective music retrieval is important in coping with the fast growth of online music data. The next study is to evaluate the performance of $DMCM$ and the competitors on the music search task. For a given music query, we use different methods to extract descriptors (feature vectors) and the system being evaluated retrieves a list of music pieces from the database that are most similar; the similarity is quantified by the distance between two descriptors with the Euclidean (l_2) distance function. We use MeanAP and MeanAROC as metrics to compare the rank list.

One of our key hypotheses for this study is that the more discriminative the information that is packed into the music signature, the more accurate the retrieval results will be. The experiments here are intended to validate the hypothesis. Table 4 summarizes the experiment results with TSII. It is clearly shown that MARSYAS which combines the feature vectors linearly demonstrates the worst performance on both metrics. Meanwhile, because DWCHs captures only low level acoustic musical properties, the related performance improvement is very marginal. Compared to DWCHs, both InMAF and CBIF take into account multiple kinds of acoustic features, which brings about substantial improvement in search effectiveness. Specifically, we observe an increase of at least 20.1% in MeanAP and 23.4% in MeanAROC. The results also show clearly that $DMCM$ leads to much better performance than the competitors, delivering around 10.9% and 23.3% improvement in MeanAP over CBIF and InMAF. The findings suggest that it is impossible to achieve accurate MIR without effectively combining musical features.

Model	MeanAP	MeanAROC
MARSYAS	0.204	0.381
DWCHs	0.267	0.423
InMAF	0.321	0.522
CBIF	0.357	0.549
$DMCM$	**0.396**	**0.591**

Table 4: Music retrieval accuracy comparison on test collection TSII.

Model	F-Measure
MARSYAS	0.314
DWCHs	0.367
InMAF	0.409
CBIF	0.433
$DMCM$	**0.524**

Table 5: Music clustering accuracy comparison on test collection TSII (Task - Artist based clustering).

Model	MeanAP			MeanAROC		
	CL	NO	DR	CL	NO	DR
MARSYAS	0.204	0.161	21.3%	0.381	0.294	22.7%
DWCHs	0.267	0.213	20.4%	0.423	0.332	21.3%
InMAF	0.321	0.275	14.2%	0.522	0.441	15.5%
CBIF	0.357	0.308	13.5%	0.549	0.473	13.7%
$DMCM$	**0.396**	**0.355**	**10.2%**	**0.591**	**0.524**	**11.3%**

Table 6: Music retrieval robustness comparison on test collection TSII. Noise type - 50% volume amplification.

6.3 On Music Clustering

Accurate music clustering process has become increasingly important for different MIR applications. Our main objective in the third study is to examine the accuracy of clustering based on the music descriptors generated by $DMCM$ versus the other approaches. We perform the performance comparison with artist based music clustering.

Table 5 shows how the various systems perform on the clustering task. Clearly, our proposed $DMCM$ significantly outperforms all the other approaches in effectiveness. In particular, the results reveal that $DMCM$ enjoys an 21% increase in F-Measure over

Model	MeanAP			MeanAROC		
	CL	NO	DR	CL	NO	DR
MARSYAS	0.204	0.171	20.3%	0.381	0.292	23.1%
DWCHs	0.267	0.221	19.4%	0.423	0.335	20.7%
InMAF	0.321	0.287	15.3%	0.522	0.448	14.1%
CBIF	0.357	0.312	14.5%	0.549	0.482	12.1%
$DMCM$	**0.396**	**0.356**	**10.0%**	**0.591**	**0.533**	**9.7%**

Table 7: Music retrieval robustness comparison on test collection TSII. Noise type - 50% volume deamplification.

Model	MeanAP			MeanAROC		
	CL	NO	DR	CL	NO	DR
MARSYAS	0.204	0.154	24.3%	0.381	0.298	21.9%
DWCHs	0.267	0.205	22.9%	0.423	0.327	22.7%
InMAF	0.321	0.269	16.2%	0.522	0.446	14.6%
CBIF	0.357	0.302	15.5%	0.549	0.478	12.9%
$DMCM$	**0.396**	**0.350**	**11.7%**	**0.591**	**0.539**	**10.9%**

Table 8: Music retrieval robustness comparison on test collection TSII. Noise type - 10 second cropping.

Model	MeanAP			MeanAROC		
	CL	NO	DR	CL	NO	DR
MARSYAS	0.204	0.142	25.3%	0.381	0.298	22.9%
DWCHs	0.267	0.201	24.9%	0.423	0.333	21.2%
InMAF	0.321	0.272	15.2%	0.522	0.440	15.7%
CBIF	0.357	0.312	12.5%	0.549	0.471	14.2%
$DMCM$	**0.396**	**0.358**	**9.7%**	**0.591**	**0.531**	**10.1%**

Table 9: Music retrieval robustness comparison on test collection TSII. Noise type - 35dB SNR mean background noise.

Model	MeanAP			MeanAROC		
	CL	NO	DR	CL	NO	DR
MARSYAS	0.204	0.139	24.1%	0.381	0.299	21.5%
DWCHs	0.267	0.189	22.9%	0.423	0.336	20.5%
InMAF	0.321	0.242	14.2%	0.522	0.447	14.3%
CBIF	0.357	0.310	13.1%	0.549	0.472	13.9%
$DMCM$	**0.396**	**0.354**	**10.5%**	**0.591**	**0.533**	**9.7%**

Table 10: Music retrieval robustness comparison on test collection TSII. Noise type - 35dB SNR white background noise.

CBIF. The gain of $DMCM$ over InMAF is even more pronounced, averaging around 24%. We believe the performance gains arise because $DMCM$ generates an effective combination of information on different acoustic features and musical dynamics, resulting in discriminative and informative signatures for the music signals.

6.4 Robustness against Audio Noise

The human hearing system possesses the robust capability to sense and identify music even in a noisy environment. This capability is very useful for real life MIR applications, where the music signals may be mixed with noise signals. Typical examples include music recorded at live concerts or at other outdoor environments. However, very few existing schemes are designed to deal with inputs that are accompanied by distortions. Thus it is important for us to evaluate the robustness of the various systems against noises. We also wish to examine how different types of audio noise may influence the music retrieval process supported by $DMCM$ and other music signature generation methods. For this study, we pollute each query music with different kinds of audio distortions. Then we carry out experiments to test the corresponding retrieval performance of our system and the competitors. We run same set of tests in Section 6.2 on TSII. In this study, we consider five different distortion cases including 50% volume amplification, 50% volume deamplification, 10 second cropping, 35dB SNR mean background noise and 35dB SNR white background noise [4].

Tables 6-10 summarize the search accuracy of the five systems for the various audio distortion cases. CL and NO denote the search accuracies obtained under clean input and noisy input, respectively. DR is the search accuracy drop ratio between clean music input and input containing noise. From the results, we observe that generally all the systems suffer certain levels of accuracy loss with noisy input. However, $DMCM$ performs more robustly than the competitors over all the noise cases. For example, $DMCM$'s MeanAP experiences a 10.2% drop when the music inputs are polluted with 50% volume amplification. In comparison, the MeanAP ratio of InMAF and CBIF decrease about 14.2% and 13.5% respectively. Moreover, in the case of 35dB SNR mean background noise, $DMCM$ only loses 10.1% in MeanAROC whereas performance degradation of 15.7% and 14.2% are observed for InMAF and CBIF. For MARSYAS and DWCHs, the performance gaps are even much wider. Thus, we conclude that $DMCM$ emerges as the more robust scheme against noise and acoustic distortion.

7. CONCLUSION

As an enabling technology for large scale MIR, music signature generation has received a lot of attention in recent years, with many different proposed approaches. Notwithstanding that, the technology is still in its infancy as the reported effectiveness are existing schemes are generally poor. The main reasons for this stagnation include 1) the lack of advanced techniques to intelligently combine multimodal and temporal information and 2) the unavailability of a comprehensive classification scheme to systematically bridge the gap between different levels of semantics. In this paper, we report a novel framework called $DMCM$ that incorporates an advanced feature extraction scheme and a composite system architecture for comprehensive music signature generation. Our system architecture contains two basic modules - 1) music preprocessing module and 2) concept dynamics modelling module in the form of an advanced two-layer classification scheme. A comprehensive empiri-

[4]We use $SNR_{dB} = 10log_{10}\frac{Si}{No}$ to calculate the signal-to-noise ratio SNR_{dB}, where Si denotes the signal power, and No denotes the noise power in dB.

cal study involving two large music collections has been conducted to compare our framework with competing methods on various MIR tasks. The experiment results show that our framework leads to significant improvements in accuracy, robustness and scalability on the MIR tasks.

The current study can be extended in several directions for further investigation: One of biggest advangtages enjoyed by $DMCM$ is the use of multiple feature about both acoustic characteristics and temporal dynamics from music. This results in more comprehensive statistical models and hence a better modelling effectiveness. One question naturally raised is how much each of these factors contributes towards accuracy and robustness improvement. In the future, we plan to have a detailed study. Further, applying the method on data from other application domains would be also very interesting.

8. REFERENCES

[1] Cal500 data set annotation, 2007. `http://cosmal.ucsd.edu/cal/pubs/annotations.txt`.

[2] Nielsen company & billboard's 2011 music industry report. *Business Wire*, 5 January 2012.

[3] F. Bach and M. I. Jordan. *A Probabilistic Interpretation of Canonical Correlation Analysis*. Technical Report 688, Department of Statistics, University of California, Berkeley, 2005.

[4] F. R. Bach and M. I. Jordan. Kernel independent component analysis. *Journal of Machine Learning Research*, 3:1–48, 2002.

[5] T. Bertin-Mahieux, D. Eck, F. Maillet, and P. Lamere. Autotagger: A model for predicting social tags from acoustic features on large music databases. *Journal of New Music Research*, 37(2), 2008.

[6] S. Bhattacharjee, R. D. Gopal, K. Lertwachara, and J. R. Marsden. Consumer search and retailer strategies in the presence of online music sharing. *J. of Management Information Systems*, 23(1), 2006.

[7] S. Bhattacharjee, R. D. Gopal, K. Lertwachara, J. R. Marsden, and R. Telang. The effect of digital sharing technologies on music markets: A survival analysis of albums on ranking charts. *Management Science*, 53(9), 2007.

[8] E. Coviello, A. B. Chan, and G. Lanckriet. Time series models for semantic music annotation. *IEEE Trans. on Audio, Speech & Language Processing*, 19(5), 2011.

[9] L. Daudet. Transients modeling by pruned wavelet trees. In *Proc. of International Computer Music Conference*, 2001.

[10] G. Doretto, A. Chiuso, Y. N. Wu, and S. Soatto. Dynamic textures. *International Journal of Computer Vision*, 51(2), 2003.

[11] R. Duda, P. Hart, and D. Stork. *Pattern Classification*. John Wiley and Sons, 2001.

[12] D. Eck, P. Lamere, T. Bertin-Mahieux, and S. Green. Automatic generation of social tags for music recommendation. In *Proc. of NIPS*, 2007.

[13] H. Green. Kissing off the big music labels. *Businessweek*, 2004.

[14] A. Haghighi, P. Liang, T. Berg-Kirkpatrick, and D. Klein. Learning bilingual lexicons from monolingual corpora. In *Proc. of ACL*, 2008.

[15] D. R. Hardoon, S. Szedmak, and J. Shawe-Taylor. *Canonical Correlation Analysis; An Overview with Application to Learning Methods*. Technical Report CSD-TR-03-02, Computer Science Dept. Royal Holloway, University of London, 2003.

[16] T. Li, M. Ogihara, and Q. Li. A comparative study on content-based music genre classification. In *Proc. of ACM SIGIR*, 2003.

[17] W. Li, Y. Liu, and X. Xue. Robust audio identification for mp3 popular music. In *Proc. of ACM SIGIR*, 2010.

[18] B. Logan. Mel frequency cepstral coefficients for music modeling. In *Proc. of ISMIR*, 2000.

[19] L. Lu, S. H. Li, and J. Zhang. Content-based audio segmentation using support vector machines. In *Proc. of IEEE ICME*, 2001.

[20] L. Lu, D. Liu, and H. Zhang. Automatic mood detection and tracking of music audio signals. *IEEE Trans. Acoust., Speech, Signal*, 2006.

[21] S. Mallat. *A Wavelet Tour of Signal Processing*. Acadamic PressAcademic Press, 3rd edition, 2008.

[22] C. D. Manning, P. Raghavan, and H. Schütze. *Introduction to Information Retrieval*. Cambridge University Press, 2008.

[23] R. Miotto and N. Orio. A probabilistic model to combine tags and acoustic similarity for music retrieval. *ACM Trans. Inf. Syst.*, 30(2), May 2012.

[24] U. Nam and J. Berger. Addressing the same but different-different but similar problem in automatic music classification. In *Proc. of ISMIR*, 2001.

[25] C. Sanden and J. Zhang. Enhancing multi-label music genre classification through ensemble techniques. In *Proc. of ACM SIGIR*, 2011.

[26] B. Scholkopf and A. J. Smola. *Learning with Kernels*. MIT Press, 2002.

[27] A. Sheh and D. Ellis. Chord segmentation and recognition using em-trained hidden markov models. In *Proc. of ISMIR*, 2003.

[28] J. Shen, B. Cui, J. Shepherd, and K. Tan. Towards efficient automated singer identification in large music databases. In *Proc. of ACM SIGIR*, 2006.

[29] J. Shen, W. Meng, S. Yan, H. Pang, and X. Hua. Effective music tagging through advanced statistical modeling. In *Proc. of ACM SIGIR*, 2010.

[30] J. Shen, J. Shepherd, and A. H. H. Ngu. Towards effective content-based music retrieval with multiple acoustic feature combination. *IEEE Trans. on Multimedia*, 8(6), 2006.

[31] Y. Song and C. Zhang. Content-based information fusion for semi-supervised music genre classification. *IEEE Trans. on Multimedia*, 10(1), 2008.

[32] D. Turnbull, L. Barrington, and G. Lanckriet. Modeling music and words using a multi-class naïve bayes approach. In *Proc. of ISMIR*, 2006.

[33] D. Turnbull, L. Barrington, G. R. G. Lanckriet, and M. Yazdani. Combining audio content and social context for semantic music discovery. In *Proc. of ACM SIGIR*, 2009.

[34] D. Turnbull, L. Barrington, D. Torres, and G. Lanckriet. Towards musical query-by-semantic-description using the CAL500 data set. In *Proc. of ACM SIGIR*, 2007.

[35] D. Turnbull, L. Barrington, D. Torres, and G. Lanckriet. Semantic annotation and retrieval of music and sound effects. *IEEE Trans. on Audio, Speech & Language Processing*, 16(2), 2008.

[36] G. Tzanetakis and P. Cook. Musical genre classification of audio signals. *IEEE Trans. on Speech and Audio Processing*, 2002.

[37] G. Tzanetakis, A. Ermolinskyi, and P. Cook. Pitch histograms in audio and symbolic music information retrieval. *Journal of New Music Research*, 2003.

[38] L. G. Valiant. The complexity of computing the permanent. *Theoretical Computer Science*, 8, 1995.

[39] B. Zhang, J. Shen, Q. Xiang, and Y. Wang. Compositemap: a novel framework for music similarity measure. In *Proc. of ACM SIGIR*, 2009.

Finding Translations in Scanned Book Collections

Ismet Zeki Yalniz
Dept. of Computer Science
University of Massachusetts
Amherst, MA, 01003
zeki@cs.umass.edu

R. Manmatha
Dept. of Computer Science
University of Massachusetts
Amherst, MA, 01003
manmatha@cs.umass.edu

ABSTRACT

This paper describes an approach for identifying translations of books in large scanned book collections with OCR errors. The method is based on the idea that although individual sentences do not necessarily preserve the word order when translated, a book must preserve the linear progression of ideas for it to be a valid translation. Consider two books in two different languages, say English and German. The English book in the collection is represented by the sequence of words (in the order they appear in the text) which appear only once in the book. Similarly, the book in German is represented by its sequence of words which appear only once. An English-German dictionary is used to transform the word sequence of the English book into German by translating individual words in place. It is not necessary to translate all the words and this method works even with small dictionaries. Both sequences are now in German and can, therefore, be aligned using a Longest Common Subsequence (LCS) algorithm. We describe two scoring functions TRANS-cs and TRANS-its which account for both the LCS length and the lengths of the original word sequences. Experiments demonstrate that TRANS-its is particularly successful in finding translations of books and outperforms several baselines including metadata search based on matching titles and authors. Experiments performed on a Europarl parallel corpus for four language pairs, English-Finnish, English-French, English-German, English-Spanish, and a scanned book collection of 50K English-German books show that the proposed method retrieves translations of books with an average MAP score of 1.0 and a speed of 10K book pair comparisons per second on a single core.

Categories and Subject Descriptors

H.3.3 [**Information Storage and Retrieval**]: Information Search and Retrieval; H.3.7 [**Digital Libraries**]: Collection, Systems Issues

General Terms

Algorithms, Experimentation

Keywords

Translation detection, sequence alignment, unique words, book collections

Permission to make digital or hard copies of all or part of this work for personal or classroom use is granted without fee provided that copies are not made or distributed for profit or commercial advantage and that copies bear this notice and the full citation on the first page. To copy otherwise, to republish, to post on servers or to redistribute to lists, requires prior specific permission and/or a fee.
SIGIR'12, August 12–16, 2012, Portland, Oregon, USA.
Copyright 2012 ACM 978-1-4503-1472-5/12/08 ...$10.00.

1. INTRODUCTION

This paper describes an approach to finding translations of documents which are long and noisy - specifically scanned books with OCR errors in large collections such as the Internet Archive (IA) or Google Books. However, it is also applicable to documents produced by governments and companies.

Finding translations is useful for many reasons. It will enable search engines to display translated versions of a book as part of the results so that for example a Spanish reader may choose a Spanish version of Goethe's Faust. By finding translations one can create parallel corpora for creating better machine translation algorithms and for cross-lingual search systems. The humanities and library communities have a great interest in aggregating works and finding translated versions of books such as Goethe's Faust. IFLA's Functional Requirements for Bibliographic Records (FRBR) requires that the next generation of cataloging systems include works aggregation [22]. This will include information on which books are translated versions of each other. However, no specific technique is proposed to do the FRBRization and it is implicitly assumed that metadata will be sufficient. Experiments show that metadata is not accurate enough to always determine which books are translations.

There are two distinct problems in the context. The first problem, which is the focus of this paper, is to decide whether given two books are translations of each other and to do it for all book pairs in the collection. Given that most book pairs are not translations, comparing all book pairs can be expensive since there are $O(nm)$ distinct book pairs in collection of n books in one language and m books in the other. Hence, there is a need for an efficient approach. The second problem is to map the portions of translated text between any two books in different languages. This is not the focus of this paper although we provide Figure 1 to illustrate translated portions of two example books.

Books and translations of books have many interesting characteristics. Books are usually much longer than web documents. Texts obtained from scanned books have also character recognition errors - in some cases substantial - and

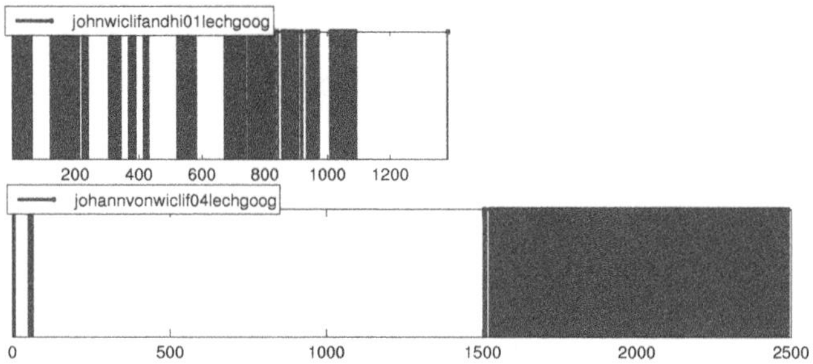

Figure 1: The figure shows the approximate overlap between an English translation (upper bar) and the German original (lower bar) as determined by a global alignment algorithm. The lengths of the bars reflect the relative sizes of the two books. Blue (black) denotes aligned portions. The German version contains the complete text while the English version is only Volume II and hence the big gap in the lower bar. The English version has additional notes and these are reflected by the gaps in the upper bar.

any algorithm must cope with them. Most translations do not have one-to-one overlap. Figure 1 shows the automatically generated overlap between Wiclif's biography in the original German and a translated version in English which only includes volume 2 with additional notes[1]. The figure shows that only a portion of the two texts overlap.

One approach is to use the book metadata to find translations of books. Our experience, however, is that metadata entries can be erroneous and therefore they are not completely reliable. This approach, therefore, does not solve the problem as discussed further in the experiments section. There are several types of errors in the metadata of scanned books. First of all, the language of books are often specified incorrect. In a test collection of 378 books, the language of several books was incorrectly specified - they are marked as English even though they are clearly in German or vice versa. Books written in multiple languages are typically not clarified too. There are books marked as English although they are in German with an English preface and/or notes. Even if the metadata is correct, it is sometimes not easy to tell whether two books are translations or not. Quite often titles do not translate exactly to other languages. Even though two books have the same title after translation, the translated version may have only the translator's or editor's name as the author. Metadata entries are manually entered to the system by the people who scan books, therefore the process is error prone. A similar problem does also exist for different Wikipedia articles. While some articles are direct translations of each other, many articles with the same title are actually written by different authors and therefore they are not translations. Therefore, Wikipedia articles can not be used for building translation detection corpora since the ground truth is not clear.

Techniques have been previously suggested for finding near

[1]The figure is generated as follows: the words which appear more than 20 times in the entire text are filtered out in both books. The remaining words in the English book are translated in place to German using a word dictionary and aligned with the remaining words in the German book using LCS. For visualization purposes we use a binning approach where each bin in the figure is colored blue (black) if there are more than a specified amount of matching words in the range. The bin size is 100 words and the horizontal axis shows the number of bins for each book.

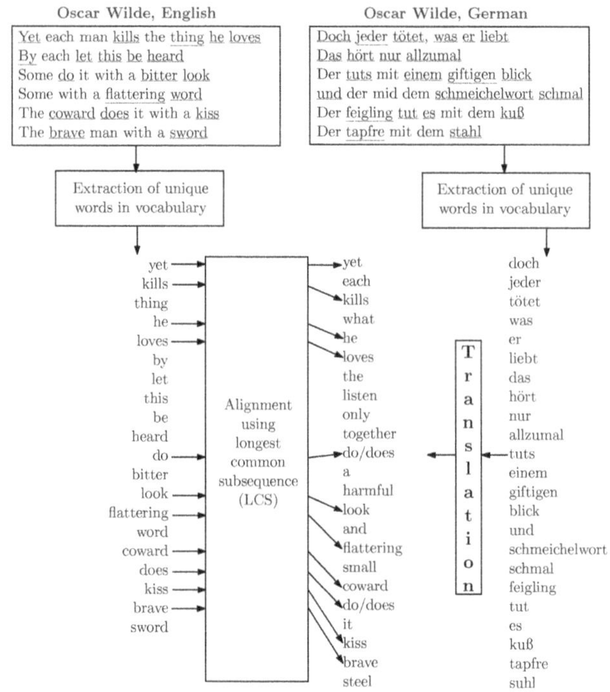

Figure 2: Illustration of the proposed framework. Unique words are underlined for two versions of a poem by Oscar Wilde. Unique words from the German version are first translated in to English using a dictionary. The resulting word sequence is aligned with the unique words extracted from the English version using LCS. The words in the LCS are indicated with single headed arrows. It is seen that a large number of words follow the same order in both sequences. This is a clear indication for texts being translations.

duplicates in the same language using shingling (n-gram overlap) [4, 5] or even partial duplicates using the alignment of "unique words" [30]. The applicability of such techniques to translation detection is not trivial. Word order is not usually preserved across languages and hence translations of individual words in a book using a dictionary do not preserve n-grams of words. Thus, traditional shingling techniques are not directly applicable for translation detection. In addition most free dictionaries available online are small. For example, the largest English-German dictionary available to us has 62K entries while a desktop edition of Merrian Webster's Collegiate dictionary has 225K entries. Due to the fact that morphological variants of words are often not found in small size dictionaries, less words get translated. Another option is to use a machine translation system to translate all the books to a common language and apply mono-lingual duplicate detection techniques as Uszkoreit et al. [29] used at Google. However, this approach requires building robust translation systems for each language and the actual translation stage is computationally expensive. Given that most researchers and organizations do not have Google's computational resources, a more practical solution is needed. Krstovski and Smith [19] use hapax words, i.e., words which are common between two different languages, to identify translation pairs in scanned book collections. They adopt a vector space representation for books and use Cosine distance as the translational similarity metric. The weakness of this approach is that there is no guarantee there exists hapax words between all pairs books. Their results also indicate that their approach fail for languages with different language families, such as English and Arabic.

To detect translations we exploit the fact that a translation must preserve the long range order of events and/or ideas. That is, chapter 5 must precede chapter 6 in both English and German versions of "The Lord of the Rings" even though individual sentences (and even paragraphs) do not preserve the word order across languages. Inspired by the work on mono-lingual partial duplicate detection of [30], we show that the sequence of words which occur only once in a book is sufficient to identify translations of books. Consider two books in two different languages, say English and German. The first step is to extract the sequence of words which occur only once in both books. Those words are referred as *unique words*. An English-German dictionary is used to transform the word sequence of the English book into German by translating individual words in place. Many words may end up being not translated since they do not exist in the dictionary. Some words may have multiple translations which are all included in the translated sequence. It turns out that a small fraction of the words being translated is sufficient for our purposes. Hapax words which are common in both sequences (examples of such words may include names which are not translated) are also included in the translated sequence. The resulting sequence is now in German and therefore can be compared with other German books. Comparison is performed using global alignment, specifically Longest Common Subsequences (LCS) algorithm. The length of LCS is a clear indication of translations. Two scoring functions are proposed: TRANS-cs and TRANS-its which normalize the LCS length by the length of the sequences in different ways. See Figure 2 for an illustrative example of our methodology.

Experiments performed on non-noisy EUROPARL documents for several languages and collections of real scanned book collections demonstrate that TRANS-its is very effective and fast in identifying translations. Three different evaluation measures are defined and very high performance scores are obtained for four language pairs of the EUROPARL dataset. English-Finnish experiments show that the technique works across language families. The technique also works on the noisy OCR output of scanned books as well. On a scanned book corpus of 2K English-German books, precision and recall score of 1.0 are achieved (outperforms Krstovski and Smith's method [19]). Retrieval experiments including a scanned book collection of size 50K indicate that TRANS-its achieves a MAP of 1.0. We compare our results to several baselines including metadata search and show that TRAN-its outperforms the baselines over all evaluation metrics. The proposed method is also quite scalable. With simple optimizations, it is seen that TRANS-its compares 10K books per second on a single core.

In the next section, we discuss the related work on translation identification and also provide a brief discussion on mono-lingual duplicate detection methods. Section 3 explains the proposed translation identification framework along with the unique word representation and the scoring functions. Evaluation measures, datasets and experiments are described next. Finally, conclusions are given along with future research directions.

2. RELATED WORK

The related problem of near duplicate detection in the same language has been well discussed especially for web documents. Most of the work uses either fingerprinting algorithms or relative frequency techniques (words with similar frequencies) [4]. Fingerprint techniques [4, 5] divide a document into distinctive chunks or shingles. The standard approach is to use n-grams of words or characters and subsample them using a variety of sampling techniques [14]. Relative frequency techniques assume that two documents with similar words and frequencies must be similar or duplicated [14, 27]. We note that n-grams are not well preserved across languages since word order in a sentence can change across translations. [30] find partial duplicates in collections of books by finding sequences of unique words and then aligning these sequences of unique words. However, their work is restricted to books in the same language. Our work is inspired by their approach.

There has been work on finding comparable corpora for machine translation. Much of this work has been done on either finding parallel sentences from small corpora [28] or web pages [23, 26, 28, 32]. Most of the work on finding web page has utilized structural information - HTML markup such anchors, links, filenames - to find [23, 26] parallel resources. Alignment was specifically rejected as being too expensive. [32] limited the alignment to titles and a translation dictionary to find parallel texts. Much of the machine translation work seems to be on the extraction of bilingual dictionaries [11] rather than finding document translations in large corpora. [28] is one of the few papers on identifying translations. The paper used several translation dictionaries and then computed the word overlap. Filtering was done based on document length for efficiency. The method was tested on a small dataset of about 1000 sentence pairs and another dataset of 325 web document pairs. [25] combined structural and content features to mine web pages for parallel corpora. [21] also used structural features paired with a content filtering scheme to find parallel corpora on the web. [18] used the idea that similar texts would have similar graph structures after compression to find translations of portions of texts.

Uszkoreit et al. [29] is one of two papers to find translations of books. They use Google's large computing resources to translate all the books in the collection to English. This transforms the problem of finding translations to monolingual duplicate detection. Next, they match chunks (n-grams) of words in translated texts to determine translation pairs. One drawback of this approach is that it requires building machine translation systems for all languages and translation of books is computationally expensive. Ideally, one should be able to find translations of books without having to translate them explicitly. The success of their approach is evaluated partially on a small dataset. Uszkoreit et al.'s method is further discussed in the experiments section. Krstovski and Smith [19] use words which are common between translations of books to find translations of books. Each book is represented in the vector space and the translational similarities between books are defined by several distance measures such as Cosine distance. They use Locality Sensitive Hashing (LSH) to efficiently compute the translational similarity scores. Our technique is compared to their approach on the publicly available datasets and we demonstrate that our approach is more accurate.

There has been extensive work on mono-lingual and cross-lingual plagiarism detection. Global alignment methods have been used to find plagiarized passages in the same language [7] but it is impractical for long documents and large collections. Most plagiarism detection techniques instead use a prefiltering stage which involves chunk overlap to detect possible duplicates before the global alignment [9]. Sequence alignment, word sampling and variants of chunking methods have also been tried for cross-lingual plagiarism detection. Please refer to [24] for a recent survey of those methods. It should be noted that cross-lingual plagiarism and translation detection for scanned book collections are different problem domains. Scanned book collections include very long documents with severe amount of OCR errors which prohibit the use of conventional approaches.

3. OUR FRAMEWORK

The first stage of our framework is to identify the language of each book in the collection. This stage can be removed in case the languages of books is known reliably. The second stage involves extracting unique word sequences from all the books. This process is performed once for each book in the collection. In the final stage, all the book pairs between the source and target languages are aligned using Longest Common Subsequences. A translation score is calculated for each book pair based on the length of the LCS. This score is later used for classification and ranking of translation pairs. The details of each stage are elaborated in the following subsections.

3.1 Language Identification

Translation identification require that the language of the book be known. One approach to detect the language is to use the metadata, which is not always reliable. Language identification has been done in the past using stopwords and letter bigrams/trigrams. While letter bigrams/trigrams tend to be more accurate for short passages, on longer texts stopword counts work equally well [12]. Here we use the stopword approach to determine the language of the book. Stopwords for each language (English, French, German, Greek, Italian, Latin and Spanish) are learned from 20 noise free e-books downloaded from the Gutenberg archive. The top five most frequent stopwords are used. A stopword is appropriate for language identification as long as it is not a stopword in another language. This approach makes the language identification process simple, fast and easily generalizable for other languages. A more accurate check on OCR errors can be done using a dictionary but this would be slower and more expensive to create. Note that this technique may fail if the book has high rates of OCR errors which corrupts a large proportion of stopwords. A quick check on a mix of 378 English-German books reveals an accuracy of 100%.

3.2 Extraction of Unique Words

Each book in the collection is represented by the sequence of words which appear only once in the entire text of the book. In this context these words are referred as "unique words". This sequence of unique words is highly descriptive of the content and flow of ideas in the book. This representation is quite compact. There are are typically a few thousands of unique words for a book of size 100K words. The number of unique words increase as the amount of document noise and the length of the text increases. In a non-noisy book, every second sentence of the document is expected to contain a unique word. The unique word representation is highly tolerant to OCR errors for duplicate and translation detection purposes.

Punctuation and numeric characters are ignored at all stages. This also eliminates false matches caused by matching page numbers which by themselves form a consistent sequence between any two books. Hyphenated words are quite common at the end of each line and they are also corrected automatically before proceeding. For efficiency, unique words are precomputed and stored in binary files. Each unique word is represented by a 32-bit hashcode which is generated using a product sum algorithm over the entire text of the string. For batch processing, the sequences of hashcodes are appended one after another in to binary files which are referred to as "barrels". A barrel containing 2K books occupies 25-35 megabytes of disk space. Alternatively, one could also index unique words and assign a term ID for each unique word. However, it would be a two-pass approach with large memory and computation requirements since the vocabulary of scanned book collections becomes arbitrarily large as the size of the collection grows.

It should be noted that a unique word in one book may not be necessarily unique in another print version of the same book. This happens due to OCR errors and/or additional or missing text in the other book. Despite these factors, it is still highly probable to find a large number of common words between the two sequences preserving the same order for mono-lingual books. Here we show that this representation is also sufficient to find translation pairs at the book level.

3.3 Translation of Word Sequences

Consider a pair of books - for example one in English and the other in German. At this point we have two unique word sequences extracted from these two books. The aim is to map the unique word sequence from the English book to German or vice versa. The first stage of mapping is to include the common words across translations (names are sometimes preserved across languages) in the translated sequence. For the remaining words, we use a dictionary to translate them in place to German word by word. If there are multiple translations for a word, then they are also included in the translated sequence. It is clear that the translated word sequence may include words repeated more than once after translation, but this is not an issue for the technique.

3.3.1 Preserving common words across translations

Names of people and places are sometimes the same in both texts (i.e. not translated). They have high discriminatory power and it is desirable to incorporate them in to the analysis. For this purpose we first intersect and find all common unique words prior to any translation. Then, the list of common words is interleaved with the translated unique word sequence and sorted based on their original location in text. Notice that names and places may be changed in the translated version of the book. In that case, we still have the translations of the unique words in the sequence which are sufficient to identify translation pairs.

3.3.2 Translation of unique words

The translation lexicon is an important component of the translation identification framework. Larger dictionaries help translate more unique words since they are more likely to be found. It is desirable that the translation lexicon has as many inflections and forms of the word as possible for best performance - since we do not do any morphological processing. Our alignment algorithm (described later) will only match two words if they have the same characters in them. Preliminary experiments on stemming and lemmatizing the words produced no significant improvements in accuracy.

Translational probabilities do not play any role in our framework. The translation lexicon is therefore regarded as a table which maps one word in the source language to one or more words in the target language. There are two ways to obtain such a translation lexicon with one-to-many entries. One option is to train it automatically from a parallel corpus [17] and ignore (or threshold) translational probabilities. However, it was found that automatically learned translation lexicons contain a considerable amount of noise. There may be dozens of words most of which are actually not associated with the source word. Further, the training process is highly sensitive to the training corpus. A translation lexicon learned from one corpus can not be generalized to another corpus.

A better option is to create a one-to-many translation lexicon using a dictionary. One can make use of all information in the dictionary. All function words are removed on both sides of each entry using a language specific stopword list. If the source entry still consists of multiple words we delete it and do not use it. If the source side of an entry has a single word remaining, then one should include it in the translation lexicon along with all its possible translations one after the other. If a source word maps translates to multiple words then each of these possible translations is listed one after the other in the sequence. If the source word maps to a phrase, the phrase is split into separate words and every word in the phrase is listed as a possible translation in the hope that one of them will map correctly. If more than one dictionary is available, one can also create a larger dictionary by merging translation entries.

3.4 Sequence Alignment

After the translating the unique word sequences of books in the source language to the target language, the next step is to compare each of them against all the books in the target language. Comparison is performed using the Longest Common Subsequence (LCS) algorithm. LCS is basically a global alignment method which gives the longest sequence preserving the long range order between two sequences. Having a large number of words in common preserving the order is a clear indication of translation.

There are a number of algorithms to compute LCS in the literature [8]. The standard dynamic programming algorithm has $O(mn)$ time and space requirements, where m and n are the lengths of the input sequences. For long input sequences, this algorithm has very large memory requirements. Therefore we adopt an $O(mn)$ time and linear space LCS algorithm [13] to calculate the LCS length without computing the actual LCS sequence itself. There is also a $O(nloglogn)$ time LCS algorithm for sequences where no element appears more than once within either input string [15]. This algorithm is not suitable for our purposes because the translated word sequence may include repeated words.

There are further improvements for fast LCS computation. It is not necessary to compute LCS over the entire input sequences. One can disregard the words which do not appear in both sequences since a word must appear in both sequences at least once in order to be in the LCS. Another improvement is to avoid LCS computation entirely when conditions apply. Given the score threshold (used for classifying books pairs to be translations) and the lengths of the sequences, it is possible to solve for a lower bound for the LCS length L. If the number of common words between two sequences is less than L, then there is no need for the alignment procedure since the resulting score is guaranteed to be lower than the threshold. These improvements provide significant speed-up. It should be noted that the intersection of elements between two sequences can be computed in linear time using a hashtable.

3.5 Scoring Functions

The length of LCS between the list of translated words and the list of unique words is used to classify or rank translation pairs. The LCS length alone can not be used for translation detection. The reason is that the number of unique words (hence the length of LCS) is a function of the book length according to Zipf's Law. Longer texts are expected to have longer lists of unique words. It is therefore desirable to normalize the LCS length based on the size of the books compared. Here we adopt the normalization techniques proposed in [30]. These approaches are elaborated in the subsections.

3.5.1 Correlation Score (TRANS-cs)

Using the analogy with correlation, the TRANS-cs score for two sequences of words X and Y is defined similar to the DUPNIQ-cs score in [30] as:

$$TRANS-cs(X,Y) = \frac{|LCS(X,Y)|}{\sqrt{|X||Y|}} \tag{1}$$

where $|LCS(X,Y)|$ is the LCS length for the aligned sequences. $|X|$ and $|Y|$ represents the length of X and Y respectively. The resulting score has a range of [0,1]. The score is maximized when the two sequences are identical.

3.5.2 Information Theoretic Score (TRANS-its)

In this context, input word sequences are defined as objects X and Y and those objects are assumed to be generated by a probabilistic model. Then, according to Lin [20], the similarity between any two objects can be defined as:

$$similarity(X,Y) = \frac{\log \Pr(common(X,Y))}{\log \Pr(description(X,Y))} \tag{2}$$

Similarity is maximized when the two objects are identical. The joint description of two objects is defined to be overall information content of both objects. In our case, the overlapping information content is defined by the longest common subsequence between X and Y and the total information content (description) is defined by the alignment produced by LCS. Once the probability of any word sequence is assumed to be inversely proportional to its length, then Lin's equation simplifies as:

$$TRANS-its(X,Y) = \frac{\log |LCS(X,Y)|}{\log(|X| + |Y| - |LCS(X,Y)|)} \tag{3}$$

TRANS-its has a range of [0,1]. The score is assumed to be zero if input sequences have no common words.

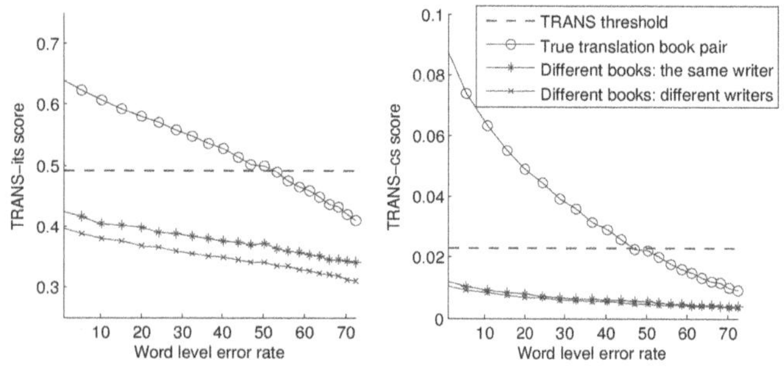

Figure 3: The effect of OCR errors on the translation scores are investigated for three different scenarios. TRANS-its (left) and TRANS-cs (right) scores are shown as a function of word level synthetic document noise. Both measures are able to classify the book pairs correctly for the given thresholds even for high rates of character level document noise.

4. SYNTHETIC EXPERIMENTS

We investigate the effect of OCR errors on translation detection by generating synthetic errors in texts. A pair of texts is created as follows: Two error-free (no OCR errors) books are downloaded from the Project Gutenberg website [2] - one in the source language (the reference text) and a second in the target language. The latter is used for generating synthetic texts by adding a specified amount of random character level document noise to simulate OCR errors. Unique words in the reference text are translated in to the target language. TRANS-its and TRANS-cs scores are computed for the reference and synthetic texts for different levels of document noise from 0% to 20% with 1% increments. Experiments are repeated one hundred times - each time with different random seeds - and the scores are averaged.

The noise model introduced in [10] is adopted for generating the synthetic texts. The model basically performs string edit operations (insertion, deletion and replacement) over the entire text for the given amount for each type of noise. The total amount of noise is defined to be the total percentage of characters deleted, replaced and inserted over the entire string. The distribution of edit operations is defined to be uniform, i.e., [1/3, 1/3, 1/3] respectively. Case is folded and all punctuations and numerals are removed. The English-German dictionary used in the synthetic experiments contains 62K words including inflections.

Three different scenarios are investigated. In the first scenario, we evaluate the effect of OCR errors for true translation pairs. In this case, the reference book is chosen to be "Egmont" which is written in German by Johann Wolfgang von Goethe and synthetic texts are generated using the English translation of the same book. In the second scenario, the same process is applied to two different books which are known not to be translations of each other but written by the same author - the German original of Goethe's "Egmont" and an English translation of 'Goethe's "Faust". The purpose of this scenario is to test the robustness of the proposed method for texts having similar style and vocabulary. The third scenario investigates the case in which two different books are written by different authors - the German version of Goethe's Egmont and an English version of "The Critique of Pure Reason" by Immanuel Kant. In a collection the most common scenario is one where the books are not translations of each other and the authors are also different.

In Figure 3, it is clear that TRANS-its and TRANS-cs scores are substantially larger for the true translation pair compared to the other two non-translation pairs. For all scenarios, the translation scores are the highest when there is no document noise and they gradually fall as the amount of noise is increased. TRANS-cs score tend to fall more drastically compared to TRANS-its. For the true translation pair, TRANS-its and TRANS-cs scores fall below the given thresholds at approximate word error rate levels 49% and 44% respectively. Notice that these word error rates are very high and unlikely to happen in practice for printed books. [31] estimate that the OCR word error rate of scanned books in the IA database is less than 15% . The proposed method is robust to the OCR errors found in scanned book collections.

Table 1 provides further detail. In all scenarios, it is seen that the number of unique words increases as the amount of noise increases. The reason is that document noise (or OCR errors) tend to produce arbitrary words which are not in the vocabulary of the book (or even the language).

It is seen that the non-translation book pair having the same author has more common words and higher translation scores compared to the third scenario where the non-translation book pair has different authors. The reason is that different books written by the same author are likely to have more common words in the vocabulary, even though one of them is translated by someone else. Despite this effect, the proposed method successfully discriminates both non-translation book pairs from the true translation pair.

The length of the sequence of words following the same order in both contexts is a clear indication of translation. This can be seen more clearly for the book pairs having the same writer (scenarios 1 and 2). See Table 1. Both book pairs have comparable numbers of common words in their representations. This information alone does not help discriminate these two cases. However, the length of the LCS is considerably higher for the true translation pair. This means that there are a large number of words following the same order for the true translation pair whereas it is not the case for the other. The sequence information of words is therefore a strong feature to detect translations. It is sufficient to have a small number of words in common preserving the same order compared to the total number of unique words in the book.

5. EVALUATION METRICS

Three different evaluation methods are defined to elucidate different aspects of the problem and also depending on what kind of ground truth is available. For large datasets, it is not possible to obtain manually labeled ground truth. In such cases, a retrieval approach must be adopted as described below.

Retrieval of Translations: In this approach, each book in the source language (English in our example) is regarded as a query and all the books written in the target language (German) are ranked according to their translational similarity score. MAP (Mean Average Precision) is calculated over the rank lists. The retrieval approach is feasible especially for large datasets since the evaluation is practical. One can adopt a pooling approach in analogy with the traditional IR ranking paradigm to obtain relevance judgments. The details are described in the experimental section.

Ranking All Book Pairs: Krstovski & Smith [19] rank all the book pairs in a single list according to some simi-

Table 1: Detailed statistics for the three pairs of books examined in Figure 3. $|X|$ and $|Y|$ corresponds to the number of unique words in books X and Y respectively. $|X \cap Y|$ corresponds to the number of common words between |X| and |Y| without any translation. $|X_T \cap Y|$ refers to the number of common words after translating the words in |X| to the language of book $|Y|$. $|LCS|$ is the length of the longest common subsequence between the word sequence representations. TRANS-its and TRANS-cs scores are also shown.

Char err. rate(%)	Word err. rate (%)	English Book X	German Book Y	|X|	|Y|	$\|X \cap Y\|$	$\|X_T \cap Y\|$	|LCS|	TRANS its	TRANS cs
0	0	Egmont	Egmont	2395	3224	32	492	251	0.643	0.090
1	5.33	Egmont	Egmont	2395	4232	34	474	235	0.623	0.074
3	15.29	Egmont	Egmont	2395	5109	34	438	209	0.593	0.055
5	24.38	Egmont	Egmont	2395	7395	33	455	187	0.570	0.044
10	43.68	Egmont	Egmont	2395	10256	30	337	128	0.514	0.026
0	0	Faust	Egmont	3706	3224	27	416	43	0.426	0.012
1	5.33	Faust	Egmont	3706	4232	29	406	42	0.415	0.011
3	15.29	Faust	Egmont	3706	5109	35	388	40	0.401	0.008
5	24.38	Faust	Egmont	3706	7395	37	363	37	0.388	0.007
10	43.68	Faust	Egmont	3706	10256	41	306	35	0.374	0.006
0	0	Kant	Egmont	2625	3224	6	270	31	0.396	0.011
1	5.33	Kant	Egmont	2625	4232	9	263	30	0.387	0.009
3	15.29	Kant	Egmont	2625	5109	10	250	30	0.374	0.007
5	24.38	Kant	Egmont	2625	7395	11	236	29	0.364	0.007
10	43.68	Kant	Egmont	2625	10256	12	205	26	0.345	0.005

larity score and compute Average Precision (AP) over the entire ranked list. This is different than the retrieval of translations approach. Consider the following list of English books E1, E2, E3 and German books G1, G2. Assume that the following ranked list is produced after comparing all the source-target book pairs (E3G1, E1G2, E2G2, E1G1, E3G2, E2G1). The retrieval of translations approach instead use E1, E2 and E3 as queries and compute the AP for each ranked list (E1G2, E1G1), (E2G2, E2G1) and (E3G1, E3G2) and average all the AP values to compute a MAP score. The ranking all book pairs approach is reasonable as long as the ground truth for the entire dataset is available. One may still go over the entire ranked list and annotate each pair manually. However, this is not feasible for large datasets since the number of book pairs to be checked is significantly larger than for the retrieval approach.

Binary Classification: This measure requires the system to classify each book pair as a translation or not. In the approaches we use this is done using a threshold over the translation scores. If the ground truth is available for the entire dataset, then precision and recall values can be generated. It should be noted that precision/recall values are the most restrictive metrics, since they require translational scores to be comparable between different book pairs and a careful selection of the score threshold. Even if MAP and AP scores are both 1.0, it is possible to get either precision or recall values below 1.0. It happens when the score threshold is either too high or too low. The least restrictive evaluation metric is the MAP score for the retrieval task since it does not require the translational scores to be comparable between different queries.

6. EXPERIMENTS

This section begins with a listing of the datasets collected and used. This is followed by a description of the translation lexicons used. Following this is a discussion of the baselines and other algorithms used for comparison. Finally, we describe a set of experiments carried out and the results obtained from them.

6.1 Datasets

Books downloaded from the Internet Archive (IA) [1] were used to construct datasets. English-German training and the 2K datasets are publicly available [2].

An English-German training set contains 30 scanned books (16 English, 14 German) from the IA database. It is manually verified that a book has at least one translation in the set. There are 31 true translation pairs in total. This set is used to estimate the translational similarity threshold for the scanned book experiments.

The EUROPARL parallel corpus is a standard collection of text documents from the proceedings of the European Parliament [16] used for machine translation. These documents are clean - since they have no OCR errors. Version 3 is used for our experiments in order to compare the results with the baseline approach described in [19]. It contains speeches from the period 04/1996-10/2006. There are over 600 documents each of which is translated in to 11 languages. Unlike the scanned book collections, these texts do not include any document noise since they are translated and typed by humans. Among these parallel corpora, we use four language-pairs: English-Finnish, English-French, English-German and English-Spanish. Notice that Finnish is from a different language family compared to the other languages. The average number of words per document in the English collection is 50360 after removing the tags. Many of these documents are much shorter than most books.

The 2K dataset is an English-German collection of 2K scanned books and is one of the datasets used by Krstovski & Smith in [19] and they refer it as the "17 book pairs" dataset. The dataset is originally created by downloading a random selection of 1K German and 1K English books from the IA website and embedding 17 book translation pairs in it. However, our approach discovered that there are actually 18 translation book pairs in the dataset. TRANS found three additional translation pairs and falsified two translation pairs which were initially in the ground truth. After

[2]http://ciir.cs.umass.edu/downloads/trans-detect/ and http://books.cs.umass.edu/downloads/trans-detect/

Table 2: Dictionary statistics after ignoring phrasal translations.

Dictionary	Words	Translation Success
English-German 62K	62242	79.8%
English-German 5K	5487	19.7%
English-Finnish	2997	11.9%
English-French	17326	54.2%
English-Spanish	23377	53.2%

manual investigation, the ground truth for this dataset has been corrected and it is used for the experiments along with the updated results obtained from Krstovski & Smith.

The 50K dataset is a collection of 50K books in German randomly selected from the the IA database. Using the language identifier, it is verified that the OCR outputs are not garbage and that the dominant language of these texts is German. This set is used only for ranking experiments. A set of 20 famous books in English are used for querying. Query books are chosen in a way that there exists at least one translation for each of them in the entire collection. The ground truth for the query set is obtained as follows: for each query book, books in the 50K collection are ranked according to the TRANS-cs, TRANS-its and metadata scores. Each of these techniques produces a ranked list for each query. The top 200 ranking entries from all three lists were pooled for each query and then manually judged. This pooling approach provide a basis to determine relative effectiveness of the systems being compared. In total, 52 translation pairs were labeled for all 20 queries.

6.2 Translation Lexicons

There are two ways to obtain a translation lexicon. The first one is to learn translations from a parallel corpus. The second one is to use a dictionary. We first tried to learn a translation lexicon for the English-German language pair using a statistical machine translation system [17]. Training was performed on the Europarl parallel corpus. However, final precision and recall figures were quite low compared to the dictionary approach. Therefore we decided to use the dictionary approach for the rest of our experiments.

Table 2 below shows statistics on the size of the dictionaries used in our experiments [3]. All the dictionaries provide translations for different forms of the word (such as plural, gerund, past participle etc.), whereas the English-German 5K and English-Finnish dictionaries lack this feature. We also provide the average percentage of unique words translated using each dictionary. The percentages are generated for the EUROPARL corpus. We also tried a number of lemmatization techniques in order to improve translation success. Even if we observed improvements in the total number of translated words, no improvement is observed in the precision and recall figures. Dictionary size and OCR error rate are the determinants of the overall success of the framework.

6.3 Baselines

Most work on creating parallel corpora has been focused on small datasets and using either structural information or the alignment of individual sentences [28] with two exceptions: Uszkoreit et al. [29] and Krstovski & Smith [19]. Uszkoreit's approach is not used as a baseline since the datasets and the translation system they used are not available to us. Here we use three baseline systems: metadata search, IBM MODEL 1 and where available numbers from Krstovski & Smith [19].

META refers to using metadata search for finding translation pairs in a collection of books. Here we use title and author information from the IA database as follows: first all the punctuation in the author and title fields are removed and all the characters are lowercased. Numeric characters are also ignored only for the author field since the date information leads to false matches. The title of the query book is also translated from English to German using the Google Translate API. The set of tokens in the author field of the query book is compared against the books in the collection of 50K German books using the Jaccard similarity. If the similarity is greater than zero, then the translated title is also compared against the title of each candidate book in the same way. The "metadata score" for a single pair of books is defined to be the average of the title and author Jaccard similarities. The metadata score is used to detect/rank books pairs for being translations. Notice that the metadata is not fully reliable since it is typed by people who scan and/or upload the book in to the IA database.

IBM M1 refers to the widely-used IBM Model 1 used for aligning words given two sentences in different languages [6]. It is used for different tasks over parallel corpora and essentially gives an estimate for the probability of a target sentence T in some language given a source sentence S in another language. There are several simplifying assumptions in this model. It does not incorporate any information about the long range order of words in the source and target sentences unlike the sequence of unique words. This approach is therefore ideal to demonstrate the effectiveness of bag-of-words models over long texts. Since this model is effective for ranking, we use it only for retrieval and ranking experiments. For fairness, the same dictionary is used for all techniques. Transition probabilities are estimated by assuming that all translations are equiprobable.

Krstovski & Smith use an approach for generating a ranked list of book translation pairs without the use of bilingual dictionary or machine translation system [19]. Each book in the collection is represented in the vector space and cosine similarity is used to rank all the book pairs in the collection. The vector representation only accounts for the words which appear in both languages without any translation. For each book, the weights of the vector representation are calculated by multiplying the frequency of the term in the book with the inverse document frequency of the term in the collection of books in the same language, i.e. (TFx-IDF). The Locality sensitive hashing (LSH) approximation algorithm is used to calculate cosine similarity to reduce the time complexity. We use their datasets and results which are publicly available.

6.4 EUROPARL Experiments

The EUROPARL dataset is used to test the effectiveness of our approach for documents with no OCR errors. There are roughly 650 documents per language each of which has a translation in the other language. For each language pair we selected 50 translation pairs at random as a training set and used the remaining as a test set. The training set is used to train the score threshold (a different threshold for each language since dictionary sizes vary significantly). For English-German, the 62K dictionary is used. The evaluations are

Table 3: Translation retrieval experiments for the EUROPARL dataset.

Dataset	TRANS-its	TRANS-cs
	MAP	MAP
Eng-Fin	1.0	1.0
Eng-Fre	1.0	1.0
Eng-Ger	1.0	1.0
Eng-Spa	1.0	1.0

Table 4: Ranking all document pairs for the EUROPARL dataset.

Dataset	TRANS-its	TRANS-cs	Krs.&Smith
	AP	AP	AP
Eng-Fin	1.0	1.0	-
Eng-Fre	1.0	1.0	-
Eng-Ger	1.0	0.994	0.986
Eng-Spa	1.0	1.0	-

done on the test set. The retrieval and ranking all pairs experiments are shown in Tables 3 and 4 respectively. Binary classification results are given in Table 5. We notice that TRANS-its has a MAP score of 1.0 and an AP of 1.0 for both the retrieval and ranking of all pairs evaluations. TRANS-cs performs slightly worse on the English-German ranking of all pairs evaluation. We also list Krstovski&Smith's result for the English-German pair from their paper (their splits are different but the results are indicative). Krstovski&Smith do not provide numbers for the other language pairs but they have graphs which clearly show that the AP score must be less than 1.0.

The binary classification experiments indicate that threshold selection is a hard problem compared to the ranking and retrieval paradigms. TRANS-its has a precision of 1.0 for all language pairs. TRANS-its also ranks all the document pairs perfectly since the AP score is 1.0. However, the recall values are slightly lower than 1.0 for English-Finnish and English-German datasets. The reason is that one pair in the English-Finnish and two pairs in the English-German dataset are below the score threshold although they are relevant. Further analysis of the results show that missing document pairs are actually very short (a few hundred words). Our technique is quite robust for longer documents. Precision and recall values for TRANS-cs are both lower than 1.0 for the English-German dataset, which indicates there are relevant documents below the score threshold while there are false positives with a score higher than the threshold. Clearly TRANS-its performs very well on all metrics.

6.5 Experiments with Real Scanned Books

Table 6 shows results for the retrieval experiments on real scanned books for the English-German datasets (Train, 2K and 50K). The best scores are shown in bold face. TRANS-its (using the large dictionary) is the most successful system among all others providing MAP scores of 1.0. Note that the results are worse when the smaller dictionary is used. Metadata search (META) performs well in ranking books for both the train and test sets but not as well for the 50K dataset (MAP = 0.821). TRANS-cs is much worse indicating the importance of LCS length normalization. IBM-M1 performs poorly. In all the tables below "Dict" refers to the size of the dictionary.

Table 5: Classification experiments for the EUROPARL dataset.

Dataset	TRANS-its		TRANS-cs	
	Precision	Recall	Precision	Recall
Eng-Fin	1.0	0.998	0.973	1.0
Eng-Fre	1.0	1.0	1.0	1.0
Eng-Ger	1.0	0.997	0.992	0.995
Eng-Spa	1.0	1.0	0.992	1.0

The evaluation for the ranking all book pairs experiment is given in Table 7. Experiments are not performed on the 50K dataset because it would require judging several thousand entries. TRANS-its again has an AP of 1.0 for the train and 2K datasets. Metadata search has a lower AP scores on both train and 2K datasets. IBM-M1 again performs poorly. Note that TRANS-its has an AP score of 1.0 even with a dictionary of size 5K. TRANS-cs performs slightly worse with a smaller dictionary. Krs.&Smith obtained an AP = 0.945 for the 2K dataset (their precision, recall and MAP results are not available for the 2K dataset).

Binary classification is performed by learning the score threshold from the train set and it is used for the 2K dataset. As seen in Table 8, TRANS-its with 62K dictionary gives perfect precision and recall values for both datasets. TRANS-cs and TRANS-its both provide perfect scores on the train set even with a small dictionary. Precision values for the 2K dataset fall if the small dictionary is used. The drastic fall in the precision figures for the 2K dataset is due to the low score threshold. This indicates that there is a need for a better threshold selection paradigm since both score functions actually perform very well in ranking all book pairs experiment, as shown in Table 7. Surprisingly metadata search does not provide perfect scores (precision = 0.739, recall = 0.944) for either the 2K set or the train set.

Uszkoreit et al. [29] best published result (using an oracle to choose the threshold) for a dataset of 103 books (English-French) with 30 matching pairs has a precision of 1.0 and a recall of 0.71. Although it is not directly comparable, we note that TRANS-its has both precision and recall 1.0 on a 2K book dataset. TRANS also does not require complete translation of books. Unfortunately, their machine translation system and datasets are not publicly available for us to be able to make a direct comparison.

7. CONCLUSIONS

A translation identification framework is presented for large scanned book collections with OCR errors. Unique words (which appear only once in the whole book) along with their actual order in the text are used to represent each book in the collection. This sampling strategy provides a compact representation and it enables efficient identification of translation pairs. A dictionary approach is adopted to translate word sequence representations. Fairly small dictionaries work well. The proposed approach is shown to be quite robust to high rates of OCR errors and it outperforms several baselines including metadata search. Retrieval experiments on several datasets including the Europarl parallel corpus with four different language pairs show that the proposed method retrieves translation pairs with a MAP score of 1.0. Future work includes further speed-ups, extensions to multiple languages and mapping translated portions.

Table 6: MAP scores for the retrieval experiments on scanned book datasets.

Approach	Dict	Dataset		
		Train	2K	50K
TRANS-its	62K	**1.0**	**1.0**	**1.0**
TRANS-cs	62K	1.0	1.0	0.717
TRANS-its	5K	1.0	1.0	0.714
TRANS-cs	5K	1.0	1.0	0.669
META	-	0.99	1.0	0.821
IBM-M1	62K	0.302	0.008	< 0.001

Table 7: AP scores for ranking all book pairs experiments for scanned book datasets.

Approach	Dict	Dataset	
		Train	2K
TRANS-its	62K	**1.0**	**1.0**
TRANS-cs	62K	1.0	1.0
TRANS-its	5K	1.0	1.0
TRANS-cs	5K	1.0	0.943
META	-	0.959	0.916
IBM-M1	62K	0.148	0.0002
Krs.&Smith	-	-	0.945

8. ACKNOWLEDGMENTS

We would like to thank David Smith and Kriste Krstovski for providing their datasets and results, Ethem F. Can for helping with the figures and Internet Archive for their book collection. This work was supported in part by the Center for Intelligent Information Retrieval and in part by NSF grant #IIS-0910884. Any opinions, findings and conclusions or recommendations expressed in this material are the authors' and do not necessarily reflect those of the sponsor.

9. REFERENCES

[1] Internet Archive. http://www.archive.org, 2012.

[2] Project Gutenberg. http://www.gutenberg.org, 2012.

[3] Wordgumbo:. http://www.wordgumbo.com, 2012.

[4] Y. Bernstein and J. Zobel. A scalable system for identifying co-derivative documents. In *SPIRE*, pages 55–67, 2004.

[5] A. Z. Broder, S. C. Glassman, M. S. Manasse, and G. Zweig. Syntactic clustering of the web. *Computer Networks*, 29(8-13):1157–1166, 1997.

[6] P. F. Brown, V. J. D. Pietra, S. A. D. Pietra, and R. L. Mercer. The mathematics of statistical machine translation: parameter estimation. *Comp. Ling.*, 19:263–311, June 1993.

[7] P. Clough. Old and new challenges in automatic plagiarism detection. National UK Plagiarism Advisory Service, http://www.ir.shef.ac.uk/cloughie/papers/pas_plagiarism.pdf, 2003.

[8] S. Deorowicz. Solving longest common subsequence and related problems on graphical processing units. *Softw. Pract. Exper.*, 40:673–700, July 2010.

[9] M. Errami, Z. Sun, A. C. George, T. C. Long, M. A. Skinner, J. D. Wren, and H. R. Garner. Identifying duplicate content using statistically improbable phrases. *Bioinformatics*, 26(11):1453–1457, 2010.

[10] S. Feng and R. Manmatha. A hierarchical, HMM-based automatic evaluation of OCR accuracy for a digital library of books. In *JCDL*, pages 109–118, 2006.

[11] P. Fung. Compiling bilingual lexicon entries from a non-parallel english-chinese corpus. In *Annual Meeting of Very Large Corpora*, 1995.

Table 8: Binary classification results on English-German datasets. "Thr", "P", "R" are threshold, precision and recall respectively.

Approach	Dict	Thr	Train		2K	
			P	R	P	R
TRANS-its	62K	0.49	**1.0**	**1.0**	**1.0**	**1.0**
TRANS-cs	62K	0.023	1.0	1.0	0.782	1.0
TRANS-its	5K	0.395	1.0	1.0	0.122	1.0
TRANS-cs	5K	0.0085	1.0	1.0	0.01	1.0
META	-	0.275	0.882	0.968	0.739	0.944

[12] G. Grefenstette. Comparing two language identification schemes. In *3rd International Conference on Statistical Analysis of Textual Data (JADT 95)*, December 1995.

[13] D. S. Hirschberg. Algorithms for the longest common subsequence problem. *J. ACM*, 24:664–675, October 1977.

[14] T. C. Hoad and J. Zobel. Methods for identifying versioned and plagiarized documents. *JASIST*, 54(3):203–215, 2003.

[15] J. W. Hunt and T. G. Szymanski. A fast algorithm for computing longest common subsequences. *Commun. ACM*, 20:350–353, May 1977.

[16] P. Koehn. Europarl: A Parallel Corpus for Statistical Machine Translation. In *The tenth Machine Translation Summit*, pages 79–86, Phuket, Thailand, 2005. AAMT.

[17] P. Koehn, H. Hoang, A. Birch, C. Callison-Burch, M. Federico, N. Bertoldi, B. Cowan, W. Shen, C. Moran, R. Zens, C. Dyer, O. Bojar, A. Constantin, and E. Herbst. Moses: Open source toolkit for statistical machine translation. In *ACL*, 2007.

[18] K. Koroutchev and M. Cebri. Detecting the same text in different languages. In *IEEE Information Theory Workshop ITW*, pages 337–341, 2007.

[19] K. Krstovski and D. A. Smith. A minimally supervised approach for detecting and ranking document translation pairs. In *6th Workshop on SMT*, pages 207–216, 2011.

[20] D. Lin. An information-theoretic definition of similarity. In *ICML '98*, pages 296–304, 1998.

[21] X. Ma and M. Liberman. Bits: A method for bilingual text search over the web. In *Machine Trans. Summit VII*, 1999.

[22] D. Mimno, G. Crane, and A. Jones. Hierarchical catalog records: Implementing a FRBR catalog. *D-Lib Magazine*, 11(10), Oct 2005.

[23] J. Y. Nie, M. Simard, P. Isabelle, and R. Durand. Cross-language information retrieval based on parallel texts and automatic mining of parallel texts from the web. In *ACM SIGIR*, pages 74–81, 1999.

[24] M. Potthast, A. Barrón-Cedeño, B. Stein, and P. Rosso. Cross-language plagiarism detection. *Language Resources and Evaluation*, 45(1):45–62, 2011.

[25] P. Resnick and N. Smith. The web as a parallel corpus. *Computational Linguistics*, 29(3), 2003.

[26] P. Resnik. Mining the web for bilingual text. In *ACL*, pages 527–534, 1999.

[27] N. Shivakumar and H. Garcia-Molina. Scam: A copy detection mechanism for digital documents. In *Ann. Conf. on the Theory and Practice of Digital Libraries*, 1995.

[28] N. Smith. From words to corpora: Recognizing translation. In *EMNLP*, pages 95–102, 2002.

[29] J. Uszkoreit, J. Ponte, A. C. Popat, and M. Dubiner. Large scale parallel document mining for machine translation. In *COLING*, pages 1101–1109, 2010.

[30] I. Z. Yalniz, E. F. Can, and R. Manmatha. Partial duplicate detection for large book collections. In *CIKM*, pages 469–474, 2011.

[31] I. Z. Yalniz and R. Manmatha. A fast alignment scheme for automatic ocr evaluation of books. In *ICDAR*, pages 754–758, 2011.

[32] C. C. Yang and K. W. Li. Automatic construction of english/chinese parallel corpora. *JASIS*, pages 730–742, 2003.

Predicting the Ratings of Multimedia Items for Making Personalized Recommendations

Rani Qumsiyeh
Computer Science Department
Brigham Young University
Provo, Utah 84602
rani_qumsiyeh@yahoo.com

Yiu-Kai Ng
Computer Science Department
Brigham Young University
Provo, Utah 84602
ng@compsci.byu.edu

ABSTRACT

Existing multimedia recommenders suggest a specific type of multimedia items rather than items of different types personalized for a user based on his/her preference. Assume that a user is interested in a particular family movie, it is appealing if a multimedia recommendation system can suggest other movies, music, books, and paintings closely related to the movie. We propose a comprehensive, personalized multimedia recommendation system, denoted MudRecS, which makes recommendations on movies, music, books, and paintings similar in content to other movies, music, books, and/or paintings that a MudRecS user is interested in. MudRecS does not rely on users' access patterns/histories, connection information extracted from social networking sites, collaborated filtering methods, or user personal attributes (such as gender and age) to perform the recommendation task. It simply considers the users' ratings, genres, role players (authors or artists), and reviews of different multimedia items, which are abundant and easy to find on the Web. MudRecS predicts the *ratings* of multimedia items that match the interests of a user to make recommendations. The performance of MudRecS has been compared with current state-of-the-art multimedia recommenders using various multimedia datasets, and the experimental results show that MudRecS significantly outperforms other systems in accurately predicting the ratings of multimedia items to be recommended.

Categories and Subject Descriptors

H.3.3 [**Information Search and Retrieval**]: Information filtering

Keywords

Multimedia recommender, rating, genre, review, popularity

1. INTRODUCTION

Current multimedia recommenders either integrate user group information extracted from social websites, consider user profiles or attributes (such as gender and age), or analyze past behavior of individual users or overall behavior of a community of users to make recommendations. These information sources are not always available to be downloaded using APIs over the Internet or social networking sites. Moreover, majority of the existing multimedia recommenders suggest only a particular type of multimedia items, which are either videos, audios, text, or images. The restricted type of recommended items is a deficient and limitation, since various types of multimedia items offer different sources of information that are appealing to extended groups of users. In this paper, we propose a personalized multimedia recommendation system, denoted MudRecS, which recommends four different types of multimedia items—movies (videos), music (audios), books (text), and paintings (images)—for its users based on their personal preferences.

MudRecS relies on neither training data, predefined knowledge bases, nor ontologies to make recommendations. It does not require any manual intervention from its users nor users' personal information. Instead, it devises recommendations solely based on users' ratings, genres, reviews, popularity of artists/authors, and readability measures on multimedia items Is that are vastly available on the Web. Besides considering the *genres* of Is, MudRecS extracts *features* from *reviews* and determines the *polarity* and general *opinions* on the features of Is. MudRecS presents a unique approach for configuring the *popularity* of role players (authors/artists) of Is that is utilized for devising the *user preference* on Is. Moreover, whenever applicable, MudRecS analyzes the *comprehension levels* of its users so that it enhances its predictions on Is that are appealing to the users.

The design of MudRecS, which compares favorably to current state-of-the-art collaborative filtering, content-based, or hybrid approaches for generating recommendations, is simple and easy to develop. It is a contribution to the area of study in multimedia recommendation, since it introduces novel measures that accurately *predict* the *ratings* of multimedia items of various domains for each individual user. Predicted ratings of items can be used for ranking the recommended items, and items with higher predicted ratings are expected to be more favorable to the users who have previously rated items of the same or a different domain, which constitute the basis for rating prediction.

We organize our paper as follows. In Section 2, we discuss previous work on multimedia recommenders. In Section 3, we detail the design of MudRecS. In Section 4, we present the experimental results which were used to evaluate the performance of MudRecS. In Section 5, we give a conclusion.

Permission to make digital or hard copies of all or part of this work for personal or classroom use is granted without fee provided that copies are not made or distributed for profit or commercial advantage and that copies bear this notice and the full citation on the first page. To copy otherwise, to republish, to post on servers or to redistribute to lists, requires prior specific permission and/or a fee.
SIGIR'12, August 12–16, 2012, Portland, Oregon, USA.
Copyright 2012 ACM 978-1-4503-1472-5/12/08 ...$15.00.

2. RELATED WORK

Machine learning, information retrieval, natural language processing, and probabilistic techniques have been adapted in the past to develop systems that recommend movies [9], song/music tracks [3], text documents [7], and images [13], to name a few. Majority of existing recommendation systems are either content-based or collaborative-filtering-based. The content-based (or cognitive) approaches [2] create a profile to capture the (items of) interest of a user U using words, phrases, and/or features. Recommenders that are content-based identify the common features of items with favorable ratings given by a user and recommend to the user other items that share the same or similar features. Recommendation systems purely based on content similarity measure, however, generally suffer from the problems of limited-content analysis and over-specialization [4]. Limited-content analysis is a result of the relatively small amount of information on users or the content of items, whereas over-specialization restricts the number and diversity of items to be recommended, since the predicted rating of an item I for a user U is *high* only if I *matches* in content (such as genres or features) with the ones that U likes.

Collaborative filtering is another well-known recommendation method [14] which identifies the group of people who share common interest or similar items with user U and recommends items to U based on the group's interests. Amazon's recommender, which applied the collaborative-filtering technique [11], suggested items to a user based on other users' previous purchase patterns and/or rated items. Such a system is differed from MudRecS, since the latter does not consider users' access patterns nor histories.

Various hybrid approaches [2] have been introduced which exploit the benefits of using both collaborative-filtering and content-based methods to improve the quality of recommendations. Contractually, MudRecS considers semantic information, such as genres, reviews, popularity, and comprehensibility of multimedia items to make recommendations.

A method that translates tags assigned to multimedia contents for cross-language retrieval is proposed in [13]. The lexical translation of annotated tags, which handles sense disambiguation of tags, however, is restricted to image retrieval only and relies on social tagging, which is not required by MudRecS. An agent-based multimedia recommendation system, which is also constrained to process image data, is presented in [10]. The recommender depends on a predefined ontology to capture the users' preferences and identifies the semantics of hypermedia images to derive their contextual information for making recommendations. MudRecS avoids constructing ontologies and accessing hyperlinks to assess multimedia items to be recommended, which eliminates the tedious setup and avoids imposed overheads.

3. OUR RECOMMENDATION SYSTEM

Multimedia items on the Web are rated using the standard "star rating system" in which an item is given a number of stars (a rating level) by web users. To predict the ratings of items previously unrated by a user U for making recommendations to U, MudRecS considers different sources of information—U's ratings, genres, reviews, role players, and text readability levels—on items, which are either movies, songs, books, and/or paintings, previously rated by U in two steps: analysis of pre-rated items and prediction.

Analysis. Given a set of multimedia items previously rated by a user U, MudRecS analyzes the preferences of U based on the genres, features, and role players of the items that U (dis)likes. The *genres* and *role players* of multimedia items can easily be extracted from representative and comprehensive multimedia websites, such as imdb.com for movies, last.fm for songs, iblist.com for books, and flickr.com for images, using a simple HTML parser, whereas *features* of multimedia items can be retrieved from reviews that are available at well-known websites, such as Epinions(.com), Consumersearch(.com), and Consumerreports(.org). All of the rating information of U are archived in MudRecS for future references. (See tables in Figures 1, 5, and 6 and Table 2 for sample archived data.) Since the number of multimedia items rated by U is only in the hundreds, or thousands the most, this analysis step is not a time-consuming nor labor-intensive process. Moreover, analysis on U is conducted once after which ratings can be predicted for items unrated by U.

Prediction. Using the set of analyzed multimedia items S rated by U, MudRecS predicts the rating of an item I unrated by U. MudRecS considers the *genres* applied to I, using previous *ratings* given by U on different genres to determine the *genre score*, denoted GS (discussed in Section 3.1), of I. MudRecS also considers each *feature* of I extracted from the reviews of I and computes the *review score*, denoted RwS, for I using *reviews* on items in S (detailed in Section 3.2). According to the *popularity* of each role player, which is either the author, actor, actress, director, or artist, of I, MudRecS assigns a *role player score*, denoted RPS, to I (see Section 3.3). Last, but not least, MudRecS calculates the *readability score*, denoted ReS, for I, if I is a book (presented in Section 3.4). MudRecS combines GS, RwS, RPS, and ReS of I to compute the *Rating_Score* of I using the *Stanford Certainty Factor* (SCF) [12] at each one of the N rating levels R_i ($1 \leq i \leq N$), where N is often in the range of 5 to 10 (as defined in Equation 1). The *rating level* with the *highest Rating_Score* is selected as the predicted rating for I, which can be used to determine the *ranking* order of recommended items unrated by U.

$$MAX_{i=1}^{N}\{Rating\_Score(R_i, I) = (GS(R_i, I) + RwS(R_i, I) + RPS(R_i, I) + ReS(R_i, I, L)) \;/\; (1 - Min\{GS(R_i, I), RwS(R_i, I), RPS(R_i, I), ReS(R_i, I, L)\})\} \quad (1)$$

where L is the readability level of I. If I is not a text document, then $ReS(R_i, I, L)$ is excluded from Equation 1 when $Rating\_Score(R_i, I)$ is computed.

3.1 The Genres of Multimedia Items

A genre is the *category* of an item I. (Table 1 shows sample genres for movies, music, books, and paintings, respectively.) The basic assumption of genres is that if two items have the *same* genre, then they are likely given *similar* ratings by the same user [6]. Besides determining the genres of I, MudRecS also considers *genre similarity* for rating prediction on I, since (i) two different genres can be highly similar, such as "suspense" and "horror" in movies, "hip hop" and "rap" in music, "dark" and "mystery" in books, and "pointillism" and "divisionism" in images, (ii) same items are sometimes assigned different genres by different experts/users, and (iii) some items have multiple genres assigned to them. *Similarities* of various genres can be determined using word-

Multimedia Items	Sample Genres
Movies	Action, Adventure, Comedy, Crime, Drama
Music	Classical, Heavy Metal, Jazz, Rap, Rock
Books	Crime, Fantasy, Fiction, Mystery, Romance
Paintings	Art, History, Landscapes, Life, Portraits

Table 1: Sample genres for different types of multimedia items considered by MudRecS

correlation factors (defined in Section 3.1.1). For each rating level of an item I, MudRecS computes the *Genre_Score* (GS) for each possible genre of I (as detailed in Section 3.1.2).

3.1.1 Similarities Among Different Genres

To determine the similarity of two genres, we employ the word-correlation factors in the *word-similarity* matrix [8], denoted *WS-matrix*. The similarity, denoted *Word_Sim*, of any two non-stop, stemmed words i and j in *WS-matrix* is computed using the (i) *frequency* of co-occurrence and (ii) relative *distances* of i and j in each document in which they occur. *WS-matrix* was constructed using the documents in the Wikipedia collection (en.wikipedia.org/wiki/Wikipedia: Databasedownload) with 930,000 documents written by more than 89,000 authors on various topics and writing styles.

Compared with WordNet (wordnet.princeton.edu) in which each pair is not assigned a similarity weight, word-correlation factors offer a more sophisticated measure of word similarity.

3.1.2 Computing Genre Scores

Using the set of multimedia items S of the same domain D previously rated by a user U and an item I of D, which is unrated by U with various genres, MudRecS assigns GS of I at the rating level R_i ($1 \leq i \leq N$) as

$$GS(R_i, I) = \frac{\sum_{G \in G_{Set}} GSG(R_i, G)}{|G_{Set}|}, \text{ where}$$

$$GSG(R_i, G) = \frac{|Items\ in\ S\ with\ G\ of\ I\ Rated\ at\ R_i\ by\ U|}{|Items\ in\ S\ Rated\ at\ R_i\ by\ U|}$$

$$+ \sum_{j=1, G_j \neq G}^{|G_{Set}|} \frac{|Items\ in\ S\ with\ G_j\ of\ I\ Rated\ at\ R_i\ by\ U|}{|Items\ in\ S\ Rated\ at\ R_i\ by\ U|} \times Word\_Sim(G, G_j) \quad (2)$$

where G_{Set} is the set of genres of I, $G_j \in G_{Set}$ ($1 \leq j \leq |G_{Set}|$), and $Word\_Sim(G, G_j)$ is the genre similarity of G and G_j. Note that $Word\_Sim(G, G_j) = Word\_Sim(G_j, G)$.

Equation 2 assigns a higher GSG to a genre G at R_i if G in S has been rated at R_i by U more frequently than at any other rating levels in S. The multiplication is used to assign weight to genres such that the *less similar* a genre G_j is to G, the *less* it is *weighted* in the computation of $GSG(R_i, G)$. Figure 1 shows an example of applying Equation 2 to a number of genres in movies, which illustrates how the 'horror' genre receives a higher score at rating level 1 than at rating level 5, since most 'horror' movies, along with genres highly similar to 'horror', i.e., 'thriller', were rated at level 1. On the other hand, 'action' and its highly similar genre, 'Adventure,' were rated higher at level 5 than at level 1.

We realize that solely relying on the genres of an item to make recommendations could yield poor rating predictions, since (i) a *large* amount of data are required to accurately determine a particular user's genre preferences, (ii) a poor

Rating	Horror (H)	Thriller (T)	Action (Ac)	Adventure (Ad)
1	50	40	6	4
2	20	9	8	4
3	4	7	7	7
4	3	8	15	5
5	1	3	25	18

$WS(H, T) = 0.93$
$WS(H, Ac) = 0.35$
$WS(H, Ad) = 0.15$
$WS(T, Ac) = 0.67$
$WS(T, Ad) = 0.33$
$WS(Ac, Ad) = 0.91$

$$GSG(1, H) = \frac{50}{100} + \left(\frac{40}{100} \times WS(H,T) + \frac{6}{100} \times WS(H,Ac) + \frac{4}{100} \times WS(H,Ad)\right) = \mathbf{0.90}$$

$$GSG(5, H) = \frac{1}{47} + \left(\frac{3}{47} \times WS(H,T) + \frac{25}{47} \times WS(H,Ac) + \frac{18}{47} \times WS(H,Ad)\right) = 0.32$$

$$GSG(1, Ac) = \frac{6}{100} + \left(\frac{50}{100} \times WS(Ac,H) + \frac{40}{100} \times WS(Ac,T) + \frac{4}{100} \times WS(Ac,Ad)\right) = 0.54$$

$$GSG(5, Ac) = \frac{25}{47} + \left(\frac{1}{47} \times WS(Ac,H) + \frac{3}{47} \times WS(Ac,T) + \frac{18}{47} \times WS(Ac,Ad)\right) = \mathbf{0.93}$$

Figure 1: Four GSG scores computed at two rating levels for an unrated movie based on movies previously rated by a user U, and WS stands for $Word\_Sim$

(good, respectively) rating value for an item I with genre G does not necessarily indicate that a user dislikes (likes, respectively) G, but may have given a poor (good, respectively) rating to I due to other factors, (iii) items can be highly similar with respect to their genres and being dissimilar with respect to other features not related to genres, such as the 'story' of a movie. MudRecS considers the genres of I as well as other features addressed in online reviews on I.

3.2 Reviews

In predicting the rating of an item I, consumer reviews, opinions, and shared experiences on I are valuable sources of information which reflect consumers' preferences on I. Unlike user ratings that simply indicate their degrees of appealing on items, *reviews* provide more detailed information. Positive/Negative opinions on different *features* (i.e., properties) of I are often included in a review of I, such as the (originality of the) story in a movie, the (innovative or mono) tone of a song, or the (surprise or predictable) ending of a book. This information can be used to enhance the accuracy of rating prediction in a recommendation system.

To utilize the valuable information included in the set of reviews RS on items previously rated by user U for predicting the rating level of I, MudRecS (i) retrieves a set of reviews on I from review search engines (as detailed in Section 3.2.1), (ii) relies on a feature-detection approach to identify features of I from retrieved reviews, and (iii) determines the *polarity* of each sentence in reviews, which has been clustered based on a particular feature, as either positive or negative (in Section 3.2.2). Hereafter, each identified feature F of I is assigned the *Polarity Feature Score* (PFS) at each rating level based on the number of positive/negative sentences in RS assigned to F at certain rating levels (in Section 3.2.3).

3.2.1 Retrieving Relevant Reviews

MudRecS retrieves reviews for I from Epinions, Consumersearch, and Consumerreports. Using a query Q with keywords in the item name of I, MudRecS selects the top-33 reviews extracted from each one of the three review repositories[1] retrieved in response to Q, which yields the set of reviews of I for identifying the (polarity of) features of I.

[1]MudRecS retrieves 33 reviews from each repository, if they exist, since a collection of a hundred reviews on I is an ideal set for analyzing the features of I [5].

The film is shot using mainly unknown **actors**, who are very good in their parts. The film works as a totally **visual experience**, which I thought was one of the best I have seen in a while. The well-chosen words of the **script** are amazing and are almost incapable of adding to the unspoken pageantry and majesty of the remarkable **cinematography**. There is really nothing much about the **plot** of the movie; you either know it or you don't, but without new or added things. The **directing** of the film was good as well as original. The director was able to mix the spiritual battle that rages between Christ and Satan, while keeping the viewer informed of the **story of the movie** in reality.

Figure 2: An Epinions.com review for the movie "Passions of the Christ" and its identified features

Visual Graphics. The film works as a totally visual experience, which I thought was one of the best I have seen in a while. Strong acting and impressive visuals make The Passion of The Christ one of the best ...

Script. The well-chosen words of the script are amazing and are almost incapable of adding to the unspoken pageantry and majesty of the remarkable cinematography. As for the script of Mel Gibson's drama, ...

Director. The directing of the film was good as well as original. ...

Story. The director was able to mix the spiritual battle that rages between Christ and Satan, while keeping the viewer informed of the story ...

Figure 3: Some features/sentences extracted from the reviews of the movie "Passions of the Christ"

3.2.2 *Detecting Item Features and Opinions in Reviews*

Since each review R in the set of 99 retrieved reviews on an item I may address various features of I, MudRecS identifies distinct *features* of I and *clusters* sentences in R based on the detected features. Sentences in a feature cluster is assigned the *polarity* of the feature. To do that, MudRecS (i) generates a set of (cluster) *labels*, which are non-stop/-numerical/-sentiment named entities, that capture the features exhibited in the set of 99 reviews, (ii) assigns each sentence S in R to a feature cluster C based on the *similarity* between S and the label of C, and (iii) identifies positive/negative opinions on each feature using its clustered sentences.

Creating (Cluster) Labels for Identified Features

Using each review R in the set of 99 reviews on I, MudRecS creates concise and accurate *labels* that reflect the *features* specified in R using a suffix array algorithm, which has been proved to be efficient and effective in discovering key phrases in large text collections [20]. The suffix array algorithm generates a list of candidate (cluster) labels by simply extracting all the suffixes in the sentences in R. Since the generated list of suffixes may include non-representative labels (i.e., non-features) in describing I in R, MudRecS removes labels that are (i) *numerical* keywords, which seldom capture a feature of I, (ii) *incomplete*, i.e., included as substrings in other labels, (iii) *sentiment* keywords, i.e., words that express a positive or negative polarity, which is not considered as a feature of I, and (iv) non-named entities, which can be identified using the Stanford Entity Tagger (nlp.stanford.edu/software/CRF-NER.shtml), since features are expressed as named entities, such as *theme* and *plot*. In addition, labels that cross *sentence boundaries*, which indicate a topical shift, and end in the *Saxon genitive form* are excluded. Moreover, candidate (cluster) labels that reference web addresses are discarded and *stopwords* at the *beginning* or at the *end* of a (cluster) label are removed to enhance the readability of the label. Figure 2 shows a review on a movie extracted from Epinions.com with the *features* identified by MudRecS **bolded** in the review.

Assigning Sentences to Clusters

To cluster sentences in reviews on I which address the same (or similar) features of I, we have developed a simple, effective clustering method. Using the set of identified cluster labels CL and each retrieved review R on I, MudRecS computes the *degree of similarity* between each sentence S in R and label L in CL, denoted $LS\_Sim(S, L)$, as defined in Equation 3, using the word-correlation factors (introduced in Section 3.1.1). This process clusters sentences that address the same or similar feature F of I, which later allows MudRecS to determine whether F receives an overall positive/negative opinion captured in the set of 99 reviews on I by counting the total number of positive/negative sentences (based on sentiments in each sentence) assigned to F.

$$LS\_Sim(S, L) = \frac{\sum_{i=1}^{|S|} \sum_{j=1}^{|L|} Word\_Sim(w_i, w_j)}{|S|} \quad (3)$$

where $|S|$ ($|L|$, respectively) is the number of distinct, non-stop, stemmed words in S (L, respectively), w_i (w_j, respectively) is a non-stop, stemmed word in S (L, respectively), and $Word\_Sim(w_i, w_j)$ is the word-correlation factor of w_i and w_j. MudRecS normalizes $LS\_Sim(S, L)$ by dividing the accumulated word-correlation factors with the number of words in S to avoid favoring long sentences.

MudRecS computes $LS\_Sim(S, L)$ for each sentence S in each review R with respect to each label L in CL and assigns S to cluster C (labeled L_C) if $LS\_Sim(S, L_C)$ is the *highest* among all the labels in CL. Figure 3 shows some features (identified by their cluster labels) that are created using a set of reviews on the movie "Passions of the Christ" extracted from Epinions.com. Also displayed in Figure 3 are some sentences that are assigned by MudRecS to a feature.

Identifying Sentiment Opinions on Sentences

To determine the positive or negative polarity of a sentence S in a cluster, MudRecS calculates the *sentiment score* of S by subtracting the *sum* of the *negative* sentiment word scores in S (determined using SentiWordNet[2]) from the *sum* of its *positive* sentiment word scores in S, which reflects the sentiment of S such that if its sentiment score is *positive* (*negative*, respectively), then S is labeled as *positive* (*negative*, respectively).

3.2.3 *Assigning Scores to Features*

MudRecS computes a score for each feature of a rated item in two steps: *Review Analysis*, which is conducted once, and *Review Score Computation*, which is applied to each item considered for rating prediction and recommendation.

Review Analysis. For each item I in a given set S of multimedia items of the same domain previously rated at a rating level R_i ($1 \leq i \leq N$) by a user U, MudRecS determines which identified feature F in S receives an overall positive (negative, respectively) feedback based on the

[2]A SentiWordNet (sentiwordnet.isti.cnr.it/search.php) score of a word is a numerical value that indicates the *positive*, *neutral*, or *negative* orientation of the word.

Movies		Features							
		Story		Plot		Visuals		Direct	
Rating Level	# of Movies	+	-	+	-	+	-	+	-
1	5	2	3	1	4	3	2	0	5
2	10	3	7	4	6	5	5	2	8
3	20	8	12	7	13	6	14	13	7
4	25	18	7	10	15	7	18	13	12
5	15	11	4	9	6	4	11	12	3
Total	75	**42**	33	31	*44*	25	*50*	**40**	35

Table 2: The ratings of 75 movies provided by a user and a number of features of the movies with positive/negative polarity at each rating level

set of 99 reviews retrieved for each I by counting the total number of *positive* and *negative* sentences in I clustered under the label of F (that represents F). If F is assigned a *larger* number of *positive* (*negative*, respectively) than *negative* (*positive*, respectively) sentiment sentences clustered by MudRecS, then the polarity of F is treated as *positive* (*negative*, respectively). Hereafter, MudRecS counts the number of times F in items of S has been assigned a positive (negative, respectively) sentiment at each rating level, which constitutes the nominator in Equation 4. (See, in Table 2, the number of polarity of the feature *Story* at each rating level.)

MudRecS computes a *Polarity Feature Score*, denoted PFS, for each feature F with polarity P_F, which is either positive ('+') or negative ('-'), at each rating level R_i ($1 \leq i \leq N$).

$$PFS(R_i, F, P_F) = \frac{\#\ of\ Items\ in\ S\ with\ F\ and\ P_F\ Rated\ at\ R_i\ by\ U}{Total\ \#\ of\ Items\ in\ S\ Rated\ at\ R_i\ by\ U} \quad (4)$$

EXAMPLE 1. Shown in Table 2 are the 75 movies rated at five different levels. The provided ratings on the 75 movies given by a user U were extracted from the Netflix dataset. Regardless of its rating level, MudRecS extracts 99 reviews retrieved for each one of the 75 movies M and determines the *polarity* of each *feature* covered in M. Table 2 shows the number of movies with an identified *feature*[3] that has been assigned a positive/negative polarity at each rating level.

The sentiments of each feature shown in Table 2 indicate that U is more interested in the *Story* and *Direct(ion)* of a movie, and less about *Plot* and *Visuals*. □

Review Score Computation. Using the items ranked by U in the Review Analysis step, the Review score (RwS) of an unrated item I is computed at each rating level R_i ($1 \leq i \leq N$) by averaging the PFS of each feature F in I with polarity P_F, which is either *Positive* or *Negative*, at R_i.

$$RwS(R_i, I) = \frac{\sum_{F \in Features} PFS(R_i, F, P_F)}{N} \quad (5)$$

where $Features$ is the set of features identified in I through the 99 reviews retrieved for I, N is the total number of features (in $Features$) ranked at R_i as computed in the Review Analysis step, and PFS is as defined in Equation 4.

[3]MudRecS has identified 11 features for the set of 75 movies, but only 4 out of 11 are displayed, since they are features of the unrated movie "War of the World" to be evaluated.

Features: *S*(tory), *P*(lot), *V*(isuals), *D*(irection)
P_{Story} = '+', P_{Plot} = '-', $P_{Visuals}$ = '-', $P_{Direction}$ = '+'
PFS(1, *S*, +) = 2/5, *PFS*(1, *P*, -) = 4/5, *PFS*(1, *V*, -) = 2/5, *PFS*(1, *D*, +) = 0/5
PFS(2, *S*, +) = 3/10, *PFS*(2, *P*, -) = 6/10, *PFS*(2, *V*, -) = 5/10, *PFS*(2, *D*, +) = 2/10
PFS(3, *S*, +) = 8/20, *PFS*(3, *P*, -) = 13/20, *PFS*(3, *V*, -) = 14/20, *PFS*(3, *D*, +) = 13/20
PFS(4, *S*, +) = 18/25, *PFS*(4, *P*, -) = 15/25, *PFS*(4, *V*, -) = 18/25, *PFS*(4, *D*, +) = 13/25
PFS(5, *S*, +) = 11/15, *PFS*(5, *P*, -) = 6/15, *PFS*(5, *V*, -) = 11/15, *PFS*(5, *D*, +) = 12/15
RwS(1, "WoW") = 2/5 = 0.4, *RwS*(2, "WoW") = 4/10 = 0.4, *RwS*(3, "WoW") = 12/20 = 0.6
RwS(4, "WoW") = 16/25 = 0.64, *RwS*(5, "WoW") = 10/15 = **0.67**

Figure 4: The *Review score* (RwS) at each rating level of the movie "War of the Worlds" (WoW) computed using PFSs based on the polarities in Table 2

EXAMPLE 2. The first two lines in Figure 4 show the features and their polarities identified by using the 99 reviews extracted for the unrated movie "War of the Worlds" (WoW). The RwS of WoW is the highest at rating level 5, which indicates that the (positive) features, i.e., *Story* and *Direction*, of WoW are regarded highly by U, which are reflected at the high levels of ranking (levels 4 and 5) of the two features as shown in Table 2. □

3.3 The Role Players of Multimedia Items

While some web users might (not) be interested in an item because of its genre(s) and/or particular features, others (dis)like the item because of its role player(s). For example, a user might enjoy movies acted by *Will Smith* regardless of the genre or visual effects of anyone of his movies. For this reason, besides analyzing the genres and reviews of multimedia items, MudRecS considers their role players.

A movie recommendation system likely suggests movies to a user U with the same actor/actress/director/producer who is highly rated by U, whereas a book recommender would suggest different books with the same authors (e.g., books published as a sequel). MudRecS uses information of role players in rating prediction by analyzing the *popularity* of a role player based on the ratings of the role player extracted from different multimedia websites (in Section 3.3.1). Hereafter, at each potential rating level of an unrated item I, MudRecS computes a *popularity* score for the role players of I, denoted *RolePlayerScore* (*RPS*) (in Section 3.3.2).

3.3.1 The Popularity of Role Players

Popularity plays an important role in rating prediction because most users are influenced by the opinions expressed by others or the degree of exposition about an author/role player in the market [1]. The *popularity* of a role player P can be determined using various measures, such as the number of sold items involving P or user reviews, which capture the *popularity* of P[4]. Each popularity ranking is a numerical value between 0 and 1 such that if P is rated (in the ascending order) n out of m role players, then the ranking of P is $\frac{n}{m}$, such that the *lower* $\frac{n}{m}$ is, the *more popular* P is. The Web is rich with lists of rated role players for different types of multimedia data.

Movies. MudRecS relies on imdb.com to determine the popularity of role players in movies. Imdb.com creates ratings of movie actors, actresses, directors, and producers. The ratings provide a snapshot of who is *popular* based on the activities involving millions of imdb users on the website, which include the number of times an actor's/actress' page is

[4]The *Popularity* of a role player P is the by-product of the unique characteristics of P, which appeal to users [1].

viewed and *statistical data* such as movie ratings, box-office gross, the number of movies a role player involved, salaries of the role players, etc. These ratings are accessible through a service, known as STARmeter, on imdb.com, which reflect the popularity of the role players in movies.

Music. To determine the popularity of music artists, MudRecS considers the ratings on music artists provided by Billboard.com and Mtvmusicmeter.com. Billboard.com, which is a premier music website and a primary source of information on trends and innovation in music, archives an extensive array of (reviews on) songs and artists. The website *rates* artists based on *users' reviews* and the number of users who *favor* an artist A (through a clickable "favorite" button on the website). Billboard.com, however, ignores the *statistical information* on A, such as the sales records of A and the number of played/downloaded streams on his/her songs. For this reason, besides the ratings on and the (un)favorability of music artists provided by Billboard.com, MudRecS also considers Mtvmusicmeter.com to determine the rating of a music artist. Mtvmusicmeter.com is a website that offers access to archived profiles of over one million music artists and allows its users to browse/play their songs. The website establishes an *artist meter* that *rates* artists based on their popularity, which is determined by tweets, blog posts, news articles, streams, and sales records. To obtain a unified popularity score for a music artist A, MudRecS averages evenly the ratings of A provided by the two music websites.

Books. MudRecS defines the ratings of book authors using the authors' popularity ratings archived at iblist.com, which is an online database that boasts entries of over 19,000 authors. Iblist.com employs a *rating* system for authors similar to the ratings of actors/actresses/directors/producers on imdb.com. The website is managed by a board of volunteer editors and administrators who ensure the quality and accuracy of posted information. To avoid spam, irrelevant, and irresponsible remarks, third-party reviews are not accepted by iblist.com. Instead, only reviews submitted by registered, well-established users, who have been approved by the board of editors and administrators, can be posted on the website.

Paintings. Since there is no well-established or well-known website that provides a rated list of popular painting artists, MudRecS defines their ratings using Wikipedia. The website maintains a list of the highest, known prices for paintings, which MudRecS uses for identifying the popularity of painters such that the *higher* the cumulative price of a set of paintings created by a painter P is, the *higher* P is *ranked*. This notion is adopted, since the prices of paintings are primarily based on the artists' popularity and vice versa.

3.3.2 Assigning Scores to Role Players

MudRecS computes the *Role Player Score* (RPS) for each role player of a multimedia item in two steps: Role Player Analysis (performed once) and Popularity Computation.

Role Player Analysis. Given a set of multimedia items S of the same domain previously rated by a user and the *popularity* of each role player in S determined in Section 3.3.1, MudRecS computes a score for S, denoted *Popularity Score* (PoS), at each rating level R_i ($1 \leq i \leq N$), which measures the average popularity of all the role players in S at R_i.

$$PoS(R_i, S) = \frac{\sum_{I \in S} \sum_{A \in I} Popularity\ of\ Role\ Player\ A\ at\ R_i}{Total\ Count\ of\ Role\ Players\ in\ S} \quad (6)$$

Set of Movies (S)	Overall Rating	*Actor 1* Ranking	*Actor 2* Ranking
Iron Man	5	5/400	16/400
Wife	2	300/400	350/400
Cars	4	60/400	40/400
Love	1	250/400	350/400
X Men	5	1/400	10/400
Prison	3	100/400	150/400

Number of distinct movie actors/actresses = 400

$PoS(1, S) = (250/400 + 350/400) / 2 = 300/400$
$PoS(2, S) = (300/400 + 350/400) / 2 = 325/400$
$PoS(3, S) = (100/400 + 150/400) / 2 = 125/400$
$PoS(4, S) = (60/400 + 40/400) / 2 = 50/400$
$PoS(5, S) = (5/400 + 16/400 + 1/400 + 10/400) / 4 = 8/400$

New, Unrated Movie I, "War of the Worlds"
Ranking of *Actor* 1 in I: 5/400, Ranking of *Actor* 2 in I: 15/400
$Avg\_Pop(I) = (5/400 + 15/400) / 2 = \underline{10/400}$, $RPS(1, I) = 1 - |Avg\_Pop(I) - PoS(1,S)| = 110/400$
$RPS(2, I) = 1 - |Avg\_Pop(I) - PoS(2,S)| = 85/400$, $RPS(3, I) = 1 - |Avg\_Pop(I) - PoS(3,S)| = 285/400$
$RPS(4, I) = 1 - |Avg\_Pop(I) - PoS(4,S)| = 360/400$, $RPS(5, I) = 1 - |Avg\_Pop(I) - PoS(5,S)| = \mathbf{398/400}$

Figure 5: The computed RPS score at each rating level for the movie "War of the Worlds", where Actor i ($1 \leq i \leq 2$) in different movies can be different

EXAMPLE 3. Figure 5 shows the ratings provided by a user U on six movies extracted from the Netflix dataset and the rankings of two main actors/actresses in each movie at various rating levels obtained from STARmeter on imdb.com[5]. $PoS(5, S) = 8/400$, the lowest value among all the rating levels, indicates that U favors *popular* actors/actresses. □

Popularity Computation. During the recommendation process, MudRecS sums the popularity score of each role player of an unrated item I. The popularity score of each role player in I is then averaged into one score, denoted *Avg_Pop*, using Equation 7, and MudRecS assigns the RPS to I at each rating level in Equation 8.

$$Avg\_Pop(I) = \frac{\sum_{A \in I} Popularity\ of\ A}{Total\ Count\ of\ Role\ Players\ in\ S} \quad (7)$$

$$RPS(R_i, I) = 1 - |Avg\_Pop(I) - PoS(R_i, S)| \quad (8)$$

where NR is the number of role players in I.

Equation 8 computes the difference between the average popularity of role players of I and the average popularity of role players of items rated at R_i by U. A *larger* RPS at R_i indicates that the popularity ranking of the role players of I is *closer* to the *popularity ranking* of role players of items previously rated at R_i, which increases the likelihood of assigning the rating level R_i to I. Equation 8 is complemented, since RPS is combined with other scores using the SCF (see Section 3), and the *higher* each *score* is at a rating level, the more likely the *rating* level is assigned to I.

EXAMPLE 4. Figure 5 shows the RPS at each rating level for the movie I, "War of the Worlds," which is played by popular actors as reflected by the averaged *Popularity Score* of role players of the movie, i.e., $Avg\_Pop(I) = 10/400$. The RPS for the movie is the *highest* at rating level 5, which increases the likelihood of the movie being rated high. □

3.4 Readability

The readability level of a book is a value between 0 and 13, i.e., Kindergarten to College. Reading can be a frustrating experience to users who struggle to understand (are not motivated to read, respectively) a book that is beyond (below, respectively) their readability levels. Analyzing the readability levels of books pre-rated by a user U can enhance

[5]An actor's/actress' ranking is the same in different movies.

Book	A	B	C	D	E	F	G	H	I	J
Reading Level (L)	11	3	9	3	12	7	11	11	3	11
Rating Level (R_i)	5	2	4	1	5	3	2	3	5	4

Unrated Book (I), "War of the Worlds"
Reading Level (L) = 11

$ReS(1, I, 11) = 0/1 \times (0/1 \times 1/11 + 0/1 \times 1/10 + 0/1 \times 1/9 + 1/1 \times 1/8 + \ldots + 0/1 \times 1/2) = 0$
$ReS(2, I, 11) = 1/2 \times (0/2 \times 1/11 + 0/2 \times 1/10 + 0/2 \times 1/9 + 1/2 \times 1/8 + \ldots + 0/2 \times 1/2) = 1/32$
$ReS(3, I, 11) = 1/2 \times (0/2 \times 1/11 + 0/2 \times 1/10 + \ldots + 1/2 \times 1/4 + \ldots + 0/2 \times 1/2) = 1/16$
$ReS(4, I, 11) = 1/2 \times (0/2 \times 1/11 + 0/2 \times 1/10 + \ldots + 1/2 \times 1/2 + \ldots + 0/2 \times 1/2) = \mathbf{1/8}$
$ReS(5, I, 11) = 1/3 \times (0/3 \times 1/11 + \ldots + 1/3 \times 1/8 + \ldots + 1/3 \times 1/1 + 0/3 \times 1/2) = 1/216$

Figure 6: The computed ReS value at each rating level for the book "War of the Worlds"

the accuracy of rating prediction on books unrated by U. MudRecS, which determines whether a book B unrated by U is appropriate for U based on the readability level of B, relies on the readability levels of books pre-rated by U.

Majority of existing readability assessment tools examine lexical, syntactic, and semantic content of a text document I to determine the readability level of I. These properties, however, are not well-designed and mostly based on observations. MudRecS relies on ReadAid [15], a fully-automated readability analyzer, to access the readability level of I.

Using a set of books S previously rated by a user U with their readability levels computed by ReadAid, MudRecS assigns a *readability score*, denoted ReS, at each rating level $R_i (1 \leq i \leq N)$ to a book I unrated by U based on the readability level L $(0 \leq L \leq 13)$ of I determined by ReadAid.

$$ReS(R_i, I, L) = \frac{Bks@R_iL}{TBks@R_i} \times \sum_{k=0, k \neq L}^{13} \frac{Bks@R_ik}{TBks@R_i} \times \frac{1}{|k-L|} \quad (9)$$

where $Bks@R_iL$ ($Bks@R_ik$, respectively) is the total number of books in S at readability level L (k, respectively) rated at R_i by U and $TBks@R_i$ is the number of books in S rated at R_i by U. The constraint "$k \neq L$" avoids a division by zero. $ReS(R_i, I, L) = 0$, if $TBks@R_i = 0$.

Equation 9 assigns a higher ReS to a book I at R_i if books in S with the same reading level L as I have been rated at R_i more frequently than at any other rating levels. $\frac{1}{|k-L|}$ assigns *higher* weight to similar, but not identical, grade levels, since users in grade levels L and $L+1$, or L and $L-1$, can usually comprehend the same materials, whereas users with grade levels 1 and 12, respectively cannot. The *smaller* the difference between two grade levels is, the *higher* it is *weighted* in a computed ReS, which is captured by $\frac{1}{|k-L|}$.

EXAMPLE 5. Figure 6 shows the ratings on 10 books given by a BookCrossing user U. The rating on an unrated book I, "War of the Worlds," is determined by using the readability levels of the 10 books pre-rated by U. The readability and rating levels of the books show that books with *high* (*low*, respectively) readability levels are often ranked at *high* (*low*, respectively) rating levels 4-5 (1-2, respectively) by U. At the readability level of 11, I is most likely to be recommended to U, which is reflected by the ReSs, since ReS for I is the *highest* at rating level 4, indicating that the readability level of I is *closer* to the readability level of books in S rated at level 4 by U than at any other rating levels. □

3.5 Utilizations of MudRecS

MudRecS can be utilized differently to make recommendations. Each of the utilizations, listed below, can easily be implemented on top of MudRecS, which only requires a user interface to be constructed that handles users' inputs.

(i) When its users provide ratings on different multimedia items, MudRecS can automatically predict the ratings for other items of the same or a different domain in its underlying database, an approach currently adapted by Netflix.com.

(ii) When a user offers an item, which is either a book that the user has read, a song that (s)he has listened, a movie or painting the user has seen, or a rating on a multimedia item, MudRecS instinctively generates a number of recommendations (with the same or higher rating) on other items.

(iii) A user can specify a multimedia item I (s)he likes and a collection of multimedia items of different domains of interest. In response, MudRecS retrieves the items in the collection closed related to I with the highest rating.

(iv) Based on the multimedia items that a user U has previously accessed, MudRecS can suggest closely related items, which is similar to a shopping recommendation system, such as EBay.com and Amazon.com, that recommends items according to previous purchases.

MudRecS can predict the rating of either a movie, song, book, or painting I that is (not) in the same domain of items that a user U has previously rated using only the title of I.

4. PERFORMANCE EVALUATION

To assess MudRecS and compare its performance with existing state-of-the-art multimedia recommendation systems, we adopted the 5-fold cross-validation scheme, which is widely-used for evaluating recommendation and IR systems. Each dataset D (introduced in Section 4.1), which is created for the evaluation purpose, is randomly split into five equal-sized, disjoint subsets D_k $(1 \leq k \leq 5)$. For each D_k, MudRecS determines the genre, review, role player, and the readability (of a book) scores of each item in $\bigcup_{l=1, l \neq k}^{5} D_l$ and computes the Root Mean Squared Error (RMSE) and Mean Absolute Error (MAE) (as defined in Section 4.2) on D_k. The RMSEs and MAEs of the five iterations are *averaged* to yield the corresponding mean error value, respectively.

We evaluate the rating predictions on unrated items determined by MudRecS and other recommendation systems on four distinct types of multimedia data: movies (videos), music (audios), books (text), and paintings (images). We compare MudRecS against four most recently proposed multimedia recommendation systems (presented in Section 4.3), each of which predicts ratings on one (or more, but not all) of the four types of multimedia data. In fact, none of the existing recommendation systems, as we are aware of, predicts ratings on all four different types of multimedia data. Besides the four recommendation systems, we also compare the rating prediction accuracy of MudRecS on movies against 20 other movie recommendation systems participated in the Netflix contest (see details in Section 4.4). Even though we have evaluated MudRecS on text, audio, video, and image documents individually and independently, the evaluation of MudRecS can easily be extended to cover cross-domain multimedia items recommended for a user, assuming that the required genres, reviews, popularity of role players, and readability (for text data), are available.

4.1 Datasets

The datasets employed to evaluate (compare, respectively) MudRecS (with others, respectively) on rating prediction are well-known and widely-used, with the exception of paintings.

Figure 7: A snapshot of images in a Facebook survey conducted for constructing the paintings dataset

Movies. The MovieLens and Netflix datasets were chosen for evaluating the rating prediction accuracy of MudRecS on movies. The MovieLens (cs.umn.edu/Research/GroupsLens) dataset was created during a 7-month period from September 19, 1997 until April 22, 1998 by the developers of MovieLens, a popular web-based recommendation system on movies. The Netflix dataset, on the other hand, was collected as part of a contest in 2008 for predicting movie ratings.

Music. The Yahoo! Music Services dataset, which was created by the Yahoo! research team, contains ratings for songs collected from two different sources: the ratings provided by Yahoo! users of the Yahoo! music services in 2006, and the ratings on randomly selected songs collected during an online survey conducted by Yahoo! Research in 2006.

Books. The popular BookCrossing dataset [21] was manually created between August and September of 2004 with data extracted from BookCrossing.com.

Paintings. To the best of our knowledge, there is no benchmark dataset available for evaluating the performance of a recommendation system on paintings. To verify the accuracy of MudRecS in rating prediction on paintings, we randomly extracted 1,000 paintings on different genres (with reviews) using the Yahoo! image search engine. To obtain user ratings on the 1,000 paintings, we relied on Facebook users. We prepared 10 different Facebook surveys, each of which includes 100 distinct paintings. (A set of 100 paintings is an ideal collection, since a larger number of paintings in a survey would overwhelm its appraisers.) Each survey required each involved user to browse through the paintings and provide star ratings (on a 1-5 scale with '5' being the highest) on 10 or more paintings, using the rating meter directly below each painting. (Figure 7 shows a snapshot of the Facebook application that includes a number of paintings in one of the surveys.) The "Not Interested" button below each painting could be clicked by the user to assign a star rating of "1" (the lowest rating) to the painting. The surveys were sent out on May 4, 2011 to different Facebook users who were asked to forward the surveys to others. By May 11, 2011, we accumulated all the responses for our study.

Table 3 shows a summary of the multimedia datasets used for evaluating and comparing the performance of MudRecS.

4.2 Evaluation Metrics

Root Mean Square Error (RMSE) and *Mean Absolute Error* (MAE) are two performance metrics widely-used for evaluating rating predictions on multimedia data. Both

Multimedia Dataset	# of Users	# of Items	# of Ratings	Rating Scale
MovieLens	943	1,682	100,000	1-5
Netflix	480,000	18,000	100,000,000	1-5
Yahoo! Music	15,400	1,000	354,000	1-5
BookCrossing	278,858	271,379	1,149,780	1-10
FB Paintings	312	964	3,312	1-5

Table 3: Datasets used for evaluating MudRecS

RMSE and MAE measure the *average magnitude* of *error*, i.e., the average prediction error, on incorrectly assigned ratings. The error values computed by RMSE are squared before they are summed and averaged, which yield a relatively *high* weight to errors of *large* magnitude, whereas MAE is a *linear* score, i.e., the absolute values of individual differences in incorrect assignments are weighted equally in the average.

$$RMSE = \sqrt{\frac{\sum_{i=1}^{n}(f(x_i) - y_i)^2}{n}}, MAE = \frac{1}{n}\sum_{i=1}^{n}|f(x_i) - y_i| \quad (10)$$

where n is the total number of items with ratings to be evaluated, $f(x_i)$ is the rating predicted by a system on item x_i ($1 \leq i \leq n$), and y_i is an expert-assigned rating to x_i.

4.3 Recommendation Systems to be Compared

In this section, we detail the recommenders to be compared with MudRecS. These recommenders were chosen, since they achieve high accuracy in rating predictions on items in their respective multimedia domains.

MF. Yu et al. [19] and Singh et al. [17] predict ratings on books, movies, songs, and paintings[6] based on matrix factorization (MF), which clusters items and users by genres so that ratings are predicted according to the rating patterns of certain groups of items on certain genres. MF can also characterize both items and users by vectors of features, which are the properties of an item. The matrix with information on users, genres, and features of an item is decomposed by features and genres, which can be combined to provide rating predictions for any user-genre-feature combination.

Yu et al. propose a non-parametric matrix factorization (NPMF) method, which does not require the model dimensionality, i.e., users, features, and ratings, to be specified apriori. Rather, the dimensionality is determined from previously rated items instead. Singh et al. introduce a collective matrix factorization (CMF) approach based on relational learning, which predicts unknown values of a relation between entities of a certain item using a given database of entities and observed relations among entities.

ML. Besides the matrix factorization methods, probabilistic frameworks have been introduced for rating predictions. Shi et al. [16] apply a supervised machine learning (ML) approach to automatically construct a ranking model/function from training data to predict ratings on movies[7]. The ML approach applies a rank-oriented strategy, which

[6]The systems were originally designed to predict ratings on *books* and *movies* only but were implemented by us for comparing their predicted ratings on *songs* and *paintings* as well.
[7]The system was originally designed to predict ratings on *movies* but was implemented by us for additional comparisons on *books*, *songs*, and *paintings* as well.

exploits pairwise preferences between *items* and *users* to generate a list of ranked items corresponding to the ratings such that the *higher* an item is ranked, the *higher* its rating.

DM. Su et al. [18] propose uMender, a music recommendation system, which predicts ratings on songs by mining musical content and context information. uMender first utilizes the *perceptual patterns* of songs, which consist of the acoustical and temporal features of a song and then clusters users who provide similar ratings to similar songs to detect patterns for acoustics and temporal features, as well as to discover new, implicit, more applicable perceptual patterns. uMender assigns a rating to an item I based on the perceptual patterns of I and the cluster to which I belongs.

Netflix. We further compare MudRecS against the 20 systems that participated in the Netflix contest in 2008. The open competition was held by Netflix, an online DVD-rental service, and the Netflix Prize was awarded to the best recommendation algorithm with the lowest RMSE score in predicting user ratings on films based on previous ratings. On September 21, 2009, the grand prize of one million dollars were given. The RMSE scores achieved by each of the twenty systems, as well as detailed discussions on their rating prediction algorithms, can be found on the Netflix website (netflixprize.com//leaderboard).

4.4 Experimental Results

Figures 8(a), 8(b), and 8(c) show the MAE and RMSE scores of MudRecS and other recommendation systems on the MovieLens, Yahoo! Music, and BookCrossing datasets, respectively. As the RMSE scores indicate, MudRecS significantly outperforms other systems on rating predictions of the respective multimedia data. Regarding the MovieLens and Yahoo! Music datasets, MudRecS achieves a RMSE score of 0.72 and 0.80, respectively, which imply that, on the average, an incorrectly assigned rating by MudRecS is less than 1 star away from its correct assignment. On the BookCrossing dataset, MudRecS achieves an RMSE score of 0.45, which indicates that the error in rating assignment is less than half a star away from the user-/expert-assigned, actual rating. The MAE scores of MudRecS are also lower than the other systems on all the corresponding datasets. On BookCrossing, the MAE scores show that an error in rating predictions is on an average of 0.2 away from the correct prediction, which indicates a very high accuracy in rating predictions on books. Among all the four multimedia domains, the MAE scores of MudRecS are at least 0.16 lower than the other compared recommendation systems.

As shown in Figure 8(d) on *Paintings*, MudRecS achieves the highest RMSE and MAE values compared with other recommenders. Comparatively, the RMSE and MAE scores of MudRecS on paintings are the highest (i.e., worst) among the respective scores on other multimedia datasets. This is probably due to the smaller number of features of paintings in their reviews compared to other types of multimedia data.

The small difference between the RMSE and MAE scores of MudRecS, as shown in Figure 8, verifies that the error in incorrect ratings predicted by MudRecS is insignificant, since the larger the errors is, the heavier they are penalized by the RMSE measure, which increases the difference between RMSE and MAE.

On the Netflix dataset, MudRecS achieves a RMSE score[8]

[8]MAE scores were not computed on the Netflix dataset due to their unavailability for the other 20 recommenders.

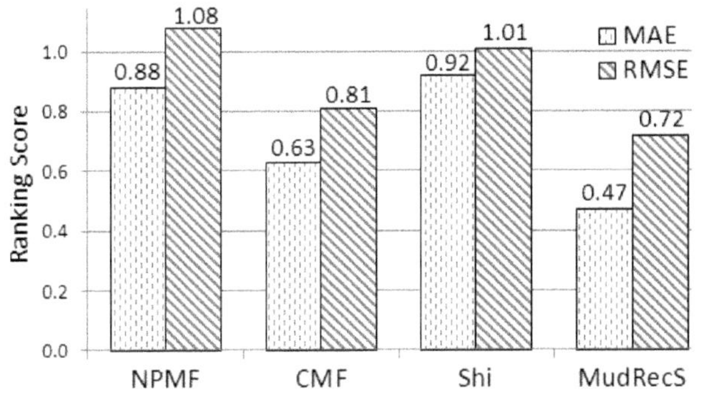

(a) The *MovieLens* dataset

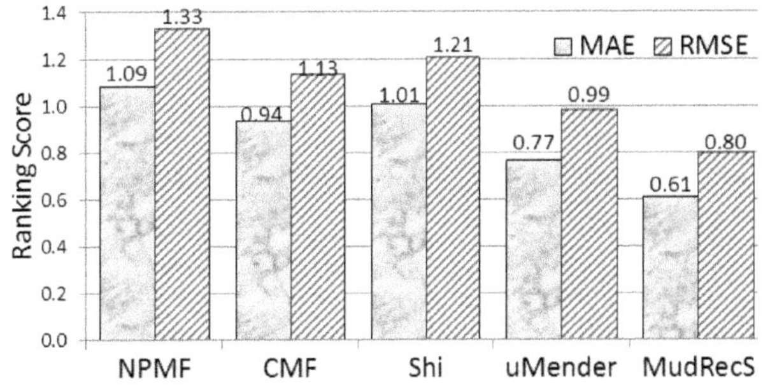

(b) The *Yahoo! Music* dataset

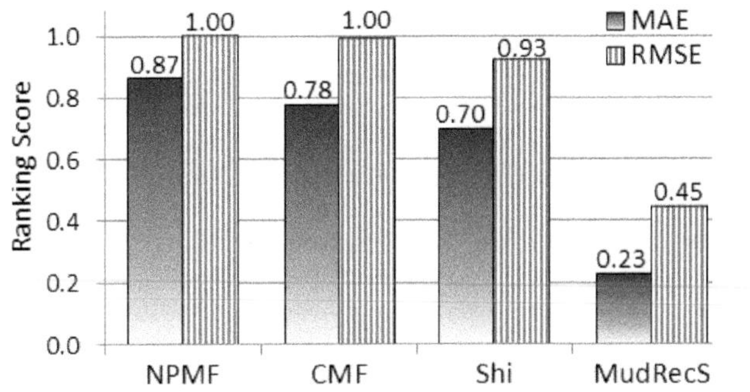

(c) The *BookCrossing* dataset

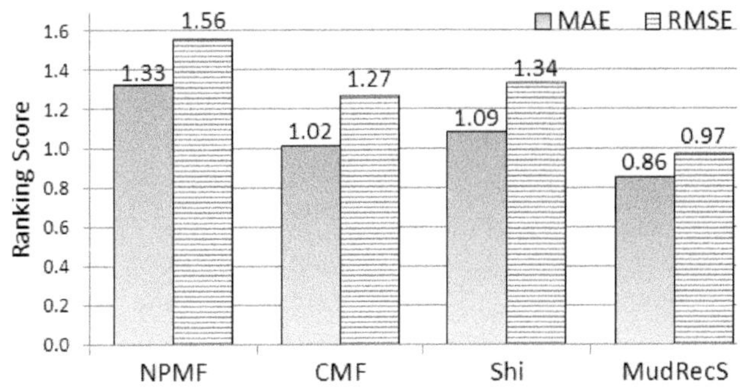

(d) The *Painting* dataset

Figure 8: The MAE and RMSE scores for various recommendation systems on different datasets

of 0.8571. MudRecS outperforms 18 recommendation systems and is only outperformed by two systems (Belkor and Ensemble), both of which achieve the same score of 0.8567, a small, insignificant fraction (0.8571 - 0.8567 = 0.0004) better than MudRecS. The reason for the slightly better RMSE score achieved by the two systems on the Netflix dataset are twofold. Unlike MudRecS, Belkor and Ensemble were specifically designed for movie rating predictions, and the construction of their algorithms focus on rating patterns found in movies which may not apply to other domains. Moreover, Belkor and Ensemble account for temporal effects, i.e., the fact that a user's preference changes over time, which may lead to different ratings for the same movie over time. The temporal effect, however, does not apply to all users and requires a larger subset of training data in order to obtain reliable results, which are the constraints. In considering a 95% confidence interval, MudRecS significantly outperforms 17 recommendation systems and is *not* significantly outperformed by *any* of the twenty systems. CineMatch, Netflix's recommender, achieves an RMSE score of 0.9514 on the Netflix dataset, which is outperformed by MudRecS.

On the average, MudRecS takes approximately two seconds to make recommendations for a user query.

5. CONCLUSIONS

It is appealing to a user who is recommended multimedia items that are closely related to items that (s)he is interested in. For example, if a user U likes the movie "The Pursuit of Happyness," it is likely that U is also interested in "Seven Pounds," which shares the same genre (i.e., drama), actor (i.e., Will Smith), and similar reviews. Instead of matching the same type of multimedia items, the recommended items, which are either in the form of movies, music, books, and/or pictures, provide more sources of information for U. Offering different types of multimedia items enriches the learning and entertaining experience for the multimedia recommender users, which can be achieved by MudRecS, our proposed multimedia recommendation system.

Given the ratings of a set of multimedia items S provided by a user U, MudRecS predicts the *rating* of an item I unrated by U based on the *genres*, *role players*, *reviews*, and the *comprehensive level* of I. Offering different types of multimedia recommendations, which include movies (videos), songs (audios), books (text), and paintings (image) of interest to a user is the uniqueness and merit of MudRecS. MudRecS does not rely on user data extracted from social websites, ontologies, access patterns, nor training data, which is simple and easy to implement, since it depends only on users' ratings, genres, role players, reviews, and readability levels of multimedia items that are widely available on the Web.

Experimental results show that MudRecS accurately predicts the rating levels of multimedia items for recommendations. The empirical study demonstrates that MudRecS significantly outperforms existing multimedia recommendation systems in making recommendations based on ratings.

6. REFERENCES

[1] E. Arnould, L. Price, and G. Zinkhan. *Consumers.* McGraw Hill, 2002.

[2] L. Campos, J. Fernandez-Luna, J. Huete, and M. Rueda-Morales. Combining Content-Based and Collaborative Recommendations: A Hybrid Approach Based on Bayesian Networks. *Approximate Reasoning*, 51(7):785–799, 2010.

[3] H. Chen and A. Chen. A Music Recommendation System Based on Music Data Grouping and User Interests. In *ACM CIKM*, pages 231–238, 2010.

[4] C. Desrosiers and G. Karypis. *Handbook on Recommender Systems.* Springer, 2009.

[5] D. Dunlavy, D. O'Leary, J. Conroy, and J. Schlesinger. A System for Querying, Clustering, and Summarizing Documents. In *IPM*, pages 1588–1605, 2007.

[6] Q. Gu, J. Zhou, and C. Ding. Collaborative Filtering: Weighted Nonnegative Matrix Factorization Incorporating User and Item Graphs. In *SDM*, pages 199–210, 2010.

[7] Z. Guan, C. Wang, J. Bu, C. Chen, K. Yang, D. Cai, and X. He. Document Recommendation in Social Tagging Services. In *WWW*, pages 391–400, 2010.

[8] J. Koberstein and Y.-K. Ng. Using Word Clusters to Detect Similar Web Documents. In *KSEM*, pages 215–228, 2006.

[9] Y. Koren. Factorization Meets the Neighborhood: A Multifaceted Collaborative Filtering Model. In *ACM SIGKDD*, pages 426–434, 2008.

[10] O. Kwon. "I Know What You Need to Buy": Context-Aware Multimedia-based Recommendation System. *Expert Systems with Applications*, 25:387–400, 2003.

[11] G. Linden, B. Smith, and J. York. Amazon.com Recommendations: Item-to-Item Collaborative Filtering. In *Internet Computing*, pages 76–80, 2003.

[12] G. Luger. *Artificial Intelligence: Structures and Strategies for Complex Problem Solving,* 6th *Ed.* Addison Wesley, 2009.

[13] T. Noh, S. Park, H. Yoon, S. Lee, and S. Park. An Automatic Translation of Tags for Multimedia Contents Using Folksonomy Networks. In *ACM SIGIR*, pages 492–499, 2009.

[14] Y. Park and K. Chang. Individual and Group Behavior-based Customer Profile Model for Personalized Product Recommendation. *Expert Systems with Applications*, 36(2):1932–1939, 2009.

[15] R. Qumsiyeh and Y.-K. Ng. ReadAid: A Robust and Fully-Automated Readability Assessment Tool. In *IEEE ICTAI*, pages 539–546, 2011.

[16] Y. Shi, M. Larson, and A. Hanjalic. List-wise Learning to Rank with Matrix Factorization for Collaborative Filtering. In *ACM RecSys*, pages 269–272, 2010.

[17] A. Singh and G. Gordon. Relational Learning via Collective Matrix Factorization. In *ACM SIGKDD*, pages 650–658, 2008.

[18] J. Su, H. Yeh, and P. Tseng. Music Recommendation Using Content and Context Information Mining. In *IEEE Intelligent Systems*, pages 16–26, 2010.

[19] K. Yu, S. Zhu, J. Lafferty, and Y. Gong. Fast Nonparametric Matrix Factorization for Large-Scale Collaborative Filtering. In *ACM SIGIR*, pages 211–218, 2009.

[20] D. Zhang and Y. Dong. Semantic, Hierarchical, Online Clustering of Web Search Results. In *ACM WIDM*, pages 69–78, 2001.

[21] C. Ziegler, S. McNee, J. Konstan, and G. Lausen. Improving Recommendation Lists Through Topic Diversification. In *WWW*, pages 22–32, 2005.

Personalized Click Shaping through Lagrangian Duality for Online Recommendation*

Deepak Agarwal†, Bee-Chung Chen†, Pradheep Elango‡, Xuanhui Wang‡
†LinkedIn, Mountain View, CA
{dagarwal, bchen}@linkedin.com
‡Facebook, Menlo Park, CA
{pradheep, xuanhui}@fb.com

ABSTRACT

Online content recommendation aims to identify trendy articles in a continuously changing dynamic content pool. Most of existing works rely on online user feedback, notably clicks, as the objective and maximize it by showing articles with highest click-through rates. Recently, click shaping [4] was introduced to incorporate multiple objectives in a constrained optimization framework. The work showed that significant tradeoff among the competing objectives can be observed and thus it is important to consider multiple objectives. However, the proposed click shaping approach is segment-based and can only work with a few non-overlapping user segments. It remains a challenge of how to enable deep personalization in click shaping. In this paper, we tackle the challenge by proposing *personalized click shaping*. The main idea is to work with the Lagrangian duality formulation and explore strong convexity to connect dual and primal solutions. We show that our formulation not only allows efficient conversion from dual to primal for online personalized serving, but also enables us to solve the optimization faster by approximation. We conduct extensive experiments on a large real data set and our experimental results show that the personalized click shaping can significantly outperform the segmented one, while achieving the same ability to balance competing objectives.

Categories and Subject Descriptors: H.3.5 [Information Storage and Retrieval]: Online Information Services

General Terms: Algorithms

Keywords: Personalization, click shaping, dual plan

1. INTRODUCTION

A significant portion of content on the web is ephemeral, new items are continuously published through various channels and obsolete ones are removed quickly. For example, content on Web portals (e.g., Yahoo!, AOL, and MSN) are refreshed frequently to recommend relevant and timely content to users. With overwhelming amount of fast changing information and unique tastes of individual users, it becomes critical to recommend interesting content to users in a personalized and timely manner.

Traditional information filtering provides personalized recommendation based on historical user ratings on items and includes both content-based filtering and collaborative filtering (e.g., [27, 13]). These methods usually work well on a relatively stable item pool, such as movies or products, but they are inferior for online content recommendation which deals with fast changing item pool such as news articles [2]. The main challenge in online content recommendation problems is to quickly identify the most interesting items (e.g., breaking news). In such a setting, it is also hard to collect a data set with explicit user ratings on items. Instead, most of online recommendation works [2, 17] rely on implicit user feedback, notably clicks, and optimize click-rates by showing articles with the highest click-through rates(CTR) that are estimated through explore/exploit techniques [16, 5].

However, using CTR as the only objective is not satisfactory because it cannot fully reflect other important engagement metrics such as number of page views or the total time-spent on a Website, which are indicative of user satisfaction [8] and also reported by third-party metric companies (e.g., comScore). Recently, click shaping [4] was introduced to tackle the problem of recommending items to jointly optimize for multiple objectives: clicks and post-click downstream utilities. The work showed that significant tradeoffs among these competing objectives can be observed and a constrained optimization formulation is an effective implementation. However, the proposed approach in [4] assumes that users are partitioned into a few coarse non-overlapping segments. In many applications a user is characterized by a high-dimensional feature vector (thousands of dimensions with large number of all possible combinations), segmented click-shaping fails to provide recommendations at such granular resolutions (user or fine grained user segments) because decisions are made at coarse user-segment resolutions in epochs — in the current epoch (e.g., 10-minute interval), a linear program (LP) is solved to decide a *serving plan* $\{x_{ij}\}$: for every (user segment i, item j) pair, x_{ij} represents the probability that the system will show item j to user segment i in the next epoch.

While it looks we can apply the LP formulation at granular user resolution by having one variable x_{uj} for each (user u, item j) pair, such a naive extension is infeasible due the

*This work was conducted when all authors were affiliated with Yahoo!

Permission to make digital or hard copies of all or part of this work for personal or classroom use is granted without fee provided that copies are not made or distributed for profit or commercial advantage and that copies bear this notice and the full citation on the first page. To copy otherwise, to republish, to post on servers or to redistribute to lists, requires prior specific permission and/or a fee.
SIGIR'12, August 12–16, 2012, Portland, Oregon, USA.
Copyright 2012 ACM 978-1-4503-1472-5/12/08 ...$15.00.

following reasons: (1) This makes the LP ill-defined in the online setting because there are *unseen* users (user segments) that are observed for the first time in the next epoch. The modified LP has to predict the set of unseen users(unseen user segments) and include corresponding variables in order to serve them in the next epoch; (2) Even if we can accurately predict which users(user segments) will be seen in the next epoch, such an extension increases the size of the LP dramatically since there are usually hundreds of thousands users(user segments) per epoch. The segmented models can bypass these issues by assigning a new user to one of the predefined segments and use the segment serving plan for the new user. Thus, there are inherent limitations to directly utilize segmented click shaping for personalization. On the other hand, when optimizing clicks is the only objective, personalized models [22, 3] usually achieve much better results than segmented models. How to enable personalization in click shaping is a challenging, but important research problem that we address in this paper.

In this paper, we propose *personalized click shaping* which combines deep personalization with click shaping for multi-objective online content recommendation. Instead of working with the *primal* serving plan x_{ij}'s, our key idea is to convert the primal problem through Lagrangian duality and obtain the *dual* serving plan. By exploiting strong convexity of our objective function, we show that the dual plan can be efficiently converted to the primal plan for online personalized serving. Furthermore, our dual formulation can also enable us to solve the optimization faster through approximation. Specifically, we make the following contributions in this paper:

- In Section 3, we propose a novel technique to solve the aforementioned unseen user problem based on Lagrangian duality. By adding some small additional terms to the original linear objective function to achieve strong convexity, we show that the large number of primal variables x_{uj}'s can be obtained as a function of a small number of *user-independent* dual variables. Thus, in each epoch, we obtain the dual plan for the next epoch and, at serving time, we efficiently convert the dual solution on the fly to obtain the primal solution x_{uj} for each user u, seen or unseen.
- In Section 4, we develop a variety of approximation methods for efficient computation. Two clustering-based methods and two types of sampling-based methods are introduced. Our results show that clustering-based methods fail to work with the dual formulation, while simple random sampling is as good as more sophisticated stratified sampling methods.
- In Section 5, we empirically show that personalized click shaping significantly outperforms and uniformly dominates segmented click shaping for all Pareto optimal points based on extensive experiments on a large real data set using a recently proposed unbiased evaluation methodology [18].

2. PRELIMINARIES

In this section, we describe the problem setting and review segmented click shaping [4].

Application setting: Consider a content recommendation module on the front page of a portal such as Yahoo!. In each bucketized time epoch t, there is a set of candidate items available for recommendation, denoted by $\mathcal{A}_t$. Each item $j \in \mathcal{A}_t$ belongs to one of K different properties of the portal (e.g., Yahoo! News, Finance, Sports, etc). Let $\mathcal{P} = \{P_1, ..., P_K\}$ denote the set of properties and $j \in P_k$ means the landing page of item j belongs to property P_k. Let $\mathcal{U}_t$ denote the set of all users in epoch t. A user $u \in \mathcal{U}_t$ visits the front page and is recommended an item from $\mathcal{A}_t$. We only consider single item recommendation in this paper; multi-item problem is more involved and left as future work. When a user clicks the recommended item, it routes her to a page in the property that the clicked item belongs to. User visits to different properties are usually significantly influenced by the clicks on the front page. For the sake of illustration, consider that the portal wants to optimize for two different objectives — (a) total number of clicks on the front page and (b) total time-spent on landing properties by users who click recommended items on the front page. Note that other objectives can be incorporated in our framework.

Explore/exploit: Content optimization is an explore/exploit problem. To optimize for any metric, we need to estimate the performance of each candidate item in terms of that metric. Without displaying an item to any user, it is difficult to know the performance of that item. The explore/exploit problem for a single objective is well studied (e.g., [3, 18]). Developing explore/exploit methods for multiple objectives that ensure certain notion of optimality is nontrivial. In this paper we assume some explore/exploit scheme is running in the system. In particular, we use a simple scheme — ϵ-greedy, which has been empirically shown to achieve good performance [26]. This scheme works as follows: We serve a small fraction of randomly selected user visits (called exploration population) with items selected uniformly at random from the current content pool in order to collect data for every item. For the remaining visits (called exploitation population), we serve the item with the highest estimated click-through rate (CTR) if the goal is to maximize clicks. With multiple objectives, the serving scheme for the exploitation population is different from that of displaying the highest CTR item as we shall see later in this paper.

Segmented models: An important assumption made in the segmented click shaping work [4] is that users are clustered into m segments. Let $\mathcal{S}$ denote the set of segments and $i \in \mathcal{S}$ denote a segment in the rest of the paper. To measure the utility of an item j, statistical models are used to estimate: (a) the probability p_{ijt} that a user in segment i would click item j when it is displayed in epoch t, and (b) the time d_{ijt} that a user in segment i would spend post-click in the landing property of item j. We call p_{ijt} CTR and d_{ijt} time-spent. Note that if the goal is to maximize clicks (or time-spent, but not both), the optimal solution is to recommend the item j with the highest p_{ijt} (or $p_{ijt} \cdot d_{ijt}$) to users in segment i.

Segmented serving scheme: We call an algorithm that recommends items to users a serving scheme. For each epoch t, a segmented serving scheme uses information obtained before the epoch to produce a *segmented serving plan* $\mathbf{x}_t = \{x_{ijt} : i \in \mathcal{S}, j \in \mathcal{A}_t\}$, where x_{ijt} is the probability that the serving scheme will recommend item j to users in segment i in epoch t. When a user visits the front page in epoch t, she is first assigned to an appropriate segment and then an item is served through a multinomial draw according to $\{x_{ijt} :$

$j \in \mathcal{A}_t\}$. It should be clear that $x_{ijt} \geq 0$ and $\sum_j x_{ijt} = 1$. Different optimization methods generate different serving plans according to different criteria. For example, the click maximization method would set x_{ij^*t} to 1, if j^* has the highest CTR item, and 0 for the remaining items. Note that the serving plan for epoch t is made before epoch t, i.e., in epoch $t-1$ in our application setting.

Objectives: Recall that we consider two objectives in this paper, number of clicks and time-spent. Let N_t denote the total number of visits during epoch t, and let $\boldsymbol{\pi}_t = (\pi_{1t}, \cdots, \pi_{mt})$ denote the fraction of visits in different user segments. Obviously, $\sum_{i \in \mathcal{S}} \pi_{it} = 1$ and $N_t \pi_{it}$ is the total number of visits of segment i. Usually, $\boldsymbol{\pi}_t$ can be estimated based on past user visits [4]. For succinctness, we drop subscript t from the notations since we always consider the current epoch t. For example, $\mathbf{x} = \{x_{ij}\}$ is the serving plan for the epoch t. Given serving plan $\mathbf{x}$, the two objectives are:

- The expected total number of clicks on the front page:

$$TotalClicks(\mathbf{x}) = N \sum_{i \in \mathcal{S}} \sum_{j \in \mathcal{A}} \pi_i x_{ij} p_{ij}. \tag{1}$$

- The expected total time-spent on property P_k:

$$TotalTime(\mathbf{x}, P_k) = N \sum_{i \in \mathcal{S}} \sum_{j \in P_k} \pi_i x_{ij} p_{ij} d_{ij}. \tag{2}$$

  We use $TotalTime(\mathbf{x}) = TotalTime(\mathbf{x}, \mathcal{A})$ to denote the total time-spent on all properties.

Click maximization scheme: The status quo algorithm is to optimize the total number of clicks. We can obtain the serving plan as $\mathbf{z} = \{z_{ij}\}$ in the following,

$$z_{ij} = \begin{cases} 1 & \text{when } j = \arg\max_{j'} p_{ij'} \\ 0 & \text{otherwise} \end{cases} \tag{3}$$

We use $TotalClicks^* = TotalClicks(\mathbf{z})$ and $TotalTime^*(P_k) = TotalTime(\mathbf{z}, P_k)$ to denote the values of the two objectives for the click maximization scheme; they are constants since $\mathbf{z}$ is a set of constants defined above.

Linear program: Although a variety of multi-objective programs (MOP) were introduced in [4], we only discuss the most flexible formulation *localized multi-objective program* (ℓ-MOP) in this paper. Formally, the optimization problem is given below.

$$\begin{aligned} \max_{\mathbf{x}} \ & TotalTime(\mathbf{x}) \\ \text{s.t. } & TotalClicks(\mathbf{x}) \geq \alpha \cdot TotalClicks^* \\ & TotalTime(\mathbf{x}, P_k) \geq \beta \cdot TotalTime^*(P_k), \ \forall k \in \mathcal{I} \end{aligned} \tag{4}$$

where $\mathcal{I}$ is a subset of $\mathcal{P}$, for which we want to ensure certain level of time-spent. This linear program seeks to maximize the total time-spent on all properties, such that the potential loss in the total number of clicks is bounded by α ($0 \leq \alpha \leq 1$) compared to the status quo click maximization scheme. For each of the key properties $P_k \in \mathcal{I}$, the total time-spent on P_k is guaranteed to be at least β ($0 \leq \beta \leq 1$) times that of the click maximization scheme.

Summary: It is important to note that any linear constraint can be added to the linear program. The above choice is useful in our application setting and serves as a running example for illustration purposes. In every epoch, we use statistical models to predict p_{ij}, d_{ij} and π_i, and then solve the linear program to obtain the serving plan $\mathbf{x}$ for the next epoch. Thus, user visits in the next epoch will be served according to the plan made before we actually see the users.

3. PERSONALIZED CLICK SHAPING

As shown above, linear programs can be effectively used to perform segmented click shaping. However, such a segmented serving scheme treats all the users in a segment in the same way — it lacks the ability of serving each individual user differently to satisfy his/her unique personal information need. In this section, we extend click shaping beyond user segments to provide personalized serving plan for individual users.

3.1 Primal Formulation

In this section, we define the primal formulation of personalized click shaping by extending the segment-based linear program in Equation 4 through redefining the form of serving plan $\mathbf{x}$.

Personalized serving plan: For personalization, we have a user-specific serving plan for each user u, instead of segment-specific ones. Thus the personalized serving plan is defined as $\mathbf{x} = \{x_{uj} : u \in \mathcal{U}, j \in \mathcal{A}\}$, where x_{uj} is the probability that user u will be served with item j in the next epoch. Since the x_{uj}'s are probabilities, we have $x_{uj} \geq 0$ and $\sum_j x_{uj} = 1$. A personalized serving scheme serves items to each individual user according to these probabilities.

Objectives: Because the form of serving plan $\mathbf{x}$ changed, the definitions of $TotalClicks(\mathbf{x})$ and $TotalTime(\mathbf{x}, P_k)$ also need to be updated.

$$\begin{aligned} TotalClicks(\mathbf{x}) &= \sum_{u \in \mathcal{U}} \sum_{j \in \mathcal{A}} x_{uj} p_{uj}, \\ TotalTime(\mathbf{x}, P_k) &= \sum_{u \in \mathcal{U}} \sum_{j \in P_k} x_{uj} p_{uj} d_{uj}, \end{aligned} \tag{5}$$

where p_{uj} is the probability that user u would click item j and d_{uj} is the length of time that user u would spend on pages in the landing property of item j after he/she clicks the item. Both the estimation of p_{uj} and d_{uj} are orthogonal to our problem formulation and any personalized statistical model such as online regression proposed in previous works [3, 2] can be plugged in. Based on CTR estimation p_{uj}, we can compute the click optimization serving scheme similarly to Equation 3 and define the status quo constants $TotalClicks^*$ and $TotalTime^*$ for personalized serving accordingly. Please note that if we instantiate p_{uj} and d_{uj} using a segment-based model (i.e., $p_{uj} = p_{ij}$ and $d_{uj} = d_{ij}$ for all u in segment i), Equation 5 will reduce to Equation 1 and Equation 2.

Challenges: With these new definitions of $\mathbf{x}$, *TotalClicks* and *TotalTime*, on the surface, Equation 4 can be trivially applied to personalized click shaping: We can solve this linear program in each epoch and use the solution to serve users in the next epoch. However, such a formulation is challenging for the following reasons:

- **Unseen users:** In the linear program, the variables x_{uj}'s are meant for all users who visit in the *next* epoch. For those next epoch users who have not visited the portal before, computing x_{uj}'s is challenging. Although we may be able to estimate the number of users (which determines the number of variables), it is difficult to predict who exactly will visit in the next epoch. But the LP input p_{uj} and d_{uj} are required to be known for all users, including unseen ones.

- **Scalability:** This linear program requires a set of variables $\{x_{uj}\}_{\forall j \in \mathcal{A}}$ for each user u, which is in fact the serving plan for that individual user. Even if we know p_{uj} and d_{uj} for all the users in the next epoch, when the number of users is large (e.g., millions), the large number of variables results in a very large linear program and thus causes scalability issues.

Key idea: To tackle these challenges, we exploit Lagrangian duality formulation of our constrained optimization problem. In the primal program of Equation 4, x_{uj}'s are the primal variables. Although we have a large number of *user-specific* primal variables, there are only a small number of nontrivial constraints in the primal formulation. Our key idea is to explore Lagrangian duality to capture the primal variables by using a small number of *user-independent* dual variables, one per constraint in the primal program. Now suppose that we can efficiently compute the optimal dual solution for the next epoch (which will be discussed in Section 4). Also suppose that in the next epoch, we can efficiently convert the dual solution on the fly to the primal solution (i.e., serving plan) for each individual user at serving time. Then the challenges are solved.

Unfortunately, linear programs do not allow easy conversion from dual solutions to primal solutions and vice versa because the derivatives of the Lagrangian vanish [7]. To ensure convertibility, we slightly modify the originally linear objective function so that it becomes strongly convex. Intuitively, let $\mathbf{q} = \{q_{uj} : u \in \mathcal{U}, j \in \mathcal{A}\}$ be some baseline serving plan. We add terms to the objective function to penalize serving plans $\mathbf{x}$ that are far away from $\mathbf{q}$. There are a few choices for the baseline $\mathbf{q}$. One is the click maximization plan $\mathbf{z}$. Another is the uniform serving plan $q_{uj} = 1/|\mathcal{A}|$, which will encourage some notion of "fairness" among items. These penalty terms can be the L2 norm or KL divergence. We focus on the L2 norm penalty term and the uniform serving plan $\mathbf{q}$ in this paper.

$$||\mathbf{x} - \mathbf{q}||^2 = \sum_{u \in \mathcal{U}} \sum_{j \in \mathcal{A}} (x_{uj} - q_{uj})^2$$

Revised primal program: After adding the penalty term, we obtain the revised primal program.

$$\begin{aligned} &\min_{\mathbf{x}} \frac{1}{2}\gamma||\mathbf{x} - \mathbf{q}||^2 - \mathit{TotalTime}(\mathbf{x}) \\ &\text{s.t. } \mathit{TotalClicks}(\mathbf{x}) \geq \alpha \cdot \mathit{TotalClicks}^* \\ &\quad \mathit{TotalTime}(\mathbf{x}, P_k) \geq \beta \cdot \mathit{TotalTime}^*(P_k), \ \forall k \in \mathcal{I}, \end{aligned} \tag{6}$$

where γ specifies the importance of the penalty. Such a modification is generic since it can be applied to any linear program based click shaping. Notice that we also change from maximization to its equivalent minimization to put the primal program in the standard form of quadratic programming problem. In some sense, the added penalty term serves as regularization and can potentially reduce the variance of the solution.

3.2 Lagrangian Duality

We now introduce the dual variables and an algorithm to efficiently convert a dual solution to its corresponding primal solution. For ease of exposition, let

$$g_0 = \alpha \cdot \mathit{TotalClicks}^* \ \text{ and } \ g_k = \beta \cdot \mathit{TotalTime}^*(P_k).$$

The Lagrangian function of the primal program is

$$\begin{aligned} \Lambda(\mathbf{x}, \boldsymbol{\mu}, \boldsymbol{\nu}, \boldsymbol{\delta}) = &\tfrac{1}{2}\gamma \textstyle\sum_u \sum_j (x_{uj} - q_{uj})^2 - \sum_u \sum_j p_{uj} d_{uj} x_{uj} \\ &- \mu_0 (\textstyle\sum_u \sum_j p_{uj} x_{uj} - g_0) \\ &- \textstyle\sum_{k \in \mathcal{I}} \mu_k (\sum_u \sum_{j \in P_k} p_{uj} d_{uj} x_{uj} - g_k) \\ &- \textstyle\sum_u \nu_u (\sum_j x_{uj} - 1) - \sum_u \sum_j \delta_{uj} x_{uj}, \end{aligned}$$

where $\mu_0 \geq 0$, $\mu_k \geq 0$, for all $k \in \mathcal{I}$ and $\delta_{uj} \geq 0$, for all u and j. This is obtained by expanding *TotalTime* and *TotalClick* according to Equation 5 and applying the Lagrange multipliers μ_0 to ensure the total click constraint, μ_k to ensure the per-property total time constraint, ν_u to ensure $\sum_j x_{uj} = 1$, and δ_{uj} to ensure $x_{uj} \geq 0$. Note that μ_0, μ_k, ν_u and δ_{uj} are also called the *dual variables.*

By setting $\frac{\partial}{\partial x_{uj}} \Lambda(\mathbf{x}, \boldsymbol{\mu}, \boldsymbol{\nu}, \boldsymbol{\delta}) = 0$, we obtain

$$x_{uj} = \frac{c_{uj} + \nu_u + \delta_{uj}}{\gamma}, \tag{7}$$

where $c_{uj} = p_{uj} d_{uj} + \mu_0 p_{uj} + \mathbf{1}_{\{j \in P_k \wedge k \in \mathcal{I}\}} \mu_k p_{uj} d_{uj} + \gamma q_{uj}$. Note that $\mathbf{1}_{\{\text{True}\}} = 1$ and $\mathbf{1}_{\{\text{False}\}} = 0$. Thus, if we have the dual solution for μ_0, μ_k, ν_u and δ_{uj}, we can reconstruct the primal solution x_{uj}. However, this does not help to solve the challenges since ν_u and δ_{uj} still depend on the users u in the next epoch. In the following, we provide an efficient algorithm that reconstructs x_{uj} from $\boldsymbol{\mu} = \{\mu_0, \mu_k\}_{\forall k \in \mathcal{I}}$ alone without the need for ν_u and δ_{uj}.

Dual serving plan: We call $\boldsymbol{\mu}$ the *dual serving plan*, which does not include any user-specific variables. The algorithm that converts a dual plan to its corresponding primal serving plan is based on the following proposition.

Proposition 1 *In the optimal solution, given user u and two items j_1 and j_2, if $c_{uj_1} \geq c_{uj_2}$ and $x_{uj_2} > 0$, then $x_{uj_1} > 0$.*

Proof sketch: According to the KKT conditions, at the optimum point, $\delta_{uj_2} = 0$ since $x_{uj_2} > 0$. Then, because $c_{uj_1} \geq c_{uj_2}$ and $\delta_{uj_1} \geq 0$, we have

$$x_{uj_1} = \frac{c_{uj_1} + \nu_u + \delta_{uj_1}}{\gamma} \geq \frac{c_{uj_2} + \nu_u}{\gamma} = x_{uj_2} > 0. \ \square$$

Without loss of generality, for each user u, we reindex items such that $c_{u1} \geq c_{u2} \cdots \geq c_{un}$, where n is the number of items. Notice that this ordering is user-specific. Based on Proposition 1, there exists a number $1 \leq t \leq n$ such that, in the optimal solution, $x_{uj} > 0$ for $j \leq t$ and $x_{uj} = 0$ for $j > t$. To find the value of t, we check from $t = 1$ to n whether the following linear system has a feasible solution:

$$\begin{aligned} &x_{uj} = \frac{c_{uj} + \nu_u}{\gamma} \ \text{ and } \ x_{uj} > 0, \text{ for } 1 \leq j \leq t \\ &\textstyle\sum_{j=1}^{t} x_{uj} = 1. \end{aligned}$$

Notice that $\delta_{uj} = 0$ if $x_{uj} > 0$. The largest t value that still gives a feasible solution is what we are looking for. By some algebra, given t, we have $\nu_u = (\gamma - \sum_{j=1}^{t} c_{uj})/t$. The above system is feasible if the smallest $x_{ut} > 0$; i.e.,

$$x_{ut} \propto c_{ut} + \frac{\gamma - \sum_{j=1}^{t} c_{uj}}{t} > 0. \tag{8}$$

Algorithm 1 Conversion algorithm

Input: dual plan $\boldsymbol{\mu}$ and an incoming user u
Output: primal plan $\{x_{uj}\}$

Predict p_{uj} and d_{uj} for each item j
Compute c_{uj} based on $\boldsymbol{\mu}$, p_{uj} and d_{uj}
Order items by c_{uj} so that $c_{u1} \geq c_{u2} \geq \dots$
Set $a = \gamma$ and $t = 1$
repeat
  if $c_{ut} + (a - c_{ut})/t \leq 0$ **then**
    $t = t - 1$ and break
  else
    $a = a - c_{ut}$ and continue
  end if
  $t = t + 1$
until $t \geq |\mathcal{A}|$
$\nu_u = a/t$
for $j = 1$ to t **do**
  $x_{uj} = (c_{uj} + \nu_u)/\gamma$
end for
return $\{x_{uj}\}$

Conversion algorithm: Given dual plan $\boldsymbol{\mu}$ and an incoming user u, the primal serving plan $\{x_{uj}\}$ for u is obtained by the conversion algorithm which is summarized in Algorithm 1.

Proposition 2 *If the input dual plan $\boldsymbol{\mu}$ is optimal for a set of users, then the output serving plan from the conversion algorithm is also optimal for the same set of users.*

Proof sketch: Based on dual variable $\boldsymbol{\mu}$, the conversion algorithm gives us $\boldsymbol{\nu}$ and $\mathbf{x}$. We can further compute δ_{uj} for all $x_{uj} = 0$ based on Equation 7. It can be verified that all these values satisfy all the KKT conditions. □

The complexity of the conversion algorithm is dominated by the prediction of p_{uj} and d_{uj} and the sorting of c_{uj}'s. Since the number of items is usually small (from hundreds to thousands), the conversion algorithm is very efficient. Furthermore, the computation can be easily paralleled by users because each user can be computed independently from others.

Discussion: By comparing the above formulation with a simple scalarization that linearly combines different objectives, their similarities lie in the weights μ_k's which can be thought as the importance for different objectives/constraints. However, scalarization is limited in its ability to obtain all the meaningful Pareto optimal points because it does not allow for fractional serving [4, 7]. The existence of ν_u in our formulation can achieve fractional serving and thus can move the Pareto optimal solutions in a more controlled way than scalarization.

4. APPROXIMATION METHODS

Since we do not observe all the users who will visit in the next epoch, we can only solve the QP approximately. The main idea is to exploit the observation that the distribution of users in the next epoch is similar to that in the current epoch. This is a mild requirement because our epoch is usually of short duration (10 minutes in our paper) and user population usually does not change significantly. It is important to note that, if we use the primal solution directly for serving, we can only serve the set of seen users because we do not have primal variables for unseen users. However, if we use the dual plan for serving, we can convert it to the per-user serving plan on the fly for all users. Our dual plan only requires that the sets of user features in the two adjacent epochs are statistically similar(we do not require users themselves to be similar). For this reason, our dual formulation can even work with a sample of users. In this section, due to the potentially large number of users in an epoch, we explore two techniques to reduce computational cost: clustering and sampling.

4.1 Clustering

Our goal is to obtain the dual solution for the QP defined in Equation 6. To reduce the QP problem size, an intuitive choice is to cluster users and then we have a small number of primal variables. Specifically, we define a set of primal variables $\{x_{ij}\}_{\forall j \in \mathcal{A}}$ for each cluster i, instead of each user u. An off-the-shelf QP solver is then used to find the dual solution $\boldsymbol{\mu}$ of the small QP problem. Finally, at serving time, $\boldsymbol{\mu}$ is used to compute the personalized serving plan $\{x_{uj}\}_{\forall j \in \mathcal{A}}$ for each individual user u using Algorithm 1. Two clustering methods are considered:

- **k-Means:** The standard k-means algorithm is applied to the set of users in the current epoch to create m clusters based on the similarity between users.
- **Top1Item:** This method puts all the users having the same highest CTR item into the same cluster. Specifically, we name clusters by item IDs. The set of users in cluster j is

$$S_j = \{u \in \mathcal{U} : j = \arg\max_{j' \in \mathcal{A}} p_{uj'}\}.$$

  For consistency, we will still use index i to refer to such a cluster in general. Please note that the number of clusters in this method does not need to be specified.

After we get the user clusters, we approximate the QP as follows: for each cluster i, we estimate p_{ij} and d_{ij} by averaging the per-user p_{uj} and d_{uj} over users u in the cluster. Also, to ensure feasibility, the baseline performance *TotalClicks** and *TotalTime** are defined based on the click maximization scheme in Equation 3. We then solve the QP to get the dual optimal values $\boldsymbol{\mu}$.

4.2 Sampling

Another way to reduce computational cost is to downsample users. We consider two types of sampling methods:

- **Random sampling:** Given a sample rate r, we randomly select $r\%$ users uniformly in the current epoch.
- **Stratified sampling:** Given a set of user clusters, we randomly sample $r\%$ users for each individual user cluster. The clusters can be created by k-means or Top1Item.

After sampling, we obtain a subset of users in the current epoch. When we solve the QP, we define a set of primal variables $\{x_{uj}\}_{\forall j \in \mathcal{A}}$ only for sampled users u. Again, we update the baseline performance *TotalClicks** and *TotalTime** by only considering the sampled users. Then, the small QP is solved to obtain the dual solution $\boldsymbol{\mu}$ which is used by the conversion algorithm for online personalized serving.

Name	Method Description
Segment-LP	Segment-based linear program, same as [4].
Clustering-based Methods (Section 4.1)	
kMeans-QP-Dual	k-means clustering and personalized serving using the dual solution
Top1Item-QP-Dual	Top1Item clustering and personalized serving using the dual solution
Sampling-based Methods (Section 4.2)	
Random-Sampling	Random sampling and personalized serving using the dual solution
Stratified-kMeans	Stratified sampling using k-means, and personalized serving using dual
Stratified-Top1Item	Stratified sampling using Top1Item, and personalized serving using dual

Table 1: Summary of the methods.

5. EXPERIMENTS

In this section, we compare different methods for click shaping as summarized in Table 1. Note that Segement-LP relies on the primal optima directly for *segmented* serving, while kMeans-QP-Dual and Top1Item-QP-Dual rely on dual optima for *personalized* serving. We report our extensive empirical results using an unbiased evaluation methodology [18] based on Yahoo! Front Page log data. We will mainly compare the personalized click shaping with the most effective segmented ones in prior work [4]. We also compare the proposed methods in terms of their abilities to enforce constraints and achieve desired tradeoff between clicks and time-spent.

5.1 Experimental Setup

Data: Our data set is derived from Yahoo! Web server logs, which record users' clicks and views of items displayed in the Today module on the Yahoo! Front Page. The data is collected from a "random bucket" of users in August 2010 for the purpose of evaluating different serving schemes. A random sample of users was assigned to the random bucket, in which each user visit was served with an item uniformly randomly picked from an editor-selected item pool. It is important to note that, based on the replay methodology described in [18], this random bucket data allows us to perform *provably unbiased* comparisons among different serving schemes. Around 2 million click and view events were collected per day. To compute downstream time-spent, we also collected post-click information on all the pages that a user visited within Yahoo! after clicking on a Today module item. Each user is identified by an anonymized browser-cookie and has a profile consisting of demographics (age and gender) and his/her affinities to different categories (such as sports, finance and entertainment) based on his/her activities throughout the Yahoo! network. No personally identifiable information is used in our experiments. To create user segments or clusters, we use the best performed method proposed in [4]. Specifically, we collect a history data of 10 days in April 2010 and create an activity vector for each user. Each entry in the vector corresponds to an item in the history data and the value is the predicted CTR of the item based on the user profile. Users are then clustered using the k-means algorithm based on the activity vectors and new users are assigned to a cluster based on cosine similarity. This applies to all k-means related methods.

Metrics: We define the time-spent d_{uj} of a user u after clicking article $j \in P_k$ as the length (in second) of the *session* of the user's events, that starts from the click and ends at the last page view inside property P_k, before the user either leaves the property or has no activity for more than 30 minutes. For confidentiality reasons, we cannot reveal the total number of clicks or total time-spent. Thus, we only report the relative CTR and relative time-spent as defined below. After running a replay experiment using serving scheme A, we compute the average number of clicks per view p_{A} (i.e., CTR) and the average time-spent per view q_{A}. Fixing one baseline algorithm B, we report the performance of algorithm A by two ratios: CTR ratio $\rho_{\text{CTR}} = \frac{p_{\mathsf{A}}}{p_{\mathsf{B}}}$ and TS ratio $\rho_{\text{TS}} = \frac{q_{\mathsf{A}}}{q_{\mathsf{B}}}$.

Age-gender model		Linear regression	
MAE	RMSE	MAE	RMSE
86.11	**119.44**	87.75	122.02

Table 2: Comparison of time-spent prediction.

Estimation of p_{ujt} and d_{ujt}: Predicted CTR p_{ujt} and time-spent d_{ujt} are necessary input to our quadratic program. The choice of statistical models for such prediction is orthogonal to the methods presented in this paper and any model can be used here. In our experiments, we use the online logistic regression (OLR) model proposed in [3] to predict CTR p_{ujt} based on the feature vector (i.e., the profile consisting of demographics and category affinities) of user u. One OLR model is trained for each item and updated per epoch, in order to quickly capture the unique behavior of each item that does not generalize well through item features. Time-spent d_{ujt} is predicted by an age-gender model. We discretize ages into 10 groups and have 3 gender groups (male, female, and unknown); this gives 30 groups in total. For each group, we use a dynamic Gamma-Poisson model to track the mean of time-spent d_{ujt} on item j by a random user u in the group. Note that because time-spent is very noisy, this simple age-gender model cuts down the variance and provides good prediction performance. More fine-grained models such as building an linear regression model on user features for each item were tested, but did not provide improvement: Table 2 compares the Mean Absolute Error (MAE) and Root Mean Square Error (RMSE) of the two methods using 2-fold cross validation. Age-gender model performs just slightly better. A better time-spent model needs further research and is not the focus of this paper.

5.2 Experimental Results

Advantage of the personalized click shaping: We first show the that personalized click shaping significantly outperforms segmented click shaping in Figure 1. We start with a simplified special case that only considers the tradeoff between total clicks and total time-spent and does not have any per-property constraint. We show the results of Random-Sampling method with sampling rate $r = 20\%$ and $\beta = 0$. The tradeoff curve is generated by varying α from 1 to 0 (where each point is produced by averaging over 5 sampling runs). In this simplified setting without per-property constraints, *scalarization* is also applicable: serving each user u with the item j that has the highest weighted sum of the two objectives: $\lambda \cdot p_{uj} + (1-\lambda) \cdot p_{uj} d_{uj}$. By varying λ from 1 to 0, we obtain a tradeoff curve for scalarization in Figure 1. Each specific value of λ or α gives us a serving scheme that,

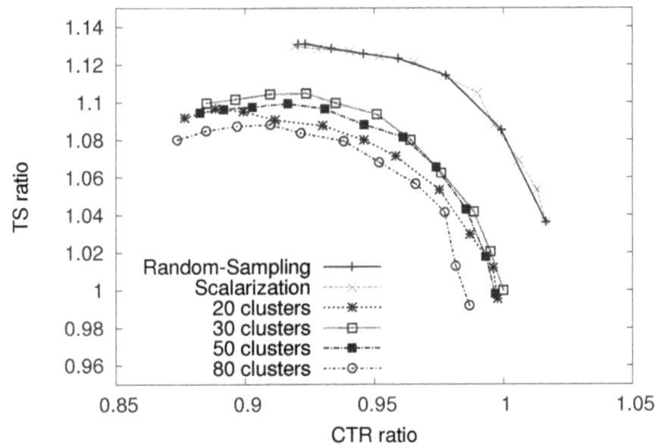

Figure 1: Personalized vs the segmented methods.

Method	CTR ratio		TS ratio	
	mean	stdev	mean	stdev
Scalarization (λ=0.50)	0.9601	0.0394	1.0796	0.0403
Random-Sampling (α=0.97)	0.9605	0.0306	1.0778	0.0322

Table 3: Temporal variance comparison.

after running through the data set, generates a pair of CTR ratio and TS ratio. To compare with segmented click shaping in this setting, we also plot the tradeoff curve using the scalarization method with different number of clusters. All the implementation details are the same as [4]. These methods are labeled as *k clusters* in the figure. From this figure, we can see that both versions of personalized click shaping outperform all the segmented click shaping on the tradeoff curves. For example, when $\lambda = 1$ and $\alpha = 1$, the personalized models achieve 2% CTR lift (statistically significant at level 0.1) and 4% TS lift (statistically significant at level 0.05). Thus working with personalized models is beneficial. Segmented click shaping achieves the best performance when the number of cluster is 30. When the number of clusters become large, the performance drops mainly because we have few users in each cluster and the component estimation of p_{ijt} and d_{ijt} (based on Gamma-Poisson) has high variance due to smaller sample size.

Figure 1 shows that both Random-Sampling and scalarization achieves similar tradeoff. This means that our dual formulation combined with sampling-based approximation is very effective to trade off competing objectives. In Table 3, we show the temporal variances of both methods on the TS ratio and CTR ratio over all the epochs. As can be seen, the variances of scalarization are much larger than those of Random-Sampling, meaning that Random-Sampling is a more stable method. This observation is similar to [4] where primal plans are used. Thus our dual formulation enjoys the same desirable property of constrained optimization, which makes sure no significant deviation from status quo performance in most epochs. It is important to note that scalarization cannot provide detailed control over per-property performance constraints (as shown in [4]). Thus, we do not further discuss scalarization in the following.

Constraint satisfaction: We have proposed a variety of approximation methods for personalized click shaping. A main question is whether they can satisfy the per-property constraints. An approximation would not be useful if it cannot satisfy the constraints well. In this set of experiments, we set $\beta = 1$. Given an α value and a property P_k, we look at the relative difference in time-spent on that property between an approximation method and the baseline click maximization scheme

$$\phi_\alpha(P_k) = \frac{TotalTime_\alpha(P_k) - TotalTime^*(P_k)}{TotalTime^*(P_k)}.$$

$\phi_\alpha(P_k) < 0$ means that the constraint on property P_k is violated and $|\phi_\alpha(P_k)|$ represents the degree of violation. We then define a satisfaction measure over all the per-property constraints as

$$\Phi_\alpha = 1 + \frac{1}{|\mathcal{V}|}\sum_{k\in\mathcal{V}} \phi_\alpha(P_k),$$

where $\mathcal{V} = \{k \,|\, \phi_\alpha(P_k) < 0, k \in \mathcal{I}\}$ is the set of properties which constraints are violated.

In Figure 2, we set $\alpha = 0.95$ and plot the satisfaction measure for each method. We set the sampling rate r = 20% for all sampling-based methods. As can be seen, all the methods except for clustering-based dual methods have $\Phi_\alpha \approx 1$ and thus satisfy the per-property constraints very well. In particular, all sampling-based dual methods satisfy the constraints well. However, clustering-based dual methods (kMeans-QP-Dual and Top1Item-QP-Dual) significantly violate the constraints. To further understand this behavior, we plot kMeans-QP-Dual and Top1Item-QP-Dual in Figure 3 for each individual property using $\phi_\alpha(P_k)$ with $\alpha = 0.95$. It can be seen that both do not respect the constraints and gives some properties more traffic than sufficient, while gives others less than necessary. This means that the clustering we tried is not a good approximation for personalized click shaping.

Tradeoff comparison: In Figure 4, we compare the tradeoff curves of different methods with per-property constraints by setting $\beta = 1$. Each curve is generated by varying α from 1 to 0. We will show that stratified sampling methods have very similar performance to Random-Sampling. Thus, for plot clarity, we only show the tradeoff curve for Random-Sampling (for which, we ran the experiments 5 times and show the average curve).

From this figure, we can see that the Random-Sampling method performs much better than the Segmented-LP method, under the per-property constraints. We can also see that Random-Sampling have the same ability to trade off the two competing objectives as Segmented-LP. Our Random-Sampling is personalized click shaping based on a dual plan,

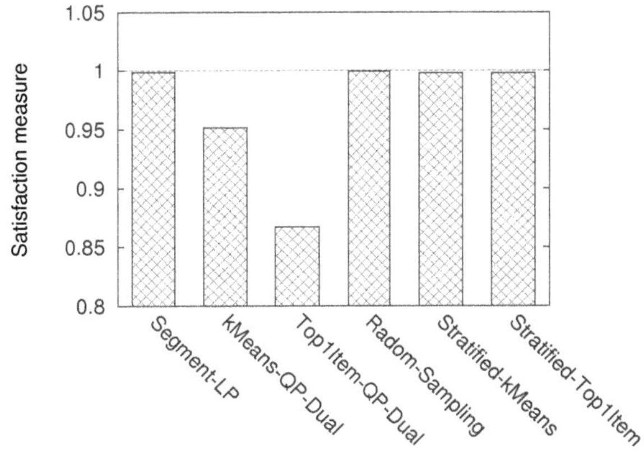

Figure 2: Satisfaction of constraints.

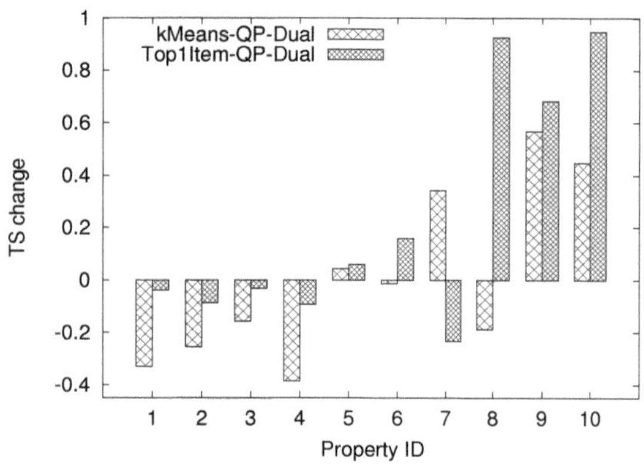

Figure 3: Per-property satisfaction for clustering.

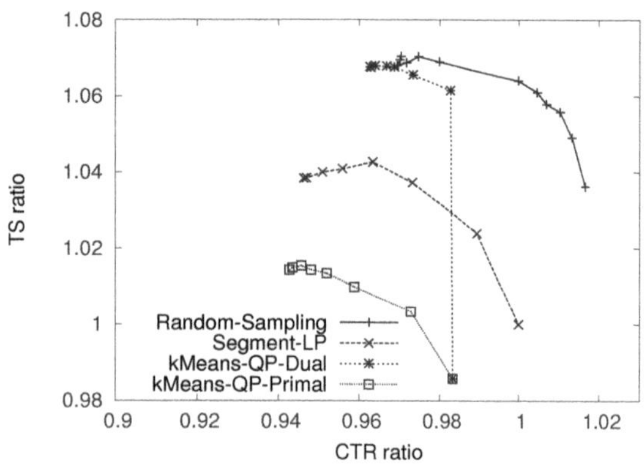

Figure 4: Tradeoff curves of different methods.

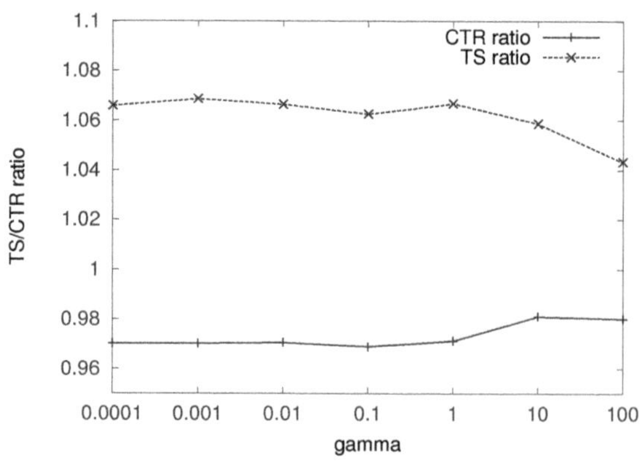

Figure 5: The impact of γ.

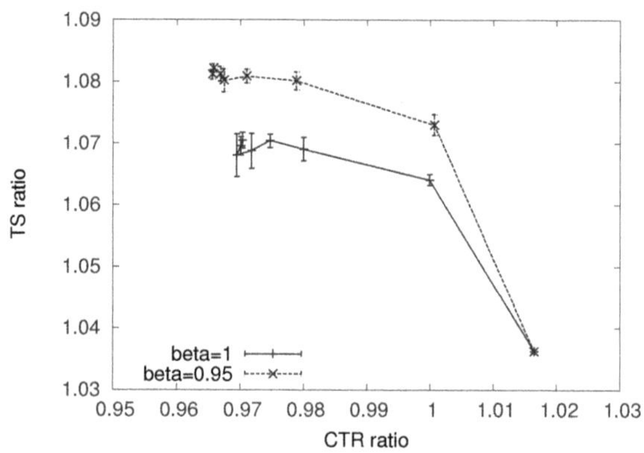

Figure 6: The tradeoff curve of different β values.

while Segmented-LP is based on a primal plan. This result confirms that our Lagrangian duality formulation is not only mathematically sound, but practically effective to incorporate personalization into click shaping.

In this figure, we also show the results of kMeans-QP-Dual for contrast. It can be seen that clustering-based approximation is not able to trade off the two objectives appropriately. The sharp jump in the tradeoff curve is a by-product of violating the per-property constraints as shown in the previous section. To confirm the correctness of our results, we also show the primal variation of k-means based approximation: kMeans-QP-Primal. This method shows a reasonable tradeoff curve. The difference between kMeans-QP-Dual and kMeans-QP-Primal is that the former uses dual plan but the latter uses the primal plan. The latter method is segmented because the primal serving plan is only for segments and each user needs to be assigned to a segment before served. This result again confirms that our clustering-based approximation is not an effective approach to approximate the Lagrangian duality.

The impact of γ: In Figure 5, we set $\alpha = 0.95$ and use the Random-Sampling method to show the impact of the parameter γ. It can be seen that when γ is less than 1, the results are not sensitive to the choice of γ. When γ is too large, the penalty term has high weight and thus the TS lift gets smaller. In all the experiments we set $\gamma = 0.001$.

Relaxation of the per-property constraints: In Figure 6, we show the tradeoff curves for $\beta = 1$ and $\beta = 0.95$. For each parameter setting, we have 5 runs of experiments and we show the mean of these 5 runs. We also plot the error bars of TS ratio. It can be see that we can achieve a better tradeoff when β is smaller because the constraints are less restrictive. We also show the $\phi_{\alpha=0.95}$ for both methods in Figure 7. It can be seen that the Random-Sampling method can roughly guarantee the per-property constraints. For $\beta = 1$, ϕ_α are almost all non-negative. For $\beta = 0.95$, ϕ_α are almost all ≥ -0.05.

Comparing different sampling methods: In Figure 8, we study the sampling ratios for Random-Sampling. As expected, when we have a larger number of samples, our approximation becomes better, thus a better tradeoff curve. In Figure 9, we show the (relative) running time needed for one run of our replay and we compare different sampling ratios. It can be seen that the running time is super-linear and this shows that sampling is necessary for our method. As shown in Figure 8, 20% sampling rate can achieve similar results as 50% sampling rate and thus sampling is an effective way of reducing the time complexity while retaining the effectiveness of our methods.

In Figure 10 and Table 4, we compare different sampling methods based on 5 sampling runs with 20% sample rate. Figure 10 shows the tradeoff curves averaged over the 5 runs and we can see that different sampling methods perform comparably with each other. In Table 4, we compute the click and TS variance as follows: For each α, we compute the standard deviation over the 5 runs. The reported re-

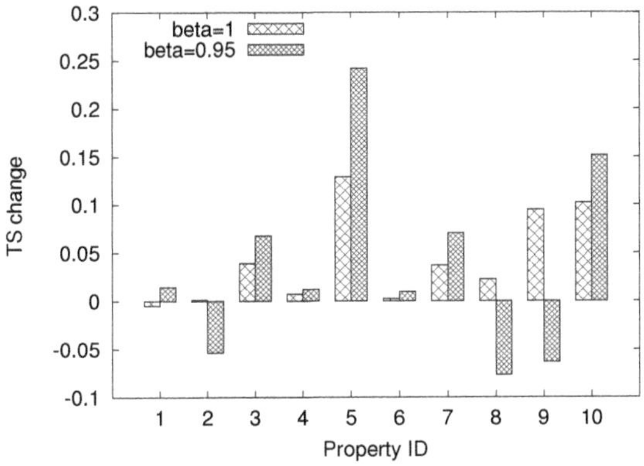

Figure 7: The impact of β on time-spent difference.

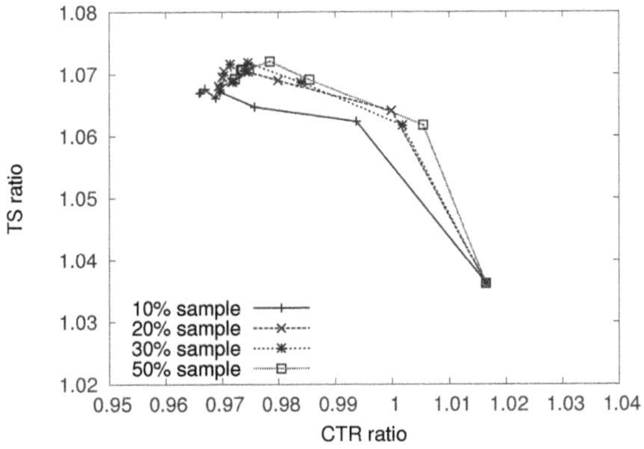

Figure 8: The impact of sample ratios.

sults are the average values of the standard deviation over all the α's. From this table, we can see that stratified methods have lower variance than random sampling. Among the two stratified methods, Stratified-kMeans has lower variance than Stratified-Top1Item. This means that k-means creates more homogeneous clusters than the Top1Item method.

Top N Properties: In Figure 11, we relax the number of per-property constraints in the Random-Sampling method and show the results when we only have the per-property constraints for the top 3, 5, and 7 properties. It can be seen that when the number of per-property constraints is reduced, we can have a better tradeoff curve. This again shows the effectiveness of dual formulation for personalized click shaping.

6. RELATED WORK

Our work is related to the broad category of Web content recommendation, which is to recommend users with *personalized* and *timely* content from a *dynamic* candidate pool such as news stories. For example, traditional collaborative filtering techniques [13, 15] have been extended to predict user clicks for news personalization [10, 20, 19]. To quickly identify interesting content, existing work such as [3, 2, 17] leverages explore/exploit methods [6, 16, 5] to actively collect user feedback (e.g., clicks) on new content in order to quickly estimate the performance of new content and maximize the number of clicks in the long run. The focus of our paper is not on accurate prediction of user clicks, but on how to jointly optimize multiple objectives. Other work such as [1, 22] uses latent factor model to combine both features and interaction activities to handle both warm-start and cold-start scenarios. Although all these methods provide *personalized* recommendation, they only consider a single objective in their problem formulations (e.g., clicks). To the best of our knowledge, there is little prior work that attempts to recommend personalized content to simultaneously optimize multiple objectives. The previous work [4] introduces the problem of click shaping. However, the proposed methods only work with user segments, instead of individual users. A main contribution of our paper is to close the gap between personalization and multi-objective optimization in Web content recommendation.

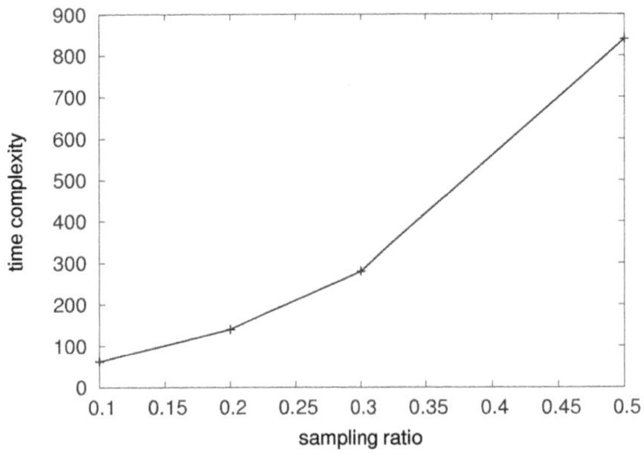

Figure 9: Time complexity vs sampling ratios.

	Random Sampling	Stratified-kMeans	Stratified-Top1Item
CTR stdev	0.00139	**0.00081**	0.00094
TS stdev	0.00187	**0.00129**	0.00156

Table 4: Average variance of sampling methods.

Our constrained optimization problem is similar to the guaranteed delivery problem [25, 9] in display advertising, where incoming users are allocated to see different ads in order to optimize ad-related utilities. For example, Vee et al. [25] consider multi-objective programming and provide techniques to simultaneously optimize for revenue of remnant inventory and overall ad quality delivered to advertisers. Our use of duality is similar to that of [25], but our content recommendation setting is very different from their advertising setting. Also, the focus of [25] is on theoretical properties, while the focus of this paper is to provide extensive experiments on real data.

Multi-objective optimization is also discussed in a number of other problem settings. For instance, auctions in sponsored search incorporate both revenue (measured by bids) and ad quality (measured by CTR) for ads ranking [11]. A common approach is simply to rank ads by the product of bid value and CTR. Sculley et al. [21] also study ad CTR and quality in sponsored search and define a new measure called *bounce rate* to capture ad quality by inferring abandonment rate on ad landing page. However, this study is exploratory and focuses on bounce rate prediction, instead of multi-objective optimization. Besides online advertising, Jambor and Wang [14] consider constraints like limited supply of the items in a collaborative filtering setting; Svore et

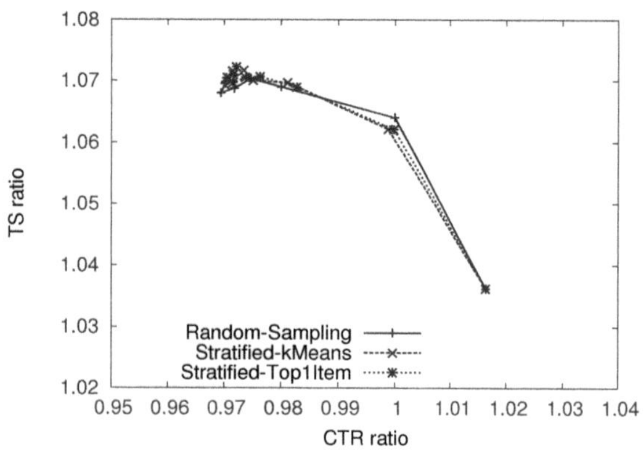

Figure 10: Comparison of different sampling methods (sampling ratio=0.2).

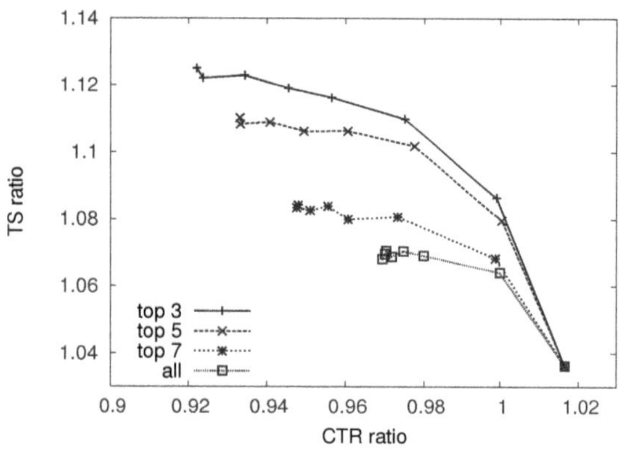

Figure 11: Impact of number of constraints.

al. [24] consider several objectives in learning to rank. These two studies are in a static setting, different from our online recommendation setting.

Finally, we note that there is a rich literature in multi-objective programming [23], convex optimization [7], and stochastic optimization [12]. Our contribution is in the application of optimization techniques to effective online personalized content recommendation.

7. CONCLUSIONS AND FUTURE WORK

In this paper, we study the problem of personalized click shaping which combines deep personalization with click shaping. We have shown that Lagrangian duality can be effectively used to solve the two challenges in applying constrained optimization to personalized serving — unseen users and scalability. By slightly modifying the objective function to achieve strong convexity, we are able to efficiently convert a *dual plan*, which consists of a small number of *user-independent* dual variables, to its corresponding primal serving plan at the time when a new user comes. Based on extensive experiments on a large real dataset, we show the set of Pareto optimal points for personalized click shaping significantly outperforms and uniformly dominates the ones for segmented click shaping.

Interesting problems for future work include how to extend our method to the scenario where multiple items can be simultaneously recommended at multiple positions on a portal page, and how to extend the current per-epoch constraints (e.g., requiring click loss to be bounded for every epoch) to long-term constraints (e.g., only requiring the total click loss in any n-epoch period to be bounded).

8. REFERENCES

[1] D. Agarwal and B.-C. Chen. Regression-based latent factor models. In *KDD*, 2009.

[2] D. Agarwal, B.-C. Chen, and P. Elango. Spatio-temporal models for estimating click-through rate. In *WWW*, 2009.

[3] D. Agarwal, B.-C. Chen, P. Elango, and et al. Online models for content optimization. In *NIPS*, 2008.

[4] D. Agarwal, B.-C. Chen, P. Elango, and X. Wang. Click shaping to optimize multiple objectives. In *KDD*, 2011.

[5] P. Auer, N. Cesa-Bianchi, and P. Fischer. Finite-time analysis of the multiarmed bandit problem. *Machine Learning*, 2002.

[6] D. A. Berry and B. Fristedt. *Bandit Problems: Sequential Allocation of Experiments.* Chapman and Hall, 1985.

[7] S. Boyd and L. Vandenberghe. *Convex Optimization.* Cambridge University Press, 2004.

[8] G. Buscher, L. van Elst, and A. Dengel. Segment-level display time as implicit feedback: a comparison to eye tracking. In *SIGIR*, 2009.

[9] Y. Chen, P. Berkhin, B. Anderson, and N. R. Devanur. Real-time bidding algorithms for performance-based display ad allocation. In *KDD*, 2011.

[10] A. Das, M. Datar, A. Garg, and S. Rajaram. Google news personalization: scalable online collaborative filtering. In *WWW*, 2007.

[11] R. Fain and J. Pederson. Sponsored search: A brief history. *Bulletin of American Society of Information and Technology*, 2006.

[12] P. V. Hentenryck and R. Bent. *Online Stochastic Combinatorial Optimization.* The MIT Press, 2006.

[13] J. L. Herlocker, J. A. Konstan, A. Borchers, and J. Riedl. An algorithmic framework for performing collaborative filtering. In *SIGIR*, 1999.

[14] T. Jambor and J. Wang. Optimizing multiple objectives in collaborative filtering. In *RecSys*, 2010.

[15] Y. Koren. Collaborative filtering with temporal dynamics. In *KDD*, 2009.

[16] J. Langford and T. Zhang. The epoch-greedy algorithm for contextual multi-armed bandits. In *NIPS*, 2008.

[17] L. Li, W. Chu, J. Langford, and R. E. Schapire. A contextual-bandit approach to personalized news article recommendation. In *WWW*, 2010.

[18] L. Li, W. Chu, J. Langford, and X. Wang. Unbiased offline evaluation of contextual-bandit-based news article recommendation algorithms. In *WSDM*, 2011.

[19] L. Li, D. Wang, T. Li, D. Knox, and B. Padmanabhan. Scene: a scalable two-stage personalized news recommendation system. In *SIGIR*, 2011.

[20] J. Liu, P. Dolan, and E. R. Pedersen. Personalized news recommendation based on click behavior. In *IUI*, 2010.

[21] D. Sculley, R. G. Malkin, S. Basu, and R. J. Bayardo. Predicting bounce rates in sponsored search advertisements. In *KDD*, 2009.

[22] D. H. Stern, R. Herbrich, and T. Graepel. Matchbox: large scale online bayesian recommendations. In *WWW*, 2009.

[23] R. Steuer. *Multi-criteria optimization: theory, computation, and application.* Wiley, 1986.

[24] K. M. Svore, M. N. Volkovs, and C. J. C. Burges. Learning to rank with multiple objective functions. In *WWW*, 2011.

[25] E. Vee, S. Vassilvitski, and J. Shanmugasundaran. Optimal online assignment with forecasts. In *EC*, 2010.

[26] J. Vermorel and M. Mohri. Multi-armed bandit algorithms and empirical evaluation. In *ECML*, 2005.

[27] Y. Zhang, J. P. Callan, and T. P. Minka. Novelty and redundancy detection in adaptive filtering. In *SIGIR*, 2002.

What Reviews are Satisfactory: Novel Features for Automatic Helpfulness Voting

Yu Hong[1] Jun Lu[2] Jianmin Yao[3] Qiaoming Zhu[4] Guodong Zhou[5]
School of Computer Science and Technology, Soochow University
No.1 Shizi Street, Suzhou City
Jiangsu Province, China
+86-18604601106
{tianxianer[1], lujun59[2]}@gmail.com, {jyao[3], qmzhu[4], gdzhou[5]}@suda.edu.cn

ABSTRACT
This paper focuses on exploring the features of product reviews that satisfy users, by which to improve the automatic helpfulness voting for the reviews on commercial websites. Compared to the previous work, which single-mindedly adopts the textual features to assess the review helpfulness, we propose that user preferences are more explicit clues to infer the opinions of users on the review helpfulness. By using the user-preference based features, we firstly implement a binary helpfulness based review classification system to divide helpful reviews and useless, and on the basis, we secondly build a Ranking SVM based automatic helpfulness voting system (AHV) which rank reviews based on their helpfulness. Experiments used a large scale dataset containing over 34,266 reviews on 1289 products to test the systems, which achieves promising performances with accuracy of up to 0.72 and NDCG@10 of 0.25, and at least 9% accuracy improvement compared to the textual-feature based helpfulness assessment.

Categories and Subject Descriptors
H.3.1 [**Information Storage and Retrieval**]: Content Analysis and Indexing – *Linguistic processing.*

Keywords
Automatic helpfulness voting, user preference, helpfulness classification.

1. INTRODUCTION
Nowadays, product reviews have become new attention-getting parts of most commercial sites[1]. In contrast to gorgeous picture or brilliant tagline in advertisement, users prefer to accept the opinions of other users, especially the experienced ones. And the user-supplied review is exactly the best medium for this interaction. However, the free network environment permits anyone to submit any review, even meaningless reply (e.g. yup, haw-haw, etc.) or disparaging remarks about competitors. Rather than enhance user experience, these reviews actually make so many noises and misapprehensions. Thus, it is crucial to have a mechanism capable of assessing the quality of reviews and shielding users from useless reviews.

Some websites already offer the mechanism for users to evaluate reviews. For example, on Amazon.com, an interface allows customers to vote for the helpfulness of each review and then ranks the reviews based on the accumulated votes. From an Amazon annotation of helpfulness: "*67 of 68 people found the following review helpful*" (Each Amazon review has this type of helpfulness annotation at the beginning part.). It specifies that 68 users voted and 67 of them thought the review is helpful. Such a voting rate (e.g. 67/68) gives a quantitative evaluation of review helpfulness, which can directly help other users select and scan high-quality reviews.

Unfortunately, the helpfulness is normally estimated by having users manually assess it. Thus it is hard to properly annotate helpfulness of newly submitted reviews and reviews with few votes as lack of manual information for the assessment. For example, for all Book products on Amazon.com, 26% reviews receive three or fewer helpfulness votes. Worse still, most websites never provide interactive function to acquire user experiences of reviews. Therefore, it is necessary to have a mechanism of automatic helpfulness voting.

Although few, there are still some pilot studies on the automatic helpfulness voting (abbr. AHV) for commercial reviews. Most of these works regard the AHV as an issue of textual-feature based classification, and verify the contributions of variety of textual features on distinguishing the helpful reviews from the useless. For example, the length of review is believed to be a simple but effective feature because a long review may offer wealth of product information.

However, AHV should be a more complex problem, which not only considers textual features (e.g. text length, language fluency and clearness), but also user preferences. As we have observed, whether a review gives the product attributes that users prefer to know, whether it wins the trust of users, and whether it has the consistent sentiments with users, all are important factors that influence the helpfulness voting. Consider the following reviews on Sony camera (from Amazon.com):

(1) *I prefer to buy the old version or Nikon.* (*3/54*)
(2) *It costs more than Nikon.* (*89/129*)
(3) *Amazing. This version offers 20x optical zoom. I even can see the sweat pores of my friends in photos.* (*125/158*)

Obviously, the review (1) cannot offer any valuable product information. This causes a very low voting rate *3/54* (6%). On the contrary, the reviews (2) and (3) show the price comparison and

*Corresponding author: Guodong Zhou

Permission to make digital or hard copies of all or part of this work for personal or classroom use is granted without fee provided that copies are not made or distributed for profit or commercial advantage and that copies bear this notice and the full citation on the first page. To copy otherwise, or republish, to post on servers or to redistribute to lists, requires prior specific permission and/or a fee.
SIGIR'12, August 12-16, 2012, Portland, Oregon, USA.
Copyright 2012 ACM 978-1-4503-1472-5/12/08...$10.00.

unique function, which are normally uppermost in most minds. This should be the reason why they achieve very high voting rates *89/129* (69%) and *125/158* (79%). Especially, the review (3) implies that the reviewer might have bought the product, which makes the words more persuasive and helpful. The examples show the textual features might be not always effective in assessing review helpfulness, e.g. the length of review (1) versus (2), but user preference learning seems to give a supplementary or even alternative method to solve the problem.

In this paper, we focus on learning three kinds of user preferences:

- Users prefer the reviews that meet their ***information needs***
- Users prefer the ***credible*** reviews
- Users prefer the reviews that have the ***mainstreaming opinion***

On the basis, we attempt to capture features that to some extent represent the preferences without any human intervention, and well use the features to improve the helpfulness-based review classification. Empirically, the textual features, e.g. the grammatical correctness, language fluency and clearness, etc., are more commonly used to detect whether the writings of reviews can make comfortable reading for users. Compared to this, our features are used to detect whether reviews can provide valuable, credible and authoritative product information for users.

The rest of the paper is organized as follows: Section 2 introduces the related work. In Section 3, we define the task of automatic helpfulness voting (AHV). In Section 4, we present the user preferences on product review and offer the quantitative evidences to support the preference-based AHV. In Section 5, we present the method of feature extraction and corresponding measurement. Section 6 gives the experimental setup. The main results are reported in Section 7. At last, we draw the conclusion in Section 8.

2. RELATED WORK

A large body of research shows the availability of product reviews in extracting product aspects[2][3] and features[4], mining user opinions[2][4] and summarizing corresponding sentiments[3]. However, there is so far a little research focusing on whether and how a product review should be determined to be helpful or useless (viz., reviews helpfulness assessment, abbr., RHA). This section specially introduces the related work on RHA.

Kim et al[1] exploited the multitude of user-rated reviews on Amazon.com, and trained an SVM regression system to learn a helpfulness function and then applied it to rank unlabeled reviews. Especially this work performed a detailed analysis of different features to study the importance of several feature classes in capturing helpfulness. Within the features, the length of reviews, unigrams, and product ratings were the most useful features, but structural features (other than length) and syntactic features had no significant impact.

Liu and Cao et al[5] studied the problem of detecting low-quality product reviews. This work firstly discovered three types of biases in the ground-truth used extensively in the previous work, and proposed a specification on the quality of product reviews. The three biases are imbalance vote bias, winner circle bias, and early bird bias. Secondly, rooting on the new ground-truth (conforming to the proposed specification), this work gave a classification-based approach to low-quality product review detection, which yields better performance of opinion summarization.

Jindal et al[6] regarded the issue as spam filtering, and gave three general types of spam reviews: 1) untruthful reviews, such as fake reviews 2) reviews on brands only which do not comment on the products but only the brands, the manufacturers or the sellers of the products and 3) non-reviews (e.g., questions, answers, and random texts). On the basis, this work detected reviews of type 2 and type 3 based on traditional classification learning using manually labeled spam and non-spam reviews, and detected type 1 by verifying whether reviews involve many opinions opposing to most other reviewers.

Cristian et al[7] confirmed that a review's perceived helpfulness depends not just on its content, but also the relation of its score to other scores. This dependence on the score contrasts with a number of theories from sociology and social psychology, but is consistent with a simple and natural model of individual bias in the presence of a mixture of opinion distributions.

Tsur et al[8] present a RevRank algorithm to rank book reviews according to review helpfulness. The RevRank is more like an adaptive Rocchio[9] algorithm when setting and modifying the "virtual core" of a set of reviews on a product. On the basis, reviews are ranked according to their distance from the "core". Although RevRank is proved to outperform a baseline imitating the Amazon user vote review ranking system, few evidences have be showed to illustrate the inevitability of the uselessness of those reviews which deviate from the "core".

Liu and Huang et al[10] et al show that the helpfulness of a review depends on three important factors: the reviewer's expertise, the writing style of the review, and the timeliness of the review. Although not clearly mentioned by Liu and Huang et al, the factors indeed reflect that the exhilarating reviews normally cater to users' tastes in the review quality (e.g. a new and well-written review from an expert is welcomed). This motivates us to explore the user-preference based review helpfulness prediction, and further search the features effectively describing user preferences.

Jo et al[11] propose an aspect and sentiment unification model to automatically discover what aspects are evaluated in reviews and how sentiments for different aspects are expressed. This work motivates us to consider whether sentiment similarity between users and reviewers affects the user preferences on reviews, and further is an effective feature to infer the determination of users for review helpfulness.

3. TASK DEFINITION

In this Section, we firstly define the task of automatic helpfulness voting (AHV), and secondly we introduce the data format of Amazon.com reviews. The data have been successfully used in previous AHV tests, so we in later Sections conduct all our analysis, illustrations and experiments on this type of data.

3.1 Task of AHV

The task of AHV firstly aims to automatically assess the review helpfulness, and secondly rank all reviews of a specific product based on their helpfulness scores. It should be performed only depending on the existing Web information without any manual intervention. For example, AHV should determine an Amazon review as helpful and highly rank it if it has the manual voting rate[1] of "*197 of 199*", and AHV should perform this under the condition of being blind to the rate. On the contrary, an Amazon review which has only "*16 of 199*" voting rate should be determined as useless and ranked lower in the ranking list of reviews.

[1] The voting rate cannot be used in automatic helpfulness voting (AHV) because it involves the manual intervention.

Therefore, given an input of a random sequence of reviews, the AHV system should output a helpfulness-based ranking list of reviews. Within this, the most key issue is to automatically assess the review helpfulness, so in this paper we firstly simplify the task of AHV, and regard it as a helpfulness-based binary classification of reviews, by which to explore the valuable features for the helpfulness assessment. On the basis, by using a Ranking SVM model[12], we finally implement a simple ranking system for product reviews.

To evaluate the system, we need two basic evaluation metrics: accuracy and NDCG@n. The accuracy is used to evaluate the performance of the helpfulness-based review classification and inspect whether every review (including both helpful and useless ones) obtain the correct decision[13]. To do this, we succeed the optimal helpfulness boundary proposed by Kim et al[1] who report the voting rate 0.6 can be used to approximately divide the helpful reviews from the useless. So we regard the boundary as the criterion to label the training and test samples for the binary classifier. The metric NDCG@n is used to evaluate the ranking system, and inspect whether its output meets the manually labeled helpfulness ranks.

Table 1: Format and availability of Amazon reviews

Review <serial number>	
<Product> *Nikon COOLPIX P300* </Product>	---Available
<Title> *Low Resolution* </Title>	---Available
<Star> *one-star* </Star>	---NA
<Time> *2011-3-4* </Time>	---Available
<Reviewer> *Unicorn John* </Reviewer>	---Available
<Content> *The photos are not clear.* </Content>	---Available
<Vote> *56/78* </Vote>	---NA
<Buyer?> Yes </Buyer?>	---NA
<Er> *The COOLPIX P300 is…* </Er>	---NA
<Pt> *9×7×6 inches …* </Pt>	---NA
<Ps> *From the manufacturer …* </Ps>	---NA
<Url> *http://www.amazon ...* </Url>	---Available

3.2 Amazon.com Data Format

In this paper, we adopt reviews on Amazon.com as our corpus to evaluate the AHV system. Amazon.com[2] provides 1,692,256 reviews on 13 types (91 subtypes) of products, such as that on Books, Kindle, Electronics, etc. An Amazon.com review normally includes following components: title, star, release time, reviewer, main content and vote. But for most reviews, especially the most recent ones, the item of <vote> is empty for lack of voters, which is the problem that should be solved by the AHV system. We standardized the format of Amazon reviews and restricted the availability of the components as the example in Table 1.

Within the review description, <Er>, <Pt> and <Ps> respectively denotes the editorial review, product detail and product description. The item <Er> is written by domain experts. The item <Pt> normally gives the specification, bestsellers rank, etc. And the item <Ps> often introduces the product functions, business analysis, and manufacturer. But not all Amazon merchandisers provide the contents of the three items, and particularly most commercial websites never involve that in reviews. Therefore, to meet the needs of the general AHV system, we restricted the use of <Er>, <Pt> and <Ps> (labeled by "NA" in Table 1). Besides, the <Star> denotes the vote on product value (from 1 to 5 stars) and the <Buyer?> records whether the reviewer is a buyer of the product. Because the two items need human intervention, we also restrict the use of them in AHV.

Actually the "Available" items in Table 1 may be all effective features to assess the helpfulness, but some of them cannot support our exploration on user-preference based AHV. For instance, the <Reviewer> provides a link to the historical reviews of a reviewer, and the corresponding voting rates can provide important reference for assessing current reviews (motivated by the hypothesis that an experienced reviewer may always give helpful reviews). But this doesn't belong to the application of user preferences in AHV, so we ignored the items in our system.

In this paper, we only regard the items <Product> and <Content> as the available local resources for AHV. The <Product> gives the product name, and the <Content> records the main contents of reviews. Other items, as discussed in the next Section, are only used to generate the quantitative evidences for our user-preference based AHV.

4. USER PREFERENCE LEARNING

In this Section, we present the user preferences on product reviews along with the quantitative evidences for their availability in assessing review helpfulness.

4.1 Needs Fulfillment

The hypothesis is that the basic user intention is to acquire the product information from reviews, by which to support the purchase decisions. If the hypothesis is true, a helpful review should have the prerequisite that it can meet the information needs. But the question is what the information needs are? By analyzing the interactive model in commercial websites, it is not hard to find the user behaviors of searching product attributes and functions before purchase. Therefore, we in this paper regard the product attribute and function as two basic information needs, and verify the possibility of using the needs fulfillment to improve review helpfulness assessment.

Table 2: Main types of products on Amazon.com

P1. Unlimited Instant Videos	P9. Movie, Music & Games
P2. MP3s & Cloud Player	P10. Electronics & Computers
P3. Amazon Cloud Drive	P11. Home, Garden & Tools
P4. Kindle	P12. Grocery, Health &Beauty
P5. Appstore for Android	P13. Toys, Kids & Baby
P6. Digital Games & Software	P14. Clothing, Shoes & Jewelry
P7. Audible Audiobooks	P15. Sports & Outdoors
P8. Books	P16. Automotive & Industrial

To prove the feasibility of the needs fulfillment in AHV, we use the items <Content>, <Er>, <Pt> and <Ps> (as shown in Table 1) to calculate the capture rate of the words of product attributes and functions in the <Content> of reviews, and generate the curve diagram of the average rates on 16 types of Amazon products (see the types in Table 2) with up to 20,000 corresponding reviews, by which to compare the distributions of needs fulfillment between the helpful and useless reviews. Thereinto, the item <Pt> provides the main words of product attributes, and the <Ps> offers that of product functions. Besides, because the item <Er> gives the review from the domain expert, we regard the capture rate in <Er> as the best measure of needs fulfillment. We show the curves and the equation of capture rate in Figure 1.

[2] http://www.amazon.com/

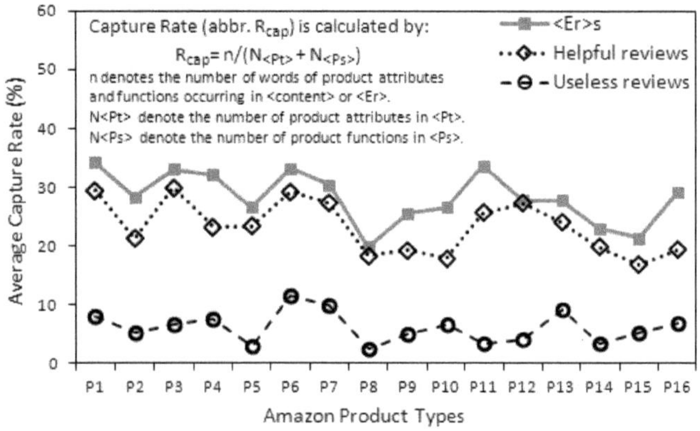

Figure 1. The capture rates of product attributes and functions in Amazon reviews

As shown in Figure 1, it is not hard to find that the capture rate curve of helpful reviews is very close to the curve of <Er>s. On the contrary, the curve of useless reviews is on the bottom of the diagram and far from the curve of <Er>. It illustrates that the helpful reviews, just like the specialist reviews, normally have the capacity to meet the user needs for product information (here only the product attributes and functions). In other words, the needs fulfillment is an important factor for helpfulness assessment. And the capture rate, as the measurement of the needs fulfillment, is a useful feature to divide helpful reviews from useless. But when using the feature in our AHV system, we will experience the problem of extracting the feature without any help from the restricted items <Er>, <Pt> and <Ps>. We will discuss this in Section 5.1.

Table 3: Uncertainties of main volitive auxiliaries

High (uncertainty)	Medium	Low
May, Maybe	Be worth	Must
Can, Could	Easy to	Have, Have to
Will, Would	Convenient to	Be ready to, Be able to
Should, Ought to	Be difficult to	Prefer to, Be willing to
Need, Need to	Hard to	Intend to, Want to, Wish to

4.2 Information Reliability

The hypothesis is that users prefer to vote for the reliable reviews because the reliability of information normally affects the correctness of purchase decision. In this Section, we focus on introducing two evidences of reliability based helpfulness voting: Volitive and Tense.

- **Volitive auxiliary based reliability determination**

At first, we think the volitive auxiliaries (along with the corresponding collocations) can give the evidence to prove the hypothesis. This is because the auxiliaries potentially represent the uncertainty (see Table 3) which can, to some extent, reflect the unreliability of reviews. Consider the reviews below:

(1) *I **prefer to** buy Sony, for it **may** have higher resolution.* (*9/68*)
(2) *It costs more than Nikon.* (*89/129*)

Compared to the review (2), the review (1) looks unreliable because without any definite information. Correspondingly, the review (1) receives a low voting rate. This shows the possibility of using the volitive auxiliary to prove the hypothesis (viz., reliability based helpfulness assessment). Therefore, we regard any sentence, which involves at least one volitive auxiliary, as an uncertainty, and use the number of uncertainties in a review to calculate the reliability score (see the equation in Figure 2). By calculating the average score for each type of Amazon product, we generated the curve diagram of average reliability scores on the 16 types of Amazon products with the corresponding 20,000 reviews, by which to compare the distribution of reliability scores between helpful and useless reviews. We show the curves in sub-figure (1) of Figure 2. Unfortunately, there is no clear discrimination between the curves. This is because the volitive auxiliaries normally have multiple pragmatic functions and senses (see the examples below).

(1) *If asked, the salespersons **have*** (**volitive auxiliary**) *said that they **had*** (**notional word**) *the detailed specification.* (Progmatics)
(2) *They **can*** (means "**may**") *come here to see this **can*** (means "**container**") *of moldy bacon? It is impossible.* (Sense)

Therefore it is not a proper measure to use the number of volitive auxiliaries to calculate the reliability score without considering pragmatics identification and word sense disambiguation. By simply using the syntactic structure (Stanford Parser[14]) and part-of-speech[15] to filter the notional words in the count of uncertainties, we improve the discrimination between the curves (see sub-figure 2 of Figure 2). Although a little weak, the volitive auxiliary indeed gives the evidence for the availability of information reliability in helpfulness assessment. But when using the feature in our AHV system, we still need to consider the influences of different levels of uncertainty in the measure of reliability. We will discuss this in Section 5.2.

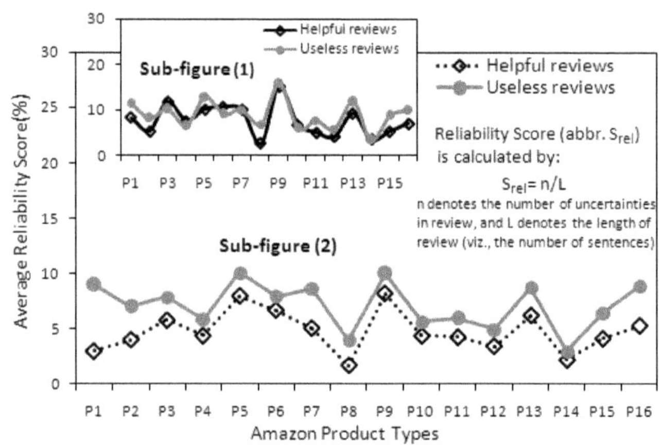

Figure 2. The reliability scores on Amazon reviews

- **Tense based reliability determination**

Secondly, we think the tenses (only past and perfect tenses here) can also give the evidence to prove the hypothesis of reliability based helpfulness voting. This is motivated by the psychology of users normally trusting the experienced reviewers and the habit of the reviewers often using past and perfect tenses in their writing. Actually the habit is reasonable because an experienced reviewer should firstly become an owner of product (normally the buyer in commercial websites) and so the corresponding opinions in reviews were mostly generated from the past experience. The direct evidence is the frequent occurrence of high voting rate in the reviews of buyers. By using the item <Buyer?> (see Table 1), we calculated the proportion of buyers in the reviewers. According to the calculation on 20,000 reviews, approximately 71.29% helpful reviews are written by the reviewers who claimed they were buyers (the item <Buyer?> == "Yes"), and only 39.05% useless reviews by visitors (<Buyer?> == "No").

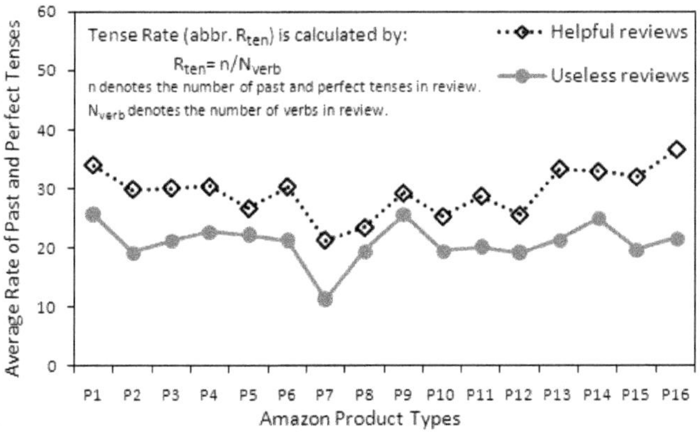

Figure 3. Tense Rate (only past and perfect tenses here) in Amazon reviews

On the basis, we calculated the rate of past and perfect tenses occurring in verbs for each review. And by calculating the average rate for each type of Amazon product, we generated the curve diagram of the average rates on the 16 Amazon products. The diagram shows that the curve of helpful reviews is easily distinguished from the useless (see Figure 3). Therefore, the tenses also give the evidence for the availability of information reliability in helpfulness assessment. As discussed in Section 3.2, we restrict the use of the item <Buyer?> to shield our AHV system from human intervention. So only the tenses, which can be obtained from the item <content>, will be used to measure the information reliability.

4.3 Mainstreaming Opinion

The hypothesis is that users prefer to vote for the reviews which are compatible with the mainstreaming opinions. In part, this is because mainstreaming opinion is normally authoritative and so more convincing.

The direct evidence to support the hypothesis is the low divergence between the star of helpful review and mainstreaming star (based on the data on Amazon.com). Here, the star (see Table 1) is a quantitative measure of product value, e.g. a five-star means "great value" but a one-star means "worthless". And the mainstreaming star is the star which occurs the most frequently in the reviews of specific product. On Amazon.com, a star is given by a reviewer through the interaction interface. Therefore, the star directly represents the opinion of reviewer on product value, and so the mainstreaming star, to some extent, reflects the mainstreaming opinion.

However, the use of the item <Star> is also restricted in our AHV system (see Table 1). The only way is to use the available item <content> to automatically detect the mainstreaming opinion and measure the divergence. The alternative for this is to adopt sentiment analysis to obtain a two-dimension opinion (positive polarity and negative polarity), and calculate the divergence based on the distribution of sentiment words in <content> of reviews. We will discuss this in Section 3.3.

5. FEATURE EXTRACTION

In this paper, we build an automatic helpfulness voting system for the reviews in common commercial websites. The system involves two functions. One is the helpfulness based review classification, and the other is review ranking. Thereinto, the classifier determines whether a review is helpful or useless, and the ranking system generates a ranking list of reviews based on their helpfulness scores. Because we directly use a current Ranking SVM model[12] to implement the review ranking, the remaining problem is only how to extract effective features for the classification. In this Section, we focus on introducing the extraction methods of our user-preference based features.

5.1 Capture Rate of Needs Fulfillment

As discussed in Section 4.1, the needs fulfillment is an important factor for helpfulness assessment, and the capture rate of product attribute and function is an effective measure of needs fulfillment. Therefore we use the rate as a feature in the classification, by which to support our AHV system.

Table 4: A type example of pseudo-feedback of Search Boss

Query_"**Nikon**"

```
<?xml> version="1.0" encoding="UTF-8" standalone="no" ?>
<ysearchresponse xmlns="http://www.inktomi.com/" responsecode ="200">
 <resultset_web count="20" start="0" totalhits ="25574196" deephits=...>
 +<result>
 </result>
 <result>
 ...
    <keyterms>
      <terms>
        <term> Nikon Store </term>
        <term> Digital Cameras </term>
        <term> Digital SLR Cameras </term>
        <term> Zoom Lens </term>
        ...
    </keyterms>
 ...
 </result>
 ...
```

The key issue of calculating the capture rate is to know what attributes and functions a product has. However, because the items <Er>, <Pt> and <Ps> are restricted to use (only <Product> and <Content> can be used), it is difficult to obtain the attributes and functions locally. An alternative way is to mine global information about product by using search engine. In this paper, we used the Yahoo!'s open search web services platform, named Search Boss[3], to mine the information. The Yahoo! Search Boss normally provides the keywords of pseudo-relevant feedbacks to a query, and if when the query is a product name, the keywords often contain plenty of product attributes and functions (see Table 4). Thus, according to the item <Product>, which denotes the product name, we can use the Search Boss to obtain the attributes and functions easily.

For each product, we use N_{fbk} top-ranked feedbacks as the global resources for the feature extraction. To obtain the optimal N_{fbk}, we randomly selected 20,000 Amazon products, and use their names as query to retrieve corresponding keywords (viz., the product attributes and functions) on the Yahoo Search Boss. And then we calculated the average overlapping rate of the keywords in editorial review (offered by the <Er> item) at every possible N_{fbk} (see Figure 4) and the average number of keywords increasing along with N_{fbk} (see Figure 5). Under the hypothesis that the editorial reviews (from domain experts) have enough product attributes and functions, by analyzing the trend curves of overlapping rate and keyword's number, we set the optimal number of N_{fbk} as 20 which just occurs at the first degression of the overlapping trend (see Figure 4) and that of the number of keywords. This illustrates that if we use more than 20 feedbacks (viz., N_{fbk}>20) to extract the keywords, we will have more noises in the keywords.

---

[3] http://developer.yahoo.com/search/boss/

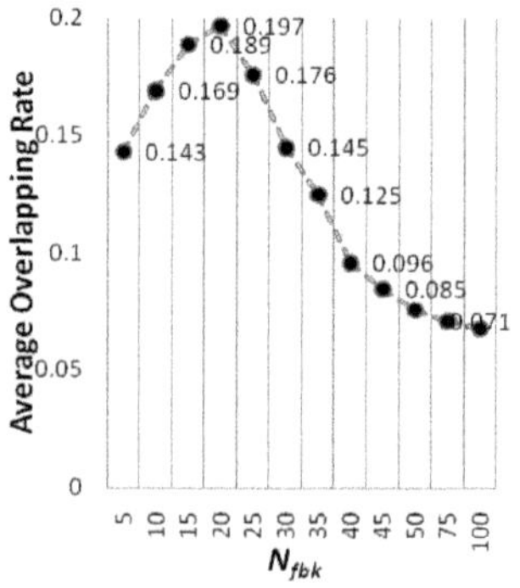

Figure 4. Overlapping trend

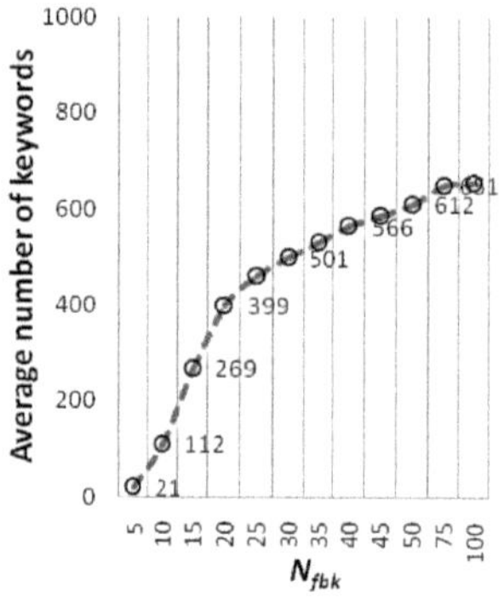

Figure 5. Increasing trend

Besides, the capture rate, as calculated in Section 4.1 (see the equation in Figure 1), neglects the distributions of product attributes and functions in global information resource. This will cause that some common attributes and functions generalize the capture-rate based measure of needs fulfillment. Therefore, according the distributions, we improve the calculation of capture rate by involving a combination weight. For an attribute or function, the weight is calculated as:

$$w_{cmb} = \alpha \cdot w_{key} + (1-\alpha) \cdot IG, \quad 0 \le \alpha \le 1 \tag{1}$$

where, α is a discount factor, IG means the mutual information of the attribute or function in training corpus, w_{key} denotes the weight in keywords. The w_{glb} is calculated as:

$$w_{key} = \frac{df}{N_{key}} \tag{2}$$

where, N_{glb} denotes the number of attributes or functions in global resource (viz., the top N_{fbk} pseudo-feedback of specific product), df denotes the number of pseudo-feedback that involving the attribute or function. On the basis, for a review, we calculate the improved capture rate as follows:

$$R'_{cap} = \frac{\sum w_{cmb} \cdot R_{cap}}{L} \tag{3}$$

where L denotes the length of review (viz., the number of words in review), R_{cap} denotes the original capture rate (see the equation in Figure 1).

In our AHV system, we use the improved capture rate as the measure of needs fulfillment. Besides, we expanded the words of product attribute and functions by using WordNet[4], by which to enhance the possibility of attribute and function word matching. And we also used the OpenNLP parser tool[5] to extract phrases from the item <content> of review.

5.2 Volition and Tense for Reliability

As discussed in Section 4.2, the information reliability is also an effective feature for helpfulness assessment. And both volition based uncertainty factor and tense based experience factor (past and perfect tenses only) can be used as the measures of reliability. In this Section, we respectively show the methods of calculating the factors.

- **Volition based uncertainty factor**

To calculate the factor, the first problem is to obtain enough priori volitive auxiliaries, by which to identify the volitive auxiliaries in content of review. Here, we adopt a cross-language collaborative mining algorithm[16] to obtain the volitive auxiliaries. The algorithm firstly use several English volitive auxiliaries as seeds, and by using a machine translation tool[17] translate the seeds into Chinese; secondly, because Chinese words can be divided into characters, and the character in Chinese volitive auxiliaries normally can combine with other characters to generate new volitive auxiliaries, the algorithm expends the Chinese auxiliaries in this way; at last it translate the new Chinese auxiliaries into English and add them into the list of seeds. The algorithm iteratively executes the operations until the number of English volitive auxiliaries never increases. After checking the auxiliaries manually, we obtained a total of 156 English volitive auxiliaries (including words and phrases).

We use the volition based uncertainty factor as the measure of information reliability, by which to support reliability based helpfulness assessment. The original uncertainty factor (see the equation in Figure 2) is calculate by the rate of sentences which involve at least one volitive auxiliary, within which syntactic structure (Stanford Parser[14]) and part-of-speech[15] is used to avoid the cases of multiple pragmatic functions and ambiguous sense. However, the original uncertainty factor neglects the influence of different uncertainty degrees of volitive auxiliaries. To improve the factor, we roughly divide volitive auxiliaries into three levels of uncertainty degree (see Table 3), and set the levels as the weighting coefficients: high uncertainty corresponds to 3, medium to 2 and low to 1, by which the improved uncertainty factor can be calculated as:

$$U_{vol} = \frac{\sum_{n} tf_v \cdot u_{max}}{N_s} \tag{4}$$

where N_s denote the total number of sentences in a review, n denotes the number of sentences which involve at least one volitive auxiliaries, u_{max} is the maximum uncertainty degree occurring in a sentence, tf_v denotes frequency of the verb adjacent to volitive auxiliary. By using tf_v, the uncertainty factor has the capacity of determining whether the uncertainty occurs at an event that a review emphasizes on (As the definition of ACE[18], an event normally is triggered by verb).

- **Tense based experience factor**

As discussed in Section 4.2, the experience factor is measured by the rate of past and perfect tenses occurring in verbs because the tenses, to some extent, reflect the possibility of reviewers having corresponding experiences to specific product. However, not all cases have the positive influence for the experience measurement. For example, the review "*I want to buy the camera because my wife **said** she **liked** its color*" has two past tenses, but only the verb "liked" can be regarded as the clue of usage experience (because "color" is normally the first user experience). Therefore, to improve the tense based experience factor, we only extract the verbs link to product attributes or functions in syntactic structure. Besides, we involve the frequencies of attributes and functions into the calculation of experience factor:

$$U_{exp} = \frac{\sum_{n} tf_p}{N_v} \tag{5}$$

where N_v denotes the total number of verbs in a review, n denotes the number of verbs link to attributes or functions in syntactic structure, and tf_p denotes the frequency of product attribute or function in review.

---

[4] http://wordnet.princeton.edu/

[5] http://incubator.apache.org/opennlp

5.3 Divergence from Mainstreaming Opinion

As discussed in Section 4.3, the divergence from mainstreaming opinion can be used to assess the helpfulness of review. Here, we propose a sentiment based divergence measurement, which only needs to use the item <content> of review.

To calculate the sentiment based divergence, the first issue is to obtain sentiment words. For this, we extract the sentiment words from WordNet Affect[19], which correspond to the WordNet synsets annotated with the six emotions: anger, disgust, fear, joy, sadness, surprise. Secondly, we roughly divided the words into two classes: positive polarity and negative polarity. Thereinto, positive-polarity class involves the words of joy, and negative-polarity class involves the words of anger, disgust, fear and sadness. But the surprise, as neutral emotion, is filtered. On the basis, we estimate the polarity of a review as:

$$P = \begin{cases} positive, & if \ \dfrac{n_{pos} - n_{neg}}{L} > \theta \\ negative, & else\,if \ \dfrac{n_{neg} - n_{pos}}{L} > \theta' \\ neutral, & else \end{cases} \qquad (6)$$

where n_{pos} denotes the number of words of positive polarity, n_{neg} denotes the number of words of negative polarity, L denotes the length of review, θ is the threshold for positive polarity determination, and θ' denotes that for negative polarity determination. By using Benchmark Corpus[20] to train the thresholds, we got their optimal values as: θ equals to 0.02 and θ' equals to 0.015. Within the equation (6), we calculate the quantitative polarity force as:

$$F = \frac{|n_{pos} - n_{neg}|}{L} \qquad (7)$$

After determining the polarity for each review, we detect the mainstreaming opinion for each product. Here, the mainstreaming opinion is either positive polarity or negative polarity. For each product, we respectively count the number of positive reviews and negative reviews, and calculate average polarity force for the two classes of reviews. And then we regard the polarity of the class which involves more reviews, as the mainstreaming opinion, and use the corresponding average polarity force as the force of mainstreaming opinion. On the basis, for each review, we calculate its divergence from mainstreaming opinion by measuring the difference between its polarity force and that of mainstreaming opinion.

6. EXPERIMENT SETUP

In this Section, we firstly introduce the dataset for our experiments, secondly we give the evaluation metrics, and at last we show the AHV systems to be tested.

6.1 Dataset

We focused our experiments on 124,878 reviews associated with Amazon products from the Multi-Domain Sentiment Dataset[6]. The dataset collected most products and reviews released on Amazon.com in 2006.

Table 5. Number of reviews of every product type

Type(P1-P8)	Num	Type(P9-P16)	Num
Un MP3s & Cloud Player	956	Movie, Music & Games	3156
limited Instant Videos	3372	Electronics & Computers	2552
Amazon Cloud Drive	1288	Home, Garden & Tools	4012
Kindle	1296	Grocery, Health &Beauty	1188
Appstore for Android	2188	Toys, Kids & Baby	616
Digital Games & Software	586	Clothing, Shoes & Jewelry	1192
Audible Audiobooks	556	Sports & Outdoors	978
P8. Books	7216	Automotive & Industrial	3116

In most commercial websites like Amazon.com, there are a large number of duplicate reviews, which often negatively influence machine learning algorithms. For this, we use a simple deduplication method to filter the redundant reviews. The method matches bigrams between each pair of reviews. And a pair of reviews is deemed duplicated if they have more than 80% bigram matching. Besides the Amazon.com also have many duplicated products, such as the products can come in black or white models, and so reviews on such product are always duplicated. We filtered out the products whose all reviews are detected to be duplicates. The filtering process discarded a total of 3,404 products and 90,612 reviews. And at last we filtered out the reviews which never received any vote.

The final dataset involves 34,266 reviews on 1289 products. The types of products and the number of reviews in each type are shown in Table 5. We followed Kim et al [1] to set the voting rate 0.6 as the boundary between helpful and useless reviews and labeled the class (helpful or useless) of reviews beforehand. On the basis, we tested our helpfulness classification system on the whole dataset.

For testing AHV systems, we labeled helpfulness ranking for the reviews on the products of Digital Games, Audiobooks, Clothing and Sports (3,311 reviews on 116 products). In evaluation process, we run 5-fold cross validation and each fold use 80% products along with their reviews as training set and the rest as test set. We didn't adopt original Amazon ranking because Amazon ranks the reviews according to the timeliness but not the helpfulness.

6.2 Evaluation Metrics

In our experiments, we used accuracy to evaluate the performance of the helpfulness based review classification, and use the NDCG metric to evaluate the performance of our AHV system.

Here, the accuracy is the rate of the reviews whose helpfulness (helpful or useless) is correctly determined. NDCG@n is widely used to evaluate the performance of pseudo-feedback ranking in the field of information retrieval. In this paper, we translate it into an evaluation of review ranking system. NDCG@n[21] means normalized discount cumulative gain, which can take into account the influence of rank to accuracy. NDCG at rank n is calculated as:

$$NDCG@n = \frac{1}{Z_n} \cdot DCG@n = \frac{\sum_{i=1}^{n} \frac{2^{r(u_i)} - 1}{\log(1+i)}}{Z_n} \qquad (8)$$

where i is the rank in the ranking list of reviews, Z_n is a normalizing factor and chosen so that for the perfect list DCG at each rank 1, and $r(u_i)$ equals 1 when u_i is a review whose helpfulness is correctly determined, else 0. In our experiments, based on the given voting rate by Amazon.com, we obtain the correct ranking list of reviews, and on the other side, AHV

[6] http://www.cs.jhu.edu/~mdredze/datasets/sentiment/

systems output the ranking list of reviews based on helpfulness. Thus, we can use the NDCG@n to evaluate their performances.

6.3 AHV Systems

In our experiments, we totally built 10 systems: four helpfulness based review classification system, four AHV systems and two improved systems. The classification systems include:

- **System1** is a baseline classification system which roughly regards all reviews in corpus as helpful reviews. Because the average priori probability of helpful review occurring (in the 5 test set) is approximately 0.55, thus the accuracy of the baseline is 0.55.
- **System2** follows the textual features based helpfulness assessment of Kim et al[1]. The system uses the LIBSVM[7] with RBF kernel function (the rest parameters are default) as the classifier, and uses length, unigram and star as the features for classification.
- **System3** follows the work of Liu and Cao et al[5] and uses the same LIBSVM as the classifier but with the features of informativeness, readability and subjectivity.
- **System4** uses our user-preference based helpfulness assessment. The system also uses the LIBSVM as the classifier but with the features of needs fulfillment, information credibility and mainstreaming-opinion divergence. Thereinto, the needs fulfillment is measured by the capture rate (see equation 3), the credibility is measured by uncertainty factors (viz., volition based factor and experience based factor, see equation 4 and equation 5) and the divergence is measured by the difference between polarity forces (see section 5.3). Besides, we trained the discount factor α of the combination weight (see equation 1) in the measure of needs fulfillment, and set its optimal value to be 1.5, by which needs-fulfillment based classification can achieve best performance.

In our experiments, the AHV systems include:

- **System5** is a baseline AHV system which randomly ranks the reviews for each product.
- **System6** is a Ranking SVM based AHV system. Thereinto, Ranking SVM employs support vector machine (SVM) to classify object pairs in consideration of large margin rank boundaries. Here, we take pairs of reviews and their relative helpfulness derived from training data as training instances and apply Ranking SVM for learning better helpfulness assessment functions, by which to obtain optimal ranking list of reviews. Besides, we use the LIBSVM with the features of Kim et al[1] to implement the pair-wise classification.
- **System7** is a Ranking SVM based AHV system. But it uses the LIBSVM with the features of Liu and Cao et al[5] to implement the pair-wise classification.
- **System8** is also a Ranking SVM based AHV system. But it uses the LIBSVM with our features to implement the pair-wise classification.

Finally, by jointly using all of the features of Kim et al, Liu and Cao et al and ours, we implement an improved classification system **(System 9)** and an improved AHV system **(System 10)**.

7 http://www.csie.ntu.edu.tw/~cjlin/libsvm

7. MAIN RESULTS

We firstly run the helpfulness based classification systems. The accuracies of the systems are shown in Table 6. Here, our system (System4) achieved promising performance with the accuracy of 71.91%. Compared to the textual feature extraction of Kim et al (System2) and Liu and Cao et al (System3), our user-preference based feature extraction additionally contributes at least 6.77% correct helpfulness assessment.

Table 6. Accuracies of helpfulness-based review classification

	System1 (baseline)	System2 (Kim)	System3 (Liu)	System4 (Ours)
Accurracy(%)	55.16	61.29	62.85	69.62

We individually used the user-preference based features and their combinations in the classifier, by which to inspect the respective contributions of the features. We show the corresponding accuracies in Table 7, within which "NF" denotes the feature of needs fulfillment, "IC_{vol}" denotes volition based information credibility, "IC_{exp}" denotes experience based information credibility, "MO" denotes divergence from mainstreaming opinion and the sign "↑" means the improvement when adding a feature into classifier. From the performances in Table 7, we can find two issues: one is that the classification accuracy when using the feature of "MO" is very low; two is that the joint use of the features of "MO" and "IC_{vol}" contributes the lowest improvement, and on the contrary, the joint use of "MO" and "IC_{exp}" contributes the most improvement.

Table 7. Respective contributions of user-preference based features and their combinations (accuracy)

Feature	Accuracy(%)	Feature Combination	Accuracy(%)
		NF+ IC_{vol}	61.68(↑3.03)
NF	58.65	NF+ IC_{exp}	64.04(↑5.39)
IC_{vol}	50.03	NF+MO	61.26(↑2.61)
IC_{exp}	51.15	MO+ IC_{vol}	52.66(↑1.51)
MO	43.43	MO+ IC_{exp}	56.19(↑6.16)
		IC_{vol} + IC_{exp}	53.43(↑2.28)

The reason for the first issue is that, in the calculation of divergence from mainstreaming opinion (viz., the feature of "MO"), the correctness of mainstreaming opinion detection is very important, and the correctness mostly relies on whether there are enough reviews to calculate a steady average polarity force. But actually the numbers of reviews for different products have very uneven distribution. Within the test dataset, there are approximately 25% products has only no more than 20 corresponding reviews. The curve of "MO" in Figure 6 illustrates the negative influence of sparse reviews for the "MO" based classifier. In the figure, the horizontal axis corresponds to different ranges of numbers of reviews a product received; the vertical axis corresponds to the average classification accuracies on different ranges. It is not hard to find, compared to other three features, the feature "MO" cannot help the classifier accurately determine the helpfulness of reviews.

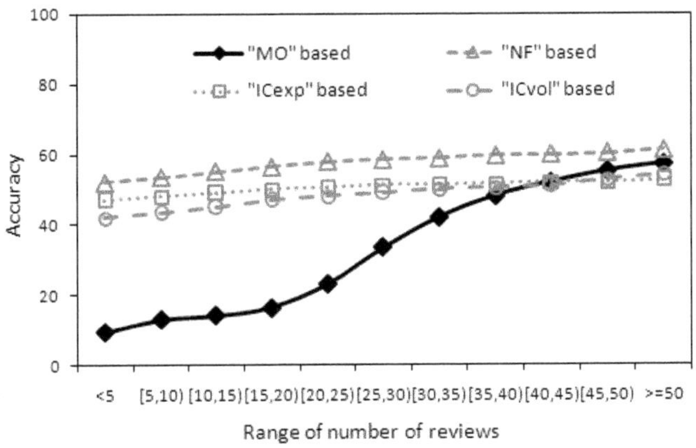

Figure 6. The accuracies of the classification systems in different ranges of numbers of reviews

The reason for the second issue is that the features "MO" and "IC_{vol}" make their classifiers have the same determination on most reviews. By analyzing the results, we found that approximately 79.2% reviews in test dataset receive the same helpfulness determination from "MO" based classifier and "IC_{vol}" based classifier. Thus, when adding the feature "IC_{vol}" into the "MO" based classifier, even if the feature has the ability to make better distinctions on review helpfulness, it has no enough space to offer this advantage. Compared to this, "MO" based classifier and "IC_{exp}" based classifier only have the same determination on 34.3% reviews. Thus the space for their respective superiority is bigger. The second issue also illustrate that the volition and sentiment normally have a compatible effect on reflecting user preference, e.g. people normally show positive sentiment to the things they preferred.

Table 8. NDCG@10 of AHV systems

	System5 (AHV baseline)	**System6** (Kim AHV)	**System7** (Liu AHV)	**System8** (Ours)
NDCG@10(%)	5.6	15.75	16.9	22.25

We secondly run the AHV systems on the test dataset. The performances of the systems are shown in Table 8. Here, NDCG@10 means the NDCG on the top 10 of ranking list, which needs that only a product with at least 10 reviews can be used as test sample. Thus we restricted the participation of products with less than 10 reviews in test, and used the rest (26,962 reviews) to evaluate the AHV systems. The results show that our AHV system achieves the optimal NDCG@10. Compared to the AHV systems of Kim et al and Liu and Cao et al, our AHV system respectively improves 6.5% and 5.35%.

At last, we run the final classification system (System9) and AHV system (System10), both of which use all existing features (including the textual features proposed by Kim et al, Liu and Cao et al, and our user-preference based features). The results show further improvements on helpfulness assessment and ranking (See Table 9).

Table 9. Performances of the improved systems

	System9 (improved classification)	**System 10** (improved AHV)
Accuracy	71.9	-
NDCG@10(%)	-	25.25

As discussed in Section 4, we use parts of items provided by Amazon.com (see Table 1) to illustrate the availability of user-preference based features in helpfulness assessment. Thereinto, the items <Er>, <Pt> and <Ps> are used to measure the feature of needs fulfillment, the item <Buyer?> is used to measure the feature of tense based information credibility, and the item <Star> is used to measure the feature of mainstreaming opinion consistency. And the capacity of the features in dividing helpful and useless reviews is obvious. But the features are restricted to use in AHV system to ensure pure automatic system without human intervention (our systems only use the items <Content> and <Product>). Here, we also use the measures to generate the review classification and AHV system for evaluating the compatibility of our only <Content> based feature extraction to the human intervention based feature extraction.

Table 10. Accuracy comparison of classification

	H(NF)	S(NF)	H(IC)	S(IC)	H(MO)	S(MO)
Accuracy	56.16	58.65	49.34	51.15	44.04	43.43

The performances of the systems are shown in Table 10 and Table 11, where "H" denotes the feature from human intervention, "S" denotes the feature only extracted from contents of review, "NF" denotes the feature of needs fulfillment, "IC" denotes information credibility (only based on tense here) and "MO" denotes mainstreaming opinion consistency. It not hard to find the performances are very compatible. The only issue is the performances of "S(NF)" and "S(IC)" are better than that by human intervention. The reason is that the measure of "NF" and "IC" have been improved based on the language information in <Content>, but it is hard for the items from human.

Table 11. NDCG@10 comparison of AHV

	H(NF)	S(NF)	H(IC)	S(IC)	H(MO)	S(MO)
NDCG@10	11.10	11.52	7.96	8.19	6.26	5.25

8. CONCLUSIONS

In this paper, we focus on discussing how to automatically assess review helpfulness and exploring the possibility of using user-preference based features to improve previous textual feature based helpfulness assessment. We respectively illustrate the availabilities of the features of needs fulfillment, information credibility and divergence from mainstreaming opinion in helpfulness assessment, and give the quantitative measures of the features. By using the features, we respectively build a helpfulness based review classification system and an automatic review ranking system. The test results on a large scale of commercial reviews (from Amazon.com) show the user-preference based features contribute substantial improvements for both review classification and ranking.

The improvements demonstrate that user preference learning is useful to review helpfulness assessment. In future, we will further explore the features that reflect the preference on commercial reviews. For example, users normally only read and vote on the reviews on the top of original ranking list by commercial websites, which will give steady voting rate to the top reviews but unreliable rate to the reviews on the bottom of ranking list. But, the similarity of contents can be used to detect the link between the relevant reviews wherever they locate. Therefore, the similarity can be used to build a collaborative helpfulness assessment, which use the steady voting rate to estimate the weak rate of the reviews which are seldom or even never seen by users on the bottom of original ranking list.

9. ACKNOWLEDGMENTS

This research is supported by the National Natural Science Foundation of China (No. 60970056, 60970057, 61003152, 90920004), Special fund project of the Ministry of Education Doctoral Program (20093211110006, 20103201110021) and Natural Science Foundation of Jiangsu Province, Suzhou City (SYG201030).

10. REFERENCES

[1] Kim, S.M., Pantel, P., and Chklovski, T., Pennacchiotti, M. 2006. Automatically Assessing Review Helpfulness. In *Proceedings of the 2006 Conference on Empirical Methods in Natural Language Processing*. Sydney, July, 423-430.

[2] Titov, I., and McDonald, R. 2008. Modeling online reviews with Multi-grain Topic Model. In *Proceedings of the 17th international conference on World Wide Web*. Beijing, China, April, 111–120.

[3] Goldensohn, S. B., Hannan, K., McDonald, R., Neylon, T., Reis, G. A., and Reynar, J. 2008. Building a sentiment summarizer for local service reviews. 2008. In *Proceedings of WWW2008 Workshop on NLP Challenges in the Information Explosion Era*. Beijing, China, April, 21-25.

[4] Popescu, A. M., and Etzioni, O. 2005. Extracting Product Features and Opinions from Reviews. In *Proceedings of Human Language Technology Conference and Conference on Empirical Methods in Natural Language Processing*. Vancouver, October, 339-346.

[5] Liu, J. J., Cao, Y. B., Lin, C. Y., Huang, Y. L., and Zhou, M. 2007. Low-Quality Product Review Detection in Opinion Summarization. In *Proceedings of the 2007 Joint Conference on Empirical Methods in Natural Language Processing and Computational Natural Language Learning* (EMNLP-CoNLL 2007). Prague, Czech Republic, June, 334-342.

[6] Jinal, N., and Liu, B. 2008. Opinion Spam and Analysis. In *Proceedings of the international conference on Web search and web data mining*. Palo Alto, California, February, 219-230.

[7] Cristian, D. N. M., Kossinets, G., Kleiinberg, Jon., and Lee, L. 2009. How Opinions are Received by Online Communities: A Case Study on Amazon.com Helpfulness Votes. In *Proceedings of the 18th international conference on World Wide Web*. Madrid, Spain, April, 141-150.

[8] Tsur, O., and Rappoport, O. 2009. REVRANK: a Fully Unsupervised Algorithm for Selecting the Most Helpful Book Reviews. In *Proceedings of the Third International AAAI Conference on Weblogs and Social Media*. San Jose, California, May, 36–44.

[9] Liu, F., Yu, C., and Meng, W. Y. 2004. Personalized web search for improving retrieval effectiveness. *IEEE Transactions on Knowledge and Data Engineering* 16(1):28–40.

[10] Liu, Y., Huang, X. J., An, A., and Yu, X. H. 2008. Modeling and predicting the helpfulness of online reviews. In *Proceedings of the 2008 Eighth IEEE International Conference on Data Mining*. Pisa, Italy, December, 443–452.

[11] Jo, Y., and Oh, A. 2011. Aspect and Sentiment Unification Model for Online Review Analysis. In *Proceedings of the fourth ACM international conference on Web search and data mining*. ACM Press, New York. February, 815-824.

[12] Cao, Y. B., Xu, J., Liu, T. Y., Li, H., Huang Y. L., and Hon, H. W. 2006. Adapting ranking svm to document retrieval. In *Proceedings of the 29th annual international ACM SIGIR conference on Research and development in information retrieval*. Seattle, Washington, USA, August, 186-193.

[13] Valizadegan, H., Zhang, R., Zhang, R., and Mao, J. 2009. In *Proceedings of the 23rd Neural Information Processing Systems* (NIPS 2009). Lake Tahoe, Nevada, USA, December.

[14] De Marneffe MC., MacCartney B., and Manning CD. 2006. Generating typed dependency parses from phrase structure parses. In *Proceedings of 5th International Conference on Language Resources and Evaluation*. Genova, May, 449-454.

[15] Giménez, J., and Màrquez, L.2004. SVMTool: A general POS tagger generator based on Support Vector Machines. In: *Proceedings of the 4th International Conference on Language Resources and Evaluation*, Lisbon, May, 43-46.

[16] Zhang, J. F., Hong, Y., Yang, Y. H., Yao, J. M., Zhu, Q. M. 2010. A grammar-based unsupervised method of mining volitive words. In *Proceedings of 2010 International Conference on Asian Language Processing*. Harbin, China, December, 137-141.

[17] Marcu, D., and Wong, W. 2002. A phrase-based joint probability model for statistical machine translation. In *Proceedings of Empirical Methods for Natural Language*. Philadelphia, PA, July, 133– 139.

[18] Doddington, G., Mitchell, A., and Przybocki. 2004. The Automatic Content Extraction (ACE) Program: Tasks, data, & evaluation. In *Proceedings of the 4th International Conference on Language Resources and Evaluation*. In Memory of Antonio Zampolli. Lisbon, May, 837–840.

[19] Strapparava, C., and Valitutti, A. 2004. Wordnet-affect: an affective extension of wordnet. In *Proceedings of the 4th International Conference on Language Resources and Evaluation*. Lisbon, Portugal, May, 1083–1086.

[20] Nasukawa, T., and Yi, J. 2003. Sentiment Analysis: Capturing Favorability using Natural Language Processing. In *Proceedings of Second International conferences on Knowledge Capture*. Sanibel Island, Florida, October, 70-77.

[21] Jarvelin, K., and Kekalainen, J. 2000. IR evaluation methods for retrieving highly relevant documents. In *Proceedings of the 23rd international ACM SIGIR conference on Research and development in information retrieval*. Athens, July, 41-48.

Automatic Refinement of Patent Queries using Concept Importance Predictors

Parvaz Mahdabi† Linda Andersson‡ Mostafa Keikha† Fabio Crestani†
†University of Lugano, Faculty of Informatics, Lugano, Switzerland
{parvaz.mahdabi, mostafa.keikha, fabio.crestani}@usi.ch
‡Vienna University of Technology, Vienna, Austria
andersson@ifs.tuwien.ac.at

ABSTRACT

Patent prior art queries are full patent applications which are much longer than standard web search topics. Such queries are composed of hundreds of terms and do not represent a focused information need. One way to make the queries more focused is to select a group of key terms as representatives. Existing works show that such a selection to reduce patent queries is a challenging task mainly because of the presence of ambiguous terms. Given this setup, we present a query modeling approach where we utilize patent-specific characteristics to generate more precise queries. We propose to automatically disambiguate query terms by employing noun phrases that are extracted using the global analysis of the patent collection. We further introduce a method for predicting whether expansion using noun phrases would improve the retrieval effectiveness.

Our experiments show that we can obtain almost 20% improvement by performing query expansion using the true importance of the noun phrase queries. Based on this observation, we introduce various features that can be used to estimate the importance of the noun phrase query. We evaluated the effectiveness of the proposed method on the patent prior art search collection CLEF-IP 2010. Our experimental results indicate that the proposed features make good predictors of the noun phrase importance, and selective application of noun phrase queries using the importance predictors outperforms existing query generation methods.

Categories and Subject Descriptors

H.3.3 [**Information Storage and Retrieval**]: Query formulation, Relevance Feedback

General Terms

Experimentation, Performance, Measurement

Keywords

Patent Search, Query Generation, Relevance Model

Permission to make digital or hard copies of all or part of this work for personal or classroom use is granted without fee provided that copies are not made or distributed for profit or commercial advantage and that copies bear this notice and the full citation on the first page. To copy otherwise, to republish, to post on servers or to redistribute to lists, requires prior specific permission and/or a fee.
SIGIR'12, August 12–16, 2012, Portland, Oregon, USA.
Copyright 2012 ACM 978-1-4503-1472-5/12/08 ...$15.00.

1. INTRODUCTION

Patent prior art search is composed of a search over previously filed patents with the aim of retrieving relevant documents, which may invalidate or at least describe prior art work in a patent application, (henceforth referred to as *query patent* in this paper). The challenges of patent prior art search are different from those of standard ad hoc text and web search. The first difference is associated to the query length: patent prior art queries are full patent applications comprising of hundreds of words as opposed to ad hoc search and web search where the queries are very short. The second issue is related to the fact that patent prior art search is a recall oriented task where the goal is to retrieve all relevant documents at early rank positions as opposed to ad hoc and web search, where the goal is to achieve high precision.

We present a solution to the patent prior art search problem allowing the user to submit a full patent document as a query and the retrieval system identifies related patent documents from a corpus accordingly. To provide such functionality, we propose two techniques to process patent documents on demand and extract terms and key phrases in order to form a query to retrieve relevant documents from the patent corpus. These two approaches can be summarized as follows: i) one approach extracts single terms from the query patent using the KL-divergence between the query patent and the collection; ii) the other approach refines the original query by expanding it with selected key concepts (i.e., bigrams or phrases) from the query patent using the global analysis of the patent collection. These two approaches are complementary to each other: the first approach extracts generic terms, favoring recall, while the second aims to find a clear focus for the query by providing more specific phrases, thus increasing precision.

However, after evaluating mean average precision (MAP) over the topic set, we observe that the expanded rank list is not statistically different from the unexpanded rank list. After performing failure analysis on a per query basis, we detected a large variation in performance for different queries; we found that while indeed the expanded rank list improves the quality of results for many queries considerably, the quality of results is poor for some other queries. One of the reasons explaining the hurting retrieval performance for some queries is attributed to the topics for which the main aspect of the query is not considered during expansion. In such cases, only important concepts describing the partial aspects of the query are extracted. This observation shows that expansion using noun phrases was not consistently beneficial for all queries. This suggests that the decision about query expansion using concepts should be taken in a query dependent way.

In this paper, we propose a method for distinguishing between queries and deciding when to selectively use the result of a refinement technique that is likely to improve the retrieval performance. Our goal is to find queries that have highly positive changes in query performance using refinement. To this end, we use query performance predictors (pre and post-retrieval) [2, 9, 1, 20] and patent-specific features in order to find highly performing queries in the expanded retrieval rank list. To decide when to use the result of the expanded list, we rely on a machine learning approach that tries to predict which one of the two competing approaches will offer the best result for a given query.

This prediction is performed in a selective query refinement framework [23, 1, 3, 8, 10]. It is desirable for us to build a robust patent retrieval system which can be used in an operational setting. We aim at quantifying the performance of the queries in order to build a robust system which can invoke different retrieval strategies in a query dependent way according to the estimated performance of a query. To the best of our knowledge no previous work have used the query performance predictors in the patent domain.

In this paper we explore extracting concepts which explicitly occur in the query patent itself. We also study extracting important concepts associated with the information need underlying the query patent through the process of query expansion by building a relevance model: 1) via pseudo relevance feedback; 2) using sample relevant documents. Our contributions are:

- Investigating different ways of estimating the query model from a query patent utilizing patent-specific characteristics.
- Presenting a method for predicting whether query expansion using concepts would improve the retrieval effectiveness.
- Investigating the impact of different types of expansion in our selective query expansion framework.

We evaluate our model on CLEF-IP 2010 collection and we report significant improvement over the strong CLEF-IP baselines. The results show that by incorporating the predicted noun phrase importance in a selective query expansion framework, we can achieve significant improvement over using query expansion for all queries.

The rest of this paper is organized as follows: Section 2 briefly reviews the related work; Section 3 and 4 define the original and the expanded query models; Section 5 describes the prediction model using query performance measures; Section 6 reports the experimental results and Section 7 reports the conclusion of the work.

2. RELATED WORK

The work performed by patent examiners involves manual query formulation from the query patent in order to find invalidating claims. They consider high term frequency in the document to be a strong indicator of a good query term. Methods to shorten a query patent have been studied for a few years and this research direction has shown to be very challenging mainly due to the presence of ambiguous terms. In the third NTCIR workshop [12], the first patent prior art search track was introduced and several patent test collections were released. Some early works [11, 13] using this collection focused on extracting keywords to form a reduced query.

A recent line of work advocates the use of the full patent application as the query to reduce the burden on patent examiners. This direction has been started by Xue and Croft [21], who conducted a series of experiments in order to examine the effect of different patent fields, and concludes with the observation that the best Mean Average Precision (MAP) is achieved using the text from the *description* section of the query patent with raw term frequencies. Fuji [6] showed that retrieval effectiveness can be improved by combining IR methods with the result of citation extraction.

The current developments in the patent search are driven by the Intellectual Property task within the CLEF[1] initiative. Several teams participated in the prior art search task of the CLEF-IP 2010 and proposed approaches to reduce the query patent by extracting a set of key terms from it. Different participating teams experimented with term distribution analysis in a language modeling setting, and they employed the document structure of the patent documents in various ways [18].

So far, one of the most comprehensive descriptions of the problem and possible solutions for the prior art search is presented by Magdy and Lopez [15]. The authors show that the best performing run of CLEF-IP 2010 uses citations extracted by training a Conditional Random Field (CRF). The second best run uses a list of citations extracted from the patent numbers within the *description* field of some patent queries. They also show that the best run employs sophisticated methods of retrieval using two complementary indices, one constructed by extracting terms from the patent collection and the other built from external resources such as Wikipedia. They compared this two approaches and conclude with an interesting observation that the second best run achieves a statistically indistinguishable performance compared to the best run.

A recent work [7] studies the effect of using Pseudo Relevance Feedback (PRF) for reducing patent queries. Authors decompose a patent application into constituent text segments and compute the language modeling similarities by calculating the probability of generating each segment from the top ranked documents. They showed that although they achieve improvement over PRF, their approach is not able to achieve statistical significance gain over the second best result of CLEF-IP 2010. As a baseline for this paper, we consider an approach which produces comparable results to the second rank participating group of CLEF-IP 2010 and we compare different variations of our proposed method to this baseline. We show that our proposed method significantly outperform the baseline.

In addition to the well known MAP metric we use the Patent Retrieval Evaluation Score (PRES) which is originally proposed by Magdy and Jones [14]. Authors showed that MAP can be a misleading metric for evaluating the performance of patent prior art search because of its inherent characteristic of favoring precision over recall. This metric measures the system recall and the quality of ranking in one score. Our experiments report an improvement in terms of MAP, recall and PRES over the baseline.

[1] http://www.ir-facility.org/clef-ip

3. ESTABLISHING A BASELINE: SINGLE TERM EXTRACTION

Patent prior art queries are full patent applications which are much longer than standard web search topics. These queries are composed of hundreds of terms and do not represent a focused information need. Thus, the success of the patent prior art search relies on the selection of good search queries.

Our goal is to estimate the query model of a query patent in a language modeling framework. This estimation enables us to identify the importance of terms and assign weights to them accordingly. By modeling the term distribution of the query patent we get a detailed representation of the query patent which allows us to expand the query, and to refine the query model by considering relationships between terms. This approach is used to bridge the vocabulary gap between the underlying information need of the query patent and the collection.

In this section, we first describe how we create a language model Θ_Q for the query patent. We use the maximum likelihood estimate smoothed by the background language model, as expressed in Equation 1 to avoid sparseness issues.

$$P(t|\Theta_Q) = (1-\lambda) \cdot P_{ML}(t|D) + \lambda \cdot P_{ML}(t|C) \quad (1)$$

where maximum likelihood estimate P_{ML} is calculated as follows:

$$P_{ML}(t|D) = \frac{n(t,D)}{\sum_{t'} n(t',D)} \quad (2)$$

We introduce a unigram query model by estimating the importance of each term according to a weighted log-likelihood based approach as expressed below:

$$P(t|Q_{orig}) = Z_t \; P(t|\Theta_Q) \; log\left(\frac{P(t|\Theta_Q)}{P(t|\Theta_C)}\right) \quad (3)$$

where $Z_t = 1/\sum_{t \in V} P(t|Q_{orig})$ is the normalization factor and is defined as the Kullback-Leibler divergence between Θ_Q and Θ_C. This approach favors terms that have high similarity to the document language model Θ_Q and low similarity to the collection language model Θ_C. For the rest of the paper Q_{orig} serves as our unigram baseline.

In order to model the query patent more precisely we need a source of additional knowledge about the information need. Patent documents are annotated with International Patent Classifications[2] (IPC). Such classes are language independent keywords assigned as metadata to the patent documents. They are categorizing the content of a patent document and reflecting the field of technology of a patent. These IPC classes resemble tags assigned to documents (henceforth referred to as *conceptual tags* in this paper).

Our goal is to build a relevance model by employing documents that have at least one conceptual tag in common with the query topic. Each relevant document from this sample is assumed to serve as evidence towards the estimation of the relevance model. Note that this relevant samples are not part of the relevance information.

Our approach to construct the relevance model Θ_{IPC} is the following. First, we estimate the level of relevance of a document D with $P(D|\Theta_{IPC})$. Then the top-k terms with the highest probability $P(t|D)$ are picked and used to build Θ_{IPC}. The sample distribution $P(t|\Theta_{IPC})$ is calculated according to Equation 4. This sampling is dependent on the original query patent as it utilizes documents with similar conceptual tags to the query patent.

$$P(t|\Theta_{IPC}) = \sum_{D \in IPC} P(t|D) \cdot P(D|\Theta_{IPC}) \quad (4)$$

Now we explain how the level of relevance of a sample document D is estimated. We can not assume documents in the relevance set to have equal importance. The reason is that documents in the relevance set can be multi-faceted and therefore not entirely relevant to the information need represented by the query patent. So we need to assign importance to the documents according to their level of relevance. We approximate the relevance of a sample document D, denoted by $P(D|\Theta_{IPC})$, based on the divergence between D and Θ_{IPC}. We measure this divergence by calculating the log-likelihood ratio between D and Θ_{IPC}, normalized by the collection C as defined below:

$$\begin{aligned} P(D|\Theta_{IPC}) &\propto H(\Theta_D, \Theta_C) - H(\Theta_D, \Theta_{IPC}) \\ &= Z_D \sum_{t \in V} P(t|\Theta_D) \log \frac{P(t|\Theta_{IPC})}{P(t|\Theta_C)} \end{aligned}$$

where $H(\Theta_D, \Theta_C)$ represents the cross entropy between the sample document D and the collection and $H(\Theta_D, \Theta_{IPC})$ represents the cross entropy between the sample document D and the topical model of relevance Θ_{IPC}. We define $Z_D = 1/\sum_{D \in IPC} P(D|\Theta_{IPC})$ as a document-specific normalization factor. This approach assigns higher scores to documents which contain specific terminology and are more similar to Θ_{IPC} and less similar to the language model of the collection Θ_C. For estimating the term importance $P(t|D)$ in Equation 4, we consider the smoothed maximum likelihood estimate of a term to avoid sparseness issues as shown in Equation 1.

We then mix the estimated relevance model using the conceptual tags and the original query in order to build an expanded query. To do this, we use a linear combination as expressed in the following:

$$P(t|Q_{ex}) = (1-\mu) \cdot P(t|\theta_{IPC}) + \mu \cdot P(t|Q_{orig}) \quad (5)$$

where $P(t|Q_{orig})$ and $P(t|\theta_{IPC})$ show the probability of term t given the original query model and the estimated relevance model, respectively. We refer to this expanded query model as EX-RM.

The performance of different unigram query models presented in this section are compared with each other in the experiment section. For comparison purposes, we also show the performance of Pseudo Relevance Feedback (PRF), as a reference baseline, and we compare this to the query models built in this section. In the experiment section we show that the relevance model constructed based on the conceptual tags (EX-RM) outperforms the result of PRF. To generate a query we pick the top-k terms with higher weights from each query model.

[2]http://www.wipo.int/classifications/ipc/en/

4. PHRASE EXTRACTION

In this section, we present our approach for extracting key phrases with similar semantics to patent query. Such phrases will be used to expand and disambiguate the initial unigram query Q_{orig} as estimated in Section 3. We then use the expanded noun phrase query Q_{expand} to retrieve relevant documents from the patent corpus. We use both corpus statistics and linguistic heuristics for finding meaningful phrases. The detail of our solution is as follows: First we identify the set of all candidate key phrases S_p for the query document d, as explained in Section 4.1. We then evaluate the significance of each candidate phrase $p \in S_p$, by assigning a score $s(c)$ between 0 and 1 to each phrase as shown in Section 4.2. Finally we select the top-k phrases to construct an expanded query. In the evaluation section, the quality of Q_{expand} is compared to the unigram query Q_{orig} by reporting the document retrieval results.

4.1 Extracting Candidate Key Phrases

We recognized and extracted candidate noun phrases with length at most 5 from the query patent, with the help of the Stanford *part of speech tagger* [19]. The part-of-speech tagger assigns part-of-speech tags (e.g., noun (NN), verb (VB), adjective (JJ), etc.) to each term $w \in d$. The part-of-speech tagger applies a pre-trained classifier on w and it's surrounding terms in d. We consider all noun phrases as candidate phrases, and compute S_p by extracting all such phrases from d. We are interested to find ordinary phrases rather than extracting named entities. The example noun phrase patterns[3] that we used are listed in Table 1.

Table 1: Example of noun phrase patterns and instances

Pattern	Instance
NN	leukocyte
JJ NN	miniature column
NN NN	blood filtration
JJ JJ NN	hydrophobic polymerizable monomer
NN NN NN	leukocyte removal performance
JJ NN NN	nonwoven polyester fabric
JJ JJ JJ NN	protonic neutral hydrophilic part
NN NN NN NN	blood transfusion side effect
...	...
NN NN NN NN NN	coating leukocyte removal filter material

4.2 Scoring Key Phrases

We used the two methods proposed in [22] for scoring phrases. We briefly revisit the two scoring approaches. The first approach employs the TF/IDF information for evaluating the importance of each phrase, while the second calculates a weight for each phrase using mutual information.

4.2.1 *Scoring Phrases based on TF/IDF*

The first scoring technique assigns a score $s_t(p)$ to a phrase p which is based on a linear combination of the total TF/IDF score of all terms in p and the degree of *coherence* of p. Coherence quantifies the likelihood of the constituting terms in forming a single concept and is a measure of stability of a phrase in the corpus. Formally, let $|p|$ denote the number of terms in phrase p; we use $w_1, w_2, ..., w_{|p|}$ to refer to the actual terms. $s_t(p)$ is formally defined as:

$$s_t(p) = \sum_{i=1}^{|p|} tf.idf(w_i) + \alpha \cdot coherence(p) \qquad (6)$$

where $idf(w_i)$ is the inverse document frequency of w_i and α is a tunable parameter. The first component in $s_t(p)$ captures the importance of each term in p by using the TF/IDF value. A rare term that occurs frequently in d is more important than a common term frequently appearing in d (with low idf). This component will reward rare phrases. The second component in $s_t(p)$ represents how coherent the phrase p is. The coherence of p is defined as:

$$coherence(p) = \frac{tf(p) \cdot (1 + \log tf(p))}{\frac{1}{|p|} \cdot \sum_{i=1}^{|p|} tf(w_i)} \qquad (7)$$

where $tf(p)$ is the number of times the phrase p appears in the document d. Equation 7 compares the frequency of p with the average tf of its terms. The additional logarithmic component give importance to phrases appearing frequently in the input document.

4.2.2 *Scoring Phrases based on Mutual Information*

The second scoring technique assigns $s_m(p)$ to a phrase p which is based on the mutual information (MI) between the terms of phrase p and the *idf* values from the background corpus. $s_m(p)$ is a linear combination of *idf* values of terms in p, frequency of p, and the point-wise mutual information among them. $s_m(p)$ is formally defined as:

$$s_m(p) = \sum_{i=1}^{|p|} idf(w_i) + \log \frac{tf(p)}{tf(POS_p)} + PMI(p) \qquad (8)$$

where $tf(p)$ and $tf(POS_p)$ are the number of times p and its part-of-speech tag sequence POS_p appear in d and its part-of-speech tag sequence POS_d, respectively. The first part represents how descriptive each term in phrase p is. The second part identifies how frequent the phrase p is at the corresponding POS tag sequence in the document. The third part captures how likely are the terms to from a phrase together. Mutual information compares the probability of observing the constituting terms in phrase p together (the joint probability) with the probabilities of observing those terms independently. The *PMI(p)* for a phrase p is defined as:

$$PMI(p) = \log\left(\frac{P(p)}{\prod_{i=1}^{|p|} P(w_i)}\right) \qquad (9)$$

where $P(w_i)$ and $P(p)$ denote the probability of occurrence of w_i and phrase p respectively at the appropriate part-of-speech tag sequence. They are formally defined as:

$$P(p) = \frac{tf(p)}{tf(POS_p)}, \; P(w_i) = \frac{tf(w_i)}{tf(POS_{w_i})} \qquad (10)$$

In order to emphasize on the importance of how frequent the phrase p occurs in the document d we weight Equation 8 by $\frac{tf(p)}{tf(POS_p)}$ as shown below:

[3]Presented instances belong to query 433 in the topic set.

$$s'_m(p) = \frac{tf(p)}{tf(POS_p)} \times \left(\sum_{i=1}^{|p|} idf(w_i) + \log \frac{tf(p)}{tf(POS_p)} + PMI(p) \right)$$

We only keep the top few highest scoring phrases to eliminate redundancy. We will do a deeper analysis on the number of selected phrases in the experimental section.

5. PREDICTING NOUN PHRASE EFFECTIVENESS

Our goal is to predict whether an expanded query using noun phrases will be more effective for retrieval than an unexpanded query. We evaluate the effectiveness of the expanded query by estimating the change in the average precision (AP) for each query. Let $AP(Q_{orig})$ and $AP(Q_{expand})$ be the AP of original unigram query and of the expanded query using noun phrases, respectively. We measure the performance change due to the Q_{expand} as expressed below,

$$chg(AP, Q) = \frac{AP(Q_{expand}) - AP(Q_{orig})}{AP(Q_{orig})} \tag{11}$$

We set a threshold at 10% for this change in AP to distinguish a good expanded query from a bad one and this indicates an effective noun phrase expansion. After identifying a good expanded query according to Equation 11, we use this estimate to decide whether the original query should be expanded or not. We then perform a selective query expansion (SQE) where we only expand effective noun phrase queries.

Before trying to estimate the effectiveness of the noun phrase query, it is interesting to know how good the SQE will perform if the true effectiveness value is used. To this end, we use the average precision of Q_{orig} and Q_{expand} to decide whether to expand a query or not. We refer to this approach as $oracle_{np}$ showing the potential upper bound of what can be achieved by combining the two rank lists based on true effectiveness. Table 2 shows the MAP for the top 1000 results with $oracle_{np}$ in comparison to the original unigram query model (baseline) and the expanded query model using noun phrases (QM-NP2). The † and ‡ symbols indicate that the improvement over the unigram baseline and QM-NP2 is statistically significant at $p<0.01$.

Table 2: Performance results using the true noun phrase effectiveness

model	MAP
baseline	0.1366
QM-NP2	0.1380
$oracle_{np}$	0.1649 † ‡

As the result of Table 2 suggests, we can achieve a 20% improvement over both unigram baseline and QM-NP2, by employing the true effectiveness of the noun phrases. We seek to reach this upper bound by a reasonable estimation of the correct AP values and the change of AP for each query according to Equation 11.

5.1 Features

In order to predict the effectiveness of an expanded query we use a set of features related to the query to estimate AP of both rank lists of Q_{orig} and Q_{expand}. These features will be explained in this Section.

The Query Clarity (QC) measure [2] quantifies the level of effectiveness of a query at retrieving a specific topic. The clarity measure is the Kullback-Leibler (KL) divergence between the query language model $P(w|Q)$ and the collection language model $P(w|C)$. Formally, the clarity score is defined as:

$$D_{KL}(Q||C) = \sum_{w \in V} P(w|Q) log \frac{P(w|Q)}{P(w|C)} \tag{12}$$

A higher clarity score indicates a clearer query with specialized vocabulary and a lower clarity score indicates a more ambiguous query with a very generic language. To calculate a clarity score in a given collection, a *relevance model* is constructed. This model captures the language usage of documents related to the query and therefore it is a collection-dependent query model.

We propose two measures inspired by the clarity measure using patent-specific characteristics. Let IPC_Q be the set of documents with similar topics to Q represented by conceptual tags. The first measure, called *Topical Clarity*, is defined as the KL-divergence between the language model of Q and the language model of IPC_Q. Formally, the Topical Clarity (TC) measure is defined as:

$$D_{KL}(Q||IPC_Q) = \sum_{w \in V} P(w|Q) log \frac{P(w|Q)}{P(w|IPC_Q)} \tag{13}$$

where $P(w|IPC_Q)$ is the relative frequency of term w in documents with similar conceptual tags to Q. We refer to this as the topical clarity. In this case, a larger KL-divergence indicates a query with fewer topics and therefore a more focused query, while a smaller KL-divergence indicates a query with a broader language use.

The second measure called *IPC-based Clarity* captures the similarity between the language usage of IPC_Q and the collection language model. This measure is defined as:

$$D_{KL}(IPC_Q||C) = \sum_{w \in V} P(w|IPC_Q) log \frac{P(w|IPC_Q)}{P(w|C)} \tag{14}$$

An alternative indication of the specificity of a query is to consider the distribution of the informative amount in the query terms [9]. This measure is defined by:

$$\gamma_1 = \sigma_{idf} \tag{15}$$

where σ represents the standard deviation of the *idf* of the terms in Q. Each query term can be associated with an inverse document frequency ($idf(w)$) describing the informative amount that a query term q carries. The $idf(w)$ is defined by:

$$idf(w) = log \frac{N - N_w + 0.5}{N_w + 0.5} \tag{16}$$

where N_w is the number of documents in which the query term w appears and N is the number of documents in the whole collection.

Another measure to predict query performance is called Query Scope (QS) [9]. This measure uses the size of the document set containing at least one of the query terms to

Table 3: Features used in the regression model for query Q

Features	
QC	Query Clarity
TC	Topical Clarity
tag-clarity	IPC-based Clarity
γ_1	Informative Amount in the Query
QS	Query Scope

infer the query performance. Formally, the query scope is defined as:

$$QS = -\log(n_Q/N) \quad (17)$$

where n_Q is the number of documents containing at least one of the query terms, and N is the number of documents in the whole collection.

These features are summarized in Table 3. Note that the length of generated queries are similar so there is no gain in considering this as a feature.

To learn a performance prediction model using these features we define the following regression problem.

$$\underset{\Phi}{argmin} \sum_{Q \in T} ||\Phi(F(Q)) - AP(Q)||^2 \quad (18)$$

where T is a set of training topics and F is a mapping from query to the feature space. F also defines a mapping from the respective rank list of the query to the feature space.

5.2 Evaluating the dependence between the predictors and AP

In this section, we will examine the correlations of the predictors with the query performance. We use AP as the focus measure indicating the query performance in our experiments. To investigate the effectiveness of the predictors, we check the Spearman rank correlation and linear regression because of their power in showing correlation between predictors and AP as suggested by previous studies [4, 9].

The linear regression assumes a linear distribution of the involved variables, which is not necessarily valid in our case. As the distribution of the involved variables is unknown, a non-parametric measure such as Spearman rank correlation which does not assume any particular structure for the relationship can find stronger relationships. However, Spearman rank correlation can not find relationships between the combinations of predictors and AP.

Table 4 summarizes the results of the linear correlations of the predictors (in isolation) with AP on the training data. We know that the relationship between predictors and AP may be nonlinear, but this allows us to compare the importance of the features by examining their coefficients. We also examine the importance of the features by examining the significance of their correlation with AP. Bold values denote statistically significant correlations with AP at the reported level of p-value using paired t-test.

In order to model the complex nonlinear relationships between combinations of predictor variables, we use Stochastic Gradient Boosting Tree (SGBT) [5]. This model produces an ensemble of weak prediction learners, i.e., decision trees. It builds additive regression models in a stage-wise manner

Table 4: Linear Regression and Spearman rank correlation coefficient of the query performance predictors with Average Precision

	LR		Spearman	
Features	r	p-value	rs	p-value
QC	**0.2180**	**0.05**	**0.3645**	**0.01**
TC	**0.2466**	**0.05**	**0.3170**	**0.01**
tag-clarity	0.0943	0.28	**0.1812**	**0.05**
γ_1	0.0491	0.61	**0.1100**	**0.05**
QS	**0.1956**	**0.05**	**0.2278**	**0.01**

and it generalizes them by allowing optimization of an arbitrary differentiable loss function. For the SGBT, we used the gbm2 package implemented in R[4]. SGBT can find a subcombination of features that may aid with the prediction of AP. With this model we can get a prediction of AP for any input. Notice that Φ in Equation 18 represents an additive model of multiple decision trees which is learnt by SGBT.

6. EXPERIMENTS

In this section, we present the results for an experimental evaluation of our proposed method of refining patent queries using concept importance predictors.

First, we describe our experimental setup and the three experimental settings used in our study. In the first setting, we compare different unigram query models built from the query patent and we show their retrieval effectiveness on CLEF-IP 2010 dataset. In the second setting, in order to find out whether we can find a clearer focus of the query patent, we expand the unigram query with extracted important key concepts (e.g., bigrams or phrases). We determine the optimal parameter settings for each query model using training data and we compare the effectiveness of expansion using noun phrases with the baseline unigram queries. In the third setting, in order to find out whether query performance predictors can indicate a successful application of phrases, we conduct an experiment where we estimate the effectiveness of using noun phrases based on the set of features proposed in Section 5. We then combine the result of the unigram query and the expanded query using the outcome of the prediction model. We show that the best performance is achieved by expansion using noun phrases in a query dependent manner.

6.1 Experimental Setup

The retrieval experiments described in this paper are implemented using Terrier[5]. We used CLEF-IP 2010 collection which consists of 2.6 million patent documents. The relevance assessment is provided for the topic set which are patent applications and have *title*, *abstract*, *description*, and *claims*. As mentioned earlier, using *description* text for query generation has been shown to achieve the best MAP in contrast to other patent fields [16]. Therefore, we use the *description* text for building the query model. Patent applications in the topic set are annotated with the metadata tags such as IPC classes. We worked with the english topic set which corresponds to 1348 topics. We note that we did

[4]http://cran.r-project.org/web/packages/gbm/
[5]http://terrier.org/

not use the citation information of the patent applications in our experiments.

During indexing and retrieval, both documents and queries are stemmed using the Porter stemmer. Stop-word removal is performed on both documents and queries using the standard Terrier stop-word list. In addition to that, we also removed all the formulas and numeric references. We used BM25 for retrieving and scoring the documents. This is because we observed that BM25 scores are slightly more effective in practice.

6.2 Experimental Evaluation

6.2.1 *Unigram Query Models*

In this section the performance comparison of different unigram query models explained in Section 3 is presented. The result of our baseline method, Q_{orig}, is comparable to the second best result of the CLEF-IP 2010 [15]. The second best participating group of CLEF-IP 2010 showed that their approach achieves a statistically indistinguishable performance compared to the best result in CLEF-IP 2010. This ensures our choice for a competitive baseline method. Therefore, Q_{orig} serves as our baseline. In our experiments, we set the smoothing parameter λ in Equation 1 to be 0.5. Table 5 reports a comparison of two query expansion models EX-RM and PRF against our baseline. The expanded query model EX-RM is constructed by building a relevance model from the sample documents with at least one conceptual tag in common with the query. The expanded query model PRF is formed based on Pseudo Relevance Feedback. We combined the original query with the expanded query, where the parameter μ controls the weight of the unigram query as shown in Equation 5. We used the training data for tuning this parameter and the optimal value for μ is set to 0.6. The result of Table 5 are obtained using 10 expansion terms extracted from the top 10 documents and the number of terms used for building the original query is set to 30. Results marked with † achieved statistically significant improvement over the baseline at p-value of 0.01 using t-test.

Table 5: Performance comparison of the unigram query models, the baseline run, relevance models using pseudo feedback documents and sample relevant documents

model	MAP	Recall	PRES
baseline	0.136	0.619	0.535
PRF	0.103	0.590	0.481
EX-RM	0.150 †	0.643	0.553

As follows from Table 5, the PRF method is not able to select the best terms for query generation and all three reported performance measurements decrease compared to the baseline. This is due to the poor quality of search results. However, the relevance model using the sample documents, EX-RM, significantly outperforms the baseline run. This suggests that using the sample documents was beneficial for building the expanded query model and EX-RM on average achieved 13% improvement over the baseline in terms of MAP.

We explore the sensitivity of each of the unigram query models, baseline run, EX-RM and PRF, to the number of query terms that need to be taken into account. We also look into the number of feedback documents that need to be taken into account for both of the expanded unigram query models EX-RM and PRF. Figure 1 presents the MAP of our techniques, for varying values of number of feedback terms, and number of feedback documents. We can see that the number of terms is not highly influential and any value higher than 30 produces the same results. However, the system is more sensitive to the number of feedback documents. It can be seen that values higher than 10 hurts the performance.

6.2.2 *Combining Unigram and Phrase Query*

We wish to examine the quality of the phrases obtained by the two different techniques explained in Section 4 in the task of prior art search. Our goal is to utilize such phrases to identify relevant documents to the query patent. We first combine the unigram query model from the query patent with the top-k concepts selected by the two scoring methods: a) TF/IDF scoring method, denoted by QM-NP1; b) mutual information-based scoring method, denoted by QM-NP2. We further examine expanded queries in which we select the top-k concepts from the pseudo feedback documents using the two scoring methods, denoted by PRF-NP1 and PRF-NP2. Finally, in order to use the evidence from the relevance set (documents with similar conceptual tags), we selected the top-k scoring noun phrases from the relevance set using the two scoring methods and we refer to this as EX-RM-NP1 and EX-RM-NP2.

The retrieval results of various combinations of unigram queries with phrases are reported in Table 6. Results marked with † are significantly better than the baseline and ‡ represents the significant improvement achieved by EX-RM-NP2 against EX-RM-NP1.

Table 6: Performance of the expanded query models using phrases

model	MAP	Recall	PRES
baseline	0.136	0.619	0.535
QM-NP1	0.131	0.600	0.521
QM-NP2	0.138	0.621	0.539
PRF-NP1	0.115	0.592	0.494
PRF-NP2	0.112	0.603	0.493
EX-RM-NP1	0.149 †	0.646 †	0.552
EX-RM-NP2	0.156 †‡	0.650 †	0.567

Our experiments indicate that expansion based on phrases extracted by the mutual information-based scoring technique most of the time outperforms TF/IDF based scoring. This suggests that using co-occurrence information is more helpful in identifying key concepts of a query patent compared to using frequency information alone.

As follows from Table 6, extracting concepts from the query patent, as done for QM-NP1 and QM-NP2, does not improve the results over the unigram baseline. As we expected, the PRF based expansion decreases the result in terms of MAP, recall, and PRES. It is clear that both relevance models built using similar conceptual tags, EX-RM-

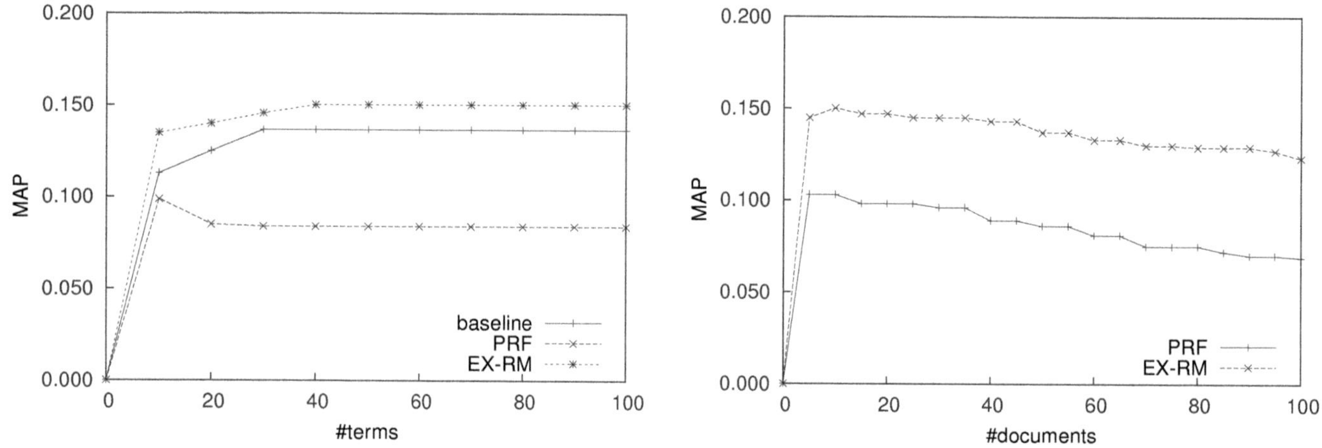

a) Number of feedback terms (MAP)

b) Number of feedback documents (MAP)

Figure 1: Sensitivity of unigram query models against (a) the number of terms and (b) the number of feedback documents used for query model construction

NP1 and EX-RM-NP2, outperform our unigram baseline significantly. This result demonstrates a positive effect of expansion using both scoring methods. In both cases these improvements hold for MAP, recall and PRES.

A very interesting conclusion which can be made by comparing the results of Table 5 and Table 6 is that despite the significant improvement of EX-RM-NP1 and EX-RM-NP2 over the baseline, the improvement over EX-RM is not significant. We performed an analysis on the query set and we found that almost 600 queries out of 1348 queries were hurt by the expansion using phrases compared to using unigrams. We therefore decided to estimate an upper bound of performance by combining these two approaches in a query dependent manner. As we already saw in Section 5, we found that by using the true effectiveness of the noun phrase queries we can achieve an increase in performance of 20% in terms of MAP. In the next section, we show how we can estimate the importance of a noun phrase query in order to decide whether to expand a given query using noun phrases or not.

In our experiments we considered proximity matches rather than exact phrases. This is due to the fact that using proximity matches gave us consistent gain in retrieval effectiveness in comparison to using exact phrases. We use a window of size 8, as suggested by previous work on proximity matching [17]. We perform a sweep (grid search) on μ to determine the optimal mixture of the original query and the expanded query according to Equation 7. The optimal value is set to 0.6 for all expansion methods.

We selected top-10 phrases and we added them to our unigram queries. We studied the sensitivity of each approach against the number of feedback documents and the number of feedback phrases that need to be taken into account. The results are shown in Figure 2. An important observation to be made from Figure 1 and Figure 2 is that using 10 pseudo relevant documents and around 40 feedback terms resulted in the best performance for all expansion methods.

6.2.3 *Selective Query Expansion Using Key Concepts*

So far we built the unigram and expanded query models using three different sources. 1) the query patent; 2) the pseudo relevant documents retrieved from PRF; 3) the relevance set which is composed of documents with similar conceptual tags to the query.

In this section, our goal is to predict whether query expansion using phrases is effective. We first predict the AP of each query in both ranked list of the expanded and unexpanded query using the features described in Section 5. We then calculate the change in AP after expansion based on the predicted values. A positive change in AP after expansion indicates an effective expansion. In the experiments, we considered a change bigger than 10% to be an effective expansion. We use this prediction value to decide which of the two competing methods will offer the best result for a given query.

We used a five-fold cross validation for our experiments. We divided the query topics into five equal parts. We trained the estimator using four out of five parts, and we applied the training model to estimate the AP of the remaining queries. We repeated the same test process on each of the five parts and we report the results on average over all five parts. The same procedure was performed for the expanded and unexpanded lists.

Table 7: Retrieval results on CLEF-IP 2010 using selective query expansion

model	MAP	Recall	PRES
baseline	0.136	0.619	0.535
QM-NP2	0.138	0.621	0.539
SQE_Q	0.152 $* \star$	0.617	0.543
PRF	0.103	0.590	0.481
PRF-NP2	0.112	0.603	0.493
SQE_{PRF}	0.122 $\uparrow \Uparrow$	0.609	0.509
EX-RM	0.150	0.643	0.553
EX-RM-NP2	0.156	0.650	0.567
SQE_{EX-RM}	0.168 $\dagger$ $\ddagger$	0.668	0.580

Table 7 shows the result of our method for selective query

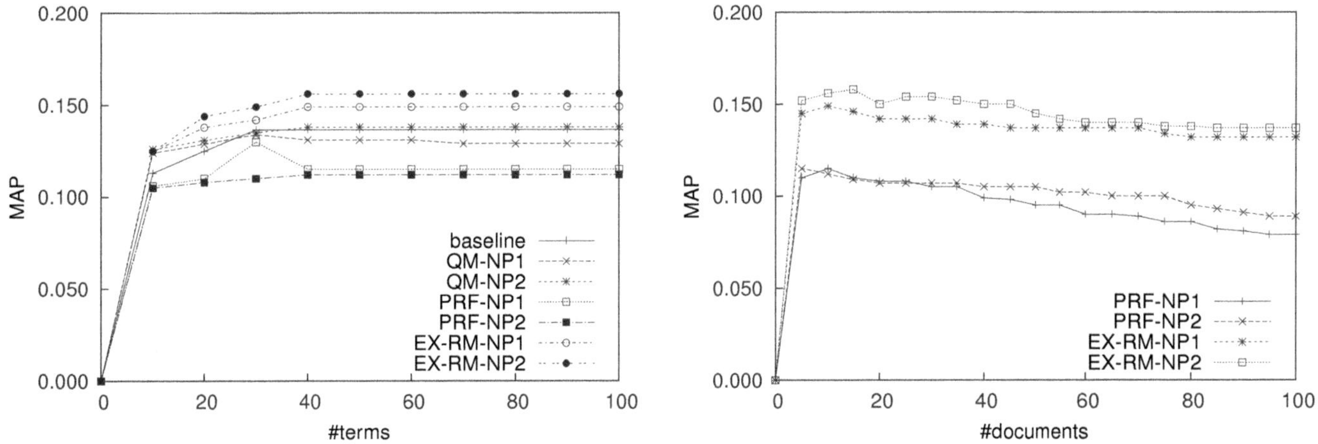

a) Number of feedback terms (MAP) b) Number of feedback documents (MAP)

Figure 2: Sensitivity of the expanded query models using noun phrases against (a) the number of terms and (b) the number of feedback documents used for expanded query model construction

expansion (SQE). The $*$ and $\star$ symbols indicate that the achieved improvement of SQE_Q over the expanded and unexpanded lists, QM-NP2 and baseline, is statistically significant at $p<0.01$. The $\uparrow$ and $\Uparrow$ symbols indicate that the achieved improvement of SQE_{PRF} over the expanded and unexpanded lists, PRF-NP2 and PRF, is statistically significant at $p<0.01$. The $\dagger$ and $\ddagger$ symbols indicate that the achieved improvement of SQE_{EX-RM} over the expanded and unexpanded lists, EX-RM-NP2 and EX-RM, is statistically significant at $p<0.01$.

As follows from Table 7, for all the three settings of our experiments, selective query expansion achieved statistically significant improvement in terms of MAP over automatic query expansion (using expansion on all queries). This indicates that the chosen features were able to accurately predict the AP for the expanded and unexpanded lists of each query. This also suggests that the predicted change in AP was a good indicator of an effective expansion. A per query analysis showed that the result of SQE method was able to detect more than half of the queries which performed well using the expansion and therefore SQE was able to effectively improve the retrieval effectiveness of those queries. The SQE method did not achieve the upper bound performance shown in Table 2, which is due to the error made by the prediction model. Despite the achieved increase in terms of MAP, there is still room for improvement which requires the choice of better features for almost all methods.

We calculated the influential features from the learnt SGBT model [5]. Query clarity, Topical clarity and IPC-based clarity are the most influential features.

7. CONCLUSION AND FUTURE WORK

In this work, we presented several versions of the unigram and the noun phrase queries for prior art search. By evaluating these query models we found that more advance IR techniques will increase performance of specific queries but the aggregated result may degrade against the baseline. To achieve consistent improvement in all queries we worked in a selective query expansion framework. The main contribution of this paper is devising a method for predicting whether expansion using noun phrases will improve the retrieval effectiveness of a query.

We experimentally determined the upper bound of what can be achieved by looking into the true effectiveness using a noun phrase query. We used a few often used features for predicting AP and we proposed some features using patent-specific characteristics. Our selective query expansion method using noun phrases obtained a statistically significant improvement over the expanded and unexpanded queries. Better features still need to be extracted which can capture the quality of the results better.

We experimented with two different scoring methods for selecting noun phrases. The scoring based on mutual information achieved better results over TF/IDF scoring. Another interesting conclusion can be made by comparing the two relevance models which were used in this study. The first relevance model was built based on PRF and the second was built by employing documents with similar conceptual tags to the query. The result of PRF method failed over initial retrieval because of the poor results, but the relevance model built based on conceptual tags outperformed the baseline.

Our work can be extended in future in several ways. First, we can improve the noun phrase extraction by using external resources related to the patent genre. Second, we can define better features so that average precision can be more accurately predicted. Third, instead of relying on the original score of the relevant documents to determine which documents should contribute in building a relevance model in a PRF scenario, we can estimate the true effectiveness of each document using a set of features employing patent-specific characteristics.

8. ACKNOWLEDGMENTS

The work of Parvaz Mahdabi was funded by the Information Retrieval Facility, through the research project "Interactive Patent Search (IPS)".

Fabio Crestani's work was partially supported by a Cátedra de Excelencia appointment at the Universidad Carlos III of Madrid (Spain), program 2011-2012, sponsored by the Banco de Santander.

9. REFERENCES

[1] G. Amati, C. Carpineto, and G. Romano. Query difficulty, robustness and selective application of query expansion. In *ECIR*, pages 127–137, 2004.

[2] S. Cronen-Townsend, Y. Zhou, and W. B. Croft. Predicting query performance. In *SIGIR*, pages 299–306, 2002.

[3] S. Cronen-Townsend, Y. Zhou, and W. B. Croft. A framework for selective query expansion. In *CIKM*, pages 236 – 237, 2004.

[4] F. Diaz and R. Jones. Using temporal profiles of queries for precision prediction. In *SIGIR*, pages 18–24, 2004.

[5] J. H. Friedman. Stochastic gradient boosting. In *Computational Statistics and Data Analysis*, volume 38, pages 367–378, 1999.

[6] A. Fujii. Enhancing patent retrieval by citation analysis. In *SIGIR*, pages 793–794, 2007.

[7] D. Ganguly, J. Leveling, W. Magdy, and G. J. F. Jones. Patent query reduction based on pseudo-relevant documents. In *CIKM*, pages 1953–1956, 2011.

[8] C. Hauff, L. Azzopardi, D. Hiemstra, and F. de Jong. Query performance prediction: Evaluation contrasted with effectiveness. In *ECIR*, pages 204–216, 2010.

[9] B. He and I. Ounis. Inferring query performance using pre-retrieval predictors. In *SPIRE*, pages 43–54, 2004.

[10] B. He and I. Ounis. Combining fields for query expansion and adaptive query expansion. *Information Processing Management*, 43(5):1294–1307, 2007.

[11] H. Itoh, H. Mano, and Y. Ogawa. Term distillation in patent retrieval. In *Proceedings of the ACL-2003 Workshop on Patent corpus processing*, volume 20, pages 41–45, 2003.

[12] M. Iwayama, A. Fujii, N. Kando, and A. Takano. Overview of the third NTCIR workshop. In *Proceedings of the ACL-2003 Workshop on Patent corpus processing*, pages 24–32, 2003.

[13] K. Konishi. Query terms extraction from patent document for invalidity search. In *NTCIR-5*, 2005.

[14] W. Magdy and G. J. F. Jones. PRES: A score metric for evaluating recall-oriented information retrieval applications. In *SIGIR*, pages 611–618, 2010.

[15] W. Magdy, P. Lopez, and G. J. F. Jones. Simple vs. sophisticated approaches for patent prior-art search. In *ECIR*, pages 725–728, 2010.

[16] P. Mahdabi, M. Keikha, S. Gerani, M. Landoni, and F. Crestani. Building queries for prior-art search. In *Proceedings of Information Retrieval Facility Conference (IRFC)*, pages 3–15, 2011.

[17] J. Peng, C. Macdonald, B. He, V. Plachouras, and I. Ounis. Incorporating term dependency in the DFR framework. In *SIGIR*, pages 843–844, 2007.

[18] F. Piroi and J. Tait. CLEF-IP 2010: Retrieval experiments in the intellectual property domain. In *CLEF-2010 (Notebook Papers/LABs/Workshops)*, 2010.

[19] K. Toutanova, D. Klein, C. Manning, , and Y. Singer. Feature-rich part-of-speech tagging with a cyclic dependency network. In *Proceedings of HLT-NAACL*, pages 252–259, 2003.

[20] M. Winaver, O. Kurland, and C. Domshlak. Towards robust query expansion: Model selection in the language modeling framework. In *SIGIR*, pages 729–730, 2007.

[21] X. Xue and W. B. Croft. Transforming patents into prior-art queries. In *SIGIR*, pages 808–809, 2009.

[22] Y. Yang, N. Bansal, W. Dakka, P. Ipeirotis, N. Koudas, and D. Papadias. Query by document. In *WSDM*, pages 34–43, 2009.

[23] E. Yom-Tov, S. Fine, D. Carmel, and A. Darlow. Learning to estimate query difficulty. In *SIGIR*, pages 512–519, 2005.

Automatic Term Mismatch Diagnosis for Selective Query Expansion

Le Zhao
Language Technologies Institute
Carnegie Mellon University
Pittsburgh, PA, USA
lezhao@cs.cmu.edu

Jamie Callan
Language Technologies Institute
Carnegie Mellon University
Pittsburgh, PA, USA
callan@cs.cmu.edu

ABSTRACT

People are seldom aware that their search queries frequently mismatch a majority of the relevant documents. This may not be a big problem for topics with a large and diverse set of relevant documents, but would largely increase the chance of search failure for less popular search needs. We aim to address the mismatch problem by developing accurate and simple queries that require minimal effort to construct. This is achieved by targeting retrieval interventions at the query terms that are likely to mismatch relevant documents. For a given topic, the proportion of relevant documents that do not contain a term measures the probability for the term to mismatch relevant documents, or the term mismatch probability. Recent research demonstrates that this probability can be estimated reliably prior to retrieval. Typically, it is used in probabilistic retrieval models to provide query dependent term weights. This paper develops a new use: Automatic diagnosis of term mismatch. A search engine can use the diagnosis to suggest manual query reformulation, guide interactive query expansion, guide automatic query expansion, or motivate other responses. The research described here uses the diagnosis to guide interactive query expansion, and create Boolean conjunctive normal form (CNF) structured queries that selectively expand 'problem' query terms while leaving the rest of the query untouched. Experiments with TREC Ad-hoc and Legal Track datasets demonstrate that with high quality manual expansion, this diagnostic approach can reduce user effort by 33%, and produce simple and effective structured queries that surpass their bag of word counterparts.

Categories and Subject Descriptors

H.3.3 [**Information Search and Retrieval**]: *Query formulation, Retrieval Models*

Keywords

Query term diagnosis, term mismatch, term expansion, Boolean conjunctive normal form queries, simulated user interactions

1. INTRODUCTION

Vocabulary mismatch between queries and documents is known to be important for full-text search. Recent research formally defined the term mismatch probability, and showed that on average a query term mismatches (fails to appear in) 40% to 50% of the documents relevant to the query [32]. With multi-word queries, the percentage of relevant documents that match the whole query can degrade very quickly. Even when search engines do not require all query terms to appear in result documents, including a query term that is likely to mismatch relevant documents can still cause the mismatch problem: The retrieval model will penalize the relevant documents that do not contain the term, and at the same time favor documents (false positives) that happen to contain the term but are irrelevant. Since the number of false positives is typically much larger than the number of relevant documents for a topic [8], these false positives can appear throughout the rank list, burying the true relevant results.

This work is concerned with the term mismatch problem, a long standing problem in retrieval. What's new here is the term level diagnosis and intervention. We use automatic predictions of the term mismatch probability [32] to proactively diagnose each query term, and to guide further interventions to directly address the problem terms. Compared to prior approaches, which typically handle the query as a whole, the targeted intervention in this work generates simple yet effective queries.

Query expansion is one of the most common methods to solve mismatch. We use the automatic term mismatch diagnosis to guide query expansion. Other forms of intervention, e.g. term removal or substitution, can also solve certain cases of mismatch, but they are not the focus of this work. We show that proper diagnosis can save expansion effort by 33%, while achieving near optimal performance.

We generate structured expansion queries of Boolean conjunctive normal form (CNF) -- a conjunction of disjunctions where each disjunction typically contains a query term and its synonyms. Carefully created CNF queries are highly effective. They can limit the effects of the expansion terms to their corresponding query term, so that while fixing the mismatched terms, the expansion query is still faithful to the semantics of the original query. We show that CNF expansion leads to more stable retrieval across different levels of expansion, minimizing problems such as topic drift even with skewed expansion of part of the query. It outperforms bag of word expansion given the same set of high quality expansion terms.

2. RELATED WORK

This section discusses how this work relates to the other research that tries to solve the mismatch problem. In particular, research on predicting term mismatch and on conjunctive normal form (CNF) structured queries forms the basis of this work.

2.1 Term mismatch and automatic diagnosis

Furnas et al. [7] were probably the first to study *vocabulary mismatch* quantitatively, by measuring how people name the same concept/activity differently. They showed that on average 80-90% of the times, two people will name the same item differently. The best term only covers about 15-35% of all the occurrences of the item, and the 3 best terms together only cover 37-67% of the cases. Even with 15 aliases, only 60-80% coverage is achieved. The

Permission to make digital or hard copies of all or part of this work for personal or classroom use is granted without fee provided that copies are not made or distributed for profit or commercial advantage and that copies bear this notice and the full citation on the first page. To copy otherwise, or republish, to post on servers or to redistribute to lists, requires prior specific permission and/or a fee.
SIGIR'12, August 12–16, 2012, Portland, Oregon, USA.
Copyright 2012 ACM 978-1-4503-1472-5/12/08...$10.00.

authors suggested one solution to be "unlimited aliasing", which led to the Latent Semantic Analysis (LSA) [6] line of research.

Zhao and Callan [32] formally defined the *term mismatch probability* to be $P(\bar{t} \mid R)$, the likelihood that term t does not appear in a document d, given that d is relevant to the topic ($d \in R$), or equivalently, the proportion of relevant documents that do not contain term t. Furnas et al. [7]'s definition of vocabulary mismatch is query independent, and can be reduced to an average case of Zhao and Callan [32]'s query dependent definition.

The complement of term mismatch is the term recall probability: $P(t \mid R)$. A low $P(t \mid R)$ means term t tends not to appear in the documents relevant to the topic. This query dependent probability $P(t \mid R)$ is not new in retrieval research. It is known to be part of the Binary Independence Model (BIM) [23], as part of the optimal term weight. Accurate estimation of $P(t \mid R)$ requires knowledge of R -- the relevant set of a topic, which defeats the purpose of retrieval, and $P(t \mid R)$ was thought to be difficult to estimate.

Recent research showed that $P(t \mid R)$ can be reliably predicted without using relevance information of the test topics [8,20,32]. Zhao and Callan [32] achieved the best predictions from being the first to design and use query dependent features for prediction, features such as term centrality, replaceability and abstractness.

Previously, $P(t \mid R)$ predictions were used to adjust query term weights of inverse document frequency (idf)-based retrieval models such as Okapi BM25 and statistical language models. Term weighting is not a new technique in retrieval research, neither is predicting term weights.

Our work is a significant departure from the prior research that predicted $P(t \mid R)$. We apply the $P(t \mid R)$ predictions in a completely new way, to automatically diagnose term mismatch problems and inform further interventions.

2.2 CNF structured expansion

Query expansion is one of the most common ways to solve mismatch. In recent years, the research community has focused on expansion of the whole query, for example using pseudo relevance feedback [17]. This form of expansion is simple to manage and effective. It also allows introduction of expansion terms that are related to the query as a whole, even if their relationship to any specific original query term is tenuous.

When *people* search for information, they typically develop queries in Boolean conjunctive normal form (CNF). CNF queries are used by librarians [16,12], lawyers [2,26] and other expert searchers [4,13,21]. Each conjunct represents a high-level concept, and each disjunct represents alternate forms of the concept. Query expansion is accomplished by adding disjuncts that cover as many ways of expressing the concept as possible.

For example, the query below from TREC 2006 Legal Track [2]

"*sales of tobacco to children*"

is expanded manually into

(*sales* OR *sell* OR *sold*) AND
(*tobacco* OR *cigar* OR *cigarettes*) AND
(*children* OR *child* OR *teen* OR *juvenile* OR *kid* OR *adolescent*)

CNF queries ensure precision by specifying a set of concepts that must appear (AND), and improve recall by expanding alternative forms of each concept. Compared to LSA or bag of word expansion, CNF queries offer control over *what query terms to expand* (*the query term dimension*) and *what expansion terms to use for a query term* (*the expansion dimension*).

However, these two dimensions of flexibility also make automatic formulation of CNF queries computationally challenging, and makes manual creation of CNF queries tedious. The few experiments demonstrating effective CNF expansion either used manually created queries or only worked for a special task. Hearst [13] and Mitra et al. [21] used ranked Boolean retrieval on manual CNF queries. Zhao and Callan [31] automatically created CNF queries for the question answering task, based on the semantic structure of the question.

Along the two directions of term diagnosis and expansion, prior research has focused on identifying synonyms of query terms, i.e. the expansion dimension. Google has patents [15] using query logs to identify possible synonyms for query terms in the context of the query. Jones and colleagues [14] also extracted synonyms of query terms from query logs. They called it query substitutions. Wang and Zhai [28] mined effective query reformulations from query logs. Dang and Croft [5] did the same with TREC Web collections. Xue, Croft and Smith [30] weighted and combined automatic whole-query reformulations, similar to the way alternative structured queries were combined in [31]. If more extensive expansions were used, the more compact CNF expansion would be a reasonable next step. Because of reasons such as suboptimal quality of expansions or insufficient number of topics for evaluation, prior research on ad hoc retrieval has not seen automatic CNF expansion to outperform keyword retrieval. Perhaps the only exception is the related problem of context sensitive stemming [27,22,3], where expansion terms are just morphological variants of the query terms, which are easier to identify and more accurate (less likely to introduce false positives).

Such prior work tried to expand any query term, and did not exploit the term diagnosis dimension, thus they essentially expanded the query terms whose synonyms are easy to find.

This work focuses on selectively expanding the query terms that really need expansion, a less well studied dimension. Exploiting this diagnosis dimension can guide further retrieval interventions such as automatic query reformulation or user interaction to the areas of the query that need help, leading to potentially more effective retrieval interventions. It also reduces the complexity of formulating CNF queries, manually or automatically. The prior research on synonym extraction is orthogonal to this work, and can be applied with term diagnosis in a real-world search system.

2.3 Simulated interactive expansions

Our diagnostic intervention framework is general and can be applied to both automatic and manual expansions. However, our experiments are still constrained by the availability of effective intervention methods. That is why we use manual CNF expansion, which is highly effective. To avoid using the expensive and less controllable online user studies, we use existing user-created CNF queries to simulate online diagnostic expansion interactions.

Simulations of user interactions are not new in interactive retrieval experiments. Harman [9] simulated relevance feedback experiments by using relevance judgements of the top 10 results, and evaluated feedback retrieval on the rest of the results. White et al. [29] also used relevance judgements and assumed several user browsing strategies to simulate users' interactions with the search interface. The interaction simulations were used as user feedback to select expansion terms. Similarly, Lin and Smucker [18] assumed a set of strategies that define how the user browses the search results, to simulate and evaluate a result browsing interface using known relevance judgements.

Compared to the prior work, our simulations never explicitly use any relevance judgements, and only make a few relatively weak assumptions about the user. We simulate based on existing user created Boolean CNF queries, which can be seen as recorded

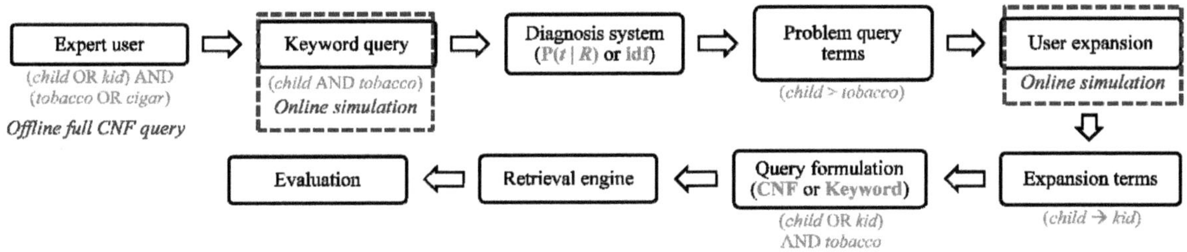

Figure 1. Simulated diagnostic expansion, with query examples in gray, simulated steps in dashed boxes and methods to test in bold red font.

summaries of real user interactions. These fully expanded queries are used to simulate selective expansion interactions.

3. DIAGNOSTIC INTERVENTION

This section discusses in more detail the diagnostic intervention framework, and shows how term diagnosis can be applied and evaluated in end-to-end retrieval experiments in an ideal setting.

We hope to answer the following questions. Suppose the user is willing to invest some extra time for each query, how much effort is needed to improve the initial query (in expansion effort, how many query terms need to be expanded, and how many expansion terms per query term are needed)? When is the best performance achieved? Can we direct the user to a subset of the query terms so that less effort is needed to achieve a near optimal performance? What's an effective criterion for term diagnosis?

3.1 Diagnostic intervention framework

The diagnostic intervention framework is designed as follows. The user issues an initial keyword query. Given the query, the system selects a subset of the query terms and asks the user to fix (e.g. expand) them. The performance after user intervention is used to compare the different diagnosis strategies.

This evaluation framework needs to control two dimensions, *the diagnosis dimension* (selecting the set of problem query terms) and *the intervention dimension* (determining the amount of intervention for each selected term). Diagnosis of terms with mismatch problems can be achieved using criteria such as low predicted $P(t \mid R)$ or high idf. The intervention dimension when implemented as query expansion can be controlled by asking the user to provide a certain number of expansion terms.

3.2 Query term diagnosis methods

We consider two term diagnosis methods, idf based term diagnosis and predicted $P(t \mid R)$ based diagnosis.

The idf based diagnosis selects the query terms that have the highest idf first. Idf is known to have a correlation with $P(t \mid R)$ [8] and has been used as a feature for predicting $P(t \mid R)$ [8,20,32]. A rare term (high idf) usually means a high likelihood of mismatch, while a frequent word (e.g. stopword) would have a high $P(t \mid R)$.

Diagnosis based on predicted $P(t \mid R)$ selects the query terms with the lowest predicted $P(t \mid R)$ first. We use the best known method to predict $P(t \mid R)$ [32], which was the first to use query dependent features for prediction. It used top ranked documents from an initial retrieval to automatically extract query dependent synonyms. These synonyms were used to create some of the effective query dependent features, e.g. how often synonyms of a query term appear in top ranked documents from the initial retrieval, and how often such synonyms appear in place of the original query term in collection documents. Section 4 describes implementation details.

3.3 Possible confounding factors

To exactly follow this ideal framework, for each query, many user interaction experiments are needed – one experiment for each possible diagnostic intervention setup, preferably, one user per setup. Many factors need to be controlled, such as users' prior knowledge of the topic, the quality of the manual interventions, users' interaction time and interaction method (whether retrieval results are examined), so that the final retrieval performance will reflect the effect of the diagnostic component instead of random variation in the experiment setup. These factors are difficult to eliminate even with hundreds of experiments per topic. We show how simulations may help in the section below.

4. EXPERIMENTAL METHODOLOGY

In this section, we design the retrieval experiments to evaluate diagnostic interventions. We explain how user simulations may be an appropriate substitute for costly online experiments with human subjects. We explain how to design the diagnostic intervention experiment so that it measures the effects of term diagnosis, minimizing effects from confounding factors such as the quality of the post-diagnosis interventions. We examine the datasets used for this simulation, in particular how well the manual CNF queries fit the simulation assumptions. We also describe the whole evaluation procedure, including the implementation of the mismatch diagnosis methods which (together with the user intervention) produce the post-intervention queries, the retrieval model behind query execution, and the evaluation metrics used to measure retrieval effectiveness.

We focus on *interactive expansion* as the intervention method, using existing CNF queries to simulate interactive expansion. This is due to both the effectiveness of query expansion to solve mismatch and the lack of user data for other types of interventions.

4.1 Simulated user interactions

As explained in Section 3.3, a large number of experiments and users are needed to evaluate diagnostic expansion using online user studies. To avoid this, we use offline automatic simulations, sketched in Figure 1. There are three players in the simulation, the *user*, the *diagnostic expansion retrieval* system and the *simulation based evaluation* system. Before evaluation, the user creates fully expanded CNF queries. These manually created CNF queries are used by the evaluation system to simulate selective expansions, and are accessible to the diagnostic retrieval system only through the simulation system. During evaluation, the simulation system first extracts a basic no-expansion keyword query from the CNF query, feeding the keyword query to the diagnosis system. The diagnostic expansion system automatically diagnoses which keywords are more problematic. Then, the simulation system takes the top several problem terms, and extracts a certain number of expansion terms for each selected query term from its corresponding conjunct in the manual CNF query. This step simulates a user expanding the selected query terms. The number of problem query terms to expand and the number of expansion terms to include are controlled by the simulation system, which will evaluate retrieval at five different selection levels and five different expansion levels. Finally, given these expansion terms for each selected query term, the diagnostic expansion system forms an expansion query and does retrieval.

For example, based on the CNF query in Section 2.2, the diagnosis method is given the keyword query *sales tobacco children*. It may see *children* as more problematic than the other terms, then a full expansion of this problem term would produce the query *sales* AND *tobacco* AND (*children* OR *child* OR *teen* OR *juvenile* OR *kid* OR *adolescent*), whose retrieval performance is evaluated as the end result of diagnostic expansion. If the evaluation system selects two query terms *sales* and *children* for expansion, with a maximum of one expansion term each, the final query would be (*sales* OR *sell*) AND *tobacco* AND (*children* OR *child*). These diagnostic expansion queries are partial expansions simulated using the fully expanded queries created by real users.

Our simulation allows us to answer the same set of questions about the diagnostic expansion system which we hope to answer through online user interactions, and requires simpler experiments. In our simulations, the same set of expansion terms is always used for a given query term, those from its corresponding CNF conjunct. Doing so minimizes the variation from the expansion terms as we measure the effects of the diagnosis component. The order in which expansion terms are added for a query term is also fixed, in the same order as they appear in the CNF conjunct. This way, we can tweak the level of expansion by gradually including more expansion terms from the lists of expansion terms, and answer how much expansion is needed for optimal performance.

Our simulation makes three assumptions about the user expansion process. We examine them below.

Expansion term independence assumption: Expansion terms from fully expanded queries are held back from the query to simulate the selective and partial expansion of query terms. This simulation is based on the assumption that the user (a random process that generates expansion terms) will produce the same set of expansion terms for a query term whenever asked to expand any subset of the query terms. Equivalently, given the topic, the expansion process for one query term does not depend on the expansion of other query terms. In reality, a human user focusing on a subset of the query terms can typically achieve higher quality expansion. Thus, selective expansion may actually do better than the reported performance from the simulations.

Expansion term sequence assumption: Controlling to include only the first few expansion terms of a query term simulates and measures a user's expansion effort for that query term. It is assumed that the user would come up with the same sequence of expansion terms for each query term, no matter whether the user is asked to expand a subset or all of the query terms. A downside of this simulation is that we do not know exactly how much time and effort the user has spent on each expansion term.

CNF keyword-query induction assumption: Instead of actually asking users to expand their initial queries, preexisting fully expanded CNF style queries are used to infer the original keyword query and to simulate the expansion process. For example, given the CNF query in Section 2.2, the original keyword query is assumed to be (*sales tobacco children*). This simulation assumes that the original keyword query can be reconstructed from the manual CNF query, which could be missing some original query terms (*of* and *to* in the example) or introduce new terms into the original keyword query. However, as long as we use highly effective CNF queries, it is safe to use the CNF induced keyword queries as the no-expansion baseline.

We also made an effort to ensure that our 'reverse-engineered' keyword query is faithful to the vocabulary of the original query. Given the TREC official topic description of a topic, we try to use the first term from each conjunct that appears in this description to reconstruct the keyword query. For conjuncts that do not have description terms, the first term in the conjunct is used.

For example, the topic described as *sales of tobacco to children*, with CNF query (*sales* OR *sell* OR *sold*) AND (*tobacco* OR *cigar* OR *cigarettes*) AND (*children* OR *child* OR *teen* OR *juvenile* OR *kid* OR *adolescent*), would have (*sales tobacco children*) as the unexpanded keyword query. If the description were *sell tobacco to children*, the keyword query would be instead (*sell tobacco children*), even when *sales* appears first in its conjunct.

4.2 Effects of confounding factors

Using user simulations instead of real users can eliminate confounding factors such as the user's prior knowledge of the topic and other details of the user interaction process.

This work tests the hypothesis that term diagnosis can effectively guide query expansion. However, two factors directly determine the end performance of diagnostic expansion, 1) the effectiveness of term diagnosis, and 2) the benefit from expansion.

Since our focus is on diagnosis, not query expansion, one of the most important confounding factors is the quality of the expansion terms, which we leave out of the evaluation by using a fixed set of high quality expansion terms from manual CNF queries to simulate an expert user doing manual expansion.

Automatic query expansion is more desirable in a deployed system, but the uncertain quality of the expansion terms can confuse the evaluation. Thus, it is not considered in this paper.

4.3 Datasets and manual CNF queries

Datasets with high quality manual CNF queries are selected to simulate and evaluate diagnostic expansion. Four different datasets have been used, those from TREC 2006 and 2007 Legal tracks, and those from TREC 3 and 4 Ad hoc tracks. They are selected in pairs, because training data is needed to train the $P(t \mid R)$ prediction model. Here, the TREC 2006 (39 topics) and TREC 3 (50 topics) datasets are used for training the baseline model parameters and the $P(t \mid R)$ prediction models, while TREC 2007 (43 topics) and TREC 4 (50 topics) are used for testing.

4.3.1 TREC Legal track datasets

The TREC Legal tracks contain Boolean CNF queries created through expert user interaction. They are fairly specific, averaging 3 conjuncts per topic, i.e., 3 concepts conjoined to form a query. The information needs of the Legal track topics are fictional, but mimic the real cases.

The lawyers who created the TREC Legal queries know what the collection is, and have expert knowledge of what terminology the corpus documents might use to refer to a concept being requested. The lawyers would give very high priority to the recall of the queries they create. They tried to fully expand every query term, so as not to miss any potentially relevant document. An effort to avoid over-generalizing the topic was also made. However, the lawyers never looked at the retrieval results when creating these CNF style queries. We call this a case of *blind user interaction*, because no corpus information is accessed during user interaction. We use the Boolean queries from [33], which achieved near best performance in TREC 2007 Legal track.

The 2006 and 2007 TREC Legal tracks share the same collection of documents. These are about 6.7 million tobacco company documents made public through litigation. They are on average 1362 words long. Many of them are OCR text, and contain spelling and spacing errors.

For relevance judgments, because of the relatively large size of the collection, a sampled pooling strategy was adopted in Legal

2007, with 555.7 judgments per topic and 101 judged relevant documents per topic.

More details about the dataset, the information needs, query formulation procedure, and relevance judgments can be found in the overview papers [2,26].

4.3.2 TREC Ad hoc track datasets

For the TREC 3 and 4 Ad hoc track datasets, high quality manual CNF queries were created by the University of Waterloo group [4]. An example query is (*responsibility* OR *standard* OR *train* OR *monitoring* OR *quality*) AND (*children* OR *child* OR *baby* OR *infant*) AND "*au pair*", where the "*au pair*" is a phrase. The information needs for the TREC 3 and 4 Ad hoc tracks are simpler (or broader), averaging 2 conjuncts per topic.

The Waterloo queries were created for the MultiText system by an Iterative Searching and Judging (ISJ) process. These queries were manually formulated with access to the results returned by the retrieval system, thesaurus and other external resources of knowledge. This constitutes a case of *user* and *corpus interaction*. Quality of the manual Boolean queries is ensured by examining the retrieval results, thus, should be better than those created from blind user interaction of the Legal tracks. Since the interaction with search results, expansion processes of the query terms may not be independent of each other. For example, in order to discover the expansion term of a query term, one may need to expand another query term first, to bring up a result document that contains the expansion term. Thus, the expansion independence assumption (of Section 4.1) is more likely to be violated by the ISJ queries than by the Legal ones.

The TREC 3 and 4 Ad hoc tracks used different collections, but they both consisted of newswire texts published before 1995. Each collection has about 0.56 million documents. The texts are non-OCR, thus cleaner than the Legal documents.

The relevance judgments of the Ad hoc tracks are deeper, because the collections are much smaller. The TREC 4 Ad hoc track made 1741 judgments per topic with 130 relevant. More details can be found in [10,11].

For all documents and queries, the Krovetz stemmer was used (more conservative than Porter), and no stopwords were removed.

4.4 Term diagnosis implementation

We explain the implementation of the diagnosis methods, idf and predicted $P(t \mid R)$, in more detail.

Idf is calculated as $\log((N - \mathrm{df})/\mathrm{df})$, where N is the total number of documents in the collection and df is the document frequency of the term. This follows the RSJ formulation [23].

For $P(t \mid R)$ prediction, we closely follow [32]'s method. Automatic features used for prediction include idf, and the three features derived from applying latent semantic analysis (LSA) [6] over the top ranked documents of an initial keyword retrieval.[1] For training purposes, $P(t \mid R)$ truth is calculated as $(r + 1)/(|R| + 2)$, where r is the number of relevant documents containing t and $|R|$ the total number of relevant documents for the query, with Laplace smoothing used. Support Vector Regression with RBF kernel is used to learn the prediction model.

There are 3 parameters: The number of top ranked documents for LSA, which is set at 180 for the Ad hoc datasets and 200 for the Legal track datasets, based on a monotonic relationship between this parameter and the total number of collection documents observed [32]. The number of latent dimensions to keep is fixed at 150, and the gamma parameter which controls the width of the RBF kernel is fixed at 1.5 (as in [32]).

[32] also used a feature that indicated whether a word in the query appears as a leaf node in the dependency parse of the query. Here, the feature is assumed to be 0 for all query terms, because the unexpanded query is usually not a natural language sentence or phrase, hence parsing may be inappropriate.

A small number of the original terms in these CNF queries are phrases, windowed occurrences or other complex structures. They are assumed to have a $P(t \mid R)$ value of 0.5. The LSA component of the Lemur Toolkit is not designed to handle these complex terms, preventing the use of [32]'s model. This is a small handicap to our $P(t \mid R)$ prediction implementation, but not to the idf method, which is based on accurate df values calculated by the Indri search engine.

4.5 The retrieval model

To achieve a state-of-the-art performance, the retrieval model needs to rank collection documents using the Boolean CNF queries. Before the mid 1990's, unranked Boolean was popular. Later research found ranked keyword to be more effective. However, to be fair, a *ranked* Boolean (e.g. soft or probabilistic) model should be used to compare with other ranking approaches.

This work adopts the language model framework, using probabilistic Boolean query execution (with Lemur/Indri version 4.10) [19]. The Boolean OR operator is still the hard OR, treating all the synonyms as if they are the same term for counting term- and document-frequencies (i.e. #syn operator in Indri query language). The Boolean AND is implemented as the probabilistic AND (the Indri #combine operator) to produce a ranking score.

Equations (1, 2) show how the retrieval model scores document d with query (a OR b) AND (c OR e). $\mathrm{tf}(a, d)$ is the number of times term a appears in document d. μ is the parameter for Dirichlet smoothing, which is set at 900 for the Ad hoc datasets and 1000 for the Legal datasets based on training.

$$\begin{aligned} &\mathrm{Score}(\,(a \text{ OR } b) \text{ AND } (c \text{ OR } e),\ d) \\ &= P(\,(a \text{ OR } b) \text{ AND } (c \text{ OR } e) \mid d) \\ &= P(\,(a \text{ OR } b) \mid d) * P(\,(c \text{ OR } e) \mid d) \end{aligned} \quad (1)$$

$$\begin{aligned} &P(\,(a \text{ OR } b) \mid d) \\ &= (\,\mathrm{tf}(a, d) + \mathrm{tf}(b, d) + \mu * (P(a \mid C) + P(b \mid C))\,) \,/\, (\mathrm{length}(d) + \mu) \\ &= P(a \mid d) + P(b \mid d) \qquad \text{(under Dirichlet smoothing)} \end{aligned} \quad (2)$$

This language model based ranked Boolean model is not the only possibility. Other ranked Boolean models include using the Boolean query as a two-tiered filter for the keyword rank list [13] [31], using the Okapi BM25 model for the conjunction [25], using probabilistic OR for the expansion terms (in Indri query language, #or instead of #syn), or using the p-norm Boolean ranking model [24]. We have tried some basic variations of the language model ranked Boolean model. Our pilot study shows that for our datasets, tiered filtering is sometimes worse than probabilistic Boolean, mostly because of the inferior ranking of the keyword queries. Probabilistic OR (#or) is numerically similar to treating all expansion terms the same as the original term (#syn), and the two methods perform similarly in retrieval. We did not try Okapi or p-norm, because the focus of this paper is $P(t \mid R)$ based diagnostic expansion, not to find the best ranked Boolean model. What is needed is one ranked Boolean model that works.

---

[1] Recently a more efficient method of predicting $P(t \mid R)$ was developed that eliminates the need for an initial retrieval [Zhao, personal communication].

4.6 Evaluation measures

We use standard TREC evaluation measures for the datasets. Traditionally, pooled judgments and precision at certain cutoffs have been used in TREC. *Mean Average Precision (MAP)* at top 1000 is a summary statistic that cares about both top precision and precision at high recall levels, and has been used as the standard measure in TREC Ad hoc and Legal tracks.

The *statAP* measure [1] is the standard measure for TREC Legal 2007. StatAP is an unbiased statistical estimate of MAP designed to work with sampled pooling. It is unbiased in the sense that if all pooled documents were judged, the MAP value would have been the same as the mean of the estimated statAP. In traditional TREC pooling, the top 50 to top 100 documents from each submitted rank list are pooled, and all pooled documents are judged. In sampled pooling, only a sampled subset of the pool is judged. The idea is to use importance sampling to judge fewer documents while maintaining a reliable estimate of MAP. Highly ranked documents from multiple pooled submissions are more likely to be relevant, and they are sampled more by importance sampling. StatAP takes into account these sampling probabilities of the judged relevant documents, so that during evaluation, a judged relevant document with sampling probability p would be counted as a total of $1/p$ relevant documents. This is because on average $1/p - 1$ relevant documents are missed during the sampling procedure, and they are being represented by that one sampled relevant document.

For topics where some relevant documents have low sampling probabilities, statAP estimates can deviate from the true AP a lot, but according to [26], when averaged over more than 20 topics, statAP provides a reliable estimate.

5. EXPERIMENTS

These experiments test two main hypotheses. ***H1***: Mismatch diagnosis can direct expansion to the query terms that need expansion. ***H2***: Boolean CNF expansion is more effective than bag of word expansion with the same set of high quality expansion terms. To test H1, the *first* experiment verifies the accuracy of idf and P(t | R)-prediction based term diagnosis against the true P(t | R). The *second* experiment shows the effects of diagnosis by evaluating overall retrieval performance along the query term dimension (5 diagnostic selection levels) and the expansion dimension (5 expansion levels). The *third* experiment compares predicted P(t | R) diagnosis with idf based diagnosis. H2 is tested by the *fourth* experiment comparing CNF and bag-of-word expansion at various levels of diagnostic expansion.

5.1 Baseline – no expansion

Listed below is the retrieval performance of the no expansion keyword retrieval baseline on the two test sets.

Dataset	Legal 2007 (MAP/statAP)	TREC 4 (MAP)
no expansion	0.0663/0.0160	0.1973

5.2 Mismatch diagnosis accuracy

Our goal is to use idf or P(t | R) predictions to diagnose query terms, to rank them in a priority order for the user to fix (expand). This section is a unit test of the diagnosis component, in which accuracy is measured by how well the diagnosis method identifies the most problematic query terms (those most likely to mismatch). We measure how well the priority order (e.g. ascending predicted P(t | R)) ranks the query term with the true lowest P(t | R), thus use Mean Reciprocal Rank (MRR) as the measure. Rank correlation measures do not distinguish ranking differences at the top vs. bottom of the rank lists, thus are less appropriate here.

On the Legal 2007 dataset, predicted P(t | R) achieves an MRR of 0.6850, significantly higher than the MRR of 0.5523 of the idf method, significant at $p < 0.026$ by the two tailed t-test. The idf method is still much better than random chance which has an MRR of 0.383, given the average 3 conjuncts per topic.

This result that P(t | R) prediction using [32]'s method is better than idf, and idf is better than random is consistent with prior research that predicted P(t | R) [8,32].

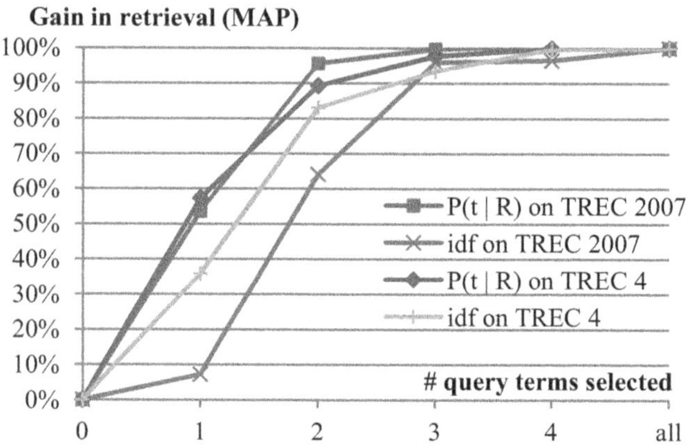

Figure 2. Relative retrieval performance gains of diagnostic expansion as the number of query terms selected for expansion increases. Calculated based on the last row of Tables 2 and 3.

5.3 Diagnostic expansion retrieval results

Tables 1 2 and 3 report the expansion retrieval performance of predicted-P(t | R) based and idf based diagnostic expansion, following the evaluation procedure detailed in Section 4.1. The results are arranged along two dimensions of user effort, the number of query terms selected for expansion, and the maximum number of expansion terms to include for a selected query term.

For example, results reported in column 2 row 2 selects 1 original query term of the highest idf for expansion, and a maximum of 1 expansion term is included for the selected query term. When the manual CNF query doesn't expand the selected query term, no expansion term will be included in the final query.

We are most concerned with the performance changes along each row of the tables, which are caused by the diagnosis methods. In Figure 2, we compare the relative performance gains of the different diagnosis methods as more query terms are being selected for expansion. Results based on the last row of Tables 2 and 3 are presented in Figure 2. No expansion is 0%, and full expansion of all query terms gets 100%. With only 2 query terms selected for expansion, predicted P(t | R) diagnosis is achieving 95% or 90% of the total gains of CNF expansion. Idf diagnosis is only achieving 64% or 83% of the total gains with 2 query terms, and need to fully expand 3 query terms to reach a performance close to the best (full expansion of all query terms). Thus, *predicted P(t | R) based diagnosis saves 1/3 of users' expansion effort while still achieving near optimal retrieval performance.*

Table 1. Retrieval performance of the two selective CNF expansion methods on TREC 2007 Legal track, as measured by *MAP*. The baseline unexpanded queries produced an MAP of 0.0663.

\ # terms selected	1		2		3		4		All
# expansions per term	idf	P(*t* | *R*)	idf	P(*t* | *R*)	idf	P(*t* | *R*)	idf	P(*t* | *R*)	(same)
1	0.0722	0.0778*	0.0802*	0.0825**	0.0892**	0.0896***	0.0893**	0.0904***	0.0901***
2	0.0780*	0.0805**	0.0825*	0.0921***	0.0916***	0.0938$^{\#}$	0.0947***	0.0961$^{\#}$	0.0971$^{\#}$
3	0.0766	0.0806**	0.0844**	0.0927***	0.0938***	0.0965$^{\#}$	0.0969***	0.0988$^{\#}$	0.0997$^{\#}$
4	0.0770	0.0809**	0.0859**	0.0948$^{\#}$	0.0968$^{\#}$	0.0993$^{\#}$	0.0996$^{\#}$	0.1015$^{\#}$	0.1024$^{\#}$
All	0.0754	0.0798*	0.0862**	0.0958***	0.0986$^{\#}$	0.1008$^{\#}$	0.1016$^{\#}$	0.1031$^{\#}$	0.1039$^{\#}$

* significantly better than the no expansion baseline by both randomization & sign tests at $p<0.05$.
** $p<0.01$ by both tests, *** $p<0.001$ by both, # $p<0.0001$ by both tests. (Same notation is used for the other tables.)

Table 2. Retrieval performance of the two selective CNF expansion methods on TREC 2007 Legal track, as measured by the TREC standard *statAP* measure. The baseline unexpanded queries produced a statAP of 0.0160. (Statistical significance tests are omitted, as they are inappropriate for the sampling based statAP measure [26].)

\ # query terms selected	1		2		3		4		All
# expansions per query term	idf	P(*t* | *R*)	idf	P(*t* | *R*)	idf	P(*t* | *R*)	idf	P(*t* | *R*)	(same)
1	0.0164	0.0233	0.0184	0.0246	0.0279	0.0282	0.0279	0.0282	0.0282
2	0.0176	0.0255	0.0189	0.0289	0.0273	0.0295	0.0288	0.0302	0.0300
3	0.0175	0.0256	0.0191	0.0290	0.0280	0.0304	0.0291	0.0307	0.0304
4	0.0176	0.0256	0.0194	0.0295	0.0292	0.0311	0.0301	0.0317	0.0314
All	0.0185	0.0345	0.0381	0.0490	0.0491	0.0504	0.0493	0.0508	0.0505

Table 3. Retrieval performance of the two selective CNF expansion methods on TREC 4 Ad hoc track, as measured by the TREC standard *MAP* measure. The baseline unexpanded queries produced an MAP of 0.1973.

\ # terms selected	1		2		3		4		All
# expansions per term\\	idf	P(*t* | *R*)	idf	P(*t* | *R*)	idf	P(*t* | *R*)	idf	P(*t* | *R*)	(same)
1	0.2087	0.2279***	0.2341*	0.2366**	0.2350**	0.2358**	0.2356**	0.2358**	0.2358**
2	0.2135	0.2392$^{\#}$	0.2503**	0.2541***	0.2552***	0.2567***	0.2578***	0.2581***	0.2581***
3	0.2187*	0.2435***	0.2538***	0.2539$^{\#}$	0.2589***	0.2608$^{\#}$	0.2619$^{\#}$	0.2622$^{\#}$	0.2622$^{\#}$
4	0.2242*	0.2489$^{\#}$	0.2654***	0.2659$^{\#}$	0.2706***	0.2731$^{\#}$	0.2753$^{\#}$	0.2756$^{\#}$	0.2756$^{\#}$
All	0.2319**	0.2526***	0.2775$^{\#}$	0.2835$^{\#}$	0.2875***	0.2916$^{\#}$	0.2935$^{\#}$	0.2938$^{\#}$	0.2938$^{\#}$

Tables 1, 2 and 3 show that the more query terms selected for expansion, the better the performance. This is not surprising, as we are using carefully expanded manual queries. Similarly, including more expansion terms (along each column) almost always improves retrieval, except for the idf method in Table 1 with only one query term selected for expansion.

The improvement over the no expansion baseline becomes significant after expanding two query terms for the idf method, and after only expanding one query term for predicted P(*t* | *R*).

Overall, P(*t* | *R*) diagnostic expansion is more stable than the idf method. This shows up in several areas. 1) Including more expansion terms always improves performance, even when only one original query term is selected for expansion. 2) Performance improvement over the no expansion baseline is significant even when only including one expansion term for one query term. These are not true for idf diagnosis. 3) Only two query terms need to be selected for expansion to achieve a performance close to the best, 33% less user effort than that of idf based diagnosis.

The statAP measure from Table 2 correlates with the MAP measure, however, the sudden increases in statAP from the 2nd last row to the last row are not present in the case of MAP. A bit of investigation shows that 1 to 2 topics benefited a lot from the extra (more than 4) expansion terms. The benefit is because of the successful matching of some relevant documents with low sampling probability, which increases statAP a lot, but not MAP. On the Legal 2007 dataset, the topic that benefited most from the more than 4 expansion terms is a topic about James Bond movies. Certainly, there are more than 4 popular James Bond movies.

Overall, predicted P(*t* | *R*) can effectively guide user expansion to improve retrieval. Expanding the first few query terms can result in significant gains in retrieval. The gain diminishes as more query terms are expanded, eventually leading to the best performance of expanding every query term.

5.4 P(*t* | *R*) vs. idf based diagnostic expansion

The subsection above shows that diagnosis can help reduce expansion effort, and that P(*t* | *R*) diagnosis results in more stable retrieval than idf. This section directly compares two retrieval experiments using predicted P(*t* | *R*) vs. idf guided expansion.

The two experiments both select 1 query term for full expansion (Table 1 last row, 2nd vs. 3rd column from the left). The MAP difference between 0.0754 of idf and 0.0798 of P(*t* | *R*) is not

Table 4. Retrieval performance of **P(*t* | *R*) guided bag of word expansion** on TREC 2007 Legal track, as measured by *MAP/statAP*. The baseline unexpanded queries produced an MAP/statAP of 0.0663/0.0160.

\ # query terms selected # expansions per query term\	1	2	3	4	All
1	0.0755**/0.0210	0.0744 /0.0172	0.0808 /0.0271	0.0768 /0.0260	0.0764***/0.0260
2	0.0795**/0.0229	0.0814** /0.0216	0.0892** /0.0242	0.0883** /0.0243	0.0867***/0.0242
3	0.0789**/0.0217	0.0829***/0.0221	0.0880** /0.0206	0.0894** /0.0207	0.0878** /0.0206
4	0.0789**/0.0217	0.0821** /0.0205	0.0908***/0.0203	0.0993***/0.0213	0.0927***/0.0214
All	0.0791**/0.0219	0.0833** /0.0217	0.1006$^{\#}$ /0.0207	0.1038$^{\#}$ /0.0211	0.1014$^{\#}$ /0.0200

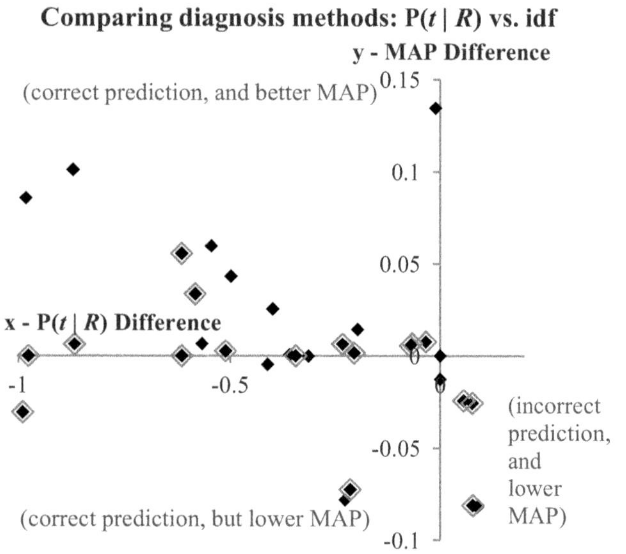

Figure 3. Difference in prediction accuracy vs. difference in MAP for the two selective query expansion methods on 43 TREC 2007 Legal Track topics. The X axis shows the difference in true P(*t* | *R*) between the first query terms selected by each method. The Y axis shows the difference in MAP between queries expanded by each method. The differences are calculated as that from predicted P(*t* | *R*) based diagnosis minus that from idf based diagnosis. Points surrounded by a diamond represent topics in which one method selected a term that had no expansions.

statistically significant. We investigate why below. According to the diagnostic expansion framework, two causes are possible, 1) the P(*t* | *R*) predictions are poor, selecting the wrong query terms to expand, or 2) the quality of the expansion terms that idf selected happen to be higher, causing the idf method to have better MAP sometimes, thus decreasing statistical significance.

To separate the effects of diagnosis and expansion, we plot the Legal 2007 topics along two dimensions in the scatter-plot Figure 3. The *x* axis represents the diagnosis dimension: the difference between the true P(*t* | *R*) of the two query terms selected by lowest predicted P(*t* | *R*) and highest idf. The *y* axis represents the expansion performance dimension: the difference between the Average Precision (AP) values of the two methods on a topic. When idf and predicted P(*t* | *R*) happen to select the same term to expand for a given topic, that topic would be plotted on the origin (x=0, y=0) – no difference in both diagnosis and expansion.

From Figure 3, firstly, most points have $x < 0$, meaning the P(*t* | *R*) predictions are better at finding the low P(*t* | *R*) terms than the idf based diagnosis. Secondly, most points are in the top left and

Table 5. Retrieval performance of **P(*t* | *R*) guided bag of word expansion** on TREC 4 Ad hoc track, as measured by *MAP*. The baseline unexpanded queries produced an MAP of 0.1973.

\#qt #exp\	1	2	3	4	All
1	0.2101**	0.2102*	0.2117**	0.2113**	0.2113**
2	0.2146***	0.2161***	0.2200**	0.2201**	0.2201**
3	0.2160***	0.2154***	0.2222***	0.2226***	0.2218**
4	0.2204$^{\#}$	0.2272***	0.2288***	0.2309**	0.2309**
All	0.2215$^{\#}$	0.2290**	0.2329**	0.2343**	0.2384**

bottom right quadrants, supporting the theory that expanding the term with lower P(*t* | *R*) leads to better retrieval performance. In the bottom right quadrant, occasionally idf method picks the right terms with lower P(*t* | *R*) to expand, and does better in retrieval.

However, there are three outliers in the bottom left quadrant, which are not fully explained by our theory. At the bottom left quadrant, predicted P(*t* | *R*) does identify the right term with a lower P(*t* | *R*), but the retrieval performance is actually worse than that of idf guided expansion.

By looking into these three topics, we found that the manual queries for topics 76 and 86 do not have any expansion terms for the query terms selected by P(*t* | *R*), while the idf selected terms do have effective expansion terms. All such topics where a query term without expansion terms is selected are annotated with diamond shaped borders in the plot. Topic 55 is because of poor expansion term quality. The P(*t* | *R*) method selects the chemical name *apatite* for expansion, which represent a class of chemicals. The manual expansion terms seem very reasonable, and are just names or chemical formulas of the chemicals belonging to the *apatite* family. However, the query is really about *apatite rocks* as they appear in nature, not any specific chemical in the apatite family. Thus, even expansion terms proposed by experts can still sometimes introduce false positives into the rank list, and this problem cannot be easily identified without corpus interaction, e.g. examining the result rank list of documents.

If these 3 topics were removed from evaluation, predicted P(*t* | *R*) guided expansion would be significantly better than idf guided expansion, at $p < 0.05$ by the two tailed sign test.

Of the 50 TREC 4 topics, similarly, 4 topics are outliers. In two cases, the P(*t* | *R*) selected query terms do not have manual expansion terms. In one topic, P(*t* | *R*) prediction did not select the right term, but MAP is higher than idf diagnosis, because the idf method selected a query term with poor expansion terms. In one topic, the retrieval performance does not differ at top ranks, and the idf method only excels after 30 documents.

Overall, most topics confirm our hypothesis that expanding the query term likely to mismatch relevant documents leads to better retrieval, and better diagnosis also leads to better retrieval.

This analysis also shows the inherent difficulty of evaluating term diagnosis in end-to-end retrieval experiments. Even with high quality manual expansion terms, there is still some variation in the quality of the expansion interventions, which can still interfere with the assessment of the diagnosis component.

5.5 Boolean CNF vs. bag of word expansion

We compare CNF style expansion with *two* advanced bag-of-word expansion methods.

For a fair comparison with manual CNF expansion, our *first* bag of word expansion baseline also uses the set of manual expansion terms selected by predicted P(t | R). Expansion terms are then grouped and combined with the original query for retrieval.

To make this baseline strong, both individual expansion terms and the expansion term set can be weighted. The individual expansion terms are weighted with the Relevance Model weights [17] from an initial keyword retrieval, with the parameter (the number of feedback documents) tuned on the training set. Manual expansion terms that do not appear in the feedback documents are still included in the final query, but a minimum weight is used to conform to the relevance model weights. Uniform weighting of the expansion terms was also tried. It is more effective than relevance model weights when expansion is more balanced, i.e. more than 3 query terms are selected for expansion. When combining the expansion terms with the original query, the combination weights are 2-fold cross-validated on the test set.

Table 4 shows *the best case* of both relevance-model-weight and uniform-weight bag of word expansion. Bag of word expansion performs worse than CNF expansion in almost all the different setups. The best performance is achieved with full expansion of 4 query terms, with a MAP of 0.1038, slightly lower than that of CNF (0.1039 in Table 1), however, the statAP value of 0.0211 is much worse than that of CNF (0.0508, Table 2).

Table 5 shows the best case bag of word expansion results on the TREC 4 Ad hoc dataset. Consistent with the statAP measure on TREC Legal 2007, CNF queries are much better than bag of word expansion. For example, with full expansion of all query terms, CNF expansion (Table 3) gets a MAP of 0.2938, 23% better than 0.2384 of the bag of word expansion with the same expansion terms, significant at $p < 0.0025$ by the randomization test and weakly significant at $p < 0.0676$ by the sign test.

Some results of bag of word retrieval at low selection levels, i.e. selecting one query term to expand, perform better than idf guided CNF expansion. But since the bag of word expansion here uses better expansion terms selected by predicted P(t | R), this does not mean that bag of word is sometimes better than CNF expansion.

The *second* bag of word expansion baseline is the standard Lavrenko Relevance Model itself [17], which uses automatic feedback terms, instead of manual ones, for expansion. Parameters trained on Legal 2006 dataset when applied to Legal 2007 lead to an MAP of 0.0606, statAP of 0.0168, worse than the no expansion baseline. On TREC 4, it gets a MAP of 0.2488, slightly better than 0.2384, the best manual bag of word expansion, but still much worse than CNF (0.2938).

In sum, given the same set of high quality expansion terms, CNF expansion works much better than bag of word expansion.

6. CONCLUSIONS

We set out with the hypothesis that term mismatch based diagnosis can successfully guide further retrieval intervention to fix 'problem' terms and improve retrieval. In this work, we applied the term mismatch diagnosis to guide interactive query expansion. Simulated interactive query expansion experiments on TREC Ad hoc and Legal track datasets not only confirmed this hypothesis, but also showed that *automatically predicted* P(t | R) probabilities (the complement of term mismatch) can accurately guide expansion to the terms that need expansion most, and lead to better retrieval than when expanding rare terms first. From the user's point of view, it usually isn't necessary to expand every query term. Guided by predicted P(t | R), expanding two terms is enough for most topics to achieve close-to-top performance, while guided by idf (rareness), three terms need to be expanded. P(t | R) guidance can save user effort by 33%.

In addition to confirming the main hypothesis, experiments also showed that Boolean conjunctive normal form (CNF) expansion outperforms carefully weighted bag of word expansion, given the same set of high quality expansion terms. The unstructured bag of word expansion typically needs balanced expansion of most query terms to achieve a reliable performance.

Although the effect from adding more expansion terms to a query term diminishes, for the query terms that do need expansion, the effects of the expansion terms are typically additive, the more the expansion the better the performance. This is consistent with prior observations on vocabulary mismatch, that even after including more than 15 aliases, the effects of mismatch can still be observed, and further expansion may still help [7].

For bag of word expansion, including more manual expansion terms also helps, but requires a balanced expansion of most query terms, and is not as effective and stable as CNF expansion.

This work is mostly concerned with automatic diagnosis of problem terms in the query, and presents them to the user for manual expansion. It is still a question whether the diagnosis can help automatic formulation of effective CNF queries. We hope to let the system suggest or select expansion terms, automatically or semi-automatically with minimal user effort. Automatic identification of high quality expansion terms would be useful when the candidate expansion terms may not be of high quality, e.g. expansion terms from result documents, thesaurus or non-expert users. Poor expansion terms in CNF queries are especially harmful, when they over-generalize the query and introduce false positives throughout the rank list. Tools such as performance prediction methods (e.g. query clarity), may help in such scenarios to detect the adverse effects of the poor expansion terms.

In the future, we also hope to diagnose precision related problems as well as mismatch problems. We can then use the diagnosis to guide disambiguation, phrasing or fielded retrieval, as well as term substitution, removal or expansion.

7. ACKNOWLEDGEMENTS

This work is supported by NSF grant IIS-1018317. Opinions in this work are solely the authors'. We thank Chengtao Wen, Grace Hui Yang, Jin Young Kim, Charlie Clarke, Gordon Cormack and NIST for helpful discussions, feedback and access to data.

8. REFERENCES

[1] J. A. Aslam and V. Pavlu. A practical sampling strategy for efficient retrieval evaluation. Report. May 2007.

[2] J. R. Baron, D. D. Lewis and D. W. Oard. TREC 2006 Legal Track Overview. In *Proceedings of the fifteenth Text REtrieval Conference (TREC '06)*, 2007.

[3] G. Cao, S. Robertson and J. Nie. Selecting Query Term Alterations for Web Search by Exploiting Query Contexts. In *Proceedings of 46th Annual Meeting of the Association for*

Computational Linguistics: Human Language Technologies (ACL-08: HLT). 148-155, 2008.

[4] C. L. A. Clarke, G. V. Cormack and F. J. Burkowski. Shortest Substring Ranking (MultiText Experiments for TREC-4). In *Proceedings of the Fourth Text REtrieval Conference (TREC-4)*. 1996.

[5] V. Dang and W. B. Croft. Query reformulation using anchor text. In *Proceedings of the 3rd ACM International Conference on Web Search and Data Mining (WSDM '10)*. 41-50, 2010.

[6] S. Deerwester, S. T. Dumais, G. W. Furnas, T. K. Landauer and R. Harshman. Indexing by latent semantic analysis. *Journal of the American Society for Information Science*, 41(6): 391-407. 1990.

[7] G. W. Furnas, T. K. Landauer, L. M. Gomez, and S. T. Dumais. The vocabulary problem in human-system communication. *Communications of ACM*, 30(11): 964-971. ACM. New York, NY. November, 1987.

[8] W. Greiff. A theory of term weighting based on exploratory data analysis. In *Proceedings of 21st Annual International ACM SIGIR Conference on Research and Development in Information Retrieval (SIGIR '98)*. 11-19, 1998.

[9] D. Harman. Towards interactive query expansion. In *Proceedings of the 11th Annual International ACM SIGIR Conference on Research and Development in Information Retrieval (SIGIR '88)*. 321-331, 1988.

[10] D. Harman. Overview of the Third Text REtrieval Conference (TREC-3). In *Proceedings of the 3rd Text REtrieval Conference (TREC '94)*, 1995.

[11] D. Harman. Overview of the Third Text REtrieval Conference (TREC-4). In *Proceedings of the 4th Text REtrieval Conference (TREC '95)*, 1996.

[12] S. Harter. *Online Information Retrieval: Concepts, Principles, and Techniques*. Academic Press. San Diego, California. 1986.

[13] M. Hearst. Improving full-text precision on short queries using simple constraints. In *Proceedings of the Fifth Annual Symposium on Document Analysis and Information Retrieval (SDAIR '96)*, 1996.

[14] R. Jones, B. Rey, O. Madani and W. Greiner. Generating query substitutions. In *Proceedings of the 15th International Conference on World Wide Web (WWW '06)*. 387-396, 2006.

[15] J. Lamping and S. Baker. Determining query term synonyms within query context. United States Patent No. 7,636,714. USPTO March, 2005.

[16] W. Lancaster. *Information Retrieval Systems: Characteristics, Testing and Evaluation*. Wiley. New York, New York, USA. 1968.

[17] V. Lavrenko and W. B. Croft. Relevance-based language models. In *Proceedings of the 24th Annual International ACM SIGIR Conference on Research and Development in Information Retrieval (SIGIR '01)*. 120-127, 2001.

[18] J. Lin and M. D. Smucker. How do users find things with PubMed?: towards automatic utility evaluation with user simulations. In *Proceedings of the 31st annual international ACM SIGIR conference on Research and Development in Information Retrieval (SIGIR '08)*. 19-26, 2008.

[19] D. Metzler and W.B. Croft. Combining the language model and inference network approaches to retrieval. *Information Processing and Management Special Issue on Bayesian Networks and Information Retrieval*, 40(5), 735-750, 2004.

[20] D. Metzler. Generalized inverse document frequency. In *Proceedings of the 17th ACM Conference on Information and Knowledge Management (CIKM '08)*. 399-408, 2008.

[21] M. Mitra, A. Singhal and C. Buckley. Improving automatic query expansion, *Proceedings of 21st annual international ACM SIGIR conference on Research and Development in Information Retrieval (SIGIR '98)*. 206-214, 1998.

[22] F. Peng, N. Ahmed, X. Li and Y. Lu. Context sensitive stemming for Web search. In *Proceedings of the 30th Annual International ACM SIGIR Conference on Research and Development in Information Retrieval (SIGIR '07)*. 639-646, 2007.

[23] S. E. Robertson and K. Spärck Jones. Relevance weighting of search terms. *Journal of the American Society for Information Science*, 27(3):129-146. 1976.

[24] G. Salton, E. A. Fox and H. Wu. Extended Boolean information retrieval. *Communications of ACM*, 26(11): 1022-1036. ACM. New York, NY. November 1983.

[25] S. Tomlinson. Experiments with the Negotiated Boolean Queries of the TREC 2006 Legal Discovery Track. In *Proceedings of the fifteenth Text REtrieval Conference (TREC '06)*, 2007.

[26] S. Tomlinson, D. W. Oard, J. R. Baron and P. Thompson. Overview of the TREC 2007 Legal Track. In *Proceedings of the sixteenth Text REtrieval Conference (TREC '07)*, 2008.

[27] E. Tudhope. Query based stemming. PhD Thesis. University of Waterloo. 1996.

[28] X. Wang and C. Zhai. Mining term association patterns from search logs for effective query reformulation. In *Proceedings of the 17th ACM Conference on Information and Knowledge Management (CIKM '08)*. 479-488, 2008.

[29] R. W. White, I. Ruthven, J. M. Jose, and C. J. Van Rijsbergen. Evaluating implicit feedback models using searcher simulations. *ACM Trans. Inf. Syst.* 23(3): 325-361. July, 2005.

[30] X. Xue, W. B. Croft and D. A. Smith. Modeling reformulation using passage analysis. In *Proceedings of the 19th ACM Conference on Information and Knowledge Management (CIKM '10)*. 2010.

[31] L. Zhao and J. Callan. Effective and efficient structured retrieval (poster description). In *Proceedings of the 18th ACM Conference on Information and Knowledge Management (CIKM '09)*. 1573-1576, 2009.

[32] L. Zhao and J. Callan. Term necessity prediction. In *Proceedings of the 19th ACM Conference on Information and Knowledge Management (CIKM '10)*. 2010.

[33] Y. Zhu, L. Zhao, J. Callan and J. Carbonell. Structured queries for legal search. In *Proceedings of the sixteenth Text REtrieval Conference (TREC '07)*, 2008

Generating Reformulation Trees for Complex Queries

Xiaobing Xue W. Bruce Croft
Center for Intelligent Information Retrieval
Computer Science Department
University of Massachusetts, Amherst, MA, 01003, USA
{xuexb,croft}@cs.umass.edu

ABSTRACT

Search queries have evolved beyond keyword queries. Many complex queries such as verbose queries, natural language question queries and document-based queries are widely used in a variety of applications. Processing these complex queries usually requires a series of query operations, which results in multiple sequences of reformulated queries. However, previous query representations, either the "bag of words" method or the recently proposed "query distribution" method, cannot effectively model these query sequences, since they ignore the relationships between two queries. In this paper, a *reformulation tree* framework is proposed to organize multiple sequences of reformulated queries as a tree structure, where each path of the tree corresponds to a sequence of reformulated queries. Specifically, a two-level reformulation tree is implemented for verbose queries. This tree effectively combines two query operations, i.e., subset selection and query substitution, within the same framework. Furthermore, a weight estimation approach is proposed to assign weights to each node of the reformulation tree by considering the relationships with other nodes and directly optimizing retrieval performance. Experiments on TREC collections show that this reformulation tree based representation significantly outperforms the state-of-the-art techniques.

Categories and Subject Descriptors

H.3.3 [**Information Storage and Retrieval**]: Information Search and Retrieval

General Terms

Algorithms, Experimentation, Performance

Keywords

Reformulation Tree, Verbose Query, Information Retrieval

Permission to make digital or hard copies of all or part of this work for personal or classroom use is granted without fee provided that copies are not made or distributed for profit or commercial advantage and that copies bear this notice and the full citation on the first page. To copy otherwise, to republish, to post on servers or to redistribute to lists, requires prior specific permission and/or a fee.
SIGIR'12, August 12–16, 2012, Portland, Oregon, USA.
Copyright 2012 ACM 978-1-4503-1472-5/12/08 ...$15.00.

1. INTRODUCTION

Although short keyword queries are still very common in web search, the increasing diversity of search applications and information needs has led to increasing complexity in queries. For example, verbose (or long) queries have become more and more popular in web search. In community-based Q&A, users pose natural language questions as queries. In patent retrieval, the whole document (patent application) is considered as the query. These complex queries help users express their information need naturally and save the effort of picking keywords. However, processing these queries poses a significant challenge for search systems.

Dealing with complex queries usually requires a series of query operations. For example, a typical process of dealing with a verbose query can be described as follows. The system first selects a subset of query words from the original query to remove noisy information. Then, the generated subset query is further modified to handle vocabulary mismatch. Finally, weights are assigned to queries generated at each step. Depending on the application, the above process could become more complicated. For example, in cross-lingual retrieval, the original verbose query needs to be translated into a foreign language query before applying any further operation. The above process will generate multiple sequences of reformulated queries, where each sequence records a way of modifying the original query using several query operations. These reformulation sequences capture the relationships between the reformulated queries. Fig. 1 displays some examples of the reformulation sequences, where the subset query is selected from the original query at the first step of the sequence and the second step further substitutes the subset query.

However, previous query representations cannot model these reformulation sequences well. The "bag of words" representation is widely used in information retrieval. Using this representation, the original query is transformed into a set of weighted words. Some extensions to this representation introduce phrases [19] and latent words [14][20].

Reformulation Sequence
Q→reductions iraqs foreign debt→reduce iraqs foreign debt
Q→iraqs foreign debt→iraqs foreign debts
Q→iraqs foreign debt→iraqs external debt

Figure 1: The reformulation sequences generated for a verbose query Q "any efforts proposed or undertaken by world governments to seek reduction of iraqs foreign debt"

This representation does not explicitly model a reformulated query, which serves as the basis of the reformulation sequences. An example of the "bag of words" representation is shown in Fig. 2 (a). Recently, the "query distribution" representation [27] was proposed to transform the original query into a set of reformulated queries. For example, Xue et al [30] represents a verbose query as a set of subset queries. This representation indeed considers a reformulated query as the basic unit, but it fails to capture the relationships between the reformulated queries. Therefore, the sequences of reformulated queries still cannot be modeled using this representation. An example of the "query distribution" representation is shown in Fig. 2 (b).

In this paper, a novel query representation is proposed to transform a complex query into a reformulation tree, where the nodes at each level of this tree correspond to the reformulated queries generated using a specific query operation. Using this representation, a reformulation sequence is naturally modeled as a path from the root node to the leaf node. The construction of the reformulation tree simulates the process of applying a series of query operations to the complex query. Furthermore, weight is assigned to each node of the reformulation tree, which indicates the importance of the corresponding reformulated query. The estimation of the weight for a node considers not only the characteristics of this node itself, but also its relationships with other nodes. Different with previous reformulation models that treat retrieval models as independent steps, we estimate the weights on the reformulation tree by directly optimizing the performance of retrieval models, which considers the reformulation model and the retrieval model in a joint view.

Verbose queries, as a typical example of complex queries, have attracted much attention recently. Previous research on verbose queries either weights the query words in the original query [16, 15, 3] or selects the best subset of query words from the original query [12]. Relatively little research considers combining multiple query operations together for improving verbose queries. Therefore, as an implementation of the reformulation tree framework, a two-level tree structure is constructed for verbose queries, where the first level corresponds to the subset query selection operation and the second level corresponds to the query substitution operation. A weight estimation method is also described, which incorporates the relationships between different reformulated queries and directly optimizes the retrieval performance.

Fig. 2 (c) shows an example reformulation tree. The first level of this tree consists of two subset queries extracted from the original query, i.e., "reductions iraqs foreign debt" and "iraqs foreign debt". At the second level, each subset query is further modified to generate query substitutions. For example, "iraqs foreign debt" has been modified to "iraqs external debt". Furthermore, weight is assigned to each node of this tree, which measures the importance of each reformulated query. Compared with other representations, the reformulation sequences as shown in Fig. 1 are captured using the reformulation tree.

The contributions of this paper can be summarized as four folds. First, a tree based query representation is proposed to deal with complex queries, which models a series of query operations and captures the relationships between the reformulated queries. Second, a specific implementation, i.e., the two-level reformulation tree, is introduced for verbose queries, which combines two important operations, subset

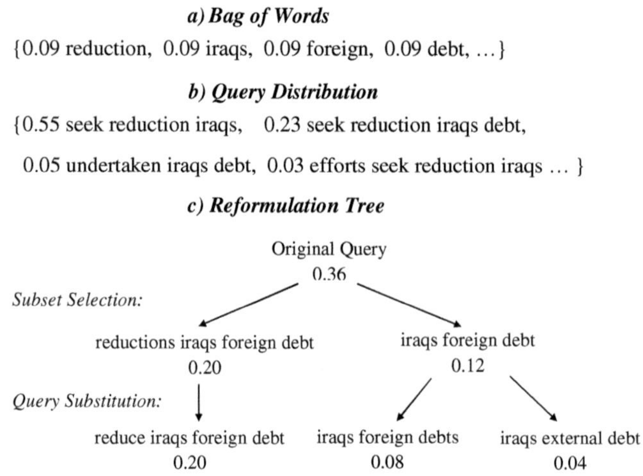

Figure 2: Different query representations for a verbose query "identify any efforts proposed or undertaken by world governments to seek reduction of iraqs foreign debt"

query selection and query substitution. Third, a weight estimation method is designed by incorporating the relationships between different reformulated queries and directly optimizing retrieval performance. Fourth, detailed experiments are conducted to show that the tree-based representation outperforms other query representations for verbose queries.

2. RELATED WORK

In this section, we first describe previous work on complex queries, especially on verbose queries and then we review previous query representation approaches.

2.1 Complex Query

As described in the introduction, complex queries have been widely used in different applications. Some examples include the verbose query, the natural language question query and the document-based query.

Kumaran and Allan [11] studied shortening a verbose query through human interaction. Bendersky and Croft [2] discovered key concepts from a verbose query. These key concepts were combined with the original query to improve the retrieval performance. Kumaran and Carvalho [12] learned to automatically select subset queries using several query quality predictors. Balasubramanian et al [1] extent [12] for web long queries.

Lease et al [16] developed a regression model to assign weights to each query word in the verbose query by using the secondary features. Lease [15] further combined their regression model with the Sequential Dependence Model, which achieved significant performance improvement. Bendersky et al [3] proposed a unified framework to measure the weights of words, phrases and proximity features underlying a verbose query.

A natural language question query is widely used in a community-based Question and Answer service such as Yahoo! Answers and Quora. Previous work [8, 9, 24] studied effectively finding previously answered questions that are relevant to a new question asked by a user. Different retrieval models have been proposed to calculate the similarity between questions. For example, a translation based retrieval model [8] were developed to deal with the vocabulary mismatch between the semantically related questions.

A document-based query allows users to directly submit a document as a query. A typical example is in patent retrieval [13], where the whole patent application is submitted to the search system in order to find the relevant patents. Many features are extracted from a patent application and these features are the basis of retrieving relevant patents.

In this paper, a tree-based representation is proposed to improve the complex query. A specific implementation for verbose queries is described. This implementation combines subset selection and query modification within the same framework, which has not been explored in previous work.

2.2 Query Representation

In this section, we review two types of query representations, "bag of words" and "query distribution".

The "bag of words" representation transforms the original query into a set of terms, either weighted or not. These terms include the words and phrases from the original query and the latent words and phrases extracted from the corpus. For example, the relevance model approach [14] adds latent words to the original query, the sequential dependency model [19] detects the phrase structure, and the latent concept expansion model [20] uses proximity features and latent words. This type of representation does not consider how to use words and phrases to form actual reformulated queries. In other words, a reformulated query is not explicitly modeled in this representation.

The "query distribution" representation transforms the original query into a set of reformulated queries, where each query is assigned a probability. This probability helps measure the importance of the query. For example, Xue et al [30] represented a verbose query as a distribution of subset queries and a modified Conditional Random Field is proposed to estimate the probability for each subset query. This type of representation indeed considers the reformulated query as the basic unit, but it assumes independence between the reformulated queries. When multiple query operations are applied, this independence assumption usually does not hold.

In this paper, the proposed "reformulation tree" representation extends the "query distribution" representation by modeling the relationships between reformulated queries using the tree structure.

Some previous work also considers the relationships between queries. Boldi et al [4] proposed to build a query-flow graph that modeled web users' search behaviors. Specifically, the directed edges between two queries indicated that they were likely to belong to the same search mission. Mei et al [17] presented a general framework to model search sequences, where a search sequence is represented as a nested sequence of search objects. The above work focuses on short keyword queries and uses query logs to capture the relationships between the queries submitted within the same search session. In contrast, in this paper, we study complex queries and model the relationships between the reformulated queries. Furthermore, the construction of the reformulation tree proposed in this paper is closely related to the final retrieval performance, while previous work studies the query graph or sequence independently from the retrieval model.

Guo et al [6] proposed a CRF-based model for query refinement, which combines several tasks like spelling correction, stemming and phrase detection. This model focuses on morphological changes of keyword queries such as spelling correction and stemming, but does not consider complex queries.

3. BACKGROUND

In this section, we summarize several basic concepts used in this paper.

A *complex query* (q) is more complicated than a short keyword query. Examples of complex queries include verbose queries, natural language question queries and document-based queries. In this paper, we will focus on verbose queries.

A *query operation* (r) indicates a query processing technique. In this paper, we focus on two query operations, i.e. subset query selection and query substitution. Subset query selection [11, 12, 1, 30] selects a subset of query words from the original query. Query substitution [10, 26, 29] replaces the original query word with a new word. Other examples of query operations include query translation, query segmentation and so on.

A *reformulated query* (q_r) is the output of applying a query operation. A *reformulation sequence* is a sequence of reformulated queries by applying a series of query operations.

A *reformulation tree* (T) is a tree structure that organizes the reformulated queries generated by different query operations. Each path of T corresponds to a reformulation sequence.

4. REFORMULATION TREE

In this section, we first describe the framework for generating the reformulation tree T. Then, we compare this tree-based representation with previous query representations. Finally, the principle of the weight estimation is described.

4.1 Framework

Suppose that n query operations $\{r_1, r_2, ..., r_n\}$ are required to process a complex query q. Then, q is transformed into a n-level tree T. Each node of T represents a reformulated query q_r. From now on, if not explicitly indicated, we use q_r to represent both a node of T and the corresponding reformulated query. The root node of T represents the original query q, which can be considered as a special reformulated query. The ith level of T are generated by applying the ith operation r_i to the nodes at the $(i-1)$th level. An arc is added between the nodes at the $(i-1)$th level and the nodes at the ith level if the latter is the output of applying r_i to the former. Therefore, each path of T corresponds to a reformulation sequence. Furthermore, weight $w(q_r)$ is assigned to each node of T, which measures the importance of the corresponding reformulated query q_r.

When T is used for retrieval, the retrieval score of a document D is calculated using Eq. 1.

$$sc(T, D) = \sum_{q_r \in T} w(q_r) sc(q_r, D) \tag{1}$$

where $w(q_r)$ is the weight assigned to the node corresponding to the reformulated query q_r and $sc(q_r, D)$ is the retrieval score of using q_r to retrieve D. In general, $sc(T, D)$ is calculated by combining the retrieval score of using each reformulated query q_r in T, where $w(q_r)$ is used as the combination weight. The calculation of $sc(q_r, D)$ depends on implementation.

4.2 Comparisons of Query Representations

In this subsection, we compare different query representations using the example in the introduction. Fig. 2 displays the "bag of words" representation, the "query distribution" representation and the "reformulation tree" representation.

In the "bag of words" representation, the basic unit is words or phrases. This representation may tell you that the important words in the original query are "reduction", "iraqs" and "debt", but how these words can be used together to form a new query is not clear.

The "query distribution" representation extends the "bag of words" representation by explicitly modeling a reformulated query. For example, this representation lists the top ranked subset queries such as "seek reduction iraqs" and "seek reduction iraqs debt". However, the relationships between the reformulated queries are not captured using this representation.

When a series of query operations are applied, we need a representation that models the reformulation sequences generated using these operations. The "reformulation tree" representation is designed to solve this problem. For example, in Fig. 2, the subset queries and the query substitutions are organized into a tree structure. This structure indicates that we need to first select subset queries and then conduct query substitution. It captures the relationships between "iraqs foreign debt" and "iraqs external debt", since the latter is the output of applying the query subsitution operation to the former.

4.3 Weight Estimation

The weight assigned to each node in the tree indicates the importance of the corresponding reformulated query. This weight should characterize both the features of this node itself and its relationships with other nodes. Therefore, the weight of q_r, i.e., $w(q_r)$, is calculated in Eq. 2.

$$w(q_r) = w(par(q_r)) \sum_k \lambda_k f_k(q_r) \tag{2}$$

where $par(q_r)$ denotes the parent node of q_r. f_k is the query feature extracted from q_r and λ_k is the parameter. Eq. 2 shows that the weight of q_r is not only decided by its own query features $\{f_k\}$ but also by the weight of its parent node $par(q_r)$. Intuitively, if q_r is important, its children should also receive high weights. In this way, the relationships between reformulated queries are incorporated into the weight estimation.

Note that Eq. 2 provides the principle of weight estimation. How to calculate $w(q_r)$ will depend on the implementation.

5. REFORMULATION TREE FOR VERBOSE QUERIES

In this section, we describe a two-level reformulation tree for verbose queries. We first describe the query operations used to construct the reformulation tree, i.e. subset query selection and query substitution. Then, we introduce a stage-based weight estimation method to assign weight to each node. Finally, the retrieval model is described.

5.1 Building Tree Structure

The construction of the reformulation tree for verbose queries consists of two steps: first, subset queries are selected from the original query; second, the subset queries generated in the previous step are further modified to generate query substitutions.

We follow Kumaran and Carvalho [12]'s method to generate subset queries. All query words from the original verbose query are considered. If the length of the verbose query is bigger than ten, we first rank all query words by their *idf* values and then pick the top ten words for the subset query generation. Then, all subset queries with length between three and six words are generated.

The passage analysis technique [29] is used to generate query substitutions. In order to replace one word from the original query, all the passages containing the rest of the query words are first extracted. Then, three methods are used to generate candidates for query substitution from these passages. **Morph** considers the morphologically similar words as candidates. **Pattern** considers the words matching the patterns extracted from the original query as candidates. **Wiki** considers the Wikipedia redirect pairs as the candidates. More details can be found in [29]. Finally, the top ranked candidates are used as query substitutions.

Given the above two query operations, the reformulation tree for the verbose query can be generated in this way. First, all subset queries with length between three to six are extracted from the original query. Each subset query is assigned a weight. How to estimate the weight will be described in the next subsection. According to this weight, we will pick the top ranked subset queries to construct the first level of the reformulation tree. *SubNum* is a parameter that controls the number of nodes at the first level. Second, among these *SubNum* subset queries, we further modify the top *ModNum* queries to generate query substitutions, which constructs the second level of the reformulation tree. *ModNum* is another parameter that controls the number of nodes that will be substituted.

For example, the reformulation tree used in the introduction (Fig. 2) can be constructed in two steps. This process is illustrated in Fig. 3. First, we pick the top two subset queries "reductions iraqs foreign debt" and "iraqs foreign debt" to construct the first level of the reformulation tree. Second, we modify these two subset queries respectively. For the first subset query, "reduce iraqs foreign debt" is generated by replacing "reduction" with "reduce". For the second subset query, two query substitutions, i.e. "iraqs foreign debt" and "iraqs external debt" are generated.

5.2 Weight Estimation

Eq. 2 indicates that the weight of a node in the reformulation tree depends on both its intrinsic features and the weight of its parent node. However, how to estimate the weight is still unclear. In this part, we describe a stage-based weight estimation method. The learning-to-rank based parameter estimation strategy [28] is used as the basis, which transforms a query feature into a corresponding retrieval feature.

In the initial stage, the root node (the original query q) is assigned the weight 1, i.e. $w(q) = 1$.

In **Stage I**, after the subset queries q_{sub} are generated, we calculate the weight of q_{sub} using Eq. 3.

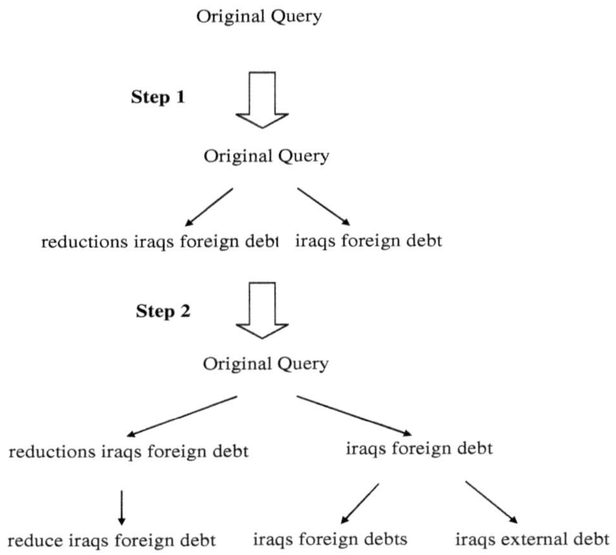

Figure 3: The process of constructing a reformulation tree

$$w(q_{sub}) = w(q) \sum_k \lambda_k^{sub} f_k^{sub}(q_{sub}) = \sum_k \lambda_k^{sub} f_k^{sub}(q_{sub}) \quad (3)$$

Eq. 3 instantiates Eq. 2 by focusing on the subset queries. f_k^{sub} is the query feature extracted from q_{sub} and λ_k^{sub} is the corresponding parameter. Since the root node is the parent of every subset query, its weight $w(q) = 1$, is used in Eq. 3.

In order to estimate $\{\lambda_k^{sub}\}$ by directly optimizing the retrieval performance, we transform each query feature f_k^{sub} into the corresponding retrieval feature F_k^{sub}, where F_k^{sub} is calculated in Eq. 4.

$$F_k^{sub}(\{q_{sub}\}, D) = \sum_{q_{sub}} f_k^{sub}(q_{sub}) sc(q_{sub}, D) \quad (4)$$

where $sc(q_{sub}, D)$ is the retrieval score of using q_{sub} to retrieve D. The calculation of $sc(q_{sub}, D)$ depends on the retrieval model. The retrieval feature F_k^{sub} combines the retrieval score of each subset query q_{sub} using their corresponding query feature $f_k^{sub}(q_{sub})$ as the combination weight. In general, F_k^{sub} indicates how well documents are ranked if f_k^{sub} is used as the weight to combine subset queries.

Now, we obtain a set of retrieval features $\{F_k^{sub}\}$. The problem of estimating $\{\lambda_k^{sub}\}$ to combine the query features $\{f_k^{sub}\}$ is transformed into the problem of combining the corresponding retrieval features $\{F_k^{sub}\}$ to achieve the best retrieval performance. The latter problem is typically solved using learning to rank techniques. In this paper, the ListNet method [5] is adopted to learn $\{\lambda_k^{sub}\}$ on the training set.

After obtaining $\{\lambda_k^{sub}\}$, we can assign the weight for each subset query according to Eq. 3.

In **Stage II**, we assign weights to the substituted queries. The weight of a substituted query q_{mod} is calculated using Eq. 5.

$$w(q_{mod}) = w(q_{sub}) \sum_k \lambda_k^{mod} f_k^{mod}(q_{mod}) \quad (5)$$

Table 1: Summary of features

Features for Subset Queries $f_k^{sub}(q_{sub})$	
MI[11]	mutual information
SQLen[12]	sub-query length
QS[7]	query scope
QC[25]	query clarity score
SOQ[12]	similarity to original query
psg	count of passages containing q_{sub}
KeyCpt[2]	whether contains the key concept
Features for Substituted Queries $f_k^{mod}(q_{mod})$	
Morph	generated using Morph
Pattern	generated using Pattern
Wiki	generated using Wiki
psg	count of passages containing q_{mod}
seg-type	the number of possible segmentations

where q_{sub} is the parent node of q_{mod}. Compared with Eq. 3, the weights of the subset queries $w(q_{sub})$ generated in Stage I are incorporated in Eq. 5.

Similarly, in order to estimate $\{\lambda_k^{mod}\}$, we transform f_k^{mod} into the corresponding retrieval feature F_k^{mod} using Eq. 6.

$$F_k^{mod}(\{q_{mod}\}, D) = \sum_{q_{mod}} w(q_{sub}) f_k^{mod}(q_{mod}) sc(q_{mod}, D) \quad (6)$$

where q_{sub} is the parent node of q_{mod}. In general, F_k^{mod} tells how well the documents are ranked if f_k^{mod} is used as the weight to combine the substituted queries. Thus, the parameters $\{\lambda_k^{mod}\}$ are learned by combining these retrieval features $\{F_k^{mod}\}$ using ListNet.

5.3 Features

In this part, we describe the query features used to characterize the subset queries and the substituted queries.

The features used to characterize the subset queries are mainly query quality predictors. This type of features have been widely used in previous research [12][30]. Examples of query quality predictors include Mutual Information [11], Query Scope [7] and Query Clarity [25]. In addition, passage information is considered. The number of passages that contain a subset query provides strong evidence for the quality of a subset query. Whether a subset query contains key concepts is also considered as a feature. These key concepts were discovered by Bendersky et al [2].

The features used to characterize the substituted queries include the type of methods of generating substituted queries. As described in Section 5.1, "Morph" indicates using the morphologically similar words as candidates, "Pattern" indicates using the pattern based method and "Wiki" indicates using the Wikipedia redirect page. The passage information is also considered as one feature. Furthermore, the number of possible segmentations of a substituted query is used as another feature. This feature can be directly obtained using the passage analysis technique [29].

The details of features are summarized in Table 1.

5.4 Retrieval Model

The retrieval score of using a reformulation tree T can be calculated using Eq. 1. For example, given the reformulation tree shown in Fig. 2, the retrieval score can be calculated as follows:

$$\begin{aligned} sc(T,D) &= 0.36 \times sc(\text{Original Query}, D) \\ &= +0.2 \times sc(\text{“reductions iraqs foreign debt”}, D) \\ &= +0.12 \times sc(\text{“iraqs foreign debt”}, D) \\ &= +0.2 \times sc(\text{“reduce iraqs foreign debt”}, D) \\ &= +0.08 \times sc(\text{“iraqs foreign debts”}, D) \\ &= +0.04 \times sc(\text{“iraqs external debt”}, D) \end{aligned}$$

In this paper, the sequential dependency model (SDM) [19] is used to calculate $sc(q_r, D)$, which has been widely used in previous work [2, 30] as a state-of-the-art technique. Using SDM, the score of a document can be calculated as follows:

$$\begin{aligned} sc(q_r, D) &= \lambda_T \sum_{t \in T(q_r)} \log(P(t|D)) + \lambda_O \sum_{o \in O(q_r)} \log(P(o|D)) \\ &+ \lambda_U \sum_{u \in U(q_r)} \log(P(u|D)) \end{aligned} \quad (7)$$

where $T(q_r)$ denotes a set of query words of q_r, $O(q_r)$ denotes a set of ordered bigrams extracted from q_r and $U(q_r)$ denotes a set of unordered bigrams extracted from q_r. λ_T, λ_O and λ_U are parameters controlling the weights of different parts and are usually set as 0.85, 0.1 and 0.05 [19]. $P(t|D)$, $P(o|D)$ and $P(u|D)$ are calculated using the language modeling approach [22, 31].

The SDM model can be easily implemented using the Indri query language [18]. Fig. 4 shows an example of Indri query for SDM model.

Figure 4: Example of Indri query.

```
q_r : iraqs foreign debt
SDM: #weight(
    0.85 #combine(iraqs foreign debt)
    0.10 #combine(#1(iraqs foreign) #1(foreign debt))
    0.05 #combine(#uw8(iraqs foreign) #uw8(foreign debt))
    )
```

Table 2: TREC collections used in experiments

Name	Docs	Topics
Gov2	25,205,179	701-850
Robust04	528,155	301-450,601-700
Wt10g	1,692,096	451-550
ClueWeb	50,220,423	1-100

6. EXPERIMENTS

Four TREC collections, Gov2, Robust04, ClueWeb (Category B) and Wt10g are used for experiments. Robust04 is a newswire collection, while the rest are web collections. The statistics of each collection are reported in Table 2. For each collection, two indexes are built, one not stemmed and the other stemmed using the Porter Stemmer[23]. Stemming transforms a word into its root form, which is conducted either during indexing or during query processing. The latter case treats stemming as a part of query reformulation, which has been shown effective for web search [21]. Both cases are considered in this paper using two types of indexes. No stopword removal is done during indexing. For each topic, the description part is used as the query. A short list of 35 stopwords and some frequent stop patterns (e.g., "find information") are removed from the description query.

The query set of each collection is split into a training set and a test set. On the training set, the parameters λ_k are learned. On the test set, the learned parameters λ_k are used to assign weight to the reformulation tree generated from each test query. Specifically, ten-fold cross validation is used, where the query set is split into ten folds. Each time nine folds are used for training and one fold is used for test. This process repeats ten times.

Several baselines are compared. QL denotes the query likelihood language model [22, 31]. SDM denotes the sequential dependence model [19]. KC denotes the key concept method proposed by Bendersky et al [2]. Note that we do not report KC on ClueWeb, since the key concept query is not provided on ClueWeb in [2]. QL+SubQL and DM+SubQL [30] are the subset query distribution methods, which combine the original query with a distribution of subset queries. QL+SubQL uses QL for both the original query and the subset queries, while DM+SubQL uses SDM for the original query and uses QL for the subset queries. In this paper, QL+SubQL and DM+SubQL are trained using the global features mentioned in [30]. SDM, KC, QL+SubQL and DM+SubQL are the state-of-the-art techniques for verbose queries. SDM and KC can be classified as the "bag of words" representation, while QL+SubQL and DM+SubQL can be considered as the "query distribution" representation. Therefore, the comparisons with these baselines help show the advantages of the "reformulation tree" representation.

The proposed reformulation tree approach is denoted as RTree, which uses SDM as the underlying retrieval model. Two parameters are used during the tree construction, *SubNum* and *ModNum*, where *SubNum* denotes how many subset queries are kept in the reformulation tree and *ModNum* denotes among those kept subset queries how many are further modified to generate query substitutions. In this paper, *SubNum* takes all subset queries generated and *ModNum* is set as 10. The effect of these parameters will be explored in the following part of this paper.

The standard performance measures, mean average precision (MAP), precision at 10 (P10) and the normalized discounted cumulative gain at 10 (NDCG10), are used to measure retrieval performance. In order to improve readability, we report 100 times the actual values of these measures. The two-tailed t-test is conducted for significance.

The *Lemur 4.10* toolkit is used to build the index and run the query. The *ireval* package provided in the toolkit is used for evaluation and significance test.

6.1 Example

In Table 3, we show some examples of the generated reformulation trees. As mentioned previously, some stopwords and stop patterns are removed from the original query. Those words are kept to improve readability. Note that they are not used for retrieval and subset query generation.

Table 3 shows that the subset queries and the substituted queries are effectively combined within the same framework. For example, given the original query "what allegations have been made about enrons culpability in the california energy crisis", the reformulation tree first generates high quality subset queries "enrons culpability california energy crisis" and "california energy crisis" and then further modifies "california energy crisis" as two substituted queries "california gas prices" and "california electricity crisis".

Table 4: Comparisons of retrieval performance. * denotes significantly different from the baseline.

	Gov2			Robust04			Wt10g			ClueWeb		
	MAP	P10	NDCG10	MAP	P10	NDCG10	MAP	P10	NDCG10	MAP	P10	NDCG10
Non-stemmed Index												
QL	22.46	49.13	35.94	22.40	39.12	39.63	16.44	28.97	27.86	10.97	21.63	14.10
SDM	23.98	51.01	38.81	23.30	40.04	40.60	16.76	31.65	29.82	11.53	22.76	15.04
KC	24.88	50.87	37.72	23.87	40.76	40.75	17.45	30.82	29.55	n/a	n/a	n/a
QL+SubQL	23.36	50.81	37.96	22.85	39.28	39.98	16.81	29.79	28.48	11.01	21.84	14.16
DM+SubQL	24.82	53.36	40.55	23.65	40.32	41.15	18.25	31.13	30.71	11.54	21.94	14.85
RTree	**26.70**	**53.96**	**40.78**	**25.07**	**42.33**	**42.64**	**19.44**	**34.02**	**32.80**	**12.94**	**26.43**	**18.05**
vs. QL	18.9%*	9.8%*	13.5%*	11.9%*	8.2%*	7.6%*	18.2%*	17.4%*	17.7%*	18.0%*	22.2%*	28.0%*
vs. SDM	11.3%*	5.8%*	5.1%*	7.6%*	5.7%*	5.0%*	16.0%*	7.5%*	10.0%*	12.2%*	16.1%*	20.0%*
vs. KC	7.3%*	6.1%*	8.1%*	5.0%*	3.9%*	4.6%*	11.4%*	10.4%*	11.0%*	n/a	n/a	n/a
vs. QL+SubQL	14.3%*	6.2%*	7.4%*	9.7%*	7.8%*	6.7%*	15.6%*	14.2%*	15.2%*	17.5%*	21.0%*	27.5%*
vs. DM+SubQL	7.6%*	1.1%	0.6%	6.0%*	5.0%*	3.6%*	6.5%	9.3%*	6.8%	12.1%*	20.5%*	21.5%*
Porter-stemmed Index												
QL	25.43	52.21	38.42	25.49	43.13	42.89	19.61	32.68	31.31	12.64	23.57	15.46
SDM	27.85	54.03	40.14	26.83	44.94	44.78	20.87	35.77	33.21	13.01	24.90	15.87
KC	27.52	53.83	39.10	25.97	41.65	42.29	21.01	34.02	32.29	n/a	n/a	n/a
QL+SubQL	26.19	53.36	39.51	25.81	43.01	43.23	20.11	32.06	30.93	12.94	25.00	16.37
DM+SubQL	28.49	55.91	**41.95**	26.99	44.86	44.94	21.98	35.05	33.45	13.29	24.08	15.58
RTree	**29.85**	**56.38**	41.84	**28.00**	**45.10**	**45.30**	**23.80**	**37.42**	**35.84**	**13.69**	**25.82**	**18.09**
vs. QL	17.4%*	8.0%*	8.9%*	9.8%*	4.6%*	5.6%*	21.4%*	14.5%*	14.5%*	8.3%	9.5%	17.0%
vs. SDM	7.2%*	4.3%*	4.2%*	4.4%*	0.4%	1.2%	14.0%*	4.6%	7.9%*	5.2%*	3.7%	14.0%*
vs. KC	8.5%*	4.7%	7.0%*	7.8%*	8.3%*	7.1%*	13.3%*	10.0%*	11.0%*	n/a	n/a	n/a
vs. QL+SubQL	14.0%*	5.7%*	5.9%*	8.5%*	4.9%*	4.8%*	18.3%*	16.7%*	15.9%*	5.8%	3.3%	10.5%
vs. DM+SubQL	4.8%*	0.8%	-0.3%	3.7%*	0.5%	0.8%	8.3%	6.8%*	7.1%*	3.0%	7.2%	16.1%*

Table 3: Examples of the reformulation tree. The top ranked nodes are displayed. In the original query Q, the stopwords and stop structures are italicized.

Q: *what* allegations *have been* made about enrons culpability *in the* california energy crisis

0.194 Q
0.133 enrons culpability california energy crisis
0.047 california energy crisis
    0.009 california gas prices
    0.008 california electricity crisis

Q: *give information on* steps *to* manage control *or* protect squirrels

0.148 Q
0.060 control protect squirrels
0.048 control squirrels
    0.013 control of ground squirrels
    0.012 control squirrel

Q: *what is the* state *of* maryland *doing to* clean up *the* chesapeake bay

0.089 Q
0.063 maryland chesapeake bay
    0.015 md chesapeake bay
    0.009 maryland chesapeake bay watershed
0.034 chesapeake bay
    0.007 chesapeake bay watershed
    0.006 chesapeake bay river

6.2 Retrieval Performance

The first experiment is conducted to compare the retrieval performance of the proposed RTree method with the baselines. The baseline methods include QL, SDM, KC, QL+Sub QL and DM+SubQL. The results are shown in Table 4. The best performance is bolded.

Table 4 shows that RTree outperforms all the baseline methods. Specifically, RTree performs better than the "bag of word" representations, SDM and KC. Using the non-stemmed index, RTree significantly improves SDM and KC on all four collections with respect to all three performance measures. For example, on ClueWeb, RTree improves SDM by 12.2% and 20.0% with respect to MAP and NDCG10, respectively. On Wt10g, RTree improves KC by 11.4% and 11.0% with respect to MAP and NDCG10, respectively. On the Porter-stemmed index, similar results are also observed. These results show that the "reformulation tree" representation is more effective than the "bag of words" representation on modeling verbose queries, since the former explicitly models the reformulated query, while the latter only considers words and phrases.

Furthermore, RTree also outperforms the "query distribution" representations, QL+SubQL and DM+SubQL. Using the non-stemmed index, RTree outperforms QL+SubQL and DM+SubQL on all four collections with respect to all three measures. Most of the improvements are significant. For example, on ClueWeb, RTree improves QL+SubQL by 17.5% and 27.5% with respect to MAP and NDCG10, respectively. Also, RTree improves DM+SubQL by 12.1% and 21.5% with respect to MAP and NDCG10, respectively. The results using the Porter-stemmed index are similar. These observations indicate that the "reformulation tree" representation is better than the "query distribution" representation,

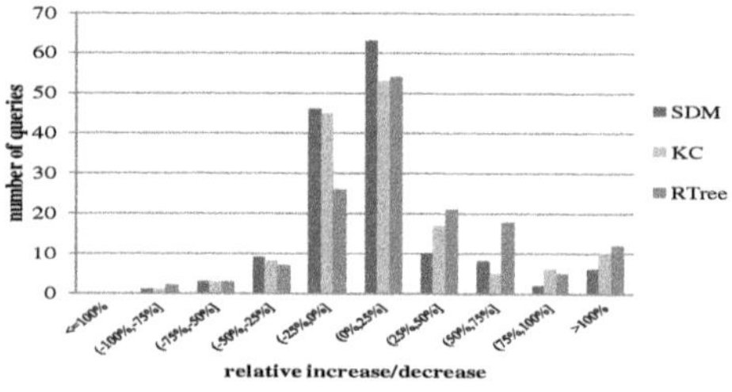

(a) Gov2

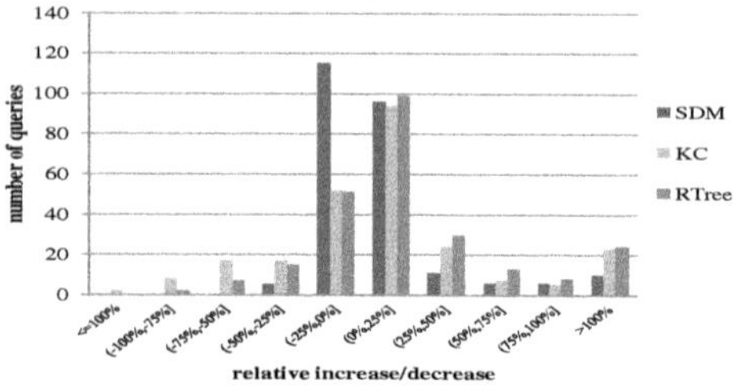

(b) Robust04

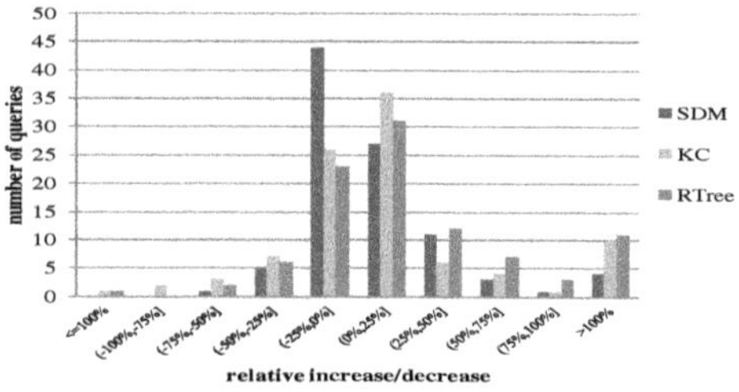

(c) Wt10g

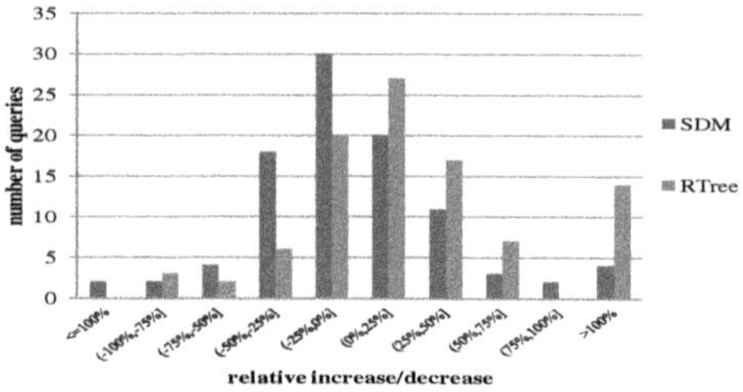

(d) ClueWeb

Figure 5: Analysis of relative increases/decreases of MAP over QL.

since the former effectively combines different reformulation operations within the same framework.

It is not surprising that RTree brings more improvements over the baselines using the non-stemmed index than using the Porter-stemmed index, since some effect of query substitutions, especially those generated using the morphologically similar words, is already provided by the Porter stemmer.

6.3 Further Analysis

Table 4 shows that RTree significantly outperforms the baseline methods. In this part, we make detailed comparisons between RTree and the baseline approaches.

First, we compare RTree with SDM and KC. Specifically, we analyze the number of queries each approach increases or decreases over QL. Fig 5 shows the histograms of SDM, KC and RTree based on the relative increases/decreases of MAP over QL. The non-stemmed index is used in Fig. 5. Similar results are observed using the Porter-stemmed index.

Table 5: Comparisons with QL+SubQL and DM+SubQL. "+", "=" and "-" denote that RTree performs better, equal or worse than QL+SubQL and DM+SubQL with respect to MAP.

RTree	vs. QL+SubQL			vs. DM+SubQL		
	+	=	-	+	=	-
Gov2	71.81%	0.67%	27.52%	63.09%	0.67%	36.24%
Robust04	68.27%	0.00%	31.73%	63.05%	0.00%	36.95%
Wt10g	62.89%	2.06%	35.05%	62.89%	1.03%	36.08%
ClueWeb	65.31%	2.04%	32.65%	70.41%	2.04%	27.55%

Table 6: The effect of subset query selection and query substitution with respect to MAP

MAP	Gov2	Robust04	Wt10g	ClueWeb
SDM	23.98	23.30	16.76	11.53
KC	24.88	23.87	17.45	n/a
QL+SubQL	23.36	22.85	16.81	11.01
DM+SubQL	24.82	23.65	18.25	11.54
RTree-Subset	25.80	24.76	18.11	11.73
RTree	26.70	25.07	19.44	12.94

Fig. 5 shows that RTree improves more queries than SDM and KC. For example, on Gov2, RTree improves 110 queries out of the total 150 queries, while SDM and KC improve 89 and 91, respectively. On Robust04, RTree improves 174 queries out of the total 250 queries, while SDM and KC improve 129 and 153 queries, respectively. At the same time, RTree also hurts less queries than SDM and KC. These observations indicate that RTree is more robust than both SDM and KC.

Furthermore, we compare RTree with QL+SubQL and DM+SubQL. QL+SubQL and DM+SubQL only consider subset query selection, while RTree combines both subset query selection and query substitution. The comparisons between them indicate whether RTree effectively combines two query operations to improve verbose queries. Specifically, we analyze the percent of queries where RTree performs better than QL+SubQL and DM+SubQL, respectively. The results using the non-stemmed index are reported in Table 5.

Table 5 shows that RTree consistently outperforms QL+SubQL and DM+SubQL for 60%-70% queries on all four collections. These results indicate that RTree provides an effective way to combine different query operations, which significantly improves the retrieval performance of verbose queries.

6.4 Subset Selection vs. Query Substitution

RTree combines subset query selection and query substitution together using a two-level reformulation tree. Previous experiments have demonstrated the general effect of this approach. In this part, we split the effect of subset query selection and query substitution. Specifically, we propose a one-level reformulation tree, which only consists of subset queries. This one-level reformulation tree is denoted as RTree-Subset. The comparisons between RTree-Subset and other approaches using the non-stemmed index are shown in Table 6.

In Table 6, RTree-Subset outperforms the baseline methods, which indicates the effect of subset queries in the reformulation tree. When query substitutions are introduced, RTree further improves RTree-Subset. Thus, both subset selection and query substitution account for the performance

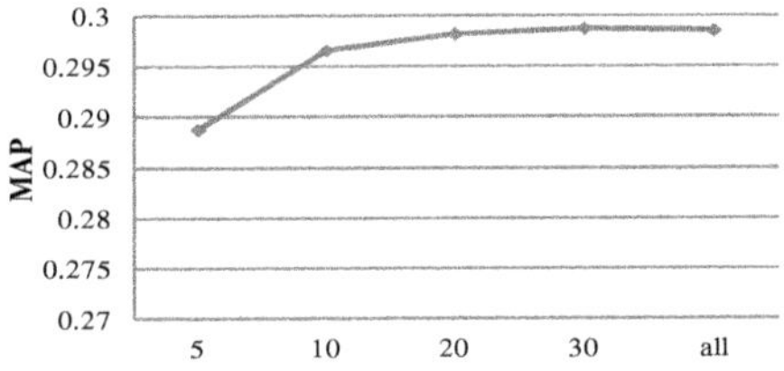

(a) Gov2

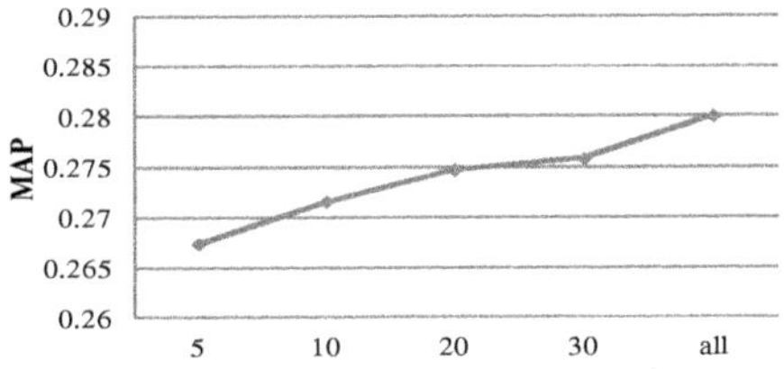

(b) Robust04

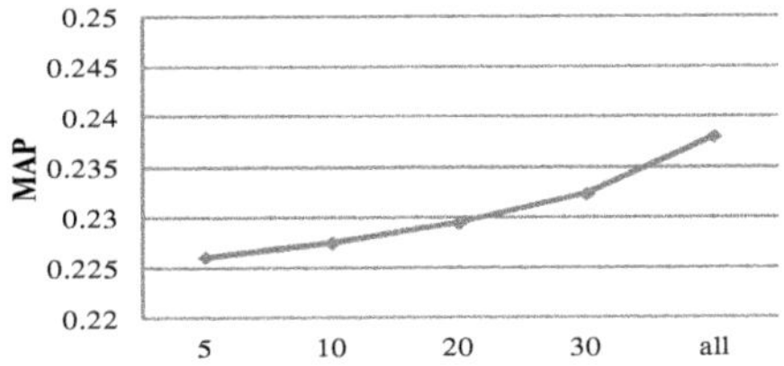

(c) Wt10g

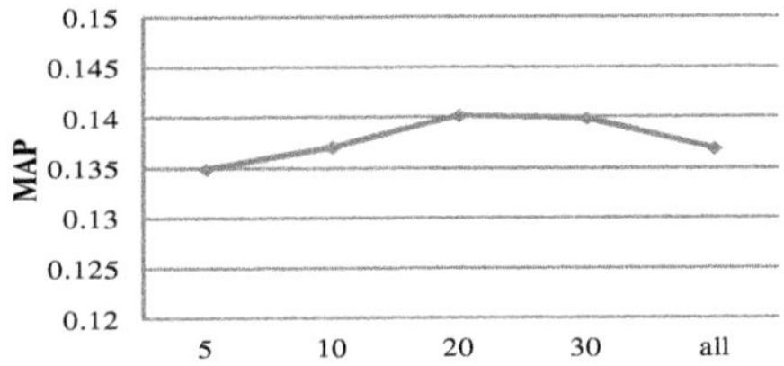

(d) ClueWeb

Figure 6: The effect of the parameter *SubNum*. x-axis denotes *SubNum* and y-axis denotes MAP.

of RTree. RTree-Subset also performs better than other subset query selection methods such as QL+SubQL and DM+SubQL.

6.5 Parameter Analysis

As described in Section 5.1, there are two parameters used during the process of constructing the reformulation tree, *SubNum* and *ModNum*. *SubNum* denotes the number of subset queries used in the reformulation tree and *ModNum* denotes the number of subset queries that are modified to generate query substitutions. In this subsection, we explore the effect of these two parameters. The Porter-stemmed index is used. Fig. 6 shows the effect of the parameter *SubNum*, where *SubNum* takes the values 5, 10, 20, 30 and "all", where *ModNum* is fixed as 10. Here, "all" indicates using all subset queries generated.

Fig. 6 shows that the best number of subset queries used in the reformulation tree is inconsistent. On Gov2, the performance becomes stable after using the top 20 subset queries. On Robust04 and Wt10g, the performance keeps increasing when more subset queries are considered. On ClueWeb, the performance drops when more than the top 20 queries are used. One possible explanation for these observations is provided. Robust04 and Wt10g are relatively small collections, thus using more subset queries is likely to retrieve more relevant documents. However, when the size of the collection becomes very large such as Gov2, using more subset queries does not help much retrieval all relevant documents. If the collection is not only big but also contains much noise such as ClueWeb, using more subset queries even hurts the performance.

Table 7: The effect of the parameter *ModNum* with respect to MAP

ModNum	Gov2	Robust04	Wt10g	ClueWeb
3	29.52	27.08	22.61	13.77
5	29.63	27.11	22.72	13.75
10	29.66	27.16	22.75	13.71

Table 7 displays the retrieval performance when *ModNum* takes three different values, i.e. 3, 5 and 10, where *SubNum* is set as 10.

Table 7 shows that there is not much performance change when *ModNum* is bigger than 3, which indicates that modifying the top three subset queries is enough to achieve most of the performance of RTree.

7. EFFICIENCY

We now discuss the efficiency of using the reformulation tree model for retrieval. The online cost of this model comes from three aspects, i.e. reformulated query generation, query feature extraction, and retrieval.

The efficiency of the reformulated query generation depends on the reformulation operations involved. For example, generating the subset queries is very efficient. In contrast, generating query substitutions using the passage analysis is more time consuming, since it needs to analyze a lot of passages.

The efficiency of the query feature extraction also depends on the query features used. Some query features are expensive such as query clarity, while some features are relatively cheap such as the frequency in query logs.

Both of these steps can be optimized if large scale query logs are available. We can limit the reformulated queries to those appearing in query logs. In this way, instead of generating queries, we simply search the query logs, which can be efficiently implemented using the index. Also, all query features can be precomputed, which speeds up the query feature extraction.

In terms of the efficiency of retrieval, Eq. 1 shows that the retrieval score of each reformulated query ($sc(q_r, D)$) is required. At first glance, this appears to be inefficient, since we need to run multiple queries. However, this can be easily optimized. Eq. 7 shows that $sc(q_r, D)$ consists of the scores of the words and bigrams in q_r. Since all the reformulated queries in the reformulation tree are generated from the same original query, they share many words and bigrams. Thus, the scores of these words and bigrams can be reused by different reformulated queries. For example, the words and bigrams in the subset queries all come from the original query. Thus, we only need to calculate the scores for every word and bigram in the original query and then reuse these scores for each subset query. Further, although query substitutions may introduce new words and bigrams, the number of these new words and bigrams is limited. For example, Table 7 shows that query substitutions generated from the top three subset queries are sufficient to achieve good retrieval performance.

8. CONCLUSION

Complex queries pose a new challenge to search systems. In order to combine different query operations and model the relationships between the reformulated queries, a new query representation is proposed in this paper, where the original query is transformed into a reformulation tree. A specific implementation is described for verbose queries, which combines subset query selection and query substitution within a principled framework. In the future, this query representation will be applied to other search tasks involving complex queries such as the cross-lingual retrieval and diversifying the search results.

Acknowledgments

This work was supported in part by the Center for Intelligent Information Retrieval and in part by ARRA NSF IIS-9014442. Any opinions, findings and conclusions or recommendations expressed in this material are those of the authors and do not necessarily reflect those of the sponsor.

9. REFERENCES

[1] N. Balasubramanian, G. Kumaran, and V. Carvalho. Exploring reductions for long web queries. In *SIGIR10*, pages 571–578, 2010.

[2] M. Bendersky and W. B. Croft. Discovering key concepts in verbose queries. In *SIGIR08*, pages 491–498, Singapore, 2008.

[3] M. Bendersky, D. Metzler, and W. B. Croft. Learning concept importance using a weighted dependence model. In *WSDM10*, New York City, NY, 2010.

[4] P. Boldi, F. Bonchi, C. Castillo, D. Donato, A. Gionis, and S. Vigna. The query-flow graph: model and applications. In *CIKM08*, pages 609–618, 2008.

[5] Z. Cao, T. Qin, T.-Y. Liu, M.-F. Tsai, and H. Li. Learning to rank: from pairwise approach to listwise approach. In *ICML07*, pages 129–136, 2007.

[6] J. Guo, G. Xu, H. Li, and X. Cheng. A unified and discriminative model for query refinement. In *SIGIR08*, pages 379–386, Singapore, 2008.

[7] B. He and I. Ounis. Inferring query performance using pre-retrieval predictors. In *SPIRE04*, pages 43–54, 2004.

[8] J. Jeon, W. B. Croft, and J. H. Lee. Finding similar questions in large question and answer archives. In *CIKM05*, pages 84–90, 2005.

[9] V. Jijkoun and M. de Rijke. Retrieving answers from frequently asked questions pages on the web. In *CIKM05*, pages 76–83, 2005.

[10] R. Jones, B. Rey, O. Madani, and W. Greiner. Generating query substitutions. In *WWW06*, pages 387–396, Ediburgh, Scotland, 2006.

[11] G. Kumaran and J. Allan. A case for shorter queries, and helping users creat them. In *ACL07*, pages 220–227, Rochester, New York, 2007.

[12] G. Kumaran and V. R. Carvalho. Reducing long queries using query quality predictors. In *SIGIR09*, pages 564–571, Boston, MA, 2009.

[13] L. Larkey. A patent search and classification system. In *DL99*, pages 179–187, Berkeley, CA, 1999.

[14] V. Lavrenko and W. B. Croft. Relevance based language models. In *SIGIR01*, pages 120–127, New Orleans, LA, 2001.

[15] M. Lease. An improved Markov random field model for supporting verbose queries. In *SIGIR09*, pages 476–483, Boston, MA, 2009.

[16] M. Lease, J. Allan, and W. B. Croft. Regression rank: learning to meet the oppotunity of descriptive queries. In *SIGIR05*, pages 472–479, Salvador, Brazil, 2005.

[17] Q. Mei, K. Klinkner, R. Kumar, and A. Tomkins. An analysis framework for search sequences. In *CIKM09*, pages 1991–1994, 2009.

[18] D. Metzler and W. B. Croft. Combining the language model and inference network approaches to retrieval. *Information Processing and Management*, 40(5):735–750, 2004.

[19] D. Metzler and W. B. Croft. A Markov random field model for term dependencies. In *SIGIR05*, pages 472–479, Salvador, Brazil, 2005.

[20] D. Metzler and W. B. Croft. Latent concept expansion using markov random fields. In *SIGIR07*, pages 311–318, Amsterdam, the Netherlands, 2007.

[21] F. Peng, N. Ahmed, X. Li, and Y. Lu. Context sensitive stemming for web search. In *SIGIR07*, pages 639–646, Amsterdam, the Netherlands, 2007.

[22] J. M. Ponte and W. B. Croft. A language modeling approach to information retrieval. In *SIGIR98*, pages 275–281, Melbourne, Australia, 1998.

[23] M. F. Porter. An algorithm for suffix stripping. *Program*, 14(3):130–137, 1980.

[24] S. Riezler, A. Vasserman, I. Tsochantaridis, V. Mittal, and Y. Liu. Statistical machine translation for query expansion in answer retrieval. In *ACL07*, pages 464–471, Prague, Czech Republic, June 2007. Association for Computational Linguistics.

[25] Y. Z. S. Cronen-Townsend and W. B. Croft. Predicting query performance. In *SIGIR02*, pages 299–306, 2002.

[26] X. Wang and C. Zhai. Mining term association patterns from search logs for effective query reformulation. In *CIKM08*, pages 479–488, Napa Valley, CA, 2008.

[27] X. Xue and W. B. Croft. Representing queries as distributions. In *SIGIR10 Workshop on Query Representation and Understanding*, pages 9–12, Geneva, Switzerland, 2010.

[28] X. Xue and W. B. Croft. Modeling subset distributions for verbose queries. In *SIGIR11*, pages 1133–1134, 2011.

[29] X. Xue, W. B. Croft, and D. A. Smith. Modeling reformulation using passage analysis. In *CIKM10*, pages 1497–1500, 2010.

[30] X. Xue, S. Huston, and W. B. Croft. Improving verbose queries using subset distribution. In *CIKM10*, pages 1059–1068, 2010.

[31] C. Zhai and J. Lafferty. A study of smoothing methods for language models applied to ad hoc information retrieval. In *SIGIR01*, pages 334–342, New Orleans, LA, 2001.

Proximity-based Rocchio's Model for Pseudo Relevance Feedback

Jun Miao[1], Jimmy Xiangji Huang[2], Zheng Ye[2]
Information Retrieval and Knowledge Management Research Lab
[1]Department of Computer Science & Engineering, [2]School of Information Technology
York University, Toronto, Canada
jun@cse.yorku.ca, {jhuang, yezheng}@yorku.ca

ABSTRACT

Rocchio's relevance feedback model is a classic query expansion method and it has been shown to be effective in boosting information retrieval performance. The selection of expansion terms in this method, however, does not take into account the relationship between the candidate terms and the query terms (e.g., term proximity). Intuitively, the proximity between candidate expansion terms and query terms can be exploited in the process of query expansion, since terms closer to query terms are more likely to be related to the query topic.

In this paper, we study how to incorporate proximity information into the Rocchio's model, and propose a proximity-based Rocchio's model, called PRoc, with three variants. In our PRoc models, a new concept (proximity-based term frequency, ptf) is introduced to model the proximity information in the pseudo relevant documents, which is then used in three kinds of proximity measures. Experimental results on TREC collections show that our proposed PRoc models are effective and generally superior to the state-of-the-art relevance feedback models with optimal parameters. A direct comparison with positional relevance model (PRM) on the GOV2 collection also indicates our proposed model is at least competitive to the most recent progress.

Categories and Subject Descriptors

H.3.3 [**Information Search and Retrieval**]: Retrieval models, Relevance feedback

General Terms

Algorithms, Performance, Experimentation

Keywords

Pseudo Relevance Feedback, Rocchio's Model, Proximity-based Term Frequency, Query Expansion

Permission to make digital or hard copies of all or part of this work for personal or classroom use is granted without fee provided that copies are not made or distributed for profit or commercial advantage and that copies bear this notice and the full citation on the first page. To copy otherwise, to republish, to post on servers or to redistribute to lists, requires prior specific permission and/or a fee.
SIGIR'12, August 12–16, 2012, Portland, Oregon, USA.
Copyright 2012 ACM 978-1-4503-1472-5/12/08 ...$15.00.

1. INTRODUCTION

Pseudo relevance feedback (PRF) via query expansion (QE) is an effective technique for boosting the overall performance in Information Retrieval (IR). It assumes that top-ranked documents in the first-pass retrieval are relevant, and then used as feedback documents in order to refine the representation of original queries by adding potentially related terms. Although PRF has been shown to be effective in improving IR performance [4, 6, 9, 13, 23, 26, 28, 30, 36, 37, 40, 42] in a number of IR tasks, traditional PRF can also fail in some cases. For example, when some of the feedback documents have several incoherent topics, terms in the irrelevant contents are likely to misguide the feedback models by importing noisy terms into the queries. This could influence the retrieval performance in a negative way. It is partially because the query itself was ignored in the process of expansion term selection. To be more specific, the term associations between candidate terms and the query terms have been ignored in traditional PRF models.

Term proximity is an effective measure for term associations, which has been studied extensively in the past few years. Most of these studies focus on the term proximity within the original query and adapt this in ranking documents [3, 5, 8, 10, 15, 24, 31, 33]. Various methods of integrating proximity information into a retrieval process are introduced in these papers, and it has proven to be useful in discriminating between the relevant and non-relevant documents.

In the field of PRF, based on the assumption that terms closer to the query terms are more likely to be relevant to the query topic, there are several studies which investigated how to give more weight to these terms in the process of pseudo relevance feedback. For example, to this end, Vechtomova *et al.* [34] imported a distance factor which combined with Mutual Information (MI) for selecting query expansion terms. Lv *et al.* [16] proposed a positional relevance model (PRM) by using position and proximity information to solve this problem and obtain significant performance.

However, as far as we are aware, there is little work done on incorporating proximity information into the traditional Rocchio's feedback model. Although the Rocchio's model has been introduced in the information retrieval field for many years, it is still effective in obtaining relevant documents. According to [41], "BM25 [27] term weighting coupled with Rocchio feedback remains a strong baseline which is at least as competitive as any language modeling approach for many tasks." This observation is also supported in our preliminary experiments of this paper. Therefore, it is promising to make an extension of the Rocchio's model to take into account the proximity information.

In addition, it is unknown how to tackle the challenge of modeling the traditional statistics of expansion terms and the relationship between expansion terms and the query terms in a unified framework. In this paper, we propose a proximity-based feedback model based on the traditional Rocchio's model, called PRoc. Unlike the PRM model, we focus on the proximity of terms rather than the positional information. In our method, we estimate the weights of candidate expansion terms by taking their distance from query terms into account. Specifically, if a term is far away from the query terms in the feedback documents, it is proposed to be punished by discounting its weight because it is likely to be irrelevant to the query topic.

The main contribution of this paper is as follows. First, we study how to adapt the traditional Rocchio's model [28] for proximity information, and propose a proximity-based feedback model, called PRoc, in which the traditional statistics of expansion terms and the proximity relationship between expansion terms and the query terms are taken into account. Second, we propose to use three proximity measures. Unlike previous methods, the importance of query terms has been taken into account to measure the proximity information by proposing a new concept, namely proximity-based term frequency. Finally, extensive experiments on standard TREC collections have been conducted to evaluate our proposed feedback model from different aspects. We compare our proposed feedback model with strong feedback baselines. Our model can achieve significantly better performance over RM3 and the classic Rocchios' model.

The remainder of this paper is organized as follows: in Section 2 we review the related work. In Section 3, three methods for measuring the proximity and our proposed model, PRoc, are presented in details. In Section 4, we introduce the settings of the experiments. In Section 5, the experimental results are presented and discussed. A direct comparison is made to compare PRoc with the most recent work PRM. Finally, we conclude our work with a brief conclusion and future research directions in Section 6.

2. RELATED WORK

2.1 Pseudo Relevance Feedback

In information retrieval, PRF via query expansion is referred to as the techniques, algorithms or methodologies that reformulate the original query by adding new terms into the query, in order to achieve a better retrieval performance. There are a large number of studies on the topic of PRF. Here we mainly review the work about PRF which is the most related to our research.

A classical relevance feedback technique was proposed by Rocchio in 1971 for the Smart retrieval system [28]. It is a framework for implementing (pseudo) relevance feedback via improving the query representation, in which a set of documents are utilized as the feedback information. Unique terms in this set are ranked in descending order of their TFIDF weights. In the following decades, many other relevance feedback techniques and algorithms were developed, mostly derived under Rocchio's framework. For example, a popular and successful automatic PRF algorithm was proposed by [26] in the Okapi system; Amati *et al.* [2] proposed a query expansion algorithm in his divergence from randomness (DFR) retrieval framework. In addition, with the development of language model [21] in IR, a number of techniques (e.g. [13, 32, 42]) have been developed to fit in the language modeling framework. In addition, Robertson [25] proposed a theoretical feedback model that supports the assumption by using of the difference of term distributions to select and re-weight the expansion terms.

For PRF in the language modeling framework, we always exploit feedback information (e.g., the top-ranked documents set, $F = D_1, D_2, \ldots, D_{|F|}$), in order to re-estimate a more accurate query language model. For example, the model based feedback approach [42] is not only theoretically sound, but also performs well empirically. The essence of model based feedback is to update the probability of a term in the query language model by making use of the feedback information. Much like model-based feedback, relevance models [13] also estimate an improved query model. The difference between the two approaches is that relevance models do not explicitly model the relevant or pseudo-relevant document. Instead, they model a more generalized notion of relevance [18]. Lv *et al.* [14] have conducted a comparable study of five representative state-of-the-art methods for estimating improved query language models in ad hoc information retrieval, including RM3 (a variant of the relevance language model), RM4, DMM, SMM (a variant of model-based feedback approach), and RMM [13, 32, 42]. They found that SMM and RM3 are the most effective in their experiments, and RM3 is more robust to the setting of feedback parameters.

However, most of these PRF approaches estimate the importance (or probability) of the candidate expansion terms based on their statistics, while the proximity information is always ignored.

2.2 Term Proximity in Previous Work

Term proximity is the co-occurrences of terms within a specified distance. Particularly, the distance is the number of intermediate terms in a document. Plenty of work has been done to integrate term proximity into both probabilistic and language models. Keen [10, 11] firstly attempted to import term proximity in the Boolean retrieval model by introducing a "NEAR" operator. Buttcher *et al.* [3] proposed an integration of term proximity scoring into Okapi BM25 and obtain improvements on several collections. Rasolofo *et al.* [24] added additional weight to the top documents which contain query term pairs appearing in a window through a two-phase process, but the improvement is somewhat marginal. Song *et al.* [31] presented a new perspective on term proximity. Query terms are grouped into phrases, and the contribution of a term is determined by how many query terms appear in the context phrases. In order to make it clear that how we could model proximity and incorporate a proximity measure, Tao *et al.* [33] systemically studied five proximity measures and investigated how they perform in the KL-divergence retrieval model and the Okapi BM25 retrieval model. Under the language modeling framework, Zhao *et al.* [45] used a query term's proximate centrality as a hyper parameter in the Dirichlet language model. Lv *et al.* [15] integrated the positional and proximity information into the language model by a different way. They defined a positional language model at each position in documents by create virtual documents based on term probation.

All the above work focuses on how to utilize the proximity information of query terms to avoid documents which contain scattered query terms. This kind of documents should be punished because they are very likely to be irrelevant. For example, a document contains both "Japan" and "Earthquake" is possible to be irrelevant to the topic "Earthquake in Japan" if these two terms are not close in the context. It could be biased to only "Earthquake" and mention some technologies in "Japan" about "Earthquake". Term proximity is effective to discriminate against these types of documents. Although there have been plenty of efforts in integrating proximity heuristic into existing retrieval models, research work about how to utilize this information for pseudo relevance feedback is still limited. Vechtomova *et al.* [34] combined several distance factors with Mutual Information for selecting query expansion terms from windows or passages surrounding query term occurrences. However, marginal improvements were observed in the experiments. Lv *et al.* [16] presented two methods to estimate the joint probability of a term w with the query Q at every position in each feedback document. This is an extension of the state-of-the-art relevance model [13], and significant improvements were obtained on two collections. Besides the work presented [16, 34], it is difficult to find other systematical work about formally modeling term proximity heuristic in the context of pseudo feedback, especially in the classic Rocchio's model.

In this paper, we propose PRoc models which integrates the proximity information of terms into the traditional Rocchio's framework. Three kinds of proximity measures are introduced to estimate relevance and importance of the candidate terms. In order to integrate term proximity into the Rocchio's model, we re-interpret the definition of term frequency and introduce a new concept, proximity term frequency. Unlike in [34], we conduct our study on a mature feedback model which has proven to be effective. Instead, the work of Vechtomova *et al.* was based on the Mutual Information which failed to perform as well as the traditional feedback model. In contrast to the work in [16], we try to employ proximity heuristic in a formalistic framework which extensively differs from the language modeling framework. Indeed, we do not concern ourselves with the position of each candidate term as in [16]. Meanwhile, to confirm the effectiveness of our model, we compare the performance of PRoc with that of PRM in Section 5. The experimental results show that our proposed PRoc is at least competitive to the most recent work, PRM.

3. PROXIMITY-BASED ROCCHIO'S MODEL

In this section, we present the proposed proximity-based Rocchio's model, called PRoc. Specifically, we first briefly introduce the traditional Rocchio's model, and present the adaption of Rocchio's model for proximity information by proposing a new concept, namely proximity-based term frequency (ptf). Then we describe in details about how to adopt ptf in three investigated proximity measures.

3.1 Adaption of Rocchio's Model

Rocchio's model [28] is a classic framework for implementing (pseudo) relevance feedback via improving the query representation. It models a way of incorporating (pseudo) relevance feedback information into the vector space model (VSM) in IR. In case of pseudo relevance feedback, the Rocchio's model without considering negative feedback documents has the following steps:

1. All documents are ranked for the given query using a particular retrieval model. This step is called *first-pass retrieval*, from which the $|R|$ highest ranked documents are used as the feedback set.
2. Each document in the feedback set R is represented as a weighted term vector, annotated by r, by a certain weighting function, for example originally by the TFIDF weights [29].
3. The representation of the query is finally refined by taking a linear combination of the initial query term vector with the feedback document vector:
$$Q_1 = \alpha * Q_0 + \beta * \sum_{r \in R} \frac{r}{|R|} \quad (1)$$
where Q_0 and Q_1 represent the original and first iteration query vectors, r is the expansion term weight vector, and α and β are tuning constants controlling how much we rely on the original query and the feedback information. In practice, we can always fix α at 1, and only study β in order to get better performance.

Many other relevance feedback techniques and algorithms [2, 4, 26] are also derived under the Rocchio's framework. For example, Carpineto *et al.* proposed to compute the weight of candidate expansion terms based on the divergence between the probability distributions of terms in the top ranked documents and the whole collection. In this paper, we also take advantage of this distributional view. But we re-interpret the definition of *term frequency* in the KLD formula 2 instead of the distribution estimated from a set of top documents. We use the following function to rank the candidate terms:
$$score(w) = P(w|d) * log(\frac{P(w|d)}{P(w|C)}) \quad (2)$$
where $P(w|d)$ is the probability of candidate expansion term w in feedback document d, $P(w|C)$ is the probability in the retrieval collection C.

Traditionally, candidate terms are ranked by their weights in the feedback documents, and the weights are affected by term frequencies in these documents extensively. However, the normal term frequency cannot capture the characteristic that whether a candidate term occurs near or far away from the query, such that the candidate term may not be relevant to the query topic. In other words, if the occurrence of a term is far away from the query terms, it should not be counted in the effective term frequency because this term is very likely to be irrelevant to the query topic. Thus, we propose a new concept, proximity term frequency (ptf), which models the frequency of a term as well as the semantics to the query in terms of proximity. In order to adapt the proximity information, we re-interpret the definition of *term frequency* by proposing three kinds of proximity measures: window-based method, kernel-based method and the hyperspace analogue to language method. The main research challenge now we are facing is how to evaluate *ptf*. In the following subsections, we introduce three measures to compute the ptf. Meanwhile, the importance of query terms is also taken into account. A very frequent query term is likely to be close to many candidate terms, which makes it difficult to distinguish the related feedback terms. Inverse document frequency (*idf*) of query terms is integrated to calculate ptf.

3.2 Window-based Method

The first method adopts a simple window-based n-gram frequency counting method, which has been popular in previous studies on using term proximity for IR (e.g. [17, 20]).

The basic idea of the window-based n-gram counting method is to segment the document into a list of sliding windows, with each window having a fixed window size *wSize*. If a document has a length of *l*, and the window size is set to *wSize*, the document is then segmented into *l-wSize* sliding windows, where each window contains *wSize* consecutive tokens. For example, if a document has four tokens A, B, C, and D, and the window size is 3, there are two windows in this document, namely A, B, C and B, C, D. The n-gram frequency is then defined as the number of windows in which all n-gram terms co-occur. There could be two variants of the n-gram models, namely the *ordered* and *unordered* n-gram models. The ordered n-gram model takes the order of occurrences of the n-gram terms into account. For the same n-gram terms, the n-grams in which the composing n-gram terms appear in different orders are considered as different n-grams. In contrast, the unordered model ignores the order of occurrences of the n-gram terms. Actually, only a rough distance between terms is considered in this measure. If two terms are in the window, they are strongly related and the co-occurrence is counted in ptf.

$$ptf(t) = \sum_{i=1}^{|Q|} C(t, q_i) IDF(q_i) \tag{3}$$

where q_i is a query term, C(t, q_i) is the number of windows in which the candidate term and the query terms co-occur, $|Q|$ is the number of query terms, and $IDF(q_i)$ equals to $log(N - N_t + 0.5)/(N_t + 0.5)$. N is the number of documents in the collection, and N_t is the number of documents that contain q_i.

The n-gram counting method has the advantage of being straight-forward, and can be easily deployed in practice. It does not take the actual distance between query terms into account directly, and any n-gram terms appear together within a window is counted as one occurrence of the n-gram. If a term is very close to a query term, its co-occurrence count with the query term will be more than that of a term far away from this query term in the sliding windows. This variant of PRoc is denoted by `PRoc1` in the rest of this paper.

3.3 Kernel-based Method

Following to previous studies [16, 44], an alternative method we use is a kernel-based method to count the term frequency in a document. There are a number of kernel functions (e.g. Gaussian, Triangle, Cosine, and Circle [44]) which were used for measuring the proximity. Gaussian kernel has been shown to be effective in most cases. In this paper, we also use the Gaussian kernel to measure the proximity between a candidate expansion term t and a query term q.

$$K(t, q) = exp[\frac{-(p_t - p_q)^2}{2\sigma^2}] \tag{4}$$

where p_t and p_q are respectively the positions of candidate term t and query term q in a document, σ is a tuning parameter which controls the scale of Gaussian distribution. In other words, σ has a similar effect as the parameter *wSize* in window-based method. In order to keep the consistency with other proximity measures, we also use *wSize* to denote σ.

Different from the window-based method, the kernel-based method is a soft proximity measure. In particular, even if the appearance of a candidate term and a query term is not in a window of *wSize*, its weight can still be slightly boosted.

In this method, beside the average proximity to the query, we also take into account the importance of different query terms. Therefore, we build a representational vector for the query, in which each dimension is the weight of a query term by the inverse document frequency formula below, and then the proximity-based term frequency ptf in the Kernel-based method is computed as follows:

$$ptf(t) = \sum_{i=1}^{|Q|} K(t, q_i) IDF(q_i) \tag{5}$$

where q_i is a query term, $|Q|$ is the number of query terms, and $IDF(q_i)$ is the same as in PRoc1. N is the number of documents in the collection, and N_t is the number of documents that contain q_i. The second variant of PRoc is denoted by `PRoc2` in the rest of this paper.

3.4 HAL Method

The Hyperspace Analogue to Language (HAL) [12] is a computational modeling of psychological theory of word meaning by considering context only as the words that immediately surround the given word. The basic motivation is that when a human encounters a new concept, its meaning is derived via other concepts occurred within the same context.

An shown in [39], the HAL Space is automatically built from a corpus of text, defined as follows: for each term in a specified vocabulary V, a $|V| \times |V|$ matrix is built by moving a sliding windows of length *wSize* across the corpus, where $|V|$ is the number of terms in vocabulary V. All words within the window are considered as co-occurring with each other with strengths inversely proportional to the distance between them. The weightings of each co-occurred terms are accumulated over the corpus. Then, a term can be represented by a semantic vector, in which each dimension is the weight for this term and other terms as follows:

$$HAL(t'||t) = \sum_{k=1}^{wSize} w(k) n(t, k, t') \tag{6}$$

where k is the distance from term t' to t, n(t, k, t') is the co-occurrence frequency within the sliding windows when the distance equals k, and $w(k) = wSize - k + 1$ denotes the strength.

In this paper, we adapt the the original HAL model similarly as in [12]. In particular, in order to measure the proximity between a candidate expansion term and the original query, we restrict the context to the query terms, not all the co-occurred terms in the feedback documents. With this adaption, the resulting vector for each candidate term denotes a proximity relationship with the entire query. Like the Kernel-based method, we also take into account the importance factor of query terms in the same way. Then, the HAL based ptf is as follows:

$$ptf(t) = vec(t) \cdot vec(Q) = \sum_{i=1}^{|Q|} HAL(t||q_i) IDF(q_i) \tag{7}$$

$IDF(q_i)$ is the as in PRoc1

In the adaption of proximity information in PRF, ptf replaces the traditional term frequency in our approach.

The weighted HAL model includes the information of term distances and co-occurrence frequencies completely. It is the first time that this linguistic model is adopted to measure the proximity. The third variant of PRoc is denoted by `PRoc3` in the rest of this paper.

4. EXPERIMENTAL SETTINGS

4.1 Test Collections

In this section, we describe four representative test collections used in our experiments: Disk4&5, WT2G, WT10G, and GOV2, which are different in size and genre. The Disk4&5 collection contains newswire articles from various sources, such as Association Press (AP), Wall Street Journal (WSJ), Financial Times (FT), etc., which are usually considered as high-quality text data with little noise. The WT2G collection is a general Web crawl of Web documents, which has 2 Gigabytes of uncompressed data. This collection was used in the TREC 8 Web track. The WT10G collection is a medium size crawl of Web documents, which was used in the TREC 9 and 10 Web tracks. It contains 10 Gigabytes of uncompressed data.

The GOV2 collection, which has 426 Gigabytes of uncompressed data, is crawled from the .gov domain. This collection has been employed in the TREC 2004, 2005 and 2006 Terabyte tracks. GOV2 is a very large crawl of the *.gov* domain, which has more than 25 million documents with an uncompressed size of 423 Gigabytes. There are 150 ad-hoc query topics, from TREC 2004 - 2006 Terabyte tracks, associated to GOV2. In our experiments, we use 100 topics in TREC 2005 - 2006. The TREC tasks and topic numbers associated with each collection are presented in Table 1. As we can see from this table, we evaluate the proposed approach with a relative large number of queries. In all the experiments, we only use the *title field* of the TREC queries for retrieval. It is closer to the actual queries used in the real application and feedback is expected to be the most useful for short queries [42].

Table 1: The TREC tasks and topic numbers associated with each collection.

Collection	Task	Queries	Docs
Disk4&5	TREC 2004, Robust	301-450	528,155
WT2G	TREC8, Web ad-hoc	401-450	247,491
WT10G	TREC9, 10, Web ad-hoc	451-550	1,692,096
GOV2	TREC04-06, Web ad-hoc	701-850	25,178,548

In the process of indexing and querying, each term is stemmed using Porter's English stemmer [22], and stopwords from InQuery's standard stoplist [1] with 418 stopwords are removed. The MAP (Mean Average Precision) performance measure for the top 1000 documents is used as evaluation metric, as is commonly done in TREC evaluations. The MAP metric reflects the overall accuracy and the detailed descriptions for MAP can be found in [35]. We take this metric as the primary single summary performance for the experiments, which is also the main official metric in the corresponding TREC evaluations.

4.2 Baseline Models

In our experiments, we compare our PRoc models with the traditional combination of BM25 and Rocchio's feedback model. In addition, we also compare the proposed models with the state-of-the-art feedback models in the KL-divergence language modeling (LM) retrieval framework. In particular, for the basic language model, we use a Dirichlet prior (with a hyperparameter of μ) for smoothing the document language model as shown in Equation 8, which can achieve good performance generally [43]. Besides, this is also utilized as the basic model in [16].

$$p(w|d) = \frac{c(w_d) + \mu p(w|C)}{|d| + \mu} \tag{8}$$

where $c(w_d)$ is the frequency of query term w in document d, $p(w|C)$ is the probability of term w in collection C and $|d|$ is the length of document d. We train the parameter in the document language model in all the experiments in order to make fair comparisons, and focus on evaluating different ways of approaching the query-related topic for PRF.

For PRF in language modeling framework, we first compare our proposed model with the relevance language model [13, 14], which is a representative and state-of-the-art approach for re-estimating query language models for PRF [14]. Relevance language models do not explicitly model the relevant or pseudo-relevant document. Instead, they model a more generalized notion of relevance R. The formula of RM1 is:

$$p(w|R) \propto \sum_{\theta_D} p(w|\theta_D)p(\theta_D)P(Q|\theta_D) \tag{9}$$

The relevance model $p(w|R)$ is often used to estimate the feedback language model θ_F, and then interpolated with the original query model θ_Q in order to improve its estimation as follows:

$$\theta_{Q'} = (1-\alpha) * \theta_Q + \alpha * \theta_F \tag{10}$$

This interpolated version of relevance model is called `RM3`. Lv *et al.* [14] systematically compared five state-of-the-art approaches for estimating query language models in ad-hoc retrieval, in which RM3 not only yields impressive retrieval performance in both precision and recall metric, but also performs steadily. In particular, we apply Dirichlet prior for smoothing document language models [42].

4.3 Parameter Settings

As we can see from all the PRF retrieval models in our experiments, there are several controlling parameters to tune. In order to find the optimal parameter setting for fair comparisons, we use the training method presented in [7] for both the baselines and our proposed models, which is popular in the IR domain for building strong baselines. In particular, first, for the smoothing parameter μ in LM with Dirichlet prior, we sweep over values from 500 to 2000 with an interval of 100. Meanwhile, we sweep the values of b for BM25 from 0 to 1.0 with an interval of 0.1. Second, for parameters in PRF models, we empirically set the number of top documents to 20 in baseline PRF approaches and our PRoc models, the number of expansion terms ($k \in 10, 20, 30, 50$), and the interpolation parameter ($\beta \in 0.0, 0.1, \ldots, 1.0$). The window size for PRoc models are from 10 to 1500 with an interval 10. To evaluate the baselines and our proposed approach, we use 2-fold cross-validation, in which the TREC queries are partitioned into two sets by the parity of their numbers on each collection. Then, the parameters learned on the training set are applied to the test set for evaluation purpose as in [19].

Table 2: BM25 vs LM on the four TREC collections

	disk4&5	WT2G	WT10G	GOV2
BM25	0.2216	0.3124	0.2055	0.3034
LM	0.2247	0.2995	0.2063	0.3040

5. EXPERIMENTS AND ANALYSIS

5.1 Comparison of Basic Retrieval Models

As we mentioned in the previous section, the results of both models are obtained by 2-fold cross-validation. Therefore, it is fair to compare them on these four collections. BM25 slightly outperforms LM with Dirichlet prior on the WT2G collection. The results of these two models are almost the same over the Disk4&5, WT10G and GOV2 collections. This comparison indicates that the classic BM25 model is generally comparative to LM, and it is reasonable to use them as the basic models of the PRF baselines and our proposed model.

5.2 Comparison with PRF Models

From Table 2 to Table 6, we can clearly see that the average performance of PRF models is superior to the basic models in most cases. The classic Rocchio's model achieves improvements of 13.31%, -0.41%, 2.34% and 4.22% over BM25 on the Disk4&5, WT2G, WT10G and GOV2 collections, while RM3 obtains significant improvements over LM (4.05%, 7.98%, 3.64% and 3.32%) on all the four collections[1]. The effectiveness of pseudo relevance feedback is reconfirmed in this set of experiments. The classic Rocchio's model, fails to obtain improvement on the WT2G collection. This indicates that the Rocchio's model is not so robust as RM3 in this case. However, the Rocchio's model outperforms RM3 on the Disk4&5 collection significantly while RM3 performs better than the classic Rocchio's model on the WT2G collection. On the WT10G and GOV2 collections, their results are very close. Therefore, the Rocchio's model is generally comparable to RM3 so that it is still competitive to be a strong baseline.

In general, the performance of our proposed PRoc models is close on all the four collections, and all of them obtain more improvements over the basic models than the Rocchio's model and RM3. Specifically, from Table 3 to Table 6, we observe that all the three proximity-based Rocchio's models outperform the classic Rocchio's model (2.00% - 11.54%) and state-of-the-art RM3 (4.78% - 12.75%) significantly on all the four collections, which demonstrates the effectiveness of the three PRoc models. Although the measures in our PRoc models are different, all of them can successfully model the proximity information to some extent. Furthermore, the PRoc models perform more robustly than the classic Rocchio's model. It indicates that proximity plays an important role in discriminating relevant expansion terms from irrelevant ones.

In addition, from Table 4 we observe that PRoc3 outperforms the other two on the WT2G collection. On the other three collections, the performance of all the three PRoc models is very close. Generally, PRoc3 is slightly more effective than the other two PRoc models.

[1]The computation of these percentages is based on the average performance of the Rocchio's model and RM3 in Table 3~6 and MAPs in Table 2.

5.3 Effectiveness of Window Size

In our proposed PRoc models, there are two important parameters: (1) β in the feedback models controlling how much we rely on the original query and the feedback information and (2) window size parameter $wSize$ in the calculation of the proximity-based frequency. In our preliminary experiments, we observed that the influence of β is similar to that in [38], which investigated this parameter thoroughly. Since we mainly focus on the study of proximity evidence, detailed discussion about β will not be made in this paper.

$wSize$ is a key parameter for most proximity measures because it determines the distance in which terms are considered to be related. Thus, how to find an appropriate window size is very important for adapting the proximity measures. In this section, we attempt to discover some useful evidence for obtaining optimal $wSize$ values. Particularly, σ in PRoc2 is also interpreted as the window size.

From Figure 1 to 4, we show how the performance of our PRoc models changes with $wSize$ on different collections. We investigate a large range of $wSize$ from 10 to 1500, and the numbers of expansion terms are 10, 20, 30 and 50. Generally, the values of $wSize$ affect the performance of all the PRoc models extensively. In the second subfigure of Figure 4, the best MAP is 0.3205 when number of expansion terms is 50, and it falls to 0.2286 when $wSize$ is 1500. Almost 30% of performance is lost in this case.

For PRoc1, PRoc2 and PRoc3, although they are based on different measures, their curves fluctuate similarly on the same collection with different numbers of expansion terms. In contrast, the curves of each PRoc model are various extensively on different collections. This demonstrates that the influence of $wSize$ is collection-based. However, the best $wSize$ values for PRoc models are not the same, not even close to each other. For example, on the disk4&5 collection, optimal $wSize$ values for PRoc1 are 80, 50, 100 and 80 over 10, 20, 30 and 50 expansion terms, and the corresponding values for PRoc1 on WT10G is 100, 30, 10 and 10. Thus, the optimal values of $wSize$ depend on the proximity measures and the collections.

Another phenomenon is that the more the expansion terms are selected, the more the performance is affected by $wSize$. Normally, the performance of PRoc models drops when $wSize$ takes a relatively large value. However, to what extent the performance is affected is determined by the number of expansion terms. Specifically, in Figure 2, while $wSize$ is relatively small, the performance of PRoc models with 50 expansion terms is the best. However, when $wSize$ is larger than 200, the curves for 50 expansion terms are constantly below all the others. As an additional example, when the number of expansion terms is 30, the performance of PRoc models is the second worst in most cases when $wSize$ is 1500.

This is reasonable because the accumulated influence of proximity information for 50 expansion terms is larger than that of the small numbers. When $wSize$ increases, it is very likely that more noise is adopted in the expansion term selection. The more expansion term are there, the more noisy information is involved. Thus, the $wSize$ must be set very carefully when the number of expansion is larger than 30 in our case.

Additionally, the influence of $wSize$ on PRoc1 is more significant than on the other two over WT10G. Meanwhile, $wSize$ affects PRoc2 more significantly over GOV2 than PRoc1 and PRoc3. Overall, the PRoc3 model is less sensi-

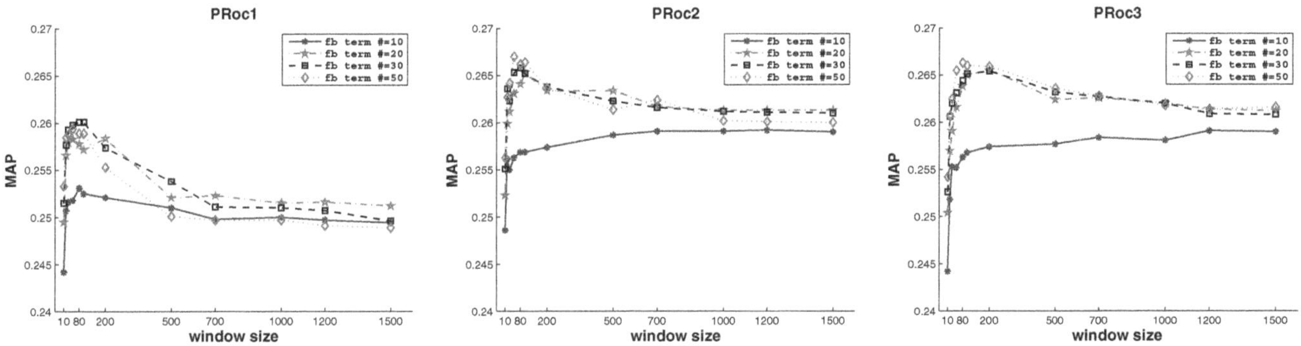

Figure 1: PRoc1, PRoc2 and PRoc3 over disk4&5 with 10, 20, 30 and 50 expansion terms

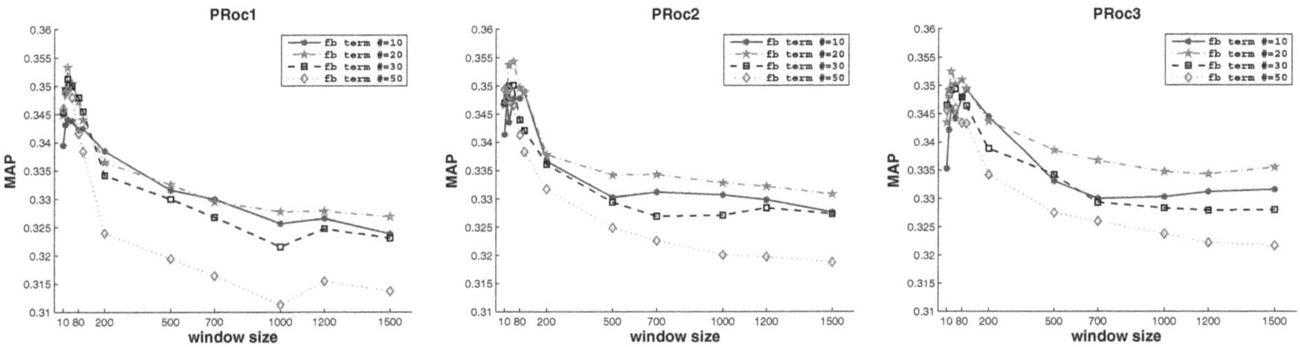

Figure 2: PRoc1, PRoc2 and PRoc3 over WT2G with 10, 20, 30 and 50 expansion terms

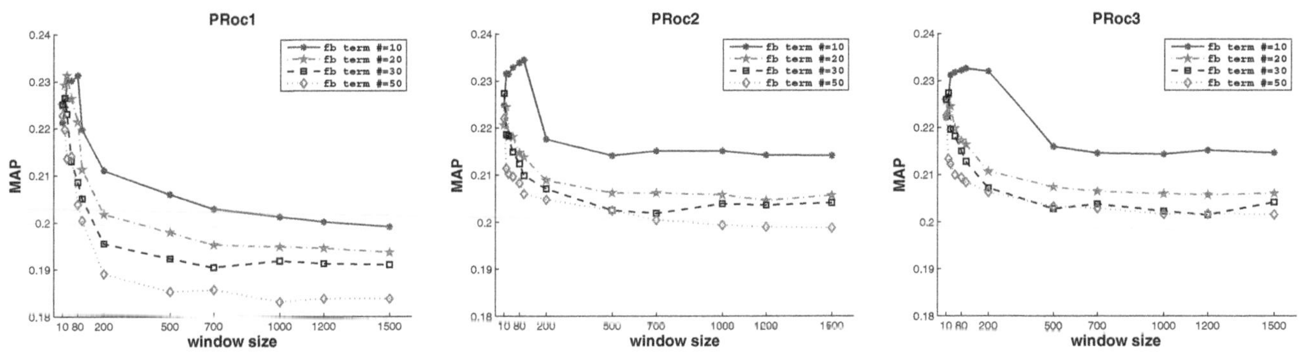

Figure 3: PRoc1, PRoc2 and PRoc3 over WT10G with 10, 20, 30 and 50 expansion terms

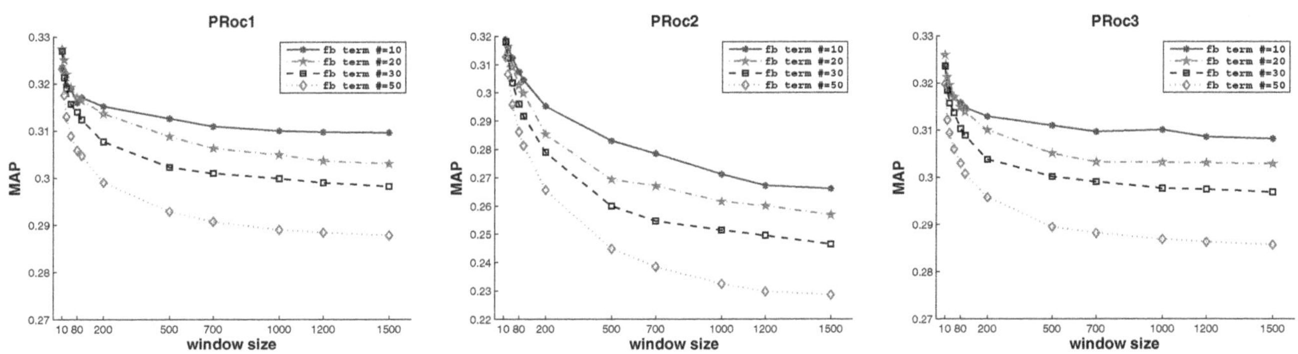

Figure 4: PRoc1, PRoc2 and PRoc3 over GOV2 with 10, 20, 30 and 50 expansion terms

Table 3: PRoc compares with BM25+Rocchio and LM+RM3 on Disk4&5. The percentages in the parenthesis are the improvement gains over the classic Rocchio's model and RM3. A "*" indicates a statistically significant improvement over the classic Rocchio's model baseline, and a "+" indicates a statistically significant improvement over the RM3 model baseline according to the Wilcoxon matched-pairs signed-ranks test at the 0.05 level. The bold phase style means that it is the best result.

# of feeback terms	PRoc1	PRoc2	PRoc3	BM25 + Rocchio	LM + RM3
10	0.2509^{+}	0.2523^{+}	$\mathbf{0.2571}^{*+}$	0.2463	0.2289
20	0.2567^{+}	0.2596^{+}	$\mathbf{0.2647}^{*+}$	0.2504	0.2326
30	0.2589^{+}	0.2595^{+}	$\mathbf{0.2662}^{*+}$	0.2545	0.2356
50	0.2578^{+}	0.2602^{+}	$\mathbf{0.2662}^{*+}$	0.2533	0.2382
Average	0.2561 (2.00%, 9.54%,)	0.2579 (2.71%, 10.31%,)	0.2636 (4.98%, 12.75%,)	0.2511	0.2338

Table 4: PRoc compares with BM25+Rocchio and LM+RM3 on WT2G

# of feeback terms	PRoc1	PRoc2	PRoc3	BM25 + Rocchio	LM + RM3
10	$\mathbf{0.3415}^{*+}$	$\mathbf{0.3415}^{*+}$	0.3385^{*+}	0.3091	0.3212
20	$\mathbf{0.3501}^{*+}$	0.3403^{*+}	0.3424^{*+}	0.311	0.3225
30	0.3452^{*+}	0.3456^{*+}	$\mathbf{0.3461}^{*+}$	0.3082	0.3255
50	0.3513^{*+}	0.3406^{*+}	$\mathbf{0.3525}^{*+}$	0.3162	0.3242
Average	0.3470 (11.54%, 7.30%,)	0.3420 (9.93%, 5.75%,)	0.3449 (10.86%, 6.65%,)	0.3111	0.3234

Table 5: PRoc compares with BM25+Rocchio and LM+RM3 on WT10G

# of feeback terms	PRoc1	PRoc2	PRoc3	BM25 + Rocchio	LM + RM3
10	0.2290^{*+}	0.2267^{*+}	$\mathbf{0.2308}^{*+}$	0.2143	0.2098
20	0.2272^{*+}	0.2219^{*+}	$\mathbf{0.2287}^{*+}$	0.2147	0.2168
30	0.2260^{*+}	$\mathbf{0.2264}^{*+}$	0.2261^{*+}	0.2084	0.2151
50	0.2202^{*+}	0.2206^{*+}	$\mathbf{0.2245}^{*+}$	0.2039	0.2136
Average	0.2256 (7.28%, 5.52%,)	0.2239 (6.47%, 4.72%,)	0.2275 (8.18%, 6.41%,)	0.2103	0.2138

Table 6: PRoc compares with BM25+Rocchio and LM+RM3 on GOV2

# of feeback terms	PRoc1	PRoc2	PRoc3	BM25 + Rocchio	LM + RM3
10	0.3271^{*+}	$\mathbf{0.3294}^{*+}$	0.3288^{*+}	0.3126	0.3071
20	0.3303^{*+}	$\mathbf{0.3325}^{*+}$	0.3315^{*+}	0.3164	0.3141
30	$\mathbf{0.3323}^{*+}$	0.3316^{*+}	0.3320^{*+}	0.3175	0.3167
50	0.3242^{*+}	$\mathbf{0.3313}^{*+}$	$\mathbf{0.3313}^{*+}$	0.3181	0.3183
Average	0.3285 (3.89%, 4.58%,)	0.3312 (4.74%, 5.44%,)	0.3309 (4.65%, 5.35%,)	0.3162	0.3141

tive than the other two PRoc models according to our experiments.

In summary, a big challenge is to find an optimal value since the value space is very large without any constraints. It is very time-consuming to try every possible values in the relevance feedback process. In order to narrow the value space of $wSize$, we attempt to find a rule to direct the searching of optimal values. Based on our experimental results, we conjecture that there are two factors affecting the choice of $wSize$: the average document length (ADL) and the size of a collection. Intuitively, if the average document length is large, it is more likely to have more than one topic in a document which leads to involve more irrelevant terms. Besides, as the increase of the size of collection, it is more likely to bring irrelevant documents into the feedback process.

In order to minimize the negative influence of noise, the values of $wSize$ should be relatively small especially when the ADL or collection size is large. Only the closest terms will be considered to avoid the selection of irrelevant terms. In our experiments, this rule is supported by some evidence. The ADL of Disk4&5 is 334 and there are only 528,155 documents in this collection. The performance of all the PRoc models is not affected by $wSize$ so extensively as that on the other collections. When there are only 10 expansion terms, the optimal value of $wSize$ can be as large as 1500. On WT10G, which has 1,692,096 documents and an average document length of 426, the optimal $wSize$ values are larger than 50 but smaller than 200. For WT2G, even it has less documents (247,491) than other collections, the optimal $wSize$ values are in a range of (30, 50) because of its long ADL (722). GOV2 is the largest collection with 25,178,548 documents in our experiments, and its ADL(679) is only smaller than that of WT2G. As a result, the optimal values of $wSize$ for GOV2 is the smallest one. It is always 10 in our case. In summary, we can use this rule to narrow the search space of optimal $wSize$ values. If a collection has plenty of documents or its ADL is large (e.g., more than 700), it is always good for us to start from 20 or smaller. Otherwise, we can try a larger starting value like 50 or more.

5.4 Comparison with PRM

We also compare our proposed model with the recently developed position relevance model (PRM) [16], which is an extension of the relevance model. In particular, PRM takes into account term positions and proximity with the intuition that words closer to query words are more likely to

Table 7: **PRoc compares with the classic Rocchio's model, RM3, PRM1 and PRM2 on Tera06 dataset. The bold phase style means that it is the best result.**

	PRoc3	Rocchio	RM3	PRM1	PRM2
MAP	0.3283	0.3156	0.3131	**0.3322**	0.3319
P@10	**0.5800**	**0.5800**	0.5043	0.5306	0.5490
P@30	**0.5260**	0.5167	0.4660	0.4884	0.4871
P@100	**0.3756**	0.3664	0.3576	0.3671	0.3741

be related to the query topic, and assigns more weights to candidate expansion terms closer to the query. To make the comparison fair, we train our parameters on the Terabyte05 topics and use Terabyte06 [2] topics on the GOV2 collection for testing as Lv. *et al.* did in [16]. Since we do not give results for the Million Query Track so far, we do not compare our method with PRM on the ClueWeb collection with the topics of this track. In [16], parameter μ in the Dirichlet smoothing is set to an optimal value of 1500, and we set b in our basic model, BM25, empirically to 0.3 [44]. As we mentioned previously, the performance of BM25 and LM with Dirichlet smoothing does not differ significantly on the GOV2 collection. Therefore, this setting will not affect the comparison. Since PRoc3 is the most robust and performs the best generally, it is selected to make this comparison. There are two versions of PRM, PRM1 and PRM2. The results of RM3, PRM1 and PRM2 are directly from [16].

In Table 7, PRoc3 outperforms the classic Rocchio's model and RM3 significantly in terms of the MAP metric, and it is only slightly inferior to PRM1 and PRM2 by 1.19% and 1.1% respectively. On the P@10, P@30 and P@100 metrics, PRoc3 obtains the best results over all the other four models and outperforms RM3, PRM1 and PRM2 significantly. All these significant tests are based on the Wilcoxon matched-pairs signed-ranks test at the 0.05 level. This shows that the retrieval accuracy of our proposed model is better than that of the PRF models in the language modeling framework in this case. Since the results of PRM1 and PRM2 are optimized, it is reasonable to state that our propose model is at least comparable to the most recent progress.

6. CONCLUSIONS AND FUTURE WORK

In this paper, a novel feedback model PRoc is proposed by incorporating proximity information into the classic Rocchio's model. Specifically, we model the statistics of expansion terms and their proximity relationship with query terms by introducing a new concept ptf. Three proximity measures, namely window-based method, kernel-based method and the HAL method, are then proposed for evaluating the relationship between expansion terms and query terms. The corresponding PRoc models based on these measures, PRoc1, PRoc2 and PRoc3, are evaluated extensively on four standard TREC collections. In general, PRoc is very effective and outperforms the state-of-the-art feedback models in different frameworks. Comparing the three variants of PRoc, PRoc3 is more effective and robust than PRoc1 and PRoc2. Meanwhile, our proposed PRoc is at least competitive to the most recent work, PRM. Additionally, we carefully analyze the influence of the parameter of $wSize$, and an empirical rule to narrow the value space of the window size is suggested.

[2] http://trec.nist.gov/data/terabyte.html

In the future, we will try to discover more about how to effectively adapt proximity into the probabilistic retrieval models. Another possible research direction is to find the exact relationship between the window size factor and the information of collections, e.g., the length distribution of documents. It is also interesting to apply our work to other retrieval frameworks, like DFR or the language modeling framework.

7. ACKNOWLEDGMENTS

This research is supported by the research grant from the Natural Sciences & Engineering Research Council (NSERC) of Canada and the Early Researcher Award/ Premier's Research Excellence Award. We thank four anonymous reviewers for their thorough review comments on this paper.

8. REFERENCES

[1] James Allan, Margaret E. Connell, W. Bruce Croft, Fangfang Feng, David Fisher, and Xiaoyan Li. INQUERY and TREC-9. In *TREC*, 2000.

[2] G. Amati. Probabilistic models for information retrieval based on divergence from randomness. *PhD thesis, Department of Computing Science, University of Glasgow*, 2003.

[3] Stefan Büttcher, Charles L. A. Clarke, and Brad Lushman. Term proximity scoring for ad-hoc retrieval on very large text collections. In *Proceedings of the 29th annual international ACM SIGIR conference*, SIGIR '06, pages 621–622, New York, NY, USA, 2006. ACM.

[4] G. Romano C. Carpineto, R. de Mori and B. Bigi. An information-theoretic approach to automatic query expansion. *ACM Transactions on Information Systems (TOIS)*, 19(1):1–27, 2001.

[5] Charles L.A. Clarke, Gordon V. Cormack, and Elizabeth A. Tudhope. Relevance ranking for one to three term queries. *Information Processing Management*, 36(2):291 – 311, 2000.

[6] Kevyn Collins-Thompson. Reducing the risk of query expansion via robust constrained optimization. In *CIKM '09: Proceeding of the 18th ACM conference on Information and knowledge management*, CIKM '09, pages 837–846, New York, NY, USA, 2009. ACM.

[7] Fernando Diaz and Donald Metzler. Improving the estimation of relevance models using large external corpora. In *SIGIR '06: Proceedings of the 29th annual international ACM SIGIR conference*, pages 154–161, New York, NY, USA, 2006. ACM.

[8] Ben He, Jimmy Xiangji Huang, and Xiaofeng Zhou. Modeling term proximity for probabilistic information retrieval models. *Inf. Sci.*, 181(14):3017–3031, 2011.

[9] Xiangji Huang, Yan Rui Huang, Miao Wen, Aijun An, Yang Liu, Josiah Poon. applying data mining to pseudo-relevance feedback for high performance text retrieval. In *IEEE ICDM 2006*, page 295–306, 2006.

[10] E. Michael Keen. The use of term position devices in ranked output experiments. *J. Doc.*, 47:1–22, 1991.

[11] E. Michael Keen. Some aspects of proximity searching in text retrieval systems. *J. Inf. Sci.*, 18:89–98, 1992.

[12] Ruth Ann Atchley Kevin Lund, Curt Burgess. Semantic and associative priming in high-dimensional semantic space. In *Proceedings of the 17th CogSci*, pages 660–665, 1995.

[13] Victor Lavrenko and W. Bruce Croft. Relevance based language models. In *Proceedings of the 24th annual international ACM SIGIR conference*, SIGIR '01, pages 120–127, New York, USA, 2001. ACM.

[14] Yuanhua Lv and ChengXiang Zhai. A comparative study of methods for estimating query language models with pseudo feedback. In *CIKM '09: Proceeding of the 18th ACM conference on Information and knowledge management*, pages 1895–1898, New York, NY, USA, 2009. ACM.

[15] Yuanhua Lv and ChengXiang Zhai. Positional language models for information retrieval. In *Proceedings of the 32nd international ACM SIGIR conference*, SIGIR '09, pages 299–306, New York, NY, USA, 2009. ACM.

[16] Yuanhua Lv and ChengXiang Zhai. Positional relevance model for pseudo-relevance feedback. In *Proceeding of the 33rd SIGIR conference*, SIGIR '10, pages 579–586. ACM, 2010.

[17] Donald Metzler and W. Bruce Croft. A markov random field model for term dependencies. In *SIGIR '05: Proceedings of the 28th annual International ACM SIGIR Conference*, pages 472–479, New York, NY, USA, 2005. ACM.

[18] Donald Metzler and W. Bruce Croft. Latent concept expansion using markov random fields. In *SIGIR '07: Proceedings of the 30th annual international ACM SIGIR conference*, pages 311–318, New York, NY, USA, 2007. ACM.

[19] Donald Metzler, Jasmine Novak, Hang Cui, and Srihari Reddy. Building enriched document representations using aggregated anchor text. In *SIGIR '09: Proceedings of the 32nd international ACM SIGIR conference on Research and development in information retrieval*, pages 219–226, New York, NY, USA, 2009. ACM.

[20] Vassilis Plachouras and Iadh Ounis. Multinomial randomness models for retrieval with document fields. In *Proceedings of ECIR*, pages 28–39, 2007.

[21] Jay M. Ponte and W. Bruce Croft. A language modeling approach to information retrieval. In *SIGIR '98: Proceedings of the 21st annual international ACM SIGIR conference*, pages 275–281, New York, NY, USA, 1998. ACM.

[22] M. Porter. An algorithm for suffix stripping. *Program*, 14:130–137, 1980.

[23] Karthik Raman, Raghavendra Udupa, Pushpak Bhattacharyya, and Abhijit Bhole. On improving pseudo-relevance feedback using pseudo-irrelevant documents. In *ECIR*, pages 573–576, 2010.

[24] Yves Rasolofo and Jacques Savoy. Term proximity scoring for keyword-based retrieval systems. In Fabrizio Sebastiani, editor, *Advances in Information Retrieval*, volume 2633 of *Lecture Notes in Computer Science*, pages 79–79. Springer Berlin, Heidelberg, 2003.

[25] Stephen E. Robertson. On term selection for query expansion. *Journal of Documentation*, 46:359–364, January 1991.

[26] Stephen E. Robertson, Steve Walker, Micheline Hancock-Beaulieu, Mike Gatford, and A. Payne. Okapi at TREC-4. In *TREC*, 1995.

[27] Stephen E. Robertson, Steve Walker, Susan Jones, Micheline Hancock-Beaulieu, and Mike Gatford. Okapi at TREC-3. In *TREC*, pages 109–126, 1994.

[28] J. J. Rocchio. Relevance feedback in information retrieval. In *G. Salton, The SMART retrieval system: Experiments in automatic document*, pages 313–323, 1971.

[29] Gerald Salton. *The SMART Retrieval System.* Prentice Hall, New Jersey, 1971.

[30] Gerard Salton and Chris Buckley. Improving retrieval performance by relevance feedback. *Journal of the American Society for Information Science*, 41:288–297, 1990.

[31] Ruihua Song, Michael Taylor, Ji-Rong Wen, Hsiao-Wuen Hon, and Yong Yu. Viewing term proximity from a different perspective. In Craig Macdonald, Iadh Ounis, Vassilis Plachouras, Ian Ruthven, and Ryen White, editors, *Advances in Information Retrieval*, volume 4956 of *Lecture Notes in Computer Science*, pages 346–357. Springer Berlin / Heidelberg, 2008.

[32] Tao Tao and ChengXiang Zhai. Regularized estimation of mixture models for robust pseudo-relevance feedback. In *SIGIR '06: Proceedings of the 29th annual international ACM SIGIR conference on Research and development in information retrieval*, pages 162–169, New York, NY, USA, 2006. ACM.

[33] Tao Tao and ChengXiang Zhai. An exploration of proximity measures in information retrieval. In *Proceedings of the 30th annual international ACM SIGIR conference*, SIGIR '07, pages 295–302, New York, USA, 2007. ACM.

[34] Olga Vechtomova and Ying Wang. A study of the effect of term proximity on query expansion. *Journal of Information Science*, 32(4):324–333, August 2006.

[35] Ellen M. Voorhees and Donna Harman. Overview of the sixth text retrieval conference. *Information Processing and Management: an International Journal*, 36:3–35, July 2000.

[36] Ryen W. White and Gary Marchionini. Examining the effectiveness of real-time query expansion. *Inf. Process. Manage.*, 43(3):685–704, 2007.

[37] Jinxi Xu and W. Bruce Croft. Improving the effectiveness of information retrieval with local context analysis. *ACM Trans. Inf. Syst.*, 18(1):79–112, 2000.

[38] Zheng Ye, Ben He, Xiangji Huang, and Hongfei Lin. Revisiting rocchio's relevance feedback algorithm for probabilistic models. pages 151–161. AIRS, 2010.

[39] Zheng Ye, Xiangji Huang, and Hongfei Lin. A bayesian network approach to context sensitive query expansion. In *SAC*, pages 1138–1142, 2011.

[40] Zheng Ye, Jimmy Xiangji Huang, and Hongfei Lin. Finding a good query-related topic for boosting pseudo-relevance feedback. *Journal of the American Society for Information Science and Technology (JASIST)*, 62(4):748-760, 2011.

[41] ChengXiang Zhai. Statistical language models for information retrieval a critical review. *Found. Trends Inf. Retr.*, 2:137–213, March 2008.

[42] Chengxiang Zhai and John Lafferty. Model-based feedback in the language modeling approach to information retrieval. In *CIKM '01: Proceedings of the tenth international conference on Information and knowledge management*, pages 403–410. ACM, 2001.

[43] Chengxiang Zhai and John Lafferty. A study of smoothing methods for language models applied to information retrieval. *ACM Trans. Inf. Syst.*, 22(2):179–214, 2004.

[44] Jiashu Zhao, Jimmy Xiangji Huang, and Ben He. CRTER: using cross terms to enhance probabilistic information retrieval. In *Proceedings of the 34th international ACM SIGIR conference*, SIGIR '11, pages 155–164, New York, USA, 2011. ACM.

[45] Jinglei Zhao and Yeogirl Yun. A proximity language model for information retrieval. In *Proceedings of the 32nd international ACM SIGIR conference*, SIGIR '09, pages 291–298, New York, USA, 2009. ACM.

Modeling User Posting Behavior on Social Media

Zhiheng Xu, Yang Zhang, Yao Wu and Qing Yang
Institute of Automation
Chinese Academy of Sciences
Beijing, 100190, China
{xuzhiheng,yagzag,wuyao,qyang}@nlpr.ia.ac.cn

ABSTRACT

User generated content is the basic element of social media websites. Relatively few studies have systematically analyzed the motivation to create and share content, especially from the perspective of a common user. In this paper, we perform a comprehensive analysis of user posting behavior on a popular social media website, Twitter. Specifically, we assume that user behavior is mainly influenced by three factors: breaking news, posts from social friends and user's intrinsic interest, and propose a mixture latent topic model to combine all these factors. We evaluated our model on a large-scale Twitter dataset from three different perspectives: the perplexity of held-out content, the performance of predicting retweets and the quality of generated latent topics. The results were encouraging, our model clearly outperformed its competitors.

Categories and Subject Descriptors

H.4 [**Information Systems Applications**]: Miscellaneous; H.3.3 [**Information Search and Retrieval**]: Information filtering—*performance measures*

General Terms

Algorithms, Experimentation

Keywords

Twitter, user modeling, user behavior, topic model

1. INTRODUCTION

With the rising popularity of social media, better understanding of user posting behavior has become crucial for many personalization and information filtering applications, as well as for better site design and advertising policies. Towards this goal, existing works have examined the workloads of various social media websites [7, 13, 21], aimed at providing a global picture of user activity patterns on these websites. There are also studies focused more on individual user behavior, by analyzing the content users have created [30, 37, 41] or inferring from their social friends [9, 14, 40], to help users find interesting information or people.

While previous works on individual user behavior [9, 14, 30, 37, 40, 41] have simply assumed that users tend to publish content they are interested in or make friends with similar interest, however, reality is much more complicated due to different usage patterns and user intentions. For example, it is reported that users are easily attracted by breaking news [1, 27], and are likely to create conversation with their intimate friends [15, 20]. On the other side, friendship on social media does not necessarily indicate similar interest, since it may arise from different sources such as influence, homophily, environment and reciprocity [4]. All these problems require a more comprehensive model of user behavior on social media, which is the task we deal with in this paper.

Inspired by those early works [1, 15, 20, 27], we believe that when a user publishes a post, he is probably influenced by three factors: breaking news happens at that moment, posts published by his friends recently and his intrinsic interest. In light of this, we equally divide our experimental time period into time intervals, and within each time interval, we compute the distribution of breaking news and friends' timeline for each user, which are assumed as two external factors that might affect his posting behavior in the same time interval. Subsequently, by modeling user interest as a distribution over latent topics, we use a mixture latent topic model to represent user posting behavior, and present the inference of our model based on collapsed Gibbs sampling.

Our experiment is based on Twitter, a popular social media website. Since Twitter has attracted thousands of individuals and organizations with business intents (e.g., news channels, online brands and social spammers), we first built a dataset of 11,358 common users, and then collected all tweets published by those users and samples of their social friends during a 70-days experimental time period. We tested our model on this dataset and showed its superiority over the competitors. Although our work has been done in the context of Twitter, we expect the same results would hold for many other similar applications, such as Facebook updates and Google Buzz.

The main contributions of our work include:

1. We build a large and reasonable dataset for analyzing user posting behavior on Twitter.

2. A simple but effective method is used to recognize breaking news from Twitter streams in a certain time period.

Permission to make digital or hard copies of all or part of this work for personal or classroom use is granted without fee provided that copies are not made or distributed for profit or commercial advantage and that copies bear this notice and the full citation on the first page. To copy otherwise, to republish, to post on servers or to redistribute to lists, requires prior specific permission and/or a fee.
SIGIR'12, August 12–16, 2012, Portland, Oregon, USA.
Copyright 2012 ACM 978-1-4503-1472-5/12/08 ...$10.00.

3. We analyze the influence of different social relationships on user posting behavior, and quantitatively measure the influence between users.

4. We propose a mixture topic model to analyze user posting behavior, and demonstrate the superiority of our model from three different tasks.

The remainder of this paper is organized as follows: section 2 provides a brief review of related work, section 3 describes the way to build our dataset, section 4 formally presents our mixture model, followed by the results of our experiments in section 5. Finally we conclude in section 6.

2. RELATED WORK

2.1 Social Media

Social media has become indispensable to users recently. A rich set of studies has been conducted on various forms of social media, such as blogs, photo and video sharing communities, question/answering portals and social bookmarking sites, focused on different properties and applications of them. For example, Gruhl et al. studied the dynamics of information propagation in blogspace [12], Leskovec et al. analyzed the network structure and evolution on different information networks [24, 25], Agichtein et al. introduced a classification framework to extract high quality content on question/answering portals [3] and Benevenuto et al. tried to discover spammers on a video sharing community [6].

Among the various successful social media websites, Twitter, a microblogging service, has attracted considerable attention from research area recently. With a limit of 140 characters for each message, Twitter enables an even faster mode of communication and information propagation. Early works [15, 20] examined the usage patterns and network properties of Twitter, and revealed that Twitter was mainly used in two different ways: as an information platform or as a social network. Subsequently, to better leverage its great wealth of both textual and social information, researchers have used Twitter to discover breaking news [28, 36], detect natural disasters [35, 39], improve realtime web search [11], characterize media events [10] and identify influential users [41] or interesting content [9].

2.2 User Modeling

The massive amount of data generated by social media users has provided researchers with insights into user behavior. For instance, by analyzing workloads from three information networks, Guo et al. showed that users' posting behavior exhibited strong daily and weekly patterns. They also pointed out that different types of content would have different characteristics [13]. Benevenuto et al. used clickstream data from a social network aggregator to compare user behavior across different online social networks, and they further investigated social interactions on those networks [7]. These macroscopic analysis of user behavior provided interesting observations about general usage patterns on social media websites, but they might lack interpretations at an individual level. To reach a better understanding of individual user behavior, work [32] investigated the causality between individual behavior and social influence by observing the information diffusion among users, work [27] predicted a user's news interest from the user activities and the news trends, work [37] proposed a user interest model based on tags generated by users and their social friends, and the SVM classification framework was leveraged in [5, 6, 23] to detect spammers and content promoters on social media.

Within the research area of Twitter, few have been done to systematically analyze individual user behavior. Previous efforts about user modeling on Twitter simply built a "bag-of-words" profile for each user based on his tweets, and extracted key words [9], entities [2], categories [30] or latent topics [17, 41] for that user. Although existing works can to some extent help recognize important information about users, however, they failed to capture the real motivation of users to publish content, as user behavior can easily be affected by some external factors other than user interest. To reach a comprehensive model of user behavior, we propose a mixture model which incorporates three important factors that might trigger user posting behavior, namely breaking news, friends' timeline and user interest. Our model is under the framework of latent topic models, since the entity-based and category-based user modeling frameworks would require external knowledge bases such as Wikipedia and AlchemyAPI [1], which are time and resources consuming. Inspired by previous works on multiple text streams modeling [8, 18, 33], we present the inference of our model based on collapsed Gibbs sampling, and further test it on a large-scale Twitter dataset from three different tasks.

3. DATASET PREPARATION

We started by using Twitter's streaming API [2] to collect a random sample of the public tweets from March 10, 2011 to May 19, 2011 (the streaming API would return about 1% of all tweets each day, and is widely used for analyzing news on Twitter). After removing non-English tweets, the stream dataset contained 56,415,430 tweets published by 9,292,345 users, with an average of 805,935 tweets each day. This stream dataset was used to extract breaking news for each time interval on Twitter. Since Twitter imposes a rate limit on crawling posts of a specific user, it is difficult for us to analyze large amount of users. Thus we would like to build a relatively small dataset of common active users.

Specifically, we assumed that a user was common and active if he had (100-3000) friends/followers, (10-200) tweets per week and has been listed (1-50) times. Most common and active Twitter users were believed to fall into this category. We randomly picked 11,358 ordinary users as our experimental users, and crawled all their tweets during the 70-days experimental time period, yielding a dataset of 7,843,190 tweets. For each user, we crawled his entire social graph, including his followees, listers (people in the user-generated lists) and listfollowees (people in the user-followed lists). As it was difficult for us to collect tweets from all those friends, we created a sample of friends for each user, including all friends that have been retweeted or mentioned more than 4 times by him (on average 30 friends were chosen for each user), and 5 randomly picked followees, listers and listfollowees respectively. Finally the entire dataset of social friends contained 179,456 unique users, and we crawled all their posts during the experimental time period, yielding a dataset of 86,815,267 tweets.

Admittedly, our samples of social friends only contain small proportion of users' friends. However, as presented

[1] http://www.alchemyapi.com/

[2] https://dev.twitter.com/docs/streaming-api/

later in this paper, users' top retweeted/mentioned friends are much more influential than other social friends. Thus we believe that our dataset (which includes users' top retweeted/mentioned friends) is still to some extent reasonable for analyzing the influence of social friends.

4. MIXTURE MODEL OF USER BEHAVIOR

Imagine the situation when a common user publishes a post about iphone, the reason behind this behavior might be: (1) he is a fan of smartphones and has a long time focus on iphone (2) he is reminded by some big events about iphone, such as the release of Iphone 4S (3) he is attracted by a discussion about iphone raised by his close social friends. In light of this, user posting behavior can be represented as a mixture model of three different factors: breaking news, posts from social friends and the user's intrinsic interest. Specifically, given a user a in time interval T, the likelihood for him to generate a word w is regarded as a sample of the following mixture model (based on the bag-of-words assumption).

$$p_{Ta}(w) = \lambda_B p(w|\theta_B) + (1-\lambda_B)(\lambda_{a2} p_T(w|\theta_N) + \lambda_{a3} p_T(w|\theta_{aF}) + \lambda_{a0} p(w|\theta_{aI})) \quad (1)$$

In the formula above, θ_B is the background smoothing model using word frequency from the entire dataset, and λ_B is the mixing weight of the background model θ_B. $p_T(w|\theta_N)$ denotes the distribution of breaking news in time interval T, and $p_T(w|\theta_{aF})$ is the distribution of friends' timeline for user a in time interval T. All breaking news and friends' posts in the same time interval are assumed to have influence on user posting behavior, since it will be computationally expensive to consider what has happened before each user behavior. $p(w|\theta_{aI})$ means the distribution of a's interest, and is represented by a distribution over latent topics in this paper. λ_{a2}, λ_{a3} and λ_{a0} are the mixing weights of breaking news, friends' timeline and user interest for a respectively.

Notice that, for each user, the model uses different mixing weights, considering the difference between users in usage patterns. For instance, some users regard Twitter as an instant messaging tool and use it to communicate with their friends (where λ_{a3} should be big). On the other hand, some people consider Twitter to be an information platform and use it to release or seek information they are interested in (where λ_{a0} should be big). As presented later in this section, all mixing weights can be automatically learned during the training process.

In the following of this section, we first separately analyze the influence of breaking news and friends' timeline on user posting behavior, and compute their corresponding distributions. Then we view user interest as a distribution over latent topics, and use a latent topic model framework to represent our mixture model of user posting behavior.

4.1 Influence of Breaking News

To identify emerging news on Twitter, we borrow the idea from TwitterMonitor [28], where news is represented by a group of bursty keywords that suddenly appear in tweets at an unusually high rate. For each time interval T, a set of bursty keywords is extracted using equation (2):

$$score(w) = \frac{NT(w)}{NT} \frac{N}{N(w)} \sqrt{NT(w)} \quad (2)$$

Table 1: Bursty Words in 3 Time Intervals

Time interval	Bursty Words
2nd	tsunami japan earthquake 90999 quake redcross hawaii tsunamis prayers tokyo
50th	kate royal wedding william middleton abbey prince duchess mcqueen wills
53th	osama laden bin obama dead abbottabad death obl islamabad 1945

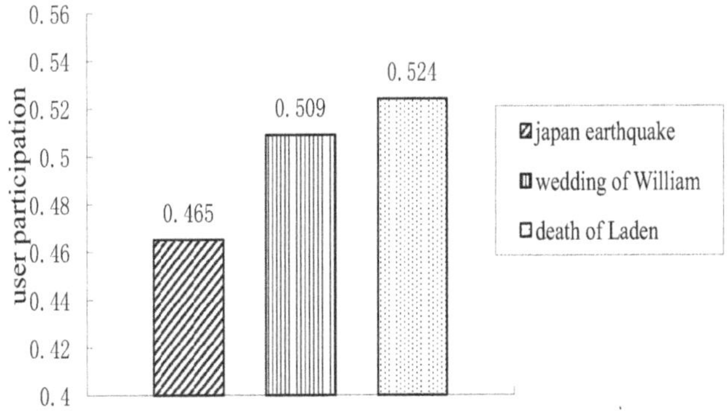

Figure 1: User Participation in 3 Events.

where $NT(w)$ represents the number of tweets containing word w in time interval T, NT is the number of tweets in T, $N(w)$ is the number of tweets containing word w in the entire dataset, and N is the number of tweets in the entire dataset. $\sqrt{NT(w)}$ is used to promote the scores of high frequency words and punish low frequency words. We set a threshold S for $score(w)$ (300 is chosen when T is 24 hours), and discard words below the threshold. It is worth to mention that we also try to set different threshold S, and find that there are no obvious change for the experimental results when S is larger than 50.

Table 1 gives the top 10 bursty words in the 2nd, 50th and 53th time intervals when T is set to be 24 hours, well represent 3 real world events: japan earthquake, wedding of prince William and the death of Osama bin Laden. Figure 1 shows user participation in the 3 events. Among the 11358 experimental users, 46.5% of users published tweets about japan earthquake in the 2nd time interval, 50.9% of users talked about the wedding of prince William in the 50th time interval and the death of Osama bin Laden attracted 52.4% of users in the 53th time interval, which demonstrate that breaking news has great impact on user posting behavior.

For each time interval T, we model the distribution of breaking news according to equation (3), where w' stands for any word that meets $score(w') \geq S$.

$$p_T(w|\theta_N) = \begin{cases} \frac{score(w)}{\sum_{w'} score(w')} & score(w) \geq S \\ 0 & score(w) < S \end{cases} \quad (3)$$

4.2 Influence of Social Friends

Twitter introduces a directed social relationship named "follow", which enables users to follow others to receive their tweets. To further help users organize their followees and filter incoming tweets, Twitter has launched another feature

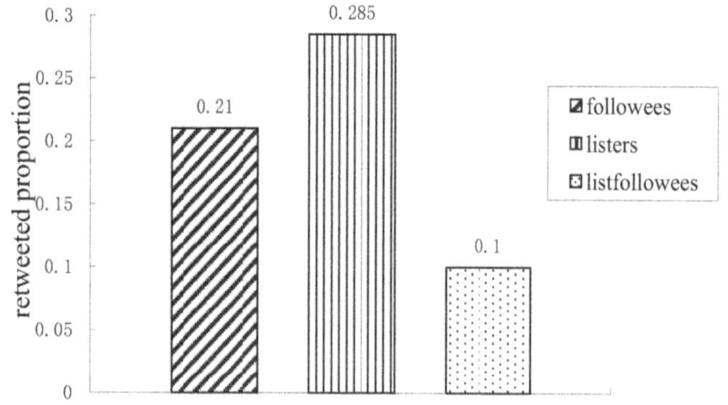

Figure 2: Influence of Friends on Retweet Behavior.

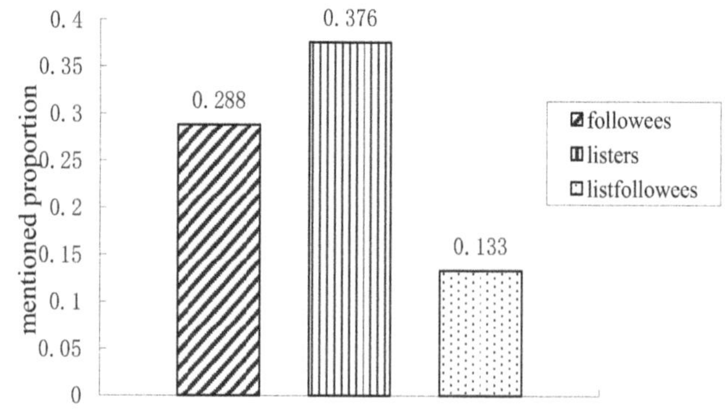

Figure 3: Influence of Friends on Mention Behavior.

named "list" since November 2, 2009, which can group sets of users into categories. Users can create their own lists, add and delete list members, or just follow other users' lists. Besides these two explicit relationships, there are two implicit relationships indicated by tweets, namely "retweet" and "mention". The retweet operates as a citation of another user's tweet, with the form "RT @username", while mention acts as a response to another user's tweet, with the form "@username". Both retweet and mention are strong signals of social influence [22].

In our dataset, on average, each user has 644 followees. 39.8% of users have created at least 1 list, with an average of 169 people in each list, 37.2% of users have followed at least 1 list, with an average of 577 people in each list. 44.7% of users do not use list, which means list has not been used as widely as follow yet. Figure 2 analyzes the influence of followees, listers and listfollowees on user retweet behavior. During the 70-days experimental time period, on average, 21% of users' followees have been retweeted by them, 28.5% of listers have been retweeted and only 10% of users' listfollowees have been retweeted by them. The influence on user mention behavior is similar, as reported in figure 3, 28.8% of followees, 37.6% of listers and 13.3% of listfollowees have been mentioned respectively. The results show that listers have a little greater impact on users than followees, but listfollowees are far less important. However, most of users' social friends have not been retweeted or mentioned, which means that the explicit relationships on Twitter do not necessarily indicate strong influence [19]. As influence mainly exsits in the form of retweet and mention on Twitter, we assume that for each user, the more times a friend is retweeted or mentioned by him, the more influence that friend has on the user. To approximately verify this assumption, we build a "bag-of-words" profile for each user based on his tweets, and use TF-IDF algorithm to determine the word weight. Only the top 200 words are selected. For each experimental user, we compute the cosine similarities with his top retweeted friends, top mentioned friends, the random sample of his friends in section 3 (i.e., 5 listers, 5 followees and 5 listfollowees) and 5 random users that are not directly connected with him. As demonstrated in Figure 4, on average, the similarities with top retweeted and top mentioned friends are clearly higher than other friends, which proves that our assumption is reasonable. On the other side, the similarities with random listers, followees and listfollowees are almost the same as random users, which is consistent with our previous conclusion that explicit relationships on Twitter are

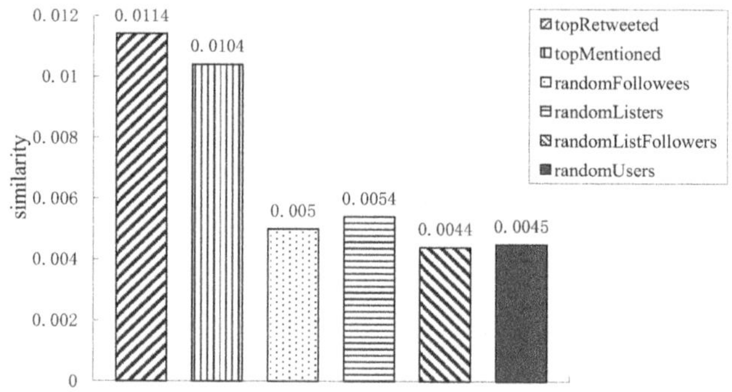

Figure 4: Similarity between Friends.

not strong symbols of influence. Based on the assumption, we use equation (4) to measure the influence of friend j on user i:

$$Influence(j,i) = \frac{X_{j,i}}{max_{j'} X_{j',i}} \quad (4)$$

Where $X_{j,i}$ is as:

$$X_{j,i} = \frac{NR(j,i) + NM(j,i) + 1}{log(N(j) + 2)} \quad (5)$$

Here $NR(j,i)$ is the number of times friend j is retweeted by user i, $NM(j,i)$ is the number of times friend j is mentioned by user i and $N(j)$ is the total number of tweets posted by user j. Due to the similar performance in figure 4, we view retweet and mention the same in equation (5).

Our measure of social influence is computationally efficient, and generally captures the strength of communications between friends, which is shown to accurately reflect the strength of relationship between friends [26, 40]. Admittedly, there are many other works on measuring influence in social networks. Since we mainly focus on modeling user posting behavior rather than computing social influence between friends, we leave it as future work to compare different measures of social influence.

For each user i in time interval T, we compute the distribution of his friends' timeline as:

$$p_T(w|\theta_{iF}) = \frac{\sum_j influence(j,i) * N_{jT}(w)}{\sum_j \sum_{w'} influence(j,i) * N_{jT}(w')} \quad (6)$$

In the equation above, $N_{jT}(w)$ means the number of times word w is tweeted by friend j during the time interval T.

If word w has never been tweeted by any friends during T, equation (6) is set to be 0.

4.3 Mixture Latent Topic Model Framework

We use a latent topic model framework to represent our mixture model of user posting behavior, where user interest is represented as a random mixture over latent topics, and can be automatically inferred during the training process.

Figure 5 shows the Bayesian graphical framework of the proposed model. The model can be viewed as an extension of author-topic model [34], a widely used variation of Latent Dirichlet Allocation (LDA) [29] to integrate authorship information of documents into topic modeling. The author-topic model assumes that each author in the document collection is represented by a distribution over topics, and each word is associated with two latent variables: an author and a topic. To generate each document from a document collection, it first chooses an author from a document's author list, samples a topic from topic distribution associated with the selected author, and then picks a word from the topic specific word distribution. As each tweet has only 1 author, the author-topic model here acts as to collect a document for each user based on all his tweets, and uses LDA to extract the topic distribution of this document.

The proposed model has a similar general structure to the author-topic model, but with additional machinery to handle the distribution of breaking news, friends' timeline and background words respectively. In particular, a latent random variable x is associated with each word, acts as a switch to determine whether the word is generated from the distribution of background model, breaking news, posts from social friends or user's intrinsic interest. x is sampled from a user-specific multinomial distribution λ_a, which in turn has a symmetric Dirichlet prior, η. A indicates the set of authors, T_1 is the set of latent topics, N_d means the length of tweet d and D is the set of tweets. The generative process of this model is as follows:

1. For each topic k, draw φ_k from Dir(β)
2. For each author a, draw θ_a from Dir(α)
3. For each author a, draw λ_a from Dir(η)
4. For the ith word w_i posted by a during T
   (a) Sample x_i from Multinomial(λ_a)
   (b) If $x_i = 0$
      A. Sample topic z_i from Multinomial(θ_a)
      B. Sample w_i from Multinomial(φ_{z_i})
   (c) Else

$$\text{Sample } w_i \text{ from } \begin{cases} p(w|\theta_B) & x_i = 1 \\ p_T(w|\theta_N) & x_i = 2 \\ p_T(w|\theta_{aF}) & x_i = 3 \end{cases}$$

4.4 Model Inference

Our inference of the latent variable x is inspired by previous works on multiple text streams modeling [8, 18, 33], where a word is "split" into different streams, and a latent variable is sampled to indicate which stream the word belongs to. For each word in a document, the assignment of the latent variable is decided by two factors: the distribution of streams in the document, and the importance of the word in each stream. Based on this idea, we view the distribution of background model, user interest, breaking news and friends' timeline as four different streams, and apply collapsed Gibbs sampling using the following updating rules:

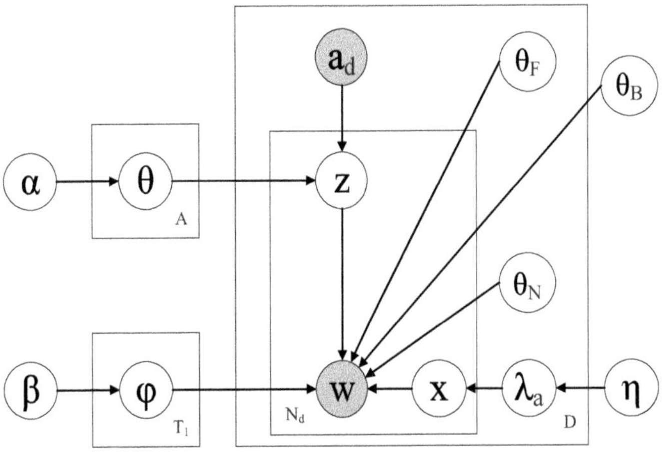

Figure 5: Bayesian Graphical Framework of the Mixture Model.

$$p(x_i = 0, z_i = t) \propto (1-\lambda_B)\frac{e_{a,0,-i}+\eta}{e_{a,-i}+3\eta}\frac{m_{a,t,-i}+\alpha}{m_{a,-i}+\alpha K}\frac{n_{t,w_i,-i}+\beta}{n_{t,-i}+\beta W} \quad (7)$$

$$p(x_i = 1) \propto \lambda_B p(w_i|\theta_B) \quad (8)$$

$$p(x_i = 2) \propto (1-\lambda_B) p_T(w_i|\theta_N)\frac{e_{a,2,-i}+\eta}{e_{a,-i}+3\eta} \quad (9)$$

$$p(x_i = 3) \propto (1-\lambda_B) p_T(w_i|\theta_{aF})\frac{e_{a,3,-i}+\eta}{e_{a,-i}+3\eta} \quad (10)$$

where $e_{a,j,-i}$and $e_{a,-i}$ are computed as:

$$e_{a,j,-i} = \frac{c_{a,j,-i}}{\sqrt{|\theta_j|}} \qquad (j = 0,2,3) \quad (11)$$

$$e_{a,-i} = \sum_j e_{a,j,-i} \qquad (j = 0,2,3) \quad (12)$$

Here $c_{a,j,-i}$ is the number of words written by a assigned to stream j (excluding the ith word), $|\theta_j|$ is the size of stream j, which means the number of non-zero words in the distribution of stream j (for the stream of user interest, we use $c_{a,0,-i}$ as an approximation). While previous works in [8, 18, 33] simply use $c_{a,j,-i}$ to denote the importance of stream j, in our work we smooth it with the size of the corresponding stream, since different streams have different size. $m_{a,t,-i}$ is the number of words posted by a assigned to topic t (excluding the ith word) and $n_{t,w,-i}$ is the number of times word w assigned to topic t (excluding the current one). m_a denotes the total number of words posted by a and n_t is the total number of words under topic t. K means the number of latent topics and W is the number of words.

The other parameters can be estimated as follows:

$$\theta_{a,t} = \frac{m_{a,t}+\alpha}{m_a+\alpha K} \quad (13)$$

$$\varphi_{t,w} = \frac{n_{t,w}+\beta}{n_t+\beta W} \quad (14)$$

$$\lambda_{a,j} = \frac{e_{a,j}+\eta}{e_a+3\eta} \qquad (j = 0,2,3) \quad (15)$$

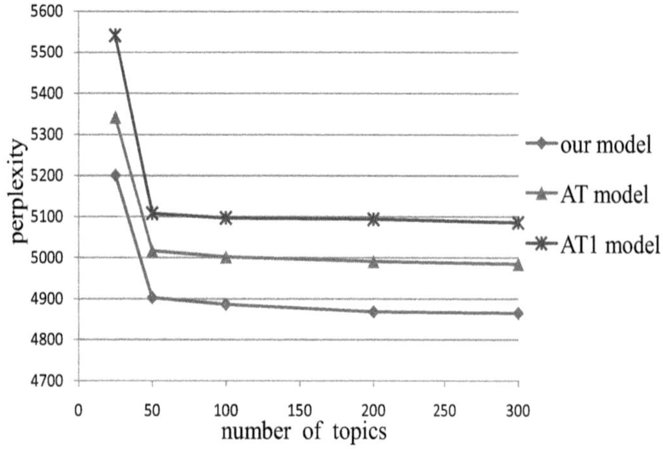

Figure 6: Perplexity of Held-out Content.

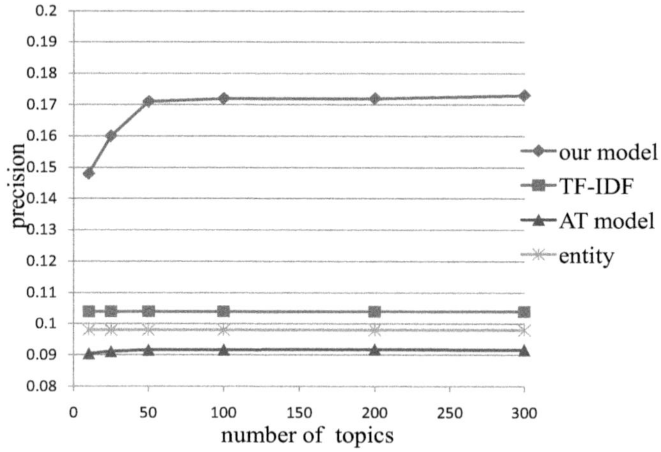

Figure 7: Precision of Predicting Retweets.

$$p(w|\theta_{aI}) = \sum_t \theta_{a,t} * \varphi_{t,w} \quad (16)$$

Hyper-parameters like α, β and η can be estimated using standard methods introduced in [31]. It is worth to mention that we also try to compute the weight of background model automatically using formula similar to (15), however the result is not as good as to set a reasonable weight before training starts (but it still outperforms our baseline).

5. EXPERIMENT

We examine the proposed model from three different perspectives: the perplexity of held-out content, the performance of predicting retweets and the quality of generated latent topics.

5.1 Perplexity of Held-out Content

The perplexity in this study means the performance of prediction for new tweets, which is a widely used method to judge the performance of a topic model. We compare the perplexities of two topic models: our model and the author-topic model. We randomly split the tweets of each user into 90% training tweets and 10% test tweets, and compute the perplexity of all test tweets according to:

$$exp(-\frac{1}{\sum_a m_a^{test}} \sum_a \sum_{w^{test}} log(p_a(w^{test}))) \quad (17)$$

where the predictive probability of a test word is denoted by $p_a(w^{test})$, and is computed by equation (1) in our model. A lower perplexity indicates better performance. We run each model five times and the perplexity of each model is average value. Figure 6 shows the results for the proposed model and author-topic model (AT model) with different number of topics. T is set to be 24 hours and λ_B is set to be 0.3 in the mixture model. As a result, the proposed model outperforms the author-topic model. We also add tweets published by users' close friends (top retweeted/mentioned friends) into the training data of author-topic model, however, as denoted by AT1 model, directly use posts from social friends even lower the performance. Notice that, the perplexities of both models do not change apparently when the number of topics is greater than 50.

5.2 Performance of Predicting Retweets

The main purpose of user modeling is to help users find interesting information from the overwhelming information streams. While in the context of Twitter, retweet is the most important signal of user interest, as users are prone to broadcast their favorite tweets to their followers. Thus, the performance of predicting retweets is a good standard to judge the performance of a user model.

Specifically, for each user in every time interval T, we randomly select a tweet that is retweeted by him (if exists), and mix it with 10 other tweets that are not retweeted by him. All the 11 tweets are published by his top retweeted/mentioned friends in the same time interval. This experiment can be seen as a real information filtering application: when a user is viewing his Twitter stream consists of 11 new tweets, he might find a tweet interesting and retweet it to his followers, on the other side, the other 10 tweets are not important to him relatively (since all the 11 tweets are published in the same time interval by his close friends, it is reasonable to assume that the user can see all of them at once). The task of a user model is to accurately predict which tweet can attract the user's attention and will be retweeted by him.

5.2.1 Compared with other user models

We first compare the performance of our model with three user models: the author-topic model in [41], the TF-IDF algorithm used in [9] and the entity-based user profile in [2] (The AlchemyAPI is used to extract entities). The predictive probability of each tweet d is computed according to equation (18) in our model, and the one with the highest probability is predicted as the retweet. T is set to be 24 hours and λ_B is set to be 0.3 again. For the three competitors, tweets are ranked based on their cosine similarities with user profiles. We repeat the experiment five times on different random sample sets and the results are the average value. Figure 7 shows the predictive precision of our model and all the other competitors.

$$p(d) = \frac{1}{N_d} \sum_{w \in d} p_a(w) \quad (18)$$

As a result, about 17.2% of retweets are correctly predicted in our model, which is clearly better than our competi-

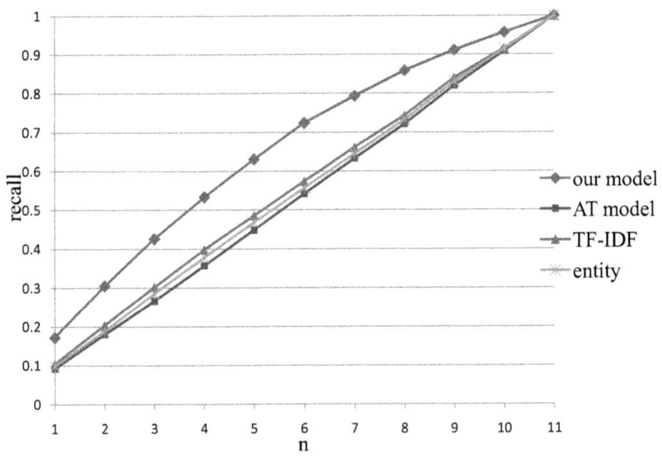

Figure 8: Recall of Predicting Retweets (5.2.1).

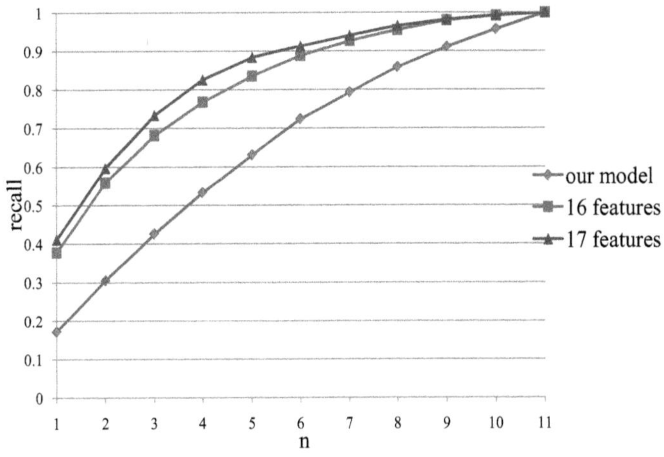

Figure 9: Recall of Predicting Retweets (5.2.2).

tors. The precision of TF-IDF algorithm, entity-based user profile and author-topic model are 10.4%, 9.8% and 9.2% respectively, which are only little better than random selection (9.1%). However, we must point out that the task is difficult since all candidate tweets are published by users' closest friends. Furthermore, all the four methods tend to reflect the similarities of tweets with users' general posting behavior, which are not especially intended for retweet prediction settings. Thus the relatively low precision of all models are reasonable. Nevertheless, the result still shows that our model can reach a better understanding of user posting behavior than the three competitors.

To avoid missing too much retweets, we should provide more candidates to increase the recall of all models. Assume that each time we provide the top n results returned by all methods, figure 8 gives the recall of retweets with different n. The number of topics is set to be 50 in our model. As demonstrated, our model outperforms the three competitors for all different n.

5.2.2 *Compared with a retweet prediction model*

We compare the performance of our model with a retweet prediction model. While retweet is recognized as the key mechanism for information diffusion on Twitter, a rich set of studies has been conducted to predict retweets [16, 38], mainly based on classification frameworks which incorporate different features related to tweets or authors.

We use logistic regression to build a retweet prediction model, leveraging 16 different features that are found to be important in previous retweet prediction models [16, 38], including author-based features (i.e., # of followers, # of followees, # of times listed, is he a verified user, his account age, # of tweets published totally and # of tweets published per day), tweet-based features (i.e., # of urls, # of hashtags, # of users mentioned, # of words, is the tweet a reply, is the tweet a retweet itself) and content-based features (i.e., the TF-IDF, entity and latent topic similarities of tweets with users' past tweets, which are the three competitors in 5.2.1).

We use the same test set in 5.2.1, and build another different training dataset based on the same method: for each group of 11 tweets, the retweet is labeled as positive example and the other 10 tweets are viewed as negative examples. To predict retweets, tweets are ranked based on their retweet probabilities returned by logistic regression.

Figure 9 gives the recall of predicting retweets with different n. The performance of our model remains unchanged to figure 8 because of the same test set. As shown in figure 9, the retweet prediction model (denoted by 16 features) indeed has large superiority over our model, since the proposed mixture model is not quite intended for retweet prediction tasks (our model only tries to reflect the likelihood of users to generate content, where other important factors associated with retweets are not considered, such as the global influence of the author and the syntactic features of tweets).

However, our mixture model can still provide an important feature for retweet models. As denoted by 17 features, the performance of the retweet model is improved after using the predictive probability of our model as a new feature (e.g., the recall of retweets is improved from 37.8% to 41.2% for top 1 result), which means that our model is of great importance for retweet prediction models. Notice that, in the 17-features retweet model, if we remove 64% tweets from a user's Twitter stream, we can still reach a recall of retweets over 80%, which is quite meaningful for social media websites like Twitter, where information overwhelming has already become a serious problem.

5.3 Impact of Model Parameters

We investigate the impact of λ_B and T on the model performance. Figure 10 shows the results of different λ_B when T is set to be 24 hours. The vertical axis on the left side of the graph is the perplexity of held-out content and the one on the right side means the precision of predicting retweets. As shown in figure 10, the model performance is generally similar when λ_B is small, and drops dramatically when λ_B is greater than 0.5. The best value for λ_B is between 0.2 and 0.3. Even if we set λ_B to be zero, the result is still satisfactory, which means the background model is not quite important to our method. We further fix λ_B to be 0.3 and analyze the influence of different time interval T in figure 11. When T is 24 hours, the model performance is the best. With T get longer, the model becomes coarse-grained and the performance drops. On the other side, the performance will also drop when T is shorter than 24 hours. According to

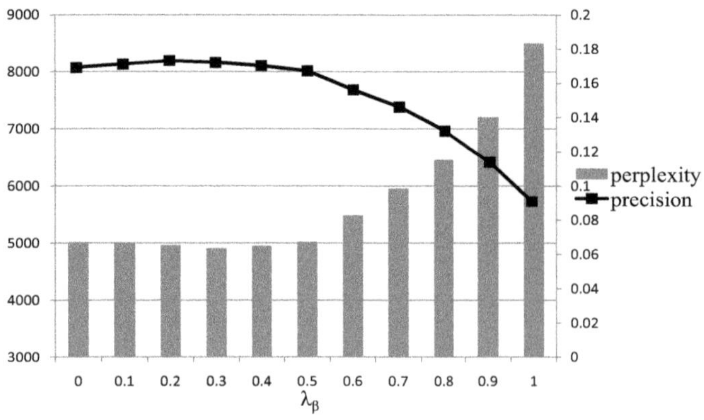

Figure 10: Influence of λ_B.

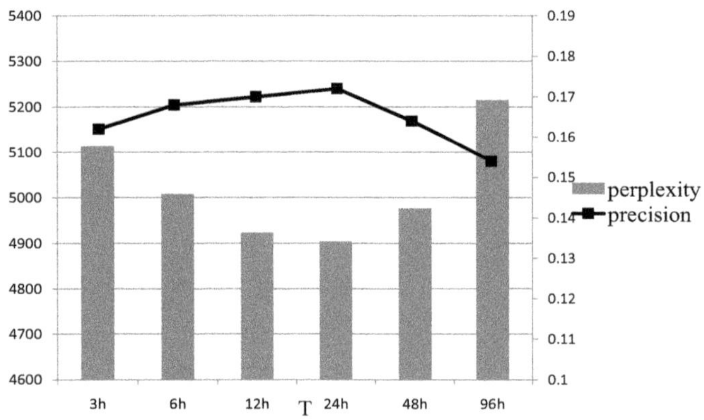

Figure 11: Influence of T.

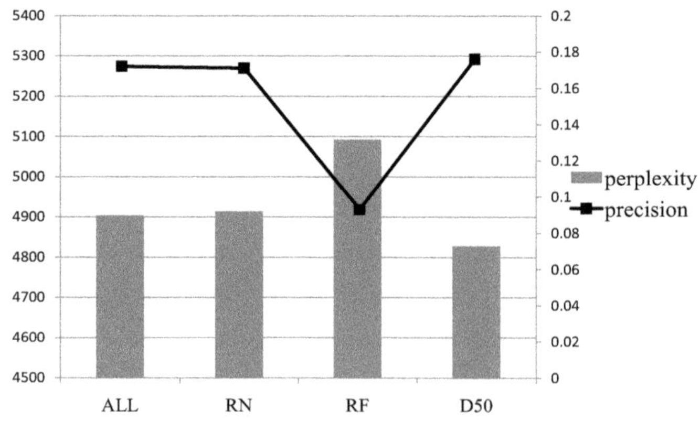

Figure 12: Importance of News and Friends' Posts.

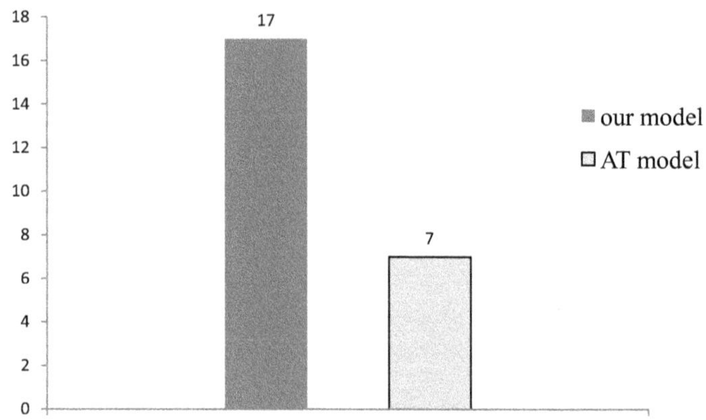

Figure 13: Labeled Result.

our observation, it might probably due to the data sparsity problem in each short time interval.

We further analyze the importance of breaking news and friends' timeline in our model respectively. As shown in figure 12, when removing breaking news from our model (denoted by RN), the performance remains almost the same, and when removing friends' timeline from our model (denoted by RF), the performance drops dramatically. This indicates that the distribution of friends' timeline contributes a lot to the mixture model, but the distribution of breaking news is of little importance. The little impact of breaking news might due to two reasons: 1. the distribution of breaking news is really sparse 2. it is quite possible that users' friends will publish posts about breaking news, which might also lower the importance of breaking news. However, the existence of breaking news is still meaningful, for example, as denoted by D50, the performance of our model is clearly better than average on the 50th day, when the wedding of prince William happened.

5.4 Quality of Latent Topics

Another typical method to judge the performance of topic models is to print top words for the latent topics and judge them by experience. We design an experiment to compare the latent topics generated by author-topic model and the proposed model. Specifically, we set the number of topics to be 50 and manually extract the same salient topics for both models. As a result, 8 latent topics are extracted, and the rest of latent topics are either meaningless topics or different topics between two models. We present the top 50 words of each latent topic to three labelers and ask them to label which one can better represent a topic. Due to the limit of space, table 2 only displays the top 10 words for each salient topic, and figure 13 gives the labeled result. On average, 71% of topics generated by the proposed model are labeled better, which shows that our model can reach a better understanding of latent topics behind Twitter streams.

5.5 Discussion

The results of our experiments prove that the proposed model clearly outperforms other user models. By comparing the perplexity of held-out content and the quality of generated latent topics, our mixture model is shown to be better than the traditional author-topic model, and within the task of predicting retweets, its superiority over other competitors is still obvious. Although our model is not comparable to retweet models in predicting retweets, however, it can still provide an important feature for them.

To reach a microscopic understanding of our mixture model, we empirically analyze how different factors work in our model based on a random sample of 30 users. First, we find that words associated with breaking news are generally well recognized. Second, for users with obvious interest (11 users are found to often publish tweets about some areas), our model can discover words related to user interest very well. Take a technology fan as an example, words such as "ipad" and "android" are easily assigned to his interest by our model. On the other side, if a user does not show strong

Table 2: Top 10 Words for Latent Topics

Topic 0		Topic 1		Topic 2		Topic 3	
mixture model	AT model	mixture model	AT model	mixture model	AT model	mixture model	AT model
film	film	libya	libya	canada	canada	game	state
movie	movie	war	people	election	vote	team	game
films	game	forces	news	canadian	election	coach	coach
screening	awesome	arab	israel	toronto	toronto	fans	draft
director	games	killed	killed	vote	harper	play	nfl
trailer	comic	gaddafi	forces	campaign	party	players	team
movies	time	military	police	government	campaign	sports	football
festival	trailer	israel	military	politics	canadian	games	players
interview	play	libyan	arab	harper	debate	basketball	ncaa
comedy	video	security	bin	vancouver	labour	season	big
Topic 4		**Topic 5**		**Topic 6**		**Topic 7**	
mixture model	AT model	mixture model	AT model	mixture model	AT model	mixture model	AT model
app	app	music	music	social	social	food	food
ipad	google	song	show	media	media	dinner	wine
iphone	ipad	album	tonight	twitter	great	wine	dinner
google	iphone	video	album	facebook	business	eat	beer
apple	apple	show	playing	blog	top	chocolate	eat
android	mobile	playing	band	post	stories	lunch	great
apps	twitter	songs	song	web	daily	cheese	lunch
data	android	listen	tour	marketing	twitter	restaurant	chocolate
code	facebook	listening	night	online	blog	delicious	love
web	video	tour	great	google	post	chicken	cheese

interest in any area, words assigned to user interest will be less reasonable, since it is difficult to model his topics of interest accurately. Third, the factor of social influence mainly captures words that are recently published by users' friends (and are not quite related to users' interest). Most words inspired by friends can be captured successfully, despite there are also many noise words included. Finally, some words out of all three factors can be handled by the background model, most of which are high-frequency words appear in daily life posts and conversations.

What is the potential value of our model for some real tweets recommendation systems? Admittedly, as demonstrated in the low accuracy of predicting retweets, it might still not be accurate enough to recommend tweets only based on our model. We believe that a good tweets recommendation system should based on classification frameworks which incorporate various of features (just like the retweet model in 5.2.2), and our model can be used as one feature to reflect the similarities of tweets with users' general posting behavior, as well as other user modeling frameworks. Furthermore, there are also many other important factors should be considered, such as the geographic information of users and their entire social graph, which we leave as future work due to the restriction of our current dataset.

Finally, we must point out that it is quite a difficult task to model user posting behavior on Twitter, since users can easily generate content with any intentions at different time and place. On account of this, our model is still a macro-level modeling of user behavior, as only three factors are included in it. Thus, the interpretation of our model at micro-level might not be good enough sometimes, especially for users with no obvious interest. Nevertheless, as shown in the results of our experiments, our model can still reach a better understanding of user posting behavior in most cases, and lay out a foundation to personalization and information filtering applications on Twitter.

6. CONCLUSION

In this paper, we propose a mixture model to analyze user posting behavior on social media. By assuming that user behavior is mainly influenced by three factors: breaking news, posts from social friends and user's intrinsic interest, our method is able to reach a more comprehensive model of user posting behavior on social media. We demonstrate the superiority of the proposed model on a popular social media website, Twitter, from three different tasks: the perplexity of held-out content, the performance of predicting retweets and the quality of generated latent topics. The results are satisfactory and our model clearly outperforms other traditional methods.

Our future work lies in several areas. First, our basic idea is not limited to latent topic models, and it will be an interesting direction to test it under other frameworks, such as the entity-based or category-based user modeling frameworks. Second, while it is widely agreed that user interest will change with time, our method does not model the change of user interest explicitly since the experimental time period is relatively short. However, to achieve a long time understanding of user posting behavior, it is necessary to incorporate time factors into user interest model. Third, there might be some special terms besides words in tweets, such as URLs, hashtags and usernames. We tend to investigate whether the presence of those terms can help improve our model performance. Finally, the distribution of breaking news and friends' timeline computed in our model are simple, and more accurate methods are worth further exploration. For example, to compute breaking news around users' geographic location, or try different measures of social influence in computing the distribution of friends' timeline.

7. REFERENCES

[1] F. Abel, Q. Gao, G.-J. Houben, and K. Tao. Analyzing temporal dynamics in twitter profiles for personalized recommendations in the social web. In *Proc. of WebSci*, 2011.

[2] F. Abel, Q. Gao, G.-J. Houben, and K. Tao. Analyzing user modeling on twitter for personalized news recommendations. In *Proc. of UMAP*, 2011.

[3] E. Agichtein, C. Castillo, D. Donato, A. Gionis, and G. Mishne. Finding high-quality content in social media. In *Proc. of WSDM*, 2008.

[4] A. Anagnostopoulos, R. Kumar, and M. Mahdian. Influence and correlation in social networks. In *Proc. of KDD*, 2008.

[5] F. Benevenuto, G. Magno, T. Rodrigues, and V. Almeida. Detecting spammers on twitter. In *Proc. of CEAS*, 2010.

[6] F. Benevenuto, T. Rodrigues, and V. Almeida. Detecting spammers and content promoters in online video social networks. In *Proc. of SIGIR*, 2009.

[7] F. Benevenuto, T. Rodrigues, M. Cha, and V. Almeida. Characterizing user behavior in online social networks. In *Proc. of IMC*, 2009.

[8] C. Chemudugunta, P. Smyth, and M. Steyvers. Modeling general and specific aspects of documents with a probabilistic topic model. In *Proc. of NIPS*, 2006.

[9] J. Chen, R. Nairn, L. Nelson, M. Bernstein, and E. H. Chi. Short and tweet: Experiments on recommending content from information streams. In *Proc. of CHI*, 2010.

[10] N. A. Diakopoulos and D. A. Shamma. Characterizing debate performance via aggregated twitter sentiment. In *Proc. of CHI*, 2010.

[11] A. Dong, R. Zhang, P. Kolari, J. Bai, F. Diaz, Y. Chang, Z. Zheng, and H. Zha. Time is of the essence : Improving recency ranking using twitter data. In *Proc. of WWW*, 2010.

[12] D. Gruhl, R.Guha, D. Liben-Nowell, and A. Tomkins. Information diffusion through blogspace. In *Proc. of WWW*, 2004.

[13] L. Guo, E. Tan, S. Chen, X. Zhang, and Y. Zhao. Analyzing patterns of user content generation in online social networks. In *Proc. of KDD*, 2009.

[14] J. Hannon, M. Bennett, and B. Smyth. Recommending twitter users to follow using content and collaborative filtering approaches. In *Proc. of RecSys*, 2010.

[15] C. Honeycutt and S. C.Herring. Beyond microblogging: Conversation and collaboration via twitter. In *Proc. of HICSS*, 2009.

[16] L. Hong, O. Dan, and B. D. Davison. Predicting popular messages in twitter. In *Proc. of WWW*, 2011.

[17] L. Hong and B. D. Davison. Empirical study of topic modeling in twitter. In *Proc. of SOMA*, 2010.

[18] L. Hong, B. Dom, S. Gurumurthy, and K. Tsioutsiouliklis. A time-dependent topic model for multiple text streams. In *Proc. of KDD*, 2011.

[19] B. A. Huberman, D. M. Romero, and F. Wu. Social networks that matter: Twitter under the microscope. 2008.

[20] A. Java, X. Song, T. Finin, and B. Tseng. Why we twitter: Understanding microblogging usage and communities. In *Proc. of WEBKDD*, 2007.

[21] H. Kwak, C. Lee, H. Park, and S. Moon. What is twitter, a social network or a news media? In *Proc. of WWW*, 2010.

[22] A. Leavitt, E. Burchard, D. Fisher, and S. Gilbert. New approaches for analyzing influence on twitter. *a publication of the Web Ecology project*.

[23] K. Lee, J. Caverlee, and S. Webb. Uncovering social spammers: Social honeypots + machine learning. In *Proc. of SIGIR*, 2010.

[24] J. Leskovec, L. Backstrom, R. Kumar, and A. Tomkins. Microscopic evolution of social networks. In *Proc. of KDD*, 2008.

[25] J. Leskovec, K. J.Lang, A. Dasgupta, and M. W.Mahoney. Statistical properties of community structure in large social and information networks. In *Proc. of WWW*, 2008.

[26] C.-Y. Lin, K. Ehrlich, V. GriffithsFisher, and C. Desforges. Smallblue: People mining for expertise search. *IEEE Multimedia Magazine*, 2008.

[27] J. Liu, P. Dolan, and E. R. Pedersen. Personalized news recommendation based on click behavior. In *Proc. of IUI*, 2010.

[28] M. Mathioudakis and N. Koudas. Twittermonitor: Trend detection over the twitter stream. In *Proc. of SIGMOD*, 2010.

[29] D. M.Blei, A. Y.Ng, and M. I.Jordan. Latent dirichlet allocation. *Journal of Machine Learning Research*, 2003.

[30] M. Michelson and S. A. Macskassy. Discovering users' topics of interest on twitter: A first look. In *Proc. of AND*, 2010.

[31] T. P. Minka. Estimating a dirichlet distribution. 2009.

[32] M. Papagelis, V. Murdock, and R. van Zwol. Individual behavior and social influence in online social systems. In *Proc. of HT*, 2011.

[33] M. Paul and R. Girju. Cross-cultural analysis of blogs and forums with mixed-collection topic models. In *Proc. of EMNLP*, 2009.

[34] M. Rosen-Zvi, T. Griffiths, M. Steyvers, and P. Smyth. The author-topic model for authors and documents. In *Proc. of UAI*, 2004.

[35] T. Sakaki, M. Okazaki, and Y. Matsuo. Earthquake shakes twitter users: real-time event detection by social sensors. In *Proc. of WWW*, 2010.

[36] J. Sankaranarayanan, H. Samet, B. E. Teitler, M. D.Lieberman, and J. Sperling. Twitterstand: News in tweets. In *Proc. of GIS*, 2009.

[37] J. Stoyanovich, S. Amer-Yahia, C. Marlow, and C. Yu. Leveraging tagging to model user interests in del.icio.us. In *Proc. of AAAI*, 2008.

[38] B. Suh, L. Hong, P. Pirolli, and E. H. Chi. Want to be retweeted? large scale analytics on factors impacting retweet in twitter network. In *Proc. of SocialCom*, 2010.

[39] S. Vieweg, A. L. Hughes, K. Starbird, and L. Palen. Microblogging during two natural hazards events: what twitter may contribute to situational awareness. In *Proc. of CHI*, 2010.

[40] Z. Wen and C.-Y. Lin. On the quality of inferring interests from social neighbors. In *Proc. of KDD*, 2010.

[41] J. Weng, E.-P. Lim, J. Jiang, and Q. He. Twitterrank: Finding topic-sensitive influential twitterers. In *Proc. of WSDM*, 2010.

Friend or Frenemy? Predicting Signed Ties in Social Networks

Shuang Hong Yang
College of Computing
Georgia Tech
shy@gatech.edu

Alex Smola
Yahoo! Research
smola@yahoo-inc.com

Bo Long
Yahoo! Labs
bolong@yahoo-inc.com

Hongyuan Zha
College of Computing
Georgia Tech
zha@cc.gatech.edu

Yi Chang
Yahoo! Labs
yichang@yahoo-inc.com

ABSTRACT

We study the problem of *labeling the edges* of a social network graph (e.g., acquaintance connections in Facebook) as either *positive* (i.e., trust, true friendship) or *negative* (i.e., distrust, possible frenemy) relations. Such signed relations provide much stronger signal in tying the behavior of online users than the unipolar Homophily effect, yet are largely unavailable as most social graphs only contain unsigned edges.

We show the surprising fact that it is possible to infer signed social ties with good accuracy *solely* based on users' behavior of decision making (or using only a small fraction of supervision information) via unsupervised and semi-supervised algorithms. This work hereby makes it possible to turn an unsigned *acquaintance network* (e.g. Facebook, Myspace) into a signed *trust-distrust network* (e.g. Epinion, Slashdot). Our results are based on a mixed effects framework that simultaneously captures users' behavior, social interactions as well as the interplay between the two. The framework includes a series of latent factor models and it also encodes the principles of balance and status from Social psychology. Experiments on Epinion and Yahoo! Pulse networks illustrate that (1) signed social ties can be predicted with high-accuracy even in fully unsupervised settings, and (2) the predicted signed ties are significantly more useful for social behavior prediction than simple Homophily.

Categories and Subject Descriptors
H.5.3 [Information Systems]: *Web-based Interaction*;
H.3.3 [Information Search and Retrieval]: *Information filtering* H.2.8 [Database Management]: *Data Mining*

General Terms: Algorithms, Performance

Keywords: Social ties, edge labeling, signed network, social behavior prediction, Homophily, sociological principles

1. INTRODUCTION

Social networks are playing an increasingly important role in shaping the business models of today's internet industry.

Permission to make digital or hard copies of all or part of this work for personal or classroom use is granted without fee provided that copies are not made or distributed for profit or commercial advantage and that copies bear this notice and the full citation on the first page. To copy otherwise, to republish, to post on servers or to redistribute to lists, requires prior specific permission and/or a fee.
SIGIR'12, August 12–16, 2012, Portland, Oregon, USA.
Copyright 2012 ACM 978-1-4503-1472-5/12/08 ...$10.00.

Not only are most emerging online services providing functionality to facilitate social interactions in their systems (e.g. last.fm, slashdot, Flikr, Yelp), but even many traditional internet systems are actively exploiting social networks to enhance their services, marketing and revenue, e.g., search engines (e.g., Bing), online retailers (e.g., Amazon), Web portals (e.g., Yahoo!). This is partly due to the widespread faith in the social effect of *Homophily* [20] that people socially acquainted tend to behave similarly. However, the extent to which this belief holds true is debatable — after all, it is unreasonable to expect two users who know each other (e.g., who are connected in Facebook) to behave alike in every aspect of their online decision making (e.g., purchase, ad click, movie rental, search intent, political view, sentimental moods). Instead, a much stronger signal of social ties is the network of trust relationships, since in many decisions we make, the opinions from the people we *trust* are what we really care about and what our decisions usually get influenced by. Unfortunately, this information is largely unavailable given the fact that the vast majority of social networks only contain acquaintance relationships, without distinguishing whom you trust from whom you don't.

Quite surprisingly, we show it is possible to infer a signed label for an acquaintance relationship — positive as trust (true friendship), negative as distrust (possible frenemy). In this way we make possible to turn an unsigned *acquaintance network* (e.g. Facebook, Myspace) to a signed *trust-distrust network* (e.g. Slashdot, Epinion). Moreover, by allowing us to tie the behavior of an online user to *whom he trusts* rather than *whom he knows*, the predicted signed relations are significantly more informative than Homophily for the purpose of behavior prediction.

1.1 Signed Social Ties

The main focus of this paper is (*i*) to predict the *signed social ties* (i.e., trust/distrust) out of the unsigned (i.e., acquaintance) relationships in social networks; and (*ii*) to examine how the predicted signed ties help behavior prediction. In particular, given that two users are socially connected (i.e., know each other), we would like to infer whether the connection is positive (e.g., trust, true friendship) or negative (e.g., distrust, possible frenemy); Furthermore, by tying the behavioral activities of online users with the inferred signed relationships, we examine how social targeting can be improved to promote online services, for example, to provide better matched search results, News articles, games, advertisements, or products [21, 18, 17, 26].

By predicting signed social ties, we enable the social connections in a traditional social network to capture much richer relationships reflecting either *positive* (e.g. trust, approval, true friendship) or *negative* (e.g. distrust, opposition, frenemy) interactions. This will substantially extend the acquaintance relationship in standard social networks (e.g. Facebook), and also the unipolar tie-strength analysis of traditional link prediction [19, 22, 5], to a meaningful new dimension — we are able to *en-sign*[1] an unsigned network by turning it to a signed network. Moreover, models designed for signed social ties also have the potential to improve our understanding of social relations and the structure of our society, shedding light to sociological principles in general [6, 22, 5, 15].

1.2 Behavior-Relation Interplay

The interplay between social relations and user's behavior of decision making is a key driving force underlying social activities [21, 18, 17]. On the one hand, social interactions can influence individual's behavior of decision making [10, 1] — for instance, users can learn from each other, following their trusted friends' good decisions and avoiding their mistakes. On the other hand, a user's behavior could in turn impact his relationships with others — for instance, a user with malicious behavior turns to get bad reputations from others. In this paper, we present a framework for predicting the signed social ties by capturing such interplay. Specifically, we explore the following "mixture of effects" assumptions about social relations and users' behavior of decision making:

1. The decision of a user is not decided solely by his own taste but also influenced by the opinions of other people whom he trusts.
2. The social relationship between two users depends not only on their intrinsic kinship but is also evolving according to the agreement between their opinions.

It is desirable to distinguish these two groups of factors when modeling behavior and social relationships. We present the *Behavior Relation Interplay* (BRI) model, a latent factor model that leverages behavioral evidence to infer social interactions and at the same time exploits the learned relations to tie users' behavior. The key idea in BRI is to associate latent factors with both users and items and to define coupled models to simultaneously characterize both the social interactions and behavioral evidences.

A key question is whether it is possible at all to infer signed ties in the absence of any labels. One of the more surprising results of our work is that it is, indeed, possible. To achieve this we design both unsupervised and semi-supervised algorithms for signed social tie prediction. In the unsupervised setting, we only observe the acquaintance connections but none of the sign labels, as is the typical case in the vast majority of the acquaintance social network sites such as Facebook. We show that BRI achieves fairly accurate predictions. The key idea is a mechanism called "*automatic sign determination*" that discovers the signs of social ties automatically from user activity data. We also examine semi-supervised prediction, where a small fraction of the sign labels are given. We show that BRI model provides comparable performance to the leave-one-out prediction results (i.e. all but one sign are observable) of the topology-based algorithm [14].

To further improve the prediction accuracy and deepen our understanding of signed social ties, we extend the BRI model to encode general sociological principles, particularly the theories of *status* and *structure balance* [6, 15]. One nice property of our model is that it naturally provides a mapping from a user to his social status and an interesting visualization of the network. We show the sociological principles are useful for signed social tie prediction.

Finally, we show that by predicting signed social ties, BRI models achieve significantly better performance in behavior prediction than models equipped with Homophily. In particular, BRI gains 5.8% improvement of RMSE in rating prediction on Epinion data, and 6.9% improvement of nDCG in top-k ranking on Yahoo! Pulse data.

As the paper consists of a series of progressive models, experimental results are presented right after each model is developed so as to motivate further enhancements. The paper is structured as follows: we first define the task and briefly reviews existing works in §2; the plain BRI model and learning algorithms are presented in §3; then §4 extends the model to encode sociological principles; §5 tests the proposed models in behavior prediction and §6 concludes.

2. BACKGROUND

2.1 Problem Definition

We consider a typical scenario in social networks where users routinely make decisions while actively interacting with one another. This motivates us to analyze the interplay between an individual user's behavior of decision making and the tie between users. Suppose we are given a set of users

$$\mathcal{U} = \{1, 2, \ldots, N\}$$

and a set of items (e.g., News articles, advertisement, retailing products, movies)

$$\mathcal{I} = \{1, 2, \ldots, M\}.$$

The users are connected by a social network represented by the graph $\mathcal{G}(\mathcal{U}, \mathcal{C})$. Here $\mathcal{C} = \{c_{uv}\}$ denotes the set of edges, i.e., $c_{uv} \in \{1, \text{missing}\}$ defines the acquaintance connection between a pair of users $(u, v) \in \mathcal{U}^2$. In the network, users actively make decisions, for example, by clicking links, purchasing products, rating movies. Formally, a decision is a mapping

$$y : \mathcal{U} \times \mathcal{I} \to \mathcal{Y}.$$

That is: user u makes a decision regarding item i with a response $y_{ui} \in \mathcal{Y}$ (e.g. u rates movie i with a score of y_{ui}). For convenience, hereafter we use u and v to index users, and i and j for items unless stated otherwise.

We are motivated by the following two tasks:

En-signing social relations. A signed social tie is a mapping $s : \mathcal{C} \subset \mathcal{U}^2 \to \{\pm 1\}$ which characterizes the overall impression (trust/distrust) of user u to user v. In essence, our aim is to *label the edges* of the graph $\mathcal{G}$ (i.e. the acquaintance relationships in a standard social network) *with signed labels* $+1$ or -1.

[1]With slight abuse of expression, here by "en-sign" we mean "to assign a sign to" something that is unsigned.

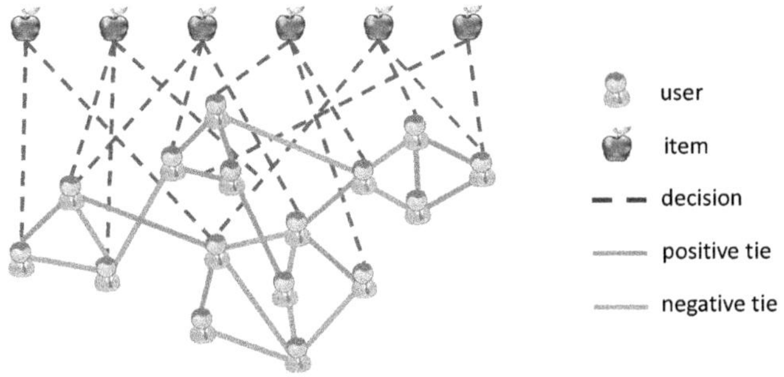

Figure 1: An illustration of decision making in social networks: users make decisions with respect to items (e.g. by rating movies); simultaneously users also interact with one another exerting positive or negative social ties.

Behavior prediction. We are also interested in predicting the users' behavior of decision making. In particular, given a user-item pair (u, i), we want to predict the response y_{ui} with high precision.

We focus on the more challenging task of sign labeling in §3 and §4, and defer the second goal to §5.

2.2 Related Work

To provide a context of our work, we briefly review existing research on behavior prediction and relation analysis.

Behavior Prediction. Behavior prediction aims at predicting future (unseen) decision responses y_{ui} of a user u w.r.t an item i. We consider collaborative filtering (CF) approaches [12, 27], which tackle the problem by learning from past behavior. A widely used approach to CF learns informative compact latent factors to uncover the dyadic interactions. The basic idea is to associate latent factors with each user and each item, and let the decision be explained by the interactions (e.g., multiplication) of these terms.

While CF approaches gain a lot success in recommender systems, they may be insufficient in the context of social networks where user interactions influence decision making dramatically [10]. For example, instead of making decisions purely by following his own taste as in recommender systems, in a social network, a user can achieve more productive decisions by learning from his friend's experiences. This aspect has been rapidly increasing in importance as many online services are starting to add a social network aspect to their system (e.g. last.fm, Yelp, Flikr) or directly rent existing social networks (e.g. Amazon, Netflix, Bing). Our recent work [26] exploited Homophily for behavior prediction, where the behavior of two socially-connected users is tied and reinforced by each other. This work further investigates a more realistic case where acquainted users are not necessarily reinforcing each other in decision making. We do so by modeling the signed social ties, a much stronger signal that allows us to tie the behavior of a user to whom he trusts rather than whom he knows.

Unsigned Relation Analysis. Traditional relation analysis [16, 23, 19, 5] focuses on unsigned relations and estimates the tie strength between two users by propagating the observed links through the network topology. For a pair of users (u, v) the observation whether they are connected (i.e., know each other) is binary $s_{uv} \in \{1, \text{missing}\}$. Many existing methods employ random walk or spectral algorithms. A random walk on the graph $\mathcal{G}$ is a reversible Markov chain on the vertices $\mathcal{U}$. Vertices are considered close whenever the hitting time is small or whenever the diffusion probability is large. In some cases spectral smoothness is used to obtain similarity via the associated graph Laplacian [24]. This yields the intrinsic kinship defined by the dominant eigenvectors of the graph [16].

Signed Relation Analysis. Social relations are complex and subtle [15, 6], reflecting interactions that could be either *positive* (e.g. trust, agreement, approval) or *negative* (e.g. distrust, disagreement, opposition). Yet until recently a number of authors began to investigate signed relations by examining the links in emerging signed social networks (e.g., Slashdot, Epinion). [6] applied random walk algorithms to propagate both positive and negative links on Epinion network. [13] conducted similar experiments on Slashdot data. [15] examined the applicability of social psychology theories at multiple signed networks. [14] further applied classification approaches to predict the sign of social relationships. While the goal of [14] is seemingly similar to the sign-labeling task we explore here, this work is still within the scope of link analysis since the focus there is solely on the network topology. Furthermore, they adopted a leave-one-out setting — a rather optimistic scenario where the sign labels for all but one edge are observable. Instead, our focus is not on network topology, but rather on discovering the interplay between relations and behavior. Also, we require no or fewer labels to obtain comparable prediction as [14].

2.3 Data

Before providing a formal description of our approaches let us briefly discuss the data, which we will use to draw intuitions for model development, test proposed models and motivate further enhancements.

Epinion We use data from `www.epinion.com` for our analysis as it is the only publicly available dataset we are aware of that contains both signed social relationship *and* user behavioral data. Epinion is a well-known knowledge and opinion sharing web site, where users post reviews and assign ratings (on a scale from 1 to 5) to various of items such as retailing products, companies, or movies. More interestingly, the site maintains a signed social network that allows each user to indicate explicitly other users that he is connected to as either positive (trust) or negative (distrust). We apply our models to predict the trust/distrust relationships. The data set contains 132 thousand users, 1560 thousand items, 13.6 million ratings and 850 thousand signed relationships. Both the user-item matrix and the user-user network are very sparse, with densities of only 0.014% and 0.0048% respectively.

Yahoo! Pulse `pulse.yahoo.com` is an unsigned social network that allows users to communicate with friends and also express their preference for items with explicit indications of "like". We examine data collected over one year, involving 10^8 users and a large collection of items, such as games, sports, News feeds, finance, travel, shopping, and local information services. Our evaluation focuses on a random subset consisting of about 400 items, 1.2 million users and 29 million "like" indications. Due to the unsigned characteristic of this network, we are not able to use this data set to evaluate

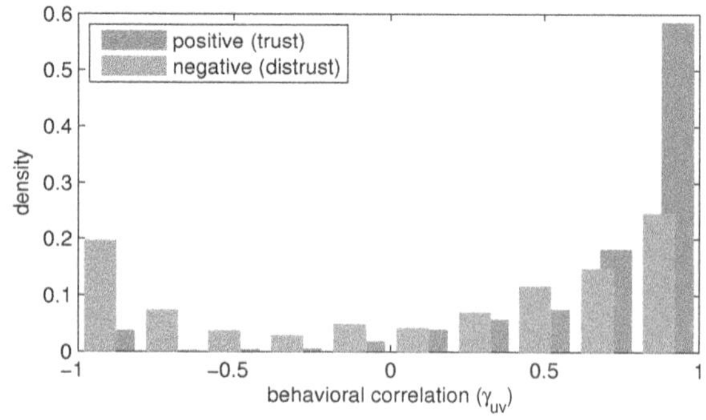

Figure 2: Histograms of behavioral correlations for positively and negatively connected users on epinion.com.

edge-sign prediction. Instead, we will use this data set for behavior prediction evaluation (Section 5).

2.4 Motivating Observations

This paper attempts to predict signed social ties by capturing the interplay between behavioral and social interactions. A key insight is that we consider the behavioral data (e.g. the ratings) to be useful for predicting signed social interactions. This is reasonable as in reality we are often willing to follow the opinions from a trusted friend and fight against those from a foe. As a result, decisions of positively-connected (i.e., trust) friends are more likely to agree, whereas for frenemies the chance of disagreement would be considerably higher. Here we empirically validate this intuition on the Epinion data, as can be seen in Figure 2.

In particular, we quantify behavioral agreement using the Pearson correlation score between the ratings of two users, and we compare this between users with positive and negative links. The Pearson score is defined as follows:

$$\gamma_{uv} := \frac{\sum_{i \in \mathcal{O}[uv]} y_{ui} y_{vi}}{\sqrt{\sum_{i \in \mathcal{O}[uv]} y_{ui}^2 \sum_{i \in \mathcal{O}[uv]} y_{vi}^2}}, \tag{1}$$

where $\mathcal{O}[uv]$ denote the set of items that both u and v rate. Figure 2 plots the distribution of γ_{uv} for positive-relationships (u trusts v) and negative-relationships (u distrusts v). We can see that the behavioral correlation is highly predictive for signed relations. Specifically, the majority (almost 90%) of the positive links indeed show positive behavioral correlations. The case for negative links is a bit more complicated — the distribution peaks at both -1 and +1, indicating that users with distrust relationships could agree or disagree with each other. But even in this case, we can still observe that for almost 40% of the negative edges, the signs of relations are consistent with the signs of behavioral correlations.

3. BEHAVIOR RELATION INTERPLAY

The nontrivial relationship between behavioral correlation and the sign of social relations motivates us to leverage both social and behavioral evidences when predicting signed social ties (and/or behavior vice versa). In this section, we present models to capture the interplay between users' behavior of decision making and social interaction in the context of social networks.

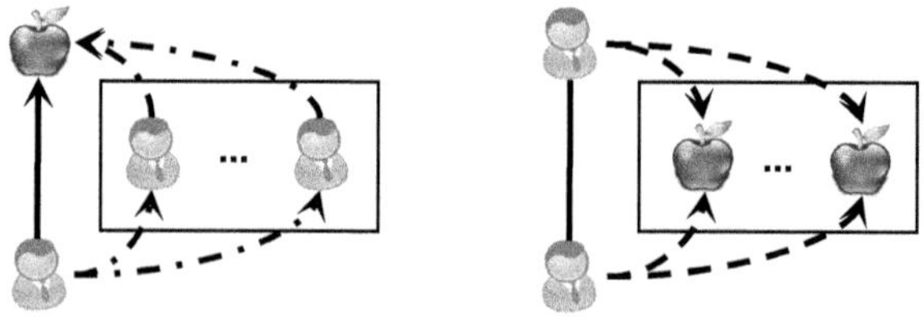

Figure 3: Illustration of behavior-relation interplay. (Left): user u makes a decision w.r.t. item i by either following his own interest in i or taking a friend v's opinion to i; (Right): social relation between u and v is a mixture of their prior impressions to each other and the calibration based on their behavioral agreement w.r.t. decision items.

3.1 The BRI Model

Similar to the latent factor CF models for behavior prediction, we devise a latent factor model for user behavior data $\{y_{ui}\}$. We associate latent factors ϕ_u with user u and ψ_i with item i. For notation convenience we require that each latent factor contains a constant component so as to absorb user/item-specific offset into latent factors. In particular, we assume the following model for behavior (The gist of our approach is captured by Figure 3):

Intrinsic taste We assume user u's interest in item i is quantified by $\phi_u^\top \psi_i$.

Trust credit Similarly, we assume user u trusts an acquainted user v with a credit $\phi_u^\top \phi_v$.

Social decision making Furthermore, we assume that user u makes decision w.r.t. item i by taking a random walk, that is: with probability p he follows his own taste $\phi_u^\top \psi_i$, or with probability $(1-p)$ he asks one of his friends, say v (with transition probability $\phi_u^\top \phi_v$) for advice, where v's opinion is captured by $\phi_v^\top \psi_i$. As a results, aspects that are favored/disliked by his friends should impact an individual user's own choices. The decision y_{ui} therefore depends on $p\phi_u^\top \psi_i + (1-p)\sum_v (\phi_u^\top \phi_v)\phi_v \psi_i$, which is achieved equivalently by "coloring" the inner product between users by a normalized variant of the correlation

$$M_y := (\operatorname{tr} C_y)^{-1} C_y \text{ where } C_y = \sum_v \phi_v \phi_v^\top \tag{2}$$

$$f_{ui} = \phi_u^\top \left[pI + (1-p)M_y\right] \psi_i \tag{3}$$

Here $p \in [0,1]$ encodes the the probability with which a user's behavior is decided by his own taste.

The same model can be applied to incorporate social relations among users. We assume a user u is fully characterized by its latent factor ϕ_u and devise the following model to characterize the relationships of user u to user v:

Prior impression We assume user u trusts an acquainted user v a priori (i.e., prior to any decision making behavior) with credit $\phi_u^\top \phi_v$.

Behavior agreement User u calibrates his impression regarding v based on the agreement[2] between his own and v's decisions, e.g., according to the correlation $\sum_i (\phi_u^\top \psi_i)(\phi_v^\top \psi_i)$.

[2]Note that a dynamic model, i.e., $h_{uv}(t)$ over time t, is possible if we have access to the time stamp of each activity.

Social tie We assume the social interaction is a mixture of both prior impression and behavior agreement with mixture parameter q, i.e.: the social tie depends on $q\phi_u^\top \phi_v + (1-q)\sum_i (\phi_u^\top \psi_i)(\phi_v^\top \psi_i)$, or equivalently:

$$M_s := (\operatorname{tr} C_s)^{-1} C_s \text{ where } C_s = \sum_i \psi_i \psi_i^\top \quad (4)$$

$$h_{uv} = \phi_u^\top [qI + (1-q)M_s]\, \phi_v \quad (5)$$

Here $q \in [0,1]$ defines the mixture probability of prior impression. Unlike in random walk models where proximity in a graph is simply used to smooth secondary estimators of parameters (e.g. reachability, hitting times), we make direct use of it to model the latent variables ϕs.

Based on the above descriptions, we specify the probabilities with spherical Gaussian distributions (extensions to other distributions are straightforward) and we summarize the overall model in the table below.

The Behavior Relation Interplay (BRI) model.	
$\forall\, u \in \mathcal{U}$	$\phi_u \sim \mathcal{N}(\phi_u \mid 0, \sigma_{\mathcal{U}}^2 I)$
$\forall\, i \in \mathcal{I}$	$\psi_i \sim \mathcal{N}(\psi_i \mid 0, \sigma_{\mathcal{I}}^2 I)$
$\forall\, u \in \mathcal{U},\ i \in \mathcal{I}$	$y_{ui} \sim \mathcal{N}(y_{ui} \mid f_{ui}, \sigma_{\mathcal{Y}}^2 I)$
$\forall\, u, v \in \mathcal{U}$	$s_{uv} \sim \mathcal{N}(s_{uv} \mid h_{uv}, \sigma_{\mathcal{S}}^2 I)$

Here $\sigma_{\mathcal{I}}$, $\sigma_{\mathcal{U}}$, $\sigma_{\mathcal{S}}$, $\sigma_{\mathcal{Y}}$ are scalars specifying the variance.

We develop inference algorithms for the proposed model, relying on three types of dyadic evidences:

1. The user behavior trace $\{y_{ui}\}$ in the form of user-item interactions such as a user's rating for a movie.
2. The unsigned user-user social connections (e.g., the acquaintance relations at Facebook) $\{c_{uv}\}$, where $c_{uv} = 1$ when u and v know each other or missing otherwise.

   Or alternatively whenever available:
3. The signed connections $\{s_{uv}\}$, $s_{uv} = \pm 1$ or missing, e.g., the trust/distrust or friend/foe relations at Epinion and Slashdot.

We refer to c_{uv} as *unlabeled tie* and to s_{uv} as *labeled tie*. Our goal is to infer the labels of social ties using none (i.e. unsupervised) or only a fraction (i.e. semi-supervised) of the label observations by fitting the latent factor model BRI on the above three sources of evidences.

3.2 Unsupervised BRI

We first consider the case where no label is observed. This is a typical setting for the majority of social network sites such as Facebook. Our key idea is to use an absolute-value link function $|\xi|$, which bridges the *hidden* signed-ties we aim to infer, h_{uv}, to the unsigned acquaintance connections we actually observed, c_{uv}. In this way, we enable the mechanism of *automatic sign determination* in the same spirit as the maximum margin clustering of [25] — we assume the objective function achieves optimality at either $h_{uv} = +1$ or $h_{uv} = -1$; through optimization, the model will automatically determine the optimal sign for h_{uv} because different signs correspond to different objective values.

Formulation. Given the observations of user-item behavioral interactions $(u,i) \in \mathcal{O}_y$ and unsigned user-user connections $(u,v) \in \mathcal{O}_c$, we have the following optimization:

$$\underset{\phi,\psi}{\text{minimize}}\ \lambda_y \sum_{(u,i)\in\mathcal{O}_y} (y_{ui} - f_{ui})^2 + \lambda_c \sum_{(u,v)\in\mathcal{O}_c} (c_{uv} - |h_{uv}|)^2 + \lambda_{\mathcal{U}} \sum_{u\in\mathcal{U}} \|\phi_u\|^2 + \lambda_{\mathcal{I}} \sum_{i\in\mathcal{I}} \|\psi_i\|^2 \quad (6)$$

where $\lambda_{\mathcal{U}}$, $\lambda_{\mathcal{I}}$, λ_c, λ_y are trade-off parameters, f_{ui} and h_{uv} are defined according to Eq(3) and Eq(5).

Prediction. Given an incoming pair of users, (u,v), we predict the sign of the social tie (i.e., trust or distrust) as follows:

$$\hat{s}_{uv} = \operatorname{sign}(h_{uv} - h_0) \quad (7)$$

Here h_0 is a threshold which suitably determines the fraction of positive and negative ties. Whenever we have access to some labels on a validation set, it is straightforward to determine h_0 via line search: simply sort h_{uv} by magnitude and compute the balanced error for each distinct value of h_{uv}. This is in complete analogy to the line search procedure of [8] for F_β scores.

Optimization. Eq(6) is minimized by stochastic gradient descent. Strictly speaking the objective does not decouple entirely in terms of ϕ and ψ due to the matrices M_y and M_s. Nonetheless we found that an approximation which performs stochastic gradient descent on ϕ and ψ while keeping M_y, M_s fixed produces good results. Also, it can be decomposed into sessions and parallelized using the MapReduce framework.

The stochastic gradient descent procedure is entirely standard: the algorithm processes all observations and updates the parameters in the direction of the negative gradient. For instance, for $\mathcal{O}_y$ the updates are as follows:

$$\phi_u \leftarrow (1 - \eta\bar{\lambda}_{\mathcal{U}})\phi_u - \eta(f_{ui} - y_{ui})(p\psi_i + (1-p)M_y\psi_i) \quad (8)$$

$$\psi_i \leftarrow (1 - \eta\bar{\lambda}_{\mathcal{I}})\psi_i - \eta(f_{ui} - y_{ui})(p\phi_u + (1-p)M_y\phi_u) \quad (9)$$

Here $\bar{\lambda}_{\mathcal{U}}$ and $\bar{\lambda}_{\mathcal{I}}$ are regularization constants suitably adjusted with respect to the prediction accuracy (they are obtained by normalizing Eq(6) in terms of size). The learning rate η is annealed with a discount factor after each iteration, as suggested by [12].

Algorithm 1 Stochastic gradient descent learning

initialize $M_y = M_s = I$, random ϕ_u and ψ_i
for $t = 1$ **to** T **do**
  Stochastic gradient descent w.r.t. ϕ_u with M_s fixed.
  Update M_s
  Stochastic gradient descent w.r.t. ψ_i with M_y fixed.
  Update M_y
end for

The absolute-value link function $|\xi|$ is approximated by a smooth variant $(\alpha^{-1} \log 2\cosh \alpha\xi)$ with $\alpha = 100$. This approximation avoids non-differentiability in the objective function and aids convergence of the optimization.

3.3 Empirical Results for Unsupervised BRI

We conducted experiments on the Epinion data set. The social relationships in Epinion are dominated by positive ones (over 85% of the edges are positive). Following the settings of [14, 6], we derive a balanced dataset containing equal numbers of positive and negative relations by randomly down-sampling the positive edges. Moreover, because

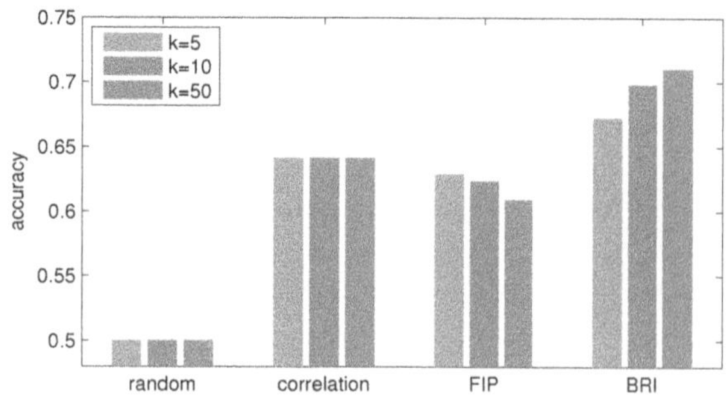

Figure 4: Unsupervised sign prediction performance on Epinion. From left to right: random guess, behavioral correlation based method, the Friendship-Interest Propagation (FIP) model [26], and the proposed BRI model. Results are reported with latent dimensionality k = 5, 10 and 50 respectively.

the behavioral data in this dataset is extremely skewed (the mean value of the ratings is around 4.6), we standardize all the ratings to the range $[-1,\ 1]$ by applying a transformation: $(y - 3.0)^{+} - 1.0$.

We evaluate the BRI model in terms of its unsupervised sign prediction accuracy. For this purpose, we hide the signs of all the relationships in the training set, i.e., all the edges are treated as "acquaintance" regardless whether they were originally trust or distrust. For comparison, we also evaluate the following three unsupervised methods:

- Random. A random guessing predictor yields 50% accuracy because the dataset is balanced.
- Correlation. The 1-dimensional classifier:

$$\hat{s}_{uv} = \text{sign}(\gamma_{uv} - \gamma_0)$$

  based on the behavioral correlations γ, where γ_0 is the optimal threshold found by line-search.
- Fip. The Friendship-Interest Propagation model [26] has been proved effective for link (tie-strength) prediction using both social and behavior data. FIP can be viewed as a special case of BRI with (1) both $p = 1$ and $q = 1$; and (2) no automatic sign determination.

Throughout this paper, all the models are evaluated by using the 1-dimensional prediction scheme Eq(7). In particular, for the output score ρ_{uv} of a model, we predict the sign as $\hat{s}_{uv} = \text{sign}(\rho_{uv} - \rho_0)$, where ρ_0 is an optimal threshold scalar found by line search on validation data.

The prediction accuracy is depicted in Figure 4, where the results of BRI and FIP are reported at latent dimensionality $k = 5$, 10 and 50 respectively. As can be seen from the figure, BRI achieves up to 71% accuracy in this unsupervised setting and it significantly outperform all the three baselines. In particular, BRI gains 42% improvement over Random, 21% over Fip and 11% over Correlation. The result is quite promising especially considering that all the signs are hidden in training. It also proves the BRI model is potentially usable in practice for en-signing unsigned social networks, given that we can predict trust/distrust from acquaintance relationships with over 70% accuracy.

One key notion that motivates our work is that we assume the behavioral data should be useful for tie-sign prediction.

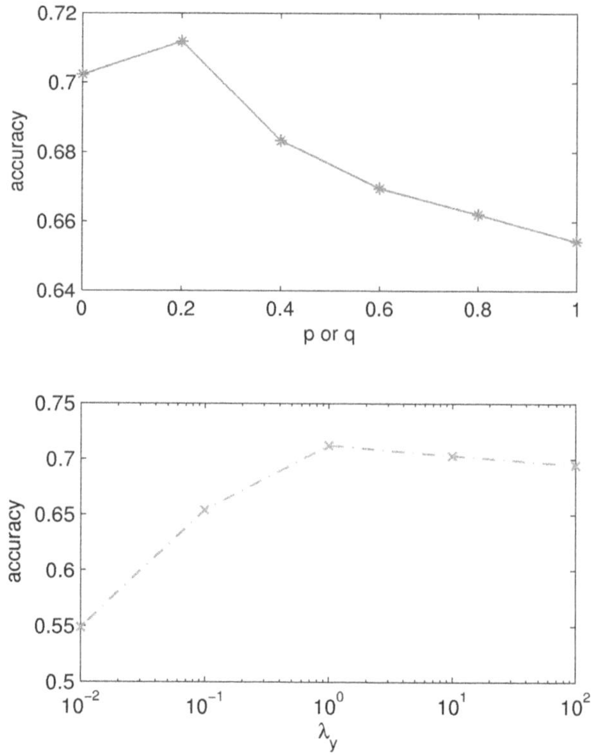

Figure 5: Top: Unsupervised sign prediction accuracy as a function of the coloring proportion $p = q$; Bottom: the same statistic for the weight for behavioral data, λ_Y.

As can be seen from Figure 4, using the behavioral data alone, the simple correlation-based predictor achieves the second best performance among all the four models. This observation validates our hypothesis and indicates that behavioral information is indeed highly predictive for signed social ties. In Figure 5 (b), we further report the accuracy of BRI as a function of the weight for behavioral data, i.e., λ_y in Eq(6). As we can see, while the best result is achieved at a moderate value of λ_y, interestingly, the performance does not degrade badly if we further increase λ_y. In contrast, if λ_y is decreasing toward 0, the performance degrades quickly towards that of random prediction — in an extreme, BRI trained on unsigned social data alone does not perform substantially better than Random. These observations reveal that, in the unsupervised setting, the behavioral information is even more predictive than the topology of the acquaintance graph.

Note that although the Fip model also leverages the behavioral data, it is ineffective in sign prediction. Fip estimates the unipolar (i.e., in the interval [0, 1]) tie-strength indicating whether two users *know each other*. Nonetheless, it is incapable to predict whether they *trust or distrust each other*, i.e. Fip cannot discern the sign of a connection. From another prespective, this comparison between Fip and Bri confirms that the proposed mechanism of *automatic sign determination* is effective for sign prediction.

The performance of the BRI model is affected by the parameters of mixture probabilities, i.e., p and q in Eq(3-5).

Table 1: Semi-supervised sign prediction performance on Epinion data. We compare five methods: random guess (RAND), Friendship-Interest propagation (FIP) [26], behavioral correlation based classifier with optimal threshold (CORR), Leave-one-out Logistic Regression based on local topology features [14] (LOO-LR), and the proposed BRI model trained with different percentages of supervision information (i.e., tie labels).

Model	RAND	FIP	CORR	LOO-LR	BRI									
Labels	0	0	0	All - 1	0	100	1%	5%	10%	20%	30%	50%	70%	90%
Accuracy	0.500	0.591	0.644	0.934	0.709	0.709	0.731	0.747	0.776	0.818	0.836	0.869	0.894	0.912

In Figure 5, we illustrate how the prediction accuracy of BRI changes with these two parameters, where for simplicity p and q are set to the same values. As can be seen from the figure, the accuracy curve is typically in a inverted U-shape with the optimal performance achieved at around 0.2. This observation suggests that both the two groups of factors (i.e. intrinsic taste vs influence, prior impression vs behavior agreement) are important and should be taken into account simultaneously as what we do in the BRI model.

3.4 Semisupervised BRI

We now consider semi-supervised formulation, where part of the labels for social ties are observed — in practice, these labels could be obtained directly from users through an online survey or simply by manual annotations. In particular, assume that in addition to the behavioral observations $\mathcal{O}_y$ and the acquaintance relations $\mathcal{O}_c$, we also have access to a small set of labeled relations (i.e., trust-distrust) on pairs $(u, v) \in \mathcal{O}_s$. In this case we add

$$\lambda_s \sum_{(u,v)\in\mathcal{O}_s} (s_{uv} - h_{uv})^2 \tag{10}$$

to the objective function of Eq(6). This formulation has a close connection with the semi-supervised classification model of [2]. It maximizes the fidelity to the *target output* (e.g. s_{uv}) of the labeled data, while approximating the target output for unlabeled data up to an arbitrary sign. A notable distinction is that we are learning latent factor models (e.g., the BRI model) rather than a global feature mapping (i.e., the classifier of the form $w^\top x + b$ in [2]).

The learning algorithm and prediction formula are similar to the unsupervised case and therefore are omitted.

3.5 Empirical Results for Semisupervised BRI

Table 1 gives the overall results of semi-supervised sign prediction on Epinion data, where we report the performance of the BRI model that are trained using progressive proportions (1% to 90%) of the labeled data. As a reference, we also report the results obtained by RANDOM guessing, CORRELATION-based 1-dimensional classifier, the Friendship-Interest Propagation (FIP) model of [26] and the leave-one-out logistic regression model (denoted LOO-LR) of [14].

Our first observation from the table is that the performance of the BRI model is approaching that of LOO-LR. As we increase the labeled data used for training, we see that the prediction accuracy of the BRI model is steadily improving, indicating that the labeled data can indeed be used to improve the prediction ability of BRI, somewhat as we expected. In particular, with 1% of labeled data, we gain over 3% improvement of accuracy; and if we use over 90% of the labeled data, BRI can achieve comparable performance as the leave-one-out prediction of [14] but using far less supervision information compared to the latter.

Interestingly, it seems that the labeled data are not always helpful for BRI. For example, the model trained using 100 (i.e. less than 0.05%) labeled edges does not perform significantly better (in some cases, even slightly worse) than the unsupervised model. This observation suggests that the amount of the labeled data should exceed a minimum threshold in order for it to take effect. This is quite different from the traditional semi-supervised learning in which labeled data, whenever available, seems to always help prediction. Nonetheless, it is reasonable in our context because we are learning a latent factor model over extremely large user/item spaces — the model is almost inevitably overparameterized and with a lot of local optima due to the nonconvexity; the labeled data cannot guarantee to drive the model toward a right direction if there is too little of it.

4. ENCODING SOCIAL PSYCHOLOGY

Theories from social psychology [6] provide profound perspectives for understanding the formation of signed relations in social networks. According to [15, 14], satisfactory sign prediction accuracy could be obtained by applying social psychology principles. For example, [14] constructed local topology-based features according to status and balance theories and employed a logistic regression classifier based on these features to predict the signed relationships. In a leave-one-out setting, their model achieves up to 93% sign prediction accuracy on Epinion data. In this section, we extend the basic BRI models to encode social psychological principles, especially the theories of status and structural balance.

4.1 Encoding Structural Balance Theory

The first theory we try to encode is that of *structural balance* [7, 15]. Roughly speaking it implies the intuition that "a friend's friend is a friend" and that "an enemy's enemy is a friend". Basically, it considers the balance of signs on a triad involving three users. It states that a triad is balanced if and only if it contains an odd number of positive edges.

BALANCE THEORY [7, 15]: *A triad (u,v,w) is balanced in either of the two cases: (1) if $s_{uv} = 1$ and $s_{uw} = 1$, then $s_{vw} = 1$; (2) if $s_{uv} = -1$ and $s_{uw} = -1$, then $s_{vw} = 1$.*

To encode the balance theory, we introduce an additional (1-dimensional) latent factor β_u for each user u. Unlike the latent profiles ϕ, β is only used to capture the structural balance of the network topology. In particular, we assume an additional component:

$$g_{uv} = \beta_u \beta_v, \tag{11}$$

The social tie is modeled using the following mixture-of-effect model:

$$h_{uv} = q_1\phi_u^\top \phi_v + q_2\phi_u^\top M_s\phi_v + q_3\beta_u\beta_v, \quad (12)$$

where $q_1,\ q_2,\ q_3 \in [0,\ 1]$ and $q_1 + q_2 + q_3 = 1$.

The new mixture component encodes the status theory because it implies: if $g_{uv} > 0$ and $g_{uw} > 0$, then $g_{vw} > 0$ (i.e. a friend's friend is a friend); if $g_{uv} < 0$ and $g_{uw} < 0$, then $g_{vw} > 0$ (i.e. an enemy's enemy is a friend). This rank-1 parametrization of structural balance matches the models used in collaborative filtering, albeit with reduced dimensionality. Effectively we are setting aside a subspace of the latent factors exclusively for social interactions.

4.2 Encoding Status Theory

In the previous sections we implicitly viewed the social network as an *undirected* graph. Here, we extend the BRI model to encode status theory [6, 15], which was developed for directed networks. That is, from now on, the social ties are viewed as asymmetric relationships. Basically, status theory assumes that there exists a partial order over the user space such that positive edges only goes from low-status nodes to nodes with higher status; therefore, the relationships are transitive, i.e., if $s_{uv} = +1$ and $s_{vw} = +1$ then $s_{uw} = +1$, and vice versa.

STATUS THEORY[6, 15]: *A positive directed link $s_{uv} = +1$ indicates that the head node u has a higher status than the tail node v; a negative link $s_{uv} = -1$ indicates that u has a lower status than v.*

To encode status theory we introduce a global user-independent parameter θ to capture the partial ordering of users. θ maps the latent user profile ϕ_u to a scalar quantity $\ell_u = \theta^\top \phi_u$, which reflects the corresponding user u's *social status*. According to status theory, we characterize social ties from u to v by modeling the relative status difference between user u and user v:

$$\ell_{uv} = \theta^\top(\phi_u - \phi_v) = \underbrace{\theta^\top \phi_u}_{=:\ell_u} - \underbrace{\theta^\top \phi_v}_{=:\ell_v}. \quad (13)$$

Note that status theory implies that the social tie is typically an antisymmetric relationship, i.e. if $s_{uv} = +1$, then $s_{vu} = -1$. This implication is, however, too strong. For example, in the Epinion case, only 2% of the bi-directional relationships are truly antisymmetric. To relax this assumption, we therefore use a mixture of effects model as in the previous section. This yields:

$$h_{uv} = q_1\phi_u^\top \phi_v + q_2\phi_u^\top M_s\phi_v + q_3(\ell_u - \ell_v). \quad (14)$$

Since ℓ_u, ℓ_v induce a total order on users it satisfies the requirements of social status theory: by transitivity $\ell_{uv} > 0$ and $\ell_{vw} > 0$ imply $\ell_{uw} > 0$.

4.3 Empirical Results

We evaluate the two extended BRI models in the semi-supervised setting and report the results in Tabel 2. As a reference, we also report the performance of the balance model and the status model on its own. As can be seen from the table, by encoding the status theory, we achieve results that are comparable with the leave-one-out prediction of [14], but we use far less supervision, i.e. observed tie labels. Also note that encoding the balance theory only leads to very marginal improvements. The latter is to be expected since adding a small subspace to an already existing multiplicative latent factor model will not change the expressive richness of the model significantly.

Table 2: Semi-supervised sign prediction performance on Epinion. We compare the following models: Structural balance (BAL), Status (STA), basic BRI model and combinations of these models, denoted by BRI+STA and BRI+BAL respectively.

%Labels	0%	1%	5%	20%	50%	90%
BAL	0.539	0.557	0.582	0.601	0.662	0.735
STA	0.617	0.719	0.757	0.799	0.824	0.843
BRI	0.709	0.731	0.747	0.818	0.869	0.912
BRI+BAL	0.711	0.734	0.751	0.821	0.870	0.912
BRI+STA	0.714	0.739	0.763	0.833	0.884	0.925

Among all the methods, the rank-1 balance model performs the worst, e.g., in the unsupervised case, it performs even much worse than FIP and the correlation-based approach. Somewhat surprisingly, the plain status model perform quite satisfactorily. In most cases, the accuracy scores achieved by the status model are very close to those obtained by the basic BRI model. This observation is consistent with the empirical insight reported in [15] that status theory turns to explain the signed relationship better. However, these results do not entirely invalidate the balance theory because we use a rank-1 model that could be too simplistic for any practical network topology.

It is worth noting that the status model provides a *status mapping* $\ell_u = \theta^\top \phi_u$ that embeds the users into a 1-dimensional space with the coordinates corresponding to users' *social status*. In Figure 6, we visualize the Epinion network by randomly sampling 0.1% edges as a bipartite graph based on this embedding. In particular, the upper and lower horizontal lines denote the embedding spaces for head nodes and tail nodes respectively; edges that match the status theory (i.e., $s_{uv} = +1$ while $\ell_u > \ell_v$ or $s_{uv} = -1$ while $\ell_u < \ell_v$) are plotted as green lines; in contrast, edges mismatch the theory are depicted as red lines; to give a clear illustration, negative edges are inverted, i.e., $s_{uv} = -1$ are replaced by $s_{vu} = +1$. This figure shows a clear picture about social status and signed relations. Over 84% of signed relations, i.e., trust/distrust, are indeed consistent with the theory, going from higher-status head nodes to lower-status tails. Noticeably, while there are confusions, they are mainly in the middle area between users with relatively small difference of social status. Also note that the confusions are becoming increasingly sparse for high-status head users, indicating that these users are more likely to be trusted by most other users, which is intuitively reasonable. An interesting investigation would be to examine how the social status discovered by this work relates to the well-known concept of *authority* [11] in social networks. We would like to leave such investigation for future research.

5. BEHAVIOR PREDICTION

A direct motivation of this work was to take advantage of signed relationships, when available, for behavior prediction purposes. The reasonable expectation in this context was that a stronger social signal would allow us to obtain better behavior prediction than what can be achieved via

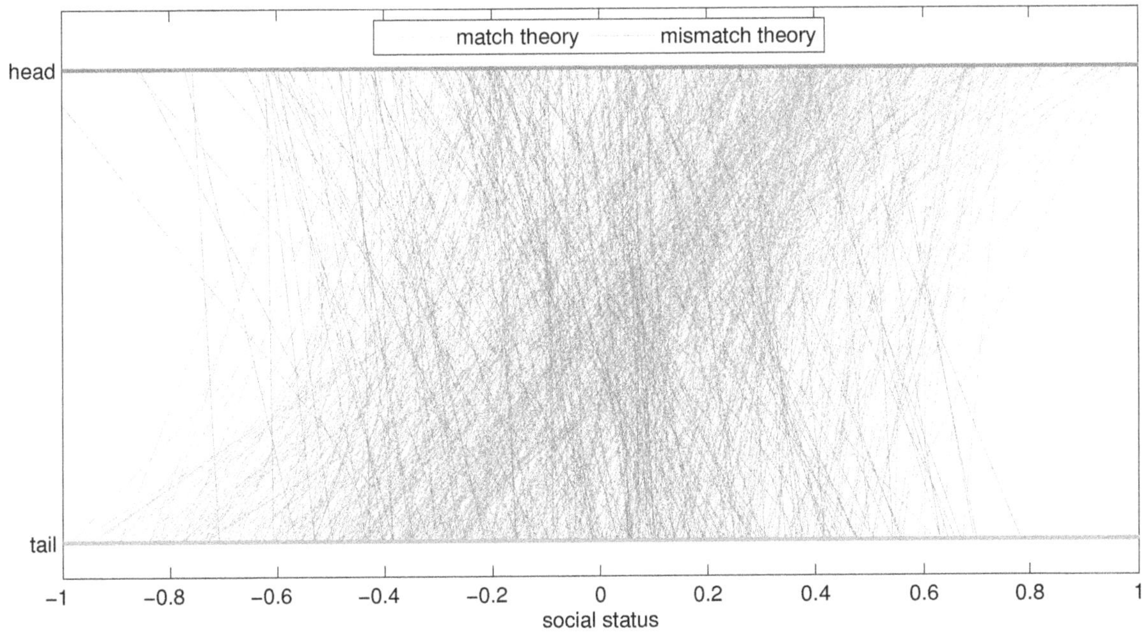

Figure 6: A visualization of social status and signed social ties for `epinion.com`. Users are embedded into a 1-dimensional space using the status scores ℓ_u as coordinates. Relationships that are consistent with the status theory are denoted as green lines, or otherwise as red lines.

Table 3: Behavior prediction performance on Epinion and Yahoo! Pulse: comparison among collaborative filtering (SVD), the FIP model [26] and our BRI model. Performance is evaluated in terms of rating prediction on Epinion, and top-k ranking on Pulse.

	Epinion		Yahoo! Pulse		
Model	RMSE	MAE	AP@5	AR@5	nDCG@5
SVD	0.556	0.387	0.726	0.208	0.734
FIP	0.553	0.386	0.761	0.225	0.767
BRI	**0.524**	**0.350**	**0.778**	**0.232**	**0.785**

unipolar Homophily. In this section, we test whether, even in the absence of explicitly available signed social ties, we are able to improve behavior prediction estimates. For this purpose, we compare three models: a plain collaborative filtering approach (SVD), the Homophily-based model (FIP) [26] and the proposed BRI model. We evaluate these models on both Epinion and Yahoo! Pulse data. For Epinion, we evaluate the rating prediction performance in terms of *root mean square error* (RMSE) and *mean absolute error* (MAE). For Pulse, because the behavior data is binary (either 1 or missing), we evaluate the top-k ranking performance, i.e. we compare the top suggestions of the model with the true actions taken by a user (i.e. whether he *liked* the item). We use the following three metrics commonly used in the IR community:

AP is the *average precision.* AP@k averages the precision of the top-k ranked list of each query (e.g. user).

AR or *average recall* of the top-k rank list of each query.

nDCG or *normalized Discounted Cumulative Gain* is the normalized position-discounted precision score.

In all three metrics we use $k = 5$ since most social networks use a similar number of items for service recommendation. For the Pulse data, we also implement the bias correction procedure suggested by [26].

The overall results are reported in Table 3. For both data sets we see that the BRI model consistently outperform the two baselines in all the measures. In particular, it improves the RMSE by 5.8% on Epinion, and the nDCG@5 score by 6.9% on Yahoo! Pulse. Note that BRI also significantly outperforms the FIP model. In terms of methodology, both FIP and BRI exploit social relations to improve behavior prediction; the difference, however, lies in how they leverage the social relations: FIP models the *unsigned tie-strength* between users which is then used to *reinforce* the decision making behavior of connected users; in contrast, BRI models the *signed ties*, distinguishing those whom we truly trust from those we do not. In this way, although behavior of two connected users is tied to each other, but not necessarily reinforcing. BRI therefore provides a mechanism that allows social users to follow the opinions from people they trust while at the same time fighting against the viewpoints of their foes. Our results suggest that signed social ties, such as trust-distrust relations, are a substantially more predictive signal in tying and regularizing social behavior than Homophily.

6. SUMMARY

We examined the problem of predicting signed social ties, such as trust and distrust, based on the acquaintance relationships in social networks. This allows us to determine, with surprising accuracy, whether a link corresponds to a trustworthy friend or rather a frenemy. We present models that infer signed ties by capturing the interplay between social relations and users' behavior of decision making, and extend the models to encode general principles from social psychology. We investigate sign prediction in both unsupervised and semi-supervised settings, conduct experiments in a variety of perspectives and report promising results. We demonstrate that the predicted signed ties are much stronger signals for relating social behavior than traditional Homophily.

Acknowledgements

We thank Su-Lin Wu for helpful discussions. Part of this work was supported by NSF Grants IIS-1049694 and IIS-1116886, and NSFC grant 61129001/F010403.

7. REFERENCES

[1] B. Awerbuch and R. Kleinberg. Competitive collaborative learning. *Journal of Computer and System Sciences*, 74(8):1271–1288, 2008.

[2] K. Bennet and A. Demiriz. Semi-supervised support vector machines. In *Advances in Neural Information Processing Systems 11*, pages 368–374, 1998.

[3] M. J. Brzozowski, T. Hogg, and G. Szabo. Friends and foes: ideological social networking. In *Proceeding of the 26th ACM CHI Conference on Human Factors in Computing Systems*, pages 817–820, 2008. ACM.

[4] Y. Chen, D. Pavlov, and J. Canny. Large-scale behavioral targeting. In *Proceedings of the 15th ACM Conference on Knowledge Discovery and Data Mining*, pages 209–218. ACM, 2009.

[5] E. Gilbert and K. Karahalios. Predicting tie strength with social media. In *Conference on Human factors in computing systems CHI*, pages 211–220, 2009. ACM.

[6] R. Guha, R. Kumar, P. Raghavan, and A. Tomkins. Propagation of trust and distrust. In *World Wide Web WWW*, pages 403–412, 2004. ACM.

[7] F. Heider. Attitudes of cognitive organization. *Journal of Psychology*, 21:107–112, 1946.

[8] T. Joachims. A support vector method for multivariate performance measures. In *Proceedings of the 22nd international conference on Machine learning (ICML '05)*, pages 377–384, 2005. ACM.

[9] O. Kallenberg. *Probabilistic symmetries and invariance principles*. Springer, 2005.

[10] T. Kameda, Y. Ohtsubo, and M. Takezawa. Centrality in sociocognitive networks and social influence: An illustration in a group decision-making context. *Journal of Personality and Social Psychology*, 73(2):296–309, August 1997.

[11] J. M. Kleinberg. Hubs, authorities, and communities. *ACM Computing Surveys*, 31, December 1999.

[12] Y. Koren, R. Bell, and C. Volinsky. Matrix factorization techniques for recommender systems. *IEEE Computer*, 42(8):30–37, 2009.

[13] J. Kunegis, A. Lommatzsch, and C. Bauckhage. The slashdot zoo: mining a social network with negative edges. In *World Wide Web* 2009, pages 741–750. ACM.

[14] J. Leskovec, D. Huttenlocher, and J. Kleinberg. Predicting positive and negative links in online social networks. In *Conference on World Wide Web WWW*, pages 641–650, New York, NY, USA, 2010. ACM.

[15] J. Leskovec, D. Huttenlocher, and J. Kleinberg. Signed networks in social media. In *Human factors in computing systems CHI*, pages 1361–1370, New York, NY, USA, 2010. ACM.

[16] D. Liben-Nowell and J. Kleinberg. The link prediction problem for social networks. In *Conference on Knowledge and Information Management CKIM*, pages 556–559, New York, NY, USA, 2003. ACM.

[17] H. Ma, M. Lyu, and I. King. Learning to recommend with trust and distrust relationships. In *ACM conference on Recommender Systems RecSys*, pages 189–196, 2009. ACM.

[18] P. Massa and P. Avesani. Trust-aware recommender systems. In *ACM conference on Recommender Systems RecSys*, pages 17–24, 2007. ACM.

[19] M. Newman. Detecting community structure in networks. *The European Physical Journal B - Condensed Matter and Complex Systems*, 38(2):321–330, 2004.

[20] M. McPherson, L. S. Lovin, and J. M. Cook. Birds of a feather: Homophily in social networks. *Annual Review of Sociology*, 27(1):415–444, 2001.

[21] J. O'Donovan and B. Smyth. Trust in recommender systems. In *Intelligent User Interfaces IUI*, pages 167–174, 2005. ACM.

[22] J. P. Onnela, J. Saramäki, J. Hyvönen, G. Szabó, D. Lazer, K. Kaski, J. Kertész, and A. L. Barabási. Structure and tie strengths in mobile communication networks. *Proceedings of the National Academy of Sciences*, 104(18):7332–7336, 2007.

[23] M. Rosvall and C. T. Bergstrom. Maps of random walks on complex networks reveal community structure. *Proceedings of the National Academy of Sciences*, 105(4):1118–1123, 2008.

[24] A. J. Smola and R. Kondor. Kernels and regularization on graphs. In *Proceeding of Annual Conference on Computational Learning Theory*, pages 144–158, 2003.

[25] L. Xu, J. Neufeld, B. Larson, and D. Schuurmans. Maximum margin clustering. In *Advances in Neural Information Processing Systems 17*. MIT Press, 2005.

[26] S.-H. Yang, B. Long, A. Smola, N. Sadagopan, Z. Zheng, and H. Zha. Like like alike – joint friendship and interest propagation in social networks. In *WWW '11: Proceedings of the 20th international conference on World wide web*, 2011. ACM.

[27] S.-H. Yang, B. Long, A. Smola, H. Zha, and Z. Zheng. Collaborative-competitive filtering: learning recommender using context of user choice In *SIGIR '11: Proceedings of the 34th ACM conference on Research and development in Information Retrieval*, 2011. ACM.

Social-Network Analysis Using Topic Models

Youngchul Cha
UCLA Computer Science Dept
Los Angeles, CA 90095
youngcha@cs.ucla.edu

Junghoo Cho
UCLA Computer Science Dept
Los Angeles, CA 90095
cho@cs.ucla.edu

ABSTRACT

In this paper, we discuss how we can extend probabilistic topic models to analyze the relationship graph of popular social-network data, so that we can "group" or "label" the edges and nodes in the graph based on their topic similarity. In particular, we first apply the well-known Latent Dirichlet Allocation (LDA) model and its existing variants to the graph-labeling task and argue that the existing models do not handle *popular nodes* (nodes with many incoming edges) in the graph very well. We then propose possible extensions to this model to deal with popular nodes.

Our experiments show that the proposed extensions are very effective in labeling popular nodes, showing significant improvements over the existing methods. Our proposed methods can be used for providing, for instance, more relevant friend recommendations within a social network.

Categories and Subject Descriptors

H.3.3 [**Information Storage and Retrieval**]: Information Search and Retrieval—*clustering*; D.2.8 [**Software Engineering**]: Metrics—*performance measures*

General Terms

Experimentation, Algorithms

Keywords

social-network analysis, topic model, Latent Dirichlet Allocation, handling popular nodes

1. INTRODUCTION

Social network services are gaining popularity. A growing number of users use major social network services, such as Facebook and Twitter, to share their thoughts and whereabouts with their friends and followers. On a social network, a user indicates that she wants to get notified of another user's updates by "following" (or making friends with) that user. Then when the followed user "updates her status" (or shares a new thought), all users who follow her are immediately notified. This "follow relationship" among users often looks unorganized and chaotic, because follow relationships are created haphazardly by each individual user and not controlled by a central entity.

In this paper, we explore techniques to provide more structure to this follow relationship (1) by "grouping" the users based on their topic interests, and (2) by "labeling" each follow relationship with the identified topic group. More formally, we consider each user in a social network as a node in a graph and each follow relationship as a directed edge between two nodes. Then our goal is to "group" a set of nodes in the graph based on their topics and "label" each edge in the graph with a topic group number.

Inferring a structure within the social-network relationship graph can be useful for many reasons. For example, a novice user on a social network often encounters the *bootstrapping* problem: discovering relevant users to connect with. To mitigate this problem, social network services may recommend potentially interesting users to new users if they can group users of similar interests and infer why the new user has decided to follow a certain initial set of other users. Similarly, we can identify a small set of "influential" users on a certain topic (say, for marketing and advertising purposes) if we can identify the users' topic interests.

Roughly, we can consider our goal as a clustering (or classification) problem, where many popular solutions such as K-means [15] and DBSCAN [6] exist. These existing methods, however, are not appropriate for our task because they either (1) associate each node with a *single* group (hard clustering) or (2) can associate each node with multiple groups (soft clustering), but require a completely separate method to label edges as well as nodes (since a node may be associated with multiple groups). Given the diversity of interest a user may have, it is too restrictive to associate a user with a single topic group. For example, Kevin Rose, one of the most popular users on Twitter, may belong to the entrepreneur group as he is the founder of Digg.com, but may also belong to the Internet commentator group since he runs a popular Internet podcast. Since many users on social networks are active in more than one community, we believe it is too unrealistic to require that every user should belong to just one group.

In this paper, we apply a well-known probabilistic topic model, called Latent Dirichlet Allocation (LDA), to the follow-relationship graph of the social network, in order to label the nodes and the edges in the graph with (possibly) multiple

Permission to make digital or hard copies of all or part of this work for personal or classroom use is granted without fee provided that copies are not made or distributed for profit or commercial advantage and that copies bear this notice and the full citation on the first page. To copy otherwise, to republish, to post on servers or to redistribute to lists, requires prior specific permission and/or a fee.
SIGIR'12, August 12–16, 2012, Portland, Oregon, USA.
Copyright 2012 ACM 978-1-4503-1472-5/12/08 ...$15.00.

topics. Unfortunately, LDA was developed for labeling *documents* and *words* with topics, (not nodes and edges in a graph) so some of the assumptions on which LDA was built are not applicable to social-network graph data. In particular, the direct application of LDA to our task requires that every node in the graph should be of roughly *equal popularity* and that we should remove nodes of high popularity from the dataset. This is particularly problematic because these popular nodes are really the ones that we want to label accurately; many users are particularly interested in identifying the topic groups of these popular users. Earlier work on the application of the LDA model to social graph [9, 26] has not addressed the handling of popular nodes.

To address the issues arising from popular nodes in the graph, we first explore existing variations of LDA. We then propose our extensions, *two-step labeling* and *threshold noise filtering*, to minimize the labeling noise introduced by popular nodes.

In summary, we make the following contributions in this paper:

- We explore the application of the well-known LDA model and its existing variations for this task and propose two extensions to make LDA suitable for the social-network relationship graph.
- We conduct extensive experiments using a real-world Twitter dataset. Through these experiments, we demonstrate that (1) the application of probabilistic topic models to social-network graphs leads to useful edge/node topic labeling and that (2) our proposed extensions significantly improve the labeling quality over existing methods.

The rest of the paper is organized as follows. In Section 2, we briefly review previous work related to our research. In Section 3, we describe LDA and justify why we use LDA to solve this labeling problem. Then we introduce four different approaches to handle the noise generated by popular users in Section 4. In Section 5, we analyze our approaches using the Twitter dataset. We summarize this paper with our conclusion in Section 6.

2. RELATED WORK

The problem that we are trying to solve can be viewed as clustering in a social network using a topic model. In this section, we briefly review related work in social-network cluster analysis and topic-model-based social-network analysis.

In his seminal work for social-network cluster analysis, Kleinberg [13] proposed Hyperlink-Induced Topics Search (HITS). In this work, he modeled the Web as a huge graph and extracted *hubs* and *authorities* in order to cluster communities on the Web. Recently, Mislove et al. [18] identified communities in Facebook based on the social graph structure and inferred unknown attributes through this community information. The methods they used to cluster communities are based on pruning edges from the whole social graph and adding edges from some seed nodes, both of which are very common and widely used approaches in social-network analysis. However, these approaches produce mutually exclusive groups and cannot support *multiple memberships*, which is important in our scenario where users have a variety of interests.

Topic models, the other class of related work, have also been extended to analyze small social-network data. Though not directly related to social-network analysis, the concept of author/user was initially introduced in the Author-Topic (AT) model [22]. It was used to extract hidden research topics and trends from CiteSeer's abstract corpus. Zhou et al. [27] modified the AT model and proposed the Community User Topic (CUT) model to capture semantic communities. McCallum et al. [16] extended the AT model and proposed the Author-Recipient-Topic (ART) model and the Role-Author-Recipient-Topic (RART) model in order to analyze the Enron e-mail corpus and an academic e-mail network. Pathak et al. [19] modified the ART model and suggested the Community-Author-Recipient-Topic (CART) model similar to the RART model. Besides these members of the AT model family, Wang et al. [24] introduced the Group Topic (GT) model and applied it to voting data from US Senate and the General Assembly of the UN. Mei et al. [17] also introduced a regularized topic modeling framework incorporating a graph structure in the data. Other LDA extensions and probabilistic topic models were also proposed for annotation data analysis [12], chat data analysis [23], tagging data analysis [8], and pairwise data analysis [2]. While most of the LDA approaches introduced above attempted to utilize the authorship information of a given text by adding the author component to the LDA's text generative model, our approach focuses on using only the social part of the data (i.e., the social graph) and is generally applicable to many large social networks.

Perhaps the work by Zhang et al. [26] and by Henderson et al. [9] is closest to our work. In both works, the authors applied LDA to academic social networks. However, their respective focus was quite different from ours. For example, [26] focused on the issue of how to convert the co-authorship information into a graph (e.g., direct co-authorship or indirect co-authorship, and edge weighting scheme based on collaboration frequency). Henderson et al. [9] addressed the issue of a large number of topic clusters generated due to *low popularity* nodes in the network, while our primary focus is the effective clustering of *high popularity* nodes.

3. APPLYING LDA TO SOCIAL-NETWORK ANALYSIS

In this section, we briefly describe LDA. Because LDA evolved from Probabilistic Latent Semantic Indexing (PLSI) [11], we first describe the concept of PLSI and then explain what differentiates LDA from PLSI. We also justify the reason why we use LDA for social-graph mining and discuss some different aspects between the standard LDA and our model.

3.1 Topic Models

Topic models assume that there are latent (hidden) topics behind words in human language. Thus, even though an author uses the word *automobile* in a document and a searcher uses the word *vehicle* in a query, topic models assume that they might have the same concept (topic) *car* in mind. Based on this assumption, topic models provide methods to infer those latent topics from visible words.

PLSI introduced a probabilistic generative model to topic

models. Equation (1) represents its document generation process based on the probabilistic generative model:

$$P(d, w) = P(d)P(w|d) = P(d) \sum_{z \in Z} P(w|z)P(z|d). \quad (1)$$

$P(d, w)$ is the probability of observing a word w in a document d and can be decomposed into the multiplication of $P(d)$, the probability distribution of documents, and $P(w|d)$, the probability distribution of words given a document. This equation describes a word selection for a document, where we first select a document then a word in that document. If we iterate this selection multiple times, we can generate a document and eventually a whole document corpus.

By assuming that there is a latent topic z, we can rewrite the equation above with the multiplication of $P(w|z)$, the probability distribution of words given a topic, and $P(z|d)$, the probability distribution of topics given a document. This equation describes adding an additional topic selection step between the document selection step and the word selection step. As there are multiple latent topics where a word may come from, we sum the multiplication over a set of all the independent topics Z.

PLSI and other probabilistic topic models support multiple memberships using the probabilities $P(w|z)$ and $P(z|d)$. For example, if $P(w_{vehicle}|z_{car}) > P(w_{automobile}|z_{car})$, the word *vehicle* is more closely related to the topic *car* than the word *automobile*, though they are all related to the topic *car*. In this way, we can measure the strength of association between a word w and a topic z by the probability $P(w|z)$. Similarly $P(z|d)$ measures the strength of association between a topic z and a document d.

Equation (2) represents the log-likelihood function of PLSI:

$$\begin{aligned} L &= \log[\prod_{d \in D} \prod_{w \in W} P(d, w)^{n(d,w)}] \\ &= \sum_{d \in D} \sum_{w \in W} n(d, w) \log P(d, w), \end{aligned} \quad (2)$$

where D and W denote a set of all d and w respectively, and $n(d, w)$ denotes the term frequency in a document (i.e., the number of times w occurred in d).

By maximizing the log-likelihood function L, we can maximize the probability to observe the entire corpus and accordingly estimate the $P(w|z)$ and $P(z|d)$ that most likely satisfy Equation (1).

3.2 Latent Dirichlet Allocation

Though PLSI is equipped with a sound probabilistic generative model and a statistical inference method, it suffers from the overfitting problem and does not cope well with unobserved words. To solve this problem, Blei et al. [4] introduced Dirichlet priors α and β to PLSI, to constrain $P(z|d)$ and $P(w|z)$, respectively. α is a vector of dimension $|Z|$, the number of topics, and each element in α is a prior for a corresponding element in $P(z|d)$. Thus, a higher α_i implies that the topic z_i appears more frequently than other topics in a corpus. Similarly, β is a vector of dimension $|W|$, the number of words, and each element in β is a prior for a corresponding element in $P(w|z)$. Thus, a higher β_j implies that the word w_j appears more frequently than other words in the corpus. As a conjugate prior for the multinomial distribution, the Dirichlet distribution can also simplify

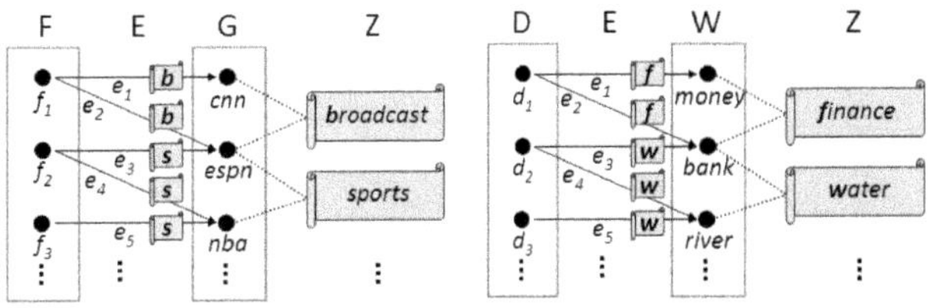

(a) Subscription graph representation of our model

(b) Subscription graph representation of the standard LDA

Figure 1: Subscription graph representation of models

the statistical inference. By placing Dirichlet priors α and β on the multinomial distributions $P(z|d)$ and $P(w|z)$, those multinomial distributions are smoothed by the amount of α and β and become safe from the overfitting problem of PLSI. It is also known that PLSI emerges as a specific instance of LDA under Dirichlet priors [7, 10].

3.3 Applying LDA to the Relationship Graph in a Social Network

Before justifying our approach, we briefly explain Twitter and a few interesting aspects of its data, which we use in our performance evaluations later in this paper. In contrast to a mutual friendship in other social networks, Twitter's relationships are unidirectional (i.e., a Twitter user does not need an approval from a user with whom she wants to make friends). Thus, we use the term *follow* when a user adds another user as her friend. Formally, when a user f follows a user g, f generates a *follow edge*, or simply an *edge*, $e(f, g)$ from a *follower* f to a *followed user* g. We also use $e'(f, g)$ to denote an edge from g to f (indicating that g is followed by f), $e(f)$ to denote the set of all outgoing edges from f, and $e'(g)$ to denote the set of all incoming edges to g. To refer to the set of all followers, the set of all followed users, and the set of all edges in the dataset we use F, G, and E, respectively.

Figure 1(a) depicts this notation using a graph that we refer to as a *subscription graph*. For example, we observe $e(f_1, cnn) = e'(cnn, f_1) = e_1$, $e(f_1) = \{e_1, e_2\}$, and $e'(espn) = \{e_2, e_3\}$ in Figure 1(a). Given this subscription graph, our goal is to label each edge with a correct label (interest) and group (label) each followed user based on those labeled edges. For example, since e_2 and e_3 are labeled with *broadcast* and *sports*, respectively, *espn* is labeled with both. Now we can frame our problem as the *graph labeling* problem of automatically associating each user g_i in G with a set of accurate interests z_k in Z based on its labeled incoming edges $e'(g_i)$. (We also label f_j in F as well.)

We can view the interest here as a topic in a document generative model. As briefly mentioned in Section 3.1, a document topic model assumes that an author has a topic in mind when selecting a word for a document. Likewise, when a user follows another user in Twitter (i.e., when a user generates a follow edge), the follower has an interest in the followed user. This interest may be caused by reasons such as sharing a common interest, having an off-line relationship, being popular, etc. Among these reasons for following someone on Twitter, the two most common reasons are sharing a common interest and being popular, since the unidirectional nature of Twitter relationships allows a user to follow another user without requiring that user to follower her in return, as in the case of a blog subscription graph.

Furthermore, we can consider a follower f to be a document d, a followed user g as a word w, and a list of followed users for the follower as the content of the document. Figure 1 illustrates this equivalence between our *edge generative model* and the standard LDA and justifies our approach of applying LDA to a relationship graph in a social network without changing LDA's generative model.

We use the same notation with LDA. z denotes a labeling of a followed user with a topic (interest), or simply a topic, $P(z|f)$ denotes the multinomial distribution of topics given a follower, and $P(g|z)$ denotes the multinomial distribution of followed users given a topic. α and β are Dirichlet priors constraining $P(z|f)$ and $P(g|z)$, respectively.

3.4 Differences between LDA and Edge Generative Model

In the previous section, we described the equivalence between our edge generative model and the standard LDA. However, there is a subtle difference between the two generative processes. While words are sampled *with replacement* in the standard LDA, followed users are sampled *without replacement* in our model. For example, in a document generative model, a document may contain the word *car* multiple times. On the other hand, in our edge generative model, a user cannot follow the same user *Barack Obama* multiple times. As a result, the probabilistic distribution in our model does not follow a multinomial distribution but follows a *multivariate hypergeometric* distribution. Fortunately, the multinomial distribution can also be used for our model because it is known that a multivariate hypergeometric distribution converges to a multinomial distribution as the sample size grows large [1]. In our case, since sampling is done on millions of nodes, the two distributions become practically indistinguishable.

Also, when we represent E in matrix form by putting F in the rows and G in the columns as $E \in B^{F \times G}$, where $B = \{0, 1\}$, some differing aspects are noticed:

1. The rows and the columns are from the same entity U, a set of all Twitter users ($F, G \subseteq U$). In a matrix formed from a document corpus, documents are located in the rows and words are located in the columns.

2. The matrix is very big and sparse. Because users follow each other, the size of the rows and columns is almost equal to that of all Twitter users ($|F| \simeq |G| \simeq |U|$). The size of the matrix becomes $|F| \times |G|$ and most of its values are 0. This aspect is different from a matrix formed from a document corpus, where the size of the columns (words) is orders of magnitude smaller than that of the rows (documents).

3. The matrix is a binary matrix, in which 1 indicates the existence of an edge and 0 indicates no edge. Each element in a matrix formed from a document corpus is the number of occurrences of each word in a document.

4. As in a matrix formed from a document corpus, the distribution of the column sums show a power-law distribution, in which some small portion of the columns accounts for a majority of the total column sum. In a document corpus, these columns correspond to words such as *the* and *is*, which we call *stop words*, and are generally removed. Those columns in our matrix, however, correspond to users such as *Barack Obama* and *Britney Spears*, which we can call *popular users*, and should be taken into account.

Among the four major differences described above, the first and the third do not affect our effort to apply LDA to the follow edge dataset. Only appropriate pre-processing is required. The second limits the size of the analysis but can be solved by adding more resources or by dividing the work into multiple machines [20].

However, the last difference has a significant effect on our analysis because it is related to the quality of our analysis results. In a document corpus analysis, the stop words are generally removed before analysis, since an analysis without removing these stop words produces a very *noisy* result where the frequent stop words are labeled with every topic [4]. However, in our analysis, popular users are very important to include in the analysis because most users are keenly interested in following famous and influential users whose topic interests are similar to theirs. Unfortunately, it is not sufficient to simply include the popular users for LDA analysis, because the inclusion of popular users produces the same noisy result seen in the text analysis case: when stop words (or popular users) are included, they get included in every topic group, producing a very noisy result.

In the following section, we explore some LDA extensions to deal with the noise generated by popular users. Note that the earlier work on the application of LDA to an authorship graph dataset [9, 26] did not address how we can handle popular users. For example, [9] focused on the issue of how to transform co-authorship relations to a graph and [26] focused on how to deal with a large number of topic groups that are produced from the nodes whose connectivity is very *low*.

Before moving to the next section, we summarize the symbols used in this paper in Table 1.

Table 1: Symbols used throughout this paper and their meanings

Symbol	Meaning
u	A Twitter user
U	A set of all u
f	A follower
F	A set of all f
g	A followed user
G	A set of all g
z	A topic (interest)
Z	A set of all z
$e(f, g)$	A follow edge from f to g
$e'(f, g)$	A follow edge from g to f
$e(f)$	A set of all outgoing edges from f
$e'(g)$	A set of all incoming edges to g
E	A set of all $e(f, g)$ $\forall f \in F$, $\forall g \in G$

4. HANDLING POPULAR USERS

As discussed in Section 3.4, popular users generate noise if they are not dealt with carefully. This section describes how to handle this issue efficiently (i.e., how to label popular

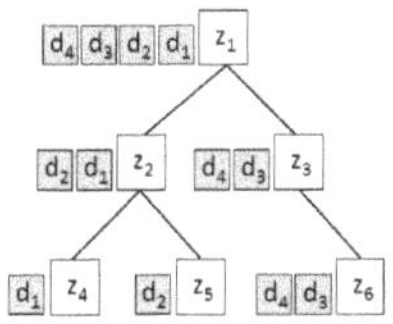

Figure 2: Topic hierarchy and documents generated in the hierarchy

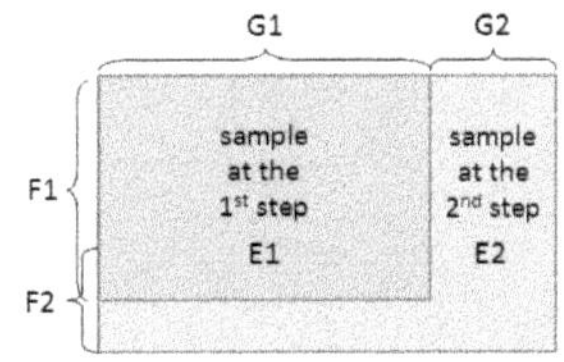

Figure 3: two-step labeling

users with correct labels). We first attempt to use the standard LDA with different settings (asymmetric priors). Then we explore the most appropriate LDA approach to this issue (Hierarchical LDA [3]) among a variety of LDA extensions we considered. Finally we propose two new LDA extensions of our own (*two-step labeling* and *threshold noise filtering*). The two new extensions can be combined together for better labeling quality.

4.1 Setting Asymmetric Priors

As mentioned in Section 3.2, LDA constrains the distributions of topics and words with Dirichlet priors α and β, respectively. Though each element of vectors α and β may take different values in principle, in the standard LDA, each element of α and β is assumed to have the same value (often referred to as the *symmetric prior assumption*). Intuitively, this assumption implies that every topic and word in a document corpus is equally likely.

Though the former sounds agreeable, the latter sounds unrealistic since it is very well known that the probability distribution of words follows a power-law distribution by Zipf's law. It is also the reason why stop words are removed before applying LDA to a document corpus, since stop words correspond to the head of the power-law distribution.

The most intuitive approach to address this issue would be to set a different prior for each followed user. Between the two priors α and β, we are only interested in β, the prior over the distribution of words given a topic, because a followed user corresponds to a word in the standard LDA. As a higher prior value implies a higher likelihood of being observed in the corpus, we set each prior value proportional to the number of incoming edges of each followed user. It is expected to associate popular users with more accurate labels as they are given adequate prior values.

We set β_{g_i}, the prior for the followed user g_i in the vector β, as in Equation (3):

$$\beta_{g_i} = \frac{0.98|e'(g_i)| + 0.01max(|e'(g)|) - 0.99min(|e'(g)|)}{max(|e'(g)|) - min(|e'(g)|)} \quad (3)$$

Note that we set the lowest value for each element in β_{g_i} as 0.01 and the highest value as 0.99 to make prior values skewed between 0 and 1.

4.2 Hierarchical LDA

Hierarchical LDA (HLDA) is also a good candidate for our problem because it generates a topic hierarchy and more frequent topics are located at higher levels. Figure 2 shows an example of topic hierarchy and document paths in the topic tree, where z_k denotes a topic and d_i denotes a document. In HLDA, when a document is generated according to Equation (1), words are chosen from topics in a document path. Since the top level topic is associated with all the documents, common words in every document (i.e., stop words) are expected to be labeled with the top level topic. On the contrary, the bottom level topics are expected to be more specific as they are associated with a small number of documents. For example, if z_2 is a topic about *network*, z_4 and z_5 would be a topic about *queueing* and *routing*, respectively. As z_1 is usually a topic consisting of the stop words, a document d_1 from the document tree path of z_1-z_2-z_4 consists of words from topic z_1, z_2, and z_4 and becomes a document about *network queueing*. Similarly in our model, z_1 is involved in every user's follow edge generation process and is expected to be associated with popular users.

This topic hierarchy is established because HLDA is based on the Nested Chinese Restaurant Process (NCRP), a tree extension to Chinese Restaurant Process, which probabilistically generates a partition of a set $\{1, 2, \ldots, n\}$ at time n. In NCRP, a document is considered as a Chinese restaurant traveler who visits L restaurants along a restaurant tree path, where L refers to the level of the tree (i.e., the length of the path).

4.3 Two-Step Labeling

In the previous sections, we explored existing LDA approaches to handle the popular user issue. Now we propose a new LDA extension: *two-step labeling*. We decompose the labeling process into two sub processes of establishing topics and labeling users with the established topics. In the first *topic establishment step*, we run LDA after removing popular users from the dataset similar to how we remove stop words before applying LDA to a document corpus. This step generates clean topics free from the noise generated by popular users. In the second *labeling step*, we apply LDA only to popular users in the dataset. As we use the collapsed Gibbs sampling algorithm [21], edges to popular users are labeled according to the pre-established topics as represented in Equation (4):

$$P(e(f_i, g_j) = z|\cdot) \propto \frac{N_{g_j z} + \beta}{\sum_{k=1}^{|G|}(N_{g_k z} + \beta)} \frac{N_{f_i z} + \alpha}{\sum_{k=1}^{|Z|}(N_{f_i z_k} + \alpha)}, \quad (4)$$

where $P(e(f, g) = z|\cdot)$ denotes the probability of labeling the edge from a follower f to the followed user g with a topic z given all conditions, N_{gz} denotes the number of times g is labeled with z, and N_{fz} denotes the number of times f is labeled with z.

This equation implies that an edge to a followed user is assigned to a topic according to how many times that user has been assigned to the topic, as well as how many times that topic has been previously assigned to the follower following that user. Thus, if some assignments are made in the first step, they affect assignments in the second step. For example, if a user f_1 follows non-popular users g_1 and g_2 and a popular user g_3, g_1 and g_2 are sampled at the first step and g_3 is sampled at the second step with a higher likelihood to

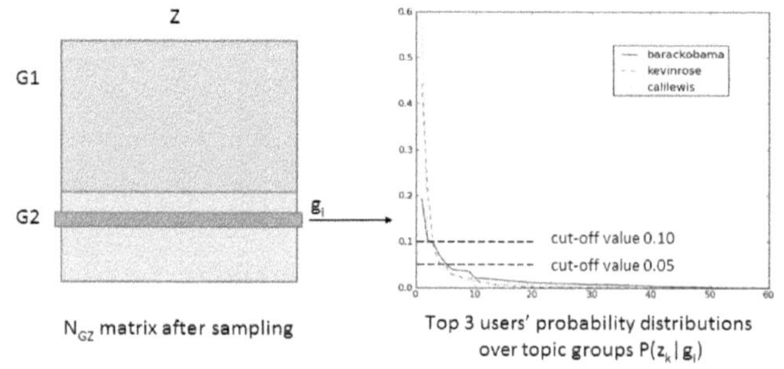

Figure 4: An example of threshold noise filtering process

be labeled with the topic that g_1 or g_2 are labeled with at the first step.

This approach is illustrated in Figure 3, where the $E1$ part of the dataset is sampled at the first step and the $E2$ part is sampled at the second step. Note that *two-step labeling* does not increase computational complexity because it samples a different part of the dataset at each sampling step. $(O(|Z| \cdot |E|) = O(|Z| \cdot (|E1| + |E2|))$

There is related research in the literature. Online LDAs introduced in [5] are designed to deal with a growing corpus and sample topics for words in a document as it comes in. Though both *two-step labeling* and online LDAs use multi-step sampling, their goals are totally different. While online LDAs try to change topics as the corpus grows over time, *two-step labeling* fixes a set of topics and labels users with this fixed set of topics. From Figure 3, $G1$ and $G2$ (words) are mutually exclusive in *two-step labeling* while $F1$ and $F2$ (documents) are mutually exclusive in online LDAs.

4.4 Threshold Noise Filtering

As briefly described in Section 3.1, the association between a user (a word) and a topic has varying association strengths represented by $P(g|z)$ ($P(w|z)$) in a probabilistic topic model. Thus, we can list users labeled with the same topic in descending order of $P(g|z)$ and regard the top entries in the list (*topic group*) as more important than the entries at the bottom because they are more strongly associated with the topic. Similarly, we can measure the association strength from the user's viewpoint using $P(z|g)$. Though *two-step labeling* may help label popular users with the right topics, popular users may take top positions even in less-relevant topic groups because even the smallest number of times a popular user is assigned to a topic group could outnumber the largest number of times a non-popular user is assigned to that topic group.

To mitigate this problem, we propose a new approach, *threshold noise filtering*, which sets a cut-off value to determine whether to label a user with each topic. By ignoring assignments below the cut-off value, we can expect smoothing and noise reduction effects as in the *anti-aliasing filter*. We set $N_{g_i z_k}$, the number of times a followed user g_i is assigned to a topic group z_k, as 0 if it is below the cut-off value C:

$$N_{g_i z_k} = \begin{cases} 0 & \text{if } P(z_k|g_i) = \frac{N_{g_i z_k}}{\sum_{j=1}^{|Z|} N_{g_i z_j}} < C \\ N_{g_i z_k} & \text{otherwise.} \end{cases}$$

As *threshold noise filtering* process is done after sampling, it does not increase computational complexity similar to *two-step labeling*. Figure 4 illustrates this process and shows the top three popular users' distributions over topic groups. (Other normal users also show similar non-linear distributions.) Alternatively, we may filter out less relevant topics by keeping only the top-K topics for each user, for a reasonably small K value. We tested both schemes (threshold noise filtering and top-K filtering), but we couldn't see any practical differences. Due to lack of space, we only report the results with the former scheme. Though *threshold noise filtering* can be used with any other approaches, we combine it with the two most representative cases, *two-step labeling* and the standard LDA in our experiments.

5. EXPERIMENTS

In this section, we experimentally compare our proposed extensions to LDA, *two-step labeling* and *threshold noise filtering*, against existing approaches. We ran experiments on a real-world dataset obtained from Twitter and compared the performance of various approaches under two evaluation metrics, *perplexity* and *quality*. As we will see from our results, our proposed extensions show performance equivalent to or significantly better than existing approaches in our experiments.

In Section 5.1, we describe our dataset and the overall experimental setup. In Sections 5.2 and 5.3, we report our results on *perplexity* and *quality*, respectively. We also provide a qualitative comparison of different approaches in Section 5.4.

5.1 Dataset and Experiment Settings

For our experiments, we use a Twitter dataset we collected between October 2009 and January 2010. The original downloaded dataset contained 273 million follow edges, but we sampled 10 million edges from this dataset to keep our experiment manageable. To ensure that all the follow edges were preserved in our sampled dataset, we first sampled *followers* randomly and included all follow edges from the sampled users, until we obtained 10 million follow edges.

Figure 5 shows the distributions of incoming and outgoing edges in the sampled dataset. The horizontal axis shows the number of edges at a node and the vertical axis shows how many nodes have the given edge count. Both axes are shown in a logarithmic scale. From the graph, it is clear that the number of incoming edges follows a power-law distribution, which is often the case for this type of dataset. Interestingly, we observe that the number of outgoing edges is quite uniform between edge counts 1 to 100, which is different from the distribution reported in [14]. We do not believe this difference is due to our sampling, because the graph from the complete dataset shows the same flat curve between the edge counts 1 and 100 [25]. It could be an interesting future work to investigate where this difference comes from. In our sampled dataset, *barackobama* has the most followers, 7410, and *zappos* follows the most users, 142,669. Table 2 shows some basic statistics of the sampled dataset.

Since we are mainly interested in investigating how different approaches handle popular users, we categorized the followed users G into two distinct sub groups according to their incoming-edge counts. One group is the *normal* user group, where $|e'(g)| \leq V$, a boundary value, and the other group is the *popular* user group, where $|e'(g)| > V$. We tested three

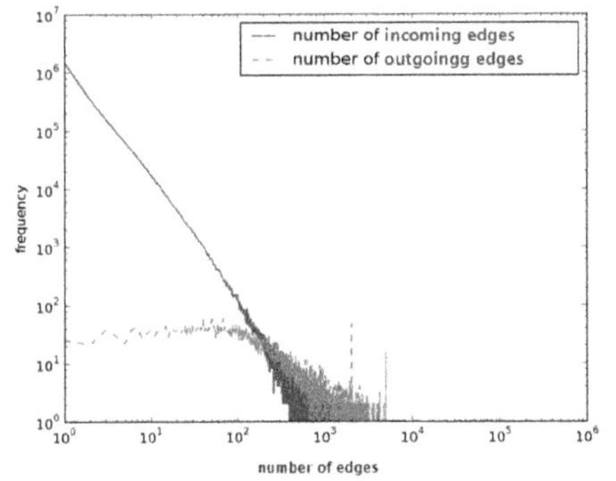

Figure 5: Distributions of incoming and outgoing edges

Table 2: Statistics of our Twitter dataset

Statistics	Value
$\|E\|$	$10,000,000$
$\|U\|$	$2,430,237$
$\|F\|$	$14,015$
$\|G\|$	$2,427,373$
$max(\|e(f)\|)$	$142,669$ (f: *zappos*)
$max(\|e'(g)\|)$	$7,410$ (g: *barackobama*)

boundary values $V = 50$, 100, and 500. Since all the results from the three boundary values show consistent patterns, we only report the result from the case when $V = 100$, where the popular user group consists of only 0.3% of all followed users but accounts for 20.2% of all follow edges.

Table 3 summarizes the eight representative experimental cases we report on in this section. *base* is the standard LDA experiment over the whole group. *non-popular* is also the standard LDA experiment but this experiment is applied only to the normal user group to remove the noise generated by popular users. For *beta*, we use asymmetric Dirichlet priors for the hyperparameter β, where we have tested proportional, inversely-proportional, and ladder-shape prior schemes. *hlda-2lv* and *hlda-3lv* are HLDA experiments with two and three levels each. *2step* is our *two-step labeling* experiment. For *threshold noise filtering*, where we have tested multiple threshold settings including $C = 0.01$, 0.05, 0.10, and $K = 1$, 2, 3, we generate *filter-base* and *filter-2step* by combining *threshold noise filtering* with *base* and *two-step labeling* each. Due to space limits and to clarify our discussion, we only report the results for a subset of our experimental settings in this paper. In particular, we report the result from proportional β priors for *beta* and $C = 0.05$ for *threshold noise filtering*. The results that are not reported in this paper are very similar to what we report here.

In all of our experiments, we generated 100 topic groups (50 groups for *hlda-2lv*) and picked the top ten entries in each topic group according to their probabilities $P(g|z)$ in each group.

5.2 Perplexity

In this section, we report our results on the *perplexity* metric, which was also used in earlier related work such as [4, 9,10,26]. *Perplexity* is a well-known standard metric used in IR. It tries to quantify the accuracy of a model by measuring

Table 3: Experimental cases and descriptions

Case	Experiment Description
base	LDA over the whole group dataset
non-popular	LDA over the normal user group dataset
beta	LDA with asymmetric β priors
hlda-2lv	HLDA with 2 levels
hlda-3lv	HLDA with 3 levels
2step	Two-step labeling
filter-base	Threshold noise filtering after *base*
filter-2step	Threshold noise filtering after *2step*

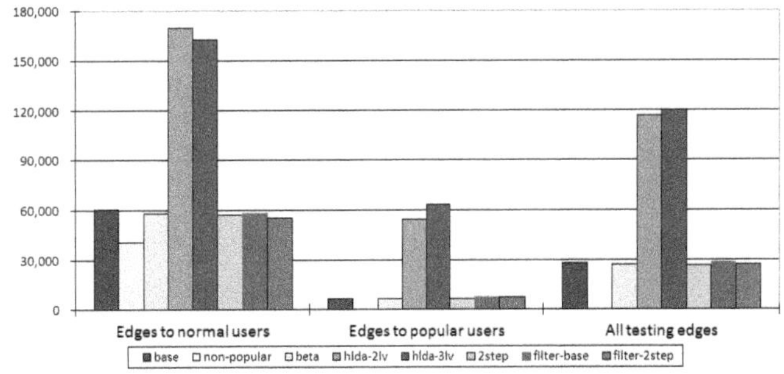

Figure 6: *Perplexity* comparison

how well the trained model deals with an unobserved test data. More precisely, perplexity is defined to be [26]:

$$Perplexity(E_{test}) = \exp^{-\frac{\sum_{e \in E_{test}} \log P(e)}{|E_{test}|}},$$

where E_{test} denotes all the edges in the test dataset.[1] We calculated *Perplexity* values for the 10% held-out dataset after training the models on the remaining 90% dataset. In general, lower perplexity means better generalizability.

Note that the original LDA model is designed to derive an optimal model that minimizes perplexity. Therefore, it is unlikely that extensions to base LDA show lower perplexity. Our primariy goal of comparing the results under the perplexity metric is to see whether our proposed extensions significantly degrade perplexity. Figure 6 compares *Perplexity* values of the eight experimental cases. The last set of bars show the *Perplexity* values on the overall test dataset. The first set of bars show *Perplexity* only on the edges to normal users and the second set of bars show *Perplexity* only on the edges to popular users.

From the graphs, we first notice that HLDA (*hlda-3lv* and *hlda-2lv*) shows significantly worse *Perplexity* than others. This is due to the fact that the standard LDA is designed to minimize *Perplexity* while HLDA is not necessarily designed for this task. We also note that the *Perplexity* value for *non-popular* is significantly lower than others. This is because we eliminate all edges to popular users in *non-popular* and do *not* include these edges in computing the *Perplexity* value. Therefore, *non-popular* had an unfair advantage of "ignoring" all noise from popular users and not being evaluated on them. Overall, we find that our *two-step labeling* and *threshold noise filtering* show similar perplexity values

[1]The *Perplexity* values of *hlda-2lv* and *hlda-3lv* are calculated with the empirical likelihood values provided by Mallet (http://mallet.cs.umass.edu).

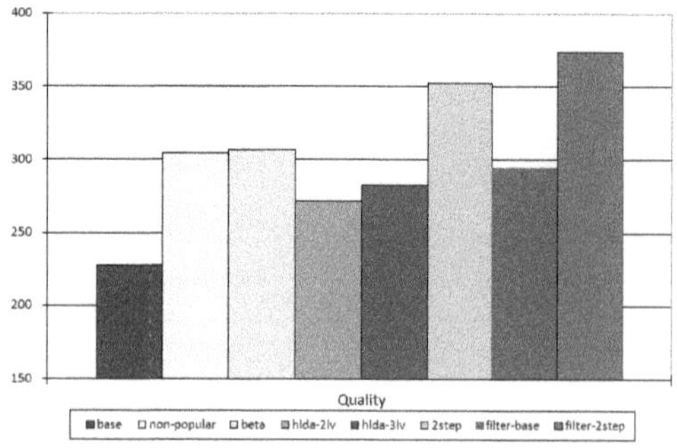

Figure 7: *Quality* comparison

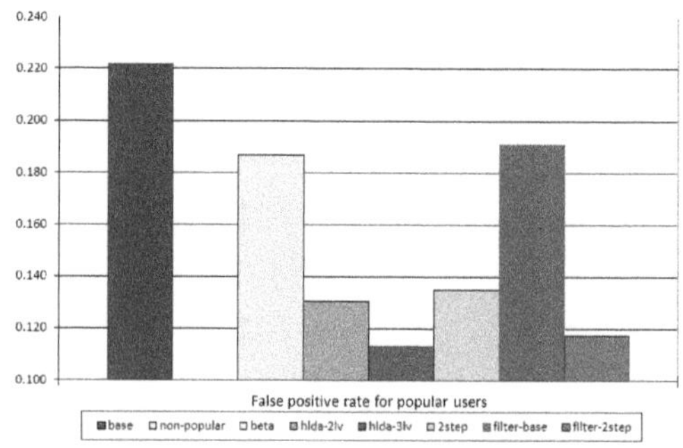

Figure 8: False positive rate of popular users

to the standard LDA model.[2] That is, our extensions to LDA do not introduce noticeable *Perplexity* degradation to the standard LDA model.

5.3 Quality

Ultimately, the effectiveness of various approaches should be determined by how users perceive the quality of the identified topic groups from each approach. To measure human-perceived quality, we conducted a survey with a total of 14 participants. The participants in our survey were presented with a random group of ten Twitter users (identified by one of the eight approaches described in Section 5.1) and were asked to indicate if each user in the topic group was relevant to the group or not. Overall, we collected 23 judged topic groups per each approach with a total of 161 judged topic groups.

Given the survey results, we computed the human-perceived *Quality* value of the topic groups Z identified by an approach as:

$$Quality(Z) = \sum_{k=1}^{|Z|}\sum_{i=1}^{|z_k|} \delta(g_i, z_k)\log(|e'(g_i)|),$$

where δ function is defined as:

$$\delta(g_i, z_k) = \begin{cases} 1 & \text{if user } g_i \text{ is related to topic group } z_k \\ -1 & \text{if user } g_i \text{ is not related to topic group } z_k. \end{cases}$$

Note that in the above *Quality* formula, the factor $\log(|e'(g_i)|)$ is added to assign higher weights to more popular users, because most people are interested in following popular users and pay more attention to the correct topic clustering of those users.

Figure 7 reports the results from this survey, where each bar shows the *Quality* value of one of the eight approaches. From this graph, we observe the following:

1. Both of our extensions, *two-step labeling* and *threshold noise filtering* are very effective in improving the human-perceived quality of identified topic groups. For example, when compared to *base*, *filter-2step* achieves a 1.64 times higher *Quality* value.

2. As *two-step filtering* initially forms clean topics free from popular user generated noise, its gain is more significant than that of *threshold noise filtering*. However, *threshold noise filtering* can be easily combined with any other approaches to improve *Quality*, as in *filter-base*.

3. If we apply the standard LDA to popular users as well without any pre-filtering, the produced topic groups are quite noisy. For example, the *Quality* value of *base* is 1.34 times lower than *non-popular*, which filters out all popular users first.

4. Using an asymmetric Dirichlet prior for the hyperparameter β improves *Quality*, but the result is still noisier compared to our extensions.

5. The HLDA model shows only marginal improvements in the *Quality* metric when compared to *base*. This low performance is because most of the low-level groups in HLDA have users with very few followers (who are less likely to be interesting when recommended) and contribute only small weights to *Quality*.

In Figure 8, we also report the false positive rates for popular users, which measures incorrect labeling of popular users. That is, whenever a user in the popular user group is placed in a topic group from our analysis, our survey participants evaluated whether the topic group is a good fit for that user. Figure 8 reports what fraction of them were considered to be a "bad fit" or an "incorrect" association. Different from Figure 7, the HLDA models seemingly perform as well as or even better than our two approaches. This is because HLDA tends to place popular users at top-level groups. When our survey participants looked at such a group, they simply considered it as a "popular user group" and determined that the popular users in the group were a good fit, even though the group itself did not exhibit any coherent topic. Therefore, even though the false positive rate for HLDA is low, it does not necessarily improve the topic-based recommendation accuracy for popular users. We can observe that our *2step* and *filter-2step* show comparably low false positive rates similar to those of the HLDA approaches.

5.4 Qualitative Comparison

In this section, we examine the topic groups generated from each approach more closely to get a better sense of the quality of produced topic groups.

Figure 9 shows the top ten users in a topic group from *base*, which we name as the *cycle* group. Together with their Twitter usernames, we show their follower counts $|e'(g)|$, and the bio of each user. By going over the users' bios, we can

[2] In fact, the *Perplexity* values of our two approaches are lower than the standard LDA in our experiments, but we expect that this is simple experimental fluctuation that does not have a significant meaning.

g	|e'(g)|	Bio
lancearmstrong	2370	7-time Tour de France winner, full time cancer fighter - LIVESTRONG!
levileipheimer	285	Pro Cyclist
ghincapie	234	*[No Bio] Professional Cyclist*
johanbruyneel	203	9X winning Tour De France Sports Director
barackobama	7410	44th President of the United States
teamradioshack	141	*[No Bio] Pro Cycle Team RadioShack*
dzabriskie	137	Professional Bike Racer
philliggett	126	Pro-cycling commentator.
christianvdv	114	Professional Cyclist
stephenfry	3384	British Actor, Writer, Lord of Dance, Prince of Swimwear & Blogger

Figure 9: Topic group *cycle* from *base* showing the popular user issue

g	|e'(g)|	Bio
googleimages	94	News, tips, and tricks direct from the Google Images team
androidandme	84	Meet your new Android friend.
androidguys	73	Your trusted source for Android news and opinion since November 5, 2007.
prethinking	66	PreThinking.com - your source for all things Palm Pre
engadgetmobile	97	Official Twitter account of Engadget Mobile!
skyfire	88	Skyfire 3.0 for Android and Skyfire 2.0 for iPhone are changing the way people browse on thier mobile devices! www.get.skyfire.com
precentral	75	All about Palm webOS devices
boygenius	95	President, General Manager, Editor-in-chief of BGR.com. Professional smack talker.
theandroidsite	71	News and reviews of Google's Android OS
nokconv	58	A team of Nokia tweeters. Follow us for various updates, info, and the occasional banal banter.

Figure 10: Topic group *mobile gadget blog* from *non-popular*

g	|e'(g)|	Bio
google	3143	News and updates from Google
twitter	3715	Always wondering what's happening.
techcrunch	3565	Breaking Technology News And Opinions From TechCrunch
tweetdeck	2649	TweetDeck is your personal browser for staying in touch with what's happening now, connecting you with your contacts across Twitter, Facebook and more.
mashable	3938	Breaking social media, tech and digital news and analysis from Mashable.com, the top resource and guide for all things web. Updates from @mashable staff.
cnnbrk	3787	CNN.com is among the world's leaders in online news and information delivery.
wefollow	2861	A user powered twitter directory located at http://wefollow.com
googlereader	691	News, tips and tricks from the Google Reader team
hootsuite	1708	Updates about the social media dashboard which allows teams to broadcast, monitor and track results. For support, follow @hootsuite_help + for news @hootwatch.
breakingnews	2210	The latest breaking news alerts around the world from hundreds of sources.

Figure 11: Topic group from *2step* corresponding to Figure 10

g	|e'(g)|	Bio
google	3143	News and updates from Google
techcrunch	3565	Breaking Technology News And Opinions From TechCrunch
tweetdeck	2649	TweetDeck is your personal browser for staying in touch with what's happening now, connecting you with your contacts across Twitter, Facebook and more.
mashable	3938	Breaking social media, tech and digital news and analysis from Mashable.com, the top resource and guide for all things web. Updates from @mashable staff.
wired	1293	Official Twitter feed for Wired magazine & Wired.com. Steering the ship this week: sports editor @erikmal
googlereader	691	News, tips and tricks from the Google Reader team
firefox	750	I make the web a little faster, safer, smarter, better.
youtube	673	Tweets on YouTube news, trends, and — of course — videos.
engadget	827	Official Twitter account of Engadget!
seesmic	1075	I make updates and announcements for Seesmic.com Send feedback/questions to @askseesmic

Figure 12: Topic group from *filter-2step* corresponding to Figure 10

see that many of the users in the group have the same interest *cycle*. However, we also observe that among the three users with the highest number of incoming edges, *barackobama*, *stephenfry*, and *lancearmstrong*, only *lancearmstrong* is related to *cycle*. The other two users, *barackobama* and *stephenfry* are included in this group simply because they are famous and followed by many users. In particular, we note that *barackobama* appears in 15 groups out of 100 topic groups produced by *base*. Among the 15 groups, only one of them is related to his specialty, *politics*, which clearly shows that the standard LDA suffers from the noise from popular users if applied directly to our social graph dataset.

Figure 10 shows an example topic group produced by *non-popular*. Note that in this group, all users have $|e'(g)|$ values of smaller than 100, because popular users are removed from the dataset. Therefore, none of the popular users will belong to a topic group under this approach. When we go over the users' bios, we see that *all* users in this group is somewhat related to *mobile gadgets*. That is, the topic group produced by *non-popular* is significantly cleaner (less noisy) than that from *base* at the expense of not being able to group any popular users.

Figure 11 shows an example topic group from *2step*. Note that many users in this group are very popular and they are mainly about the same topic, *tech media*, indicating that *2step* is able to group popular users into the right topic group in general. However, we observe that *2step* still suffers from the presence of a few popular, yet less relevant users in the group (in this example, *cnnbrk* and *breakingnews* may be considered less relevant to the group than others).

With *threshold noise filtering*, we achieved less noisy results. Figure 12 shows a result topic group from *filter-2step* corresponding to the group in Figure 11 from *2step*. We observe that *cnnbrk* and *breakingnews*, popular users on general media, are now removed from Figure 11 and more technology-centric media such as *firefox*, *youtube*, and *engadget* are added. Note that *firefox* and *youtube* are Twitter accounts publishing news related to FireFox and YouTube. As we pick only a few most probable topics for popular users in *filter-2step*, they have less chance to appear in less-relevant topic groups.

6. CONCLUSION

In this paper, we applied LDA to analyze the relationship graph in a large social network. Different from the usual approaches that extract topics from textual data, such as bio and tweets, our approaches rely purely on the social-network graph consisting of follow edges. Even with this relatively limited type of data compared to those of previous approaches, our approaches generated very well-organized results and showed the great potential of applying LDA to these kinds of clustering applications. Our approaches are especially useful when only linkage data is available.

We also dealt with popular user generated noise, which is inevitable in a large social network. Unlike the stop words in the standard LDA applications, popular users have important meanings and should be dealt with carefully. We explored four extensions to the standard LDA and quantitatively and qualitatively analyzed their results using a Twitter dataset. Our proposed approaches, two-step labeling and threshold noise filtering, are very effective in handling this popular user issue, showing 1.64 times improvement in the quality of the produced topic groups, compared to the standard LDA model.

7. ACKNOWLEDGEMENTS

We would like to thank Jong Han Park, and Christopher Moghbel for their help and feedback throughout this research.

8. REFERENCES

[1] Multinomial distribution. `http://en.wikipedia.org/wiki/Multinomial_distribution`.

[2] E. M. Airoldi, D. M. Blei, S. E. Fienberg, and E. P. Xing. Mixed membership stochastic blockmodels. In *J. Mach. Learn. Res.*, 2008.

[3] D. M. Blei, T. L. Griffiths, M. I. Jordan, and J. B. Tanenbaum. Hierarchical topic models and the nested chinese restaurant process. In *Neural Information Processing Systems*, 2003.

[4] D. M. Blei, A. Y. Ng, and M. I. Jordan. Latent dirichlet allocation. *Journal of Machine Learning Research*, 3:993–1022, 2003.

[5] K. R. Canini, L. Shi, and T. L. Griffiths. Online inference of topics with latent dirichlet allocation. In *Artifical Intelligence and Statistics*, 2009.

[6] M. Ester, H. peter Kriegel, J. S, and X. Xu. A density-based algorithm for discovering clusters in large spatial databases with noise. In *Proceedings of 2nd International Conference on Knowledge Discovery and Data Mining*, pages 226–231. AAAI Press, 1996.

[7] M. Girolami and A. Kaban. On an equivalence between plsi and lda. In *SIGIR*, 2003.

[8] M. Harvey, I. Ruthven, and M. J. Carman. Improving social bookmark search using personalised latent variable language models. In *WSDM*, 2011.

[9] K. Henderson and T. Eliassi-Rad. Applying latent dirichlet allocation to group discovery in large graphs. In *Proceedings of the 2009 ACM symposium on Applied Computing*, 2009.

[10] M. D. Hoffman, D. M. Blei, and F. Bach. Online learning for latent dirichlet allocation. In *In NIPS*, 2010.

[11] T. Hofmann. Probabilistic latent semantic indexing. In *SIGIR*, 1999.

[12] T. Iwata, T. Yamada, and N. Ueda. Modeling social annotation data with content relevance using a topic model. In *NIPS*, 2009.

[13] J. M. Kleinberg. Authoritative sources in a hyperlinked environment. *Journal of the ACM*, 1999.

[14] H. Kwak, C. Lee, H. Park, and S. Moon. What is twitter, a social network or a news media? In *Proceedings of the 19th international conference on World wide web*, WWW '10, pages 591–600, New York, NY, USA, 2010. ACM.

[15] S. Lloyd. Least squares quantization in pcm. *IEEE Transactions on Information Theory*, pages 129–137, 1982.

[16] A. Mccallum, X. Wang, and A. Corrada-Emmanuel. Topic and role discovery in social networks with experiments on enron and academic email. *Journal of Artificial Intelligence Research*, 30:249–272, 2007.

[17] Q. Mei, D. Cai, D. Zhang, and C. Zhai. Topic modeling with network regularization. In *Proceedings of the 17th international conference on World Wide Web*, WWW '08, pages 101–110, New York, NY, USA, 2008. ACM.

[18] A. Mislove, B. Viswanath, K. P. Gummadi, and P. Druschel. You are who you know: Inferring user profiles in online social networks. In *WSDM*, 2010.

[19] N. Pathak, C. DeLong, A. Banerjee, and K. Erickson. Social topic models for community extraction. In *The 2nd SNA-KDD Workshop*, 2008.

[20] A. Smola and S. Narayanamurthy. An architecture for parallel topic models. In *VLDB*, 2010.

[21] M. Steyvers and T. L. Griffiths. Probabilistic topic models. *Handbook of Latent Semantic Analysis*, 2007.

[22] M. Steyvers, P. Smyth, M. Rosen-Zvi, and T. Griffiths. Probabilistic author-topic models for information discovery. In *SIGKDD*, 2004.

[23] V. Tuulos and H. Tirri. Combining topic models and social networks for chat data mining. In *In Proc. of the 2004 IEEE/WIC/ACM International Conference on Web Intelligence*, 2004.

[24] X. Wang, N. Mohanty, and A. Mccallum. Group and topic discovery from relations and text. In *In Proc. 3rd international workshop on Link discovery*, pages 28–35. ACM, 2005.

[25] M. J. Welch, U. Schonfeld, D. He, and J. Cho. Topical semantics of twitter links. In *WSDM*, 2011.

[26] H. Zhang, B. Qiu, C. L. Giles, H. C. Foley, and J. Yen. An lda-based community structure discovery approach for large-scale social networks. In *In IEEE International Conference on Intelligence and Security Informatics*, pages 200–207, 2007.

[27] D. Zhou, E. Manavoglu, J. Li, C. L. Giles, and H. Zha. Probabilistic models for discovering e-communities. In *World Wide Web Conference*, 2006.

Cognos: Crowdsourcing Search for Topic Experts in Microblogs

Saptarshi Ghosh*
IIT Kharagpur, India
MPI-SWS, Germany

Naveen Sharma*
IIT Kharagpur, India
MPI-SWS, Germany

Fabricio Benevenuto
UFOP, Brazil

Niloy Ganguly
IIT Kharagpur, India

Krishna P. Gummadi
MPI-SWS, Germany

ABSTRACT

Finding topic experts on microblogging sites with millions of users, such as Twitter, is a hard and challenging problem. In this paper, we propose and investigate a new methodology for discovering topic experts in the popular Twitter social network. Our methodology relies on the wisdom of the Twitter crowds – it leverages Twitter `Lists`, which are often carefully curated by individual users to include experts on topics that interest them and whose meta-data (List names and descriptions) provides valuable semantic cues to the experts' domain of expertise. We mined List information to build `Cognos`, a system for finding topic experts in Twitter. Detailed experimental evaluation based on a real-world deployment shows that: (a) Cognos infers a user's expertise more accurately and comprehensively than state-of-the-art systems that rely on the user's bio or tweet content, (b) Cognos scales well due to built-in mechanisms to efficiently update its experts' database with new users, and (c) Despite relying only on a single feature, namely crowdsourced Lists, Cognos yields results comparable to, if not better than, those given by the official Twitter experts search engine for a wide range of queries in user tests. Our study highlights Lists as a potentially valuable source of information for future content or expert search systems in Twitter.

Categories and Subject Descriptors: H.3.3 [Information Search and Retrieval]: selection process; H.3.5 [On-line Information Services]: Web-based services

General Terms: Algorithms, Design, Experimentation.

Keywords: Twitter, topic experts, Lists, crowdsourcing, hubs, authorities.

1. INTRODUCTION

Microblogging sites, out of which Twitter is the most popular, have emerged as an important platform for exchanging real-time information on the Web. Recent estimates suggest that 200 million active Twitter users post 150 million tweets (messages) daily [1]. These messages contain a wide variety of information, varying from conversational tweets to highly relevant information on niche topics. The users posting these messages range from globally popular news organizations and celebrities to locally popular community organizers or activists and from domain experts in fields like computer science and astrophysics to spammers that fake the identities of well-known users.

As a result, the quality of information posted in Twitter is highly variable and finding the users that are recognized sources of relevant and trustworthy information on specific topics (i.e., topic experts) is an important challenge. Identifying topic experts is also the first step towards finding authoritative information on the topic. Recognizing this, Twitter itself has created a topical expert search system (known as the Twitter Who To Follow (WTF) service [16]). However, as we show later in this paper, the results from this service leave a lot of scope for improvement.

In this paper, we present **Cognos**, a system for finding topic experts in Twitter. Cognos is based on a new methodology for inferring users' expertise. Traditional approaches to identify topical experts in Twitter rely either on the information provided by the user herself (e.g., in the 'bio' or short autobiography of the Twitter account) [17] or on analyzing the network characteristics and tweeting activity of users [10, 19]. Cognos takes an entirely different approach to identify topical experts in Twitter utilizing *crowdsourced* topical annotation of experts. Specifically, Cognos exploits the *Lists* feature in Twitter, using which any user can group Twitter accounts that tweet on a topic that is of interest to her, and follow their collective tweets. We observe that many users carefully create Lists to include other Twitter users who they consider as experts on a given topic. Furthermore, they generate meta-data, such as List names and descriptions, that provide valuable semantic cues to the topical expertise of the users included in the List. Our key idea is to analyze the meta-data of the Lists containing a user to infer the user's topics of expertise, which in turn enables us to identify topical experts.

To build Cognos, we address three key challenges: (1) How to accurately and comprehensively infer an individual user's topics of expertise from Lists? (2) How to rank the relative expertise of different users identified as experts on a given topic?, and (3) How to crawl the Lists meta-data for hundreds of millions of Twitter users efficiently and scalably?

*Authors contributed equally to this work.

Permission to make digital or hard copies of all or part of this work for personal or classroom use is granted without fee provided that copies are not made or distributed for profit or commercial advantage and that copies bear this notice and the full citation on the first page. To copy otherwise, to republish, to post on servers or to redistribute to lists, requires prior specific permission and/or a fee.
SIGIR'12, August 12–16, 2012, Portland, Oregon, USA.
Copyright 2012 ACM 978-1-4503-1472-5/12/08 ...$10.00.

The main contributions of this paper lie in the methodologies we propose to tackle the above challenges.

We present an extensive evaluation of Cognos based on user feedback obtained using a real-world deployment, which can be accessed at `http://twitter-app.mpi-sws.org/whom-to-follow/`. We summarize here a few highlights from our evaluation: We find that Cognos performs as well as or better than the official Twitter WTF service for more than 52% of the queries. Cognos yields particularly better search results in those cases in which experts do not provide account bios, or whose bios do not contain information about the user's topic of expertise. Moreover, Cognos rarely produces entirely irrelevant results, unlike the Twitter WTF service whose top results, at times, include a few users who are not at all related to the given query, but whose names or bios contain the terms in the query. Furthermore, as Cognos is based on the use of a single and simple feature (Twitter Lists), it is more scalable than prior approaches, which use computationally intensive machine learning algorithms over graph and content-based metrics [10, 19].

2. RELATED WORK

As the number of users and information shared in Twitter grows exponentially, information retrieval techniques, such as search and recommender systems, are increasingly being used to find trending topics, interesting users, and valuable content [14, 16]. A critical component of such systems consists of identifying users who are important sources of information on specific topics (topical experts).

There have been several attempts to measure the influence of Twitter users and thereby identify influential users or experts [3, 4, 8, 12]. However, none of these efforts attempts to identify experts in any *specific topic*. To our knowledge, there have been only two notable efforts that have approached the problem of identifying experts in *specific topics* [10, 19]. Weng *et. al.* [19] proposed a Page-Rank like algorithm TwitterRank that uses both the Twitter graph and processed information from tweets to identify experts in particular topics. On the other hand, Pal *et. al.* [10] used clustering and ranking on more than 15 features extracted from the Twitter graph and the tweets posted by users.

Apart from the above research studies, there also exist some *services* for identifying topical experts in Twitter. Recognizing the importance of searching for experts on specific topics, Twitter itself provides an official "who to follow" (WTF) service [16] where one can search for experts on a given topic (query). Though the exact details of implementation of the service are not publicly known, it is reported [17] that Twitter WTF uses several factors such as the profile information (e.g., name and bio) of users, their social links, their level of engagement in Twitter, and so on to identify topical experts.

All the above approaches primarily rely on the information provided by the user herself (e.g., her account name and bio, the tweets posted by her) and her social graph to infer the topics in which she is an expert. In contrast, the present work relies on the 'wisdom of the Twitter crowd' (i.e., how others describe this user), collected through crowdsourced Lists. Further, all of the above mentioned research studies use fixed Twitter datasets collected at a certain point in time. To the best of our knowledge, this study is the first to address the practical challenge of keeping an OSN-based search / recommender system up-to-date, a challenge that has become essential given the phenomenal growth rate of user populations in today's OSNs [2].

Finally, a few prior studies have used Twitter Lists for different purposes, such as, to identify popular users in a few specific topics (e.g., celebrities, bloggers) and study how they interact with the rest of the Twitter population [20], or to serve as seed nodes for algorithms like topic-sensitive Pagerank [18], or to contextualize individual users [11]. The present study uses Lists for a fundamentally different purpose, which is to find topic experts. In a prior workshop paper [13], we described how we can use Lists to infer topics of expertise for individual Twitter users. In this paper, we not only extend the work to build a fully functional search system, but also present an in-depth evaluation of the quality of List-based expertise inference and ranking.

3. METHODOLOGY AND CHALLENGES

In this section, we first propose our methodology for finding topic experts using Twitter `Lists`. Later we identify the key design challenges in designing a search system based on the methodology.

3.1 Methodology: Leverage Twitter Lists

Twitter introduced Lists in late 2009, to help users organize their followings (i.e., the people whom a user follows) and the information they post [7]. By creating a List, a user can group other Twitter users, and view the aggregated tweets posted by all the listed users in the List timeline. When creating a List, a user typically provides a List name (free text, limited to 25 characters) and optionally adds a List description. For instance, a user can create a List named "celebrities" and add celebrities to this List. Then, the user can view tweets posted by these celebrities in the List timeline.

Table 1 presents illustrative examples of Lists, extracted from our dataset (to be detailed in Section 5.2). The key observation here is that the List names and descriptions provide valuable semantic cues to the topics of expertise of the members of the Lists. For example, using List meta-data, we can associate BarackObama with *politics* and *politicians*, Eminem with *music* and *musicians*, and Daniel Tunkelang with *SIGIR*. Thus, Lists provide a way to annotate Twitter users with their topics of expertise. Interestingly, these annotations are generated by arbitrary Twitter users and so they reflect the collective wisdom of the crowds.

Our methodology relies on *extracting the information contained in the crowdsourced Lists to build an expert search system*. Specifically, it has three parts: (i) gather crowd-created Lists for all Twitter users, (ii) mine List meta-data to infer the topical expertise of individual Twitter users, and (iii) for a given query topic, rank the relative expertise of the users whose topical expertise matches the query.

3.2 Key open questions and design challenges

Our proposed methodology for building a search system for experts in Twitter raises a number of important questions and key design challenges, which we enumerate below:

1. How to infer users' topics of expertise from Lists? Do Lists contain sufficient information to infer the various topics of expertise of individual Twitter users both accurately and comprehensively?

List Name	Description	Members
News	News media accounts	nytimes, BBCNews, WSJ, cnnbrk, CBSNews
Music	Musicians	Eminem, britneyspears, ladygaga, rihanna, BonJovi
Tennis	Tennis players and Tennis news	andyroddick, usopen, Bryanbros, ATPWorldTour
Politics	Politicians and people who talk about them	BarackObama, nprpolitics, whitehouse, billmaher
SIGIR2010	People tweeting from SIGIR 2010	Daniel Tunkelang, Maria Grineva, Ian Soboroff, James Caverlee

Table 1: Examples of Lists, their description, and some members

2. How to rank the relative expertise of different users identified as experts on a given topic?

3. How to crawl the Lists meta-data for tens of millions of Twitter users (experts) created by hundreds of millions of other users? How to keep the Lists data up-to-date as several hundreds of thousands of new users join and create new Lists every single day [2]?

We address the above research challenges in each of the subsequent sections. In Section 4, we describe how we use Lists to infer the topics of expertise of individual Twitter users. Section 5 presents Cognos, a topical expert search system for Twitter that leverages the topical expertise inferred using Lists to identify experts on a given topic and rank them. In Section 6, we propose efficient strategies that minimize the number of Lists that we need to crawl to keep the Cognos system up-to-date. We conduct an extensive evaluation of our proposals by comparing their performance with two systems: (i) the state-of-the-art research system for identifying topical experts in Twitter [10], and (ii) the official Twitter Who-To-Follow service [16].

4. USING LISTS TO INFER EXPERTISE

In this section, we first describe our methodology of inferring the expertise of individual Twitter users and then evaluate the accuracy and expressiveness of the inferred expertise.

4.1 Mining List meta-data to infer expertise

As described in our prior workshop paper [13], our strategy consists of extracting frequently occurring topics (words) from the List meta-data (names and description) and associating these topics with the listed users. The intuition behind our strategy is that a user listed by many other users under a certain topic is very likely to be an expert on that topic. Previous efforts that analyzed Twitter Lists showed that *nouns* and *adjectives* in List names and descriptions are particularly useful for this purpose [11]. So our strategy to extract topics from List meta-data consists of the following steps:

1. Since List names cannot exceed 25 characters, users often combine multiple words using *CamelCase* (e.g., TennisPlayers). We separate these into individual words.
2. We apply common language processing techniques such as case-folding, stemming, and removal of stop-words. In addition to the common stop-words, a set of domain-specific stop-words are also filtered out, e.g., Twitter, List, and Formulist (a tool frequently used to automatically create Lists).
3. Then, we identify nouns and adjectives using a part-of-speech tagger.
4. As a significant fraction of List names and descriptions are in languages other than English, we group together words that are very similar to each other based on edit-distance among words, e.g., politics and *politica*, journalist and *jornalistas*, etc. It can be noted that these words are not unified even by a standard stemmer.
5. As List names and descriptions are typically short, we consider only unigrams and bigrams as topics.

The above strategy produces a set of topics for each user, as well as the frequency with which a topic appears in the names and descriptions of the Lists containing the user.

4.2 Evaluating quality of expertise inference

When evaluating the quality of inferred topics of expertise, we check for two metrics: (i) accuracy – is the user really an expert in the inferred topics? (ii) expressiveness – do Lists comprehensively capture all the different topics in which a user has expertise?

For our evaluation, we need to gather ground truth information about some Twitter users' expertise. Since such ground truth is difficult to obtain for a random set of Twitter users, we consider the following strategies: First, we evaluate for a select set of *popular* users whose true topics of expertise are generally well-known or easily verifiable. Second, for a given set of topics, we collect the top experts identified by the state-of-the-art research system for identifying topical authorities [10], and by the official Twitter WTF service [16]. We then check if our methodology identifies these users as experts in the given topics. The results not only demonstrate the high quality of our expertise inference, but they also uncover drawbacks of the competing state-of-the-art methods.

4.2.1 Inferred expertise for selected popular users

Table 2 shows the top 10 topics (inferred using our List-based method) for a few Twitter users whose expertise is well-known. Our inference is accurate and comprehensive not only for users with millions of followers, but also for users with hundreds or thousands of followers. For instance, for Mark Sanderson (Program Committee Chair at SIGIR 2012), even though his Twitter account is included in only *12 Lists*, the inferred topics identify that he is a researcher in computer science ("cs"), specializing in information retrieval, machine learning ("ml"), search and so on. Again, for US senators (two examples shown in Table 2 – Chuck Grassley and Claire McCaskill), our methodology could accurately identify a variety of topics, such as, their political party (Republicans / Democrats), their state, their gender ('women' in case of Claire McCaskill), their political ideology (conservative / progressive) and even a number of the senate committees of which each senator is a member ('health' in case of Chuck Grassley). We verified the accuracy of our inference using the Wikipedia pages for these people, and found them to be almost always accurate (see [13] for details). Thus, List meta-data is often sufficiently rich to yield high quality expertise inference for a variety of users.

4.2.2 Comparing Cognos with state-of-the-art research system

Next we compare the extent to which the experts identified by a state-of-the-art research system built by Pal *et. al.* [10] can be recalled by our methodology. Pal *et. al.* use more

User	# followers	Most frequent topics
Barack Obama	12,481,245	politics, celebs, government, famous, president, news, leaders, noticias, current events
Ashton Kutcher	9,479,352	celebs, actors, famous, movies, stars, comedy, funny, music, hollywood, pop culture
Mark Sanderson	320	information retrieval, ir, cs, ml, semantic, analysis, search, research, nlproc, tech
Chuck Grassley	34,710	politics, senator, congress, government, republicans, iowa, gop, officials, conservative, health
Claire McCaskill	63,687	politics, senator, government, congress, democrats, missouri, dems, officials, progressive, women
BBC News	574,035	media, news, noticias, journalists, politics, english, newspapers, current, periodicos, london
Linux Foundation	46,718	linux, tech, open, software, libre, gnu, computer, developer, ubuntu, unix
Yoga Journal	71,689	yoga, health, fitness, wellness, magazines, media, mind, meditation, body, inspiration

Table 2: The most common topics of expertise of some well-known Twitter users, as identified from Lists. All topic-words are case-folded to lower case.

User	Extracts from Bio
Query: iphone	
macworld	Mac, iPod, iPhone experts
TUAW	Unofficial Apple Weblog
Query: oil spill	
kate_sheppard	Reporter covering energy, environment
LATenvironment	Environmental news from California
Query: world cup	
FIFAWorldCupTM	FIFA soccer world cup tweets
itvfootball	News from ITV football

Table 3: Some of the top 10 results reported by Pal *et. al.* [10], for whom the topics inferred using Lists include the query-topic (iphone / oil spill / world cup)

than 15 features extracted from the Twitter social graph and the content of the tweets posted by users to identify topical experts. Though an implementation of this system is not publicly available, their paper lists the top 10 experts identified for three specific topics – "iphone", "oil spill" and "world cup". We test whether the topics inferred by our methodology for these experts match with the topic reported by Pal *et. al.*

We find that for a majority of the top 10 experts – 8 out of 10 for "iphone", 7 out of 10 for "world cup", and 6 out of 10 for "oil spill" – in each of the three topics, the set of topics inferred by us includes the topic for which they are reported by Pal *et. al.* Table 3 shows some of these experts, along with their bio.

However, for the rest of the cases, the topics inferred using Lists do *not* contain the topic reported by Pal *et. al.*. Table 4 lists these users along with their bios. Examining their bio, it is evident that these users are, in fact, *not* specifically related to the topic of the corresponding query. For example, a social media entrepreneur and technology blogger *teedubya* was identified as an expert on "iphone", even though he is not a specialist on Apple products. Similarly, *Reuters*, *CBSNews* and *channel4news* are popular news media that report on a variety of topics, including those that are not related to "oil spill" or "world cup". It is likely that the algorithm used by Pal *et. al.* identified these users as experts because a number of their tweets were related to the topic in question during the period when the evaluation was done.

It is worth noting that Pal *et. al.* had explicitly set out to discover topical experts that are not just overtly general and highly followed authorities like popular news media accounts. They highlight the discovery of dedicated specialists that mostly post tweets related to their specialization. Interestingly, our methodology has successfully recalled all such experts (i.e., 100% recall) even though it relies only on one feature, namely Lists. In comparison, Pal *et. al.* rely on 15 features, which indicates the relative advantages of using crowdsourced Lists to identify users' expertise.

User	Extracts from Bio
Query: iphone	
teedubya	Social Strategy Shaman, SEO
macTweeter	*Account no longer exists in Twitter*
Query: oil spill	
Reuters	latest news from around the world
CBSNews	official Twitter feed of CBS News
TIME	Breaking news and current events
huffingtonpost	The Internet Newspaper
Query: world cup	
nikegoal	marketing, music, education, sport
Flipbooks	News, Random Information
channel4news	exclusive stories & breaking news

Table 4: The top 10 results reported by Pal *et. al.* [10], for whom the topics inferred using Lists does *not* include the query-topic (iphone / oil spill / world cup)

4.2.3 Comparing Cognos with Twitter WTF

The official Twitter Who-To-Follow (WTF) service [16] helps to search for topical experts for a given topic (query), and is reported to use several factors, such as, the profile information (e.g., name and bio) of users, their social links, and their level of engagement in Twitter [17]. As part of a user survey to evaluate our system (detailed in Section 5.3.3), we obtained the top 20 experts returned by the Twitter WTF service for a few hundred queries generated by users. We investigated the extent to which our methodology could recall these experts.

Out of the 3,495 distinct users returned by Twitter as top 20 results for some given query, the topics inferred using Lists include the corresponding topic (word in the given query) for 83.4% (2,916) of the users. However, the topics inferred by the List-based methodology for the other 16.6% (579) users did *not* contain the topic (word) in the query. To understand these missing experts better, we manually verified 50 randomly selected users out of the 579 users.

We found 9 out of these 50 users (i.e., 18%) to be relevant experts on the query topics. Our List-based methodology infers topics very similar to the query, but none matching the exact query-word. Table 5 shows two such examples. For the Twitter account of the *dineLA* restaurant, the inferred topics include 'food' and 'restaurant' but not the query-word 'dining' (for which it was returned by Twitter WTF). Similarly, for the Twitter user *HubbleHugger77* who is a space explorer and has directed the film 'Saving Hubble', we identify 'space', 'cosmology' and 'nasa' but not the query-word 'hubble'. This would appear to suggest that a user's name and bio contain clues to the user's expertise.

However, in 29 out of the 50 cases (i.e., 58%), we found that the official Twitter WTF service returns *wrong* results, i.e., the returned user is not at all related to the topic of the query for which she is returned. We conjecture that this is because the query-word appears in the name or bio of the

Query	User	Extracts from Bio	Major topics obtained from Lists
Users for whom topics inferred from Lists contain very similar words but not the exact query-word			
dining	dineLA	official Twitter account of dineLA	restaurant, food, los angeles, chefs, recipes
hubble	HubbleHugger77	Space Explorer, Director of Film Saving Hubble	science, tech, space, universe, cosmology, nasa
Wrong results in Twitter WTF top 20 results			
astrophysicist	jimmyfallon	astrophysicist	celebs, comedy, funny, actors, famous, humor
cooking	danecook	When I tweet, I tweet to kill	celebs, comedy, funny, famous, actors
origami	ScreenOrigami	Web developer from Germany	webdesign, webkrauts, html, designers

Table 5: Examples of (i) users for whom topics inferred from Lists contain semantically very similar words but not the exact query-word (ii) wrong results within Twitter WTF top 20 results.

user. For instance, the well-known comedian Jimmy Fallon has (mockingly) described himself as an astrophysicist in his bio, as a result of which he shows up in the top 20 Twitter WTF results for the query 'astrophysicist'. Table 5 shows other examples of users who are wrongly included within the top 20 results returned by Twitter WTF. We were not able to infer the relevance of the expert to the query in the remaining 12 out of the 50 (24%) manually verified user accounts, as we found the query to be ambiguous.

Thus, not only does our methodology recall a vast majority (83.4%) of the experts identified by Twitter WTF, but also a majority of the missing experts were incorrectly identified by Twitter. Our List-based methodology fails to recall only a small fraction of experts who are actually related to the given query, and even in those cases, we identify topics that are semantically quite similar to the query word.

4.2.4 Summary

Our evaluation demonstrates that our proposed methodology of utilizing crowdsourced List meta-data provides an accurate and comprehensive inference of topics of expertise of individual Twitter users. We also show that in many cases, the List-based methodology is more accurate compared to the existing techniques of inferring topics of a user from her profile or her tweets. In the next section, we describe how we utilize the topics inferred using Lists, to build a search system for topical experts in Twitter.

5. COGNOS EXPERT SEARCH SYSTEM

In this section, we leverage our previously discussed methodology to infer users' expertise to build *Cognos*[1], a search system for topical experts in Twitter. Cognos uses crowdsourced Lists as the *only* source of information and so its performance illustrates the potential uses of Lists in finding experts. We first describe how we rank experts in Cognos and then present an extensive evaluation of the Cognos system.

5.1 Ranking experts

Ranking of users related to a given topic is a well-studied problem, and over the years, several ranking algorithms have been proposed for the Web [6], online topical communities [21], and even for topical experts in Twitter [10,19]. The expert ranking schemes in Twitter take into account several metrics extracted from the social graph and the content of the tweets posted by users. In contrast, we decided to evaluate a ranking scheme that is based solely on the Lists feature, since one of our objectives is to evaluate crowdsourced Lists as the *only* source of information for topical experts – we have already shown that Lists can be used to accurately infer topics of expertise, now we investigate whether Lists are also an effective metric to rank topical experts.

The method described in Section 4.1 gives for each individual user, a topic vector $\{(t_i, f_i)\}$, where t_i are the set of topics inferred for the user, and f_i is the frequency of occurrence of topic t_i in the names and descriptions of the Lists containing the user. Given a query, we compute a topical similarity score between this topic vector for a user and the given query vector, using the algorithm in [5] which computes the *cover density ranking* between the vectors. We chose this similarity score (which is suited to queries containing one to three terms) since queries to expert search systems are almost always short, hence using cosine similarity on tf-idf based representations may not be very effective [9,10]. Finally, we multiply the topical similarity score for a user with the logarithm of the number of Lists containing the user – the intuition behind this is that a user who is included in more number of Lists (by other users) is likely to be more popular in Twitter.

Thus, given a query (topic), Cognos identifies the set of experts related to the topic using the List-based methodology discussed in Section 4.1, and then ranks them using the algorithm described above. In the remainder of this section, we evaluate this List-based methodology of identifying and ranking topical experts in Twitter.

5.2 Building the Cognos experts database

To populate the Cognos expertise database, we started to crawl all the Lists containing all Twitter users. We quickly realized that a brute-force crawl of all Lists for all users would be prohibitively expensive and would not scale. So we only crawled the Lists containing all the 54 million Twitter users in a complete snapshot of the Twitter social network taken in August 2009 [4]. This is only a small fraction of the estimated 465 million Twitter users as of January 2012 [2]. We address the challenge of crawling Lists efficiently and scalably to include experts that joined after 2009, in Section 6.

Of the 54 million Twitter users, we found that 6,843,466 users have been listed at least once. In order to reliably infer topical expertise of a user from Lists, it is important that a user has been listed at least a few times. So we considered only those users who were listed at least 10 times. There were 1,333,126 users listed more than 10 times. Some of these users were listed more than a hundred thousand times. Due to rate-limitations in accessing the Twitter API, we limited our data collection to at most 2000 Lists per user. Overall, for the 1.3 million users, we gathered a total of 88,471,234 Lists. Out of these, 30,660,140 (34.6 %) Lists had a description, while the others only had the List name.

[1]The name is derived from the word *cognoscenti*, i.e., people who are considered to be especially well informed about a particular topic.

Category	Sample queries
News	politics, sports, entertainment, science, technology, business
Journalists	politics, sports, entertainment, science, technology, business
Politics	conservative news, liberal politicians, USA / German / Brasilian / Indian politicians
Sports	F1, baseball, soccer, poker, tennis, NFL, NBA, Bundesliga, LA Lakers
Entertainment	celebrities, movie reviews, theatre, music
Hobbies	hiking, cooking, chefs, traveling, photography
Lifestyle	wine, dining, book club, health, fashion
Science	biology, astronomy, computer science, complex networks
Technology	iPhone, mac, linux, cloud computing
Business	markets, finance, energy

Table 6: The 55 sample queries used for evaluation of Cognos.

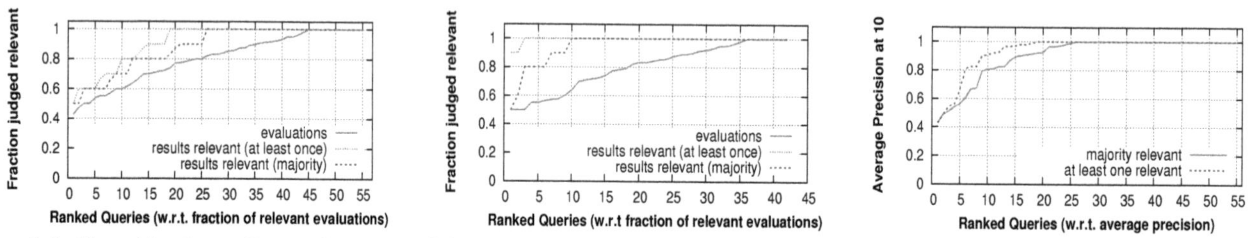

(a) Considering all results (b) Considering only results that are evaluated at least twice (c) Average precision at 10

Figure 1: Fraction of evaluations / individual Cognos results that were judged relevant (queries ranked w.r.t. fraction of relevant judgments) (a) considering all results, and (b) considering only those results for a query, which were evaluated at least twice; (c) Average precision for the top 10 results returned by Cognos

5.3 Evaluating Cognos expert search system

Judgments on the quality of the results returned by a search system are to an extent subjective. So we chose to evaluate Cognos through an user study where a set of human evaluators judged the relevance of the results returned by Cognos, using a web-based feedback service (available at `http://twitter-app.mpi-sws.org/whom-to-follow/`). We also gathered another set of user evaluations where the results returned by Cognos were directly compared with those returned by the official Twitter WTF service [16]. We also compared the top experts returned by Cognos with those returned by the state-of-the-art research system [10].

The above URL was publicly advertised to a few hundred people at each of the three home institutions of the authors, which are located across three different continents. We preferred such an *in-the-wild* evaluation (instead of a controlled evaluation with a fixed set of evaluators and few selected queries, as used by [10]) as it resembles a real-world deployment of the search system.

5.3.1 Evaluating quality of Cognos results

In this evaluation, an evaluator issues a query, for which she is shown the top 10 results returned by Cognos. Then the evaluator gives a binary judgment on each of the top 10 results as to whether it is relevant to the given query. The queries used for the evaluations could be selected from a given set of 55 sample queries spread over the 10 categories shown in Table 6. In the rest of this section, we use the term 'evaluation' to indicate a relevant / non-relevant judgment for an individual result (topical expert) given by Cognos for a particular query.

Overall, we obtained 2,136 relevance judgments[2] over the top 10 results for the 55 sample queries, out of which 1,680 (i.e., 78.7%) judged the result to be relevant to the query.

[2]Despite our request, some of the evaluators did not evaluate all 10 results for a particular query.

We found that the fraction of evaluations that judged a result as relevant, for each individual rank out of the top 10 (i.e., considering the results shown at a certain rank for any of the 55 queries) to be largely invariant – the top 4 results were judged to be relevant in more than 80% of the evaluations, while the results ranked 5–10 were judged relevant in more than 75% of the evaluations.

Next we examined the Cognos results that received the 456 (i.e., 21.3%) 'non-relevant' judgments. We found a large amount of subjectivity in these judgments driven by whether a particular evaluator recognizes a Twitter user as a top expert on a given topic. We found a number of cases where the same result for the same query was judged relevant by some evaluators and non-relevant by others. For example, for the query 'cloud computing', Werner Vogels, who is one of the principal architects of Amazon's approach to cloud computing, was rated as relevant in 4 evaluations, and as non-relevant in 6 evaluations, possibly because his name was not known to these evaluators.

To understand the subjectivity in judgments, we consider for each particular query, (i) what fraction of evaluations judged a result for this query as relevant, (ii) what fraction of the top 10 results were judged relevant at least once, and (iii) what fraction of the top 10 results were judged relevant in the *majority* of evaluations. Fig. 1(a) shows the distribution of these fractions for all queries (where queries are ranked by the fraction of evaluations that judged a result as relevant). It can be seen that for 37 out of the 55 queries, every result was judged relevant by at least one evaluation, and for 30 out of the 55 queries, every result was judged relevant by the majority of the evaluations for that particular result.

The effects of subjectivity can be seen even more clearly in Fig. 1(b) where we plot the above three fractions for each query, considering only those results that were evaluated at least twice. Note that there are 13 queries (out of the 55)

Cognos results			Results by Pal *et. al.*		
User	Extracts from bio	followers	User	Extracts from bio	followers
Query: oil spill					
BP_America	BP America	35,505	NWF	National Wildlife Federation	76,796
TheOilDrum	energy, peak oil, sustainability	26,257	TIME	Breaking news, current events	3,231,359
GOHSEP	Emergency Preparedness	5,295	huffingtonpost	The Internet Newspaper	1,574,848
usoceangov	National Ocean Service	37,866	NOLAnews	Latest news and updates	29,433
USCG	US Coast Guard	20,513	Reuters	Latest news	1,491,852
Query: iphone					
p0sixninja	iPhone Hacker	127,631	macworld	Mac, iPod, iPhone experts	182,248
iH8sn0w	made f0recast, iREB, iFaith	105,015	Gizmodo	Technologies that change	347,667
chronicdevteam	Hax	107,541	macrumorslive	Updates from Apple events.	170,813
MuscleNerd	iPhone hacker	330,625	macTweeter	*Account no longer exists in Twitter*	
iPhone_News	iPhone news and notes	153,024	engadget	Twitter account of Engadget	419,583
Query: world cup					
worldcupscores	Live 2010 World Cup Scores	10,866	TheWorldGame	Australia's football website	11,541
EdsonBuddle	Soccer playerFC Ingolstadt	30,808	GrantWahl	Sports Illustrated writer	180,290
thefadotcom	Website for England Football	102,536	owen_g	Guardian's Olympics editor	14,930
nytimesgoal	New York Times Soccer Blog	11,699	guardian_sport	Sport news from Guardian	121,095
herculezg	US National Team Forward	31,454	itvfootball	News from ITV football	54,395

Table 7: Top 5 results by Cognos and by Pal *et. al.* [10] for the three queries evaluated by Pal *et. al.*, along with their bio and number of followers

for which no individual result was evaluated twice, hence Fig. 1(b) shows the other 42 queries. For as many as 40 out of these 42 queries, every result (that was evaluated at least twice) was judged relevant by at least one evaluation, and for 33 out of these 42 queries, every result (that was evaluated at least twice) was judged relevant by the majority of the evaluations for that result.

Finally, we computed the average precision of the top 10 results returned by Cognos. Fig. 1(c) shows the average precision for all 55 queries, considering two cases – (i) a result is said to be relevant if it is judged relevant in the *majority* of evaluations, and (ii) a result is said to be relevant if it is judged relevant in at least one evaluation. For 30 out of the 55 queries, all the top 10 results were voted relevant (i.e., average precision of 1) in the majority of the evaluations. Also, for 45 out of the 55 queries, the average precision was above 0.8 in both cases. The Mean Average Precision (MAP) for the top 10 Cognos results, considering all 55 queries, was 0.905 in case (i) and 0.939 in case (ii).

The above statistics show that a vast majority of the results returned by Cognos were judged topically relevant to the given query (topic) by at least some evaluators. Thus, Cognos can successfully identify relevant experts over a wide variety of topics.

5.3.2 Comparing Cognos with state-of-the-art research system

As discussed in Section 4, Pal *et. al.* [10] give the top 10 experts identified by their algorithm for three specific queries: *oil spill*, *iphone*, and *world cup*. For these queries, Table 7 compares the top 5 results from Cognos and the top 5 results reported by Pal *et. al.*, along with the bio and number of followers of each result. Note that while the top results reported by Pal *et. al.* contain some general news media sites (as also discussed in Section 4.2.2), the top Cognos results are much more topic-specific, even if they are not as popularly followed as the news media sites. Interestingly, in their paper, Pal *et. al.* explicitly set out to discover such specialized topic-specific experts, even if they are not as highly visible as globally popular celebrities or media accounts. Cognos achieves this goal better than the state-of-the-art system.

5.3.3 Comparing Cognos with Twitter WTF

In this evaluation, when an evaluator issues a query, she is simultaneously shown the top 10 results returned by Cognos as well as the top 10 results returned by the official Twitter WTF service for the same query. The results are anonymized, i.e., the evaluator is not told which result-set is from which service, in order to prevent bias in judgment. Then the evaluator indicates which set of results is better for the given query, or whether both result-sets are equally good or equally bad.[3] Since Cognos uses a Twitter dataset crawled in 2009 (see Section 5.2), we filtered out from the Twitter WTF results those user-accounts that were created *after* 2009, in order to make the comparison fair.[4] In order to test the performance of Cognos 'in-the-wild', we allowed the evaluators to issue any query of their choice.

We obtained relevance judgments for a total of 325 queries, out of which 259 are distinct. These queries are evaluator-chosen and they cover a wide variety of topics. Given the high subjectivity observed in user relevance judgments in the previous section, we choose to focus our evaluation on the 27 distinct queries that were asked at least two times. In total, these 27 queries were asked 93 times.

Table 8 shows the 27 queries that were asked at least twice. For each query, we consider the verdict – Cognos better / Twitter WTF better / tie – based on majority voting. The queries for which there was a unanimous verdict (i.e., all evaluations for this query agreed that one or the other was better) are italicized in Table 8. Cognos was judged to be better for 12 out of the 27 queries, while Twitter WTF was judged better for 11, and there was a tie for 4 queries. The fact that Cognos was judged to be better than the official Twitter WTF service for 44% of the queries, clearly indicates the potential of crowdsourced Lists (the only feature used in Cognos) in identifying topical experts in Twitter. It can be noted that a significant fraction of the cases where Twitter WTF was unanimously judged better are names of individuals (celebrities) or organizations. Since such names

[3]The search engines corresponding to the result-sets are revealed to the evaluators *after* the evaluation is done.
[4]The date on which an account was created is available from the profile information.

	Cognos better	Twitter WTF better	Tie
Queries	Linux, computer science, mac, India, Apple, Facebook, *internet*, ipad, markets, *windows phone*, photography, politic journalist	politic news, music, *Sachin Tendulkar*, Twitter, *Alka Yagnik*, *Anjelina Jolie*, cloud computing, *Delhi*, *Harry Potter*, metallica, *IIT Kharagpur*	Microsoft – Cognos better: 1, Twitter better: 1, both good: 1, both bad: 1 Dell, Kolkata – Cognos better: 1, Twitter better: 1 Sanskrit as an official language – both bad: 2
Average overlap in top 10 results	**1.83**	**2.1**	**3.0**

Table 8: Evaluator-chosen queries (which were asked at least two times) for comparison of Cognos and Twitter WTF, where the verdict (Cognos better / Twitter better / tie) is given by majority voting. Queries in italics are the ones for which there was a unanimous verdict.

Cognos results			Twitter WTF results		
User	Extracts from bio	followers	User	Extracts from bio	followers
		Query: music			
Katy Perry	i kissed a girl ...	15,016,823	iTunes Music	Music updates for U.S.	1,903,343
Lady Gaga	mother monster	19,203,867	YouTube	YouTube news, trends, videos	9,220,791
taylorswift13	*Bio not written*	10,994,066	SonyMusicGlobal	home of Sony Music	102,753
jtimberlake	Official Justin Timberlake	8,451,967	50cent	It's the kid 50 Cent	5,861,243
Pink	it's all happening	7,128,708	guardianmusic	Squashing music	107,167
		Query: windows phone			
BrandonWatson	developers on Windows Phone	12,462	Windows Phone	Official Windows Phone	130,925
wmpoweruser	Windows Phone Power Users	10,402	pocketnow.com	Windows Phone news	42,134
Charlie Kindel	Founder, CTO, Mentor	8,026	WP Dev Team	Windows Phone Dev Team	37,344
joebelfiore	Runs team doing W. Phone 7	15,542	WindowsPhoneNL	Windows Phone in Nederland	2,785
pocketnow.com	Windows Phone news	42,134	WPCentral	All thing Windows Phone 7	18,266

Table 9: Top 5 results by Cognos and Twitter WTF for queries "music" and "windows phone". While top Cognos results mostly contain personal accounts, top Twitter WTF results mostly contain organizations / business accounts.

appear very rarely in the List names / descriptions, Cognos does not handle these queries well.

Table 8 also shows that the top 10 Cognos results have very low overlap with top 10 Twitter WTF results across all queries. This is in spite of the fact that 83.4% out of the Twitter WTF top 20 results for some query (topic) were inferred by our List-based methodology to be related to the same topic (as was reported in Section 4.2.3). This implies that the low overlap between the top Cognos results and top Twitter WTF results is primarily due to the List-based *ranking* used in Cognos.

In general, we observe that the top Twitter WTF results mostly include organizations / business accounts while the top Cognos results mostly include personal accounts. This is possibly because the Twitter WTF considers the name and bio of users [17], and organizational / business accounts are more likely (compared to personal accounts) to have names or bios containing terms related to their topics of expertise. We present some examples in Table 9 for the queries 'music' (for which the majority voted Twitter WTF better), and 'windows phone' (for which the majority voted Cognos better). As such, these examples again bring out the subjective nature of human judgment, where some evaluators preferred the personal accounts while others preferred the organizational accounts.

5.3.4 Summary

Our evaluation of the Cognos search system shows that a vast majority of its results are relevant for a wide variety of topics. In fact, Cognos rarely produces entirely irrelevant results for queries. Comparing Cognos with state-of-the-art research system by Pal *et. al.* and the official Twitter WTF service highlights the advantages of relying on crowdsourced Lists to identify experts. Cognos yields particularly better search results in the cases when the bio or tweets posted by a user does not correspond to or contain information about the user's topic of expertise. In fact, Cognos performs as good as or better than the official Twitter WTF service for more than 52% of the queries, even though it is based on a single and simple feature (Lists).

6. FINDING EXPERTS EFFICIENTLY

In this section, we address the practical challenge of keeping our Cognos system up-to-date, even as hundreds of thousands of new Twitter accounts and new Lists are created every day.

6.1 Scalability problem with crawling Lists

We begin by analyzing the scalability of a simple updation strategy that relies on periodically crawling all the Twitter users and the Lists that contain them. Recent reports indicate that 200 million new users joined Twitter in the last 9 months [2], which roughly amounts to 740,000 new users joining per day. For each user, we would need to make at least one extra request to crawl her Lists. Thus, just to keep the system up-to-date by crawling the newly joining users everyday, a lower-bound rate limit would be of at least 1,480,000 requests per day. Twitter normally rate-limits the number of API requests from a single machine (IP address) to 150 per hour [15], i.e., to 3600 user profile crawls per day. Fortunately, three of our machines were *white-listed* by Twitter, which allows each of them to crawl at a significantly higher rate of 20,000 API requests per hour. Thus, we can make at most 1,440,000 ($20{,}000 \times 3 \times 24$) API requests per day from all three of our white-listed machines. Note that our maximum crawl rate is still lower than the lower-bound rate we would need to gather the profiles and Lists of all new users joining Twitter every day. Given that we would need to periodically crawl the new Lists for the already existing 465 million Twitter users [2], it becomes quite evident that the strategy of crawling all users' Lists would not scale.

Next, we estimated the number of highly listed users amongst the 465 million Twitter accounts as of January 2012. Since Twitter assigns userids in an integer sequence starting from 1, we took a random sample of 300,000 integers in the range 1 to 465 million, and attempted to crawl the profiles of Twitter userids in the sample. The distribution of experts within this large random sample can be expected to be similar to the distribution of experts among all Twitter users. For instance, only 363 out of the 300,000 sampled users (i.e., 0.12%) were listed 100 or more times; hence we expect the total number of Twitter users who are listed 100 or more times to be 0.12% of the entire Twitter population. Thus, only a small fraction of all Twitter users are highly listed experts and once they are identified, it would be possible to crawl the Lists containing them periodically. The key challenge, however, lies in efficiently identifying these experts from the large Twitter user population.

6.2 Crawling experts efficiently

Our discussion above shows that we cannot exhaustively crawl Lists for all Twitter users. However, we can crawl Lists for the small fraction of *expert* users, if we somehow identified them from the Twitter user population. We now propose and evaluate a strategy to efficiently identify expert users.

We begin by observing that the Twitter social network consists of a number of *hubs*, users who follow a large number of popular experts and include them in Lists. Our strategy is to first identify popular hubs in an older snapshot of the network (when the network was considerably smaller) and then leverage the Lists created by the top hubs in order to find new authorities. It can be noted that this strategy also relies on crowdsourcing – we expect the Twitter crowd (in particular, the top hubs) to discover experts who newly join Twitter, and we can utilize their discovery by periodically crawling the Lists created by the top hubs.

We used the well-known HITS algorithm to identify the top hubs in the snapshot of the Twitter network gathered in 2009 [4] (introduced in Section 5.2), when the network had only 54 million users. We then crawled the Lists created by the top *1 million* hubs in the network to efficiently discover experts. In all, the top 1 million hubs had created 479,129 Lists, which taken together contained 4,100,367 distinct users. Out of these, 2,064,373 (i.e., 50.3%) have been included in 10 or more Lists. In comparison, only 1.13% of all the users in our large random sample of Twitter users are listed 10 or more times. The difference clearly indicates that our strategy is effective in focusing our crawls on experts in Twitter. The crawl for the Lists created by the top 1 million hubs took about 3 weeks (January 20 – February 8, 2012) using three machines white-listed by Twitter, and hence, it can be repeated every month to discover new experts.

6.3 Evaluating coverage of our crawls

In this section, we estimate the fraction of experts covered by our strategy to crawl Lists created by top hubs.

6.3.1 Coverage of most listed users

We measure the fraction of most listed users in Twitter that is covered by our methodology as follows. First, we estimate the number of Twitter users listed at least K times by computing the number of such users in our random sample of 300,000 users, and then scaling it to the total Twitter population of 465 million users. Next we calculate the fraction of the estimated number of users listed at least K times, that is actually discovered by crawling the Lists created by the top hubs.

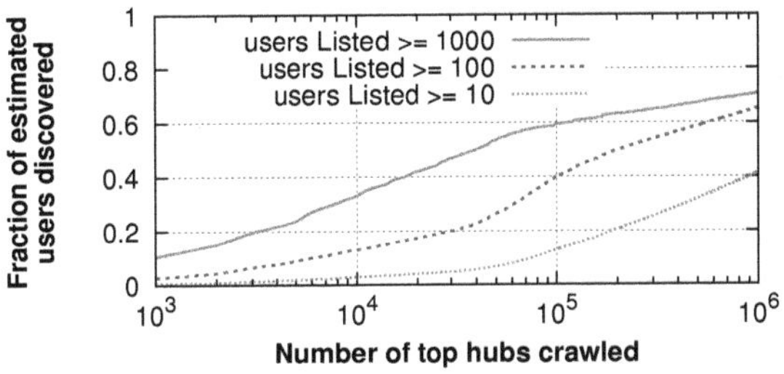

Figure 2: Fraction of estimated number of experts who are included in at least K Lists, that is discovered in the hub-based crawl, for $K = 10, 100, 1000$.

Figure 2 plots the fraction of experts discovered against the number of top hubs crawled. By crawling the Lists created by the top 1 million hubs, we discover 25,887 experts who are listed 1000 or more times, which is 70.6% of our estimated total number of experts listed at least 1000 times in Twitter. Further, we find that crawling the Lists created by only the top 100,000 hubs is sufficient to discover 53.3% of the estimated number of experts listed 1000 or more times. Thus, the hub-based updation methodology can be used to efficiently discover a large fraction of experts in Twitter.

6.3.2 Coverage of newly joined experts

Our expert discovery strategy is also effective in discovering newly joined experts. Even though our top hubs were selected using a 2009 snapshot of the Twitter network, more than 42.3% of the 4,100,367 users in the Lists created by these hubs have joined Twitter after 2009. Further, we show some examples of very recently created Twitter accounts that our hub-based crawl could discover, in Table 10. Our crawl of Lists created by the top 1 million hubs, which ended on February 8, 2012, discovered some experts who joined Twitter as recently as Feb 6 or Feb 4 (i.e., while the crawl was going on). This not only validates our hypothesis that the top hub nodes quickly discover newly joined experts and add them to their Lists, but it also shows the effectiveness of the hub-based updation strategy.

Account	Bio / Description	Listed	Created
MartiRiverola	F.C.Barcelona	67	Feb 6
annekirkbride	English Actress	23	Feb 4
AaronAStanford	Canadian Actor	32	Feb 1
Shay Given	Ireland goalkeeper	107	Jan 27
CourteneyCox	American actress	294	Jan 24
PMOIndia	Prime Minister India	309	Jan 23

Table 10: Examples of very recently created expert accounts discovered by our Hub-based crawl (which ended on Feb 8, 2012)

6.3.3 Coverage of experts identified by other systems

We evaluate whether our updation methodology can discover topical experts returned by the Pal *et. al.* research system and Twitter WTF service. Out of the 30 topical experts stated by Pal *et. al.* (for the three topics "oil spill", "world cup" and "iPhone"), 29 are included in the crawls of Lists created by the top 1 million hubs (the 1 remaining account no longer exists in Twitter). Next, we consider the

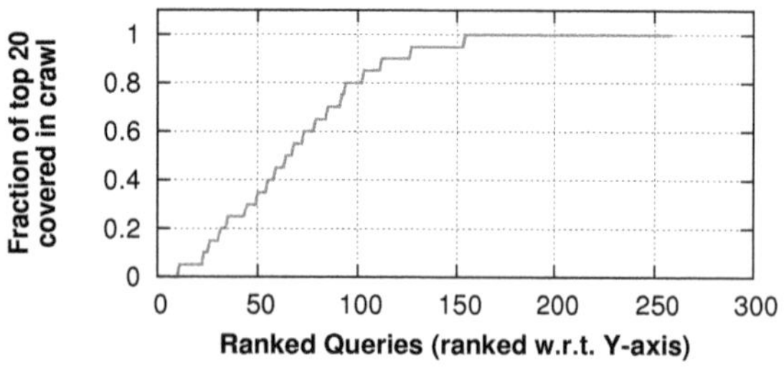

Figure 3: Distribution of the fraction of Twitter WTF top 20 results that is covered in our hub-based crawl (for the queries discussed in Section 5.3.3)

top 20 experts returned by Twitter WTF for each of the 259 queries obtained by our user-survey (see Section 5.3.3) and calculate what fraction of these experts are covered by our hub-based crawls. Figure 3 plots the distribution of the fraction of Twitter WTF top 20 results included in our hub-based crawls, across all queries. It can be seen that our crawls include all Twitter WTF top 20 results for more than 50% of the queries and at least 15 out of the Twitter WTF top 20 results for close to 80% of the queries.

The above results indicate that our hub-based strategy – periodically discovering experts through the Lists created by top hubs – can be used to efficiently discover newly joined experts, and keep our expert search system up-to-date in the face of rapid increase in the Twitter population.

7. CONCLUSION

As Twitter emerges as a popular platform for finding real-time information on the Web, an important research challenge lies in identifying experts in specific topics. In this paper, we show that an effective solution to this hard problem lies in exploiting the wisdom of the Twitter crowds. Specifically, we observe that individual Twitter users, for their own convenience, annotate and classify experts in various topics using the Lists feature. By aggregating the List information for individual Twitter users, we can obtain an extremely rich characterization of their topical expertise as perceived by the Twitter crowds. We leverage this insight to build and deploy Cognos, a topical expert search system. Through extensive evaluation, we demonstrate that even though Cognos is built utilizing *only* the Lists feature, it can compete with the commercial who-to-follow system deployed by Twitter itself. We believe that crowdsourced Lists provide a valuable foundation for building future content search / recommendation / discovery services in Twitter.

Our current List-based methodology is vulnerable to List spamming, where malicious users can create fake Lists including a target user to manipulate the inferred attributes for the user. To date, we did not find much evidence of such attacks. However, such attacks can easily be launched in the future. Defending against such attacks would require the List-based methodology to consider the reputation of the users who create the Lists – a crucial challenge that we plan to address in future work.

Acknowledgment

The authors thank the anonymous reviewers whose suggestions helped to improve the paper. This research was supported in part by a grant from the Indo-German Max Planck Centre for Computer Science (IMPECS).

8. REFERENCES

[1] There Are Now 155m Tweets Posted Per Day, Triple the Number a Year Ago. http://rww.to/gv4VqA, April 2011.

[2] Twitter to hit 500 million accounts by February. http://bit.ly/twitpopulation, Jan 2012.

[3] E. Bakshy, J. M. Hofman, W. A. Mason, and D. J. Watts. Everyone's an influencer: quantifying influence on Twitter. In *Proceedings of ACM Conference on Web Search and Data Mining (WSDM)*, 2011.

[4] M. Cha, H. Haddadi, F. Benevenuto, and K. P. Gummadi. Measuring User Influence in Twitter: The Million Follower Fallacy. In *Proceedings of AAAI Conference on Weblogs and Social Media (ICWSM)*, May 2010.

[5] C. Clarke, G. Cormack, and E. Tudhope. Relevance ranking for one to three term queries. *Information Processing and Management*, 36(2), 2000.

[6] T. H. Haveliwala. Topic-sensitive pagerank. In *Proceedings of ACM Conference on World Wide Web (WWW)*, 2002.

[7] N. Kallen. Twitter blog: Soon to Launch: Lists. http://blog.twitter.com/2009/09/soon-to-launch-lists.html, Sep 2009.

[8] C. Lee, H. Kwak, H. Park, and S. Moon. Finding influentials based on the temporal order of information adoption in Twitter. In *Proceedings of ACM Conference on World Wide Web (WWW)*, 2010.

[9] D. Metzler, S. Dumais, and C. Meek. Similarity measures for short segments of text. In *Proceedings of European Conference on Information Retrieval*, 2007.

[10] A. Pal and S. Counts. Identifying topical authorities in microblogs. In *Proceedings of ACM Conference on Web Search and Data Mining (WSDM)*, 2011.

[11] R. Pochampally and V. Varma. User context as a source of topic retrieval in Twitter. In *Proceedings of Workshop on Enriching Information Retrieval (with ACM SIGIR)*, 2011.

[12] D. M. Romero, W. Galuba, S. Asur, and B. A. Huberman. Influence and passivity in social media. In *Proceedings of ACM Conference on World Wide Web (WWW)*, 2011.

[13] N. Sharma, S. Ghosh, F. Benevenuto, N. Ganguly, and K. Gummadi. Inferring Who-is-Who in the Twitter Social Network. In *Proceedings of Workshop on Online Social Networks (with ACM SIGCOMM)*, 2012.

[14] J. Teevan, D. Ramage, and M. R. Morris. #twittersearch: a comparison of microblog search and web search. In *Proceedings of ACM Conference on Web Search and Data Mining (WSDM)*, 2011.

[15] Rate Limiting | Twitter Developers. https://dev.twitter.com/docs/rate-limiting.

[16] Twitter: Who to Follow. http://twitter.com/#!/who_to_follow.

[17] Twitter Improves "Who To Follow" Results & Gains Advanced Search Page. http://selnd.com/wtfdesc.

[18] M. J. Welch, U. Schonfeld, D. He, and J. Cho. Topical semantics of Twitter links. In *Proceedings of ACM Conference on Web Search and Data Mining (WSDM)*, 2011.

[19] J. Weng, E.-P. Lim, J. Jiang, and Q. He. Twitterrank: finding topic-sensitive influential twitterers. In *Proceedings of ACM Conference on Web Search and Data Mining (WSDM)*, 2010.

[20] S. Wu, J. M. Hofman, W. A. Mason, and D. J. Watts. Who says what to whom on Twitter. In *Proceedings of ACM Conference on World Wide Web (WWW)*, 2011.

[21] J. Zhang, M. S. Ackerman, and L. Adamic. Expertise networks in online communities: Structure and algorithms. In *Proceedings of ACM Conference on World Wide Web (WWW)*, 2007.

Author Index

www.ingramcontent.com/pod-product-compliance
Ingram Content Group UK Ltd.
Pitfield, Milton Keynes, MK11 3LW, UK
UKHW051455290926
15471UKWH00008B/1222

9 781450 320009